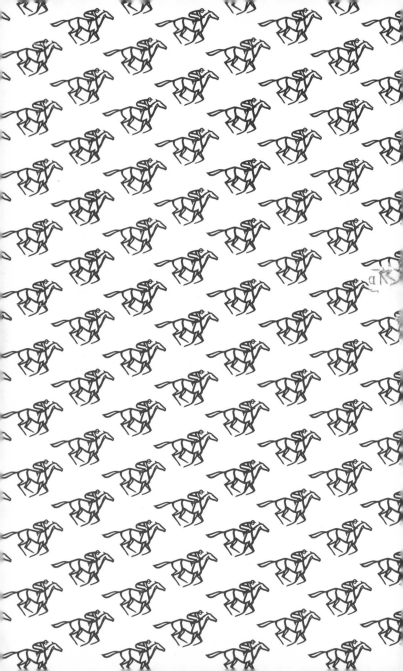

AGE, WEIGHT & DISTANCE TABLE

Distance	Age	Jan	Feb	March	April	May	June
2m	5	12—7	12—7	12—7	12—7	12—7	12—7
	4	11–13	12—0	12—1	12—2	12—3	12—4
2¼m	5	12—7	12—7	12—7	12—7	12—7	12—7
	4	11–12	11–13	12—0	12—1	12—2	12—3
2½m	5	12—7	12—7	12—7	12—7	12—7	12—7
	4	11–11	11–12	11–13	12—0	12—1	12—2
2¾m	5	12—6	12—7	12—7	12—7	12—7	12—7
	4	11–10	11–11	11–12	11–13	12—0	12—1
3m	5	12—6	12—6	12—7	12—7	12—7	12—7
	4	11–8	11–10	11–11	11–12	11–13	12—0

Distance	Age	Jul	Aug	Sept	Oct	Nov	Dec
2m	5	12—7	12—7	12—7	12—7	12—7	12—7
	4	12—4	12—5	12—5	12—6	12—6	12—7
	3	11—5	11—6	11—8	11—9	11–11	11–12
2¼m	5	12—7	12—7	12—7	12—7	12—7	12—7
	4	12—3	12—4	12—5	12—5	12—6	12—6
	3	11—4	11—5	11—7	11—8	11—9	11–10
2½m	5	12—7	12—7	12—7	12—7	12—7	12—7
	4	12—2	12—3	12—4	12—5	12—6	12—6
	3		11—4	11—6	11—7	11—8	11—9
2¾m	5	12—7	12—7	12—7	12—7	12—7	12—7
	4	12—2	12—3	12—4	12—5	12—5	12—6
	3					11—7	11—8
3m	5	12—7	12—7	12—7	12—7	12—7	12—7
	4	12—1	12—2	12—3	12—4	12—5	12—5
	3					11—6	11—7

For 6-y-o's and older, use 12-7 in all cases

Note Race distances in the above tables are shown only at ¼-mile intervals. For races of 2m 1f use the 2¼-mile table weights; for races of 2m 3f use 2½ miles; and so forth. For races over odd distances, the nearest distance shown in the table should be used. RACES OVER DISTANCES longer than 3 miles should be treated as 3-mile races.

1

The Sporting Life

BEST RUNNER OF ALL EVERY YEAR

YOU'RE LIFELESS WITHOUT IT

CHASERS & HURDLERS
1992/93

Price £58.00

A TIMEFORM PUBLICATION

Compiled and produced by

G. Greetham, B.A., G. F. Walton, Dip.A.D. (Directors), J. D. Newton, B.A. (Editor-in-Chief), E. K. Wilkinson (Editor), S. D. Rowlands, B.A. (Handicapper), R. J. C. Austen, B.A., G. Crowther, M. T. Greenwood, W. Hughes, G. M. Johnstone, D. Sheard, J. Willoughby and C. Wright, B.A.

© **Portway Press Limited 1993**

ISBN 0 900599 65 0

CONTENTS

1 Age, Weight and Distance Table

7 Introduction

15 Timeform Champion Jumpers 1992/93

16 Timeform 'Top Hundred'

18 Explanatory Notes

22 The Form Summaries and Rating Symbols

23 Chasers & Hurdlers 1992/93

842 Big Race Results 1992/93

879 Index to Photographs

887 1992/93 Statistics

889 Timeform Champions

893 Fixtures 1993/94

National ends in fiasco

Race void after double start

National disaster

From false start to false finish, Aintree's race that never was stuns Britain

Sunday Telegraph

NEWS OF THE WORLD

Britain's Most Popular Newspaper

THE BANNED NATIONAL

BAD NEWS False starts ruin race — it won't be run again

GOOD NEWS Lamont won't get his hands on £6m bets tax!

FUNNY DJ KENNY IN AIDS RIDDLE: PAGES 14 & 15

THE GRAND SHAMBLES

The Mail ON SUNDAY

DELIA SMITH'S SUMMER RECIPES

Big race is void after two false starts

THE GRAND FARCICAL

People

What a Grand National disgrace

Sunday Mirror

FORWARD WITH BRITAIN

FREE EYE SHADOW WORTH £2.35

NATIO DISGR

£112 million shambles at Aintree

THE INDEPENDENT ON SUNDAY

Shambles at Aintree ■ 30 horses in race that wasn't ■ Bookies to return £75m bets

Chaos at Grand National reduces spectacle to farce

Sunday EXPRESS

BRITAIN'S RICHEST
HOW WE FEEL ABOUT OUR WEALTH

SAVE UP TO £130 ON GREAT DAYS OUT

NATIONAL DISGRACE

● Bedlam at bookies
● Flag man blamed
● Lamont loses £6m

Chasers & Hurdlers 1992/93

Introduction

The 1992/3 jumps season was an eventful one, off the course as well as on. As ever, the weather played a significant part in dictating the shape of the campaign with conditions largely conducive to competitive, uninterrupted racing. There was rain aplenty until well into the New Year, followed by a spell of several weeks in which little fell at all. The Cheltenham and Aintree Festivals in the spring were run on ground firmer than usual, and certainly firmer than that which prevailed for many of the championship trials, but they still attracted plenty of runners. There were more races during the latest season than in any other.

It is ironic, therefore, that the season will be remembered as much for a race that wasn't officially run as for any other single incident. 'The Grand National that never was' put racing on the front pages and was the day's main item on television and radio news, though the publicity wasn't the type the sport would have wished for. A bizarre set of circumstances caused the great race to be declared void after two false starts, the second of which was not recalled properly. Perceived impracticalities ruled out running the contest at a later date. **Esha Ness** 'won' the unofficial Grand National, his jockey being one of several who seemed unaware of what had happened at the time. Naturally, much of the essay on Esha Ness in this Annual is given over to the events and ramifications of that extraordinary day in April.

There was much for racing in general to be optimistic about, though. A new governing body for the sport, the British Horseracing Board, slowly began to take shape; a further experiment with Sunday racing took place at Cheltenham in November; evening opening of betting offices was legalised and, on the opening day of the Cheltenham Festival, the Chancellor Norman Lamont gave the industry as a whole an amazing boost with his provision of VAT relief for many owners, trainers and breeders. Details of the last of these can be found in the essay on the appropriately-named **Givus A Buck**, winner of the Ritz Club Chase which was being run at the time of the budget statement.

Stars were born, and, sadly, some died. The losses of **Mighty Mogul** and **Rushing Wild**, both of whom achieved so much in a relatively short space of time, along with that of the reigning Champion Hurdler **Royal Gait**, were particularly keenly felt by supporters of the winter game. So too, of course, was the death in December of the outstanding northern trainer Arthur Stephenson. Another very popular figure champion jockey Peter Scudamore retired from race-riding after success on **Sweet Duke** at Ascot in April.

Scudamore's premature departure meant that a first jump jockey's title became a foregone conclusion for Richard Dunwoody, who held a handy lead at the time anyway. It also prompted quite a shake-up in riding arrangements with the leading stables for the 1993/4 season. After some deliberation Dunwoody opted to take the place of Scudamore as stable jockey to Martin Pipe (champion trainer for the fifth season running) while the talented young Adrian Maguire will step into Dunwoody's shoes at David Nicholson's. It must have been a difficult decision for Dunwoody to make, for Nicholson himself had by some way his most successful season, finishing second in the trainers' championship.

On the equine front, the 1992/3 season was the familiar story of rise and fall. One of the most pleasing features was the emergence of several staying chasers of note, chiefly the Tote Cheltenham Gold Cup winner and Timeform Champion Jumper of 1992/3 **Jodami**. Given a faultless preparation by his trainer Peter Beaumont and handled with sympathy and skill throughout the season by his new jockey Mark Dwyer, Jodami progressed through the ranks, landing the Mandarin, the Peter Marsh and Leopardstown's Hennessy Cognac Gold Cup along the way, before crowning his campaign with victory in chasing's 'blue riband'. What really impressed was the manner and merit of his success at Cheltenham. The moment going to the last fence when Dwyer looked round for non-existent dangers before asking Jodami for his final effort, will remain one of the abiding memories of the season. In beating Rushing Wild by two lengths, the pair clear in a field well up to standard, Jodami put up a performance worthy of his rating of 174p, the highest achieved in the race itself since Burrough Hill Lad nine years previously. What's more, at the age of eight, Jodami is as young as any winner of the Gold Cup since Little Owl in 1981. Time is on Jodami's side, and, with luck, he should be thrilling racing fans for some years to come.

With Carvill's Hill side-lined the old guard of staying chasers was represented by the first three home in the 1992 Gold Cup. While **Cool**

The Gold Cup, a two-horse race at the last, Jodami and Rushing Wild

Docklands Express and Run For Free, two grand servants to their stables, fight out the finish of the Martell Cup

Ground made relatively little impact, **The Fellow**, and to a lesser extent **Docklands Express**, provided stern resistance and a bench mark by which to judge the new generation. The second successive victory of the French-trained The Fellow in the King George VI Chase at Kempton on Boxing Day was one of the season's most popular, although it probably wasn't a vintage performance by the race's, or the horse's, high standards. Docklands Express was under a cloud for part of the season but re-emerged to run a tremendous race under top weight in the Racing Post Chase and to gain a deserved success in the valuable Martell Cup Chase at Aintree. His chief victim on this last-named occasion was one of the best of the second-season chasers **Run For Free**, who had earlier led home a Pipe-trained one-two-three-four in the Coral Welsh National at Chepstow.

By comparison the two-mile chasing division was noticeably weak. The previous season's champion **Remittance Man** had only two races before sustaining an injury that ruled him out for the remainder of the campaign. His old rivals **Katabatic** and **Waterloo Boy** were troubled with physical problems also, and they didn't always show their form (both were well below form in the Queen Mother Champion Chase). No authentic replacements materialised. As a result, on the day, the Queen Mother Champion Chase took less winning than any of the previous dozen, **Deep Sensation** running to a rating of only 148 in beating the in-and-out **Cyphrate** narrowly.

Prospects for the future do look bright though. The leading two-mile novice chasers were an especially good bunch, with **Sybillin** (who beat Deep Sensation impressively in the Victor Chandler Chase at Ascot in

9

The Champion Hurdle . . . . .
Peter Scudamore and Granville Again have victory in their grasp

January), **Travado, Wonder Man** and **Viking Flagship** seeming the best of them. It was Travado who landed the most prestigious race for horses in this particular division, the Waterford Castle Arkle Chase, but Sybillin put up the best efforts of all. Viking Flagship posted his claims towards the season's close with two convincing victories at the Punchestown Festival in late-April. It's difficult to predict which of these up-and-coming chasers will come out on top in the future but not difficult at all to see them collectively establishing a new era in two-mile chasing.

The leading staying novice chasers of 1992/3 will have their work cut out to do likewise over longer distances. Our idea of the best of them was **Cab On Target**, who missed the Cheltenham Festival and then put the winner of the Sun Alliance Chase, the admirably tough and consistent **Young Hustler**, firmly in his place when the pair met at Aintree. A fast jumper with a good turn of foot, Cab On Target at this stage looks the one most likely to develop into the chief rival to Jodami for the 1994 Cheltenham Gold Cup. We doubt that Young Hustler will make it to the very top, but he was definitely one of the stars of the 1992/3 season. At times it almost seemed as if he was in action every other day, and getting better and better for it, too! He made a substantial contribution to what was a remarkably successful season for his trainer, Nigel Twiston-Davies.

One of the chief protagonists in the latest Gold Cup, Rushing Wild, who sadly sustained a fatal injury in the Jameson Irish Grand National a month later, had been the best hunter chaser of the previous year. There were several promising performers among the hunter chasers of 1993, too, notably **Double Silk** who achieved the Cheltenham-Aintree Foxhunters double, emulating Grittar in 1981. Grittar went on to win the Grand National in the following year, and such a target looks a realistic one for Double Silk in 1994. Let's hope that Double Silk doesn't share the fate of a horse we made similar predictions for at the end of 1990/1, Esha Ness!

Jump racing lost another horse of considerable note when the highly impressive BonusPrint Christmas Hurdle winner **Mighty Mogul** was put down as a result of an injury sustained during a race at Cheltenham in January. Nothing that happened in the Champion Hurdle subsequently caused a revision of the view that he'd have been the one they'd all have had to beat in that contest. By the season's end Mighty Mogul's performance at Kempton was still entitled to be regarded as the best by a hurdler during the campaign. In his absence **Granville Again** wrested the spoils in the Smurfit Champion Hurdle, thus making amends for his misfortune in the same contest the previous year. That regular in top hurdling events in recent years **Royal Derbi** ran the race of his life to finish a length down in second, followed not far behind by the Arlington Bula Hurdle winner **Halkopous**, the Tote Gold Trophy winner **King Credo**, the previous year's Champion runner-up **Oh So Risky** and **Vintage Crop**. The last-named did particularly well in view of his inexperience as a hurdler (it was only his third race) and the fact that conditions did not bring his stamina (proven at a high level on the Flat) fully into play. The Irish again had a shortage of high-class performers in open competition, and Vintage Crop's effort at Cheltenham was probably the best by any of them during 1992/3.

Granville Again went on to the Martell Hurdle at Aintree over an extra half a mile, but was eclipsed there by his older brother, the 1991 Champion Hurdler **Morley Street**. Morley Street became something of a notorious character in the latest season. He was anything but predictable and seemed to turn it in on at least one occasion, in the Racecall Ascot Hurdle in November. The decision to attach a § to his Timeform rating, indicating the horse's unreliability, scandalized some. There was never any question that Morley Street was still a force to be reckoned with at the highest level on his day though, and for a performance of merit it is difficult to top his in that Aintree race. Ridden with great confidence and judgement by Graham Bradley, Morley Street joined issue on the bridle going to the last and quickened instantly when finally loosed halfway up the run-in, going away from Granville Again at the line a length and a half to the good. It's a shame that the display by horse and rider didn't receive the attention at the time that it deserved, overshadowed as it was by events later on Grand National day.

The leading staying hurdlers were a substandard lot, and, with their taking it in turns to win the big races, no undisputed champion emerged. The BonusPrint Stayers' Hurdle at Cheltenham went to the outsider **Shuil Ar Aghaidh**, one of six winners at the Festival for Irish stables and one of four for Irish champion jockey Charlie Swan.

Graham Bradley and Morley Street (left) set to pounce in the Aintree Hurdle

Having said that the Irish had a shortage of high-class performers in open competition once again, they can derive considerable encouragement from events at the Festival. Not only was it their most successful since 1982 in terms of winners, but it also showed that they have a number of highly promising horses. The Irish novice hurdlers were a particularly strong collection, and **Montelado**, runaway winner of the Trafalgar House Supreme Novices' Hurdle, is a horse of immense potential. Montelado was not seen out again, but provided all is well with him he looks every inch Champion Hurdle material. His only defeat in three starts was a narrow one at the hands of the tough mare **Bayrouge**, chief standard bearer for the prolific Ann O'Brien stable. The only horse to have beaten Montelado earlier in his career, **Tiananmen Square**, also deserves mention as a novice hurdler of note. He ran only twice before being side-lined, but the second of his wins, at the chief expense of Bayrouge at Navan in December, showed him to be a most exciting prospect.

The leading British-trained novice hurdlers achieved less. Arguably the best of them was **Lord Relic**, whose defeat at Cheltenham might have owed something to the good to firm going or to an interrupted preparation. We retain faith in Lord Relic (who had easily accounted for the Cheltenham winner **Gaelstrom** previously) and see him as an excellent prospect for the top staying hurdles in the coming season.

The Irish also dominated the juvenile hurdling scene. **Shawiya** won a closely-fought Daily Express Triumph Hurdle, the first of her sex to win the race, and went on to put up an even better performance when winning a valuable contest at Punchestown in April. If there is a realistic Champion Hurdle contender amongst the leading juveniles of 1992/3 then it is probably her. Truth to tell, though, they were a poor group otherwise (even Shawiya, rated 141p, is not up to the usual standard for a leader of the generation), and the next best **Bold Boss** actually put up his best effort in defeat in a handicap. Perhaps something will emerge from the ruck in the next season. It usually does!

These then are some of the leading events, issues and characters of the past National Hunt season, all of them dealt with at greater length in the main body of **Chasers & Hurdlers 1992/93**. It is only to be expected that the reader will put his or her own interpretation on some of the issues discussed, and that he or she will have personal favourites among the thousands of horses listed. Be it a run-of-the-mill performer around 'the gaffs' or a Cheltenham Festival winner, you will find each horse's achievements recorded accurately and in context for posterity.

'**Chasers & Hurdlers 1992/93**' deals individually, in alphabetical sequence, with every horse that ran over the sticks in the 1992/3 season (including on the all-weather tracks), plus a number of Irish and French horses that did not race here. For most of these horses is given (1) its age, colour and sex, (2) its breeding, (3) a form summary giving details of all its performances during the past season, (4) a rating of its merit, (5) a commentary upon its racing or general characteristics as a racehorse, with some suggestions, perhaps, regarding its prospects for 1993/4 and (6) the name of the trainer in whose charge it was on the last occasion it ran.

The book is published with a twofold purpose. Firstly, it is intended to have permanent value as a review of the exploits and achievements of the more notable of our chasers and hurdlers in the 1992/3 season. Thus, while the commentaries upon the vast majority of the horses are, of necessity, in note form, the best horses are more critically examined, and the short essays upon them are illustrated by half-tone portraits and photographs of some of the races in which they ran. Secondly, the book is designed to help the punter to analyse races, and the Explanatory Notes which follow this Introduction contain instructions for using the data. A Companion volume accompanies 'Chasers & Hurdlers', providing among other things, for the first time, statistics on trainers and sires, adapted for easy reference and use.

The objective of the '**Chasers & Hurdlers 1992/93 Statistical Companion**' is explained in the introduction to that volume. Some reference material traditionally featured in 'Chasers & Hurdlers' now appears in the Companion, which has allowed us to improve the readability of the main volume by increasing type size. We hope you will find '**Chasers & Hurdlers 1992/93**' and the '**Chasers & Hurdlers 1992/93 Statistical Companion**' an informative and entertaining combination.

October 1993

TIMEFORM
CHAMPION JUMPERS
1992/93

CHAMPION JUMPER
BEST STAYING CHASER
(RATED AT 174p)
JODAMI
8 b.g. Crash Course – Masterstown Lucy (Bargello)
Owner Mr J. N. Yeadon   Trainer P. Beaumont

BEST TWO-MILE CHASER (RATED AT 161?)
KATABATIC
10 br.g. Strong Gale – Garravogue (Giolla Mear)
Owner Pell-mell Partners   Trainer A. Turnell

BEST NOVICE CHASER (RATED AT 156)
SYBILLIN
7 b.g. Henbit – Tea House (Sassafras)
Owner Marquesa de Moratalla   Trainer J. FitzGerald

BEST HUNTER CHASER (RATED AT 122p)
DOUBLE SILK
9 b.g. Dubassof – Yellow Silk (Counsel)
Owner Mr R. C. Wilkins   Trainer R. C. Wilkins

BEST TWO-MILE HURDLER (RATED AT 170)
MIGHTY MOGUL
6 ch.g. Good Thyne – Deep Shine (Deep Run)
Owner Mrs Shirley Robins   Trainer D. Nicholson

BEST STAYING HURDLER (RATED AT 161)
SWEET DUKE (FR)
6 b.g. Iron Duke – Sweet Virginia (Tapioca II)
Owner Mr A. Mavrou   Trainer N. Twiston-Davies

BEST NOVICE HURDLER (RATED AT 150P)
MONTELADO
6 b.g. Montelimar – Misippus (Green God)
Owner Mr F. O. Hannon   Trainer P. J. Flynn

BEST JUVENILE HURDLER (RATED AT 141p)
SHAWIYA (IRE)
4 b.f. Lashkari – Shaiyra (Relko)
Owner Miss G. Maher   Trainer M. O'Brien

THE TIMEFORM
TOP CHASERS AND HURDLERS

Here are listed the 'Top 100' Chasers and Hurdlers in the annual

Chasers

174p	Jodami
172	Rushing Wild
171	The Fellow
166	Royal Athlete
165	Docklands Express
163	Remittance Man
163	Run For Free
163	Ucello II
161p	Sibton Abbey
161?	Katabatic
161	Chatam
160	Another Coral
160	Ubu III
159?	Waterloo Boy
157	Twin Oaks
156	Cool Ground
156	Party Politics
156	Pat's Jester
156	Sybillin
155	Blazing Walker
154p	Cab On Target
154?	Arctic Call
154	Cahervillahow
154	Gold Options
153	Garamycin
153	General Idea
153	Kings Fountain
153	Tipping Tim
152p	Travado
152	Garrison Savannah
152	Miinnehoma
151	Bradbury Star
151	Sabin du Loir
151	Wonder Man
150?	Brown Windsor
150	The Illywhacker
149	Romany King
149	Second Schedual
149	Young Hustler
149	Zeta's Lad
148	Captain Dibble
148	Deep Sensation
148	Topsham Bay
147?	Wingspan
147§	Cyphrate
147	Givus A Buck
147	Ryde Again
145p	Black Humour
145?	Bonanza Boy
145	Cherrykino
145	Uncle Ernie
144p	General Pershing
144p	Viking Flagship
144	Cavvies Clown
144	Classical Charm
144	Mutare
143p	Country Member
143p	Storm Alert
143§	Henry Mann

143	Armagret
143	Beech Road
143d	Joyful Noise
143	Space Fair
142p	Barton Bank
142§	Espy
142	Ebony Jane
142	River Tarquin
141?	Redundant Pal
141	Blitzkreig
141	King of The Lot
141	Last 'o' The Bunch
141	Moment of Truth
141	Tinryland
141	Young Benz
140	Riverside Boy
140	Soft Day
140	Young Pokey
139d	Clever Folly
139	Flashing Steel
139	Forest Sun
139	How's The Boss
138§	Clay County
138	Bishops Hall
138	Gambling Royal
138	Sure Metal
137p	Capability Brown
137p	Very Very Ordinary
137p	Wind Force
137?	Atlaal
137?	Esha Ness
137x	Boraceva
137	Belmount Captain
137	Danny Harrold
137	Gale Again
137d	Nos Na Gaoithe
136p	Cogent
136p	Dakyns Boy
136	Cushinstown
136	Whats The Crack
135p	Antonin
135?	Al Hashimi
135?	Ida's Delight
135	For The Grain
135	Freeline Finishing
135	Valiant Boy

Hurdlers

170	Mighty Mogul
169§	Morley Street
167	Granville Again
166	Royal Derbi
165§	Flown
165§	Ruling
165	Muse
164	Halkopous
164	Staunch Friend
161p	King Credo
161	Sweet Duke
160	Pragada

160	Ubu III
159p	Vintage Crop
159	Oh So Risky
158§	Burgoyne
157	Coulton
157	Mole Board
157	Shuil Ar Aghaidh
156	Baydon Star
156	Crystal Spirit
156	Sweet Glow
156	True Brave
156	Vagog
156	Valfinet
155	Jinxy Jack
154	Native Mission
153§	Tyrone Bridge
153	Flakey Dove
153	Lift And Load
152	Eyelid
151P	Spinning
151	Kribensis
150P	Montelado
150?	Lonesome Glory
149	Ambuscade
149	Better Times Ahead
149	Dee Ell
149	The Fellow
147	Duke of Monmouth
146	Ucello II
145p	Hawthorn Blaze
145	Balasani
145	Super Sense
144	Dara Doone
144	Jungle Knife
143p	Belvederian
143	Beech Road
142?	Boro Eight
142	Absalom's Lady
142	Al Mutahm
142	Castle Secret
142	The Widget Man
141p	Shawiya
141p	Tiananmen Square
141	Deb's Ball
141	Grace Card
140p	Bold Boss
140p	Lord Relic
140	Bayrouge
140	Bitofabanter
140	Bollin William
140	Boscean Chieftain
140	Rodeo Star
139	Athy Spirit
139	Jopanini
139	Kilcash
138p	Hebridean
138	Bucks-Choice
138	Lady Olein
137p	Amazon Express
137p	Brackenfield
137p	Fissure Seal

16

137	Capability Brown	136p	Roll A Dollar	135p	Majed
137	Glen Lochan	136p	Simpson	135	Beachy Head
137	Novello Allegro	136p	Winter Squall	135	Gaelstrom
137	Princess Casilia	136?	One More Dream	135	Gallateen
137	Satin Lover	136	Cardinal Red	135	Major Bugler
137	Second Schedual	136	Cock Cockburn	135	Olympian
136p	Avro Anson	136	Marlin Dancer	135	Peanuts Pet
136p	High Alltitude	136	Mudahim	134p	Giventime
136p	High Baron	136	Muir Station	134?	Big Matt

THE TIMEFORM TOP NOVICES, JUVENILES AND HUNTER CHASERS

Here are listed the 'Top 20' Novice Hurdlers, Novice Chasers, Juvenile Hurdlers and Hunter Chasers

Novice Hurdlers

150P	Montelado
143p	Belvederian
142?	Boro Eight
141p	Tiananmen Square
140p	Lord Relic
140	Bayrouge
138p	Hebridean
138	Bucks-Choice
137p	Brackenfield
137p	Fissure Seal
137	Glen Lochan
137	Princess Casilia
137	Satin Lover
136p	High Alltitude
136p	Roll A Dollar
136p	Winter Squall
136	Cardinal Red
136	Muir Station
135p	Majed
135	Gaelstrom

Juvenile Hurdlers

141p	Shawiya
140p	Bold Boss
137p	Amazon Express
135	Major Bugler
134	Judicial Field
132p	Lemon's Mill
132p	Titled Dancer
132	Dare To Dream
131p	Beauchamp Grace
131p	Nadjati
130p	Indian Quest
130	Autumn Gorse
130	Dominant Serenade
129p	Kiveton Tycoon
129	Storm Dust
128p	Cariboo Gold
128	Bo Knows Best
128	Loshian
127	Her Honour
126	Clurican
126	Ivor's Flutter
126	Mohana
126	Top Spin

Novice Chasers

156	Sybillin
154p	Cab On Target
152p	Travado
151	Wonder Man
149	Young Hustler
144p	Viking Flagship
142p	Barton Bank
140	Soft Day
139	Flashing Steel
139	Forest Sun
139	How's The Boss
137p	Capability Brown
137?	Atlaal
136p	Cogent
136p	Dakyns Boy
135p	Antonin
135	Valiant Boy
134p	Flashthecash
133	Superior Finish
132	Deep Heritage
132	Gay Ruffian

Hunter Chasers

122p	Double Silk
120p	Radical Views
117p	Sheer Jest
117	Assaglawi
117	Generals Boy
117	Moorcroft Boy
116p	Kerry Orchid
116	Dark Dawn
116	Mount Argus
116	Once Stung
115	Davy Blake
114 +	Teaplanter
114	Royle Speedmaster
112	Tenesaint
111	Gold Shot
111	No Escort
111	Tartan Trix
110P	Elegant Lord
110	Celtic Leisure
110	Fifth Amendment
110	Mandraki Shuffle
110	The Red One

EXPLANATORY NOTES

The aim of this annual and of Timeform (Chasing Edition) is to supply accurate information as to the merit and the racing character of every horse racing over the sticks, and to present it in a form in which it may be of the greatest practical use in assessing the prospects of the runners in a race.

TIMEFORM RATINGS

The merit of each horse is given as a rating, in pounds, the rating being the number of pounds which the horse's performances would entitle it to receive in a universal handicap embracing all horses worth a rating in training, in which the ratings range from around 175 (12st 7lb) for the very best horses down to around 55 for the worst horses. A horse rated at 155 is thus approximately 20 lb below the top of the handicap; and a horse rated at 168 is to be regarded as 4 lb better than another rated at 164. Ratings preceded by a c relate to steeplechasing, the others, in a lighter type-face, to hurdle racing.

THE LEVEL OF THE RATINGS

At the close of each season all the horses that have raced are re-handicapped from scratch, and each horse's rating is revised. It is also necessary to adjust the general level of the handicap, so that the mean of all the ratings is kept at the same standard level from year to year. This explains why, in this book, the ratings are, in general, different from those in the final issue of the 1992/93 Timeform Chasing series.

USING THE RATINGS

In using Timeform to assess the prospects of the various runners in any race, the first proceeding is to find out which of them are most favoured by the weights by using the ratings to evaluate the chances of all the runners purely on a handicap basis. This involves adjusting each horse's rating to take into account its age and actual weight it has to carry. The second proceeding is to examine the comments on the horses with a view to considering what factors, other than weight, might also affect the outcome of the race.

Steeplechase ratings, preceded by c, should not be confused with hurdle ratings. A steeplechase rating should never be used to assess the chance of a horse in a hurdle race, and hurdle ratings should never be used when the race being dealt with is a steeplechase. Where a horse has raced over fences and also over hurdles its ratings as a chaser and hurdler are printed one above the other, the steeplechase rating (c) being placed above the hurdle rating. Thus with

REGALITY c**157**
                                                                    143

the top figure, 157, is the rating to be used in steeplechases, and the one below, 143, is for use only in hurdle races. The procedure for making age and weight adjustments to the ratings (i.e. for the calculation of Race Ratings) is as follows:-

A.   Horses of the Same Age

If the horses all carry the same weight there are no adjustments to be made, and the horses with the highest ratings have the best chances. If the horses carry different weights, jot down their ratings, and to the rating of each horse add one point for every pound the horse is set to carry less than 12st 7lb, or subtract one point for every pound it has to carry more than 12st 7lb. When the ratings have been adjusted in this way the highest resultant figure indicates the horse with the best chance at the weights.

Example (any distance: any month of the season)

Teucer	5 yrs (11-0) . .	Rating 140 . .	add 21	161
Kiowa	5 yrs (10-7) . .	Rating 125 . .	add 28	153
Golden Age	5 yrs (10-4) . .	Rating 120 . .	add 31	151

Teucer has the best chance, and Golden Age the worst

B.   Horses of Different Ages

In this case reference must be made to the Age, Weight and Distance Table. This is printed on the page facing the front cover and also on the bookmark. Use the Table for steeplechasers and hurdlers alike. Treat each horse separately, and compare the weight it has to carry with the weight prescribed for it in the Table, according to the age of the horse, the distance of the race and the month of the year. Then, add one point to the rating for each pound the horse has to carry less than the weight given in the Table: or, subtract one point from the rating for every pound it has to carry more than the weight prescribed by the table. The highest resultant figure indicates the horse most favoured by the weights.

Example (2¾m steeplechase in January)

(Table Weights: 8-y-o 12-7; 7-y-o 12-7; 5-y-o 12-6)

Black Book	8 yrs (12-8) . .	Rating 140 . .	subtract 1 . .	139
Pressman	7 yrs (12-3) . .	Rating 132 . .	add 4	136
Copyright	5 yrs (12-7) . .	Rating 150 . .	subtract 1 . .	149

Copyright has the best chance, and Pressman the worst

Example (3m hurdle race in March)

(Table Weights: 9-y-o 12-7; 5-y-o 12-7; 4-y-o 11-11)

Oxer	9 yrs (10-12) . .	Rating 110 . .	add 23	133
Clairval	5 yrs (10-7) . .	Rating 119 . .	add 28	147
Gallette	4 yrs (10-7) . .	Rating 128 . .	add 18	146

Clairval has the best chance, and Oxer the worst

JOCKEYSHIP AND RIDERS' ALLOWANCES

There is just one further point that arises in evaluating the chances of the horse on the basis of their ratings: the question of jockeyship in general, and riders' allowances in particular. The allowance which may be claimed by a rider is given to enable such riders to obtain race-riding experience against experienced jockeys. For the purposes of rating calculations it should, in general, be assumed that the allowance the rider is able to claim (3lb, 5lb or 7lb) is nullified by his or her inexperience. Therefore, *the weight adjustment to the ratings should be calculated on the weight allotted by the handicapper, or determined by the conditions of the race,* and no extra addition should be made to a rating because the horse's rider claims an allowance.

The above is the general routine procedure. But of course there is no reason why the quality of jockeyship should not be taken into account in assessing the chances of horses in a race. Quite the contrary. Nobody would question that the jockeyship of a first-class rider is worth a pound or two, and occasionally a claiming rider comes along who is riding quite as well as the average jockey long before losing the right to claim. It should be noted, however, that if a horse is regularly ridden by a claimer the fact will have been taken into account by the Timeform handicapper when assessing it.

WEIGHING UP A RACE

The ratings tell you which horses in a particular race are most favoured by the weights; but complete analysis demands that the racing character of each horse, as set out in the commentary upon it, is also studied carefully to see if there is any reason why the horse might be expected not to run up to its rating. It counts for little that a horse is thrown in at the weights if it has no pretensions whatever to staying the distance, or is unable to act on the prevailing going.

These two matters, suitability of distance and going, are, no doubt, the most important points to be considered. But there are others. For example, the ability of a horse to accommodate itself to the conformation of the track. Then there is the matter of pace versus stamina: as between two stayers of equal merit, racing over a distance suitable to both, firm going, or a small field with the prospect of a slowly-run race, would favour the one with the better pace and acceleration, whereas dead or soft going, or a big field with the prospect of a strong gallop throughout the race, would favour the sounder stayer. There is also the matter of the horse's ability and dependability as a jumper and of its temperament: nobody would be in a hurry to take a short price about a horse with whom it is always an even chance whether it will get round or not, or whether it will consent to race.

A few minutes spent checking up on these matters in the commentaries upon the horses concerned will sometimes put a very different complexion on a race from that which is put upon it by the ratings alone. We repeat, therefore, that the correct way to use Timeform, or this annual volume, in the analysis of individual races is, first to use the ratings to find out which horses are most favoured by the weights, and second, to check through the comments on the horses to see what factors other than weight might also affect the outcome of the race.

Incidentally, in setting out the various characteristics, requirements and peculiarities of each horse in the commentary upon him, we have always expressed ourselves in as critical a manner as possible, endeavouring to say just as much, and no whit more than the facts seem to warrant. Where there are clear indications, and definite conclusions can be drawn with fair certainty, we have drawn them: if it is a matter of probability or possibility we have put it that way, being careful not to say the one when we mean the other; and where real conclusions are not to be drawn, we have been content to state the facts. Furthermore, when we say that a horse *may not* be suited by hard going, we do not expect the reader to treat it as though we had said that the horse *is not* suited by hard going. In short, both in our thinking and in the setting out of our views we have aimed at precision.

THE FORM SUMMARIES

The form summaries enclosed in the brackets list each horse's performances in sequence, and show three items of information for each outing. The race distance is given in furlongs, steeplechase form figures are prefixed by the letter 'c' and N.H. Flat race form figures by the letter 'F', the others relating to form over hurdles, that on an all-weather surface being prefixed by the letter 'a'. Runs in N.H. Flat races are not recorded in the ratings.

The going is symbolised as follows: h = hard or very firm; f = firm (turf) or fast (all-weather); m = on the firm side of good; g = good (turf) or standard (all-weather); d = dead, or on the soft side of good; s = soft, sticky or holding (turf) or slow (all-weather); v = heavy, very heavy or very holding.

Placings are indicated, up to sixth place, by the use of superior figures, an asterisk being used to denote a win; and superior letters are used to convey what happened to the horse during the race: F = fell (F³ denotes remounted and finished third); pu = pulled up; ur = unseated rider; bd = brought down; r = refused; su = slipped up; ro = ran out; co = carried out.

Thus, [1992/3 F16g 16s* c18g^pu 16f² c20v^F] states that in the 1992/93 jumping season the horse ran five times; unplaced in a 2m N.H. Flat race on good going, winning a 2m hurdle race on soft going, being pulled up in a 2¼m steeplechase on good going, running second in a 2m hurdle race on firm going and falling in a 2½m steeplechase on heavy going; all races on turf.

Where sale prices are given they are in guineas unless otherwise stated. The prefix IR denotes Irish guineas.

THE RATING SYMBOLS

The following symbols, attached to the ratings, are to be interpreted as stated:-

p   the horse is likely to make more than normal progress and to improve on its rating.

P   there is convincing evidence, or, to say the least, a very strong presumption that the horse is capable of form much better than it has so far displayed.

+   the horse's form may be rather better than we have rated it.

d   the horse appears to have deteriorated, and might no longer be capable of running to the rating given.

§   a horse who is unreliable, either for temperamental or for other reasons; one who may run up to its rating on occasions, but cannot be trusted to do so.

§§   an arrant rogue or thorough jade; so temperamentally unsatisfactory as to be not worth a rating.

x   moderate or sketchy jumper.

xx   a very bad jumper, so bad as to be not worth a rating.

?   the horse's rating is suspect. If used without a rating the symbol implies that the horse's merit is impossible to assess with confidence, or that the horse is out of form.

CHASERS & HURDLERS 1992/93

Horse	Commentary	Rating

A A BAMBA 4 b.f. Slip Anchor – Enchanting Dancer (FR) (Nijinsky (CAN)) [1992/3 17m] half-sister to one-time useful hurdler and winning chaser Folk Dance (by Alias Smith): modest staying handicapper on Flat: tailed off in juvenile hurdle in September: sold 3,200 gns Doncaster January Sales. *N. A. Callaghan*

–

AAH JIM BOY 10 ch.g. Riboboy (USA) – Parrot Fashion (Pieces of Eight) [1992/3 c21f4] sturdy gelding: novice hurdler: fair pointer: remote fourth in novice hunter chase in May. *J. Sprake*

c72
–

AAHSAYLAD 7 b.h. Ardross – Madam Slaney (Prince Tenderfoot (USA)) [1992/3 22v* 20d* 24spu 24d* 22g* 27d2] sturdy horse: tough and quite useful stayer on Flat: sold out of F. Lee's stable 20,000 gns Newmarket Autumn Sales: successful in novice hurdles at Worcester, Newcastle (handicap), Hexham and Ayr (handicap) after turn of year, showing fairly useful form: below best for amateur final outing: stays well: acts on heavy ground: blinkered last 3 starts. *J. White*

124

AAL EL AAL 6 br.h. High Top – Last Card (USA) (Full Out (USA)) [1992/3 F14d* 16d2] leggy horse: won NH Flat race at Perth in September: second in novice hurdle at Wincanton following month: sold 2,000 gns Ascot November Sales. *P. J. Hobbs*

88

AARDVARK 7 ch.g. On Your Mark – Vaguely Jade (Corvaro (USA)) [1992/3 17d 16g a16gpu 16mF 16fpu] close-coupled gelding: poor 2m novice hurdler: pulled up lame final outing (blinkered). *N. Tinkler*

73

ABBENOIR 11 br.g. Radical – White Abbess (Atlas) [1992/3 21d c27d5 c21s5 c26spu c24s6 c17d5 c27d4] winning hurdler/chaser: poor form in 1992/3: stays 3m: acts on soft going and good to firm: blinkered once. *Mrs M. A. Kendall*

c75
–

ABBEY'S LAST MARCH 4 b.f. Marching On – Abbey Rose (Lorenzaccio) [1992/3 F12d] leggy filly: half-sister to 2 minor winners by Cawston's Clown: dam second over 7f and 1m at 2 yrs: well beaten in NH Flat race at Windsor in February: yet to race over hurdles. *A. W. Jones*

ABBOT OF FURNESS 9 b.g. The Parson – Chestnut Fire (Deep Run) [1992/3 16s 21g3 20g* 22s* 16s3 20s* 21s4 17sF 21s* 17s3 17g 22d] leggy, workmanlike gelding: fairly useful chaser in 1991/2: useful hurdler: won handicaps at Ayr, Haydock and Newcastle in first half of season: effective at 2m and stays 2¾m: acts well with give in the ground: makes the odd bad mistake over fences: usually forces pace. *G. Richards*

c–
134

ABBOTSHAM 8 b.g. Ardross – Lucy Platter (FR) (Record Token) [1992/3 c27m2 c24f2] angular gelding: one-time useful hunter chaser: modest form when runner-up in small fields of handicappers in 1992/3: stays well: acts on any going: races up with pace: not a fluent jumper. *O. J. Carter*

c99
–

ABDICATOR 13 ch.g. Levanter – Saffron Princess (Thriller) [1992/3 c21m3] big, deep-girthed gelding: staying handicap chaser: very lightly raced in recent seasons: tailed off in August: sketchy jumper. *L. Lungo*

c–

ABELONI 4 ch.g. Absalom – Agreloui (Tower Walk) [1992/3 16g6 16s4 16g2 16s 17d5 18m4 17d 17s6] compact, sturdy gelding: modest and inconsistent at around 1m on Flat: sold out of J. Glover's stable 2,600 gns Doncaster November Sales: modest juvenile hurdler: well below form last 5 starts: not sure to stay much beyond 2¼m: acts on soft ground. *W. Williams*

89

ABERCROMBY CHIEF 8 br.g. Buckskin (FR) – Free For Ever (Little Buskins) [1992/3 c26spu c24gF3 c28d5 c24d3 c26g5 c32d4 c24d5 c33gpu c24dpu] big, leggy, workmanlike gelding: modest handicap chaser: suited by test of stamina: acts on heavy going: blinkered last 2 starts: sketchy jumper. *J. K. M. Oliver*

c90
–

ABERCROMBY COMET 8 br.g. Strong Gale – Star-Pit (Queen's Hussar) [1992/3 18g c17g4 c17mF3 c21dpu c16s5 c16mF c22mpu] lengthy gelding: poor novice hurdler/chaser: trained until after third start by K. Oliver: only form at around 2m on good ground: poor jumper of fences. *B. Mactaggart*

c80 x
–

ABERFOYLE (IRE) 5 b.g. Vision (USA) – Princess John (Run The Gantlet (USA)) [1992/3 a22g* a18g4 a24g5] leggy, sparely-made gelding: modest handicap hurdler: has gained 3 of his 4 wins at Lingfield, won there in January: stays 2¾m: acts on good to firm ground and both all-weather surfaces. *Miss Gay Kelleway*

94

ABERNETHY PEARL 7 gr.m. Warpath – Verona Queen (Majestic Streak) [1992/3 27dpu] pulled up in 2 points and a novice hurdle: dead. *G. R. Dun*

–

ABEROY 14 ch.g. Abercorn – Maroyal (Rage Royal) [1992/3 22d 17m4 c24g4 c18d5 a18g] sturdy, workmanlike gelding: carries condition: poor hurdler/chaser nowadays: stays 3¼m: yet to show his form on very soft ground, acts on any other. *M. J. Ryan*

c–
74

ABITBIZARRE 7 ch.g. Sunyboy – Minor Furlong (Native Bazaar) [1992/3 c22g5 c21m6] leggy gelding: poor novice hurdler/chaser: no form in 1992/3: stays 2½m: acts on heavy ground. *M. Bloom*

c–
–

ABITMORFUN 7 ch.g. Baron Blakeney – Mary Mile (Athenius) [1992/3 c21g4 c26gpu] fair pointer: fourth at Uttoxeter, better effort in hunter chases in May. *S. A. Brookshaw*

c76
–

ABLE LEADER 7 b.g. Beldale Flutter (USA) – Buckham Barn (Lorenzaccio) [1992/3 17s6] robust gelding: winning hurdler: best form at up to 2¼m: acts on soft going: blinkered last 3 starts: looked ungenuine only start in 1992/3 (October). *M. C. Pipe*

– §

ABLE PLAYER (USA) 6 b. or br.g. Solford (USA) – Grecian Snow (CAN) (Snow Knight) [1992/3 16d4 16m* 16g* 17g6 20g* 21s2 16gF 20g] leggy gelding: fairly useful handicap hurdler: won at Southwell, Wetherby (twice) and Edinburgh in first half of season (sold out of C. Thornton's stable 32,000 gns Doncaster November Sales after fifth outing): not raced after January: effective at 2m and stays 21f: acts on good to firm and soft ground. *Mrs S. A. Bramall*

123

ABNEGATION 8 b.g. Abednego – Autumn Magic (Arctic Slave) [1992/3 17g3 22v* 25s2 24spu 25d2 20g5 21m4] close-coupled gelding: fairly useful handicap hurdler: won at Cheltenham in December: ran creditably when in frame afterwards: well suited by a test of stamina: acts on good to firm and heavy ground. *J. H. Johnson*

126

ABSAILOR 9 b.g. Kambalda – Tarsilogue (Tarqogan) [1992/3 c16m3 c25g2 c21dpu c21d2 c25gpu c24g5 c20g c24d5 c26g3 c21g5 c21g c24dpu c20f2 c22v] tall, lengthy gelding: modest handicap chaser: stays 25f: acts on firm and dead ground: occasionally blinkered or visored: unenthusiastic and none too consistent. *Mrs S. C. Bradburne*

c89 §
–

ABSALOM'S LADY 5 gr.m. Absalom – High Point Lady (CAN) (Knightly Dawn (USA)) [1992/3 17s²] leggy, unfurnished mare: useful hurdler: good second in handicap at Chepstow in October: suited by testing conditions at around 2m and should stay beyond 19f: acts on soft going. *G. B. Balding*   142

ABSENT RELATIVE 5 ch.m. Absalom – Relatively Smart (Great Nephew) [1992/3 17m² 17m³ 18d* 16g⁴ a16g² a20g* a20g³ 16f* 18g* 17g²] sparely-made mare: fairly useful handicap hurdler: won at Fontwell early in season and Lingfield, Windsor and Fontwell in second half: effective at 2m to 2½m: probably acts on any ground: genuine and consistent. *Miss B. Sanders*   120

ABSOLATUM 6 ro.g. Absalom – Omnia (Hill Clown (USA)) [1992/3 24gᵖᵘ] compact gelding: winning pointer: no sign of ability over hurdles. *P. M. Rich*   –

ABSOLUTELY RIGHT 5 ch.g. Absalom – Sun Worshipper (Sun Prince) [1992/3 16v⁵ 22vᵖᵘ 26sᵖᵘ 21gᵖᵘ] neat gelding: half-brother to winning hurdler See The Light (by Relkino): poor middle-distance performer on Flat: no form over hurdles. *J. White*   –

ABSOLUTLEY FOXED 4 gr.f. Absalom – May Fox (Healaugh Fox) [1992/3 16vᵖᵘ] neat filly: half-sister to winning 2¾m hurdler Moorland Lady (by Swing Easy): poor maiden on Flat: showed nothing in January on hurdling debut. *B. A. McMahon*   –

ABU MUSLAB 9 b. or br.g. Ile de Bourbon (USA) – Eastern Shore (Sun Prince) [1992/3 20d 16g⁴ c17m² c18g³ c17g² c17mᵘʳ c18m] sturdy gelding: modest hurdler/novice chaser: probably stays 2½m: acts on good to firm going and equitrack. *G. F. Edwards*   c84 97

ACE OF DIAMONDS 7 ch.m. Spur On – Seven Diamonds (Turnpike) [1992/3 22f] smallish mare: poor hurdler: usually runs in sellers: tailed off in September: stays 2½m: acts on any turf going (ran moderately on fibresand). *F. S. Storey*   –

ACE OF SPIES 12 b.g. He Loves Me – Belle Bergere (Faberge II) [1992/3 22g c24dᵖᵘ c24g³ c20sᵖᵘ c20s⁵ c25s⁵ c20d⁵ c29gᵖᵘ c34dᵖᵘ] tall, leggy gelding: fairly useful staying chaser in 1991/2: fair form at best in 1992/3, last 2 starts in Britain: tried blinkered and visored. *Mrs Gill E. Jones, Ireland*   c106 –

ACE REPORTER 4 b.f. Double Schwartz – Strapless (Bustino) [1992/3 16g] modest maiden, stays 1¼m, on Flat: visored, tailed off in novice hurdle at Hexham in March. *B. Beasley*   –

ACERTAINHIT 9 b.g. Ascendant – Hit The Button (Red Alert) [1992/3 c21g⁴ c21m² c25g³ c25m⁴] compact gelding: poor novice chaser: stays 3m: acts on good to firm ground: sketchy jumper. *S. R. Bowring*   c76

ACHELOUS 6 b.g. Dominion – Siren Sound (Manado) [1992/3 16s²] small gelding: moderate middle-distance performer on Flat: second in seller at Leicester in February on hurdling debut. *J. A. Glover*   80

ACHIEVED AMBITION (IRE) 5 gr.g. Derring Rose – In Paris (Last Fandango) [1992/3 F16d F17m] rangy gelding: has scope: first foal: dam unraced half-sister to useful hurdler Boardmans Crown: mid-division in NH Flat races in February and April: yet to race over hurdles or fences. *J. A. C. Edwards*   –

ACHILTIBUIE 9 b.g. Roscoe Blake – Gorgeous Gertie (Harwell) [1992/3 c16g³ c18mᵖᵘ c19g³ c16d⁵] leggy, good-topped gelding: poor handicap chaser: not raced after November: stays 2½m: best on a sound surface. *F. J. Yardley*   c81 –

ACKERS WOOD 5 b.g. Castle Keep – Gloria Maremmana (King Emperor (USA)) [1992/3 16f 16m 16d a16gᵖᵘ] of little account on Flat nowadays: bad novice hurdler: headstrong: sold 1,200 gns Ascot February Sales. *K. R. Burke*   63

ACQUISITION 6 b.g. Petorius – Steady The Buffs (Balidar) [1992/3 18g^{pu} 17d 16g 17m 17d] compact, good-bodied gelding: of little account on Flat nowadays: no sign of ability over hurdles: sold 1,000 gns Doncaster June Sales. *S. G. Payne* –

ACRE HILL 9 gr.g. Alias Smith (USA) – Acolyte (Roan Rocket) [1992/3 c124 c17g² c16g* c17d³ c17m c21g² c22m⁵] strong, workmanlike gelding: carries – condition: fairly useful handicap chaser: won at Kempton in October: off course all winter, creditable second at Southwell in May: barely stays 21f: seems suited by a sound surface: has broken blood vessels. *N. J. Henderson*

ACROSS THE CARD 5 b.g. Lir – Cornish Susie (Fair Season) [1992/3 18f² 20g² 20m³ 18g^{wd} 22d² 22s 23v 20g 22m³ 22g⁵ 24f] plain, rather 73 sparely-made gelding: poor novice hurdler: stays 2¾m: acts on firm and dead going: visored first 2 outings 1992/3, blinkered last two. *A. Moore*

ACROSS THE LAKE 9 b.g. Over The River (FR) – Golden Highway c89 (Royal Highway) [1992/3 c25d⁴ c25m³] angular, leggy gelding: winning – hurdler: only form in steeplechases when fourth in hunter chase at Kelso in April: stays well: best form with give in the ground. *Mrs A. L. Farrell*

ACROW LINE 8 b.g. Capricorn Line – Miss Acrow (Comedy Star (USA)) [1992/3 21v 24s 22m 26m⁴ 24s² 25g³ 26v*] leggy, close-coupled gelding: 122 fairly useful handicap hurdler: ran well in the spring and improved effort when winning at Cartmel in May: suited by good test of stamina: acts on good to firm ground, particularly well on heavy: blinkered once: runs in snatches. *D. Burchell*

ACT OF PARLIAMENT (IRE) 5 br.g. Parliament – That's Show Biz (The Parson) [1992/3 F17f⁵] first foal: dam won at around 2m over hurdles and fences in Ireland: favourite, fifth of 15 in NH Flat race at Hereford in May: yet to race over hurdles or fences. *K. C. Bailey*

ACT OF UNION (IRE) 4 b.c. Green Desert (USA) – Carnival Dance (Welsh Pageant) [1992/3 a16g^{pu} 17d^{pu} 17d^{pu} 17m^{pu}] lengthy colt: half- – brother to winning hurdler Safe (by Kris): fair 6f and 7f winner at best: no sign of ability over hurdles: blinkered last 2 outings. *D. J. Bell*

ADAJOKE 4 b.g. Sulaafah (USA) – Our Horizon (Skyliner) [1992/3 F16g] first foal: dam, disqualified 7f seller winner, no form over hurdles: well beaten in NH Flat race at Chepstow in June: yet to race over hurdles. *Mrs A. Knight*

ADANAR (USA) 6 gr.g. Irish River (FR) – Adjanada (Nishapour (FR)) [1992/3 16f] close-coupled gelding: of little account: blinkered once. *N. A.* – *Twiston-Davies*

ADDINGTON BOY (IRE) 5 br.g. Callernish – Ballaroe Bar (Bargello) [1992/3 F16d⁴] fifth foal: dam unraced half-sister to several winning jumpers: fourth in NH Flat race at Haydock in February: yet to race over hurdles or fences. *G. Richards*

ADDINGTON LAD 8 b.g. Le Moss – Santimwen (Cassim) [1992/3 21s⁴ 21s 17f] leggy, lengthy gelding: hobdayed: poor novice hurdler nowadays: 78 stays 3m: acts on soft ground. *G. Richards*

ADEN APOLLO 12 ch.g. Apollo Eight – Fuchsia Cottage (Ossian II) c– [1992/3 c24g^{pu} c16g⁵ c20g^{pu} c25s c25g⁵] tall gelding: winning chaser: no – form since 1990/1: blinkered once. *T. Craig*

ADMINISTER 5 b.m. Damister (USA) – Apply (Kings Lake (USA)) [1992/3 18m^{pu}] small, angular mare: one-time fair middle-distance – performer on Flat: showed nothing in seller in March on hurdling debut. *L. J. Codd*

ADMIRAL GRAY (NZ) 6 gr.g. Captain Jason (NZ) – Larksleve (NZ) (Grey Bird (NZ)) [1992/3 F17f] New Zealand-bred gelding: behind in NH Flat race at Hereford in May: yet to race over hurdles or fences. *Mrs J. R. Renfree-Barons*

ADMIRALS ALL 10 br.g. Julio Mariner – Double Finesse (Double c– Jump) [1992/3 c21s⁵ c21d c23m^{pu} c24g⁴] leggy, good-topped gelding: –

one-time fair hurdler/chaser: lightly raced in recent years: no form, including in hunter chases, in 1992/3: blinkered last outing. *P. T. Walwyn*

ADMIRAL'S LEAP 9 ch.g. Quayside – Sailor's Will (Laurence O) [1992/3 c26s4 c24spu c24vpu c26s4 c25gpu] workmanlike gelding: handicap chaser: generally ran poorly in 1992/3: stays well: acts on heavy going and good to firm: blinkered nowadays: irresolute. *T. Thomson Jones*

c84 §
– §

ADMIRAL'S MISTRESS (IRE) 5 ch.m. Sexton Blake – Little Cygnet (My Swanee) [1992/3 17d 16v6 a18g6 a18g2] lengthy, unfurnished mare: fifth foal: dam, placed in NH Flat race and over hurdles in Ireland, is half-sister to smart jumpers Royal Dipper and Henry Mann: poor novice hurdler: well beaten last 2 outings: will stay at least 2½m. *P. J. Makin*

72

ADMIRALS SECRET (USA) 4 ch.c. Secreto (USA) – Noble Mistress (USA) (Vaguely Noble) [1992/3 17g3 16g3] strong colt: fair form at up to 1½m on Flat: third in juvenile hurdles at Huntingdon (better effort) in February and Worcester in March: jumps none too fluently. *C. F. Wall*

101

ADMIRALTY WAY 7 b.g. Petorius – Captive Flower (Manacle) [1992/3 17g4 16d4 a16g* 17d* 16d3 17s4 17g* 16f 17g5 17f] leggy gelding: much improved after joining present trainer (trained first 2 outings by R. Brotherton), winning handicap at Southwell, novice event at Hereford and novice handicap at Bangor in second half of season: excellent seventh in Swinton Handicap Hurdle at Haydock on eighth start: best at around 2m: acts on firm and dead ground, and fibresand: pulls hard and is held up. *W. Clay*

118

ADMIRAL VILLENEUVE 5 b.g. Top Ville – Great Tom (Great Nephew) [1992/3 21g] rangy, unfurnished gelding: seventh foal: half-brother to middle-distance winners Five Farthings (by Busted) and Warning Bell (by Bustino); dam, useful 2-y-o, half-sister to top 1981 2-y-o filly Circus Ring: showed promise when tenth of 15 finishers in novice hurdle at Newbury in February: sure to improve. *C. R. Egerton*

75 p

ADVENT LADY 6 ch.m. Kemal (FR) – Armantine (Brave Invader (USA)) [1992/3 c21gpu c21gpu] workmanlike mare: second foal: dam never ran: no sign of ability. *M. Sams*

c–
–

AEDEAN 4 ch.g. Risk Me (FR) – Finlandaise (FR) (Arctic Tern (USA)) [1992/3 17m5 18m3 17g2 17g5 17d* 17d* 16m6 17f2 17mF] leggy gelding: half-brother to winning Irish hurdler Ingmar (by Seymour Hicks): modest 6f/7f performer on Flat: won juvenile hurdle at Hereford in November: ran well both completed starts afterwards: yet to race beyond 2¼m: acts on firm and dead ground. *C. A. Horgan*

94

AFARISTOUN (FR) 9 b.g. Top Ville – Afrique (FR) (Exbury) [1992/3 17v 21v 22d 17spu 17f 17d] lengthy, sparely-made gelding: one-time useful 2m hurdler, has lost his form completely: second in novice chase in 1991/2: blinkered fifth outing: sold 1,800 gns Malvern June Sales. *J. A. C. Edwards*

c–
–

AFFA 4 b.f. Local Suitor (USA) – Pine (Supreme Sovereign) [1992/3 17d5 16spu] leggy, lengthy filly: half-sister to winning hurdler Flying (by Head For Heights): placed at up to 1¼m on Flat: no form in juvenile hurdles. *T. Thomson Jones*

–

AFFAIR OF HONOUR (IRE) 5 ch.g. Ahonoora – Good Relations (Be My Guest (USA)) [1992/3 21g 22d 24gpu] smallish, good-bodied gelding: fair hurdler at best: well beaten 1992/3: stays 2½m: acts on good to firm and dead ground. *J. J. O'Neill*

–

AFFIRMED'S DESTINY (USA) 4 b.g. Affirmed (USA) – Grand Destiny (USA) (Grand Central) [1992/3 a18g a16gF a18g 17fpu] sparely-made gelding: poor maiden on Flat (sold out of J. Dunlop's stable 3,700 gns Ascot November Sales): no form over hurdles. *W. Clay*

–

AFORE JANE 4 b.f. Lomond (USA) – Dabbiana (CAN) (Fappiano (USA)) [1992/3 18g2 17m2] half-sister to winning hurdler Alton Bay (by Al Nasr): modest staying maiden on Flat: poor form in early-season juvenile hurdles: will stay at least 2½m: blinkered second start. *G. Harwood*

81

A FORTIORI (IRE) 5 b.g. Denel (FR) – Sofa River (FR) (Riverton
(FR)) [1992/3 F17s* F16g] first foal: dam, ran 4 times on Flat in France,
half-sister to several French Flat winners, notably very smart sprinter Trio
Boy: won NH Flat race at Newbury in January: soundly beaten in similar
race at Kempton in February: yet to race over hurdles or fences. *M. C. Pipe*

AFRICAN SAFARI 9 b.g. Daring March – African Berry (African Sky)
[1992/3 c18s⁴ c16m⁵ c17d c16s⁶ a16g a16g⁶ c19m⁵] tall, rather dipped-backed
gelding: novice selling hurdler: winning chaser: ran poorly in 1992/3: stays
2½m: acts on good to firm going: blinkered once: looks reluctant nowadays.
Mrs S. J. Smith

c– §
– §

AFTER FOUR 9 gr.g. Roselier (FR) – Caherelly Cross (Royal Buck)
[1992/3 c26dᵖᵘ c24d⁵ c25d² c24d³ c24s] workmanlike gelding: modest
novice chaser: not raced after January: sold 4,200 gns Doncaster May Sales:
thorough stayer: probably acts on any going. *J. J. O'Neill*

c86

AFTERKELLY 8 b.g. Le Moss – Vamble (Vulgan) [1992/3 18g⁵ 24s²
c20sᵖᵘ 25sᵖᵘ 21sᵖᵘ] leggy, angular gelding: poor novice hurdler: no show on
chasing debut: suited by good test of stamina: acts on soft going. *A. J. K.
Dunn*

c–
83

AFTER THE FIRE 4 ch.g. Dunbeath (USA) – Cinderwench (Crooner)
[1992/3 18gᵖᵘ] no sign of ability on Flat (trained by A. Lee) or in
early-season juvenile hurdle. *J. White*

–

AFTER THE NUMBER 8 b.g. Le Moss – Fly Fuss (Little Buskins)
[1992/3 17m³ 16d 25dᵖᵘ 22d³] strong, close-coupled gelding: winning
hurdler: only form of 1992/3 when third in selling handicap at Sedgefield in
October: probably stays 2¾m. *M. J. Charles*

71

AFTICA 6 ch.g. Cardinal Flower – Maudie's Choice (Nebbiolo) [1992/3
F17d] third foal: dam poor Irish maiden: tailed off in NH Flat race at Ascot in
April: yet to race over hurdles or fences. *J. S. Moore*

AGARB (USA) 8 b.g. Key To The Mint (USA) – Knight's Promise (USA)
(Sir Ivor) [1992/3 c23s⁵ c25mᵖᵘ] good-bodied gelding: winning hurdler:
little promise in 2 starts over fences: sold 1,400 gns Ascot December Sales:
stays 25f: acts on dead ground: blinkered 3 times, including both outings
1992/3. *K. C. Bailey*

c–
–

A GENTLEMAN TWO 7 b.h. All Systems Go – Solar Honey (Roi
Soleil) [1992/3 16s³ 20s⁵ 16s 16m] neat horse: poor hurdler: stays 2½m:
probably acts on any going. *J. L. Eyre*

78

AGWA 4 b.c. Local Suitor (USA) – Meissarah (USA) (Silver Hawk (USA))
[1992/3 16d 16d⁶ 16gᶜᵒ 16d⁶ 16m 16m] small colt: brother to novice hurdler
Magic Secret: no form on Flat (sold out of B. Hanbury's stable 500 gns
Newmarket July Sales) or over hurdles: pulls hard. *J. C. Gillen*

–

AHERLOW 13 b.g. Brave Invader (USA) – Cant Pet (Cantab) [1992/3
c24fᵖᵘ c24f c26f⁴] big, rangy gelding: hunter chaser: sold 3,100 gns
Doncaster August Sales: no form in 1992/3: resold 1,100 gns Ascot 2nd June
Sales: needs a thorough test of stamina: acts on soft ground and good to
firm: occasionally blinkered. *G. L. Humphrey*

c–
–

AHERLOW GLEN 9 b.g. Le Bavard (FR) – Bit of Fashion (Master
Owen) [1992/3 c22f c33m⁴] rangy gelding: modest hunter chaser: stays long
distances: acts on good to firm and heavy ground: usually blinkered prior to
1992/3. *M. C. Pipe*

c84

AH JIM LAD 9 b.g. Jimsun – Gigante Rossa (Mount Hagen (FR)) [1992/3
c21dᵖᵘ c20g⁶ c20m³] leggy gelding: poor novice hurdler/chaser: stays
2¾m: acts on soft and good to firm ground. *A. Bailey*

c69
–

AIDE MEMOIRE (IRE) 4 b.f. Don't Forget Me – Pharjoy (FR) (Pharly
(FR)) [1992/3 16s 17d⁵ 16f] modest stayer on Flat: sold out of C. Booth's
stable 4,500 gns Doncaster November Sales: best effort over hurdles on
second start. *Mrs B. K. Broad*

82

AIOLI 7 b.m. Tyrnavos – Coco de Mer (Homing) [1992/3 16g 26dᵖᵘ 21vᵖᵘ
a22g⁴] workmanlike mare: selling hurdler: lightly raced in recent seasons,

71

and first form for long time when fourth at Southwell in January: stays 2¾m: acts on soft going, probably on fibresand. *R. G. Brazington*

AIR BROKER (NZ)   12 b.g. Oakville – Sweet Canyon (NZ) (Headland II) [1992/3 c26m² c23g] small gelding: hunter chaser nowadays: second at Folkestone in May: suited by 3m and more: acts on any going. *Mrs S. Clarke* — c90 —

AIR COMMANDER   8 br.g. Strong Gale – Southern Slave (Arctic Slave) [1992/3 c17m* c16mᵘʳ c16g⁴ c18m* c21g² c17d⁶ c18mᵖᵘ a18g⁶ c18d² c20f* c20f* c20mᶠ c17m c18g⁴] angular, light-bodied gelding: modest chaser: won handicaps at Newton Abbot (seller, sold out of R. Buckler's stable 8,400 gns) and Stratford early in season and Doncaster (novices) and Stratford in March: effective at 2m and stays 21f: acts on firm and dead ground: tends to hang left: blinkered once. *Mrs P. M. Joynes* — c96 —

AIR SMILES   6 gr.m. Scallywag – Carmarthen Honey (Eborneezer) [1992/3 16s³ 22d⁵] big, workmanlike mare: half-sister to 2 winning hurdlers, including top-class Cruising Altitude (by Celtic Cone): dam fairly useful though rather wayward pointer: poor form in novice hurdles: dead. *O. Sherwood* — 88

AIR SUPREMACY   4 b. or br.c. Skyliner – Runasca (Runnymede) [1992/3 17dᵖᵘ] well beaten at 2 yrs: pulled up in early-season juvenile hurdle. *S. Coathup* — —

AISHOLT   8 ch.m. Avocat – Bryophila (FR) (Breakspear II) [1992/3 22d³ 17s⁴ 20d 23dᵖᵘ c21dᵘʳ] rather sparely-made mare: poor novice hurdler: unseated rider second on chasing debut: stays 2¾m: acts on soft ground. *K. Bishop* — c– 65

AISLING OG   6 ch.m. Feelings (FR) – Wand of Youth (Mandamus) [1992/3 17g⁵ 16g 17s⁶ 16g 18d] lengthy, sparely-made mare: first foal: dam, lightly-raced half-sister to several winning jumpers, is daughter of very smart staying chaser Young Ash Leaf: poor novice hurdler: will be suited by further than around 2m: best efforts on good ground: blinkered fourth start. *R. McDonald* — 73

AIYBAK (IRE)   5 b.g. Lashkari – Aytana (FR) (Riverman (USA)) [1992/3 16sᵘʳ 17m] close-coupled, angular gelding: fairly useful novice hurdler: creditable eighth to Montelado in Trafalgar House Supreme Novices' Hurdle at Cheltenham in March: raced only at around 2m but will be suited by further: acts on good to firm ground: sometimes finds little under pressure. *D. K. Weld, Ireland* — 125

AKIMBO   6 ch.g. Bold Lad (IRE) – Western Gem (Sheshoon) [1992/3 20dᵖᵘ 21m⁴ 17vᵖᵘ] good-topped gelding: modest hurdler at best: no form in 1992/3: suited by sharp 2m: acts on firm going. *William Price* — —

AKRASH VALLEY   8 gr. or ro.g. Ardross – Haloom (Artaius (USA)) [1992/3 24dᵖᵘ 26g⁶ 24s⁵ c22s⁵] well-made gelding: poor novice hurdler: tailed off on chasing debut: stays 25f: acts on heavy going. *P. M. McEntee* — c– 71

AKURA (IRE)   4 b.f. Vision (USA) – Bebe Altesse (GER) (Alpenkonig (GER)) [1992/3 17m² 18m³ 17m 18m⁶] good-topped filly: modest performer at around 1m on Flat: sold out of M. Johnston's stable 6,200 gns Doncaster June Sales: poor form in juvenile hurdles: visored final outing (September, saddle slipped). *A. L. Forbes* — 69

A LAD INSANE   12 br.g. Al Sirat (USA) – Endora (Royal Palm) [1992/3 c26g⁴ c24m⁵ c27g] compact gelding: handicap chaser: no form in 1992/3: stays 25f: yet to race on heavy going, acts on any other: visored once: moody. *K. C. Bailey* — c– § — §

ALAICBRUN   8 b.g. Golden Love – Carrigal (Deep Run) [1992/3 22f⁵ 25sᵖᵘ c25gᵖᵘ] leggy, lengthy gelding: novice hurdler/chaser: no form for a long time: trained until after second start by M. Dods: blinkered twice: poor jumper of fences. *M. Sams* — c– x —

ALAMIR (USA)   5 b.g. Shadeed (USA) – Glamour Girl (FR) (Riverman (USA)) [1992/3 16vᵖᵘ 18vᵖᵘ 17g⁵ 18d 17d 17g 16g] sturdy gelding: once-raced — 62

on Flat: poor form over hurdles: sold out of N. Henderson's stable 2,400 gns
Ascot March Sales after second start, blinkered last three. *Mrs A. Swinbank*

ALAMSHAH (IRE)   5 b.h. Lashkari – Alannya (FR) (Relko) [1992/3 2 1g
22s 16v⁵] angular horse: half-brother to several winners, including fair Irish   – §
hurdler Altountash (by Labus): poor maiden on Flat: no form over hurdles,
and looks reluctant: blinkered. *H. Willis*

ALAN BALL   7 b.g. Broadsword (USA) – Keshoon (Sheshoon) [1992/3   **c99**
c18m³ c16d² c16sʳᵒ c17g² c20g⁴ c17m* c18m*] big, leggy gelding: modest   –
handicap chaser: improved in the spring and won at Taunton and Market
Rasen: best form at around 2m: acts on soft and good to firm ground:
blinkered nowadays: sketchy jumper: races up with pace. *Miss S. J. Wilton*

ALANERRY   13 br.g. Alanrod – Kerry B (Paddy's Birthday) [1992/3   c–
c25dF c26mᵖᵘ] compact gelding: poor novice jumper: blinkered nowadays.   –
Mrs Jacqueline Breeden

ALASKAN GOODWILL   10 b.g. Snow Warning – Runaway Bay   c–
(Punchinello) [1992/3 c25g c26g] big gelding: no sign of ability over fences.
Mrs R. Birtwistle

AL BADETO   6 b.m. Hays – Atedaun (Ahonoora) [1992/3 16m 16dᵘʳ 16d]
sparely-made mare: bad novice selling hurdler. *J. Norton*   57

ALBEMINE (USA)   4 b.g. Al Nasr (FR) – Lady Be Mine (USA) (Sir Ivor)
[1992/3 17g⁶ 16f* 17f* 17g* 16fF] fair miler on Flat: took well to hurdling,   113 p
and won novice events at Windsor and Huntingdon and quite valuable
juvenile handicap at Newbury, all in March: every chance when falling 2 out
in juvenile handicap at Haydock in May: acts on firm ground: usually jumps
well: races up with pace: should improve further. *Mrs J. Cecil*

ALBERTITO (FR)   6 b.g. Esprit du Nord (USA) – Aranita (Arctic Tern
(USA)) [1992/3 17d* 16d⁴ 17f 17m⁴ 16f] leggy gelding: fairly useful hurdler: 117
won handicap at Stratford in February: also ran creditably fourth outing,
below form otherwise: best at around 2m: acts on good to firm and dead
ground: held up. *R. Hollinshead*

ALBERT THE GREAT   10 ch.g. Meldrum – Bath Miss (Appiani II)
[1992/3 18d 18d 16s 20d⁶] compact gelding: poor handicap hurdler: stays   84
2½m: acts on any going: tried blinkered in 1986/7. *Mrs S. Taylor*

ALBURY GREY   6 gr.m. Petong – Infelice (Nishapour (FR)) [1992/3
20m⁶ 18s 16d 20g² 17d a20gᵘʳ a22g³ a20g 22f] leggy mare: poor selling   68
hurdler: trained until after fifth start by R. Curtis: stays 2¾m: acts on firm
going and equitrack: blinkered once. *P. M. McEntee*

ALCOY (IRE)   4 b.g. Glow (USA) – Organdy (Blakeney) [1992/3 17g
a18g* a18g* a18g* 17g⁶ a16g* 20f* a18g* a16gF] tall, leggy gelding: modest   118
maiden at best on Flat: fair form over hurdles: won 5 novice hurdles at
Lingfield and another at Southwell in second half of season: stays 2½m:
acts on firm ground and all-weather: jumps well: claimer ridden: takes good
hold and races up with pace. *P. A. Kelleway*

ALDAHE   8 ch.g. Dalsaan – Alanood (Northfields (USA)) [1992/3 17s⁵
17d⁶ 17v a20g* a20gF a20g³] workmanlike gelding: lightly raced over   69
hurdles: won novice handicap at Lingfield in January: stays 2½m: acts on
equitrack. *B. Forsey*

ALDAVERA   4 ch.g. Executive Man – Springle (Le Johnstan) [1992/3
16sᵖᵘ 17vᵖᵘ 17g] angular gelding: no form on Flat or over hurdles: visored   –
final outing: sold 1,400 gns Ascot May Sales. *M. Dixon*

ALDERBROOK   4 b.c. Ardross – Twine (Thatching) [1992/3 17s] leggy
colt with scope: sold 38,000 gns Newmarket Autumn Sales: shaped   – P
promisingly when in mid-division in 18-runner juvenile hurdle at Newcastle
in December: multiple middle-distance winner on Flat in 1993 for Mrs J.
Cecil: should do considerably better. *Miss S. E. Hall*

ALDINGTON BABY MAE   5 ch.g. Creetown – Mae Mae
(Communication) [1992/3 17sᵖᵘ 16s 16sᵘʳ 17g 17f a18gᵖᵘ] rather sparely-   64

made gelding: poor maiden plater over hurdles: sold out of C. Trietline's stable 780 gns Doncaster March Sales after fifth start. *J. L. Eyre*

ALDINGTON BELL 10 b.g. Legal Eagle – Dear Catalpa (Dear Gazelle) [1992/3 c18g⁵ c20m⁴ c16g³ c21d³ c16d³ c21s c20sᵖᵘ c16s² c20d⁴ c16m* c17f* c16g² c20f* c18m² c16m²] leggy gelding: modest form over fences: won novice events at Hereford and Ludlow and claimer at Taunton in March: good efforts last 2 outings 21f: probably acts on any going: usually blinkered. *C. C. Trietline*   c91 –

ALDINGTON CHAPPLE 5 b.g. Creetown – Aldington Miss (Legal Eagle) [1992/3 17d 17d⁶ 17dᵖᵘ 17gᵖᵘ 16gᵖᵘ 16f a18gᵖᵘ a21gᶠ 21mᵖᵘ] leggy gelding: no form over hurdles: sold out of C. Trietline's stable 2,600 gns Doncaster March Sales after fifth start: blinkered last 2 outings. *B. Preece*   –

ALDINGTON MILLPOND 5 b.g. Creetown – Dear Catalpa (Dear Gazelle) [1992/3 17d⁴ 16sᵖᵘ 17s 16s 17f⁵] leggy, angular gelding: poor novice hurdler: sold 2,100 gns Doncaster March Sales: yet to race beyond 17f: acts on soft ground. *C. C. Trietline*   78

ALDINGTON PEACH 4 ch.f. Creetown – Aldington Cherry (Legal Eagle) [1992/3 17s³ 18d⁴ 16d⁵ 16g* 17mᵖᵘ] deep-girthed filly: no form on Flat: made running when winning selling hurdle at Nottingham (bought in 6,000 gns) in March, easily best effort. *P. D. Evans*   87

ALDRA BOND 8 ch.g. Gold Song – Petite Case (Upper Case (USA)) [1992/3 20gᵖᵘ] sparely-made gelding: fair hurdler at best/winning chaser: lightly raced in recent seasons: stays 2½m: acts on firm ground: visored once. *K. R. Burke*   c– –

ALEDAN 12 b.g. Raise You Ten – Melodic Beat (Melodic Air) [1992/3 c26m⁶] big, angular gelding: poor novice staying chaser: blinkered once. *Mrs D. M. Grissell*   c– –

ALEGBYE 7 b.g. Buckskin (FR) – Slave Run (Deep Run) [1992/3 c21gᶠ c20gᶠ] rangy gelding with scope: modest novice hurdler, lightly raced: would have finished second but for falling 2 out in novice chase at Wincanton in October: fell first later in month: should stay beyond 2½m: has raced mainly on good ground. *R. J. O'Sullivan*   c82 –

ALERT THE BOYS 4 ch.g. Norwick (USA) – Red Gay (Red Alert) [1992/3 16vᵖᵘ a16g a16g⁶ 16g] leggy gelding: third foal: dam, plating-class maiden on Flat, behind in 2 races over hurdles: poor form over hurdles: sold 825 gns Ascot March Sales: pulls hard. *R. J. Hodges*   72

ALEXA'S BOY 9 b.g. African Sky – Regal Step (Ribero) [1992/3 c22gᵖᵘ] leggy gelding: poor novice jumper: form only at around 2m: acts on heavy going. *T. B. Hallett*   c– –

ALEX THUSCOMBE 5 ch.g. Takachiho – Portate (Articulate) [1992/3 aF16g 17g 18s 18m 16g⁵ 22m] smallish, close-coupled gelding: seventh foal: brother to winning jumper Ben Tirran and novice jumper Wayward Edward: dam, poor hurdler/chaser, stayed well: poor novice hurdler: best effort at 2m on good ground. *Mrs S. Lamyman*   66

ALGAIHABANE (USA) 7 b.g. Roberto (USA) – Sassabunda (Sassafras (FR)) [1992/3 c24sᵖᵘ] leggy gelding: novice hurdler: winning pointer: signs of a little ability prior to being pulled up in hunter chase at Chepstow in April: stays 2¾m: acts on firm and dead ground: sold 1,300 gns Ascot 2nd June Sales. *Ms Kay Rees*   c– –

ALGARI 6 b.g. Petitioner – Jill Somers (Will Somers) [1992/3 18g⁴ c17fᵇᵈ c16m² c16g² c17m* c17d⁴ c16s⁴ c17d² c20f* c18dᵘʳ c18v*] tall gelding: novice hurdler: won novice chases at Kelso, Newcastle and Cartmel in the spring: stays 2½m: acts on any ground. *G. Richards*   c98 –

AL HAAL (USA) 4 b.c. Northern Baby (CAN) – Kit's Double (USA) (Spring Double) [1992/3 16s⁴ 16v a16g* a18g⁴ 17d] lengthy, sparely-made colt: fair middle-distance maiden on Flat: sold out of P. Walwyn's stable 5,800 gns Newmarket July Sales: won novice hurdle at Lingfield in January: 86

31

ran poorly final outing: easily best form on equitrack: usually races prominently. *J. Joseph*

AL HASHIMI 9 b.g. Ile de Bourbon (USA) – Parmesh (Home Guard c135 ?
(USA)) [1992/3 c17v³ c16s² c16s⁶ c17m⁴ c16g² c17f³ c16s²] big, lengthy –
gelding: has been hobdayed and had soft palate and tie-back operations, and
runs tubed nowadays: useful chaser: below form last 2 outings, running
poorly on final one: sold only 4,400 gns Ascot May Sales: effective at 2m and
stays 2½m: acts on any going. *D. Nicholson*

ALIAS GRAY 6 b.g. Alias Smith (USA) – Gray Loch (Lochnager) [1992/3
17dᵖᵘ 17gᵖᵘ 17d 17d] big, workmanlike gelding: third foal: half-brother to 2m –
Flat winner Fallowfield Lad (by Anax) and novice hurdler Fallowfield Lass
(by Some Hand): dam 1m winner: tailed off in novice hurdles. *Mrs S. Taylor*

ALIAS SILVER 6 gr.g. Alias Smith (USA) – Duresme (Starry Halo) c–
[1992/3 16s³ 17g 16s⁵ 26s⁵ a22g² a24g³ 22d c27gᵖᵘ a20g4] neat gelding: poor 79
novice hurdler: no show on chasing debut: stays 3m: acts on soft going and
fibresand. *J. W. Curtis*

ALICE'S BOY 12 b.g. Tycoon II – Small Dragon (Pendragon) [1992/3 c–
c21s⁶ c21dᵘʳ c21g c24v c24dᵖᵘ] sturdy gelding: winning chaser: no form for a –
long time. *A. W. Jones*

ALICE'S MIRROR 4 gr.f. Magic Mirror – Pousdale-Tachytees
(Tachypous) [1992/3 17m 18g* 17g² 16g⁴ 20s⁴ 18v² 17d² 17m⁵ 17g*] 86
sparely-made filly: lightly-raced maiden on Flat: won juvenile hurdle at
Fontwell in September and novice event at Plumpton in March: stays 2¼m
(respectable effort over 2½m): acts on heavy ground. *T. P. McGovern*

ALICE SMITH 6 gr.m. Alias Smith (USA) – Dancing Jenny (Goldhill)
[1992/3 F17v⁴ F17v 23s 20m³ 20g³ 20v 18d] big, workmanlike mare: poor 78
novice hurdler: stays 2½m: acts on good to firm going. *B. J. Eckley*

ALICE SPRINGS 4 ch.f. Prince of Peace – Alice Woodlark (Sir Lark)
[1992/3 F16g] lengthy, unfurnished filly: first foal: dam placed in points: –
mid-division in 21-runner NH Flat race at Worcester in March: yet to race
over hurdles. *L. G. Cottrell*

ALIF (IRE) 4 b.c. Ajdal (USA) – Pilot Bird (Blakeney) [1992/3 16d 16f⁵
16m] no form on Flat: sold out of J. Dunlop's stable 5,600 gns Newmarket 75
Autumn Sales: poor novice hurdler: best effort on second outing. *W. Clay*

ALIZARI (USA) 4 b.c. Topsider (USA) – Alia (Sun Prince) [1992/3 18m⁴
18s⁴ 18m 22vᵖᵘ 22m] neat colt: half-brother to winning hurdler Cognizant 74
(by Known Fact): modest staying maiden on Flat: sold out of G. Harwood's
stable 2,400 gns Newmarket September Sales: poor form over hurdles:
trained until after third start by G. Fleming. *C. Smith*

AL-KHALIDA 9 br.m. Kala Shikari – Sea Daisy (Mossborough) [1992/3 c–
c21dᵘʳ c21g c24m] smallish, sparely-made mare: winning chaser: tailed off –
in hunter chases in 1992/3: stays 2¼m: acts on hard going: usually
blinkered nowadays. *Mrs Gillian A. Russell Holmes*

ALKINOR REX 8 ch.g. Welsh Pageant – Glebehill (Northfields (USA)) c126
[1992/3 c16gF c16d² c17v* c17v² c16g³ c17mF] rather sparely-made –
gelding: fairly useful chaser: won handicap at Towcester in December: ran
creditably next 3 starts: races only at around 2m: acts on heavy going (well
beaten when falling on good to firm final outing): has won when blinkered:
sketchy jumper. *G. Harwood*

ALKIONIS 7 b.h. Dominion – Norfolk Gal (Blakeney) [1992/3 16g 17d⁵
17d⁶] smallish, sparely-made horse: poor novice over hurdles: occasionally –
blinkered: dead. *W. G. M. Turner*

ALLAZARE 5 b.m. Alias Smith (USA) – Lazarette (Welsh Saint) [1992/3
22f⁵] light-framed mare: of little account. *N. B. Thomson* –

ALLEGRAMENTE 4 b.c. Music Maestro – Eastern Romance (Sahib)
[1992/3 18m 18g] sparely-made colt: plating-class maiden at around 1m on –
Flat: no form in early-season juvenile hurdles. *R. O'Leary*

ALLEGRO CON BRIO 5 b.g. Alleging (USA) – Diami (Swing Easy (USA)) [1992/3 F 17s aF 16g 16mᵖᵘ] tall gelding: first foal: dam, 5f winner at 2 yrs, jumped badly in 2 races over hurdles: soundly beaten in NH Flat races and when pulled up in novice hurdle: sold 950 gns Ascot June Sales. *T. Thomson Jones* —

ALL ELECTRIC 8 b.g. Electric – Miss Tweedie (Aberdeen) [1992/3 18s 18g 17f⁵ 21s 17mᵖᵘ] sturdy gelding: novice hurdler, poor form in 1992/3: sold 1,250 gns Ascot June Sales: best form at around 2m: probably acts on any going. *C. C. Elsey* 74

ALLEZMOSS 7 b.g. Le Moss – Allitess (Mugatpura) [1992/3 c22s² c20v⁶ c20s⁴ c22s² c24s² c21d² c25mF c29s⁴ c20dᵇᵈ] workmanlike gelding: fair hurdler: fairly useful novice over fences in 1992/3, won at Limerick in December: creditable fourth in Jameson Irish Grand National at Fairyhouse in April: every chance when falling 6 out in valuable amateurs handicap at Cheltenham: stays well: acts on heavy going: blinkered third and fourth starts. *E. Bolger, Ireland* c123 +

ALL FOR LUCK 8 b.g. Kemal (FR) – Lisgarvan (Walshford) [1992/3 c20v² c21v²] non-thoroughbred Irish gelding: fairly useful hurdler: showed promise when second in novice chases at Down Royal and Perth in April: stays 21f: acts on heavy going. *J. F. C. Maxwell, Ireland* c88 p

ALL GREEK TO ME (IRE) 5 b.g. Trojan Fen – Do We Know (Derrylin) [1992/3 18d³ 18dF 17s² 20d⁶] leggy gelding: fair handicap hurdler: not raced after December: stays 2¼m: acts on soft ground. *C. W. Thornton* 108

ALLIED'S TEAM 6 b.m. Teamwork – Allied Beaumel (Jimmy Reppin) [1992/3 16s 17s 18gᵖᵘ 17d] small, angular mare: second foal: dam poor winning hurdler: no sign of ability in novice hurdles. *J. Joseph* —

ALLIMAC NOMIS 4 b.g. Daring March – Game For A Laugh (Martinmas) [1992/3 18m* 18g³ 16g³ 18d⁴ 18g*] leggy gelding: brother to winning hurdler Good For A Loan: plater on Flat (stays 1¼m): sold out of N. Callaghan's stable 1,800 gns Newmarket July Sales: won juvenile hurdles at Market Rasen in September and April (claimer, improved effort): stays 2¼m: acts on good to firm ground: retained 900 gns Ascot December Sales. *I. Campbell* 101

ALL JEFF (FR) 9 b.g. Jefferson – Fromentel (FR) (Timour II) [1992/3 c25g³ c33d* c24vᵘʳ c25gᵖᵘ] neat gelding: has had soft palate operation: fairly useful chaser: successful in handicap at Haydock in December: ran poorly in March on final start (first for 2 months): suited by thorough test of stamina: acts on any going: occasionally blinkered prior to 1992/3: sometimes wears tongue strap. *C. P. E. Brooks* c127

ALLO GEORGE 7 ch.g. Buckskin (FR) – Dodgy Lady (Royal Avenue) [1992/3 c18fᵘʳ c18fF 16g⁵ 19m⁴ 17sᵖᵘ 25s² 22v⁶ 25d³ 23d³ 22m³ 18g³ 22d* 21m⁴] plain gelding: trained until after eleventh start by Mrs J. Wonnacott: won novice handicap hurdle at Newton Abbot in May: let down by his jumping over fences: stays 25f: acts on good to firm and soft ground. *M. Williams* c– x 83

ALL OVER THE WORLD 9 b.g. Kind of Hush – Bosworth Moll (Henry The Seventh) [1992/3 25mᵖᵘ] workmanlike gelding: poor hurdler: no aptitude for chasing: best form at around 3m: acted on hard going: dead. *J. R. Fort* c– —

ALL PRESENT (IRE) 5 b.g. Reach – Mar Del Plata (Crowned Prince (USA)) [1992/3 16dᵖᵘ 17d 22m⁶] leggy gelding: winning hurdler: no form in 1992/3: best form at 2m: acts on dead going. *D. R. Gandolfo* —

ALL TALK NO ACTION (IRE) 4 ch.g. Orchestra – Clarrie (Ballyciptic) [1992/3 20dᵖᵘ 16v 22gᵖᵘ] rather leggy gelding: brother to 5-y-o No Pain No Gain and half-brother to winning hurdler/chaser Dickie Murray (by Brave Invader) and an Irish NH Flat race winner by Wolverlife: dam won 2m hurdle: no sign of ability over hurdles. *B. J. Curley* —

ALL THE JOLLY 5 b.m. Bay Express – Whisper Gently (Pitskelly) [1992/3 17gᵖᵘ] half-sister to winning hurdler Spanish Whisper (by Aragon): —

poor maiden on Flat at 3 yrs: tailed off when pulled up in novice hurdle in April. *Miss C. J. E. Caroe*

ALL WELCOME 6 b.g. Be My Guest (USA) – Pepi Image (USA) (National) [1992/3 17m⁴ 17d c16m 16g⁴ 18spu] lengthy gelding: modest hurdler nowadays: not raced after November: once-raced over fences: usually races around 2m: acts on any ground: blinkered second and final outings: sometimes wears tongue strap. *G. M. Moore*   c– 98

ALLYFAIR 8 gr.m. Scallywag – Spartan Blonde (Spartan General) [1992/3 17s⁴ c24vpu 22d⁶ 17f⁶ 22f 26s² 24s⁴ 22d³ 25m] leggy mare: moderate novice hurdler: showed nothing on chasing debut: stays well: acts on soft ground: reportedly broke blood vessel once. *Mrs J. G. Retter*   c– 90

ALMANZORA 9 ch.g. Proverb – Serrulata (Raise You Ten) [1992/3 17g* 17m] big, leggy, lengthy gelding: lightly-raced hurdler: won novice event at Stratford in March: hampered after fourth when behind in Trafalgar House Supreme Novices' Hurdle at Cheltenham later in month: has raced only at 2m but will stay further: may be capable of better. *Mrs J. Pitman*   93 +

ALMARREEKH (FR) 8 b.g. Glint of Gold – Formulate (Reform) [1992/3 18g 16g 18g⁵ 20s 22s³] leggy gelding: poor novice hurdler: stays 2¾m: acts on heavy ground: blinkered once. *P. Monteith*   75

ALMERIMAR 9 b.g. Home Guard (USA) – Melaleuca (Levmoss) [1992/3 c20gpu c21dpu c19g² c19s c22mpu] good-topped gelding: poor novice chaser: stayed 19f: acted on firm ground: dead. *Christopher Wright*   c84 –

ALMOST A PRINCESS 5 b.m. Alleging (USA) – Rabab (Thatching) [1992/3 16m] leggy mare: maiden plater over hurdles: has raced only at around 2m: acts on soft ground: won over 1½m on Flat in May for W. G. M. Turner. *J. Akehurst*   – §

AL MUTAHM (USA) 5 b.g. Green Dancer (USA) – Musical Medicine (FR) (Margouillat (FR)) [1992/3 17d² 22v² 21spu] rangy gelding: useful hurdler: second in minor events at Cheltenham in November and December: destroyed after severing tendon at Newbury: stayed 2¾m: acted on heavy going. *J. A. B. Old*   142

ALNASRIC PETE (USA) 7 b.g. Al Nasr (FR) – Stylish Pleasure (USA) (What A Pleasure (USA)) [1992/3 16vpu 16vpu 17d] workmanlike gelding: modest form at around 1m on Flat: sold out of D. Wilson's stable 4,400 gns Newmarket Autumn Sales: raced too freely and no form in novice hurdles. *G. L. Humphrey*   –

ALOSAILI 6 ch.g. Kris – Vaison La Romaine (Arctic Tern (USA)) [1992/3 16d⁴ 16d* 17s² 17s 16s⁴ 17d* 18g⁵ 17m 17s³ 17dpu 17m² 16d²] lengthy, angular gelding: moderate hurdler: awarded seller at Ludlow in November and won conditional jockeys selling handicap at Taunton (bought in 2,800 gns) in February: good second in non-selling handicap penultimate outing: races only at around 2m: acts on good to firm and soft ground: often finds little off bridle, and best held up: inconsistent. *B. Stevens*   98 §

ALPHA ONE 8 ch.g. Belfalas – Clonaslee Foam (Quayside) [1992/3 c25v* c25g* c26g²] won hunter chases at Towcester in February and Wolverhampton in March: good second at Uttoxeter in May: sold 10,000 gns Ascot June Sales: stays well: acts on heavy ground. *Miss C. Saunders*   c98

ALPINE TROOPER 6 ch.g. Burslem – Alpina (King's Troop) [1992/3 18spu] once-raced on Flat: no sign of ability in novice hurdle in November. *B. Stevens*   –

ALREEF 7 b.g. Wassl – Joey (FR) (Salvo) [1992/3 17g⁶ 17s⁶ a16g⁴ a18g* a20g² a18g³ 17f² 22f³] leggy gelding: fair handicap hurdler: won amateurs event at Lingfield in January: ran creditably next 3 outings: stays 2½m: acts on any going, except possibly heavy. *T. Thomson Jones*   110

AL SAHIL (USA) 8 b.g. Riverman (USA) – Tobira Celeste (USA) (Ribot) [1992/3 20v⁵ 17d³ 22s* 21s² 27g] smallish, workmanlike gelding: selling hurdler: won at Newton Abbot (no bid) in April: stays 2¾m: acts on soft going: usually blinkered. *J. White*   92

AL SHANY 7 ch.m. Burslem – Paradise Regained (North Stoke) [1992/3 17v³ 16vᵖᵘ 18sᵖᵘ] small mare: poor novice hurdler: trained until after second start by W. Carter: sold 1,050 gns Ascot May Sales: has raced only at around 2m: acts on heavy ground. *T. G. Mills*   79

AL SKEET (USA) 7 b.g. L'Emigrant (USA) – Processional (USA) (Reviewer (USA)) [1992/3 16g*] leggy gelding: won selling handicap hurdle at Worcester (no bid) in October: no promise in novice chases: races only at around 2m: best efforts on good ground: tried blinkered: inconsistent in 1991/2. *R. J. Price*   c–
78

ALTAR POINT 9 b.m. Persian Bold – Ida (Jukebox) [1992/3 18gᵖᵘ] neat mare: poor novice hurdler, very lightly raced. *Mrs L. C. Jewell*   –

ALTEREZZA (USA) 6 b.g. Alleged (USA) – Hester Bateman (USA) (Codex (USA)) [1992/3 16s⁶ 20d⁶ 16d 22d* 16d 21m 24g] sparely-made gelding: useful hurdler: disappointed after winning handicap at Leopardstown in January (at Cheltenham on penultimate outing): stays 2¾m: acts on soft ground: blinkered final outing. *D. K. Weld, Ireland*   133

ALTERNATION (FR) 4 ch.f. Electric – Alanood (Northfields (USA)) [1992/3 17g⁵ 16s⁴ 17v 16v⁶ 22s⁴ 21g⁶ 22d³ 23m³ 23m² 23g* 25m²] workmanlike filly: modest middle-distance performer on Flat: bought out of P. Cole's stable 5,200 gns Newmarket September Sales: improved form last 2 starts over hurdles, winning conditional jockeys novice handicap hurdle at Stratford in May: suited by a test of stamina: best form on a sound surface. *J. Webber*   106

ALTISHAR (IRE) 5 b.g. Darshaan – Altiyna (Troy) [1992/3 20g⁴ 16g 16d 17g⁵] leggy ex-Irish gelding: lightly-raced 1½m winner on Flat: poor novice hurdler: stays 2½m: acts on dead ground. *D. R. Gandolfo*   73

ALTO 4 ch.g. Superlative – Rose Music (Luthier) [1992/3 18m 18m³] lengthy gelding: poor maiden on Flat: blinkered, poor form when third in early-season juvenile hurdle at Market Rasen. *J. G. FitzGerald*   74

ALTON BAY 5 b.g. Al Nasr (FR) – Dabbiana (CAN) (Fappiano (USA)) [1992/3 22m² 22g⁵ 22d² 21m⁵ 20v² 20g² 22vꟳ a18gᵘʳ] leggy gelding: moderate handicap hurdler: retained 6,000 gns Doncaster November Sales: stayed 2¾m: acted on any going: visored third and fourth starts: dead. *Mrs D. Haine*   88

ALTO PRINCESS 4 b.f. Noalto – Queen of The Hills (Connaught) [1992/3 17f⁴ 17g⁶ 18d] sparely-made filly: poor maiden on Flat and over hurdles. *A. P. Jones*   61

AL-TORFANAN 9 b.g. Taufan (USA) – Powder Box (Faberge II) [1992/3 16s 16d] tall, leggy gelding: one-time modest miler on Flat, usually visored: tailed off in novice hurdles. *T. Kersey*   –

ALUM BAY 4 b.g. Reference Point – Bella Colora (Bellypha) [1992/3 16d* 16sᵖᵘ] maiden on Flat, fairly useful on his day: sold out of H. Cecil's stable 20,000 gns Newmarket Autumn Sales: won maiden hurdle at Edinburgh in January: destroyed after breaking a leg at Catterick later in month. *N. Tinkler*   91

ALWAYS ALEX 6 b.m. Final Straw – Two High (High Top) [1992/3 18g* 16fᵖᵘ] smallish mare: modest hurdler: won selling handicap at Worcester (no bid) in August: not seen out after September: stays 2¼m: suited by a sound surface. *P. D. Evans*   90

ALWAYS ALLIED (IRE) 5 b.g. Dalsaan – Novesia (Sir Gaylord) [1992/3 17m⁴ 17m⁶ 20m⁶ 16sᵖᵘ 17vᵖᵘ] workmanlike gelding: poor novice hurdler: best form at around 2m: acts on heavy ground. *J. Joseph*   61

ALWAYS AWAY 9 ch.g. Quayside – Safe Return (Canisbay) [1992/3 16s 16s c16dᴿ] workmanlike gelding: little promise in novice hurdles: made mistakes and refused on chasing debut. *J. White*   c–
–

ALWAYS READY 7 b.g. Tyrnavos – Merchantmens Girl (Klairon) [1992/3 16d* 17d³ 17s⁴ 17v⁶ 16s⁴ 16v³ a16g* a16g³ 16d³ 17d⁶] sturdy gelding: won novice hurdle at Uttoxeter in October and conditional jockeys   95 handicap at Lingfield in January: poor efforts last 2 outings: likely to prove best at around 2m: acts on good to firm, heavy ground and equitrack. *R. Lee*

ALWAYS ROYAL 4 b.g. Dara Monarch – Shoshoni (Ballymoss) [1992/3 16dur 18g] sparely-made gelding: half-brother to 3 Flat winners, including Macho Man (by Mummy's Game), also successful over hurdles and fences: dam, 1½m winner, half-sister to Warpath and Dakota: no show in juvenile claiming hurdle in February: sold 1,650 gns Doncaster March Sales. *C. W. Thornton* –

AMADEUS (FR) 5 b.g. Pamponi (FR) – Katy Collonge (FR) (Trenel) [1992/3 F16d² F17d 24s] French-bred gelding: half-brother to novice hurdler/chaser Turoldus (by Toujours Pret): second in NH Flat race in March: well beaten in similar event and a maiden hurdle afterwards. *M. D. Hammond* –

AMARANTHINE 6 b.m. Sunley Builds – Warm Up (Hot Brandy) [1992/3 21vpu 21gpu 25fpu] fifth foal: dam winning pointer: seems of little account. *Miss D. J. Baker* –

AMARI KING 9 b.g. Sit In The Corner (USA) – Maywell (Harwell) [1992/3 c17d5 c17s² c16v4 c21f³ c21g* c17m] workmanlike gelding: usually fails to impress in appearance: quite useful chaser: generally well below his best in 1992/3, though won at Sandown in March: stays 21f when conditions aren't testing: acts on any ground: unreliable. *Capt. T. A. Forster* c124 § –

AMARI PRINCE 8 ch.g. Rarity – Polyxena (FR) (Pretendre) [1992/3 c25mF c24g³] big ex-Irish gelding: half-brother to winning Irish hurdler Sports Edition (by Music Boy) and NH Flat race winner Oats A Plenty (by Oats): dam placed at up to 1½m on Flat in Ireland: maiden hurdler: modest pointer/novice hunter chaser in Britain: stays 3m: has broken blood vessels. *D. E. Fletcher* c83 –

AMAZON EXPRESS 4 b.c. Siberian Express (USA) – Thalestria (FR) (Mill Reef (USA)) [1992/3 17g* 17g5 16g* 17m²] 137 p

Amazon Express proved a bargain after being bought out of Clive Brittain's stable for a mere 3,400 guineas after winning a seller on the Flat at Folkestone in September. That win was only the second in fourteen starts for the leggy Amazon Express, who seemed fully exposed as an ordinary performer. Yet he went on to win two handicaps on the Flat, showing fair form, then developed into one of the season's leading juvenile hurdlers, earning almost £30,000 in prize money for his new owner.

Tote Placepot Hurdle, Kempton—
improving Amazon Express (centre) wins this Grade 2 contest

Mrs Jill Moss's "Amazon Express"

Amazon Express (b.c. 1989)	Siberian Express (USA) (gr 1981)	Caro (gr 1967)	Fortino II
			Chambord
		Indian Call (b or br 1966)	Warfare
			La Morlaye
	Thalestria (FR) (b or br 1982)	Mill Reef (b 1968)	Never Bend
			Milan Mill
		Sweep Up (b 1975)	Relko
			Salocar

Amazon Express made his mark over hurdles immediately, winning a juvenile event at Fakenham in October impressively by fifteen lengths. That he failed to step up on that effort when tackling much stronger opposition in the Stroud Green Hurdle at Newbury four months later was disappointing at the time, but in retrospect the run was probably needed. A sharper Amazon Express gave a much improved display when reappearing in the Tote Placepot Hurdle at Kempton later in February, winning by a neck from Top Spin. Both horses came from off the pace in a strongly-run race, with Amazon Express, who'd made good headway to lead between the last two, keeping on gamely to hold Top Spin's strong late challenge, the pair drawing twelve lengths clear. Although Amazon Express' jumping left something to be desired, on form he had to be considered a serious contender for the Daily Express Triumph Hurdle at Cheltenham, and only Beauchamp Grace and Indian Quest, first and second respectively in the Stroud Green Hurdle, started at shorter odds for the race. Amazon Express looked in fine shape and easily turned the tables on that pair, coming out best of the British-trained runners. He hurdled with much greater fluency than at Kempton, and travelled comfortably in the middle of the field until briefly denied a clear run when attempting to improve his position after two out. Running on strongly once clear in the straight, he took second place from Major Bugler halfway up the run-in, drifting left as he did so, and got to within three quarters of a length of Shawiya, his run appearing to be coming to an end as he neared the finish. Amazon Express, who won again on the Flat in June, will continue on the upgrade when returned to hurdling but is unlikely to improve sufficiently to trouble the very best.

Thalestria, the dam of Amazon Express, was a useful seven-furlong winner in England at two years and subsequently won over eleven furlongs in France. Amazon Express is Thalestria's second foal. Her first, School Teacher (by Never So Bold), won three times over middle distances in France in 1992. The second dam Sweep Up was a maiden but the third dam Salocar was a winning daughter of that grand mare Barwin, who won ten races and was placed twice in the Cambridgeshire in the early -'sixties. Amazon Express, who will stay beyond seventeen furlongs, acts on good to firm going and has yet to race on ground softer than good over hurdles. He has won on good to soft on the Flat. *R. Akehurst*

AMBASSADOR ROYALE (IRE)   5 gr.g. Pennine Walk – Hayati (Hotfoot) [1992/3 17d 17dᵖᵘ 17f⁵ 18g³ 17m² 16d* 18m* 16m²] leggy gelding: fairly useful middle-distance performer on Flat at best: sold out of P. Cole's stable only 3,800 gns Newmarket September Sales: claimed out of D. R. Tucker's stable £5,100 fifth start: successful in novice hurdles at Ludlow (seller, no bid) and Exeter in the spring: good second final start: stays 2¼m: acts on good to firm and dead going: visored fifth outing, blinkered afterwards: sometimes wears tongue strap. *M. Williams* — 88

AMBER GLOW (IRE)   4 ch.g. Glow (USA) – Sea Queen (FR) (Le Fabuleux) [1992/3 16dᶠ] leggy gelding: no form on Flat: beaten when falling in juvenile selling hurdle in October. *L. J. Codd* — –

AMBER REALM   5 ch.m. Southern Music – Thrupence (Royal Highway) [1992/3 F16g F18g] half-sister to modest chaser Goodfellow's Folly (by New Brig): dam, well beaten in novice hurdles, is daughter of half-sister to top-class hunter chaser Credit Call: well beaten in NH Flat races: yet to race over hurdles or fences. *R. H. Buckler* — –

AMBLESIDE HARVEST   6 b. or br.g. Decent Fellow – Watch The Birdie (Polyfoto) [1992/3 25m⁴ 20s* 22s 25d] rather leggy, unfurnished gelding: fairly useful handicap hurdler: won at Ayr in January: well below form afterwards: should stay beyond 2½m: acts on soft ground. *J. J. O'Neill* — 116

AMBROSE   6 b.g. Ile de Bourbon (USA) – Famous Band (USA) (Banderilla (USA)) [1992/3 c17dᵘʳ c17s² c19v³ c20mᵇᵈ c18mᶠ c20f²] lengthy gelding: fairly useful hurdler: modest novice chaser: stays 2½m: acts on any going: not an accomplished jumper, but has the ability to win a race over fences. *R. F. Johnson Houghton* — c94 + –

AMBUSCADE (USA)   7 ch.g. Roberto (USA) – Gurkhas Band (USA) (Lurullah) [1992/3 25g* 25s³ 20d² 24vᵖᵘ] small, workmanlike gelding: improved into a very useful hurdler in 1992/3: won handicap at Ayr in November: placed in Akzo Long Distance Hurdle at Newbury and Waterloo Hurdle at Haydock: suited by test of stamina: ran poorly on heavy going final start (January), acts on any other ground. *Mrs M. Reveley* — 149

AMERICAN HERO   5 ch.g. Persian Bold – American Winter (USA) (Lyphard (USA)) [1992/3 16sᶠ 16d³ 18g⁴] moderate miler on Flat: poor novice hurdler: best effort final outing (October). *R. Allan* — 75

AMIGOS   5 ch.g. Nordance (USA) – Hi Gorgeous (Hello Gorgeous (USA)) [1992/3 17g²] leggy, good-topped gelding: fair hurdler: broke down when good second in handicap at Fakenham in October: likely to prove best at around 2m: has raced only on good ground. *P. Mitchell* — 110

AMLAK (USA)   4 b.c. Riverman (USA) – Ruwiyda (USA) (In Reality) [1992/3 16sᵖᵘ 17g a16g⁴ 17fᵖᵘ] sturdy colt: lightly-raced maiden on Flat, stays 1¼m: sold 3,200 gns Newmarket Autumn Sales: no form over hurdles. *J. E. Banks* — –

AMONG FRIENDS 8 b.g. Green Shoon – Lin-A-Dee (Linacre) [1992/3 **c96** x
c21g³ c21mᵇᵈ c21sᵖᵘ] rather unfurnished gelding: modest chaser: stays –
2¾m: acts on good to firm and dead ground: let down by his jumping. *G. B.
Balding*

AMOUR DU SOIR (USA) 6 b.g. L'Emigrant (USA) – Evening Kiss
(USA) (Saggy) [1992/3 17s² 16d] sparely-made gelding: very lightly-raced 83
novice hurdler: will prove best at around 2m: acts on equitrack and soft
ground. *R. Lee*

AMOUREUSE (IRE) 4 b.f. Petorius – Amorak (Wolver Hollow)
[1992/3 17d⁴ 17sᶠ 16s⁵ 16d] leggy, sparely-made filly: half-sister to winning 73
jumpers Escribana (by Main Reef) and Tap Dancing (by Sallust):
temperamental plating-class sprinter on Flat: novice selling hurdler: only
form on first outing. *T. H. Caldwell*

AMOUR ROYAL 6 gr.g. Mendez (FR) – Allez Royale (Artaius (USA))
[1992/3 16s⁵ 16gᵖᵘ] well-made gelding: has been hobdayed: winning 2m §§
hurdler: blinkered both starts 1992/3: usually temperamental at start (has
refused to race twice). *Denys Smith*

AMPHIGORY 5 b.g. Gorytus (USA) – Peculiar One (USA) (Quack
(USA)) [1992/3 19h³ 20g⁴ 17d⁵ 18f* 22dᵖᵘ 18d³ 17d⁵ 22d 17v⁶ 18s⁶ a18g² 88 §
20d² 18m⁵ 18g⁴ 20m² 18d² 22f²] leggy gelding: half-brother to winning
hurdler Hats High (by High Top): maiden on Flat: modest hurdler: won
novice claimer at Exeter in September: ran well on several occasions
afterwards: stays 2¾m: acts on any going: best blinkered: thoroughly
irresolute. *P. R. Rodford*

AMTRAK EXPRESS 6 ch.g. Black Minstrel – Four In A Row
(Cracksman) [1992/3 F17g* F16d⁵ 17s* 16v³ 16d* 16m* 17g] IR 7,400 4-y-o: 115
third foal: brother to winning Irish pointer Mighty Atom: dam, unraced,
from successful jumping family: leggy, sparely-made gelding: won NH Flat
race at Cheltenham in October: fairly useful novice hurdler: won at Taunton
in December and Wincanton in February (valuable auction event) and
March: long way below form final outing: will stay beyond 17f: acts on good
to firm and heavy going: jumps soundly. *N. J. Henderson*

AMY'S MYSTERY 12 b. or br.g. Bivouac – Mystery Trip (Kadir Cup) **c75**
[1992/3 c25g⁴] deep-bodied gelding: poor novice hunter chaser: stays 3m: –
acts on good to firm ground. *Mrs S. Thompson*

ANARUKA (USA) 5 b.g. Roberto (USA) – Tea And Roses (USA) (Fleet
Nasrullah) [1992/3 16g 20d 16s a18g] leggy gelding: modest novice hurdler –
at best: well beaten in 1992/3: sold 1,050 gns Ascot June Sales: races mainly
at around 2m but should prove suited by further: form only on good going:
sometimes wears tongue strap. *S. Mellor*

AN BUCHAILL LIATH (IRE) 4 gr.g. Roselier (FR) – Buckette Lady
(Buckskin (FR)) [1992/3 F17f] first foal: dam never ran: behind in NH Flat –
race at Sandown in March: yet to race over hurdles. *T. B. Hallett*

ANCHOR BAY 6 ch.g. Tug of War – Leeann (Pitpan) [1992/3 21dᵖᵘ]
smallish, rather unfurnished gelding: fourth foal: brother to winning –
hurdler/chaser Military Secret: dam unraced: no promise in maiden in
November on hurdling debut: sold 3,000 gns in May. *W. A. Stephenson*

ANDALUCIAN SUN (IRE) 5 ch.g. Le Bavard (FR) – Sun Spray (Nice
Guy) [1992/3 F17d] close-coupled, unfurnished gelding: half-brother to –
numerous winning jumpers, notably very useful Forest Sun (by Whistling
Deer): dam lightly raced: seventh of 18 in NH Flat race at Ascot in April: yet
to race over hurdles or fences. *G. B. Balding*

ANDERMATT 6 b.h. Top Ville – Klarifi (Habitat) [1992/3 20sᵖᵘ 22s 25v²
21s* 22d 23d* 20g² 21m 21v² 24g³] compact horse: fairly useful hurdler: 121
won handicaps at Wetherby (novice event) in December and Uttoxeter in
February: ran well afterwards: stays 25f: acts on heavy and good to firm
ground: blinkered once: usually held up. *J. Mackie*

ANDERSON ROSE 5 b.m. Kind of Hush – Fille de Bourbon (Ile de
Bourbon (USA)) [1992/3 17g 18gᶠ 17s² 17m] small mare: selling hurdler: not 62

raced after September: sold 1,100 gns Ascot May Sales: stays 2¼m: acts on soft ground and fibresand. *D. J. Wintle*

ANDITISITIS (USA)   4 gr.c. Verbatim (USA) – Enamor (USA) (Drone) [1992/3 18v³ 18s 17v⁵ 17d⁵] modest middle-distance maiden on Flat: sold out of D. Arbuthnot's stable 7,600 gns Newmarket September Sales: easily best run in juvenile hurdles on third outing. *D. W. Browning*   75

AND ME   4 ch.f. Don't Forget Me – Nicola Wynn (Nicholas Bill) [1992/3 18f⁴ 17s* 16v² 17vᵖᵘ a20gᵖᵘ 18d 21sᵖᵘ] angular filly: bad maiden on Flat: won selling hurdle at Huntingdon (bought in 2,300 gns) in November: ran poorly last 4 starts: should stay beyond 17f: acts on heavy ground: visored sixth outing, blinkered final one: sold out of D. Thom's stable 1,700 gns Ascot February Sales after penultimate start. *D. N. Carey*   71

ANDRELOT   6 b.h. Caerleon (USA) – Seminar (Don (ITY)) [1992/3 16s³ 23s 17s 16g³ c21m² c20s⁴ 22d 21d³ 27fᵖᵘ] close-coupled, rather angular horse: modest hurdler/novice chaser: stays 21f: acts on good to firm and soft ground: usually visored or blinkered: inconsistent: sold 5,000 gns Malvern June Sales. *K. White*   **c85** §
   85 §

ANDRETTI'S HEIR   7 ch.g. Andretti – Mounemara (Ballymore) [1992/3 c26sF 21dᵖᵘ] unfurnished gelding: third foal: dam unraced: placed in Irish points in 1991: fell first on steeplechasing debut, showed little on hurdling debut. *P. Beaumont*   c–
   –

ANDREW   10 b.g. Le Coq d'Or – Turkish Suspicion (Above Suspicion) [1992/3 c24mᵖᵘ] strong, plain gelding: hunter chaser: stays well: acts on soft and good to firm going: suited by forcing tactics: blinkered once. *G. McGuinness*   c–
   –

ANDREW'S FIRST   6 br.g. Tender King – Dame Kelly (Pitskelly) [1992/3 18g³ 17g⁴ 21d³ 22s* 22s³ 21g* 20d* 21mᵇᵈ 25f* 22m⁴] progressed into fairly useful hurdler in 1992/3: successful in handicaps at Nottingham in December, Newbury and Haydock in February and Aintree (valuable event) in April: given plenty to do and ran well in circumstances final outing: effective at 2½m to 25f: acts on any ground: blinkered once: held up: genuine: should improve further. *M. J. Wilkinson*   127 p

Ladbroke Racing Handicap Hurdle, Haydock —
Andrew's First lands a gamble; the grey Mazmoor comes second

100 Pipers Hurdle (Handicap), Aintree—
Andrew's First leads over from Metal Oiseau (blinkers), Pashto and Dawadar (rails)

ANDREWS MINSTREL   6 br.g. Black Minstrel – Lucky Pace (Lucky Brief) [1992/3 17v* 17v² a22gF] light-framed gelding: won novice hurdle at Plumpton in November: acted on heavy going: dead. *J. R. Jenkins*   93

ANDROS PRINCE   8 b.g. Blakeney – Ribamba (Ribocco) [1992/3 c24m² c25d⁴ c24d³ c24d³] good-bodied gelding: modest novice chaser: trained first 3 starts by J. McConnochie: stays 3¼m: acts on soft going, ran respectably on good to firm. *M. W. Easterby*   **c93**

ANDY BOY   9 b.g. Mr Fordette – Killonan Lass (The Parson) [1992/3 c16v³c16g⁵c17mc21furc17m⁶] good-topped, workmanlike gelding: winning chaser: no form in 1992/3: stays 2½m when conditions aren't testing: probably acts on any going: sometimes blinkered: refused once. *T. Casey*   c– –

ANDY JACK   4 ch.g. Risk Me (FR) – Gemma Kaye (Cure The Blues (USA)) [1992/3 18d 16dpu 16gF] sparely-made gelding: poor maiden on Flat: sold 1,050 gns Ascot July Sales: no sign of ability in selling hurdles: sold out of B. Forsey's stable 1,600 gns Ascot December Sales after second start, resold 1,400 gns Ascot 2nd June Sales. *J. A. Bennett*   –

ANFIELD SALLY   7 b.m. Anfield – Bargain Line (Porto Bello) [1992/3 a16gpu 16s 22d 18d⁴ 22g] sparely-made mare: poor novice selling hurdler. *Mrs P. A. Barker*   63

ANGELICA PARK   7 b.m. Simply Great (FR) – Rosana Park (Music Boy) [1992/3 20f³ 20f²] small mare: moderate handicap hurdler: creditable second at Haydock in May: stays 3m: acts on firm and good to soft going. *J. Wharton*   97

ANGELO'S DOUBLE (IRE)   5 b.h. M Double M (USA) – Bebe Altesse (GER) (Alpenkonig (GER)) [1992/3 16d⁵ 16g² 17dF 17v² 17v³] well-made horse: fair 7f winner at 3 yrs: fair novice hurdler: not raced after January: yet to race beyond 17f: acts on heavy ground: sketchy jumper. *G. A. Ham*   97

ANGELS KISS (SWE)   8 b. or br.g. Atlantic Boy – Cielo-Azzurro (He Loves Me) [1992/3 16m³ 18gF 17sF 20m² 18s³ 16g⁶ 17v*] tall gelding: 97

41

Miss J. Semple's "Annio Chilone"

selling hurdler: won at Newton Abbot (no bid) in November: stayed 2½m when conditions weren't testing: acted on good to firm and heavy ground: sketchy jumper: dead. *M. C. Pipe*

ANGEL TRAIN (IRE)   5 ch.m. Burslem – Senama (FR) (Sanctus II) [1992/3 16d a18gᵖᵘ] poor and inconsistent handicapper on Flat, stays 1m: has shown nothing in seller and claimer (blinkered) over hurdles: sold 1,300 gns Doncaster January Sales. *J. Parkes*   –

ANGLESEY RAMBLER   11 b.g. Le Johnstan – May Slave (Arctic Slave) [1992/3 c25gᵖᵘ] of little account. *J. A. Hewitt*   c– –

ANISESNO   6 ch.m. Mansingh (USA) – Missive (FR) (Bold Lad (USA)) [1992/3 18gᵖᵘ] behind in 2 sellers on Flat at 3 yrs: tailed off when pulled up in novice event in April on hurdling debut. *N. A. Callaghan*   –

ANKUD (IRE)   4 b.f. Dominion – Wurud (USA) (Green Dancer (USA)) [1992/3 17s* 16gᵖᵘ 17mᶠ] leggy, sparely-made filly: half-sister to winning hurdler Thuhool (by Formidable): modest form at up to 1m on Flat in Ireland: sold out of K. Prendergast's stable 1,700 gns Newmarket Autumn Sales: made most when winning novice selling hurdle at Newton Abbot (no bid) in February: beaten long way out next time and weakening when falling 2 out final start: headstrong: sketchy jumper. *M. C. Pipe*   80

ANNA VALLEY   7 b.m. Gleason (USA) – Paperchain (Articulate) [1992/3 22d3 18d2 24v3 20d2 21vᶠ 20s4 18v2 22d2 21g4] leggy mare: modest novice hurdler: best at distances shorter than 3m: acts on heavy going: consistent, but looks none too keen under pressure. *G. B. Balding*   86

ANNE'S BANK (IRE)   5 b.m. Burslem – West Bank (Martinmas) [1992/3 17v6 16f4] small mare: poor novice selling hurdler. *A. Moore*   63

ANNICOMBE RUN   9 b.m. Deep Run – Purcella (Straight Lad) [1992/3 21g* 21s5 24d2 22vᵖᵘ 20g 21m 17g6] smallish, workmanlike mare: fairly   121 useful handicap hurdler: won at Kempton in October: poor efforts last 4 starts: stays 3m: acts on good to firm and soft ground: has broken blood vessels. *R. Lee*

ANNIE DE POMME   9 ch.m. Leander – Pomme (Polic) [1992/3 c25d³   **c83** c27spu c24s⁶] lengthy, sparely-made mare: winning chaser: not raced after   – December: stays 25f: acts on good to firm and dead ground. *N. A. Twiston-Davies*

ANNIE KELLY   5 b.m. Oats – Deep Moppet (Deep Run) [1992/3 F16s] unfurnished mare: first living foal: dam winning Irish hurdler: tailed off in NH Flat race at Warwick in February: yet to race over hurdles or fences. *J. Wharton*

ANNIE'S DAUGHTER   9 b.m. Majestic Maharaj – Aldington Honey   **c–** (Cawston's Clown) [1992/3 c19hur c26gpu] modest pointer: failed to   complete in 2 novice chases in August. *Mrs S. M. Farr*

ANNIES ROSE   8 br.g. Soldier Rose – Easy Action (Negotiation) [1992/3   **c76** c25g³ c26mpu] sparely-made gelding: winning pointer: poor novice   – otherwise. *Ms Kim Matthews*

ANNIO CHILONE   7 b.h. Touching Wood (USA) – Alpine Alice **c117** (Abwah) [1992/3 17d c18d² c24d² c25d* c24v⁴ c24s⁴ c26v* c26v² c25d*   – c25m⁴ c26m] well-made horse: carries plenty of condition: fair hurdler: successful in novice chases at Ascot (handicap), Folkestone and Sandown (handicap) in mid-season, showing fairly useful form: creditable fourth in Sun Alliance Chase at Cheltenham in March: suited by thorough test of stamina and forcing tactics: acts on good to firm and heavy going: sound jumper: sometimes runs in snatches, but goes well for claimer P. Hide. *J. T. Gifford*

ANONA CROSS (IRE)   5 b.m. Swan's Rock – Anona-Anona (Alcide) [1992/3 aF16g 25vpu 24gpu] half-sister to winning chaser Beau Charm (by   – Beau Chapeur): dam won 3 races at up to 1¾m on Flat: no sign of ability. *R. T. Juckes*

ANOTHER BARNEY   9 ch.g. Stetchworth (USA) – Another Reef (Take   **c73** A Reef) [1992/3 18g⁵ c17f⁴ c16d³ c16m⁴] workmanlike gelding: winning   – hurdler/chaser in 1990/1: only form since on second start: races at around 2m: acts on firm going: usually races freely. *M. Dixon*

ANOTHER BOLUS   11 gr.g. Yankee Gold – Pretty Candy (Candy Cane)   **c– x** [1992/3 c24g] leggy gelding: fairly useful chaser at his best: no form since   – 1990/1: sometimes blinkered: poor jumper of fences: sold 2,800 gns Malvern June Sales. *B. J. Heffernan*

ANOTHER CANFORD   8 ch.g. Humdoleila – Little Tot (Flush Royal)   **c82** [1992/3 c21sF c26v³ c26vpu c24d⁵ c24spu] compact gelding: maiden hurdler: – poor novice chaser: stays 3¼m: acts on heavy ground: blinkered final outing. *P. G. Murphy*

ANOTHER COLUMBUS   10 b.m. St Columbus – Milk River (Another   **c–** River) [1992/3 21gpu c24fpu] leggy mare: no sign of ability. *W. John Smith*

ANOTHER CORAL   10 br.g. Green Shoon – Myralette (Deep Run) **c160** [1992/3 c21g² c21d² c21v* c20s* c26s2]   –
    Another Coral was a morning withdrawal from the Tote Cheltenham Gold Cup after he was found to have a slight strain in his off-fore tendon. He'd earned a tilt by running at least as well as ever in the Timeform Hall of Fame Chase over the course at the end of January. Patiently ridden as usual, Another Coral was just run out of it by Sibton Abbey after being produced with a well-timed run to lead soon after the last. The Timeform Hall of Fame Chase showed that Another Coral was effective at three and a quarter miles —he'd previously done nearly all his racing at up to two and a half—and it wouldn't have been a surprise if he'd given a good account of himself in the Gold Cup, especially as he was one of those proven on top-of-the-ground, conditions which prevailed on the day. Another Coral has a particularly fine record at Cheltenham and again ran well in the two big pre-Christmas

43

Tripleprint Gold Cup (Handicap Chase), Cheltenham—
Another Coral holds on well from Second Schedual and Tipping Tim (stars)

handicap chases, the Mackeson Gold Cup and its twin run under various titles since the days when it was well known as the Massey-Ferguson Gold Cup. Another Coral won the Mackeson in 1991 and finished a creditable second in a good field for the latest edition, beaten seven lengths by the progressive Tipping Tim. Both were in the field a month later for the race over the same course and distance run under the title of the Tripleprint Gold Cup, a sponsorship taken up by the film developing and processing company when A.F. Budge withdrew at the last moment because of financial difficulties. On terms 8 lb better than in the Mackeson, Another Coral, second in the same race the previous year, turned the tables comfortably on Tipping Tim, the pair divided at the finish by Irish-trained Second Schedual. The Tripleprint Gold Cup was Another Coral's fifth victory over the Cheltenham fences, but he showed that he isn't just a Cheltenham specialist when putting up an even better performance in the Hungerford Handicap Chase at Newbury in January. Another Coral won in the style of a horse capable of holding his own outside handicap company, beating the improving Very Very Ordinary, giving him 21 lb, by a length and a half, the pair of them thirty lengths clear.

Another Coral (br.g. 1983)	Green Shoon (b 1966)	Sheshoon (ch 1956)	Precipitation
			Noorani
		Chrysoprase (gr 1957)	Arctic Star
			Emerald Green
	Myralette (ch 1978)	Deep Run (ch 1966)	Pampered King
			Trial By Fire
		Evening Society (b 1968)	Even Money
			Teafield

Another Coral used to have a reputation as an edgy horse—an aversion to brass bands being one of his foibles—but he remained calm in the preliminaries in the latest season. His trainer told us in a *Timeform Interview* that Another Coral benefited from the move to his new training complex at Jackdaw's Castle high on the Cotswolds, from where Nicholson enjoyed a

Mr M. R. Deeley's "Another Coral"

magnificent season, finishing second in the trainers' table and joining the select band of jumping trainers who have reached the hundred-winner mark in a season (only Arthur Stephenson, Martin Pipe, Gordon Richards and Michael Dickinson had done so in the post-war era). Jackdaw's Castle is surrounded by its own purpose-built gallops and there isn't another stable or string in sight. 'All the horses are very relaxed and Another Coral, a nervous horse who had problems holding his form for long periods, is completely switched off here and has kept in great form,' said Nicholson. The tall, lengthy Another Coral is a good jumper and a genuine type who acts on any going. He is suited by waiting tactics and is effective at two and a half miles to three and a quarter. Another Coral's admirable versatility will give connections a wide range of options in the next season. There's little to add to the comprehensive pedigree details that appeared in Another Coral's essay in the previous edition of *Chasers & Hurdlers* except to report that his younger half-brother Raymylette (by Le Moss) won two bumpers in Ireland in the latest season before joining Henderson's yard for whom he shaped most encouragingly on his only start, when second to Trainglot in a quite valuable novice hurdle at Warwick. *D. Nicholson*

ANOTHER CORNER 10 b.g. Normandy – Liberdad (Matador) [1992/3   **c77** c23d c25g⁵ c27gᵘʳ c26dᵖᵘ c24g⁵ 25m⁶ 27g c26m⁴ c23m] compact gelding: **83** poor hurdler/chaser: stays 25f: acts on firm and dead ground: tried visored and blinkered. *T. W. Donnelly*

ANOTHER DETAIL 7 b.g. Details Galore – Milk River (Another River) [1992/3 17fᵖᵘ] sturdy gelding: of little account. *W. John Smith*   **–**

ANOTHER DYER 9 ch.g. Deep Run – Saint Society (Saint Denys)   **c– x** [1992/3 c25dᵖᵘ] big, lengthy gelding: winning hurdler: modest novice chaser   **–** at best: stays 2¾m: acts on soft going: blinkered once: poor jumper of fences. *G. Richards*

ANOTHER EARL (USA) 9 ch.g. Belted Earl (USA) – Aloran (USA) (Prince John) [1992/3 16d 16s a16gF 16s 18g 26m3 20m4 21f] rather sparely-made gelding: poor novice hurdler: effective at 2m and stays 3¼m: probably acts on any going: blinkered once. *E. Weymes*   66

ANOTHER FOUNTAIN 7 b.g. Royal Fountain – Another Joyful (Rubor) [1992/3 18g5] compact, workmanlike gelding: poor novice hurdler: stiff task only start in 1992/3: stays 2½m: best form with plenty of give in ground. *J. E. Dixon*   –

ANOTHER MARCH 7 b.g. Marching On – River Sirene (Another River) [1992/3 18m6 16m6] leggy gelding: poor 2m maiden plater over hurdles: sold 2,100 gns Doncaster January Sales, resold 1,350 gns Doncaster March Sales: blinkered once. *J. J. Birkett*   60

ANOTHER MEADOW 5 b.g. Meadowbrook – Another Joyful (Rubor) [1992/3 16dpu 20spu 16g 16dpu 17dpu] smallish, well-made gelding: third foal: half-brother to novice hurdlers Dark Fountain and Another Fountain (both by Royal Fountain): dam winning 2m hurdler: no sign of ability. *J. E. Dixon*   –

ANOTHER NICK 7 ch.g. Nicholas Bill – Another Move (Farm Walk) [1992/3 24s6 20s 24d3] leggy gelding: lightly-raced novice hurdler: stays 3m: acts on dead ground. *J. M. Jefferson*   88

ANOTHER NUT 4 b.f. Blushing Scribe (USA) – Manageress (Mandamus) [1992/3 17m5] maiden plater on Flat: tailed off in early-season juvenile hurdle. *P. D. Evans*   –

ANOTHER SCALLY 10 b.m. Scallywag – Gouly Duff (Party Mink) [1992/3 20gpu] poor plater over hurdles: sold 1,300 gns Doncaster August Sales. *J. Mackie*   –

ANOTHER SCHEDULE 12 ch.g. Beau Tudor – Mo Sgeal Fein (Kabale) [1992/3 c21fpu] strong, deep-girthed gelding: winning chaser: pulled up lame in September: stays 25f: probably acts on any going: pulls hard, and is suited by racing up with the leaders: tends to sweat. *C. P. E. Brooks*   c–

ANOTHER STRIPLIGHT 10 ch.g. Pauper – Hill Invader (Brave Invader (USA)) [1992/3 c28gpu c26gpu c24g c26mpu] big, lengthy gelding: tubed: shows traces of stringhalt: modest handicap chaser at best: showed nothing in 1992/3: blinkered once. *R. Brotherton*   c–

ANOTHER TROUP 11 b.g. Beau Charmeur (FR) – Ballinabranna (Vivi Tarquin) [1992/3 c21v5 c26spu c24v4 c24v5 c26sF c26g4 c26g6 c27gF c21g6 c21f6] strong, lengthy gelding: poor chaser: stays well: acts on heavy going: sometimes blinkered: reluctant, and needs plenty of driving. *R. D. Townsend*   c80 §

ANOTHER VINTAGE 4 ch.g. Risk Me (FR) – Meanieminymoe (Star Appeal) [1992/3 16v 18s5 18d5 16v3 16gpu 17g2 16m] leggy gelding: sprint maiden on Flat: poor form in juvenile hurdles: changed hands 1,550 gns Ascot February Sales: stays 2¼m: probably acts on heavy going. *P. D. Cundell*   82

ANSHEGEE 8 b. or br.m. Strong Gale – Fairy Queen (Prefairy) [1992/3 18gpu] lengthy, sparely-made mare: novice selling hurdler: ungenuine: sold 2,300 gns Malvern June Sales. *R. J. Price*   – §

ANSTEY GADABOUT 7 ch.g. Sixpenny Moon – Tikiland (Pedigree Unknown) [1992/3 22s 18m] leggy gelding: first foal: dam never ran: seems of little account over hurdles: won a point in March. *W. G. Turner*   –

ANSTON SPIRIT 8 b.m. Brianston Zipper – Flashy Joe (Vicky Joe) [1992/3 c21dpu] small mare: let down by her jumping in 2 points and on steeplechasing debut. *T. M. Jones*   c– x

ANTAGONIST 6 b.g. Aragon – Princess Story (Prince de Galles) [1992/3 17g5 17g] close-coupled gelding: poor maiden on Flat: well beaten in novice hurdles. *R. M. Stronge*   –

ANTARCTIC CALL 6 b.g. Callernish – Polarogan (Tarqogan) [1992/3 F17d] strong gelding: first foal: dam, unplaced in 3 NH Flat races in Ireland, half-sister to several winners, notably very smart staying chaser Arctic Call (by Callernish) and fair out-and-out staying chaser Polar Nomad: seventh of 21 in NH Flat race at Sandown in October: yet to race over hurdles or fences. *O. Sherwood*

ANTE UP (IRE) 5 b.h. Sharpen Up – Petillante (USA) (Riverman (USA)) [1992/3 16s⁵ 17dᴿ 16sᴿ] tall, close-coupled horse: bad novice hurdler, temperamental to boot: blinkered twice. *J. Akehurst* §§

ANTHONY BELL 7 b.g. Carlingford Castle – Birthday Offering (Pitpan) [1992/3 c21g⁴ c16mᶠ c17sᵘʳ 22m 22dᵖᵘ c17m* c17g*] workmanlike gelding: novice hurdler: improved over fences on last 2 outings and won novice events at Sedgefield (handicap) and Hexham in May: best efforts at around 2m on a sound surface: headstrong, suited by waiting tactics. *T. J. Carr* **c96** –

ANTICO NATIVO (IRE) 5 b.g. Be My Native (USA) – David's Pleasure (Welsh Saint) [1992/3 18g⁴ 20m⁵] leggy, narrow gelding: modest hurdler: creditable efforts early in season: barely stays 2½m: acts on good to firm ground, and extremely well on equitrack: suited by waiting tactics. *S. Dow* **101**

ANTIGUAN FLYER 4 b.c. Shirley Heights – Fleet Girl (Habitat) [1992/3 16s² a16g* a16g⁵ 17f⁶ 17g² 21g² 17d⁴ 18d 25m³] angular colt: fair at around 1½m on Flat: sold out of B. Hills's stable 12,500 gns Newmarket Autumn Sales: modest form over hurdles: won juvenile event at Southwell in January: ran creditably when placed afterwards: effective at around 2m and stays 25f: acts on good to firm and soft going, and on fibresand. *J. R. Bostock* **89**

ANTIGUAN SMILE 8 ch.g. Croghan Hill – Evan's Love (Master Owen) [1992/3 20m 2 1mʳᵗʳ] big, leggy gelding: poor hurdler: fell second only start over fences: often mulish at start. *M. D. Hammond* **c–** **– §**

ANTIGUAN SOL 5 ch.m. Nearly A Hand – Solhoon (Tycoon II) [1992/3 16d 22d 22fᵖᵘ] lengthy mare: half-sister to winning hurdler Solerof (by Averof): dam won sellers over 6f and 7f: no sign of ability. *Mrs P. N. Dutfield*

ANTI MATTER 8 b.g. Kings Lake (USA) – Firyal (Nonoalco (USA)) [1992/3 16f² 16f³] leggy, angular gelding: fair hurdler/chaser, lightly raced nowadays: creditable efforts over hurdles in May: stays 2½m: possibly unsuited by heavy going, acts on any other. *Mrs J. G. Retter* **c–** **115**

ANTINOUS 9 ch.g. Hello Gorgeous (USA) – Marthe Meynet (Welsh Pageant) [1992/3 c16g³ c18dᶠ c16d³ c16s² c21s⁵ c18dᶠ] smallish gelding: fair chaser nowadays: not raced after January: sold 2,600 gns Doncaster May Sales: best at around 2m: acts on any going: poor jumper: held up and often finds little under pressure. *M. H. Easterby* **c108 x** –

ANTONIN (FR) 5 ch.g. Italic (FR) – Pin'hup (FR) (Signani (FR)) [1992/3 17g 26m 25spᵘ 22d c16s² c16g* c17s* c17s² c17f* c20s* c16g²] **c135 p** –

Golden Eagle Novices' Chase, Ascot—Antonin continues to improve

sparely-made gelding: poor form over hurdles: very much better over fences and put up a useful performance when second to Viking Flagship in valuable novice event at Punchestown in April: earlier won at Edinburgh, Huntingdon (2, one a handicap) and quite valuable event at Ascot: best form at around 2m, but should stay further: acts on any ground: jumps well and races with zest. *Mrs S. A. Bramall*

ANTRIM COUNTY 8 ch.g. Deep Run – Gothic Arch (Gail Star) [1992/3 c25d4 c24d5 c20s5 c18s2 c24s5 c20vF c24d2 c20vF c20d3 c22vur c16d6 c25f5 c20s2 c25v2 c21dur] fairly useful chaser: ran creditably considering bad mistake 4 out in valuable handicap at Aintree in April on twelfth start: stays 25f: probably acts on any going: blinkered third and fourth starts. *Patrick Mullins, Ireland* **c115**
–

ANY DREAM WOULD DO 4 b.f. Efisio – Pasha's Dream (Tarboosh (USA)) [1992/3 16g4 18d2 16spu 16f* 16g2] rather sparely-made filly: half-sister to fair hurdler/winning chaser Obeliski (by Aragon): poor 1m winner on Flat: won juvenile hurdle at Wetherby in May: creditable second in novice event on same course later in month: yet to race beyond 2¼m: acts on firm and dead going. *P. Beaumont* **84**

ANY GOSSIP 10 b.g. Proverb – Bartina (Bargello) [1992/3 c22g c17d c22gur c16g* c18dpu c21d5 c17d c16dpu c16fpu] angular, workmanlike gelding: half-brother to winning hurdler/chaser Bartina's Star (by Le Bavard): dam winning Irish hurdler/chaser at up to 2¼m: winning hurdler: fair chaser: won at Tramore (trained until after then by E. O'Grady) in August: ran poorly afterwards: effective at 2m and probably stays 2¾m: acts on good to firm and dead ground. *J. J. O'Neill* **c107 d**

ANYONE'S FANCY 8 ch.m. Callernish – Madam Helen (Shackleton) [1992/3 22s5] sparely-made mare: lightly-raced hurdler: once-raced over fences: probably stays 2¾m: acts on soft going: headstrong. *D. R. Gandolfo* **c–**
85

ANYTHINGYOULIKE 4 b.g. Lighter – Mill Miss (Typhoon) [1992/3 F16s F17m] unfurnished gelding: half-brother to winning pointer Miss Cone (by Celtic Cone): dam of no account: mid-division in NH Flat races: yet to race over hurdles. *C. A. Smith*

APACHE BRAVE 8 gr.g. Warpath – Et Tu (Marcus Brutus) [1992/3 16d* 20msu 16g6 21v5 21s6 20s] small, leggy gelding: won novice hurdle at Hexham in October: generally ran creditably afterwards (not raced after January): sold only 820 gns Doncaster May Sales: stays 21f: acts on heavy going. *J. L. Goulding* **88**

APARECIDA (FR) 7 b. or br.m. Direct Flight – Doll Poppy (FR) (Carmarthen (FR)) [1992/3 c27vF 17vpu 22vpu] ex-Irish mare: half-sister to winning French jumper Gaastra (by Le Pontet): winning pointer: no sign of ability over hurdles: fell first on steeplechasing debut. *T. B. Hallett* **c–**
–

APOLLO KING 7 b.g. Indian King (USA) – Mehudenna (Ribero) [1992/3 17f4 20s] compact gelding: fairly useful hurdler in 1991/2: well beaten 1992/3: stays 2½m: probably acts on any going: sometimes breaks blood vessels: often amateur ridden: usually goes well at Plumpton. *P. Mitchell* **–**

APOLLO RED 4 ch.g. Dominion – Woolpack (Golden Fleece (USA)) [1992/3 16spu] modest maiden at around a mile on Flat: sold 2,100 gns Ascot November Sales: tailed off when pulled up in juvenile hurdle in December. *P. W. Harris* **–**

APPLIANCEOFSCIENCE 6 b.g. Bairn (USA) – Moonlight Serenade (Crooner) [1992/3 a16g] compact gelding: selling hurdler: will prove best at 2m: acts on dead ground, below form on heavy and fibresand: wears blinkers. *A. S. Reid* **–**

APPLIED GRAPHICS (IRE) 5 br.m. Bulldozer – Welsh Wise (Welsh Saint) [1992/3 17g 16vpu 18dpu a22g5 a24gF 23d4] lengthy, sparely-made mare: bad novice hurdler. *J. Mackie* **61**

APRIL'S BABY 9 b.m. Paico – Manhattan Brandy (Frankincense) [1992/3 c21vur c21gpu c21f4] leggy mare: poor novice hurdler/chaser: occasionally wears hood: formerly temperamental. *Miss C. J. E. Caroe* **c69**

APRIL SHADOW 4 b.f. Shardari – X-Data (On Your Mark) [1992/3 16s 18d^{pu}] sparely-made filly: poor maiden on Flat: sold out of C. Thornton's stable 2,500 gns Doncaster October Sales: showed nothing in mid-season juvenile hurdles. *Mrs P. Sly*   –

APRIL'S MODEL LADY 7 b.m. Shaab – Dream Lady (Kalimnos) [1992/3 22f⁴ 22g 17m⁴ 16m⁵ c16g²] poor novice hurdler: second in novice event at Hereford in May on chasing debut: stays 2¾m: acts on firm ground: will probably improve over fences. *N. A. Twiston-Davies*   c78 p / 71

APSIMORE 6 ch.m. Touching Wood (USA) – Balgreggan (Hallez (FR)) [1992/3 22d 25s 18s 23s³ 26d⁵ 24s⁴ 23d⁴ 24f² 22f³] neat mare: modest novice hurdler: stays 3m: acts on any going. *J. C. Tuck*   88

AQUILIFER 13 ch.g. Deep Run – Gentle Eagle (Symbol) [1992/3 c26v⁴] big, rather plain gelding: smart chaser: finished lame only start of 1992/3 (December): needs testing conditions when racing at 3m nowadays, and is well suited by a thorough test of stamina: acts on heavy going and is unsuited by top-of-the-ground: tough and genuine. *M. C. Pipe*   c–

ARABIAN BOLD (IRE) 5 br.g. Persian Bold – Bodham (Bustino) [1992/3 17f^F 17s⁶ 16f³ 16f* 16m*] small, workmanlike gelding: useful hurdler: won minor event at Warwick and handicap at Uttoxeter in May: raced only at around 2m: acts on firm going: hard puller, suited by forcing tactics and strong handling. *N. J. Henderson*   131

ARAGONA 4 b.f. Aragon – Polly Worth (Wolver Hollow) [1992/3 16g 16g 16s 16v⁴] leggy, sparely-made filly: poor peformer on Flat (7f winner) and over hurdles: retained 800 gns Ascot November Sales. *P. D. Cundell*   66

ARAGON AYR 5 b. or br.g. Aragon – Brig of Ayr (Brigadier Gerard) [1992/3 17d 16g⁶ 17d 16g⁶ 18g⁶ 17m² 17s*] workmanlike gelding: maiden plater on Flat: won claiming hurdle at Perth in April: yet to race beyond 2¼m: acts on good to firm and soft ground. *P. Monteith*   97

ARAGON COURT 5 b.g. Aragon – Balatina (Balidar) [1992/3 18m⁵] compact gelding: winning 1¼m plater on Flat: fifth in early-season selling hurdle at Market Rasen: sold 2,700 gns Ascot November Sales. *J. Pearce*   67

ARAGON MIST 4 b.f. Aragon – Feathers Fly (Busted) [1992/3 F16g] second foal: dam never ran: behind in NH Flat race at Worcester in March: yet to race over hurdles. *Mrs N. S. Sharpe*

ARANY 6 b.g. Precocious – Bellagio (Busted) [1992/3 17v 17d⁶ 16g⁵ 16d*] angular gelding: fairly useful miler on Flat nowadays: improved form over hurdles when winning novice handicap at Uttoxeter in April comfortably by 12 lengths: likely to prove best at around 2m: acts on dead ground: open to further improvement. *M. H. Tompkins*   93 p

ARCADIAN PRINCESS 4 b.f. Teenoso (USA) – Top Shot (Grundy) [1992/3 17v^{pu} 18m⁴ 17s] small, leggy filly: no sign of ability on Flat: sold out of Miss A. Whitfield's stable 600 gns Newmarket Autumn Sales: poor juvenile hurdler. *B. Byford*   61

ARCHIE BROWN 6 b.g. Deep Run – Fairgoi (Baragoi) [1992/3 21v² 16g* 20g^{pu}] strong, angular gelding with scope: very much a chasing type: second foal: half-brother to winning Irish hurdler/chaser Gnome's Tycoon (by Strong Gale): dam, NH Flat race winner in Ireland, placed over hurdles: ran promisingly in novice hurdle in January on debut, and 3 months later won similar event at Ayr by 15 lengths: swerved badly left fifth, soon well behind and pulled up 3 out when long odds on at Ascot next time (found to have chipped knees and is to undergo surgery): stays 21f: acts on heavy ground. *S. E. Sherwood*   122

ARCOT 5 b.g. Formidable (USA) – Pagan Queen (Vaguely Noble) [1992/3 16d* 17d² 17d* 16d^{ur} 16g⁶] close-coupled gelding: successful in novice hurdles at Uttoxeter in November and Newcastle in January: ran as though something amiss final start: will prove best at around 2m: acts on dead   123

Shoveler Novices' Hurdle, Newcastle—Arcot has quickened clear by the last

ground: pulls hard, tends to hang left and idles in front: not an accomplished jumper as yet: has good turn of foot and is held up. *J. A. Glover*

ARCROSS 7 b.g. Vision (USA) – Heidi Von Allmen (Ballymore) [1992/3 18gpu] behind in NH Flat race and when pulled up in a selling hurdle. *S. Dow* —

ARCTIC BARON 8 b.g. Baron Blakeney – Learctic (Lepanto (GER)) [1992/3 c27m³ c26f³ c26f³ c27d⁴ c24f⁵] lengthy gelding: moderate handicap chaser: stays well: probably acts on any going: sometimes blinkered: needs keeping up to his work. *Mrs J. C. Dawe* **c92** —

ARCTIC BLOOM 7 gr.m. Scallywag – Constant Rose (Confusion) [1992/3 c21gF] leggy mare: no sign of ability: blinkered once. *C. I. Ratcliffe* **c—** —

ARCTIC CALL 10 b.g. Callernish – Polar Lady (Arctic Slave) [1992/3 c28d²] tall gelding: has had 2 soft-palate operations: very smart chaser: finished lame when second of 4 at Cheltenham in November: stays well: acts on any going: usually blinkered but has run well when not: usually makes running: sometimes let down by his jumping. *O. Sherwood* **c154 ?** —

ARCTIC CIRCLE (IRE) 4 ch.g. Northern Baby (CAN) – High Quail (USA) (Blushing Groom (FR)) [1992/3 16m* 17m* 17g* 17v⁶] rather unfurnished gelding: plating-class maiden on Flat: won juvenile hurdles at Worcester, Huntingdon and Ascot and finished creditable sixth at Cheltenham in first half of season: will stay further than 17f: acts on good to firm and heavy going. *Miss A. J. Whitfield* 105

ARCTIC COURSE (IRE) 5 ch.g. Crash Course – Polar Vixen (Arctic Slave) [1992/3 F16g F17d³] half-brother to winning hurdler Arpal Conquest (by Brave Invader): dam sister to 2 winning jumpers, notably useful staying chaser Yanworth: successful in 2 points in Ireland, including in January: third in NH Flat race at Ascot in April: yet to race over hurdles or in a steeplechase. *D. Nicholson*

ARCTICFLOW (USA) 8 ch.g. Arctic Tern (USA) – Bold Flora (USA) c–
(Bold Favorite (USA)) [1992/3 25d a22g³ 21gᵖᵘ 25m⁶ 25g c18g⁶ c18m⁵] –
good-bodied gelding: poor novice hurdler/chaser: usually blinkered. *N. B. Thomson*

ARCTIC KINSMAN 5 gr.g. Relkino – Arctic Advert (Birdbrook)
[1992/3 F17d* F17mˢᵘ F16f⁴] lengthy, unfurnished gelding: third foal: dam,
lightly-raced maiden, from successful jumping family: won NH Flat race at
Ascot in April: fourth at Haydock in May: yet to race over hurdles or fences.
N. A. Twiston-Davies

ARCTIC LINE 5 b.g. Green Ruby (USA) – Sally Ann III (Port Corsair)
[1992/3 F17g F17m] leggy non-thoroughbred gelding: half-brother to
winning hurdler Always Dangerous (by Celtic Cone): in rear in early-season
NH Flat races and 2 maidens on Flat in the spring: yet to race over hurdles
or fences. *J. M. Bradley*

ARCTIC OATS 8 ch.m. Oats – Arctic Festival (Arctic Slave) [1992/3
22m⁵] leggy mare: fair hurdler, lightly raced: stays 3m: acts on firm going: –
visored twice. *W. W. Haigh*

ARCTIC PADDY 10 ch.g. Paddy's Stream – Chorabelle (Choral Society) c–
[1992/3 c21g⁵] strong gelding: novice hunter chaser: will stay very long
distances: acts on firm and dead ground: sketchy jumper. *Miss C. Saunders*

ARCTIC RED 6 ch.g. Deep Run – Snow Sweet (Arctic Slave) [1992/3
F16v⁴ F17m] rangy gelding: has plenty of scope: brother to poor maiden
jumper Snowy Run: dam won NH Flat race in Ireland: signs of a little ability
in NH Flat races: yet to race over hurdles or fences. *D. Nicholson*

ARCTIC ROSE 9 b.m. Soldier Rose – Cool Gipsy (Romany Air) [1992/3 c–
c26gᵖᵘ] winning pointer: tailed off when pulled up in maiden hunter chase in
May. *Mrs R. C. Matheson*

ARCTIC RULER 7 ch.g. Deep Run – Artic Leap (Arctic Slave) [1992/3 c–
25s⁴ 22vᵖᵘ c21vᵖᵘ] compact gelding: poor novice hurdler: showed little on 71
chasing debut: stays 25f: acts on soft going. *D. J. G. Murray-Smith*

ARCTIC SKYLIGHT 9 ch.g. Lighter – Arctic Dawn (Arctic Slave) c113
[1992/3 18g³ c21d* c16m* c18m² c18d*] workmanlike gelding: fair hurdler: 113
successful in novice chases at Perth, Carlisle and Bangor early in season:
stayed 2½m: acted on good to firm and heavy going: dead. *G. Richards*

ARCTIC TEAL 9 b.g. Town And Country – Arctic Warbler (Deep Run) c114 §
[1992/3 c24g³ c26s⁴ c23v² c24s⁴ c26v³ c26s³ c28g c26d⁴ c27d⁴ c26m⁴] –
good-bodied gelding: fair handicap chaser: stays 3¼m: acts on heavy and
good to firm going: usually blinkered or visored: needs plenty of driving and
is a difficult ride: unreliable. *O. Sherwood*

ARDBRIN 10 ch.g. Bulldozer – Hazels Fancy (Prefairy) [1992/3 c16d³ c125
c16s⁶ c21v* c21d⁴ c21f* c18d²] leggy, close-coupled gelding: fairly useful –

Fulwell Handicap Chase, Kempton—the grey Calapaez's mistake lets in Ardbrin

chaser: successful in handicaps at Kempton (quite valuable event) in January and Wincanton (3 ran) in March: effective at 2m and probably stays 3m: acts on any going: blinkered once: front runner: jumps well. *T. P. Tate*

ARDCRONEY CHIEF 7 ch.g. Connaught – Duresme (Starry Halo) [1992/3 c18g² c17d* c16g³ c16d⁴ c21d* c22s⁶ c20g c24s² c20g⁴ c26m² c26m³ c20sᵖᵘ] big, workmanlike gelding: winning hurdler: won novice chases at Towcester and Huntingdon in first half of season: generally below form afterwards: stays 21f: probably needs an easy surface: blinkered fourth and final outings. *D. R. Gandolfo* **c96**
–

ARDEARNED 6 b.m. Ardross – Divine Penny (Divine Gift) [1992/3 22d 20fᵇᵈ 22d 18s 16s] small, compact mare: novice selling hurdler: no form for a long time. *Mrs J. A. Young* –

ARDESEE 13 ch.g. Le Coq d'Or – Katie Little (Nulli Secundus) [1992/3 c24s* c26d⁴ c27g⁴ c33m⁶] plain gelding: fairly useful hunter chaser on his day: won at Chepstow in February: creditable fourth at Taunton in April 2 starts later, easily best effort afterwards: out-and-out stayer: acts on heavy going: sometimes blinkered: usually jumps soundly. *D. J. Wintle* **c100**
–

ARDGLASS BOY 10 b.g. Black Minstrel – My Mela (Alibi II) [1992/3 23g³ 28d⁴ 22s⁵] won 2 points in Ireland in 1989: poor form over hurdles, including in a seller. *J. L. Eyre* 67

ARDILES 9 b.g. Windjammer (USA) – Primmy (Primera) [1992/3 18g 22d*] smallish, sparely-made gelding: collapsed and died after winning selling handicap hurdle at Sedgefield in October: stayed 2¾m: acted on dead ground. *R. O'Leary* 72

ARDLUSSA BAY 5 b.m. Miramar Reef – Coliemore (Coliseum) [1992/3 21g 21d⁴ 20s* 23dᵇᵈ 21s⁴ 21v² 25g* 21s* 25d 20g²] leggy, workmanlike mare: improved hurdler: won novice events at Carlisle in November and Wetherby (mares event) in March and handicap at Ayr in between: effective at 2½m and stays 25f: acts on heavy going. *J. M. Jefferson* 112

ARD T'MATCH 8 b.g. Ardross – Love Match (USA) (Affiliate (USA)) [1992/3 25f⁴ 22g c25d⁴ c25d* c33v³ c30s⁵ c27g⁴ c25s³ c25g²] sturdy gelding: fair hurdler: won novice handicap chase at Wolverhampton in November: generally ran creditably afterwards: well suited by thorough test of stamina: acts on heavy ground: has worn blinkers, usually visored nowadays. *A. L. Forbes* **c95**
–

AREMEF (USA) 4 b. or br.g. Northern Baby (CAN) – Bambina Linda (ARG) (Liloy (FR)) [1992/3 17d* 17g² 17f³ 17g² 17g*] leggy gelding: fair form over middle distances on Flat: won juvenile hurdle at Stratford in February and novice hurdle on same course in May: ran creditably in between: will stay beyond 17f: acts on dead and firm ground: takes a good hold. *Mrs J. Cecil* 118

ARE-OH 4 ch.g. Noalto – Miss Racine (Dom Racine (FR)) [1992/3 21f] fourth foal: half-brother to winning hurdler Master Ofthe House (by Kind of Hush): dam won over 1m in Ireland: tailed off in novice hurdle at Wetherby in May. *W. G. Reed* –

ARFER MOLE (IRE) 5 b.g. Carlingford Castle – Sharpaway (Royal Highway) [1992/3 F16g⁵] half-brother to 3 winning jumpers by Deep Run, notably high-class Mole Board: dam Irish NH Flat race winner: fifth of 22 in NH Flat race at Kempton in February: yet to race over hurdles or fences. *J. A. B. Old* –

ARGAKIOS 6 b.g. Busted – Salamina (Welsh Pageant) [1992/3 16v⁴ a16g³ 25vᶠ 17g²] leggy, sparely-made gelding: modest novice hurdler: sold 2,100 gns Ascot May Sales: should stay beyond 17f (pulled hard and was beaten when falling 2 out over 25f): acts on dead and good to firm ground, probably on fibresand: visored last 2 outings. *D. Burchell* 91

ARIADLER (IRE) 5 b.g. Mister Lord (USA) – Arianrhod (L'Homme Arme) [1992/3 21v] first foal: dam ran once: tailed off in novice hurdle at Hexham in November: sold 4,800 gns in May. *W. A. Stephenson* –

ARISTOCRATIC PETER (USA)   6 b.g. Sir Ivor – Glimmer Glass (USA) (The Axe II) [1992/3 18g⁶ 17m 17d a16gᵖᵘ 17g] sturdy, good-bodied gelding: poor maiden plater over hurdles: blinkered twice: sold 2,000 gns Ascot July Sales. *D. W. Browning*   60

ARISTOCRAT VELVET   11 b.g. Bold Lad (IRE) – Majestic's Gold (Rheingold) [1992/3 16mᵖᵘ] leggy gelding: very lightly-raced novice hurdler. *Mrs A. Swinbank*   –

ARLEY GALE   5 ch.m. Scallywag – Lady Letitia (Le Bavard (FR)) [1992/3 F17m] lengthy mare: second foal: dam, winning Irish hurdler, half-sister to Wayward Lad: seventh of 17 in early-season NH Flat race at Bangor: yet to race over hurdles or fences. *D. McCain*   –

ARMAGRET   8 b.g. Mandrake Major – Friendly Glen (Furry Glen) [1992/3 c21d² c21m c21g³ c26s⁴ c20g⁴ c20d* c21d* c20g* c21m³ c21s⁵ c23d²] lengthy, workmanlike gelding: improved into a useful chaser in 1992/3, winning at Newcastle (twice) and Wetherby (Marston Moor Chase (Limited Handicap)) in second half of season: good third to Second Schedual in Cathcart Challenge Cup at Cheltenham on ninth outing: effective at around 2½m and stays 3m: acts on any going. *B. E. Wilkinson*   c143 –

ARMALA   8 ch.g. Deep Run – Bardicate (Bargello) [1992/3 c21s⁶ c17s³ c22sᵖᵘ c16d c21g* c21f*] strong, lengthy gelding: trained until after fourth start by A. Blackmore: much improved afterwards, winning handicap chase at Lingfield and novice event at Huntingdon in March: stays 21f: acts on firm ground: jumps fences soundly: should progress further. *J. T. Gifford*   c97 p –

ARMATEUR (FR)   5 b.g. Miller's Mate – Artistically (USA) (Ribot) [1992/3 F16d⁴ aF16g³ 16v³] in frame in NH Flat races (trained by J. White until after first start) and a novice hurdle at Worcester in April (promising third): should improve. *J. C. McConnochie*   85 p

ARMED FORCE   6 b.g. Shernazar – Skittish (USA) (Far North (CAN)) [1992/3 23m⁶ 22f⁵] poor staying maiden on Flat: poor form in novice hurdles in May. *F. Gray*   72

ARM IN ARM   8 b.h. Pas de Seul – Social Partner (Sparkler) [1992/3 23s⁴ 23s⁶ 24v 23v 24vᵖᵘ] leggy horse: lightly-raced novice hurdler, poor form: stays 3m: acts on soft going: blinkered final outing. *F. Gray*   76

Marston Moor Chase (Limited Handicap), Wetherby—the winner Armagret (D. Byrne)

AROUND THE HORN 6 b. or br.g. Strong Gale – Tou Wan (Grand Roi) **c99**
[1992/3 c20g² c16g* c16s* c16vᵖᵘ] good-topped gelding: novice hurdler: –
won novice chases at Hereford and Wetherby in first half of season: ran
poorly final outing (January): stays 2½m: acts on soft ground: not yet an
accomplished jumper. *Andrew Turnell*

ARPAL BREEZE 8 ch.g. Deep Run – Arpal Magic (Master Owen) **c82**
[1992/3 c24f²] well-made gelding: winning hurdler: novice chaser: sold –
10,000 gns Doncaster August Sales: second in hunter chase at Lingfield in
March: probably stays 3m and acts on any ground. *J. M. Turner*

ARRAN VIEW 7 br.g. Aragon – Shadow Play (Busted) [1992/3 21d*
21mᵖᵘ] leggy gelding: ran easily best race for a long time when 50/1-winner 92
of selling handicap hurdle at Uttoxeter (no bid) in April: ran as though
something amiss next time: stays 21f: acts on firm and dead ground. *B. J.
Llewellyn*

ARRASTRA 5 b.m. Bustino – Island Mill (Mill Reef (USA)) [1992/3 a16g⁵
16d⁶ 16g⁶ 18g* 22sᵖᵘ] sparely-made mare: moderate middle-distance 85
performer on Flat: sold out of I. Balding's stable 7,000 gns Newmarket
Autumn Sales: won conditional jockeys selling handicap hurdle at
Folkestone (bought in 6,600 gns) in March: sold 6,200 gns Doncaster May
Sales: stays 2¼m: best form on good going. *R. Lee*

ARR EFF BEE 6 b.g. Crooner – Miss Desla (Light Thrust) [1992/3 21f⁶
21d⁴ 22g* 21f⁴ 25m²] close-coupled gelding: selling hurdler: bought in 3,100 93
gns after winning at Market Rasen in April: good second in non-seller final
outing: stays 25f: acts on dead and good to firm ground: blinkered nowadays.
J. P. Smith

ARROW DANCER 7 b.g. Gorytus (USA) – Rose And Honey (Amber
Rama (USA)) [1992/3 17m⁵ 17m*] leggy gelding: lightly-raced 2m hurdler: 83
won seller at Carlisle (no bid) in September: acts on good to firm ground. *J. J.
O'Neill*

ARSONIST 8 ch.g. Ardross – Dragonist (Dragonara Palace (USA)) **c–**
[1992/3 c17sᵖᵘ 20fᵖᵘ] lengthy gelding: one-time fair handicap hurdler: no –
show in 1992/3, including on chasing debut: stays 2½m: acts on firm
ground: front runner. *A. G. Blackmore*

ARTFUL ABBOT 9 ch.g. The Parson – She's Clever (Clever Fella) **c100**
[1992/3 c22g³ c25g* c28d⁴ 21d* 22v⁴ 25s 23g⁶ 21dᵖᵘ 25m⁴] lengthy, 113 d
well-made gelding: usually impresses in appearance: fair hurdler/chaser:
won handicaps over fences at Southwell and over hurdles at Cheltenham
(conditional jockeys) in first half of season: ran poorly last 4 starts: stays
3m: probably acts on any going: front runner: refused once: best in blinkers
over fences. *S. E. Sherwood*

ARTFUL ARTHUR 7 b.g. Rolfe (USA) – Light of Zion (Pieces of Eight) **c–**
[1992/3 c21sᵖᵘ c24dᵖᵘ] workmanlike gelding: poor hurdler: no sign of ability –
over fences: shapes like a thorough stayer: acts on dead ground: usually
blinkered nowadays. *J. C. McConnochie*

ARTHURLILY 4 b.f. Norwick (USA) – Quite Lucky (Precipice Wood)
[1992/3 F17sᵖᵘ F16s 16gᵖᵘ] workmanlike filly: third foal: dam, winning 2m
hurdler, stayed 2½m: no sign of ability in NH Flat races and a novice hurdle.
C. D. Broad

ARTHUR'S MINSTREL 6 ch.g. Black Minstrel – Jadida (FR) (Yelapa **c97**
(FR)) [1992/3 c21f² c21g² c24d² c21s² c24g⁴] tall, sturdy gelding with plenty –
of scope: winning hurdler: modest novice chaser: trained until after fourth
start by W. A. Stephenson: not raced after January: stays 3m: acts on any
ground: jumps soundly in the main. *P. Cheesbrough*

ARTHURS STONE 7 ch.g. Kings Lake (USA) – Two Rock (Mill Reef
(USA)) [1992/3 18m 18f³ 16f² 18s²] angular, workmanlike gelding: selling 92
hurdler: sold 2,500 gns Ascot September Sales: pulled up in a point in April:
resold 2,100 gns Malvern June Sales: stays 2¼m: acts on soft and firm
ground: races with head high: visored once: formerly inconsistent (used to
break blood vessels). *O. Brennan*

ARTIC WINGS (IRE) 5 b.m. Mazaad – Evening Flight (Northfields (USA)) [1992/3 F14s F17g 17f⁵ 18s⁴ 16m³ 16m⁵] sturdy mare: second foal: dam poor Irish Flat maiden: poor novice hurdler: acts on good to firm and soft going. *O. Brennan*   76

ARTIFICER 7 b.g. Sexton Blake – Sea Pills (Quayside) [1992/3 22g 21spu] rather leggy gelding: poor novice selling hurdler: blinkered once: looks none too keen. *Mrs S. Taylor*   – §

AS ALWAYS (IRE) 5 ch.m. Hatim (USA) – Red Magic (Red God) [1992/3 21m] compact mare: modest stayer at best on Flat when trained by G. Lewis: behind in early-season novice hurdle: sold 1,850 gns Ascot February Sales. *D. T. Thom*   –

ASARGAR 7 b.g. Gorytus (USA) – Astara (Nishapour (FR)) [1992/3 16s 16m 18v² 17d 18f³ 17g⁶ 16g 20m² 16d³] sparely-made gelding: moderate handicap hurdler: stays 2½m: acts on any ground. *J. P. Smith*   94

ASBAAB 8 b.g. Young Generation – The Yellow Girl (Yellow God) [1992/3 c21spu 16dpu 17v a18g 17m] compact gelding: poor novice hurdler/chaser. *Mrs J. Wonnacott*   c– / –

ASCOT DELPHINIUM 6 b.m. Baron Blakeney – Aunt Livia (Royalty) [1992/3 16vpu 16vpu] leggy mare: no sign of ability. *J. Webber*   –

ASCOT LAD 8 ch.g. Broadsword (USA) – Aunt Livia (Royalty) [1992/3 c16dF c21s⁵] tall, close-coupled gelding: winning hurdler: modest form when fifth in novice chase at Bangor in December: will stay beyond 21f: best form on a sound surface: jumps fences none too fluently. *J. Webber*   c91 / –

AS D'EBOLI (FR) 6 b.g. What A Guest – Ana d'Eboli (FR) (King of The Castle (USA)) [1992/3 17s⁵ 20d³ 16g 20d⁵ 20g² 17d⁵ 21s³ 16m³ 22m³ 21g*] neat gelding: selling hurdler: sold out of J. FitzGerald's stable 1,600 gns Doncaster March Sales after fifth outing: won at Hexham (no bid) in May: stays 2¾m: probably acts on any going: blinkered (ran creditably) fourth and fifth outings. *M. D. Hammond*   90

AS DU TREFLE (FR) 5 ch.g. Petit Montmorency (USA) – Gall de Marsalin (FR) (Roi de Perse II) [1992/3 16v* 17s⁴ 22s* 20d* 25f³] unfurnished gelding: won twice at around 11f on Flat in French Provinces in 1991: took well to hurdling and won novice events at Leicester, Newton Abbot (conditional jockeys) and Haydock in second half of season: ran well when third in quite valuable novice event at Aintree in April: stays 25f: probably acts on any going: front runner: jumps well in main. *M. C. Pipe*   124

AS GOOD AS GOLD 7 ch.g. Oats – Goldyke (Bustino) [1992/3 c17f⁴ c21gpu c27dpu 22vpu] workmanlike gelding: winning hurdler: no form for some time, including over fences: blinkered once. *T. M. Jones*   c– / –

ASHBOURNE LAD 11 b. or br.g. Persian Bold – In The Clover (Meadow Mint (USA)) [1992/3 a18gF] neat gelding: lightly-raced winning hurdler: dead. *G. A. Ham*   –

ASHDREN 6 b.h. Lochnager – Stellaris (Star Appeal) [1992/3 17s³ 17f⁶ 17d³ a16g³ 17g* 17f²] workmanlike horse: moderate form over hurdles: won amateurs novice event at Fakenham in May: ran well next time: unlikely to stay beyond 17f: acts on any ground. *A. Harrison*   94

ASHFOLD COPSE 7 ch.g. Broadsword (USA) – Celtic Well (Celtic Cone) [1992/3 c17gur c21m* c21s* c24vpu c21s² c24g* c25mF] workmanlike gelding: useful hurdler: similar form to win novice chases at Windsor and Huntingdon in November and Kempton in February: suffered a fatal fall at Cheltenham in March: stayed 3m: acted on good to firm and soft ground. *G. Harwood*   c124

ASHMAE 11 b.g. Anax – Solentown (Town Crier) [1992/3 c19vpu c21gF c27g⁴ c18sF] leggy, sparely-made gelding: poor hurdler/novice chaser: dead. *A. S. Neaves*   c– / –

ASHPIT 12 b.g. Pitpan – Baobab (Bargello) [1992/3 c25d³] strong gelding: novice hunter chaser: stays 25f: probably acts on any going: blinkered once. *A. B. Garton*   c83

ASK FOR MORE 8 b.g. Proverb – Primrose Walk (Charlottown) [1992/3 22s² 23s* 26d⁶ 25vᵖᵘ] leggy gelding: has been fired: won conditional jockeys novice hurdle at Wolverhampton in January: struggling from a long way out both outings afterwards: stays 3m: acts on any ground. *J. A. C. Edwards*   98

ASK FRANK 7 b.g. Seymour Hicks (FR) – West Bank (Martinmas) [1992/3 c27vᵖᵘ c26s² c27s c29vᶠ] strong gelding: fairly useful chaser: not raced after heavy fall in January: stays well: acts on soft going: jumps none too fluently. *G. B. Balding*   c116 –

ASKINFARNEY 6 ch.g. Deep Run – Coolbawn Lady (Laurence O) [1992/3 c25s* c26v³ c25v² c26v⁵ c26d³] smallish, sturdy ex-Irish gelding: half-brother to winning hurdler/chaser Gold Haven (by Pollerton) and winning chaser Postman's Path (by Over The River): dam behind in 2 NH Flat races: won novice chase at Towcester in November: disappointed badly on last 3 outings: suited by thorough test of stamina: acts on heavy ground: sometimes breaks blood vessels. *John R. Upson*   c106 ?

ASK MOSS 8 ch.g. Le Moss – Triple Fire (Deep Run) [1992/3 24s 17g⁶ 21d⁶ 23s* 25v 25sᵖᵘ 21sᵖᵘ 22v] workmanlike gelding: handicap hurdler: fairly useful form when winning at Kelso in November: poor efforts afterwards: sold 1,200 gns Ascot June Sales: should stay beyond 3m: probably acts on any going. *G. B. Balding*   125 d

ASK THE GOVERNOR 7 b.g. Kambalda – Roman Run (Deep Run) [1992/3 22v* 22v⁵ 17sˢᵘ 18g⁴ 20m² 22d* 17g⁶ 21m* 21s² 20g⁶] leggy gelding: winning pointer: fair hurdler: won novice event at Fontwell in December and handicaps at Wincanton and Warwick in the spring: probably needs at least 2½m and should stay beyond 2¾m: acts on good to firm and heavy going. *G. B. Balding*   110

ASLAN (IRE) 5 gr.g. Ela-Mana-Mou – Celestial Path (Godswalk (USA)) [1992/3 F18d* F17s* F17v* F17m⁴] rangy gelding: fourth foal: half-brother to Karazan (by Nishapour), fairly useful at up to 1¼m on Flat, and 2 other winners: dam Irish 5f to 7f winner: won NH Flat races at Sedgefield, Carlisle and Chepstow (quite valuable event) in first half of season: close-up fourth to Rhythm Section in Guinness Festival Bumper at Cheltenham in March: sometimes sweats: races with head high: yet to race over hurdles or fences. *J. G. FitzGerald*

ASOLUS 7 ch.g. Pollerton – Miss Breta VII (Pedigree Unknown) [1992/3 20m²] good-bodied ex-Irish gelding: poor hurdler: second in novice selling hurdle at Hereford in March: stays 2½m: acts on good to firm ground. *I. R. Jones*   77

ASPIRANT 5 b.g. High Top – Yen (AUS) (Biscay (AUS)) [1992/3 18mᵖᵘ] took very strong hold when pulled up in early-season maiden hurdle. *K. G. Wingrove*   –

ASSAGLAWI 11 b.g. Troy – Queen's Counsellor (Kalamoun) [1992/3 c21m* c23f* c21g³ c25gᵖᵘ c26m* c24m* c23f*] good-bodied gelding: fairly useful chaser: winner of 2 handicaps at Worcester early in season and hunter chases at Wincanton, Exeter and Worcester in the spring: stays 3¼m: acts on firm and dead ground. *Miss H. C. Knight*   c117 –

ASSURING (IRE) 5 b.g. Sure Blade (USA) – Exciting (Mill Reef (USA)) [1992/3 16d⁵ 16s* 16s 16d* 17m⁶ 16s 16d 16g³ 17f⁵] leggy gelding: useful handicap hurdler: won at Naas in January and February: good sixth in valuable event at Cheltenham in March: raced only around 2m: probably acts on any going: blinkered last 2 outings (fair efforts): sometimes has tongue tied down. *J. S. Bolger, Ireland*   130

ASTERIX 5 ch.g. Prince Sabo – Gentle Gael (Celtic Ash) [1992/3 16s 16g 17f⁵] successful at up to 7f on Flat: poor novice hurdler: will prove best over sharp 2m. *J. M. Bradley*   61

ASTINGS (FR) 5 b.g. Brezzo (FR) – Osca (FR) (Taj Dewan) [1992/3 16g 16d³ 16d 16d³ 21s² 18m⁴ 22v*] tall French-bred gelding with scope: 90

moderate hurdler: odds-on winner of novice event at Cartmel in May: stays 2¾m: acts on heavy going. *J. G. FitzGerald*

ASTON AGAIN 7 br.g. Furry Glen – Mrs Day (Master Owen) [1992/3 c17f² c16m⁴ c17gF] lengthy, shallow-girthed, dipped-backed gelding: winning hurdler: modest form in early-season novice chases: stays 2½m: acts on firm going: sketchy jumper of fences. *G. M. Moore*

c89
–

ASTON EXPRESS 10 b.g. Decent Fellow – Kilbride Lady VI (Menelek) [1992/3 22g c17gᵘʳ c17dᵖᵘ] good-bodied gelding: fairly useful staying chaser at best: no form in 1992/3: sometimes blinkered: looks reluctant nowadays. *G. M. Moore*

c§§
–

ASTON WARRIOR 6 ch.m. Roman Warrior – Steeple Delight VII (Pedigree Unknown) [1992/3 16gᵖᵘ 16mᵖᵘ] workmanlike mare: first foal: dam unraced: no sign of ability over hurdles: sold 1,500 gns Malvern June Sales. *M. J. Charles*

–

ASTRALEON (IRE) 5 b.g. Caerleon (USA) – Noah's Acky Astra (USA) (Ack Ack (USA)) [1992/3 F14d 17mᵖᵘ 17d 16m⁴ 16g² 17m³ 18g² 17f²] leggy gelding: modest novice hurdler: yet to race beyond 2¼m: acts on firm going. *R. Allan*

87

ASTRE RADIEUX (FR) 8 b.g. Gay Mecene (USA) – Divine Etoile (USA) (Nijinsky (CAN)) [1992/3 c21d³ c21s⁵ c16s⁴ c21d c20g⁴ c18sᵘʳ c16f] workmanlike gelding: fair chaser at up to 21f at his best: unreliable nowadays: blinkered twice. *Mrs S. J. Smith*

c– §
– §

ASTROAR 12 b.g. Indiaro – Astrador (Golden Catch) [1992/3 c21g⁵ c21gF] leggy gelding: winning hunter chaser: stays 25f: acts on firm ground. *J. Perry*

c–

AS YOU WERE 11 b.g. Beau Charmeur (FR) – Leaney Escort (Escart III) [1992/3 c24d² c26m³ c24g²] fair pointer: maiden hunter chaser: stays 3¼m: acts on firm and dead ground: blinkered last 3 outings. *J. M. Turner*

c98

ATATURK (USA) 5 ch.g. Ankara (USA) – Wattle It Be (USA) (Bold Commander (USA)) [1992/3 16dᵖᵘ 16d] small, sparely-made gelding: poor 2m novice hurdler: ran badly in 1992/3 (not raced after November): best effort on good ground. *G. Barnett*

–

ATHAR (IRE) 4 b.f. Master Willie – Walladah (USA) (Northern Dancer) [1992/3 17v⁵ 17sᵘʳ 18s³ 18v² 16v² 16d⁴ 16g² 17v⁵] light-framed filly: fair middle-distance performer on Flat: modest juvenile hurdler: acts on heavy going. *R. J. Baker*

89

ATHASSEL ABBEY 7 b.g. Tender King – Pearl Creek (Gulf Pearl) [1992/3 17g⁵ c16mᵖᵘ c18sᵖᵘ c19fᵖᵘ 16f] smallish gelding: poor novice jumper: usually blinkered nowadays. *Miss L. Bower*

c–
–

ATHENE NOCTUA 8 b.m. Aragon – Lady Lorelei (Derring-Do) [1992/3 20s a16g 16vᵖᵘ 16g] sparely-made mare: poor novice hurdler. *R. Hollinshead*

–

ATHOS 8 br.g. High Season – Keen Lass (Andrea Mantegna) [1992/3 22dᵖᵘ 23dʳᵗʳ] angular gelding: poor novice hurdler, lightly raced: refused to race final outing. *G. L. Roe*

– §

ATHY SPIRIT 8 b.g. Furry Glen – Gweedore (Prince Hansel) [1992/3 16g⁶ 22s⁶ 16d 17m] small, stocky gelding: one-time smart hurdler: useful form at best in 1992/3: behind in Smurfit Champion Hurdle at Cheltenham final outing: best form at 2m: acts on good to firm and dead ground. *W. Fennin, Ireland*

139

ATLAAL 8 b.g. Shareef Dancer (USA) – Anna Paola (GER) (Prince Ippi (GER)) [1992/3 16d³ 16d c21sF c16v³ c16v² c16d² c16vF² c16d* c21g² c16m⁶ c17sF] tall, close-coupled gelding: one-time useful hurdler: showed a similar level of form in novice chases in second half of 1992/3: won 4-runner James Capel Novices' Chase at Ascot in February by ¾ length from Wonder Man: would have finished a good second to Viking Flagship at Chepstow

c137 ?
–

Mr Oliver Donnelly's "Atlaal"

final outing but for falling last: best form at 2m: probably acts on any going: races up with pace: jumps soundly in the main. *J. R. Jenkins*

ATONE 6 b.g. Peacock (FR) – Forgello (Bargello) [1992/3 16d 16s* 16s* 16d⁵ 16d³ 16d* 16d* 21m⁵ 16s³ 16d⁴] compact gelding: useful hurdler: had a fine season and won minor events at Fairyhouse and Punchestown, 2 handicaps at Leopardstown (one a novice event) and EBF Johnstown Hurdle at Naas: creditable efforts last 3 starts, including when fifth in Sun Alliance Novices' Hurdle at Cheltenham in March: effective at 2m to 21f: acts on good to firm and soft going: genuine. *J. R. Cox, Ireland*   **133**

AT PEACE 7 b.g. Habitat – Peace (Klairon) [1992/3 c18m⁴] compact gelding: selling hurdler: fourth in early-season novice event at Bangor on chasing debut: likely to prove best around 2m: acts on good to firm ground and fibresand: has broken blood vessel. *J. White*   **c73** **–**

ATROPOS (FR) 5 b.g. Le Riverain (FR) – Herbe Fine (FR) (Francois Saubaber) [1992/3 c18d³ c17s³ c21v²] smallish ex-French gelding: 11f winner on Flat: trained on first start by M. Rolland: signs of ability in novice chases afterwards: difficult to assess. *C. P. E. Brooks*   **c?** **–**

ATTADALE 5 b.g. Ardross – Marypark (Charlottown) [1992/3 20s⁶ 20g³ 16gᶠ 20g* 25s* 21g* 22g* 21s* 20f*] leggy, workmanlike gelding: modest stayer on Flat: in very good form in novice hurdles in second half of season, successful at Newcastle (twice), Wetherby (handicap), Carlisle, Sedgefield and Hexham: effective at 2½m and stays 25f: probably acts on any going: a credit to his trainer: will continue on the upgrade. *L. Lungo*   **120 p**

ATTIC WIT (FR) 7 b.g. Shirley Heights – Laughing Matter (Lochnager) [1992/3 21vᵖᵘ 16vᵖᵘ] no sign of ability in novice hurdles: sold 800 gns Ascot June Sales. *T. J. Etherington*   **–**

EBF Johnstown Hurdle, Naas—Atone and Charlie Swan take the last

ATTYRE 6 ch.m. Riberetto – Pteridium (Royal Palm) [1992/3 F17g⁵ 16v 17d⁵ 17m⁵ 20g⁵ 23m] sturdy mare: poor novice hurdler: may prove best at around 2m: acts on dead and good to firm ground. *J. N. Dalton*   68

AUBURN BOY 6 ch.g. Sexton Blake – Milan Union (Milan) [1992/3 16s⁶] strong gelding: third foal: dam lightly-raced half-sister to high-class Half Free: signs of ability when sixth in novice hurdle at Catterick in January: will stay beyond 2m: sure to improve. *M. W. Easterby*   – p

AUBURN CASTLE 4 b.c. Good Times (ITY) – Glorious Jane (Hittite Glory) [1992/3 F17g F17m⁵ F16g² 16g⁴ 16s² 21s] compact colt: fourth foal: dam fairly useful Irish hurdler at around 2m: modest form when in frame first 2 outings over hurdles: ran badly final start: should stay beyond 17f: acts on soft ground. *M. W. Easterby*   91

AUCTION KING (IRE) 4 b.g. Auction Ring (USA) – Brigadina (Brigadier Gerard) [1992/3 16m 16s a16g³ a16g⁶] strong, workmanlike gelding: modest 1m winner on Flat: only form in juvenile hurdles on third outing. *A. Smith*   74

AUCTION LAW (NZ) 9 ch.g. Pevero – High Plateau (NZ) (Oncidium) [1992/3 c25sꟳ c26d³ c26vᵖᵘ c26dᵖᵘ c28g² c34dᵖᵘ] lengthy, workmanlike gelding: fairly useful chaser: in-and-out form in 1992/3: stays 3½m: acts on soft going: sometimes runs in snatches. *D. H. Barons*   c121 –

AUDE LA BELLE (FR) 5 ch.m. Ela-Mana-Mou – Arjona (GER) (Caracol (FR)) [1992/3 16g] small, sparely-made mare: fair stayer on Flat: – p

Dennys Juvenile Hurdle, Leopardstown—
Titled Dancer and Arctic Weather are about to be caught by Autumn Gorse (behind leader)

behind in valuable novice hurdle at Kempton in February: will be better off in ordinary company. *Mrs A. Knight*

AUGER BORE (IRE) 5 ch.g. Torus – Aurora Moss (Quisling) [1992/3 F18s F17f] third live foal: dam ran once: behind in NH Flat races: yet to race over hurdles or fences. *B. Forsey*

AUGUST FOLLY 13 b.m. Idiot's Delight – Highway Holiday (Jimmy Reppin) [1992/3 c19dpu c21gur c19v3 c24dF c18g3 c19d3 c18f5] workmanlike mare: modest chaser: trained until after fourth outing by P. Andrews: stays 2½m: acts on dead ground. *R. J. Price*

c90
–

AUGUST TWELFTH 5 b.g. Full of Hope – Espanita (Riboboy (USA)) [1992/3 21d] sparely-made gelding: poor novice hurdler. *D. C. O'Brien*

–

AUGUST (USA) 12 b.g. Sensitive Prince (USA) – Polynesian Charm (USA) (What A Pleasure (USA)) [1992/3 18dbd 17d 16g 18g6 18g6 16s 22g4 22m 25m4 22m 16g] good-bodied gelding: poor selling hurdler: stays 2¾m: acts on any going: blinkered final outing. *J. R. Fort*

62

AUK EYE (NZ) 9 b.g. Auk (USA) – Horafama (NZ) (Patron Saint) [1992/3 c22dF c21d*] plain gelding: lightly-raced handicap hurdler: collapsed and died after winning novice chase at Wolverhampton in November: stayed 3m: acted on soft ground. *K. White*

c89
–

AUNT ADA 4 ch.f. Adonijah – Balidilemma (Balidar) [1992/3 F17s5 F16s] half-sister to 3 winners, including pointer Strong Point (by Castle Keep):

dam fair miler, is half-sister to high-class 6f to 1m winner Joshua: signs of a little ability in NH Flat races: retained 750 gns Ascot May Sales: yet to race over hurdles. *R. Rowe*

AURORA LAD   6 ch.h. Free State – Hawthorne Vale (Richboy) [1992/3   87
21gᵖᵘ 16d 17s 16d⁴ 21m³] small horse: modest novice hurdler: stays 21f: acts on dead and good to firm ground. *Mrs S. J. Smith*

AUSPICIOUSOCCASION   11 ch.g. Deep Run – Cool Amanda (Prince   c–
Hansel) [1992/3 c23dᵘʳ] rangy, workmanlike gelding: poor hunter chaser nowadays. *G. C. Evans*

AUSTHORPE SUNSET   9 b.g. Majestic Maharaj – Kings Fillet (King's   c–
Bench) [1992/3 22m⁵ 23g² 22s⁴ 16g⁴ 20g⁶ 18s⁵] rather sparely-made   106
gelding: handicap hurdler: sold out of M. Hammond's stable 2,100 gns Ascot September Sales after first outing: not raced after December: fell only start over fences: stays 23f when conditions aren't testing: acts on any going: visored twice, blinkered once: front runner. *T. W. Donnelly*

AUTHORSHIP (USA)   7 b. or br.g. Balzac (USA) – Piap (USA)   107
(L'Aiglon (USA)) [1992/3 21m³] leggy, rather sparely-made gelding: fair hurdler: first race for 2 seasons when close third in handicap at Chepstow in March: will stay beyond 2¾m: acts on firm ground: held up. *W. J. Musson*

AUTONOMOUS   8 b.g. Milford – Mandrian (Mandamus) [1992/3 26mᵖᵘ   93
16g⁵ 22s³ 21f 21m⁴ 23fᵖᵘ] sturdy gelding: moderate hurdler: stays 2¾m: probably acts on any ground. *K. S. Bridgwater*

AUTUMN GORSE (IRE)   4 ch.g. Salmon Leap (USA) – Nous (Le   130
Johnstan) [1992/3 16s³ 16sᶠ 16d* 16d] big, plain gelding with plenty of scope: type to make a chaser: half-brother to 3 winners, including Irish NH

John Geraghty's "Autumn Gorse"

Flat race winner by The Noble Player: dam fair winning sprinter: fair 11f winner on Flat: won Dennys Juvenile Hurdle at Leopardstown in December: ran well when seventh to Royal Derbi in AIG Europe Champion Hurdle on same course following month (reportedly injured off-fore knee): in lead when tried to run out and fell last on second start: yet to race beyond 2m: acts on soft ground. *Mrs A. M. O'Brien, Ireland*

AUTUMN LEAF 5 b.m. Afzal – Autumn Ballet (Averof) [1992/3 F12d F17f] unfurnished mare: second foal: dam selling hurdler: behind in NH Flat races: yet to race over hurdles or fences. *C. D. Broad*

AUTUMN ZULU 14 gr.g. Wishing Star – Autumn Lulu (London Gazette) [1992/3 c21vᵖᵘ c18vᵖᵘ c17v⁵ c21s³] workmanlike, shallow-girthed gelding: poor chaser: stays 21f: acts on heavy ground. *Miss L. Bower*   c74 –

AUVILLAR (USA) 5 br.g. Temperence Hill (USA) – Exquisita (USA) (Cougar (CHI)) [1992/3 17m 20g⁶ 26d4 17s* a20g⁴ a16g⁶ 17d 16s³ a16g² a20g⁴ c17s² c19d c18v² c18f] compact gelding: poor hurdler: won claiming handicap at Wolverhampton in November: only form over fences when second in 2¼m novice event at Cartmel in May: best at up to 2½m: acts on heavy going and fibresand: visored nowadays. *D. Burchell*   c84 84

AVENA 6 b.m. Oats – Premier Susan (Murrayfield) [1992/3 F17m*] first foal: dam, winning hurdler, effective at 2m and stayed well: 10-length winner of 15-runner NH Flat race at Hereford in May: yet to race over hurdles or fences. *S. Christian*

AVENUE FOCH (IRE) 4 gr.g. Saint Estephe (FR) – Marie d'Irlande (FR) (Kalamoun) [1992/3 16d] unfurnished gelding: won 1m maiden from 3 starts on Flat in Ireland in 1992: little promise in juvenile maiden hurdle at Ludlow in February. *D. J. G. Murray-Smith*   –

AVERON 13 b.g. Averof – Reluctant Maid (Relko) [1992/3 a16gᵖᵘ 16v 17d a20g⁶] winning hurdler: novice chaser: no form in 1992/3: stays 2¼m: acts on heavy going. *C. P. Wildman*   c– –

AVISHAYES (USA) 6 b.g. Al Nasr (FR) – Rose Goddess (Sassafras (FR)) [1992/3 16d4] sturdy, workmanlike gelding: no form in novice hurdles. *M. D. Hammond*   –

AVONBURN (NZ) 9 ch.g. Tawfiq (USA) – Bid Hali (NZ) (Trelay (NZ)) [1992/3 c24s* c25s⁵ c21d*] big, lengthy gelding: fair chaser: successful 4 times at Windsor, including in handicaps in November and January: stays 3m: probably acts on any going: sound jumper: sometimes wears blinkers, better without: held up nowadays. *P. R. Hedger*   c112 –

AVONMOUTHSECRETARY 7 b.m. Town And Country – Star Display (Sparkler) [1992/3 c26gᵖᵘ c26g⁴ c26g⁵ c24gᵖᵘ c24d] workmanlike mare: carries condition: winning chaser: ran badly in 1992/3: trained until after first start by R. Holder: stays 25f: probably acts on any going: blinkered last 3 outings. *P. G. Murphy*   c– –

AVRO ANSON 5 b.g. Ardross – Tremellick (Mummy's Pet) [1992/3 17m* 17g* 16v³ 17m² 17f⁴] tall, leggy gelding: progressive hurdler: successful in 2 handicaps at Newcastle in first half of season: ran well afterwards, fourth in Sunderlands Imperial Cup at Sandown in March on final outing: effective at 2m but will be suited by further: acts on any ground: won over 17f on Flat in April. *M. J. Camacho*   136 p

AWAY GAME 5 b.m. Idiot's Delight – Young Mistress (Young Emperor) [1992/3 F14gᵖᵘ] sturdy mare: fourth foal: half-sister to 2-y-o 5f winning plater Ucanbid (by Penmarric): dam never ran: broke down halfway in NH Flat race in April: dead. *C. P. E. Brooks*

AWKAS 8 b.g. Busted – Moreno (Varano) [1992/3 c21dꟳ 18d c16g³ c17sꟳ c16s* c16g c16dᵘʳ c16g⁶ c26mᵘʳ c21sᵘʳ c21sᵖᵘ 22m] compact, workmanlike gelding: winning hurdler: won novice chase at Catterick in December: ran poorly afterwards: form only at around 2m: probably acts on any going: poor jumper of fences. *G. M. Moore*   c87 x –

AXEL 6 b.g. Rymer – Carousel (Pamroy) [1992/3 F14g] leggy gelding: fourth foal: dam never ran: well beaten in NH Flat race at Market Rasen in April: yet to race over hurdles or fences. *M. H. Tompkins*

AYANDEE 11 ch.g. Vital Season – Jemquo (Quorum) [1992/3 16f^{pu} 18f^{pu}] winning pointer: no sign of ability over hurdles. *N. R. Mitchell* — —

AYIA NAPA 6 b.g. Known Fact (USA) – Folgoet (FR) (Pharly (FR)) [1992/3 18g^{pu} 16m^6 18g] leggy ex-Irish gelding: third foal: half-brother to 2 winners in Italy, including jumper Texas Rich (by Jalmood): dam, maiden, stayed 1m: poor novice hurdler. *Mrs S. C. Bradburne* — 66

AZUREUS (IRE) 5 ch.g. Horage – Effortless (Try My Best (USA)) [1992/3 17m^6 21m*] compact gelding: modest hurdler: won handicap at Southwell in October: stays 21f: acts on good to firm ground: sometimes unreliable at start: won on Flat in 1993. *Mrs M. Reveley* — 101

AZURLORDSHIPLEASES 7 b.g. Gleason (USA) – Geeaway (Gala Performance (USA)) [1992/3 c21m^{pu}] poor maiden pointer: blinkered, no show in novice hunter chase in June. *Richard Collins* — c–

B

BABAROOMS PARADISE (NZ) 6 b.m. Babaroom (USA) – Our Paradise (NZ) (Belmura) [1992/3 c18m^5 c21m^6] compact mare: winning hurdler: well beaten in 2 early-season novice chases: seems not to stay 2½m: acts on firm ground. *J. R. Jenkins* — c–

BABA'S LADY (NZ) 6 b.m. Babaroom (USA) – Windsor Lady (NZ) (Silver Dream) [1992/3 c16f^2 c21m^2 c18g^{ur}] small, good-quartered mare: winning hurdler: poor form in early-season novice chases: races mainly at around 2m: acts on hard ground: blinkered once. *J. R. Jenkins* — c60 ?

BABCOCK BOY 8 b.g. Prince Bee – Gail Borden (Blue Chariot) [1992/3 23d* 20g 28d^2 25s^3 23m*] leggy gelding: lightly-raced hurdler: won novice events at Kelso in November and March: stays well: acts on good to firm and soft ground. *Mrs M. Reveley* — 100

BABY ALEX 9 br.g. Derrylin – Nello (USA) (Charles Elliott (USA)) [1992/3 a18g^6 a16g] neat gelding: novice selling hurdler: tried blinkered: unreliable and one to avoid. *I. A. Balding* — §

BABY ASHLEY 7 b.m. Full of Hope – Nello (USA) (Charles Elliott (USA)) [1992/3 17g a16g^3 a16g* a16g^3 a16g^2 16s 17m^5 a16g*] lengthy, dipped-backed mare: poor hurdler: won at Southwell in February (seller, no bid) and May (claimer): races only at 2m: acts on good to firm going and fibresand. *D. Morris* — 79 +

BABY WIZZARD 4 b.f. Scottish Reel – Wizzard Art (Wolver Hollow) [1992/3 17f*] poor middle-distance performer on Flat: won novice hurdle at Plumpton in March by 8 lengths, left clear last: should improve. *R. Rowe* — 82 p

BACK BEFORE DAWN 6 b.g. Marching On – Willow Path (Farm Walk) [1992/3 F14d^5 16g^4 16g^5 21v 16g^2 16d^4 18d^6 16g^4 17v^2 17d^4] close-coupled, workmanlike gelding: second living foal: half-brother to winning hurdler/chaser Back Before Dark (by Silly Prices): dam, poor staying novice hurdler, sister to winning jumper Willow Walk and half-sister to very useful hunter chaser Jaunty Jane: poor novice hurdler: best form at around 2m but should stay further: acts on heavy ground: usually forces pace. *P. Monteith* — 83

BACK FROM THE DEAD 7 br.g. Miner's Lamp – Four Shares (The Parson) [1992/3 24v^6 25s^{pu}] smallish, angular gelding: lightly-raced novice staying hurdler: no form in 1992/3. *John R. Upson* — —

BACKPACKER 13 b.g. New Brig – Preston Deal (Straight Deal) [1992/3 c23h^2 c24f^5 c25g^4 c24g] leggy, angular gelding: modest handicap chaser: stays well: acts on hard and dead ground: poor jumper. *G. P. Enright* — c87 x

Mr M. D. Smith's "Balasani"

BACK TO FORM 8 ch.g. Homing – Alezan Dore (Mountain Call)
[1992/3 25g 18d] sturdy gelding: poor novice selling hurdler: refused once. – §
W. G. M. Turner

BADASTAN (IRE) 4 b.c. Shardari – Badalushka (Rex Magna (FR))
[1992/3 16d⁴ 16g⁵ 20s² 22d* 22dᵖᵘ 17m 21d³ 24f³ 21f⁴] leggy, angular colt: 101
half-brother to fairly useful hurdler Bakhtaran (by Mouktar): dam fair 1½m
winner: twice-raced on Flat in Ireland, winning over 1½m: fair form over
hurdles: won novice event at Sedgefield in February: best subsequent effort
penultimate start: probably needs further than 2m, and stays 3m: acts on
firm and dead ground. *T. P. Tate*

BADBURY LAD 7 br.g. Strong Gale – Cherish (Bargello) [1992/3 22g⁵ c93
c23s⁶ c26dF c25g⁵ c25s⁴ c24v c24d⁴ c27d² c26g³ c27g³ c24m²] –
workmanlike gelding: novice hurdler: modest form at best over fences:
suited by a thorough test of stamina: best effort on dead ground: sometimes
blinkered. *J. S. King*

BADGERS GIFT 7 br.g. Warpath – Bravade (Blast) [1992/3 16m]
lengthy gelding: novice selling hurdler (often visored or blinkered): – §
sometimes looks none too keen over hurdles and refused both starts in
points in 1993. *A. Bailey*

BADIHAR (USA) 9 ch.g. Nijinsky (CAN) – Mofida (Right Tack) [1992/3 c– x
c21d⁵] big, good-topped gelding: poor novice chaser: sold 3,200 gns Malvern –
June Sales: probably stays 3m: acts on heavy and good to firm going:
blinkered 4 times in 1991/2: often let down by jumping. *T. Long*

BADRAKHANI (FR) 7 b.g. Akarad (FR) – Burnished Gold (Breton) c?
[1992/3 c21sᵖᵘ c16dF 17s*] small, close-coupled gelding: fairly useful 126

hurdler: won handicap at Huntingdon in November: showed ability in second of 2 novice chases: sold only 1,600 gns Ascot February Sales: best at 2m: acts on any going. *N. J. Henderson*

BAD TRADE   11 ch.g. Over The River (FR) – Churchtown Lass (Master   c113 §
Owen) [1992/3 c21d² c21d³ c20s* c23s² c21s³ c16v⁴] strong gelding: fair   –
handicap chaser: won conditional jockeys event at Haydock in November:
trained until after next outing by W. A. Stephenson: sold 3,900 gns in May:
stays 2½m: best form with give in the ground: held up: often fails to go
through with his effort. *P. Cheesbrough*

BAHRAIN QUEEN (IRE)   5 ch.m. Caerleon (USA) – Bahrain Vee
(CAN) (Blushing Groom (FR)) [1992/3 16d⁴ 21d 26d³ 28v⁶ 21d 22m*]   82
sparely-made mare: poor hurdler: won selling handicap at Market Rasen
(bought in 3,700 gns) in May: stays 3¼m: acts on hard and dead going. *C.
Smith*

BAKHTARAN   6 b.g. Mouktar – Badalushka (Rex Magna (FR)) [1992/3
18m* 16g* 17f² 17g] tall, workmanlike gelding: fairly useful hurdler: won   122
handicaps at Market Rasen and Southwell early in season (not raced after
October): best around 2m on a sound surface: held up. *John R. Upson*

BALAAT (USA)   5 b.g. Northern Baby (CAN) – Bar J Gal (USA) (Key To
The Mint (USA)) [1992/3 18m 22m⁴ 18dᶠ 20m² 16s⁴ 22m 22s 16f] leggy   104 d
gelding: handicap hurdler: ran poorly in second half of season: stays 2½m:
acts on any going. *M. C. Chapman*

BALADEE PET   4 gr.g. Petong – Baladee (Mummy's Pet) [1992/3
18mᵖᵘ] leggy gelding: plating-class sprint maiden on Flat: no promise on   –
hurdling debut in August. *Mrs V. A. Aconley*

BALADIYA   6 b.m. Darshaan – Bayazida (Bustino) [1992/3 20g⁶ 22s   c91
c16m* c16dᶠ c16d a16g² a16g⁴] leggy mare: poor novice hurdler: form over   75
fences only when successful in novice event at Windsor in November:
trained until after fifth start by T. Keddy: effective from 2m to 2½m: acts on
good to firm ground and fibresand: sometimes blinkered: not yet a fluent
jumper of fences: won at 1½m on Flat in 1993. *D. Morris*

BALASANI (FR)   7 b.g. Labus (FR) – Baykara (Direct Flight) [1992/3
22s⁴ 17g 21d² 21m] smallish, lengthy gelding: very useful hurdler: generally   145
ran creditably in 1992/3, including when short-headed by Boscean Chieftain
in handicap at Chepstow in February: effective at 17f to 21f, should stay
further: acts on good to firm and soft ground: won on Flat in 1993, including
in Ascot Stakes. *M. C. Pipe*

BALHERNOCH   4 b.g. Lochnager – Penumbra (Wolver Hollow) [1992/3
F17g² F14s²] half-brother to winning jumpers Cantabile (by Bustino) and   –
Denberdar (by Julio Mariner): dam useful sprinter: second in NH Flat races
at Bangor and Market Rasen in the spring: yet to race over hurdles. *M. H.
Easterby*

BALISTEROS (FR)   4 b.g. Bad Conduct (USA) – Oldburry (FR) (Fin
Bon) [1992/3 F16g F17d] well beaten in NH Flat races: yet to race over   –
hurdles. *T. P. Tate*

BALLAD RULER   7 ch.g. Ballad Rock – Jessamy Hall (Crowned Prince   c–
(USA)) [1992/3 c16gᵖᵘ c20dᵖᵘ F13m 22f³ 21dᵖᵘ 22f⁶ c21f⁵ 21mᵖᵘ 23fᵖᵘ]   68
angular gelding: poor novice hurdler/chaser: stays 2¾m: acts on firm
ground: visored twice. *P. A. Pritchard*

BALLERINA ROSE   6 b.m. Dreams To Reality (USA) – Ragtime Rose
(Ragstone) [1992/3 17s 17m⁶ 21s³ 16g³ 16f⁵ 17fᵖᵘ] leggy, angular mare: 91
moderate handicap hurdler: trained until after second start by O. O'Neill:
stays 21f: best form with give in the ground. *D. Burchell*

BALLIMINSTER   8 b.g. Balinger – Merry Minuet (Trumpeter) [1992/3   c?
c25gᶠ c25dᵖᵘ c20dᶠ c21vᶠ] strong, sturdy gelding: novice hurdler: yet to   –
complete over fences, but looked set to win amateurs handicap at
Folkestone in January on final start when falling 3 out: stays 2¾m: acts on
good to firm and heavy ground: blinkered 1992/3. *C. T. Nash*

BALLINAMOE 8 b.g. Rymer – Superdora (Super Slip) [1992/3 22gᵖᵘ 16vᵖᵘ c18mF] strong gelding: half-brother to several winning jumpers: dam showed a little ability in Irish NH Flat races: no sign of ability: sold out of T. Hallett's stable 2,300 gns Ascot November Sales after first start. *R. H. Buckler*   c– –

BALLINHASSIG 9 b.g. Slippered – Rathcreevagh (Harwell) [1992/3 c21d6] well-made gelding: novice chaser: suited by test of stamina: probably acted on any going: dead. *John R. Upson*   c–

BALLOO HOUSE 8 ch.g. Le Moss – Forgello (Bargello) [1992/3 21s5 26s2 26dᵖᵘ 26g* 25s4 26m*] leggy ex-Irish gelding: half-brother to useful jumper Music Be Magic (by Brave Invader) and to 3 other winning jumpers by Peacock: dam won on Flat and over hurdles in Ireland: point winner: won novice hurdles at Catterick in February and March (handicap): suited by thorough test of stamina: best form on a sound surface: visored last 5 outings. *Mrs P. Sly*   96

BALLYANTO 8 b.g. Lepanto (GER) – Ballyarctic (Arcticeelagh) [1992/3 19m* 20g2 17s 21d3 21v6 18s5 20s 21m 18g2 18m 16g5] lengthy gelding: handicap hurdler: won at Exeter in September: trained until after third start by R. Holder, sold out of P. Murphy's stable 4,100 gns Doncaster January Sales after seventh: well below form afterwards: stays 2½m well, and should stay 3m: probably acts on any going. *C. Parker*   99 d

BALLYBELL 8 ch.g. Prince Mab (FR) – Lydien (Sandford Lad) [1992/3 c22gF] well-made gelding: poor novice hurdler: has fallen both outings in steeplechases. *J. L. Gledson*   c– –

BALLYCASTLE MARY (IRE) 4 ch.f. Music Boy – Apple Rings (Godswalk (USA)) [1992/3 17mᵖᵘ] no sign of ability on Flat or in early-season juvenile hurdle: sold 775 gns Ascot November Sales. *T. J. Naughton*   –

BALLY CLOVER 6 ch.g. Deep Run – Miss de Jager (Lord Gayle (USA)) [1992/3 18d* 17d* 17v3 21g2 21m] rather leggy, unfurnished gelding: won novice hurdles at Fontwell and Cheltenham (handicap) in first half of season: ran very well on third outing, creditable efforts afterwards: stays 21f: acts on heavy and good to firm ground. *N. J. Henderson*   124

BALLY CRUISE 6 br.m. Cruise Missile – Ballynore (News Item) [1992/3 22dᵖᵘ] angular non-thoroughbred mare: second foal: dam unraced: tailed off when pulled up in early-season novice hurdle. *K. Bishop*   –

BALLYEDEN 9 br.m. Beau Charmeur (FR) – Mac's Wish (Three Wishes) [1992/3 c24g6 c26sᵖᵘ c21gᵖᵘ] sturdy mare: fair hunter chaser in 1991/2: ran badly in handicaps in 1992/3: stays well: acts on soft going. *C. T. Nash*   c– –

BALLY FLAME 7 b.g. Balliol – Flame (Firestreak) [1992/3 18gF 17d 21sᵘʳ] brother to winning hurdler Va Utu: no sign of ability on Flat or over hurdles. *Mrs M. A. Kendall*   –

BALLYKILTY 8 b.g. Beau Charmeur (FR) – Clonamona (Karabas) [1992/3 c21d4 16s5 21v5] workmanlike gelding: winning hurdler: well beaten in 1992/3, including on chasing debut: stays 2¾m: acts on soft ground. *T. T. Bill*   c– –

BALLYLORD 9 ch.g. Lord Ha Ha – Bally Decent (Wrekin Rambler) [1992/3 21s2 16d* 21v* 16s 17s5 25d 21m2 18d6 17d2 21s6 16s3 21g5] close-coupled gelding: shows traces of stringhalt: modest hurdler: won handicaps at Haydock (conditional jockeys) and Uttoxeter in December: inconsistent afterwards: stays 21f: acts on heavy and good to firm going: jumps well: sometimes idles in front. *J. J. O'Neill*   99

BALLYMGYR (IRE) 4 ch.g. Town And Country – Channel Breeze (Proverb) [1992/3 F17d4] first foal: dam fair staying chaser: fourth in NH Flat race at Hereford in May: yet to race over hurdles. *S. Mellor*   –

BALLYMONEYBOY 4 ch.g. Ballacashtal (CAN) – Honeybuzzard (FR) (Sea Hawk II) [1992/3 17v2] leggy, sparely-made gelding: half-brother to   ?

useful hurdler Jopanini (by Homing): modest 1m winner on Flat: second in weakly-contested novice hurdle at Lingfield in February: sold 1,200 gns Newmarket July Sales: difficult to assess. *M. H. Tompkins*

BALLY MURPHY BOY 8 b.g. Rare One – Royal Dress (Perspex) [1992/3 c21mF] modest pointer: fell sixth on steeplechasing debut. *Mrs D. M. Grissell* c–
–

BALLYNICK 9 ch.g. Balinger – Ellen Mavourneen (Tiepolo II) [1992/3 c16gᵘʳ c17mF] smallish, sturdy gelding: poor novice hurdler: no form in points and has failed to complete in steeplechases: barely stays 2¾m: acts on dead ground. *N. J. Henderson* c–
–

BALLY PARSON 7 b.g. The Parson – Ballyadam Lass (Menelek) [1992/3 16d c22dᵘʳ c21dᵖᵘ c17s³c20sᵖᵘ c16g⁴c18g³c20gᵘʳ] tall, good-bodied gelding: poor novice hurdler/chaser: stoutly bred and likely to need much further than 2m: blinkered once. *J. Chugg* c81
–

BALLYROE LADY 7 ch.m. Over The River (FR) – Must Ramble (Wrekin Rambler) [1992/3 c21s² c21g* c25dF c25s³ c21g* c20g⁴ c21d⁴] lengthy ex-Irish mare: winning hurdler: won novice chases at Wincanton (mares event) in November and Huntingdon in February: ran well in valuable mares novice handicap at Uttoxeter in March on final start: stays 25f: acts on soft ground: not an accomplished jumper as yet. *D. R. Gandolfo* c103
–

BALLYSTATE 5 ch.m. Ballacashtal (CAN) – Brandenbourg (Le Levanstell) [1992/3 19g* 18d*] leggy, sparely-made mare: fair handicap hurdler: successful at Exeter in October and November: effective at around 2m and stays 2¾m: acts on dead ground: has run creditably when sweating: jumps well: often makes running. *C. James* 105

BALLYWILLWILL 7 b.g. Wolver Hollow – Nuageuse (Prince Regent (FR)) [1992/3 c21d³ c25dᵖᵘ c20d⁵ c21s c20sᵖᵘ] compact, workmanlike gelding: winning hurdler: poor novice chaser: stays 21f: acts on good to firm and dead ground: blinkered final start. *Miss S. J. Wilton* c81
–

BALMORAL DRIVE 6 br.m. Roscoe Blake – Nikancy (Castlenik) [1992/3 c21dᵖᵘ] of little account. *A. Bailey* c–
–

BALMY BREEZE 6 b.m. Idiot's Delight – Modom (Compensation) [1992/3 23s⁶ 17v 17v a16g⁵ 18g⁶ 22f⁵] smallish, plain mare: poor novice hurdler: best at up to 2¼m: acts on heavy going and equitrack. *W. G. R. Wightman* 66

BALVENIE 9 ch.g. Le Bavard (FR) – Arctic Free (Master Buck) [1992/3 c21gᵖᵘ c20sᵖᵘ] rangy gelding: lightly-raced staying novice hurdler/chaser: has run blinkered: sometimes looks reluctant. *J. J. Whelan* c– §
–

BALZAC BOY (IRE) 5 ch.g. Deep Run – Woodford Princess (Menelek) [1992/3 17g 16s² 16v* 16v⁶ 18g 16m³] well-made gelding: type to make a chaser: won novice hurdle at Wincanton in January: ran creditably final outing: should stay further than 2m: acts on heavy and good to firm going: tends to wander under pressure. *Mrs J. Pitman* 97

BAMAN POWERHOUSE 5 b.g. Bold Owl – Bella Abzug (Karabas) [1992/3 17dᵖᵘ] small, lightly-made gelding: no sign of ability: sold 1,500 gns Ascot 2nd June Sales. *M. Scudamore* –

BANAIYKA (IRE) 4 b.f. Shernazar – Banasiya (Mill Reef (USA)) [1992/3 16s⁶ 16d 16d² 16v³ 16s* 16d* 25f⁵] lengthy, workmanlike filly: 1½m winner on Flat: won juvenile hurdles at Gowran Park and Clonmel in second half of season: looked a difficult ride but possibly unsuited by firm ground when well beaten at Aintree final start: should stay beyond 2m: acts on soft going. *Patrick Mullins, Ireland* 114

BANANA CUFFLINKS (USA) 7 b.g. Peterhof (USA) – Heather Bee (USA) (Drone) [1992/3 18m* 16m² 18m² 16g³] leggy gelding: won maiden hurdle at Market Rasen in August: acted on good to firm ground and fibresand: visored first and last 2 starts: dead. *M. H. Tompkins* 84

BANBRIDGE 10 ch.g. Paddy's Stream – Glenroid (Polaroid) [1992/3 c16g* c16g³ c19g² c16dᵖᵘ c16fᵖᵘ] tall gelding: fairly useful handicap chaser: c124 §
–

won at Ludlow in October: ran badly last 2 outings: stays 19f: acts on any going: jumps soundly: sometimes none too keen: sometimes breaks blood vessels. *D. Nicholson*

BANCHORY 4 ch.c. Dunbeath (USA) – Filwah (High Top) [1992/3 F17g⁴ aF16g³ aF16g²] third foal: dam never ran: in frame in NH Flat races: yet to race over hurdles. *M. W. Easterby*

BAND OF HOPE (USA) 6 ch.m. Dixieland Band (USA) – Reflection (Mill Reef (USA)) [1992/3 16f² 16d* 18d⁴ 16v⁴ a16g⁴ 17s* 17d⁶ 17m³ 16d² 16f⁴ 17m⁶ 16m²] small mare: modest hurdler: won claimers at Uttoxeter in November and Bangor in February: ran creditably afterwards: stays 2¼m: acts on any going: blinkered last 2 outings. *W. Clay*   88

BAND SARGEANT (IRE) 4 b.g. Nashamaa – Indian Honey (Indian King (USA)) [1992/3 17m⁴ 18g⁴ 18f^co 17g² 17g³ 16g^pu] strong, lengthy gelding: showed ability at 2 yrs: fair juvenile hurdler: not raced after October: best efforts on good ground. *G. Richards*   95

BANGAGIN 7 b.g. Balinger – Rapagain (Deep Run) [1992/3 c16g⁴ c16s⁴] neat gelding: lightly-raced 2m novice hurdler/chaser: has shown signs of only a little ability. *J. Webber*   c–
–

BANG ON TARGET 5 ch.g. Cruise Missile – Airy Fairy (Space King) [1992/3 17s⁶ 20d⁶ 16f] sturdy gelding: sixth foal: dam winning hurdler at up to 2½m: soundly beaten over hurdles, including in sellers. *A. P. Jarvis*   –

BANKER'S GOSSIP 9 b.g. Le Bavard (FR) – Gracious View (Sir Herbert) [1992/3 c26d c24d² c24s⁴ c26d^R a24g] good-quartered gelding: has been hobdayed: fair chaser: generally well below form in 1992/3 (not raced after January): sold 4,000 gns Ascot March Sales: suited by good test of stamina: acts on firm and dead going: sometimes breaks blood vessels: occasionally looks none too keen and refused once. *D. Nicholson*   c104 §
– §

BANK PLACE 6 ch.g. Sheer Grit – Shatana (Tarboosh (USA)) [1992/3 F16s³ F16s⁴ F16s* 22m²] fourth foal: dam never ran: placed in points in 1992: successful in 25-runner NH Flat race at Naas in December, when trained by M. Hourigan: second of 7 in novice hurdle at Worcester in March: will stay beyond 2¾m: should improve. *S. E. Sherwood*   94 p

BANKROLL 6 b.g. Chief Singer – Very Nice (FR) (Green Dancer (USA)) [1992/3 c18f 23s⁶ 22m*] good-topped gelding: fair hurdler: won handicap at Wincanton in March by 15 lengths: tailed off in novice event on chasing debut: stays 2¾m: acts well on firm going: sometimes breaks blood vessels. *P. J. Hobbs*   c–
111

BANNISTER 8 b.g. Known Fact (USA) – Swiftfoot (Run The Gantlet (USA)) [1992/3 19g^pu] sparely-made gelding: progressive form over hurdles early in 1991/2 (trained by M. Pipe last 3 starts): evidently difficult to train since and was pulled up lame in October: stays 21f, at least when conditions aren't testing: acts on hard going: headstrong. *M. Williams*   –

BANOUR (USA) 5 b.g. Arctic Tern (USA) – Banana Peel (Green Dancer (USA)) [1992/3 17g³ 22g 17g⁶ 18d 18d* 21g² 19d 18s⁴ 20g⁵ 21s^pu 20g 20g] Irish gelding: second foal: half-brother to a minor winner in USA: dam, minor winner, half-sister to very smart middle-distance winner Beaune: fairly useful hurdler: won handicap at Fairyhouse in October: below form last 6 outings, including at Ayr and Perth: stays 21f: acts on good to firm and dead going: best form blinkered. *J. F. C. Maxwell, Ireland*   127

BANTEL BARGAIN 4 b.f. Silly Prices – Yellow Peril (Mljet) [1992/3 F16g F17d] first foal: dam never ran: behind in NH Flat races: yet to race over hurdles. *R. Allan*   –

BANTON LOCH 6 br.g. Lochnager – Balgownie (Prince Tenderfoot (USA)) [1992/3 c24m^pu] lengthy gelding: modest novice hurdler in 1990/1: no show on steeplechasing debut: probably stays 2½m: acts on soft ground: visored over hurdles. *J. D. Hankinson*   c–
–

BAPTISMAL FIRE 9 ch.g. Baptism – Levi's Star (Levmoss) [1992/3 c22g² c22g² c23s² c18g* c24g⁴ c24d^pu c25f⁵] strong, good-topped gelding: c126
–

fairly useful chaser: trained until after second start by P. Mullins in Ireland: won handicap at Fontwell in September: creditable fourth at Kempton following month, best effort in similar events subsequently: stays 3m: acts on any going. *J. Ffitch-Heyes*

BARAHIN (IRE)   4 b.g. Diesis – Red Comes Up (USA) (Blushing Groom (FR)) [1992/3 17s 17v 22d 16d] leggy, useful-looking gelding: modest and ungenuine at up to 1¼m on Flat, winner in 1993: sold 13,500 gns Doncaster November Sales: no form over hurdles: springer in market last time: may be capable of better. *R. J. O'Sullivan*   –

BARAOORA   11 gr.g. Bruni – Tory Island (Majority Blue) [1992/3 20dˢᵘ 25dᵖᵘ 17d] tall, well-made gelding: winning hurdler: maiden chaser: seems of little account nowadays: blinkered once. *M. J. Smith*   c–
–

BARBARA'S CUTIE   5 ch.m. Tina's Pet – Eucharis (Tickled Pink) [1992/3 a16gᶠ] poor sprinter on Flat: showed nothing in selling hurdle at Southwell in February. *M. Blanshard*

BARBARY REEF (IRE)   5 b.g. Sarab – Brown's Cay (Formidable (USA)) [1992/3 18f⁶] half-brother to winning selling hurdler Superetta (by Superlative): quite modest 1¼m winner on Flat at his best: tailed off in novice hurdle at Fontwell in August. *G. H. Eden*   –

BARCHAM   6 b.g. Blakeney – La Pythie (FR) (Filiberto (USA)) [1992/3 a18g² 17f⁴ 17g* 17g* 16m² 17fᶠ] smallish gelding: selling hurdler: won 2 handicaps at Huntingdon in April, second a conditional jockeys event (bought in 5,100 gns): claimed £5,300 final start: has raced only at around 2m: probably acts on any turf going, possibly on equitrack. *G. A. Pritchard-Gordon*   90

BARDESAN   7 b.g. Kambalda – Early Start (Wrekin Rambler) [1992/3 22d* 19m² 26g⁵ 23g⁵ a18gᶠ a18g* a16g* 20f² 16s²] tall gelding: fair hurdler: won novice events at Exeter in September and Southwell in February and March (handicap): good second on penultimate start, well below form on last: effective from 2m to 2¾m: acts on dead and firm going and fibresand: front runner: blinkered once: sometimes looks temperamental. *O. Sherwood*   107

BARE FISTED   5 ch.g. Nearly A Hand – Ba Ba Belle (Petit Instant) [1992/3 17vᵖᵘ 16d 16m 17gᶠ 18d] rather unfurnished gelding: second foal: dam winning hunter chaser: has shown nothing in novice hurdles. *J. S. King*   –

BARELY BLACK   5 br.g. Lidhame – Louisa Anne (Mummy's Pet) [1992/3 16v⁵ 20v³ 16d 21s 17v² 16vᵖᵘ] leggy, sparely-made gelding: poor novice hurdler: probably stays 2½m: acts on heavy ground: courage under suspicion. *N. M. Babbage*   75

BARFORD LAD   6 b.g. Nicholas Bill – Grace Poole (Sallust) [1992/3 17d⁴ 17d 16s] rather sparely-made gelding: fairly useful at up to 1¼m on Flat, winner twice in 1992: promising fourth in novice event at Ascot in November on hurdling debut, but failed to reproduce that form. *J. R. Fanshawe*   89

BARGA   4 b.f. Dancing Brave (USA) – Sylvatica (Thatching) [1992/3 16d 16d 16s 17mᵖᵘ] smallish, leggy filly: of little account. *W. Clay*   –

BARGAIN AND SALE   8 br.g. Torenaga – Miss Woodville (Master Buck) [1992/3 c25mᴿ c24s⁶ c23f² c28fᵖᵘ] compact gelding: only sign of ability in hunter chases when second at Worcester in May: blinkered last outing: usually a poor jumper. *D. J. Minty*   c95 x

BARGE BOY   9 b.g. Jimsun – Barge Mistress (Bargello) [1992/3 17g⁴ c16g² 17g³ 21f³] sturdy gelding: fairly useful hurdler: creditable efforts when in frame in 1992/3: clear of remainder when never-nearer 2 lengths second to Dis Train in novice event at Warwick in March on chasing debut: stays 21f: best form on a sound surface: jumps soundly: sure to improve and win a run-of-the-mill novice chase. *J. A. B. Old*   c101 p
122

BARGEE (USA)   4 b.g. Riverman (USA) – North Mist (USA) (Far North (CAN)) [1992/3 17sᵖᵘ 17d 16d 16gᵖᵘ] leggy gelding: lightly raced on Flat: –

sold out of P. Cole's stable 4,300 gns Newmarket Autumn Sales: no sign of ability over hurdles: resold 1,700 gns Doncaster June Sales. *W. Bentley*

BARKIN 10 b.g. Crash Course – Annie Augusta (Master Owen) [1992/3 c33s4 c24s4 c30s2 c32dur c27dpu c26f4 c22v*] lengthy gelding: moderate handicap chaser: won amateurs event at Cartmel in May: stays extremely well: acts on heavy ground: usually a poor jumper. *G. Richards* **c99 x**
–

BARKISLAND 9 b.g. Prince Regent (FR) – Satlan (Milan) [1992/3 c18d4 c18m3 c16d* c16m3 c16d2 c16v5 c20g* c21gur c21s c21f5] leggy, close-coupled gelding: modest handicap chaser: won at Southwell in October and Edinburgh (amateurs) in February: well below form last 2 starts: stays 2½m: acts on good to firm and soft going: takes good hold: sometimes blinkered in 1991/2. *P. Beaumont* **c91**
–

BARLEY MOW 7 b.g. Wolverlife – Ellette (Le Levanstell) [1992/3 18d3 18s6 17d 16g3 17mpu 17g5 22d 18f] leggy, close-coupled gelding: poor hurdler: once-raced over fences: stays 2¼m: acts on good to firm and dead ground. *Mrs Barbara Waring* **c–**
82

BARMBRACK 4 ch.g. Doulab (USA) – Irish Cookie (Try My Best (USA)) [1992/3 16dpu] lengthy gelding: poor maiden on Flat, stays 1m: tailed off when pulled up in juvenile selling hurdle at Uttoxeter in October. *R. M. Whitaker* –

BARNABY BENZ 9 b.g. Lochnager – Miss Barnaby (Sun Prince) [1992/3 c26m3] dipped-backed, good-quartered gelding: novice hurdler/hunter chaser: best form up to 3m: probably acts on any going: visored once. *K. Cumings* **c76**
–

BARNABY BOY 5 b.g. Ayyabaan – Owen's Hobby (Owen Anthony) [1992/3 F17d 16d a22g4] smallish gelding: third foal: half-brother to moderate staying hurdler Driver (by Motivate): dam placed in points: no sign of ability. *M. Brown* –

BARNEY RUBBLE 8 b. or br.g. Politico (USA) – Peak Princess (Charlottown) [1992/3 c25dbd c25g3 c25g4] leggy gelding: winning pointer: modest novice hunter chaser: stays 25f. *D. W. Whillans* **c82**
–

BARN STRIPPER 5 ch.m. Germont – Copper Tinsell (Crooner) [1992/3 F16vpu] third foal: dam lightly-raced 2m hurdler: tailed off when pulled up in NH Flat race at Hexham in December: yet to race over hurdles or fences. *M. A. Barnes* –

BARONESS BELLE 7 gr.m. Baron Blakeney – My Belleburd (Twilight Alley) [1992/3 F17g 16spu] smallish, deep-girthed mare: fifth foal: dam unraced: seventh of 17 in NH Flat race in December: reluctant to go to post and showed nothing following month on hurdling debut. *R. J. Hodges* –

BARONESS BLAKENEY 4 gr.f. Blakeney – Teleflora (Princely Gift) [1992/3 F16s F16g F18g] small, lengthy filly: sister to very useful jumper Baron Blakeney and plating-class 1m winner Blakeney's Gift, also half-sister to 2 winners on Flat: dam sprinting half-sister to high-class stayer Grey Baron: tailed off in NH Flat races: yet to race over hurdles. *M. C. Pipe* –

BARONESS ORKZY 7 ch.m. Baron Blakeney – General's Daughter (Spartan General) [1992/3 22dF 20sF] workmanlike mare: poor novice hurdler. *W. G. M. Turner* –

BARON MANA 8 b.g. Baron Blakeney – Manalane (Manacle) [1992/3 c21m4] winning pointer: fourth in novice hunter chase at Folkestone in May. *Richard J. Hill* **c65**
–

BARONNEY 7 b.h. Tycoon II – Karandala (Above Suspicion) [1992/3 21vpu a16gpu 17m] leggy horse: of little account. *B. A. McMahon* –

BARON TWO SHOES 7 gr.g. Baron Blakeney – Win Shoon Please (Sheshoon) [1992/3 c25g6 c21s4 c25d5] compact, workmanlike gelding: moderate handicap hurdler/novice chaser: stays 2¾m: probably acts on any going: blinkered 3 times, including on last 2 starts: sketchy jumper of fences. *N. A. Gaselee* **c86**
–

BARRICA   6 b.m. Main Reef – Devon Defender (Home Guard (USA))   **c92**
[1992/3 c16s³ c19d* c22g⁴ c21m⁴ c21dᵖᵘ] tall, lengthy mare: winning   –
hurdler: successful in mares novice chase at Hereford in February: ran
respectably 2 starts later: probably stays 2¾m: acts on dead and good to
firm ground: has run in snatches. *D. Nicholson*

BARRY OWEN   7 b.g. Owen Anthony – Tacita (Tacitus) [1992/3 18s⁴   79
22vᵖᵘ 17s⁴ 16v⁵ 16d] leggy, sparely-made gelding: poor novice selling
hurdler: sold 1,900 gns Doncaster March Sales, resold 1,050 gns same
venue in May: best effort at 17f on soft going. *B. A. McMahon*

BAR THREE (IRE)   4 b.g. Lafontaine (USA) – El Prat (Royal Match)   –
[1992/3 18sᵖᵘ] lightly-raced maiden on Flat: tailed off when pulled up in
juvenile hurdle at Market Rasen in September. *L. J. Codd*

BARTOLOMEO (USA)   4 b.g. Vaguely Noble – Stonechurch (USA)   87
(Naskra (USA)) [1992/3 18m² 17m²] good-topped gelding: poor and
inconsistent handicapper on Flat, stays 1½m: runner-up in early-season
juvenile hurdles at Market Rasen and Perth (claimer): sold 7,000 gns
Newmarket Autumn Sales. *Mrs J. R. Ramsden*

BARTON BANK   7 br.g. Kambalda – Lucifer's Daughter (Lucifer (USA))   **c142 p**
[1992/3 c21s* c23v* c21v* c24sᶠ c26m* c25mᵖᵘ]   –
Only one of the season's staying novice chasers impressed us more
overall than Barton Bank, and that was Cab On Target. Both, we feel, will go
on to reach the top flight although Barton Bank's career suffered a set-
back when he dropped out with a circuit left in the Sun Alliance Chase at
Cheltenham in March. It transpired that he had broken a blood vessel. Big
things were predicted for Barton Bank over fences even while he was a
hurdler, especially after he won the Heidsieck Dry Monopole Novices'
Hurdle at Aintree, and he went so far towards fulfilling those predictions in
five outings that he started favourite for the Sun Alliance ahead of Young
Hustler: 7/4 against 9/4. Barton Bank had won three novice chases by
Christmas, the first two at Worcester the third at Cheltenham. He made the
most striking of debuts in accounting for Forest Sun and Cogent, followed
up by beating Superior Finish effortlessly, then comfortably kept his
unbeaten record intact against an improved Young Hustler in a race in
which Forest Sun fell. Thus far Barton Bank's jumping had been quick and
fluent, although he showed a tendency to keep rather low. On his next
outing, even-money favourite in the Feltham Novices' Chase at Kempton on
Boxing Day, he put in some tremendous leaps out in front and gained

Whitlenge Novices' Chase, Warwick — easy for Barton Bank

Mrs J. Mould's "Barton Bank"

ground at most of the fences, and looked well in command until he got too close to the third last and came down, leaving Dakyns Boy to run out the winner. As planned, Barton Bank completed his preparation for the Sun Alliance with just one race after Kempton. He came in for an easy opportunity at Warwick in February when Superior Finish was withdrawn, and won by a distance in a canter, getting the third last wrong again but in the main jumping soundly and boldly.

Barton Bank (br.g. 1986)	Kambalda (b 1970)	Right Royal V (br 1958)	Owen Tudor
			Bastia
		Opencast (br 1957)	Mossborough
			Coal Board
	Lucifer's Daughter (b 1976)	Lucifer (ch 1966)	Crimson Satan
			La Joliette
		Fiorina (b 1964)	Javelot
			Fiora

Barton Bank could well develop into a Gold Cup candidate if he keeps sound. He is, incidentally, by the same sire as the 1992 Sun Alliance Chase winner Miinnehoma who failed to make the Gold Cup line-up in the latest season but may do so one day. Barton Bank's family has been fairly successful in recent generations. The third dam Fiora won numerous races on the Flat and over hurdles including the Naas November Handicap. Her daughter Fiorina, also a Flat winner, produced the useful Killamonan who finished third in a Waterford Crystal Supreme Novices' Hurdle. Barton Bank's dam, a lightly-raced sister to Killamonan, had previously thrown the point-to-point winner Sandalay's Daughter (by Sandalay). Her six-year-old is Barton Bank's brother Case Harden, the winner of a maiden hurdle at Warwick in March. The lengthy Barton Bank is suited by a test of stamina. He has done most of his racing on soft or heavy going but he put up that very useful performance at Aintree on good; the first time he encountered firmer than good was at Warwick, the second time was at the Cheltenham Festival. Anyone seeing him skip round at Warwick would find it hard to believe that the ground had anything to do with his disappointing last time. Mainly because he is such a quick and fluent jumper, he usually makes the running. *D. Nicholson*

BARTONDALE 8 br.m. Oats – Miss Boon (Road House II) [1992/3 c20gF c24spu c24d6 c19d c20m* c20f3 c21m5 c23dpu c18m4 c24g4 c21f4] angular, plain mare: poor chaser: won maiden at Edinburgh in February: best effort afterwards on penultimate outing: stays 3m: acts on firm ground: visored once.*J. M. Bradley*   c80

BARTRES 14 ch.g. Le Bavard (FR) – Gail Borden (Blue Chariot) [1992/3 c24g5 c24f3 c22f c26f2 c24g4] lengthy, plain, raw-boned gelding: fair hunter chaser nowadays: stays well: acts on any going: usually held up: has worn blinkers (not for some time). *D. J. G. Murray-Smith*   c93

BARUD (IRE) 5 b.g. Persian Bold – Pale Moon (Jukebox) [1992/3 16g2 17grtr 16grtr a16grtr] leggy gelding: poor maiden hurdler: trained until after third outing by D. Burchell: often refuses to race and is one to avoid.*J. D. Thomas*   74 §

BAS DE LAINE (FR) 7 b.g. Le Pontet (FR) – La Gaina (FR) (New Chapter) [1992/3 21g4 16g5 17d6] tall gelding: fairly useful hurdler: best effort of season on second start: wasn't seen out after November: should stay beyond 21f: acts on good to firm and soft ground. *O. Sherwood*   125

BASHAMAH (IRE) 4 b. or br.f. Nashamaa – Raja Moulana (Raja Baba (USA)) [1992/3 17vpu a16gpu 20spu] leggy, lightly-made filly: plating-class middle-distance maiden on Flat: sold out of C. Brittain's stable 2,100 gns Ascot November Sales: has shown nothing over hurdles: blinkered last outing.*I. R. Jones*   –

BASILEA 10 b.g. Strong Gale – Katie Kumar (Silver Kumar) [1992/3 c21d2 c21d2 c26fF c23f] well-made gelding: one-time fair chaser: well below form in 1992/3: stays 3m: acts on heavy going: blinkered once: has refused 3 times and is best left alone. *Capt. T. A. Forster*   c§§ – §

BASILICUS (FR) 4 b.c. Pamponi (FR) – Katy Collonge (FR) (Trenel) [1992/3 F16g4 F16d] French-bred colt: brother to 5-y-o Amadeus and half-brother to novice hurdler/chaser Turoldus (by Toujours Pret): showed ability in mid-season NH Flat races: yet to race over hurdles. *Mrs S. J. Smith*   –

BASIL THYME 13 ro.g. Scallywag – Savette (Frigid Aire) [1992/3 c21d4 c21g4 c21gur c23g5] tall gelding: poor chaser: stays 21f: acts on any going: poor jumper. *Miss P. M. Whittle*   c85 x –

BASSE TERRE 9 b.g. Mill Reef (USA) – Land Ho (Primera) [1992/3 c21g4] good-topped gelding: very lightly-raced novice hurdler: some promise when fourth at Sandown in March on chasing debut: stays 21f: best form on a sound surface.*N. A. Twiston-Davies*   c94 –

BASSETJA (IRE) 4 b.f. Lashkari – Belle Doche (FR) (Riverman (USA)) [1992/3 18d3 16g6 18v 17v5 18m*] lightly-raced maiden on Flat in France for A. de Royer-Dupre: won maiden hurdle at Downpatrick in May: ran at Perth previous outing: stays 2¼m: acts on good to firm going. *J. F. C. Maxwell, Ireland*   93

BASSO PROFUNDO 6 ch.g. Kind of Hush – Rosaceae (Sagaro) [1992/3 28dpu 16g 20d6 26s] sturdy, workmanlike gelding: poor form in novice hurdles: stays 3m: acts on good to firm and soft ground. *W. G. Reed*   78

BASTIDE (IRE) 5 b.g. Burslem – Spadilla (Javelot) [1992/3 F17g] leggy gelding: half-brother to winning hurdlers Good Lord (by Lord Gayle) and Storm Warrior (by Main Reef): ninth of 24 finishers in NH Flat at Cheltenham in October: yet to race over hurdles or fences. *M. H. Tompkins*   –

BATABANOO 4 ch.g. Bairn (USA) – For Instance (Busted) [1992/3 16d* 17g3 16g* 17g5 16m* 17m* 17g3 16f3] small, sparely-made gelding: brother to winning hurdler Forbearance: fair winner at up to 1¼m on Flat: fairly useful over hurdles and was successful at Wetherby, Edinburgh (twice) and   124

Newcastle (quite valuable handicap): also ran well last 2 starts: not sure to stay much beyond 2m: acts on firm and dead ground: usually held up. *Mrs M. Reveley*

BATHWICK BOBBIE 6 b.g. Netherkelly – Sunwise (Roi Soleil) [1992/3 16v⁵ 17v³ 18g⁶] big, good-topped gelding: chasing type: second foal: dam never ran: has shown ability in novice hurdles and will do better in due course. *Andrew Turnell*   89 p

BATTERY FIRED 4 ch.g. K-Battery – Party Cloak (New Member) [1992/3 F17d⁴ F17m] workmanlike gelding: second living foal: dam lightly-raced maiden on Flat and over hurdles: showed ability in NH Flat races in April: yet to race over hurdles. *N. B. Mason*

BATTLE BLAZE 10 ch.g. Glorified – General's Daughter (Spartan General) [1992/3 c19f⁴ c18dᵘʳ c19gᶠ c17s c20g] angular gelding: poor novice hurdler/chaser: trained until after fourth start by W. G. M. Turner: stays 21f: acts on dead going: tends to make mistakes. *P. D. Cundell*   c–
–

BATTLE STANDARD (CAN) 6 b.g. Storm Bird (CAN) – Hoist Emy's Flag (USA) (Hoist The Flag (USA)) [1992/3 18g⁴ 16m* 17d* 16d⁶ 16s⁴ 17s 18g 17m⁴ 17m⁶ 16s⁴ 17s] lengthy gelding: fair performer at up to 1¼m on Flat: selling hurdler: won at Catterick (bought in 4,200 gns) and Bangor (bought in 5,250 gns) in October: generally ran respectably afterwards: should stay beyond 17f: acts on good to firm and soft ground: blinkered last outing (ran badly). *Mrs S. A. Bramall*   90

BATTLE STING 9 b.g. Hard Fought – Mrs Bee (Sallust) [1992/3 20d] close-coupled gelding: poor hurdler: barely stays 2½m: acts on any going, except possibly heavy. *Mrs S. A. Ward*   –

BATTUTA 4 ch.f. Ballacashtal (CAN) – Valpolicella (Lorenzaccio) [1992/3 16m] leggy filly: plating-class maiden on Flat: behind in juvenile hurdle at Wetherby in October. *R. Earnshaw*   –

BAVANTER 7 ch.g. Le Bavard (FR) – My Lily (Levanter) [1992/3 c20m⁵] ex-Irish gelding: half-brother to fair chaser It's Only A Joke (by Dominion Day): maiden pointer: poor form when fifth in novice chase at Market Rasen in September: sold 1,600 gns Doncaster May Sales. *B. S. Rothwell*   c72

BAVARD BAY 9 b. or br.g. Le Bavard (FR) – Winterwood (Bargello) [1992/3 c20g² c21s³ c25g³ c33v⁵ c26spᵘ c26s* c27gᶠ c26g⁴ c24d c21sᵘʳ 25vpᵘ 21s* 25m 22m] rangy, good sort: moderate performer: successful over fences at Catterick in January and in selling hurdle at Hexham (bought in 3,200 gns) in May: stays well: acts on soft going: visored 3 times in 1992/3 (including when successful), blinkered final outing: poor jumper of fences: inconsistent. *G. Richards*   c98 §
86 §

BAWNRUADH 8 ch.g. Wrens Hill – Oldtown Princess VI (Chou Chin Chow) [1992/3 c24gᶠ c23dᶠ 20g 28g c24dpᵘ c21vᶠ 25m] lengthy gelding: poor hurdler/novice chaser: blinkered fifth outing. *T. Dyer*   c–
–

BAYBEEJAY 6 b.m. Buzzards Bay – Peak Condition (Mountain Call) [1992/3 18m⁵ 16sᵘʳ 16d* 16d⁴ 20vᶠ 18s⁴ 16v⁴ 23d⁴ 17d⁵ 21f² 26v⁴ 16m⁵] small, sparely-made mare: selling hurdler: won at Uttoxeter (no bid) in November: well beaten last 2 starts: stays 23f: acts on any ground. *R. Brotherton*   76

BAYDON STAR 6 br.g. Mandalus – Leuze (Vimy) [1992/3 17g* 21g* 17d* 17s* 16s² 25g* 25m³]   156

It was asking too much of Baydon Star to fill the void left by Mighty Mogul, but if there was something of a second-best feel to Baydon Star in 1992/3, the story could be very different in twelve months time. Nothing can be taken for granted in racing—his connections will know that—but Baydon Star should have a big say in the destination of novice chasing honours. This strapping individual is very much a chasing type, and has shown very smart form over hurdles. Just six years old, he already has a deserved reputation for enthusiasm and consistency, and has caught the eye with his fast and

Rendlesham Hurdle, Kempton—
Baydon Star is left clear as Sweet Glow crashes out at the last

fluent jumping. In short, Baydon Star is one of the best chasing prospects around.

Following a novice campaign under Mrs Pitman which yielded wins at Windsor and Chepstow, Baydon Star began his second season over hurdles on a mark of 113 in a handicap at Ascot in October, justifying favouritism. Well placed and progressing in leaps and bounds, Baydon Star was made favourite in all his seven starts in 1992/3. An impressive performance in beating Sweet Duke by four lengths in the Tom Masson Trophy at Newbury made him look a good thing, unpenalised, in the £17,200 Ladbroke November Handicap Hurdle at Aintree seventeen days later, and a seven-length success there was followed by another in the H.S.S. Hire Shops Hurdle at Ascot in which his nearest pursuers were Corrin Hill and a below-form Flown. Twelve days after that Ascot victory (and little more than two months after his reappearance) Baydon Star was back in a handicap, this time on a mark of 145, for the New Year's Day Hurdle at Windsor. Mighty Mogul had put himself at the head of the Champion Hurdle betting earlier in the week with his win in the Christmas Hurdle but within six weeks he was dead and the same connections' Baydon Star was put forward as a Champion Hurdle replacement. In his favour, Baydon Star had again shown markedly improved form at Windsor, to a standard which entitled him to consideration in a very open Champion Hurdle field, but he had been beaten; receiving weight and having had every chance, Baydon Star just couldn't get the better of Muse, eventually going down by a length.

75

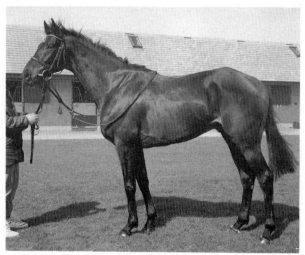

Mrs Shirley Robins' "Baydon Star"

The Stayers' Hurdle had seemed the more likely Cheltenham option at that stage, before Mighty Mogul's sad demise, an option to which connections returned when it became clear that top-of-the-ground conditions would prevail at the Festival. To help them overcome the temptation of a Champion Hurdle challenge they had the evidence of Baydon Star's sixth run of the season, in the four-runner Rendlesham Hurdle at Kempton in February over three miles and half a furlong. The outcome looked far from certain when Sweet Glow crashed upsides at the last, but Baydon Star's performance, making smooth headway from the turn and still not called upon to make his final effort when left alone, nonetheless lent plenty of encouragement for his prospects in the Stayers'. Baydon Star started 3/1 favourite at Cheltenham despite not taking the eye particularly in the preliminaries, and he went on to give supporters a good run for their money. Coming to the last he was bang in contention with Shuil Ar Aghaidh and Pragada, but failed to take it cleanly and that signalled the end of his challenge; he lost five and a half lengths on Shuil Ar Aghaidh up the hill.

Baydon Star (br.g. 1987)	Mandalus (b 1974)	Mandamus (br 1960)	Petition
			Great Fun
		Laminate (gr 1957)	Abernant
			Lamri
	Leuze (b 1963)	Vimy (b 1952)	Wild Risk
			Mimi
		Over The Border (b 1945)	Scottish Union
			Lapel

Like Mighty Mogul, Baydon Star was purchased as an unbroken three-year-old by Mrs Pitman at the Tattersalls Derby Sale, fetching IR 52,000 guineas to Mighty Mogul's 19,000. A glance at the record of Baydon Star's dam explains why he was valued so highly. Unraced herself, Leuze

BAY

has produced a string of winners including the 1979 Grand National winner Rubstic (by I Say), the useful chaser Bennachie (by Firestreak) and the smart hunter chaser Barstick (by Bargello). One of the very few of her foals which failed to win was Lettuce (by So Blessed) and she has made amends at stud with the Lincoln and Royal Hunt Cup winner Mighty Fly and the Derby third Mighty Flutter. The best of Leuze's previous foals, though, ends his career as a chaser just as Baydon Star begins his. After career victories including the Sun Alliance Chase and Jim Ford Challenge Cup, and places in such as the Whitbread Gold Cup and King George, Kildimo added the Becher Chase at Aintree to his list of successes at the age of twelve in November. It now looks as if his final appearance was as one of the nine who never jumped a fence in the void Grand National. Baydon Star is the last reported foal out of Leuze, who died in 1990. His sire Mandalus showed very useful form in winning thirteen races on the Flat. None of those was beyond a mile and a quarter and the vast majority at a mile, but in his final season new connections ran him in the two-and-three-quarter-mile Queen Alexandra Stakes and he finished a good third. David Nicholson has trained a couple of well-above-average chasers by Mandalus in the two-milers Long Engagement and Springholm. Baydon Star has already demonstrated that he stays better than them, although his form with testing conditions at two miles is on a similar level to what he has shown at three. He acts on soft ground and good to firm. All in all, there are plenty of options open for Baydon Star. He has a bright future. *D. Nicholson*

BAY-EM-VAY 11 ch.g. Derrylin – Forest Flower (Fine Blade (USA)) [1992/3 24s^{pu} c16v^{pu} c24d^{pu}] workmanlike gelding: little sign of ability. *Graham Richards*

c–
–

BAYFORD ENERGY 7 ch.g. Milford – Smiling (Silly Season) [1992/3 c25d^{pu} c21m^5] lengthy gelding: winning hurdler: sold 1,200 gns Ascot November Sales: no sign of ability over fences: should stay beyond 2½m: acts on good to firm ground. *Miss J. du Plessis*

c–
–

BAYIN (USA) 4 b.c. Caro – Regatela (USA) (Dr Fager) [1992/3 17s^F] leggy colt: behind in maidens on Flat: sold out of R. Armstrong's stable 5,200 gns Newmarket Autumn Sales: behind when falling last in juvenile hurdle at Newbury in November. *M. D. I. Usher*

–

BAYPHIA 5 ch.g. Bay Express – Sophie Avenue (Guillaume Tell (USA)) [1992/3 17d* 18f* 17d 18d] leggy gelding: won novice hurdles at Newton Abbot and Exeter in August: not seen out after November: will stay beyond 2¼m: acts on firm and dead ground. *Mrs F. Walwyn*

93

BAYRAM (FR) 11 br.g. Blakeney – Zarin (GER) (Arjon) [1992/3 c24v^{pu} c26s^{pu} c26d^{pu}] compact gelding: winning hurdler/chaser: showed nothing in 1992/3: sold 950 gns Ascot June Sales: poor jumper: sometimes wears tongue strap. *T. J. Etherington*

c– x
–

BAYROUGE (IRE) 5 br.m. Gorytus (USA) – Bay Tree (FR) (Relko) [1992/3 16v^3 16s* 16s* 16s* 16d* 19d* 22s* 16v^2 16d* 19d^2 16v* 22s^3 19s^2 16d*]

140

'If we could get the best out of her, she would be very good. She just saves a bit sometimes' was an honest if somewhat surprising appraisal of Bayrouge by her owner after this remarkable mare had won the Country Pride Champion Novice Hurdle at Punchestown in April. Bayrouge had seemed more deserving of the epithets tough, game and consistent after this, her fourteenth race of the season over hurdles of which she'd won nine and been placed in the other five. Seven of those wins had been gained by the turn of year, in a maiden at Listowel, handicaps at Tipperary, Punchestown, Naas and Fairyhouse, and novice events at Galway and Leopardstown, the last-named at the chief expense of Montelado. When winning her eighth race, the Naas Supporters Hurdle, Bayrouge had Princess Casilia a length and a half behind her in second place, and the same two mares also dominated the Country Pride Champion Novice Hurdle three months later. The race had been weakened by the absence of Montelado, who'd won the

77

1st Choice Novices' Hurdle, Leopardstown—Bayrouge (near side) beats Montelado

Trafalgar House Novices' Hurdle since his defeat by Bayrouge. And with both the favourite Boro Eight and Bucks-Choice, who'd twice beaten Bayrouge, failing to give their running it became even less competitive. Nevertheless, in winning by four lengths from Princess Casilia, Bayrouge put up a smart performance, her best to date. Ridden by Richard Dunwoody in place of her usual partner the 7-lb claimer Kieran Gaule, Bayrouge gave an improved display of jumping, making her only mistake at the first. Moving smoothly past the leader Boro Eight approaching the third last, Bayrouge kept on too strongly for Princess Casilia who was her only challenger after Big Matt had fallen two out when in third place.

			Nijinsky	Northern Dancer
	Gorytus (USA)		(b 1967)	Flaming Page
	(b 1980)		Glad Rags II	High Hat
Bayrouge (IRE)			(ch 1963)	Dryad
(br.m. 1988)			Relko	Tanerko
	Bay Tree (FR)		(b 1960)	Relance III
	(b 1969)		The Blonde	Wild Risk
			(ch 1958)	Kisaki

Bayrouge, bred by her owner, is a half-sister to seven winners. They include the useful staying chaser Duntree (by Day Is Done) and Ravaro (by Raga Navarro). The latter, another tough and versatile performer, won the Irish Cesarewitch and also showed very useful form over hurdles, finishing second in the 1986 Waterford Crystal Stayers' Hurdle. Bayrouge, a fairly useful winner over eleven furlongs on the Flat as a three-year-old, is a daughter of the mile-and-a-half maiden race winner Bay Tree. Her grandam The Blonde, who never ran, produced five winners, notably the 1967 Derby

Mr Joseph Crowley's "Bayrouge"

fourth Royal Sword. Bayrouge was the chief contributor to a tremendous season enjoyed by her stable run by Mrs Anne Marie O'Brien, the daughter of Bayrouge's owner. Mrs O'Brien, who sent out more winners than any other trainer in Ireland in 1992/3 with fifty-three, handed in her licence at the end of the season. Her husband, a former Irish champion amateur rider, has taken over. Bayrouge is effective at two miles and will stay beyond two and three quarter miles. She showed form on top-of-the-ground on the Flat but has raced only on a soft surface over hurdles. The leggy, angular Bayrouge was due to be schooled over fences the day after winning, and it's likely that she'll be running in novice chases in 1993/4. *Mrs A. M. O'Brien, Ireland*

BAY TERN (USA)   7 b.h. Arctic Tern (USA) – Unbiased (USA) (Foolish Pleasure (USA)) [1992/3 21g² 23g* 17s² 17d* 17m* 22d² 20m] sparely-made horse: fairly useful handicap hurdler: trained until after first start by M. H. Easterby: successful at Kelso in October and April and at Perth (conditional jockeys event) in May: saddle slipped last outing: effective at 2m and stays 23f: acts on firm and dead ground: visored once: usually races up with pace: genuine and consistent. *T. Dyer*   119

BAZZROY (IRE)   4 ch.g. King Persian – Miss Noora (Ahonoora) [1992/3 17mpu 18g³ 18dpu] sparely-made gelding: behind only outing on Flat, at 2 yrs: showed a little ability in juvenile claiming hurdle at Fontwell in September: pulled up lame only subsequent outing (November): blinkered last 2 starts. *J. S. Moore*   51

79

BEACHAMWELL 11 b.g. Record Run – Mishabo (Royalty) [1992/3 c– c20mᵖᵘ] strong, lengthy gelding: winning 2m hurdler: well beaten only completed outing over fences: acts on dead going. *M. C. Pipe* —

BEACH BUM 7 gr.g. Scallywag – St Lucian Breeze (Vivify) [1992/3 16v 16vᵖᵘ 16d 17g 16f⁴] fourth foal: half-brother to 2 poor novice hurdlers: dam once-raced half-sister to useful hurdler/fair chaser Rutley and to Topham Trophy winner Canit: little sign of ability in novice hurdles. *Mrs J. A. Young* —

BEACH PATROL (IRE) 5 b.g. Thatching – Waveguide (Double Form) [1992/3 17d 17dᶠ 16m 17dᵖᵘ] leggy gelding: no sign of ability over hurdles: trained until after third outing by A. Batey. *W. Storey* —

BEACHY HEAD 5 gr.g. Damister (USA) – No More Rosies (Warpath) [1992/3 16v² 17s⁴ 21v⁴ 21s* 22dᶠ] leggy, sparely-made gelding: useful hurdler: won at Perth in April: tailed off when falling last in Prix La Barka at Auteuil in June: effective at 2m and stays 21f: acts on heavy and good to firm ground: usually jumps well: forces pace. *J. J. O'Neill* 135

BEADS 8 ch.m. Noalcoholic (FR) – Siouxsie (Warpath) [1992/3 17f] half-sister to 5 winners by Mandrake Major: dam 2-y-o 6f winner: has been to stud: well beaten in novice hurdle at Newcastle in May. *M. A. Barnes* —

BE AMBITIOUS (IRE) 5 ch.g. Arapahos (FR) – Hilarys Mark (On Your Mark) [1992/3 21g] plain gelding: second foal: dam never ran: well beaten in novice hurdle at Carlisle in March. *S. G. Payne* —

BEAM ME UP SCOTTY (IRE) 4 br.g. Orchestra – Bright Path (He Loves Me) [1992/3 17m⁶ 18g⁵ 17g 17g⁴ 17f] leggy gelding: 1½m winner on Flat: poor maiden over hurdles: sold 3,400 gns Ascot June Sales. *P. Mitchell* 74

BEAN DREAMS 8 b.g. Prince Bee – Travelling Fair (Vienna) [1992/3 c– c23gᵖᵘ c21gᵖᵘ] leggy, good-topped gelding: winning selling hurdler: poor novice chaser: stays 2½m: acts on firm ground. *M. P. Muggeridge* —

BEAN KING 7 gr.g. Ardross – Meanz Beanz (High Top) [1992/3 17v³ 22s 26mᶠ 21sᶠ 21m] good-topped gelding: fairly useful hurdler: easily best effort of season on first start: should stay beyond 17f: acts on heavy ground. *N. J. Henderson* 118

BEANLEY BROOK 5 ch.m. Meadowbrook – The Bean-Goose (King Sitric) [1992/3 F16v 21v⁶ 17d⁴ 18d*] first foal: dam of little account: won mares novice hurdle at Exeter in April: should stay beyond 2¼m: yet to race on a sound surface. *K. C. Bailey* 87

BEANZ MEANZ 7 b.g. Torenaga – Kinneagh Queen (Le Prince) [1992/3 24s²] modest novice hurdler: stayed 3m: acted on any going: dead. *J. H. Johnson* 91

BEATLE SONG 5 b.m. Song – Betyle (FR) (Hardicanute) [1992/3 17d⁶ 17fᵖᵘ] inconsistent miler on Flat: no form over hurdles, in seller last time. *R. J. Hodges* —

BEAUCADEAU 7 b.g. Alzao (USA) – Pretty Gift (Realm) [1992/3 16f* c– p 18m² 16m⁴ 18d⁴ 16d⁵ 18s² c17vᶠ c16sᶠ 17d⁴ 16d³ 16d⁶ 16s⁵ 16f² 17m³ 18m* 107 16g²] neat, good-quartered gelding: fair handicap hurdler: won at Hexham in August and Cartmel in May: fell both starts in novice chases, but showed promise: races only at around 2m: probably acts on any going: usually wears tongue strap. *M. A. Barnes*

BEAUCHAMP EXPRESS 6 b.g. Castle Keep – Jubilee (Reform) [1992/3 18dʳᵗʳ 16d² 17d⁴ 22v* 22v* 21vᵖᵘ 21sᵖᵘ 21mᵖᵘ] angular gelding: 105 § useful middle-distance stayer on Flat at 3 yrs: won novice hurdles at Newton Abbot (handicap) in December and Worcester in January: ran poorly last 3 outings: will stay 3m: acts on heavy ground: refused to race on hurdling debut, looked reluctant final start: one to treat with caution. *O. Sherwood*

BEAUCHAMP GRACE 4 b.f. Ardross – Buss (Busted) [1992/3 17v* 131 p 16v* 16v* 17g* 17m] good-topped filly: half-sister to fairly useful staying hurdler Torbole (by Reliance II): fair stayer on Flat: sold out of J. Dunlop's stable 14,500 gns Newmarket Autumn Sales: winner of first 4 starts in

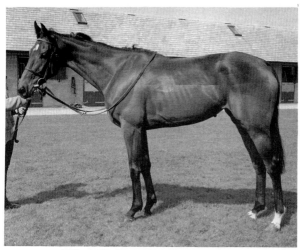

Million In Mind Partnership's "Beauchamp Grace"

juvenile hurdles, at Cheltenham, Towcester, Warwick and Newbury (Stroud Green Hurdle, by ½ length from Indian Quest): favourite when below form in Daily Express Triumph Hurdle at Cheltenham: sold 28,000 gns Doncaster May Sales: will stay beyond 17f: acts on heavy going and possibly unsuited by good to firm: worth another chance. *D. Nicholson*

BEAU CHARM   9 b.g. Beau Charmeur (FR) – Anona-Anona (Alcide) **c114 ?** [1992/3 c25g c27v[5] c27v[ur] c25v[pu] c26v[pu] c25s[2] c24s[4] c26g c26g[2] c33g[5]] **–** leggy gelding: novice hurdler: handicap chaser: jumped better than usual, after being hampered start, when excellent fifth to Run For Free in Stakis Scottish National at Ayr in April on last start: stays well: acts on heavy going. *J. T. Gifford*

BEAUFAN   6 br.g. Taufan (USA) – Beaume (FR) (Faraway Son (USA)) [1992/3 17g[pu] 16f 16d[6] 17s[pu] 17s[5] 21d[pu]] neat gelding: poor hurdler: best **72** effort of season on third start: form only at around 2m: acts on dead going: has twice run blinkered, and had tongue tied down. *C. F. C. Jackson*

BEAU PARI   9 b.g. Beau Charmeur (FR) – Raised-In-Paris (Raise You **c103** Ten) [1992/3 c19f[2]] compact gelding: fairly useful hurdler at his best: **–** winning chaser: second in handicap at Fontwell in October: sold 2,500 gns Ascot June Sales: stays 3m: acts on firm and dead going: sketchy jumper of fences. *J. T. Gifford*

BEAU ROSE   10 b.g. Beau Charmeur (FR) – Rosantus (Anthony) [1992/3 **c–** c24d[pu] c24d[pu] c25g[pu]] well-made gelding: hunter chaser: ran poorly in 1993: **–** stays well: acts on firm ground. *C. C. Trietline*

BEAUTIFUL DREAM   5 b.m. Kalaglow – Question Mark (High Line) [1992/3 F17v[3] F17v[2] F17v[su] 20s[ur] 22v[4] 22v* 24s[pu]] angular mare: fifth foal: **96** half-sister to Flat winners Taiga (by Northfields) and The Betsy (by Imperial Fling): dam, sister to Park Hill winner Quay Line, won twice over

*S. W. Showers Silver Trophy Chase, Cheltenham—Beech Road makes all;
Katabatic hangs on over the second last*

1½m: won novice hurdle at Wincanton in January: stayed 2¾m: acted on heavy going: dead. *R. J. Baker*

BECCY BROWN 5 b.m. Rabdan – Sarona (Lord of Verona) [1992/3 F16d 25dᵖᵘ 21g⁶] half-sister to fair 2m chaser Marejo (by Creetown) and winning pointer Nellies Well (by Royal Fountain): dam useful hurdler/chaser: no sign of ability. *F. T. Walton* —

BECK COTTAGE 5 b.g. Celtic Cone – Ellen Greaves (Deep Run) [1992/3 F16dˢᵘ 16d⁴ 17s⁵ 20dᵖᵘ] rangy gelding with scope: showed some ability in novice hurdles at Haydock and Carlisle in November: subsequently off course 3 months and out of depth on return: should prove suited by further than 2m. *R. F. Fisher* 80

BECKLEY FOUNTAIN (IRE) 5 br.g. Royal Fountain – Sweet Mystery (Floriferous) [1992/3 20g 21f²] leggy, workmanlike gelding: second foal: dam poor maiden hurdler: nearest finish when second in novice hurdle at Wetherby in May: will stay beyond 21f. *J. H. Johnson* 88

BECTIVE BOY 11 ch.g. Wolverlife – Al Radegonde (St Alphage) [1992/3 c21vᵖᵘ c17d⁶ c24g³ c18s⁴ c20gᴿ c21fᵖᵘ c18fᵖᵘ] leggy gelding: poor novice hurdler/chaser: stays 2½m: acts on heavy going. *Miss L. Bower* c–
–

BEDFIELD (IRE) 5 b.g. Buckskin (FR) – McNutt (Weavers' Hall) [1992/3 17dᵇᵈ 17s 21m] leggy, lengthy gelding: third foal: dam, placed over hurdles, from family of useful chaser Cuddy Dale: well beaten in novice hurdles at Sandown and Cheltenham (Sun Alliance): looks sort to do better, particularly over fences. *F. Murphy* – p

BEDOUIN PRINCE (USA) 6 b.h. Danzig (USA) – Regal Heiress (English Prince) [1992/3 18m²] compact horse: first form over hurdles when second in maiden at Market Rasen in May: should stay beyond 2¼m. *B. Richmond* 86

BEEBOB 5 b.m. Norwick (USA) – Anzeige (GER) (Soderini) [1992/3 22v³ 21v 22s 20d⁴ 18g² 17fᵖᵘ] sparely-made mare: fairly useful hurdler: placed at Cheltenham in December and Worcester in March: reportedly injured her back last outing: stays 2½m: acts on soft going: jumps none too fluently. *M. C. Pipe* 121

BEECH GROVE 12 b.g. Random Shot – Fauteuil (Faubourg II) [1992/3 c24f⁴ c26m* c21g³] strong, workmanlike gelding: fair hunter chaser: won at c90 x
–

Cheltenham in May: probably needs a good test of stamina: acts on soft and good to firm going: often let down by his jumping. *Miss C. Gordon*

BEECH ROAD 11 ch.g. Nearly A Hand – North Bovey (Flush Royal) [1992/3 c21d3 c20dur c21s* c21s2 c20g4 c21g* 21f2 c22m* 16f2 23f2] leggy, sparely-made gelding: won Champion Hurdle at Cheltenham in 1989: best effort over hurdles of 1992/3 and only useful form when runner-up at Uttoxeter on seventh outing: useful chaser: won handicap at Warwick, 4-runner S. W. Showers Silver Trophy Chase at Cheltenham and handicap at Stratford (dead-heated) in second half of season: stays 2¾m: acts on any going: formerly unreliable at start: has broken blood vessels. *G. B. Balding*　**c143**
143

BEE DEE BOY 5 b.g. Julio Mariner – H And K Gambler (Rheingold) [1992/3 23g4 23d 23dur 22g4 20s5 17m3 21d2 24s3 20g5 24g*] trained until after fifth start by Miss L. Perratt: improved effort when winning amateurs maiden hurdle at Hexham in May: suited by 3m. *G. Richards*　86

BEE GARDEN 12 b.g. Giolla Mear – Regency View (Royal Highway) [1992/3 c21s2 c19d3 c21g2 c21g* c19v5] strong, compact gelding: fairly useful hunter chaser: won at Sandown in March: headstrong and best form at up to 2lf: acts on soft going: usually blinkered. *Mrs J. Litston*　**c103**
–

BEE-KAY-ESS 10 b.g. Porto Bello – Penny Bazaar (Native Bazaar) [1992/3 c17m3 c21gpu] leggy, close-coupled gelding: winning pointer: poor novice otherwise. *R. W. Savery*　c–
–

BEERA QUEST 14 br.g. Caballero – Kellsboro Rocket (Master Rocky) [1992/3 c24m6 c24gpu] smallish, compact gelding: winning hunter chaser: no form since 1991. *S. C. Horn*　c–
–

BEETEE YOU 10 b.g. Royalty – Jinkin (King's Troop) [1992/3 c16m6 c21spu] tall gelding: handicap chaser: no form since 1989/90: stays 2½m: acts on hard ground. *T. T. Bill*　c–
–

BEIJA FLOR 6 gr.g. Busted – Rusticello (Rusticaro (FR)) [1992/3 16d 16m] good-topped gelding: no form over hurdles, including in sellers. *F. Jordan*　–

BELAFONTE 6 br.g. Derrylin – Ulla Laing (Mummy's Pet) [1992/3 22g5 20g* 21sF 21s6 22v3 25spu 22s 21m6 18g2] neat gelding: fairly useful handicap hurdler: trained until after first start by R. Holder: won conditional jockeys event at Ascot in October: second of 11 at San Siro in May: stays 2¾m: acts on any going: tried in blinkers: none too consistent. *C. P. E. Brooks*　124

BELARIUS 5 b.g. Bellypha – Celebrity (Troy) [1992/3 18dpu 16gpu 16mro] lengthy, angular gelding: of little account: sold 1,500 gns Doncaster January Sales. *R. E. Barr*　–

BEL BARAKA (IRE) 4 ch.g. Bering – Typhoon Polly (Lord Gayle (USA)) [1992/3 17d 18spu] compact gelding: modest maiden on Flat: no sign of ability in selling hurdles, pulling too hard: sold 2,500 gns Doncaster January Sales. *D. R. C. Elsworth*　–

BEL COURSE 11 b.g. Crash Course – Belen (Milesian) [1992/3 c16s3 c16d2 c21s* c21m4 c22fpu c21d4 c23f c21fF] tall, rather leggy gelding: fair chaser: sixth course win when scoring at Worcester in February: poor efforts afterwards: effective at 2m and stays 25f: seems to act on any going: blinkered twice: has worn a pricker: unreliable. *J. Webber*　**c102** §
–

BELDINE 8 gr.g. Belfort (FR) – Royal Celandine (Royal Palace) [1992/3 c16m* c16dF c20g3] lengthy, angular gelding: winning hurdler: fair handicap chaser: won seller at Perth (no bid) in August: creditable third at Ayr in October: stays 2½m: yet to race on heavy ground, acts on any other. *P. Monteith*　**c106**
–

BELFRY LAD 5 b.g. Ayyabaan – Sarah's Joy (Full of Hope) [1992/3 F17g F16d] smallish, plain gelding: third foal: dam twice-raced maiden: mid-division in NH Flat race in October: sold 2,200 gns Ascot November Sales: yet to race over hurdles or fences. *C. D. Broad*　–

BELIEVE IT 4 b.c. Bellypha – Hasty Key (USA) (Key To The Mint (USA)) [1992/3 17g⁵ 17g 16g 17mᵖᵘ 16g⁵ 17m⁴ 18m³ 18v⁵] leggy colt: half-brother to winning selling hurdler Cixi (by Far Out East): lightly-raced maiden on Flat: sold out of C. Brittain's stable 4,200 gns Newmarket July Sales: poor form over hurdles: acts on good to firm ground, well below form on heavy. *N. Waggott* 80

BELLAGIO BILL 8 br.g. Billion (USA) – Nikancy (Castlenik) [1992/3 18g⁶ 22sᵖᵘ] close-coupled gelding: of little account. *C. Bridgett* –

BELLAGROVE (IRE) 5 ch.m. Yashgan – Lamya (Hittite Glory) [1992/3 a18gᵖᵘ] ex-Irish mare: fifth foal: half-sister to a poor Flat maiden and to a winner in Belgium (both by Welsh Term): dam ran here at 2 yrs, later won in Sweden: modest maiden on Flat: won 2 juvenile hurdles in 1991/2 when trained by D. Murphy: jumped badly and showed nothing in handicap at Southwell in February: yet to race beyond 2¼m: best form on good going: sometimes blinkered in 1991/2. *B. S. Rothwell* –

BELLA RUN 4 ch.f. Commanche Run – Bonne de Berry (Habitat) [1992/3 18v 16vᵖᵘ 17fᵖᵘ] lengthy, workmanlike filly: maiden on Flat: no sign of ability over hurdles: blinkered last start. *R. J. Hodges* –

BELLE BRIDGETTE (IRE) 5 b.m. Il Pontevecchio – Hanseletta (Prince Hansel) [1992/3 F16d] fourth foal: dam maiden hurdler and winning pointer in Ireland: well beaten in NH Flat race at Ludlow in December: yet to race over hurdles or fences. *P. M. McEntee* –

BELLE ISLE BILL 8 b.g. Chantro – Hannah's Song (Saintly Song) [1992/3 c20f] leggy, workmanlike gelding: of little account: sometimes blinkered. *W. J. Smith* c– –

BELLEZZA 6 b.m. Ardross – Bobo Ema (Auction Ring (USA)) [1992/3 20g⁴ 20d* 20s² 23s 20d 20f* 20f] lengthy mare: fair hurdler: successful in 2 handicaps at Taunton (first an amateurs event) in first half of season, and returned to form after 2 poor efforts to win similar event at Lingfield in March: effective at 2½m and should stay 3m: probably acts on any going. *A. Moore* 113

BELLING BELLING (IRE) 5 b.m. Soughaan (USA) – Dame Ross (Raga Navarro (ITY)) [1992/3 a16g 20v⁶ 16s⁵ 18g 17f 17d 16v³ 16d 18m⁴ 16m⁴] small, light-framed mare: novice selling hurdler: best form at 2m on a sound surface. *C. H. Jones* 65

BELLMAN 8 b.g. Barley Hill – Bellote (Seven Bells) [1992/3 c33mᵖᵘ] fair pointer: tailed off when pulled up in hunter chase at Cheltenham in May. *N. M. Lampard* c– –

BELLOFAGUS 8 b.g. Liberated – Courdelle (Coup de Myth) [1992/3 c16mᶠ c23gᶠ 16g 17d] leggy, sparely-made gelding: poor novice hurdler/chaser. *J. K. M. Oliver* c– –

BELL ONE (USA) 4 ch.g. Lightning Leap (USA) – Ambrose Channel (USA) (Key To The Mint (USA)) [1992/3 aF13g² F17m] lengthy gelding: first foal: dam unraced daughter of sister to Diamond Shoal and Glint of Gold: refused to enter stalls only outing on Flat: sold out of I. Balding's stable 3,200 gns Ascot November (1991) Sales: second in NH Flat race at Lingfield in February: in mid-division in valuable similar race at Cheltenham in March: yet to race over hurdles. *A. J. K. Dunn* –

BELL STAFFBOY (IRE) 4 b.g. Phardante (FR) – Trumpster (Tarqogan) [1992/3 F16s⁵ F17g* F17m²] good-topped gelding: first foal: dam, moderate Irish hurdler, from successful jumping family: won 17-runner NH Flat race at Bangor in March: close second at Cheltenham following month: yet to race over hurdles. *C. D. Broad* –

BELLS YEW GREEN 11 ch.g. Captain James – Mexican Two Step (Gay Fandango (USA)) [1992/3 a20g a20gᵖᵘ a20g c16dᶠ] lengthy, angular gelding: novice hurdler: no form for a long time: has fallen both starts over fences. *J. R. Bosley* c– –

BELLTON 5 gr.g. Bellypha – Celestial Air (Rheingold) [1992/3 17d⁶ 16d²
16g* 18g² 16s*] tall gelding with scope: won novice hurdles at Nottingham
in February and Wetherby in April: creditable second in quite valuable
novice event at Kelso in between: will stay beyond 2¼m: acts on soft going:
will improve further and win more races. *J. G. FitzGerald*   118 p

BELMOREDEAN 8 ch.g. Be My Guest (USA) – Hanna Alta (FR) **c 100**
(Busted) [1992/3 c17d* c17g² c17f* c16v⁴ c16f³] lengthy, angular gelding: –
fair hurdler: successful in early-season novice chases at Newton Abbot and
Taunton: creditable third in similar race at Lingfield in March: suited by
sharp 2m: acts on firm and dead ground. *R. J. O'Sullivan*

BELMORE ROCK 6 b. or br.g. Oats – Direct Call (Menelek) [1992/3
18f⁴ 22d 17s⁴] rather unfurnished gelding: easily best effort in novice   83
hurdles when fourth at Huntingdon on last start: should stay
beyond 17f: acts on soft going. *R. J. O'Sullivan*

BELMOUNT CAPTAIN 8 ch.g. Le Bavard (FR) – The Brown Link **c 137**
(Rugged Man) [1992/3 c24s* c25g³ c28d* c25d² c30s⁶ c25s²] lengthy
gelding: usually looks very well: useful chaser: won Mercedes Benz
Handicap at Chepstow in October and Flowers Original Handicap at
Cheltenham in November: also ran creditably on his other starts: a
thorough stayer: acts on soft going: jumps soundly: consistent. *G. B.
Balding*

BELPENEL 7 ch.g. Pharly (FR) – Seldovia (Charlottown) [1992/3 25sᵖᵘ
16g 20g 21v 22d⁴ a20g³ a20g 22g⁵ 28gᵖᵘ] sparely-made gelding: selling   75
hurdler: stays 2½m: acts on soft going and fibresand: sometimes blinkered,
visored last 4 starts. *C. A. Smith*

*Flowers Original Handicap Chase, Cheltenham —
the winner Belmount Captain (Richard Guest)*

BELSTONE FOX 8 br.g. Buckskin (FR) – Winter Fox (Martinmas) **c115 x**
[1992/3 c21s² c16d² c18d³ c16v⁵ c17g* c17g* c21m c16fᵖᵘ] rangy, rather –
sparely-made gelding: fair hurdler: successful in novice chases at
Doncaster in January and Newbury in February: badly let down by his
jumping subsequently: best form at around 2m: acts on soft going: takes
good hold and races up with pace. *D. Nicholson*

BELTANE THE SMITH 13 ch.g. Owen Anthony – North Bovey **c–**
(Flush Royal) [1992/3 c21d⁴] angular gelding: moderate hurdler/novice –
chaser: well-beaten fourth in hunter chase at Huntingdon in February:
successful in 2 points subsequently: should stay 2½m: acts on any going:
blinkered once: not an accomplished jumper of fences. *J. C. Sweetland*

BELVEDERIAN 6 b.g. Deep Run – Arctic Shine (Arctic Slave) [1992/3
16d* 18g² 20d³ 21s* 24s* 22d* 24v⁴ 18s* 21m 20s*] 143 p
Belvederian failed to do himself justice on his two visits to Britain,
finishing well beaten in both the Premier Long Distance Hurdle at Haydock
in January and the Sun Alliance Novices' Hurdle at Cheltenham in March.
He should be judged on his Irish form, the best of which entitles him to be
rated second only to Montelado among the season's novice hurdlers. It's a
possibility, though we wouldn't want to put it any stronger, that Belvederian
was unsuited by the heavy ground at Haydock and the firmish going at
Cheltenham. He's done virtually all his racing in Ireland on dead and soft
ground, and his record over hurdles there stands at six wins from eight
starts. The first four of those wins, at Roscommon, Navan, Fairyhouse and
Leopardstown, came before the turn of the year, the fifth, in the Red Mills
Trial Hurdle at Gowran Park, between visits to Britain. And when returned
to Fairyhouse in April, Belvederian crowned a fine season by winning the
Festival Novices' Hurdle. A lack-lustre effort from the favourite Bucks-
Choice made Belvederian's task easier, but in winning by seven lengths
from Muir Station he confirmed himself a smart novice.

Festival Novices' Hurdle, Fairyhouse—a smart performance from Belvederian

Mr A. J. O'Reilly's "Belvederian"

Belvederian (b.g. 1987)	Deep Run (ch 1966)	Pampered King (b 1954)	Prince Chevalier / Netherton Maid
		Trial By Fire (ch 1958)	Court Martial / Mitrailleuse
	Arctic Shine (b 1967)	Arctic Slave (b 1950)	Arctic Star / Roman Gallery
		Shining Clare (ch 1959)	Greek Star / Castle Clare

Belvederian, bought for IR 15,000 guineas at Fairyhouse in November, 1990, fetched 20,000 guineas when re-submitted at Doncaster Sales the following May. He's a brother to the useful jumper Belgrove Lad and the winning pointer Shining Run, and a half-brother to the fair chaser Sheba's Boy (by Menelek). Their dam Arctic Shine, a full sister to five winners, four of them jumpers, won three races over hurdles and one over fences, all at around two miles. Belvederian himself has won from two miles to three miles, putting up his best performance at two and a half. His trainer was reported to have said before Cheltenham that Belvederian was the best horse he had sent to the Festival meeting, high praise indeed from one who sent out Buck House to win both the Trafalgar House Supreme Novices' Hurdle and Queen Mother Champion Chase and Trapper John the Stayers' Hurdle. Belvederian has some way to go to justify his trainer's opinion, but time is on his side and it's on the cards that Belvederian, an angular, workmanlike individual, will prove even more effective over fences than over hurdles. He's a good prospect. *M. F. Morris, Ireland*

BE MY ERA (IRE) 5 b.g. Be My Guest (USA) – Ribera (FR) (Wittgenstein (USA)) [1992/3 17g 16d 16m] leggy gelding: poor form at best over hurdles. *A. W. Denson*

   –

BE MY HABITAT 4 ch.g. Be My Guest (USA) – Fur Hat (Habitat) [1992/3 16d⁴ 17d 17d³ 17d* 17v⁴ 21d⁵ 20s* 17sᵖᵘ 22sᵖᵘ 17d⁶ 21m 20d 21f* 22m⁵] stocky gelding: maiden on Flat: successful in juvenile hurdles at Ascot in November and January and novice event at Wetherby in May: stays 21f: acts on any going: best with forcing tactics: inconsistent. *Miss L. C. Siddall*

   107

BEN 7 ch.g. Seymour Hicks (FR) – Kirin (Tyrant (USA)) [1992/3 c17fᶠ c16g⁴ c19gᶠ c18sᶠ c17sᵖᵘ] workmanlike gelding: poor novice hurdler/chaser: sold 825 gns Ascot May Sales: blinkered once: bad jumper of fences. *Mrs A. Knight*

   cxx
   –

BEN ADHEM 11 b.g. Hotfoot – Heaven Chosen (High Top) [1992/3 18d² 16g*] leggy gelding: won handicap hurdle at Windsor in November: best around 2m: acts on good to soft ground. *S. Dow*

   121

BENDICKS 11 b.g. Young Generation – Mint (Meadow Mint (USA)) [1992/3 c17s⁴ c18d c17sᶠ c16v⁴] rangy, workmanlike gelding: modest chaser at best in 1991/2: showed nothing in 1992/3: best at around 2m: acts on good to firm and heavy going. *A. Moore*

   c–
   –

BENGAIRN 10 br.g. Pitpan – Star Deb (Star Gazer) [1992/3 c17vᵖᵘ c16sᵖᵘ c16sᵘʳ c16g³ c16g] rangy gelding: very lightly-raced winning 2m hurdler: no sign of ability in novice chases: acts on heavy going. *G. Richards*

   c–
   –

BENGAL TIGER (IRE) 5 b. or br.g. Petoski – Heart 'n' Soul (Bold Lad (IRE)) [1992/3 18d³ 16d³ 17d⁵ 16m²] workmanlike gelding: 9f winner on Flat in 1992: sold out of J. Akehurst's stable 2,000 gns Newmarket Autumn Sales: maiden hurdler: ran creditably in selling company last 3 starts: likely to prove best at around 2m: acts on good to firm and dead ground: blinkered once in 1991/2, visored last outing. *P. D. Evans*

   87

BENGAZEE (IRE) 5 b.g. Abednego – Sazek (Brave Invader (USA)) [1992/3 F17s F16v 25d] lengthy gelding: first foal: dam never ran: mid-division in NH Flat races: seventh of 10 finishers in novice hurdle at Uttoxeter in February: should improve. *N. A. Twiston-Davies*

   – p

BENGHAZI 9 b. or br.g. Politico (USA) – Numerous (New Brig) [1992/3 c24dᵘʳ c21g⁵ c25gᵖᵘ 25d² 22g⁵ 27d*] tall gelding: improved hurdler in the spring and won amateurs novice event at Kelso: novice chaser: stays 27f: acts on heavy going. *A. M. Thomson*

   c–
   108

BENISA RYDER 10 ch.g. Stanford – Bamstar (Relko) [1992/3 c16sᶠ] short-backed gelding: handicap hurdler, form only at around 2m: poor form in points: suffered a fatal fall in novice chase at Southwell in September: acted on firm ground and was possibly unsuited by very soft. *M. C. Pipe*

   c–
   –

BENJAMIN 5 b.g. Relkino – Combe Hill (Crozier) [1992/3 16v² 17s³ 16s² 17g³] rather unfurnished gelding: type to jump fences: first foal: dam, winning hurdler/chaser, barely stayed 3m: best effort in novice hurdles when strong-finishing third in valuable novice handicap at Cheltenham in April on last outing: effective at 2m but will be well suited by further: acts on heavy ground: likely to improve further and sure to win a race. *N. A. Gaselee*

   103 p

BENJAMIN LANCASTER 9 b.g. Dubassoff (USA) – Lancaster Rose (Canadel II) [1992/3 c17v³ c19sᶠ c17vᵖᵘ c17v c17s² c21d⁶] sparely-made gelding: maiden chaser: little form: races mainly at around 2m: poor jumper. *T. B. Hallett*

   c– x
   –

BENNAN MARCH 6 br.g. Daring March – Sweet And Shiny (Siliconn) [1992/3 22g⁵ 20g] first foal: dam, poor maiden on Flat, showed little in 2 races over hurdles: yet to complete in points: automatic top weight when fifth in novice handicap hurdle at Ayr in January: well beaten in maiden event 6 days later. *P. Monteith*

   ?

BEN'S BEAUTY 5 b.g. Aragon – Aunt Charlotte (Charlottown) [1992/3 17gᵘʳ c19dᵖᵘ] probably of little account: trained first start by Mrs S. Oliver, blinkered second. *F. L. Matthews*

   c–
   –

BEN TIRRAN 9 b. or br.g. Takachiho – Portate (Articulate) [1992/3 c91 d
a16gF c21g* c21g4 c26g3 c22g3 c21gpu c21g2 c21m3 c21f5 c21g5] leggy –
gelding: modest chaser: won handicap at Sedgefield in February: below
form afterwards: stays 2½f: acts on hard ground: visored last 2 outings. *Mrs
S. Lamyman*

BENTLEY MANOR 4 ch.g. M Double M (USA) – Sally Chase (Sallust)
[1992/3 17g 17s6 17g6 22s* 22gpu] stocky gelding: fourth foal: half-brother 80
to several Flat winners, notably quite useful 1m to 1¼m performer Super
Sally (by Superlative): dam useful sprint 2-y-o: dead-heated for first place in
novice selling hurdle at Ludlow (no bid) in April: stays 2¾m: suited by soft
going: game.*John R. Upson*

BENTON'S PRIDE 5 b.m. Julio Mariner – Coxmoor Maid (Royal
Pennant) [1992/3 17g 20g 16spu 20vpu 26dpu] small mare: sister to poor –
novice hurdler Mariners Mol and half-sister to winning hurdler/chaser
Celtic Story (by Celtic Cone): dam winning hurdler/chaser: of little account:
blinkered fourth start. *R. T. Juckes*

BEN ZABEEDY 8 b.g. Gone Native – Intense (FR) (Sassafras (FR))
[1992/3 16g3 a22g4 18v2 20d3 20f5 17f3 18f3] leggy gelding: fair handicap 111
hurdler on his day: below best after fourth start, in seller final one: stays
2½m: acts on any going: usually held up. *R. Akehurst*

BE PATIENT MY SON 12 b.g. Stanford – Try My Patience (Balliol) c–
[1992/3 c18sbd c17mpu] workmanlike gelding: poor maiden hurdler/chaser. –
Miss C. J. E. Caroe

BERESFORDS GIRL 8 b.m. Furry Glen – Hansel's Queen (Prince c103
Hansel) [1992/3 c24d6 c26d6 c27vpu c24s* c26v6 c24v* c29s3 c28g5 c24s3 c24d2] –
workmanlike mare: fair handicap chaser: won at Exeter in December and
Leicester in January: good second at Exeter in April: stays 29f: acts on
heavy going and good to firm. *P. G. Murphy*

BERKANA RUN 8 ch.g. Deep Run – Geraldine's Pet (Laurence O) c72
[1992/3 c24sF c21m3] sparely-made gelding: poor maiden hurdler/hunter –
chaser.*J. M. Turner*

BERKELEY HILL BOY 6 ch.g. Castle Keep – Brown Velvet
(Mansingh (USA)) [1992/3 16s 16d4 21d5 16s] lengthy, workmanlike gelding: 80
plating-class sprinter on Flat: poor novice hurdler: best effort on second
outing: likely to prove best around 2m. *R. Hollinshead*

BERRY'S SKY LARK 6 ch.m. Crested Lark – Quick Walk (Farm Walk)
[1992/3 F17m 14dpu 16vpu 17dpu 16dF] leggy mare: fourth foal: dam unraced: –
no sign of ability: sold 825 gns Ascot 2nd June Sales. *F. Jordan*

BERTIE BOY 8 ch.g. Balinger – Ambatina (Articulate) [1992/3 c21s* c106
c20s2 c24s c21spu] strong, lengthy gelding: fair chaser: won conditional
jockeys handicap at Wetherby in January: ran poorly last 2 starts: effective
at 2½m and stays 3m: acts on soft going: jumps soundly. *Mrs M. Reveley*

BERVIE HOUSE (IRE) 5 br.g. Strong Gale – Bramble Hill (Goldhill)
[1992/3 F16s4 F16d4 22g3] second foal: dam never ran: signs of a little ability 74 p
in NH Flat races and in amateurs maiden hurdle at Ayr: should improve. *Mrs
M. Reveley*

BERYL'S JOKE 9 b.g. Double Form – Rockeater (Roan Rocket) [1992/3
22vpu a22g3 a22gpu 23g 21d5 23f6] good-topped gelding: poor novice staying 62 §
hurdler: trained until after third outing by R. Baker: often blinkered: not one
to trust. *P. J. Hobbs*

BEST GUN 4 b.g. K-Battery – Ribonny (FR) (Fast Hilarious (USA))
[1992/3 16s5] angular gelding: fair middle-distance stayer on Flat: fifth of 20 85 p
in juvenile hurdle at Catterick in January: should improve. *C. W. C. Elsey*

BE SURPRISED 7 ch.g. Dubassoff (USA) – Buckenham Belle (Royben) c–
[1992/3 c24mpu] angular gelding: moderate chaser: stiff task only outing of –
season: stays 21f: acts on good to firm and soft going. *A. Moore*

BETALONGABILL 4 b. or br.g. Lir – Cornish Susie (Fair Season)
[1992/3 17g4 18g4 16g] leggy, sparely-made gelding: brother to novice 77

hurdler Across The Card: poor maiden on Flat, placed at up to 1m: poor form in early-season juvenile hurdles. *M. Madgwick*

BE THE BEST 5 b.g. Rousillon (USA) – Shadywood (Habitat) [1992/3 18g] middle-distance staying maiden on Flat: behind in selling hurdle at Sedgefield in October. *M. P. Naughton* —

BETSY BOOP 8 b.m. Pauper – Day Fiddle (Harwell) [1992/3 22dᵖᵘ c– c25sᴿ] leggy mare: poor maiden jumper: trained first outing by R. O'Leary: — tried blinkered. *Donald Merchant*

BETTA WIN 9 b.m. Tower Walk – Floor Show (Galivanter) [1992/3 20gᵖᵘ 22f 17gᵖᵘ] big, lengthy mare: of little account. *D. L. Williams* —

BETTER STILL (IRE) 4 b.f. Glenstal (USA) – That's Better (Mourne) [1992/3 16m] small filly: soundly beaten on Flat and in a juvenile hurdle. *P. C. Haslam* —

BETTER TIMES AHEAD 7 ro.g. Scallywag – City's Sister **c117** (Maystreak) [1992/3 25g³ 21s⁴ 25s* c21s* 24v² c25fᵖᵘ c25gᵖᵘ c26d*] **149** compact gelding: very useful hurdler: good second to Pragada at Haydock in January: won novice chases at Bangor in November and December and Cartmel in May, showing quite useful form: stays well: best form with plenty of give in the ground: races up with pace: jumps none too fluently. *G. Richards*

BETTY BARLOW 7 ch.m. Sagaro – Mattie Ross (Midsummer Night II) [1992/3 F18d 16v 20s 20dᵖᵘ] angular mare: little sign of ability over hurdles. — *M. F. Barraclough*

BETTY ELSTON 5 ch.m. Hell's Gate – Pretty Penny (Naucetra) [1992/3 F18v 16d 18d 22mᶠ] small, plain mare: no sign of ability. *J. G. Thorpe* —

BETTY HAYES 9 b. or br.m. Jimsun – Damside (Shackleton) [1992/3 **c96** c26m* c23f³] sparely-made mare: winning hurdler: won hunter chase at — Folkestone in May: good third at Worcester later in month: suited by a good test of stamina: acts on any ground: has won when sweating profusely: front runner. *H. Wellstead*

BETWEEN THE SHEETS 8 b.g. Crooner – Miss Chianti (Royben) **c–** [1992/3 c21sᴿ 26dᵖᵘ] leggy gelding: winning hurdler: maiden chaser: no — form for long time: blinkered twice. *N. R. Mitchell*

BEY D'AO (FR) 5 b.g. Baillamont (USA) – Ondoa (FR) (President (FR)) [1992/3 16v] lengthy gelding: well beaten on Flat at 3 yrs: sold out of C. — Cyzer's stable 1,700 gns Newmarket Autumn (1991) Sales: tailed-off last in novice hurdle at Kempton in January. *M. C. Humby*

BEYOND MOMBASA 6 br.m. Silly Prices – Elitist (Keren) [1992/3 20dᵖᵘ] compact mare: probably of little account: ran out once and refused — once in points. *N. Chamberlain*

BEYOND OUR REACH 5 br.g. Reach – Over Beyond (Bold Lad (IRE)) [1992/3 22s³ 25sᵘʳ] angular gelding: moderate novice hurdler: will prove **96** suited by a test of stamina. *R. J. Hodges*

BEYOND REASON 7 b.g. Kemal (FR) – Smooth Lady (Tarqogan) **c86** [1992/3 22sᵖᵘ 25s* 28dᵖᵘ 25d⁶ c20d³ c23g² c26m²] sturdy, lengthy gelding: **86** brother to 1988 Grand National winner Rhyme 'N' Reason and to 2 other winning jumpers, including fairly useful staying chaser Outside Edge: dam unraced sister to very useful 2m chaser Menehall and half-sister to 1984 Grand National winner Hallo Dandy: won novice hurdle at Carlisle in November: placed in novice chases, showing modest form: suited by test of stamina: probably acts on any going: blinkered last 2 outings. *G. Richards*

BIBENDUM 7 b.g. Furry Glen – Bibs (Royal And Regal (USA)) [1992/3 **c118** 16v⁴ c16s* c20g² c20g* c20s² c20gᶠ c21m⁵] strong gelding: fairly useful **118** hurdler: took well to chasing and won novice events at Nottingham in February and Stratford in March: ran well on most of his other completed starts: stays 2½m: acts on heavy ground: jumps soundly in the main. *R. Waley-Cohen*

BICK BENEDICT   9 b.h. Try My Best (USA) – Western Star (Alcide) [1992/3 20m6 22f2 21m4 c21g c23dF] compact horse: lightly raced: poor novice hurdler/chaser: stays 2¾m: acts on firm ground. *R. Earnshaw*   c– 70

BICKERMAN   10 b.h. Mummy's Pet – Merry Weather (Will Somers) [1992/3 16s 16d4 17s3 18s3 22m3 16g 21m] lightly-made horse: moderate handicap hurdler: best efforts of season on third and fifth outings: probably stays 2¾m: pulls hard and forces pace: acts on any going: successful with and without blinkers. *J. L. Spearing*   89

BIDDERS CLOWN   8 b.g. Ring Bidder – Lucky Joker (Cawston's Clown) [1992/3 a21gF] lengthy, sparely-made gelding: winning hurdler: fell fourth only outing of season (May): stays 2½m: acts on good to firm ground. *B. R. Cambidge*   –

BID FOR SIX (USA)   4 br.g. Saratoga Six (USA) – Savage Bunny (USA) (Never Bend) [1992/3 17dpu 17gpu] compact gelding: half-brother to winning hurdler Alleged Savage (by Alleged): fairly useful miler at best when trained by R. Hannon: showed nothing over hurdles: sold 900 gns Ascot May Sales. *G. Thorner*   –

BIDWEAYA (USA)   6 b.m. Lear Fan (USA) – Sweet Snow (USA) (Lyphard (USA)) [1992/3 20g] lightly-raced handicapper at up to 1¼m on Flat: behind in novice hurdle at Doncaster in December. *J. L. Eyre*   –

BIGANARD   12 b.g. Hard Fact – Sweet Chance (Chance Meeting) [1992/3 c16g4 c23fpu] probably of little account. *H. J. Manners*   c–

BIG BAD WOLF (IRE)   5 gr.g. Orchestra – Perato (Nishapour (FR)) [1992/3 F17d] first foal: dam fairly useful Irish hurdler: mid-division in NH Flat race at Ascot in April: yet to race over hurdles or fences. *J. A. C. Edwards*   –

BIG BEAT (USA)   5 br.g. Super Concorde (USA) – Embroglio (USA) (Empery (USA)) [1992/3 18s* 17v* 16s2 17v4 16g5] workmanlike gelding: improved into a fairly useful novice hurdler and won at Folkestone in November and Sandown (handicap) in December: best effort next start, when second to Satin Lover at Kempton on Boxing Day: well below form last 2: stays 2¼m: acts on heavy going: headstrong and makes running. *D. R. C. Elsworth*   128

BIG BEN DUN   7 b.g. The Parson – Shanban (Shackleton) [1992/3 20s c21s* c24v5 c21vF c24v* c25d3 c23g* c24g* c26m2] tall, leggy ex-Irish gelding: fifth foal: dam, NH Flat race winner, poor maiden hurdler: novice hurdler: had a good season over fences and won handicaps at Punchestown (landed big gamble, trained until after then by J. G. O'Neill) in January, Lingfield in February, Worcester in April and Stratford in May: stays 3¼m: acts on good to firm and heavy going. *John R. Upson*   c104 –

BIG CHANCE   4 ch.g. Sharpo – Cherry Ridge (Riva Ridge (USA)) [1992/3 22spu 17gpu] compact gelding: first foal: dam, smart miler, half-sister to high-class middle-distance performer Red Glow: modest 1m winner in Ireland at 3 yrs when trained by J. Byrne: behind when pulled up in competitive novice and juvenile hurdles at Huntingdon in February. *J. Ffitch-Heyes*   –

BIG COUNTRY   10 b.g. Town And Country – Top Soprano (High Top) [1992/3 21vpu] big, plain, dipped-backed gelding: winning hurdler: backward only outing of season (December): stays 3m: acts on fibresand. *B. J. McMath*   –

BIG DIAMOND (FR)   9 b.g. Bikala – Diathese (FR) (Diatome) [1992/3 c21s c16vpu 17g 17m* 18s3 17g4 17fpu] leggy, sparely-made gelding: moderate hurdler: very easy winner of claimer at Wolverhampton in March: below form subsequently: has shown little over fences: best at around 2m: acts on soft going and good to firm: visored last start, blinkered previous three. *I. Campbell*   c– 94

BIGGLES BOY   4 b.g. Sunley Builds – Solent Flyer (Undulate (USA)) [1992/3 F17m] useful-looking gelding: first foal: dam novice selling hurdler: well beaten in NH Flat race at Cheltenham in April: yet to race over hurdles. *K. C. Bailey*   –

BIGHAYIR 6 gr.g. Petong – Nook (Julio Mariner) [1992/3 17v⁵ 20d*] small, sturdy gelding: fair hurdler: didn't have to run to his best when easy winner of claimer at Haydock (claimed £12,101 and exported to race in Sweden) in December: stays 2½m: acts well with plenty of give in the ground: visored early in 1991/2, blinkered nowadays. *M. C. Pipe*   103 +

BIG MAC 6 gr.g. Warpath – Susan McIntyre (Double Jump) [1992/3 21m* 17m⁶ 20g⁶ 21v] rangy gelding with scope: won novice hurdle at Carlisle in September: below form afterwards: will be well suited by further than 21f: acts on dead and good to firm ground: blinkered last outing. *G. Richards*   85

BIG MATT (IRE) 5 b.g. Furry Glen – Stoirin (Mart Lane) [1992/3 F16m² F16m* F16g* 16v* dis 16d⁴ 16d⁵ 19s⁴ 16dF] leggy gelding with scope: second foal: dam poor maiden hurdler: successful in NH Flat races at Naas and Galway: first past post in maiden hurdles at Navan (disqualified) in November and Leopardstown in December: would have finished excellent third to Bayrouge but for falling 2 out in valuable event at Punchestown in April: should stay beyond 2m: acts on heavy going: won 1¾m maiden in July, 1993, on Flat debut. *P. Burke, Ireland*   134 ?

BIGSUN 12 b.g. Sunyboy – Stella Roma (Le Levanstell) [1992/3 c25m⁵] sturdy gelding: carries plenty of condition: one-time useful chaser: modest form when successful in 2 points in April: well beaten in hunter chase following month: suited by a thorough test of stamina and ideally by a sound surface: blinkered twice. *P. Venner*   c–
–

BILBERRY 4 b.f. Nicholas Bill – Snow Tribe (Great Nephew) [1992/3 16s⁶ 17s⁶ 16s⁶ a18g] sparely-made filly: half-sister to high-class hurdler Past Glories (by Hittite Glory) and useful jumper Snow Blessed (by So Blessed): 1¾m winner on Flat: easily best effort in juvenile hurdles on second start: will stay beyond 17f: unenthusiastic. *C. W. C. Elsey*   82 §

BILBO BAGGINS (IRE) 5 ch.g. Beau Charmeur (FR) – Hiking (Royal Highway) [1992/3 20d⁶ 16v 17s 20m⁴ 23f⁴ 17d] well-made gelding: poor novice hurdler: will prove suited by a test of stamina: best efforts on a sound surface: blinkered fifth start. *Mrs J. Pitman*   73

BILBROOK 11 b.g. Pardigras – Gay Heath (Langton Heath) [1992/3 c26mᵖᵘ c21g² c19v⁶ c22m⁴] leggy, sparely-made gelding: was blind off side: fair hunter chaser: second at Sandown in March, easily best effort of season: stayed 25f: acted on heavy going: dead. *R. M. Fear*   c92
–

BILDESTON 5 b.g. Teenoso (USA) – Sue Grundy (Grundy) [1992/3 F16d F14m³ F16d³] first foal: dam won at up to 1¼m: third in NH Flat races in March: yet to race over hurdles or fences. *K. A. Morgan*

BILL AND COUP 8 br.m. Nicholas Bill – Counter Coup (Busted) [1992/3 c21g c24sᵘʳ c22v⁶ c21d⁵ c21g³ c18m* c17g⁵ c21g⁵ c20gᵖᵘ c21f³ c18g² c18f²] small, workmanlike mare: modest chaser: won conditional jockeys handicap at Market Rasen in March: good second in claimer and handicap at Stratford afterwards: best at up to 2¾m: probably acts on any going: sometimes wears tongue strap: poor jumper. *K. A. Morgan*   c86 x
–

BILLHEAD 7 b.g. Nicholas Bill – Time-Table (Mansingh (USA)) [1992/3 c25gF c21m⁵] tall, leggy gelding: poor novice hurdler: fifth of 6 finishers in novice hunter chase at Uttoxeter in June. *Miss J. Thomas*   c70
–

BILLION MELODY 11 b.g. Billion (USA) – Thistle (Highland Melody) [1992/3 c23vᵖᵘ 16d 24sᵖᵘ a20g² a20g³ 22m⁶] leggy, sparely-made gelding: moderate hurdler: ran creditably when placed at Southwell fourth and fifth starts: no show on chasing debut: stays 3m: acts on firm ground and fibresand. *C. Cowley*   c–
88

BILL OF RIGHTS 5 b.g. Nicholas Bill – Cold Line (Exdirectory) [1992/3 F16d F17v] first foal: dam, modest 1½m winner, half-sister to several winners, notably high-class hurdler Past Glories: seventh in NH Flat races in first half of season: yet to race over hurdles or fences. *G. A. Ham*

BILL QUILL 9 ch.g. Nicholas Bill – Bobette (King Bob) [1992/3 17m² c16m³ c17s* c16g* c21s² c16mF 17v³ c16v² c18v² c17v⁴ c18s⁵] workmanlike   c94
73

gelding: poor novice hurdler: better over fences and won claimer (claimed out of P. Hobbs's stable £3,250) at Newton Abbot and conditional jockeys handicap at Worcester in September: ran creditably most starts afterwards: effective at 2m and stays 21f: acts on good to firm and heavy ground. *R. G. Frost*

BILLY BATHGATE 7 ch.g. Gala Performance (USA) – Royal River (Another River) [1992/3 c16d* c16dur c16s F c16d c16d3 c16f4 c19f* c21m2] strong, rangy gelding: has had soft palate operation: fair hurdler: won novice chases at Kempton in October and Hereford in May: also good fourth to Valiant Boy at Aintree and second to Flashthecash at Warwick: effective at 2m and stays 21f: probably acts on any going: sometimes breaks blood vessels: not yet an accomplished jumper. *N. J. Henderson*   **c125** –

BILLYBITME 6 b.g. Homing – Love Beach (Lorenzaccio) [1992/3 c16dur c16v6 c21v3] no sign of ability: tried visored/blinkered. *P. R. Hedger*   **c–** –

BILLY BORU 5 b.g. Magnolia Lad – Mingwyn Wood (Pirate King) [1992/3 F17d2 F17v3 16v2] leggy gelding: NH Flat race winner: promising staying-on second in novice event at Towcester in January on hurdling debut: will be suited by further: likely to improve. *A. R. Davison*   **92 p**

BILLY LOMOND (IRE) 5 b.g. Lomond (USA) – Relko's Belle (FR) (Relko) [1992/3 17d6 20g4 17g5] winning middle-distance plater on Flat: best effort over hurdles when fourth in claimer at Exeter in May: blinkered last outing. *P. J. Hobbs*   **75**

BILLY TORY 7 ch.g. Netherkelly – Hasty Kate (Hasty Word) [1992/3 16s] first foal: dam, winning selling hurdler, stayed 25f: tailed off in novice hurdle at Nottingham in December. *P. D. Evans*   –

BILOXI BLUES 11 gr.g. Blue Refrain – Haunting (Lord Gayle (USA)) [1992/3 c26f* c21m* c27f*] strong, close-coupled gelding: fairly useful chaser at best: won hunter chases at Hereford, Folkestone and Fontwell in May: stays 27f: best on a sound surface. *Andrew Turnell*   **c96** –

BINDER 6 b.g. Oats – Drom Lady (Royalty) [1992/3 20d4 22dpu] rangy gelding: fourth of 7 in novice hurdle at Market Rasen in November: tailed off when pulled up nearly 5 months later: stoutly bred. *Mrs D. Haine*   **80**

BIN LID (IRE) 4 b.f. Henbit (USA) – Our Ena (Tower Walk) [1992/3 16g 16d3 16d6 17mF 18g4 17m] lengthy, workmanlike filly: fifth foal: half-sister to 6f winner Right Path (by Ya Zaman) and Irish 2-y-o 1m winner Furena (by Furry Glen): dam second over 5f at 3 yrs in Ireland: poor form over hurdles: retained 5,400 gns Doncaster May Sales: stays 2¼m: acts on good to firm and dead ground: visored fifth outing. *G. Richards*   **66**

BINNY GROVE 7 b.m. Sunyboy – Gold Gift (Gold Rod) [1992/3 18vpu 18g] workmanlike mare: only form over hurdles when second early in 1991/2: should stay beyond 17f. *P. J. Hobbs*   –

BIRCHALL BOY 5 br.g. Julio Mariner – Polarita (Arctic Kanda) [1992/3 16d 16g] fourth foal: dam winning staying hurdler: behind in maiden hurdle at Uttoxeter and novice event at Worcester, both in April. *J. C. McConnochie*   –

BIRD OF SPIRIT 13 b.g. Hot Brandy – Bird of Honour (Dark Heron) [1992/3 c24v6 c24v3 c26dpu c23g4 c26m* c25m* c26mpu] tall, good-quartered gelding: modest chaser: won handicaps at Hereford and Southwell in May: pulled up, reportedly lame, last start: stays 3¼m: acts on good to firm and heavy going. *M. Scudamore*   **c95** –

BIRLING JACK 12 b.g. Bronze Hill – Fortilage (Fortina) [1992/3 c26dpu] big, strong gelding: fairly useful chaser at best: tailed off when pulled up only outing of season (November): stays well: acts on heavy and good to firm going: occasionally let down by his jumping. *J. A. C. Edwards*   **c–** –

BIRONI 4 b.g. Scorpio (FR) – Stern Lass (Bold Lad (IRE)) [1992/3 16s 16d] leggy, sparely-made gelding: first foal: dam, modest 1m winner, stayed 1¼m: signs of ability, never placed to challenge, in juvenile hurdles at Catterick and Haydock in December. *G. Richards*   **– p**

Pierse Contracting John P. Harty Memorial Handicap Chase, Punchestown—
Bishops Hall (right), Second Schedual (left) and Ebony Jane at the last

BISHOPS HALL 7 br.g. Pimpernels Tune – Mariner's Dash (Master **c138**
Buck) [1992/3 c20s⁶ c24g⁵ c24g* c27spu c24d⁴ c21d⁵ c24d³ c29s c25g* –
c22s] plain gelding: useful chaser: won handicaps at Leopardstown in
October and Punchestown (valuable event) in April, latter waited with by
2½ lengths from Second Schedual: pulled up in Hennessy Cognac Gold Cup
at Newbury on fourth start: best form up to 25f: acts on soft going. *H. de
Bromhead, Ireland*

BISHOPS ISLAND 7 b.g. The Parson – Gilded Empress (Menelek) **c124 x**
[1992/3 c20s⁵ c20dF c23v* c21sF c26v² c21sF 21m⁴ 21m] strong, 124 +
close-coupled gelding: fairly useful hurdler: creditable last of 4 in Grade 2
event at Warwick: easily won novice chase at Uttoxeter earlier, but
otherwise let down by his jumping over fences: stays 25f: acts on heavy
going. *D. Nicholson*

BISHOP'S TIPPLE 7 b.g. Monksfield – Fair Vic (Fair Turn) [1992/3
18s⁴ 20d 28d* 26g² 22g² 21d⁵ 28g²] tall gelding: won novice hurdle at 100
Sedgefield in February: ran well when second afterwards: suited by test of
stamina: acts on soft ground. *T. J. Carr*

BISHOPSTONE BILL 4 b.g. Skyliner – Sybilly (Nicholas Bill) [1992/3
17mpu] poor sprint maiden on Flat: tailed off when pulled up in juvenile –
hurdle at Huntingdon in August: sold 950 gns Ascot September Sales
following day. *S. Mellor*

BISHTHORN 8 b. or br.g. Uncle Pokey – Heavenly Pride (Goldhills **c–**
Pride) [1992/3 17gpu 22gpu] of little account in points: unseated rider only –
outing over fences: little promise in 2 races over hurdles. *John Whyte*

BITOFABANTER 6 ch.g. Celtic Cone – Little Ginger (Cawston's
Clown) [1992/3 16d 17g³ 17m 16f⁵] lengthy, rather angular gelding: useful 140
handicap hurdler: ran well first 3 starts, including in Tote Gold Trophy at
Newbury and County Hurdle at Cheltenham on second and third outings:
yet to race beyond 17f: acts on good to firm and soft ground: usually held up.
A. L. T. Moore, Ireland

BIT OF A CLOWN 10 b.g. Callernish – Gusserane Lark (Napoleon **c113**
Bonaparte) [1992/3 c28d³ c22s* c33vur c25v* c22v² c25v* c29g⁴] rangy –
gelding: fair handicap chaser: goes particularly well at Towcester and won
there in November, December and February, taking total to 6: suited by a
thorough test of stamina: has form on good to firm going but ideally suited
by plenty of give: occasionally blinkered: game. *Mrs I. McKie*

BITOFANATTER 5 ch.g. Palm Track – Little Ginger (Cawston's
Clown) [1992/3 F16g 16g 16g] good-bodied gelding: tailed off in novice –
hurdles. *R. H. Goldie*

94

BIXIO 9 gr.g. Absalom – Brescianina (Hugh Lupus) [1992/3 25m⁶] small,   c–
plain gelding: winning pointer: poor novice hurdler/steeplechaser: suited by   –
test of stamina: acts on hard and dead ground: blinkered 5 times in 1989/90.
Miss J. L. Rae

BLACK ARROW 6 br.g. Full of Hope – Snow Damsel (Mandamus)
[1992/3 F17m] half-brother to 2 poor maiden jumpers: dam lightly-raced
half-sister to Derby winner Snow Knight: unseated rider in a point in April:
behind in NH Flat race in May: yet to race over hurdles or in a steeplechase.
D. C. O'Brien

BLACKDOWN 6 b.h. Rainbow Quest (USA) – Cider Princess (Alcide)
[1992/3 16dᵖᵘ 17dᵖᵘ 17s² 18m] leggy horse: modest hurdler: creditable   88
second in claimer at Perth in April, best effort of season: pulls hard and
likely to prove suited by 2m: probably acts on any ground. *T. Dyer*

BLACKGUARD (USA) 7 ch.g. Irish River (FR) – Principle (USA)
(Viceregal (CAN)) [1992/3 24sᵖᵘ 22s 17m] well-made gelding: winning   –
hurdler: no worthwhile form in 1992/3: unlikely to stay beyond 2m: acts on
good to firm ground: usually blinkered nowadays. *R. J. Manning*

BLACK HORSE LAD 9 ch.g. Orchestra – Little Peach (Ragapan)   c–
[1992/3 c24vᵖᵘ c19vᴿ c27vᵖᵘ c24m⁶ c21d c24gᵖᵘ c26d5 21m] sturdy ex-Irish   –
gelding: trained until after first start by A. Keane, and on next outing by P.
Nicholls: novice hurdler: behind in selling handicap last start: has shown
nothing over fences: best form at 2m: acts on heavy and good to firm ground.
Mrs J. G. Retter

BLACK H'PENNY 5 b.m. Town And Country – Black Penny (West
Partisan) [1992/3 F16s 21v⁵] sturdy mare: third foal: half-sister to useful   –
hurdler Simpson (by Royal Match): dam, fair hurdler, well suited by a good
test of stamina: remote eighth of 22 in NH Flat race at Warwick in February:
tailed off in mares novice hurdle at Towcester week later. *J. A. B. Old*

BLACK HUMOUR 9 b.g. Buckskin (FR) – Artiste Gaye (Artist's Son) **c145** p
[1992/3 c21s² c23v* c25s² c26s* c27mᶠ c25f*]

Peter Scudamore won the jockeys' championship in 1990/1 despite ten
weeks off with a broken leg: his total of 422 rides was easily the lowest in
the eight title-winning seasons, but a strike rate of one in three saw him
comfortably home. While Scudamore has now retired from the saddle Black
Humour, the horse whose fall in a Market Rasen hurdle race in November
1990 put him out of action, is still in training and has come on so much since
then that he is going to be a force to reckon with in some of the big
long-distance handicap chases in 1993/4, the Grand National to name but
one. Black Humour ran well in all his races in the latest season, his second
over fences, not least when put in apparently out of his depth in the
Cheltenham Gold Cup. On that occasion he was keeping on steadily at the
back of the main bunch, around ten lengths behind the leader, when he fell
three out. Probably what persuaded connections to run him there was his
six-length defeat of Bradbury Star at level weights at Warwick in January on
his previous start, when he produced some spectacular jumping and a
strong finish. They would also have been encouraged by his previous
efforts, in two handicaps at Worcester (he finished second to Cherrykino
the first time and won by twenty-five lengths the second) and in a minor
race at Sandown (he finished four lengths second to Country Member).

Black Humour had a choice of engagements at Aintree two weeks after
the Gold Cup. In the end it was decided to go for the Perrier Jouet Chase, a
fairly valuable handicap run over the Mildmay fences, rather than take on
top stayers again in the Martell Cup on the same course or tackle the
Grand National. He was 33/1 with 9-8 for the National immediately after
Cheltenham, there being the doubt whether he would run. Black Humour
started second favourite with top weight for the Perrier Jouet. They bet 4/1
the field, but the eleven-runner race looked much less open than that after
half a circuit. The favourite Sikera Spy and Side of Hill set off at a scorching
pace, with the result that the runners became spread fifty lengths between
first and last. Black Humour, normally a front-runner although ridden with

Perrier Jouet Chase (Handicap), Aintree—
the astutely-ridden Black Humour takes over at the last

restraint in the Gold Cup, began sluggishly and was soon a long way behind the leaders, nursed along by his rider Bradley in an attempt to get him jumping. The horse looked to have no earthly chance until starting out onto the final circuit. Then he began to work his way towards the leaders—still Sikera Spy and Side of Hill—down the back straight and seemed to grow stronger and stronger as the race went on. Sikera Spy got the better of the duel up front on the home turn, but Black Humour continued to make ground through the field and he caught her between the last two fences. He was ahead over the last, and ran on to win well on top by three lengths. Black Humour's deliberate jumping on the first circuit might have been a consequence of his heavy fall in the Gold Cup. At this stage there's no cause for concern; usually he jumps well.

Black Humour (b.g. 1984)	Buckskin (FR) (b 1973)	Yelapa (br 1966)	Mossborough
			Your Point
		Bete A Bon Dieu (b 1964)	Herbager
			Caralline
	Artiste Gaye (b 1961)	Artist's Son (br 1936)	Gainsborough
			Centeno
		Goldiane (ch 1936)	Golestan
			Hunter's Cloud

A win for Black Humour in one of jumping's major races would extend one of the longest, fullest broodmare records of recent times. He is the last foal produced by Artiste Gaye, the dam of the brothers Gaye Brief and Gaye Chance (by Lucky Brief) who between them won thirty-five races including a Champion Hurdle and a Stayers' Hurdle, and other multiple winners in Royal Gaye (by Arcticeelagh) and Artistic Prince and The Fencer (both by Indigenous). Black Humour is Artiste Gaye's second foal by Buckskin. The previous year's mating produced the National Hunt Flat race winner Gaye Memory who is now a broodmare herself. Most of Artiste Gaye's runners have been stayers, and Black Humour, although he was tried only once

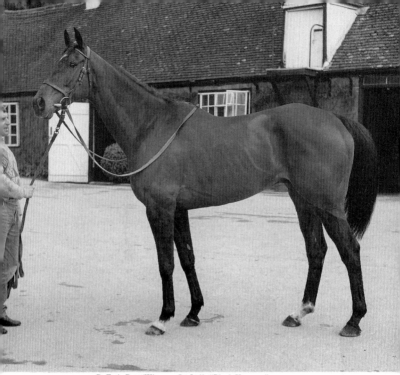

R. E. A. Bott (Wigmore St) Ltd's "Black Humour"

beyond two and a half miles as a hurdler, has proved no exception; very likely he will stay beyond three and a quarter. A rangy gelding, he acts on any going. *C. P. E. Brooks*

BLACK JEWEL 10 b.g. Welsh Captain – New York Rose (Pieces of Eight) [1992/3 16m* 17s* 16d⁵ 17d² 16s²] lengthy, good-topped ex-Irish gelding: wide-margin winner in October of conditional jockeys selling handicap hurdle at Southwell (no bid) and novice seller at Newton Abbot (sold out of M. Usher's stable 5,200 gns): also ran well last 2 starts: sold 1,400 gns Doncaster March Sales: will stay beyond 17f: probably acts on any going. *R. Hollinshead*   94

BLACK JOKER 7 br.g. Lord Ha Ha – Edwina-Marie (Sir Herbert) [1992/3 17dᵖᵘ 17d³ 16s⁴ 16v² 16d³ 16d⁴ 17g⁴ 16d] moderate novice hurdler: generally ran creditably in 1992/3: sold 6,600 gns Ascot June Sales: will stay beyond 17f: best form with give in the ground and acts on heavy. *A. J. Wilson*   89

BLACK SAPPHIRE 6 ch.g. Lomond (USA) – Star of India (General Assembly (USA)) [1992/3 21s c21sᶠ c22sᶠ 23s] sturdy gelding: fair hurdler at his best: well beaten both starts in 1992/3: let down by his jumping both outings over fences: sold 5,700 gns Ascot February Sales: should stay beyond 21f: acts on soft and good to firm going: visored last start. *M. H. Tompkins*   c– –

BLACK SPUR 11 br.g. Spur On – Ravenside (Marcus Superbus) [1992/3 **c101**
c17g³ c21s* c16s* c21s⁶ c20g c21s³ c17spu] workmanlike, angular gelding: –
fair chaser: won 2 handicaps at Carlisle in November: below form
subsequently, pulling up lame last outing: effective at testing 2m and stays
3¼m: acts on any going: usually makes running and jumps well: game. *J. I.
A. Charlton*

BLACKWATER PANTHER (IRE) 4 b.g. Palace Panther – Temple
Goddess (USA) (Naskra (USA)) [1992/3 16s] workmanlike gelding: modest –
form on fibresand on Flat at 2 yrs, tailed off only outing since: showed little
in juvenile hurdle at Wetherby in January. *C. N. Allen*

BLAKEINGTON 7 b.g. Baron Blakeney – Camina (Don Carlos) [1992/3 c–
c24vpu c24vpu c27dpu c23g⁵ c21d⁵ c21dur c21dpu] compact gelding: little –
sign of ability: tried blinkered. *N. R. Mitchell*

BLAKELIN 7 gr.m. Baron Blakeney – Voolin (Jimmy Reppin) [1992/3 **c93**
c25d³] small mare: no sign of ability over hurdles: modest pointer, winner in –
May: third in hunter chase at Towcester later in May. *Mrs S. Gill*

BLAKENEYS GIFT 7 gr.g. Blakeney – Teleflora (Princely Gift) c–
[1992/3 19m⁵ 24spu c17vpu 16d] smallish, sparely-made gelding: poor novice –
hurdler: no show in 1992/3, including on chasing debut: should stay beyond
17f: acts on soft ground. *N. R. Mitchell*

BLAKE'S FINESSE 6 gr.m. Baron Blakeney – True Finesse (True
Song) [1992/3 22vpu] workmanlike mare: no sign of ability. *R. H. Alner* –

BLAKES SECRET 7 b.g. Roscoe Blake – Decode (Tangle) [1992/3 c–
16m⁵ 16g⁵ 17m³ 21f] angular, rather sparely-made gelding: hard-pulling 2m 66
selling hurdler: no promise on only start over fences: acts on firm ground
and fibresand: often makes running. *A. L. Forbes*

BLAKEWAY 6 gr.m. Baron Blakeney – Provoking (Sharp Edge) [1992/3
aF16g² F16s 22f] first thoroughbred foal: dam novice selling hurdler/chaser: –
showed a little ability in NH Flat races: behind in mares novice hurdle at
Wincanton in March. *P. F. Nicholls*

BLANC SEING (FR) 6 b.g. Shirley Heights – Blanche Reine (FR)
(Nureyev (USA)) [1992/3 16v³ 20g⁴] good-topped gelding: modest soft- 92
ground middle-distance stayer on Flat (best blinkered): in frame in
mid-season novice hurdle at Towcester and maiden event at Edinburgh,
better effort in former: should prove well suited by further than 2m: may
benefit from blinkers. *M. W. Easterby*

BLASKET HERO 5 gr.g. Kalaglow – Glory Isle (Hittite Glory) [1992/3
22s 17s⁵ 18d⁴ 17d 22spu 20d³ 20m* 16g⁴ 18g⁶] lengthy gelding: won novice 92
handicap hurdle at Bangor in March: good fourth in similar event at
Towcester following day (carried head high): stays 2½m: acts on good to
firm and soft going: usually blinkered. *Mrs S. D. Williams*

BLAZING JOKER 6 b.g. Idiot's Delight – Romany Empress (Roman
Warrior) [1992/3 17dpu 17spu 17m⁶ 17vpu 17m] lengthy gelding: poor form 59
over hurdles, including in a selling handicap. *R. Lee*

BLAZING PEARL 5 b.m. Blazing Saddles (AUS) – Ring of Pearl
(Auction Ring (USA)) [1992/3 18m] small, sparely-made mare: no form over –
hurdles, including in sellers. *J. L. Harris*

BLAZING WALKER 9 ch.g. Imperial Fling (USA) – Princess Kofiyah **c155**
(High Line) [1992/3 c21d³ c24g⁶] tall, lengthy gelding: top-class chaser in –
1990/1 when trained by W. A. Stephenson: only very smart form in valuable
mid-season handicaps at Wetherby and Kempton in 1992/3, reportedly
sustaining minor injury on second occasion: sold privately (remains in
stable) 40,000 gns in May: effective at 2m to 3m: acts on good to firm and
soft going: has fine turn of foot and is held up: usually sweats: has shown
tendency to jump to the right. *P. Cheesbrough*

BLIMPERS DISCO 4 gr.c. Grey Desire – In A Spin (Windjammer
(USA)) [1992/3 16d 16s] workmanlike colt: maiden on Flat, showed a little –

ability at 2 yrs: well beaten in juvenile hurdles at Haydock and Nottingham in December: pulls hard. *E. H. Owen jun*

BLIND SHOT 6 b.h. Kris – Shuteye (Shirley Heights) [1992/3 18gᵖᵘ] lightly raced and no worthwhile form on Flat: no promise in October on hurdling debut. *T. Craig* —

BLINKIN' NORA 9 gr.m. Winden – Fully-Charged (King's Coup) [1992/3 c21sᵖᵘ] modest pointer: no promise in novice hunter chases. *Mrs R. W. Lewis* c–

BLITZKREIG 10 gr.g. General Ironside – Tyrone Typhoon (Typhoon) [1992/3 c18s⁶ c20s⁶ c17d² c16s c20d³] lengthy Irish gelding: very smart chaser in 1990/1: second in quite valuable handicap at Leopardstown in December, best effort of season: reportedly found to be suffering from respiratory distress final start: effective at 2m when conditions are testing and stays 2½m: acts on good to firm and heavy ground. *E. J. O'Grady, Ireland* c141

BLUEBELL TRACK 7 b.m. Saher – Douriya (Brave Invader (USA)) [1992/3 20s⁶ 28dᵖᵘ 24g] leggy mare: poor novice hurdler: stays 3m: acts on any ground: wears blinkers. *V. Thompson* —

BLUE BOURBON 9 b.g. Ile de Bourbon (USA) – Habanna (Habitat) [1992/3 c19d c21gᵘʳ c19vᵖᵘ] rangy, attractive gelding: winning chaser: sold 5,400 gns Doncaster October Sales: no form in 1992/3: best form at 2m: acts on heavy going: makes mistakes. *Paul Bradley* c– x

BLUE BUCCANEER 10 b.g. Fine Blue – Port Dancer (Port Corsair) [1992/3 c17sᶠ c20m³ c17m⁶ c17mᵘʳ] sturdy gelding: maiden hurdler: modest chaser: best effort of season at Towcester in May on last completed outing: best form at 2m: acts on good to firm and dead going. *Capt. T. A. Forster* c94

BLUECHIPENTERPRISE 7 br.m. Blakeney – Hey Skip (USA) (Bold Skipper (USA)) [1992/3 c19h* c21s⁴ c23m³ c23d⁴ c19m⁶ c26d⁴ c24g⁶ c21f³ c24g] rather leggy mare: half-sister to winning jumper Cosmic Ray (by Comedy Star): lightly raced and no sign of ability on Flat: poor form at best over fences: successful in novice event at Exeter in August: stays 3m: acts on any ground: blinkered last outing. *A. J. Cottrell* c75

BLUE DANUBE (USA) 9 ch.g. Riverman (USA) – Wintergrace (USA) (Northern Dancer) [1992/3 c26m² c26g²] rather sparely-made gelding: winning chaser: clear second in hunter chases at Cheltenham and Uttoxeter in May: stays 3¼m: acts on heavy going and good to firm: usually visored or blinkered in 1989/90, visored twice in 1991/2. *S. G. Allen* c98

BLUE DART 13 ch.g. Cantab – Maisie Owen (Master Owen) [1992/3 c20g³ c21d⁶ c25f c22f c25v] strong gelding: one-time fairly useful staying chaser: no form since 1990/1. *Capt. T. A. Forster* c–

BLUE DISC 8 br.g. Disc Jockey – Kaotesse (Djakao (FR)) [1992/3 a20g⁴ a18g* a16g⁴ 21d 17d⁴ 16s⁵ 25m 21mᵖᵘ] sturdy gelding: modest hurdler: no bid after winning sellers at Southwell in February and Carlisle (conditional jockeys handicap) in April: well below best last 3 outings: sold out of R. Hollinshead's stable 2,200 gns Doncaster May Sales after penultimate start: effective from 2m to 2½m: acts on firm, dead ground and fibresand: blinkered fourth and last starts. *A. L. Forbes* 97

BLUE DUN 4 b.g. Petong – Glyn Rhosyn (Welsh Saint) [1992/3 17dᵖᵘ 18s 20sᵖᵘ] small gelding: plating-class form at 2 yrs: no sign of ability over hurdles: sold 1,350 gns Ascot February Sales. *Mrs J. Wonnacott* —

BLUE ENSIGN 8 b.g. Beldale Flutter (USA) – Blue Rag (Ragusa) [1992/3 c16g² c16g⁶ c16gᶠ] small, sparely-made gelding: maiden plater over hurdles: modest novice chaser: barely stays 2m: often blinkered: held up. *M. P. Muggeridge* c86

BLUE HAZEZZO 10 ch.g. Remezzo – Double Blue II (Double Red) [1992/3 c21sᵘʳ] lightly-raced maiden pointer: unseated rider fourth in novice hunter chase in February. *Mrs P. A. Hemmings* c–

BLUE POINT (IRE) 4 b.f. On Your Mark – Littoral (Crash Course) [1992/3 F12d] small filly: half-sister to 3 winners, including fairly useful hurdler Steveadon (by Don): dam, half-sister to Kribensis, won over 1½m in Ireland: mid-division in NH Flat race at Windsor in February: yet to race over hurdles. *N. A. Callaghan*

BLUE ROSETTE 4 b.g. Lucky Wednesday – Cadenette (Brigadier Gerard) [1992/3 18d] second foal: dam, 1¼m winner on Flat, poor novice over hurdles: behind in juvenile hurdle at Sedgefield in October. *M. W. Easterby* –

BLUES BALIDAR 5 ch.g. Balidar – Kimble Blue (Blue Refrain) [1992/3 16v] poor maiden on Flat: behind in selling hurdle at Warwick in December. *G. Thorner* –

BLUFF KNOLL 10 b.g. New Brig – Tacitina (Tacitus) [1992/3 c25g³ c30m⁴ c28s* c28dᵘʳ c30d⁴ c28d² c33g³ c24v³ c23d*] tall, strong, close-coupled gelding: fairly useful chaser nowadays: won handicaps at Kelso in November and April: stays very well: suited by give in the ground. *R. Brewis* **c121**

BLUNHAM EXPRESS 4 b.f. Never So Bold – Park Parade (Monsanto (FR)) [1992/3 18mᵖᵘ] placed at up to 1m on Flat: tailed off when pulled up in juvenile hurdle at Market Rasen in September: sold 1,200 gns Ascot October Sales. *T. Fairhurst* –

BLURRED VISION (IRE) 4 b.g. Vision (USA) – Yvonne's Choice (Octavo (USA)) [1992/3 F18s⁶ 16d 16g] robust gelding: second foal: dam 9f winner: soundly beaten in NH Flat race and juvenile hurdles. *J. E. Collinson* –

BLUSHING BELLE 5 b.m. Local Suitor (USA) – Shuteye (Shirley Heights) [1992/3 21spᵘ 23s 16v a20g* 17f*] sturdy mare: middle-distance handicapper on Flat: sold out of P. Cole's stable 3,800 gns Newmarket Autumn Sales: successful in mares novice hurdle at Lingfield in February and seller at Plumpton (no bid) in March: stays 2½m: acts on equitrack and probably on any turf going: blinkered last 2 starts. *J. White* 84

BLUSHING GOLD 4 ch.f. Blushing Scribe (USA) – Nonpareil (FR) (Pharly (FR)) [1992/3 18dᵖᵘ 16dF 16s⁵ 22s⁶ 16s 18g⁵ 16g 17d⁶ 17f 18m⁶ 16g⁴] leggy, sparely-made filly: fourth foal: sister to winning hurdler Mister Lawson: poor novice hurdler: sometimes blinkered. *Mrs J. Jordan* 66

BLUSHING TIMES 8 b.g. Good Times (ITY) – Cavalier's Blush (King's Troop) [1992/3 21f 17d 21g] rather dipped-backed gelding: novice hurdler: no form in 1992/3: usually visored or blinkered. *A. P. Stringer* –

BLUSTERY FELLOW 8 b.g. Strong Gale – Paulas Fancy (Lucky Guy) [1992/3 c16g* c18d⁵ c16d³ c17f² c20f² c20f⁵] well-made gelding: has been hobdayed: maiden hurdler (blinkered once): fair handicap chaser: won at Worcester in October: also ran well third to fifth starts: suited by strongly-run race at 2m and stays 2½m: acts on firm and dead ground. *J. Chugg* **c104** –

B'N'B LADY 5 b.m. Vin St Benet – Combe Grove Lady (Simbir) [1992/3 F17v 16s 16sᵘʳ 21v 20s⁵ 17fpᵘ] leggy mare: seventh foal: half-sister to Flat winners Lawnswood Lad (by Runnymede) and Predestine (by Bold Owl), latter also successful over hurdles: dam lightly-raced half-sister to disqualified French Gold Cup winner Tulip II: no sign of ability. *R. Evans* –

BOARDING SCHOOL 6 b.g. Glenstal (USA) – Amenity (FR) (Luthier) [1992/3 c18mF c16d² c16g⁵ c16g c16d³ c16m* c16g* c18m³ c22m² c20m*] workmanlike gelding: fairly useful hurdler: fair form in novice chases, winning at Wolverhampton, Ayr and Market Rasen in the spring, last 2 in handicaps: stays 2¾m: acts on good to firm and soft ground: has had tongue tied down. *C. Parker* **c98** –

BOARD THE TRAIN 12 b.g. Gunner B – Great Blue White (Great Nephew) [1992/3 c27s c24m⁶ c27s] workmanlike gelding: poor staying novice chaser: lightly raced and no form for long time: visored last 2 starts. *G. A. Ham* **c–** –

BOBBY SOCKS 7 b. or br.g. Blakeney Point – Countesswells **c106**
(Behistoun) [1992/3 c16vFc17sur 17s⁵ 16d⁵a18g³a20g⁵c20m²c16m*c21g* 75
c21g*c17f⁴] stocky gelding: poor novice hurdler: completed a hat-trick over
fences when winning handicap at Huntingdon in April very easily: also ran
well next time: successful earlier in maiden chase at Wolverhampton and
novice handicap chase at Huntingdon: stays 21f: acts on firm and dead going.
R. Lee

BOB'S REQUEST (IRE) 5 b.g. Spin of A Coin – Candark VII
(Pedigree Unknown) [1992/3 27d⁴ 24s²] non-thoroughbred gelding: first 98
foal: dam winning pointer in Ireland: clear second in maiden hurdle at
Hexham in May, better effort: shapes like a thorough stayer. *J. I. A. Charlton*

BOB TISDALL 14 ch.g. Deep Run – Amphibian (Zarathustra) [1992/3 **c96**
c23d⁵ c25f³ c22f⁵] strong, lengthy, plain gelding: hunter chaser nowadays: –
creditable fifth in Martell Fox Hunters' at Aintree in April on last start:
stays well: probably acts on any ground: blinkered once. *Miss C. L. Dennis*

BOCA CHIMES 8 b.g. Welsh Saint – Howzat (Habat) [1992/3 20m³
25spu] small gelding: no sign of retaining ability in early-season selling –
hurdles. *Grenville Richards*

BODFARI 8 b.m. Lighter – Connaughts' Trump (Connaught) [1992/3 **c–** x
c25vur c25mur c24s] leggy mare: fair pointer: poor jumper in hunter chases. –
P. H. Morris

BODINNICK (IRE) 5 ch.g. Glen Quaich – Clonaslee Foam (Quayside)
[1992/3 F16m] fourth foal: half-brother to fair hunter chaser Alpha One (by
Belfalas): dam won NH Flat race in Ireland: mid-division in NH Flat race at
Warwick in May: yet to race over hurdles or fences. *O. Brennan*

BO KNOWS BEST (IRE) 4 ch.g. Burslem – Do We Know (Derrylin)
[1992/3 17v 16v⁵ 16g 17m* 17m] workmanlike gelding: half-brother to fair 128
hurdler All Greek To Me (by Trojan Fen): fair performer on Flat, stays
1½m: won quite valuable juvenile hurdle at Chepstow in March: didn't
impress in appearance but ran very well to finish seventh in Daily Express
Triumph Hurdle at Cheltenham later in month: yet to race beyond 17f: acts
on good to firm ground, shaped well on heavy. *J. Sutcliffe*

BOLD AMBITION 6 br.g. Ela-Mana-Mou – Queen of The Dance
(Dancer's Image (USA)) [1992/3 16d² 17g⁵ 17d⁵ 20v³ 20g² 20d⁶ 20m⁴ 22s] 111
leggy, close-coupled gelding: poor form on Flat: fair form in novice hurdles:
well below form in handicap last start: suited by forcing tactics at 2m, and
stays 2½m: acts on heavy and good to firm ground. *T. Kersey*

BOLD ANSWER 10 b.g. Bold Owl – Subtle Answer (Stephen George) **c–**
[1992/3 17m 16mpu] smallish, workmanlike gelding: winning hurdler: of –
little account nowadays: has been tried blinkered and visored. *C. R. Beever*

BOLD BOSS 4 b.g. Nomination – Mai Pussy (Realm) [1992/3 16g* 17s*
17s⁴ 17gpu 17d* 16d* 16g* 17f 16g* 16f²] 140 p
Bold Boss achieved a higher rating than any other British-trained
juvenile hurdler in 1992/3 when finishing runner-up under 12-0 in a four-
year-old handicap at Haydock in May. Left in the lead two out, when
Albemine fell upsides, Bold Boss was worn down close home by the in-form
Thinking Twice, who received 18 lb. It was a very useful effort from a horse
with a fine record. That said, Bold Boss certainly didn't stand out among a
far from vintage crop of British juveniles, and he has a long way to go before
he can be considered a major contender for top honours in 1993/4, when
he'll be trained by Martin Pipe. Bold Boss, a sturdy, good sort, does have
more scope for improvement than most of the leading juveniles, though, and
he'll surely improve his already fine record over hurdles.
Bold Boss had earned his big weight at Haydock, having won no fewer
than six races including the Petros Victor Ludorum Hurdle on the same
course in February. Bold Boss, conceding weight all round, was most impressive in beating Glaisdale by five lengths in the Victor Ludorum,
travelling well throughout and showing an excellent turn of foot to go clear
after two out. Successful earlier in juvenile events at Edinburgh and

Petros Victor Ludorum Hurdle, Haydock — Bold Boss impresses

Newcastle and a novice event at Ascot, Bold Boss then picked up another juvenile event, at Ayr, before tackling the Glenlivet Anniversary Hurdle at Aintree in April. Bold Boss appeared to hold an excellent chance of winning this very valuable event, and started a short-priced favourite, but he ran his only poor race of the season and finished last of eight. A bad mistake had resulted in Bold Boss being pulled up on his fourth start, but there appeared to be no excuses for his performance at Aintree. Any suspicions that Bold Boss was past his best for the season were dispelled when he gave lumps of weight and a comprehensive beating to five opponents in a juvenile handicap at Ayr just over two weeks later, while his performance at Haydock on his final start put paid to the idea that he might have been unsuited by the firm ground at Aintree. He probably acts on any going.

Bold Boss (b.g. 1989)	Nomination (b 1983)	Dominion (b 1972)	Derring-Do
			Picture Palace
		Rivers Maid (br 1977)	Rarity
			Takette
	Mai Pussy (ch 1975)	Realm (b 1967)	Princely Gift
			Quita II
		Broad River (b 1967)	Chieftain II
			Immensely

Bold Boss is the seventh foal of the fairly useful sprinter Mai Pussy, whose other winners include the smart seven-furlong to mile-and-a-quarter performer Beau Sher (by Ile de Bourbon) and the fair hurdler Gulsha (by Glint of Gold). Bold Boss, like his dam, showed quite useful form on the Flat. Unraced at two years, he did most of his racing at seven furlongs and a mile in 1992 when trained by Ben Hanbury, winning once and also finishing a very close second in the Britannia Stakes at Royal Ascot. Bold Boss, who races keenly and has a turn of foot, will prove best at around two miles. His fluent jumping will stand him in good stead when he tackles more experienced opposition. *G. M. Moore*

BOLD CHOICE 7 b.g. Auction Ring (USA) – Inner Pearl (Gulf Pearl) c87
[1992/3 c16m² c23g* c23m²] workmanlike gelding: moderate hurdler: won –
novice chase at Worcester in August: finished lame in September and
wasn't seen out again: stays 23f: acts on firm ground, possibly unsuited by
soft: has been tried blinkered and visored. *R. G. Frost*

BOLD HONEY (IRE) 5 ch.m. Nearly A Nose (USA) – White Honey –
(Bold Lad (IRE)) [1992/3 a16gᵖᵘ a16gᵖᵘ] third foal: dam lightly-raced Irish –
maiden: showed nothing over hurdles in February. *F. Sheridan*

BOLD IMP 8 bl.g. Dubassoff (USA) – Woodlands Girl (Weepers Boy) c–
[1992/3 16f²⁄₄u] compact gelding: poor novice hurdler: showed nothing only –
start over fences: stays 2¼m: acts on dead ground: blinkered once. *P. Leach*

BOLD IN COMBAT 10 b.g. Junius (USA) – Malmsey (Jukebox) [1992/3 c87 §
c22m³ c24g³ c33m c26f4 c24f] small gelding: hunter chaser nowadays: stays – §
well: suited by a sound surface and acts on hard going: sometimes
blinkered, visored final outing: inconsistent and sometimes takes little
interest. *T. Casey*

BOLD KING'S HUSSAR 10 ch.g. Sunyboy – Oca (O'Grady) [1992/3 c–
c22f] big, lengthy gelding: one-time fairly useful hurdler: winning –
pointer/steeplechaser: stays 2½m: acts on any going: sometimes sweating
and edgy in preliminaries. *Mrs David Plunkett*

BOLD MAC 7 b.g. Comedy Star (USA) – Northern Empress (Northfields
(USA)) [1992/3 17gᵖᵘ] very lightly raced and no sign of ability over hurdles. –
M. Blanshard

BOLD MAN (NZ) 6 b.g. So Bold (NZ) – If It Wishes (NZ) (Zamazaan)
[1992/3 20s] angular gelding: behind in 2 novice hurdles. *Mrs J. R.
Renfree-Barons*

BOLD MELODY 4 b.f. Never So Bold – Broken Melody (Busted)
[1992/3 16f* 18g] leggy filly: modest miler on Flat: easy winner of 3-runner ?
juvenile hurdle at Hexham in August: soundly beaten at Cartmel 5 days
later: difficult to assess. *P. C. Haslam*

BOLD MONK (NZ) 11 ch.g. Pag-Asa (AUS) – Chatalia (NZ) (Rocky c– §
Mountain (FR)) [1992/3 c24s] sparely-made gelding: has been fired: fair but –
irresolute chaser at his best: no form for a long time: sometimes blinkered
or visored. *D. H. Barons*

BOLD MOOD 4 br.g. Jalmood (USA) – Boldie (Bold Lad (IRE)) [1992/3
16g 18g³ 17m⁵] leggy, sparely-made gelding: placed over 6f at 2 yrs: sold out 83
of J. Berry's stable 1,300 gns Doncaster August Sales: best effort over
hurdles when fifth in claimer at Newcastle in March: acts on good to firm
ground. *J. J. Birkett*

BOLD'N 6 ch.g. Ardross – Princess Dina (Huntercombe) [1992/3 20m
17d] big, strong gelding: third living foal: brother to winning Irish hurdler –
Rosshire and half-brother to fair hurdler Family Line (by High Line) and fair
miler Labelon Lady (by Touching Wood): dam in frame at up to 9f: well
beaten in novice hurdles but showed signs of ability last time. *N. B. Mason*

BOLD REINE (FR) 4 b.f. Policeman (FR) – Labold (Bold Lad (IRE))
[1992/3 F17dˢᵘ] half-sister to several winners on Flat in France: dam
successful on Flat in France: slipped up after 4f in NH Flat race at Hereford
in May: yet to race over hurdles. *R. J. Hodges*

BOLD SETKO (IRE) 4 b.g. Bold Arrangement – Ribamba (Ribocco)
[1992/3 a16gᵖᵘ] half-brother to winning hurdler Andros Prince (by –
Blakeney): plating-class maiden on Flat: sold out of J. Eustace's stable 3,100
gns Newmarket Autumn Sales: tailed off when pulled up in juvenile hurdle
at Southwell in January. *C. T. Nash*

BOLD SPARK 5 br.g. Electric – Boldie (Bold Lad (IRE)) [1992/3 20d
17gᵖᵘ 17mᵖᵘ] small gelding: of little account: visored once. *J. M. Bradley* –

BOLD SPARTAN 10 b.g. Bold Owl – Spartan's Girl (Spartan General) c101
[1992/3 c28d² c30d² c33g c28g⁶] rangy gelding: fair handicap chaser: good –

103

second at Kelso in December and Newcastle in January: stiff task third outing, ran poorly last: stays very well: acts on any going. *J. K. M. Oliver*

BOLD STEVE 4 ch.g. Never So Bold – Vian (USA) (Far Out East (USA)) [1992/3 17v 17s⁴ 18m⁶] close-coupled gelding: modest maiden on Flat when trained by L. Cumani, placed at 1m: best effort over hurdles final start: dead. *M. H. Tompkins*   79

BOLD STREET BLUES 6 b.g. Bold Owl – Basin Street (Tudor Melody) [1992/3 17g² 16g⁵ 20g⁵ 20g³ 22s 17d³ 17dᵖᵘ] sturdy, close-coupled gelding: poor novice hurdler: stays 2½m: acts on any going. *J. Allen*   82

BOLGHERI 5 b.g. Nicholas Bill – Barrie Baby (Import) [1992/3 16s³ 16s⁵ 17sᵖᵘ 22gˢᵘ] workmanlike gelding: modest hurdler: stayed 2½m: acted on soft ground: dead. *Mrs M. Reveley*   89

BOLLINGER 7 ch.g. Balinger – Jolly Regal (Jolly Good) [1992/3 21s² 20v⁶ 21v³ 25d* 24d³ 24g⁶] lengthy gelding: useful hurdler: won handicap at Wetherby in February: good third to Sweet Duke in similar event at Ascot 2 months later: effective at around 2½m and stays 3m: acts on heavy going. *J. T. Gifford*   131

BOLLIN MAGDALENE 5 b.m. Teenoso (USA) – Klairlone (Klairon) [1992/3 21g*] leggy, angular mare: half-sister to useful hurdler and fair chaser Ambassador (by General Assembly): plating-class staying handicapper on Flat, often visored or blinkered: jumped soundly when winning novice hurdle at Wetherby in October: will stay beyond 21f. *M. H. Easterby*   90

BOLLIN PATRICK 8 b.g. Sagaro – Bollin Charlotte (Immortality) [1992/3 16g² 21s 17d⁵ 20d³ 16d³ 20gᵖᵘ 17f²] sturdy gelding: fairly useful hurdler: creditable efforts when placed in handicaps at Wetherby (2), Newcastle and Aintree (valuable event) in 1992/3: effective at 2m and stays 21f: acts on any going. *M. H. Easterby*   126

BOLLIN WILLIAM 5 b.h. Nicholas Bill – Bollin Charlotte (Immortality) [1992/3 17d* 17s* 20s* 20d³ 16s² 22s 21m³ 20f] tall, close-coupled horse: improved into a useful hurdler, winning handicaps at Bangor, Chepstow and Haydock in first half of season: good second on last-named course in January: below form final 3 starts: effective at 2m and stays 2½m: acts on good to firm and soft ground: jumps well in the main. *M. H. Easterby*   140

BOLL WEEVIL 7 b.g. Boreen (FR) – Lavenham Lady (Precipice Wood) [1992/3 c17gᶠ 21g 21v*] moderate handicap hurdler: won at Uttoxeter in April: showed promise on chasing debut: should stay beyond 21f: acts on heavy going. *O. Sherwood*   c– p 99

BOLT OF GOLD 5 b.m. Glint of Gold – Habutai (Habitat) [1992/3 22vᵖᵘ 17sᵖᵘ 21g 17f 18g⁴ 18mᵘʳ 18gᵖᵘ] sparely-made mare: of little account. *L. Waring*   –

BOLTON FLYER 7 b.m. Aragon – Linda's Romance (USA) (Restless Restless (USA)) [1992/3 20gᵖᵘ] poor form on Flat: started slowly and always tailed off (eventually pulled up) in selling handicap hurdle in October. *O. O'Neill*   –

BONANZA 6 ch.g. Glenstal (USA) – Forliana (Forli (ARG)) [1992/3 c21d* c21d* c21dᶠ c23d* c21d² c21gᵘʳ c21g⁶ c21gᶠ 24d 22g] small, angular gelding: fair hurdler at his best, well below form last 2 outings: won 2 novice chases at Sedgefield in first half of season and handicap at Market Rasen in January: stays 23f: acts on any going: blinkered once: needs plenty of driving, and sometimes takes little interest. *Mrs M. Reveley*   c114 –

BONANZA BOY 12 b.g. Sir Lark – Vulmid (Vulgan) [1992/3 c24v³ c30s⁴ c29v³ c30s²] sparely-made, smallish gelding: one-time high-class chaser: still capable of useful form on his day, as he showed when fourth in Coral Welsh National at Chepstow in December: well below that form afterwards: suited by good test of stamina and plenty of give in the ground: blinkered twice: looks a difficult ride. *M. C. Pipe*   c145 ? –

BONNIE ARTIST 9 ch.g. Caruso – Bonnie Ribema (Three Dons) [1992/3 c23m6 c25m3 c27d4] leggy, rather lightly-made gelding: staying handicap chaser: jumps poorly and seems to have lost interest. *W. A. Stephenson*   c– §

BONSAI BUD 10 b.g. Tug of War – Keep The Day (Master Buck) [1992/3 c24d* c26s* c26s2 c27s6 c35sF c30spu c34d c26v5] rangy gelding: fairly useful handicap chaser: successful at Kempton and Warwick in first half of season: below form last 2 starts: dyed-in-the-wool stayer: acts on soft ground. *D. J. G. Murray-Smith*   c120

BONZER 4 br.g. Electric – Lady Doubloon (Pieces of Eight) [1992/3 18s3] brother to winning hurdler Bright-One: lightly raced and signs of ability on Flat: third in juvenile hurdle at Market Rasen in September. *J. G. FitzGerald*   85

BOOGIE BOPPER (IRE) 4 b.g. Taufan (USA) – Mey (Canisbay) [1992/3 16v* 18s2 18d2 18v* 16v4 16s2 16s 17gpu 17g4 17v] small, leggy, close-coupled gelding: modest middle-distance maiden on Flat: sold out of M. Bell's stable 7,500 gns Newmarket Autumn Sales: won conditional jockeys selling handicap at Nottingham (bought in 6,800 gns) in December and juvenile hurdle at Folkestone in January: ran poorly last 4 outings: sold 2,300 gns Ascot June Sales: stays 2¼m: suited by plenty of give in the ground: blinkered last 2 outings: possibly none too genuine. *M. C. Pipe*   97

BOOKCASE 6 b.g. Siberian Express (USA) – Colourful (FR) (Gay Mecene (USA)) [1992/3 17d 17d 16s 17f] leggy gelding: fairly useful hurdler in 1991/2: well beaten in handicaps in 1992/3: should stay further than 2m: acts on good to firm going: blinkered last 3 starts: takes a good hold: winner on Flat in 1993. *D. R. C. Elsworth*   –

BOOKER EXPRESS 4 ch.f. Oats – Lingfield Lady (Julio Mariner) [1992/3 aF16g] first foal: dam won two 17f selling hurdles: tailed off in NH Flat race at Lingfield in March: yet to race over hurdles. *P. Howling*

BOOKIE BASHER 10 b. or br.g. Derring Rose – Wine Spy (Quisling) [1992/3 18gpu 17vbd 16d 17s a16g] poor novice hurdler: races mainly at around 2m. *R. Curtis*   –

BOOK OF DREAMS (IRE) 5 b.g. Mandalus – Hare Path (Private Walk) [1992/3 F17m] second foal: dam won on Flat and over hurdles in Ireland: well beaten in NH Flat race at Cheltenham in April: yet to race over hurdles or fences. *D. Nicholson*

BOOK OF MUSIC (IRE) 5 b.g. Orchestra – Good Loss (Ardoon) [1992/3 17v3 17s 17s5 17m5] strong gelding: chasing type: third foal: brother to winning Irish hurdler Daintree Lady: dam unraced: fair form in novice hurdles: will stay at least 2½m: acts on heavy and good to firm going: has scope, type to do better in time and sure to win a race. *J. T. Gifford*   111 p

BOOK OF RUNES 8 b.g. Deep Run – Wychelm (Allangrange) [1992/3 16s4 16v3 20d5 16d* 20v* 17g3 20g4] tall, leggy gelding: chasing type: won novice handicap hurdles at Uttoxeter in March and Hereford in April: probably needs testing conditions at around 2m and stays 2½m: acts on heavy going: visored last 4 starts: usually forces pace. *J. A. C. Edwards*   96

BOOM TIME 8 br.g. Strong Gale – Karin Maria (Double Jump) [1992/3 c20s2 c20s4 c24d* c24s2 c25vpu c25v5 c22d* c25d4 c22f c23s3] tall, lengthy gelding: trained until latest season by N. Henderson: fair handicap chaser: won at Naas in October and Fairyhouse in February: ran respectably in John Hughes Memorial Trophy at Aintree in April, penultimate start: should stay beyond 25f: probably acts on any going. *Mrs J. Harrington, Ireland*   c110 –

BOON HILL 4 b.g. Green Ruby (USA) – Nyota (Reform) [1992/3 18dpu] poor maiden on Flat: tailed off when pulled up in juvenile hurdle at Sedgefield in October. *M. W. Ellerby*   –

BOOTH'S BOUQUET 5 b.g. Ginger Boy – Lismore (Relkino) [1992/3 17v4 17d 16g] leggy, close-coupled gelding: second foal: dam modest middle-distance maiden: signs of ability in novice hurdles. *Miss B. Sanders*   – p

Crudwell Cup (Handicap Chase), Warwick—
Boraceva (right) gets off the mark for the season, at Do Be Brief's expense

BOOTSCRAPER 6 ch.g. Doc Marten – Impish Ears (Import) [1992/3 22v²] compact gelding: fair hurdler: first race for 16 months when short-head second at Newton Abbot in April: suited by 2½m to 2¾m: acts on any going. *R. J. Baker* — 119

BORACEVA 10 b.g. Salluceva – Boreen Queen (Boreen (FR)) [1992/3 c26g² c26d² c28sur c26vur c27s c35sur c27v⁴ c27mur c29g* c25m³ c25gᵇᵈ c33g⁶ c24d* c25d*] workmanlike, good-quartered gelding: useful handicap chaser: won at Warwick in March and Perth and Towcester in May: stayed very well: acted on good to firm and heavy going: tended to make the odd bad mistake: dead. *G. B. Balding* — c137 x

BORDER ARCHER 9 br.g. Lighter – Inishdooey (Bargello) [1992/3 c27spu c21v² c23g] lengthy gelding: moderate chaser: creditable second at Worcester in April, easily best effort of season: stays 3¼m: acts on heavy going. *P. J. Hobbs* — c98 –

BOREEN JEAN 9 ch.m. Boreen (FR) – Kitty Quin (Saucy Kit) [1992/3 25f* 25m 26f⁴] sturdy mare: fair hurdler: won handicap at Uttoxeter in September: twice well beaten 8 months later: winning chaser, but makes mistakes: stays well: acts on any ground. *K. S. Bridgwater* — c– 106

BOREEN OWEN 9 b.g. Boreen (FR) – Marble Owen (Master Owen) [1992/3 c25g⁵ c27d* c27d* c28sᶠ c24spu c24d c27m² c27d* c24d⁴] big gelding: fair handicap chaser: easily best efforts of season at Sedgefield, winning in November (twice, one an amateurs minor event) and April: suited by long distances: acts on good to firm and heavy going: has been tried blinkered and visored, but didn't wear them in 1992/3. *J. J. O'Neill* — c113 –

BORING (USA) 4 ch.g. Foolish Pleasure (USA) – Arriya (Luthier) [1992/3 16g⁵ 17g 18m⁵ 18d] quite modest on Flat, stays 1¼m: poor form over hurdles. *W. Storey* — 79

BORLEAFRAS 13 b.g. Sassafras (FR) – Levers Leap (King's Leap) [1992/3 a21gᶠ] sturdy gelding: poor performer nowadays: usually let down by his jumping in steeplechases: stays 2½m: acts on any going. *J. Carden* — c– x –

BORN DEEP 7 ch.g. Deep Run – Love-In-A-Mist (Paddy's Stream) [1992/3 16v 22v³ 19s* 20s⁶ 24d² 24v 24v* 20v⁵ 24g] second foal: dam won NH Flat race and 2m maiden hurdle: won maiden hurdle at Naas in January and minor event at Clonmel in April: ran poorly final start: stays 3m: acts on heavy going: useful novice. *Anthony Mullins, Ireland* — 132

BORN WITH A VEIL   7 b.g. Thatching – Star Harbour (St Paddy) [1992/3 17g⁴ 22g⁵ 18m⁴] leggy, workmanlike gelding: novice selling hurdler: sold 1,200 gns Ascot December Sales: suited by around 2m: acts on firm and dead ground: blinkered once. *M. Williams*   75

BORO EIGHT   7 b.g. Deep Run – Boro Nickel (Nicolaus) [1992/3 20d 16gᶠ 16v* 18d* 17m⁴ 16s⁵ 16d]   142 ?

If there was an award for the most impressive performance of the season, Boro Eight's win in the Deloitte And Touche Novice Hurdle at Leopardstown in February would earn a nomination at least. It was a display of bold-jumping, front-running which his eight rivals never looked anywhere near able to cope with, and, in a race where he was clear virtually throughout, Boro Eight won by thirteen lengths—value for double—from Time For A Laugh. The second, who started favourite at level weights, went on to show himself a useful novice. Boro Eight, however, failed to enhance his reputation with three defeats from three subsequent starts, all in top novice events. He performed respectably when favourite for the Trafalgar House Supreme Novices' Hurdle at Cheltenham on ground a good deal faster than he'd met at Leopardstown, finishing eighteen lengths fourth behind twelve-length winner Montelado, unable to quicken turning for home. He was beaten on merit there; however, his later failures at Fairyhouse in the Jameson Gold Cup and Punchestown in the Country Pride Champion Novice Hurdle were due to a physical problem which undermines confidence in his ability to fulfil his potential. He broke a blood vessel at Fairyhouse where he weakened tamely into a well-beaten fifth place behind Princess Casilia, and ran as if he did at Punchestown where he performed similarly to be a remote seventh behind Bayrouge. Boro Eight was ridden at Punchestown by Horgan instead of his usual rider Maguire who missed all three days of the Festival due to a seven-day whip ban, a harsh punishment

Deloitte And Touche Novice Hurdle, Leopardstown—
Boro Eight (A. Maguire) is clear virtually throughout

Mr J. P. Hill's "Boro Eight"

for trying too hard. Boro Eight ended his novice season with two wins from seven starts (a maiden at Gowran Park preceded Leopardstown) and a severely dented reputation. Control of his physical problem seems the key to the future prospects of an undeniably talented horse.

		Deep Run (ch 1966)	Pampered King (b 1954)	Prince Chevalier
Boro Eight (b.g. 1986)				Netherton Maid
			Trial By Fire (ch 1958)	Court Martial
				Mitrailleuse
		Boro Nickel (b 1963)	Nicolaus (b 1939)	Solario
				Nogara
			Moneyfinder (b 1952)	Boro Boudour
				Albuera

The sturdy Boro Eight, a typical example of the type of horse favoured by his trainer, is, appropriately, the eighth and last foal of Boro Nickel. Of the six previous living foals two were above-average performers—the Galway Plate winner Boro Quarter (by Normandy) and Boro Eight's brother Boro Smackeroo, a useful hurdler/chaser who raced in Britain in the latest season. A half-sister Boro Cent (by Little Buskins) is the dam of the successful staying hurdler Tallywagger. Boro Nickel herself won six point-to-points. Boro Eight should stay beyond two and a quarter miles. Boro Smackeroo stays two and a half and Boro Eight gives the impression that he'd stay at least as well as his brother. Boro Eight acts on heavy going and good to firm, though may prove better with give in the ground than on top-of-the-ground. It's to be hoped he can produce some more displays on a par with the one at Leopardstown in 1993/94. *Patrick Mullins, Ireland*

108

BORO SMACKEROO 8 b.g. Deep Run – Boro Nickel (Nicolaus) **c133**
[1992/3 c22s⁶ c20d* 17v⁶ c16s³ c17m³ c16m⁵ c16fᵖᵘ] sturdy gelding: useful   133
hurdler/chaser: won handicap chase at Listowel in September: sold out of P.
Mullins' stable 19,000 gns Goffs October Sales after third start: good efforts
first 3 outings in Britain: effective from 2m to 2½m: acts on good to firm and
heavy going: front runner: sometimes breaks blood vessels. *J. H. Johnson*

BORRAM (IRE) 4 b.g. Persian Bold – Silken Topper (High Hat) [1992/3
16m⁶ 17g⁴ 17f] poor maiden on Flat: no sign of ability over hurdles, including   –
in sellers. *D. Nicholson*

BORRETO 9 b. or br.g. Treboro (USA) – Fiji Express (Exbury) [1992/3
20g 22v⁴ 18s⁶ 21v 20v² 23d⁶ 21sᵖᵘ] lengthy, workmanlike gelding: novice   88
selling hurdler: easily best effort when second in claimer at Lingfield in
February: acts on heavy going: looks a difficult ride: sometimes
blinkered or visored. *C. James*

BORROKINO 8 b.m. Relkino – Market Melody (Highland Melody)
[1992/3 22f 18d⁵] workmanlike, plain mare: novice hurdler: no worthwhile   –
form for a long time: has been blinkered and visored. *Mrs Y. E. Stapleton*

BOSCEAN CHIEFTAIN 9 b.g. Shaab – Indian Stick (Indian Ruler)
[1992/3 25s* 22d* 24s⁴ 24d² 21d* 24d⁴ 24f*] leggy gelding: useful hurdler: 140
had a fine season, winning handicaps at Taunton and Wincanton in
December and Chepstow in February, and Dean Moor Long Distance
Hurdle at Haydock (beat Cardinal Red 3½ lengths) in May: stays 3¼m: acts
on any going: races prominently: tough and genuine. *Mrs J. G. Retter*

BOSSBURG 6 b.m. Celtic Cone – Born Bossy (Eborneezer) [1992/3   **c84**
c18d⁵ c20dᶠ c16v⁴ c16s³ c16d³ c19d c21dᵖᵘ c16s³ c17s* c16f² c16g⁴] small   –
mare: maiden chaser: modest chaser: amateur ridden, won mares novice
event at Hexham in April: ran well next outing, poorly last: should stay
beyond 17f: acts on any going: usually blinkered nowadays. *D. McCain*

Dean Moor Long Distance Hurdle, Haydock—25/1-shot Boscean Chieftain belies his odds

BOSTON EXPRESS 4 ch.g. Ballacashtal (CAN) – Disco Diamond (Le Coq d'Or) [1992/3 16dᵖᵘ 16d] big, lengthy, unfurnished gelding: second foal: dam of little account: no sign of ability in juvenile hurdles in November. *R. D. E. Woodhouse* –

BOSTON ROVER 8 b.g. Ovac (ITY) – Vulgan Ten (Raise You Ten) c109 [1992/3 c16dᶠ c17g⁴ c16m² c18d* c17s* c16dᶠ c20m* c20g⁵ c17m² c21f⁵ c17d*] smallish, plain gelding: fair handicap chaser: won at Market Rasen and Towcester in November, Stratford in April and Towcester in May: stays 2½m: acts on heavy and good to firm going: game, genuine and consistent. *O. Brennan*

BOSWORTH BAY 11 b.g. Orange Bay – Bosworth Moll (Henry The Seventh) [1992/3 17vᵖᵘ] sparely-made gelding: novice selling hurdler: no form for long time: sometimes blinkered. *T. Casey* –

BOTMOOR WAY 6 gr.g. Blakeney – Belinda Mede (Runnymede) [1992/3 16g 18dᵖᵘ 16d5] lengthy gelding: novice selling hurdler: blinkered second outing. *C. R. Egerton* –

BOUGHT THE ACES (IRE) 5 gr.g. Flash of Steel – Soubrette (Habat) [1992/3 17sᵖᵘ 17s] unfurnished gelding: fifth foal: half-brother to winning Irish hurdler Slow Start (by Wassl): dam, French provincial 10.8f winner, half-sister to 3 good-class middle-distance performers: no sign of ability in 2 novice hurdles. *G. A. Ham* –

BOUNDEN DUTY (USA) 7 b.g. His Majesty (USA) – Inward Bound c126 (USA) (Grey Dawn II) [1992/3 c16g³] big, well-made, good sort: fairly useful chaser: creditable third in handicap at Worcester in October, only outing of season: best form at 2m but shapes like he'll be suited by further: acts on firm ground: has worn tongue strap: races up with pace. *G. Harwood*

BOUNDER ROWE 6 b.g. Henbit (USA) – Arita (FR) (Kronzeuge) c– [1992/3 18v] medium-sized gelding: has been tubed: poor novice hurdler: – tailed off in selling handicap in January: jumped badly on chasing debut: has pulled hard and worn net muzzle. *J. Ffitch-Heyes*

BOUTZDAROFF 11 ch.g. Dubassoff (USA) – Love Seat (King's Bench) c134 [1992/3 c16g⁴ c16d² c16s c16s5 c17d⁴ c17g* c16f* c16g³ c18m²] lengthy, workmanlike gelding: formerly a smart chaser: useful form at best in 1992/3: won handicaps at Sedgefield in March and Aintree (valuable event, by 2½ lengths from Fragrant Dawn) in April: suited by a sharp 2m: best form on a sound surface and acts on firm going. *J. G. FitzGerald*

BOWBERRY 4 ch.f. Mossberry – If You Must VII (Pedigree Unknown) [1992/3 18gᵖᵘ] non-thoroughbred filly: first foal: dam unraced: tailed off – when pulled up in juvenile hurdle at Fontwell in September. *R. Rowe*

BOWCAP 9 ch.m. Capricorn Line – Springbow (Silent Spring) [1992/3 c– c27d5] no sign of ability in hunter chases. *B. R. J. Young* –

BOW HANDY MAN 11 ch.g. Nearly A Hand – Bellemarie (Beau c103 d Chapeau) [1992/3 c26g⁶ c25m³ c24m⁴ c27d³ c27g³ c26mᶠ c27d³ c26d² c26s* c24s³ c29s³ c27d³ c27g³ c28g⁶ c27m⁴] compact gelding: handicap chaser: jumped better than usual when winning at Catterick in December: below form otherwise: out-and-out stayer: acts on good to firm and soft going: has been tried blinkered and visored: usually poor jumper. *Denys Smith*

BOWLAND CONNECTION 6 ch.g. Crash Course – Bonnemahon (Polyfoto) [1992/3 21s 21f⁶ 17g⁶ 22vᵖᵘ] plain gelding: poor novice hurdler: 78 stays 21f: acts on firm ground. *J. L. Eyre*

BOWLAND GIRL (IRE) 4 b.f. Supreme Leader – El Marica (Buckskin (FR)) [1992/3 aF16g⁵ aF16g⁶ F16m² 22d 21fᵖᵘ] lengthy, unfurnished filly: – first foal: dam unraced: second in NH Flat race at Nottingham in March: showed little in 2 novice hurdles. *R. Hollinshead*

BOWLANDS HIMSELF (IRE) 5 b.g. The Parson – Yellow Canary (Miner's Lamp) [1992/3 F17m] first foal: dam never ran: behind in NH Flat race at Carlisle in October: yet to race over hurdles or fences. *C. Parker*

Martell Aintree Chase (Limited Handicap)—
Boutzdaroff (ahead of Fragrant Dawn) finds conditions in his favour

BOWLANDS WAY   9 b.g. Al Sirat (USA) – Kilbride Lady VI (Menelek)   **c75**
[1992/3 c21d4] big gelding: fair winning hurdler: completing for first time   –
over fences when remote fourth in novice event at Carlisle in April: stays
3m: acts on good to firm and soft going: visored twice in 1990/1. *C. Parker*

BOWL OF OATS   7 ch.g. Oats – Bishop's Bow (Crozier) [1992/3 c20s3   **c104**
c21dpu c20v* c24d c24s c21v* c22v*] compact gelding: maiden hurdler: –
won handicap chases at Market Rasen (novices) in December, Lingfield in
February and Towcester in April: stays 2¾m well: acts on heavy going:
blinkered last 2 starts. *Andrew Turnell*

BOXING MATCH   6 b.g. Royal Boxer – Mutchkin (Espresso) [1992/3
a20g5 16s 16g] leggy gelding: poor plater over hurdles. *J. M. Bradley*   –

BOX OF DELIGHTS   5 br.g. Idiot's Delight – Pretty Useful
(Firestreak) [1992/3 F16s] fourth living foal: dam won on Flat and over
hurdles: behind in NH Flat race at Ludlow in January: yet to race over
hurdles or fences. *R. Dickin*

BOYCOTT   6 b.g. Buckskin (FR) – Natanya (Menelek) [1992/3 16v* 16d2
20d2] sturdy, workmanlike gelding: chasing type: half-brother to several   **129 p**
winning jumpers, including top-class hunter chaser Eliogarty (by Lucky
Brief): dam never ran: impressive winner of novice hurdle at Windsor in
February: useful performance when second to Hebridean in well-contested
similar event at Ascot in April on last start, staying on strongly: will prove
suited by a good test of stamina: acts on heavy going: will win more races. *S.
E. Sherwood*

BOY PAINTER   10 ch.g. Gunner B – Sister Anne (Mourne) [1992/3 18d   **c–** §
c16d4 16s 18d] tall gelding: selling hurdler: no form in 1992/3, including on   – §
only outing over fences: form only at around 2m: acted on any going:
blinkered once: looked temperamental: dead. *J. H. Johnson*

111

BOYS ROCKS 5 ch.g. Lighter – Nelodor (Nelcius) [1992/3 16g⁶ 20g⁶ 17d⁴ 16vᶠ a16g] brother to winning pointers Funnyfoot and Kate's Girl, latter also a successful steeplechaser: dam winning 2½m hurdler: tailed off only start on Flat (at 2 yrs): poor form over hurdles. *J. A. C. Edwards*   71

BRABINER LAD 9 ch.g. Celtic Cone – Bit of A Madam (Richboy) [1992/3 28d⁵ 25spu 20g⁴ 21f³ 21m³] sturdy gelding: lightly-raced modest novice hurdler: best efforts at around 2½m: acts on firm and dead ground. *T. Laxton*   88

BRACKENFIELD 7 ch.g. Le Moss – Stable Lass (Golden Love) [1992/3 21m* 24s* 24v* 20s* 24s* 20g*]   137 p

Brackenfield hasn't put a foot wrong since making an inauspicious start to his hurdling career in a novice event at Sedgefield in March, 1992. The winner of both his starts in National Hunt Flat races, Brackenfield started second favourite at Sedgefield but gave a lack-lustre performance, jumping deliberately and trailing in last of the seven finishers. Brackenfield could only get better, but the extent to which he improved in the latest season, having changed stables in the meantime, must have surprised even the most optimistic of his supporters. He ran in six novice hurdles and won them all, notably the Philip Cornes Saddle Of Gold Final at Chepstow in February. Brackenfield, with victories at Carlisle, Market Rasen (two) and Ayr already under his belt, started favourite at Chepstow, where his chief rivals appeared to be the two other promising northern-trained novices Lo Stregone and Thistle Monarch and the tough and genuine mare Gaelstrom. A distance of three miles and a combination of soft ground and a sound gallop, set by Gaelstrom, made for a very stiff test of stamina, and most of the runners were in trouble a long way from the finish. At the last flight in the back straight, five from home, Gaelstrom was almost joined by Bracken-field, and turning for home this pair began to draw well clear of Lo Stregone and Thistle Monarch. Gaelstrom looked to be travelling the better at this stage and went a couple of lengths up, but Brackenfield, sticking gamely to his task, was able to take full advantage when the leader blundered at the

Albert Bartlett & Sons 'Future Champions' Novices' Hurdle, Ayr— a bloodless victory for Brackenfield

Guy Faber's "Brackenfield"

fourth last. Brackenfield always held the upper hand from there, though he had to be driven right out to hold off the rallying Gaelstrom by one and a half lengths. On her next start Gaelstrom won the Sun Alliance Novices' Hurdle at Cheltenham, whereas a less adventurous policy was adopted with Brackenfield. He made just one other appearance, in a three-runner novice event at Ayr in April for which he started at odds-on. With the second favourite Frickley running poorly, Brackenfield was left with a simple task and made all for an easy win. The disconcerting aspect of Brackenfield's performance was that he jumped to the right throughout, something which, if repeated, might cause problems when he tackles fences in the next season. That apart, it's hard to see why Brackenfield, a big, lengthy, good sort, shouldn't do very well and he appeals as one to follow in novice chases.

Brackenfield (ch.g. 1986)	Le Moss (ch 1975)	Le Levanstell (b 1957)	Le Lavandou Stella's Sister
		Feemoss (b 1960)	Ballymoss Feevagh
	Stable Lass (b 1982)	Golden Love (b 1967)	Above Suspicion Syncopation
		Kilcoran Lass (br 1975)	Straight Lad Shean Lass

Brackenfield is the first foal of Stable Lass, who like her dam and grandam was unraced. Stable Lass's second foal Shean Alainn, a full sister to Brackenfield, and also trained by Mrs Reveley, won a mares novice hurdle at Towcester in the latest season. The third dam Shean Lass produced no fewer than nine winners, including the very useful jumpers Donohill, No Hill, Shean Lad and Winter Rain. Brackenfield is effective at two and a half miles and he'll stay beyond three. He acts on good to firm and heavy going. *Mrs M. Reveley*

BRADBURY ROSE   6 b.m. Bradbury Master – Gillian Rosemary (John Splendid) [1992/3 F16m F16d F16dᵖᵘ] second foal: dam winning pointer: has shown nothing in NH Flat races: yet to race over hurdles or fences. *T. J. Price*

BRADBURY STAR   8 b.g. Torus – Ware Princess (Crash Course)   **c151**
[1992/3 c25d* c20d³ c24s⁴ c26s² c21d² c24g³]   –

Bradbury Star was a popular choice for a chaser to follow at the start of 1992/3. A high-class hurdler in his day, he'd been an instant success over fences in 1991/2 and eventually wound up the winner of seven races in nine starts at two miles to three miles, notably the Mumm Mildmay Novices' Chase at Aintree from Jodami and Run For Free. He'd also gone down only narrowly to Miinnehoma in a memorable Sun Alliance Chase at the Cheltenham Festival, while on the other occasion he'd unseated his rider at the first at Ascot. But Bradbury Star proved unrewarding, not to say frustrating, to follow. The only race he won in 1992/3 was the first of his six, the Steel Plate And Sections Young Chasers Final at Cheltenham in November, for which he started at 2/1 on with all his five opponents at least a stone out of the handicap. His form afterwards was uneven, and never reached the level once anticipated. To cap it all, he was found to be lame on the morning of Gold Cup day, had to be withdrawn from the event, and didn't run again.

To be honest, Bradbury Star's chances of a Gold Cup win were looking somewhat remote long before his withdrawal. He'd cut little ice in the King George VI Chase at Kempton on Boxing Day when expectations of a Grade 1 win were considerably higher following a close third place behind his stable-companion Deep Sensation under top weight in the H&T Walker Gold Cup at Ascot second time up. The Fellow beat him the best part of thirty lengths in the King George; Bradbury Star weakened into fourth behind Pat's Jester

*Steel Plate And Sections Young Chasers Championship Final
(Limited Handicap), Cheltenham—
Bradbury Star (left) and Le Piccolage at the last*

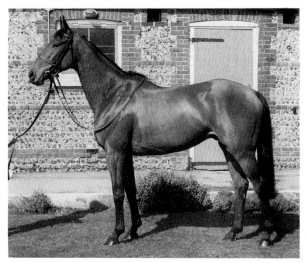

James Campbell's "Bradbury Star"

and The Illywhacker from the second last. Bradbury Star's next effort was his worst of the season—he couldn't get to grips with Black Humour at level weights when odds on for a minor chase at Warwick—and fortunately he left it well behind in running Cherrykino to two lengths in another minor chase at Wincanton four weeks later. As he'd been conceding 8 lb to the improving Cherrykino, that performance raised hopes of a win in the Racing Post Chase at Kempton towards the end of February, in which he had a lower handicap mark than in the Young Chasers Final or the H&T Walker. He started 11/4 favourite in a good-class field, in fact. However, while he ran a sound race, he found Zeta's Lad and Docklands Express just too strong in the straight; Gold Cup entry Docklands Express edged him out of second spot by a neck, conceding 18 lb.

		Ribero	Ribot
	Torus	(b 1965)	Libra
	(b 1976)	Lighted Lamp	Sir Gaylord
Bradbury Star		(b 1967)	Chandelier
(b.g. 1985)		Crash Course	Busted
	Ware Princess	(b 1971)	Lucky Stream
	(b 1979)	Peppardstown	Javelot
		(b 1965)	East Africa

Having forecast big things for Bradbury Star at the end of his novice chasing season, it is with a certain amount of reluctance that we confess to being unable now to see his developing into a top-class chaser. Unless that first season, and the Sun Alliance in particular, took more out of him than was appreciated and he needs another summer to recover, it is hard to see where the necessary improvement to take him beyond smart handicapper grade can come from. Not from the jumping department, surely—he is an excellent jumper already. However, he will probably be able to improve on his form in the H&T Walker and at Wincanton, his best in 1992/3, if ridden with more restraint. He is a horse who tends to idle in front, yet showed up from the start and had the lead a long way out in both races. There is also a school of thought which holds that Bradbury Star would do better kept away from really soft ground, such as he came across in the King George and at Warwick. That's a possibility, although he has shown he acts on any other, including dead. As for distance—he is versatile, effective at two and a half miles to twenty-five furlongs. Bradbury Star is the unraced Ware Princess' second foal; the fourth foal, Drumdeels Star (by Le Bavard) won a National Hunt Flat race and a hurdle race in Ireland in the latest season. The next dam, a half-sister to the well-known National Hunt sire Harwell, produced numerous jumping winners, including three above average by Raise You Ten in Aces Wild, Baies and Okeetee. *J. T. Gifford*

BRADMORE'S VISION 7 b.g. Vision (USA) – Plum Run (USA) (Run The Gantlet (USA)) [1992/3 20mᴾᵘ] sparely-made gelding: winning selling hurdler: no form for a long time: blinkered once in 1991/2, visored only outing 1992/3. *L. J. Barratt* —

BRAIDA BOY 7 b.g. Kampala – Braida (FR) (Tissot) [1992/3 16g 21s* 22v⁴ 22s⁶ 23g⁴ 21m*] rangy gelding: won novice hurdles at Fakenham (conditional jockeys handicap) in December and Uttoxeter in June: stays 2¾m: acts on good to firm and heavy going. *M. Bradstock* — 89

BRAMBLEBERRY 4 gr.c. Sharrood (USA) – Labista (Crowned Prince (USA)) [1992/3 16g⁴ 16d² 16g² 16s⁵ 17v 17d² 16s* 17m⁴ 16sᶠ] close-coupled colt: half-brother to winning hurdler Rushluan (by Kalaglow): placed at up to 1¼m on Flat: won juvenile hurdle at Wetherby in February: disqualified after finishing good second (placed fourth) in quite valuable juvenile handicap at Newcastle following month: will stay further than 17f: acts on soft and good to firm ground: blinkered fifth start: races up with the pace. *Mrs S. J. Smith* — 100

BRAMBLE PINK 7 b.m. Brando – Celtic Pink (Dumbarnie) [1992/3 17m³ 18d] in frame in NH Flat races in 1991/2: never-dangerous third in maiden at Taunton in April, better effort over hurdles. *B. Forsey* — 72

BRAMBLES WAY 4 ch.g. Clantime – Streets Ahead (Ovid) [1992/3 18d³ 16gᵘʳ 16d⁶] smallish gelding: plating-class maiden on Flat and over hurdles. *W. L. Barker* — 77

BRAMBLE TWIG 8 b.g. Monksfield – Bramble Mill (Master Buck) [1992/3 25sᴾᵘ] lengthy gelding: pulled up both starts over hurdles: dead. *Lady Eliza Mays-Smith* —

BRANDESTON 8 b.g. Northern Treat (USA) – Fussy Budget (Wolver Hollow) [1992/3 c22g* c20g* c21d⁵] compact, good-bodied gelding: fairly useful handicap chaser: successful at Stratford and Newbury (Glynwed International Chase) early in season: finished lame in Mackeson Gold Cup at Cheltenham in November: stays 2¾m: acts on any ground: front runner: jumps boldly but makes the odd mistake. *F. Murphy* — c128 —

BRANDON GROVE 5 b.m. Welsh Captain – Cottagers Lane (Farm Walk) [1992/3 a16g* 16s] fifth foal: sister to 6-y-o Celtic Lane: dam lightly-raced half-sister to fairly useful jumper River Sirene: won novice hurdle at Southwell in January: well beaten but not knocked about facing stiffer task next time: bred to stay beyond 2m: acts on fibresand: jumps soundly. *T. D. Barron* — 86

BRANDON PRINCE (IRE) 5 b.g. Shernazar – Chanson de Paris (USA) (The Minstrel (CAN)) [1992/3 17g² 20d² 17m] close-coupled gelding: half-brother to winning hurdler Reilton (by Cure The Blues): fairly useful stayer on Flat: second in competitive novice hurdle at Newbury in February, but below that form both subsequent starts, blinkered final one: should stay at least 2½m. *I. A. Balding* — 118

BRANDY HAMBRO 12 b.g. Hot Brandy – Ice Bird (Fighting Charlie) [1992/3 c25g⁴] big, lengthy, rather plain gelding: poor staying chaser nowadays. *C. Parker* — c—

BRAVE BEN 8 b. or br.g. Tanfirion – Cherry Gal (El Gallo) [1992/3 16vᵖᵘ 24vᵖᵘ a24gᵖᵘ] close-coupled, good-bodied gelding: no form over hurdles. *D. J. Bell* —

BRAVE BUCCANEER 6 ch.g. Buckskin (FR) – Not So Dear (Dhaudevi (FR)) [1992/3 21s⁴ 25s* 24v² 26d²] rangy gelding with scope: chasing type: fair form over hurdles: won novice event at Newbury in January: good second next time but below form last start: suited by a thorough test of stamina and plenty of give in the ground. *D. J. G. Murray-Smith*   112

BRAVE DEFENDER 9 ch.g. Niniski (USA) – Hirsova (Gulf Pearl) [1992/3 c24m² c24sᵖᵘ c21d⁵ c26sᶠ³ c24v² c21g* c29f*] workmanlike gelding: fair chaser: won handicap at Sedgefield in February and dead-heated with Farm Week in similar race at Windsor in March: effective at around 2½m and stays very well: acts on any going: tends to run in snatches: twice blinkered: usually goes well at Windsor. *J. White*   c104 —

BRAVE HIGHLANDER (IRE) 5 b.g. Sheer Grit – Deerpark Rose (Arapaho) [1992/3 16d²] second foal: dam, half-sister to fairly useful chaser Retail Runner, won a point in Ireland: made an encouraging debut when second in novice hurdle at Wincanton in April: likely to improve and win a race. *J. T. Gifford*   95 p

BRAVO STAR (USA) 8 b.g. The Minstrel (CAN) – Stellarette (CAN) (Tentam (USA)) [1992/3 16g 26g³ 22s⁴ 19m³ 18f* 24d² 26g* 19g³] small, strong gelding: fair handicap hurdler: won at Exeter in September (amateurs) and Ludlow in October: finished lame later in October, and wasn't seen out again: stays 3¼m, effective at much shorter: acts on firm and dead ground: has run well blinkered and visored (hasn't worn either since 1989/90): front runner, jumps well. *P. Leach*   108

BRAZEN GOLD 7 b.g. Boreen (FR) – Flashy Gold (Le Bavard (FR)) [1992/3 c24dᵖᵘ c25m³ c24f³ c2 1m⁵ c26d⁵] big, workmanlike gelding: modest form in hunter chases: stays 3m: acts on firm going (ran badly on dead last start). *Sir John Barlow*   c81

BRAZIER BOY 8 b.g. Combine Harvester – Dunmurry Girl (Perdu) [1992/3 17s c17vᵖᵘ c17vᵖᵘ c17sᵖᵘ a16g] workmanlike gelding: no sign of ability. *A. P. Jarvis*   c— —

BREAKDANCER (IRE) 4 b.g. Fabulous Dancer (USA) – Bennetta (FR) (Top Ville) [1992/3 17mᵖᵘ 17f² 17d⁶] fair performer on Flat, winner 4 times at 1½m early in 1993: second in juvenile seller at Taunton in October, best effort over hurdles: retained 3,500 gns Newmarket Autumn Sales. *W. R. Muir*   79

BREAKFAST CAR 11 b.g. Oats – Drawing Room Car (Chingacgook) [1992/3 c22mᵖᵘ c16s c18dᵖᵘ c16dᵖᵘ] leggy, narrow gelding: one-time fair chaser: of little account nowadays. *D. L. Williams*   c— —

BREAKING DAWN 8 b.g. Deep Run – Arctic Moonshine (Arctic Slave) [1992/3 c23gᶠ 21dᵖᵘ 28gᵖᵘ 17gᶠ 16mᶠ] leggy gelding: poor winning hurdler: broke a leg and destroyed after falling at Catterick in March: showed little aptitude for chasing: stayed 2¾m. *N. B. Mason*   c— —

BREAK THE CHAIN 8 b. or br.g. Callernish – Lovely Daisy (Menelek) [1992/3 c21g⁴ c23gᶠ c21d⁴ c23s* c23d² c24g² c27d* c21g* c20f³ c24s²] small, lightly-made gelding: fairly useful hurdler: won novice chases at Kelso in November (trained until after then by W. A. Stephenson) and Sedgefield (handicap) in January and handicap on latter course in March: sold privately 27,000 gns in May: effective at around 2½m and stays 27f: acts on any going: tough and genuine. *P. Cheesbrough*   c107

BREAK THE HABIT (FR) 6 gr.h. Habitat – Hippodrone (USA) (Drone) [1992/3 20sᵘʳ 17d 22d 22gᵖᵘ] compact horse: well beaten in novice hurdles. *T. M. Gibson*   —

BREENAMORE 11 b.g. Push On – Icydora (Arctic Slave) [1992/3 c21dᵖᵘ] rangy gelding: winning hunter chaser: little show in February: stays   c— —

3¼m, at least when conditions aren't testing: acts on any going: visored: used to be temperamental. *Mrs S. Clarke*

BREEZY SAILOR 7 ch.g. Tumble Wind (USA) – Bouganville (Gulf Pearl) [1992/3 16m^pu 17m] small, sparely-made gelding: lightly-raced selling hurdler: often blinkered or visored. *R. Thompson* —

BRENDA HUNT (IRE) 4 gr.f. Huntingdale – Brenda (Sovereign Path) [1992/3 21s³ 17m⁶ 18m^pu] lengthy filly: of little account on Flat: showed a little ability first 2 starts over hurdles. *J. S. Moore* 72

BRESIL (USA) 4 ch.c. Bering – Clever Bidder (USA) (Bold Bidder) [1992/3 16g^F] leggy, quite good-topped colt: moderate maiden on Flat, placed at up to 1¼m: weakening when falling 3 out in juvenile hurdle at Worcester in March. *A. P. Jarvis* —

BRIAR'S DELIGHT 5 b.g. Idiot's Delight – Briar Park (Timolin (FR)) [1992/3 F17s 17g 16d 21d⁶ 18d^F] close-coupled gelding: first foal: dam winning pointer: narrow lead and probable winner when falling last in novice handicap hurdle at Kelso in April, first sign of ability. *J. K. M. Oliver* 77

BRICANA 10 b.g. Bonne Noel – Duty (Le Prince) [1992/3 16f 17m^pu] close-coupled gelding: fourth live foal: brother to Irish point-to-point winner Rathpoleen: dam placed over 1½m on Flat and in 2½m maiden hurdle: won 2 NH Flat races in Ireland in 1987/8: well beaten in novice hurdle at Uttoxeter in September: dead. *W. A. Stephenson* —

BRIDGE PLAYER 6 ch.m. The Noble Player (USA) – Auction Bridge (Auction Ring (USA)) [1992/3 17d⁶ 17s⁵ 22d³ 26g⁵ 20m⁵ 21v³ 25d*] sparely-made mare: half-sister to winning hurdler Auction Fever (by Hello Gorgeous): plating-class stayer on Flat: modest form over hurdles: 4-length winner of maiden at Perth in May: stays 25f: acts on dead ground. *D. Moffatt* 86

BRIEF CASE 7 ch.g. The Parson – Bookmark (Shackleton) [1992/3 c20s^F c24s³ c24s⁴ c24d² c20d* c32m⁵] tall, lengthy gelding: third foal: dam won NH Flat race, 25f steeplechase and a point in Ireland: in frame in his 3 completed races over fences prior to winning novice event at Navan in March: jumped poorly when tailed off in valuable amateurs event over 4m at Cheltenham later in month: stays 3m: acts on soft going. *A. L. T. Moore, Ireland* c92

BRIEF ENCOUNTER (NZ) 9 b.g. Foreign Affair – Euphemia (NZ) (Piccolo Player (USA)) [1992/3 c21s^pu c27v² c22v³ c35s^R] leggy gelding: fair chaser: creditable efforts when placed in November and January: refused later in January: suited by good test of stamina: acts on heavy ground. *P. F. Nicholls* c102 —

BRIERY HILL 7 br.g. Furry Glen – Sweetly Stung (Master Rocky) [1992/3 c27d^F] no sign of ability in 2 novice hurdles: fell fatally on chasing debut. *N. J. Henderson* c– —

BRIGADIER BILL 8 ch.g. Nicholas Bill – Sailing Brig (Brigadier Gerard) [1992/3 16v 18g 20g^F 22f 17f^F] leggy gelding: winning 2m selling hurdler: no form in 1992/3: acts on firm ground. *J. White* —

BRIGAND GIRL 11 b.m. New Brig – Tillside (Lucky Brief) [1992/3 27m⁶ 26g 20g⁶ 23m] sparely-made mare: has been tubed: novice hurdler/chaser: more sign of temperament than ability: blinkered once in 1991/2: visored last 2 outings. *M. W. Eckley* c– — §

BRIGG MELODY 12 ch.m. Oedipus Complex – In For A Penny (Soletra) [1992/3 18v 25d^pu 18g⁵ 28m 18s^pu] of no account nowadays. *J. G. Thorpe* —

BRIGGS BUILDERS 9 b.g. Absalom – Quenlyn (Welsh Pageant) [1992/3 c17d^pu c17g⁶ c16d* c17g*] rangy gelding: fair chaser: blinkered, won handicaps at Plumpton and Huntingdon in February: likely to prove best at around 2m: acts on good to firm and dead going: usually makes running. *M. P. Muggeridge* c103

BRIGGS LAD (IRE) 4 ch.g. Be My Native (USA) – Zestino (Shack (USA)) [1992/3 17s 16v⁵ 16f² 23m⁴ 16f* 20m* 16m⁴] workmanlike gelding: 98

fair form at up to 1¾m on Flat: sold out of W. Jarvis' stable 8,600 gns Newmarket Autumn Sales: won juvenile hurdles at Uttoxeter and Hereford in May: effective at 2m and stays 23f: best form on top-of-the-ground: blinkered last 3 starts: carries head high and appears less than keen. *K. C. Bailey*

BRIGHT BEAT 6 gr.g. Glasgow Central – Crowebrass (Crowned Prince (USA)) [1992/3 c20mpu] unplaced in NH Flat races at Southwell: no promise on chasing debut. *R. Hollinshead* c–

BRIGHTLING BOY 8 ch.g. Deep Run – Susan La Salle (Master Owen) [1992/3 18d 17vur 20v4 20v3 23f* 20fpu 22g* 22f5] leggy, angular gelding: won novice hurdle (4 ran) at Windsor in March and conditional jockeys selling handicap at Fontwell (no bid) in April: stays 2¾m: acts on any going. *D. M. Grissell* 94

BRIGHT POLLY 7 ch.m. Politico (USA) – Bright Night (Cagirama) [1992/3 16s 18d 18d c17gF c16s4 c16mF c26dpu] no sign of ability: looks a difficult ride. *J. S. Haldane* c–
–

BRIGHT SAPPHIRE 7 b.g. Mummy's Pet – Bright Era (Artaius (USA)) [1992/3 20g 26d 17g6 23spu] small, sparely-made gelding: poor hurdler nowadays: stays 3m: acts on good to firm and soft ground and equitrack. *J. D. Thomas* 73

BRIGHT SEA (USA) 5 b.g. Secreto (USA) – Muriels Dream (USA) (Blue Prince II) [1992/3 18m 17spu 23gpu] small gelding: has run tubed: of little account. *Billy Williams* –

BRIGINSKI 4 b.f. Myjinski (USA) – Raunchy Rita (Brigadier Gerard) [1992/3 17g 17fF 18d] no worthwhile form on Flat (trained by K. Burke) or over hurdles, including in sellers. *Miss J. Southall* –

BRIG'S GAZELLE 11 b.m. Lord Nelson (FR) – Cliburn New Cut (New Brig) [1992/3 c26dpu] leggy, sparely-made mare: handicap chaser: little show only outing of season (November): suited by good test of stamina: acts on hard and dead ground: sound jumper. *I. Park* c–
–

BRIGTINA 5 b.g. Tina's Pet – Bristle-Moss (Brigadier Gerard) [1992/3 17m2 20g* 20d6 17g4 20g3 17g3 21f3] rather sparely-made gelding: selling hurdler: won handicap at Hereford (no bid) in October: fair efforts most subsequent outings: unlikely to stay much beyond 2½m: acts on firm ground. *J. M. Bradley* 74

BRILLIANT DISGUISE 4 ch.f. Ballacashtal (CAN) – Davemma (Tachypous) [1992/3 18g3] leggy, sparely-made filly: winning 1m plater at 2 yrs, placed at 1½m in August: finished lame when third in juvenile hurdle at Cartmel later in month. *P. Monteith* 81

BRILLIANT FUTURE 8 b.m. Welsh Saint – Autumn Gift (Martinmas) [1992/3 17spu 17d3 17d4 16m3 17f6] leggy, sparely-made mare: lightly-raced hurdler: poor form in 1992/3: races at around 2m: acts on good to firm and dead going. *P. J. Hobbs* 82

BRIMPTON BERTIE 4 ch.g. Music Boy – Lady of Bath (Longleat (USA)) [1992/3 17f2 17g4] angular gelding: well beaten on Flat: modest form when in frame in juvenile hurdles at Taunton and Newbury in March: likely to prove best at around 2m: acts on firm going. *Major D. N. Chappell* 91

BROAD BEAM 13 b.g. Averof – Angel Beam (SWE) (Hornbeam) [1992/3 c16m2 c16g c19dpu] rangy gelding: modest chaser: trained until after second start by P. Hobbs: stays 2½m: probably acts on any going: takes strong hold: usually finds little under pressure. *Mrs T. White* c95 §
–

BROAD HEART 4 ch.g. Broadsword (USA) – Pamkins Hart (Pamroy) [1992/3 F17g] third foal: half-brother to lightly-raced novice hurdler Grey Bertino (by Neltino): dam moderate staying hurdler: tailed off in NH Flat race at Bangor in March: yet to race over hurdles. *J. P. Smith* –

BROAD STREET 10 br.g. Balliol – Ballyarctic (Articeelagh) [1992/3 c25m4] rangy gelding: poor novice hurdler/chaser: best at up to 2½m: acts on good to firm and dead going. *R. Green* c–
–

BROADWELL 9 ch.g. Floriferous – Dromos (Cracksman) [1992/3 16v⁶   c–
c21gᶠ c20g⁶ c21mᵖᵘ] rangy gelding: little sign of ability: dead. *Capt. T. A.   –
Forster*

BROCKLESBY 5 ch.g. Sunyboy – Changatre (Malinowski (USA))
[1992/3 F16m] third foal: dam, 1¼m seller winner on Flat, tailed off only
start over hurdles: behind in NH Flat race at Warwick in May: yet to race
over hurdles or fences. *Mrs M. Reveley*

BROCTUNE BAY 4 b.g. Midyan (USA) – Sweet Colleen (Connaught)
[1992/3 F16g* F17g F14g*] compact gelding: third foal: half-brother to 1988
2-y-o 6f seller winner Colleens Daughter (by Aragon): dam winning 2m
hurdler and half-sister to useful jumper Brave Hussar: won NH Flat races at
Edinburgh in January and Market Rasen in April: yet to race over hurdles.
Mrs M. Reveley

BROCTUNE GREY 9 gr.m. Warpath – Hitesca (Tesco Boy) [1992/3
25gᵖᵘ] small, plain, sparely-made mare: fair hurdler: collapsed and died 2   –
out at Perth in September: was suited by a test of stamina: acted on firm and
soft going. *Mrs M. Reveley*

BRODESSA 7 gr.g. Scallywag – Jeanne du Barry (Dubassoff (USA))
[1992/3 22g³] lengthy, rather sparely-made gelding: won NH Flat race in   92
1990/1: better than ever on Flat in 1992, winning over 13.6f: raced freely and
jumped untidily when third in novice hurdle at Cheltenham in October:
needs to settle better. *Mrs M. Reveley*

BROKE THE BANK 6 b.g. Idiot's Delight – Waterside (Shackleton)
[1992/3 22s⁵ 18m 17d 21m³ 25d] angular gelding: third in weak novice   ?
hurdle at Carlisle in October, only sign of ability: sold 1,800 gns Ascot
December Sales. *W. T. Kemp*

BROMO (USA) 8 b.g. Sir Ivor – Ciao (USA) (Silent Screen (USA))   c–
[1992/3 c22sᵖᵘ c22vᵖᵘ 24s c23g⁶ c22gᵖᵘ c21vᵖᵘ 24gᵖᵘ] lengthy, rather   –
sparely-made gelding: novice hurdler/chaser: no form for a long time:
visored sixth start. *P. A. Pritchard*

BROMPTON ROAD 10 b.g. Derring Rose – London Gem (London c112
Gazette) [1992/3 c27vᵖᵘ c33s* c24s² c26vᶠ c30s³ c25v² c25g⁶]   –
workmanlike gelding: fair chaser: successful in handicap at Bangor in
December: best efforts third and fifth starts: stays 4m: acts on heavy going:
game front runner: sketchy jumper. *R. Lee*

BROMWICH BILL 8 b.g. Headin' Up – Bilbao (Capistrano) [1992/3 16g
17dᵖᵘ] smallish, workmanlike gelding: poor maiden on Flat, placed over 6f in   –
Ireland in 1991: no promise in early-season novice hurdles at Ludlow and
Stratford. *J. Cosgrave*

BRONZE FINAL 10 br.g. Track Spare – Bronze Foliage (Bois Le Roi)   c– x
[1992/3 c24dᵖᵘ c23vᶠ c21s⁵ c21s⁴ c26v⁵ c21g⁵] leggy, close-coupled   –
gelding: fair chaser in 1991/2: no worthwhile form in 1992/3: effective at
2½m and should stay 3m: acts on good to firm and soft ground: often makes
mistakes. *J. T. Gifford*

BROOM ISLE 5 b.m. Damister (USA) – Vynz Girl (Tower Walk) [1992/3
17s 20f*] lengthy, quite good-topped mare: moderate hurdler: trained by   96
Mrs A. Knight until after first start: improved form when winning 5-runner
mares handicap at Haydock in May, left in lead last: stays 2½m: suited by
top-of-the-ground. *D. Burchell*

BRORA ROSE (IRE) 5 b.m. Drumalis – Run Swift (Run The Gantlet
(USA)) [1992/3 18f 16f 22d³ 18g³ 16s² 17s³ 18s* 22v³ 22d 22f³ 18g⁵ 22gᵖᵘ   85
17g⁴ 22f⁶] sparely-made mare: half-sister to winning jumper Hard To Hold
(by He Loves Me): poor handicapper on Flat for J. Bethell, stays 1¾m:
trained first 6 outings over hurdles by R. Frost, next 3 by Mrs F. Walwyn:
won novice handicap at Exeter in January: ran creditably next start, below
form afterwards: sold 5,000 gns Ascot June Sales: should stay beyond 2¾m:
best form with give in the ground and acts on heavy: sometimes looks none
too keen. *J. Joseph*

BROTHER ANDREW 7 ch.g. Sandalay – Dusky Smile (Dusky Boy) [1992/3 c21dpu] tall, narrow gelding: poor novice hurdler: showed little in novice event on chasing debut. *Denys Smith* c– –

BROTHER BILL 8 ch.g. Sovereign Bill – Queen's Brook (Daybrook Lad) [1992/3 c27spu] lengthy gelding: poor winning pointer: made several mistakes and was pulled up in novice chase at Newton Abbot in October. *D. Bloomfield* c–

BROTHERLYAFFECTION 4 ch.g. Brotherly (USA) – Lady Peggy (Young Nelson) [1992/3 a16g a16g5] modest form on fibresand on Flat, stays 1m: has shown little over hurdles. *R. Hollinshead* –

BROUGHTON BLUES (IRE) 5 ch.g. Tender King – Princess Galicia (Welsh Pageant) [1992/3 18m 16m5 16f 17g 17f] smallish gelding: middle-distance plater on Flat: no form over hurdles, including in sellers. *W. J. Musson* –

BROUGHTON MANOR 8 b.m. Dubassoff (USA) – Welcome Honey (Be Friendly) [1992/3 c21d5 c19sbd 20s2 c16d* c16v* c16v* c21g5] rather leggy mare: fair chaser: won handicaps at Wincanton in December and January, and Kempton in between: lightly-raced novice hurdler: stays 21f: acts on any going: races up with pace: jumps well: tough, genuine and consistent. *Mrs J. G. Retter* c114 99

BROUGHTON'S TANGO (IRE) 4 b.g. Tender King – Topless Dancer (Northfields (USA)) [1992/3 17v 17s 16v5 17d3 17g*] neat gelding: half-brother to a winning Italian jumper by Gay Fandango: modest performer on Flat: sold out of W. Musson's stable 6,000 gns Newmarket Autumn Sales: showed ability over hurdles prior to winning juvenile event at Taunton in March: will stay beyond 17f. *M. J. Heaton-Ellis* 98

BROWN AS A BERRY (IRE) 5 b.g. Glow (USA) – Sun Bed (Habitat) [1992/3 16d 18dpu 16gF] sturdy gelding: no sign of ability: trained by W. Storey first outing: blinkered last start. *R. Gray* –

BROWN BABY 7 br.m. Full of Hope – Funny Baby (Fable Amusant) [1992/3 c21g4 c21m] workmanlike mare: poor pointer: well beaten in hunter chases. *S. J. Gilmore* c–

BROWNED OFF 4 br.g. Move Off – Jenifer Browning (Daring March) [1992/3 F16dpu] first foal: dam poor maiden on Flat and over jumps: saddle slipped and pulled up in NH Flat race at Hexham in March: yet to race over hurdles. *J. E. Swiers* –

BROWN REBEL 7 b.g. Royal Boxer – Brown Rose (Rose Knight) [1992/3 22d 23v6 c21mur] lengthy gelding: well beaten in novice hurdles: showed nothing on chasing debut. *P. J. Hobbs* c– –

BROWN SAUCE (NZ) 7 b.g. Wolverton – Gold Leaf (NZ) (Princely Note) [1992/3 16m3 16g] small, sturdy gelding: modest hurdler: easily better effort in handicaps in 1992/3 when creditable third at Ludlow in October: sold 1,800 gns Ascot June Sales: will stay further than 2m: acts on good to firm going. *N. J. Henderson* 93

BROWNSIDE BRIG 8 b.g. Goldhill – Tumlin Brig (New Brig) [1992/3 16d 16fur 16f*] angular gelding: very lightly raced over hurdles: won novice seller at Worcester (bought in 3,000 gns) in May: races only at 2m: acts on firm going. *M. H. Tompkins* 88

BROWN WINDSOR 11 b.g. Kinglet – Cauldron (Kabale) [1992/3 c25d2 c30spu] angular gelding: smart chaser: seemed to run creditably when second in 4-runner handicap at Sandown in October: pulled up in January, only subsequent start: stays really well: acts on firm and dead going, but is almost certainly unsuited by very soft: blinkered twice in 1991/2: usually a fine jumper. *N. J. Henderson* c150 ? –

BRUCE BUCKLEY 5 b.g. Julio Mariner – Petal Princess (Floribunda) [1992/3 F16d 16s 17v 17d 18g5 17g4 22gpu 17gpu] workmanlike gelding: 73 half-brother to several winners, including fairly useful staying hurdler/chaser Royal Cedar (by Celtic Cone): dam stayed 1m: poor novice hurdler: should stay beyond 2¼m: acts on dead going. *J. R. Jenkins*

BRUCE'S CASTLE   7 b.g. Beau Charmeur (FR) – Maid In The Mist (Pry) [1992/3 c17s^{ur} c21s⁵ c24g^{pu}] big, leggy gelding: poor novice hurdler/chaser: sold 3,200 gns Doncaster May Sales. *B. S. Rothwell*   c78 –

BRUFF ACADEMY   12 b. or br.g. Crash Course – My Dayan (Palestine) [1992/3 c16m⁶ c21d] tall gelding: has stringhalt: poor handicap chaser: let down by his jumping on occasions: stayed 2½m: acted on firm going: dead. *R. Paisley*   c–

BRUSHFORD   9 b.g. Dublin Taxi – Polymart (Polyfoto) [1992/3 c27d⁶ c25m^F c25d⁵ c21g⁶ c27g⁵] compact, workmanlike gelding: poor novice staying chaser: sold privately 2,100 gns in May. *J. Wade*   c78 –

BRYANSBI   9 b.m. Golden Passenger – Psidium's Gal (Psidium) [1992/3 22d⁵ c23f^{pu} 22d 17d] sparely-made mare: poor novice selling hurdler: trained until after third start by T. Hallett, sold 1,000 gns Ascot May Sales: no promise on chasing debut and poor form in points in 1993: blinkered once. *Mrs J. Wonnacott*   c– –

BRYNHILL ALERT   7 ch.g. Croghan Hill – Brynhurst Court (Red Alert) [1992/3 18g] leggy, sparely-made gelding: no form in novice hurdles: sold 1,400 gns Ascot September Sales, resold 4,500 gns Malvern June Sales. *Mrs S. Minns*   –

BUCKANNARA   8 ch.g. Baptism – Penny Maes (Welsh Saint) [1992/3 c16d^F 18d⁴ 24g^{pu}] tall gelding: poor 2m novice hurdler/chaser. *Miss L. A. Perratt*   c– –

BUCK COMTESS (USA)   4 b.f. Spend A Buck (USA) – Comtesse Anne (USA) (Secretariat (USA)) [1992/3 18s 16v⁵ a16g^{ur} 16g 22s⁶] big, rangy filly: second foal: dam won at up to 1½m in France: useful winner at around 1¼m on Flat in France when trained by Mme C. Head: little worthwhile form over hurdles. *J. R. Jenkins*

BUCKELIGHT (IRE)   5 b.g. Buckskin (FR) – Yvonne's Delight (Laurence O) [1992/3 16v 17g⁵ 16g³] smallish, robust gelding: seventh foal: half-brother to winning hurdler/chaser Iron Gray (by General Ironside): dam never ran: easily best effort in novice hurdles when staying-on third in   91

Irish National Novices' Hurdle Series Final, Punchestown—
Bucks-Choice is clear at the last

Mr T. Mullins' "Bucks-Choice"

20-runner event at Worcester in April: will be suited by further than 2m. *Capt. T. A. Forster*

BUCKINGHAM GATE 7 gr.g. Tap On Wood – Place Dauphine (Sea Hawk II) [1992/3 22s³ c20d* c24s³ c24s 21v² 23d⁶] compact, good-bodied gelding: moderate hurdler: won novice handicap chase at Ludlow in December: stays 3m: acts on good to firm and heavy ground: poor jumper of fences. *D. R. Gandolfo* — c91 x / 94

BUCKLE IT UP 8 b.g. Buckskin (FR) – The Hofsa (Varano) [1992/3 c25g² c27d² c25sᵘʳ c24d⁴ c24dᵖᵘ c24sᶠ] leggy gelding: modest chaser: ran creditably on his completed starts in 1992/3: stays 27f: acts on heavy going: blinkered 4 times in 1991/2: amateur ridden: tends to hang. *A. H. Mactaggart* — c84

BUCKNALL GIRL 5 br.m. Town And Country – Dear Jem (Dragonara Palace (USA)) [1992/3 F12d⁵ 17m 18dᵖᵘ] small mare: half-sister to a winner in Sweden and to winning hurdler Dear Miff (by Alias Smith): dam 5f winner at 2 yrs: fifth of 18 in NH Flat race at Windsor: showed little over hurdles. *R. Brotherton* — –

BUCK OWENS 8 ch.g. Buckskin (FR) – Kassina (Laurence O) [1992/3 20g 21s c17g² c27m*] workmanlike gelding: handicap hurdler: won novice chase at Sedgefield in March by 12 lengths: stays 27f: acts on good to firm ground: should improve further over fences. *J. H. Johnson* — c95 p / –

BUCKRA MELLISUGA 9 b.g. Tumble Wind (USA) – Bedouin Dancer (Lorenzaccio) [1992/3 18m³ 16m* 17m² 17m² 18d² 20m³ 17m] smallish, robust gelding: handicap hurdler: won conditional jockeys event at Worcester and ran creditably most other starts early in season: sold privately 3,600 gns in May: effective at 2m and stays 2½m: acts on hard and dead ground: best in blinkers (has found little). *W. A. Stephenson* — 105

BUCKS-CHOICE 6 b.g. Buckskin (FR) – Ursula's Choice (Cracksman) [1992/3 20s* 16v³ 19d* 20v* 19s* 21m 20s⁵ 16d³] big, good-bodied gelding: — 138 chasing type: developed into a very useful novice in 1992/3, winning twice each at Naas and Punchestown: well below his best on firmish ground when seventh in Sun Alliance Novices' Hurdle at Cheltenham in March: reportedly finished very distressed penultimate start and jumped badly when well beaten on last: will stay beyond 2½m: acts on heavy going. *Patrick Mullins, Ireland*

BUCKS COUNTY   9 b. or br.g. Strong Gale – Viva Amore (Red Alert)   c– [1992/3 c17gF c19spu] good-topped gelding: poor maiden pointer: failed to complete in 2 hunter chases. *C. N. Nimmo*

BUCKSHEE BOY   11 ch.g. Buckskin (FR) – Old Hand (Master Owen)   c– [1992/3 c21gF 22d c25d4] lengthy, rather sparely-made gelding: fair 2½m/3m chaser on his day: has lost his form: tried blinkered. *J. Pilkington*

BUCKSHOT (IRE)   5 b.g. Le Moss – Buckfast Lass (Buckskin (FR))   – [1992/3 F18v5 F16v 23f4 22fpu] workmanlike gelding: second foal: dam unraced: no sign of ability in NH Flat races and novice hurdles: trained by G. Eden first outing. *C. N. Williams*

BUCKSKIN CLOVER (IRE)   5 b.g. Buckskin (FR) – Dewy Clover   – (Green Shoon) [1992/3 F16s] smallish gelding: fifth foal: dam maiden Irish hurdler: in rear in NH Flat race at Warwick in February: yet to race over hurdles or fences. *P. Burgoyne*

BUCK THE TREND   7 b.g. Buckskin (FR) – Dawn Rambler (Wrekin   – Rambler) [1992/3 21dF 22dpu 20vpu] angular gelding: poor novice hurdler: sometimes blinkered: sold 1,500 gns Ascot December Sales. *G. Thorner*

BUCK TO   8 b.m. Buckskin (FR) – Laurebon (Laurence O) [1992/3 16gF   – 21mur 21spu] workmanlike, angular mare: little sign of ability. *R. H. Goldie*

BUCKWHEAT LAD (IRE)   5 br.g. Over The River (FR) – Buckwheat   – p Lass (Master Buck) [1992/3 17s] sturdy gelding: first foal: dam unraced: needed race, ran green but showed some ability in novice hurdle at Newcastle in December: sold privately 8,200 gns in May. *W. A. Stephenson*

BUDDINGTON   8 b.g. Celtic Cone – Goolagong (Bargello) [1992/3   c109 c26d2 c27v* c26s* c27v5 c24v2 c26vur] rangy gelding: fair handicap chaser: won at Newton Abbot in November and Folkestone in December: ran creditably fifth start: suited by a thorough test of stamina: acts on heavy ground: sound jumper: suited by forcing tactics: carries head high and sometimes flashes tail under pressure. *Capt. T. A. Forster*

BUDDY HOLLY (NZ)   8 b.g. Leader of The Band (USA) – Annie Day   c95 (NZ) (Battle-Waggon) [1992/3 22d c25g2 c26g4 24f6 c27d* c25dur] compact,   83 workmanlike gelding: poor novice hurdler: moderate handicap chaser: came from behind when winning at Newton Abbot in May: stays 27f: acts on dead ground. *J. A. B. Old*

BUDGET   5 ch.g. Bustino – Australia Fair (AUS) (Without Fear (FR))   – [1992/3 17gpu 20vpu] sparely-made gelding: seems of little account. *A. J. Chamberlain*

BUD'S BET (IRE)   5 b.g. Reasonable (FR) – Pearl Creek (Gulf Pearl)   [1992/3 17g4 16d4 a18g2] compact gelding: modest hurdler: best effort of   93 season when second at Southwell in January: stays 2¼m: acts on dead ground and fibresand. *J. C. McConnochie*

BULLAFORD FAIR   5 b.g. Sergeant Drummer (USA) – Clifton Fair   (Vimadee) [1992/3 F14srtr] third foal: half-brother to 2 poor animals: dam, fair hurdler/chaser, best at distances short of 2½m: blinkered, refused to race in NH Flat race at Market Rasen in April: sold 1,600 gns Doncaster May Sales: yet to race over hurdles or fences. *Mrs A. Swinbank*

BULLANGUERO (IRE)   4 ch.g. Be My Guest (USA) – Timid Bride   (USA) (Blushing Groom (FR)) [1992/3 16g6 17m] 43,000Y: compact gelding: 75 third foal: closely related to fair 1989 2-y-o 6f and 7f winner Kerama (by Glenstal): dam 10.4f winner out of useful 5f and 1m winner Miss Zadig: sixth of 10 finishers in juvenile hurdle at Hexham in October, when trained by J.

FitzGerald: blinkered, behind in similar event at Killarney in May. *M. A. McCullagh, Ireland*

BULLY BOY   10 ch.g. Margouillat (FR) – Chere Madame (Karabas) [1992/3 c20gpu 16f] angular, sparely-made gelding: poor chaser: no worthwhile form since 1989/90, including over hurdles: visored once. *M. D. I. Usher*

c–
–

BULLY PRINGLE   8 b.g. Mr Fordette – Princess Caroline (Red Pins) [1992/3 a22gpu] good-topped gelding: brother to winning Irish jumper Best Vintage and half-brother to another, Bridgetown Lad (by Super Slip): dam unraced: in frame in Irish points in 1990: pulled up in a point and a novice hurdle (reportedly lame) since. *K. White*

–

BUMPTIOUS BOY   9 b.g. Neltino – Bellardita (Derring-Do) [1992/3 c16s4c17dFc16dpu 17g 16dc17m] compact gelding: handicap hurdler: novice chaser: poor form in 1992/3: races only at around 2m: acts on good to firm and dead ground. *A. J. Wilson*

c83
–

BUNDLE OF LUCK   6 ch.m. Touching Wood (USA) – Best Offer (Crepello) [1992/3 22d5 18m4 22d5 17g6 22d3 a20g6] neat mare: poor form over hurdles: stays 2¾m: acts on firm and dead going (ran poorly on equitrack). *K. Bishop*

68

BUONARROTI   6 b.g. Ela-Mana-Mou – Amiel (Nonoalco (USA)) [1992/3 17v3 20v* 21s4 21v2 21v3 21d5 22d6 24g*] strong, lengthy gelding: handicap hurdler: improved form when winning at Ascot in April: successful earlier at Lingfield: suited by a test of stamina: acts on heavy going. *J. A. B. Old*

125

BURFORDS DELIGHT   4 b.f. Idiot's Delight – Lylas Pleasure VII (Pedigree Unknown) [1992/3 F17mF] small non-thoroughbred filly: first foal: dam unraced: behind when falling 4f out in NH Flat race at Cheltenham in April: yet to race over hurdles. *R. Dickin*

BURFORD (USA)   6 ch.g. Time For A Change (USA) – Windrush Lady (USA) (Unconscious (USA)) [1992/3 17v 17v] sparely-made gelding: no form over hurdles. *B. J. Heffernan*

–

BURGOYNE   7 b.g. Ardross – Love Match (USA) (Affiliate (USA)) [1992/3 25g* 25s2 26s2 24v3 25m 24f5]

158 §

Burgoyne was Peter Easterby's sole runner at the Cheltenham National Hunt Festival, bidding to give the trainer his first winner at the meeting since Jobroke in the County Hurdle in 1986. There was hardly a moment, however, when Burgoyne looked like improving on his fourth in the 1992 Stayers' Hurdle, let alone winning—a big disappointment in a campaign which had begun with his promising to progress into a high-class performer. Burgoyne's reappearance at the end of October had brought a win in almost the best possible style, a five-length defeat of the 1992 Stayers' Hurdle winner Nomadic Way in the Tote West Yorkshire Hurdle at Wetherby, Burgoyne looking in fine shape and, in receipt of 7 lb, making virtually every yard, ridden along approaching the second last but never seriously challenged. Four weeks later he produced a performance that was better still, but in a case of endeavour without its due reward, in the Akzo Long Distance Hurdle at Newbury. As at Wetherby, Burgoyne was always either first or second. It was a clear first both entering the straight and at the last, but with half a furlong to travel he began to drift badly left under right-handed driving, carrying Tyrone Bridge, who'd begun to close, with him. At the post, Burgoyne had hung on by a neck but the two horses were on the far rails and it was no surprise when Burgoyne lost the race in the stewards' room, Lorcan Wyer receiving a ban for careless riding. The form shown by Burgoyne, giving 4 lb to Tyrone Bridge with another ten lengths back to Ambuscade, was amongst the best shown by any staying hurdler in Britain or Ireland in 1992/3.

This hard race was an obvious disappointment to his connections and backers, though, and from his record in the remainder of the season one could be forgiven for thinking that it had much the same effect on Burgoyne. His two-and-a-half-length second to Vagog in the Long Walk Hurdle at

Ascot, ridden along at an early stage, was a respectable effort, but from there on the endeavour was more conspicuous from his jockey. Dwyer took the ride in the Long Distance Hurdle on heavy ground at Haydock in January, Maguire in the Stayers' Hurdle at Cheltenham and the Dean Moor Long Distance Hurdle at Haydock on top-of-the-ground, but the outcome was the same, the jockey having to show Burgoyne the whip about a circuit too soon and the partnership finishing well beaten. Blinkers were applied at Cheltenham. A visor had been worn when Burgoyne was below form on his final start in 1991/2.

	Ardross (b 1976)	Run The Gantlet (b 1968)	Tom Rolfe First Feather
Burgoyne (b.g. 1986)		Le Melody (ch 1971)	Levmoss Arctic Melody
	Love Match (USA) (b 1980)	Affiliate (ch 1974)	Unconscious Swinging Doll
		Nanny Tammy (b 1971)	Tim Tam Nandine

Burgoyne, his sire Ardross and dam Love Match all ran for Henry Cecil on the Flat, Burgoyne winning two middle-distance claimers on his only starts as a three-year-old and being claimed for £21,001 to join his present stable, for whom he also ran on the Flat as a four-year-old, but without success. Love Match had two runs at two years, showing fair form in seven-furlong maidens. She is a daughter of the unraced American-bred Nanny Tammy and a granddaughter of the German winner Nandine who was a sister to Neckar and Naxos, German classic winners in the 1950s. Burgoyne is Love Match's second foal, following the staying hurdler/chaser Ard T'Match (also by Ardross), and one of her later produce is Valatch (by Valiyar), a modest winner over a mile and a half yet to get off the mark over hurdles. The rather leggy Burgoyne jumps well and is suited by a thorough test of stamina, acts on soft ground and, as we said earlier, ran poorly on his only starts on top-of-the-ground and heavy. He now looks a very hard ride, needing plenty of driving. A winner on his second start in the 1990/1 season and first time out in both since, let's hope that Burgoyne can regain his enthusiasm in 1993/4. *M. H. Easterby*

Tote West Yorkshire Hurdle, Wetherby—Burgoyne makes all

BURGUNDY BOY 9 ch.g. Black Minstrel – Miss Hi-Land (Tyrant (USA)) [1992/3 c17dF c21d4 c16gur c16d3 c16vpu c21dF] tall gelding: winning hurdler: easily best effort in novice chases when third at Nottingham in November: suffered a fatal fall at Wetherby in February: was effective at 2m and stayed 21f: acted on heavy going. *A. P. Jarvis*   c95 –

BURLINGTON SAM (NZ) 5 b.g. Veloso (NZ) – Bees Knees (NZ) (Bardall (NZ)) [1992/3 F17m] angular New Zealand-bred gelding: ran green when in mid-division in NH Flat race at Cheltenham in April: yet to race over hurdles or fences. *D. H. Barons*   –

BURN BRIDGE (USA) 7 b.g. Linkage (USA) – Your Nuts (USA) (Creme Dela Creme) [1992/3 16f4 18d* 17f6 17m2 18g2 16d5 20d4 20d 17d] lightly-made gelding: moderate hurdler: won seller at Cartmel (bought in 5,000 gns) in August: sold out of M. Hammond's stable 1,550 gns Doncaster March Sales after eighth start, ran poorly final 2: stays 2½m: acts on any ground: often blinkered, visored once. *T. H. Caldwell*   98

BURNDITCH GIRL 7 ch.m. Raga Navarro (ITY) – Queen of The Nile (Hittite Glory) [1992/3 17g] sparely-made mare: 2m novice hurdler: little worthwhile form. *Mrs N. S. Sharpe*   –

BURNET 8 b.g. Be My Guest (USA) – Burghclere (Busted) [1992/3 c21m* c20m* c23gur] good-bodied gelding: maiden hurdler: won novice chases at Worcester and Market Rasen in August: unseated rider second later in month, and wasn't seen out again: stays 2¾m: acts on dead and good to firm ground. *T. P. McGovern*   c95 –

BURSANA 7 b.m. Burslem – Lady of Surana (Shirley Heights) [1992/3 17d 16g2 17m 20d6] sparely-made mare: moderate handicap hurdler: good second at Worcester in April: tailed off both subsequent starts: form only at 2m: acts on good to firm and dead ground: sometimes carries head high under pressure. *J. L. Spearing*   91

BUSHFIRE MOON 5 ch.g. Julio Mariner – Flea Pit (Sir Lark) [1992/3 20g 23dpu 22vpu] angular gelding: half-brother to winning hurdler/chaser Mrs Peopleater (by Ancient Monro): poor maiden on Flat: no form in novice hurdles. *N. A. Twiston-Davies*   –

BUSHTUCKER 5 ch.g. Say Primula – Kerosa (Keren) [1992/3 17m 22mpu] fourth foal: half-brother to novice hurdler Greenfield Manor (by Move Off): dam well beaten in 2 races on Flat: no sign of ability in novice hurdles in March and May. *Miss S. J. Turner*   –

BUSMAN (IRE) 4 ch.g. Be My Guest (USA) – Cistus (Sun Prince) [1992/3 17s2 16s6] close-coupled, sparely-made gelding: half-brother to ungenuine winning hurdler Celcius (by Ile de Bourbon): fair 1¼mm winner on Flat in 1992: sold out of R. Hern's stable 13,500 gns Newmarket Autumn Sales: second in juvenile hurdle at Newbury in November: well below that form only subsequent start (January). *W. R. Muir*   93

BUSTED ROCK 8 b.h. Busted – Mexican Two Step (Gay Fandango (USA)) [1992/3 17g6 17d3] angular horse: half-brother to winning hurdler Mexican Vision (by Vision): tough, genuine and quite useful 1¼m to 1½m handicapper on Flat: better effort in novice hurdles when third at Doncaster in December: finished lame and has been retired to stud. *Mrs L. Piggott*   104

BUSTED SPRING 12 b.g. Crash Course – Rose of Spring (Golden Vision) [1992/3 c24mpu] big, strong gelding: one-time quite useful hunter chaser: pulled up lame only outing in 1993: stays 3m: probably acts on any going: poor jumper. *Miss I. Dady*   c– x

BUSTINELLO (IRE) 5 br.g. Bustineto – Rich Belle (Goldhill) [1992/3 22g 16g] third foal: brother to a bad animal: dam unraced half-sister to winning hurdler/staying chaser Greenore Pride: won a point in Ireland in February: better effort in novice hurdles in April when eighth of 20 at Worcester on last start: should prove suited by further than 2m. *F. Murphy*   76

BUSTLING AROUND 6 b.m. Bustino – Waltz (Jimmy Reppin) [1992/3 17dpu 16dpu 16s 16d5 17d6 16s 17s5 c16vF c16s4 c16spu] leggy mare: poor novice hurdler/chaser. *J. R. Bosley*   c70 70

BUSTONIAN 7 br.g. Bustineto – Andonian (Road House II) [1992/3 18s^{pu} 17v^{pu} a16g^6 c16s^{pu} c17m^{pu} 17v^4] sturdy, lengthy gelding: sold 2,000 gns Ascot November Sales: poor novice hurdler/chaser: resold 2,100 gns Ascot May Sales. *C. L. Popham*
  c–
  –

BUSTON KING 8 b.g. Lafontaine (USA) – King's Chase (King's Leap) [1992/3 17m^2 23g^F 17s] tall, leggy gelding: lightly-raced poor novice hurdler: should prove suited by further than 17f. *Major W. N. Sample*
  70

BUSY BOY 6 b.g. Dominion – Baidedones (Welsh Pageant) [1992/3 23s^3 24v^2 23d^{bd} 20d^4 25d^2 21s^4 28g^5] compact gelding: novice hurdler: best effort when second at Ayr in January on fifth outing: suited by 3m: yet to race on top-of-the-ground. *R. R. Lamb*
  91

BUTLERS PET 14 b.g. Mummy's Pet – Reluctant Maid (Relko) [1992/3 21d^{pu} c21v^3 c18d^5 c18g^5] rangy gelding: moderate chaser at best: well beaten in 1992/3: pulled up in selling hurdle first outing: stays 2¼m: acts on any going: blinkered once: has looked irresolute. *T. B. Hallett*
  c–
  –

BUTTON BOX 7 ch.m. Horage – Arriva (USA) (Disciplinarian) [1992/3 22s^{pu} 22d^{pu} 20f^3 16d 17s^{pu}] angular mare: third of 4 finishers in novice hurdle at Taunton in October, only form: blinkered last 3 starts. *A. Barrow*
  67

BUZBOUR 5 ch.g. Kabour – Mrs Buzby (Abwah) [1992/3 16d^{pu}] leggy, workmanlike gelding: won 6f claimer on Flat in January: claimed out of D. Chapman's stable £3,201 following month: tailed off when pulled up in novice event in February on hurdling debut. *D. J. Wintle*
  –

BUZZARDS CREST 8 ch.g. Buzzards Bay – Diamond Talk (Counsel) [1992/3 16m 16s^{pu} 16v^{pu}] close-coupled gelding: very lightly raced and no form over hurdles. *Bob Jones*
  –

BWANA KALI 11 b.g. Kala Shikari – Modom (Compensation) [1992/3 20g^{pu}] close-coupled gelding: poor hurdler/novice chaser: best form at around 2m on a sound surface: visored once in 1991/2. *J. A. Bennett*
  c–
  –

BWANA SIMBA 8 b.g. Mljet – Uzuri (Cagirama) [1992/3 17d 27d^F 25d^{pu}] stocky gelding: no sign of ability. *J. K. M. Oliver*
  c–
  –

BY FAR (USA) 7 b.m. Far North (CAN) – Countess Babu (USA) (Bronze Babu) [1992/3 17m^3 22g^4 16s^6 17v 16s^F a16g^F 20g^3 17g^5 20d^{pu}] leggy, sparely-made mare: modest hurdler: poor efforts last 2 outings, generally ran creditably earlier: stays 2¾m: acts on any going: usually held up: sketchy jumper. *O. O'Neill*
  93

BY THE BYE 6 ch.m. Bybicello – Reel Keen (Firestreak) [1992/3 27d^{pu}] third foal: sister to quite useful staying hurdler Fettucine: dam placed in 7f seller at 2 yrs: tailed off when pulled up in amateurs novice hurdle at Kelso in April. *R. R. Lamb*
  –

BYZANTINE 5 b.g. Damister (USA) – Rustle of Silk (General Assembly (USA)) [1992/3 20m^4 18m* 16f* 17d^{pu} 18g^3 16d^6 16g 17g 17m^3 21g^3 17f^4] tall gelding: modest form over hurdles: won novice events at Sedgefield and Uttoxeter early in season: creditable efforts when placed afterwards: probably stays 2 1f: acts well on firm ground: usually visored or blinkered. *G. Richards*
  88 +

C

CABBIE'S BOY 7 ch.g. Dublin Taxi – Petriva (Mummy's Pet) [1992/3 c21m^6 c16m^5 c16g^{pu}] tall gelding: of little account: blinkered once. *R. E. Barr*
  c–
  –

CABIN HILL 7 ch.g. Roselier (FR) – Bluejama (Windjammer (USA)) [1992/3 17m^3 17m 20g^4] smallish, strong gelding: moderate hurdler: retained 3,600 gns Ascot September Sales: should stay beyond 2½m: best efforts on dead going. *S. Christian*
  88

CABOCHON 6 b.g. Jalmood (USA) – Lightning Legacy (USA) (Super Concorde (USA)) [1992/3 17s^2 22d^5 17s* 16d* 16g^3 26m 20d^4] lengthy
  127

Mr Jack Joseph's "Cabochon"

gelding: fair stayer on Flat: sold out of D. Morley's stable 17,000 gns
Newmarket Autumn Sales: useful novice hurdler: successful at Ascot and
Ludlow and ran well when in frame at Kempton and Ascot in second half of
season: should stay beyond 2½m: acts on soft going: front runner. *R. G.
Frost*

CAB ON TARGET   7 br.g. Strong Gale – Smart Fashion (Carlburg)   **c154** p
[1992/3 c20g* c22s* c20d* c20g² c25f* c20g*]   –
    The case for Cab On Target grows ever more formidable. He's looked a
cracking chasing prospect since his early days as a novice hurdler and, on
the evidence of his first season over fences, he has the potential to go right
to the top. He was the pick of the season's staying novice chasers and has
most of the qualities we look for in a potential Gold Cup winner. Cab On
Target faced his stiffest cross-examination in the Mumm Mildmay Chase at
Aintree in April, up against, principally, the Sun Alliance Chase winner
Young Hustler and the very useful Forest Sun. He put them both firmly in
their place, winning most impressively by twelve lengths and six from
Forest Sun and a below-par Young Hustler, moving smoothly throughout
and gaining ground at most of his fences; time may show that even a top-
form Young Hustler would have faced a well-nigh impossible task conceding
6 lb to Cab On Target. Cab On Target's winning time was a record for the
course and distance, over four seconds inside the existing one put up only
the previous day by Docklands Express in the Martell Cup Chase. The very
firm going at Aintree had reportedly caused Cab On Target's connections
some heart-searching before they decided to let him take his chance. Cab
On Target showed he'd come to no harm when following up in the valuable
Edinburgh Woollen Mill's Future Champion Novices' Chase at Ayr a

Forgive'N Forget Novices' Chase, Doncaster—Cab On Target goes clear from Dusty Miller

fortnight later, when he didn't need to run to anything like his best to win comfortably by eight lengths from Persian House. That victory took his racing record to thirteen wins in sixteen races since he made his debut in a National Hunt Flat race at Kelso as a four-year-old.

The latest Gold Cup winner Jodami also made his debut—a successful one like Cab On Target's—in a National Hunt Flat race at Kelso in the 1989/90 season. Both progressed very well in novice hurdles the next

Mumm Mildmay Novices' Chase, Aintree—
Cab On Target shows himself a high-class novice chaser;
Young Hustler and Better Times Ahead (grey) try to keep tabs,
eventual second Forest Sun is just behind

season, Cab On Target remaining unbeaten until the White Satin Novices' Hurdle at Aintree where, taking on some of the season's best staying novices, he managed only seventh, giving the impression that twenty-five furlongs on softish ground may have overtaxed his stamina at that stage, though he had also been off the course for two and a half months. Whilst Jodami was sent chasing in 1991/2—and took high rank among that season's new recruits—Cab On Target was kept over hurdles. He had another interrupted campaign, this time not being seen out after his only defeat in four starts, by Forest Sun when odds on in the Rendlesham Hurdle at Kempton in February. By that time, however, Cab On Target had shown himself a good-class hurdler, picking up the West Yorkshire Hurdle over three miles at Wetherby, the Newbury Long Distance Hurdle over a more testing three miles, and the Spa Hurdle over two and a half at Cheltenham.

Cab On Target has been unlucky with illnesses and injuries in his time and he missed the Cheltenham Festival again in the latest season. He suffered an overreach when beaten at odds on in a novice chase at Stratford in early-March, an outing intended to tune him up for his Festival target, reportedly more likely to have been the Cathcart Challenge Cup than the Sun Alliance Chase. The Stratford race itself—in which Cab On Target was beaten eight lengths by Bibendum—was Cab On Target's first since mid-December. He'd been kept off the course first by a punctured sole and then by a throat infection. His first three races over fences had all produced impressive victories. A highly satisfactory debut at Ayr in November, achieving a simple task without coming off the bridle, was followed by another facile success at Nottingham later the same month. Cab On Target jumped well in both races, looking an excellent recruit to steeplechasing. His first real test came in the Forgive'N Forget Novices' Chase at Doncaster where he was opposed by Dusty Miller, a useful hurdler who also seemed likely to make a major impact over fences, judged on a comfortable success in a fairly strong novice chase at Newbury in November. Cab On Target and Dusty Miller had the Forgive'N Forget Chase to themselves

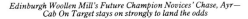

Edinburgh Woollen Mill's Future Champion Novices' Chase, Ayr—
Cab On Target stays on strongly to land the odds

from the home turn until Cab On Target asserted himself going to the last for an impressive ten-length victory. Even at this stage Cab On Target seemed sure to take high rank among the season's novice chasers and appeared a most exciting prospect, looking even further ahead. The very genuine Cab On Target jumps fences extremely well and isn't beholden to the state of the going. He stays twenty-five furlongs well, but is by no means short of speed and is effective at two and a half miles. If he keeps clear of illness and injury he looks bound to have a big say in the destination of the staying steeplechasers' championship. If he were ours he'd be aimed at the King George VI Chase—a race tailor-made for him—as well as the Cheltenham Gold Cup.

Cab On Target (br.g. 1986)	Strong Gale (br 1975)	Lord Gayle (b 1965)	Sir Gaylord
			Sticky Case
		Sterntau (br 1969)	Tamerlane
			Sterna
	Smart Fashion (b 1976)	Carlburg (b 1964)	Crepello
			Bacchanalia
		Smart Money (b 1964)	Even Money
			Intelligence

The lengthy Cab On Target, very much a chasing type on looks, is by Strong Gale who has proved himself a top-class sire of jumpers, especially chasers. He sires winners throughout the distance range. At the latest Cheltenham Festival, for example, three of his offspring were successful—Travado in the Arkle Chase over two miles, Gaelstrom in the Sun Alliance Novices' Hurdle over two miles five furlongs and Strong Beau in the Fulke Walwyn Kim Muir Chase over three miles one furlong. The Queen Mother Champion Chase winner Katabatic and the Hennessy Gold Cup winner Sibton Abbey are among the other notable steeplechasers sired by Strong Gale who looks set to take over the star role in National Hunt breeding from

Mrs J. G. Fulton's "Cab On Target"

the deceased Deep Run. Strong Gale, who stands at the Rathbarry Stud in County Cork, sired the winners of 96 races and over £479,000 in Britain in the latest season when he finished runner-up in the sires' table to Deep Run. He'd finished runner-up in 1990/1 and third in 1991/2. Cab On Target's dam the bumper winner Smart Fashion, who was also placed over hurdles and in point-to-points, has bred one other winner so far, the fair chaser Strong Approach, a year-older full brother to Cab On Target, who is also versatile so far as distance goes. He is effective at two miles when conditions are testing and stays three miles well. Smart Fashion, a full sister to the very smart staying chaser Everett, was bred for stamina, by Carlburg, a fair performer on the Flat who needed long distances, out of the lightly-raced maiden Smart Money, the product of a mating between the highly successful sire of jumpers Even Money and the winning stayer Intelligence. *Mrs M. Reveley*

CACHE FLEUR (FR)   7 ch.g. Kashneb (FR) – Blanche Fleur (FR) (Mont Blanc II) [1992/3 c21d3 c26s5 c24v* c25d3 c21g4 c25m4] leggy gelding: quite useful chaser: won conditional jockeys handicap at Kempton in January: ran creditably next and final outings: stays 25f: acts on good to firm and heavy ground: blinkered nowadays: poor jumper. *M. C. Pipe*   c129 x –

CADDLESTOWN   9 b. or br.g. Derring Rose – Quick Romance (Lucky Brief) [1992/3 c25dF 23dF 17gpu] well-made gelding: lightly-raced novice hurdler: fell eighth on chasing debut: sketchy jumper. *D. McCain*   c– –

CADDY   12 ch.g. Candy Cane – Maddy (George Spelvin (USA)) [1992/3 c24fur] small, sturdy gelding: handicap chaser: unseated rider third in October: stays 3m: acts on any going. *S. Christian*   c– –

CADENCY   5 b.g. Teenoso (USA) – Mullet (Star Appeal) [1992/3 17s4 17g2 17g* 17g6] small, sturdy gelding: fairly useful handicap hurdler: won at Huntingdon in October: not raced after following month: races only at around 2m: unsuited by testing conditions: pulls hard, and is usually held up. *M. H. Tompkins*   121

CADFORD BALARINA   6 ch.m. Adonijah – Jarama (Amber Rama (USA)) [1992/3 17d5 22spu 22v a20g6 a22gF] compact mare: poor maiden plater over hurdles: blinkered once, visored last 2 starts. *Mrs P. M. Joynes*   –

CADOLIVE   5 b.m. Royal Vulcan – Cissac (Indian Ruler) [1992/3 21v 22vpu 21v3 22m] leggy mare: half-sister to 5f winner Tou Fou (by Royben) and winning 2m hurdler Don Jacobo (by Neltino): dam of little account: no form over hurdles. *G. A. Ham*   –

CAETANI   9 b.g. Busted – Spring In Rome (USA) (Forli (ARG)) [1992/3 18d3 22g2 25spu 17m] sturdy, dipped-backed gelding: poor novice hurdler: stays 2¾m: acts on dead ground. *M. W. Easterby*   81

CAHERVILLAHOW   9 b. or br.g. Deep Run – Bargara (Bargello) [1992/3 c25g5 c25sF c20s4 c24d2 c26v c24d5 c27s3 c27m c30d3] workmanlike gelding: smart chaser at best nowadays: second to General Idea in valuable event at Leopardstown in December, best effort of 1992/3: soundly beaten in Tote Cheltenham Gold Cup in March on eighth start, fair third in Whitbread Gold Cup at Sandown on final one: close second to Esha Ness in void Grand National: suited by test of stamina: acts on any going: blinkered 3 times, including on seventh and eighth starts: sketchy jumper. *M. F. Morris, Ireland*   c154 –

CAHIROWEN   10 b.g. Derring Rose – Dawn Goddess (St Chad) [1992/3 18dpu] quite good-topped ex-Irish gelding: winning hurdler/chaser: pulled up lame in November: stays 2½m: acts on heavy going. *C. R. Beever*   c– –

CAIPIRINHA (IRE)   5 br.m. Strong Gale – Arctic Moonshine (Arctic Slave) [1992/3 F17g] half-sister to 4 winning jumpers: dam dead-heated in maiden hurdle: mid-division in 18-runner NH Flat race at Doncaster in January: yet to race over hurdles or fences. *S. Christian*   –

Peregrine Handicap Chase, Ascot—Calapaez leads Strong Approach, the pair well clear

CAIRNCASTLE 8 b.g. Ardross – Brookfield Miss (Welsh Pageant) [1992/3 22m⁴ 24g* 27d* 24g³ 23d* 26d² 22d³ 24v⁵ 26m] small, leggy gelding: fair handicap hurdler: won at Worcester, Newton Abbot and Stratford in first half of season, below form both outings in second half: refused on only outing over fences: stays very well: acts on hard and dead ground: below form in blinkers. *C. R. Barwell*   c– 114

CAIRNEYMOUNT 7 b.g. Croghan Hill – Glentoran Valley (Little Buskins) [1992/3 21g⁶ 22d c24gpu c21gur c20m³ c24dpu] good-topped gelding: poor novice hurdler/chaser: form only at around 2½m, should stay further: acts on good to firm ground: sold 3,300 gns Ascot June Sales. *J. A. C. Edwards*   c75 75

CAITHNESS CLOUD 5 ch.h. Lomond (USA) – Moonscape (Ribero) [1992/3 16gur 16g⁴ 16g²] angular horse: half-brother to fairly useful hurdler Lemhill (by He Loves Me): fair 1½m winner on Flat at 3 yrs: moderate novice hurdler: not raced after February: will stay beyond 2m: has raced only on good ground. *C. Parker*   93

CAITHNESS PRINCE 7 b.g. Prince Tenderfoot (USA) – Lavenham Rose (Floribunda) [1992/3 16g³ 17spu 16g⁵ 17d* 22dpu 17d] sturdy, lengthy gelding: chasing type: won novice hurdle at Carlisle in February: poor efforts afterwards: should stay beyond 17f: acts on dead ground. *C. Parker*   88

CAITHNESS ROCK 4 ch.g. Ballad Rock – Thessaloniki (Julio Mariner) [1992/3 17m³ 17m⁶ 16g⁵ 16d 16d⁵ 17mpu] close-coupled gelding: poor maiden on Flat (trained by M. Jarvis) and over hurdles: dead. *C. Parker*   76

CA-KNOWE (IRE) 4 b.f. Coquelin (USA) – Tumble Ria (Tumble Wind (USA)) [1992/3 17s 18d 16dur] angular filly: second foal: half-sister to plater Stane Street (by Gorytus), winner on Flat and over hurdles: dam, winner in Belgium, half-sister to Kribensis: little sign of ability over hurdles. *A. C. Whillans*   –

CALABRESE 8 ch.g. Monsanto (FR) – Salsafy (Tudor Melody) [1992/3 c19v* c25s³ c20sur 24s 22s c27m³ c25f³] smallish, leggy, lengthy gelding: fairly useful chaser nowadays: won handicap at Hereford in November: below form last 4 starts, including over hurdles: effective at around 2½m in   c123 –

134

very testing conditions and stays very well: needs give in the ground: blinkered nowadays: races up with pace: not an accomplished jumper. *N. J. Henderson*

CALAPAEZ 9 gr.g. Nishapour (FR) – Charter Belle (Runnymede) [1992/3 16g⁴ c21v* c21s* c21d² c20s² c21v² c25d² c24g c20s* c21g²] big, leggy, workmanlike gelding: useful hurdler/chaser: successful over fences in handicap at Plumpton and minor event at Kempton in November, and handicap at Ascot in March: good second in valuable race at Cheltenham final outing: effective from 2½m to 3m: acts on any going: usually held up: blinkered once: consistent. *Miss B. Sanders* **c131** 131

CALICON 7 ch.g. Connaught – Calgary (Run The Gantlet (USA)) [1992/3 16d² 16vᵖᵘ] tall, angular gelding: useful hurdler: second in minor event at Warwick in October: ran poorly 3 months later: sold only 1,100 gns Ascot June Sales: will stay further than 2m: acts on firm and dead ground. *I. A. Balding* 130 ?

CALLABAWN 6 ch.g. Callernish – Meelabawn (Abednego) [1992/3 25gᶠ] lengthy gelding: first foal: dam never ran: well behind when falling in novice hurdle in March. *L. Lungo* –

CALLAS ELECTRIC 6 b.m. Deep Run – La Flamenca (Brave Invader (USA)) [1992/3 22sᵘʳ 20g 22s⁵ 22d⁴ 23d² 26g³ 22f² 23mᵇᵈ] workmanlike mare: modest novice hurdler: stayed well: acted on firm and dead going: dead. *D. Nicholson* 91

CALLEROSE 6 b.g. Callernish – Tarqogan's Rose (Tarqogan) [1992/3 22v³] workmanlike gelding: chasing type: poor novice hurdler, lightly raced: staying type: acts on heavy going. *Capt. T. A. Forster* 65

CALL HOME (IRE) 5 b.g. Callernish – Easter Beauty (Raise You Ten) [1992/3 F16f* F17m*] useful-looking gelding with scope: third foal: half-brother to useful chaser Flashthecash (by Torus): dam unraced: won NH Flat races at Wincanton in March and Cheltenham in April: yet to race over hurdles or fences. *J. T. Gifford*

CALL KENTONS 7 ch.g. Ovac (ITY) – South Park (Sandford Lad) [1992/3 16g² 16g] close-coupled gelding: poor novice hurdler: sold out of J. FitzGerald's stable 2,300 gns Doncaster November Sales after first start: not raced after following month: should stay beyond 2m: acts on good to firm ground. *D. A. Nolan* 72

CALL ME DICKINS 4 gr.g. Rusticaro (FR) – Bad Start (USA) (Bold Bidder) [1992/3 17d] well beaten on Flat and in novice hurdle in February: sold 1,500 gns Ascot 2nd June Sales. *R. Hollinshead* –

CALL ME EARLY 8 ch.g. Callernish – Mi Na Meala (Party Mink) [1992/3 c16m⁴ c21g⁵ c25d² c22sᵘʳ c26sᵘʳ] big, lengthy, good-topped gelding: moderate handicap chaser: not raced after December: stays 25f: acts on heavy ground: tends to jump to the right. *B. S. Rothwell* **c90**

CALLYR 6 b.h. Julio Mariner – Midnight Pansy (Deadly Nightshade) [1992/3 F16v⁶ F16s³ 21d] tall, leggy horse: half-brother to several winners, notably useful hurdlers Jimsintime and Jimbalou (both by Jimsun): dam placed over hurdles: third in NH Flat race in February: well beaten in novice hurdle following month. *R. G. Brazington* –

CALMATA 12 br.m. Dubassoff (USA) – Raging Calm (Salvo) [1992/3 c17vᵖᵘ c26dᵖᵘ c21g c25sᵖᵘ c20gᵖᵘ c21g⁴ c20f⁵ c25m² c18mᶠ] lengthy mare: poor novice chaser: suited by test of stamina: best efforts on a sound surface. *Lady Ann Bowlby* **c85** –

CALORA (USA) 6 b.m. Private Account (USA) – Cristalina (FR) (Green Dancer (USA)) [1992/3 c21s⁵ c16d c21dᵖᵘ c18vᵖᵘ 21v⁶ c17v 17s] sturdy ex-French mare: half-sister to 3 winners, notably Chatam (by Big Spruce): dam 1m winner: winning hurdler/chaser: no form in 1992/3: stays 19f: blinkered fourth to sixth starts. *Martyn Meade* **c–** –

CAL'S BOY 4 b.g. Green Ruby (USA) – Green Gypsy (Creetown) [1992/3 16sᵖᵘ] tall, close-coupled gelding: poor maiden on Flat: showed little in juvenile hurdle in January. *J. P. Smith* –

CAMBO (USA) 7 b.g. Roberto (USA) – Cameo Shore (Mill Reef (USA)) [1992/3 16d* 20d3 17v 22s6 16g2 17s2 22d* 22m5] compact gelding: won novice handicap hurdles at Haydock in November and Sedgefield in April: effective at 2m and stays 2¾m: acts on good to firm and soft ground, well beaten on heavy. *M. C. Banks*   95

CAMDEN BELLE 11 gr.m. Camden Town – Haut Lafite (Tamerlane) [1992/3 c21d6 c27vpu c21g3 c25f3 c25g5] tall, workmanlike mare: shows traces of stringhalt: moderate chaser: stays 3m: acts on firm and dead ground: sometimes wears tongue strap: inconsistent. *M. P. Muggeridge*   c92 –

CAMDEN GROVE 5 b.m. Uncle Pokey – Camden (David Jack) [1992/3 17dF 18g4] lengthy, unfurnished mare: has shown little over hurdles. *R. McDonald*   –

CAMDEN KNIGHT 8 b.g. Camden Town – Motionless (Midsummer Night II) [1992/3 21dpu 16v 16s 22dpu 20g3] leggy gelding: winning hurdler: form in 1992/3 only when blinkered in seller final start: stays 2½m: acts on dead ground. *N. Bycroft*   83

CAMDORE BOY 13 b.g. Anax – Paddy's Daughter (St Paddy) [1992/3 16m] compact gelding: lightly-raced selling hurdler: stays 2½m. *R. Lee*   –

CAME DOWN 10 gr.g. Nearly A Hand – Bellentina (Rugantino) [1992/3 c16s5 c18d4 c16d5 c26vpu c17f* c16f3] big gelding: modest chaser: won 2-finisher handicap at Chepstow in March: best at around 2m: acts on any going: inconsistent. *R. J. Hodges*   c96 § –

CAMELOT KNIGHT 7 br.g. King's Ride – Jeanette Marie (Fighting Don) [1992/3 c21s* c24s* c26v2 c25s5 c21d c22vpu c26m3] tall, leggy gelding: maiden hurdler: much better over fences, and won novice events at Newton Abbot and Kempton in first half of season: creditable efforts when placed afterwards: sold to join N. Twiston-Davies 35,000 gns Ascot June Sales: suited by good test of stamina: acts on heavy and good to firm ground: jumps soundly in the main. *Miss H. C. Knight*   c112 –

CAMPSEA-ASH 9 gr.g. Rusticaro (FR) – Lady d'Arbanville (FR) (Luthier) [1992/3 17f4 c17g4 c16g2 c17d3 c16d2] big, lengthy gelding: has been hobdayed: fairly useful handicap chaser: best effort of season when second at Ascot on third start: not raced after November: best at 2m: best form on a sound surface: tends to wander under pressure and has found little. *F. Murphy*   c128 –

CANAAN VALLEY 5 ch.g. Absalom – My Pink Parrot (Pirate King) [1992/3 18m3 18m6] lengthy gelding: poor performer on Flat nowadays: poor form in early-season events over hurdles: pulls hard (wears net muzzle): sold 2,500 gns Doncaster November Sales. *J. G. FitzGerald*   72

CANAL STREET 4 b.f. Oats – Murex (Royalty) [1992/3 F16v6 F16g3] first foal: dam won 2 NH Flat races: third of 21 in mares NH Flat race at Worcester in March: yet to race over hurdles. *P. J. Hobbs*   –

CANBRACK (IRE) 4 b.g. Glenstal (USA) – Cottage Style (Thatch (USA)) [1992/3 18dpu] plating-class maiden on Flat: behind when pulled up in juvenile hurdle in November: sold 2,200 gns in May. *W. A. Stephenson*   –

CANCALE (IRE) 5 b.g. Strong Gale – Ginosa (Kalamoun) [1992/3 F16s F16s 17g] fourth foal: half-brother to a Flat winner in Italy by Burslem: dam middle-distance Flat maiden: well beaten in NH Flat races: showed a little ability in novice hurdle at Taunton in April. *C. L. Popham*   74

CANDLE GLOW 5 ch.m. Capitano – Fused Light (Fury Royal) [1992/3 22s4 21vpu a18gpu 22d 17g4 18g5 17m2] small, rather sparely-made mare: poor novice hurdler: sold 3,400 gns Ascot June Sales: stays 2¾m: acts on soft and good to firm ground. *Mrs F. Walwyn*   73

CANDLE KING (IRE) 5 b.g. Tender King – Candelaria (FR) (Touch Paper) [1992/3 17g3 17g* 17g 17sF 16g3 17m3 17d 16g a18g5 a18gpu a16g3 a18g3 16g2 17f4] sparely-made gelding: modest miler at best on Flat: poor form over hurdles: won seller at Hereford (sold out of M. Fetherston-Godley's stable 3,200 gns) in August: inconsistent afterwards: yet to race   72 beyond 2¼m: acts on good to firm, soft going and equitrack: blinkered second and last 2 outings. *H. J. Manners*

CANDY TUFF   7 b.g. Candy Cane – Pixelated (Mon Capitaine) [1992/3 c21s² c25g* c25s* c25d²] leggy, angular gelding: fair hurdler: won novice chases at Ayr and Wetherby in January: creditable second in quite valuable event at Ayr later in month: effective at around 2½m and stays 25f: has won on firm going but possibly best with give in the ground: not yet an accomplished jumper of fences: sometimes sweats. *Mrs M. Reveley*   **c110**
–

CANNING'S COLLEGE   7 b.m. Sunyboy – Only Members (New Member) [1992/3 16d 20m 22dᵖᵘ 23m⁴ 20f 21f²] tall mare: poor novice hurdler: stays 23f: acts on firm ground. *R. Hawker*   77

CANNY CHRONICLE   5 b. or br.g. Daring March – Laisser Aller (Sagaro) [1992/3 17m³ 16f 16f⁵] lengthy gelding: very useful juvenile hurdler in 1991/2: long way below form in 1992/3: likely to prove best at around 2m on a sharp track: best form on good going. *M. H. Tompkins*   –

CANON CLASS   12 b.g. The Parson – Pallatess (Pall Mall) [1992/3 c24m⁵ c23f² c24gᵘʳ c22d* c24f³] sturdy gelding: handicap chaser: won amateurs event at Towcester in October: finds 2½m on short side and stays 3m: acts on any going. *D. Nicholson*   **c90**
–

CANOSCAN   8 ch.g. Grey Ghost – Canny's Tudor (Tudor Cliff) [1992/3 c21g⁴] rangy, workmanlike gelding: winning hurdler: little promise in novice chases, including October: best form at 2m: acts on soft going: blinkered nowadays: tail swisher. *Lady Herries*   **c–**
–

CANOWINDRA   8 ch.m. Pony Express – Irish Flo (Cassanant) [1992/3 16vᵖᵘ 21sᵖᵘ 17mF 22dᵖᵘ 20mF 16dᵖᵘ] sturdy mare: of no account: blinkered twice. *C. H. Jones*   –

CAN'T DISCLOSE   12 b.g. Bonne Noel – Lady Aylmer (Nice Guy) [1992/3 c23d⁵ c21g⁸ c20d³ c24dᵖᵘ c19vᵘʳ c18m⁵ 27g] lengthy, good-quartered gelding: winning hurdler: poor novice chaser: stays 3m: acts on   **c79**
–

Culroy Novices' Chase, Ayr—not foot perfect, but Candy Tuff is clear

firm and dead ground: usually blinkered or visored: sketchy jumper. *Miss H. C. Knight*

CANTGETOUT 7 b.m. Furry Glen – Brave Light (Brave Invader (USA))   **c70**
[1992/3 c24m⁴ c21gᵖᵘ c21s⁴ c25s⁶ c17d⁵ c21d⁴ c21g⁵] poor novice   **–**
hurdler/chaser: stays 27f: acts on soft going: blinkered once. *Mrs S. J. Smith*

CANTORIS FRATER 6 ch.g. Brotherly (USA) – Decoyanne (Decoy
Boy) [1992/3 18d³ 16v⁶ 20d] lengthy, unfurnished gelding: poor novice   **82**
hurdler: should stay beyond 2¼m (stiff task at 2½m in February): probably
acts on heavy going. *P. J. Hobbs*

CAPABILITY BROWN 6 b.g. Dominion – Tomfoolery (Silly Season)   **c137** p
[1992/3 24v³ 22d c23v* c20v* c24vF* c25d* c25mᵘʳ]   **137**
   'M. Pipe's selected' is a safe long-range tip nowadays for the Coral
Welsh National. The stable has won the race four times in the last five
seasons—with Bonanza Boy (twice), Carvill's Hill and Run For Free—and
its four runners in the latest edition filled the first four places. Capability
Brown, the stable's best staying novice chaser in the latest season, looks
just the type for the Welsh National, a tough, front runner who should stay
all day. Front runners do well at undulating Chepstow where there are five
fences in the straight, the first part of which is downhill. Capability Brown
gained an extraordinary victory when favourite in a novice chase on the
track in January. He ran his rivals into the ground and was clear when falling
at the third last; his rider Scudamore had time to remount and set off again
still in front for a thirty-length victory over second favourite Rufus, Capability Brown surviving another blunder at the last.
   Capability Brown was a useful staying hurdler before having his atten-
tions turned to steeplechasing after his first two races in the latest season.
An impressive debut at Worcester in January was followed by a comfortable
victory at Haydock a little over a fortnight later in a qualifier in the Steel
Plate And Sections Young Chasers series. Capability Brown jumped boldly
and accurately in both races, though he nearly came down at the first at

*Aspiring Champions Novices' Chase, Chepstow—
second success in four days for Capability Brown*

Reynoldstown Novices' Chase, Ascot—
Capability Brown has Channels Gate for company at the fourth last

Haydock when slipping awkwardly on landing. The victory at Chepstow followed three days after Haydock, and Capability Brown was out again the next week at Ascot where he was one of only four runners in the valuable Reynoldstown Chase. The Reynoldstown, a Grade 2 event, was effectively a two-horse race between Capability Brown and another very useful recruit to chasing Dakyns Boy, successful in four of his five races over fences up to that time, including the Tripleprint Feltham Novices' Chase at Kempton and the Peter Ross Novices' Chase at Ascot. Capability Brown, receiving 7 lb from Dakyns Boy, led virtually throughout and drew clear from the second last for a ten-length victory. Capability Brown met his only defeat over fences in the Sun Alliance Chase at the Cheltenham Festival where he ran a fine race until blundering and unseating his rider six from home. He'd had a tremendous duel with the eventual winner Young Hustler up to that point, the pair of them forcing a very strong gallop from the start and soon racing clear of the rest.

		Derring-Do	Darius
	Dominion	(b 1961)	Sipsey Bridge
	(b 1972)	Picture Palace	Princely Gift
Capability Brown		(b 1961)	Palais Glide
(b.g. 1987)		Silly Season	Tom Fool
	Tomfoolery	(br 1962)	Double Deal
	(br 1973)	Rouge Royale	Fidalgo
		(b 1965)	Indian Melody

The rather leggy Capability Brown was bred for the Flat, by the very tough and genuine miler Dominion out of the fair maiden two-year-old Tomfoolery. Tomfoolery, whose dam was a winner over a mile and a daughter of Irish Oaks second Indian Melody, was bred to stay a mile and a quarter. The best Flat horse bred by the now-deceased Tomfoolery was the fairly useful and versatile handicapper Springs Welcome (by Blakeney) who stayed two

Mr David S. Lewis' "Capability Brown"

miles and was effective at a mile and a quarter. Capability Brown, himself, was raced at a mile and a quarter as a two-year-old, finishing fifth to Rock Hopper in a listed race at Newmarket, but he was only a fair maiden on the Flat, tried at up to a mile and three quarters as a three-year-old. After being purchased out of D. Morley's stable for 13,000 guineas at the Newmarket Autumn Sales, Capability Brown won juvenile hurdles at Leicester and Wolverhampton for J. M. Bradley before being sent to be trained by Pipe. Capability Brown is prone to the odd bad mistake over fences, and that may well prevent his graduating to the highest level. But he seems sure to develop into a smart staying handicapper at least. He probably acts on any going. *M. C. Pipe*

CAPE COTTAGE 9 ch.g. Dubassoff (USA) – Cape Thriller (Thriller) [1992/3 c25d⁴ c2 1m³ c23f⁴] novice hunter chaser: stays 25f: acts on firm and dead ground. *D. J. Caro* **c90**

CAPELI CONE 11 b.g. Celtic Cone – Capelena (Mon Fetiche) [1992/3 c33s² c30d⁶ c24vᶠ c26g⁴ c26d⁵] strong gelding: poor chaser nowadays: sold 1,000 gns Malvern May Sales: thorough stayer: acts on heavy going: blinkered once: poor jumper. *Mrs H. Parrott* **c83 x
–**

CAPENWRAY (IRE) 4 br.g. Supreme Leader – Godetia (Be Friendly) [1992/3 F16d* F17g⁴] half-brother to 6f winner Whitsun (by Divine Gift): dam never ran: won 21-runner NH Flat race at Hexham in March: fourth in similar event at Bangor later in month: yet to race over hurdles. *R. F. Fisher*

140

CAPICHE (IRE) 4 b.g. Phardante (FR) – Sainthill (St Alphage) [1992/3 F17g⁵ F14g⁶ F16g*] lengthy, angular gelding: half-brother to Flat winner Knockglas (by Hardgreen) and to maidens on Flat and over jumps: dam twice-raced sister to top sprinter Sandford Lad: won 11-runner NH Flat race at Chepstow in June: yet to race over hurdles. *J. Etherington*

CAPITAL LAD 4 ch.g. Dublin Lad – Wellington Bear (Dragonara Palace (USA)) [1992/3 18f] no form on Flat (may be ungenuine) or in early-season juvenile hurdle. *M. Avison*

CAPITAL PUNISHMENT 7 ch.g. Capitano – Loophole (London   c88
Gazette) [1992/3 c18f⁴ c20g⁴ c25g² c26g^F c26g^ur c24m²] workmanlike   –
gelding: novice hurdler: modest novice chaser: sold 9,200 gns Ascot June
Sales: stays 25f: acts on dead, good to firm going and equitrack:
inconsistent. *Mrs F. Walwyn*

CAPPAHOOSH (IRE) 4 ch.f. Salmon Leap (USA) – Tagik (Targowice   72
(USA)) [1992/3 16s⁵ 16v⁴] angular filly: half-sister to winning hurdler Home
Or Away (by Homing): poor handicapper at up to 1¼m on Flat: showed a
little ability in selling hurdle and juvenile event in mid-season: sold 6,200
gns Doncaster January Sales. *H. J. Collingridge*

CAPPUCCINO GIRL 6 ch.m. Broadsword (USA) – Coffee Bob   90
(Espresso) [1992/3 17s⁴ 18s² 16v² 20g*] sturdy mare: modest form when
winning novice hurdle at Plumpton in March: will stay beyond 2½m: best
effort on good ground. *F. Gray*

CAPRICORN BLUE 10 b.g. Blue Cashmere – Aqua Nimba (Acropolis)   c–
[1992/3 22s⁶ c21m⁵ c24m^F c25g⁴ c21d^pu] small, lightly-made gelding: –
novice hurdler/chaser: stays 25f: acts on good to firm and dead
ground: sometimes visored or blinkered. *W. L. Barker*

CAPRICORN KING 7 b.g. Capricorn Line – Queen's Rose (Queen's
Hussar) [1992/3 16s^pu] leggy gelding: winning 2m hurdler: was best with
give in the ground: dead. *D. McCain*

CAPRONI 6 b.g. Lomond (USA) – Helaplane (USA) (Super Concorde   –
(USA)) [1992/3 25d⁵] behind in NH Flat race (visored) in 1990/1 and novice
claiming hurdle in September. *Miss L. A. Perratt*

CAPSIZE 7 ch.g. Capitano – Fused Light (Fury Royal) [1992/3 c16m   c93
c21s^pu c21v³ c17f⁴ c16f4] leggy, good-topped gelding: winning hurdler: –
modest novice chaser: should prove suited by further than 17f: probably acts
on any going. *A. Moore*

CAPTAIN AHAB 9 b.g. Balinger – Sea Rambler (Menelek) [1992/3   c–
21s^pu 21v 21v⁵ 28g³ 27d] sparely-made gelding: poor hurdler nowadays: no   84
aptitude for chasing: stays well: acts on heavy and good to firm going. *J. White*

CAPTAIN BARNEY 10 b.g. Welsh Saint – Psidial (FR) (Psidium)   77
[1992/3 16d 21g⁴ 22s⁴ 21s⁵ 21v* 23v⁴ 26d^pu] leggy gelding: seventh foal:
half-brother to winning Irish jumper Donadea (by Mugatpura): dam poor
maiden: poor hurdler: won selling handicap at Towcester (no bid) in
January: pulled up lame final outing (February): usually gets behind, and
needs a good test of stamina: acts on heavy going: blinkered last 3 outings:
claimer ridden. *J. E. Long*

CAPTAIN BRAMSTAN (IRE) 5 b.g. Fayruz – Abroad (Takawalk II)
[1992/3 F14m] half-brother to several winners, including very useful jumper
Nos Na Gaoithe (by Strong Gale): dam lightly-raced maiden: tailed off in NH
Flat race at Market Rasen in March: yet to race over hurdles or fences. *Mrs S. A. Bramall*

CAPTAIN BRANDY 8 ch.g. Step Together (USA) – Manhattan Brandy   c128
(Frankincense) [1992/3 c17d⁶ c19s* c20v⁴ c19d³ c21d* c20d³ c21s* c24d⁴   –
c22f c29s^co c21d³] workmanlike gelding: fair hurdler: fairly useful form over
fences: successful in novice event at Listowel and handicaps at
Leopardstown and Punchestown in 1992/3: always behind in John Hughes
Memorial Trophy at Aintree in April on ninth start: best form at around
2½m: acts on heavy going: genuine. *F. Flood, Ireland*

CAPTAIN CHROME 6 b.g. Welsh Captain – Chrome Mag (Prince de Galles) [1992/3 23mᵖᵘ 16s 16d⁶ 16d 21sᵖᵘ] leggy gelding: poor hurdler: stays 2½m: acts on soft going: blinkered fourth outing. *K. S. Bridgwater* –

CAPTAIN COGNAC 7 ch.g. Sunyboy – Spanish Harpist (Don Carlos) [1992/3 c24dᵖᵘ c26vꟳ c26vᵖᵘ] big, lengthy gelding: novice hurdler/chaser: no form: tried blinkered. *P. J. Hobbs* c–

CAPTAIN CUTE 8 gr. or ro.g. Absalom – Cute (Hardicanute) [1992/3 c17d² c17v² c16s⁴ c21dᵖᵘ c17d⁵ c21gꟳ c21sᵖᵘ c21gꟳ 21g⁶] compact gelding: poor novice hurdler/chaser: form only at around 2m: acts on heavy ground: visored eighth outing. *D. T. Garraton* c81 –

CAPTAIN DIBBLE 8 b.g. Crash Course – Sailor's Will (Laurence O) [1992/3 c25g² c26g* c27s c25s* c30s⁵ c25s³ c25d³ c30d] c148 –

'A proper jumper and a horse with a lovely temperament' is how Peter Scudamore described his Grand National mount Captain Dibble. Scudamore chose to partner Captain Dibble, on whom he'd won the Scottish National the previous season, in preference to one of the Pipe-trained pair Chatam and Riverside Boy. The saga of the two false starts and subsequent voiding of the Grand National is recounted elsewhere, but the fiasco wasn't without its humourous side. Captain Dibble was one of those that completed a circuit before being pulled up, one weighing-room colleague suggesting that Scudamore, looking for an elusive victory in steeplechasing's most famous race, had pulled up when he spotted Chatam still at the start and saw the opportunity to switch to a fresh horse for the re-run!

Captain Dibble has plenty of qualities that would make him a good Grand National prospect another year. He's a thorough stayer, usually a

SGB Handicap Chase, Ascot—Captain Dibble and Miinnehoma are well clear at the last

Mrs R. Vaughan's "Captain Dibble"

sound jumper and isn't beholden to the state of the going, having shown his form on going ranging from good to firm to soft. He might be an even more interesting prospect with his training geared to producing him at his peak for Aintree. Judged on Captain Dibble's lack-lustre performance in the Whitbread Gold Cup on his final outing of another tough campaign—he appeared to drop himself out from halfway—considerate handling and a measured build-up to the National might suit him in the next season. Blinkers might also help to rekindle his flagging enthusiasm. Captain Dibble also had a hard season as a novice though he was most progressive, a fair second in the Arlington Premier Chase Final and a creditable fifth in the Sun Alliance Chase being among some noteworthy performances before winning the Scottish National. He started the latest season open to further improvement. However, the handicapper took his measure after he'd won two of his first four races, including the SGB Handicap Chase at Ascot in December, and he faced mostly uphill work in the second half of the season, during which he gave the impression more than once that he was losing some of his zest for the game.

Lately-perceived shortcomings in Captain Dibble's racing character, however, mustn't be allowed to overshadow his achievements in what, taken overall, was another good season. After shaping well on his reappearance, he went on to take the Badger Beer Chase, a limited handicap at Wincanton in November, confirming that he was suited by the forcing tactics that had served him so well in the Scottish National. However, on his next appearance he was a major disappointment in the Hennessy Cognac Gold Cup at Newbury where some untypically shoddy jumping early on resulted in his being unable to take up a position up with the pace. It transpired that Captain Dibble returned with bruised heels after the Hennessy which necessitated standing him in ice for long periods and equipping him with leather wedges between his feet and shoes to absorb impact. When he won the SGB Handicap Chase, Captain Dibble travelled to the course with bags of frozen peas strapped to his feet—his success prompting the memorable line 'Captain Birds Eye helps Captain Dibble to keep his cool'. Captain Dibble stayed on gamely, recovering from a mistake six out, to beat Miinnehoma by two and a half lengths at Ascot, the pair of them drawing a long way clear. Captain Dibble's best efforts after the SGB were fifth to Run For Free in the Coral Welsh National at Chepstow in December and a creditable last of three to Country Member and Rushing Wild in the Agfa Diamond Chase at Sandown in February.

Captain Dibble (b.g. 1985)	Crash Course (b 1971)	Busted (b 1963)	Crepello
			Sans Le Sou
		Lucky Stream (b 1956)	Persian Gulf
			Kypris
	Sailor's Will (ch 1976)	Laurence O (ch 1965)	Saint Crespin III
			Feevagh
		Some Will Say (b 1970)	Will Somers
			Say The Word

The tall, angular Captain Dibble is bred to be suited by a thorough test of stamina, being by the now-deceased Crash Course, also sire of the Cheltenham Gold Cup winner Jodami, out of a granddaughter of an Irish Cesarewitch winner. Captain Dibble's dam Sailor's Will won at up to twenty-one furlongs over hurdles in Ireland and is also the dam of Admiral's Leap (by Quayside), a fair staying hurdler/chaser at his best. *N. A. Twiston-Davies*

CAPTAIN DOLFORD   6 ch.g. Le Moss – Niatpac (Royal Highway) [1992/3 18v* 20d4] close-coupled, rather unfurnished gelding: fourth foal: dam winning Irish hurdler: 50/1-winner of novice hurdle at Fontwell in February: again finished strongly when fourth in similar event at Ascot following month: will prove well suited by a thorough test of stamina: should improve further. *D. M. Grissell*   108 p

CAPTAIN FRISK   10 bl. or br.g. Politico (USA) – Jenny Frisk (Sunacelli) [1992/3 c25d2 c25d* c25d2 c26v4 c24dur c26d* c25g2] tall gelding: retained 3,200 gns Ascot July Sales: fair form over fences: won novice chases at Cheltenham (amateurs) in November and Uttoxeter in February: good second in handicap at Nottingham later in February: will stay beyond 3¼m: acts on soft going (well below best on heavy): sound jumper. *K. C. Bailey*   c114

CAPTAIN KRAYYAN   7 b.g. Krayyan – Cap d'Antibe's (Furry Glen) [1992/3 c18g2 c17fF] tall, lengthy gelding: novice selling hurdler: no form in novice chases: probably stayed 2½m: acted on good to firm and soft going: blinkered once: dead. *R. Rowe*   c–
–

CAPTAIN MANNERING (USA)   8 b.g. Tina's Pet – Independentia (Home Guard (USA)) [1992/3 20d3] good-bodied gelding: novice selling hurdler: well beaten in novice chases: stays 2½m: acts on good to firm and dead ground: sometimes wears visor or blinkers. *T. J. Price*   c–
71

CAPTAIN MOR   11 b.g. Welsh Captain – Oona More (Straight Deal) [1992/3 c21gsu c21f*] lengthy gelding: fair chaser: won handicap at Sedgefield in September: sold 5,800 gns in May: stays 2¾m: acts on any going: once blinkered. *W. A. Stephenson*   c117
–

CAPTAIN MY CAPTAIN (IRE)   5 ch.g. Flash of Steel – Amanzi (African Sky) [1992/3 17d* 17s4 21s4 25v2 21m 20v3] rangy, unfurnished gelding: poor middle-distance staying maiden on Flat: won novice hurdle at Wolverhampton in November: ran creditably third and fourth outings: stays 25f: acts on heavy ground. *R. Brotherton*   93

CAPTAIN STOCKFORD   6 b.g. Grey Ghost – Stubbin Moor (Kinglet) [1992/3 F17g F16m6] second foal: dam never ran: unplaced in early-season NH Flat races: yet to race over hurdles or fences. *A. L. Forbes*

CAPTAIN TANCRED (IRE)   5 b.g. The Parson – Tudor Lady (Green Shoon) [1992/3 18g5 16s* 16g4 16s a16g5 16s* 17s3 17v6] IR 5,700Y: small,   92

lightly-made gelding: second foal: dam, from family of useful staying chaser Church Warden, ran once: won novice hurdle at Southwell in September (sold out of T. Tate's stable 4,200 gns Doncaster October Sales before next start) and selling handicap at Wetherby (bought in 5,800 gns) in April: effective at 2m but will prove suited by further: acts on soft ground. *J. J. Birkett*

CAPTAIN TEACH 7 b.g. Relkino – Pirate's Cottage (Pirate King) [1992/3 16d 17m 23d 16g 24g4 20g 24dpu 24g 16g 25m 21g3] good-topped gelding: poor maiden hurdler: sold 2,200 gns Doncaster June Sales: stays 3m: best efforts on good ground: visored twice. *P. Monteith*   66

CAPTAIN TOM 10 b.g. Blue Refrain – Icy Look (Arctic Time) [1992/3 c21g] leggy gelding: very lightly-raced maiden jumper. *Mrs E. J. Miller*   c–\
–

CAPULET 10 b.g. Henbit (USA) – Lady Juliet (USA) (Gallant Man) [1992/3 22m2] good-topped gelding: moderate handicap hurdler: fair second at Newton Abbot in March: sold 1,000 gns Ascot May Sales: stays 2¾m: acts on heavy going, probably on good to firm. *Mrs J. Wonnacott*   91

CARABALI DANCER 5 ch.g. Ballacashtal (CAN) – Lillicara (FR) (Caracolero (USA)) [1992/3 21s*] tall, leggy, lengthy gelding: modest form over hurdles: won handicap at Hexham in April in good style: stays 21f: acts on soft ground and on fibresand: may improve further. *D. T. Garraton*   97

CARABUCK 6 b.g. Buckskin (FR) – Caralgo (Miralgo) [1992/3 18s 16v4 16vpu 22m4 21g4 22g5] workmanlike gelding: half-brother to winning Irish jumper Van-Riel (by Distinctly): dam, winner twice at around 1¾m on Flat in Ireland, placed over hurdles: modest novice hurdler: will stay beyond 2¾m: acts on good to firm and heavy ground. *R. Rowe*   86

CARAGH BRIDGE 6 ch.g. Kambalda – Halcyon Years (Royal Highway) [1992/3 17v3 16vpu 21g 22d4 20g] compact gelding: half-brother to winning hurdlers Seabright Smile (by Pitpan) and Westway (by Paddy's Stream), latter useful stayer: dam never ran: modest novice hurdler: will stay beyond 2¾m: effort on dead ground. *M. J. Wilkinson*   91

CARA MUFFIN 9 b.g. Dramatic Bid (USA) – Speedy Valley (Wolver Hollow) [1992/3 c16gpu c21dpu] tall, angular gelding: poor novice hurdler/chaser: not raced after October: suited by sharp 2m: probably acts on any going: sometimes blinkered or visored: sometimes looks ungenuine. *J. Mackie*   c– §\
– §

CARATS MAJOR 11 b.g. Mandrake Major – Miss Carats (Le Dieu d'Or) [1992/3 c25m4] fair pointer: fourth in novice hunter chase at Southwell in May. *D. Applewhite*   c78

CARAT STICK 13 b.m. Gold Rod – Slipper Satin (Lord of Verona) [1992/3 c25dpu 20d 26spu] lengthy mare: winning hurdler: poor novice chaser: suited by acres of stamina: acts on heavy going: poor jumper of fences. *F. T. Walton*   c– x\
–

CARBISDALE 7 ch.g. Dunbeath (USA) – Kind Thoughts (Kashmir II) [1992/3 c20d3 c25fpu c20g2] workmanlike gelding: carries condition: fairly useful chaser: never-dangerous second of 4 in handicap at Ayr in April: will stay beyond 2½m: acts on good to firm and heavy ground: visored once: often jumps none too fluently. *Mrs M. Reveley*   c128\
–

CARBONATE 8 b.g. Mr Fluorocarbon – Girl On A Swing (High Top) [1992/3 c16g* c16g4 c19gF c17vF c16d2 c16v* c16s* c16vF] lengthy, workmanlike gelding: fair hurdler: won novice chase at Hereford in October and handicaps at Worcester and Ascot (conditional jockeys) in January: clear when falling last in handicap at Wincanton later in January on final start: unlikely to stay much beyond 19f: acts on good to firm and heavy ground: held up. *R. H. Buckler*   c111\
–

CARBON LADY 8 ch.m. Mr Fluorocarbon – Lady Marmalade (Hotfoot) [1992/3 20g] leggy, close-coupled mare: selling hurdler: sold 725 gns Ascot November Sales: suited by around 2½m: yet to race on heavy going, acts on any other. *R. A. Bennett*

CARDENDEN (IRE) 5 b.g. Bustomi – Nana (Forlorn River) [1992/3 F17m F16g 17d 18g³ 17s⁴ 17d] leggy gelding: half-brother to several winners, including hurdler/chaser Nathan Blake (by Sexton Blake): dam 2-y-o 5f winner: poor novice hurdler: likely to stay beyond 2¼m: best effort on good ground. *Mrs S. C. Bradburne* · 76

CARDINAL BIRD (USA) 6 b.g. Storm Bird (CAN) – Shawnee Creek (USA) (Mr Prospector (USA)) [1992/3 20d 16v* 17d² 16v² 17s⁶ 16v* 17s 16d⁶ 17s 17mpᵘ] compact gelding: won handicap hurdles at Worcester (novice event) in November and Windsor in February: ran poorly afterwards: stays 2¼m: acts on heavy ground: blinkered nowadays: reluctant. *S. Mellor* · 91 §

CARDINAL RALPH 9 b.g. Ovac (ITY) – Alice Minkthorn (Party Mink) [1992/3 c26m⁴] big, angular gelding: hunter chaser nowadays: stays 25f: acts on good to firm and soft ground. *Mrs S. N. J. Embiricos* · c–
–

CARDINAL RED 6 b.g. The Parson – Rose Ravine (Deep Run) [1992/3 16gpᵘ 22s* 22d³ 22v⁴ 25s⁴ 21m² 25f* 24f²] · 136

Cardinal Red, first foal of the very talented and notably genuine racemare Rose Ravine, hardly looked a chip off the old block during the early stages of his racing career, when his wayward tendencies easily over-shadowed his achievements. After confirming the promise shown in his first season by winning a novice hurdle at Worcester in October, Cardinal Red went off the rails both literally and metaphorically. On his next start he lost a huge amount of ground by running extremely wide turning into the back straight at Wincanton, and when tried in blinkers at Sandown he swerved violently left at the ninth and looked reluctant. It's probably significant that both races were on right-handed courses. Cardinal Red did at least manage to keep straight when going left-handed in his remaining starts, though on his next outing at Newbury early in January he once again looked a difficult ride and clearly still had his problems. It was two and a half months before Cardinal Red was seen on a racecourse again. He reappeared in the Sun

Belle Epoque Sefton Novices' Hurdle, Aintree—
Cardinal Red (right) turns the tables on Cheltenham winner Gaelstrom

Mrs F. Walwyn's "Cardinal Red"

		[Aureole	[Hyperion
	[The Parson	(ch 1950)	[Angelola
	(b 1968)	[Chanteur II	
Cardinal Red		[Bracey Bridge	[Rutherford Bridge
(b.g. 1987)		(b 1962)	
	[Deep Run	[Pampered King	
	[Rose Ravine	(ch 1966)	[Trial By Fire
	(b 1979)	[Dandyville	[Vulgan
		(br 1965)	[Dandybash

Alliance Novices' Hurdle at Cheltenham, a surprising choice of engagement
for a horse with his record. Cardinal Red couldn't reasonably be expected to
make his presence felt up against the pick of the young staying hurdlers and
was sent off at 150/1 in the nineteen-runner field, but he belied those odds
by finishing an excellent second to Gaelstrom. A combination of factors help
explain the dramatic improvement shown by Cardinal Red. Paddock
inspection revealed that he'd done well physically during his lay-off, and the
race itself showed that he'd also matured mentally. After looking as though
he might drop out of contention when outpaced at the third last, Cardinal
Red rallied gamely to get to within two and a half lengths of the winner.
Another factor to be taken into account was the going, for Cardinal Red had
never raced on top-of-the-ground before. He went on to prove just as
effective on an even firmer surface on his last two starts, both of which were
run at around three miles. In the Belle Epoque Sefton Novices' Hurdle at
Aintree, Cardinal Red turned the tables on Gaelstrom on terms 6 lb better,

forging clear on the run-in to beat her by one and a half lengths. And when pitched in against much more experienced performers in the Dean Moor Long Distance Hurdle at Haydock, Cardinal Red ran another fine race to finish three and a half lengths second to Boscean Chieftain.

Kept to hurdling Cardinal Red could develop into a leading contender for the Stayers' Hurdle at Cheltenham, but at the time of writing the plan is for him to go chasing in the New Year. The Stayers' Hurdle is a race which was won by Rose Ravine in controversial circumstances in 1985. Rose Ravine beat her stable-companion Crimson Embers, who was also in the same ownership, by a neck, and was allowed to keep the race despite having severely hampered the second on the run-in. That was the last race won by Rose Ravine, whose other victories included those in the Hoechst Regumate Mares Final at Newbury, the Bishops Cleeve Hurdle at Cheltenham and the Fernbank Hurdle at Ascot. Rose Ravine, whose second foal Lie Detector (by Nearly A Hand) finished a close fifth in a Cheltenham National Hunt Flat race in April, is out of a daughter of a half-sister to the dam of the Gold Cup winner Glencaraig Lady. Her grandam Dandybash, a stayer, won on the Flat and over hurdles and fences in Ireland. This is also the family of Maid of Money and Ten of Spades. Fences didn't figure in any plans for the small, light-bodied Rose Ravine in her racing days, but Cardinal Red, although unfurnished at present, is a more prepossessing type and he'll surely make a name for himself as a staying chaser. Rose Ravine wasn't beholden to the state of the ground, and while Cardinal Red has put up easily his best performances on a firm surface he may prove as effective under different conditions when he strengthens up. The ground was soft when he gained his first success. Cardinal Red has so far been trained by his owner Cath Walwyn, who took over Saxon House stables on the retirement of husband Fulke, trainer of Rose Ravine, in 1990. Mrs Walwyn herself relinquished her licence at the end of the latest season, and Cardinal Red is to join a newcomer to the training ranks Ben de Haan, rider of the 1983 Grand National winner Corbiere. *Mrs F. Walwyn*

CARD PARTY 8 ch.g. Lucky Wednesday – Hutton Barns (Saintly Song) [1992/3 18d^{pu} c20g^{pu} 16s^{pu} c17d^6 c20g c20g^F c17g c17d^F 17d] leggy gelding: poor novice hurdler/chaser: stays 2½m: sketchy jumper. *N. Waggott* — c73 —

CAREFREE TIMES 6 b.g. Good Times (ITY) – Danaka (FR) (Val de Loir) [1992/3 21m^2 24g^5 26m^{ur} 25g 24s a20g^6 22g 22m^4 25s^4 22g^6 28m^{pu}] dipped-backed gelding: poor novice hurdler: generally ran poorly after first start: stays 21f: acts on good to firm ground: has been tried blinkered and visored. *J. Norton* — 79 d

CARELESS KISS 9 ch.m. Persian Bold – More Kisses (Morston (FR)) [1992/3 16d 16s^2 18s^3] sparely-made mare: modest handicap hurdler: not raced after November: stays 2¼m: acts on soft ground. *A. Moore* — 98

CARELESS LAD 7 ch.g. Precocious – Mousquetade (Moulton) [1992/3 18f*] compact gelding: very lightly-raced hurdler: won novice event at Fontwell in August: stays 2¾m: acts on firm ground. *J. Joseph* — 102

CARFAX 8 ch.g. Tachypous – Montana Moss (Levmoss) [1992/3 20v^6 23s 20v^5 18s^5 a20g^3 a24g* a22g* 25g^{pu} a24g^2 a24g* a24g^5 20s^{pu} a24g^4] small gelding: fair hurdler: won 2 handicaps and a claimer at Lingfield in second half of season: effective from 2½m to 3m: acts on heavy going and goes well on all-weather surfaces: sometimes blinkered: often set plenty to do. *R. P. C. Hoad* — 105

CARIBBEAN PRINCE 5 ch.g. Dara Monarch – My Ginny (Palestine) [1992/3 16s 17d^5 17s* 17s^3 16s^5 17v^2 17v^4 17s 16g^6 17g^3 24s^{pu} 17g^{pu}] leggy gelding: handicap hurdler: won at Newton Abbot in October: below form last 6 outings: sold 4,000 gns Ascot 2nd June Sales: should stay beyond 17f: seems well suited by plenty of give in the ground: sometimes blinkered in 1991/2, usually visored nowadays. *M. McCourt* — 104 d

CARIBOO GOLD (USA) 4 b.c. Slew O' Gold (USA) – Selket's Treasure (USA) (Gleaming (USA)) [1992/3 17s^3 21d^{pu} 16g 16d* 17m^2 17g*] good-topped colt with scope: fair maiden on Flat when trained by J. Gosden: — 128 p won maiden hurdle at Uttoxeter and juvenile handicap at Ascot in April: easily best effort and fairly useful form when ½-length second to Her Honour in juvenile event at Cheltenham in between: should stay beyond 17f: acts on soft and good to firm going: blinkered third start: should improve and win more races. *K. C. Bailey*

CARLA ADAMS 7 ch.m. Billion (USA) – Jupiters Jill (Jupiter Pluvius) [1992/3 18d⁶ 21d³ 16gᵖᵘ] sparely-made mare: poor novice hurdler: not raced after October: stays 21f. *W. Storey* — 63

CARLINGFORD BELLE 7 ch.m. Carlingford Castle – Swiftly Belle (Deep Run) [1992/3 21m⁶ 25dᵖᵘ 23m] plain mare: poor novice hurdler: should stay beyond 2½m: acts on good to firm and soft ground. *J. L. Needham* — –

CARLINGFORD LIGHTS (IRE) 5 ch.g. Carlingford Castle – Chinese Queen (Tarim) [1992/3 16s 17s⁵ 17gᵖᵘ 18d 18g⁶] tall, unfurnished gelding: second foal: brother to a poor performer: dam winning Irish hurdler/chaser: novice hurdler: seemed to run very well final start: will stay further than 2¼m: acts on soft going. *O. O'Neill* — 83 ?

CARLINGFORD WINTER 7 ch.g. Carlingford Castle – Winter Serenade (Whistling Wind) [1992/3 20mᵖᵘ] stocky gelding: carries condition: poor novice hurdler: sold 1,750 gns Doncaster March Sales: stays 3m: best efforts on good to soft going: visored twice in 1991/2. *D. Moffatt* — –

CARLING WOOD 7 ch.g. Carlingford Castle – Elsea Wood (Eborneezer) [1992/3 c16gᵖᵘ c20vᵘʳ] strong, good-topped gelding: poor novice hurdler/chaser: dead. *J. P. Leigh* — c–

CARLSAN 7 ch.g. Carlingford Castle – Lovely Sanara (Proverb) [1992/3 F17gᵖᵘ] first foal: dam maiden Irish pointer: tailed off when pulled up in NH Flat race in October: yet to race over hurdles or fences. *Mrs A. Price* — –

CARNETTO 6 b.m. Le Coq d'Or – Carney (New Brig) [1992/3 17d 18d⁵ 21s⁶ 18d⁴] workmanlike mare: third foal: dam once-raced sister to quite useful staying chaser Solo Sam: has shown ability in novice hurdles, and should do better with more of a test of stamina. *R. Brewis* — 71 p

CARN MAIRG 6 b.m. Oats – Hardwick Sun (Dieu Soleil) [1992/3 21sᵖᵘ 22m⁴] no sign of ability over hurdles: dead. *J. M. Jefferson* — –

CAROGROVE 10 b.g. Rusticaro (FR) – Heather Grove (Hethersett) [1992/3 21gᵖᵘ 25m⁴ 27g 27fᵖᵘ] small gelding: moderate handicap hurdler: broke down final start: won 2 novice chases in 1991/2: stays 3¼m: suited by a sound surface and acts on hard ground: blinkered once. *E. T. Buckley* — c–, 91

CAROLES CLOWN 7 gr.m. Another Realm – Show Business (Auction Ring (USA)) [1992/3 16d⁵ 20d⁵ a18g] leggy mare: modest handicap hurdler: ran poorly after first outing (not raced after January): best at up to 2½m: acts on dead ground and all-weather surfaces. *M. J. Haynes* — 93

CAROLE'S RISK 4 b.f. Risk Me (FR) – Gold Duchess (Sonnen Gold) [1992/3 F12d] neat filly: second foal: dam modest 5f winner: last of 18 in NH Flat race in February: yet to race over hurdles. *R. Ingram* — –

CAROLINE RUA 7 ch.m. Lord Ha Ha – Ballinlough (Prince Hansel) [1992/3 16g 16g⁴ 20gF 26d³ 22s³ 21v³ 17vᵖᵘ] compact ex-Irish mare: first foal: dam, placed in NH Flat races, poor maiden hurdler: poor novice hurdler: not raced after December: stays 3¼m: acts on soft ground. *C. C. Trietline* — 75

CAROMANDOO (IRE) 5 b.g. Simply Great (FR) – Tanimara (Sassafras (FR)) [1992/3 16g⁴ 16d⁵ 17d⁶ 17s 18s a16g⁴a20g⁵a18g³ 17m⁵ 18d⁴ 18m*] leggy gelding: moderate hurdler on his day: won handicap at Exeter in May: stays 2¼m: acts on good to firm, dead ground and fibresand: occasionally blinkered/visored (visored at Exeter): inconsistent. *A. Barrow* — 92

CAROUSEL CALYPSO 7 ch.g. Whistling Deer – Fairy Tree (Varano) [1992/3 c24s* c23dF c27d⁵ c24d⁵ c26g* c26g² c27m² c24m²] leggy, lightly-built gelding: fair chaser: won novice event at Newcastle in December and handicap at Catterick in February: ran creditably afterwards: — c100, –

suited by long distances: acts on good to firm and heavy going. *M. D. Hammond*

CAROUSEL CROSSETT 12 b.m. Blind Harbour – Grange Classic (Stype Grange) [1992/3 28d] strong, compact mare: poor novice hurdler/ chaser: stays 3¼m: acts on soft ground. *E. M. Caine*

c–
–

CAROUSEL MUSIC 6 b.m. On Your Mark – Diana's Choice (Tudor Music) [1992/3 16d²] modest middle-distance performer on Flat: second in 16-runner maiden at Uttoxeter in April on hurdling debut: will improve. *J. Akehurst*

87 p

CAROUSEL ROCKET 10 ch.g. Whistling Deer – Fairy Tree (Varano) [1992/3 c28d³ c30d⁵ c29s⁴ c24d* c33gᵖᵘ c28g⁵ c26g* c27dᵖᵘ c24d* c24dᵖᵘ] sparely-made gelding: fair handicap chaser: successful at Carlisle in February, March and April: suited by good test of stamina: acts on heavy going and good to firm: blinkered once. *M. D. Hammond*

c103
–

CARPET CAPERS (USA) 9 b.g. Dance Bid (USA) – Cofimvaba (FR) (Verrieres) [1992/3 22s⁴ 18g 20sᵖᵘ 18f⁶] small gelding: one-time fair hurdler: poor form, including in sellers, in 1992/3: stays 2¾m: acts on any going: has won 6 times at Plumpton. *J. Ffitch-Heyes*

82

CARRICK LANES 6 b.g. Oats – Once Bitten (Brave Invader (USA)) [1992/3 21s² 20s* 25s⁵ 21g 24s² 26g*] workmanlike gelding: won novice hurdles at Bangor in December and Huntingdon in April: thorough stayer: acts on soft going. *D. Nicholson*

103

CARRICKMINES 8 ch.g. Deep Run – Gallant Breeze (USA) (Mongo) [1992/3 c26mᵖᵘ c25dᵖᵘ c21m² c24m* c25dᶠ c28fᵖᵘ] angular gelding: won novice hunter chase at Stratford in May: stays 3m: acts on firm and dead ground. *Lee Bowles*

c95
–

CARRICKROVADDY 7 ch.g. Deroulede – Ballybeg Maid (Prince Hansel) [1992/3 c24s² c27v³ c24g³ c32mᵖᵘ c25s³ c25d c24m* c25mᵘʳ c26m²] big, strong gelding: won novice chase at Stratford in May, best effort: stays well: acts on good to firm and soft ground: blinkered last 3 outings. *B. Smart*

c99
–

CARRIGEEN HERO 9 b. or br.g. Good Thyne (USA) – Shutter Speed (Polyfoto) [1992/3 21m 26mᵖᵘ] workmanlike gelding: of little account: tried blinkered. *R. O'Leary*

c–
–

CARRIGEEN LAD 6 b.g. Mandalus – Monread (Le Tricolore) [1992/3 22g³ 20v* 22v 22gᵖᵘ 23m*] rather unfurnished gelding: third foal: dam of little account: won novice hurdles at Plumpton in November and Stratford (improved form) in April: stays 23f: acts on good to firm and heavy ground. *N. J. Henderson*

104

CARRIGLAWN 8 ch.g. Buckskin (FR) – Sonlaru (Deep Run) [1992/3 c22vᵖᵘ c21sʳᵒ c25sᵘʳ c24dᶠ] compact gelding: first foal: dam unraced: winning pointer in Ireland: failed to complete in novice chases. *G. B. Balding*

c–
–

CARRIKINS 6 b.m. Buckskin (FR) – Carrigello (Bargello) [1992/3 18f² 20d* 20gᵖᵘ] won novice hurdle at Plumpton in October: ran badly 5 months later: stays 2½m: acts on dead ground. *D. M. Grissell*

90

CARRINGTONS HILL (IRE) 4 b.g. Tender King – Dorcetta (Condorcet (FR)) [1992/3 F14m⁶] third foal: half-brother to winning hurdler High Stoy (by My Top) and useful Irish novice chaser Force Seven (by Strong Gale): dam, French 1½m winner, half-sister to a winning hurdler: sixth of 20 in NH Flat race at Market Rasen in March: yet to race over hurdles. *Miss S. J. Wilton*

CARSETHORN 6 ch.m. Feelings (FR) – Raver (Runnymede) [1992/3 F16d] tailed off in 2 NH Flat races: yet to race over hurdles or fences. *J. Colston*

CARSON CITY 6 ch.g. Carlingford Castle – Even More (Even Money) [1992/3 21g⁵ 20d³ 24g² 22g²] rangy, rather unfurnished gelding with scope: moderate novice hurdler: sold out of J. FitzGerald's stable 11,500 gns

90

Doncaster November Sales after second outing: not raced after January: probably stays 3m: acts on dead ground: tends to run in snatches and looks a difficult ride. *Mrs M. Reveley*

CARSWELL'S CHOICE   10 ch.g. Belfalas – Santal Air (Ballyciptic) [1992/3 c21s² c27s² c23f⁵ c23d c17s² c27d³ c24dᵖᵘ 22v 22v⁵ 18sᵘʳ c25d c27sᵘʳ 27d] good-topped gelding: winning selling hurdler: poor maiden over fences: trained until after eighth start by C. Popham: stays 3¼m: probably acts on any going: blinkered twice: moody. *J. Honeyball*   **c86 §**
– §

CARZARA   6 b.m. Zambrano – Miss Appleyard (Bronze Hill) [1992/3 17sᵖᵘ 25dᵖᵘ 25gᵖᵘ] robust, deep-bodied mare: second foal: sister to novice hurdler Zarbano: dam unraced half-sister to winning hurdler Burn Wood out of tip-top pointer Maeve: no sign of ability in novice hurdles. *B. Mactaggart*   **–**

CASA BELLA   6 b.m. Belfort (FR) – Cassiar (Connaught) [1992/3 16s 16d a16g⁵ a24gᵘʳ a20g³ a24gᵖᵘ 18m⁵ 28m² 16v* 22m 22f* 26dᵖᵘ] leggy mare: claimed out of J. FitzGerald's stable £2,000 after fourth start: won selling handicap hurdles at Towcester (bought in 3,000 gns) and Huntingdon (novices, no bid) in the spring: pulled up lame final start: effective at 2m under very testing conditions and stays 3½m: acts on any going: none too consistent: ran poorly when tried blinkered. *B. Richmond*   **73**

CASE HARDEN   6 ch.g. Kambalda – Lucifer's Daughter (Lucifer (USA)) [1992/3 F17s² 21g* 24s⁴] tall, unfurnished gelding: fourth foal: brother to very useful hurdler/promising chaser Barton Bank and half-brother to winning Irish pointer Sandalays Daughter (by Sandalay): dam, lightly-raced maiden, sister to 2 winning jumpers, including useful Killamonan: won maiden hurdle at Warwick in March: rather disappointing later in month: should stay beyond 21f. *N. J. Henderson*   **104**

CASH CRISIS   13 ch.g. Hell's Gate – Pound Foolish (Cash And Courage) [1992/3 c21m³ c23fᵖᵘ c17s³] sparely-made gelding: poor chaser: stayed 21f: acted on any going: inconsistent: dead. *A. Barrow*   **c75**
–

CASHEW KING   10 b.g. Faraway Times (USA) – Sinzinbra (Royal Palace) [1992/3 c21m³ c20gᵖᵘ] tall, leggy gelding: one-time useful chaser: not raced after October: stays 2½m: best form with give in the ground: has won when sweating. *D. McCain*   **c117**
–

CASH POINT   6 b.g. Sweet Monday – Kindling (Psidium) [1992/3 22sᵖᵘ 17s 23sᵖᵘ 16d c22gᵖᵘ] big, lengthy gelding: no sign of ability. *Miss J. Eaton*   **c–**
–

CASHTAL DAZZLER   6 b.g. Ballacashtal (CAN) – Miss Meg (John Splendid) [1992/3 16d⁵ 17s⁵ 16m⁵ 16g] leggy gelding: poor form over hurdles: barely stays 2m: blinkered second and final outings: sold 1,500 gns Doncaster May Sales. *N. Tinkler*   **73**

CASHTAL RUNNER   4 ch.c. Ballacashtal (CAN) – Woodrush (Mummy's Pet) [1992/3 17m⁵ 17gᵖᵘ] angular colt: plating-class maiden at 2 yrs: showed nothing in 2 novice hurdles at Bangor in March. *E. H. Owen jun*   **–**

CASIENNE (IRE)   5 ch.m. Doulab (USA) – Borshch (Bonne Noel) [1992/3 18mᶠ 21s² 21v⁴ 16d 20g 21f* 20m] small mare: selling hurdler: trained until after first start by R. Holder: no bid after winning conditional jockeys handicap at Chepstow in March: stayed 21f: probably acted on any ground: blinkered last 2 starts: dead. *P. G. Murphy*   **84**

CASINO MAGIC   9 b.g. Casino Boy – Gypsy Girl (Marmont) [1992/3 c21dᵖᵘ c20d a20g c21d* c21s* c19m* c19g⁵ c20d⁶] workmanlike gelding: novice hurdler: modest handicap chaser: won at Huntingdon (conditional jockeys), Folkestone and Hereford in second half of season: effective at around 2½m and probably stays 3m: acts on any going: blinkered once. *J. L. Spearing*   **c88**

CASNIKTONY   4 b.g. Ilium – Scottish Belle (Scottish Rifle) [1992/3 17g⁵] fourth foal: dam, winning hurdler, stayed 2½m: lightly-raced maiden on Flat: tailed off in early-season juvenile hurdle. *A. Moore*   **–**

CASPIAN FLYER   10 br.g. Persian Bold – Orapa (Aureole) [1992/3 c21mᵘʳ] workmanlike gelding: winning pointer: poor novice chaser: tried blinkered: makes mistakes. *A. C. Maylam*   **c– x**
–

Lady Mary Mumford's "Castle Courageous"

CASPIAN PRINCE 7 b.g. The Brianstan – Bouboulina (Hornbeam) [1992/3 F17m⁶ 17s 17vᵖᵘ] half-brother to quite useful staying hurdler Peter Martin (by Monsanto): dam won in Greece: no sign of ability over hurdles: sold 1,400 gns Ascot May Sales. *Miss H. C. Knight* —

CASS 6 ch.g. Stanford – Autumn Supreme (Supreme Sovereign) [1992/3 c20mᵘʳ c25sꟳ 23d⁶ 24vᵖᵘ] sturdy gelding: poor novice jumper: tried blinkered: reluctant. *N. A. Twiston-Davies* c– § 71 §

CASSIE SINGS 5 b.m. Battle Hymn – Spartan Doll (Country Retreat) [1992/3 17dᵖᵘ] sixth foal: dam never ran: tailed off when pulled up in early-season novice hurdle. *T. B. Hallett* —

CAST ADRIFT 6 b.m. Balinger – Growing Wild (Free State) [1992/3 F17m] workmanlike mare: second foal: dam, plating-class middle-distance maiden on Flat, showed no form over hurdles: well beaten in NH Flat race at Cheltenham in April: yet to race over hurdles or fences. *G. C. Maundrell* —

CASTALINO 7 b.m. Carlingford Castle – Barfly (Avocat) [1992/3 24s 20v³ 20s⁴ 18s⁵ 22vꟳ 20v³ 24s² 24d* 24d* 25f⁶ 24g] fair hurdler: won handicaps at Thurles in February and Navan in March: ran creditably in valuable handicap at Aintree on tenth start: suited by good test of stamina: probably acts on any going. *Jeremiah Ryan, Ireland* 106

CASTELLANI 8 b.g. Castle Keep – Asteria (Tycoon II) [1992/3 20mᵖᵘ] stocky gelding: winning hurdler: pulled up lame in July: easily best efforts at 2m on good to firm ground: usually visored nowadays. *M. W. Eckley* —

CASTING TIME (NZ) 9 br.g. Drums of Time (USA) – In Haste (NZ) (In The Purple (FR)) [1992/3 c25s⁵ c26v⁴ c24sᵖᵘ c23vᵘʳ c21f* c20fᵘʳ c24mᵖᵘ] c98 —

leggy, angular gelding: poor novice hurdler: 33/1, improved form to win novice chase at Sandown in March: ran creditably in similar event in April until pulling up lame approaching last: acts on firm going. *D. H. Barons*

CASTLEACRE 7 ch.g. Mr Fluorocarbon – Misfired (Blast) [1992/3 18g] small, lightly-made gelding: winning selling hurdler: pulls hard and best at 2m: acts on firm and dead going: blinkered twice. *C. A. Smith* –

CASTLEBAY LAD 10 br.g. Crozier – Carbery Star (Kemal (FR)) [1992/3 25v 24d² 24s⁵] sturdy gelding: fair hurdler: failed to complete in 2 novice chases: sold privately 1,500 gns Ascot June Sales: stays 3m: acts on heavy ground: blinkered once. *J. A. B. Old* c– 105

CASTLE BLUE 6 b.g. Carlingford Castle – Blue Lagoon (Forlorn River) [1992/3 22v 21s⁴ 20g⁶ 26s⁴ 22d⁶] rather leggy gelding: modest novice hurdler: stays 3¼m: acts on soft going. *N. J. Henderson* 89

CASTLE CLOWN 8 ch.g. Castle Keep – Peteona (Welsh Saint) [1992/3 16d] leggy, dipped-backed gelding: brother to fairly useful hurdler Castle Courageous and half-brother to winning hurdler/chaser Kingholm Quay (by Scottish Rifle): one-time fair middle-distance handicapper on Flat: behind in early-season novice hurdle. *Lady Herries* –

CASTLE COURAGEOUS 6 b.g. Castle Keep – Peteona (Welsh Saint) [1992/3 18s* 22d* 17d* 21d²] workmanlike gelding: half-brother to winning hurdler/chaser Kingholm Quay (by Scottish Rifle): fairly useful staying handicapper on Flat, winner in May, 1993: took well to hurdling, winning novice events at Fontwell and Wincanton in November and Plumpton in February: best effort when second to High Alltitude in quite valuable novice event at Chepstow in February: stays 2¾m: acts on soft going. *Lady Herries* 130 p

CASTLE CROSS 6 ch.g. Carlingford Castle – Siba Vione (Dusky Boy) [1992/3 23d⁵ 25spu] leggy gelding: fourth foal: half-brother to a poor animal by Boreen: dam ran twice: signs of ability first start in novice hurdles in first half of season. *J. I. A. Charlton* 72

CASTLE DIAMOND 6 ch.g. Carlingford Castle – Miss Diamond (Diamonds Are Trump (USA)) [1992/3 20m³ 16s⁵ 24s⁶ c20d⁶ c17f² 21f 17f² 22f²] leggy, shallow-girthed gelding: modest hurdler: better effort over fences when second in novice event at Newbury in March: stays 2¾m: best efforts on a sound surface: sketchy jumper of fences. *H. M. Kavanagh* c95 95

CASTLEFERGUS 6 b.h. Over The River (FR) – Money Buck (Master Buck) [1992/3 c21m²] first foal: dam winning Irish pointer: lightly-raced winning pointer in Ireland: gambled on when second of 3 finishers in novice chase won by Young Hustler at Bangor in September. *G. M. Moore* c89

CASTLE GALAH 6 b.m. Castle Keep – My Pink Parrot (Pirate King) [1992/3 17mpu] sparely-made mare: of little account. *S. Woodman* –

CASTLE JESTER 8 gr.g. Castle Keep – Peters Pleasure (Jimsun) [1992/3 c21spu] lengthy gelding: selling hurdler: poor winning chaser: form only at 2m: acts on good to firm ground: sometimes blinkered. *Mrs C. F. Elliott* c–

CASTLE KING 6 b.g. Crash Course – Caherelly Cross (Royal Buck) [1992/3 c21s² c20g* c20g⁶ c20m* c20m* c20f⁶] lengthy, quite good-topped gelding: carries plenty of condition: fairly useful chaser: trained until after first start by W. A. Stephenson: won handicaps at Doncaster in December, February and March: jumped markedly right when tailed off final start: sold 62,000 gns in May: will stay beyond 21f: acts on good to firm and soft ground: jumps soundly. *P. Cheesbrough* c116 –

CASTLE MAID 6 b.m. Castle Keep – Village Lass (No Mercy) [1992/3 16gpu] leggy mare: poor sprint maiden on Flat: tailed off when pulled up in early-season novice hurdle. *R. J. Hodges* –

CASTLE ORCHARD 9 br.g. Lepanto (GER) – Cora (Current Coin) [1992/3 21g] leggy, lengthy gelding: no sign of ability. *P. Hayward* c–

CASTLE REUBEN 5 br.g. Green Ruby (USA) – Penny Venus (Comedy Star (USA)) [1992/3 16vpu 16s c16d⁵ c19s c21g] big, workmanlike gelding: c68

poor novice hurdler/chaser: best effort at 2m on dead ground: tried blinkered. *R. Dickin*

CASTLERICHARDKING 8 b. or br.g. Matching Pair – Dont Rock (Rugged Man) [1992/3 17g* 20g³ 18g⁵ 17g 17g 16f 22dᵖᵘ 18d⁶] workmanlike gelding: poor hurdler: won novice handicap at Hereford in August: below form afterwards: well beaten only completed outing over fences: should stay beyond 17f: best effort on good going: blinkered fourth and seventh outings: unreliable. *R. T. Juckes*

c–
70 §

CASTLE SECRET 7 b.g. Castle Keep – Baffle (Petingo) [1992/3 24sᵖᵘ 21f³] leggy, rather sparely-made gelding: useful hurdler: creditable last of 3 (close up) behind Flakey Dove in valuable event at Uttoxeter in May: effective at 2m and stays 25f: best form on a sound surface: sometimes wears hood. *D. Burchell*

142

CASUAL PASS 10 ch.g. Formidable (USA) – Pitapat (Shantung) [1992/3 20g⁵ 26sᵖᵘ c24dᵖᵘ 17mʳᵗʳ 17m² 18g* 17d* 17d² 16s* 17f³ 18m 16gʳᵗʳ 21g*] small, sturdy gelding: carries plenty of condition: fair hurdler: successful in claimer at Kelso and handicaps at Carlisle and Hexham (2) in the spring: pulled up on chasing debut: stays 21f: acts on any going: sometimes blinkered and ridden in spurs (was when successful): sometimes refuses to race and looks unenthusiastic. *L. Lungo*

c–
103 §

CATAKIL (FR) 4 b.g. Bikala – Catacomb (USA) (Halo (USA)) [1992/3 F16m] brother to winning jumper Clear Call and half-brother to a French Flat winner by Sharpman: dam French 7f 2-y-o winner: well beaten in NH Flat race in May: yet to race over hurdles. *T. P. Tate*

CATCHAPENNY 8 br.g. True Song – Quickapenny (Espresso) [1992/3 c25d⁶ c25dᵖᵘ c24s³ c26v³ c24g c25d* c26d² c28g⁴ c26d* c25s* c26m⁴]

c96
–

Bet With The Tote Novices' Handicap Chase (Final), Uttoxeter—
Catchapenny is about to be hard pressed by Rathvinden House

compact gelding: improved chaser: had a good season over fences: successful in novice events at Wolverhampton (claimer) in February, Uttoxeter (valuable event) in March and Market Rasen in April, last 2 handicaps: stays well: acts on good to firm and soft ground: blinkered nowadays. *M. J. Wilkinson*

CATCHA THIEF 5 b.g. Final Straw – Honey Thief (Burglar) [1992/3 F16s F16s] half-brother to 3 winning sprinters, notably smart Prince Reymo (by Jimmy Reppin): dam won over 5f at 2 yrs: tailed off in NH Flat races: sold 1,700 gns Ascot March Sales: yet to race over hurdles or fences. *Mrs V. S. Hickman*

CATCH THE CROSS 7 gr.g. Alias Smith (USA) – Juliette Mariner (Welsh Pageant) [1992/3 c21v* c21s² c24mF c24gpu 25fpu c21m* c21m⁵] deep-girthed, workmanlike gelding: useful hurdler: fairly useful handicap chaser: won at Warwick in December and Newton Abbot in May: best form at up to 3m, though has won at 3¼m: acts on any going: used to wear blinkers, visored nowadays: suited by waiting tactics: sometimes looks unenthusiastic. *M. C. Pipe*   c124 –

CATEL RING (IRE) 4 b.c. Auction Ring (USA) – Dame Kelly (Pitskelly) [1992/3 18m] half-brother to fairly useful hurdler Andrew's First (by Tender King): maiden plater on Flat: tailed off in early-season juvenile hurdle. *I. Campbell*   –

CATHGAL 8 b.g. Crozier – Mawnie (Mon Capitaine) [1992/3 c17fur c17d⁴ c21mur c17gpu] leggy, sparely-made gelding: no sign of ability over hurdles: poor novice chaser. *V. Thompson*   c72 –

CATHOS (FR) 8 b.g. Bellman (FR) – Charming Doll (Don (ITY)) [1992/3 18gwd 23spu 17v 18vrtr] neat gelding: novice hurdler: ungenuine (often reluctant to race) and one to avoid. *D. A. Wilson*   §§

CATHS FOLLY 6 b.m. Humdoleila – Salvo's Grace (FR) (Salvo) [1992/3 20s 22m 21vpu] angular, plain mare: no sign of ability. *J. H. Peacock*   –

CATUNDRA (IRE) 5 ch.m. Far North (CAN) – 'tis A Kitten (USA) (Tisab (USA)) [1992/3 17m 17m 17d] workmanlike mare: maiden plater over hurdles: ran poorly in 1992/3: races at around 2m: acts on good to firm ground and fibresand. *Mrs A. Knight*   –

CAUTIOUS REBEL 6 ch.g. Shy Groom (USA) – Riot Girl (Right Boy) [1992/3 20d⁴ 17v 22d⁴ 24f⁵ 20g²] sturdy, angular ex-Irish gelding: half-brother to 4 Irish Flat winners: dam Irish 11f winner: winning pointer: moderate novice hurdler: will probably prove suited by further than 2½m, and stays 3m: acts on any ground. *G. B. Balding*   93

CAVAK (IRE) 5 b.g. Indian King (USA) – Blyth's Folly (Prince Tenderfoot (USA)) [1992/3 18m 18f 18dro 18m] quite good-topped gelding: poor novice selling hurdler: blinkered nowadays: temperamental. *Mrs J. Jordan*   – §

CAVALINO VINO 6 b.g. Joshua – Snippet (Ragstone) [1992/3 F16d 17spu 17gpu] third foal: half-brother to 23f selling hurdle winner Snappit (by Billion): dam, from good family, of little account: no sign of ability in NH Flat race and novice hurdles. *D. McCain*   –

CAVO GRECO (USA) 4 b.g. Riverman (USA) – Cypria Sacra (USA) (Sharpen Up) [1992/3 17m 18s 16v 17d* 17m³ 17f³ 18gF 17g⁶] small gelding: poor maiden on Flat (sold out of P. Cole's stable 3,100 gns Newmarket July Sales): won selling handicap hurdle at Hereford (bought in 4,400 gns) in February and would have won similar event at Fontwell in March but for falling last: likely to stay beyond 2¼m: acts on firm and dead ground. *J. Joseph*   85 +

CAVOLERIE 6 br.g. Ovac (ITY) – Where's Vallee (Skymaster) [1992/3 F16m F17d] half-brother to poor novice chaser Cushy File (by Even Say): dam never ran: well beaten in NH Flat races: sold 3,200 gns Doncaster May Sales: yet to race over hurdles or fences. *J. G. FitzGerald*

Jim Ford Challenge Cup (Chase), Wincanton—
Cavvies Clown leads Garrison Savannah, Ghofar (right) and Cool Ground

CAVVIES CLOWN   13 b.g. Idiot's Delight – Cavallina (Vulgan) [1992/3 **c144**
c21d⁵ c26d* c25mᵘʳ c25fᵘʳ c33gᵖᵘ] small, rather sparely-made gelding: –
top-class chaser at best: useful form when winning Jim Ford Challenge Cup
at Wincanton in February for third time (by 2 lengths from Garrison
Savannah): failed to complete afterwards: stays very well: acts on any going:
suited by forcing tactics: tends to be mulish and led in at start. *Mrs J. Pitman*

CAWARRA BOY   5 b.g. Martinmas – Cawarra Belle (Crimson Beau)
[1992/3 F16d³ F17v 16v 17g⁶] compact gelding: poor form in 2 novice   69
hurdles. *C. James*

CAWKWELL DEAN   7 b.g. Boco (USA) – Cawkwell Duchess (Duc   **c–**
d'Orleans) [1992/3 c26gᵖᵘ] modest pointer: well beaten when pulled up in
hunter chase in May. *C. D. Stamp*

CAWKWELL TOM   9 b.g. Boco (USA) – Cawkwell Duchess (Duc   **c92**
d'Orleans) [1992/3 c24g⁵ c24g⁴ c26g* c24gᵖᵘ] strong, lengthy gelding: won
maiden hunter chase at Uttoxeter in May: stays 3¼m: acts on dead ground.
C. D. Stamp

CAWSTON BAY   8 b.m. Cawston's Clown – Princess Davinia (Saintly
Song) [1992/3 20gᵘʳ 22mᶠ a20gᵖᵘ] sparely-made mare: poor novice hurdler: – §
refused to race once. *J. Norton*

CAXTON (USA)   6 b.g. Halo (USA) – Printing Press (USA) (In Reality)
[1992/3 20m] sparely-made gelding: modest hurdler: stiff task only start in   –

1992/3 (March): likely to prove suited by sharp 2m: acts on good to soft and good to firm going: blinkered once. *W. Bentley*

CEDAR RUN 10 b.g. Billion (USA) – Sapele (Decoy Boy) [1992/3 c19d5 c25g3] rather sparely-made gelding: selling hurdler/chaser: best form at around 2m: probably acts on any going: blinkered twice: twice refused to race and should be treated with caution. *G. F. H. Charles-Jones*   c80 §
– §

CEDARS ROSSLARE 8 b.g. Black Minstrel – Sea Guest (Arctic Que) [1992/3 21vpu c20dur c27d5 c25gur c24fpu 25f4 22s 25gF 27d] ex-Irish gelding: poor novice hurdler/chaser: stays 27f: form only on dead ground: blinkered last 2 outings. *R. G. Frost*   c–
71

CEFFYL DU 4 br.c. Mandabo – Rusty Fern (Rustingo) [1992/3 F16f5 16dpu] smallish colt: first foal: dam winning 2m hurdler/chaser: looked reluctant in novice selling hurdle in April. *D. Burchell*   – §

CEILIDH BOY 7 b.g. Oats – Charlotte's Festival (Gala Performance (USA)) [1992/3 20g2 23g* 23d2 23s* 23d* 20d] plain gelding: ran out only start over fences: won 3 novice hurdles at Kelso in first half of season, showing fairly useful form, well beaten only outing in second (February): stays well: best form on an easy surface, and acts on soft ground. *Mrs J. D. Goodfellow*   c–
114

CELCIUS 9 b.g. Ile de Bourbon (USA) – Cistus (Sun Prince) [1992/3 17d5 17g2 22s3 17d 16s* 16dF 18s4 17v2 20s* 21vpu 20d4 21m 18g2 22s 18d6 18f2] small, light-framed gelding: fair hurdler: won handicap at Leicester in November and claimer at Haydock in January: effective at 2m and stays 2¾m: acts on any going: wears blinkers: usually held up: sometimes refuses to go through with his effort. *M. C. Pipe*   c–
107 §

CELERY RISE (NZ) 9 b.g. Palm Beach (FR) – Golden Wedding (NZ) (Sucaryl) [1992/3 17v 23vpu 23vpu] compact gelding: of no account nowadays. *G. L. Humphrey*   c– x
–

CELESTIAL STREAM 6 ch.g. Paddy's Stream – Starlight Beauty (Scallywag) [1992/3 F17f] first foal: dam never ran: well beaten in NH Flat race in May: yet to race over hurdles or fences. *L. J. Williams*

CELTIC BANJO 8 br.m. Celtic Cone – Allende (Grand Roi) [1992/3 19mF 22dpu 17vpu] small, lengthy mare: third foal: half-sister to winning selling hurdler Cervante Sovereign (by Sovereign Bill): dam winning hurdler: seems of little account. *J. D. Roberts*   –

CELTIC BARON 8 ch.g. Billion (USA) – Celtic View (Celtic Cone) [1992/3 16dF 17s 17s5 20mF 16dpu] tall, workmanlike gelding: second foal: brother to ungenuine winning jumper Sillian: dam unraced half-sister to 2 winners over jumps, including useful Welton Lad: novice hurdler: form only on third start: should stay further than 17f: acts on soft going. *Mrs A. R. Hewitt*   72

CELTIC BIZARRE 5 b.m. Celtic Cone – Charity Bazzar (Native Bazaar) [1992/3 22s5] lengthy mare: bad novice hurdler: sold 875 gns Ascot February Sales. *C. T. Nash*   60

CELTIC BOB 13 ch.g. Celtic Cone – Quaife Sport (Quayside) [1992/3 17d6 18g6 17m 17f] small, robust gelding: one-time fairly useful hurdler: no form since 1990/1: stays 2½m: acts on any going: sometimes visored. *O. O'Neill*   –

CELTIC BREEZE 10 b.g. Celtic Cone – Sipped (Ballyciptic) [1992/3 23g4 23g 25g5 21s5 28v5 26s6 c24gpu 21v4 21s3 25g* 24g2 25dF 25m 25m3] sturdy gelding: fair handicap hurdler: won at Ayr in March: ran creditably when placed after: retained 3,800 gns Doncaster May Sales: maiden chaser: out-and-out stayer: acts on good to firm ground, particularly well on heavy: visored. *M. P. Naughton*   c–
105

CELTIC BRIDGE 5 ch.m. Celtic Cone – Bridge Ash (Normandy) [1992/3 F16s4 F17m] small mare: second foal: half-sister to winning pointer Rusty Bridge (by Rustingo): dam quite useful chaser, needed good test of

stamina: signs of ability in NH Flat races: yet to race over hurdles or fences.
Mrs S. M. Johnson

CELTIC BUNNIE 8 b.m. Celtic Cone – Charlotte's Festival (Gala Performance (USA)) [1992/3 21g 17m 20g 22g⁶ 24m⁶] lightly raced over hurdles, little sign of ability: sold 2,300 gns Doncaster May Sales. *Mrs J. D. Goodfellow* –

CELTIC CATCH 7 br.g. Celtic Cone – Eyecatcher (Doubtless II) [1992/3 17sꟳ a16g⁵ c16s⁴ c17s⁴ c16m³ c16g³] rangy gelding: poor hurdler/novice chaser: will stay further than 2m: acts on soft and good to firm going. *J. R. Bosley* — c73 73

CELTIC CHIEF 10 b.g. Celtic Cone – Chieftain's Lady (Border Chief) [1992/3 c18v³ c21vᵖᵘ 24d⁴ 17sᵖᵘ] strong gelding: one-time top-class hurdler: novice chaser, form only when third at Market Rasen in December: stays 2½m: suited by give in the ground and acts on heavy: sketchy jumper of fences. *M. C. Pipe* — c94 —

CELTIC CHIMES 9 ch.m. Celtic Cone – Dyna Bell (Double Jump) [1992/3 c21g² c21m³ c16v² c17vᵇᵈ c16s³ c17vᵖᵘ] small mare: poor hurdler/novice chaser: not raced after January: best form at up to 2¼m: acts on any ground: sometimes visored in 1989/90. *G. P. Enright* — c79 —

CELTIC DIAMOND 8 b.m. Celtic Cone – Eight of Diamonds (Silent Spring) [1992/3 c27s* c27g* c27s] leggy mare: fair handicap chaser: won at Newton Abbot and Fontwell early in season (not raced after October): stays 3¼m: acts on good to firm and heavy ground. *Mrs J. G. Retter* — c110

CELTIC EMERALD 5 ch.m. Celtic Cone – Emerald Flight (Cantab) [1992/3 F17d F17m] lengthy mare: second foal: half-sister to poor novice hurdler Rustic Flight (by Rustingo): dam, of little account, is granddaughter of very useful hurdler Flight's Orchid: well beaten in NH Flat races: yet to race over hurdles or fences. *R. J. Eckley* —

CELTIC FLAME 12 ch.g. Celtic Cone – Dandy's Last (Prefairy) [1992/3 c25mꟳ] leggy, short-backed gelding: poor performer nowadays: poor jumper. *Rob Murrell* — c– x —

CELTIC GAMBLE 6 ch.g. Celtic Cone – Hayley (Indian Ruler) [1992/3 18g] sturdy gelding: tailed off in novice event in March on hurdling debut. *Mrs Gill E. Jones, Ireland* —

CELTIC HAMLET 14 ch.g. Celtic Cone – Royal Gertrude (Royal Buck) [1992/3 c27g³] lengthy, sparely-made gelding: poor handicap chaser: stays 3¼m: acts on any going: sometimes blinkered. *J. E. Long* — c– —

CELTIC LAIRD 5 ch.g. Celtic Cone – Anitacat (No Argument) [1992/3 16v] strong, good sort: third foal: dam fair chaser, winner from 2m to 3m: not knocked about unduly when mid-field in 16-runner novice hurdle at Wincanton in January: should improve. *Mrs J. Pitman* — – p

CELTIC LANE 6 b.m. Welsh Captain – Cottagers Lane (Farm Walk) [1992/3 F18d F16s 26g] fourth foal: sister to winning hurdler Brandon Grove: dam lightly-raced half-sister to fairly useful jumper River Sirene: behind in NH Flat races and novice hurdle. *Mrs A. Swinbank* —

CELTIC LEISURE 9 b.g. Celtic Cone – Leisure Bay (Jock Scot) [1992/3 c27m² c33mᵖᵘ] good-topped gelding: hunter chaser: much improved effort when second to Double Silk at Cheltenham in April: jumped and ran poorly following month: stays 27f: acts on good to firm ground. *Mrs R. A. Vickery* — c110

CELTIC PRINCE 7 ch.g. Celtic Cone – Lothian Countess (New Brig) [1992/3 c24d* c26gꟳ c23s* c25g² c25d³ c24dᵖᵘ c35s⁴ c30sᵖᵘ] tall, leggy, plain gelding: fairly useful hurdler: fair chaser: won handicap at Perth and novice event at Uttoxeter early in season: ran creditably when in frame afterwards (not raced after February): thorough stayer: acts on soft ground: blinkered twice in 1991/2 and first 2 outings in 1992/3. *N. A. Twiston-Davies* — c104

CELTIC REMORSE 11 b.m. Celtic Cone – Armagnac Bay (Armagnac Monarch) [1992/3 c27s³ 26g c27s² c26gᵖᵘ] smallish mare: poor chaser: — c79 —

trained until after third start by J. Thomas: stays 27f: acts on any going: best form without blinkers. *T. L. Jones*

CELTIC RHYME 6 ch.m. Celtic Cone – Rhymarc (Rymer) [1992/3 23s⁵ 24g⁴ 23m 25m] leggy, plain mare: poor novice hurdler: stays 3m: best effort on good ground. *P. T. Dalton* — 70

CELTIC ROMPER 6 ch.g. Celtic Cone – Amber Palace (Sallust) [1992/3 16v⁴ 17f⁵] lengthy gelding: poor novice hurdler, lightly raced: yet to race beyond 2m: best effort on heavy ground. *T. J. Houlbrooke* — 79

CELTIC SAGE 6 b. or br.g. Celtic Cone – In A Dream (Caruso) [1992/3 22d² 20g 22m⁵] angular gelding: poor novice hurdler: will stay beyond 2¾m: acts on dead and good to firm ground. *D. Esden* — 80

CELTIC SONG 6 ch.m. Celtic Cone – Lor Darnie (Dumbarnie) [1992/3 16g³ 21d³ 20g³ 20s² 20gᵖᵘ 23d² 16g³ 21s* 20d³ 25g² 21sᵖᵘ 24gF 21d⁵ 21s⁵] sturdy mare: moderate form over hurdles: won novice event at Carlisle in January: out of form in the spring: stays 25f: acts on good to firm and soft going. *W. G. Reed* — 96

CELTIC SPARK 5 ch.g. Celtic Cone – Kohinoor Diamond (Roman Warrior) [1992/3 17v⁴ 16sᵖᵘ 24s 16f⁴ 20m⁴ 17g⁵] stocky gelding: first foal: dam winning hurdler: poor novice hurdler: should stay beyond 17f: best effort on heavy going: blinkered last 2 outings. *K. C. Bailey* — 79

CELTIC TOKEN 4 ch.c. Celtic Cone – Ready Token (SWE) (Record Token) [1992/3 F17f F17m] second foal in Britain: dam won over jumps in Sweden: well beaten in NH Flat races: should stay to race over hurdles. *F. Jordan*

CELTIC TOWN 5 ch.g. Celtic Cone – Booterstown (Master Owen) [1992/3 16s 17d] sixth foal: half-brother to novice hurdler Nicsamlyn (by Julio Mariner): dam poor novice hurdler: tailed off in novice hurdles. *O. Sherwood* — –

CELTIC TRUST 10 ch.g. Celtic Cone – Trust Ann (Capistrano) [1992/3 c27g⁴ c21m⁴ c27mᵖᵘ] strong, workmanlike gelding: staying chaser: well beaten in 1992/3. *Simon J. Robinson* — c– –

CELTIC WATERS 8 ch.m. Celtic Cone – Moonbreaker (Twilight Alley) [1992/3 c21dᵘʳ c23gF c25gᵖᵘ c20gF c20s⁶ c20g⁴ c24g² c25gᵖᵘ c24g c23dF c24m⁴ c25g⁵ c24s³ 27d⁶] leggy mare: poor novice hurdler/chaser: stays 3m: acts on soft ground: poor jumper of fences. *Mrs D. Thomson* — c83 x –

CELTIC WILLIAM 10 b.g. Celtic Cone – By Midnight (By Rights) [1992/3 c21gᵖᵘ] poor pointer: no show in maiden hunter chase in May. *Mrs J. A. Skelton* — c–

CELTIC WIND 6 ch.m. Celtic Cone – Cool Wind (Windjammer (USA)) [1992/3 17g⁶ 16f 17d⁵ 21s⁴ 17sᵖᵘ 17gᵖᵘ] small mare: bad novice hurdler. *T. Morton* — 65

CELTINO 5 ch.g. Relkino – Celtic Slave (Celtic Cone) [1992/3 F17f⁵] first foal: dam fair hurdler and fairly useful chaser: fifth of 18 in NH Flat race at Sandown in March: yet to race over hurdles or fences. *Capt. T. A. Forster*

CENANNUS BOY 4 b.g. All Systems Go – Natina-May (Mandrake Major) [1992/3 F17d] first foal: dam poor novice selling hurdler: tailed off in NH Flat race at Carlisle in April: yet to race over hurdles. *F. S. Storey*

CENTRAL LASS 5 gr.m. Glasgow Central – Fast Gold (Goldfella) [1992/3 F16s F17m] compact mare: second foal: half-sister to a poor animal by Spanish Bold: dam probably of little account: well beaten in NH Flat races in the spring: yet to race over hurdles or fences. *K. White*

CENTRE ATTRACTION 14 b.g. Little Buskins – Money For Fun (Even Money) [1992/3 c24m² c20s³ c21v³] close-coupled gelding: fair hunter chaser nowadays: stays 3m: acts on good to firm and heavy ground: visored once. *N. B. Mason* — c91 –

CENTURY PORT (FR) 8 b.g. Iron Duke (FR) – Lots of Money (Hook Money) [1992/3 16d] leggy gelding: modest novice hurdler at best: will stay beyond 19f. *D. McCune* — 75

CERTAIN LADY 4 ch.f. Absalom – Bold Duchess (Persian Bold) [1992/3 17d⁵ a 16gᵖᵘ a 16gᶠ] small, sparely-made filly: useful 7f plater on Flat for G. Blum: showed nothing over hurdles: tried blinkered: dead. *R. T. Juckes*　　　　－

CERTAIN LIGHT 15 br.g. Lucifer (USA) – Fool Proof (Primera) [1992/3 c21s*] small, angular, workmanlike gelding: high-class hunter chaser at best: first form since 1990/1 when winning at Huntingdon in February: needs testing conditions at 2½m and stays 3¼m: acts on soft ground. *Mrs Angus Campbell*　　c104　　－

CERTAIN LOOK 6 b.h. Yawa – Best Lady (Try My Best (USA)) [1992/3 18vᵖᵘ] second foal: half-brother to a lightly-raced Flat maiden by Tender King: dam, maiden, stayed 1m: showed nothing in novice event in February on hurdling debut. *A. S. Neaves*　　　　－

CERTAIN STYLE 10 b.g. Connaught – Nushka (Tom Fool) [1992/3 16g³ 21frtr c16f³ 17s³ c17mrtr c24g] good-bodied gelding: winning hurdler: one-time fairly useful chaser at up to 2½m: sometimes blinkered: thoroughly irresolute and one to leave well alone. *J. A. B. Old*　　c§§　　§§

CEVA PARK 8 b.g. Salluceva – South Park (Sandford Lad) [1992/3 c27mᵖᵘ] tall, rather angular gelding: poor novice hurdler/chaser: stayed 3m: acted on good to firm ground: dead. *R. Earnshaw*　　c－　　－

CHADWICK'S GINGER 5 ch.m. Crofthall – Knight Hunter (Skyliner) [1992/3 16s a16g² a16g* a16g⁵ 17m] close-coupled mare: poor hurdler: won maiden hurdle at Southwell in February: ran creditably after: races only at around 2m: acts on good to firm ground and fibresand: blinkered once: sometimes finds little under pressure, and best held up. *B. C. Morgan*　　77

CHAFOLD COPSE 8 ch.g. Deep Run – Yellow Idol (Yellow God) [1992/3 17gᵖᵘ] big, rangy gelding: chasing type: type to carry condition: fair winning hurdler: ran as though something amiss in October: yet to race beyond 17f: has raced only on good ground. *G. Harwood*　　　　－

CHAGHATAI (USA) 7 ch.g. Sir Ivor – Clutch Hitter (USA) (Nodouble (USA)) [1992/3 17sᵖᵘ 16v a20g a20g 16g⁶ c16d⁶ c16f³ c16mᵖᵘ] lengthy, angular gelding: poor novice hurdler/chaser: best form at around 2m: acts on good to firm and dead ground: tried blinkered. *W. Clay*　　c72　　－

CHAIN SHOT 8 b.g. Pas de Seul – Burnished (Formidable (USA)) [1992/3 c18mur c18m³ c18m* c16d* c17d² c16m⁴] compact gelding: fair handicap chaser: won at Market Rasen and Perth early in season (not raced after October): races only at around 2m: acts on hard and dead ground: takes good hold: tough. *M. H. Easterby*　　c107　　－

CHALIE RICHARDS 6 b.g. Furry Glen – Polar Princess (Prince Hansel) [1992/3 F16v⁶ 16s⁵ c16d³] big, strong gelding: chasing type: sixth foal: dam, half-sister to useful hurdler/chaser Dublin Express, placed over hurdles in Ireland: showed promise in novice hurdle at Leicester and novice chase (close last of 3 finishers) at Haydock in February: will stay beyond 2m. *D. McCain*　　c93 ?　　－ p

CHALKIEFORT 4 gr.g. Belfort (FR) – Cutler Heights (Galivanter) [1992/3 F16g] third foal: half-brother to winning Flat plater Bantel Bowler (by Beverley Boy): dam well beaten over hurdles: showed nothing in NH Flat race at Catterick in March: yet to race over hurdles. *R. McDonald*　　　　－

CHAMBROS 6 ch.g. Krayyan – Chilcombe (Morston (FR)) [1992/3 16vur 17d²] strong, compact gelding: fair middle-distance winner on Flat: showed plenty of ability both starts in novice hurdles, given a lot to do when second at Hereford in February: reportedly broke down on Flat in June. *N. A. Twiston-Davies*　　110

CHAMOIS BOY 9 ch.g. Buckskin (FR) – Levandia (Le Levanstell) [1992/3 22fᵖᵘ c27vᵖᵘ 23s⁵ 25v 21v 18g⁴ 22g] compact ex-Irish gelding: winning hurdler: trained first 5 starts by R. Frost: only form in Britain when fourth in handicap at Fontwell in March: has shown nothing over fences: stays well: acts on soft ground: blinkered third to fifth outings. *R. J. O'Sullivan*　　c－　　94

CHAMPAGNE GOLD 6 ch.g. Bairn (USA) – Halkissimo (Khalkis) [1992/3 17s 16v 20s 17s 16d² 16d⁵ 17m] leggy gelding: moderate handicap hurdler nowadays: should stay beyond 2m: acts on dead going: blinkered last 3 starts. *J. C. McConnochie*   90

CHAMPAGNE LAD 7 ch.g. Hawaiian Return (USA) – Bohemian Girl (Pardao) [1992/3 c17g³ c21d² c19dF c21v⁶ c21s² c21d* c21f³ c21f* c20s*] short-backed, sparely-made gelding: useful hurdler: won novice chases at Windsor and Wincanton and handicap chase at Chepstow in second half of season: stays 21f: acts on any going with possible exception of heavy: sometimes hangs and finds nothing under pressure. *J. T. Gifford*   c116 –

CHAMPAGNE RUN 8 b.g. Runnett – Tolaytala (Be My Guest (USA)) [1992/3 20f 26g⁶ 22s³ 22s c21dpu 17v² 18s 21v a20g 17d³dis 22s⁶] lengthy gelding: modest hurdler: trained until after penultimate start by W. G. M. Turner: jumped badly on only outing over fences: stays 3¼m: acts on any going: occasionally blinkered or visored: inconsistent. *L. G. Cottrell*   c– 95

CHAMPENOISE 5 b.m. Forzando – Migoletty (Oats) [1992/3 a16gF] half-sister to winning hurdler Jabrut (by Young Generation): plating-class miler on Flat: sold out of M. Bell's stable 3,300 gns Newmarket Autumn Sales: behind when falling in novice hurdle in January. *R. E. Barr*   –

CHANCE BUY 10 b.g. Rolfe (USA) – Astonishment (Blast) [1992/3 c24g] smallish, sparely-made gelding: novice hunter chaser: stays 3m: acts on dead ground: blinkered once. *Mrs S. Nash*   c– –

CHANCERY BUCK 10 ch.g. Pauper – What Vision (Golden Vision) [1992/3 c27s³ c27d² c24g³ c22m² c22spu c26vpu c26fpu c18g³ c25d⁵ c24f⁶] leggy gelding: moderate handicap chaser: trained until after sixth start by G. Balding: stays 3¼m: acts on good to firm and soft going. *R. G. Frost*   c94

CHANDIGARH 5 br.g. High Top – Lady Zi (Manado) [1992/3 17d³ 17s 16s 16drtr 16gpu] sturdy gelding: modest maiden at around 1m on Flat: third at Wolverhampton in November, only form in novice hurdles: most unlikely to stay beyond 2m: temperamental. *R. Lee*   80 §

CHANGE THE ACT 8 b.g. Furry Glen – Raise The Standard (Distinctly (USA)) [1992/3 c21vpu c21s² c21m³ c16m* c17v³] long-backed, angular gelding: fair chaser: won handicap at Worcester in March: effective at 2m to 21f: acts on soft and good to firm going: blinkered last 3 starts. *O. Sherwood*   c111 –

CHANGE WEAR 7 b.g. Alzao (USA) – Piccadilly Lil (Pall Mall) [1992/3 c17spu] sparely-made gelding: tubed: winning 2½m selling chaser: lightly raced and no form since 1990/1. *B. Scriven*   c– –

CHANNEL PASTIME 9 b.g. Turn Back The Time (USA) – Channel Ten (Babu) [1992/3 c25spu c24spu c24vpu c24dur c27spu] sturdy, lengthy gelding: yet to complete in novice chases. *D. L. Williams*   c–

CHANNELS GATE 9 b.g. Fine Blue – Collies Pet (Clear Run) [1992/3 c26g* c27s* c23g² c27s³ c24d² c25d³ c32mur c22f⁴] good-topped gelding: third foal: half-brother to novice hurdler Bit of Space (by Space King): dam fair pointer: former eventer: won novice chases at Hereford and Newton Abbot early in season: ran creditably afterwards: stays very well: probably acts on any ground: forces pace and jumps well. *J. A. C. Edwards*   c104

CHANTILLY DAWN 9 b.m. Gunner B – Liscannor Lass (Burglar) [1992/3 18g] smallish, sparely-made mare: poor novice selling hurdler: blinkered twice. *J. C. Haynes*   –

CHANTRY BARTLE 7 ch.g. Say Primula – Sallametti (USA) (Giacometti) [1992/3 17m* 21m² 21g² 17v³ 17s⁴ 16g⁴ 17s* 17f³ 18m²] smallish gelding: fair handicap hurdler: won at Carlisle in October and January: stays 21f: acts on any going: consistent. *C. W. Thornton*   108

CHAPEL HILL (IRE) 5 b.m. The Parson – Hazy Hill (Goldhill) [1992/3 17g² 16s³ 16d² 16v 16d⁵ 20m⁴ 17m] lengthy mare: third foal: half-sister to Irish NH Flat winner Hazy Rose (by Roselier): dam never ran: modest novice hurdler: should stay beyond 17f: acts on soft ground (well below best on heavy and good to firm). *Andrew Turnell*   87

CHAPEL OF BARRAS (IRE) 4 b.g. Bob Back (USA) – Gay Honey (Busted) [1992/3 F 12d* F 17f] workmanlike gelding with plenty of scope: half-brother to winning hurdler Green Spider (by Gay Fandango) and Flat winner Petropower (by Petorius): dam unraced: won NH Flat race at Windsor in February: showed further signs of ability when behind in valuable similar event at Aintree in April and in 3 races on Flat afterwards: yet to race over hurdles. *P. J. Hobbs*

CHARCOAL BURNER 8 br.g. Royal Match – Resist (Reliance II) [1992/3 16v⁵ 17d 17g⁶ 17s⁵ 17d⁴] small gelding: poor hurdler: trained until after fourth start by R. Callow: races mainly at around 2m: acts on heavy going. *Mrs J. G. Retter* 87

CHARGED 4 ch.g. Scottish Reel – Abielle (Abwah) [1992/3 F 16g F 14m] half-brother to 2 winners on Flat, notably ungenuine Northern Amethyst (by Imperial Fling): dam stayed well: behind in NH Flat races: yet to race over hurdles. *W. Jarvis*

CHARLAFRIVOLA 5 br.g. Persian Bold – Tattle (St Paddy) [1992/3 17m³] close-coupled, sparely-made gelding: poor 2m novice hurdler. *T. R. Greathead* 66

CHARLIE ATLAS (IRE) 5 b.g. Strong Gale – Lynwood Lady (Malicious) [1992/3 F 16d 17s⁴ 16s 16g] strong, good sort: third foal: brother to novice hurdler Paper Star: dam winning selling hurdler at up to 2½m: well beaten in novice hurdles. *S. Mellor* –

CHARLIE BURTON 11 b.g. My Chopin – Judy Burton (Mummy's Pet) [1992/3 18m² 17gᵖᵘ 16f 22g⁶ 17dᵖᵘ] compact gelding: winning 2m hurdler: lightly raced: seems to have lost his form: usually blinkered. *G. E. Jones* 90 d

CHARLIE DICKINS 9 b.g. Free State – Time of Your Life (Mount Hagen (FR)) [1992/3 16g³ 17m³ 17f³ 22s⁵ 22d 16f 16f⁴] workmanlike gelding: modest hurdler: showed ability only completed start over fences (1991/2): stays 2¾m: seems suited by give in the ground: inconsistent and sometimes reluctant. *J. L. Harris* c– § 98 §

CHARLIE McCARTHY 5 b.g. Tudor Rhythm – Impatience (Kibenka) [1992/3 c24mᵖᵘ] leggy, sparely-made gelding: pulled up in a point and a maiden hunter chase in February. *M. McCarthy* c–

CHARLIE NOSE 10 ch.g. Stetchworth – Pride of Hatton (Gulf Pearl) [1992/3 20mᵖᵘ] workmanlike gelding: novice hurdler/winning 2½m chaser, very lightly raced. *C. Weedon* c– –

CHARLIE'S DARLING 5 b.m. Homing – Kip's Sister (Cawston's Clown) [1992/3 18s 23s² a22g² a20gᵖᵘ] leggy mare: poor hurdler: pulled up lame final start (January): stays 23f: acts on soft, good to firm going and equitrack. *J. White* 80

CHARLOTTE'S EMMA 6 b.m. Oats – Charlotte's Festival (Gala Performance (USA)) [1992/3 23g⁵ 26d* 23s 24d⁵ 25d⁴] close-coupled, sparely-made mare: fair handicap hurdler: won at Catterick in November: below form afterwards (not raced after February): stays 3¼m: acts on any going. *Mrs J. D. Goodfellow* 105

CHARLTON YEOMAN 8 b.g. Sheer Grit – Bell Walks Breeze (Flaming Breeze (CAN)) [1992/3 c21f4 c21f*] leggy gelding: fair hurdler at best: won weakly-contested novice chase at Huntingdon in May: stays 21f: acts on dead and firm ground: blinkered once. *R. Rowe* c90 –

CHARLYCIA 5 b.m. Good Times (ITY) – Gallic Law (Galivanter) [1992/3 18g 16m³ 18d⁵ 18d⁶ 16s⁴ 16s a16g⁴ a20g³ 16d³ 17m³ 18m* 18sᵇᵈ 17s⁵ 18m⁴ 17f⁵] neat mare: won selling hurdle at Market Rasen (bought in 5,200 gns) in March: below form afterwards: stays 2½m: acts on good to firm, soft going and fibresand: sometimes visored, including when successful. *T. J. Carr* 88

CHARLY PHARLY (FR) 6 b.g. Pharly (FR) – Burnished (Formidable (USA)) [1992/3 17f³ 16s 16d 17d 17m* 18f*] workmanlike gelding: improved form when winning selling hurdles at Newton Abbot (sold out of B. Llewellyn's stable 3,700 gns) and Fontwell (handicap, retained 3,200 gns) in 97

May: stays 2¼m: acts well on a firm surface: tried in blinkers, better without: front runner. *R. G. Frost*

CHARMED I'M SURE 6 ch.m. Nicholas Bill – Farandella (English Prince) [1992/3 17g⁵ 20vᵘʳ 18s* 20s 22d⁴ 24s 20g⁴] workmanlike mare: won selling handicap hurdle at Exeter (no bid) in December: creditable efforts when fourth afterwards: stays 2¾m: acts on good to firm and soft ground: blinkered nowadays. *P. G. Murphy*   87

CHARMED LIFE 4 b.c. Legend of France (USA) – Tanagrea (Blakeney) [1992/3 18sᵖᵘ] sturdy, angular colt: claimed out of H. Cecil's stable £8,007 after winning 1½m claimer in September, well beaten on Flat since: little sign of aptitude for hurdling in juvenile event at Exeter in January. *A. Barrow*   –

CHARMERS WISH 9 b.m. Beau Charmeur (FR) – Velvet's Wish (Three Wishes) [1992/3 c20g c22m c25m² c25v⁵ c20s⁵ c20s c24d c21gᵖᵘ c27dᶠ] good-topped ex-Irish mare: poor novice chaser: trained until after seventh start by J. Rossiter: stays 25f: acts on good to firm and dead ground. *David F. Smith*   c76

CHARMING GALE 6 b. or br.m. Strong Gale – Evas Charm (Carlburg) [1992/3 25m⁵ c21d² c23g* c25g² c23g³ c23d* c23s⁴ c24gᵖᵘ c21g³ c21g⁴ c24m* c24s² c21f³ c21g³] angular, sparely-made mare: winning hurdler: won 2 novice chases at Kelso in first half of season and a novice handicap chase at Carlisle in March: stays 25f: acts on firm and dead ground. *Mrs S. C. Bradburne*   c93
                                                                                     –

CHARMONIX 4 ch.f. Scottish Reel – Sand Valley (FR) (Arabian) [1992/3 17mᵖᵘ 17d* 16d 16v⁴ a18gᵖᵘ] tall, leggy filly: poor maiden on Flat: won novice selling hurdle at Stratford (no bid) in October: poor efforts afterwards (not raced after February): yet to race beyond 17f: acts on dead going. *J. Joseph*   78

CHARTER SPRINGS 7 b.h. Miami Springs – Little Charter (Runnymede) [1992/3 17mᵖᵘ 16dᵖᵘ 24gᵖᵘ 21f⁵] half-brother to winning hurdler Charmeleon Girl (by New Member) and winning pointer Chevanter (by Levanter): dam won 1m seller: has shown nothing over hurdles. *Miss C. Horler*   –

CHASING GOLD 7 gr.m. Sonnen Gold – Royal Huntress (Royal Avenue) [1992/3 c22mᵖᵘ c18fᵘʳ c21gᵖᵘ] workmanlike mare: no sign of ability. *A. J. K. Dunn*   c–
                                                                                     –

CHASMARELLA 8 b.m. Yukon Eric (CAN) – Miss Polly Peck (March Past) [1992/3 25d³ 21f] small, sparely-made mare: moderate hurdler: trained until after first start by A. Davison: suited by 3m: acts on firm and dead ground. *Miss S. L. Gallie*   90

CHAT-A-LONG 7 ch.g. Le Bavard (FR) – Cool Blue (Deep Run) [1992/3 F17g c21gᵖᵘ c21m³ c24gᵖᵘ] leggy gelding: second foal: dam won 2m maiden hurdle in Ireland: no sign of ability in early-season novice chases: blinkered last 2 starts: won a point in April. *D. H. Brown*   c–

CHATAM (USA) 9 b.g. Big Spruce (USA) – Cristalina (FR) (Green Dancer (USA)) [1992/3 c27s⁴ c24d² c27m]   c161
      The 1991 Hennessy Cognac Gold Cup winner Chatam was returned to   –
Newbury in November after an eleven-month absence from the track, facing a considerably stiffer task than when winning the previous year from Party Politics and Docklands Express. His fitness, however, could be taken on trust—Pipe's horses are nearly always as fit as they can be made first time—and Chatam started joint-second favourite behind Jodami, to whom he had to concede 16 lb. Chatam did very well to finish fourth behind Sibton Abbey, Jodami and The Fellow, especially as his jumping let him down on the day. Another eleven weeks elapsed before Chatam was seen out again, during which time Jodami won the Mandarin Handicap Chase at Newbury (a race won by Chatam the previous year) and the Peter Marsh Chase at Haydock. When the pair met at level weights in the Hennessy Cognac Gold Cup at Leopardstown in mid-February Jodami started favourite, ahead of

Dr B. Nolan's "Chatam"

Chatam, the pair comprising a very strong British challenge for what is the Irish equivalent of the Cheltenham Gold Cup, a level-weights championship event for staying chasers. British-trained horses won five of the first six runnings—the race was inaugurated in 1987—and Jodami and Chatam dominated the latest edition. Chatam was just run out of it by Jodami after leading two out but he jumped much better than at Newbury and confirmed himself a high-class chaser, one who looked to have a fair chance on form in the Gold Cup. He was Scudamore's preferred mount at Cheltenham—the stable also ran Rushing Wild and Run For Free—but he ran poorly, never travelling or jumping well after blundering at the first. Scudamore deserted Chatam in favour of Captain Dibble in the Martell Grand National; Chatam was one of those who did not start the race which was declared void after two false starts. Chatam looked none too keen to line up at Aintree and wasn't seen out again, though he was kept in training for a crack at the Grand Steeple-Chase de Paris in June, an engagement he missed after reportedly showing an aversion to French-style fences.

Chatam, whose pedigree has been dealt with in earlier Annuals, is a tall gelding who usually impresses in appearance. He has a round action, which some theorists would have taken as a sign that he was likely to be at a disadvantage in top-of-the-ground conditions such as those which prevailed on Gold Cup day. Whether Chatam is *unsuited* by a firm surface—the Gold Cup is the only time he has run on one over jumps—isn't something that can be concluded from the evidence available at the moment; but his Gold Cup performance is certainly something to bear very much in mind before

Chatam (USA) (b.g. 1984)	Big Spruce (USA) (b or br 1969)	Herbager (b 1956)	Vandale II / Flagette
		Silver Sari (b 1961)	Prince John / Golden Sari
	Cristalina (FR) (gr 1978)	Green Dancer (b 1972)	Nijinsky / Green Valley
		Crix (gr 1964)	Major Portion / Covert Side

backing him under similar conditions next time. There's more substance to the theory that Chatam needs a left-handed track: he has an ingrained tendency to jump left and has run badly both times he has been on a right-handed course over jumps. Chatam stays well and goes well fresh. *M. C. Pipe*

CHEAP METAL 8 br.g. Sonnen Gold – Economy Pep (Jimmy Reppin) [1992/3 22gF 20m* 20g5 21mpu a20g a24g5 a20g3 a22g4 24f] sparely-made gelding: poor hurdler: won novice handicap at Plumpton in September: stays 3m: acts on good to firm ground and equitrack: tried visored, blinkered nowadays: tends to hang and carry head high: unreliable. *R. Ingram*   85 §

CHEAP 'N' NICE 6 ch.m. Julio Mariner – Double Cousin (Dalesa) [1992/3 16g] close-coupled, angular mare: well beaten in novice hurdles. *C. Parker*   –

CHEEKA 4 ch.g. Dawn Johnny (USA) – Lallax (Laxton) [1992/3 18g5 18dpu 16d2 16d5 a18gpu a16g4 a18g3 a16g3] lightly-raced maiden on Flat: poor novice hurdler: yet to race beyond 2¼m: acts on dead going and equitrack: races up with pace: sometimes looks none too keen. *C. Smith*   81

CHEEKY POT 5 b.g. Petoski – Pato (High Top) [1992/3 18d2 17m 16g5 18s* a16g 16s3 20m* 22g4 18m 16g4] smallish, good-topped gelding: modest hurdler: won novice handicaps at Sedgefield in December and Edinburgh in February: best effort final start: effective at 2m and stays 2¾m: acts on good to firm and soft ground (soon behind on fibresand): usually visored/blinkered. *Denys Smith*   90

CHEERFUL TIMES 10 b.g. Faraway Times (USA) – Chevulgan (Cheval) [1992/3 17d 16spu 16v5 16s 16s6 17d6 16g4 17f5 22f2 21v3 22d6] compact gelding: fair hurdler nowadays: stays 2¾m: probably acts on any going: held up. *B. A. McMahon*   109

CHELSEA MAN 12 b.g. Idiot's Delight – River Spell (Spartan General) [1992/3 c26f2] sparely-made gelding: hunter chaser: stays 3¼m: acts on firm going: usually blinkered or visored nowadays: deliberate jumper. *M. C. Ashton*   c81 / –

CHELWORTH RAIDER 7 ch.g. Oats – Driven Snow (Deep Run) [1992/3 16d3 17d* 17g2 16d 17m2 17g 16f2 20g2] leggy, lengthy gelding: fair handicap hurdler: won at Huntingdon in November: ran well most starts afterwards: stays 2½m: acts on good to soft and firm going. *J. L. Spearing*   102

CHEQUE BOOK 5 ch.g. Nestor - Vulgan's Joy (Vulgan Slave) [1992/3 16grtr 17fpu 16fF 17f] lightly-made gelding: no sign of ability over hurdles: temperamental (refused to race once): blinkered once. *W. G. Mann*   – §

CHEREN BOY 4 ch.g. Swing Easy (USA) – Shades of Autumn (Double Form) [1992/3 17spu 16dpu] close-coupled gelding: maiden plater on Flat: no sign of ability over hurdles. *J. Honeyball*   –

CHERGO 8 b.g. Abednego – Cheramble (Wrekin Rambler) [1992/3 c22g2 c25m* c25d3 c25m2] workmanlike gelding: third foal: half-brother to winning Irish pointer Cheiranthus (by Cantab): dam won on Flat and over hurdles: won hunter chase at Bangor in March: good third at Ascot later in month: stays 25f: acts on good to firm and dead ground. *Miss C. Saunders*   c97

CHERRY BOB 4 ch.f. Adonijah – Cherry Picking (Queen's Hussar) [1992/3 17m3] poor plater on Flat, stays 1½m: third in early-season juvenile claiming hurdle at Bangor: sold 700 gns Doncaster October Sales. *C. W. Thornton*   51

CHERRYGROVE   7 ch.g. Roman Warrior – Soldiers Dream (Spartan   c–
General) [1992/3 c23mᵖᵘ c21gF c21mᵖᵘ] lengthy gelding: no sign of ability in
steeplechases: blinkered last 2 starts. *R. Curtis*

CHERRYKINO   8 b.g. Relkino – Cherry Stack (Raise You Ten) [1992/3   **c145**
c21s* c21d* c20v* c21d* c27mF]
            The death of four horses at jumping's great show-piece the Chelten-
ham Festival was a stark reminder that injury and death are perennial
threats in National Hunt racing. Ashfold Copse suffered a fatal fall in the Sun
Alliance Chase, the mare Emily's Star broke her knee in a fall at the first in
the National Hunt Chase, Milford Quay broke his off-hind on landing over
the sixth in the Mildmay of Flete, and Cherrykino fractured his near-fore
when falling at the seventh in the Tote Cheltenham Gold Cup. Cherrykino's
demise robbed steeplechasing of one of its most exciting prospects, a horse
who seemed certain to improve into a good-class chaser, possibly a top-
class one. Cherrykino had won his last six races and looked well worth his
place in the Gold Cup field on the strength of a victory over some more
established performers in the Racing In Wessex Chase at Wincanton in
February. He'd been successful earlier in the season in a handicap at
Worcester, a qualifier in the Arlington Premier Chase series at Uttoxeter
and another handicap at Chepstow, jumping well and winning in excellent
style each time. Cherrykino hadn't been raced beyond two and three
quarter miles over fences, but he'd won at three over hurdles and, though
not short of speed, looked sure to be suited by the Gold Cup trip. He
acted on heavy going and hadn't encountered top-of-the-ground before
Cheltenham.

Cherrykino (b.g. 1985)	Relkino (b 1973)	Relko (b 1960)	Tanerko / Relance III
		Pugnacity (b 1962)	Pampered King / Ballynulta
	Cherry Stack (b 1972)	Raise You Ten (br 1960)	Tehran / Visor
		Cherry Tang (br 1952)	Mustang / Bright Cherry

            The workmanlike Cherrykino was erroneously tagged in some news-
papers as 'the last relative of the immortal Arkle still racing', or similar. His
dam Cherry Stack was a daughter of Cherry Tang, a half-sister to Arkle.
Cherry Tang was sold by Arkle's breeder for only 380 guineas as a
five-year-old, before Arkle reached the racecourse. A poor hurdler, she was
later acquired by Arkle's owner Anne Duchess of Westminster for whom
her last foal—after three barren years—was the Raise You Ten filly Cherry
Stack. Cherry Stack, now dead, won over fences in Ireland and had two foals
before Cherrykino, Cherry Brave (by Le Bavard) and Gaelic Cherry (by
Gleason), both winning hunter chasers. Gaelic Cherry won the Duke of
Gloucester Memorial Hunters' Chase and the Royal Artillery Gold Cup,
both at Sandown, in the latest season. Cherrykino's owner sold his
year-younger half-sister Cherry Country (by Town And Country) when she
decided to give up breeding. Cherry Country is now at stud in Ireland.
Arkle's only other half-sister, Cherry Bud, produced an Irish Grand
National winner in Colebridge and an Aintree Grand National runner-up in
Vulture. That branch of the family was represented on the racecourse in the
latest season by the novice chasers Squeeze Play (out of Cherry Bud's
daughter Cherry Leaf) and Muirfield (out of Cherry Bud's daughter Cherry
Tart). The very good point-to-pointer Fort Hall (also out of Cherry Tart)
was second in a hunter chase at Huntingdon in May. *Capt. T. A. Forster*

CHERRYWOOD LASS   5 br.m. Belfort (FR) – Rainbow Vision (Prince
Tenderfoot (USA)) [1992/3 18m5] leggy mare: no form on Flat: tailed off in   –
claimer in February on hurdling debut. *R. Curtis*

CHERYLS PET (IRE)   5 b.m. General Ironside – Kilmanahan (Arctic
Slave) [1992/3 21v2 16d4 22v a20gF 17d 18d2 16s3 20d4] angular mare: 71 §
twelfth foal: dam unraced sister to a winning hurdler and half-sister to smart
hurdler Troyswood: poor novice hurdler: blinkered, claimed £5,050 final

start (February): stays 21f: acts on heavy going: sometimes looks ungenuine. *P. Burgoyne*

CHESAPEAKE BAY 8 b. or br.g. Rusticaro (FR) – Gulf Girl (Welsh Saint) [1992/3 17g² 16g c18m⁴ c16vᶠ c16s⁴] workmanlike gelding: maiden hurdler: moderate chaser: not raced after November: races only at around 2m: acts on good to firm and soft ground: pulls hard and best allowed to stride on: jumps fences none too fluently. *G. B. Balding* **c86**
90

CHESTER BELLE 4 b.f. Ballacashtal (CAN) – Cascabel (Matahawk) [1992/3 17mᵖᵘ] of little account on Flat: saddle slipped in early-season juvenile hurdle. *P. C. Haslam* –

CHESTER TERRACE 9 ch.g. Crofter (USA) – Persian Mourne (Mourne) [1992/3 a16g] small, compact gelding: winning hurdler: races only at 2m: acts on dead going. *J. L. Spearing* –

CHESWOLD LASS 9 ch.m. Derek H – Fashionable Lady (Prince Rois) [1992/3 18mᵖᵘ] sparely-made mare: of no account. *B. Richmond* –

CHEVELEY DANCER (USA) 5 b.g. Northern Baby (CAN) – Alwah (USA) (Damascus (USA)) [1992/3 16dᵖᵘ 16sᵖᵘ 16m 16s* 17dᵖᵘ] 50/1-winner of novice handicap hurdle at Worcester in March, only form of 1992/3: raced only at 2m: acts on soft going. *A. W. Denson* 82

CHIAROSCURO 7 b.g. Idiot's Delight – Lampshade (Hot Brandy) [1992/3 20v* 22d5] lengthy gelding: won novice handicap hurdle at Hereford in November: ran moderately following month: stays 2½m: acts on heavy going. *P. J. Hobbs* 85

CHIASSO FORTE (ITY) 10 b.g. Furry Glen – Cassai (FR) (Molvedo) [1992/3 17s² 17d³ 17d6 c16v² c21s³ c17g⁴ c21g⁴ c17v² c21f⁴ c19g⁴] sturdy gelding: fair hurdler/chaser: ran creditably most starts: stays 21f: acts on any going. *P. J. Hobbs* **c112**
112

CHICA MIA 9 b.m. Camden Town – Backwoodsgirl (Young Emperor) [1992/3 17m6 17m] leggy mare: no form over hurdles. *G. A. Ham* –

CHIC AND ELITE 6 b.m. Deep Run – Elite Lady (Prince Hansel) [1992/3 16gᵖᵘ 17m* 17m* 17g⁴ 16v⁴ 17s³ 21s a16g 17m⁴ c17g6] sturdy mare: won 2 novice hurdles at Carlisle early in season: showed some promise in novice event on chasing debut: should stay further than 17f: acts on good to firm and heavy going: takes good hold and makes running: should improve over fences. *J. J. O'Neill* **c– p**
94

CHICHELL'S HURST 7 ch.m. Oats – Milly Kelly (Murrayfield) [1992/3 21g 20s³ 18v6 21v* 21s³ 21s5 22mᵖᵘ] leggy, workmanlike mare: fair handicap hurdler: won at Leicester in January: ran well next time: stays 21f: best form with give in the ground and acts on heavy. *Mrs P. Sly* 107

CHICKABIDDY 5 b.m. Henbit (USA) – Shoshoni (Ballymoss) [1992/3 F17m 16g 20g 18d 16g 20g 16g 17m] small, sparely-made mare: poor novice hurdler: sold out of C. Thornton's stable 2,800 gns Doncaster November Sales after first start and resold 1,900 gns same venue in May: best efforts at around 2m: acts on good to firm ground. *J. K. M. Oliver* 62

CHIEF CELT 7 ch.g. Celtic Cone – Chieftain's Lady (Border Chief) [1992/3 22gᵖᵘ 21s* 22v³ 22s³ 22v 25s² 25s⁴ 24g*] strong, lengthy gelding: won novice hurdles at Towcester in November and Worcester (improved form) in April: showed little only start over fences: suited by a good test of stamina: acts on heavy ground. *J. S. King* **c–**
110

CHIEF IN COMMAND 5 ch.h. Celtic Cone – Chieftain's Lady (Border Chief) [1992/3 F16g] brother to one-time top-class hurdler Celtic Chief and to winning hurdler Chief Celt and half-brother to other winners: dam unraced: well beaten in NH Flat race at Kempton in February: yet to race over hurdles or fences. *M. C. Pipe* –

CHIEF MOLE (USA) 8 gr.g. Caro – Head Spy (USA) (Chieftain II) [1992/3 16d5 16dᶠ c16m³] rangy gelding: poor novice hurdler: made mistakes when third in maiden at Edinburgh in February on chasing debut: **c81 §**
81 §

167

sold 1,400 gns Doncaster May Sales: best at 2m: acts on good to firm and dead ground: ungenuine. *J. H. Johnson*

CHIEF RAIDER (IRE) 5 br.g. Strong Gale – Lochadoo (Lochnager) [1992/3 21d* 21s⁵ 22d 22g⁶] sturdy gelding: won novice hurdle at Hexham in November (trained until after then by W. A. Stephenson): well below form last 2 outings: sold 18,000 gns in May: stays 21f: acts on soft going. *P. Cheesbrough*   95

CHILD OF THE MIST 7 b.g. Lomond (USA) – Lighted Lamp (USA) (Sir Gaylord) [1992/3 17spu 23s 23s 16s³ 21v*dis 17g* 17f² 17g⁴ 20f 21f 21f⁵ 17g*] lengthy gelding: fairly useful hurdler: first past the post in claimer at Towcester (disqualified) and 2 handicaps at Fakenham in second half of season: effective at around 2m and stays 2¾m: acts on any going: blinkered once: sometimes looks irresolute. *John Whyte*   124

CHILL WIND 4 gr.c. Siberian Express (USA) – Springwell (Miami Springs) [1992/3 17m* 20g⁵ 16spu 17m*] big, lengthy colt: poor maiden on Flat: won juvenile hurdle at Carlisle in September and novice handicap on same course in March: effective at 17f and will stay beyond 2½m: acts on good to firm ground. *N. Bycroft*   86

CHILTERN WAY 7 b.g. Radical – Summerello (Bargello) [1992/3 25d⁴ c26vpu c23v⁴ c23vpu 26dpu] close-coupled gelding: of little account: blinkered final start. *K. R. Burke*   c– –

CHIMES OF THE DAWN 9 ch.g. Tower Walk – Neptia's Word (Great Nephew) [1992/3 c16dpu c16dur] angular gelding: selling hurdler: jumped none too fluently both starts over fences: races only at around 2m: acts on dead going. *J. Mackie*   c– –

CHINAMAN 4 b.g. Noalto – Diorina (Manacle) [1992/3 18v 17v³ 16d 16d 17f² 17m³] leggy, good-topped gelding: half-brother to winning hurdler Disport (by Import): poor maiden on Flat and over hurdles: retained 4,800 gns Ascot May Sales: yet to race beyond 2¼m: probably acts on any ground: blinkered last 3 outings. *W. G. R. Wightman*   80

CHINA SKY 5 b.g. Tina's Pet – Buy G'S (Blakeney) [1992/3 17m 16vpu a18gpu] leggy gelding: winning miler on Flat: showed nothing over hurdles: sold out of C. Allen's stable 1,400 gns Newmarket Autumn Sales after first start. *R. M. Stronge*   –

CHIP AND RUN 7 b.g. Strong Gale – Pampered Run (Deep Run) [1992/3 c16g* c20g* c21g* c17g³ c18gF] ex-Irish gelding: first foal: dam winning 2m hurdler: won 2 novice chases at Down Royal in October when trained by F. Flood and 3-runner handicap at Wolverhampton in March: better suited by 2½m than 2m: has raced mainly on good ground: jumps well. *Mrs J. G. Retter*   c110 –

CHIPAROPAI (IRE) 5 b.m. Commanche Run – Violino (USA) (Hawaii) [1992/3 17m⁴ 17s² 16v³ 17s* 20d] smallish mare: poor form over hurdles: trained by W. Storey first outing: won novice handicap at Bangor in December: not raced after following month: sold 2,200 gns Doncaster May Sales: should stay further than 17f: acts on heavy and good to firm going. *M. D. Hammond*   76

CHIPCHASE 13 b.g. New Brig – Tillside (Lucky Brief) [1992/3 22m c21m⁴ c26mpu] compact, good-bodied gelding: poor hurdler/chaser nowadays: stays 25f: probably acts on any going: tried blinkered in 1986/7. *B. E. Wilkinson*   c– –

CHIRKPAR 6 b.g. Shernazar – Callianire (Sir Gaylord) [1992/3 16d 25m] leggy gelding: smart hurdler at best: below form in 1992/3, including in Stayers' Hurdle at Cheltenham: stays 2¾m: acts on good to firm and soft ground. *J. S. Bolger, Ireland*   –

CHOCTAW 9 gr.g. Great Nephew – Cheyenne (Sovereign Path) [1992/3 c26d² c26s² c29s² c26g² c28g³ c27d² c27m*] strong gelding: moderate handicap chaser: won at Sedgefield in May: stays well: acts on any going: tried blinkered (not in 1992/3): often makes running: sometimes looks ungenuine, but is consistent. *P. Beaumont*   c94

CHOICE CHALLANGE 10 ch.g. Deep Run – Geraldine's Pet   **c97 x**
(Laurence O) [1992/3 c25mF c21d4 c21v5 c24g4 c21s2] lengthy gelding: **–**
modest handicap chaser: not raced after January: stays 3m well: probably
acts on any going: blinkered nowadays: often let down by his jumping, and
sometimes looks none too genuine. *M. D. Hammond*

CHOICE LOT 6 b.g. Auction Ring (USA) – More Candy (Ballad Rock)
[1992/3 16d] no sign of ability over hurdles: sold 1,100 gns Doncaster   **–**
September Sales. *T. H. Caldwell*

CHOIR'S IMAGE 6 br.m. Lochnager – Choir (High Top) [1992/3 17m3
16dF 18g] leggy mare: only sign of ability when third in novice hurdle at   **79**
Newcastle in October. *J. L. Eyre*

CHRIS'S GLEN 4 ch.g. Librate – Misty Glen (Leander) [1992/3 F16m
F16g6] third foal: half-brother to 2 poor maiden jumpers: dam winning   **–**
hurdler who stayed 3m: well beaten in NH Flat races: yet to race over
hurdles. *J. M. Bradley*

CHRISTIAN LAD 5 gr.g. Belfort (FR) – California Split (Sweet
Revenge) [1992/3 17dpu 17gpu] leggy gelding: winning sprinter: no form   **–**
over hurdles. *R. G. Frost*

CHRISTMAS GORSE 7 b.g. Celtic Cone – Spin Again (Royalty)   **c–**
[1992/3 c20dpu] big, rangy gelding: poor novice hurdler: showed nothing on   **–**
chasing debut in December. *N. A. Gaselee*

CHRISTMAS HOLLY 12 b.g. Blind Harbour – Holly Doon (Doon)   **c–**
[1992/3 16d6 22g6 28gpu 17f5 a21g c25g] workmanlike gelding: winning   **85**
hurdler/chaser: poor performer nowadays: stays 3m: probably acts on any
going. *R. S. Wood*

CHRISTMAS HOLS 7 b.g. Young Generation – Foston Bridge   **c–**
(Relkino) [1992/3 21g5 c21m6] compact gelding: novice selling hurdler: **–**
trained first start by Miss L. Bower: tailed off on chasing debut: best form at
around 2m: acts on hard ground: usually blinkered/visored nowadays. *J. S. Greatrex*

CHUCK CURLEY (USA) 5 b.g. Gregorian (USA) – Bishop's Fling
(USA) (King's Bishop (USA)) [1992/3 16g2 16s* 17g2 17s3 17g5] big, good   **98 p**
sort with plenty of scope: every inch a chaser: won novice hurdle at
Nottingham in December: creditable efforts afterwards: likely to prove best
around 2m: acts on soft going: pulls hard, is held up and tends to find little:
open to further improvement. *B. J. Curley*

CHUCKLESTONE 10 b.g. Chukaroo – Czar's Diamond (Queen's
Hussar) [1992/3 24d4 26g2 24f*] neat gelding: fair handicap hurdler: won at   **109**
Chepstow in May: stays 3¼m: acts on firm and dead ground: needs plenty of
driving. *J. S. King*

CHUKKARIO 7 b.g. Chukaroo – River Damsel (Forlorn River) [1992/3
16s 23s a20g5] leggy gelding: no sign of ability. *P. Mitchell*   **–**

CHURCH STAR 9 b.m. Cajun – Lady of Rathleek (Furry Glen) [1992/3
18g5 18gpu 16d2 17f2 17v a20g4] workmanlike mare: novice selling hurdler: **69 §**
stays 2¼m: acts on firm and dead ground: tried visored, blinkered
nowadays: tail swisher: ungenuine. *J. J. Bridger*

CIRCLE BOY 6 b.g. Carlingford Castle – Magic User (Deep Run) [1992/3
18g5 22g 18d] sparely-made gelding: bad novice hurdler. *R. R. Lamb*   **59**

CIRCUIT COURT (IRE) 5 gr.g. Law Society (USA) – Spindle Berry
(Dance In Time (CAN)) [1992/3 16v5] fourth foal: brother to Irish Flat   **–**
winner Coalition and half-brother to 2 other Flat winners: dam 5f winner at
2 yrs: 1¾m Flat winner in Ireland in 1991: well-beaten fifth in novice event
at Worcester in April on hurdling debut. *J. R. Jenkins*

CIRCUIT RING 7 b.g. Electric – Brookfield Miss (Welsh Pageant)
[1992/3 17d3 23d6 17s2 16d6 a18g 20d2 22g5] sparely-made gelding: **87**
half-brother to fair staying hurdler Cairncastle (by Ardross): moderate
staying handicapper on Flat: modest novice hurdler: stayed 2½m: acted on
soft going: dead. *T. H. Caldwell*

CIRCULATION 7 b.g. Town And Country – Veinarde (Derring-Do) [1992/3 c16m⁴ c16d³ c20sF³ c16v⁴ c16d⁶ c21g² c18s* c17d² c16m³ c18d⁴] strong, good-bodied gelding: carries plenty of condition: modest handicap chaser: won at Market Rasen in April: ran creditably next 2 outings: best form at up to 2¼m: acts on good to firm and heavy ground. *D. McCain*

c98
–

CISTOLENA 7 ch.m. Cisto (FR) – Keep Shining (Scintillant) [1992/3 21vᵖᵘ c25m⁴ c23mᵖᵘ] sparely-made mare: lightly raced: poor maiden hurdler/chaser. *W. Clay*

c66
–

CITY ENTERTAINER 12 br.g. Tycoon II – Border Mouse (Border Chief) [1992/3 c26d c27dᵖᵘ] one-time fairly useful staying chaser, lightly raced: sold 5,600 gns Ascot June (1992) Sales: no form in 1992/3. *D. McCain*

c–
–

CITY INDEX (USA) 7 b.g. J O Tobin (USA) – Fannie Annie (USA) (L'Enjoleur(CAN)) [1992/3 16d⁵ 21m⁶ c21v⁶ c20v² c16v⁶ c20dᵖᵘ 18f⁴] leggy, angular gelding: poor hurdler/chaser: probably stayed 3m: acted on any ground: sometimes looked none too keen: dead. *N. A. Smith*

c71
75

CITY KID 8 br.g. Black Minstrel – Glenarold Lass (Will Somers) [1992/3 21d⁶ 23s³ 22vᵖᵘ 23vᵖᵘ c18vF c21g* c21d³ c21d*] close-coupled, sturdy gelding: novice hurdler: won novice chases at Folkestone in February and Newton Abbot (handicap) in April: stays 3m: acts on soft ground: sometimes wears tongue strap. *J. T. Gifford*

c97
–

CITY LINE 4 b.g. Capricorn Line – Racine City (Dom Racine (FR)) [1992/3 17g a18g² 16m³ 18g²] neat gelding: moderate stayer on Flat: modest juvenile over hurdles: will stay beyond 2¼m: acts on good to firm going and equitrack. *D. R. Laing*

94

CIXI 5 b.m. Far Out East (USA) – Hasty Key (USA) (Key To The Mint (USA)) [1992/3 20vᵖᵘ 17gF 18v] sparely-made mare: winning selling hurdler: no form in 1992/3 (not raced after January): best form at around 2m: acts on hard going: front runner. *M. C. Pipe*

–

CLAIRON JUNIOR (FR) 6 b.g. Rose Laurel – La Gaina (FR) (New Chapter) [1992/3 21gᵖᵘ] unfurnished gelding: modest novice hurdler at best: will stay beyond 2½m: acts on dead ground. *Mrs F. Walwyn*

–

CLAIR SOLEIL (USA) 4 b.g. Conquistador Cielo – Parissaul (Saulingo) [1992/3 17g⁶ 17vᵖᵘ 17f⁵] neat gelding: half-brother to fairly useful hurdler Silken Fan (by Lear Fan): lightly-raced middle-distance maiden on Flat: no form over hurdles. *A. Moore*

–

CLAN REEL 4 ch.g. Move Off – Let's Dance (Mansingh (USA)) [1992/3 17s 17m] fourth living foal: brother to a poor animal: dam won from 7f to 1½m: tailed off in juvenile hurdles in the spring. *R. H. Goldie*

–

CLARE COAST 7 ch.g. Deep Run – Clare's Sheen (Choral Society) [1992/3 18d² 16g 22s⁵ 16g⁶] lengthy, angular gelding: seventh foal: half-brother to a winner in Belgium by Touch Paper: dam no show in 2 races over hurdles: poor novice hurdler: should stay beyond 2¼m: best effort on dead ground. *J. Wade*

81

CLARE LAD 10 ch.g. Garda's Revenge (USA) – Sea Dike (Dike (USA)) [1992/3 22d* 23m⁵ 21f 26s 17v⁵ 21s 21v³ 21v³ c21s⁶ c20g⁵ c26g² c25s⁶ c21d c21g² 21d²] sturdy gelding: selling hurdler: won handicap at Newton Abbot (bought in 2,000 gns) in August: poor novice chaser: stays 3¼m: acts on any going: blinkered seventh and final outings: jumps fences poorly. *D. J. Wintle*

c80 x
80

CLARES HORSE 6 b.g. Deep Run – At Random (Random Shot) [1992/3 22m³ 26gF 24g⁵ 23m c23f⁴ c23g* c23dF c26g³ c25g² c24dᵖᵘ c24m⁶] lengthy, dipped-backed gelding: poor maiden hurdler: won novice chase at Worcester in September: ran poorly afterwards: stays well: acts on good to firm ground: blinkered second and third outings: looks reluctant. *John R. Upson*

c89 §
79 §

CLARES OWN 9 b.g. Al Sirat (USA) – Andonian (Road House II) [1992/3 c18s* c21d⁴ c16g* c16s* c16g³ c16g⁵ c20d c18m² c18d²] workmanlike gelding: moderate chaser: won handicaps at Market Rasen, Ayr (conditional jockeys) and Nottingham in first half of season: also ran well last 2 starts, in

c94
–

May: effective from 2m to 3m: probably unsuited by heavy ground, acts on any other: often makes running: sometimes blinkered in 1989/90. *J. Wade*

CLASH OF CYMBALS   4 gr.g. Orchestra – Woodland View (Precipice Wood) [1992/3 aF16g4] first foal: dam, winning hurdler/chaser, stayed 2¾m: well-beaten fourth in NH Flat race at Lingfield in March: yet to race over hurdles. *P. J. Jones*

CLASS ATTRACTION (USA)   4 b.f. Northern Baby (CAN) – Chellingoua (USA) (Sharpen Up) [1992/3 F17f4 F16m] second foal: half-sister to a graded stakes-placed performer in USA by Hilal: dam lightly-raced maiden in France, placed over 1m: bought 5,300 gns Newmarket Autumn Sales: fourth at Hereford in May, probably better effort in NH Flat races: yet to race over hurdles. *M. C. Pipe*

CLASSEY BOY   10 ch.g. Celtic Cone – Trespassing (Poaching) [1992/3 c21v5 c22vpu c25spu c25v4] heavy-topped gelding: handicap chaser: no form in 1992/3: suited by a thorough test of stamina. *G. A. Ham*   c– –

CLASSICAL BLUE   7 ch.g. Fine Blue – Classical Air (Melodic Air) [1992/3 16g 17d4] very tall, lengthy gelding: fourth foal: half-brother to winning selling hurdler King's Classic (by Kinglet): dam never ran: poor form when fourth in late-season novice hurdle. *R. G. Frost*   78

CLASSICAL CHARM   10 b.g. Corvaro (USA) – Mahe Reef (Be Friendly) [1992/3 c16s4 c16d2 c16gF] tall, angular Irish gelding: top-class hurdler in 1987/8: one of the best novice chasers of 1991/2: best effort of 1992/3 on first start: acted on any going, but went particularly well in the mud: front runner: dead. *J. A. O'Connell, Ireland*   c144 –

CLASSIC BART   9 b.g. Class Distinction – Sea Farmer (Cantab) [1992/3 c25spu] modest pointer: no show in maiden hunter chase in April. *C. Graham*   c– –

CLASSIC CONTACT   7 b.g. Whistling Top – Fosseway Folly (Saucy Kit) [1992/3 20dF 22m3] leggy gelding: lightly-raced novice hurdler: modest form: stays 2¾m: acts on good to firm and soft going. *N. B. Mason*   87

CLASSIC EXHIBIT   4 b.g. Tate Gallery (USA) – See The Tops (Cure The Blues (USA)) [1992/3 18m6 17m3 17f2 17m2 16d* 17f3 16dF 16f4 16m3] small, sparely-made gelding: poor maiden on Flat: sold out of S. Woods's stable 3,600 gns Newmarket September Sales after second outing over hurdles: won juvenile selling hurdle at Uttoxeter (no bid) in October: ran well afterwards: likely to prove best at around 2m: acts on firm and dead ground: sometimes looks reluctant, and isn't one to trust. *A. L. Forbes*   79 §

CLASSIC HUNTER (NZ)   5 b.g. Ivory Hunter (USA) – Classic Lass (NZ) (Rapanni) [1992/3 F16d F17v2 F17v 21g6 22m4 23m5] sparely-made gelding: poor maiden hurdler: stays 23f: acts on good to firm ground. *D. H. Barons*   77

CLASSIC MINSTREL   9 br.g. Black Minstrel – Mariners Mate (Windsor Test) [1992/3 23g6 23d c20g2 c16s3 c24g*] big gelding: poor novice hurdler: won novice chase at Edinburgh in February: stays 3m: acts on soft ground. *Mrs S. C. Bradburne*   c87 67

CLASSIC RING (IRE)   5 b.m. Auction Ring (USA) – Classic Choice (Patch) [1992/3 17m5 18g6 21d] small, plain mare: poor novice hurdler: sold 2,100 gns Doncaster January Sales: stays 21f: acts on good to firm and dead ground. *J. I. A. Charlton*   63

CLASSICS PEARL (IRE)   5 gr.m. Reasonable (FR) – Zanskar (Godswalk (USA)) [1992/3 17g3 17d* 18f 25s6 19gF 16s3 20s* 23dpu] neat mare: maiden on Flat: attracted no bid after winning selling hurdles at Newton Abbot in September and Bangor in February: stays 2½m: acts on soft ground, ran badly on firm. *N. A. Twiston-Davies*   84

CLASSIC STATEMENT   7 ch.h. Mill Reef (USA) – Lady Graustark (USA) (Graustark) [1992/3 22m 25g6 23d5 a24g3 25m4 23m2 24s 22d] smallish, well-made horse: fair handicap hurdler nowadays: stays well: acts   109 on good to firm, heavy ground and equitrack: blinkered (ran creditably)/visored last 3 starts. *R. Lee*

CLASS MATE   6 br.m. Decent Fellow – Top Marks (Breakspear II) [1992/3 17v 16s 18v 18s 23f3] leggy mare: no sign of ability. *R. D. Townsend*   –

CLAXTON GREENE   9 b.g. Bon Chat – Pippy Greene (Yellow God) **c116** [1992/3 c24s* c25vF c25s2 c26v3 c24d3 c27d* c24g* c32m2 c25dpu] – sparely-made gelding: half-brother to winning sprint plater Creetown Lady (by Creetown): dam stayed 7f: useful pointer in 1992: sold 16,500 gns Doncaster August Sales: won novice chases at Chepstow in December and Taunton in February and March: short-head second to Ushers Island in valuable amateurs event at Cheltenham later in March: stays very well: probably acts on any going: front runner: game and consistent. *M. C. Pipe*

CLAY COUNTY   8 b.g. Sheer Grit – Make-Up (Bleep-Bleep) [1992/3 **c138** § c17g* c16d4 c17s2 c16d3 c17m c17d* c16g* c16g4 c16s4] well-made gelding: – useful handicap chaser: won at Kelso in November and February (minor event) and at Ayr in March: poor efforts otherwise: barely stays 2m under testing conditions: acts on any going: tends to jump to the right: front runner who needs to dominate: unreliable. *R. Allan*

CLEANING UP   11 b.g. Carlburg – The Charwoman (Menelek) [1992/3 **c72** c21m3 c21m4 c19m5 c17f5 c23spu c25mF c19d c24f] workmanlike gelding: – poor chaser: trained until after fifth start by D. Gandolfo, next time by M. Milne: stays 2¾m: acts on firm going: tried blinkered. *A. J. Chamberlain*

CLEAN SINGER   4 b.f. Chief Singer – Rosalka (ITY) (Relko) [1992/3 16d* 17g 24d 18dF] close-coupled filly: poor maiden on Flat: won seller at 69 Hexham (no bid) in November, only worthwhile form over hurdles. *N. Bycroft*

CLEAR COMEDY (IRE)   5 br.m. Jester – Clear Belle (Klairon) [1992/3 18s 18s6 a20g6 17d 17m4] leggy, lengthy mare: 6f winner as 2-y-o: poor 64 plater over hurdles: best efforts at around 2m: acts on soft and good to firm ground. *R. G. Frost*

CLEAR IDEA (IRE)   5 ch.g. Try My Best (USA) – Sloane Ranger (Sharpen Up) [1992/3 20g2 16f2 16s 17g4 17d2] rangy gelding: plating-class 88 maiden on Flat: modest novice hurdler: probably stays 2½m: acts on firm going and good to soft: takes strong hold and races prominently. *Mrs F. Walwyn*

CLEEVELAND LADY   6 b.m. Turn Back The Time (USA) – Nurse Pat (Rolfe (USA)) [1992/3 F17m* F16d4 F17v5 17v6 16vur 17s5 17d2 17g* 17f3] 83 small mare: first foal: dam behind in a NH Flat race: won NH Flat race at Bangor in October and maiden hurdle at Plumpton in March: likely to stay beyond 17f: acts on any going. *W. G. M. Turner*

CLERIC ON BROADWAY (IRE)   5 b.m. The Parson – L O Broadway (Crash Course) [1992/3 F16d5 F14g4] unfurnished mare: first foal: sister to 4-y-o Cudder Or Shudder: dam fair hurdler who stayed 2¾m: showed ability both starts in NH Flat races: sold out of D. Moffatt's stable 8,200 gns Doncaster January Sales in between: yet to race over hurdles or fences. *S. E. Kettlewell*

CLERIHUE   4 br.f. Rymer – Funny Baby (Fable Amusant) [1992/3 17d6] sister to useful hurdler/winning pointer Rymster and half-sister to 2 other – p jumping winners: dam useful 2m chaser: never dangerous or knocked about when sixth in novice hurdle at Newton Abbot in April: should improve. *P. J. Hobbs*

CLEVER DICK   8 b.g. Cosmo – Princess Albertina (FR) (King of The Castle (USA)) [1992/3 16v 16d2 20sur 22f] lengthy gelding: modest hurdler: 90 stays 2½m: acts on good to firm and dead ground: usually visored/blinkered nowadays. *A. Moore*

CLEVER FOLLY   13 b.g. Idiot's Delight – Lilac Veil (Dumbarnie) **c139** d [1992/3 c17m* c21m c20m3 c16gF3 c21mpu c17g5 c20gpu c16f] angular, – workmanlike gelding: useful chaser at best: won early-season handicaps at Newton Abbot and Bangor: subsequently off course 6 months and ran poorly afterwards: stays 21f (not 3m): suited by a sound surface: goes well with forcing tactics: visored once: usually jumps well. *G. Richards*

CLEVER SHEPHERD 8 b.g. Broadsword (USA) – Reluctant Maid (Relko) [1992/3 c21v³ c26v² c24v² c24v⁶ c23g² c26g³ c27g² c24d*] leggy, workmanlike gelding: fair handicap chaser: won at Exeter in April: suited by a test of stamina: acts on heavy ground: twice blinkered: consistent. *P. J. Hobbs*   c107   –

CLIFFALDA 10 ch.g. Young Man (FR) – Hampsruth (Sea Hawk II) [1992/3 c33sᵖᵘ] smallish, sturdy, dipped-backed gelding: carries condition nowadays: one-time useful hurdler: won 2 novice chases in 1991/2: pulled up after a bad mistake only outing 1992/3 (December): stays 3m: probably needs give in the ground, and acts on soft: sometimes blinkered in 1988/9. *G. Richards*   c–   –

CLIFTON CRUISER (USA) 4 ch.g. Miswaki (USA) – Atomic Juice (USA) (Sauce Boat (USA)) [1992/3 17dᵖᵘ 17dᵖᵘ] neat gelding: no form on Flat (for C. Nelson) or in early-season juvenile hurdles. *Mrs F. Walwyn*   –

CLIFTON HAMPDEN 5 b.g. Blakeney – Red Ruby (Tudor Melody) [1992/3 18f³ 19m] neat gelding: maiden hurdler: not raced after September: should stay beyond 2¾m: acts on firm ground, possibly unsuited by heavy: moody. *Lady Herries*   – §

CLIPPER ONE 5 b.m. Dreams To Reality (USA) – Sleekit (Blakeney) [1992/3 17g² 17m⁴ 18m² 18f⁴ 17g³ 18g² 16g 17m a16g² a16g² a16g³ a16gᶠ] smallish mare: poor novice hurdler: retained 600 gns Newmarket Autumn Sales: stayed 2¼m: acted on good to firm ground and on equitrack: consistent: dead. *K. O. Cunningham-Brown*   80

CLOGHRAN LAD 6 ch.g. Millfontaine – Lady Pitt (Pitskelly) [1992/3 16s 18d 16g 16s 16v⁵ 16v⁶ 20s² 16d² 18vᶠ 18d 17g² 21f⁴] ex-Irish gelding: third foal: half-brother to winning sprinter Deep In The Valley (by Wolver Hollow): dan never ran: fair handicap hurdler at best: trained until after tenth outing by T. O'Neill: poor form in selling company in Britain last 2 outings: stays 2½m: best form with plenty of give in the ground: successful with and without blinkers. *D. J. Wintle*   105

CLONADRUM 9 ch.g. Le Bavard (FR) – Broken Dream's (Hail Titan) [1992/3 25s 21vᵖᵘ 20g] compact ex-Irish gelding: no form over hurdles or fences: blinkered once. *T. Dyer*   c–   –

CLONMACOGUE 12 br.g. Mandalus – Elusive Dream (Majority Blue) [1992/3 17sᵖᵘ 23dᵖᵘ c16s⁵ c21dᵘʳ c21gᵖᵘ c27mᵘʳ] lengthy gelding: of little account nowadays: sold 750 gns Ascot May Sales. *B. Stevens*   c– x   –

CLONMILL 8 ch.g. Don – Sapristi (Psidium) [1992/3 16s 21s² 21v⁶ c20v⁵ c24sᵇᵈ c24v c24dF 21s³ 22g⁶ 28g³] workmanlike ex-Irish gelding: moderate novice hurdler/chaser: trained until after seventh start by A. L. T. Moore: stays 3½m: acts on soft ground: sketchy jumper of fences. *J. W. Curtis*   c–   97

CLONONY CASTLE 7 ch.g. Lord Gayle (USA) – Early Morn (Sassafras (FR)) [1992/3 c20s⁴ c21s² c20v³ 21g c24d⁵ c27g⁴] angular ex-Irish gelding: half-brother to 2 poor animals: dam twice-raced half-sister to Main Reef: novice hurdler/chaser: modest form at best: stays 3m: acts on soft going: tried blinkered: ungenuine. *J. J. O'Neill*   c89 §

CLONROCHE DRILLER 8 b. or br.g. Pauper – Lady Abednego VII (Pedigree Unknown) [1992/3 c23g c25g⁴ c24m³ c25d c21d⁵ c23s³ c21s² c21dᵖᵘ c21s³ c21g* c20m² c21d⁶ c21s* c21fᵘʳ c21d³] workmanlike gelding: moderate chaser: won amateur handicaps at Leicester in March and Perth in April: stays 23f: acts on good to firm and soft going: blinkered once: usually races up with pace. *Mrs S. A. Bramall*   c97

CLOSEBUTNOCIGAR 9 b.g. Paddy's Stream – Churchtown Breeze (Tarqogan) [1992/3 c23gᶠ c20sᴿ] workmanlike gelding: ungenuine maiden pointer/chaser. *J. A. Pickering*   c– §

CLOUD HOPPER 6 ch.m. Scallywag – Grecian Cloud (Galivanter) [1992/3 F17g] behind in NH Flat races: yet to race over hurdles or fences. *J. A. Pickering*

CLOVERMILL 5 b.m. Sayf El Arab (USA) – Opinion (Great Nephew) [1992/3 22f^{pu}] sparely-made mare: selling hurdler: stayed 2½m: acted on any going: best visored: dead. *W. Bentley* –

CLURICAN (IRE) 4 ch.g. Dara Monarch – Jane Bond (Good Bond) [1992/3 16g^4 17d* 17d^2 17v* 17v^3 17s^3 16d^2 17m 16g^6] compact gelding: half-brother to useful Irish jumper Jennycomequick (by Furry Glen) and to fair hurdler Majestic Lad (by Royalty): fair 1¼m winner on Flat: won juvenile hurdles at Sandown and Hereford in first half of season: creditable efforts afterwards, in valuable events at Cheltenham and Punchestown last 2 outings: sold to join N. Tinkler 15,000 gns Doncaster May Sales: will stay 2½m: acts on good to firm and heavy going: keen type who is often on toes: usually held up. *D. Nicholson* 126

CLWYD LODGE 6 b.g. Blakeney – High Caraval (High Top) [1992/3 20g^{pu}] small, stocky gelding: bad novice hurdler: tried blinkered. *R. T. Juckes* –

CLYDE RANGER 6 b.g. Kemal (FR) – Clyde Avenue (Peacock (FR)) [1992/3 24s* 24v* 25s^3 24d^3 25s 25d] small, sturdy gelding: fair hurdler: won novice handicaps at Newcastle and Hexham in December: below form last 2 starts: out-and-out stayer: suited by plenty of give in the ground: races prominently. *M. D. Hammond* 104

COASTING 7 b.g. Skyliner – Shantung Lassie (FR) (Shantung) [1992/3 c21d^6] workmanlike gelding: winning hurdler: signs of ability in novice event at Warwick in October on chasing debut (dislocated a hind joint, but said to have recovered): best form at up to 21f: acts on good to firm going. *G. B. Balding* c– p
–

COBB GATE 5 b.h. Creetown – Glazepta Final (Final Straw) [1992/3 16s^{pu} 17s^3 17m 17f 17s^3 17d* 16f^4 17f^6] sturdy horse: selling hurdler: very fortunate winner (beaten third when left in lead last) of conditional jockeys handicap at Newton Abbot (no bid) in April: has raced only at around 2m: probably acts on any ground: blinkered last 2 outings. *B. Stevens* 75

COBBLERS CROSS 8 ch.m. Hasty Word – Stormation (Compensation) [1992/3 c21v^4 c18g^5] big, robust mare: no sign of ability. *R. E. Peacock* c–
–

COBBLERS HILL 4 gr.g. Another Realm – Morning Miss (Golden Dipper) [1992/3 17m] fairly useful plater on Flat (stays 1m), winner in 1993: tailed off in early-season juvenile hurdle: sold 1,000 gns Doncaster September Sales. *J. White* –

COBBLERS LAD (NZ) 7 b.g. Drums of Time (USA) – Parfum (NZ) (Copenhagen) [1992/3 22v^{pu}] unplaced in NH Flat races and novice hurdles: dead. *J. White* –

COBB RUN 7 ch.g. Deep Run – Inneen Alainn (Prince Hansel) [1992/3 16g^6 18g^5 22d c26d^{pu}] good-bodied gelding: poor novice hurdler: only form on first start: no show on chasing debut: sold 1,050 gns Ascot March Sales. *R. H. Alner* c–
70

COBO BAY 8 ch.g. General Assembly (USA) – Top Hope (High Top) [1992/3 c16g^2 c16d^F c16d^{ur} c16d c18d^3 c16m^4 c16s^5] strong, compact gelding: winning hurdler: modest novice chaser: should stay further than 2¼m: acts on dead and firm ground: jumps fences poorly. *K. White* c88 x

CO-CHIN (IRE) 4 gr.c. Coquelin (USA) – Whiffswatching (USA) (Sassafras (FR)) [1992/3 17d* 16g^2 16s* 17d^2 16d^5 16g^3 16f^2] smallish colt: fair handicapper at up to 1m on Flat when trained by G. Lewis: won juvenile hurdles at Bangor in October and Catterick in January: ran well afterwards: has plenty of pace and will prove best at around 2m: probably acts on any going: held up. *D. Moffatt* 112

COCK-A-DOODLE-DO 7 b.g. Petorius – Bertida (Porto Bello) [1992/3 21m^4 18g^5 17d^6 22d^3] smallish, angular gelding: winning selling hurdler: not raced after September: sold 750 gns in May: probably stays 2¾m: acts on firm and dead ground: blinkered once. *J. Wade* 69

COCK A LEEKIE (NZ) 10 b.g. Mayo Mellay (NZ) – Summermayo (NZ) c– x
(Summer Magic II) [1992/3 17vᵖᵘ 16v] rather leggy gelding: fair hurdler at –
best: failed to get past fifth in 3 novice chases: sold 700 gns Ascot June
Sales: best form at up to 2½m: acts on firm ground, yet to show his form on
heavy. *D. H. Barons*

COCK COCKBURN 7 ch.g. Sheer Grit – Merry Mirth (Menelek) c?
[1992/3 16g 17g* c21g 16d⁶ 16dᶠ] angular, sparely-made gelding: useful 136
hurdler: won handicap at Tralee in August: not raced after January: well
beaten in Breeders' Cup Chase in USA, only outing over fences: stays
2½m: acts on good to soft ground: usually held up. *J. Queally, Ireland*

COCK-OF-THE-ROCK 12 b.g. Cantab – Cherry Bounce (Vulgan) c–
[1992/3 c21m] modest pointer: novice hunter chaser: stays 3¼m. *Mrs S.* –
Clarke

COCKSTOWN LAD 7 b.g. Main Reef – Pasadena Girl (Busted) [1992/3 c–
17f⁵ 22dᵖᵘ] rather angular gelding: winning hurdler: once-raced over –
fences: no form since 1990/1: placed in points in 1993: tried in blinkers, visor
and a hood. *J. R. Jenkins*

CODDINGTON VILLAGE 8 b.g. Bonnova – Hidden Melody (Melodic
Air) [1992/3 22dᵖᵘ 20d⁶] rather sparely-made gelding: maiden hurdler: no –
form since 1990/1: sold 2,100 gns Ascot November Sales: tried blinkered/
visored. *S. E. Sherwood*

COE 7 b. or br.g. Coquelin (USA) – Gully (Dike (USA)) [1992/3 c21d³ c111 x
c21dᵖᵘ c21dᶠ c24f* c24f² c24f⁴] sparely-made gelding: fair chaser: won –
handicap at Lingfield in March: ran creditably afterwards: stays 3m: acts on
firm and dead ground: usually blinkered: poor jumper. *R. Akehurst*

COGENT 9 b.g. Le Bavard (FR) – Cottstown Breeze (Autumn Gold) c136 p
[1992/3 c21s³ c21sᶠ c20s* c21d* c21v* c20g² c20gᶠ] rangy gelding: fairly –

Pell-mell Partners' "Cogent"

175

useful hurdler: smart novice chaser: successful in minor events at Newbury and Wincanton in first half of season and novice event at Kempton in January: good second to Young Hustler in Arlington Premier Series Chase Final at Newbury in February: effective at around 2½m and stays well: probably acts on any going: jumps soundly though rather low: consistent: should continue to do well. *Andrew Turnell*

COINAGE 10 gr.g. Owen Dudley – Grisbi (Grey Sovereign) [1992/3 c19gᵖᵘ 16m c26mᵖᵘ] leggy gelding: winning hurdler/chaser: no form for a long time: blinkered nowadays: poor jumper. *R. F. Johnson Houghton* c– x

COIN GAME (IRE) 5 b.m. Dalsaan – Canhaar (Sparkler) [1992/3 16sᵖᵘ 17dᵖᵘ] small, angular mare: lightly raced and no form on Flat: pulled up both starts over hurdles. *Graeme Roe* –

COL BUCKMORE (IRE) 5 b.g. King's Ride – Mugra (Mugatpura) [1992/3 F16s⁵ F16g⁵] fourth live foal: half-brother to winning Irish chaser Dysart Lass (by Buckskin): dam never ran: fifth in NH Flat races at Navan and Ayr: yet to race over hurdles or fences. *J. F. C. Maxwell, Ireland*

COLD MARBLE (USA) 8 b.g. Told (USA) – Coney Dell (Ercolano (USA)) [1992/3 18gᵖᵘ 18fᵖᵘ 22vᵖᵘ 18s 22v 17d 17mᵖᵘ] small gelding: poor maiden hurdler: tried visored/blinkered. *D. R. Tucker* –

COLERIDGE 5 gr.g. Bellypha – Quay Line (High Line) [1992/3 25g⁵] close-coupled, sparely-made gelding: fairly useful staying handicapper on Flat: blinkered, some promise when fifth in novice hurdle at Doncaster in January (tended to run in snatches): should do better. *D. Shaw* 84 p

COLFAX SAM 6 b.h. Norwick (USA) – Alwen (Blakeney) [1992/3 18d 16dᵘʳ] small, angular horse: no sign of ability over hurdles. *B. S. Rothwell* –

COLLABORATE (IRE) 4 b.g. Shareef Dancer (USA) – Royal Saint (USA) (Crimson Satan) [1992/3 17s⁶ 20s⁴ a20g⁴] strong gelding: once-raced on Flat: no form over hurdles: sold 775 gns Ascot February Sales. *G. Harwood* –

COLNE VALLEY KID 8 ch.g. Homing – Pink Garter (Henry The Seventh) [1992/3 c16g⁴ c21sᵖᵘ c21dᵖᵘ c16vᵘʳ c18vᵖᵘ] seems of little account nowadays: tried blinkered. *A. Moore* c– –

COLONEL FAIRFAX 5 gr.g. Alias Smith (USA) – Mistress Meryll (Tower Walk) [1992/3 17d⁵ 17gᵖᵘ] smallish gelding: poor and irresolute maiden on Flat: showed nothing in novice hurdles: sold out of N. Henderson's stable 2,200 gns Ascot February Sales in between, resold 1,600 gns Ascot 2nd June Sales. *R. P. C. Hoad* –

COLONEL GAY 8 ch.g. Scorpio (FR) – My Sweetie (Bleep-Bleep) [1992/3 c17fF 16m c17gᵖᵘ 17m] small, workmanlike gelding: winning 2m hurdler: no form over fences: sold 780 gns Doncaster August Sales, resold out of K. Wingrove's stable 620 gns Ascot November Sales after second start. *B. Scriven* c– –

COLONEL KENSON 7 ch.g. Avocat – Bryophila (FR) (Breakspear II) [1992/3 c21gᵖᵘ c21s⁶ c27v⁴ c26vᵖᵘ c25dᵖᵘ] tall gelding: only sign of ability when fourth in novice chase in December: blinkered last 4 starts. *R. Champion* c75

COLONEL O'KELLY (NZ) 9 br.g. Kirrama (NZ) – Gold Coast (NZ) (Palm Beach (FR)) [1992/3 c24s⁶ c24s³ c25d* c23g³ c21s⁶ c27g c26f⁶] lengthy gelding: modest handicap chaser: won at Wolverhampton in February: ran poorly last 3 outings: stays 25f: acts on soft going. *D. H. Barons* c89 –

COLONEL POPSKI 11 ch.g. Niniski (USA) – Miss Jessica (Milesian) [1992/3 c17g] small, lightly-made gelding: selling hurdler/novice chaser: no form since 1989/90: occasionally blinkered. *R. E. Barr* c– –

COLONIAL BEAUTY (FR) 4 b.f. In Fijar (USA) – Exceptional Beauty (Sallust) [1992/3 17dᵖᵘ 16vᵖᵘ] angular filly: once-raced on Flat: no sign of ability in juvenile hurdles. *G. F. H. Charles-Jones* –

COLONNA (USA) 7 b.g. Run The Gantlet (USA) – Evolutionary (USA) (Silent Screen (USA)) [1992/3 a16g⁰ʳ 17g 17d 17g] leggy, sparely-made gelding: winning 2m hurdler: no form in 1992/3: blinkered once. *B. Richmond* — –

COLOUR COST (IRE) 5 b.g. Roi Guillaume (FR) – Wilden (Will Somers) [1992/3 16g⁰ʳ 21d⁴ 17d⁵ 17s* 16d⁵ 21d⁰ᵘ] leggy, sparely-made gelding: won novice hurdle at Carlisle in January: stayed 2 1f: acted on soft ground: dead. *M. D. Hammond* — 87

COLOUR POLICY 6 ch.m. Politico (USA) – Hoar Frost (Doubtless II) [1992/3 18v⁰ᵘ] lengthy, sparely-made mare: no sign of ability in novice hurdles. *Miss N. Berry* — –

COLSAN BOY 6 b.g. Remainder Man – Wimbledon's Pet (Mummy's Pet) [1992/3 16s 17d] small gelding: lightly raced 6f winner on Flat: no form in novice hurdles. *Mrs S. D. Williams* — –

COLVIN LAD 6 gr.g. Rusticaro (FR) – Twice Regal (Royal Prerogative) [1992/3 17s⁰ᵘ 17f⁰] leggy, smallish gelding: poor novice hurdler: sold 2,000 gns Ascot November Sales: blinkered twice: dead. *C. L. Popham* — –

COLWAY PRINCE (IRE) 5 b.g. Prince Tenderfoot (USA) – El Cerrito (Tribal Chief) [1992/3 17d⁰ 16v a16g 16d* 16s* 16g 17m³ 17d² 17m⁰ᵘ 17f⁰ʳ 16m⁴ 17f] smallish gelding: selling hurdler: bought in after winning handicaps at Ludlow (2,400 gns) and Worcester (5,200 gns) in February: races at around 2m: probably acts on any ground: ran poorly in visor ninth start: often held up. *A. P. Jones* — 80

COMANECI (IRE) 5 b.m. Ahonoora – Church Mountain (Furry Glen) [1992/3 16d 16d a16g⁶ 22d a16g* a16g² a16g⁴] lengthy mare: poor hurdler: won claimer at Lingfield in February: best at around 2m: acts on good to soft going and equitrack: blinkered twice. *R. T. Juckes* — 82

COMBAT ZONE 9 b.g. Brigadier Gerard – Tantot (Charlottown) [1992/3 20pm⁰ᵘ 17m 17d⁶] smallish, well-made gelding: second foal: half-brother to Flat winner/novice hurdler Kentucky Quest (by Darby Creek Road): dam, middle-distance maiden, is half-sister to 2000 Guineas winner Mon Fils and very smart Son of Silver: no form over hurdles. *P. Leach* — –

COMEDY BASIN 10 b.g. Comedy Star (USA) – Porcupine Basin (Lucifer (USA)) [1992/3 c24v⁰ᵘ c25f⁰ʳ c24f⁰ᵈ c21g] workmanlike gelding: winning staying chaser: no form since 1989/90: blinkered twice. *A. G. Sims* c– –

COMEDY RIVER 6 br.g. Comedy Star (USA) – Hopeful Waters (Forlorn River) [1992/3 17d 16m³ 16d 17g³ 17d²] compact gelding: modest hurdler, lightly raced: yet to race beyond 17f: acts on good to firm, good to soft ground and equitrack. *J. L. Spearing* — 88

COMEDY ROAD 9 br.g. Old Jocus – Blue Flash (Blue Lightning) [1992/3 c21gp⁰ᵘ c26d c22gp⁰ᵘ c25m⁰ʳ c25mF c21d³ c17m c21g³ c26m³ c21f² c21m*] sturdy gelding: modest handicap chaser: won at Uttoxeter in June: effective at around 2½m, and stays well: acts on firm and dead ground: blinkered second to eighth outings. *R. Lee* c95 –

COMEDY SPY 9 gr.g. Scallywag – Ida Spider (Ben Novus) [1992/3 c20dF c21sF c23v³ c21vF c21vF 25d³ 20d⁴ 25v* 22m] leggy, good-topped gelding: moderate hurdler: won novice event at Uttoxeter in April: has shown similar ability over fences but is badly let down by his jumping: stays 25f: acts on heavy ground. *Mrs A. R. Hewitt* c99 x 99

COME HOME ALONE 5 ch.g. Sayf El Arab (USA) – Apprila (Bustino) [1992/3 22g⁴ 21d⁵ 23gF 22d* 22v⁶ 22g] close-coupled gelding: won novice handicap hurdle at Ludlow in December: below form afterwards (not raced after February): will stay beyond 2¾m: acts on dead ground: blinkered last 3 starts. *N. A. Gaselee* — 89

COME OFF IT 4 b.f. Uncle Pokey – Daleena (Dalesa) [1992/3 21mp⁰ᵘ 18d 21sp⁰ᵘ] angular filly: fourth foal: half-sister to winning hurdler Old Mill — –

Stream (by Rapid River): dam winning pointer: no sign of ability in novice hurdles. *W. Raw*

COME ON CUDDLES 5 b.m. Rymer – The Ceiriog (Deep Diver) [1992/3 F18s F16vᵖᵘ] no sign of ability in NH Flat races: yet to race over hurdles or fences. *E. F. Birchall*

COMETTI STAR 9 ch.g. Giacometti – Hotazur (Hotfoot) [1992/3 c21sᶠ c20g⁴ c18mᶠ c17f⁶] lengthy gelding: modest chaser: stays 2½m: acts on firm ground. *J. Wharton*   **c95** –

COMIC LINE 8 b.g. Old Jocus – Straight Lane (Straight Lad) [1992/3 c21fᶠ] no form in novice hurdles: poor pointer: blinkered, well behind when falling last in novice hunter chase in May. *Mrs Gillian Lane*   **c–** –

COMING ALIVE 6 gr.g. Saher – Misty Light (Bustino) [1992/3 22m 21d³ 22d⁶ 23s³] quite good-topped gelding: modest handicap hurdler: not raced after November: sold 13,000 gns in May: stays 23f: acts on soft and good to firm ground: sketchy jumper. *W. A. Stephenson*   **99**

COMMANCHE BRAVE 10 ch.g. Royal Blend – Billie Jean (Sweet Revenge) [1992/3 c21m] lengthy, angular gelding: no form over hurdles or in a steeplechase: temperamental winning pointer. *Marco Cusano*   **c–** –

COMMANCHE DRIFTER 5 b.m. Commanche Run – Ivelostmyway (Relko) [1992/3 F17g F14s aF16g 18dᵖᵘ] small mare: fourth foal: dam won 4 races, 3 at 1¾m: no sign of ability in NH Flat races or a novice hurdle. *J. R. Bostock*

COMMANCHERO 6 gr.g. Telsmoss – Count On Me (No Mercy) [1992/3 c24dᵖᵘ c18v² c21dᵘʳ c19mᵘʳ c20fᵘʳ 24f³ 25g³ 20m³ 21d*] leggy, close-coupled gelding: poor hurdler: no bid after winning selling handicap at Towcester in May: novice chaser: stays well: probably acts on any going. *R. J. Hodges*   **c75 ?** 75

COMMANCHE SIOUX (IRE) 5 b.m. Commanche Run – Papsie's Pet (Busted) [1992/3 18d 16s⁴ 17d⁵] small, good-quartered mare: poor winning hurdler: best form at around 2m: acted on soft going: visored twice: dead. *K. A. Morgan*   **69**

COMMERCIAL ARTIST 7 b.g. Furry Glen – Blue Suede Shoes (Bargello) [1992/3 22s* 20d⁵ 19d c20v* c17d² c17d² c24v² c21d⁵] rather leggy gelding: useful hurdler: won handicap at Listowel in September: similar level of form in novice chases: successful at Punchestown in December: ran well next 2 starts, well below form last 2: stays 2¾m: acts on heavy going. *V. Bowens, Ireland*   **c131** 131

COMMON COUNCIL 4 gr.g. Siberian Express (USA) – Old Domesday Book (High Top) [1992/3 16sᵖᵘ] sturdy gelding: fair form on Flat, winner at 1¼m in 1993: no show in juvenile hurdle in March. *M. D. Hammond*   –

COMPANY SECRETARY 5 b.m. Julio Mariner – Dancing Jenny (Goldhill) [1992/3 F17d] second foal: half-sister to 6-y-o Alice Smith (by Alias Smith): dam twice-raced daughter of fair hurdler/useful chaser Vikrom: tailed off in NH Flat race at Carlisle in April: yet to race over hurdles or fences. *T. Dyer*

COMSTOCK 6 ch.g. Coquelin (USA) – Maura Paul (Bonne Noel) [1992/3 16d³ 16g* 16s⁵] useful-looking gelding: fairly useful middle-distance handicapper at best on Flat: made mistakes when winning novice hurdle at Edinburgh in December: creditable fifth in handicap at Wetherby following month: should progress, particularly over further. *N. Tinkler*   **88 p**

CONCERT PAPER 9 b.g. Over The River (FR) – Good Surprise (Maelsheachlainn) [1992/3 c21d² c24m³ c25d⁴ c25s² c24g³ c21s³ c21vᵖᵘ c27gᵘʳ c25m c26dᶠ] leggy gelding: winning hurdler: moderate novice chaser: stays 25f: acts on good to firm and soft ground: often blinkered: ungenuine. *R. O'Leary*   **c90 §** –

CONEY DOVE 8 b.m. Celtic Cone – Shadey Dove (Deadly Nightshade) [1992/3 17s⁵ 17m⁵ 16s 21d²] small mare: modest hurdler: not raced after November: stays 21f: probably acts on any going. *R. J. Price*   **91**

CONEY ROAD 4 gr.g. Grey Desire – Miss Diaward (Supreme Sovereign) [1992/3 F17d2] fourth foal: half-brother to winning hurdler Divilmint (by Absalom): dam winning middle-distance stayer: second in NH Flat race at Hereford in May: yet to race over hurdles. *Miss S. E. Hall*

CONFOUND (IRE) 4 b.g. Wolverlife – Arachosia (Persian Bold) [1992/3 16m] no form on Flat: tailed off in early-season juvenile selling hurdle. *J. Akehurst* –

CONNABEE 9 b.g. Connaught – Sera Sera (Hill Clown (USA)) [1992/3 18f] workmanlike gelding: bad novice hurdler: fell only outing in steeplechase. *J. C. Poulton* c–
–

CONNAUGHT CRUSADER 5 b.g. Relkino – Yellow Iris (Le Bavard (FR)) [1992/3 F17d*] third foal: half-brother to 2 lightly-raced animals: dam, modest novice hurdler, half-sister to useful staying chaser Glyde Court and from good jumping family: won 18-runner NH Flat race at Ascot in April: yet to race over hurdles or fences. *P. J. Hobbs*

CONNOR THE SECOND 5 b.g. Pollerton – Pinkworthy Pond (Le Bavard (FR)) [1992/3 F17m] first foal: dam, of little account, is daughter of half-sister to Irish Grand National winner Sweet Dreams: tailed off in early-season NH Flat race: yet to race over hurdles or fences. *P. F. Nicholls*

CONSTRUCTION KING 7 br.g. Score Twenty Four (USA) – Teleprity (Welsh Pageant) [1992/3 c19mpu c21dpu] close-coupled, good-topped gelding: poor novice hurdler/chaser: often blinkered, visored once: won a point in March. *R. Dickin* c–
–

CONSTRUCTIVIST (IRE) 4 b.c. Fools Holme (USA) – Spire (Shirley Heights) [1992/3 17g4 17f4 16d 18vpu] sparely-made colt: modest middle-distance maiden at best on Flat: sold out of B. Hills's stable 7,000 gns Newmarket Autumn Sales: poor juvenile hurdler: best effort on first start. *M. F. Barraclough* 70

CONTACT KELVIN 11 br.g. Workboy – Take My Hand (Precipice Wood) [1992/3 c21vpu c21vpu c21sur c21d6 c20g c21g c21g 17d 22g] big, workmanlike gelding: handicap chaser: no form in 1992/3, including over hurdles: best at up to 2½m: acts on soft going and good to firm. *N. Bycroft* c–
–

CONTINUITY 4 b.f. Celestial Storm (USA) – Tamassos (Dance In Time (CAN)) [1992/3 16d 22g3] small, sparely-made filly: first foal: dam, 1¼m winner, is half-sister to Halkopous: sold out of M. Tompkins' stable 5,200 gns Newmarket December Sales: third in maiden hurdle at Sedgefield in February: winning stayer on Flat in 1993. *E. J. Alston* 75

CONTRACTORS DREAM 5 b.g. Librate – Opal Lady (Averof) [1992/3 16spu 17dbd a20gpu] neat gelding: bad plater over hurdles: sometimes visored. *J. M. Bradley* –

COOCHIE 4 b.f. King of Spain – York Street (USA) (Diamond Shoal) [1992/3 18g 18d5 17d4 17s 20mpu 20d 16m5 17d3] sparely-made filly: poor maiden plater on Flat and over hurdles: best form at around 2m: acts on dead ground: blinkered last 3 outings. *R. J. Baker* 62

COOL AND EASY 7 b.g. King's Ride – Princess Grand (Kashiwa) [1992/3 c21g3 c24d* c26v3 c24d3 c25s4 c26d2 c26d2 c25g4] good-topped, angular gelding: winning hurdler: won novice handicap chase at Taunton in November: ran well most starts afterwards: stays 3¼m well: acts on heavy ground: jumps soundly in the main. *J. T. Gifford* c99
–

COOL APOLLO (NZ) 6 b.g. Gay Apollo – Maple Leaf (NZ) (King's Troop) [1992/3 21vpu 17d 22m 25gpu] workmanlike gelding: of little account. *D. H. Barons* –

COOL CLOWN 6 b.g. Idiot's Delight – Fabice (Vonice) [1992/3 16s2 24v2 25s2 23v* 21v* 22f2] leggy, unfurnished gelding: won novice hurdles at Folkestone in January and Towcester in February: jumped left throughout when good second at Sandown in March: stays well: acts on any going: suited by forcing tactics: sketchy jumper. *M. C. Pipe* 115

COOL DAY 6 b.g. Kemal (FR) – Nicky's Guess (Three Dons) [1992/3 20g^{pu}] rangy gelding: type to make a chaser: poor novice hurdler: sold 3,000 gns Doncaster November Sales. *T. P. Tate*   –

COOL DUDE 7 b.g. Furry Glen – Gemma's Fridge (Frigid Aire) [1992/3 22m⁴ 16d* 16s* 16s³ 16d² 18g³ 18m⁶ 17s⁶] sparely-made, close-coupled gelding: sold out of O. Brennan's stable 2,000 gns Doncaster September Sales after first start: won selling handicap hurdle (no bid) and claimer at Catterick in first half of season: poor efforts last 2 starts: little promise over fences: best form at around 2m: acts on good to firm and soft going. *J. H. Johnson*   c– 97

COOLE DODGER 8 gr.g. Scallywag – Coole Streak (Perspex) [1992/3 c18v⁴ c24s c21g² c21mᶠ c26f* c24g⁵ c26f^{pu}] rangy gelding: fair chaser: won handicap at Wincanton in March: stays 3¼m: acts on any going: usually races prominently. *G. A. Ham*   c105 –

COOLEY'S VALVE (IRE) 5 b.g. Pennine Walk – First Blush (Ela-Mana-Mou) [1992/3 16s⁴ 16g 17g* 18g^{pu}] angular, workmanlike gelding: fairly useful juvenile hurdler in 1991/2: sold 26,000 gns Newmarket Autumn Sales: only form of 1992/3 and still below best when winning novice event at Newbury in March: yet to race beyond 2¼m: raced mainly on good ground: has broken blood vessels and sometimes finds little under pressure. *N. J. Henderson*   116

COOL FLIGHT 4 ch.f. Absalom – Fancy Flight (FR) (Arctic Tern (USA)) [1992/3 16s^{pu}] lengthy, sparely-made filly: twice-raced on Flat: saddle slipped in juvenile hurdle in November: sold 1,050 gns Doncaster January Sales. *R. Thompson*   –

COOL GROUND 11 ch.g. Over The River (FR) – Merry Spring (Merry-mount) [1992/3 c25g⁴ c27dᶠ c24v⁴ c25s c30s² c26s³ c26d³ c27m c29sᶠ c27g²]   c156 –

Conditions were all against Cool Ground's attempt to hold on to the Cheltenham Gold Cup, and he never looked remotely like succeeding. But there was nothing in his record since that surprise, grindingly hard-won short-head victory over The Fellow in 1992 to suggest he could have managed it had the heavens opened. On his only subsequent outing in 1991/2 he'd faded into tenth behind Party Politics in the Grand National, seeming not to adapt fully to the fences and running way below Gold Cup form. In 1992/3 he'd been having a disappointing season, and although, as anticipated, his form began to pick up after the turn of the year it never reached any great heights. The first signs of improvement appeared in the Anthony Mildmay, Peter Cazalet Memorial Chase at Sandown in January, when his second to the easy winner Rushing Wild at a disadvantage of 27 lb reduced his Gold Cup odds to 16/1 in places. That was already his fifth start. Later in the month, at Cheltenham in the Timeform Hall of Fame Chase, he ran what turned out to be his best race of the season to finish around six lengths third to Sibton Abbey. There followed a reasonable effort for third place behind Cavvies Clown in a moderately-run Jim Ford Challenge Cup at Wincanton, a ninth place behind Jodami in the Gold Cup, an early fall in the Irish Grand National at Fairyhouse and a lack-lustre second to Le Piccolage off a considerably reduced handicap mark in an uncompetitive Golden Miller Trophy at Cheltenham in April.

		Luthier	Klairon
	Over The River (FR)	(b or br 1965)	Flute Enchantee
	(ch 1974)	Medenine	Prudent II
Cool Ground		(b 1967)	Ma Congaie
(ch.g. 1982)		Merrymount	Charlottown
	Merry Spring	(b 1970)	Merry Mate
	(ch 1977)	Rose of Spring	Golden Vision
		(ch 1971)	Springville Rose

It is too much to expect that Cool Ground will come back to his best now. However, if he can keep Anno Domini at bay he will probably be given another shot at the Grand National. On a second look at the fences, in the Becher Chase in November, he was handling them better than the first time until he failed to rise high enough at the thirteenth and took one of the rare falls in his long career. He was travelling well just behind the leaders, and should, in theory, have been thereabouts at the finish, as only he and the eventual winner Kildimo were carrying their correct weight in the handicap. Cool Ground will get the National trip, whatever his run in 1992 might suggest to the contrary. Like so many by Over The River, staying is his game. He needs give in the ground to be seen to advantage, and acts on heavy going. *G. B. Balding*

COOL SOCIETY (USA)   4 ch.g. Imp Society (USA) – Icy Friend (USA)   79
(It's Freezing (USA)) [1992/3 18m 16g⁶ 22dᵖᵘ 17g⁵ 16f³ 16m⁶ 17f³] leggy
gelding: modest at best, stays 1¼m, on Flat: poor novice hurdler: form only
at around 2m: acts on firm going: blinkered penultimate outing. *W. J. Musson*

COOMBESBURY LANE   7 b.m. Torus – Nimble Rose (Furry Glen)   c–
[1992/3 18f³ 20g⁴ 19f* 18m² 22d² 22d* 22d 21g 18dF] small, sparely-made   85
mare: modest hurdler: won novice events at Exeter (handicap) and Ludlow
in first half of season: once-raced over fences: unlikely to stay much beyond
2¾m: acts on firm and dead going: blinkered twice in 1991/2. *P. J. Jones*

COONAWARA   7 b.g. Corvaro (USA) – Why Don't Ye (Illa Laudo)
[1992/3 16d⁶ F16d* 17v* 17v* 16s*]   130 p

Not too much should be made of the statistics which show that Tim Forster sent out more winners over hurdles than over fences in the latest season. It doesn't signify a change in policy by someone who has always been first and foremost a trainer of steeplechasers, perfectly willing to allow his charges all the time they need to develop, mature and learn their job thoroughly. You can be sure that the majority of those horses who were winning over hurdles will be tackling fences before too long, including Coonawara who looks a very good prospect. Coonawara, a seven-year-old, has certainly been allowed plenty of time to develop. Prior to joining his present stable he had run only five times in Ireland for Enda Bolger, winning a point-to-point and a National Hunt Flat race, the latter at Tipperary in October. And he's had just three outings for Forster, creating a highly favourable impression when making all in two novice hurdles at Lingfield in January and one at Warwick the following month. Coonawara jumped well and put up a useful performance on the latter course, where the promising Sparkling Sunset, receiving 10 lb, was the only runner remotely to threaten him from halfway. Coonawara, maintaining a strong gallop all the way to the line, beat him by four lengths.

	Corvaro (USA) (b 1977)	Vaguely Noble (b 1965)	Vienna
Coonawara (b.g. 1986)			Noble Lassie
		Delmora (br 1972)	Sir Gaylord
			Penitence
	Why Don't Ye (b 1974)	Illa Laudo (b 1967)	Lauso
			Four Twos
		Warble Bird (br 1969)	Tarqogan
			Windsor Blue

Coonawara, bought for IR 9,000 guineas as a three-year-old, is by the very smart French middle-distance performer Corvaro, sire also of the top-class hurdler and smart chaser Classical Charm, put down after breaking a shoulder when falling in March. The dam Why Don't Ye, a twice-raced maiden, is a daughter of an unraced half-sister to the Lockinge Stakes winner Bluerullah, sire of the very smart jumpers Potato Merchant and Chinrullah. Why Don't Ye has produced two other winners, namely Uisce Noire (by Condorcet), successful in a two-mile hurdle, and Little Shepherd (by Guillaume Tell), a winner over seven furlongs and a mile. Coonawara, a well-made gelding, acts on heavy going and has yet to race on a firm surface. He's done all his racing over hurdles at around two miles but will stay further. *Capt. T. A. Forster*

COOPERS SPOT-ON (IRE)   5 b.g. Glenstal (USA) – Shikari Rose   83
(Kala Shikari) [1992/3 21g³ 18g⁴ 23g⁴ 16d⁴ 17s³ 16g³ 20dᵖᵘ] small, compact

Betterton Chase, Newbury—Copper Mine makes all in this three-runner event

ex-Irish gelding: blinkered when 2m winner on Flat in 1992: poor novice hurdler: stayed 21f: best form on good ground: visored once: dead. *P. Monteith*

COPELAND LAD   11 b.g. Radical – No Dice (No Argument) [1992/3 c26gF] big, workmanlike gelding: winning hurdler: maiden chaser: stays well: probably acts on any going. *P. Seagrave*

    c–
    –

COPFORD   6 b.g. Teenoso (USA) – Chalkey Road (Relko) [1992/3 16vpu 26dF] sturdy gelding: yet to complete in novice hurdles. *D. J. Wintle*

    –

COP FOR THAT   11 gr.g. Meldrum – Splendid Lines (John Splendid) [1992/3 21s 22spu c16d5 c21g4 c22g3 c21m4 23m3 c21gF] tall, plain gelding: poor novice hurdler/chaser: stayed 2¾m: acted on heavy ground: dead. *Miss J. Eaton*

    c80
    62

COPPER BEACH LADY   7 b.m. Andretti – Mon Chapeau (High Hat) [1992/3 22d5 18f 16mur] no form over hurdles. *D. R. Gandolfo*

    –

COPPER CABLE   6 ch.g. True Song – Princess Mey (Country Retreat) [1992/3 16s4] tall, good-topped gelding: chasing type: first form in novice hurdles when fourth at Haydock in November: will stay beyond 2m. *C. Smith*

    85

COPPER HALL   7 ch.g. Mr Fluorocarbon – Helping Hand (Right Boy) [1992/3 c16sF] fourth foal: brother to NH Flat race-placed Tommy Owt and half-brother to hurdles-placed Skerne Spark (by Hotfoot): dam winning hurdler: fell first in novice chase in December on debut: sold 1,200 gns Doncaster January Sales. *M. J. Camacho*

    c–

COPPER MINE   7 b.g. Kambalda – Devon Lark (Take A Reef) [1992/3 c16g3 c17d2 c16d3 c17g4 c18d* c17m* c20f* c21g5 c21f* c21f* c22f2] tall, close-coupled gelding: fairly useful hurdler: similar level of form over fences: successful at Stratford, Doncaster, Newbury and Worcester (twice, both handicaps) in second half of season: ran poorly final start: stays 21f:

    c115
    –

acts on dead and firm ground: blinkered fourth outing: tends to jump left: sometimes idles in front. *O. Sherwood*

COPPER STREAK 11 ch.g. Streak – Copper Cloud (Foggy Bell) [1992/3 22g⁴ c21fᵘʳ 21d] compact gelding: winning hurdler: novice chaser: probably stays 2¾m: acts on soft going and good to firm: blinkered twice: poor jumper of fences: has refused on several occasions in points. *P. J. Jones*   c– x 69

COPY LANE (IRE) 4 b. or br.g. Runnett – Airy Queen (USA) (Sadair) [1992/3 18f² 17g* 18m² 17m⁵ 17g* 16g⁴ 18g*] leggy gelding: inconsistent maiden on Flat, stays 1¼m: successful in juvenile hurdles at Plumpton, Taunton and Exeter early in season: stays 2¼m: acts on firm ground: sold 6,000 gns Newmarket Autumn Sales. *M. R. Channon*   103

COQUET ISLAND 11 ch.g. Politico (USA) – Coquetdale (St Satur) [1992/3 c25gᵘʳ c21sᵘʳ c25fF c17m³] plain gelding: completing for first time in steeplechases when third in novice event at Kelso in March. *G. Richards*   c72

COQUI LANE 6 ch.g. Le Coq d'Or – Gala Lane (Gala Performance (USA)) [1992/3 F16g⁶ F16g 16g⁴ 18m³ 21s⁶] poor novice hurdler: should stay at least 2½m: acts on good to firm ground: amateur ridden. *G. R. Dun*   85

CORACO 6 br.g. Oats – Coral Delight (Idiot's Delight) [1992/3 F16d F17d 17v³ 16v* 21g³] leggy, close-coupled gelding: won novice hurdle at Kempton in January: creditable third at Newbury following month: effective at 2m when conditions are testing and will stay beyond 21f: acts on heavy going: should progress. *Mrs T. D. Pilkington*   99 p

CORAL PINK 6 b.m. Miramar Reef – Wharton Manor (Galivanter) [1992/3 F16v 16d 17f⁴ 17g 20g³ 22dF] workmanlike mare: sixth foal: half-sister to several winners, including French hurdler Old Man Mose (by Simply Great): dam, fair Flat performer, stayed 1m: poor novice hurdler: easily best effort on penultimate start. *K. C. Bailey*   83

CORALS DREAM (IRE) 4 b.g. Petorius – Walkyria (Lord Gayle (USA)) [1992/3 17d⁶] useful at up to 1m at 2 yrs, fair form for C. Wall in 1993: some promise in novice event at Wolverhampton in February. *J. J. O'Neill*   – p

CORBALLY BESS 13 br.m. Saulingo – Pretty Janey (Hardicanute) [1992/3 17gᵖᵘ] lengthy mare: selling hurdler: novice chaser: lightly raced and no form for a long time. *Miss L. Bower*   c–
–

CORBY CROWN 8 br.m. Royal Fountain – Carney (New Brig) [1992/3 c24sᵖᵘ] rather leggy mare: once-raced over hurdles: modest pointer: pulled up in hunter chase in April. *H. W. Lavis*   c–
–

CORBY KNOWE 7 b.g. Pragmatic – Easter Noddy (Sir Herbert) [1992/3 25s⁵] leggy gelding: winning pointer in Ireland: signs of only a little ability in 2 races over hurdles: sold 1,100 gns Doncaster January Sales. *C. Parker*   –

CORDIGLIA 9 ch.m. Newski (USA) – Pack Ice (Arctic Slave) [1992/3 22dᵖᵘ] rangy mare: fair pointer: let down by her jumping in steeplechases, and no promise on hurdling debut. *R. H. Alner*   c– x
–

CORINTHIAN GOD (IRE) 4 b.c. Red Sunset – Rathcoffey Duchy (Faberge II) [1992/3 17s 17vᵖᵘ 18v⁴ 16g*] leggy colt: well backed, first form over hurdles when winning selling handicap at Fontwell (no bid) in March: poor middle-distance performer (best form on a sound surface) on Flat, winner in June. *D. A. Wilson*   84

CORLEY FLOWER 4 b.f. Sizzling Melody – Dame Corley (L'Enjoleur (CAN)) [1992/3 17mᵖᵘ] neat filly: poor sprint maiden plater on Flat: no promise in September on hurdling debut. *P. D. Cundell*   –

CORLY SPECIAL 6 b.g. Lyphard's Special (USA) – Courreges (Manado) [1992/3 21dF 21vᵖᵘ 17s 16v²] sparely-made gelding: poor selling hurdler: stays 2¾m: acts on heavy and good to firm ground: blinkered once (ran creditably). *L. J. Codd*   70

CORNET 7 b.g. Coquelin (USA) – Corny Story (Oats) [1992/3 c21g³ c20g* c20m³ c20g* c20g c21v⁴ 17d⁴ c24m* c20gᵘʳ c20g⁴] compact gelding: winning hurdler: fairly useful chaser: won 2 handicaps at Ayr in first half of season and Edinburgh (seventh course win) in February: let down by his   c129 §
–

jumping last 2 starts: stays 3m: acts on heavy going and good to firm: best visored, blinkered third outing: moody, and no easy ride. *Denys Smith*

CORN EXCHANGE 5 b.g. Oats – Travellers Cheque (Kibenka) [1992/3 F16s 21g^{pu}] plain gelding: sixth foal: dam lightly-raced daughter of fair staying chaser Lira: no sign of ability in NH Flat race in January and maiden hurdle in May: sold 1,000 gns Malvern May Sales. *T. H. Caldwell* — —

CORNISH COSSACK (NZ) 6 br.g. Wolverton – Cotton Bud (NZ) (Balkan Knight (USA)) [1992/3 22s^3 19f^5 22s^4 22v 22d^{ur} 18s 17v^2 17s^5 22m^4 c17m^3 c21d^4] leggy gelding: poor form in novice hurdles and in 2 starts over fences: stays 2¾m: acts on heavy going and good to firm. *D. H. Barons* — c75 75

CORN LILY 7 ch.m. Aragon – Ixia (I Say) [1992/3 17g^4] leggy, workmanlike mare: fair handicap hurdler: respectable fourth at Cheltenham in October, only outing of season: should prove suited by further than 2m: acts on firm going: jumps soundly. *Mrs M. Reveley* — 113

CORPORATE MEMBER 6 ch.g. Exhibitioner – Sciambola (Great Nephew) [1992/3 23m^F] close-coupled, workmanlike gelding: tailed off in novice hurdles. *G. Barnett* — —

CORPORATE TYPE (IRE) 5 b.g. Last Tycoon – Sherkraine (Shergar) [1992/3 16g 18d^4 16m 16d 18d 17s 17f^R 16g] sturdy gelding: poor novice selling hurdler: sold out of G. Kelly's stable 1,500 gns Doncaster September Sales after second start: blinkered twice. *J. C. Haynes* — 58 §

CORPUS 4 ch.c. Ballacashtal (CAN) – Millingdale (Tumble Wind (USA)) [1992/3 17d^{pu} 16d 17v^{pu} 18s] leggy, lightly-made colt: half-brother to moderate winning jumpers Out of Stock (by Neltino) and Norstock (by Norwick): no form on Flat or over hurdles. *R. J. Hodges* — —

CORRADO 9 ch.g. Creative Plan (USA) – Bali (Ballymoss) [1992/3 c25d^{pu}] ex-Irish gelding: moderate novice hurdler: poor form over fences: stays 3m: acts on dead ground: blinkered once. *Mrs G. M. Gladders* — c– —

CORRARDER 9 ch.g. True Song – Craig Maigy (Idiot's Delight) [1992/3 c21v^{pu} c17d* c18f^4] leggy gelding: useful hunter chaser at best: first form since 1991 when winning amateurs handicap at Newton Abbot in April: not discredited next time: stays 2¾m: acts on firm and dead ground. *J. A. B. Old* — c100 —

CORRAVORRIN 8 ch.g. Garda's Revenge (USA) – Pearl Creek (Gulf Pearl) [1992/3 c24g^2 c26m^{pu} c25d^{pu} c23m^F] compact, workmanlike gelding: winning chaser: first race for nearly 18 months when good second in handicap at Taunton in April: failed to complete in 3 subsequent races: stays 3m: acts on good to firm and dead ground. *S. Christian* — c92 —

CORRIE LASS 11 ch.m. Funny Man – Space Project (Space King) [1992/3 c22m^{pu}] sparely-made mare: winning hurdler: no show on chasing debut: stays 3m: probably acts on any going. *C. Bridgett* — c– —

CORRIN HILL 6 b.g. Petorius – Pete's Money (USA) (Caucasus (USA)) [1992/3 17s* 17g^3 17s^2 21s^{pu} 16g^3 17m 18s*] small, leggy gelding: fair at best on Flat, stays 7f: changed hands 1,400 gns Newmarket Autumn Sales: won novice hurdles at Market Rasen in November and April: much better form when placed in valuable events on second and third starts: sold 9,400 gns Doncaster May Sales: form only at around 2m: acts on soft going: stiff task when blinkered sixth outing. *P. A. Kelleway* — 128

CORRUPT COMMITTEE 10 ch.g. Henbit (USA) – The Bungalow (Habitat) [1992/3 c22m^3 c20m* c20s^F] workmanlike gelding: winning hurdler: won novice chase at Market Rasen in September: seemed not to stay 25f: was possibly unsuited by soft ground: dead. *K. C. Bailey* — c88 —

CORSTON RACER 5 ch.g. Scallywag – Corston Lass (Menelek) [1992/3 17d^3] sturdy gelding: poor novice hurdler: third at Perth in September: stays 2½m: acts on good to firm and dead going. *Denys Smith* — 79

CORSTON SPRINGS 11 gr.g. Bruni – Corston Lass (Menelek) [1992/3 c24m^3 c24f^5] workmanlike gelding: fair pointer: poor form in hunter chases: finished lame last start: stays 25f: form only on a sound surface. *M. P. Jones* — c82 —

COS I'M HANDY 4 b.c. Nearly A Hand – Cosmic (Foggy Bell) [1992/3 aF16g5] first foal: dam successful pointer: last of 5 in NH Flat race at Lingfield in February: yet to race over hurdles. *W. G. M. Turner*

COSMIC DANCER 6 ch.g. Horage – Royal Cloak (Hardicanute) [1992/3 26g4 25dpu 24s a24g2 a22g* a22g* a22g* a24g] light-framed gelding: fair handicap hurdler: successful 3 times at Southwell in 1992/3 (winner there 7 times in all): stays 3m: acts on good to firm going and particularly well on fibresand: often blinkered: sometimes finds little, and is usually held up. *S. P. C. Woods*

112

COSMIC FORCE (NZ) 9 b.g. Diagramatic (USA) – Cosmic Lass (NZ) (Roselander) [1992/3 20m* c16dur 20d5] angular gelding: lightly-raced hurdler: trained by N. Smith, easily best effort when winning novice handicap at Bangor in October: not raced after following month, no promise only start over fences: stays 2½m: acts on good to firm going. *C. D. Broad*

c–
83 ?

COSMIC FUTURE 4 gr.c. Siberian Express (USA) – Bourgeonette (Mummy's Pet) [1992/3 17d3 16s a16g4 a16g2] half-brother to fair hurdler Silks Domino (by Dominion): modest middle-distance performer on Flat: placed in juvenile hurdles at Ascot and Southwell: sold only 550 gns Ascot June Sales: yet to race beyond 17f: acts on dead going and fibresand. *S. P. C. Woods*

98

COSMIC RAY 8 b.g. Comedy Star (USA) – Hey Skip (USA) (Bold Skipper (USA)) [1992/3 c21m2 c21f4 c26mpu 18d 16d4 16d* 18d2 16f6 20m] leggy gelding: handicap hurdler/chaser: won conditional jockeys event over hurdles at Hexham in March: effective at 2m and stays 21f: probably acts on any going: visored 5 times in 1988/9. *Mrs V. A. Aconley*

c95
95

COSSACK NOIR 5 b.g. Lidhame – Almeda (Martinmas) [1992/3 17spu 18m] seems of little account. *N. R. Mitchell*

COTAPAXI 8 gr.g. John de Coombe – Go Gently (New Member) [1992/3 c16g3 c17d3 c16gpu c17gFc17f3 c16g3 c16vpu c17v4 c16v6 c17m* c16f* c17m] lengthy, workmanlike gelding: modest chaser: won novice events at Newton Abbot and Lingfield (handicap) in March: well below form last outing: best at 2m: acts on dead and firm ground. *R. J. Hodges*

c90
–

COT LANE 8 ch.g. Remainder Man – Smokey Princess (My Smokey) [1992/3 c25g] strong, compact gelding: carries condition: winning pointer: poor novice hurdler/steeplechaser: stays well: visored once. *J. W. Walmsley*

c–
–

COTSWOLD CASTLE 7 ch.g. Carlingford Castle – Last Trip (Sun Prince) [1992/3 16v 16s6 21g 17g3 18g 16s] tall gelding: poor novice hurdler: probably needs further than 2m and stays 21f: visored last outing: tried to run out once. *R. Dickin*

82

COTTAGE WALK (NZ) 6 b.g. War Hawk – Chocolate's Girl (NZ) (Bright Brocade (NZ)) [1992/3 22spu 18d] lengthy gelding: showed ability in NH Flat races: poor form in novice hurdle at Exeter in November. *D. H. Barons*

63

COUGAR 7 ch.g. Song – Flying Milly (Mill Reef (USA)) [1992/3 17m3 18d3 16g6 16d6 a20g4 a20g c16mpu 16m5 a18g5] small, sturdy gelding: poor novice hurdler: showed nothing on chasing debut: stays 2½m: acts on good to firm, dead ground and fibresand: tried blinkered and visored: thoroughly unreliable. *Mrs S. M. Austin*

c– §
71 §

COULDNT BE BETTER 6 br.g. Oats – Belle Bavard (Le Bavard (FR)) [1992/3 16d2 17v* 20gpu] rangy, good sort: chasing type: first foal: dam, winning 2m hurdler, from good jumping family: all out to land the odds in novice hurdle at Lingfield in December: broke a blood vessel following month, only subsequent start: effective at around 2m but will be very well suited by further: acts on heavy going. *C. P. E. Brooks*

106

COULTON 6 ch.g. Final Straw – Pontevecchio Due (Welsh Pageant) [1992/3 17g4 16v2 16g* 17m]
  Coulton's bid for the Champion Hurdle came to nothing and he now goes chasing. Reportedly he has schooled so well over fences that his

157

trainer described him as 'the next Desert Orchid'. Stranger things have happened but we'll limit ourselves to a more modest prediction, that Coulton will at least emulate the great horse one day by developing into a better chaser than he was a hurdler. That in itself is saying a lot, for Coulton has some good form to his credit over the smaller obstacles, notably a win over established horses in a Grade 2 event at Uttoxeter on his last start as a novice in the 1991/2 season and a half-length second to Jinxy Jack, giving him 3 lb, in the Haydock Park Champion Hurdle Trial in February on his second start in 1992/3. Haydock put him back on course for the Champion Hurdle after a modest effort on his reappearance in the Fighting Fifth Hurdle at Newcastle, and he kept there by doing all that was necessary in the Tote City Trial at Nottingham in February, when beating his only serious rival Duke of Monmouth two lengths in a slowly-run, five-runner limited handicap. Indeed, from the beginning of February he disputed favouritism in the ante-post lists. In view of this, his performance at Cheltenham was rather a let-down. Perhaps it had something to do with his failure to take the eye in the paddock beforehand. In the race he jumped with less fluency than usual, and although he was able to mount some sort of challenge on the outside downhill from the top turn, it fizzled out quickly approaching the second last. He is definitely better than that.

		Thatch	Forli
	Final Straw	(b 1970)	Thong
	(ch 1977)	Last Call	Klairon
Coulton		(b 1964)	Stage Fright
(ch.g. 1987)		Welsh Pageant	Tudor Melody
	Pontevecchio Due	(b 1966)	Picture Light
	(b 1982)	Silvera	Ribero
		(b 1974)	Silver Bede

Looking at Coulton's style of racing, his record, his pedigree, it is hard to see where the confidence in his ability to stay the Gold Cup distance comes from. The logical target at the next Festival must surely be the Arkle Trophy, not the Sun Alliance Chase. The horse pulls hard (he is usually held up); he had no difficulty coping with the return to two miles in 1992/3 after winning four times at two and a half, indeed his best form is at two miles and he seemed to be only just lasting home at two and a half as a novice; and he is bred to be a miler on the Flat. Coulton is by the high-class miler Final

Tote City Trial Handicap Hurdle, Nottingham—
Coulton keeps himself in the Champion Hurdle picture;
Duke of Monmouth chases him home

Straw out of a mare who showed plenty of ability at two and three years, winning three races at Lingfield and another at Epsom at distances between six furlongs and eight and a half furlongs, the last one the longest she ever tackled. Coulton is Pontevecchio Due's first foal. Her third Ponte Cervo (by Hadeer) has run a few times at up to seven furlongs without showing anything, while her fourth is Pontevecchio Moda (by Jalmoud), a winner over six furlongs and an extended seven furlongs as a two-year-old in 1992. Coulton is physically a chasing type, a workmanlike, angular individual. He acts on good to firm and heavy going. As intimated, he is a good jumper of hurdles as a rule. *M. W. Easterby*

COUNTERBID 6 gr.g. Celio Rufo – Biddy The Crow (Bargello) [1992/3 **c92** §
23g³ 24g⁵ 21d c24d⁴ c25g² c20fᶠ² c20g⁴ c21f²] workmanlike gelding: fair **105**
hurdler: would have won novice chase at Ludlow in March but for falling 2
out (remounted): jumped moderately and was irresolute under pressure
when second in similar event at Worcester in May: stays 23f: best form on a
sound surface (acts on firm going): blinkered once over hurdles and at
Worcester, visored third and fourth starts over fences: front runner: isn't
one to rely on. *J. A. C. Edwards*

COUNTER BLAST 4 b.f. Valiyar – Trading (Forlorn River) [1992/3
18sᵖᵘ] lightly raced and no sign of ability on Flat: tailed off when pulled up in   –
juvenile hurdle at Folkestone in December. *W. Holden*

COUNTERPUNCH 9 b.g. Torus – Candy Belle (Candy Cane) [1992/3   **c–** §
17dᵖᵘ c17g c19s⁶ c17s³ c16v⁴ c17dʳᵗʳ c17m⁶ c16mʳᵗʳ] well-made gelding: **–** §
winning hurdler: poor novice chaser: trained second start only by M. Smith:
temperamental, and sometimes refuses to race. *A. M. Forte*

COUNTORUS 7 b.g. Torus – Gay Countess (Master Buck) [1992/3 16f³
21g³] rangy gelding: moderate handicap hurdler: creditable third at   **98**
Wetherby in May, first and better effort of season: effective at 2m and stays
3m: acts on firm and dead ground. *J. H. Johnson*

COUNT ROBERT (USA) 5 ch.g. Roberto (USA) – Domludge (USA)
(Lyphard (USA)) [1992/3 16g⁶ 16s 17g 16gᵖᵘ 18m] small gelding: poor plater   –
over hurdles: tried blinkered: carries head high. *Miss Jacqueline S. Doyle*

COUNTRY BARLE 5 b.g. Town And Country – Pelant Barle (Prince
Barle) [1992/3 F17d] fourth foal: half-brother to quite useful hurdler Celtic
Barle (by Celtic Cone): dam quite useful pointer: behind in NH Flat race at
Ascot in April: yet to race over hurdles or fences. *H. B. Hodge*

COUNTRY KEEPER 5 b.g. Town And Country – Mariban (Mummy's
Pet) [1992/3 F17g] rangy gelding: first foal: dam winning hurdler:
never-nearer seventh of 16 in NH Flat race at Newbury in March: yet to race
over hurdles or fences. *B. J. M. Ryall*

COUNTRY KIZZIE 4 b.f. Ballacashtal (CAN) – Better Try Again (Try
My Best (USA)) [1992/3 F17f F17fᵖᵘ] first foal: dam poor maiden: showed
nothing in NH Flat races in March and May: yet to race over hurdles. *N. K. Thick*

COUNTRY LAD (IRE) 5 b.g. M Double M (USA) – Kundrie (GER)
(Luciano) [1992/3 17s² 22v 17v³ 17s* 17dᶠ 17s⁶ 17g*] strong, workmanlike   **110 p**

*EBF 'National Hunt' Novices' Handicap Hurdle (Final), Cheltenham —
33/1-shot Country Lad springs a surprise*

gelding: chasing type: carries plenty of condition: won novice handicap hurdles at Cheltenham in January and April (EBF National Hunt Novices' Hurdle Final, impressively by 10 lengths): best form at 17f: acts on soft ground: races prominently: progressive, and will win more races. *Mrs S. D. Williams*

COUNTRY MEMBER 8 ch.g. New Member – Romany Serenade **c 143** p (Romany Air) [1992/3 c26d* c24d* c25s* c27s c25d* c25m²] –

The stable companions Country Member, Katabatic and Storm Alert each looked to hold an excellent chance in their respective races at the Cheltenham Festival, but all three had to settle for a minor placing. Country Member came closest to winning. He was just touched off by Givus A Buck in a driving finish, which also involved Boraceva and Cache Fleur, to the Ritz Club National Hunt Handicap Chase. Country Member, encountering firmish ground for the first time, ran well enough and we have to accept that he is effective on such a surface. However, he did come back rather sore from Cheltenham and wasn't seen out again, and it's possible that he may prove ideally suited by give in the ground when he returns to action in 1993/4. All of Country Member's other completed starts over fences took place on dead or soft ground, and apart from a lack-lustre effort at Newbury in January his record was one of continuous improvement. By mid-season Country Member had picked up handicaps at Wincanton and Newbury and a minor event at Sandown, and he put his disappointing effort well behind him when returned to Sandown in February for the Agfa Diamond Chase. Country Member had only two opponents in this very valuable limited handicap, but they were formidable ones in Captain Dibble and Rushing Wild. The latter had run away with the Anthony Mildmay, Peter Cazalet Memorial on the same course the previous month, and he started at odds on to follow up despite his considerable rise in the weights. Country Member, in receipt of 21 lb, proved too good for him on the day, though. The pair shook off Captain Dibble before the second last, and with the front-running Rushing Wild having no more to give Country Member stormed clear on the run-in to win by six lengths.

Most of Country Member's relatives have made their mark either in point-to-points or hunter chases, or both. They include his brothers What's Yours, Wadswick Lad and Senator of Rome, the last-named also a fair

Agfa Diamond Handicap Chase, Sandown—
Country Member (right) challenges Rushing Wild

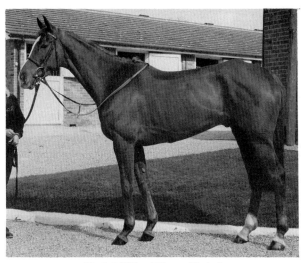

Mrs C. C. Williams' "Country Member"

Country Member (ch.g. 1985)	New Member (ch 1965)	Alcide (b 1955)	Alycidon
			Chenille
		Maiden Speech (b 1959)	Relic
			Gracious Speech
	Romany Serenade (b 1967)	Romany Air (ch 1951)	Tambourin
			Windwhisper
		Right Choice (b 1949)	Tiberius
			Wedding Belle

handicap chaser, and his half-sister Smoke Serenade (by Royal Smoke). His half-brother Govenor's Last (by Armagnac Monarch) showed useful form in handicap chases. Country Member's dam Romany Serenade, an unraced daughter of the winning pointer Right Choice, is a half-sister to four winning jumpers, notably the 1971 Cheltenham Foxhunter winner Hope Again. Country Member himself began his career over hurdles, finishing runner-up on the first of three outings. A late starter—he was just turned six when he made his debut—with just fifteen races under his belt, Country Member is unlikely to have reached his peak yet and he should continue to do well in handicap chases over three miles and more. The Hennessy Gold Cup at Newbury is said to be his first objective. He's a sound jumper. *Andrew Turnell*

COUNTRY MISTRESS 6 b.m. Town And Country – Barge Mistress (Bargello) [1992/3 F17d a16g 16f⁶] rather unfurnished mare with scope: little sign of ability in novice hurdles: bred to stay at least 2½m. *J. A. B. Old* –

COUNTRY RAMBLER 5 b.g. Relkino – Vacuna (Bargello) [1992/3 16v 18gᵖᵘ 16s⁵ 20m⁶] leggy, close-coupled gelding: second foal: dam poor novice hurdler/chaser: poor novice hurdler himself. *P. J. Hobbs* 80

COUNTRY SINGER   10 b.m. Town And Country – Song Without Words (Spartan General) [1992/3 21vᴾᵘ 21f⁶ 22fᴾᵘ] lengthy mare: lightly-raced novice hurdler: blinkered once. *P. M. McEntee* –

COUNTRY SPIDER   8 b.m. Country Retreat – Lolly Spider (Rugantino) [1992/3 c24sꟻ] lengthy mare: maiden pointer: would have finished fourth but for falling last in hunter chase at Chepstow in April: should improve. *Mrs R. Atkinson* **c74** p

COUNT SURVEYOR   6 ch.g. Corawice – Miss Magello (Bargello) [1992/3 c17v⁶] eighth foal: half-brother to winning jumpers Bit of Order (by Choral Society) and Nuaffe (by Abednego): dam never ran: remote sixth in novice chase at Hexham in November on debut. *W. A. Stephenson* **c–**

COUNTY CONTRACTOR   6 gr.g. Capricorn Line – Blue Wonder (Idiot's Delight) [1992/3 17dᴾᵘ 17g 16dᴾᵘ a16g a24g c16m⁶ c17mᴾᵘ c16mꟻ] of little account: blinkered last 2 outings. *C. L. Popham* **c–** **–**

COURAGEOUS CHARGER (USA)   11 ch.g. Bold Bidder – Charger's Star (USA) (Pia Star) [1992/3 c17g⁶] good-bodied gelding: poor novice chaser: stays 25f: acts on firm ground: blinkered twice. *G. Piper* **c–** **–**

COURSE OF ACTION   8 b.g. Crash Course – Narita (Narrator) [1992/3 c25d⁵ c27d⁴ c25vꟻ c26sᵘʳ c27dᴾᵘ 28g⁶] leggy, workmanlike gelding: poor novice hurdler/chaser: stays 27f: acts on dead ground: blinkered last 2 outings. *P. Beaumont* **c–** **–**

COURT CIRCULAR   4 b.c. Miswaki (USA) – Round Tower (High Top) [1992/3 a16gᵘʳ a16g* 17g⁶ 22g⁶ a20g* a16g* 17m⁴ 22m a18g² 20g⁶ 17d² 17f*] angular colt: half-brother to winning hurdler Windsor Park (by Bold Forbes): maiden on Flat: sold out of Lord Huntingdon's stable 7,000 gns Newmarket Autumn Sales: fair form over hurdles: won juvenile event and 2 novice events at Southwell and novice handicap at Stratford in second half of season: effective at 2m and stays 2½m: acts on firm, dead ground and fibresand: blinkered last 4 outings. *W. Clay* **107**

COURT OF KINGS   4 b.g. Green Desert (USA) – Abbeydale (Huntercombe) [1992/3 16g⁴ 18s² 17d⁵ 16d 16m] leggy, close-coupled gelding: no form on Flat: sold out of P. Cole's stable 3,200 gns Newmarket Autumn Sales: modest form first 2 starts in juvenile hurdles: ran badly on good to firm ground final outing (February). *J. M. Bradley* **92**

COURT RAPIER   11 ch.g. Pardigras – Weepers Laura (Weepers Boy) [1992/3 c19g³ c21g⁵ c18d c17m c20f³ c19d⁵] leggy gelding: handicap chaser: poor form in 1992/3: suited by around 2½m: probably acts on any going. *Mrs H. Parrott* **c81** **–**

COURT ROOM   4 b.g. Aragon – Ladysave (Stanford) [1992/3 18f⁵ 16s⁴ 17d⁵ a16g 18v² 17g 17s] poor maiden on Flat and over hurdles: stays 2¼m: acts on any going. *A. Moore* **71**

COUTURE INNOVATORS   6 b.g. Music Boy – Miss Couture (Tamerlane) [1992/3 21dᴾᵘ] compact gelding: half-brother to winning hurdler/chaser Couture Stockings (by Free State): plating-class staying handicapper on Flat: tailed off when pulled up in novice hurdle at Uttoxeter in October. *J. Mackie* **–**

COUTURE STOCKINGS   9 b.g. Free State – Miss Couture (Tamerlane) [1992/3 22s⁵] small gelding: winning chaser: fair handicap hurdler: bit backward, shaped as though retaining all ability when fifth of 20 at Nottingham in February, but wasn't seen out again: stays 3m: possibly best on a sound surface. *J. Mackie* **c–** **102** +

COWDEN COTTAGE   9 ch.g. Connaught – Forty Lines (Fortino II) [1992/3 c22v² c24dᴾᵘ c21sꟻ c24dꟻ] strong, workmanlike gelding: lightly raced: winning hurdler: promising second in novice event at Towcester in December on chasing debut, but failed to complete subsequently: stays 2¾m well: acts on heavy ground: jumps boldly in main but inclined to make the odd mistake. *Dr D. Chesney* **c104** **–**

COWGATE FOUNTAIN 7 b.m. Royal Fountain – Cowgate Lady (Most
Secret) [1992/3 c20s^F c26s^{pu}] moderate hurdler: tailed off when pulled up in
novice chase: seemed barely to stay 3m: acted on good to firm and soft
going: dead. *Mrs M. Reveley*

c–
–

COXANN 7 b.g. Connaught – Miss Nelski (Most Secret) [1992/3 23m^4
26d 24d^4 23s^2 28v^4 22v^4 26d^4 23d 23d^3 a24g^4 a24g^{pu} c24m^{pu} 21s^2 a21g^3]
compact gelding: modest handicap hurdler: has failed to complete in 2
outings over fences: stays very well: acts on heavy and good to firm going:
has worn blinkers (not when successful): unreliable. *J. C. McConnochie*

c– §
89 §

COZZI (FR) 5 gr.g. Cozzene (USA) – Land Girl (USA) (Sir Ivor) [1992/3
18m 17g 17f] angular gelding: poor novice hurdler. *J. M. Bradley*

69

CRABBY BILL 6 br.g. Blakeney – Dancing Kathleen (Green God)
[1992/3 21g] small, rather leggy gelding: modest handicap hurdler: stiff task
in October, only outing of season: will stay further than 2¾m: acts
particularly well on equitrack: blinkered nowadays. *Miss B. Sanders*

–

CRACKLING ANGELS 6 b.m. Martinmas – Freeze Frame (Averof)
[1992/3 22d 18d^2] leggy mare with scope: best effort in novice hurdles when
staying-on second in mares race at Exeter in April: should stay beyond
2¼m. *R. H. Buckler*

86

CRAFT EXPRESS 7 b.g. Bay Express – Lydia Rose (Mummy's Pet)
[1992/3 a16g^{pu}] small gelding: one-time useful sprinter on Flat when trained
by M. Johnston: no show on either first start over hurdles, trained by N. Meade
in Ireland on first occasion. *Miss S. J. Wilton*

–

CRAFTY CHAPLAIN 7 ch.g. The Parson – She's Clever (Clever Fella)
[1992/3 22s 17s^4 17s^4 c21s^F c20s c21v^4 c22g^F c16m^3 c18g^5 c16m^3 c18m^{pu}]
sturdy, close-coupled gelding: poor novice hurdler/chaser: trained until
after ninth start by P. Bevan: whipped round last final outing: stays 2½m:
visored last start over hurdles: poor jumper of fences. *D. McCain*

c77 x
77

CRAFTY COPPER 9 b.g. Henbit (USA) – Quatemala (Welsh Saint)
[1992/3 c21m^2 c21s* c22g^2 c22m^{pu} c23f^3 c23d* c25g^4 c24g^3 c25g^2 c25g^3
c33m^5 c26g^3] leggy gelding: winning hurdler: won novice chase at Newton
Abbot in August (trained until after fifth start by A. Jarvis) and hunter chase
at Uttoxeter in February: ran creditably afterwards, particularly so on ninth
outing: stays 4m: probably acts on any ground. *P. Bradley*

c90 +
–

CRANK SHAFT 6 b.g. Strong Gale – Tullow Performance (Gala
Performance (USA)) [1992/3 F17d^6 F16s F16s 18g^5 22d^6 26g^2] workmanlike
gelding: second foal: brother to An Bothar Dubh and half-brother to Cuilin
Bui (by Kemal), both winning Irish hurdlers: dam dual NH Flat race and
hurdles (at up to 3m) winner, also placed over fences: easily best effort in
novice hurdles when second at Huntingdon in April, though ran in snatches
and looked none too a easy a ride: stays 3¼m. *F. J. Yardley*

95

CRAWFORD SAYS 8 b.g. Kemal (FR) – Xandor (Songedor) [1992/3
c18d^3 c18s^4 c26s^3 c24v^2 c20s^3 c25d* c24v c27s^2 c25d* c34d c29s^6 c25g^6]
rangy, good-topped gelding: fairly useful handicap chaser: won at
Punchestown in December and Fairyhouse in February: ran well in
Jameson Irish Grand National at Fairyhouse in April on eleventh outing,
below form starts either side (former at Uttoxeter): stays well: acts on
heavy going. *J. H. Scott, Ireland*

c119
–

CRAWN HAWK 8 br.g. Croghan Hill – Gin An Tonic (Osprey Hawk)
[1992/3 20s^{pu}] tailed off when pulled up in 2 novice hurdles at Bangor in
1990/1 and December: sold 1,650 gns Doncaster January Sales. *T. P. Tate*

–

CRAZY DAISY 6 ch.m. Turn Back The Time (USA) – Nicaline (High
Line) [1992/3 20v^4 17s^{pu} 17v^{pu} a20g] NH Flat race winner: no form over
hurdles: blinkered last start. *W. G. M. Turner*

–

CRAZY HORSE DANCER (USA) 5 b.g. Barachois (CAN) – Why
Pass (USA) (Pass (USA)) [1992/3 17g^4 20m^5 17d 16d^3 16s^6 21v^4 22g^3 23m^3
21d^F 27d^{pu}] strong, close-coupled gelding: moderate hurdler: creditable
efforts last 3 completed starts, including in a seller: stays 23f: acts on good
to firm and heavy going. *F. Jordan*

89

CRAZY RIVER 6 b.g. Vision (USA) – Etty (Relko) [1992/3 c21grtr] workmanlike gelding: fair hurdler: similar level of form in 2 completed points in 1993: refused to race on one occasion, and did so again in novice hunter chase at Uttoxeter in May: stays 3m: acts on dead ground, unsuited by heavy: best in blinkers: not one to trust. *Denis McCarthy*

c– §
– §

CREAG DHUBH 4 br.g. Petong – Hawthorne Vale (Richboy) [1992/3 F17f] second foal: half-brother to novice hurdler Aurora Lad (by Free State): dam, bad plater at 2 yrs, sister to Burrough Hill Lad: mid-division in NH Flat race at Sandown in March: yet to race over hurdles. *M. C. Pipe*

CREAM AND GREEN 9 b.g. Welsh Chanter – Jumana (Windjammer (USA)) [1992/3 16s² 16d² 17s 17dF] sparely-made gelding: modest 2m handicap hurdler: suffered a fatal fall at Wolverhampton in February: pulled up only outing over fences: acted on good to firm and dead ground. *K. White*

c–
89

CREAM BY POST 9 b.m. Torus – Lady Manta (Bargello) [1992/3 c24fur] rather angular mare: winning hurdler: has shown nothing in steeplechases but is a fair chaser (winner 4 times in 1993): probably stays 2¾m: acts on firm and dead ground. *R. Barber*

c–
–

CREAM OF THE CROP (IRE) 5 ch.g. Milk of The Barley – Hua Hin (Night Star) [1992/3 16dpu] good-topped gelding: behind in NH Flat races and when pulled up in a novice selling hurdle. *J. Wharton*

–

CREDIT CALL (IRE) 5 br.g. Rhoman Rule (USA) – Maiacote (Malacate (USA)) [1992/3 F17d F17m] small, leggy gelding: first living foal: dam never ran: tailed off in NH Flat races in the spring: yet to race over hurdles or fences. *R. G. Brazington*

–

CREEAGER 11 b.g. Creetown – Teenager (Never Say Die) [1992/3 20d 17g⁵ 21s⁴ 20g] strong, compact gelding: fair hurdler: best efforts of season first 2 starts: winning chaser: stays 3m: probably acts on any going. *J. Wharton*

c–
106

CREESHLA 6 b.g. Bustomi – Mattress (Silver Cloud) [1992/3 c26d*] successful in a point prior to winning maiden hunter chase at Cartmel in May by 15 lengths: stays 3¼m: acts on dead ground. *R. Bewley*

c95 p

CREETOWN SARAH 5 ch.m. Creetown – Sara's Light (Precipice Wood) [1992/3 16v a18gpu] no promise over hurdles. *W. G. Mann*

–

CREPT OUT (IRE) 4 ch.c. On Your Mark – Valbona (FR) (Abdos) [1992/3 17dF 16s a16g⁶ 18d] compact colt: modest 6f/7f performer on Flat: sold out of Miss S. Hall's stable 3,000 gns Doncaster September Sales: no form over hurdles, including in a selling handicap. *J. L. Harris*

–

CRESTWOOD LAD (USA) 4 ch.g. Palace Music (USA) – Sweet Ellen (USA) (Vitriolic) [1992/3 18d⁶ 18d⁵ 17s⁶ 16dur 16d⁴ 16f⁶ 17f] plating-class maiden on Flat: poor form over hurdles: best efforts fifth and sixth starts (claimer and selling handicap): should stay beyond 2m: sold 1,600 gns Doncaster June Sales. *Mrs M. Reveley*

74

CRETOES DANCER (USA) 4 br.g. Secreto (USA) – Mary Read (USA) (Graustark) [1992/3 17g] sturdy gelding: modest maiden on Flat: well beaten in juvenile hurdle at Newbury (wore tongue strap) in October. *W. R. Muir*

–

CROBEG 8 b.g. Furry Glen – Windsor Reef (Take A Reef) [1992/3 25gpu 21m³ 25dpu c21mpu] big, workmanlike gelding: winning pointer in Ireland: only sign of ability in Britain, including on steeplechasing debut, when third of 5 in slowly-run handicap hurdle at Carlisle in September. *J. J. O'Neill*

c–
71

CROCK-NA-NEE 12 b.g. Random Shot – Saucy Slave (Arctic Slave) [1992/3 c24f⁶ c19v² c24d² c27m³ c26f² c24g⁶] workmanlike gelding: fair hunter chaser nowadays: stays 3¼m: acts on any going. *Mrs Fiona Vigors*

c93
–

CROESONEN 9 ch.m. Balinger – Rock Rose (Rockavon) [1992/3 20s 17d c16m⁶] workmanlike mare: no sign of ability. *G. Richards*

c–
–

CROFTER'S CLINE 9 b. or br.g. Crofter (USA) – Modena (Sassafras (FR)) [1992/3 20spu] sturdy gelding: takes keen hold and doesn't stay over hurdles. *A. Bailey*

–

CROFT MILL 7 b.g. Furry Glen – Aplomb (Ballymore) [1992/3 17s³ 23s* 22s² 23s 22s⁵] leggy gelding: has stringhalt: won novice hurdle at Windsor in November: creditable second in similar event at Nottingham later in month but below form subsequently: stays 23f well: acts on soft going: wore tongue strap penultimate start. *Miss H. C. Knight*　　90

CROFTON LAKE 5 ch.g. Alias Smith (USA) – Joyful Star (Rubor) [1992/3 F17s F17g⁶ F16d] good-topped gelding: second foal: half-brother to 6-y-o Joyful Imp (by Import): dam modest staying chaser: behind in NH Flat races: yet to race over hurdles or fences. *J. E. Dixon*

CROFT PARK 5 b.g. Elegant Air – Session (Reform) [1992/3 F17d F16g] second foal: half-brother to a winner in Italy: dam fair 7f winner out of half-sister to High Line: behind in NH Flat races: yet to race over hurdles or fences. *W. L. Barker*

CROGHAN STAR 12 br.m. Furry Glen – Star Treasure (Levmoss) [1992/3 c16sᵖᵘ] leggy, lengthy mare: poor chaser, lightly raced nowadays: stays well: acts on firm going. *Alf Watson*　　c–

CROIX VAL MER 6 b. or br.m. Deep Run – Bold Penny (Beau Chapeau) [1992/3 17d² 22s⁶ 16s 20d] plain mare: third foal: sister to winning chaser Mint-Master and half-sister to winning hurdler/chaser Jodi's Money (by The Parson): dam winning hurdler at up to 21f in Ireland: second in novice hurdle at Stratford in November, best effort: bred to be well suited by further than 17f: acts on dead ground. *Mrs I. McKie*　　82

CROMER'S EXPRESS 4 ch.c. Mansingh (USA) – Sallusteno (Sallust) [1992/3 16g 17m 18sʳᵗʳ] close-coupled colt: maiden sprinter on Flat: no sign of ability over hurdles: visored last 2 outings, refusing to race on latter occasion. *T. Kersey*　　– §

CRONKSBANK 5 ch.g. Superlative – Rosinante (FR) (Busted) [1992/3 F16s] workmanlike gelding: half-brother to a minor 2-y-o winner by Dunbeath and to winning pointer Hill Ryde (by Junius): dam, placed at 7f, is daughter of smart sprinter Rambling Rose: tailed off in NH Flat race at Wetherby in January: sold 1,500 gns Doncaster March Sales: yet to race over hurdles or fences. *L. Lungo*

CRONK'S COURAGE 7 ch.g. Krayyan – Iresine (GER) (Frontal) [1992/3 16dᵖᵘ] good-topped gelding: sprinter on Flat, moderate winner in 1992: tailed off when pulled up in novice hurdle at Haydock in December. *E. J. Alston*

CROPDATE 10 b.g. Lucifer (USA) – Chamowen (Master Owen) [1992/3 c21d⁵ c24dᵖᵘ] deep-girthed, workmanlike gelding: modest novice hurdler/ chaser: stays 3m: possibly unsuited by firm ground: blinkered last 3 starts in 1990/1. *J. L. Spearing*　　c81

CROSA'S DELIGHT 6 b.g. Idiot's Delight – Crosa (Crozier) [1992/3 F17s⁴ F17d F16v] tall, leggy gelding: first foal: dam quite useful staying chaser: best effort in NH Flat races first start: unruly to post next time: yet to race over hurdles or fences. *A. P. Jones*

CROSSOFSPANCILHILL 7 ch.g. Duky – Cappahard (Record Run) [1992/3 c21s³ c21v⁵ c24d⁵ c27vᵖᵘ c17v⁴ c20d³ c25mᵖᵘ] plain, workmanlike gelding: moderate chaser at best: easily best effort of season on penultimate start: pulled up lame final outing: stays 27f: acts on good to firm and heavy ground: seems suited by forcing tactics: raced too freely when blinkered once. *C. C. Trietline*　　c84

CROSS REFERENCE 5 b.m. Oats – Crosswise (Firestreak) [1992/3 F16d 25gᵖᵘ] smallish mare: half-sister to several winning jumpers, including smart staying hurdler/chaser A Kinsman (by Rubor) and one-time fairly useful staying chaser Pampering (by Pamroy): dam daughter of useful chaser Brand X: behind in NH Flat race and when pulled up in a novice hurdle (raced freely). *J. E. Brockbank*

CROSSROAD LAD 7 b.g. Beldale Flutter (USA) – Croda Rossa (ITY) (Grey Sovereign) [1992/3 a16g] leggy, lengthy, sparely-made gelding:

modest hurdler at best: lightly raced and little worthwhile form for long time: best at 2m: acts on firm going. *Miss K. M. George*

CROSULA   5 br.g. Sula Bula – Crosa (Crozier) [1992/3 F17g 16d 17vᵖᵘ] leggy, unfurnished gelding: second foal: dam quite useful staying chaser: no sign of ability in NH Flat race and novice hurdles. *A. P. Jones* —

CROWDED HOUSE (IRE)   5 b. or br.g. Mazaad – Standing Ovation (Godswalk (USA)) [1992/3 16d³ 16dᶠ 16d 20f⁵] tall, rather angular gelding: useful hurdler: not quite so good in 1992/3 as previously: stiff task in Martell Aintree Hurdle in April: should stay beyond 2m: acts on good to soft going: has had tongue tied down: blinkered first time at Aintree. *B. V. Kelly, Ireland*   132

CROWECOPPER   14 b.g. Netherkelly – Cammy (Sing Sing) [1992/3 c25m⁵] leggy gelding: poor chaser: stays 25f: suited by a sound surface. *B. Preece*   c– —

CROWN BALADEE (USA)   6 b. or br.g. Chief's Crown (USA) – Naseem Baladee (Kris) [1992/3 17v a16g⁴ a18g² a20g* a20g³ a20g⁴ 18g⁶ 20d⁴] sturdy gelding: won novice handicap hurdle at Lingfield in January: ran creditably next time: reportedly broke blood vessel sixth start: stays 2½m: goes particularly well on equitrack. *M. D. I. Usher*   89

CROWN ROYALE   8 b.m. Some Hand – Lady Rerico (Pamroy) [1992/3 c25vᵖᵘ] fair pointer: novice hunter chaser: stays 2¾m: acts on good to firm going. *Mrs G. England*   c– —

CROXDALE GREY   6 gr.m. Alias Smith (USA) – La Fille (Crooner) [1992/3 c20fᵘʳ] leggy, plain mare: fifth foal: dam winning selling hurdler: of little account on Flat and in points: jumped poorly on steeplechasing debut. *P. Needham*   c– —

CRU EXCEPTIONNEL   5 b.g. Scottish Reel – Elton Abbess (Tamerlane) [1992/3 17mᶠ] fair handicapper on Flat, stays 9f: sold out of P. Makin's stable 20,000 gns Newmarket Autumn Sales: showed ability before falling last in valuable 5-y-o hurdle at Chepstow in March: sure to do better. *P. J. Hobbs*   — p

CRUISE ALONG   6 ch.m. Cruise Missile – If And When (Balliol) [1992/3 21vᶠ 16v 22v 21v² 22g³ 22d] rather unfurnished mare: easily best effort when second in mares novice hurdle at Towcester in February: should stay beyond 21f: possibly needs plenty of give in the ground. *N. A. Twiston-Davies*   84 +

CRUISE CONTROL   7 b.g. Cruise Missile – Kenda (Bargello) [1992/3 c22g] rangy gelding: poor novice hurdler/chaser: seventh of 8 finishers in novice hunter chase at Nottingham in February. *Kerry Hollowell*   c– —

CRUISE PARTY (IRE)   5 b.g. Slip Anchor – Cider Princess (Alcide) [1992/3 16v⁶ 17g⁶ 22gᵖᵘ] leggy, lengthy gelding: has been tubed: poor form over hurdles: headstrong. *Mrs D. Haine*   72

CRUISER TOO   6 b.g. Cruise Missile – Delegation (Articulate) [1992/3 F17v F17d F17m 20mᶠ] tall gelding with scope: fourth foal: brother to a poor animal: dam moderate pointer: well beaten in NH Flat races: fell fourth on hurdling debut. *S. N. Cole*   —

CRYSTAL BEAR (NZ)   8 b.g. Veloso (NZ) – Euphemia (NZ) (Piccolo Player (USA)) [1992/3 17d³ 16m⁴ 21m* 17d⁶ 22m] leggy gelding: useful hurdler: won handicap at Chepstow in March: fair effort next time, long way below form last outing: stays 21f: acts on soft going and good to firm. *Capt. T. A. Forster*   132

CRYSTAL COMET   9 gr.m. Cosmo – Neezerbel (Eborneezer) [1992/3 17sᵖᵘ] tall mare: lightly-raced winning 2¼m hurdler: acts on heavy going. *Mrs J. G. Retter*   —

CRYSTAL CONE   7 b.g. Celtic Cone – Queen's Crystal (Royal Palace) [1992/3 19m⁶ 17v* 21d⁵] rather leggy gelding: only form when winning 6-runner novice handicap hurdle at Chepstow in February: well out of depth next start: should stay beyond 17f: acts on heavy going. *A. M. Forte*   77

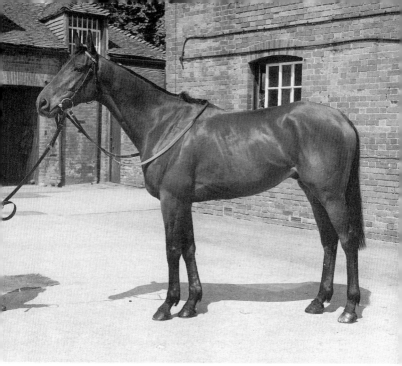

Mr Paul Mellon's "Crystal Spirit"

CRYSTAL HEIGHTS 7 ch.g. Wolver Heights – Crystal's Solo (USA) (Crystal Water (USA)) [1992/3 c26vF c21s² c27s² c25g² c24fpu] angular gelding: fairly useful hurdler: second in novice chases, showing fair form: pulled up lame last start (March): probably stays 27f: acts on soft going: not yet an accomplished jumper of fences. *Mrs J. G. Retter*   c96 –

CRYSTAL HEIGHTS (FR) 5 ch.g. Crystal Glitters (USA) – Fahrenheit (Mount Hagen (FR)) [1992/3 17gpu 17s 17gF 16f] lengthy gelding: fair performer on Flat, best efforts at 7f: sold out of W. O'Gorman's stable 5,000 gns Newmarket Autumn Sales: looks a doubtful stayer over hurdles: resold 1,500 gns Ascot May Sales. *J. Joseph*   –

CRYSTAL MINSTREL 7 b.g. Black Minstrel – Cool Girl (Menelek) [1992/3 25d 25d 23d] sturdy gelding: poor novice hurdler: stays 2¾m: acts on dead going: jumps none too fluently. *J. A. C. Edwards*   –

CRYSTAL SPIRIT 6 b.g. Kris – Crown Treasure (USA) (Graustark) [1992/3 21fur 25m 24s³ 24f³] rangy, good-looking gelding with scope: usually looks well: very much type to make a chaser: smart hurdler: best effort of season when third in valuable event won by Sweet Duke at Ascot in March on third start: effective at around 2½m and stays 25f: probably acts on any going: front runner. *I. A. Balding*   156

C SHARP 6 ch.g. Song – Simply Jane (Sharpen Up) [1992/3 17dpu] workmanlike gelding: of little account on Flat nowadays: pulled up in   –

November on hurdling debut: sold 2,000 gns Ascot February Sales, resold 1,800 gns Ascot 2nd June Sales. *W. R. Muir*

CUCKOO IN THE NEST 10 br.g. Imperial Fling (USA) – Nest Builder c– x
(Home Guard (USA)) [1992/3 c18m^{ur} 17m4] good-topped gelding: poor 2m –
hurdler: let down by his jumping over fences: often blinkered or visored and
has also worn a hood. *R. Hollinshead*

CUDDER OR SHUDDER (IRE) 4 b.f. The Parson – L O Broadway
(Crash Course) [1992/3 F16f] second foal: sister to 5-y-o Cleric On
Broadway: dam fair hurdler who stayed 2¾m: well beaten in NH Flat race at
Haydock in May: yet to race over hurdles. *D. Moffatt*

CUILEANN 8 b. or br.g. Caerleon (USA) – Manfilia (Mandamus) [1992/3
21d4] neat gelding: modest hurdler: not disgraced only outing of season 92
(November): stays 3m (seemingly not 3¼m): acts on firm and dead going.
D. J. Deacon

CULTURED 4 b.g. Saint Cyrien (FR) – Made of Pearl (USA) (Nureyev 116 p
(USA)) [1992/3 16s6 16v* 17d2 16f2 17s* 17g4] smallish, sparely-made
gelding: fair middle-distance stayer on Flat: sold out of M. Stoute's stable
15,000 gns Newmarket Autumn Sales: successful in novice hurdle at
Windsor in February and juvenile event at Perth in April: good fourth in
juvenile handicap at Ascot later in month: ideally needs testing conditions at
around 2m and will stay further: acts on heavy going (long way below form
on firm): sketchy jumper: should continue to progress. *J. White*

CULTURE SHOCK (IRE) 4 ch.f. Hatim (USA) – Rock Singer (Ballad
Rock) [1992/3 aF16g4 22d^{pu} a16g4] sturdy filly: second foal: dam never ran: –
well beaten in NH Flat race in March: little promise in claiming hurdle at
Southwell in May. *M. Johnston*

CUMBRIAN CLASSIC 4 b.g. Glint of Gold – Blubella (Balidar) [1992/3
17m] no sign of ability on Flat: soon tailed off in August on hurdling debut: –
sold 900 gns Doncaster November Sales. *L. Lungo*

CUMREW 13 b.g. Gunner B – Almadena (Dairialatan) [1992/3 c24d6 c–
c24s^{pu}] compact, workmanlike gelding: staying chaser: showed nothing in 2 –
races in November: wears blinkers. *Capt. T. A. Forster*

CUMREWS NEPHEW 5 ch.g. Enchantment – Carrapateira (Gunner
B) [1992/3 F17f F17d] second foal: half-brother to fair hurdler/chaser Pink
Gin (by Tickled Pink): dam unraced sister to one-time fairly useful staying
chaser Cumrew: behind in NH Flat races in the spring: yet to race over
hurdles or fences. *R. Brotherton*

CUNNINGHAMS FORD (IRE) 5 b.g. Pollerton – Apicat (Buckskin
(FR)) [1992/3 F17m4] first foal: dam unraced half-sister to high-class
staying chaser Simon Legree: fourth in NH Flat race at Doncaster in
February: yet to race over hurdles or fences. *O. Sherwood*

CUPID'S COURAGE (IRE) 4 gr.f. Bold Arrangement – God's Kiss
(Godswalk (USA)) [1992/3 18v^{pu} 17s^{pu}] lengthy filly: fourth foal: half-sister –
to Irish NH Flat race winner Exile On Main St (by Scorpio): dam poor
middle-distance Flat maiden in Ireland: modest maiden at around 1m on Flat
in Ireland when trained by M. Halford: tailed off when pulled up in juvenile
hurdles in January and April. *Mrs L. C. Jewell*

CURAHEEN BOY 13 b.g. Tepukei – Curraheen Lady (Master Buck) c97
[1992/3 c22d*^{dis} c20g2 c21s2 c20f* c24f2 c22f^{pu} c24d6 c26m* c23g6 c21g3]
lengthy gelding: fairly useful hunter chaser: first past the post at Stratford
(demoted) in February, Doncaster in March and Hereford in May: effective
at 2½m and stays 3¼m: probably acts on any going. *C. C. Trietline*

CURSNEH DECONE 8 ch.m. Celtic Cone – Decorum (Quorum)
[1992/3 22d4 22g5 22d^{pu}] lengthy mare: lightly-raced novice hurdler: stays 73
2¾m: best form on a sound surface. *J. M. Bradley*

CURTAIN FACTORY 4 ch.g. Jupiter Island – Dalchroy (Hotfoot)
[1992/3 16d^{pu} 16s 16d 17g* 16g6 17m] compact gelding: half-brother to 86
modest miler Asitappens (by Music Maestro): dam, poor maiden, ran only at

2 yrs: best effort over hurdles when winning novice event at Newcastle in February: stiffish task in handicap final start. *M. H. Easterby*

CUSHINSTOWN 10 ch.g. Callernish – Bean An Ti (Festive) [1992/3 c26s³ c27v] workmanlike gelding: useful chaser: first race for 12 months when creditable third in handicap at Warwick in November: dropped out tamely in straight when favourite for similar race at Chepstow following month, and wasn't seen out again: will stay beyond 3¼m: acts well in the mud. *M. C. Pipe*   **c136**

CUTE ENCHANTRESS 6 b.m. Enchantment – Chalk Your Cue (Pals Passage) [1992/3 20gᵖᵘ 22m 25m c27vᵘʳ] leggy mare: no form over hurdles: well beaten when unseating rider in novice event on chasing debut: blinkered last 2 outings. *T. B. Hallett*   **c–**   **–**

CUTSDEAN CROSS (IRE) 5 br.g. Roselier (FR) – Holy Cross (Arcticeelagh) [1992/3 F16v⁶ 22g⁵ 25d³ 21m⁶] fourth foal: half-brother to winning hurdler/chaser Regent Cross (by Prince Regent): dam, winning Irish pointer, half-sister to several winning jumpers, including top-class hunter Eliogarty: best effort over hurdles when third in maiden at Perth in May: will prove suited by good test of stamina: acts on dead going. *D. Nicholson*   **86**

CWM ARCTIC 6 b.m. Cisto (FR) – Menel Arctic (Menelek) [1992/3 F16m F17v⁵ 22v 17s³ 16d 26d⁴ 20m] plain, leggy mare: half-sister to winning hurdler Desperate (by Saxon Farm): dam NH Flat race winner/maiden hurdler in Ireland: poor novice hurdler: best effort over 3¼m on dead going. *Mrs A. Price*   **81**

CWM GWAUN 9 ch.g. Le Bavard (FR) – Glenbawn Lady (Orchardist) [1992/3 c19d² c25dᶠ c19sᵖᵘ c19vᵖᵘ] lengthy gelding: only form over fences when second in hunter chase at Hereford in February: stays 25f: acts on good to firm and dead ground: blinkered last outing. *Mrs A. Price*   **c86**   **–**

CYPHRATE (USA) 7 b. or br.g. Saint Cyrien (FR) – Euphrate (FR) (Royal And Regal (USA)) [1992/3 c20d⁶ c16s* c16s⁴ c17g³ c16g² c16m² c16f⁵ c16dᵖᵘ]   **c147 §**   **–**

The best and worst performances of the enigmatic Cyphrate are poles apart. An impressive victory in the Frogmore Handicap Chase at Ascot in December and an excellent second in the Queen Mother Champion Chase at the Cheltenham Festival contrast sharply with several most disappointing efforts. Cyphrate's courage came under suspicion on more than one occasion in the latest season and he's not one to rely on. Cyphrate's victory in the Frogmore Handicap marked him down as a high-class two-miler in the making. He travelled well from the start, cruised up on the bridle in the straight and soon drew clear when Scudamore, who had bided his time, kicked him clear on the run-in. Confirmation of the promise in Cyphrate's Ascot victory was a long time coming, though he ran well, going strongly and looking a danger early in the straight, when third to Waterloo Boy and Katabatic in the Game Spirit Chase at Newbury in February. Cyphrate had both Waterloo Boy and Katabatic behind him in the Queen Mother Champion Chase where Scudamore sent him on much sooner than usual—three out on this occasion—only for the patiently-ridden Deep Sensation to loom up going better at the last. Cyphrate couldn't hold Deep Sensation on the flat and went down by three quarters of a length, with a below-form Katabatic two lengths back in third. On his previous start Cyphrate had been beaten by Emsee-H, who is no more than fairly useful, at Kempton in the Emblem Chase, the conditions of which treated Cyphrate very favourably. On both his starts after the Festival meeting Cyphrate was well beaten. He followed a disappointing fifth in the Martell Aintree Chase with a very poor effort in the BMW Drogheda Handicap at Punchestown in April when he found little ridden along and dropped right out after a mistake three out, his rider pulling him up before the last.

The tall Cyphrate was bred for the Flat. Like his stable-companion Chatam, he raced for Mme Head in France before being transferred to his present trainer for a jumping career. His pedigree was outlined in *Chasers &*

Alias Smith & Jones Racing's "Cyphrate"

Cyphrate (USA) (b. or br.g. 1986)	Saint Cyrien (FR) (b 1980)	Luthier (b or br 1965)	Klairon Flute Enchantee
		Sevres (b 1974)	Riverman Saratoga
	Euphrate (FR) (b 1976)	Royal And Regal (b or br 1970)	Vaguely Noble Native Street
		On The Wing (b 1970)	Tanerko Nellie Fleet

Hurdlers 1991/92. Cyphrate is best at around two miles and acts on soft and good to firm going. He has a useful turn of foot and is usually held up. Cyphrate's tendency to make the odd bad mistake, and the fact that he sometimes wears a tongue strap, are also worth recording. *M. C. Pipe*

CYPRUS (FR) 5 b. or br.g. Crystal Glitters (USA) – Sihame (Crystal Palace (FR)) [1992/3 16g* 17g⁵ 16g⁴ 17m 17f* 17s⁵ 17m⁴ 23gᵇᵈ] good-topped gelding: won novice hurdles at Wincanton in October and Stratford in March: will stay beyond 17f (brought down fourth at 2¾m): acts on firm ground: blinkered fifth and sixth outings. *Miss Jacqueline S. Doyle*   96

CYRANO'S LAD (IRE) 4 b. or br.g. Cyrano de Bergerac – Patiala (Crocket) [1992/3 F17f⁶ F16m] leggy gelding with some scope: half-brother to several winners, including useful Irish sprinter Dubel Boy (by On Your Mark), later successful in USA: dam lightly-raced maiden: showed a little ability in NH Flat races: yet to race over hurdles. *J. A. Glover*

CYRILL HENRY (IRE) 4 b.g. Mister Majestic – Stamina (Star Appeal) [1992/3 18f⁴ 17m⁴ 18d 16s⁴ 16g² a16g 18g³ 16g] sturdy, rather dipped-backed gelding: modest plater on Flat and over hurdles: stays 2¼m: probably acts on any going. *M. Dods*   77

CYTHERE 9 gr.g. Le Soleil – Vinotino (Rugantino) [1992/3 c26g² c27dᵘʳ c27s* c25s² c24v⁵ c25v* c35s³ c27d* c25mᵘʳ c33g] workmanlike gelding: **c111** –

improved chaser in 1992/3 and was successful in novice events at Fontwell and Towcester and handicap at Chepstow in mid-season: suited by a thorough test of stamina: acts on any going: races prominently. *J. T. Gifford*

CZAR NICHOLAS 4 ch.g. Nicholas Bill – Cateryne (Ballymoss) [1992/3 aF16g² aF16g⁵ F14s⁴] half-brother to winning hurdler Deep Water Bay (by Lochnager): dam ran only once: showed ability in NH Flat races: sold 9,000 gns Doncaster May Sales: yet to race over hurdles. *Miss S. E. Hall*

CZERMNO 10 br.g. Strong Gale – Aquamanda (Bleep-Bleep) [1992/3 c26g⁵] leggy, workmanlike gelding: fair pointer: well beaten in hunter chases. *M. A. Lloyd*   c–
–

D

DADDY'S DARLING 8 b.m. Mummy's Pet – Annie Get Your Gun (Blakeney) [1992/3 20m³ 20m 20m⁵] small, leggy mare: poor novice hurdler: not raced after September: stays 2½m: acts on good to firm and dead going. *R. Evans*   71

DAGAZ 7 b. or br.g. Pragmatic – Little Bride (Tarqogan) [1992/3 24d* 24gᵖᵘ] leggy, close-coupled gelding: fairly useful hurdler who was progressing well until pulled up lame in October on last start (blinkered): had won handicap at Cheltenham previous month: stays well: best run on good to soft ground: still has something to learn about jumping. *N. A. Twiston-Davies*   115

DAGOBERTIN (FR) 7 ch.g. Roi Dagobert (FR) – Regalla (FR) (Viceregal (CAN)) [1992/3 20d² c19d² c19d* c18d⁴ c22v³ c20sꟳ c16v⁴ c19v*   c119 p
119

Mr P. A. Leonard's "Dagobertin"

c21s^{F3} 21f^4 17d 22m^5 21f^3] leggy, rather sparely-made ex-French gelding: fairly useful chaser: successful at Auteuil in October: trained until after fifth start by G. Bonnaventure: very easily landed the odds in novice event at Fontwell in February and would have won in similar fashion at Worcester later in month but for falling last (remounted): ran over hurdles afterwards, showing fairly useful form on first occasion, but below that subsequently: stays 2¾m: probably acts on any ground: blinkered last start: has tongue tied down: sketchy jumper. *M. C. Pipe*

DAILY SPORT AUGUST   4 gr.f. Risk Me (FR) – Susie Hall (Gold Rod) [1992/3 18mpu 18mpu] small filly: winning sprint plater on Flat at 2 yrs, has become one to avoid: no promise over hurdles. *M. C. Chapman* –

DAILY SPORT GIRL   4 b.f. Risk Me (FR) – Net Call (Song) [1992/3 16g^5 17s^3 17s^4 17v^4 17v 16d^4 17s^2 17g* 17f^6 16d^6] sparely-made filly: modest plater at around 1m on Flat: moderate form over hurdles, including in sellers: won juvenile claimer at Stratford in March: best effort on heavy ground. *B. J. Llewellyn*   81

DAISY GIRL   7 b.m. Main Reef – Mellow Girl (Mountain Call) [1992/3 16m^2] sturdy mare: in good form on Flat in 1992, winning three 1½m handicaps: improved form when returned to hurdling, finishing second in handicap at Wetherby (wore tongue strap) in October: looked capable of better still, particularly if tried over further, but wasn't seen out again. *J. Mackie*   113

DAKYNS BOY   8 ch.g. Deep Run – Mawbeg Holly (Golden Love) [1992/3 c25g^3 c26v* c22v* c24s* c25s* c25d^2 c33g^{ur}]   **c136** p –

If ever a horse looked to possess the physical attributes to make a better chaser than a hurdler it was Dakyns Boy, and his first season over fences went so well that he started favourite for the Scottish National on only his seventh run. However, physique isn't everything in chasing. Suspicions that Dakyns Boy might not be fluent enough a jumper to emulate his stable-companion Captain Dibble, who won the race as a novice in 1992 on his seventh start, proved well founded when a mistake at the eighth fence put him out; and he needs to brush up in the jumping department if he is to do well, as we anticipate he eventually will, in good long-distance handicaps in future, even the Grand National one day. Dakyns Boy had been having a fine season before Ayr, his only defeat apart from on his debut coming when he had to concede 7 lb to Capability Brown and went down by ten lengths in the Reynoldstown Novices' Chase at Ascot in February.

Tripleprint Feltham Novices' Chase, Kempton—third win over fences for Dakyns Boy

Mr Alan Parker's "Dakyns Boy"

Kept to racing against other novices he won in succession at Warwick, Towcester, Kempton and Ascot, valuable prizes at the last two courses, the Tripleprint Feltham Novices' Chase on Boxing Day and the Peter Ross Novices' Chase three weeks later. The Feltham attracted two other very promising recruits in Barton Bank and Forest Sun but neither got round. Barton Bank hadn't been asked for an effort when he fell in the lead three out and was an unlucky loser. Dakyns Boy, who seemed booked for a good second place at the time the leader fell, was left a distance clear when Forest Sun fell independently at the same fence, and he survived a blunder of his own at the next to run home unchallenged from the only other finisher Ardcroney Chief. The Peter Ross turned into a thorough test of stamina on the soft ground when the front-running Claxton Greene was taken on for the lead. That suited Dakyns Boy who, having hit three of the first eight fences, came to take it up going to four out, soon got well on top, and sauntered home by fifteen lengths.

		Pampered King (b 1954)	Prince Chevalier
			Netherton Maid
	Deep Run (ch 1966)	Trial By Fire (ch 1958)	Court Martial
			Mitrailleuse
Dakyns Boy (ch.g. 1985)		Golden Love (b 1967)	Above Suspicion
			Syncopation
	Mawbeg Holly (ch 1979)	Hansels Pride (ch 1971)	Prince Hansel
			Slave Light

Dakyns Boy showed plenty of ability before he was sent chasing, winning three National Hunt Flat races and a novice hurdle at up to two miles for John Edwards' stable; he was transferred from Edwards to Twiston-Davies after his first start of 1992/3. Two miles would be much too short for him nowadays; the further off the better, really. He acts well on soft or heavy going. The rangy, good-looking Dakyns Boy is the first foal of an unraced mare Mawbeg Holly. His brother Castle Court has been placed in National Hunt Flat races in Ireland. The next two dams are also unraced winner-producers. The older of them, Slave Light, has produced a couple of staying chasers in the high-class Simon Legree and the useful Bashful Lad. Added to that, she is a full sister to Dawn Run's dam Twilight Slave (Dawn Run was by Deep Run, as is Dakyns Boy). *N. A. Twiston-Davies*

DALBEATTIE 4 b.f. Phardante (FR) – Kemoening (Falcon) [1992/3 F16m F17m] half-sister to several winning hurdlers, notably Triumph Hurdle winner Saxon Farm (by Hittite Glory): dam modest Flat maiden: eighth in NH Flat races at Warwick and Hereford in May: yet to race over hurdles. *N. A. Twiston-Davies*

DALEHOUSE LANE 5 b.g. Ring Bidder – Anniversary Token (Record Token) [1992/3 F16s 21gF 24dpu] leggy gelding: second foal: dam won 1¼m seller: mid-division in NH Flat race: showed nothing over hurdles: jumps poorly at present. *R. D. E. Woodhouse* —

DALE PARK 7 b.h. Kampala – Coshlea (Red Alert) [1992/3 21gpu c17v4] c80 sparely-made horse: fair hurdler: poor form when fourth in novice event at — Hexham in November on chasing debut: stays 2½m: suited by plenty of give in the ground. *N. Tinkler*

DALLISTON (NZ) 7 br.g. March Legend (NZ) – Auklyn (NZ) (Auk c91 (USA)) [1992/3 c16s2 c17s2 c16dF c17f6] leggy gelding: winning hurdler: — moderate novice chaser: sold 3,400 gns Ascot June Sales: effective at 2m and should stay further: acts on soft going: sometimes breaks blood vessels. *N. J. Henderson*

DAL MISS 6 b.m. Dalsaan – Loyal And Regal (Royal And Regal (USA)) [1992/3 17spu] leggy mare: of little account on Flat: tailed off when pulled up — in novice hurdle at Wolverhampton in January. *R. E. Peacock*

DALRYMPLE 10 br.g. Tanfirion – Dark Gold (Raise You Ten) [1992/3 18g] won 2¼m claiming hurdle on equitrack at Lingfield in 1990/1: tailed off — in handicap at Exeter in March, only outing since. *B. Palling*

D'ALTAGNAN 7 ch.g. Dalsaan – Fresh As A Daisy (Stanford) [1992/3 17gpu] lengthy gelding: well beaten over hurdles. *S. G. Payne* —

DAMANOUR (USA) 7 gr.g. Lypheor – Damana (FR) (Crystal Palace (FR)) [1992/3 17m* 21m2 18d3] small gelding: selling hurdler: won 94 conditional jockeys event at Bangor (bought in 2,750 gns) in August: twice ran creditably later in month: stays 2f: acts on firm and dead ground: has found nothing: sold 1,100 gns Doncaster October Sales. *G. Richards*

DAMART (USA) 9 b.g. Verbatim (USA) – Ice Wave (USA) (Icecapade (USA)) [1992/3 16g 17g 17d 16d2 16s 18d 16d 16g6 16m 16s] small gelding: 82 poor hurdler: second in seller at Catterick in November, best effort of — season: races only at around 2m: acts on good to firm and dead ground (yet to show his form on soft): blinkered last start. *Miss L. C. Siddall*

DAMCADA (IRE) 5 b. or br.g. Damister (USA) – Tiptoe (Dance In Time c– (CAN)) [1992/3 16d 18d 16g5 16d2 16spu 16v 16d 16s 16dc22vpuc21fpuc21gpu 98 d c17d5] compact gelding: moderate novice hurdler in Ireland: well below form when blinkered eighth start (trained until after then by E. Lynam): no promise over fences: should stay beyond 2m: acts on dead ground. *D. J. Wintle*

DAMERS CAVALRY 10 b.g. Stanford – Margery (FR) (Cadmus II) c115 [1992/3 c25m2 c26d6 c26vpu c27mF c26m*] lengthy, workmanlike gelding: — fairly useful handicap chaser: returned to form and won 4-runner event at Doncaster (fourth course win) in March: sold 2,600 gns Doncaster May Sales: stays well: probably acts on any going: occasionally blinkered: sometimes looks unenthusiastic. *R. Lee*

DAMERS TREASURE 7 ch.g. General Ironside – Dalmond (Diamonds c79 Are Trump (USA)) [1992/3 c21m2 c26gF] big ex-Irish gelding: maiden —

hurdler: second in novice hunter chase at Warwick in May: stays 21f: acts on good to firm ground. *B. R. Summers*

DAMES RUBY 5 b.m. Green Ruby (USA) – Dame Caroline (Wollow) [1992/3 18g^{pu}] tailed off on Flat at 3 yrs: well behind when pulled up in novice hurdle at Worcester in October. *D. J. Wintle* —

DAMIER BLANC (FR) 4 b.g. Damister (USA) – Roche Blanche (FR) (Great Nephew) [1992/3 17v* 16d^4 16s^4 17g] leggy, useful-looking gelding: won 3 times at 1½m and once over 1¾m on Flat in French Provinces in 1992, when trained by H. Pantall: very easy winner of weakly-contested novice hurdle at Lingfield in February, but showed little subsequently: should stay beyond 17f: blinkered: difficult to assess. *M. C. Pipe* ?

DANBURY LAD (IRE) 5 b.g. Bustineto – Clyzari (Pinzari) [1992/3 F16v^5 F17g 21s^{pu} 24s^{pu}] half-brother to winning Irish jumpers Babazar, Zarigal (both by Regular Guy) and Ballinarahy (by Al Sirat): dam ran once: no sign of ability. *M. D. Hammond* —

DANCER'S LEAP (IRE) 5 ch.m. Salmon Leap (USA) – Villars (Home Guard (USA)) [1992/3 16f 16s] no promise in claimers on Flat and early-season novice hurdles. *J. E. Banks* —

DANCERS REVENGE 7 ch.g. Michael's Revenge – Vivyiki (Kirtonian) [1992/3 F17m] sturdy, lengthy gelding: half-brother to plating-class middle-distance winner Baldingstone Boy (by Seaepic): dam unraced: behind in NH Flat race at Bangor in October: yet to race over hurdles or fences. *P. T. Dalton* —

DANCING BOAT 4 b.g. Shareef Dancer (USA) – Sauceboat (Connaught) [1992/3 18d 16s^{pu} a16g^3 18s^{ur} a16g^{pu}] sturdy gelding: poor novice hurdler: trained until after second start by K. Morgan: sold 2,100 gns Ascot February Sales before next outing. *J. L. Harris* 72

DANCING CHIEF 5 br.g. Lidhame – Darlinga (Derring-Do) [1992/3 16d^{pu} 18m^{pu}] leggy gelding: of little account: sold 1,550 gns Doncaster May Sales. *T. J. Carr* —

DANCING DANCER 4 b.f. Niniski (USA) – Verchinina (Star Appeal) [1992/3 18s^5 18v^6 17d^5] leggy filly: half-sister to winning hurdler Romola Nijinsky (by Bustino): maiden on Flat: sold out of N. Wright's stable 980 gns Newmarket Autumn Sales: has shown only a glimmer of ability over hurdles. *R. G. Frost* —

DANCING DAYS 7 ch.g. Glenstal (USA) – Royal Agnes (Royal Palace) [1992/3 20m^{ur} 18d^3 24g 22d^6 22d* 18d^3 26s a20g* 20d^5 a20g^2 a22g^3 a22g^3 a20g^2 22g^5 18d^6 22m^{pu} a21g^2 21g^5 20m] small, good-bodied gelding: modest hurdler: won selling handicap at Sedgefield (no bid) in November and novice handicap at Southwell in January: ran creditably most outings afterwards: maiden chaser: best at up to 2¾m: acts on good to firm, dead going and fibresand: usually blinkered, occasionally visored: sometimes finds little. *J. Parkes* c–86

DANCING EYES 8 b.m. Jester – Le Chat (Burglar) [1992/3 22d^3 26g^F 18f^6 18f] leggy, sparely-made mare: maiden selling hurdler: stays 21f: seems suited by top-of-the-ground and acts on hard: blinkered twice. *M. C. Pipe* —

DANCING GEM 4 b.g. Librate – Opal Lady (Averof) [1992/3 16f^{pu}] probably of little account on Flat: showed nothing in novice selling hurdle at Ludlow in March. *J. M. Bradley* —

DANCING GEORGE (CAN) 9 b.g. Russian George (FR) – Dancing Sadie (USA) (Dancer's Image (USA)) [1992/3 21f] ex-Irish gelding: winning hurdler: in need of race and always behind in selling handicap in September: novice chaser: stays 2½m: acts on heavy going. *S. Coathup* c–—

DANCING HOLLY 6 br.g. Mufrij – Holly Doon (Doon) [1992/3 18g^6 16m 20d* 21d^3 24s 16s^2 16s^4] small, sparely-made gelding: won novice hurdle at Market Rasen in November: also ran well when in frame subsequently: should stay further than 2½m (well beaten at 3m): acts on soft ground: game. *R. S. Wood* 93

DANCING LEGEND (IRE) 5 b.g. Lyphard's Special (USA) – Princess Nabila (USA) (King Pellinore (USA)) [1992/3 16mF 18d 16d 17g5] leggy gelding: poor hurdler: sold 850 gns Doncaster March Sales: races at around 2m: acts on soft going: tried blinkered: reluctant. *J. Parkes*   78 §

DANCING PADDY 5 b.h. Nordance (USA) – Ninotchka (Niniski (USA)) [1992/3 21s3 18v*dis 20v2 17s4 17s* 18mF 17m 17d*] leggy horse: useful handicap hurdler: first past post at Fontwell (disqualified on technical grounds) in December, Cheltenham in January and Ascot (quite valuable event) in April: probably stays 2½m: needs plenty of give in the ground: races up with pace: sometimes wears tongue strap: progressive. *K. O. Cunningham-Brown*   132 p

DANCING REEF 4 b.f. Miramar Reef – Facing (Quiet Fling (USA)) [1992/3 F12d F16g 18mF 18m6] light-framed, angular filly: second foal: dam poor maiden plater on Flat and over hurdles: behind in NH Flat races and a novice hurdle. *Mrs J. Jordan*   –

DANCING RIVER 7 b.g. Niniski (USA) – River Chimes (Forlorn River) [1992/3 c18d* c21f* c21m* c21g5] small, leggy gelding: winning hurdler: progressed well in handicap chases when winning at Cartmel in August, Uttoxeter in September and Bangor in October, but ran poorly later in October and wasn't seen out again: stays 21f: acts on firm and dead going: game: held up. *W. A. Stephenson*   c116 –

DANCING SENSATION (USA) 6 b.m. Faliraki – Sweet Satina (USA) (Crimson Satan) [1992/3 a16g4 c17f2 c16g3] tall mare: modest form over hurdles: well beaten in 2 novice handicap chases when 3-y-o: races at around 2m: acts on good to firm going and fibresand: 3 times a winner at around 7f on Flat in 1993. *J. Wharton*   c– p 89

DANCING SOL 7 b.m. Lepanto (GER) – Solo Waltz (Quiet Fling (USA)) [1992/3 F16m5 22dpu] workmanlike mare: signs of ability in 2 NH Flat races at Ludlow, none in mares novice hurdle at Wincanton. *J. S. King*   –

DANCING STREET 5 ch.m. Scottish Reel – Florence Street (Final Straw) [1992/3 17s 20g 16g3 16g 16d] workmanlike mare: poor novice hurdler: sold 3,000 gns Doncaster September Sales: third at Edinburgh in December, best effort of season: should stay beyond 2m: acts on firm going. *T. Craig*   79

DAN DE LYON 5 ch.g. Broadsword (USA) – Little Primrose (Master Owen) [1992/3 F16d 16sF 17dbd 17g 17g4 17f2 17m] rangy gelding: has scope: easily best effort in novice hurdles when never-nearer second at Stratford in March: will stay further than 2m: acts on firm ground. *D. Nicholson*   86

DANDY MINSTREL 9 br.g. Black Minstrel – Julanda (Tarboosh (USA)) [1992/3 c23vpu c26vpu 25s c21d c24v* c24s* c26d2 c26g* c34d4 c25g2 c24d5] lengthy gelding: modest hurdler: fair chaser: trained until after fourth start by E. Wheeler: in fine form subsequently, winning handicaps over fences at Windsor and Huntingdon in February and Folkestone in March: suited by 3m and more: probably acts on any going: sometimes blinkered (not since joining current trainer): makes mistakes over fences: well ridden by D. Bridgwater. *N. A. Twiston-Davies*   c107 x

DANDY REASON 9 br.g. Abednego – Drumrainey (Arctic Slave) [1992/3 c25gF] poor maiden pointer: fell sixth on steeplechasing debut. *Mrs Pat Mullen*   c–

DANGEROSA 4 b.f. Aragon – Faster Still (Giolla Mear) [1992/3 aF16g4] third foal: dam, half-sister to useful chaser Misty Fort, won 2½m novice chase: fourth of 7 in NH Flat race at Lingfield in March: yet to race over hurdles. *A. Moore*   –

DANISH CHIEF 12 b.g. Brave Invader (USA) – Just Darina (Three Dons) [1992/3 21d] leggy, sparely-made gelding: poor staying hurdler/novice chaser: has run blinkered (with hood on final start 1991/2) and visored: looks reluctant nowadays. *W. Clay*   c– § – §

DANISH DITTY 4 ch.g. Viking (USA) – Irish Limerick (Try My Best (USA)) [1992/3 aF16g4 aF16g] third foal: dam fairly useful 6f winner at 2 yrs:

fourth in NH Flat race at Lingfield in February: well beaten next time: yet to race over hurdles. *M. C. Banks*

DAN MARINO   11 ch.g. Condorcet (FR) – Ascalon (Levmoss) [1992/3   c–
20dᵖᵘ] angular, smallish gelding: winning chaser: one-time fairly useful   –
hurdler: showed nothing only outing in 1992/3: stays 3m: acts on soft going:
races up with pace. *M. C. Pipe*

DANNY CONNORS   9 b.g. Furry Glen – Steady Lady (Lord Gayle   c129
(USA)) [1992/3 c21dᶠ c25g² c21s* c23dᵖᵘ] workmanlike gelding: useful   –
hurdler/chaser: won handicap over fences at Bangor in November: stayed
25f: acted on soft ground: dead. *J. J. O'Neill*

DANNY HARROLD   9 b.g. Deep Run – Chillaway (Arctic Slave) [1992/3   c137
c20d² c24mᵖᵘ] rangy, good-quartered gelding: very useful hurdler: useful   –
chaser: good second to Deep Sensation in H & T Walker Gold Cup Chase
(Limited Handicap) at Ascot in November: successful at 3m but best form at
2½m: unraced on firm ground, acted on any other: a difficult ride (carried
head high and tended to hang): best in blinkers: retired due to recurrent
broken blood vessels. *Andrew Turnell*

DAN O'TULLY   14 b.g. Danjovan – The Bird O'Tully (The Padisha)   c–
[1992/3 c24f⁵ c22gᶠ c21g c21mᵖᵘ] tall gelding: poor maiden hunter chaser.   –
C. N. Nimmo

DANRIBO   10 b.g. Riboboy (USA) – Sheridans Daughter (Majority Blue)   c–
[1992/3 c24gᵘʳ c27dᵖᵘ] strong, lengthy gelding: pointer, successful 3 times   –
in 1992: no form in steeplechases. *John Whyte*

DANTE'S DELIGHT   5 b.m. Idiot's Delight – Super Princess (Falcon)
[1992/3 17d a16g⁴] better effort over hurdles when fourth of 9 finishers in   70
poor maiden at Lingfield in January. *O. Sherwood*

DANTE'S INFERNO   7 ch.g. Orchestra – Trekking (Homing) [1992/3   c116
16g³ 17gᵖᵘ c21dᶠ c20gᶠ c16g³ c21s c16sᶠ c16d* c16d* c16g* c16fᵖᵘ c16g²   78
c21d* c25g³] tall, good-bodied gelding: novice hurdler: fairly useful form
over fences: successful in novice events at Ayr (3, two of them handicaps)
and Perth in second half of season: effective at 2m, barely stays 25f: acts on
good to firm and soft going. *Mrs S. C. Bradburne*

DANTE'S NEPHEW   6 b.g. Le Moss – Candy Coated (Candy Cane)
[1992/3 17s⁶ 17v⁴ 20s⁴ 17g⁶] tall, useful-looking gelding: chasing type: 100
fourth foal: dam never ran: fair form in novice hurdles: best form at around
2m but should prove suited by further: acts on heavy going. *J. T. Gifford*

DANUM LAD   9 b.g. Uncle Pokey – Honey Season (Silly Season) [1992/3   c–
17gᵖᵘ] leggy, angular gelding: poor novice hurdler/chaser: twice blinkered.   –
R. T. Juckes

DANZA HEIGHTS   7 br.g. Head For Heights – Dankalia (Le
Levanstell) [1992/3 17g⁴ 16m] leggy gelding: fair handicap hurdler: fourth at   105
Kelso in October, better effort of season: should stay further than 2¼m.
Mrs M. Reveley

DAPHNIS (USA)   4 b.c. Lead On Time (USA) – Dancing Vaguely (USA)
(Vaguely Noble) [1992/3 F14s* F17d] third foal: half-brother to useful
hurdler Reve de Valse (by Conquistador Cielo): dam French middle-
distance winner: won 15-runner NH Flat race at Market Rasen in April: well
beaten, again making most, at Sandown later in month: sold 8,400 gns
Doncaster May Sales: yet to race over hurdles. *C. R. Egerton*

DAPPING   9 b.m. Beldale Flutter (USA) – Sass-Go (Sassafras (FR))   c75
[1992/3 c18mᶠ c21mᵖᵘ 26g c16g² c21mᵘʳ c26gᵖᵘ c20gᵖᵘ] smallish mare: poor   –
hurdler: only form of season when second in poor chase at Hereford in
August: blinkered third and last outings. *A. P. James*

DARA DOONE   7 b.g. Dara Monarch – Lorna Doone (USA) (Tom Rolfe)
[1992/3 17g⁴ 21s³ 20d⁵ 24s³] sturdy, workmanlike gelding: useful hurdler: 144
put up his best performance yet when third, clear of remainder, to Sweet
Glow in valuable handicap at Ascot in January on last start: needs further
than 2m and stays 3m: acts on soft going. *R. Akehurst*

DARA MELODY (IRE)   4 b.g. Dara Monarch – Ascensiontide (Ela-Mana-Mou) [1992/3 18d³ 16d² 16s⁶ 18d a16g*] tall, leggy gelding: maiden on Flat: won selling handicap hurdle at Southwell (bought in 3,000 gns) in February: sold 4,000 gns Doncaster March Sales: stays 2¼m: acts on dead ground and fibresand: blinkered once: looks none too keen under pressure, and best held up. *J. G. FitzGerald*   84

D'ARCYS GOLD   4 b.f. Jalmood (USA) – Primrose Way (Young Generation) [1992/3 20mᵖᵘ] no sign of ability on Flat or in selling handicap hurdle. *R. J. Hodges*   –

DARE DAGO   9 b.g. Homeboy – Tallishire Beverly (The Go-Between) [1992/3 c25g³ c24mᵖᵘ 25dᵖᵘ c24gᵖᵘ a22gᵖᵘ a20g a22g⁶] strong, close-coupled gelding: poor novice hurdler/chaser: has run in sellers: trained until after third start by R. Weaver: blinkered fifth and sixth outings: sold 875 gns Ascot 2nd June Sales. *R. W. Emery*   c81 –

DARE SAY   10 b.g. Kris – Pampered Dancer (Pampered King) [1992/3 c18m² c18m² c19d³ c16m² c19g*] tall, leggy, close-coupled gelding: moderate chaser: ran creditably in handicaps in first half of 1992/3, though fortunate winner of 4-runner event at Hereford in November (2-length leader fell at the last): stays 19f: yet to race on very soft ground, acts on any other: often held up. *Mrs H. Parrott*   c97 –

DARE TO DREAM (IRE)   4 b.g. Baillamont (USA) – Tears of Allah (FR) (Troy) [1992/3 17v* 17v* 17s* 16g]   132

It's rare for the winner of a seller to hit the headlines, but Dare To Dream did just that when successful at Leicester in October. His win clinched a substantial gamble for Geoff Lewis' stable, who'd backed themselves to send out the winners of fifty races on the Flat in 1992. Dare To Dream, having emerged from relative obscurity, continued to be in the spotlight

Finale Junior Hurdle, Chepstow—
Dare To Dream (right) jumps the last marginally better than Mohana

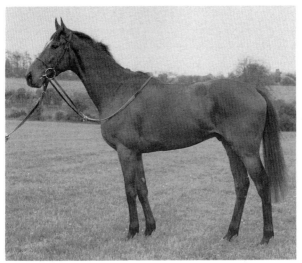

Miss Judy Smith's "Dare To Dream"

Dare To Dream (IRE) (b.g. 1989)	Baillamont (USA) (b 1982)	Blushing Groom (ch 1974)	Red God
			Runaway Bride
		Lodeve (b 1972)	Shoemaker
			Locust Time
	Tears of Allah (FR) (ch 1983)	Troy (b 1976)	Petingo
			La Milo
		Firyal (ch 1977)	Nonoalco
			Neriad

following a change of trainer and a switch to hurdling. By the turn of the year he was unbeaten in three outings over hurdles and had established himself as a leading juvenile. After easily justifying favouritism at Plumpton in November, Dare To Dream tackled much stronger opposition in the Summit Junior Hurdle at Lingfield and the Finale Junior Hurdle at Chepstow. There was no doubting Dare To Dream's superiority at Lingfield, where he drew six lengths clear on the run-in, but he had little to spare at Chepstow and was possibly fortunate to win. Driven along to stay in touch on the home turn, Dare To Dream was almost upsides the leader Mohana four out and, continuing to respond to his jockey's urgings, began to draw clear with Mohana approaching the second last. Mohana still held a narrow lead at the last but she met it all wrong, allowing Dare To Dream, none too fluent himself, to go a couple of lengths up, the outcome virtually decided. Dare To Dream, keeping on gamely, held the renewed challenge of Mohana by three quarters of a length. It was Dare To Dream's fifteenth race of the year and probably his toughest, and a break of four months followed. Outwardly the lay-off appeared to have benefited Dare To Dream, who looked fit and well when reappearing in the Champion Four-Year-Old Hurdle at Punchestown in April. But his appearance wasn't reflected in his performance. He made a mistake at the fourth, lost touch after the next and trailed in eleventh of the twelve finishers. Dare To Dream, who'd raced on soft or heavy going on his first three starts, might require more testing conditions than those he encountered at Punchestown but we wouldn't use that as the sole excuse for his poor run.

The leggy Dare To Dream is the first foal of Tears of Allah, a half-sister to the fairly useful jumper Anti Matter. Tears of Allah, placed over a mile and a quarter in France, is a daughter of Firyal who showed very useful form at up to the same distance there. Firyal is one of nine winners out of the unraced Neriad, the best of them the 1974 Prix de l'Arc de Triomphe runner-up Comtesse de Loir. Dare To Dream has won three races on the Flat, showing himself effective at up to a mile and three quarters on ground ranging from firm to dead. He has raced only at around two miles over hurdles but his style of running—he takes time to warm to his task—suggests that he may well prove even better over further. Dare To Dream isn't an accomplished jumper as yet but should improve as he gains experience. He is to be trained by P. J. Hobbs in 1993/4. *R. Akehurst*

DARING CLASS 7 b.m. Class Distinction – Darymoss (Ballymoss) [1992/3 17m³ 16m² 18f* 17g⁵ 16f⁵ 17g 18m⁵ 16d⁶c 18gc 16sc 17mc 18m³c 16m 18f^pu] lengthy mare: poor hurdler: won handicap at Exeter in August, easily best effort: only form over fences when third in novice claimer at Exeter in May: stays 2¼m: acts on firm going: keen sort, races prominently. *P. R. Rodford*   c76 / 88 d

DARING TROUBLE 4 b.f. Tremblant – Daring Damsel (Daring March) [1992/3 17g 16s 16v⁶ 20d 16f³] workmanlike filly: well beaten only start on Flat: first worthwhile form over hurdles when third in seller at Windsor in March: acts on firm ground. *G. F. H. Charles-Jones*   70

DARI SOUND (IRE) 5 b.g. Shardari – Bugle Sound (Bustino) [1992/3 21d⁴ 22d² 21s⁵ 20g² 21s² 22m* 21s^ur] angular gelding: fair handicap hurdler: comfortable winner at Market Rasen in March: running a creditable race when unseating rider at the last at Wetherby in April: stays 2¾m: acts on good to firm and soft ground: usually jumps well: consistent. *J. G. FitzGerald*   113

DARKBROOK 6 b.g. Green Shoon – Pitpan Lass (Pitpan) [1992/3 20g^F 22s³ 21d⁵ 25d⁴ c21s² c26v² c21s⁴ 22m² c25s^ur 22g⁴] leggy, rather plain ex-Irish gelding: moderate novice hurdler/chaser: suited by test of stamina: acts on good to firm and heavy going. *D. R. Gandolfo*   c99 / 99

DARK DAWN 9 b.g. Pollerton – Cacador's Pet (Chinatown) [1992/3 c21d² c21g* c22f² c21v* c23g* c25g^F] workmanlike gelding: useful hunter chaser: won at Leicester, Perth and Uttoxeter in 1993: also good second to Double Silk in Martell Fox Hunters' at Aintree: stays 2¾m: acts on any going: jumps well. *P. Cheesbrough*   c116 / –

DARK DEEP DAWN 6 ch.m. Deep Run – Swinging Sovereign (Swing Easy (USA)) [1992/3 17d F12d 22s⁴ 20g⁴ 16v⁴ c21v c16dF c16d⁵ c21d^pu] lengthy mare: poor novice hurdler: let down by her jumping over fences: stays 2¾m: acts on soft ground. *John R. Upson*   c– x / 77

DARK EMPEROR 12 br.g. Park Spirit – Pin Up Girl (Workboy) [1992/3 c20d⁶ c25s^pu c19m³ c16d^pu] good-bodied gelding: winning hurdler/chaser: third in claiming chase at Catterick in March, easily best effort of season: stays 2½m: probably acts on any going. *Mrs E. Slack*   c77 / –

DARK FOUNTAIN 6 br.g. Royal Fountain – Another Joyful (Rubor) [1992/3 16v 18g 24d^pu 16g³] second foal: brother to novice hurdler Another Fountain: dam winning 2m hurdler: third at Hexham in May, best effort in novice hurdles. *J. E. Dixon*   73

DARK MIDNIGHT (IRE) 4 br.g. Petorius – Gaelic Jewel (Scottish Rifle) [1992/3 18g 18dF 17s^pu] leggy gelding: half-brother to winning 2m hurdler Irish Emerald (by Taufan): plating-class sprinter on Flat: no sign of ability over hurdles. *R. R. Lamb*   –

DARK VISION 4 br.f. Noalto – Valeur (Val de Loir) [1992/3 16s 16v 17m⁵] leggy, workmanlike filly: half-sister to several winners, including   –

hurdlers Able Vale (by Formidable) and Vision of Wonder (by Tyrnavos): maiden on Flat: no form over hurdles, including in seller: sold 1,500 gns Ascot 2nd June Sales. *J. S. King*

DARLING ELLEN   8 b.m. Leading Man – Queen Maeve (Connaught) [1992/3 c19s c17d³ c17m⁵ c2 1m⁵] showed a little ability first 2 starts in hunter chases, tailed off last two. *T. Fowler*   c82

DARTINGTON BLAKE   9 b.g. Roscoe Blake – Princess Hot Fire (Hotfoot) [1992/3 18m⁴ 22mᵖᵘ 22f⁴ 20sᵖᵘ a22g a20g] leggy gelding: bad maiden hurdler/chaser: sometimes blinkered. *J. Dooler*   c– 58

DARTON RI   10 b.g. Abednego – Boogie Woogie (No Argument) [1992/3 c25dᵖᵘ] good-topped gelding: very lightly-raced novice chaser: stays 3m: best run on dead ground. *Mrs S. Maxse*   c– –

DASHING APRIL   5 b.m. Daring March – Ritruda (USA) (Roi Dagobert) [1992/3 16d 16m] leggy mare: poor maiden at best on Flat: no promise in novice hurdle and a seller. *D. T. Thom*   –

DASHING MARCH   4 b.f. Daring March – Miss Casanova (Galivanter) [1992/3 17s 17v³ 16d 18g 16d⁵] leggy filly: half-sister to several winning jumpers, notably very smart hurdler Ra Nova (by Ragstone) and quite useful chaser Jody's Boy (by Full of Hope): dam 2-y-o 6f winner: poor form over hurdles: likely to stay beyond 17f: acts on heavy going. *M. S. Saunders*   77

DASTARDLY DALE   7 b.g. Baron Blakeney – Rue Talma (Vigo) [1992/3 c17gᵖᵘ] half-brother to several winning jumpers, including fairly useful chaser The Antartex (by Vital Season): showed nothing in novice chase at Sedgefield in March. *J. R. Adam*   c–

DAUNOU (FR)   7 b.g. Fabulous Dancer (USA) – Dourdan (Prudent II) [1992/3 16m⁶ 18g³ 24sᵖᵘ] rather leggy gelding: moderate handicap hurdler: stayed 2½m: probably acted on any going: dead. *D. J. Wintle*   96

DAVARA   7 gr.g. Dawn Johnny (USA) – News Belle (London Gazette) [1992/3 18dᵖᵘ 17m 16g 18g³ 23mᵖᵘ] lengthy gelding: poor novice hurdler: stays 23f: acts on good to firm ground: tried blinkered. *S. J. Leadbetter*   68

DAVERNS   6 b. or br.g. Dalsaan – Molly Pitcher (Hul A Hul) [1992/3 16m] of little account: sold 1,400 gns Ascot November Sales. *F. Jordan*   –

DAVES DELIGHT   7 ch.m. Lighter – The Deer Hound (Cash And Carry) [1992/3 22dᶠ 17v² 25s⁵ 17v 17v⁴ 22d 25d⁶ 17s² 18d⁴ 18g] poor novice hurdler: effective under testing conditions at 17f and should stay further than 2¾m: suited by plenty of give in the ground. *Miss S. Waterman*   79

DAVE'S LASS   4 ch.f. Crever – Monagram (Mon Fetiche) [1992/3 17dᵖᵘ 16vᵖᵘ] signs of ability on Flat for D. Burchell: no show in selling hurdles. *R. J. Price*   –

DAVID JOHN   6 b.g. Furry Glen – Brave Polly (Brave Invader (USA)) [1992/3 17g⁴ 22sᵖᵘ 25g³] 7,500 4-y-o: big, rangy, good sort: chasing type: third foal: brother to NH Flat race winner Dark Glen: dam, successful in NH Flat race, is half-sister to Welsh National winner Charlie H: in frame in novice hurdles at Newbury in November and Doncaster (best effort, running on) in January: suited by a test of stamina: ran badly on soft ground: should improve further. *S. Christian*   93 p

DAVID'S DUKY   11 ch.g. Duky – Cross Pearl (Pearl Orient) [1992/3 21s² c30dᵖᵘ 21s⁵] sturdy, dipped-backed gelding: useful chaser at his best: tailed off when pulled up 3 out in Whitbread Gold Cup at Sandown on second start: fair handicap hurdler: suited by good test of stamina: acts on heavy going. *J. White*   c– 109

DAVID'S OWN   4 b.g. Petong – Carvery (Milford) [1992/3 17m⁴ 16m 17f 18g] seems of little account on Flat nowadays: little better over hurdles: sold 1,350 gns Ascot November Sales. *S. Mellor*   60

DAVY BLAKE   6 b.g. Cool Guy (USA) – True Grit (Klairon) [1992/3 c16mᵘʳ 21g² 16d⁵ c25g* c25m* c25g³ c21vᶠ c25d² c24s³] leggy, useful-looking gelding: half-brother to winning jumpers Rooster Cogburn and La Boeuf (both by Bing II): dam 1¼m winner: novice hurdler: useful   c115 85

hunter chaser: won twice at Kelso in March: good second on same course in April: stays 25f: acts on good to firm and heavy ground. *T. N. Dalgetty*

DAVY'S WEIR   13 ch.g. Paddy's Stream – Tevie (Le Levanstell) [1992/3 c21m^pu c20f c24m^6 c21g^3 c20s^6 c21g^pu] dipped-backed gelding: winning hurdler/chaser: has lost his form: blinkered twice in 1989/90. *B. Thornley*   c–
–

DAWADAR (USA)   6 b.h. Exceller (USA) – Damana (FR) (Crystal Palace (FR)) [1992/3 20g* 22s^5 24m* 25f^4] sturdy horse: fairly useful hurdler: simple task when successful in claimers at Doncaster (conditional jockeys) in January and Edinburgh (claimed out of N. Tinkler's stable £6,525) in February: good fourth in valuable handicap at Aintree in April: stays 3m: acts on firm and dead ground. *J. S. Goldie*   120

DAWN CHANCE   7 gr.g. Lighter – Main Chance (Midsummer Night II) [1992/3 c16d^5 c16d] good-bodied gelding: no form over hurdles or fences. *R. J. Hodges*   c–
–

DAWN COYOTE (USA)   10 ch.g. Grey Dawn II – Beanery (USA) (Cavan) [1992/3 20g c21d c21s^pu 25m^5] moderate hurdler at best, well beaten in 2 sellers in 1992/3: poor novice chaser: stays 3¼m: acts on heavy going: blinkered once. *Mrs S. Taylor*   c–
–

DAWN MELODY   5 b.m. Lighter – True Melody (Pardigras) [1992/3 F16s F17m] sturdy mare: fourth foal: half-sister to novice hurdlers Riddlemeroo (by Chuckaroo) and Five Stars (by Majestic Maharaj): dam, third in NH Flat race, behind both completed starts over hurdles: well beaten in NH Flat races in April: yet to race over hurdles or fences. *J. Colston*

DAWSON CITY   6 ch.g. Glint of Gold – Lola Sharp (Sharpen Up) [1992/3 c20d^2 c16d* c20d* c21s* c17s^2 c20d* c21d^2] smallish, leggy gelding: very useful hurdler: won novice chases at Nottingham, Aintree and Wetherby in first half of season and Newcastle (Dipper Novices' Chase) in January: good second to Young Hustler in valuable event at Sandown last start: best form   c123 p
–

Stanley Leisure Children In Need Novices' Chase, Aintree—
Dawson City jumps the last ahead of Strong Beau (right) and Scole

Dipper Novices' Chase, Newcastle—Dawson City is clear at the last

around 2½m, likely to stay further: acts on good to firm and heavy ground: tough and consistent: usually jumps well: should make a useful handicap chaser. *M. H. Easterby*

DAYS OF THUNDER   5 ch.g. Vaigly Great – Silent Prayer (Queen's Hussar) [1992/3 16d² 17vᶠ 16v⁶ 16s 16d² 17d*] sturdy gelding: modest hurdler: won selling handicap at Plumpton (no bid) in February: suited by sharp 2m: acts on dead ground: held up. *J. White*   94

D C FLYER   9 ch.m. Record Token – Take My Hand (Precipice Wood) [1992/3 c21d³ c23g² c24mᶠ c24m⁵ c23s] rangy mare: winning pointer: poor novice chaser. *N. B. Mason*   c–

DEADLINE   10 br.g. Strong Gale – Countess Charmere (Chamier) [1992/3 c23sᶠ c16spᵘ c21s⁶ c20g c21gpᵘ c16g c21gpᵘ c21sᵘʳ c21fpᵘ c21mpᵘ 26m c22v⁴] sturdy gelding: modest chaser: sold 5,900 gns Doncaster August Sales: clear when unseating rider 3 out in amateurs handicap at Perth in April: ran poorly otherwise in 1992/3: stays a sharp 3m: acts on soft going: usually blinkered nowadays: sometimes jumps badly and to his right: unreliable. *S. G. Chadwick*   c89 §
                                                                                                                                                                        –

DEAL WITH HONOR   4 b.f. Idiot's Delight – Vulgan's Honor (Paddy's Birthday) [1992/3 F16v 17gpᵘ] second foal: half-sister to winning selling hurdler Debt of Honor (by Deep River): dam, selling hurdler, stayed 21f: tailed off in NH Flat race in April and when pulled up in novice hurdle in May. *K. S. Bridgwater*

DEBACLE (USA)   4 b.c. Raft (USA) – Kuala (USA) (Hawaii) [1992/3 17d³ 16gᵇᵈ] smallish colt: won 9.7f maiden race on Flat in August: third of 5 finishers in juvenile hurdle at Sandown in October: in midfield when brought down 4 out in similar event at Windsor in November: sold 7,600 gns Newmarket July Sales. *G. Harwood*   98

Kepak Boyne EBF Hurdle, Navan—
nothing much in it at the last;
from left to right, Shuil Ar Aghaidh, Bayrouge and the winner Dee Ell

DEB'S BALL   7 b.m. Glenstal (USA) – De'b Old Fruit (Levmoss) [1992/3 17m* 18g* 17m² 17m³ 16d² c17dᶠ 16s⁴ 16f 22d* 23f*] workmanlike mare: useful handicap hurdler: won at Bangor and Cartmel in August and on latter course and at Stratford (beat Beech Road a neck in minor event) late in season: jumped deliberately and fell seventh on chasing debut: stays 2¾m: acts on any going: tends to get behind and suited by a strongly-run race. *D. Moffatt*   c– 141

DEBT OF HONOR   5 ch.g. Deep River – Vulgan's Honor (Paddy's Birthday) [1992/3 20m² 21d⁶ 22d³ 22d² a22g* a20g⁵] sparely-made gelding: won selling hurdle at Southwell (no bid) in January: stays 2¾m: acts on dead going, good to firm and fibresand: blinkered last 3 starts: looks a difficult ride. *K. S. Bridgwater*   79

DECANNA   8 ch.m. Decoy Boy – Louisianalightning (Music Boy) [1992/3 c21gᶠ c21mᵖᵘ] workmanlike mare: no form over hurdles: poor pointer: failed to complete in hunter chases. *Miss P. M. Whittle*   c– –

DECCAN PRINCE   9 b.g. Decoy Boy – Queen's Herald (King's Leap) [1992/3 18mᵖᵘ] leggy, lengthy gelding: very lightly-raced selling handicap hurdler: very stiff task and in need of race only outing of season (October): ran poorly over 2½m: acts on firm going. *D. R. Tucker*   –

DECENT GOLD   10 b. or br.g. Decent Fellow – Blaze Gold (Arizona Duke) [1992/3 c21gᴿ] smallish, sturdy gelding: poor novice hurdler (blinkered once): inconsistent pointer, modest at best: tailed off when refusing in maiden hunter chase in March. *Mrs Sally Norris*   c– § –

DECENT MAN   10 b.g. Derring Rose – Addies Lass (Little Buskins) [1992/3 c25m⁴ c25g³ c26s³ c23d³ c26sᶠ c27g* c25d* c26g² c26m* c27mᵖᵘ] well-made gelding: fair chaser: won handicaps at Sedgefield and Market Rasen in February and Catterick (finished alone) in March: pulled up lame last outing: stays 27f: acts on good to firm and soft ground: blinkered once. *P. Beaumont*   c102 –

DECIDED (CAN)   10 b.g. Affirmed (USA) – Expediency (USA) (Vaguely Noble) [1992/3 21g⁶ c21dᵖᵘ 21d] well-made gelding: fairly useful hurdler/chaser at best but showed nothing in 1992/3: stays 2½m: acts on heavy   c– –

212

going: broke blood vessel once: blinkered once: moody: won 2m seller on Flat in May. *R. Lee*

DECIDEDLY DUTCH   6 br.g. Dutch Treat – Indecisive (Lombard (GER)) [1992/3 a20g^{pu} a20g^{pu} c17s³ c21g^{pu}] leggy gelding: poor hurdler/novice chaser: stays 2¼m: acts on fibresand: jumps fences none too fluently. *Miss Gay Kelleway*   c75
–

DECIDING BID   7 ch.g. Valiyar – Final Call (Town Crier) [1992/3 18g 20g⁵ 17d 16s 17v a16g⁶ a24g^F a16g³ a16g² a20g² 18g⁴ 16g^F 20s⁵ 17d⁵ 18f] rather sparely-made gelding: poor hurdler: trained fourth to twelfth starts by Mrs M. Long: effective from 2m to 2½m: acts on dead going and equitrack: occasionally blinkered. *J. E. Long*   73

DECRETO   12 ch.g. Touch Paper – Tacora (Cernobbio) [1992/3 c16f⁶ c20s^{pu} c17g c19g^{ur} c19s^{pu}] poor novice hurdler/chaser: trained until after second start by E. Wheeler. *Mrs Jackie Kendall-Davis*   c–
–

DEE ELL   7 ch.g. Little Wolf – Sagora (Sagaro) [1992/3 22d³ 18v³ 22s* 20s² 21d⁵] Irish gelding: very useful hurdler: won quite valuable event at Navan in February by head from Shuil Ar Aghaidh: runner-up in smart company at Auteuil in April, and finished fifth there in May: will stay beyond 2¾m: has raced only on a soft surface. *A. L. T. Moore, Ireland*   149

DEE EM AITCH   4 b.g. Lightning Dealer – Some Say (I Say) [1992/3 F12d F17f F16g] tall, leggy gelding: fourth known foal: dam apparently of little account: well beaten in NH Flat races: yet to race over hurdles. *C. H. Jones*

DEE JAY PEE   7 ch.g. Electric – Lady Gaston (Pall Mall) [1992/3 17g^{pu}] workmanlike gelding: poor novice hurdler: showed nothing in seller in April. *B. Preece*   –

DEEP CALL   6 br.g. Callernish – Rise An Run (Deep Run) [1992/3 24s² 20s 21s⁴ 28d³] big gelding: modest form when in frame in novice hurdles: stays 3m well (appeared not to get 3½m): jumps none too fluently. *T. P. Tate*   91

DEEP CHANCE   7 b.g. Deep Run – Sweet Slievenamon (Arctic Slave) [1992/3 16d^{pu} 17d 18m] rangy, chasing type: lightly raced and no worthwhile form over hurdles: sold 6,500 gns Doncaster May Sales. *J. W. Curtis*   –

DEEP COLONIST   11 ch.g. Deep Run – New Colonist (Colonist II) [1992/3 c20g⁵ c25s³] big, workmanlike gelding: one-time fairly useful chaser: well beaten both starts in 1992/3: stays 3½m well: acts on soft going: possibly suited by left-handed track: jumps soundly in the main. *T. P. Tate*   c–
–

DEEP DAWN RUN   7 ch.m. Deep Run – Geraldine's Pet (Laurence O) [1992/3 22d 16g^{pu} 17f 21d] compact mare: poor novice selling hurdler: trained by Mrs J. Retter first outing. *A. P. James*   57

DEEP DECISION   7 b.g. Deep Run – Another Dutchess (Master Buck) [1992/3 18d 20d 16d 17d⁴ 21f⁵ 21g⁴] tall, workmanlike gelding: poor novice hurdler: should stay beyond 21f: best effort on firm ground: type to do better over fences. *P. Cheesbrough*   79

DEEP DELIGHT   6 b.m. Idiot's Delight – Browne's Return (Deep Run) [1992/3 22g^{rtr}] tailed off in NH Flat race on debut: refused to race both outings since, in novice selling hurdle in October: sold 2,100 gns Doncaster November Sales, resold 2,000 gns Doncaster June Sales. *R. J. Eckley*   – §

DEEPENDABLE   6 ch.g. Deep Run – Hester Ann (Proverb) [1992/3 17v³ 16v^{pu} 21g² 22g] tall, useful-looking gelding with scope: modest novice hurdler: stays 21f: acts on heavy ground. *N. J. Henderson*   88

DEEP HERITAGE   7 ch.g. Deep Run – Bunkilla (Arctic Slave) [1992/3 c20s⁴ c20v² c19d* c16v* c21d^{pu} c20d²] tall, good-topped gelding: fairly useful hurdler: took well to chasing in 1992/3, winning at Leopardstown in   c132
–

DEE

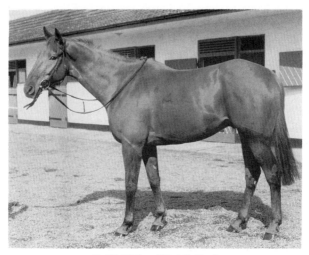

Mr J. P. McManus' "Deep Heritage"

December (minor event) and Navan in January (beat Galevilla Express in novice event): stays 2½m: acts on heavy ground. *A. L. T. Moore, Ireland*

DEEP LEGEND   8 b.g. Deep Run – Hansel's Trouble (Prince Hansel)   c–
[1992/3 c24dF] big, rangy gelding: of little account: dead. *F. L. Matthews*   –

DEEP RELATIONS   4 b.f. Stanford – Dads Run (Deep Run) [1992/3 F17d] first foal: dam ran once: tailed off in NH Flat race at Carlisle in April: yet to race over hurdles. *J. S. Wainwright*

DEEP SELECTION (IRE)   5 b.m. Deep Run – Random Select (Random Shot) [1992/3 17dpu] no sign of ability on Flat and in novice hurdle   –
in February. *F. G. Smith*

DEEP SENSATION   8 ch.g. Deep Run – Bannow Bay (Arctic Slave) c148
[1992/3 c16g² c17d² c20d* c16s² c24s⁵ c16s² c21d² c16m* c20f*]   –

Prize money isn't always an effective barometer of racing merit. Take Deep Sensation, for example. His three victories—in the H & T Walker Gold Cup, the Queen Mother Champion Chase and the Mumm Melling Chase—earned £134,854 for his connections, the highest earnings of any horse over the sticks during the season in Britain. But Deep Sensation is no champion in terms of form. Far from it. He's no more than a smart chaser and we'll be surprised to see him have anything like such a successful season again. His performance in the Queen Mother Champion Chase fell a long way short of what is normally required to win the race, and it's impossible to rate highly his victory in the Mumm Melling Chase, a Grade 1 event like the Queen Mother Champion Chase for which the turnout was most disappointing. Frankly, the mark of 160 allotted to Deep Sensation by the Jockey Club handicapper on the strength of an eight-length defeat of Redundant Pal at Aintree is much higher than is warranted on the evidence of the form-book, the way we read it anyway.

Deep Sensation started the season on the mark of a useful handicapper, having established himself among the leaders of a none-too-distinguished crop of two-mile novice chasers in 1991/2. He'd won three of his five completed races and started favourite at Cheltenham for the Arkle Challenge Trophy in which Young Pokey, Tinryland and Space Fair all finished in front of him. Nothing Deep Sensation achieved on his first two outings—when runner-up in handicaps at Wetherby and Chepstow—could have caused anyone to challenge the view expressed in *Chasers & Hurdlers 1991/92* that Deep Sensation would 'have to improve a good deal to be up to troubling the best two-mile chasers at anything like level weights'. In fact, it came as a surprise to most when stable-jockey Murphy chose to ride Deep Sensation in preference to the favourite, the Sun Alliance Chase runner-up Bradbury Star, in the H & T Walker Gold Cup at Ascot in November. The H & T Walker Gold Cup, a handicap with a limited weight range, is designed to bring together up-and-coming young chasers and draws its field largely from the ranks of the second-season chasers. The race was inaugurated in 1981 and replaced the Buchanan Whisky Gold Cup, a highly successful two-mile conditions event, which had started life as the Black & White Whisky Gold Cup, and been won in its time by Flyingbolt, Dicky May, Pendil, Bula, Night Nurse and Anaglogs Daughter. Changing weight-for-age events into limited handicaps doesn't always lead to bigger fields, one of the aims when the race was revamped. The Black & White/Buchanan averaged seven runners in its fifteen runnings. The H & T Walker has fared only marginally better and the field for the latest edition was only the third to reach double figures in twelve runnings. It was a good-class field, though, with Cyphrate, Beech Road, The Illywhacker, Deep Sensation, Irish-trained Second Schedual, Danny Harrold and Far Senior next in the weights behind Bradbury Star. Most had shown plenty of ability as novices, Beech Road had finished third in the Mackeson and Far Senior had also progressed well in the current season, winning his last two starts in handicap company. Young Hustler, nearly two stone out of the handicap and a 100/1-shot, was the only novice among the ten runners. Deep Sensation had done nearly all his racing, over hurdles and fences, at two miles but he'd run creditably when tried at two and a half and had given the impression as a novice chaser that he might have a more rewarding second season over fences campaigned at the longer trip. He won the H & T Walker in good style, jumping soundly and making smooth headway, after being held up in rear, to lead on the

H & T Walker Gold Cup (Handicap Chase), Ascot—Deep Sensation clears the last ahead of Second Schedual (noseband) and Bradbury Star

Queen Mother Champion Chase, Cheltenham—
Deep Sensation is poised to challenge the leader Cyphrate at the last;
they are followed over by Katabatic (left) and Fragrant Dawn

bridle after the second last. His rider needed to push him out on the run-in
to hold off Danny Harrold by two lengths with Bradbury Star and Second
Schedual close up in third and fourth.

Deep Sensation lost all his four races between the H & T Walker Gold
Cup and the Queen Mother Champion Chase, running over a variety of
distances. He finished runner-up in both his races at two miles, to Waterloo
Boy (who gave him 21 lb) in the Tingle Creek Trophy at Sandown and to the
novice Sybillin (who beat him ten lengths, receiving 1 lb) in the Victor
Chandler Handicap at Ascot. Deep Sensation failed to make the frame over
three miles in soft ground in the King George VI Chase, though he wasn't
disgraced in fifth, facing a stiff task over a distance which almost certainly
stretches his stamina, at least when conditions are testing. Deep Sensation's last race before the Cheltenham Festival was in the valuable Marston
Moor Chase, a limited handicap over two miles five furlongs at Wetherby in
February. Deep Sensation should have won. He moved effortlessly into the
lead after the third last and drew clear going to the final fence, only to throw
the race away. Armagret, 19 lb out of the handicap and held at the last, got up
in the last seventy-five yards as Deep Sensation downed tools. On this
showing Deep Sensation was no longer one to trust implicitly—he'd previously shown a tendency to wander under pressure—and he started at 11/1
in a Queen Mother Champion Chase generally viewed as a virtual match
between Katabatic and Waterloo Boy. The pair had finished second and
third to the side-lined Remittance Man the previous year and had had the
finish of the Game Spirit Chase, seemingly the most significant Cheltenham
trial, to themselves. Katabatic, a close second to Waterloo Boy at Newbury,
started favourite for the Champion Chase at 6/5; Waterloo Boy was 7/4, with

Deep Sensation and Cyphrate (third in the Game Spirit) the only others in the field of nine, most of whom were out of their depth, at odds shorter than 16/1. With Katabatic and Waterloo Boy running well below form, the Champion Chase took much less winning than usual. Deep Sensation's three quarters of a length victory over Cyphrate didn't represent top-class form—third-placed Katabatic wasn't at his best by a long chalk—and in our view either of the first two in the previous day's Arkle, Travado and Wonder Man, would have given the Champion Chase principals a good run for their money. Exaggerated waiting tactics were adopted on Deep Sensation in the Champion Chase, Murphy keeping him on a tight rein as Cyphrate led, going well, from the third last until the run-in where Deep Sensation quickened to lead and then found enough, though clearly idling once in front, to hold on. It was noticeable that Murphy—who afterwards described Deep Sensation as 'the most frustrating horse you could ever put your leg across'—never went for his whip. Waterloo Boy ran as if something went amiss with him, finishing a distant sixth, but he started joint favourite with Deep Sensation when the pair met in the two-and-a-half-mile Mumm Melling Chase, from which Katabatic was a late withdrawal. Waterloo Boy again failed to give his running at Aintree and was pulled up after breaking a blood vessel. Deep Sensation, jumping soundly as usual, made mincemeat of his two remaining opponents, leading on the bridle at the last and drawing clear of the enigmatic Redundant Pal with the minimum of fuss, showing no tendency to idle once in front on this occasion. The other survivor Gold Options, who just failed to catch the weakening Redundant Pal for second, is more of a stayer and was outpaced by the first two from the second last; he'd seemed unlikely to be suited by the firm going, which placed the emphasis on speed. Deep Sensation himself acts on any going, by the way.

The rangy Deep Sensation always looked the type to make a chaser, the job for which he was bred. His dam Bannow Bay was a fair performer over hurdles and fences and a sister to the very smart chaser The Benign Bishop, as well as to the fairly useful hurdler Ballyowen; she was also a half-sister to the very useful chaser Chandigar. Deep Sensation's grandam Honeytown won over hurdles and fences and his great grandam Sanvina won the Scottish Grand National. Deep Sensation's achievements in the latest season helped to put his remarkable sire Deep Run at the top again. Deep Run was champion sire over jumps in Britain for the fourteenth

Mumm Melling Chase, Aintree —
Deep Sensation has the measure of Redundant Pal at the last

Mr R. F. Eliot's "Deep Sensation"

Deep Sensation (ch.g. 1985)	Deep Run (ch 1966)	Pampered King (b 1954)	Prince Chevalier Netherton Maid
		Trial By Fire (ch 1958)	Court Martial Mitrailleuse
	Bannow Bay (ch 1969)	Arctic Slave (b 1950)	Arctic Star Roman Galley
		Honeytown (ch 1954)	Fortina Sanvina

successive season, being responsible also for Run For Free (Welsh and Scottish Nationals), Granville Again (Champion Hurdle), Morley Street (Elite Hurdle and Aintree Hurdle), Waterloo Boy and the smart novice chaser Dakyns Boy, among others. Weight of numbers is often cited as the main reason for Deep Run's dominance—it's estimated that he sired over 1,400 thoroughbred foals—but there has been plenty of quality mixed in with the quantity. The numerical advantage Deep Run enjoyed also ensures that his name will remain prominent in National Hunt breeding until well into the next century. He has already been leading broodmare sire twice. 'Doing what comes natur'lly' wasn't a problem for the prodigious Deep Run who regularly covered more mares than any other stallion in Britain and Ireland until his final season in 1987. He monopolised the cream of Ireland's jumping mares in his later years by which time he was covering around two hundred thoroughbred mares a season. Deep Run's youngest stock are now five and there will almost certainly be more good winners in the pipeline

218

before Deep Run has to rely entirely on his daughters to keep up the good work. *J. T. Gifford*

DEER CREST 13 b.g. Deep Run – Skiporetta (Even Money) [1992/3 c25f^{pu}] sturdy, short-legged gelding: fair hunter chaser in 1992: ran poorly in March: stays 3m when conditions aren't testing: acts on any going: suited by forcing tactics: often sweats. *Capt. W. H. Bulwer-Long*   c– –

DEER FENCER 11 br.g. Mandalus – Boolaben (Arctic Slave) [1992/3 c18g²] ex-Irish gelding: winning 2m hurdler/chaser: lightly raced of late: second over fences at Fontwell in September: acts on soft going. *M. Madgwick*   c82 –

DEERNESS SPOOK 10 ro.g. Grey Ghost – Part Rum (Parthian Star) [1992/3 c17d⁴ c21s⁶ c17f^{pu}] lengthy, plain gelding: fair handicap chaser at best: destroyed after breaking a leg at Chepstow in March: best form at around 2m: probably acted on any going: visored once. *T. Thomson Jones*   c– §

DEERS LEAP 4 ch.f. Ore – Kimble Lady (Averof) [1992/3 F16v F16s F16g] first foal: dam, behind in 3 races on Flat, sister to winning jumper Thetchu and half-sister to very useful jumpers Sprowston Boy and Young Benz: soundly beaten in NH Flat races in second half of season: yet to race over hurdles. *R. D. E. Woodhouse* –

DEHAR BOY 7 b.g. Buzzards Bay – Nahawand (High Top) [1992/3 16v^{pu}] compact gelding: poor novice over hurdles, very lightly raced: visored in seller only outing in 1992/3. *T. H. Caldwell* –

DE JORDAAN 6 br.g. Callernish – Gorge (Mount Hagen (FR)) [1992/3 F16s⁶ 18g² 18g^F 18m³] second foal: dam a maiden: best effort in novice hurdles second at Sedgefield in February: pulled hard for conditional jockey next start: sold 5,000 gns Doncaster June Sales. *Mrs M. Reveley*   90

DE LA BILLIERE (IRE) 5 b.h. King of Clubs – Crazyfoot (Luthier) [1992/3 18d 16f] small horse: poor maiden on Flat and over hurdles: blinkered first start in 1991/2. *H. Willis* –

DELGANY RUN 9 ch.g. Deep Run – Miss Reindeer (Reindeer) [1992/3 c22s*] compact gelding: novice hurdler: fair handicap chaser: having first race for over a year, won at Nottingham in November: will stay 3m: acts on soft going: forces pace: tends to jump to the right. *Miss H. C. Knight*   c100 –

DELIGHTFUL MISS 6 b.m. Idiot's Delight – Miss Inigo (Sagaro) [1992/3 F17g aF16g] second in NH Flat race at Lingfield in 1991/2: soundly beaten in similar events in 1992/3: yet to race over hurdles or fences. *H. J. M. Webb* –

DELPIOMBO 7 br.g. Lochnager – Precious Petra (Bing II) [1992/3 16v⁵ 17g³ 16m* 18s^F] good-quartered gelding: lightly-raced hurdler: won selling handicap at Catterick (no bid) in March: running good race when falling last (held length lead) in claimer at Market Rasen following month: keen-running type, best at around 2m: acts on good to firm and soft ground: dual 1m winner on Flat in May. *J. G. FitzGerald*   98

DELTA FOXTROT (USA) 4 b.g. Seattle Dancer (USA) – Dame du Nil (FR) (Targowice (USA)) [1992/3 16v^{pu} 18d² 22g⁶] sparely-made gelding: modest maiden on Flat: sold out of D. Arbuthnot's stable 10,000 gns Newmarket Autumn Sales: second of 4 finishers at Market Rasen in February, best effort in juvenile and novice hurdles. *M. C. Banks*   85

DEL TOBOSO (IRE) 5 br.g. Nordico (USA) – Lady Dulcinea (ARG) (General (FR)) [1992/3 F16m⁴ 17d⁵ 17s 22v⁴] second foal: dam won 5 races at 3 and 4 yrs in Peru: no form over hurdles. *J. White* –

DEMOCRATIC BOY 11 b.g. Free State – Klaire (Klairon) [1992/3 22g c21d³ c24d⁴ c21v² c21s⁶ c23g⁵] close-coupled, workmanlike gelding: poor chaser: probably stays 3m: acts on any going: unreliable. *J. S. King*   c82 § – §

DEMOKOS (FR) 8 ch.g. Dom Racine (FR) – Eagletown (FR) (Dictus (FR)) [1992/3 16g⁵ 16s 16s³ 16d 17m] leggy, sparely-made gelding: poor hurdler: will stay beyond 2m: best form on firm ground. *A. P. Stringer*   83

DENBERDAR 10 b.g. Julio Mariner – Penumbra (Wolver Hollow) **c80**
[1992/3 c16spu c22g5 c21f5] leggy, lightly-made gelding: winning hurdler: –
poor novice chaser: best effort over fences when fifth at Sandown in March
on last outing: stays 21f: acts on firm ground. *M. F. Barraclough*

DENBY HOUSE LAD (CAN) 6 br.g. Assert – Queens Club (USA)
(Cyane) [1992/3 24s4] big, workmanlike gelding: novice hurdler: ran poorly –
only outing of season (November): should be suited by further than 2½m:
acts on soft ground. *C. Parker*

DENCAST 6 b.g. Battle Hymn – Ishiyama (Owen Anthony) [1992/3 17gpu
17g] lightly raced and no sign of ability: sold 1,350 gns Ascot November –
Sales. *H. J. Manners*

DENIM BLUE 4 ch.c. Mandrake Major – Delphinium (Tin King) [1992/3
16g 17d 16f4 17m3 18m2] modest form at around 1m on Flat: in frame in 81
juvenile hurdles in May, showing poor form: stays 2¼m: acts on firm going.
W. G. Reed

DENNINGTON (IRE) 5 ch.g. Deep Run – La Flamenca (Brave Invader
(USA)) [1992/3 17s a16g 17s3 22d3 22s5 22g* 17g4 22v4] rangy, rather 81
unfurnished gelding with scope: fourth foal: brother to winning hurdler My
Key Silca: dam winner over hurdles at up to 2¾m in Ireland: won novice
handicap hurdle at Huntingdon in February: creditable effort last outing:
needs further than 2m and stays 2¾m: acts on heavy going: yet to race on a
firm surface. *F. Murphy*

DENTICULATA 5 ch.g. Domynsky – Melody Song (Saintly Song)
[1992/3 16v 20d 20g] smallish, strong gelding: poor novice hurdler. *P.* 65
Spottiswood

DERAB (USA) 7 b.g. Alleged (USA) – Island Charm (USA) (Hawaii) **c100**
[1992/3 c20s5 21s c20d* c16d* 17s6 21v4 25g4 21g c22d4 17g6] strong 126
gelding: fairly useful hurdler: won novice chases at Ludlow in November
and December: effective at 2m and stays 25f: acts on good to firm and heavy
ground: jumps well: usually blinkered: wears tongue strap: runs the odd
poor race (has broken blood vessels). *S. E. Sherwood*

DERECHEF 6 ch.m. Derrylin – Songe d'Inde (Sheshoon) [1992/3 17g6
16d3 17m* 17fF] angular mare: won novice handicap hurdle at Stratford in 88 +

Wensleydale Hurdle, Wetherby—
the blinkered Desert Mist leads Lonesome Train (No. 5) and Take By Storm over the last

May: close up and still travelling well when falling 2 out in similar race on same course in June: acts on good to firm ground. *Mrs J. G. Retter*

DERISTONE 8 b.g. Rustingo – Deriside (Saucy Kit) [1992/3 17gpu 22dpu 20dpu a18g4] leggy gelding: poor novice hurdler: sold 1,300 gns Malvern June Sales. *M. W. Davies* –

DERRING VALLEY 8 b.g. Derrylin – Chalke Valley (Ragstone) [1992/3 c25g* c25sF c26vur c23gR 25dpu c22v2 c24d3 c22m*] smallish, lengthy gelding: one-time useful hurdler: modest form over fences: won novice events at Exeter in October and Towcester in May: suited by test of stamina: acts on good to firm and heavy ground: blinkered last 4 outings: refused fourth start and ran in snatches seventh. *A. P. Jones* c97 –

DERRY LOVE 6 gr.m. Derrylin – Rough Love (Abwah) [1992/3 17d] tailed off in novice hurdles. *L. J. Barratt* –

DERRYMOSS 7 b.g. Le Moss – Derrynaflan (Karabas) [1992/3 F16m F16g F16s F16g 20s 21s5 16fpu 20gpu] ex-Irish gelding: second foal: half-brother to a lightly-raced novice hurdler by Deep Run: dam twice-raced half-sister to useful Irish staying chaser Seskin Bridge: no sign of ability: trained by M. Bowe until after fifth start: blinkered third and last 3 outings. *M. C. Pipe* –

DERRY PRINCESS 7 b.m. Workboy – Derry Island (Varano) [1992/3 c22gur c21gur] won a point in May: yet to complete in hunter chases. *Robert Robinson* c–

DERRYWOOD 11 ch.g. Roselier (FR) – Delphine Rousseau (FR) (Burglar) [1992/3 c24s5] compact gelding: poor maiden jumper. *Rodger Farrant* c– –

DESERT FORCE (IRE) 4 b.c. Lomond (USA) – St Padina (St Paddy) [1992/3 16g2 16s6 16d6 18s* 16gpu 17g3 18g3] small, sparely-made colt: half-brother to fairly useful hurdler/winning chaser Invasion (by Kings Lake): fair maiden at best on Flat: won juvenile hurdle at Folkestone in February: good third in similar race at Taunton 2 outings later, jumped poorly and well below form on last: stays 2¼m: acts on soft going: blinkered fourth and fifth starts, visored last 2: has worn tongue strap: sometimes looks none too keen. *Miss Gay Kelleway* 103

DESERT HEIGHTS (IRE) 4 b.g. Head For Heights – Sahara Goddess (Realm) [1992/3 F18spu] closely related to useful 1982 Italian 2-y-o Shirley Reef (by Shirley Heights): dam 2-y-o 5f winner: showed nothing in NH Flat race at Exeter in January: yet to race over hurdles. *M. J. Heaton-Ellis* –

DESERT MIST 4 gr.f. Sharrood (USA) – Misty Halo (High Top) [1992/3 17m* 18g2 17m2 17g3 17g* 17g3 16g* 17v 24d3 24d* 28g3 26m* 26v5] big filly: quite modest stayer on Flat: had a good first season over hurdles and showed quite useful form: successful in juvenile events at Perth, Kelso and Wetherby (Grade 2 Wensleydale Juvenile Hurdle), novice event at Market Rasen and amateurs handicap at Cartmel: stays well: acts on good to firm and dead ground, below form on heavy: blinkered: needs plenty of driving. *Denys Smith* 110

DESERT PALM 8 b.m. Palm Track – Diascia (Dike (USA)) [1992/3 17v 20g6 20f2 17f2 20s4 21f] angular mare: poor hurdler nowadays: creditable efforts when in frame in 1992/3: stays 2¾m: probably acts on any going: sometimes blinkered (not last 4 outings): inconsistent. *R. J. Hodges* 84 §

DESERT SPLENDOUR 5 b.h. Green Desert (USA) – Lost Splendour (USA) (Vaguely Noble) [1992/3 16s 17s6] sturdy, good-bodied horse: half-brother to winning hurdler Persian Splendour (by Persian Bold): fair 7f to 9f performer on Flat (won in May): sold out of C. Brittain's stable 5,800 gns Newmarket Autumn Sales: no form over hurdles. *B. R. Cambidge* –

DESERT WARBLER (USA) 6 ch.h. The Minstrel (CAN) – Thats The Reason (USA) (Bold Reason) [1992/3 16d] angular, sparely-made horse: tailed off in novice event and a seller over hurdles. *N. Waggott*

DESIGN WISE   9 b.g. Prince Bee – Wollow Princess (Wollow) [1992/3 26s 22d 17d] small gelding: inconsistent selling hurdler: no form in 1992/3: stays 2¾m: acts on hard ground: has run blinkered, often visored. *R. Earnshaw*   –

DESPERATE   5 ch.g. Saxon Farm – Menel Arctic (Menelek) [1992/3 16g⁵ 21s* 24g* 24g 27g*] sturdy gelding: made up into a quite useful handicap hurdler, winning at Chepstow, Bangor and Stratford (finished lame) in the spring: needs further than 2m and stays 27f: acts on heavy going (ran poorly on good to firm). *N. A. Twiston-Davies*   116

DESPERATE MAN   4 b.g. Ballacashtal (CAN) – Priors Dean (Monsanto (FR)) [1992/3 17dᵖᵘ 16sᵖᵘ] workmanlike gelding: plating-class maiden at 2 yrs: pulled up in mid-season novice event and a claimer (claimed by N. Smith £5,100) over hurdles. *R. Thompson*   –

DE VALERA   5 b.m. Faustus (USA) – Dame du Moulin (Shiny Tenth) [1992/3 18m⁶ 28f⁴ 21v⁴ 26s⁶ 28s 22d c17dᶠ 22m 26d³] sparely-made mare: poor winning hurdler: jumped poorly on chasing debut: stays 3m: acts on hard going: visored once. *W. Bentley*   c–
68

DEVIL'S CORNER   5 b.g. Relkino – Just Jolly (Jolly Jet) [1992/3 F12d F17d F16f] good-topped gelding: half-brother to winning hurdlers Brockley Belle (by Track Spare) and Dreamers Delight (by Idiot's Delight), latter useful novice: dam won at up to 2m on Flat and up to 3m over hurdles: behind in NH Flat races in second half of season: yet to race over hurdles or fences. *H. J. M. Webb*   –

DEVIL'S SOUL   5 b.g. Faustus (USA) – Ragged Moon (Raga Navarro (ITY)) [1992/3 16s⁴ 17d⁴ 16v a18g⁵ a16g⁴ 17mᵇᵈ 17m⁴ 16g⁴ 16s⁶ 22g⁵] sparely-made gelding: modest when in the mood on Flat: novice hurdler: poor form at best (including in selling handicaps): sold out of R. Akehurst's stable 2,100 gns Ascot February Sales after third start: best form at around 2m: acts on good to firm and soft going: held up: probably temperamental: sold 1,700 gns Doncaster June Sales. *J. Parkes*   75 §

DEVIL'S VALLEY   10 ch.g. Lucifer (USA) – Barrowvale (Valerullah) [1992/3 24s⁶ 24v⁴ c16s* c17vᵖᵘ c17dᵖᵘ c16vᶠ] rangy gelding: fairly useful hurdler and useful chaser at best: only form in a long time when winning 6-runner conditional jockeys handicap chase at Folkestone in December: best at distances shorter than 3m: acts on any going: usually blinkered: takes good hold and races prominently: ungenuine. *R. Rowe*   c115 §
– §

DEVIOSITY (USA)   6 b.g. Spectacular Bid (USA) – Reinvestment (USA) (Key To The Mint (USA)) [1992/3 18s] lengthy gelding: moderate novice hurdler in 1991/2 when trained by B. Hills: tailed off only outing in 1992/3: should prove better at 2½m than 2m: acts on dead ground and equitrack: blinkered last 3 starts in 1991/2. *N. G. Ayliffe*   –

DEVONGALE   7 br.g. Strong Gale – Smart Money (Even Money) [1992/3 c21s³ c20g⁵ c25s⁴] smallish, workmanlike gelding: half-brother to several winning jumpers, notably very smart staying chaser Everett, and to NH Flat race winner Smart Fashion (both by Carlburg), latter dam of Cab On Target (by Strong Gale): dam maiden hurdler: won a point in 1992: modest form when in frame in novice chases at Wetherby in December and January: stays 25f: acts on soft going: sketchy jumper. *Mrs H. Bell*   c84

DEVONIAN (USA)   4 ch.g. Affirmed (USA) – Domludge (USA) (Lyphard (USA)) [1992/3 F16g F14m⁴ F17g⁶] sparely-made gelding: second foal: dam once-raced half-sister to high-class middle-distance mare Mrs Penny: showed some ability in NH Flat races in March: yet to race over hurdles. *Miss Jacqueline S. Doyle*   –

DEVON PRIDE (NZ)   6 b.g. Kutati (NZ) – Lyrical Rose (NZ) (Roselander) [1992/3 22sᵖᵘ 18m 17v⁵ 20dᵖᵘ] angular, plain gelding: of little account: sometimes blinkered. *M. R. Churches*   c–
–

DEVON ZIPPER   8 b.g. Brianston Zipper – Salmon Spirit (Big Deal) [1992/3 c17sᵇᵈ c18m⁶ c16g] rangy, workmanlike gelding: poor novice hurdler: showed nothing over fences: tried blinkered. *G. L. Roe*   c–

DEXTER CHIEF 4 b.g. Elegant Air – Emblazon (Wolver Hollow) [1992/3 17m² 17m³] modest maiden on Flat, stays 1¼m: sold out of I. Balding's stable 10,500 gns Newmarket July Sales: better effort over hurdles in August when third in juvenile claimer at Perth. *J. White* 90

DEXTEROUS LADY 7 b.m. Vital Season – Skilla (Mexico III) [1992/3 18m* 18d⁴ 20s 16gᵖᵘ 22f 22s 20g] leggy mare: won novice selling hurdle at Exeter (no bid) in October: poor efforts last 5 outings: stays 19f: acts on good to firm and dead ground: tried blinkered: poor jumper. *C. James* 76 x

DEXTRA DOVE 6 gr.g. Julio Mariner – Grey Dove (Grey Love) [1992/3 18d² 21g⁶ 16f* 17s* 17g² 20g⁴ 16f² 18f²] leggy gelding: fairly useful hurdler: won handicaps at Wincanton in March and Chepstow following month: good second 3 times afterwards: stays 2¼m, seemingly not 2½m: probably acts on any going. *P. J. Hobbs* 119

DHARAMSHALA (IRE) 5 b.g. Torenaga – Ambitious Lady (Status Seeker) [1992/3 F14s⁴ F18v⁴] fifth foal: half-brother to fair Irish hurdlers Glamorous Gale and Ambitious Gale (both by Strong Gale): dam, sprint maiden, twice-raced over hurdles: fourth in NH Flat races at Market Rasen in November and December: yet to race over hurdles or fences. *O. Brennan*

DIAMOND CUT (FR) 5 b.g. Fast Topaze (USA) – Sasetto (FR) (St Paddy) [1992/3 17s⁵ 17g² 21g⁴ 16s² 17m] leggy gelding: fairly useful hurdler: generally ran creditably in first half of season: first race for 4 months when tailed off last start: stays 2¼m, not 21f: probably acts on any ground: sometimes pulls hard. *M. C. Pipe* 128

DIAMOND FORT 8 b.g. Mirror Boy – Fortina Lass (Schomberg) [1992/3 c21v³ c24v² c24v* c25g⁴ c26dᵖᵘ c26v² c24d⁴] leggy, workmanlike gelding: fair handicap chaser: won at Lingfield in January: also ran well on fourth and sixth starts: suited by good test of stamina: acts on heavy going: usually jumps soundly. *J. C. McConnochie* c107

DIAMOND INTHE DARK (USA) 5 b.h. Diamond Prospect (USA) – Implicit (Grundy) [1992/3 16g⁵ 16g] brother to winning hurdlers Diamond 71

Welsh Handicap Hurdle, Chepstow—Dextra Dove draws clear of Easy Buck

Sprite and Magic At Dawn, latter also successful over fences: modest 7f winner on Flat: fifth in novice event at Edinburgh in December, better effort in novice hurdles: visored second start: sold 2,600 gns Doncaster May Sales. *C. Tinkler*

DIAMOND LIGHT 6 ch.g. Roman Warrior – Another Jo (Hotfoot) [1992/3 17g^{pu}] first foal: dam winning selling hurdler: tailed off when pulled up in novice hurdle at Hereford in May on debut. *V. R. Bishop* —

DIAMOND PROSPECTOR 4 b.g. Jalmood (USA) – Lady Andrea (Andrea Mantegna) [1992/3 F16v aF16g⁴ F17g* F17d] sturdy gelding: fifth foal: half-brother to Flat winners Likeable Lady (by Piaffer) and Logical Lady (by Tina's Pet), latter also a successful hurdler: dam never ran: best effort in NH Flat races when making all at Newbury in March: yet to race over hurdles. *A. Hide*

DIANES DESTINY 9 b.g. Kambalda – Kinsella's Choice (Middle Temple) [1992/3 c25m³ 26g⁶ c25g² c23f⁵ c23v² c22v³ c20g² c21g^{ur}] smallish, workmanlike gelding: modest handicap chaser: stayed well: acted on any going: dead. *John R. Upson* c99 —

DIANE'S PRIDE (IRE) 4 b.f. Strong Gale – Money Run (Deep Run) [1992/3 F17m] angular, unfurnished filly: first foal: dam winning 2m hurdler/chaser in Ireland: tailed off in NH Flat race at Cheltenham in April: yet to race over hurdles. *W. Clay*

DIBLOOM 5 b.g. Nomination – Tosara (Main Reef) [1992/3 17d 17g⁵ 16s* 16v^{pu}] lengthy gelding: made all in novice handicap at Warwick in November: pulled up following month and wasn't seen out again: will prove best over sharp 2m: acts on soft ground: amateur ridden last 3 starts. *J. D. Thomas* 91

DICKIE'S GIN 9 b.g. Mr Fordette – Gin An Tonic (Osprey Hawk) [1992/3 c20d⁵ c25g⁵ 21v⁶] leggy, workmanlike gelding: poor novice hurdler/chaser: stayed 2½m: acted on good to firm ground: dead. *J. Wade* c—

DIDDLEY (IRE) 5 ch.h. Sandhurst Prince – Regal Rhapsody (Owen Dudley) [1992/3 20g⁵ 16f 18g^{ur} 17d^{pu} 20s^{pu} a18g^F] novice hurdler: no worthwhile form: trained until after fourth start by J. Bridger: blinkered last outing. *Mrs M. E. Long*

DIDSBURY RED 6 b.m. Chantro – Sirene River (Another River) [1992/3 F16d 16s^{ro} 18g^{pu}] small, dipped-backed mare: no sign of ability. *W. J. Smith* —

DIE IN THE SKY 12 ch.g. Welsh Pageant – Heaven And Earth (Midsummer Night II) [1992/3 c18m c20g^{pu}] workmanlike gelding: poor chaser: stays 2¾m: acts on any going. *Mrs T. J. McInnes Skinner* c— —

DIGGER DOYLE 4 b.g. Cragador – Chaconia Girl (Bay Express) [1992/3 17f³] modest miler on Flat: third in juvenile maiden hurdle at Lingfield in March: sold 3,700 gns Doncaster Sales later in month: dead. *C. N. Allen* 90

DILKUSH 4 b.g. Dunbeath (USA) – Good Try (Good Bond) [1992/3 16m 22d^{pu} 22g^{pu} 22f^{pu}] tall gelding: half-brother to winning hurdler Trumps (by Grundy): no form on Flat (sold out of J. Holt's stable 1,100 gns Newmarket Autumn Sales) or over hurdles: blinkered last outing: resold 1,050 gns Ascot June Sales. *Mrs P. Sly* —

DILLEACHTA 6 b.m. Mandalus – Jadini (Gombos (FR)) [1992/3 F17v⁴ F16v³ F16v* 17d^{pu}] big, good-topped mare: third foal: sister to NH Flat race and point winner Springmount: dam won over 1¾m on Flat and over 2m over hurdles in Ireland: trained by J. Moore first outing: won NH Flat race at Warwick in January: broke leg on hurdling debut: dead. *D. Nicholson* —

DI MODA 6 ch.g. Buzzards Bay – Diamond Talk (Counsel) [1992/3 21d c16s^{pu} c21s⁶ c21s⁴ c25g⁴] lengthy, workmanlike gelding: poor maiden hurdler/chaser: stays 21f: acts on soft going: tried visored. *J. R. Bosley* c73 —

DINNER SUIT 9 b.g. Enchantment – Fancy Feathers (AUS) (Pipe of Peace) [1992/3 c24f^{pu} c26m⁴] well-made gelding: winning hunter chaser: c— —

ran badly in March and May, but won a point in between: stays 25f: acts on firm going: blinkered twice (not when successful). *Mrs P. Grainger*

DINSDALE LAD 7 ch.g. Sweet Monday – Forgets Image (Florescence) [1992/3 c17f5 c17g c17dur c17d6 c17d4 c16sur c16d6 17d] angular gelding: poor novice hurdler/chaser: easily best effort of season when fourth at Newcastle in January: races only at around 2m: acts on soft ground: blinkered once. *M. A. Barnes* — c80 —

DINZEO 6 b.g. Buckskin (FR) – Laurolin (Laurence O) [1992/3 F18d] fourth live foal: half-brother to winning hurdler/pointer Self Aid (by Fine Blade): dam unraced sister to fair chaser Harvest: well beaten in NH Flat race at Sedgefield in October: yet to race over hurdles or fences. *Mrs S. J. Smith*

DIPLOMATIC 4 b.g. Ardross – Lizarra (High Top) [1992/3 F16d F16v* F16s2 F17m5] good-topped gelding with scope: second foal: dam placed over 6f at 2 yrs: easily landed the odds in 4-runner NH Flat race at Navan in January: staying-on fifth in valuable event at Cheltenham in March: yet to race over hurdles. *M. A. O'Toole, Ireland*

DIRECT 10 b.g. The Parson – Let The Hare Sit (Politico (USA)) [1992/3 c24s3 c27v* c25v2 c24sF c26v2 c29s* c24s2 c24dpu] tall gelding: fairly useful handicap chaser: won at Chepstow in December and Warwick in February: suited by test of stamina: acts on any going, but goes particularly well in the mud: usually races prominently: jumps soundly in the main. *J. A. C. Edwards* — c116 —

DIRECT INTEREST 10 ch.g. Al Sirat (USA) – Honey Come Home (Timobriol) [1992/3 c18mur c18m3 c21f* c25g3 c21f3 c21m3 c17d4 c25g4 c21d c21d c27dpu c26gpu c16g c19m4 c21g] strong, dipped-backed gelding: poor handicap chaser: won at Hexham in August: ran creditably on occasions afterwards but sometimes took little interest: stays 25f: acts on hard and dead going: blinkered once, visored twice. *Denys Smith* — c83 § —

Jack Brown Handicap Chase, Chepstow —
Direct and the grey Farm Week take the third last together

225

DIRECTOR PLEASE   10 ch.g. Whealden – Dyna Bell (Double Jump)   c– x
[1992/3 c25f] sturdy gelding: poor novice chaser: stays 2½m: poor jumper   –
of fences. *J. Webber*

DISCAIN BOY   13 b.g. Bargello – Another Romney (Malfaiteur) [1992/3   c–
c21m⁶] compact gelding: poor pointer/hunter chaser nowadays: stays 27f: –
acts on firm going: visored twice. *G. Evans*

DISCO DUKE   8 b.g. Record Token – Grandgirl (Mansingh (USA))   c– x
[1992/3 c21d³] lengthy, workmanlike gelding: moderate hurdler: poor   –
novice chaser, often makes mistakes: probably stays 25f: possibly unsuited
by firm going, acts on any other. *A. Moore*

DISSIDENT DANCER   4 b.g. The Dissident – Someway (Dublin Taxi)
[1992/3 aF16g F17m] leggy gelding: first foal: dam poor plater: tailed
off in NH Flat races in March and April: yet to race over hurdles. *J. H.
Peacock*

DISSIMULATEUR (FR)   4 b.c. Legend of France (USA) – Dartana
(FR) (Roi Dagobert) [1992/3 17v² 17g* 17g 17m] compact ex-French colt: 116
second foal: dam ran twice: useful middle-distance performer on Flat when
trained by F. Boutin: won juvenile hurdle at Doncaster in January: tailed off
both starts afterwards: subsequently sold, reportedly to race back in
France, 18,000 gns Doncaster May Sales: probably needs forcing tactics at
2m, and will be suited by further: blinkered last outing. *O. Sherwood*

DISTANT CHERRY   8 gr.m. General Ironside – Cherry Token (Prince   c81 x
Hansel) [1992/3 c21dᵇᵈ 24s c21s⁶ c24g⁴ c20g³ c26sᵖᵘ a24gᵖᵘ c24m² c27m²   65
25s³ c25g⁵ c25fᵘʳ c25mᵖᵘ 24g] leggy, workmanlike mare: poor novice
hurdler/chaser: stays 27f: best form on a sound surface: sometimes
blinkered or visored: poor jumper of fences. *D. Lee*

DISTANT HOME   5 b.g. Homeboy – Distant Sound (Faraway Times
(USA)) [1992/3 16m⁴ 17g⁴ 17g⁶ 16g³ 16m⁶ a20g] angular gelding: poor   69
novice hurdler: best form at around 2m: acts on good to firm going: best
form without blinkers. *C. H. Jones*

DISTANT MEMORY   4 gr.g. Don't Forget Me – Canton Silk
(Runnymede) [1992/3 16m 18m³ 17f⁵ 17g] poor maiden on Flat: poor form in   63
selling hurdles: pulls hard and suited by sharp 2m: blinkered second and
third outings. *P. J. Hobbs*

DISTANT MILL (IRE)   5 b.g. Millfontaine – Distant Breeze (London
Bells (CAN)) [1992/3 F16sˢᵘ] second foal: dam unraced: slipped up in NH

Saint Systems Risograph Hurdle, Doncaster—
Dissimulateur is strongly pressed by Great Max (No. 8)

Flat race at Nottingham in February: yet to race over hurdles or fences. *R. Dickin*

DISTILLATION   8 b.g. Celtic Cone – Cauldron (Kabale) [1992/3 c27s⁵   **c?** c26g* c25dᶠ c24d⁶ c21v⁴ c27vᵖᵘ] sturdy gelding: sixth foal: half-brother to fair chaser Premier Charlie (by Prince de Galles) and smart staying chaser Brown Windsor (by Kinglet): dam winning hunter from good chasing family: won maiden point in 1992 and 4-finisher novice chase at Cheltenham in October: let down by his jumping subsequently: suited by a thorough test of stamina. *G. F. Edwards*

DISTINCTIVE (IRE)   4 ch.g. Orchestra – Zimuletta (Distinctly (USA)) [1992/3 F16m⁵ F17m⁴] compact gelding: second foal: dam winning Irish hurdler/chaser: signs of ability in NH Flat races at Nottingham in March and Cheltenham in April: yet to race over hurdles. *M. J. Wilkinson*

DIS TRAIN   9 ch.g. Deep Run – Bunkilla (Arctic Slave) [1992/3 c16s³ **c120** c17d⁴ c16vᵣₒ c16d² c16g* c20sᵇᵈ c21d*] rangy gelding: useful hurdler at   – best: won novice chases at Warwick in March and Newton Abbot in April: best effort on fourth start, when second to Viking Flagship at Wolverhampton: effective at 2m and stays 21f: seems to act on any going: ran out third outing, but did nothing wrong subsequently. *S. E. Sherwood*

DI THAVED (IRE)   5 ch.g. Balboa – Our Foxbar (Swinging Junior) [1992/3 F16g] third foal: dam moderate sprinter: behind in NH Flat race at Ayr in March: yet to race over hurdles or fences. *J. C. Haynes*

DIVINE CHANCE (IRE)   5 b.g. The Parson – Random What (Random Shot) [1992/3 17dᵘʳ 16v 17g⁶] sturdy gelding: third foal: half-brother to 6-y-o   **75 p** Marrob (by Deep Run), placed in NH Flat race: dam, unraced half-sister to winning hurdler Noble Yeoman, from family of Mr What and L'Escargot: sixth in novice hurdle at Taunton in April, showing a little ability: will be suited by further than 17f. *N. A. Gaselee*

DIZZY DEALER   6 b.m. Le Bavard (FR) – Dizzy Dot (Bargello) [1992/3   **c82** x 18h⁴ c20mᶠ c18fᵘʳ c18s⁴ c17f⁴ c17dᵘʳ c17f⁵ c21d⁵ c16d² c16sᵘʳ c21sᵘʳ c16sᵘʳ   – a20g⁵ c16s⁵ c19mᶠ c17d⁵ 17d c17s⁴ c21s⁴ c17g⁴] smallish mare: novice jumper: stays 21f: best form with give in the ground: poor jumper of fences. *Mrs J. Jordan*

DIZZY (USA)   5 gr.m. Golden Act (USA) – Bergluft (GER) (Literat) [1992/3 18s⁵ 17d⁶ 16g² 16g* 20s⁶ 17d² 18g* 20g⁶ 18m* 17g² 17f² 16g⁶]   **126** good-topped mare: fairly useful hurdler: won handicaps at Edinburgh in January and twice at Kelso in March: stays 2¼m (not 2½m): acts on firm and dead going: game, genuine and consistent. *P. Monteith*

DJEBEL PRINCE   6 b.g. Ile de Bourbon (USA) – Noirmont Girl (Skymaster) [1992/3 17d⁶ 16s² 17v* 17vᶠ 17v* 17v 16d⁵] sturdy gelding: **103** improved hurdler in first half of season: winner of 2 handicaps at Newton Abbot in December: well below form last 2 starts: ideally suited by sharp 2m: acts on heavy going: held up: jumps soundly. *C. R. Egerton*

DO A RUNNER   6 ch.g. Le Moss – Polarville (Charlottesvilles Flyer) [1992/3 F16v⁴ 16g 20s 25d 16g 22g⁵ 21d 27d⁵ 25d] leggy, lengthy gelding: **72** poor novice hurdler: easily best effort on sixth start. *J. Love*

DO BE BRIEF   8 ch.g. Le Moss – Right Performance (Gala Performance **c118** (USA)) [1992/3 c24v c24v c24g* c29g² c34d³ c25d²] strong gelding: useful   – hurdler: fairly useful staying chaser: won handicap at Huntingdon in February: ran respectably afterwards: possibly doesn't stay 4¼m: acts on heavy going: jumps none too fluently on occasions: usually blinkered. *Mrs J. Pitman*

DOCKLANDS EXPRESS   11 b.g. Roscoe Blake – Southern Moss (Sea **c165** Moss) [1992/3 c26d³ᵈⁱˢ c24s⁶ c21v³ c24g² c27m⁶ c25f* c30d⁴ c26m*   – c22g*]

    'No foot, no horse'. Problems with a crumbling pedal bone caused anxiety for the connections of Docklands Express in the first part of the latest season. The horse didn't see a racecourse until just before Christmas and looked a long way off recapturing his best form on each of his first three starts, including the King George VI Chase in which he'd run The Fellow to a length and a half the previous season. But, just as some were writing him off, Docklands Express, wearing plastic shoes, re-established himself with an excellent effort under 12-0 in the Racing Post Chase at Kempton in February, a race he had won in each of the two previous seasons. He gave the resolute type of performance which had become his hallmark, keeping on with the utmost gameness to edge out Bradbury Star for second, a length and a half behind Zeta's Lad. After a slightly disappointing sixth to Jodami in the Tote Cheltenham Gold Cup—where he looked in excellent shape and had the ground in his favour—Docklands Express resumed winning ways in the Martell Cup Chase at Aintree. The small field included two others who had run in the Gold Cup, seventh-placed Run For Free and Very Very Ordinary who had been pulled up. The sound-jumping Docklands Express beat Run For Free by a length and a half, leading on the bit at the second last and tending to idle once in front. The Whitbread Gold Cup, which Docklands Express won in controversial circumstances in 1991, was next on the agenda. The good to soft ground wasn't ideal for him, however, and he managed only a fair fourth behind Givus A Buck, Topsham Bay and Caher-villahow (who had been disqualified after passing the post first in 1991). Docklands Express completed the season with odds-on victories in minor events at Warwick and Fakenham (ridden by the trainer's wife in an amateur race) in May; he'd have had a race on his hands at Warwick if Rowlandsons Jewels hadn't broken down approaching the last when going well.

		Blakeney	Hethersett
	Roscoe Blake	(b 1966)	Windmill Girl
	(b 1975)	Rhodie	Rasper
Docklands Express		(br 1962)	Ria Mooney
(b.g. 1982)		Sea Moss	Ballymoss
	Southern Moss	(ch 1963)	Thebas II
	(ch 1972)	Beare Green	Eastern Venture
		(ch 1958)	Furthermore

Docklands Express isn't an imposing individual—he's a smallish, sturdy gelding—but he's made of the right stuff. You couldn't wish for a more genuine racehorse. There's nothing to add to the details of his pedigree provided in previous editions of *Chasers & Hurdlers*. Docklands Express stays very well and is a good jumper. He acts on any going but goes particularly well on a sound surface. He's been a splendid servant to his stable over the years. *K. C. Bailey*

Martell Cup Chase, Aintree—
Docklands Express (No. 2) collars long-time leader Run For Free at the second last

American Express F.X. Veterans Chase, Warwick—
Docklands Express jumps the fourth last ahead of the eventual third-placed Gala's Image

DOC LODGE 7 b.m. Doc Marten – Cooling (Tycoon II) [1992/3 18f⁵ 17f]
leggy mare: poor novice hurdler: has run in a seller: races freely and will
prove suited by sharp 2m: blinkered once. *J. White* — 67

DOC'S COAT 8 b.g. Tower Walk – Gold Loch (Lochnager) [1992/3 17s⁶
17s* 17d⁴ 17gᶠ 17m 20g⁵] stocky gelding: fairly useful handicap hurdler: — 117

Kestrel Handicap Hurdle, Ascot—
a mud-spattered Adrian Maguire and Doc's Coat jump the last ahead of Flakey Dove

won at Ascot in March: creditable fourth on same course following week: stays 2½m: acts on any going: reportedly broke blood vessel once in 1990/1. *C. P. Wildman*

DOCTOR BRIGGS (IRE) 4 ch.g. King of Clubs – Great Meadow (Northfields (USA)) [1992/3 16gpu a16g⁵ 18d⁵ 18m] tall, unfurnished gelding: half-brother to Rathbrides Joy (by Kafu), a winner on Flat and placed over hurdles in Ireland: dam never ran: no sign of ability: has worn a tongue strap. *Mrs J. Jordan*   –

DOCTOR DUNKLIN (USA) 4 b.g. Family Doctor (USA) – Mis Jenifer's Idea (USA) (Capital Idea (USA)) [1992/3 F16s F16g² F16m] first foal: dam placed once from 9 starts in USA: close second in NH Flat race at Catterick in February: badly hampered next start: yet to race over hurdles. *Mrs V. C. Ward*

DOCTOR FOSTER (IRE) 5 b.g. Rymer – Ash Copse (Golden Love) [1992/3 16s⁴] IR 5,000 3-y-o: fourth foal: dam lightly-raced daughter of winning half-sister to The Dikler: promising debut when fourth in novice hurdle at Southwell in September, but wasn't seen out again: bred to prove well suited by further than 2m. *Mrs S. J. Smith*   82

DOES IT MATTER 8 b.g. Le Moss – Miss Argument (No Argument) [1992/3 c24spu] rangy gelding: winning pointer/hurdler in Ireland: showed plenty of ability in novice chases in 1991/2: pulled up in November: was best at distances short of 3m: dead. *R. Akehurst*   c–

DOLIKOS 6 b.g. Camden Town – Wolveriana (Wolver Hollow) [1992/3 c16d⁴ c17s* c16d* c18gF] leggy, quite good-topped gelding with scope: winning hurdler: made all when winning handicap chases at Huntingdon (novice event) in December and Carlisle in April: form only at around 2m: acts on soft ground: jumps soundly in the main: should improve further and win more races over fences. *J. M. Jefferson*   c100 p   –

DOLITINO 9 gr.m. Neltino – Sandoli (Sandford Lad) [1992/3 c16m² c17f³ c24g⁴ c21d⁵ c17d⁵ c17g c24m⁶ c26g³ c21g c26d⁴ c16s³ c17s⁵ c16m³ c22mF c26d] small, sparely-made mare: poor novice chaser: effective at 2m and stays 25f: probably acts on any going. *Miss Z. A. Green*   c71   –

DOLLAR SEEKER (USA) 9 b.h. Buckfinder (USA) – Syrian Song (USA) (Damascus (USA)) [1992/3 20m*] close-coupled, rather sparely-made horse: won novice hurdle at Bangor in August: stays 2½m: acts on good to firm ground (blinkered only time over hurdles, would probably have won on dead in 1990/1 but for unseating rider). *A. Bailey*   89

DOLLAR WINE (IRE) 4 b.g. Alzao (USA) – Captain's Covey (Captain James) [1992/3 17m³ 17f³ 18f⁶ 18g² 18m 17gro 16g² 18g³ 17d⁴] quite modest handicapper on Flat, stays 1m: plater over hurdles: not seen out after October: stays 2¼m: visored second outing, trained until after fifth by J. Moore. *J. J. Birkett*   75

DOLLY BOD 5 b.m. Kabour – Argostone (Rockavon) [1992/3 18g 16mpu 16d] sturdy mare: half-sister to winning hurdler Little Miss Horner (by Sit In The Corner): no sign of ability on Flat or over hurdles. *M. H. Easterby*   –

DOLLY OATS 7 ch.m. Oats – Royaldyne (No Argument) [1992/3 17d 17sF 20d⁴ 22v⁴] tall, leggy mare: poor novice hurdler: best effort of season on last start: stays 2¾m: acts on heavy going. *R. J. Eckley*   79

DOLLY PRICES 8 b.m. Silly Prices – Miss Friendly (Status Seeker) [1992/3 16d 22d 16d 18d² 16d 17s² 22s⁴ 17d⁴ a16g 16d 18d³ 18dF 16g 16g 17f 18g 21g] smallish mare: poor novice hurdler: well below form last 5 starts: stays 2½m: suited by plenty of give in the ground. *W. J. Smith*   82 d

DOLLY WARDANCE 10 gr.m. Warpath – April (Silly Season) [1992/3 21v⁶ 25v³ 23d] sturdy mare: moderate hurdler: easily best effort of season on second start: stays 25f: acts on heavy going. *T. W. Donnelly*   96

DOLPHIN TOWN 4 b.f. Neltino – Swag Jacket (Laurence O) [1992/3 F16g F17f] first foal: dam poor novice chaser: behind in NH Flat races in February and March: yet to race over hurdles. *M. P. Muggeridge*

DOMAIN 5 b.h. Dominion – Prelude (Troy) [1992/3 a16g³] leggy horse: selling hurdler: not disgraced in claimer at Southwell in May: should stay beyond 2m: best form on fibresand: wears blinkers. *R. J. Weaver*   77

DOMAN 4 ch.g. Domynsky – Mantina (Bustino) [1992/3 18g 17g] neat gelding: fifth foal: half-brother to fairly useful 7f/1m performer Yearsley (by Anfield): dam never ran: signs of ability in juvenile hurdle at Cartmel in August and novice event at Newcastle in February. *J. G. FitzGerald*   72

DOM EDINO 10 b.g. Dominion – Edna (Shiny Tenth) [1992/3 26s⁶ 25g³] rangy gelding: has been hobdayed: one-time useful hurdler: remote third in conditional jockeys handicap at Perth in September: winning chaser: blinkered last start 1991/2. *M. Avison*   c– –

DOMINANT FORCE 4 b.g. Primo Dominie – Elan's Valley (Welsh Pageant) [1992/3 16s⁵ 17v³] leggy gelding: modest maiden on Flat, stays 1¼m: modest form in juvenile hurdles at Kempton and Plumpton in November: jumps sketchily. *R. Hannon*   89

DOMINANT SERENADE 4 b.g. Dominion – Sing Softly (Luthier) [1992/3 17g² 16g* 17g* 17v* 16d* 17m 17f⁵] small gelding: staying maiden on Flat: took well to hurdling and won juvenile events at Hexham, Kelso and Cheltenham (valuable event, by ½ length from Storm Dust) in first half of season and Ayr in January: creditable fifth in valuable event at Aintree in April: will stay beyond 17f: probably acts on any going: tail swisher. *M. D. Hammond*   130

DOMINION TREASURE 8 b. or br.h. Dominion – Chrysicabana (Home Guard (USA)) [1992/3 20s 21v 23g⁴ 22spu 18d² 21m 20g 21d] small horse: moderate hurdler: second at Exeter in April, best effort of season: stays 21f, probably not 3¼m: acts on any going. *R. J. Baker*   87

DONEGAL STYLE (IRE) 5 b. or br.g. Kemal (FR) – Donegal Lady (Indigenous) [1992/3 F16g 20g⁴ 16d⁶ 16m 20m⁴] unfurnished gelding: half-brother to 4 winning jumpers, including fairly useful hurdler Donegal Hope (by Will Somers): dam never ran: poor novice hurdler: stays 2½m: acts on dead and good to firm ground. *J. H. Johnson*   80

DONE INSTANTLY 8 b.g. Day Is Done – Instanter (Morston (FR)) [1992/3 18d⁵ 16v* 18d⁴ 18s⁴ 17m⁵ 17f⁴ 16s⁴] lengthy, plain gelding: fairly useful hurdler: won maiden at Punchestown in January: also ran well in valuable handicaps at Cheltenham, Aintree and Fairyhouse last 3 starts: should stay beyond 17f: acts on any going. *Patrick Mullins, Ireland*   123

DONIA (USA) 4 ch.f. Graustark – Katrinka (USA) (Sovereign Dancer (USA)) [1992/3 16d 17g²] leggy filly: fair maiden on Flat when trained by P. Cole, placed from 1m to 1½m in 1992: only poor form when close second of 6 in novice hurdle at Plumpton in March. *N. J. Henderson*   74

DON KEYDROP 9 b.g. Don – Tomrousse (FR) (Diatome) [1992/3 c21s c24d a24gpu a24g⁶] leggy gelding: fair handicap hurdler and modest novice chaser at his best: showed nothing in 1992/3: seems better suited to 3m than shorter: usually goes well on equitrack, possibly unsuited by soft ground. *Miss B. Sanders*   c– –

DONNA'S TOKEN 8 br.m. Record Token – Lyricist (Averof) [1992/3 16g 17g⁶ 16d³ 17v³ 17d⁴ 16m* 17g² 18f* 17g⁵ 22v² 16g⁶ 22f³] small, sparely-made mare: improved form to win handicap hurdles at Warwick (novices) in February and Worcester in March: below form subsequently: stays 2¼m: ideally suited by firm going: blinkered once. *R. L. Brown*   94

DONOSTI 9 b.g. Rusticaro (FR) – Blue Flame (USA) (Crimson Satan) [1992/3 17m 17vpu a16g* a16g* 17m⁴ 16f⁵ 17m³] strong, workmanlike gelding: fair hurdler: won handicaps at Lingfield in January (conditional jockeys) and February: no form over fences: best at around 2m: acts on firm, dead ground and equitrack. *R. Lee*   c– 103

DON'T BUCK 6 b.g. Slippered – I'm A Buck (Master Buck) [1992/3 23s² 26g³ 25dpu] deep-girthed gelding with scope: chasing type: fourth foal: brother to winning Irish pointer Harold Michel: dam never ran: showed plenty of promise in 2 Irish points in 1991: placed in novice hurdles at   91

Uttoxeter and Huntingdon in October: ran poorly following month, and wasn't seen out again: suited by test of stamina. *John R. Upson*

DON'T GIVE UP   5 b.h. Nomination – Tug Along (Posse (USA)) [1992/3 16g] fair form at up to 7f at 2 yrs, below best on Flat since: automatic top weight, tailed off in handicap at Worcester in April on hurdling debut. *R. A. Bennett*   –

DON'T LIGHT UP   7 b.g. Lighter – Hannah's Bar (Babu) [1992/3 21s* 24v⁴ 26dᶠ 22d 20g² 26g⁴] workmanlike gelding: chasing type: won novice hurdle at Leicester in January: good efforts next time and fifth outing, below best otherwise: sold to join P. Nicholls 9,700 gns Ascot June Sales: stays well: acts on heavy ground: visored fifth outing, blinkered last. *J. A. C. Edwards*   100

DON'T TELL JUDY (IRE)   5 b.g. Strong Gale – Two In A Million (Rarity) [1992/3 17g 22g 21spu] tailed off in NH Flat race and over hurdles. *A. J. Wight*   –

DONT TELL THE WIFE   7 br.g. Derring Rose – Dame Sue (Mandamus) [1992/3 21d³ 25d² c21s² c17v³ c21s⁶ c17sᶠ c21dᶠ 22d* 22m] compact gelding: won novice hurdle at Worcester in March: ran creditably in novice handicap following month: fair novice chaser: suited by further than 2m and stays 25f: acts on soft and good to firm going: visored sixth outing. *Mrs D. Haine*   c100
100

DON'T WORRY (IRE)   4 ch.f. Hatim (USA) – Nadja (Dancer's Image (USA)) [1992/3 17fpu] angular filly: plater on Flat, form at up to 1m: tailed off when pulled up in juvenile hurdle at Plumpton in August. *M. H. Tompkins*   –

DON'T YER KNOW   9 b.g. Kala Shikari – Modom (Compensation) [1992/3 c16vpu c19vpu c16spu 18m] workmanlike gelding: no sign of ability: tried visored and blinkered. *P. R. Hedger*   c–
–

DON VINCENTO   7 b.g. Don – Fourth Degree (Oats) [1992/3 16v³ 17m³ 24v*] lengthy, rather plain gelding: very lightly raced: won NH Flat race in 1990 and maiden hurdle at Ballinrobe in April: third in novice hurdle at Bangor on second outing: very tenderly handled there (reportedly returned lame) and trainer and rider each fined £650: stays 3m: acts on heavy ground. *P. F. Lehane, Ireland*   108 ?

DOOLAR (USA)   6 b.g. Spend A Buck (USA) – Surera (ARG) (Sheet Anchor) [1992/3 17m⁴ 17d⁵ 16d* 16g 21f* 21m] angular gelding: quite useful hurdler: easy winner of handicaps at Uttoxeter in April and May: ran poorly last outing: stays 21f: acts on firm and dead ground. *P. T. Dalton*   118

DOONLOUGHAN   8 b.g. Callernish – Cora Swan (Tarqogan) [1992/3 c24m² c25fur c26g*] lengthy gelding: maiden hurdler: moderate chaser: highly fortunate winner of handicap at Cheltenham in October, held in third when left clear 2 out: stays well: acts on firm going: jumps soundly. *G. B. Balding*   c99
–

DORA D'OR   7 br.m. Le Coq d'Or – Katie Little (Nulli Secundus) [1992/3 22fpu] no sign of ability in points and novice hurdles. *G. F. White*   –

DORADUS   5 br.g. Shirley Heights – Sextant (Star Appeal) [1992/3 18g* 16m⁵ 17f³ 18g*] workmanlike gelding: won novice handicap hurdles at Sedgefield in February and March: looked none too keen under pressure both starts in between: should stay beyond 2¼m: not one to trust implicitly. *J. G. FitzGerald*   98

DORAN'S TOWN LAD   6 b.g. Tumble Gold – Thomastown Girl (Tekoah) [1992/3 16g⁵ 16s* 17g 17d 20s⁵ 18d⁶ 16d⁴ 17m] leggy gelding: first foal: dam, NH Flat race winner and poor maiden hurdler in Ireland, half-sister to 1982 Champion Hurdle winner For Auction and fairly useful jumper The A Train: fairly useful hurdler: won handicap at Listowel in September: best effort subsequently (behind at Cheltenham fourth and last starts) on seventh outing: stays 2¼m: probably acts on any going. *Anthony Mullins, Ireland*   128

DOREEN'S PRIDE 7 ch.m. Celtic Cone – Quae Supra (On Your Mark) **c62** x
[1992/3 16vpu 16dur c16vF6 c20d5 c19dF] lengthy mare: modest novice –
hurdler at best: poor novice chaser: sold 1,050 gns Doncaster March Sales:
best runs at 2m on good ground: poor jumper of fences. *P. G. Murphy*

DORLIN CASTLE 5 b.g. Scorpio (FR) – Gorgeous Gertie (Harwell)
[1992/3 20s 25g2 24s5] close-coupled gelding: second live foal: half-brother 76
to winning hurdler/chaser Achiltibuie (by Roscoe Blake): dam, winning
hurdler/chaser, stayed 2½m: second in novice hurdle at Carlisle in March,
best effort: jumped to his right next time: stays 25f: yet to race on a firm
surface. *L. Lungo*

DORNVALLEY LAD 12 ch.g. Anax – Lovely Diana (Supreme **c–**
Sovereign) [1992/3 c16g3 c17f6 c16g 21g] good-topped gelding: poor 2m –
chaser: acts on firm ground. *D. T. Garraton*

DOROBO (NZ) 5 b.g. Ivory Hunter (USA) – Mountain Hi (NZ) (Rocky
Mountain (FR)) [1992/3 F16d6 17d6 16v6 21v4 24s] angular gelding: has 85
shown a little ability in NH Flat race and novice hurdles: should stay beyond
21f: acts on heavy going. *Capt. T. A. Forster*

DORONICUM 14 ch.g. Deep Run – May Foliage (Barman II) [1992/3 **c–**
c16m5 c16g4 c23spu] strong, deep-girthed gelding: poor chaser nowadays: –
stays 25f: best form over fences on a sound surface. *C. R. Beever*

D'OR'S GEM 10 b.g. Brigadier Gerard – Siraf (Alcide) [1992/3 c24sur **c–**
c21spu] small, workmanlike gelding: moderate chaser: stays 3m: acts on –
good to firm and soft going: visored when gaining last success, has also won
blinkered. *P. J. Bevan*

DO THE RIGHT THING 5 ch.m. Busted – Taniokey (Grundy) [1992/3
18m6] angular mare: poor form over hurdles: should stay beyond 2m. *J. A. B.* –
Old

DOTS DEE 4 ch.f. Librate – Dejote (Bay Express) [1992/3 18g 18mpu
18d] maiden plater on Flat, placed over 1¼m: no promise over hurdles, –
including in a seller: visored second start. *J. M. Bradley*

DOT'S JESTER 4 b.c. Jester – Taylors Renovation (Frimley Park)
[1992/3 16spu] leggy colt: second foal: dam winning hurdler: no sign of –
ability at 2 yrs or in a juvenile hurdle at Haydock in November. *E. J. Alston*

DOTTEREL (IRE) 5 b.g. Rhoman Rule (USA) – Miysam (Supreme
Sovereign) [1992/3 18g 16s 16d 20vpu 16vpu 16f 17fpu 17f] leggy gelding: of –
little account. *R. G. Brazington*

DOUBLE COUNT (NZ) 7 b.g. Dual Kingdom (AUS) – Countess Fuego
(NZ) (Tierra Fuego) [1992/3 22spu 20gpu 16vpu a16gpu] small New –
Zealand-bred gelding: of little account. *J. Mackie*

DOUBLE DOSE 8 br.m. Al Sirat (USA) – Gilded Empress (Menelek)
[1992/3 26gpu 23g 17s5 18s] small, angular mare: poor novice hurdler: 61
should prove suited by further than 17f. *J. L. Eyre*

DOUBLE LARK 4 b.c. Bairn (USA) – Straffan Girl (Sallust) [1992/3
17mpu] plating-class sprint maiden Flat: no promise in July on hurdling –
debut: sold 700 gns Ascot September Sales. *R. Hollinshead*

DOUBLE SILK 9 b.g. Dubassoff (USA) – Yellow Silk (Counsel) [1992/3 **c122** p
c21d3 c26g* c27m* c22f* c27m* c27m*]
   Double Silk achieved the notable Cheltenham Foxhunter-Aintree Fox
Hunters' double in 1993, the first horse to do so in the same season since
Grittar in 1981. Only eight horses have pulled it off since the war—Lucky
Purchase (1947), Colledge Master (1961), Credit Call (1972) and Bullock's
Horn (1973) when the Cheltenham race was run over four miles, Spartan
Missile and Rolls Rambler in the two years preceding Grittar. Like Spartan
Missile, the outstanding hunter chaser of the past twenty years, and Grittar,
who went on to win the 1982 Grand National, Double Silk is being talked of
as a live National candidate. At the time of writing his owner-trainer has yet
to decide whether to make the move to open competition. Double Silk has a
style of racing—he's a bold-jumping, front runner—and a relish for a test of

stamina which make him an ideal National type. His form is not yet of a sufficient level to make him an outstanding proposition—he isn't a Spartan Missile or even a Grittar just yet—but he has the potential for further improvement and it would be a pity if he was denied his chance outside hunter chase company.

Double Silk, a progressive hunter in 1992, began the season with a defeat at Wincanton; however, he wasn't fully fit and was facing an insufficient test of stamina anyway. He then won his pre-Cheltenham race, at Warwick, by a rapidly-reducing neck from Moorcroft Boy (receiving 7 lb) and went for the Christies Foxhunter Chase with seemingly only average prospects. Seven horses featured in front of him in the betting—Kerry Orchid from Ireland and The Red One were joint-favourites ahead of Toureen Prince, a formerly-useful handicapper who'd impressed in point-to-points, and four who'd been in good form in Radical Views, Once Stung, Seven of Diamonds and Tartan Trix. In spite of the absence of the injured Teaplanter and Sheer Jest (regarded as too inexperienced) the Foxhunter was the best contested hunter chase of the season. The test of stamina the race provided brought out the best in Double Silk. He set a sound pace, jumped boldly and well and stayed on resolutely from three out to withstand all his challengers. Kerry Orchid was almost on terms after a good leap at the last but could do no more on the flat and went down by a length and a half. Once Stung held every chance but was one-paced after a mistake two out and finished five lengths further back in third. Toureen Prince was a non-staying fourth, Warwick second Moorcroft Boy fifth. Radical Views fell at the first bringing down The Red One. Double Silk's four pursuers all performed well subsequently—Kerry Orchid won at the Punchestown Festival, Once Stung won his next three, Moorcroft Boy his next two and Toureen Prince both his subsequent two.

Aintree provided much less exacting company. The Martell Fox Hunters' Chase is a race where too many of the runners are there just to get round these days. Twenty-seven took part in 1993, fifteen of them aged twelve or over. Few of them came into the race in much form. Double Silk, 5/2 favourite this time, dominated the race, jumping the unfamiliar fences with particular flair. His regular rider Ron Treloggan needed only hands and heels to maintain the idling Double Silk's lead on the long run-in. Dark Dawn, winner of his next two races, was six lengths second with the ordinary ex-handicapper Mandraki Shuffle a further seven back in third. Double Silk ran twice after Aintree, both times at Cheltenham, and was both times successful against limited opposition.

Christies Foxhunter Challenge Cup, Cheltenham—
Double Silk makes all to beat the grey Kerry Orchid and Once Stung

Martell Fox Hunters' Chase, Aintree—Double Silk lands in front over the Chair

Double Silk (b.g. 1984)	Dubassoff (USA) (b 1969)	Sea-Bird II (ch 1962)	Dan Cupid
			Sicalade
		Love Lyric (b 1955)	Prince Chevalier
			Riding Rays
	Yellow Silk (br 1972)	Counsel (b 1952)	Court Martial
			Wheedler
		Gorse (ch 1966)	Tangle
			Genista

Double Silk, a tall, good-topped gelding, has yet to race on very soft going. He has winning form on dead but his best form is on top-of-the-ground. There isn't much to say about his breeding. The last foal of his unraced dam, he is the first horse of any consequence from his family in recent times. However, the family has another Aintree Fox Hunters' Chase winner among its members. Minto Burn, the winner back in 1967, was out of a fair hunter chaser called Cousin Kate; Double Silk's great-grandam Genista, a winner of three point-to-points herself, was a sister to Cousin Kate. *R. C. Wilkins*

DOUBLE THE BLACK 8 ch.m. Black Minstrel – Oweena Jay (Double-U-Jay) [1992/3 20d^{pu} 22g^{pu}] plain, angular ex-Irish mare: fourth foal: sister to French jumping winner Ballyard Crystal: dam, poor novice over jumps, won at up to 1½m on Flat in Ireland: winning pointer: no signs of ability otherwise: sold 1,800 gns Ascot June Sales. *Miss C. J. E. Caroe*   c–
–

DOUBLE TRICKS 10 gr.g. Peacock (FR) – Mourne Lass (Hereford) [1992/3 c20s⁵ c35s^{pu} c24v c26d^{pu}] angular gelding: handicap chaser: raced with little zest in 1992/3: sold 1,500 gns Ascot February Sales: thorough stayer: acts on good to firm and soft going: tried in blinkers and a hood (not when successful). *D. Burchell*   c–
–

DOUBLE TURN 12 b.g. Comedy Star (USA) – Pearl River (NZ) (Bourbon Prince) [1992/3 c22f] compact, good-bodied gelding: carries plenty of condition: long-priced winner of 1991 Seagram Fox Hunters' Chase at Liverpool: well below form since: stays 3m: acts on any going: unreliable. *Mrs J. Read*   c– §
–

DOUBLE U DEE 10 b.g. Rapid Pass – Abbyrama (Abyss) [1992/3 26g 18m 17f⁶ 20g⁵ 20m 22f a21g^{ur}] workmanlike gelding: winning pointer: has shown nothing over hurdles. *H. E. Haynes*   –

235

DOUBTING DONNA 7 gr.m. Tom Noddy – Dewy's Quince (Quorum)   **c82**
[1992/3 c24s* c24d4] good-topped mare: once-raced over hurdles: won   –
hunter chase at Chepstow in April: jumped none too fluently but not
disgraced at Ludlow later in month: stays 3m: acts on soft ground. *Mrs D.
Hughes*

DOUCE ECLAIR 7 b.m. Warpath – Sweet Clare (Suki Desu) [1992/3   73
22d3 16g 25gpu] workmanlike mare: fourth reported foal: sister to a maiden
pointer and half-sister to winning 2½m hunter chaser John Corbet (by
Ascertain): dam never ran: poor maiden pointer: best effort in novice
hurdles when third at Sedgefield in September: pulled up, reportedly lame,
following month and wasn't seen out again: will prove suited by test of
stamina. *Mrs M. Reveley*

DOUCE INDIENNE 8 gr.m. Warpath – Sweet Clare (Suki Desu)
[1992/3 2 1spu] lightly-raced maiden pointer: no promise in April on hurdling   –
debut. *Mrs M. Reveley*

DOUGAL'S BIRTHDAY 7 br.g. Glen Quaich – Ramla Bay (Rarity)
[1992/3 22mpu 21d 17f 21gpu] first foal: dam maiden Irish hurdler: no form   –
over hurdles. *G. M. R. Coatsworth*

DOUGHMAN 4 b.g. Runnett – Trila Love (Lomond (USA)) [1992/3
17mpu] little worthwhile form on Flat: tailed off when pulled up in juvenile   –
claiming hurdle at Carlisle in September. *J. Norton*

DOVEDON PRINCESS 6 gr.m. Baron Blakeney – Grace of Langley
(Foggy Bell) [1992/3 F17g a24gpu] behind in NH Flat races and maiden   –
hurdle (blinkered). *J. R. Bostock*

DOVEHILL 7 gr.g. Pragmatic – Arconist (Welsh Pageant) [1992/3 18g4   71
18g6] sparely-made gelding: poor novice hurdler. *R. D. Townsend*

DOVETTO 4 ch.g. Riberetto – Shadey Dove (Deadly Nightshade) [1992/3
F17m] sparely-made gelding: fourth foal: half-brother to winning hurdler   –
Coney Dove (by Celtic Cone) and to smart hurdler Flakey Dove (by Oats):
dam, from good jumping family, showed useful form over hurdles: tailed off
in NH Flat race at Cheltenham in April: yet to race over hurdles. *R. J. Price*

DOWN DALE 8 br.g. Hillandale – Indian Madness (Indian Ruler) [1992/3   c–
c21m] maiden pointer: tailed off in novice hunter chase at Newton Abbot in   –
May. *Mrs L. Bloomfield*

DOWN THE ROAD 6 br.g. Roi Guillaume (FR) – Killanny Bridge   **c87**
(Hallez (FR)) [1992/3 c21d2 c23g3 c17dF c21s3] tall, leggy gelding:
half-brother to NH Flat race winner/novice jumper Sir Dubel (by Al Sirat):
dam behind in 3 NH Flat races: won 2 points in Ireland in 1992: modest
novice chaser: probably stays 23f: acts on soft ground: not yet an
accomplished jumper. *J. H. Johnson*

DOWRY SQUARE (IRE) 5 b. or br.g. Strong Gale – Bavette (Le
Bavard (FR)) [1992/3 F16s F17g] unfurnished, angular gelding: first foal: –
dam, unraced, comes from very successful jumping family: soundly beaten
in NH Flat races: yet to race over hurdles or fences. *P. G. Murphy*

DOXFORD HUT 9 b.g. Class Distinction – Tillside Brig (New Brig)   c–
[1992/3 21s c17s5 c20dpu c17d] sturdy gelding: poor novice hurdler/chaser: –
trained until after third start by C. Nash: sold 2,200 gns Doncaster May
Sales: should be suited by further than 2m. *C. H. P. Bell*

DRAG ARTIST 8 br.g. Artaius (USA) – Drag Line (Track Spare) [1992/3   c–
17v6 16v 20d c16m5] angular gelding: novice selling hurdler: showed   –
nothing on chasing debut: stays 2½m: acts on good to firm ground. *M.
Scudamore*

DRAGONADE 12 b. or br.g. Dragonara Palace (USA) – La Sarmate (FR)   c–
(Hard Sauce) [1992/3 20vpu] leggy gelding: winning pointer: novice selling   –
hurdler/chaser: little form of late: sometimes blinkered or visored. *B. R. J.
Young*

DRAGONS DEN 7 b.g. Furry Glen – Ballygriffin (Deep Run) [1992/3   **c104**
22g 21d* 21s4 22v c21g3 c25g* c24m6 c21f*] won novice hurdle at   104

Uttoxeter in October and novice chases at Southwell in March and Worcester in May: effective at 2 1f and stays 25f: acts on soft and firm going: usually forces pace: not yet an accomplished jumper of fences. *S. E. Sherwood*

DRAGON SPIRIT 4 gr.g. Absalom – Fair Eleanor (Saritamer (USA)) [1992/3 17g 17d 17s² a16g³] sparely-made gelding: maiden on Flat, stays 7f: sold out of S. Woods's stable 2,600 gns Newmarket September Sales: placed in selling hurdle at Taunton in December and novice hurdle at Lingfield in January: resold 1,300 gns Ascot June Sales: acts on soft ground. *R. G. Frost* 82

DRAWN'N'QUARTERED 6 b.g. Decent Fellow – Pencil Lady (Bargello) [1992/3 F17g] fourth living foal: half-brother to fair staying chaser Hotplate (by Buckskin): dam, a winner several times over hurdles and fences in Ireland, stayed 3m: mid-division in NH Flat race at Doncaster in January: yet to race over hurdles or fences. *J. Chugg*

DRAW POKER 8 b.g. Uncle Pokey – Hejera (Cantab) [1992/3 c21vᵖᵘ a24gᵖᵘ] lengthy gelding: modest novice hurdler in 1990/1: pulled up both starts since, in novice chase (jumped poorly) first time: stays 19f. *O. Sherwood* c– –

DR DANGEROUS 7 b.g. Politico (USA) – Newgrove (Cantab) [1992/3 21dᵖᵘ] lengthy, angular gelding: first foal: dam winning pointer: tailed off when pulled up in maiden hurdle at Carlisle in November. *W. Storey* –

DREADNOUGHT 13 gr.g. Rugantino – Thwarted (The Ditton) [1992/3 F10d 16d a18gᵖᵘ] selling hurdler: has failed to complete course over fences: stays 2¾m: probably acts on any going. *J. Carden* c– –

DREAMAGO 10 br.m. Sir Mago – Dreamadee (Vimadee) [1992/3 c21s⁴] modest pointer: tailed off in hunter chase at Wetherby in March. *D. G. Atkinson* c–

DREAM CARRIER (IRE) 5 b.g. Doulab (USA) – Dream Trader (Auction Ring (USA)) [1992/3 17s] compact gelding: fair 7f performer on Flat, successful in 1993 for T. Barron: tailed off in novice hurdle at Newbury in November. *R. Hannon* –

DREAMCOAT (USA) 12 gr. or ro.g. Jig Time (USA) – Restless Polly (USA) (Restless Wind) [1992/3 c20dᵖᵘ c24fᵖᵘ c26mᵖᵘ] leggy gelding: selling hurdler: winning chaser: has lost his form. *R. Lee* c– –

DREAMERS DELIGHT 7 b.g. Idiot's Delight – Just Jolly (Jolly Jet) [1992/3 F12d* 17s* 17s* 17v² 17v² 17g² 17mᶠ 17f⁶] rangy gelding: chasing type: successful in novice hurdles at Aintree and Newbury in November: had earlier won novelty event on Flat at Uttoxeter: found little under pressure on his other completed starts, including when good sixth to Roll A Dollar at Aintree last time: should stay beyond 17f: probably acts on any going: blinkered last 2 outings: a shirker. *D. Nicholson* 126 §

DREAMSIDE 6 ch.m. Quayside – Dreamello (Bargello) [1992/3 22d⁴ 24sᵖᵘ 24gᶠ] workmanlike mare: unlucky loser of novice handicap hurdle at Nottingham in November on first start (4 lengths clear when almost falling 2 out), only sign of ability: should stay beyond 2¾m. *B. S. Rothwell* 80 ?

DRESS UP 9 b.g. Cajun – Prink (USA) (Stage Door Johnny) [1992/3 22s 27d 20mᵖᵘ] good-bodied gelding: novice hurdler: no form since 1990/1: let down by his jumping over fences: tried blinkered or visored. *N. G. Ayliffe* c– x –

DREWITTS DANCER 6 b.g. Balboa – Vermillon (FR) (Aureole) [1992/3 a18gᵖᵘ 16d⁶ 18g⁶] angular gelding: poor novice hurdler: sold 850 gns Ascot June Sales: should stay beyond 2m: acts on firm going: visored last outing. *F. Gray* –

DRINKS PARTY (IRE) 5 b.m. Camden Town – Holy Water (Monseigneur (USA)) [1992/3 17m 18dᶠ 18v³ a20g 18g] sparely-made mare: won 11f seller on Flat in October: sold out of J. Wharton's stable 2,000 gns Doncaster Sales later in month: poor plater over hurdles: stays 2¼m: acts on heavy going. *M. J. Charles* 69

DRIVING FORCE 7 ch.g. Be My Native (USA) – Frederika (USA) (The **c109**
Minstrel (CAN)) [1992/3 c17s* c20s⁴ c18d² c16s² c22g³ c21s⁵ c17m⁶ c17m⁵ –
c18g⁴] sparely-made, hollow-backed gelding: fair chaser: won handicap at
Fakenham in December: creditable efforts on occasions afterwards:
effective at 2m and stays 2¾m when conditions aren't testing: probably acts
on any going: jumps well: usually held up. *Mrs M. McCourt*

DR JEKYLL 8 b.g. Karlinsky (USA) – Woodbank Jewel (Fidel) [1992/3 **c73**
c18mᵇᵈ c16m³ c16g⁶ c20dᵖᵘ] sturdy gelding: winning pointer: poor form –
over hurdles and in steeplechases: trained until after third start by R.
Weaver: sold 1,200 gns Ascot 2nd June Sales. *R. W. Emery*

DR MACCARTER (USA) 6 gr.g. Dr Carter (USA) – Now Voyager 92
(USA) (Naskra (USA)) [1992/3 17gᵖᵘ 17g⁴ 17mᶠ 16f⁶ 16f25s* 25d*] compact
gelding: fair form over middle distances on equitrack at 3 and 4 yrs, trained
most of time by W. O'Gorman: visored/blinkered all starts prior to showing
improved form to win selling handicap hurdle (bought in 5,800 gns) and a
handicap at Uttoxeter in October: suited by good test of stamina: acts on
soft going: ridden by claimer. *A. L. Forbes*

DROMIN ACE 7 b.g. Torus – Dinsdale (Menelek) [1992/3 c21sᵘʳ c26dᵖᵘ **c–**
c25sᵘʳ 21gᵖᵘ] sturdy gelding: fifth foal: half-brother to winning staying –
chaser Majic Rain (by Northern Value): dam never ran: placed in points in
Ireland in 1991 and in Britain in 1992: failed to complete course in novice
chases and a maiden hurdle. *D. Esden*

DROMINA STAR 12 b.g. Pauper – Kitty The Hare (Hardicanute) **c75** x
[1992/3 c16m⁴ c18vᵘʳ] sturdy, plain gelding: poor novice chaser, let down by –
his jumping. *Mrs S. C. Bradburne*

DROMIN FOX 7 b.g. The Parson – Kilcor Rose (Pitpan) [1992/3 c16dᵘʳ **c–**
c16m⁵ c26gᵖᵘ 20m] good-topped, plain gelding: no sign of ability. *Denys* –
Smith

DROMIN LEADER 8 b.g. Crash Course – Astral Fairy (Prefairy) **c82**
[1992/3 c17dᶠ c21m² c24gᶠ] modest pointer/steeplechaser: creditable –
second in hunter chase at Folkestone in May: should stay beyond 21f: acts
on good to firm going. *J. M. Turner*

DROMIN MIST 6 ch.g. Over The River (FR) – Ten-Cents (Taste of **c91**
Honey) [1992/3 c24g² c23v³ c26d³] lengthy gelding: half-brother to winning –
jumpers Kyle Wood (by Daybrook Lad) and Green Marble (by Green
Shoon): dam winning 2m hurdler: won a point in Ireland: sold 12,000 gns
Doncaster May (1992) Sales: modest form in novice chases on first and last
starts: stays 3¼m: acts on dead ground (stiff task on heavy): jumps soundly.
J. Mackie

DROPS OF GOLD 9 ch.g. Le Bavard (FR) – Caroline's Money (Even
Money) [1992/3 16g 18v] sparely-made gelding: very lightly-raced winning –
hurdler: sold out of A. Mactaggart's stable 700 gns Doncaster September
Sales: no show in November and December: probably stays 2¾m and acts
on any ground. *G. Fleming*

DR ROCKET 8 b.g. Ragapan – Lady Hansel (Prince Hansel) [1992/3 **c113**
c17v²c17v³c16s³c16sᵘʳc16v*c16dᶠc17gᵘʳc18d⁴c17g*c21sᶠc17v*c16v² –
c17m³ c18d⁶ c21f³ c19g²] leggy gelding: fair handicap chaser: won at
Uttoxeter in January and Towcester (conditional jockeys event) in March
and April: pulls hard, but probably stays 21f: acts on any going: sometimes
let down by his jumping. *R. Dickin*

DRUMCEVA 7 b. or br.g. Salluceva – Drumvision (Brave Invader (USA))
[1992/3 21s⁴ 22s 26d⁵ 25f²] workmanlike gelding: easily best effort in 95
novice hurdles when runner-up at Newbury in March: stays well. *G. B.*
Balding

DRUMSTICK 7 ch.g. Henbit (USA) – Salustrina (Sallust) [1992/3 c16d⁴ **c110** p
c16s⁵ a16g⁴ c18s* c18gᵘʳ c16m* c16m* c17f* c18f*] leggy gelding: 86
modest hurdler: improved over fences in the spring, winning novice events
at Market Rasen (amateurs), Hereford and Southwell and handicaps at

Huntingdon and Stratford: stays 2¼m: acts on any ground: likely to improve further. *K. C. Bailey*

DRU RI'S BRU RI 7 b.g. Kafu – Bru Ri (FR) (Sir Gaylord) [1992/3 20d⁶ 16s 22d a16g a16g⁶ 16g² 18g] neat gelding: poor hurdler: easily best effort of season sixth start: probably stays 2¾m: acts on any going: sometimes has tongue tied down: wears blinkers. *W. J. Smith* — 78

DRUSO (USA) 9 b.g. Raise A Cup (USA) – Pretty Pride (USA) (Kentucky Pride) [1992/3 18dᵖᵘ 22s a20g a24g⁴ a20g⁵ a24g* a24g⁶ 28mᵖᵘ] rangy gelding: poor hurdler: won handicap at Southwell in February: ran poorly afterwards: stays 3m: acts on good to firm, dead ground and fibresand: sometimes blinkered or visored. *R. F. Marvin* — 83

DRY GIN 10 ch.g. Grundy – Karajinska (USA) (Nijinsky (CAN)) [1992/3 F12d 17v c25s³ c22sᵖᵘ c33vᵖᵘ c24s⁶ c18d⁵ c21d c25s c25dᵖᵘ c25mᵖᵘ c22v⁶ c23mᵖᵘ] leggy, plain gelding: moderate chaser at his best: generally out of form in 1992/3: stays 3m: acts on any going: has worn visor, better without. *M. C. Chapman* — c– –

DRY TIME 5 ch.g. Alias Smith (USA) – Amirati (Amber Rama (USA)) [1992/3 16g 16d 24v 16s a18g⁵] tall, sparely-made gelding: half-brother to 2 minor winners on Flat: dam temperamental plater: bad novice hurdler: blinkered last start. *M. H. Easterby* — 57

DUART 13 b.g. Saunter – Traverser (Spiritus) [1992/3 c19sᵘʳ a20gᵖᵘ] tall, shallow-girthed gelding: poor staying handicap chaser: showed nothing in handicap hurdle in February. *Mrs J. Scrivens* — c– –

DUBACILLA 7 b.m. Dubassoff (USA) – Just Camilla (Ascertain (USA)) [1992/3 c24sᶠ c16v* c19s* c21dᵘʳ c24d* c24g² c21d* c25g*] good-topped mare: novice hurdler: much better over fences and put up fairly useful performance when winning Royal Fern Novices' Handicap at Ascot in April on last start impressively by 20 lengths: earlier successful in novice handicap chases at Wincanton and Taunton, handicap on latter course and Tattersalls Mares Only Novices' Chase Final (Limited Handicap) at Uttoxeter: effective at around 2½m when conditions are testing and stays 3m well: acts on heavy ground: held up: jumps soundly: sure to win more races over fences. *H. T. Cole* — c124 p –

DUBALEA 10 b.g. Dubassoff (USA) – Thirkleby Kate VII (Bivouac) [1992/3 c25d² c16m* c16g⁵ c17g⁶ c21v⁴ c18m⁴ c18d⁵] tall, close-coupled gelding: modest chaser: won handicap at Edinburgh in February: ran poorly — c86 –

Tattersalls Mares Only Novices' Chase Final, Uttoxeter—
in the air together early in the home straight are, from left to right,
Dubacilla, Duo Drom and River Pearl

after next start, including in a hunter chase: seems best at 2m: probably acts on any going. *J. S. Haldane*

DUBIOUS JAKE 10 b.g. Dubassoff (USA) – Coliemore (Coliseum) [1992/3 c26s^{pu} c21v^2 c28s^F c33v* c33s^{ur} c20d^5 c29v^4 c30s^4 c33g c29g^{ur} c32d^3] smallish gelding: fair handicap chaser: won at Market Rasen in December: best subsequent efforts sixth and eighth starts: effective at 2½m when conditions are testing and stays very long distances: acts on heavy going and good to firm: used to wear blinkers. *R. D. E. Woodhouse*

   c104
   –

DUBLIN FLYER 7 b.g. Rymer – Dublin Express (Tycoon II) [1992/3 c23g^4 c20d^2 c20s^4 c24g* c24s^2 c24s^2 c26d*] big, well-made gelding: winning hurdler: easy winner of novice chases at Doncaster in December and Uttoxeter in April, making all: twice creditable second in between: suited by a thorough test of stamina: acts on soft ground: jumps boldly, though rather erratically on occasions: should make up into a useful handicapper. *Capt. T. A. Forster*

   c118 p
   –

DUBLIN INDEMNITY (USA) 4 b.g. Alphabatim (USA) – Sailongal (USA) (Sail On-Sail On) [1992/3 17m 17f^3 17g* 16g^2 17g^4 16g^{pu} 16v a16g^6] leggy gelding: poor miler on Flat: modest form over hurdles: won seller at Hereford (bought in 4,000 gns) in September: sold 1,400 gns Doncaster March Sales, resold 1,400 gns Doncaster May Sales: not sure to stay much beyond 17f: acts on firm ground: takes good hold, and races prominently. *N. A. Callaghan*

   81 +

DUCHESS OF TUBBER (IRE) 5 b.m. Buckskin (FR) – Unforgetabubble (Menelek) [1992/3 22g] fourth foal: half-sister to 2 winning jumpers, including fair Irish performer Opryland (by Deep Run): dam, poor maiden Irish pointer, placed in NH Flat race: won a point in Ireland in January: poor form when seventh in amateurs maiden hurdle at Ayr in March. *R. F. Fisher*

   65

DUCKHAVEN 10 b.g. Duky – Fair Haven (Fair Seller) [1992/3 24s^4 21s 21v^2 23d 24s 22s^{pu} 27d^2 c21d^{pu}] leggy gelding: winning hurdler: second in sellers at Uttoxeter in January and Newton Abbot (handicap) in April: no form over fences: stays well: suited by give in the ground and acts on heavy: often blinkered. *R. J. Baker*

   c–
   87

DUCK OR GROUSE 8 b.g. Mandalus – Kenga (Roman Warrior) [1992/3 c23m*] big, rangy gelding: won poor novice chase at Market Rasen in August: stays 3¼m: best form on good to firm going. *John R. Upson*

   c78

DUHARRA (IRE) 5 ch.g. Flash of Steel – Mrs Walmsley (Lorenzaccio) [1992/3 16g^3 16d^3 16d^2 16d^4 16d* 17m^{ur} 16d 20d^4] lengthy, good-bodied gelding: fairly useful handicap hurdler: won at Punchestown in October: close second but under pressure when unseating rider 2 out in valuable event at Cheltenham in March: probably stays 2½m: acts on good to firm and dead going, seems unsuited by soft: usually blinkered/visored. *D. K. Weld, Ireland*

   126

DUKE OF APROLON 6 ch.g. Duky – Aprolon Lady (Mon Capitaine) [1992/3 18s^3 17d^3 17g* 20d^6 17g^{pu} 18f^4] compact gelding: half-brother to fairly useful hunter chaser Many A Slip (by Slippered) and to several other winning pointers: dam unraced sister to top-class staying chaser Captain John: won novice hurdle at Sandown in February, making most: saddle slipped fifth outing: will be suited by further than 2½m: ran poorly on firm going: type to do better. *J. T. Gifford*

   99 p

DUKE OF MONMOUTH (USA) 5 b.g. Secreto (USA) – Queen For The Day (USA) (King Emperor (USA)) [1992/3 17d^3 17s^6 16s^4 16g^2 17m 17f c17g* c17g* c21m^{pu}] strong, good-bodied gelding: usually looks well: very useful hurdler on his day: jumped quite well when very easy winner of novice chases at Taunton and Huntingdon in April: let down by his jumping in more competitive race on last outing: sold, reportedly to race in USA, 22,000 gns Doncaster May Sales: form only at around 2m: acts on good to soft going: best in blinkers over hurdles (hasn't worn them over fences). *S. E. Sherwood*

   c112 +
   147

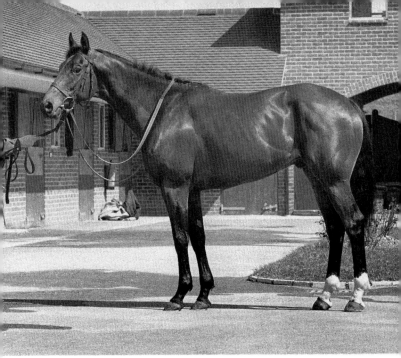

Mr Ali Saeed's "Duke of Monmouth"

DUKE'S WHISTLE   10 gr.g. Whistling Deer – Ruemaro (Peacock (FR)) [1992/3 c24g⁴ c25d⁶ c24dᵖᵘ] smallish, good-quartered gelding: handicap chaser: well beaten in 1992/3: stayed 25f: acted on firm ground: reportedly retired. *D. Nicholson*   c– –

DULZURA   5 b.m. Daring March – Comedy Lady (Comedy Star (USA)) [1992/3 16m 18g² 17m c17v⁵] leggy mare: poor plater over hurdles: soundly beaten in selling handicap in January on chasing debut. *A. P. Jarvis*   c– 68

DUNBRODY ABBEY   10 ch.m. Proverb – Sprats Hill (Deep Run) [1992/3 c21sᵖᵘ c24dᶠ c26f c23f] plain, rather sparely-made mare: winning 3m chaser: showed nothing in 1992/3. *Capt. T. A. Forster*   c– –

DUNCAN   8 b.g. Cut Above – Tristan du Cunha (USA) (Sir Ivor) [1992/3 c22dᵘʳ c20g* c24dᵖᵘ c27mᵖᵘ c20sᵖᵘ c17mᶠ c23g] strong gelding: hunter chaser: fairly useful form when winning at Newbury in February: ran badly afterwards: stays 25f: acts on good to firm and soft going. *Miss C. Saunders*   c105 d

DUNCAN IDAHO   10 b.g. Busted – Riboreen (Ribero) [1992/3 16s 21d 24d⁴ 23s⁴ 24dᶠ 25v* 23d² 20d⁵ 25dᵖᵘ] tall, lengthy gelding: fair hurdler: won handicap at Uttoxeter in January: creditable efforts next 2 starts: suited by a test of stamina and plenty of give in the ground: usually held up: tail swisher, sometimes finds little under pressure. *R. Callow*   109

DUNDEE PRINCE (NZ)   5 ch.g. Defecting Dancer – Camelot Queen (NZ) (Danseur Etoile (FR)) [1992/3 F17s⁶ F16v] New Zealand-bred gelding:

sixth of 15 in NH Flat race at Newbury in January: tailed off in similar event 3 months later: yet to race over hurdles or fences. *K. C. Bailey*

DUNDROMA 7 b.g. Callernish – River Dodo (Over The River (FR)) [1992/3 c23d³ c25d³ c22s³ c25d³ c24gF] workmanlike gelding: lightly-raced novice hurdler: modest form in novice chases: sold out of O. Sherwood's stable 1,200 gns Doncaster November Sales after second start: was suited by stamina test: acted on soft ground: dead. *R. Champion*   **c89** –

DUNDYVAN 11 ch.g. Crimson Beau – Flora Day (Floribunda) [1992/3 c25g c26dᵖᵘ] sturdy gelding: poor form in maiden hunter chases. *S. J. Leadbetter*   **c–** –

DUNEPRE (IRE) 5 b.g. Derring Rose – Shuil Suas (Menelek) [1992/3 F16v a24g⁶] third foal: dam, Irish NH Flat race winner, unplaced only outing over hurdles: tailed off in NH Flat race in January and novice claiming hurdle in February. *D. J. G. Murray-Smith*   –

DUNKERY BEACON 7 b.g. Casino Boy – Crown Member VII (Pedigree Unknown) [1992/3 c21sF c26vᵖᵘ c24dᵖᵘ c20f⁴ 23m⁶ 20m⁶ 23g] leggy gelding: no sign of ability over fences: novice hurdler: form only on good to firm going: trained until after second start by J. Roberts. *H. S. Howe*   **c–** **72**

DUNMAGLASS 6 b.g. Sayf El Arab (USA) – Stubble (Balidar) [1992/3 20dᵖᵘ] very lightly-raced maiden on Flat, little form: showed nothing in well-contested novice event in April on hurdling debut. *R. Ingram*   –

DUNMAIN GALE 8 b. or br.m. Strong Gale – Dunmain Stream (Paddy's Stream) [1992/3 c21mᵖᵘ c23gᵖᵘ c23dF] lengthy, workmanlike mare: third foal: dam unraced: no promise in steeplechases. *G. H. Peter-Hoblyn*   **c–**

DUNNICKS VIEW 4 b.g. Sula Bula – Country Magic (National Trust) [1992/3 16d⁵ 17m⁵] lengthy gelding: first foal: dam winning pointer: showed little in juvenile hurdles in February and March. *F. G. Tucker*   –

DUNNICKS WELL 4 ch.g. Sula Bula – Celtic Beauty (Celtic Cone) [1992/3 17vᵖᵘ] first foal: dam, winning hurdler/chaser, stayed well: showed nothing in juvenile hurdle at Newton Abbot in November. *F. G. Tucker*   –

DUNNOHALM 4 gr.f. Kalaglow – Counter Coup (Busted) [1992/3 F14m] half-sister to winning jumpers Halmajor (by Mandrake Major) and Bill And Coup (by Nicholas Bill) and NH Flat winner Amari Queen (also by Nicholas Bill): dam lightly raced: mid-division in NH Flat race at Market Rasen in March (whipped round start): yet to race over hurdles. *C. W. C. Elsey*   –

DUNRAVEN BAY 7 gr.g. Bay Express – Lydiate (Tower Walk) [1992/3 F14s³ F17d 16s 17m⁴ 16g⁶] big, good-bodied gelding: chasing type: easily best effort over hurdles when fourth in claimer at Newcastle in March: sold 5,200 gns Doncaster May Sales: will stay beyond 2m: acts on good to firm ground: sketchy jumper. *Mrs M. Reveley*   **96**

DUNRAVEN ROYAL 10 b.g. Le Bavard (FR) – Vulstar (Vulgan) [1992/3 c24vᵖᵘ c21vᵖᵘ c21v⁵ c26gᵖᵘ c29f³ c26g⁵] tall, leggy gelding: winning out-and-out stayer: has lost his form: usually blinkered: looks a difficult ride. *R. Curtis*   **c–**

DUNSTABLE (IRE) 5 b.g. Formidable (USA) – Dunoof (Shirley Heights) [1992/3 16f 16gᵖᵘ] sturdy gelding: of no account. *B. S. Rothwell*   –

DUNTREE 8 ch.g. Day Is Done – Bay Tree (FR) (Relko) [1992/3 c26v* c24dF c30sᵘʳ c29vF c29s⁴ c33gᵘʳ] tall gelding: put up useful performance when winning valuable sponsored handicap chase at Cheltenham in December, but failed to complete in 4 of his 5 subsequent starts: suited by good test of stamina: acts on heavy going: prone to bad mistakes. *D. Nicholson*   **c131 x**

DUO DROM 8 ch.m. Deep Run – Lady Dromara (Lord of Verona) [1992/3 c21sᵖᵘ c21s² c16v² c16s² c17s² c24g* c21d² c23d² c22d²] lengthy mare: fair hurdler: moderate form over fences: won novice event at Fakenham in February: also ran well on her other completed starts: effective at 2m to 3m: **c95**

acts on good to firm and heavy ground: sound jumper: consistent. *Mrs D. Haine*

DURHAM SUNSET 6 b.m. Callernish – Decent Downs (Decent Fellow) [1992/3 c20s pu] first foal: dam unraced half-sister to a winning chaser: pulled up before fourth in mares novice chase in November on debut. *J. H. Johnson*

c–

DURLEY SONG 7 gr.g. Cree Song – Donrae (Don (ITY)) [1992/3 20s pu 16s 16d 18g 17m] tall gelding: seems of little account. *Miss S. J. Turner*

–

DURRINGTON 7 b.g. Crooner – Glanfield (Eborneezer) [1992/3 17s* 24v4 18s 22v6 16d6 25d5 22v pu] leggy, workmanlike gelding: won novice hurdle at Newton Abbot in October: generally ran creditably afterwards, but poorly last start: effective around 2m and stays 3m: acts on heavy going. *M. J. Bolton*

85

DURSHAN (USA) 4 ch.c. Shahrastani (USA) – Dukayna (Northfields (USA)) [1992/3 18g5] middle-distance winner on Flat in Ireland, when trained by J. Oxx: showed some promise in novice event at Folkestone in March on hurdling debut: quite useful form on Flat afterwards: will improve over hurdles. *J. R. Jenkins*

– p

DUSKOMI 7 b.g. Bustomi – Damaring (USA) (Saidam) [1992/3 17g pu 17g ur 17d6] half-brother to several winners, including hurdler Personal Call (by Personality): dam 2-y-o 6f winner in USA: no sign of ability in novice hurdles. *G. A. Ham*

–

DUSTY MILLER 7 b.g. Current Magic – Royal Barb (Barbin) [1992/3 c20d* c20d2 c21s*] angular, workmanlike gelding: useful hurdler: showed progressive form in his 3 races over fences in 1992/3, winning novice chases at Newbury in November and Kempton (narrowly from Ashfold Copse) in December: reportedly suffered slight leg injury afterwards and wasn't seen out again: will stay beyond 2 1f: acts on heavy and good to firm going: sound jumper: will win more races over fences provided he makes a full recovery. *S. E. Sherwood*

c124 p
–

DUTCH AUCTION 9 b.g. Taufan (USA) – Mock Auction (Auction Ring (USA)) [1992/3 22m pu 2 1f pu] poor novice hurdler: has run in sellers: visored last 3 outings. *R. Johnson*

–

DUTCH BLUES 6 b.g. Dutch Treat – My Polyanna (Polyfoto) [1992/3 18d3 16v2 28d pu 2 1s pu] close-coupled, workmanlike gelding: winning selling hurdler: creditable efforts when placed in non-sellers in 1992/3: should stay beyond 2¼m: acts on heavy ground: blinkered once. *Mrs S. M. Austin*

77

DUTCH RHYMES 8 b.m. Rymer – Dutch Princess (Royalty) [1992/3 22v5 23v5] plain mare: very lightly raced over hurdles: better effort of 1992/3 on first start: should stay beyond 2¾m: acts on heavy going. *G. P. Enright*

73

DUTEST 6 b.h. Aragon – Indian Call (Warpath) [1992/3 F12d3 16d 16v3 17d5 17g2 16d5] smallish horse: fair 9f winner as 3-y-o for A. Stewart: poor novice hurdler: has raced only at around 2m: acts on heavy ground: blinkered last 2 starts. *M. C. Pipe*

80

DWADME 8 b.g. High Top – Durun (Run The Gantlet (USA)) [1992/3 c27s*] compact gelding: fairly useful staying hurdler when trained by O. Sherwood: won novice chase at Newton Abbot in October (dismounted after line, and wasn't seen out again): acts on good to firm and soft going: blinkered once in 1991/2. *R. J. O'Sullivan*

c96

DYD 5 b.m. Sulaafah (USA) – Wrekin Belle (Dance In Time (CAN)) [1992/3 16s 16v pu 17d6 16d] workmanlike gelding: poor form over hurdles. *F. Jordan*

–

DYFLIN 7 b.g. Red Sunset – Melka (Relko) [1992/3 c16f* c17d3 c16g3] workmanlike gelding: moderate hurdler: won novice chase at Worcester in September: creditable third at Cheltenham later in month, next and better subsequent effort: likely to prove best at around 2m: acts on firm and good to soft going: jumps fences soundly. *K. R. Burke*

c100
–

DYNAVON   7 b.m. Dynastic – Avon Melody (Bilsborrow) [1992/3 28m⁶] well beaten in 2 NH Flat races and a novice selling hurdle. *T. J. Carr*   –

E

EAGLE BID (IRE)   5 b.g. Auction Ring (USA) – Gay Folly (Wolver Hollow) [1992/3 16g 22g 20dᶠ 18d⁶ 23s⁵ a20g] good-bodied gelding: best effort in novice hurdles when sixth in novice event at Fontwell in October: stays 2¼m, not 23f. *S. Dow*   75

EAGLE CHATTER   5 b.m. Backchat (USA) – Joseagle (Jock Scot) [1992/3 F14s] half-sister to very smart 2m hurdler Humberside Lady (by Jellaby): dam never ran: well beaten in NH Flat race at Market Rasen in April: yet to race over hurdles or fences. *A. A. Hambly*

EAGLE ROCK (USA)   5 b.g. Green Dancer (USA) – Village Jazz (USA) (Stage Door Johnny) [1992/3 F16s* F16d* F16d³ F17m] close-coupled gelding: half-brother to a winner in USA by Topsider: dam won in USA: won NH Flat races at Listowel in September and Naas in November: in mid-division in valuable similar race at Cheltenham in March: yet to race over hurdles or fences. *L. Young, Ireland*

EAGLE TRACE   10 b.g. Derring Rose – Vulvic (Vulgan) [1992/3 c25gᵖᵘ] strong gelding: staying maiden hurdler/steeplechaser. *P. L. Southcombe*   c–
–

EALING COURT   4 ch.g. Blazing Saddles (AUS) – Fille de General (Brigadier Gerard) [1992/3 F16d⁴ F16d² F16d* F17f⁶ F16d⁴] workmanlike gelding: half-brother to 2 winners abroad: dam unraced: won NH Flat race at Navan in March: sixth of 15 in valuable similar event at Aintree in April: yet to race over hurdles. *Declan Gillespie, Ireland*

EARLHAM   7 ch.g. Kambalda – Arctic Raheen (Over The River (FR)) [1992/3 20d⁵ 22d³ c17sᴿ a22g³ a24g* 25gᶠ] moderate form over hurdles: won maiden at Southwell in March: refused at the fourth on chasing debut: was effective from 2¾m to 3m: acted on fibresand: sometimes visored (was unsuccessful): dead. *O. Brennan*   c–
85

EARLY BREEZE   7 b.g. Tumble Wind (USA) – Dawn Hail (Derring-Do) [1992/3 17d⁴ 16d⁶ 17s³ 17v a16g a16g⁵ 17g 17d³ 17g³ 16m] small gelding: poor hurdler nowadays: third in 2 sellers in April: suited by a sharp 2m: probably acts on any ground: often held up. *Mrs M. McCourt*   81

EARLY DRINKER   5 gr.g. Gabitat – Blow My Top (Some Hand) [1992/3 aF16g* F14g] leggy, unfurnished gelding: first foal: dam, 1m winner on Flat, moderate 2m novice hurdler: won 5-runner NH Flat race at Lingfield in February: seventh in 19-runner event at Market Rasen 2 months later: yet to race over hurdles or fences. *O. Sherwood*

EARLY GALES   4 b.f. Precocious – Galesa (Welsh Pageant) [1992/3 17dᵖᵘ] leggy filly: well beaten in 2 races on Flat: showed nothing in January on hurdling debut. *J. Pearce*   –

EARLY MAN   6 b.g. Mandalus – Early Start (Wrekin Rambler) [1992/3 23s* 23s² 25v* 20v* 20dᵖᵘ] lengthy gelding: chasing type: brother to Dat Train and half-brother to several other winning jumpers: dam unraced half-sister to useful chaser Southerly Buster: won novice hurdle at Folkestone in November and handicaps at Kempton in January and Plumpton in February: ran as though something amiss last start: effective at 2½m and stays 25f: acts on heavy going: not a fluent jumper as yet. *D. M. Grissell*   110

EARLY STAR   4 b.c. Precocious – Staritsa (USA) (Alleged (USA)) [1992/3 17d] quite good-topped colt: fair performer on Flat at around 1m when trained by T. Barron: always behind in juvenile hurdle at Taunton in February. *K. Bishop*   –

EARTHQUAICH   9 ch.g. Glen Quaich – City Red (Coppi) [1992/3 17vᵖᵘ c19dᶠ] of little account. *Mrs S. D. Williams*   c–
c–

EARTH SUMMIT 5 b.g. Celtic Cone – Win Green Hill (National Trust) [1992/3 F17g² F17m 25d⁶ 26d⁴ 21g 24s* 24gᵘʳ 24f] leggy gelding: third foal: half-brother to winning pointer Winnie Lorraine (by St Columbus): dam winning 17f chaser: won novice hurdle at Chepstow in April: stays well: acts on soft going, probably unsuited by firm. *N. A. Twiston-Davies*   101

EASBY HOPES 7 b.g. Full of Hope – Linden Dolly (Gulf Pearl) [1992/3 22m⁵ 22d* 22dᶠ 20vᵖᵘ] big, leggy gelding: type to make a chaser: won novice hurdle at Huntingdon in November: sold 4,600 gns Doncaster May Sales: effective at 2¾m and should stay 3m: acts on soft going: pulls hard: blinkered last start (ran badly). *S. E. Kettlewell*   85

EASBY JOKER 5 b.g. Idiot's Delight – Be Spartan (Spartan General) [1992/3 F17s F16v* F16s³ F17m] good-topped gelding: fifth foal: half-brother to NH Flat race winner Pennethorne Place (by Deep Run) and winning staying hurdler Baron Safeguard (by Baron Blakeney): dam unraced half-sister to a winning staying chaser: won NH Flat race at Hexham in December: third of 20 in similar event at Wetherby following month and seventh of 24 in valuable race at Cheltenham in March: yet to race over hurdles or fences. *S. E. Kettlewell*

EASBY MANDRINA 6 b.m. Mandalus – Deep Cristina (Deep Run) [1992/3 17d 16g 16sᵖᵘ 17m⁴] angular mare: modest hurdler: will stay further than 17f: suited by plenty of give in the ground. *S. E. Kettlewell*   87

EASBY ROC (IRE) 5 b.g. Bulldozer – Lady Mell (Milan) [1992/3 F14s⁶ aF16g F14s] fourth foal: half-brother to winning Irish jumpers Dismell (by Distinctly) and Mount Falcon (by Paico): dam won 2m hurdle in Ireland: has shown only a glimmer of ability in NH Flat races: yet to race over hurdles or fences. *S. E. Kettlewell*

EASTER BABY 7 ch.m. Derrylin – Saintly Miss (St Paddy) [1992/3 16v* 16sᵖᵘ] sparely-made mare: changed hands 625 gns Ascot December Sales: only form when winning mares novice hurdle at Towcester later in month. *P. D. Cundell*   91

EASTER LEE 13 b.g. Idiot's Delight – Stacy Lee (French Beige) [1992/3 c17m⁴ c18g⁴ c19mᶠ c24f⁵ c21gᶠ] tall, leggy gelding: fair hunter chaser in 1992: ran poorly in 1992/3, in handicaps first 3 starts when trained by R. Hodges: stays well: probably acts on any going. *J. W. Dufosee*   c– –

EASTERN EVENING 8 gr.g. Runnett – Sacola (Busted) [1992/3 c19gᵘʳ] lengthy, angular gelding: poor and inconsistent novice hurdler: third in a maiden point in February: unseated rider third following month on steeplechasing debut. *J. C. Poulton*   c– –

EASTERN MAGIC 5 b.h. Faustus (USA) – Hithermoor Lass (Red Alert) [1992/3 16s³ 17d² 16s² 17s² 18s³ a16g³ 16v] small, angular horse: fair handicap hurdler: ran creditably in 1992/3 until final start (first for 3 months): has raced only at around 2m: acts on soft going and equitrack: held up. *J. Akehurst*   103

EASTERN OASIS 10 b.g. Anax – Casbar Lady (Native Bazaar) [1992/3 17m⁵ 25g² 22g² c24g* c25d³ c25g²] small, short-backed gelding: fair hurdler nowadays: won novice handicap chase at Edinburgh in January: first race for 4 months, ran as though something amiss last outing: stays 3m: acts on any going. *J. Andrews*   c110 114

EASTERN PHOEBE 4 ch.f. Pharly (FR) – Damiya (FR) (Direct Flight) [1992/3 16sᵘʳ a16gᵖᵘ 18g 18g 16s] lengthy, sparely-made filly: half-sister to winning jumpers Scotoni (by Final Straw) and Kingfisher Bay (by Try My Best): behind in 2 outings on Flat: sold out of A. Stewart's stable 1,200 gns Nemarket Autumn Sales: no sign of ability over hurdles: resold 1,350 gns Doncaster June Sales. *R. E. Barr*   –

EASTERN PLEASURE 6 gr.g. Absalom – First Pleasure (Dominion) [1992/3 16d² 16g⁵ 23g³ 21v³ 26s³ 22d² 16v²] sturdy gelding: poor form over hurdles: close second in selling handicap last start (January): effective at 2m and stays 2¾m: acts on heavy going. *M. D. Hammond*   76

EASTERN STATESMAN 8 gr.h. El-Birillo – Eastern Faith (Crown Again) [1992/3 21dpu c22sur c24spu] workmanlike horse: third reported foal: half-brother to one-time smart hunter chaser Eastern Destiny (by Gay Baron): dam well beaten on Flat and over hurdles: showed little in novice hurdle and novice chases in first half of season. *R. J. Weaver* — c–

EASTERN WHISPER (USA) 6 gr.h. Arctic Tern (USA) – Mazyoun (USA) (Blushing Groom (FR)) [1992/3 17m] neat horse: winning 2m hurdler: no worthwhile form for a long time: blinkered final outing in 1991/2. *A. Moore* — —

EASTER TERM 5 b.m. Welsh Term – Silly Woman (Silly Season) [1992/3 17dpu 20gpu] probably of little account. *M. R. Channon* — —

EAST GALE 5 b.m. Oats – Rock Dodger (Sovereign Bill) [1992/3 17s3 16dpu] compact mare: first foal: dam unraced: some promise when third in novice hurdle at Bangor in November: pulled up lame at Windsor in February: wasn't seen out again. *S. Christian* — 74

EASTHORPE 5 b.g. Sweet Monday – Crammond Brig (New Brig) [1992/3 16g6 16spu 17s2 17g 17d* 17g2 16m6] smallish, sturdy gelding: first foal: dam fair staying hurdler: trained by M. W. Easterby first outing: modest form over hurdles: won novice event at Wolverhampton in February: creditable second there next start: acts on soft going: jumps well. *Miss H. C. Knight* — 98

EAST RIVER 9 b.g. Midland Gayle – French Note (Eton Rambler) [1992/3 c27gF c27f2] leggy, sparely-made gelding: inconsistent chaser: creditable second in amateurs handicap at Fontwell in October: stays 27f: acts on any going. *G. B. Balding* — c85 —

EASTSHAW 11 b.g. Crash Course – What A Duchess (Bargello) [1992/3 c24dpu c26dpu] lengthy gelding: useful chaser in 1991/2: ran badly both starts in 1992/3: effective at 2½m and stays 25f: acts on soft going and good to firm. *Capt. T. A. Forster* — c– —

EASY BUCK 6 b.g. Swing Easy (USA) – Northern Empress (Northfields (USA)) [1992/3 17d6 17d* 17v 17s3 17s2 16f 17g4 16f*] tall, good-topped gelding: type to make a chaser: useful hurdler: won handicaps at Ascot (valuable event) in November and Warwick (made all) in May: good efforts when placed in between: effective at 2m and will stay 2½m: acts on any ground, with possible exception of heavy. *N. A. Gaselee* — 131

EASY LIFE (IRE) 4 ch.c. Boyne Valley – Manna Rose (Bonne Noel) [1992/3 F14g] leggy, close-coupled colt: first foal: dam placed in Irish NH Flat races: well beaten in NH Flat race at Market Rasen in April: yet to race over hurdles. *D. E. Cantillon* — —

EASY OVER (USA) 7 ch.g. Transworld (USA) – Love Bunny (USA) (Exclusive Native (USA)) [1992/3 c22g3] leggy, workmanlike gelding: modest hurdler/novice chaser: ran creditably in hunter chase at Fakenham in March: won a point later in month: stays 2¾m: acts on any going: blinkered once. *Mrs Lucy Wadham* — c90 —

EASY PURCHASE 6 br.g. Swing Easy (USA) – Dauphiness (Supreme Sovereign) [1992/3 16m] tall gelding: plating-class middle-distance performer on Flat: no promise in novice hurdles: sold 925 gns Ascot September Sales after reappearance, resold 1,000 gns Ascot May Sales. *R. J. Holder* — —

EASY RHYTHM 6 b.g. Tudor Rhythm – Tiebell (Foggy Bell) [1992/3 F16s aF16g 22g] leggy gelding: second foal: brother to 5-y-o Just Woody: dam, fair hurdler, stayed 2¾m: unplaced in NH Flat races: showed nothing in maiden hurdle at Sedgefield. *B. M. Temple* — —

EAU D'ESPOIR 4 b.f. Monsanto (FR) – Hopeful Waters (Forlorn River) [1992/3 18f3 18f 18f3 17d2 16d* 16s3 20s2] small filly: half-sister to winning hurdler Comedy River (by Comedy Star): poor maiden on Flat, stays 1¼m: modest form over hurdles: won seller at Nottingham (bought in 4,800 gns) in November: ran creditably final start: stays 2½m: best form with plenty of give in the ground. *J. L. Spearing* — 87

EBONY GALE 7 br.g. Strong Gale – Vanessa's Princess (Laurence O) [1992/3 22v* 25s4 25vpu 25d5 22d] rather leggy, workmanlike gelding: improved form when winning handicap hurdle at Fontwell in December: below that afterwards: suited by good test of stamina: acts on heavy going: sometimes runs in snatches and may benefit from blinkers. *Mrs J. Pitman*   115

EBONY ISLE 4 gr.f. Grey Desire – Clairwood (Final Straw) [1992/3 16gpu 16g6] small, close-coupled filly: seems of little account: sold 1,450 gns Doncaster March Sales. *Miss L. A. Perratt*   –

EBONY JANE 8 br.m. Roselier (FR) – Advantage (Perspex) [1992/3 c18s4 c24v2 c24dF c26v2 c24d2 c25d2 c29s* c25g4]   **c142**

Sixth to Vanton in 1992, Ebony Jane won the Jameson Irish Grand National at the second attempt, holding on well by a length from the fast-finishing outsider Rust Never Sleeps after racing prominently from the start, jumping into the lead at the third last and repelling a challenge from the favourite Zeta's Lad who eventually came third. Thirteen of the twenty-seven starters completed the course but the event turned out rather less competitive than it promised to be, for most of the better-fancied horses apart from Zeta's Lad and Ebony Jane (she was co-second favourite with Rushing Wild) failed to complete. Royal Athlete and Cool Ground were among the early casualties; front-running Rushing Wild broke his pelvis and was pulled up before the sixteenth; Sibton Abbey, never a factor, lasted a bit longer before he, too, was pulled up. Nevertheless, take nothing away from the genuine and consistent Ebony Jane. She had been in great form and had finished a close second in four of her previous five races, including a couple of Irish jumping's important handicaps, the Thyestes Chase at Gowran Park and the Harold Clarke Leopardstown Chase; there was only a short head between Zeta's Lad and her at Gowran Park, only half a length between Garamycin and her at Leopardstown where the winner, one of the best chasers in Ireland, conceded 21 lb. A fall interrupted the sequence of

Jameson Irish Grand National, Fairyhouse—Ebony Jane is clear at the last

Mr James Lynch's "Ebony Jane"

seconds, but usually Ebony Jane can be relied upon to get round, and she jumped soundly throughout in the Irish National. Tough, as well as genuine and consistent, Ebony Jane was pulled out again at Punchestown two weeks after running at Fairyhouse and finished an excellent fourth to Bishops Hall under a penalty in another valuable chase.

			Misti IV	Medium
	Roselier (FR)		(br 1958)	Mist
	(b 1973)		Peace Rose	Fastnet Rock
Ebony Jane			(gr 1959)	La Paix
(br.m. 1985)			Perspex	Persian Gulf
	Advantage		(ch 1958)	Tropical Sun
	(ch 1969)		Countess Charmere	Chamier
			(br 1963)	Marennes

Ebony Jane's dam Advantage is a half-sister to the 1984 Grand National fifth Earthstopper, a very useful horse who unfortunately collapsed and died after that race. Several other winning jumpers come from the same mare, Countess Charmere, and Advantage herself won eight point-to-points. Ebony Jane became Advantage's second winner when she also won a point-to-point in 1990; her half-sister Sexton's Service (by The Parson) had set the ball rolling in a two-and-a-half-mile hurdle at Tralee two years earlier. A good test of stamina suits Ebony Jane. Regarded as needing some give in the ground by connections, she has done all her racing so far on an easy surface, plenty of it on soft or heavy ground. She races up with the pace. Reportedly, her next campaign will be geared towards a bid for the Martell Grand National at Aintree. *F. Flood, Ireland*

EBONY SWELL 12 b.g. Eborneezer – Jenysis (Compensation) [1992/3 c22s c33v6 c24s5 c25s] sparely-made gelding: fair chaser at his best: well beaten in 1992/3: stays 3m: acts on any going. *S. W. Campion*

c–

EBORNEEZER'S DREAM 10 ch.g. Eborneezer – Portate (Articulate) [1992/3 c18g6 c25m5 c17g] workmanlike gelding: poor novice hurdler/chaser: probably stays 3m: blinkered once. *Mrs S. Lamyman*

c–
–

EBORNY JACK 11 b.g. Eborneezer – Cliff House (Articulate) [1992/3 c23m4 c26g5 c23g5 c25g6] sturdy gelding: poor form in early-season novice chases. *J. R. Bosley*

c74

EBRO 7 ch.g. Aragon – Caribbean Blue (Blue Cashmere) [1992/3 c21dpu c16dpu] lengthy gelding: seems of little account. *V. Thompson*

c–
–

ECOSSAIS DANSEUR (USA) 7 ch.g. Arctic Tern (USA) – Northern Blossom (CAN) (Snow Knight) [1992/3 a16gpu a16g5] small, angular gelding: modest hurdler in 1991/2: showed nothing in 1992/3: best form at 2m: acts on good to firm and good to soft ground: blinkered last 5 starts. *E. T. Buckley*

–

EDBERG 9 b. or br.g. Strong Gale – White Shoes (Tiepolo II) [1992/3 c21d* c21d6 c16s5] lengthy gelding: useful chaser: impressive winner of handicap at Sandown in October: below form afterwards: effective from 2m to 3m: acted on any going: usually jumped well: was game and genuine: dead. *J. H. Johnson*

c132
–

EDDIE KYBO 8 ch.g. Cidrax (FR) – Claragh Run (Deep Run) [1992/3 18f5 19m2 18f2 18drtr 22s 20f6 17vpu] sparely-made gelding: moderate handicap hurdler: runner-up twice in September, but gave trouble at start afterwards and refused to race once: stays 2½m: acts on any ground: held up: one to treat with caution. *G. F. Edwards*

98 §

EDDIES FELLA 8 b.g. New Member – Daniel's Fancy (Cheveley Lad) [1992/3 c17dur 17s c25gF c25spu 23spu] tall, leggy gelding: poor novice selling hurdler: yet to complete over fences. *A. P. Jones*

c–
–

EDDIES WELL 10 ch.m. Torus – Random Belle (Random Shot) [1992/3 c20g6 c24d6 c20m4 c26g5 c24d] lengthy, sparely-made mare: poor chaser nowadays: sold 4,000 gns Doncaster October Sales. *Miss Z. A. Green*

c–
–

EDDIE WALSHE 8 b.g. Smackover – Ashmore Lady (Ashmore (FR)) [1992/3 16m5 16m6 16g6 16m2 c16d 16g3 20g2 16g 16spu 17g6 18gpu] close-coupled, well-made ex-Irish gelding: first foal: dam ran once: handicap hurdler: sold out of D. Kiely's stable 4,000 gns Doncaster October Sales after sixth start: creditable second at Ayr in November, best effort in Britain: poor form on chasing debut: sold 2,800 gns Doncaster May Sales: pulls hard and barely stays 2½m: acts on good to firm ground. *D. Moffatt*

c–
99 d

EDENGEM 5 b.g. Green Ruby (USA) – Step Softly (St Chad) [1992/3 F17m 16dpu] leggy gelding: seventh living foal: half-brother to 4 winners, including hurdler Doucement (by Cheval), who stayed well: dam won 3m novice chase: behind in NH Flat race and a novice hurdle. *M. A. Barnes*

–

EDEN'S CLOSE 4 ch.g. Green Dancer (USA) – Royal Agreement (USA) (Vaguely Noble) [1992/3 17g4 17g* 17g2 17v 17s5 17g4 16g3 17m] leggy, angular gelding: fair middle-distance performer on Flat: quite a useful hurdler: won at Newbury in October: good efforts in well-contested events fifth to seventh starts: yet to race beyond 17f: acts on soft going: visored seventh outing. *M. H. Tompkins*

119

EDEN STREAM 6 b.g. Paddy's Stream – Surplus Silk (Redundant) [1992/3 F16d] first foal: dam of little account: tailed off in NH Flat race at Haydock in February: yet to race over hurdles or fences. *B. C. Morgan*

–

EDEN SUNSET 7 ch.g. Over The River (FR) – Last Sunset (Deep Run) [1992/3 c26d2] workmanlike gelding: poor maiden hurdler/pointer: second in maiden hunter chase at Cartmel in May, showing fair form. *Richard Collins*

c84
–

Mr S. R. Webb's "Egypt Mill Prince"

EDGE OF THE GLEN 5 b.g. Alleging (USA) – Scotch Bonnet
(Supreme Sovereign) [1992/3 17v* 17s^{pu} 20m⁵] seems of little account on
Flat: won conditional jockeys selling hurdle at Plumpton (no bid) in
February: respectable effort last outing: probably stays 2½m: acts on heavy
and probably on good to firm going. *R. J. Hodges*   76

EDIMBOURG 7 b.h. Top Ville – Miss Brodie (FR) (Margouillat (FR))
[1992/3 c16v^F c16v³ c21d c24g^{pu}] tall, light-framed, narrow horse: poor
novice hurdler/chaser: should prove suited by further than 2m: acts on
heavy ground: pulled hard when visored once. *T. J. Etherington*   c79
–

EDIREPUS 5 b.g. Lightning Dealer – Pentland Beauty (Remainder Man)
[1992/3 16s³ F10d³ 17d³] leggy, workmanlike gelding: maiden on Flat:
better effort in novice hurdles on second start, at Stratford in November:
will prove best over sharp 2m: has room for improvement in his jumping.
Mrs M. Reveley   83

EDWARD LEAR (USA) 7 b.g. Lear Fan (USA) – Coed (USA) (Ribot)
[1992/3 16d^{pu}] angular, sparely-made gelding: selling hurdler: no form since
1990/1: blinkered last 2 starts 1991/2. *J. G. FitzGerald*   –

EDWARD SEYMOUR (USA) 6 b.g. Northern Baby (CAN) – Regal
Leader (USA) (Mr Leader (USA)) [1992/3 16d 17s² 16v⁵ 16s* 17s³ 16d 17m²]   93

leggy gelding: won conditional jockeys selling hurdle at Ludlow (bought in 6,800 gns) in January: ran well when placed in non-sellers afterwards: raced only at around 2m: acts on good to firm and heavy going. *W. Jenks*

EDWINA'S DELIGHT 4 b.f. Idiot's Delight – Edwina's Dawn (Space King) [1992/3 18gpu] eighth living foal: half-sister to NH Flat race winner/novice jumper Gymcrak Dawn (by Rymer): dam unraced daughter of a successful staying chaser: no promise in juvenile hurdle at Cartmel in August: sold 1,800 gns Doncaster September Sales. *D. McCain* —

EGYPT MILL PRINCE 7 b.g. Deep Run – Just Darina (Three Dons) [1992/3 c18d² c16d* 17v⁵ c17m* c21m³] big, rangy gelding: useful hurdler: impressive winner of Coventry Novices' Chase at Cheltenham in November, but unimpressive when landing odds at Towcester in May (first race for 5 months): good third in valuable novice event at Warwick later in May: stays 21f when conditions aren't testing: acts on good to firm and heavy going: pulls hard, tends to hang and sometimes finds little: blinkered last 4 starts. *Mrs J. Pitman* **c120** —

EID (USA) 4 b.g. Northern Baby (CAN) – Millracer (USA) (Le Fabuleux) [1992/3 17m⁴ 17d³ 16g² 18g³ 16g⁶ 17m³ 17m] small, good-topped gelding: fair handicapper at around 1m on Flat: sold out of D. Morley's stable 14,000 gns Newmarket July Sales: easily best efforts in juvenile hurdles on third and fifth starts, both at Kempton: out of depth when blinkered last outing: unreliable. *Martyn Meade* **111 §**

EIGHTEENTHIRTYFOUR (IRE) 5 b.h. Ballad Rock – Weavers' Tack (Weavers' Hall) [1992/3 16vpu] smallish, close-coupled horse: lightly raced and no worthwhile form on Flat: no sign of ability in novice event in February on hurdling debut. *A. Moore* —

EIGHTY EIGHT 8 b.g. Doctor Wall – Pennulli (Sir Nulli) [1992/3 c16d c20spu c21spu c20dpu c19f⁴ c21f⁶] plain gelding: of no account. *Mrs H. B. Dowson* **c–** —

ELABJER (USA) 4 b.g. Shadeed (USA) – Glamour Girl (FR) (Riverman (USA)) [1992/3 16m² 17m² 16m³ 17mpu] small gelding: lightly-raced maiden on Flat: modest form when placed over hurdles: dead. *P. D. Evans* **90**

ELAINE TULLY (IRE) 5 b.m. Persian Bold – Hanna Alta (FR) (Busted) [1992/3 17g⁵] neat mare: half-sister to winning jumper Belmoredean (by Be My Guest): fairly useful middle-distance stayer on Flat, successful in 1993: well beaten in quite well-contested novice event at Newbury in March on hurdling debut: should do better. *M. J. Heaton-Ellis* **– p**

ELDER PRINCE 7 ch.g. Final Straw – Particular Miss (Luthier) [1992/3 16m 18d 18d 20s] sparely-made gelding: fair hurdler at his best: ran poorly in 1992/3: sold 4,100 gns Doncaster May Sales: winning chaser but is often let down by his jumping: best around 2m: acts on good to firm and soft ground. *M. H. Easterby* **c– x** —

ELECKYDO 4 ch.f. Electric – Deed (Derring-Do) [1992/3 18d² 16g⁶ 18spu] poor maiden on Flat and over hurdles. *R. J. Hodges* **67**

ELECTRA LAD 7 ch.g. Le Moss – Rekin Gold (Wrekin Rambler) [1992/3 c24sF] strong, deep-girthed gelding: behind in 2 NH Flat races in Ireland: fair pointer: had just been headed by winner when falling 3 out in hunter chase at Ludlow (would have finished second) in April: jumped well prior to departing and should do better. *J. N. Cheatle* **c85 p**

ELECTRIC BUCK 5 b.m. Electric – Buckbe (Ragstone) [1992/3 20v² 18v⁴ 22mF] good-topped mare: first foal: dam useful jumper who stayed 29f: would have run well but for falling last in novice hurdle at Fontwell in February: will prove suited by test of stamina. *R. H. Alner* **83**

ELECTRIC VALLEY (IRE) 5 gr.m. Electric – Trois Vallees (Ile de Bourbon (USA)) [1992/3 F17v] second foal: half-sister to a poor animal by Persian Bold: dam, granddaughter of smart sprinter Bas Bleu, 1¼m winner: tailed off in NH Flat race at Newton Abbot in November: yet to race over hurdles or fences. *W. G. M. Turner*

ELECTROJET 5 b.m. Electric – Shy Talk (Sharpen Up) [1992/3 17dpu] sturdy mare: showed a little ability in 2m selling hurdles in 1991/2, none in November: pulls hard. *A. W. Jones* –

ELEGANT BERTIE 4 ch.g. Relkino – Arctic Elegance (Articulate) [1992/3 F16f⁴ F17f] sixth foal: dam well beaten in juvenile hurdle: fourth of 6 in NH Flat race at Wincanton in March: well beaten in similar race in May: yet to race over hurdles. *J. L. Spearing*

ELEGANT FRIEND 5 ch.g. Music Boy – Cardinal Palace (Royal Palace) [1992/3 17gᵖᵘ 17sᵘʳ 17gᵇᵈ 16v² a18g³ 18d* 17g* 17d³ 17gF] sparely-made gelding: half-brother to winning hurdler/chaser Sharp Order (by Sharpo): modest performer on Flat, stays 1¼m: retained 2,400 gns Newmarket Autumn Sales after first start over hurdles: successful in selling handicaps at Market Rasen (bought in 5,000 gns) in January and Fakenham (no bid) in March: good third in novice handicap last completed start: unlikely to stay beyond 2¼m: acts on dead going and fibresand. *M. H. Tompkins* 96

ELEGANT LASS 7 ch.m. Adonijah – Elegante (Frankincense) [1992/3 17g] compact mare: no form over hurdles, including in seller. *B. Smart* –

ELEGANT LORD (IRE) 5 ch.g. Lord Ha Ha – Giolla Sheen (Giolla Mear) [1992/3 c25d²] sturdy gelding: fifth foal: half-brother to a winning jumper in Italy by General Ironside: dam unraced daughter of a winning chaser: sold IR 22,000 gns Fairyhouse June Sales after winning only start in points in 1992: won another point in Ireland in March: made tremendously promising hunter chase debut at Punchestown following month, running odds-on Kerry Orchid to ¾ length after joining winner on bridle at the last: looks a good hunter chaser in making. *E. Bolger, Ireland* c110 P

ELEGANT MARY 9 gr.m. Grey Ghost – Mary McQuaker (Acer) [1992/3 c16s c24gᵘʳ c21g⁶] strong mare: winning 2m hurdler: very lightly raced and no worthwhile form for a long time, including over fences. *W. L. Barker* c– –

ELEGANT STRANGER 8 b.g. Krayyan – Tumvella (Tumble Wind (USA)) [1992/3 c21m² c22gF] smallish, workmanlike gelding: fair hurdler: modest novice chaser: stayed 2 1f: acted on any going: visored twice: dead. *J. M. Turner* c70 +

ELEGANT TOUCH 4 b. or br.f. Elegant Air – Teye (Mummy's Pet) [1992/3 18d⁴ 16g 16s⁶ 17d² 16v³ 17m⁶] leggy, sparely-made filly: half-sister to winning hurdler Aber Cothi (by Dominion): modest handicapper, stays 1¼m, on Flat: novice selling hurdler: ran badly last outing (blinkered first time): changed hands 3,300 gns Ascot June Sales: likely to prove best around 2m: acts on heavy going: sometimes wears tongue strap. *M. C. Pipe* 73

ELFAST 10 b.g. Neltino – Niagara Rhythm (Military) [1992/3 c21v c21d⁶ c16s³] rather leggy gelding: handicap chaser, quite useful form at best in 1992/3: seemed to take little interest when held up last outing (January): seems suited by 2m to 2½m: probably acts on any going: usually jumps well. *J. Webber* c125 –

ELFIE'S SON 9 b.h. Sonnen Gold – Elf Trout (Elf-Arrow) [1992/3 c21sᵇᵈ 23sᵖᵘ 16vᵖᵘ] sturdy horse: poor novice hurdler: showed nothing in 1992/3, including in seller: sold 2,000 gns Ascot June Sales: has failed to complete course over fences. *Miss K. M. George* c– –

ELGIN 4 b.g. Lochnager – Targos Delight (Targowice (USA)) [1992/3 18d 16g* 16s⁵ 16g⁶ 20g] workmanlike gelding: half-brother to selling hurdler Miami Holiday (by Miami Springs): poor maiden on Flat, suited by 7f, when trained by A. Bailey: made all in 7-runner juvenile hurdle at Ayr in November: well below that afterwards: difficult to assess. *J. K. M. Oliver* 98 ?

ELIOT 5 b.m. Silly Prices – Elitist (Keren) [1992/3 16s 21g 22dᵖᵘ] compact mare: no sign of ability over hurdles: dead. *N. Chamberlain* –

ELISSA 7 ch.m. Tap On Wood – Blakewood (Blakeney) [1992/3 18dʳᵒ 18d 16s c17sᵘʳ a16gᵖᵘ] leggy, plain mare: of little account: has twice run out. *G. P. Kelly* c– – §

ELITE BOY 11 ch.g. Deep Run – Elite Lady (Prince Hansel) [1992/3 c90
c21gᵖᵘ c16d4 c19g* c20s4 c21gᵖᵘ c19g3] lengthy, shallow-girthed gelding: –
moderate handicap chaser: made all at Hereford in March: easily best
subsequent effort on last outing: stayed 2½m: acted on firm and dead going:
sound jumper: dead. *D. McCain*

ELITE DESIGN 6 b. or br.g. Tender King – Lanata (Charlottown)
[1992/3 21g2 24f3 20s2 25d6 20g2 21d] leggy, sparely-made gelding: modest   85
novice hurdler: stays 3m: acts on firm and soft ground: visored second to
fourth starts: none too consistent. *O. Brennan*

ELITE LEO 8 b.g. Longleat (USA) – Abielle (Abwah) [1992/3 17s2 17g3   c– p
c16gF c18sF c16sᵘʳ] sturdy gelding: poor novice hurdler: showed promise   75
but failed to complete over fences: effective at 2m and stays 2¾m: acts on
soft going. *P. J. Hobbs*

ELITE REG 4 b.g. Electric – Coppice (Pardao) [1992/3 18d2 17s* 16v*   122
17g* 21d4 17sᵖᵘ 17d2 20f* 17f* 22f* 22f2] sparely-made gelding:
half-brother to winning hurdler Parbold Hill (by Carwhite): poor maiden on
Flat: claimed out of C. Egerton's stable £6,001 first start over hurdles: did
well subsequently and won selling hurdle at Aintree (no bid), juvenile event
at Warwick and novice handicap at Doncaster in first half of season, and
claimers at Haydock and Chepstow and novice handicap at Worcester in
May: effective at 2m and stays 2¾m: acts on any going: blinkered: tough:
front runner. *M. C. Pipe*

ELIZABETHAN AIR 4 b.f. Elegant Air – Lizabeth Chudleigh (Imperial
Fling (USA)) [1992/3 16vᵖᵘ 17d3 17gF] leggy, lengthy filly: half-sister to   71
winning Irish hurdler Jonja's Chudleigh (by Aragon): modest miler on Flat:
sold out of A. Lee's stable 600 gns Newmarket Autumn Sales: poor form
when third in juvenile hurdle at Taunton in February. *A. J. Chamberlain*

ELLAFITZETTY (IRE) 4 b.f. Ela-Mana-Mou – Etty (Relko) [1992/3
16m3] half-sister to winning hurdler Aunt Etty (by Record Token): dam   72
1¼m winning half-sister to useful staying jumper Sporting Mariner:
claimed out of F. J. Houghton's stable £3,430 after winning 2m claimer on
Flat in July: poor form when third in juvenile selling hurdle at Worcester in
August: sold 750 gns Newmarket Autumn Sales. *M. C. Pipe*

ELLERTON HILL 10 br.g. Potent Councillor – Kenny (Royal Pennant) c102 +
[1992/3 c21g* c24m* c22m2 c25m* c28fᵘʳ] angular gelding: successful in   –
hunter chases at Leicester (maiden), Newcastle and Market Rasen (both
novices) in 1993: only defeat in completed starts by Sheer Jest at Stratford:
stays 25f: acts on good to firm going: forces pace: jumps well. *Mrs Jean
Brown*

ELLTEE-ESS 8 ch.g. Lighter – Verosina (Lord of Verona) [1992/3   c86 x
c21m4 c20mF c23g3 c22m4 c23f* c23gᵖᵘ c26gᵖᵘ c21g3 c17g2 c21dᵖᵘ a20g6]   –
close-coupled gelding: handicap hurdler: jumped poorly over fences except
when 20-length winner of novice event at Worcester in September: ran well
when placed afterwards: needs further than 2m and stays 23f: acts on firm
ground and fibresand: best without blinkers over hurdles, wore them third
to sixth and last 3 starts over fences. *R. J. Weaver*

ELMO 7 b.m. Sunyboy – Elmolyn (St Elmo) [1992/3 21vᵖᵘ 22f] lengthy
mare: no sign of ability over hurdles: sold 1,400 gns Ascot May Sales. *S. E.   –
Sherwood*

ELSA 4 gr.f. Green Ruby (USA) – Classey (Dubassoff (USA)) [1992/3
16m5 20m* 21f3 22f] poor plater on Flat: trained first start over hurdles by   80
R. Holder: won maiden hurdle at Exeter in May: below that last 2 outings:
stays 2½m: acts on good to firm ground: visored last 3 starts. *P. G. Murphy*

ELSHARH (IRE) 4 br.c. Sure Blade (USA) – Urjwan (USA) (Seattle
Slew (USA)) [1992/3 17m4] poor maiden on Flat, third at 1m: fourth of 8   65
finishers in selling hurdle at Bangor in July: sold 1,400 gns Ascot September
Sales. *J. A. Glover*

ELVERCONE 12 b.g. Celtic Cone – Capelena (Mon Fetiche) [1992/3   c– §
22gᵖᵘ c25f4 c22f] lengthy gelding: staying chaser: no form in 1992/3 (trained   – §

first start by A. J. Wilson), though won a point in April: best visored, blinkered once: reluctant. *D. Mills*

ELVER SEASON   10 b.m. Vital Season – Capelena (Mon Fetiche) [1992/3 24s] fairly useful hunter chaser at best: tailed off in novice event in April on hurdling debut: stays 25f: unsuited by firm going, acts well on soft. *R. H. Alner*

c–
–

ELVETT BRIDGE (IRE)   5 b.g. Sallust – Mamie's Joy (Prince Tenderfoot (USA)) [1992/3 18mᵖᵘ] compact gelding: novice hurdler: has run in a seller: pulled up only outing of season (September): races only at around 2m: acts on dead and good to firm ground. *D. R. Franks*

–

EL VOLADOR   6 br.h. Beldale Flutter (USA) – Pharjoy (FR) (Pharly (FR)) [1992/3 16s² 17d* 17d² 18m*] workmanlike horse: lightly-raced hurdler: won novice events at Taunton in November and Fontwell (comfortably) in March: also ran well in between: stays 2¼m: acts on soft and good to firm going: should continue to progress. *R. J. O'Sullivan*

99 p

ELWADI   6 b.g. Vaigly Great – Final Act (Decoy Boy) [1992/3 18sᵖᵘ 23s⁶ a20g³ a24gᶠ a22g a18g⁵ c24fᵘʳ c21gᵖᵘ] poor novice hurdler: has failed to complete over fences: tried visored, blinkered last start. *R. P. C. Hoad*

c–
70

ELWAZIR (USA)   4 b. or br.c. The Minstrel (CAN) – Romeo's Coquette (USA) (Gallant Romeo (USA)) [1992/3 16vᵖᵘ a16gᴿ 18mᵘʳ] small colt: modest maiden at best on Flat, sold out of P. Walwyn's stable 4,000 gns Newmarket July Sales: no form over hurdles: temperamental. *D. Marks*

§§

ELZEE'S LIABILITY (USA)   5 b.g. Cormorant (USA) – Raise The Bridge (USA) (Raise A Cup (USA)) [1992/3 17mᵘʳ] rangy gelding: no sign of ability in NH Flat race and novice hurdle. *A. J. K. Dunn*

–

EMERALD CHARM (IRE)   5 b.m. Mister Lord (USA) – Ko Mear (Giolla Mear) [1992/3 F16d] fourth foal: dam no sign of ability in NH Flat race and 2 races over hurdles: behind in NH Flat race at Ayr January: yet to race over hurdles or fences. *J. I. A. Charlton*

EMERALD HILL   8 b.g. Wolverlife – Emmerdale (Star Gazer) [1992/3 21f 22g 20gᵖᵘ 21d] lengthy, angular gelding: lightly-raced winning 2m hurdler in Ireland: behind all starts in 1992/3: sold 1,000 gns Ascot May Sales: tried blinkered/visored. *B. Stevens*

–

EMERALD MOON   6 b.g. Auction Ring (USA) – Skyway (Skymaster) [1992/3 19g³ 17g* 17d] sparely-made gelding: won selling handicap hurdle at Taunton (no bid) in November: ran poorly in non-seller later in month and wasn't seen out again: stays 19f: acts on good to firm and soft ground. *W. G. Turner*

72

EMERALD RULER   6 b.g. Tender King – Blue Gulf (Gay Fandango (USA)) [1992/3 16g* c18gᶠ 22s² 22v³ 17d² 22v⁶] sturdy gelding: chasing type: won novice hurdle at Worcester in September: better efforts when placed subsequently: fell eighth on chasing debut: not seen out after December: stays 2¾m: acts on good to firm and heavy going: blinkered twice in 1991/2: races up with pace. *J. Webber*

c–
104

EMERALD STORM   6 br.g. Strong Gale – Emerald Flair (Flair Path) [1992/3 16s* 17s³ 22d³ 18f³ 17g] lengthy gelding: first foal: dam, successful at around 1½m on Flat in Ireland, half-sister to 2 winning jumpers, notably very useful chaser Southern Minstrel: odds on, easy winner of novice hurdle at Warwick in December: best subsequent effort on third start: stays 2¾m: acts on soft going. *N. J. Henderson*

93

EMERALD SUNSET   8 b.g. Red Sunset – Kelly's Curl (Pitskelly) [1992/3 24s⁶ 25g* 26dᶠ 25s 25v⁵ 25g] sparely-made gelding: fair handicap hurdler: won at Newbury in October: below form subsequently (trained until after fifth start by A. Davison): suited by long distances and give in the ground. *Miss S. L. Gallie*

115 d

EMERALD VENTURE   6 b.g. Seclude (USA) – No Time For Tears (Grange Melody) [1992/3 20g³ 22s² 16f³ 16d⁴ 16d⁵] leggy gelding: poor

83

novice hurdler: stays 2¾m: probably acts on any going: visored nowadays. *T. H. Caldwell*

EMILY'S STAR 6 b.m. Comedy Star (USA) – Emily Kent (Royal Palace) [1992/3 21g* 22s* 22m2 25g* 24d3 c22v* c23vpu c24s4 c26v4 c27d3 c32mF] lengthy, workmanlike mare: fair hurdler/chaser: successful in novice hurdles at Perth, Newton Abbot and Wetherby and novice handicap chase at Nottingham in first half of season: destroyed after falling at Cheltenham in March: was suited by thorough test of stamina: acted on good to firm and heavy going: needed plenty of driving: blinkered last 4 outings. *N. A. Twiston-Davies*

c101
104

EMMA VICTORIA 5 b.m. Dominion – Gwiffina (Welsh Saint) [1992/3 16v a20gpu 17s4 16gF 17v4 20d5 20mpu] leggy mare: poor novice hurdler: tailed off when pulled up in a seller last start: sold out of Miss L. Siddall's stable 2,600 gns Doncaster January Sales after third outing. *R. Brotherton*

62

EMPEROR ALEXANDER (IRE) 5 b.g. Tender King – Persian Apple (USA) (No Robbery) [1992/3 a18g5 17dur] sparely-made gelding: middle-distance performer on Flat, fair at best: showed some ability when fifth of 15 in novice hurdle at Southwell in January. *N. A. Smith*

78

EMPEROR BUCK (IRE) 5 b.g. Buckskin (FR) – Gilded Empress (Menelek) [1992/3 F16s4 F17m2 F17f* F17f5] rather unfurnished gelding: has scope: half-brother to 2 winning jumpers, including quite useful hurdler/chaser Bishops Island (by The Parson): dam lightly-raced maiden: won 18-runner NH Flat race at Sandown in March: fifth of 15 in similar event at Aintree in April: yet to race over hurdles or fences. *D. Nicholson*

EMPEROR CHANG (USA) 6 b.g. Wavering Monarch (USA) – Movin Mitzi (USA) (L'Heureux (USA)) [1992/3 20m5 20m2 20gpu 17d4 21s3 22g3 22g*] sturdy gelding: game winner of novice handicap hurdle at Nottingham in March: trained until after third start by R. Hollinshead: stays 2¾m: suited by a sound surface. *G. Barnett*

93

EMPERORS WARRIOR 7 ch.g. High Line – Cocoban (Targowice (USA)) [1992/3 22g2 20g5] lengthy gelding: moderate novice hurdler: poor form in sellers in October: suited by around 2¾m: acts on good to soft and good to firm ground: blinkered final outing in 1991/2, visored last start. *C. D. Broad*

81

EMRAL MAID 6 b.m. Royal Palace – Morstons Maid (Morston (FR)) [1992/3 F16d 23spu] light-framed mare: tailed off in NH Flat races: made mistakes and was tailed off when pulled up in conditional jockeys novice hurdle in January. *R. E. Peacock*

–

EMRAL MISS 5 b.m. Scorpio (FR) – Sugar Loch (Lochnager) [1992/3 F16d F17g] fourth foal: dam 1m winner: well beaten in NH Flat races: yet to race over hurdles or fences. *G. Richards*

EMRYS 10 ch.g. Welsh Pageant – Sun Approach (Sun Prince) [1992/3 17m3 17m3 c16f* c17d4 c18mpu c16g* c17m4 c18m*] sparely-made gelding: winning hurdler: modest form over fences, winner of handicaps at Worcester in September, Hereford (novices) in March and novice claimer at Exeter in May: suited by around 2m: acts on firm and dead ground: pulls hard and makes running. *D. Burchell*

c97
–

EMSBOY 5 b.g. Lidhame – Fille de Phaeton (Sun Prince) [1992/3 17g4 17s* 23g 16sF 18s3 a18g 18m2 20m* 17d* 17m3 18dpu] small, sparely-made gelding: modest hurdler: won novice event at Newton Abbot in October and novice sellers (no bid both times) at Hereford in March and April: stayed 2½m: acted on good to firm and soft going: often blinkered: sometimes looked none too keen: dead. *P. D. Cundell*

93 §

EMSEE-H 8 br.g. Paddy's Stream – Kincsem (Nelcius) [1992/3 c21d3 c16g5 c17g* c21d2 c21d* c21s2 c21dpu c16s* c20spu c16d4 c16g* c21mur c20s3 c16g] workmanlike gelding: fairly useful chaser: won handicaps at Huntingdon (2) in first half of season and Sandown in January, and minor event at Kempton in February: well below form last 2 outings: effective from 2m to 2½m: acts on any going: jumps to the right (has won only on

c123
–

255

Emblem Chase, Kempton—
Emsee-H (centre) rallies to beat Cyphrate (right) and Setter Country

right-handed tracks): usually forces pace: sometimes breaks blood vessels: genuine. *F. Murphy*

ENBORNE LAD 9 gr.g. Celtic Cone – Blue Delphinium (Quorum) [1992/3 21d⁶ 25v 22v 21s⁵ 21f 22f 21m] small, sturdy gelding: moderate hurdler: best effort of season on sixth start: probably stays 3m and acts on any going: often blinkered. *G. P. Enright* — 87

ENCHANTED FLYER 6 b.g. Doulab (USA) – Enchanted (Song) [1992/3 18mᶠ 16g⁵ 17m⁵ 18s⁵ 16m² 16d 16s 17g³ 17gᶠ 16f] leggy, close-coupled gelding: poor maiden on Flat and over hurdles: best efforts on a sound surface: jumps none too fluently. *T. W. Donnelly* — 68

ENCHANTED MAN 9 b.g. Enchantment – Queen's Treasure (Queen's Hussar) [1992/3 c21g² c25sᶠ c24sᵘʳ c24sᵖᵘ c16s³ c20d* c21m³] leggy gelding: winning hurdler: moderate chaser: won claimer at Stratford in February: creditable third at Wolverhampton following month: stays 2½m: probably acts on any going: best in a hood over hurdles: sometimes looks a difficult ride. *R. Lee* — c88 —

ENFANT DU PARADIS (IRE) 5 b.m. Shernazar – Fille de L'Orne (FR) (Jim French (USA)) [1992/3 16g* 17g* 17g² 16d³ a16g] small, leggy mare: won claiming hurdle at Ludlow and selling handicap at Fakenham (no bid) in October: ran well next 2 starts: should stay beyond 17f: acts on dead ground, ran poorly on fibresand: front runner. *P. D. Evans* — 79

ENIGMATIC (USA) 5 b.h. Green Dancer (USA) – Inscrutable Lady (USA) (Exclusive Native (USA)) [1992/3 16d⁴] successful at up to 1¼m on Flat in France, when trained by A. Fabre: modest form when fourth of 25 in novice hurdle at Wetherby in February: should improve. *K. A. Morgan* — 91 p

ENKINDLE 6 b.m. Relkino – Nelion (Grey Sovereign) [1992/3 21f³ 16v² 16s⁶ 18d] leggy, angular mare: novice selling hurdler: best effort of season on second start: form only at 2m: acts on heavy and good to firm ground. *B. W. Murray* — 73

ENSHARP (USA) 7 b.g. Sharpen Up – Lulworth Cove (Averof) [1992/3 c16m² c18d⁶] strong, workmanlike gelding: modest chaser: easily better — c94 —

effort of season when second at Southwell in May: not sure to stay much beyond 2m: acts on good to firm going: blinkered twice in 1991/2. *S. Gollings*

ENTERPRISE LADY (FR)   6 ch.m. Gorytus (USA) – Calder Hall (Grundy) [1992/3 17d6] sparely-made mare: poor novice hurdler, has run in sellers: better suited by 19f than 2m. *M. Williams*   –

ENTERTAINMENT PARK   7 b.g. Park Row – Feodora (Songedor) [1992/3 16gF] smallish, workmanlike gelding: won NH Flat race in 1991/2: no worthwhile form in novice hurdles: dead. *B. Preece*   –

ENTIRE   9 ch.g. Relkino – Tactless (Romulus) [1992/3 18m 18spu 17m 26m6 c21mpu c24fur] workmanlike gelding: winning top-of-the-ground 2m hurdler: no worthwhile form in 1992/3, including over fences. *J. D. Hugill*   c–
–

ENVOPAK MAJOR   6 ch.g. Ovac (ITY) – Mariner's Leap (King's Leap) [1992/3 17v 18gpu] rather leggy gelding: no sign of ability: dead. *G. L. Humphrey*   –

ENVOPAK TOKEN   12 ch.g. Proverb – Luck Token (Festive) [1992/3 c26vF c21spu] strong, rangy gelding: fairly useful chaser in 1990/1 when trained by J. Gifford: has failed to complete both starts since: suited by test of stamina: acts on soft going and good to firm. *G. L. Humphrey*   c–
–

EPILENY   9 br.g. Random Shot – Charming Hostess (Khalkis) [1992/3 c21g2 c28fF] leggy gelding: only form in steeplechases when second in novice hunter chase at Uttoxeter in May: blinkered last 2 starts 1991/2. *Miss P. M. Whittle*   c81
–

EQUATOR   10 ch.g. Nijinsky (CAN) – Sound of Success (USA) (Successor) [1992/3 17d 16g 20s c21d c20g6 c23g5 c25g6 c17m2 c21v3 c17d3 c24m5 c18v4] tall gelding: winning hurdler: modest novice chaser: effective at 2m and stays well: acts on heavy and good to firm going: blinkered once. *J. S. Haldane*   c80
–

EQUINOCTIAL   8 b.g. Skyliner – Night Rose (Sovereign Gleam) [1992/3 23gpu 22d 21s 28spu c21s c27d3 c21d2 c21g2 c25mpu] tall gelding: inconsistent winning hurdler: modest form when placed in novice chases: ran as though something amiss last outing (March): stays 27f: acts on dead ground: sometimes blinkered. *M. Dods*   c85
–

EQUINOR   6 b.h. Norwick (USA) – Cithern (Canisbay) [1992/3 17s 22s 17m 24gpu] sturdy horse: fair hurdler as a juvenile in 1990/1: no form in 4 handicaps since: form only at 2m: acts well on firm ground: usually races with tongue tied down. *R. A. Bennett*   –

EQUITY CARD (IRE)   5 b.g. King of Clubs – Carntino (Bustino) [1992/3 23d 17m 24g6 24g2] leggy gelding: modest novice hurdler: best efforts of season on last 2 starts: stays 3m: acts on dead going. *L. J. Barratt*   87

ERCALL MILLER   6 b.g. Van Der Linden (FR) – Salica (ITY) (Hogarth (ITY)) [1992/3 23d3 24s* 24s5 23s5 26g* 24s5] close-coupled, workmanlike gelding: successful in novice hurdles at Bangor in November and Wolverhampton (handicap) in March, showing modest form: stays very well: acts on soft going: sometimes jumps none too fluently. *K. White*   97

ERIC'S TRAIN   7 b.g. Strong Gale – Star-Pit (Queen's Hussar) [1992/3 c21d c19gF] well-made gelding with scope: winning hurdler when trained by Mrs J. Pitman: has shown promise both outings in novice chases: travelling like a winner when falling 3 out at Taunton in November: probably stays 21f: acts on good to firm and dead going: takes strong hold: not a fluent jumper as yet. *G. B. Balding*   c89
–

ERINY (USA)   4 b.g. Erins Isle – Memorable Girl (USA) (Iron Ruler (USA)) [1992/3 16s3 16dur 16m 16m5] workmanlike gelding: modest 1m and 9f winner on Flat: sold out of S. Norton's stable 8,400 gns Newmarket Autumn Sales: poor form in juvenile hurdles: best effort on soft going. *J. F. Bottomley*   82

ERLEMO   4 b.c. Mummy's Game – Empress Catherine (Welsh Pageant) [1992/3 16d 16s 21v 16g 23d] tall, leggy colt: poor staying maiden on Flat: 73 sold out of J. Benstead's stable 4,500 gns Ascot November Sales: poor form first 2 starts over hurdles: blinkered subsequently. *W. Clay*

EROSTIN FLOATS   9 ch.g. Paddy's Stream – Zeta's Daughter (Master   **c102** Owen) [1992/3 c24m⁶ c24f² c27g⁴] tall gelding: fair staying handicap chaser: – creditable second at Huntingdon in September: well below form later in month, only subsequent start: stays 3m: acts on firm going: sketchy jumper. *John R. Upson*

EROSTINS SWAN   7 b.g. Strong Gale – Kindello (Bargello) [1992/3   c– c25dᵘʳ c21sᶠ 22d⁵ 23f²] lengthy gelding: poor staying novice hurdler: yet to   70 get past the sixth over fences. *John R. Upson*

ERRANT KNIGHT   9 ch.g. Deep Run – Dame Lucy (Prince Hansel) **c113** [1992/3 c26gᶠ c21vᵇᵈ c27v² c24mᵘʳ c21s c22g*] lengthy gelding: fair   – handicap chaser: won at Stratford in March: stays 3¼m: acts on heavy and good to firm going: sketchy jumper. *M. C. Pipe*

ESCADARO (USA)   4 b.g. Liloy (FR) – Mlle Chanteuse (USA) (The Minstrel (CAN)) [1992/3 16s³ a18g 21v 16s⁵ 21g 28m⁴] leggy, sparely-made   84 gelding: poor maiden on Flat and over hurdles (trained by S. Norton first start): should stay further than 2m: form only on soft ground: visored last 3 outings. *Mrs V. C. Ward*

ESCAPE TALK   6 gr.m. Gabitat – Getaway Girl (Capistrano) [1992/3 28f⁵] small, sparely-made mare: bad novice selling hurdler. *J. Dooler*   –

ESHA NESS   10 b.g. Crash Course – Beeston (Our Babu) [1992/3 c26d* **c137** ? c26s³ c26v⁵ c27s² c24m⁵ c25m⁵ c33g⁴]   –

If there were a Richter scale for sporting disasters the happenings at the 1993 Grand National would surely almost defy measurement. A worse mess outside farce would be hard to imagine. The race was declared void—and around £30m in bets returned—after a number of horses completed a circuit or more after a second false start. On a wet and windy day, the thirty-nine runners arrived ten minutes early at the start and were kept waiting for a similar period, after coming under starter's orders, while around fifteen demonstrators near the first fence were removed. By the time the starter let the field go for the first time, some of the horses—including Chatam, Roc de Prince and Royle Speedmaster—had become reluctant to line up while others seemed too close to the tape, which in the method used for the National rises above the heads of the jockeys. The tape broke after catching New Mill House and Direct, the starter immediately shouting 'False start, false start' and waving his fluttering flag above his head. Most of the jockeys heard the starter while others became entangled in the tape. The whole field pulled up well before the first fence and returned to the start. The false start was announced over the public address system. The horses were lined up once more after the tape was repaired but Chatam and Royle Speedmaster again hung back, reluctant to line up. As with the first false start, the starter had to ask some jockeys to move their mounts back from the tape. As the tape went up—the starter shouting 'Come on, come on', as he released it—some of the horses were still too close and the tape became caught under the neck of Formula One and round the body of Dunwoody, rider of Wont Be Gone Long. The starter's calls of 'False start, false start' weren't clearly heard this time, partly because he had moved his microphone—connected to loudspeakers on either side of the jockeys—to one side before releasing the tape. Much was made at the time of the fact that the starter did not unfurl his flag after the second false start was called. Nine of the jockeys pulled up before the first fence but the others continued, believing it was a real race. The Jockey Club's committee of inquiry—whose report, which appeared in June, was labelled a 'whitewash' in the popular press—concluded that the advance flag man, positioned a hundred yards down the course, did not wave his recall flag on either false start. He has denied the allegation, though the jockeys were adamant they saw no recall flag the second time. To add to the confusion, no message was relayed over the public address system immediately after the second false start, though the jockeys probably wouldn't have heard it in any

Martell Grand National Handicap Chase, Aintree—the first false start . . . . .

case. Even if some of the jockeys suspected something was amiss it was understandable that they didn't risk pulling up, in the absence of any clear instruction to the contrary. There is no Jockey Club rule or instruction that provides for a race to be stopped once the field has passed the advance flag man, but Aintree officials did try to stop the runners at the Chair—the jockeys ignored them believing them to be protestors—and then again at the bend after the water jump and as they approached the starting point again. Those connected with some of the horses also tried to wave down the riders, and ten of the runners were stopped at around the halfway point. In a futile exhibition, a dozen carried on and seven completed the course, led by Esha Ness, Cahervillahow, Romany King, The Committee and Givus A Buck. After an unnecessary delay, the Aintree stewards announced the inevitable outcome: the race was void, in accordance with Rule 28 which dictates that, when the recall flag is not raised after a false start, a race over jumps is void if all the horses are not pulled up before completing a circuit. The latest National could, arguably, have been even more controversial had the attempts to stop the field in time been successful. Except for those who had fallen on the first circuit—the well-backed Royal Athlete among

. . . . . and the second

Esha Ness (left), The Committee (centre) and Romany King take the last together

them—all the runners would have been eligible for the re-run. All bets would have stood, adding to the quandary of those connections whose horses had already covered two miles.

The Grand National fiasco was a humiliation for racing. The biggest sporting audience of the year—there were around sixteen million television viewers in Britain alone—saw the world's most famous race reduced to a stunning shambles. Just how it came to happen must be a matter of some shame for the blundering officials involved. The advance flag man and the starter—who is responsible for the efficient conduct of the start and should therefore bear the brunt of the blame for what happened on the day— were both in the dock afterwards. But they were at the end of a chain of incompetence which also included the Aintree executive and the Jockey Club (whose disciplinary stewards considered its committee's report and predictably recommended that no action should be taken). Viewed with hindsight, the starting system used for the Grand National—known as the 'Grey Gate'—was inappropriate. It was outdated, and concerns had been expressed about its efficiency at various times. The Jockey Club should not have approved it for the Grand National. Since 1991 a man had been stationed at either side of the course to operate a pulley to help the tape to rise (something which had no relevance to events in 1993 but was indicative of shortcomings). After the 1991 Grand National, the starter had recommended that the start should be reduced in width because the seventy-five-yard span (significantly more than is needed to accommodate the maximum forty runners) resulted in the tape sagging in the middle and being slow to rise at around that point, something which gave more problems in wet and windy weather. The starter also recommended that the starter's rostrum be moved to the inside of the course where most of the runners lined up and where the starter would be better positioned to hear the jockeys. The recommendation to move the starter's rostrum was acted upon by the Aintree executive, but it did not reduce the width of the Grand National start, seemingly because it would have encroached onto the hurdle track which would have had to be made narrower at that point, reducing the scope for moving the plastic running rail in particularly wet weather.

Lessons are learned by mistakes, and changes are certain to be made in the starting system and procedure for the 1994 National.

The 1993 National will inevitably be remembered as 'the race that never was' and, when the embarrassment has passed, will be absorbed into the rich folklore of the event. But the occasion will always remain a poignant one for the connections of the thirty-nine runners who went to post, most of them trained especially for this race. Esha Ness was part of a strong team representing Mrs Pitman's stable, which also included the Cheltenham Gold Cup third Royal Athlete, and Garrison Savannah (who was pulled up at halfway). The latter had looked in command in the 1991 National until faltering on the run-in. Esha Ness was a horse who had had his problems and had become something of a disappointment. He'd won at Wincanton on his reappearance in November and shown useful form on his day, including when runner-up to Jodami in the Mandarin Handicap Chase at Newbury. But he was inconsistent and had been well below form in the Fulke Walwyn Kim Muir Challenge Cup at the Cheltenham Festival meeting on his latest start. He was sent to Ayr for the Scottish National after the Aintree fiasco, looking well treated on his Aintree 'form', but managed only fourth, never in contention.

Esha Ness (b.g. 1983)	Crash Course (b 1971)	Busted (b 1963)	Crepello
			Sans Le Sou
		Lucky Stream (b 1956)	Persian Gulf
			Kypris
	Beeston (b 1966)	Our Babu (b 1952)	My Babu
			Glen Line
		Sprite (ch 1948)	Jamaica Inn
			Bibs

The strong, rangy Esha Ness is by Crash Course, sire of the Gold Cup winner Jodami and 1992 Grand National runner-up Romany King among others. He was bought by his trainer for IR 17,000 guineas as an unbroken three-year-old at the Tattersalls Derby Sale, following Garrison Savannah (led out unsold but later purchased privately) into the sale-ring. Esha Ness's dam Beeston, a winner on the Flat and over hurdles and the dam of four winners over jumps including the useful hurdler/chaser Sports Reporter (by Jukebox), is a half-sister to a number of winners including the Irish St Leger third Avril Sprite. Another of her half-sisters Winged Sprite was the dam of that splendid chaser Sandy Sprite who looked set for victory

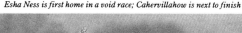

Esha Ness is first home in a void race; Cahervillahow is next to finish

Mr Patrick Bancroft's "Esha Ness"

in the 1971 Grand National, leading over the last until breaking down on the run-in and finishing fifth to Specify. Esha Ness stays very long distances and acts on any going. In case he is returned to Aintree for the 1994 National it should be recorded that he took really well to the fences and completed the course hand-timed by our representative in 9m 1.13sec, the second-fastest time recorded over the Grand National course. *Mrs J. Pitman*

ES MOLI 6 b.m. Sunyboy – Upham Jubilee (Murrayfield) [1992/3 17mF 16f] second foal: dam winning pointer/maiden hunter chaser: tailed off in novice hurdle in September: dead. *J. Webber* —

ESPERO (CHI) 12 ch.g. El Oriental (ARG) – Elfish (CHI) (Proposal) **c75** [1992/3 c18dpu c17gur c21s c21v5 c17vF] sturdy gelding: novice hurdler/ chaser: only form of season when fifth over fences at Leicester in January: stays 3m: acts on heavy and good to firm going: visored last outing. *C. J. Vernon Miller* —

ESPRIT DE FEMME (FR) 7 b.m. Esprit du Nord (USA) – Bustelda (FR) (Busted) [1992/3 18d2 18s2] small mare: improved form when second **96** in novice hurdles at Fontwell in October and November: should stay beyond 2¼m: acts on soft ground. *D. W. Browning*

ESPRIT FORT (USA) 4 b.f. Last Tycoon – Spirit of The Wind (USA) (Little Current (USA)) [1992/3 16spu] leggy, sparely-made filly: modest —

262

middle-distance maiden on Flat: tailed off when pulled up in juvenile hurdle at Warwick in January. *P. W. Chapple-Hyam*

ESPY 10 b.g. Pitpan – Minorette (Miralgo) [1992/3 c20g³ c26g⁴ c24d³ c21vᵖᵘ c24d² c25f²] neat gelding: useful chaser when in the mood: generally ran creditably in 1992/3, best effort when second at Sandown in March on last outing: stays 3¼m, not 29f: has won on dead going but ideally suited by a sound surface: sometimes let down by his jumping: has been blinkered and visored. *C. P. E. Brooks* **c142 §**
–

ESSAYEFFSEE 4 b.g. Precocious – Floreal (Formidable (USA)) [1992/3 18g 18s⁶] workmanlike gelding: modest maiden on Flat, stays 11f: poor form in early-season juvenile hurdles: joined Mrs M. Reveley. *M. H. Easterby* **68**

ESSDOUBLEYOU (NZ) 5 ch.g. Sambuk – Gardone (Petingo) [1992/3 F17d] strong gelding: dam, lightly raced, showed no form in Britain: eighth of 18 in NH Flat race at Ascot in April: yet to race over hurdles or fences. *Mrs J. R. Renfree-Barons* **–**

ESS EL AR 5 b.m. Say Primula – Muskcat Rambler (Pollerton) [1992/3 F16v F16v² aF16g* F17m 17sF 18d⁵ 18g⁴] lengthy, unfurnished mare: first foal: dam, daughter of winning hurdler, seemed of little account: won NH Flat race at Southwell in March: clear when falling 3 out in maiden hurdle at Newton Abbot in April: poor form in novice events subsequently: pulls hard. *M. C. Pipe* **81**

ESSEN AITCH 4 b.f. Lochnager – Eamon's Girl (Irish Star) [1992/3 17d 16s] angular, workmanlike filly: second foal: dam unraced: well beaten in juvenile hurdles in October and January. *Mrs H. Parrott* **–**

EURIDICE (IRE) 4 ch.f. Woodman (USA) – Arctic Kite (North Stoke) [1992/3 16d⁶ 16g F 17f³] leggy, angular filly: modest middle-distance performer on Flat when trained by L. Cumani: best effort in juvenile hurdles when sixth at Wincanton in February. *W. G. M. Turner* **86**

EUROFLIGHT 4 b.f. Natroun (FR) – Bustling Nelly (Bustino) [1992/3 17g 16g] lengthy, plain filly: half-sister to fair hurdler/winning chaser Silk Degrees (by Dunbeath): placed over 1¼m on Flat: no promise in 2 runs over hurdles early in season. *D. R. Tucker* **–**

EUROTWIST 4 b.g. Viking (USA) – Orange Bowl (General Assembly (USA)) [1992/3 16s² 16s² 16d*] small, close-coupled gelding: modest middle-distance performer on Flat: runner-up in juvenile hurdles prior to winning novice event at Catterick in February: will stay beyond 2m: acts on soft going: jumps soundly: open to further improvement. *T. D. Barron* **94 p**

EVENING DRESS 4 ch.f. Night Shift (USA) – Maple Rock (Music Boy) [1992/3 16d 17d⁶] small filly: poor maiden on Flat: gave impression barely stayed when sixth in novice selling hurdle at Stratford in October: sold 1,000 gns Ascot November Sales. *I. Campbell* **61**

EVENING SESSION (IRE) 4 ch.g. Burslem – Icefield (Northfields (USA)) [1992/3 16g 16g 16s⁶] no sign of ability on Flat or in novice hurdles. *J. Norton* **–**

EVENING SUNSET 7 b.g. Red Sunset – Princess Elinor (Captain James) [1992/3 18g³ c18sF⁴ c25gᵖᵘ c25mᵘʳ c25mᵘʳ] small gelding: novice selling hurdler: has shown nothing over fences: trained until after second start by G. Fleming: probably stays 2½m: usually blinkered or visored. *C. Smith* **c–**
–

EVENLODE 9 b.g. Netherkelly – Miss Curiso (Master Spiritus) [1992/3 c24g c23vᵖᵘ c22g⁶ c22g³] good-bodied gelding: no sign of ability in novice hurdles: poor novice chaser: suited by test of stamina. *C. J. Vernon Miller* **c73**
–

EVERALDO (FR) 9 b.g. Top Ville – Floressa (FR) (Sassafras (FR)) [1992/3 25g⁴] tall, angular gelding: backward when below-form fourth in Grade 2 event at Wetherby in October: wasn't seen out again: effective at 2½m and stays 25f: acts on heavy ground: jumps well: game. *N. J. Henderson* **?**

263

EVER SMILE (FR) 6 ch.g. Be My Guest (USA) – Smiling (FR) (Great Nephew) [1992/3 17v^{pu} 20s 16s^{pu} 22g^5 17d^4 22m^3] leggy, lightly-made gelding: modest hurdler nowadays: best effort of season when fourth at Stratford in February: effective from 2m to 2½m: acts on firm and dead ground. *M. C. Pipe*   99

EVERSO IRISH 4 b.g. Hatim (USA) – Ever So (Mummy's Pet) [1992/3 18g 16d 16m^4] angular gelding: poor maiden on Flat: sold out of M. Tompkins' stable 1,000 gns Newmarket Autumn Sales after second start over hurdles: easily best effort when fourth in novice event at Worcester in March. *P. D. Evans*   85

EWHONOSEBEST 6 ch.g. Lir – Cornish Susie (Fair Season) [1992/3 18f^{pu}] small gelding: no sign of ability in 3 outings over hurdles. *B. R. J. Young*   –

EXACT ANALYSIS (USA) 7 b. or br.g. Verbatim (USA) – Mity Nice Girl (USA) (Handsome Boy) [1992/3 17v^2 17s 17s* 16g^5 16m 17s^{pu} 20g^{pu}] sturdy gelding: moderate hurdler: won novice handicap at Newton Abbot in February: ran poorly last 3 starts: should stay beyond 17f: acts on heavy going: usually races up with pace. *N. R. Mitchell*   92

EXARCH (USA) 4 b.c. His Majesty (USA) – Velvet (USA) (Sir Ivor) [1992/3 18s^4 17v^2] sturdy, useful-looking colt: behind in maiden races on Flat: blinkered, better effort over hurdles when second in juvenile event at Chepstow in January: sold 4,400 gns Ascot March Sales. *M. J. Heaton-Ellis*   87

EXCELLED (IRE) 4 gr.f. Treasure Kay – Excelling Miss (USA) (Exceller (USA)) [1992/3 17d 16g^4 16d^5] angular, close-coupled filly: probably of little account. *C. J. Drewe*   –

EXCISE MAN 5 ch.g. Import – Super Satin (Lord of Verona) [1992/3 F16v^6 17d^{pu} 16g] brother to 6-y-o Super Sandy and half-brother to 3 winning staying jumpers: dam placed over hurdles and fences: no sign of ability in NH Flat race and novice hurdles. *F. T. Walton*   –

EXCITING PROSPECT 9 ch.g. North Summit – Hopefull Polly (Polyfoto) [1992/3 c24f^4] leggy, rather sparely-made gelding: has stringhalt: fair hurdler in 1989/90: bit backward, well beaten in hunter chase at Newbury in March but shaped as though retaining some ability: probably stays 2½m: acts on firm ground. *P. Caudwell*   c– p   –

EXECUTIVE JET 11 ch.g. Monseigneur (USA) – Starlit Way (Pall Mall) [1992/3 22m] ex-Irish gelding: lightly-raced maiden on Flat and over hurdles. *J. J. Birkett*   –

EXPANSIONIST 4 b.g. Midyan (USA) – Dastina (Derring-Do) [1992/3 16m^5 16s 16s^5 16s^4 16d 18g^6 22d^{pu}] small, leggy gelding: stayer on Flat, successful 4 times in 1992 (claimed out of S. Woods's stable £8,010 in August): poor juvenile hurdler: found little fifth outing: should stay beyond 2m: acts on soft going. *Mrs J. R. Ramsden*   79

EXPLORATION (USA) 6 b.g. Explodent (USA) – Molly Moon (FR) (Kalamoun) [1992/3 22s 16g 18m^4 17m^2 18m* 17f^F] good-topped gelding: won 3 times over middle distances on Flat in French Provinces in 1992, when trained by H. Pantall: sold 2,800 gns Newmarket Autumn Sales: progressive form over hurdles up to winning novice event at Cartmel in May by 10 lengths: stays 2¼m: acts on good to firm going. *K. A. Morgan*   92

EXPLOSIVE SPEED (USA) 5 b.g. Exceller (USA) – Strait Lane (USA) (Chieftain II) [1992/3 17s^6 17m^2 17g^2 17d^6] small gelding: fair hurdler: good second in handicaps at Newcastle in October and November: not seen out after December: races mainly at around 2m: acts on dead and good to firm ground: not a fluent jumper. *M. D. Hammond*   113

EXPOUND (USA) 8 b.g. Far North (CAN) – Speaking of Sweets (USA) (Elocutionist (USA)) [1992/3 c16v^6 22d^{pu} 17v c16d^F a22g^4 c16m^2 c20f^4 c21g^4 c24f^4] leggy gelding: selling hurdler: poor novice chaser: stays 2½m well: best form with plenty of give in the ground: sometimes blinkered. *R. T. Juckes*   c–   –

EXPRESS REALE 8 b.g. Al Sirat (USA) – Real Path VII (Pedigree Unknown) [1992/3 c21s^{pu} c21s^6 c26v^{pu} 25v^3 24v^3 25v* 25d^2 28m^{pu} 24v^2 25m^{pu}] sturdy gelding: won novice handicap hurdle at Uttoxeter in January: ran creditably both completed outings subsequently: no form over fences (poor jumper): suited by thorough test of stamina: acts on heavy going and seems unsuited by good to firm: tried visored, blinkered nowadays: lazy and needs plenty of driving. *T. Thomson Jones*   **c– x** 102

EXPRESS SIGNMAKER (IRE) 4 b.f. Paean – Moment of Weakness (Pieces of Eight) [1992/3 16m^2] quite moderate plater on Flat at 2 yrs, little form in 1992: jumped sketchily when second in juvenile selling hurdle at Worcester in August: sold 640 gns Doncaster September Sales. *J. White*   73

EXTRA BEAT 6 ch.g. Carlingford Castle – Safe Run (Deep Run) [1992/3 16d 22s^3 25d^3 20d^2 25s 25s^2] sturdy, angular gelding: chasing type: sixth foal: dam unraced: modest form in novice hurdles: below form last 2 starts: stays 25f: acts on soft ground. *G. Richards*   90

EXTRA GRAND 7 b.g. Oats – Booly Bay (Le Prince) [1992/3 c21s^{pu} c21s^{pu} c25s^F c21g* c25f^3 c21f^2 c23m*] big, good-bodied gelding: modest novice hurdler: won novice handicap chase at Worcester in April and novice chase at Uttoxeter following month: stays 25f: acts on firm ground: blinkered third outing. *O. Sherwood*   **c93** –

EXTRA HIGH (USA) 5 ch.g. Nepal (USA) – Evening Scarlet (USA) (Bold Commander (USA)) [1992/3 16d 21m^5 18g 16m 16d 24g^5] tall, leggy, lengthy gelding: poor maiden hurdler: not a fluent jumper: blinkered nowadays. *V. Thompson*   67

EYELID 7 b.h. Roscoe Blake – Pie Eye (Exbury) [1992/3 17g^2 16d^2 16d^5 16d^2 17m 16d^3] stocky horse: smart hurdler: ran well in 1992/3, notably   152

Mrs Seamus Purcell's "Eyelid"

when tenth to Granville Again in Smurfit Champion Hurdle at Cheltenham (hampered early on) in March: effective at 2m to 19f: acts on good to firm and dead ground: consistent. *Michael Purcell, Ireland*

F

FAARIS 12 b.g. Troy – Real Snug (Realm) [1992/3 c21d6 c22fF c21m3] strong, workmanlike gelding: hunter chaser nowadays: poor third at Folkestone in May: stays 21f: acts on any going: tends to sweat and to swish tail under pressure. *Mrs D. M. Grissell*   c74 –

FABULOUS QUEEN (FR) 10 b.m. Fabulous Dancer (USA) – Moquerie (FR) (Beaugency (FR)) [1992/3 c20f c21m] strong, sturdy mare: winning pointer: well beaten in hunter chases. *P. Venner*   c– –

FACILITY LETTER 6 gr.g. Superlative – Facetious (Malicious) [1992/3 17m4 16g 18spu 16s2 a16g 16s 18dur] stocky gelding: winning hurdler: only poor form in 1992/3, including in sellers: barely stays 2½m: probably acts on any going. *G. M. Moore*   81

FACT OR FICTION 7 br.g. Known Fact (USA) – Noble Wac (USA) (Vaguely Noble) [1992/3 a16g3 a16gur a20g4] handicap hurdler: best effort of season when third at Lingfield in February: stays 2½m: has raced only on equitrack. *Miss B. Sanders*   90

FACTOR TEN (IRE) 5 b.g. Kemal (FR) – Kissowen (Pitpan) [1992/3 F17d5 F17d3 F17s6 17d3 16g* 16d3 22d*] tall, unfurnished gelding: chasing type: first foal: dam unraced half-sister to Kissane and another winning jumper: fair form when winning novice hurdles at Kempton in February and Ludlow in April: will stay beyond 2¾m: acts on dead ground: should progress. *Miss H. C. Knight*   104 p

FACTOTUM 10 b.g. Known Fact (USA) – Blue Shark (Silver Shark) [1992/3 17g5 16dpu 18f6 17f] compact gelding: modest handicap hurdler: stays 2¼m: acts on firm and dead going. *R. Akehurst*   87

FAIR BROTHER 7 ch.g. Le Bavard (FR) – Fair People (Varano) [1992/3 17s2 16s5 17d* 17v c21v2 c19sF c20dF 25fF] workmanlike gelding: successful in novice hurdle at Taunton in November: narrowly-beaten second in novice event at Newton Abbot in December on chasing debut: jumped sketchily there and fell in 3 subsequent outings: will stay 3m: acts on heavy going: blinkered last 2 starts. *D. J. G. Murray-Smith*   c95 x / 95

FAIR CROSSING 7 ch.g. Over The River (FR) – Golden Chestnut (Green Shoon) [1992/3 c20g4] tall, good-bodied gelding: carries plenty of condition: winning hurdler: made numerous mistakes when remote fourth in novice chase at Ascot in October: stays 21f: yet to race on a firm surface. *C. P. E. Brooks*   c89 –

FAIRFIELD'S BREEZE 8 b.m. Buckskin (FR) – Mistic Breeze (Master Owen) [1992/3 22s 16m 18d] lengthy, rather dipped-backed mare: well beaten in novice hurdles. *R. Dickin*   –

FAIRFIELDS CONE 10 ch.m. Celtic Cone – Bond's Best (Good Bond) [1992/3 22g* 22s* 22d3 21d2 20d2 21v* 22s 22s5 21s6 21mur 22m] lengthy mare: fair handicap hurdler: won at Cheltenham (conditional jockeys), Newton Abbot and Warwick in first half of season: good fifth at Sandown in February, but well below form last 2 completed starts: should stay beyond 2¾m: best form with give in the ground: genuine. *R. Dickin*   113

FAIR PLUME (NZ) 7 b.g. Royal Plume – Fair Carlyle (NZ) (Zamazaan) [1992/3 17d 16s6 17d 21gpu 17m 17vF 17m 17d4 16m5] small, workmanlike gelding: bad novice hurdler: blinkered/visored nowadays. *Mrs A. L. M. King*   60

FAIR PROSPECT 7 b.g. Shirley Heights – Sans Blague (USA) (The Minstrel (CAN)) [1992/3 c20d2 c20d5 c23gF c26d5] leggy, angular gelding: fair hurdler/chaser: stays 2½m: acts on good to firm and heavy going: has been tried in blinkers, but is better without: poor jumper. *P. J. Hobbs*   c101 x / –

266

FAIR ROWANNA 5 b.m. Prince of Peace – Miss Tidy (Gang Warily) [1992/3 24s^{pu}] non-thoroughbred mare: first foal: dam never ran: tailed off when pulled up in maiden hurdle at Hexham in May: sold 1,800 gns Malvern June Sales. *Mrs M. Stirk* —

FAIRSPEAR 4 b.g. Faustus (USA) – Emma's Star (Comedy Star (USA)) [1992/3 18s a20g a16g^4] poor maiden on Flat, stays 1¼m: no worthwhile form over hurdles: tried blinkered. *J. White* —

FAIRWAYS ON TARGET 7 b.g. Billion (USA) – Aileen's Belle (The Parson) [1992/3 c21g^F 20d^5] leggy, workmanlike gelding: fair hurdler: creditable fifth at Doncaster in December: stays 2 1f: acts on good to firm and dead going: usually races up with pace: tends to make the odd mistake over hurdles, and jumped poorly only start over fences. *Mrs M. Reveley* c– 113

FAIT ACCOMPLI (FR) 4 ch.g. Fayruz – Artipiar (Tyrant (USA)) [1992/3 18m 17m^{pu}] smallish gelding: no promise in 2 runs over hurdles in August, first a seller: sold 820 gns Doncaster September Sales. *J. J. O'Neill* —

FAITHFUL STAR 8 b.g. Tilden – Star Relation (Star Gazer) [1992/3 c21f* c20g* c17g* c22g4 c19g* c19d^2 c18m* c20g c25v^F c21v^3 23s^2 21s* 17g^2 20g^5] leggy, close-coupled ex-Irish gelding: fairly useful handicap chaser: successful in 1992/3 at Kilbeggan, Wexford, Killarney (trained until after then by W. Roper), Hereford and Exeter: also successful in novice hurdle at Leicester in February: sold 9,200 gns Ascot June Sales: stays 23f: probably acts on any ground: blinkered last 2 starts over fences (ran creditably second time): none too fluent a jumper over fences. *M. C. Pipe* c126 97

FALCONBRIDGE BAY 6 ch.g. Buzzards Bay – Swaynes Princess (St Chad) [1992/3 F12d^3 aF16g^2 17d] strong gelding: half-brother to modest 7f winner Frivole (by Comedy Star): dam ran twice: placed in NH Flat races: behind in novice hurdle at Newton Abbot in April. *C. P. Wildman* —

FALCON FLIGHT 7 ch.g. Tampero (FR) – Kemoening (Falcon) [1992/3 a16g* a18g^2] neat gelding: fair hurdler at his best: won claimer at Lingfield in January: creditable second in similar event there following month (reportedly finished lame): suited by sharp 2m: acts on good to soft going and equitrack. *R. Simpson* 101

FALCONS DAWN 6 b.g. Exhibitioner – African Bloom (African Sky) [1992/3 17g^2] sparely-made gelding: novice hurdler: good second at Stratford in May: visored last 2 starts in 1991/2, running creditably final one: will prove best at 2m. *L. J. Codd* 89

FALSE ECONOMY 8 ch.g. Torus – Vulvic (Vulgan) [1992/3 c24g^2 c26g^3 c26d^F c25v* c34d c22v^2 c24d^5] rangy gelding: fair chaser: won handicap at Towcester in February: easily best effort subsequently when second on same course in April: stays 25f: acts on heavy ground. *J. A. C. Edwards* c111 —

FALSIDE 9 b.g. Alias Smith (USA) – High Caraval (High Top) [1992/3 c25d c26s^{pu} c24m^5] fair pointer: no form otherwise (blinkered twice over hurdles): sold 5,800 gns Ascot March Sales. *G. L. Humphrey* c–

FAMBRIDGE 4 b.g. Baron Blakeney – Tye Bridge (Idiot's Delight) [1992/3 F16s^6 F17m 16d] non-thoroughbred gelding: fourth foal: dam ran once: signs of a little ability in NH Flat races: bad mistake fifth when well beaten in maiden hurdle at Uttoxeter in April. *D. Nicholson* —

FAMILY LINE 5 b.g. High Line – Princess Dina (Huntercombe) [1992/3 17d* 17g^2 17m^5 17g^4 18d^4 16g^3 16d^5 17d^4 16g^3 16g^5 17s 17s^5 16g* 17m* 16g* 17g^5 16g*] sturdy gelding: fair hurdler: won handicap at Perth early in season, claimers at Nottingham and Doncaster in February and handicaps at Ayr in March and April: races at around 2m, but should stay further: acts on heavy and good to firm ground: sometimes wears tongue strap: genuine and consistent. *Miss L. A. Perratt* 108

FAMOUS LAD 10 b.g. Bold Lad (IRE) – Famous Band (USA) (Banderilla (USA)) [1992/3 F12d c16v^3] compact gelding: handicap chaser: ran poorly only outing of season over jumps (December): best at around 2m: acts on soft going: tried blinkered and visored: poor jumper. *R. Lee* c– x —

FAMOUS RUN 13 ch.g. Deep Run – Milwaukee Famous (Blue Lightning) [1992/3 c23m3 c27spu c25gpu] strong gelding: poor chaser: stayed 3m: acted on hard ground: dead. *B. Richmond*   **c79** –

FANILLE 7 b.g. Top Ville – Flying Fantasy (Habitat) [1992/3 c22vpu c24dpu] small, workmanlike gelding: poor handicap hurdler/maiden chaser: stays 2½m: acts on firm and dead going: ran poorly when tried blinkered: looks a difficult ride. *D. J. Bell*   **c–**

FANLIGHT 5 b.h. Beldale Flutter (USA) – Carib Flash (Mill Reef (USA)) [1992/3 17g5 18f4] leggy horse: best effort over hurdles when winning juvenile event in 1991/2: sold out of R. Akehurst's stable 3,500 gns Ascot February Sales: only poor form in 2 races in the spring, one of them a seller: should prove suited by further than 2m: acts on soft ground. *A. Moore*   **83**

FANTASTICAL 5 br.g. Vision (USA) – April (Silly Season) [1992/3 F17m 16g* 16d] close-coupled, sparely-made gelding: won novice hurdle at Edinburgh in December: ran as though something amiss in novice handicap on same course following month. *J. J. O'Neill*   **87**

FANTASY WORLD 7 ch.m. Kemal (FR) – Rockford Lass (Walshford) [1992/3 21v4 22v3 18v* 21vpu 22d* 21gpu] lengthy mare: chasing type: won mares novice hurdle at Fontwell in January and novice handicap at Sandown (better effort) following month: ran poorly last start: effective at 2¼m and stays 3m: acts on heavy going: best with forcing tactics. *J. T. Gifford*   **97**

FARAH 4 b. or br.f. Lead On Time (USA) – Muznah (Royal And Regal (USA)) [1992/3 16s2 16s a16gpu 16dpu 16g 22mF 22d4] compact filly: half-sister to winning hurdlers Nahar (by Known Fact) and Fayafi (by Top Ville): sold out of H. Thomson Jones's stable 1,600 gns Newmarket July Sales: best form over hurdles when second in seller in November, but would probably have finished good second but for falling last in mares novice handicap at Nottingham in March: will stay at least 2¾m: acts on good to firm and soft ground. *J. R. Turner*   **78**

FARAT (USA) 5 ch.h. Woodman (USA) – Solac (FR) (Gay Lussac (ITY)) [1992/3 16s3 25g4] smallish horse: fairly useful on Flat for J. Dunlop, suited by a test of stamina: promising third in novice hurdle at Kempton in December, but failed to confirm that effort (wandered under pressure) following month: should stay much further than 2m. *N. J. Henderson*   **100 ?**

FARM STREET 6 b.g. Henbit (USA) – Mill Hill (USA) (Riva Ridge (USA)) [1992/3 18m3 16spu 16g c16mur] leggy gelding: poor novice hurdler: showed little on chasing debut: sold 1,700 gns Ascot December Sales: 7f winner on Flat for C. Broad in February. *T. P. McGovern*   **c– 68**

FARM WEEK 11 gr.g. General Ironside – News Letter (London Gazette) [1992/3 26g* c26d c25v2 c25d4 c27v2 c24s5 c35s5 c29f* c34d c26f2] strong, compact gelding: fair handicap chaser: won at Wincanton in October and Windsor (dead-heated) in March: sold 5,000 gns Ascot June Sales: out-and-out stayer: acts on any going: visored once: inconsistent: makes mistakes. *G. B. Balding*   **c113 x** –

FARNWORTH 10 b.g. Quayside – Brave Trudy (Brave Invader (USA)) [1992/3 c27gur c21s3 c32d5 c27dpu c21s4 c24sF c24v4 c21fpu] lengthy, workmanlike gelding: modest chaser: best efforts of season on second and fifth starts: stays 3m: acts on heavy going and good to firm: blinkered once: has broken blood vessel. *G. M. Moore*   **c90** –

FAR OUT 7 b.g. Raga Navarro (ITY) – Spaced Out (Space King) [1992/3 21d4] sparely-made gelding: winning hurdler: sold 3,400 gns Doncaster August Sales: remote last of 4 finishers in October: resold 1,600 gns Doncaster March Sales: stays 21f: acts on firm and dead going: blinkered 3 times in 1990/1, including when successful. *K. G. Wingrove*

FARRANRORY 9 br.m. Mandalus – Caisepuca (Lucky Guy) [1992/3 c21dF] small, workmanlike mare: winning hunter chaser: fell at the seventh in handicap in November: stays 25f: acts on good to firm and dead going. *Mrs J. C. Breese*   **c–**

FAR RUN 6 b.g. Farhaan – Ballynavin Run (Deep Run) [1992/3 16s⁵ 16s⁶ c16v⁵] leggy gelding: half-brother to winning hurdler Teniente (by Smooth Stepper): dam lightly-raced Irish maiden hurdler: poor form in novice hurdles: behind in a novice chase (jumped none too fluently). *R. Rowe* c– 73

FAR SENIOR 7 ch.g. Al Sirat (USA) – Ross Lady (Master Buck) [1992/3 c26d⁵ c24g* c25d* c20dᵖᵘ] tall, leggy gelding: useful chaser: won Charisma Gold Cup (Handicap) at Kempton and 4-runner handicap at Sandown in October: ran as though something amiss last start (November): will stay beyond 3m: acts on good to firm and dead ground: tends to idle in front, and is held up: very sound jumper. *K. C. Bailey* c132 ? –

FAR TOO LOUD 6 b.g. Taufan (USA) – Octet (Octavo (USA)) [1992/3 21s² 21f*] workmanlike gelding: fair handicap hurdler: won at Newbury in March: will stay beyond 2¾m: acts on any going: blinkered once: looked unco-operative twice in 1991/2. *Mrs J. G. Retter* 105

FAR VIEW (IRE) 4 ch.g. Phardante (FR) – Whosview (Fine Blade (USA)) [1992/3 F16s 17f⁶ 20dᵖᵘ 22gᵖᵘ] leggy, unfurnished gelding: third foal: half-brother to winning hurdler Heathview (by Pitpan): dam, unraced, from successful jumping family: no sign of ability. *H. B. Hodge* –

FASHION PRINCESS 7 gr.m. Van Der Linden (FR) – Pendle's Secret (Le Johnstan) [1992/3 18h³ 22dᵖᵘ] small mare: inconsistent selling hurdler: stays 19f: acts on hard ground. *Mrs A. Knight* 80

FASSADININ 12 ch.g. Condorcet (FR) – Engadina (Alcide) [1992/3 18gᵖᵘ 22fᶠ 18g⁴ 16s] angular gelding: one-time useful Irish 2m hurdler: poor nowadays: used to be blinkered, visored last 2 outings. *W. L. Barker* 65

Charisma Gold Cup Chase, Kempton—Far Senior shows the best pace in the closing stages

FASTBIT 6 ch.h. Henbit (USA) – Fastidious (Guillaume Tell (USA)) c–
[1992/3 17s⁵ 16s 16v⁵ 16s 20s⁴ 17v² 17d⁴ c16gᶠ 17fᵖᵘ 17m] close-coupled 75
horse: poor novice hurdler: claimed out of C. Jackson's stable £4,000 after
seventh outing: in lead when falling sixth at Southwell in May on chasing
debut: stays 2½m: acts on good to firm and heavy ground: sometimes
breaks blood vessels. *K. C. Bailey*

FAST CRUISE 8 b.m. Cruise Missile – Speeder (Space King) [1992/3 c89
c21g c25dᵖᵘ c21sᶠ c28s⁴ c24d c24s⁶] angular mare: modest hurdler/chaser: –
best effort of season on fourth start: stays 3½m: needs give in the ground
and acts on heavy. *E. H. Owen jun*

FAST FUN 5 b.h. Germont – Fearful Fun (Harwell) [1992/3 21m⁴ 23g] no
sign of ability over hurdles. *C. Parker*

FAST STUDY 8 b.g. Crash Course – Mary May (Little Buskins) [1992/3 c102
c23g² c24s* c21sᶠ c27v* c24v³ c26dᶠ] workmanlike gelding: fair form over –
fences: won novice events at Leicester in November and Newton Abbot in
January: sold 3,200 gns Ascot June Sales: suited by a thorough test of
stamina: acts on heavy going: sketchy jumper. *D. Nicholson*

FAST THOUGHTS 6 b.g. Feelings (FR) – Heldigvis (Hot Grove)
[1992/3 22g*] sparely-made gelding: fair hurdler: kept on strongly to win 111
handicap at Worcester in October: wasn't seen out again: should stay 3m:
acts on dead ground: front runner. *D. R. Gandolfo*

FATACK 4 b.g. Kris – Ma Petite Cherie (USA) (Caro) [1992/3 17v⁶ 16g⁴
17f⁵] lightly-raced maiden on Flat: sold out of M. Stoute's stable 1,200 gns 88
Newmarket Autumn Sales: best effort over hurdles when fourth in novice
event at Worcester in April. *Miss Jacqueline S. Doyle*

FATHER DAN (IRE) 4 ch.c. Martin John – Sonia John (Main Reef)
[1992/3 18m³] lightly raced and no form on Flat at 3 yrs for D. Moffatt: poor 73
form when third of 5 in selling hurdle at Market Rasen in June. *Miss Gay
Kelleway*

FATHER DOWLING 6 br.g. Teofane – Stream Flyer (Paddy's Stream) c93
[1992/3 c26g² c27s² c27d* c27s² c24dᶠ c27v² c21d c27vᵖᵘ c19m³ c24m² –
c26f² c27g⁴] smallish, rather leggy ex-Irish gelding: first foal: dam never
ran: modest form over fences: won novice chase at Fontwell in October: ran
creditably in the spring on last 4 starts: thorough stayer: probably acts on
any going: visored eighth and last starts. *G. B. Balding*

FATHER FORTUNE 5 b.g. The Parson – Irish Mint (Dusky Boy)
[1992/3 16sᵖᵘ 17d 17g] smallish, good-bodied gelding: second foal: 76 p
half-brother to winning hurdler Sorbiere (by Deep Run): dam, poor novice
hurdler/chaser, half-sister to Corbiere: showed some promise and wasn't
unduly knocked about when beaten in novice hurdles at Huntingdon in
January and Cheltenham in April: will improve further. *O. Sherwood*

FATHER JOHN 9 ch.g. Viking (USA) – Theban Queen (Pindari) [1992/3 c– §
c24vᵖᵘ c25vᴿ c26gᵖᵘ 28m⁴ c27gᵖᵘ] strong gelding: carries plenty of – §
condition: poor hurdler/chaser: stays 3¼m: acts on hard ground: usually
blinkered nowadays: unreliable at start. *M. P. Muggeridge*

FATHER RALPH 7 ch.g. Rolfe (USA) – Quelliney (High Line) [1992/3
16s* 17s 17d⁶ 22d² 17dᵖᵘ] sturdy gelding: won novice hurdle at Windsor in 89
January: creditable efforts next 3 starts: probably needs testing conditions
when racing at 2m and should stay beyond 2¾m: acts on soft ground. *D. R.
Gandolfo*

FATHER TIME 9 ch.g. Longleat (USA) – Noddy Time (Gratitude) c100
[1992/3 c20d³ c23v²] sturdy, workmanlike gelding: useful hurdler at his –
best: jumped none too fluently but showed promise in competitive novice
chases at Doncaster and Uttoxeter in December: stays 3m: probably acts on
heavy going. *M. H. Tompkins*

FATHOM FIVE (IRE) 4 b.f. Slip Anchor – Sheer Luck (Shergar)
[1992/3 17dᵖᵘ] leggy, angular filly: sold out of I. Balding's stable 4,900 gns –
Newmarket Autumn Sales: showed nothing in juvenile hurdle at Taunton in
February: successful in 6f selling handicap on Flat in May. *M. Williams*

FAUSTNLUCE LADY 4 b.f. Faustus (USA) – Miss Friendly (Status Seeker) [1992/3 18s a16gᵖᵘ] leggy filly: half-sister to novice hurdler Dolly Prices (by Silly Prices): no form on Flat or in juvenile hurdles. *G. A. Ham* –

FAUX PAVILLON 9 ch.g. Alias Smith (USA) – Beech Tree (Fighting Ship) [1992/3 18m* 18g*] big gelding: won 2 novice handicap hurdles at Exeter (second for conditional jockeys) in October: should stay beyond 2¼m: acts on good to firm ground: tried none too fluent a jumper: tried blinkered: formerly unreliable. *Mrs J. G. Retter* 90

FAVOURED VICTOR (USA) 6 ch.g. Diesis – Northern Walk (CAN) (Nijinsky (CAN)) [1992/3 18d 16d⁴ 17g 17d⁵ 16d* 17g* 18d² 16s 17d⁵] strong gelding: won novice hurdles at Catterick (handicap) and Fakenham in February: good second at Market Rasen later in February, but well beaten last 2 starts: stays 2¼m: acts on dead going: pulls hard and seems best forcing pace. *K. A. Morgan* 95

FAVOURITE SONG 5 ch.m. Scallywag – Saucy Eater (Saucy Kit) [1992/3 F17d] fifth foal: half-sister to a poor maiden jumper by Balinger: dam winning staying hurdler: fell in a point in April: mid-division in 17-runner NH Flat race at Hereford in May: yet to race over hurdles or in a steeplechase. *P. Bradley*

FAYNAZ 7 ch.h. Tumble Wind (USA) – Ceduna (FR) (Right Tack) [1992/3 16g a16g* a16g³ a16gᵘʳ] small, angular horse: modest form over hurdles: claimer ridden, came from well off pace to win novice event at Lingfield in January: races at around 2m: acts on firm ground and on equitrack. *W. R. Muir* 91

FEARLESS FRED 6 ch.g. Crever – Most Appealing (Majority Blue) [1992/3 20g⁴ 18s 16v⁵ 16v⁵ 20d*] lengthy, sparely-made gelding: moderate form over hurdles: successful in novice handicap at Hereford in February: stays 2½m: acts on good to firm and heavy going. *Mrs J. G. Retter* 95

FEARLESS KING 7 b.g. Kings Lake (USA) – Intrepid Lady (USA) (Bold Ruler) [1992/3 23d 24s 24gʳᵗʳ 20sᵖᵘ 26g⁶ 25g³ 23g⁵ c27g c20f] workmanlike gelding: poor novice hurdler/chaser: stays 3m: acts on firm ground. *E. H. Robson* c72 / 76

FEARSOME 7 gr.g. Formidable (USA) – Seriema (Petingo) [1992/3 17s⁵ 16g 17v⁵ 17v* 17v³ 25d⁶ 22v* 22d] sturdy gelding: fair hurdler: won handicaps at Newton Abbot in December (seller, no bid) and April: sold out of Mrs J. Wonnacott's stable 4,000 gns Ascot February Sales after sixth outing: effective at 2m when conditions are testing and stays 2¾m well: probably acts on any going: sometimes blinkered in 1990/1. *K. R. Burke* 101

FEASIBLE 9 b.g. Kampala – Rajang (Sharpen Up) [1992/3 16g] leggy gelding: poor hurdler: shaped with promise in November, but wasn't seen out again: stays 2¼m: acts on dead going, goes well on fibresand. *S. B. Avery* –

FEDNEYHILL 9 b.g. Northern Value (USA) – Harwell Lady (Harwell) [1992/3 c24m*] lengthy gelding: fair pointer: won maiden hunter chase at Doncaster in February: stays 3m: acts on good to firm ground. *Miss C. Saunders* c85

FEELING FOOLISH (IRE) 4 ch.g. Fools Holme (USA) – Felin Geri (Silly Season) [1992/3 17dᶠ] inconsistent middle-distance handicapper on Flat, when trained by T. Fairhurst: would have finished a remote fourth of 13 in juvenile selling hurdle at Taunton in November but for falling at the last. *B. Forsey* 64

FEELING ROSEY 11 b.m. Uncle Pokey – Rose's Code (True Code) [1992/3 c21s⁵ c22vᵖᵘ c26s c21d c26d³ c25m] compact, good-quartered mare: winning hurdler: poor novice chaser: stays well: acts on any going: inconsistent. *D. T. Todd* c64 / –

FEILE NA HINSE 10 b.g. Cidrax (FR) – Hildamay (Cantab) [1992/3 c24s³ c26vᶠ c29d* c33gᵘʳ c25d⁵] workmanlike gelding: fair handicap chaser: won at Catterick in February: ran creditably at Punchestown in April: stays well: probably acts on any going. *R. Champion* c100 / –

FELL MIST 10 b.g. Silly Prices – Minimist (Bilsborrow) [1992/3 c24f⁵] c–
compact gelding: modest novice hurdler: no form in steeplechases, but is a –
fairly useful pointer: acts on heavy going. *Mrs Elizabeth A. March*

FELL WARDEN 5 br.g. Norwick (USA) – Kuwait Taxi (Dublin Taxi) 76
[1992/3 16s⁴ 16d 16d⁵ 16g a16g 22g a18g²] close-coupled, plain gelding:
second foal: dam, well beaten in selling hurdles, half-sister to fair hurdler
Aniece: poor novice hurdler: has run in sellers. *J. A. Hellens*

FELSINA (IRE) 4 b.f. Slip Anchor – Sepideh (Habitat) [1992/3 16d 16dᵖᵘ –
16g] little sign of ability on Flat or over hurdles. *W. Storey*

FELSPAR 7 gr.g. Coquelin (USA) – Candide (Bustino) [1992/3 17d 16g –
16sᵖᵘ 23mᶠ] lengthy, sparely-made gelding: tubed: no sign of ability: dead.
P. Hayward

FENCE JUDGE 11 b.g. Green Shoon – Bramble Belle (Vulgan) [1992/3 c98
c21d c25v⁴] compact gelding: hunter chaser nowadays: stays 3¼m: –
probably acts on any ground: tends to sweat: usually blinkered in 1991/2. *R.
W. Heyman*

FENNORHILL 9 b. or br.g. Al Sirat (USA) – Choralgina (Choral c70
Society) [1992/3 c19h³ c26gᵖᵘ c20m⁵ c26d³] poor maiden chaser: stays –
3¼m: acts on dead ground. *A. P. James*

FENOUILLE 6 b.g. Ile de Bourbon (USA) – Foreseen (Reform) [1992/3 –
26sᵖᵘ 21sᵖᵘ] angular gelding: poor novice hurdler: tried blinkered/visored.
Mrs V. Teal

FEN PRINCESS (IRE) 5 b.m. Trojan Fen – Cenerentola (FR) (Caro) –
[1992/3 18m⁶] close-coupled mare: modest staying handicapper on Flat:
jumped poorly and ran in snatches in early-season seller on hurdling debut.
P. C. Haslam

FENTON BRIDGE 9 b.g. Gleason (USA) – Divine Drapes (Divine Gift) c95
[1992/3 c25d* c25d⁴ c24dᵖᵘ c24d c24m* c20s³ c24fᵖᵘ] workmanlike –
gelding: won novice chases at Bangor (handicap) in October and Chepstow
in March: sold 6,200 gns Ascot June Sales: stays 3m: acts on soft and good to
firm going: blinkered last 3 starts: sometimes looks reluctant. *Andrew
Turnell*

FENWICK 6 b.g. Magnolia Lad – Isobel's Choice (Green God) [1992/3 –
21g⁵] smallish, angular gelding: winning selling hurdler: sold 3,100 gns in
May: stays 2½m: acts on heavy ground. *W. A. Stephenson*

FERENS HALL 6 b.g. Pollerton – String of Pearls (Pall Mall) [1992/3 91
16d³ 16g 17sᵖᵘ] unfurnished gelding: third in novice hurdle at Uttoxeter in
October: raced too freely afterwards (not seen out after January). *A. J.
Wilson*

FERMAIN 4 ch.g. Bustino – Trail of Blues (Cure The Blues (USA)) 72
[1992/3 17v⁵ 17v a16g 20s⁴ 17g⁵] close-coupled gelding: well beaten on Flat:
sold out of Lord Huntingdon's stable 3,400 gns Ascot November Sales: poor
novice hurdler: stays 2½m: acts on soft ground. *A. Barrow*

FERN HEIGHTS 6 b.g. Runnett – Jenny's Baubee (Busted) [1992/3 –
17d] no sign of ability over hurdles. *C. D. Broad*

FERODA 12 b.g. Ashmore (FR) – Dedham Vale (Dike (USA)) [1992/3 16d c132
c17s³ c20sᵖᵘ c24d c21dᶠ c17g⁴ c16g c20s⁴ c21d⁶] lengthy, powerful gelding: –
one-time very smart chaser: useful form at best in 1992/3: stays 21f: acts on
any going. *A. L. T. Moore, Ireland*

FERROMYN 8 b.g. Green Shoon – Ferrajo (Pretendre) [1992/3 c20s⁶ c104
c20s⁵ c18s⁵ 24d⁶ c24s* c21d 20d⁵ 26m c29sᶜᵒ c25d] tall, leggy, lengthy 120
gelding: fairly useful handicap hurdler: behind in valuable event at
Cheltenham on eighth outing: won novice chase at Punchestown in January:
stays 3m: acts on soft ground. *E. J. O'Grady, Ireland*

FERRUFINO (IRE) 5 b.h. Montekin – Fauchee (Busted) [1992/3 17g⁵ 100 d
16g⁴ 16g³ 16g² 16d 20sᵖᵘ 21sᵖᵘ 16dᵖᵘ 22vᵖᵘ] sparely-made ex-Irish horse:
seventh foal: brother to winning hurdler Cares of Tomorrow: dam
lightly-raced 1½m winner: 9f winner on Flat: moderate novice at best over

hurdles: trained by J. Bolger until after fourth start, next 2 by T. Morgan: no form in Britain: should stay further than 2m: form only on good ground. *D. J. Wintle*

FERRYCROSTHEMERSEY (IRE) 4 b.f. Red Sunset – Glomach (USA) (Majestic Light (USA)) [1992/3 16d] smallish filly: of little account on Flat: tailed off in early-season juvenile selling hurdle. *G. Fleming* –

FERRY ROAD 7 ch.g. Deep Run – Tarmar (Sayfar) [1992/3 17d⁴ 20d⁵ 17d] leggy gelding: no form over hurdles. *R. Rowe* –

FESTIVAL FANCY 6 ch.m. Le Coq d'Or – Rabbit Patrol (Guide) [1992/3 23g⁴ 28d³ 25d 28g⁴ 24m² 24g³ 25d³ 28mF 26m² 27f⁶] leggy, shallow-girthed mare: fair hurdler: ran creditably most starts in 1992/3: stays well: best form with give in the ground. *Mrs M. Reveley* 107

FETTLE UP 5 ch.g. Lyphard's Special (USA) – Fire Risk (Thatch (USA)) [1992/3 21dF 20vᵖᵘ a20g² a20g³ 20f a20g*] lengthy gelding: poor hurdler: won novice event at Southwell in May: stays 2½m: best form on fibresand: sometimes blinkered, and was when successful: sometimes looks reluctant. *J. Wharton* 77

FETTUCCINE 9 ch.g. Bybicello – Reel Keen (Firestreak) [1992/3 22m* 25m* 26s* 25gᵘʳ 24g* 25g c20g⁴ c23gF c25g⁴ 25s² 21sᵖᵘ 26v⁴ 27f*] compact gelding: fairly useful handicap hurdler: trained until after sixth start by W. A. Stephenson: had a good season and won at Market Rasen, Perth (amateurs), Cartmel, Cheltenham and Stratford: only poor form in novice chases: stays very well: acts on any going: sometimes runs in snatches: jumps fences none too fluently. *P. Cheesbrough* **c80**
126

FICHU (USA) 5 b.g. Sharpen Up – Mousseline de Soie (FR) (Riverman (USA)) [1992/3 F17g F10d⁴ 16d 16fᵖᵘ] sturdy gelding: signs of ability when seventh in novice hurdle at Ludlow in December: ran poorly on firm ground 3 months later. *G. Thorner* 78

FIDDLE A LITTLE 8 b.g. Deep Run – Brideweir (Chandra Cross) [1992/3 c26g³ c22g² c21g²] quite good-topped gelding: moderate handicap chaser: stayed 2¾m: acted on firm and dead ground: dead. *F. Murphy* **c108**
–

FIDDLER'S DRUM 6 b.g. Fidel – Timpany Lass (Dalesa) [1992/3 F16s 16g 16g⁶ 21m⁶ 17g] tall gelding: fifth foal: dam maiden Irish jumper: poor novice hurdler: stays 21f: acts on good to firm ground: not a fluent jumper: pulls hard. *G. Richards* 77

FIDDLERS PIKE 12 b.g. Turnpike – Fiddlers Bee (Idiot's Delight) [1992/3 c26s⁴ c29v* c30s* c29d² c34d⁵ c30dᵖᵘ] rangy gelding: useful **c132**
–

John Hughes Grand National Trial Chase, Chepstow—Fiddlers Pike continues in fine form

handicap chaser: won quite valuable events at Warwick in January and Chepstow (John Hughes Grand National Trial) in February: excellent second to Party Politics in Greenalls Gold Cup at Haydock and not disgraced in Midlands National at Uttoxeter: suited by a test of stamina: acts on heavy ground: trainer ridden: front runner: jumps well. *Mrs R. G. Henderson*

FIDDLERS THREE 10 ch.g. Orchestra – Kirin (Tyrant (USA)) [1992/3 c21s3 c22v3] tall, good-bodied gelding: fair chaser: suited by a test of stamina: acts on heavy going. *Capt. T. A. Forster* — **c103**

FIDEL EXPRESS 7 ch.g. Fidel – Spanish Empress (Don (ITY)) [1992/3 c20m4 c20sF c23g] half-brother to Queen's Vase winner Evzon (by English Prince), NH Flat winner Drumscap (by Remainder Man) and winning hurdler Pointer Man (by Major Point): dam placed over 1¼m: winning pointer in Ireland: poor form in early-season novice chases: sketchy jumper. *W. A. Stephenson* — **c75**

FIELD CONQUEROR 12 b.g. Busted – Divine Thought (Javelot) [1992/3 c29vpu c21s5 c26dpu] compact gelding: one-time useful chaser: no form in 1992/3: stays 3m: acts on heavy going: best blinkered. *M. Bradstock* — **c–**

FIELDHAVEN 4 b.f. Little Wolf – Keshoon (Sheshoon) [1992/3 F16f] fourth foal: half-sister to winning chaser Alan Ball (by Broadsword): dam fair staying hurdler: tailed off in NH Flat race at Haydock in May: yet to race over hurdles. *Miss S. J. Wilton*

FIELDRIDGE 4 ch.g. Rousillon (USA) – Final Thought (Final Straw) [1992/3 17g] workmanlike gelding: fairly useful on Flat, won 1¼m event in May, 1993: no show in quite well-contested juvenile hurdle at Doncaster in January: should do better. *C. P. E. Brooks* — **– p**

FIELDS MAN 11 b.g. Old Lucky – Rusty Lowe (Rustam) [1992/3 c19dpu] workmanlike gelding: novice hunter chaser: stayed 3m: acted on dead ground: dead. *G. W. Lewis* — **c–**

FIERCE 5 ch.g. Carwhite – Nosey (Nebbiolo) [1992/3 17s5 17s3 17v5 16s2 25v6 17s* 18s4 22f3 17f* 18v2] leggy gelding: fair handicap hurdler: won at Huntingdon in February and Newbury in March: stays 2¾m, not 25f in testing conditions: acts on any going: visored nowadays. *J. R. Jenkins* — **108**

FIERY FRED 6 b.g. Strong Gale – Princess Wager (Pollerton) [1992/3 22g6 23g 22dpu] workmanlike gelding: poor novice hurdler: form only on first outing, pulled up lame final one (December). *S. E. Sherwood* — **73**

FIERY SUN 8 b.g. Sexton Blake – Melanie Jane (Lord Gayle (USA)) [1992/3 17m 16m 17g 16g2 a20g5 a16g6 17g a18g* a16g5 20m3 18m* 16f4 a21g6] small gelding: fair handicap hurdler: won at Southwell (amateurs event) in February and Sedgefield in March (trained until after then by R. Barr): stays 2½m when conditions aren't testing: acts on firm, dead ground and fibresand: effective visored or not. *S. E. Kettlewell* — **111**

FIESTA DANCE 10 b.g. Record Token – Presumptuous (Gay Fandango (USA)) [1992/3 c20m6 c27m4 c18s5 26dpu c22v] rangy handicap chaser: no form in 1992/3: trained by G. Fleming until after third outing: stays 3m: acts on firm going: blinkered final outing. *C. Smith* — **c–** **–**

FIFFA'S BOY 10 gr.g. Sunyboy – Fiffa (Town Crier) [1992/3 c21m] workmanlike gelding: no form over hurdles: fair pointer: well beaten in novice hunter chase at Cheltenham in May. *Christopher Hooley* — **c–** **–**

FIFTH AMENDMENT 8 b.g. The Parson – Biowen (Master Owen) [1992/3 c24s6 c25gpu c24v4 c21d* c24g* c25f c25g2 c22mpu c30dpu] well-made gelding: fair chaser: trained by A. Turnell first 2 starts: won hunter chases at Windsor in February and Stratford in March: suited by around 3m: probably acts on any ground: wears blinkers. *Mrs F. Walwyn* — **c110**

FIFTY WINKS 7 b.g. Bulldozer – Chartreuse (Ionian) [1992/3 F16dpu] useful-looking gelding: unplaced in 3 NH Flat races: yet to race over hurdles or fences. *John R. Upson*

FIGHTING CHRISTINE (USA) 6 ch.m. Fighting Fit (USA) – Born Anew (USA) (Avatar (USA)) [1992/3 17gpu 18spu 17m 17d3 16d4 17s a22gpu — **79**

a18g4 a16gpu] workmanlike mare: poor hurdler: form only at around 2m: acted on good to firm, dead ground and equitrack: often blinkered: dead. *R. T. Juckes*

FIGHTING DAYS (USA)   7 ch.g. Fit To Fight (USA) – August Days (USA) (In Reality) [1992/3 c2 1m* c23d c19f3 c2 1d2 c19g2 c19mpu c16g3 c16s6 c19f3 c2 1mpu] sparely-made, plain gelding: winning hurdler: won novice chase at Plumpton in September: ran poorly in second half of season: stays 2 1f: acts on hard and dead ground: blinkered last 2 outings. *A. Moore*   **c91**
—

FIGHTING JESSICA   8 b.g. Slippered – Daffydown Lady (Menelek) [1992/3 c25d2 c22g4 c22s4 c24g 20gF c25d2 c24m6 c24f2 c22d3] leggy, workmanlike gelding: modest handicap hurdler/chaser: stays 25f: probably acts on any ground: sketchy jumper of fences. *John R. Upson*   **c99**
—

FIGHTING WORDS   7 ch.g. Prince Bee – How Hostile (Tumble Wind (USA)) [1992/3 c16m* c16g* c16d4 c21s3 c21d3 c21g* c21g3 c20s4] workmanlike gelding: fairly useful hurdler: won 2 novice chases at Wetherby in October and one at Sandown in February: barely stays 2¾m: acts on good to firm and soft ground: sound jumper: useful handicap chaser in making. *J. T. Gifford*   **c122** p
—

FIGHT TO WIN (USA)   5 b.g. Fit To Fight (USA) – Spark of Life (USA) (Key To The Mint (USA)) [1992/3 22g4 19g5 22v4 17s3 21s a20g2 c26d6 c2 1f* c20f3 c2 1g* c24m*] compact gelding: fair hurdler: won novice chases at Windsor, Plumpton and Taunton in the spring: sold 12,000 gns Ascot June Sales: stays 3m: acts on any going: usually visored nowadays. *I. A. Balding*   **c103**
112

FILE CONCORD   9 br.g. Strong Gale – Lady Reporter (London Gazette) [1992/3 17v4 17s c22gpu c21d5 c23spu] big, rangy gelding: fairly useful hurdler/chaser at best: form only on first start in 1992/3 (broke blood vessel third): will stay beyond 2 1f: acts on heavy going. *Mrs J. Pitman*   **c–**
126

FILE JET   7 b.g. Candy Cane – Never-Cot-Napping (Even Money) [1992/3 23d] tall gelding: poor novice hurdler: dead. *Mrs J. Pitman*
—

FILE VESTRY (IRE)   5 b.g. Torus – Reynella (Royal Buck) [1992/3 16vpu] leggy, unfurnished gelding: fourth foal: half-brother to winning staying hurdler Scandalous Rumour (by Le Bavard): dam Irish NH Flat race winner: showed nothing in novice hurdle at Kempton in January. *Mrs J. Pitman*
—

FILM LIGHTING GIRL   7 ch.m. Persian Bold – Mey (Canisbay) [1992/3 16d a18g a20g] poor novice hurdler: trained until after first outing by R. Weaver. *R. W. Emery*   62

FINAL ACE   6 ch.g. Sharpo – Palmella (USA) (Grundy) [1992/3 a16g4] leggy gelding: poor maiden plater over hurdles: best efforts at 2m on equitrack. *Miss S. J. Wilton*
—

FINAL CHANT   12 br.g. Joshua – Chantfour (Chantelsey) [1992/3 c25d* c25g2 c25m2 c25d5] good-topped gelding: very useful hunter chaser at best, fairly useful form in 1992/3: won at Kelso in February: stays 25f: acts on any ground: sometimes jumps sketchily. *D. A. D. Brydon*   **c104**

FINAL HOPE (IRE)   5 ch.g. Burslem – Mesnil Warren (Connaught) [1992/3 24g5] angular, unfurnished gelding: winning pointer: poor maiden hurdler: stays 3m. *R. Tate*   67

FINALLY FANTAZIA   4 ch.f. True Song – Catherine Bridge (Pitpan) [1992/3 F17d*] first foal: dam, winning hurdler, stayed 2½m: 50/1, won 17-runner NH Flat race at Hereford in May: yet to race over hurdles. *Mrs I. McKie*

FINAL SPRING   9 b.g. Hubble Bubble – Final Answer (Honour Bound) [1992/3 c25m3 c25dpu] good-topped gelding: winning hunter chaser: stays 3m: acts on firm and dead ground. *Mrs J. C. Breese*   **c89**
—

FINE AS FIVEPENCE   4 b.f. Sulaafah (USA) – Shes Broke (Busted) [1992/3 18mF 18dF 18g4 17s] small filly: of little account on Flat: poor form in juvenile hurdles in first half of season. *Mrs A. Knight*   75

FINE HARVEST   7 b.g. Oats – Kayella (Fine Blade (USA)) [1992/3 20s   c–
c16vᵖᵘ c16d4 c16g4 c20f5 c16mF c21vᵖᵘ c20gᵖᵘ] good-topped gelding: poor   –
novice hurdler/chaser. *B. A. McMahon*

FINE LACE   9 b.m. Palm Track – Grecian Lace (Spartan General) [1992/3   c90
c21mᵘʳ c28f4] prolific winner in points: best effort in hunter chases when
fourth at Stratford in June: stays 3½m: acts on firm ground. *G. B. Tarry*

FINE OAK   6 br.m. Point North – Fidessa (Fine Blade (USA)) [1992/3 16g
20sᵖᵘ 16g] workmanlike mare: no sign of ability. *D. Robertson*   –

FINE THYNE (IRE)   4 ch.g. Good Thyne (USA) – Bring Me Sunshine
(Wolverlife) [1992/3 F17m*] rangy, rather plain gelding: first foal: dam won
2m maiden hurdle in Ireland: narrow winner of 23-runner NH Flat race at
Cheltenham in April: yet to race over hurdles. *G. Harwood*

FINE TIMING   6 b.g. Roscoe Blake – Off The Pill (Marshal Pil) [1992/3   c–
c17fᵖᵘ] pulled up in steeplechases. *M. McCormack*

FINE TUDOR   7 b.g. Jimsun – Mill Haven (Mannion) [1992/3 c17dᵖᵘ]   c–
close-coupled gelding: poor novice hurdler: yet to complete in points and a   –
hunter chase. *Mrs E. H. Heath*

FINGERS CROSSED   9 b.m. Touching Wood (USA) – La Pythie (FR)
(Filiberto (USA)) [1992/3 21f* 26s5 28f2 25m* 25d5 24mᵖᵘ] neat mare: 94
modest handicap hurdler: won at Hexham (seller, bought in 4,700 gns) and
Carlisle early in season: suited by test of stamina: acted on any going with
possible exception of fibresand: blinkered once: front runner: dead. *M. D.
Hammond*

FINKLE STREET (IRE)   5 b. or br.g. Strong Gale – Super Cailin
(Brave Invader (USA)) [1992/3 17g] smallish, leggy gelding: half-brother to   –
winning jumpers Mr Optimist (by Pollerton) and Grace Moore (by Deep
Run): dam never ran: tailed off in novice event at Huntingdon in February
on hurdling debut. *F. Murphy*

FINNEGAIS   6 b.g. Floriferous – Marline (Captain James) [1992/3 F12d   c–
c16gᵖᵘ] workmanlike gelding: third foal: brother to poor novice jumper
Floline: dam twice-raced half-sister to several winners including very
useful Irish 7f winner Dempsey, subsequently successful over hurdles:
behind in NH Flat race: pulled up after bad mistake third in novice chase in
March. *P. Butler*

FINNERAN'S FANTASY   4 b.g. Cree Song – Mab (Morston (FR))
[1992/3 17gᵖᵘ a16g5 18vᵖᵘ a16gᵖᵘ] lengthy, angular gelding: twice-raced on   66
Flat: poor form at best over hurdles. *D. Morris*

FIRE AND REIGN (IRE)   5 b.g. Sandhurst Prince – Fine Form (USA)
(Fachendon) [1992/3 F17g] plain, leggy gelding: first foal: dam lightly-raced
maiden: behind in NH Flat race at Newbury in March: yet to race over
hurdles or fences. *P. F. Nicholls*

FIRE AT WILL   10 br.g. Random Shot – Kindly (Tarqogan) [1992/3   c–
c22sᵖᵘ] close-coupled, angular gelding: fair chaser in 1991/2: out-and-out   –
stayer: acts well on a soft surface. *Capt. T. A. Forster*

FIREAWAY FLANAGAN   6 b.g. King's Ride – Cahore (Quayside)   c–
[1992/3 c21vᵖᵘ c20m5] workmanlike gelding: first foal: dam unraced
half-sister to the dam of Jodami: third in an Irish point in 1992: sold 20,000
gns Doncaster May (1992) Sales: showed little in novice chases: dead. *O.
Sherwood*

FIRED EARTH (IRE)   5 b.g. Soughaan (USA) – Terracotta (GER)
(Nebos (GER)) [1992/3 16s* 16d2 16d3] good-topped gelding: second foal: 95 +
dam winner on Flat in Germany: easily won novice hurdle at Leicester in
January: creditable efforts afterwards without showing expected
improvement: will stay 2½m: acts on soft going. *J. R. Fanshawe*

FIREFIGHTER   4 ch.c. Sharpo – Courtesy Call (Northfields (USA))
[1992/3 16s3 16d5 a16g6 16v4 16d5 21g] close-coupled colt: half-brother to   84
winning Irish jumper Joshua Tree (by Hello Gorgeous): fair winner from 9f
to 1½m on Flat: modest form over hurdles: trained until after fifth start by

R. Hollinshead: best form at 2m: acts on heavy ground: visored final start. *B. P. J. Baugh*

FIREHALMS 6 b.g. Reesh – Halmsgiving (Free State) [1992/3 c25m5] sparely-made gelding: no form over hurdles: modest pointer: signs of ability in hunter chase at Nottingham in March. *A. W. Pickering* c66 –

FIRE RUN 6 b.m. Deep Run – Palazon (Laurence O) [1992/3 17v] lengthy mare: no sign of ability. *P. Butler* c– –

FIRE STREET 7 b.g. Gleason (USA) – Ross Maid (Random Shot) [1992/3 c21g5] winning pointer in Ireland: made mistakes when fifth in novice event at Sedgefield in October on steeplechasing debut. *J. H. Johnson* c–

FIREWATER STATION 10 br.g. Buckskin (FR) – Gamonda (Gala Performance (USA)) [1992/3 c21m5] ex-Irish gelding: modest pointer in Britain in 1993: fifth in novice hunter chase at Folkestone in May. *Mrs D. B. A. Silk* c63

FIRM PRICE 12 b.g. Our Mirage – Strip Poker (Raise You Ten) [1992/3 23g2 22d* 20d 22s* 20f* 20g2 22g5] tall, sparely-made gelding: fair chaser: fairly useful hurdler: won handicap at Sedgefield in November and claimers at Huntingdon in February and Doncaster in March: stays 27f: acts on any going: blinkered twice: poor jumper of fences. *Mrs M. Reveley* c– x 121

FIRST COMMAND (NZ) 6 b.g. Captain Jason (NZ) – Lady of The Dawn (NZ) (Princely Note) [1992/3 17s 17v4 16v3 20dpu] compact gelding: modest form at best in novice hurdles: should prove well suited by further than 17f: acts on heavy going. *Capt. T. A. Forster* 85

FIRST CRACK 8 b.m. Scallywag – Furstin (Furry Glen) [1992/3 17d5 20d3 21v 16v3 22d3 23d* 22m2 25d 24gF 22dpu] compact, workmanlike mare: novice chaser: fair handicap hurdler: won at Wolverhampton in February: effective from 2m to 23f: probably acts on any going: sometimes finds little under pressure, and is best held up: poor jumper of fences. *F. Jordan* c– x 103

FIRST DESIGN 6 b.g. Rustingo – Designer (Celtic Cone) [1992/3 c25vpu c23v4] lengthy, unfurnished gelding: poor novice hurdler: winning pointer: well beaten in hunter chases: stays 21f: acts on soft ground. *P. D. Jones* c–

FIRST DIVISION (FR) 10 b.g. Wolver Hollow – Home And Away (Home Guard (USA)) [1992/3 17s 17s6 17d2 20d 18g4 17m2 21d5 22f4 17g] angular, workmanlike gelding: modest handicap hurdler nowadays: has run in sellers: best at up to 2¼m: acts on soft and good to firm going: blinkered last 2 starts. *W. Jenks* 89

FIRST DRIVE 6 ch.g. Le Moss – Kanturk Lady (Tarqogan) [1992/3 F17g] ex-Irish gelding: fifth foal: half-brother to winning Irish 3m chaser Kanturk Warrior (by Riot Helmet): dam twice-raced in Irish points: tailed off in NH Flat races: sold 3,200 gns Malvern February Sales: won a point in May: yet to race over hurdles or in a steeplechase. *J. A. C. Edwards*

FIRST EVER (IRE) 4 b.g. Welsh Term – Simone's Luck (Malinowski (USA)) [1992/3 21s 16g4] second foal: half-brother to fair 2m hurdler Simone's Son (by Hatim): dam poor maiden on Flat and over hurdles: poor form when fourth in novice hurdle at Hexham in May. *R. R. Lamb* 71

FIRST EXHIBITION 6 b.m. Claude Monet (USA) – All Hail (Alcide) [1992/3 22m4] leggy, sparely-made mare: poor novice selling hurdler: sold 600 gns Ascot November Sales: stays 2½m: acts on any ground. *Mrs A. Knight* –

FIRST LESSON (NZ) 7 b.g. Church Parade – Horafama (NZ) (Patron Saint) [1992/3 16d3 17gur] sparely-made gelding: poor novice hurdler, lightly raced: should stay beyond 2m: acts on soft ground. *P. J. Hobbs* 86

FIRST LORD 7 b.g. Lord Gayle (USA) – Touquaise (FR) (Takawalk II) [1992/3 c20s2 c25g2] workmanlike gelding: winning hurdler: novice chaser: only poor form early in 1992/3: needs a test of stamina: acts on soft going and good to firm. *Mrs V. A. Aconley* c84

FISHERMAN'S QUAY   9 ch.g. Music Boy – Golconda (Matador)   c–
[1992/3 c21mᵖᵘ c24gᵖᵘ c23gᵘʳ] poor pointer: no sign of ability in
steeplechases. *Miss J. L. Rae*

FISHIN' TACKLE (USA)   5 b.g. Sportin' Life (USA) – Perilune (USA)   77
(Soy Numero Uno (USA)) [1992/3 2 ld 16g 17g⁶] leggy, close-coupled
gelding: poor novice hurdler: not raced after October: unlikely to stay much
beyond 2m: acts on good to firm and heavy ground. *L. Lungo*

FISHKI   7 b.m. Niniski (USA) – Ladyfish (Pampapaul) [1992/3 c25g*   c96
c25vᶠ c21s³ c26dᶠ c21dᵖᵘ] sparely-made mare: fair hurdler: won novice   –
chase at Ayr in November, and would probably have won similar events
following month and in February but for falling in latter stages: something
looked amiss final start: suited by 3m and give in the ground: front runner.
M. D. Hammond

FISH QUAY   10 ch.g. Quayside – Winkle (Whistler) [1992/3 c21v² c25dʳᵒ   c96   x
c24s⁵] lengthy, workmanlike gelding: hunter chaser nowadays: stays well: –
probably acts on any going: blinkered once: has broken blood vessel: poor
jumper. *Mrs K. M. Lamb*

FISIANNA   4 b.f. Efisio – Jianna (Godswalk (USA)) [1992/3 17vᵖᵘ 17v a16g   –
17vᵘʳ 18vᵘʳ a20g⁵ 18g 17g] small filly: lightly-raced sprint maiden on Flat for
A. Davison: no sign of ability over hurdles. *Mrs M. E. Long*

FISSURE SEAL   7 ch.g. Tug of War – Annies Pet (Normandy) [1992/3   c131 p
c25vᵖᵘ c24d* c20s* c24s⁴ c24v* 24d* 24d³ 20d* 26m* 22s⁴ c25d*]   137 p
   Apart from winning a point-to-point Fissure Seal had little to show for
three seasons' racing, but his fortunes improved dramatically after a change
of stables between his first and second starts in 1992/3. Fissure Seal made
remarkable progress and won seven races worth over £70,000, showing
himself to be not only a tough and genuine performer but also a versatile and
useful one. Fissure Seal's first three wins were gained over fences, at
Wexford and Clonmel (two of them); his next three over hurdles, at
Leopardstown, Fairyhouse and Cheltenham. And he won a novice handicap
at the Punchestown Festival when returned to chasing on his final start.
Fissure Seal's performance in very valuable and strongly-contested events
at Cheltenham and Punchestown are worth singling out. At Cheltenham,
where he was one of only two Irish challengers for the American Express
Gold Card Handicap Hurdle Final, Fissure Seal didn't appear on the scene
until the second last, one of eight still in with a chance at that stage. Fissure

American Express Gold Card Handicap Hurdle Final, Cheltenham—
Fissure Seal isn't fluent at the last but proves too strong for Jakarrdi (left) and Kings Rank

Seal continued to make significant progress, moving through between Kings Rank and Jakarrdi to take a narrow lead at the last, where an untidy jump lost him some momentum. Soon back on an even keel, Fissure Seal stayed on strongly under pressure to forge two and a half lengths clear of Jakarrdi. Fissure Seal had to work even harder to win the Heineken Gold Cup at Punchestown, again coming from off the pace in a race run at a good gallop. He and Son of War were engaged in a tremendous battle from the second last, Fissure Seal prevailing by a head. Fissure Seal's jumping wasn't particularly fluent but it should improve as he gains experience.

Fissure Seal (ch.g. 1986)	Tug of War (ch 1973)	Reliance II (b 1962)	Tantieme / Relance III
		Pirate Queen (ch 1966)	Pirate King / Cantus
	Annies Pet (b 1977)	Normandy (b 1965)	Vimy / Stone Crop
		Clever Pet (br 1969)	Menelek / Cool Pet

The three mares on the bottom line of Fissure Seal's pedigree were all unraced. Cool Pet produced three winners, including the fairly useful chaser Outstanding, while Clever Pet is the dam of a winning pointer. As yet Fissure Seal is Annies Pet's only winner, but that should be rectified before too long provided Fissure Seal's brother Yeoman Warrior fulfils the promise he showed in novice hurdles in the latest season. The leggy Fissure Seal isn't a very prepossessing individual, but he's an admirable racehorse and one who should continue to do well over hurdles and fences when stamina is at a premium. He acts on good to firm and heavy ground. *H. de Bromhead, Ireland*

FISTFUL OF BUCKS 7 b.g. Lochnager – Crimson Ring (Persian Bold) [1992/3 20g 25g4 20g2] leggy gelding: fair handicap hurdler: stays 2½m: acts on soft going. *T. Dyer*   106

FIT FOR FIRING (FR) 9 b.m. In Fijar (USA) – Elizabeth Wales (Abernant) [1992/3 c21d* c21v* c26d2] tall, leggy mare: fair handicap chaser: won at Wincanton and Newton Abbot and finished creditable second   **c114** –

Regency Hurdle, Warwick—Flakey Dove stays on strongly

on former course in first half of season: effective at 2½m and stays 3¼m: acts on any going. *D. R. C. Elsworth*

FITNESS FANATIC 5 b.g. Nishapour (FR) – Bustling Nelly (Bustino) [1992/3 18f⁵ 17m] half-brother to fair hurdler/winning chaser Silk Degrees (by Dunbeath): of little account on Flat nowadays: signs of a little ability in early-season novice hurdles. *J. T. Gifford* —

FIT THE BILL 5 b.g. Nicholas Bill – Golden Windlass (Princely Gift) [1992/3 F12d⁴ F10d² a16g^bd] angular, workmanlike gelding: modest hurdler: raced only at 2m: acted on good to firm going: dead. *C. Tinkler* —

FIVE CASTLES 5 b.g. Castle Keep – Teftu (Double Jump) [1992/3 18f* 20m⁵] angular gelding: won novice selling handicap at Fontwell (bought in 3,100 gns) in August, clearly best effort over hurdles. *G. P. Enright* 69

FIVE LAMPS 13 b.g. Paddy's Stream – Ballinarose (Arctic Slave) [1992/3 17d² 17v] rangy gelding: fairly useful hurdler: failed to get beyond second in 2 outings over fences: stayed 2½m: acted on good to firm and heavy going: thoroughly genuine: dead. *R. Dickin* c– / 118

FIVELEIGH BUILDS 6 b.g. Deep Run – Giolla Donn (Giolla Mear) [1992/3 24s² 25v³] unfurnished gelding: fairly useful hurdler: not raced after December: stays 25f: acts on good to firm and heavy ground. *John R. Upson* 118

FIVELEIGH FIRST (IRE) 5 b.g. Furry Glen – Ballygriffin (Deep Run) [1992/3 21s 16s⁶ 17v⁶ 22s 24s³] strong, lengthy gelding: chasing type: modest novice hurdler: suited by a test of stamina: acts on soft going. *John R. Upson* 89

FIVE STARS 6 br.m. Majestic Maharaj – True Melody (Pardigras) [1992/3 F17m 16d 20m 16f²] very dipped-backed mare: first sign of ability when second in novice hurdle at Worcester (blinkered) in March. *J. Colston* 78

FIXBY 4 ch.g. Nicholas Bill – Muninga (St Alphage) [1992/3 17g^pu 16d 16s] 2,700Y: close-coupled, workmanlike gelding: half-brother to Flat —

winner/novice hurdler Mr Kewmill (by Homing) and to a winner abroad: dam useful 5f performer: no form in juvenile hurdles: dead. *J. J. O'Neill*

FLAKEY DOVE 7 b.m. Oats – Shadey Dove (Deadly Nightshade) [1992/3 17d² 17g⁵ 21m* 21f² 17m 17s² 21f* 16f] close-coupled, sparely-made mare: smart hurdler: successful in Regency Hurdle at Warwick (by 5 lengths from Lift And Load) in February and St Modwen Staffordshire Hurdle at Uttoxeter (beat Beech Road a length) in May: ran best race when never-nearer seventh to Granville Again in Smurfit Champion Hurdle at Cheltenham on fifth outing: effective from 2m to 21f, and may stay further: possibly unsuited by soft ground, acts on any other: tends to idle and suited by waiting tactics: jumps well. *R. J. Price*   153

FLAME OF ARAGON 7 ch.m. Aragon – Enlighten (Twilight Alley) [1992/3 16m 17mⁿ 28g] close-coupled, good-bodied mare: modest maiden at best on Flat: no sign of ability over hurdles. *W. T. Kemp*   –

FLAMEWOOD 4 b.f. Touching Wood (USA) – Alan's Girl (Prince Hansel) [1992/3 F16v⁴ F17g] fifth foal: half-sister to winning hurdler Threewaygirl (by Rymer) and 7-y-o Sworded Knight (by Broadsword): dam, winning hurdler, probably stayed 3m: signs of ability in NH Flat races: yet to race over hurdles. *Mrs D. Haine*

FLAPPING FREDA (IRE) 5 ch.m. Carlingford Castle – Just Darina (Three Dons) [1992/3 F17m] sturdy mare: eighth foal: half-sister to useful 2m hurdler/winning chaser Egypt Mill Prince (by Deep Run) and winning 3m hurdler Danish Chief (by Brave Invader): dam once-raced half-sister to good hunter chaser Credit Call: seventh in 24-runner NH Flat race at Cheltenham in April: yet to race over hurdles or fences. *J. R. Jenkins*

FLASHING STEEL 8 b.g. Broadsword (USA) – Kingsfold Flash (Warpath) [1992/3 c22s* c18sᶠ c21d* c22d* c25d]   **c139**

Irish novice chasing was under-represented at Cheltenham in March: no Flashing Steel, no How's The Boss, no Soft Day, no Son of War, no Deep Heritage, no Table Rock; and, while present, Fissure Seal was there to win the big handicap hurdle Final. The absentees weren't an outstanding bunch of novices, admittedly, but amounted to as good as the Irish stables had in 1992/3. Flashing Steel was one of the best of them and looked an excellent prospect until he ran poorly in the Heineken Gold Cup at Punchestown in April. For some reason he wasn't himself that day. He looked well beforehand but had already come off the bridle when he made a bad mistake at the tenth; he could make no progress afterwards and finished tailed off, reportedly showing 'respiratory distress'. Flashing Steel carried clear top weight in the handicap at Punchestown, 13 lb more than the principals Fissure Seal and Son of War, following three clear-cut wins from three completed rounds over fences. We were particularly impressed by the second one, in the WinElectric Novice Chase Series Final at Leopardstown in February. Most of the leading home-trained novices turned out, Soft Day being a notable exception. Flashing Steel, a very nice type, a big, rangy chasing sort with smart hurdling form, lacked experience. He was making his first appearance since falling in a race won by Soft Day at Punchestown in early December and only his third in all over fences (the first had resulted in a twenty-length win at Fairyhouse in November). Nevertheless he jumped better than anything else, took the lead two out after moving well in a handy position from the start then stayed on strongly to pull thirteen lengths clear of Allezmoss and Galevilla Express, two horses who, incidentally, came to grief at Cheltenham. Two weeks later Flashing Steel won another Final, the six-runner EBF Novices' Chase Series at Fairyhouse, unchallenged by fifteen lengths from Buckboard Bounce. He was already getting on top when Solar Symphony's fall left him clear three out.

Flashing Steel put up his best performance as a hurdler over two and three quarter miles; his steeplechase wins have come over the same distance or thereabouts. The Heineken Chase was his first race over further, so it remains to be seen whether he gets three miles. He will almost certainly show that he does. His breeding is interesting. He's by the

EBF Novices' Chase Series Final, Fairyhouse—
Flashing Steel easily lands the odds

Champion Hurdle runner-up Broadsword, who stayed at least two and a half miles, out of the one-mile plater Kingsfold Flash. The dam's previous foals were fillies of contrasting abilities, the winning hurdler/chaser Four Sport (by Swing Easy) who just about stayed two and a half miles, and the useful one-mile to one-and-a-quarter-mile handicapper Kingsfold Flame (by No Loiterer). She has had other runners in Wensleydalewilliam (by Tudorville) and On The Sauce (by Kala Shikari), both of them hurdles winners, the one at two and a half miles, the other at up to three and a quarter, and Miltonfield (by Little Wolf), placed in a National Hunt Flat race at Fairyhouse in April. The second dam Piccadilly Rose stayed a mile and a half on the Flat, the third dam Folk Song won over five furlongs as a two-year-old, her only season to race. Piccadilly Rose produced a winner over jumps in Old Eros, very useful in his days as a juvenile hurdler.

		Ack Ack	Battle Joined
	Broadsword (USA)	(b 1966)	Fast Turn
	(b 1977)	Cutting	Bold Ruler
Flashing Steel		(ch 1966)	Sarcastic
(b.g. 1985)		Warpath	Sovereign Path
	Kingsfold Flash	(gr 1969)	Ardneasken
	(ch 1977)	Piccadilly Rose	Reform
		(ch 1972)	Folk Song

It is to be hoped that all is well with Flashing Steel, so that he has the chance to fulfil his promise over fences and stiffen Irish chasing ranks led at present by the likes of Cahervillahow, General Idea and Garamycin. Flashing Steel should have plenty of racing left in him. He didn't start until

282

he was six years old and has run just thirteen times, including three times unbeaten in National Hunt Flat company. Twelve of those races were on dead ground or softer, the other, Thetford Forest's Sun Alliance Novices' Hurdle at Cheltenham in which he made several mistakes and was beaten going to three out, on good ground. However, the prevailing firmish ground was not the reason for his missing Cheltenham in 1993—other objectives had been announced well before then. *J. E. Mulhern, Ireland*

FLASH OF REALM (FR)   7 b.h. Super Moment (USA) – Light of Realm (Realm) [1992/3 16g 17g³ 17s⁴] rangy horse: modest novice hurdler, lightly raced: raced only at around 2m: acts on soft going. *P. Monteith*   88

FLASHTHECASH   7 b.g. Torus – Easter Beauty (Raise You Ten)   **c134** p
[1992/3 20g⁵ c20s⁴ 17d² c24sᶠ c18v* c21sᶠ c21sᶠ c24d* c20mᵇᵈ c20f* c20f*   95
c26m* c21m*]

The Godiva Kingmaker Novices' Chase, a valuable Grade 2 event run at Warwick in May, looks likely to prove a welcome addition to the programme. Following a low-key start in 1991 when Anti Matter landed the odds from three opponents, the race has progressed in terms of quantity and quality. Milford Quay and Beech Road occupied the first two places in a seven-runner field in 1992, and in the latest season nine horses, each of them successful at least twice over fences, went to post. They included the 1992 Daily Express Triumph Hurdle winner Duke of Monmouth, an easy winner of both his starts in novice chases, Shu Fly and Billy Bathgate, second and fourth respectively in the valuable two-mile novice chase at Aintree the previous month, Egypt Mill Prince, the impressive winner of Cheltenham's Coventry Novices' Chase, and the fast-improving Flashthecash, who started favourite. The fences had proved something of a problem for Flashthecash in his early races, but for which he'd have had a better record than two wins, in a handicap at Fontwell and a novice handicap at Stratford, from his first seven starts in chases.

Flashthecash learned from his mistakes, and as his jumping became consistently good so his form improved and he picked up further wins at Chepstow, Aintree and Cheltenham. In the Chivas Regal Amateur Riders Novices' Handicap Chase at Aintree Flashthecash made most of the running, but the usual waiting tactics were adopted at Cheltenham where, under a confident ride, Flashthecash was hugely impressive in beating Indian Tonic by six lengths. The Godiva Kingmaker Novices' Chase provided Flashthecash, conceding weight all round, with by far his stiffest test, but he proved more than equal to it. He travelled strongly as Egypt Mill Prince set a good pace which had most of the field in trouble a long way from home, and after taking over from the tiring leader approaching the second last he was ridden out to win by five lengths from Billy Bathgate.

Flashthecash (b.g. 1986)	Torus (b 1976)	Ribero (b 1965)	Ribot Libra
		Lighted Lamp (b 1967)	Sir Gaylord Chandelier
	Easter Beauty (b 1981)	Raise You Ten (br 1960)	Tehran Visor
		Easter Vigil (b 1971)	Arctic Slave Pet Jackdaw

Flashthecash, a small, compact gelding, not many people's idea of an ideal chasing type, was bought for IR 10,000 guineas at Tattersalls Derby Sale in 1990. Runner-up in a point-to-point in Ireland the following year, Flashthecash then joined his present stable and won a novice hurdle at Fontwell in his first season. He's the first foal of the unraced Easter Beauty, a sister to two winning jumpers and half-sister to three others. Easter

Chivas Regal Amateur Riders' Novices' Handicap Chase, Aintree—
Flashthecash holds off Tres Amigos

Godiva Kingmaker Novices' Chase, Warwick —
Flashthecash takes over from Egypt Mill Prince at the second last

Beauty's third foal Call Home (by Callernish) was successful on both his starts in National Hunt Flat races in the latest season, the second of them at Cheltenham on the same day that Flashthecash won there. Flashthecash's grandam Easter Vigil, also unraced, is a daughter of a winning sister to Ormond King, a very useful performer over hurdles and fences in Ireland in the 'seventies. Connections will be spoilt for choice when they come to plan Flashthecash's campaign for the next season, for he's effective at around two and a half miles and is likely to stay beyond three and a quarter miles which leaves them with plenty of options. Races such as the Mackeson Gold Cup and H & T Walker Gold Cup could well figure on his agenda in the first part of 1993/4. There seems no reason why the progressive Flashthecash, a winner also on ground ranging from firm to heavy, shouldn't have another very successful season. *G. B. Balding*

FLASHY DANCER   8 ch.g. Young Man (FR) – Gem-May (Mansingh (USA)) [1992/3 22d6 24g6 23g5 22d] rather leggy gelding: poor form in early-season novice hurdles: best effort on second outing, visored final one. *W. L. Barker*   72

FLASS VALE   5 b.g. Final Straw – Emblazon (Wolver Hollow) [1992/3 20m 22d5] close-coupled gelding: moderate hurdler: not raced after September: changed hands 1,250 gns Ascot February Sales: stays 2¾m: acts on hard ground: usually blinkered: sometimes makes mistakes. *T. Fairhurst*   –

FLAXON WORRIOR   9 ch.g. Roman Warrior – Domino Smith (White Speck) [1992/3 17spu 21s4 a18gpu] leggy gelding: poor novice hurdler: stays 2¾m: acts on good to firm and soft ground. *A. J. Le Blond*   67

FLEMISH FUDGE   11 b.g. Candy Cane – Leuze (Vimy) [1992/3 c24sF] rangy gelding: fair handicap chaser, lightly raced: suited by around 3m and give in the ground: jumps well: game. *Miss H. C. Knight*   c–
–

FLETCHER'S BOUNTY (IRE)   4 b.c. Glenstal (USA) – Maimiti (Goldhill) [1992/3 16m] small colt: sold 3,300 gns Newmarket Autumn   67

Sales: modest maiden on Flat, probably stays 1¼m: behind in juvenile hurdle at Catterick in March. *Mrs M. Reveley*

FLIGHT HILL 9 br.g. Relkino – Firella (Firestreak) [1992/3 c20gF c18d² c20gF c20g c20g c21g* c21mF] leggy, workmanlike gelding: fairly useful chaser: disappointing before winning by 30 lengths at Sedgefield in April: probable winner when falling last on same course following month: effective from 2m to 2 1f: acts on firm and dead ground: best with forcing tactics: reportedly broke blood vessel once. *Mrs M. Reveley*   c127 –

FLIGHT OF SONG 6 ch.m. Busted Fiddle – Why Bird (Birdbrook) [1992/3 17g⁶ 18f 17g⁴ 16g 17m⁶] sparely-made mare: poor maiden plater over hurdles. *D. J. Wintle*   63

FLIGHT OF STEEL 8 ch.g. Le Moss – Mary Deen (Avocat) [1992/3 c18m* c21mpu] very lightly-raced novice hurdler: dead-heated in novice chase at Bangor in July: stayed 21f: acted on good to firm going: dead. *Martyn Meade*   c76 –

FLIGHTY DOVE 4 b.f. Cruise Missile – Another Dove (Grey Love) [1992/3 F16s] fourth foal: sister to winning hurdler/chaser Another Cruise: dam, fair 2m hurdler, from a very successful jumping family: tailed off in NH Flat race at Bangor in February: yet to race over hurdles. *R. J. Price*

FLIGHTY GUEST 5 gr.m. Be My Guest (USA) – Julia Flyte (Drone) [1992/3 18gF] lengthy, sparely-made mare: selling hurdler: fell in August: should stay beyond 2¼m: possibly suited by sound surface: blinkered once. *Miss S. J. Wilton*   –

FLING IN SPRING 7 b.g. Last Fandango – Lovely Season (Silly Season) [1992/3 22g c16d² c18v⁵ a20g³ a22g³ a20g³ a20g³ 17m⁵ c19s c18g⁵ 17m] compact gelding: poor novice hurdler/chaser: sold 1,500 gns Doncaster May Sales: stays 2½m: acts on heavy, good to firm ground and fibresand: blinkered last 3 outings. *J. C. McConnochie*   c70 68

FLINTERS 6 b.g. Deep Run – En Clair (Tarqogan) [1992/3 F17s⁵] half-brother to useful hurdler/chaser Dudie (by Karabas) and high-class chaser Twin Oaks (by Raise You Ten): showed ability in 2 NH Flat races: yet to race over hurdles or fences. *D. McCain*

FLOATS 7 b.m. Oats – Lets Fly (Birdbrook) [1992/3 c19g] no sign of ability. *N. Thomas*   c– –

FLOOD MARK 9 ch.g. High Line – Crystal Fountain (Great Nephew) [1992/3 c24fsu c24f⁵] workmanlike gelding: carries condition: poor novice hurdler/chaser: stays 3m: acts on hard ground. *R. A. Ford*   c– –

FLORAL BOUQUET 4 ch.f. Never So Bold – My Fair Orchid (Roan Rocket) [1992/3 18g³] poor maiden on Flat: sold 1,650 gns Doncaster June Sales: third in early-season novice selling hurdle at Southwell. *O. Brennan*   –

FLORALIA 5 b.m. Auction Ring (USA) – Norpella (Northfields (USA)) [1992/3 16m⁶ 17g] compact mare: fair miler at best: showed nothing in novice hurdles. *D. R. Gandolfo*   –

FLORIDA GOLD 6 b.g. Hard Fought – Klairelle (Klairon) [1992/3 a18gpu] poor novice hurdler. *Miss L. Bower*   –

FLOWING RIVER (USA) 7 b.h. Irish River (FR) – Honey's Flag (USA) (Hoist The Flag (USA)) [1992/3 17d⁴ 17g³ 17g³ 16g³ 16g² 18m³ 17g* 17gF 16gbd] leggy, short-backed horse: fair handicap hurdler: won at Kelso in April: races only at around 2m: acts on good to firm and heavy going: sometimes wears tongue strap: held up and usually finds little. *R. Allan*   104

FLOWN 6 b.g. Hotfoot – My Own II (El Relicario) [1992/3 17s⁵ 17s³ 16d² 18m* 17m 20f³ 16g⁶]   165 §

Few of the present-day top hurdlers, certainly not Flown, are shining examples of reliability. Flown is a good horse on his day, good enough to start favourite for the Champion Hurdle, but has seldom been seen at his best since he shot to the fore in the Supreme Novices' Hurdle at Cheltenham in 1992. His only other win since then came in a minor race at Fontwell

'National Spirit' Challenge Trophy Hurdle, Fontwell—Flown completes a simple task

in February; his only pieces of top-class form in the Christmas Hurdle at Kempton, when five lengths second to Mighty Mogul, and in the Aintree Hurdle, when three and a half lengths third to Morley Street. There may well be more than one reason for his inconsistency. One that suggests itself after a very disappointing last-of-six finish behind Staunch Friend in the Scottish Champion Hurdle on his final outing is temperament. He seemed to resent being taken on for the lead by Jinxy Jack and appeared to lose interest once headed at the fourth, so that no amount of pushing and shoving could persuade him back into contention. Accordingly, for the time being caution is advised so far as Flown is concerned.

Flown's second in the Christmas Hurdle was an excellent run, well in advance of his form in his previous two races of the season. He had four Champion Hurdle contenders behind him that day, and in the absence of Mighty Mogul he started the heavily-backed 7/2 favourite in a field of eighteen for the big race at Cheltenham. However, three of the four—Granville Again, King Credo and Oh So Risky—turned the tables on him there, while he finished a respectable eighth, beaten just under ten lengths. To give him his due, on this occasion he ran on after being strongly challenged two out and squeezed on the turn, and he also did in his only other race before Ayr, when tackling two and a half miles for the first time in the Aintree Hurdle. At Aintree he set a strong gallop and held on to his lead until reaching the run-in. Apart from at Fontwell, Flown had no respite from facing high-class opposition. Perhaps he would have had more to show from his season had connections availed themselves of an astonishingly lenient Jockey Club handicap mark after the Christmas Hurdle which put him in the Tote Gold Trophy at Newbury on 10-10, 18 lb below the top-weight Ruling. As we know, the race went to the Christmas Hurdle fourth King Credo from 3 lb out of the handicap.

Flown will probably need to be switched to chasing if he is to start to win races out of turn, and at the time of writing he is said to be going for the

Flown (b.g. 1987)	Hotfoot (br 1966)	Firestreak (br 1956)	Pardal
			Hot Spell
		Pitter Patter (br 1953)	Kingstone
			Rain
	My Own II (ch 1964)	El Relicario (ch 1953)	Relic
			Saponite
		Bees And Honey (b 1952)	Chanteur II
			Fair Honey

Breeders' Cup Chase in America in the autumn. He is the sort to jump fences, a sturdy, good-topped individual who jumps hurdles very well. As for distance and ground—he is effective at two miles to two and a half miles and on firm to dead ground. His trainer regards him as unsuited by soft, and the form-book supports that opinion. Flown, best ridden up with the pace over hurdles although he has won coming from behind on the Flat, wears blinkers. The horse is one of seven Flat winners produced by My Own II, herself a winner at a mile to eleven furlongs. The dam died six months after producing Flown. Among her winners were Flown's sister, the useful and genuine staying filly Fleeting Affair, and, best of the lot, the 1979 Champion Stakes third Haul Knight (by Firestreak) who, incidentally, used to show his best form in blinkers. Fleeting Affair's first foal is the winning juvenile hurdler Trump. *N. J. Henderson*

FLUIDITY (USA) 5 b.g. Robellino (USA) – Maple River (USA) (Clandestine) [1992/3 a16g⁵ a16g⁶ a16g* a16g⁴ 17f⁴ 16f* 17f⁴ 17f⁶] won selling handicap hurdles at Lingfield, Stratford (no bid either time) and Ludlow (bought in 2,800 gns) in second half of season: will prove best at around 2m: acts on firm ground and all-weather surfaces: blinkered final outing (ran poorly): sometimes flashes tail under pressure. *E. T. Buckley* — 89

FLYAWAY (FR) 8 ch.g. Touching Wood (USA) – Flying Sauce (Sauce Boat (USA)) [1992/3 17m⁴ 18d⁶ 26d] lengthy gelding: winning pointer/hurdler: pulled up only outing in a steeplechase: form only at around 2m: possibly suited by a sound surface. *R. J. Weaver* — c–

FLY BY NORTH (USA) 5 b.h. Northern Horizon (USA) – Lazy E (CAN) (Meadow Court) [1992/3 17g³ 18d⁴ 16g³ 20g* 20s* 20s⁴ 20s³ 18d⁴ 16d² 16g⁵ 20v 17s⁶ 20m² 18m⁵] fair form over hurdles: won handicaps at Down Royal and Downpatrick in first half of season: well beaten in Scotland on tenth and twelfth outings: stays 2½m: acts on soft and good to firm going: blinkered 3 times, including last 2 starts. *J. F. C. Maxwell, Ireland* — 106

FLY FOR GOLD (IRE) 4 b.f. Simply Great (FR) – Golden Pheasant (Henbit (USA)) [1992/3 16s* 17v⁵ 16vᵖᵘ a20g² 17f³] leggy filly: modest middle-distance performer on Flat: won selling hurdle at Nottingham (bought in 7,200 gns) in November: ran creditably over 2½m, but may prove suited by shorter distances: acts on soft going and equitrack. *D. W. P. Arbuthnot* — 88

FLY GUARD (NZ) 6 gr.g. Imperial Guard – Fly (IRE) (Three Legs) [1992/3 16s⁵ 16m⁴] leggy gelding: fourth in novice hurdle at Ludlow in March: will stay further than 2m: acts on good to firm ground: should progress further. *D. H. Barons* — 87 p

FLYING CONNECTION 5 b.g. Never So Bold – Gunner's Belle (Gunner B) [1992/3 16d⁶] sparely-made gelding: poor novice hurdler: likely to prove best at around 2m: acts on good to soft ground. *W. Clay* — –

FLYING DOWN TO RIO (IRE) 5 b.h. Try My Best (USA) – Gay France (FR) (Sir Gaylord) [1992/3 17d² 16d 16s 18sᵖᵘ] close-coupled horse: 9f seller winner on Flat: sold out of M. Naughton's stable 3,400 gns Doncaster October Sales: remote second in novice hurdle at Wolverhampton in November: no form afterwards: likely to prove best around 2m: acts on dead going. *A. L. Forbes* — 74

FLYING FINISH 8 gr.g. Junius (USA) – Blue Alicia (Wolver Hollow) [1992/3 c27sᵖᵘ c2 1sᵖᵘ c16v c19v⁴ c18s²] leggy gelding: poor novice chaser: first sign of ability on final start: tried blinkered. *G. R. Graham* — c79 —

FLYING FREEHOLD 8 b.g. Callernish – Flying Music (Little c100
Buskins) [1992/3 c26d³] leggy, workmanlike gelding: lightly-raced winning –
chaser: suited by a test of stamina: acted on soft going: dead. *John R. Upson*

FLYING LION 8 b.g. Flying Tyke – Comedy Spring (Comedy Star c–
(USA)) [1992/3 c25gF c25gF] workmanlike gelding: probably of little –
account. *Mrs A. Swinbank*

FLYING PROMISE 5 ch.h. Stanford – Impailand (Imperial Fling –
(USA)) [1992/3 17f⁵] poor maiden miler on Flat: automatic top weight, tailed –
off in novice handicap at Lingfield in March on hurdling debut. *R. A. Bennett*

FLYING SPEED (USA) 5 b.g. Far North (CAN) – Diatoma (FR)
(Diatome) [1992/3 19g² 17d³ 16v* 20g⁴ 16d a16g³ 16d* 16f*] angular 125
gelding: fairly useful hurdler: successful in claimers at Uttoxeter in
December and Wincanton in April and handicap at Worcester in May:
effective at 2m to 2½m: acts on any going. *M. C. Pipe*

FLYING ZIAD (CAN) 10 ch.g. Ziad (USA) – Flying Souvenir (USA) c95 d
(Flying Relic) [1992/3 c21m* c18f² c21m* c21spu c16f⁴ c20f³ c21gpu c25g³ –
c25mur c24f⁴] tall, workmanlike gelding: fair hurdler: won handicap chase at
Newton Abbot and novice event at Huntingdon very early in season:
generally ran poorly afterwards: stays 21f: probably acts on any going: front
runner. *R. Curtis*

FLY THE STREAM 6 b.m. Paddy's Stream – Fly Blackie (Dear –
Gazelle) [1992/3 17fF] leggy mare: no sign of ability over hurdles. *P. J. Hobbs*

FOCUS ON FOSTER 11 ch.g. Warpath – April (Silly Season) [1992/3 c78
c21f² c21g⁴ c21d c19vpu] close-coupled, good-quartered gelding: carries –
plenty of condition: poor chaser: trained until after third outing by J.
Webber: stays well: probably acts on any going: has been visored, usually
blinkered nowadays. *J. F. King*

FOGAR (USA) 11 ch.g. Transworld (USA) – Laced Up (USA) (Winged T) c88 §
[1992/3 c17m² c16f* c16g³ c16gpu] lengthy gelding: modest handicap –
chaser: won at Plumpton in August: not raced after October: form only at
around 2m: probably acts on any going: moody. *J. White*

FOLK DANCE 11 b.g. Alias Smith (USA) – Enchanting Dancer (FR) c93 §
(Nijinsky (CAN)) [1992/3 21d c21v³ c26spu c25s* c24d c21g⁵ c20d² c25f –
c26dF 24gur] sparely-made, rather dipped-backed gelding: winning hurdler:
modest chaser nowadays: trained second to seventh starts by G. Richards:
won claiming chase at Ayr in January: stays 25f: probably acts on any going:
winner visored and not: isn't one to trust, and suited by strong handling. *G.
B. Balding*

FOODBROKER FLYER (NZ) 9 b.g. In The Purple (FR) – Disguise c100
(NZ) (Hermes) [1992/3 c24s⁵ c24vF] sturdy gelding: winning hurdler: –
lightly-raced chaser: stays 3m: probably acts on any going. *R. Akehurst*

FOOLISH AFFAIR 9 b.g. Decent Fellow – Silly Carina (Silly Season) c94
[1992/3 c21g*] lengthy gelding: once-raced over hurdles and having only –
second race over fences when winning novice event at Southwell in August:
stays 3m: acts on good to firm ground: visored/blinkered over fences. *O.
Brennan*

FOOLISH FANTASY 5 b.g. Idiot's Delight – In A Dream (Caruso) –
[1992/3 22d⁶ 20s 17s 20d] leggy gelding: well beaten in novice hurdles: sold
2,400 gns Ascot June Sales. *Mrs A. E. Ratcliff*

FOOLISH SOPRANO 7 b. or br.m. Idiot's Delight – Indian Diva
(Indian Ruler) [1992/3 16s³ 17f³ 17g³ 18d⁶] lengthy mare: chasing type: poor 84
novice hurdler: will stay further than 2¼m: probably acts on any ground. *N.
J. Henderson*

FORBEARANCE 5 ch.m. Bairn (USA) – For Instance (Busted) [1992/3
17s⁴ 16gF 17s⁵ 16g²] lengthy, unfurnished mare: winning hurdler: good 91
second in claiming handicap at Nottingham in February (claimed £5,050):
yet to race beyond 17f: best form on a sound surface. *Mrs M. Reveley*

Bradstock Insurance Novice Chase, Punchestown—
Force Seven looks a useful chaser in the making

FORCE   6 ch.g. Oats – Springbow (Silent Spring) [1992/3 F17s F18s] fourth foal: half-brother to winning pointer Bowcap (by Capricorn Line): dam, modest hurdler/chaser, stayed 2½m: behind in NH Flat races: yet to race over hurdles or fences. *Mrs P. M. Joynes*

FORCE EIGHT   6 b.g. Strong Gale – Belle Kisco (Ballyciptic) [1992/3 21g 16m5] poor form when fifth at Nottingham, better effort in novice hurdles in March. *J. Chugg*   72

FORCELLO (USA)   10 b.g. Forli (ARG) – Heavenly Bow (USA) (Gun Bow) [1992/3 16g 22v5 17v6 21v 17d 22s 27d] smallish, strong gelding: poor hurdler: showed nothing in 2 runs over fences: stays 2¾m: probably acts on any going. *F. G. Hollis*   c–
74

FORCE SEVEN   6 b.m. Strong Gale – Dorcetta (Condorcet (FR)) [1992/3 c18s* c20d*] compact mare: useful hurdler: promising over fences and won quite valuable novice events at Fairyhouse and Punchestown in April: successful on Flat following month: stays 21f: acts on soft and good to firm going: sure to progress and win more races over fences. *Patrick Mullins, Ireland*   c123 p
–

FOREST FAWN (FR)   8 b. or br.m. Top Ville – Red Deer (FR) (Kirkland Lake) [1992/3 17v 17v5 a18g5 17s 16g a16gpu] sparely-made mare: winning 2m hurdler: has lost her form: tried blinkered. *E. A. Wheeler*   –

FOREST FLAME (USA)   8 ch.g. Green Forest (USA) – Flavia Miss (USA) (His Majesty (USA)) [1992/3 17s2 20m2 23g 20f4 16d*] rather   108 sparely-made gelding: fair handicap hurdler: won at Wincanton in October: best form at around 2m: ran poorly on heavy going, seems to act on any other: best held up: usually blinkered prior to 1992/3. *Mrs J. G. Retter*

FOREST LORD 9 br.g. Lord Gayle (USA) – Heart 'n' Soul (Bold Lad (IRE)) [1992/3 16f⁴ 16dᵖᵘ 17g 17g⁶ 17g] workmanlike, good-quartered gelding: poor novice hurdler. *D. McCain* 70

FOREST PRIDE (IRE) 4 b.f. Be My Native (USA) – Woodforest (Scorpio (FR)) [1992/3 F16s² F17d] leggy filly: first foal: dam unraced: second in mares NH Flat race at Ludlow in April: last of 13 later in month: yet to race over hurdles. *K. C. Bailey* –

FOREST RANGER 11 b.g. The Parson – Nora Grany (Menelek) [1992/3 c26g³ c22fᵘʳ c33m²] strong, close-coupled gelding: fair hunter chaser nowadays: stays very well: acts on any going. *J. Porter* c94 –

FOREST SUN 8 ch.g. Whistling Deer – Sun Spray (Nice Guy) [1992/3 c21s² c21v* c21vᶠ c24sᶠ c21s* c24v² c21d⁶ c21m⁴ c25f²] workmanlike gelding: sometimes looks dull in coat: very useful hurdler: smart novice chaser: won at Cheltenham in November and Sandown in January: good efforts when in frame behind Second Schedual in Cathcart Chase at Cheltenham and Cab On Target in Mildmay Chase (Novices') at Aintree on last 2 starts: needs further than 2m nowadays and stays 25f: acts on any ground: jumps soundly in the main. *G. B. Balding* c139 –

FOREVER TWEEKY 4 ch.f. Crever – Joyeuse (Biskrah) [1992/3 18gᵖᵘ] neat filly: tailed off both starts on Flat and when pulled up in early-season juvenile hurdle. *P. R. Hedger* –

FORGE 5 ch.g. Formidable (USA) – Red Shoes (Dance In Time (CAN)) [1992/3 17m 17m 18f⁵ 19gᶠ a18g⁵ a18g* a20g² a16g³ a18g*] close-coupled, workmanlike gelding: poor maiden on Flat: trained until after third start over hurdles by P. Cundell: won novice handicaps at Lingfield in January and March: stays 2½m: acts on equitrack. *K. O. Cunningham-Brown* 96

FOR HEAVEN'S SAKE (FR) 8 br.g. Be My Guest (USA) – Woolf (FR) (Roi Dagobert) [1992/3 22s] angular gelding: fair hurdler in 1991/2: –

Steel Plate And Sections Young Chasers Novices' Chase (Qualifier), Cheltenham — Forest Sun revels in the mud

well beaten in April: stays 3¼m: acts on firm going: blinkered once: sometimes looks none too genuine: racing in Channel Islands. *B. Preece*

FORMAL   7 b.g. Cidrax (FR) – Late Challange (Tekoah) [1992/3 c25vᵖᵘ]   c–
good-topped, workmanlike gelding: poor novice hurdler/chaser: stays   –
2¾m: best efforts on dead ground: sold 3,000 gns Ascot June Sales. *Mrs D. M. Grissell*

FORMAL INVITATION (IRE)   4 ch.g. Be My Guest (USA) – Clarista   124
(USA) (Riva Ridge (USA)) [1992/3 17d³ 17d² 16d² 16m* 17m* 17g⁴] tall,
lengthy gelding: modest middle-distance handicapper on Flat when trained
by G. Lewis: won novice hurdles at Ludlow and Wolverhampton in March
and ran very well in juvenile handicap at Newbury later in month: pulls hard
and will prove best at around 2m: acts on good to firm and dead going: tends
to carry head high. *D. Nicholson*

FORM-ER-SELF   6 ch.g. Hello Handsome – Waterbeck (Weathercock)
[1992/3 26d⁶] brother to winning sprinter Que Bella and half-brother to 2   –
other winners, including hurdler Dick's Revenge (by Martinmas): dam won
at up to 3m over hurdles: maiden pointer: blinkered, showed nothing in
novice event in February on hurdling debut: sold 1,300 gns Doncaster May
Sales. *Mrs A. Swinbank*

FORMULA ONE   11 b.g. Ardoon – Little Dipper (Queen's Hussar)   c–
[1992/3 c29s⁴ c33s³ c24sᵖᵘ c30s c26v⁴ c24s³] strong, lengthy gelding: –
winning hurdler/chaser: no worthwhile form in 1992/3: occasionally
blinkered. *J. A. C. Edwards*

FOR PETER   8 b.g. Bulldozer – Canada (Milesian) [1992/3 21gᵖᵘ 20dᵖᵘ   c–
c27gF] workmanlike gelding: winning pointer: novice hurdler/chaser: dead.   –
G. H. Peter-Hoblyn

FORT DIANA   7 br.g. Julio Mariner – Blue Delphinium (Quorum)
[1992/3 18d 20dF 22vᵖᵘ 23vᵖᵘ] no sign of ability: blinkered final outing. *P. J. Hobbs*

FORT-GALAS PRIDE   5 br.m. Belfort (FR) – Lingala (Pinturischio)
[1992/3 17d 16f] sparely-made mare: no form on Flat: poor form in novice   59
hurdles. *P. J. Hobbs*

FORT HALL   14 b.g. Raise You Ten – Cherry Tart (Vulgan) [1992/3 c24f²   c91
c24g³] strong gelding: prolific winner in points: moderate hunter chaser
nowadays: stays 3¼m: acts on firm going. *Mrs Lucy Wadham*

FORTH AND TAY   11 b.g. New Brig – Shine Bright (Scintillant) [1992/3   c94
c24dᵖᵘ c25g² c25d³ c24d* c24s* c24m⁴] close-coupled gelding: novice
hurdler: won novice chases at Carlisle and Perth in April: stays 25f: acts on
heavy going (respectable effort on good to firm final start). *Mrs S. C. Bradburne*

FOR THE GRAIN   9 b.g. Nishapour (FR) – Some Dame (Will Somers)   c135
[1992/3 c20s² c21v⁵ c21d*] tall, leggy gelding: useful chaser: won handicap   –
at Kempton in December: stays 21f: acts on heavy going: tends to sweat and
be on toes: usually waited with and needs plenty of driving: consistent. *D. Nicholson*

FORTINA'S SONG   6 ch.g. True Song – Free Fortina (Free Boy)
[1992/3 F17m 17d 21spᵘ 17dᵖᵘ 21s] first foal: dam never ran: no sign of   –
ability. *S. G. Griffiths*

FORT NOEL   10 br.g. Bonne Noel – Fortellina (Fortino II) [1992/3 c20s*   c106 ?
c21s⁴ c25dᵖᵘ] tall, good-bodied gelding: has had a soft palate operation:
fairly useful hurdler: impressively won novice chase at Chepstow in
October: something amiss both subsequent starts, finishing lame on final
one (November): should stay 3m: acts well on heavy going. *P. J. Hobbs*

FORT RANK   6 br.m. Ranksborough – Foxy Fort (Ampney Prince)
[1992/3 F18g⁵] first foal: dam, very lightly-raced novice hurdler, comes from
a successful jumping family: fifth in NH Flat race at Exeter in March: yet to
race over hurdles or fences. *R. G. Frost*

FORT RUN 4 gr.g. Belfort (FR) – High Run (HOL) (Runnymede) [1992/3 16g3 18dF 17g 16g a16gpu] tall, angular gelding: half-brother to very useful French middle-distance filly Lady Tamara (by Kenmare): dam won twice in Holland and was second in Dutch 1000 Guineas and Dutch Oaks: poor juvenile hurdler: dead. *N. B. Mason*   80

FORTUNATA 5 b.m. Van Der Linden (FR) – Dectette (Quartette) [1992/3 F14s F14g] leggy mare: second foal: dam lightly-raced maiden pointer: tailed off in NH Flat races: yet to race over hurdles or fences. *Lady Ann Bowlby*

FORTUNES COURSE (IRE) 4 b.f. Crash Course – Night Rose (Sovereign Gleam) [1992/3 F16v5 F16s5 F17d] fourth foal: half-sister to winning jumpers Night Guest (by Northern Guest) and Equinoctial (by Skyliner): dam never ran: has shown only a little ability in NH Flat races: yet to race over hurdles. *J. S. King*

FORTUNE STAR (IRE) 4 b.c. Glow (USA) – Lucky For Me (Appiani II) [1992/3 16dpu 16vpu] angular colt: half-brother to winning hurdlers Busted Luck (by Busted) and Bushido (by Great Nephew): fair middle-distance stayer on Flat: sold out of J. Dunlop's stable 16,500 gns Newmarket Autumn Sales: tailed off when pulled up in juvenile hurdles: sold 900 gns Ascot June Sales. *O. Sherwood*   –

FORTY WATTS 8 b.m. Sparkler – Forty Lines (Fortino II) [1992/3 22d] small mare: very lightly-raced novice hurdler: stays 21f: acts on soft ground. *Dr D. Chesney*   –

FORWARD GLEN 6 br.g. Sexton Blake – Daring Glen (Furry Glen) [1992/3 21v6 21s4 22d5] leggy, lengthy gelding: fair hurdler in 1991/2: well below form in 1992/3: changed hands 14,500 gns in May after second outing: stays 25f: acts on good to firm and soft going. *P. Cheesbrough*   –

FOSBURY 8 b.g. Kambalda – Joyful Luck (Master Buck) [1992/3 c20gpu c24m2 c21dF c30m3 c29sF] leggy gelding: third foal: dam unraced: winning hurdler/chaser in Ireland: fair form when placed in Newcastle handicaps in first half of season: probably stays 3¾m: acts on soft and good to firm ground. *Mrs S. A. Bramall*   c103 –

FOTOEXPRESS 5 ch.g. Librate – Rosefox (Owen Anthony) [1992/3 17v 17v6 18d 20v* 20d* 18g* 17m4 20s* 17g] workmanlike gelding: had a good season over hurdles in 1992/3, winning at Lingfield (claimer), Plumpton (2 handicaps) and Folkestone in second half of season: stays 2½m well: acts on heavy and good to firm ground: amateur ridden nowadays: wears tongue strap. *R. Rowe*   117

FOUNTAIN OF FIRE (IRE) 5 b.m. Lafontaine (USA) – Mil Pesetas (Hotfoot) [1992/3 17m 17d 24d5 26v2 27g] lengthy, leggy mare: poor novice hurdler: stays well: acts on heavy ground: visored fourth outing, blinkered final one. *L. J. Codd*   68

FOURCEES 8 b.g. Balidar – Star Duchess (Duke of Ragusa) [1992/3 c21m2] compact gelding: once-raced over hurdles: modest pointer: second in novice hunter chase at Folkestone in May. *M. H. Wood*   c74 –

FOUR DEEP (IRE) 5 ch.g. Deep Run – I'm Grannie (Perspex) [1992/3 F17s3 F16d4 F16g5 16s3 17g 18g 21s] leggy, workmanlike gelding: fourth foal: half-brother to winning chaser Who's In Charge (by Proverb): dam maiden hurdler: third in novice hurdle at Catterick in January: failed to reproduce that form: should stay beyond 2m: acts on soft going. *J. H. Johnson*   84

FOUR FROM THE EDGE 10 b.g. Pollerton – Honeytoi (Carlburg) [1992/3 c25spu c24dpu c16v2 c21d4] workmanlike gelding: poor novice chaser: best effort at 2m on heavy going. *Dr P. Pritchard*   c75 –

FOUR RIVERS 8 b.g. Relkino – Crystal Fountain (Great Nephew) [1992/3 17m c16f3 c26g4 c22d3] robust gelding: poor novice hurdler/chaser: in frame in early-season events, and also in points in 1993: stays 3¼m: acts on firm and dead going. *Mrs I. McKie*   c81 –

Mr W. H. O'Gorman's "Fragrant Dawn"

FOUR STAR LINE 8 ch.g. Capricorn Line – Florida Girl (Owen
Dudley) [1992/3 22m⁶] workmanlike gelding: winning hurdler: once-raced –
since 1990/1: stays 21f: acts on good to firm and dead going. *W. G. M. Turner*

FOURTH IN LINE (IRE) 5 b.g. Horage – Littoral (Crash Course)
[1992/3 16d⁵] half-brother to 2 winners, including hurdler Steveadon (by   83
Don): dam, half-sister to Kribensis, won over 1½m in Ireland: NH Flat race
winner: showed ability in novice hurdle at Ludlow in December: looked
likely to improve, but not seen out again. *Mrs V. S. Hickman*

FOUR TRIX 12 gr. or ro.g. Peacock (FR) – Merry Chariot (Blue Chariot) **c121**
[1992/3 c22g³ c21s² c25m* c24d⁶ c26sᶠ² c20g⁴ c27d² c33d³ c29dᵖᵘ c25m²]   –
neat gelding: fairly useful chaser nowadays: won handicap at Bangor in
September: ran creditably when placed afterwards: effective at 2¾m and
stays long distances: seems to act on any going: visored fifth outing (would
have won but for falling 2 out): usually jumps soundly: sent to race in
Ireland. *G. Richards*

FOX CHAPEL 6 b.g. Formidable (USA) – Hollow Heart (Wolver
Hollow) [1992/3 16s 16s⁶ 17g 21s* 20d 21mᵘʳ 22sᵖᵘ 22g² 20m⁴] smallish,   **114 §**
workmanlike gelding: fair hurdler: retained 6,100 gns Doncaster November
Sales: won handicap at Warwick in February: ran creditably last 2 starts:
stays 2¾m: acts on good to firm and soft ground: sometimes takes little
interest and not one to trust. *J. G. FitzGerald*

294

FOXGROVE 7 b.m. Kinglet – Foxbury (Healaugh Fox) [1992/3 c24s² c80
c23vᵖᵘ] neat mare: once-raced over hurdles: fair pointer: second in hunter –
chase at Ludlow in April, but failed to confirm that effort next time. *P. G.
Warner*

FOXY BOY 10 b.g. Chantro – La Sirene (Pinturischio) [1992/3 c20d⁶] c–
strong, workmanlike gelding: poor novice staying hurdler/chaser: sold –
1,300 gns Doncaster March Sales. *J. P. Leigh*

FOYLE FISHERMAN 14 b.g. No Argument – Cute Peach c–
(Hardicanute) [1992/3 c26g⁵ c26d⁵ c24v⁵ c30sᵖᵘ] big gelding: one-time very –
useful staying chaser: no form in 1992/3. *J. T. Gifford*

FRAGONARD (IRE) 4 b.g. Pharly (FR) – Girl On A Swing (High Top)
[1992/3 16sᶠ 17sᵖᵘ 16v 18d] good-topped gelding: half-brother to winning –
hurdler/chaser Carbonate (by Mr Fluorocarbon): 7f winner at 2 yrs: sold out
of G. Pritchard-Gordon's stable 2,000 gns Newmarket Autumn Sales: no
form over hurdles (blinkered once): sold 2,000 gns Doncaster January
Sales, resold 1,500 gns Doncaster March Sales. *J. J. O'Neill*

FRAGRANT DAWN 9 br.g. Strong Gale – Aridje (Mummy's Pet) c134
[1992/3 c17d* c16d⁶ c16s³ c16d² c17f* c16m⁴ c16f² c17m² c16g⁶] –
workmanlike gelding: useful chaser: won handicaps at Newbury in
November and March and ran well most other starts 1992/3, including
fourth in Queen Mother Champion Chase at Cheltenham: races at around
2m: acts on any going: jumps boldly, though sometimes makes mistakes. *D.
R. C. Elsworth*

FRAGRANT PATH 6 b.m. Warpath – Fragrant Story (Sweet Story)
[1992/3 25gᵖᵘ 24d⁶ 24m⁵] angular mare: third foal: half-sister to 2 poor –
novice hurdlers: dam, unraced daughter of fair out-and-out staying chaser
Fragrant Flyer, is half-sister to winning hurdler Fragrant Friday: no form
over hurdles. *W. G. Reed*

FRAMPTON HOUSE 11 b.g. Fine Blue – Frampton Close c–
(Punchinello) [1992/3 c21d⁴c16s⁵ c20v⁶ a20g c21m⁶ c21g c22v⁵ c21gᵖᵘ] –
lengthy, sparely-made gelding: poor hurdler/novice chaser: no worthwhile
form in 1992/3: often sweats. *M. J. Charles*

FRAMSDEN 7 b.g. Le Moss – Storybook Child (Raise You Ten) [1992/3
17d] big, rangy gelding: third foal: half-brother to a poor animal by Prominer: –
dam maiden hurdler: tailed off in novice hurdle at Huntingdon in January. *F.
Murphy*

FRANK DALE 10 b.g. Space King – Mileceptic (Preciptic) [1992/3 16g
22d⁵] sparely-made gelding: staying selling hurdler: tried visored. *G. H.* –
Jones

FRANK RICH 6 b.g. King's Ride – Hill Invader (Brave Invader (USA))
[1992/3 F16d² 16sᵖᵘ 16vᵖᵘ 16m³ 17g²] close-coupled, useful-looking gelding: 90
modest novice hurdler: will stay beyond 17f: acts on good to firm going. *S. E.
Sherwood*

FRANK'S THE NAME 4 br.g. Sweet Monday – Lady Shikari (Kala
Shikari) [1992/3 F16g F17fF17d 18f⁶] second foal: dam unraced half-sister to –
fair hurdler The Grifter: signs of a little ability in NH Flat races and a novice
hurdle. *M. Madgwick*

FRANKUS 4 b.g. Nicholas Bill – Sigh (Highland Melody) [1992/3 17d⁵
16v⁵ a16g² 17f⁴ 16s 17f⁴] neat gelding: plating-class maiden on Flat and over 82
hurdles: likely to stay beyond 17f: easily best effort on firm ground on final
start. *S. Mellor*

FRANS GIRL 10 b.m. Take A Reef – March Maid (Marmaduke) [1992/3 c–
c21mᵘʳ] compact mare: winning selling hurdler: yet to get past the fourth in –
2 steeplechases: stays 3m: acts on soft going: blinkered once. *C. L. Popham*

FREDDY OWEN 7 b.g. Le Moss – Arctic Snow Cat (Raise You Ten)
[1992/3 25sᵖᵘ 16d 17g] big, lengthy gelding: of little account: blinkered last 2 –
starts. *L. J. Codd*

South Wales Electricity Handicap Chase, Chepstow—
Freeline Finishing (near side)
is more fluent than Deep Sensation at the last

FRED KELLY 7 b.g. Pitskelly – Suffred (African Sky) [1992/3 c16d c—
c20gF c21s4 c23vpu] lengthy gelding: second foal: half-brother to winning
Irish hurdler Visions Sky (by Vision): dam 5f winner: tailed off in novice
chases. *B. S. Rothwell*

FREDS MELODY 8 br.g. Dubassoff (USA) – Sovereign Melody c—
(Fortino II) [1992/3 18d6 22d2 22v4 18s4 22v4 21f3] good-bodied gelding: 93
modest novice hurdler/chaser: stays 2¾m: best form with give in the
ground. *F. G. Tucker*

FRED SPLENDID 10 b.g. Piaffer (USA) – How Splendid (John c94
Splendid) [1992/3 c16g5 c19g3 c16v5 c24sur c18s5 c17v* c16v* c16d2 c16g2 —
c19m2 c17s* c17m3 c17d4] strong, good-bodied gelding: modest chaser: won
handicaps at Newton Abbot (2, first a seller) and Plumpton in second half of
season: races mainly at around 2m: acts on any going: sometimes wanders
under pressure, and suited by strong handling. *R. J. Hodges*

FRED THE TREAD 11 br.g. Radetzky – Sun Queen (Lucky Sovereign) c—
[1992/3 c21g6 c21g5 c21m4] tall gelding: shows traces of stringhalt: winning —
2m hurdler/chaser: well beaten in hunter chases in 1992/3: sometimes
blinkered. *Miss Amanda J. Rawding*

FREDWILL 6 ch.g. Red Johnnie – Will Tack (Will Scarlet) [1992/3
aF16g5] brother to fairly useful Irish hurdler/chaser Stigon: dam 6f winner:
showed little in NH Flat race at Lingfield in March: yet to race over hurdles
or fences. *A. Moore*

FREE EXPRESSION 8 b.m. Kind of Hush – Liberation (Native Prince) c70
[1992/3 18f c17s4 c17d c17g3 c17d c17vbd c19d4 c17vpu c21m5 c17m4 —

296

c18g c19spu c17spu c17m5 c18g6] tall mare: poor novice hurdler/chaser: races mainly at around 2m: acts on any going: blinkered twice. *Mrs E. M. Brooks*

FREE JUSTICE   9 br.g. Impecunious – Old Brief (Lucky Brief) [1992/3 16s 16g 21s4 21v4 22s4 18s 16v2 16d5 16m3 17f 22d] leggy gelding: moderate hurdler: no form over fences: needs testing conditions at 2m and stays 2¾m: acts on heavy and good to firm going. *A. J. Wilson*

c–
93

FREELINE FINISHING   9 b.g. Furry Glen – Superday (Straight Deal) [1992/3 c18g* c17d* c16d2 c21v4 c16sF] leggy, close-coupled gelding: useful handicap chaser: won at Exeter and Chepstow in first half of season (not raced after January): effective at 2m and stays 21f: probably acts on any going: makes the odd bad mistake. *N. J. Henderson*

c135
–

FREEMANTLE   8 ch.g. Welsh Pageant – Reno (USA) (Pronto) [1992/3 24v6 16d] leggy gelding: winning hurdler: no form in 1992/3: probably stays 2¾m: acts on heavy going. *R. H. Buckler*

–

FREE MINX   7 b.g. Free State – Musical Minx (Jukebox) [1992/3 22frtr] compact gelding: winning 2½m hurdler: usually reluctant and has twice refused to race: one to leave well alone. *Mrs V. A. Aconley*

§§

FREEPHONE (CAN)   4 b.g. Phone Trick (USA) – Flying Aristocrat (USA) (Prince John) [1992/3 16gpu 17g 16g 16spu 18spu] sturdy gelding: poor maiden on Flat: no form in juvenile hurdles: blinkered last 3 starts: sold 575 gns Ascot February Sales. *J. Akehurst*

–

FREE STYLE   7 b.m. Liberated – Coquet Lass (Bing II) [1992/3 16gpu] lengthy mare: pulled up in novice hurdles. *P. Beaumont*

–

FREE TRANSFER (IRE)   4 b.c. Dara Monarch – Free Reserve (USA) (Tom Rolfe) [1992/3 17s 18g6 18d3 18g 20m] sturdy colt: half-brother to winning staying hurdler Metal Oiseau (by Ela-Mana-Mou): maiden on Flat: sold out of P. Tulk's stable 11,500 gns Doncaster November Sales: third in juvenile event at Market Rasen in February, best form over hurdles: blinkered second start. *J. S. Wainwright*

78

FRENCH CHARMER   8 b.g. Beau Charmeur (FR) – Shreelane (Laurence O) [1992/3 c23vpu c16s2 c21s2 c19s4 c20gpu c20m2] leggy gelding: novice hurdler/chaser: should stay 3m: acts on soft and good to firm going: may be better than we've rated him and should win races over fences. *J. T. Gifford*

c95 +

FRENCHMANS FANCY   12 b.g. Le Bavard (FR) – Lady Nessa (Prince Hansel) [1992/3 c25v c27m6] tall gelding: fairly useful hunter chaser in 1991: tailed off in 1993: blinkered once. *R. J. Jenks*

c–

FRENCH PLEASURE   7 gr.m. Dawn Johnny (USA) – Perfect Day (Roan Rocket) [1992/3 22g] half-sister to fair pointers Lady Blizzard (by Snow Warning) and Space Man (by True Song): fair pointer: well beaten in novice event at Fontwell in April on hurdling debut. *D. R. Gandolfo*

–

FRENDLY FELLOW   9 b.g. Grundy – Relfo (Relko) [1992/3 20m2] small, sturdy gelding: modest hurdler: not seen out after July: little aptitude for chasing: stays 21f: goes well on top-of-the-ground: wears blinkers: irresolute. *F. Jordan*

c–
96

§
§

FRENI   4 b.f. Primo Dominie – F Sharp (Formidable (USA)) [1992/3 17g6] maiden plater on Flat: tailed off in early-season juvenile hurdle. *J. White*

–

FRESH-MINT   9 b.g. Giacometti – What A Mint (Meadow Mint (USA)) [1992/3 18dpu 18m] sparely-made gelding: modest hurdler: poor efforts in 1992/3: stays 2½m: acts on hard and dead going: tried blinkered. *B. Forsey*

–

FRICKLEY   7 b. or br.g. Furry Glen – Shallow Run (Deep Run) [1992/3 16g* 16g* 16g2 17d* 16g* 17g* 17m6 17f4 20g2] sturdy gelding: useful novice hurdler, who won at Ayr (twice, including handicap), Hexham and Doncaster (twice, including Rossington Main): good efforts in valuable events at Cheltenham and Aintree seventh and eighth outings: best form at

134

Charles Sidney Novices' Hurdle, Doncaster—
Frickley is on his way to the third of his five wins

around 2m (ran lack-lustre race over 2½m): acts on firm and dead ground:
jumps extremely well, and is type to make a chaser. *G. Richards*

FRIENDLY BANKER (AUS)   9 b.g. Old Crony (USA) – Doubly Bold   c71
(AUS) (Home Guard (USA)) [1992/3 c20d⁴ c20dᵖᵘ] leggy, workmanlike   –
gelding: poor novice hurdler/chaser: sold 1,800 gns Doncaster May Sales.
Capt. T. A. Forster

FRIENDLY FELLOW   4 b.g. Idiot's Delight – G W Supermare (Rymer)
[1992/3 F17g⁵] compact gelding: first foal: dam won 2¾m novice hurdle:
fifth in NH Flat race at Newbury in March: yet to race over hurdles. *D. R. C.
Elsworth*

FRIENDLY HENRY   13 ch.g. Be Friendly – Henrys Lady (Henry The   c?
Seventh) [1992/3 c25f⁵] strong, workmanlike gelding: winning chaser: –
appeared to run very well in amateurs event at Sandown in March: stays
well: probably acts on any going: tried blinkered: inconsistent. *Mrs Sally
Mullins*

FRIENDLY LADY   9 b.m. New Member – Friendly Glow (Pal O Mine)   c96
[1992/3 c28f*] fairly useful pointer: having second race in steeplechases
when winning novice hunter chase at Stratford in June by 1½ lengths from
Moorcroft Boy, showing fairly useful form: stays 3½m: acts on firm ground.
J. G. Cann

FRIENDLYPERSUASION (IRE)   5 b.g. Legend of France (USA) –
Waladah (Thatch (USA)) [1992/3 17vꜰ 16dᵖᵘ] small gelding: half-brother to   –
winning jumper Dream Merchant (by Welsh Pageant): modest form over
middle distances on Flat: no sign of ability in selling hurdles. *Miss J. Southall*

FRIENDLY SAINT   12 b.g. Kemal (FR) – Cinnamon Saint (Be Friendly)   c–
[1992/3 17sᵖᵘ 18v 20vᵖᵘ] workmanlike gelding: winning hurdler/chaser: –
showed nothing in 1992/3: usually blinkered. *J. E. Long*

FRIENDLY SOCIETY   7 ch.g. Le Moss – Panetta (USA) (Pantene)
[1992/3 22s 23d 24m] sparely-made gelding: half-brother to several   –

winners, including hurdler Martinelli (by Martinmas): dam ran only twice: well beaten over hurdles. *R. R. Lamb*

FRISCO CITY (CHI) 7 b.g. Domineau (USA) – Farrerita (CHI) (Crivelli) [1992/3 c18f[ur] c20g* c20d6 c20d c16v5 c18g* c16g3 c18g3] tall gelding: won novice chases at Ludlow in October (trained first 4 outings by S. Christian) and Bangor (handicap) in April: suited by around 2½m: best form on a sound surface: amateur ridden: sometimes hangs under pressure. *Mrs M. R. T. Rimell*   c90 –

FRISKNEY DALE LAD 8 b.g. Side Track – Midi Run (Deep Run) [1992/3 c21m*] leggy gelding: has been fired: winning hurdler: won novice event at Sedgefield in September on chasing debut: stays 21f: acts on firm and dead ground: front runner: looked likely to improve over fences, but wasn't seen out again. *Mrs M. Reveley*   c101 –

FROG HOLLOW (IRE) 5 b.g. Lafontaine (USA) – Glens Hansel (Prince Hansel) [1992/3 F16s 16d 16g] fifth foal: dam, winning pointer, half-sister to useful staying chaser Glen Owen: no sign of ability. *Capt. T. A. Forster*   –

FROGNAL 6 b.g. Broadsword (USA) – Belle of Sark (Daybrook Lad) [1992/3 20g[pu]] no sign of ability. *R. H. Buckler*   –

FROME BOY 8 ch.g. New Member – Groundsel (Reform) [1992/3 c25v4 c23v5 c26m3] poor form in hunter chases: stays 25f: acts on heavy ground. *Mrs Roger Guilding*   c73 –

FRONT PAGE 6 ch.g. Adonijah – Recent Events (Stanford) [1992/3 16s* 17d* 18v* 17v4] stocky gelding: fair handicap hurdler: won conditional jockeys events at Windsor and Stratford, and was awarded race at Fontwell in first half of season: stays 2¼m: acts on heavy ground: takes good hold and races prominently. *J. Akehurst*   105

FRONT STREET 6 b.g. Idiot's Delight – Nakomis (USA) (Sky High (AUS)) [1992/3 16g 16d*] lengthy gelding: much improved form when winning novice handicap hurdle at Wincanton in December: will prove best at 2m: acts on dead ground: looked likely to progress further but wasn't seen out again. *S. E. Sherwood*   89

FROSTY RECEPTION 8 ch.g. What A Guest – Stormy Queen (Typhoon) [1992/3 18h[ur] 18f[pu] c17f4 a20g5 a22g3 a24g2] leggy, workmanlike gelding: fair hurdler: poor form only outing over fences: stays 3m: acts on firm going and equitrack: blinkered nowadays. *R. J. Baker*   c72 101

FROZEN FLAME 8 ch.m. Pollerton – Polar Flame (Roan Rocket) [1992/3 c21sF c21sF a24g[pu]] workmanlike mare: poor novice hurdler: fell both starts in novice chases. *R. Hollinshead*   c–

FROZEN MINSTREL 9 b.g. Black Minstrel – Arctic Sue (Arctic Slave) [1992/3 16m c17d3 c16d[pu] c16g[ur] c16s* c17d3 c16m[ur] c17m4 c16f5 c18dF] leggy, plain gelding: modest chaser: won at Catterick in January: sold 3,600 gns Ascot June Sales: headstrong and unlikely to stay much beyond 2m: acts on good to firm and soft going: sketchy jumper. *J. H. Johnson*   c96 –

FROZEN STIFF (IRE) 5 ro.g. Carlingford Castle – Run Wardasha (Run The Gantlet (USA)) [1992/3 F16d F17d] fifth foal: half-brother to fairly useful Irish hurdler Emperors Pride (by Cut Above) and very useful Irish novice chaser Son of War (by Pragmatic): dam never ran: well beaten in NH Flat races: yet to race over hurdles or fences. *M. D. Hammond*   –

FRUHMAN 7 b.g. Strong Gale – Honeytoi (Carlburg) [1992/3 20m[pu] c25g[pu] c21s[pu] c16g2 c16m2] tall, angular gelding: half-brother to winning pointers Four From The Edge and Manawatu (both by Pollerton): dam winning Irish pointer: no sign of ability over hurdles: second in 2 novice handicap chases at Southwell in May, showing poor form: best form at 2m: acts on good to firm ground. *Mrs S. J. Smith*   c79 –

FRUITFUL AFFAIR (IRE) 4 b.f. Taufan (USA) – Lucky Engagement (USA) (What Luck (USA)) [1992/3 17s] lightly-raced 6f winner on Flat: behind in juvenile hurdle at Newbury in January. *T. Thomson Jones*   –

FUEGO BOY (NZ)   13 b.g. Tierra Fuego – Silver Melody (NZ) (Silver   c– §
Fish) [1992/3 c16d6] rangy gelding: shows traces of stringhalt: inconsistent   –
handicap chaser: best at 2m: acts on heavy going and good to firm: often
finds little and isn't one to trust. *A. J. Wilson*

FULL ALIRT   5 ch.m. Lir – Full Tan (Dairialatan) [1992/3 F17v 17sF 22d
22m 18gF] sparely-made mare: second foal: half-sister to a poor animal by   –
Bay Spirit: dam of no account: no sign of ability. *B. R. J. Young*

FULL MONTY   7 ch.g. Raga Navarro (ITY) – Miss Quay (Quayside)
[1992/3 18m4 22m2 16g2] leggy, lightly-made gelding: fair handicap hurdler: 105
not raced after August: stays 2¾m: acts on any going: visored once. *Denys
Smith*

FULL OF FIRE   6 b.h. Monksfield – Sheila's Flame (Reformed
Character) [1992/3 F16d2 F16d5] third foal: brother to Irish hurdles winner
The Bird O'Donnell: dam unraced: showed ability in NH Flat races: yet to
race over hurdles or fences. *G. Richards*

FULL OF TRICKS   5 ch.g. Mossberry – Duchess of Hayling VII   c–
(Pedigree Unknown) [1992/3 16vpu 18v 17g c21fpu] rangy gelding: no sign of   –
ability. *M. Madgwick*

FULL O'PRAISE (NZ)   6 br.g. Church Parade – Adios Belle (NZ)
(Adios) [1992/3 17m5 17d5 18d3 18d* 17m* 17g 17f4] rangy, good sort with   99
plenty of scope: every inch a chaser: won novice hurdles at Market Rasen in
February and Newcastle in March: takes good hold and has raced only at
around 2m: acts on dead and firm ground: usually held up. *P. Calver*

FULL SHILLING (USA)   4 b. or br.c. Sovereign Dancer (USA) – Full
Virtue (USA) (Full Out (USA)) [1992/3 17d4 17d4 16s] leggy colt: poor   73
maiden on Flat and over hurdles: best effort on first outing, blinkered next
time. *R. Curtis*

FULL SIGHT (IRE)   4 b.g. Vision (USA) – Peaches And Cream (FR)
(Rusticaro (FR)) [1992/3 16g 17s6 16v5 a20g2 a21g4] compact gelding: poor   76
middle-distance stayer on Flat: sold out of M. Tompkins' stable 4,100 gns
Newmarket September Sales: poor novice hurdler: stays 2½m: best effort
on fibresand: visored last 2 starts: weak finisher. *I. Campbell*

FUNDEGHE (USA)   4 b.g. Rainbow Quest (USA) – Les Biches (CAN)
(Northern Dancer) [1992/3 16d 16vpu] quite attractive gelding: poor maiden   61
on Flat and over hurdles. *J. E. Banks*

FUN MONEY   6 b.g. Balinger – Cover Your Money (Precipice Wood)
[1992/3 22v4 22vur] good-topped gelding: NH Flat race winner: promising   92
fourth in novice hurdle at Worcester in November: unseated rider third
following month: will stay further than 2¾m. *A. J. Wilson*

FUN 'N' GAMES   8 br.g. Kemal (FR) – Smooth Lady (Tarqogan) [1992/3   c106
c18sF c20v5 c20dF c18d4 c25g3 c18v* c25s3 c25dF c24g c19dur] compact   –
gelding: fair hurdler/chaser: won novice chase at Downpatrick and finished
good third in handicap chase at Fairyhouse in April: third in novice event at
Ayr previous month: stays 25f: acts on heavy going: blinkered final start. *J.
F. C. Maxwell, Ireland*

FUNNY OLD GAME   6 ch.g. Deep Run – June's Friend (Laurence O)   c96
[1992/3 20m 21d c26dF c26spu c20s* c25dF c25g3 c25gur c24d2 c24sur   –
c25g4] small, stocky ex-Irish gelding: third foal: half-brother to winning
Irish chaser Conna Ramble (by General Ironside): dam useful Irish jumper:
modest chaser: won handicap at Ayr in January: ran well when completing
afterwards: no sign of ability in 2 races over hurdles: should stay beyond
3m: acts on soft going. *D. McCune*

FURRY BABY   6 b.m. Furry Glen – Another Bless (Random Shot)
[1992/3 21g4 25d* 28g* 23g6 28v* 28s3 22s4 26m 25spu 27d3 26m5] leggy   103
mare: fair hurdler: successful in novice events at Southwell and Sedgefield
(handicap) and handicap at Nottingham in first half of season: ran creditably
when in frame afterwards: suited by thorough test of stamina: acts on heavy
ground: genuine. *M. Avison*

FURRY FOX (IRE) 5 b.g. Furry Glen – Pillow Chat (Le Bavard (FR)) [1992/3 F 16m] second foal: dam unraced: mid-division in 24-runner NH Flat race at Warwick in May: yet to race over hurdles or fences. *G. B. Balding*

FURRY KNOWE 8 b.g. Furry Glen – I Know (Crespino) [1992/3 c21g² c24d⁴ c25s⁶ c21dF c23g³ 21fᵖᵘ c25m⁴] big, rangy gelding: fair handicap chaser: would have won at Uttoxeter in April but for falling 2 out: probably stays 25f: probably acts on any ground: poor jumper. *Mrs F. Walwyn*   **c106 x** / –

FURRY LOCH 7 b.g. Furry Glen – Loreto Lady (Brave Invader (USA)) [1992/3 18f c17gᵘʳ 17dF 22d] rather leggy gelding: of little account. *H. M. Kavanagh*   **c–** / –

FURRYVALE 8 b.m. Furry Glen – Sun Raker (Vivadari) [1992/3 18g⁵ 17m² 20m⁴ 25dᵖᵘ 21v 26m⁴ 25mᵖᵘ] leggy mare: novice selling hurdler: ran poorly after second start: effective at 17f and stays 3m: form only on a sound surface: blinkered once. *C. C. Trietline*   **74**

FURZEN HILL 14 b.g. Jimsun – Lady Maggie (Distinctive) [1992/3 c26gᵖᵘ c24d⁴ c27gᵖᵘ] tall gelding: staying chaser: no form since 1989/90: tried blinkered. *J. S. King*   **c–** / –

FUSION 9 b.g. Mill Reef (USA) – Gift Wrapped (Wolver Hollow) [1992/3 17m] rangy gelding: poor 2m novice hurdler, very lightly raced. *R. Earnshaw*   –

FU'S LADY 11 b.m. Netherkelly – Cindyr (Ritudyr) [1992/3 c17d⁴ c16d⁵ c17s³ c17v³ c16sF c21m⁴] tall, leggy mare: one-time very useful chaser: fairly useful form at best in 1992/3: stays 2½m, not 3m: acts on any going: usually a front runner. *M. C. Pipe*   **c124** / –

FUTURE GAMBLE 8 b.g. Auction Ring (USA) – Silja (FR) (Masetto) [1992/3 17g 20dᵖᵘ] sparely-made gelding: poor novice hurdler. *Mrs G. S. Plowright*   –

FUTURE KING 6 b.g. Dynastic – Forthcoming (New Brig) [1992/3 16d] tall, leggy gelding: winning hurdler: stays 21f: acts on good to soft going. *A. P. Jarvis*   –

G

GABISH 8 b.g. Try My Best (USA) – Crannog (Habitat) [1992/3 c16f² c16g* c16f⁴ c18g² c21d⁴ c16v⁴ c21f² c17mᵖᵘ c16sᵖᵘ] small gelding: poor chaser: won handicap at Plumpton in September: trained until after sixth outing by R. Voorspuy (ran well on next start, in March): stays 21f: acts on any going: blinkered once. *J. Ffitch-Heyes*   **c81** / –

GABRIELLA MIA 8 b.m. Ranksborough – Gin And Lime (Warpath) [1992/3 21s⁵ 21s³ 24v* 25d³] tall mare: won novice hurdle at Leicester in January: creditable third in handicap at Wetherby following month: suited by 3m: acts on heavy ground. *A. P. Jarvis*   **102**

GADBROOK 11 b.g. Rymer – Quelles Amours (Spartan General) [1992/3 c25s⁵ c25g³ c22f c25g⁵] lengthy, plain gelding: winning chaser: stays 27f: acts on any going: usually visored or blinkered. *R. Lee*   **c90** / –

GAELGOIR 9 gr.g. Godswalk (USA) – Sagosha (Irish Love) [1992/3 22d³ 16v* 20v⁴ 17g⁴ 24f⁵] compact gelding: poor hurdler: won novice handicap at Warwick in December: ran well last 2 starts, in the spring: suited by testing conditions at around 2m and stays 3m: acts on any ground. *C. F. C. Jackson*   **76**

GAELIC CHERRY 10 b.g. Gleason (USA) – Cherry Stack (Raise You Ten) [1992/3 c25sF c25f* c25g* c27m³ c26mF c26fᵘʳ c25d⁶] lengthy, angular gelding: fairly useful hunter chaser: won twice (including Royal Artillery Gold Cup) at Sandown in March: stays 25f: probably acts on any ground: blinkered once. *D. E. Fletcher*   **c103** / –

GAELIC FROLIC 10 ch.g. Connaught – Frivolity (Varano) [1992/3 20m⁴ 27m⁴ 26g² c22m* c23m* c21f* c21g²] rangy, sparely-made gelding: fair chaser: won novice events at Stratford, Exeter and Uttoxeter early in season (not raced after October): stays well: acts on firm going. *P. D. Cundell*   **c104** / **104**

The Byrcor Syndicate's "Gaelic Myth"

GAELIC MYTH (USA) 6 b.g. Nijinsky (CAN) – Irish Valley (USA) (Irish River (FR)) [1992/3 16v⁵ 16s* 16v³ 16d⁵ 16d² 17m⁵ 17f² 16s⁶] small, good-quartered gelding: useful middle-distance performer on Flat: similar level of form over hurdles: won novice event at Limerick in December: ran creditably most starts afterwards, including when fifth to Montelado in Trafalgar House Supreme Novices' Hurdle at Cheltenham and second to Roll A Dollar in Seagram Top Novices' Hurdle at Aintree on sixth and seventh outings: will stay beyond 17f: probably acts on any going: tends to wander under pressure and looks a difficult ride. *T. Stack, Ireland*   132 +

GAELIC SILVER 10 gr.g. Celtic Cone – Blue Delphinium (Quorum) [1992/3 c22d 26dᵖᵘ 21vᵖᵘ] smallish, lengthy gelding: winning hurdler: lightly raced and no form since 1990/1: jumped badly on chasing debut. *J. C. McConnochie*   c– –

GAELSTROM 6 b.m. Strong Gale – Armonit (Town Crier) [1992/3 17g* 21s* 22gᶠ 21d* 26d* 25s⁵ 22v² 21s² 24s² 21m* 25f²]   135

No great stretch of the imagination was required to convince many of those present at the Newbury New Year meeting that they had just seen a future Cheltenham Festival winner. Jodami had carried 12-0 to victory in the Mandarin Handicap Chase, but an even more striking performance was put up in the Challow Hurdle in which Lord Relic turned Gaelstrom into a toiling also-ran in a few strides shortly after the third last. The eventual margin between the two was ten lengths—and it could have been considerably more. When the pair met again at Cheltenham in the Sun Alliance Novices' Hurdle, Lord Relic was 5/2 favourite and Gaelstrom 16/1. A fair assessment on what had transpired at Newbury, but there the going had been soft, at Cheltenham it was good to firm.

302

Quite who these very different conditions would suit in a nineteen-runner field for the Sun Alliance was far from clear, only five of the nineteen having run on top-of-the-ground before. Gaelstrom was one of those five, and her one outing on good to firm had resulted in a poor effort on the last of seven outings, in which she'd shown modest form, in 1991/2. Since then, Gaelstrom had made great progress. The Challow Hurdle had demonstrated as much, despite her being beaten so comprehensively, and before that she'd won novice events at Stratford, Chepstow, Uttoxeter and Cheltenham and shown useful form in defeat in Grade 2 races at Newbury and Sandown. Whereas Lord Relic arrived at Cheltenham without another run after the Challow, Gaelstrom had run in the £10,800 Philip Cornes Saddle of Gold Stayers' Novices' Hurdle at Chepstow, and again run well. In fact, she probably would have won but for making a blunder at the fourth last which handed the initiative to Brackenfield. In the Sun Alliance, Gaelstrom once more set out to make all and only eight were still in contention turning downhill, Gaelstrom being closely attended by the Irish 10/1-shot Bucks-Choice and the outsiders Martomick and Cardinal Red, with Lord Relic, Hebridean, Atone and Giventime only just behind them. Approaching the third last, Scudamore and Lord Relic threw down their challenge, quickening on the inside to take the lead, but Lord Relic could never get more than a couple of lengths clear, a fine jump at the last put Gaelstrom right back on terms, and it was the mare who stayed on much the stronger up the hill. Her winning margin was two and a half lengths with Lord Relic failing to hold on to second by one and a half lengths from the 150/1-shot Cardinal Red, Giventime fourth and Atone fifth, seven lengths clear of the remainder. It was a typically game performance from Gaelstrom, the highlight of her superb season. Not that she did herself or her connections anything but credit on her one remaining start, her eleventh of the season, in the Belle Epoque Sefton Novices' Hurdle at Aintree. On terms 6 lb worse than in the Sun Alliance, Gaelstrom found Cardinal Red too strong by a length and a half, headed at the second last but sticking to her task in fine style.

Sun Alliance Novices' Hurdle, Cheltenham —
Gaelstrom (left) rallies gamely to overhaul Lord Relic on the run-in;
Cardinal Red (right) stays on for second

Mrs J. K. Powell's "Gaelstrom"

		⌈Lord Gayle	⌈Sir Gaylord
	⌈Strong Gale	│ (b 1965)	⌊Sticky Case
	│ (br 1975)	⌊Sterntau	⌈Tamerlane
Gaelstrom	⌊	(br 1969)	⌊Sterna
(b.m. 1987)	│	⌈Town Crier	⌈Sovereign Path
	⌊Armonit	│ (gr 1965)	⌊Corsley Bell
	(ch 1980)	⌊Wasdale	⌈Psidium
		(b 1964)	⌊Helen Rosa

A private purchase for 6,000 guineas at Doncaster as a three-year-old, Gaelstrom is the first foal out of Armonit, the second being Jenerate (by Electric) who is also trained by Twiston-Davies and started favourite for a bumper at Ascot in April, finishing, however, down the field. Armonit was a winner at two, three, four and five years, over seven furlongs and an extended mile and a quarter on the Flat in the first two of those seasons, then five times, including twice in Ireland, over hurdles. She won at up to two and a half miles and, like Gaelstrom, was a front-runner. Her dam Wasdale was a useful sprinter and grandam Helen Rosa an even better one, showing smart form at two, three and four years in the 'fifties. The presence of Town Crier as her maternal grandsire reinforces the impression of speed in Gaelstrom's pedigree, but there's no doubt that Gaelstrom is seen to best effect with a test of stamina. Another strength—that lapse at Chepstow was a rare one—is her jumping, and, while on the leggy side, Gaelstrom has the scope to do well over fences. She acts on any going, and is tremendously tough and genuine. *N. A. Twiston-Davies*

GAILY DANCE 5 b.m. Monsanto (FR) – Step You Gaily (King's Company) [1992/3 17g] lengthy mare: no sign of ability over hurdles. *N. G. Ayliffe* –

GALADINE 11 gr.g. Gaberdine – Spring Gala (Ancient Monro) [1992/3 **c93**
c17d² c24g² c25s³ c24sᵖᵘ] lengthy gelding: winning hurdler/chaser: modest –
form in handicaps over fences in 1992/3, twice finishing lame: stays 25f: acts
on heavy going. *M. H. Easterby*

GALAGAMES (USA) 6 ch.g. Lyphard (USA) – Morning Games (USA) **c85**
(Grey Dawn II) [1992/3 17v 16v 16dᵖᵘ c17sᶠ c17g c16m⁵ c18g⁴ c16g*] robust –
gelding: carries condition: winning hurdler, no form since 1990/1: won
novice chase at Hereford in May: races mainly at 2m: acts on soft ground:
blinkered once. *R. H. Buckler*

GALA'S IMAGE 13 br.g. Gala Performance (USA) – Chilita (Tarqogan) **c107**
[1992/3 c26d* c27g⁴ c26m³ c21f⁵ c24f³] compact, robust gelding: fair –
handicap chaser nowadays: won at Wincanton in April: stays 3½m: acts on
any going. *J. C. McConnochie*

GALA WATER 7 ch.m. Politico (USA) – Royal Ruby (Rubor) [1992/3 **c83**
c20g⁴ c25v* c25g⁴] lengthy, good-topped, plain mare: finished alone in –
novice chase at Hexham in December: ran creditably following month: stays
3m: acts on heavy going. *T. D. C. Dun*

GALAXY ABOUND (NZ) 5 b.g. Galaxy Bound (NZ) – Petite d'Amour
(NZ) (Minnamour) [1992/3 F17d] workmanlike gelding: well beaten in NH
Flat race at Ascot in April: yet to race over hurdles or fences. *D. H. Barons*

GALAXY HIGH 6 b.g. Anita's Prince – Regal Charmer (Royal And
Regal (USA)) [1992/3 17v² 21d³ 17g 17gᵖᵘ] sparely-made gelding: fairly **127**
useful hurdler: ran creditably first 2 starts: stays 2¾m, at least when
conditions aren't testing: acts on good to firm and heavy going. *N. J.
Henderson*

GALE AGAIN 6 br.g. Strong Gale – Going Again (Giolla Mear) [1992/3 **c137**
c21m* c21dᵖᵘ c17s* c20s* c20s² c17d² c20d*] –
Northern racing lost one of its legendary characters when Arthur
Stephenson died in December. Though he never won the jumping trainers'
championship—which is decided on prize money—Stephenson saddled a
hundred winners or more in a season on a record nine occasions. Farming
minor races in the North was his stock in trade—'little fish are sweet' was
one of his oft-quoted remarks—and in a career spanning almost half a
century, first as a permit holder and then from 1959 as a licenced trainer, he

East Lancs Chase, Haydock—Gale Again stays on strongly ahead of Milford Quay

sent out around 3,000 winners. That leading racing statistician John Randall traced 2,989 wins in Britain, though his research was hampered by the discovery that some of Stephenson's winners as a little-known permit holder were almost certainly credited incorrectly in some sources to his famous cousin Willie Stephenson. Randall claims Stephenson's total—including 344 wins on the Flat—as a record for a trainer in Britain, surpassing the previous best score of 2,950 by Arthur Yates who dominated the National Hunt scene in the late-Victorian era. The Thinker's Gold Cup triumph in 1987—one of only three Cheltenham Festival successes for Stephenson—and the July Cup and Nunthorpe victories of 1967 champion sprinter Forlorn River were among the biggest training successes of Stephenson's career. Kinmont Wullie gave him his first big winner in the 1961 Scottish National and the performances of such as Pawnbroker (Mackeson Gold Cup), Rainbow Battle (Welsh National), Celtic Gold and Supermaster kept his name to the fore in the 'sixties until he reached his first century in the 1969/70 season. Sea Merchant, Villierstown, Blazing Walker, Southern Minstrel and Durham Edition were among the best-known winners trained by 'W.A.' in recent years. Durham Edition was runner-up twice in the Grand National, a race in which O'Malley Point, Hawa's Song, Mr Jones and The Thinker were also placed for Stephenson.

Gale Again was Stephenson's last winner, in a two-mile handicap chase at Newcastle in December, after which the licence was transferred to his nephew Peter Cheesbrough. Gale Again, who had progressed well in a splendid first season over jumps in 1991/2, had looked an exciting young chaser when winning a well-contested handicap at Wetherby on his reappearance. In view of the style of his win that day, he had been a disappointment in the Mackeson Gold Cup, jumping badly and always in the rear, before picking up the winning thread at Newcastle with a five-length victory over Clay County. Gale Again won two of his remaining four races, completing a relatively straightforward task in a three-runner handicap at Newcastle and winning the East Lancs Chase (formerly the Timeform Chase) at Haydock's good late-February meeting. Gale Again may not have fully lived up to his promise but he was a decisive winner of the East Lancs Chase from Milford Quay, racing with zest and jumping soundly.

	Strong Gale (b 1975)	Lord Gayle (b 1965)	Sir Gaylord
			Sticky Case
Gale Again		Sterntau (br 1969)	Tamerlane
(br.g. 1987)			Sterna
	Going Again (b 1976)	Giolla Mear (b 1965)	Hard Ridden
			Iacobella
		Favoured (b 1964)	Pampered King
			Machete

The well-made Gale Again, whose pedigree was covered in *Chasers & Hurdlers 1991/92*, wasn't included in the dispersal sale in the spring of the horses which Stephenson owned or in which he had an interest. Gale Again ran in the colours of leading owner Peter Piller who had him in partnership with the trainer. We understand Gale Again will be based in Ireland with Tommy Stack in the next season. Gale Again needs testing conditions at around two miles and should stay beyond two and three quarters, the longest distance at which he has so far been raced. He acts on good to firm and soft going. Gale Again sometimes idles and is best held up. He's a useful chaser and should win more races. *P. Cheesbrough*

GALEVILLA EXPRESS 6 br.m. Strong Gale – Canute Villa **c126** (Hardicanute) [1992/3 18d^4 c16d^4 c18s^2 c17d^{3dis} c18d* c16v^2 c19d^4 c21d^3 **?** c16d* c16m^F c18s^2 c16g^3] lengthy mare: useful hurdler: won quite valuable novice chases at Fairyhouse and Naas in second half of season: close up when falling 4 out in Waterford Castle Arkle Challenge Trophy Chase at Cheltenham in March: stays 21f: acts on heavy and good to firm ground. *V. Bowens, Ireland*

GALLANT EFFORT (IRE) 5 b.h. Thatching – Meeting Adjourned (General Assembly (USA)) [1992/3 18g^6 16d^2 20d^3 20v* 21s 18s^2 a22g^2 **107**

Mrs S. Doyle's "Galevilla Express"

a22g² 22v² 23g³ 21d] tall horse: fair hurdler: won handicap at Plumpton in November: ran creditably most starts afterwards: stays 2¾m: acts on heavy ground and on equitrack. *S. Dow*

GALLANTRY BANK 8 b.g. Buckskin (FR) – Sayanarra (King's Leap) [1992/3 c26dᵖᵘ] big, strong gelding: lightly-raced novice hurdler/chaser, poor at best. *D. McCain*   c–
–

GALLATEEN 5 gr.g. Touching Wood (USA) – Lune de Minuit (USA) (Caro) [1992/3 18d³ 16s² 18s* 20d 17g⁶ 20d* 20g³ 21mᶠ 20f* 20g³ 21s*]   135

Oddbins Handicap Hurdle, Aintree—the grey Gallateen halts Olympian's winning run

good-bodied gelding: chasing type: useful handicap hurdler: had a good season, winning at Kelso in November, Ayr in February, Aintree (Oddbins Hurdle from Olympian, showing much improved form) in April and Perth in May: will stay 3m: acts on any going: effective with or without blinkers: jumps well. *G. Richards*

GALLEY BAY 7 b.m. Welsh Saint – Locust Grove (Sassafras (FR)) [1992/3 c16vᵖᵘ 21d a20g² 22mᵖᵘ 18m⁵ 22d] workmanlike mare: modest hurdler: jumped poorly on chasing debut: stays 21f: acts on soft, good to firm going and equitrack: ran poorly when blinkered twice. *Mrs P. N. Dutfield*
c–
89

GALLIC BELLE 7 b.m. Roman Warrior – Belle Lutine (Relkino) [1992/3 c21g⁶] lengthy mare: no form over hurdles (blinkered once): modest pointer: well beaten in maiden hunter chase in May. *B. R. Hughes*
c–
–

GALLOWAY BREEZE 8 b.g. Day Is Done – Whispering Breeze (Caliban) [1992/3 18m⁶ 22f⁶ 21g 21d⁵ c24mᵖᵘ c21mᵖᵘ] strong, lengthy gelding: poor novice hurdler: sold out of D. Smith's stable 1,800 gns Doncaster October Sales after fourth outing: tailed off when pulled up in hunter chases: stays 2¾m: acts on firm and dead ground: visored/blinkered last 3 starts. *S. I. Pittendrigh*
c–
64

GALLOWAY RAIDER 9 br.g. Skyliner – Whispering Breeze (Caliban) [1992/3 a20g c16g⁴] close-coupled gelding: modest winning hurdler: some promise when fourth in novice event at Edinburgh in February on chasing debut: effective at 2m and stays well: acts on any going. *Denys Smith*
c78 p
–

GALLOW'S DALE GIRL 5 b.m. Reesh – Teresa Way (Great White Way (USA)) [1992/3 F14g] smallish mare: half-sister to fair 7f performer Brizlincote and quite useful sprinter Master Cawston (both by Cawston's Clown): dam placed over 5f at 2 yrs: tailed off in NH Flat race at Market Rasen in April: yet to race over hurdles or fences. *C. B. Beever*

GALWAY GAL 9 b.m. Proverb – Tengello (Bargello) [1992/3 c20m² c21m⁵ c21mF c21d⁴ c25g⁶ 26m⁵ 24g⁵] small mare: poor hurdler/novice chaser: stays 3m: acts on firm going. *F. S. Storey*
c78
–

GALWAY STAR 6 b.h. Kampala – Lady Kiara (Monseigneur (USA)) [1992/3 17m* c17s* c17d⁴ 17gᵖᵘ] leggy, workmanlike horse: fairly useful hurdler: won handicap at Newton Abbot in August: successful in novice chase on same course in September: raced only at around 2m: acted on firm and soft ground: blinkered once: often found little, and needed exaggerated waiting tactics: dead. *M. C. Pipe*
c89
129

GAMBLING PEER 6 b.g. Pia Fort – Gambling Lady (Entanglement) [1992/3 F17g 22sᵖᵘ] angular gelding: fourth foal: dam lightly-raced novice hurdler: no sign of ability in NH Flat race and a novice hurdle. *C. A. Smith*
–

GAMBLING ROYAL 10 ch.g. Royal Match – Chance Belle (Foggy Bell) [1992/3 c24s* c27s⁵ c25sᵘʳ c24m] leggy, rather sparely-made gelding: useful chaser: won limited handicap at Kempton in November: reportedly damaged a suspensory ligament when running poorly final start (January): stays 27f: acts on soft going: usually a sound jumper. *D. Nicholson*
c138
–

GANDOUGE GLEN 6 b.g. Furry Glen – Gandouge Lady (Keep The Peace) [1992/3 16s⁴ 17s⁵ 17sF 21gF 18g* 18g* 18g*] leggy, unfurnished gelding: progressive hurdler, won maiden at Folkestone and 2 novice events at Fontwell in the spring, showing quite useful form: will stay at least 2½m: acts on soft going, won NH Flat race on good to firm. *J. T. Gifford*
116 p

GANOON (USA) 10 ch.g. Northern Baby (CAN) – Tropical Island (USA) (Raise A Native) [1992/3 18f² 22s⁵ 17g⁶ 16g c18s⁶ c16v⁴ c17vᵖᵘ] rangy gelding: moderate hurdler/chaser: trained until after fourth start by W. G. M. Turner, sold 1,050 gns Ascot May Sales: stays 2¾m: acts on any going: visored once: races up with pace. *J. Akehurst*
c92
92

GARAMYCIN 11 b.g. Pitpan – Cacador's Pet (Chinatown) [1992/3 c25s³ c20s³ c24d³ c21dᵘʳ c24d*] c153
–

'He has been entered for Cheltenham in each of the past three years and every time something has gone wrong with him' is what Garamycin's

Harold Clarke Leopardstown Chase, Leopardstown—
Garamycin holds off Ebony Jane; For William (far side) finishes fourth

trainer said after the horse had won the Harold Clarke Leopardstown Chase in January. Three years is now four years. Garamycin sustained an injury to his heel in winning the race under 12-0 for the second time in succession, and he not only missed Cheltenham again but also the remainder of the season. The Leopardstown Chase is usually a very competitive handicap, and the latest running produced a thrilling finish with less than two lengths covering the first four finishers. The patiently-ridden Garamycin made steady progress from early on the second circuit and was running away going to three out. But his rider kept him in check until after the last, which he jumped fractionally ahead of Ebony Jane and For William, and when shaken up he battled on gamely to hold off that pair, and the rallying Joe White. At the line Garamycin had half a length to spare over the subsequent Irish Grand National winner Ebony Jane, who was receiving 21 lb, with Joe White edging into third place. As in 1991/2 we've rated Garamycin's performance in the Leopardstown Chase as one of the best of the season by an Irish-trained staying chaser. We have him only a pound behind Cahervillahow and level with General Idea, even though he finished some way behind both when third in the Ericsson Chase at Leopardstown in December on his third start. Garamycin was a better horse a month later.

Garamycin
(b.g. 1982)
- Pitpan (b 1969)
  - Pampered King (b 1954)
    - Prince Chevalier
    - Netherton Maid
  - Pitter Patter (br 1953)
    - Kingstone
    - Rain
- Cacador's Pet (ch 1973)
  - Chinatown (b 1967)
    - Dicta Drake
    - Cheongsam
  - Cacador's Darling (ch 1957)
    - Cacador
    - Golden Lace

Each of the three dams on the bottom line of Garamycin's pedigree was unraced. Cacador's Pet, who died in 1988, has bred two other winners. Garamycin's brother Afford A King showed quite useful form over fences and won the 1988 Galway Plate, while his half-brother Dark Dawn (by Pollerton) is a fairly useful hunter chaser nowadays. The second dam Cacador's Darling bred several winning jumpers and also Calamity Jane, the dam of the 1989 William Hill Golden Spurs Handicap Chase winner Proverity and Tom Bob, runner-up in the 1988 Maryland Hunt Cup.

Garamycin, who stays three miles and acts on any going, jumps soundly in the main though he is prone to making the odd bad mistake. He's done all his racing in Ireland and has a particularly good record at Leopardstown, where he's won seven times. It would be good to see him outside of his native country, but, as he's rising eleven, time is running out. Let's hope he makes it to Cheltenham in 1994. *W. Deacon, Ireland*

GARDA'S GOLD 10 b.g. Garda's Revenge (USA) – Mielee (Le Levanstell) [1992/3 17m] smallish, sparely-made gelding: selling hurdler nowadays: maiden chaser: best at around 2m with plenty of give in the ground: visored twice. *R. Dickin*
c–
–

GARDEN CENTRE BOY 9 ch.g. Riboboy (USA) – Miss Topaz (Pitcairn) [1992/3 c22g²] sparely-made gelding: winning pointer: novice hunter chaser: blinkered when second at Fakenham in May: sold 4,200 gns Malvern June Sales: stays 3m: acts on dead ground: sometimes gives trouble at start, and has run out in points: one to treat with caution. *B. J. Heffernan*
c81 §
– §

GARDENERS BOY 5 ch.g. Ballacashtal (CAN) – Rockery (Track Spare) [1992/3 17d 18f 18spu] plating-class maiden at 2 yrs: tailed off over hurdles. *T. B. Hallett*
–

GARRISON SAVANNAH 10 b.g. Random Shot – Merry Coin (Current Coin) [1992/3 c21vF c26s⁵ c21d³ c26d² c27m c30d⁶ c26m²] good-topped gelding: won 1991 Tote Cheltenham Gold Cup: still capable of smart form, seventh to Jodami in latest running of that race: ran poorly last 2 starts: best form at around 3¼m: acts on any going: wears blinkers: usually jumps well. *Mrs J. Pitman*
c152
–

GARRYDUFF MOVER 9 b.g. Rarity – Hansel's Trouble (Prince Hansel) [1992/3 c21s⁶ c16s³ c17v³] sturdy, angular ex-Irish gelding: winning chaser: no worthwhile form in 1992/3 (not raced after December): stays 2½f: acts on heavy ground. *M. D. Hammond*
c–
–

GARRY ODDER 9 ch.g. Garryowen – Deceptive Day (Master Buck) [1992/3 24dpu 26spu 28g² 28gpu] leggy gelding: winning hurdler: lightly raced and only form since 1989/90 when second in handicap at Sedgefield in February: thorough stayer: acts on dead ground. *J. H. Johnson*
88

GARSTON LA GAFFE 8 b.g. Le Moss – Tipperary Special (Wrekin Rambler) [1992/3 19m³ 22v 20d³ 26d³ 22g⁶ 24s³ 23m* 22d² 25m⁵] workmanlike gelding: type to make a chaser: won novice hurdle at Uttoxeter in May: best form at 2¾m/3m: acts on good to firm and soft going: blinkered twice, including fifth start: none too consistent. *M. Bradstock*
97

GASCOIGNE WOOD 5 b.h. Petoski – Be My Queen (Be My Guest (USA)) [1992/3 17m 20g] lengthy horse: no sign of ability on Flat or in novice hurdles. *R. Tate*
–

GASSON GIRL 7 br.m. Golden Dipper – Golden Columbine (Column (USA)) [1992/3 18s] small mare: fifth foal: sister to poor novice jumper All Gold Boy: dam poor hurdler: tailed off in novice event at Fontwell in November on hurdling debut. *G. P. Enright*
–

GATHERING TIME 7 ch.g. Deep Run – Noble Gathering (Artaius (USA)) [1992/3 c20d⁴ c19g⁵ c22s* c24gR c22s c22vF 24d 22v 22d³] ex-Irish gelding: trained by D. Hughes prior to final start: fair handicap hurdler: won novice chase at Galway in October: suited by a test of stamina: acts on soft going: sometimes blinkered over hurdles. *J. H. Johnson*
c97
109

GATTERSTOWN 10 ch.g. Over The River (FR) – Larkins Mills (Master Owen) [1992/3 c26mpu] compact gelding: winning staying chaser: pulled up lame in March. *Mrs N. Goffe*
c–
–

GAVASKAR (IRE) 4 b.g. Indian King (USA) – Sovereign Bloom (Florescence) [1992/3 F17g] half-brother to several winners, including hurdler Lihbab (by Ballad Rock): dam Irish 6f winner: behind in NH Flat race at Newbury in March: yet to race over hurdles. *G. B. Balding*
–

Mr Frank Jones's "Gay Ruffian"

GAVEKO (USA)   4 b.g. Al Nasr (FR) – Corolina (USA) (Nashua) [1992/3 16m³ 18d³ 18d² 17g* 16s 16s⁵ 16m* 17s³ 20fF] leggy, close-coupled gelding: well beaten on Flat: won juvenile hurdles at Newcastle in November and Catterick in March: stays 2¼m: acts on good to firm and soft ground: blinkered nowadays: front runner: usually jumps well: tail swisher. *J. G. FitzGerald*   97

GAYLIGHT   6 b.g. Gay Meadow – Pladda Light (Silent Spring) [1992/3 16v a20gᵖᵘ 20dᵖᵘ] third foal: dam poor novice hurdler/chaser: no sign of ability in novice hurdles. *J. Holcombe*   –

GAYNOR'S BOY (IRE)   4 ch.c. Hatim (USA) – Corista (Tudor Music) [1992/3 16sᵖᵘ] smallish colt: no sign of ability on Flat or in a selling hurdle. *T. Kersey*   –

GAY RUFFIAN   7 b.g. Welsh Term – Alcinea (FR) (Sweet Revenge) [1992/3 c16v* c20s* c21v* c21d⁴ c21g² c20f⁴ c19g*] small, sparely-made gelding: useful hurdler: won novice chases at Worcester, Ludlow and Uttoxeter in January and handicap at Hereford in May, best effort and useful performance on last-named course: best form at up to 21f but should stay further: suited by plenty of give in the ground: not a fluent jumper of fences as yet. *M. C. Pipe*   c132 –

GEBLITZT   9 b.g. Tumble Wind (USA) – Tatty Kay (Tarqogan) [1992/3 16vᵖᵘ 16v 17g] angular gelding: 2m novice hurdler, no form for a long time. *J. E. Long*   –

GEE-A   14 br.g. Arapaho – Arctic Daisy (Arctic Slave) [1992/3 c22f c24d³] workmanlike, rather sparely-made gelding: fairly useful hunter chaser   c105 –

nowadays: stays 3m: probably acts on any going: sometimes blinkered: usually races up with pace. *G. A. Hubbard*

GEE UP 10 b.g. Buckskin (FR) – Sarah Gee (Goldhill) [1992/3 c21d6 c21d] leggy, shallow-girthed gelding: winning pointer: poor novice hurdler/chaser: stays 2½m: acts on hard ground. *D. R. Greig*

c–
–

GEMBRIDGE JUPITER 15 b.g. Jupiter Pluvius – Some Ana (Neron) [1992/3 c25dur c22g2 c24g2 c24f* c21m4 c23fur c25g2] lengthy gelding: hunter chaser nowadays: won at Stratford in March: stays 25f: acts on any going: sound jumper. *C. C. Trietline*

c97
–

GEMDOUBLEYOU 5 b.m. Magnolia Lad – Amber Windsor (Windjammer (USA)) [1992/3 17m5 17g 16s 16mpu] close-coupled mare: of little account. *F. Jordan*

–

GEMINI STAR 6 ch.m. Castle Keep – Teftu (Double Jump) [1992/3 17spu 17dpu 18f 22s] first foal: dam quite moderate at up to 7f: of little account. *T. B. Hallett*

–

GENERAL BRANDY 7 b.g. Cruise Missile – Brandy's Honour (Hot Brandy) [1992/3 17v5 21vpu 17g 20g 21f6 24spu] sturdy gelding: chasing type: brother to a poor novice hurdler: dam failed to complete in points: modest form at best in novice hurdles: should stay at least 21f: best effort on heavy ground. *J. T. Gifford*

89 ?

GENERAL DIXIE (USA) 4 b.g. Dixieland Band (USA) – Bold Example (USA) (Bold Lad (USA)) [1992/3 17v 17s 17v] good-topped gelding: fair form in 2 runs on Flat: signs of ability in juvenile hurdles: sold 4,400 gns Doncaster January Sales: races with tongue tied down. *R. Hannon*

– p

GENERAL HARMONY 10 ch.g. True Song – Spartando (Spartan General) [1992/3 c25g c25d2 c28d5] strong, lengthy gelding: modest chaser: not raced after December: stays 25f: acts on good to firm and dead ground: usually blinkered nowadays. *Miss G. S. Jennings*

c86
–

GENERAL HINTON 9 b.g. General Assembly (USA) – Cherry Hinton (USA) (Nijinsky (CAN)) [1992/3 c19s6 c24spu] workmanlike gelding: once-raced over hurdles: maiden pointer/hunter chaser. *J. R. Jones*

c69
–

Ericsson Chase, Leopardstown—
General Idea (near side) is about to get the better of Cahervillahow

GENERAL IDEA   8 ch.g. General Assembly (USA) – Idealist (Busted) **c 153**
[1992/3 c20g* c22g^{ur} c18d* c21d^4 c20s^2 c24d* c24d^3 c21m^2]   –

What was yet another successful season for the smart Irish chaser
General Idea could so easily have been even more rewarding, for he was
beaten by only a head in both the Punchestown Chase in December and the
Cathcart Challenge Cup at Cheltenham in March. The difference in prize
money between winning and finishing second in those races amounted to
around £25,000. General Idea, who'd earlier landed the odds in minor
events at Killarney and Punchestown, soon gained compensation for the
first of those narrow defeats, inflicted by Gold Options. Three weeks later
he started favourite for the Grade 1 Ericsson Chase at Leopardstown and
won it by two lengths from Cahervillahow, who conceded 3 lb. On his only
previous attempt at three miles General Idea had appeared not to stay, but
even under relatively testing conditions the distance posed no problems for
him at Leopardstown. Patiently ridden, he moved through to challenge
Cahervillahow for the lead going to the last, soon gained the upper hand and
forged clear on the run-in. At this stage the plan was to go for the
Cheltenham Gold Cup with General Idea, but that was shelved after he
finished a remote third behind Jodami and Chatam in the Hennessy Cognac
Gold Cup at Leopardstown in February. While he couldn't have been
expected to beat the first two General Idea should have finished closer,
especially as he was still in with every chance going to two out. When
General Idea appeared at Cheltenham in March it was for the Cathcart, in
which he looked to have good prospects of registering his first course win.
He'd run three times at Cheltenham previously, on the last occasion in
November finishing fourth in the Mackeson Gold Cup. General Idea
performed creditably once again but just failed to peg back the front-running
Second Schedual, edging right under strong pressure on the run-in.

General Idea is the third foal and second winner produced by Idealist.
Her second foal Fact Finder (by Known Fact) won the 1989 William Hill
Lincoln Handicap. Idealist, successful twice over a mile and a half, is a

Dr Michael Smurfit's "General Idea"

		Secretariat	Bold Ruler
	General Assembly (USA)	(ch 1970)	Somethingroyal
	(ch 1976)	Exclusive Dancer	Native Dancer
General Idea		(ro 1967)	Exclusive
(ch.g. 1985)		Busted	Crepello
	Idealist	(b 1963)	Sans Le Sou
	(b 1979)	Small World	Levmoss
		(b 1972)	Royal Words

daughter of Small World, a smart performer at up to a mile and a quarter, and a great granddaughter of the Irish One Thousand Guineas winner Royal Danseuse. General Idea, a strong, deep-girthed gelding, is effective at two and a half miles and stays three. He acts on soft ground and good to firm. *D. K. Weld, Ireland*

GENERAL JAMES 10 ch.g. General Ironside – Royal Bonnet (Beau Chapeau) [1992/3 c16g³ c16g³ c18gᵖᵘ c20fᵖᵘ] rangy, good sort: winning chaser at up to 2½m: no form in 1992/3, pulling up lame final outing. *J. T. Gifford*

c–
–

GENERAL MERCHANT 13 br.g. Legal Tender – Elissa Cheng (Chinese Lacquer) [1992/3 c18v* c18s³ c18v² c17v* c21s³ c19m² c17g³ c16f* c18g² c16s³ c17m*] tall, workmanlike gelding: modest chaser: a grand old campaigner who had his most successful season to date: won sellers (no bid) at Fontwell and Towcester and handicaps at Lingfield and Towcester in 1992/3: effective at around 2m and stays 3m: acts on any going: usually blinkered: tough and consistent: a credit to his trainer. *R. J. Hodges*

c89
–

GENERAL PERSHING 7 br.g. Persian Bold – St Colette (So Blessed) [1992/3 c21sᵖᵘ c21sᵖᵘ c20g* c21s² c25d* c20d* c24d² c21d* c25s* c24v*]
A useful and progressive young chaser who according to his trainer will make a Grand National horse one day, General Pershing looks to have a very bright future. Not that his past has been dull. Unplaced twice for Michael Stoute's stable as a two-year-old, General Pershing won a mile-and-a-half maiden at Catterick the following season when trained by David Morley and then had a season's hurdling with Frank Jordan before joining his present stable. General Pershing's first season over hurdles will be remembered chiefly for his most unlucky defeat in a televised juvenile

c144 p
–

Mitsubishi Shogun Trophy Handicap Chase, Uttoxeter—
General Pershing gains the fourth of his six wins at the chief expense of Lake Teereen

event at Sandown. He was around twenty lengths clear when falling at the last, and then proceeded to hamper the new leader Coe, putting paid to Coe's chance of winning, before being remounted to take fourth place. General Pershing went on to show quite useful form in handicaps in his second season, winning three times, but since then he's raced only over fences. An impressive winner of a novice event at Bangor in August, 1991, on his chasing debut, General Pershing returned with heat in a leg and missed the remainder of the season. But he's more than made up for lost time since, winning no fewer than six races following an inauspicious start to the latest season. General Pershing was pulled up at Bangor on his first two outings. His performance on his reappearance in November was the subject of a stewards' inquiry, for General Pershing was in touch and apparently still going well when pulled up approaching the last, his rider seemingly under the impression that something had gone amiss. General Pershing's fitness gave no cause for concern in nine subsequent outings. He'd probably have been successful but for almost falling two out when returned to Bangor nineteen days later, and by season's end he'd won handicaps at Ayr (three of them), Uttoxeter and Wetherby, and a minor event at Perth. General Pershing put up his best performance in the Wetherby Handicap Chase in April on his penultimate start, having the race won a long way out and passing the post thirty lengths clear. General Pershing will face much stiffer tasks in 1993/4, but he may improve enough to keep one step ahead of the handicapper for some time yet.

		Bold Lad	Bold Ruler
	Persian Bold	(b 1964)	Barn Pride
	(br 1975)	Relkarunner	Relko
General Pershing		(b 1968)	Running Blue
(br.g. 1986)		So Blessed	Princely Gift
	St Colette	(br 1965)	Lavant
	(br 1978)	Sans Le Sou	Vimy
		(b 1957)	Martial Loan

General Pershing, a compact gelding, is the fifth foal of St Colette, an unraced half-sister to the top-class middle-distance performer and very successful sire Busted. St Colette's first foal, Dudley's Impact (by Owen Dudley), won over one and a half miles in Ireland. General Pershing is effective at two and a half miles to twenty-five furlongs. He has plenty of form on top-of-the-ground, but, having suffered damage on firmish going on his chasing debut, it's unlikely that he'll be risked again under those conditions. Indeed, he was taken out of the Perrier Jouet Chase at Aintree on the morning of the race because the ground was considered to be too firm. General Pershing races with zest and is usually allowed to bowl along in the lead, making the best use of his bold and fluent jumping. *G. Richards*

GENERALS BOY 11 b.g. General Ironside – Even More (Even Money) **c117**
[1992/3 c28f*] compact gelding: useful pointer: having second race in –
steeplechases since 1989/90 when winning Horse And Hound Cup (Hunter Chase) at Stratford in June by 10 lengths from Sheer Jest: stays 3½m: acts on any going with possible exception of heavy: has been tried in blinkers: sure to win more races. *P. F. Craggs*

GENERAL WOLFE 4 ch.g. Rolfe (USA) – Pillbox (Spartan General)
[1992/3 F17m6] rangy gelding with scope: fourth foal: half-brother to fairly useful hurdler Spartan Times (by Official): dam winning 3m chaser: sixth in 24-runner NH Flat race at Cheltenham in April: yet to race over hurdles. *Capt. T. A. Forster*

GENEROUS SCOT 9 b.g. Rarity – Galloping Santa (Santa Claus)
[1992/3 2 1g 17d 24s⁴ 22s⁶ 26d] leggy gelding: modest novice hurdler: stays 85
3m: acts on firm and dead ground, possibly unsuited by soft. *A. P. James*

GENIE SPIRIT 4 gr.f. Nishapour (FR) – A'Dhahirah (Beldale Flutter
(USA)) [1992/3 17m 17sᵖᵘ 17d 17m² 17mᵖᵘ 20d] lengthy, rather unfurnished 61
filly: second foal: half-sister to Row Ree (by Ore), winner of 1½m maiden and 2 NH Flat races: dam unraced half-sister to smart 7f to 1¼m performer

Beau Sher: poor juvenile hurdler: blinkered fifth outing. *N. A. Twiston-Davies*

GEN-TECH   6 b.g. Star Appeal – Targa (GER) (Stani) [1992/3 16g⁴ 20gᵖᵘ 16s 22d 25sᵖᵘ c20m⁶ c25g³ 22v⁵ 22m] leggy, lengthy, plain gelding: of little account: sold out of A. James's stable 3,600 gns Malvern May Sales after seventh outing: blinkered/visored last 3 starts. *T. H. Caldwell*   c–
–

GENTLEMAN ANGLER   10 ch.g. Julio Mariner – San Salvador (GER) (Klairon) [1992/3 c21f⁶ c25m* c27f³ c24fᵖᵘ] leggy, angular gelding: lightly raced in recent seasons: winning hurdler: won novice chase at Southwell in May by a distance: poor efforts afterwards: stays 25f: acts on any going. *S. E. Sherwood*   c99
–

GEORGE BUCKINGHAM   8 b.g. Royal Palace – Flying Idol (Acrania) [1992/3 23s³ 25s c24s⁴ 22mᵖᵘ] lengthy gelding: winning hurdler: pulled up lame final start: little promise over fences: stays 3m: acts on heavy going. *G. A. Ham*   c–
95

GEORGE LANE   5 b.g. Librate – Queen of The Kop (Queen's Hussar) [1992/3 17d 16s 16m⁵ 17m] neat gelding: modest novice hurdler: form only on third start: sometimes hangs left under pressure. *F. Jordan*   86

GER OFF   4 b.g. Buzzards Bay – Foot Sure (Hotfoot) [1992/3 F17g F16sᵇᵈ 16sᵖᵘ 16g⁶] dipped-backed, sparely-made gelding: first foal: dam showed no sign of ability on Flat: blinkered, first form when sixth in selling hurdle at Catterick in March. *F. Gibson*   67

GERRANS BAY (IRE)   4 b.g. Stalker – Goggle Box (Song) [1992/3 16s a16g] compact gelding: first foal: dam never ran: no sign of ability over hurdles. *Mrs P. N. Dutfield*   –

GET STEPPING   7 ch.g. Posse (USA) – Thanks Edith (Gratitude) [1992/3 c21mᵘʳ] maiden pointer: unseated rider seventh in novice hunter chase in June: sold 7,000 gns Malvern Sales later in month. *B. J. Heffernan*   c–

GHIA GNEUIAGH   7 b. or br.g. Monksfield – Kindly (Tarqogan) [1992/3 20d 26sᵖᵘ 25sᵖᵘ 23d² 17d* 24g* 20g³] close-coupled gelding: type to make a chaser: sold out of C. Trietline's stable 7,400 gns Doncaster March Sales after fourth start: subsequently returned to best and won novice hurdles at Newton Abbot and Bangor in April: effective at around 2m and stays 3m: acts on good to firm and dead ground: front runner. *N. A. Twiston-Davies*   98

GHOFAR   10 ch.g. Nicholas Bill – Royale Final (Henry The Seventh) [1992/3 c21dᴿ 26dᵖᵘ c20s³ c24d³ c30sᴿ c27v³ c26d⁴ c22fᵖᵘ] leggy, workmanlike gelding: fairly useful chaser nowadays: suited by test of stamina: acts on any going: best in blinkers: sound jumper: has become unreliable. *D. R. C. Elsworth*   c130   §
–

GIANO   5 ch.g. True Song – Lavenham Rose (Floribunda) [1992/3 F16s² F17f] lengthy, good-topped gelding: chasing type: half-brother to several winners, notably high-class chaser Cybrandian (by Prince Regent): dam 1m winner: second of 22 in NH Flat race at Warwick in February: tailed off in valuable similar event at Aintree in April: yet to race over hurdles or fences. *R. Rowe*

GIDDY HEIGHTS (IRE)   4 b.f. Head For Heights – Blaze of Light (Blakeney) [1992/3 16sᵖᵘ 17vᵖᵘ] small, lightly-made filly: poor 7f maiden on Flat: sold out of J. Leigh's stable 580 gns Doncaster October Sales: showed nothing in juvenile hurdles (blinkered on first occasion) in first half of season. *R. F. Stone*

GILBERT (IRE)   5 br.g. Dalsaan – Pennyala (Skyliner) [1992/3 16g c18d 21sᵖᵘ 16f 20mᵖᵘ 17fᵖᵘ] leggy ex-Irish gelding: first foal: dam, Irish Flat maiden, placed at up to 1½m: trained until after second outing of season by M. McCausland: no sign of ability: often blinkered. *D. N. Carey*   c–
–

GILMANSCLEUCH (IRE)   5 b.m. Mandalus – Wreck-Em-All (Wrekin Rambler) [1992/3 18gᵖᵘ] no promise in 2 runs over hurdles. *J. K. M. Oliver*   –

GILPA VALU 4 ch.g. Ovac (ITY) – More Cherry (Bargello) [1992/3 F17m] sturdy gelding: third foal: dam lightly-raced sister to smart jumpers Colebridge and Vulture, is granddaughter of half-sister to Arkle: mid-division in 24-runner NH Flat race at Cheltenham in April: yet to race over hurdles. *Mrs J. Pitman*

GILSTON LASS 6 b.m. Majestic Streak – Cannes Beach (Canadel II) [1992/3 c16f² c18g⁴ c19f² c21g⁵ c20d⁴ c16f² c19f² c16m⁴ c21f³ c21f²] sturdy mare: poor novice chaser: stays 21f: acts on firm and dead going: occasionally blinkered: front runner. *J. S. King* c82 –

GILT BRONZE 9 b.g. Glint of Gold – Girandole (FR) (Sir Gaylord) [1992/3 c17spᵘ] angular gelding: modest hurdler in 1990/1: no show on chasing debut in February: stays 21f: best form on soft going: blinkered once. *M. C. Banks* c– –

G'IME A BUZZ 5 ch.m. Electric – Marshalla (Cawston's Clown) [1992/3 F17v³ F17g² 16d⁵] NH Flat race winner: blinkered, showed some promise despite jumping poorly in fillies novice hurdle at Wincanton in December. *M. C. Pipe* – p

GIN AND ORANGE 7 b.g. Mummy's Pet – Amberetta (Supreme Sovereign) [1992/3 17v 18v⁶ 18s] good-quartered gelding: poor 2m novice selling hurdler: visored twice. *J. R. Jenkins* –

GINA'S CHOICE 7 b.m. Ile de Bourbon (USA) – Modern Romance (Dance In Time (CAN)) [1992/3 c16f⁴ 17g c20gpᵘ 17d a20gF] angular mare: winning 2m selling hurdler: poor novice chaser: acted well on firm going: sometimes wore net muzzle and tongue strap: dead. *P. A. Pritchard* c– –

GINGER DIP 11 ch.m. Golden Dipper – Medway Melody (Romany Air) [1992/3 c26g⁴] compact, workmanlike mare: winning pointer: poor maiden steeplechaser. *Miss N. Berry* c– –

GINGER PINK 7 b.g. Strong Gale – Zitas Toi (Chinatown) [1992/3 c25gᵘʳ c24mF c20g⁴ c24g c16sF 24g⁴ 26g 20m³ 17d] workmanlike gelding: poor novice hurdler/chaser: sold 5,400 gns Doncaster May Sales: stays 3m: acts on good to firm ground: blinkered final outing: sketchy jumper of fences. *J. H. Johnson* c76 76

GINGER TRISTAN 7 ch.g. Ginger Boy – Also Kirsty (Twilight Alley) [1992/3 F17d⁶ 22v² 20v³ 23v³ 22d⁶ 22g*] good-bodied gelding: chasing type: second foal: dam lightly-raced novice hurdler: showed plenty of ability in novice hurdles, winning one at Fontwell in April: stays well: acts on heavy ground. *D. M. Grissell* 100

GIOVANNI 11 gr.g. Star Appeal – Pasty (Raffingora) [1992/3 c21gF] sparely-made gelding: of little account nowadays. *P. Winkworth* c– –

GIPSY DAWN 7 gr.m. Lighter – Half A Minute (Romany Air) [1992/3 21g⁶ 25v] small mare: retained 8,400 gns Ascot July Sales: winning hurdler: not raced after December: should stay further than 2½m: acts on good to soft ground. *C. R. Barwell* –

GIPSY RAMBLER 8 gr.g. Move Off – Gipsy Silver (Pongee) [1992/3 c17spᵘ] smallish, angular gelding: poor winning hurdler: no sign of ability over fences. *N. Chamberlain* c– –

GIPSY REW 6 ch.m. Andy Rew – Loxley Air (Romany Air) [1992/3 22dF 20mpᵘ 24gpᵘ] lengthy, unfurnished mare: no sign of ability in novice hurdles. *M. J. Heaton-Ellis* –

GITCHE GUMME 12 b.g. Warpath – Enchanting (Behistoun) [1992/3 c27g⁵ c26g⁵ c26dpᵘ] soundly beaten in hunter chases. *Mrs T. R. Kinsey* c–

GIVE HIM TIME 4 ch.g. May Be This Time – Miss Eutopia (Dunphy) [1992/3 F14m] first foal: dam unraced: behind in NH Flat race at Market Rasen in March: yet to race over hurdles. *D. Lee*

GIVE IT A BASH (IRE) 5 b.m. Gianchi – Marzia Fabbricotti (Ribero) [1992/3 F18d F17g] seventh foal: half-sister to a winner in USA by Wolver Hollow: dam unraced: well beaten in NH Flat races: yet to race over hurdles or fences. *G. Fleming*

GIVEITAGO 7 b.g. Mandalus – Knockscovane (Carlburg) [1992/3 16v
17d² 21f³] tall, lengthy ex-Irish gelding: half-brother to winning Irish
pointer Kipp Chuggy (by Laurence O): dam won over hurdles and fences:
successful pointer: novice hurdler: modest form at least when placed at
Stratford and Newbury: stays 21f: probably acts on any ground. *Andrew
Turnell*

92 +

GIVE ME AN ANSWER 7 ch.m. True Song – Spartan Daisy (Spartan
General) [1992/3 18v⁴ 21f*] smallish, angular mare: second foal: dam,
winning jumper, effective at 2½m and stayed well: won NH Flat race in
1990/1 and novice hurdle at Warwick in May: will stay beyond 21f: acts on
firm going: sure to improve further. *N. J. Henderson*

89 p

GIVE ME HOPE (IRE) 5 b.m. Be My Native (USA) – Diamond Gig
(Pitskelly) [1992/3 17d⁴ 24spu 16v⁶ 20d F13m 17g⁵ 17d] leggy mare:
plating-class middle-distance handicapper on Flat: novice hurdler: easily
best effort at 2m on heavy ground. *R. J. Price*

85

GIVENTIME 5 ch.g. Bustino – Duck Soup (Decoy Boy) [1992/3 16s*
16d² 17v* 20v* 17sco 17s² 21m⁴]

134 p

Giventime was one of the season's unluckiest losers. The even-money
favourite for the Racegoers Club Hall of Fame Novices' Handicap Hurdle at
Cheltenham in January, Giventime looked all set for his fourth win over
hurdles when he was forced out by the leader Gandouge Glen at the
penultimate flight. Giventime's claiming rider Daniel Fortt failed to pull up
his mount, although he did manage to steer him round the final flight, and
Giventime went on to pass the post full of running, just a couple of lengths
behind the hard-ridden winner Country Lad. Fortt was fined £75 for not
pulling up, but the stewards quite rightly dealt much more severely with
Gandouge Glen's rider Declan Murphy. Murphy, who had moved his mount
across to the left as the favourite challenged on his inside, was found guilty
of intentional interference and suspended for fourteen days. To add to
Murphy's troubles, he injured his right shoulder when the tiring Gandouge
Glen fell at the last and missed the winning ride on Sibton Abbey in the
Timeform Hall of Fame Chase later that afternoon. Fortt, who'd won two
novice hurdles at Uttoxeter and a novice handicap at Lingfield on Giventime, was again on board when the horse finished a good second to Winter
Squall in a novice event at Sandown a week after Cheltenham. Understand-
ably, he was replaced when Giventime returned to Cheltenham for the Sun
Alliance Novices' Hurdle, as he'd have been unable to draw his allowance.
In the Sun Alliance Giventime showed further improvement to take fourth
place behind Gaelstrom, beaten five and a half lengths, finishing best of all
having been only eighth turning for home. This was the first time Giventime
had raced on firmish ground since his debut over hurdles in October, 1991.
He jarred himself that day and was subsequently off the course for a year,
winning on soft going on his return and then gaining his other two victories
on heavy.

Giventime (ch.g. 1988)	Bustino (b 1971)	Busted (b 1963)	Crepello / Sans Le Sou
		Shipyard (ch 1963)	Doutelle / Paving Stone
	Duck Soup (b 1978)	Decoy Boy (b 1967)	Tin Whistle / Scargill
		Coup (ch 1962)	Hook Money / Touch

Giventime, bought as a yearling by his trainer for 6,000 guineas, had
seven races on the Flat in two seasons, winning a ten-furlong maiden at
Pontefract during the second of them. Duck Soup's previous five foals were
winners on the Flat, too, namely Crete Cargo, Soupcon and Really Squid-
gely (all by King of Spain), Joseph (by Rolfe) and Melody Mill (by Milford).
Soupcon and Joseph were also successful over hurdles. Duck Soup, a
modest seven-furlong winner, is out of the useful middle-distance stayer
Coup, herself a daughter of the useful if somewhat temperamental middle-
distance performer Touch. The sturdy, compact Giventime should make his
mark over fences eventually, but there are more races to be won with him

over hurdles first, probably in handicap company. A genuine sort who races with enthusiasm, he's effective at around two miles when conditions are very testing and will stay three miles. *Andrew Turnell*

GIVUS A BUCK   10 br.g. Buckskin (FR) – My Pet (Phalorain) [1992/3   **c147** c18v* c26v² c30sᵖᵘ c24f* c25m* c30d²]   —

When some prominent racehorse owners finish counting their money and begin counting their blessings, they might give thanks to the deposed Chancellor of the Exchequer Norman Lamont. Coinciding with the appro-privately-named Givus A Buck's passing the post first in the Ritz Club National Hunt Handicap Chase at the Cheltenham Festival, Mr Lamont announced in Parliament an amazing concession for racehorse owners, most of whom will now be allowed to reclaim VAT on the cost of their racing activities. What odds would have been offered against any Government giving VAT relief to racehorse owners in the same budget as they imposed it on the fuel which everybody needs to keep warm? The concession represented an about-turn for the Government which the previous year had responded to appeals to alleviate racing's economic problems by replying that it would be 'politically unacceptable' to levy a lower rate of VAT on bloodstock than on any other commodity. In other words, the Government couldn't be seen, with the country in the deepest recession for a generation, to be arranging for some of the very rich to pay less tax on their hobby. The change of heart followed a direct appeal to the Prime Minister and Mr Lamont from representatives of racing and breeding and from Tory MPs in rural constituencies who warned that the British bloodstock industry was in decline and would be crippled by the effects of European Community VAT laws which were due to lead to bloodstock sold in Britain being subject to 17.5% VAT, compared to special rates of 2.7% in Ireland and 5.5% in France. When Mr Lamont's new scheme is introduced it may well be the Irish and French that are complaining! However, even after the budget announce-ment, there were still owners campaigning for the Government to take a smaller cut from the betting tax to enable extra money to be diverted into prize money. Some are never satisfied.

Givus A Buck has had a somewhat chequered career and has taken some time to live up to his trainer's expectations. Elsworth predicted in a *Timeform Interview* that 'Givus A Buck is going to be a very good horse one day and will make a chaser'. Givus A Buck, winner of a bumper as a five-year-old, had just started out as a hurdler. 'At the moment his mind is working a bit fast, and he needs more time and more schooling, because he's

Ritz Club National Hunt Handicap Chase, Cheltenham —
a cracking race between Givus A Buck (centre), Country Member (blaze) and Boraceva

jumped terribly on both his outings . . . . . but he could be a star one day'. Elsworth's faith in Givus A Buck, a strong, rangy, good sort who looked a chasing type from the day he first set foot on a racecourse, has looked misplaced at times. But patience paid off when Givus A Buck put past disappointments behind him and developed into a smart chaser in the latest season, improving by leaps and bounds on his return from a mid-season break. The Ritz Club National Hunt Handicap Chase attracted a field of only seven in which Givus A Buck, a comfortable winner of a weakly-contested handicap at Newbury earlier in the month, started third favourite behind the progressive performers Country Member and Stirrup Cup. The race produced the closest finish of the Festival meeting, Givus A Buck leading from quite early and holding off Country Member and Boraceva by a short head and a neck, despite drifting left under the whip. Givus A Buck is game but sometimes races lazily and has looked a difficult ride. His idiosyncrasies contributed to his downfall in the Whitbread Gold Cup at Sandown in April, after he had completed in fifth in the void Grand National in the meantime. Givus A Buck showed he'd suffered no ill-effects from his exertions at Aintree by excelling himself at Sandown where, a stone out of the handicap, he drew clear from three out with the 1992 winner Topsham Bay. Givus A Buck kept on gamely to get home by a head but was demoted after hanging left on the run-in and bumping his rival as he veered away from the whip.

Givus A Buck (br.g. 1983)	Buckskin (FR) (b 1973)	Yelapa (br 1966)	Mossborough
			Your Point
		Bete A Bon Dieu (b 1964)	Herbager
			Caralline
	My Pet (ch 1966)	Phalorain (ch 1945)	Precipitation
			Phalaris Girl
		Princess Ana (ch 1960)	Prince Richard
			Black Ana

Givus A Buck, whose dam My Pet was unraced, is a half-brother to three winning jumpers: the prolific winning chaser My Buck (by Master Buck), the winning hurdler Fifty Bucks (also by Master Buck) who became a successful though temperamental point-to-pointer, and the winning chaser and fairly useful point-to-pointer Mister Skip (by Never Slip). My Buck was versatile so far as distance goes, winning at two miles to twenty-five furlongs. Givus A Buck is essentially a stayer but he won over two and a quarter miles under testing conditions at Fontwell on his reappearance in the latest season and is by no means slow. He acts on any going. He is blinkered nowadays. *D. R. C. Elsworth*

GLADONIA 6 gr.m. Godswalk (USA) – Aingeal (Fordham (USA)) [1992/3 18d 26s^{pu} 16s^{pu}] small mare: poor maiden plater at best over hurdles: often visored in 1991/2, blinkered once. *J. Parkes*　　　　–

GLADTOGETIT 7 br.m. Green Shoon – Hill Sixty (Slippered) [1992/3 **c98** c22s³ c21s² c26s^{pu} c21d² c22v^{pu} 22d c24g* c22g⁵ c21g⁵] small, lengthy　– mare: moderate handicap chaser: ran poorly after winning at Fakenham in February: effective at 2 1f and stays 3m: acts on soft ground: occasionally blinkered: sometimes finds little, and best held up. *D. R. Gandolfo*

GLADYS EMMANUEL 6 b.m. Idiot's Delight – Indian Whistle **c–** (Rugantino) [1992/3 c21f⁶] smallish mare: poor 2m novice hurdle　– (blinkered once): maiden pointer: well beaten in novice hunter chase. *R. E. Pocock*

GLAISDALE (IRE) 4 b.g. Lomond (USA) – Glass Slipper (Relko) [1992/3 16v* 16d2] leggy, good-topped gelding: fairly useful stayer on Flat: **121 p** sold out of H. Cecil's stable 33,000 gns Newmarket Autumn Sales: won novice hurdle at Towcester in February: ran good race to finish second to Bold Boss in Petros Victor Ludorum Hurdle at Haydock later in month: will stay at least 2½m: acts on heavy ground: sure to improve further and win more races. *M. H. Tompkins*

GLASGOW 4 b.g. Top Ville – Glasson Lady (GER) (Priamos (GER)) [1992/3 16v^{rtr}] disappointing and unsatisfactory maiden on Flat: sold out of **§§**

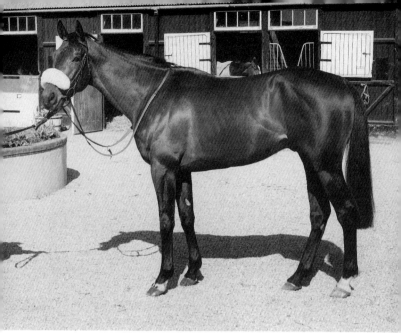

Oceala Limited's "Glaisdale"

E. Alston's stable 1,500 gns Ascot December Sales: refused to race in April on hurdling debut and bolted and withdrawn from next start: one to leave severely alone. *G. E. Jones*

GLASS CASTLE (FR)   9 b.g. Crystal Palace (FR) – Halliana (USA)   **c–**
(Bold Reason) [1992/3 c16v^{bd} c17s^F c16v^{pu} c17s^F] rather leggy gelding: poor middle-distance maiden on Flat in 1990: no form over fences. *R. F. Johnson Houghton*

GLASS MOUNTAIN   11 gr.g. Scallywag – Miss Maskin (Sikandar)   **c82**
[1992/3 c23s^2 c25g^2 c21v^4 c21g^3 c21m^4 c23m] strong gelding: carries plenty   **–**
of condition: poor chaser nowadays: stays 3¼m: acts on any going: usually blinkered nowadays: has broken blood vessels. *J. White*

GLASTONDALE   7 b.g. Beldale Flutter (USA) – Glastonbury (Grundy)
[1992/3 17m^2 16g 17s] close-coupled, sparely-made gelding: poor middle-   **83**
distance handicapper on Flat: sold out of T. Barron's stable 3,600 gns Doncaster June Sales: only form over hurdles since 1989/90 when second in early-season claimer at Perth. *J. J. Birkett*

GLEBELANDS GIRL   6 b.m. Burslem – Genzyme Gene (Riboboy
(USA)) [1992/3 20g^4 25s^3 18d* 26d^{rtr} 18s^2 22v^2 23s^2 24d^{rtr} 24v 17v^2 22g^6 **99 §**
27m^{rtr} 24s^2] compact mare: modest hurdler: won seller at Fontwell (bought in 3,100 gns) in October: runner-up several times afterwards: effective at around 2m under testing conditions and stays 3m: acts on good to firm and heavy ground: inconsistent: unreliable at start and sometimes refuses to race. *R. Rowe*

GLEBE PRINCE 13 b.g. Brave Invader (USA) – Once More (Even   **c84**
Money) [1992/3 c21g³ c26m² c26g³ c27f* c26d² c27f⁵ c27f] leggy gelding: –
poor chaser: won amateurs handicap at Fontwell in October: stays 27f: acts
on firm and dead ground. *R. Rowe*

GLEMOT (IRE) 5 br.g. Strong Gale – Lady Nethertown (Windjammer
(USA)) [1992/3 16d⁶ 16m 16d³ 17s* 18s⁵ 16d² 18g⁴] tall, unfurnished   **77**
gelding: poor hurdler: won novice handicap at Kelso in November: ran
creditably last 2 starts: yet to race beyond 2¼m: acts on soft going. *J. H.
Johnson*

GLENAVEY 12 b.g. Cantab – Dancing Flame (Dead Ahead) [1992/3   **c–**
c24gᵘʳ c22fᶠ] strong, deep-bodied gelding: hunter chaser: stays well: acts
on good to firm and good to soft going. *Mike Roberts*

GLENBROOK D'OR 9 b.g. Le Coq d'Or – Wedderburn (Royalty) **c122**
[1992/3 c26d² c25d⁴ c26s* c33d² c27v² c26s³ c30sᵖᵘ] small gelding: carries   –
condition: fairly useful chaser: won handicap at Warwick in November: ran
particularly well fifth and sixth starts, something looked amiss final one
(February): dyed-in-the-wool stayer: suited by plenty of give in the ground.
A. J. Wilson

GLEN CHERRY 7 b.g. Furry Glen – Our Cherry (Tarqogan) [1992/3 **c104**
c21gᶠ c21d* c21d c26vᵖᵘ] big, rangy gelding: fair handicap chaser: won at   –
Uttoxeter in November: ran poorly afterwards (not raced after January):
likely to prove suited by good test of stamina: acts on dead going. *Capt. T. A.
Forster*

GLENCLOUD (IRE) 5 b.g. Glenstal (USA) – Clouded Issue (Manado)
[1992/3 18d⁶ 16s⁴ 20d² 16d* 17g 17m 16s⁵ 16d] neat gelding: useful hurdler: **133**
won The Ladbroke at Leopardstown in January by neck from Kilcash: below
form in valuable events in Britain next 2 starts: effective at 2m and stays
2½m: acts on soft going: blinkered last 2 starts, running creditably first
time. *N. Meade, Ireland*

GLENCOMMON 12 ch.g. Forties Field (FR) – Deep Pearl (Deep Run)
[1992/3 18h² 22dᵖᵘ 18f* 19m] good-bodied gelding: inconsistent hurdler: **97**
won selling handicap at Exeter (no bid) in August: stays 21f, probably not
3m: acts on hard and dead ground: blinkered twice. *R. J. Baker*

GLENELIANE (IRE) 5 b.m. Glenstal (USA) – Sweet Eliane
(Birdbrook) [1992/3 18m² 16g*] leggy mare: won novice claiming hurdle at   **81**

The Ladbroke, Leopardstown—
Glencloud (extreme left) still has plenty to do as Native Mission leads over the last

Mr D. Tierney's "Glencloud"

Southwell in August: likely to prove best at around 2m: acts on good to firm ground. *J. L. Harris*

GLEN FINNAN 5 ch.m. Ballacashtal (CAN) – Glen Kella Manx (Tickled Pink) [1992/3 17m] lengthy mare: poor 2m maiden plater over hurdles. *M. P. Muggeridge* —

GLENFINN PRINCESS 5 ch.m. Ginger Boy – Lady Amazon (Spartan General) [1992/3 F16m6 F16g3] second foal: dam never ran: third in NH Flat race at Chepstow in June: yet to race over hurdles or fences. *K. S. Bridgwater*

GLENGOOLE 10 b.g. Glen Quaich – Blush (Twice Worthy (USA)) [1992/3 c18f2 17v6 a22g a18g2] well-made gelding: modest hurdler/novice chaser: stays 21f: acts on hard going and equitrack. *B. Smart*   c83
89

GLENGRIFFIN 8 b.g. Furry Glen – Ballygriffin (Deep Run) [1992/3 c21dpu c22vpu c21v6 c21gur c21g3] sturdy gelding: winning hurdler: no form over fences: stays 2¾m: raced only on an easy surface. *J. T. Gifford*   c–
–

GLEN LOCHAN 13 b.g. Mr Bigmore – Freuchie (Vulgan) [1992/3 c27mpu] close-coupled gelding: winning hunter chaser: stiff task in March: well suited by a distance of ground: acts on soft and good to firm going. *J. D. Jemmeson*   c–
–

GLEN LOCHAN (NZ) 8 gr.g. Three Legs – La Bruyere (NZ) (Le Fripon (NZ)) [1992/3 17d3 19m* 21d* 20d* 22v* 21spu] good-topped gelding: much improved novice hurdler who won at Exeter, Kempton, Ascot and Sandown in first half of season: useful performance when beating Gaelstrom by 10 lengths in quite valuable 4-runner event on last-named course: stayed 2¾m: acted on good to firm and heavy going: dead. *Miss H. C. Knight*   137

GLEN LUSS 6 gr.m. Scallywag – Fernez (Fez) [1992/3 22v 22s 21vpu a24g5] compact mare: novice hurdler: poor form. *C. R. Egerton*   66

GLEN MIRAGE   8 b.g. Furry Glen – By Mistake (Miralgo) [1992/3 16s³   **c75**
25s³ 21s c21vur c21s³ c21g 20g² 21s³] leggy, workmanlike gelding: poor   85
novice hurdler/chaser: sold out of M. Wilkinson's stable 2,500 gns Ascot
February Sales after fifth outing: stays 25f: acts on soft ground: blinkered
twice over fences: sometimes looks none too keen. *Mrs F. E. White*

GLEN MOSELLE   7 gr.g. Celtic Cone – Hunters Glen (Tiger Shark)
[1992/3 23mpu] second foal: dam lightly-raced novice hurdler: showed   –
nothing in novice hurdle at Uttoxeter in May. *B. R. Cambidge*

GLENORAN   6 b.g. Celio Rufo – Two In A Million (Rarity) [1992/3 22fpu
17m⁶ 16m 20m⁵ 22g 17m 16g 18d] sturdy gelding: poor novice hurdler: 81 §
trained until after third start by V. Thompson: best efforts at around 2m:
acts on good to firm ground: temperamental. *S. I. Pittendrigh*

GLEN PARISH   8 b.m. Furry Glen – Priestcroft Star (Saintly Song)
[1992/3 17s 22v 23vpu 20d] leggy ex-Irish mare: fourth foal: half-sister to   –
winning Irish hurdler Shabra Star (by Balinger): dam, winning 2m hurdler,
stayed 2½m: maiden pointer: no sign of ability over hurdles: sold 1,600 gns
Ascot May Sales. *G. L. Humphrey*

GLEN PENNANT   6 b.g. Furry Glen – Raise The Standard (Distinctly
(USA)) [1992/3 17gpu] big, rangy gelding: fifth foal: brother to fairly useful   –
jumper Change The Act and half-brother to winning jumper St Andrew's
Bay (by Rymer): dam never ran: showed nothing in novice hurdle at
Newbury in February. *T. J. Etherington*

GLENROWAN (IRE)   5 b.g. Euphemism – Deity (Red God) [1992/3
F17f] half-brother to winning Irish jumper Hi Harry (by Fidel): dam poor   –
maiden at 2 yrs: behind in NH Flat race at Hereford in May: yet to race over
hurdles or fences. *P. G. Murphy*

GLENSHANE LAD   7 b.g. Fidel – Molly Dancer (Choral Society)   **c95**
[1992/3 18g 20g* c17d² c20mF 17v⁵ 17s⁶ 20v 21v⁶ 17g* 22d³ 17g⁴ 18m⁴   108
22d⁵] sturdy ex-Irish gelding: first foal: dam unraced half-sister to winning
hurdler New Gold Dream: fair handicap hurdler: won at Sligo in August
(trained until after then by I. Ferguson) and Hereford in March: second in
novice event at Towcester in October on chasing debut (fell next time):
stays 2¾m: acts on dead ground. *K. C. Bailey*

GLENSIDE JERRY   13 b.g. Chas Sawyer – Ruckinge Girl (Eborneezer)   **c–   x**
[1992/3 c23hpu] workmanlike gelding: handicap chaser: pulled up lame in
August: thorough stayer: acts on any going: sometimes visored or
blinkered: poor jumper. *R. G. Frost*

GLENSTAL PRIORY   6 b.m. Glenstal (USA) – Jumbolia (Wolver
Hollow) [1992/3 16g a20g⁴ 16g 22m⁵ 22d⁵ 20g⁴ a24g⁵ 22f 21mpu]   76
sparely-made mare: modest stayer on Flat: poor novice hurdler: stays 3m:
acts on fibresand: blinkered final start. *F. Gibson*

GLENTOWER (IRE)   5 b.g. Furry Glen – Helens Tower (Dual) [1992/3
F17d] half-brother to 3 winners, including Irish hurdler Face To Face (by
The Parson): dam winning Irish hurdler/chaser: eighth of 21 in NH Flat race
at Ascot in April: yet to race over hurdles or fences. *N. J. Henderson*

GLITTERBIRD   6 br.m. Glint of Gold – Dovetail (Brigadier Gerard)
[1992/3 20s⁶ 22vpu 22v² 18d] leggy mare: poor novice hurdler: stays 2¾m: 66
acts on heavy going: occasionally blinkered. *K. Bishop*

GLITTER GREY   7 gr.m. Nishapour (FR) – Saraday (Northfields (USA))   **c102**
[1992/3 c20d* c20gur c20s⁴ c20s² c20s⁴ c24sur c25v c20s³ c22d c18d³ c21s⁶   –
c28d⁴ c28d⁴ c24s² c21d c25s⁶ c20m* c24g] leggy mare: winning hurdler:
fair handicap chaser: won at Roscommon in September and Down Royal in
May: well beaten in valuable mares novice handicap at Uttoxeter on
fifteenth start: effective at 2½m and stays well: acts on soft and good to firm
going. *J. H. Scott, Ireland*

GLOSSY   6 ch.g. Derrylin – Floor Show (Galivanter) [1992/3 16d 16d⁶
16vpu 16spu a16g* a16g³ 16g⁶ 17mpu] sparely-made gelding: sold 5,200 gns   65
Doncaster August Sales: poor hurdler: won novice handicap at Southwell in

January: races at 2m: acts on dead ground and fibresand: jumps none too fluently: takes good hold and forces pace. *B. A. McMahon*

GLOVE PUPPET 8 ch.g. Nearly A Hand – April Belle (Grisaille) c97
[1992/3 c21d² c25d* c25d⁴] workmanlike gelding: winning hurdler: won –
novice chase at Sandown in October: respectable fourth at Ascot following
month: stays 25f: acts on dead going: suited by forcing tactics. *G. B. Balding*

GLOWING DARKNESS 8 gr.m. Kalaglow – Guama (Gulf Pearl)
[1992/3 18d] no sign of ability in NH Flat race and a novice selling hurdle. *J.* –
M. Carr

GLOWING MANTLE (IRE) 5 ch.m. Glow (USA) – Dismantle
(Aureole) [1992/3 16m] sparely-made mare: poor 2m maiden plater over –
hurdles. *R. E. Peacock*

GOADBY VENTURE 6 ch.m. Saxon Farm – Pixie's Party (Celtic
Cone) [1992/3 17g³ 16gpu] lengthy mare: lightly-raced 2m maiden plater 73
over hurdles. *Miss S. J. Wilton*

GODERSMISTAKE 10 b.g. New Member – Lafitte (Lucky Sovereign) c–
[1992/3 c21g⁶] rangy gelding: poor pointer/novice hunter chaser. *Miss J.* –
Eaton

GODOUNOV 10 b.g. Godswalk (USA) – Grilse Run (Stupendous) c–
[1992/3 c17d 16d c16g⁵ 22g c17m⁵] close-coupled gelding: winning hurdler: –
poor novice chaser: no form in 1992/3: sometimes blinkered or visored. *T.*
Fairhurst

GOING PUBLIC 6 br.g. Strong Gale – Cairita (Pitcairn) [1992/3 18g
16g⁵ 17g 16d 16g⁶] leggy, good-topped gelding: poor novice hurdler: trained 75
by W. A. Stephenson until after fourth start: yet to race beyond 17f: acts on
hard ground. *P. Cheesbrough*

GOLD BONNET 4 br.f. Heights of Gold – Church Belle (Spartan
General) [1992/3 F16m] fifth foal: half-sister to winning pointer
Churchmere and winning hurdler/chaser Moze Tidy (both by Rushmere):
dam winning staying hurdler: last of 24 in NH Flat race at Warwick in May:
yet to race over hurdles. *G. P. Enright*

GOLD CAP (FR) 8 ch.g. Noir Et Or – Alkmaar (USA) (Verbatim (USA)) c111
[1992/3 c24s² c25gur c27d² c25d³ c24v³ c27v* c32m⁴ c25dpu] angular –
gelding: fair chaser: won handicap at Fontwell in February: creditable fourth
in valuable amateurs event at Cheltenham in March: thorough stayer:
probably acts on any ground: blinkered fourth and fifth outings: sketchy
jumper. *P. J. Hobbs*

GOLD DIGGER 6 b.m. True Song – Gold Thief (Goldfella) [1992/3
F16v] first foal: dam pulled up both starts over hurdles: tailed off in NH Flat
race at Uttoxeter in April: yet to race over hurdles or fences. *W. G. Mann*

GOLDEN ANCONA 10 ch.g. London Bells (CAN) – Golden Darling
(Darling Boy) [1992/3 16d 16d⁴ 16v 16s⁶ 16s 17g⁶] sparely-made gelding: 68
poor at up to 1m on Flat: novice selling hurdler: barely stays 2m when
conditions are very testing: acts on dead ground. *M. Brittain*

GOLDEN CELTIC 9 b.g. Rare One – Cooleen (Tarqogan) [1992/3 c–
c21dpu 22d] workmanlike gelding: fairly useful hurdler/chaser at best: no –
form in 1992/3: best form at around 2½m: acts on soft going: has reportedly
broken blood vessels. *Miss H. C. Knight*

GOLDEN CHESNEY 6 ch.g. Remezzo – Golden Vanity (Golden
Surprise) [1992/3 F16g] third foal: half-brother to winning pointer Gilt
Image (by Rapid Pass): dam winning pointer: behind in NH Flat race at
Kempton in February: yet to race over hurdles or fences. *B. R. Millman*

GOLDEN CROFT 10 ch.g. Crofter (USA) – Rossian (Silent Spring) c–
[1992/3 16d c16vpu c21spu 21v 17s 17g] strong, close-coupled gelding: –
winning chaser: maiden hurdler: no form for a long time: tried blinkered:
sold 1,000 gns Malvern June Sales. *D. McCain*

GOLDEN FARE 8 ch.g. Scallywag – Katie Fare (Ritudyr) [1992/3 c16g² c86
c16d³ c20d⁴ c16d² c17s² c20m³ c24dF c20m⁴] good-topped gelding: –

moderate novice chaser: stays 2½m: acts on soft and good to firm ground. *R. Lee*

GOLDEN FRAME 6 ch.h. White Christmas – Can Bowl (Bowling Pin) [1992/3 F17d 26d^{pu} 24v^{pu} 17s 16d4] tall, rather unfurnished horse: first foal: dam unraced half-sister to fairly useful hurdler/fair pointer Timlyn: winning pointer in Ireland: poor novice hurdler: best efforts at 2m but should be suited by further: acts on soft ground. *D. J. G. Murray-Smith* — 78

GOLDEN FREEZE 11 b.g. Golden Love – Freezeaway (Vulgan) [1992/3 c18d3 c21d^{pu} c20s5 c20s2 c21g6] big, rangy gelding: impresses in appearance: fairly useful chaser at best nowadays: suited by around 2½m: acts on heavy going: takes good hold and best allowed to stride on: jumps boldly: blinkered second start: often finds little in a finish. *Mrs J. Pitman* — c123 § —

GOLDEN GUNNER (IRE) 5 ch.g. Mazaad – Sun Gift (Guillaume Tell (USA)) [1992/3 18d3 16g3 16s* 16g6 17s2] close-coupled gelding: fair handicap hurdler: won at Worcester in October: not raced after December: stays 2½m: acts on good to firm, soft ground and equitrack. *M. McCourt* — 102

GOLDEN ISLE 9 b.h. Golden Fleece (USA) – Dunette (FR) (Hard To Beat) [1992/3 16g4 17s4 16v6 16g3 16s 16g* 18g3 17s 16g3 16f* 17g2 16g2] smallish, sturdy horse: won maiden hurdle at Ayr in February and novice event at Haydock in May: good second in handicaps afterwards: stays 2¼m: suited by a sound surface. *J. I. A. Charlton* — 113

GOLDEN LARK 6 b.m. Crested Lark – Golden Valley (Hotfoot) [1992/3 F17v F16v 16s 20s6 c20f^F] quite good-topped mare: first foal: dam unraced half-sister to winning staying jumper Ambergate: no sign of ability: blinkered once. *D. McCain* — c–

GOLDEN MADJAMBO 7 ch.h. Northern Tempest (USA) – Shercol (Monseigneur (USA)) [1992/3 22g 20g^F 22v] leggy, sparely-made horse: novice hurdler: no form. *F. Jordan* — –

GOLDEN MAIN 7 b.g. Glint of Gold – Sea Venture (FR) (Diatome) [1992/3 20g^{pu}] compact gelding: very lightly-raced maiden (stayed 1¾m) on Flat: collapsed after being pulled up in early-season novice hurdle: dead. *S. Mellor* — –

GOLDEN MINSTREL 14 ch.g. Tudor Music – Ethel's Delight (Tiepolo II) [1992/3 c21d4 c26g4 c22f] hunter chaser nowadays: suited by around 3m: acts on any going. *Mrs S. N. J. Embiricos* — c95 —

GOLDEN MOSS 8 ch.g. Le Moss – Call Bird (Le Johnstan) [1992/3 18g] lengthy gelding: chasing type: fair winning hurdler in 1991/2: finished lame in September: needs at least 2½m, and should stay 3m: acts on soft ground. *J. Ffitch-Heyes* — –

GOLDEN PELE 12 b.g. Golden Love – Feale-Side Nook (Laurence O) [1992/3 c26m^{pu}] modest pointer: pulled up in novice hunter chase in May. *Mrs B. Ansell* — c–

GOLDEN PROPOSAL 4 gr.f. Nomination – Jellygold (Jellaby) [1992/3 16g 18f 18d6] angular filly: half-sister to winning hurdler Harpley (by Beldale Flutter): poor maiden on Flat: sold out of M. Bell's stable 3,900 gns Newmarket July Sales: no sign of ability over hurdles in first half of season. *M. J. Bolton* — –

GOLDEN REVERIE (USA) 5 b.g. Golden Act (USA) – Our Reverie (USA) (J O Tobin (USA)) [1992/3 20g 16d 22d5 20g* 18g^{bd} 17f^F] small gelding: poor hurdler: won selling handicap (no bid) at Ayr in February, easily best form over hurdles: visored once, blinkered once. *B. Mactaggart* — 80

GOLDEN SICKLE (USA) 4 b.g. Amazing Prospect (USA) – Marisickle (USA) (Maris) [1992/3 18v^{pu} 16v^{pu}] sparely-made gelding: plating-class sprint maiden on Flat: no sign of ability in juvenile hurdles in January. *M. J. Ryan* — –

GOLDEN SPINNER 6 ch.g. Noalto – Madame Russe (Bally Russe) [1992/3 F17s* F16s F17d3] rather unfurnished gelding: sixth foal by a thoroughbred stallion: half-brother to very smart jumper The Tsarevich, fair jumper Tsarella and NH Flat race winner Tsaritsyn (all by Mummy's Pet): won NH Flat race at Newbury in January: third in similar event at Ascot in April: yet to race over hurdles or fences. *N. J. Henderson*

GOLDEN SUPREME 7 ch.g. Deep Run – Good Calx (Khalkis) [1992/3 21dpu 16sur 16s 21spu] rangy gelding: half-brother to useful staying hurdler/chaser Master Bob (by Pitpan): dam won 2 points in Ireland: very lightly raced and no sign of ability. *J. W. Curtis* —

GOLDFINGER 10 ch.g. Billion (USA) – Old Hand (Master Owen) [1992/3 c16v4 c20d6 c25d4 c20f3] angular, workmanlike gelding: modest novice chaser: stays 2½m: acts on dead and firm going. *J. Pilkington* **c90** —

GOLD GLEN (IRE) 5 ch.g. Red Sunset – Park Lady (Tap On Wood) [1992/3 22s 18m2 20f3] angular gelding: poor novice hurdler: stays 2½m: probably acts on any going: blinkered 3 times, including last 2 starts. *P. J. Makin* **84**

GOLD HAVEN 9 ch.g. Pollerton – Coolbawn Lady (Laurence O) [1992/3 c21dco c21dpu c21dpu] rangy gelding: fairly useful chaser: would have run well but for being carried out first outing: showed nothing subsequently (not raced after November): stays 3m: acts on good to soft and firm going. *Andrew Turnell* **c?** —

GOLDINGO 6 ch.g. Rustingo – Ruths Image (Grey Love) [1992/3 F16v2 17s* 17v* 17g 21f4] smallish, workmanlike gelding: won novice hurdles at Taunton in January and Hereford in April: best form at 17f with plenty of give in the ground. *G. M. Price* **98**

GOLD MEDAL (FR) 5 gr.g. Saint Cyrien (FR) – Golden Glance (FR) (Crystal Palace (FR)) [1992/3 18h* 18f6 17g 17s* 17d4 21d2 21s*] small, leggy gelding: fair hurdler: won claimers at Exeter and Warwick and amateurs handicap at Chepstow in 1992/3 (not raced after November): needs testing conditions at around 2m and stays 21f well: acts on any ground: jumps well: makes running: tough. *M. C. Pipe* **113**

GOLD OPTIONS 11 ch.g. Billion (USA) – Foggy Park (Foggy Bell) [1992/3 c24dpu c21d* c25s4 c20s* c20s* c24v3 c24g5 c20f3 c21g4 c25g] **c154** —

Gold Options is a fine advertisement for holidays in Ireland. He's spent each summer there since joining his present stable in Yorkshire at the start of the 1987/8 season, usually returning better than ever. Gold Options' latest visit turned into a working holiday which proved very rewarding.

Narraghmore Handicap Chase, Punchestown—Gold Options gets off the mark for the season

Mitsubishi Shogun Newton Chase, Haydock—
Gold Options (far side) still has two to catch as he jumps the last upsides Twin Oaks

In four outings for Peter McCreery's stable Gold Options won twice at
Punchestown, on the second occasion in December beating General Idea by
a head in the Durkan Brothers International Punchestown Chase. Gold
Options, who'd been receiving 10 lb from General Idea, faced a stiffer test on
his return to Britain, set to meet such as Katabatic, Kings Fountain and
Twin Oaks at level weights in the Mitsubishi Shogun Newton Chase at
Haydock in January. Gold Options' chances of winning it appeared little
better than they had twelve months earlier, when he'd finished third, and he
was sent off at 14/1. Turning for home those odds looked singularly
unattractive for Gold Options was under pressure in fourth place, around
fifteen lengths behind Kings Fountain who was continuing to run on
strongly in the lead chased by Twin Oaks and Katabatic. On the long run to
the second last, the first fence in the straight having been omitted, Twin
Oaks gave way to Katabatic, and the latter appeared set to take full
advantage when Kings Fountain began to send out distress signals going to
the last. At this stage Gold Options, who'd finally collared the tiring Twin
Oaks, looked unlikely to finish any closer than third, but the picture
changed dramatically on the run-in. Whereas Kings Fountain and Katabatic,
who'd blundered at the last, could barely raise a gallop Gold Options
continued to stay on, making up ground hand over fist. Gold Options caught
the leaders halfway up the run-in and, despite drifting left, drew clear to win
by three lengths from Katabatic, in turn two and a half lengths ahead of
Kings Fountain. To an extent Gold Options had been flattered, having come
from off a very strong pace to pass tiring rivals, but he put up an unquestionably smart performance on his next start. Returned to Haydock later in
January for the Peter Marsh Chase, a limited handicap in which he was set
to receive weight from only Run For Free, Gold Options finished six lengths
third to Jodami. Gold Options ran close to form in only one of his four
subsequent starts, when fifth in the Racing Post Chase at Kempton. Lack-

lustre displays in his last two races left the strong impression that Gold Options was ready for his summer's rest again. He'd more than earned it.

Gold Options (ch.g. 1982)	Billion (USA) (ch 1974)	Restless Wind (ch 1956)	Windy City
			Lump Sugar
		Festiva (b 1955)	Espace Vital
			Flaming Beauty
	Foggy Park (br 1972)	Foggy Bell (b 1965)	Golden Vision
			Milium
		Kenya Park (br 1958)	Neron
			Ulamambri

Gold Options is the third of four foals produced by Foggy Park and the only one of any note. Foggy Park, tailed off in three novice hurdles, is a daughter of the very useful point-to-pointer Kenya Park. The good-topped Gold Options, who wears blinkers, is effective at two and a half miles to twenty-five furlongs and acts on any going, though he is ideally suited by give. He's a sound jumper. To date Gold Options has won sixteen races, including two National Hunt Flat and four hurdles, earning over £140,000 in win and place money. He'll surely be adding to that total when he returns refreshed in 1993/4. *J. G. FitzGerald*

GOLD SHAFT 10 b.g. Kambalda – Golden Goose (Prince Hansel) [1992/3 c21dF c2 1vpu c2 1d c2 1s5 c2 1g5 c22dpu c18f3] leggy gelding: winning hurdler/chaser: no form for long time: tried blinkered: faint-hearted. *R. R. Ledger*   c– §

GOLD SHOT 7 ch.g. Hard Fought – Cartridge (FR) (Jim French (USA)) [1992/3 c25m2 c24m* c23v* c25g2 c26f* c28fpu] lengthy gelding: won hunter chases at Taunton, Worcester (valuable event) and Warwick in 1992/3, showing useful form: ran poorly final outing: stays well: acts on any ground. *P. Bowen*   c111

GOLFER'S SUNRISE 8 b.g. Red Sunset – Miss Stradavinsky (Auction Ring (USA)) [1992/3 c18gF] small gelding: 2m selling hurdler: fell on chasing debut: acted on dead going: pulled hard, and often found little: dead. *H. M. Kavanagh*   c– §

GO MARY 7 b.m. Raga Navarro (ITY) – Go Perrys (High Hat) [1992/3 20m5 20g 16s6] sparely-made mare: third foal: sister to poor novice hurdler Peerglow: dam won 2m hurdle and 2m hunter chase: poor novice hurdler: stays 2½m: acts on good to firm and soft ground. *Miss C. Phillips*   73

GO MILETRIAN 9 b.g. Sonnen Gold – Chestnut Hill (Sassafras (FR)) [1992/3 c26d5 c25mpu] compact, workmanlike gelding: no form in steeplechases. *Fred Kirby*   c–

GONE ASTRAY 8 ch.m. The Parson – Merry Missus (Bargello) [1992/3 c21d4 c2 1m2 c23gF c17s3 c2 1sur c24m6 c2 1gF] sparely-made mare: winning hurdler: modest novice chaser: trained until after sixth start by F. Walton: needs further than 2m and stays 2¾m: acts on dead and good to firm ground. *J. I. A. Charlton*   c86

GONER HOUSE 8 ch.g. General Ironside – Slavesville (Charlottesvilles Flyer) [1992/3 c27g3 c20f c27gF c25g5] workmanlike gelding: winning 2½m chaser: no form in Britain. *M. McCarthy*   c–

GONE'S GIRL 7 ch.m. Green Shoon – Gone (Whistling Wind) [1992/3 17g] sister to staying jumpers Green Tops and Shoon Wind, latter useful: dam maiden hurdler/pointer in Ireland: tailed off in novice hurdle at Taunton in April: sold 750 gns Ascot June Sales. *D. R. C. Elsworth*   –

GOOD BLOW (IRE) 5 br.g. Strong Gale – Gerise (Nishapour (FR)) [1992/3 F16s] first foal: dam 1½m Flat winner and 2m hurdle winner in Ireland: tailed off in NH Flat race at Ludlow in January: yet to race over hurdles or fences. *A. J. Wilson*   –

GOODBYE ROSCOE 8 b.m. Roscoe Blake – Sugar Loch (Lochnager) [1992/3 c26gpu] of little account. *Miss J. Eddy*   c–

GOOD EGG 7 ch.m. Tachypous – Get Involved (Shiny Tenth) [1992/3 c2 1mᵖᵘ c18m⁶] leggy mare: very lightly raced and no form. *R. Hollinshead*

c–
–

GOOD FOR A LOAN 6 b.g. Daring March – Game For A Laugh (Martinmas) [1992/3 16g² 16g a20g* 17m* 17m] leggy gelding: fair handicap hurdler: won at Lingfield and Doncaster in February: effective at 2m and stays 2½m: acts on good to firm going and equitrack: usually a front runner. *R. Lee*

108

GOODHEAVENS MRTONY 6 b.g. Carwhite – Golden October (Young Generation) [1992/3 F16d F16v 16sᵖᵘ 25d 16dᵖᵘ 22g 26m⁴ 23mʳᵒ 21d] leggy gelding: of little account and temperamental to boot: visored final outing. *M. P. Naughton*

– §

GOOD PROFILE (USA) 5 b.h. Liloy (FR) – I Sparkle (USA) (Gleaming (USA)) [1992/3 16sᵖᵘ 16d⁴] leggy, workmanlike horse: fairly useful hurdler as a juvenile (rated at 124): ran as though something amiss in 2 starts in 1992/3, reportedly lame second one: unlikely to stay much beyond 2m: acts on soft ground: to join M. Pipe. *G. M. Moore*

–

GOOD SECRET 6 ch.g. Good Thyne (USA) – Etta Girl (Bay Express) [1992/3 F17s 20gᵖᵘ] third in NH Flat race in 1990/1: well beaten in similar event and a novice hurdle in 1992/3. *R. F. Fisher*

–

GOOD SEOUL 9 b.g. Good Times (ITY) – Olympic Visualise (Northfields (USA)) [1992/3 c16d³ c16s³ c20v⁴ c17s c16s⁶ c23dᵘʳ] workmanlike, good-bodied gelding: poor novice chaser: stays 2½m: acts on good to firm and heavy ground: sometimes blinkered or visored. *K. A. Morgan*

c79
–

GOOD SESSION 6 ch.g. Milk of The Barley – Rapid Rhythm (Free State) [1992/3 18sᵖᵘ 22g 28gᵖᵘ] leggy, close-coupled gelding: of little account nowadays. *A. W. Potts*

–

GOODSHOT RICH 9 b.g. Roscoe Blake – Hunter's Treasure (Tudor Treasure) [1992/3 c27s* c24v* c22vᵖᵘ c26vᵖᵘ c34dF] well-made gelding: fairly useful chaser: won handicaps at Newton Abbot and Lingfield in first half of season: failed to complete afterwards, but ran well for a long way in valuable handicap at Uttoxeter final start: stays well: acts on heavy going: sometimes looks irresolute. *C. P. E. Brooks*

c115
–

GOOD TONIC 10 b.g. Goldhill – Quinine's Girl (Deep Run) [1992/3 c21d⁵ c20s⁴ c21d⁴ c21s⁴ c24v⁴ c20g² c25dF c20f³ c25g² c26dᵖᵘ] sturdy, workmanlike gelding: fairly useful chaser: not so good as previously, but ran creditably on several occasions in 1992/3: stays 25f: acts on any going: sometimes blinkered: usually jumps well. *T. J. Etherington*

c120
–

GOOD WATERS 13 b. or br.g. Paddy's Stream – Good Surprise (Maelsheachlainn) [1992/3 c25m² c25d⁴] close-coupled gelding: fair hunter chaser: stays well: acts on good to firm and dead going: jumps soundly in the main. *W. J. Warner*

c89
–

GOOD WORD 11 ch.g. Proverb – Good Calx (Khalkis) [1992/3 c20gᵘʳ] lengthy, workmanlike gelding: winning hunter chaser: should stay beyond 2¾m: acts on dead ground. *Mrs Fiona Vigors*

c–
–

GORDANO 6 ch.g. Muscatite – Coral Star (Tarboosh (USA)) [1992/3 19h³ 22gᵖᵘ] neat gelding: inconsistent selling hurdler: probably stays 2¼m: suited by a sound surface. *D. C. Jermy*

–

GORDON PASHA 7 gr.g. Oats – Another Spring (Town Crier) [1992/3 F17s³ 16s 17s⁵ 17d³] 20,000 4-y-o: workmanlike gelding: half-brother to very useful hurdler Buck Up (by Buckskin): dam won on Flat and over hurdles: sold 5,700 gns Doncaster May Sales: poor novice hurdler: acted on soft ground: dead. *O. R. Prince*

75

GORT 5 b.g. Teenoso (USA) – Stemegna (Dance In Time (CAN)) [1992/3 F17d⁴ F17v* F17v⁶ 22v⁴ 21g 21s³ 20dᵖᵘ 25g⁵] smallish gelding: fourth foal: half-brother to a winner over jumps in Italy: dam unraced: won NH Flat race at Newton Abbot in November: poor novice hurdler: stays 2¾m: acts on heavy going: blinkered penultimate start. *Miss K. S. Allison*

79

GO SOUTH 9 b.g. Thatching – Run To The Sun (Run The Gantlet (USA)) [1992/3 23sᴿ 24dᴾᵘ] lengthy gelding: capable of fair form over hurdles but is thoroughly unreliable and sometimes refuses to race: blinkered twice, visored once: one to avoid. *J. R. Jenkins* §§

GOTAGETON 6 b.m. Oats – Palace Pet (Dragonara Palace (USA)) [1992/3 F17g F16m² 17s 17dᴾᵘ 16f] unfurnished mare: third foal: half-sister to 2 poor animals: dam ran once: no form in novice selling hurdles. *D. J. G. Murray-Smith* –

GOTTA BE JOKING 5 ch.g. Funny Man – Palimony (Communication) [1992/3 16v² 17v 22d⁴ 20d] close-coupled gelding: novice hurdler: easily best effort at 2m on heavy ground. *Miss H. C. Knight* 93

GOTT'S DESIRE 7 ch.g. Sweet Monday – Steel Lady (Continuation) [1992/3 17mᴾᵘ] poor on Flat, best at around 1m: showed nothing in maiden hurdle at Taunton in April. *C. D. Broad* –

GO UNIVERSAL (IRE) 5 br.g. Teofane – Lady Dorcet (Condorcet (FR)) [1992/3 17s 16sꜰ 16d³ 16d4] rather unfurnished gelding: third foal: dam won over 9f in Ireland: moderate novice hurdler: will stay beyond 17f: acts on dead going. *M. Bradstock* 85

GRACE CARD 7 b.g. Ela-Mana-Mou – Val de Grace (FR) (Val de Loir) [1992/3 25s* 24s² 25g²] sparely-made gelding: developed into a useful hurdler in 1992/3: won handicap at Wetherby in December: second in valuable events at Ascot (handicap) and Kempton and also a winner on Flat (April) afterwards: thorough stayer: best with plenty of give in the ground. *Mrs M. Reveley* 141

GRACEFUL VULCAN 4 ch.f. Royal Vulcan – Grand Central (Grand Roi) [1992/3 18d⁶ 16d] lengthy filly: sixth foal: half-sister to 3 winners, including hurdlers Grand Palace (by Royal Palace) and fairly useful Lady Mantegna (by Andrea Mantegna): dam fair miler: poor form over hurdles. *K. A. Morgan* 68

GRACELAND LADY (IRE) 5 b.m. Kafu – Theda (Mummy's Pet) [1992/3 16mᴾᵘ] smallish mare: of little account on Flat nowadays: no promise on hurdling debut early in season. *Mrs S. M. Austin* –

GRAHAM GOOCH 7 b.g. Record Run – Loch Ailsh (Owen Anthony) [1992/3 16v²] workmanlike gelding: promising second in novice event at Worcester in April on hurdling debut: will improve. *G. B. Balding* 87 p

GRAIN MERCHANT 7 b.g. Blakeney – Epilogue (Right Royal V) [1992/3 22g 17s³ 18d⁶ 22d⁵ 23s⁵ 24vᴾᵘ 26m³ 26v³ 20d²] small, leggy, angular gelding: novice selling hurdler: probably stays 3¼m: best efforts with give in the ground: visored final outing (ran well). *F. J. Yardley* 78

GRAMINIE (USA) 7 gr.g. Graustark – Etoile d'Orient (Targowice (USA)) [1992/3 23g⁵] lengthy gelding: very lightly-raced novice hurdler: stays 23f: acts on dead going. *P. J. Hobbs* 93

GRAN ALBA (USA) 7 gr.h. El Gran Senor (USA) – Morning Games (USA) (Grey Dawn II) [1992/3 16d 17s⁴ 16g⁴] good-topped horse: very smart and thoroughly genuine 2m hurdler in 1991/2: disappointed in 1992/3: acts on good to firm and dead ground: blinkered final outing. *R. Hannon* –

GRAND FELLOW (IRE) 4 br.g. Thatching – Concave (Connaught) [1992/3 16v² 18s⁶ 22v⁶ 20sᴾᵘ 17sᴾᵘ 18g⁵ 17dᴾᵘ 17d³] neat gelding: poor maiden on Flat (trained by J. Bethell) and over hurdles: best efforts at around 2m with plenty of give in the ground: blinkered twice. *A. M. Forte* 67

GRAND FRERE 7 br.g. Gorytus (USA) – Balista (Baldric II) [1992/3 17s* 17m⁴ 17g* 18dᴾᵘ 17d⁵ 16f* 20g] lengthy, rather plain gelding: fair hurdler: won at Newton Abbot and Taunton early in season and Wincanton in May: will prove best at around 2m: acts on any ground: held up. *M. C. Pipe* 114

GRAND HAWK (USA) 5 b.g. Silver Hawk (USA) – Ginger Lass (USA) (Elocutionist (USA)) [1992/3 17g² 18d* 16s* 16v² 20s* 21v* 22s³ 21g* 20d⁵] smallish, workmanlike gelding: fair middle-distance performer for M. Moubarak on Flat: took well to hurdling in 1992/3, winning novice events at 133

Mr Malcolm B. Jones's "Grand Hawk"

Exeter, Leicester, Ascot and Kempton (2): useful efforts on last 2-named courses: stays 2¾m: acts on heavy going: blinkered last 2 outings: front runner. *M. C. Pipe*

GRAND INQUISITOR 11 b.g. Pry – Sassenach Girl (Sassafras (FR)) [1992/3 c25f] rather leggy gelding: one-paced maiden chaser: poor jumper. *Mrs Sally Mullins*

c– x
–

GRAND VALUE 10 ch.g. Kambalda – Candy Slam (Candy Cane) [1992/3 c25mᵖᵘ c26gᵘʳ c25mᶠ 18gᵇᵈ 25sᶠ] good-topped gelding: maiden hurdler/winning chaser: no form for a long time: sold 1,800 gns Ascot 2nd June Sales: blinkered twice: poor jumper. *D. McCain*

c– x
– x

GRANGE BRAKE 7 b.g. Over The River (FR) – Arctic Brilliance (Arctic Slave) [1992/3 c24g* c25d³ c20vᶠ³ c24v⁶ c20s² c24sᵇᵈ c20v² c21s³ c26d² c20f* c20fˢᵘ c20s* c21g³ c25g³] leggy gelding: fair hurdler: successful in novice chases at Perth early in season, Newbury (quite valuable handicap) in March and Ascot (Bollinger Champagne Novices' Handicap) in April: effective at around 2½m and stays well: acts on any going: twice wore hood in 1991/2, blinkered nowadays: sketchy jumper. *N. A. Twiston-Davies*

c110
–

GRANGE CHIEF (IRE) 5 b.g. Lafontaine (USA) – Lisaniskey Lady (Varano) [1992/3 21dᵘʳ 16d⁴ 23s⁴] unfurnished gelding: second foal: dam winning pointer and maiden steeplechaser: poor novice hurdler: not raced

83

Bollinger Champagne Novices' Handicap Chase, Ascot—
Grange Brake has the measure of Nevada Gold at the last

after November: sold 27,000 gns in May: should stay further than 2m: acts on dead ground. *W. A. Stephenson*

GRANGEDEAL ILLEGAL   5 b.g. Town And Country – Burley Hill Lass (Crimson Beau) [1992/3 21d⁴ 25d⁵] lengthy gelding: modest novice hurdler: not raced after November: stays 25f: acts on dead ground. *Miss S. J. Wilton*   87

GRANNY'S GIRL   5 b.m. Mummy's Game – Michaelmas (Silly Season) [1992/3 a16g⁴ a16g a18g⁴ a16gᵖᵘ] leggy mare: poor novice hurdler: races at around 2m, mainly on all-weather surfaces. *J. L. Harris*   55

GRANNY'S LAD   6 ro.g. Scallywag – Beech Melba (Saucy Kit) [1992/3 F17s aF16g 16sᵖᵘ] workmanlike gelding: chasing type: first foal: dam, lightly raced, showed little on Flat or in points: no sign of ability. *Mrs S. M. Johnson*   –

GRANNY'S PRAYER   12 br.g. Boreen (FR) – Ace Blue (Pardal) [1992/3 c21gᵖᵘ c25m⁵ c24s c24gᵘʳ c26g⁵ c25g⁵ c25g² c26dᵖᵘ] big, workmanlike gelding: poor chaser nowadays: stays 25f: acts on any going. *Miss R. J. Patman*   c83
                                                                                    –

GRANVILLE AGAIN   7 ch.g. Deep Run – High Board (High Line) [1992/3 17v² 17v² 16d³ 17m* 20f²]   167
    A long, tortuous run-up to the Smurfit Champion Hurdle ended in a very open-looking contest going on merit to Granville Again, ante-post favourite until he lost the winning habit in the first half of the season. The run-up to the big race began at the previous Cheltenham Festival when the novice Royal Gait became Champion Hurdler, with defending champion Morley Street only sixth behind him. What a prospect Royal Gait was: if he could achieve so much in only his fourth race over hurdles how much more would he be capable of in another twelve months? The field he beat in 1992 was regarded as substandard, but contained at least one other very promising horse in Granville Again. Granville Again made his move with Royal Gait three out, travelling at least as well, and was poised a length behind the leaders when he fell at the second last. He would probably have won had he stood up. Had he won, that would have been five out of five for the season. Granville Again went on to take the Scottish Champion Hurdle the following month with his best performance up to that point in his career. Morley Street went on to take the Aintree Hurdle with a performance of similar merit, while Royal Gait was put by for 1992/3.

The first half of the 1992/3 season saw much happen that had a bearing on the Champion Hurdle, notably the rise of Mighty Mogul and the death of Royal Gait. It saw three defeats in as many starts for Granville Again, culminating in a straightforward five-length and three-length reverse behind Mighty Mogul and Flown in the BonusPrint Christmas Hurdle at Kempton which seemed to suggest that he had been overtaken by the younger horses. The general level of his form approximated to his best of 1991/2. First time up he was beaten a length by Morley Street in the Coral-Elite Hurdle at Cheltenham in November, beaten for speed on the flat after losing momentum at the last. Morley Street was giving him weight, but the small field had pottered round in very heavy ground and the result wasn't taken too much at face value. Granville Again's second run was also at Cheltenham, in the Arlington Bula Hurdle in similar conditions. He started favourite to turn the tables on Morley Street at levels and did so, only to find Halkopous, receiving 6 lb, too strong in the straight. For those holding ante-post vouchers on him, their best hope seemed to rest in the rain keeping clear of the Festival: one of Granville Again's main assets was a good turn of foot which seemed likely to prove a more potent weapon under less extreme conditions than he encountered in the Elite Hurdle and the Bula Hurdle.

On the day, conditions were fast, similar to those in the 1992 Scottish Champion Hurdle. By then events had moved on apace in the hurdling world. Mighty Mogul had met with the same fate as Royal Gait, as a result of a leg injury sustained in the Wyko Power Transmission Hurdle at Cheltenham in January won easily by Muse, who himself went temporarily wrong soon after. Nothing came out of a confusing set of trials to rival Mighty Mogul's form at Kempton. Some of the trialists, such as Coulton, King Credo, former champion Kribensis, Ruling and Valfinet, seized the opportunity to advance their claims, while others, notably Halkopous, Morley Street, Royal Derbi and Staunch Friend, ran well below their best on their most recent appearance although they still took their chance in the big race. Three of the eighteen-strong Champion Hurdle field, Granville Again, Oh So Risky and Vintage Crop, hadn't been seen out at all in the second half of the season for one reason or another, the very inexperienced Vintage Crop

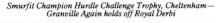

Smurfit Champion Hurdle Challenge Trophy, Cheltenham —
Granville Again holds off Royal Derbi

Mr Eric Scarth's "Granville Again"

not since he'd hacked up in the Cesarewitch in October. Granville Again, according to his trainer, had had 'niggling problems', whatever that meant. In the circumstances it was no surprise that the Kempton runner-up Flown should start favourite, although his odds of 7/2 following heavy support seemed cramped. Granville Again, Scudamore's choice ahead of the much-improved Kingwell Hurdle winner Valfinet, started second favourite at 13/2. Next on 9/1 came Coulton, Halkopous and the sponsor's Vintage Crop, a point ahead of Oh So Risky, who'd reportedly injured his back in the Christmas Hurdle. Four of the runners started at 50/1 or more, among them Royal Derbi.

Had there been betting on how the race would take shape, Royal Derbi would have been one of the favourites for pacemaker. However, he was held up. Otherwise the race settled down much as anticipated, Valfinet attempting to dominate pressed by Flown and Jinxy Jack, while most of the jockeys, including those on Granville Again, Oh So Risky, Morley Street, Kribensis and none-too-fluent Coulton, were biding their time. Ruling, third in 1991 and 1992 but uncooperative when so minded, soon became detached and eventually got so far behind he was pulled up. Valfinet failed to dominate, giving way to Jinxy Jack and Flown going to the fifth, but his efforts resulted in a truly-run affair which, as usual in the Champion Hurdle, came rapidly to the boil at the second last. Jinxy Jack still held the lead there, but only narrowly from a whole line of opponents. Granville Again, for one, rose almost with him, and it was Granville Again and Royal Derbi who went on after straightening up for home, chased by Halkopous. All three principals had travelled well throughout; Royal Derbi had looked to be going particularly well at the second last, but Granville Again virtually settled

335

matters by producing a good turn of foot on the run to the last. Safely over in front, he kept on up the hill to win driven out by a length from Royal Derbi. Two and a half lengths away came Halkopous, followed by King Credo and Oh So Risky, the last-named closely attended by Vintage Crop, Flakey Dove and Flown. Little more than nine lengths covered the eight horses, suggesting the race was substandard as well as unusually open.

Both former champions faded out of contention up the hill, the subsequently-retired Kribensis into eleventh, Morley Street into twelfth. In his current form Morley Street seemed to stand little chance of turning the tables on Granville Again or Flown on similar ground in the Martell Aintree Hurdle three weeks later, although his record in the event was outstanding. However, he it was that produced the decisive turn of foot, as at Cheltenham in November. The event turned out to be primarily a show-case for the talents of Morley Street and his jockey Graham Bradley. For his part Granville Again confirmed himself superior to Flown—who finished a good third—and produced a determined challenge on the flat before Morley Street settled the issue in a matter of strides and beat him a length and a half. While connections of other top-class or potentially top-class hurdlers must have been impressed, they will draw encouragement from the fact that the winner is rising ten and had provided further proof that Granville Again is beatable. The next season could well be one of great opportunity for the likes of Vintage Crop, Montelado, Tiananmen Square, Spinning and Roll A Dollar, and while Granville Again will win his share of trials he may well need to improve to retain the title.

			Deep Run (ch 1966)	Pampered King (b 1954)	Prince Chevalier Netherton Maid
Granville Again (ch.g. 1986)				Trial By Fire (ch 1958)	Court Martial Mitrailleuse
		High Board (b 1977)	High Line (ch 1966)	High Hat Time Call
			Matchboard (br 1963)	Straight Deal Royal Alliance

As everyone in racing must know by now, Morley Street and Granville Again are brothers, by the dominant jumping sire of his era Deep Run out of an unraced daughter of the tip-top staying hunter Matchboard, the last-named a close relative of the good Irish chaser Royal Bond. The details have been set out several times previously in *Chasers & Hurdlers* but seem bound to need updating in years to come as three mares out of High Board—Deep Line and Running Board (both by Deep Run) and Balancing Act (by Balinger)—have been retired to the paddocks, and there are more foals of hers coming along. As noted in *Chasers & Hurdlers 1991/92* the rather angular Granville Again is probably less stout a stayer than his brother; he has yet to tackle further than two and a half miles, the distance of the Aintree Hurdle. He is effective from two to two and a half. While on the subject of distances, a note of explanation about that of the Champion Hurdle which has now become seventeen furlongs again. No mystery—the course has been remeasured, along with all the others in Britain, and, like so many, has been found to be longer than previously believed. Granville Again is particularly well suited by a sound surface. He has an excellent turn of foot. *M. C. Pipe*

GRAVITATE 5 b.g. Song – Sheer Bliss (St Paddy) [1992/3 17g^{pu} 17g^{pu}] leggy gelding: of little account. *R. M. Stronge*   –

GRAY ROSETTE 4 b.f. Scallywag – Lady St Clair (Young Generation) [1992/3 F17g] first foal: dam, Flat winner and placed in 2m hurdles, half-sister to several winning jumpers, including very useful hurdler The Grey Bomber (by Scallywag): tailed off in NH Flat race at Bangor in March: yet to race over hurdles. *E. H. Owen jun*

GRAY'S ELLERGY 7 b.m. Oats – Glistening (Aureole) [1992/3 23g^F] leggy mare: modest staying novice hurdler: fell only outing of 1992/3 (September): acts on dead ground. *D. R. Gandolfo*   –

GRAZEMBER 6 b.g. Oats – Mellie (Impecunious) [1992/3 23d^F 22s^6 20v^6 18d 18d^6 17g 21f] workmanlike gelding: novice hurdler: no form in 1992/3. *R. Earnshaw* —

GREAT GUSTO 7 b.g. Windjammer (USA) – My Music (Sole Mio (USA)) [1992/3 c21m*] rather sparely-made gelding: winning hurdler: won novice hunter chase at Newton Abbot in May on steeplechasing debut: stays 2 1f: acts on good to firm going: should improve. *Miss L. Blackford* c88 p

GREAT HEIGHTS 6 b.g. Shirley Heights – As You Desire Me (Kalamoun) [1992/3 16g^{rtr} 16g^2 18m^2] one-time useful stayer on Flat: blinkered when second in maiden hurdle and novice event in Scotland in March: will stay beyond 2 1/4m: acts on good to firm ground: refused to race on hurdling debut (has also done so in blinkers on Flat). *J. J. O'Neill* 85

GREAT IMPOSTOR 5 ch.g. Vaigly Great – Lady Waverton (Huntercombe) [1992/3 19h^4 17g^6 17s^3 18m 20m^4 17d^{F2} 17m^4 17d^3 20g^6] plating-class middle-distance maiden on Flat and over hurdles: would have won conditional jockeys selling handicap at Newton Abbot in April but for falling last (remounted): stays 2 1/2m: acts on soft and good to firm ground: blinkered third and fourth starts. *R. J. Hodges* 76

GREAT MAX (IRE) 4 b. or br.g. Simply Great (FR) – Lockwood Girl (Prince Tenderfoot (USA)) [1992/3 16g 17g^2 17s^2 17g^2 16g] workmanlike gelding: fair form over middle distances on Flat: sold out of Sir Mark Prescott's stable 23,000 gns Newmarket September Sales: quite useful form in juvenile hurdles: will prove best around 2m: acts on soft going: races up with pace: visored last 2 starts (best effort on first occasion). *M. A. Jarvis* 115

GREAT ORME (NZ) 6 b.g. Captain Jason (NZ) – Two Lettres (NZ) (Aureate) [1992/3 F16d F17d] New Zealand-bred gelding: half-brother to poor novice hurdler Afterthought (by Prince Simbir): well behind in NH Flat races: yet to race over hurdles or fences. *D. H. Barons* —

GREAT POKEY 8 b. or br.g. Uncle Pokey – Mekhala (Menelek) [1992/3 c16m c17d^4 c16s^2 c16d^4 c16g^{ur} c17g^4 c16d^{pu}] good-topped gelding: poor chaser: races at around 2m: acts on soft ground: blinkered fifth outing. *A. S. Corner* c79

GREAT SALING 8 b.g. Vaigly Great – Goosie-Gantlet (Run The Gantlet (USA)) [1992/3 17d^{ur} 22d^{pu} 17v] sturdy, good-bodied gelding: winning 2m hurdler: no form in 1992/3: blinkered nowadays. *F. Jordan* —

GREAT SERVICE 6 ch.g. Vaigly Great – Janlarmar (Habat) [1992/3 c21d^{pu}] sturdy gelding: novice selling hurdler: no show on chasing debut (October): blinkered twice 1991/2. *M. Dods* c—

GREEK FLUTTER 8 b.g. Beldale Flutter (USA) – Greek Blessing (So Blessed) [1992/3 c21g^5 c16s* c16s^2 c20d^2 c16s^2] leggy gelding: has been fired: fairly useful hurdler: won novice chase at Haydock in November: runner-up all starts subsequently (not raced after February): stays 2 1/2m: probably acts on any ground. *J. G. FitzGerald* c116 —

GREENFIELD LADY 5 b.m. Town And Country – Lakshmi Lady (Kala Shikari) [1992/3 17s] first foal: dam, sprint plater on Flat, placed over hurdles: tailed off in early-season novice hurdle. *P. G. Murphy* —

GREENHAM COMMON 4 b.g. Cruise Missile – Willmon (Willipeg) [1992/3 F16v^{pu}] third foal: dam unplaced both starts: tailed off when pulled up in NH Flat race at Uttoxeter in April: yet to race over hurdles. *J. H. Peacock* —

GREENHEART 10 br.g. Green Shoon – Giollaretta (Giolla Mear) [1992/3 c16g^F c17g^3 c17d^4 c16v^3 c17s^F c16f^{F3} c16m^{ur} 18g 17f^{pu}] rangy gelding: useful handicap chaser at best: well beaten most starts 1992/3, including in novice hurdles: free-running sort, best at 2m: ideally suited by top-of-the-ground: reckless jumper. *R. D. Townsend* c— —

GREENHILL GO ON 8 b. or br.m. Oats – Ballylaneen (Master Buck) [1992/3 24s 17d] fifth foal: half-sister to 2 poor novice jumpers by Celtic Cone: dam placed over hurdles: tailed off in novice hurdles. *B. R. Millman* —

GREENHILL RAFFLES 7 ch.g. Scallywag – Burlington Belle c– (Galivanter) [1992/3 18g* 22m* 20d³] workmanlike gelding: fair winning 109 p chaser in 1991/2: successful in novice hurdles at Worcester in October and Newton Abbot in March: good third in similar event at Ascot later in March: stays 2¾m: probably acts on any going: capable of further improvement over hurdles. *P. J. Hobbs*

GREENHILLS PRIDE 9 b.g. Sparkling Boy – Soheir (Track Spare) c– [1992/3 c16s c18v⁵ a20g* a20g 22g] good-topped gelding: selling hurdler: 84 won at Southwell (no bid) in January, easily best effort of season: winning chaser: stays 2½m: probably acts on any going: blinkered once. *J. R. Jenkins*

GREENHIL TARE AWAY 5 b.g. Oats – Burlington Belle (Galivanter) [1992/3 F16v F17m⁵] rangy gelding: half-brother to useful hurdler and smart chaser Mr Moonraker (by Idiot's Delight): dam unraced: signs of ability in NH Flat races: yet to race over hurdles or fences. *P. J. Hobbs*

GREENHITHE 4 b.g. Green Desert (USA) – Anegada (Welsh Pageant) [1992/3 F14m] half-brother to numerous winners, including good 7f to 1½m winner John French (by Relko) and very useful middle-distance performer Flamingo Pond (by Sadler's Wells): dam, who showed ability at 2 yrs, is half-sister to Derrylin: showed nothing in NH Flat race at Market Rasen in March: yet to race over hurdles. *M. C. Chapman*

GREEN ISLAND (USA) 7 b.g. Key To The Mint (USA) – Emerald c113 p Reef (Mill Reef (USA)) [1992/3 c16g* c19m* c20f² c18d* c18g*] small – gelding: winning hurdler: progressive chaser: won handicaps at Worcester in August and Exeter in September, April and May: stays 2½m: acts on any going: blinkered once: sometimes whips round at start. *A. J. K. Dunn*

GREEN'S EXHIBIT 4 b.g. Song – Scotch Thistle (Sassafras (FR)) [1992/3 18f⁴ 18d⁴ 18f² 18d] leggy gelding: half-brother to winning hurdler Mr 83 Bennington (by Diligo): plating-class maiden on Flat: easily best effort over hurdles in first half of season when second in seller at Fontwell. *K. O. Cunningham-Brown*

GREEN'S GAME 5 ch.g. Vital Season – Iced Lolly (Master Stephen) [1992/3 16v 17d⁵] smallish, workmanlike gelding: third foal: dam winning – pointer: showed nothing in novice hurdles. *N. R. Mitchell*

GREEN SHEEN (IRE) 5 ch.g. Green Shoon – Hill Sixty (Slippered) [1992/3 25g 25s⁴ 28d⁶] sturdy gelding: brother to winning chaser 76 Gladtogetit and half-brother to other winning jumpers: dam unraced half-sister to staying chaser Carndonagh: poor form in novice hurdles: sold 2,000 gns in May: looks a thorough stayer: acts on soft ground. *W. A. Stephenson*

GREEN SILVER 11 gr.g. Hardgreen (USA) – Spring Silver (Palestine) c– [1992/3 24mᵖᵘ] lengthy gelding: modest hurdler/chaser: suited by test of – stamina: acted on good to firm and soft going: dead. *L. Lungo*

GREEN'S SEAGO (USA) 5 ch.g. Fighting Fit (USA) – Ornamental (USA) (Triple Crown (USA)) [1992/3 16m⁶ 17dᵖᵘ 16d a20g⁴ a16g 16s 16g 16f⁴ 67 17m⁵ 17f] small gelding: poor novice hurdler: stays 2½m: acts on fibresand, best efforts on turf on a sound surface (acts on firm). *J. L. Harris*

GREEN'S STUBBS 6 b.g. Ballad Rock – Aventina (Averof) [1992/3 17m⁶ 20g⁵ 18mᵇᵈ 17g 18dᵖᵘ 17fᵖᵘ 16f 17g⁶] of little account on Flat 56 nowadays: bad novice hurdler. *A. Barrow*

GREEN'S THORBURN (USA) 5 b. or br.g. Vaguely Noble – Halo Again (USA) (Halo (USA)) [1992/3 16dᶠ 17s 17v⁴ 23s² 21v³ 21v 18v⁴] 79 § sparely-made gelding: novice selling hurdler: stays 23f: acts on heavy going: blinkered once, visored once: tail swisher: ungenuine. *A. Moore*

GREEN'S TRILOGY (USA) 5 b.g. Lyphard's Wish (FR) – Capitol Caper (USA) (Senate Whip (USA)) [1992/3 17g 17s 17v⁴ 16vᵖᵘ 17d 17g] 72 sparely-made gelding: fair winner at up to 1m on Flat at 2 yrs: poor maiden hurdler: yet to race beyond 17f: easily best effort on heavy going. *K. F. Clutterbuck*

GREEN'S VAN GOYEN (IRE) 5 b.g. Lyphard's Special (USA) – Maiden Concert (Condorcet (FR)) [1992/3 17s 20d*] lengthy, angular gelding: fairly useful hurdler: won handicap at Plumpton in October: better suited by 2½m than 2m: acts on soft and good to firm going: game. *R. Akehurst* 117

GREEN TRIX (IRE) 5 b.g. Denel (FR) – Blue Trix (Blue Chariot) [1992/3 17m 21d 24g³] ex-Irish gelding: half-brother to several winning jumpers, including fair performers Tartan Trix (by Pitpan) and No More Trix (by Kemal): dam lightly-raced maiden: first sign of ability over hurdles when third in maiden at Edinburgh in February: suited by 3m. *C. Parker* 78

GREEN WALK 6 b.m. Green Shoon – Princess Charmere (Tepukei) [1992/3 c21spu 22gpu 20g⁴ 22f³ 22f⁴] rangy mare: half-sister to winning jumper Owen (by Pollerton): no sign of ability in hunter chase (trained by M. Pinto): poor staying novice selling hurdler. *R. Rowe* c–
56

GREENWICH BAMBI 5 b.m. Music Boy – Coca (Levmoss) [1992/3 18d⁴ 20d³ 21v³ 21s² 18s* 17f4] small, sparely-made mare: trained until after fourth start by W. Carter: won novice hurdle at Folkestone in February: by no means disgraced facing insufficient test of stamina next time: stays 21f: acts on any going. *T. G. Mills* 93 +

GREEN WILLOW 11 ch.g. Callernish – Kilwillow (Fray Bentos) [1992/3 c17dpu c21dpu c17vF c20s4] big, rangy, angular gelding: fairly useful chaser at his best: no form in 1992/3: stays 21f: probably acts on any going: sketchy jumper. *J. T. Gifford* c–
–

GREENWINE (USA) 7 br.g. Green Dancer (USA) – Princesse Margo (Targowice (USA)) [1992/3 c17s² c18gpu c16mF c16s⁶ c16v² c16spu c16d⁵ c16g* c18g² c19fpu 18f[F]] leggy gelding: winning hurdler: modest chaser: won novice event at Plumpton in March: stays 2¼m: acts on good to firm and heavy ground: ran poorly when blinkered twice: jumps none too fluently: unreliable. *Mrs L. Richards* c90 §
–

GRENAGH 12 ch.g. Rouser – All Blarney (Blarney Stone) [1992/3 21s² 24v* 24d* 25f] smallish, workmanlike gelding: lightly-raced handicap hurdler: fairly useful: won at Chepstow in January and February: stays 3m: acts on heavy going, ran poorly both starts on top-of-the-ground: genuine. *V. R. Bishop* 121

GREY ANCONA (IRE) 4 gr.c. Double Schwartz – Pete's Money (USA) (Caucasus (USA)) [1992/3 F17g F17d F16f] half-brother to useful novice hurdler Corrin Hill (by Petorius) and modest novice chaser Pete's Sake (by Scorpio): dam never ran: well beaten in NH Flat races (visored final start), and on Flat in 1993: yet to race over hurdles. *C. Tinkler*

GREY BUT ROSY (IRE) 4 gr.f. Kafu – Rossaldene (Mummy's Pet) [1992/3 17dpu 17gpu] leggy filly: plating-class maiden on Flat, stays 1m: no sign of ability in early-season juvenile hurdles (blinkered last time): sold 900 gns Ascot December Sales. *P. M. McEntee* –

GREY COMMANDER 5 gr.h. Grey Desire – Melowen (Owen Dudley) [1992/3 18m³] sparely-made horse: better effort over hurdles when third in maiden claimer at Market Rasen in March. *M. Brittain* 88

GREY CPHAS 4 gr.g. Grey Desire – Malindi (Mansingh (USA)) [1992/3 17m 21s⁵ 20dpu 17m⁵] leggy gelding: no form on Flat (for M. McCormack) or in selling hurdles: blinkered final outing. *Mrs S. D. Williams* –

GREYFRIARS BOBBY 7 ch.g. Hard Fought – Victorian Pageant (Welsh Pageant) [1992/3 16v 21g⁶ 22d] sparely-made gelding: fair hurdler in 1991/2: modest form at best in 1992/3: barely stays 2¾m: acts on soft ground. *Mrs J. G. Retter* –

GREY HUSSAR (NZ) 7 gr.g. War Hawk – Poi (NZ) (Native Turn (USA)) [1992/3 16v⁶ 23v* 23f²] leggy gelding: won novice handicap hurdle at Windsor in February: broke blood vessel and finished lame following month: sold 2,200 gns Ascot June Sales: suited by a test of stamina: acts on heavy going. *N. J. Henderson* 90

GREY ILLUSIONS 5 gr.g. Nishapour (FR) – Morica (Moorestyle) [1992/3 16s 22s 17spu 17f3] sturdy gelding: poor maiden on Flat and over hurdles: best effort at 17f on firm ground: blinkered third outing. *C. L. Popham*　72

GREY MERLIN 6 gr.g. Derrylin – Sea Kestrel (Sea Hawk II) [1992/3 16mpu 17g 20g3 17d 17s 18g 20g4 21s 21g4] small, strong gelding: winning hurdler: no form in 1992/3: stays 2½m: acts on soft going: unreliable. *Mrs S. Taylor*　– §

GREY POWER 6 gr.m. Wolf Power (SAF) – Periquito (USA) (Olden Times) [1992/3 22m* 21d* 21spu F13m2 16d 21f] sturdy mare: won novice hurdles at Sedgefield and Wetherby (conditional jockeys handicap) in first half of season: ran poorly over hurdles afterwards: retained 23,000 gns Doncaster June Sales: stays 2¾m: acts on good to firm and dead ground. *Mrs M. Reveley*　113

GREY REALM 5 ch.m. Grey Desire – Miss Realm (Realm) [1992/3 18m 22f5 20s 18g 23g a22g] compact mare: poor novice hurdler: best efforts over 2¾m: acts on firm ground. *R. E. Barr*　63

GREY RUM 8 gr.g. Absalom – Cuba Libre (Rum (USA)) [1992/3 17mpu 18gpu] lengthy gelding: winning hurdler: ran poorly early in season: once-raced over fences: best at 2m: acts on good to firm ground: blinkered twice. *J. J. Birkett*　c– –

GREY SALUTE (CAN) 10 gr.g. Vice Regent (CAN) – Night Out (USA) (Bustino) [1992/3 16d4 20dpu c16v4] big, strong, good sort: one-time smart 2m hurdler: no form in 1992/3, including on chasing debut. *J. R. Jenkins*　c– –

GREYSBY 11 gr.g. General Ironside – Kiskadee (Seven Bells) [1992/3 c17v5 c16s6 c17vpu c21g4 c25g3 c21g] workmanlike gelding: winning 2¾m chaser: no form in 1992/3: usually visored nowadays, blinkered once. *O. Brennan*　c– –

GREY SEASON 4 gr.g. Belfort (FR) – Cherry Season (Silly Season) [1992/3 F14m F17g] fourth foal: dam 7f winner: soundly beaten in NH Flat races: yet to race over hurdles. *T. W. Donnelly*

GREY TORNADO 12 gr.g. Rugantino – Tornadora (Typhoon) [1992/3 c19g4 c18g3 c19m4 c16g4 c24g* c26g3 c24fur c27mur c19g2 c19m5 c24f4 c20fF c24gpu] small, compact gelding: modest chaser nowadays: won weakly-contested handicap at Taunton in September: good second at Hereford in March but below that form subsequently: stays 3m: acts on firm ground: blinkered 3 times in 1991/2. *Mrs S. D. Williams*　c89 –

GREY TOUPE'E 7 gr.g. Kala Shikari – Peggy Wig (Counsel) [1992/3 22spu 16m 23dpu] close-coupled gelding: half-brother to fairly staying hurdler/chaser Longriver Lady (by Town And Country): dam winning plater on Flat: winning pointer: no sign of ability over hurdles. *G. W. Giddings*

GREY TRIX (IRE) 5 gr.g. Le Moss – Moll of Kintire (Politico (USA)) [1992/3 F16d6] fifth living foal: dam fairly useful Irish hurdler: remote sixth of 20 finishers in NH Flat race at Hexham in March: yet to race over hurdles or fences. *T. P. Tate*

GRIFFINS BAR 5 b.g. Idiot's Delight – Milly Kelly (Murrayfield) [1992/3 17s 17s 16spu] smallish, lengthy gelding: half-brother to winning jumpers Singlesole (by Celtic Cone) and Chichell's Hurst (by Oats): dam won 2m novice hurdle: no sign of ability in novice hurdles. *Mrs P. Sly*　–

GRINDLEY BROOK 8 b.g. Over The River (FR) – Cullagh's Girl (Tepukei) [1992/3 c24dpu] tall, lengthy gelding: no promise in novice hurdles or a hunter chase. *D. McCain*　c– –

GRIS ET VIOLET (FR) 6 ch.g. Iron Duke (FR) – Darkeuse (FR) (Dark Tiger) [1992/3 18g2 21g 16gur 18v* 20d*] strong, workmanlike gelding: handicap hurdler: won at Market Rasen in December and Newcastle in January, showing much improved form on latter course: stays 2½m: acts on good to firm and heavy ground: forces pace. *J. G. FitzGerald*　110

GROG (IRE) 4 b.g. Auction Ring (USA) – Any Price (Gunner B) [1992/3 17m6 17s4 18v5] compact gelding: fair handicapper on Flat, winner 3 times at up to 1½m in 1992 (claimed out of M. Channon's stable £11,556 in August): fair effort when fourth of 24 in juvenile hurdle at Newbury in January: reportedly broke a blood vessel when well-backed favourite for similar race later in month. *S. E. Sherwood*   103

GRONDOLA 6 b.m. Indian King (USA) – Trysting Place (He Loves Me) [1992/3 c16m4 c16g6 c17d6 a16gpu c16mrtr c16sF c17gpu 16f] leggy mare: poor winning hurdler/maiden chaser: sold 1,050 gns Ascot June Sales: pulls hard and usually races at around 2m: probably acts on any going: sometimes wears hood: inconsistent: refused to race fifth outing. *D. Burchell*   c73 §
–

GROUSEMAN 7 gr.g. Buckskin (FR) – Fortina's General (General Ironside) [1992/3 c20dF 23s 20s* 22d* 22g 22g2] leggy gelding: fair handicap hurdler: won at Taunton in January and Ludlow in February: would have finished in frame in novice handicap chase at Ludlow in December but for falling 2 out: should stay beyond 2¾m: acts on soft ground. *Miss H. C. Knight*   c– p
107

GROUSE MOOR 14 b.g. Wabash – Jyppy (Phebus) [1992/3 c25g c26f3] rather sparely-made gelding: no form in hunter chases. *R. R. Collier*   c–

GROVE SERENDIPITY (IRE) 5 b.g. Glenstal (USA) – Huppel (Huntercombe) [1992/3 17s* 16v4 17d2 17g* 18g 17d2 a20g3 22fwd] compact gelding: modest middle-distance performer at best on Flat: fair form over hurdles: won novice events at Wolverhampton in January and March: acted on heavy going (poor effort on fibresand): blinkered: dead. *M. C. Pipe*   101

GUIBURN'S NEPHEW 11 ch.g. National Trust – Arran Sunset (Miracle) [1992/3 c20g2 c24d5 c21d2 c21v4 c21v* c20f* c20f2 c20m2 c16g*] rangy gelding: usually carries plenty of condition: fairly useful handicap chaser: won at Newton Abbot in January, Chepstow in March and Ascot (quite valuable event) in April: best form at up to 21f: acts on any going: races up with pace: sometimes makes mistakes: genuine and consistent. *P. J. Hobbs*   c125
–

GUILD STREET 8 b.m. Hasty Word – Mickley Vulstar (Sea Moss) [1992/3 c25m2 c24f2 c24s4] smallish, well-made mare: fair hunter chaser: creditable efforts in March on first 2 starts, well below form on last: stays 25f: acts on firm ground. *Paul Jones*   c86

Ostler Handicap Chase, Chepstow—Guiburn's Nephew makes all from Sirrah Jay

GUILDWAY 10 b.g. Bulldozer – Lucky Favour (Ballyciptic) [1992/3 c–
c26v] moderate chaser at his best: well beaten in handicap in April: stays –
3¼m: acts on firm going. *Mrs M. R. T. Rimell*

GULFLAND 12 ch.g. Gulf Pearl – Sunland Park (Baragoi) [1992/3 17v³]
runner-up in 2 of his 4 races over hurdles in 1984/5: fit from Flat, remote 74
third of 11 in novice event at Plumpton in November. *G. A. Pritchard-Gordon*

GULL POND 5 b.m. Coronash – Royal Tudor (Tudor Treasure) [1992/3
17vᵖᵘ 22vᵖᵘ] sister to winning jumpers Arish Mel and Red Shah: dam poor –
maiden: no sign of ability in novice hurdles. *R. J. Hodges*

GULSHA 7 b.m. Glint of Gold – Mai Pussy (Realm) [1992/3 c20sᶠ c18m² c108
c17g4] leggy mare: fair hurdler: second in novice event at Bangor, best –
effort over fences early in season: stays 2½m: acts on soft going. *N. A.
Twiston-Davies*

GUNMETAL BOY 9 b.g. Warpath – Geranium (Ragusa) [1992/3 c25g* c89
c25mᵖᵘ] sturdy gelding: hunter chaser: sold 12,000 gns Doncaster August –
Sales: won maiden event at Kelso (despite rider losing irons close home) in
April: showed nothing following month: stays 25f: acts on firm ground. *Miss
Lucinda V. Russell*

GUNNER JIM 9 b.g. Gunner B – Well Lined (Straight Lad) [1992/3 c–
c26mᵖᵘ] rangy gelding: little sign of ability. *J. C. Peate* –

GUNNERSBURY ROAN 6 ro.g. Oats – Goldaw (Gala Performance
(USA)) [1992/3 22dᵖᵘ 18f6 17v6 17v 18v³] sparely-made gelding: poor novice 61
hurdler: should be suited by further than 2¼m. *R. Voorspuy*

GUNNER'S FLIGHT 9 ch.m. Celtic Cone – Lady Lucy (Hardraw Scar) c105
[1992/3 c26d²] lengthy mare: useful hunter chaser: creditable second at –
Plumpton in February: stays 3m: acts on dead ground: blinkered twice
over hurdles: sold 10,000 gns Malvern June Sales. *H. Wellstead*

GUNNER STREAM 9 ch.g. Gunner B – Golfers Dream (Carnoustie) c– x
[1992/3 c24d4 c28sᶠ c26vᵖᵘ] workmanlike gelding: modest chaser at his –
best: well below form, let down by his jumping, in 1992/3: stays 3m: best
effort on good going. *P. G. Murphy*

GUSHKA 6 b.g. Le Moss – Saucy Serene (Tarqogan) [1992/3 F17d]
second foal: dam won a point in Ireland: well beaten in NH race at –
Hereford in May: yet to race over hurdles or fences. *Mrs J. G. Retter*

GUTE NACHT 10 ch.g. Laurence O – Cherry Branch (Menelek) [1992/3 c81
16sᶠ 24vᵖᵘ 22s 24d4 c25m² c27m6 c25sᵖᵘ] small gelding: winning pointer: 81
poor novice hurdler/chaser: stays well: acts on good to firm and dead going.
S. W. Campion

GYDAROS 8 b.g. Ardross – Handy Dancer (Green God) [1992/3 20g
17sᵇᵈ 20g a20g6] well-made gelding: lightly raced and no form over hurdles. –
Denys Smith

GYMCRAK CYRANO (IRE) 4 b.f. Cyrano de Bergerac – Sun Gift
(Guillaume Tell (USA)) [1992/3 17f 17m²] half-sister to winning hurdler 73
Golden Gunner (by Mazaad): quite modest 7f winner at 2 yrs: better effort
over hurdles when second in juvenile claimer at Carlisle in September. *M.
H. Easterby*

GYMCRAK FORTUNE (IRE) 5 b.g. Kafu – Forlorn Chance (Fighting
Don) [1992/3 17dᵖᵘ] tall gelding: sold 600 gns Ascot February Sales: well –
beaten both starts over hurdles. *P. D. Cundell*

GYMCRAK GAMBLE 5 b.g. Beldale Flutter (USA) – Baridi (Ribero)
[1992/3 17m 22g² 17d4 21d4 26d² 28v 24d4 20g4 25d² 25d6 25v³ 28m² 21s³ 94
26m4 26v³] lengthy gelding: moderate handicap hurdler: generally ran
creditably in 1992/3: stays 3¼m: probably acts on any going on turf (below
form on fibresand): visored once. *T. Dyer*

GYMCRAK SOVEREIGN 5 b.g. Ballacashtal (CAN) – Get Involved
(Shiny Tenth) [1992/3 16g 16s6 16s* 17d 17d4 a16g*] tall, lengthy gelding 103
with some scope: fair handicap hurdler: won at Nottingham in January and

Southwell in May: stays 2¼m: acts on soft ground and fibresand: usually a front runner. *M. H. Easterby*

GYMCRAK STARDOM   7 gr.g. Comedy Star (USA) – Chemin de Guerre (Warpath) [1992/3 17d 2 1s⁶ 16s* 17sᶠ 17d* 17f² 20f] close-coupled, good-topped gelding: chasing type: fairly useful handicap hurdler: won at Catterick in January and Sandown following month: good second to Olympian in Sunderlands Imperial Cup on latter course in March: best form at around 2m: probably acts on any going. *M. H. Easterby*   127

GYPSY TRAIL (USA)   5 br.g. Darby Creek Road (USA) – Majestic Nature (USA) (Majestic Prince) [1992/3 18f] small, close-coupled, sparely-made gelding: plater over hurdles: below form only outing of season (August): stays 2½m: usually blinkered or visored nowadays. *P. J. Hobbs*   –

H

HABTON WHIN   7 b.g. Le Bavard (FR) – Bob's Hansel (Prince Hansel)   c 100
[1992/3 22d² 24g* 25g² c21d* c24sᶠ c23d c25sᶠ 24dᵖᵘ] lengthy gelding: 100
won novice hurdle at Market Rasen in October and novice chase at Sedgefield in November: let down by his jumping over fences subsequently and ran in snatches returned to hurdling: stays 25f: acts on good to firm and soft ground: tends to idle in front. *M. H. Easterby*

HADLEIGHS CHOICE   6 b.g. Fairy King (USA) – Jillette (Fine Blade (USA)) [1992/3 18d 18gᵇᵈ 16m 18s⁶ a18gᵘʳ] sparely-made gelding: poor form   56
in selling hurdles. *G. Fleming*

HAGLER   10 br.g. Silly Prices – Reigate Head (Timber King) [1992/3 21g⁴   78
2 1f⁶ 25s 24g² 26d⁶ 22d 16d a20g a24gᵖᵘ] small, workmanlike gelding: selling hurdler: sold 3,100 gns Doncaster August Sales: trained first outing by R. Hollinshead: best effort of season on fourth start: barely stays 3m: acts on good to firm and soft ground: blinkered once. *G. Fierro*

HAITHAM   6 b.h. Wassl – Balqis (USA) (Advocator) [1992/3 2 1vᵖᵘ 22f   107
22d⁶ 18f*] leggy horse: fair hurdler: amateur ridden, won handicap at Fontwell in May: should stay beyond 2¼m: easily best form on a sound surface. *R. H. Buckler*

P.Z. Mower EBF Chase, Thurles—
Haki Saki is clear at the last

HAKI SAKI   7 ch.g. Tug of War   c 130
– Shannon Lek (Menalek) [1992/3 20v⁴ c20s* 24d⁵ c20d* c29sᵖᵘ] fair hurdler: useful chaser: won handicap at Limerick in December and P.Z. Mower Chase at Thurles (beat New Mill House by 6 lengths) in February: stays 2¾m: acts on heavy going. *A. Leahy, Ireland*

HALE'S MELODY   8 b.m.   c–
Dubassoff (USA) – Hale Lane (Comedy Star (USA)) [1992/3 c24f4] winning pointer: tailed off in NH Flat races and a hunter chase. *Mrs P. Townsley*

HALF BROTHER   11 br.g.   c102
Faraway Times (USA) – Sinzinbra   –
(Royal Palace) [1992/3 c22m³ c21s² c22vᵖᵘ c17v³ c20gᵖᵘ c22g³] leggy, angular gelding: fair handicap chaser on his day: has become disappointing: suited by 2½m and forcing tactics: acts on

heavy going and good to firm: sometimes gives impression something amiss: trained until after penultimate start by Mrs J. Pitman. *J. T. Gifford*

HALFWAY TAVERN 6 b.m. Town And Country – Copper Cloud (Foggy Bell) [1992/3 18m] rather unfurnished mare: poor plater over hurdles. *Capt. T. A. Forster* –

HALKOPOUS 7 b.g. Beldale Flutter (USA) – Salamina (Welsh Pageant) [1992/3 17g* 17v* 16d 17m3] 164

Halkopous came through well in his second season over timber, on the last of just four starts finishing a close third in the Champion Hurdle and putting himself on our short list for the 1994 renewal. Whereas many a good novice never makes it, Halkopous—runner-up to Flown in the Supreme Novices' Hurdle at Cheltenham and to Carobee in the Top Novices' Hurdle at Aintree in 1991/2—quickly established himself in the senior ranks. He won two Grade 2 races before Christmas, in so doing accounting for half a dozen championship contenders. He made his reappearance in the Bellway Homes Fighting Fifth Hurdle at Newcastle in November, co-favourite with another northern-trained second-season prospect Coulton in a field of six. Coulton failed to do himself justice, and the main challenge to Halkopous, who was on top from the second last despite a mistake at the last, came from the previous year's winner Royal Derbi. There was six lengths between them at the finish. The Arlington Bula Hurdle at Cheltenham the following month promised a much stiffer examination of Halkopous' credentials. He started fourth favourite at 8/1 behind Granville Again, Morley Street and Oh So Risky, receiving 6 lb from each; Kribensis and Boro Smackeroo completed the line-up at long odds. As at Newcastle Halkopous came to the second last clearly going best. He'd always been well placed in a race run at a fair pace in very testing conditions, and he quickened away with enthusiasm in the straight to win easily by ten lengths and six from Granville Again and Morley Street. It was a very convincing performance, whatever excuses might be made for the others, and, in the absence of the well-touted Cesarewitch winner Vintage Crop, Halkopous, now favourite for the Champion Hurdle, started at odds on next for the AIG Europe Champion Hurdle at Leopardstown in January. However, the outcome of the latter race, as of a fair few in the hurdles pattern in the latest season, seemed to do more to cloud than clarify the Champion Hurdle picture. Royal Derbi led all the way, the odds-on shot came nowhere; in fact, Halkopous beat only one home. However, he was in trouble too far out for there to be nothing wrong with him. Sure enough, the vet afterwards reported that 'the gelding was found

Bellway Homes Fighting Fifth Hurdle, Newcastle—Halkopous smashes through the last

Arlington Bula Hurdle, Cheltenham—a much better jump from Halkopous as he storms clear

to be in respiratory distress'. In spite of this reverse, and the fact that the ground at the Festival was not only very different from that on which the Bula was decided but firmer than any on which he had previously shown form over hurdles, Halkopous was one of the shorter-priced horses in the Champion Hurdle, starting third favourite along with Coulton and Vintage Crop at 9/1. He gave his supporters an excellent run, improving to have every chance going to the last after being waited with.

Halkopous (b.g. 1986)	Beldale Flutter (USA) (b 1978)	Accipiter (b 1971)	Damascus Kingsland
		Flitter Flutter (b or br 1966)	Cohoes Ellerslie
	Salamina (ch 1978)	Welsh Pageant (b 1966)	Tudor Melody Picture Light
		Femme Elite (ro 1969)	Young Emperor Fairy Flax

Although not quite able to get to grips with the first two in the Champion Hurdle on the run-in, Halkopous has a good turn of foot. He is a mile-and-a-quarter horse on the Flat, a quite useful one at that, winner of the Magnet Cup at York as a five-year-old. There's very little of jumping in his background. His dam, grandam and great-grandam on the female side all won on the Flat (Fairy Flax the King's Stand Stakes at Royal Ascot), and to Ile de Bourbon Salamina produced the high-class middle-distance performer Ile de Chypre. However, another of Halkopous' half-brothers Argakios (by Busted) has been placed in novice hurdles. Halkopous has been raced only at two miles over hurdles; he is likely to be kept to that distance, and also to hurdling, for another season although he will be sent chasing eventually. He is a fine jumper. An angular gelding, he acts on good to firm and clearly very well on heavy going. *M. H. Tompkins*

HALLBOROUGH 8 ch.g. Warpath – Bargain Line (Porto Bello) [1992/3 c–
21spu c25spu a16gF 16dpu] rangy gelding: modest hurdler in 1990/1: no sign –

of retaining ability, including on chasing debut: stays 2½m: acts on fibresand: tried blinkered and visored. *Mrs P. A. Barker*

HALL END LADY (IRE) 5 b.m. Tumble Wind (USA) – Avise La Fin (Scottish Rifle) [1992/3 aF16g³ aF13g⁵] half-sister to Flat winners Ayrshire Lass (by High Top) and Laharna Girl (by Star Appeal), latter also a winning selling hurdler: dam 7f winner at 2 yrs: showed little in NH Flat races at Lingfield in January and February: yet to race over hurdles or fences. *J. White*

HALLO FOUNTAIN 10 b.g. Royal Fountain – Artlight (Articulate) [1992/3 28dᵖᵘ c24gᵖᵘ] workmanlike gelding: no sign of ability. *Mrs S. Taylor*   c–
–

HALLO MAM (IRE) 4 br.f. Tender King – Fruit of Passion (High Top) [1992/3 16s⁴ 16s 16s 17m² 16g² 16g² 18g³ 16f* 16m 16f* 16m*] lengthy filly: second foal: sister to winning hurdler Royal Romper: dam unraced: lightly-raced middle-distance maiden on Flat in Ireland: won selling hurdles at Uttoxeter (handicap, bought in 2,800 gns) and Worcester (novice event, no bid) and non-selling novice handicap on former course late in season: best form at 2m on a sound surface: waited with. *O. Brennan*   86

HAL'S PRINCE 6 b.g. Le Moss – Hal's Pauper (Official) [1992/3 F17g] well beaten in NH Flat races: yet to race over hurdles or fences. *J. L. Needham*

HALSTON PRINCE 6 b.g. Petorius – Repicado Rose (USA) (Repicado (CHI)) [1992/3 16d 20g 16g 16d 16g 17m 17sᵖᵘ] compact gelding: modest nowadays on Flat, winner over 1¼m in 1992: sold out of Mrs J. Ramsden's stable 2,000 gns Doncaster September Sales: poor form in novice hurdles. *B. Mactaggart*   68

HAMANAKA (USA) 4 b.f. Conquistador Cielo (USA) – Tastefully (USA) (Hail To Reason) [1992/3 16s³ 16d* 16s⁵ 17m⁴ 16s⁴] tall, leggy filly: modest maiden at around 1m on Flat: sold out of J. Fanshawe's stable 6,200 gns Newmarket Autumn Sales: won novice hurdle at Wetherby in February: easily best effort subsequently when good fourth on fourth outing: acts on dead and good to firm ground. *M. D. Hammond*   97

HAMPER 10 ch.g. Final Straw – Great Care (Home Guard (USA)) [1992/3 c19vᵖᵘ c19sᵖᵘ c26vᵖᵘ c19v³ c16d³ c18m³ c19mᵖᵘ c17mᵖᵘ c17sᵖᵘ 17m 16f⁴ 17f⁶ 20g 18f] close-coupled gelding: poor handicap hurdler/novice chaser: stays 2¼m: acts on any going: sometimes blinkered: looks a difficult ride. *N. R. Mitchell*   c80
80

HAND IN GLOVE 7 b.g. Star Appeal – Cash Limit (High Top) [1992/3 17d* 17s⁶ 18s 16s] strong gelding: won conditional jockeys novice claiming hurdle at Wolverhampton in November: tailed off subsequently: stays 17f: acts on dead going: blinkered last start (gave impression something amiss). *R. Brotherton*   80

HAND OUT 9 b.m. Spare A Dime – Stolen Ember (Burglar) [1992/3 c23dF c21gᵖᵘ c17v³ c24d² c24s⁴] leggy, shallow-girthed mare: poor chaser: good second in novice handicap at Taunton in November: running creditably in similar event on same course following month when bad mistake 3 out: wasn't seen out again: needs further than 17f and stays 3m: acts on heavy going. *R. H. Buckler*   c82

HANDSOME GENT 4 b.g. Dunbeath (USA) – French Surprise (Hello Gorgeous (USA)) [1992/3 16g] fairly useful at best, stays 11f, on Flat: sold out of Lord Huntingdon's stable 6,400 gns Ascot November Sales: some promise when ninth of 13 in juvenile hurdle at Edinburgh in January: should improve. *L. Lungo*   78 p

HANDSOME NED 7 br.g. Netherkelly – Beau Wonder (Veiled Wonder (USA)) [1992/3 17d* 18d 17v² 18s* 17f⁵] smallish, workmanlike gelding: modest form over hurdles: won novice event at Plumpton in October and handicap at Folkestone in February: ran poorly last start: should stay further than 2¼m: acts on heavy ground: races prominently. *D. M. Grissell*   95

HANDY DOVE 6 b.m. Palm Track – Saucy Dove (Saucy Kit) [1992/3 17m³ 17g² 17gʳᵒ 22f* 16g* 17g* 20d² 17d⁴] lengthy, sparely-made mare: 89

won novice hurdles at Worcester in September and Ludlow and Hereford (handicap) in October: stays 2¾m: acts on firm and dead ground: ran out third start. *R. J. Price*

HANDY LASS 4 b.f. Nicholas Bill – Mandrian (Mandamus) [1992/3 17v a16g⁶ 17s⁴ 17f² 16s⁵ 17v² 18d⁶ 18m²] half-sister to winning hurdlers Santo Boy (by Monsanto) and Autonomous (by Milford): 1¼m winner on Flat when trained by J. Wharton: sold 1,800 gns Doncaster October Sales: poor juvenile hurdler: likely to stay beyond 2¼m: acts on any going. *Mrs A. Knight* — 79

HANDY TRICK 12 ch.g. Duky – Deep Sea (Deep Run) [1992/3 c25gᵖᵘ c25dᵘʳ c25d⁵ c26d⁵ c25sᵖᵘ c26sᵘʳ c29sᵖᵘ] one-time very useful staying chaser, has lost his form completely: blinkered last 2 starts. *Mrs H. Bell* — c– –

HANDY VENTURE 5 ch.m. Nearly A Hand – Kath's Venture (St Columbus) [1992/3 F17g 21s] leggy, sparely-made mare: second foal: half-sister to Irish NH Flat race winner Idiots Venture (by Idiot's Delight): dam unraced sister to Grand National winner Maori Venture and fairly useful staying chaser Rock Saint: little sign of ability in NH Flat race and a novice hurdle. *B. S. Rothwell* — –

HANNAH BEE 6 gr.m. Humdoleila – Heron's Mirage (Grey Mirage) [1992/3 17sᶠ 21vᵖᵘ a20g] small, strong mare: well beaten over hurdles. *W. Clay* — –

HANNAH BROWN (IRE) 5 ch.m. Carlingford Castle – Liebeslied (Dike (USA)) [1992/3 17mᵖᵘ 16fᵖᵘ] of little account: visored last start. *J. G. M. O'Shea* — –

HANNAH MILLIE NICK 8 b.m. Balinger – Saucy Eater (Saucy Kit) [1992/3 c22dᵖᵘ c22mᵖᵘ c21mᵖᵘ] lengthy, angular mare: poor novice selling hurdler: no show over fences. *F. L. Matthews* — c– –

HAPPY BREED 10 b.g. Bustino – Lucky Realm (Realm) [1992/3 c18dᵖᵘ c16s⁴] lengthy gelding: winning 2m hurdler/chaser: very lightly raced nowadays, and something possibly amiss in 1992/3. *O. Brennan* — c– –

HAPPY HIGGINS 9 b.g. Strong Gale – Quayville (Quayside) [1992/3 c21g²] rangy gelding: maiden hurdler: moderate pointer: second in maiden hunter chase at Uttoxeter in May: sold 4,200 gns Ascot June Sales. *R. K. Aston* — c86 –

HAPPY HORSE (NZ) 6 ch.g. Gaiter (NZ) – Silver Valley (NZ) (Retained) [1992/3 22g⁶ 22v³ 25s³ 24v 23d* 26g² 17f⁴ 22g³ 18d] stocky, well-made gelding: won novice handicap hurdle at Stratford in February: ran well next 3 outings (especially so on eighth start), long way below his best last: stays 3¼m: acts on any going: sometimes needs plenty of driving. *D. H. Barons* — 92

HAPPY PADDY 10 ch.g. Paddy's Stream – Inch Tape (Prince Hansel) [1992/3 c21gᵖᵘ c21g⁶] sparely-made gelding: very lightly-raced maiden jumper: should stay at least 2½m: acts on dead ground. *B. R. Summers* — c– –

HARAKA SASA 5 ch.m. Town And Country – Quite Lucky (Precipice Wood) [1992/3 16d 17d 21v 21vᵖᵘ] plain, rather sparely-made mare: second foal: dam, winning 2m hurdler, stayed 2½m: behind in novice hurdles in first half of season. *J. Webber* — –

HARDIHERO 7 b.g. Henbit (USA) – Hardirondo (Hardicanute) [1992/3 25m⁴ 22m 28f³ 25m³ 23s⁴ 28s⁵ 26s* 25d 24m² 28g⁵ 25d⁴ 25s⁶] leggy, rather sparely-made gelding: modest hurdler: won handicap at Catterick in December: creditable efforts when in frame subsequently: stays well: acts on any going: ran poorly when visored once. *G. F. White* — 92

HARD SELL 6 ch.g. Hard Fought – Misoptimist (Blakeney) [1992/3 16vᵖᵘ a16gᵖᵘ] strong gelding: modest 7f/1m performer on Flat at best: showed nothing in a claimer and a novice event over hurdles. *J. G. FitzGerald* — –

HARD TO GET 6 b.g. Rousillon (USA) – Elusive (Little Current (USA)) [1992/3 18m⁶ 18mᵇᵈ 17g³ 19m 21f 18d⁵ a20g a16gᵖᵘ] small gelding: poor — 74 hurdler: below form last 4 starts: stays 2½m: acts on firm going: best blinkered. *M. F. Barraclough*

HARD TO HOLD 10 b.g. He Loves Me – Run Swift (Run The Gantlet (USA)) [1992/3 a20g* a20g* a20g* 22d a18g² 22s² 22d⁶ a24gᵘʳ] shallow-girthed gelding: winning chaser: fairly useful handicap hurdler: won 3 times on all-weather at Southwell in January: ran creditably most outings afterwards, and was unlucky at Southwell on final one, unseating rider at the last when 5 lengths clear: stays 3m: acts on any going: blinkered once: suited by forcing tactics: amateur ridden: tough and genuine. *A. A. Hambly*   c– 116

HARD TO RESIST 8 b.g. Oats – Anchor Lady (The Brianstan) [1992/3 22vᵖᵘ 16vᵖᵘ c21sᵖᵘ] angular, workmanlike gelding: poor novice hurdler/chaser. *D. J. Wintle*   c– –

HARLEY 13 ch.g. Cranley – Harmony Rose (Drumbeg) [1992/3 c25sᵖᵘ c25gᵖᵘ c22f c25g⁴ c33m* c25g⁴] strong gelding: fairly useful hunter chaser at his best: well below form in 1993 except when winning at Cheltenham in May by 12 lengths: needs a thorough test of stamina nowadays: acts on heavy going and good to firm: usually jumps soundly: blinkered once over hurdles. *Miss J. Eaton*   **c99** –

HARPLEY 6 gr.g. Beldale Flutter (USA) – Jellygold (Jellaby) [1992/3 21s⁴ 20v²] smallish, lengthy gelding: moderate hurdler at his best: sold out of S. Kettlewell's stable 2,700 gns Ascot September Sales: only poor form in November, in seller on second occasion: stays 3m: probably acts on any going: visored last start, blinkered previous three. *M. Castell*   80

HARRISTOWN (IRE) 5 b.g. Orchestra – Maynooth Belle (Busted) [1992/3 F17g F17f²] lengthy gelding: half-brother to winning hurdlers Captain Webster (by Sandford Lad) and Qualitair King (by Tumble Wind): dam unraced: second in NH Flat race at Doncaster in March: sold to join K. Bailey 28,000 gns Doncaster May Sales: yet to race over hurdles or fences. *J. Hanson*

HARRY HASTINGS (USA) 14 b.g. Vaguely Noble – Country Dream (USA) (Ribot) [1992/3 c22gᶠ] big, strong, rangy gelding: one-time useful 2m hurdler: poor pointer nowadays: weakening when falling 5 out in hunter chase at Ayr in March: acts on any going. *Miss Heather Galbraith*   c– –

HARRY LIME 8 b.g. Beldale Flutter (USA) – Zither (Vienna) [1992/3 21dᵖᵘ 16f 22m⁶ 26dᵖᵘ] sturdy gelding: selling hurdler: best effort of season on penultimate start: stays 25f: acts on any going: blinkered once/visored once in 1991/2. *C. Bridgett*   85

HARRYS CASTLE 7 b.g. Carlingford Castle – Cloneen Lady (Master Owen) [1992/3 16g 24vᵖᵘ] lengthy gelding: third foal: dam winning pointer and in frame over hurdles in Ireland: little promise in novice hurdles in first half of season. *J. S. Wainwright*   –

HARRY'S GEM (IRE) 5 br.g. Green Ruby (USA) – Miami Blues (Palm Track) [1992/3 17d] lengthy, narrow gelding: no sign of ability in claiming hurdle early in 1991/2 and novice selling hurdle in May. *Miss A. J. Whitfield*   –

HARRY'S JOY 5 b.m. Aragon – Happy Donna (Huntercombe) [1992/3 17sᵖᵘ 18sᵖᵘ] half-sister to winning hurdler Happy Cash (by Blue Cashmere): no form on Flat when trained by C. Hill: tailed off when pulled up in selling hurdles in December and January. *D. R. Tucker*   –

HARRY THE CAB 4 ch.c. Hadeer – Hilly (Town Crier) [1992/3 aF16g² aF13g* aF16g³] first reported foal: dam quite useful 2-y-o 6f winner: won NH Flat race at Lingfield in February: third of 5 on same course following month: sold 6,400 gns Doncaster May Sales: yet to race over hurdles. *Dr J. D. Scargill*   –

HARRY THE HORSE 5 ch.g. Capricorn Line – Laureppa (Jimmy Reppin) [1992/3 F17m²] big gelding: third foal: half-brother to novice hurdlers by Little Wolf and Milford: dam, winning hurdler/chaser, half-sister to quite useful chaser Laundryman: dead-heated for second in 23-runner NH Flat race at Cheltenham in April: yet to race over hurdles or fences. *M. Bradstock*

HARVEST SPLENDOUR (USA) 6 b.m. Solford (USA) – Autumn
Splendour (AUS) (Luskin Star (AUS)) [1992/3 22d 17m^{ur}] leggy mare: won a
point in March: novice selling hurdler: probably stays 2½m: acts on any
ground: visored once. *H. C. Harper*

—

HASHAR (IRE) 5 b.h. Darshaan – Hazy Idea (Hethersett) [1992/3 18v^2
17s^4 16s^2 17s^5 17m^4] smallish, well-made horse: fairly useful handicap
hurdler: good fourth in County Hurdle at Cheltenham in March on last start:
yet to race beyond 2¼m: acts on good to firm and soft going. *D. R. C.
Elsworth*

119

HASTY DIVER 12 ch.g. Crash Course – Tara Babu (Garland Knight)
[1992/3 c26g c21g^R] workmanlike gelding: has run tubed: winning staying
chaser: no form for a long time. *Paul Maine*

c–
—

HASTY SALVO 9 ch.m. Hasty Word – Salvo's Grace (FR) (Salvo)
[1992/3 c21m^3] sparely-made mare: fair pointer: poor novice steeplechaser.
H. Wellstead

c–
—

HASTY SPARK 5 b.g. Shardari – Fire And Ice (FR) (Reliance II) [1992/3
17d^{pu}] leggy, close-coupled gelding: only sign of ability on Flat when fifth in
1¼m seller in 1992: tailed off when pulled up in novice hurdle at Huntingdon
in January. *C. F. Wall*

—

HATHERDEN TOMBOY (IRE) 5 ch.g. Carlingford Castle – Queen
Hadrian (Golden Love) [1992/3 F17d] workmanlike gelding: fourth foal: dam
winning Irish pointer: behind in NH Flat race in October: sold 3,000 gns
Ascot June Sales: yet to race over hurdles or fences. *J. W. Mullins*

—

HATS HIGH 8 b.g. High Top – Peculiar One (USA) (Quack (USA))
[1992/3 17s^6 17d 17s^5 20v^3 c21v^{ur} c21v^F 20v 17v^4 20s] lengthy, lightly-made
gelding: moderate hurdler: has shown nothing over fences: stays 2¼m: acts
on heavy going: usually blinkered or visored: probably ungenuine. *F. Gray*

c– §
88 §

HATTON'S FESTIVAL 6 b.m. Ring Bidder – The Festival Chat
(Saucy Kit) [1992/3 a18g^6] leggy, angular mare: poor novice hurdler. *R.
Champion*

—

HAUT-BRION (IRE) 4 br.g. Alzao (USA) – Romanee Conti (Will
Somers) [1992/3 16d 17d 16s] rather leggy gelding: poor maiden on Flat and
over hurdles. *W. Storey*

—

HAVE A NIGHTCAP 4 ch.g. Night Shift (USA) – Final Orders (USA)
(Prince John) [1992/3 17f 18g* 16d5 16d^2 16v^6 a16g^2 a16g^5 a16g^2 a16g* a16g^F
a16g^{pu}] close-coupled gelding: in frame at up to 1m on Flat: sold out of M.
Jarvis' stable 2,500 gns Newmarket July Sales: modest hurdler: won seller
at Market Rasen (bought in 3,800 gns) in October and handicap at Southwell
in February: stays 2¼m: acts on dead ground and fibresand: inconsistent. *J.
L. Harris*

96

HAVERTON 6 b.g. Carwhite – Rosie Pug (Mummy's Pet) [1992/3 18g^{pu}
17g 16d 18d5] compact gelding: poor plater over hurdles. *T. Casey*

59

HAWAIIAN YOUTH (IRE) 5 ch.g. Hawaiian Return (USA) – Eternal
Youth (Continuation) [1992/3 F17m^4 F16m^3] sturdy gelding: eighth foal:
half-brother to winning Irish sprinter Trendy Youth (by Be Friendly) and to
a poor novice jumper by Le Moss: dam Irish 7f winner: close up in NH Flat
races at Cheltenham in April and Warwick in May: yet to race over hurdles
or fences. *R. Rowe*

—

HAWKSWOOD (NZ) 5 b.g. War Hawk – Miss Rosewood (NZ) (Le
Fripon (NZ)) [1992/3 F17d] leggy New Zealand-bred gelding: behind in NH
Flat race at Sandown in October: dead. *D. H. Barons*

—

HAWTHORN BLAZE 7 br.g. Alzao (USA) – Konigin Kate (GER)
(Authi) [1992/3 17v* 21s* c21v* c21s*] tall, workmanlike gelding:
progressive hurdler who won handicaps at Cheltenham in December and
Newbury in January, putting up very useful performance in latter: created
very favourable impression when trotting up in small fields in novice chase
at Lingfield (jumped to the right) and minor chase at Leicester (jumped

c126 P
145 p

Mr Clive D. Smith's "Hawthorn Blaze"

well) in February: stays 2lf: acts on heavy going: front runner: sure to go on to much better things over fences. *M. C. Pipe*

HAWTHORNE GLEN 6 b.g. Furry Glen – Black Gnat (Typhoon) [1992/3 18s 18v³ 25g] leggy, workmanlike gelding: poor novice hurdler: creditable third at Folkestone in January: stays 2¼m, not 25f: acts on heavy going. *A. R. Davison*   77

HAWWAR (USA) 6 b. or br.g. Lypheor – Berkeley Court (Mummy's Pet) [1992/3 a20g⁴ a22g⁶ a24g⁵ a24g⁴ a22g³ c24m c24f⁵ c23m²] close-coupled gelding: poor hurdler: best effort over fences when second of 5 finishers in novice event at Market Rasen in May: stays well: acts on good to firm ground and on all-weather surfaces: visored once. *Mrs A. L. M. King*   c81   81

HAZEL CREST 6 b.g. Hays – Singing Wren (Julio Mariner) [1992/3 17s⁴] tall, lengthy gelding: NH Flat race winner: showed promise when fourth in novice hurdle at Newcastle in December, but wasn't seen out again. *J. G. FitzGerald*   73 p

HAZEL HILL 7 ch.m. Abednego – Severine (Jukebox) [1992/3 F17m⁴ F16d⁵ 23d 24vᵖᵘ 21vᵖᵘ] sturdy mare: won a point in Ireland in 1992: no sign of ability in novice hurdles. *J. K. Cresswell*   –

HAZEL LEAF 7 b.m. Le Moss – Camden (David Jack) [1992/3 17m² 20g⁵ 16g 17g⁵ 16g 17g⁶ 21s⁴ 17d*] sparely-made mare: improved form when   93

winning novice hurdle at Perth in May by 12 lengths: best with plenty of give in the ground at around 2m. *R. McDonald*

HAZLEWOOD GLEN 7 b.g. Furry Glen – Woodford Princess (Menelek) [1992/3 F16v² 21s⁵] angular, sparely-made gelding: won 2 NH Flat races in 1990/1: second in similar event at Hexham in December: soundly beaten but some promise when fifth in novice hurdle at Wetherby in January. *T. P. Tate* — p

HAZZARD'S BOY 8 ch.g. Dubassoff (USA) – Sleepline Spartan (Spartan General) [1992/3 c16v c19v⁵] good-topped gelding: of little account: tried blinkered. *Mrs J. C. Dawe* c–
–

HEAD FOR HOME 8 gr.m. Grey Ghost – Reigate Head (Timber King) [1992/3 18dᵖᵘ 21dᵖᵘ 18g 21sᵖᵘ 16g⁵ 20m 16gF] lengthy, good-topped mare: poor novice hurdler: dead. *B. Bousfield* 70

HEADIN' ON 13 b.g. Headin' Up – Olisa (Bally Russe) [1992/3 c23hᵖᵘ c21m² c19g³ c21m³ c24f⁴ c22g² c20m² c21f³ c20sᵖᵘ c24m c22f³] lengthy gelding: poor chaser: well below form last 4 outings: barely stays 3m: acts on hard going: has broken blood vessels. *Mrs P. M. Joynes* c83
–

HEAD LAD 10 ch.g. Headin' Up – Authors Daughter (Charlottown) [1992/3 c25sᵖᵘ c25gᵖᵘ] workmanlike gelding: poor novice hurdler/chaser: blinkered once. *F. Lloyd* c–
–

HEAD TURNER 5 b.m. My Dad Tom (USA) – Top Tina (High Top) [1992/3 19h⁵ 22f⁵ 17m 18f³ 17g* 18d² 18m² 16dᵖᵘ 17d] sparely-made mare: selling hurdler: won at Taunton (no bid) in September: ran well when runner-up at Exeter later in month and in October: best at around 2m: acts on good to firm and dead ground: blinkered third outing. *C. P. Wildman* 74

HEARD IT BEFORE (FR) 8 b.h. Pharly (FR) – Lilac Charm (Bustino) [1992/3 22d⁶ 20g⁵ 17dᵖᵘ] small horse: selling hurdler: best efforts at around 2m. *R. P. C. Hoad* –

HEARTS ARE WILD 6 ch.g. Scallywag – Henry's True Love (Random Shot) [1992/3 17g*] well-made gelding: type to make a chaser: improved form when winning novice hurdle at Huntingdon in October: should stay beyond 17f: acts on dead ground. *Capt. T. A. Forster* 97

HEATHER MOTH 11 b.g. Candy Cane – Rumdora (Rum (USA)) [1992/3 c26g⁶] rangy gelding: poor novice hurdler/chaser: blinkered once. *John Mackley* c–
–

HEATHFIELD GALE 6 b. or br.m. Strong Gale – Erskine Melody (Melody Rock) [1992/3 F17vF F17g* 22v 22d² 22m² 21g* 20fF] leggy mare: first foal: dam won 2¾m hurdle: successful in NH Flat race at Doncaster in December: progressive hurdler: won Hoechst Panacur Mares Only Final (Handicap) at Newbury in March and would have won mares handicap at Haydock in May but for falling last: will stay beyond 2¾m: acts on firm ground. *M. C. Pipe* 106 p

HEATHVIEW 6 b.g. Pitpan – Whosview (Fine Blade (USA)) [1992/3 F16v³ 21sᵘʳ 22s⁶ 22g² 22g⁴ 24m² 17d⁶ 18g*] small, stocky gelding: modest hurdler: won conditional jockeys novice event at Sedgefield in April: ran creditably most previous starts: effective at 2m and stays 2¾m: best form on good ground: sometimes flashes tail and finishes weakly. *J. G. FitzGerald* 87

HEAVENLY HOOFER 10 b.g. Dance In Time (CAN) – Heavenly Chord (Hittite Glory) [1992/3 16dᵖᵘ 17g⁴ 17m 16g 17f 16g⁵] smallish, workmanlike gelding: poor hurdler: once-raced over fences: suited by around 2m and a sound surface. *J. L. Goulding* c–
64

HEAVENLY PEACE 10 b.g. Welsh Saint – Sweet Accord (Balidar) [1992/3 17vᵖᵘ] half-brother to useful middle-distance performer Rock Chanteur (by Ballad Rock): dam won over 1m and 1¼m in Ireland: winning 2m hurdler in Ireland in 1988/9: having first race since that season when pulled up in handicap at Newton Abbot in January: suited by a sound surface. *A. P. Jarvis* –

Mr P. A. Deal's "Hebridean"

HEBRIDEAN   6 b.g. Norwick (USA) – Pushkar (Northfields (USA))
[1992/3 17v* 17s² 22s* 21m 20d*]   138 p
   Not seen out until April, 1992, when turned five, Hebridean made up
for lost time in the next twelve months, running a dozen times and showing
no sign of the problems which had kept him off the course. A bright future
on the Flat beckoned when, on only his second start, Hebridean finished
third in the Aston Park Stakes, a listed event run at Newbury. Hebridean
didn't quite fulfil the promise of that run but he did go on to show useful
form on occasions for Henry Candy's stable, including when winning a
two-mile minor event at Goodwood in October. Whatever he'd achieved on
the Flat the well-made Hebridean looked the type to do even better over
jumps and, after changing stables, he lived up to expectations, winning
three of his five starts and showing himself a smart novice. Hebridean easily
justified favouritism at Newton Abbot on his hurdling debut, and he was just
as impressive when accounting for much stronger opposition at Huntingdon, in the Sidney Banks Memorial Novices' Hurdle, and Ascot. He won by
twelve lengths from High Alltitude at Huntingdon and by four from Boycott
at Ascot, on each occasion travelling well and showing a good turn of foot to
go clear in the closing stages. Lack of experience contributed to Hebridean's defeat on his second start when his jumping let him down, while the
firmish ground was probably the reason for his finishing a well-beaten
eighth in the Sun Alliance Novices' Hurdle at Cheltenham on his other
outing. Hebridean, who acts well in the mud, would have gone close at
Cheltenham if he'd been able to reproduce his best form.
   Given suitable conditions Hebridean should make a greater impression at the next Cheltenham Festival, when he's likely to be contesting the
Stayers' Hurdle. The distance of just over three miles will pose no problems

		Far North	Northern Dancer
	Norwick (USA)	(b 1973)	Fleur
	(b 1979)	Shay Sheery	A Dragon Killer
Hebridean		(b or br 1969)	Annie K
(b.g. 1987)		Northfields	Northern Dancer
	Pushkar	(ch 1968)	Little Hut
	(b 1980)	Chippings	Busted
		(b 1972)	Chip

for Hebridean, who finished strongly over an extended twenty-one furlongs in testing ground at Huntingdon. Hebridean, by the very smart middle-distance stayer Norwick, is the fourth foal of Pushkar, an unraced half-sister to the twelve-furlong Group 3 winner Red Chip. The second dam Chippings, also unraced, is a half-sister to the good sprinter Silver God out of the five-furlong winner Chip. Pushkar has produced four other winners besides Hebridean, easily the best of them being the smart middle-distance performer Eradicate, winner in 1990 of the Zetland Gold Cup and Magnet Cup. *D. Nicholson*

HECTOR'S RETURN 5 ch.h. True Song – Ol' Blue Eyes (Bluerullah) [1992/3 F16s⁴] second foal: dam won points after birth of first foal: fourth in 20-runner NH Flat race at Nottingham in February: yet to race over hurdles or fences. *R. Brotherton*

HEDDON HAUGH (IRE) 5 br.g. Seclude (USA) – Miss Kambalda (Kambalda) [1992/3 F17m] first foal: dam lightly-raced maiden: mid-division in 25-runner NH Flat race at Carlisle in October: sold privately 15,500 gns in May: yet to race over hurdles or fences. *W. A. Stephenson*

HEDGEHOPPER (IRE) 5 b.g. Henbit (USA) – Selham (Derring-Do) [1992/3 16g 17v a20g²] tall gelding: easily best effort over hurdles when second in novice handicap at Lingfield in January: stays 2½m: acts well on equitrack. *C. Weedon* — 86

HEIGHT OF FUN 9 b.g. Kambalda – Moongello (Bargello) [1992/3 c23f³ c27s⁵ c21s* c21g³ c24fF c18d² c25d² c24g² c26v⁵ c26vᵖᵘ c20f³ c19m⁶ c27g c26f* c23f² c26m c25m⁵] leggy gelding: handicap chaser: won at Southwell (conditional jockeys) in September and Hereford in May: stays 3¼m: probably acts on any going: sometimes blinkered (including last 4 starts): lazy and needs plenty of driving: inconsistent. *C. L. Popham* — c93 §, – §

HEILEN LULLABYE 7 ch.m. True Song – Princess Mey (Country Retreat) [1992/3 16sᵖᵘ] leggy, lightly-made mare: no sign of ability: tried blinkered. *C. Smith* — –

HEIST 4 ch.g. Homeboy – Pilfer (Vaigly Great) [1992/3 F16d* F17m² F16s²] angular gelding: third foal: dam, placed over 7f at 2 yrs, is half-sister to Waterford Crystal Stayers' Hurdle winner Rustle: won NH Flat race at Leopardstown in January: favourite, strong-finishing second in Guinness Festival Bumper at Cheltenham in March: long odds on when beaten at Fairyhouse in April: yet to race over hurdles. *N. Meade, Ireland* — –

HELENUS (USA) 5 b.g. Danzig (USA) – Helen Street (Troy) [1992/3 16dᵖᵘ] close-coupled gelding: no sign of ability over hurdles: blinkered once. *T. Craig* — –

HELIOPSIS 5 b.g. Shirley Heights – If (FR) (Kashmir II) [1992/3 17s² 24d* 21s*] quite attractive gelding: fair hurdler: won handicaps at Haydock and Wetherby in December: effective at 2m when conditions are testing and stays 3m: acts on good to firm and soft ground: not a fluent jumper as yet. *M. D. Hammond* — 113

HELL OF A GUY 6 b.g. Absalom – Outward's Gal (Ashmore (FR)) [1992/3 17g⁶] NH Flat race winner: no form over hurdles. *A. Moore* — –

HELLO GRANDAD 9 b.g. Hello Gorgeous (USA) – Emerin (King Emperor (USA)) [1992/3 c21v⁶ c21vF c18v³] third foal: half-brother to winning hurdler Lucky Knight (by Rarity): dam won twice over 6f: won a point in Ireland in 1989: little sign of ability in novice chases: sold 850 gns Ascot June Sales: sketchy jumper. *C. P. E. Brooks* — c–

HELLO LADY 6 b.m. Wolverlife – Lady Cromer (Blakeney) [1992/3 a22g⁵] leggy mare: no sign of ability over hurdles. *D. J. G. Murray-Smith*   –

HELLO LIZ 5 b.m. Meadowbrook – Piper's Knoll (Bing II) [1992/3 18g 23g] sparely-made mare: third foal: dam of little account: no form in novice hurdles at Kelso in October: should stay well. *C. Parker*

HELLO SAM 10 ch.g. Hello Gorgeous (USA) – Samra (Welsh Saint)   c– x
[1992/3 22spu 17v⁶ 21g² 17g³ 17g⁵] leggy gelding: best effort for a long time   69
when third in conditional jockeys selling handicap at Bangor in March: let
down by his jumping over fences: stays 3m: acts on any going. *J. A. Bennett*

HELLO VANOS 5 b.g. King of Spain – Flaming Peace (Queen's Hussar)
[1992/3 18d 18s 18v] workmanlike gelding: novice selling hurdler: no show
in 1992/3: visored once. *C. R. Beever*

HELMAR (NZ) 7 b.g. Gay Apollo – War Field (NZ) (War Hawk) [1992/3   c81
c20g³ c16gF c16mF c20d⁵ c20dpu c20m c16g⁴ c20m²] workmanlike gelding:
winning hurdler: poor novice chaser: stays 2½m: acts on dead and good to
firm going: sometimes breaks blood vessel. *F. Jordan*

HELMSLEY PALACE 4 b.f. Dominion – Queen Midas (Glint of Gold)
[1992/3 17fF 17m 17fpu] lightly-raced maiden on Flat: sold out of Mrs J.
Cecil's stable 1,900 gns Newmarket July Sales: no sign of ability in
early-season juvenile hurdles, including a seller. *J. White*

HEMUST 9 br.g. True Song – Shewill (Evening Trial) [1992/3 c26dpu   c–
c21m⁴ c25spu] workmanlike gelding: of little account. *S. Dow*

HENBURY HALL (IRE) 5 gr.g. Bellypha – Rustic Stile (Rusticaro
(FR)) [1992/3 18m² 16spu 18m³ 16g³ 18s 16m⁶] good-bodied gelding: selling   90 d
hurdler: sold out of Mrs M. Reveley's stable 3,600 gns Doncaster
September Sales after first outing: below form subsequently: stays 2¼m:
acts on good to firm ground, unsuited by soft: carries head high and
sometimes looks unenthusiastic. *M. F. Barraclough*

HENLEY REGATTA 5 br.g. Gorytus (USA) – Straw Boater (Thatch
(USA)) [1992/3 17d³ 18fpu 16f² 16g³ 17d⁴ 17m⁶ a20g⁴ 18g⁴ 18g⁵ 16dF 20m⁵   83
17m⁵] leggy gelding: novice hurdler, poor nowadays: stays 2¼m: acts on
firm and dead ground: visored once: sometimes looks none too keen. *P. R.
Rodford*

HENRY MANN 10 br.g. Mandalus – Little Dipper (Queen's Hussar)   c143 §
[1992/3 c24d c26s⁴ c21s²] good-topped gelding: useful chaser: good fourth   –
in Timeform Hall of Fame Chase at Cheltenham in January: well below form
both other starts in 1992/3: suited by good test of stamina: acts on any going:
jumps well: best efforts when blinkered: needs plenty of driving, and takes
little interest on occasions. *S. Christian*

HENRY WILL 9 b.g. Nicholas Bill – Silver Cygnet (My Swanee) [1992/3   c– x
16m⁴ c16d c16gF] angular gelding: poor novice hurdler: let down by his   72
jumping over fences: suited by sharp 2m: acts on good to firm going. *T.
Fairhurst*

HERBALIST 4 b.c. Mandrake Major – Mohican (Great Nephew) [1992/3
F16m² F16g*] first foal: dam modest 1½m winner: won NH Flat race at Ayr
in March: sold to join J. Hellens 20,000 gns Doncaster May Sales: yet to race
over hurdles. *C. W. Thornton*

HERE COMES TIBBY 6 b.m. Royal Fountain – Miss Hubbard (New
Brig) [1992/3 16d 23g 23g² 21v² 16v* 22g³ 17s 17d] small mare: won novice   84
hurdle at Hexham in December: good third at Ayr in January: well below
form last 2 starts: effective at 2m when conditions are very testing and stays
2¾m: acts on heavy going. *W. G. Reed*

HERE HE COMES 7 b.g. Alzao (USA) – Nanette (Worden II) [1992/3
17v* 17v* 16vpu 17g] smallish, leggy gelding: progressive form when   129 +
winning handicap hurdles at Lingfield in December and January: stiff task,
met trouble in running and did very well in Tote Gold Trophy at Newbury on
last start: twice successful on Flat subsequently: takes good hold and best
at around 2m: acts on heavy going. *R. Akehurst*

HERE'S MARY   9 b.m. Amoristic (USA) – Pitpans Star (Pitpan) [1992/3
22f6 22g5] dipped-backed mare: maiden pointer: tailed off in novice hurdles   –
in August. *C. R. Barwell*

HERESY (IRE)   4 b.f. Black Minstrel – Swiftly Belle (Deep Run) [1992/3
F16s F16g] rather unfurnished filly: half-sister to fairly useful Irish hurdler
Billy Bligh (by Buckskin): dam half-sister to several winners, including
staying chaser The Langholm Dyer: tailed off in NH Flat races: yet to race
over hurdles. *R. Mathew*

HER HONOUR   4 b.f. Teenoso (USA) – Burning Ambition (Troy)
[1992/3 16d* 16s2 16v6 17d* 17m 17f2 17m*]   127
        The Grand National fiasco wasn't the only incident that exposed
officialdom to ridicule in the latest season. The handling of the Her Honour
'nobbling' case provided a feast for those with an appetite for the farce of
Jockey Club incompetence. Rightful indignation was expressed about the
withholding of information that Her Honour had tested positive to the
quick-acting tranquiliser drug acetylpromazine after she was beaten over
forty lengths when 6/4 favourite for a novice hurdle at Kempton in January.
The Jockey Club's flimsy defence, when the story became public over a
month after the event, was that hushing up was necessary to enable its
security officers and the police to carry out their inquiries 'without the glare
of publicity'. The news about Her Honour and the further revelation that
another heavily-backed runner Flash of Straw had been 'got at' in a Flat race
at Yarmouth the previous August had a more damaging effect on the image
of racing than if disclosures had been made as quickly as possible at the
time. Her Honour and Flash of Straw were the first proven cases of horses
being doped to lose since those of Bravefoot, Norwich and Flying Diva in
September 1990. Acetylpromazine was used in those three cases and, as
with Her Honour, was almost certainly administered at the racecourse
stables. Detomidine was the drug detected in tests taken from Flash of
Straw. Claims that doping is more widespread than is generally acknowledged were made in a controversial BBC programme *On The Line*
broadcast in July. The programme featured 'a mystery man'—recognised by
some in racing—who claimed that 'people working for bookmakers' were
prepared to pay upwards of £5,000 to have a target horse 'nobbled'. The man
claimed to have doped 'at least' twenty racehorses—including Bravefoot,

*Clark Whitehill Juvenile Novices' Hurdle, Cheltenham —
Her Honour (right) has to work hard to beat Cariboo Gold*

Mrs Alison C. Farrant's "Her Honour"

Norwich and Flying Diva—by injecting acetylpromazine, working with a team who discovered where the horse was stabled and helped 'the needle man' to breach racecourse security to get at the horse. A tightening of racecourse security and an increase in the number of horses dope tested after below-par performances seems sure to follow. A Jockey Club inquiry held in late-July, following a criminal investigation by Devon and Cornwall police, concluded that it wasn't possible to establish the source of the prohibited substance found in Her Honour's sample. Trainer Pipe was fined £200 under rule 53.

Her Honour suffered no lasting ill-effects from her experience at Kempton. She went on to confirm the impression, gleaned from an easy victory at Haydock on her hurdling debut in December, that she would prove herself one of the better recruits to the ranks of the juveniles. She resumed winning ways at Taunton in February—before the news leaked out that she had tested positive at Kempton—and put up a good effort when second to Titled Dancer in the Glenlivet Anniversary Hurdle at Aintree. Her Honour had done best of the three Glenlivet Hurdle runners who had contested the Daily Express Triumph Hurdle at Cheltenham, finishing a fair ninth to Shawiya who had just got the better of Titled Dancer in a competitive event at Punchestown in February. Her Honour had shown signs of temperament at Cheltenham—being mulish at the start and running in snatches—but did nothing wrong at Aintree, leading after the fifth and rallying on the run in to go down by half a length. Her Honour ended the season on a winning note at Cheltenham's April meeting, though she had to work quite hard to justify heavy market support in an above-average juvenile hurdle.

Her Honour (b.f. 1989)	Teenoso (USA) (b 1980)	Youth (b 1973)	Ack Ack
			Gazala
		Furioso (b 1971)	Ballymoss
			Violetta III
	Burning Ambition (ch 1983)	Troy (b 1976)	Petingo
			La Milo
		Singe (b 1972)	Tudor Music
			Trial By Fire

The tall, sparely-made Her Honour was claimed out of Lord Huntingdon's stable for £15,501 after winning at Salisbury in September. She showed fairly useful form over middle distances on the Flat before being switched to jumping. Her Honour is by the Derby winner Teenoso out of Burning Ambition, a half-sister to the One Thousand Guineas winner One In A Million. Burning Ambition herself showed nothing in four races on the Flat but her first two foals to reach the racecourse—the other was the modest miler Dance On Sixpence (by Lidhame)—have both won. Her Honour's grandam Singe was an unraced half-sister to Deep Run. Her Honour will stay beyond seventeen furlongs and acts on firm and dead going. She usually races up with the pace but did equally well ridden more conservatively on her final start. *M. C. Pipe*

HERLIN 5 b.g. Relkino – Copper Cloud (Foggy Bell) [1992/3 F17g* 16d6 16dF 17g4] workmanlike gelding: half-brother to winning hurdler Copper Streak (by Streak): dam poor novice hurdler: won NH Flat race at Hereford in October: will stay further than 17f. *Capt. T. A. Forster*   85

HERMES HARVEST 5 b.g. Oats – Swift Messenger (Giolla Mear) [1992/3 17d 21s3 20s6 26gpu] tall gelding: form only when distant third in novice hurdle at Chepstow in December: tried visored. *D. L. Williams*   72

HEROES SASH (USA) 8 b.h. Lypheor – Salish (USA) (Olden Times) [1992/3 17v 17g] formerly useful miler on Flat, no form in 1992: well beaten over hurdles: trained first outing by A. Moore. *J. D. Thomas*   –

HERR GARSIDE 4 b.g. Mashhor Dancer (USA) – Dash (Connaught) [1992/3 16s] small gelding: second foal: dam ran once: jumped sketchily and tailed off in juvenile hurdle at Catterick in December. *M. W. Easterby*   –

HE WHO DARES WINS 10 b.g. Le Bavard (FR) – Brave Air (Brave Invader (USA)) [1992/3 c26g4 c25m2 c25gF c25m2 c25g*] tall, lengthy gelding: fair chaser: won handicap at Hexham in October: also ran creditably on his other completed starts: stays 3½m: acts on hard and dead ground: blinkered last 7 outings in 1990/1: needs plenty of driving and looks a difficult ride. *W. A. Stephenson*   c114

HEYFLEET 10 b.g. Tachypous – Heyford (Blakeney) [1992/3 17s6 c17v4 c20s c21v* c24s5 c26g2 c26dpu c26gF] smallish, workmanlike gelding: fair handicap chaser: won at Plumpton in February: good second on same course in March: stays 3¼m: best form with give in the ground: blinkered nowadays: sometimes looks reluctant: inconsistent. *Mrs J. Pitman*   c100 § –

HEY RAWLEY 8 b.g. Sagaro – Silly Games (Siliconn) [1992/3 c23d3 c25s4 c20g3 c21d*] workmanlike gelding: moderate chaser: tubed, won handicap at Sedgefield in January: stays 3m and is effective at shorter distances: acts on firm and dead ground: tends to carry head high: usually let down by his jumping. *Mrs M. Reveley*   c96 x –

HEZEKIAH 5 b.h. Swing Easy (USA) – Way of Life (Homeric) [1992/3 F14d] sixth foal: half-brother to winning 2¼m selling hurdler Ganger Camp (by Derrylin): dam 1m winner: mid-division in 18-runner NH Flat race at Perth in September: yet to race over hurdles or fences. *J. White*   –

HICKELTON LAD 9 ch.g. Black Minstrel – Lupreno (Hugh Lupus) [1992/3 c18fpu] tall, shallow-girthed gelding: modest chaser at his best: tailed off when pulled up in handicap at Fontwell in August: stays 2½m: ideally suited by a sound surface. *D. L. Williams*   c–

HICKORY WIND 6 ch.g. Dalsaan – Derrain (Prince Tenderfoot (USA)) [1992/3 20g^{pu} 17d³ 18d 23d^{pu}] rather sparely-made gelding: lightly-raced novice hurdler: third at Stratford in October, easily best effort of season. *J. Allen*   80

HICKSONS CHOICE (IRE) 5 br.g. Seymour Hicks (FR) – Gentle Rain (Tower Walk) [1992/3 F17m 18d⁵] unfurnished gelding: behind in NH Flat races: showed some promise when fifth in novice event at Market Rasen in February on hurdling debut. *J. Wade*   73

HIDDEN FLOWER 4 b.f. Blakeney – Molucella (Connaught) [1992/3 17f 18d 17v^{pu} 22f⁵] small filly: poor maiden on Flat and over hurdles: trained first 3 starts by J. Roberts. *H. S. Howe*   70

HIDDEN OATS 6 ch.g. Oats – Pharaoh's Lady (Pharaoh Hophra) [1992/3 17s⁴ 17s⁴ 17d^{pu} 16g² 17m* 16f⁵] leggy gelding: fair hurdler: ran creditably most starts in 1992/3 and won handicap at Stratford in May: will stay beyond 17f: acts on good to firm and soft ground. *Mrs J. Pitman*   102

HIDDEN PLEASURE 7 b.g. Furry Glen – Baloney (Balidar) [1992/3 c17s^F c18d c22s c16m^{ur}] close-coupled, workmanlike ex-Irish gelding: trained until after third outing by C. Magnier: no form over hurdles: would have won maiden chase at Wolverhampton in March but for unseating rider last: acts on good to firm going. *S. Christian*   c93 ?   –

HIGH ALLTITUDE (IRE) 5 b.g. Coquelin (USA) – Donna Cressida (Don (ITY)) [1992/3 16g 21d* 20s* 20g* 20s² 21s² 22s² 21d*]   136 p

High Alltitude was retired for the season after winning the Persian War Premier Novices' Hurdle at Chepstow in February by three lengths from Castle Courageous. By that stage he had become well worth a place in the Sun Alliance Novices' Hurdle field, but there was the future to think about: he looks a good prospect, especially for chasing, and connections were understandably wary of asking too much too soon. High Alltitude, in only his first season as a hurdler in 1992/3 following three runs and two wins in National Hunt Flat races, was kept busy, making eight starts from the end of October despite being given a rest through December. He won consecutively at Carlisle, Haydock (idling markedly) and Newcastle in November, and continued on the upgrade after the turn of the year although he failed to win again until Chepstow. Brackenfield just ran him out of it in a novice event at Ayr; Robingo beat him three lengths in a sprint finish to a tactical affair at Leicester; then Hebridean outpaced him by twelve lengths in the Sidney Banks Memorial at Huntingdon. A small yet interesting field lined up for the Persian War, with Now Your Talkin, Sun Surfer, High Alltitude and the unbeaten Castle Courageous seeming likely to prove well matched, though the issue was complicated by the fact that the value of the race precluded High Alltitude's rider claiming his 3 lb allowance and Now Your Talkin's claiming his 7 lb. The four horses jumped the fourth last, at the entrance to the straight, almost in line after the early pace had been steady. Things began to change at the next. Now Your Talkin and Sun Surfer each made a mistake, handing the initiative to Castle Courageous and High Alltitude. Going to the second last Castle Courageous seemed strongest, but High Alltitude outjumped him, piled on more pressure at the last and forged clear on the flat. Now Your Talkin took third a further ten lengths behind, with Sun Surfer taking fourth ahead of the only other starter, the outclassed Crystal Cone.

High Alltitude (IRE) (b.g. 1988)	Coquelin (USA) (ch 1979)	Blushing Groom (ch 1974)	Red God
			Runaway Bride
		Topolly (ch 1969)	Turn-To
			Polly Girl
	Donna Cressida (br 1972)	Don (gr 1966)	Grey Sovereign
			Diviana II
		Cresca (b 1963)	Saint Crespin III
			Djidda II

Report has it that High Alltitude will spend a further season over hurdles before he goes chasing, but presumably plans could change if the handicapper gets a hold of him or if he is difficult to place in conditions

*Persian War Premier Novices' Hurdle, Chepstow —
High Alltitude shows further improvement*

events. The way he jumps hurdles and the way he is built (he jumps soundly
and is a rangy, quite imposing individual) he will definitely make a chaser
whenever his chance comes. As to distance and ground—High Alltitude is
effective at two and a half miles and will stay further than two and three
quarters; thus far in his career he has raced only on an easy surface. High
Alltitude's sire Coquelin showed smart form at up to a mile and a half on the
Flat in France and Italy. His dam Donna Cressida was almost as good on the
Flat in Ireland, at up to a mile and a quarter, and won the Group 2 Player-
Wills Stakes at Leopardstown. The family has made an impact on the classic
scene in its time—Cresca is a half-sister to the Irish One Thousand Guineas
winner Wenduyne and her maternal grandam is the Irish Oaks winner
Djebellica, ancestress of such as Cambremont and Bon Mot III. By
comparison Donna Cressida's record as a broodmare is fairly ordinary, and
High Alltitude was picked up for 6,000 guineas at the Newmarket October
Yearling Sales. A year-older full sister to High Alltitude called Cresalin won
over middle distances in Ireland in 1990. *G. M. Moore*

HIGH BACCARAT 4 ch.g. Formidable (USA) – By Surprise (Young
Generation) [1992/3 17g] maiden plater on Flat: held up, made a couple of
mistakes and finished lame in juvenile hurdle at Taunton in September. *A. J.
Chamberlain*

–

HIGH BARON 6 gr.g. Baron Blakeney – High Finesse (High Line)
[1992/3 18sᵘʳ 18s* 16v* 16v* 17m² 17d 22m⁶] strong, lengthy gelding:
carries plenty of condition: developed into a useful hurdler in 1992/3,
winning handicaps at Exeter and Wincanton (2, first a conditional jockeys

136 p

event): good second to Thumbs Up, finishing fast, in County Hurdle at Cheltenham in March and would have gone close to winning on same course last start but for mistake at the last: effective at 2m and stays 2¾m: acts on good to firm and heavy going: likely to improve further. *R. H. Alner*

HIGH BEACON 6 ch.g. High Line – Flaming Peace (Queen's Hussar) [1992/3 17vᵖᵘ 16s 20dᵘʳ 17gᵖᵘ] small gelding: half-brother to winning hurdlers Paradise Straits (by Derrylin) and Fiesole (by Sharpo): useful middle-distance stayer on Flat at 4 yrs (trained by H. Candy), but lost his form in 1992: no form over hurdles: blinkered last 3 starts. *K. C. Bailey* —

HIGHBROOK (USA) 5 b.m. Alphabatim (USA) – Tellspot (USA) (Tell (USA)) [1992/3 16g* 16g²] workmanlike mare: fairly useful middle-distance performer on Flat: impressive winner of novice hurdle at Catterick in February: clear second to Lemon's Mill in mares novice event at Warwick following month: jumps well: will progress further and win more races. *M. H. Tompkins* 111 p

HIGH BURNSHOT 6 br.g. Cardinal Flower – Andonian (Road House II) [1992/3 F17d] fourth foal: half-brother to winning chaser Clares Own (by Al Sirat): dam placed in a maiden hurdle in Ireland: well beaten in NH Flat race at Carlisle in April: yet to race over hurdles or fences. *C. Parker*

HIGH CASTE 6 ch.g. Carwhite – Brazen (Cash And Courage) [1992/3 25g a22g] leggy gelding: poor novice over hurdles: sometimes visored or blinkered. *B. C. Morgan* —

HIGHCLIFFE JESTER 4 b.g. Jester – Canty Day (Canadel II) [1992/3 18sᵖᵘ] no sign of ability on Flat or in a juvenile hurdle. *P. Beaumont* —

HIGHEST MOUNTAIN 4 ch.g. Superlative – Montania (Mourne) [1992/3 F17m] half-brother to several winners, including hurdler Relief Map (by Relkino): dam won over 7f: well beaten in NH Flat race at Doncaster in February: yet to race over hurdles. *M. W. Easterby*

HIGHFIELD PRINCE 7 b.g. Prince Tenderfoot (USA) – Parler Mink (Party Mink) [1992/3 c20fᵖᵘ c24m⁵] sparely-made gelding: winning hurdler/chaser: showed nothing in 2 hunter chases in March: unlikely to stay much beyond 2m: acts on firm going (possibly unsuited by soft): visored once. *Donald Merchant* c– —

HIGH FINANCE 8 ch.g. Billion (USA) – Miss Plumes (Prince de Galles) [1992/3 22m 20g³ 17g* 21dᵖᵘ a16g a20g a24g³ a16gᶠ] leggy, sparely-made gelding: moderate handicap hurdler: won at Fakenham in October: easily best effort subsequently when third at Southwell in May: effective at around 2m and stays 3m: acts on firm ground and fibresand. *R. J. Weaver* 91

HIGHGATE MILD 8 br.g. Homeboy – Lady Jewel (Kibenka) [1992/3 c25sᵖᵘ] strong gelding: maiden pointer/hurdler/steeplechaser. *Miss S. J. K. Scott* c– —

HIGH GRADE 5 b.g. High Top – Bright Sun (Mill Reef (USA)) [1992/3 17s³ 17d³ 20d⁶ F13m³ a20g⁵ 21v⁴] neat gelding: fair hurdler: ran creditably first 3 starts, below best last 2: stays 2½m: acts on soft going, goes particularly well on equitrack: tail flasher, and sometimes looks none too keen: blinkered third and fifth starts. *Miss S. J. Wilton* 101 §

HIGHLAND AIR 5 b.g. Elegant Air – Calgary (Run The Gantlet (USA)) [1992/3 16s] lengthy gelding: no sign of ability: dead. *I. A. Balding* —

HIGHLAND BOUNTY 9 b.g. High Line – Segos (Runnymede) [1992/3 17vᵖᵘ 20v⁴ 17s⁴ 18m³] plain gelding: unreliable hurdler nowadays: best effort of season on second start: out of depth final one: stays 21f: acts on any going. *S. Dow* 98 §

HIGHLAND BRAVE 6 b.g. Crofter (USA) – Calling Bird (Warpath) [1992/3 22fᵘʳ 23d 16sᵖᵘ] lengthy gelding: lightly raced and little sign of ability: blinkered once. *J. Colston* —

HIGHLAND ECHO 10 b.g. Impecunious – Scotchemup (Raisin)   c95
[1992/3 c25d² c24f² c27m⁵ c27m⁴ c27d⁴] workmanlike gelding: fair hunter
chaser: stays 3¼m: acts on firm and dead going. *Mrs John C. Edwards*

HIGHLAND FRIEND 5 ch.g. Highlands – Friendly Wonder (Be
Friendly) [1992/3 F18d F17s 28d³ 26s 24mᵘʳ] workmanlike gelding: first   78
foal: dam well beaten on Flat: third in novice event at Sedgefield in
November, only form over hurdles. *F. Watson*

HIGHLAND LAIRD 9 b.g. Kampala – Bonny Hollow (Wolver Hollow)   c–
[1992/3 c17d⁵] well-made gelding: poor maiden hurdler/pointer/hunter   –
chaser. *H. Hill*

HIGHLANDMAN 7 b.h. Florida Son – Larne (Giolla Mear) [1992/3 17d⁶
20m² 23d⁴ 23sꟳ 17d³ 18d⁴ 17g² 18g 17m 17v⁴] lengthy, workmanlike horse: 88
chasing type: modest novice hurdler: effective at 17f with give in the ground
and stays 23f: acts on good to firm and soft ground (below form on heavy). *J.
S. Haldane*

HIGHLAND POACHER 6 ch.g. Netherkelly – Spartiquick (Spartan
General) [1992/3 17d⁶ 16s* 20vᵖᵘ 17s⁴ 16d⁵ 17g] sturdy gelding: won novice   90
hurdle at Haydock in November: below form subsequently: should stay
beyond 2m: acts on soft going. *D. McCain*

HIGHLAND RALLY (USA) 6 b.g. Highland Blade (USA) – Fast Trek
(FR) (Trepan (FR)) [1992/3 21s 25g⁶] rangy gelding: sold 4,200 gns   78
Doncaster November Sales: poor novice hurdler. *M. Avison*

HIGHLAND RIVER 6 b.m. Salmon Leap (USA) – Sigtrudis (Sigebert)
[1992/3 22g 17d⁵ 21s⁴ 26m⁶ 24g³] angular mare: poor novice hurdler: stays   71
3¼m: acts on good to firm and soft ground. *T. A. K. Cuthbert*

HIGHLAND SON 12 b.g. Sunyboy – Highland Path (Jock Scot) [1992/3   c89
c25dᵖᵘ c24f* c27f⁵] leggy, close-coupled gelding: won 2 points in April and   –
3-runner novice hunter chase at Chepstow in May: stays 25f: acts on any
going. *R. J. Smith*

HIGHLAND SPIRIT 5 ch.m. Scottish Reel – Salacious (Sallust)
[1992/3 17m 20g* 17g* 19m* 20g* 16m* 18d* 16g 20f* 20m* 17g² 20g*   119
21f* 22m²] sparely-made mare: fairly useful form over hurdles: won more
races in 1992/3 than any other jumper, namely novice events at Hereford
(2), Exeter, Taunton, Ludlow and Exeter in first half of season, and
handicaps at Taunton (2) and novice events at Market Rasen (mares) and
Chepstow in the spring: effective from 2m to 2½m: acts on firm and dead
ground: best held up: tough. *M. C. Pipe*

HIGHLANE LAD 9 b.g. Flair Path – Rathmoon Road (Royal Captive)
[1992/3 16s⁶ 16v³] lengthy, angular gelding: poor novice hurdler, has run in   78
sellers: best form at 2m: acts on soft going: sometimes wears tongue strap.
T. W. Donnelly

HIGHLY DECORATED 8 b.g. Sharpo – New Ribbons (Ribero)
[1992/3 17m³ 16s] sturdy gelding: lightly-raced winning selling hurdler: 85
third in claimer at Carlisle in March, easily better effort of season: stays
2½m: acts on any going: ran poorly when blinkered once: sometimes
swishes tail: often finds little. *Mrs S. J. Smith*

HIGHLY INFLAMMABLE (USA) 5 b.m. Wind And Wuthering
(USA) – Heat Haze (USA) (Jungle Savage (USA)) [1992/3 16d⁶ 22vᵖᵘ]   –
lengthy mare: little sign of ability over hurdles. *C. R. Barwell*

HIGH MARINER 7 ch.m. Julio Mariner – High Lee (Will Hays (USA))   c–
[1992/3 c17fᵖᵘ 23g⁶ 22gᵖᵘ] leggy mare: winning selling hurdler: no promise   72
on chasing debut: sold 825 gns Ascot May Sales: stays 23f: acts on dead
ground: ran poorly when blinkered. *K. G. Wingrove*

HIGH MIND (FR) 4 br.g. Highest Honor (FR) – Gondolina (FR)
(Vaguely Noble) [1992/3 16d 16d³ 16g 16d⁶ 16g² 16m 16m³] workmanlike   95
gelding: no worthwhile form on Flat: easily best effort over hurdles when
second in novice event at Catterick in February: races up with pace:
possibly ungenuine. *Miss L. C. Siddall*

HIGH PADRE 7 b.g. The Parson – High Energy (Dalesa) [1992/3 c20d³ **c109** c25d* c24sᶠ c25s* c26dᵖᵘ c28g* c28m²] strong gelding: fair hurdler: won – novice chase at Wetherby in November and handicaps at Nottingham in February and March: suited by a good test of stamina: best form with give in the ground and acts on soft going: jumps soundly in the main. *J. G. FitzGerald*

HIGH PENHOWE 5 ch.m. Ardross – Spritely (Charlottown) [1992/3 F17g⁶ F16g 17g 24dᵖᵘ 2 1d⁴] leggy mare: fifth live foal: half-sister to winning 72 Irish 1986 2-y-o Arabian Princess (by Taufan): dam poor Flat maiden: first form in novice hurdles when fourth at Carlisle in April. *Mrs V. A. Aconley*

HIGH PLATEAU (USA) 6 ch.g. Raise A Native – Soft Horizon (USA) (Cyane) [1992/3 16v⁵ 20m⁵] good-topped gelding: fair maiden at best on 82 Flat: fifth in novice hurdles at Leicester (better effort) in January and Doncaster in February. *O. Sherwood*

HIGH POST 4 b.g. Lidhame – Touch of Class (FR) (Luthier) [1992/3 16s²] leggy gelding: plater on Flat, successful twice over 1¼m in 1992: clear 101 of remainder when second of 14 in juvenile hurdle at Kempton in November. *D. Marks*

HIGH STREET BLUES 6 b.g. White Prince (USA) – Crendle Hill **c–** (French Beige) [1992/3 20gᵖᵘ c25sᶠ] compact gelding: behind in novice – hurdles: fell first on chasing debut. *T. Keddy*

HIGHTOWN FONTANA 12 b.m. Gunner B – Fountain (Reform) – [1992/3 17v 16g 20g 18g⁶] tall mare: winning hurdler: has produced 2 foals: little form since her return. *R. J. Hodges*

HIGHTOWN-PRINCESS (IRE) 5 gr.m. King Persian – Ambient – (Amber Rama (USA)) [1992/3 18gᵖᵘ] placed over 7.6f on Flat: tailed off when pulled up in novice event in April on hurdling debut. *M. P. Muggeridge*

HIGHWAY LIGHT 6 b.m. Lighter – Hilda's Way (Royal Highway) – [1992/3 18g] half-sister to fairly useful chaser Highway Express (by Pony Express): dam winning pointer: has shown nothing in points or a novice hurdle. *R. J. Hodges*

HILL ROYALE 7 b.g. Mister Lord (USA) – Lucky Lace (Brocade **c90** p Slipper) [1992/3 c24sᶠ] workmanlike gelding: moderate pointer: would have finished second in hunter chase at Chepstow in April but for falling 2 out: should improve. *W. K. Rhead*

HILL RYDE 10 br.g. Junius (USA) – Rosinante (FR) (Busted) [1992/3 **c72** c20mᶠ c21m⁴ c22g⁴ c26g] good-bodied gelding: winning pointer: poor – novice hurdler/steeplechaser: stays 3m. *R. Shiels*

HILLS OF HOY 7 b.g. Teenoso (USA) – Fairy Tern (Mill Reef (USA)) – [1992/3 17s 17fᵖᵘ] well-made gelding: sold out of K. Bailey's stable 1,650 gns Ascot September Sales: no form over hurdles. *D. N. Carey*

HILL STREET (FR) 11 b.g. Grandchant (FR) – Tetlin (FR) (Apollo **c–** Eight (FR)) [1992/3 c20fᵘʳ] sparely-made, angular gelding: modest chaser – nowadays: won 2 points in April: stays 21f: acts on heavy going: broke blood vessel once in 1989/90: sketchy jumper of fences. *M. C. Ashton*

HILLTOP BLUE 8 br.g. Meldrum – Aqua Blue (Blue Cashmere) **c–** [1992/3 c26g] once-raced over hurdles: modest pointer: tailed off in novice – hunter chase in March. *Mrs G. Strickland*

HILLTOWN BLUES 4 gr.g. Le Solaret (FR) – Herminda (King of Spain) [1992/3 16m 17mᵖᵘ 16gᵘʳ 18g⁶ 17g⁴ 16g⁴ 16d* 17s⁵ 16d 17d⁴ 16d* 17g⁴ 87 16g 17v* 20f⁴ 18m⁴ 18v] leggy gelding: plating-class maiden on Flat: trained first 2 starts over hurdles by M. H. Easterby: subsequently won seller at Catterick (no bid), juvenile claimer at Ayr and novice handicap at Perth: stays 2¼m: acts on heavy and good to firm ground: blinkered ninth outing: usually forces pace. *T. Dyer*

HILLTOWN (IRE) 5 b.g. Camden Town – Chaconia (Record Run) [1992/3 F16m 16g³ 17dᵖᵘ] first foal: dam, winner on Flat and over hurdles, is 86 half-sister to very smart hurdler and fairly useful chaser Major Thompson: modest form when third in novice hurdle at Catterick in March. *J. H. Johnson*

HILL TRIX 7 b.g. Le Moss – Up To Trix (Over The River (FR)) [1992/3 c26vᵖᵘ c24g³ c25s² c25gᵖᵘ] strong, sturdy gelding: second foal: dam unraced half-sister to numerous jumping winners, including useful Brown Trix: won both starts in Irish points in 1992: placed in novice chases at Taunton in March and Ascot in April, showing fair form: suited by good test of stamina. *K. Bishop*　　c99

HILLWALK 7 b.g. Croghan Hill – Bell Walks Fancy (Entrechat) [1992/3 22d² 20d* 19d² 20v⁴ 21v⁵ 16v³ 20g⁴ 21m 22d⁵] leggy, angular gelding: second foal: dam, unraced, from successful jumping family: won maiden hurdle at Punchestown in October: trained until after third start by Mrs A. M. O'Brien: best efforts in Britain when third at Towcester in February and eleventh in Sun Alliance Novices' Hurdle at Cheltenham in March: suited by testing conditions around 2m and stays 2¾m: acts on heavy and good to firm ground. *R. Curtis*　　114

HIMLAJ (USA) 8 b.g. Far North (CAN) – Lusaka (USA) (Tom Rolfe) [1992/3 17g⁴ 20g³ 18f⁶ 16g 16d 22vᵖᵘ] neat gelding: reportedly blind near eye: won selling hurdle (no bid) at Hereford in August: below form in non-sellers subsequently: best form at around 2m on good ground. *S. Mellor*　　90 d

HINTON HARRY (IRE) 4 b.g. Kafu – Rosy O'Leary (Majetta) [1992/3 16g 16sᵖᵘ a16g] angular gelding: of little account: sold 1,200 gns Ascot February Sales. *S. Mellor*　　–

HINTON LADY 4 b.f. Ilium – Lavender Rose (Beau Lavender) [1992/3 F16v] half-sister to poor novice hurdler Hinton Mariner (by Julio Mariner): dam unraced: tailed off in NH Flat race at Warwick in January: yet to race over hurdles. *C. R. Egerton*　　–

HINTON MARINER 6 b.g. Julio Mariner – Lavender Rose (Beau Lavender) [1992/3 17s 16gʳᵗʳ] rather unfurnished gelding: poor novice hurdler: sold 1,000 gns Ascot March Sales: sometimes blinkered or visored: refused to race twice, including on last start. *W. G. Turner*　　– §

HIRAM B BIRDBATH 7 b.g. Ragapan – At The King's Side (USA) (Kauai King) [1992/3 20m 21g³ 22f³ c21g* 21g³ c21m² c21dᶠ a20g c21d⁶ c24g³ c24dᵖᵘ] smallish, close-coupled gelding: moderate hurdler/chaser: won novice event over fences at Southwell in October: ran creditably when placed otherwise, including over hurdles: stays 3m: acts on good to firm ground, goes particularly well on fibresand (probably unsuited by dead): blinkered: tends to idle in front, and is held up. *J. A. Glover*　　c95
95

HITCHIN A RIDE 6 b.g. Dublin Taxi – Farmers Daughter (Red Slipper) [1992/3 17dᶠ] sprint handicapper on Flat: refused to settle, and showed no promise in novice hurdle at Newton Abbot in September. *M. P. Muggeridge*　　–

HIT THE BOX 8 ch.g. Quayside – Three Dieu (Three Dons) [1992/3 16sᵖᵘ 21s a22g] workmanlike gelding: of little account. *C. R. Beever*　　–

HIZEEM 7 b.g. Alzao (USA) – Good Member (Mansingh (USA)) [1992/3 18m] well beaten in 2 selling hurdles. *M. P. Naughton*　　–

HOBBYS GIRL 8 b.m. Straight Knight – Owen's Hobby (Owen Anthony) [1992/3 c25dᶠ 25dᵖᵘ c21gᴿ] lengthy mare: poor maiden jumper: trained until after first start by Miss S. Rettie. *Mrs S. C. Bradburne*　　c–
–

HOGMANAY (CAN) 11 b.g. Halo (USA) – Annie Laurie (CAN) (Kennedy Road (CAN)) [1992/3 c17g c16g³ c18d⁵] tall, leggy, sparely-made gelding: fairly useful front-running chaser nowadays: won United House Construction Handicap Chase at Ascot in 1991/2: best effort of 1992/3 when third in latest running of that event in October: stays 21f, probably not 3m: acts on firm ground: tail swisher: sometimes led in at start nowadays: usually jumps well. *R. F. Casey*　　c125
–

HOISTTHESTANDARD 6 ch.m. Stanford – Precious Mite (Tambourine II) [1992/3 16m⁴ 18gᶠ 18g c20f c25mᵖᵘ] smallish ex-Irish mare: poor maiden jumper: trained until after third start by H. Cleary. *Mrs I. H. Hadden*　　c–

HOLD COURT (IRE) 5 ch.g. The Noble Player (USA) – Sindos (Busted) [1992/3 17d 17spu] lengthy, good-quartered gelding: only worthwhile form when winning selling hurdle on equitrack in 1991/2: yet to race beyond 17f. *N. A. Callaghan* —

HOLDENBY 8 b.g. Henbit (USA) – Isadora Duncan (Primera) [1992/3 16g³ 18d⁵ 17d² 16g c17g³ c16d* c17gpu] leggy, close-coupled gelding: fair handicap hurdler: won novice chase at Catterick in February: was best at around 2m: acted on hard and good to soft ground: dead. *Mrs M. Reveley* c102
115

HOLD FAST (IRE) 5 b.g. Dara Monarch – No Flight (Nonoalco (USA)) [1992/3 16vpu F13m⁶ 17f 17g⁶] poor 7f winner on Flat: sold out of H. Candy's stable 3,200 gns Newmarket Autumn Sales: of little account over hurdles. *C. T. Nash* —

HOLDFORTH 6 b.g. Sayyaf – Chief Dilke (Saulingo) [1992/3 16d 21v⁵ c16s a22g a22g4] sturdy gelding: winning selling hurdler: well beaten on chasing debut: suited by test of stamina: acts on firm ground: sometimes visored or blinkered. *W. W. Haigh* c–
77

HOLD IM TIGHT 5 b.g. Teamwork – Holdmetight (New Brig) [1992/3 16vpu 18g] fourth foal: half-brother to 2 poor performers by Battlement: dam poor novice hurdler/chaser: no sign of ability in 2 novice hurdles. *R. G. Frost* —

HOLD ON TIGHT 8 ch.m. Battlement – Holdmetight (New Brig) [1992/3 17dpu] compact mare: novice selling hurdler: pulled up lame in September and wasn't seen out again: stays 2¼m: acts on firm going. *R. G. Frost* —

HOLD YOUR HAT ON 4 ch.g. Celestial Storm (USA) – Thatched Grove (Thatching) [1992/3 F14m* F17f] sturdy gelding: second foal: dam unraced half-sister to several winners, including fair hurdler Gods Will: won 20-runner NH Flat race at Market Rasen in March: ninth of 15 in valuable similar event at Aintree in April: sold 10,000 gns Doncaster May Sales: yet to race over hurdles. *C. W. Thornton* —

HOLD YOUR RANKS 6 b.g. Ranksborough – Holdmetight (New Brig) [1992/3 18g⁶] third foal: half-brother to 2 poor performers by Battlement: dam poor novice hurdler/chaser: always behind in novice hurdle at Exeter in March. *R. G. Frost* —

HOLIDAY ISLAND 4 ch.g. Good Times (ITY) – Green Island (St Paddy) [1992/3 17g⁴ 17v 18s] leggy gelding: fair handicapper at up to 1½m on Flat, winner twice in 1992 when trained by C. Brittain: fourth in juvenile hurdle at Newbury in October: tailed off both subsequent starts. *R. Akehurst* 81

HOLLY BROWN 10 br.m. Derrylin – Friday Brown (Murrayfield) [1992/3 17sF 17spu 16g⁶ c17vur c18spu] short-backed mare: produced a foal in 1991: modest handicap hurdler: creditable effort only completed outing of season, in lead when falling last on first start: tailed off when pulled up in novice claiming chase at Exeter in December: will stay beyond 2¼m: acts on good to firm and soft ground. *P. J. Hobbs* c–
91

HOLLY MARTIN'S (IRE) 5 ch.g. Buckskin (FR) – Dungourney Lady (Tarqogan) [1992/3 23dpu a20g²] workmanlike gelding: fourth foal: dam maiden half-sister to several winning jumpers: visored, second of 4 finishers in novice hurdle at Southwell in May: sold 3,200 gns Ascot 2nd June Sales. *C. P. E. Brooks* 71

HOLT PLACE 10 b.g. Be My Guest (USA) – Ya Ya (Primera) [1992/3 24gpu 21dpu a20g a20g⁵ a24gpu] smallish, good-bodied gelding: fair hurdler in 1991/2: well below form in 1992/3: stays 3m: acts on firm and dead ground. *N. A. Smith* —

HOLY FOLEY 11 b.g. The Parson – En Clair (Tarqogan) [1992/3 c21s* c24m* c27mpu] smallish, lengthy gelding: sold 1,000 gns Ascot November Sales: successful in hunter chases at Newton Abbot (novices) in February and Ludlow in March: stiff task last time: will stay beyond 3m: acts on soft and good to firm ground. *Miss Susan Pitman* c99
—

HOLY JOE 11 b.g. The Parson – Doonasleen (Deep Run) [1992/3 22v⁴ 21v⁵ 22s 21d⁴ 17d²] workmanlike gelding: fairly useful handicap hurdler: creditable fifth at Kempton in January and second at Hereford in April: 129

effective at 17f and stays 3m when conditions aren't testing: acts on heavy and good to firm going: usually races up with pace. *A. J. Wilson*

HOLY MACKEREL 6 ch.g. The Parson – Shallow Run (Deep Run) [1992/3 16g 22s⁶ 21g³ 23fᵖᵘ 24gᵖᵘ] strong gelding: novice hurdler: best effort when never-nearer third in maiden at Towcester in March: should stay beyond 2 1f. *N. J. Henderson*   86

HOLY WANDERER (USA) 4 b.g. Vaguely Noble – Bronzed Goddess (USA) (Raise A Native) [1992/3 17sᵘʳ 17v³ 17s⁵ 18v³ 17dᶠ 17d⁴ 16g* 17m] sturdy, compact gelding: carries condition: moderate 1½m winner on Flat in 1992: retained by trainer 3,800 gns Newmarket Autumn Sales: quite useful form on occasions over hurdles: won juvenile event at Worcester in March and ran well in Daily Express Triumph Hurdle at Cheltenham later in month: will prove best at around 2m: acts on heavy and good to firm going: pulls hard, and sometimes finds little off bridle: inconsistent. *D. W. P. Arbuthnot*   119

HOME COUNTIES (IRE) 4 ch.g. Ela-Mana-Mou – Safe Home (Home Guard (USA)) [1992/3 16v³ 17s² 16d³ 17v* 16f2] quite good-topped gelding with scope: fairly useful at up to 1¼m on Flat in Ireland when trained by J. Oxx: similar level of form when placed in juvenile hurdles: didn't have to be anywhere near his best to land the odds in similar race at Newton Abbot in April: sold 12,000 gns Doncaster May Sales: yet to race beyond 17f: acts on heavy ground: blinkered last 2 starts: finds little under pressure, and turned it in last time. *N. J. Henderson*   117 §

HOME POOL 8 ch.g. Habitat – Rossitor (Pall Mall) [1992/3 16fᵖᵘ] angular, sparely-made gelding: lightly raced and of little account. *D. J. Wintle*   –

HOME REVIEW 5 ch.m. Day Is Done – Little Lea VII (Pedigree Unknown) [1992/3 F18g] second foal: dam never ran: tailed off in mares NH Flat race at Exeter in March: yet to race over hurdles or fences. *Mrs J. C. Dawe*   –

HOME TO ROOST 13 b. or br.g. Peacock (FR) – La Belle Dame (Super Sam) [1992/3 21s 28sᵖᵘ 25d a22g⁵ a24g 28g 28g⁶ 25d 21s] compact gelding: poor staying novice hurdler/chaser (poor jumper): blinkered last 3 starts. *F. Jestin*   c– x 61

HOMME D'AFFAIRE 10 br.g. Lord Gayle (USA) – French Cracker (Klairon) [1992/3 c21v² c21s² c24v⁴ c21vᶠ c21s⁴] smallish gelding: moderate handicap chaser: creditable efforts first 2 starts but below form afterwards in 1992/3: stays 2¾m: acts on any going. *R. J. O'Sullivan*   c99 –

HONEST FRED 7 br.g. Mandalus – Quayside Fairy (Quayside) [1992/3 24sᵖᵘ 24v 22v 17d⁶ 16v⁴ 21sᶠ 22g³ 22f⁵ 24g] small gelding: poor novice hurdler: sold 2,800 gns Ascot June Sales: probably stays 3m: acts on dead ground: usually blinkered/visored: irresolute. *J. A. C. Edwards*   78 §

HONEYBEER MEAD 11 ch.g. Le Bavard (FR) – Midnight Oil (Mene-lek) [1992/3 c26d⁴] leggy, lengthy gelding: fair handicap chaser at his best: bit backward when below form only outing of season (October): suited by a test of stamina: acts on soft going: tends to make mistakes. *B. J. M. Ryall*   c– –

HONEY SNUGFIT 4 ch.f. Music Boy – Buy G'S (Blakeney) [1992/3 18m] workmanlike filly: modest plater on Flat at best: tailed off in selling hurdle at Market Rasen in August: sold 875 gns Ascot September Sales. *M. W. Easterby*   –

HOOK LINE'N'SINKER 7 b.g. Kabour – Valpolicella (Lorenzaccio) [1992/3 c25gᵖᵘ] close-coupled, workmanlike gelding: novice hurdler: successful in a point in May, well behind when pulled up in hunter chase later in month. *M. E. Sowersby*   –

HOPE DIAMOND 10 b. or br.g. Sparkler – Canaan (Santa Claus) [1992/3 c21d³ c26gᵖᵘ c25vᵖᵘ c26g⁴ c21mᵖᵘ] sparely-made gelding: winning chaser: probably stays 3m: best form with give in the ground: usually blinkered: deliberate jumper. *C. C. Trietline*   c82 –

HOPEFUL ALDA 8 b. or br.m. Kambalda – Hopeful Bar (Bargello) [1992/3 c21m⁶] small mare: moderate hurdler: no form over fences: should   c– –

stay beyond 21f: seems to need give in the ground: visored once. *E. T. Buckley*

HOPE HALL (IRE)   5 b.g. Fairy King (USA) – Burren Star (Hardgreen (USA)) [1992/3 F16m F14m] IR 16,000Y: second foal: dam lightly-raced maiden: well beaten in NH Flat races in February and March: yet to race over hurdles or fences. *R. M. Whitaker*

HORATIAN   8 b.g. Horage – Assurance (FR) (Timmy Lad) [1992/3 18h3] rather sparely-made gelding: winning 2m hurdler: no form for a long time. *Mrs J. Wonnacott*   –

HORCUM   8 b. or br.g. Sweet Monday – Charlie's Sunshine (Jimsun) [1992/3 c24dpu c27dpu c25gpu c22mpu] leggy gelding: of little account: visored last start. *P. A. Pritchard*   c–
–

HOSTILE ACT   8 b.g. Glenstal (USA) – Fandetta (Gay Fandango (USA)) [1992/3 16d2] close-coupled gelding: lightly-raced novice hurdler: creditable second in 21-runner event at Wetherby in November: form only at 2m: acts on dead ground. *Miss P. Hall*   92

HOTDIGGITY   5 ch.g. Grey Desire – Heldigvis (Hot Grove) [1992/3 17d] angular gelding: showed a modicum of ability in novice hurdle at Perth in September. *P. Monteith*   68

HOT LASS   7 ch.m. Class Distinction – Hot Tramp (Country Retreat) [1992/3 18fpu 16s c16vpu c16d a16g6 c16gF c16gpu c18sF] small, lengthy mare: no sign of ability. *J. J. Bridger*   c–
–

HOTME   8 b.m. Jolly Me – Verona Brandy (Hot Brandy) [1992/3 20gpu a20gpu] fourth foal: sister to 5-y-o I'm-A-Tot: dam, winning selling hurdler/novice chaser, stayed 2½m: no sign of ability in claiming hurdles in August and January. *H. J. Manners*   –

HOTPLATE   10 ch.g. Buckskin (FR) – Pencil Lady (Bargello) [1992/3 c25mpu] sparely-made gelding: fair chaser: tailed off when pulled up in October, and wasn't seen out again: stays very well: acts on any going: tends to sweat and be on toes: usually jumps soundly. *D. McCain*   c–
–

HOT PROSPECT   4 b.f. Damister (USA) – Smelter (Prominer) [1992/3 16spu 17gpu 18g 18g4] leggy, shallow-girthed filly: poor form at up to 11f on Flat: sold out of J. Etherington's stable 2,000 gns Doncaster November Sales: little sign of ability in juvenile hurdles: resold 1,900 gns Malvern June Sales. *Mrs P. A. Russell*   –

HOT STAR   7 b.g. Hotfoot – La Camargue (Wollow) [1992/3 20g4 20s4 22s5 25d3 25s5] leggy gelding: moderate novice hurdler: blinkered, best effort when third in conditional jockeys handicap at Carlisle in February: suited by a test of stamina: acts on soft ground. *G. M. Moore*   98

HOT TIP   4 b.f. Beldale Flutter (USA) – Summer's Darling (Final Straw) [1992/3 17g6 16d 16d 17s4 17g3 16d a16g] leggy filly: poor maiden on Flat and over hurdles: yet to race beyond 17f: best effort on good going. *J. L. Eyre*   70

HOUGHTON   7 b.g. Horage – Deirdre Oge (Pontifex (USA)) [1992/3 c16d2 c21dpu c21dF c16d2 c20g2 c16g3 c20m*] rangy, good sort: winning hurdler: placed in novice chases prior to winning one at Newcastle in March: stays 2½m: acts on soft and good to firm ground: sometimes wanders and flashes tail under pressure: blinkered second outing. *M. W. Easterby*   c97
–

HOUXTY LAD   7 b.g. Full of Hope – Cupid's Delight (St Paddy) [1992/3 c26spu c24s4] big, plain gelding: poor hurdler/chaser: needs further than 2½m and stays 25f: acts on heavy ground: poor jumper. *J. I. A. Charlton*   c–   x
–

HOWARD'S POST   4 b.g. Dunbeath (USA) – Broad Horizon (Blakeney) [1992/3 17m4 17m4 16g4] leggy gelding: half-brother to several winners, including hurdler Great Aspect (by Great Nephew): dam 2-y-o 7f winner stayed 1¾m, is closely related to Rarity: poor form in early-season juvenile hurdles. *J. J. O'Neill*   79

HOWARYADOON   7 b.g. Good Thyne (USA) – Butler's Daughter (Rhett Butler) [1992/3 22s4 23g4 21s5 25s* 22v3 c21sur c21g4 25dpu] workmanlike gelding: winning pointer: fair hurdler: won conditional jockeys   c99
104

handicap at Newbury in January: unseated rider last (had just been left in lead) in novice event at Worcester in February on chasing debut: broke blood vessel next time: suited by a thorough test of stamina and plenty of give in the ground. *R. Rowe*

HOWARYAFXD 6 ch.g. Green Shoon – Pandos Pet (Dusky Boy) [1992/3 17s² 16s 23s³ c20dᵖᵘ] sturdy, lengthy gelding: chasing type: third foal: dam a maiden: winning pointer: best effort in novice hurdles when second at Newton Abbot in October: broke blood vessel on chasing debut: should stay beyond 17f: acts on soft going: forces pace. *Miss H. C. Knight* — c– / 84

HOWCLEUCH 6 b.m. Buckskin (FR) – Swiftly Belle (Deep Run) [1992/3 21d³] rangy mare: poor novice hurdler: creditable third at Hexham in November: will stay beyond 2½m: acts on heavy going. *J. K. M. Oliver* — 78

HOW DOUDO 6 b.m. Oats – Galah Bird (Darling Boy) [1992/3 20s³ 22v⁶ 25v⁴ 21s*] leggy mare: won maiden claiming hurdle at Chepstow in April: should prove suited by good test of stamina: acts on soft going. *S. Christian* — 81

HOWE STREET 10 gr.g. Torus – Jim's Fancy (Walshford) [1992/3 c21m³ c21dᵘʳ c17s* c17v⁵ c20g² c21m] workmanlike gelding: fairly useful chaser: won handicap at Newbury in November: also ran well when placed in 1992/3: stays 2½m: acts on good to firm and heavy ground: usually a sound jumper: forces pace. *J. H. Johnson* — c129 / –

HOWGILL 7 b.g. Tower Walk – In Form (Formidable (USA)) [1992/3 16s³ 16d a 16g a 16g⁴ a 18g a 18gᶠ c16d⁴ c16sᵖᵘ] close-coupled, robust gelding: winning hurdler: poor novice chaser: form only at 2m but worth another try over further: acts on firm going and fibresand. *R. Hollinshead* — c80 / 80

HOW HUMBLE (IRE) 4 b.f. Phardante (FR) – How Hostile (Tumble Wind (USA)) [1992/3 F17dᵖᵘ] fifth foal: half-sister to fairly useful hurdler/chaser Fighting Words (by Prince Bee): dam, poor Irish maiden, half-sister to smart stayer Barley Hill: tailed off when pulled up in NH Flat race at Hereford in May: yet to race over hurdles. *B. P. J. Baugh*

HOW'S THE BOSS 7 b.g. Ragapan – Barradan Lass (Deep Run) [1992/3 c19s* c16d³ c17d³ c17d* c19d² c21dʳᵒ c18s* c16g] — c139 / –

The potential rewards are great but there are trials along the way for anyone associated with the fickle How's The Boss, most obviously for his jockey. In the 1991/2 season his win in The Ladbroke was the performance which put twenty-one-year-old Jason Titley firmly on the map. Twelve months on and Titley had lost the ride. The partnership had justified favouritism at Listowel on How's The Boss's first venture in novice chases but two defeats followed. On the second of those, showing useful form behind Soft Day in a Grade 2 race at Leopardstown on Boxing Day, How's The Boss had got to the front at the fifth of the eleven fences then faded on the run-in, his trainer reportedly commenting that he had been in the lead far too soon. Mark Dwyer took over.

The new partnership got off to a winning start, How's The Boss leading at the last and going on to land the odds by four lengths from Commercial Artist at Leopardstown, but this was followed by two efforts which Dwyer must have found exasperating in the extreme. In the Baileys Arkle Perpetual Challenge Trophy, again at Leopardstown, at the end of January, How's The Boss had the third of five encounters in 1992/3 with Soft Day. Soft Day had finished in front of him on their previous two meetings, Titley's last two appearances on How's The Boss, but a reversal looked a near-certainty as they came round the final turn this time, the pair having made steady headway from the rear to dispute the lead, the difference being that Soft Day had been ridden along from the third last whereas How's The Boss was still on the bridle. At the post, however, Soft Day was a length and a half to the good, Dwyer having delayed his effort on How's The Boss until about a third of the way up the run-in only to receive a negligible response. There was the possibility, of course, that the slightly longer trip of two miles and three furlongs had found out How's The Boss, but his next start (interestingly over a longer trip again) in a Grade 2 event at Leopardstown left no doubt that there was a temperamental kink there as well. A fair

Fitzpatricks Hotel Group Chase, Leopardstown—How's The Boss and Mark Dwyer

*Power Gold Cup Chase, Fairyhouse—the leader Soft Day is about to fall,
leaving How's The Boss to win from Galevilla Express*

amount of the post-race publicity concentrated on the fact that there was no continuous running rail on the approach to the last fence, rather than that How's The Boss had decided to jump the hurdle wing that was there. At the time of his 'running out', How's The Boss had closed on Allezmoss and Galevilla Express but Flashing Steel had gone clear. How's The Boss would have finished second.

			Ragusa	Ribot
	Ragapan		(b 1960)	Fantan II
	(b 1970)		Panaview	Panaslipper
How's The Boss			(b 1960)	April View
(b.g. 1986)			Deep Run	Pampered King
	Barradan Lass		(ch 1966)	Trial By Fire
	(b 1975)		Money Even	Even Money
			(br 1971)	Killea

Soft Day had missed that race but was back for the Power Gold Cup at Fairyhouse in April and on this occasion it was How's The Boss who emerged on top. However, in light of what had gone before, it is surely less than prudent to state categorically that he would still have done so had the crowd not been robbed of a tremendous spectacle, Dwyer later promising that he would have 'waited until the death if I had to', when Soft Day fell at the last holding a slight lead. Some enlightenment on the issue was due to be provided sixteen days later in what promised to be one of the highlights of the Punchestown Festival, the pair starting co-favourites at level weights in the Bank of Ireland Colliers Novice Chase, but it failed to materialise. Soft Day broke a leg at the second and had to be put down. How's The Boss, ridden by Charlie Swan, finished the course but was virtually pulled up in

Mr Edward Farrell's "How's The Boss"

last place, reportedly suffering from a shoulder injury. A sad end to a most engaging series between two of Ireland's top novice chasers.

How's The Boss is the third foal out of Barradan Lass, following the winning pointers Guici's Rag (by Ragapan) and Proverbial Luck (by Proverb), the latter also a three-mile hunter chase winner in March 1992. A winning point-to-pointer herself, Barradan Lass has had only one return registered with Weatherbys since How's The Boss, dead twins by Ragapan in 1988. The leggy, useful-looking How's The Boss acts on good to firm and soft going, but was below form on heavy. He is effective at two miles and his performance, as far as it went, in giving 6 lb to Flashing Steel in that two-mile five-furlong race at Leopardstown suggests that he probably stays that distance as well. He's obviously no easy ride, but How's The Boss's sound jumping and sheer ability are bound to see him win more races. *J. Brassil, Ireland*

HTHAAL (USA) 5 b. or br.g. Caro – Endurable Heights (USA) (Graustark) [1992/3 17m2 18g3 20g3 16d2 17d* 20g2 20g5 24dpu 17m4] poor maiden on Flat: won novice hurdle at Kelso in November: ran creditably most other starts: stays 2½m: acts on good to firm and dead ground: blinkered fifth to eighth starts. *L. Lungo*   89

HUDSON BAY TRADER (USA) 6 b.g. Sir Ivor – Yukon Baby (USA) (Northern Dancer) [1992/3 20g* 21d3 18d2 20s* 20s* 20v2 20d4 22m2 22s* 20f4] close-coupled, workmanlike gelding: fairly useful hurdler: won novice events at Market Rasen and Newcastle (2) in first half of season, and handicap on former course in April: should stay beyond 2¾m: acts on good to firm and heavy going: visored twice in 1991/2: genuine. *P. Beaumont*   125

HUGLI 6 ch.g. Relkino – Hors Serie (USA) (Vaguely Noble) [1992/3 24d3 24g6 26g4] smallish, lightly-made gelding: fair handicap hurdler: best effort of season when fourth at Hereford in October: stays 3¼m: acts on good to firm and dead: best forcing pace: has looked ungenuine: blinkered/visored. *S. E. Sherwood*   102

HULA 5 b.g. Broadsword (USA) – Blakes Lass (Blakeney) [1992/3 F16d 27dpu] sixth foal: brother to winning pointer No Fizz and half-brother to 2 other winners, including hurdler In Contention (by Hittite Glory): dam second at 1¼m: behind in NH Flat race in January and when pulled up in amateurs novice hurdle in April. *Mrs S. Taylor*   –

HUNG OVER 7 b.m. Smackover – Passionate (Dragonara Palace (USA)) [1992/3 20f2] workmanlike mare: poor maiden on Flat and in points (ungenuine): blinkered, second of 3 in poor novice hurdle at Plumpton in August. *R. Champion*   58 ?

HUNMANBY GAP 8 ch.g. Flying Tyke – Another Mufsie (Tehran Court) [1992/3 22dpu 20m5 22m2 22d4 22g* 22m] lengthy, angular gelding: won selling handicap hurdle at Sedgefield (no bid) in April: blinkered, ran poorly in similar event on same course following month: will stay beyond 2¾m: acts on firm ground. *P. Beaumont*   75

HUNTED 6 ch.g. Busted – Madam Cody (Hot Spark) [1992/3 22spu 23spu] small, sturdy gelding: no worthwhile form over hurdles, including in a seller. *A. R. Davison*   –

HUNTERS CLUB 5 b.m. Amerian (USA) – Demo's Lady (Status Seeker) [1992/3 F16v 22fpu 16fpu] no sign of ability. *G. A. Pritchard-Gordon*   –

HUNTING DIARY 7 b.g. Town And Country – Royal Dialogue (Royal Buck) [1992/3 c24sF c21vpu c26d c24g5 c21dF c23g] lengthy gelding: poor staying novice chaser. *J. W. Mullins*   c–

HUNTING GROUND 5 b.h. Dancing Brave (USA) – Ack's Secret (USA) (Ack Ack (USA)) [1992/3 18f* 22m3 24f*] neat horse: fair handicap hurdler: successful at Fontwell (blinkered only time, made mistakes) and Worcester prior to being sold 5,000 gns Ascot September Sales: stays 3m: acts well on firm ground: sometimes wears tongue strap: races lazily and needs plenty of driving: winning stayer on Flat for A. Bailey in 1993. *G. Harwood*   102

HUNTWORTH 13 ch.g. Funny Man – Tamorina (Quayside) [1992/3 **c**112
c26g² c25gᵖᵘ] big, plain gelding: fairly useful chaser in 1991/2: well-beaten
second at Cheltenham, better effort in October: stays very well: acts on any
going: often makes running: often amateur ridden: jumps boldly and well in
the main. *M. C. Pipe*

HURDY 6 ch.g. Arapahos (FR) – Demelza Carne (Woodville II) [1992/3
16g* 16d³ 21s² 20g* 17f* 21m] rather leggy, close-coupled gelding: 111 p
progressive form in novice hurdles: won at Wetherby in October and
Doncaster in January and March: also ran well in Sun Alliance Novices'
Hurdle at Cheltenham later in March: sold 50,000 gns Doncaster May Sales:
will stay beyond 21f: probably acts on any going: sometimes hangs left and
carries head high. *J. Hanson*

HURRICANE ANDREW (IRE) 5 ch.g. Hawaiian Return (USA) –
Viable (Nagami) [1992/3 28d] half-brother to winning chaser Remember –
Josh (by Rusticaro): dam placed in NH Flat race: tailed off in novice hurdle at
Sedgefield in November: sold 3,800 gns in May. *W. A. Stephenson*

HURRICANE BLAKE 5 b.g. Blakeney – Nibelunga (Miami Springs)
[1992/3 23g* 20d² 25g² 22m³ 22f* 25g²] angular gelding: won novice 120
hurdles at Windsor in November and Sandown in March: better efforts when
second in handicaps at Newbury and Cheltenham on third and last starts:
thorough stayer: best form on a sound surface: blinkered last 2 outings. *D.
M. Grissell*

HURRICANE HORACE 6 br.g. Strong Gale – Arctic Tack (Arctic
Slave) [1992/3 22sᵖᵘ 16g³ 20s 17d 20m³ 16g⁵] compact gelding: eighth foal: 92
brother to useful Irish hurdler/chaser Soft Day and half-brother to winning
pointer/novice chaser Sharp Opinion (by Le Bavard): dam unraced: trained
until after third start by W. A. Stephenson: modest form in novice hurdles:
sold 52,000 gns in May: should stay beyond 2½m: acts on good to firm
going. *P. Cheesbrough*

HURRICANE RYAN (IRE) 5 b.g. Lafontaine (USA) – Etesian
(Tumble Wind (USA)) [1992/3 F16v³] fifth foal: half-brother to a winner in –
Italy by Kampala: dam 5f winner at 2 yrs: third of 16 in NH Flat race at
Uttoxeter in April: yet to race over hurdles or fences. *M. Bradstock*

HUTNER 8 b.g. Henbit (USA) – Fountain (Reform) [1992/3 c16s³ c16g⁴ **c**104
c17d² c21d³ c17g* c17m* c17d³ c21s* c21f²] good-topped gelding: winning –
hurdler: fair form over fences: successful in novice events at Sedgefield and
Newcastle in March and Wetherby in April: good second in handicap on
last-named course in May: stays 21f: acts on any going: genuine. *M. Dods*

HYDROPIC 6 b.g. Kabour – Hydrangea (Warpath) [1992/3 a16g⁵ 22vᵖᵘ]
poor maiden on Flat, stays 11f: moderate winning pointer: no form in novice –
hurdles: blinkered last outing. *D. W. Chapman*

HYMN BOOK (IRE) 4 b.f. Darshaan – Divina (GER) (Alpenkonig
(GER)) [1992/3 18f⁵ 18m⁴] quite modest maiden on Flat: sold out of M. 69
Stoute's stable 4,100 gns Newmarket July Sales: poor form in early-season
juvenile hurdles at Exeter. *R. J. Manning*

HYMNE D'AMOUR (USA) 5 b.m. Dixieland Band (USA) – La
Francaise (USA) (Jim French (USA)) [1992/3 17d* 17d³ 17s* 16s³ 17s 17g* 104
22m* 17d²] neat mare: modest middle-distance handicapper on Flat:
successful over hurdles in 2 novice events and a handicap at Wolverhampton and 2¾m mares novice handicap at Nottingham: good second in
handicap at Newton Abbot on last start: effective at 17f and stays 2¾m: acts
on good to firm and soft going: sound jumper: game. *Miss H. C. Knight*

I

IAMA ZULU 8 ch.g. Son of Shaka – Quick Sort (Henry The Seventh) **c**–
[1992/3 c23sᵖᵘ c20sᵖᵘ c21mᶠ] rangy gelding: modest chaser at his best: –

failed to complete in 1992/3: stays 3m: acts on firm and dead ground. *P. J. Hobbs*

IBN SINA (USA)　6 b.g. Dr Blum (USA) – Two On One (CAN) (Lord　c–
Durham (CAN)) [1992/3 c25gpu] sparely-made gelding: novice selling　–
hurdler: placed in points but showed nothing in steeplechase in 1993: has
been tried blinkered. *P. H. Morris*

IBN ZAMAN (USA)　7 b.g. Graustark – Wake Robin (Summer Tan)　–
[1992/3 20g⁴ 21f] lengthy, good-bodied gelding: selling hurdler: no show in
August and September: stays 19f: best blinkered. *D. N. Carey*

ICARUS (USA)　7 b.g. Wind And Wuthering (USA) – Cedar Waxwing c119
(USA) (Tom Fool) [1992/3 c21f⁴ c17g⁶ c20g³ c20d* c21vF c20d³ c21g*　–
c20fur c21s³ c20g c22m* c22v² c22f²] compact gelding: fairly useful
handicap chaser: won at Edinburgh, Bangor (trained until after tenth start
by M. H. Easterby) and Stratford (dead-heated with Beech Road) in second
half of season: has won from 2m to 3m, ideally suited by around 2½m: acts
on any going: usually visored or blinkered: jumps boldly and well. *D. H. Brown*

ICE GOLD　6 ch.g. Le Moss – Slave Light (Arctic Slave) [1992/3 20g]　–
well-made gelding: modest novice hurdler at his best: stayed 2½m: acted
on heavy ground: dead. *J. H. Johnson*

ICE WALK　4 gr.f. Kalaglow – Krishnagar (Kris) [1992/3 18s 17f⁶ 17fpu]　–
lengthy, rather unfurnished filly: no form on Flat: sold out of W. Jarvis'
stable 2,100 gns Newmarket Autumn Sales: little worthwhile form in novice
hurdles. *M. J. Wilkinson*

ICY RULLAH (IRE)　4 b.g. Callernish – Icy Lou (Bluerullah) [1992/3　79
16d 16g] smallish, angular gelding: second foal: dam won Irish point: poor
form in juvenile hurdles in November and December: likely to prove suited
by further than 2m. *J. Wade*

IDA'S DELIGHT　14 br.g. Idiot's Delight – Ida Spider (Ben Novus) c135 ?
[1992/3 c21m c25g³] leggy gelding: veteran chaser, useful at best: returned　–
to form when never-dangerous third in Grade 2 Charlie Hall Chase at
Wetherby (usually goes well there) in October: wasn't seen out again:
suited by stiff 2½m and stays 25f: acts on any going: genuine, though often
gets well behind early on. *J. I. A. Charlton*

I DID IT MY WAY　8 b.g. The Parson – Entry Hill (Menelek) [1992/3　69 ?
22g³] lengthy gelding: half-brother to winning pointers Corpse Reviver (by
Pollerton) and Les Parvenus (by Smartset): let down by his jumping in
points, but has shown a little ability: shown form when third of 7 in novice
hurdle at Worcester in August: sold 1,150 gns Ascot November Sales: will
be suited by 3m. *G. H. Peter-Hoblyn*

IDIOM　6 b.g. Idiot's Delight – Squiffy (Articulate) [1992/3 F16d 16s 16d]　76
sturdy gelding: half-brother to 3 winning jumpers: dam successful staying
chaser: showed some promise in novice hurdle at Ludlow in January but
well beaten in similar race there in February: sold to join Mrs J. Retter 6,000
gns Ascot June Sales. *J. A. C. Edwards*

IDLEIGH'S RUNON　10 gr.g. Deep Run – Zion (Palestine) [1992/3　c–
c17mF 17g] leggy gelding: poor novice hurdler/chaser: trained first start by　–
J. Joseph: likely to prove best at around 2m: has worn a net muzzle. *R. G. Frost*

IDLEIGH'S STAR　9 b.g. Torus – Safari Queen (Halsafari) [1992/3　c–
c26dF c27dF 22d4 20v4] good-topped gelding: poor form in novice chases:　–
has failed to complete in novice chases, though signs of ability. *A. Moore*

IDLEIGH'S TUDOR　8 b.g. Tudorville – Green Monkey (Court　–
Harwell) [1992/3 17d4 16spu] close-coupled, good-bodied gelding: little sign
of ability in novice hurdles. *D. Nicholson*

IDLING BY　7 b.g. Carlingford Castle – Hanslein (Prince Hansel) [1992/3　76
16v5 25spu 22vpu 22d 20d5 25g2] unfurnished gelding: winning pointer in

Ireland: novice selling hurdler: sold 2,700 gns Ascot June Sales: suited by a test of stamina: acts on heavy going. *D. R. Gandolfo*

IDONI 4 b.g. Bustino – Miranda Julia (Julio Mariner) [1992/3 17d^{ur} 17g²] compact gelding: half-brother to 5-y-o Marine Society (by Petoski): fair form when placed in 1¼m maiden on Flat: sold out of C. Brittain's stable 5,800 gns Newmarket Autumn Sales: would have finished second but for unseating rider last in juvenile hurdle at Taunton in February: close second in similar event on same course following month: will stay beyond 17f. *R. Curtis* — 97

IF YOU SAY SO 7 ch.g. Say Primula – Vinovia (Ribston) [1992/3 20m 20m⁴ 23g* 25s^{pu}] workmanlike gelding: easy 10-length winner of amateurs maiden hurdle at Kelso in November when trained by W. A. Stephenson: ran poorly in novice event at Wetherby following month: sold 6,000 gns in May: suited by a test of stamina: acts on firm ground. *P. Cheesbrough* — 85 +

IL BAMBINO 5 ch.g. Bairn (USA) – Trapani (Ragusa) [1992/3 17g⁴ 16d⁴ 17g³ 20m³ 17g³ 21m²] sparely-made gelding: modest maiden hurdler: stays 2½m: acts on good to firm ground. *H. J. Manners* — 89

ILDERTON ROAD 6 br.m. Noalto – Mac's Melody (Wollow) [1992/3 16v 16d 21g⁶] tall, lengthy mare: modest performer on Flat: poor novice hurdler: best effort at 2m on heavy going. *Mrs Barbara Waring* — 68

ILEWIN 6 br.g. Ile de Bourbon (USA) – City Swinger (Derrylin) [1992/3 18g² 17g 20v⁴ 17d³ 16s^F 18v³ a16g³ 16v a18g³ 17g⁵ 17f² 17d² 16m* 16f] compact gelding: moderate hurdler: easy winner of seller at Towcester (bought in 4,000 gns) in May: best at up to 2¼m: acts on dead, firm ground and fibresand: visored once: suited by waiting tactics. *J. R. Jenkins* — 96

I LIKE IT A LOT 10 ch.g. Proverb – Jupiters Jill (Jupiter Pluvius) [1992/3 c19d^{pu} c20m c18d⁶] lengthy, sparely-made gelding: handicap chaser: no show in 1992/3: stays 2½m: acts on firm ground. *P. J. Hobbs* — c– –

ILLOGICAL 6 br.m. Ile de Bourbon (USA) – Modern Romance (Dance In Time (CAN)) [1992/3 16s 17d^{bd} 16g³ 17g⁴] rather leggy mare: poor hurdler: has raced only at around 2m: visored last start (below form). *J. A. Glover* — 70

IMA DELIGHT 6 b.m. Idiot's Delight – Milly Kelly (Murrayfield) [1992/3 22s² 21v* 22d^{pu} 22s³ 21s³ 21g^F] workmanlike mare: modest hurdler: won mares novice event at Warwick in December: good third in handicap at Nottingham in January and mares novice event at Wetherby in March: stays 2¾m: acts on heavy going: looked very temperamental third start. *Mrs P. Sly* — 97

IMAGE BOY (IRE) 5 br.g. Flash of Steel – Gay Pariso (Sir Gaylord) [1992/3 17f 17f³] no show in 3 races at 2 yrs: first sign of ability when remote third of 8 finishers in novice hurdle at Huntingdon in May. *J. A. Bennett* — 68

I'M A MISS 7 ch.m. Le Coq d'Or – Star Attention (Northfields (USA)) [1992/3 18g 22d] small, sturdy mare: poor form over hurdles, including in sellers: sold 2,400 gns in May: should prove suited by further than 2m. *W. A. Stephenson* — 62

IMA RED NECK (USA) 4 b.g. Dixieland Band (USA) – Bright Reply (USA) (Gleaming (USA)) [1992/3 18s^{pu} 17s 18v³ 17v⁴ 16d^{pu}] compact gelding: sold out of J. Gosden's stable 6,400 gns Newmarket Autumn Sales: best effort in juvenile hurdles when third at Fontwell in January: stays 2¼m: acts on heavy ground: won over 1½m on Flat in 1993, wearing visor. *J. S. Moore* — 86

I'M-A-TOT 5 br.m. Jolly Me – Verona Brandy (Hot Brandy) [1992/3 18f^{pu}] sixth foal: sister to 8-y-o Hotme: dam, winning selling hurdler/novice chaser, stayed 2½m: pulled up in selling hurdle in September: sold 700 gns Ascot February Sales. *H. J. Manners* — –

IMBIBER 7 b.g. Alias Smith (USA) – The High Dancer (High Line) [1992/3 16f^{pu} 16g 17d 21s^{pu} 16f⁵ 17m 17f^{pu}] compact gelding: of little account. *H. E. Peachey* — –

IMC

I'M CONFIDENT 9 b.g. Stetchworth (USA) – Mrs Baggins (English c–
Prince) [1992/3 20v 21v⁶ 16v] workmanlike ex-Irish gelding: one-time fairly –
useful hurdler/chaser: no show in handicap hurdles in 1992/3: blinkered
once. *N. M. Babbage*

I'M CURIOUS 4 b.f. Kirchner – The Dupecat (Javelot) [1992/3 16s 22f⁵
24gpu 22f⁶ 21dpu 24gF] sparely-made filly: of little account on Flat: 58
plating-class novice hurdler. *R. Thompson*

I'M FINE 8 b. or br.m. Fitzwilliam (USA) – Quick Thinking (Will Somers)
[1992/3 16d 16d³ 16s*] sparely-made mare: won novice hurdle at Catterick 74
in December (finished lame): will stay beyond 2m: acts on soft ground. *P.
Beaumont*

IMGONNAWIN 5 b.m. Meadowbrook – Spring Gala (Ancient Monro)
[1992/3 17d 21spu 16gur] angular mare: fourth foal: half-sister to winning
jumpers Galadine (by Gaberdine) and Gala Loch (by Lochnager) and to 4-y-o
Young Gala (by Young Man): dam tailed-off last only start: no sign of ability
over hurdles. *S. G. Payne*

IMHOTEP 6 gr.g. Claude Monet (USA) – Miss Melmore (Nishapour
(FR)) [1992/3 16g* 18m*] modest and lightly-raced miler on Flat: created 102 p
favourable impression when easy winner of novice hurdles at Catterick and
Kelso in March, making running on both occasions, but finishing lame on
latter course: will prove best around 2m: acts on good to firm ground. *Mrs
M. Reveley*

IMPALE 9 b. or br.g. Crash Course – Show Rose (Coliseum) [1992/3 c–
c26vF c21vF 24spu 23gpu] leggy gelding: winning hurdler/chaser: lightly –
raced and no form since 1990/1. *D. R. Greig*

IMPANY 14 br.g. Parasang – Swift Imp (Swift Flight) [1992/3 c18m² c82
c16m⁴ c16g⁶ c17d⁵ c16m* c16m⁶ c17d³] strong, compact gelding: poor
chaser: won selling handicap (no bid) at Ludlow in October: good third in
non-seller at Sedgefield following month: effective at 2m and stayed 3m:
acted on firm and dead ground: blinkered twice: usually jumped well:
retired. *J. J. O'Neill*

IMPECCABLE TIMING 10 ch.g. Paddy's Stream – Wynchy Comby c81
(Royal Buck) [1992/3 26d c25s⁴ c27v⁵ c24spu c17v c23gpu c27d³ a21g] big,
lengthy gelding: poor hurdler/novice chaser: stays 27f: acts on good to firm
and dead going: blinkered once. *O. O'Neill*

IMPERIAL FLAME 7 b.m. Imperial Lantern – Three Terns (Seaepic
(USA)) [1992/3 22mpu 16gur] small mare: no sign of ability on Flat or over –
hurdles. *Mrs J. Carr Evans*

IMPERIAL FLIGHT 8 b.g. Pampabird – Queen of Time (Charlottown) c–
[1992/3 16g 16g* 16m⁴] close-coupled, quite good-topped gelding: moderate 95
hurdler: won claimer at Wincanton in February: ran creditably in handicap
there following month: let down by his jumping in novice chases: best at
around 2m: acts on good to firm and dead ground. *J. S. King*

IMPERTAIN 13 br.g. Ascertain (USA) – Swift Imp (Swift Flight) [1992/3 c68
c21gpu c21g c20gpu c16f c20f4] big, lengthy gelding: carries plenty of –
condition: poor handicap chaser: stays 3m: acts on any going: inconsistent:
visored last 2 starts. *W. S. Cunningham*

IMPORTANT RISK 4 ch.g. Risk Me (FR) – Miss Import (Import)
[1992/3 17mpu 18vF] no sign of ability on Flat or over hurdles. *B. Mactaggart* –

I'M SPECIAL (IRE) 5 ch.m. Lyphard's Special (USA) – Doon Belle
(Ardoon) [1992/3 17g⁴ 17g² 22f4] poor novice selling hurdler: visored twice, 68
blinkered once in 1991/2. *J. R. Jenkins*

I'M TOBY 6 b.g. Celtic Cone – Easter Tinkle (Hot Brandy) [1992/3 21s²
25g* 25d* 25s⁶ 25v²] sturdy, lengthy, good sort: chasing type: seventh foal: 104 p
half-brother to high-class hunter chaser Sweet Diana (by Bivouac): dam
winning hurdler: won novice hurdles at Doncaster in January and Uttoxeter
in February: good second in similar race at Perth in April: stays 25f: acts on
heavy ground: has scope and is type to do better. *J. G. FitzGerald*

374

INAN (USA) 4 b.c. El Gran Senor (USA) – Assez Cuite (USA) (Graustark) [1992/3 16d6 17g 16d 18d 16v6 16d2 18d4 16s3 17s4 16f3 18v2] well-made colt: fair but disappointing middle-distance performer on Flat: sold out of J. Dunlop's stable 15,500 gns Newmarket Autumn Sales: modest form at best over hurdles: yet to race beyond 2¼m: probably acts on any going: possibly not to be trusted. *R. O'Leary* — 90

INCHCAILLOCH (IRE) 4 b.c. Lomond (USA) – Glowing With Pride (Ile de Bourbon (USA)) [1992/3 17vpu 16d 16g6] rangy, useful-looking colt: fair middle-distance stayer on Flat: set strong pace until 3 out in juvenile hurdles on last 2 starts: probably capable of better. *J. S. King* — 79 p

INCONCLUSIVE 6 b.g. Roselier (FR) – Kilbride Madam (Mandalus) [1992/3 c21d* c20gpu c21spu] leggy, close-coupled gelding: no worthwhile form over hurdles: won novice event at Wetherby in January on chasing debut: pulled up both starts afterwards: should stay beyond 21f. *Mrs S. A. Bramall* — c86 —

IN COUNCIL 6 b. or br.h. Blakeney – Regal Lady (FR) (Relko) [1992/3 17spu 17d 17d 17m2 17gpu] compact horse: once-raced on Flat: runner-up in selling handicap hurdle at Newton Abbot in March: dead. *D. N. Carey* — 75

IN DEEP WATER 6 ch.m. Over The River (FR) – Deepdecending (Deep Run) [1992/3 18g4 20g2 20m3 22d2 a22g3 a22g* a24g4] small mare: poor form over hurdles: claimed out of Mrs V. Aconley's stable £5,000 fifth outing: won novice event at Southwell in January: well below form only subsequent start: should stay beyond 2¾m: acts on good to firm, dead ground and fibresand. *D. J. Wintle* — 78

INDIAN CHARMER 5 b.g. Indian King (USA) – Sweet Colleen (Connaught) [1992/3 F17m 16m] leggy, workmanlike gelding: behind in NH Flat races, and a novice hurdle at Catterick in October: sold 2,800 gns Doncaster November Sales. *M. W. Easterby* — —

INDIAN FIGHTER 7 b.g. Indian King (USA) – Condoree (Condorcet (FR)) [1992/3 c17gpu] workmanlike gelding: failed to complete in points and hunter chases. *G. H. Wagstaff* — c–

INDIAN HEATHER (IRE) 5 b.m. Indian King (USA) – Yellow Plume (Home Guard (USA)) [1992/3 18g] lengthy mare: seventh foal: half-sister to modest 1989 staying 2-y-o Toucan (by King of Clubs): dam won at around 1m at 2 yrs in Ireland: well beaten on Flat, and in selling hurdle in October. *J. Parkes* — —

INDIAN HILL 8 b.g. Jalmood (USA) – Montania (Mourne) [1992/3 17vpu 21spu] very lightly raced and no sign of ability: blinkered first outing. *B. J. M. Ryall* — —

INDIAN KNIGHT 8 b.g. Kinglet – Indian Whistle (Rugantino) [1992/3 c24m2 c28fur] useful pointer: shaped well when close second to Carrickmines in novice hunter chase at Stratford in May: unseated rider ninth following month: should improve and win races. *C. A. Green* — c98 p

INDIAN MAESTRO 7 b.g. Music Maestro – Indian Wells (Reliance II) [1992/3 17dpu 16m F10d6] sparely-made gelding: poor novice jumper: sold 1,250 gns Doncaster May Sales. *Mrs A. Swinbank* — c– —

INDIAN ORCHID 6 b.m. Warpath – Flower Child (Brother) [1992/3 F16d3] half-sister to Desert Orchid (by Grey Mirage) and winning chaser Peacework (by Workboy): dam winning chaser: third in 11-runner NH Flat race at Catterick in November: yet to race over hurdles or fences. *Mrs M. Reveley* — —

INDIAN QUEST 4 b.g. Rainbow Quest (USA) – Hymettus (Blakeney) [1992/3 17v4 16s* 16v* 17g2 17m 16g4] leggy, close-coupled gelding: once-raced on Flat: sold out of R. Hern's stable 15,000 gns Newmarket Autumn Sales: won juvenile hurdles at Nottingham and Kempton around turn of year: ran well when in frame in well-contested races at Newbury in February and Punchestown in April: will stay at least 2½m: acts on heavy — 130 p

going (not disgraced on good to firm): usually races up with pace: should do well in 1993/4. *N. A. Gaselee*

INDIAN RIVER (IRE) 5 b.g. Indian King (USA) – Chaldea (Tamerlane) [1992/3 F14s² F16s] half-brother to several winners, including very useful Flat performer Kahaila (by Pitcairn), dam of useful jumper Kiichi: dam unraced: second in NH Flat race at Market Rasen in November: tailed off in similar race in February: yet to race over hurdles or fences. *J. G. FitzGerald*

INDIAN RUN (IRE) 4 b.g. Commanche Run – Excitingly (USA) (Val de L'Orne (FR)) [1992/3 F16s⁵ 16d² 17g* 17m 20d⁵] compact, workmanlike gelding with plenty of scope: fourth foal: half-brother to a poor Irish Flat maiden by Full Pocket: dam unraced: won juvenile hurdle at Sandown in February: better effort when staying-on eleventh of 25 in Daily Express Triumph Hurdle at Cheltenham following month: should prove well suited by further than 17f (never going well over 2½m last start): acts on good to firm going: worth another chance to confirm Cheltenham run. *R. J. Hodges*   123

INDIAN SWALLOW (FR) 4 b.f. Shirley Heights – Swift And Sure (USA) (Valdez (USA)) [1992/3 17v⁴ 16d 17s² 17m⁶] sturdy filly: third foal: sister to a Flat maiden and closely related to another: dam useful 5f and 1¼m winner: poor form in juvenile hurdles: will stay further than 17f. *D. Nicholson*   71

INDIAN TONIC 7 br.g. Ovac (ITY) – Green Hedge (Goldhill) [1992/3 c110 p
c20f² c25s* c26m² c24m²] tall, workmanlike gelding: poor novice hurdler: –
much better over fences and won Fairview New Homes Novices' Chase at
Ascot in April by 15 lengths: good second in novice events at Cheltenham
(handicap) later in month and at Stratford in May: will stay beyond 3¼m:
acts on good to firm and soft ground: front runner: jumps well, and should
make into quite a useful handicapper. *N. A. Twiston-Davies*

INFERRING 5 b.g. Alleging (USA) – Be My Darling (Windjammer
(USA)) [1992/3 22g 18m³ 17g 20m] leggy gelding: plating-class maiden on 78
Flat: no better over hurdles. *J. S. Wainwright*

INGLEBY FLYER 5 b.m. Valiyar – Fardella (ITY) (Molvedo) [1992/3
F16d F16g] sister to winning hurdler Solitary Reaper: dam minor 11f winner
in France: tailed off in NH Flat races at Catterick in November and
February: yet to race over hurdles or fences. *Mrs S. Frank*

IN-KEEPING 7 b.m. Castle Keep – Primmy (Primera) [1992/3 18m 17fᵖᵘ
17m⁶] sparely-made mare: front-running 2m handicap hurdler: no form for a –
long time. *R. C. Spicer*

INNOCENT PRINCESS (NZ) 6 ch.m. Full On Aces (AUS) – Kia
Court (NZ) (Barcas (USA)) [1992/3 22s* 24f³ 23g* 24g 25s 23dᵖᵘ 22m 103 d
22m⁵] small mare: won handicap hurdles at Newton Abbot and Stratford
early in season: well below form subsequently: stays 3m: acts on any
ground. *D. H. Barons*

IN NO DOUBT 4 b.g. Precocious – Global Lady (Balliol) [1992/3 17g⁴
16d² 17s] unfurnished gelding: poor maiden on Flat: best effort over hurdles 101
when second in juvenile event at Haydock in December: ran as though
something amiss following month. *J. J. O'Neill*

INTARSIA 9 b.g. Smartset – London Fancy (London Gazette) [1992/3 c– §
c19vᴿ] strong, workmanlike gelding: poor novice hurdler/chaser: seems –
not to stay 3m: blinkered once, visored twice: has refused twice. *R.
Williams*

INTEC (NZ) 7 b.g. Sir Avon (NZ) – Ride The Storm (NZ) (Crest of The c82
Wave) [1992/3 c21m² c28fᵖᵘ] fair pointer: second in novice hunter chase at
Newton Abbot in May. *W. W. Dennis*

INTEGRITY BOY 6 b.g. Touching Wood (USA) – Powderhall (Murray- c–
field) [1992/3 c21gᵖᵘ] small, leggy gelding: winning selling hurdler: showed –
nothing in October on chasing debut: suited by further than 2m, and stays
3m: best form with give in the ground and acts on soft: usually blinkered
over hurdles. *R. O'Leary*

Fairview New Homes Novices' Chase, Ascot—Indian Tonic makes all and jumps well

Tote Eider Handicap Chase, Newcastle—
a thorough test of stamina brings out the best in Into The Red

INTERIM LIB 10 b.g. Lighter – Ballinew (New Brig) [1992/3 c20g⁵ **c115**
c24m* c25g² c20g² c27d⁵ c20d³ c20g² c22f c20g³ c23dᵖᵘ c24f³] tall, leggy —
gelding: fairly useful handicap chaser: won at Newcastle in October:
creditable efforts most subsequent starts: broke blood vessel penultimate
outing, tailed off last: effective at 2m, barely stays 25f: acts on any going:
takes a good hold and usually races up with pace: jumps well: amateur or
claimer ridden: tough and genuine. *Mrs S. C. Bradburne*

INTERNAL AFFAIR 5 gr.m. Aragon – Alicia Markova (Habat) [1992/3
17dᵖᵘ] poor form at around 1m on Flat: no promise in November on hurdling —
debut. *C. Cowley*

INTERPRETATION (NZ) 7 b.g. Uncle Remus (NZ) – Misinterprate **c102**
(NZ) (None Better) [1992/3 c20m* c21mᶠ c22s² c21fᵖᵘ] close-coupled —
gelding: winning hurdler: successful on chasing debut in novice event at
Ludlow in October: good second in similar race at Fakenham in December:
ran as though something amiss only subsequent outing: stays 2¾m: acts on
good to firm and soft ground: blinkered last 2 starts. *N. J. Henderson*

IN THE CREASE (USA) 5 b.g. Sportin' Life (USA) – Crinoline
(Blakeney) [1992/3 F17g] rangy, good-looking gelding: has plenty of scope: —
second foal: dam, 1½m winner who stayed 2m, is out of half-sister to good
sprinter Shiny Tenth: behind in NH Flat race at Newbury in March: yet to
race over hurdles or fences. *N. J. Henderson*

IN THE FASHION 11 br.g. Never Slip – Smashing Style (Harwell) **c–**
[1992/3 c25g⁵ c26dᵖᵘ c26sᵖᵘ c26gᵖᵘ] leggy, close-coupled gelding: fair 3m —
chaser at best: has lost his form completely. *Mrs H. Bell*

IN THE GAME (IRE) 4 b.f. Mummy's Game – Carado (Manado)
[1992/3 17s 17m 16d 17f⁶] leggy, sparely-made filly: modest handicapper on —
Flat, stays 7f and goes well on equitrack (sometimes looks temperamental):
changed hands 740 gns Newmarket Autumn Sales: well beaten over
hurdles. *Miss A. J. Whitfield*

IN THE SPOTLIGHT (IRE) 5 b.h. The Noble Player (USA) – On Her Own (Busted) [1992/3 22d⁴ 20g² 16f⁵ 22g 22mᵖᵘ] angular horse: selling hurdler: stays 2½m: acts on dead and firm going: best blinkered. *R. Curtis* 73

IN THE ZONE 8 b.g. Martinmas – Modom (Compensation) [1992/3 a16g³ c21d³ c18g⁴ c19sᵖᵘ c21dᵖᵘ c19f*] big gelding: novice hurdler: easily best effort over fences when winning novice event at Fontwell in May: stays 19f: best efforts on firm and good to firm going. *W. G. R. Wightman* c91
82

INTO THE FUTURE 6 b.g. Mummy's Game – Valley Farm (Red God) [1992/3 18m 16g⁴ 16m⁵ 17d² 16d⁴ 16g 16m 18v³] small, rather sparely-made gelding: selling hurdler: ran creditably most starts in 1992/3: stays 2¼m: probably acts on any going: successful blinkered and not. *A. P. Stringer* 78

INTO THE RED 9 ch.g. Over The River (FR) – Legal Fortune (Cash And Courage) [1992/3 c26d⁴ c27v⁴ c30d* c29v² c33g* c34d²] fairly useful handicap chaser: in good form in 1992/3 and won at Newcastle in January and February (Tote Eider Chase, from Ushers Island): very good second in Midlands National at Uttoxeter in March: stays extremely well: acts on heavy going: jumps soundly. *J. White* c124
–

INTO THE TREES 9 b.g. Over The River (FR) – Diana's Flyer (Charlottesvilles Flyer) [1992/3 c20m² c20s* c25gᵇᵈ c24m* c24m⁴ c24gᶠ c25d⁴ c24g c20fᵖᵘ c22m³ c23m⁶] lengthy gelding: winning hurdler: easy winner of novice chases at Market Rasen and Newcastle in first half of season: only modest judged on form in second half: stays 3m: acts on soft and good to firm going: blinkered once: amateur ridden. *R. Tate* c90 +
–

INTREPID FORT 4 br.g. Belfort (FR) – Dauntless Flight (Golden Mallard) [1992/3 18g 16g] tall, lengthy, sparely-made gelding: poor maiden on Flat: poor form in seller on second outing over hurdles. *B. W. Murray* 59

INTREPID LASS 6 b.m. Wassl – Risk All (Run The Gantlet (USA)) [1992/3 24v⁵ 26d] sparely-made mare: novice hurdler: easily better effort of season when fifth at Leicester in January: stays 3m: acts on heavy ground. *H. Candy* 80

INTRICACY 5 b.m. Formidable (USA) – Baffle (Petingo) [1992/3 17d⁴] half-sister to useful hurdler Castle Secret (by Castle Keep): fair handicapper on Flat, winner at 1¾m in 1992: last of 4 finishers in novice hurdle at Sandown in February. *C. C. Elsey* 73

IN TRUTH 5 ch.g. Dreams To Reality (USA) – Persian Express (Persian Bold) [1992/3 20g 16s⁶ 16s² 16d 18g* 18s³ 20m⁵] rather sparely-made gelding: poor handicapper on Flat, stays 1½m: won novice hurdle at Southwell in March: creditable efforts at Market Rasen afterwards: stays 2½m: acts on good to firm and soft ground. *J. P. Leigh* 101

INVERINATE 8 b.g. Lomond (USA) – Major Concession (Major Portion) [1992/3 21d 26d 21s⁴ 28s⁶ c23dᶠ 26sᵖᵘ c23gᶠ] sturdy gelding: winning hurdler: fell both starts over fences: suited by a test of stamina: has won on good to firm going, goes particularly well on heavy: best with forcing tactics: often amateur ridden: blinkered last 3 starts: unreliable. *L. Lungo* c–
93 §

INVERTIEL 9 b.g. Sparkling Boy – Phyl's Pet (Aberdeen) [1992/3 16g c17vᵖᵘ c17sᶠ 16g³ 16g⁶ 20s⁵ 16d⁵ c16d] workmanlike gelding: modest hurdler: poor novice chaser: best form at 2m: acts on firm ground. *P. Monteith* c–
96

INVISIBLE ARMOUR 4 gr.g. Precocious – Haunting (Lord Gayle (USA)) [1992/3 17m²] poor middle-distance maiden on Flat: second of 9 finishers in juvenile hurdle at Perth in August. *P. C. Haslam* 85

INVITE D'HONNEUR (NZ) 11 ch.g. Guest of Honour (NZ) – Jillian's Joy (NZ) (Khan Sahib) [1992/3 17sᵖᵘ 21v 21d³ 22g² 22gᵘʳ 26d* 21m⁴] sturdy gelding: modest hurdler: won selling handicap (bought in 3,000 gns) at Cartmel in May: good fourth in similar race at Uttoxeter later in month: stays 3¼m: acts on good to firm and dead ground: blinkered once. *C. D. Broad* 87

I PERCEIVE 6 b.g. Vision (USA) – Wavetree (Realm) [1992/3 20g] half-brother to several winners, including hurdler Military Salute (by Sandhurst Prince): fair performer but unreliable on Flat, winner 3 times at – p up to 1½m in 1992: showed some promise in novice hurdle at Doncaster in December, but wasn't seen out again. *F. H. Lee*

IRENE LOCK 5 b.g. Lock And Load (USA) – Porto Irene (Porto Bello) [1992/3 18m⁴] lightly raced and no sign of ability on Flat: remote fourth in novice selling hurdle at Exeter in September. *D. C. Tucker* —

IRIDOPHANES 7 ch.g. Import – Grouse (March Past) [1992/3 c21m⁴] big, rangy gelding: behind in NH Flat race in 1990/1: poor maiden pointer: well beaten in novice hunter chase in May. *Mrs P. Robeson* c–

IRISH BAY 7 b.g. Derrylin – Sea Kestrel (Sea Hawk II) [1992/3 16v* 21s⁵ 17d⁴ 22m* 21mᵖᵘ 24d⁶] sturdy, good sort: chasing type: fair hurdler: won novice events at Towcester in December and Fontwell in February: creditable sixth at Ascot in April: probably stays 3m: acts on good to firm and heavy ground. *N. J. Henderson* 108

IRISH DITTY (USA) 6 ch.g. Irish River (FR) – Devon Ditty (Song) [1992/3 16d⁶ 16s³ 17g⁶ 16s* 16d* 17g³ 17gᵖᵘ] neat gelding: modest hurdler: won handicaps at Catterick in January and February: ran creditably next start, poorly last: races only at around 2m: acts on good to firm and soft ground: front runner. *K. A. Morgan* 96

IRISH EMERALD 6 b.g. Taufan (USA) – Gaelic Jewel (Scottish Rifle) [1992/3 17d²] fair handicap hurdler: creditable second at Bangor in October: wasn't seen out again: likely to prove best at 2m: acts on good to firm and dead ground. *G. C. Bravery* 113

IRISH GENT 7 br.g. Andretti – Seana Sheo (Seana Sgeal) [1992/3 c23gᴿ c25v²] workmanlike gelding: modest winning hurdler: second in novice chase at Hexham in November: sold 12,500 gns in May: suited by a test of stamina: acts on good to firm and heavy ground. *W. A. Stephenson* c89 —

IRISH LIL 6 b.m. Paddy's Stream – Thistle Blue (Lepanto (GER)) [1992/3 17d⁶ 17d 23sᵖᵘ 18v 18g] lengthy mare: tailed off in novice hurdles. *M. J. Smith* —

IRISH STAMP (IRE) 4 b.g. Niniski (USA) – Bayazida (Bustino) [1992/3 17v] half-brother to winning chaser Baladiya (by Darshaan): fairly useful at up to 1¾m on Flat, winner in 1992: showed ability in well-contested juvenile hurdle at Cheltenham in December, but wasn't seen out again. *J. Pearce* 91

IRISH TAN 6 br.g. Tanfirion – Anglesea Market (Sea Hawk II) [1992/3 16g 17g] modest novice hurdler at his best: yet to race much beyond 2m. *A. R. Aylett* —

IRISH VELVET 7 b.g. Ballacashtal (CAN) – Normandy Velvet (Normandy) [1992/3 16f⁵ c21f* c22fF] good-topped gelding: of little account on Flat: won novice event at Worcester in May on steeplechasing debut: fell 4 out next time: showed some promise in novice selling hurdle on first start: stays 21f: acts on firm ground. *R. G. Frost* c88 p – p

IRON BARON (IRE) 4 b.c. Sure Blade (USA) – Riverine (FR) (Riverman (USA)) [1992/3 a16g⁶] half-brother to winning hurdler Perjury (by Try My Best): modest middle-distance performer on Flat: showed nothing in juvenile hurdle at Lingfield in February: sold 6,200 gns Ascot 2nd June Sales. *R. Hollinshead* —

IRON PRINCE 7 gr.g. General Ironside – Pry Princess (Pry) [1992/3 c23g c23gᵖᵘ c23dF³ c25vᵖᵘ c23d c25gᵖᵘ 22gᵖᵘ] big, strong gelding: poor novice hurdler/chaser: trained until after sixth start by K. Oliver: stays 2½m: poor jumper of fences. *A. C. Whillans* c– x

ISABEAU 6 b.m. Law Society (USA) – Elodie (USA) (Shecky Greene (USA)) [1992/3 21g* 22f² 24d²] neat mare: fair hurdler: didn't have to be anywhere near her best to win amateur riders event at Southwell in August: better efforts when second at Worcester in September and Hexham in October: best at 2½m to 3¼m: acts on good to firm and heavy going: usually held up: visored once in 1991/2. *K. A. Morgan* 108

ISHRAAQ (USA) 5 ch.g. Alydar (USA) – Water Lily (FR) (Riverman (USA)) [1992/3 17v⁵ 18s⁵ 17g⁵ 22g 16m 17f²] close-coupled gelding: brother to Grade 1 stakes winner Talinum and half-brother to other Flat winners, notably useful Gharam (by Green Dancer): dam very useful French 2-y-o, subsequently winner in USA: poor form in 2 races on Flat for D. Weld in Ireland: best effort over hurdles when second of 12 finishers in selling handicap at Huntingdon in May: acts on firm going: blinkered last 3 starts. *R. Akehurst*   81

ISLAND DESERT (IRE) 5 b.m. Green Desert (USA) – Salote (USA) (Forli (ARG)) [1992/3 17m 18f⁵] leggy mare: of little account: has been tried blinkered and visored. *R. Callow*   –

ISLAND GALE 8 br.g. Strong Gale – Island Varra (Deep Run) [1992/3 c25g³ c24m² c24m⁶ c25g³ c24d³ c25s² c25d⁶ c24d c25f⁴] big, rangy gelding: poor novice hurdler/chaser: stays 25f: acts on any ground. *D. McCune*   c84 –

ISLAND JETSETTER 7 ch.g. Tolomeo – Baridi (Ribero) [1992/3 c16g c16s⁴ c20g c16d³ c16g⁴ a16g⁵ c18s² c16g³ c16f³ c16m* c17f⁵] rangy, angular gelding: fair handicap chaser: won at Southwell in May: tailed off over hurdles sixth start: takes good hold and unlikely to stay much beyond 2m: probably acts on any ground: sometimes wears tongue strap: races up with pace. *Mrs S. J. Smith*   c101 –

ISLAND JEWEL 5 ch.g. Jupiter Island – Diamond Talk (Counsel) [1992/3 17sᶠ 16d 16s⁴ 16v⁴ 16v* 16g] leggy gelding: lucky winner of novice handicap hurdle at Towcester in February: will stay beyond 17f: acts on heavy ground: visored once (ran creditably). *J. R. Bosley*   84

ISLAND PEARL 13 ch.g. Gulf Pearl – Island Woman (King's Troop) [1992/3 26sᵖᵘ 22d 17d⁶ c24mᵖᵘ] leggy, lightly-made gelding: winning hurdler/poor novice chaser: stayed 2¾m: acted on firm and good to soft ground: dead. *W. T. Kemp*   c– –

ISLE-O-VALLA 7 br.m. Fitzpatrick – Island More (Mugatpura) [1992/3 17s⁴ 18d c17v² c18sᵖᵘ] lengthy mare: novice hurdler/chaser: acted on heavy ground: dead. *T. B. Hallett*   c79 –

ISOBAR 7 b.g. Another Realm – Lady Eton (Le Dieu d'Or) [1992/3 27m⁵ 22m 26s² 24f⁶ 20m 20m 26m] neat gelding: handicap hurdler/chaser: easily best effort over hurdles in 1992/3 when second at Cartmel in August: stays 3¼m: acts on any going: has run blinkered or visored (not since 1990/1): sometimes looks none too keen. *M. C. Chapman*   c– 88

ISSYIN 6 ch.g. Oats – Spiders Web (Big Deal) [1992/3 c17v³ c16s² c17sᶠ] tall, angular gelding with scope: second foal: dam most genuine and consistent chaser in her prime, effective from 2m to 3m: showed ability in novice chases at Hexham and Wetherby in December: fell heavily following month, and wasn't seen out again: will stay beyond 17f: acts on heavy ground: sketchy jumper. *M. W. Easterby*   c87 –

ITALIAN TOUR 13 ch.g. Coliseum – Follow Me (Guide) [1992/3 21d 22g a21g 26d] big, lengthy gelding: winning hurdler: no worthwhile form in 1992/3: maiden chaser: stays 2¾m: acts on good to firm ground. *Mrs G. S. Plowright*   c– –

ITHKURNI (USA) 4 b.f. Green Forest (USA) – Queen's Visit (Top Command (USA)) [1992/3 17g] leggy filly: lightly-raced maiden on Flat, modest form at best: showed nothing in novice hurdle at Newbury in February. *P. Hayward*   –

ITS A CRACKER 9 b.g. Over The River (FR) – Bob's Hansel (Prince Hansel) [1992/3 16d⁶ 19d³ 24s⁴ c20v⁴ c20v² c22d² c24sᵇᵈ c16v² c21d⁴ c25m³] leggy gelding: fairly useful handicap hurdler: has also shown plenty of ability over fences: jumped deliberately and well behind until running on in latter stages when third to Young Hustler in Sun Alliance Chase at Cheltenham in March on last start: stays 25f: acts on good to firm and heavy going: sure to win a race over fences. *J. A. Berry, Ireland*   c122 116

ITS A DEAL 7 b.g. Lochnager – J J Caroline (Track Spare) [1992/3 c27g² c25sᶠ] brother to winning hurdler/chaser J J Jimmy: dam ran twice at 2 yrs: c76 second of 3 in hunter chase at Sedgefield in February: close up when falling 6 out in similar company at Hexham 2 months later. *S. I. Pittendrigh*

ITS ALL OVER NOW 9 b.g. Martinmas – Devon Lark (Take A Reef) [1992/3 a20g4 20m 17d4 17f] workmanlike gelding: poor and inconsistent hurdler: stays a sharp 2¼m: acts on firm ground: often blinkered or visored: sometimes looks temperamental. *Mrs A. L. M. King*   81 §

ITS ALL VERY FINE 12 ch.g. Deep Run – Flat Refusal (Raise You Ten) [1992/3 c16s6] lengthy, good-quartered gelding: winning chaser: behind in conditional jockeys handicap in October: poor form in points in 1993: stays 3¼m: acts on soft and good to firm going: usually jumps well. *J. Perrett*   c–

ITS GRAND 4 b.g. Sula Bula – Light of Zion (Pieces of Eight) [1992/3 F17d] third live foal: half-brother to a poor animal by New Member: dam poor plater on Flat and over hurdles: behind in NH Flat race at Ascot in April: yet to race over hurdles. *R. J. Manning*

ITS NEARLY TIME 10 b.g. Newski (USA) – Lavenanne (Tacitus) [1992/3 c16v* c16v* c20d2 c17sF c16g2] workmanlike gelding: fairly useful chaser: comfortable winner of handicaps at Uttoxeter (trained until after then by Mrs R. Brackenbury) in December and Warwick in January: good second at Chepstow and Worcester subsequently: effective at 2m and stays 2¾m: acts on heavy going and not discredited on good to firm: genuine: usually sound jumper. *P. F. Nicholls*   c118 –

IT'S NOT MY FAULT (IRE) 5 b.g. Red Sunset – Glas Y Dorlan (Sexton Blake) [1992/3 16s 18v4 16v3 17v3 18v2 16v3 a20g2 16s2 22m5 22s* 22s3 25g4] small, light-framed gelding: showed more resolution than usual when dead-heating for first place in novice selling hurdle at Ludlow (no bid) in April: suited by a test of stamina: acts on heavy ground and fibresand: sometimes blinkered. *D. J. Wintle*   79 §

IT'S SO (USA) 7 b.h. Vaguely Noble – Halo Dotty (USA) (Halo (USA)) [1992/3 24spu 25spu 18s 21spu 21vur] ex-Irish horse: handicap hurdler: no form in Britain: stays 2½m: acts on good to firm and soft ground: blinkered last outing. *W. G. Turner*   –

IT'S THE PITS 6 b.g. Tender King – Pithead (High Top) [1992/3 17d3 21s* 17g2 21g*] sturdy gelding: won maiden hurdle at Perth in April and novice event at Hexham in May: will stay beyond 21f: acts on soft going: should improve further. *L. Lungo*   102 p

IT'S VARADAN 9 ch.h. Rabdan – Miss Casanova (Galivanter) [1992/3 20v5 18v5 16v6 17g4 17d* 16dF 17d3 16g 21m] lightly-made, close-coupled horse: moderate handicap hurdler: narrow winner at Stratford in February: creditable effort 2 outings later, well beaten last 2: best at around 2m: acts on heavy going. *T. J. Etherington*   100

ITYFUL 7 gr.g. Bellypha – Tants (Vitiges (FR)) [1992/3 c21m3 c16m5 c16m6 c20dpu c20spu c20g* c20g* c24g3 c20gpu] big, leggy gelding: modest chaser: won maiden and novice event at Edinburgh in December and January: creditable third on same course in February: stays 3m: visored last 6 outings. *B. E. Wilkinson*   c94 –

IVANOV (USA) 5 b.h. Nijinsky (CAN) – Fine Spirit (USA) (Secretariat (USA)) [1992/3 20m 18gpu] lengthy horse: novice hurdler: no show in 1992/3 (broke blood vessel when favourite for seller on second occasion). *J. White*   –

IVEAGH LAD 7 br.g. Irish Star – Lady McQuaid (Mick McQuaid) [1992/3 F16g4 c17f3 c20s3 c18g3 c17g3 c24m4 c21g] rangy ex-Irish gelding: poor maiden hurdler/chaser: trained until after first outing by I. Ferguson, next 4 by J. Jenkins: won a point in April: may prove best at distances short of 3m: acts on firm ground. *Miss J. Sawney*   c76 –

IVE CALLED TIME 5 b.h. Sergeant Drummer (USA) – Alice Rairthorn (Romany Air) [1992/3 aF16g] second foal: dam winning pointer: soundly beaten in NH Flat race at Southwell in February: yet to race over hurdles or fences. *P. F. Nicholls*

IVINGHOE 5 b.g. Taufan (USA) – Upper Sister (Upper Case (USA)) [1992/3 17sᵖᵘ 16f] neat gelding: no sign of ability in 2 runs on Flat and 2 over hurdles: sold 1,100 gns Ascot May Sales. *Mrs H. Fullerton* —

IVOR'S FLUTTER 4 b.g. Beldale Flutter (USA) – Rich Line (High Line) [1992/3 17d⁴ 17s² 17g³ 16g 17m] leggy, angular gelding: fairly useful middle-distance stayer on Flat: has also shown plenty of ability over hurdles, best efforts when second in well-contested juvenile event at Cheltenham in January and staying-on eighth of 25 in Daily Express Triumph Hurdle on same course in March on last start: will be well suited by 2½m: acts on good to firm and soft going: blinkered fourth start: needs plenty of driving: should win races over hurdles. *D. R. C. Elsworth* 126

IVORS GUEST 7 b.g. Be My Guest (USA) – Ivor's Date (USA) (Sir Ivor) [1992/3 21v c23vᶠ c16s³ c21s² c16d⁶ 25fᵖᵘ] leggy gelding: one-time fairly useful hurdler: pulled up lame on last start: moderate form at best in novice chases: probably stays 2½m: probably acts on any going: usually blinkered or visored: none too keen: sketchy jumper of fences. *R. Lee* c88 §
— §

IVYCHURCH (USA) 7 ch.g. Sir Ivor – Sunday Purchase (USA) (T V Lark) [1992/3 22m⁵ 22m² c21s³ c27s⁴ c21m⁴ c21s⁶ c26dᵖᵘ 22d 22g c21fᵖᵘ] strong gelding: carries condition: poor novice hurdler/chaser: stays 25f: yet to race on extremes of going, acts on any other: blinkered sixth and seventh starts (trained by M. Pipe). *J. Joseph* c76
76

IVY HOUSE (IRE) 5 b.g. Orchestra – Gracious View (Sir Herbert) [1992/3 F17d] half-brother to fair staying hurdler/chaser Banker's Gossip (by Le Bavard) and useful chaser The Gooser (by Torus): dam won 2½m hurdle in Ireland: well beaten in NH Flat race at Carlisle in April: yet to race over hurdles or fences. *J. J. O'Neill*

IXOR (FR) 9 ch.g. Yours – Brouette (FR) (Makalu) [1992/3 c24gᵖᵘ] lengthy gelding: fair pointer: moderate handicap chaser: stayed 3m: acted on good to soft ground: dead. *C. T. Nash* c—
—

J

JACK BE BRIEF 8 b.g. Duky – Golden Mela (Golden Love) [1992/3 c24dᵖᵘ] tall gelding: first foal: dam won a point and finished in frame in a maiden hurdle in Ireland: jumped poorly in novice chase at Windsor in January on debut. *R. Rowe* c—

JACK DIAMOND 5 ch.g. Seven Hearts – Barlinnie Blossom (Broadmoor) [1992/3 aF16g⁶ 16v³ 22gᵖᵘ 16mʳᵒ 16fᵖᵘ] second foal: dam showed nothing in 2 points: no sign of ability. *Mrs R. Williams* —

JACK DWYER 9 br.g. Mr Fordette – Daraheen Gate (Arcticeelagh) [1992/3 c21m⁶] angular, close-coupled gelding: maiden hurdler: modest pointer: has shown nothing in steeplechases: poor jumper. *M. J. R. Bannister* c— x
—

JACK PRESTO 5 ch.g. Cisto (FR) – Haselbech (Spartan General) [1992/3 20dᵖᵘ] third foal: half-brother to winning pointer Sam Pepper (by Turn Back The Time): dam placed in points: tailed off when pulled up in novice selling hurdle in April on debut. *Mrs S. M. Farr* —

JACK'S BARN 9 b.g. St Columbus – Dane Hole (Past Petition) [1992/3 23d c20dᵖᵘ c24d⁵ c24g² c22m⁵] rather leggy gelding: poor novice hurdler/chaser: stays 3m: visored last 3 outings. *J. R. Bosley* c75
—

JACK SNIPE 6 br.g. Shaab – Florence Court (Le Patron) [1992/3 18d 17s³ 16d⁵ 18s⁵ c16v⁴ c22vᶠ c20f⁶] good-bodied gelding: poor novice hurdler: has shown little over fences: probably stays 2½m: acts on any going. *R. G. Frost* c—
78

JACKSON FLINT 5 b.g. Nishapour (FR) – Scamperdale (French Beige) [1992/3 17g 21s² 20m*] good-bodied gelding: fairly useful performer on Flat, stays 1¾m: first race for 3½ months, confidently ridden, idled run-in when 96 p

Yorkshire Handicap Hurdle, Doncaster—Jakarrdi quickens away from Dari Sound

winning novice hurdle at Doncaster in March: stays 21f: acts on good to firm and soft going: should progress. *H. Thomson Jones*

JACKSON SQUARE (IRE)   5 b.g. Prince Tenderfoot (USA) – Double Habit (Double Form) [1992/3 16g] lengthy gelding: lightly raced and no form on Flat: behind in novice hurdle at Worcester in September. *W. G. M. Turner* —

JACK THE HIKER   10 b.g. Rare One – Royal Dress (Perspex) [1992/3 c17m³ c17s⁴ c17s* c16sᵖᵘ 17fᵖᵘ] big, close-coupled, workmanlike gelding: modest chaser: best effort when winning conditional jockeys selling handicap at Newton Abbot (no bid) in October: sold out of R. Baker's stable 625 gns Ascot March Sales after next outing: best at around 2m: acts on any going: reportedly breaks blood vessels: sketchy jumper. *Mrs J. Wonnacott* **c86** —

JADEHARA   6 b.m. Crystal Glitters (USA) – Jawhara (Upper Case (USA)) [1992/3 17gᵖᵘ 21sᵖᵘ] good-topped mare: fourth foal: half-sister to fairly useful 2-y-o winners Jad (by Riboboy) and Garnet (by Thatch): dam won from 5f to 7f: looked thoroughly ungenuine in early-season novice hurdles. *D. Burchell* §§

JADIDH   5 b.m. Touching Wood (USA) – Petrol (Troy) [1992/3 18m³ 22s* 22v³ 25s³ 23s⁶ 25v 16v³ 16d⁴ 20d² 20g* 22m² 18g³ 22d] sparely-made mare: modest hurdler: generally ran creditably in 1992/3: won handicaps at Newton Abbot (amateurs) in October and Taunton (mares) in March: effective at around 2½m and stays 25f: acts on good to firm and heavy ground: occasionally blinkered, visored once: usually soon off bridle, and is a difficult ride. *Mrs J. C. Dawe* 95

JAILBREAKER   6 ch.g. Prince of Peace – Last Farewell (Palm Track) [1992/3 18v⁶ 17v⁵ 21s² 21v³ c17s* c16g⁵ c27v* c27d⁵] leggy, close-coupled gelding: fair hurdler: ran creditably when placed at Warwick and Leicester **c107** 110

384

in January: won handicap chase in February and novice chase (made all) in April, both at Newton Abbot: effective at 17f and stays very well: acts on heavy ground. *B. R. Millman*

JAKARRDI   7 ch.g. Torus – Honey Come Back (Master Owen) [1992/3 18v² 16s² 21v² 22d⁴ 20g* 20d 26m² 25f⁵] lengthy gelding: chasing type: useful handicap hurdler: won at Doncaster in January: good second to Fissure Seal in valuable event at Cheltenham in March: stays 3¼m: acts on good to firm going, probably on heavy. *Mrs J. Pitman*   131

JALINGO   6 ch.g. Jalmood (USA) – Linguistic (Porto Bello) [1992/3 16v⁴] leggy gelding: lightly-raced fair hurdler: respectable fourth in handicap at Wincanton in January: should stay further than 2m: needs give in the ground, and acts well on heavy. *P. J. Makin*   102

JALORE   4 gr.g. Jalmood (USA) – Lorelene (FR) (Lorenzaccio) [1992/3 a22g a20g] small gelding: half-brother to winning hurdler/chaser Leon (by Niniski): poor form at around 1¾m on Flat: well beaten over hurdles in January. *R. Hollinshead*   –

JAMES MY BOY   13 ch.g. Jimmy Reppin – College Brief (Lucky Brief) [1992/3 c17d² c21s* c20gᵘʳ c21s* c21s³ c20sᵘʳ] strong, workmanlike gelding: winning hurdler: modest chaser: won handicaps at Bangor in November (novices) and December: not seen out after January: stays 21f: acts on heavy going. *M. D. Hammond*   c93 –

JAMES THE FIRST   5 ch.g. Wolver Heights – Juliette Mariner (Welsh Pageant) [1992/3 17m* 17d* 16d² 17s⁶ 17d* 16d* 17g³ 17g] lengthy gelding: fair hurdler: successful in novice events at Stratford and Hereford in first half of season and handicaps at Wolverhampton and Haydock (novices) in February: will stay at least 2½m: acts on good to firm and probably on soft going: should make up into a useful handicapper. *P. F. Nicholls*   108 p

JAMESTOWN BOY   5 b.g. King of Clubs – Jhansi Ki Rani (USA) (Far North (CAN)) [1992/3 17m³ 16g⁴ 17d⁵ 17d² 16d⁶ 17s* a16g² 22m 17g 17m 16d⁵ 17f²] leggy, angular gelding: modest hurdler: won seller at Bangor (bought in 2,250 gns) in November: good second in claimer at Stratford in June, easily best subsequent effort: best at around 2m: probably acts on any going: usually blinkered: not one to rely on. *B. Preece*   94 §

JAMMY JIMMY   5 gr.g. Slim Jim – Katie Grey (Pongee) [1992/3 F16d 16g] third foal: brother to fair hurdler Mils Mij: dam winning hurdler: showed nothing in NH Flat race and a novice hurdle at Hexham in March. *J. Hurst*   –

JAM TOMORROW   7 b.g. Kemal (FR) – Peter's Pet (Bahrain) [1992/3 21m 23g² 21s⁶ 21s⁵ c25f⁵] good-topped gelding: poor novice hurdler: modest last of 5 finishers in novice event at Wetherby in May on chasing debut: stays 25f: probably acts on any going. *Mrs S. A. Bramall*   c84 77

JANE'S DELIGHT   9 b.g. Royal Palace – Violate (Continuation) [1992/3 16d c23vᵖᵘ c19sᵖᵘ] strong, compact gelding: winning hurdler: poor novice chaser: stays 2½m: acts on good to firm and dead ground. *Mrs A. Price*   c–

JANET SCIBS   7 b.m. Dubassoff (USA) – Luckley Brake (Quiet Fling (USA)) [1992/3 17s⁴ 17v⁴ 20s 17v⁶ a18gᵘʳ 17d 20m⁶ 26s] small mare: poor novice hurdler: stays 2½m: acts on soft and good to firm going. *N. G. Ayliffe*   72

JAN-RE   9 ch.g. Deep Run – Khalketta (Khalkis) [1992/3 c17fᵖᵘ] leggy, workmanlike gelding: moderate hurdler: broke down run-in in novice chase at Huntingdon (led eighth until last) in September, and wasn't seen out again: stays 2½m: acts on dead ground: broke blood vessel second start. *F. Murphy*   c–

JANUARY DON   8 b.g. Hold Your Peace (USA) – Meg's Pride (Sparkler) [1992/3 c26mᵘʳ c28fᵖᵘ] smallish, angular gelding: novice hunter chaser: stays 25f: acts on dead ground: sometimes blinkered: ungenuine. *J. S. Warner*   c– §

JARRAS   8 b.g. Touching Wood (USA) – Hilary's Hut (Busted) [1992/3 17g] sturdy gelding: winning hurdler, very lightly raced nowadays: 65

blinkered, showed he retains some ability when eighth in seller at Hereford in September: seemed not quite to stay 2 1f in testing conditions: acts on soft going. *C. A. Smith*

JARRWAH 5 ch.m. Niniski (USA) – Valiancy (Grundy) [1992/3 17v a22g a20g3 a20g* a24g2 a24g* 21spu] sparely-made mare: much improved form when winning 2 handicap hurdles at Lingfield in second half of season, awarded first one: ran poorly returned to turf last outing: effective at 2½m to 3m: acts well on equitrack. *J. L. Spearing* — 95

JARZON DANCER 5 br.g. Lidhame – Long Valley (Ribero) [1992/3 16spu 16v5 16s5 20v 16v2 18g2 17m2 17f4 20f6 22fpu 17f5] smallish, leggy gelding: poor maiden on Flat and over hurdles: stays 2¼m: acts on any ground. *D. A. Wilson* — 71

JASMIN PATH 8 ro.m. Warpath – Jasmin (Frankincense) [1992/3 18m5 22m3 23m4 18s* 20g6 20f5 17f6 18m5 16s] leggy, lengthy mare: moderate hurdler at her best: won selling handicap at Southwell (no bid) in September: trained until after next start by J. Leigh: stays 2¾m: acts on any going: blinkered last 2 outings: irresolute (sometimes reluctant to race). *S. Gollings* — 94 §

JASON'S QUEST 9 gr.g. Golden Fleece (USA) – Carose (Caro) [1992/3 20grtr] strong gelding: one-time fairly useful hurdler: poor maiden pointer/hunter chaser: blinkered once: often refuses to race and is one to leave alone. *K. Bishop* — c§§ / §§

JATHAAB (IRE) 4 b.g. Ajdal (USA) – Etoile de Nuit (Troy) [1992/3 17m3 22dpu 18s5 16f3 18m2] close-coupled gelding: fairly useful form on Flat: sold out of M. Stoute's stable 4,000 gns Newmarket Autumn Sales: only poor form over hurdles: acts on firm and soft going: visored last outing. *I. Campbell* — 81

JATINGA (IRE) 5 .g. Bulldozer – Lady Talisman (Continuation) [1992/3 F16g F18ssu 16v F16s* 16g] leggy gelding: half-brother to winning Irish hurdler/chaser Altnabrocky (by Ovac): dam poor Irish maiden: won NH Flat race at Down Royal in December (trained until after then by J. Maxwell): no worthwhile form in novice hurdles: pulled hard and jumped none too fluently on second occasion. *M. C. Pipe* — –

JAUNTY GIG 7 b.g. Dunphy – Hazel Gig (Captain's Gig (USA)) [1992/3 28fpu] leggy gelding: fair handicap hurdler: pulled up lame in September: sold 2,600 gns in May: suited by a thorough test of stamina: acts on firm and soft ground: blinkered once in 1990/1: has run in snatches. *W. A. Stephenson* — –

JAWANI (IRE) 5 b.g. Last Tycoon – Fabled Lady (Bold Lad (IRE)) [1992/3 20m* 21g3 22f* 23m4] close-coupled gelding: plating-class stayer on Flat: won novice hurdles at Doncaster in February and Ludlow in May: stays 2¾m: acts on firm ground. *Dr J. D. Scargill* — 92

JAY AITCH 4 b.g. Lightning Dealer – Spartan Sprat (Spartan General) [1992/3 17mpu 17v6 16vpu] leggy gelding: third reported foal: dam poor novice hurdler: no sign of ability over hurdles. *C. H. Jones* — –

JAYEFFTEE 9 b.m. Ovac (ITY) – Bright Company (King's Company) [1992/3 16v6 20g] leggy mare: first foal: dam little sign of ability in Irish Flat races: well beaten in novice hurdles in April. *John R. Upson* — –

JAY JAY'S VOYAGE 10 b.g. Saunter – Traverser (Spiritus) [1992/3 a16g 17g 18g5 25mur 24gpu 20m 16f6] close-coupled gelding: poor form over hurdles: best effort over 2¼m. *Mrs J. Scrivens* — 72

JAZZY JUMPER 11 b. or br.g. Smooth Stepper – Choralgina (Choral Society) [1992/3 c21d] leggy gelding: lightly-raced chaser: blinkered and wore a tongue strap when behind in hunter chase in February: best at up to 2½m: acts on heavy going: jumps none too fluently. *J. G. O'Neill* — c–

JEASSU 10 b.g. Whistlefield – Menhaden (Menelek) [1992/3 17g5] leggy gelding: useful hurdler at his best: needed race only start in 1992/3 (October): has fallen in 4 of his 8 races over fences, but jumped soundly and — c– / –

showed fair form when completing: seems suited by around 2½m: acts on good to firm and soft going. *A. J. Wilson*

JEBALI 6 ch.g. Good Times (ITY) – Penitent (Sing Sing) [1992/3 18v 18mF] rather sparely-made gelding: disputing third when falling last in 6-runner claimer at Fontwell in February, first sign of ability over hurdles. *D. W. Browning*

?

JEFFERBY 6 b.g. Roscoe Blake – Darling Eve (Darling Boy) [1992/3 c20d4 c24sF c22s3] workmanlike gelding: winning hurdler: poor form when in frame in novice chases: mistakes prior to falling fifth in between and needs to brush up his jumping: stays 3m: acts on dead ground: often sweats: sometimes blinkered or visored: looked most reluctant final start in 1991/2. *J. A. Glover*

c76

– §

JELBLEND 11 b.g. Jellaby – Just Janie (John Splendid) [1992/3 c16g4 c20g5] big, workmanlike gelding: poor novice hurdler/chaser: stays 3m: acts on dead ground. *V. Thompson*

c–

–

JELLYBAND 5 ro.g. Baron Blakeney – General's Daughter (Spartan General) [1992/3 F17g] lengthy gelding: fifth foal: brother to poor novice hurdler Baroness Orkzy: dam poor pointer: behind in NH Flat race at Cheltenham in October: yet to race over hurdles or fences. *W. G. M. Turner*

JELLY JILL 10 ro.m. Jellaby – Petoria (Songedor) [1992/3 c17f2 c17fpu c25g3] angular, sparely-made mare: poor novice chaser: trained until after second start by R. Allan: reportedly finished lame in maiden hunter chase in April: stays 25f: sometimes blinkered. *Mrs J. Seymour*

c73

–

JELLY MORTON 8 b.g. Cure The Blues (USA) – Molly Pitcher (Hul A Hul) [1992/3 17d5 16vpu a20g2 17s] workmanlike gelding: poor maiden hurdler/chaser: creditable second in claiming hurdle on equitrack on third outing: stays 2½m: poor jumper of fences. *M. Williams*

c– x
67 +

JENDEE (IRE) 5 b.g. Dara Monarch – Bunch of Blue (Martinmas) [1992/3 21m2 25d3] leggy, close-coupled gelding: modest novice hurdler: creditable efforts at Perth in August and September: stays 25f: acts on good to firm and dead ground. *J. A. Hellens*

84

JENERATE 5 br.g. Electric – Armonit (Town Crier) [1992/3 F17d] second foal: half-brother to useful staying hurdler Gaelstrom (by Strong Gale): dam won 5 races at up to 2½m over hurdles: favourite, well beaten in NH Flat race at Ascot in April: yet to race over hurdles or fences. *N. A. Twiston-Davies*

JERVANDHA 5 b.m. Strong Gale – Belcraig (Foggy Bell) [1992/3 22spu 17spu] smallish, leggy mare: no form over hurdles. *Mrs H. Parrott*

–

JESSOP 8 b.g. Gleason (USA) – Perusia (Pirate King) [1992/3 c18d5 c27spu c16vpu c24gpu c20d c27dF] rangy, good sort: little promise over hurdles and fences. *S. Mellor*

c–
–

JESTER'S GEM 4 ch.f. Jester – Tresanna (Treboro (USA)) [1992/3 17f] maiden plater on Flat: well beaten in juvenile selling hurdle at Huntingdon in September. *B. W. Murray*

–

JESTERS PROSPECT 9 b.g. Idiot's Delight – Miss Prospect (Sweet Story) [1992/3 c20g3] leggy gelding: fair chaser in 1991/2: well below his best only outing in 1992/3 (November): effective at 2m when conditions are testing, and stays 2¾m: acts on any going but ideally suited by plenty of give: poor jumper. *Mrs J. D. Goodfellow*

c– x
–

JET 7 br.g. Gorytus (USA) – Red Berry (Great Nephew) [1992/3 17s6 20f6 18g 22s 25gur 20m] close-coupled gelding: poor novice hurdler: stays 21f: acts on good to firm and soft ground: sometimes blinkered. *C. L. Popham*

–

JET JOCKEY 4 b.g. Relkino – Fen Mist (Deep Run) [1992/3 F16s F17f F16m] unfurnished gelding: first foal: dam unraced daughter of half-sister to Cheltenham Gold Cup winner Royal Frolic: behind in NH Flat races: yet to race over hurdles. *R. C. Spicer*

JEWEL OF THE NILE 5 b.m. Glenstal (USA) – Miller's Daughter (Mill Reef (USA)) [1992/3 17g 16d] small mare: plating-class maiden at 3 yrs: – §

387

no sign of ability over hurdles in first half of season: looked reluctant in seller second occasion. *J. D. Thomas*

JIGGING 5 ch.g. Scottish Reel – Kesarini (USA) (Singh (USA)) [1992/3 18m⁴] angular gelding: selling hurdler: fourth at Market Rasen in August: gives impression will prove best at 2m. *Mrs A. L. M. King*   71

JILLY WOOD 9 gr.m. Pragmatic – Bartlemy Fair (Town Crier) [1992/3 c17vᵖᵘ c26vᵖᵘ c19d] plain, close-coupled mare: selling hurdler: no sign of ability in 5 races over fences: best effort at 2m: acts on firm ground and unsuited by a soft surface. *Dr P. Pritchard*   c–
–

JIMBALOU 10 b.g. Jimsun – Midnight Pansy (Deadly Nightshade) [1992/3 21sᶠ 22sᵖᵘ 21d⁶ 20d 23g³ 26m 24s⁵ 25m] tall, leggy, rather plain gelding: fair hurdler nowadays: barely stays 3m under testing conditions: acts on soft and good to firm ground. *R. G. Brazington*   107

JIM BOWIE 10 b.g. Yukon Eric (CAN) – Mingwyn Wood (Pirate King) [1992/3 18s c21s⁴ c27v² c26sᵖᵘ] workmanlike gelding: selling hurdler: poor novice chaser: stays 3¼m: acts on any going. *A. R. Davison*   c82
–

JIM-JOE 8 b.g. Royal Fountain – Sugar Maple (Sweet Story) [1992/3 c24gᶠ c21g⁶ c21dᵇᵈ c23d² 23s⁵ 20g⁶ a18g² a20gᶠ] good-topped gelding: poor novice hurdler/chaser: probably stays 2¾m: acts on dead ground and fibresand. *N. B. Mason*   c74
74

JIMMY MAC JIMMY 6 b.g. Carriage Way – Tuthill Bello (Porto Bello) [1992/3 16v⁶ 18s⁴ c17v* c16s² c16g c21s c17g⁴ c16gᵖᵘ c21s³ 21s⁶] lengthy, rather sparely-made gelding: winning selling hurdler: won novice chase at Hexham in December: ran creditably next time, generally well below form subsequently: effective at 2m and stays 2½m: acts on heavy going: poor jumper of fences. *Miss L. A. Perratt*   c89 x
–

JIMMY O'DEA 6 br.g. Funny Man – Premier Nell (Mandamus) [1992/3 c24mᵖᵘ c26d⁴ c24s⁴ c24dᵖᵘ c24mᶠ c25g³ c24f² c20sᵖᵘ c21vᶠ c20gᵘʳ c25m² c25m* c23m² c22f*] lengthy gelding: novice hurdler: won maiden chase at Southwell and 3-runner novice chase at Stratford late in season: stays 25f: acts on any going: visored nowadays: has been blinkered: formerly ungenuine. *T. T. Bill*   c93
–

JIMMY RIVER 10 br.g. Young Man (FR) – Mary Fox (Mummy's Pet) [1992/3 c25dᶠ c24d⁶ c25d³ c24s*] sturdy, close-coupled gelding: useful hunter chaser: beat Moorcroft Boy a head, pair distance clear, at Perth in May: stays well: acts on heavy going. *K. Anderson*   c109
–

JIMMY THE GILLIE 7 b. or br.g. Sunley Builds – Lac Royale (Lochnager) [1992/3 16d* 16d³ 17d⁴] rangy, good sort with scope: chasing type: fairly useful hurdler: won handicap at Kempton in October: good efforts at Wincanton in November and Doncaster (hung left under pressure) in December: yet to race beyond 17f: acts on good to soft and good to firm going: jumps soundly. *S. Christian*   125

JIM'S JEWEL 5 ch.m. Slim Jim – Malandot (Malicious) [1992/3 F16d] second foal: dam unplaced in NH Flat races: tailed off in NH Flat race at Catterick in November: yet to race over hurdles or fences. *T. J. Carr*

JIMS LASS 11 ch.m. Slim Jim – Highmoor Lass (Rubor) [1992/3 c23m⁴ c26g⁵ c23fᶠ c20m⁶ c24m³ c25gᶠ c27d³ c25d⁶ c26dᵘʳ] small mare: novice hurdler/chaser: jumps fences erratically. *C. W. Pinney*   c67 x
–

JIMSTER 11 b.g. Jimsun – Merry Minuet (Trumpeter) [1992/3 c24s² c21d⁶ c26m² c25m³ c25d⁶] big, strong, deep-girthed gelding: moderate handicap chaser: generally ran creditably in 1992/3: stays 3¼m: acts on good to firm and soft going: usually races prominently and jumps well. *C. T. Nash*   c94
–

JIMSTRO 8 b.g. Jimsun – Bistro Blue (Blue Streak) [1992/3 c24g* c24d⁴ c24s*] workmanlike gelding: won novice chases at Huntingdon in October and December, showing fair form: thorough stayer: acts on soft going: below form when blinkered. *J. Pearce*   c99
–

JIM'S WISH (IRE) 5 b.h. Heraldiste (USA) – Fete Champetre (Welsh Pageant) [1992/3 16m 16g 17g 17d⁶ 18mᵘʳ 16g³] smallish, sturdy horse: modest novice hurdler in 1991/2: best effort in 1992/3 when third from long way out of handicap at Hexham in May: races at around 2m: acts on good to firm going: usually blinkered nowadays. *T. A. K. Cuthbert*   81

JIM VALENTINE 7 b. or br.g. Furry Glen – Duessa (Linacre) [1992/3 c18d⁴ c20d* c17v² c21s⁴ c20g³ c20sᵖᵘ] angular, lengthy ex-Irish gelding: fourth foal: dam maiden hurdler: trained until after reappearance by G. Farrell: winning hurdler: won novice chase at Stratford in November: better efforts when placed at Newton Abbot in December and Stratford in March: effective at around 2m when conditions are testing and stays 2½m: acts on heavy going. *D. J. Wintle*   c94 –

JINGA 8 b.g. Castle Keep – Eldoret (High Top) [1992/3 18fᵇᵈ 21d⁵ 20g* 20f³] smallish, good-bodied gelding: fair handicap hurdler: won at Plumpton in March: fair third on same course later in month: stays 2¾m: acts on dead ground, probably on firm. *Lady Herries*   107

JINSKY'S JEWEL 5 b.g. Myjinski (USA) – Song of Pride (Goldhills Pride) [1992/3 17v 17d] no sign of ability. *R. Thompson*   –

JINXY JACK 9 b.g. Random Shot – True Or False (Varano) [1992/3 17m* 16g* 16d* 17d³ 16v* 17d* 17m 17f⁵ 16g⁴ 16f]   c– 155
    With the claims of a succession of young pretenders to the Champion Hurdle title looking decidedly tenuous, the run-up to Cheltenham saw some publicity given to the each-way chance of an old one in Jinxy Jack. He had beaten Coulton in the Haydock Park Champion Hurdle Trial, and in many lists Coulton was the Champion Hurdle favourite. The actual title 'Champion Hurdler' would, of course, seem something of a misnomer if held by Jinxy Jack as the art of jumping, over hurdles or fences, has not always looked his strong point. More important for his prospects was the question of merit. Jinxy Jack had performed to a similar level of form in his previous three seasons, one that did not look good enough even in 1993, and he did not have to improve on it to win at Haydock. He was receiving 3 lb from

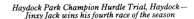

Haydock Park Champion Hurdle Trial, Haydock —
Jinxy Jack wins his fourth race of the season

Coulton, who looked some way off peak fitness, and was made favourite to register his fourth win of the season. The previous three had come in September and October in a handicap at Bangor and minor events at Kempton and Warwick—by eight, then fifteen lengths—followed by a creditable third to the favourably-treated Baydon Star in a valuable event at Aintree in November. His success at Haydock was gained in typical style. Taking a good hold, Jinxy Jack was soon at the head of affairs then, challenged by Coulton at the last, he battled back to prevail by half a length. A remote third, fourth and fifth were Royal Derbi, Ruling and Rodeo Star.

After a bloodless fourth consecutive victory in the Morebattle Hurdle (sponsored in 1993 by the Ship Hotel) at Kelso, Jinxy Jack duly took his chance at Cheltenham. Putting in an unusually good round of jumping, he led from going to the fifth and still held the advantage turning for home, but he was swallowed up shortly afterwards and eventually beaten about eleven lengths, the ninth of seventeen finishers. He ran well. He is a smart animal, and a pretty dependable one as well these days, but has a fair bit to find if he's to figure prominently in the result of a Champion Hurdle. His latest effort followed a sixth of sixteen finishers behind Kribensis and eleventh of twenty-one to Morley Street. One month later Jinxy Jack performed well again to be fourth of six to Staunch Friend in the Scottish Champion Hurdle. The only blemishes on his 1992/3 record came before and after that race, in a quite valuable handicap at Aintree and the Swinton at Haydock, on both occasions never getting to the front (having been reluctant to line up at Aintree) and not given a hard race when he was clearly held.

Jinxy Jack (b.g. 1984)	Random Shot (b 1967)	Pirate King (b 1953)	Prince Chevalier
			Netherton Maid
		Time And Chance (b 1957)	Supreme Court
			Foxtrot
	True Or False (br 1973)	Varano (b 1962)	Darius
			Varna II
		True (b or br 1964)	Straight Lad
			Parkadotia

The big, rangy Jinxy Jack is the second foal out of the Irish National Hunt Flat race and hurdle race winner True Or False. The first (by Le Bavard) had one run in an Irish point-to-point, unseating his rider, and True Or False has had only two living foals since Jinxy Jack and only one named, that being the poor novice hurdler True Dilemma (by Salluceva). Jinxy Jack is effective from two miles to two and a half, acts on good to firm and heavy ground but was well beaten on firm going in the Swinton. He was visored once in 1990/1. It was March, 1992, that Jinxy Jack last ran over fences, showing useful form, and perhaps his still rather haphazard jumping will mean that he is kept to the smaller obstacles. The latest season showed that there are still plenty of races to be won with him. *G. Richards*

J J JIMMY 9 b.g. Lochnager – J J Caroline (Track Spare) [1992/3 c16m³ c20d⁴ c20f* c21f²] small, good-topped gelding: handicap chaser: won at Chepstow in May: good second at Warwick later in month: stays 21f: acts on firm and dead ground. *S. Christian* — c97 —

JOBURN 10 b.m. Shua Jo – Glassburn (St Georg III) [1992/3 c20s⁵ c22v³ c23d⁵ c22vᵇᵈ] leggy, angular mare: poor form in novice chases: stays 2¾m: acts on heavy going. *S. E. Sherwood* — c80 —

JOCK'S BURN 7 ch.g. Paddy's Stream – Fairyslave (Arctic Slave) [1992/3 22s³ 21d* 20g* 25dF 25s⁶] smallish, sturdy gelding: made most when winning novice hurdles at Hexham (handicap) and Ayr: not seen out after November: best form at around 2½m: acts on heavy ground. *G. Richards* — 91

JODAMI 8 b.g. Crash Course – Masterstown Lucy (Bargello) [1992/3 c24s² c27s² c27s* c24v* c24d* c27m*] — c174 p —

The emergence of eight-year-old Jodami as a top-notch staying steeplechaser should have implanted fresh hope in those who talk about the decline in the standard of our best chasers. An 'old-fashioned' type of

Mandarin Handicap Chase, Newbury—Jodami comes to take it up from Esha Ness

chaser, bred for the job, Jodami is a superb jumper with excellent stamina. He went from strength to strength in the latest season, winning his final four races, his smooth victory in the Tote Cheltenham Gold Cup ensuring that 1992/3 will be remembered as Jodami's season. Jodami was virtually unopposed in the ballot for the National Hunt Horse of the Year award, receiving twenty-four of the twenty-five votes cast by the Press selection committee.

It is a generalisation of considerable merit that the best races attract the best horses and represent the best form. However, that hasn't always been so with the Cheltenham Gold Cup which—for all its prestige and for all that it is widely acknowledged as *the* championship race—has produced some surprising results over the years. There was no doubting, however, that Jodami's winning performance was right up to championship standard. He really showed his worth on the day, coming home an emphatic two-length winner from the front-running Rushing Wild after being confidently ridden. The only anxious moment came when Jodami lost his footing entering the straight as Dwyer shook him up to go in pursuit of Rushing Wild. Third-placed Royal Athlete, a top-class novice back in 1989/90 and lightly raced since, finished seven lengths further back, just in front of the King George VI Chase winner The Fellow who had been runner-up in the last two Gold Cups. Another of the up-and-coming brigade Sibton Abbey, winner of the Hennessy, came fifth and Docklands Express, third in the previous year's Gold Cup, finished sixth. The 1992 winner Cool Ground, who, in any case had been largely disappointing in the current season, was outpaced and managed only ninth. Chatam, unproven on firm going, and Run For Free, whose saddle slipped, were leading fancies who failed to give their running on the day, but Jodami deserves full credit for his Gold Cup winning display. He won with something in hand too, quickening well on the flat after his rider had allowed himself the luxury of a look round approaching the final fence. On the form-book, Jodami put up the best performance seen in the Gold Cup since Burrough Hill Lad, in 1984. Gold Cup winners often seem to find it much more difficult to stay on top than to get there—only five

*Peter Marsh Handicap Chase, Haydock—Jodami continues on the upgrade;
Run For Free is about to be overhauled this time*

horses have won the Gold Cup more than once—but Jodami almost
certainly has more improvement in him and we fully expect him to maintain
his supremacy for at least the next season. Unless illness, injury or loss of
form intervene, he could well become the first since L'Escargot in 1971 to
stage a repeat success in Cheltenham's greatest race.

Notwithstanding the poor record of favourites—only four have won in
twenty-two runnings since L'Escargot—the Gold Cup is the sort of race you
would expect to go to a form-horse. The runners meet at weight-for-sex and
most of them are fully exposed. Jodami and Rushing Wild were among those
in the field in 1993 that weren't. Both had progressed all season, particularly
Jodami who had shaped from an early stage as a horse who could win a Gold
Cup. However, even after he had won the Grade 1 Hennessy Cognac Gold
Cup at Leopardstown in February, on his first outing of the season outside
handicap company, Jodami still looked to have something to find on form
with the proven top-class performers in the Gold Cup line-up. Jodami
started the season on the mark of a useful chaser—he'd shown good form as
a novice, winning the first three of his six races—and was beaten in his first
two races, starting in the Edward Hanmer Memorial Chase, a limited
handicap at Haydock where he finished second to Run For Free. Jodami
looked sure to be better for the outing and his jumping, which wasn't all it
might have been in his first season, was most encouraging in the hands of
new jockey Mark Dwyer. A measure of the progress Jodami still had to
make to reach the top class came in his second race, the Hennessy Cognac
Gold Cup at Newbury at the end of November when Jodami just came off
worse in a close finish with Sibton Abbey, with The Fellow, conceding 25 lb
and 27 lb respectively to the first two, a magnificent third, six lengths
behind Jodami. While The Fellow went on to take his second King George
VI Chase, the mid-season staying chasers' championship, Jodami and Sibton
Abbey waited for handicaps in the New Year. Jodami started a heavily-

backed favourite for the Mandarin Chase at Newbury and, after making a mistake four out, won in workmanlike style, being brought with a well-timed run and forging ahead under pressure on the flat. Sibton Abbey came fourth the next weekend to Rushing Wild in the Anthony Mildmay, Peter Cazalet Chase at Sandown, the pair of them receiving lumps of weight from second-placed Cool Ground. Jodami was much more impressive on his final start in handicap company in the Peter Marsh Chase at Haydock at the end of January. He jumped soundly and ran on in excellent style after travelling very strongly behind front-running Run For Free all the way up the straight. Gameness, sound jumping and staying power are three highly desirable attributes in a Gold Cup prospect, and Jodami displayed them all in the Peter Marsh in which he also showed a good turn of foot for a stayer, responding well when shaken up after the last. Despite coming out second best at the weights, Jodami looked a more impressive Gold Cup prospect than runner-up Run For Free, not least because of his superior jumping. Jodami carried on in the same vein, facing his toughest task to date, in the Hennessy Cognac Gold Cup at Leopardstown where, confidently ridden, he just got the better of a level-weights duel with Chatam. The race provided an illustration of how much progress Jodami had made; Chatam had finished seven and a half lengths behind Jodami, conceding 16 lb, in the Hennessy at Newbury in November. Jodami's narrow victory had a less dramatic effect on his odds for the Gold Cup—he remained second favourite behind The Fellow at around 4/1—than the prolonged spell of dry weather leading up to the Cheltenham Festival. High pressure dominated the British weather for nearly a month and the weekend before Cheltenham most of the country was bathed in unseasonal sunshine and blue skies, which brought out most of the paraphernalia of a summer's day. In the face of considerable criticism from some sources, Cheltenham's clerk of the course Philip Arkwright had taken a calculated risk—one that proved justified—by beginning 'selective watering' at Cheltenham some time in advance of the Festival meeting. But the prospect of firm or good to firm ground changed the complexion of things as most of the Cheltenham trials had been run on an easy or a soft surface, including all the races which Jodami had contested during the

Hennessy Cognac Gold Cup, Leopardstown—a good finish in prospect; Jodami and Chatam are a distance clear

Tote Cheltenham Gold Cup, Cheltenham—Jodami crowns a fine season; Rushing Wild has a slight advantage at the last

season. Jodami eased to 8/1 on the day, joint-second favourite with Docklands Express, but he wasn't at all inconvenienced by the firmish conditions and proved that he probably acts on any going.

Jodami's Gold Cup triumph provided a famous victory for a small, family-run Yorkshire stable and was a splendid advertisement for National Hunt racing. Unlike the Flat, which is dominated by the bloodstock empires of a relatively few very wealthy owners, the winter game gives much more chance to those in racehorse ownership, or breeding, in a small way. Jodami went through the ring at Tattersalls Derby Sale for IR 12,500 guineas as a four-year-old before being bought by his trainer, a former point-to-point trainer, on a buying mission in Ireland, reportedly for around £16,000. Jodami didn't make his debut until he was five and was ridden in his first race, a bumper at Kelso which he won, by the trainer's daughter, and then, until the latest season, mostly by the trainer's son-in-law. Jodami's progress in his first season over hurdles was impressive. He was beaten only once in six outings and slammed a useful field in a novice handicap at Ayr's Scottish National meeting on his final outing. Jodami was sent chasing the next season, and the rest is history.

As we have said, Jodami is a chasing type in appearance, a deep-girthed, good sort who usually takes the eye in the paddock. He is by the now-deceased Crash Course, a high-class stayer on the Flat who has proved to be a good sire of chasers, responsible for some notable stayers including the commendably consistent Irish Grand National winner Maid of Money,

Mr J. N. Yeadon's "Jodami"

Jodami (b.g. 1985)	Crash Course (b 1971)	Busted (b 1963)	Crepello Sans Le Sou
		Lucky Stream (b 1956)	Persian Gulf Kypris
	Masterstown Lucy (b or br 1978)	Bargello (b 1960)	Auriban Isabelle Brand
		Lucille (b 1969)	Master Owen Pretty Show

the Scottish National winner Captain Dibble and the Grand National runner-up Romany King. Jodami's dam Masterstown Lucy didn't reach the racecourse but is a full sister to the fairly useful staying chaser Hurry Up Henry and a half-sister to Rugged Lucy, a tough mare successful in a National Hunt Flat race and over hurdles and fences (she won the 1981 Galway Plate) in Ireland; Jodami's grandam the unraced Lucille also bred a Norwegian Oaks winner in Lumax, who went on to be successful over jumps, and another winning Irish hurdler Bold Penny. Both Masterstown Lucy and Lucille were sired by influential jumping stallions, Bargello and Master Owen respectively. Further back, Jodami's once-raced great grandam Pretty Show, the dam of Cambridgeshire runner-up Dance All Night (herself dam of Lockinge winner Scottish Reel) was a daughter of After The Show, runner-up in the Irish One Thousand Guineas and fourth in the Irish Oaks. Jodami is the second foal of Masterstown Lucy, who has since produced five fillies, two by Crash Course and one each by Over The River, King's Ride and Satco. Jodami's year-younger full sister Crashtown Lucy won a two-mile novice chase at Thurles and was a winning point-to-pointer. *P. Beaumont*

JODY'S GAMBLE 4 b.g. Scorpio (FR) – Forgets Image (Florescence) [1992/3 16s] leggy gelding: half-brother to 3 winners, including hurdler Excavator Lady (by Most Secret): pulled up lame in seller only outing on Flat: wasn't knocked about when in rear in juvenile hurdle at Catterick in January. *G. M. Moore* —

JOE QUALITY 6 b.g. Smackover – Whangarei (Gold Rod) [1992/3 22dpu 16s a16g a20g6 20mpu 22spu] leggy gelding: of little account. *B. Preece* —

JOG-ALONG 4 b.g. Cool Guy (USA) – South Dakota (Patch) [1992/3 F16d 17f 16g] first foal: dam unraced: tailed off in NH Flat race and novice hurdles. *G. M. R. Coatsworth* —

JOGALOT 7 b.g. Lochnager – Key Harvest (Deep Diver) [1992/3 c22gpu c21spu c17gpu] strong, compact gelding: no sign of ability. *Fred Kirby* c–

JOHN CORBET 10 b.g. Ascertain (USA) – Sweet Clare (Suki Desu) [1992/3 c20f3 c24m3 c23gpu c21g*] leggy, workmanlike gelding: moderate hunter chaser: stays 21f: acts on hard ground. *Mrs Jean Brown* c83 —

JOHN NAMAN (IRE) 4 b.g. Phardante (FR) – Wolverham (Wolver Hollow) [1992/3 16d5 17s6 16g6 16d* 16d2 17g6 16g5 17m4 16g] leggy ex-Irish gelding: third foal: dam unraced: modest staying maiden on Flat: trained by W. Mullins first start: won maiden hurdle at Edinburgh in January: generally ran creditably afterwards, though well beaten in seller last outing: will stay beyond 17f: acts on dead and good to firm ground. *P. Monteith* 82

JOHNNY'S SLIPPER 8 b.g. Slippered – Mudinuri (Little Buskins) [1992/3 c24d5 c26v3] big, strong, lengthy gelding: winning chaser: tailed off in handicaps in February and April: should prove suited by good test of stamina: acts on good to firm and soft going: jumps soundly in the main. *P. Cheesbrough* c–

JOHNNY WILL 8 b.g. Salluceva – Hellfire Hostess (Lucifer (USA)) [1992/3 c17d2 c21g3 c20g5 c20s3 c17g2] sturdy gelding: fairly useful hurdler in 1990/1: fair novice chaser: stays 2½m: acts on soft going and yet to race on top-of-the-ground. *Miss H. C. Knight* c102 —

JOHN O'DEE 10 b.g. Kambalda – Lady Parkhill (Even Money) [1992/3 c22g5 c25d4 c24d3 c27dpu c21s6 c24s c24g2 c24g3 c22g4 c21g3] lengthy, rather sparely-made gelding: fair handicap chaser: poor efforts last 3 starts: stays 3¼m: acts on any going: has won when blinkered: sometimes wears tongue strap: inconsistent. *F. Murphy* c116 d —

JOHN SHAW (USA) 5 b.h. L'Emigrant (USA) – Ivory Wings (USA) (Sir Ivor) [1992/3 17s2 a16g* 16s2 a16g3 18g3 17f4 16f 18d3 20m*] compact horse: modest middle-distance stayer on Flat: similar ability over hurdles: claimed out of C. Tinkler's stable £6,300 after first outing: won novice event at Southwell in January and dead-heated for first in handicap at Market Rasen in June: stays 2½m: acts on soft, good to firm going and fibresand: wears tongue strap. *R. O'Leary* 97

JOHNS JOY 8 b.g. Martin John – Saybya (Sallust) [1992/3 17g2] one-time fair handicapper at up to 1¼m on Flat: much better effort over hurdles when second in novice event at Taunton in November. *D. R. C. Elsworth* 75

JOHNSTED 7 ch.g. Red Johnnie – Busted Love (Busted) [1992/3 17msu 18g3 18m5 21v4 20d3 a24g2 a16g* 21g* 16d 16dur 17gur a18g* 17d* 21m2] close-coupled, sparely-made gelding: won selling hurdle (no bid) and claimer at Southwell in March and sellers on same course (bought in 4,200 gns) and at Hereford (no bid) in May: effective from 2m to 3m: acts on good to firm and dead ground, and on fibresand: often blinkered (wasn't last 3 starts). *W. Clay* 94

JOHNS THE BOY 7 b.g. Kambalda – Liskennett Girl (Master Owen) [1992/3 16g] first foal: dam disqualified after winning maiden hurdle in Ireland: signs of ability, not knocked about, in novice event at Catterick in February on hurdling debut: should improve. *G. Richards* – p

JOKER JACK 8 ch.g. Garryowen – Deceptive Day (Master Buck) [1992/3 20d 17v³ 22s³ 23s⁴ 17s 18s⁴ 21s³ 18v⁵ 20v* 20v³ 20d² 22g⁵ 20g⁴ 27m* 17g³ 20s⁴ 20g³ 22f³ 26f³] leggy gelding: moderate hurdler: won handicaps at Lingfield (novices) in January and Fontwell in March: effective at 2½m and stays 27f: acts on any going: ridden up with pace: jumps well. *R. Dean* 91

JOKERS PATCH 6 ch.g. Hotfoot – Rhythmical (Swing Easy (USA)) [1992/3 22vᵖᵘ] neat gelding: has given some very temperamental displays since winning novice hurdle in November, 1991: tried blinkered to no avail. *Billy Williams* §§

JOKESTER 6 b.g. Impecunious – Merry Minuet (Trumpeter) [1992/3 17g⁴ 16s² 16v* 16vˢᵘ] lengthy, angular gelding: won novice handicap hurdle at Nottingham in December: in lead when slipping up on home turn in similar event at Uttoxeter later in month: should stay further than 2m: acts on heavy going. *C. T. Nash* 84

JOLI EXCITING 8 b.m. Tepukei – Merry Leap (Stephen George) [1992/3 22g 21s 22g 20m⁵ 21g⁵ 24s⁶] smallish mare: poor novice hurdler: best form at 3m on soft going. *J. R. Adam* 66

JOLI'S GREAT 5 ch.m. Vaigly Great – Jolimo (Fortissimo) [1992/3 16s a20gᵘʳ a18g* a16g* 23d⁵ 17d*] small mare: half-sister to several winners, notably good hurdler Osric (by Radetzky): moderate 11f winner on Flat in 1992: won 2 claiming hurdles at Lingfield in March and a novice handicap at Fakenham in April: best at around 2m: acts on dead ground and equitrack. *M. J. Ryan* 88

JOLIZAL 5 ch.m. Good Times (ITY) – New Central (Remainder Man) [1992/3 a16gᵖᵘ] poor plater on Flat, placed over 1m: showed nothing in maiden hurdle at Lingfield in January. *D. Morris* –

JOLLY GHOST 4 b.g. Grey Ghost – Pamolie (Pamroy) [1992/3 21gᵖᵘ] third live foal: dam showed nothing in 2 races: no show in novice hurdle at Hexham in May. *R. E. Barr* –

JOLLY JAUNT 8 ch.g. St Columbus – Jaunting (Jolly Jet) [1992/3 21g⁵ 21d 23m² 23g] leggy, workmanlike gelding: moderate novice hurdler: creditable second at Stratford in May: ran poorly on same course later in month: stays 23f: acts on good to firm and dead ground. *M. J. Wilkinson* 86

JOLLY ROGER 6 br.g. Swan's Rock – Treasure Ship (Sovereign Lord) [1992/3 17dᵖᵘ 21sᵖᵘ 26s⁵ 20g c25s⁴ c24fᶠ c21g³] lengthy gelding: winning hurdler: poor novice chaser: sold 4,600 gns Doncaster May Sales: stays 3m: acts on any going. *J. Hanson* c80 –

JOMANA 7 ch.m. Roman Warrior – Tina's Magic (Carnival Night) [1992/3 c18m* c16g* c16f c17gᶠ] lengthy mare: maiden hurdler: won 4-runner novice chases at Bangor and Hereford (best effort) in August: stayed 2½m: acted on good to firm going: dead. *J. M. Bradley* c90 –

JON'S CHOICE 5 b.g. Andy Rew – Whangarei (Gold Rod) [1992/3 F16m 17sᵖᵘ 16sᵖᵘ a16gᵖᵘ a16gᵖᵘ 16mᵖᵘ 16f⁴ 20mᵖᵘ 16d²] lengthy gelding: novice hurdler: blinkered when second at Towcester in May, easily best effort: ran in seller time before: acts on dead going. *B. Preece* 89

JOPANINI 8 b.g. Homing – Honeybuzzard (FR) (Sea Hawk II) [1992/3 17d⁴ 17v* 17d² 17v⁶ c21s³ 22m 24f⁶] compact, good-bodied gelding: useful hurdler: won handicap at Cheltenham in November: below form last 2 starts: made mistakes when last of 3 finishers in novice event at Warwick in February on chasing debut: effective at around 2m when conditions are testing and should stay beyond 21f: acts on any going: best ridden up with pace. *N. J. Henderson* c90 139

JORDANSTOWN HOUSE 11 b.g. Stubbs Gazette – Rumdoo (Rum (USA)) [1992/3 25g c25g c25sᵖᵘ] big, close-coupled gelding: well beaten in hunter chases. *A. J. Barnett* c–

JOTO 6 b.g. Le Johnstan – Too Do (Manado) [1992/3 16m⁶] angular gelding: lightly-raced poor novice hurdler. *O. R. Prince* –

JOVEN TOP 5 gr.g. Mansingh (USA) – Jovenita (High Top) [1992/3 F17g 16s 16vᵖᵘ 16sᵖᵘ] workmanlike gelding: half-brother to winning chaser Tough Cookie (by Lochnager) and to a winner in Belgium: dam ran twice: no sign of ability in novice hurdles. *Mrs I. McKie* —

JOVIAL MAN (IRE) 4 b.g. Ela-Mana-Mou – Jovial Josie (USA) (Sea Bird II) [1992/3 18m⁵] no worthwhile form on Flat or in juvenile hurdle at Exeter in September. *S. Mellor* —

JOYFUL IMP 6 b.m. Import – Joyful Star (Rubor) [1992/3 2 1vᵖᵘ 17d 16g²] sturdy mare: poor novice hurdler: visored once. *J. E. Dixon* 68

JOYFULNESS (FR) 8 b.m. Cure The Blues (USA) – Jermaric (Great Nephew) [1992/3 16g] sparely-made mare: 2m hurdle winner in 1989/90: well beaten since: has run blinkered and visored. *P. J. Bevan* —

JOYFUL NOISE 10 b.g. Lighter – Roadway Mistress (Mandamus) [1992/3 20g* c22g c20sᵖᵘ c18d* c20g* c16g⁴ c18s³ c21s⁴ c21d⁴ c24gᵘʳ c21g⁴] good-topped ex-Irish gelding: useful performer at best: won hurdle race at Roscommon and handicap chases at Fairyhouse and Navan early in season: trained until after seventh start by A. L. T. Moore: below form in Britain subsequently, looking unenthusiastic last start: best form at up to 2½m: seems to act on any going: blinkered once in 1991/2. *A. P. Jarvis* c143 d 122

J P MORGAN 5 b. or br.g. Law Society (USA) – Queen of The Brush (Averof) [1992/3 16g³ 17s³ 16g* 16gᶠ] leggy, sparely-made gelding: half-brother to fairly useful hurdler and novice chaser Imperial Brush (by Sallust): poor handicapper on Flat (a difficult ride), effective from 1m to 2m: won novice hurdle at Edinburgh in December: running creditably when falling last at Ayr following month: will stay beyond 17f: acts on soft ground: visored: makes mistakes. *M. P. Naughton* 93

J R JONES 6 b.g. Blakeney – Bonne Baiser (Most Secret) [1992/3 18d³ 22g⁴] small gelding: poor handicap hurdler: stays 2¾m: below form on soft going, probably acts on any other. *Mrs A. R. Hewitt* 79

JR'S PET 6 b.m. Auction Ring (USA) – What A Pet (Mummy's Pet) [1992/3 2 1f 17s 17fᶠ] no sign of ability. *D. H. Barons* —

JUBILATA (USA) 5 ch.m. The Minstrel (CAN) – All Gladness (USA) (Alydar (USA)) [1992/3 17s³ 16v⁵ 16d² 16s 16m³ 18v⁶ 17f⁴] leggy, close-coupled mare: poor middle-distance handicapper on Flat: poor maiden over hurdles: trained until after fourth start by M. Naughton: barely stays 2m under very testing conditions: acts on good to firm and dead ground. *Martyn Wane* 73

JUDGE AND JURY 4 br.g. Law Society (USA) – Full of Reason (USA) (Bold Reason) [1992/3 17s 18v⁵] half-brother to fairly useful hurdler/novice chaser Magnus Pym (by Al Nasr): won 1¾m seller on Flat (has looked unco-operative) in October: sold out of M. Fetherston-Godley's stable 6,200 gns Ascot November Sales: showed nothing in mid-season juvenile hurdles: sold 2,000 gns Ascot June Sales. *O. Sherwood* —

JUDGES FANCY 9 b.g. Monksfield – Knollwood Court (Le Jean) [1992/3 25gᶠ 26d⁶ 20d² 22s 25g 24gᶠ] sparely-made gelding: very useful staying hurdler in 1990/1: best effort in 1992/3 when second in handicap at Newcastle on dead going in January: sold out of C. Trietline's stable 20,000 gns Doncaster March Sales after next outing: used to be best on firm ground. *N. A. Twiston-Davies* 131

JUDICIAL FIELD (IRE) 4 b.g. Law Society (USA) – Bold Meadows (Persian Bold) [1992/3 16d⁴ 16v* 16d² 16d² 17m⁴ 16s* 16g³] 134

Judicial Field returned to Ireland after changing hands for 22,000 guineas at the Newmarket Autumn Sales, his trainer possibly surprised to get him back. As one of the best Flat racers on offer at Newmarket, Judicial Field seemed sure to attract plenty of interest, especially from those in search of a hurdler, and the chances were high that he'd be sold and moved on. Anyone who turned him down is no doubt regretting it now. Judicial Field took really well to hurdling, and on his next appearance in England he

Stablemate Racing Plc's "Judicial Field"

Judicial Field (IRE) (b.g. 1989)	Law Society (USA) (br 1982)	Alleged (b 1974)	Hoist The Flag
			Princess Pout
		Bold Bikini (b 1969)	Boldnesian
			Ran-Tan
	Bold Meadows (b 1981)	Persian Bold (br 1975)	Bold Lad
			Relkarunner
		Spare Filly (b 1961)	Beau Sabreur
			La Pucelle

finished fourth in the Daily Express Triumph Hurdle at Cheltenham, ahead of five others sold at the Autumn Sales, namely Indian Quest (15,000 guineas), Holy Wanderer (3,800 guineas), Beauchamp Grace (14,500 guineas), Robingo (26,000 guineas) and Top Spin (52,000 guineas). Judicial Field was always prominent at Cheltenham and kept on strongly all the way to the line, where he was three and a half lengths adrift of the winner Shawiya. Judicial Field had run well in all his previous races, winning at Gowran Park on the second of them, and he continued in good form after Cheltenham. Following a short-head defeat of Pennine Tune at Fairyhouse, Judicial Field went on to finish third behind Shawiya and Titled Dancer in the Champion Four-Year-Old Hurdle at Punchestown. Shawiya beat him by twelve and a half lengths this time. The leggy Judicious Field has less scope for improvement than several of the other leading juveniles, but he's a reliable sort who should continue to give a good account of himself, probably in handicap company.

Judicial Field is the third foal of Bold Meadows, a fair winner over seven furlongs and a mile and a quarter. Bold Meadows, whose fourth foal Field of Vision (by Vision) has won at up to seven furlongs, is from a very successful family. Her dam Spare Filly, a fairly useful stayer and sister to the smart hurdler Samothraki, produced a host of winners, including Van Houten, a Group 2 winner in Italy, and the useful Manfilia. The latter is the dam of Kilijaro, a high-class filly at six furlongs to a mile and a quarter. Judicial Field, as we've said, is no slouch himself on the Flat. He won at seven furlongs and a mile at two years and twice over a mile and a half at three, showing useful form. Usually blinkered on the Flat, Judicial Field wore them in four of his last five starts over hurdles. On the other occasion, at Cheltenham, he was visored. Judicial Field will stay beyond seventeen furlongs; he has shown his form on ground ranging from good to firm to heavy. *D. K. Weld, Ireland*

JUDICIOUS CAPTAIN 6 b.g. New Member – Injudicious (Quorum) [1992/3 18g⁶ 17m⁴ 21d* 22g] good-topped gelding: half-brother to winning chaser Light Sentence (by No Mercy): dam, half-sister to very useful stayer Cornuto, won over 1m: easily best effort when impressive winner of novice hurdle at Carlisle in April: much better suited by 2½f than shorter: acts on dead ground. *J. R. Adam*   107

JUDYS LINE 9 b.m. Capricorn Line – Gold Braid (Martial) [1992/3 c27vᵇᵈ c21v⁵ c26dᵖᵘ c17mᵘʳ 22s] tall, workmanlike mare: moderate hurdler at best: poor novice chaser: no form in 1992/3: stays well: ideally suited by plenty of give in the ground. *Miss S. Waterman*   c– –

JUKE BOX BILLY (IRE) 5 ch.g. Kemal (FR) – Friendly Circle (Crash Course) [1992/3 22d 21s] unfurnished gelding: first foal: dam Irish NH Flat race winner: little show in novice hurdle in February and maiden hurdle in April. *J. H. Johnson*   –

JULIETSKI 5 gr.m. Niniski (USA) – Plum Blossom (USA) (Gallant Romeo (USA)) [1992/3 21m* 25d* 22g⁵ 23m⁶ 20g 23d* 25v⁶ 26d⁶] small, leggy, sparely-made mare: modest hurdler: successful in selling handicap (no bid) and novice claimer at Perth early in season, and a claimer at Uttoxeter in March: tailed off last 2 starts: suited by 2½m and more: acts on firm and dead going: blinkered once, usually visored nowadays. *M. D. Hammond*   88

JULIOS GENIUS 6 br.h. Julio Mariner – Legal Genius (Crown Law) [1992/3 18v⁶ 16g⁶ 17g³] leggy, unfurnished horse: fifth foal: dam won 2 points and a 19f hunter chase: has shown ability in novice hurdles: will stay beyond 2¼m. *J. T. Gifford*   84

JUMBEAU 8 ch.g. Beau Charmeur (FR) – My Hansel (Prince Hansel) [1992/3 18d c16dᶠ c16v²] big, robust gelding: modest novice hurdler/chaser: should stay beyond 2m: acts on heavy going: jumps fences soundly. *J. T. Gifford*   c93 –

JUMP 8 gr.g. General Ironside – Maroon Well (Wrekin Rambler) [1992/3 c24mᵖᵘ c21gᵖᵘ] lengthy, good-bodied gelding: poor novice hurdler/chaser: sold 1,600 gns Ascot May Sales: sketchy jumper. *Fred Kirby*   c– –

JUMPING CACTUS 4 b.c. Song – Marguerite Gerard (Rheingold) [1992/3 17mˢᵘ 18g⁶ 18m⁶ 18d² 18g²] brother to winning hurdler Strike A Chord and half-brother to 2 Flat winners: dam won over 1¼m and stayed 13f: sold 2,000 gns Doncaster March Sales: second in selling hurdles at Sedgefield in September and October. *J. A. Hellens*   78

JUMPING JUDGE 6 b.g. Salmon Leap (USA) – Quack Shot (USA) (Quack (USA)) [1992/3 a16g 17g] leggy gelding: tailed off in novice hurdles in January and April. *T. Thomson Jones*   –

JUMPIN' JIMINY 5 ch.g. Buzzards Bay – Model Lady (Le Bavard (FR)) [1992/3 F17f F17m] tall, unfurnished gelding: first foal: dam, NH Flat race winner, fair novice hurdler: mid-division in NH Flat races in March and April: yet to race over hurdles or fences. *R. Brotherton*

JUMP N FLY 5 b.m. Pitpan – Henrietta Honey (Henry The Seventh) [1992/3 17m^{pu} 23m^{pu} 17g^{pu}] second foal: dam finished last in seller at 2 yrs: probably of little account. *Mrs L. C. Jewell* —

JUNGLE HIGHWAY 4 b.f. Java Tiger – Amber Highway (Royal Highway) [1992/3 F16m F17m] never ran: well behind in NH Flat races in May: yet to race over hurdles. *D. Nicholson*

JUNGLE KNIFE 7 b.g. Kris – Jungle Queen (Twilight Alley) [1992/3 17d^2 16s* 17v 16s^6 16v^6 16f^2] leggy gelding: useful hurdler: easily landed the odds in 2-runner minor event at Warwick in November: returned to form when second to Spinning in Swinton Handicap Hurdle at Haydock in May: races only at around 2m: probably acts on any going: suited by sharp track. *M. H. Tompkins* 144

JUNGLE RITES (IRE) 5 b.g. Indian King (USA) – Spring Step (Tepukei) [1992/3 F16g^6] third foal: half-brother to The Fax Man (by Rusticaro), a NH Flat race winner and poor novice hurdler: dam never ran: sixth of 12 in NH Flat race at Catterick in March: yet to race over hurdles or fences. *J. G. FitzGerald*

JUNIOR (BEL) 8 ch.g. Dernier Bingo (BEL) – Lune de Miel (BEL) (Boulou) [1992/3 c20s^R] lengthy gelding: poor maiden hurdler/pointer: refused eighth on steeplechasing debut (visored): stays 2¾m. *Mrs C. Day* c– §
—

JUNIORS CHOICE 10 br.g. Bivouac – Lucky Number II (Lucky Sovereign) [1992/3 c22g^2 c25g^6 c24s^6] fair pointer, successful in May: second at Ayr in March, best effort in hunter chases. *John Threadgall* c77

JUNO AWAY 6 b.m. Strong Gale – Lepida (Royal Match) [1992/3 20s^4 22v^2 22s] good-bodied mare: poor novice hurdler: will stay 3m: acts on heavy going. *K. White* 67

JUNO'S SPECIAL (IRE) 5 b.m. Lyphard's Special (USA) – Hasty Goddess (Nebbiolo) [1992/3 F16s F16f] angular mare: third foal: dam fair middle-distance winner who stayed well: well beaten in NH Flat races at Ludlow and Haydock in the spring: yet to race over hurdles or fences. *A. A. Hambly*

JUPITER MOON 4 b.c. Jupiter Island – Troy Moon (Troy) [1992/3 17d 17m* 18d^5 16d 21s^4 17g^4 21g^3] sturdy colt: modest middle-distance stayer on Flat, not one to rely on: sold out of C. Brittain's stable 15,500 gns Newmarket September Sales: won juvenile hurdle at Bangor in October: generally ran creditably afterwards: stays 21f: acts on good to firm and soft ground. *Mrs A. Swinbank* 85

JURANSTAN 8 b.g. Furry Glen – Atlantic Hope (Brave Invader (USA)) [1992/3 c25v^5 c24s^2 c28f^{pu}] leggy gelding: poor novice chaser: stays 27f: acts on good to firm and soft going: blinkered on several occasions, but not in 1992/3: sketchy jumper: refused to race once. *J. C. Collett* c83 §
—

JURIST (USA) 9 b. or br.g. Alleged (USA) – Connie Knows (USA) (Buckpasser) [1992/3 22m^{pu} 22d^{pu} 17m 20f] good-bodied gelding: poor hurdler: no form in 1992/3: stayed 2½m: acted on good to firm ground: was sometimes blinkered: dead. *G. L. Roe*

JURZ (IRE) 5 b.h. Pennine Walk – Kawkeb (USA) (Vaguely Noble) [1992/3 16d^2 16m*] rangy horse with scope: lightly-raced hurdler: fairly useful form when winning handicap at Warwick in February, despite jumping poorly (finished lame): yet to race beyond 2m: acts on good to firm and dead going. *R. J. Hodges* 117

JUST A LIGHT (IRE) 5 ch.g. Jester – Beach Light (Bustino) [1992/3 F17g F17d^6] lengthy gelding: fourth foal: half-brother to 3 winners, including fairly useful Irish hurdler Magic Million (by Gorytus): dam, 1¼m winner, is daughter of smart sprinter Street Light: sixth in NH Flat race at Carlisle in April: yet to race over hurdles or fences. *L. Lungo*

JUST A MEMORY 7 b.g. Kafu – Souveniers (Relko) [1992/3 17s^{pu} 16s 16g⁴ 17m 18s c16f^{ur} c16g^{pu}] sturdy gelding: selling hurdler: ran poorly in 1992/3: yet to complete over fences: sold 950 gns Ascot June Sales: seems suited by a sharp 2m: acts on good to firm and dead going: sometimes blinkered. *C. C. Trietline* c–

JUST A SECOND 8 b.m. Jimsun – Saroan Meed (Midsummer Night II) [1992/3 24v² 24v⁶ 24v³ 26d³ c23g² 24g⁴ 24g 23g] leggy mare: moderate novice hurdler at best: ran badly last 2 starts: poor form when second in novice chase at Worcester in March: stays 3¼m: acts on heavy going: blinkered once. *C. J. Drewe* c74 98 d

JUSTASERFF 11 b.g. Czarist – Follow Me (Guide) [1992/3 c16g² c16s* c20f⁶] angular gelding: won maiden chase at Perth in April: form only at 2m: acts on soft going, well beaten on firm. *L. Lungo* c91

JUST AS HOPEFUL (NZ) 9 b.g. In The Purple (FR) – Bighearted (NZ) (Better Honey) [1992/3 20s⁴ 25s^{pu} c21d^{ur} c23g^R 27m² 28m²] tall gelding: fair handicap hurdler: second at Fontwell and Nottingham in March: no aptitude for fences, and one to leave alone: suited by a test of stamina: acts on good to firm and heavy going: sometimes blinkered and visored: difficult ride: inconsistent. *D. H. Barons* c§§ 115 §

JUST A SONG 7 br.m. Song – Atoka (March Past) [1992/3 16g^{pu}] seems of little account. *Mrs E. Moscrop* –

JUST A TRIFLE 11 gr.m. Jellaby – Just Jolly (Jolly Jet) [1992/3 22d^{pu} c16d^{pu} c21m^R] plain mare: has been hobdayed: showed nothing over hurdles or in steeplechases: very temperamental. *G. Stickland* c§§ –

JUST A WONDER 9 b.m. Comedy Star (USA) – Gretna Wonder (Elopement) [1992/3 20g² 19m⁵ 22g 21m^{pu}] small, sparely-made mare: poor hurdler: ran well first 2 starts: stays 2¾m: acts on firm going: usually blinkered or visored. *S. Christian* 85

JUST BALLYTOO 6 b.g. Fidel – Baringle (Bargello) [1992/3 17d⁵ 22m⁶ 22m 23f³ 25m] compact gelding: brother to winning jumpers Ballyeamon and Air Supply: dam unraced: blinkered only time and only form in novice hurdles when third at Stratford in March. *P. J. Jones* 63

JUST BLAKE 12 b.g. Blakeney – Just A Dutchess (USA) (Knightly Manner (USA)) [1992/3 22m² 22m³ 22g 22s⁶ 20s 22f^F] close-coupled gelding: fair handicap hurdler at best: trained until after fourth start by J. Roberts: novice chaser: stayed 2¾m: acted on good to soft and good to firm ground: dead. *R. P. C. Hoad* c– 102

JUST BROOK 14 b.g. Country Retreat – Rissole (Woodcut) [1992/3 c26d^{ur}] sparely-made, angular gelding: poor maiden pointer/hunter chaser. *Dennis Hutchinson* c–

JUST CHARLIE 4 b.g. Bustino – Derring Miss (Derrylin) [1992/3 F16s 20v⁵ 16d 16d] sturdy gelding: third foal: dam fairly useful 2-y-o 6f winner: little sign of ability. *M. W. Easterby* –

JUST CRACKER 8 ch.g. Monsanto (FR) – Pertune (Hyperion's Gurls) [1992/3 20g 20g⁴ 17g⁵ 17s³ 17s* 16g² 18g³ 26d* 17g* 22v^F] sparely-made gelding: improved hurdler in 1992/3, successful in selling handicaps at Newton Abbot (conditional jockeys, no bid) and Hereford (bought in 2,600 gns) and novice event at Taunton in first half of season: was effective at 17f and stayed 3¼m: acted on soft ground: was genuine: dead. *P. Leach* 91

JUST DONALD 6 b.g. Politico (USA) – Brox Treasure (Broxted) [1992/3 c19d^F] poor maiden pointer: fell fifth in a hunter chase in February. *Mrs P. Grainger* c–

JUST EVE 6 gr.m. Alias Smith (USA) – Cupid's Delight (St Paddy) [1992/3 17m 17m³ 20m⁵ 16g 17m^{pu} 17d 17s⁵ 18d] leggy mare: poor novice hurdler: stays 2½m: acts on good to firm going. *J. L. Gledson* 69

JUST FOR A LAUGH 6 b.m. Idiot's Delight – Mekhala (Menelek) [1992/3 F17g F16s] workmanlike mare: sister to useful Irish 2m chaser Good For A Laugh and half-sister to winning chaser Great Pokey (by Uncle

Pokey): dam won 2m novice chase: behind in NH Flat races at Cheltenham in October and Bangor in February: yet to race over hurdles or fences. *J. L. Needham*

JUST FOR KICKS 7 br.g. Saher – Kix (King Emperor (USA)) [1992/3 25mF 26s] fair winning hurdler in 1990/1: no form in 1992/3: form only at 2m: acts on soft going: blinkered once. *J. J. O'Neill* —

JUST (FR) 7 b.g. The Wonder (FR) – Just A Beauty (FR) (Kenmare (FR)) [1992/3 17d* 16v³ 17v⁶ 17d³ 20mᵖᵘ 17f² 21d² 17v² 22d 23g³ 17g⁴] tall, lengthy gelding: modest hurdler: won novice handicap at Taunton in November: often ran with credit subsequently, including in selling handicaps: stays 21f: probably acts on any ground: blinkered fourth and fifth starts, visored afterwards. *M. C. Pipe* — 90

JUST FRANKIE 9 ch.g. Tepukei – Harpalyce (Don't Look) [1992/3 c17g* c16m* c18d⁴ c16d² c17g³ c18m³ c17m³ c16f⁶] lengthy, workmanlike gelding: fair chaser: won handicaps at Hexham and Catterick in first half of season: generally ran creditably afterwards: stays 2¼m: acts on firm and dead ground: races up with pace. *Mrs M. Reveley* — c106

JUST-GO-AGAIN 4 ch.g. All Systems Go – Argostone (Rockavon) [1992/3 17m 18d a18gᵖᵘ] leggy gelding: half-brother to winning hurdler Little Miss Horner (by Sit In The Corner): seems of little account: blinkered last start. *J. M. Jefferson* —

JUSTICE LEA 13 b.g. Kinglet – Evada (Eborneezer) [1992/3 25m² 24d³ 26m² 26d 21m] strong, lengthy gelding: modest hurdler: ran creditably first 3 starts in 1992/3: winning pointer/maiden hunter chaser: suited by long distances: acts on any going: usually claimer ridden. *T. A. K. Cuthbert* — c– / 89

JUST INCREDIBLE 7 b.g. Auction Ring (USA) – Elated (Sparkler) [1992/3 c16g⁴ c16sᵖᵘ c22sᵖᵘ] sturdy gelding: poor novice hurdler/chaser: sold 1,750 gns Doncaster March Sales: jumps fences poorly. *J. P. Leigh* — c84 x / –

JUST LIKE TRIGGER 8 ch.g. Deep Run – Elsea Wood (Eborneezer) [1992/3 18vᵖᵘ] lengthy, sparely-made gelding: well beaten in novice hurdles: has given trouble at start. *J. T. Gifford* —

JUST MICK 12 b.g. Tycoon II – Vulrory (Vulgan) [1992/3 c24d³ c24m⁵ c26f³ c23fᵖᵘ] smallish, sturdy gelding: fair hunter chaser nowadays: creditable efforts first 2 starts in 1993: stays 3m: acts on dead and good to firm going. *Mrs H. B. Dowson* — c82

JUST MOLLY 6 b.m. Furry Glen – Hansel's Trouble (Prince Hansel) [1992/3 F16g F16s⁶ 21s⁴] workmanlike mare: seventh foal: half-sister to winning jumpers Developer's Run (by Deep Run) and Garryduff Mover (by Rarity): dam won at 2m on Flat and over hurdles in Ireland: signs of ability in NH Flat races and a Wetherby mares novice hurdle in second half of season: should improve over hurdles. *J. G. FitzGerald* — 78 p

JUST MOSS 7 b.g. Le Moss – Just Reward (Choral Society) [1992/3 c21vᵖᵘ c24v* c26v³ c25vᵘʳ c24s* c25dF c21gF] rangy, workmanlike gelding: once-raced over hurdles: won handicap chases at Lingfield in December and Leicester in February: stayed 3¼m: acted on heavy ground: dead. *R. Rowe* — c114 / –

JUST MY BILL 7 ch.g. Nicholas Bill – Misnomer (Milesian) [1992/3 21m⁵ 21g³ 21d⁶] workmanlike gelding: half-brother to several winners, including fair hurdlers York Cottage (by Royal Palace) and Half Asleep (by Quiet Fling): modest middle-distance stayer on Flat: modest form in novice hurdles in first half of season: jumps none too fluently: visored first and last starts, blinkered in between. *N. Tinkler* — 84

JUST NELLY 7 ch.m. Noalto – Moss Pink (USA) (Levmoss) [1992/3 20d⁵ 22g 20s c16v⁶ a20g a22g² c23dᵖᵘ c17g⁵ c27f² c22m⁴ c27f⁶] poor novice hurdler/chaser: stays 27f: acts on firm going. *J. W. Mullins* — c67 / 67

JUST PATRIMONY 9 br.g. Petrassi (GER) – Quilpee Mai (Pee Mai) [1992/3 c26m² c26mF] close-coupled, good-quartered gelding: fair pointer: second in hunter chase at Warwick in February: disputing lead when falling — c84 / –

4 out at Cheltenham in May: shapes like a thorough stayer: acts on good to firm ground: blinkered once over hurdles. *D. M. Baxter*

JUST PERKINS 8 ch.g. Bold Owl – Buckenham Belle (Royben) [1992/3 c19s⁵ c21m] lengthy gelding: poor novice hurdler/chaser: modest pointer: stays 2½m: probably acts on any going. *N. J. Reece*

c75
–

JUST PRETEND 9 b. or br.m. Sayyaf – Lovely Pretense (USA) (Pretense) [1992/3 c25sᵖᵘ c17d c20g c27g⁵ 22g c25d⁴ c24m c27dᵖᵘ 25s c27gᵖᵘ] small, lengthy mare: poor staying hurdler/chaser: little worthwhile form in 1992/3: tried visored/blinkered. *V. Thompson*

c–
–

JUST PULHAM 8 b.g. Electric – Lady Acquiesce (Galivanter) [1992/3 17g 16s 17dᵖᵘ 16d⁵ 18gF 16d⁶ 17fur 18m] compact gelding: poor hurdler: races at around 2m: acts on soft ground. *S. G. Payne*

82

JUST ROSIE 4 b.f. Sula Bula – Rosa Ruler (Gambling Debt) [1992/3 F16v 16v⁴ 17f* 18g* 17gF] sparely-made filly: second foal: half-sister to a poor novice hurdler by Oats: dam, fair hurdler, seemed to stay 3m: behind in NH Flat race when trained by T. Keddy: won novice hurdles at Hereford and Exeter in May: every chance when falling final start: will stay beyond 2¼m: acts on firm going. *Andrew Turnell*

95

JUST SO 10 br.g. Sousa – Just Camilla (Ascertain (USA)) [1992/3 c26d⁴ c27v⁴ c30s c35s² c33g c27s³] tall, workmanlike gelding: fairly useful chaser: good second to Riverside Boy at Taunton in January: well below that subsequently: needs very long distances and testing conditions: visored twice in 1991/2, blinkered third to fifth starts in 1992/3: looks a difficult ride. *H. T. Cole*

c128

JUST WOODY 5 b.g. Tudor Rhythm – Tiebell (Foggy Bell) [1992/3 F16s⁵ F17m F17d⁶ 21s² 21f] third foal: brother to 6-y-o Easy Rhythm: dam, fair hurdler, stayed 2¾m: second in novice event at Hexham in April, better effort in novice hurdles: likely to stay beyond 21f: acts on soft going. *B. M. Temple*

82

JYMJAM JOHNNY (IRE) 4 b.g. Torus – Inventus (Pitpan) [1992/3 F17d] leggy gelding: second foal: dam, sister to 2 winning jumpers, well beaten in NH Flat race: ninth of 18 in NH Flat race at Ascot in April: yet to race over hurdles. *J. Akehurst*

K

KABAYIL 4 b.f. Dancing Brave (USA) – Psylla (Beldale Flutter (USA)) [1992/3 17v* 17d* 16v⁵] smallish, workmanlike filly: fair middle-distance performer on Flat: sold out of P. Walwyn's stable 17,000 gns Newmarket December Sales: comfortable winner of 2 juvenile hurdles at Plumpton in February: fair fifth in handicap at Towcester in April: likely to stay beyond 17f: acts on heavy going: jumps soundly. *C. R. Egerton*

92

KABELIA 5 b.m. Kabour – Belhill (Beldale Flutter (USA)) [1992/3 F16g F17g] first foal: dam, poor maiden, stayed 1¼m: behind in NH Flat races in March: yet to race over hurdles or fences. *S. Coathup*

KACHINA MAID 8 b.m. Anfield – Grey Twig (Godswalk (USA)) [1992/3 17g] well beaten in 2 sellers over hurdles. *Mrs A. Knight*

–

KADAN (GER) 9 b.g. Horst-Herbert – King Lady (GER) (Marduk (GER)) [1992/3 17s² 18fF] angular, sparely-made gelding: useful hurdler at best: lightly raced recently, and showing first worthwhile form in over 2 years when second of 4 finishers in handicap on soft ground at Newton Abbot in August: stays 2¼m: best form on a sound surface (acts on firm ground): usually held up. *W. G. Turner*

113

KADARI 4 b.f. Commanche Run – Thoughtful (Northfields (USA)) [1992/3 16s² 20g⁵] leggy, sparely-made filly: half-sister to high-class hurdler Muse (by High Line): modest stayer on Flat: better effort over hurdles when second in juvenile event at Wetherby in December (flashed

88

tail): sold 10,000 gns Doncaster March Sales: should stay beyond 2m. *A. Harrison*

KADI (GER) 4 b.g. Shareef Dancer (USA) – Kaisertreue (GER) (Luciano) [1992/3 17v* 17s³ 17g* 17m 17f] leggy, light-bodied gelding: fairly useful, lightly-raced middle-distance performer on Flat in Ireland when trained by J. Oxx: won juvenile hurdles at Sandown in January and Huntingdon in February: good efforts subsequently in valuable events at Cheltenham and Aintree: likely to prove best around 2m: acts on any going: sketchy jumper. *D. Nicholson*   125

KAFUBA (IRE) 5 br.g. Kafu – Rabuba (Connaught) [1992/3 aF 16g aF 13g 21gᵖᵘ 21gᵖᵘ] angular gelding: second foal: half-brother to a poor animal by Dominion: dam, placed twice over 1½m, half-sister to Irish 2000 Guineas second Brother Philips: behind in NH Flat races and when pulled up over hurdles in second half of season. *R. M. Flower*   –

KAHAROA (NZ) 7 gr.g. Ironclad (NZ) – In Haste (NZ) (In The Purple (FR)) [1992/3 c21sᶠ 24sᵖᵘ 25s 22vᵖᵘ 22v 23d 21sᵖᵘ] robust gelding: no sign of ability: sold 1,650 gns Ascot June Sales: sometimes blinkered. *D. H. Barons*   c–

KAHER (USA) 6 b.g. Our Native (USA) – June Bride (USA) (Riverman (USA)) [1992/3 17s⁵ 16s⁵ a16g 18d] leggy gelding: fairly useful 2m hurdler in 1991/2: well below form in 1992/3 (broke a blood vessel last start): sold out of N. Callaghan's stable 7,800 gns Doncaster March Sales after third outing: acts on good to firm going: pulls hard and is held up: usually jumps well. *N. A. Twiston-Davies*   –

KAHHAL (IRE) 5 gr.m. Doulab (USA) – Queen's Counsellor (Kalamoun) [1992/3 a16gᵖᵘ] no sign of ability over hurdles: sold 1,700 gns Ascot May Sales. *N. M. Babbage*   –

KAHIN 6 br.g. Diesis – Kawkeb (USA) (Vaguely Noble) [1992/3 20vᵖᵘ] close-coupled gelding: second in novice hurdle in August, 1991: showed nothing in similar event at Plumpton in November. *D. R. Gandolfo*   –

KALABERRY 5 gr.m. Kalaglow – Moberry (Mossberry) [1992/3 16sᶠ] showed a little ability in NH Flat races in 1991/2: fell third in September on hurdling debut: sold 2,000 gns Doncaster Sales later in month. *W. W. Haigh*   –

KALA BRAVE 6 b.g. Kala Shikari – Suffield Park (Wolver Hollow) [1992/3 F 18v] fourth foal: dam won selling hurdle: soundly beaten in NH Flat race at Market Rasen in December: yet to race over hurdles or fences. *M. C. Pipe*

KALABUCK 6 gr.g. Kalaglow – Buckhurst (Gulf Pearl) [1992/3 18m 16d a16g⁶] leggy gelding: poor maiden hurdler. *D. C. Tucker*   63

KALAMOSS 4 ch.f. Kalaglow – Moss Pink (USA) (Levmoss) [1992/3 16m⁵ 17s³ 18f² 16g⁶ 18g⁵ 18d³ 25d 22m⁴ 20f⁵ 18g 20m* 22fᵖᵘ 18g⁵] small filly: sister to winning hurdler Abigail's Dream and half-sister to winning chaser Mr Murdock (by Last Fandango): no worthwhile form on Flat: won selling handicap at Taunton (no bid) in April: ran well final start: stays 2½m: acts on good to firm going. *N. R. Mitchell*   86

KALANSKI 7 ro.g. Niniski (USA) – Kalazero (Kalamoun) [1992/3 16g 16s⁵ 16g 17d⁵ 16d] compact gelding: fairly useful hurdler: below form at Ascot in November on penultimate start and ran as though race was needed when next seen out in April:sold to join C. Egerton 9,600 gns Doncaster May Sales: should stay further than 2m: acts on soft going. *A. L. T. Moore, Ireland*   121

KALKO 4 b.c. Kalaglow – Salchow (Niniski (USA)) [1992/3 16s³ 16g² 16d² 17d* 16d³ 17g* 16g² 16g⁴] small, close-coupled colt: modest at up to 1½m on Flat: sold out of C. Brittain's stable 5,000 gns Newmarket Autumn Sales: won novice hurdle at Kelso in February and juvenile event on same course in March: also ran well last 2 starts: will stay beyond 17f: acts on soft ground. *M. D. Hammond*   102

KALOGY 6 gr.m. Kalaglow – Coyote (Welsh Pageant) [1992/3 17s² 17f⁶] tall, leggy mare: quite useful hurdler: ran well in handicaps at Ascot in January and Sandown (valuable event) in March: stays 21f: acts on firm and soft going. *Mrs J. G. Retter* — 118

KALZARI (USA) 8 b.g. Riverman (USA) – Kamisha (FR) (Lyphard (USA)) [1992/3 17g 17d² 16d⁶ 17v⁵ 16v⁵ a16g³ 20d⁵ 18g³] compact gelding: poor handicap hurdler: generally ran creditably in 1992/3: stays 2½m: acts on good to firm, heavy ground and equitrack. *D. J. Deacon* — 83

KAMART 5 gr.m. Belfort (FR) – Practicality (Weavers' Hall) [1992/3 16s 16g 17s 17d⁶ 16d c17g³ c17d⁴ c17g* c17s² c17m² c18m³] lengthy mare: poor novice hurdler: won novice chase at Hexham in March: ran well afterwards, particularly final start: yet to race beyond 2¼m: probably acts on any ground: visored once. *M. A. Barnes* — c84 + —

KAMBALDA RAMBLER 9 b. or br.g. Kambalda – Stroan Lass (Brave Invader (USA)) [1992/3 c21v⁶ c17v⁷ᵖᵘ c20s³ c20g⁴ c21s⁴ c24d c24dᵖᵘ] leggy, close-coupled gelding: handicap chaser: best efforts of season on third and fourth starts: probably stays 3m: well suited by plenty of give in the ground: best with forcing tactics and strong handling. *C. Parker* — c99 —

KAMEO STYLE 10 b.g. Kambalda – Smashing Style (Harwell) [1992/3 c21g c22s³ c21v⁴ c21sᵘʳ c21sᶠ 21v c25d⁶ c25mᵖᵘ c19g⁶] compact, good-topped gelding: modest handicap chaser: only form in 1992/3 on second and third outings: stays 3m: needs plenty of give in the ground: best blinkered. *F. Jordan* — c86 —

KAMOGUE 6 b.m. Carlingford Castle – Fair Invader (Brave Invader (USA)) [1992/3 22s⁶ 22g⁴ 17d⁶ 22m⁴] workmanlike mare: moderate novice hurdler: fourth at Wincanton in November, second and best effort of season: stays 2¾m: acts on soft going, possibly unsuited by good to firm. *D. R. Gandolfo* — 85

KAMSEL 10 b.g. Kambalda – My Hansel (Prince Hansel) [1992/3 c19dᵖᵘ c21dᵘʳ c24s c21gᵘʳ c23gᵖᵘ] lengthy gelding: winning hurdler/chaser: lightly raced and no form for long time: poor jumper. *Miss J. Southall* — c– x —

KANNDABIL 6 gr.h. Nishapour (FR) – Katana (FR) (Le Haar) [1992/3 17g⁵ 16g⁵ c16g² c16g⁵ c17d* c16s² c16d⁴ 16d³ c17m³ 16d² 21s⁵ 16f⁵ c17g²] strong, stocky horse: fair hurdler: won novice handicap chase at Newcastle in January: well below form last 3 starts over fences: stays 2½m: acts on good to firm and soft ground: blinkered nowadays: sometimes races with tongue tied down (has reportedly had problems with his wind): inconsistent and not one to trust. *N. Tinkler* — c105 § 115 §

KANOOZ (IRE) 5 br.g. Wassl – Countess Candy (Great Nephew) [1992/3 18m³ 23m* 21f² 20m] workmanlike gelding: bought in 3,800 gns after winning conditional jockeys selling handicap hurdle at Stratford in September: sold out of S. Mellor's stable 1,100 gns Ascot November Sales after third start (ran well): below form when next seen out in April: stays 23f: best form on top-of-the-ground: probably best blinkered (races lazily). *A. J. K. Dunn* — 95

KANO WARRIOR 6 b.g. Furry Glen – Last Princess (Le Prince) [1992/3 21s⁶ 16d 22vᵖᵘ 25d 22m³ 20g⁵ 22d² 22f³ 23m* 23g⁶] good-topped gelding: chasing type: third foal: brother to winning hurdler Strath Royal: dam won over 2m on Flat and a 2½m novice chase: moderate form over hurdles: won novice event at Stratford in May: well beaten for conditional jockey later in month: should stay beyond 23f: acts on good to firm and dead ground. *N. A. Twiston-Davies* — 92

KARAKTER REFERENCE 11 br.g. Reformed Character – Windtown Beauty (Laser Light) [1992/3 c23sᴿ 22d⁴ c21gᵖᵘ c24dᵖᵘ c21f] small, strong, short-backed gelding: novice hurdler: quite a useful chaser at his best: refused in valuable handicap in Belgium on first start and ran poorly subsequently: stays 25f: acts on firm and good to soft going: usually jumps well. *R. J. O'Sullivan* — c– 83

KARNATAK 12 b.g. Artaius (USA) – Karera (Kalamoun) [1992/3 c21m⁵ c16m⁴ c21g⁵ c25g⁴ 22gᵖᵘ] small, lightly-made gelding: top-of-the-ground chaser at up to 2¾m, a shadow of his former self: tried blinkered/visored over hurdles. *Mrs P. M. Joynes*

c–
–

KASAYID 6 br.g. Niniski (USA) – Raabihah (Shirley Heights) [1992/3 16d² 16m⁶] leggy, close-coupled gelding: moderate form in novice hurdles at Ludlow in February and March: should prove suited by further than 2m: acts on good to firm and dead going. *S. Christian*

90

KASHAN (IRE) 5 b.g. Darshaan – Kamanika (FR) (Amber Rama (USA)) [1992/3 20g 22m⁶ 22s 22d⁵ 18m] leggy gelding: fairly useful hurdler in 1991/2: only modest form in 1992/3: should stay beyond 2m: blinkered twice. *J. M. Bradley*

88

KASISI (IRE) 4 b.f. Bluebird (USA) – Inchmarlo (USA) (Nashua) [1992/3 17d⁴ 17g³ 16f 16d 23m⁴ 21f⁵] leggy, workmanlike filly: half-sister to winning hurdler Marlingford (by Be My Guest): modest middle-distance performer on Flat when trained by A. Stewart: modest form over hurdles: probably stays 23f: acts on good to firm and dead ground. *J. Webber*

84

KATABATIC 10 br.g. Strong Gale – Garravogue (Giolla Mear) [1992/3 c161 c16g* c18d² c16s* c20s² c17g² c16m³ c21g³]

c161 ?
–

'Too many repeats' is a criticism often made, particularly of British television. Armchair followers of jumping have become increasingly familiar with the encounters of those hardy perennials Katabatic and Waterloo Boy. They had met six times before the latest season—Katabatic coming out on top on each occasion—and there were a further three meetings in the latest season before the two old rivals met in the Queen Mother Champion Chase at the Festival meeting, where they appeared to stand out in a field of nine. Katabatic had won the Champion Chase in 1991 and come second to Remittance Man in 1992; Waterloo Boy had been placed in the last three runnings of the race. Katabatic lost out to Waterloo Boy in the Plymouth Gin

United House Construction Handicap Chase, Ascot—
Katabatic makes a successful reappearance

Pell-mell Partners' "Katabatic"

Haldon Gold Cup at Exeter (Katabatic returned off colour) and in the closest race of the season between the pair in the Game Spirit Chase at Newbury, where Katabatic ran well, beaten a length conceding 3 lb. Their encounter in between, in the Castleford Chase at Wetherby, didn't live up to expectations. Katabatic gained a hollow ten-length victory as Waterloo Boy put in an uncharacteristically poor round of jumping; Boro Smackeroo was the only other runner. Despite a somewhat in-and-out season, in which his only other victory came under top weight on his reappearance in the United House Construction Handicap at Ascot, Katabatic looked the one to beat in the Queen Mother Champion Chase and started 6/5 favourite. But he didn't show his form and went down by three quarters of a length and two to Deep Sensation and the Game Spirit third Cyphrate, making little impression after being niggled along some way from home and coming under strong pressure approaching the last (Waterloo Boy ran as if something amiss). Katabatic again started favourite on his only subsequent outing, in the S.W. Showers Silver Trophy Chase at Cheltenham in April, when he managed only third of four to Beech Road, a result which reportedly left connections considering retiring Katabatic.

Katabatic (br.g. 1983)	Strong Gale (br 1975)	Lord Gayle (b 1965)	Sir Gaylord
			Sticky Case
		Sterntau (br 1969)	Tamerlane
			Sterna
	Garravogue (b 1973)	Giolla Mear (b 1965)	Hard Ridden
			Iacobella
		Fashion's Frill (b 1962)	Black Tarquin
			Dress Parade

The rangy Katabatic has been a grand servant to his stable over the years. His fifteen victories (all except one of them over fences) also include those in the Martell Aintree Chase, the Grand Annual Challenge Cup and the S.W. Showers Silver Trophy Chase, in addition to the two championship races for the two-milers, the Queen Mother Champion Chase and the Castleford Chase. Katabatic isn't a specialist two-miler, however. He stays two and a half miles well and there's enough stamina further back in his family—his grandam is a half-sister to the very good staying chaser Height O'Fashion—to suggest he'd have a fair chance of staying three. Katabatic is a sound jumper who acts on any going. He has a good turn of foot and is usually held up. *Andrew Turnell*

KATHY FAIR (IRE)   4 b.f. Nicholas Bill – Fair Flutter (Beldale Flutter (USA)) [1992/3 17fᵣₒ 16g 17s⁶ 17dF 17fF] sparely-made filly: poor maiden on Flat and over hurdles: ran out first outing: pulls hard. *R. J. Baker* — 58 §

KATIE ANN   5 b.m. Full of Hope – Princess Gardens (Majetta) [1992/3 F14s F17g] first foal: dam unraced: behind in NH Flat races in November and December: yet to race over hurdles or fences. *J. P. Leigh* — —

KATIESIMP   4 gr.f. Import – Katie Grey (Pongee) [1992/3 16g⁵ 17sᵖᵘ 16g 20dᵖᵘ] tall, sparely-made filly: fourth foal: half-sister to useful hurdler/novice chaser Mils Mij (by Slim Jim): dam won novice hurdle: no sign of ability on Flat or over hurdles. *J. Hurst* — —

KATIE'S JOKER   7 b.g. Idiot's Delight – Roller Skate (Saratoga Skiddy) [1992/3 17d² 17s³ 16s⁵ a18g 17g 17g⁵ 18d²] leggy gelding: moderate form over hurdles: easily best efforts when second in novice events at Cheltenham in September and Cartmel in May: stays 2¼m: acts on dead ground. *O. O'Neill* — 88

KATY'S LAD   6 b.g. Camden Town – Cathryn's Song (Prince Tenderfoot (USA)) [1992/3 16s² 16v 16vᵖᵘ] small, close-coupled gelding: modest middle-distance performer on Flat, suited by give in the ground: second in novice hurdle at Leicester in January: failed to reproduce that effort in 2 subsequent starts. *B. A. McMahon* — 87

KAUSAR (USA)   6 b.h. Vaguely Noble – Kozana (Kris) [1992/3 16g² 24sᵖᵘ 22s] sturdy horse: modest staying handicapper on Flat: second in novice event at Ayr in November, easily best effort over hurdles: should be well suited by further than 2m. *G. M. Moore* — 93

KAYARTIS   4 b.f. Kaytu – Polyartis (Artaius (USA)) [1992/3 17g⁴ 18d* 16g² 16sF 16s⁴ 20f²] leggy filly: staying handicapper on Flat, winner in 1993: won juvenile hurdle at Sedgefield in October: ran creditably when in frame subsequently: will prove suited by at least 2½m: probably acts on any going: should make a fair handicapper. *Mrs M. Reveley* — 94 p

KAYFAAT (USA)   5 b.g. Spend A Buck (USA) – Duped (USA) (On The Sly (USA)) [1992/3 leggy, sparely-made gelding: fair winner over hurdles in 1991/2: tailed off in handicap in December, and wasn't seen out again: will stay further than 2m: acts well on soft ground. *M. C. Pipe* — —

KAYMONT   5 b.m. Germont – Kaymay (Maystreak) [1992/3 17gᵖᵘ] well beaten in claimers at 2 yrs: showed nothing in seller in April on hurdling debut. *Capt. J. Wilson* — —

KAYRUZ   5 b.g. Fayruz – Rheinbloom (Rheingold) [1992/3 17d 17d] half-brother to one-time fairly useful stayer/smart pointer Rhusted (by Busted): dam won over 1½m: behind in novice hurdles in November: headstrong. *D. Burchell* — —

KAYTAK (FR)   6 b.g. Mouktar – Kaythama (Run The Gantlet (USA)) [1992/3 17g² 16d⁴ 17s⁶ 16s⁶ 20g 16g* 17fF] leggy, sparely-made gelding: fair handicap hurdler at his best: won 4-runner event at Nottingham in March: should stay beyond 2¼m: acts on dead and good to firm ground: visored last 2 outings. *J. R. Jenkins* — 110

K C'S DANCER   8 ch.g. Buckskin (FR) – Lorna Lass (Laurence O) [1992/3 c25d c21gᵖᵘ c19s⁴ c21v³ c24g⁵ c26d* c27f*] workmanlike gelding: modest chaser: won novice events at Hereford and Fontwell in May: stays 27f: acts on firm and soft ground: below form when blinkered in seller fourth start. *R. Dickin* — c98 —

KEE KEE'S DREAM 9 gr.m. Strong Gale – Sun Empress (Young Emperor) [1992/3 21v^F 22d c16v^5 c24s^{ur} 17d] lengthy mare: poor novice hurdler/chaser: stays 19f: blinkered twice. *F. Jordan* — c–

KEELBY 8 b.g. Kemal (FR) – Peter's Pet (Bahrain) [1992/3 25g^5 25d 20g^{pu} 22d^{pu}] big, workmanlike gelding: chasing type: won 2 novice hurdles in 1990/1: no form in 1992/3: stays 25f: acts on good to firm and soft ground. *J. G. FitzGerald* — –

KEEN VISION (IRE) 5 b.g. Vision (USA) – Calvino (Relkino) [1992/3 a18g* a16g^2 a20g*^{dis} a18g* 17f] smallish, workmanlike gelding: always going well when first past post in 3 handicap hurdles at Lingfield, disqualified on second occasion (lost weight cloth) in second half of season, showing fair form: below best last outing: effective from 2m to 2½m: acts on good to firm ground, goes well on all-weather surfaces: takes good hold and is held up. *D. W. P. Arbuthnot* — 111

KEEP OUT OF DEBT 7 b.g. Castle Keep – Deep In Debt (Deep Run) [1992/3 c21s^F] sturdy gelding: won 2 novice hurdles in 1991/2: fell tenth on chasing debut: stayed 2¾m: dead. *J. T. Gifford* — c– –

KEEP SHARP 7 b.g. Broadsword (USA) – Castle Donato (Donato di Niccolo) [1992/3 21v 16s^5 16s a16g^3 c17g c16g^6 c16g^2 c17m^2 c17m^{F3} c16g^F] lengthy, sparely-made gelding: poor novice hurdler: has shown ability in small fields over fences but is difficult to assess: races mainly at around 2m: acts on good to firm going: sometimes has tongue tied down. *Mrs S. J. Smith* — c? 56

KEEP STRAIGHT 7 b.g. Castle Keep – Straight To Bed (Dominion) [1992/3 c21d^{pu} 16d] sparely-made gelding: selling hurdler/poor novice chaser: visored twice: unreliable. *K. A. Morgan* — c– § – §

KEEP TALKING 8 b.g. Le Bavard (FR) – Keep Faith (Raise You Ten) [1992/3 c24d^{pu} c27s^5 c30s^{pu}] rangy, good sort: fairly useful chaser: jumped to his right but always to the fore when creditable fifth in quite valuable handicap at Newbury in January: ran poorly on his other 2 starts in 1992/3: stays extremely well: acts on soft and good to firm going: usually a sound jumper. *T. Thomson Jones* — c129

KELLING 6 b.g. Blakeney – Domicile (Dominion) [1992/3 22s 17s^2] angular gelding: won NH Flat race in 1991/2 when trained by Mrs J. Retter: clear of remainder when second of 13 in novice hurdle at Taunton in December: should stay beyond 17f. *P. F. Nicholls* — 95

KELLY OWENS 8 ch.g. Kemal (FR) – Jill Owens (Tarqogan) [1992/3 c20d a20g c24g^6 c22g^2 c24d^4 c24f^3] big, plain gelding: poor novice hurdler/chaser: creditable second in maiden chase at Towcester in March: should stay beyond 2¾m: blinkered last 2 outings. *N. A. Smith* — c79 –

KELLY'S BLOOM 11 b. or br.g. Netherkelly – Buck's Bloom (Master Buck) [1992/3 c17g^{pu}] compact gelding: no sign of ability in steeplechases. *D. R. Bloor* — c–

KELLY'S COURT 7 gr.m. Netherkelly – Moll (Rugantino) [1992/3 18v^{pu}] leggy mare: no sign of ability in hunter chase and novice hurdles. *D. J. Wintle* — c– –

KELLY'S SPUR 6 b.m. Spur On – Kelly's Move (Lord Nelson (FR)) [1992/3 F14d] fourth live foal: dam temperamental novice hurdler: behind in NH Flat race at Perth in September: yet to race over hurdles or fences. *F. S. Storey* —

KELLY THE BUCK 5 b.h. Netherkelly – Buck's Bloom (Master Buck) [1992/3 F17m] sixth foal: dam lightly-raced daughter of a winning chaser: well beaten in NH Flat race at Doncaster in February: yet to race over hurdles or fences. *J. Wharton* —

KEMALS DELIGHT 6 ch.m. Kemal (FR) – Sheena's Delight (Whistling Top) [1992/3 16v^6 17s 26v^F 25g^{pu}] lengthy ex-Irish mare: second foal: dam unplaced in NH Flat race: poor maiden hurdler: has run in sellers. *C. D. Broad* — –

KEMMY DARLING   6 b.m. Kemal (FR) – Dream Away (Dusky Boy) [1992/3 F16v aF16g 21vᵖᵘ] second live foal: half-sister to NH Flat race winner Never Let On (by Denel): dam lightly-raced maiden in Ireland: no sign of ability in NH Flat races and a mares novice hurdle. *M. P. Muggeridge* —

KENILWORTH (IRE)   5 b.g. Kemal (FR) – Araglin Dora (Green Shoon) [1992/3 F16v²] second foal: dam winning Irish pointer: second of 16 in NH Flat race at Uttoxeter in April: yet to race over hurdles or fences. *J. G. FitzGerald* —

KENILWORTH LAD   5 br.g. Ring Bidder – Lucky Joker (Cawston's Clown) [1992/3 18d² 18g⁴ 17d²] leggy, sparely-made gelding: won 2 NH Flat races last season: moderate form when second in novice hurdles at Kelso in February and Perth in May: made mistakes in between: stays 2¼m: acts on dead ground. *Mrs M. Reveley* 94

KENTISH PIPER   8 br.g. Black Minstrel – Toombeola (Raise You Ten) [1992/3 c22m* c24d² c20gᵖᵘ c21s²ᵈⁱˢ c21s* c23d² c21m⁶ c21dᵘʳ c20s⁵] big, close-coupled gelding: fairly useful handicap chaser: won at Stratford in October and Leicester in February: good second at Uttoxeter later in February: effective at around 2½m and stays 3m: successful on good to firm ground but best form with plenty of give: takes time to warm to his task. *N. A. Gaselee* c116 —

KENTON (USA)   5 b.h. Blushing Groom (FR) – Sylph (USA) (Alleged (USA)) [1992/3 20d² 21dᵖᵘ 16v 20vᵖᵘ] neat horse: half-brother to middle-distance winners Nesaah (by Topsider) and Mingus (by The Minstrel), latter also successful over hurdles: dam very useful middle-distance performer: once-raced on Flat: second in novice hurdle at Plumpton in October: showed nothing subsequently: stays 2½m: acts on dead ground. *R. Akehurst* 95

KENTUCKY CHICKEN (USA)   4 b.f. Secreto (USA) – Stark Ice (USA) (Icecapade (USA)) [1992/3 18dᵖᵘ 16dᵖᵘ 18g⁴ 21sᵖᵘ] leggy filly: no form on Flat or over hurdles: trained by F. J. Houghton first outing, blinkered third: sold 1,400 gns Doncaster June Sales. *D. G. Swindlehurst* —

KENYATTA (USA)   4 b.g. Mogambo (USA) – Caranga (USA) (Caro) [1992/3 16g³ 17d⁴ 17f] sparely-made gelding: poor maiden on Flat, stays 13f: in frame in juvenile hurdles at Windsor in November and Taunton (saddle slipped) in March, showing modest form. *A. Moore* 87

KEONI   8 ch.m. Vaigly Great – Stockingful (Santa Claus) [1992/3 25sᵖᵘ 25vᵖᵘ 22sᵖᵘ c19dᶠ] poor novice hurdler/chaser. *J. Mackie* c— —

KERRY MY HOME   6 ch.g. Le Moss – Sno-Sleigh (Bargello) [1992/3 21g 18s⁶ 17s] smallish, angular gelding: second foal: dam, maiden jumper in Ireland, half-sister to 3 winning jumpers, notably high-class Ten Plus and fairly useful The Milroy: soundly beaten in novice hurdles in first half of season. *B. J. Curley* —

KERRY ORCHID   5 gr.g. Absalom – Matinata (Dike (USA)) [1992/3 F16s³ c24d* c27m² c25d*] c116 p

Kerry Orchid did remarkably well for one so young and inexperienced to finish a length and a half second to Double Silk in the Christies Foxhunter Chase at Cheltenham in March. Five years of age is very young to be tackling a championship race over the Cheltenham fences. His previous experience amounted to starts in Ireland in a point-to-point and a National Hunt Flat race as a four-year-old and in two point-to-points and a Thurles hunter chase early in 1993. However, he was unbeaten over jumps and there was enough confidence behind him for him to start at 11/2 for the Foxhunter, joint-favourite in a field of eighteen. In the race he travelled strongly from the start, jumping well in the main, and challenged Double Silk for the lead from two out to the line, sticking to his task gamely and producing a superb leap at the last which put him almost level.

Kerry Orchid missed Aintree and Fairyhouse but wasn't finished for the season. He turned out in a race full of interest at Punchestown in April, the Sean Macklin Champion Hunters Chase, where, improbably, a five-

*Sean Macklin Champion Hunters Chase, Punchestown—
young hunter Kerry Orchid continues to impress*

year-old hunter-chase debutant opened up at 6/4 to beat him. This other
young horse, Elegant Lord, had won his two point-to-points. Kerry Orchid
came out on top but, conceding 5 lb, with little to spare. Always handy,
tending to fiddle in a steadily-run affair, he went on at the thirteenth of the
eighteen fences then had to fend off a strong challenge from Elegant Lord,
who came through on the bridle and looked the more likely to win until that
little extra experience of Kerry Orchid's told on the flat. Less than a length
separated them at the finish. Kerry Orchid and Elegant Lord are obviously
two individuals that could go places in the next few years, not just in the
world of hunter chasing but beyond. However, they have time on their side
and future plans already announced for Kerry Orchid reveal that he won't be
hurried. He is to remain a hunter chaser for another season, with Cheltenham and Aintree his principal objectives.

		Abwah	Abernant
Kerry Orchid	Absalom	(gr 1969)	The Creditor
(gr.g. 1988)	(gr 1975)	Shadow Queen	Darius
		(ch 1965)	Shadow
	Matinata	Dike	Herbager
	(b 1972)	(ch 1966)	Delta
		Hash Amato	Vigo
		(gr 1961)	Catherine de Valois

Hunter chase pedigrees lack nothing in variety; the range is classic to
carthorse. Kerry Orchid would have been a sprinter had he taken after his
sire Absalom or his grandam Hash Amato, a five-furlong sprinter in the
latter case. His dam Matinata ran once, as a two-year-old. Of her five
previous foals, four won on the Flat here or abroad and they included Early
Call (by Kind of Hush), a useful filly at up to a mile and a half. Her seventh
foal is Second Call (also by Kind of Hush), three times a winner over hurdles
in the latest season. If not bred for chasing Kerry Orchid is built for
it—rangy and workmanlike. In his short career he has already shown that he
acts on good to firm and good to soft ground. Improvement from him looks
certain. *E. J. O'Grady, Ireland*

KERRYS EYE 9 b.g. Gladden – Swinging Time (High Treason) [1992/3   c–
22s 25d 22m6 c24fF c27v3 c24mur c18m] lengthy, sparely-made gelding: –
poor novice jumper. *P. R. Rodford*

KERRY TO CLARE 7 gr.m. Step Together (USA) – Creagh (Sky Boy)
[1992/3 22dpu 21dpu] leggy mare: poor novice hurdler: stays 3m. *T. M.*   –
Gibson

412

Mr Peter Curling's "Kerry Orchid"

KETTI   8 br.m. Hotfoot – Nigrel (Sovereign Path) [1992/3 17s^F 24s³ 25g⁴
17d² 17d 16s⁴ 21v* 22s 18m² 21f³ 25m 16d⁵] small, workmanlike mare: fairly   128
useful hurdler: won handicap at Kempton in January: well below her best
last 2 outings: effective at 2m and stays 3m: acts on any going: often
blinkered or visored (wasn't at Kempton). *D. L. Williams*

KEV'S LASS (IRE)   5 ch.m. Kemal (FR) – Nellie's Dream (Over The
River (FR)) [1992/3 F16g⁴ F16g 18g 18s 20v⁶ 16d³ 18d² 18s⁴ 16v* 26g⁵   94
22f^{pu}] medium-sized ex-Irish mare: first foal: dam unraced sister to staying
chaser Gatterstown: pulled up in a point in 1992: made all in novice hurdle at
Worcester in April on British debut (previously trained by P. Banville):
should stay beyond 2¼m: possibly needs plenty of give in the ground, acts
on heavy. *F. Murphy*

KEY DEAR (FR)   6 ch.g. Darly (FR) – Keep Happy (FR) (Red
Vagabonde) [1992/3 17s³ 18f² 17g² 18d^{pu} 17f* 16d a16g⁶ a18g⁵ 17f² 17m^F   87
20m 20g³] leggy, shallow-girthed gelding: modest hurdler: won conditional
jockeys novice event at Taunton in October: ran well when placed
otherwise: sold to join R. Juckes 4,200 gns Ascot June Sales: stays 2½m:
acts on firm and dead going: usually blinkered nowadays: jumps none too
fluently: pulls hard and races up with pace. *P. F. Nicholls*

KEYLU   4 b.f. Sula Bula – Key Biscayne (Deep Run) [1992/3 F16s] plain
filly: fifth foal: dam winning hurdler/chaser at around 2m: tailed off in NH
Flat race at Warwick in February: yet to race over hurdles. *G. W. Giddings*

KHAKI LIGHT 5 b.g. Lighter – Blue Speckle (Tom Noddy) [1992/3 F16d F17s] second foal: dam moderate staying chaser: tailed off in NH Flat races in October and December: yet to race over hurdles or fences. *M. J. Charles*

KHALLOOF (IRE) 4 b.g. Ballad Rock – Tapiola (Tap On Wood) [1992/3 16g a18gᵖᵘ] angular, workmanlike gelding: 7f winner on Flat: sold out of M. Jarvis' stable 2,200 gns Newmarket July Sales: showed nothing over hurdles in January and February. *Denys Smith* –

KHARIF 9 b.g. Formidable (USA) – Pass The Rulla (USA) (Buckpasser) [1992/3 c17gᵘʳ c16m² c17d⁵ c16g c16g³ 16d 24m⁴ 24m⁴ 18g⁵] sturdy gelding: poor hurdler nowadays/novice chaser: stays 2¾m: unsuited by heavy going, acts on any other: blinkered fifth and last 2 outings. *R. Allan*   c80 80

KHARTOUM FLYER 8 ch.g. Alanrod – Ginnett (Owen Anthony) [1992/3 c21gᶠ] angular gelding: maiden pointer: fell seventh in maiden hunter chase in March. *E. B. De Giles*   c–

KHOJOHN 5 ch.g. Chief Singer – Pirate Lass (USA) (Cutlass (USA)) [1992/3 18m⁵ 16f 18m⁵ 20g⁶ a20g² a20g⁴ a24g* 25g² 21g* 25s* a24g*] sparely-made gelding: trained first 4 outings by R. Woodhouse: won novice handicap hurdles at Southwell, Hexham and Wetherby and handicap at Southwell in second half of 1992/3: stays 25f: acts on good to firm, soft ground and fibresand: sometimes runs in snatches: claimer ridden. *Mrs V. A. Aconley*   98

KIBREET 6 ch.g. Try My Best (USA) – Princess Pageant (Welsh Pageant) [1992/3 20vᶠ 17s c16s² c17g³ c16d c17f³ c20s c17g⁴] lengthy gelding: fairly useful hurdler at best: moderate form over fences: should stay further than 17f: acts on good to firm ground, probably on soft: has looked unenthusiastic and is one to treat with caution over fences. *D. R. C. Elsworth*   c93 § –

KICKING BIRD 6 b.m. Bold Owl – Sodina (Saulingo) [1992/3 21sᵖᵘ] leggy mare: behind in NH Flat race and when pulled up in a novice hurdle. *K. C. Bailey*   –

KICK ON MAJESTIC (IRE) 4 b.g. Mister Majestic – Avebury Ring (Auction Ring (USA)) [1992/3 18f 18gᶠ] small gelding: poor and inconsistent handicapper on Flat, suited by 7f: blinkered, seventh of 10 in juvenile hurdle at Sedgefield in September. *N. Bycroft*   62

KIDLAW 5 b.g. Good Times (ITY) – Bedfellow (Crepello) [1992/3 17m² 17m* 17d* 17d⁵ 17g⁴ 18g⁴] leggy, lengthy, unfurnished gelding with scope: won novice hurdles at Newcastle (conditional jockeys, trained until after then by W. A. Stephenson) in November and Kelso in December: creditable efforts on his other starts: will be well suited by a stiffer test of stamina: acts on good to firm and dead ground. *P. Cheesbrough*   94

KIKIS 6 ch.g. Saher – Rose Almond (Stanford) [1992/3 23gᵖᵘ 17s⁵ 17v⁴ 16s 18v] smallish gelding: poor novice hurdler: not raced after January: best form at 17f: acts on heavy going. *J. S. Moore*   76

KILCASH (IRE) 5 b.g. Salmon Leap (USA) – Roblanna (Roberto (USA)) [1992/3 19m 16d² 17s* 17d* 16d² 17v² 16s³ 16d²] tall gelding: useful handicap hurdler: won at Chepstow and Sandown in October: remained in excellent form, and finished close second to Glencloud in The Ladbroke at Leopardstown in January final start despite a bad mistake at the last: effective at 2m and will stay beyond 19f: well suited by give in the ground and acts on heavy: best blinkered: sometimes wears tongue strap: often hangs left, and is suited by strong handling: tough and consistent. *P. R. Hedger*   139

KILCLOONEY FORREST 11 b.g. King's Equity – Carrig-An-Neady (Orchardist) [1992/3 c25g c25d⁵ c25dᵖᵘ c25vᵘʳ c25s² c25dᶠ c24s³ c25sᶠ c25dᵘʳ c25sᵖᵘ c24d³] sturdy gelding: novice chaser: easily best effort in 1992/3 on fifth start: suited by a thorough test of stamina: acts on soft going: sketchy jumper. *Mrs S. J. Smith*   c94 d

KILCOLGAN 6 ch.g. Le Bavard (FR) – Katula (Khalkis) [1992/3 22s⁴ 22d⁴ 23g⁶ 24s⁵] leggy gelding: poor novice hurdler: sold 8,200 gns in May: best effort over 17f on good to firm ground. *W. A. Stephenson*   63

KILCONNEY PRINCE 11 br.g. Martinmas – Dark Gold (Raise You Ten) [1992/3 c19vF] lengthy gelding: poor novice jumper. *Miss Linda Morgan*   c– –

KILCOURSEY 8 ch.g. Lucifer (USA) – Be An Angel (Be Friendly) [1992/3 c21f⁴] compact gelding: poor maiden hurdler/chaser: sketchy jumper: visored fourth start in 1991/2, blinkered since. *B. Stevens*   c– –

KILDIMO 13 b.g. Le Bavard (FR) – Leuze (Vimy) [1992/3 c24m⁴ c25g c27d* c24d⁴ c25s⁵ c30s⁵ c25d⁶ c29dpu] big gelding: high-class chaser at his best, fairly useful in later years: won Crowther Homes Becher Chase (Handicap) at Aintree in November by 7 lengths from Four Trix: ran lack-lustre races last 2 starts: stayed well: best on ground no softer than dead: jumped well: suited by forcing tactics: became unreliable: has been retired. *Mrs S. J. Smith*   c128 §

KILDONAN 6 b.g. Welsh Captain – Madam Import (Import) [1992/3 17m 21g⁴ 21d⁶ 24s⁵ 21g c18gF c17m⁵] workmanlike gelding: quite modest handicapper at up to 1¼m on Flat at best: poor novice jumper: dead. *B. S. Rothwell*   c– 70

KILDOWNEY HILL 7 b.g. Kemal (FR) – Nadine's Pride (Double-U-Jay) [1992/3 F16g⁴ F20d³ 22g⁶ 23d⁵] workmanlike ex-Irish gelding: won a point in 1992: in frame in NH Flat races when trained by E. Bolger: poor form in novice hurdles in October and November: sold 5,800 gns Ascot June Sales. *Miss H. C. Knight*   66

KILFORD 13 b.g. Northfields (USA) – Ashaireez (Abernant) [1992/3 c21g] compact gelding: poor novice chaser: visored once, blinkered once. *P. R. M. Philips*   c– –

KILFRANCIS LAD 16 b.g. Milan – Wandering Princess (Prince Hansel) [1992/3 c23m⁴] sturdy gelding: fairly useful hunter chaser in 1990: poor form in handicap only start in 1992/3 (August): stays 3m: acts on hard ground. *Mrs S. M. Johnson*   c79 –

KILHALLON CASTLE 10 b.g. Town And Country – Castell Memories (Tacitus) [1992/3 c26dpu c21s⁶ c25g* c26m² c26g² c24m² c21g²] smallish, sturdy gelding: fair handicap chaser: won at Ayr in February: ran creditably next 3 starts: stays 3¼m: acts on soft and good to firm going. *G. Richards*   c100 –

KILKILMARTIN 11 b.g. Rarity – Kilkilwell (Harwell) [1992/3 c17v⁵ c17vpu c23g⁶ c20m³ c20f⁵ c17v³ c18mpu c17m³ c22gpu] lengthy, deep-   c84 x –

Crowther Homes Becher Handicap Chase, Aintree —
Kildimo (left) takes the feature race at the November meeting

girthed gelding: modest novice chaser: stays 2½m: acts on soft and good to firm going: poor jumper. *H. J. Manners*

KILKNOCKIN 11 ch.g. Boreen (FR) – Ceylon Fort (Fortina) [1992/3 c26m^{pu} c26g] big, strong gelding: modest hunter chaser at best: showed nothing in 1992/3: stays 3¼m: acts on heavy going. *Miss C. Saunders* — c–

KILLARNEY MAN 7 br.g. Pragmatic – Lilly of Killarney (Sunny Way) [1992/3 21f^{pu} 26s^{pu}] leggy, angular gelding: sold 1,800 gns Ascot June Sales: no form in novice hurdles. *T. J. Etherington* — –

KILLBANON 11 b.g. Imperius – Flail (Hill Gail) [1992/3 c24d^F c24d^4 c25m^4] tall, strong, lengthy gelding: useful chaser at best: has run poorly last 4 completed starts: suited by a test of stamina: probably acts on any going. *C. C. Trietline* — c–

KILLESHIN 7 bl.g. Al Sirat (USA) – Spin Off (Wrekin Rambler) [1992/3 c27f^4] lengthy gelding: maiden hurdler/chaser: sold 1,550 gns Ascot March Sales: stays 25f: acts on good to firm going: sketchy jumper. *K. R. Burke* — c–

KILLTUBBER HOUSE 7 ch.g. Deep Run – Astrella Celeste (Menelek) [1992/3 16s] ex-Irish gelding: poor novice hurdler. *J. Cosgrave* — 70

KILLULA CHIEF 6 b.g. Strong Gale – Lolos Run VII (Pedigree Unknown) [1992/3 16d^2 26g^4 17m^4 c20g^3 22d^3 17f^F 17g* 20g^2 16m^2] leggy gelding: made most when winning novice hurdle at Bangor in May: ran creditably after: some promise on chasing debut: trained until after then by T. Tate and until after eighth outing by K. Bailey: best at up to 2½m: acts on dead ground: blinkered last 5 starts. *J. G. M. O'Shea* — c– p / 99

KILLULA KING 6 br.g. Black Minstrel – Ski Cap (Beau Chapeau) [1992/3 c17g* c21s^4 c16g^5 c16s^3 c16s^F c16g^5] angular, quite good-topped gelding: maiden hurdler: won novice chase at Kelso in October: ran well next 2 starts (trained until after then by W. A. Stephenson): should stay beyond 21f: acts on any going: poor jumper of fences. *P. Cheesbrough* — c101 x / –

KILLURA (IRE) 5 b.g. Royal Fountain – Hill Side Glen (Goldhill) [1992/3 21g^4] leggy gelding: first foal: dam lightly-raced maiden: second in a point in Ireland in 1992: carrying condition when promising fourth of 21 in novice hurdle at Newbury in February. *K. C. Bailey* — 91 p

KILMINFOYLE 6 b.g. Furry Glen – Loreto Lady (Brave Invader (USA)) [1992/3 F17g^6 17g 20m 22m^3] rangy gelding: has scope: second foal: brother to a poor novice jumper: dam unraced half-sister to 3 winners, including fair jumper Royal Thrust: poor novice hurdler: stays 2¾m: acts on good to firm going. *Mrs M. Reveley* — 75

KILTONGA 6 b. or br.g. Indian King (USA) – Miss Teto (African Sky) [1992/3 22m 21d^{pu} 27d^{pu}] sturdy, close-coupled gelding: selling hurdler: showed nothing in 1992/3: stays 2¼m: acts on good to firm going. *P. Leach* — –

KILTROUM (FR) 4 gr.g. Courtroom (FR) – Kiltie (Habat) [1992/3 17m^4 18f^6 18s^5 18g 16m^3 18d^{ur}] strong, close-coupled gelding: maiden on Flat, some ability at 2 yrs: modest plater over hurdles: stays 2¼m: acts on any going. *C. Tinkler* — 72

KIMBERS (IRE) 5 b.g. Lomond (USA) – Take Your Mark (USA) (Round Table) [1992/3 16f^3] sturdy gelding: one-time useful 1½m performer on Flat, has gone wrong way: third in novice event at Windsor in March on hurdling debut: sold 2,400 gns Ascot May Sales. *S. Mellor* — 74

KINCARDINE BRIDGE (USA) 4 b.g. Tiffany Ice (USA) – Priestess (USA) (Time To Explode (USA)) [1992/3 F16d 17s^{pu}] first foal: dam unraced: tailed off in NH Flat race and when pulled up in a juvenile hurdle in the spring. *Mrs S. C. Bradburne* — –

KINDA GROOVY 4 b.g. Beveled (USA) – Tory Blues (Final Straw) [1992/3 17s 16s 22d^5 22g^3] compact gelding: second foal: dam, no form in 3 races on Flat, sister to Skinnhill and half-sister to Tresidder, both fairly useful chasers at best: best effort over hurdles when third of 15 in novice event at Sedgefield in March: will be suited by further than 2¾m. *I. Park* — 89

KIND'A SMART 8 ch.g. Kind of Hush – Treasure Seeker (Deep Diver) c101
[1992/3 c16g² c18d³ c16s* c20gᵇᵈ c21d³ c18dᵘʳ c17dᶠ c16g* c21g⁴ c16g⁴ –
c21f⁴] smallish, lengthy gelding: fair handicap chaser: won at Windsor in
November and Catterick in February: retained 7,000 gns Doncaster May
Sales: effective at 2m to 2½f: probably acts on any going: best without visor:
has tongue tied down: held up: sometimes let down by his jumping. *K. A.
Morgan*

KINDLY LADY 5 b.m. Kind of Hush – Welcome Honey (Be Friendly)
[1992/3 17s 17m⁵ 17d⁴] half-sister to fair chaser Broughton Manor (by 76
Dubassoff): of little account on Flat: showed a little ability over hurdles in
April and May. *Mrs J. G. Retter*

KINDRED CAMEO 4 ch.f. Risk Me (FR) – First Experience (Le
Johnstan) [1992/3 18m 17m] lengthy filly: plating-class maiden on Flat: sold –
out of G. Lewis' stable 750 gns Ascot July Sales: no promise over hurdles in
August. *K. F. Clutterbuck*

KINFAUNS DANCER 5 b.m. Celtic Cone – New Dawning (Deep Run)
[1992/3 23d³ 20s 26gᵖᵘ] sparely-made, small mare: first foal: dam unraced 82
half-sister to several winning jumpers: promising third in novice hurdle at
Kelso in November but ran as though something amiss 2 subsequent starts.
Mrs M. Reveley

KING CASH 7 b.g. Kambalda – Lisgarvan Highway (Dusky Boy) [1992/3 c–
c24mᶠ] leggy, workmanlike ex-Irish gelding: first foal: dam winning Irish –
pointer: fair hurdler: sold out of A. L. T. Moore's stable 27,000 gns
Doncaster May (1992) Sales: fell eleventh in novice event in November on
chasing debut: stays 3m: acts on heavy going. *Mrs S. A. Bramall*

KING CREDO 8 b.g. Kinglet – Credo's Daughter (Credo) [1992/3 17v⁴
16d⁴ 17g* 17m⁴] 161 p
The pre-publicity suggested that King Credo had virtually been
wheeled out from the sick bay to take his place in the Tote Gold Trophy. A
runny nose had prevented him being sent to Ireland for The Ladbroke five
weeks earlier and had been followed in quick succession by colic and a foot

*Tote Gold Trophy (Handicap Hurdle), Newbury—King Credo (left) lands the valuable prize;
Native Mission finishes runner-up for the second year in succession*

injury which still had his connections worrying on the day of the race at Newbury. None of this stopped King Credo winning by five lengths in a sixteen-runner field, positively bolting in, with a further four lengths back to the third. Racing towards the outside, King Credo made smooth headway into mid-division at the cross flight, tracked the pace-setting favourite Royal Derbi at the fourth last and was so full of running approaching the last that Native Mission was the only conceivable danger. That obstacle safely if rather awkwardly negotiated, King Credo sprinted clear. Third was the Irish challenger Bitofabanter.

It was immediately announced that King Credo would take his chance in the Champion Hurdle. He had a lot to find on form, despite the ease of his win, as he'd carried only 10-0 in the Tote Gold Trophy (the dual Champion Hurdle third Ruling had 12-0), an assessment which looked decidedly lenient beforehand as well as afterwards. The performance that gave King Credo such a good chance at Newbury (and, for that matter, in The Ladbroke) was his eighteen-length fourth to Mighty Mogul in the Christmas Hurdle at Kempton. King Credo was a 33/1-chance that day and his effort represented a marked improvement. That should not have caused too much surprise—he'd been a progressive type in his previous two seasons over hurdles despite seemingly regular physical set-backs, winning five of his eight races, including the Imperial Cup—and the promise of better still after his troubled preparation for Newbury made King Credo an interesting outsider in the Champion. So it proved. Starting at 20/1, King Credo was always within striking distance of the leaders, turned into the straight in sixth or seventh then stayed on at the one pace to finish an excellent fourth of seventeen finishers, six and a half lengths off the winner Granville Again. A run in the Cordon Bleu Handicap Hurdle at Aintree was mooted, but his trainer had stated that he would not be tested again on ground as firm as at Cheltenham, and the Champion Hurdle was King Credo's last race of the season.

		Pampered King (b 1954)	Prince Chevalier
	Kinglet (b 1970)		Netherton Maid
		War Ribbon (br 1955)	Anwar
King Credo (b.g. 1985)			Last Rank
		Credo (ch 1960)	Crepello
	Credo's Daughter (b 1966)		Marsyaka
		Spring Campaign (b 1960)	Vic Day
			Halador

To say that King Credo is the standard bearer for his stable would be a severe understatement. His Tote Gold Trophy was its sole victory of the season; in fact, it had only two runners and two runs besides King Credo, one pulled up and the other tailed off. Steve Woodman had eight horses listed in his care in the 1993 *Horses In Training*, three of them, including King Credo, out of the mare Credo's Daughter who represented Woodman's father with distinction in the 'seventies. The winner of four races on the Flat in Ireland, Credo's Daughter proceeded to win nine over jumps, eight in steeplechases. In her final season she finished in the frame in the Mackeson, Hennessy, Massey-Ferguson and the SGB Chase and made a winning end to her career, all in November and December. She'd not done too badly before King Credo at stud either, with three winners, including Have Faith (by Sunyboy) who looked particularly promising when fifth in the 1987 Supreme Novices' Hurdle but had an injury-blighted career thereafter. Credo's Daughter is a half-sister to Driella, the dam of the Irish Grand National runner-up Seskin Bridge and smart chaser Comeragh King. Comeragh King was an instantly recognizable individual with his low head carriage and, coincidentally, King Credo tends to catch the eye carrying his head high and awkwardly in a finish. The closing stages also often see him wandering under pressure, but there is no doubt about his resolution. In terms of form, King Credo just gets better and better. A rangy, sparely-made gelding who is progressing physically, he is reported to go novice chasing and is clearly a good prospect although his hurdling tends to be punctuated by the odd clumsy error. One such blunder came at the second last when he was making a promising reappearance in the William Hill

Handicap Hurdle on heavy going at Sandown. The ground at Cheltenham for the Champion was good to firm. King Credo has won at two and a quarter miles and will stay further. *S. Woodman*

KINGFISHER BAY 8 b.g. Try My Best (USA) – Damiya (FR) (Direct Flight) [1992/3 27m³ c26g² c26m* c23s² c26d* c26v² c21v⁴ c25d c27m³ c26g³ c26s³] leggy gelding: winning hurdler: moderate chaser: won 2 novice events at Plumpton early in season: stays 27f: probably acts on any ground. *J. White*   c93 –

KING FLIPPER 7 b.g. King's Ride – Natasha Ann (Allangrange) [1992/3 c16vᵖᵘ] tall, lengthy gelding: of no account. *J. R. Jenkins*   c– –

KINGFORD 14 ch.g. Supreme Sovereign – Florrie Ford (Kelly) [1992/3 c26m] compact gelding: modest pointer: winning hunter chaser: stays 21f: acts on heavy going. *S. R. Green*   c– –

KING OF NORMANDY (IRE) 4 ch.g. King of Clubs – Miss Deauville (Sovereign Path) [1992/3 17d 16s² 17v³ 18v* 17g⁶ 18g 17g 22fᵖᵘ] workmanlike gelding: reluctant and of little account on Flat: poor form over hurdles: won 3-finisher seller at Fontwell (no bid) in February: stays 2¼m: best form with plenty of give in the ground: visored once, blinkered once. *J. Ffitch-Heyes*   74

KING OF SHADOWS 6 b. or br.g. Connaught – Rhiannon (Welsh Pageant) [1992/3 a18g a18gᵖᵘ c26dᶠ a21gᶠ] close-coupled gelding: modest hurdler at best: no form in 1992/3: fell on chasing debut: stays 3m: acts well on fibresand. *J. Carden*   c– –

KING OF STEEL 7 b.g. Kemal (FR) – Black Spangle (Black Tarquin) [1992/3 25g⁴ 25s² 24d² 26s* 25d⁵ 26m²] small gelding: trained first start by N. Bycroft: won novice hurdle at Catterick in January: suited by long distances and forcing tactics: best efforts with plenty of give in the ground. *M. D. Hammond*   96

KING OF THE LOT 10 br.g. Space King – Nicola Lisa (Dumbarnie) [1992/3 c16g* c16d* c17s²] tall, sparely-made gelding: useful chaser: won handicaps at Wetherby and Cheltenham in first half of season: also ran well final start (November): best at 2m: acts on any going: has run well when sweating. *D. Nicholson*   c141 –

KING OF ZURICH 6 b.g. Alzao (USA) – Perfect Choice (Bold Lad (IRE)) [1992/3 16s⁵ 18g] compact gelding: fair novice hurdler in Ireland in 1990/1: no worthwhile form in 1992/3 but shaped as though retaining some ability: yet to race beyond 2¼m: acts on soft ground. *R. Rowe*   – p

KING OPTIMIST 4 ch.g. King Persian – Misoptimist (Blakeney) [1992/3 18f*] poor maiden plater on Flat: won juvenile hurdle at Sedgefield in September: stays 2¼m: acts on firm ground. *A. Smith*   86

KINGS BROMPTON 7 b.h. Latest Model – Idson Lass (Levanter) [1992/3 17vᵖᵘ 18g] sturdy horse: no sign of ability. *J. R. Payne*   –

KINGS CHARIOT 6 b.g. King's Ride – Royalement (Little Buskins) [1992/3 F16g⁶] first foal: dam never ran: sixth of 22 in NH Flat race at Kempton in February: yet to race over hurdles or fences. *Lady Eliza Mays-Smith*   –

KINGS DAWN 5 b.m. Dawn Johnny (USA) – Old Currency (Lucky Brief) [1992/3 22sᵖᵘ] compact mare: sixth foal: half-sister to a poor animal by Rambah: dam plating-class maiden on Flat: soon tailed off in maiden hurdle in February on debut. *G. Fleming*   –

KING SEAR 11 br.g. Dubassoff (USA) – Noble Device (El Cid) [1992/3 c19s² c21m⁶] compact gelding: fair pointer: novice hunter chaser: stays 2½m: acts on good to firm and soft ground. *Mrs Yvonne Allsop*   c87 –

KINGSFOLD PET 4 b.g. Tina's Pet – Bella Lisa (River Chanter) [1992/3 18gᵖᵘ 16gᵖᵘ] tall gelding: half-brother to winning hurdlers Es-Port (by Mummy's Game) and Strictly Business (by Song): seems of little account. *M. J. Haynes*   –

KINGS FOUNTAIN 10 br.g. Royal Fountain – K-King (Fury Royal) c153
[1992/3 c21d2 c21dF c24sur c20s3 c21d5] tall, rather leggy gelding: very –
smart chaser at best: placed in small fields in valuable events at Wincanton
and Haydock: ran poorly final start: effective around 2½m and stays 25f: yet
to show his very best form on soft ground, acts on any other: races up with
the pace: prone to the odd bad mistake: blinkered last 2 outings. *K. C. Bailey*

KING'S GUEST (IRE) 4 b.g. Tender King – Saintly Guest (What A
Guest) [1992/3 16m3 16g 16g5 16m4] compact gelding: one-time fair 82
performer at around 1m on Flat: poor form over hurdles: keen type and
barely stays 2m: acts on good to firm ground. *G. M. Moore*

KINGS GUNNER 6 ch.g. Kings Lake (USA) – Resooka (Godswalk c85
(USA)) [1992/3 c24s3 c2 1m4] compact gelding: modest pointer: better effort –
in hunter chases when fourth in novice event at Cheltenham in May: should
stay beyond 21f: acts on good to firm ground. *Mrs J. Litston*

KINGS HATCH 7 ch.g. Down The Hatch – Lady Hapsburg
(Perhapsburg) [1992/3 18g 20mpu 17gpu] leggy, close-coupled gelding: of –
little account: blinkered final start. *A. P. Jones*

KING'S MAVERICK (IRE) 5 b.g. King's Ride – Lawless Secret
(Meadsville) [1992/3 F17s5 aF16g5 F17f] third foal: half-brother to 6-y-o –
Secret Law (by Celio Rufo): dam unraced: signs of ability in NH Flat races:
yet to race over hurdles or fences. *T. Thomson Jones*

KINGS RANK 8 br.g. Tender King – Jhansi Ki Rani (USA) (Far North c101 §
(CAN)) [1992/3 22s5 c18s2 c24v5 21v6 22v4 26m6 25f 22v4 c18m5 c24fur 124 §
25m5] sparely-made gelding: fairly useful hurdler when in the mood: novice
chaser, fair form at best: retained 8,200 gns Ascot June Sales: stays 3¼m:
acts on any going: usually blinkered, visored final outing: isn't one to trust.
M. C. Pipe

KING'S RARITY 7 b.g. King's Ride – Kilim (Weavers' Hall) [1992/3
18s] rangy gelding: chasing type: winning hurdler: should stay beyond 2m: –
acts on good to firm going. *A. J. Wilson*

KING'S SHILLING (USA) 6 b.g. Fit To Fight (USA) – Pride's
Crossing (USA) (Riva Ridge (USA)) [1992/3 20gpu 16s5 16m5 17d6 17m* 121
17g2 17d* 17m* 16g* 16f 17g* 16f 16m3 17f4] workmanlike gelding: fairly
useful hurdler: trained by Mrs S. Oliver on first outing and by J.
Cosgrave next 3 starts: much improved subsequently, winning at Hereford
(twice), Stratford, Worcester and Bangor in the spring: best at around 2m:
acts on firm and dead ground, and on fibresand: held up. *C. D. Broad*

KINGSTHORPE 5 ch.g. Brotherly (USA) – Miss Kewmill (Billion
(USA)) [1992/3 17dF 16v 17s 16mpu 16mF] leggy, sparely-made gelding: of –
little account. *G. H. Yardley*

KING'S TREASURE (USA) 4 b.g. King of Clubs – Crown Treasure
(USA) (Graustark) [1992/3 17d4 16s2 16s4 17mur 17g3] good-topped gelding: 111
half-brother to several winners, including very smart hurdler Crystal Spirit
(by Kris): fair maiden on Flat (stayer) and over hurdles: will stay beyond 17f:
acts on soft going. *I. A. Balding*

KINGS WILD 12 b.g. Mandalus – Queens Trip (Mon Capitaine) [1992/3 c–
c22fF c2 1fpu c23gpu c17fpu] workmanlike gelding: winning chaser: no form –
since 1990/1: blinkered once. *A. P. Jones*

KINGSWOOD KITCHENS 13 b.g. General Ironside – Tyrone c83 §
Typhoon (Typhoon) [1992/3 c25v5 c27m4 c26m4 c24g] workmanlike, rather – §
angular gelding: poor chaser: stays well: probably acts on any ground:
blinkered once: ungenuine: sold 1,500 gns Ascot 2nd June Sales. *P. C.
Clarke*

KING WILLIAM 8 b.g. Dara Monarch – Norman Delight (USA) (Val de c–
L'Orne (FR)) [1992/3 17g3 17f* 17g 17g2 17m5 17g6 16d4] sturdy gelding: fair 109
handicap hurdler: won at Huntingdon in September: also ran well late on:
once-raced over fences: best form at around 2m: suited by a sound surface
(acts on hard ground): held up. *J. L. Spearing*

KINNESTON 9 b.g. Night Porter – Dysie Mary (Apollonius) [1992/3   **c76**
c23g^F c17d c23s^5 c23d^6 c25g^{pu} c25s^3 c23d^{ur} c20g^5 c23g^{ur} c24m^5 c21d]   –
good-topped gelding: poor novice chaser: stays 25f: acts on soft ground. *N. W. Alexander*

KINO 6 b.g. Niniski (USA) – Relkina (FR) (Relkino) [1992/3 c18f^5 c18g*   **c96**
c16g^R 17s^2 c21d^F c22s^F 17v^3 a20g^6 16v 23d^4 16g 25m^3 27g] smallish   **91**
gelding: moderate handicap hurdler: won novice chase at Stratford in September: effective at around 2m and stays 25f: acts on heavy and good to firm going (ran poorly on equitrack): best in blinkers: sometimes looks temperamental: sketchy jumper. *S. E. Sherwood*

KINOKO 5 ch.g. Bairn (USA) – Octavia (Sallust) [1992/3 17m^4 16v* 16g^2]   **101**
lengthy gelding: modest middle-distance stayer on Flat, winner twice in 1993: won novice hurdle at Uttoxeter in December: good second in similar event at Catterick in March: will stay beyond 17f: acts on heavy going. *K. W. Hogg, Isle of Man*

KINROYAL 8 br.g. Royal Fountain – Most Kind (Tudenham) [1992/3   **c–**
c24m^6] leggy gelding: of little account. *F. Jestin*   –

KIRBY OPPORTUNITY 5 ch.m. Mummy's Game – Empress   –
Catherine (Welsh Pageant) [1992/3 20g 22d] modest middle-distance performer on Flat (claimed out of J. Pearce's stable £8,001 in June): behind in novice hurdles in September and March. *P. Leach*

KIRCHWYN LAD 5 b.g. Kirchner – Gowyn (Goldhill) [1992/3 16d 16g   **73**
17f] half-brother to several winners, including hurdler/chaser Richards Bay (by Record Run): dam never ran: poor form in novice hurdles: best effort on final start. *S. J. Leadbetter*

KIRKCALDY (IRE) 4 b.g. Glad Dancer – Rosabuskins (Little Buskins)   **76**
[1992/3 18m 23g^3 21s] fourth foal: dam well beaten in Irish NH Flat races: third in poor novice hurdle at Kelso in April, only form. *Mrs S. C. Bradburne*

KIRKLEES ROCK 6 br.m. Kala Shikari – Lady Farrier (Sheshoon)   –
[1992/3 21s^{pu}] small, well-made mare: winning staying selling hurdler: sold 1,300 gns Doncaster May Sales. *W. Bentley*

KIRKMAN'S KAMP 8 b.g. Royal Palace – The Guzzler (Behistoun)   **82 p**
[1992/3 22m^4] one-time modest stayer on Flat: showed ability when fourth in late-season seller at Cartmel on hurdling debut: should improve. *P. D. Evans*

KIRSTENBOSCH 6 b.g. Caerleon (USA) – Flower Petals (Busted)   **94**
[1992/3 18g^2 16m^2 17m* 17d^3 22m* 18v^4] compact gelding: modest hurdler: won claimer at Carlisle and seller at Cartmel (bought in 2,800 gns) in the spring: effective at 2m and stays 2¾m when conditions aren't testing: acts on good to firm and heavy ground. *L. Lungo*

KIRSTY'S BOY 10 b.g. Majestic Streak – Cute Peach (Hardicanute)   **c123**
[1992/3 c24m^6 c25g^4 c24m^4 c25m^4 c24f* c24g^4 c25g*] small gelding: fairly   –
useful chaser: won 3-runner handicaps at Newcastle and Wetherby in May: stays 25f: probably acts on any going: sometimes wears blinkers or visor (didn't in 1992/3). *Miss L. A. Perratt*

KIRSTY'S PEACH (IRE) 4 b.f. Miramar Reef – Cute Peach
(Hardicanute) [1992/3 F16g] half-sister to smart chaser Foyle Fisherman (by No Argument) and fairly useful jumper Kirsty's Boy (by Majestic Streak): dam unplaced in 2 outings at 2 yrs: behind in NH Flat race at Ayr in March: yet to race over hurdles. *Miss L. A. Perratt*

KISSANE 12 br.g. Kemal (FR) – Chamowen (Master Owen) [1992/3   **c110**
c19g* c21s^2 c26g^3 c19v^{pu} c21d c21d^6 c19m^{ur}] strong, rangy gelding: fair   –
handicap chaser: won at Hereford in September and would probably have won on same course in March but for unseating rider (returned lame): suited by around 2½m: acts on heavy and good to firm ground: front runner: safe jumper. *C. D. Broad*

KISU KALI 6 ch.g. Kris – Evita (Reform) [1992/3 c17m^3 c16f^F c16g^4 **c84**
c21m^2 c18g* c19f^{pu} c16v^5 c16v^3 c17v* c19v^4 c16v^2 c16s^6 c21f* c18g^3]   –

compact gelding: selling hurdler: won novice chases at Fontwell and Newton Abbot (handicap) in first half of season and Lingfield (valuable event in which his sole opponent finished lame) in March: probably stays 2½m: acts on any going. *J. Ffitch-Heyes*

KITCHI KOO 9 b.m. Imperial Fling (USA) – Hard To Follow (Roi Lear (FR)) [1992/3 21v⁴ 21s 21s*] rangy mare: modest handicap hurdler: won at Warwick in January: jumped poorly both starts over fences: will stay beyond 2¾m: acts on good to firm and heavy ground. *A. J. Wilson* — c– x 100

KITTINGER 12 b.g. Crash Course – Mandaloch (Mandamus) [1992/3 c21d⁴ c21v³ c19s* c21d c22g² c21s⁴ c23f³ c24g] lengthy, workmanlike gelding: fair chaser: won handicap at Taunton in December: stays 3m: probably acts on any going. *P. J. Hobbs* — c101 –

KITTY BUTLER 7 b.m. Tampero (FR) – Lady Piersfield (Mugatpura) [1992/3 17dᵖᵘ 17vᶠ 22s c16v⁴ c21v c16v³ c17sᵖᵘ c16g⁴ c16fᶠ] sparely-made mare: no form over hurdles: poor novice chaser: dead. *P. Butler* — c71 –

KIVETON TYCOON (IRE) 4 b.c. Last Tycoon – Zillionaire (USA) (Vaguely Noble) [1992/3 16d* 16s* 16g⁴ 17m⁶] strong, sturdy colt: carries condition: fair maiden on Flat: won 2 juvenile hurdles at Nottingham in November: nearest at finish when good sixth to Shawiya in Daily Express Triumph Hurdle at Cheltenham (blinkered) in March: will stay beyond 17f: acts on good to firm and soft going: should improve further. *J. A. Glover* — 129 p

KIWI LAKE (NZ) 7 b.h. Balkan Knight (USA) – Tempest True (NZ) (Tempest Boy) [1992/3 21g 16g 24sᵖᵘ] no form in novice hurdles: sold 2,000 gns Doncaster May Sales. *N. A. Twiston-Davies* — –

KIWI L'EGLISE (NZ) 7 br.g. Church Parade – Llantilly Lass (NZ) (Llananthony (NZ)) [1992/3 22g 22vᵖᵘ] leggy gelding: modest novice hurdler at around 2m at best: no form in 1992/3. *D. H. Barons* — –

KIWI VELOCITY (NZ) 6 b.m. Veloso (NZ) – Eumenides (NZ) (Head Hunter) [1992/3 22v² 24v* 22v² 22d* 21g⁴] leggy mare: won novice hurdles at Worcester in January and February: suited by good test of stamina: acts on heavy going. *P. J. Hobbs* — 112

KLINGON (IRE) 4 b.g. Formidable (USA) – Melbourne Miss (Chaparral (FR)) [1992/3 20s⁵ 16s³ 16v³ a16g² a16g³] strong gelding: half-brother to winning jumpers Lake Tiberias (by Kings Lake) and Taroudant (by Pharly): modest maiden on Flat (stayer) and over hurdles: sold 3,500 gns Doncaster March Sales: best form at 2m but should stay further: acts on heavy ground and fibresand. *R. Hollinshead* — 94

KNAVE OF CLUBS 6 ch.g. King of Clubs – La Calera (GER) (Caracol (FR)) [1992/3 22s* 22m* 21f*] good-bodied gelding: in tremendous form over hurdles in the spring, winning handicaps at Ludlow (first start for stable), Cheltenham and Towcester: stays 2¾m: acts on any going: sometimes blinkered prior to 1992/3: genuine: likely to improve further. *N. A. Twiston-Davies* — 121 p

KNAYTON PROSPECT 5 br.g. Strong Gale – Shuil Ard (Quayside) [1992/3 F17d⁵ F16v 21sᵖᵘ 16d 20m² 20m* 21g] sturdy, workmanlike gelding: chasing type: first foal: dam unraced: successful in novice hurdle at Newcastle in March: will stay beyond 2½m: form only on good to firm going: sometimes wears tongue strap. *M. W. Easterby* — 97

KNIGHT IN SIDE 7 ch.g. Tachypous – Miss Saddler (St Paddy) [1992/3 18m⁴ 17s³ 16f⁶ 17g] leggy gelding: modest hurdler: should stay beyond 2¼m: acts on good to firm and soft going. *R. Callow* — 90

KNIGHTLY ARGUS 6 ch.g. Le Moss – Cala San Vicente (Gala Performance (USA)) [1992/3 16d³ 22m³ 20d³ 25sᶜᵒ 18s 24f⁶ 22d⁵] sturdy gelding: modest novice hurdler: stays 2¾m: acts on good to firm and dead ground. *S. E. Sherwood* — 90

KNIGHT OF HONOUR 5 ch.g. Touching Wood (USA) – Nobly Born (USA) (The Minstrel (CAN)) [1992/3 20g⁵ 28g⁴] close-coupled gelding: poor form over hurdles (tried blinkered) and in points. *M. Dods* — –

KNIGHT OIL 10 b.g. Miner's Lamp – Fair Argument (No Argument) c126 §
[1992/3 c21g⁴ c24s⁴ c21v² c25v² c25v² c24f² c25m] sturdy, good sort: fairly –
useful chaser: stays well: acts on any going: usually blinkered: often jumps
deliberately: sometimes runs in snatches: not one to trust. *O. Sherwood*

KNIGHTON COOMBE (NZ) 7 ch.g. The Expatriate – Sashay (NZ)
(Showoff) [1992/3 17s³ 23d 22d⁴ 22d³ 25mᶠ] sparely-made, angular gelding: 105
fair hurdler: stays 2¾m: acts on good to soft ground. *Capt. T. A. Forster*

KNIGHT PAWN 4 b.g. Uncle Pokey – Lady Carol (Lord Gayle (USA))
[1992/3 16g 16s 16sᵖᵘ] workmanlike gelding: signs of ability on Flat, none in –
juvenile hurdles: dead. *J. P. Leigh*

KNIGHTSBRIDGE BC 6 b.g. Bulldozer – Golden Annie (Le
Tricolore) [1992/3 17s 24vᵖᵘ 21g 20v⁶] tall, workmanlike gelding: second –
foal: dam behind in 3 Irish NH Flat races: no form in novice hurdles:
blinkered final outing. *K. C. Bailey*

KNIGHTS (NZ) 7 br.g. Vice Regal (NZ) – Montrose Lass (AUS) (Gay c80
Gambler (USA)) [1992/3 18d* 20d³ 16g⁶ 17s 17d c16d⁴ 21d⁶ c21g⁴ 22g* 107
25m*] neat, quite attractive gelding: fair handicap hurdler: won at
Sedgefield in November (ladies event) and April and Uttoxeter in May: poor
form in novice chases: effective at around 2m and stays 25f: acts on good to
firm and dead going: poor efforts when tried blinkered/visored. *C. D. Broad*

KNIGHT'S SPUR (USA) 6 b.g. Diesis – Avoid (USA) (Buckpasser) c98
[1992/3 c17d⁵ c18mᵇᵈ c16d² c16s³ c16dᵖᵘ c17f* c16d* c18g² c17m³ c21f⁶] –
sturdy gelding: fair hurdler: successful in novice chases at Newbury and
Uttoxeter in March: best form at up to 2¼m: probably acts on any going. *J. Webber*

KNOCKELLY CASTLE 13 ch.g. Deep Run – Laganore (Will Somers) c103
[1992/3 c21s³ c21d* c25f² c22f c19v*] big, workmanlike gelding: carries –
plenty of condition: one-time useful chaser: won hunter chases at Sandown
in February and Hereford in April: effective at around 2½m, and probably
stays 3m: acts on any going. *Jon Trice-Rolph*

KNOCK KNOCK 8 ch.g. Tap On Wood – Ruby River (Red God) [1992/3
17f³] compact gelding: handicap hurdler: good third at Newbury in March: 113 p
will prove suited by sharp 2m: acts on firm going: should improve further. *I. A. Balding*

KNOCK RANK 8 b.g. Ranksborough – Knockabitoff (Raise You Ten)
[1992/3 23s² 23d³] sturdy, workmanlike gelding: placed in novice hurdles at 96
Kelso in first half of season: stays 23f: acts on soft ground. *Mrs M. Reveley*

KNOCK THRICE 11 b.g. Ballynockan – Quibba (Bandolier) [1992/3 c–
c18m] workmanlike gelding: winning 2m chaser: no form since 1989/90. *B. E. Wilkinson*

KNOCK TO ENTER (USA) 5 b.g. Diesis – Privy (USA) (Tisab (USA))
[1992/3 17gᵘʳ] sold out of M. Stoute's stable 11,500 gns Newmarket Autumn – p
Sales: unseated rider fifth in novice hurdle at Taunton in November: useful
at 6f to 1m on Flat, winner in 1993: likely to do better over hurdles. *M. Williams*

KNOCKUMSHIN 10 ch.g. Kambalda – Vina's Last (Royal Buck) [1992/3 c103
c26m² c24f* c24fʳᵒ c27g* c24d* c27m² c26m* c26f³] strong, workmanlike –
gelding: fairly useful hunter chaser: won at Taunton (2), Ludlow and
Folkestone in 1993: would also have won at Ludlow on third start but ran out
last: stays 27f: acts on dead and firm going: tried blinkered in 1989/90.
Sidney J. Smith

KNOWAFENCE 7 b.m. Idiot's Delight – Master Suite (Master Owen) c–
[1992/3 c25mᵖᵘ] once-raced over hurdles: poor maiden pointer: pulled up on –
steeplechasing debut. *Miss Scarlett J. Crew*

KNOWE HEAD 9 b.g. Beau Charmeur (FR) – Niagara Lass (Prince c85
Hansel) [1992/3 c25m²] close-coupled, deep-girthed gelding: modest –
maiden chaser: stays 25f: acts on any going: blinkered once. *Miss C. A. Blakeborough*

KNOWING 6 gr.m. Lochnager – Caroline Lamb (Hotfoot) [1992/3 20g⁴ 21d] well beaten in novice hurdles: sold 2,000 gns Doncaster January Sales. *M. D. Hammond* –

KNOW-NO-NO (IRE) 4 ch.g. Balboa – Simply Marvellous (Mon Capitaine) [1992/3 F16g³ F16g⁶] fourth foal: half-brother to 5f winner Woodman Weaver (by Balidar): dam showed little sign of ability: third at Catterick in February, probably better effort in NH Flat races: yet to race over hurdles. *M. D. Hammond*

KNOX'S CORNER 8 ch.g. Green Shoon – Sister Fiona (Tepukei) [1992/3 c23dF⁴ c25spu c24s c26gpu c25fpu] big, strong, workmanlike ex-Irish gelding: winning hunter chaser: no form in Britain: stays well: acts on soft going. *R. Curtis* c–

KNUCKLE DOWN 12 b.g. Kambalda – Fair Rullagh (Bluerullah) [1992/3 c24dro c24m⁶ c25gpu c25g⁵] chunky gelding: winning hurdler in Ireland: close third when running out 2 out in hunter chase at Ludlow in February: failed to reproduce that effort: should stay 3m: probably acts on any ground. *Miss A. J. Green* c? –

KOBYRUN 7 ch.g. Deep Run – Kobylka (David Jack) [1992/3 17d² 18vpu] workmanlike gelding: second in novice hurdle at Plumpton in October, only form. *D. M. Grissell* 89

KOLINSKY 7 ch.g. Dunbeath (USA) – Kolomelskoy Palace (Royal Palace) [1992/3 17s a20g] workmanlike gelding: poor staying novice hurdler at best: no form in 1992/3. *C. R. Beever* –

KONRAD WOLF (FR) 9 ch.g. Irish River (FR) – Orangette (ITY) (Bonconte di Montefeltro) [1992/3 c26mpu] leggy, rather sparely-made gelding: one-time fair hunter chaser: ran poorly in February, but subsequently ran well in points: stays 3m: acts on good to firm going. *S. A. Brookshaw* c– –

KONVEKTA CONTROL 6 ch.g. Deep Run – Mill Shine (Milan) [1992/3 F16g* F17v⁴ 20s³] rangy gelding with scope: dual NH Flat race winner, including at Ayr in November: promising third in novice event at Newcastle in December: should do better. *J. J. O'Neill* 96 p

KONVEKTA KING (IRE) 5 br.g. Mandalus – Realma (Realm) [1992/3 F16m* F17g⁵] IR 16,000Y: half-brother to several winners, including high-class hurdler and useful chaser Bonalma (by Bonne Noel): dam unraced: won NH Flat race at Ludlow in October: well beaten in similar event later in month: yet to race over hurdles or fences. *J. J. O'Neill*

KORITSAKI 8 br.m. Strong Gale – Grecian Tan (Tantivy) [1992/3 c24dpu c19d³ c21m²] sparely-made mare: winning hurdler: modest novice chaser: stays 21f: acts on firm and dead ground. *Miss H. C. Knight* c90 –

KOULOURA 7 b.m. True Song – Lady Bess (Straight Lad) [1992/3 17srtr 17v⁵ 18drtr] trained until after second start by Mrs J. Retter: refused to race in 2 of her 3 races over hurdles. *R. G. Frost* §§

KOVALEVSKIA 8 ch.m. Ardross – Fiordiligi (Tudor Melody) [1992/3 23s³ a20g⁴ 17v* a20g* 18g] smallish, sturdy mare: modest hurdler: no bid after winning selling handicaps at Lingfield (conditional jockeys) and Southwell in January: effective at 2m when conditions are testing and probably stays 23f: acts on all-weather surfaces and heavy going: often jumps sketchily and gets behind. *D. A. Wilson* 94

KRIBENSIS 9 gr.g. Henbit (USA) – Aquaria (Double-U-Jay) [1992/3 17v⁵ 16d⁶ 16g² 17m] lengthy gelding: top-class hurdler at best, winner of 1990 Waterford Crystal Champion Hurdle: difficult to train (has broken blood vessels) and lightly raced since: smart form when second in Kingwell Hurdle at Wincanton in February and when eleventh in Smurfit Champion Hurdle at Cheltenham in March: races only at around 2m: has won on soft going but best form on a sound surface. *M. R. Stoute* 151

KRISSOS 6 b.g. Good Times (ITY) – Chrysicabana (Home Guard (USA)) [1992/3 16d⁵ a18g⁴] soundly beaten on Flat: changed hands 2,400 gns 86

Newmarket Autumn Sales: better effort in novice hurdles when fourth at Southwell in January: blinkered. *Denys Smith*

KRONPRINZ (IRE)   5 b.g. Local Suitor (USA) – Kaiserchronik (GER) (Cortez (GER)) [1992/3 18gF 17g3 18v4 17s4 22m4 17m 20m3 17m 18m5 18v] close-coupled, sparely-made gelding: moderate handicap hurdler: stays 2¾m, at least when conditions aren't testing: acts on good to firm and dead ground (ran respectably first start on heavy): blinkered twice: possibly irresolute. *M. C. Chapman*   90

KUSHBALOO   8 b.g. Kambalda – Cushla (Zabeg) [1992/3 c16m3 c21m* c25g* c23g* c24g2 c25d* c24m* c21g2 c24d4] tall gelding: winning hurdler: successful in novice chases at Carlisle, Hexham and Kelso in first half of season and Ayr and Doncaster in February: good second in quite valuable event at Carlisle in March, but ran poorly final outing: will probably prove suited by further than 2½m and stays 25f: acts on good to firm and good to soft going: usually jumps soundly. *C. Parker*   c120 –

KWACHA   7 b.g. Reesh – Madame Quickly (Saint Crespin III) [1992/3 16g 17sF 18s 20s4 c17d4 c16dpu 21g6 22g3 17d 17spu] close-coupled, workmanlike gelding: poor maiden hurdler/chaser: probably stays 2¾m: acts on firm and dead going: visored final outing. *W. Williams*   c– 66

KYTTON CASTLE   6 ch.m. Carlingford Castle – Ballykytton (Signa Infesta) [1992/3 17m4 17d6 17s6 17s3 16sbd 16d4 18d4] compact mare: poor novice hurdler: will stay beyond 2¼m: acts on soft going. *R. Dickin*   77

L

LAABAS   10 br.g. Ile de Bourbon (USA) – Lyric Dance (Lyphard (USA)) [1992/3 23spu 25vpu 20v 22v 20g] good-bodied, dipped-backed gelding: winning 2m hurdler: no form in 1992/3. *J. E. Long*   –

LACIDAR   13 b. or br.g. Radical – No Dice (No Argument) [1992/3 c20f2 c27g3 c22f] fairly useful chaser at best: modest form in hunter chases in 1993: probably stays 27f: acts on any going with possible exception of heavy: usually ridden up with the pace. *P. Seagrave*   c95 –

LA CIENAGA   9 ch.g. Cheval – Clashdermot Lady (Shackleton) [1992/3 c20dpu c21d2 c20sur c21srtr 17s c19vrtr c16d5 c21m* c21dR] leggy gelding: fairly useful hurdler/modest chaser: won novice event over fences at Bangor in March: stays 21f: acts on firm and dead going: sketchy jumper of fences: often refuses to race or is reluctant to do so: best left alone. *G. B. Balding*   c99 §§

LACKENDARA   6 ch.g. Monksfield – Driven Snow (Deep Run) [1992/3 16s3 17g3 16sF 17v4 16d3 16d* 17f4] small, close-coupled ex-Irish gelding: won novice hurdle at Windsor in February: broke blood vessel following month: should stay further than 17f: acts on soft ground: usually races prominently. *Miss H. C. Knight*   100

LADDIE BALLINGER   11 br.g. Balinger – Stella Hedera (Star Signal) [1992/3 c21g] rangy gelding: novice hurdler: poor pointer: well beaten in maiden hunter chase in May. *P. J. A. Bomford*   c– –

LAD LANE   9 b. or br.g. Proverb – Quarry Lane (Bargello) [1992/3 c22gpu c22m3 c25m6 c22g4] tall gelding: winning hurdler: poor novice chaser: no form since 1990/1: often blinkered prior to 1992/3. *John Whyte*   c– –

LAD OF LANGTON   4 b.g. Head For Heights – Al Nuwaibi (USA) (Sir Ivor) [1992/3 aF16g aF16g6] second foal: dam 6f winner at 2 yrs: showed nothing in NH Flat races: yet to race over hurdles. *R. F. Stone*

LADY ALYS   5 gr.m. Enchantment – Alison Grey (Jellaby) [1992/3 F17g F17s aF16g4] first foal: dam once-raced half-sister to several winners, including quite useful staying hurdler Wonder Wood: behind in NH Flat races (blinkered final outing): yet to race over hurdles or fences. *R. J. Hodges*

LADY BE BRAVE 10 b.m. Laurence O – Miss Argument (No Argument) [1992/3 21d 20s³ 20d] lengthy, angular mare: winning pointer: only sign of ability otherwise when third in novice hurdle at Carlisle in November. *W. Storey* — c–70

LADY BLAKENEY 7 gr.m. Baron Blakeney – Queen of The Bogs (Straight Rule) [1992/3 F16g⁴ F20m³ F17g⁴ 16d⁵ 22s⁵ 25s⁴] leggy ex-Irish non-thoroughbred mare: second foal: half-sister to a poor animal by Latest Model: dam winning 2m chaser: winning pointer: poor novice hurdler: trained until after fourth start by P. Lenihan. stays 25f: acts on soft ground. *B. S. Rothwell* — 69

LADY BLIZZARD 11 gr.m. Snow Warning – Perfect Day (Roan Rocket) [1992/3 c26vᵖᵘ c16d⁴ c21s c16vᶠ c19sᵖᵘ] plain mare: poor novice chaser: best effort at 2m but should be well suited by further: acts on dead ground. *A. J. Mason* — c69

LADY BUCHAN 4 b.f. Elegant Air – Regain (Relko) [1992/3 16d 17g⁵ 16g] good-topped filly: half-sister to several winners, including hurdler White River (by Pharly): fair maiden on Flat, placed at up to 1¼m: sold out of Mrs J. Cecil's stable 9,800 gns Newmarket December Sales: poor form over hurdles: easily best effort on second start. *N. Tinkler* — 74

LADY BUNTING 6 b.m. Well Decorated (USA) – Lady's Flag (USA) (Fifth Marine (USA)) [1992/3 17f² 20m² 18m²ᵈⁱˢ 17d³ 17vᶠ 18g⁶ 18m⁵ 17g⁵] leggy, sparely-made mare: poor maiden hurdler: best efforts at around 2m: acts on firm and dead ground. *R. Voorspuy* — 81

LADY CHAN 5 b.m. Town And Country – Sand Lady (Sandford Lad) [1992/3 16f⁶ 17g⁶ 21d 16d³] sparely-made mare: poor novice hurdler: should stay further than 2m: acts on heavy going: best effort in blinkers final start (November). *Miss S. J. Wilton* — 75

LADY DONOGHUE (USA) 4 b.f. Lyphard's Wish (FR) – It's High Time (High Line) [1992/3 18d⁴] modest on Flat, won at around 1m in May, 1993: showed promise when fourth in juvenile hurdle at Sedgefield in November: should improve. *Mrs M. Reveley* — 68 p

LADY GHISLAINE (FR) 6 b.m. Lydian (FR) – Planeze (FR) (Faraway Son (USA)) [1992/3 17d 17s* a20g³ 16v⁴] plain mare: half-sister to a winning hurdler in France: no form on Flat: won conditional jockeys selling hurdle at Huntingdon (sold out of A. Reid's stable 2,500 gns) in December: stays 2½m: acts on equitrack and soft ground (ran poorly on heavy). *J. White* — 83

LADY GWENMORE 5 b.m. Town And Country – Ment More (Sahib) [1992/3 23g³ 22d⁶ 20g² 20f²] leggy mare: poor novice hurdler: stays 23f: best form on sound surface: mostly blinkered in 1991/2 and on final outing. *R. Akehurst* — 87

LADY IN GOLD 7 ch.m. Torus – Miss Mallard (Crash Course) [1992/3 18m 22fᶠ] lengthy, plain mare: no sign of ability over hurdles: blinkered once. *I. Campbell* — –

LADY LLANFAIR 7 b.m. Prince Tenderfoot (USA) – Picnic Time (Silly Season) [1992/3 c21m*] leggy mare: improved into fairly useful pointer in 1993: won 20-runner novice hunter chase at Cheltenham in May: stays 21f: acts on good to firm ground: should improve further. *W. D. Oakes* — c93 p

LADY OF STRATTON 6 b.m. Enchantment – Disco Diamond (Le Coq d'Or) [1992/3 F16v] tailed off in 2 NH Flat races: sold 1,300 gns Ascot June Sales: yet to race over hurdles or fences. *B. Stevens* — –

LADY OLEIN (IRE) 5 b.m. Alzao (USA) – Katie Cecil (Princely Gift) [1992/3 16d 17g⁵ 16d² 16d⁴ 16s* 16s* 16d³ 16dᶠ 16d 16s 16d²] close-coupled mare: useful hurdler: won 2 handicaps at Fairyhouse in November: good second to Time For A Run at Punchestown in April: not sure to stay much beyond 2m: acts on soft going: usually held up: blinkered (ran badly) tenth outing: sometimes has tongue tied down. *Mrs J. Harrington, Ireland* — 138

LADY POLY 5 b.m. Dunbeath (USA) – First Temptation (USA) (Mr Leader (USA)) [1992/3 17m 18d a20g⁴ a22gᵘʳ a16gᵖᵘ a18g a16g⁵ 17g³ 17g⁶] — 73

22g^3 20m^5 21d 23f^5] small mare: selling hurdler: sold out of Miss B. Sanders' stable 900 gns Ascot November Sales after second start: stays 2¾m: acts on equitrack. *R. F. Stone*

LADY QUAKER 5 b.m. Oats – Sweet Optimist (Energist) [1992/3 F 17g] close-coupled mare: first foal: dam, half-sister to useful chaser Bold Agent, won novice hurdle: well beaten in NH Flat race at Doncaster in January: yet to race over hurdles or fences. *B. S. Rothwell*

LADY RANDOLPH 4 b.f. Elegant Air – Cara Rose (Rheingold) [1992/3 17f 18f 17g 16d^6 18v 16f 18g^3 16m^6 22f] sparely-made filly: poor maiden on Flat and over hurdles: visored/blinkered 4 times: irresolute. *I. Campbell*   65 §

LADY REMAINDER 6 ch.m. Remainder Man – My Aisling (John de Coombe) [1992/3 c21d^3 c20s^2 c22v^3 c26v^{pu} c25s^5 c27d^4 a22g^{pu} c21g^5] compact mare: poor novice chaser: stays long distances: acts on heavy ground: blinkered twice: sketchy jumper. *B. S. Rothwell*   c78 –

LADY RISK ME 4 gr.f. Risk Me (FR) – Donrae (Don (ITY)) [1992/3 18g^2 17f 18f^6] of little account on Flat: bad form in early-season selling hurdles. *J. R. Bostock*   59

LADY ROSEMOUNT 4 ch.f. Morston (FR) – Miss Cervinia (Memling) [1992/3 F 16m F 14g] small filly: half-sister to several poor animals: dam modest middle-distance performer: signs of a little ability in NH Flat races: yet to race over hurdles. *J. A. Pickering*

LADY'S DAY 7 ch.m. Al Sirat (USA) – Last Day (Night And Day II) [1992/3 c19f^5 c24g^{pu} c21g^{pu} c19g^{pu}] workmanlike ex-Irish mare: half-sister to winning jumper Gerry Doyle (by Al Sirat): poor form at best in novice chases: showed nothing in Britain (trained first 2 starts by J. Gifford): blinkered once. *W. Smith*   c–

LADYSIBELOU 5 gr.m. Alias Smith (USA) – Bargello's Lady (Bargello) [1992/3 20s^{pu} 16g 2 1m 17f] small mare: fourth foal: half-sister to quite useful chaser Sword Beach (by Scallywag): dam winning staying hurdler/chaser: no form in novice hurdles. *Mrs A. Hamilton*   –

LADY'S ISLAND (IRE) 5 br.m. Over The River (FR) – Banner Lady (Milan) [1992/3 c20g^4 c20m^4] third living foal: dam never ran: showed ability in novice chases: will stay beyond 2½m: acts on good to firm ground. *J. I. A. Charlton*   c76

LADY TOKEN 9 b.m. Roscoe Blake – Princess Token (Khalkis) [1992/3 c25m^4 c26g* c20g^6 c26m^3] sturdy, close-coupled mare: modest chaser: won handicap at Catterick in March: ran well final start: stays 3¼m: acts on firm and good to soft ground. *H. J. Gill*   c94

LADY WIMS 4 ch.f. Undulate (USA) – Biddy Charley (Peacock (FR)) [1992/3 aF 16g^5] second foal: half-sister to a bad novice hurdler by Oats: dam, winning chaser, stayed well: fifth of 10 in NH Flat race at Lingfield in March: yet to race over hurdles. *P. F. Nicholls*

LAFHEEN (IRE) 5 b.g. Lafontaine (USA) – Curraheen (Crash Course) [1992/3 F 16d 18d 16s^{pu} 20v^{pu} 18v 18g^5 16f^{pu} 16s 22v^6] stocky gelding: bad novice hurdler: blinkered once. *Miss R. J. Patman*   57

LAFKADIO 6 b.g. Gay Mecene (USA) – Lakonia (Kris) [1992/3 18g^2 26s 20d 24v^{pu} 22s^{pu} 25m^5 26m 22s^4 26m^3 26v^{pu}] small gelding: fair handicap hurdler: stays 3¼m: acts on firm ground: needs plenty of driving: refused to race once in 1991/2. *M. C. Chapman*   102

LA FONTAINBLEAU (IRE) 5 gr.g. Lafontaine (USA) – Alsong (Al Sirat (USA)) [1992/3 F 18d F 16d 20m^3 22f^2 22m^3 21s^2] tall, leggy gelding: fourth foal: dam never ran: modest novice hurdler: stays 2¾m: probably acts on any going: amateur ridden. *D. H. Brown*   88

LAGATURNE LADY 4 ch.f. Kaytu – Read 'n' Rite (High Line) [1992/3 17d 16s^6 17g^5 17f^{pu}] lengthy, sparely-made filly: third foal: dam lightly-raced maiden on Flat and over hurdles: poor form in juvenile hurdles: easily best effort on soft ground. *M. J. Charles*   73

LAHARNA GIRL 9 b.m. Star Appeal – Avise La Fin (Scottish Rifle) –
[1992/3 17d^{pu}] small, sparely-made mare: selling hurdler: sold privately
1,300 gns Doncaster August Sales: probably stays 3m and acts on any going:
sometimes visored or blinkered and looks none too keen. *Mrs A. E. Ratcliff*

LAKE DOMINION 4 b.g. Primo Dominie – Piney Lake (Sassafras 89
(FR)) [1992/3 16s 17d a16g* a16g² 16m⁵] smallish, close-coupled gelding:
half-brother to a winning jumper in Belgium by Milford: moderate maiden
on Flat, stays 1¼m: changed hands 10,500 gns Newmarket Autumn Sales:
won juvenile hurdle at Lingfield in February: yet to race beyond 17f: best
form on equitrack, ran respectably on good to firm ground. *P. W. Harris*

LAKE MISSION 8 b.g. Blakeney – Missed Blessing (So Blessed) c113
[1992/3 c19d⁴ c18g² c21g⁵ c20g² c20s⁶ c21d* c20f² c21d³ c24g^{pu}] sturdy,
good-bodied gelding: fair handicap chaser: won at Sandown in February: ran
poorly last 2 starts: effective around 2½m and should stay 3m: acts on firm
and dead going: races prominently: jumps soundly in main. *S. E. Sherwood*

LAKE TEEREEN 8 ch.g. Callernish – Gusserane Lark (Napoleon c116
Bonaparte) [1992/3 c21s* c21m² c21s* c20s³ c21s² c21d c20d⁵ c21d² c21g²
c21m^{pu}] lengthy gelding: useful hurdler: won novice chases at Worcester
and Folkestone in first half of season: ran well when placed afterwards:
effective at 2½m to 25f: acts on good to firm and soft ground: jumps soundly
in the main: races up with pace. *R. Rowe*

LAKINO 11 b.g. Relkino – Lake Naivasha (Blakeney) [1992/3 c24f^{pu}] c–
leggy gelding: winning 2m hurdler/chaser, lightly raced. *K. A. Morgan*

LAMASTRE 4 b.f. Jalmood (USA) – Daring Lass (Bold Lad (IRE)) –
[1992/3 18v^{ur} 17d^{pu}] won 6f seller at 2 yrs but no form on Flat for a long time:
showed nothing in juvenile hurdle at Plumpton in February. *C. Weedon*

LAMBSON 6 b.g. Petorius – Julie Be Quick (USA) (Selari) [1992/3 16d⁶] –
rather sparely-made gelding: winning hurdler: best efforts at around 2m:
acts on good to firm going: looks none too enthusiastic: usually visored
(wasn't only start of 1992/3, in October). *R. M. Whitaker*

LAMORE RITORNA 4 br.f. Lidhame – Arbor Lane (Wolverlife) 78
[1992/3 16g^{pu} a16g² a20g³ a18g³ 16m⁵] leggy filly: modest 1m winner on

Evesham Conditional Jockeys' Novices' Hurdle, Cheltenham—
the much improved Land Afar trots up

Mr T. J. Ford's "Land Afar"

Flat: retained 600 gns Newmarket Autumn Sales: poor novice hurdler: stayed 2½m: acted on equitrack: visored on debut: dead. *K. O. Cunningham-Brown*

LAND AFAR   6 b.g. Dominion – Jouvencelle (Rusticaro (FR)) [1992/3 16s⁵ 16d 16d* 17d* 17f³ 17g* 16f] compact gelding: trained until after second start by J. O'Shea: greatly improved afterwards, winning novice hurdles at Uttoxeter (handicap) and Stratford in February and Cheltenham (conditional jockeys) in April: easily best effort and useful performance when third to Roll A Dollar in Seagram Top Novices' Hurdle at Aintree: raced only at around 2m: successful on dead ground but best form on firm: occasionally visored (only on second start in 1992/3). *J. Webber*   131

LANDED GENTRY (USA)   4 b.c. Vaguely Noble – Phydilla (FR) (Lyphard (USA)) [1992/3 16s* 16v² 21d²] compact colt: fair maiden on Flat, stays 1¾m: sold out of P. Chapple-Hyam's stable 6,200 gns Newmarket Autumn Sales: won juvenile hurdle at Leicester in November: ran well both starts following month: suited by testing conditions at 2m and should stay beyond 21f: acts on heavy going. *C. D. Broad*   108

LAND OF THE FREE   4 b.f. Valiyar – L'Americaine (USA) (Verbatim (USA)) [1992/3 17v² 17v² 17v² 20s* 16v* 17s³ 17f⁴ 17f* 17s³ 17m² 18d⁵] leggy filly: first foal: dam 9f winner in France: 1½m winner on Flat in France: claimed out of H. Pantall's stable 121,111 francs (approx £14,300) in October: won juvenile hurdles at Taunton (2) and Wincanton in second half of season (2 of them claimers): stays 2½m: acts on any ground: best held up: jumps soundly in the main. *M. C. Pipe*   107

429

LAND OF WONDER (USA) 6 b.g. Wind And Wuthering (USA) – Heat Haze (USA) (Jungle Savage (USA)) [1992/3 c25v6] leggy, angular gelding: of little account over hurdles: modest pointer: sixth in hunter chase at Towcester in April. *Mrs C. Hicks* c83 –

LANDSKER OATS 7 b.m. Oats – Gemmerly Jane (Bally Russe) [1992/3 28v 26spu 26dpu 28mpu 21d c25gpu] leggy, sparely-made mare: winning staying hurdler: no form in 1992/3, including on chasing debut: sold 1,000 gns Ascot 2nd June Sales: very temperamental and best left alone. *Mrs P. Sly* c– §§

LANE LAD 9 ch.g. Creative Plan (USA) – Crinken Lane (Sterling Bay (SWE)) [1992/3 17m5 17f4 18f4 17s6 18f5 16g 17g 18s a16g 17m5 20m 18mF 17d] lengthy gelding: poor hurdler: generally out of form in 1992/3: stays 2½m: probably acts on any going. *Mrs J. Wonnacott* –

LANGLANDS LAD 5 b.g. Karlinsky (USA) – Queen's Bronze (King's Troop) [1992/3 16d] small gelding: no signs of ability in NH Flat race and a novice hurdle. *H. S. Howe* –

LANGROVE 9 b.g. Cleon – Dear Lady (Dear Gazelle) [1992/3 c21m4 c23g c27d2 c27dur] workmanlike gelding: ungenuine maiden chaser: stays well: acts on hard and dead ground: blinkered twice. *Mrs V. A. Aconley* c81 § –

LANSDOWNE 5 b.h. High Top – Fettle (Relkino) [1992/3 20g 24s2] neat horse: poor novice hurdler: not raced after November: suited by test of stamina: acts on soft going. *O. O'Neill* 84

LA PEREET (IRE) 5 b.m. Vision (USA) – Great Alexandra (Runnett) [1992/3 18mpu 16g6 18s 17dpu 18d 18spu 18d a20g4 a16g 22g 21dpu 17gpu 22gpu] angular mare: winning 2m selling hurdler: bad form in 1992/3: usually blinkered nowadays. *B. Richmond* 51

LAPIAFFE 9 b.g. Piaffer (USA) – Laval (Cheval) [1992/3 c23f* c23f3 c25s2 c25gF 24d6 c26d5 c20g* c20d4 c21d3 c16d4 c21s2 c26f c20fur c21m2 c25mur c21m3 c23mF] leggy, sparely-made gelding: winning hurdler: modest chaser: won claiming chases at Exeter (claimed out of R. Hodges' stable £9,089) and Edinburgh in first half of season: stays 3m: acts on any going. *A. Harrison* c94 –

LA PRINCESSE 6 b.m. Le Bavard (FR) – Morry's Lady (The Parson) [1992/3 21s* 16v2 22v* 21v2] useful-looking mare with scope: chasing type: won novice hurdles at Warwick in November and Newton Abbot in January: good second in similar event at Towcester in February on final start: suited by further than 2m and will stay beyond 2¾m: acts on heavy going: jumps soundly. *O. Sherwood* 111

LARAPINTA (IRE) 5 b.g. Montelimar (USA) – Shapely (Parthia) [1992/3 F16g F16d3 16v4 17g 16d 17m 18d] leggy ex-Irish gelding: half-brother to 3 Flat winners, including useful Red Emerald (by Red God): dam, fair on Flat, stayed 1¾m: novice hurdler: trained until after third start by P. Burke: below best thereafter: will stay beyond 2m: acts on heavy ground. *J. H. Johnson* 90 ?

LA RAPTOTTE 6 b.m. Alzao (USA) – Maypole Hie (Bold Lad (IRE)) [1992/3 17g3 16d* 16s4 16s] sparely-made mare: modest handicap hurdler: won at Towcester in October: not raced after November: races only at 2m: acts on soft going and on fibresand: tough. *M. J. Charles* 99

LARA'S BABY (IRE) 5 ch.m. Valiyar – Tapiola (Tap On Wood) [1992/3 18g* 18m4 17m4 F13m4] neat mare: fair middle-distance performer at best on Flat: poor hurdler: won selling handicap at Cartmel (bought in 3,000 gns) in August: not discredited next 2 starts: stays 2¼m: acts on good to firm ground. *N. Tinkler* 80

LARCH IMAGE GIRL 8 b.m. Rolfe (USA) – Seaknot (Perhapsburg) [1992/3 c19g] seems of little account. *Mrs D. Buckett* c– –

LARGE ACTION (IRE) 5 b.g. The Parson – Ballyadam Lass (Menelek) [1992/3 F17g* F17m F17d*] tall, unfurnished gelding with scope: seventh foal: half-brother to fair hurdler/useful chaser One More Knight (by

Roselier): dam never ran: won NH Flat races at Doncaster in January and Sandown (quite valuable event, in good style) in April: midfield in valuable contest at Cheltenham in between: yet to race over hurdles or fences. *O. Sherwood*

LARK RISE (USA) 5 ch.g. The Minstrel (CAN) – Glowing Prospect (USA) (Mr Prospector (USA)) [1992/3 17g³ 17dᵘʳ 17d⁵ 17v a20g* 17mᶠ] leggy gelding: poor form over hurdles: won maiden at Lingfield in February: stayed 2½m: acted on equitrack: dead. *C. Weedon* 79

LARKSMORE 8 br.m. Royal Fountain – Newtonmore (Game Rights) [1992/3 c26dᵖᵘ c22v* c30sᵖᵘ c25v³ c25m] sturdy mare: modest chaser: 50/1, improved effort when winning handicap chase at Towcester in January: well beaten afterwards: stays very well: acts on heavy going. *Miss D. J. Baker* c98 –

LARLOCH 9 br.g. Young Generation – Black Fire (Firestreak) [1992/3 18g] workmanlike gelding: very lightly raced: winning pointer: poor 2m novice hurdler. *T. Craig* –

LARNACA 6 b.g. Shernazar – Checkers (Habat) [1992/3 16s² 16d⁴ 16dᶠ 16s 17f] leggy, angular gelding: useful hurdler: ran poorly last 2 starts, in valuable handicap at Aintree on final one: races only at 2m: acts on heavy going: usually held up. *B. V. Kelly, Ireland* 132

LASCAR (USA) 5 ch.g. Riverman (USA) – Meteoric (High Line) [1992/3 16d F12d⁶ a20g³ 16s⁶] sturdy gelding: poor novice hurdler: trained by G. Thorner until after third start: stays 2½m: act on dead ground and equitrack. *D. T. Turner* 68

LAST EXTRAVAGANCE 12 b.g. Bluerullah – Queen Hansel (Prince Hansel) [1992/3 c23g] workmanlike gelding: winning hunter chaser: stays 3m well: acts on soft and good to firm going. *H. Wellstead* c– –

LAST HOUSE 10 ch.m. Vital Season – Parkhouse (Spartan General) [1992/3 c26gᵖᵘ c27vᵖᵘ c24vᵖᵘ 22dᵖᵘ] close-coupled mare: one-time fairly useful staying chaser: no form since 1990/1. *M. P. McNeill* c– –

LASTING MEMORY 7 b.m. Ardross – Irreprochable (Mount Hagen (FR)) [1992/3 24g² 27d² 24d⁶ 26g⁵ 22s* 25s⁶ a20g² 27m⁵ c18g c27gᵖᵘ 22m²] leggy, sparely-made mare: fair handicap hurdler: won at Fontwell in November: no form in novice chases: stays well: probably acts on any going: inconsistent. *R. G. Frost* c– 104

LAST JEWEL 10 b.m. Vitiges (FR) – Welsh Jewel (Welsh Pageant) [1992/3 17sᵖᵘ] very lightly raced and of little account over hurdles: won a point in May. *D. Burchell* –

LAST MAN IN 6 br.g. Balinger – Wealthy (Gold Rod) [1992/3 c25dᵖᵘ c21g⁵] smallish, workmanlike gelding: no sign of ability. *Mrs A. L. M. King* c– –

LAST MATCH 5 b.g. Final Straw – Light Duty (Queen's Hussar) [1992/3 16sᵖᵘ 20m³ 20g 24sᵖᵘ 22d] lengthy gelding: no sign of ability. *B. Preece* –

LAST OF MOHICANS 5 b.g. Warpath – Gemima Tenderfoot (Prince Tenderfoot (USA)) [1992/3 22fᵖᵘ 20g⁶ 18g 17m⁶ 17dᵖᵘ 17gᵖᵘ] smallish gelding: of little account: sold out of C. Weedon's stable 2,200 gns Ascot September Sales after third start, resold 975 gns Ascot November Sales before next outing. *C. L. Popham* –

LAST OF THE FLIES 12 ch.g. Kemal (FR) – Gledswing (Reynard Volant) [1992/3 c25g⁴ c25v⁴ c23s³ c23d⁵ c26s³ c24d⁵] rangy, workmanlike gelding: poor novice chaser: stays 3¼m: acts on heavy going: amateur ridden. *A. H. Mactaggart* c81

LASTOFTHEVIKINGS 8 ch.g. Cisto (FR) – Vivyiki (Kirtonian) [1992/3 c22d⁴ c23d⁴ c24mᵘʳ c24mᵖᵘ 26sᵖᵘ] sparely-made gelding: poor novice hurdler/chaser: trained until after fourth start by Miss U. McGuinness: stays 23f: acts on soft ground: poor jumper of fences. *J. L. Needham* c77 x –

LAST 'O' THE BUNCH 9 ch.g. Meldrum – Golden Royalty (Royalty) [1992/3 c21g⁴ c16s* c16d* c16s² c20sᵖᵘ c20s³ c16f⁴ c21s* c20g* c16s² c141 –

Leigh Handicap Chase, Haydock —
a mistake at the last doesn't stop Last 'o' The Bunch

c22m3] workmanlike gelding: useful chaser: successful in 2 handicaps at Haydock in first half of season and one at Wetherby and Ayr in April: effective at 2m to 21f: acts on good to firm and soft ground: suited by forcing tactics. *G. Richards*

LA STRAVAGANZA 5 b.m. Slip Anchor – St Isadora (Lyphard (USA)) [1992/3 16spu 17spu 16dF a18gpu] neat mare: of little account on Flat nowadays and over hurdles: visored twice. *B. P. J. Baugh* —

LAST SHOWER 8 ch.m. Town And Country – Rainbow's End (My Swallow) [1992/3 22m3 23m] sparely-made mare: novice hurdler: no worthwhile form since 1988/9. *Miss R. J. Patman* —

LA SWANN 8 ch.m. Leander – Mrs Swann VII (Pedigree Unknown) [1992/3 c2 1m] poor maiden pointer: well beaten in novice hunter chase in May. *Miss J. Edginton* c–

LATE CUT 8 b.g. Tap On Wood – Sometime Lucky (Levmoss) [1992/3 20s6 25s 22v5 c19spu] modest novice hurdler at best: no form in 1992/3: blinkered, pulled up on chasing debut in January. *M. C. Pipe* c–
—

LATENT TALENT 9 b.g. Celtic Cone – Fra Mau (Wolver Hollow) [1992/3 c25g* c27spu c24d4 c24m4 c25g2 c33gpu] big, lengthy, angular gelding: useful chaser: won quite valuable handicap at Ascot in October: good second at Sandown in February: stays 25f: acts on good to firm and dead ground: races up with the pace: usually a bold jumper. *S. E. Sherwood* c133

LATIN MASS 5 ch.m. Music Boy – Omnia (Hill Clown (USA)) [1992/3 a18gpu] sparely-made mare: of little account over hurdles. *A. Barrow* —

LATIN QUARTET 5 b.g. Chief Singer – Pampas Miss (USA) (Pronto) [1992/3 a16g^{pu}] strong, sturdy gelding: poor 2m novice hurdler: best efforts on good ground: sometimes visored. *K. R. Burke* — –

LATOUR 5 b.g. Lafontaine (USA) – Lucky Omen (Queen's Hussar) [1992/3 22d 25d 24d^2 21d^6 21s^6] smallish, good-bodied gelding: half-brother to winning hurdler Lucky Blake (by Blakeney): one-time fair middle-distance performer on Flat: sold 9,800 gns Newmarket Autumn Sales: modest novice hurdler: stays 3m: acts on dead ground: blinkered fourth outing: looked reluctant final one. *Mrs A. Swinbank* — 92 §

LATVIAN 6 gr.g. Rousillon (USA) – Lorelene (FR) (Lorenzaccio) [1992/3 18g 16m] sturdy, workmanlike gelding: half-brother to winning hurdler/chaser Leon (by Niniski): behind in early-season novice hurdles: fair middle-distance performer on Flat, winner in 1993. *R. Allan* — –

LAUDER SQUARE 5 gr.g. Pragmatic – Royal Ruby (Rubor) [1992/3 27d 24s 25d] second foal: half-brother to winning chaser Gala Water (by Politico): dam of little account: tailed off all starts over hurdles. *T. D. C. Dun* — –

LAUGHING GAS (IRE) 4 ch.g. Lord Ha Ha – Magic Deer (Whistling Deer) [1992/3 17v^6 17d^6] first foal: dam Irish 1¾m winner: well beaten in juvenile hurdles. *John R. Upson* — –

LAUNCH PAD 7 br.g. Score Twenty Four (USA) – Rocket Alert (Red Alert) [1992/3 22f^3] fifth foal: half-brother to useful 1¼m winner Ardlui (by Lomond): dam 5f to 7f winner: failed to complete in points in 1991: remote last of 3 finishers in novice event at Worcester in March on hurdling debut. *Dr P. Pritchard* — –

LAUNDRYMAN 10 b.g. Celtic Cone – Lovely Laura (Lauso) [1992/3 c20g^4 c26g^{pu} 23d^4 c24v^{pu} 21g^5 21f^3] lengthy, angular gelding: modest novice hurdler: fairly useful chaser at best: ran poorly last 2 outings over fences 1992/3: should stay beyond 21f: probably acts on any going: tends to race lazily. *S. Mellor* — c– 102

LAURA'S BEAU 9 b.g. Beau Charmeur (FR) – Laurabeg (Laurence O) [1992/3 c24d c26v 19v c27s^{pu} c29s c25g] close-coupled gelding: useful chaser in 1991/2, third in Martell Grand National at Liverpool: well beaten in 1992/3, including in void running of same race: suited by extreme test of stamina: ideally suited by plenty of give in the ground: best in blinkers. *F. Berry, Ireland* — c– –

LAUREL CONNECTION 4 b.g. Precocious – Becky Sharp (Sharpen Up) [1992/3 16m^{pu} 16d^F 16d^{pu}] good-bodied gelding: of little account. *Mrs A. R. Hewitt* — –

LAURIE-O 9 b.g. Deep Run – Eight of Diamonds (Silent Spring) [1992/3 c21d* c21v^6 c26s^{pu} c24m^5 c28g^5 c27d^{pu} c21g^3 c21m^2 c25g^{pu}] tall, lengthy gelding: fair handicap chaser at best: won at Hexham in November: generally well below form afterwards: stays 3m: acts on any going: jumps none too fluently: unreliable. *R. R. Lamb* — c108 §

LAVA FALLS (USA) 7 b. or br.g. Riverman (USA) – In Triumph (USA) (Hoist The Flag (USA)) [1992/3 16g 16g^4 17f^5 22g^6 21f 26f^5 22f^5] angular, sparely-made gelding: modest handicap hurdler: stays 2½m: acts on firm going. *M. C. Banks* — 91

LAVALIGHT 6 b.g. Lighter – Laval (Cheval) [1992/3 17g 17d 17f* 25m^2 20m^4 22f* 22d^{pu}] leggy gelding: poor hurdler: won novice handicaps at Taunton and Wincanton in the spring: effective at around 2m and stays 25f: well suited by top-of-the-ground. *R. J. Hodges* — 76

LAW CHAMBERS 6 b.g. Law Society (USA) – Amata (USA) (Nodouble (USA)) [1992/3 16m] angular gelding: poor 2m novice hurdler: blinkered once. *P. R. Haley* — –

LAW FACULTY (IRE) 4 b.g. Law Society (USA) – Ask The Wind (Run The Gantlet (USA)) [1992/3 16m^{ur} 17m^{pu}] of little account on Flat nowadays: no sign of ability in early-season juvenile hurdles. *G. A. Ham* — –

LAWLEY 11 br.g. Humdoleila – Cloudari (Pindari) [1992/3 c 19g5] lengthy   c–
gelding: winning hunter chaser: stays 2½m: acts on heavy going: blinkered   –
twice. *Mrs Angus Campbell*

LAWNSWOOD PRINCE (IRE) 4 b.g. Anita's Prince – La Croisette
(Nishapour (FR)) [1992/3 17fpu 17f] plating-class maiden on Flat, stays 7f: no   –
sign of ability in early-season juvenile hurdles. *J. L. Spearing*

LAWNSWOOD SUN 7 b.g. Broadsword (USA) – Lawnswood Miss   c–
(Grey Mirage) [1992/3 c21d3 c20vur c21vpu c20dur c16d] good-topped
gelding: no form in novice chases: sold 7,200 gns Doncaster May Sales. *R.
Hollinshead*

LAWSON PRINCESS 9 b. or br.m. Latest Model – Calamity (Haven)
[1992/3 22mpu] small, sparely-made mare: very lightly raced and no sign of   –
ability. *A. Barrow*

LAY IT OFF (IRE) 4 br.f. Strong Gale – Give Her The Boot (Little
Buskins) [1992/3 F16g 16v6] leggy filly: first foal: dam winning Irish hurdler: –
soundly beaten in NH Flat race and juvenile hurdle. *J. G. O'Neill*

LAZZARETTO 5 b.g. Ballacashtal (CAN) – Florence Mary (Mandamus)
[1992/3 F16s F16s] fourth foal: dam poor novice hurdler: well beaten in NH   –
Flat races: sold 2,000 gns Doncaster May Sales: yet to race over hurdles or
fences. *Capt. J. Wilson*

LEACROFT 9 b.g. Domitor (USA) – Whitmarsh (Hessonite) [1992/3 20m   c–
c16g5] compact gelding: winning 2m hurdler/chaser: ran badly in 1992/3. *A.   –
W. Jones*

LEADER SAL (IRE) 4 br.g. Supreme Leader – Repetitive (USA) (Tell
(USA)) [1992/3 17m 18mpu 16s 16d] compact gelding: first foal: dam winning   –
selling hurdler at up to 2¼m: no sign of ability in juvenile hurdles. *J. Wade*

LEADING PROSPECT 6 b.g. Idiot's Delight – Miss Prospect (Sweet   99
Story) [1992/3 18g* 17g2 20g 20g2 18d* 18g 20g4] lengthy, sparely-made,
angular gelding: modest hurdler: won novice events at Kelso in October and
February: stays 2½m: acts on dead going: game. *Mrs J. D. Goodfellow*

LEADING ROLE 9 ch.g. Rolfe (USA) – Paravant (Parthia) [1992/3   95
22m6 25m3 21g2 22m4 21s2 21m3 21d3 24m2 22d 26d6 26s4 20d3 22d* 18d
20g4] small, sturdy gelding: modest hurdler: won selling handicap at
Sedgefield (no bid) in January: stayed 25f: acted on soft and good to firm
ground: blinkered once: dead. *A. Harrison*

LEAGAUNE 11 br.g. Over The River (FR) – Cora Princess (Laurence O)   c95
[1992/3 c20spu c25v3 c26fbd c25dpu] smallish, rather sparely-made gelding:
fair chaser at best: third in hunter chase at Towcester in April, only form
since 1990/1: out-and-out stayer: acts on heavy going. *T. Casey*

LEAH JAY 6 ch.g. Sayyaf – Patriots Day (Red Regent) [1992/3 16s 17s
17vpu 17gpu] small, compact gelding: of little account: blinkered once. *E. A.   –
Wheeler*

LEANDER LAD 8 b.g. Paico – Miss Leander (Leander) [1992/3 c16dF   c–
c18gF 18m 16m6] leggy, workmanlike gelding: 2m novice hurdler: no form   –
since 1989/90, including in 2 novice chases (fell both times). *D. McCain*

LEAN ON ME 10 ch.g. Laurence O – Colshaw Lass (Border Chief)   c–
[1992/3 c21spu c26m5 c24g6] lengthy gelding: no sign of ability in hunter   –
chases. *J. N. Cheatle*

LEAPIN 5 b.g. Peter Wrekin – Leawell (Leander) [1992/3 F17s] second
foal: dam winning 2m selling hurdler: behind in NH Flat race at Newbury in   –
January: yet to race over hurdles or fences. *J. N. Dalton*

LEARNED STAR 8 b.g. Bustiki – Learned Lady (Crozier) [1992/3 21m   66
17g 16d5 24spu] leggy, workmanlike gelding: poor novice hurdler: only form
on third start. *J. L. Eyre*

LEARNER DRIVER 6 b.g. Crash Course – Broken Mirror (Push On)
[1992/3 F17d F16g2 22g] workmanlike gelding: first foal: dam unraced sister   –
to winning jumper Montgomery and half-sister to useful jumper Admiral's

Cup: second in NH Flat race at Edinburgh in January: showed nothing on hurdling debut following month: sold 2,700 gns Doncaster May Sales. *J. G. FitzGerald*

LEAVENWORTH 9 ch.g. Bustino – Hide The Key (USA) (Key To The Mint (USA)) [1992/3 24s 24v⁴ 22s 24s³] workmanlike gelding: fair handicap hurdler: novice chaser: stays 25f: acts on heavy going: blinkered twice. *Mrs J. G. Retter*   c– 111

LE BUCHERON 7 b.g. Vaigly Great – Couteau (Nelcius) [1992/3 c16v² c21v³ c17sᵖᵘ c21mᵘʳ c25gᵘʳ] big, rather leggy gelding: winning hurdler: modest novice chaser: barely stays 21f in testing conditions: acts on heavy ground. *M. J. Ryan*   c86 –

LE CAROTTE 11 ch.g. Balinger – Camargue (Combat) [1992/3 22fᵖᵘ] lengthy, workmanlike gelding: fairly useful staying hurdler in 1989/90: pulled up lame both outings since: novice chaser: poor jumper of fences. *A. Barrow*   c– x –

LE CHAT NOIR 10 br.g. Paico – June (Pendragon) [1992/3 18f⁴ 25d² c21s* 17v² 18v³ 22g²] tall gelding: fairly useful hurdler/chaser: won handicap over fences at Folkestone in November: effective at 2m and stays 25f: acts on any going: genuine and consistent. *D. M. Grissell*   c118 118

LE DENSTAN 6 b.g. Valuta – Sweet Canyon (NZ) (Headland II) [1992/3 F17d 16d 22vᵖᵘ 22m⁵] leggy gelding: brother to staying novice hurdler/chaser Spikey and half-brother to winning staying jumpers Chemist Broker and Air Broker (both by Oakville): dam half-sister to top-class jumper Grand Canyon: no form in novice hurdles. *P. R. Hedger*   –

LEESWOOD 5 b.g. Little Wolf – Tina's Gold (Goldhill) [1992/3 F16v³ 16sᵖᵘ 17s* 17m* 16d⁴ 17g²] close-coupled gelding: won novice hurdles at Bangor in February and March: ran creditably in handicaps after: will stay beyond 17f: acts on good to firm and soft going. *R. Lee*   91

LEFT HANDED 10 br.g. Strong Gale – Gleann Buidhe (Pampered King) [1992/3 c22gᵖᵘ] lengthy, rather sparely-made gelding: poor novice jumper. *J. M. Bulman*   c– –

LEGAL LEGACY 5 b.m. Norwick (USA) – Jambalaya (Amboise) [1992/3 21sᵖᵘ a18g⁵ a22g³] leggy, rather sparely-made mare: poor novice hurdler: stays 2¾m: best efforts on equitrack. *Mrs F. E. White*   74

LEGAL WIN (USA) 5 ch.h. Arctic Tern (USA) – Banker's Favorite (USA) (Lyphard (USA)) [1992/3 19h* 17m⁶ 21f² 23m 18m 25s a18g⁴ a20gᵖᵘ 17gᵖᵘ] small, sparely-made horse: poor hurdler: won selling handicap at Exeter (no bid) in August: sold out of F. Jordan's stable 1,500 gns Ascot November Sales after sixth start: stays 21f: acts on hard ground: blinkered nowadays. *M. D. I. Usher*   67

LE GINNO (FR) 6 ch.g. Concorde Jr (USA) – Fromentel (FR) (Timour II) [1992/3 F16v*] sixth foal: half-brother to 4 winning jumpers, notably useful stayer All Jeff (by Jefferson): dam unraced: 20/1, 6-length winner of 16-runner NH Flat race at Uttoxeter in April: yet to race over hurdles or fences. *C. P. E. Brooks*

LEGION OF HONOUR 5 b.g. Ahonoora – Shehana (USA) (The Minstrel (CAN)) [1992/3 16d 16m³ 16g³] fair middle-distance handicapper on Flat, winner in May, 1993: sold 5,000 gns Newmarket Autumn Sales: best run over hurdles when third in maiden at Ayr in March on final start. *M. P. Naughton*   82

LEGITIM 4 br.g. Move Off – Eliza de Rich (Spanish Gold) [1992/3 16g 17s 16m⁵ 16m² 17f] leggy gelding: poor sprint maiden on Flat: poor novice hurdler: will stay beyond 2m: acts on good to firm ground (ran poorly on firm). *J. M. Jefferson*   74

LEGUARD EXPRESS (IRE) 5 b.h. Double Schwartz – All Moss (Prince Tenderfoot (USA)) [1992/3 17d 17s 17s² 20m] small, sparely-made horse: maiden plater over hurdles: unlikely to stay much beyond 17f: acts on soft going: blinkered last 2 starts, best effort on first occasion. *O. O'Neill*   76

Martell Mersey Novices' Hurdle, Aintree—
Lemon's Mill can afford to be careless at the last; she's twenty-five lengths clear

LEIGH CROFTER 4 ch.g. Son of Shaka – Ganadora (Good Times (ITY)) [1992/3 16g] compact gelding: modest and inconsistent performer on Flat, stays 7f: no promise in early-season juvenile claiming hurdle. *R. J. Holder* —

LEINTHALL DOE 7 b.m. Oats – Cover Your Money (Precipice Wood) [1992/3 21m⁵] smallish mare: showed ability when fifth in novice event at Carlisle in March on hurdling debut: stoutly bred: should improve. *J. L. Needham* 71 p

LEINTHALL FOX 7 b. or br.m. Deep Run – Winter Fox (Martinmas) [1992/3 17g² 18g 20g⁴ 20mᵖᵘ 17d 17m] leggy, shallow-girthed mare: easily best effort in novice hurdles when second at Stratford early in season: should be well suited by further than 2m: poor jumper. *J. L. Needham* 94 x

LEINTHALL PRINCESS 7 b.m. Prince Regent (FR) – Due Consideration (Sir Herbert) [1992/3 17d 21dᵖᵘ] well beaten in novice hurdles. *J. L. Needham* —

LE JACOBIN 10 br.g. Rare One – Cooleen (Tarqogan) [1992/3 c26dᵖᵘ] compact gelding: winning pointer: no form otherwise (blinkered twice). *Miss C. L. Dennis* c–
—

LELLAJES 4 b.f. Welsh Term – Santa Magdalena (Hard Fought) [1992/3 F16m F16g⁵] first foal: dam won in Belgium: mid-division in NH Flat races: yet to race over hurdles. *R. Hollinshead* —

LE METAYER (FR) 5 b.g. Le Nain Jaune (FR) – Tawendo (FR) (Tamelo (FR)) [1992/3 18gᶠ 17g³ 16s* 16d* 17g² a18g³] leggy ex-Irish gelding: progressive form when winning novice hurdles at Ludlow and Wincanton in April and finishing good second to Country Lad in valuable 115

novice handicap at Cheltenham later in month: ran poorly on fibresand final outing: should stay further than 17f: acts on soft ground. *K. C. Bailey*

LEMON'S MILL (USA) 4 b.f. Roberto (USA) – Mill Queen (Mill Reef (USA)) [1992/3 16d* 16g* 17m² 20f* 16g] 132 p

Although he seems able to get the best out of any horse, trainer Martin Pipe has done particularly well with fillies bought off the Flat as three-year-olds. Prior to the latest season Sea Island and Hopscotch were the most notable examples, but three of the most recent recruits have also made names for themselves. Lemon's Mill, Mohana and Her Honour all showed useful form over hurdles in 1992/3, winning twelve races between them. Mohana and Her Honour had already won before Lemon's Mill appeared over hurdles for the first time in a juvenile maiden at Ludlow in February. Lemon's Mill soon made up for lost time, easily landing the odds at Ludlow and following up in a mares only novice event at Warwick, where she had to work hard to get the better of the promising five-year-old Highbrook. Lemon's Mill also took on older horses in her next two races, the first of them at the Cheltenham Festival. Instead of joining Mohana and Her Honour in the Triumph Hurdle, Lemon's Mill was sent for the Trafalgar House Supreme Novices' Hurdle in which she was one of only two four-year-olds in a field of fifteen. Lemon's Mill fared much better than her stable companions did. Though no match for the impressive twelve-length winner Montelado, Lemon's Mill finished a clear second, racing up with the pace and staying on gamely up the hill having been outpaced before the home turn. Lemon's Mill gave the impression that she'd do even better over

Mr Stuart M. Mercer's "Lemon's Mill"

a longer trip, and next time out she was tried over two and a half miles in the Martell Mersey Novices' Hurdle at Aintree. As things turned out Lemon's Mill would have won that race whatever the distance. One of her opponents, One Man, ran a lack-lustre race while the other, Leotard, who'd been some way behind her at Cheltenham, never threatened to finish any closer this time. Lemon's Mill, a 2/1-on shot, was soon around fifteen lengths clear and won by twenty-five without coming off the bridle. Lemon's Mill failed to distinguish herself when returned to two miles for the Champion Four-Year-Old Hurdle at Punchestown later in April, dropping away quickly once headed two out and finishing seventh behind Shawiya.

		Roberto (USA)		Hail To Reason		Turn-To
		(b 1969)		(br 1958)		Nothirdchance
Lemon's Mill (USA)				Bramalea		Nashua
(b.f. 1989)				(b 1959)		Rarelea
		Mill Queen		Mill Reef		Never Bend
		(b 1979)		(b 1968)		Milan Mill
				Passer Queen		Buckpasser
				(br 1972)		Northern Queen

Lemon's Mill will probably prove better suited by two and a half miles than two, and she is likely to stay further. She stayed quite well on the Flat, winning over a mile and a half on her debut and being placed over a mile and three quarters before being sold out of John Gosden's stable for 13,500 guineas at the Newmarket December Sales. Lemon's Mill's half-sisters Rebuke and Golden Mill (both by Mr Prospector) won on the Flat, the former at up to fifteen furlongs in France and the latter over a mile and a half. Her half-brother Millers Tale (by Nureyev) was successful over seven furlongs. Lemon's Mill's dam Mill Queen, a fairly useful winner at up to nine furlongs, is out of a winning daughter of the Canadian Oaks winner Northern Queen. Lemon's Mill obviously has a future at stud, but there are more races to be won with her over hurdles first. Unlike many of the fillies her trainer takes on, Lemon's Mill has physical scope and it's in her favour that she had a relatively light first season over hurdles. A tall filly, who acts on firm and dead ground, she looks sure to improve. *M. C. Pipe*

LENINGRAD (USA) 9 ch.g. Nureyev (USA) – Diorama (USA) (Secretariat (USA)) [1992/3 c23h³ c27s⁵ c16g⁶ c25f^pu c27f⁶] workmanlike gelding: poor chaser: stays 23f: acts on hard ground. *P. R. Rodford*   c69 –

LEONADIS POLK 4 ch.g. Hadeer – Brokelsby Anne (Dunphy) [1992/3 18m⁶ 16s 16g⁴ 18g] workmanlike gelding: modest form at up to 1m on Flat when trained by W. Pearce: poor form over hurdles, including in a seller: unlikely to stay much beyond 2¼m: acts on good to firm ground. *J. H. Johnson*   62

LEOTARD 6 b.g. Lyphard's Special (USA) – Tondbad (Furry Glen) [1992/3 16d* 21d4 17v^pu 16v² 17d² 17m 20f² 16g*] sturdy gelding: first foal: dam won on Flat (1¾m) and over hurdles (smart juvenile) in Ireland: one-time fairly useful performer on Flat: won novice hurdles at Uttoxeter in October and Worcester in April: best efforts at Ascot and Cheltenham on fifth and sixth starts: best form around 2m: probably acts on any ground. *O. Sherwood*   121

LE PELLEY'S ISLE 6 b.g. Pitskelly – Belitis (Tudor Melody) [1992/3 22f4 21d² 16d5 16d² 22s² 16v* 20d³ 22dF] leggy gelding: selling hurdler: won at Hexham (no bid) in December: effective at 2m when conditions were very testing and stayed 2¾m: acted on any ground: dead. *M. A. Barnes*   79

LE PIAT D'OR 12 ch.g. Le Coq d'Or – Game Gypsy (Game Rights) [1992/3 c24m^pu] workmanlike gelding: winning hurdler/chaser: very lightly raced and no form since 1988/9. *R. M. Whitaker*   c–

LE PICCOLAGE 9 b.g. The Parson – Daithis Coleen (Carnival Night) [1992/3 c21d² c25d² c22v* c24d² c27g*] rangy gelding: progressive chaser, fairly useful already: won handicaps at Nottingham in December and Cheltenham (Mitsubishi Shogun Golden Miller Trophy) in April, beating   c123 p –

Cool Ground 8 lengths in latter: stays 27f: acts on good to firm and heavy going: jumps boldly: front runner. *N. J. Henderson*

LE QUARANTIEME 4 b.f. Looking Glass – Theresa (Tanfirion) [1992/3 F17d] half-sister to several winners in Germany, notably German Derby winner Temporal (by Surumu): dam, plating-class maiden in Britain, later successful in Germany: behind in NH Flat race at Hereford in May: yet to race over hurdles. *T. H. Caldwell*

LER CRU (IRE) 4 b.c. Lafontaine (USA) – Kirsova (Absalom) [1992/3 17v^{ur} 18v^4 17s 18v 17g 17s^3] good-bodied colt: carries condition: modest and inconsistent at around 1m on Flat: sold out of C. Brittain's stable 5,200 gns Newmarket Autumn Sales: first form in juvenile hurdles when third at Plumpton in April. *J. Ffitch-Heyes*   75

LESBET 8 b.m. Hotfoot – Remeta (Reform) [1992/3 18m^2 24d^3 25v^4 23s a24g^6 25v^4 25g a24g^5 26m 22s 27d] small, workmanlike mare: fair handicap hurdler on her day: well out of form, including in sellers, in second half of season: suited by test of stamina: acts on any going: inconsistent and sometimes looks unenthusiastic. *C. P. Wildman*   117 d

LE TEMERAIRE 7 b.h. Top Ville – La Mirande (FR) (Le Fabuleux) [1992/3 c18g^2 c16m* c16d^4 c18v^2 16s] sturdy horse: fairly useful hurdler at best: won novice chase at Catterick in October: ran creditably next 2 starts: should stay beyond 2¼m: acts on good to firm and heavy ground: sketchy jumper of fences: placed on Flat in summer. *N. Tinkler*   c102 –

LETHAL WEAPON 9 b.g. Prominer – Hammer And Tongs (Politico (USA)) [1992/3 c26g c24m^4 c27d^{pu} c25s c26d] big gelding: bad maiden hunter chaser. *Simon J. Robinson*   c–

LETTERFORE 6 br.m. Strong Gale – Ruby Girl (Crash Course) [1992/3 c22v^6 c21v^3 c21s* c24v^3 c26v^3 c24v* c26m^{pu}] lengthy, sparely-made mare: winning hurdler: won novice chases at Folkestone in December and Windsor in February: pulled up lame later in February: suited by a good test of stamina: acts on heavy ground: sketchy jumper of fences. *John R. Upson*   c103 –

LETTS GREEN (IRE) 5 ch.g. Exhibitioner – Cress (Crepello) [1992/3 18d 21g 23s^{pu}] sturdy, compact gelding: poor novice hurdler: stays 21f: form only on a sound surface: blinkered 3 times, including last 2 outings: sometimes looks none too keen. *M. J. Haynes*   –

Mitsubishi Shogun Golden Miller Trophy (Handicap Chase), Cheltenham— front-runner Le Piccolage sees off the opposition in good style

Berkshire Hurdle, Newbury—
Lift And Load (right) is too good for the favourite Flakey Dove

LEVEL QUAY   10 ch.m. Quayside – Marbles (Levanter) [1992/3 c25d⁵   c–
c26g⁵ c25s] poor novice hunter chaser at best. *J. W. Barker*

LEVEL UP   4 ch.f. Beveled (USA) – Haiti Mill (Free State) [1992/3 17dᵖᵘ]   –
compact filly: modest 7f winner on Flat when trained by R. Guest: no
promise in early-season juvenile hurdle. *C. D. Broad*

LEVEN BABY   6 br.m. Blazing Saddles (AUS) – Farababy (FR) (Faraway   93
Son (USA)) [1992/3 17d⁵ 24dᵖᵘ 20g] small, angular mare: moderate hurdler:
ran badly in seller final start: sold 1,300 gns Doncaster March Sales: stays
2½m: acts on soft and good to firm going. *Mrs M. Reveley*

LIABILITY ORDER   4 b.g. Norwick (USA) – Starky's Pet (Mummy's   104
Pet) [1992/3 16m² 16g⁶ 17v⁴ 16s* 17s 18d* 16m² 16dᵖᵘ 16g² 16fᵖᵘ] leggy,
good-topped gelding: brother to fairly useful hurdler Sunset And Vine: fair
handicapper on Flat for R. Boss, stays 1¼m: won juvenile hurdles at
Catterick in December and Market Rasen in January: injured when almost
falling at the last final start: will stay beyond 2¼m: best form with give in
the ground (acts on heavy). *M. D. Hammond*

LIAM OG (IRE)   5 gr.g. Sexton Blake – Pranburi (Mount Hagen (FR))   –
[1992/3 F17d] tall, rather unfurnished gelding: second foal: dam never ran:
tailed off in NH Flat race at Ascot in April: yet to race over hurdles or
fences. *T. P. McGovern*

LIAMS PRIDE   10 ch.g. Mart Lane – Miss Manhattan (Bally Joy) [1992/3   c85
c16g* c21f³ c16d c16g⁴ c16mᶠ c21sᶠ] angular gelding: modest chaser: won   –
claimer at Southwell in August: sold out of C. Trietline's stable 2,000 gns
Ascot December Sales after fifth outing: best at 2m: acts on dead going:
blinkered once. *P. Riddick*

LIBERTY GLEN   4 b.f. Glenstal (USA) – Liberation (Native Prince)   –
[1992/3 16dᵘʳ] sparely-made filly: unseated rider first in
early-season juvenile selling hurdle. *J. L. Eyre*

LIBERTY JAMES   6 ch.g. Remezzo – Lady Cheval (Cheval) [1992/3   69
16m⁵ 17sᵖᵘ 17m³ 18g 17f] leggy gelding: poor novice hurdler. *Mrs E. M.*
Brooks

LIBERTY RANGE   5 b.m. Liberated – Inrange (Connaught) [1992/3   –
17sᵖᵘ] no sign of ability in 2 races over hurdles. *R. Johnson*

LIDDINGTON BELLE 4 b.f. Reesh – Stephouette (Stephen George) [1992/3 F16g F16s 20d^{pu}] sparely-made filly: fourth foal: half-sister to NH Flat race winner/poor novice jumper Tee Qu (by Jimsun): dam won at 2½m over hurdles: well beaten in NH Flat races and when pulled up in novice selling hurdle. *J. S. King* —

LIE DETECTOR 5 b.g. Nearly A Hand – Rose Ravine (Deep Run) [1992/3 F17m⁵] well-made gelding: second foal: half-brother to useful staying hurdler Cardinal Red (by The Parson): dam smart staying hurdler: fifth of 23 in NH Flat race at Cheltenham in April: yet to race over hurdles or fences. *O. Sherwood* —

LIFT AND LOAD (USA) 6 b.g. Lyphard's Wish (FR) – Dorit (USA) (Damascus (USA)) [1992/3 20d⁴ 17s³ 16g 21m² 21f* 24s^{pu}] rather sparely-made gelding: smart hurdler: won Berkshire Hurdle at Newbury in March by 6 lengths from Flakey Dove: running creditably when pulled up lame final start: will stay beyond 21f: acts on any ground: tends to sweat: consistent. *R. Hannon* 153

LIGHTEN THE LOAD 6 b.g. Lighter – Princess Charybdis (Ballymoss) [1992/3 24v^{pu}] sturdy gelding: little sign of ability in NH Flat race and a novice hurdle. *R. H. Buckler* —

LIGHT GENERAL 9 ch.g. Lighter – Spartan Anna (Spartan General) [1992/3 c18m^F] leggy gelding: novice chaser: no form since 1989/90. *H. M. Kavanagh* c–

LIGHTNING SPARK 4 b.f. Electric – Hot Money (Mummy's Pet) [1992/3 18g³ 16d² 16g 17g^{pu}] leggy, lengthy filly: poor maiden on Flat and over hurdles: stayed 2¼m: acted on dead ground: blinkered once: dead. *M. Avison* 74

LIGHT O'THE MILL 4 b.f. Electric – Furrette (Furry Glen) [1992/3 F12d 18g^{pu} 17s^{pu}] lengthy filly: second foal: half-sister to poor novice hurdler Dukes Hope (by Idiot's Delight): dam moderate hurdler: no sign of ability in NH Flat race or over hurdles. *Miss L. Bower* —

LIGHT SLIPPERS (IRE) 4 b.f. Ela-Mana-Mou – Golden Thread (Glint of Gold) [1992/3 F12d F17f⁴] smallish, leggy filly: first foal: dam never ran: fourth of 18 in NH Flat race at Sandown in March: yet to race over hurdles. *R. Curtis* —

LIGHT VENEER 8 ch.g. Touching Wood (USA) – Oscilight (Swing Easy (USA)) [1992/3 22g⁵ c25g* c25s² c26v* c25s* c24s* 25f* c21s* c21m^{pu}] sturdy gelding: handicap hurdler: won 2-runner event at Newbury in March: successful in 5 of his 7 races in novice chases, scoring at Wolverhampton, Hereford, Nottingham, Exeter and Hexham: stiff task final start: ideally needs further than 2½m and stays 3¼m: acts on any going: sound jumper: should continue to progress. *Mrs M. A. Jones* c113 p ?

LIMBALI 5 b.h. Touching Wood (USA) – Sizzler (Blakeney) [1992/3 22f^{pu}] no sign of ability on Flat and in a novice hurdle. *S. Gollings* —

LIME STREET 5 b.g. Idiot's Delight – Dealers Dream (Whistlefield) [1992/3 F17s 17s² 17d³ 21g^F] smallish, sparely-made gelding: first foal: dam failed to complete in points and behind in NH Flat race: poor novice hurdler: will stay beyond 17f: acts on soft going. *N. A. Twiston-Davies* 87

LIME STREET LIL 5 br.m. Precocious – Merchantmens Girl (Klairon) [1992/3 17g^{pu} 16d^{pu} 18s^{pu} 18v^{pu} a16g^{pu}] workmanlike mare: half-sister to winning hurdlers Lady Windmill (by Milford) and Always Ready (by Tyrnavos): poor maiden on Flat: of little account over hurdles: blinkered final start: sold 1,150 gns Ascot March Sales. *Mrs L. C. Jewell* —

LINCHMERE LAD (IRE) 5 b.g. Petorius – Adamantos (Yellow God) [1992/3 19h²] sturdy gelding: poor novice hurdler: best efforts at around 2m on good ground. *T. R. Greathead* 76

LINCOLN LIEDER 6 ch.g. Balinger – Metaxa (Khalkis) [1992/3 23s^{ur} 22v^{pu} 23s^{pu} 23v⁶] workmanlike gelding: brother to winning jumper Blue —

Rainbow and half-brother to winning jumpers Cheerful Days (by Kinglet) and Met Officer (by Sunyboy): dam half-sister to very smart hunter chaser False Note and fair staying chaser Napoleon Brandy: no sign of ability in novice hurdles. *Mrs L. C. Jewell*

LINDANJAN 9 b.m. Radetzky – Cherio Honey (Macherio) [1992/3 23mᵖᵘ] sparely-made mare: of little account. *Mrs A. Knight*   –

LINDA'S FEELINGS 5 b.m. Feelings (FR) – Salvage Girl (Military) [1992/3 F16g] first foal: dam unraced: behind in NH Flat race at Edinburgh in January: yet to race over hurdles or fences. *T. Dyer*

LINDEMAN 4 b.g. Reach – Montana Moss (Levmoss) [1992/3 16gᵖᵘ] tall, leggy gelding: half-brother to winning hurdlers Carfax (by Tachypous) and Joe Bumpas (by Noalto): dam quite useful hurdler in Ireland: plating-class maiden miler on Flat: tailed off when pulled up in early-season juvenile hurdle: dead. *S. Dow*   –

LINEBACKER 9 b.g. High Line – Gay Trinket (Grey Sovereign) [1992/3 c24m⁵ c26g*] sturdy gelding: won novice hunter chase at Catterick in March, making most: stays 3¼m. *David F. Smith*   **c90** –

LINGDALE LASS 4 gr.f. Petong – Our Mother (Bold Lad (IRE)) [1992/3 17gᵖᵘ 17mᵖᵘ 17d] angular filly: 6f winner at 2 yrs, well beaten on Flat in 1992: no form over hurdles. *M. W. Eckley*   –

LINGER HILL 6 br.g. Netherkelly – Ballyvelour (Ballyciptic) [1992/3 17s 16d] workmanlike gelding: chasing type: sixth foal by a thoroughbred stallion: dam, 1½m seller winner, is half-sister to smart Lord Helpus: behind in novice hurdles. *J. Webber*   –

LINGHAM BRIDE 11 b.m. Deep Run – Bride View (Chinatown) [1992/3 c27gᵖᵘ c27dᵘʳ c27dᵖᵘ c21v⁴ c26sᵖᵘ] small, lightly-made mare: winning hurdler/chaser: a light of other days: blinkered last 2 starts. *J. E. Swiers*   **c–** –

LINGHAM MAGIC 8 b. or br.m. Current Magic – Old Mill Lady (Royal Goblin) [1992/3 c20f⁶ c21g² c27dᵖᵘ c17m⁴ c21g* c21g²] smallish, workmanlike mare: poor chaser: won maiden hunter chase at Uttoxeter in May: stays 21f: acts on firm going: often blinkered prior to 1992/3: poor jumper. *J. E. Swiers*   **c83** x

LING (USA) 8 b. or br.g. Far North (CAN) – Zabolina (Busted) [1992/3 18v* 18d 22f³ 18f] compact gelding: lightly-raced hurdler: won 3-runner handicap at Worcester in April: ran creditably 2 starts later: stays 2¾m: acts on any going. *R. G. Frost*   98

LINK COPPER 4 ch.g. Whistlefield – Letitica (Deep Run) [1992/3 17m⁵ 16gᵖᵘ] sturdy gelding: first foal: dam of little account: no sign of ability. *H. M. Kavanagh*   –

LINKSIDE 8 b.g. Good Thyne (USA) – Laurel Wood (Laurence O) [1992/3 17d² 17sᵇᵈ 20d³ 16g*] leggy gelding: lightly raced: third in novice hurdle at Haydock in February, easily best effort: odds on, workmanlike winner of maiden hurdle at Ayr following month: will stay beyond 2½m: acts on dead ground. *D. Moffatt*   103

LINN FALLS 8 br.m. Royal Fountain – Border Gloria (Border Chief) [1992/3 c25g³] lengthy, angular mare: poor novice hurdler/hunter chaser: stays 25f: acts on dead ground: blinkered once. *Miss C. E. J. Dawson*   **c76** –

LINNGATE 4 b.f. Silver Season – Private Path (Warpath) [1992/3 F16g³ F16d* F16s³ F17f³] rather unfurnished filly: third foal: half-sister to winning hurdler Thistleholm (by Hello Handsome): dam never ran: won NH Flat race at Ayr in January: third to Native Field in valuable similar event at Aintree in April on final outing: yet to race over hurdles. *L. Lungo*

LINPAC EXPRESS 4 b.g. Siberian Express (USA) – North Page (FR) (Northfields (USA)) [1992/3 16sᵖᵘ a16gᶠ 16d⁴] leggy gelding: poor maiden on Flat: sold 3,000 gns Doncaster October Sales: first form over hurdles when fourth in novice selling hurdle at Ludlow (visored) in April. *P. T. Dalton*   68

LINRED 8 b.g. Politico (USA) – Denwick Bambi (Hamood) [1992/3 c25m4] rangy gelding: fair pointer: fourth in hunter chase at Nottingham in March. *Mike Roberts* — **c67**

LION OF VIENNA 6 b.g. Bulldozer – Lucky Favour (Ballyciptic) [1992/3 21d 28d2 24spu 21d2 25v*] quite good-topped, leggy gelding: improved effort when winning novice hurdle at Perth in April, making most: suited by good test of stamina: acts well on heavy going. *T. J. Carr* — **95**

LIRELLA 6 ch.m. Lir – Barry's Girl (Silly Answer) [1992/3 F16d a20g 21vpu 17s] lengthy, sparely-made mare: no sign of ability. *P. R. Rodford* — —

LIRIE LAD 7 ch.g. Lir – Barry's Girl (Silly Answer) [1992/3 21s3 22v5 22v6 a22g5 c22v4 c21s2 c23g3 c22g* c22v3 c26m6 c26d4] leggy, sparely-made gelding: modest novice hurdler: won maiden chase at Towcester in March: stays 3¼m: acts on good to firm and heavy going. *P. R. Rodford* — **c83 88**

LISALEEN PRINCE 8 b.g. Duky – Gild Over (Red Slipper) [1992/3 c24vpu] lengthy, robust gelding: winning pointer: maiden hurdler/chaser: dead. *N. J. Henderson* — **c– –**

LISA ROSA 6 b.m. Ardross – Macaw (Narrator) [1992/3 21v5 23d3 24s] leggy mare: selling hurdler: stays 3m: needs give in the ground. *Miss S. J. Wilton* — **84**

LISSADELL LADY 4 gr.f. Sharrood (USA) – Clouded Vision (So Blessed) [1992/3 17d] smallish, lengthy filly: fair 9f winner on Flat (wore blinkers) in Ireland: no promise on hurdling debut: sold 1,400 gns Ascot 2nd June Sales. *F. Jordan* — —

LITMORE DANCER 5 br.m. Mashhor Dancer (USA) – Daring Charm (Daring March) [1992/3 18g 16g6 16sF 17g3] lengthy mare: poor miler on Flat: poor novice hurdler: takes strong hold and will prove best around 2m. *J. M. Bradley* — **59**

LITTLE BIG 6 b.g. Indian King (USA) – Route Royale (Roi Soleil) [1992/3 17m2 17g2 22m4 19g* 16d3 20g3 22m 20f5] compact gelding: modest hurdler: won novice event at Exeter in October: stays 2¾m: acts on good to firm and dead ground. *C. D. Broad* — **85**

LITTLE BROMLEY 6 ch.m. Riberetto – Bromley Rose (Rubor) [1992/3 F16s2 F16d6 17dpu 16g] compact non-thoroughbred mare: first foal: dam unraced: showed ability in NH Flat races: no promise over hurdles. *A. Eubank* — —

LITTLE BRYMA 11 b.g. Rymer – Saucy Walk (Saucy Kit) [1992/3 c21g6 c25gpu 21s c21gpu] tall gelding: poor novice hurdler/chaser: poor jumper: blinkered once. *I. L. Curson* — **c– x –**

LITTLE CLARE 6 b.m. Oats – County Clare (Vimadee) [1992/3 F17g 16d 24vpu 22mF] small, sparely-made mare: no sign of ability. *F. Jordan* — —

LITTLE CONKER 5 ch.g. All Systems Go – L'Irondelle (On Your Mark) [1992/3 18d4 16m4 21dur a16gF 18m5 17m 16s5 22m2] small gelding: poor novice hurdler: stays 2¾m: acts on good to firm, soft ground and fibresand: visored sixth outing. *A. Smith* — **72**

LITTLEDALE (USA) 7 b.g. Lypheor – Smeralda (Grey Sovereign) [1992/3 16dur 16v6 a18g5 a22g2 22g5 23d 24f 22f4 c23m4] leggy, sparely-made gelding: poor form in novice hurdles and on chasing debut: stays 2¾m: acts on good to firm ground and equitrack. *M. J. Wilkinson* — **c68 71**

LITTLE ERNIE 7 b.g. Idiot's Delight – Allende (Grand Roi) [1992/3 17vpu 20gpu 17mur] no sign of ability over hurdles: trained first start by R. Baker. *M. C. Pipe* — —

LITTLE FREDDIE 4 ch.g. Roman Warrior – Dawns Ballad (Balidar) [1992/3 F16g4 F16d F16f] second foal: dam unraced: signs of a little ability in NH Flat races: yet to race over hurdles. *J. I. A. Charlton* — —

LITTLE GENERAL 10 ch.g. General Ironside – Coolentallagh (Perhapsburg) [1992/3 c21dur c26gpu c26vpu c27vF c25s c26sur c27m2 c28m*] stocky, compact gelding: modest chaser: won handicap at — **c92**

Nottingham in March: withdrawn lame the folowing month: stays long distances: best on top-of-the-ground. *R. Rowe*

LITTLE IVOR 4 b.g. Kings Lake (USA) – Ange Gris (USA) (Grey Dawn II) [1992/3 18m] sparely-made gelding: poor middle-distance maiden on Flat: soundly beaten in early-season selling hurdle: sold 1,300 gns Ascot September Sales. *Denys Smith*

LITTLE LEMON 9 b.m. Spartan Jester – Port'n Lemon (Hot Brandy) [1992/3 c27d*] fair pointer: won hunter chase at Newton Abbot in May: stays 27f: acts on dead going: should improve. *D. Luxton*

c78 p

LITTLE LONDON 14 br.g. Pieces of Eight – Whistler's Princess (King Emperor (USA)) [1992/3 27mpu] small, lengthy gelding: winning staying hurdler/chaser: no form for a long time: usually blinkered. *T. Morton*

c–
–

LITTLE MIGHT 7 ch.g. Sir Patrick – Dawn Express (Pony Express) [1992/3 c27spu c23mpu c23d c27spu c19mF] lengthy, workmanlike gelding: half-brother to 3 winning pointers, one of them also successful in a hunter chase: winning pointer: no form in steeplechases. *Mrs J. Wonnacott*

c–

LITTLE-NIPPER 8 ch.g. Derrylin – Emily Kent (Royal Palace) [1992/3 c20s6 c20s4 c21s4 c21v2 c21s* c20gur] rangy gelding: has scope: fairly useful hurdler: won novice handicap chase at Cheltenham in January in good style: unseated rider fourth following month: stays 21f: acts on heavy going: held up: should improve over fences. *D. Nicholson*

c102 p
–

LITTLE NOD 4 ch.c. Domynsky – Vikris (Viking (USA)) [1992/3 16m2 17g2 17msu 16f2 16m4 17f2] poor maiden miler on Flat: moderate form over hurdles: yet to race beyond 17f: acts on good to firm going (respectable efforts on firm). *J. White*

95

LITTLE SAIL 7 ch.m. Little Wolf – Sarasail (Hitting Away) [1992/3 18g 24s] lengthy mare: won 2 NH Flat races in 1989/90: tailed off in novice hurdles. *N. A. Twiston-Davies*

–

LITTLE TOM 8 b.g. Nearly A Hand – Lost In Silence (Silent Spring) [1992/3 c17g3 c20m2 c20f4 c16s3 c21g4 c21f* c19d*] tall gelding: moderate handicap chaser: won at Huntingdon and Hereford in May: effective at 2m to 21f: acts on firm and dead going: usually a sound jumper: races up with pace. *J. S. King*

c92
–

LITTLETON LULLABY 8 ch.m. Milford – Littleton Song (Song) [1992/3 17v 17vpu 17dpu] small, lengthy mare: probably of little account. *B. J. Meehan*

–

LITTLE TORMENT 4 b.g. Jalmood (USA) – Head First (Welsh Pageant) [1992/3 F17g F14s] smallish gelding: half-brother to winning jumpers Rahiib and Hello Steve (both by Final Straw) and Domarc (by Moorestyle): dam quite useful 1½m winner: well beaten in NH Flat races: yet to race over hurdles. *T. Kersey*

LITTLE TORO 11 b.g. Torus – Little Echo (Little Buskins) [1992/3 24d 25d c21dpu] leggy, sparely-made gelding: inconsistent and irresolute hurdler: no sign of ability over fences: stayed 2¾m: acted on any going: tried blinkered and visored: dead. *C. R. Barwell*

c–
– §

LIVE ACTION 6 b.g. Alzao (USA) – Brig O'Doon (Shantung) [1992/3 17d5] sturdy, angular gelding: has been hobdayed and had soft palate operation: winning 2m hurdler: well beaten in October: acts on dead ground. *Miss H. C. Knight*

–

LIVE AND LET LIVE 9 b.g. Comedy Star (USA) – Maid of Warwick (Warwick) [1992/3 c21dpu c16d3 c16m] compact gelding: no sign of ability. *R. Tate*

c–
–

LIVE IN HOPE 11 b.g. Condorcet (FR) – Hopefull Polly (Polyfoto) [1992/3 20f 26d 18s] sparely-made gelding: winning hurdler/chaser at up to 2½m: sold 1,700 gns Ascot September Sales: no form in 1992/3. *P. S. Madgwick*

c–
–

LIZZIES LASS 8 br.m. Sandalay – Kiltegan (Charlottesvilles Flyer) [1992/3 23s^{pu} 22v^{pu} 22g^{pu} 22f 22g] plain mare: poor novice hurdler at best. *F. Gray* –

LLACCA PRINCESS 5 b.m. Rymer – Karyobinga (So Blessed) [1992/3 17s^{pu} 17s^{pu} 16d^{pu} 16m] sparely-made mare: of little account. *M. W. Eckley* –

LLANELLY (FR) 6 gr.m. Kenmare (FR) – Grey Valley (USA) (Vigors (USA)) [1992/3 16v^5 16s 22d^{pu} 17g^5 17g^4 26v^{pu}] light-framed mare: of little account: sometimes blinkered. *Graeme Roe* –

LLES LE BUCFLOW 5 ch.h. Little Wolf – Elsell (Grey Mirage) [1992/3 F16m^3 F16d 22d^{pu} 16s^{pu} 17s^F 20d^F 17m^{ur} 17v^{pu} 16f^6] sparely-made horse: of little account: blinkered once. *F. Jordan* –

LLOYDS DREAM 4 b.g. Lidhame – Christines Lady (Roman Warrior) [1992/3 17g 17s^6] neat gelding: no sign of ability on Flat or over hurdles. *D. Shaw* –

LOANINGDALE 8 ch.g. Lomond (USA) – Aliceva (Alcide) [1992/3 c17g^{pu} c21m^6 c24m^{bd} 24g^{pu} 21m 22f^3] leggy gelding: one-time fairly useful hurdler: no form since 1989/90, including in novice chases: wears blinkers: ungenuine. *R. Akehurst* c– § — §

LOBRIC 8 b.g. Electric – Light O'Battle (Queen's Hussar) [1992/3 23d^4 22s c21s^3 c24s^4 c24gF] workmanlike gelding: fair handicap hurdler: poor novice chaser: not raced after December: stays 3m: acts on any going: usually blinkered nowadays, visored once. *J. R. Jenkins* c83 104

LOCAL CUSTOMER 8 b.g. Le Bavard (FR) – Penny Bar (Bargello) [1992/3 c21f^5 c17f^3 c23s^3 c24d^{pu} c25g^2 c23g^4 c23m^2] lengthy gelding: modest chaser: trained until after third outing by M. Hammond: second in hunter chase and handicap late in season: probably needs further than 2m, and stays well: suited by a sound surface (acts on firm): sometimes blinkered (only once in 1992/3). *P. Bradley* c89

LOCAL DEALER 5 ch.g. Scottish Reel – Green Pool (Whistlefield) [1992/3 18d 16d 18v^{ur} 17f^6] sturdy gelding: would have won novice selling handicap hurdle at Market Rasen in December but for unseating rider 2 out: ran poorly 5 months later: yet to race beyond 2¼m. *J. F. Bottomley* 78

LOCAL FLYER 4 b.g. Local Suitor (USA) – Noirmont Girl (Skymaster) [1992/3 16s^5 16s^5 16v^6 a16g^2 a16gF a16g* a18g^4 a16g^5] leggy, angular gelding: half-brother to several Flat winners, notably smart and very speedy 1977 2-y-o Noiritza (by Young Emperor) and to winning hurdler Djebel Prince (by Ile de Bourbon): dam ran only at 5f, winning twice: won juvenile hurdle at Southwell in February: ran poorly afterwards: yet to race beyond 2¼m: acts well on fibresand. *J. E. Banks* 101

LOCH BLUE 11 b.g. Lochnager – La Sinope (FR) (Thatch (USA)) [1992/3 c27v^F c24s^{pu}] big, leggy gelding: winning hurdler/chaser: jumped poorly in 1992/3: should stay 3m: acts on heavy going and good to firm. *S. Dow* c–

LOCH DUICH 7 ch.h. Kris – Sleat (Santa Claus) [1992/3 16s^{pu} 17d^6] tall, leggy horse: poor winning hurdler: no form in 1992/3 (trained first start by R. Baker): raced only at around 2m: acts on good to firm and dead ground. *R. J. Hodges* –

LOCHEARNHEAD (USA) 6 b.h. Lomond (USA) – Carmelize (USA) (Cornish Prince) [1992/3 18s 17s^{pu} a16g^{pu}] lengthy, angular horse: lightly raced on Flat in Ireland, stays 1¼m: no sign of ability over hurdles. *B. Byford* –

LOCHEART LADY 6 b.m. Lochnager – Cross Your Heart (Busted) [1992/3 16g 16g 16s 17m^6] poor hurdler: yet to race beyond 17f: acts on good to soft going. *A. P. Stringer* 77

LOCHERRE 9 gr.g. Lochnager – Chemin de Guerre (Warpath) [1992/3 a20g a20g 21v a22g^2 a24g^{pu} 25m 21d^{pu}] lengthy, workmanlike gelding: poor hurdler: only form in 1992/3 when second at Southwell in February: stays 2¾m: acts on soft going and fibresand: sometimes visored: reluctant. *B. P. J. Baugh* 80 §

445

LOCH GARANNE 5 br.m. Lochnager – Raperon (Rapid River) [1992/3 16d* 17s² 17s* 17d³ 16d* 18g] angular, good-topped mare: won novice hurdles at Wetherby and Newcastle in first half of season and handicap on former course in February: ran as though something amiss final outing: likely to prove best at around 2m: acts on soft ground: not an accomplished jumper as yet. *M. J. Camacho* — 112

LOCHNAGRAIN (IRE) 5 b. or br.g. Strong Gale – Mountain Sedge (Goldhill) [1992/3 F16d] half-brother to winning jumpers Wild Argosy (by Lucifer), Mountain Mear (by Giolla Mear) and Ronans Birthday (by Furry Glen): dam won on Flat at 1½m and over hurdles in Ireland: soundly beaten in NH Flat race at Ayr in January: yet to race over hurdles or fences. *Miss L. A. Perratt*

LOCH SCAVAIG (IRE) 4 b.f. The Parson – Regent Star (Prince Regent (FR)) [1992/3 F16s* F16s² F16v⁵] leggy filly: sixth foal: dam won at 7f on Flat and in frame over hurdles in Ireland: won NH Flat race at Wetherby in January: yet to race over hurdles. *D. Moffatt*

LOCK KEEPER (USA) 7 b.g. Riverman (USA) – Jamila (Sir Gaylord) [1992/3 16g* 16g 16m⁶] smallish gelding: poor hurdler: won claiming handicap at Southwell in August: unlikely to stay much beyond 2m: acts on good to firm and soft ground: won on Flat in January and February (for C. J. Hill). *J. Mackie* — 77

LODESTAR (IRE) 5 b.h. Rainbow Quest (USA) – Air Distingue (USA) (Sir Ivor) [1992/3 18g² 16d6 16d] good-topped horse: modest novice hurdler: ran badly last 2 outings: yet to race beyond 2¼m: acts on dead ground: ungenuine. *N. Tinkler* — 94 §

LODGING 6 ch.g. Longleat (USA) – Mollified (Lombard (GER)) [1992/3 18d5 c16gF c17vur c20vur] workmanlike gelding: poor novice hurdler: let down by his jumping over fences: should stay beyond 17f: acts on dead and good to firm ground: usually blinkered prior to 1992/3. *B. Ellison* — c– x / –

LO-FLYING MISSILE 5 gr.g. Cruise Missile – Lo-Incost (Impecunious) [1992/3 16s⁵ 16s² 22dᵖᵘ] good-topped gelding: chasing type: no worthwhile form in novice hurdles. *R. Dickin* — –

LOGAMIMO 7 b.g. Lord Gayle (USA) – Miss Morgan (Native Prince) [1992/3 c21m⁴ c18d² c18mᵣᵒ c21m⁶ c21d³ c17d* c16s* c21s* c27s c20d⁶ c24m⁴ c21g³] neat gelding: fairly useful handicap chaser: won at Sedgefield, Aintree (conditional jockeys) and Wetherby in first half of season: effective at 2m and probably stays 27f: acts on any going: blinkered in 1989/90: sometimes wears tongue strap: jumps soundly. *J. A. Hellens* — c123 / –

LOMBARD OCEAN 4 ch.g. Ballacashtal (CAN) – Realm Gift (Realm) [1992/3 17s⁵] modest sprinter on Flat at best: tailed off in selling hurdle in November. *A. Bailey* — –

LONESOME GLORY (USA) 5 ch.g. Transworld (USA) – Stronghold (FR) (Green Dancer (USA)) [1992/3 17g* 12f* 20f* 16d* 20d² 20f* 19g³ 22v* 24f*] angular gelding: winner at least 6 times over hurdles in USA: put up very useful performance when leading close home to beat Al Mutahm in quite valuable 4-runner event at Cheltenham in December on eighth start: stays 3m: acts on any going. *F. Bruce Miller, USA* — 150 ?

LONESOME TRAIN (USA) 4 ch.g. Crafty Prospector (USA) – Alaki Miss (USA) (Olden Times) [1992/3 17m* 17m² 17g* 16g² 17v³ 17g³] strong gelding: modest middle-distance maiden on Flat: sold out of J. Gosden's stable 4,200 gns Ascot July Sales: won 2 juvenile hurdles at Perth early in season: ran well afterwards, especially so on last 2 starts (not raced after January): will stay beyond 17f: acts on good to firm and heavy ground. *C. Weedon* — 114

LONGGHURST 10 b.g. Camden Town – Olanrose (Kythnos) [1992/3 c23g³ c26gF] leggy, sparely-made gelding: poor hurdler/novice chaser: stayed 25f: acted on any going: sometimes blinkered: poor jumper of fences: dead. *B. Forsey* — c77 x / –

LONG LANE LADY 7 ch.m. Longleat (USA) – Teresa Way (Great White Way (USA)) [1992/3 16v] lengthy mare: poor and inconsistent 6f/7f handicapper on Flat: no sign of ability in seller in December on hurdling debut: sold 1,100 gns Doncaster January Sales. *J. Mackie* —

LONTANO (GER) 11 b.g. Pentathlon – Lodina (GER) (Hodell) [1992/3 c23vᵖᵘ c22dF c23m5] dipped-backed, sparely-made gelding: winning hurdler: modest novice chaser at best: no form in 1992/3: stays 2½m: ideally suited by give in the ground: blinkered once. *M. J. Ryan* c– —

LOOKINGFORARAINBOW (IRE) 5 ch.g. Godswalk (USA) – Bridget Folly (Crofter (USA)) [1992/3 16f] leggy gelding: fair middle-distance stayer on Flat, winner early in 1993: behind in early-season novice event on hurdling debut. *Bob Jones* —

LOOK LIVELY (USA) 8 b.g. Smarten (USA) – Danseuse (USA) (Jig Time (USA)) [1992/3 18f c21mᵘʳ c21s c24s5 c22vᵖᵘ] rather leggy, sparely-made gelding: winning hurdler: maiden chaser: no form since 1990/1: sold 800 gns Ascot February Sales. *J. T. Gifford* c– —

LOON 5 ch.g. Bairn (USA) – Patois (I Say) [1992/3 17dᵖᵘ 17g 17s a16g4 a18g3 a16g a16g4 17f4] workmanlike gelding: poor novice hurdler: trained by P. Hobbs first start: races only at around 2m: acts on dead ground and equitrack: headstrong front runner: temperamental, and sometimes reluctant to race. *J. Joseph* 66 §

LOOSE ENDS 6 ch.h. Persian Bold – Crimson Royale (High Line) [1992/3 24m 17m 22g] ex-Irish horse: fair hurdler: trained until after first start by E. O'Grady: below form both outings in Britain: stays 3m: acts on good to firm going. *T. H. Caldwell* —

LOOSE FLING 8 b.g. Imperial Fling (USA) – In Leiu (Tutankhamen) [1992/3 22g6 17m5 21g4 25d2 24gᵖᵘ] tall gelding: very lightly-raced novice over hurdles: broke down final start: suited by good test of stamina: acts on dead ground. *Mrs B. Butterworth* 87

LOOSE WHEELS 7 b.g. Strong Gale – Kylogue Daisy (Little Buskins) [1992/3 24m F21g c21s4 c25m6] leggy, lengthy ex-Irish gelding: third foal: dam unraced half-sister to several winning jumpers, notably fairly useful Irish chaser Kylogue Lady and good-class hunter chaser Three Counties: poor novice hurdler/chaser: probably stays 3m: acts on good to firm and soft ground: blinkered second start (trained until after then by D. Hughes). *Mrs P. Sly* c– —

LORD BELMONTE (IRE) 4 b.g. Cyrano de Bergerac – Noble Nancy (Royal And Regal (USA)) [1992/3 17g2 17mᵖᵘ 17g6 16d4 17v 16v a20g6] no form on Flat: sold out of C. Cyzer's stable 1,300 gns Ascot July Sales: poor novice hurdler: form only at around 2m: acts on dead ground. *P. M. McEntee* 59

LORD FAWSLEY 8 b. or br.g. St Columbus – Ducal Gold (Solar Duke) [1992/3 c21m2] fair pointer: second in novice hunter chase at Uttoxeter in June: should improve. *G. J. Tarry* c83 p

LORD LEITRIM (IRE) 4 b.c. Nordico (USA) – Brave Louise (Brave Shot) [1992/3 17g] sparely-made colt: poor maiden miler on Flat: no promise in early-season juvenile hurdle. *N. A. Callaghan* —

LORD MUSTARD 10 ch.g. Lord Ha Ha – Royal Cloak (Hardicanute) [1992/3 25d 22s] smallish, sturdy gelding: winning hurdler/chaser: very lightly raced and no form since 1989/90, though won a point in February. *J. A. C. Edwards* c– —

LORD NEPTUNE 4 gr.g. Petong – Odile (Green Dancer (USA)) [1992/3 16s 17g a16g a16g3 a16g4] neat gelding: of little account on Flat: easily best run over hurdles when third in juvenile event at Lingfield in February: barely stays 2m: acts on equitrack: usually visored or blinkered. *J. R. Jenkins* 73

LORD PURNA 11 ch.g. Sir Mago – Lady Annapurna (High Perch) [1992/3 c25m* c25mF] sparely-made gelding: fairly useful hunter chaser: won at Market Rasen in March: suited by 3m and more: acts on hard ground, possibly unsuited by a yielding surface: forces pace. *M. E. Sowersby* c105

LORD RELIC (NZ)   7 b.g. Zamazaan (FR) – Morning Order (NZ)
(Bismark) [1992/3 21v* 21s* 21s* 21m³ 26s]   140 p

The Grade 1 Challow Hurdle at Newbury in early-January spotlighted a
potential Cheltenham Festival winner in Lord Relic, a New Zealand-bred
with good Flat form down-under who was able to coast home for his third
success over hurdles despite some unpolished, occasionally hesitant,
jumping. It was the third time in a row that Lord Relic had impressed as a
horse with a bright future. He had previously won other novice events at
Uttoxeter and Chepstow in December. The opposition at Newbury was by
far the strongest he had faced and provided as good a test of a Cheltenham
candidate as could be expected at that stage of the season. The six other
runners in the Challow Hurdle—in race card order Corrin Hill, Glen
Lochan, Irish Bay, Mr Matt, Yorkshire Gale and Gaelstrom—were also
winners, all of them except Corrin Hill and Gaelstrom winners last time out,
too. The betting suggested a close finish between Lord Relic and the other
New Zealand-bred in the field, Glen Lochan, but the latter was beaten on the
home turn and was pulled up along with Corrin Hill. Gaelstrom offered the
stiffest resistance. She took them along at a fair pace, tracked by Lord Relic,
until giving way to Lord Relic at the sixth. She hung on for a while but was
really stretched when the winner quickened and simply couldn't live with
him in the straight. Lord Relic strode right away, and though eased
considerably on the flat he had a good ten lengths to spare at the line.

Lord Relic didn't race again before the Sun Alliance Novices' Hurdle,
for which he started 5/2 favourite in a field of nineteen and was beaten four
lengths into third place behind Gaelstrom. He ran like a horse needing the
run, flagging under pressure up the hill and being overtaken by Cardinal
Red as well as re-overtaken by Gaelstrom after looking assured of victory
when he quickened on from Gaelstrom approaching two out. However, it is
rare for any of Pipe's to want for fitness (eleven weeks off proved no bar to
success at the meeting for stable-companion Granville Again) and the

Challow Hurdle, Newbury—Lord Relic spreadeagles a useful field

Mrs H. J. Clarke's "Lord Relic"

reason for defeat may just as well lie elsewhere: in the firmish ground, for instance, or in his again less-than-fluent jumping. Another fifteen weeks went by before Lord Relic was seen out again, in the Grande Course de Haies d'Auteuil run over a testing three and a quarter miles in Paris. He faced a mammoth task, against most of the leading staying hurdlers in France. In the circumstances he ran respectably, racing up with the leaders until three out and eventually coming eighth of fourteen behind that fine horse Ubu III, beaten twenty-three lengths.

Lord Relic's Flat form sets him well apart from the usual recruit from New Zealand. Among his eight wins is one in the listed Oliver Nicholson Handicap (ten and a half furlongs on heavy going at Ellerslie), and among his fourteen places is a third in the Group 2 Wrightson Bloodstock Guineas at the same course. From a New-Zealand point of view he is a very well-bred horse, too. His sire, the good French stayer Zamazaan, proved to be an inspired acquisition, in twenty prolific years at stud in Auckland being responsible for a notable percentage of winners to runners and stakes winners to runners. Zamazaan's son Beau Zam was Australasian champion in 1987/8. Lord Relic's dam Morning Order produced a winner in Australia

449

called Zambrelic to a previous covering by Zamazaan. Morning Order failed to win, unlike her dam Morning Star (thrice successful in New Zealand) and grandam Mayrah (thrice successful in Australia). Neither mare was a black-type winner, but a filly out of Morning Star, a half-sister to Morning Order called Princess Dram, achieved that status in 1984/5—the season she was rated joint-third best three-year-old filly in New Zealand.

Lord Relic (NZ) (b.g. 1986)	Zamazaan (FR) (ch 1965)	Exbury (ch 1959)	Le Haar
			Greensward
		Toyama II (b 1955)	Tulyar
			Rose O'Lynn
	Morning Order (NZ) (b 1979)	Bismark (b 1967)	Relic
			Gun Play
		Morning Star (ch 1965)	Wilkes
			Mayrah

Lord Relic's reappearance in the coming season is something to look forward to. Once he gets his jumping right he is going to be top class at two and a half miles and upwards over hurdles. It is on account of his inexperience that we say 'once' rather than 'if', and it is on account of his need to gain experience that we expect him to spend at least another season over hurdles before he is sent chasing. Lord Relic should stay three miles even though to date he has always taken a good hold. His precise ground requirements remain to be determined, though he clearly handles the mud. *M. C. Pipe*

LORD'S FINAL 6 ch.g. Royal Match – White Cone (Celtic Cone) [1992/3 18f³ 19f³] small, compact gelding: lightly-raced novice hurdler, poor form: stays 19f: acts on firm ground. *C. R. Barwell* — 83

LORD TIM (IRE) 5 ch.g. Hatim (USA) – Lady Harford (Great Heron (USA)) [1992/3 22gpu 25vpu 24s 25d⁶] neat gelding: no sign of ability over hurdles. *J. A. Hellens* — –

LORD TRILBY (IRE) 4 b.g. The Noble Player (USA) – Little Trilby (Tyrant (USA)) [1992/3 17mF 18dpu 16v 22d] small gelding: half-brother to fair Flat winner Stelby (by Stetchworth): dam useful at up to 7f: tailed off over hurdles: visored last 2 starts. *Mrs V. C. Ward* — –

LORENTEGGIO (USA) 8 b.g. Al Nasr (FR) – Clairvoyance (USA) (Round Table) [1992/3 22m⁴ 18f⁶ 22s⁵] smallish gelding: lightly-raced novice hurdler: poor form: stays 2¾m: best efforts on top-of-the-ground. *Mrs J. Wonnacott* — 75

LOS BUCCANEROS 10 br.g. Neltino – Pirella (Pirate King) [1992/3 c16s⁴] useful-looking gelding: fair hurdler: first race since 1989/90 when promising fourth in novice event at Ludlow in April on chasing debut: unlikely to stay much beyond 2m: probably acts on any ground: should improve sufficiently to win a similar race. *S. Christian* — c85 p –

LOSHIAN (IRE) 4 ch.f. Montelimar (USA) – Fair Chance (Young Emperor) [1992/3 16s⁵ 16s* 16s* 16d* 17m⁵] workmanlike filly: 1½m winner on Flat: took well to hurdling and won juvenile events at Limerick (2) in December and Leopardstown (Diners Club Stillorgan Hurdle) in January: good fifth to Shawiya in Daily Express Triumph Hurdle at Cheltenham in March: will stay beyond 17f: acts on good to firm and soft going: edgy type who tends to be on toes: jumps well. *Mrs A. M. O'Brien, Ireland* — 128

LO STREGONE 7 b.g. The Parson – Somers Castle (Will Somers) [1992/3 20s² 22d* 22s* 20v* 24s³ 20dpu] rangy, useful-looking ex-Irish gelding: chasing type: won 3 novice hurdles at Haydock around turn of year: below-form third in valuable event at Chepstow in February, ran poorly later in month: should stay beyond 2¾m: acts on heavy ground: races up with pace: jumps well in the main. *T. P. Tate* — 132

LOTHIAN ADMIRAL 11 b.g. Roscoe Blake – Lothian Lady (New Brig) [1992/3 c23sF c24gur 28g⁵] sturdy gelding: winning hurdler: poor novice — c– x –

chaser: trained until after second start by C. Nash, sold 1,750 gns Doncaster May Sales: stays 25f: acts on heavy going: poor jumper. *C. H. P. Bell*

LOTHIAN PILOT 6 ro.g. Alias Smith (USA) – Lothian Lightning (Lighter) [1992/3 c21m³ c25g^F] leggy gelding: winning hurdler: third in novice event at Carlisle in October on chasing debut: stays 21f: acts on soft and good to firm ground. *L. Lungo*   c85 –

LOTHIAN SULTAN 9 b.g. Roscoe Blake – Lothian Lady (New Brig) [1992/3 c25f] workmanlike gelding: winning 2m hurdler: no form over fences: dead. *G. Harwood*   c–

LOT OF MOXIE (IRE) 4 ch.f. Muscatite – Canebrake Lady (Formidable (USA)) [1992/3 17d^{pu}] small filly: first foal: dam of little account on Flat: no sign of ability in early-season novice selling hurdle. *P. R. Hedger*   –

LOUANDY 9 b.g. Furry Glen – Boreen Queen (Boreen (FR)) [1992/3 21g^{ur}] rather leggy gelding: twice-raced novice hurdler: close up when unseating rider 2 out in 21-runner event at Newbury in February. *K. C. Bailey*   – p

LOUDEST WHISPER 5 b.g. Reach – Dancela (Ela-Mana-Mou) [1992/3 16f] soundly beaten in 2 novice hurdles. *K. S. Bridgwater*   –

LOUGH BROWN 10 ch.g. Ardoon – Nayleen (Petingo) [1992/3 21s^{pu} 22v⁶ 16v⁴ 18v* 22d^{pu}] lengthy gelding: lightly-raced hurdler: won novice handicap at Folkestone in January: stayed 2¼m: acted on heavy going: dead. *T. Casey*   83

LOUIS FARRELL 8 br.g. Furry Glen – Brave Light (Brave Invader (USA)) [1992/3 23s a22g⁵ 17v⁵ 23v a16g^{pu} 20d⁴ 22m⁶] rather sparely-made gelding: poor novice hurdler: once-raced over fences: trained by D. Burchell until after fifth outing: stays 2¾m: acts on good to firm and soft going: sometimes wears a hood. *D. J. Wintle*   c– 69

LOUNGING 4 gr.f. Pragmatic – Deep Coach (Deep Run) [1992/3 17d] second foal: half-sister to a poor maiden hurdler by Oats: dam 2m selling hurdle winner: tailed off in amateurs maiden hurdle at Carlisle in April. *J. S. Haldane*   –

LOVE ANEW (USA) 8 b.g. Sensitive Prince (USA) – Armure Bleue (FR) (Riverman (USA)) [1992/3 c16m³ c16g³ c18m⁵ c17g⁵ c16g² c22g* c16s³ c21g⁴ c22g* c21g² c22d^{ur} c19f³ c21f] sturdy gelding: moderate chaser: won handicaps at Fakenham in October (trained until after seventh start by O. Sherwood) and March: effective from 2m to 2¾m: acts on good to firm and good to soft going: tried blinkered in 1991/2: sometimes finds little, and needs exaggerated waiting tactics: tends to flash tail under pressure. *M. Dixon*   c97 §

LOVE ON THE ROCKS 8 b.m. Martinmas – Love Is Blind (USA) (Hasty Road) [1992/3 18g⁴ c21g³ c17v* c21s⁴ c21s 21v c25d⁴ c19d⁶ c20d] close-coupled mare: poor novice hurdler: won mares novice handicap chase at Newton Abbot in November: ran poorly most starts afterwards: stays 21f: acts on heavy going. *R. J. Price*   c88 d

LOVER BILL 11 b.g. Golden Love – Billeragh Girl (Normandy) [1992/3 c21s c24d^{pu} c24d^{ur} c25d c20f^F c21m² c21s c24f^F] workmanlike gelding: poor novice hurdler/chaser: stays 3m: acts on good to firm and soft ground: blinkered nowadays. *M. J. Wilkinson*   c83 –

LOVER'S LOCK 11 b.g. Golden Love – Payne's Lady (Lock Diamond) [1992/3 c25d^F c25s^{pu}] winning pointer: yet to complete in hunter chases: trained first start by S. Pittendrigh, visored second. *M. Wanless*   c–

LOVER'S MOON 6 b.h. Ela-Mana-Mou – Ce Soir (Northern Baby (CAN)) [1992/3 21g 18d] sturdy horse: one-time fairly useful out-and-out stayer on Flat: behind both starts in novice hurdles: sold 1,000 gns Ascot December Sales. *N. Tinkler*   –

LOVING AROUND (IRE) 5 b.m. Furry Glen – Shannon Ville (Deep Run) [1992/3 F16s] rangy mare with scope: third foal: sister to fairly useful hurdler and winning chaser Shannon Glen: dam, winning hurdler/chaser,

451

from successful jumping family: well beaten in NH Flat race at Ludlow in April: yet to race over hurdles or fences. *N. J. Henderson*

LOVING OMEN 6 ch.g. Touching Wood (USA) – Etoile d'Amore (USA) (The Minstrel (CAN)) [1992/3 17m⁵ 16g⁶ 20g24v³ 17mF 17d⁶ 21s³ 18d* 17d⁴ 18m⁵] good-topped gelding: moderate form over hurdles: won novice handicap at Kelso in April: best form with give in the ground: blinkered last 4 outings. *Miss Z. A. Green* — 89

LOVISTE BAY 4 b.f. Mummy's Game – Miss Maina (Thatching) [1992/3 17f⁴] of little account on Flat: no sign of ability in early-season juvenile hurdle: sold 525 gns Ascot March Sales. *J. Ffitch-Heyes* — –

LOWAWATHA 5 b.g. Dancing Brave (USA) – Shorthouse (Habitat) [1992/3 17sᵖᵘ a16gᵖᵘ] leggy gelding: poor 2m novice hurdler: won on Flat in February. *D. Morris* — –

LOWLANDS 7 br.g. Strong Gale – Gleann Buidhe (Pampered King) [1992/3 c21dᵖᵘ c21mᵖᵘ c21g² c20dF] workmanlike gelding: poor maiden hurdler: second in novice event at Sedgefield in October, only form over fences: sold out of G. Richards' stable 8,400 gns Doncaster October Sales before next start: stays 21f: acts on soft ground: jumps fences none too fluently. *Lady Eliza Mays-Smith* — c88

LOWLANDS BOY 4 b.c. Claude Monet (USA) – Aquarian Star (Cavo Doro) [1992/3 18m] unfurnished colt: of little account on Flat nowadays: no sign of ability in early-season juvenile hurdle: sold 1,200 gns Doncaster October Sales. *T. Fairhurst* — –

LOXLEY RANGE (IRE) 5 ch.g. Hatim (USA) – Chantal (Charlottesville) [1992/3 16g² 18m² 16d 16m⁶ 18d² 16d⁴ 18s³ 18v² 18d⁴ 16s* 16sF 16m⁴ 17fF 17m 17g] sparely-made gelding: selling hurdler: won handicap at Catterick (no bid) in January: races at around 2m: acts on good to firm and soft ground (ran respectably on heavy): blinkered once, usually visored: irresolute. *O. Brennan* — 80 §

LOYAL NOTE 5 ch.g. Royal Vulcan – Maynote (Maystreak) [1992/3 a16g⁵] no sign of ability in NH Flat race and maiden hurdle. *Mrs E. M. Andrews* — –

LOYAL SPIRIT 9 b.g. True Song – Wilspoon Hollow (Wolver Hollow) [1992/3 c26gᵖᵘ] workmanlike gelding: no form over jumps. *Mrs P. M. Pile* — c– –

LT PINKERTON 6 ch.g. Julio Mariner – Miss Evelin (Twilight Alley) [1992/3 21v 20g] tailed off in novice hurdles: dead. *T. P. Tate* — –

LUCCA 4 b.f. Sure Blade (USA) – Lucayan Princess (High Line) [1992/3 F18s] first foal: dam very useful on Flat at up to 1½m: behind in NH Flat race at Exeter in January: yet to race over hurdles. *Miss P. O'Connor* —

LUCIES KAPER 4 b.f. Royben – Greek Glance (Athenien II) [1992/3 F18g] half-sister to poor novice hurdler/chaser Balinglance (by Balinger): dam of little account: tailed off in NH Flat race at Exeter in March: yet to race over hurdles. *J. Honeyball* —

LUCKACTIVE 7 ch.g. Lucky Wednesday – Swakara (Porto Bello) [1992/3 17s] angular gelding: no form in novice hurdles. *G. H. Jones* — –

LUCK MONEY 7 b.g. Gleason (USA) – Candy Princess (Candy Cane) [1992/3 c24m⁴ c22dF c25sᵖᵘ c25sᵖᵘ c23vᵖᵘ a20gF] no sign of ability. *R. Mathew* — c– –

LUCKY AGAIN 6 br.h. Ile de Bourbon (USA) – Soft Pedal (Hotfoot) [1992/3 17mF 17s⁶ 17m⁶ c17g* c17fF c16m⁵ c16d³ c16d² c16v] big, lengthy horse: poor novice hurdler: won novice chase at Taunton in September: ran well when placed afterwards (not raced after January): unlikely to stay much beyond 2m: acts on firm and dead going. *C. L. Popham* — c98 –

LUCKY BLUE 6 b.g. Blue Cashmere – Cooling (Tycoon II) [1992/3 16d⁵ 16d⁶ 17sᵘʳ 16m⁴ 17g 17m³ 17d 20f³ 17m⁶] good-topped gelding: poor novice hurdler: best form at around 2m: acts on good to firm and dead ground: blinkered once. *R. J. Hodges* — 72

LUCKY HARVEST 6 b.m. Oats – Lucky Janie (Dual) [1992/3 25s^{rtr} 22d⁴ 21v 22d 26m⁶] workmanlike mare: poor novice hurdler: stays 2¾m: acts on dead ground. *Mrs A. E. Ratcliff* — 67

LUCKY HELMET 9 b.g. Riot Helmet – Lucky Pace (Lucky Brief) [1992/3 c21s c21s c27v³ c26v^F c27v^{pu} c22v^{pu} 23d 17d 21m⁵ 21s^{pu} 21f] leggy gelding: poor hurdler/novice chaser: blinkered once: poor jumper of fences. *W. G. McKenzie-Coles* — c– x —

LUCKY MAY 6 b.m. Baron Blakeney – Learctic (Lepanto (GER)) [1992/3 22v^{pu} c19d c24g⁴ c24f²] third foal: sister to winning chaser Arctic Baron: dam ran 3 times over hurdles: pulled up in novice hurdle: no worthwhile form in novice chases. *Mrs J. C. Dawe* — c– —

LUCKY OLE SON 6 b.g. Old Lucky – Drake's Beauty (Captain Drake) [1992/3 c24s^F] compact gelding: novice hurdler: poor pointer: yet to complete in steeplechases. *David Brace* — c– —

LUCKY THROW 7 b.g. Lucky Wednesday – Sodance (So Blessed) [1992/3 22g^{pu}] compact gelding: of little account. *N. G. Ayliffe* — —

LUCKY VILLAIN 8 b.g. Roselier (FR) – Menvone (Menelek) [1992/3 c24s* c27v⁶ c25d^F c24m⁵] tall gelding: poor novice hurdler: won novice handicap at Taunton in December, only form over fences: stays 3m: acts on soft ground. *N. J. Henderson* — c87 —

LUCY BELLE (IRE) 4 b. or br.f. Nashamaa – Bella Lucia (Camden Town) [1992/3 16d⁶ 16v^{pu} 17m^{pu}] ex-Irish filly: second foal: dam won over 7f at 2 yrs and stayed 1½m: poor maiden on Flat: no form over hurdles: trained first outing by D. Gillespie. *E. A. Wheeler* — —

LUDOVICIANA 4 b.f. Oats – Crafty Look (Don't Look) [1992/3 F16g⁶ F17m] lengthy, unfurnished filly: third foal: half-sister to novice hurdler/chaser Craftsman (by Balinger): dam won 3m chase: sixth in NH Flat race in March: tailed off next time: yet to race over hurdles. *J. Pearce* — —

LUGER (IRE) 5 b.g. Farhaan – Divine Wonder (Divine Gift) [1992/3 16d⁶ 16d⁶ 16v⁴] fifth foal: brother to poor performer Carriganore: dam never ran: novice selling hurdler: trained by W. A. Stephenson first 2 starts: not raced after December: barely stays 2m under testing conditions. *P. Cheesbrough* — 73

LUKE'S BRAVE BOY 5 ch.g. Prince Ragusa – Golden Baby (Sharpen Up) [1992/3 20d 21s^{pu} 20s 17s] lengthy, workmanlike gelding: winning hurdler: sold 16,000 gns Doncaster August Sales: form only at 2m: acted on soft ground: dead. *Mrs V. C. Ward* — —

LULA PATTIE 9 b. or br.m. Ascertain (USA) – Royal Barb (Barbin) [1992/3 c26g^F] poor pointer: behind when falling in novice hunter chase in March. *T. H. Pounder* — c– —

LUMBERJACK (USA) 9 b.g. Big Spruce (USA) – Snip (Shantung) [1992/3 c18d* c18d² c21d* c21v² c20g^{pu} c21d⁵ c21s² c22f^F 22m^{pu}] close-coupled, sparely-made gelding: fairly useful handicap chaser: won at Stratford and Wetherby prior to being sold out of J. FitzGerald's stable 21,000 gns Doncaster November Sales: below form last 5 outings: barely stays 21f when conditions are very testing: acts on heavy and good to firm going: sometimes races with tongue tied down: best in blinkers. *C. R. Egerton* — c127 —

LUMUMBA DAYS 7 gr.g. Neltino – Bright Swan (Will Hays (USA)) [1992/3 17s² 17v⁶ 17d² 16s⁴ 17m* 17m* 17m^{pu}] sparely-made gelding: modest hurdler: won novice events at Wolverhampton in March and Taunton in April: ran as though something amiss final start: best at around 2m: acts on soft and good to firm ground: sometimes has tongue tied down. *Martyn Meade* — 96

LUNABELLE 5 b.m. Idiot's Delight – Barbella (Barolo) [1992/3 16d³ 16d* 18v⁵] leggy mare: won fillies novice hurdle at Wincanton in December: ran poorly following month: should stay further than 2m: acts on dead going. *I. A. Balding* — 95

LUNAR LUNACY (IRE) 5 b.m. Ahonoora – Flinging Star (USA) (Northern Fling (USA)) [1992/3 17m^{pu}] half-sister to winning hurdler You Are A Star (by Persian Bold): no promise in 2 races on Flat: no promise in early-season novice hurdle. *K. F. Clutterbuck* –

L'UOMO CLASSICS 6 b.g. Indian King (USA) – Sperrin Mist (Camden Town) [1992/3 21d 16s^5] leggy gelding: poor novice hurdler: blinkered twice. *R. Rowe* –

L'UOMO PIU 9 b.g. Paddy's Stream – Easter Vigil (Arctic Slave) [1992/3 c16m* c18g^6 c19s^5] workmanlike gelding: fair hurdler: won novice chase at Worcester in August: ran poorly afterwards (not raced after January): best form at around 2m: acts on soft going and good to firm. *A. Barrow* c92

LUPY MINSTREL 8 br.g. Black Minstrel – Lupreno (Hugh Lupus) [1992/3 c24m* c25g^3 c26s^4 c26d^{ur} c28s^3 c26g^3] leggy gelding: modest handicap chaser: won at Carlisle in September: ran creditably last 2 starts: suited by a thorough test of stamina: acts on good to firm and soft ground. *C. Parker* c97

LUSTREMAN 6 ch.g. Sallust – Miss Speak Easy (USA) (Sea Bird II) [1992/3 17g* 16f^2 18g^5 16s^4 17d^4 16f^F] workmanlike gelding: modest handicap hurdler: won at Hereford in August: trained until after fourth start by M. Channon: ran creditably next time: will stay beyond 17f: acts on firm and dead going. *J. H. Peacock* 93

LUSTY LAD 8 b.g. Decoy Boy – Gluhwein (Ballymoss) [1992/3 18f^F 18d^{pu}] small, sparely-made gelding: fairly useful hurdler in 1991/2: ran badly in early-season events in 1992/3: stays 2½m: acts on hard, dead going and particularly well on equitrack: has broken blood vessels. *M. J. Haynes* –

LUSTY LIGHT 7 b.g. Strong Gale – Pale Maid (Rise'n Shine II) [1992/3 16d* 17m^2 22g^2 25s^{pu} 22d* 22g^4] useful-looking gelding: chasing type: won novice hurdles at Towcester in October and Huntingdon (handicap) in January: should stay beyond 2¾m: acts on dead and good to firm ground. *Mrs J. Pitman* 104

LUTHIOR (FR) 7 gr.g. Carwhite – Luthiana (FR) (Luthier) [1992/3 20f*] leggy, sparely-made gelding: finished badly lame when winning 3-runner novice hurdle at Plumpton in August: probably stays 2½m: acts on dead and firm ground: blinkered once. *J. E. Long* 70 ?

LUVANKISS 11 ch.m. Chance Meeting – Alice-Emma (Kolper) [1992/3 c19d^5] novice hunter chaser: probably stays 2½m: acts on dead ground. *H. J. Manners* c–

LYCIAN MOON 4 b.f. Norwick (USA) – Brigannie Moon (Brigadier Gerard) [1992/3 17f^{pu}] no sign of ability on Flat or in early-season juvenile selling hurdle. *Mrs J. C. Dawe* –

LYNCH LAW (IRE) 5 b. or br.h. Law Society (USA) – Hogan's Sister (USA) (Speak John) [1992/3 16d^5 16g* 17d*] half-brother to winning jumper Al Misk (by Dewan): fairly useful winner at up to 1½m (including when blinkered) on Flat in Ireland in 1991: successful in novice hurdles at Hexham in March and Carlisle (stayed on strongly) in April: sold to join M. Pipe 40,000 gns in May: will stay beyond 17f: acts on dead ground: has further improvement in him and should win more races. *P. Cheesbrough* 112 p

LYNELLY 7 br.m. Netherkelly – Lyns Legend (Marengo) [1992/3 26g 18g^3 22g 23m 20v^4 25s 24v^{pu}] small mare: poor novice hurdler: probably stays 3m and acts on any ground: blinkered final start (January): sweats. *G. M. Price* 66

LYN'S RETURN (IRE) 4 b.c. Nordico (USA) – Salmas (FR) (Right Royal V) [1992/3 a16g* a16g* a16g* a16g* a16g* 17f] small colt: modest on Flat, stays 1¾m: took very well to hurdling and won maiden, juvenile event, novice event and 2 handicaps at Lingfield in second half of season: ran well in valuable novice event at Aintree on final start: likely to prove best at around 2m: acts on firm ground and equitrack: usually jumps well: tough and reliable. *R. Simpson* 117

LYPHENTO (USA) 9 b.h. Lyphard's Wish (FR) – Hasty Viento (USA) **c121** (Gallant Man) [1992/3 c21m[5] c24d[F]] tall, leggy, angular horse: has been to – stud: fairly useful chaser: creditable fifth at Wetherby early in season: stays 2½m: possibly unsuited by very firm ground, acts on any other: jumps well in the main. *J. T. Gifford*

LYPHEORIC (USA) 8 b.g. Lypheor – Fabulous Salt (USA) (Le **c–** Fabuleux) [1992/3 c20v[pu]] leggy gelding: winning hurdler: poor novice – chaser at best: stays 2½m: acts on dead going. *Mrs J. R. Ramsden*

LYPH (USA) 7 b.g. Lypheor – Scottish Lass (Scotland) [1992/3 16s[pu] **c–** x 22v[pu] a20g[2] 20s[6]] smallish gelding: poor hurdler: won selling **85** handicap at Lingfield (no bid) in March: jumped poorly both outings over fences: stays 2½m: acts on any going: sometimes blinkered. *P. R. Hedger*

M

MAAMUR (USA) 5 gr.g. Robellino (USA) – Tiger Trap (USA) (Al Hattab (USA)) [1992/3 20g* 17v[3] 20s[3]] workmanlike gelding: half-brother **128** to winning hurdler/chaser OK Corral (by Malinowski): fair 1½m winner on Flat: won novice hurdle at Hereford in September: quite useful form when third in William Hill Handicap Hurdle at Sandown in December and in novice event at Ascot in January: effective at 2m and stays 2½m: acts on heavy going: drifted right under pressure last 2 starts. *D. Burchell*

MABEL BROWN 5 b.m. Enchantment – Charlotte Daughter (Brigadier Gerard) [1992/3 17g[pu] 20v[pu]] of little account: blinkered last start. *W. G. M.* – *Turner*

MABTHUL (USA) 5 b.g. Northern Baby (CAN) – Persuadable (USA) (What A Pleasure (USA)) [1992/3 16g 17d[3] 17d[3] 17d 17s[2] a16g 17d 17g 17f[6] **81 §** 17d[4] 17f*] well-made gelding: modest at 2 yrs, no form on Flat since: selling hurdler: sold 2,400 gns after winning novice handicap at Huntingdon in May: acts on firm and soft going: irresolute. *K. C. Bailey*

MACARTHUR 8 b.g. Ardross – Polly Peachum (Singing Strand) [1992/3 **c121** c16s* c16v[2] c16s[4] c16g[2] c20f[3]] workmanlike gelding: fairly useful handicap chaser: won at Catterick in December: creditable efforts when placed subsequently: best at up to 2½m: probably acts on any ground: suited by forcing tactics: races with tongue tied down: jumps well: genuine. *M. W. Easterby*

MACCONACHIE 6 b.g. Good Times (ITY) – High Point Lady (CAN) **c80** (Knightly Dawn (USA)) [1992/3 16g c17g[3]] leggy, close-coupled gelding: – novice hurdler: jumped poorly when third in novice event at Kelso in October on chasing debut: likely to prove best at around 2m. *M. Dods*

MACEDONAS 5 b.h. Niniski (USA) – Miss Saint-Cloud (Nonoalco (USA)) [1992/3 16s[5] 16s[3] 16s* 16v[2] 20g[3] 18s[2] 16d[4] 17f* 20f] leggy horse: fair **112** hurdler: won conditional jockeys handicap at Warwick in January and amateurs handicap at Sandown in March: generally ran creditably in between, but poorly last start: best form at around 2m: probably acts on any going. *T. Casey*

MACHO MAN 8 br.g. Mummy's Game – Shoshoni (Ballymoss) [1992/3 **c90** 16s[6] 22v[6] c18v[3] c21v[pu]] smallish, sparely-made gelding: winning hurdler/ – chaser: sold out of J. J. O'Neill's stable 7,200 gns Doncaster August Sales: creditable efforts first and third starts: stays 2¾m: probably acts on any going: sometimes blinkered. *T. J. Etherington*

MACKINNON 8 b.g. Broadsword (USA) – Salambos (Doon) [1992/3 **c95** + c16d* c17d[2] c24m[F] c21s[ur] c20g[4]] big, lengthy gelding: novice hurdler: won – novice chase at Haydock in February: ran creditably next time and still travelling well when parting company with rider third and fourth starts: stiff task last one: will stay 3m: acts on dead and good to firm ground. *G. Richards*

MACMURPHY 8 ch.g. Deep Run – Millymeeta (New Brig) [1992/3 24g⁴ 22m] modest pointer: showed only a little ability over hurdles late in season. *A. M. Thomson*   68

MAC RAMBLER 6 b.g. Hotfoot – Arkengarthdale (Sweet Story) [1992/3 16v] lengthy, workmanlike gelding: novice hurdler: well below form only outing of season (December): stays 2½m: acts on firm ground. *N. Bycroft*   –

MAC'S BOY 4 b.g. Macmillion – Tender Manx (Owen Dudley) [1992/3 F16s F17m] third foal: dam of little account: mid-division in NH Flat races in February and April: yet to race over hurdles. *B. Palling*

MAC'S LEAP 5 ch.g. Homeboy – Miss Sunblest (Whistler) [1992/3 F16g] brother to 6-y-o Manaboutthehouse and half-brother to several winners, including useful middle-distance performer and hurdler Jondi (by The Parson): dam won over 5f at 2 yrs: behind in NH Flat race at Kempton in February: yet to race over hurdles or fences. *Mrs I. McKie*

MAC THE BAT (IRE) 5 gr.g. Court Macsherry – Grey Willow (Willowick (USA)) [1992/3 17f⁴] fifth foal: dam Irish Flat maiden: remote fourth of 8 finishers in maiden hurdle at Huntingdon in May on debut. *W. A. Murphy, Ireland*   67

MADAGANS GREY 5 gr.g. Carwhite – Cheri Berry (Air Trooper) [1992/3 22g² 22gF] rather leggy, close-coupled gelding: retained 3,700 gns Doncaster October Sales: moderate novice hurdler: second at Huntingdon in April: stays 2¾m: has run mainly on good ground: running poorly when falling next time: takes good hold. *R. Boss*   92

MADAM BEE 9 ch.m. Funny Man – Sister Broncho (Three Dons) [1992/3 26g] sparely-made mare: no sign of ability in novice hurdles. *G. Richards*   –

MADAME SULAAFAH 5 b.m. Sulaafah (USA) – Madame Rochas (Midsummer Night II) [1992/3 21fpu] beaten in sellers on Flat: tailed off when pulled up in novice event in May on hurdling debut. *B. Palling*   –

MADAM MARGEAUX (IRE) 4 b.f. Ardross – Madam Slaney (Prince Tenderfoot (USA)) [1992/3 F18g] third foal: sister to winning hurdlers Aahsaylad and Sweet George: dam 1m to 1¼m winner: tailed off in mares NH Flat race at Exeter in March: yet to race over hurdles. *Mrs J. G. Retter*

MADAM PICASSO (IRE) 4 gr.f. Anita's Prince – Perbury (Grisaille) [1992/3 16s 16s³ 16s³ 17g⁶ 17g 17v⁴ 17m⁵ 17d³] leggy ex-Irish filly: eighth foal: half-sister to several winners, including useful hurdler General Breyfax (by Sweet Revenge): dam quite useful 2-y-o: 1m winner on Flat: juvenile hurdler: trained until after third start by A. Taylor in Ireland: only poor form over here: has raced only at around 2m: acts on heavy ground. *N. R. Mitchell*   77 +

MAD CASANOVA 8 b.g. Scorpio (FR) – Parveen (FR) (Kouban (FR)) [1992/3 c18d* c18sur c24s c21v* c21v⁶ c21v⁴ c21v⁴ c20f⁴ 22dpu 18d 16f³] rangy gelding: fair handicap chaser: won at Fontwell (conditional jockeys) and Lingfield in first half of season: fair effort in handicap hurdle last start: successful at 25f but ideally suited by around 2½m: probably acts on any ground: effective with and without blinkers or visor: reluctant, and one to treat with caution. *R. J. O'Sullivan*   c105 § 105 §

MADFA 8 b.g. Prince Tenderfoot (USA) – Vectis (Quorum) [1992/3 c24vpu c26vpu 21v⁶ 23gpu] rangy gelding: winning hurdler: maiden chaser: lightly raced and no form for long time: blinkered last start. *R. Akehurst*   c– –

MADRAJ (IRE) 5 b. or br.h. Double Schwartz – Poka Poka (FR) (King of Macedon) [1992/3 21v⁶ 17v 18s 20d 16f³ 17m] leggy, good-topped horse: handicap hurdler: only modest form at best in 1992/3: trained until after fourth start by R. Baker: best form at around 2m: acts on firm going. *R. J. Hodges*   85

MAD THYME 6 b.g. Idiot's Delight – Another Breeze (Deep Run) [1992/3 21sur 21v² 22s² 21mF 20d 20dpu] angular, unfurnished gelding: fair novice hurdler on his day: would have won at Newbury in November, but   104 §

hung badly left run-in and unseated rider: will stay beyond 2¾m: acts on heavy going: difficult ride and not one to trust. *N. A. Gaselee*

MAELKAR (FR) 9 b.g. Maelstrom Lake – Karabice (Karabas) [1992/3 24s⁵] tall, leggy, narrow gelding: lightly-raced, very useful hurdler at his best: well below-form fifth at Chepstow in October, and wasn't seen out again: broke blood vessel on chasing debut, unseated rider fourth only other start over fences: stays 25f: acts on any going: jumps hurdles well. *J. J. O'Neill* c– –

MAESTROSO (IRE) 4 b.c. Mister Majestic – That's Easy (Swing Easy (USA)) [1992/3 17g² 17gᵘʳ 17v 17s³ 17v⁵ 17s⁴ 16d 17m 21f²] neat colt: fair middle-distance stayer on Flat: fair maiden over hurdles: best form at around 17f: acts on good to firm and soft ground: blinkered last 3 starts: inconsistent and sometimes find little. *R. F. Johnson Houghton* 104 §

MAGGOTS GREEN 6 ch.m. Pas de Seul – Fabled Lady (Bold Lad (IRE)) [1992/3 17mᵖᵘ 16f⁶ 16s⁵ 18f³ 17s 16g⁴] angular mare: poor novice hurdler: probably stays 2¼m and acts on any going. *J. M. Bradley* 72

MAGICAL MORRIS 11 ch.g. Balinger – River Spell (Spartan General) [1992/3 c21g³ c24g³ c25dᵖᵘ] lengthy gelding: maiden hunter chaser: creditable efforts first 2 starts: won a point in April: barely stays 3m. *W. R. Hacking* c87

MAGIC AT DAWN (USA) 8 ch.g. Diamond Prospect (USA) – Implicit (Grundy) [1992/3 c16m* c21m³ c21mF] strong, compact gelding: modest hurdler: successful in novice event at Perth in August on chasing debut, and ran creditably when third in similar race on same course following day: best form at up to 21f: acts on hard going. *B. M. Moore* c85 –

MAGIC BLOOM 7 br.m. Full of Hope – Mantavella (Andrea Mantegna) [1992/3 18d⁵ 18s 18g⁵ 17m* 17f³ 16g* 20m⁴] improved in spring and won conditional jockeys claiming handicap hurdle at Newcastle and novice event at Wetherby: also ran well last outing: stays 2½m: acts on firm going. *A. P. Stringer* 91

MAGIC SECRET 5 b.g. Local Suitor (USA) – Meissarah (USA) (Silver Hawk (USA)) [1992/3 16s² 21d³ 21v 16s⁶ a22g⁴] neat gelding: won two 13f handicaps on Flat in 1992: claimed out of P. Haslam's stable £8,005 in August: below form third and fourth starts: stays 2¾m: acts on soft going, good to firm and fibresand. *P. J. Bevan* 91

MAGIC SOLDIER 8 br.g. Mandrake Major – Dior Queen (Manacle) [1992/3 c25g² c24dF] strong, rangy gelding: modest chaser: creditable second in hunter chase at Ayr in February: stays 25f: acts on heavy going and good to firm: tends to carry head high. *Ronnie A. Bartlett* c86 –

MAGNETIC PRINCE 4 b.g. Tina's Pet – Miss Magnetism (Baptism) [1992/3 17fᵖᵘ 18sᵖᵘ 17g] leggy gelding: first foal: dam winning hurdler: maiden plater on Flat: no promise over hurdles. *G. Blum* –

MAGNOX 12 ch.g. Keren – So Blue (Espresso) [1992/3 c20m³] lightly-built gelding: poor staying novice hurdler/chaser: blinkered once. *J. E. Swiers* c– –

MAGNUS PYM 8 b.g. Al Nasr (FR) – Full of Reason (USA) (Bold Reason) [1992/3 17d c16v⁴ c19d³ c17vᵖᵘ 20sᵖᵘ 20sF 20v⁶ 16vᵖᵘ 17g 16f⁵] good-topped gelding: fair hurdler in 1991/2, no worthwhile form in 1992/3: fourth in handicap at Worcester in November, easily best effort over fences: best at around 2m: acts on heavy going and good to firm: sometimes blinkered, but not when successful: ungenuine: sold 2,000 gns Ascot 2nd June Sales. *G. B. Balding* c94 § – §

MAHAASIN 5 b.m. Bellypha – Dame Ashfield (Grundy) [1992/3 20mᵖᵘ] half-sister to fair hurdler Valiant Dash (by Valiyar): poor middle-distance maiden on Flat: no promise in juvenile hurdle at Bangor in August. *L. J. Codd* –

MAHAFEL 9 b.g. Kris – Royal Meath (Realm) [1992/3 c16dᵖᵘ] lengthy, angular gelding: little sign of ability. *N. A. Twiston-Davies* c– –

MAHATMACOAT 6 ch.g. Prince of Peace – Avec Amour (Jolly Jet) [1992/3 F17g 17s4] lengthy gelding: mid-division in NH Flat races: remote fourth in maiden event at Newton Abbot in April on hurdling debut. *Mrs J. G. Retter* — 71

MAHIR (USA) 5 ch.h. Sharpen Up – Vie En Rose (USA) (Blushing Groom (FR)) [1992/3 18gpu 16f] sturdy colt: of little account: blinkered once. *D. J. Bell* — –

MAIDEN OF IRON (IRE) 5 ch.m. Flash of Steel – Takastroll (Hello Gorgeous (USA)) [1992/3 22d] workmanlike mare: novice hurdler: well beaten in October, only outing of 1992/3: blinkered last 4 starts 1991/2. *J. C. McConnochie* — –

MAID MARINER 11 br.m. Julio Mariner – Molly Polly (Molvedo) [1992/3 24gpu] small mare: inconsistent handicap hurdler: pulled up lame in October, and wasn't seen out again: stays 25f: form only on a sound surface: has been tried blinkered and visored: looks a difficult ride. *M. C. Chapman* — – §

MAILCOM 7 b.g. Strong Gale – Poll's Turn (Le Tricolore) [1992/3 21g3 24dF 22vF 22mpu 22g* 21f* 27gF] big, lengthy gelding: chasing type: fairly useful hurdler: successful in handicaps at Huntingdon in April and Towcester in May: stays 3m: acts on firm and good to soft going. *Mrs J. Pitman* — 119

MAJED (IRE) 5 b.h. Wolverlife – Martin Place (Martinmas) [1992/3 16g* 16d* 16g* 17d2 16g2 18g* 17d2] leggy horse: best effort over hurdles when second in quite valuable handicap at Ascot in April on last outing: earlier successful in novice events at Ayr (twice), Haydock and Kelso: yet to race beyond 2¼m: acts on dead ground: jumps soundly: has a turn of foot and is usually waited with: tough and consistent: likely to improve further. *Mrs M. Reveley* — 135 p

MAJESTIC DREAM 9 b.m. Majestic Maharaj – Floating Dreams (Bonheur) [1992/3 17s 22d] small, lengthy mare: tailed off in novice hurdles. *C. W. Mitchell* — –

MAJESTIC GAMBLER 5 b.g. Enchantment – Wessex Kingdom (Vaigly Great) [1992/3 18m 18gpu] no promise in novice hurdles: blinkered last start. *N. B. Mason* — –

MAJESTIC GOLD 5 b.g. Majestic Maharaj – Balas (Goldfella) [1992/3 F16d 16s] workmanlike gelding: behind in NH Flat races, but showed some — 76 p

Dalrymple Novices' Hurdle, Ayr—an easy success for the improving Majed

ability in novice hurdle at Ludlow in April after 5-month break: will improve. *F. Jordan*

MAJESTIC MELODY 5 ch.m. Crooner – Royal Birthday (St Paddy) [1992/3 17g 16g 17d 16v^{ur}] sparely-made mare: half-sister to top-class 2m hurdler Royal Derbi (by Derrylin): poor maiden on Flat and over hurdles. *W. Carter*

70

MAJESTIC RIDE 9 b.g. Palm Track – Lakeland Lady (Leander) [1992/3 c21g^{pu} c21m³] tall, angular gelding: poor novice hurdler/chaser: makes mistakes over fences. *J. C. Peate*

c69 x
–

MAJIC RAIN 8 bl.g. Northern Value (USA) – Dinsdale (Menelek) [1992/3 c27d⁵ c25g⁶ c26m⁵ c30m⁵ c26d⁴ c30d c24d c28g^{pu} c32d² c27m³ c24d c21f^{pu} c25g⁵ c21g⁴ c23m^{pu}] tall, leggy gelding: moderate handicap chaser: thorough stayer: probably acts on any ground: blinkered twice in 1991/2: very unreliable. *G. M. R. Coatsworth*

c89 §

MAJOR BELL 5 br.g. Silly Prices – Melaura Belle (Meldrum) [1992/3 20s⁴ 20s⁵ 21s³ 16g⁵ 20g⁴ 18g⁵] unfurnished gelding: first foal: dam fair sprinter: modest novice hurdler: stays 2½m: acts on soft ground. *A. C. Whillans*

93

MAJOR BUGLER (IRE) 4 b.g. Thatching – Bugle Sound (Bustino) [1992/3 17v 17s* 17s³ 17v⁴ 17s* 17g³ 17m³ 16g^{pu}]

135

Major Bugler is 'bred to be anything'. The term usually refers to class, but for Major Bugler there was a wide range of imponderables. In what area would he find his niche? The breeding clues were the top-class sprinter Thatching as his sire and a dam, the useful Bugle Sound, who won at a mile and a quarter and stayed a mile and three quarters. The mating had been tried before and produced the Irish six-furlong winner Sound of Victory. Bugle Sound had thrown another couple of winners as well, including the hurdler Dari Sound (by Shardari), but what really appealed to the imagination was her being a half-sister to, among others, the three-time Champion Hurdler See You Then and the dual Oaks-placed Dubian, dam of the latest One Thousand Guineas winner Sayyedati. It is easy to see how Major Bugler, a colt with plenty of scope who made 16,000 guineas as a yearling, might have caught the eye of a dual-purpose trainer such as Toby Balding. Under his tutelage Major Bugler has come through as a fairly useful

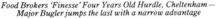

Food Brokers 'Finesse' Four Years Old Hurdle, Cheltenham —
Major Bugler jumps the last with a narrow advantage

middle-distance performer on the Flat and one of the latest season's best juvenile hurdlers.

Major Bugler (IRE) (b.g. 1989)	Thatching (b 1975)	Thatch (b 1970)	Forli Thong
		Abella (ch 1968)	Abernant Darrica
	Bugle Sound (b 1977)	Bustino (b 1971)	Busted Ship Yard
		Melodina (br 1968)	Tudor Melody Rose of Medina

Major Bugler embarked on a hurdling campaign after one win (in a £9,500 handicap) from eleven starts on the Flat. Eleventh of fifteen on heavy ground in a £14,200 event at the Cheltenham Sunday meeting was not an overly promising start for one of the early favourites for the Triumph Hurdle—he also disappointed on similar going on his fourth outing—but with rather less testing conditions on his next two runs he won by fifteen lengths at Newbury and was third in the Finale Junior Hurdle at Chepstow. Further useful performances came when winning the 'Finesse' at Cheltenham from Ivor's Flutter and when seven and a half lengths third to Beauchamp Grace in the Stroud Green Hurdle at Newbury. It was Beauchamp Grace from the latter who attracted most of the favourable notices with regard to the Triumph Hurdle, but Major Bugler who ultimately emerged best. For a long way in the Triumph it looked as if he might emerge best of all. He made good headway to chase the leaders at the third last and turned into the straight pressing Shawiya for the lead with none going better. The pair were clear, but Major Bugler began to hang left and made a mess of the last, continuing to hang and carry his head high as he weakened on the run-in to end up beaten two and three quarter lengths into third. A rangy sort, he looked in fine condition that day and, with an eye to the future, was one of only a few in the field who impressed in terms of physique. Our enthusiasm for Major Bugler's prospects, however, is tempered by the less than whole-hearted attitude he seems to have displayed on more than one occasion in the closing stages, and by his poor efforts in April when returned to the Flat for one race then tailed off (from the fourth) in the Murphys Irish Stout Champion 4-Y-O Hurdle at Punchestown. He has an excuse for that run in Ireland, though, as he was coughing afterwards. He has since been gelded. *G. B. Balding*

MAJOR BUSH   6 b.g. Julio Mariner – Peperino (Relko) [1992/3 F17d 16s⁶ 16d 16f² 17s* 17d³ 16f³ 23m³ 21mᵖᵘ] tall gelding: won maiden hurdle at Newton Abbot in April: creditable efforts next 3 starts, as though something amiss last: effective at around 2m and stays 23f: probably acts on any going. *Mrs J. Pitman*   94

MAJOR INQUIRY (USA)   7 b.g. The Minstrel (CAN) – Hire A Brain (USA) (Seattle Slew (USA)) [1992/3 20f² 17d 22m] lengthy gelding: useful hurdler on his day: easily best effort in 1992/3 when second in handicap at Plumpton in March: not fluent and no form in 2 races over fences: should stay beyond 2½m: acts on firm and dead ground: broke blood vessel once. *D. R. C. Elsworth*   c–
128

MAJORITY HOLDING   8 b.g. Mandrake Major – Kirkby (Midsummer Night II) [1992/3 16sᵖᵘ 18s⁴ 16g* 17sᵘʳ 16f⁶] rather leggy gelding: poor form at best on Flat: bought in 3,000 gns after winning selling hurdle at Towcester in March by 20 lengths: well below form only completed outing afterwards. *J. White*   90

MAJORITY MAJOR (IRE)   4 b.g. Cheval – La Perla (Majority Blue) [1992/3 17m³ 17g] half-brother to several winners, including hurdlers Jupiter Express (by Jupiter Pluvius) and Snowy Pearl (by Golden Love), former once quite useful: dam moderate at up to 7f: poor form in early-season juvenile hurdles: sold 8,800 gns in May. *W. A. Stephenson*   71

MAJOR KINSMAN   8 b.g. Nepotism – Noon Hunting (Green Shoon) [1992/3 c21dᵖᵘ 26dᵖᵘ 21s c21sF⁴ c21s* c21v* c21s* c21v³ c21s³ c21g*] workmanlike gelding: fair handicap chaser: successful at Sedgefield,   c111
–

Lingfield, Wolverhampton and Huntingdon in 1992/3: best form at around 2½m: acts on heavy going: usually jumps soundly. *R. Lee*

MAJOR MATCH (NZ) 11 b.g. Frassino – Burks Rainbow (NZ) (Weyand (USA)) [1992/3 c19g² c21f² c24g c21d c24m⁵ c20f⁵] lightly-made gelding: fairly useful handicap chaser at best: ran creditably first 2 starts, below form subsequently: stays 3¼m, at least in a slowly-run race: ideally suited by a sound surface: blinkered twice in 1989/90 and once in 1990/1. *Capt. T. A. Forster*   c125 –

MAJOR NOVA 4 b.g. Ra Nova – Phyllis Jane (Lepanto (GER)) [1992/3 F16s F17m] third foal: dam unraced: well beaten in NH Flat races in February: yet to race over hurdles. *N. A. Smith*

MAJOR PLAYER 8 ch.m. Some Hand – Fursena (Fury Royal) [1992/3 19h⁶ c18fF] sturdy mare: poor novice hurdler: fell at the third in August on chasing debut. *M. C. Pipe*   c– –

MAJOR RISK 4 ch.g. Risk Me (FR) – Brampton Grace (Tachypous) [1992/3 16d³ 17gᵖᵘ] rather sparely-made gelding: plater on Flat, placed at 1½m: made running when showing poor form in juvenile selling hurdle at Uttoxeter in October: sold 4,000 gns Newmarket Autumn Sales. *P. A. Kelleway*   79

MAJOR ROUGE 11 ch.g. Mandrake Major – Red Form (Reform) [1992/3 c27d³] deep-girthed gelding: winning chaser: remote third in hunter chase at Sedgefield in April: stays 3m: acts on firm going: usually blinkered. *Mrs S. Herdman*   c83 –

MAJOR'S LAW (IRE) 4 b.c. Law Society (USA) – Maryinsky (USA) (Northern Dancer) [1992/3 16g³ 16s⁵ 18v² 17d³ a16g² 17g* 17g⁵ a16g²] small, sturdy colt: fair performer on Flat, stays 1½m well: sold out of C. Brittain's stable 16,500 gns Newmarket Autumn Sales: won novice hurdle at Plumpton in April: creditable efforts last 2 starts: should stay beyond 2¼m: acts on fibresand, probably on heavy going. *I. Campbell*   99

MAJOR TOM 16 b.g. Cantab – Ice Folly (Arctic Slave) [1992/3 c18dᵖᵘ] compact gelding: poor staying chaser: backward only outing of season (October): makes mistakes. *H. Willis*   c– x –

MAJOR WAGER 8 br.g. Dubassoff (USA) – Cape Mandalin (Mandamus) [1992/3 24gᵖᵘ] tall, rangy gelding: no sign of ability. *D. H. Barons*   c– –

MAKE ME PROUD (IRE) 4 b.f. Be My Native (USA) – Miami Life (Miami Springs) [1992/3 17s⁵ 16d³ 16d² 17d⁴ 17g³ 18g 17g* 16d 16g² 18d⁵] sparely-made filly: plating-class maiden on Flat: sold out of R. Armstrong's stable 2,000 gns Newmarket Autumn Sales: best effort over hurdles when winning conditional jockeys handicap at Carlisle in March: creditable second in novice event at Hexham later in month: probably needs a testing 2m and will stay 2½m: acts on soft ground: visored sixth to eighth and last starts. *W. Bentley*   94

MALLYAN 6 b.m. Miramar Reef – Charlie's Sunshine (Jimsun) [1992/3 17g 18m⁶ 22g] bad plater over hurdles. *P. A. Pritchard*   –

MALLYPHA (FR) 9 b.g. Bellypha – Marzala (USA) (Honest Pleasure (USA)) [1992/3 c19mᵖᵘ 18gᵖᵘ 22gᵖᵘ] good-bodied gelding: winning 2m handicap hurdler: has lost his form entirely: blinkered once: sold 1,200 gns Ascot 2nd June Sales. *P. Howling*   c– –

MALTBY BOY 10 b.g. Royal Palace – Assel Zawie (Sit In The Corner (USA)) [1992/3 c26m³ c24f⁴] fairly useful pointer, successful 7 times in 1993: moderate form in hunter chases at Folkestone and Huntingdon in May. *Mrs A. Hickman*   c82

MALTESE FLAME 4 br.f. Bay Spirit – Lym Millie Maid VII (Pedigree Unknown) [1992/3 F16s] non-thoroughbred filly: dam unraced: tailed off in NH Flat race at Nottingham in February: yet to race over hurdles. *A. M. Forte*

MALVERNIAN 7 b.g. Fine Blade (USA) – Nesford (Walshford) [1992/3 c–
22v 24v 22s⁴ 17m⁴ 16s c21d⁶ c21f⁶] tall gelding: poor novice hurdler/chaser: 82
stays 2¾m: acts on good to firm and heavy ground. *Mrs H. Parrott*

MALVERN MADAM 6 b.m. Reesh – Creta (Grundy) [1992/3 20m 18d³
16d] leggy, lengthy mare: only sign of ability when close third in novice 76
hurdle at Marken Rasen in November: stays 2¼m: acts on dead going. *J. L.
Eyre*

MAMALAMA 5 ch.m. Nishapour (FR) – Gauloise (Welsh Pageant)
[1992/3 18f⁵ 17m² 16g 17g³ 16d⁴ 17sᵘʳ a16g² a16g⁴ 17g² 17fᶠ 18g⁵ 17g⁵ 83
16mᵘʳ] compact mare: maiden on Flat: poor novice hurdler: ran creditably
most starts in 1992/3: will stay further than 2¼m: acts on firm and dead
ground and on equitrack. *J. J. Bridger*

MANABOUTTHEHOUSE 6 b.g. Homeboy – Miss Sunblest
(Whistler) [1992/3 16g⁶ 16f² 17f³ 16d³] ex-Irish gelding: half-brother to 93
several winners, including useful middle-distance performer Jondi (by The
Parson): dam 5f winner at 2 yrs: modest form when placed in novice hurdles
at Wincanton, Huntingdon and Towcester in May. *Mrs I. McKie*

MANAGEMENT 5 b.h. Faustus (USA) – Rosana Park (Music Boy)
[1992/3 a20gᵖᵘ 24gᵖᵘ] lengthy, unfurnished horse: no sign of ability. *R. –
Allan*

MANAIR (IRE) 4 b.c. Elegant Air – Romantic Overture (USA) (Stop
The Music (USA)) [1992/3 17m 18m] leggy colt: lightly raced and no form on –
Flat: sold out of A. Stewart's stable 2,000 gns Ascot June Sales: well beaten
in early-season juvenile hurdles. *W. Clay*

MANCHANT (IRE) 5 b. or br.m. Mandalus – Enchanting (Behistoun)
[1992/3 F16d F17d] half-sister to several winners, including hurdler –
Warchant (by Warpath): dam 10.6f winner: well beaten in NH Flat races in
the spring: yet to race over hurdles or fences. *Mrs M. Reveley*

MANDALAY PRINCE 9 b.g. Nishapour (FR) – Ops (Welsh Saint) c§§
[1992/3 20m⁴ 22m* 22f* 24f* 25g² 27d⁴ 25d⁴ c21gᴿ c26dᴿ F12d 22s] 96 §
workmanlike gelding: modest hurdler: won novice events at Newton Abbot
(conditional jockeys), Fontwell (claimer) and Hexham in August: lost
enthusiasm afterwards (refused both outings over fences): sold 1,000 gns
Ascot November Sales: stays well: acts on firm and dead ground: visored
final start: not one to trust. *J. G. M. O'Shea*

MANDER'S WAY 8 b.g. Furry Glen – Art Mistress (Master Owen) c104 §
[1992/3 c21s³ c24d³ c24s⁴ c21s³ c24sᵘʳ c25dᵖᵘ c24d³] well-made gelding: –
fair chaser: ran creditably most completed starts in 1992/3: sold 16,000 gns
Ascot June Sales: best at up to 3m: acts on soft going: blinkered third outing:
lazy and needs strong handling: sometimes looks reluctant. *Miss H. C.
Knight*

MANDIKA 5 b.g. Flash of Steel – Bushti Music (Bustino) [1992/3 22s⁴
21v a20g⁶] strong gelding: fair hurdler at best: below form in 1992/3: will be –
suited by further than 2¾m: acts on soft going. *M. A. Jarvis*

MANDRAKI SHUFFLE 11 b.g. Mandalus – Indictment (Desert Call) c110
[1992/3 c24v² c26d³ c26g⁵ c22f³ c24d* c33mᶠ] strong, workmanlike
gelding: useful hunter chaser nowadays: won at Fakenham in April: third in
Martell Fox Hunters' at Aintree previous start: stays well: acts on any
ground: usually blinkered: has tried to run out twice. *O. Sherwood*

MANDRAY 10 br.g. Mandalus – Kimin (Kibenka) [1992/3 c16d⁶] strong, c–
rangy gelding: one-time fairly useful chaser but lightly raced in recent –
seasons: was best in strongly-run race around 2m: probably acted on any
going: dead. *John R. Upson*

MANDYS SPECIAL 7 ch.m. Roman Warrior – Petite Mandy c–
(Mandamus) [1992/3 c24sᵖᵘ] lengthy, angular mare: second foal: dam useful
pointer/hunter chaser: modest pointer: pulled up in hunter chase at
Chepstow in April. *I. R. Brown*

MANENDA 6 br.m. Mandalus – Verenda (Roman Gift) [1992/3 22g² 22d⁴ 20d² 21v⁵ 20d² 26m⁵ 25g] leggy, sparely-made mare: fair handicap hurdler: generally ran with credit in 1992/3: stays 3¼m: acts on dead and good to firm ground, possibly unsuited by heavy. *D. Nicholson*   111

MANEREE 6 b.m. Mandalus – Damberee (Deep Run) [1992/3 17v 17s 20d 20d 16g² 17f² 20d*] unfurnished mare: odds on when 12-length winner of novice hurdle at Hereford in May: best efforts previous 3 starts: stays 2½m: acts on firm and dead going: takes strong hold. *N. A. Callaghan*   90

MANETTIA (IRE) 4 b.f. Mandalus – Disetta (Distinctly (USA)) [1992/3 F16g⁴ F17d*] third living foal: half-sister to fair Irish hurdler Toretta (by Torus): dam winning Irish hurdler: won 25-runner NH Flat race at Carlisle in April: yet to race over hurdles. *Mrs M. Reveley*

MAN FROM MARS 7 b.g. Wolver Hollow – Arcticmars (Arctic Chevalier) [1992/3 a22g⁵ 20g³] leggy, close-coupled gelding: modest hurdler at best: below form in February and March: stays 3m: acts on good to firm going and fibresand. *P. J. Hobbs*   80

MANGROVE 9 b.g. Mandalus – Pine Princess (Neron) [1992/3 c20g⁵ c17g⁴ c19v] lengthy, good-quartered gelding: winning hurdler: novice chaser: well beaten in hunter chases in 1993: best form at 2m: acts on soft going. *Mrs J. M. Bailey*   c–

MANGROVE GREEN 5 ch.m. Royal Vulcan – Royal Feature (King's Equity) [1992/3 F17d 22gᵖᵘ] first foal: dam placed in NH Flat race and novice hurdle: behind in NH Flat race and when pulled up in a maiden hurdle in April. *Mrs E. M. Andrews*   –

MANGROVE MIST (IRE) 5 b.m. Nishapour (FR) – Antiguan Cove (Mill Reef (USA)) [1992/3 21m² 23g⁵] tall, leggy mare: modest hurdler: creditable second in handicap at Cartmel in September, easily better effort of season: stays 2½m: acts well on top-of-the-ground: usually ridden by 7-lb claimer. *P. Monteith*   90

MANHATTAN BOY 11 b.g. Oats – Into Harbour (Right Tack) [1992/3 17f³ 20g* 17m³ 18g³ 20d² 20v³ 17v* 17v 22v⁵ 20g² 20g⁴ 20s³] neat gelding: selling hurdler: generally ran creditably in 1992/3: no bid after winning at Plumpton in August and November (conditional jockeys handicap): stays 2½m: acts on any going: visored once: tough and consistent: has won 12 times at Plumpton. *J. Ffitch-Heyes*   95

MANHATTAN CHASE 10 b.g. Deep Run – Price Rise (Raise You Ten) [1992/3 c21dᵖᵘ c27dᵖᵘ c26sᶠ c24dᵖᵘ] lengthy, workmanlike gelding: fair chaser at best: ran poorly in 1992/3: stays well: acts on heavy going. *G. Richards*   c–

MANJACK 5 b.g. Good Times (ITY) – Miss Deed (David Jack) [1992/3 aF16g] tailed off in NH Flat races: yet to race over hurdles or fences. *D. E. Cantillon*

MAN OF MOREEF 6 b.g. Miramar Reef – Coliemore (Coliseum) [1992/3 16g 17d 17d⁶] brother to fair staying hurdler Ardlussa Bay and half-brother to 2 winning jumpers: dam won NH Flat race and 2m hurdle: well beaten over hurdles. *J. K. M. Oliver*   –

MAN OF MYSTERY 7 b.g. Torus – Queens Folly (King's Bench) [1992/3 c20sᵖᵘ c21sᵖᵘ c24sᵖᵘ c24d⁵ c19s* c22v⁴ c21gᵖᵘ c21f⁵ c22g³] workmanlike gelding: winning hurdler: easily best effort in novice chases when winning at Hereford in April: trained prior to then by C. Trietline: stays 21f: evidently suited by plenty of give in the ground: blinkered last 2 starts: sometimes looks a difficult ride. *N. A. Twiston-Davies*   c99 –

MAN OF THE WEST 10 b.g. Mandalus – Belle of The West (Royal Buck) [1992/3 c16d² c17d⁵ c16v⁵ c16vᵖᵘ] sturdy, lengthy, good sort: useful hurdler in 1989/90: only poor as novice chaser nowadays: sold 1,450 gns Ascot May Sales: pulls hard and has raced only at around 2m: suited by give in the ground. *K. C. Bailey*   c92 ? –

MAN O MINE (IRE) 4 b.g. Strong Gale – Caffra Mills (Pitpan) [1992/3 F16m*] second foal: dam runner-up in Irish NH Flat race on only start: narrow winner of 24-runner NH Flat race at Warwick in May: yet to race over hurdles. *F. Murphy*

MAN ON THE LINE 10 ch.g. Whistling Deer – Black Tulip (Pals Passage) [1992/3 c20d5 c21dpu 22m] compact, workmanlike gelding: fairly useful hurdler/chaser at best, still a maiden over fences: no form in 1992/3: stays 2 1f: acts on good to firm and dead going: none too resolute and best left alone. *R. Akehurst* c– §
–

MANOR COURT (IRE) 5 ch.g. Remainder Man – Court Fancy (Little Buskins) [1992/3 20s] fourth foal: dam never ran: tailed off in novice hurdle at Ayr in January on debut. *R. R. Lamb* –

MANOR MAN 6 ch.g. New Member – Gamlingay (Rosyth) [1992/3 17s5 21s4] close-coupled gelding: poor form in 3 novice hurdles. *M. Williams* 73

MANOR RANGER 7 b.g. Deep Run – Tanarpa (Dusky Boy) [1992/3 21m 16s5 22spu 23mpu] big, strong gelding: little worthwhile form over hurdles. *J. W. Curtis* –

MANSBER (IRE) 4 b.g. Mansooj – Our Bernie (Continuation) [1992/3 16d 17g] neat gelding: plating-class maiden on Flat: no promise in early-season juvenile hurdles. *Pat Mitchell* –

MAN'S BEST FRIEND 6 b.g. Mandalus – Tara Weed (Tarqogan) [1992/3 c25v* c24d4 c21s4 c24d c28g3 c32d*] smallish, sturdy gelding: fair hurdler/chaser: successful over fences at Hexham in November (novice event) and March (handicap): suited by a thorough test of stamina: acts on heavy going. *T. P. Tate* c101
–

MANSE KEY GOLD 6 ch.m. Vaigly Great – Carafran (Stanford) [1992/3 18m 18g6 18v a16gpu] small, compact mare: poor novice hurdler: best effort over 2m on soft ground: blinkered once in 1991/2. *J. Dooler* 66

MANSFIELD HOUSE 8 ch.g. Swing Easy (USA) – Pollinella (Charlottown) [1992/3 18vpu] won over 1½m on Flat at 4 yrs: blinkered, showed nothing in novice hurdle at Fontwell in February. *P. N. Upson* –

MANULIFE 4 b.g. King of Spain – Try G'S (Hotfoot) [1992/3 17s 17v5 17d 17d4 16d5 16fF] neat gelding: plating-class maiden on Flat (sold out of B. Beasley's stable 2,500 gns Doncaster October Sales) and over hurdles: should stay beyond 17f: acts on heavy ground: blinkered last start. *R. Brotherton* 72

MANWELL 6 br.g. Tudor Rhythm – Tiemandee (Mandrake Major) [1992/3 21s 17f] rather sparely-made gelding: no sign of ability. *B. M. Temple* –

MANY A SLIP 8 ch.g. Slippered – Aprolon Lady (Mon Capitaine) [1992/3 c24d4 c25g2 c27d* c23vro] lengthy gelding: fairly useful hunter chaser: won at Sedgefield (wore a tongue strap) in April: slight lead when running out 4 out at Worcester later in month: stays 27f: acts on dead and good to firm ground: usually jumps well and forces pace. *T. D. Walford* c106
–

MANZOOR SAYADAN (USA) 5 b.g. Shahrastani (USA) – Icing (Prince Tenderfoot (USA)) [1992/3 16dpu 16d2 22s5] lengthy gelding: moderate handicap hurdler: still looked as though race would do him good when fair second at Uttoxeter in March: should stay beyond 2m, but ran as though didn't stay 2¾m: acts on dead ground. *Mrs J. Pitman* 96

MAOUJOUD 5 b.g. Green Desert (USA) – Anne Stuart (FR) (Bolkonski) [1992/3 18g4] half-brother to winning hurdler/chaser Mighty Prince (by Pharly): no show in sellers on Flat in August and September: tailed-off last in selling hurdle later in September. *R. P. C. Hoad* –

MARAADY (USA) 4 b.g. Alydar (USA) – Ma Petite Jolie (USA) (Northern Dancer) [1992/3 17f] showed nothing on Flat: sold out of M. Stoute's stable 3,100 gns Newmarket July (1992) Sales: jumped none too fluently when behind in juvenile maiden hurdle at Lingfield in March. *G. P. Enright* –

MARANDISA 6 ch.m. Pharly (FR) – Marissiya (Nishapour (FR)) [1992/3 61
16d 16d 16v⁵ 16dᵖᵘ] poor middle-distance performer on Flat: poor form in
selling hurdles in first half of season. *M. P. Naughton*

MARANO 5 b.g. Julio Mariner – Rapenna (Straight Lad) [1992/3 F17f –
17g⁴] half-brother to winning hurdler Celtic Sands (by Celtic Cone): dam,
lightly-raced pointer, sister to fair chaser Rapallo: behind in NH Flat race
and novice hurdle at Hereford in May. *Mrs N. S. Sharpe*

MARCELLINA 11 ch.m. Welsh Pageant – Connarca (Connaught) c89
[1992/3 c28d c25s² c20sᵖᵘ] sturdy mare: modest chaser: stayed 25f: acted –
on good to firm and soft ground: dead. *E. J. Alston*

MARCH ABOVE 7 ch.g. Cut Above – Marchesana (March Past) [1992/3
20v 23s⁵ 23s⁴ 21v⁶ 21v 23g⁴ 22m³ 22s] workmanlike gelding: moderate 94 §
hurdler: easily best effort of season penultimate start: stays 2¾m: acts on
soft and good to firm ground (tailed off on equitrack): usually visored or
blinkered: unreliable. *B. Stevens*

MARCH AHEAD 7 gr.g. Aristocracy – Pollyfaster (Polyfoto) [1992/3 c– x
c22g⁵ c16m⁶ 16s⁵ 20dF] rather leggy gelding: winning hurdler: novice –
chaser: trained all bar final start by W. A. Stephenson: stayed 2½m: showed
form only on a sound surface: jumped fences poorly: dead. *P. Cheesbrough*

MARCH LANE 6 b.g. Battle Hymn – Empress Chanda (King Emperor
(USA)) [1992/3 16vᵖᵘ 16sᵖᵘ 17dᵖᵘ] strong, good-bodied gelding: fourth foal:
brother to a poor Flat maiden: dam showed some ability at 2 yrs: no sign of
ability in novice hurdles. *J. Webber*

MARCONDA (IRE) 4 b.f. Colonel Godfrey (USA) – Sun Patch (Patch)
[1992/3 F18s F16v³ aF16gᵖᵘ] fourth foal: dam unraced: third in NH Flat race
at Warwick in January: pulled up lame following month: yet to race over
hurdles. *G. A. Ham*

MARCO-PIERRE (IRE) 4 b.g. Bon Sang (FR) – Miss Tehran
(Manacle) [1992/3 F17d 17s] half-brother to Flat and hurdles winner –
Timsolo (by Remainder Man): dam modest miler: well beaten in NH Flat
race and a juvenile hurdle in April. *N. W. Alexander*

MARDEF 5 ch.g. Ahonoora – Zeyneb (Habitat) [1992/3 aF16g³] third foal:
half-brother to Known Lady (by Known Fact), winning plater on Flat: dam
half-sister to very smart stayer General Ironside: third in NH Flat race at
Lingfield in February: yet to race over hurdles or fences. *B. Byford*

MARDIOR 5 b.m. Martinmas – Diorina (Manacle) [1992/3 18s a18g⁶]
leggy mare: half-sister to winning hurdler Disport (by Import): won 1m –
seller on Flat in 1992: has shown nothing over hurdles: blinkered last start.
W. G. R. Wightman

MARDOOD 8 b.g. Ela-Mana-Mou – Tigeen (Habitat) [1992/3 22fᵖᵘ 18v³
21v 22d* 18d* 22d*] lengthy gelding: progressive hurdler: sold 10,000 gns 116 p
Doncaster August Sales: won at Newton Abbot and Exeter in April and on
former course in May: stays 2¾m: acts on firm and dead ground: in fine
form on Flat in 1993. *P. Leach*

MARIAN EVANS 6 b.m. Dominion – Kindjal (Kris) [1992/3 21m⁵]
small, workmanlike mare: poor 2m novice hurdler: tailed off only start in –
1992/3 (August). *T. Craig*

MARIDADI 7 ch.g. True Song – Themopolli (Spartan General) [1992/3
22d³ 21s] big, lengthy gelding: chasing type: promising third in novice 88
hurdle at Haydock in December, but failed to confirm that effort in similar
event at Leicester following month: will be suited by further than 2¾m:
acts on dead ground. *M. J. Wilkinson*

MARIE BABY 9 br.m. King of Spain – Sonseeahray (March Past)
[1992/3 17d] smallish, leggy mare: no form over hurdles for a long time: –
tried blinkered and visored. *Graeme Roe*

MARIE SWIFT 8 b.m. Main Reef – Sarus (Amber Rama (USA)) [1992/3 c–
17d 22gᵘʳ 20g 17v⁶] lengthy, sparely-made mare: poor winning pointer: poor

465

novice hurdler/chaser: likely to prove suited by further than 2m. *B. J. Llewellyn*

MARINER'S AIR 6 ch.m. Julio Mariner – Havon Air (Celtic Cone) [1992/3 F16s F16g⁵ 17m] close-coupled mare: first foal: dam, winning hurdler/novice chaser, stayed 2½m: fifth of 21 in mares NH Flat race at Worcester in March: showed nothing in maiden hurdle at Wolverhampton later in month. *J. L. Spearing*

MARINER'S BOW 6 ch.g. Julio Mariner – Bishop's Bow (Crozier) [1992/3 F17v F17s 16gᵘʳ] tall gelding: second foal: half-brother to winning chaser Bowl of Oats (by Oats): dam useful chaser, stayed 2¾m: well beaten in NH Flat races: backward, tailed off when unseating rider fourth in claimer in February on hurdling debut. *G. Stickland*

MARINERS COVE 5 br.g. Julio Mariner – Ionian Isle (FR) (Jim French (USA)) [1992/3 F17g aF16g F16f 16f23m⁶ 21f⁶] second foal: dam winning selling hurdler: behind in NH Flat races: well beaten in novice hurdles in May. *R. G. Brazington*

MARINERS DANCE 5 ch.m. Julio Mariner – Fullstop (Salvo) [1992/3 F17f] sister to NH Flat race-placed Mariners Pet and half-sister to winning hurdler Assumption (by Jimsun): dam poor maiden on Flat and over hurdles: tailed off in NH Flat race at Hereford in May: yet to race over hurdles or fences. *R. G. Brazington*

MARINERS LEGEND 7 ch.m. Julio Mariner – Firs Park (Crozier) [1992/3 c22v⁵ c21v³ c26sᵖᵘ a24g⁴ c25d⁵ a24g⁶] smallish ex-Irish mare: fifth foal: half-brother to novice hurdler/winning pointer Woodhay Hill (by Oats): dam, fair hurdler and winning chaser, stayed 3m: winning pointer: poor novice hurdler/chaser: sold 5,000 gns Doncaster March Sales: sketchy jumper. *R. Hollinshead* — c–57

MARINERS LOVE 7 b.m. Julio Mariner – Love of Kings (Golden Love) [1992/3 18g 20g] close-coupled mare: poor novice hurdler: no promise on chasing debut. *Miss S. J. Wilton* — c––

MARINERS MEMORY 5 b.h. Julio Mariner – Midnight Pansy (Deadly Nightshade) [1992/3 F16s] close-coupled horse: half-brother to several winners, notably useful hurdlers Jimsintime and Jimbalou (both by Jimsun): dam placed over hurdles: tailed off in NH Flat race at Warwick in February: yet to race over hurdles or fences. *R. G. Brazington*

MARINERS MIRROR 6 b.m. Julio Mariner – Sujono (Grey Mirage) [1992/3 21v⁵] close-coupled mare: fairly useful hurdler at best: tailed off only outing of season (December): stays 2½m: yet to race on firm ground, acts on any other: front runner: game: has won when sweating. *M. Scudamore* — –

MARINERS SECRET 7 b.m. Julio Mariner – Midnight Pansy (Deadly Nightshade) [1992/3 22g⁶ 21d 22d² a20g 21s 22d⁵] neat mare: modest handicap hurdler: best efforts of season on third and last starts: effective at 2¾m and should stay 3m: acts on good to soft going and fibresand. *R. G. Brazington* — 94

MARINER'S WALK 6 ch.h. Julio Mariner – Nunswalk (The Parson) [1992/3 16d 17s] tall, unfurnished horse: no promise in novice hurdles in first half of season. *J. M. Bradley* — –

MARINE SOCIETY 5 b.g. Petoski – Miranda Julia (Julio Mariner) [1992/3 17s⁶ 16s³ 16s⁵] smallish, sparely-made gelding: fair maiden on Flat: stays 1¾m: sold out of P. Walwyn's stable 8,200 gns Newmarket September Sales: modest form in novice hurdles: visored second outing. *R. Lee* — 84

MARIOLINO 6 b.g. Buzzards Bay – Banking Coyne (Deep Diver) [1992/3 16d 16d 16s 17v 23d* 20g* 17mᵖᵘ 16f⁴ 20g³ 20g⁶] fair hurdler: trained until after third start by R. Jennings in Ireland: won sellers at Stratford (no bid) in February and Taunton (bought in 5,200 gns) in March: ran well when in frame in non-selling handicaps at Ludlow and Exeter in May: effective at 2m and stays 23f: acts on firm and dead ground: blinkered once in 1991/2. *P. Leach* — 100

MARJONS BOY 6 ch.g. Enchantment – Nevilles Cross (USA) (Nodouble (USA)) [1992/3 c16f c17f^{pu}] leggy, sparely-made gelding: no sign of ability: blinkered in 1992/3. *C. D. Broad*   c–

MARKED CARD 5 b.g. Busted – Winter Queen (Welsh Pageant) [1992/3 17m 18g 18g^6 16g^5 21g^5 17m^2 17d^2 18d^5] sturdy gelding: poor novice hurdler: best form at around 2m: acts on good to firm and dead ground: blinkered once. *Mrs M. A. Kendall*   78

MARKET FORCES 10 b.g. Soldier Rose – Cover Your Money (Precipice Wood) [1992/3 c24v^{pu}] leggy, good-topped gelding: fair chaser at best: pulled up only outing of season (January): stayed 3¼m: acted on heavy going: dead. *N. A. Gaselee*   c–

MARKET LEADER 13 b. or br.g. Kala Shikari – Natflat (Barrons Court) [1992/3 c18m* c18m* c19g^4 c18m^4 c16g^4 c18m^5 c19g^4 c17m^4 c17m^3] lengthy gelding: modest chaser: successful twice at Market Rasen early in season: mostly below form subsequently: effective around 2m and stays 2½m: acts on firm and dead going. *R. Lee*   c84

MARLEFIELD 11 ch.g. Le Bavard (FR) – Ballyowen (Arctic Slave) [1992/3 c23g^F c25g^{pu} c23d c25g^{pu}] tall, leggy gelding: ungenuine novice hurdler/chaser: probably stays 3m: visored all bar third start in 1992/3. *J. K. M. Oliver*   c– §

MARLIN DANCER 8 b.g. Niniski (USA) – Mullet (Star Appeal) [1992/3 17v^4 21d* 21s^{pu} 20d^{bd} 21g^2 22f*] close-coupled, rather sparely-made gelding: useful handicap hurdler: won in good style at Kempton in December and narrowly in slowly-run race at Sandown in March: stays 2¾m: acts on any going: has a foot infirmity which sometimes causes him to run poorly. *Miss B. Sanders*   136

MARLINGFORD 6 ch.g. Be My Guest (USA) – Inchmarlo (USA) (Nashua) [1992/3 18s^6 17d 18d 17d^3 17s^4 20m] rangy gelding: fair hurdler: trained first 2 starts by Mrs M. Reveley: easily best effort in 1992/3 when third at Carlisle in April: stays 2½m: acts on soft and good to firm ground: front runner: blinkered fifth start: not one to trust implicitly. *Mrs J. Jordan*   110

MAROWINS 4 ch.g. Sweet Monday – Top Cover (High Top) [1992/3 16d 16s] lengthy gelding: modest form at up to 1½m on Flat: tailed-off last in juvenile hurdles at Haydock and Nottingham in December: successful on Flat subsequently. *E. J. Alston*   –

MARPATANN (IRE) 4 b.c. Vision (USA) – Eimkar (Junius (USA)) [1992/3 16m^4 18g^6] seems of little account. *A. S. Reid*   –

MARQUEE CAFE 9 ch.g. Sallust – Royal Sensation (Prince Regent (FR)) [1992/3 22d 24d^5 22m* 22g^4 22d^{pu} 21f] smallish, angular gelding: moderate handicap hurdler: won at Newton Abbot in March: ran poorly last 2 starts: stays 25f: acts on dead going and good to firm. *J. Kirby*   95

MARRADONG BROOK 8 ch.g. Giacometti – Freuchie (Vulgan) [1992/3 26g^3 c25s^3 c22v^{pu} 25s^6] workmanlike gelding: fairly useful hurdler: modest third only completed start over fences: stayed 3¼m: acted on good to firm and soft going: blinkered last outing: dead. *Capt. T. A. Forster*   c89   118

MARRA'S ROSCOE 7 b. or br.g. Roscoe Blake – British Pet Queen (High Table) [1992/3 F17s^6 23d^2 20s^5 25d* 25g^3 28g*] sparely-made gelding: fair form over hurdles: won novice events at Ayr in January and Sedgefield in April: stays very well: acts on dead ground: edgy type. *Mrs M. Reveley*   101

MARROB 6 ch.h. Deep Run – Random What (Random Shot) [1992/3 F16v F17s^2 F16s] workmanlike horse: second foal: dam, unraced half-sister to winning hurdler Noble Yeoman, from family of Mr What and L'Escargot: best effort in NH Flat races when second of 14 at Newbury in January: yet to race over hurdles or fences. *R. Akehurst*   –

MARSDEN ROCK 6 b. or br.m. Tina's Pet – Take My Hand (Precipice Wood) [1992/3 F14d^6 17m 16v^3 17s^2 16d 24s] leggy mare: fourth foal: half-sister to winning jumpers Contact Kelvin (by Workboy), Gunner Mac   79 (by Gunner B) and D C Flyer (by Record Token): dam poor maiden: poor form when placed in mid-season novice hurdles at Hexham and Carlisle: soundly beaten last 2 starts: form only at around 2m: acts on heavy ground. *N. B. Mason*

MARSHALL SPARKS 6 ch.g. Electric – Marshalla (Cawston's Clown) [1992/3 F16s*] sister to NH Flat winner G'ime A Buzz: second outing in NH Flat races when winning at Ludlow in January: yet to race over hurdles or fences. *M. C. Pipe*

MARSHLANDER 14 b.g. Sheshoon – Dinamarsh (Nelcius) [1992/3   **c81** c21g4 c24f6 c28d6 c24d4] tall gelding: veteran handicap chaser: stays well: acts on any ground: front runner: visored once in 1991/2, blinkered last start. *D. R. Gandolfo*

MARSH'S LAW 6 br.g. Kala Shikari – My Music (Sole Mio (USA)) [1992/3 18m* 16d4 18s* 21f6 22f2 16d*] angular gelding: lightly raced: won   **106** claiming hurdles at Market Rasen in March (maiden event) and April and novice hurdle at Towcester in May: acts at up to 2¼m: acts on good to firm and soft ground: visored fifth outing. *O. Brennan*

MARSH WARBLER 5 b.g. Wattlefield – Be Lyrical (Song) [1992/3 17dpu 18mF 17sur 16spu] workmanlike gelding: novice 2m selling hurdler: **–** pulls hard: blinkered third start. *R. G. Frost*

MARTELLA 11 b.g. Martinmas – Columbella (Jukebox) [1992/3 c17mF   **c–** c21m] winning pointer: no sign of ability in hunter chases. *G. T. Ingleton*

MARTELL BOY (NZ) 6 b.g. Princes Gate – Amorae (NZ) (Arragon) [1992/3 21d 24v5 22v 22v3 24v4 24s* 24s6] good-topped gelding: will make a   **104** chaser: easily best effort over hurdles when winning novice event at Worcester in March: stays 3m: acts on soft going: tends to run in snatches. *D. H. Barons*

MARTELL SPIRIT (NZ) 6 br.g. Racing Is Fun (USA) – Royal Tryst (NZ) (Sir Tristram) [1992/3 22g2] strong, lengthy New Zealand-bred   **86** gelding: won 2 NH Flat races in 1991/2: jumped none too fluently when staying-on second in novice hurdle at Cheltenham in October (looked sure to improve but wasn't seen out again): will be suited by a stiffer test of stamina. *D. H. Barons*

MARTHA'S SON 6 b.g. Idiot's Delight – Lady Martha (Sidon) [1992/3 18f* 17g3 16d4 17s* 16vpu] lengthy, rather unfurnished gelding: fairly useful   **128** handicap hurdler: won at Fontwell, Wincanton and Newbury (quite valuable event) in 1992/3, but ran as though something amiss last outing (January): bred to stay beyond 2¼m though takes strong hold: probably acts on any going: usually held up. *Capt. T. A. Forster*

MARTI BROWN 6 br.m. Martinmas – Sister Brown (Murrayfield) [1992/3 F17s aF16g] fourth foal: half-sister to a poor animal by Import: dam, half-sister to Townley Stone and from a successful jumping family, won 2 NH Flat races and finished fourth only outing over hurdles: last in NH Flat races at Newbury in January and Lingfield in March: yet to race over hurdles or fences. *Miss H. C. Knight*

MARTINA 5 b.m. Tina's Pet – Tin Tessa (Martinmas) [1992/3 17d] fair sprinter on Flat: jumped sketchily and always behind in novice hurdle at   **–** Doncaster in December. *J. Wharton*

MARTINI EXECUTIVE 5 b.h. King of Spain – Wigeon (Divine Gift) [1992/3 16g 17d2] half-brother to winning hurdler Spring Wigeon (by Miami   **87** Springs): fairly useful miler on all-weather surfaces on Flat (usually blinkered): blinkered, forced pace, when second in novice event at Perth in May: better effort over hurdles: likely to prove best at around 2m: acts on dead going. *B. E. Wilkinson*

MARTIN'S LAMP 6 b.g. Martinmas – Lampstone (Ragstone) [1992/3 16s* 17v6 16v* 16v2] tall, leggy, angular gelding: easy winner of novice   **124 p** hurdles at Towcester in November and January: put up quite useful performance when second in similar event on same course in February: may prove best at around 2m at present: acts on heavy going: races up with the pace: should progress further. *J. T. Gifford*

MARTIN THOMAS 10 br.g. Auction Ring (USA) – Canelle (Sassafras (FR)) [1992/3 c24s^{pu} c25d^{ur} c26m^6] angular gelding: won poor novice hunter chase in 1991: has shown nothing since: stays 25f: acts on soft going. *D. Powell*   c–

MARTOMICK 6 br.m. Montelimar (USA) – Be My Joy (Be My Guest (USA)) [1992/3 21s^{pu} 25s^3 20s^2 21v^3 21m^6 22f* 24g] unfurnished mare: winning pointer in Ireland: good sixth to Gaelstrom in Sun Alliance Novices' Hurdle at Cheltenham and landed the odds in mares novice event at Wincanton (didn't need to run up to her best), both in March: best efforts at up to 2¾m: probably acts on any going. *K. C. Bailey*   122

MARTRAJAN 6 br.g. Miner's Lamp – Another Cailin (Master Buck) [1992/3 17s^3 16s 16m^2 21d^3 17g] good-bodied gelding: chasing type: modest novice hurdler: stays 21f: acts on soft and good to firm going. *Mrs J. Pitman*   91

MARY BOROUGH 7 gr.m. Baron Blakeney – Risello (Raise You Ten) [1992/3 17g^{pu} 23d^{pu} 21v 22v^{pu} a18g a20g^{pu} 22f 25m^{pu} 18d^{pu}] smallish mare: no sign of ability: blinkered eighth outing. *Mrs J. A. Young*   c–

MARY KNOLL (IRE) 5 b.m. Crash Course – Bonnemahon (Polyfoto) [1992/3 F17f] half-sister to 2 winners, including selling hurdler Esker House (by Raga Navarro): dam placed at up to 7.5f in Ireland: tailed off in NH Flat race at Hereford in May: yet to race over hurdles or fences. *J. L. Needham*

MARYLAND FARMER 6 b.g. The Parson – Fubar (Crash Course) [1992/3 22d^5 22v c21d^{pu}] good-topped, workmanlike gelding with scope: showed some ability in NH Flat races in 1991/2, and when fifth in novice hurdle at Wincanton in November: tailed off when pulled up in April on chasing debut: likely to prove suited by test of stamina. *P. F. Nicholls*   c–

MARY O'REILLY 8 br.m. Callernish – Monavalla (Kabale) [1992/3 17g 21v c21g^6 c25g^4 c21f^5 c18m^4] poor novice hurdler/chaser. *W. G. Mann*   c–

MARY'S MUSIC 5 b.m. Southern Music – Hi Mary (High Line) [1992/3 16d^3 16v^{pu} a18g 16d^F 17f^6] leggy, plain mare: best effort over hurdles when remote third in fillies novice event at Wincanton in December. *Mrs J. C. Dawe*   74

MARZOCCO 5 ch.g. Formidable (USA) – Top Heights (High Top) [1992/3 17s^3 18d 17v* 16s^2 17d^4 18g^3] neat gelding: won maiden hurdle at Lingfield in January: also ran well afterwards: likely to prove best at around 2m: acts on heavy ground: sometimes looks none too keen. *J. Ffitch-Heyes*   88

MASAI MARA (USA) 5 ch.g. Mogambo (USA) – Forever Command (USA) (Top Command (USA)) [1992/3 18m^F 17m] leggy gelding: won 2 juvenile hurdles in 1991/2, when trained by P. Haslam: sold 3,200 gns Doncaster November Sales: close up when falling 2 out in minor event at Fontwell in February: still bit backward when no show in valuable handicap at Cheltenham following month: should stay further than 2¼m: acts on good to firm going. *J. Ffitch-Heyes*   ?

MASCALLS LADY 8 b.m. Nicholas Bill – Whisper Gently (Pitskelly) [1992/3 a20g a16g] sparely-made mare: poor novice hurdler. *N. B. Thomson*   –

MASH THE TEA (IRE) 4 b.g. Mazaad – Tassie (Lochnager) [1992/3 17m 17s^4 21g^{pu} 17g] neat gelding: no form on Flat or over hurdles. *H. J. Collingridge*   –

MASNOON (USA) 10 ch.g. Sharpen Up – A Twinkling (USA) (Prince John) [1992/3 22g^{pu}] tall gelding: formerly a useful chaser but has lost his form and enthusiasm: pulled up lame in handicap hurdle in October: tried blinkered. *J. L. Eyre*   c– §

MASROUG 6 b.g. Dunbeath (USA) – Fleur Rouge (Pharly (FR)) [1992/3 17v^5 18v 17v^2 17v^4 17d^2 18m^3 17g^4 20s* 18f^2 23m 18f^4] lengthy, workmanlike gelding: modest hurdler: won selling handicap at Plumpton in April (no bid): stays 2½m: acts on any going, including equitrack. *A. Moore*   89

MASTER BAVARD (IRE) 5 ch.g. Le Bavard (FR) – Honey Come Back (Master Owen) [1992/3 aF16g² aF16g* aF16g*] fifth foal: brother to winning Irish jumper Rosewood Honey and half-brother to useful hurdler Jakarrdi (by Torus): dam winning hurdler/chaser in Ireland: won 2 NH Flat races at Lingfield in March: yet to race over hurdles or fences. *M. S. Saunders*

MASTER BOSTON (IRE) 5 gr.g. Soughaan (USA) – Ballinoe Lass (Captain James) [1992/3 16s 17g 16d⁶ 21f 21g²] angular gelding: second foal: dam, half-sister to useful jumper Norton Cross, placed over hurdles in Ireland: best effort in novice hurdles when second at Hexham in May: stays 21f. *R. D. E. Woodhouse*   85

MASTER BRACKEN 4 ch.g. Grey Desire – Maha (Northfields (USA)) [1992/3 F14g] compact gelding: third foal: dam behind in NH Flat race: mid-division in NH Flat race at Market Rasen in April: yet to race over hurdles. *T. D. Barron*

MASTER CAVERS (IRE) 5 b.g. Farhaan – Open Return (Never Return (USA)) [1992/3 18g⁶] second foal: dam never ran: last of 6 in novice hurdle at Sedgefield in February. *B. Mactaggart*   –

MASTER COMEDY 9 b.g. Comedy Star (USA) – Romardia (Romulus) [1992/3 c18d³ c18s* c21s³ c18v³ c21v c18v⁴ c21d⁶ c18v⁴ c16s⁴ c18g⁴] leggy, sparely-made gelding: poor chaser: won handicap at Fontwell in November: in-and-out form afterwards: effective at around 2m and stays 3¼m: acts on heavy going: blinkered nowadays: races up with pace. *Miss L. Bower*   c80
       –

MASTER CORNET 8 ch.g. Celtic Cone – Yogurt (Saint Denys) [1992/3 c26m* c25d* c26dur c26d⁶ c29d³ c25g³ c26mF] workmanlike gelding: modest chaser: won handicaps at Catterick in October and Market Rasen in November: not disgraced on last 2 completed starts: suited by good test of stamina: acts on good to firm and dead ground: blinkered last outing: usually makes running. *B. S. Rothwell*   c97
       –

MASTER DANCER 6 b.g. Mashhor Dancer (USA) – Silent Dancer (Quiet Fling (USA)) [1992/3 24f² 24d 26g⁵ a22g³ a24g³ a22g²] close-coupled gelding: fair handicap hurdler: generally ran creditably in 1992/3: stays 3m: acts on firm and dead ground and goes well on all-weather surfaces: amateur ridden: usually races up with pace: consistent. *M. Blanshard*   110

MASTER D DEE 5 gr.g. Absalom – Elizabeth Howard (Sharpen Up) [1992/3 20gF 24vpu 20m] smallish gelding: no sign of ability. *H. J. Collingridge*   –

MASTER ERYL 10 gr.g. Anax – Blackberry Hill (Sovereign Path) [1992/3 c19d⁴ c26m³ c24f*] tall gelding: fair hunter chaser: left clear last when winning at Ludlow in March: stays 3¼m: acts on firm ground: makes mistakes. *Mrs Roger Guilding*   c90 x

MASTER FLASHMAN 4 ch.g. Swing Easy (USA) – Yashama (Supreme Red) [1992/3 F16d F16m 16g⁵] sixth foal: half-brother to fair hurdler/chaser The Slater (by Town And Country) and winning pointer/hunter chaser The Motcombe Oak (by Brotherly): dam never ran: little sign of ability in NH Flat races and a juvenile hurdle. *Mrs S. C. Bradburne*   –

MASTER FOODBROKER (IRE) 5 br.g. Simply Great (FR) – Silver Mantle (Bustino) [1992/3 22sur] workmanlike gelding: won 2½m juvenile hurdle in 1991/2: sold out of D. Elsworth's stable 2,600 gns Newmarket Autumn Sales: virtually refused last 2 outings over hurdles: wears blinkers: one to leave alone. *W. J. Musson*   §§

MASTER FRITH 5 gr.g. Dutch Treat – Dromeden Janice (Andrea Mantegna) [1992/3 F16d F14s 16v 22vpu] lengthy gelding: first foal: dam unraced: no sign of ability in NH Flat races and novice hurdles. *K. S. Bridgwater*   –

MASTER JOLSON 5 b.g. Sunyboy – Lady De-Lacy (Pitpan) [1992/3 18d 16s³ 18s² 22s² 22g* 24s² 24g²] leggy, lengthy, unfurnished gelding: fair form over hurdles: won novice handicap at Nottingham in February: good   106

second in novice events at Worcester in March (hung left under pressure) and April: stays 3m: acts on soft going. *D. Nicholson*

MASTER KIWI (NZ) 6 b.g. Bagwis (AUS) – Veela (NZ) (Oakville) [1992/3 F18s⁵ F16s F17g] unfurnished New Zealand-bred gelding: well beaten in NH Flat races: yet to race over hurdles or fences. *M. C. Pipe*

MASTER MISCHIEF 6 br.g. Zambrano – Merry Missus (Bargello) [1992/3 17m⁶ 16v⁴ 22g c17d⁶ c17g c23g³ c24sᵖᵘ c16m² 18m⁵ 22v³] lengthy gelding: poor novice hurdler/chaser: stays 23f: acts on good to firm and heavy ground: blinkered seventh to ninth outings. *F. T. Walton*   **c84** 77

MASTER MUCK 10 b.g. Sagaro – Emperor's Gift (Menelek) [1992/3 c24dᵘʳ c25sᵘʳ c20m⁴ c24m⁴ c25s c20g³ c22m* c24f³] rather leggy gelding: won 4-runner novice hunter chase at Towcester in May: only poor judged on other form in 1992/3: stays well: probably acts on any ground: usually a poor jumper of fences. *N. A. Twiston-Davies*   **c96** ?

MASTER MURPHY 4 b.c. Aragon – Magnifica (Sandy Creek) [1992/3 17d 16v 16v] leggy colt: first foal: dam placed at up to 1½m on Flat in France: no sign of ability over hurdles. *P. G. Murphy*   –

MASTER OF HOUNDS 7 b.g. Kind of Hush – Jambalaya (Amboise) [1992/3 c23m² c20mF c21m* c21m³] lengthy, workmanlike gelding: second foal: dam poor staying maiden: won novice chase at Perth in August: ran poorly in similar event at Sedgefield following month, and wasn't seen out again: stays 21f: acts on good to firm going. *T. D. Barron*   **c94**

MASTER OF THE HUNT (IRE) 4 b.c. Huntingdale – Lady Juliet (USA) (Gallant Man) [1992/3 16d⁶ 17f⁶] leggy colt: half-brother to winning hurdler Capulet (by Henbit): poor plater on Flat at 2 yrs: tailed off in juvenile hurdles in February and March. *R. A. Bennett*   –

MASTER OF THE ROCK 4 b.c. Alzao (USA) – Come True (FR) (Nasram II) [1992/3 16d⁵ 16d⁴ 17s² 17s* 18d 16s³ 18d* 18g⁴ 16g³ 16s²] leggy, close-coupled colt: poor maiden on Flat, stays 1½m: sold out of P. Makin's stable 8,200 gns Newmarket Autumn Sales: selling hurdler: won at Bangor (bought in 5,000 gns) in December and Sedgefield (no bid) in February: will stay beyond 2¼m: acts on soft ground: usually visored or blinkered: consistent. *Mrs P. A. Barker*   85

MASTER OF TROY 5 b.g. Trojan Fen – Gohar (USA) (Barachois (CAN)) [1992/3 21mF] neat gelding: fair handicap hurdler at best: probably in need of race, fading when falling 2 out, at Carlisle in October, only outing of season: stays 2½m: acts on any going. *C. Parker*   –

MASTER PEPPER 12 b.g. Latest Model – Miss Pepper (Arctic Chevalier) [1992/3 c21f] little sign of ability over hurdles and in steeplechases: moderate winning pointer. *D. D. Scott*   c– –

MASTER PLAN (FR) 7 b.g. Carwhite – Manene (FR) (Tapioca II) [1992/3 17sᵖᵘ 22s 16g 22v 21vᵖᵘ] sturdy gelding: of little account. *D. L. Williams*   –

MASTER RAJH 9 b.g. Majestic Maharaj – Miss Medina (St Elmo) [1992/3 16g² c16g⁶ c21d] leggy, workmanlike gelding: smart chaser at best: long way below form in 1992/3: novice over hurdles: form only at around 2m nowadays: acts on firm and dead going: usually jumps soundly, though rather low. *J. Chugg*   c– 81

MASTER REACH 4 br.g. Reach – Lady Donaro (Ardoon) [1992/3 17d⁴ 17v 17g 17d⁴ 18g⁵ 17f* 17g] workmanlike gelding: maiden on Flat: won juvenile maiden hurdle at Lingfield in March: well beaten last start: likely to stay beyond 17f: acts on firm ground. *Miss K. S. Allison*   99

MASTER SACHA 5 b.g. Jupiter Island – Snow Chief (Tribal Chief) [1992/3 F16s F17g] half-brother to a 5f winner by Young Generation and to 2 poor novice jumpers: dam fairly useful miler: tailed off in NH Flat races: yet to race over hurdles or fences. *D. McCain*   –

MASTER SALESMAN 10 b.g. Torenaga – Madam Milan (Milan) [1992/3 c18m⁵ c18s³ c16mF c17s³ c16d³ c16g* c16g⁴ c16g³ c16sF c16mᵘʳ   **c97** – §

c18m⁴ c18m⁴] sturdy gelding: fair chaser: won claimer at Edinburgh in December: well below best last 2 starts: sold 4,000 gns Doncaster May Sales: best at up to 2½m: acts on firm and dead ground: usually held up: none too consistent: usually goes well at Edinburgh. *B. S. Rothwell*

MASTER SANDY (USA) 6 b.g. Master Willie – Whose Broad (USA) (Hoist The Flag (USA)) [1992/3 21m²] well beaten on Flat at 3 yrs: promising second of 11 in novice event at Carlisle in March on hurdling debut: will improve. *W. G. Reed* — 85 p

MASTER'S CROWN (USA) 5 ch.g. Chief's Crown (USA) – Mastoora (USA) (Raise A Native) [1992/3 22m 18d* 16f* 18s³ 20g* 18d² 17v⁶ 18v] well-made gelding: handicap hurdler: in good form in first half of season and won at Cartmel (conditional jockeys), Worcester and Market Rasen (ladies): should stay beyond 2½m: seems unsuited by heavy ground, probably acts on any other: sometimes blinkered, including on second and fourth starts. *M. C. Chapman* — 103

MASTER SHIKARI 4 b.g. Kala Shikari – La Bambola (Be Friendly) [1992/3 16m⁴ 17g² 18g* 17m* 16g³] poor maiden on Flat when trained by J. Banks: won novice selling hurdle (bought in 3,000 gns) at Southwell and juvenile claiming hurdle at Carlisle early in season: stays 2¼m: acts on good to firm going. *N. Tinkler* — 89

MASTER SOUTH LAD 9 b.g. Shrivenham – Miss Rosewyn (Wynkell) [1992/3 c18f* c19m⁴] tall gelding: modest novice hurdler: won novice chase at Exeter in September: below that form in similar event there following month: best at up to 2½m: possibly needs a sound surface: blinkered final outing in 1991/2. *N. R. Mitchell* — c94 / –

MASTER TIM 9 ch.g. Timolin (FR) – Straight Beauty (Straight Lad) [1992/3 c26dᵖᵘ c25s c25gᵖᵘ] good-topped, lengthy gelding: no sign of ability over hurdles or in steeplechases: sold 4,000 gns Doncaster May Sales. *Capt. T. A. Forster* — c– / –

MASTER TREASURE 11 ch.g. Fair Turn – Real Treasure (Master Owen) [1992/3 c22g⁴] compact gelding: little form over hurdles or in steeplechases: has been blinkered and visored. *R. Wilson* — c– / –

MASTER WILLIAM 9 b.g. Pollerton – Ballyea Jacki (Straight Lad) [1992/3 27m⁴ 25f² 21sᶠ³ 24g* 28g⁶] smallish, sturdy gelding: carries plenty of condition: modest handicap hurdler: won at Southwell in October: ran poorly 4 months later, only subsequent start: stays 25f: acts well on firm ground: usually visored. *J. A. C. Edwards* — 87

MATAWAI (NZ) 6 b.g. Prince Simbir (NZ) – Tudor Maid (NZ) (Monitor) [1992/3 20g] compact gelding: little sign of ability. *D. H. Barons* — –

MATERIAL GIRL 7 b.m. Busted – First Huntress (Primera) [1992/3 c21sᶠ c22g* c21s* c19s* c21g³ c24mᵖᵘ] compact mare: poor novice hurdler: won hunter chases at Nottingham (novices) in February, Wetherby in March and Hereford (novices) in April: creditable third in handicap chase penultimate start, let down by jumping final one: should stay beyond 2¾m: acts on soft going. *C. R. Egerton* — c109 / –

MATRACE 8 ch.m. Mummy's Game – Sospirae (Sandford Lad) [1992/3 c25s] winning pointer: no sign of ability otherwise. *K. Little* — c– / –

MA TRAVERS 5 b.m. Pragmatic – Personality Plus (Master Owen) [1992/3 20vᵖᵘ] first foal: dam fair staying chaser: showed nothing in novice hurdle at Plumpton in November: sold 675 gns Ascot February Sales. *R. F. Stone* — –

MATRIC 12 b. or br.g. Mandalus – Bel Arbre (Beau Chapeau) [1992/3 c23gᶠ c24g] good-topped gelding: one-time fair chaser: little form since 1989/90, though won a point in March. *D. E. Ingle* — c– / –

MATTS BOY 5 b.g. Runnett – Thatchville (Thatch (USA)) [1992/3 16gᵖᵘ] modest miler on Flat nowadays: tailed off when pulled up in novice hurdle at Catterick in March. *Miss S. E. Hall* — –

MAUDLINS CROSS 8 ch.g. Vaigly Great – Pepin (Midsummer Night c 115 II) [1992/3 c16m* c18d4 c17d² c17d* c16gF c17d* c17g* c18m5] rangy – gelding: handicap chaser: developed into a fairly useful performer in 1992/3, winning at Southwell and Sedgefield in first half of season and on latter course in February and Kelso in April: races only at around 2m: acts on good to firm and dead ground: usually held up: jumps well. *Mrs M. Reveley*

MAUDS THYNE 6 b.g. Good Thyne (USA) – Katherine Maud (Choral Society) [1992/3 F16m] half-brother to winning Irish hurdlers Pronoun (by Proverb) and Vitamin Maud (by Energist): dam won on Flat and over hurdles: sixteenth of 24 in NH Flat race at Warwick in May: yet to race over hurdles or fences. *J. T. Gifford*

MAUNDY MIST 9 ch.m. Foggy Bell – Fair Ches (Pedigree Unknown) [1992/3 17gpu 16gpu 17mpu] angular, plain mare: lightly raced and no sign of – ability. *C. H. Jones*

MAUREEN'S FANCY 8 ch.g. Stetchworth (USA) – Tep's Choice c– (Arctic Slave) [1992/3 c24gpu c22vpu 24dpu 25g3 17m5 21g6 21s5 25v 22m 81 24g² c18mF] workmanlike ex-Irish gelding: third foal: half-brother to winning Irish hurdler Atomic Lady (by Over The River): dam little worthwhile form: novice hurdler/chaser: easily best effort in Britain when second in amateurs maiden event over hurdles at Hexham in May: stays 3m. *J. Parkes*

MAX CLOWN 10 b.g. Cawston's Clown – Maxine's Here (Copte (FR)) c– [1992/3 c25mF] leggy, lightly-made gelding: poor novice hurdler: showed – little in points and a claiming chase: dead. *R. J. Jackson*

MAX MILLER 5 ch.g. Funny Man – Sizzle (High Line) [1992/3 F17d – 21spu] workmanlike gelding: first foal: dam, from good jumping family, showed plenty of promise on only start over hurdles: tenth of 21 in NH Flat race at Sandown in October: pulled up lame following month on hurdling debut: dead. *N. A. Twiston-Davies*

MAYBE O'GRADY (IRE) 4 b.g. Strong Gale – Rosie O'Grady – (Barrons Court) [1992/3 F17f³] workmanlike gelding: brother to novice hurdler Zilljo's Star and half-brother to several minor winners: dam won on Flat and over hurdles: third of 11 in NH Flat race at Doncaster in March: yet to race over hurdles. *Mrs M. Reveley*

MAY-DAY-BABY 7 ch.g. Le Moss – Sirrahdis (Bally Joy) [1992/3 24v4 89 23s* 22vpu 23vpu] workmanlike gelding: best effort when winning novice hurdle at Folkestone in December: suited by test of stamina: acts on heavy going: sometimes wears a tongue strap. *John R. Upson*

MAYFAIR MINX 9 b.m. St Columbus – Belgrave Queen (Sheshoon) c– [1992/3 25g² 26dpu c20mpu c22gF 22d4 24f² 22f 27f4] rather leggy mare: fair 118 § handicap hurdler: showed nothing either start over fences: stays 25f: acts well on firm ground: sometimes looks ungenuine. *S. Christian*

MAYFIELD PARK 8 b.g. Park Row – Arctic Lee (Arctic Judge) [1992/3 c– c26vpu c24vsu c26vF 25d c23gur] sparely-made gelding: poor novice – hurdler: has failed to complete over fences: visored last outing. *C. R. Barwell*

MAYO MAN (IRE) 4 ch.g. Master Willie – Kuwaiti (Home Guard – (USA)) [1992/3 16s³] compact gelding: poor maiden on Flat, probably stays 85 1½m: jumped none too fluently when third in juvenile hurdle at Haydock in November: will be suited by further than 2m. *Mrs M. Reveley*

MAYORAN (NZ) 9 b.g. Mayo Mellay (NZ) – Bundoran (NZ) (Bally c 107 Royal) [1992/3 c24s³ c25g6 c28d c27vpu c26g³ c26dpu c24d c24g5] leggy, angular gelding: fair chaser: creditable third at Chepstow in October and Exeter in March: ran poorly otherwise in 1992/3: sold 10,000 gns Ascot June Sales: stays 25f: acts on heavy going: usually visored over hurdles, blinkered last 2 starts. *D. H. Barons*

MAYOR OF LISCARROL 8 ch.g. Red Regent – Cairita (Pitcairn) c– [1992/3 c17d5 c21f c21gpu] ex-Irish gelding: third foal: half-brother to novice hurdler Going Public (by Strong Gale): dam unraced half-sister to winning hurdler Aqaba Prince: successful pointer: modest novice at best in steeplechases: tailed off both completed outings in 1992/3: best effort over 2½m on dead ground. *M. Smith*

MAY OVER 8 ch.g. Smackover – May Bond (Good Bond) [1992/3 c26m⁴] 9f winner on Flat: once-raced over hurdles: modest maiden pointer: showed ability when fourth in hunter chase at Cheltenham in May. *Miss Sharon Baldwin* — **c86**

MAY RUN 7 b.m. Cruise Missile – Trial Run (Deep Run) [1992/3 17g 25g* 24dᵖᵘ 23g⁴ 23mᵖᵘ] small mare: won poor novice hurdle at Carlisle in March: only other form when fourth in similar event at Kelso following month: stays well. *J. I. A. Charlton* — **75**

MAY SQUARE (IRE) 5 ch.g. Nicholas Bill – Casa Rosada (Known Fact (USA)) [1992/3 17m⁵] good-bodied gelding: winning novice hurdler: stiff task in handicap only outing of season (August): will prove best at 2m: acts on good to firm and dead ground. *Mrs A. Knight* — **–**

MAYTOWN 7 ch.g. Town And Country – Mayotte (Little Buskins) [1992/3 17g 24vᵖᵘ c24sᵖᵘ c20sᶠ c20d c20m⁴ c21fᵘʳ c24f⁴ c24dᵖᵘ] workmanlike gelding: fourth in novice chase at Ludlow in March, only sign of ability: sold 2,100 gns Ascot June Sales: sometimes visored or blinkered: reluctant to race penultimate start. *P. G. Murphy* — **c74 §**

MAZMOOR 7 gr.m. Zambrano – Highmoor Lass (Rubor) [1992/3 17g⁵ 16s⁴ 20g* 20d²] good-topped mare: fairly useful hurdler: won quite valuable handicap at Newcastle in February: excellent second in similar event at Haydock week later: suited by 2½m: acts on soft ground: game: usually amateur ridden and forces pace. *A. Eubank* — **127**

MCNAB (IRE) 4 b.g. Treasure Kay – Finlarrig (Thatching) [1992/3 17f] lightly-raced maiden on Flat: behind in juvenile selling hurdle at Taunton in October. *C. P. Wildman* — **–**

MEADOW GAME (IRE) 4 ch.f. Stanford – Rose Meadow (Mummy's Game) [1992/3 18m 18fᵖᵘ] sturdy filly: lightly-raced maiden on Flat: no promise in juvenile hurdles in August. *W. G. M. Turner* — **–**

MEADOWVALE 8 b.g. Furry Glen – In View Lass (Tepukei) [1992/3 c24m⁶ c27d⁶ c27g⁴] rangy gelding: moderate chaser: creditable fourth at Sedgefield in October: sold 6,200 gns Doncaster Sales later in month: stays well: acts on good to firm ground. *G. Richards* — **c87**

MEAT THE FOULKES (NZ) 12 b.g. Sea Anchor – Divinity (NZ) (Holy Smoke II) [1992/3 c27dᵖᵘ] lengthy gelding: tubed: novice hurdler: handicap chaser: pulled up (reportedly lame) only outing in 1992/3: suited by test of stamina and plenty of give in the ground. *J. E. Collinson* — **c–**

MECADO 6 b.g. Ballacashtal (CAN) – Parma Nova (Dominion) [1992/3 18s⁵ 21vᵖᵘ 18v* 17v³ 16s⁶ 16g² 21d* 16d² 18d] leggy gelding: no bid after winning selling handicap hurdles at Fontwell in January and Uttoxeter in March: good second on latter course in April, better effort in non-sellers subsequently: stays 21f: acts on heavy ground: visored last 4 outings. *F. J. Yardley* — **79**

MEDBOURNE (IRE) 4 b.f. Alzao (USA) – Dress In Spring (Northfields (USA)) [1992/3 a16g a20gᵖᵘ] temperamental maiden plater on Flat: showed nothing over hurdles. *J. L. Harris* — **–**

MEDIA MESSENGER 4 b.g. Hadeer – Willow Court (USA) (Little Current (USA)) [1992/3 16g 16g⁴ 16d³] angular gelding: 9f winner on Flat: best effort over hurdles when fourth in juvenile event at Edinburgh. *Denys Smith* — **87**

MEDIATOR 4 b.g. Valiyar – Blushing Cousin (Great Nephew) [1992/3 16d⁵ 17g⁶ 17f] lightly-raced staying maiden on Flat: little worthwhile form over hurdles: blinkered second start. *A. Moore* — **–**

MEDINAS SWAN SONG 5 b.g. Nearly A Hand – Miss Medina (St Elmo) [1992/3 F16d⁶] brother to winning 2m chaser Nearly Medina and half-brother to smart 2m chaser Master Rajh (by Majestic Maharaj): dam, fair chaser, successful at up to 21f: sixth of 17 in NH Flat race at Ludlow in December: yet to race over hurdles or fences. *R. J. Hodges*

MEDRONHEIRA 8 ch.g. Le Moss – Monaleigh (Sir Herbert) [1992/3 F16g F19m² 22v 23s c27s⁵ c24gᵖᵘ c24fᵖᵘ] lengthy ex-Irish gelding: third foal: dam winning hurdler/chaser at up to 3m in Ireland: trained until after second outing by P. Berry: placed in NH Flat races but has shown nothing over hurdles and fences: blinkered final start 1991/2. *R. J. Hodges*

c–
–

MEESON CODE 6 b.g. Coded Scrap – Meeson Secret (Most Secret) [1992/3 17gᵖᵘ 17g] neat gelding: selling handicap hurdler: ran poorly in April: raced only at around 2m: acts on dead going. *R. Champion*

–

MEGA BLUE 8 gr.m. Scallywag – Town Blues (Charlottown) [1992/3 c18d³ c16d* c17g* c16g⁴ c18d² c17d⁶ c21g* c16s² c21gᶠ] workmanlike mare: fair chaser: winner of handicaps at Catterick and Doncaster (conditional jockeys) in first half of season and at Southwell in March: 4 lengths clear when falling 3 out on last-named course in May: effective at 2m to 21f: probably acts on any going: visored once over hurdles: usually makes running. *Mrs V. A. Aconley*

c 106
–

MEIGLE STREET 8 b.m. Balgaddy – Golden Owen (Master Owen) [1992/3 c17s⁶] poor maiden pointer: well beaten in mares novice event at Hexham in April on steeplechasing debut. *J. S. Haldane*

c–

MEKSHARP 6 ch.g. Slim Jim – Baru (Rubor) [1992/3 21v⁶ 23s 23d⁵ 21gᵖᵘ 20g 20f a18g⁴ a21g³] close-coupled gelding: poor novice hurdler: stays 23f: acts on heavy ground and fibresand: blinkered last 5 outings. *J. P. Smith*

75

MELDON 6 b.g. Paddy's Stream – Enchanted Evening (Warpath) [1992/3 16d⁶ 18s² 18s 22vᵖᵘ 25d* 26g⁴] compact gelding: won novice handicap hurdle at Taunton in February: stays 25f: acts on soft ground: inconsistent. *Mrs J. G. Retter*

81

MELDON SONG 5 b.m. Pitskelly – Daughter of Song (Song) [1992/3 16g 17dᵖᵘ] half-sister to winning hurdler Classical Quartet (by Relkino): poor form at 2 yrs: seems of little account as a hurdler. *C. Cowley*

–

MELEAGRIS 9 b.g. True Song – Fritillaria (Bargello) [1992/3 22v⁵ 22s* 26d² 26d*] leggy gelding: improved form over hurdles and won novice events at Ludlow (handicap) in January and Wolverhampton (easily) in February: suited by a test of stamina: best form with plenty of give in the ground: sometimes gives trouble at start: should improve further. *D. Nicholson*

114 p

MELKONO 9 br.g. Meldrum – Ivory Coast (Poaching) [1992/3 24f² 16m] sturdy gelding: lightly-raced poor novice hurdler: second of 4 at Hexham in August: stays 3m: acts on hard ground. *Denys Smith*

?

MELLION PRIDE (IRE) 5 b.g. Sheer Grit – Saucy Slave (Arctic Slave) [1992/3 F17d] good-topped gelding with scope: half-brother to several winners, including fair chaser Crock-Na-Nee (by Random Shot): dam, twice a winner over hurdles at around 2m in Ireland, half-sister to smart hurdler Troyswood: well beaten in NH Flat race at Ascot in April: yet to race over hurdles or fences. *J. A. B. Old*

MELLOW GOLD 6 br.m. Meldrum – Golden Royalty (Royalty) [1992/3 F17s F16d] sister to useful chaser Last 'o' The Bunch: dam poor maiden on Flat: behind in NH Flat races at Carlisle and Catterick in November: yet to race over hurdles or fences. *G. Richards*

MEL'S ROSE 8 ch.g. Anfield – Ragtime Rose (Ragstone) [1992/3 17s² 16v³ 16s⁶ 17g* 17g⁴] sparely-made gelding: fair form in novice hurdles: didn't have to be at his best to win at Plumpton in March: unlikely to stay much beyond 17f: acts on heavy ground. *Dr J. D. Scargill*

97

MEMBERS' REVENGE 12 b.g. New Member – Aileens Revenge (Sweet Revenge) [1992/3 c21s³ c21d⁴] lengthy gelding: handicap chaser: third to Sacre d'Or at Uttoxeter, easily better effort early in season: effective at 2m and stays 21f: acts on any going. *S. Christian*

c 113
–

MEN

MENADARVA 12 b.g. Golden Passenger – Mena Lodge (Menelek) [1992/3 c21sF c16s4 c21vpu] compact gelding: lightly-raced pointer: very lightly raced in steeplechases, showing poor form at best. *R. R. Ledger*

c–

MENDIP MUSIC 9 br.g. Sousa – Track Music (Track Spare) [1992/3 c24fsu] leggy, shallow-girthed gelding: modest pointer: yet to complete in hunter chases, though has shown signs of ability. *Mrs Gillian Lane*

c–

MENEBUCK 7 b.g. Buckskin (FR) – Meneplete (Menelek) [1992/3 20g* 24g c20d3 c21d* c21dur c21d* c26vF c24sF c26dF 23g* 27m3 20g* 17g* 20s2] lengthy, leggy ex-Irish gelding: half-brother to 2 winning jumpers, including fairly useful Blacksburg (by Black Minstrel): dam, unraced, from successful jumping family: fairly useful hurdler: won at Clonmel in June (trained until after third outing by E. M. O'Sullivan), Folkestone in February and Plumpton in March and April: also successful in 2 novice chases at Wincanton, showing fair form: effective at 2m and stays 23f: acts on heavy ground: poor jumper of fences: genuine. *Lady Herries*

c105 x
128

MENINGI 12 ch.g. Bustino – Miss Filbert (Compensation) [1992/3 c21g 22v 23s c24s6 c25m3] leggy, rather narrow gelding: modest handicap hurdler/chaser in 1991/2: well below form in 1992/3: stays 21f: ideally suited by give in the ground and acts on heavy going: blinkered once. *K. Bishop*

c–
–

MERANDI SPECIAL 6 b.g. Coquelin (USA) – Mountain Chase (Mount Hagen (FR)) [1992/3 18g4 16spu 18s 22d a18gpu c21f 17f3 17g6] sparely-made gelding: poor hurdler nowadays: sold out of J. Thomas' stable 825 gns Ascot February Sales after fifth outing: tailed off on chasing debut: stays 19f: best form on top-of-the-ground: blinkered fourth start. *R. F. Stone*

c–
82

MERANO (FR) 10 ch.g. Tip Moss (FR) – Association (FR) (Margouillat (FR)) [1992/3 c24s* c24s3 c25m2] lengthy, plain gelding: useful chaser: won handicap at Newcastle in December: ran very well both subsequent starts, particularly when second to Strong Beau in valuable amateurs handicap at

c130
–

Grouse Handicap Chase, Newcastle—Merano makes a winning reappearance

Cheltenham in March: stays 25f well: acts on good to firm and soft going. *M. W. Easterby*

MERCERS MAGIC (IRE) 5 ch.g. Dalsaan – Rixensart (Credo) [1992/3 22g 22f⁵ a21gᵖᵘ] sturdy gelding: bad novice selling hurdler. *K. G. Wingrove* —

MERCHANT HOUSE (IRE) 5 ch.g. Salmon Leap (USA) – Persian Polly (Persian Bold) [1992/3 18f²] first outing for present stable and first form over hurdles when second in novice event at Exeter in August: stays 2¼m: acts on firm going. *M. C. Pipe* 88

MERE CHANTS 4 b.f. Kings Lake (USA) – Rengaine (FR) (Music Boy) [1992/3 16sᶠ 17dᶠ] leggy, lightly-made filly: modest maiden on Flat, stays 1m: no sign of aptitude for hurdling: sold 825 gns Ascot February Sales. *C. Weedon* —

MERE CLASS 7 b.g. Class Distinction – Cuckmere Grange (Floriana) [1992/3 c16vᶠ c20d* c24sᶠ c21v³ c24m* c25g²] rangy gelding: once-raced over hurdles: won novice chases at Haydock in December and Stratford (impressively) in April: good second in novice handicap at Ascot later in April: stays 3m: acts on good to firm and dead ground: on the upgrade and will win more races. *C. P. E. Brooks* c110 p

MERITMOORE 10 b.g. Moorestyle – More Treasure (Ballymore) [1992/3 c21s⁶ c24s⁴ c21d⁶ c21sᶠ c17s²] rangy gelding: handicap chaser: would have won at Hexham in April but for falling last: ran creditably there following month: barely stays 3m: acts on heavy ground: blinkered last 2 outings. *G. M. Moore* c92 +

MERLIN ROCKET 5 b.g. Pony Express – Polly Bird (Pharaoh Hophra) [1992/3 aF13g F16f² F17m] workmanlike gelding: first foal: dam, winning pointer/novice hurdler, half-sister to Foxhunter Chase winner The Drunken Duck: second of 6 at Wincanton in March, only sign of ability in NH Flat races: yet to race over hurdles or fences. *R. Callow* —

MERLINS GIRL 7 ch.m. Feelings (FR) – Raver (Runnymede) [1992/3 F17g c24gᵘʳ] sparely-made mare: sister to 6-y-o Carsethorn: dam sprint plater: placed in a point in 1992: behind in NH Flat race in December and when unseating rider eleventh in novice chase at Fakenham in February. *D. Esden* c–

MERLINS WISH (USA) 4 ch.g. Yukon (USA) – Dear Guinevere (USA) (Fearless Knight) [1992/3 17s⁴] compact gelding: fairly useful at up to 1m on Flat, winner in 1993: promising fourth to Major Bugler in juvenile hurdle at Newbury in November. *R. Hannon* 91 p

MERRY HILL 5 b.m. Barley Hill – Merebimur (Charlottown) [1992/3 17g⁵ 22dᶠ 16sᵖᵘ] angular mare: third foal: half-sister to a poor animal: dam, half-sister to 2 winning jumpers, winner over hurdles: of little account. *D. R. Gandolfo* —

MERRY JERRY 7 b. or br.g. Montreal Boy – Very Merry (Lord of Verona) [1992/3 c25g⁶] big gelding: half-brother to useful pointer/winning hunter chaser Ready Steady (by Bivouac): dam from successful jumping family: won a point in March: well beaten in hunter chase at Kelso earlier in month. *Clive Storey* c–

MERRYLEE 6 br.m. Royal Fountain – Whitmarsh (Hessonite) [1992/3 18g 17m] small mare: fourth foal: half-sister to winning 2m hurdler/chaser Leacroft (by Domitor): dam in frame over 7f and 1m from only 3 starts: no sign of ability in novice hurdle at Cartmel in August and seller at Carlisle in September. *S. G. Payne* —

MERRY MAGGIE 6 b.m. Stanford – Piercing Glances (Patch) [1992/3 20m] unfurnished mare: poor novice hurdler: stays 19f: acts on dead ground: visored final start in 1991/2. *O. Brennan* —

MERRY MASTER 9 br.g. Le Coq d'Or – Merry Missus (Bargello) [1992/3 c25m* c25g* c25s* c30sᶠ c25d² c33g⁵ c25m⁶ c33g²] leggy gelding: fairly useful chaser: successful in 3 handicaps at Wetherby in first half of c128 + —

season: good second to Run For Free in Stakis Scottish National at Ayr in April on last start: suited by a thorough test of stamina: has won on good to firm ground but best efforts with give: usually jumps soundly: front runner. *R. C. Armytage*

MERRY MATIC 10 gr.g. Pragmatic – Victor's Valley (Deep Run) [1992/3 16g 17s⁶ 17gᵖᵘ] good-bodied gelding: lightly-raced novice hurdler, poor form at best: sold 725 gns Ascot February Sales: tried blinkered. *F. Gray*   –

MERRY SCORPION 4 ch.g. Scorpio (FR) – Merry Jane (Rymer) [1992/3 F16s 16d³ 16d⁶] good-topped gelding with scope: first foal: dam, fairly useful hurdler, stayed 25f: still carrying plenty of condition when third in juvenile hurdle at Ayr in January: very stiff task next time: will be suited by further than 2m. *E. H. Owen jun*   81

MERRY WAND 8 ch.g. Merrymount – Royal Kate (Royal Trip) [1992/3 24vᵖᵘ c21vᵖᵘ] fifth foal: brother to winning hunter chaser Calder Bridge and to fair Irish hurdler Ballybrit Boy: dam half-sister to useful chaser Kenlis: no sign of ability. *R. Lee*   c– –

METAL OISEAU (IRE) 5 ch.g. Ela-Mana-Mou – Free Reserve (USA) (Tom Rolfe) [1992/3 16s⁴ 17s³ 20v⁴ 21s⁵ a24g 24v² 22v* 21g² 20d⁴ 21m 25f² 24v* 25g* 24g] sturdy gelding: fairly useful handicap hurdler: won at Fontwell in February and Towcester and Cheltenham in April: long way below best at Punchestown later in April: stays 25f: acts on any going: blinkered: tough. *J. S. Moore*   123

METTERNICH 8 b.g. Habitat – Sarah Siddons (FR) (Le Levanstell) [1992/3 16d 16s³ 16v⁴ a22g] sturdy gelding: half-brother to 2 good Flat winners and successful hurdler Star Quest (by Rainbow Quest): dam won Irish 1000 Guineas and Yorkshire Oaks: Irish NH Flat race winner: successful in 2 claimers on Flat in Britain in 1992: poor form in claiming hurdles and sellers: beaten long way out when tried at 2¾m: possibly unsuited by fibresand. *M. H. Tompkins*   77

MEZIARA 12 b.g. Dominion – Abertywi (Bounteous) [1992/3 c27gᵖᵘ] small, good-bodied gelding: handicap hurdler: failed to complete in 2 outings in steeplechases, but is a winning pointer: stays extremely well: acts on heavy going and possibly unsuited by top-of-the-ground: sometimes blinkered or visored: has looked a difficult ride. *Paul O. J. Hosgood*   c– –

George Duller Handicap Hurdle, Cheltenham—
Metal Oiseau jumps the last just behind the runner-up Hurricane Blake

MIAMI BEAR 7 b.g. Miami Springs – Belinda Bear (Ragstone) [1992/3 **c101** x
c20s³ c20dᵘʳ c25sᵘʳ c20gᶠ c25d c20dᶠ 17g] good-bodied gelding: fair –
hurdler/chaser at best: ran poorly last 2 completed outings: stays 2¾m:
acts on good to firm and soft ground: poor jumper over fences. *Mrs S. J.
Smith*

MIAMI IN SPRING 10 ch.g. Miami Springs – Fado (Ribero) [1992/3
17s] workmanlike gelding: fairly useful hurdler in 1991/2: wore tongue –
strap, never dangerous in November, only outing of 1992/3: better suited by
2½m than 2m: acts on dead and good to firm ground. *Miss B. Sanders*

MIAMI SPLASH 6 ch.g. Miami Springs – Splash of Red (Scallywag)
[1992/3 16d4 16g* 17v² 18s* 17s² 17s⁵ 16d* 17f⁵] big, good-bodied gelding: **121**
chasing type: fairly useful handicap hurdler: won at Wincanton in
November, Exeter in December and Wincanton in February, first 2 for
amateurs: stays 2¼m: acts on heavy going (ran badly on firm last start): has
turn of foot and is held up: jumps well. *P. J. Hobbs*

M I BABE 8 ch.m. Celtic Cone – Cover Your Money (Precipice Wood) **c106**
[1992/3 c16s*] lengthy mare: fair chaser: first race for a year when winning
handicap at Nottingham in January: best form at 2m: acts on good to firm and
soft ground: genuine: goes well fresh. *Mrs I. McKie*

MICHELLE CLARE 7 b.m. Good Times (ITY) – Paradise Island
(Artaius (USA)) [1992/3 18f 16fᵖᵘ] little promise in selling and novice –
hurdles. *P. Butler*

MICKEEN 6 b.g. Le Bavard (FR) – Autumn Queen (Menelek) [1992/3
F16s⁶ 20d 16g⁴ 17d 17gᵖᵘ 23m* 23m³] ex-Irish gelding: second live foal: **107**
half-brother to winning hurdler Snowy Autumn (by Deep Run): dam
unraced sister to several winners, including fairly useful staying hurdler
Woodford Prince: trained until after third outing by D. Weld: easily best
effort in Britain when winning novice hurdle at Stratford in April: stays 23f:
acts on good to firm ground. *Miss H. C. Knight*

MICKEY GOODMAN 6 b.g. Exhibitioner – Aria (Saintly Song) [1992/3
F16g F16g² F18g⁴ 17gᵖᵘ] fifth foal: brother to winning Irish hurdler Same As
That and half-brother to 1m winner African Opera (by Kampala): dam won
over middle distances in Ireland: showed ability in Irish NH Flat races but
none over hurdles: trained until after third outing by J. Queally: dead. *F.
Murphy*

MICK'S TYCOON (IRE) 5 b.g. Last Tycoon – Ladytown (English
Prince) [1992/3 19h⁶ 21f 25s⁵ 26d² 23s* 28v³ 23s* 21v² 21v³ 27m⁴ 20mᵖᵘ **93**
22g] small, leggy gelding: selling hurdler: bought in 4,000 gns after winning
handicaps at Folkestone in November and December: fair effort in
non-seller tenth start (trained until after then by M. Pipe): stays 3¼m:
probably acts on any going: usually blinkered or visored: held up: looks a
difficult ride. *T. P. McGovern*

MICRONOVA 7 ch.g. Homing – Tula Music (Patch) [1992/3 a20g⁴ a22g⁴
a24g² 24gᵖᵘ 24f 22fᵖᵘ] leggy, sparely-made gelding: poor novice hurdler: **69**
stays 3m: acts on firm ground and fibresand: usually blinkered in 1991/2. *T.
Thomson Jones*

MIDAS WELL 4 b.g. Midyan (USA) – Sobriquet (Roan Rocket) [1992/3
18f³ 18d⁵ 18f 18d 17g⁶ 17mᵖᵘ] leggy gelding: of little account at 2 yrs: poor **68**
plater over hurdles: blinkered third start: looked none too resolute on fifth.
G. A. Ham

MIDDAY SHOW (USA) 6 b.h. Roberto (USA) – Worlds Fair (USA)
(Our Hero (USA)) [1992/3 17m 18g* 20s³ 22d] compact horse: modest form **92**
over hurdles: won novice seller at Worcester (no bid) in September: ran
well next start but poorly on last (January): stays 2½m: acts on any ground:
sometimes wears tongue strap: best held up: occasionally looks
temperamental. *J. R. Jenkins*

MIDDLEHAM CASTLE 4 b.g. Lafontaine (USA) – Superfina (USA)
(Fluorescent Light (USA)) [1992/3 F16g] first foal: dam unraced: behind in

NH Flat race at Ayr in March: subsequently showed signs of ability on Flat: yet to race over hurdles. *M. Johnston*

MIDDLETON TINY   12 b.g. Pony Express – Rambling Rolls (Silver Cloud) [1992/3 c21m^{ur}] lightly-raced winning pointer, successful in May: tailed off when unseating rider eleventh in novice hunter chase at Newton Abbot earlier in month. *H. J. Widdicombe*   c–

MIDDLEWICK   8 b.g. Ballacashtal (CAN) – Thunder Bay (Canisbay) [1992/3 16f⁴ 17f*] sturdy gelding: modest hurdler: won handicap at Stratford in June: seems suited by around 2m: acts on any going. *S. Christian*   99

MIDFIELDER   7 ch.g. Formidable (USA) – Pampas Flower (Pampered King) [1992/3 16g⁵ c21d² c20g^{pu} c20s⁵ c21m⁶ 22s⁶ 22m] neat gelding: useful hurdler and fairly useful chaser at best: well below form after second outing in 1992/3: stays 2 1f: acts on firm and dead going. *P. J. Hobbs*   c107   ?
—

MIDLAND GLENN   9 ch.g. Midland Gayle – Dawn Dreamer (Avocat) [1992/3 25s⁴ 24d* 22sF 25g³ 26m] angular, sparely-made gelding: fairly useful hurdler: won handicap at Market Rasen in January: fair third at Nottingham in March, best effort subsequently: stays 3m: acts on any ground: usually jumps well. *J. L. Eyre*   126

MIDLAND LAD   8 br.g. Midland Gayle – Dikaro Lady (Dike (USA)) [1992/3 26s⁴ 28f* 24d⁵ 25d² 23g³ 22d³ 23s⁵ 28s² 25m² 28m* 25f 25s⁵ 25m] compact, good-quartered gelding: fair handicap hurdler: won at Sedgefield in September and Nottingham in March: thorough stayer: acts on any ground: blinkered eleventh outing. *J. L. Eyre*   114

MIDNIGHT CALLER   7 br.g. Callernish – Miss Pitpan (Pitpan) [1992/3 c21s* c24v* c24sF c27s*] workmanlike ex-Irish gelding: second foal: dam unraced sister to a winning jumper: maiden hurdler: successful in novice chase at Windsor and Lowndes Lambert December Novices' Chase at Lingfield in first half of season and handicap chase at Newton Abbot in April: suited by good test of stamina: acts on heavy going: front runner: jumps soundly in the main, though occasionally to the left: should progress. *S. E. Sherwood*   c112   p
—

MIDNIGHT FLOTILLA   7 b.m. Balinger – Foglet (Foggy Bell) [1992/3 22d³ 18s⁵ 22g⁶ 22m] sparely-made mare: poor novice hurdler: stays 2¾m: acts on good to firm ground: headstrong. *J. G. FitzGerald*   66

MIDNIGHT MADNESS   15 b.g. Genuine – Indian Madness (Indian Ruler) [1992/3 c24m³ c26f^{ur}] sparely-made gelding: one-time useful chaser: third in hunter chase at Exeter in May: was a thorough stayer: was possibly not at his best on heavy going, acted on any other: dead. *Mrs L. Bloomfield*   c78
—

MIDNIGHT MYSTIC   6 b.m. Black Minstrel – Magic Blaze (Carnival Night) [1992/3 16s^{pu} 21v^{pu}] of little account. *Dr P. Pritchard*   —

MIDNIGHT SECRET   9 b.m. Scallywag – Politely (Polic) [1992/3 16v 16g] seventh foal: half-sister to fair hurdler Bonny Gold (by Goldhill) and winning chaser Smiling Cavalier (by Cavo Doro) who both stayed 2½m: dam 1m winner on Flat: well beaten in novice hurdles at Worcester in April. *W. Clay*   —

MIDNIGHT STORY   8 gr.g. Pragmatic – Midnight Oil (Menelek) [1992/3 c17g⁶ c21s⁴] big, strong gelding: poor novice hurdler/chaser: easily better effort of season first outing: will stay at least 2½m: acts on dead going. *Miss S. L. Gallie*   c–
—

MIDNIGHT STRIKE (USA)   9 b.g. Topsider (USA) – Revels End (Welsh Pageant) [1992/3 18g⁶ 20m 22d 18m² 22d³ 20gF] rather sparely-made gelding: fair hurdler at best nowadays: refused only start over fences: stays 2¾m: acts on good to firm and dead going: usually blinkered: usually finds little, and isn't one to trust. *M. Williams*   c–   §
102   §

MIDNIGHT ZEBEE   12 b.g. Lindbergh – Wishful Miss (Three Wishes) [1992/3 c25s³ c25m^{pu} c21g^{ur}] has shown nothing in novice hunter chases: blinkered twice. *R. Green*   c–

MIDORI 5 b.m. State Diplomacy (USA) – Predora (Premonition) [1992/3 2 1s^pu] smallish, sparely-made mare: well beaten in novice hurdles. *Mrs A. Tomkinson* –

MIG 8 b.m. Sagaro – Lady Gaylord (Double Jump) [1992/3 c21s^pu] leggy, lengthy mare: winning hurdler/chaser: first race for 14 months, little show in handicap in January: stays 2¾m: form only on good going. *N. B. Mason* c– –

MIGHTY CHANCE 8 b.g. Furry Glen – Cant Pet (Cantab) [1992/3 24g^pu 16d] big gelding: novice hurdler/chaser: no form for long time: sold 1,600 gns Malvern May Sales. *F. Jordan* c– x

MIGHTY FROLIC 6 b.m. Oats – Mighty Nice (Vimadee) [1992/3 c20s^F c21s3 c25v^ur c24f* c23d3 c27g3] leggy, angular mare: no form in novice hurdles: won maiden chase at Lingfield in March: ran creditably on her other completed starts: stays well: probably acts on any going. *M. McCormack* c91 –

MIGHTY MARK 14 b.g. Rebel Prince – White Net (Monet) [1992/3 c25m* c28f4] tall gelding: one-time useful chaser: 30-length winner of hunter chase at Towcester in May: well beaten in valuable event in June: stays very well: acts on any going. *F. T. Walton* c105 –

MIGHTY MERC 5 ch.g. Shaab – Cornish Saffron (Spitsbergen) [1992/3 F16g] third foal: dam never ran: behind in NH Flat race at Ayr in March: yet to race over hurdles or fences. *Mrs B. K. Broad*

MIGHTY MICHAEL 7 br.g. Furry Glen – Swan of The Bride (Orchardist) [1992/3 c20f] big, workmanlike gelding: half-brother to winning jumpers Paka Lolo (by Menelek) and Golden Czar (by Deep Run): backward and green, soundly beaten in novice chase at Newbury in March. *A. P. Jarvis* c–

MIGHTY MOGUL 6 ch.g. Good Thyne (USA) – Deep Shine (Deep Run) [1992/3 17g* 21s* 17s* 20d* 16d* 22s^pu] 170

Two events over the last weekend in January shook the Champion Hurdle market. On the Saturday the ante-post favourite for the race, Mighty Mogul, was pulled up lame after the third last in the Wyko Power Transmission Hurdle at Cheltenham, and on the Sunday the second favourite, Halkopous, finished well beaten behind Royal Derbi at Leopardstown. As a result the two market leaders were taken out of the betting. Halkopous was eventually reinstated, but not Mighty Mogul. The latter had fractured his

Tote Silver Trophy (Handicap Hurdle), Chepstow—Mighty Mogul proves a handicap snip

Waterloo Hurdle, Haydock—
Mighty Mogul gets the better of Ambuscade in one of the bizarrest races of the season

off-fore knee, and after attempts were made to save him—he underwent surgery to pin the carpal joint—he was put down for humane reasons.

Prior to the accident, after he'd put up a top-class performance to win the BonusPrint Christmas Hurdle at Kempton, Mighty Mogul stood out on his own as short as 5/2 for the Champion Hurdle. He'd been having a tremendous season. He began it in a new stable, very much in the shadow of his new stable-companion Carobee—who eventually missed the whole of the season through injury. Mighty Mogul showed very useful form as a lightly-raced novice in 1991/2 for Mrs Pitman but on his final start was beaten easily by Carobee in the Swish Hurdle at Chepstow, and to begin with he was aimed at handicap hurdles by Nicholson. However, in the second of them, the valuable and well-contested Tote Silver Trophy at Chepstow in November, he followed up a Newbury win in a manner that pointed to his being a good-class animal in the making, quickening clear on the bridle from three out before being eased right up on the flat with any amount in hand of the pursuing Petosku and Dara Doone. Three weeks later, dropped back half a mile and upgraded considerably in the BonusPrint Gerry Feilden Hurdle at Newbury, he came through at the chief expense of the favourite Staunch Friend, showing admirable resolution. So much had Mighty Mogul improved by now that the Waterloo Hurdle at Haydock in December looked a formality with Ambuscade and Bollin William his only significant rivals in a field of four. He duly landed the odds with a great deal to spare in farcical circumstances: the runners missed out the second hurdle, which had been dolled off by mistake, and covered about a mile before returning to jump it and resume their journey after being allowed a short breather. Haydock wasn't much of a preparation for a race like the Christmas Hurdle, and it remained to be seen how Mighty Mogul would cope with a group of established hurdlers over a sharp two miles. At times he hadn't been particularly fluent in his last two races, and there were plenty who expected Granville Again to find him out. Granville Again started favourite at 11/10; Mighty Mogul was second favourite at 3/1, ahead

BonusPrint Christmas Hurdle, Kempton—
Mighty Mogul's blunder at the last is the only blot on a tremendous performance

of Oh So Risky (7/1), Gran Alba (9/1), Flown (10/1), Kribensis (12/1), King Credo (33/1) and Regent Lad (200/1). Mighty Mogul's performance was thoroughly convincing although he made a bad mistake at the last. The race was all over bar a fall some way from home. He went on from the front-running Flown three out, having travelled smoothly in a prominent position from the start, and readily kept hold of his lead in the straight, shrugging off his blunder to go on to win by five lengths and three from Flown and the favourite. The very useful handicapper King Credo ran well to come out best of the rest, another ten lengths back. This was undoubtedly the best hurdle race run in the first half of the season, and it was run in a good time under the conditions, too. To underline the scale of Mighty Mogul's loss, by the end of the second half no horse had shown better form, not even Granville Again or Morley Street.

Mighty Mogul (ch.g. 1987)	Good Thyne (USA) (br 1977)	Herbager (b 1956)	Vandale II
			Flagette
		Foreseer (b 1969)	Round Table
			Regal Gleam
	Deep Shine (b 1974)	Deep Run (ch 1966)	Pampered King
			Trial By Fire
		Shinaro (br 1967)	Straight Deal
			Valley of Roses

Mighty Mogul, bought by Mrs Pitman as an unbroken three-year-old at the Derby Sale, was by the stayer Good Thyne out of a mare with good jumping credentials. The mare Deep Shine was bred to win a hurdle race, and she obliged over two miles in modest company at Limerick Junction as a four-year-old, having previously lost a similar contest at Roscommon on a disqualification. Her dam produced several other winners, including Deep Shine's brother, the useful hurdler Marshell Key, and the 1982 Waterford Crystal Supreme Novices' Hurdle winner Miller Hill. Mighty Mogul is not

Deep Shine's only winner. The first of her four earlier foals, Platonic Affair (by Kemal), was successful on the Flat in Ireland as a six-year-old and has since brought his total of victories over hurdles to six. A more recent foal, a sister to Mighty Mogul called Deep Thyne, won a National Hunt Flat race at Naas in March. Mighty Mogul, a lengthy, chasing type, was effective at distances from two miles to twenty-one furlongs. He acted well on soft going. *D. Nicholson*

MIGHTY RANDOLPH   5 ch.g. Electric – Lettuce (So Blessed) [1992/3 2 1s⁵ 20f⁴ 18d⁵ 2 1s⁶ 24vᵖᵘ 17mᵖᵘ] rather unfurnished gelding: half-brother to Lincoln Handicap and Royal Hunt Cup winner Mighty Fly and fair chaser Mighty Falcon (both by Comedy Star) and Derby third Mighty Flutter (by Rolfe): dam half-sister to Rubstic and Kildimo: poor novice hurdler: should be suited by further than 2¼m: blinkered fifth outing. *R. H. Alner*   77

MIINNEHOMA   10 b. or br.g. Kambalda – Mrs Cairns (Choral Society)   c 152
[1992/3 c24v² c25s² c30s³ c26sᵖᵘ]   –

One of the season's biggest certainties was that Martin Pipe would be leading trainer for the fifth successive time, equalling the post-war feat of Fred Winter who achieved five of his eight championships in successive seasons from 1970/1. But even the powerful Pipe stable had its share of disappointments, one of the biggest being the failure of Miinnehoma to develop into a Gold Cup horse. Miinnehoma had proved himself the best staying novice chaser of 1991/2 with a hard-fought victory over Bradbury Star in the Sun Alliance Chase at the Festival meeting; Run For Free was ten lengths back in third and the subsequent Scottish National winner Captain Dibble fifth in a vintage field in which seven of the eighteen starters were unbeaten in their completed outings over fences, including Miinnehoma, Bradbury Star and Run For Free. Miinnehoma was beaten twelve lengths by Run For Free in the Rehearsal Chase at Chepstow on his reappearance, looking unlikely from some way out to land the odds. The pair reproduced their running three weeks later in the Coral Welsh National in similar conditions on the same course, Miinnehoma finishing third to Run For Free in an historic 1,2,3,4 finish for Pipe-trained runners. Miinnehoma's jumping wasn't so fluent as it might have been in his second season over fences and he gave a particularly erratic display in the SGB Handicap Chase at Ascot on his outing between the Rehearsal Chase and the Welsh National. Miinnehoma lost ground at almost every fence that day and was hanging markedly left from six out, running particularly wide after three out; Scudamore was at his strongest and most determined as Miinnehoma stayed on well for second to Captain Dibble, the pair twenty lengths clear. Miinnehoma wasn't seen out after being pulled up lame—reportedly struck into—in the Timeform Hall of Fame Chase at Cheltenham in January on his only other start.

		Right Royal V	Owen Tudor
	Kambalda	(br 1958)	Bastia
	(b 1970)	Opencast	Mossborough
Miinnehoma		(br 1957)	Coal Board
(b. or br.g. 1983)		Choral Society	Pinza
	Mrs Cairns	(b 1959)	Tessa Gillian
	(b or br 1974)	Arctic Mint	Arctic Slave
		(b 1962)	Ballinagre Walk

The leggy, sparely-made Miinnehoma has had relatively little racing for a ten-year-old. Two Irish point-to-points and three National Hunt Flat races was the sum of his racing experience before he joined his present stable in 1989/90. He has run only twelve times in four seasons with Pipe, though he missed the whole of his second one through injury. Miinnehoma is a thorough stayer and is suited by give in the ground and forcing tactics. Following his somewhat wayward display in the SGB Handicap Chase—one which tended to suggest, among other things, that he might be best on a left-handed track—Miinnehoma was equipped with a visor in the Welsh National and wore blinkers on his final start. *M. C. Pipe*

MIKES BOYS   9 ch.g. Record Run – Our Denise (Bend A Bow (USA))   c–
[1992/3 c 16sᵖᵘ] big, angular gelding: of little account. *P. Butler*   –

MILAN FAIR 9 b.g. Mill Reef (USA) – Fairweather Friend (USA) (Forli (ARG)) [1992/3 18g^{pu} 17m 17g^5 16d^6 16m^5] lengthy gelding: poor plater over hurdles: may prove best over sharp 2m. *Miss K. M. George*   62

MILBIRD 12 ch.g. Milford – Gulf Bird (Gulf Pearl) [1992/3 c26d^{pu} c26m^6] sturdy gelding: has been tubed: winning hunter chaser: no form since 1991: stays 3¼m: acts on good to firm and dead going. *Denis McCarthy*   c–

MILCLERE 7 ch.m. Milford – Great Lass (Vaigly Great) [1992/3 21g^3 18g] angular mare: poor novice hurdler, lightly raced: tried blinkered. *J. Wharton*   –

MILFORD QUAY 10 ch.h. Milford – Miss Quay (Quayside) [1992/3 c21d^2 c21d^F c20v* c21v^F c21d^2 c21v^F c20g^5 c20d* c20d^2 c21m^{pu}] sparely-made horse: very useful hurdler/chaser at his best: won minor events over fences at Chepstow in December and February: was suited by around 2½m and give in the ground: front runner: sometimes unruly at start: prone to bad mistakes: dead. *M. C. Pipe*   c134 –

MILITARY ACTION (IRE) 5 b.g. Venetian Gate – Ridansky (Stetchworth (USA)) [1992/3 2 1m^{pu} 17s 23d] rangy gelding: has scope: third foal: dam placed over 5f at 2 yrs in Ireland: trained by W. A. Stephenson first outing: no form in novice hurdles. *J. I. A. Charlton*   –

MILITARY EXPRESS 10 b.g. Pony Express – Millstar (Military) [1992/3 17d^4 22v^6 a20g] rather sparely-made gelding: poor novice hurdler: tailed off on equitrack last start. *L. C. Corbett*   69

MILITARY HONOUR 8 b.g. Shirley Heights – Princess Tiara (Crowned Prince (USA)) [1992/3 c2 1g^{pu} c21d^4 c17v* c17s^5 c17d^F 21s^6 c17d c20f^4 c16g^5 c21s^3] rather sparely-made gelding: winning hurdler: successful in novice chase at Hexham in November: ran creditably most starts afterwards: effective at 2m when conditions are testing and should stay 3m: usually blinkered. *J. E. Swiers*   c84 –

MILITARY SECRET 7 ch.g. Tug of War – Leeann (Pitpan) [1992/3 c23s^F c25g^2 c25d* c25d^4] tall, close-coupled gelding: moderate hurdler: c94 –

Arlington Premier Series Chase (Qualifier), Chepstow—
Milford Quay is not hard pressed to prevail; Grange Brake is remounted after falling

landed the odds in novice chase at Hexham in November: also ran creditably on both other completed starts: sold 3,200 gns in May: suited by good test of stamina: acts on firm and dead going. *W. A. Stephenson*

MILITARY TWO STEP   11 b.g. Rarity – Jasusa (Cantab) [1992/3 c24f3 c28fpu] smallish gelding: novice hurdler: fair pointer: third in hunter chase at Huntingdon in May: stays 3m: acts on firm ground, possibly unsuited by very soft. *Mrs Teresa Elwell*   **c88 –**

MILIYEL   4 ch.f. Rousillon (USA) – Amalee (Troy) [1992/3 17g5 17g6 16g5 16s2 16g* 18g2 18g* 17g3 18g2 16f2 16m2 17g*] workmanlike filly: modest hurdler: won claimer at Edinburgh in February and selling handicaps at Sedgefield (bought in 5,400 gns) in March and Fakenham (bought in 3,600 gns) in May: claimed out £4,251 in between first 2 wins: will stay beyond 2¼m: suited by give in the ground and acts on soft: won over 17f on Flat in July. *Miss Gay Kelleway*   **97**

MILLADOR   4 b.f. Glint of Gold – Tsar's Bride (Song) [1992/3 16m2 18m* 16m* 16g5 17v 17d4 16f5] good-topped filly: poor middle-distance staying maiden on Flat: won juvenile hurdles at Market Rasen and Wetherby early in season: creditable efforts in selling handicaps last 2 starts: should stay 2½m: acts on firm and dead ground: visored fifth outing. *M. H. Tompkins*   **107**

MILL BURN   4 ch.g. Precocious – Northern Ballerina (Dance In Time (CAN)) [1992/3 16d6 17g6] leggy gelding: maiden on Flat: retained 700 gns Doncaster June (1992) Sales: set plenty to do both outings over hurdles, doing well to finish sixth of 19 after being badly hampered in Doncaster seller in December on second start: one to keep an eye on. *I. Campbell*   **76 p**

MILL DE LEASE   8 b.g. Milford – Melting Snows (High Top) [1992/3 22d6 20gpu 22m6 21d6 22s6 22g] leggy, sparely-made gelding: modest selling hurdler: stays 2½m well: acts on any going. *J. Dooler*   **85**

MILLEFIORI   4 b.f. Battle Hymn – Lane Patrol (Hopton Lane) [1992/3 17fpu] appears to be of little account on Flat: tailed off when pulled up in juvenile selling hurdle at Huntingdon in September. *K. S. Bridgwater*   **–**

MILLIE BELLE   7 ch.m. Milford – Charter Belle (Runnymede) [1992/3 a18g a22g c18m2 c19mpu c21f3 c27g2 c21g3 c25gpu c27f5] leggy mare: winning hurdler: placed in novice chases, showing modest form at best: effective at around 2½m and stays well: acts on firm ground: visored last 2 outings, blinkered previous 2: sometimes looks reluctant. *Miss B. Sanders*   **c86 –**

MILLIES OWN   6 ch.g. Deep Run – The Cardy (Chou Chin Chow) [1992/3 16s 16s4 17d 16gur 16dpu] robust gelding: poor form in novice hurdles. *S. Mellor*   **–**

MILLIE (USA)   5 ch.m. Master Willie – La Zonga (USA) (Run The Gantlet (USA)) [1992/3 16g5 22d] small, leggy mare: poor novice hurdler: stays 2½m: acts on equitrack. *G. Fleming*   **–**

MILLROUS   5 b.m. Rousillon (USA) – Brookfield Miss (Welsh Pageant) [1992/3 16v* 17v4 20d* 16m* 17d5 17g 17f3] lengthy mare: half-sister to fair staying hurdler Cairncastle (by Ardross): poor maiden on Flat when trained by R. Guest: won selling hurdles at Towcester (bought in 5,000 gns), Exeter (novices, no bid) and Warwick (bought in 3,400 gns) in 1992/3, 2 of them for conditional jockeys: stays 2½m: acts on good to firm and heavy going: blinkered last 4 outings: irresolute. *M. C. Pipe*   **86 §**

MILLTOWN BRIDGE   9 b.g. Pitpan – Just Killiney (Bargello) [1992/3 c16mur] tall gelding: of little account. *R. J. Hodges*   **c– –**

MILLY BLACK (IRE)   5 b.m. Double Schwartz – Milly Lass (FR) (Bold Lad (USA)) [1992/3 18s*] neat mare: sold out of J. Harris' stable 1,050 gns Ascot September Sales: showed improved form to win novice selling hurdle at Exeter in January (bought in 4,300 gns): should stay beyond 2¼m: evidently suited by soft going. *J. Akehurst*   **89**

MILPARSHOON   6 b.m. Green Shoon – Milparinka (King's Equity) [1992/3 20v2 20vpu 20vpu 18v4] sparely-made mare: poor novice selling hurdler. *J. O'Donoghue*   **63**

MILS MIJ   8 br.g. Slim Jim – Katie Grey (Pongee) [1992/3 25g 25g³ 20s³ 21s⁶ c16g² c20dᶠ c25d⁴] compact gelding: carries plenty of condition: fairly useful hurdler nowadays: shaped promisingly first 2 starts over fences and would have won valuable Dipper Novices' Chase at Newcastle in January but for falling 2 out: ran poorly in similar event at Ayr later in month, and wasn't seen out again: probably stays 25f: acts on any going: usually amateur ridden over hurdles. *J. Hurst*   c122 ?
129

MILTON BRYAN   8 ch.g. Red Sunset – Priddy Moun (Kalamoun) [1992/3 c2 1vᵖᵘ a24g a22g⁵ a22gᶠ 22g 22fᵖᵘ] smallish, plain gelding: no form over hurdles for a long time: once-raced over fences: stays 2½m: acts on any going: tried blinkered. *R. Voorspuy*   c–
–

MILTON ROOMS (IRE)   4 ch.c. Where To Dance (USA) – Raga Rine (Raga Navarro (ITY)) [1992/3 16sᶠ 16sᵖᵘ 16s 16d 16g²] stocky colt: maiden on Flat for C. Booth: easily best effort over hurdles when second in seller at Catterick in March: likely to prove best at 2m: visored third start. *D. T. Garraton*   81

MILZIG (USA)   4 b.c. Ziggy's Boy (USA) – Legume (USA) (Northern Baby (CAN)) [1992/3 17g² 17d² 17v⁵] good-bodied colt: quite useful middle-distance performer on Flat: fair form in juvenile hurdles: yet to race on top-of-the-ground over hurdles (acts on good to firm on Flat): blinkered second start. *D. R. C. Elsworth*   105

MINDY (IRE)   5 b.g. Salmon Leap (USA) – Malija (FR) (Malicious) [1992/3 18g³ 16s⁶ 17vᵖᵘ] workmanlike gelding: poor selling hurdler: acts on good to firm and soft going: usually blinkered or visored. *G. Stickland*   72

MINELLA MAN   6 b.g. The Parson – Poula Scawla (Pollerton) [1992/3 F16s* F16s* F16d² 20s* 20v* 22d* 20d*]   133 p

Minella Man's first season came to a close on March 17th, not as might have been expected at Cheltenham, where he'd have been a leading contender for the Sun Alliance Novices' Hurdle, but at Leopardstown in the Castrol GTX3 Hurdle. The going at Cheltenham was considered too firm for Minella Man, who'd raced only on ground softer than good in Ireland. Under more familiar conditions at Leopardstown, the progressive Minella Man retained his unbeaten record over hurdles and put up a useful performance in winning by a length from Rogerdor. Minella Man's earlier wins over hurdles had come in qualifiers in the I.N.H. Stallion Owners Novice Hurdle Series, a series designed for future chasers, at Punchestown and Tipperary; and in the Final itself at Navan where he had his five rivals well strung out at the end of two and three quarter miles. As in his other races, all at two and a half miles, Minella Man raced up with the pace at Navan and stayed on strongly under pressure. He'll prove well suited by a thorough test of stamina, something which could have been predicted from his pedigree.

		Aureole	Hyperion
	The Parson	(ch 1950)	Angelola
	(b 1968)	Bracey Bridge	Chanteur II
Minella Man		(b 1962)	Rutherford Bridge
(b.g. 1987)		Pollerton	Rarity
	Poula Scawla	(b 1974)	Nilie
	(b or br 1981)	Chihuahua	Mustang
		(b 1963)	St Bride

Minella Man's sire The Parson, who died in 1990, is very much an influence for stamina and his numerous winners include Trapper John and Shuil Ar Aghaidh, both of whom have won the Stayers' Hurdle at Cheltenham. The dam Poula Scawla is an unraced half-sister to five winning jumpers, notably the useful hurdler/chaser Mac's Chariot, winner of the Lloyds Bank Champion Novice Hurdle at Cheltenham in 1977. The grandam Chihuahua, also unraced, is a sister to three winning jumpers, including the top-class hunter chaser Poulakerry. Minella Man is the third foal of Poula Scawla. Her first two foals Maul-More and Granary Grain, both by Deep Run, have also won over hurdles, the latter at up to three miles. The only other produce of Poula Scawla, who died in 1991, is Minella Man's five-year-old brother Monkton. He showed some promise on his debut when seventh of twenty-three in a National Hunt Flat race at Cheltenham in April. But for being affected by a virus Minella Man would have begun his racing career in point-to-points in 1992. As it was he made his debut in a National Hunt Flat race at Tipperary in October, justifying favouritism that day and also at Fairyhouse on his next start. Minella Man will be tackling fences next, and he seems sure to prove a formidable opponent in novice events when stamina is at a premium. *Mrs A. M. O'Brien, Ireland*

MINER JACKSON 6 b.g. Miner's Lamp – London Daisy VII (Pedigree Unknown) [1992/3 16g 23dF 21v* 23d5 25d4 25s] smallish, angular gelding: won novice hurdle at Hexham in November: creditable fourth at Ayr in January, easily best effort afterwards: stays 25f: acts on heavy going. *M. D. Hammond*   97

MINERS REST 5 b.m. Sula Bula – Miners Lodge (Eborneezer) [1992/3 16g 16f4 22d 20m] compact mare: second foal: dam fairly useful hurdler at up to 21f: poor novice hurdler: form only at 2m: acts on firm ground. *P. J. Hobbs*   72

MINE'S AN ACE (NZ) 6 br.g. Full On Aces (AUS) – Endure (NZ) (Causeur) [1992/3 17d* 17g3 18m3 22spu 17d2 16d 17d3 17m* 18g2] leggy gelding: won novice hurdles at Newton Abbot in September and March (handicap): good second in novice handicap at Exeter later in March: stays 2¼m well: acts on dead and good to firm ground, ran poorly on soft. *D. H. Barons*   95

MING BLUE 4 ch.f. Primo Dominie – Burnt Amber (Balidar) [1992/3 17d6 18spu 17g3 17m3 22s 18m2 22m4] sturdy filly: plating-class maiden on Flat (sold out of P. Makin's stable 950 gns Newmarket Autumn Sales) and over hurdles (best efforts at up to 2¼m on a sound surface). *J. M. Bradley*   60

MINGUS (USA) 6 b.g. The Minstrel (CAN) – Sylph (USA) (Alleged (USA)) [1992/3 a16g4 22m* 21g5] poor middle-distance stayer on Flat: sold out of Mrs J. Ramsden's stable 7,600 gns Newmarket Autumn Sales: won novice hurdle at Sedgefield in May: ran poorly later in month: stays 2¾m: acts on good to firm ground and fibresand. *R. F. Fisher*   84

MINSTRALS BOYO 6 ch.g. Black Minstrel – Sweater Girl (Blue Cashmere) [1992/3 aF16g6 F17m] rather plain gelding: third foal: dam won over 1½m: well beaten in NH Flat races: yet to race over hurdles or fences. *F. Sheridan*

MINT FRESH 6 b.g. Sunley Builds – Coin All (All Tan) [1992/3 c21mur] good-topped gelding: of little account over hurdles: failed to complete in points and novice chase. *C. James*   c– –

MINT-MASTER 8 ch.g. Deep Run – Bold Penny (Beau Chapeau) [1992/3 c19g5 c25dF c21d3 c28d c25d] sturdy gelding: poor chaser: no worthwhile form in 1992/3: sold 2,100 gns Ascot May Sales: stays 3m: acts on good to firm going: blinkered third start. *Mrs I. McKie*   c– –

MINTY MUNCHER 5 b.m. Idiot's Delight – By The Lake (Tyrant (USA)) [1992/3 17d 25gF] leggy, unfurnished mare: fourth foal: half-sister to poor animal Southend Flutter (by Beldale Flutter): dam poor staying maiden: little sign of ability in novice hurdles. *N. B. Mason*   –

MIRACLE MAN 5 b.g. Kemal (FR) – Knockeevan Girl (Tarqogan) [1992/3 F17g 17g4 22mF] tall, leggy gelding: has scope: second foal: dam lightly-raced sister to a winning jumper and half-sister to smart chaser Father Delaney: showed promise in novice hurdle at Sandown in February: would have won similar event at Newton Abbot following month but for falling last: likely to prove suited by a test of stamina: sure to win an ordinary novice hurdle. *C. Weedon*   92 p

MIRAGE OF WINDSOR (IRE) 5 b.g. Bulldozer – Lucky Favour (Ballyciptic) [1992/3 16sur 17d 20fpu] sturdy gelding: brother to winning hurdler/chaser Guildway and winning staying hurdler Lion of Vienna: dam, half-sister to an Irish NH Flat race winner, poor Irish maiden: showed a   75

little ability in novice hurdle at Huntingdon in January: stiff task over 2½m on firm ground only subsequent start (should stay trip). *B. J. Curley*

MIRAMAC 12 br.g. Relkino – Magical (Aggressor) [1992/3 c22d6 24s5 c18s3 c17vpu c21s6 c27m4 22s5 27d* 21dpu] compact, sturdy gelding: modest hurdler nowadays: attracted no bid after winning selling handicap at Newton Abbot in April: modest form at best over fences (poor jumper): stays well: probably acts on any going: has run well visored. *R. G. Frost*   c85 x / 93

MIRANDINHA 9 ch.g. Nicholas Bill – Matsui (Falcon) [1992/3 c26m5] workmanlike gelding: winning hurdler/chaser: fairly useful pointer nowadays: tailed off in hunter chase at Cheltenham in May: stays 2¾m: acts on dead going: tried blinkered. *Ken James*   c– / –

MISCHIEVOUS GIRL 5 ch.m. Funny Man – Marnie's Girl (Crooner) [1992/3 F14g] unfurnished mare: third foal: half-sister to 2 poor animals: dam placed in selling hurdles: well beaten in NH Flat race at Market Rasen in April: yet to race over hurdles or fences. *R. Tate*

MISHRIF 11 b.g. Sonnen Gold – Blue Queen (Majority Blue) [1992/3 c24v6] angular gelding: winning hunter chaser: was usually blinkered over hurdles, once over fences: dead. *Mrs L. P. Baker*   c– / –

MISHY'S STAR 11 b.m. Balliol – Conte Bleu (Jan Ekels) [1992/3 22d 22s4 22d4 28g5 24v 17v4 22s 18g 17s5 22v3 25g6 c21dpu] tall mare: bad novice hurdler/chaser: often blinkered: sometimes wears tongue strap: looks a difficult ride. *A. M. Forte*   c– § / – §

MISS BOBBY BENNETT 6 b.m. Kings Lake (USA) – Karen Lee M (USA) (Roman Line) [1992/3 21d 20dur 17vpu] smallish, leggy mare: useful novice hurdler in 1991/2: lost her enthusiasm in 1992/3 and is best left alone: blinkered once. *M. C. Pipe*   – §

MISS BROWN 5 b.m. Relkino – Gadabout (Galivanter) [1992/3 F17g] fifth foal: half-sister to 2 poor animals by Rymer: dam poor novice hurdler: mid-division in NH Flat race at Doncaster in December: yet to race over hurdles or fences. *E. H. Owen jun*

MISS CAPULET 6 b.m. Commanche Run – Judy Burton (Mummy's Pet) [1992/3 20m6 c18gF c17dur 21d 22d* 20s 25v* 25v3 23d] angular mare: modest form over hurdles: won novice events at Nottingham in November and Uttoxeter (handicap) in December: ran poorly last start: hasn't got beyond the fourth over fences: stays 25f: acts on good to firm and heavy going: successful only when blinkered. *T. W. Donnelly*   c– / 87

MISS CONSTRUE 6 b.m. Rymer – Miss Behave (Don't Look) [1992/3 c22gF] sturdy mare: tailed off over hurdles: poor form when winning a point in February: behind when falling thirteenth in hunter chase at Fakenham in March. *Capt. W. H. Bulwer-Long*   c– / –

MISS CORVARO 6 b.m. Corvaro (USA) – Secret Isle (USA) (Voluntario III) [1992/3 20s] rather leggy mare: plating-class novice hurdler: form only at 2m: acts on soft ground. *J. S. Wainwright*

MISS CRESTA 4 b.f. Master Willie – Sweet Snow (USA) (Lyphard (USA)) [1992/3 16vpu 18dpu 17dpu 16gF] small, plain filly: poor maiden on Flat: sold out of H. Candy's stable 1,100 gns Newmarket Autumn Sales: seems of little account over hurdles. *D. R. Wellicome*

MISS DOODY 4 b.f. Gorytus (USA) – Kittycatoo Katango (USA) (Verbatim (USA)) [1992/3 17v2 16s6 17d4] smallish filly: modest form, stays 1¼m, on Flat: second in juvenile hurdle at Plumpton in November: off course 3 months subsequently and failed to reproduce that form: acts on heavy going: sketchy jumper. *M. R. Channon*   93

MISS EMO 6 b.m. Fine Blade (USA) – Weavers Vision (Weavers' Hall) [1992/3 21mF 21gpu] close-coupled mare: well beaten over hurdles: blinkered last start. *Mrs S. C. Bradburne*   –

MISS ENRICO 7 b.m. Don Enrico (USA) – Mill Miss (Typhoon) [1992/3 c23gpu c26mur 22g 22gur 22dpu] leggy mare: no sign of ability over hurdles   c– / –

or in steeplechases: won a point in May: sold 3,000 gns Doncaster June Sales. *C. L. Popham*

MISS EQUILIA (USA) 7 ch.m. Crystal Glitters (USA) – Warwara (Roan Rocket) [1992/3 20d* 17g⁶ a16g⁶ 17d* 16f² 17g² 17f²] small, sparely-made mare: won claiming hurdle at Hereford in February and novice hurdle at Newton Abbot in May: creditable second on last 3 outings, including in sellers: stays 2½m: acts on firm and dead ground: none too easy a ride and probably suited by waiting tactics. *M. C. Pipe*   98

MISS FERN 8 b.m. Cruise Missile – Fernshaw (Country Retreat) [1992/3 c24gᶠ c26g* c25v³ c24d³ c25v⁵ c24v³ c25s c26g⁵ c26dᵖᵘ c21g⁴ c24g² c23m⁵] leggy, sparely-made mare: moderate handicap chaser: won at Hereford in November: below form fifth to tenth starts: stays 3¼m: probably acts on any going. *R. Dickin*   c96

MISS GROSSE NEZ (IRE) 4 b.f. Cyrano de Bergerac – Fait Dodo (On Your Mark) [1992/3 17m 18g⁴] plating-class maiden on Flat: no worthwhile form in novice hurdles, one a seller. *C. W. Thornton*   –

MISS HYDE (USA) 4 br.f. Procida (USA) – Little Niece (Great Nephew) [1992/3 16g* 16d³ 22d⁶ 18g] sparely-made filly: half-sister to winning hurdler Straw Blade (by Final Straw): quite modest on Flat (usually visored), stays 1¼m: won juvenile hurdle at Windsor in November: good third next start, but poor efforts final 2, visored when running a moody race last time: acts on dead ground. *J. A. Glover*   94 §

MISS JEDD 6 gr.m. Scallywag – Leckywil (Menelek) [1992/3 20gᵖᵘ 20s⁶] workmanlike mare: more sign of temperament than ability over hurdles. *W. G. Young*   – §

MISS KEIRA 5 ch.m. Cruise Missile – Keira (Keren) [1992/3 F17s 23s⁶ 26s⁶] angular mare: second foal: dam fair middle-distance handicapper on Flat: tailed off in mid-season novice hurdles. *R. Paisley*   –

MISS LAWN (FR) 5 ch.m. Lashkari – Miss Jonquiere (FR) (Dictus (FR)) [1992/3 a22g⁴] angular mare: fair winning form over hurdles in 1991/2: well beaten in March, only outing of 1992/3: stays 2½m: acts well on fibresand. *D. Burchell*   –

MISS MAC 6 ch.m. Smackover – Stewart's Rise (Good Bond) [1992/3 17d 16d 17sᵖᵘ] leggy, lightly-made mare: bad plater on Flat: behind in novice hurdles. *E. J. Alston*   –

MISS MARIGOLD 4 b.f. Norwick (USA) – Kiki Star (Some Hand) [1992/3 17f 17d⁵ 17s³ 18s³ 16g⁴ 17m* 18gᵘʳ 17mʳᵗʳ] tall, leggy, angular filly: well beaten on Flat: best effort over hurdles when wide-margin winner of juvenile fillies seller at Wolverhampton (no bid) in March: refused to race last outing: acts on good to firm going. *R. J. Hodges*   81 §

MISS MARULA 6 br.m. Ascendant – Jacaranda (Marcus Superbus) [1992/3 22dʳᵗʳ 22sᵖᵘ] small mare: second foal: dam lightly-raced maiden pointer: tailed off when pulled up in novice hurdle in October: refused to race previous start. *J. E. Collinson*   – §

MISS MATTERS 6 b.m. Strong Gale – Miss Filbert (Compensation) [1992/3 16gᵘʳ 16d⁶] no worthwhile form in 3 races over hurdles: blinkered on debut: tried to refuse and unseated rider third first outing in 1992/3. *Miss T. A. White*   –

MISS MELBURY 8 gr.m. Baron Blakeney – Sunny Breeze (Roi Soleil) [1992/3 18g] angular mare: no sign of ability in points or over hurdles. *D. C. Jermy*   –

MISS MOODY 7 ch.m. Jalmood (USA) – Ice Galaxie (USA) (Icecapade (USA)) [1992/3 c16gᵖᵘ a16g 17mᵖᵘ] workmanlike mare: won novice claiming hurdle early in 1991/2: has run poorly since: little show in claimer on chasing debut. *J. M. Bradley*   c–

MISS MOONBEAM 4 ch.f. Little Wolf – Smallwood Twilight (Twilight Alley) [1992/3 aF16g⁵ 22g] fourth foal: dam never ran: no sign of ability in NH Flat race in February or novice hurdle following month. *M. W. Easterby*   –

MISS NICHOLAS 8 b.m. Old Jocus – Sweet Orchid (Border Chief) [1992/3 c21gpu] poor maiden pointer: tailed off when pulled up in a maiden hunter chase in March. *M. Sams*

c–

MISS NOSEY OATS 5 b.m. Oats – Miss Poker Face (Raise You Ten) [1992/3 F17s] sister to winning hurdler/staying chaser Master Oats and half-sister to 2 other winners: dam fairly useful hurdler: behind in NH Flat race at Huntingdon in December: yet to race over hurdles or fences. *R. Curtis*

MISS PRECOCIOUS 5 b.m. Precocious – Hissy Missy (Bold Lad (IRE)) [1992/3 16g5] smallish, stocky mare: little form over sprint distances on Flat: pulled hard when tailed-off last of 5 finishers in mares novice hurdle at Warwick in March. *D. Shaw*

–

MISS SARAHSUE 7 br.m. Van Der Linden (FR) – Blakesware Dancer (Dance In Time (CAN)) [1992/3 20f3] lengthy mare: probably of no account on Flat: bad last of 3 in novice hurdle at Plumpton in August. *J. E. Long*

–

MISS SCHWARTZKOPF 4 ch.f. War Hero – Miss Metro (Upper Case (USA)) [1992/3 17s4] second foal: dam winning hurdler: poor maiden at 2 yrs: tailed off in juvenile hurdle at Newton Abbot in August. *C. L. Popham*

–

MISS SHAW 7 b.m. Cruise Missile – Fernshaw (Country Retreat) [1992/3 c18m3 c20s3 c20d3 21s3 21v6 c21sF c19d4 c32mur 24g5] lengthy, rather sparely-made mare: modest novice hurdler/chaser: easily best efforts on second, fourth and seventh starts in 1992/3: effective at 2½m and should stay 3m: acts on soft ground. *E. H. Owen jun*

c84
84

MISS SIMONE 7 b.m. Ile de Bourbon (USA) – Nanga Parbat (Mill Reef (USA)) [1992/3 16m5 17g3 17s* 22d* 19f2 22g6 20mpu 23m2 20d* 21s4 20v6 25spu 22m2] sparely-made mare: improved hurdler and won novice events at Newton Abbot (2) and Hereford in first half of season: good second in novice handicap at Cheltenham in April: stays 2¾m: probably acts on any going: usually blinkered (wasn't last 2 starts): sometimes looks most ungenuine. *N. A. Twiston-Davies*

92 §

MISS SOUTER 4 b.f. Sulaafah (USA) – Glenn's Slipper (Furry Glen) [1992/3 17d6 16d4 17f5 17f2 17v3 17m2 17fur] leggy filly: poor maiden on Flat: modest form over hurdles: races only at around 2m: acts on firm and dead going, below form on heavy. *H. S. Howe*

86

MISS TIMBER TOPPER 9 b.m. Liberated – Tacitina (Tacitus) [1992/3 c24gpu 26spu c24gF c26sF a22gpu 24m6] sparely-made mare: poor hurdler: yet to complete over fences: stays well: acts on firm ground. *Mrs V. A. Aconley*

c–
72

MISS TINO 5 b.m. Relkino – Miss Horatio (Spartan General) [1992/3 20gpu] leggy mare: no form on Flat: showed nothing in February on hurdling debut. *Mrs S. C. Bradburne*

–

MISS VAGABOND 5 b.m. Scallywag – Once Bitten (Brave Invader (USA)) [1992/3 F16s F16v F16g5 18mpu] strong, good-topped mare: second foal: half-sister to fair hurdler Carrick Lanes (by Oats): dam, half-sister to useful chaser Greenwood Lad, won selling hurdle: soundly beaten in NH Flat races: reluctant to line up and showed nothing on hurdling debut: sold 2,300 gns Doncaster March Sales. *J. G. FitzGerald*

–

MISS WAG 6 gr.m. Scallywag – Night Profit (Carnival Night) [1992/3 16d 21s 25d 22g 28m5] smallish, close-coupled mare: of little account. *W. G. Young*

–

MISTER BUTLER 14 b.g. Menelek – Golden Number (Goldhill) [1992/3 c24dpu c23g c27f2] sturdy gelding: hunter chaser: close second at Fontwell in May, only form of season: stays 27f: possibly unsuited by very soft ground, acts on any other. *G. D. Blagbrough*

c89
–

MISTER BYBLOS 7 b.g. Lomond (USA) – Current Jargon (USA) (Little Current (USA)) [1992/3 21d6 17g6] small, sparely-made gelding: moderate hurdler at best: well beaten in sellers in April: stays 19f: acts on firm and dead going: usually blinkered prior to 1992/3. *R. J. Price*

–

MISTER CHIPPENDALE 6 b.g. Floriferous – Midi Skirt (Kabale) —
[1992/3 17s 17g 18m] IR 5,000 3-y-o: big, rangy gelding with plenty of scope:
half-brother to several modest performers: dam lightly-raced half-sister to
good Irish chaser Height O'Fashion: tailed off in novice hurdles: trained by
A. Turnell first outing. *C. Smith*

MISTER CHRISTIAN (NZ) 12 b.g. Captain Jason (NZ) – Grisette **c100**
(NZ) (Arctic Explorer) [1992/3 c27s4 c25v6 c26v c24v3 c26d c27d] leggy, —
shallow-girthed gelding: fair handicap chaser on his day: best effort of
season when third at Lingfield in February: stays very well: acts on heavy
going and good to firm: has found little: usually blinkered, visored once:
suited by racing up with the pace and needs plenty of driving. *P. F. Nicholls*

MISTER CUMBERS 6 b.g. Bulldozer – Baltic Star (Ballyciptic) [1992/3 **c75**
F16s 22g 25g4 24d c17g5 c21vur c16sF] smallish, sturdy gelding: seventh —
foal: brother to Irish NH Flat winner/maiden hurdler Dozing Star: dam 2m
Flat winner in Ireland: has shown nothing over hurdles: showed a little
ability in novice event at Hexham in March on chasing debut: let down by
his jumping both starts subsequently: sold 1,900 gns Doncaster May Sales.
Miss L. C. Plater

MISTER ED 10 ch.g. Monsieure Edouarde – Are You Poaching **c127**
(Poaching) [1992/3 c24mpu c24v3 c24s c25s4 c24v5 c27m* c29fF c34d* —
c33g3] smallish, sparely-made gelding: fairly useful handicap chaser: won at
Fontwell in February and at Uttoxeter (Midlands National, by 15 lengths) in
March: creditable third in Stakis Scottish National at Ayr in April: needs a
thorough test of stamina and plenty of driving: acts on dead and good to firm
going. *R. Curtis*

MISTER FEATHERS 12 b.g. Town And Country – Nikali (Siliconn) **c102** §
[1992/3 c21g3 c22d2 c20m* c24d6 c20d c21g6 c17g3 c21g3 c19m* c20d5 c19f2 —
c17m4] sturdy gelding: fair chaser: won handicaps at Ludlow (amateurs) in
October and Taunton in April: stays 2¾m: acts on firm and dead ground: has
run blinkered and hooded, but not for long time: unreliable. *J. S. King*

MISTER GEBO 8 b.g. Strong Gale – Miss Goldiane (Baragoi) [1992/3 **c100**
c27s2 c26g3 c23f4] small, lightly-made gelding: fair hurdler/chaser: —
respectable efforts in early-season events in 1992/3: suited by test of
stamina: acts on firm ground and probably on soft: blinkered twice in 1991/2.
J. A. C. Edwards

Tetley Bitter Midlands National (Handicap Chase), Uttoxeter—
Mister Ed causes an upset in some style

MISTER HALF-CHANCE 7 b.g. Nearly A Hand – Lavilla (Tycoon II) [1992/3 22s*] big, rather leggy, close-coupled gelding: moderate novice hurdler in 1990/1 when trained by D. Elsworth: having only race since that season, improved form when winning maiden at Nottingham in February: will stay 3m: acts on soft going. *M. C. Pipe*   109

MISTER HARTIGAN 13 b.g. Menelek – Fortrition (David Jack) [1992/3 c24v² c24s c24v c24v² c27gᵖᵘ] strong, good-bodied gelding: has been fired: fair handicap chaser: best efforts of season on first and penultimate starts: pulled up lame on last in February: stays well: acts on heavy going: poor jumper. *J. A. C. Edwards*   c102 x –

MISTER JOE 6 gr.g. Warpath – Misty Twist (Foggy Bell) [1992/3 18d 21dᵖᵘ] first foal: dam never ran: tailed off in novice hurdles: sold 1,200 gns Doncaster June Sales. *S. G. Payne*   –

MISTER JOLLY 7 b.g. Le Moss – Santimwen (Cassim) [1992/3 24s⁶ 17v³] leggy, lengthy gelding: best effort in novice hurdles when third at Hereford in April: sold 2,000 gns Malvern June Sales. *A. P. James*   74

MISTER LAWSON 7 ch.g. Blushing Scribe (USA) – Nonpareil (FR) (Pharly (FR)) [1992/3 17g 16g a16g² a16g⁵ a16g³ 16f⁵ 17m*] modest hurdler nowadays: won handicap at Taunton in April: races at around 2m: acts on good to firm going and equitrack. *B. Forsey*   91

MISTER MAJOR 5 ch.g. Absalom – Gay Tamarind (Tamerlane) [1992/3 21g² 18d⁴ 21s² 21s³ 22v⁵ 21vᵖᵘ 21g⁶ 21g⁴ 21g³ 20f⁵ 22g³] neat gelding: fair handicap hurdler: ran creditably most starts in 1992/3: stays 2¾m: acts on any going. *G. B. Balding*   116

MISTER MOODY (FR) 8 ch.h. Master Thatch – Moonly (FR) (Lionel) [1992/3 c27d³ c27d² c26s³ 28s⁴ c28g⁴ c27m* c24d⁶ c24sᵘʳ c27m⁵ c24fᵖᵘ] leggy, plain horse: maiden hurdler: modest handicap chaser: won at Sedgefield in March: sold out of J. Johnson's stable 5,600 gns Doncaster May Sales after ninth outing: stayed 3½m: probably acted on any ground: dead. *B. P. J. Baugh*   c90 87

MISTER NOVA 4 b.g. Ra Nova – Homing Hill (Homing) [1992/3 F16m⁴] second foal: dam, half-sister to fairly useful sprinter All Agreed, won NH Flat race on only start: close fourth of 24 in NH Flat race at Warwick in May: yet to race over hurdles. *N. J. Henderson*   –

MISTER ODDY 7 b.g. Dubassoff (USA) – Somerford Glory (Hittite Glory) [1992/3 16d² 16s³ 16s² 17v⁶] leggy gelding: fair handicap hurdler: creditable efforts in conditional jockeys events first 3 starts in 1992/3: races only at around 2m: acts on soft going. *J. S. King*   104

MISTER TICKLE 8 b.g. Deep Run – Desert Maid (Proverb) [1992/3 c21f⁵ c24dᵖᵘ 25dᵖᵘ c19dᵖᵘ c32dᵘʳ c25v³] sturdy, workmanlike gelding: winning staying hurdler/chaser: showed nothing in 1992/3: trained for fourth start by Miss S. Scott: poor jumper of fences: tried blinkered and visored: moody and one to leave alone. *L. J. Codd*   c– § – §

MISTER TUFTIE 8 b.g. Black Minstrel – Articinna (Arctic Slave) [1992/3 c24gᵘʳ c24m² c25g* c25g⁵ c25g² c23d² c25dᶠ c25g³ c21s⁶] workmanlike gelding: winning hurdler: won novice chase at Ayr in October: good efforts when placed subsequently: sold 13,000 gns Doncaster May Sales: stays 25f: acts on any going with possible exception of heavy: none too fluent a jumper. *G. Richards*   c95 –

MISTER TYSON 6 b.g. Carriage Way – Pepina (Shoolerville (USA)) [1992/3 F16d] second foal: dam rare 7f winner: tailed off in NH Flat race at Warwick in October: yet to race over hurdles or fences. *D. R. Gandolfo*   –

MISTIC GLEN (IRE) 4 b.f. Mister Majestic – Northern Glen (Northfields (USA)) [1992/3 16v⁴ 17s 16s 22d³ 22d 18m² 20m* 22g* 18d 22m⁴] neat filly: no worthwhile form on Flat: moderate hurdler: won novice events at Newcastle (handicap) in March and Huntingdon in April: suited by 2½m or more: best form on a sound surface. *J. Parkes*   95

MISTI MAC (IRE) 5 b.g. Roselier (FR) – Graig Island (Furry Glen) [1992/3 aF16g F17g] first foal: dam unraced daughter of a winning hurdler: tailed off in NH Flat races: yet to race over hurdles or fences. *R. O'Leary*

MISTRAL GIRL (IRE) 5 b.m. Tumble Wind (USA) – Arthashat (Petingo) [1992/3 17mᵖᵘ 17sᵖᵘ] sparely-made mare: no worthwhile form over hurdles: trained first start by J. Joseph. *R. G. Frost* —

MISTRAL STORY 8 b.g. Pitpan – Flashy Flake (Candy Cane) [1992/3 21d⁶ 22d⁴ 25sᵖᵘ c16vᵘʳ c26gᵖᵘ c24f⁴ c20g⁶] tall, leggy gelding: poor novice hurdler/chaser: probably stays 2¾m and acts on dead ground: blinkered sixth outing. *J. T. Gifford* | c– 79

MISTRESS MCKENZIE 7 ch.m. Deep Run – Unforgetabubble (Menelek) [1992/3 22s⁵ 24vᵖᵘ 22v c27vᵖᵘ] lengthy mare: novice hurdler: tailed off when pulled up in novice event on chasing debut: should stay beyond 21f: acts on soft going. *K. Bishop* | c– –

MISTS OF TIME 10 gr. or ro.g. Grey Dawn II – Hyroglyph (USA) (Northern Dancer) [1992/3 22m 24sᵖᵘ 22dᵖᵘ 21f] big, workmanlike gelding: poor hurdler/chaser: stays 2¾m: acts on firm and dead ground: blinkered once, visored 4 times: jumps fences poorly. *C. J. Vernon Miller* | c– x –

MISTY GREY 4 gr.g. Scallywag – Finwood (Ashmore (FR)) [1992/3 F17f F16m] rangy gelding with scope: fifth foal: dam won 2½m hurdle: well beaten in NH Flat races in March: yet to race over hurdles. *G. Fierro*

MISTY NIGHT 5 gr.m. Grey Desire – Maha (Northfields (USA)) [1992/3 17s 17d 17s 22d 20g] leggy mare: poor novice hurdler: no form in 1992/3: should stay beyond 2m. *P. Monteith* | –

MISTY (NZ) 6 b.g. Ivory Hunter (USA) – Our Loaming (NZ) (Sovereign Edition) [1992/3 20g³ 22d² 21s² 22d⁵] unfurnished gelding: modest novice hurdler: should stay beyond 2¾m: acts on soft going: blinkered last 2 starts. *Capt. T. A. Forster* | 86

MISTY VIEW 4 gr.f. Absalom – Long View (Persian Bold) [1992/3 18vᵖᵘ 16d 16d 16f³] neat filly: fair middle-distance performer on Flat: sold out of M. Jarvis' stable 13,000 gns Newmarket Autumn Sales: poor form over hurdles: winner on Flat in 1993. *J. White* | 75

MIXIES JIM 10 b.g. Royal Match – Borecca (Boreen (FR)) [1992/3 23gᵖᵘ 17d 20dᶠ 16gᵖᵘ] smallish, close-coupled gelding: poor maiden jumper: blinkered last 2 outings. *D. G. Swindlehurst* | c– –

MIZYAN (IRE) 5 b.g. Melyno – Maid of Erin (USA) (Irish River (FR)) [1992/3 17s² 17d³ a18g* 20g⁴ 20f⁴] leggy, rather plain gelding: fairly useful handicap hurdler: won at Southwell in February: good fourth at Newcastle later in month and at Aintree in April: stays 2½m: probably acts on any turf ground, and on fibresand: broke blood vessel once: takes good hold. *J. E. Banks* | 120

MOAT LEGEND 8 b.g. Red Regent – Natflat (Barrons Court) [1992/3 c18gᵘʳ c21gᵖᵘ c21f⁴ c18gᶠ] sturdy gelding: maiden hurdler/chaser/pointer: let down by his jumping in steeplechases: sold 1,150 gns Ascot December Sales after second start, resold 2,800 gns Ascot 2nd June Sales. *D. R. Greig* | c66 x

MOBILE MESSENGER (NZ) 5 b.g. Ring The Bell (NZ) – Sleepy Slipper (NZ) (Avaray (FR)) [1992/3 F17g⁶ F16d 16d 17d⁶] New Zealand-bred gelding: first sign of ability when never-nearer sixth of 15 in novice hurdle at Wolverhampton in February: will stay beyond 17f: may improve. *D. H. Barons* | 77

MODEL NURSE 6 b.m. Exhibitioner – Majestic Nurse (On Your Mark) [1992/3 17mᶠ 17s 17d⁴ 17g⁵] leggy mare: novice hurdler: form only on last 2 starts: yet to race beyond 17f: acts on dead going. *Mrs A. Knight* | 57

MODEST LADY 7 gr.m. Fujiwara – Cullen Castle (Dear Gazelle) [1992/3 18g 22m⁴] compact mare: third foal: half-sister to winning hurdler Hascombe Hill (by Smartset): dam lightly-raced maiden: no sign of ability in early-season novice hurdles: sold 3,000 gns in May. *W. A. Stephenson*

Pipe Scudamore Racing Club's "Mohana"

MODULATOR 11 b.g. Celtic Cone – Ballylaneen (Master Buck) [1992/3   **c77**
c17g⁵ 20m c22g 22gᶠ c21dᵖᵘ c16sᵖᵘ] small gelding: poor novice hurdler/   –
chaser: stays 2¾m: acts on soft going: tried blinkered. *T. Dyer*

MOGUL DANCER 7 b.g. Workboy – Lillies Brig (New Brig) [1992/3   –
23g 23d 18gᵖᵘ] big, plain gelding: chasing type: no sign of ability over
hurdles. *N. W. Alexander*

MOHANA 4 br.f. Mashhor Dancer (USA) – The Ranee (Royal Palace)
[1992/3 17m* 17s* 17s* 17m* 17d* 16g³ 17d* 17s² 16s² 18v² 16d⁴ 17m]   **126**
leggy filly: modest maiden on Flat, second in 1½m claimer in June (claimed
out of J. Dunlop's stable £4,521): won juvenile hurdles at Newton Abbot (3),
Bangor and Cheltenham (2) prior to finishing good second in Finale Junior
Hurdle at Chepstow in December on eighth start: ran poorly afterwards:
will stay 2½m: acts on good to firm and soft ground: front runner. *M. C. Pipe*

MOHELI 6 b.m. Ardross – Mayotte (Little Buskins) [1992/3 17d⁶ 21d⁵
22v² 21v³ 25s] workmanlike mare: modest handicap hurdler: not raced after   **93**
January: should stay further than 2¾m: acts on good to firm and heavy
ground. *P. G. Murphy*

MO ICHI DO 7 b.g. Lomond (USA) – Engageante (FR) (Beaugency (FR))   **c75**
[1992/3 a22g³ a22g⁴ c21v²] small gelding: poor hurdler: second in selling   **83**
handicap at Uttoxeter in April on chasing debut: stays 3m: probably acts on
any going: blinkered nowadays: often forces pace. *Miss S. J. Wilton*

Agfa Hurdle, Sandown—Mole Board is poised to pounce as Valfinet tires in front

MOLE BOARD   11 br.g. Deep Run – Sharpaway (Royal Highway) [1992/3 17s*]

157

In *Chasers & Hurdlers 1990/91* we reported that 100/1 had been available on the Champion Hurdle fourth Mole Board, and attached the comment 'O ye of little faith!'. A Bristol cash punter's decision to invest £1,000 each-way when offered the same odds in late-December 1992, however, seemed to be taking things too far. Mole Board hadn't had a race in the interim. His last run had been a victory, his first for over three years, in the Keith Prowse Long Distance Hurdle at Ascot in April, 1991. In the meantime, Keith Prowse had gone under and Mole Board had been laid low with a tendon injury. In the end, it was 668 days before Mole Board was able to return to racecourse action. What a return it was!—one of the most astounding races of the season. His five opponents in the Agfa Hurdle on soft ground at Sandown in February were Valfinet, on a five-timer and the 6/5 favourite; Morley Street and Ruling, who had been first and third in that 1991 Champion Hurdle; and Gran Alba, another trying to come back from injury. Valfinet set a scorching pace; he was a good ten lengths clear beginning the final turn and had increased the advantage to at least fifteen entering the straight. Scanning back through the field, each of his rivals seemed to be toiling to no effect, until one came to the 33/1-shot Mole Board who'd been held up last and was on the bridle. Switched to the outside, Mole Board went a clear second before the second last and, putting in a prodigious leap, began to make ground on the leader hand over fist. A combination of

496

Valfinet tying up and Mole Board finishing like a train saw the lead change hands in the last hundred and fifty yards and Mole Board go on to win by six lengths, the pair twenty lengths clear. In the revised Champion Hurdle betting, Mole Board was as low as 10/1, surely his shortest price in the five years that he had been considered for the race. The trainer's view of his chance was that 'he's a better horse now and it's a worse race'. But it was all academic. After an extremely wet spell leading up to that Sandown race, near-drought conditions followed, and with top-of-the-ground at Cheltenham Mole Board could not run. Nor did he run in any other race in Britain, and an appearance in Ireland, where easy ground was much easier to find, was apparently ruled out by his being a bad traveller.

Mole Board (br.g. 1982)	Deep Run (ch 1966)	Pampered King (b 1954)	Prince Chevalier
			Netherton Maid
		Trial By Fire (ch 1958)	Court Martial
			Mitrailleuse
	Sharpaway (br 1974)	Royal Highway (b 1955)	Straight Deal
			Queen's Highway
		Sharp Awakening (br 1959)	King Hal
			Broken Dawn

No twelve-year-old has ever won the Champion Hurdle, and Hatton's Grace and Sea Pigeon are the only eleven-year-olds. Mole Board has the option of the Stayers' Hurdle, in which the twelve-year-olds have done no better, but statistics and age aside, the seemingly increasing frequency in recent years of top-of-the-ground may well mean that Mole Board doesn't even get a chance to improve his Festival record, currently standing at an eighth (when 7/4 favourite) in the 1988 Sun Alliance Novices' Hurdle, then sixth and fourth in the 1989 and 1991 Champion Hurdles. Connections do, however, have the possibility of a five-year-old half-brother to Mole Board, the IR 20,000-guinea acquisition Arfer Mole (by Carlingford Castle) who shaped promisingly in a National Hunt Flat race at Kempton in February. Mole Board is Sharpaway's first produce and although two of her other foals (his brothers Deep Dawn and the ungenuine Sound of Islay) are winners, none has shown anything like his ability. A greater pity is that this enigmatic individual has had such limited opportunities himself. Small in stature and a seemingly regular sufferer from leg trouble, Mole Board has been a very exciting racehorse in his day. *J. A. B. Old*

MOMENT OF PASSION (IRE)   5 b.m. Tumble Gold – Lightfoot Lady (Tekoah) [1992/3 F17d F14g] smallish mare: fourth live foal: half-sister to Irish NH Flat race winner Our River (by River Beauty): dam won 2m maiden hurdle in Ireland: tailed off in NH Flat races: yet to race over hurdles or fences. *F. Jestin*

MOMENT OF TRUTH   9 b.g. Known Fact (USA) – Chieftain Girl (USA) (Chieftain II) [1992/3 17m* c17g* c16g⁴ c17g² c16d⁴ c20g³ 16g⁴ c16mᶠ] compact gelding: fairly useful hurdler (won at Perth in August), but was better known as a useful chaser: won handicap at Cheltenham in October: stayed 2½m: best on a sound surface: jumped well: tough and consistent: dead. *P. Monteith*   c141 122

MOMSER   7 ch.g. Mr Fluorocarbon – Jolimo (Fortissimo) [1992/3 21d 22f⁴ 20m*] smallish, sparely-made gelding: fair handicap hurdler: won at Market Rasen in May: stays 2½m: probably acts on any going. *M. J. Ryan*   111

MONARU   7 b.g. Montekin – Raubritter (Levmoss) [1992/3 26s³ 26s* 24m³] smallish, angular gelding: fairly useful handicap hurdler: won at Catterick in January: creditable third at Newcastle in March: suited by a good test of stamina: acts on any going: usually visored or blinkered in 1989/90: suited by waiting tactics. *Mrs M. Reveley*   121

MONASIRA   8 ch.m. Lord Ha Ha – Westburn VII (Pedigree Unknown) [1992/3 c16g c16dᶠ c16vᵖᵘ] workmanlike, close-coupled mare: poor 2m novice hurdler/chaser. *R. Dickin*   c– –

MONA'S PRINCE   6 b. or br.g. Class Distinction – Princess Mona (Prince Regent (FR)) [1992/3 20vᵖᵘ 18sᵖᵘ a16gᶜᵒ a16g 17g 18f] lengthy gelding: no sign of ability. *D. A. Wilson*   –

William Hill Handicap Hurdle, Uttoxeter—Montagnard (near side) pops up at a long price

MONAUGHTY MAN 7 br.g. Tower Walk – Springdamus (Mandamus) [1992/3 16g 21dro 16dpu 17s] good-topped, workmanlike gelding: first foal: dam, moderate hurdler/chaser, stayed 21f: no sign of ability in novice hurdles. *E. M. Caine* —

MONDAY CLUB 9 ch.g. Remezzo – Jena (Brigadier Gerard) [1992/3 c17sF a16g2 c16d3 17d6 16g] leggy, angular gelding: fair hurdler: moderate novice chaser: best form at 2m: probably acts on any ground: poor jumper of fences: weak finisher. *J. C. Tuck* — **c88** x **112**

MONETARY FUND 9 br.g. Red Sunset – Msida (Majority Blue) [1992/3 21dpu 22spu 17dF c20vpu] compact gelding: fair hurdler at best: twice-raced over fences: tried visored: one to leave alone nowadays. *Mrs P. M. Joynes* — **c–** **–**

MONEY FROM AMERICA 14 ch.g. Deep Run – Artic Leap (Arctic Slave) [1992/3 c25g2] winning hurdler/novice chaser in Ireland: fair pointer in Britain nowadays: second in hunter chase at Towcester in March: stays 25f: acts on soft ground. *Mrs Pauline Adams* — **c82** **–**

MONIAIVE 4 b.g. Son of Shaka – Lady Bounty (Hotfoot) [1992/3 18g 17d 16d 17s a16gpu 16g] small gelding: no form on Flat: poor form at best over hurdles. *W. Clay* — **59**

MONKEY RUN 6 ch.g. Monksfield – Sound Run (Deep Run) [1992/3 F18d] first foal: dam poor maiden hurdler in Ireland: behind in NH Flat race in October: fair form when winning 4 points in the spring: yet to race over hurdles or in a steeplechase. *M. W. Easterby* —

MONK'S MISTAKE 11 ch.g. Monksfield – Hardyglass Lass (Master Owen) [1992/3 c16g5 c16sF c16g2 c16s3 17v3 16d4 21d] compact, rather sparely-made gelding: winning 2m hurdler/chaser: poor form in 1992/3. *A. L. Forbes* — **c80** **–**

MONKTON (IRE) 5 ch.g. The Parson – Poula Scawla (Pollerton) [1992/3 F17m] brother to useful Irish hurdler Minella Man and half-brother to 2 other winning hurdlers, including fair stayer Granary Grain (by Deep Run): dam unraced half-sister to 5 winning jumpers, notably useful Mac's Chariot: seventh of 23 in NH Flat race at Cheltenham in April: yet to race over hurdles or fences. *Capt. T. A. Forster* —

MONOLULUS SURPRISE (IRE)   5 b.m. Primo Dominie – Atilla The Hen (Hot Spark) [1992/3 16s^F 18g^{pu}] workmanlike mare: seems of little account over hurdles. *S. B. Avery*   –

MONSCOMA (IRE)   5 b.h. Montelimar (USA) – Scoma (Lord Gayle (USA)) [1992/3 17g^{pu} a16g^{ur}] workmanlike horse: no worthwhile form over hurdles: blinkered final outing. *R. Ingram*   –

MONSIEUR LE CURE   7 b.g. The Parson – Caramore Lady (Deep Run) [1992/3 16s^2 17v* 18g^2] good-topped gelding: chasing type: highly impressive winner of novice hurdle at Newton Abbot in January: hung right when second at Worcester in March: will stay beyond 2¼m: acts on heavy going: jumps well: forces pace: sure to improve and win more races. *J. A. C. Edwards*   123 p

MONTAGNARD   9 b.g. Strong Gale – Louisa Stuart (FR) (Ruysdael II) [1992/3 21v^{pu} 22s 25d* 25s^{pu} 22d^{pu}] small, rather sparely-made gelding: fairly useful hurdler on his day: won handicap at Uttoxeter in March: ran poorly afterwards: suited by good test of stamina: acts on heavy going: races up with pace: game: jumps well. *M. Bradstock*   119

MONTAGNE   4 br.f. Midyan (USA) – La Masse (High Top) [1992/3 17v 16g 22g 17g 17d 17g^{pu}] light-framed filly: half-sister to a winning French jumper by Carwhite: poor maiden on Flat and over hurdles: sold out of H. Candy's stable 2,500 gns Newmarket Autumn Sales. *S. Coathup*   –

MONTALINO   10 gr.g. Neltino – Montage (Polyfoto) [1992/3 c16v^{ur} c16v^5 c17g^2 c17g^2 c16g* c17m^2] workmanlike gelding: fair handicap chaser: won at Folkestone in March: ran well next time: best form at 2m: acts on good to firm and dead ground: poor jumper. *G. L. Humphrey*   c100 x –

MONTEBEL (IRE)   5 br.g. Montelimar (USA) – Be My Joy (Be My Guest (USA)) [1992/3 22v^6] tall, leggy, close-coupled gelding: has scope: fairly useful as a juvenile hurdler: well beaten in December: effective at 2m and should stay beyond 2½m: has won on dead ground but best form on a sound surface. *N. A. Twiston-Davies*   –

MONTELADO   6 b.g. Montelimar (USA) – Misippus (Green God) [1992/3 20g* 16d^2 17m*]   150 P

What a magnificent season Charlie Swan had! Apart from becoming champion jockey in Ireland for the fourth time, in the process matching his previous season's record-breaking achievement by riding more than a hundred winners, Swan also enjoyed great success in the top races, notably at the Cheltenham Festival where he was the leading rider. Swan's four wins at Cheltenham were all gained on hurdlers, namely Montelado, Fissure Seal, Shawiya and Shuil Ar Aghaidh, but he's just as good a rider of chasers, as he demonstrated when winning the Irish Grand National on Ebony Jane. Small wonder, then, that Swan's name appeared on the short-list for the job of stable jockey to Martin Pipe following the retirement of Peter Scudamore in April. Swan missed out on that job and with it the chance to team up with the Champion Hurdler Granville Again, but we doubt if he lost very much sleep over it. He'll have plenty of good horses to ride in the next season, among them a possible future champion hurdler in Montelado who looked a most exciting prospect when winning the Trafalgar House Supreme Novices' Hurdle at Cheltenham in March.

Montelado had come to the fore at Cheltenham twelve months earlier when he won the inaugural running of the Festival Bumper, and much was expected of him in his first season over hurdles. Montelado lived up to expectations. Three days after winning a two-mile event on the Flat in October Montelado made his hurdling debut in a maiden at Limerick, where he landed the odds with little difficulty. A much sterner test faced him when he reappeared two months later in a quite valuable novice event at Leopardstown, and although beaten at odds of 9/4-on he put up the best performance by a novice hurdler in the first half of the season. The useful and far more experienced Bayrouge, beat Montelado by a length, the pair finishing a distance clear of the remainder. Montelado was clearly going to be a major contender for the Supreme Novices' Hurdle, but plans to give him more experience over hurdles before then had to be shelved as the horse failed to please his trainer with his well-being. Swan rode the fully-recovered Montelado for the first time at Cheltenham, taking over from Richard Dunwoody who was claimed to ride Dreamers Delight. With Dunwoody now under contract to the Pipe stable it's almost certain that Swan will continue his association with Montelado, especially after such a successful start to the partnership. Swan can have had few more comfortable rides. Montelado, taken wide in order to give him a good view of his hurdles, didn't put a foot wrong. Ridden with much more restraint than at Leopardstown, where he'd tried to make all, Montelado travelled strongly in the mid-division as the favourite Boro Eight, pressed by the four-year-old Lemon's Mill, set a strong pace. Montelado, still under restraint, moved into fourth place on the downhill run to three out and then joined Boro Eight in the lead two out where Dreamers Delight, in touch and going well, fell. Shaken up on the turn for home, Montelado produced a breathtaking turn of speed to go clear in a few strides and the race was all over bar the shouting. Six lengths up jumping the last Montelado, kept up to his work, stormed up the hill to win by twelve lengths, the same margin by which he'd won the Festival Bumper. Lemon's Mill stayed on to take second place, two and a half lengths ahead of Satin Lover with Boro Eight in fourth. It was a most impressive performance from Montelado, one which evoked memories of the ill-fated Golden Cygnet who'd also won this event in scintillating style fifteen years earlier. As had been the case with Golden Cygnet, Montelado was immediately hailed as a future champion. The enthusiasm was understandable. While the field for the Supreme Novices' Hurdle lacked strength in depth, several of the runners did have useful performances to their credit. Yet they were made to look very ordinary by a horse running for just the third time over hurdles and having only his seventh race in all. With scope for much more than normal improvement, Montelado has all the credentials to go right to the top. Montelado suffered sore shins after Cheltenham and wasn't seen out again, but following pin-firing on his forelegs he'll be back in action in 1993/4 when the Smurfit Champion Hurdle will be his main objective. A hat-trick of victories for Montelado at the Cheltenham Festival is a distinct possibility. Following Granville Again's defeat at Aintree in

*Trafalgar House Supreme Novices' Hurdle, Cheltenham—
the hugely impressive winner Montelado takes the last in front;
Lemon's Mill (striped cap) and Satin Lover (left) chase him home*

Mr F. O. Hannon's "Montelado"

April, Montelado was promoted to 6/1 favourite for the 1994 Champion Hurdle by William Hill.

	Montelimar (USA) (b 1981)	Alleged (b 1974)	Hoist The Flag
			Princess Pout
		L'Extravagante (b 1973)	Le Fabuleux
Montelado (b.g. 1987)			Fanfreluche
	Misippus (b 1974)	Green God (ch 1968)	Red God
			Thetis II
		Honest Scot (b 1969)	Aberdeen
			Eternal Truth

Montelado is by the well-bred Montelimar, the winner of a maiden event and the Group 2 Gallinule Stakes, both over a mile and a quarter, on his only two starts. He's the eighth foal of Misippus, a bad plater who gained her only placing over seven furlongs. Misippus, out of a winning half-sister to the Lincoln winner Sovereign Bill, has bred two other winners, notably the useful hurdler Strokestown Lad (by Tanfirion). Strokestown Lad stayed two and a half miles, as does Montelado who gained his first win over hurdles at the trip. It's unlikely that Montelado will be campaigned beyond two miles in the foreseeable future, though. Montelado, a tall, quite good-topped gelding who took the eye in the paddock at Cheltenham, put up his best performance on firmish ground but it's too early to draw any definite conclusions about his going requirements. The ground was good to soft when he ran against Bayrouge, and he appeared not to be inconvenienced by the heavy going when he finished second to Tiananmen Square, giving him weight, on his final appearance in National Hunt Flat races. *P. J. Flynn, Ireland*

MONTGOMERY 12 b.g. Push On – Mirror Back (Master Owen) [1992/3 **c80**
c25dᵖᵘ c25dᶠ c24s c26s⁴ c24sᵘʳ c25v⁴ c25f] lengthy, workmanlike gelding: –
poor chaser: stays 3¼m: acts on any going: often blinkered. *W. G.
McKenzie-Coles*

MONT MIRAIL 7 b.g. Buckskin (FR) – Woodcliffe (Harwell) [1992/3
21d³] half-brother to winning chaser Deep Cliff (by Deep Run): dam, lightly 85 p
raced, from good jumping family: 25/1, shaped quite well when third in
novice event at Carlisle in April on hurdling debut: will improve. *G.
Richards*

MONTPELIER LAD 6 br.g. Elegant Air – Leg Glance (Home Guard **c112**
(USA)) [1992/3 21g⁶ 17g⁵ 17d c16g* c16s* c17g² c16d² 17m* c16f⁵ c16d⁶ 134
c20g³ c21d² c18g* c18m*] well-made gelding: useful handicap hurdler: won
at Doncaster in March: won novice chases at Ayr (2) and Bangor and
handicap at Cartmel in second half of season: best form at up to 2¼m: acts
on good to firm and soft ground: blinkered seventh outing (ran creditably).
G. Richards

MONTRAVE 4 ch.g. Netherkelly – Streakella (Firestreak) [1992/3 16g
17g 16g³ 17m⁵] tall, plain gelding: half-brother to winning hurdler Legal 89
Streak (by Mr Fluorocarbon): once-raced on Flat: modest juvenile hurdler:
acts on good to firm ground. *P. Monteith*

MONTYKOSKY 6 b.g. Montekin – Reliable Rosie (Relko) [1992/3 17m²
23m³ 21f 25sᵖᵘ 20g⁴] neat gelding: untrustworthy selling hurdler: stays 23f: 67 §
acts on good to firm, dead ground and fibresand: blinkered once: won a point
in February. *B. Preece*

MONTYS GUNNER 9 ch.g. Gunner B – Montcall (Mountain Call) **c–**
[1992/3 c33m] behind in novice hurdles: maiden pointer: tailed off when –
pulled up in hunter chase in May. *D. E. S. Smith*

MONUMENTAL LAD 10 ro.g. Jellaby – Monumental Moment (St **c116**
Paddy) [1992/3 c21s⁴ c24g⁵ c21dᵖᵘ c16s] big, strong, plain gelding: fairly –
useful chaser: ran badly final outing (January): stays 2½m: acts on soft
going: usually a sound jumper. *Mrs H. Parrott*

MOONLIGHT CRUISE 5 b.m. Cruise Missile – Saucy Moon (Saucy
Kit) [1992/3 22g⁶ 24s] leggy, unfurnished mare: second foal: dam, winning –
chaser, probably stayed 2½m: no form over hurdles. *P. Beaumont*

MOON MONKEY (IRE) 5 b.g. Derring Rose – Paiukiri (Ballyciptic)
[1992/3 17g⁴] half-brother to winning jumpers Glen George (by Furry Glen) –
and Betty's Pearl (by Gulf Pearl): dam staying maiden: distant fourth in
novice hurdle at Wolverhampton in March. *Mrs A. L. M. King*

MOON REEF 7 ch.m. Main Reef – Malmsey (Jukebox) [1992/3 a20g] **c–**
workmanlike mare: of little account: sold 1,800 gns Malvern June Sales: – §
sometimes blinkered or visored: temperamental. *D. J. Wintle*

MOON SPIN 4 b.f. Night Shift (USA) – Hors Serie (USA) (Vaguely
Noble) [1992/3 16d 17fᵖᵘ] half-sister to several winning jumpers, notably – p
useful Bespoke (by Relkino) and quite useful Wick Pound (by Niniski): fair
performer at up to middle distances on Flat, winner several times in 1993:
signs of ability on first start over hurdles: saddle slipped next time: should
do better. *Major W. R. Hern*

MOORBRIDGE 8 ch.g. Rontino – Ballinlonig Lass (Diritto) [1992/3 **c–** §
c24mᵖᵘ c25d⁶ c17vᶠ c20gᴿ] sturdy gelding: half-brother to 3 minor winning
Irish jumpers: no sign of ability in novice chases (refused final outing). *Mrs
S. J. Smith*

MOORCROFT BOY 8 ch.g. Roselier (FR) – Well Mannered (Menelek) **c117**
[1992/3 c26g² c27m⁵ c25d* c24g* c24g² c24s² c28f²] sturdy gelding: useful –
hunter chaser: won novice events at Ascot and Huntingdon and also ran well
on his other starts (especially so on penultimate outing) in 1992/3: stays
well: probably acts on any ground, goes particularly well on soft: sometimes
takes time to warm to his task. *D. Nicholson*

MOOR LODGE (USA) 4 b.g. Hero's Honor (USA) – Prospector's Star (USA) (Mr Prospector (USA)) [1992/3 18f* 17m* 18m*] leggy gelding: modest 1½m winner on Flat: won early-season juvenile hurdles at Exeter (2) and Stratford: stays 2¼m: acts on firm ground: sold to race in USA. *M. H. Tompkins*   110

MOOR SCOPE 11 ch.g. Whistlefield – Horoscope (Romany Air) [1992/3 c21s³ c26g⁶ c25v²] strong, lengthy gelding: fairly useful hunter chaser: placed at Warwick and Towcester: effective at around 2½m and stays well: acts on any going. *J. F. F. White*   c102

MOOT POINT (USA) 5 b.h. Sharpen Up – Gaelic Logic (USA) (Bold Reason) [1992/3 F12d²] modest stayer on Flat, ran creditably in February: yet to race over hurdles or fences. *J. R. Jenkins*

MOPHEAD KELLY 4 ch.c. Netherkelly – Trois Filles (French Marny) [1992/3 F16v] first foal: dam tailed off in selling hurdles: tailed off in NH Flat race at Uttoxeter in April: yet to race over hurdles. *W. Clay*

MORCINDA 7 ch.g. Ballacashtal (CAN) – Montelimar (Wolver Hollow) [1992/3 c16mF c17gF c16m c17dpu F10d⁵] tall, angular gelding: no sign of ability. *P. Monteith*   c– –

MORE LARKS (IRE) 5 b. or br.g. Godswalk (USA) – Charmeuse (Cut Above) [1992/3 16fpu] sparely-made gelding: poor maiden on Flat: no sign of ability on hurdling debut in September. *M. B. James*   –

MORGANS ACE 4 ch.c. Morgans Choice – Adjals Ace (London Glory) [1992/3 18d⁶ 17fro] seems of little account on Flat and over hurdles. *B. R. Millman*   –

MORGANS HARBOUR 7 br.g. Radical – Parsfield (The Parson) [1992/3 c26v² c27vur c24d⁴ c26d⁶ c25s⁴ c27g²] workmanlike gelding: fair novice chaser: needs thorough test of stamina: best with plenty of give in the ground: none too consistent. *K. R. Burke*   c95

MORGANS MAN 4 b.c. Morgans Choice – Mandover (Mandamus) [1992/3 17g*] third foal: half-brother to a maiden pointer by Spitsbergen: dam winning pointer: 25/1, won novice hurdle at Hereford in May: will stay further than 17f: should improve. *Mrs S. D. Williams*   91 p

MORIARTY 6 b.g. Martinmas – Love Is Blind (USA) (Hasty Road) [1992/3 17g] poor novice selling hurdler. *R. J. Price*   –

MORLEY STREET 9 ch.g. Deep Run – High Board (High Line) [1992/3 17v* 20d² 17v³ 17s⁵ 17m 20f*]   c– 169 §

However strong an impression the Sunday papers managed to give to the contrary, Grand National day had more to it than the events which blighted the famous steeplechase. We still got some superb racing, notably in a Martell Aintree Hurdle which breathtakingly upstaged a memorable opener won by Spinning. The previous three Aintree Hurdles had been won by Morley Street. As he lined up for the fourth year his chance of extending his run appeared none too bright. He'd not been in the best of form since outsprinting Granville Again in the Coral-Elite Hurdle at Cheltenham on their seasonal reappearance back in November, and had looked a shadow of his former self in his last two races, when finishing last behind Mole Board in the Agfa Hurdle at Sandown and twelfth behind Granville Again in the Champion Hurdle. But Morley Street responded to a remarkably confident ride from Graham Bradley to turn the tables on Granville Again at Aintree, and won the race with his best performance since his own Champion Hurdle-winning season of 1990/1.

Morley Street was ridden with finesse as well as confidence, and although it might be true that most races come down almost entirely to the ability of the horse, this one featured jockeyship much more prominently. There probably hasn't been a more artistic rider over jumps than Bradley since John Haine retired, and he was seen to great advantage on Morley Street, a horse who is best held up as long as possible. On this occasion Morley Street wasn't allowed to go on until halfway up the run-in. Held up last of six, well back from Flown who set a scorching gallop, he made such effortless progress from four out that he could have had the lead at any time from two out. Flown still led on sufference at the last, where a characteristically good jump took Morley Street almost alongside, cruising under restraint. The signal for action came when Granville Again, prominent throughout, began to press on the outside. One tap behind the saddle and Morley Street lengthened immediately to settle the issue in a matter of strides; at the line he'd gone a length and a half up, three and a half lengths up on third-placed Flown. There was a curious sequel to the race: the winner joined the second at the top of the Jockey Club's hurdle ratings. The decision not to promote Morley Street above Granville Again was officially defended on the very odd grounds that 'it would be invidious to have either horse rated superior'. However, just before the end of the season the handicappers did take courage, more accurately reflecting the situation by reducing Granville Again's rating.

By the time Bradley first got the ride on Morley Street in the latest Champion Hurdle, taking over from Dunwoody who'd replaced long-serving Frost after the previous one, the horse's propensity to do little in front was well established. He'd twice shown it markedly in 1991/2, when handing the Leopardstown Champion Hurdle to Chirkpar and when almost being caught by Minorettes Girl in the Aintree Hurdle. A further example came in the Racecall Ascot Hurdle, in his second race in 1992/3. Having had his effort delayed until going to the last, he quickened ahead like the 5/2-on shot he was, then failed to run on and was caught near the line by Muse. Before, we'd always described this behaviour of his as idling, but failure to run on has an implication of unreliability about it. And whether the root of the problem was temperamental or physical (he has a history of breaking blood vessels) Morley Street was definitely becoming an unreliable betting proposition. We felt obliged to alert subscribers in the usual way, through use of the *Timeform* 'squiggle' (for a horse, however good on its day, who may run up to its rating on occasions, but cannot be trusted to do so). Morley Street finished a disappointing third behind Halkopous and Granville Again in his race after Ascot, the Arlington Bula Hurdle at Cheltenham in December. Then came Sandown, Cheltenham, and the revival at Aintree. He remains an unreliable betting proposition.

Coral-Elite Hurdle, Cheltenham—
Morley Street (left) has his younger brother Granville Again
in his sights as he jumps the last

504

Martell Aintree Hurdle—
Morley Street is pulling double at the last, with only Flown ahead of him;
Granville Again follows them on the inside

Morley Street is said to be set to resume his chasing career next, starting with the Breeders' Cup Steeplechase in America. Morley Street has won two Breeders' Cup Chases already but his record over the bigger British fences is none too encouraging. He made three quick appearances in his Champion Hurdle season. He looked good against token opposition on his debut at Worcester, but was comprehensively outjumped by Remittance Man in the Rovacabin Noel Novices' Chase at Ascot and pulled up before three out after continually jumping left and seeming to lose confidence in the Feltham Novices' Chase at Kempton. Maybe he'll take to it second time round, as did Beech Road. If not, he can always be returned to hurdling: a fifth Aintree Hurdle win would surely be a record to stand for ever. Oddly enough, the latest season produced two other hurdlers who succeeded in winning the same race for the fourth time: Jinxy Jack continued to monopolise the Morebattle Hurdle at Kelso and Manhattan Boy won his fourth Peacehaven Selling Hurdle at Plumpton in August (though his victories haven't come in successive seasons).

Morley Street (ch.g. 1984)	Deep Run (ch 1966)	Pampered King (b 1954)	Prince Chevalier / Netherton Maid
		Trial By Fire (ch 1958)	Court Martial / Mitrailleuse
	High Board (b 1977)	High Line (ch 1966)	High Hat / Time Call
		Matchboard (br 1963)	Straight Deal / Royal Alliance

The rangy Morley Street is an excellent jumper of hurdles, fast, fluent and sure. Even at nine he is still also one of the fastest between them, and possesses a fine turn of finishing speed, especially for one who stays at least twenty-one furlongs. Furthermore, although connections claim that he is suited by a sound surface he is fully effective on any type of going—there could hardly be two more contrasting surfaces than those he won on at

Michael Jackson Bloodstock Ltd's "Morley Street"

Cheltenham (as heavy as seen all season) and Aintree (so firm it caused a rash of withdrawals). There is little to say about his pedigree that hasn't been said before, since there have been many opportunities to dissect it on account of his feats and those of his brother Granville Again. There can be no more quite like the pair, for Deep Run died in 1987, but the dam produced a colt by the champion sire's heir apparent Strong Gale in 1992. *G. B. Balding*

MORSHOT 6 b.g. Oats – Duckdown (Blast) [1992/3 17v 17v 16v] workmanlike gelding: sixth foal: brother to winning Irish staying hurdler Magic Oats and half-brother to Celtic Shot and 5-y-o Sister Shot (both by Celtic Cone): dam winning hurdler from good jumping family: little promise over hurdles. *C. P. E. Brooks* –

MOSCOW DYNAMO 6 br.g. Siberian Express (USA) – County Line (High Line) [1992/3 20dpu 17mpu] poor novice at best over hurdles. *Mrs A. Knight* –

MOSS BEE 6 br.g. Zambrano – Brown Bee III (Marcus Superbus) **c88**
[1992/3 20m c16d⁵ c25dpu c23sF c24d⁵ c25s⁵ c24d c16m² c17g³ c21d⁵ c21s⁵ c16m* c17g³ c21g⁴] strong gelding: poor novice hurdler: won maiden chase at Perth in May: stays 21f: best on a sound surface. *W. G. Reed* –

MOSSGARA 8 b.g. Le Moss – Bargara (Bargello) [1992/3 21s² 25v⁵ 25s²] rangy, chasing type: quite useful handicap hurdler: second at Warwick 118

506

in November and Kempton in December: suited by test of stamina: acts on heavy going: takes good hold and races prominently. *Mrs J. Pitman*

MOSSIE GOLD 6 b.m. Oats – Arctic Fern (Arcticeelagh) [1992/3 17s^{bd} 16s^4 16g 18d 16d^6 21s 22g^4 23m^4] sparely-made mare: poor novice hurdler: stays 2¾m: acts on soft ground. *M. P. Naughton*   73

MOSSIMAN (IRE) 5 b.g. Le Moss – Suparoli (Super Sam) [1992/3 21d] half-brother to several winning jumpers, including very useful hurdler Tara Lee (by Tarqogan): dam poor Irish sprint maiden: well beaten in novice hurdle at Carlisle in April on debut. *N. W. Alexander*   –

MOSS PEAT 8 b.g. Le Moss – Andara (Hugh Lupus) [1992/3 22s^6 c25d^F] dipped-backed gelding: poor novice hurdler: fell on chasing debut: only form over 2½m on good ground: blinkered once. *R. G. Frost*   c–

MOSSY FERN 7 b.m. Le Moss – Deep Fern (Deep Run) [1992/3 c26d^5 c25v^{pu} c21v^4 c26d* c24g^{ur} c23m^2 c23s* c26v* c27d^4] leggy, workmanlike mare: fairly useful handicap chaser: won at Hereford, Worcester and Uttoxeter in second half of season: stays well: ran respectably on good to firm going sixth start, best form with plenty of give in the ground. *O. Sherwood*   c123 –

MOSSY RUN 6 ch.m. Le Moss – Kaminaki (Deep Run) [1992/3 21g^{pu} c22v^F] angular mare: no sign of ability: dead. *J. Wharton*   c– –

MOST INTERESTING 8 b.m. Music Boy – Quick Glance (Oats) [1992/3 17s^5 17d^4 16m^F 17g^3] smallish mare: modest hurdler: form only at around 2m: acts on good to firm and soft ground: usually held up. *G. H. Jones*   85

MOST RICH (IRE) 5 b.g. Dalsaan – Boule de Soie (The Parson) [1992/3 16s^6 17s^4 22v^3 22g] workmanlike gelding, rather unfurnished at present: sold 32,000 gns Doncaster August Sales: progressive form in novice hurdles first 3 starts: stays 2¾m: acts on heavy going. *Capt. T. A. Forster*   90

MOST SURPRISING (IRE) 4 b.g. Runnett – Blue Elver (Kings Lake (USA)) [1992/3 17m 17d^{pu}] lengthy gelding: modest 7f performer on Flat: showed nothing in early-season juvenile hurdles. *B. P. J. Baugh*   –

MOTLEY 5 br.m. Rainbow Quest (USA) – Sans Blague (USA) (The Minstrel (CAN)) [1992/3 17s^{pu}] smallish mare: seems of little account on Flat: no promise only start over hurdles. *J. Akehurst*   –

MOTOR CLOAK 7 b.g. Motivate – Cavalry Cloak (Queen's Hussar) [1992/3 16d^{pu} 17s^4 20s^2 22s^{pu} 17d 21s^4 17f^2] small gelding: poor novice hurdler: stays 2½m: probably acts on any going. *R. L. Brown*   80

MOTTRAM'S GOLD 8 ch.g. Good Times (ITY) – Speed The Plough (Grundy) [1992/3 20s^6 16v^F 16d 17g^{pu} 17g] small gelding: modest handicap hurdler: ran poorly in 1992/3: maiden chaser: stays 19f: acts on heavy going: blinkered once. *Mrs J. G. Retter*   c– –

MOU-DAFA 13 br.g. Mugatpura – Fanny O'Dea (Sadler's Wells) [1992/3 c22m^{pu}] small, narrow gelding: one-time fairly useful 2m chaser. *R. Lowe*   c– –

MOULTON BULL 7 ch.g. Chabrias (FR) – Welsh Cloud (Welsh Saint) [1992/3 c17v c21g^2 c23g^{bd} c20f^3 c22m^F c21g*] leggy, workmanlike gelding: won novice chase at Hexham in May: should stay beyond 21f: acts on firm ground: sketchy jumper. *S. J. Leadbetter*   c86

MOUNTAIN CABIN 11 ch.g. Patch – Sweet Mountain (Whistling Wind) [1992/3 c25g*] leggy gelding: winning hurdler: won hunter chase at Bangor in May: stays 25f: acts on good to firm and dead going: blinkered twice: temperamental. *G. D. Hanmer*   c81 § – §

MOUNTAIN GLOW 6 gr.g. Siberian Express (USA) – Bombshell (Le Levanstell) [1992/3 17g 18m] compact gelding: poor 2m novice hurdler: tried visored/blinkered. *B. Richmond*   –

MOUNTAIN KINGDOM (USA) 9 b.h. Exceller (USA) – Star In The North (USA) (Northern Dancer (CAN)) [1992/3 21g^{pu} 16d^3 17d 16s^2 20s^2] strong horse: fairly useful hurdler: not raced after December: suited by   122 testing conditions at 2m and stays 3m: acts on good to firm and soft ground. *N. Tinkler*

MOUNTAIN MASTER 7 b.g. Furry Glen – Leney Girl (Seminole II) [1992/3 22g⁴] leggy gelding: lightly-raced novice hurdler: stays 2¾m: acts on good to firm ground. *N. J. Henderson* — 85

MOUNTAIN RETREAT 7 br.g. Top Ville – Tarrystone (So Blessed) [1992/3 18fF 16gᵖᵘ 17g 16s² 18m* 16m⁴ 18d³ 18f²] leggy gelding: fair hurdler: won handicap at Exeter early in season: ran creditably later on: best at around 2m: acts on any going, including all-weather: front runner: none too fluent a jumper. *M. Williams* — 107

MOUNT ARGUS 11 ch.g. Don – Pendula (Tamerlane) [1992/3 c23d² c24d² c22f⁶ c26g*] strong gelding: useful hunter chaser: fifth course victory when winning at Uttoxeter in May: suited by a thorough test of stamina and give in the ground. *S. A. Brookshaw* — c116 / –

MOUNT EATON FOX 10 b.g. Buckskin (FR) – Town Fox (Continuation) [1992/3 c21s² c21g* c24f³ c25dᵖᵘ c27f] big, plain gelding: won maiden hunter chase at Folkestone in February: ran well next time: stays 3m: best form on a sound surface (respectable effort on soft): blinkered once. *P. F. Henderson* — c90 / –

MOUNTEBOR 9 b.g. Prince Regent (FR) – Land (Baldric II) [1992/3 c26d⁴ c24s² c24s⁵ c25s⁵ c24m⁴ c26mᵇᵈ] tall, lengthy gelding: fair handicap chaser: stays 3¼m: probably acts on any going: best form going right-handed: tends to carry head high and sometimes runs in snatches. *P. C. Haslam* — c102 / –

MOUNT FALCON 11 br.g. Paico – Lady Mell (Milan) [1992/3 c23gᵖᵘ] sturdy gelding: winning chaser: sold 875 gns Ascot November Sales: no form since 1989/90: resold 1,500 gns Malvern June Sales: occasionally blinkered: refused to race once. *R. D. Griffiths* — c– §

MOUNT KINABALU 6 b.g. Head For Heights – Kaisersage (FR) (Exbury) [1992/3 17d² 17f³] long-backed gelding: poor novice hurdler: placed twice late on, including in seller: races at around 2m: acts on firm, dead going and fibresand. *S. Christian* — 76

MOUNT PATRICK 9 b.g. Paddy's Stream – Hills of Fashion (Tarqogan) [1992/3 c21m⁵] workmanlike gelding: no form in 2 races over hurdles: modest pointer: fifth in novice hunter chase at Folkestone in May. *N. W. Padfield* — c60 / –

MOUNTSHANNON 7 b.g. Pry – Tara Ogan (Tarqogan) [1992/3 c21vF c24d⁴ c21gF 22gᵖᵘ 22m³ 26f⁶] workmanlike gelding: winning hurdler: let down by his jumping over fences: stays 2¾m: acts on dead and good to firm ground. *C. C. Trietline* — c– x / 91

MOURNE WARRIOR 10 b.g. Le Bavard (FR) – Glenallen (Carnatic) [1992/3 c21mᵖᵘ c21m⁵ c26g⁴ c23g⁴ c23f² c23g⁴ 22f⁵ 21f⁶] leggy gelding: poor maiden hurdler/chaser: stays 3¼m: acts on firm ground: usually visored or blinkered nowadays. *K. White* — c73 / –

MOVING FORCE 6 b.g. Muscatite – Saint Simbir (Simbir) [1992/3 18d 16g 16s⁶ a16gᵖᵘ] lengthy gelding: poor over middle distances on Flat and over hurdles: sold 1,200 gns Ascot March Sales: yet to race beyond 2¼m: acts on soft ground. *E. A. Wheeler* — 68

MOVING OUT 5 b.g. Slip Anchor – New Generation (Young Generation) [1992/3 16d⁵ 21v⁴ 25s 17d* 20g 16d⁵ 18d³ 16m*] leggy gelding: second foal: dam half-sister to good jumpers Mazel Tov and High Knowl: fair stayer on Flat: sold out of Sir Mark Prescott's stable 37,000 gns Newmarket Autumn Sales: made all in novice hurdles at Wolverhampton in February and Warwick (handicap) in May: very best form around 2m: acts on good to firm and dead ground: fair effort when blinkered seventh outing. *Miss H. C. Knight* — 96

MOWTHORPE 8 ch.g. Ballad Rock – Simeonova (Northfields (USA)) [1992/3 18g⁵ 16m³ c17dF 16s⁵ 18d 16d 16m⁶ 17m 16g 16g⁶] dipped-backed — c– / 87 gelding: modest hurdler: novice chaser: races mainly at around 2m: acts on good to firm and soft going: sometimes blinkered. *M. W. Easterby*

MOYDRUM PRINCE 7 ch.g. Carlingford Castle – Chinese Queen (Tarim) [1992/3 c16m5 c21m6] ex-Irish gelding: maiden hurdler: well beaten both outings in steeplechases (trained until after first start by G. Cully): best form at 2m: acts on heavy ground. *R. W. Crank* c– –

MOYMET 7 b.g. Jester – Majesta (Majority Blue) [1992/3 21g 23dpu 16g 16f2] compact, workmanlike gelding: novice hurdler/chaser: second in seller at Worcester in May: stays 2½m: acts on any ground: blinkered last 2 starts. *K. R. Burke* c– 85

MOYNSHA HOUSE (IRE) 5 b.g. Carlingford Castle – Verbana (Boreen (FR)) [1992/3 16spu 23spu 17v6] smallish, sturdy gelding: half-brother to 3 winning jumpers, notably useful staying chaser Cuddy Dale (by Deep Run): dam well beaten on Flat: no form in novice hurdles in first half of season: bred to stay well. *B. J. Curley* –

MOYODE REGENT 9 b.g. Prince Regent (FR) – Sylvarna (Seminole II) [1992/3 c17d4 c20g c20f c21s c20fpu] close-coupled gelding: poor novice hurdler/chaser: stays 2½m: acts on soft ground. *R. R. Lamb* c73 –

MOZEMO 6 ch.g. Remezzo – Mo Storeen (Abednego) [1992/3 16d 20s] tall, sparely-made gelding: behind in novice hurdles. *A. Bailey* –

MOZE TIDY 8 b.g. Rushmere – Church Belle (Spartan General) [1992/3 c26s5 c21dF c21d c26g6 c23m5] rather leggy, quite good-topped gelding: has had soft palate operation: handicap chaser: generally ran poorly in 1992/3: stays 3m: acts on soft ground: usually wears tongue strap. *R. Rowe* c– –

MR BOSTON 8 b.g. Halyudh (USA) – Edith Rose (Cheval) [1992/3 c21d6 c25d3 c27spu c28d4 c24s2 c30d3 c25s5 c28d3 c33g6 c25gF c26f*] lengthy, workmanlike gelding: fairly useful handicap chaser: trained until after ninth outing (blinkered only time) by R. Woodhouse: easy winner at Uttoxeter in May: would also have been easy winner at Ayr previous start but for falling 2 out: stays very well: acts on any going. *Mrs M. Reveley* c123 –

MR BRISKET 11 ch.g. Import – Argostone (Rockavon) [1992/3 c24mpu] workmanlike gelding: novice hurdler/chaser: no form for a very long time. *Mrs Corrina Hirst* c– –

MR BUSKER (IRE) 4 b.g. Orchestra – Kavali (Blakeney) [1992/3 F16m] half-brother to fairly useful Irish chaser Market Mover (by Lord Gayle): dam unraced: seventh of 24 in NH Flat race at Warwick in May: yet to race over hurdles. *D. J. G. Murray-Smith* –

MR CLANCY (IRE) 5 b.g. Over The River (FR) – Buskin's Dream (Little Buskins) [1992/3 F17d6 F17m2] smallish gelding: sixth live foal: dam unraced: won point in Ireland in March: second in 24-runner NH Flat race at Cheltenham following month: yet to race over hurdles or in a steeplechase. *T. G. Mills* –

MR DORMOUSE 7 b.g. Comedy Star (USA) – Tea-Pot (Ragstone) [1992/3 c21s3 c21mpu] sparely-made gelding: winning hurdler: moderate novice chaser: not raced after November: stays 25f well: acts on any going: best efforts over hurdles in visor (not visored last 4 starts over fences). *I. A. Balding* c96 –

MR DYNAMIC 11 b.g. Over The River (FR) – Rita's Star (Star Gazer) [1992/3 c20d6 c27v* c27vpu c35spu c22vpu c27d6] lengthy, workmanlike gelding: novice hurdler: poor form over fences: fortunate winner of novice chase at Newton Abbot in December: stays 27f: acts on heavy ground: tried blinkered. *D. J. Deacon* c81 –

MR ELK 4 gr.g. Bellypha – Shuteye (Shirley Heights) [1992/3 17m5 18g 22d3 21vpu] poor staying maiden on Flat: easily best effort over hurdles when third in selling handicap at Sedgefield in November: will stay beyond 2¾m: acts on dead ground: blinkered first start. *Mrs M. Reveley* 75

MR ENTERTAINER 10 gr.g. Neltino – Office Party (Counsel) [1992/3 c21gF c20s4 c20g* c24g c20sF c21f2] good-topped gelding: fairly useful c129 –

chaser: won handicap at Newbury in February: creditable second at Uttoxeter in May: effective at around 2½m and probably stays 3m: acts on dead and firm ground: races up with pace. *N. A. Gaselee*

MR FELIX 7 b.g. Camden Town – Mohila (Busted) [1992/3 c18mF c16g5 c17f* c16v* c16s4] close-coupled gelding: improved chaser: won claimer at Huntingdon and handicap at Plumpton prior to running extremely well when fourth in valuable event at Sandown in December: best at around 2m: acts on any ground: blinkered 3 times in 1990/1: sometimes gives trouble at start. *R. Champion* — c92 +

MR FENWICK 9 ch.g. Domitor (USA) – Topsey Lorac (St Columbus) [1992/3 20m 27g 26vpu] good-topped, workmanlike gelding: one-time fair staying hurdler: very lightly raced and no form since 1988/9. *J. L. Eyre* — –

MR FIVE WOOD (IRE) 5 ch.g. Denel (FR) – Beau Lady (Beau Chapeau) [1992/3 F16d5 F16d5 22g* 25v3] fifth foal: dam winning Irish jumper: won amateurs maiden hurdle at Ayr in March: creditable third in novice event at Perth following month: stays 25f: acts on heavy ground: to join G. Richards. *J. F. C. Maxwell, Ireland* — 95 p

MR FLANAGAN 7 b.g. Idiot's Delight – Here We Go (Hallez (FR)) [1992/3 25spu 22v2 24s4 21d* 20d] workmanlike gelding: chasing type: sixth foal: half-brother to 2m Flat winner/novice hurdler Full Speed Ahead (by Hotfoot): dam won over 7.5f at 2 yrs in Ireland: showed plenty of ability prior to making all in novice hurdle at Uttoxeter in March: stiff task following month: effective at 21f and stays well: acts on heavy ground: should do better. *C. P. E. Brooks* — 109 p

MR FLUTTS 7 b.g. Derrylin – Madam Flutterbye (Quiet Fling (USA)) [1992/3 20gF 20g2] lightly-raced winning hurdler: creditable second in handicap at Hereford in May: stays 2½m: acts on good to firm going. *J. C. Tuck* — 100

MR FUDGE 6 gr.g. Broadsword (USA) – Blades (Supreme Sovereign) [1992/3 F17d F16s aF16g3 18s2 18m] sturdy, workmanlike gelding: half-brother to winning jumpers Oakgrove and Not So Sharp (both by Roan Rocket): dam ran only at 2 yrs: second in novice hurdle at Market Rasen in April: will stay beyond 2¼m: acts on soft ground. *O. Brennan* — 95

MR GEE 8 b.g. Crooner – Miss Desla (Light Thrust) [1992/3 c26vur c27s3] rangy gelding: poor staying novice chaser: no form in first half of season: blinkered twice. *R. Curtis* — c–

MR GLEN 8 ch.g. The Parson – Park Blue (Levanter) [1992/3 c25vF 23g* 25v4 28g4] tall, leggy gelding: lightly-raced hurdler: won novice event at Kelso in April: easily best effort next time: fell third on chasing debut (trained until after then by G. Richards): stays 25f: acts on heavy ground. *N. B. Mason* — c– 92

MR GOSSIP 11 b.g. Le Bavard (FR) – Regency View (Royal Highway) [1992/3 c24dur] leggy gelding: fairly useful hurdler in 1991/2: sold 7,300 gns Doncaster October Sales: one-time fair chaser: placed in points in 1993: out-and-out stayer: acts on good to firm and soft ground: tried blinkered in 1989/90: tends to run in snatches and is a difficult ride. *Mrs V. Wales* — c–

MR HAPPY FEET 6 b.g. Julio Mariner – Sarasail (Hitting Away) [1992/3 17dur 22v6 24spu] leggy gelding: lightly raced and no sign of ability. *A. P. James* — –

MR INVADER 6 br.g. Le Moss – Bruna Magli (Brave Invader (USA)) [1992/3 16s 23v4 22g2 22f4] good-topped gelding: chasing type: poor novice hurdler: will stay beyond 2¾m: best efforts on a sound surface (acts on firm). *N. A. Gaselee* — 84

MR JAMBOREE 7 b.g. Martinmas – Miss Reliant (Reliance II) [1992/3 c16g* c16dF c21s4 c16v3 c16d3 c16d6 c24f* c21g* c21g6] leggy gelding: maiden hurdler: won novice chases at Kempton in October and Newbury and Sandown in March: stays 3m: probably best on a sound surface (acts on firm going): usually jumps well. *J. T. Gifford* — c112

MR JERVIS (IRE) 4 b.g. M Double M (USA) – Amorosa (GER) (Frontal) [1992/3 17s⁵] big, strong, workmanlike gelding: chasing type: half-brother to a winner in Germany by Horst-Herbert: dam lightly-raced half-sister to successful French jumper Mister Gay: tailed-off last in juvenile hurdle at Sandown in February. *J. T. Gifford* —

MR KIRBY 11 b.g. Monksfield – Mayfield Grove (Khalkis) [1992/3 c26mᵖᵘ c21gᵘʳ] tall gelding: staying hurdler/maiden chaser: no form since 1989/90: tried blinkered/visored. *A. P. Jones* c– —

MR KNITWIT 6 ch.g. Kambalda – Clonaghadoo (Perspex) [1992/3 18g² 17d²] sturdy gelding: modest form when placed in early-season novice hurdles (finished lame final outing): takes good hold but will stay further than 2¼m: acts on dead ground. *G. Richards* 96

MR LE MOSS 7 b.g. Le Moss – Peaceful Pleasure (Silent Whistle) [1992/3 20v 20vᵖᵘ] tall gelding: chasing type: very lightly-raced novice hurdler: pulled up lame in February: should stay well. *M. C. Pipe* —

MR MAD 5 b.g. Good Times (ITY) – Mistress Bowen (Owen Anthony) [1992/3 21sᵖᵘ] lengthy gelding: tailed off in novice hurdles. *J. D. Thomas* —

MR MATT (IRE) 5 b.g. Bustineto – Princesspry (Pry) [1992/3 21d² 20v* 20v* 21s⁴ 23gˢᵘ] workmanlike gelding: first foal: dam unraced: winning pointer in Ireland: won novice hurdle at Plumpton and handicap at Lingfield in first half of season: every chance when slipping up after 4 out final start (February): effective at around 2½m and will stay 3m: acts on heavy going. *D. M. Grissell* 111

MR MAYFAIR 10 b.g. The Parson – Doe Royale (Royal Buck) [1992/3 25sᵖᵘ c23v⁴ c23g⁴ c24m³ c22g² c26d² c23m³] lengthy, workmanlike gelding: winning hurdler: moderate maiden chaser: stays 3¼m: acts on good to firm and dead ground: visored final start (below form). *J. A. C. Edwards* c87 —

MR MCGREGOR 11 b.g. Formidable (USA) – Mrs Tiggywinkle (Silly Season) [1992/3 16dᵖᵘ 17vᵖᵘ 17fᵖᵘ] neat gelding: lightly-raced selling hurdler: no form in 1992/3. *K. R. Supple* —

MR MULKEEN 6 b.g. Lucky Wednesday – Swakara (Porto Bello) [1992/3 21sᵖᵘ 16vᵖᵘ 17d] angular gelding: no sign of ability. *G. H. Jones* —

MR MURDOCK 8 b.g. Last Fandango – Moss Pink (USA) (Levmoss) [1992/3 c24f* c24mᵘʳ c21f* c28f³] angular, sparely-made gelding: fairly useful hunter chaser: won at Lingfield and Wincanton (novices) and also ran well when third at Stratford in 1992/3: stays 3½m: probably acts on any going. *H. Wellstead* c96

MR NEWS (IRE) 4 b.c. Trojan Fen – Princess Biddy (Sun Prince) [1992/3 18d* 16d* 17g²] close-coupled colt: brother to winning selling hurdler Pushy Lover: poor maiden on Flat: sold 1,050 gns Doncaster October Sales: won selling hurdle at Market Rasen (bought in 3,500 gns) and juvenile claiming handicap hurdle at Ludlow: claimed for £6,101 (probably for export) in December on final start: stays 2¼m: acts on dead going: held up. *S. E. Kettlewell* 86

MR OPTIMIST 12 b.g. Pollerton – Super Cailin (Brave Invader (USA)) [1992/3 17s] tall, rather finely-made gelding: poor hurdler: let down by his jumping over fences: stays 21f: acts on soft going (seems unsuited by firm). *Miss T. A. White* c– —

MR PANACHE 11 ch.g. Dublin Taxi – Becalmed (Right Tack) [1992/3 21sᵘʳ c18dᵖᵘ] compact, good-bodied gelding: very lightly raced: novice selling hurdler: poor chaser: no form since 1990/1. *J. S. Hubbuck* c– —

MR-PAW 10 b.g. Deep Run – Khalketta (Khalkis) [1992/3 c17s⁴ c17s³ c21s c25sᵘʳ c21d c17sᵖᵘ c21g² c17g² 22fᵖᵘ c17f³ c18m*] tall, leggy gelding: modest chaser: won maiden event at Market Rasen in June: stays 21f: probably acts on any going: blinkered once. *F. Murphy* c87 —

MR PICKPOCKET (IRE) 5 b.g. Roselier (FR) – Gusserane Princess (Paddy's Stream) [1992/3 F16v* F16s³ F17m F17d] leggy gelding: has scope: third foal: half-brother to promising hunter chaser Overheard (by Over The River): dam signs of ability in maiden hurdles and NH Flat races in Ireland: won NH Flat race at Towcester in January: behind in well-contested similar events last 2 outings: yet to race over hurdles or fences. *J. Akehurst*

MR PIPKIN 7 b.g. Casino Boy – True Minstrel (Prince Hansel) [1992/3 c17spu c17mF 20g] strong gelding: no sign of ability. *R. J. Hodges* c– –

MR POD 7 b.g. Grey Ghost – Forlorn Lady (Forlorn River) [1992/3 c24gpu c27dpu c21s] angular gelding: poor maiden hurdler/chaser at best: no form in 1992/3. *R. R. Lamb* c– –

MR POPPLETON 4 ch.c. Ballacashtal (CAN) – Greenstead Lady (Great Nephew) [1992/3 21dpu] leggy colt: no promise in juvenile hurdle in December: won 1½m maiden on Flat in February: sold 7,300 gns Doncaster May Sales. *D. W. P. Arbuthnot* –

MR REINER (IRE) 5 br.g. Vision (USA) – Yvonne's Choice (Octavo (USA)) [1992/3 18m5 17m4 18m* 22f* 18d* 18g2 22spu 18d* 22d4 18s3 16s 18m3 18d4 22m6 22m2 18m6] compact gelding: fair hurdler: won 4 races at Sedgefield in first half of season, 2 sellers (no bid), novice handicap and handicap: generally ran creditably afterwards: effective at 2¼m and stays 2¾m: probably acts on any going: excellent mount for a claimer: tough and genuine. *J. Wade* 101

MR ROYAL 7 b.g. Royal Match – Bel Ria (Gay Fandango (USA)) [1992/3 20s6] sturdy gelding: first foal: dam placed at up to 1½m on Flat: very green, signs of ability when sixth in novice hurdle at Newcastle in December: sold to M. Hammond 14,000 gns in May: will improve. *W. A. Stephenson* 69 p

MRS BAS 6 br.m. Oats – Polarita (Arctic Kanda) [1992/3 20m6 16g4 17d4 21f 16s] leggy mare: poor maiden plater: best form at around 2m: acts on dead ground. *W. Clay* 66

MR SETASIDE 8 br.g. Royal Fountain – Cregg Park (Orchardist) [1992/3 c23s3 c25d4 c24d5 c24s2 c26v* c24s* c24v2 c33g4] tall, angular gelding: poor novice hurdler: better over fences, and won handicaps at Uttoxeter (novice event) in December and Leicester in January: not raced after February: suited by good test of stamina: acts on heavy going: blinkered once: sound jumper. *J. Mackie* c107 –

MRS JAWLEYFORD (USA) 5 b.m. Dixieland Band (USA) – Did She Agree (USA) (Restless Native) [1992/3 18g2 18d* 18d 16v3 18vpu a16g2 a16g3 a16g* a16g* a16g2 17spu] leggy, angular mare: fair handicap hurdler: won at Sedgefield in October and Southwell in February and March: form only at around 2m: acts on heavy going and fibresand. *C. Smith* 110

MR SLATE 7 b.g. Uncle Pokey – Irma Flintstone (Compensation) [1992/3 c17f6] little sign of ability. *J. H. Johnson* c– –

MRS MAYHEW (IRE) 5 ch.m. Deep Run – Gortroe Queen (Simbir) [1992/3 17g5 20g5 16v* 16g] lengthy, unfurnished mare: third foal: dam won on Flat and over jumps (at up to 2½m) in Ireland: won novice hurdle at Worcester in April: ran poorly later in month: should stay 2½m: acts well on heavy ground. *F. Murphy* 83

MR SMILEY 6 b.g. Pharly (FR) – Yelming (Thatch (USA)) [1992/3 17fpu] no sign of ability. *R. J. Baker* –

MR SNAIL 5 b.g. Petorius – Spring Lane (Forlorn River) [1992/3 17d 17dpu 16d] sturdy gelding: fair 7f winner on Flat in 1991, no form in 1993 including in novice hurdles. *S. E. Kettlewell* –

MR SNIPE 7 gr.h. Sit In The Corner (USA) – Grey Bird (Eastern Venture) [1992/3 F18d3 F16g4 16sF 22dpu] leggy horse: sixth foal: brother to useful hurdler Mr Woodcock and half-brother to winning hurdler Poaching Pocket (by Some Hand): dam fair staying hurdler: signs of a little ability in NH Flat races and novice hurdles: dead. *Mrs M. Reveley* –

MRS NORMAN 4 b.f. Lochnager – Economy Pep (Jimmy Reppin) [1992/3 16d 16g 16mF] leggy filly: half-sister to winning hurdler Cheap –

Metal (by Sonnen Gold): of little account on Flat and in novice hurdles: blinkered final outing. *A. W. Potts*

MRSUNVALLEYPEANUTS 7 b.g. Le Moss – Quit The Hassle (Deep Run) [1992/3 a16g4] no sign of ability. *Capt. J. Wilson* –

MR TAYLOR 8 b.g. Martinmas – Miss Reliant (Reliance II) [1992/3 24d c21spu c22s4 c24gur a22g6 a24g 21v* 21s* 21s5 21f4 22f] leggy, close-coupled gelding: fair handicap hurdler: successful at Towcester in February and Wetherby in March: no form over fences: stays 3m: probably acts on any ground: unreliable. *H. J. Collingridge* c–
108 §

MR TITTLE TATTLE 7 b.g. Le Bavard (FR) – Mille Fleurs (Floribunda) [1992/3 c21g2 c27dF c24spu c24d6 c24g2 c24fpu c21d4] strong gelding: winning hurdler: modest novice chaser: stays 3m: form only on good ground: blinkered nowadays. *K. C. Bailey* c87
–

M R TWO 6 b.g. Andy Rew – Small Hope Bay (The Brianstan) [1992/3 17dF 16d 16d 20d 16m] leggy gelding: of little account. *P. D. Evans* –

MR VERGETTE 9 ch.g. Mr Fordette – Ark's Vision (Golden Vision) [1992/3 c23d2 c21gpu] tall, leggy gelding: winning hurdler: maiden chaser: stayed 2½m: acted on good to firm and dead ground: dead. *Mrs J. G. Retter* c78
–

MR WESTCLIFF 5 b.g. Sonnen Gold – Dyna Drueni (Law of The Wise) [1992/3 F16d6 16g 20g a16g5] rather unfurnished gelding: first foal: dam winning hurdler out of half-sister to smart hunter chaser Snowdra Queen: no sign of ability over hurdles. *Denys Smith* –

MR WOODLARK 6 b.g. Ranksborough – Presceena Wood (Precipice Wood) [1992/3 F18s2 F16g4 F17m] big, rangy gelding: second foal: half-brother to winning Wood Corner (by Sit In The Corner): dam won over fences at 2½m and 25f: in frame in NH Flat races: yet to race over hurdles or fences. *R. G. Frost* –

MR ZIEGFELD (USA) 4 b.g. Fred Astaire (USA) – I Assume (USA) (Young Emperor) [1992/3 16spu 16d6 16d] angular gelding: modest middle-distance performer at best on Flat: sold 10,000 gns Newmarket Autumn Sales: showed nothing in juvenile hurdles: blinkered last 2 starts. *R. J. Baker* –

MTOROSHANGA 4 b.f. Ascendant – Jacaranda (Marcus Superbus) [1992/3 F18s 17d6 16fpu] sparely-made, close-coupled filly: third foal: sister to temperamental 6-y-o Miss Marula: dam lightly-raced maiden pointer: no sign of ability. *J. E. Collinson* –

MUBAARIS 10 ch.g. Hello Gorgeous (USA) – Aloft (High Top) [1992/3 21g3 23m 22f3 25s 24gF 26s* 24s* 25spu a24gpu 26s4] compact gelding: carries condition: modest hurdler: won handicaps at Catterick (seller, sold out of B. Richmond's stable 3,800 gns) and Bangor in first half of season: not raced after January: sold 1,600 gns Doncaster May Sales: stays very well: acts on any going: sometimes blinkered: often hangs left (has worn pricker on near side) and is suited by left-handed courses: ungenuine. *Mrs A. Swinbank* 93 §

MUBADIR (USA) 5 ch.g. Nodouble (USA) – Hapai (Nijinsky (CAN)) [1992/3 16g* 16g* 16d5 18s2 16d2 17m 16m2] angular gelding: useful hurdler: won maiden at Galway and minor event at Tipperary early in season: ran well when second afterwards, poorly at Cheltenham on penultimate outing: stays 2¼m: acts on soft and good to firm going: blinkered once. *N. Meade, Ireland* 132

MUCH 6 ch.g. Morston (FR) – Podzola (Royal Prerogative) [1992/3 16m 20g 16s6 17dF] unfurnished gelding: no form in novice hurdles. *Mrs A. Price* –

MUDAHIM 7 b.g. Shareef Dancer (USA) – Mariska (FR) (Tanerko) [1992/3 22s3 21d3] close-coupled gelding: smart hurdler in 1991/2: only useful form in mid-season events in 1992/3: stays well: successful on good to firm ground but ideally suited by plenty of give. *C. D. Broad* 136

MUDDY LANE 5 b.g. Ilium – Monstrosa (Monsanto (FR)) [1992/3 17g 22fur 22s3 20m 17d*] lengthy gelding: no bid after winning novice selling 79 hurdle at Newton Abbot in May: every chance when trying to run out and unseating rider last on second outing: stays 2¾m: probably acts on any going. *P. F. Nicholls*

MUFID (USA) 4 ch.g. Woodman (USA) – Princess Laika (USA) (Blushing Groom (FR)) [1992/3 17f] lightly-raced maiden on Flat, stays 1m: sold out of R. Hern's stable 2,200 gns Newmarket Autumn Sales: well behind in novice hurdle at Newcastle in May. *R. R. Lamb* —

MUIRFIELD 7 ch.g. Hawaiian Return (USA) – Cherry Tart (Vulgan) c74 [1992/3 c23g³ c23g⁴ c17d⁴ c16g c20gᵘʳ c24gᴿ c20g] strong, lengthy gelding: — poor novice chaser: stays 23f: acts on dead ground: blinkered final start. *J. K. M. Oliver*

MUIRFIELD VILLAGE 7 b.g. Lomond (USA) – Ukelele (USA) (Riva Ridge (USA)) [1992/3 18f] small, lengthy gelding: poor hurdler nowadays: — stays 2¾m: acts on any ground: visored once. *C. T. Nash*

MUIR STATION (USA) 5 b.h. Darby Creek Road (USA) – Donna Inez (USA) (Herbager) [1992/3 17s* 16d* 16d³ 16s² 16d² 16d³ 16d* 16s³ 20s² 136 21g³] leggy, close-coupled horse: usually looks well: useful hurdler: won maiden at Tralee and minor events at Listowel and Leopardstown (quite valuable event) in 1992/3: effective at 2m under testing conditions, and will stay beyond 2lf: acts on heavy going: wears blinkers: tough and consistent. *J. S. Bolger, Ireland*

MUIZENBERG 6 b.g. Mashhor Dancer (USA) – Allotria (Red God) [1992/3 17d² 17d*] good-topped gelding: won novice hurdle at Stratford in 95 October: will prove best at around 2m: acts on dead ground. *J. A. C. Edwards*

MULAWIH (USA) 5 b.g. Secreto (USA) – 'n Everything Nice (USA) (Damascus (USA)) [1992/3 F14s⁵ F16g⁶] fourth foal: half-brother to 2

Miss Catriona M. Keating's "Muir Station"

winners in North America: dam unraced half-sister to Alydar: bought for 5,200 gns Newmarket Autumn (1991) Sales: signs of ability in NH Flat races: yet to race over hurdles or fences. *Mrs V. A. Aconley*

MULBANK 7 b.g. Sit In The Corner (USA) – Hidden Treasure (Tudor Treasure) [1992/3 17v⁶ 20s² c17s* c20g³ c16f²] tall gelding: fair hurdler: won novice event at Chepstow in February on chasing debut: ran respectably afterwards: effective at 2m and will stay beyond 2½m: acts on any going: races up with pace: likely to make quite useful handicap chaser. *P. J. Hobbs*   c105 p / 105

MULBEN (NZ) 13 ch.g. San Mellay (NZ) – Dollie (NZ) (Even Stevens) [1992/3 c21sᵖᵘ] lengthy, rather narrow gelding: novice hurdler/chaser: lightly raced and no form since 1988/9. *J. E. Grey*   c– / –

MULBERRY HARBOUR (IRE) 5 b.g. Orchestra – Turbo Lady (Tumble Wind (USA)) [1992/3 F14d 17sᵖᵘ 22sᵖᵘ] 1,550 3-y-o: close-coupled gelding: fourth foal: dam unraced half-sister to 2 winning jumpers: no sign of ability: blinkered final outing: sold 1,500 gns Doncaster March Sales. *C. C. Trietline*   –

MULCIBER 5 b.g. Head For Heights – Quisissanno (Be My Guest (USA)) [1992/3 18s⁶] leggy gelding: lightly-raced novice hurdler: likely to prove best at around 2m: fair middle-distance performer on Flat (goes well on equitrack), winner twice early in 1993. *G. Harwood*   84

MULLINGAR CON (IRE) 5 gr.g. Orchestra – Kilross (Menelek) [1992/3 17g 17d 17s] leggy, good-topped gelding: fourth foal: half-brother to winning Irish 2¾m hurdler Ross Gale (by Strong Gale): dam poor maiden jumper in Ireland: poor form in 2m novice hurdles: bred to do better over further. *B. J. Curley*   73 p

MULTUM IN PARVO 10 b.g. Proverb – Kova's Daughter (Brave Invader (USA)) [1992/3 c25dᵖᵘ c20sᶠ⁵ c21v³ c21dᵖᵘ c21s⁴ c21dᵖᵘ] lengthy gelding: one-time useful chaser: fairly useful form at best in 1992/3: best form at around 2½m: acts on any going: visored final start. *J. A. C. Edwards*   c124 / –

MUMMY'S SONG 8 b.g. Mummy's Pet – Welsh Miniature (Owen Anthony) [1992/3 26gᵖᵘ 16fᵖᵘ 17d] angular, sparely-made gelding: winning 2m selling hurdler: no form since 1989/90: refused to race once. *J. Harriman*   – §

MUNDAY DEAN 5 ch.g. Kind of Hush – Nancy Brig (Brigadier Gerard) [1992/3 21sᵖᵘ 17v⁵ 17v a16g* a16g² a18g² a16g³ 17g³] workmanlike gelding: poor hurdler: won maiden at Lingfield in January: won at 1½m on Flat in May: best form around 2m but should stay further: acts on good to firm ground and equitrack: blinkered last 4 starts. *R. J. O'Sullivan*   79

MUNIR (USA) 4 b. or br.c. Fappiano (USA) – Naval Orange (USA) (Hoist The Flag (USA)) [1992/3 16d⁵ 16s⁴ a16g³ a18g* a20g* a20g* 22m⁵] tall, leggy colt: modest middle-distance maiden on Flat in Ireland: sold out of K. Prendergast's stable 2,300 gns Newmarket Autumn Sales: successful in 3 novice hurdles at Southwell in second half of season, first 2 handicaps: stays 2¾m: acts on good to firm, soft going and fibresand: sometimes needs plenty of driving. *J. L. Harris*   97

MUNKA 7 b.g. Tachypous – Canterbury Lace (Golden Vision) [1992/3 17g* 17s⁴ 16d² 18g² 17g] compact gelding: chasing type: eighth reported foal: dam once-raced half-sister to Bula: won novice hurdle at Newbury in November: generally ran creditably afterwards: effective at 2m, but will be well suited by further: acts on soft ground: should prove capable of better. *P. J. Hobbs*   96 p

MURPHAIDEEZ 6 b.g. Le Moss – Toombeola (Raise You Ten) [1992/3 20m⁶ 21d 24s⁴ 21s 22d* 25vᵖᵘ] small gelding: easily best effort over hurdles when winning novice handicap at Market Rasen in January by a distance: should stay beyond 2¾m: acts on dead going. *R. Earnshaw*   93

MURPHY STREET 7 b.g. Buckskin (FR) – Orinda Way (Deep Run) [1992/3 22g⁵ 21d 20d c21dᶠ] sturdy gelding: poor novice hurdler: only a little promise on chasing debut: stays 2¾m. *N. A. Twiston-Davies*   c– / 81

MURPHYS WAY 4 br.f. Ardross – Choir (High Top) [1992/3 F16s*
F17m F17m] angular filly: fifth foal: half-sister to 6-y-o Choir's Image (by
Lochnager): dam behind in 4 races on Flat: 33/1, won 16-runner NH Flat
race at Bangor in February: soundly beaten in better contests afterwards:
yet to race over hurdles. *J. L. Eyre*

MUSCADINE 6 b.m. Muscatite – Bee Hawk (Sea Hawk II) [1992/3
22mpu 17g 16d] sparely-made mare: of no account. *A. J. Chamberlain*

MUSE 6 ch.g. High Line – Thoughtful (Northfields (USA)) [1992/3 20d*
26s⁶ 16s* 22s* 16g³]   165

Muse provided plenty of food for thought in his third season over
hurdles. Too much for the odds-on Morley Street in the Racecall Ascot
Hurdle in November. That race saw Muse, straight out of the novice class,
exceed our expectations for him at the first opportunity. A small individual,
he was not an obvious choice for top hurdling honours despite his smart
novice form (including a second to the ill-fated Thetford Forest in the Sun
Alliance) and although he had seen off five of his six rivals approaching the
last at Ascot, it looked as if Morley Street would still put Muse firmly in his
place. It was 9/1-shot Muse, however, who stuck his neck out on the run-in,
winning by a head, with another eight lengths back to the third, Tyrone
Bridge. Morley Street was conceding 8 lb and the pace had been a pretty
steady one, but no matter, this was clearly a much improved performance
from Muse all the same.

His next success came giving weight all round. In the meantime he'd
come sixth of eight finishers in the Long Walk Hurdle at Ascot, effectively
disproving the theory that he was an out-and-out stayer. Muse reverted to
two miles for the first time in 1992/3 in the Cheveley Park Stud New
Year's Day Hurdle at Windsor. Changed from a conditions event to a limited
handicap, the latest renewal was decided in a stirring finish. Muse was
pressed on both sides going to the second last; Duke of Monmouth, the
even-money favourite Baydon Star, Jungle Knife and Lift And Load were the
ones snapping at his heels. Baydon Star (receiving 8 lb) and Lift And Load
(receiving 17 lb) drew level on the run-in but in the last hundred yards Muse
and his 5 lb-claiming jockey Tony Procter were again on top. This turned
out to be the best performance in a handicap hurdle all season, one that
made 25/1 quotes for the Champion Hurdle look generous at the time. The
last big moves in the Champion market, however, owed most to misfortune.
The biggest shake-up came after Muse's fourth start of the season, in the
Wyko Power Transmission Hurdle at Cheltenham at the end of January; in a
four-runner race, Muse demonstrated what good form he was in, storming
clear of Nomadic Way to take the £27,000 first prize by twenty-five lengths,
but as much attention was focused at the top of the hill on the stricken
Mighty Mogul. Muse was now sharing Champion Hurdle favouritism, but he

*Cheveley Park Stud New Year's Day Hurdle (Limited Handicap), Windsor—
Muse (No. 1) battles on gamely to victory, just ahead of Baydon Star and Lift And Load*

Wyko Power Transmission Hurdle, Cheltenham—
Muse (P. Holley) jumps the last a long way clear

too failed to make the line-up. Attempting to give 8 lb to principal rival Valfinet in the Kingwell Hurdle at Wincanton on his warm-up for Cheltenham, Muse was beaten a long way into third, returning with a knee injury. Thankfully, Muse lived to fight another day, and he returned to action on the Flat in June. And fight, of course, is what he does best. Muse is a racehorse of great enthusiasm, a most genuine front runner reminiscent of his late stable-companion Floyd.

		High Line (ch 1966)	High Hat (ch 1957)	Hyperion / Madonna
Muse (ch.g. 1987)			Time Call (b 1955)	Chanteur II / Aleria
		Thoughtful (ch 1979)	Northfields (ch 1968)	Northern Dancer / Little Hut
			Wishful Thinking (ch 1960)	Petition / Musidora

Muse has yet to show that he stays so well as Floyd did, but gives the impression that he is strong enough in stamina to need conditions testing when he's at two miles. At the time, it was the general view that he faced a stiff task conceding weight to Valfinet over two miles on good ground at Wincanton and he started at 7/4 to Valfinet's 5/4 on. Muse's earlier runs in 1992/3 were all on a soft surface, but his novice record and Flat career suggest that he acts on top-of-the-ground as well. Muse's dam is the fairly useful mile-and-a-quarter winner Thoughtful, a half-sister to Heavenly Thought (the dam of top-class miler Homing and St Leger second Water Mill) and a granddaughter of the 1949 One Thousand Guineas and Oaks winner Musidora. Of Thoughtful's two previous foals, one, Meditator (by High Line), is a winning hurdler best at up to two and a half miles, and her fourth is the winning Flat stayer Kadari (by Commanche Run), placed over hurdles. We will probably have to travel to Germany to see any more of Thoughtful's produce, however, following her sale for 5,400 guineas at Newmarket in December, 1989. The first of her foals born there is already a winner, the imaginatively-named Master Willie colt Thoughtful's Willie. *D. R. C. Elsworth*

MUSICAL MONARCH (NZ)   7 ch.g. Leader of The Band (USA) – Cheelbrite (NZ) (Head Hunter) [1992/3 21v* 21s³ 24s² 21g* 25d⁴ 22d] 112 compact gelding: fair handicap hurdler: successful at Chepstow in December and Warwick in March: stays 3m: acts on heavy going: races up with the pace. *D. H. Barons*

MUSICAL MONK 5 ch.g. True Song – Princess Iona (St Columbus) [1992/3 16s^F] non-thoroughbred gelding: first foal: dam unraced: behind when falling last in novice hurdle at Warwick in November on debut: dead. *J. Webber*

—

MUSICAL TREND (IRE) 5 br.g. Whistling Top – Alta Moda (FR) (Snob II) [1992/3 F16g] half-brother to winning Irish jumpers Blue Ring (by Young Barnaby) and Ring Princess (by Whistling Top): dam placed on Flat in France: behind in NH Flat race at Kempton in February: yet to race over hurdles or fences. *O. Sherwood*

—

MUSIC BE MAGIC 14 b.g. Brave Invader (USA) – Forgello (Bargello) [1992/3 c20f4 c21m3] good-topped, workmanlike gelding: one-time useful chaser and fair hurdler: in frame in hunter chases in March: stays 2½m: seems to act on any going: blinkered twice, visored once: irresolute. *N. B. Mason*

c79 §
— §

MUSIC BOX 7 ch.g. Orchestra – Pearl Locket (Gulf Pearl) [1992/3 17g3 16m* 18g 24g5 c20g c19s c16dF c16vur 16v] sturdy ex-Irish gelding: won handicap hurdle at Naas in July: no form after, including over fences: sold out of W. Browne's stable 11,500 gns Doncaster October Sales after fifth outing: should stay beyond 2m: acts on good to firm and dead ground. *R. J. Hodges*

c–
98 d

MUSIC DANCER 4 b.g. Music Boy – Stepping Gaily (Gay Fandango (USA)) [1992/3 17gro] unfurnished gelding: modest sprinter on Flat: sold 6,400 gns Newmarket Autumn Sales: ran out second (saddle slipped) in selling hurdle in December. *R. J. Hodges*

—

MUSKET SHOT 5 br.g. Zambrano – Now You Know (Scottish Rifle) [1992/3 16d 17m 17g 16m 21d] small, leggy gelding: poor maiden on Flat and over hurdles: blinkered final outing. *V. Thompson*

—

MUSKORA (IRE) 4 b.g. Muscatite – Singing Wren (Julio Mariner) [1992/3 F17m] unfurnished gelding: fourth foal: half-brother to NH Flat race winner Hazel Crest (by Hays): dam ran twice: eighth of 23 in NH Flat race at Cheltenham in April: yet to race over hurdles. *G. H. Peter-Hoblyn*

—

MUSTAHIL (IRE) 4 gr.g. Sure Blade (USA) – Zumurrudah (USA) (Spectacular Bid (USA)) [1992/3 17m3 17g 16g5 16g 16d5] small gelding: modest handicapper on Flat, winner at 1m in 1993: modest form at best over hurdles: easily best effort on good to firm going: sometimes looks reluctant. *R. J. Hodges*

96

MUST BE MAGICAL (USA) 5 ch.g. Temperence Hill (USA) – Honorine (USA) (Blushing Groom (FR)) [1992/3 17g5 16dsu 16d5 17g6] tall, workmanlike gelding: poor middle-distance stayer on Flat (goes well on fibresand): sold 2,200 gns Doncaster November Sales: only form over hurdles when fifth in maiden at Uttoxeter in April on third start: should stay beyond 2m: acts on dead ground: sometimes wears tongue strap. *J. Mackie*

82

MUST B HAVON 7 b.m. Deep Run – Fugue (Le Prince) [1992/3 17mpu] second foal: dam won NH Flat race and placed at up to 3m over hurdles: showed nothing in maiden hurdle in April on debut. *G. H. Yardley*

—

MUSTHAVEASWIG 7 gr.g. Croghan Hill – Gin An Tonic (Osprey Hawk) [1992/3 21d2 21gur 26d2 c26vpu c20s2 c24g* c25g* c24f2 c25g* c25g2 c23f4] well-made gelding: novice hurdler: successful in handicap chases at Doncaster (novices), Nottingham and Sandown in second half of season: stays well: probably acts on any going: not yet an accomplished jumper of fences. *D. Nicholson*

c117
101

MUTARE 8 b.g. Boreen (FR) – Slave Trade (African Sky) [1992/3 c20spu c25sF c25dF] well-made gelding: very useful hurdler/chaser: showed he'd retained his ability until falling at the last on final 2 starts: stayed 3m: acted on heavy and good to firm going: usually forced pace: dead. *N. J. Henderson*

c144
—

MUTARID (USA) 8 ch.h. Kris – Voie Lactee (FR) (Amber Rama (USA)) [1992/3 16s5 c17vpu 17d c25mpu] angular horse: poor hurdler/maiden chaser: best form at 2m: acts on soft going. *K. A. Morgan*

c–
—

MUTUAL AGREEMENT 6 ch.m. Quayside – Giolla's Bone (Pitpan) [1992/3 F17v 22v 22f6 20d3 17m2 16d4] fourth foal: half-sister to winning hurdler/chaser Mutual Trust (by Pollerton): dam behind in NH Flat races and a maiden hurdle in Ireland: novice selling hurdler: stays 2½m: acts on dead and good to firm ground. *R. G. Frost*　　76

MUTUAL TRUST 9 ch.g. Pollerton – Giolla's Bone (Pitpan) [1992/3 c20g c21sur c25d* c20s4 c21g* c21v* c21m* c22m*] lengthy ex-Irish gelding: first foal: dam behind in NH Flat races and a maiden hurdle in Ireland: trained until after first start by A. Geraghty: winning hurdler: took well to chasing, winning novice events at Hexham, Bangor, Perth (2, both handicaps) and Cartmel in the spring: effective at 2½m and stays 25f: acts on good to firm and heavy ground: jumps soundly: should improve further. *G. Richards*　　c110 p —

MUZO (USA) 6 b.g. Irish River (FR) – Dance Flower (CAN) (Northern Dancer (CAN)) [1992/3 c17m4 c18m4] compact gelding: poor novice hurdler/chaser: sold 1,100 gns Ascot September Sales: form only at around 2m: acts on good to firm ground: visored once. *M. Bradley*　　c–

MWEENISH 11 b.g. Callernish – No Trix (No Argument) [1992/3 c25mpu c21gur c21d5 c19gF c19v2 c26vur c25vpu c24sur c24v4 c25s c23d5 c25m2 c26d* c25g3] rangy gelding: fair handicap chaser on his day: won at Uttoxeter in March: suited by good test of stamina: acts on heavy going: poor jumper: unreliable. *J. Webber*　　c108 §

MY BOOKS ARE BEST (IRE) 4 gr. or br.f. Sexton Blake – Rozifer (Lucifer (USA)) [1992/3 17v 18m3 17gpu] smallish, sparely-made filly: second foal: dam won over hurdles and fences in Ireland: third of 6 in claiming hurdle at Fontwell in February, only sign of ability. *H. Willis*　　?

MY CHIARA 7 b.m. Ardross – My Tootsie (Tap On Wood) [1992/3 23s] compact mare: fair handicap hurdler in 1991/2: ran poorly in November: suited by a test of stamina: acts on dead going: usually visored nowadays. *P. J. Bevan*　　–

MY CUP OF TEA 10 b.g. Porto Bello – Aravania (Rarity) [1992/3 c17vpu c17vpu c17vpu c17fur c20fpu c18f] angular, sparely-made gelding: one-time fairly useful 2m chaser: no form since 1989/90. *M. C. Pipe*　　c–

MY CZECH MATE 4 ch.g. Risk Me (FR) – Legal Sound (Legal Eagle) [1992/3 17d] sturdy gelding: poor maiden sprinter on Flat: sold out of R. Hannon's stable 600 gns Ascot July Sales: little sign of ability in juvenile hurdle at Stratford in February. *K. F. Clutterbuck*　　–

MY DAD FRANK 7 gr.g. Scallywag – Noble For Stamps (Deep Run) [1992/3 16s 21spu 16s 20d] big, good-topped gelding: no sign of ability in novice hurdles. *J. Mackie*　　–

MY DESIRE 5 ch.m. Grey Desire – Another Move (Farm Walk) [1992/3 24g2 21d2 28d* 20g2 26s4] leggy, sparely-made mare: half-sister to quite useful hurdler Tancred Sand (by Nicholas Bill): fair stayer on Flat, winner in 1993: won novice hurdle at Sedgefield in November: saddle slipped final outing: effective at 2½m and stays very well: acts on dead ground: needs to brush up her jumping: should progress. *Mrs M. Reveley*　　97 p

MY DUCATS (IRE) 5 b.m. Red Sunset – Saulonika (Saulingo) [1992/3 17m 16g 17dpu] sturdy mare: half-sister to winning Irish hurdler Fiddlers Green (by Orchestra): no worthwhile form on Flat or over hurdles. *T. Casey*　　–

MY FIRE QUACKERS (USA) 10 b.g. Quack (USA) – Legendary Lover (USA) (Bold Legend) [1992/3 c21mpu] poor maiden on Flat in Ireland at 3 yrs: seems of little account in points and a novice hunter chase. *J. Hurst*　　c–

MY GIRL FRIDAY 4 b.f. Scorpio (FR) – Nikancy (Castlenik) [1992/3 16m] half-sister to winning hurdler Lucy Lastic (by Tycoon II): dam modest hurdler: lightly raced and no form on Flat: tailed off in early-season juvenile hurdle. *W. Clay*　　–

MY GRAIN 4 ch.f. Ballacashtal (CAN) – Sequoia (Sassafras (FR)) [1992/3 17v 16f6 17f] poor maiden sprinter on Flat: no form over hurdles. *T. Thomson Jones*　　–

MYHAMET 6 b.g. Gorytus (USA) – Honey Bridge (Crepello) [1992/3 22d* 20g6 18s* 20d* 22m5 20g5] leggy gelding: modest form over hurdles: won novice event at Exeter and claiming handicap at Fontwell in first half of season and handicap at Taunton in February: stays 2¾m: best form with plenty of give in the ground: blinkered 4 times, only time 1992/3 on second start: inconsistent. *P. J. Hobbs*   98

MY KEY SILCA 8 ch.g. Deep Run – La Flamenca (Brave Invader (USA)) [1992/3 20v5 22d5 23s a24gF 22m3 22v3 22f4 25mpu] sparely-made gelding: modest hurdler: stays 2¾m: acts on any ground: visored once. *C. T. Nash*   94

MY KIND OF GIRL 6 b.m. Royal Vulcan – Dracons Girl (Cave of Dracan) [1992/3 21vpu] no sign of ability in NH Flat race and a novice hurdle. *John R. Upson*   –

MYLIEGE 9 b.g. Lord Gayle (USA) – My Natalie (Rheingold) [1992/3 c27gpu] leggy gelding: winning staying selling hurdler: no sign of aptitude for chasing: sometimes blinkered. *P. Leach*   c– –

MY LINDIANNE 6 gr.m. Alias Smith (USA) – Lindrick Passion (Silly Season) [1992/3 22m3 22m 21gF 22d5 20g F10d 16v* 18d5 a20g5 16g4 17f 18gpu 16g3] small, plain mare: poor hurdler: won conditional jockeys selling handicap at Leicester (no bid) in January: best efforts at 2m: acts on heavy ground: blinkered once. *J. Dooler*   71

MY MELLOW MAN 10 ch.g. Malicious – Mincy (No Mercy) [1992/3 c24g2 c24f2 c27g2 c26m2] compact gelding: fairly useful hunter chaser: best effort at Taunton on penultimate start: stays 27f: acts on soft and good to firm going: blinkered 3 times, including final outing. *Mrs J. Litston*   c100

MY NEW BEST FRIEND 9 b.g. Prince Bee – Tender Song (Pretendre) [1992/3 21f* 25dpu a20g2 a22g5] leggy, angular gelding: fair hurdler: won selling handicap (no bid) at Uttoxeter in September: looked reluctant final start (February): stays well: acts on firm going and equitrack: visored in 1989/90. *R. Lee*   108 ?

MY NEW WAY 9 b.m. Newski (USA) – Good Way (Good Apple) [1992/3 22g 22dpu] leggy, lengthy mare: no sign of ability over hurdles. *Mrs V. A. Aconley*   –

MY NOMINEE 5 b.g. Nomination – Salala (Connaught) [1992/3 c26mur] modest 7f winner at 3 yrs: fair maiden pointer: close up and travelling well when unseating rider 6 out in hunter chase at Cheltenham in May. *Miss A. J. Green*   c– p

MY PILOT 9 b.g. Al Sirat (USA) – Dandyville (Vulgan) [1992/3 c23gpu c21dpu 20m 22f] robust, workmanlike gelding: lightly raced: poor novice hurdler at best: pulled up all starts in steeplechases: sold 1,200 gns Ascot 2nd June Sales. *J. S. Moore*   c– –

MY PREROGATIVE 4 gr.f. Sula Bula – Lavender Lace (Blue Refrain) [1992/3 F17g] first foal: dam unraced: tailed off in NH Flat race at Bangor in March: yet to race over hurdles. *D. J. Deacon*   –

MYROSS 9 b.g. Habitat – Rosy Dew (Red God) [1992/3 c16m4 16m c16g3 c20g4 c23gpu] ex-Irish gelding: modest chaser: trained until after fourth outing by T. Walsh: stays 2½m: acts on good to firm ground. *M. Pepper*   c92 ? –

MY ROSSINI 4 b.g. Ardross – My Tootsie (Tap On Wood) [1992/3 F16d* F16v4 F17d3] brother to fair staying hurdler My Chiara: dam useful winner from 7f to 1¼m: won NH Flat race at Haydock in February: in frame in similar events afterwards: yet to race over hurdles. *P. J. Bevan*   –

MY SENOR 4 b.g. Jalmood (USA) – San Marguerite (Blakeney) [1992/3 17m4 17g4 17g3 17g* 17v 18v* 21d6 17v2 17g 17g] neat gelding: poor middle-distance maiden on Flat: won juvenile hurdles at Newbury and Fontwell in first half of season: ran badly last 2 outings: should stay beyond 2¼m: acts on heavy going: looks a difficult ride. *M. Madgwick*   101

MY SKIWAY 10 b.g. Newski (USA) – Good Way (Good Apple) [1992/3 c24d* c26d3 c24g2 c24m5 c23s5 c21g* c26m2 c25mpu] stocky gelding: fair chaser: won handicaps at Huntingdon in November and Bangor (conditional   c106

jockeys) in April: stays well: acts on any going: usually a bold jumper. *T. W. Donnelly*

MY SON JOHN 10 ch.g. Plenty Spirit – Lady Keeper (Worden II) [1992/3 22d 21v c24s] lengthy gelding: of little account. *J. H. Peacock*

c–
–

MY SPARKLING RING 7 b.g. Sparkling Boy – Bells of St Martin (Martinmas) [1992/3 17f^{pu}] workmanlike gelding: no sign of ability in novice hurdles. *C. T. Nash*

–

MYSTIC MARTINET 7 ch.m. Scallywag – Mystic Mintet (King Log) [1992/3 c21g^R] poor maiden pointer: tailed off when refusing in novice hunter chase in May. *Mrs E. N. Wilson*

c–

MYSTIC MEMORY 4 b. or br.f. Ela-Mana-Mou – Mountain Memory (High Top) [1992/3 16d^4 16g^3 16s^2 20m^2 17m* 21g*] sparely-made filly: modest stayer on Flat: won juvenile maiden hurdle at Perth and novice handicap at Wetherby (improved effort) in May: better suited by 21f than shorter: best efforts on a sound surface. *Mrs M. Reveley*

101

MY SWAN SONG 8 b.g. Soul Singer – Palmaria (Be Friendly) [1992/3 18d^3 21s^5 20d 22m^3 24s 22f^5] small, close-coupled gelding: moderate handicap hurdler: stays 2¾m: probably acts on any going. *J. P. Smith*

95

MYTHICAL STORM 6 b.m. Strong Gale – Jupiter Miss (USA) (Hawaii) [1992/3 F17s 16d^3 18d* 21s 21g^2 22g^3] angular mare: won mares novice hurdle at Sedgefield in January: best effort when second in valuable mares novice handicap at Newbury in March: has won at 2¼m, but will prove suited by a good test of stamina: acts on dead ground: likely to improve. *Mrs M. Reveley*

96 p

MY TOBIAS 6 ch.g. Muscatite – Lady Kimberley (Salvo) [1992/3 17g 16s] workmanlike gelding: chasing type: seventh live foal: half-brother to winning Irish hurdler Boreen Deas (by Boreen): dam never ran: behind in novice hurdles: sold 1,800 gns Ascot February Sales. *Andrew Turnell*

MY TURN NEXT 5 b.m. King of Spain – Its My Turn (Palm Track) [1992/3 22m^2 21m^5 16v^5] of little account on Flat nowadays: poor novice hurdler. *K. W. Hogg, Isle of Man*

62

MYVERYGOODFRIEND 6 b.g. Swing Easy (USA) – Darymoss (Ballymoss) [1992/3 17s^2 22s* 22d^4 23d^{pu}] plain gelding: winning chaser: successful in novice hurdle at Newton Abbot in September: ran poorly in March on final start (first for 6 months): sold 1,950 gns Ascot June Sales: stays 2¾m: acts on good to firm and soft ground: sometimes blinkered. *M. C. Pipe*

c–
87

N

NACONA 7 b.g. Noalto – Party Girl (Pardao) [1992/3 16v 16d] workmanlike gelding: tubed: winning 2m hurdler in 1990/1: no other form. *J. S. King*

–

NADIAD 7 b.g. Darshaan – Naveen (Sir Gaylord) [1992/3 16v^{pu} 16s^2 c16d^4 c16d^2 c20s^6 c18s^2 c18g^2] rangy gelding: winning hurdler: moderate novice chaser: barely stays 2½m: probably acts on any ground. *D. McCain*

c87
97

NADJATI (USA) 4 ch.g. Assert – Najidiya (USA) (Riverman (USA)) [1992/3 17m^3 17f^3] sparely-made gelding: fairly useful 1½m winner on Flat in Ireland: 25/1, ran very good race to finish third to Titled Dancer in Glenlivet Anniversary Hurdle at Aintree in April on second start: will stay beyond 2m: acts on firm ground: will improve further, and is sure to win races over hurdles. *D. R. Gandolfo*

131 p

NAGOBELIA 5 b. or br.h. Enchantment – Lost Valley (Perdu) [1992/3 F17m^2 F17d F17s^6 17d] leggy horse: second foal: dam winning selling hurdler: signs of ability in NH Flat races, none on hurdling debut. *J. Pearce*

NAHAR 8 b. or br.g. Known Fact (USA) – Muznah (Royal And Regal (USA)) [1992/3 17s^5 17g 21m^5] neat gelding: fairly useful hurdler, very

117

No 1 Bourbon Street Champion National Hunt Flat, Aintree—
Native Field (No. 4) stays on well to get the better of Ned The Hall

lightly raced: stays 21f: below form on heavy going, seems to act on any other. *S. Dow*

NAJEB (USA) 4 b.g. Chief's Crown (USA) – Modiste (USA) (Sir Ivor) [1992/3 17d⁴ 16g 18m⁴ 21d] smallish, angular gelding: 2-y-o winner, of little account on Flat nowadays: sold out of B. Hanbury's stable 1,300 gns Newmarket Autumn Sales: poor form over hurdles, including in sellers: sketchy jumper. *P. D. Evans*   76

NAMOOS 12 br.g. Thatching – Little Firefly (USA) (Bold Ruler) [1992/3 c24vR] good-bodied gelding: winning hunter chaser in 1991: no other form over fences: tried blinkered: temperamental. *Denis McCarthy*   c– §, –

NAN'S BOY 5 b.h. Blakeney – Classy Nancy (USA) (Cutlass (USA)) [1992/3 22v* 21s³ 25s] good-bodied horse: won novice hurdle at Worcester in November: stayed 2¾m: acted well with plenty of give in the ground: dead. *P. G. Murphy*   104

NARE POINT 8 ch.g. Floriferous – Rather Grand (Will Somers) [1992/3 16spu c16d⁴ c16dF c17s⁶] well-made gelding: no sign of ability. *J. R. Bosley*   c–, –

NASEER (USA) 4 b.g. Hero's Honor (USA) – Sweet Delilah (USA) (Super Concorde (USA)) [1992/3 16gpu 17g² 17v 17s⁵] lengthy, workmanlike gelding: modest middle-distance handicapper on Flat (possibly irresolute): second in juvenile event at Newbury, best effort over hurdles in first half of season: ran in a seller final start. *N. A. Callaghan*   92

NASHOON (IRE) 4 b.c. Nashamaa – Nistona (Will Somers) [1992/3 18dpu 16d 16dpu] leggy colt: half-brother to 2 winning hurdlers, including fair performer Royal Estimate (by Tender King): of little account on Flat and over hurdles. *T. Kersey*   –

NASTY BOSS 5 b.g. Nicholas Bill – Dark Finale (Javelot) [1992/3 16sF] leggy gelding: poor maiden on Flat: fell first in January on hurdling debut. *Mrs F. E. White*   –

NATHAN BLAKE 8 gr.g. Sexton Blake – Nana (Forlorn River) [1992/3 c26g* c23gF c27s² c24s c28g⁶ c25mF c26f² c24f*] close-coupled gelding: winning hurdler: won novice chases at Hereford in September and Ludlow (handicap) in May: sold 11,500 gns Ascot June Sales: stays 3¼m: goes particularly well on a sound surface: usually blinkered. *K. C. Bailey*   c99, –

NATHIR (USA) 7 b.h. Diesis – As You Would (USA) (Fleet Nasrullah) [1992/3 c16v³ c16v* c16v² c16s² c21g³ c17g²] lengthy gelding: poor novice hurdler: won novice chase at Folkestone in February: generally ran creditably afterwards: best form at 2m: acts on good to firm and heavy ground. *P. Butler*   c93, –

NATIVE CROWN (IRE) 5 b.g. Be My Native (USA) – Crystal Halo (St Chad) [1992/3 24m* 20g⁵] leggy, close-coupled gelding: fair hurdler: won handicap at Newcastle in November: ran badly later in month: suited by 3m: acts on dead and good to firm ground. *Mrs S. C. Bradburne* 104

NATIVE FIELD (IRE) 4 b.g. Be My Native (USA) – Broomfield Ceili (Northfields (USA)) [1992/3 F17m* F17f* F17f*] leggy gelding: eighth foal: half-brother to winning 2m hurdler Saceili (by Saher): dam won twice at 1m: won NH Flat races at Doncaster in February and March and valuable event at Aintree in April, last named by neck from Ned The Hall: yet to race over hurdles. *J. G. FitzGerald*

NATIVE MISSION 6 ch.g. Be My Native (USA) – Sister Ida (Bustino) [1992/3 17d 16d⁴ 17g² 16g²] tall, workmanlike gelding: smart hurdler: very good second to Staunch Friend (gave 8 lb) in Friendly Hotels Scottish Champion Hurdle at Ayr in April on final start: earlier in frame in The Ladbroke at Leopardstown and Tote Gold Trophy at Newbury: races at around 2m: acts on good to firm and dead ground: fluent jumper: often finds little under pressure and best held up as long as possible. *J. G. FitzGerald* 154

NATIVE PRIDE 6 ch.g. Be My Native (USA) – Blue Regalia (Royal And Regal (USA)) [1992/3 c17d* c20g³ c24d* c25spu] lengthy, good-topped gelding: fair hurdler: won novice chases at Cheltenham in September and Windsor in January, quite useful performance in latter: ran badly later in January on final start: will stay beyond 3m: acts on dead ground: not a fluent jumper as yet: goes well fresh. *K. C. Bailey* c120 –

NATIVE SCOT 7 ch.m. Be My Native (USA) – Bunduq (Scottish Rifle) [1992/3 c22d⁵ c17vF c21v⁵ c17s⁶ c25d² c24dpu c23d⁴ c21v* c21g⁴ c23mF] leggy mare: novice hurdler: poor chaser: won selling handicap at Uttoxeter (no bid) in April: probably stays 3m: acts on heavy ground: visored 3 times over hurdles. *K. R. Burke* c80 –

NATRAL EXCHANGE (IRE) 4 b.c. Natroun (FR) – Aladja (Mill Reef (USA)) [1992/3 18g*dis 17m* 18s* 17g⁵] angular colt: modest staying maiden on Flat: first past post in juvenile hurdles at Fontwell (claimer, disqualified on technical grounds), Plumpton and Market Rasen: ran well final start (October): will stay 2½m: acts on good to firm and soft ground: visored. *J. W. Hills* 108

NAUGHTY NICKY 9 b.m. Monksfield – Mary Escart (Escart III) [1992/3 c26v³ c26dpu c26dpu c24gpu] lengthy mare: poor chaser: will stay beyond 3¼m: acts on heavy going. *K. Bishop* c78 –

NAUPLIOS 4 b.g. Oedipus Complex – Lombard Street (Naucetra) [1992/3 F14m F14g] leggy, unfurnished gelding: first foal: dam never ran: tailed off in NH Flat races: yet to race over hurdles. *J. G. Thorpe*

NAVAL BATTLE 6 ch.g. Lepanto (GER) – Annie Louise (Parthia) [1992/3 F16d* F17v⁵ F16s] workmanlike gelding with scope: brother to winning hurdler/chaser Pantomime Prince: dam 1¾m winner: won NH Flat race at Warwick in October: mid-division in similar events afterwards: yet to race over hurdles or fences. *J. S. King*

NAVAL RAID 6 b.m. Julio Mariner – London Blitz (Home Guard (USA)) [1992/3 17mpu 16d 22gur 20g 20d 20m 16g⁵ 18g] small, light-framed mare: poor novice hurdler: sold 2,000 gns Doncaster May Sales: stays 2½m: acts on dead ground. *Mrs J. D. Goodfellow* 62

NAZZARO 4 b.g. Town And Country – Groundsel (Reform) [1992/3 17d³ 17v² 17s⁶] half-brother to winning hurdler Frome Girl (by Balinger) and pointer Frome Boy (by New Member): dam third over 9f at 2 yrs: poor form in 17f juvenile hurdles and a seller in first half of season: acts on heavy ground. *W. G. M. Turner* 77

NEARCTIC BAY (USA) 7 b.g. Explodent (USA) – Golferette (USA) (Mr Randy) [1992/3 17d 17g⁴ 17f² 16g 18f³ 17f] big gelding: modest handicap hurdler: once-raced over fences: stays 2½m: acts on firm, dead ground and fibresand: wears tongue strap. *T. T. Bill* c– 85

NEARLY A QUEEN 9 b.m. Nearly A Hand – Sovereign Piece (Sovereign Bill) [1992/3 16s^{pu} a20g^{ur}] lengthy mare: winning pointer: showed nothing over hurdles. *W. G. R. Wightman* —

NEARLY AT SEA 4 ch.f. Nearly A Hand – Culm Port (Port Corsair) [1992/3 F16m] first foal: dam fairly useful staying chaser: tailed off in NH Flat race at Warwick in May: yet to race over hurdles. *L. G. Cottrell* —

NEARLY FIVE TOO 6 b.m. Lepanto (GER) – Five To (Nearly A Hand) [1992/3 F17v 18v 22d^{pu}] leggy, rather unfurnished mare: second foal: dam unraced: no sign of ability. *A. P. Jones* —

NEARLY HONEST 5 ch.m. Nearly A Hand – Miss Saddler (St Paddy) [1992/3 17d^F 17s 17v^{pu} a16g² a16g] sister to useful 2m hurdler Teletrader and half-sister to 2 other winning jumpers: dam, winning hurdler, stayed 2¾m: no form on Flat: easily best effort over hurdles when second in maiden at Lingfield in January: likely to stay beyond 2m: acts on equitrack. *R. J. Hodges* 73

NEASHAM TIME (FR) 4 br.c. Lead On Time (USA) – Neasham Queen (FR) (Roi Dagobert) [1992/3 F14m⁵ F14s] half-brother to a winner in France by Kenmare: dam, from very successful family, placed twice in France: signs of a little ability in NH Flat races: yet to race over hurdles. *J. L. Eyre* —

NEAT AND TIDY 8 b.g. Dubassoff (USA) – Spic And Span (Crisp And Even) [1992/3 22m⁶ 20d^{pu} 24g^{pu}] big gelding: lightly-raced novice hurdler: no form. *N. H. Davis* —

NEBRASKA 7 b.g. Mandalus – Dark Dear (Master Buck) [1992/3 F16s⁴ F16s³ c35d* c20s* c26v c24s c27s c32m^{pu} c32g^R] rangy, workmanlike gelding: fair chaser: won quite valuable chases at Punchestown and Limerick in first half of season: ran poorly last 4 starts, including at Cheltenham (took little interest) on eighth outing: stays very well: acts on soft going: blinkered once: sketchy jumper. *E. Bolger, Ireland* **c108** §

NED THE HALL (IRE) 5 b. or br.g. Callernish – Dream Daisy (Choral Society) [1992/3 F16d² F16d F16g² F17f² F16d] fourth foal: dam winning Irish pointer: won a point in January prior to finishing runner-up in 3 NH Flat races, beaten neck by Native Field in valuable event at Aintree on fourth start: sold to join K. Bailey 27,000 gns Doncaster May Sales: yet to race over hurdles or in a steeplechase. *P. M. J. Doyle, Ireland* —

NEEDWOOD FOREST 10 b.m. Tycoon II – Arctic Lion (Arctic Slave) [1992/3 c24g^{ur} c26d^{pu}] angular mare: poor novice hurdler/chaser: stays 2¾m: form only on good ground. *B. C. Morgan* c– —

NEEDWOOD LEADER 12 b.g. Averof – The Doe (Alcide) [1992/3 c16s⁵ a22g⁶] sparely-made gelding: novice selling hurdler: poor winning chaser: best at around 2m on sound surface: often blinkered over hurdles: poor jumper of fences: ungenuine. *Dr P. Pritchard* c– § — §

NEEDWOOD MUPPET 6 b.g. Rolfe (USA) – Sea Dart (Air Trooper) [1992/3 21s] smallish, workmanlike gelding: fair hurdler: not raced after shaping well in November: will stay beyond 2¾m: acts on good to firm and heavy ground. *B. C. Morgan* —

NEEDWOOD NATIVE 5 b.g. Rolfe (USA) – The Doe (Alcide) [1992/3 17d 17g^{pu}] leggy gelding: second in NH Flat race: no promise in novice hurdles. *B. C. Morgan* —

NEEDWOOD POPPY 5 b.m. Rolfe (USA) – Needwood Nap (Some Hand) [1992/3 16d⁵ 18d⁵ 21v 20v⁴ 22g⁴ a24g³ 26m²] leggy mare: novice selling hurdler: stays 3¼m: acts on heavy and good to firm going. *B. C. Morgan* 74

NEEDWOOD SPRITE 7 ch.m. Joshua – Sea Dart (Air Trooper) [1992/3 20g⁶ 23d⁵ 23d² 23m*] sparely-made mare: fair handicap hurdler: won at Wolverhampton in March by 12 lengths: stays 23f: acts on good to firm and dead ground: usually visored. *B. C. Morgan* 107

NEGATORY (USA) 6 ch.g. Secreto (USA) – Negation (USA) (Mongo) [1992/3 22d 20m⁵] rather sparely-made gelding: fair hurdler in 1991/2: no —

form in 2 late-season events in 1992/3: stays 3m: acts on dead ground. *M. C. Chapman*

NELADAR 6 b.m. Ardar – Caravan Centre (Nelcius) [1992/3 F 17m] first foal: dam winning hurdler, stayed 3m: behind in early-season NH Flat race: yet to race over hurdles or fences. *R. E. Barr*

NELL'S IMAGE 5 ch.m. Town And Country – Elegant Nell (Free State) [1992/3 F16d 16dpu] second foal: dam winning 2m selling hurdler: no sign of ability in NH Flat race and a selling hurdle. *Miss S. J. Wilton* —

NELLYBAAN 5 ch.m. Ayyabaan – Nippy Nelly (St Alphage) [1992/3 F16g] third foal: dam maiden sprint plater: tailed off in NH Flat race at Chepstow in June: yet to race over hurdles or fences. *Mrs R. Harry*

NELSAC 9 gr.g. Neltino – Cissac (Indian Ruler) [1992/3 c25spu c24d4 c27vpu c25vpu] strong, workmanlike gelding: poor novice staying chaser: blinkered twice. *G. A. Ham* c–
—

NELSON'S LASS (IRE) 5 b. or br.m. Carwhite – Praise The Lord (Lord Gayle (USA)) [1992/3 20dur 17spu] small mare: no sign of ability over hurdles. *Mrs S. M. Austin* —

NELTAMA 9 gr.g. Neltino – Tarama (Tamerlane) [1992/3 c22g c17g2 c22g* c24gpu c22m2 c25m5] small, good-bodied gelding: winning hurdler: won novice hunter chase at Fakenham in March: should stay at least 3m: acts on soft going, probably on good to firm. *Miss C. Saunders* c94
—

NELTEGRITY 4 b.g. Neltino – Integrity (Reform) [1992/3 17m3 16s* 20s2 17vF] leggy, angular gelding: modest at up to 1¼m on Flat: won juvenile hurdle at Towcester in November: ran well next time and would have run creditably but for falling last on final outing (also in November): effective at 2m when conditions are testing and stays 2½m: acts on heavy going. *T. H. Caldwell* 100

NEPAL STAR (USA) 4 ch.g. Nepal (USA) – Oblivious Star (USA) (Star de Naskra (USA)) [1992/3 F14s F14g] strong gelding: brother to a winner and half-brother to another in USA: dam won in USA: well beaten in NH Flat races: yet to race over hurdles. *J. G. FitzGerald*

NERAK SENGA 11 ch.g. Crimson Beau – Ballinkillen (Levmoss) [1992/3 c24d5] workmanlike gelding: winning chaser, hunter nowadays: stays 3m: acts on good to firm and dead ground. *M. Bloom* c80
—

NESSFIELD 7 b.m. Tumble Wind (USA) – Ceiling (Thatch (USA)) [1992/3 c20s* c22v4 c16sur c16d2 c26d* c25sF c25dpu c21g c21f3] sparely-made, angular mare: one-time fair hurdler: won mares novice chases at Market Rasen in November and Catterick in February: stays 3¼m: acts on any going: usually wears tongue strap. *K. A. Morgan* c86
—

NETHERBRIDGE 15 b.g. Netherkelly – Bream Bridge (Manicou) [1992/3 c25m4] small, lengthy, lightly-made gelding: poor chaser: stays 3¼m: acts on any going. *D. R. Gandolfo* c77
—

NEVADA GOLD 7 ch.g. Kemal (FR) – French Note (Eton Rambler) [1992/3 c16s4 c17d6 c23vF c21s* c20d3 c21f* c20s2 c21g*] big, lengthy gelding: winning hurdler: sold 5,600 gns Ascot September Sales: won novice chases at Warwick, Worcester and Cheltenham (quite valuable event, improved effort) in second half of season: will probably stay 3m: probably acts on any going: should improve further and win more races over fences. *F. J. Yardley* c117 p
—

NEVENTER (FR) 4 b.g. Lead On Time (USA) – Tysfjord (FR) (Silly Season) [1992/3 aF 16g 18m 16f 18vpu 18m5] leggy gelding: modest maiden at around 1m on fibresand on Flat: no sign of ability over hurdles. *M. C. Chapman* —

NEVER A PENNY 10 b.g. Nearly A Hand – Pilicina (Milesian) [1992/3 c18f* c18gpu c27g2] workmanlike gelding: fair handicap chaser: gained fourth course success at Fontwell in August: effective at 2¼m and stays 3m: acts on any going: wears blinkers: inconsistent and reluctant. *J. P. D. Elliott* c90 §
—

NEVER FORGOTTEN   8 ch.g. The Parson – Our Gale (Dusky Boy) [1992/3 17m* 16f³ 18g* 20g⁵ 17d⁴ 16f³ 17m] small, compact gelding: fair hurdler at best: won novice event at Huntingdon and handicap at Fontwell early in season: below form afterwards: best form at around 2m on a sound surface: sometimes reluctant to race. *R. Akehurst*   104

NEVER LET ON (IRE)   5 ch.g. Denel (FR) – Dream Away (Dusky Boy) [1992/3 F17g⁴ F16g* 17g⁶] smallish, plain ex-Irish gelding: third live foal: dam lightly-raced maiden in Ireland: won NH Flat race at Down Royal in July when trained by J. Maxwell: signs of ability when sixth in novice hurdle at Newbury in November. *M. Bradstock*   77 p

NEVER TOUCHED ME   6 b. or br.m. Belfort (FR) – Realm Gift (Realm) [1992/3 16vᵖᵘ 16sᵖᵘ] sixth foal: sister to a winner in Denmark and half-sister to a winner in Belgium: dam, 5f-placed at 2 yrs, half-sister to dam of Roland Gardens: showed nothing over hurdles: sold 1,000 gns Doncaster March Sales. *M. F. Barraclough*   –

NEVER TYRED   7 b.g. Tanfirion – Ivy Crest (Bluerullah) [1992/3 F16d c21sᵖᵘ c16v⁴ c21f⁶] eighth foal: half-brother to several Irish middle-distance winners on Flat: dam poor Flat maiden: no form over fences: trained until after third start by J. White. *G. L. Humphrey*   c–

NEWARK ANTIQUEFAIR   5 b.g. Rolfe (USA) – Sea Dart (Air Trooper) [1992/3 16f⁴ 16s⁶ 17g²] neat gelding: brother to fair hurdler Needwood Muppet and half-brother to winning hurdler Needwood Sprite (by Joshua): poor staying handicapper on Flat: easily best effort in early-season novice hurdles when second at Huntingdon: will stay 2½m. *B. C. Morgan*   93

NEW CHARGES   6 b.g. Shernazar – Wise Blood (Kalamoun) [1992/3 21g² 18d⁴ 21v⁴ 20g³ 21s³ 24g² 25sᵖᵘ 21f⁴] smallish, good-topped gelding: modest novice hurdler: best form at up to 21f: acts on soft ground. *P. Beaumont*   98

NEW GAME   11 b.m. New Member – Rare Game (Raise You Ten) [1992/3 c24dᵘʳ] lengthy mare: poor chaser: won 2 points prior to unseating rider in hunter chase in April: stays 3¼m: acts on firm ground. *M. P. Fear*   c– –

NEW HALEN   12 br.g. Dikusa – Miss Pear (Breakspear II) [1992/3 c22g c21m²] leggy, rather sparely-made gelding: fairly useful chaser on his day: finished lame when second at Bangor in August: stays 25f: acts on any going: suited by forcing tactics: blinkered once: formerly irresolute. *A. P. James*   c121

NEWHALL PRINCE   5 b.g. Prince Ragusa – Doyles Folly (Rheingold) [1992/3 F16v⁴ F16s 17gᶠ 16sᵖᵘ 16g 17m 16m] leggy gelding: poor novice hurdler: will stay beyond 17f. *J. P. Smith*   80

NEWHOLME FARM   10 ch.g. Mart Lane – Aplomb (Ballymore) [1992/3 25gᵖᵘ] lengthy gelding: modest novice hurdler at best, lightly raced: stays 2½m: acts on any going. *J. G. FitzGerald*   –

NEWLANDS-GENERAL   7 ch.g. Oats – Spartiquick (Spartan General) [1992/3 c16v² c20gᵘʳ] tall, leggy gelding: lightly raced: fair hurdler: promising second in novice chase at Nottingham in December: unseated rider third following month: will stay further than 2m: probably acts on heavy ground: should improve over fences. *J. G. FitzGerald*   c90 p –

NEWMARKET SAUSAGE   12 ch.g. Owen Dudley – Manoeuvre (Mountain Call) [1992/3 20m] small, sturdy gelding: poor performer nowadays: tried in blinkers. *T. Kersey*   c– –

NEW MILL HOUSE   10 ch.g. Tobique – Ascess (Eastern Venture) [1992/3 c17s⁶ c16g c24sᵖᵘ c24d c26vᵖᵘ c20d² c25gᴿ] strong, workmanlike gelding: useful chaser: in lead when running out 3 out in valuable event at Punchestown in April: took part in void Martell Grand National earlier in month: stays 3¼m: acts on heavy going: blinkered fifth and sixth (ran well) outings. *A. L. T. Moore, Ireland*   c130

NEW PROBLEM 6 b.m. New Member – Light of Zion (Pieces of Eight) [1992/3 17g 16s] sparely-made mare: poor maiden hurdler: best efforts at around 2m, but should stay further: acts on fibresand. *R. J. Manning* —

NEWS REVIEW 10 b.g. Pony Express – Channel Ten (Babu) [1992/3 c24m3 c25d2 c24s4 c21s c24sur c26vF c24d* c26d4 c24g3 c24f3 c26dpu c27m3] lengthy gelding: modest form over fences: won novice event at Stratford in February: ran creditably when third: stays 3m: acts on firm and dead ground. *D. G. Williams* **c98**

NEW STATESMAN 5 br.g. Politico (USA) – Nova Ray (Ben Novus) [1992/3 F16m] second foal: dam unraced: mid-division in 24-runner NH Flat race at Warwick in May: yet to race over hurdles or fences. *C. R. Barwell* —

NEWTON POINT 4 b.g. Blakeney – Assertive (USA) (Assert) [1992/3 17g* 17v 18g4 16f5] workmanlike gelding: fair staying handicapper on Flat: won juvenile hurdle at Cheltenham in October: well below that form afterwards (off course 5 months before third start): sold 6,800 gns Ascot June Sales: should stay further than 17f: blinkered final start: jumps none too fluently. *G. A. Pritchard-Gordon* **109**

NEW YORK BOY 5 b.g. Sergeant Drummer (USA) – Auction Ring (Track Spare) [1992/3 17s 16g5 16g5 16v5] third foal: dam poor plater: poor form in novice hurdles: yet to race beyond 17f: best effort on good ground. *R. G. Frost* **85**

NGERU 7 b.g. Mummy's Pet – Great Optimist (Great Nephew) [1992/3 c22dF] lengthy gelding: brother to 3 Flat winners, including sprinter Matou: dam middle-distance winner: modest 2m maiden hurdler in Ireland in 1990: fell third on steeplechasing debut in February: subsequently placed in a point: acts on good to firm ground. *R. Heathfield* **c–**
—

NICHOLAS JAMES (IRE) 5 ch.g. Torus – Candy Belle (Candy Cane) [1992/3 F17d4 F17d] brother to moderate hurdler Counterpunch: dam, unplaced in Irish NH Flat races, half-sister to several winners over jumps: fourth in NH Flat race at Ascot in April: well beaten later in month: yet to race over hurdles or fences. *G. B. Balding* —

NICHOLAS MARK 9 ch.g. Gunner B – Bargain Line (Porto Bello) [1992/3 17m 16g6] good-topped gelding: winning hurdler: ran badly in first half of season: should stay beyond 17f: acts on good to firm ground. *J. G. FitzGerald* —

NICHOLAS PLANT 4 ch.g. Nicholas Bill – Bustilly (Busted) [1992/3 F16d3 F16d] half-brother to a winner in Austria: dam won at 1¼m: third in NH Flat race at Ayr in January: behind in March: yet to race over hurdles. *L. Lungo* —

NICKLARE 7 b.m. Palm Track – Foolish Hooley (Idiot's Delight) [1992/3 22spu 25g] small, light-framed mare: of little account. *R. J. Price* **c–**
—

NICKLE JOE 7 ro.g. Plugged Nickle (USA) – Travois (USA) (Navajo (USA)) [1992/3 21gpu 16s5 20d 21m 24spu] lengthy gelding: fair hurdler at best: generally ran badly in 1992/3: suited by around 2½m: acts on good to firm and dead ground. *M. Tate* —

NICKLUP 6 ch.m. Netherkelly – Voolin (Jimmy Reppin) [1992/3 18d 17d4 22s* 20s* 23v 21vpu] angular mare: won mares novice hurdles at Huntingdon and Exeter (handicap) in first half of season, ran as though something amiss in 2 starts in second: will stay 3m: acts on soft going. *Capt. T. A. Forster* **94**

NICKNAVAR 8 ch.g. Raga Navarro (ITY) – Bay Girl (Persian Bold) [1992/3 22v c24vur c24v c21sur c21g3 c18gpu] small, angular gelding: modest chaser in 1991/2: only poor form in 1992/3: suited by around 2½m: acts on any going. *Mrs P. A. Tetley* **c79**

NICK THE BRIEF 11 b.g. Duky – Roman Twilight (Romulus) [1992/3 c30s3 c24d] big, strong, lengthy gelding: high-class chaser at his best: won Irish Gold Cup twice: no form in 1992/3: suited by a good test of stamina, **c–**
—

plenty of give in the ground and forcing tactics: game: has been retired. *John R. Upson*

NICKY'S BELLE 8 ch.m. Nicholas Bill – Raging Calm (Salvo) [1992/3 22g^{pu}] big, workmanlike mare: no sign of ability in novice hurdles. *Lady Ann Bowlby* —

NICOGHAN (NZ) 11 b.g. Claudio Nicolai (USA) – Afghan Lady (Afghanistan) [1992/3 c20g⁶] compact, angular gelding: novice hurdler/chaser: lightly raced and no form since 1990/1. *T. Dyer* c–

NICSAMLYN 6 ch.m. Julio Mariner – Booterstown (Master Owen) [1992/3 aF16g⁶ 21v⁴ 16d 17d] poor novice hurdler: only form on third start. *C. A. Smith* 74

NIDOMI 6 ch.g. Dominion – Nicholas Grey (Track Spare) [1992/3 18s⁴ 17v⁶ a16g⁴ 17d⁴] leggy gelding: poor novice hurdler: yet to race beyond 2¼m: acts on soft, good to firm going and equitrack. *G. P. Enright* 75

NIGHT CLUBBING (IRE) 4 b.c. Dance of Life (USA) – Tigeen (Habitat) [1992/3 17v^F 16v² 18s² 16d³] smallish, sturdy ex-Irish colt: half-brother to several winners, including hurdler Mardood (by Ela-Mana-Mou): second in well-contested juvenile hurdle at Kempton in January on second start: well below that form afterwards, hanging badly under pressure: should stay beyond 2m: acts on heavy ground: useful form on Flat in 1993, winning 3 times at up to 1½m. *R. Akehurst* 118

NIGHT CLUB (GER) 9 ch.g. Esclavo (FR) – Nightlife (GER) (Priamos (GER)) [1992/3 a16g⁶] lengthy gelding: poor novice hurdler: best form at 2m: acts on fibresand: blinkered nowadays. *J. P. Smith* —

NIGHT FANCY 5 ch.g. Night Shift (USA) – Smooth Siren (USA) (Sea Bird II) [1992/3 22s 23g] sturdy gelding: lightly-raced novice hurdler, poor form at best. *Mrs A. M. Woodrow* —

NIGHT GUEST 11 br.g. Northern Guest (USA) – Night Rose (Sovereign Gleam) [1992/3 c17g⁵ c21s⁵ c23s* c21s² c23d* c25s⁴ c16g* c25m³ c21g^{ur} c21g²] tall, close-coupled gelding: fair chaser: won conditional jockeys claimer and handicap at Kelso in first half of season and claimer at Carlisle in March: effective at 2m and stays 25f: acts on any going. *P. Monteith* c104 —

NIGHT OF MADNESS 6 br.g. Black Minstrel – Margeno's Love (Golden Love) [1992/3 21d² 21s 20m⁵] smallish gelding: poor novice hurdler: will stay 3m: acts on dead going. *G. Richards* 84

NIGHT WIND 6 b.g. Strong Gale – Kylogue Lady (London Gazette) [1992/3 17d⁵ 16d⁴ 17d* 16m] angular gelding: won novice hurdle at Huntingdon in January: will stay at least 2½m: acts on dead ground (ran respectably on good to firm): should progress. *Andrew Turnell* 94 p

NIJMEGEN 5 b.g. Niniski (USA) – Petty Purse (Petingo) [1992/3 23d³ 16d² 16v* 16s* 16v² 16d* 17f 17d] smallish, good-bodied gelding: fairly useful handicap hurdler: won at Uttoxeter, Wetherby and Haydock in mid-season: ran poorly last 2 outings: should stay beyond 2m but appears not to stay 23f: acts on heavy ground: blinkered 3 times in 1991/2: jumps well. *J. G. FitzGerald* 122

NIKITAS 8 b.g. Touching Wood (USA) – Hi There (High Top) [1992/3 17m* 16d² 17m* 16d* 17s* 17d³ 17s 17f⁶ 17f³ 17m³ 16f⁶ 22d⁴] workmanlike gelding: fairly useful handicap hurdler: won at Stratford (twice), Haydock and Newbury in first half of season: best form at around 2m: probably acts on any ground: best ridden up with pace: tough and consistent. *Miss A. J. Whitfield* 119

NINEOFUS 7 b.g. Lochnager – Mountain Child (Mountain Call) [1992/3 c21g^F 21g⁶ 22d⁵ 23s² 20g⁴ 21s 20g⁵ 22s 20d] workmanlike, good-quartered gelding: one-time useful hurdler: ran poorly after fourth outing in 1992/3: winning chaser: stays 25f: probably acts on any ground: races up with pace: makes mistakes over fences. *M. H. Easterby* c– x 125 d

NINETEEN SHILLINGS 14 br.g. Giolla Mear – Perry's Bride (Perspex) [1992/3 c24d^{pu} c33m^{pu}] lengthy, workmanlike gelding: winning chaser: of little account nowadays. *Keith Thomas*

c– x
–

NINFA (IRE) 5 b.m. The Parson – Lulu's Daughter (Levanter) [1992/3 F17s^4 16g^4 17s^6 17d^3] leggy, unfurnished mare: half-sister to 3 winners by Deep Run, notably useful hurdler/chaser Highfrith: dam unraced half-sister to I'm A Driver: showed plenty of promise in novice hurdles, notably when eye-catching third at Carlisle in February, finishing very strongly without being at all knocked about: will stay further than 17f: acts on dead ground: will improve considerably and win a similar event. *G. Richards*

84 P

NINO AZUL 4 b.g. Today And Tomorrow – Jill Somers (Will Somers) [1992/3 22f^{pu}] half-brother to winning chaser Algari (by Petitioner): dam second over 5f at 2 yrs: showed nothing in novice hurdle in March. *H. Sawyer*

NIPOTINA 7 b.m. Simply Great (FR) – Mothers Girl (Huntercombe) [1992/3 F12d^5] poor winning stayer on Flat: ran in celebrity event at Uttoxeter in November: yet to race over hurdles or fences. *R. Hollinshead*

NIPPER SMITH 10 b.g. Chantro – Alice Springs (Coronation Year) [1992/3 18g 16m] small, sparely-made gelding: selling hurdler: novice chaser: no form since 1987/8: sometimes blinkered. *J. Skelton*

c–
–

NIRVANA PRINCE 4 ch.g. Celestial Storm (USA) – Princess Sunshine (Busted) [1992/3 F17f* F17m^3] third foal: half-brother to NH Flat race-placed Sunlight Express (by Homing): dam, well beaten, out of half-sister to top-class Flat performers Double Jump and Rarity: won NH Flat race at Hereford in May: third in similar race on same course later in month: yet to race over hurdles. *B. Preece*

NISHKINA 5 b.g. Nishapour (FR) – Varishkina (Derring-Do) [1992/3 16f^6 18s* 17m^4 22d^4 18d^3 18s^3 18v^3 21m^5 c18s^3 c18g^4] angular, sparely-made gelding: modest handicap hurdler: won at Market Rasen in September: mistakes and no form in 2 races over fences: effective at around 2m and stays 2¾m: probably acts on any ground: blinkered sixth and seventh outings (ran creditably both times). *M. H. Easterby*

c–
91

NITRE (CAN) 5 b.h. Blushing Groom (FR) – Night Light (CAN) (Northern Dancer) [1992/3 F16s^2 F14m^2 F16m^3 F17f] compact horse: half-brother to several winners in North America, including Canadian Oaks winner Playlist (by Miswaki): dam twice-raced maiden: placed in NH Flat races: yet to race over hurdles or fences. *G. H. Jones*

NIYAKA 6 b.g. Le Bavard (FR) – Another Adventure (Dual) [1992/3 F16s F16s^5 aF16g* F17m 20g^6 24g^3] workmanlike gelding: eighth foal: dam second in two 2m maiden hurdles in Ireland: won NH Flat race at Southwell in February: poor form in novice hurdles in April: likely to need a test of stamina. *Capt. J. Wilson*

76

NO ASHES 6 ch.g. Noalto – Bryony Ash (Ribero) [1992/3 F17m 17d 22s^{pu}] workmanlike gelding: no sign of ability. *Mrs V. C. Ward*

–

NOBLE AUK (NZ) 5 br.g. Le Grand Seigneur (CAN) – Lady Auk (NZ) (Auk (AUS)) [1992/3 F17s F17d] New Zealand-bred gelding: soundly beaten in NH Flat races: yet to race over hurdles or fences. *D. H. Barons*

NOBLE BEN (NZ) 9 b.g. Vaguely Tender (USA) – Malaika (NZ) (Silver Dream) [1992/3 c16s^{ur} c16d* c16g^{ur}] leggy gelding: winning hurdler: won novice handicap chase at Wolverhampton in February by 20 lengths: leading when unseating rider 3 out in novice event at Plumpton following month: likely to prove best at up to 2½m: acts on dead ground: front runner: should improve further over fences. *K. C. Bailey*

c101 p
–

NOBLE BID 9 b.h. Kings Lake (USA) – First Round (Primera) [1992/3 22d a20g a24g^6 21d 26d^5] sturdy horse: poor hurdler: stays 3m: acts on firm ground and fibresand: usually blinkered nowadays. *Miss S. J. Wilton*

79

NOBLE BRONZE 5 b.m. Sonnen Gold – Gouly Duff (Party Mink) [1992/3 F17m F18d^6 28d^{pu}] fifth foal: half-sister to winning staying hurdler

–

Noble Scamp (by Scallywag): dam placed in points: little sign of ability. *Mrs V. A. Aconley*

NOBLE EYRE 12 br.g. Aristocracy – Jane Eyre (Master Buck) [1992/3 16s c16g* c16v³ 17v 18spu] smallish, workmanlike gelding: modest chaser: won claimer at Wolverhampton in November: ran badly over hurdles last 2 starts (not raced after December): stays 3m, but races mainly at around 2m: probably acts on any going: visored once. *D. R. Gandolfo*   **c89** –

NOBLE FELLOW 6 b.g. The Noble Player (USA) – Fravelot (Javelot) [1992/3 18gF] angular gelding: no form over hurdles: blinkered once. *P. M. McEntee*   –

NOBLE FORESTER (IRE) 5 b.g. Lord Ha Ha – Diana Harwell (Harwell) [1992/3 F17m] half-brother to winning pointer Eloot Brigade (by Light Brigade): dam unraced: eighth in 24-runner NH Flat race at Cheltenham in April: yet to race over hurdles or fences. *Major D. N. Chappell*

NOBLE INSIGHT 6 ch.g. The Noble Player (USA) – Instanter (Morston (FR)) [1992/3 18m6 17v4 20v 16s* 17s 16v 17g 20g³ 17f 17f 18m³ 22d 27gpu 22f4] small, sparely-made gelding: fairly useful effort when winning handicap hurdle at Kempton in December: mostly well below form afterwards: probably stays 2½m and acts on any going: usually wears blinkers or visor: usually gets behind: ungenuine. *M. C. Pipe*   **116 §** –

NOBLE QUESTION 9 b.m. Scallywag – Gouly Duff (Party Mink) [1992/3 c20m² c22g4 c25dpu c21g4] compact, good-bodied mare: poor maiden jumper: stayed 2½m: acted on good to firm ground: dead. *J. I. A. Charlton*   **c72** –

NOBLE YEOMAN 9 b.g. King's Ride – Baronston (Boreen (FR)) [1992/3 16f] rangy, good-topped gelding: once-raced over fences: fair hurdler in 1991/2: well below his best in September: will stay beyond 17f: acts on soft ground. *R. Dickin*   **c–** –

NO BONUS 9 ch.g. Baragoi – Lillytip (Tepukei) [1992/3 17m4 17gpu 18d5 17d a16g a16gur 17m 16f 17dpu] lengthy gelding: winning hurdler: no form in   –

BonusPrint Handicap Hurdle, Kempton—
Noble Insight (right) wins this competitive race from Hashar (left) and Kilcash

1992/3, ran in a seller final start: best at around 2m: acts on hard ground: tried blinkered in 1990/1. *R. J. Baker*

NO BOUNDARIES 7 b.g. Pitskelly – Santa Chiara (Aztec) [1992/3 20m] poor winning pointer: well beaten in maiden in May on hurdling debut: sold 2,500 Ascot June Sales. *L. J. Williams* —

NOCATCHIM 4 b.g. Shardari – Solar (Hotfoot) [1992/3 17g 16d* 17d* 16f* 17m4] good-topped gelding: half-brother to winning jumper Harbour Bridge (by Blakeney): modest maiden on Flat, stays 1¼m: sold out of B. Hills's stable 12,500 gns Newmarket Autumn Sales: won juvenile hurdles at Wincanton and Stratford and novice event at Ludlow in second half of season: ran as though something amiss final start: yet to race beyond 17f: acts on firm and dead going: jumps well: blinkered all bar hurdling debut: front runner. *S. E. Sherwood* 118

NODDYS EXPRESS 8 ch.g. Pony Express – Toddy Noddy (Three Wishes) [1992/3 22vpu 24v 23v5 24fpu] sturdy gelding: third foal: half-brother to a poor novice hurdler by Sharp Deal: dam winning pointer: no form over hurdles. *R. H. Buckler* —

NODFORMS INFERNO 4 b.g. Idiot's Delight – River Linnet (Forlorn River) [1992/3 F17g F17d] fourth foal: dam 1½m winner: well beaten in NH Flat races: sold 8,000 gns Doncaster May Sales: yet to race over hurdles. *D. Eddy* —

NODFORM WONDER 6 b.g. Cut Above – Wonder (Tekoah) [1992/3 18gF 20m6 17m5 21g* 23g* 24d*] rather unfurnished gelding: fairly useful handicap hurdler: in fine form in first half of season, winning at Wetherby, Kelso and Ascot: sold 10,500 gns Doncaster May Sales: stays 3m and is effective at shorter distances: acts on good to firm and dead ground: front runner. *D. Eddy* 125

NODOFF 5 ch.g. Dubassoff (USA) – Coincidence Girl (Manacle) [1992/3 F17m F17s 17spu] tall, lengthy, workmanlike gelding: seventh foal: dam unraced: no sign of ability. *S. J. Leadbetter* —

NOEL LUCK 13 ch.g. Deep Run – Monavalla (Kabale) [1992/3 c22f c24dur] leggy, sparely-made gelding: winning chaser: no show in hunter chases in 1993: stays 3¼m: acts on good to firm and soft ground. *Mrs H. M. Dee* c– –

NO ESCORT 9 b.g. Pitpan – Royal Escort (Royal Highway) [1992/3 c21s2 c22g* c26m* c25m3] strong, tall gelding: useful hunter chaser: won at Fakenham in February and Hereford in March: effective at 21f and stays 3¼m: acts on good to firm and soft ground: forces pace: jumps boldly: runs the odd poor race (often broke blood vessels in 1992). *Miss C. Saunders* c111

NOGGINS (IRE) 4 b.g. Cyrano de Bergerac – Coshlea (Red Alert) [1992/3 18m4 17m5 17m 16g 17spu] compact gelding: half-brother to winning hurdler Dale Park (by Kampala): modest maiden at best on Flat: poor novice hurdler: trained first 2 starts by N. Tinkler: yet to race beyond 2¼m: best effort on good ground: blinkered final outing. *Mrs E. Moscrop* 76

NO GRANDAD 9 br.m. Strong Gale – Blue Bleep VII (Pedigree Unknown) [1992/3 c24d2 c26s* c26d3 c24s* c33v2 c28s5 c25s c24s2 c24g2 c27g4 c27d*] angular mare: fair handicap chaser: won at Uttoxeter and Huntingdon in first half of season and Newton Abbot (amateurs) in April: suited by test of stamina: probably needs give in the ground (acts on heavy). *John R. Upson* c103 –

NO GUTS NO GLORY 6 b.g. Mansingh (USA) – Lyn Affair (Royal Palace) [1992/3 18spu 16vpu 17d c24mpu c21dpu] third reported foal: half-brother to winning selling hurdler Sedgewell Orchid (by John de Coombe): dam, placed over 1½m on Flat, poor novice hurdler: no sign of ability. *W. G. Turner* c– –

NOHALMDUN 12 b.g. Dragonara Palace (USA) – Damsel (Pampered King) [1992/3 c17m c20m5 c17m2 c17g2 c18s4 c17m5] leggy, workmanlike gelding: very useful chaser at best: fairly useful form in 1992/3: best at 2m: acts on any going: suited by waiting tactics. *M. H. Easterby* c120 –

NO LIGHT 6 gr.g. Celio Rufo – Lady Templar (Lord Gayle (USA)) [1992/3 F16g F16g* F16s³ 16d* 20g 21v* 18v 17f^pu] half-brother to a winning hurdler by Tug of War: dam unraced sister to useful hurdler and fair chaser Midland Gayle: won NH Flat race at Tipperary, maiden hurdle at Listowel and handicap at Navan in first half of season: trained until after seventh start by A. Mullins: no show on British debut: stays 21f: acts on heavy ground. *Mrs I. McKie*   115

NOMADIC ROSE 4 b.f. Nomination – Tina Rosa (Bustino) [1992/3 18f⁴ 18g* 18g² 17g³ 16s* 17d a16g³ a20g⁴] small, angular filly: plating-class maiden on Flat: won selling hurdle at Fontwell (bought in 2,900 gns) in September and juvenile event at Kempton (easily best effort) in first half of season: not raced after January: effective at 2m under testing conditions and should stay 2½m: acts well on soft going. *T. J. Naughton*   103

NOMADIC WAY (USA) 8 b.h. Assert – Kittyhawk (Bustino) [1992/3 25g² 25s 22s²] small, lengthy horse: very smart hurdler at best, winner of Stayers' Hurdle in 1992 and second in Champion Hurdle in 1991 and 1990 at Cheltenham: second to Burgoyne in West Yorkshire Hurdle at Wetherby in October: ran poorly afterwards: stayed well: acted on any going: best in blinkers: jumped well and raced up with pace: retired due to leg injury. *B. W. Hills*   ?

NOM DE FORT 8 gr.g. Belfort (FR) – French Strata (USA) (Permian (USA)) [1992/3 c23d^pu c22g^pu c21f⁵ c22m³ c25s^pu] sparely-made gelding: poor novice hurdler/chaser: stays 2¾m: acts on good to firm ground. *R. C. Spicer*   c73 –

NOMELAP 8 b.g. Palemon – Coronation Heath (Coronation Year) [1992/3 c24m c21m⁴] lengthy, shallow-girthed gelding: of little account over hurdles: poor form in hunter chases: stays 3m: acts on good to firm ground. *Jamie Poulton*   c66 –

NO MORE THE FOOL 7 ch.g. Jester – Prima Bella (High Hat) [1992/3 c22g* c16s² c17d² c16d³ c16g^F c20g⁵ c18g² c22m⁵] lengthy gelding: modest chaser: won novice event at Cartmel in August: lost form after third start: stays 2¾m: acts on good to firm and soft ground: blinkered final outing. *J. Berry*   c90 –

NO MORE TRIX 7 b.g. Kemal (FR) – Blue Trix (Blue Chariot) [1992/3 c24g³ c26s^ur c21d* c21g* c23d³] smallish, lengthy gelding: winning hurdler: won 2 novice chases at Sedgefield in February: jumped poorly when tailed off late in month: effective at 21f and should stay 3¼m: acts on good to firm and soft ground: forces pace. *T. P. Tate*   c102 –

NONCOMMITAL 6 b.h. Mummy's Pet – Shadow Play (Busted) [1992/3 16s⁶ 16s^F 16d³] angular horse: closely related to winning hurdlers My Buddy (by Mummy's Game) and Arran View (by Aragon): poor staying maiden plater on Flat: third in seller at Catterick in November, best effort over hurdles: yet to race beyond 2m: acts on dead ground. *J. Mackie*   75

NONE SO BRAVE 5 b.h. Dancing Brave (USA) – So Fine (Thatching) [1992/3 17g⁴] sparely-made horse: useful juvenile hurdler in 1991/2: well beaten only outing in 1992/3 (October): raced only at around 2m: acted on good to firm and soft ground: dead. *R. Akehurst*   –

NONE SO WISE (USA) 7 ch.g. Believe It (USA) – Nonesuch Bay (Mill Reef (USA)) [1992/3 c20s² c21s⁶ c24d^F c25d² c25d² c26v^pu] leggy gelding: winning hurdler: fair novice chaser: stays 25f: acts on soft going: sketchy jumper of fences. *N. R. Mitchell*   c100 –

NO PAIN NO GAIN (IRE) 5 ch.g. Orchestra – Clarrie (Ballyciptic) [1992/3 16f²] rangy gelding: has scope: brother to poor novice hurdler All Talk No Action and half-brother to winning hurdler/chaser Dickie Murray (by Brave Invader) and an Irish NH Flat race winner by Wolverlife: dam won 2m hurdle: jumped none too fluently when second in selling hurdle at Windsor in March on debut: will stay beyond 2m: should improve. *B. J. Curley*   85 p

NORDANSK 4 ch.g. Nordance (USA) – Free On Board (Free State) [1992/3 17v6 17v 16v 16f* 16d2 18f*] compact gelding: modest middle-distance maiden on Flat: no bid after winning selling hurdles at Windsor in March and Fontwell in May: yet to race beyond 2¼m: acts on firm and dead ground. *M. Madgwick*　87

NORDEN (IRE) 4 ch.g. M Double M (USA) – Papukeena (Simbir) [1992/3 F17m] medium-sized gelding: half-brother to fair hurdler Papajoto (by Ahonoora): dam Irish 13f winner: behind in NH Flat race at Cheltenham in April: yet to race over hurdles. *R. J. Hodges*　–

NORDIC FLASH 6 b.g. Nordico (USA) – Rosemore (Ashmore (FR)) [1992/3 17m2 17g3 17f3] smallish gelding: moderate hurdler: best form at around 2m: best on a sound surface (acts on firm going). *T. J. Naughton*　97

NORDIC FLIGHT 5 b. or br.g. Julio Mariner – Last Flight (Saucy Kit) [1992/3 F17v F18s aF16g 17mpu] half-brother to winning jumpers Celtic Flight and Ruby Flight (both by Celtic Cone), latter useful staying hurdler: dam unraced daughter of very useful hurdler Flight's Orchid: no sign of ability: visored third start. *R. J. Eckley*　–

NORDIC SAVAGE 11 b.g. John de Coombe – Jet Beam (Jolly Jet) [1992/3 c23spu c16vpu c16v] workmanlike gelding: of no account. *J. E. Long*　c–
–

NORDROSS 5 b.m. Ardross – Noreena (Nonoalco (USA)) [1992/3 22gpu 16f 16g 20d 20v4 16s 20s3 a20gpu] sturdy mare: half-sister to winning hurdler Yamanouchi (by Hard Fought): dam ran only twice: only form over hurdles when third in seller in February. *J. H. Peacock*　67

NO REBASSE 11 b.g. Over The River (FR) – Good Surprise (Maelsheachlainn) [1992/3 c26m*] compact, workmanlike gelding: novice hurdler: won novice hunter chase at Folkestone in May: stays 3¼m: acts on good to firm going. *M. A. Johnson*　c85

NO REPLY 7 br.g. Tumble Gold – Santa Luna (Saint Crespin III) [1992/3 F18v c20gF c26spu c25dpu c21gur] half-brother to very smart hurdler/chaser Boreen Prince and winning jumper Loanan (both by Boreen): dam unraced half-sister to useful hurdler Never Lit Up: no sign of ability in novice chases. *Mrs H. Bell*　c–

NORFOLK THATCH 7 b.g. Thatching – Pellarosa (Crepello) [1992/3 17m4 17gur 17s4 17m5] leggy gelding: novice selling hurdler: barely stays 2m: acts on good to firm going: blinkered twice, including final outing (September). *K. S. Bridgwater*　82

NORHAM CASTLE 10 b.g. Scott Joplyn – Gay Amanda (Counsel) [1992/3 17f5 22gpu] big, strong gelding: bad novice hurdler/chaser. *R. R. Ledger*　c–
–

NORMAN CONQUEROR 8 br.g. Royal Fountain – Constant Rose (Confusion) [1992/3 c21dro c25d* c21v2 c21vF c21v3 c21v2 c24g2 c25f2] workmanlike gelding: fairly useful handicap chaser: won amateurs event at Ascot in November: stays 25f: acts on any going: blinkered last 2 outings: races up with pace: consistent. *T. Thomson Jones*　c117
–

NORMANDY BILL 6 br.g. Golden Love – Billeragh Girl (Normandy) [1992/3 F17g 26dpu] good-bodied gelding: brother to useful hurdler/smart chaser Second Schedual: dam half-sister to smart jumper Troyswood: no sign of ability. *D. McCain*　–

NORMEAD LASS 5 b.m. Norwick (USA) – Meads Lass (Saritamer (USA)) [1992/3 17gpu 18d 16spu a22ga 18g6 c18sur c18gc17dF] leggy mare: of little account. *Miss P. Hall*　c–
–

NORNAX LAD (USA) 5 b.h. Northern Baby (CAN) – Naxos (USA) (Big Spruce (USA)) [1992/3 17m* 20g* 22f* 22g2 21g5 22m4 21g4 22f*] sparely-made, close-coupled horse: successful in novice hurdles at Newton Abbot, Plumpton and Huntingdon early in season and handicap at Ludlow in March: will stay beyond 2¾m: acts on firm going. *Martyn Meade*　109

NORSE COUNTRY   6 b.m. Town And Country – Norsemen's Lady   c– §
(Habat) [1992/3 c25g^{ro}] small, rather sparely-made mare: poor maiden   –
plater over hurdles: ran out first on steeplechasing debut. *A. G. Sims*

NORSTOCK   6 b.m. Norwick (USA) – Millingdale (Tumble Wind (USA))   c82
[1992/3 c16m^3 c17v^{bd} c2 1s^6 a18g^4 17v* 2 1v* 17s^2 16v* a16g^3 20s 26d^2 26v^2]   102
leggy mare: fair hurdler: winner of sellers at Chepstow (conditional jockeys
event, no bid), Uttoxeter (bought in 3,500 gns) and Towcester (bought in
3,000 gns) in second half of season: poor form in novice chases: effective
from 2m to 3¼m: acts on any going: tough and game. *J. White*

NORTH BANNISTER   6 br.g. Baron Blakeney – Freuchie (Vulgan)   c–
[1992/3 20m^2 c21m^F c21s^F 22m^{pu}] sturdy gelding: poor novice hurdler: 77 §
faller on both starts over fences: sold 2,800 gns Ascot May Sales: should
stay beyond 2½m: acts on good to firm ground: irresolute. *Capt. T. A.
Forster*

NORTHERN CODE   6 br.g. Funny Man – Dialling Code (Don't Look)   –
[1992/3 16d^{pu} 22g^{pu}] workmanlike gelding: first foal: dam unplaced in NH
Flat race: no sign of ability in novice hurdles. *P. J. Dennis*

NORTHERN CONQUEROR (IRE)   5 ch.g. Mazaad – Gaylom (Lord
Gayle (USA)) [1992/3 17s 17g^3] small gelding: first form over hurdles when   82
third in amateurs novice event at Fakenham in May: won at 1¼m on Flat in
1993: likely to prove best at around 2m. *T. J. Naughton*

NORTHERN EMPEROR (IRE)   4 b.g. The Noble Player (USA) –   –
Staderas (Windjammer (USA)) [1992/3 16m] leggy gelding: of little account
on Flat: well behind in early-season juvenile hurdle. *M. H. Easterby*

NORTHERN GUEST (NZ)   6 ch.g. Faith Guest – Zamiya (NZ) (Trelay
(NZ)) [1992/3 19m^5 22s^{pu} 23s^{pu}] compact gelding: no form in novice   –
hurdles. *D. H. Barons*

NORTHERN JINKS   10 b.m. Piaffer (USA) – Miss Merida (Midsummer   c115
Night II) [1992/3 c16s^5 c16v* c2 1s^3 c21v^6 c16s^4 c17d^2 c18d* c16s* c16g^2 –
c19d^4] big, workmanlike mare: fairly useful handicap chaser: won at
Worcester in November and Stratford and Worcester in February: effective
at 2m and stays 21f: acts on good to firm and heavy ground: suited by forcing
tactics. *R. Dickin*

NORTHERN LION   10 br.g. Northfields (USA) – Pride of Kilcarn   c–
(Klairon) [1992/3 c17m^{pu}] angular, workmanlike gelding: modest chaser in   –
1991/2: showed nothing in May: stays 2¼m: acts on any going: front runner.
R. Thompson

NORTHERN MEADOW   12 b.g. Northern Value (USA) – Babaville   c102
(Meadsville) [1992/3 c2 1f^2 c26g* c24m^3 c25g^F] angular, workmanlike   –
gelding: game and genuine handicap chaser: won at Cartmel in August:
stayed well: acted on any going: sound jumper: dead. *S. G. Chadwick*

NORTHERN NATION   5 b.g. Nomination – Ballagarrow Girl (North
Stoke) [1992/3 16g^3 16f^5 17g^4 16g^2 a16g* a16g* a16g^2 a16g^2 a16g* 16g^5 102
a16g^F 18m] neat gelding: fair handicap hurdler: won 3 times at Southwell in
second half of season: raced only at around 2m: acts on dead going and
especially well on fibresand: consistent. *W. Clay*

NORTHERN OPTIMIST   5 b.m. Northern Tempest (USA) – On A Bit
(Mummy's Pet) [1992/3 21s^{pu} 17m^5 17d^6 21s^3 20v^3 21v^2 23d^5 17d^4 23g 26m^5 86
24s^6 21s^2 20d^2 20m*] small mare: selling hurdler: bought in 2,700 gns after
winning at Hereford in May: stays 21f: acts on good to firm and heavy
ground. *B. J. Llewellyn*

NORTHERN RAINBOW   5 b.g. Rainbow Quest (USA) – Safe House
(Lyphard (USA)) [1992/3 2 1d^{pu} 17g 22s^{pu} 18d] angular gelding: lightly-raced   –
maiden on Flat, stays 1¼m: sold out of P. Cole's stable only 2,000 gns
Newmarket September Sales: little worthwhile form over hurdles,
including when favourite for a seller: headstrong. *I. Campbell*

NORTHERN RARITY (USA)   4 gr.g. Northern Baby (CAN) – The
Rarest (Rarity) [1992/3 aF16g^4 aF16g* F16g* F17m] leggy gelding:

half-brother to several winners on Flat, notably high-class 2-y-o Exclusively Raised (by Exclusive Native): dam Irish 5f winner: bought for 1,600 gns Newmarket July Sales: won NH Flat races at Southwell and Catterick in February: dead. *J. Norton*

NORTHERN SADDLER 6 ch.g. Norwick (USA) – Miss Saddler (St Paddy) [1992/3 c17f² c16dᴾᵘ c16m² c19g* c24dᶠ c24sᶠ 18s³ 17f* 16m⁶ 16g³ 17s* 17g] good-topped gelding with scope: won novice handicap chase at Taunton in November and novice handicap hurdles at Doncaster and Ascot in March: stays 19f: probably acts on any ground. *R. J. Hodges*   c90 99

NORTHERN SAINT 10 b.g. Northern Guest (USA) – Red Rose (Saint Denys) [1992/3 c21m⁶] winning hunter chaser in Ireland: tailed off in May: stays 3m: acts on firm ground: blinkered once. *Mrs T. J. Hills*   c–

NORTHERN SECURITY 9 b.g. Workboy – Northern Venture (St Alphage) [1992/3 17dᴾᵘ] leggy, close-coupled gelding: of little account. *J. S. Haldane*   –

NORTHERN SOCIETY (USA) 10 b.g. Norcliffe (CAN) – Te Ve Society (USA) (Te Vega) [1992/3 c25dᴾᵘ] leggy gelding: winning pointer: lightly-raced novice hunter chaser. *Peter Scott*   c–

NORTHERN SQUIRE 5 b.g. Uncle Pokey – Kit's Future (Saucy Kit) [1992/3 16s⁶ 17s⁵ 16g⁵ 16g 17m⁶ 17sᴾᵘ 16m] tall, useful-looking gelding: chasing type: third foal: half-brother to winning hurdler/chaser Potato Picker (by Celtic Cone) and maiden jumper Potato Man (by Zambrano): dam, from successful jumping family, placed once over hurdles: poor novice hurdler: yet to race beyond 17f: acts on good to firm and soft ground: visored sixth outing. *J. M. Jefferson*   80

NORTHERN STEEL 7 b.g. Wolver Hollow – Aggrapina (St Alphage) [1992/3 16m 20vᴾᵘ 17dᴾᵘ] lengthy gelding: lightly raced and no sign of ability. *Graham Richards*   –

NORTHERN VILLAGE 6 ch.g. Norwick (USA) – Merokette (Blast) [1992/3 22v³ 21d⁴ a18g² a20g* 22s⁶ 20g 24sᴾᵘ 22f³ 26f²] rather sparely-made, close-coupled gelding: fair handicap hurdler: won at Lingfield in January: ran well last 2 starts: effective at 2¼m and stays 3¼m: acts on any going: visored sixth start (blinkered next time). *S. Dow*   108

NORTHERN VISION 6 b.g. Vision (USA) – Smelter (Prominer) [1992/3 17d 16d 16s 18g 16g c17dᴾᵘ c20fᶠ c17g] sturdy gelding: novice hurdler: no form over fences: races mainly at around 2m: acts on dead ground: blinkered once. *R. R. Lamb*   c–

NORTH ESK (USA) 4 ch.g. Apalachee (USA) – Six Dozen (USA) (What A Pleasure (USA)) [1992/3 16m⁶] rangy gelding: fair handicapper at up to 1¼m on Flat, winner twice in June, 1993, for D. Wilson: midfield in early-season juvenile hurdle, pulling hard: probably capable of better. *Denys Smith*   – p

NORTH FLYER 4 b.g. Norwick (USA) – Minuetto (Roan Rocket) [1992/3 17dᴾᵘ] plating-class maiden on Flat, stays 1m: sold 1,800 gns Doncaster October Sales: no sign of ability in juvenile selling hurdle in November. *D. Burchell*   –

NORTHLANDS WAY 8 ch.g. Orchestra – Nessie B (Star Gazer) [1992/3 17d⁶ 25s⁶] leggy, lengthy gelding: little sign of ability in novice hurdles. *P. J. Hobbs*   –

NORTHUMBRIAN KING 7 b.g. Indian King (USA) – Tuna (Silver Shark) [1992/3 c24mᶠ c24sᴾᵘ] workmanlike gelding: useful hunter chaser in 1992: ran poorly final start: stays 3m: acts on hard and dead going. *Mrs K. Walton*   c–

NORTH WOLD PARK 9 ch.g. Vitiges (FR) – Sesta (Artaius (USA)) [1992/3 c25f c24f³ c24d³ c26mᴾᵘ] strong, good-bodied gelding: novice hunter chaser: stays 3m: acts on firm and dead ground. *D. E. Fletcher*   c88 –

NORTINO 5 ch.g. Norwick (USA) – Soft Chinook (USA) (Hitting Away) [1992/3 17d² 17s* 17d c16g c16d 17d 17s⁴ 16m* 16g⁵] leggy gelding: poor   c– 83

hurdler: won claimers at Carlisle in November and Uttoxeter (novices) in May: jumped deliberately and no form in novice chases: will stay beyond 17f: probably acts on any going. *J. I. A. Charlton*

NORTON'S COIN 12 ch.g. Mount Cassino – Grove Chance (St Columbus) [1992/3 c21d⁴ c17d⁵ c20gᴿ] lengthy gelding: winner of 1990 Tote Cheltenham Gold Cup: showed nothing in 1992/3 (had soft palate, tie-back and hobday operations after second start) and has been retired. *S. G. Griffiths*

c–
–

NORTON'S KNIFE 5 ch.g. Scorpio (FR) – Royal Pam (Pamroy) [1992/3 aF16g⁵] fifth living foal: half-brother to novice jumpers Mountain Muse (by Sunyboy) and Simply Joyful (by Idiot's Delight): dam, unraced, comes from successful jumping family: well beaten in NH Flat race at Southwell in March: yet to race over hurdles or fences. *J. G. FitzGerald*

NORVAL 11 b.g. King's Equity – Helenium (Khalkis) [1992/3 26m⁴] compact, workmanlike gelding: fair chaser in 1991/2: winning hurdler: fourth in handicap at Catterick in October: suited by a test of stamina: acts on any going: blinkered once: jumps deliberately and often gets well behind over fences. *N. B. Mason*

c–
108

NO SID NO STARS (USA) 5 ch.g. Diamond Shoal – Side Saddle (USA) (Codex (USA)) [1992/3 17mᶠ 18m3 22f* 21m3 22d* 18g* 18d5 22d² 20d5] smallish, workmanlike gelding: successful in 3 novice hurdles at Sedgefield in first half of season: not raced after February: effective at 2¼m and stays 2¾m: has won on firm ground, best form with give: blinkered first 2 outings: held up. *G. M. Moore*

103

NOS NA GAOITHE 10 br.g. Strong Gale – Abroad (Takawalk II) [1992/3 c21m² c21g² c21d c21s² c21vᵖᵘ c20m⁴ c21d⁴ c22f3 c25sᶠ] workmanlike gelding: useful chaser at best: generally well below form after second start: barely stays 3m: acts on heavy going and good to firm: often blinkered: has tongue tied down: held up: usually jumps well: inconsistent: weak finisher: not one to rely on. *M. H. Easterby*

c137 d
–

NOTABLE EXCEPTION 4 b.g. Top Ville – Shorthouse (Habitat) [1992/3 17m 16d* 16s 17g* 17m²] leggy, unfurnished gelding: modest staying maiden on Flat: won juvenile hurdles at Catterick in November and Newcastle (claimer) in February: good third (promoted a place) in quite valuable juvenile handicap on latter course in March: will stay beyond 17f: acts on dead and good to firm ground: should continue to progress. *Mrs M. Reveley*

96 p

NOT ALL BLISS 5 ch.m. Kabour – Wedded Bliss (Relko) [1992/3 F10d F14s] fourth foal: sister to winning pointer Gan Awry: dam won on Flat and over hurdles: tailed off in NH Flat races in November: yet to race over hurdles or fences. *G. P. Kelly*

NOTARIUS (FR) 5 b.g. Deep Roots – Lady Ring (Tachypous) [1992/3 17m⁵ 18m 22sᵖᵘ 20g 28d⁴ c16g⁴ c17g⁴ c17g 18g] shallow-girthed, angular gelding: half-brother to a Flat and jumps winner in France by In Fijar: dam maiden half-sister to useful chaser Silent Valley: of little account: blinkered once. *J. Wade*

c–
–

NOTARY-NOWELL 7 b.g. Deep Run – Hamers Flame (Green Shoon) [1992/3 22f⁴ 23g⁴ 25d3 21g* 26g* 22d² c21d² c21sᶠ 21s⁶ c21f c21f5] rangy gelding: fair hurdler: won amateurs event at Fakenham and novice event at Huntingdon early in season: modest novice chaser: effective at 21f and stays well: acts on good to firm and soft going: tends to sweat: successful with and without blinkers. *F. Murphy*

c88
107

NOT GORDONS 4 b.c. All Systems Go – Lady Abernant (Abwah) [1992/3 17gᵖᵘ 16g3 17g 16g] workmanlike colt: no form on Flat: third in claimer at Edinburgh in February, only form over hurdles. *J. H. Johnson*

75

NOTHINGBUTPLEASURE 7 b.g. Deep Run – Vamble (Vulgan) [1992/3 c17dᵘʳ c19m5 c21dʳᵒ c19gᶠ 20v5 a20g] lengthy, sparely-made gelding: poor novice hurdler at best: no form over fences. *C. L. Popham*

c–
–

NOTHINGBUTTROUBLE   9 ch.g. Roselier (FR) – Continuity Lass   c–
(Continuation) [1992/3 c21spu c21spu c20dpu 24v] compact gelding: poor   –
novice hurdler at best: no form over fences. *Mrs H. Parrott*

NOTHING DOING (IRE)   4 b.g. Sarab – Spoons (Orchestra) [1992/3   –
16s] close-coupled, sparely-mare gelding: plating-class maiden on Flat,
barely stays 1¼m: tailed off in claiming hurdle in February. *W. J. Musson*

NOT SO SOON   8 b.g. Beau Charmeur (FR) – Willie's Sister (Even   c95
Money) [1992/3 c21d² c25g⁴ c22s* c24vpu c24dpu c25s² c25g²] sturdy,   –
close-coupled gelding: maiden hurdler: modest form over fences: won
novice event at Fakenham in December: good second twice at Market
Rasen in April: effective at 21f under testing conditions and stays 25f: acts
on soft ground. *K. C. Bailey*

NOT YET   9 b.g. Connaught – Ritratto (Pinturischio) [1992/3 16m 17m⁵   76
16d 18m] small, good-bodied gelding: poor middle-distance performer on
Flat nowadays: poor novice hurdler: yet to race beyond 2¼m: acts on good
to firm and dead ground. *E. Weymes*

NOUGAT RUSSE   12 b.g. Sweet Story – Natasha VI (Blue Cliff) [1992/3   c102
c24d* c24d³ c24spu c24s⁶ c24v⁴ c24d² c24m³ c23m* c23s² c24d* c25gur
c24f² c24g] tall, workmanlike gelding: fair chaser: won handicaps at Ludlow
(amateurs) in November and Worcester and Ludlow (novices) in the spring:
suited by a test of stamina: probably acts on any ground: sometimes
blinkered prior to 1992/3: not a fluent jumper: usually soon off bridle. *N. A.
Twiston-Davies*

NOUSHY   5 ch.m. Ahonoora – Bolkonskina (Balidar) [1992/3 16f 18gF 17g]   54
small mare: bad 2m novice selling hurdler. *K. S. Bridgwater*

NOUVELLE CUISINE   5 b.m. Yawa – Radigo (Ragstone) [1992/3   87 p
F14d³ F17m² F17s² 16dF 16g⁴ 17f* 17g⁵ 16g*] small, leggy mare: fifth foal:
dam won twice over 1¼m: won novice hurdles at Newcastle and Hexham in
May: will stay at least 2½m: acts on firm going: likely to progress. *G. M.
Moore*

NOVA SPIRIT   5 b.m. Electric – Miss Casanova (Galivanter) [1992/3   98
22vpu 17v⁵ 17v² 17g² 18g* 17spu 18d] close-coupled mare: modest hurdler:
won handicap at Exeter in March: effective at around 2m and stays 21f well:
suited by give in the ground and acts on heavy. *M. S. Saunders*

NOVELLO ALLEGRO (USA)   5 b.g. Sir Ivor – Tants (Vitiges (FR))   137
[1992/3 16s⁴ 20v* 16d* 16d² 20f⁶ 16dF] good-topped gelding: has been

Bookmakers Hurdle, Leopardstown—
Novello Allegro takes the last alongside runner-up Muir Station (blinkers);
the race was marred by the subsequent death of Royal Gait (white sleeves)

Mrs Rita Polly's "Novello Allegro"

hobdayed: useful hurdler: won minor event at Navan and Bookmakers Hurdle at Leopardstown in December: ran creditably next 2 starts, including when sixth in Martell Aintree Hurdle in April: effective from 2m to 2½m: probably acts on any going: blinkered once: occasionally finds little, and usually held up. *N. Meade, Ireland*

NOW BOARDING 6 b.m. Blazing Saddles (AUS) – Strictly Swing (Swing Easy (USA)) [1992/3 17dᵖᵘ 20gᶠ 20dᵖᵘ] poor performer, stays 1¼m, on Flat: no form over hurdles: sold out of R. Hodges' stable 1,250 gns Ascot March Sales after first outing. *Mrs J. Wonnacott*   –

NOWHISKI 5 b.h. Petoski – Be Faithful (Val de Loir) [1992/3 21g⁴ 16f⁵ 18m³ 16g⁴ 17d³ 18s* 16vᵖᵘ] workmanlike horse: selling hurdler: bought in 2,700 gns after winning handicap at Market Rasen in November: ran poorly following month: should stay further than 2¼m: acts on good to firm and soft ground. *K. A. Morgan*   81

NOW YOUR TALKIN 7 b.g. Furry Glen – Butty Miss (Menelek) [1992/3 21s² 22m* 21d* 23d* 20d* 22v³ 21d³ 21m 25fᵖᵘ] smallish gelding: useful novice hurdler: won at Ludlow (handicap), Warwick, Wolverhampton and Aintree (handicap) in first half of season: stayed well: acted on good to firm and soft going: dead. *D. Nicholson*   129

NUDGE DOUBLE UP 8 b.g. Hays – Bonny Bertha (Capistrano) [1992/3 c23g² c27s⁴ c23gᵘʳ c26g⁴] workmanlike gelding: winning hurdler: poor novice chaser: stays 3¼m: acts on firm ground: blinkered once: jumps none too fluently: ungenuine. *P. J. Hobbs*   c79 §
– §

NUNS JEWEL 7 ch.m. Julio Mariner – Nunswalk (The Parson) [1992/3 26g⁵ 21g* 22s³ 19m⁴ 22gᵖᵘ 22g 26g³ 21d 22s 25m 22fᶠ] small mare: modest hurdler at best: won conditional jockeys handicap at Southwell in August: ran poorly last 4 starts: stays 3¼m: probably needs a sound surface (acts on firm ground): takes good hold and usually races prominently. *J. M. Bradley* — 89 d

NUN SO GAME 6 b.m. The Parson – Hardy Polly (Pollerton) [1992/3 18s 21v 18v 20d⁴] lengthy mare: bad novice hurdler. *S. Mellor* — 59

NUTACRE 8 b.m. Julio Mariner – Misacre (St Alphage) [1992/3 16d 16m c17d⁶ c20s³ c22vᵖᵘ] lengthy mare: lightly-raced novice hurdler/chaser: no form. *G. P. Kelly* — c– –

NUTCASE 4 b.f. Idiot's Delight – Real Beauty (Kinglet) [1992/3 F16m F16v] first foal: dam well beaten only start over hurdles: mid-division in NH Flat races: yet to race over hurdles. *J. A. Pickering* — –

NUT TREE 8 b.m. King of Spain – Grandpa's Legacy (Zeus Boy) [1992/3 a22g⁶ 23m⁴ 28m³ 17g] angular mare: modest hurdler: stays 3½m: acts on good to firm and dead ground, and on fibresand: blinkered third outing (ran creditably): runs in snatches. *D. R. Wike* — 86

NYIKA 5 br.m. Town And Country – Nikali (Siliconn) [1992/3 16d 16s⁶] neat mare: sister to winning jumper Mister Feathers: dam second twice over sprint distances at 2 yrs: well beaten in novice hurdles. *J. Webber* — –

O

OAKLANDS WORD 4 br.g. Hasty Word – Salvo's Grace (FR) (Salvo) [1992/3 F16s 17mᵖᵘ 21d] narrow, close-coupled gelding: half-brother to winning hurdler/chaser Gardeners Choice (by Mossberry): dam won twice over hurdles after birth of first foal: no sign of ability. *D. G. Williams* — –

OAK PARK (IRE) 5 br.g. Prince Tenderfoot (USA) – Louisa Stuart (FR) (Ruysdael II) [1992/3 16m 16s 17g²] small gelding: fair hurdler: yet to race beyond 17f: acts on good to soft going: sometimes wears tongue strap. *J. A. Pickering* — 102

OANIK (FR) 13 b.g. Le Verglas – Baby Mauries (FR) (Cirio) [1992/3 c25vᵖᵘ] workmanlike ex-French gelding: maiden hurdler/chaser. *Guy Luck* — c– –

Liverpool Novices' Handicap Hurdle, Aintree—Now Your Talkin wins with plenty in hand

OAT COUTURE 5 b.h. Oats – Marjoemin (Import) [1992/3 F17d⁵] first foal: dam of little account on Flat: fifth of 25 in NH Flat race at Carlisle in April: yet to race over hurdles or fences. *L. Lungo*

OATIS REGRETS 5 b.g. Oats – Joscilla (Joshua) [1992/3 F16d* 16d* 16v* 21g* 17m⁶] unfurnished gelding: first foal: dam, winning hurdler, is daughter of useful staying chaser Princess Camilla: won NH Flat race at Warwick and novice hurdles at Ludlow, Wincanton and Newbury in 1992/3: also ran creditably final start: effective at 2m with give in the ground and will stay beyond 21f: acts on heavy and good to firm going: will improve and win more races. *Miss H. C. Knight* — 110 p

OATS FOR LAUGHTER 5 b.m. Oats – Sound of Laughter (Hasty Word) [1992/3 F16g] compact mare with scope: second foal: sister to novice hurdler More Laughter: dam, fair hurdler, stayed 2½m: behind in NH Flat race at Worcester in March: yet to race over hurdles or fences. *D. R. Gandolfo*

OATS N BARLEY 4 b.g. Oats – Doon Silver (Doon) [1992/3 F18s³ F16s F17f 20d 20m²] leggy gelding: third foal: dam selling hurdler: second in maiden at Exeter in May, first form over hurdles. *P. R. Rodford* — 82

OBELISKI 7 b.g. Aragon – Pasha's Dream (Tarboosh (USA)) [1992/3 18g⁴ 18d³ c16g*] angular, rather sparely-made gelding: fair hurdler at best: won claiming chase at Southwell (claimed £9,560, to race abroad) in October: stays 2½m: acts on soft ground: visored 4 times in 1990/1, blinkered at Southwell. *P. C. Haslam* — c110 109

OBIE'S TRAIN 7 ch.g. Buckskin (FR) – Whisper Moon (Chinatown) [1992/3 17s⁶ c21d⁵ c24s² c18s* c18s* c25d² c21s² c27dF c26dpu c21f³] tall, leggy gelding: winning hurdler: won novice claiming chases at Exeter in December (claimed out of G. Balding's stable £10,001) and January: effective at around 2m, barely stays 3m: best form on soft going. *M. C. Pipe* — c105 –

OBLATION (USA) 8 b.g. Master Willie – Bold Caress (Bold Lad (IRE)) [1992/3 c19gpu] sturdy, compact gelding: poor novice jumper. *Miss S. Barraclough* — c– –

OBOLOV 6 ch.g. Vaigly Great – Dortia (Martinmas) [1992/3 16m 22dpu a18g³ a18g] lengthy gelding: bad maiden hurdler. *F. Coton* — 59

OCEAN DAY 10 b.g. Balinger – Vimaday (Vimadee) [1992/3 c26m³ c24g⁴] sturdy, long-backed gelding: poor novice hunter chaser: probably stays 3¼m and acts on good to firm ground. *B. Heywood* — c78

OCEAN LEADER 6 b.g. Lord Ha Ha – Rough Tide (Moss Court) [1992/3 20d² 20g 16s³ 21d⁵] stocky gelding: first foal: dam winning pointer in Ireland: modest novice hurdler: will stay 3m: acts on soft ground. *Mrs D. Haine* — 92

OCEAN LINK 9 gr.g. Cunard – La Chatelaine (Border Chief) [1992/3 c21sF c24gpu c24m²] leggy, sparely-made gelding: first form in hunter chases when second at Exeter in May. *H. Wellstead* — c79 –

OCEAN ROGUE 12 b. or br.g. Scallywag – Ocean Rock (Rockavon) [1992/3 20m⁵ c21g² 20mpu] rangy gelding: winning hurdler: poor novice chaser: stays 3m: acts on firm ground: tried in blinkers/visor. *P. D. Evans* — c74 –

OCEAN ROSE 6 gr.m. Baron Blakeney – Deep Ocean (Deep Run) [1992/3 17s 18d 17d 22g 22g 22m] small mare: poor novice hurdler: best effort at 2¾m on good ground. *Mrs B. Butterworth* — 64

OCO ROYAL 4 b.c. Tinoco – Queen's Royale (Tobrouk (FR)) [1992/3 17f*] close-coupled colt: modest middle-distance maiden on Flat: won juvenile hurdle at Plumpton in August: sold 1,000 gns Ascot March Sales. *J. Ffitch-Heyes* — 78

OCTOBER WINDS (NZ) 7 b.g. Balkan Knight (USA) – Rawhiti (NZ) (Acharacle) [1992/3 16drtr 17vrtr 17s 16vpu 17dpu] compact gelding: of little account over hurdles and very unreliable at start to boot: blinkered once. *P. J. Hobbs* — §§

ODILEX 6 b.g. Mummy's Pet – Odile (Green Dancer (USA)) [1992/3 16g 16g³ 16d⁶ 16v⁵ 17g 17g] sturdy gelding: modest miler at best at 4 yrs: poor form in novice hurdles: raced only at around 2m: acts on dead going. *N. A. Gaselee*   84

ODSTONE PEAR 8 b.m. Kemal (FR) – Loughan-Na-Curry (No Argument) [1992/3 23s] lengthy mare: winning hurdler: suited by a test of stamina: acts on firm going and equitrack. *P. Leach*   –

ODYSSEUS 7 b. or br.g. Deep Run – Russian Wings (Zabeg) [1992/3 16s 17g] rangy gelding: no sign of ability. *R. Waley-Cohen*   –

OFFICER CADET 6 b.g. Shernazar – Selection Board (Welsh Pageant) [1992/3 22g² 24d 22s⁴ 25s 26d* 23d⁴ 24d³] small, leggy gelding: fair hurdler: sold out of R. Curtis' stable 6,000 gns Ascot December Sales after fourth outing: won handicap at Huntingdon in January: needs a thorough test of stamina: best form with give in the ground: blinkered third and fourth outings (ran poorly both times). *D. A. Wilson*   100

OFF THE BRU 8 b.g. General Ironside – Amelieranne (Daybrook Lad) [1992/3 c24d⁴ c25g² c25g⁵ c27d⁶ c28s⁵ c33d⁴ c30d c25dᶠ c28dᵘʳ c33gᵘʳ c28g² c25m* c33g c24d³ c25gᶠ] strong, workmanlike gelding: fair handicap chaser: won at Kelso in March: out-and-out stayer: acts on good to firm and dead ground: blinkered/visored eighth and ninth outings: jumps none too fluently. *Mrs S. C. Bradburne*   c104 –

OGENDEBA 13 b.g. Abednego – Shady Tree (Three Wishes) [1992/3 c22sᵖᵘ c26sᵖᵘ c27vᶠ] sturdy gelding: carries condition: winning chaser: no form since 1990/1. *J. S. Moore*   c–

OHCUMGACHE 5 b.g. Little Wolf – Baliview (Balidar) [1992/3 17dᵖᵘ 17f⁶] leggy gelding: first foal: dam of little account: seems no better himself. *R. J. Hodges*   –

OH MOTHER 8 b. or br.m. Uncle Pokey – Chumolaori (Indian Ruler) [1992/3 c26gᵖᵘ c21m³ c18m³] lengthy mare: moderate pointer: poor novice chaser: stays 21f: acts on good to firm ground: visored twice over hurdles. *R. Tate*   c72 –

OH SO BOLD 6 ch.g. Royal Boxer – Staryllis Girl (Star Moss) [1992/3 c21m⁵ c19s c24dᵘʳ c21m⁴ c24f² c25m³ c24f⁵] workmanlike gelding: poor hurdler/novice chaser: stays 25f: acts on firm and dead ground. *J. M. Bradley*   c79 –

OH SO CUTE 6 b.m. Kings Lake (USA) – Shirley's Joy (Shirley Heights) [1992/3 24g] second foal: dam won over 1m on Flat in Ireland: well beaten in late-season amateurs maiden at Hexham on hurdling debut. *P. Beaumont*   –

OH SO HANDY 5 b.g. Nearly A Hand – Geordie Lass (Bleep-Bleep) [1992/3 18gᵖᵘ 18f 17gᵖᵘ 16g] no sign of ability. *R. Curtis*   –

OH SO RISKY 6 b.g. Kris – Expediency (USA) (Vaguely Noble) [1992/3 17v³ 17v⁴ 16d⁵ 17m⁵]   159

Oh So Risky hasn't won over hurdles since he routed the opposition in the Daily Express Triumph Hurdle in 1991. And he won't have many opportunities to put matters right in 1993/4 if, as in the previous two seasons, his campaign is geared towards the Smurfit Champion Hurdle at Cheltenham in March, taking in a few of the trial races along the way. He's also due to tackle the Breeders' Cup Chase before starting his British campaign. Oh So Risky is a very smart performer, but there are several hurdlers around who are more than a match for him at level weights. The 1992 Champion Hurdle, in which Oh So Risky finished a close second to Royal Gait, was a sub-standard one, and Oh So Risky's standing among the top hurdlers can be better gauged from his performance in the latest running at Cheltenham in March. A horse who goes well fresh, Oh So Risky was having his first race for almost three months at Cheltenham, where for the first time during the season ground conditions were in his favour. Although Oh So Risky has form in the mud a sound surface suits him ideally, and on going which was on the firm side of good he acquitted himself well in finishing fifth behind Granville Again, Royal Derbi, Halkopous and King

Credo. Oh So Risky, held up in the rear as usual, was pushed along from the top of the hill and came through to deliver his challenge on the outside of the field at the second last. Put under stronger pressure turning for home, Oh So Risky could keep on at only one pace to the finish, where he was eight and a half lengths adrift of Granville Again. Oh So Risky had also finished behind Granville Again in his previous three starts, when the latter was placed. In an unsatisfactory race for the Coral-Elite Hurdle at Cheltenham in November Oh So Risky, having his first race since being gelded, shaped well when third to Morley Street; and he then finished a respectable fourth to Halkopous in the Bula Hurdle on the same course. But he was some way below form in the Christmas Hurdle at Kempton, his last outing before the Champion Hurdle.

		Sharpen Up	Atan
Oh So Risky	Kris	(ch 1969)	Rocchetta
(b.g. 1987)	(ch 1976)	Doubly Sure	Reliance II
		(b 1971)	Soft Angels
	Expediency (USA)	Vaguely Noble	Vienna
	(b or br 1976)	(b 1965)	Noble Lassie
		Gazala II	Dark Star
		(br 1964)	Belle Angevine

Oh So Risky is a half-brother to four winners, notably the one-time useful hurdler/chaser Decided (by Affirmed) and Bin Shaddad (by Riverman), the latter a useful miler in Britain who went on to show even better form in Germany. Their dam Expediency, placed twice at around a mile and a quarter, is a full sister to Mississippian, the top-rated two-year-old in France in 1973, and to the 1980 Irish St Leger winner Gonzales; and she's a half-sister to the top-class middle-distance performer Youth. Oh So Risky himself has shown useful form over middle distances on the Flat, including when winning at Newmarket in July. He's done all his racing over hurdles at around two miles, and that is always likely to be his optimum trip. Oh So Risky, a leggy, quite good-topped gelding who usually looks very well, has his share of temperament. Led in at the start last time out, having played up on his previous two appearances at Cheltenham, he sometimes looks none too keen at the business end of a race. *D. R. C. Elsworth*

OH SO WINDY 6 b.m. Oats – Tempest Girl (Caliban) [1992/3 16s 18d⁴ 16s⁴ 22g³ 20vᵖᵘ] smallish, leggy mare: lightly-raced novice hurdler: poor form: stays 2¾m: acts on soft ground. *Mrs A. L. M. King*   75

OK CORRAL (USA) 6 gr.g. Malinowski (USA) – Tiger Trap (USA) (Al Hattab (USA)) [1992/3 c24d⁵ c25d⁶ c25v⁴ c21v* c21v² c26s² c25f⁶ c26g* c25g³ c26g* c27m³ c24g³ c24f²] sturdy gelding: fair handicap chaser: won at Folkestone (amateurs) and Plumpton (twice) in second half of season: stays 27f: acts on any going: successful with blinkers and without. *J. White*   c108 –

OK RECORDS 6 b.g. Cure The Blues (USA) – Last Clear Chance (USA) (Alleged (USA)) [1992/3 16s 16d⁶ 20g² 22f² 24g⁶ c17sᵘʳ 17f 17d 18v²] lengthy, sparely-made gelding: novice selling hurdler: unseated third on chasing debut: suited by around 2½m: acts on any ground: visored both outings 1990/1. *O. O'Neill*   c– 76

O K SOHFAR 6 ch.m. Rolfe (USA) – Royale Final (Henry The Seventh) [1992/3 22d⁶ 23gᵖᵘ] small mare: of no account. *G. F. H. Charles-Jones*   –

OLANTHE (USA) 4 ch.g. Blushing Groom (FR) – Olamic (USA) (Nijinsky (CAN)) [1992/3 16v³ 17f⁶ 20gᵖᵘ] lengthy, useful-looking ex-French gelding: useful middle-distance performer on Flat: only poor form over hurdles: sold, reportedly back to France, 8,200 gns Doncaster May Sales: blinkered. *C. P. E. Brooks*   80

OLD APPLEJACK 13 ch.g. Hot Brandy – Windfall VI (Master Owen) [1992/3 c20m* c25g⁶ c21s⁴ c20s² c20d⁴ c26s² c24mᵖᵘ] lengthy, angular gelding: fairly useful and most genuine chaser: eighth course victory when successful in handicap at Newcastle in October: effective at 2½m and stayed extremely well: probably acted on any going: usually raced prominently and jumped well: dead. *J. H. Johnson*   c129

OLD BRIDGE (IRE) 5 ch.g. Crash Course – What A Duchess (Bargello) [1992/3 17v² 18g³ 17gᵖᵘ 16v²] unfurnished gelding: seventh foal: brother to winning jumpers Eastshaw and Social Climber, former useful, and half-brother to novice hurdler What A Noble (by Deep Run): dam, unraced, from excellent jumping family, including L'Escargot, What A Buck and The Pilgarlic: fair form in novice hurdles, though looked wayward third start: will stay at least 2½m: acts on heavy ground. *Andrew Turnell*   98

OLD BRIG 7 br.g. Roscoe Blake – Hunter's Treasure (Tudor Treasure) [1992/3 22g* 23d³ 17v⁴ 18s c24d c21f²] leggy gelding: modest form over hurdles: won novice event at Wincanton in November: blinkered when second in novice chase at Worcester in March: better at around 2¾m than 2m: acts on firm and dead going: races up with pace. *M. C. Pipe*   c99
99

OLD EROS 9 ch.g. Bold Owl – Piccadilly Rose (Reform) [1992/3 c16g² c16g²] smallish, sparely-made gelding: one-time fairly useful hurdler: lightly-raced novice chaser, modest form: stays 21f: probably acts on any going: front runner, suited by a sharp track. *Mrs M. Reveley*   c93
–

OLD FATHER TIME 6 b.g. The Parson – Scotch News (London Gazette) [1992/3 F17d F17s 21g⁵ 22m⁴] big, rangy gelding: fifth foal: half-brother to NH Flat race winner Andero (by Tug of War) and Where Am I Going (by Le Bavard), placed in NH Flat races and points: dam unraced: poor form in novice hurdles: type to do better, particularly over fences. *K. C. Bailey*   78 p

OLD GLORY 5 ch.g. Valiyar – Old Kate (Busted) [1992/3 20g] leggy gelding: well beaten over hurdles. *M. S. Saunders*   –

OLD MILL STREAM 7 br.g. Rapid River – Daleena (Dalesa) [1992/3 c16m c21m⁴ c16m⁴ c17d⁴ c16dᵘʳ c16sᵖᵘ c17d] big, rangy gelding: winning hurdler: poor novice chaser: stays 21f: best efforts on a sound surface (acts on hard ground). *W. Raw*   c82
–

OLD MORTALITY 7 b.g. Uncle Pokey – Speed Trap (Pontifex (USA)) [1992/3 16gᵃ18gᵖᵘ 20g⁶ 16d c20m⁴ 18dᵖᵘ 17f⁵ 17gᵖᵘ 18m* 16g³] tall gelding: made all in novice hurdle at Cartmel in May, best effort: well beaten only start over fences: stays 2¼m: best on a sound surface. *R. Allan*   c–
87

OLD PEG 5 b.m. Reach – Lizarra (High Top) [1992/3 16g 16s⁶ 16s⁴ a18gᵖᵘ 16d] leggy mare: poor hurdler: sold 4,200 gns Newmarket September Sales: raced at around 2m: acted on soft and good to firm going: usually blinkered, visored once: dead. *R. J. Manning*   77

OLD REDWOOD 6 b. or br.g. Scallywag – China Bank (Wrekin Rambler) [1992/3 c16sᶠ⁴ c20dᶠ⁴ c20vᶠ³ 21s⁵ c20fᶠ] leggy, good-topped gelding: modest novice hurdler/chaser: stays 2½m: acts on heavy ground: let down by his jumping over fences. *D. McCain*   c88 x

OLD ROAD (USA) 7 b.g. Regal And Royal (USA) – Raise Me (USA) (Mr Prospector (USA)) [1992/3 c21s⁵ c23fF c21g⁴ c20g⁵ c20d³ c16v* c24dᵖᵘ c18vᵖᵘ c20dᵖᵘ c17m² c22m⁵] smallish, sparely-made gelding: modest chaser: claimed out of Mrs J. Wonnacott's stable £6,500 after second start: won novice event at Plumpton in November: likely to prove best at up to 2½m: best effort on heavy ground. *D. J. Wintle*   c90

OLD SPECKLED HEN 5 ch.m. The Noble Player (USA) – Making Tracks (Sagaro) [1992/3 c16fF c16mᵖᵘ] sparely-made mare: novice hurdler/chaser: no form. *T. Casey*   c–
–

OLD STEINE 5 b.g. Elegant Air – Brightelmstone (Prince Regent (FR)) [1992/3 17mᵘʳ 16g 17g 17d³ 22m²] leggy gelding: lightly-raced maiden on Flat: moderate novice hurdler: best effort at 2¾m on good to firm ground: blinkered third and fourth starts: pulls hard. *P. J. Hobbs*   99

OLEJ (USA) 4 b.g. Danzig Connection (USA) – Smarted (USA) (Smarten (USA)) [1992/3 16v⁵ 16g 18fᵖᵘ] sparely-made gelding: poor maiden on Flat: sold out of Lord Huntingdon's stable 1,150 gns Ascot November Sales: probably of little account over hurdles: blinkered final start. *C. D. Broad*   –

OLE OLE 7 br.g. Boreen (FR) – Night Caller (Middle Temple) [1992/3 c25d^{bd}] tall gelding: winning hunter chaser: stays 3m: acts on good to firm and dead ground. *Mrs E. Moscrop*

c–

OLIVIPET 4 b.f. Sula Bula – Gamlingay (Rosyth) [1992/3 F17m] leggy filly: half-sister to winning pointer Miss Rughill (by New Member): dam poor novice hurdler/chaser: tailed off in NH Flat race at Cheltenham in April: yet to race over hurdles. *F. Gray*

OLLIVER DUCKETT 4 b.g. Bustino – Tatiana (Habitat) [1992/3 16s^F 17d^{ur} 17d 16m⁶] unfurnished gelding: no form on Flat: poor novice hurdler: yet to race beyond 17f: acts on good to firm ground, probably on soft. *P. Calver*

72

OLVESTON (NZ) 9 b.g. Sea Anchor – Statira (NZ) (Imperial March (CAN)) [1992/3 16v* 17s³ a16g⁴ F13m* 16m⁵ 17s^{pu} c16v⁴ 20g^{pu}] well-made, workmanlike gelding: winning chaser: handicap hurdler: won at Worcester in January: generally ran poorly afterwards, though won weakly-contested celebrity race on Flat at Ludlow in March: sold 1,600 gns Ascot June Sales, resold 2,800 gns Malvern June Sales: best form at around 2m: acts on good to firm and heavy ground: pulls hard and is often held up: sometimes hangs left under pressure: poor jumper of fences. *P. F. Nicholls*

c– x
114 d

OLYMPIAN 6 ch.g. High Line – Elysian (Northfields (USA)) [1992/3 23g* 17f* 21m* 20f² 16f]
Handicap hurdler Olympian won over £100,000 for his connections in the space of five days in March, his victories in the Sunderlands Imperial Cup and the Coral Cup landing a £50,000 bonus on offer if the Imperial Cup winner followed up by winning a race at the Cheltenham Festival. Olympian, transferred from McGovern's yard after a disappointing season in 1991/2, didn't have his first outing for Pipe until seen out at Stratford in early March, by which time the weights for the Imperial Cup and for the early-closing Cheltenham Festival handicaps were already out. Olympian hadn't won in eleven starts the previous season and had plummeted down the handicap. He looked extremely well treated on his form as a juvenile—when he'd won four times and come fifth in the Triumph Hurdle—especially after he disposed impressively of a field of largely out-of-form handicappers at Stratford. Olympian was 10 lb out of the handicap at the five-day stage in the two-mile Imperial Cup but, clearly revitalised, looked to have a good chance at the weights, even so. He started a very heavily-backed 6/4 favourite, looking a 'good thing' after the weights were raised 10 lb at the overnight stage. Olympian made all, setting a scorching gallop and jumping fluently, to win going away by three lengths in course record time, his task eased when eventual third Spinning blundered while looking very dangerous at the

135

*Sunderlands Imperial Cup (Handicap Hurdle), Sandown—
short-priced favourite Olympian is too good for Gymcrak Stardom (grey) and Spinning (right)*

*Coral Cup (Handicap Hurdle), Cheltenham—four days later,
Olympian wins the inaugural running of this valuable event*

second last. Olympian was entered for both the Coral Cup and the County
Hurdle at Cheltenham. He had always looked more of a staying type and it
was no surprise to see connections opt for the Coral Cup over an extra five
furlongs. On a stiffer mark than at Sandown, though carrying the same
weight, ten stone, Olympian again dominated from an early stage, jumping
fast and fluently. He kept up a tremendous gallop, over a dozen lengths clear
of his twenty rivals much of the way, and held on up the finishing hill to win
by two and a half lengths from Sillars Stalker. Mission accomplished! Pipe
had certainly made the most of Olympian's lenient handicap mark, but could
expect no mercy from the handicapper in forthcoming races. Olympian went
next to Aintree where, racing off a mark 13 lb higher than at Cheltenham, he
lost nothing in defeat in the Oddbins Handicap Hurdle, hanging on to the
lead until the last flight and finding only Gallateen too good for him. The
Oddbins Handicap is over two and a half miles and Olympian has shown his
very best form at around that trip. Back at two miles in the Swinton Handicap Hurdle at Haydock in May he set a strong gallop but was swallowed up
once in line for home. Olympian, who is usually blinkered nowadays, acts on
firm and dead going. He jumps well and is suited by forcing tactics.

Olympian (ch.g. 1987)	High Line (ch 1966)	High Hat (ch 1957)	Hyperion
			Madonna
		Time Call (b 1955)	Chanteur II
			Aleria
	Elysian (br 1980)	Northfields (ch 1968)	Northern Dancer
			Little Hut
		Elizabethan (br 1973)	Tudor Melody
			Ash Lawn

Olympian, a deep-girthed gelding, has essentially a Flat-racing pedigree. He is by the notably tough and genuine stayer High Line who made a
name for himself as a sire both Flat and jumping (Muse and the brothers
Bobsline and Barrow Line are among his most notable jumpers). Olympian's
dam was a fairly useful racemare at her best, successful over six furlongs as
a two-year-old and placed in the ten-furlong Nassau Stakes as a three-year-
old when she seemed to stay a mile and a half. Olympian is still a maiden on
the Flat but Elysian has bred three winners in that sphere, two of them by
Derby winner Slip Anchor, namely the fairly useful staying handicapper Sea
Goddess and the useful middle-distance performer Anchorite, and Circe (by
Main Reef) a fair mile winner who stayed a mile and a quarter. Olympian's
grandam Elizabethan won at a mile on her only start and was from a famous
Childwick Bury Stud family, being out of a half-sister to the Two Thousand
Guineas and Derby winner Royal Palace. *M. C. Pipe*

545

OMORSI 6 b.m. Prince Tenderfoot (USA) – Her Name Was Lola (Pitskelly) [1992/3 F12d 16s^F 16v] good-topped mare: poor maiden on Flat, stays 1½m: well beaten in novice hurdle at Towcester in December. *J. White* —

ON ALERT (NZ) 6 ch.g. Double Trouble (NZ) – Stand By (NZ) (Oakville) [1992/3 17s^5 22d^2 22dF] leggy gelding: poor novice hurdler: not raced after September: stays 2¾m: acts on soft ground. *D. H. Barons* 78

ONAWING ANDAPRAYER 6 b.m. Energist – Mary's Double (Majetta) [1992/3 F17d 24v^{pu} a20g] lengthy mare: second foal: half-sister to winning 2¾m hurdle winner Cainsbridge Queen (by Crash Course): dam won 2½m hurdle in Ireland: tailed off in NH Flat race and over hurdles: sold 2,300 gns Ascot 2nd June Sales. *J. W. Mullins* —

ONCE STUNG 7 br.g. Sandalay – Nenana (Menelek) [1992/3 c25d^2 c25s^2 c24f* c27m^3 c25g* c25d* c26g* c28f^3] angular gelding: useful hunter chaser: had a good season and won at Newbury, Kelso (twice) and Uttoxeter: also third in Foxhunter Chase at Cheltenham: below form in valuable event at Stratford final outing: effective at 3m and stays long distances: probably acts on any going: jumps soundly. *P. Cheesbrough* c116

ON CUE 6 gr.g. Magic Mirror – Tug Along (Posse (USA)) [1992/3 a20g^6 a24g^{pu} a24g^{pu} 17m^2 20g^6 24s^{pu} 17g^5 24g] angular, close-coupled gelding: poor novice hurdler: easily best run at 17f on good to firm going: blinkered once: temperamental. *K. S. Bridgwater* 79 §

ONE FOR IRENE 6 gr.m. Hotfoot – Vila Real (Town Crier) [1992/3 16g 16gF] sparely-made mare: poor hurdler: barely stays 2m: best form on good going: tried visored. *R. J. Price* —

ONE FOR THE CHIEF 5 b.g. Chief Singer – Action Belle (Auction Ring (USA)) [1992/3 21s 20d a24g^{ur} 25s 28g^2 22m 25m^2] workmanlike gelding: poor maiden hurdler: sold 4,600 gns Doncaster May Sales: stays 3½m: acts on good to firm and heavy ground. *R. M. Whitaker* 79

ONE FOR THE POT 8 ch.g. Nicholas Bill – Tea-Pot (Ragstone) [1992/3 c16s* c16d^4 c16g^2 c16dF 16d^3 16g^3 c17d* c20s^6 c21s^2 c16f*] small, sturdy gelding: fairly useful hurdler: won novice chases at Catterick, Hexham and Uttoxeter (amateurs) in second half of season: probably stays 21f: acts on any going: usually held up. *M. P. Naughton* c103 123

ONE MAN (IRE) 5 gr.g. Remainder Man – Steal On (General Ironside) [1992/3 16d 21m^2 20m* 26d^3 20gF 22s* 20m* 20f^3 22g^2] sturdy gelding: chasing type: first foal: dam never ran: ran out in an Irish point: won novice hurdles at Newcastle in October (trained until after fifth start by W. A. Stephenson), Nottingham (handicap) in January and Ayr in February: excellent second in novice handicap at Ayr in April: sold 68,000 gns in May: stays 2¾m: acts on good to firm and soft ground (soon tailed off on firm). *P. Cheesbrough* 126 p

ONE MORE DREAM 6 ch.g. Deep Run – Rare Dream (Pollerton) [1992/3 16g^2 17d^4 17v^{pu}] workmanlike gelding: has scope: winning hurdler: in frame in small-field minor events at Kempton and Cheltenham first 2 starts, showing useful form: ran poorly final outing (December): should stay beyond 17f: acts on dead ground. *G. B. Balding* 136 ?

ONE MORE RUN 6 ch.g. Deep Run – Mawbeg Holly (Golden Love) [1992/3 17s 21g] workmanlike gelding: third foal: brother to promising (already useful) staying chaser Dakyns Boy: dam never ran: showed ability in novice event at Ascot in January on hurdling debut: should stay at least 2½m (well beaten when tried at trip): worth another chance. *G. B. Balding* 87 p

ONE TO NOTE 9 br.g. Star Appeal – Town Lady (Town Crier) [1992/3 17g^3 22g] lengthy gelding: modest hurdler: not raced after October: should stay further than 17f: acts on heavy going. *M. P. Muggeridge* 93

ONEUPMANSHIP 8 ch.g. Derrylin – Lucky Janie (Dual) [1992/3 21g^3 20d^3 20f^3 20f^6] small, leggy gelding: useful hurdler: good third in handicaps at Newbury and Haydock in February and Lingfield in March: stays 21f: probably acts on any going. *Mrs J. R. Renfree-Barons* 132

ONLY A ROSE 4 br.f. Glint of Gold – No More Rosies (Warpath) [1992/3   110
18d* 20s* 16s² 16v⁴ 14s* 16s³] leggy, close-coupled, light-framed filly:
half-sister to useful hurdler Beachy Head (by Damister): no form on Flat:
won juvenile hurdles at Sedgefield and Haydock in November and Ayr
(claimer) in January: effective at 2m under testing conditions and will stay
beyond 2½m: acts on soft ground. *C. W. Thornton*

ONLY FOR PLEASURE 5 b.g. Idiot's Delight – Sarasail (Hitting   –
Away) [1992/3 17dᵖᵘ 17dᵖᵘ] angular gelding: no sign of ability in novice
hurdles. *J. R. Jenkins*

ONLY IN IRELAND 7 b.g. Bulldozer – Welsh Wise (Welsh Saint)   c–
[1992/3 17vᵖᵘ c16dᵖᵘ c17sᵖᵘ] leggy gelding: lightly raced and no form over   –
hurdles or fences. *P. F. Nicholls*

ONLY THE LONELY 6 b.g. Mummy's Game – Izobia (Mansingh   c–
(USA)) [1992/3 c25vᶠ c24sᵖᵘ c21mᵖᵘ] workmanlike gelding: poor 2m   –
hurdler: no sign of ability in hunter chases: sometimes blinkered, visored
once. *D. W. Parker*

ON TAP 9 ch.g. Tap On Wood – Joshua's Daughter (Joshua) [1992/3 c21d² c106
c16g⁴ c20d* c20s² c21dᵖᵘ] strong, workmanlike gelding: winning hurdler: –
successful in novice handicap chase at Haydock in November: stayed 2½m:
acted on good to firm and soft ground: dead. *M. H. Easterby*

ON THE HOOCH 8 ch.m. Over The River (FR) – Bit of Fashion c106 ?
(Master Owen) [1992/3 23g³ c20s⁴ c21s⁵ c20s⁴ c16d³ c21g² c21g² c21g³   106
c21m* c22f c21s³ c24v² c20f⁵ c21mᵖᵘ] close-coupled mare: fair hurdler/
chaser: won handicap over fences at Carlisle in March: stays 3m: acts on any
going: usually amateur or claimer ridden: inconsistent. *Mrs S. C. Bradburne*

ON THE JAR (IRE) 5 gr.g. Entre Nous – Hot Canary (Tepukei) [1992/3   –
F14s 16s 17dᵖᵘ 17fᵖᵘ] leggy gelding: no sign of ability. *C. C. Trietline*

ON THE LINE 5 b.g. Belfort (FR) – Queen's Parade (Sovereign Path)   95
[1992/3 20v 16d² 16m² 18g* 17gᶠ 18fᵖᵘ] leggy, close-coupled gelding:
modest hurdler: won handicap at Worcester in March: stayed 2¼m: acted
on good to soft and good to firm ground: dead. *C. R. Barwell*

ON THE OTHER HAND 10 b.g. Proverb – Saltee Star (Arapaho) c125
[1992/3 21g c24d³ c20d⁵ c21s c25f*] leggy, lengthy ex-Irish gelding: fairly   –

Horse And Hound Grand Military Gold Cup, Sandown—
On The Other Hand (left) lifts this prestigious race for amateurs

useful chaser: trained until after fourth outing by J. Mulhern: won amateurs event at Sandown in March: stays 25f: possibly unsuited by heavy going, acts on any other. *G. Richards*

ON THE SAUCE   6 b.g. Kala Shikari – Kingsfold Flash (Warpath) [1992/3 24s^{pu} 25d^F 22m* a22g^2 21d^3 25m^3 26v* 27d^6 18m* 20g* 21m*] sturdy gelding: fair hurdler: had a good season and won claimers at Fontwell and Exeter and sellers at Hereford (no bid), Exeter (bought in 3,400 gns) and Uttoxeter (handicap, bought in 5,500 gns): effective at 2¼m and stays 3¼m: acts on good to firm and heavy going: visored once, blinkered nowadays: front runner. *M. C. Pipe*   102

ON THE TEAR   7 br.g. The Parson – Queen Menelek (Menelek) [1992/3 c16g^{pu} c17m^{F4} c18s^2 c16s^F c16s^4 c20m^{ur} c22g^{pu}] rather leggy gelding: poor novice chaser: sold 8,400 gns Doncaster May Sales: stays 2¼m: acts on soft and good to firm ground: poor jumper. *J. Hanson*   c82   x

ON THE TWIST   11 b.g. Callernish – Irish Beauty (Even Money) [1992/3 c24d^{pu} c25s^4] angular gelding: useful chaser in 1991/2: showed nothing in 1992/3: suited by 3m and more: acts on good to firm and soft ground: best with forcing tactics: jumps soundly, but to the right. *F. Murphy*   c–

ON YOUR WAY   11 b.g. Ragapan – Fourteen Carat (Sterling Bay (SWE)) [1992/3 c22g^4 c21d^{bd} c24d c22v^2 c24s^4 c21d^{pu} c25g^F c25d^F c21g^5 c22g^5 c21g^2 c20g^{pu} c21g^5] leggy gelding: handicap chaser: easily best effort in 1992/3 on fourth start: sold 3,400 gns Doncaster May Sales: stays 2¾m: acts on heavy ground: blinkered last 3 starts: poor jumper. *J. P. Leigh*   c111   d

OOZLEM (IRE)   4 b.g. Burslem – Fingers (Lord Gayle (USA)) [1992/3 16g^{pu} 18g] leggy gelding: half-brother to winning hurdler Hallow Fair (by Wolver Hollow): bad maiden on Flat and over hurdles: blinkered final start. *C. A. Horgan*   –

OPAL'S TENSPOT   6 b.g. Royal Boxer – Opal Lady (Averof) [1992/3 20g^2 23s^3 18m*] lengthy gelding: modest hurdler: won novice event at Southwell in October: stays 23f: acts on soft and good to firm ground. *J. M. Bradley*   88

OPENING OVERTURE (USA)   7 b.m. At The Threshold (USA) – Rhine Queen (FR) (Rheingold) [1992/3 22f^2 20g 21s^{pu}] close second of 2 finishers on first start, but otherwise seems of little account. *C. R. Beever*   ?

OPEN SESAME   7 b.g. Be My Guest (USA) – Syrian Sea (USA) (Bold Ruler) [1992/3 21v^{pu} 21s 16s^3 20d 17g^3 16d] lengthy gelding: poor novice hurdler: best form at around 2m: acts on good ground. *M. Bradstock*   79

OPERATION WOLF   7 ch.g. Adonijah – Sesta (Artaius (USA)) [1992/3 16s 17d^3 16g^4 16m* 17s* 16g^4] stocky gelding: type to carry condition: one-time useful performer at around 1¼m on Flat: won novice hurdles at Worcester and Perth in the spring: ran well in handicap final start: yet to race beyond 17f: acts on soft and good to firm ground. *N. Tinkler*   101

ORATEL FLYER   6 gr.g. Kirchner – Hyperion Princess (Dragonara Palace (USA)) [1992/3 17m^{pu}] bad sprint maiden on Flat: no sign of ability in early-season novice event on hurdling debut. *R. Thompson*   –

ORCHIPEDZO   8 ch.g. Le Moss – Jupiters Jill (Jupiter Pluvius) [1992/3 c16m* c21g^2 c16f^3 c16g^5 c16m^3 c16s^3 22d a18g c16m^4] angular gelding: poor handicap chaser/novice hurdler: won over fences at Worcester in August: trained until after seventh start by R. Dickin: barely stays 2½m: acts on good to firm and soft ground: sometimes wears tongue strap. *C. Cowley*   c80

ORDER OF MERIT   8 b.g. Cut Above – Lady Habitat (Habitat) [1992/3 17d 18f 19m c27d^{ur} 20g^{pu}] small, sturdy gelding: poor novice hurdler: let down by his jumping in 2 races over fences: best form at around 2m: acts on hard and dead ground. *S. F. Turton*   c–
–

ORGANIC (IRE)   5 b.g. Orchestra – Art Mistress (Master Owen) [1992/3 F17s] seventh foal: half-brother to 3 winning jumpers, including fair Mander's Way (by Furry Glen): dam, winning hurdler at up to 2½m in Ireland, sister to good chaser Artifice: won NH Flat race in Ireland in 1991/2:

sold 46,000 gns Doncaster May (1992) Sales: seventh in similar race at Carlisle in November: yet to race over hurdles or fences. *O. Brennan*

ORIEL DREAM 6 br.m. Oats – Ellen Greaves (Deep Run) [1992/3 24d² 21s* 24d² 24s² 20d⁶ 20f4] workmanlike mare: carries condition: fair hurdler: won handicap at Carlisle in November: ran poorly last 2 outings: stays 3m: acts on good ground, possibly unsuited by firm: reportedly breaks blood vessels. *R. F. Fisher*   113

ORIENTAL NATIVE (USA) 6 ch.g. Raise A Native – Etoile d'Orient (Targowice (USA)) [1992/3 16dᵖᵘ] leggy gelding: no sign of ability in 2 races over hurdles and looks ungenuine to boot. *G. M. Graham*   – §

ORIENTAL SONG 4 ch.f. Battle Hymn – Miss Kung Fu (Caliban) [1992/3 16gᵖᵘ] rather sparely-made filly: no form on Flat or in a novice hurdle. *K. S. Bridgwater*   –

ORIENTEER 4 b.g. Reference Point – Optimistic Lass (USA) (Mr Prospector (USA)) [1992/3 18mᵘʳ 17m] once-raced on Flat: sold out of L. Cumani's stable 3,400 gns Newmarket July Sales: well beaten in early-season juvenile hurdle: resold 1,900 gns Doncaster May Sales. *Mrs A. Swinbank*   –

ORPEN (IRE) 5 gr.g. Caerleon (USA) – Caring (Crowned Prince (USA)) [1992/3 16gᵘʳ] sparely-made gelding: no form in novice hurdles: dead. *C. Cowley*   –

ORTON HOUSE 6 b.g. Silly Prices – Who's Free (Sit In The Corner (USA)) [1992/3 16s 17d 26g⁴ 24m³ 25d⁵ 24g⁶] angular, rather close-coupled gelding: poor novice hurdler: stays well: best efforts on a sound surface. *J. I. A. Charlton*   84

OSGATHORPE 6 ch.g. Dunbeath (USA) – Darlingka (Darling Boy) [1992/3 17m* 17m³ 16d 18g a16g⁵] modest hurdler: won novice event at Perth in August: ran poorly after second start: sold out of G. Richards' stable 3,400 gns Doncaster October Sales after fourth: races at around 2m: acts on good to firm going. *M. D. I. Usher*   91

OSMOSIS 7 b.g. Green Shoon – Milparinka (King's Equity) [1992/3 c21d c24g⁵ c25s⁵ c24g c16s] rangy gelding: form in novice chases only on second start. *D. J. G. Murray-Smith*   c78

OSSIE 4 b.c. Nicholas Bill – Ozra (Red Alert) [1992/3 16d 17g⁴] neat colt: poor maiden on Flat: claimed out of B. Palling's stable £5,500 in April on first start over hurdles: fourth in novice event following month. *N. A. Twiston-Davies*   86

OSTURA 8 b.g. Sir Ivor – Casual (USA) (Caro) [1992/3 18s⁶ c16dᵘʳ c16v⁴ 21v² c16s⁴] rather leggy gelding: winning hurdler, lightly raced: some promise in novice chases: should stay beyond 2m: acts on heavy going. *J. White*   c– p / –

OTHER RANKS (IRE) 5 b.g. Trojan Fen – Wernlas (Prince Tenderfoot (USA)) [1992/3 16s³ 16d⁵ 16s⁴ 16g 17d³] ex-Irish gelding: poor maiden hurdler: trained until after third start by P. Phelan: yet to race beyond 17f: acts on soft ground. *P. J. Dennis*   72

OTHET 9 b.g. Thatch (USA) – Hot Pad (Hotfoot) [1992/3 16v⁶ 17d³ 20g⁴ 18m² 17m³ 18g⁴ 20m⁵ 16f² 17g*] lengthy gelding: selling hurdler: won at Hereford (no bid) in May: failed to complete over fences: effective from 2m to 2½m: acts on firm and dead ground: consistent. *Mrs S. D. Williams*   c– / 87

OTTERBURN HOUSE 9 b.g. Proverb – High Energy (Dalesa) [1992/3 c26d* c29s³ c26s² c24s* c24m² c29dᵖᵘ] leggy, workmanlike gelding: fairly useful chaser: won handicaps at Uttoxeter in November and Haydock in January: good second to Young Hustler in Great Yorkshire Chase at Doncaster later in January: not seen out after February: suited by a test of stamina: acts on soft and good to firm going: usually makes running: jumps very well. *J. G. FitzGerald*   c123 / –

OTTER BUSH 4 b.g. Daring March – Rhythmical (Swing Easy (USA)) [1992/3 17g 17d⁴ 16s⁵ 17s³ 17s³ 16v⁵ a16g 16s⁵ 16m² 16sʳᵒ] strong, plain   89 §

gelding: half-brother to ungenuine winning hurdler Jokers Patch (by Hotfoot): of little account on Flat: modest novice hurdler: sold out of G. Blum's stable 2,100 gns Doncaster January Sales after seventh outing: raced only at around 2m: acts on good to firm and soft ground: visored fourth to seventh outings: reluctant. *Mrs S. J. Smith*

OTTER MILL 5 b.g. Harvest Spirit – Jolly Music (Money Business) [1992/3 c17sF 17dpu 20m c27dpu c26mF] brother to winning jumper Harvest Hymn and half-brother to several others: dam won 2m hurdle: no promise over hurdles or fences. *O. J. Carter*

c–
–

OTTERWAY LADY 7 ch.m. Harvest Spirit – Penny Change (Money Business) [1992/3 c21mpu c21mpu] very lightly raced: yet to complete. *O. J. Carter*

c–
–

OTTOMAN EMPIRE 6 b.g. Kemal (FR) – Vulgan Ten (Raise You Ten) [1992/3 F17d2 F16s F17f5 22g6] rangy gelding: half-brother to moderate hurdler and fair chaser Boston Rover (by Ovac): dam won bumpers event: showed ability in NH Flat races and a Huntingdon maiden hurdle: should do better. *O. Brennan*

– p

OUBLIER L'ENNUI (FR) 8 b.m. Bellman (FR) – Cassoway (Kashmir II) [1992/3 c26g3 c24g4] leggy mare: modest handicap chaser at best: ran poorly in 1992/3: should stay beyond 21f: acts on firm and dead ground. *D. H. Barons*

c–
–

OUNAVARRA MILL 7 b.g. Deep Run – Miss Cheeky (Master Buck) [1992/3 26gpu 22spu 27dpu] smallish gelding: fair staying hurdler in 1991/2: ran badly in 1992/3: sometimes visored. *M. S. Saunders*

–

OUR ARNOLD 6 b.g. Julio Mariner – Old Hand (Master Owen) [1992/3 F17d F17m6] sixth foal: half-brother to winning jumper Buckshee Boy (by Buckskin) and novice jumper Goldfinger (by Billion): dam behind in novice hurdles: sixth of 15 in NH Flat race at Hereford in May: yet to race over hurdles or fences. *J. Pilkington*

OUR BILLY BOY 7 b.g. Baron Blakeney – Bonne Baiser (Most Secret) [1992/3 c21mpu c27dpu] small, plain gelding: poor maiden jumper. *F. R. Bown*

c–
–

OUR EDDIE 4 ch.g. Gabitat – Ragusa Girl (Morston (FR)) [1992/3 17m 17f6 16g5] leggy, sparely-made gelding: modest maiden on Flat, stays 1¼m: modest form in early-season juvenile hurdles: will prove best over sharp 2m: best effort on good ground. *B. Gubby*

98

OUR EILEEN 4 b.f. Claude Monet (USA) – Have Form (Haveroid) [1992/3 17g] no form on Flat: tailed off in early-season juvenile hurdle. *B. Smart*

–

OUR FELLOW 11 br.g. Boreen (FR) – Suspicious Vulvic (Above Suspicion) [1992/3 c24s c21d c27vpu c25s3 c25d4 c22f c26fpu] big, rangy gelding: modest chaser: stays 3¼m: acts on soft and good to firm going. *G. B. Balding*

c90

OUR HERO 10 ch.g. Posse (USA) – Blonda (Exbury) [1992/3 17spu 17m6 25dpu] leggy, sparely-made gelding: winning 2½m hurdler: no form since 1990/1, including over fences: visored nowadays. *W. Storey*

c–
–

OUR JACKIE 8 b.g. Pony Express – Corniche Rose (Punchinello) [1992/3 c25gpu] winning pointer: failed to complete in 2 novice chases. *R. J. Hodges*

c–
–

OUR LITTLE GEM 5 br.m. Star Appeal – Targa (GER) (Stani) [1992/3 16d 18f 22dpu] lengthy, plain mare: sister to poor novice jumper Gen-Tech and half-sister to winning Irish stayer Tintoretto (by Dschingis Khan) and 1981 2-y-o 1m seller winner Tarawera (by Royben): dam won in Germany: bad novice hurdler: dead. *J. White*

–

OUR MAN IN HAVANA 4 ch.g. Never So Bold – Bellagio (Busted) [1992/3 a16g 18d6 16dur 16g4 16g3 16d2] lengthy gelding: no form on Flat: sold out of P. Cole's stable 3,300 gns Newmarket Autumn Sales: modest

92

form over hurdles: yet to race beyond 2¼m: acts on dead ground. *Mrs A. Swinbank*

OUR NOBBY 11 br.g. McIndoe – Fair Arctic (Bally Russe) [1992/3 c17v⁶ c20sᵘʳ c21s⁶ c21g⁶ c21m c21f² c24gᵖᵘ] lengthy, workmanlike gelding: fairly useful chaser at best: second of 3 at Wincanton, well beaten other starts 1992/3: sold 1,600 gns Ascot June Sales: stays 3m: acts on any going: blinkered once, visored once. *D. R. C. Elsworth*

c?
–

OUR SLIMBRIDGE 5 b. or br.g. Top Ville – Bird Point (USA) (Alleged (USA)) [1992/3 16s* 18d* 20d⁴ 17g* 21s⁴ 17gᵖᵘ 17fᵖᵘ] sparely-made, leggy gelding: fair hurdler: won seller (bought in 5,000 gns) at Worcester in October, and handicaps at Market Rasen in December and Doncaster in January: ran badly last 2 outings: effective at 2m and stays 2½m: acts on soft going: held up and suited by good gallop. *C. N. Williams*

112

OUR SURVIVOR 9 b.g. Trimmingham – Lougharue (Deep Run) [1992/3 c21d⁵ c25vᵖᵘ 26s⁵ c20g⁴ 16s⁶ c24g⁴ c21sᵖᵘ c16sᶠ a18g⁴ a20g* a24gᵖᵘ a20g* a20gᵖᵘ c17m² c17mᶠ c21g² c21d³ c18g* c16mᵖᵘ c22mᵖᵘ c17g⁵] rangy gelding: poor hurdler: won claimers at Southwell in February (claimed out of M. W. Easterby's stable £2,025) and March (handicap): modest chaser: won novice handicap at Market Rasen in April: ran badly last 3 starts: stays 2½m: acts on good to firm, soft ground and fibresand: often blinkered: formerly reluctant. *J. Parkes*

c87
80

OUTCROP 5 br.m. Oats – Night Out III (Metropolis) [1992/3 F17s F16v 16dᵖᵘ] leggy, unfurnished mare: dam maiden hurdler/pointer: no sign of ability. *Miss H. C. Knight*

–

OUTFIELD 7 b.m. Monksfield – Pedalo (Legal Tender) [1992/3 16d⁴ 21vᵖᵘ c16v c17sᵖᵘ c16s⁶ 16g³ 17m² 16s 16m 23mᶠ] sparely-made mare: poor novice hurdler: no form over fences: best form at around 2m: acts on good to firm and dead going. *J. Webber*

c–
80

OUT N'OUT (IRE) 5 b.m. Hard Fought – Out Re (Blakeney) [1992/3 F16g F18g⁴ F16d 17dᵘʳ 17vᵖᵘ a20g⁶ c22mᵘʳ c21fᵖᵘ] ex-Irish mare: second foal: dam unraced: trained until after third start by I. Ferguson: no sign of ability. *J. R. Jenkins*

c–
–

OUT THE GAP 10 ch.g. Cheval – Clashdermot Lady (Shackleton) [1992/3 c16mᶠ c17g⁶ c21dᵘʳ c21dᵖᵘ 17s² 22d³ 25g⁵ 21m⁴ 25dᵇᵈ] close-coupled, lightly-made gelding: moderate hurdler: poor novice chaser: stayed 2¾m: acted on soft going: dead. *S. G. Payne*

c75
99

OVER AND ABOVE 11 b. or br.g. Mandalus – Killotteran Lass (Kabale) [1992/3 c24g² c24m³ c24s² c33s⁵] workmanlike gelding: fair handicap chaser: not raced after December: stays 3¼m (probably not 4m): acts on any going: blinkered once. *N. J. Henderson*

c106
–

OVERHEARD 6 ch.g. Over The River (FR) – Gusserane Princess (Paddy's Stream) [1992/3 c24s* c25g*] rangy ex-Irish gelding: promising hunter chaser, fairly useful already: won at Ludlow and Bangor (novice event) in April, finishing lame when beating Gold Shot ¾ length in latter: stays 25f: acts on soft ground: should win more races. *Miss C. Saunders*

c109 p

OVERHEREOVERTHERE 10 ch.g. Green Shoon – Cool Madam (Master Owen) [1992/3 c24gᵇᵈ c26d* c25dᶠ c25s* c24v] big, rangy gelding: fair chaser: won novice events at Uttoxeter and Towcester in first half of season: stays well: acts on soft ground: game. *John R. Upson*

c100

OVERLORD 4 b.g. Faustus (USA) – Hi Love (High Top) [1992/3 F16s* F17m F17d⁵] strong, workmanlike gelding: chasing type: third foal: dam fair 1½m and 2m winner: won NH Flat race at Nottingham in February: mid-division in similar events at Cheltenham and Sandown afterwards: yet to race over hurdles. *W. R. Muir*

OVERMAN 5 ch.g. Official – Shesheen (Lauso) [1992/3 23mᵖᵘ] first reported foal: dam winning hurdler/pointer: no sign of ability in novice hurdle in April on debut. *P. J. Hobbs*

–

OVERPOWER 9 b.g. Try My Best (USA) – Just A Shadow (Laser Light) [1992/3 18f4] fair at 1m to 1¼m on Flat, winner in 1993: second outing over hurdles when fourth in early-season novice event: will prove suited by sharp 2m. *M. H. Tompkins*   81

OVER THE DEEL 7 ch.g. Over The River (FR) – Cahernane Girl (Bargello) [1992/3 c24m2 c27g5 c27d* c30m* c25vF c28s c26vpu c32dpu c22fur c30dpu] compact gelding: fair handicap chaser: won at Sedgefield and Newcastle in first half of season: trained until after sixth start by W. A. Stephenson: no form last 5 starts: sold 18,000 gns in May: suited by good test of stamina: acts on good to firm and dead ground. *P. Cheesbrough*   c110

OVER THE ODDS (IRE) 4 ch.g. Over The River (FR) – Run of Luck (Lucky Brief) [1992/3 17m6 17g 22d 22g4 22g5 17m6] lengthy, plain gelding: fifth live foal: half-brother to poor novice hurdler Running Lucky (by Le Moss): dam unraced half-sister to top-class hunter chaser Eliogarty: poor form over hurdles: will stay long distances: best efforts on good ground. *J. Wade*   77

OVER THE POLE 6 b.g. Cruise Missile – Arctic Lee (Arctic Judge) [1992/3 17g 20d5 16v3 17d3] tall, rangy gelding, with plenty of scope: chasing type: third foal: half-brother to poor novice jumper Mayfield Park (by Park Row): dam, poor novice hurdler/steeplechaser, won a point: progressive form over hurdles, staying-on third in novice event at Ascot in February on final start: probably acts on heavy ground: will progress further and is sure to win races. *J. T. Gifford*   114 p

OVER THE STREAM 7 b.g. Over The River (FR) – Bola Stream (Paddy's Stream) [1992/3 20s6 25g6 25s2 24s3 21s5 24vpu c27g2 c24f* c27m4 c24d6 c25f2 c26d3] good-bodied gelding: poor novice hurdler: won novice chase at Doncaster in March: ran well last 2 starts: stays well: probably acts on any ground: blinkered fifth start (ran creditably). *M. D. Hammond*   c92 / 83

OVER THE STYX 8 br.g. Over The River (FR) – My Dear Good Woman (Lucifer (USA)) [1992/3 c16g5 c17d3 c18g4 c25spu c21 1s2 c21m3 c21g6 c18vF] lengthy, dipped-backed gelding: no form over hurdles: modest novice chaser: should stay beyond 21f: best efforts on a yielding surface. *G. Richards*   c85 / –

OWD HENRY 10 b.g. Rymer – Jo-Marie (Master Buck) [1992/3 c24mur c25g5] lengthy, workmanlike gelding: modest chaser at best: tailed off in quite valuable hunter chase in April: stays 27f: acts on soft and good to firm ground: sketchy jumper. *N. E. H. Hargreave*   c–

OWEN 9 b.g. Pollerton – Princess Charmere (Tepukei) [1992/3 c21g* c19v6 c19s4 c21d3 c21g5 c26g2 c26g2 c21g* c23g5 c21fpu] close-coupled gelding: modest handicap chaser: successful at Worcester in September and Plumpton in April: stays 3¼m: acts on any going. *B. Smart*   c92 / –

OWLANDISH 5 b.g. Bold Owl – Whipalash (Stephen George) [1992/3 20d6 17s5 16s 17g4] sturdy gelding: poor novice hurdler: best efforts at around 2m on good ground. *D. McCain*   73

OWT ON 6 ch.g. Sweet Monday – Young April (Young Man (FR)) [1992/3 17d4 16g3 18g6] poor novice hurdler: raced only at around 2m: best effort on good ground. *J. R. Fort*   81

OXFORD PLACE 9 br.g. Derrylin – Garden Party (Reform) [1992/3 c25mur] tall, workmanlike gelding: selling hurdler: no form over fences: sometimes blinkered or visored. *C. Lawson*   c– / –

OXYMERON (USA) 9 ch.g. Temperence Hill (USA) – Luv Luvin' (USA) (Raise A Native) [1992/3 19h2 22dpu] workmanlike gelding: poor hurdler/maiden chaser: stays 21f: acts on hard ground: often blinkered: no battler. *K. C. Bailey*   c– § / 76 §

P

PACIFIC GEM 6 br.g. Valiyar – Mary Martin (Be My Guest (USA)) [1992/3 c16mF c18dpu] leggy gelding: poor maiden hurdler/winning chaser: c– / –

sold 1,550 gns Doncaster January Sales: stays 2¼m: acts on good to soft and good to firm ground. *R. Curtis*

PACIFIC RUN 8 ch.g. Deep Run – Little Welly (Little Buskins) [1992/3 c21g⁵ c19f^pu] lengthy gelding: of little account. *S. Dow*   c–

PACIFIC SOUND 10 b.g. Palm Track – Pacific Dream (Meldrum) [1992/3 c16d^ur c25m⁴ c25g c21d⁴ c22s⁴ c25s⁴ c28s c21s⁵] good-bodied gelding: fair handicap chaser at best: easily best effort in 1992/3 on fifth outing: stays 25f: acts on good to firm and soft going: tends to make mistakes. *Mrs S. J. Smith*   c100

PACO'S BOY 8 b.g. Good Thyne (USA) – Jeremique (Sunny Way) [1992/3 c25d² c29s² c33d⁵ c24s^pu c27v^pu c20d] rangy, good-topped gelding: fairly useful handicap chaser at best: ran poorly after second start: stays 29f: acts on any going: best blinkered (visored once). *M. C. Pipe*   c121 –

PACTOLUS (USA) 10 b.g. Lydian (FR) – Honey Sand (USA) (Windy Sands) [1992/3 24g 21s 22s⁶ 26m 23f³] angular, rather sparely-made gelding: useful hurdler at best: not so good in 1992/3: barely stays 3m: acts on any going: blinkered second start. *S. Christian*   120

PADAVENTURE 8 b.g. Belfalas – Cardamine (Indigenous) [1992/3 c21d² c24d² c25s* c25d^pu] lengthy gelding: fairly useful chaser: won handicap at Wetherby in January: ran poorly following month: stays 3¼m well: acts on heavy and good to firm ground: jumps soundly. *Mrs M. Reveley*   c115 –

PADDYBORO 15 ch.g. Paddy's Progress – Kellsboro (Coxcomb) [1992/3 c19d c21d⁵ c21g³ c22m⁵] rangy, good sort: poor hunter chaser nowadays: has broken blood vessels. *Miss W. G. Evans*   c75 –

PADDY BUCK 13 ch.g. Caribo – Buck's Rose (Royal Buck) [1992/3 c27s^pu c27f³ c20m c25s⁵ c24d 24v⁶ c27v³ c27d⁵] rangy gelding: staying chaser: on the downgrade. *J. Honeyball*   c93 d –

PADDY HAYTON 12 br.g. St Paddy – Natenka (Native Prince) [1992/3 c25d c25g^ur c24m³ c27g⁶ c24m⁴ c25d^pu] good-topped gelding: quite useful hunter chaser in 1992: only modest form in 1993: stays well: acts on any going: tried blinkered. *S. J. Leadbetter*   c86

PADDY IN PARIS 10 ch.g. Paddy's Stream – Wrekin Rose (Master Owen) [1992/3 c21m⁶] workmanlike gelding: poor novice chaser. *Miss U. McGuinness*   c– –

PADDY MORRISSEY 6 b.g. Strong Gale – Reynoldstown Rose (Caribo) [1992/3 21d] workmanlike gelding: poor novice hurdler: best effort only start in 1992/3 (November). *J. S. Haldane*   80

PADDY'S DREAM 13 b.g. Paddy's Stream – Fairyslave (Arctic Slave) [1992/3 c22v^pu] lengthy gelding: winning hurdler/chaser: no form since 1990/1. *Miss P. O'Connor*   c–

PADDY'S GOLD (IRE) 5 b.g. Kemal (FR) – Thai Nang (Tap On Wood) [1992/3 17d 17d^pu] leggy gelding: of little account: sold 1,850 gns Ascot February Sales. *C. D. Broad*   –

PADDY'S POND 15 ch.g. Paddy's Stream – Clerihan (Immortality) [1992/3 c24d⁵ c26m²] tall gelding: winning hunter chaser: only form since 1991 when second at Hereford in May: stays well: acts on soft and good to firm ground. *N. J. Reece*   c87 –

PADDYSWAY 6 b.g. Paddy's Stream – Lastway (The Ditton) [1992/3 22v* 22v* 22s⁶ 24f* 22m* 27g⁴] leggy, good-topped gelding: won novice handicap hurdles at Wincanton, Chepstow and Cheltenham in second half of season: stays 27f: acts on any going. *G. A. Ham*   96

PADIORD 6 ch.g. Caerleon (USA) – Osmunda (Mill Reef (USA)) [1992/3 17m² 18f² 18f² 20m³] angular, plain gelding: modest hurdler: not raced after September: sold 1,400 gns Ascot May Sales: stays 2¾m: acts on good to soft and firm going: has broken blood vessels: held up. *D. J. Wintle*   99

PADISHAH (IRE) 4 ch.c. Kris – Aunty (FR) (Riverman (USA)) [1992/3 F17f² F17m⁴] fourth foal: half-brother to useful Irish Flat performer Kyra (by Sadler's Wells): dam French 1¼m winner: in frame in NH Flat races at Hereford in May: yet to race over hurdles. *W. R. Muir*

PADRIGAL 10 ch.m. Paddy's Stream – Peaceful Madrigal (Blue Cliff) [1992/3 c21s⁶ c25d* c24g⁴ c22v²] workmanlike mare: fair hunter chaser: won at Wolverhampton in February, only form in 1992/3: stays 25f: acts on dead ground (well below form on softer). *J. N. Cheatle* — c94

PAKENHAM 7 b.g. Deep Run – Hazy Dawn (Official) [1992/3 16s⁵ 17d² 24dᵖᵘ] 60,000 4-y-o: rangy gelding with scope: chasing type: first foal: dam fairly useful hurdler/chaser, well suited by test of stamina: modest form in novice hurdles: ran badly final start: should stay at least 2½m. *G. Richards* — 86

PALACEGATE KING 4 ch.g. King Among Kings – Market Blues (Porto Bello) [1992/3 17s* 17s² 17s⁶ 17d⁶ 20d⁴ 17g 17d² 16g⁵ 20f³] sparely-made gelding: modest 6f/7f performer on Flat: sold out of J. Berry's stable 2,000 gns Doncaster October Sales: variable form over hurdles: won claimer at Newcastle in December: similar form in second half of season only on seventh start: best form at around 2m with plenty of give. *A. C. Whillans* — 110

PALANQUIN 11 ch.g. Royal Palace – Duresme (Starry Halo) [1992/3 24m³ 26dᵖᵘ 24d⁶ 22s 25d 24m* 25m*] leggy, close-coupled gelding: fair handicap hurdler: won at Edinburgh in February and Doncaster in March: poor novice chaser: stays well: best on a sound surface (acts on hard going): races up with pace: usually blinkered: ridden in spurs last 2 starts: poor jumper of fences. *W. G. Reed* — c– x / 102

PALMAS PRIDE 6 b.g. Dalsaan – Sabirone (FR) (Iron Duke (FR)) [1992/3 17d 16g² 16d 20mᵖᵘ] good-bodied gelding: winning hurdler: raced mainly at around 2m: acted on good to firm ground: dead. *M. D. Hammond* — 90

PALM COURT 5 b.g. Miramar Reef – Palm Cross (Palm Track) [1992/3 F16d] first foal: dam winning staying chaser: tailed off in NH Flat race at Haydock in February: yet to race over hurdles or fences. *Miss J. Eaton*

PALMER'S GOLD 12 b.g. Palm Track – Golden Pinelopi (Sovereign Lord) [1992/3 c25mᵖᵘ c26fᵖᵘ] sturdy gelding: winning staying chaser, has lost his form: trained first start by T. Caldwell. *B. E. L. Howard* — c–

PALM HOUSE 8 ch.g. Coquelin (USA) – Kew Gift (Faraway Son (USA)) [1992/3 20m* 22m 22m* 20m* 25g⁴ 18d⁴ 18g* 23g c16g² c16dᵘʳ c16g² 18m⁴ c16dᵖᵘ] leggy, angular gelding: successful over hurdles at Bangor (2 conditional jockeys events, second a seller), Sedgefield and Kelso (claimer) in first half of season: ran poorly last 3 starts, trained until after eleventh by G. Richards: acts on good to firm and dead going: sometimes blinkered or visored. *W. Storey* — c100 d / 104 d

PALM READER 9 b.g. Palm Track – Carbia (Escart III) [1992/3 c21m* c21m* c21s⁵ c20m² c17g³ c16d³ c20g²] smallish, well-made gelding: fairly useful handicap chaser: successful at Perth and Sedgefield early in season: trained until after sixth outing by W. A. Stephenson: not raced after January: sold 24,000 gns in May: suited by around 2½m: seems best on a sound surface: genuine: usually held up. *P. Cheesbrough* — c127

PALMRUSH 9 b.g. Tepukei – Vulrusika (Vulgan) [1992/3 c20f⁵ c21g* c21f* c21f*] leggy gelding: fair handicap chaser: won at Hexham, Wetherby and Warwick in the spring: stays 21f: acts on hard and dead ground: front runner: jumps well. *M. D. Hammond* — c103

PAMBER PRIORY 10 b.g. Balinger – Miset (Right Royal V) [1992/3 c26d c26d³ c26s* c25v³ c27sᵘʳ c24s² c29s² c26g³ c25v* c24d] rather leggy gelding: fair handicap chaser: won at Folkestone in November and Towcester in April: stays well: has form on good to firm but seems best with give in the ground (acts on heavy): poor jumper. *T. Thomson Jones* — c114 x

PAMELA'S LAD 7 ch.g. Dalsaan – La Margarite (Bonne Noel) [1992/3 c21g³] leggy, lengthy gelding: poor maiden hurdler: fair pointer: third in maiden hunter chase at Uttoxeter in May: stays 2¾m: acts on good to firm and dead ground. *M. A. Lloyd* — c82

PAMPERED GEM   5 b.m. Pitpan – Fidelight (Fidel) [1992/3 F 14s] first foal: dam, novice hurdler/chaser, seemed to stay 2½m: tailed off in NH Flat race at Market Rasen in April: yet to race over hurdles or fences. *T. J. Carr*

PAMPERING   12 b.g. Pamroy – Crosswise (Firestreak) [1992/3 c21s² c24s c30s⁶ c27d⁴ c19m⁵ c27g⁶ c26f⁵ c24g⁶] workmanlike gelding: modest chaser nowadays: suited by a thorough test of stamina: acts on heavy going: blinkered final start. *Martyn Meade* — **c88**

PAMVAC (IRE)   5 b.m. Ovac (ITY) – Pamrina (Pamroy) [1992/3 23gᶠ 23dᵖᵘ 24g⁶ 20d 18d⁵ 21g 22gᵖᵘ 22mᵖᵘ] leggy, useful-looking mare: first foal: dam, winning hurdler/chaser, stayed 3m: poor novice hurdler: should stay beyond 2½m: form only on dead ground: visored last 2 starts. *Mrs M. Reveley* — **64**

PANATHINAIKOS (USA)   8 b.g. Nodouble (USA) – Faisana (ARG) (Yata Nahuel) [1992/3 16g a24g a20g⁶ a24g 22f⁴ 17g] sparely-made gelding: poor hurdler: needs further than 17f and stays 2¾m: acts on firm going and equitrack: blinkered final outing: sometimes wears tongue strap. *G. A. Ham* — **72**

PANDESSA   6 b.m. Blue Cashmere – Jeanne du Barry (Dubassoff (USA)) [1992/3 21s* 22g⁴ 21d² 20d* 20g³ 17g³ 16g*] rather sparely-made mare: fair hurdler: won handicap at Southwell, conditional jockeys claimer at Edinburgh and claimer at Wetherby in 1992/3: effective at 2m and stays 2½m: acts on any going: consistent. *Mrs M. Reveley* — **106**

PANDORA'S PRIZE   7 ch.m. Royal Vulcan – Semi-Colon (Colonist II) [1992/3 25d⁶ 21d 22s⁶ c21s³ c22vᵘʳ c18s c20d⁴ c24f³ c21m⁴ c16s⁶ c21gᵖᵘ c18mᵖᵘ] sparely-made mare: selling hurdler: poor novice chaser: stays 3m: probably acts on any going: visored twice, blinkered once. *Mrs P. M. Joynes* — **c78**

PANDY   7 b.g. Thatching – Hot Stone (Hotfoot) [1992/3 16s² 17v⁶ 16d³ 17d² 21f⁵ 17g² 17f² 17g³] compact gelding: modest novice hurdler: should stay beyond 17f: probably acts on any going. *G. Thorner* — **92**

PANICSUN   8 b.g. Sunyboy – Midnight Panic (Panco) [1992/3 c24m⁶] modest pointer: sixth in hunter chase at Taunton on steeplechasing debut. *M. B. Bent* — **c69**

PANTECHNICON   13 b.g. Pitpan – Avatea (Arctic Slave) [1992/3 c17m³ c19g⁵ c18g* c21gᵖᵘ c24gᵘʳ c19f⁴ c18sᵖᵘ c19m³ c17g⁵ c18g⁴ c19m c17mᵖᵘ c20fᵖᵘ] big, rangy gelding: handicap chaser: won at Fontwell in September: ran badly last 5 starts: best at distances short of 2½m: acts on any going: blinkered once: front runner. *A. Barrow* — **c88 d**

PANT LLIN   7 b.g. Mummy's Pet – Goosie-Gantlet (Run The Gantlet (USA)) [1992/3 17m⁴ 16m⁶ c16gᶠ c16d⁵ c17v³ c16s⁴ c17v 16d 16m⁵] strong, compact gelding: poor hurdler/novice chaser: best around 2m: acts on any ground: sometimes blinkered: inconsistent and ungenuine. *F. Jordan* — **c81 §**
81 §

PANTO PRINCE   12 br.g. Lepanto (GER) – Native Wings (Al-'alawi) [1992/3 c21d³ c17v⁴ c16v³ c23d⁶ c20f* c20m* c20s⁴] leggy gelding: has — **c123**

*Rocking Horse Nursery Handicap Chase, Newbury—
Panto Prince (right) and Lake Mission battle it out*

been fired: fairly useful chaser nowadays: won handicaps at Newbury and Chepstow in March: stays 25f, at least when conditions aren't testing: acts on any going: races up with the pace: normally a fine jumper: genuine. *C. L. Popham*

PAPAJOTO 8 b.g. Ahonoora – Papukeena (Simbir) [1992/3 c18dᵖᵘ c18v⁴] angular gelding: fair 2m hurdler: no form in novice chases: blinkered once. *K. R. Burke*

c—
–

PAPER CLIP 4 b.f. Jalmood (USA) – Westonepaperchase (USA) (Accipiter (USA)) [1992/3 16s a16g⁵ a16g² 17m⁴ 21m⁴ 22gᵖᵘ a21g²] small, close-coupled filly: modest miler at best on Flat: poor novice hurdler: better suited by 21f than shorter: acts on good to firm ground and fibresand: blinkered sixth outing. *J. K. Cresswell*

77

PAPER'S PET 6 br.m. Hawaiian Return (USA) – Longevity (Wolverlife) [1992/3 F16m F16g] second foal: dam unraced: last in NH Flat races: yet to race over hurdles or fences. *D. A. Nolan*

PAPER STAR 6 br.m. Strong Gale – Lynwood Lady (Malicious) [1992/3 16f⁴ 17g⁴ 22g³ 22gᶠ 21s⁴] unfurnished mare: poor novice hurdler: not raced after November: will stay further than 2¾m: probably acts on any going. *M. P. Muggeridge*

78

PAPERWORK BOY 8 ch.g. Buckskin (FR) – Orinda Way (Deep Run) [1992/3 21g 24d⁵ 26d 16s 26sᵖᵘ] lengthy, good sort: winning hurdler: no form in 1992/3: sold 1,150 gns Doncaster May Sales: stays 2½m: acts on soft going: blinkered third start: resold 1,100 gns Ascot 2nd June Sales. *M. H. Easterby*

–

PAPPA DONT PREACH (IRE) 5 b.g. Carlingford Castle – Ballyoran Princess (The Parson) [1992/3 F14d 21d 17g⁵ 16s⁴ 22g 16m] rather unfurnished gelding: first foal: dam lightly-raced pointer: winning Irish pointer: only worthwhile form over hurdles when fifth in novice event in October: should stay further than 17f. *John R. Upson*

87

PARADIGM'S VISION (IRE) 5 b.m. Vision (USA) – Echo Repeating (Ballymore) [1992/3 18mᶠ] lightly-made mare: twice-raced over hurdles: dead. *A. Harrison*

–

PARADISE BEACH 8 b.g. Skyliner – Looks A Million (Wollow) [1992/3 c22gᵖᵘ c24gᵖᵘ] tall, leggy gelding: one-time fair 2m hurdler: showed nothing in hunter chases: sold 2,400 gns Ascot 2nd June Sales. *S. Mellor*

c—
–

PAR AVION 8 b.g. Beldale Flutter (USA) – Pitroyal (Pitskelly) [1992/3 25dᵖᵘ] tall, plain gelding: lightly-raced novice hurdler, modest form at best: only form at 2½m on good ground. *A. W. Denson*

–

PARBOLD HILL 5 ch.g. Carwhite – Coppice (Pardao) [1992/3 16f 17gᵖᵘ] close-coupled gelding: easily best effort when winning 2¼m selling hurdle on equitrack in 1991/2 (visored only time): tried blinkered. *K. R. Burke*

–

PARDON ME MUM 8 ch.g. The Parson – Please Mum (Kabale) [1992/3 20g* 24g⁵ 22s* 22s⁵ 21v⁴ 22dᵖᵘ 22d* 22mᵖᵘ a21g⁴ 20d* 20g³] smallish, sturdy gelding: fairly useful hurdler: successful in maiden at Galway (trained until after next outing by N. Madden in Ireland) and handicap at Newton Abbot (amateurs) early in season and handicaps at Ludlow and Hereford (conditional jockeys) late on: best form at around 2½m: acts on soft ground, possibly unsuited by good to firm: blinkered nowadays. *K. C. Bailey*

119

PARDON ME SIR 9 b.g. North Summit – Peaceful Pleasure (Silent Whistle) [1992/3 17m 17s⁵ 17s⁴ 17g⁵] well-made, chasing type: winning hurdler: lightly raced of late, but still capable of fair form: stays 2½m: acts on soft going and good to firm. *M. C. Humby*

115

PARISIENNE KING (USA) 4 b.g. Key To The Kingdom (USA) – Paris Dawn (USA) (Mr Redoy (USA)) [1992/3 16s 17g a18gᵖᵘ 18d⁶ a16gᵖᵘ] small gelding: bad maiden on Flat (sold out of F. Lee's stable 720 gns Doncaster September Sales) and over hurdles: sold out of R. Marvin's

55 §

stable 1,100 gns Doncaster March Sales after fourth outing: visored/blinkered last two: probably ungenuine. *R. F. Marvin*

PARIS OF TROY 5 b.h. Trojan Fen – Little Loch Broom (Reform) [1992/3 20g* 22f* 22g*] neat horse: made into a useful hurdler early in season, winning claimer at Hereford and 2 handicaps at Worcester: much better suited by around 2½m than 2m: acts on dead, firm ground and fibresand: front runner: consistent. *N. A. Twiston-Davies*   132

PARK DRIFT 7 ch.g. Say Primula – Kerera (Keren) [1992/3 c21gpu] poor staying maiden hurdler: poor pointer: no show in maiden hunter chase in May. *G. Thornton*   c–
–

PARKING BAY 6 b.g. Bay Express – Sophie Avenue (Guillaume Tell (USA)) [1992/3 17dpu] good-topped gelding: no form over hurdles. *G. A. Pritchard-Gordon*   –

PARKINSON'S LAW 5 b.g. Idiot's Delight – Morgan's Money (David Jack) [1992/3 F17m] smallish, lengthy gelding: third foal: half-brother to winning pointer Scally's Choice (by Scallywag): dam winning staying chaser, from good jumping family: tailed off in NH Flat race at Cheltenham in April: yet to race over hurdles or fences. *G. B. Balding*

PARK SHADE 14 b.g. Jupiter Pluvius – Shady Tree (Three Wishes) [1992/3 c25gpu c26mpu] rangy gelding: poor hunter chaser nowadays. *R. Mathew*   c–
–

PARKY PETE 12 ch.g. Peter Wrekin – Cabarita (USA) (First Landing) [1992/3 c19spu c26vpu c27dpu c24g5 c21dur] sturdy gelding: of little account. *B. Scriven*   c–
–

PARLEBIZ 4 b.f. Parliament – That's Show Biz (The Parson) [1992/3 F16g] second foal: dam fair Irish hurdler/chaser: well beaten in NH Flat race at Ayr in March: yet to race over hurdles. *A. J. Wight*

PARLEMENTAIRE 7 ch.g. Coquelin (USA) – Sunblast (Roan Rocket) [1992/3 17gpu] compact gelding: of no account over hurdles. *R. J. Weaver*   –

PARR (IRE) 5 b.g. Salmon Leap (USA) – Mums (Mummy's Pet) [1992/3 16m6 18g5 17m] leggy gelding: of no account: sold 1,500 gns Doncaster September Sales. *J. Mackie*   –

PARSON FLYNN 6 b.g. Mandalus – Flynn's Field (The Parson) [1992/3 c24m5 c25g5] strong gelding: third foal: dam never ran: maiden pointer: no promise and jumped poorly in steeplechases. *Capt. T. A. Forster*   c–

PARSONS GREEN 9 b.g. The Parson – Move Along Gypsy (Menelek) [1992/3 c20s* c25s6 c27sF c24m6 c33gur] tall gelding: useful chaser: won handicap at Newbury in November: below form both completed starts afterwards: suited by test of stamina: acts on soft and good to firm ground: usually blinkered nowadays (visored once): best ridden up with pace. *N. J. Henderson*   c133

PARSONS PLEASURE 10 b.g. Pry – Will Preach (Will Somers) [1992/3 c26d5] workmanlike gelding: modest chaser: ran creditably in October: suited by test of stamina: acts on dead ground: sometimes runs in snatches. *M. J. Wilkinson*   c95
–

PARTING MELODY 5 ch.m. True Song – Maries Party (The Parson) [1992/3 F17d5] second foal: dam, poor maiden jumper, half-sister to fairly useful Irish chaser Vulelek: fifth in NH Flat race at Hereford in May: yet to race over hurdles or fences. *R. Lee*

PARTY MAGIC 11 br.m. Lord of Arabia – Party Night (Evening Trial) [1992/3 c24fpu c21vpu] half-sister to 2 poor animals: dam poor hunter chaser: showed nothing in novice chases. *Miss D. J. Baker*   c–

PARTY POLITICS 9 br.g. Politico (USA) – Spin Again (Royalty) [1992/3 c27spu c26spu c29d* c33g]   c156

Had the Grand National not been void the 1992 winner Party Politics would have been returned as favourite, probably at 7/1 which was the price generally available about him at the time of the first false start. Party

Politics' price was as high as 33/1 when the weights were published early in February, his participation in some doubt at that stage for he'd been pulled up on both his outings in the latest season, reportedly breaking a blood vessel on the second occasion. He was also suffering further problems with his breathing, something for which he'd already undergone two operations, both of them before he won the National. Apparently his oxygen supply was now being reduced by paralysis to part of the left side of his larynx. In order to try to overcome the problem it was decided to tube Party Politics. This last-resort but straightforward operation involves inserting a tube into the horse's throat, enabling air to pass directly to the lungs, bypassing the damaged part of the larynx. It proved an immediate success. Around three weeks afterwards Party Politics put himself right back in the Grand National picture by winning the Greenalls Gold Cup Handicap Chase at Haydock under top weight. For a race worth over £27,000 to the winner the Greenalls Gold Cup wasn't strongly contested and Party Politics was given most to do by Fiddlers Pike who was running from 12 lb out of the handicap. Party Politics collared Fiddlers Pike going to the last and forged clear on the run-in to win by four lengths. Party Politics was denied the opportunity to emulate Tipperary Tim, the only tubed horse to have won the Grand National, although he did complete a circuit of the fences before being pulled up, once again making light of the fences. Turned out a couple of weeks later for the Scottish National at Ayr, Party Politics looked in very good shape but ran poorly, never getting into the race. It would seem that his problems are far from being behind him.

Party Politics (br.g. 1984)	Politico (USA) (b 1967)	Right Royal V (br 1958)	Owen Tudor
			Bastia
		Tendentious (b 1959)	Tenerani
			Ambiguity
	Spin Again (br 1975)	Royalty (br 1968)	Relko
			Fair Bid
		Spin A Yarn (br 1967)	Doubtless II
			Spinning Coin

Party Politics, a very tall, rangy gelding who tends to sweat, is the first foal of Spin Again and far and away the best of her three foals which have

Greenalls Gold Cup (Handicap Chase), Haydock —
Party Politics returns to form; Fiddlers Pike finished second

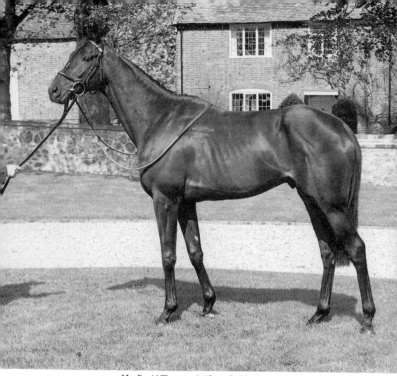

Mrs David Thompson's "Party Politics"

made it to the racecourse. Spin Again, a fair hurdler/chaser, is out of Spin A Yarn, a winning sister to the useful chasers High Havens and Copperless. A relentless galloper and a fine jumper, Party Politics is suited by a good test of stamina and give in the ground. *N. A. Gaselee*

PARTY PRINCE   9 b.g. Lord Gayle (USA) – Merrie Moira (Bold Lad (IRE)) [1992/3 c16d] leggy gelding: winning 2m hurdler: poor novice at best over fences: blinkered once. *C. Weedon*   c–
–

PASHTO   6 b.g. Persian Bold – Epure (Bellypha) [1992/3 21v⁶ 21g 25d3 25f3 25g4] sturdy gelding: fairly useful handicap hurdler: ran well last 3 starts: stays well: acts on any ground: jumps well. *N. J. Henderson*   123

PASSAGE HOME   6 b.m. Blakeney – Maze (Silly Season) [1992/3 17mF 17m 17d 16g 20d 23d] leggy mare: maiden on Flat: of little account over hurdles: tried visored. *D. J. Bell*   –

PASSAGE TO FREEDOM   11 gr.m. Pals Passage – Arctic Freedom (Arctic Chevalier) [1992/3 c16g 16s c26d2 c26gbd c25dpu c23dpu c25g6 16g6 c18m2] workmanlike mare: poor novice hurdler/chaser: stays 3¼m: acts on dead and good to firm ground: visored final outing. *Mrs S. Lamyman*   c70
–

PASSED PAWN   6 b.g. Blakeney – Miss Millicent (Milesian) [1992/3   117
27m* 26g* 22s⁶ 27d⁵ 24s⁴ 21s² 25s² 22v² 25s² 24d⁵ 24v³ 25g⁶ a20g⁵ 22m⁵
22f*] small, leggy gelding: fairly useful handicap hurdler: won at Newton
Abbot and Hereford (amateurs) in August and Fontwell in May: stays well:
acts on any ground: races up with pace: genuine and consistent. *M. C. Pipe*

PASSING THOUGHT   6 b.g. Pollerton – Royal Willow (Royal Buck)   71
[1992/3 23g⁵ 21vᵖᵘ 18s⁶] leggy, workmanlike gelding: poor novice hurdler:
sold 2,600 gns Doncaster January Sales: best effort over 23f. *T. P. Tate*

PASSO ALL'ERTA (ITY)   10 b. or br.g. Furry Glen – Janis Ian (Never   c82
Say Die) [1992/3 c20d³ c17v⁵ c17v² c21sF a18g⁴ 17d² 17d² 20g³ 17g⁴ 22s   82
17g⁶ 16f c18gᵖᵘ] leggy, lengthy gelding: poor hurdler/novice chaser: stays
2½m: acts on good to firm and heavy going: blinkered once, sometimes
visored: jumps none too fluently. *D. J. Deacon*

PASS THE KEY (IRE)   4 b.g. Treasure Kay – Piney Pass (Persian   83
Bold) [1992/3 18m⁴ 18g 17f⁴ 16d³ 16s³ 17g 16g*] workmanlike gelding:
modest 7f winner on Flat: bought in 4,600 gns after winning selling hurdle at
Catterick in March: sold 1,000 gns Ascot May Sales: suited by sharp 2m:
acts on dead ground. *N. Tinkler*

PAST GLORIES   10 b.h. Hittite Glory – Snow Tribe (Great Nephew)   c–
[1992/3 c16dF c16gF 20m] lengthy horse: high-class 2m hurdler at his best: –
faller on both starts over fences. *J. Hetherton*

PASTORAL PRIDE (USA)   9 b.g. Exceller (USA) – Pastoral Miss   c–
(Northfields (USA)) [1992/3 c20gᵖᵘ c17g⁵ c20s⁵] small, compact gelding: –
smart front-running hunter chaser in 1992: ran as though something badly
amiss in 1993 (broke blood vessel first start): most unlikely to stay beyond
21f: acts on heavy going: to be trained by D. Wintle. *Miss Polly Curling*

PASTREL   6 b.m. Van Der Linden (FR) – Lewesdon Lady (My Lord)   –
[1992/3 a22gᵖᵘ] leggy mare: probably of little account. *Mrs A. Tomkinson*

PATCHOULI'S PET   10 b.m. Mummy's Pet – Primage (Primera)   c§§
[1992/3 c25g⁶ c21mR c23fR] small, lightly-made mare: staying selling   §§
hurdler/novice chaser: blinkered once, visored once: unreliable. *F. L.
Matthews*

PAT CULLEN   8 b.g. The Parson – Duhallow Hazel (Major Point)   c71 x
[1992/3 c20d⁵ c24sF c20v⁵ c25sᵖᵘ c18s a20g⁶ c20dᵖᵘ c21g⁶ c22g⁵ c19sᵖᵘ]
leggy gelding: poor maiden hurdler/chaser: sold 1,300 gns Ascot June Sales:
stays 21f: acts on heavy ground: occasionally blinkered: poor jumper of
fences. *Mrs P. M. Joynes*

PATHFINDER FORCE (IRE)   5 b.g. Tate Gallery (USA) – Sister   –
Eucharia (Oats) [1992/3 17s a18g] no form in 2 races on Flat and in 2 novice
hurdles. *P. R. Hedger*

PATROL   4 b.c. Shirley Heights – Tender Loving Care (Final Straw)   90
[1992/3 17g 16m⁴ 17g⁵ 17m] leggy colt: modest staying maiden on Flat: sold
7,200 gns Newmarket Autumn Sales: modest form in juvenile hurdles: will
stay further than 17f: acts on good to firm ground. *J. H. Johnson*

PATRUSIKA   7 b.m. Full of Hope – Vulrusika (Vulgan) [1992/3 c26dᵖᵘ]   c–
leggy mare: winning pointer: no form otherwise: sold to join S. Kettlewell   –
5,000 gns Doncaster June Sales. *T. R. Beadle*

PAT'S JESTER   10 ch.g. Orchestra – Owey (Sovereign Gleam) [1992/3   c156
c25g² c24d² c24s²]   –
     Only The Fellow came between Pat's Jester and a big prize for a small
stable in the King George VI Chase at Kempton in December. Pat's Jester,
who on several occasions had hinted that he'd make his mark in top
company, ran a fine race and looked the likely winner from being left in front
four out until The Fellow came there travelling very strongly going to the
last. Unable to quicken on the flat, Pat's Jester went down by eight lengths.
It might not have been the best King George ever seen, but in this form the
horse seemed to have winning a good chase in him. However, before he
could run again he had a training set-back and was ruled out until 1993/4,

leaving connections with thoughts of what might have been and the consolation of £24,610 in prize money for his effort at Kempton plus seconds in the Charlie Hall Chase at Wetherby and the Tommy Whittle Chase at Haydock on his other outings.

Pat's Jester's run in the Charlie Hall in October was his first over fences for his former trainer Dick Allan and his first for the stable for three seasons. He'd had all 1989/90 off, followed by two seasons with Gordon Richards who during that time, in just a few races, made him into as good a chaser as he'd been a hurdler with Allan, that's to say a smart one. As a young horse Pat's Jester had won the Ekbalco Hurdle at Newcastle, the Bula Hurdle at Cheltenham and the Scottish Champion Hurdle at Ayr in a single season. His best run over fences had been a win from Katabatic in the Newton Chase at Haydock on his second start in 1991/2. He ended that season under a cloud, finishing tailed off behind Remittance Man at Aintree, but was obviously back to form in the Charlie Hall. For most of the way he went like the best horse in the race but after jumping notably well he put in a short one at the last when looking as if he'd win narrowly, handed the advantage to Tipping Tim, and despite rallying couldn't quite get back up. He was conceding the improving Tipping Tim, who had the benefit of a previous race, 8 lb. After such a promising reappearance Pat's Jester's twelve-length defeat by Twin Oaks in the Tommy Whittle came as rather a let-down, although the course specialist Twin Oaks, also receiving 8 lb, did start favourite ahead of him. Pat's Jester travelled with little fluency from halfway and couldn't get to grips. The rider dismounted at the finish, reportedly feeling his mount had 'gone a bit short on him'. We saw a different horse at Kempton.

Pat's Jester (ch.g. 1983)	Orchestra (ch 1974)	Tudor Music (br 1966)	Tudor Melody / Fran
		Golden Moss (ch 1965)	Sheshoon / Muscosa
	Owey (b 1973)	Sovereign Gleam (b 1968)	Sovereign Path / Tudor Gleam
		Lake Lavandou (b 1951)	Le Lavandou / Lake Tanganyika

The Cheltenham Gold Cup was on Pat's Jester's agenda in each of the last two seasons. However, he is more of a King George horse than a Gold Cup horse; while he stays well enough he is not an out-and-out slogger in, say, the Cool Ground mould. The going for the last two runnings of the Gold Cup would have helped him get the trip, but in point of fact although he has won on good to firm he is ideally suited by some give (it was soft underfoot at Kempton). The tall Pat's Jester usually jumps fences very well, and is well equipped to tackle courses such as Cheltenham and Haydock. Astonishingly, considering what he is now, Pat's Jester made his racecourse bow in an early-season five-furlong dash when not quite two years old; he was trained by Pat Rohan in those days. He's Flat bred, and eventually, given time and distance, he managed to win races on the Flat, albeit at a considerably lower level than in his present sphere of operation. His brother, the winning hurdler Lovely Band, is one of three previous foals out of the unraced Owey to win at sprint distances on the Flat. A younger sister, Vanuatu, appeared over hurdles in the latest season but she seems to have little future on the track. *R. Allan*

PATS MINSTREL 8 b.g. Black Minstrel – Lohunda Park (Malinowski (USA)) [1992/3 c26g⁴ c25d⁵ c25dᵖᵘ c25s⁴ c24v c19v⁵ c24dᵖᵘ c16g* c16f* c16s⁴] workmanlike gelding: fair chaser: won novice events at Plumpton and Sandown in March: probably best at around 2m and acts on any going: blinkered nowadays: jumps none too fluently. *R. Champion*   **c100**

PATSY'S PET 5 b.m. Tina's Pet – Emperor Star (King Emperor (USA)) [1992/3 18g a16g⁶] leggy, rather sparely-made mare: poor novice hurdler: yet to race beyond 2¼m: acts on fibresand. *T. Fairhurst*

PAULINUS 5 b.g. Nomination – New Ribbons (Ribero) [1992/3 16g] sturdy gelding: little sign of ability. *Denys Smith*

PAY HOMAGE 5 ch.g. Primo Dominie – Embraceable Slew (USA) (Seattle Slew (USA)) [1992/3 16g] sturdy gelding: useful miler on Flat, in good form and won 3 times in May, 1993: soundly beaten in valuable novice event at Kempton in February on hurdling debut but wasn't unduly knocked about: sure to do better. *I. A. Balding* — p

PAY TO DREAM (IRE) 5 b.g. Runnett – Pursue (Auction Ring (USA)) [1992/3 22dF 17m 17d] sparely-made gelding: selling hurdler: stayed 2½m: went well on fibresand: dead. *W. Storey* —

PEACEFUL POLLY (IRE) 5 b.m. Pollerton – Rule The Waves (Deep Run) [1992/3 F16d F17v F16d 17gpu 17gpu 20dpu 17fpu] smallish, workmanlike mare: third live foal: dam, Irish NH Flat race winner, poor maiden hurdler: no sign of ability. *M. Tate* —

PEACE KING 7 ch.g. Adonijah – Flaming Peace (USA) (Lyphard (USA)) [1992/3 17f² 17m³ 18g* 20m⁴ 17g 18f³] strong, compact gelding: fairly useful handicap hurdler: won at Fontwell in September: sold 4,400 gns Newmarket Autumn Sales: stays 2¼m: acts on firm going: often held up: inconsistent. *G. Harwood* 126 §

PEACEMAN 7 b.g. Martinmas – Miss Posy (Pitskelly) [1992/3 16s* 17s* 16v* 16g⁴ 17fro 17d] rather sparely-made gelding: won novice hurdles at Warwick, Huntingdon and Kempton prior to finishing good fourth in valuable event on last-named course in February: ran poorly final outing: raced only at around 2m: acts on heavy going: front runner. *Mrs D. Haine* 122

PEACE OFFICER 7 br.g. Strong Gale – Peace Woman (Pitpan) [1992/3 c23mur c18s² c16g² c19d* c16s² c16dF c20mpu] rangy gelding: novice hurdler: won novice chase at Taunton in November: no form afterwards (not raced after January): best form at around 2½m: probably acts on any going: sometimes breaks blood vessels: inconsistent. *P. R. Hedger* c114 —

PEACH LEAF 12 b.g. Brave Invader (USA) – Cant Pet (Cantab) [1992/3 c24v c26m⁵ c25d] chunky, plain gelding: carries condition: winning hunter chaser: no form since 1990/1: visored last 2 outings. *N. J. Pewter* c— —

PEACOCK FEATHER 5 b.m. Bustino – Wide of The Mark (Gulf Pearl) [1992/3 16d⁴ 16m⁴a 16g³ a20g³ 17v* 17d³] poor hurdler: no bid after winning selling handicap at Newton Abbot in April: stays 2½m: best form on a yielding surface on turf, also acts on fibresand. *K. R. Burke* 77

PEAJADE 9 b.g. Buckskin (FR) – Kaminaki (Deep Run) [1992/3 c22s² c24d* c29vur c26v* c27d³ c26v² c25g⁴] leggy, workmanlike gelding: fair chaser: won handicaps at Stratford in November and Uttoxeter in January: suited by long distances and plenty of give in the ground: blinkered once: carries head high, and occasionally looks none too keen. *D. Nicholson* c108 —

PEAK DISTRICT 7 b.g. Beldale Flutter (USA) – Grand Teton (Bustino) [1992/3 20g* 16d³ 18g⁵ 16s⁵ 16dF a16g⁴ a16g 16s 16d a16gpu] smallish gelding: handicap hurdler: won conditional jockeys event at Hereford in September: generally ran poorly afterwards: effective from 2m to 2½m: acts on soft going and fibresand: sometimes blinkered/visored. *K. S. Bridgwater* 92 d

PEAK ROYALE (NZ) 7 ch.g. Royal Fencer (NZ) – Royal Service (NZ) (Alcimedes) [1992/3 22d⁶ 22s² 26dpu 22d] close-coupled gelding: only sign of ability over hurdles when second in novice event at Newton Abbot in October. *D. H. Barons* 84

PEANUTS PET 8 b.h. Tina's Pet – Sinzinbra (Royal Palace) [1992/3 c17gpu 16g⁴ 17m* 17d³ 20s³ 21s³ 21vur 22s³ 20g 21m] close-coupled horse: winning chaser: useful hurdler: won 2-finisher limited handicap at Newcastle in November: also ran well in more-competitive events: ran badly last 2 outings: stays 2¾m: probably acts on any going: poor jumper of fences. *T. P. Tate* c— x 135

PEARLED (USA) 6 b.g. Affirmed (USA) – Snow Pearl (USA) (Boldnesian) [1992/3 F16g] leggy gelding: behind in NH Flat races: yet to race over hurdles or fences. *J. R. Bostock* —

PEARL PROSPECT 10 br.g. Kambalda – Georgette (Neron) [1992/3 16m 24g³] leggy, workmanlike gelding: winning hurdler: well beaten early in season, including in a seller: stays 2¼m: possibly unsuited by very soft going, acts on any other. *D. J. Bell* –

PEARLY FLIGHT 6 b.g. Rustingo – Last Flight (Saucy Kit) [1992/3 F17d F17mᵇᵈ 23m 21fᶠ] workmanlike gelding: well beaten in NH Flat races and a novice hurdle. *R. J. Eckley* –

PEARLY WHITE 4 b.f. Petong – White's Pet (Mummy's Pet) [1992/3 17d a16g⁵ a16g⁵ 17mᶠ 17m⁵ 16vᵖᵘ] small, sparely-made filly: plating-class maiden on Flat and over hurdles: not sure to stay much beyond 17f: acts on dead and good to firm ground. *H. J. Manners* 69

PEAT STACK 4 gr.g. Petong – Delnadamph (Royal Palace) [1992/3 F16d F17d] second foal: dam lightly-raced maiden: tailed off in NH Flat races: yet to race over hurdles. *W. G. Reed* –

PEATSWOOD 5 ch.h. Rolfe (USA) – Cathy Jane (Lauso) [1992/3 22g³ 24s² 21s*] small horse: fairly useful handicap hurdler: won at Towcester in November: suited by good test of stamina: acts on soft ground. *M. R. Channon* 130

PECCAVI 9 ch.g. Hard Fought – Princess Sinna (Sun Prince) [1992/3 c16mᵖᵘ c16gᵖᵘ] novice chaser: no form since 1989/90. *V. R. Bishop* c–

PECHE D'OR 9 ch.g. Glint of Gold – Fishermans Bridge (Crepello) [1992/3 16v 24d⁶ 22d 21f 27g 20g⁵] angular, sparely-made gelding: modest hurdler at best: no form in 1992/3: stays 2¾m: acts on any going: sometimes blinkered. *H. E. Haynes* –

PECTORUS (IRE) 5 b.g. Denel (FR) – Pretty Damsel (Prince Hansel) [1992/3 16v 16s³ 16s² 21g² 21m] tall gelding: seventh foal: half-brother to 2 winning jumpers by Midland Gayle, including staying hurdler Pretty Gayle: dam placed over hurdles: NH Flat race winner in Ireland: fair novice hurdler: will stay further than 21f: acts on soft and good to firm going: blinkered second start: sometimes wears tongue strap: not yet an accomplished jumper: sure to win a race. *M. C. Pipe* 102

PEDE GALE (IRE) 5 b.m. Strong Gale – Deep Adventure (Deep Run) [1992/3 F17g² 17d⁵ 16d 16s 22g 17m] sturdy mare: poor novice hurdler: probably stays 2¾m: acts on dead and good to firm ground: blinkered final start. *J. C. McConnochie* 64

PEGMARINE (USA) 10 b.g. Text (USA) – Symbionese (USA) (Bold Reason) [1992/3 c20d² c16dᵖᵘ c20gᵖᵘ c21gᵖᵘ] compact gelding: poor novice hurdler/chaser: stays 2½m: acts on dead ground. *Mrs A. M. Woodrow* c82 –

PEMBROKE BAY 10 b.g. Paddy's Stream – Tudor Gello (Bargello) [1992/3 c25sᵖᵘ] leggy gelding: modest novice hurdler: once-raced over fences: stayed 2¾m: acts on soft ground. *R. Lee* c– –

PENIARTH 7 b.m. Oats – Rapenna (Straight Lad) [1992/3 21v⁶ 25vᵖᵘ 25vᵖᵘ] leggy mare: no sign of ability. *Mrs N. S. Sharpe* –

PENNANT COTTAGE (IRE) 5 b.m. Denel (FR) – The Hofsa (Varano) [1992/3 F16v] smallish mare: half-sister to winning jumpers Boxit (by General Ironside) and Buckle It Up (by Buckskin): dam, maiden hurdler, is half-sister to several winning jumpers, including useful Denys Adventure: mid-division in 18-runner NH Flat race at Towcester in January: yet to race over hurdles or fences. *P. D. Evans*

PENNETHORNE PLACE 8 ch.m. Deep Run – Be Spartan (Spartan General) [1992/3 18g⁴ 18g² 18g² 22g²] small, lengthy mare: modest maiden hurdler: stays 2¾m: best efforts on good going. *D. M. Grissell* 93

PENNY HOLME 5 br.m. State Diplomacy (USA) – Harpalyce (Don't Look) [1992/3 23sᵖᵘ 17vᵖᵘ] angular mare: half-sister to fair 2m chaser Just Frankie (by Tepukei): dam of little account: no sign of ability in novice hurdles. *R. J. Baker* –

PENNYS GIFT 6 b.g. Full of Hope – Queen's Penny (Queen's Hussar) [1992/3 17mpu 22f6] good-bodied gelding: no sign of ability over hurdles: blinkered final start. *D. C. O'Brien* –

PENSIONER PATCH 11 ch.g. Grey Ghost – Final Edition (Derek H) [1992/3 c16vpu] stocky gelding: poor novice hurdler/chaser: no form since 1990/1. *R. J. O'Sullivan* c–

PENTLAND DANCER (IRE) 4 ch.f. Pennine Walk – La Duse (Junius (USA)) [1992/3 F17g F16m 22gF 21g] small, plain filly: second foal: dam, from excellent family, placed over 1½m: no sign of ability. *R. R. Lamb* –

PENULT 8 ch.g. New Member – Miss Stalbridge (Eastern Venture) [1992/3 c24mF] brother to useful chaser Memberson: fair pointer: fell fatally on steeplechasing debut. *J. W. Dufosee* c–

PENULTIMATE HAND 5 ch.m. Nearly A Hand – Freuchie (Vulgan) [1992/3 F18g* F16s5] angular mare: half-sister to several winning jumpers, including fairly useful For Good (by Good Bond) and Marradong Brook (by Giacometti): dam winning hurdler: won mares NH Flat race at Exeter in March: fifth in similar event at Ludlow following month: yet to race over hurdles or fences. *Capt. T. A. Forster* –

PEOPLE'S CHOICE 8 br.g. Strong Gale – Carrig-An-Neady (Orchardist) [1992/3 c25f2 c24s5 c26gpu] small gelding: modest handicap chaser: pulled up lame final start (October): suited by around 3m: acts on firm ground. *N. R. Mitchell* c95 –

PEPPERON 7 ch.m. Heroic Air – Dunlean (Leander) [1992/3 21d6 28g6] sparely-made mare: no sign of ability. *Mrs M. Reveley* –

PERCY SMOLLETT 5 br.g. Oats – Misty Sunset (Le Bavard (FR)) [1992/3 F16d 16d 17d2 17d 20g* 26s5] well-made gelding, chasing type: first foal: dam, winning 2½m hurdler, half-sister to several winning jumpers, notably very smart chaser Western Sunset: improved form when 40/1-winner of novice hurdle at Hereford in March: should stay further than 2½m (tailed off over 3¼m). *J. C. McConnochie* 88

PERE BAZILLE 6 ch.g. Claude Monet (USA) – Western Line (High Line) [1992/3 c16sF 16g3 a16g5 20g 17gF 16f3 16d3 18mpu] leggy gelding: modest hurdler: sometimes runs in sellers: fell on chasing debut: stays 19f: acts on dead and firm going: usually visored nowadays (blinkered once). *P. F. Nicholls* c– 98

PERFAY (USA) 5 ch.h. Nodouble (USA) – Perfect Example (USA) (Far North (CAN)) [1992/3 16s* 17g5 17d] sparely-made horse: fairly useful miler at best on Flat: won novice hurdle at Leicester in January: ran poorly final start: likely to prove best at around 2m: acts on soft going. *J. R. Fanshawe* 101

PERFECT LIGHT 4 b.c. Salmon Leap (USA) – Sheer Gold (Yankee Gold) [1992/3 18s] second foal: dam smart staying hurdler: poor maiden on Flat: behind in early-season juvenile hurdle. *Mrs S. J. Smith* –

PERFORATE 4 b.g. Teenoso (USA) – Bag Lady (Be My Guest (USA)) [1992/3 17spu 17d6] poor stayer on Flat: sold 6,000 gns Newmarket Autumn Sales: no form over hurdles: blinkered second start. *R. J. Baker* –

PERNICKETY 13 b.g. Proverb – Royal Rally (Royal Record II) [1992/3 c24g3 22s] workmanlike gelding: no form since 1990/1: sometimes blinkered. *N. R. Mitchell* c– –

PER QUOD (USA) 8 b.g. Lyllos (FR) – Allegedly (USA) (Sir Ivor) [1992/3 16v4 17g4] sturdy gelding: half-brother to fair hurdler Prosequendo (by Robellino): one-time smart middle-distance stayer on Flat: forced pace when fourth in novice hurdles at Kempton in January and Newbury in February: will stay beyond 2m: acts on heavy ground: should improve again and win a race over hurdles. *N. J. Henderson* 98 p

PERRY WELL 9 b.g. Maculata – Magic Minstrel (Pitpan) [1992/3 24gur 28v a24g4 a24g3 26d 21f5 28m3 26fur 27gbd 27f2] workmanlike gelding: novice chaser: modest handicap hurdler: suited by good test of stamina: cxx 98

probably acts on any ground: sometimes blinkered: bad jumper of fences. *K. C. Bailey*

PERSIAN BUD (IRE)   5 b. or br.g. Persian Bold – Awakening Rose (Le Levanstell) [1992/3 18f^{pu}] sparely-made horse: no sign of ability in 2 races over hurdles, visored in latter. *J. R. Bosley*   –

PERSIAN HOUSE   6 ch.g. Persian Bold – Sarissa (Reform) [1992/3 c18g* c16g^2 c16s^2 c17s^3 c16s^4 c17s^{ur} c21g* c20g^2 c20g^2 c21m^4] tall, angular gelding: fair hurdler: won novice chases at Market Rasen in October and Carlisle (quite valuable event) in March: ran well, including in a handicap, last 3 starts: stays 21f: acts on soft ground, particularly well on a sound surface: has broken blood vessels. *J. M. Jefferson*   c114 –

PERSIAN LION   4 br.g. Reesh – Parijoun (Manado) [1992/3 16s 16g^6 16m] leggy gelding: well beaten on Flat (sold 2,500 gns Doncaster August Sales) and over hurdles. *F. Watson*   –

PERSIAN LUCK   7 br.g. Persian Bold – Ansedonia (Captain's Gig (USA)) [1992/3 18g^2] angular gelding: winning hurdler: first form since 1989/90 when second in handicap at Fontwell in March: stays 2¼m: best form on a sound surface. *D. Welsh*   94

PERSIAN SWORD   7 b.g. Broadsword (USA) – Sorraia (El Ruedo) [1992/3 16s* 16v* 16s 16m] leggy gelding: lightly-raced hurdler: modest form: won 2 novice handicaps at Warwick in January: effective at 2m under testing conditions and probably stays 2¾m: acts on heavy going, probably unsuited by good to firm. *D. Nicholson*   92

PERSIAN VALLEY   8 b.g. Persian Bold – Empress Valley (Gay Fandango (USA)) [1992/3 18g^5 16s^3 16d 21d^F 16g^6 a18g^{pu} 17s 17d 17g^F 16g^4 17d^F] neat ex-Irish gelding: fair hurdler at best: trained until after fifth start by M. Grassick: no form in Britain: stays 2¼m: probably acts on any going: usually blinkered nowadays: temperamental. *F. Jordan*   – §

PERSIAN WOLF   5 gr.h. Little Wolf – Persian Water (Waterfall) [1992/3 aF16g 17g^{pu} 17s^6] half-brother to winning hurdler Steveyvul (by Whistlefield): dam unraced half-sister to fairly useful pointer Eagle Moonday: no sign of ability. *O. O'Neill*   –

PERSONAL HAZARD   4 ch.g. Risk Me (FR) – Princess Lily (Blakeney) [1992/3 16d^3 17s^3 16s* 16s* 17s^5 17g^3] leggy, quite good-topped gelding: fair handicapper on Flat, stays 1¼m: won juvenile hurdles at Wetherby in December and January: acts on soft ground: visored fifth outing (fair effort): not yet an accomplished jumper. *M. H. Easterby*   104

PERSUASIUS (IRE)   5 b.g. Petorius – Be A Dancer (Be Friendly) [1992/3 20m] tall gelding: modest at around 1m on Flat, blinkered when successful: sold out of B. Beasley's stable 4,800 gns Doncaster November Sales: last of 8 in novice event at Doncaster in March on hurdling debut. *W. L. Barker*   –

PERSUASIVE   6 b.m. Sharpo – Queen's Eyot (Grundy) [1992/3 16g^2 16s* 16g* 16s^3 16g^5 16g^4 16d 16s 16d^4 16g^2 17s* 16f^4] sparely-made mare: fairly useful handicap hurdler: successful at Haydock and Catterick in November and Perth in April: later a winner on Flat: unlikely to stay much beyond 2m: probably acts on any going: tough and genuine. *Miss L. A. Perratt*   127

PERTEMPS JOBSHOP   7 b.g. Busted – Green Bonnet (FR) (Green Dancer (USA)) [1992/3 22s^{pu} 16d] rangy gelding: chasing type: no promise in novice hurdles. *D. Nicholson*   –

PERU   5 b.g. Conquistador Cielo (USA) – Dance Flower (CAN) (Northern Dancer (CAN)) [1992/3 17f^3] modest performer at up to 1¼m on Flat at 3 yrs: third in early-season novice event at Taunton on hurdling debut. *Mrs J. G. Retter*   74

PESIDANAMICH (IRE)   5 b.g. Mummy's Treasure – Bay Supreme (Martinmas) [1992/3 16g] fair 7f performer on Flat, best on all-weather   –

when blinkered: tailed off in novice event at Catterick in March on hurdling debut: sold 3,500 gns Doncaster June Sales. *J. P. Leigh*

PESSOA   6 b.g. Crash Course – Charming Simbir (Simbir) [1992/3 18m⁵ 17vᵖᵘ 16d4] second foal: dam poor Irish maiden on Flat: poor novice hurdler: will stay 2½m: acts on good to firm and dead ground. *Mrs S. J. Smith*   74

PETER MARTIN TWO   4 b.g. Farajullah – Transonic (Continuation) [1992/3 16gᵖᵘ] no sign of ability only outing on Flat and on hurdling debut. *J. C. Gillen*   –

PETER PUMPKIN   5 b.g. Tickled Pink – Wild Pumpkin (Auction Ring (USA)) [1992/3 18gᵖᵘ] compact gelding: lightly-raced novice hurdler, poor at best: pulled up lame in September. *R. Voorspuy*   –

PETE'S SAKE   8 b.g. Scorpio (FR) – Pete's Money (USA) (Caucasus (USA)) [1992/3 c24dᵖᵘ c25d3 c24v3 c26gF c25sᵖᵘ] good-bodied gelding: poor novice chaser: suited by test of stamina: acts on heavy ground: blinkered last 2 outings: sometimes wears tongue strap. *N. J. Henderson*   c84

PETITE AMIE   5 gr.m. Petoski – Amourette (Crowned Prince (USA)) [1992/3 17mᵖᵘ 19h 26gᵘʳ 22g6] leggy mare: of little account over hurdles: tried blinkered and visored. *Mrs P. M. Joynes*   –

PETMER   6 b.g. Tina's Pet – Merency (Meldrum) [1992/3 17d3 17g2 17s* 19g2 18v5] leggy gelding: poor form over hurdles: won claimer at Newton Abbot in October: trained by R. Curtis third and fourth starts: likely to prove best at around 2m: acts on soft going: irresolute and looks a difficult ride. *G. B. Balding*   82 §

PETOSKU   5 b.g. Petoski – House Maid (Habitat) [1992/3 25g* 17s3 21s2 22v2] good-topped gelding: fairly useful hurdler: won conditional jockeys handicap at Perth in September: ran well afterwards (not raced after December): effective at 2m when conditions are testing, and stays 25f: acts on heavy and good to firm going: genuine and consistent. *N. A. Twiston-Davies*   129

PETRULLO   8 b.h. Electric – My Therape (Jimmy Reppin) [1992/3 16s3 16d4] small, sturdy horse: one-time very useful middle-distance performer on Flat: signs of ability both starts over hurdles and should do better. *R. F. Casey*   – p

PETS PRIDE   9 br.g. Goldhills Pride – Peticienne (Mummy's Pet) [1992/3 c17gᵖᵘ] angular gelding: yet to complete. *Ian Gilbert*   c–

PETTAUGH (IRE)   5 b.g. The Parson – Bright Record (Royal Record II) [1992/3 17s6 a20g6 20s5] brother to fairly useful hurdler/winning chaser Book of Gold and half-brother to other winning jumpers, notably quite useful hurdler/very useful hunter chaser Gratification (by Gala Performance): dam maiden half-sister to top-class 1971/2 juvenile hurdler Official: novice hurdler: only form on first start. *F. Murphy*   73

PETTICOAT RULE   5 b.m. Stanford – Scottish Rose (Warpath) [1992/3 F14d F17m 18d 20g 16d 17sᵖᵘ] sparely-made mare: first foal: dam, one-paced maiden on Flat, well beaten only start over hurdles: no sign of ability in novice hurdles. *F. T. Walton*   –

PETTY BRIDGE   9 b.g. Weavers' Hall – Royal Cup (Politico (USA)) [1992/3 24g2 23d2 c23v3 c26vF c24d4 c24s6 22sᵖᵘ 18g5 26m 25g 24g2 22d 27g5 22d4 27f5] leggy gelding: fairly useful handicap hurdler: creditable efforts when runner-up in 1992/3, well below form otherwise: showed plenty of promise on first 2 starts over fences, but failed to confirm it: suited by test of stamina: acts on heavy and good to firm ground: blinkered once: jumps fences none too fluently. *A. P. James*   c103 132 d

PEWTER PETA   9 gr.m. Chukaroo – Silmira (Grey Mirage) [1992/3 21vᵖᵘ 21sᵖᵘ 22dᵖᵘ 20dᵖᵘ 23dᵖᵘ 24gᵖᵘ 23g 17g 23fᵖᵘ] lengthy, plain mare: of little account: sometimes blinkered. *Graeme Roe*   –

PHAETONS GLORY   9 b.g. Hittite Glory – Fille de Phaeton (Sun Prince) [1992/3 18vᵖᵘ] sturdy gelding: lightly-raced 2m novice hurdler, poor form at best. *P. D. Cundell*   –

PHARAOH BLUE 9 ch.g. Blue Cashmere – Phaedima (Darius) [1992/3 c27s³ 24f⁵ 25s 20f 26g* c24sF c24dᵖᵘ] angular gelding: fair hurdler: won handicap at Hereford in October: novice chaser: not raced after November: stays 3¼m: suited by top-of-the-ground: blinkered/visored last 3 starts: poor jumper of fences. *M. C. Pipe* — c– x 110

PHARGOLD (IRE) 4 ch.g. Phardante (FR) – Mallee (Malinowski (USA)) [1992/3 17m* 16m⁶ 17m⁶ 17g⁵ 18d 17g] compact gelding: poor form over hurdles: won claimer at Bangor in July: sold out of P. Haslam's stable 1,700 gns Doncaster September Sales after third outing, trained next 2 by R. Weaver: not seen out after December: races freely and best over sharp 2m: acts on good to firm going. *R. W. Emery* — 74

PHARLY STORY 5 b.h. Pharly (FR) – Certain Story (Known Fact (USA)) [1992/3 16d⁴ 16d⁴ 18g* 17m² 17f* 17g² 16d* 16f³] leggy horse: fairly useful hurdler: won novice events at Worcester, Chepstow and Wincanton in the spring: yet to race beyond 2¼m: acts on firm and dead ground: blinkered nowadays: held up: sometimes turns it in. *M. C. Pipe* — 117 §

PHAROAH'S GUEST 6 ch.g. Pharly (FR) – Exuberine (FR) (Be My Guest (USA)) [1992/3 16d 20d 23g² 21g²] angular gelding: modest hurdler: stays 23f: acts on good to firm, dead going and equitrack. *N. A. Twiston-Davies* — 90

PHAROAH'S LAEN 12 b.g. Laen – Pharoah's Lady (Pharaoh Hophra) [1992/3 c26d⁴ c30sᵖᵘ c24mᵖᵘ] tall, leggy gelding: useful staying chaser in 1991/2: well beaten in 1992/3. *Mrs J. Pitman* — c–

PHIL-BLAKE 6 br.g. Blakeney – Philogyny (Philip of Spain) [1992/3 16m] poor 2m hurdler: no form since 1990/1: refused to race once. *S. Mellor* — – §

PHILCO'S ANGEL 4 gr.f. Habs Lad – Regal Whim (Lord of Arabia) [1992/3 F14m] first foal: dam of little account: behind in NH Flat race in March and on Flat in May: yet to race over hurdles. *Mrs A. L. M. King* — –

PHILHARMONIC (IRE) 5 b.g. Orchestra – High Fi (High Hat) [1992/3 F17g³ aF16g² F16f*] compact gelding: half-brother to several winners, including hurdler End of Era (by Patch): dam unraced half-sister to useful hurdler Royal Illusion: won 15-runner NH Flat race at Haydock in May: yet to race over hurdles or fences. *J. G. FitzGerald* — –

PHILIPPONNAT (USA) 7 b.g. Sensitive Prince (USA) – August Bride (USA) (Chieftain II) [1992/3 c25vR] leggy gelding: modest pointer: behind when refusing tenth in hunter chase in February. *R. Jones* — c– –

PHILIP'S WOODY 5 b.g. Sula Bula – Pine Gypsy (Workboy) [1992/3 16gF 17v⁴ a16g* 16g² 16fF 16s³] close-coupled, rather unfurnished gelding: won maiden hurdle at Lingfield in February: easily best effort when second at Kempton later in month: will stay beyond 17f: acts on equitrack, best turf form on good ground. *N. J. Henderson* — 107

PHIL-MAN 4 b.c. Tina's Pet – Pakpao (Mansingh (USA)) [1992/3 18dᵖᵘ] angular colt: plating-class maiden at around 1m on Flat: no promise in selling hurdle: sold 720 gns Doncaster November Sales. *T. Fairhurst* — –

PHILOSTRA 5 b.m. Final Straw – Philogyny (Philip of Spain) [1992/3 17dᵖᵘ] unfurnished mare: no sign of ability over hurdles. *Martyn Meade* — –

PHILS PRIDE 9 b.g. Sunotra – La Furze (Winden) [1992/3 c16s* c18v* c16d³ c16vᵖᵘ c21d⁵ c20d⁴ 16d³] leggy, sparely-made gelding: quite useful hurdler nowadays: similar form over fences: successful in novice events at Catterick and Market Rasen in December: stays 21f: probably acts on any going: sketchy jumper of fences. *J. G. FitzGerald* — c115 115

PHOEBELLE 7 gr.m. Scallywag – Rodway Belle (Phebus) [1992/3 24sᵖᵘ 24gᵖᵘ] sister to a poor maiden pointer and half-sister to winning pointer: dam winning chaser: unseated rider in a point and showed nothing in novice hurdles in the spring. *C. D. Broad* — –

PHYRIAFAIR 12 b.g. Rouser – Brazen Lady (Bold As Brass) [1992/3 18f 20mᵖᵘ] strong, sturdy gelding: winning hurdler: pulled up lame in September: novice chaser. *R. Lee* — c– –

PICADOR 9 b.g. Piaffer (USA) – Go Gently (New Member) [1992/3 c21spu c21g6 c20gur c26dpu] tall, angular gelding: fair chaser in 1991/2: ran poorly in 1992/3: stays 3¼m: acts on firm going: successful in blinkers (worn them only once since 1989/90). *P. J. Hobbs*

c–
–

PICKETSTONE 6 b.g. Cornishman – Delrouge (Delaunay) [1992/3 22g 21d 16s4 16v3 c17spu c16m5 21f2] sturdy gelding: modest novice hurdler: poor novice chaser: stays 21f: easily best effort on firm going. *J. Webber*

c70
89

PIECEMEAL 7 gr.m. Baron Blakeney – Maria's Piece (Rose Knight) [1992/3 22d a16g 26spu 27dpu] sturdy mare: maiden pointer: tailed off over hurdles. *W. G. R. Wightman*

–

PIERRE BLANCO (USA) 4 b.g. Sovereign Don (USA) – Kiss Off (USA) (Princely Native (USA)) [1992/3 16s] modest middle-distance maiden on Flat in Ireland: well beaten in juvenile hurdle at Wetherby in December. *M. Bradstock*

–

PIGALLE WONDER 5 br.h. Chief Singer – Hi-Tech Girl (Homeboy) [1992/3 16g 17fF] small horse: signs of a little ability in early-season novice hurdles: modest winner at up to 1¼m on equitrack on Flat in 1993, including blinkered. *R. J. O'Sullivan*

71

PIGEON ISLAND 11 b.g. General Ironside – Brown Cherry (Master Buck) [1992/3 c21s6 c23f2 c21g* c26mrtr 22srtr c27f6] rather leggy gelding: novice hurdler: won novice chase at Plumpton in August: stays 3¼m: acts on firm ground: blinkered twice: sometimes refuses to race and is best left alone. *G. F. H. Charles-Jones*

c80 §
§§

PIKE'S CAROLORRE 6 b.m. Royal Boxer – Lady Zeta (Marengo) [1992/3 F18s aF16g F16g 16f5 16dF] small, sparely-made mare: third foal: sister to 2 poor animals: dam 2½m chase winner: no sign of ability. *J. M. Bradley*

–

PILGRIMS WAY (NZ) 6 ch.g. Prince Simbir (NZ) – Lady Fenella (NZ) (Della Porta) [1992/3 16s 16v 17f4] sturdy gelding: novice hurdler: easily best effort when fourth at Huntingdon in May: probably open to further improvement. *J. T. Gifford*

89 p

PIMPERNEL KING 7 b.g. Pimpernels Tune – Katie's Princess (Prince Hansel) [1992/3 a20gpu] ex-Irish gelding: third foal: dam unraced half-sister to several winning jumpers: no sign of ability: blinkered once. *P. Burgoyne*

c–
–

PIMS CLASSIC 5 gr.g. Absalom – Musical Maiden (Record Token) [1992/3 18s 16f5 17g 17f5] strong, close-coupled gelding: poor handicapper on Flat, stays 1½m: poor novice hurdler: yet to race beyond 17f: acts on firm ground. *J. L. Harris*

64

PIMS GUNNER (IRE) 5 b.g. Montelimar (USA) – My Sweetie (Bleep-Bleep) [1992/3 c16f c16d4 16g5 c20d2 c20s4 c20d4 c20m* c20m* c20s5 c21f3] neat gelding: handicap hurdler: successful in novice chases at Ludlow and Chepstow (handicap) in March: sold 10,000 gns Ascot June Sales: stays 2½m: acts on good to firm and dead ground. *D. Burchell*

c101 +
–

PINECONE PETER 6 ch.g. Kings Lake (USA) – Cornish Heroine (USA) (Cornish Prince) [1992/3 16sF] sparely-made gelding: modest handicap hurdler: looked probable winner when falling last at Nottingham in January: barely stays 19f: acts on any going: usually visored or blinkered. *O. Brennan*

93

PINEMARTIN 10 b.g. Pry – Sassenach Girl (Sassafras (FR)) [1992/3 c26g2] rangy gelding: fair chaser: creditable second in handicap at Cartmel early in season: stays 3¼m (not 3½m): probably acts on any ground: sound jumper. *G. Richards*

c110
–

PINISI 8 ch.g. Final Straw – Bireme (Grundy) [1992/3 22mur] strong gelding: poor winning hurdler: will stay 3m: acts on dead ground. *J. Wharton*

–

PINK GIN 6 ch.g. Tickled Pink – Carrapateira (Gunner B) [1992/3 c16d* c20g* c20dF c21g3 c25d2 c24m2 c25g* c25m6] sturdy gelding: modest hurdler: won novice chases at Carlisle and Newcastle in first half of season

c98
–

and Southwell in May: stays 25f: acts on good to firm, soft ground and fibresand: sometimes visored. *M. D. Hammond*

PINKJINSKI (IRE) 4 b.g. Petoski – Winterlude (Wollow) [1992/3 17m] of little account on Flat nowadays: tailed off in early-season juvenile hurdle. *D. Burchell*

PINTAIL BAY 7 b.g. Buzzards Bay – Pin Hole (Parthia) [1992/3 c16v³ c17vᶠ c16f⁵ c17s* c21dᵖᵘ c17mᵖᵘ] good-bodied gelding: winning hurdler: won novice chase at Newton Abbot in April: poor efforts afterwards: best form at around 2m: probably acts on any going: visored once, blinkered nowadays: not yet an accomplished jumper of fences: probably none too genuine. *C. P. E. Brooks*   c88 ?   –

PIONEER PETE 6 b.g. Prince of Peace – Bingley Sharlene (Good Apple) [1992/3 F17g 17v⁵ 16v] sixth foal: dam never ran: no sign of ability (trained first start by P. Nicholls). *R. G. Frost*   –

PIPER O'DRUMMOND 6 ch.g. Ardross – Skelbrooke (Mummy's Pet) [1992/3 20m 21d⁶ 21d⁴ 20g c23d* c25gᵖᵘ c25sᵖᵘ c23d³ c20d² c23g* c21f⁴ c23gᵇᵈ c21v³ c20d⁵] leggy, close-coupled gelding: poor novice hurdler: successful in novice chases at Kelso in December and March: ran well at Punchestown final start: stays 23f: acts on dead ground: inconsistent. *Mrs S. A. Bramall*   c100 85

PIPER'S SON 7 b.g. Sagaro – Lovely Laura (Lauso) [1992/3 26sᵖᵘ 21g⁴] lengthy, sparely-made gelding: fairly useful novice hurdler: fourth in handicap at Newbury in February: stays well: best runs on good going. *M. Bradstock*   118

PIPS PROMISE 4 b.g. Doc Marten – Little Muff (Potent Councillor) [1992/3 18m] compact gelding: no sign of ability on Flat or on hurdling debut. *J. M. Jefferson*   –

PIRATE BOY 6 ch.g. Turn Back The Time (USA) – Dream of Fortune (Barbary Pirate) [1992/3 F16m] behind in 2 NH Flat races: yet to race over hurdles or fences. *W. G. M. Turner*

PIRATE HOOK 5 b.g. Julio Mariner – London Blitz (Home Guard (USA)) [1992/3 F16m F16g² F17f] lengthy, useful-looking gelding: second foal: brother to poor novice hurdler: dam ran once: second in NH Flat race at Ayr in March: ran well long way in valuable similar event at Aintree in April: yet to race over hurdles or fences. *Mrs J. D. Goodfellow*

PIRATE OF PENZANCE 5 ch.g. Shaab – Lady of Penzance (My Swanee) [1992/3 18dᵖᵘ 17v 17vᵖᵘ] unfurnished gelding: no sign of ability. *S. C. Horn*   –

PITHY 11 ch.g. Orange Bay – Pranky (Bold Lad (IRE)) [1992/3 c16s* c21g³ c17v² c16v² c20s* c16v² c18d⁴ c21g⁴ c19m³] close-coupled, angular gelding: modest handicap chaser: won at Worcester (conditional jockeys) in October and Ludlow in January: effective at 2m when conditions are very testing and stays 25f: acts on good to firm and heavy ground: sometimes visored or blinkered prior to 1992/3: usually held up. *R. J. Price*   c99

PIT PONY 9 b.g. Hittite Glory – Watch Lady (Home Guard (USA)) [1992/3 17d⁵ 22g⁶ 17g 20g⁴ c21s c16dᶠ c16d⁴ c16g⁴ 17d c21s⁵ c20f⁶ c16m⁵ 16g³] small, compact gelding: poor hurdler/novice chaser: stays 2½m: suited by plenty of give in the ground: sometimes visored: inconsistent. *Miss L. A. Perratt*   c80 § 80 §

PLACID LAD 6 b.g. Bustomi – Worling-Pearl (Radetzky) [1992/3 20g* 17d⁵ 20s⁶ 22s] useful-looking gelding: lightly-raced hurdler: easily best effort when winning novice event at Hereford in October: ran as though something amiss afterwards (not raced after January): should stay further than 2½m: best form on good going. *J. Webber*   104 d

PLAN OF ATTACK (USA) 9 ch.g. Staff Writer (USA) – Eagle's Course (USA) (Montparnasse II) [1992/3 c22gᵘʳ c24m c17gᵖᵘ] strong gelding: no sign of ability: tried visored. *M. Sams*   c–

Beachley Handicap Chase, Chepstow —
Plastic Spaceage's good season continues; here he gets the better of Direct

PLASTIC SPACEAGE   10 b.g. The Parson – Chestnut Fire (Deep Run)   c127
[1992/3 c21vF c16v2 c21v2 c20v2 c20s* c22vF c24s* c27d*] tall, leggy   –
gelding: fairly useful handicap chaser: won at Chepstow (twice) and Newton
Abbot in second half of season: stays 27f: acts on heavy going: genuine and
consistent. *J. A. B. Old*

PLAT REAY   9 b.g. Uncle Pokey – Hejera (Cantab) [1992/3 c21d6 c21s3   c–
c20gF c20spu c21m5 c21m5] strong gelding: fairly useful chaser in 1991/2:
generally ran poorly in 1992/3: stays 2¾m: acts on good to soft going: jumps
none too fluently. *Capt. T. A. Forster*

PLAYFUL JULIET (CAN)   5 b.m. Assert – Running Around (USA)
(What A Pleasure (USA)) [1992/3 22v6 22s a20g a22g5] sturdy, close-   –
coupled mare: winning hurdler: ran poorly in 1992/3: stays 2¾m: acts on
fibresand and soft going. *B. R. Cambidge*

PLAY GAMES (USA)   5 ch.g. Nijinsky (CAN) – Playful Queen (USA)
(Majestic Prince) [1992/3 16s] good-topped gelding: one-time fair 1½m   –
winner on Flat: showed nothing in novice event at Kempton in December on
hurdling debut. *Lady Eliza Mays-Smith*

PLAYING TRUANT   5 b.g. Teenoso (USA) – Elusive (Little Current
(USA)) [1992/3 16s2 16g* 16s2] sturdy gelding: won novice hurdle at   95
Wincanton in November: creditable second in similar event at Haydock
later in month: will stay beyond 2m: acts on soft ground: looks a difficult
ride. *D. R. Gandolfo*

PLAYPEN   9 b.g. Sit In The Corner (USA) – Blue Nursery (Bluerullah)   c101 x
[1992/3 c18f3 c27d* c25sur c24f2 c27sF c24sF c21v5 c21v* c21s2 c26f4 c21v2   88
c21m3 22f3 23f2] small gelding: modest novice hurdler: fair chaser: won
handicap at Newton Abbot in September and claimer at Lingfield in January:
effective at 21f and stays well: acts on any going: occasionally looks
ungenuine: poor jumper of fences. *R. G. Frost*

PLAY THE BLUES   6 gr.m. Cure The Blues (USA) – Casual Pleasure   c84
(USA) (What A Pleasure (USA)) [1992/3 c19h2 c18f2 c18f* c18f6 c16s4 a16g4   84
17dbd] leggy, lengthy mare: poor hurdler/chaser: won novice event over
fences at Exeter in August: ran creditably over hurdles late on: stays 2½m:
probably acts on any ground. *R. G. Frost*

PLEASE PLEASE ME (IRE)   5 b.m. Tender King – Tacama (Daring
Display (USA)) [1992/3 17m* 16f 17g2 17m a16g5 a16g4 a18g3 a16g5 16g*   79

570

17f3] small mare: poor hurdler: successful in claimers at Stratford in September and Warwick (handicap) in March: races at around 2m: acts on firm ground and equitrack. *K. O. Cunningham-Brown*

PLECTRUM   5 b.m. Adonijah – Cymbal (Ribero) [1992/3 20m5 25gur] poor novice hurdler. *J. L. Spearing*   –

PLENARY   10 b.g. Proverb – Sinarga (Even Money) [1992/3 c21m6 c24m] leggy, angular gelding: poor staying novice hurdler: no form over fences. *J. Wharton*   c–   –

PLENTIFUL   7 b.m. Young Generation – Pundy (Grundy) [1992/3 18v 17vF 18s 16f3 23mpu] lengthy, rather dipped-backed mare: poor novice hurdler: form only at 2m: acted on firm ground: dead. *A. Moore*   66

PLENTY CRACK   10 b.g. Deep Run – Perspex-Pride (Perspex) [1992/3 c26s3 c28s4 c33dpu c24s* c28d* c29dF] strong gelding: carries plenty of condition: fairly useful chaser: won handicaps at Carlisle in January and Kelso in February: stays very well: suited by give in the ground: none too consistent: sometimes let down by his jumping: sometimes looks a difficult ride. *B. Mactaggart*   c129   –

PLUCKY PUNTER   5 b.g. Idiot's Delight – Birds of A Feather (Warpath) [1992/3 16g 16d5 17s 16s6 16m2] smallish, workmanlike gelding: second foal: dam of little account: poor novice hurdler: will stay beyond 17f: acts on dead and good to firm ground. *M. H. Easterby*   83

PLUM LINE   4 ch.g. Rymer – Dunoon Court (Dunoon Star) [1992/3 aF16g] half-brother to winning jumpers Warren Gorse (by Lucky Sovereign) and Pamrina (by Pamroy): dam novice hurdler: well beaten in NH Flat race at Lingfield in March: yet to race over hurdles. *Mrs L. C. Jewell*   –

POACHER'S DELIGHT   7 ch.g. High Line – Moonlight Night (FR) (Levmoss) [1992/3 25s5 25s c24f* c24mF c24f* c27f2] leggy, lengthy gelding: moderate handicap hurdler: trained until after second start by Mrs J. Retter: won novice chases at Taunton in March and Chepstow in May and would have won on former course in between but for falling 2 out: stays 27f: probably acts on any going. *M. C. Pipe*   c101   97

POCKET WATCH   4 b.g. Good Times (ITY) – Votsala (Tap On Wood) [1992/3 F17g] first foal: dam 6f winner at 2 yrs: tailed off in NH Flat race at Bangor in March: yet to race over hurdles. *D. Esden*   –

PODRIDA   7 gr.m. Persepolis (FR) – Pot Pourri (Busted) [1992/3 27d3] sturdy mare: winning hurdler, lightly raced: stays 27f: acts on soft ground. *R. J. O'Sullivan*   92

POETIC GEM   8 b.g. Rymer – Pearlyric (Eastern Lyric) [1992/3 c21s4 c21d c20g5 c16s5 c20d5 c20g6 c20g6 c21g3 c26mpu] close-coupled gelding: fair handicap chaser nowadays: best form at around 2½m: acts on good to firm and heavy ground: inconsistent. *Mrs S. J. Smith*   c103   –

POINT MADE   10 b.g. Tycoon II – Cala Conta (Deep Run) [1992/3 17g6 17s3 c20m3 c26g2 c25d* c26v3 c24s3 c24v c24gF] close-coupled gelding: modest handicap hurdler/chaser: won over fences at Nottingham in November: stayed 3¼m: probably acted on any going: visored once: sketchy jumper: dead. *J. R. Bosley*   c92   94

POINT TAKEN (USA)   6 b.g. Sharpen Up – Furry Friend (USA) (Bold Bidder) [1992/3 17s5 18v 17s6 16g 17g5 21gF 22gpu] workmanlike gelding: novice selling hurdler: best efforts at around 2m: acts on soft going: ungenuine. *K. A. Morgan*   67 §

POKEY'S PRIDE   10 b.g. Uncle Pokey – Strawberry Ice (Arctic Storm) [1992/3 21gpu 17s6 20g a18gpu] lengthy gelding: one-time quite useful middle-distance stayer on Flat: no sign of ability over hurdles. *J. R. Bostock*   –

POLAR GLEN   12 gr.g. Polaroid – Glenallen (Carnatic) [1992/3 c26m2] smallish, sparely-made gelding: fairly useful hunter chaser nowadays: suited by a good test of stamina: acts on any going: tried blinkered, but not for some time. *J. W. Dufosee*   c99   –

POLAR HAT 5 ch.g. Norwick (USA) – Sky Bonnet (Sky Gipsy) [1992/3 F18v³ F17s 17s³ 16mᶠ] leggy, sparely-made gelding: half-brother to a winner in Hong Kong by Rising River and 1m seller winner Frisco (by Absalom): dam won at 1m and 1¼m: signs of ability in 2 NH Flat races and 2 novice hurdles: likely to stay beyond 17f: should do better. *M. C. Pipe*   92 p

POLARIS 7 ro.g. Move Off – Toadpool (Pongee) [1992/3 c17dᵘʳ c17dᵘʳ c16g c16s4] big, lengthy gelding: poor novice hurdler: no form over fences. *N. Chamberlain*   c–

POLAR REGION 7 br.g. Alzao (USA) – Bonny Hollow (Wolver Hollow) [1992/3 c26d5 c24g c25sᶠ c27d² c24d* c27g* c28g* c26d c24s* c27g* c24m³] smallish, sparely-made gelding: fair hurdler: took well to fences and won 3 times at Sedgefield (2 novice events and a handicap) and once each at Carlisle (novices) and Perth (handicap) in second half of season: suited by a good test of stamina: probably acts on any ground: forces pace. *J. G. FitzGerald*   c112 –

POLDER 7 b.g. Lochnager – Dutch Girl (Workboy) [1992/3 16vᵖᵘ 16s4 16d5 17d6 16g* 17g6 c17m* c18g5 c17d² c16g3] lengthy gelding: modest performer: won conditional jockeys claiming handicap over hurdles at Catterick and novice event over fences at Newton Abbot in second half of season: best at around 2m: probably acts on any going: visored once. *D. L. Williams*   c87 80

POLECROFT 10 b.g. Crofter (USA) – Grange Kova (Allangrange) [1992/3 c16g4 c21s4 21v] leggy, sparely-made gelding: moderate hurdler at best: signs of ability in 2 handicap chases early in season: stays 25f: acts on heavy going: blinkered once. *D. Burchell*   c83 –

POLICEMANS PRIDE (FR) 4 bl.g. Policeman (FR) – Proud Pet (Petingo) [1992/3 F12d] rather leggy gelding: half-brother to several winners on Flat in France, including middle-distance performer Proud Master (by Master Thatch): dam successful over 1¾m in Ireland: behind in NH Flat race at Windsor in February: yet to race over hurdles. *P. S. Madgwick*

POLICY MAKER 6 br.g. Politico (USA) – May Moss (Sea Moss) [1992/3 F16dᵖᵘ] non-thoroughbred gelding: second foal: dam winning pointer: pulled up in NH Flat race in December: dead. *N. A. Twiston-Davies*

POLISH 15 gr.g. Tycoon II – Preshine (Specific) [1992/3 24sᵖᵘ] small, close-coupled gelding: staying handicap hurdler/novice chaser: no form since 1990/1: blinkered once. *K. S. Bridgwater*   c– x –

POLISHING 6 ch.g. Touching Wood (USA) – Loveshine (USA) (Gallant Romeo (USA)) [1992/3 16d 17g4 16s* 20sᵖᵘ 20gᵖᵘ 20g6 20m* 21s² a24gᵘʳ 21s4] close-coupled gelding: fairly useful hurdler: won handicaps at Wetherby in December and Newcastle in March: generally poor efforts otherwise (reportedly broke blood vessel fourth start): suited by testing conditions at 2m and stays 2½m: acts on good to firm and soft going: blinkered final outing, visored previous four: tends to get behind: not one to trust. *M. D. Hammond*   119 §

POLISH RIDER (USA) 5 ch.h. Danzig Connection (USA) – Missy T (USA) (Lt Stevens) [1992/3 18s 17d5 17v a16g4] compact horse: once-raced on Flat: poor novice hurdler: yet to race beyond 2¼m: easily best effort on fibresand. *Mrs D. Haine*   83

POLITICAL ISSUE 9 b.g. Politico (USA) – Red Stockings (Red Pins) [1992/3 c25d4 c24mᵖᵘ] strong, workmanlike gelding: winning hunter chaser: stays 3m: acts on soft ground: sketchy jumper. *T. L. A. Robson*   c– –

POLITICAL KING 9 b.g. Politico (USA) – Kiku (Faberge II) [1992/3 c27mᶠ] fourth foal: dam no form in novice hurdles: fell fatally in novice chase on debut. *J. I. A. Charlton*   c–

POLITICAL MAN 9 b.g. Mandalus – Worth A Vote (Vilmoray) [1992/3 c21m] plain, angular gelding: no sign of ability in steeplechases. *Mrs T. J. Hills*   c–

POLLERTON'S PRIDE   6 b.m. Pollerton – Arctic Snow Cat (Raise You Ten) [1992/3 22d⁵ 16f⁵ 21d² 20g⁴ 16d² 16d* 23d* 28v² 25v 20g³ 25dᵘʳ 22m⁵ 24g⁵ 25m² 25m⁶] smallish mare: modest hurdler: won novice events at Nottingham and Stratford in November: ran well when second late on: successful at 2m but suited by much longer distances: probably acts on any going: game. *W. Clay*   95

POLLIBRIG   9 br.m. Politico (USA) – Taras Brig (New Brig) [1992/3 c25d³ c25g* c24m⁴ c22g* c25m³] workmanlike mare: hunter chaser nowadays: won at Ayr in February and March: stays 3m: acts on good to firm and soft going. *W. Hamilton*   c82

POLLITTS PRIDE   7 ch.m. Crash Course – Fotopan (Polyfoto) [1992/3 28mᵖᵘ 22m 21g⁴] bad novice hurdler nowadays. *G. M. Moore*   57

POLLOCK (FR)   10 b.g. Arctic Tern (USA) – Golden Gleam (FR) (Lyphard (USA)) [1992/3 c17mᶠ] leggy, angular gelding: fair hurdler: let down by his jumping both outings over fences: stays 2½f: has won on hard going, but best form with give: blinkered nowadays. *Miss Linda Wonnacott*   c–
–

POLLY PENORA   6 ch.m. Crested Lark – Allied Cardiff (Import) [1992/3 22f² 17g] compact mare: only sign of ability when second in early-season novice claiming hurdle at Fontwell. *R. G. Frost*   73

POLLY'S LASS   9 b.m. Tom Noddy – Sporting Polly (Sporting Offer) [1992/3 17g 18g⁶ 18d 16d 16v a16g⁶ a20g³ a22g⁶ 23dᵖᵘ c21mᶠ] plain, rather sparely-made mare: poor maiden hurdler: fell third on steeplechasing debut: stays 2½m: acts on heavy ground. *J. R. Bosley*   c–
62

POLLY VERRY   11 br.m. Politico (USA) – Merry Leap (Stephen George) [1992/3 c24mᶠ] angular mare: winning pointer: novice hunter chaser: stays 3¼m: acts on firm ground. *J. R. Adam*   c–

POLYDEUCES   7 b.g. Swan's Rock – Mary Morison (Ragusa) [1992/3 16d⁶ 16g] well-made gelding: 2m novice hurdler: no form in 1992/3. *J. S. King*   –

POLYGONUM   11 b.g. Kemal (FR) – Wacoty (Typhoon) [1992/3 c21s⁶ c24d⁵ c22f] strong, sturdy gelding: quite useful hunter chaser at best: ran poorly in 1993: stayed 3m: acted on heavy going: blinkered once: dead. *W. M. Burnell*   c–
–

POLYNIXOS   7 b.g. Raga Navarro (ITY) – Whistler's Princess (King Emperor (USA)) [1992/3 16m⁵ 16fᵖᵘ 16gᵖᵘ] leggy, sparely-made gelding: bad novice hurdler. *R. Thompson*   51

POLYNOGAN   7 b.g. Pollerton – Wrekenogan (Tarqogan) [1992/3 F16d 21gᵖᵘ 20dᵖᵘ] plain gelding: third foal: brother to maiden jumper Hursthill and half-brother to fair Irish hurdler Cooleogan (by Proverb): dam, unraced half-sister to fair jumper Parsons Law, out of half-sister to Ekbalco: no sign of ability over hurdles. *R. H. Buckler*   –

PONDERED BID   9 b. or br.g. Auction Ring (USA) – Ponca (Jim French (USA)) [1992/3 18gᵖᵘ 16v³ 16s⁵ 21vᵖᵘ 18g] angular gelding: poor hurdler: changed hands 2,100 gns Doncaster January Sales after first outing, resold 675 gns Ascot June Sales: best at around 2m with give in the ground: blinkered nowadays: moody. *Pat Mitchell*   78 §

PONENTINO   7 b.g. Strong Gale – Milan United (Milan) [1992/3 a18gᵖᵘ 16gᵖᵘ c18mᶠ] workmanlike gelding: of little account: visored final outing. *G. P. Kelly*   c–
–

PONTEUS PILOT   12 ch.g. Levanter – Quelle Pas (Kelling) [1992/3 c27f⁴] tall, lengthy gelding: winning hunter chaser: stays well: acts on hard ground. *H. Wellstead*   c76
–

PONTOON BRIDGE   6 ch.g. Carlingford Castle – Lumax (Maximilian) [1992/3 F17d* 17s 17s 17g³ 17f* 17g] rangy gelding with plenty of scope: chasing type: first foal: dam, Norwegian Oaks winner and successful hurdler, half-sister to 3 winning jumpers, and to the dam of Jodami: won NH Flat race at Sandown in October (trained by Miss H. Knight) and novice hurdle there   99 p in March: will be suited by further than 17f: acts on firm ground: will improve. *G. Harwood*

PONTYNYSWEN 5 b.g. Ballacashtal (CAN) – Tropingay (Cawston's Clown) [1992/3 17d⁵ 16s⁵ 17d* 16f³ a16g*] rather sparely-made gelding: 127 fairly useful hurdler: won novice events at Chepstow in February and Southwell in May: excellent third to Spinning in Swinton Handicap at Haydock in between: stays beyond 17f: probably acts on any going: sometimes runs in snatches. *D. Burchell*

POOR FARMER 7 b.g. Burslem – My Veterinary Pal (Pals Passage) – [1992/3 16d] no sign of ability over hurdles: blinkered once. *J. S. Wainwright*

POORS WOOD 6 b.g. Martinmas – Lyaaric (Privy Seal) [1992/3 16s* 109 p 17v⁶ 17d⁴ 16g³ 18g* 17g⁴] tall, unfurnished gelding: chasing type: fifth foal: half-brother to winning hurdlers Metman (by Fair Season) and Metannee (by The Brianstan): dam never ran: won novice hurdles at Kempton in November and Folkestone in March: good fourth in valuable novice handicap at Cheltenham in April: yet to race beyond 2¼m: acts on soft ground: has further improvement in him. *J. T. Gifford*

POP ABROAD 8 b. or br.m. Broadsword (USA) – Lady Poppy (Sahib) 80 [1992/3 16s 21v⁴ 21s² 16d⁶ 25m 25mᵖᵘ] leggy, lengthy mare: poor novice hurdler: stays 21f: acts on heavy ground: usually forces pace. *P. J. Bevan*

POP A PRINGLE (NZ) 6 gr.g. Khairpour – Starlana (NZ) (Super Gray c– (USA)) [1992/3 c21sᵖᵘ] lengthy gelding: twice raced and no sign of ability. *D. – H. Barons*

POPESWOOD 10 b.g. Nicholas Bill – Villarrica (FR) (Dan Cupid) c81 § [1992/3 c19f³ c18s² c19s² c24v⁵ c21d c24v³ c24v⁴ c26g² c26g³ c26g⁴] leggy – gelding: poor handicap chaser: stays 3¼m: acts on any ground: sometimes blinkered prior to 1992/3: not one to trust. *W. G. R. Wightman*

POP FESTIVAL 4 b.f. Electric – Vino Festa (Nebbiolo) [1992/3 F16g⁴ – F18g⁴ F16f 16m] first foal: dam fairly useful hurdler, effective from 2m to 3m: signs of ability in NH Flat races, none in novice hurdle. *P. T. Dalton*

POPPLE 10 ch.g. Country Retreat – Poppy Lansdowne (Levmoss) – [1992/3 22sᵖᵘ] strong, lengthy gelding: no sign of ability in novice hurdles. *N. A. Twiston-Davies*

POPSI'S LEGACY 6 ch.m. Little Wolf – Popsi's Poppet (Hill Clown – (USA)) [1992/3 20dᵖᵘ] twice-raced novice over hurdles, poor at best. *M. J. Haynes*

POP SONG 9 b.g. High Season – Top of The Pops II (Hanover) [1992/3 c98 c27v³ c26s⁴ c27v⁶ c24s²] sparely-made, close-coupled gelding: moderate – chaser: suited by a good test of stamina: acts on any going: jumps none too fluently: sometimes has tongue tied down. *G. L. Roe*

PORTAVOGIE 9 b.g. Kambalda – Mary's Honour (Honour Bound) c86 [1992/3 16g c20g⁵ c27g² c24d c17s³ c20f* c21m³ c22v⁵ c23m] compact – gelding: modest handicap chaser: won amateurs event at Newcastle in May: stays well: acts on any ground: sometimes blinkered. *C. Parker*

PORTER'S SONG 12 ch.g. True Song – Spartan Clover (Spartan c91 General) [1992/3 c22d³ c25dᵖᵘ c17g³] strong, good-bodied gelding: fair hunter chaser: stays 3m: acts on soft and good to firm ground. *R. Hutsby*

PORT IN A STORM 4 b.c. Blakeney – Crusader's Dream (St Paddy) 68 [1992/3 16d 17sᵖᵘ 17g⁴] compact colt: half-brother to winning hurdler King's Crusade (by Reform): modest maiden on Flat, placed at up to 1¼m: sold out of W. Jarvis' stable 8,400 gns Newmarket Autumn Sales: poor form in selling hurdles in first half of season. *N. Tinkler*

PORTKNOCKIE 5 b.m. Rymer – Vulpine Lady (Green Shoon) [1992/3 82 F17m F16g 23d⁴ a22gᶠ] small, angular mare: first foal: dam lightly-raced pointer: fourth in novice hurdle in December: showed nothing on fibresand month later: sold 2,200 gns Doncaster March Sales: will need good test of stamina. *Mrs M. Reveley*

PORTO HELI 6 b.g. Precocious – Coral Heights (Shirley Heights) [1992/3 16s³ 17s³ 16g⁴] small, compact gelding: modest hurdler nowadays: sold 950 gns Ascot June Sales: best form at around 2m: acts on any going: blinkered nowadays: tends to carry head high. *M. C. Pipe* 92

PORTONIA 9 b.m. Ascertain (USA) – Hardwick Sun (Dieu Soleil) [1992/3 c25s⁴ c27d* c27g² c26m³ c27d⁴ c26d* c26s* c29s* c29d² c28g² c27d³] smallish, lengthy mare: fairly useful handicap chaser: won at Sedgefield and Catterick (twice) in first half of season and on latter course in January: stays very well: probably acts on any going: claimer ridden nowadays: front runner. *Mrs M. Reveley* c115 –

POSITIVE ACTION 7 b.g. Croghan Hill – Auragne (FR) (Crowned Prince (USA)) [1992/3 c16d² c16m² c16d⁴ c16d⁴ c17v* c16s³ c16g c16s³ c16d c16d² c21s⁴ c17s* c16f⁴ c21m⁴] leggy, lightly-made gelding: modest handicap chaser: won at Hexham in December and May: best form at around 2m: acts on good to firm and heavy going: inconsistent. *M. A. Barnes* c90 –

POSTAGE STAMP 6 ch.g. The Noble Player (USA) – Takealetter (Wolver Hollow) [1992/3 22d⁶ 25v] good-topped gelding: fairly useful hurdler in 1991/2: stiff tasks in 1992/3: should stay beyond 2¾m: acts on dead and good to firm ground: usually a front runner. *J. Pearce* –

POSTMAN'S KNOCK 8 b.g. Town And Country – Record Surprise (Record Run) [1992/3 c25g⁵ᵘ] winning pointer: novice chaser, modest at best. *N. E. H. Hargreave* c– –

POSTMAN'S PATH 7 ch.g. Over The River (FR) – Coolbawn Lady (Laurence O) [1992/3 16s c23gᶠ c21v* c21g⁴] sturdy gelding: poor novice hurdler: won novice chase at Uttoxeter in April: downed tools next time: should prove suited by test of stamina: acts on heavy going: one to be wary of. *Capt. T. A. Forster* c99 § –

POTATO MAN 7 gr.g. Zambrano – Kit's Future (Saucy Kit) [1992/3 c21d⁴ c23gᵖᵘ] strong, compact gelding: novice chaser, poor at best. *Mrs S. Taylor* c– –

POTATO PICKER 12 b.g. Celtic Cone – Kit's Future (Saucy Kit) [1992/3 c16d⁵ c21d c26dᵖᵘ c26sᵘʳ c20dᵖᵘ] sturdy gelding: winning hurdler/chaser: no form since middle of 1991/2. *Mrs S. Taylor* c– –

POULSTONE 6 ch.g. Over The River (FR) – Mourne Lass (Hereford) [1992/3 F18v² F18s* F16s 21sᶠ] IR 9,500 3-y-o: half-brother to winning jumpers Wrens Lass (by Wrens Hill) and Double Tricks (by Peacock): dam placed over hurdles and in a point: won NH Flat race at Exeter in January: fell fatally in novice hurdle at Leicester in February. *J. A. C. Edwards* –

POWDER BOY 8 ch.g. Tarrago (ITY) – Powder Princess (Prince Hansel) [1992/3 c24f* c24g* c24sᵖᵘ c26vᵖᵘ c25mᵘʳ c21f³ c26dᵖᵘ c24m⁴ c24fᵘʳ c24mᵖᵘ] angular, lightly-made gelding: moderate chaser: won 2 handicaps at Taunton in first half of season: ran well once on same course late on: stays 3¼m: acts on firm and dead ground. *Mrs J. C. Dawe* c95 –

POWER HAPPY 8 ch.m. Instant Fame – Dawn Dreamer (Avocat) [1992/3 23d⁴ 20s⁴ 23sᵖᵘ 17s² 22sᵖᵘ 21g 16f* 20v⁵] good-bodied mare: won novice hurdle at Worcester (jumped right) in March, easily best effort: should stay beyond 2m: evidently acts well on firm ground. *F. J. Yardley* 84

POWER OF PRAYER 6 ch.m. The Noble Player (USA) – Sandra's Choice (Sandy Creek) [1992/3 17dᵖᵘ] poor maiden on Flat: no sign of ability in early-season novice event on hurdling debut. *R. F. Johnson Houghton* –

POWERSURGE 6 b.h. Electric – Ladysave (Stanford) [1992/3 20d³ 18d² 22s²] smallish horse: novice selling hurdler: not raced after November: stays 2¾m: acts on soft ground: blinkered final outing. *A. Moore* 79

PRAGADA 10 b.g. Pragmatic – Adare Lady (Varano) [1992/3 24s 24v* 25m² 24s² 24f⁴] c– 160
    We learned in the latest season that Pragada doesn't need give in the ground in order to show his best form. Though he failed to do himself justice on very firm going on his final start, Pragada did put up a very smart

Jim Ennis Construction Premier Long Distance Hurdle, Haydock—
Pragada revels in the testing conditions and is too good for Better Times Ahead

performance on good to firm when two and a half lengths second to Shuil Ar Aghaidh in the Stayers' Hurdle at Cheltenham in March. Pragada, third in the same event two years earlier, has a very good record at the Cheltenham Festival, having won and finished second in the Coral Golden Hurdle on his other visits there. He's achieved plenty elsewhere, too, and a couple of months before the latest Festival he won the Jim Ennis Construction Premier Long Distance Hurdle at Haydock. The ground at Haydock was barely raceable but Pragada made light of the conditions, setting a gallop which had all except Better Times Ahead in trouble well before the second last. Better Times Ahead was still in with a chance at the last but Pragada, staying on resolutely under hard driving, forged clear to beat him by five lengths. Pragada also ran well immediately after Cheltenham in the Letheby & Christopher Long Distance Hurdle at Ascot, a race he'd won in 1992. This time round he had to settle for second place, seven lengths behind Sweet Duke to whom he was conceding 7 lb.

	Pragmatic	Relko	Tanerko
	(gr 1975)	(b 1960)	Relance III
Pragada		Paracelle	Vimy
(b.g. 1983)		(gr 1961)	Palsaka
	Adare Lady	Varano	Darius
	(ch 1975)	(b 1962)	Varna II
		Go Fort	Fortina
		(ch 1966)	Letgo

Two seasons ago when trained by Josh Gifford Pragada showed useful form in novice chases, winning twice. But he took a heavy fall on his final outing and that appeared to have affected his confidence when he reappeared in a handicap the following season, for he made mistakes and was tailed off when pulled up. Now rising eleven, it's unlikely that Pragada will be asked to tackle fences again. Not that he needs to, for he'll continue to make his presence felt in the top long-distance events over hurdles. Pragada's pedigree has been well documented in previous annuals, and we need only add that his four-year-old half-sister Wyjume (by Phardante), trained by Gifford, finished third in a National Hunt Flat race in March on her debut. The workmanlike Pragada, a thorough stayer, is well suited by forcing tactics. He wears blinkers nowadays. *M. C. Pipe*

PREACHERS POPSY   7 ch.m. The Parson – Ballycold (Arctic Slave)   –
[1992/3 22gᵖᵘ] half-sister to a winning pointer by Beau Chapeau: dam,

half-sister to very useful Irish hunter Colonel Heather and useful chaser Fudge Delight, won over hurdles and fences: no sign of ability in novice event at Huntingdon in April on hurdling debut. *O. Sherwood*

PREAMBLE 4 b.f. Baillamont (USA) – Luth Celtique (FR) (Thatch (USA)) [1992/3 16d⁵ 17g 17d 17dᵖᵘ] tall, lengthy, sparely-made mare: poor plater on Flat and over hurdles: sold out of Mrs J. Ramsden's stable 3,200 gns Doncaster November Sales after first start. *S. G. Chadwick* 63

PREBEN FUR 16 b.g. Mon Capitaine – Flashing Beauty (Straight Lad) [1992/3 c25mᵖᵘ c21d] handicap chaser: seems of little account nowadays. *P. Salmon* c– –

PRECIOUS JUNO (IRE) 4 b.f. Good Thyne (USA) – Crashing Juno (Crash Course) [1992/3 F16s*] sturdy filly: half-sister to several winning jumpers, including fairly useful staying chaser Macroom (by Furry Glen) and hurdler Whippers Delight (by King Persian): dam never ran: won 17-finisher mares NH Flat race at Ludlow in April: yet to race over hurdles. *Mrs J. Pitman*

PRECIOUS MEMORIES 8 br.g. Kabour – Kings Fillet (King's Bench) [1992/3 c24gᵖᵘ c24mᶠ c25sᵖᵘ c17gᵘʳ c20mᶠ c17g 21s⁶ c23m*] lightly-made gelding: modest chaser: returned to form when winning novice event at Market Rasen in May: barely stays 3m: acts on good to firm and dead ground: sometimes blinkered or visored prior to 1992/3. *M. P. Naughton* c89 –

PRECIOUS WONDER 4 b.c. Precocious – B M Wonder (Junius (USA)) [1992/3 17v³ 18sᵖᵘ 16gᵖᵘ] leggy colt: fair 7f performer on Flat: third in juvenile event at Plumpton in February, only form over hurdles. *P. Butler* 77

Mrs Margaret McGlone's "Pragada"

PRECIPICE RUN 8 ch.g. Deep Run – Lothian Lassie (Precipice Wood) [1992/3 17s 16d* 17d⁴ 20g* 16s² 18d*] workmanlike gelding: chasing type: won novice hurdles at Hexham, Bangor and Cartmel in the spring: will stay beyond 21f: acts on soft ground. *G. Richards*   111

PRECIS 5 b.m. Pitpan – Ottery News (Pony Express) [1992/3 22m 18g⁴ 17s* 18d³] second live foal: dam very good hunter chaser: won maiden hurdle at Newton Abbot in April: improved form next time: should stay further than 2¼m: acts on soft going. *O. J. Carter*   90

PREDESTINE 8 b.g. Bold Owl – Combe Grove Lady (Simbir) [1992/3 16s 17v⁴ a16gᵖᵘ 17v⁴ 17dᵖᵘ] small gelding: poor hurdler: sold 1,000 gns Ascot May Sales: races only at around 2m: acts on heavy ground. *M. Madgwick*   81

PREDICTABLE 7 ch.g. Music Boy – Piccadilly Etta (Floribunda) [1992/3 17vᵖᵘ] lengthy, robust gelding: no form over hurdles. *Mrs A. Knight*   –

PREMIER LADY 6 b.m. Red Sunset – Be A Dancer (Be Friendly) [1992/3 17m 17g 25d⁵] neat mare: novice hurdler, poor at best: sold 500 gns Newmarket July Sales. *K. G. Wingrove*   –

PREMIER PRINCESS 7 b.m. Hard Fought – Manntika (Kalamoun) [1992/3 24f⁴ 26g⁶ 24g 25g 25m 24f⁶] small, sparely-made mare: fair staying handicap hurdler at best: no form after first start: acts on firm and dead ground: sometimes has tongue tied down: racing in Channel Islands. *G. A. Ham*   115 d

PREOBLAKENSKY 6 b.g. Blakeney – Preobrajenska (Double Form) [1992/3 16d 17m³ 17d³ c16d³ c20s⁵ c20g² 21m* 17d 16g⁵ 17d³ 26vᵖᵘ] leggy gelding: fairly useful handicap hurdler: best effort when winning at Carlisle in March: moderate novice chaser: probably needs further than 2m and stays 21f: acts on good to firm and dead ground. *G. Richards*   c91 120

PRE PAINT 4 b.c. Sizzling Melody – Chalet Girl (Double Form) [1992/3 17s⁵ a16g⁵ 16gᵖᵘ] small colt: no form in 2 races at 2 yrs: poor form first 2 starts over hurdles: yet to race beyond 2m. *J. Akehurst*   69

PRESENT TIMES 7 b.g. Sayf El Arab (USA) – Coins And Art (USA) (Mississipian (USA)) [1992/3 17s⁵ 16s 16v 17g 18g 17f³ 17g⁴ 16mᶠ] leggy gelding: modest hurdler: best form at around 2m: acts on good to firm and soft going: often goes well at Windsor. *A. Moore*   86

PRESET 6 ch.g. Homing – Constanza (Sun Prince) [1992/3 c16gᶠ c21s⁴] sturdy gelding: poor 2m novice hurdler (visored once): fairly useful pointer in 1993 for Mrs P. Russell: showed promise when fourth in novice chase at Hexham in April: sure to improve. *J. A. Hellens*   c– p

PRESSURE GAME 10 b.g. Miami Springs – Cheena (Le Levanstell) [1992/3 c16m²] small gelding: poor hurdler/chaser: races at around 2m: acts on firm ground: tried in blinkers and visor. *B. Mactaggart*   c78 –

PRETTY BOY GEORGE 4 ch.g. St Columbus – Sea Farmer (Cantab) [1992/3 F14s] fifth foal: dam failed to complete course in 3 outings: tailed off in NH Flat race at Market Rasen in April: yet to race over hurdles. *K. F. Clutterbuck*   –

PRETTY GAYLE 11 ch.m. Midland Gayle – Pretty Damsel (Prince Hansel) [1992/3 28gᵖᵘ] sparely-made mare: staying handicap hurdler: lightly raced in recent seasons and no form since 1990/1: blinkered once. *J. L. Eyre*   –

PRICELESS HOLLY 5 b.g. Silly Prices – Holly Doon (Doon) [1992/3 20sᵖᵘ] lengthy, unfurnished gelding: half-brother to 3 winning hurdlers, notably smart stayer Yorkshire Holly (by Bivouac): no sign of ability on Flat or in novice event at Newcastle in December on hurdling debut. *R. S. Wood*   –

PRIDEAUX PRINCE 7 b.g. Prince Regent (FR) – Fairy (Prefairy) [1992/3 c26gᶠ c21g³ c26d² c25s⁶ c26d] lengthy gelding: maiden hunter chaser: blinkered when tailed off last 2 starts: stays 3¼m: acts on dead ground. *Miss C. L. Dennis*   c80 –

PRIDE OF PENDLE 4 ro.f. Grey Desire – Pendle's Secret (Le   83
Johnston) [1992/3 16m 17g³ 16spu 16s⁶ 17g² 16s³20m⁶] leggy, close-coupled
filly: half-sister to 2 winning hurdlers, including fair Rivers Secret (by
Young Man): modest at up to 9f on Flat, winner several times in 1993 for P.
Calver: poor form over hurdles: will prove best at around 2m: acts on soft
ground. *B. E. Wilkinson*

PRIDEWOOD GOLDING 6 ch.g. Soldier Rose – Quick Reply   84
(Tarqogan) [1992/3 17m³ 22g 20v⁵ 16vpu 22d 17g 17m 17d] smallish gelding:
poor novice hurdler: may prove best at around 2m. *R. J. Price*

PRIDEWOOD PICKER 6 b.g. Joshua – Guinea Feather (Over The   –
River (FR)) [1992/3 F16s 17spu] leggy gelding: first foal: dam, lightly raced
in novice hurdles after birth of foal, half-sister to 2 winning jumpers,
including useful hurdler Westway: no sign of ability. *R. J. Price*

PRIMA AURORA 5 br.m. Primo Dominie – Alumia (Great Nephew)   79
[1992/3 18s⁶ 16d⁶ a21g*] lengthy mare: selling hurdler: won at Southwell
(bought in 3,600 gns) in May: stays 21f: acts on dead ground and fibresand.
A. A. Hambly

PRIME DISPLAY (USA) 7 ch.g. Golden Act (USA) – Great Display   c–
(FR) (Great Nephew) [1992/3 c21vF c21s 21mpu 24d⁵ 24g² 24g⁴] robust,   130
stocky gelding: handicap hurdler: second at Bangor in April, best effort in
1992/3: let down by his jumping in 2 novice chases: stays 3m well: acts on
good to firm and soft going. *O. Sherwood*

PRIME MOVER 5 b.g. Mummy's Game – Feast-Rite (Reform) [1992/3   74
16g 16s 17v 16d³ 16m* 17fur] leggy gelding: fair at up to 1m on Flat, winner in
1993: won selling handicap hurdle at Uttoxeter (sold out of D. Burchell's
stable 4,400 gns) in May: will prove best at around 2m: acts on good to firm
and dead ground: visored last 2 starts. *I. Campbell*

PRIMERA BALLERINA 5 ch.m. Primo Dominie – Yankee Special   57
(Bold Lad (IRE)) [1992/3 18gF 17s⁵ 22d a16g] sparely-made, rather plain
mare: bad novice hurdler: trained until after third start by K. Cunningham-
Brown. *J. White*

PRIMITIVE SINGER 5 b.g. Chief Singer – Periquito (USA) (Olden   c94
Times) [1992/3 21s⁵ 21v² 21g c21d³] strong, workmanlike gelding: fair   108
hurdler: third in novice handicap at Newton Abbot in April on chasing debut:
sold only 800 gns Ascot June Sales: stays 21f: has won on good to firm going,
but best form with give in the ground and acts on heavy. *Miss H. C. Knight*

PRINCE ALI 4 b.g. Tina's Pet – Ribbons of Blue (Jimmy Reppin) [1992/3   –
18gpu] no sign of ability only outing on Flat and on hurdling debut (both
sellers). *B. Ellison*

PRINCE HAL 10 b.g. Just A Monarch – Madame Meilland (Florio)   c§§
[1992/3 c20dpu] smallish gelding: maiden pointer: has looked reluctant in 2
steeplechases: blinkered once. *R. T. Juckes*

PRINCE JAKATOM 6 ch.g. Ballad Rock – Ballysnip (Ballymore)   62
[1992/3 17g⁶] angular gelding: twice raced in selling hurdles, poor form. *J. D.
Thomas*

PRINCE JUAN 6 b.g. Kampala – Ceduna (FR) (Right Tack) [1992/3 16s   –
17s⁶ 17gpu 16f] smallish gelding: half-brother to several winners, including
hurdlers Gerise (by Nishapour) and Faynaz (by Tumble Wind): dam never
ran: winning hurdler in Ireland: no form in 1992/3: raced only at 2m: acts on
dead ground: sometimes blinkered and has tongue tied down: returned to
Ireland. *M. Bradstock*

PRINCE KESAR (USA) 9 b.g. Majestic Light (USA) – Kesar Queen   c–
(USA) (Nashua) [1992/3 c21gpu] workmanlike gelding: bad maiden pointer:
showed nothing on steeplechasing debut. *Miss P. Sutton*

PRINCE KILINOIS 9 b.g. Tina's Pet – Solea (Gay Fandango (USA))   c–
[1992/3 c21gpu 19m 16g] workmanlike gelding: poor novice hurdler/chaser: –
blinkered once. *Mrs H. Parrott*

PRINCE KLENK 12 b.g. Random Shot – Delia Ross (Dalesa) [1992/3 c–
25s 22dF 21s6] plain, lengthy gelding: winning staying hurdler: no form in –
1992/3: unseated rider only outing over fences. *A. R. Davison*

PRINCE NEPAL 9 b.g. Kinglet – Nepal (Indian Ruler) [1992/3 c24dpu]
big, rangy gelding: winning hunter chaser: stays 25f: acts on soft and good to
firm ground. *Steve Hulse*

PRINCE OF PREY 5 ch.g. Buzzards Bay – Sleepline Princess (Royal
Palace) [1992/3 F17g F17m2] leggy gelding: fourth foal: brother to Sleepline
Fantasy and Sleepline Royale, both successful on Flat and latter also over
hurdles: second of 15 in NH Flat race at Hereford in May: yet to race over
hurdles or fences. *T. Thomson Jones*

PRINCE OF SALERNO 6 ch.g. Slippered – Daffydown Lady
(Menelek) [1992/3 20g6] workmanlike gelding: no form in novice hurdles. –
N. A. Gaselee

PRINCE RUA 7 ch.g. Wrens Hill – Oldtown Princess VI (Chou Chin c–
Chow) [1992/3 c21mpu c27fpu] poor maiden hurdler (in Ireland)/winning
pointer: no form in hunter chases. *Mrs K. M. Martin*

PRINCE'S COURT 10 b.g. Kinglet – Court Scene (Royal Levee (USA)) c88
[1992/3 c21dF c21mF c21s2 c20d6 c21g3 c19m4 c24m4 c26f3] workmanlike –
gelding: winning hurdler: moderate novice chaser: stays 3¼m: probably
acts on any going: blinkered last 2 starts (ran creditably): jumps none too
fluently. *Andrew Turnell*

PRINCESS BUSTER 9 b.m. Gilmore Prince – Busters Chance
(Armagnac Monarch) [1992/3 23mpu 17m4] of little account. *J. W. Mullins* –

PRINCESS CASILIA 8 ch.m. Croghan Hill – Ballybeg Maid (Prince
Hansel) [1992/3 F16s3 F16s3 16s 16v3 16v* 20s* 17v* 16v2 18d2 18s2 16s* 137
20s4 16d2]

The 1992/3 season was a particularly successful one for Willie Mullins.
Not only did he become champion amateur rider in Ireland for the fifth time,
but he also had the good fortune to train the smart novice hurdler Princess

*Jameson Gold Cup (Novices' Hurdle), Fairyhouse—
Princess Casilia clouts the last but has plenty in hand*

Mr M. O'Dowd's "Princess Casilia"

Casilia. Mullins wasn't on board when Princess Casilia got off the mark over hurdles in a handicap at Clonmel in December. But he rode her in all her subsequent races, the partnership being successful in further handicaps at Limerick and Gowran Park and, more significantly, in the Jameson Gold Cup Hurdle at Fairyhouse in April. With the favourite Boro Eight breaking a blood vessel and Gaelic Myth running badly Princess Casilia's task in the Jameson Gold Cup wasn't so tough as it might have been, but no-one could quibble with the manner of her victory. Princess Casilia took up the running two out, quickly recovered from a mistake at the last and went on to beat Winds of War by eight lengths. Princess Casilia, who has run twenty-four times in the past two seasons, is as tough as that other grand Irish mare Bayrouge, though in terms of ability the latter just has the edge. The pair have met twice with Princess Casilia finishing second to Bayrouge each time. She was beaten by one and a half lengths in the Naas Supporters Hurdle on her eighth start of the season, and by four lengths in the Champion Novices' Hurdle at Punchestown on her final one.

Princess Casilia (ch.m. 1985)	Croghan Hill (b 1975)	Lord Gayle (b 1965)	Sir Gaylord
			Sticky Case
		Good Report (ch 1961)	Golden Cloud
			Signal Gun
	Ballybeg Maid (ch 1974)	Prince Hansel (ch 1961)	The Phoenix
			Saucy Wilhelmina
		No Hunting (b 1971)	No Time
			Hunter's Hut

Princess Casilia, a lengthy, rather sparely-made mare, has put up her best performances at two miles, but she did win over two and a half at Limerick. She possibly hadn't recovered from her exertions in the Jameson

Gold Cup just two days earlier when below form on her latest attempt at the latter trip. Princess Casilia, with two wins in National Hunt Flat races under her belt, cut little ice over three miles on her hurdling debut in 1991/2. Whether she'll stay three miles is debatable. Her half-brother Carrick-rovaddy (by Deroulede), a winner of a novice chase at Stratford in May, is suited by a distance of ground but her half-sister Baunfaun Rose (by Roselier), successful over hurdles and fences in Ireland, was best at two miles. Princess Casilia is from the first crop of Croghan Hill, a very useful winner at up to two miles on the Flat and successful in three hurdle races over the same distance. Her dam Ballybeg Maid is an unraced half-sister to three winning jumpers. Princess Casilia acts on heavy going and has yet to race on a firm surface. *W. P. Mullins, Ireland*

PRINCESS JO   4 b.f. Prince of Peace – Avec Amour (Jolly Jet) [1992/3 17d] fifth live foal: dam winning hurdler: tailed off in juvenile selling hurdle at Taunton in November. *Mrs A. Knight* —

PRINCESS MOODYSHOE   5 ch.m. Jalmood (USA) – Royal Shoe (Hotfoot) [1992/3 22m3] sparely-made mare: modest hurdler in 1991/2: well below form only outing in 1992/3 (August): best at up to 19f: acts on dead ground. *M. C. Pipe* —

PRINCETHORPE   6 b.g. Ring Bidder – Sparkling Jenny (Sparkler) [1992/3 F17m5 F16d 16s 17m 16d] leggy, unfurnished gelding: first foal: dam moderate staying hurdler: no form over hurdles. *B. R. Cambidge* —

PRINCE TINO   5 b.g. Bustino – Northern Empress (Northfields (USA)) [1992/3 17g 16m2 16d2 16s3 17g2 18g3 17m* 16f2 17g4] good-bodied gelding: fair hurdler: won novice handicap at Stratford in April: will stay further than 2¼m: probably acts on any going: sometimes finds little. *N. A. Gaselee* — 101

PRINCE VALMY (FR)   8 br.g. Mill Reef (USA) – Princesse Vali (FR) (Val de L'Orne (FR)) [1992/3 17s6 18d5 17s5 17v2 21v a20g 17v2 17s4 21s6 18m3] lengthy, angular gelding: poor novice hurdler: best form at around 2m: acts on heavy and good to firm ground: sometimes blinkered: none too enthusiastic on occasions. *N. G. Ayliffe* — 71 §

PRINCE YAMADORI   9 b.g. Riboboy (USA) – Orange Tip (Orange Bay) [1992/3 c20dpu c27spu 24v] tall, angular gelding: winning pointer: little sign of ability otherwise. *H. Willis* — c– –

PRINCE ZEUS   14 br.g. Prince de Galles – Zeus Girl (Zeus Boy) [1992/3 c27f] sparely-made gelding: winning chaser: modest pointer nowadays. *Mrs T. J. Hills* — c– –

PRIOR CONVICTION (IRE)   4 b.g. Monksfield – Locked Up (Garda's Revenge (USA)) [1992/3 17m3 16g 20s6 22dpu 25d 28gpu] good-topped gelding: first foal: dam, poor Irish Flat maiden, last only outing over hurdles: juvenile hurdler: only form on debut. *G. M. Moore* — 71

PRIORY PIPER   4 b.g. Maris Piper – Priory Girl (Rugantino) [1992/3 17gpu 16g5 17f 21spu 20m3 17f] leggy, angular gelding: well beaten on Flat: only worthwhile form over hurdles when third in seller in May. *J. A. Pickering* — 73 ?

PRISCILLIAN   9 b.g. Runnett – Douala (GER) (Pentathlon) [1992/3 22v c18spu] angular, good sort: novice hurdler: modest handicap chaser in 1990/1: no show in 1992/3: best form at around 2m: acts on good to firm ground. *J. A. B. Old* — c– –

PRIVATE AUDITION   11 b.g. Crimson Beau – Loren (Crocket) [1992/3 c20spu c17d* c17g4 c17m6 c16v* c16gF] tall, lengthy gelding: fairly useful handicap chaser: won at Huntingdon in January and Worcester (conditional jockeys) in April: best form at up to 2½m: acts on any going: sketchy jumper: sometimes looks temperamental. *F. Murphy* — c118 –

PRIVATE JET (IRE)   4 b.g. Dara Monarch – Torriglia (USA) (Nijinsky (CAN)) [1992/3 F17s4 F16s F16s] half-brother to several winners abroad, including very successful French jumper Monsieur Mystere (by Top Ville):

dam placed on Flat in France: signs of ability in NH Flat races: yet to race over hurdles. *J. Ffitch-Heyes*

PRIZE MATCH   4 ch.f. Royal Match – Prize Melody (Remezzo) [1992/3 17v*] first foal: dam, lightly raced, placed over hurdles and fences: 20-length winner of juvenile hurdle at Newton Abbot in November on debut: will stay beyond 17f: likely to improve. *N. A. Gaselee*   89 p

PROCTORS ROW   6 b.g. Rymer – Cytisus (Above Suspicion) [1992/3 20s 16s^6 c16g^3 c16m^2 c18g^6 c16v^3 c21g^4] workmanlike gelding: poor novice hurdler/chaser: should stay beyond 2m: acts on good to firm and soft ground: visored final start. *D. McCain*   c81 –

PRODIGAL MISS   5 b.m. Carwhite – Devadara (Royal Levee (USA)) [1992/3 17m^2 17d^4 17g^5 16g 17m 17d] close-coupled mare: no form on Flat: poor maiden plater over hurdles: sold 575 gns Ascot November Sales: yet to race beyond 17f: acts on good to firm and dead ground. *Mrs A. Knight*   63

PROGRAMMED TO WIN   6 b.g. Pollerton – Fair Corina (Menelek) [1992/3 20g* 24s^2 21s* 20g^5 22g 21s^{pu}] leggy, unfurnished gelding: fair hurdler: won novice events at Ayr (handicap) in November and Wetherby in January: something possibly amiss final 2 starts: effective at 2½m and stays 3m: acts on soft ground. *Mrs M. Reveley*   110

PROJECT'S MATE   6 br.g. Rustingo – Lyricist (Averof) [1992/3 F17g 17d 22d 17g^6 16s] brother to moderate hurdler Rusty Music: dam never ran: well beaten in novice hurdles. *R. L. Brown*   –

PROMPTER   7 ch.g. Hasty Word – Trewenol (Goldhill) [1992/3 c25g^{pu} c21d^6 c26d^{pu} c21v^{pu} 23s 22s^{pu}] compact gelding: novice hurdler/chaser: no form: looks ungenuine: blinkered last 2 starts. *W. T. Kemp*   c– § – §

PRONOUNCED   6 b.g. Deep Run – Lovely Bio (Double-U-Jay) [1992/3 F16v^5 21s 22s^{pu} 21s^3] IR 15,500 3-y-o: small gelding: half-brother to fair hurdler/novice chaser Black Moccasin (by Buckskin): dam, useful winner on Flat and over hurdles in Ireland, half-sister to Yorkshire Cup winner Alto Volante: first form over hurdles when third in amateurs event at Hexham in May: sold 4,200 gns Ascot June Sales. *J. A. C. Edwards*   77

PROPAGANDA   5 b.g. Nishapour (FR) – Mrs Moss (Reform) [1992/3 18g 17g*] well-made gelding: half-brother to numerous winners, including very smart middle-distance stayer Jupiter Island (by St Paddy) and high-class 1983 2-y-o sprinter Precocious (by Mummy's Pet): once-raced on Flat: won 9-runner novice hurdle at Newbury in March by a neck from Sohrab, pair clear: will stay beyond 17f: should improve further. *N. J. Henderson*   108 p

PROPERO   8 b.g. Electric – Nadwa (Tyrant (USA)) [1992/3 c20d^3 c21v^3 c20s^2] sturdy, good-bodied gelding: useful hurdler: fair form in novice chases in first half of season: stays 2½m: suited by give in the ground and acts on heavy: should win a race over fences. *J. T. Gifford*   c109 –

PROPLUS   11 ch.g. Proverb – Castle Treasure (Perspex) [1992/3 c25m^2 c23m^2 c25g* c24f^3 c25s* c25m^3 c25m^2 c24d^5 c28g^3 c34d c25f^{pu} c24f*] rangy, sparely-made gelding: fair handicap chaser: won at Southwell in August and September and Ludlow in May: suited by good test of stamina: probably acts on any going: blinkered 3 times. *J. A. C. Edwards*   c107 –

PROSEQUENDO (USA)   6 b.g. Robellino (USA) – Allegedly (USA) (Sir Ivor) [1992/3 20d^4 17d^2 16s* 17v^4 17v*] successful in handicap hurdles at Towcester in November and Lingfield (conditional jockeys) in December, on latter course showing improved form when scoring by 15 lengths: best form at around 2m but should stay at least 2½m: acts on heavy ground, won on firm on Flat in 1993. *M. Dixon*   107

PROSPECTING   5 b.g. Damister (USA) – Copt Hall Royale (Right Tack) [1992/3 21g^2] close-coupled, workmanlike gelding: won 2 points in 1993: poor novice hurdler: ran well at Wetherby in May: stays 21f: acts on good to firm ground. *M. W. Easterby*   81

PROSPECT OF WHITBY 7 ch.m. True Song – Looking For Gold (Goldfella) [1992/3 17dᵖᵘ 17d⁶ a16g 16f 17f] angular mare: of no account. *P. A. Pritchard* –

PROUD BISHOP 14 b.g. The Parson – Maximum Bonus (Wrekin Rambler) [1992/3 c26g] workmanlike gelding: one-time fair hurdler/chaser in Ireland: won a point in Britain in 1991: tailed off in hunter chase in March: sold 1,000 gns Ascot June Sales. *C. N. Nimmo* c–

PROUD CROZIER 11 b.m. Crozier – Lady Actress (Arctic Slave) [1992/3 c20sᵖᵘ c16s⁶ c27dᵖᵘ] leggy mare: no sign of ability in steeplechases. *S. G. Chadwick* c–

PROUD DRIFTER 6 br.g. Crash Course – Purlane (FR) (Kashmir II) [1992/3 25s 22v 20f] workmanlike ex-Irish gelding: brother to a winning Irish hurdler and half-brother to several minor winners: dam seemed to need long distances on Flat: placed in NH Flat races in 1991/2, when trained by N. Madden: no worthwhile form over hurdles. *K. C. Bailey* –

PROUD POINT 8 b.m. Over The River (FR) – High Town Jackie (David Jack) [1992/3 c26v⁴ c26vᶠ c27v² c24v² c27s³] rangy mare: modest novice chaser: sold 5,000 gns Doncaster May Sales: stays 27f: acts on heavy going. *Mrs P. N. Dutfield* c80 –

PROVING 9 ch.g. Proverb – Golden Strings (Perspex) [1992/3 20sᶠ 21v⁴ 22sᵖᵘ 22m] rangy gelding: lightly-raced novice hurdler: signs of ability only on second start, but ran poorly both subsequent starts: bred to stay well. *J. T. Gifford* –

PRUDENT PEGGY 6 br.m. Kambalda – Arctic Raheen (Over The River (FR)) [1992/3 22s² 22dᵖᵘ c21g⁴ 20s⁵ 22v² c16v³ 21v³ a20g² 22mᵖᵘ 21g⁵ 17s² 17d² 22dᵖᵘ] smallish, angular mare: second foal: sister to winning hurdler Earlham: dam unraced half-sister to a winning jumper: modest novice hurdler: poor novice chaser: effective at 2m and will stay beyond 2¾m: suited by plenty of give in the ground. *R. G. Frost* c73 84

PRUSSIAN GUARD 7 b.g. Lomond (USA) – Friedrichsruh (FR) (Dschingis Khan) [1992/3 17d⁵ 18s 22v 22v³ 22s³] good-topped gelding: half-brother to modest hurdler Baltic Sea (by Northfields): well beaten on Flat at 3 yrs: has shown ability over hurdles, best effort when third in conditional jockeys novice event at Newton Abbot in February on last start: will be suited by 3m: yet to race on a sound surface. *Mrs J. G. Retter* 90

PRY'S-JOY 9 b.g. Pry – Charmaines Joy (London Gazette) [1992/3 c24f* c24g* c21d³ c24g⁵ c26gᵖᵘ c21v* c21gᵖᵘ c21f⁴ c24f² c23m⁴] big, workmanlike gelding: modest handicap chaser: won at Huntingdon and Stratford early in season and at Worcester in April: stays 3m well: acts on any ground: usually held up. *F. Murphy* c96 –

PTOLEMY (FR) 6 gr.g. Persepolis (FR) – Rivoltade (USA) (Sir Ivor) [1992/3 20m² 20s] good-topped gelding: novice hurdler: best effort when second at Bangor in July: blinkered, tailed off at Tralee following month: stays 2½m: acts on good to firm ground. *Miss H. C. Knight* 82

PUCKS PLACE 12 ch.g. Midsummer Night II – Pirate's Cottage (Pirate King) [1992/3 22m] well-made gelding: fairly useful chaser at best, but sometimes refuses: novice hurdler: backward, well beaten in September, only outing of season: stays well: probably acts on any going: has refused 3 times (blinkered once). *Mrs S. J. Smith* c§§

PUFF PUFF 7 b.m. All Systems Go – Harmonious Sound (Auction Ring (USA)) [1992/3 17g⁴] winning 2¼m hurdler: no form for a long time: refused to race once. *Miss B. Sanders* – §

PUFFY 6 ch.g. Wolverlife – Eskaroon (Artaius (USA)) [1992/3 18d] smallish, sturdy gelding: lightly raced over hurdles: ran as though very much in need of race in November: likely to prove best at 2m. *M. Dods* –

PUKKA MAJOR (USA) 12 gr.g. Le Fabuleux – Pakeha (FR) (Zeddaan) [1992/3 c22vᴿ c27v⁵ c27mᴿ c27m⁵ 24vᵖᵘ] tall, rather lightly-made gelding: c§§ §§

one-time useful chaser: usually reluctant to race nowadays, and is one to leave alone. *T. Thomson Jones*

PUKKA SAHIB 6 b.g. Jalmood (USA) – So True (So Blessed) [1992/3 F16d2 F16s F17d] angular gelding: second foal: half-brother to fair miler and novice hurdler Keep Your Word (by Castle Keep): dam, very smart middle-distance performer, is half-sister to fair staying hurdler Accuracy: second in 17-runner NH Flat race at Ludlow in December, best effort: yet to race over hurdles or fences. *G. B. Balding*

PUNCHBAG (USA) 7 b.g. Glint of Gold – Cassy's Pet (Sing Sing) [1992/3 22s 18s3 17v* 17v* 21v 17d5 23d 17s* 16g 17d] leggy gelding: modest hurdler: won handicaps at Newton Abbot in December (seller, no bid), January and April: well below form last 2 starts: once-raced over fences: effective at 2m and stays 2½m: goes particularly well in the mud. *G. A. Ham*

c–
98

PUNCH'S HOTEL 8 ch.g. Le Moss – Pops Girl (Deep Run) [1992/3 c24d2 c26dF c25dF c26g2 c26dF] rather leggy ex-Irish gelding: half-brother to winning chaser Traprain Law (by Politico): dam, sister to very useful staying chaser Bob Tisdall, won NH Flat race and a point: maiden hurdler: winning pointer: second in novice chases, showing fair form: let down by his jumping otherwise over fences: stays well: blinkered first 2 starts 1991/2. *R. Rowe*

c90 x
–

PUNKY KNAVE 7 br.g. Rough Lad – Prince's Daughter (Black Prince) [1992/3 16g 22v5 20d] tall, workmanlike gelding: no worthwhile form over hurdles. *W. G. M. Turner*

–

PURA MONEY 11 b.g. Mugatpura – Bell Money (Even Money) [1992/3 c16g2 c18m4] strong, rangy gelding: fair handicap chaser: reportedly suffered laceration of hind leg in December, and wasn't seen out again: stays 2½m: acts on any going. *G. Richards*

c103
–

PURBECK DOVE 8 gr.g. Celtic Cone – Grey Dove (Grey Love) [1992/3 c21dpu c27s6] workmanlike gelding: novice hurdler: winning chaser: no show in handicaps in October: likely to prove best at around 2½m: acts on soft going: blinkered once in 1990/1. *K. Bishop*

c–
–

PURITAN (CAN) 4 b.c. Alleged (USA) – Conform (CAN) (Blushing Groom (FR)) [1992/3 21d3] leggy colt: thorough stayer on Flat, fair form: sold out of G. Harwood's stable 25,000 gns Newmarket Autumn Sales: promising first race over hurdles when third in juvenile event at Kempton in December: below best on Flat in 1993: will prove suited by test of stamina. *N. Tinkler*

95 p

PUSEY STREET BOY 6 ch.g. Vaigly Great – Pusey Street (Native Bazaar) [1992/3 16m* 17g 17m3 a16g 16f5] leggy, sparely-made gelding: has been tubed: won novice hurdle at Worcester in August, best effort: races only at around 2m: acts on good to firm going: winner over 1m on Flat in May. *J. R. Bosley*

80

PYEWACKET 5 gr.m. Belfort (FR) – Spartan Flutter (Spartan General) [1992/3 F16s F17m] half-sister to winning hurdler and novice chaser Spartan Ranger (by Lochnager): dam winning pointer: tailed off in mid-season NH Flat races: yet to race over hurdles or fences. *N. Tinkler*

Q

QAJAR 9 gr.g. Nishapour (FR) – Gravina (Godswalk (USA)) [1992/3 c27s4] smallish, sturdy gelding: winning hurdler/chaser: poor fourth over fences at Newton Abbot in August, only outing of season: suited by 3m: acts on heavy and good to firm going: sometimes blinkered. *K. C. Bailey*

c–
–

QANNAAS 9 br.g. Kris – Red Berry (Great Nephew) [1992/3 c24f*] sturdy gelding: one-time fairly useful hurdler: fair pointer, winner in May: 7-length winner of hunter chase at Huntingdon later in month: stays 3m: acts on firm and dead going: blinkered: suited by forcing tactics. *W. Smith*

c97
–

Sea Pigeon Handicap Hurdle, Doncaster—Qualitair Sound goes for home

Q-EIGHT (IRE)   5 b.h. Vision (USA) – Warning Sound (Red Alert) [1992/3 16m⁴ 17d⁶] placed over middle distances on Flat in 1991: poor form in novice hurdles at Worcester and Newton Abbot in August. *A. P. Jarvis*   –

QUADRIREME   4 b.g. Rousillon (USA) – Bireme (Grundy) [1992/3 16d⁵ 16f* 17m³ 17m* 16m*] leggy gelding: half-brother to winning hurdlers Dhoni (by Bustino), Pinisi (by Final Straw) and Trireme (by Rainbow Quest): fair middle-distance stayer on Flat: sold out of R. Hern's stable 27,000 gns Newmarket Autumn Sales: easy winner of novice hurdles at Wincanton in March and Newton Abbot and Uttoxeter in May: fairly useful form on last-named, and when finding little third start: will stay beyond 17f: acts on firm ground: type to make a useful handicapper. *J. A. B. Old*   123 p

QUAI D'ORSAY   8 b.g. Be My Guest (USA) – Noblanna (USA) (Vaguely Noble) [1992/3 20gᵖᵘ 20f* 20f⁴] smallish, well-made gelding: handicap hurdler: successful 5 times at Plumpton, including in March: ran creditably at Lingfield later in month: stays 2½m: acts on any going: sometimes blinkered: unreliable. *F. J. O'Mahony*   102 §

QUAKER BOB   8 b.g. Oats – Bobette (King Bob) [1992/3 22s⁵ 22s² c27vᵖᵘ] leggy gelding: lightly-raced novice hurdler: creditable second in handicap at Fontwell in November: pulled up lame in novice chase on same course in December: will be suited by further than 2¾m: acts on good to firm and heavy going. *P. J. Hobbs*   c–
93

QUALITAIR IDOL   4 b.f. Dreams To Reality (USA) – Village Idol (Blakeney) [1992/3 16vᵖᵘ 17f⁴ 18gᶠ 17mᶠ 20m 18m³] half-sister to winning hurdlers Hickling Squires (by Tachypous) and Sporting Idol (by Mummy's Game): poor maiden on Flat: sold out of J. Bottomley's stable 1,300 gns Doncaster October Sales: no worthwhile form over hurdles, including in sellers. *Mrs A. Knight*   –

QUALITAIR MEMORY (IRE)   4 ch.g. Don't Forget Me – Whist Awhile (Caerleon (USA)) [1992/3 16v* 16v² a16g⁴ 16s 16g³ 16g 17g² 16f² 22f² 21m³] leggy gelding: ungenuine maiden on Flat: won conditional jockeys novice selling hurdle at Warwick (no bid) in December: ran creditably most starts subsequently: probably stays 2¾m and acts on any going. *J. Akehurst*   80

QUALITAIR SON   5 b.g. Lochnager – Qualitairess (Kampala) [1992/3 16g⁶ 17sᵖᵘ 18m⁶] good-topped gelding: first foal: dam plating-class 1m winner on Flat: only a little sign of ability over hurdles. *B. Mactaggart*   –

QUALITAIR SOUND (IRE)   5 b.g. Mazaad – A Nice Alert (Red Alert) [1992/3 17s 17d* 16s 16v⁵ 16d² 17g 17m⁶ 17f⁶ 16g⁴ 16gᶠ] compact gelding: 128

carries condition: fairly useful handicap hurdler: won at Doncaster in December: in-and-out form subsequently: yet to race beyond 17f: acts on good to firm and dead going: held up: visored ninth start (respectable effort). *J. F. Bottomley*

QUARNDON 8 ch.g. Deep Run – Dame Lucy (Prince Hansel) [1992/3 c16gpu] lengthy, angular gelding: no sign of ability: sold 1,600 gns Ascot November Sales. *F. Coton* c– –

QUARRINGTON HILL 4 b.g. Mansingh (USA) – Stonebow Lady (Windjammer (USA)) [1992/3 17dpu] leggy gelding: half-brother to winning hurdler Wild Atlantic (by Welsh Saint): well beaten in 3 races on Flat: blinkered, no promise in novice selling hurdle at Stratford in October. *K. S. Bridgwater* –

QUARRY HOUSE (IRE) 5 b.g. The Parson – April Sal (Sallust) [1992/3 F17g4] leggy gelding: fourth foal: brother to winning staying chaser Red Amber: dam, poor maiden, stayed 1¼m: fourth of 16 in NH Flat race at Newbury in March: yet to race over hurdles or fences. *Major D. N. Chappell* –

QUARTZ HILL (USA) 4 b.g. Crafty Prospector (USA) – Mom's Mia (USA) (Great Mystery (USA)) [1992/3 17s] half-brother to several winners in North America: dam showed signs of a little ability: has been hobdayed and had soft palate operation: tailed off in juvenile hurdle at Perth in April. *R. R. Lamb* –

QUASSIMI 9 gr.g. Ahonoora – Silk Empress (Young Emperor) [1992/3 c20g4 c17g6 c21d5 c16s5 c24gpu] compact gelding: moderate handicap chaser: stayed 2½m: acted on any going: dead. *G. Richards* c90 –

QUAYAGE 10 ch.g. Quayside – Reaper's Pride (Artist's Son) [1992/3 c16f5 c16s3 c21d2 c24s2] sturdy, close-coupled gelding: winning hurdler/pointer: best effort in novice chases at Kempton in November, last outing: stayed 3m: acted on any ground: dead. *Mrs F. Walwyn* c95 –

QUEEN'S CHAPLAIN 9 b.g. The Parson – Reginasway (Flair Path) [1992/3 c26g2 c21g* c25s* c22mpu c26m5] strong, good-bodied gelding: hunter chaser nowadays: won maiden at Hexham in March and novice event at Wetherby in April: poor efforts last 2 starts: stays 3¼m: acts on good to firm and soft ground: blinkered once. *Mrs A. Swinbank* c92 –

QUEEN'S FAVOURITE 5 b.m. Sunyboy – Fit For A King (Royalty) [1992/3 16spu 17d] rather unfurnished mare: first foal: dam winning 2m hurdler: no sign of ability in novice hurdles. *J. Webber* –

QUEENS TOUR 8 b.h. Sweet Monday – On Tour (Queen's Hussar) [1992/3 22g 18spu 22m] small horse: sold 1,500 gns Doncaster October Sales: third in 2½m maiden on hurdling debut in 1991/2: has shown nothing since. *T. Kersey* –

QUELLE CHEMISE 7 b.m. Night Shift (USA) – Quaranta (Hotfoot) [1992/3 17spu 20dpu] workmanlike, deep-girthed mare: no sign of ability in novice hurdles: blinkered both starts in 1992/3. *G. H. Yardley* –

QUENTIN DURWOOD 7 gr.g. Mr Fluorocarbon – Donallan (No Mercy) [1992/3 17s4 16v2 c17gur c17s2 c17s3 c17g3] workmanlike gelding: fair hurdler, lightly raced: placed in small fields of novice chasers, showing modest form at best and jumping none too fluently: best at around 2m: acts on heavy going. *Mrs J. Pitman* c92 107

QUERRIN LODGE 7 b.g. Furry Glen – Opel Kadett (Steel Heart) [1992/3 c17fF c21f3 c20s4 c21dpu c21m5 23g] small, sturdy gelding: poor maiden hurdler/chaser: only form in 1992/3 on second outing: sold 2,100 gns Doncaster October Sales: blinkered twice in 1992/3. *Mrs A. Swinbank* c73 –

QUETTA'S GIRL 6 b.m. Orchestra – Quetta's Dual (Dual) [1992/3 18g 18m3] sturdy mare: fourth foal: half-sister to winning hurdlers Restandbethankful (by Random Shot) and Woodland Flower (by Furry Glen), latter also successful over fences: dam won over hurdles and fences in Ireland: third of 4 in poor novice hurdle at Southwell in October. *Mrs S. Lamyman* 67

QUICK AFFAIR 8 ch.g. Feelings (FR) – Unmentionable (Vulgan) [1992/3 c21g] lightly-raced pointer, modest form: well beaten in maiden hunter chase in May. *W. J. Tolhurst*　　c–

QUICK RAPOR 8 b.g. Rapid Pass – Dark Sensation (Thriller) [1992/3 c25s6 c24spu c26vbd c24f2] tall gelding: behind in novice hurdles: modest novice chaser: stays 3m: acts on firm going. *Capt. T. A. Forster*　　c83 –

QUICK REACTION 10 b.g. Main Reef – Swift Response (No Argument) [1992/3 c21s4 c24g3 c26g4 c24d4] smallish, well-made gelding: in frame in hunter chases in 1992/3, showing fair form: stays 3m: acts on firm and soft ground: blinkered nowadays: sometimes wears tongue strap. *Mrs E. H. Heath*　　c90 –

QUIDEST 10 ch.g. Ovac (ITY) – Gothic Arch (Gail Star) [1992/3 c25mpu c26mpu a22gpu] angular gelding: maiden hurdler: poor winning chaser: stays 3m: acts on firm ground: occasionally blinkered: poor jumper of fences. *A. Fowler*　　c– x

QUIET DAWN 7 b.m. Lighter – Lost In Silence (Silent Spring) [1992/3 25d c21mur c22vur 26m*] lengthy, sparely-made mare: poor hurdler: won seller at Wolverhampton (no bid) in March: let down by her jumping both starts over fences: stays 3¼m: suited by a sound surface. *J. S. King*　　c– 84

QUIETLY IMPRESSIVE (IRE) 5 b.m. Taufan (USA) – Way Ahead (Sovereign Path) [1992/3 16s 16s 16s4 16m3 16f5] small, leggy mare: moderate middle-distance performer at best on Flat: sold out of M. Bell's stable 2,400 gns Newmarket Autumn Sales: poor novice hurdler: best effort on good to firm ground. *Mrs P. Sly*　　75

QUIET MISS 4 b.f. Kind of Hush – Miss Acrow (Comedy Star (USA)) [1992/3 17m4 16m* 17s2 18m6 18f* 16d3 17v a20gpu 16d 16g6 22f 18g4] neat filly: half-sister to winning hurdlers Acrow Line (by Capricorn Line) and Acrow Lord (by Milford): dual 7f winner on equitrack at 2 yrs: attracted no bid after winning early-season juvenile selling hurdles at Worcester and Fontwell: ran poorly after sixth start: sold 1,100 gns Newmarket July Sales: likely to prove best around 2m: probably acts on any ground. *Mrs A. Knight*　　86

QUIET RIOT 11 b.g. Hotfoot – Tuyenu (Welsh Pageant) [1992/3 17g6 16d3 22s] strong, workmanlike gelding: lightly-raced novice hurdler: third in seller at Towcester in October: stays 21f: acts on any going: blinkered last 2 starts: won seller on Flat in 1993. *J. White*　　71 §

QUINBERRY 5 ch.m. Mossberry – Miss Harlequin (Manor Farm Boy) [1992/3 F16vpu 17dpu 17f 16f] angular mare: first foal: dam, poor maiden plater on Flat, no sign of ability in 2 races over hurdles: of little account. *R. C. Pugh*　　–

QUINTANA 11 ch.g. Quayside – Clerihan (Immortality) [1992/3 c21m3 c23gpu c21g3] close-coupled gelding: winning hurdler: poor novice chaser: took little interest second start, reportedly finished lame next time: sold 820 gns Doncaster October Sales: stays 2¾m: acts on dead ground, ran badly on soft: often visored or blinkered. *P. J. Bevan*　　c75 § –

QUIRINUS (CZE) 11 b.g. Hugben – Quartela (CZE) (Lyon) [1992/3 c34g* c29f4] tall Slovakian gelding: won Velka Pardubicka in October: jumped moderately, tailed off in handicap at Windsor in March: automatic top weight in void Martell Grand National, tailed off when pulled up after a circuit: stays extremely well. *K. A. Morgan*　　c?

QUORN COUNTRY 5 b.g. Lochnager – Periplus (Galivanter) [1992/3 F17g4 F16d] big, plain gelding: brother to NH Flat race winner Scottish Mountain: dam at her best at 2 yrs: showed a little ability in NH Flat races at Carlisle and Hexham in March: yet to race over hurdles or fences. *G. M. Moore*　　–

R

RAAWI 5 b.g. Be My Guest (USA) – Fast Motion (Midsummer Night II) [1992/3 20s3 20gpu 21vpu 20f4 21dpu 16s3 22g3 17g2 22m5 17g5] tall, leggy,　　89 §

angular gelding: modest hurdler: ran creditably when in frame in 1992/3, including in selling company: stays 2½m: probably acts on any ground: sometimes wears tongue strap: found nothing off bridle seventh outing: blinkered final one: inconsistent. *J. A. Glover*

RABA RIBA 8 gr.g. Oats – Erica Alba (Yukon Eric (CAN)) [1992/3 23d a24g² a22g* a20g* a22gᵘʳ a22g* a20g* 24s 22dᵖᵘ] leggy, good-topped gelding: improved form over hurdles when winning handicap at Lingfield in March: earlier an easy winner of 3 novice events on same course, last a conditional jockeys event: poor-jumping novice chaser: effective at 2½m and stays 3m: acts on firm ground (has run poorly on soft), goes really well on equitrack. *J. L. Spearing*

c– x
117

RABBIT'S FOOT 5 b.m. Touching Wood (USA) – Royal Custody (Reform) [1992/3 21sᵖᵘ 17s⁵ 20v a22g a20g⁴ 22m 22f 25g] small mare: poor middle-distance maiden on Flat: poor novice hurdler: best run at 17f on soft ground. *R. J. O'Sullivan*

–

RABSHA (IRE) 5 b.m. Taufan (USA) – Serraj (USA) (Seattle Slew (USA)) [1992/3 16d* 16g⁴] lengthy, shallow-girthed mare: won selling hurdle at Hexham in October: good fourth in novice hurdle at Ayr later in month: has raced only at 2m: acts on dead ground. *D. McCune*

77

RACECAGE GOLD CARD 6 ch.g. Camden Town – Polly Royal (Music Boy) [1992/3 18sᵖᵘ] angular gelding: novice hurdler: blinkered twice in 1990/1: looked thoroughly ungenuine once in 1991/2: one to leave alone. *T. Kersey*

– §

RACE TO THE RHYTHM 6 gr.m. Deep Run – Mother Cluck (Energist) [1992/3 F17g³ F16v 21s⁵ 24s⁵ 21v⁴ 24g⁶] sturdy mare: third in NH Flat race: poor form in novice hurdles: stays 3m: yet to race on top-of-the-ground. *J. A. C. Edwards*

78

RACING RASKAL 6 b.g. Dunphy – Raskaska (Aureole) [1992/3 16mᶠ] small gelding: winning stayer on Flat: poor novice hurdler: dead. *Capt. J. Wilson*

–

RADAR KNIGHT 5 b.h. Beldale Flutter (USA) – Eurynome (Be My Guest (USA)) [1992/3 22g⁴ 16v 18s] tall, shallow-girthed horse: maiden over hurdles: no form in 1992/3, ran as though something amiss first outing and moved badly to post last: stays 2¾m: acts on dead ground. *R. A. Bennett*

–

RADICAL LADY 9 b.m. Radical – Peaceful Madrigal (Blue Cliff) [1992/3 c23d² c28s⁶ c21s⁴ c24s⁴ c24d c25g² c24m⁶ c24d³ c25g⁵ c24d⁴ c25g²] sparely-made mare: fair chaser nowadays: creditable efforts when placed in 1992/3: stays well: acts on any going: blinkered sixth and seventh starts. *G. M. Moore*

c106
–

RADICAL REQUEST 10 br.g. Derring Rose – Kitty Laurence (Laurence O) [1992/3 c17v² c18s⁴ c18vᵖᵘ c17v² c21s² c21d⁵] close-coupled gelding: moderate chaser: generally ran creditably in 1992/3: stays 2½m: suited by give in the ground and acts on heavy going: blinkered once. *K. R. Burke*

c86
–

RADICAL VIEWS 8 b.g. Radical – Regency View (Royal Highway) [1992/3 c21s* c24d* c27mᶠ] robust gelding: type to carry condition: progressive hunter chaser, very useful already: successful at Warwick and Haydock (beat Mount Argus by 4 lengths) in February: will stay beyond 3m: acts on good to firm and soft ground: blinkered once: front runner: jumps soundly: will win more races. *Mrs A. M. Murray*

c120 p

RADIO CAROLINE 5 b.g. All Systems Go – Caroline Lamb (Hotfoot) [1992/3 18g] smallish gelding: pulled hard and tailed off 2 outings over hurdles. *M. Tate*

–

RADIO CUE 10 b.g. Wolverlife – Tell The Bees (Narrator) [1992/3 c17m² c23fᵘʳ] winning hurdler/hunter chaser: creditable second at Cheltenham in May: subsequently won a point: effective at around 2m and stays 25f: acts on firm ground: has won blinkered. *P. Bowen*

c94

RAEHILL   6 ch.m. Celtic Cone – Groundsel (Reform) [1992/3 F17v 20s
16s 17s] compact, rather plain mare: tailed off in novice events and claimer
over hurdles. *Mrs A. R. Hewitt*   –

RAFFLES TOWER   12 b.g. Tower Walk – Cloister Rose (Track Spare)   **c79**
[1992/3 c21g⁴ c16g² c17f c16g³ c17gᵘʳ c16gᶠ a16gᵖᵘ] leggy gelding: poor
novice hurdler/chaser: trained until after third start by B. Richmond. *I. L.
Curson*

RAFIKI   8 br.g. Show-A-Leg – Drink Time (Forlorn River) [1992/3 c23vᶠ   **c98**
c27vᶠ c16v* c17s³ c20fᵘʳ c17s² c21f³ c18g* c26m*] lengthy gelding: –
winning hurdler: moderate chaser: successful over fences in novice events
at Warwick and Exeter and handicap at Uttoxeter in 1992/3: effective at 2m
and stays 3¼m: acts on good to firm and heavy ground. *Mrs J. G. Retter*

RAGALOO   7 ch.g. Ragapan – Tangmalangaloo (Laurence O) [1992/3 21d   **c–**
c26vᵖᵘ c27v⁴ c27sᶠ c24gᶠ c26g³] sturdy gelding: novice hurdler/chaser: no   –
form: blinkered last 2 outings. *C. D. Broad*

RAGE   6 ch.g. Final Straw – Nasty Niece (CAN) (Great Nephew) [1992/3
16v 16g 20m⁴] workmanlike gelding: poor winning hurdler: has lost his
form: tried blinkered/visored. *D. A. Nolan*   –

RAGLAN LADY   6 ch.m. Carlingford Castle – Kate's Wish (Wishing
Star) [1992/3 20g 16d² 17g⁴] close-coupled mare: poor novice hurdler: ran   73
creditably in sellers last 2 starts: should stay beyond 17f: acts on dead
ground. *A. Bailey*

RAGLAN ROAD   9 b.g. Furry Glen – Princess Concorde (Great Heron   **c95**
(USA)) [1992/3 c23d* c21g* c25g⁴ c20d⁴ c21d⁴ c20f³ c25f⁶ c21g⁴] rangy   –
gelding: fair chaser: won novice events at Exeter in September and
Wincanton in October: ran creditably on several occasions subsequently:
sold 15,500 gns Doncaster May Sales: stays well: acts on good to firm and
dead ground. *Mrs P. N. Dutfield*

RAGTIME   6 b.g. Pas de Seul – Boldella (Bold Lad (IRE)) [1992/3 21gᵖᵘ]
neat gelding: winning hurdler: pulled up lame in August, and wasn't seen
out again: stays 2½m: acts on heavy ground. *A. S. Reid*   –

RAG TIME BELLE   7 ch.m. Raga Navarro (ITY) – Betbellof (Averof)   **c–**
[1992/3 16g 16m² 16d² 17d 16g⁶ 17m⁴ 17f⁶] leggy, lightly-made mare: 89
handicap hurdler/chaser: ran creditably when in frame early in season and at
Stratford in May: suited by sharp 2m: acts on good to firm and dead going:
has won when sweating: genuine: occasionally let down her jumping over
fences. *Miss A. J. Whitfield*

RAGTIME BOY   5 b.g. Sunyboy – Ragtime Dance (Ragstone) [1992/3
F17g³ F17d⁶] first foal: dam never ran: showed ability in NH Flat races at
Newbury in March and Sandown following month: yet to race over hurdles
or fences. *C. R. Barwell*   –

RAGTIME COWBOY JOE   8 gr.g. Alias Smith (USA) – Repel
(Hardicanute) [1992/3 17d 20d 23d⁵ 24v⁶ 24vᵖᵘ a20g* a22g* 23dᵖᵘ] sturdy   84
gelding: poor hurdler: won maiden claimer at Southwell in January and
novice handicap on same course following month: stays 2¾m: best on
fibresand: usually gets well behind early on. *J. Allen*

RAGTIME SONG   4 b.g. Dunbeath (USA) – Kelowna (USA) (Master
Derby (USA)) [1992/3 18gᵖᵘ] tailed off when pulled up in maiden hurdle at
Folkestone in March: won over 1½m on Flat subsequently. *R. Akehurst*   –

RAIKES RUSTLER   9 b.g. Ascertain (USA) – Lucky Apple (Levmoss)   **c76**
[1992/3 c25d³ c27dᵖᵘ c25v⁵ c26v⁴ c24d] rather sparely-made gelding: poor
novice chaser: stays well: acts on heavy going. *J. D. Hugill*   –

RAINBOW STRIPES   6 ch.g. Rainbow Quest (USA) – Pampas Miss
(USA) (Pronto) [1992/3 16g 16g⁵ 20fᵖᵘ] leggy gelding: modest hurdler at
best: no show in claimers in 1992/3, looking ungenuine in blinkers last time:
stays 2¾m: acts on dead going and fibresand. *B. S. Rothwell*   –

RAIN CHASER (NZ) 12 b.g. Reindeer – Neralate (NZ) (Stipulate) c–
[1992/3 c24s^{ur} c25d^6] lengthy, workmanlike gelding: winning pointer: of –
little account otherwise (blinkered 3 times over hurdles). *Philip Andrews*

RAIN DOWN 6 b. or br.g. Miner's Lamp – Queen McQuaid (Mick
McQuaid) [1992/3 21s^5 23s^5] sixth foal: half-brother to winning jumpers 78
Young River and Sid McQuaid (both by Over The River) and Castlesaffron
(by Laurence O): dam, lightly-raced novice hurdler, placed in NH Flat races:
showed ability in novice hurdles at Towcester in November and Folkestone
in December: will prove suited by a good test of stamina. *Mrs I. McKie*

RAINHAM 6 b.g. Sadler's Wells (USA) – Edge of Town (Habitat) [1992/3
16d 16s^3 17s^2 16s^3 16s^4 17d* 16d^6 17g^3 16s] good-bodied gelding: won novice 89
hurdle at Wolverhampton in February: ran poorly next and last starts: races
at around 2m: acts on soft ground: tends to sweat. *D. McCain*

RAIN MAN (NZ) 8 b.g. Noble Car (USA) – Lyoney (NZ) (Bally Royal) c79
[1992/3 c20g^3] well-made gelding: first sign of ability when third in maiden –
chase at Edinburgh in December. *M. D. Hammond*

RAIN MARK 12 b.g. Politico (USA) – Rightful Ruler (Sovereign Lord) c91
[1992/3 c21s^4 c21d^5 c21s^F c20s^6] lengthy, rather sparely-made gelding: fair –
hunter chaser: creditable effort on second start, well below form otherwise
in 1993: barely stays 3m: acts on good to firm and soft going. *M. G.
Chatterton*

RAIN-N-SUN 7 gr.g. Warpath – Sun Noddy (Tom Noddy) [1992/3 16g*
17g 16d^4 17g a20g 20f] plain gelding: won novice claiming hurdle at 80
Southwell in October: ran creditably next 2 starts, poorly last 3: best form at
around 2m: acts on dead ground: visored on 3 occasions, including
penultimate outing. *J. L. Harris*

RAIN SHADOW 4 b.f. Nearly A Hand – Rainbow Springs (Silly Season)
[1992/3 F16g^{pu}] close-coupled filly: first live foal: dam selling hurdler, best
at 2m: showed nothing in NH Flat race at Worcester in March: yet to race
over hurdles. *B. R. Millman*

RAISEAMILLION 5 b.g. Macmillion – Firbeck (Veiled Wonder (USA))
[1992/3 F16m^5 18g* 18g 17m^5 22d^3 20g*] useful-looking gelding: won 94 p
novice hurdles at Sedgefield in February and Bangor (handicap) in May:
effective at 2¼m and will stay beyond 2¾m: acts on dead ground: should
improve further. *G. M. Moore*

RAISE AN ARGUMENT 14 b.g. No Argument – Ten Again (Raise You c103
Ten) [1992/3 c23d^3 c24g^3 c20s] workmanlike, good-bodied gelding: shows –
traces of stringhalt: fairly useful hunter chaser nowadays: best effort of
season when third at Stratford in March on second start: stays 3¼m: suited
by give in the ground. *Mrs J. H. Docker*

RAITH HOMES 7 ch.g. Import – Gay Dawn (Gay Fandango (USA)) c–
[1992/3 18m 24s^4 c24d^F] rangy gelding: poor novice hurdler: winning –
chaser: doesn't stay 3m. *N. R. Mitchell*

RAITH PC 4 ch.g. Aragon – All Fine (Fine Blade (USA)) [1992/3 17m^5
18g^{pu} 16g 17s^{pu}] close-coupled gelding: behind in 2 races on Flat: signs of a 67
little ability over hurdles. *G. Richards*

RAKAIA RIVER (NZ) 6 b.g. Veloso (NZ) – Talon (NZ) (War Hawk)
[1992/3 21d^4] twice-raced novice hurdler: still green but showed ability 85
when fourth at Warwick in October: will be suited by further than 21f. *Capt.
T. A. Forster*

RALLEGIO 4 b.g. Alleging (USA) – Radigo (Ragstone) [1992/3 F16g
F16d] sixth foal: half-brother to winning hurdler Nouvelle Cuisine (by
Yawa): dam won twice over 1¼m: unplaced in NH Flat races in January: yet
to race over hurdles. *P. Monteith*

RALLYE STRIPE 9 gr.g. Buckskin (FR) – Petit Bleu (Abernant) c73
[1992/3 c18g^4 c17g c16m^F c21d^{pu} 16s^6 a20g^{pu} c16g c16g^{pu}] tall, leggy –
gelding: poor novice hurdler/chaser. *Mrs S. A. Bramall*

RALLYING CRY (IRE) 5 b.h. Last Tycoon – Clarina (Klairon) [1992/3 F17m4 F16g3 17g6 16g5 18m] good-bodied horse: poor form over hurdles: carries head high. *R. Allan* — 78

RAMALLAH 4 b.g. Ra Nova – Anglophil (Philemon) [1992/3 F17d2] seventh living foal: half-brother to a poor novice jumper by Neltino: dam, 2-y-o 6f winner, behind in selling hurdles: clear second of 21 in NH Flat race at Ascot in April: yet to race over hurdles. *J. White*

RAMBLE (USA) 6 ch.m. Highland Park (USA) – Hill Pleasure (USA) (What A Pleasure (USA)) [1992/3 a18g*] lengthy mare: won novice event at Southwell in January on second start over hurdles in fairly good style, but wasn't seen out again: likely to stay beyond 2¼m. *J. A. B. Old* — 87

RAMBLING SONG 13 ch.g. True Song – Tenella (Wrekin Rambler) [1992/3 c21g2 c19m2] strong gelding: carries plenty of condition: fairly useful chaser: good second at Exeter in September, second and better effort of season: best form at around 2½m: acts on heavy and good to firm ground: usually jumps well. *Capt. T. A. Forster* — c118

RAMLOSA (NZ) 9 b.g. Uncle Remus (NZ) – Sereniwai (NZ) (Golden Plume) [1992/3 c26grtr c25g3 c27sF c26vpu c27s4 c24dpu c24f3 22s4 27d3 22d4] rangy gelding: novice hurdler: has run in sellers: has shown ability over fences but is temperamental and one to be wary of: stays well: blinkered seventh outing. *D. H. Barons* — c82 § / 82

RAMOVA 4 b.f. Ra Nova – Maid of The Manor (Hotfoot) [1992/3 18vpu] third foal: dam never ran: showed nothing in juvenile hurdle at Fontwell in December. *R. Curtis* — –

RAMPAL (IRE) 4 b.g. Dancing Brave (USA) – Zinzara (USA) (Stage Door Johnny) [1992/3 18d 18vpu 16v6 17d 17m a21gpu] modest maiden on Flat: sold out of G. Wragg's stable 8,000 gns Newmarket Autumn Sales: seems of little account over hurdles and temperamental to boot: blinkered last outing. *D. J. Wintle* — – §

RAMPALLION 10 b.g. Riboboy (USA) – Rampage (Busted) [1992/3 c16m4 c16g3 c17g*] lengthy gelding: fair hurdler at his best: in frame in novice chases prior to winning one at Taunton in March: best form around 2m: acts on any going: blinkered once. *R. Rowe* — c94 / –

RAMSEY STREET 6 b.m. Mummy's Game – Green Jinks (Hardgreen (USA)) [1992/3 16vpu 17v 17v5 17vpu 17v5 23d3 21d] leggy mare: novice selling hurdler: easily best effort of season when third in claimer at Uttoxeter in March: stays 23f: acts on good to firm and dead ground. *B. J. Llewellyn* — 70

RAMSTAR 5 ch.g. Import – Meggies Dene (Apollo Eight) [1992/3 F17s 17s 16d 17m6] sturdy gelding: third foal: dam, winning hurdler/chaser, stayed 3m: poor form in novice hurdles: best effort on soft going. *Mrs J. Pitman* — 75

RANDOLPH PLACE 12 br.g. Pitpan – French Cherry (Escart III) [1992/3 c27mur] big, good-topped gelding: useful hurdler/chaser when trained by G. Richards: fairly useful form in points in 1993: frequently let down by his jumping in steeplechases (travelling comfortably when unseating rider 8 out in valuable hunter chase at Cheltenham in March): stays 25f: acts on heavy and good to firm going. *Ian D. Stark* — c– x / –

RANDOM CHARGE 12 ch.g. Random Shot – Patricia Brant (Reverse Charge) [1992/3 c21spu c21mpu] small, sturdy gelding: poor novice hurdler /chaser: won a point in May: blinkered once. *R. J. Alford* — c– / –

RANDOM PLACE 11 ch.g. Random Shot – Sicilian Princess (Sicilian Prince) [1992/3 c26m* c25gur c25mpu] compact gelding: hunter chaser: 100/1-winner at Warwick in February: failed to complete both subsequent starts: stays 3¼m: acts on soft and good to firm going. *Mrs R. Pocock* — c85

RANDOM PUSH 8 b.g. Push On – Artalla (USA) (Nantallah) [1992/3 c25gpu c21m] moderate winning pointer (temperamental): no promise in novice hunter chases. *P. Lewis* — c–

RAPID BOY 9 b. or br.g. Rapid River – Silver Thread (Sayfar) [1992/3 21g5 25fpu 16d c25gpu] workmanlike, plain gelding: of little account. *Mrs E. B. Scott* c– –

RAPID MOVER 6 ch.g. Final Straw – Larive (Blakeney) [1992/3 21vpu 17s 16g 16d3 20d6 20m2 16m* 18g 16g6] rather leggy gelding: won maiden hurdle at Edinburgh in February: ran well both subsequent outings: effective at 2m and should stay beyond 2½m: acts on soft and good to firm ground: blinkered last 3 starts: 11f winner on Flat in June. *D. A. Nolan* 84

RAPID ROSIE 5 ch.m. Noalto – Cora (Current Coin) [1992/3 17v 18spu a16gpu a22g4 a16g4 16g] leggy, sparely-made mare: poor novice hurdler: has run in sellers: tried blinkered/visored. *D. R. Laing* 67

RAPIER THRUST 11 ch.g. Fine Blade (USA) – Zoom Zoom (Bargello) [1992/3 c25g2 c25g5] leggy, angular gelding: one-time useful hurdler/ chaser: very lightly raced in recent seasons, but retains ability: better effort of 1992/3 when second at Market Rasen in October: stays 3m when conditions aren't testing: acts on any going: suited by forcing tactics: tends to jump to his right. *J. G. FitzGerald* c117 –

RAP UP FAST (USA) 4 b.g. Eskimo (USA) – Naomi's Flash (USA) (Ray Jeter (USA)) [1992/3 17m3 16gF 16g 16g 17m 16gpu 17d21spu 17f 17mF 18vpu 18m4] angular gelding: poor maiden on Flat: form over hurdles only on first start (trained until after then by C. Thornton): blinkered ninth to eleventh outings. *N. Waggott* 66

RARE BID (NZ) 10 br.g. Balak – So Rare (NZ) (Sobig) [1992/3 c23h* c19g* c19g3 c19m3] leggy, sparely-made gelding: comfortable winner of handicap chases at Exeter and Hereford in August: not raced after September: stays 25f: probably acts on any going: sketchy jumper: has found little. *R. J. Hodges* c102 –

RARE FIRE 9 ro.g. Rarity – El Diana (Tarboosh (USA)) [1992/3 c17d* c17d3 c26d3 c24g] workmanlike gelding: first form in steeplechases when winning novice handicap at Hexham in November: below that form subsequently: should stay beyond 17f: acts on dead going. *Mrs M. Reveley* c90 –

RARE LUCK 10 b.m. Rare One – Silly Millie (Menelek) [1992/3 c26g2 c26d3 c24g3 c26v2 c27vpu] smallish, sturdy mare: modest handicap chaser: best efforts of season on second and fourth starts: suited by test of stamina: acts on any going. *P. J. Jones* c91 –

RARFY'S DREAM 5 b.g. Dreams To Reality (USA) – Elbandary (Shirley Heights) [1992/3 17f a16g* a18g5] workmanlike gelding: best effort over hurdles when winning handicap at Lingfield in January: subject of stewards inquiry next time (made significant late progress under tender handling): subsequently reported to have sustained a leg injury: will prove best at around 2m: acts well on all-weather surfaces. *J. E. Banks* 101

RASCALETTO 6 b.m. Scallywag – Happy Returns (Saucy Kit) [1992/3 F17d] sister to a poor animal and half-sister to another by Bali Dancer: dam, fair pointer and winning hunter chaser, stayed well: ran out in a point in May: behind in NH Flat race at Hereford later in month: yet to race over hurdles or in a steeplechase. *A. P. James*

RASTA MAN 5 b.g. Ore – Bellino (Andrea Mantegna) [1992/3 F16s5 F17d5] leggy, unfurnished gelding: first foal: dam fair staying hurdler: fifth in NH Flat races at Warwick in February and Ascot in April: yet to race over hurdles or fences. *W. J. Musson*

RATHER SHARP 7 b.g. Green Shoon – Rather Special (Varano) [1992/3 c16vpu c24fF c18gpu c17v* c19f2 c20f4 c16m3] workmanlike gelding: sold 2,700 gns Ascot November Sales: won novice handicap chase at Towcester in April: good second at Hereford following month, best subsequent effort: stays 19f: acts on any going. *C. L. Popham* c82 –

RATHMORE 7 b.g. Carlingford Castle – Red-Leria (Red Regent) [1992/3 c21dpu c25spu c27vF c24v4 c26v4 c24g* c26g* c26d3 c26mur] plain, robust gelding: moderate hurdler: won novice chases at Lingfield in February and c101 –

Folkestone in March: thorough stayer: best form on a sound surface: dead. *N. A. Gaselee*

RATHVINDEN HOUSE (USA) 6 b.g. Hostage (USA) – Great c107 Verdict (USA) (Le Fabuleux) [1992/3 25d* 21s4 c22vur c21s* c21v2 c24d2 110 c26d2 c20s3] tall gelding: fair hurdler: won handicap at Kempton in October: also fair form over fences: won novice chase at Warwick in January: runner-up in similar events subsequently, good run in valuable novice handicap at Uttoxeter in March on penultimate start: stays 3¼m: acts on heavy going. *T. Thomson Jones*

RATIFY 6 br.g. Shirley Heights – Rattle (FR) (Riverman (USA)) [1992/3 16s4 16s6 16d2 17g*] small, well-made gelding: improved effort when 101 winning 5-runner handicap hurdle at Fakenham in March: ran in seller time before: likely to prove best at around 2m: acts on dead ground: sometimes wears tongue strap. *K. A. Morgan*

RAVECINO 4 ch.f. Ballacashtal (CAN) – Lemelasor (Town Crier) [1992/3 16g 16g 16gro 18g] sparely-made filly: poor performer on Flat and 71 § over hurdles: ran out third outing: barely stays 2m. *J. S. Haldane*

RAVEN'S GREEN 5 br.m. Relkino – Aingers Green (Nicky's Double) [1992/3 F16v F16g] first foal: dam winning hurdler/hunter chaser: well beaten in NH Flat races: yet to race over hurdles or fences. *D. Nicholson*

RAW COMMODITY (IRE) 5 b.g. Commonty (USA) – Warren Row (USA) (Balzac (USA)) [1992/3 F17g] good-topped gelding: first foal: dam, half-sister to a winning jumper, modest maiden here earlier won novice in Italy: tailed off in NH Flat race in March: yet to race over hurdles or fences. *S. E. Sherwood*

RAWHIDE 9 ch.g. Buckskin (FR) – Shuil Eile (Deep Run) [1992/3 c24gR c– 24d 24s c24dpu c24dpu 25g 22m4 24f5 27f] small, sturdy ex-Irish gelding: 104 one-time useful chaser: trained until after fifth start by M. Morris: fair form when fourth in handicap hurdle at Newton Abbot in May: stays well: acts on heavy going and good to firm: occasionally blinkered: reportedly broke blood vessel once. *Mrs J. G. Retter*

RAWYARDS BRIG 10 b.g. New Brig – Moonbreaker (Twilight Alley) c– [1992/3 c25dF c24mF] rangy, good sort: smart Irish hunter chaser in 1991, when trained by I. Ferguson: fell in early stages both starts in Britain: stays 3m: acts on heavy going. *Ronnie A. Bartlett*

RAYLES SAMARA 5 b.m. Prince of Peace – My Samantha (Pampered King) [1992/3 F18g 21vpu] non-thoroughbred mare: showed nothing in – mares NH Flat race and mares novice hurdle in the spring. *P. J. Hobbs*

RAYMYLETTE 6 ch.g. Le Moss – Myralette (Deep Run) [1992/3 20s 22d F16s* F20s* 21m2] rangy ex-Irish gelding: has scope: half-brother to 116 p very smart chaser Another Coral (by Green Shoon): dam, winning hurdler, from successful jumping family: won NH Flat races at Naas and Limerick in December: trained until after fourth start by M. Morris: shaped most encouragingly and quite useful effort when second to Trainglot in quite valuable novice hurdle at Warwick in February: likely to stay beyond 21f: sure to improve and win races over hurdles. *N. J. Henderson*

RAYON VERT (USA) 10 b.g. Green Dancer (USA) – Lerida (FR) c– (Riverman (USA)) [1992/3 c24fpu c26m3] big, leggy gelding: 2m novice – hurdler: no form over fences: acts on firm ground. *Mrs T. J. Millard*

RAZOO 6 b.g. Decent Fellow – Alice Johnston (Majetta) [1992/3 F18d 20g 25g4] brother to Irish NH Flat winner Achfairy and half-brother to 3 80 winners, including fair hurdler Churches Green (by Sassafras): poor form in novice hurdles: sold 4,200 gns Ascot June Sales: jumps sketchily. *J. A. C. Edwards*

RAZZLE DAZZLE BOY 11 ch.g. Some Hand – Fair Georgina (Silver c– Cloud) [1992/3 c19d6 c20fpu] compact gelding: winning hurdler/chaser: little – show in hunter chases in 1993: stays 21f: acts on firm going. *Ms L. H. Sheedy*

REACH ME NOT (IRE) 4 ch.f. Reach – Injaz (Golden Act (USA)) [1992/3 16s^{pu} 22s^{pu} 16v 17g^F] small, lightly-made filly: well beaten on Flat and over hurdles. *Mrs N. S. Sharpe* –

READY OR NOT 7 ch.g. Sunyboy – Flammula (Wrekin Rambler) [1992/3 c20s⁶ c21g²] fourth in maiden hurdle in 1990/1: having only second outing since when second in novice chase at Folkestone in February: stays 21f. *Andrew Turnell* **c90**

READY STEADY 11 ch.g. Bivouac – Very Merry (Lord of Verona) [1992/3 c25d⁵] workmanlike gelding: winning pointer/hunter chaser: well beaten at Kelso in February: stays 3m: acts on any going: jumps sketchily. *S. Friar* **c–**

READY TO DRAW (IRE) 4 ch.c. On Your Mark – Mitsubishi Art (Cure The Blues (USA)) [1992/3 18d⁴ 16s³] sparely-made colt: useful middle-distance plater on Flat: in frame in juvenile hurdle at Sedgefield in October and selling hurdle at Nottingham in November: stays 2¼m: acts on soft going. *Ronald Thompson* 79

REAL CLASS 10 b.g. Deep Run – Our Cherry (Tarqogan) [1992/3 c25g^{pu} c21s³ c24s³ c25g³ c25g³ c24s^F 21s*] strong, rangy gelding: type to carry condition: fair chaser, best effort of season on second start: won amateurs event over hurdles at Hexham in May: sold 8,000 gns Doncaster Sales later in month: stays well: acts on soft going: blinkered sixth outing: sometimes takes little interest. *G. Richards* **c106** 84

REAL HARMONY 7 ch.g. Le Bavard (FR) – Winning Wink (Milan) [1992/3 18d 26d⁴ c27v⁵ c21v^{pu}] lengthy ex-Irish gelding: fourth foal: dam unraced: NH Flat race winner: novice hurdler/chaser: well beaten in 1992/3. *R. J. O'Sullivan* **c–**

REALLY A RASCAL 6 b.g. Scallywag – Rockefillee (Tycoon II) [1992/3 F17g³] rangy gelding: first foal: dam, lightly-raced novice hurdler, daughter of a winning hurdler: in frame in a point in Ireland in 1992: third in 25-runner NH Flat race at Cheltenham in October: yet to race over hurdles or in a steeplechase. *D. R. Gandolfo* –

REALLY HONEST 12 b.g. He Loves Me – Whitethorn (Gulf Pearl) [1992/3 c17g^{ur}] leggy, sparely-made gelding: moderate 2m hurdler: behind when unseating rider sixth in hunter chase in March: acts on good to firm and dead ground. *D. Mills* **c–**

REAL PROGRESS (IRE) 5 ch.g. Ashford (USA) – Dulcet Dido (Dike (USA)) [1992/3 F17g⁴ 22g⁵ 16s* 17s² 17s² 21d² 17s] workmanlike, unfurnished gelding with scope: sixth foal: half-brother to Irish NH Flat race winner No Shouting (by Sayyaf) and a winner in Hong Kong: dam placed over 1¼m in Ireland: won 2 points in Ireland in 1992 and novice hurdle at Windsor in November: good second in novice hurdles afterwards, one of them a handicap: stays 21f: acts on soft ground: idles in front, and sometimes wanders under pressure. *P. J. Hobbs* 102

RECEIVE DOUBLE 6 b.g. Lighter – Levanter Rose (Levanter) [1992/3 16v^{pu} 17g^{pu}] small, compact gelding: tubed last start: no sign of ability. *Mrs S. D. Williams* –

RECIDIVIST 7 b.m. Royben – On Remand (Reform) [1992/3 c16d^{pu} c21g^{pu} 20d⁵ c16v⁴ c16s³ c17f³ c16s^F c17g^{pu} c17m⁴] workmanlike mare: winning hurdler: poor novice chaser: stays 2½m: acts on good to firm and soft ground: blinkered nowadays. *R. J. Hodges* **c80** 80

RECORD EDGE 6 ch.g. Roman Warrior – Record Red (Record Run) [1992/3 17d⁵] workmanlike gelding: poor novice hurdler/chaser: dead. *Mrs P. M. Joynes* **c–** 64

RECORDING CONTRACT 5 b.g. Song – Port Na Blath (On Your Mark) [1992/3 16f² 17g² 16g 18d 16d 16d^{ro} 16v⁵ 17g*] leggy, close-coupled ex-Irish gelding: first foal: dam won over 6f from 2 starts on Flat in Ireland: poor form over hurdles: trained until after third outing by B. Kelly: won seller at Doncaster (sold 5,000 gns, probably for export) in December: raced only at around 2m: best form on a sound surface. *J. Parkes* 82

RECTILLON 6 b.h. Rousillon (USA) – Rectitude (Runnymede) [1992/3 16m 17m⁴ 16g] smallish horse: only worthwhile form over hurdles when fourth in novice event at Huntingdon in August: blinkered, wandered under pressure last outing. *T. P. McGovern*   72

RED AMBER 7 ch.g. The Parson – April Sal (Sallust) [1992/3 c21g³ c24gᵘʳ c25s³ c27v* c24vᵖᵘ c24dF c23g* c26dF] tall, leggy, lengthy gelding: maiden hurdler: moderate form over fences: successful in novice events at Fontwell in December and Worcester (very fortunate) in March: suited by long distances: acts on heavy ground: blinkered last 2 starts. *S. E. Sherwood*   c91 –

RED BEACON 6 b.g. Red Sunset – Mount of Light (Sparkler) [1992/3 21g] poor form on Flat at 2 yrs: showed nothing in March on hurdling debut. *J. L. Goulding*   –

RED BEAN 5 ch.g. Ginger Boy – Pharona (Pharaoh Hophra) [1992/3 17v⁵ a16g³ a16g* 17g⁵ 16f³ 17f²] strong, rangy gelding: chasing type: moderate form over hurdles: won maiden at Lingfield in February: good efforts in 3 subsequent starts: should stay beyond 17f: acts on firm ground and on equitrack. *J. O'Donoghue*   86

RED BEAVER 5 ch.g. Nearly A Hand – Water Eaton Gal (Legal Eagle) [1992/3 17v 22vᵖᵘ] sturdy, angular gelding: first foal: dam, winning selling hurdler, best at 2m: no sign of ability in novice hurdles in December and January. *P. R. Hedger*   –

REDCLYFFE (USA) 5 b.g. Secreto (USA) – Regal Heiress (English Prince) [1992/3 17v 22v 18v] compact gelding: little promise over hurdles, including in a selling handicap. *R. G. Frost*   –

RED COLUMBIA 12 ch.g. St Columbus – Red Tan (Crespin Rouge) [1992/3 c25m⁵ c17d³ c27dF c17mᵖᵘ a24gᵖᵘ c22g² c23m] tall, good-bodied gelding: handicap chaser: sold out of M. Wilkinson's stable 4,000 gns Ascot November Sales after first start: placed in amateur events at Sedgefield in January and Fakenham in May, easily best efforts of season: stays well: acts on good to firm and soft ground: usually a sound jumper: sometimes blinkered in 1990/1. *F. Coton*   c82 –

REDGRAVE GIRL 11 b.m. Deep Run – Cool Girl (Menelek) [1992/3 18fᵇᵈ c16fᵖᵘ 16gᵇᵈ 17g 16d 20d⁶ 16v³ 16v 16d 17g* 18d⁵] small, good-quartered mare: fair hurdler nowadays: won mares handicap at Taunton in April: showed nothing on chasing debut: probably stays 2¾m: acts on any going: sometimes finds little and hangs left. *K. Bishop*   c– 103

RED INK 4 ch.g. Blushing Scribe (USA) – Pink Robber (USA) (No Robbery) [1992/3 17d a16g² a16g³ a16g⁴] neat gelding: maiden plater on Flat when trained by J. Sutcliffe: best effort over hurdles when second in maiden at Lingfield in January: yet to race beyond 17f: acts on equitrack. *J. R. Jenkins*   84

RED JACK (IRE) 4 b.g. Red Sunset – Rockeater (Roan Rocket) [1992/3 17g 18dF 16s* 18s⁴ 16s³ 20vᵖᵘ] leggy gelding: plating-class maiden at best on Flat: won selling hurdle at Towcester (no bid) in November: ran well in non-sellers next 2 starts, poorly on last (February): stays 2¼m: acts on soft going. *J. Akehurst*   96

RED JAM JAR 8 ch.g. Windjammer (USA) – Macaw (Narrator) [1992/3 17m⁶ 16f* 16g⁴] sturdy gelding: won novice hurdle at Worcester in September: ran creditably (though put head in air under pressure) later in month: seems suited by sharp 2m: acts on firm going: sold 2,000 gns Doncaster June Sales. *J. Mackie*   95

RED RING 6 br.g. Auction Ring (USA) – Rosalie II (Molvedo) [1992/3 c17d³ c20g c21m³ c26v⁵] workmanlike gelding: fair hurdler: poor form in novice chases: best form at 2m: acts on good to firm and soft ground. *J. Webber*   c80 –

RED RONDO 9 ch.g. Rontino – Ivy Hill (Cantab) [1992/3 c21d⁶ c23v³ c21s⁴ c21s⁴ c24d² c25m²] sturdy gelding: modest handicap chaser: c96 ?

generally ran creditably in 1992/3: sold 7,500 gns Ascot June Sales: stays 25f, at least when conditions aren't testing: acts on heavy and good to firm going: usually front runner: jumps boldly but inclined to make the odd mistake. *J. A. C. Edwards*

RED SCORPION 9 b.g. Furry Glen – Glamorous Night (Sir Herbert) [1992/3 c18m3 c18s2 c21mF c17fF 18gpu 23g2 23d6 20g 22gpu] leggy gelding: poor novice hurdler/chaser: trained first start by T. Caldwell: sold 3,200 gns Doncaster May Sales: stays 23f: acts on good to firm and soft ground: sometimes visored. *W. Williams*   c75   68

RED SOMBRERO 4 ch.g. Aragon – Hat Hill (Roan Rocket) [1992/3 16sF 16d 17g 17f] small gelding: half-brother to winning hurdler Nore Hill (by Town And Country): plating-class form on Flat: sold privately out of G. Cottrell's stable 2,800 gns Ascot November Sales: of little account over hurdles. *R. Brotherton*   –

RED TEMPEST (IRE) 5 b.g. Red Sunset – Msida (Majority Blue) [1992/3 16g 18g 21s 17dpu] close-coupled gelding: poor novice hurdler. *J. S. Goldie*   72

REDUNDANT PAL 10 ch.g. Redundant – Palesa (Palestine) [1992/3 c16spu c20spu c16s5 c21g4 c20f2 c20spu] leggy, plain ex-Irish gelding: very useful performer on his day: only form of season when second of 3 finishers in Melling Chase at Aintree in April: effective from 2m to 2½m: probably acts on any going: blinkered nowadays: doesn't find much off bridle and needs holding up for as long as possible. *Martyn Meade*   c141 ?   –

RED UNDER THE BED 6 b.g. Cardinal Flower – Roman Flyer (Perhapsburg) [1992/3 c27g* c27d2 c23vur c24s4] workmanlike gelding: no sign of ability over hurdles: won hunter chase at Sedgefield in February: easily best effort when clear second on same course in April: stays 27f: acts on dead ground. *Mrs S. A. Bramall*   c103   –

REEDFINCH 4 b.g. Rabdan – Tangara (Town Crier) [1992/3 F16m] first foal: dam unraced: mid-divison in 24-runner NH Flat race at Warwick in May: yet to race over hurdles. *O. Sherwood*   –

REEF LARK 8 b.g. Mill Reef (USA) – Calandra (USA) (Sir Ivor) [1992/3 17d3 22g3 22d2 22d5 c16d3 c16d3 c21d5 c20g3 c17g6 22m6] angular, sparely-made gelding: selling hurdler: modest novice chaser: needs further than 2m nowadays and stays 2¾m: probably needs give in the ground: well beaten when blinkered: consistent. *D. McCune*   c87   84

REEL OF TULLOCH (IRE) 4 b.g. Salmon Leap (USA) – Miss Sandman (Manacle) [1992/3 16g6 17s3 16v2 17s] leggy gelding: changed hands 8,000 gns Newmarket Autumn Sales: poor form in juvenile events and seller first 3 starts over hurdles: will stay further than 17f: blinkered third start: winner over 15f on Flat in 1993. *P. C. Haslam*   79

REGAL ESTATE 9 ch.g. Royal Palace – Salira (Double Jump) [1992/3 c27g* c27d2 c26s* c33vbd c27d* c33gF c27d4] tall gelding: winning hurdler: fair handicap chaser: successful at Sedgefield in October and February and Carlisle in between: thorough stayer: acts on heavy and good to firm going. *R. Earnshaw*   c104   –

REGAL ROMPER (IRE) 5 b.h. Tender King – Fruit of Passion (High Top) [1992/3 16s 16d3 16g* 17d4 16d* 16s5 16d6 17d 16s3 16g] small, sturdy horse: poor maiden on Flat: successful in handicap hurdles at Hexham in October (conditional jockeys seller, no bid) and November (novice event): ran creditably most other starts: raced only at around 2m: acts on soft ground. *Mrs S. J. Smith*   96

REGAN (USA) 6 b.m. Lear Fan (USA) – Twice A Fool (USA) (Foolish Pleasure (USA)) [1992/3 25m2 c21m2 24d4 21d c21d2 c21s* c26s6 c16d* c24m3 c21g6] sparely-made mare: modest hurdler: won mares novice chases at Sedgefield in December and Wetherby (handicap) in February, showing modest form: effective at 2m and stays 25f: acts on good to firm and soft ground: jumps soundly. *J. H. Johnson*   c92   92

REGARDLESS 11 b.g. Quayside – Bel Arbre (Beau Chapeau) [1992/3 **c100** c24g*] close-coupled gelding: successful in 2 points prior to winning hunter – chase at Fakenham in May: stays 25f: acts on soft going. *C. D. Dawson*

REGENT CROSS 8 b.g. Prince Regent (FR) – Holy Cross **c–** (Arcticeelagh) [1992/3 c24fur] strong, good-bodied gelding: winning – hurdler/chaser: fairly useful form in points in 1993: behind when unseating rider thirteenth in hunter chase in May: stays 2½m: acts on firm and dead going. *Mrs R. Wormall*

REGENT LAD 9 b.g. Prince Regent (FR) – Red Laser (Red God) [1992/3 17d* 17d2 17d 16d 16sF] leggy, angular gelding: fair handicapper at around **100** 1m on Flat: won novice hurdle at Stratford in October: ran well when second in similar event at Ascot following month, easily best effort subsequently: likely to prove best around 2m: yet to race on a sound surface. *Miss L. C. Siddall*

REGGAE BEAT 8 b.g. Be My Native (USA) – Invery Lady (Sharpen Up) **c108** [1992/3 c16g* c17d* c16s3 c21g3 c18g] leggy gelding: fair hurdler: – successful in novice chases at Catterick and Doncaster in first half of season: ran badly in 2 of his 3 subsequent starts: barely stays 2½m: acts on firm and dead ground: sometimes has tongue tied down: jumps well. *I. Campbell*

REGGIE 11 b.g. Impecunious – Vixens Surprise (Eastern Venture) **c77** [1992/3 c21gpu c26m4 c27f3] rangy gelding: modest pointer/maiden hunter – chaser: visored, in frame at Folkestone and Fontwell in May: stays 27f: acts on firm going. *R. H. Wilkinson*

REHAB VENTURE 9 ch.g. Deep Run – Hansel's Princess (Prince **c96** Hansel) [1992/3 c22g3 c21d2 c22spu] leggy, rather sparely-made gelding: – moderate handicap chaser: creditable second at Uttoxeter in November: pulled up lame later in month, and wasn't seen out again: stays 2¾m: acts on soft going. *D. Esden*

REILTON 6 b.g. Cure The Blues (USA) – Chanson de Paris (USA) (The Minstrel (CAN) [1992/3 18m3 17m2 18g* 17d2 18d5 16v3] modest hurdler: **88** won conditional jockeys seller at Sedgefield (no bid) in October: sold out of J. Parkes's stable 2,600 gns Doncaster November Sales after fifth outing: stays 2¼m: acts on heavy and good to firm going: consistent. *A. L. Forbes*

REJOINUS 8 ch.g. Blue Refrain – Teesdale (Aggressor) [1992/3 c20s3 **c104** c20dF c21s3 c17s* c21s4 c20g3 c21s3] big, workmanlike gelding: – lightly-raced novice hurdler: fair chaser: won maiden event at Leicester and handicap at Carlisle in January in good style: below form last 3 starts: effective at 17f and 21f: acts on soft ground: jumps soundly. *A. P. Stringer*

REKLAW 6 b.g. Hard Fought – Rubina Park (Ashmore (FR)) [1992/3 18g5 16m2 16d 18d 17d 20m4 25mpu] plating-class maiden on Flat: poor form, **74** including in sellers, over hurdles: sold out of M. Hammond's stable 1,500 gns Doncaster January Sales after fourth start: stays 2½m: best form on a sound surface: blinkered fourth and last 2 outings. *S. G. Chadwick*

RELATED SOUND 7 b.g. Uncle Pokey – Darling June (Midsummer Night II) [1992/3 21g* 20m4 20s4 20g3 22m6] angular, plain gelding: won **72** novice handicap hurdle at Southwell in August: ran creditably next 3 starts: not seen out after October: stays 21f: acts on good to firm ground: blinkered twice in 1989/90: front runner. *M. F. Barraclough*

RELEKTO 11 b.g. Relko – Heaven Knows (Yellow God) [1992/3 c21d2 **c109** c21d3 c21g3 c20s2 c27gpu] good-topped, workmanlike gelding: useful – hunter chaser: ran creditably all completed starts in 1993: broke down badly last outing: stays 2½m: acts well with plenty of give in the ground. *M. J. Felton*

RELKONI 6 b.g. Relkino – Only Miranda (Typhoon) [1992/3 20m 21fpu] no sign of ability. *M. Williams* –

RELTIC 6 b.g. Celtic Cone – Releta (Relkino) [1992/3 22dpu 20spu 21v4 20v5 a24g5 21sur 25g* 24f2 25m4] workmanlike gelding: poor form over **78**

hurdles: won conditional jockeys novice selling handicap at Taunton (no bid) in April: ran well in non-sellers subsequently: stays well: acts on any ground: tried visored. *C. D. Broad*

RELUCTANT SUITOR 4 ch.g. Shy Groom (USA) – Belaka (Beldale Flutter (USA)) [1992/3 F16m* F17m6 F17f4] 4,600 2-y-o: close-coupled gelding: first foal: dam fair maiden best at 2 yrs: won NH Flat race at Edinburgh in February: subsequently ran well in valuable similar events at Cheltenham and Aintree: yet to race over hurdles. *M. D. Hammond*

RELUGAS 6 b.g. Relkino – Galosh (Pandofell) [1992/3 F17g F17g] strong gelding: brother to modest hurdler/chaser Ink Splash and half-brother to 3 winners: dam needed long distances: fell at the first in a point in 1992: behind in NH Flat races: yet to race over hurdles or in a steeplechase. *Mrs A. Price*

REMIND ME ON (IRE) 5 b.g. Remainder Man – Bettons Rose (Roselier (FR)) [1992/3 21m3] compact gelding: has shown little over hurdles. *J. Wade*

REMITTANCE MAN 9 b.g. Prince Regent (FR) – Mittens (Run The c163 Gantlet (USA)) [1992/3 c21d* c21s*]

Race number thirteen over fences proved unlucky for the Champion Two-Miler Remittance Man. While warming up for Boxing Day's King George VI Chase in the Peterborough Chase at Huntingdon in November he

Peterborough Chase, Huntingdon —
Remittance Man has to work hard to land the spoils
and is subsequently found to be injured

injured his off-fore tendon and, as a result, was laid off for the rest of the season. The injury is thought not to be serious, but it was felt that he's too good a horse to take risks with. Remittance Man has won twelve of his races over fences, including the Arkle Challenge Trophy in 1991 and the Queen Mother Champion Chase in 1992, the latter from those two stalwarts Katabatic and Waterloo Boy. His one defeat came behind The Fellow and Docklands Express in the King George of 1992, not in the Peterborough Chase, although he wasn't impressive in the latter and would probably have been beaten had Uncle Ernie kept his feet at the last. Prior to Huntingdon, Remittance Man had begun his season well, easily accounting for his only serious rival Kings Fountain in the Desert Orchid South Western Pattern Chase at Wincanton.

Remittance Man (b.g. 1984)	Prince Regent (FR) (br 1966)	Right Royal V (br 1958)	Owen Tudor
			Bastia
		Noduleuse (b 1954)	Nosca
			Quemandeuse
	Mittens (b 1977)	Run The Gantlet (b 1968)	Tom Rolfe
			First Feather
		Aunt Eva (b 1971)	Great Nephew
			Calleva

That Remittance Man sustained an injury at some stage of the race may be enough to explain his performance at Huntingdon. It is worth noting, though, that the ground was softer than any on which he has shown his best form, and we would have grave reservations about backing him in a major race run on soft. He is almost certainly suited by a sound surface. Others would have reservations about him over three miles, in view of his performance in the 1992 King George. Made favourite, he looked all over the winner turning for home having gone on five out, only to be caught approaching the last and eventually beaten three and a half lengths by The Fellow. However, he might have needed the run. His preparation hadn't been trouble free, and his sole previous public outing had turned into nothing more than an exhibition round. We've no doubts about his staying three miles; judged on his pedigree he has a reasonable chance of staying further, but connections give the strong impression that the Queen Mother Champion Chase rather than the Gold Cup will be the Cheltenham target again. Remittance Man's sire the Irish Derby winner Prince Regent died in 1993. He had a quiet season with his jumpers, the pick of them after Remittance Man being stable-companion Tinryland. Mittens, the dam of Remittance Man, was also represented in the latest season by the much-improved Sillars Stalker (by the sprinter Stalker), three times a winner and a very good second in the Coral Cup at Cheltenham: there's a horse that will stay three miles for you. *N. J. Henderson*

RENAGOWN   10 b.g. Pragmatic – Midnight Oil (Menelek) [1992/3 c17g² c24mᶠ c25g⁶ c17g⁵ c21m* c22f c21vᵘʳ c20fᶠ] rangy gelding: fairly useful chaser in Ireland: sold out of J. FitzGerald's stable 9,600 gns Doncaster November Sales after first start: won hunter chase at Carlisle in March: stayed 3m: probably acted on any going: blinkered final outing: dead. *S. G. Chadwick*   c104 –

RENTA KID   4 b.f. Swing Easy (USA) – Dewberry (Bay Express) [1992/3 18mᵖᵘ] winner over 5f at 2 yrs, but well beaten on Flat since: blinkered, no promise in juvenile hurdle at Exeter in September. *P. J. Hobbs*   –

RENT DAY   4 b.f. Town And Country – Notinhand (Nearly A Hand) [1992/3 F18s] second foal: dam, unraced, from successful jumping family: soundly beaten in NH Flat race at Exeter in January: yet to race over hurdles. *J. W. Mullins*   –

REPEAT THE DOSE   8 b.g. Abednego – Bahia de Palma (No Argument) [1992/3 c16d⁵ c25s⁵ c24vᵖᵘ c20s* c21s³ c24d³ c21mᵖᵘ c20sᵖᵘ] lengthy gelding: useful chaser: returned to form to win handicap at Ascot in January: also ran well next 2 starts, but no other form in 1992/3: stays 3m: acts on good to firm and soft ground: sometimes let down by his jumping. *T. J. Etherington*   c134 –

RE-RELEASE 8 ch.m. Baptism – Release Record (Jukebox) [1992/3 c 106
c20v⁴ c21v* c26d⁵ c25m⁴ c25fᵘʳ c24g³] workmanlike mare: useful hurdler: –
fair chaser: won conditional jockeys handicap at Windsor in February, best
effort of season: stays 21f: acts on good to firm and heavy ground:
sometimes visored or blinkered: sketchy jumper. *M. C. Pipe*

RESISTING (USA) 5 b.g. Desert Wine (USA) – Fool's Miss (USA)
(Saltville) [1992/3 24dᵖᵘ 18m 18s 22gᵖᵘ] leggy gelding: of little account and – §
temperamental to boot: blinkered last outing. *M. C. Chapman*

RESTLESS MINSTREL (USA) 4 b.g. The Minstrel (CAN) –
Dismasted (USA) (Restless Native) [1992/3 17f a16g⁶] modest middle- –
distance maiden on Flat: sold out of L. Cumani's stable 4,700 gns
Newmarket September Sales: well beaten in novice hurdles in May. *J. E.
Banks*

RESTOWEST 6 ch.g. Hotfoot – Mondoodle (Monsanto (FR)) [1992/3
17d 19m 22dᵖᵘ 22s] small gelding: of little account: blinkered last start. *Mrs –
J. Wonnacott*

RETAIL RUNNER 8 b.g. Trimmingham – Deep Rose (Deep Run) c 118
[1992/3 c20g* c20d c20s* c20s³ c21d] tall, close-coupled gelding: maiden –
hurdler: won 2 novice chases at Ascot in first half of season: also ran well
when third in handicap there in January: stays 2½m: acts on soft ground:
headstrong and best allowed to bowl along: usually a bold and accurate
jumper. *J. T. Gifford*

REVE DE VALSE (USA) 6 ch.h. Conquistador Cielo (USA) – Dancing
Vaguely (USA) (Vaguely Noble) [1992/3 22m⁶] compact horse: smart –
juvenile hurdler in 1990/1: well below that form since: beaten long way out
in September, only outing of 1992/3: should stay further than 2¼m: acts on
good to firm and soft ground. *Denys Smith*

REVE EN ROSE 7 b.m. Revlow – Bois de Rose (Indian Ruler) [1992/3
23s⁵ 21v³ 18s] leggy mare: moderate hurdler: effective at 2m and stays 23f: 90
acts on good to firm and heavy going. *M. D. McMillan*

Grosvenor Insurance Handicap Chase, Ascot—
Repeat The Dose (No. 3) about to go clear

Guinness Festival Bumper, Cheltenham—
Rhythm Section (near side) leads home an Irish 1-2-3

REVEL   5 ch.g. Sharpo – Waltz (Jimmy Reppin) [1992/3 17d 21spu] modest sprinter at best on Flat, no form in 1992: tailed off in amateur events over hurdles in the spring. *T. M. Gibson* —

REVILLER'S GLORY   9 b.g. Hittite Glory – Zulaika Hopwood (Royalty) [1992/3 c21d3 c23s6 c21s2 c25g3 c23m4] tall gelding: novice hurdler: moderate novice chaser: may prove best at around 2½m: acts on soft going, possibly unsuited by good to firm: sometimes sweating and edgy. *P. Beaumont*   c88 —

REVTON   6 ch.m. Michael's Revenge – Vivyiki (Kirtonian) [1992/3 25dpu 21s] NH Flat race winner: no form over hurdles: blinkered last start. *P. T. Dalton* —

REX TREMENDA   8 b.g. Bustino – Elfinaria (Song) [1992/3 c25g4 c25spu] strong gelding: winning pointer: poor maiden hurdler/steeplechaser. *J. D. Telfer*   c74 —

REXY BOY   6 b.g. Dunbeath (USA) – Coca (Levmoss) [1992/3 20s* 20g4 20g* 20g4 20m6 22d 22s 21g5] sturdy gelding: won novice handicap hurdles at Market Rasen and Edinburgh in first half of season: twice ran creditably in second half: stays 2¾m: acts on soft going. *W. L. Barker*   80

REZA   5 gr.g. Superlative – Moon Charter (Runnymede) [1992/3 17mrtr 17d 18g 18d 17g 20d a20g2 a20g 17m5 a16g5] workmanlike gelding: poor novice hurdler: stays 2½m: acts on fibresand and good to firm ground: irresolute, and needs to dominate. *J. L. Eyre*   73 §

RHODE ISLAND RED   10 ch.g. Henbit (USA) – Embarrassed (Busted) [1992/3 c24gpu c24m4 c24spu c24g4 c27m6 c24f3 c27f3 c22m6] sturdy, close-coupled gelding: modest handicap chaser: third in amateurs event at Fontwell in May, penultimate and easily best effort of season: stays 3¼m: acts on any going: visored once: inconsistent. *A. Moore*   c84 § — §

RHOMAN COIN (IRE)   5 br.g. Rhoman Rule (USA) – Kylemore Abbey (Junius (USA)) [1992/3 17d4 21s3 22d3 26spu a24g 22g2 18m2 17d2 22g2 21f3]   93 smallish, angular gelding: modest hurdler: generally ran creditably in 1992/3, including in sellers: sold 8,200 gns Doncaster May Sales: stays 2¾m: acts on dead and firm ground: blinkered last 5 starts: sometimes looks none too keen. *B. S. Rothwell*

RHOSSILI BAY 5 b.g. Idiot's Delight – Hitting Supreme (Supreme Sovereign) [1992/3 F16f²] fifth foal: brother to winning Chaser Punching Glory: dam unraced: second in 15-runner NH Flat race at Haydock in May: yet to race over hurdles or fences. *Mrs M. Reveley*

RHU NA HAVEN 9 b. or br.g. Le Bavard (FR) – Shuil Dubh (Black   **c78** Tarquin) [1992/3 c18m³ c22g³ c25s⁴ c24m³ c22g⁵ c25g⁵ c25g³] leggy   **–** gelding: poor novice chaser: trained until after second start by D. McCain: sold 6,000 gns Ascot June Sales: stays 3m: acts on soft and good to firm ground. *R. K. Aston*

RHYMING PROSE 5 b.m. Rymer – Emerin (King Emperor (USA)) [1992/3 F17d] half-sister to several winners, including Irish jumper Lucky Knight (by Rarity): dam won twice over 6f: tailed off in NH Flat race at Ascot in April: yet to race over hurdles or fences. *J. A. B. Old*

RHYTHM SECTION (IRE) 4 ch.g. Where To Dance (USA) – Lady Fandet (Gay Fandango (USA)) [1992/3 F16d² F16d* F17m*] 21,000Y: compact gelding: fourth foal: half-brother to fair Irish middle-distance maiden Zoria (by Tender King): dam, from family of Oaks winner Circus Plume, ran 4 times at 2 yrs: won NH Flat races at Leopardstown in January and Cheltenham (Guinness Festival Bumper, by ½ length from Heist) in March: yet to race over hurdles. *J. H. Scott, Ireland*

RIBOKEYES BOY 11 b.g. Riboboy (USA) – Molvitesse (Molvedo) [1992/3 17m 17vᵖᵘ] sparely-made gelding: inconsistent selling hurdler: **–** showed nothing in 1992/3: stays 2¼m: acts on good to firm and heavy going. *A. R. Davison*

RIBOVINO 10 b.g. Riboboy (USA) – The Guzzler (Behistoun) [1992/3   **88** 16d⁶ 17v² 22d* 21s 16v] leggy, sparely-made gelding: selling hurdler nowadays: won handicap at Ludlow (no bid) in December: ran poorly afterwards: stays 2¾m: acts on any going. *P. J. Jones*

RICH AND RED 7 b.m. Rubor – Bit of A Madam (Richboy) [1992/3 22g] lengthy mare: third foal: dam won novice hurdle and placed in points: placed   **–** in 2 maiden points in 1992: no promise in novice hurdle at Wincanton in November. *K. C. Bailey*

RICHARD HUNT 9 b.g. Celtic Cone – Member's Mistress (New   **c88** Member) [1992/3 c24g² c24fᶠ c26m³] angular gelding: fair pointer: also fair   **–** form when placed in hunter chases at Leicester (maiden) in March and Cheltenham in May: will stay long distances. *V. H. Rowe*

RICHARDS KATE 9 b.m. Fidel – Baroness Vimy (Barrons Court)   **c86 ?** [1992/3 c20s c20vᵖᵘ c20sᶠ c21s⁴ c16d⁴] smallish mare: winning hurdler: **–** modest novice chaser: trained in 1991/2 by M. Bradstock in Britain, first 4 starts in 1992/3 by I. Ferguson in Ireland: below-form last of 4 finishers in novice handicap at Wetherby in February, final outing: stays 2½m: acts on heavy going. *M. Bradstock*

RICH DESIRE 4 b.f. Grey Desire – Richesse (FR) (Faraway Son (USA))   **82** [1992/3 F12d⁶ F16g* F17m 16v³ 16g⁵ 16f³ 20m² 21f³] light-framed, dipped-backed, plain filly: sixth foal: half-sister to 3 winners, including hurdler Rabirius (by Mandrake Major): dam ran once: won mares NH Flat race at Worcester in March: poor form in juvenile and novice hurdles afterwards: stays 21f: acts on any going. *R. A. Bennett*

RICH HEIRESS (IRE) 4 b.f. Last Tycoon – Lamya (USA) (Alydar (USA)) [1992/3 18v³ 18g 17mᵖᵘ] half-sister to winning Irish hurdler   **–** Bellagrove (by Yashgan): poor maiden on Flat and over hurdles: sold out of A. Moore's stable 1,150 gns Ascot February Sales after first start. *V. Thompson*

RICHMOND (IRE) 5 ch.g. Hatim (USA) – On The Road (On Your   **83** Mark) [1992/3 16g² 16m² 18d* 16d 17s⁶] lengthy gelding: modest form at around 1m on Flat for S. Norton and B. Beasley: won novice hurdle at Market Rasen in November: ran poorly last 2 starts: sold 1,100 gns Doncaster May Sales: likely to prove best around 2m: acts on good to firm and dead going: blinkered all bar second outing. *N. Tinkler*

RICH PICKINGS 4 b.f. Dominion – Miss By Miles (Milesian) [1992/3 18g⁶ 18d⁴ 17d* 16v⁵ 20d⁵ 25d⁴ 24f⁴ 25m⁴ 22d⁵] small, sparely-made filly: half-sister to winning hurdlers Devisdale (by Swing Easy) and Torwada (by Troy), latter fairly useful: staying plater on Flat, winner in 1993: sold out of C. Cyzer's stable 4,800 gns Newmarket September Sales: won juvenile selling hurdle at Taunton (bought in 5,000 gns) in November: best effort when fourth in novice handicap at Taunton in February on sixth start: stays 25f: acts on firm and dead going. *D. R. Tucker*   83

RICH REMORSE 14 b.g. Tycoon II – Kero Code (Straight Lad) [1992/3 c25v⁵ c25vᵖᵘ c28gᵖᵘ c26g³] strong, compact gelding: fair staying chaser at best: no form in 1992/3: makes mistakes. *R. Curtis*   c– x

RICHVILLE 7 b.g. Kemal (FR) – Golden Ingot (Prince Hansel) [1992/3 c20d⁶ c21s⁵ c19v* c21f⁴ c19s² c20sF] sturdy gelding: fair hurdler/chaser: won novice event over fences at Fontwell in January: good second at Hereford in April: best form around 2½m, should stay further: acts on heavy and good to firm ground: blinkered fourth and fifth outings. *K. C. Bailey*   c101

RICMAR (USA) 10 ch.g. Lydian (FR) – Regency Tale (CAN) (Vice Regent (CAN)) [1992/3 22m* 22s² 25fᵖᵘ] workmanlike gelding: modest hurdler: won handicap at Newton Abbot in August: pulled up lame in September, and wasn't seen out again: poor form in novice chases: stays 2¾m: acts on any going: tried blinkered, but not in 1992/3. *Mrs J. G. Retter*   c– 96

RIDDLEMEROO 8 b.g. Chukaroo – True Melody (Pardigras) [1992/3 20sᵖᵘ 17s 22g 25gF 16dᵖᵘ 22vᵖᵘ 20g] stocky gelding: little sign of ability: visored last outing. *A. L. Forbes*   –

RIDE THE WIND 9 ch.g. Windjammer (USA) – Madam Clare (Ennis) [1992/3 c24mᵖᵘ] leggy gelding: once-raced over hurdles: poor pointer: no show in hunter chase at Exeter in May. *D. W. Heard*   c– –

RIDWAN 6 b.g. Rousillon (USA) – Ring Rose (Relko) [1992/3 22g³ 21g⁴ c25d² c24gF c25sᵘʳ 26dᵖᵘ 21s⁴ 21g⁵ 24s⁴ 25s³ 25mʳᵒ 27g² 27fᵖᵘ] sparely-made gelding: fair handicap hurdler: modest form on only completed start over fences: effective at 2½m and stays 27f: acts on soft going: blinkered sixth outing: tends to race with head in air: sketchy jumper of fences. *K. A. Morgan*   c91 101

RIFFLE 6 b.g. Crash Course – Rifflealp (Sterling Bay (SWE)) [1992/3 17s⁵] fourth foal: dam won over 6f and 7f in Ireland: tailed-off last of 5 in novice hurdle at Ascot in January. *J. T. Gifford*   –

RIFLE RANGE 10 b.g. Torus – Miss Bavard (Le Bavard (FR)) [1992/3 c21d³ c25g* c20d* c21d⁵] rangy, sparely-made gelding: fairly useful chaser: won handicaps at Ayr in November and Haydock in December in good style: disappointing fifth at Kempton later in December: effective at 2½m and stays 27f: acts on soft going: sound jumper: front runner. *J. J. O'Neill*   c124

RIG STEEL 13 ch.g. Welsh Pageant – Fir Tree (Santa Claus) [1992/3 c23d⁶ c25gᵖᵘ c24g⁵ c26vF] lengthy, workmanlike gelding: races mainly in hunter chases nowadays: ran poorly in 1992/3: suited by a test of stamina: acts on any going: sketchy jumper. *B. C. Morgan*   c–

RIMOUSKI 5 b.h. Sure Blade (USA) – Rimosa's Pet (Petingo) [1992/3 16d 17d⁵ 18g³ 25v² 24g³ 25m*] smallish, good-bodied horse: moderate form over hurdles: narrow winner of novice handicap at Uttoxeter in May: suited by good test of stamina: acts on good to firm and heavy going: held up: whipped round start first outing: poor middle-distance winner on Flat in 1993. *B. R. Cambidge*   98

RINANNA BAY 6 b.m. Good Thyne (USA) – Devon Royale (Le Prince) [1992/3 c21d 22v⁵ 22vᵇᵈ 25d c23dᵘʳ c24m³] lengthy, angular ex-Irish mare: second foal: dam winning 2m hurdler/chaser in Ireland: poor novice   c79 79

hurdler/chaser: stays 3m: acts on heavy and good to firm ground: blinkered once. *K. Bishop*

RI-NA-RITHANN   8 b.g. Deep Run – Casacello (Punchinello) [1992/3 17d⁵ 16d⁶] rangy, good sort: every inch a chaser on looks: useful novice hurdler in 1989/90: well below form in 2 handicap hurdles in February: stays 2½m: acts on any going. *Mrs J. Pitman*

RING CORBITTS   5 b.g. Politico (USA) – Penny Pink (Spartan General) [1992/3 F16g 21s⁶ 20g pu 20g⁶ 21d³ 25v² 28m⁴] rangy gelding: modest novice   84 hurdler: sold 10,000 gns Doncaster May Sales: stays 3½m: acts on heavy and good to firm ground: sketchy jumper. *D. Eddy*

RINGLAND (USA)   5 b.h. Gate Dancer (USA) – Tinnitus (USA) (Restless Wind) [1992/3 17g* 17d 16g* 17g⁵ 18g 17g 18m²] good-topped   100 horse: quite useful at up to 1m on Flat: sold out of P. Haslam's stable 12,000 gns Doncaster September Sales: won novice hurdles at Kelso in October and Ayr in January: good second in handicap at Cartmel in May: unlikely to stay much beyond 2¼m: acts on good to firm ground: tends to hang badly left (sometimes wears pricker on near side). *D. Moffatt*

RINGMORE   11 ch.g. Porto Bello – Dirrie Star (Dunoon Star) [1992/3   c88 c16m c17d pu c16g³ c20g² c21s c16s* c17v³ c16g⁵ c16g³ c19m² c21g c16d pu 17s pu] strong, good-bodied gelding: has been tubed: winning hurdler: moderate chaser: won conditional jockeys selling handicap at Catterick (no bid) in January: at least fair efforts when placed subsequently: best form at around 2m: acts on any going: sound jumper: sometimes wears tongue strap. *J. Parkes*

RING OF FORTUNE (FR)   5 b.g. Fast Topaze (USA) – Forgata (FR)   c– (Bolkonski) [1992/3 c21d ur c17m 24f pu] good-bodied gelding: fairly useful   – hurdler in 1991/2: not fluent in novice chases in May, taking little interest on second occasion: stays 2¾m: acts on soft ground: blinkered nowadays. *M. C. Pipe*

RING OF THE SOUTH   6 b.g. Jalmood (USA) – Saturne (Bellypha) [1992/3 17g 17g ur 17d F] compact gelding: of no account: dead. *P. M. McEntee*   –

RINGYBOY   8 b.g. Runnett – Graunuaile (Proud Chieftain) [1992/3 17v pu   c– a20g pu c16s c21g⁵ c24d pu 17f 18f] of no account nowadays: sold 1,150 gns   – Ascot June Sales. *J. A. Bennett*

RINKY DINKY DOO   7 b.g. Oats – County Clare (Vimadee) [1992/3   c– c23s ur c25g F c20s pu c21s pu a22g⁴] leggy gelding: of little account. *C. Cowley*   –

RINTINTIN   6 ch.g. Tina's Pet – Countess Down (Roan Rocket) [1992/3 21d pu] workmanlike gelding: poor novice hurdler: sold 1,200 gns Ascot   – February Sales. *N. M. Babbage*

RIO HAINA   8 ch.g. St Columbus – Kruganko (Arctic Slave) [1992/3   c109 c26d² c26d* c26s² c26d pu c26g c23g⁶] workmanlike hunter: fair handicap chaser: won at Warwick in October: good second there following month, only subsequent form: stays 3¼m: acts on good to firm and soft going: jumps soundly. *Capt. T. A. Forster*

RIP THE CALICO (IRE)   5 b.m. Crash Course – Rocky's Dream (Aristocracy) [1992/3 18v 23s 20m ur 16d⁵ 17g pu 17f] sparely-made ex-Irish   – mare: first foal: dam, 1½m Flat winner in Ireland, poor maiden over hurdles: won a point in 1992: soundly beaten over hurdles: blinkered in seller final outing. *P. Burgoyne*

RISE OVER   7 ch.m. Smackover – Stewart's Rise (Good Bond) [1992/3 16d pu] leggy mare: poor novice hurdler: visored, tailed off when pulled up in   – claiming hurdle at Uttoxeter (looked headstrong) in November. *P. D. Evans*

RISING DEXY   8 b.g. Bay Express – Maladie d'Amour (Fidalgo) [1992/3 17g pu] novice hurdler: only form over 2m on good to firm going. *J. White*   –

RISING MEMBER   8 ch.g. New Member – Sharon (Sunny Way) [1992/3 16s pu] workmanlike gelding: half-brother to winning hurdler/chaser   – Belliver Prince (by Rugantino): dam never ran: backward and no show in novice hurdle at Windsor in January. *R. Champion*

RISING TEMPO (IRE) 5 b.g. Lomond (USA) – May Hill (Hill Clown (USA)) [1992/3 17d a16g^{pu} a16g³ a16g⁴ a16g³ 17f⁵ 17g³] fair form at up to 1¾m on Flat, winner in 1993: poor form at best over hurdles: will stay beyond 17f: acts on equitrack: sometimes visored: looked none too keen sixth start. *B. P. J. Baugh* — 78

RISK FACTOR 7 b.g. Auction Ring (USA) – Flying Anna (Roan Rocket) [1992/3 17s⁵ 16d⁶ 22v*] close-coupled, good-topped gelding: modest hurdler: won novice handicap at Worcester in April: stays 2¾m: acts on heavy ground. *R. Lee* — 82

RIVAGE BLEU 6 b.g. Valiyar – Rose d'Aunou (FR) (Luthier) [1992/3 F17s 18g 21f] strong gelding: little sign of ability. *J. S. King* — –

RIVA (NZ) 6 ch.g. Beechcraft (NZ) – Bronze Penny (NZ) (Patron Saint) [1992/3 17v* 20v²] plain, angular gelding: impressive winner of novice hurdle at Lingfield in December: weakened close home when second in similar race on same course in January: sure to win more races at up to 2½m provided all is well with him. *Mrs J. R. Renfree-Barons* — 116 p

RIVA'S TOUCH (USA) 10 b.g. Riva Ridge (USA) – Touch (USA) (Herbager) [1992/3 c18m⁶ c16g c16g⁶ c20m c21d^{pu} c18m⁶] poor chaser: seems best at up to 2¼m on a sound surface. *Mrs A. L. M. King* — c– –

RIVE-JUMELLE (IRE) 5 b.m. M Double M (USA) – Riverwave (USA) (Riverman (USA)) [1992/3 17d² 16v³ 17v⁶ 17d⁵ 18s⁵ 17f⁴ 17d] sparely-made mare: modest 1¼m performer on Flat when trained by M. Bell: showed best form first 2 starts in novice hurdles: below that form subsequently: acts on heavy ground. *J. R. Jenkins* — 83

RIVER BED (FR) 9 ch.g. Sharpman – River Craft (Reliance II) [1992/3 c16g^{pu}] angular, sparely-made gelding: winning hurdler/chaser: no worthwhile form for a long time: reluctant to race and tried to refuse final start in 1991/2. *K. A. Morgan* — c– §

RIVERBOAT QUEEN 10 br.m. Rapid River – Royal Barb (Barbin) [1992/3 c25s⁵ c25s⁵ c25g*] moderate hunter chaser: best effort of season when winning at Wetherby in May: stays 25f: form only on good ground. *T. H. Pounder* — c86

RIVER BOUNTY 7 ch.g. Over The River (FR) – Billie Gibb (Cavo Doro) [1992/3 c25g⁴] smallish, sturdy gelding: winning hurdler: fairly useful chaser: shaped well when creditable fourth in handicap at Ascot in October, but wasn't seen out again: stays 25f: acts on good to firm and dead going (well beaten on soft). *John R. Upson* — c115 –

RIVER CHASE (IRE) 5 ch.m. Salmon Leap (USA) – Amboselli (Raga Navarro (ITY)) [1992/3 20m^{pu}] lengthy mare: no sign of ability over hurdles: pulls hard. *D. J. Wintle* — –

RIVER CONSORT (USA) 5 bl.g. Riverman (USA) – Queens Only (USA) (Marshua's Dancer (USA)) [1992/3 16g⁴ 17s 17s 17d⁴ 16f⁵ 21f⁴] smallish, lengthy gelding: 7f winner at 2 yrs for G. Harwood: moderate novice hurdler: ran particularly well final start: stays 21f. *A. J. K. Dunn* — 91 +

RIVER FLY 8 ch.g. Over The River (FR) – Diana's Flyer (Charlottesvilles Flyer) [1992/3 21d⁵ 24v^{pu} c25s^F c20d^{pu} c21f* c21g² c19f^{pu}] lengthy gelding: poor form over hurdles: completing first time over fences when winning novice event at Plumpton in March: good second on same course following month, ran poorly last start: should stay 3m: acts on firm and dead going. *J. White* — c90 84

RIVER GALAXY 10 ch.g. Billion (USA) – River Severn (Henry The Seventh) [1992/3 c24m⁴] smallish, sparely-made gelding: 2m novice hurdler (blinkered twice): lightly-raced pointer nowadays: tailed off in novice hunter chase in May. *Mrs Ann Taylor* — c– –

RIVER HOUSE 11 ch.g. Over The River (FR) – Kinsella's Choice (Middle Temple) [1992/3 c21f³ c25m⁶ c26m² c23d* c26d⁶ c24g⁶ c20g⁴ c24m³ c26g⁴ c24m* c25f^{pu} c25g^{pu} c22v³ c22f*] angular gelding: fair handicap chaser: won at Kelso in November (trained until after fifth outing — c105 §

by W. A. Stephenson), Newcastle in March and Stratford (finished lame) in June: sold out of P. Cheesbrough's stable 5,000 gns in May after twelfth outing: stays 27f: acts on hard and dead ground: sometimes takes little interest, and is unreliable. *J. White*

RIVERILLON 5 ch.g. Rousillon (USA) – Dance Lover's (FR) (Green Dancer (USA)) [1992/3 16d⁴ 17f³] 9f maiden race winner on Flat when trained in Ireland by J. J. McLoughlin: better effort in novice hurdles when third of 7 finishers at Hereford in May. *Martyn Meade*   84

RIVER ISLAND (USA) 5 b.g. Spend A Buck (USA) – Promising Risk (USA) (Exclusive Native (USA)) [1992/3 18g⁴ 17s* 17v 17d* 17d⁵ 21m³ 17m³ 17s² 17d³ 17d³] smallish gelding: reportedly had wind operation after first start: won novice hurdles at Taunton in December and Huntingdon in January and ran well most other starts, showing fairly useful form: best form at around 2m: acts on soft and good to firm going. *J. A. B. Old*   116

RIVER LOSSIE 4 b.g. Bustino – Forres (Thatch (USA)) [1992/3 F17g² F17m³] tall, rather unfurnished gelding: half-brother to 2 winners, including fairly useful 1985 2-y-o Loch Hourn (by Alias Smith): dam unraced: placed in NH Flat races at Doncaster in January and February: sold 24,000 gns Doncaster May Sales: yet to race over hurdles. *W. Jarvis*

RIVER ORCHID 4 b.f. Mashhor Dancer (USA) – Summer Sky (Skyliner) [1992/3 17d³ 20s³ 16v⁶ 17s⁶ 17f*] workmanlike filly: poor maiden at 2 yrs: won novice selling hurdle at Taunton (sold 3,500 gns) in March: resold 2,500 gns Ascot June Sales: stays 2½m: well beaten on heavy ground but acts on any other. *P. F. Nicholls*   80

RIVER PEARL 8 b.m. Oats – Dark Pearl (Harwell) [1992/3 22g* c21g⁶ c20g² c20s⁶ c23s² c23d⁴ c16d² c24d² 21s^pu c21d⁵] lengthy mare: fair hurdler: won handicap at Ayr in October: modest form in novice chases: effective at 2m to 3m: acts on soft ground: jumps soundly in the main and should win a race over fences. *G. Richards*   c92   108

RIVER RED 7 ch.g. Over The River (FR) – Monasootha (Paddy's Stream) [1992/3 23g² 23s⁴ 16s⁵ a22g^F 23f^pu] compact gelding: best effort in novice hurdles when second in November: needs further than 2m and should stay beyond 23f. *J. White*   91

RIVER REEF 7 b. or br.g. Dunphy – Zarinia (FR) (Right Royal V) [1992/3 c21s^ur c21m⁵ c21d^pu c19d^F 18s⁶ 17v] leggy, sparely-made gelding: novice hurdler/chaser: no worthwhile form: blinkered last outing. *M. P. Muggeridge*   c–   –

RIVERSIDE BOY 10 ch.g. Funny Man – Tamorina (Quayside) [1992/3 c33v^ur c30s² c35s* c30s^ur c29d⁴ c33g^F c27d^pu] leggy gelding: useful handicap chaser on his day: won quite valuable event at Taunton in January: below form only completed outing subsequently: suited by a good test of stamina: acts on soft going: forces pace: sometimes runs in snatches. *M. C. Pipe*   c140

RIVERSIDE MOSS (IRE) 5 ch.g. Le Moss – Arctic Chatter (Le Bavard (FR)) [1992/3 F16v] half-brother to winning hurdler Sound of Jura (by Deep Run): dam unraced half-sister to fair staying chaser Arctic Slogan: tailed off in NH Flat race at Uttoxeter in April: sold 1,500 gns Ascot May Sales: yet to race over hurdles or fences. *P. J. Hobbs*   –

RIVER SPIRIT (USA) 8 ch.g. Arts And Letters – Norma Teagarden (Jukebox) [1992/3 c19s³ c24m³] leggy, lengthy gelding: novice hurdler: third in novice hunter chases in April (easily best effort) and May: won a point in between: stays 19f: probably acts on any going. *W. J. Warner*   c82   –

RIVER STREAM 6 b.m. Paddy's Stream – River Belle (Divine Gift) [1992/3 18d^pu] light-framed mare: twice-raced novice over hurdles: no form. *L. G. Cottrell*   –

RIVER TARQUIN 9 b.g. Over The River (FR) – Tarqogan's Rose (Tarqogan) [1992/3 c24s² c25s^F c24d* c26v⁴ c24d^F c24d c29s^pu] workmanlike gelding: useful chaser: won Findus Handicap at Leopardstown in December: fair fourth next time but below form subsequently: stays very   c142   –

Findus Handicap Chase, Leopardstown—River Tarquin has the race in the bag at the last

well: acts on heavy going: races to the fore: blinkered nowadays. *J. T. R. Dreaper, Ireland*

RIVERWISE (USA) 5 b.h. Riverman (USA) – Village Sass (USA) (Sassafras (FR)) [1992/3 17s^pu] smallish horse: poor novice hurdler: ran badly in October on only outing of season. *N. R. Mitchell* —

RIYADH LIGHTS 8 b.g. Formidable (USA) – Rivers Maid (Rarity) [1992/3 a20g*] neat gelding: modest hurdler: made running when winning 5-runner claimer at Lingfield in January: well beaten only start over fences: stays 3¼m: acts on hard ground and equitrack. *M. D. I. Usher* c– 87 ?

ROAD BY THE RIVER (IRE) 5 ch.g. Over The River (FR) – Ahadoon (Gulf Pearl) [1992/3 25v⁵ 25v⁵] seventh foal: half-brother to winning 7f plater Lady Grim (by Status Seeker): dam never ran: won a point in Ireland in 1992: showed promise in novice hurdles late in season: should do better. *P. Cheesbrough* – p

ROAD TO AU BON (USA) 5 b.g. Strawberry Road (AUS) – Village Lady (USA) (Crimson Satan) [1992/3 18g^pu] leggy gelding: poor hurdler: showed no zest in novice handicap at Exeter in October. *R. J. Baker* –

ROAD TO FAME 6 b.g. Trimmingham – Go Artistic (Go-Tobann) [1992/3 F17g⁵ 16d⁵] sturdy gelding: half-brother to winning Irish jumper 73 p

608

Quarry Machine (by Laurence O) and several maiden jumpers: dam never ran: fifth of 18 in NH Flat race at Doncaster in January: showed some promise when fifth in novice event at Windsor in February on hurdling debut. *D. R. Gandolfo*

ROAD TO RICHES 7 b.g. Al Sirat (USA) – Royal Niece (Blue Chariot) [1992/3 21v 21s] leggy gelding: fair hurdler in 1991/2: well beaten in handicaps in December: stays 2½m: acts on dead going. *T. Thomson Jones* —

ROAD TO THE WEIR 6 b. or br.g. Maculata – Any Old Road (Giolla Mear) [1992/3 17mpu 28dpu 25spu 23d 22gF a22gpu 16dpu] leggy gelding: first foal: dam maiden hurdler: of little account. *Mrs S. A. Bramall* —

ROARK 11 ch.g. Relkino – Hurlingham (Harken) [1992/3 21vpu] big, lengthy gelding: lightly raced, and only form for long time when winner of handicap hurdle in 1991/2: backward and showed nothing in January: fell only start over fences: stays 21f: acts on heavy going. *R. F. Stone* c–

ROBBIE BURNS 7 br.h. Daring March – Gangawayhame (Lochnager) [1992/3 c26dpu c26v3 c27spu c18vpu] winning 2m selling hurdler: has shown nothing over fences: sold 2,100 gns Doncaster January Sales: acts on good to firm going: tried blinkered. *J. Ffitch-Heyes* c–

ROBBIE'S BOY 6 b.g. Sunley Builds – Lucys Willing (Will Hays (USA)) [1992/3 23d 17s3 16s6 a20g5] sparely-made gelding: poor novice hurdler: best effort when third in seller at Bangor in December: sometimes visored. *M. Brown* 70

ROBERT'S REJECT (USA) 6 ch.m. Assert – Bold Sands (USA) (Wajima (USA)) [1992/3 21spu 16v a20g4] lightly-raced novice hurdler: poor form. *Mrs M. E. Long* 63

ROBINGO (IRE) 4 b.c. Bob Back (USA) – Mill's Girl (Le Levanstell) [1992/3 17v3 17v2 18s* 17v* 21s* 17m] small, leggy colt: useful stayer on Flat (wears blinkers): sold out of C. Brittain's stable 26,000 gns Newmarket Autumn Sales: best effort over hurdles when winning 3-runner novice event at Leicester in February from High Alltitude and Sun Surfer: had landed odds in juvenile events at Exeter and Chepstow previous month: will stay beyond 21f: acts on heavy going (always behind in Daily Express Triumph Hurdle on good to firm): visored first 4 starts, blinkered last 2: jumps none too fluently. *M. C. Pipe* 125

ROBINS CHOICE 9 b.m. Scallywag – Chumolaori (Indian Ruler) [1992/3 c25m* c26g3] won novice hunter chase at Southwell in May: good third at Uttoxeter later in month: stays 3¼m: acts on good to firm going. *R. Tate* c88

ROBINS FIND (IRE) 5 b.g. Reasonable (FR) – Skyway (Skymaster) [1992/3 17d5] modest middle-distance maiden on Flat: remote fifth of 11 in novice hurdle at Newton Abbot in August. *R. G. Frost* —

ROBINS LAD 7 b.g. Beldale Flutter (USA) – Piemonte (Nebbiolo) [1992/3 20mpu] shallow-girthed gelding: poor form in novice hurdles. *Mrs A. Swinbank* —

ROBINS SON 6 b.g. Krayyan – Fleam (Continuation) [1992/3 18gpu] lengthy gelding: quite moderate novice hurdler at best: pulled up lame in seller in October: unlikely to stay beyond 2m. *N. Tinkler* —

ROCCO 6 b.g. King's Ride – Ladycastle (Pitpan) [1992/3 c21d2 c24sF c21v2] leggy, good-topped gelding: useful novice hurdler in 1991/2 for Mrs J. Pitman: showed plenty of ability in novice chases at Warwick, Kempton and Lingfield in 1992/3: stays 3m: best form with give in the ground: not yet a fluent jumper of fences but should win races. *S. E. Sherwood* c106 p

ROC COLOR (FR) 4 b.g. Cimon – Lynley (FR) (Kimberley) [1992/3 15d2 15d4 17m4 17g4 17s 18v* 17f3 22v3 c18v6 17d* 17f5] leggy, workmanlike gelding: has had soft-palate operation: once-raced on Flat: fair form over hurdles: trained first 2 starts by J. Ortet in France: won juvenile event at Fontwell in January and novice handicap at Hereford in May: sixth in c? 102

steeplechase in Turin in May: stays 2¼m: acts on any going: blinkered last outing: sometimes wears tongue strap. *C. P. E. Brooks*

ROC DE PRINCE (FR) 10 br.g. Djarvis (FR) – Haute Volta II (FR) (Beau Fixe) [1992/3 c26v c25v c24dF c27s c25mᵘʳ] tall, sparely-made ex-Irish gelding: useful chaser at best: well below form in 1992/3: trained until after fourth start by T. Walsh: suited by test of stamina: has won on good to firm going but best form with plenty of give: front runner. *M. C. Pipe* **c–** / –

ROCHESTER 7 gr.g. Entre Nous – Satan's Daughter (Lucifer (USA)) [1992/3 c16dᵇᵈ c16sF c16d⁶ c16v³ c16s* c17sF 16s⁴ 17g*] leggy gelding: moderate form over hurdles and fences: won novice handicap chase at Wolverhampton in January and novice hurdle at Taunton (improved form) in April: best at around 2m: suited by give in the ground. *R. Lee* **c92** / 99

ROCHESTOWN LASS 7 b.m. Deep Run – Knockatippaun (Bahrain) [1992/3 20s⁵ 23s* 25d⁴ 25d* 24s* 24vᵖᵘ] lengthy mare: fair hurdler: successful in 2 novice events at Uttoxeter and handicap at Towcester in first half of season: ran poorly last outing (December): suited by test of stamina: acts on soft ground: visored last 3 starts. *P. T. Dalton* 106

ROCHESTOWN RUN 8 b.g. Deep Run – Rochestown Lady (Khalkis) [1992/3 21gpu] angular gelding: fourth foal: dam winning pointer: showed a little ability in points in 1991: tailed off when pulled up in maiden in March on hurdling debut. *Mrs P. Sly* –

ROCK BAND (IRE) 4 b.c. Ballad Rock – Bobs (Warpath) [1992/3 16g] quite modest maiden on Flat, best short of 1m: sold out of L. Cumani's stable 6,400 gns Newmarket September Sales: behind in juvenile hurdle at Windsor in November. *T. M. Jones* –

ROCKET LAUNCHER 7 b.g. Strong Gale – Adell (Fordham (USA)) [1992/3 16g³ 16d⁴ 16v² c16v* c16d⁴ c20f* c32mᵖᵘ c20f² c21dF] well-made gelding: moderate novice hurdler: won novice chases at Plumpton in February and Newbury in March: very good second in quite valuable novice handicap at Newbury later in March: stays 2½m (jumped poorly for amateur over 4m): acts on any going: sometimes has tongue tied down: usually jumps soundly. *D. R. C. Elsworth* **c106** / 93

ROCKET RUN (IRE) 5 b.g. Orchestra – Roselita (Deep Run) [1992/3 17vᵖᵘ 16g 16m⁴ 17fᵖᵘ] close-coupled gelding: third foal: half-brother to fair jumper Wolver Run (by Furry Glen) and winning Irish hurdler Tara Mill (by Petorius): dam won over 5f at 2 yrs: fourth in novice hurdle at Wincanton in March, only form. *M. S. Saunders* 84

ROCK HARD 4 ch.g. Ballad Rock – Norska (Northfields (USA)) [1992/3 17d² 17v⁴ 16s³ 16v⁴ 17d⁴ 17f⁵] leggy gelding: lightly-raced modest maiden on Flat: sold out of W. Jarvis' stable 5,600 gns Newmarket July Sales: moderate form over hurdles: acted on soft going: dead. *William Price* 93

ROCK LEGEND 5 ch.h. Legend of France (USA) – Two Rock (Mill Reef (USA)) [1992/3 16v⁴ 17d³ 21g⁵] small horse: half-brother to winning hurdler Arthurs Stone (by Kings Lake): middle-distance performer on Flat, fair at best: fair form when fourth in novice event at Kempton in January, but failed to confirm that promise in 2 subsequent runs: takes strong hold: jumps sketchily. *D. Shaw* 102

ROCKMOUNT ROSE 8 b.m. Proverb – Wandering Gal (Prince de Galles) [1992/3 c26vF c16v c21g² c27d c27fᵘʳ c21f* c24f3] smallish, sparely-made mare: won point in Ireland in 1991 and novice handicap chase at Huntingdon in May, latter by 15 lengths: best form at up to 21f: acts on firm ground. *R. Rowe* **c82** +

ROCK SONG (IRE) 4 ch.g. Ballad Rock – Mrs Tittlemouse (Nonoalco (USA)) [1992/3 16sᵖᵘ 17mᵖᵘ] leggy, angular gelding: modest 7f winner on Flat: sold out of P. Cole's stable 2,100 gns Doncaster November Sales: pulled up in 2 juvenile hurdles in March. *J. Mackie* –

ROCKTOR (NZ) 8 b.g. Shy Rambler (USA) – Sobina (NZ) (Sobig) [1992/3 c26gF c24g³ c26g³ c26d⁶ c24m* c25f³ c27gᵘʳ c27d²] close-coupled, workmanlike gelding: fairly useful chaser: successful in handicap at Ludlow **c122** / –

in March: ran well most other completed starts: suited by a good test of stamina: acts on firm and dead ground: sometimes jumps sketchily. *D. H. Barons*

ROCKY VULGAN 10 b.g. Hildenley – Phayre Vulgan (Vulgan) [1992/3 c27spu c27s4 c22spu c24vpu c26spu c27gpu] rather sparely-made gelding: poor novice hurdler/chaser: stays 3m: acts on dead ground: blinkered. *Miss L. Bower*

c–
–

ROCQUAINE 7 ch.g. Ballad Rock – Lola Sharp (Sharpen Up) [1992/3 16spu] angular gelding: lightly-raced winning hurdler: pulled up at Worcester in October, only outing of season: stays 2¼m. *K. White*

–

RODEO STAR (USA) 7 ch.h. Nodouble (USA) – Roundup Rose (USA) (Minnesota Mac) [1992/3 16v5 17g6 16d2] workmanlike horse: useful hurdler: fair sixth in Tote Gold Trophy Handicap at Newbury in February: second in 4-runner minor event at Haydock later in month: in very good form on Flat subsequently (won Chester Cup): best form at around 2m but should stay further: acts on good to firm and soft ground: jumps well: races up with the pace: tough and genuine. *N. Tinkler*

140

ROGERDOR (USA) 5 b.g. Tom Rolfe – Grand Bonheur (USA) (Blushing Groom (FR)) [1992/3 16g* 17g* 16g4 16d 16d* 24d 20d2] fairly useful stayer on Flat (blinkered) at 3 yrs, when trained by G. Harwood: successful over hurdles at Killarney, Dundalk and Listowel early in season: good second to Minella Man at Leopardstown in March: should stay beyond 2½m (first outing for over 5 months when well beaten over 3m): acts on dead ground: useful. *N. Meade, Ireland*

130

ROGER RABBIT (FR) 4 b.g. Rusticaro (FR) – Bustelda (FR) (Busted) [1992/3 17vpu 22vpu 20spu 17g5 a16g6 16g 17gpu 22f] tall gelding: half-brother to novice hurdler Esprit de Femme (by Esprit du Nord): poor maiden on Flat: sold out of R. Boss's stable 2,600 gns Newmarket September Sales: no worthwhile form over hurdles: trained first 3 starts by R. Frost: resold 1,100 gns Ascot June Sales: blinkered third outing. *J. Joseph*

–

ROGERSON 5 ch.g. Green-Fingered – Town Belle (Town Crier) [1992/3 16spu 16d] smallish gelding: sixth foal: half-brother to winning pointer Owensville (by Owen Anthony): dam unraced: little show in novice hurdles at Windsor in January and February. *A. Moore*

–

ROGER'S PAL 6 ch.h. Lir – Amberush (No Rush) [1992/3 16d5 16s3 17g3 17g* 16f6 17f3 17g2 16m2 18f5] close-coupled horse: won selling handicap hurdle at Plumpton (no bid) in March: mainly creditable efforts afterwards: best at around 2m: acts on any ground: blinkered once in 1991/2. *A. Moore*

87

ROGEVIC BELLE 5 ch.g. Swing Easy (USA) – Betbellof (Averof) [1992/3 17f4 16mpu 17f5] leggy, lengthy gelding: bad novice selling hurdler: blinkered first start, visored second. *M. W. Eckley*

53

ROLL A DOLLAR 7 b.g. Spin of A Coin – Handy Dancer (Green God) [1992/3 17d3 17g3 17g* 16g* 17f*]

136 p

Roll A Dollar struck form with a vengeance in 1993. A useful middle-distance stayer on the Flat but below form in 1992, he'd made a promising debut over hurdles at the age of six at Ascot in November, twelve lengths behind Satin Lover. Six months on and there were problems choosing between the pair on their novice form and very little doubt in our view that Roll A Dollar is the better prospect. Satin Lover's best form came when third to Montelado in the Supreme Novices' Hurdle at the Cheltenham Festival, a meeting which Roll A Dollar missed. He hadn't even been entered. That's most unlikely to be repeated in 1994. Roll A Dollar's second meeting with Satin Lover in their novice season, in the Seagram Top Novices' Hurdle at Aintree, had a very different outcome to the first. The nine-strong field included, besides Satin Lover, the Supreme Novices' runners Gaelic Myth (fifth), Frickley (sixth) and Dreamers Delight (unseated rider when close up two out), and the impressive Beaufort Hurdle winner Winter Squall. It was Roll A Dollar, however, who started favourite. He had had two races since Ascot, at Newbury and Kempton in February, and

Dovecote Novices' Hurdle, Kempton—
Roll A Dollar comes out on top in a well-contested event

won them both. The Grade 2 Dovecote Novices' Hurdle at Kempton had demanded a useful performance for him to forge three lengths clear from Winter Squall, with the next four home Cabochon, Peaceman, Big Beat and

Seagram Top Novices' Hurdle, Aintree—
Roll A Dollar leads Land Afar and Frickley,
and just holds on from the strong-finishing Gaelic Myth (striped sleeves)

Arcot. Peaceman was another who contested the Top Novices' at Aintree, though not for long, as he ran out dramatically at the fifth when in the lead, leaving the race to be run at just a fair pace. Roll A Dollar, who had been held up in rear as usual, made a challenging move sooner than connections thought ideal, being on the heels of the leaders entering the straight, but his chance was prejudiced more obviously by his jumping. Having been awkward at the first, he flattened the second last when disputing the lead, and landed askew at the last as well. Meanwhile, Gaelic Myth had been creeping closer, despite steering a somewhat erratic course, and mounted a strong challenge, the pair going past the post almost together, three quarters of a length ahead of the 50/1-shot Land Afar. Roll A Dollar got the verdict by a head. Satin Lover was last of the eight finishers on what turned out to be his last appearance of the season. Roll A Dollar did not appear over hurdles again either, but this was far from the last that was seen of him. Returned to the Flat, he showed himself to be an improved horse in that department as well, winning the Sagaro Stakes and finishing third in the Yorkshire Cup. Now connections have their sights set firmly on the Champion Hurdle.

Roll A Dollar is one of only two winners to have emerged so far from the seven crops at stud by Spin of A Coin. The other is C'An Botana who won a maiden hurdle in Ireland in 1991. From a total of ninety-two registered foals, Spin of A Coin has had two other placed horses. A fairly useful handicapper on the Flat, Spin of A Coin had thirty-one starts in four seasons and won five of them, including the Bessborough at Royal Ascot. Roll A Dollar's owner/breeder also owned Spin of A Coin. Roll A Dollar's dam Handy Dancer was another fairly useful performer on the Flat, winning

Mr K. Higson's "Roll A Dollar"

three times at a mile and a quarter before being sold for 4,700 guineas and having a far less fruitful spell over hurdles, finishing lame on the last of five starts in which she'd shown only a little ability. Handy Dancer has a most presentable record at stud. Indeed, it's questionable whether Roll A Dollar is her best produce because her next foal is Karinga Bay (by Ardross), winner of the Gordon Stakes in 1990 and fourth in the Eclipse in 1993. Two Flat winners of much less ability by The Brianstan and Ardross preceded Roll A Dollar (Handy Dancer's fourth foal) and another, by Aragon, has followed him. The latest of her foals to see the racecourse are the maidens Flying Wind (by Forzando) and Tickerty's Gift (by Formidable). Handy Dancer's dam and grandam showed ability comparable to her's, but less stamina; Miss Golightly won over five furlongs as a two-year-old and Gracious Gal was best at six or seven furlongs.

	Spin of A Coin (br 1978)	Boreen (b 1968)	Tamerlane / Scyllinda
Roll A Dollar (b.g. 1986)		Lovely Linan (b 1964)	Ballylinan / Heart Throb
	Handy Dancer (ch 1977)	Green God (ch 1968)	Red God / Thetis II
		Miss Golightly (ch 1972)	Jimmy Reppin / Gracious Gal

The leggy, useful-looking Roll A Dollar will stay two and a half miles over hurdles. He won on firm going at Aintree and was below form on his one outing on soft on the Flat. He still has something to learn about the jumping game, having had just four starts, and will surely continue his progress in a second season. Will Roll A Dollar be worth his place in the Champion Hurdle field? Well, Montelado and Tiananmen Square stand out amongst the latest batch of two-mile novices, but it's hard to name another with a better chance of making the grade. One can only be enthusiastic about his prospects. *D. R. C. Elsworth*

ROLLING THE BONES (USA) 4 b.g. Green Dancer (USA) – Davelle's Bid (USA) (Bold Bidder) [1992/3 16sᵘʳ 17s 16s 16g⁵ 16s] leggy gelding: thorough stayer on Flat, modest at best: best effort in juvenile hurdles when fifth at Edinburgh in January: will prove suited by further than 17f. *M. P. Naughton*   86

ROLSTER PRINCESS 4 ch.f. Right Regent – Sharp Lass (Sharpen Up) [1992/3 F17d] fourth foal: dam tailed off only start: behind in NH Flat race at Hereford in May: yet to race over hurdles. *A. M. Forte*

ROMAN DART 9 b.g. Roman Warrior – Angodeen (Aberdeen) [1992/3 c16vᵖᵘ c16d⁴ c18dᵖᵘ c17vᵖᵘ] strong gelding: moderate chaser in 1991/2: no form in 1992/3: races only at around 2m: acts on soft going and fibresand. *M. Scudamore*   c– –

ROMANIAN (IRE) 5 ch.h. Sallust – Cailin d'Oir (Roi Soleil) [1992/3 18m] workmanlike gelding: has shown nothing in 2 starts over hurdles: modest 13f winner on Flat in January. *R. Akehurst*   –

ROMAN ROMANY 4 ch.g. Sir Patrick – Roman Lass (Roi Soleil) [1992/3 F16s 16d 17f⁴] lengthy gelding: first foal: dam once-raced half-sister to fair chaser Roman Bistro: ninth of 18 in NH Flat race: poor form when fourth in juvenile hurdle at Lingfield in March. *J. T. Gifford*   81

ROMANSH 4 b.g. Shernazar – Romara (Bold Lad (IRE)) [1992/3 17g⁶] leggy gelding: fair form at up to 1½m on Flat for G. Wragg: sold 5,000 gns Newmarket Autumn Sales: well beaten sixth in novice event at Newbury in March on hurdling debut. *Miss Jacqueline S. Doyle*   –

ROMAN WOOD 11 b.m. St Columbus – Weywood (Coliseum) [1992/3 c22vᴿ c33mᵖᵘ] maiden pointer: no sign of ability in hunter chases. *Mrs T. J. Hill*   c– –

ROMANY KING 9 br.g. Crash Course – Winsome Lady (Tarqogan) [1992/3 c24g⁶ c25d* c24s³ c25s⁴ c20g³ c24g c21d⁵] workmanlike gelding: very useful chaser: second in 1992 Grand National and third in void running   c149 –

of 1993 event: won handicap at Exeter in November: generally fair efforts subsequently: effective at 2½m and stays extremely well: acts on soft and good to firm ground: genuine, though tends to idle in front and is waited with: jumps well. *G. B. Balding*

ROMANY SPLIT 8 b.g. Official – Romany Park (Romany Air) [1992/3 22vpu 16s5 16v5 16s a18g3 a18g a16g4 17g] sturdy gelding: poor novice hurdler/chaser: stays 2¼m: acts on fibresand: tried blinkered: sketchy jumper. *D. Nicholson*
c–
71

ROMFUL PRINCE 10 b.g. White Prince (USA) – Romfultears (Romany Air) [1992/3 c21s5 c23vpu c26vF c26d4 c25dR c26m5 c21d3 c21f*] lengthy, sparely-made gelding: fair hurdler: moderate form over fences: short-head winner of novice handicap at Wincanton in May: best form at up to 3m: acts on any going. *C. W. Mitchell*
c95
–

ROMOLA NIJINSKY 5 b.m. Bustino – Verchinina (Star Appeal) [1992/3 17m4 20g5 18m* 16g3 20g3 17d5 17g2] smallish, workmanlike mare: selling hurdler: bought in 3,400 gns after winning handicap at Market Rasen in September: ran creditably afterwards, and also won 3 times on Flat early in 1993: stays 2½m: acts on good to firm and dead ground: blinkered last outing in 1991/2. *P. D. Evans*
71

ROMOOSH 4 b.f. Formidable (USA) – Missed Blessing (So Blessed) [1992/3 16s4 17v5] half-sister to winning jumper Lake Mission (by Blakeney): fair 1¼m winner on Flat: sold out of C. Brittain's stable 7,600 gns Newmarket Autumn Sales: poor form in selling hurdles in November and February: jumps none too fluently. *N. A. Callaghan*
68

RONANS BIRTHDAY 11 b.g. Furry Glen – Mountain Sedge (Goldhill) [1992/3 22s6 c25v c24g3 c26v4 c24g3 c24m2 c24f2 c25g6] big, lengthy gelding: fair chaser at best: in-and-out form in 1992/3: stays 25f when conditions aren't testing: acts on good to firm and soft ground. *P. J. Hobbs*
c105
–

RONANS GLEN 6 b. or br.g. Glen Quaich – Willabelle (Will Somers) [1992/3 F16gsu 16v 17s3 20s4 21v5 22g2 21g* 22m* 20d2] lengthy ex-Irish gelding: chasing type: first foal: dam unraced: won a point in 1991: trained until after second start by W. Burke: improved hurdler in the spring who won maiden at Towcester and novice event at Worcester: ran another good race when second in novice event at Ascot on last start: will stay beyond 2¾m: acts on good to firm and heavy going. *M. J. Wilkinson*
111

RONGWHEEL 11 b.g. Furry Glen – Monday's Pet (Menelek) [1992/3 22spu 18f] sparely-made gelding: poor form in points and over hurdles. *Mrs J. Wonnacott*
–

RONOCCO 11 ch.g. Baptism – Kilteelagh Lady (King's Leap) [1992/3 c16g5 c16m2 c18dsu c17f4 c16f2 c17d5 c17m] leggy, sparely-made gelding: poor chaser nowadays: suited by 2m and top-of-the-ground: front runner: jumps boldly. *Mrs S. D. Williams*
c75
–

ROONEY 7 b.g. Glen Quaich – Dashing Bird (Dominion) [1992/3 c18s3 c20vpu] leggy, lengthy gelding: tubed: of little account. *A. Smith*
c–
–

ROPE 7 b.g. Rolfe (USA) – Mountain Rescue (Mountain Call) [1992/3 18s a16g* a18g5 c16g5 a16g3 17f 16vpu a21g*] compact gelding: modest hurdler: won handicaps at Southwell in January and May: showed nothing on chasing debut: sold 5,000 gns Ascot June Sales: stays 21f: acts on good to firm, dead ground and all-weather surfaces: sometimes gets behind: inconsistent. *Mrs F. Walwyn*
c–
98

ROSATEEN 5 br.m. Teenoso (USA) – Red Roses (FR) (Roi Dagobert) [1992/3 17dF 16v4 21v 16vpu a24g3] sturdy mare: bad novice hurdler: tried blinkered: looks reluctant. *R. T. Juckes*
52 §

ROSCOE HARVEY 11 br.g. Roscoe Blake – Hunter's Treasure (Tudor Treasure) [1992/3 c19d* c20m4 c24d2 c24g5 c20d2 c26vF] strong gelding: fair handicap chaser: won at Exeter in September: generally ran creditably afterwards: not seen out after January: stays 3m: acts on soft and good to firm going: takes a good hold and usually makes running. *C. P. E. Brooks*
c108
–

ROSCOES DINKY   6 br.m. Roscoe Blake – Minibus (John Splendid) [1992/3 c 19d] seems of little account: blinkered once. *Mrs A. Turner*   c–
–

ROSE CUT (USA)   6 ch.g. Diesis – Sweet Ramblin Rose (USA) (Turn-To) [1992/3 20g³] angular, sparely-made gelding: poor novice hurdler: sold 1,200 gns Ascot November Sales: best form at 2m on a sound surface. *D. J. S. Cosgrove*   74

ROSE EDGE   4 b.c. Kris – Butterfly Rose (USA) (Iron Ruler (USA)) [1992/3 17s⁴] no form on Flat for J. Hills: tailed-off last of 4 finishers in juvenile hurdle at Newton Abbot in August. *G. F. H. Charles-Jones*   –

ROSEHIP   8 b.g. Derring Rose – Fairy Island (Prince Hansel) [1992/3 25v⁶ 25d⁵ 25s^F 25m³ 25d^ur c24m⁴ c24d^pu c27g⁶ c25f^F c26d³ c26m⁴] sturdy gelding: poor hurdler/novice chaser: stays 3m: acts on firm and dead ground: blinkered once, visored twice: sketchy jumper. *P. Cheesbrough*   c74
–

ROSE KING   6 b.g. King's Ride – Choral Rose (Blue Refrain) [1992/3 F16v² 17s] sturdy, useful-looking gelding: first foal: dam unraced: second of 18 in NH Flat race at Towcester in January: pulled hard when last of 10 in novice hurdle at Sandown month later: type to do better in due course. *J. T. Gifford*   – p

ROSE LANCASTER   10 b.m. Oh Henry – Lancaster Rose (Canadel II) [1992/3 c27v^pu c26d^pu c27s^pu] lengthy mare: often sweats: no form over hurdles: poor chaser: showed nothing in 1992/3: stays 3¼m: sometimes blinkered. *T. B. Hallett*   c–
–

ROSEN THE BEAU (IRE)   5 gr.g. Roselier (FR) – Dunderry Class (Dusky Boy) [1992/3 16s 17v] sturdy, close-coupled gelding: half-brother to fairly useful Irish hurdlers Coolerin Boy (by Politico) and Gangabal (by Prominer), former also a winning chaser: dam unraced sister to fair Irish hurdler Regent's Rose and half-sister to useful staying hurdler Vulmegan: tailed-off last in novice hurdles in November and December. *N. A. Gaselee*   –

ROSE OF GOLDEN   7 b.m. Bustineto – North Rose VII (Urami) [1992/3 c16g⁵ c17f^pu] sparely-made mare: no sign of ability. *R. Champion*   c–
–

ROSE OF THE GLEN   7 ch.m. Respighi – Ruckinge Girl (Eborneezer) [1992/3 21g^pu] plain mare: fourth in NH Flat race in 1990/1: pulled up and dismounted fourth in novice hurdle at Newbury in February. *P. M. McEntee*   –

ROSES HAVE THORNS   6 ch.m. Ela-Mana-Mou – Cienaga (Tarboosh (USA)) [1992/3 17v a24g] sparely-made mare: winning hurdler: soundly beaten in handicaps in December and January: best form at 2m: acts on good to firm going and fibresand. *D. J. Wintle*   –

ROSE'S MATE (IRE)   4 br.g. Roselier (FR) – Charlies Mate (Prince Regent (FR)) [1992/3 16g^pu 21s^pu] half-brother to winning hurdler/chaser Glen Maye (by Maystreak): dam ran once: pulled up in early stages both starts over hurdles. *N. W. Alexander*   –

ROSE'S ORPHAN   7 gr.g. Scallywag – Rose's Code (True Code) [1992/3 F17d] half-brother to winning jumpers Feeling Rosey (by Uncle Pokey) and Warriors Code (by Roman Warrior): dam useful pointer and winning hunter chaser: behind in NH Flat race at Doncaster in December: yet to race over hurdles or fences. *D. T. Todd*   –

ROSE TABLEAU   10 ch.m. Ballymore – Princess Pageant (Welsh Pageant) [1992/3 21m² 26m* 25g² 26d c21s² c24g 25g⁶ 25s⁴ 28m⁵] leggy, sparely-made, plain mare: fair handicap hurdler: won at Catterick in October: better effort over fences when second in mares novice event at Sedgefield in December: stays 3¼m: acts on good to firm and soft ground: tried blinkered (below best). *J. J. O'Neill*   c79
100

ROSGILL   7 ch.g. Mill Reef (USA) – Speedy Rose (On Your Mark) [1992/3 17s³ 22v² 21s 17s³ 16s⁴ 17f* 17g] sturdy gelding: quite useful handicap hurdler: won at Newbury in March: creditable efforts when placed earlier: effective at 2m and stays 2¾m: acts on any going: visored fifth outing. *M. H. Tompkins*   117

ROSIN THE BOW (IRE) 4 gr.g. Roselier (FR) – Pastinas Lass (Bargello) [1992/3 16g 16s 17s5 18m5 21d] fifth foal: dam unraced half-sister to high-class Irish hurdler Slaney Idol: juvenile hurdler: fifth at Perth and Downpatrick in the spring: stays 2¼m: best effort on good to firm ground. *J. F. C. Maxwell, Ireland* — 80

ROSSA PRINCE 15 br.g. Pitpan – Santa Belle (Delirium) [1992/3 c18gF] winning pointer: maiden hurdler/chaser: very lightly raced nowadays: sold 700 gns Ascot September Sales. *J. P. D. Elliott* — c– –

ROSS GRAHAM 5 gr.g. Macmillion – Play It Sam (Mandamus) [1992/3 17s3 20m6 17gpu 17g] leggy, lengthy gelding: poor staying maiden on Flat: promising third in novice event at Sandown in February on hurdling debut, but failed to confirm that effort: should stay beyond 17f. *Mrs Barbara Waring* — 100

ROSS VENTURE 8 b.g. Monksfield – Fitz's Buck (Master Buck) [1992/3 c22g c19g2 c25mF c24m* c25d4] leggy gelding: quite useful handicap chaser: successful at Windsor in November: one-paced when fourth in valuable event at Ascot in February: sold to join L. Lungo 11,500 gns Ascot June Sales: stays 25f: ideally suited by a sound surface: sometimes jumps to the right: front runner: has won for amateur. *J. A. C. Edwards* — c129 –

ROSSVILLE 8 ch.g. Kemal (FR) – Golden Ingot (Prince Hansel) [1992/3 c16g3] strong, good-topped gelding: very temperamental chaser: refuses as often as not, did so only outing in 1992/3 (continued). *J. I. A. Charlton* — c§§ –

ROSTREAMER 10 b.g. Paddy's Stream – Tarqogan's Rose (Tarqogan) [1992/3 c26m3] leggy, short-backed gelding: fair hurdler/pointer: maiden chaser (not a fluent jumper): suited by a thorough test of stamina: acts on heavy and good to firm ground: tried blinkered: moody. *Miss A. Newton-Smith* — c87 § – §

ROTHKO 12 b.g. Ile de Bourbon (USA) – Scala di Seta (Shantung) [1992/3 20g 20d] angular gelding: improved into a fairly useful hurdler in 1991/2: long way below form in 2 handicaps in February: suited by good test of stamina: acts well on soft ground. *Mrs S. J. Smith* — –

ROUCELLIST BAY 5 ch.g. Rousillon (USA) – Cellist (USA) (Bagdad) [1992/3 16g] no sign of ability on Flat: tailed off in novice hurdle at Edinburgh in December. *V. Thompson* — –

ROUGH CUT 8 ch.g. Krayyan – Angelic Appeal (Star Appeal) [1992/3 23spu 22d 17v 21spu 17gpu 21spu 17dpu] angular, sparely-made gelding: novice hurdler: no form for long time: usually blinkered nowadays. *R. T. Juckes* — –

ROUGH QUEST 7 b.g. Crash Course – Our Quest (Private Walk) [1992/3 c21s2] good-topped gelding: smart novice chaser in 1991/2: looked and ran as though in need of race when below-form second at Kempton in November, only outing in 1992/3: has form at 25f, but likely to prove ideally suited by around 2½m: acts on soft going, yet to encounter a firm surface: likely to prove best with waiting tactics: jumps well. *T. J. Etherington* — c121 + –

ROUTE MARCH 14 ch.g. Queen's Hussar – Wide of The Mark (Gulf Pearl) [1992/3 23m2 25fpu] small, lightly-made gelding: poor hurdler, lightly raced: stays 3m: acts on any going: has been blinkered and visored. *P. A. Pritchard* — 63

ROUYAN 7 b.g. Akarad (FR) – Rosy Moon (FR) (Sheshoon) [1992/3 c22d3] leggy, lengthy gelding: useful hurdler: has jumped soundly and shown promise both starts in novice chases: third at Stratford in October: stays 25f: acts on dead going and good to firm. *Mrs J. Pitman* — c93 + –

ROVING REPORT 6 gr.g. Celio Rufo – Black Rapper (Le Tricolore) [1992/3 c21m*] modest pointer, winner twice early in 1993: won novice hunter chase at Folkestone in May: will stay beyond 21f: acts on good to firm going: should improve. *H. Wellstead* — c85 p

Constant Security Handicap Chase, Doncaster—
Rowlandsons Jewels takes over from long-time leader Sooner Still

ROVING SEAL 11 br.m. Privy Seal – Roving Belle (Wrekin Rambler) [1992/3 c26v⁴ c18v³ c24sᵖᵘ c18sᵖᵘ] workmanlike mare: fair hunter chaser in 1992: well beaten in handicaps in first half of 1992/3: stays well: acts on any ground. *W. G. M. Turner*

c–
–

ROVING VAGABOND 9 b.g. Newski (USA) – Proven Gypsy (Ampney Prince) [1992/3 17d 18g] yet to complete in points: no sign of ability in novice hurdles. *B. R. J. Young*

–

ROVULENKA 5 b.g. Royal Vulcan – Natenka (Native Prince) [1992/3 17s⁶ 16s*] lengthy, rather sparely-made gelding: half-brother to several winning jumpers, including quite useful hunter chaser Paddy Hayton (by St Paddy): dam unraced half-sister to useful jumper Hill of Slane: made running when winning novice hurdle at Leicester in February quite impressively: will be suited by further than 2m: sure to progress and win more races. *M. C. Pipe*

107 p

ROWHEDGE 7 ch.g. Tolomeo – Strident Note (The Minstrel (CAN)) [1992/3 23m⁵ 21f 27g 21dᵖᵘ] small, lightly-made gelding: selling hurdler: well below form in 1992/3: stays 2¾m: acts on firm and dead ground. *Miss Jacqueline S. Doyle*

–

ROWLANDSONS GEMS 8 ch.g. Enchantment – Lillicara (FR) (Caracolero (USA)) [1992/3 17s⁵ 16v⁴ 20d³ 21g² 17mᵖᵘ] workmanlike gelding: fair handicap hurdler: ran creditably when in frame in 1992/3: stiff task last outing: stays 21f: acts on good to firm, heavy going and equitrack: blinkered once, visored once. *P. Leach*

108

ROWLANDSONS JEWELS 12 br.g. Avocat – Coolavane (David Jack) [1992/3 c27s⁶ c26d* c25s³ c24m³ c25d⁵ c24g c25f* c30d c26mᵖᵘ] leggy gelding: useful chaser: won handicaps at Doncaster in December and

c131
–

Sandown in March: running fine race (travelling best) when pulled up lame approaching last in minor event at Warwick in May: seems ideally suited by around 3m: acts on any going: tends to sweat: has won 5 times at Sandown. *D. J. G. Murray-Smith*

ROXKELLY BLUES 7 ch.g. Cree Song – Pitskelly Blues (Pitskelly) c–
[1992/3 a16gpu 16gpu] workmanlike gelding: failed to complete in points and –
a steeplechase: modest second in novice hurdle in 1991/2, no show in 2 races
in May: usually blinkered: sold 1,500 gns Doncaster June Sales. *T. D. Barron*

ROXTON HILL 8 br.g. Croghan Hill – Norhamina (Tyrone) [1992/3 c87
c16d3] rangy gelding: very much a chasing type: modest novice hurdler: –
promising third of 4 finishers in novice event at Kempton in October on
chasing debut, but wasn't seen out again: should stay further than 2m: has
reportedly broken blood vessels. *C. P. E. Brooks*

ROYAL APPROVAL 10 ch.g. Privy Seal – Delilah Dell (The Dell) c84 §
[1992/3 c24m2 c25gro c25dpu c26gur c28f5] lengthy gelding: novice hunter
chaser: trained until after first start by Miss D. Stanhope: stays 3½m: acts
on firm ground: ran out second outing: sketchy jumper. *S. A. Blyth*

ROYAL ATHLETE 10 ch.g. Roselier (FR) – Darjoy (Darantus) [1992/3 c166
25s5 23s* 24s c24g4 c27m3 c29sur 24g] 129
    Royal Athlete finally took his place in the top flight of steeplechasers,
but old habits die hard and occasional jumping errors reduced that position
to a rather precarious toehold. A first-circuit fall when 5/4 favourite in the
Sun Alliance Chase had marred his otherwise excellent novice season way
back in 1989/90. In 1993, he was a faller in the void Grand National and
unseated rider in the Irish National, on both occasions when the weights
gave him a fine chance. The performance which made Royal Athlete look so
well handicapped and marked his belated emergence as a top-class chaser
came in the Cheltenham Gold Cup. Immediately after his novice season, he
would have been on most Gold Cup short-lists, but when in 1993 he finally
did make it to the field, Royal Athlete was sent off at 66/1. He had only
one race over fences in the interim. That run, preceded by three (including a
win off a Jockey Club mark of only 108 at Windsor) over hurdles, was when
eight and three quarter lengths fourth of eleven to Zeta's Lad in the Racing
Post Chase at Kempton less than three weeks earlier. Given the insufficient
test of stamina, his Racing Post run was a promising effort, but hardly one to
herald his bold showing in the Gold Cup. Looking extremely well, Royal
Athlete put in a virtually faultless round of jumping at Cheltenham and was
only about three lengths off the leader four out. He lost his winning chance
when outpaced coming down the hill, but rallied strongly to move into third
at the last, eventually being beaten nine lengths behind Jodami.

Tote Credit Handicap Hurdle, Windsor—
Royal Athlete wins from a large field on only his second outing since 1989/90

Mr G. & L. Johnson's "Royal Athlete"

		Misti IV (br 1958)	Medium Mist
Royal Athlete (ch.g. 1983)	Roselier (FR) (b 1973)	Peace Rose (gr 1959)	Fastnet Rock La Paix
	Darjoy (br 1976)	Darantus (b 1960)	Buisson Ardent Duranta
		Our Joy (b 1957)	Vulgan Jess Figaro

As trials go for horses with 10-4 in the Grand National, this was about as good as they get. The chief question mark over him was probably whether the short period of just over two weeks was long enough for him to recover from his exertions in the Gold Cup. It was a question that was never resolved. The merits of most of the field for this race were as open to debate afterwards as they had been before, but not in the case of Royal Athlete who took a heavy fall at the fence after Valentines first time round, the only one of the seriously fancied runners whose failure to complete could not be blamed on a man with a red flag. Nine days later, his retrieving mission in the Irish Grand National at Fairyhouse ended in a similar vein when he hit the fifth fence too hard to give Mark Pitman any chance of remaining in the saddle. With Pitman preferring Garrison Savannah, Royal Athlete's rider at Cheltenham and Aintree had been Ben de Haan, the winning jockey on the

620

same stable's Corbiere in the Grand National ten years earlier, who retired at the end of the season to take up training. De Haan took the ride again for Royal Athlete's final outing of 1992/3 but there was no transforming this very downbeat end to the season. Returned to hurdles for a £5,000 contest at Ascot in late-April, Royal Athlete was beaten over thirty-five lengths off another lenient mark.

Royal Athlete's dam Darjoy was unraced and her produce besides Royal Athlete have failed to make much of an impact; Dis Fiove (by Le Bavard) was successful in a bumper, and over both hurdles and fences while Do Be Have (also by Le Bavard) was placed in two NH Flat races here as a four-year-old in 1992 for Mrs Pitman but has not run since. The family has recently seen considerably better days in the Grand National, however, as West Tip is out of a sister to the winning point-to-pointer Our Joy, Royal Athlete's grandam. Whether Royal Athlete will run in the race again remains to be seen, but he is obviously most unlikely to be so well handicapped. The thorough test of stamina will suit him extremely well and he acts on ground as diverse as heavy and good to firm; his only run on firm was when falling in the Sun Alliance. Let's hope that Royal Athlete's health and jumping allow him to consolidate his position among the top chasers—a ten-year-old now, 1993/4 will be only his fourth season on the racecourse. *Mrs J. Pitman*

ROYAL BATTERY (NZ)   10 br.g. Norfolk Air – All At Sea (NZ) (Man The Rail) [1992/3 c26d4 c26d4 c25v4 c27s2 c27d3] smallish, workmanlike, good-quartered gelding: fairly useful chaser on his day: good second at Newton Abbot in April, below that form on same course later in month: suited by very long distances: acts on any going: has shown tendency to jump to right: sweats. *D. H. Barons*   c120 –

ROYAL BATTLE   5 b.m. Broadsword (USA) – Non Such Valley (Colonist II) [1992/3 18gpu] half-sister to fair chaser Prince Carlton (by Autre Prince): dam in rear in novice hurdles: tailed off when pulled up in maiden hurdle at Folkestone in March. *Mrs J. Bloom*   –

ROYAL BEAR   11 gr.g. Rupert Bear – Queens Leap (King's Leap) [1992/3 c17m4 c2 1mpu] rangy gelding: very lightly-raced maiden jumper: no worthwhile form. *K. E. Deen*   c– –

ROYAL CEDAR   12 br.g. Celtic Cone – Petal Princess (Floribunda) [1992/3 c28d c25s5 c22v4 c26dF c24spu c28gpu c28gpu] well-made gelding: one-time fairly useful chaser: best effort of season when fourth in handicap at Nottingham in December: trained until after fifth start by J. McConnochie: stays 3½m: acts on any going: makes the odd mistake. *J. W. Curtis*   c99 –

ROYAL CHARGE (USA)   12 b.g. King Pellinore (USA) – Reload (FR) (Relko) [1992/3 24spu 28gpu] leggy, close-coupled gelding: moderate handicap hurdler at best: pulled up lame last outing: stays well: acts on any going, except perhaps on all-weather. *D. R. Wellicome*   –

ROYAL CIRCUS   4 b.g. Kris – Circus Ring (High Top) [1992/3 16d 18d 16d 16s3 16v6 17s a16g2 a18g4 a18g* a22g2] lengthy gelding: poor maiden on Flat: sold out of P. Harris' stable 625 gns Ascot July Sales: won selling hurdle at Lingfield in February: good second in claiming handicap there later in month: stays 2¾m: acts well on equitrack. *P. W. Hiatt*   91

ROYAL CRAFTSMAN   12 b. or br.g. Workboy – Royal Huntress (Royal Avenue) [1992/3 c24m4 c25f3 c24gpu] strong gelding: moderate handicap hurdler/chaser: ran creditably when in frame in September: stays 3m: acts on firm going: tried blinkered/visored: sometimes takes little interest and is one to be wary of. *A. J. K. Dunn*   c93 § –

ROYAL CUPID (IRE)   5 b.g. Royal Fountain – Margeno's Love (Golden Love) [1992/3 F17mpu F16g2 F16d2 23spu] leggy gelding: seventh foal: half-brother to NH Flat race winner/novice hurdler Night of Madness (by Black Minstrel): dam unraced: close second in NH Flat races: destroyed after breaking leg on hurdling debut. *G. M. Moore*   –

ROYAL DAY   7 ch.g. Deep Run – Lady Perkins (Little Buskins) [1992/3   **c84**
c25v² c26m4 c21g³ c22v* c23v³ c25m³] rather sparely-made gelding:
brother to winning jumper Noble Run: dam winning hurdler: winning
pointer in Ireland: fair hunter chaser: successful at Towcester in April:
stays 25f: acts on heavy and good to firm ground. *Miss C. Saunders*

ROYAL DERBI   8 b.g. Derrylin – Royal Birthday (St Paddy) [1992/3 16g³
17g² 16v³ 16d* 17g 21f4 17m² 16g⁵]   166

Outsiders have had their moments in the Champion Hurdle in the last
few years. The latest to excel himself was Royal Derbi who produced a
career-best performance to finish second to Granville Again at 50/1 in
March. Royal Derbi's career has been a long one, and he had already had two
shots at the race, coming ninth to Morley Street in 1991 and eleventh to
Royal Gait in 1992. On neither occasion did he run to form, but there was
little reason to suppose he would have reached a place had he done so (he
started at 66/1 against Morley Street, 50/1 against Royal Gait), and he began
the latest season seemingly fully exposed. Nothing happened before Cheltenham in 1992/3 to suggest that third time round would be radically different for Royal Derbi. He'd been having a quiet season, if anything looking
not quite the force of old. Following three defeats, including one behind
Champion Hurdle contenders Halkopous (in the Fighting Fifth Hurdle at
Newcastle) and another behind Jinxy Jack and Coulton (in the Haydock Park
Trial), he got off the mark in the A.I.G. Europe Champion Hurdle at
Leopardstown in late-January. Vintage Crop's withdrawal at Leopardstown
appeared to smooth the way for another win for the Bula Hurdle winner
Halkopous. He started at odds on in a field of eleven, while Royal Derbi
drifted out to 14/1 as better support came for the Irish runners Novello
Allegro, Crowded House, Autumn Gorse and Muir Station. However, Royal
Derbi made all. Having set a good pace, he was given a breather round the

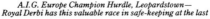

A.I.G. Europe Champion Hurdle, Leopardstown—
Royal Derbi has this valuable race in safe-keeping at the last

Mr M. Tabor's "Royal Derbi"

home turn then quickened to go four lengths clear running towards the last. He had to be ridden to hold on afterwards, but did so, gamely, by two and a half lengths from Novello Allegro who himself was closely attended by Muir Station and Irish Peace. Halkopous was in trouble a long way out and finished next to last.

Royal Derbi's win earned him an immediate quote of 20/1 for the Champion Hurdle, Halkopous and the injured Mighty Mogul being removed from the betting. He didn't hold his market position for long. Two weeks later he ran moderately when favourite with 10-8 for the Tote Gold Trophy at Newbury, dropping away quickly having set a sound pace to three out. And a first attempt at two and a half miles, in the Berkshire Hurdle at Newbury ten days before the Cheltenham Festival, ended in his finishing a well-beaten last of four behind Lift And Load; held up, he was in trouble as soon as the pace quickened a mile from home. Holding Royal Derbi up was a radical change of tactics understandable in the circumstances. At two miles front-running had always been his game. However, he was waited with again in the Champion Hurdle and, surprisingly, appeared on the scene two from home pulling double behind Jinxy Jack. Sent about his business, he responded strongly, he and Granville Again going on from Halkopous. And although Granville Again showed the better turn of foot on the run to the last, Royal Derbi kept on responding very stoutly all the way to the line to keep the margin between them down to a length. Royal Derbi came close enough to reproducing the form in the Scottish Champion Hurdle in April to give further credence to the idea that after five seasons and forty-odd races he was better than ever. Because of the tactics, perhaps. Held up once more, he improved from three out, came off the bridle going to the last then kept on to finish around four lengths fifth of six to Staunch Friend.

		Derrylin (b 1975)	Derring-Do (b 1961)	Darius
Royal Derbi (b.g. 1985)				Sipsey Bridge
			Antigua (ch 1958)	Hyperion
				Nassau
		Royal Birthday (b 1976)	St Paddy (b 1957)	Aureole
				Edie Kelly
			Laroyso (ch 1967)	Lauso
				Royal China

Season 1993/4 is likely to see Royal Derbi in pursuit of more two-mile hurdles. He's done connections proud down the years in the trials, and in his record are wins in the Bula Hurdle, the Fighting Fifth Hurdle, the New Year's Day Hurdle and the Punchestown Champion Four-Year-Old Hurdle. Smallish but workmanlike, he hasn't been seen out over fences although he jumps hurdles very well as a rule. He acts on good to firm as well as heavy ground. While consistency wasn't a strong point in 1992/3, no-one could deny his toughness. There seems little point in re-raking over Royal Derbi's pedigree at this stage of his career. The knowledge that his dam is stoutly bred, by a St Leger winner out of a staying mare, will probably point the punter in the wrong direction should he be tried over longer distances again. The dam was still producing in 1992; she threw a colt by Blakeney that year following a brother to Royal Derbi the year before. Royal Derbi's half-sister Majestic Melody (by Crooner) had a few runs over hurdles in 1992/3, turning out to be just a plater. *N. A. Callaghan*

ROYAL ESTIMATE 7 br.g. Tender King – Nistona (Will Somers) [1992/3 c16gᵖᵘ] strong, close-coupled gelding: fairly useful 2m hurdler in 1990/1: prominent when pulled up lame in closing stages of novice chase at Wetherby in October, and wasn't seen out again: acts on dead and good to firm going: best blinkered. *M. W. Easterby*

          c?
          –

ROYAL FIFE 7 br.m. Royal Fountain – Aunt Bertha (Blandford Lad) [1992/3 21sᵖᵘ 22gᵖᵘ 16gᵇᵈ 21dᵖᵘ 17f 16g⁶] bad novice hurdler. *Mrs B. K. Broad*

          59

ROYAL FIREWORKS 6 ch.g. Royal Vulcan – Bengal Lady (Celtic Cone) [1992/3 16sᵖᵘ 16s] deep-girthed gelding: first foal: dam maiden pointer: pulled up in 2 points: eighth of 23 in novice hurdle at Nottingham in December. *J. Webber*

          –

ROYAL FLAMINGO 7 gr.m. Deep Run – Crown Bird (Birdbrook) [1992/3 16v* 16v³ 16v³ c16d⁵ c22m* c22d* c21g³ c22g*] sparely-made mare: won novice hurdle at Towcester in December: did well over fences subsequently, winning novice events at Nottingham in March and Stratford in May, and handicap at Fakenham in between: effective at 2m under testing conditions and stays 2¾m: acts on heavy and good to firm going. *G. C. Bravery*

          c94
          94

ROYAL FOOL 7 b.g. Idiot's Delight – Royal Celandine (Royal Palace) [1992/3 16f⁴ 17gᵖᵘ] leggy gelding: poor form in novice hurdles: sold 900 gns Ascot May Sales. *O. Sherwood*

ROYAL GAIT 10 b.g. Gunner B – High Gait (High Top) [1992/3 16d⁴]
    'Why does it have to happen to the good ones?' Sadly, Martin Pipe's question on losing Rushing Wild in the Irish Grand National had to be asked on other occasions during the season. The Champion Hurdler Royal Gait died in action at Leopardstown in December, survived only a month by his heir-apparent Mighty Mogul who injured a knee beyond repair in the Wyko Power Transmission Hurdle at Cheltenham. Royal Gait collapsed just after the line in the Bookmakers Hurdle at Leopardstown, as a result of heart failure brought on by a massive internal haemorrhage; he'd gone very well in the race until faltering into fourth place on the run-in. So ended a remarkable tale of the Turf—about a thoroughly likeable horse who rose

          ?

from nowhere to become a top-class stayer on the Flat and then, late in life, was brought out of retirement to win the Champion Hurdle as a novice in only his fourth race; there could well have been more to tell had Royal Gait made it to Cheltenham again, for he would probably have been better then than when he beat Oh So Risky and Ruling in 1992. One thing is certain, a clash there between him and Mighty Mogul would have been worth going a long way to see, and the event was much the poorer for their absence. *J. R. Fanshawe*

Royal Gait (b.g. 1983)	Gunner B (ch 1973)	Royal Gunner (ch 1962)	Royal Charger
			Levee
		Sweet Councillor (b 1968)	Privy Councillor
			Sugarstick
	High Gait (b 1977)	High Top (b 1969)	Derring-Do
			Camenae
		Gay Charlotte (b 1971)	Charlottown
			Merry Mate

ROYAL GAIT (NZ) 5 b.g. Gaiter (NZ) – Heather Carlyle (NZ) (Faux Tirage) [1992/3 F17d⁴] neat gelding: fourth of 18 in NH Flat race at Ascot in April: yet to race over hurdles or fences. *D. H. Barons*

ROYAL GARDEN 4 ch.g. Royal Vulcan – Park Covert (On Your Mark) [1992/3 F16m⁴ F17g²] leggy, sparely-made gelding: half-brother to fair sprinter Park Springs (by Brigadier Gerard): dam stayed 1m: in frame in NH Flat races at Edinburgh in February and Carlisle in March: yet to race over hurdles. *P. Calver*

ROYAL GIOTTO 7 br.h. Royal Fountain – Mount Fairy VI (Prefairy) [1992/3 F16v 21fF 24spu] lengthy horse: second foal: dam, winning Irish pointer, showed signs of ability in long-distance hunter chases: tailed off in NH Flat race and no promise in 2 starts over hurdles. *W. G. McKenzie-Coles*

ROYAL GLINT 4 b.f. Glint of Gold – Princess Matilda (Habitat) [1992/3 16v 20mF 17g 17g²] poor maiden on Flat (trained by I. Balding and M. Heaton-Ellis): first form over hurdles when second in novice event at Hereford in May. *H. E. Haynes*   85

ROYAL GUY 8 b.g. Royal Fountain – Cayle Guide (Guide) [1992/3 20g c26vpu c24s4 a24g⁴ a22gpu] leggy gelding: winning pointer: poor novice hurdler/steeplechaser. *D. Morris*   c–
67

ROYAL HAVEN 7 br.g. Royal Fountain – Tax Haven (Quayside) [1992/3 c20spu c20d² c21d² c25spu c21gpu] big, rangy, good sort: poor form in novice hurdles: promising second in novice chase at Ludlow in February on second start, but failed to confirm it: stays 2½m: acts on dead going: blinkered last outing. *S. E. Sherwood*   c82
–

ROYAL HONEY BEE 5 ch.m. Royal Match – Honey Gamble (Gambling Debt) [1992/3 17spu 17mpu 20mpu] first foal: dam no sign of ability over hurdles: pulled up in maiden hurdles in the spring. *P. Wakely*   –

ROYAL INVADER 9 b.g. Silly Prices – Fishermans Lass (Articulate) [1992/3 c21d⁶ c25vur c25v³ c24d⁴ c25s⁶ c21dur 20g⁵ 28gpu] angular gelding: poor hurdler/modest novice chaser: stays 3m: form only with give in the ground. *M. Dods*   c86
76

ROYALIST (CAN) 7 b.g. Commemorate (USA) – Hangin Round (USA) (Stage Door Johnny) [1992/3 c25s³] close-coupled gelding: poor novice hurdler: won 2 points prior to finishing third in maiden hunter chase at Hexham in April: stays 25f: acts on heavy going and good to firm, possibly unsuited by fibresand: visored once, blinkered twice. *R. J. Kyle*   c81
–

ROYAL JESTER 9 b.g. Royal Fountain – Tormina (Tormento) [1992/3 c22g³ c25g² c25s*] workmanlike gelding: once-raced over hurdles: won maiden hunter chase at Hexham in April: stays 25f: acts on soft ground. *Clive Storey*   c89
–

ROYAL MAZI 6 b.m. Kings Lake (USA) – Seven Seas (FR) (Riverman (USA)) [1992/3 21f a18g⁶] leggy, lengthy mare: poor selling hurdler: probably stays 2¾m: acts on firm and dead going: has run blinkered and visored: ungenuine. *C. R. Beever*   – §

ROYAL MILE 8 b.g. Tyrnavos – Royal Rib (Sovereign Path) [1992/3 c25s^{pu} c24d] tall, leggy gelding: winning hurdler: modest handicap chaser at best: showed nothing in 1992/3: sold 2,500 gns in May: stays well: probably acts on any ground. *P. Cheesbrough*

c–
–

ROYAL PIPER (NZ) 6 br.g. Piperhill – Blue Ice (NZ) (Balkan Knight (USA)) [1992/3 20d^{ro} 17v^2 16v* 22v^2 17s^5 21g^6 22m^4 20d^{ur} 20d 23m^2] deep-girthed, workmanlike gelding: carries condition: fair hurdler: won novice handicap at Uttoxeter in December: also ran well in novice events last 2 starts: stays 23f: acts on heavy and good to firm going: suited by strongly-run race: sometimes sweats and shows signs of temperament. *D. H. Barons*

111

ROYAL PRINT (IRE) 4 ch.g. Kings Lake (USA) – Reprint (Kampala) [1992/3 16m^3 18f^3 17f* 17g^3 16g* 16g^6 17g^6 17m^2 17g] lengthy gelding: plating-class staying maiden on Flat: won juvenile selling hurdle at Huntingdon (bought in 2,900 gns) and juvenile claimer at Wincanton early in season: ran very well next 3 starts: will stay at least 2½m: acts on firm ground. *W. R. Muir*

100

ROYAL PROGRESS 7 b.g. King's Ride – Saucy Melody (Malicious) [1992/3 c20m^3 c25g^{ur} c24m^{pu} 26g^{rtr}] modest novice hurdler/chaser at best: has become very unreliable at start: one to avoid. *G. C. Bravery*

c§§
§§

ROYAL QUARRY 7 b.g. Royal Fountain – True Friend (Bilsborrow) [1992/3 21s^{pu} 16d 16d 21d^{pu}] sturdy, lengthy gelding: has shown nothing in novice hurdles. *J. L. Goulding*

–

ROYAL REFRAIN 8 ch.g. True Song – Polaris Royal (Fury Royal) [1992/3 22v^3 23s^4 22g^4] rangy, workmanlike gelding: very lightly-raced novice hurdler: best effort when fourth at Wolverhampton in January on second start: will be suited by long distances: acts on soft ground. *Capt. T. A. Forster*

86

ROYAL SAXON 7 b.g. Mandalus – La Campesina (Arctic Slave) [1992/3 c24g^3 c21m* c21d^{pu} c24d^5 c22m^F] strong gelding: winning hurdler: tried to run out at second last when winning novice chase at Windsor in November: blinkered, running well when falling last in similar race at Nottingham in March: sold 10,000 gns Ascot June Sales: should stay beyond 21f: acts on good to firm and dead going, possibly unsuited by soft. *Miss H. C. Knight*

c92

ROYAL SHEPHERD 10 br.g. Red Regent – Shepherds Bush (Shooting Chant) [1992/3 21d^4] smallish, leggy gelding: poor hurdler: tried blinkered. *M. P. McNeill*

64

ROYAL STANDARD 6 b.g. Sadler's Wells (USA) – Princess Tiara (Crowned Prince (USA)) [1992/3 24f^{pu}] tall, leggy gelding: untrustworthy maiden hurdler, has fair amount of ability but disinclined to use it: visored. *P. M. Rich*

– §

ROYAL STING 7 b.g. Prince Bee – Dolly-Longlegs (Majority Blue) [1992/3 c26m^5] sparely-made, angular gelding: modest form in points, successful in March: winning hunter chaser: poor fifth at Folkestone in May: stays 2½m: acts on good to firm ground: often blinkered. *J. M. Turner*

c–

ROYAL STREAM 6 br.g. Royal Fountain – Struide (Guide) [1992/3 20d 24d^3] workmanlike gelding with scope: chasing type: poor novice hurdler: should stay beyond 2½m (stiff task over 3m): acts on soft going. *C. Parker*

ROYAL SULTAN 4 b.g. Destroyer – Hopeful Subject (Mandamus) [1992/3 18d] well beaten on Flat and in a juvenile hurdle. *Denys Smith*

–

ROYAL SURPRISE 6 b.g. Royal Fountain – Miss Craigie (New Brig) [1992/3 18m 24f^3] brother to novice chaser Shiona Anne and half-brother to fair chasers Mr Coggy (by Fez) and Brownhill Lass (by Sunyboy): dam useful hunter chaser: well beaten in novice hurdles in August: sold 4,000 gns in May. *W. A. Stephenson*

–

ROYAL SWINGER 5 ch.m. Royal Match – Easy Swinger (Swing Easy (USA)) [1992/3 F17g 17s^{pu} 16v^{pu} 16d 17s^6 16d] sparely-made mare: seems of little account. *Dr P. Pritchard*

–

ROYAL TRIBUTE 8 ch.g. Ribdale – Dizzy Day (My Boy Willie) [1992/3 c–
c26gᵘʳ] big, lengthy gelding: poor novice hurdler/chaser: stayed 2¾m: –
acted on hard ground: blinkered once: dead. *J. H. Johnson*

ROYAL VACATION 4 b.g. King of Spain – Crane Beach (High Top)
[1992/3 18f³ 17m² 18d 16d⁴ 16gᵘʳ 18g⁵ 18g³ 17m²] sparely-made gelding: 82
fourth foal: half-brother to 7f seller winner Cassibella (by Red Sunset): dam
never ran: showed ability in varied company most completed starts over
hurdles: stays 2¼m: acts on firm and dead going. *G. M. Moore*

ROYAL VERSE (FR) 6 b.h. Recitation (USA) – Sauce Royale (Royal
Palace) [1992/3 22f⁴] leggy horse: twice-raced over hurdles, little sign of
ability. *R. Curtis*

ROYAL WONDER 7 b.m. Welsh Saint – Collectors' Item (Run The
Gantlet (USA)) [1992/3 22g³ 20g² 23s³] leggy mare: fair hurdler: creditable 101
efforts all 3 starts in 1992/3: stays 23f: acts on any going: blinkered
nowadays: showed signs of temperament in 1989/90: has been to stud. *M. C.
Pipe*

ROYLE SPEEDMASTER 9 ch.g. Green Shoon – Cahermone Ivy c114
(Perspex) [1992/3 c21g* c24m* c25f* c26d* c26s³ c26d⁶ c24d* c25g c27f² –
c26fᵖᵘ] lengthy, workmanlike gelding: fair chaser: won handicaps at
Worcester, Stratford, Exeter and Cheltenham early in season and hunter
chase at Ludlow in February: stays 3¼m: acts on any going. *O. Sherwood*

ROY'S DREAM 10 b.g. Down The Hatch – Promising Dream (Dreamy c89
Eyes) [1992/3 c23d c21s⁶ c23d* c24dᵖᵘ] rangy gelding: won novice handicap
chase at Kelso in February: stayed 3m: acted on heavy and good to firm
going: dead. *S. J. Leadbetter*

ROY'S HILL 7 b.g. Royben – Magic Sky (Alto Volante) [1992/3 17g 16d⁵
18g³] strong, compact gelding: lightly-raced modest novice hurdler: sold 91
4,400 gns Ascot June Sales: stays 19f: best efforts on good going. *Mrs F.
Walwyn*

RUBICON WATCH 4 b. or br.f. Green Ruby (USA) – Watch Lady
(Home Guard (USA)) [1992/3 18sᵖᵘ 16d] lengthy filly: half-sister to winning –
hurdler Pit Pony (by Hittite Glory): once-raced on Flat: showed nothing
over hurdles in January and February. *C. R. Barwell*

RUBINS BOY 7 ch.g. Riberetto – Gaie Pretense (FR) (Pretendre) c– p
[1992/3 c23d⁶ c22dᶠ c24gᶠ 23s 26d² 22d⁶ 23mᵖᵘ 24s⁶ 21f] workmanlike 100
gelding: modest hurdler: easily best effort of season when second at
Huntingdon in January: some promise in novice chases though not yet an
accomplished jumper: stays 3¼m: acts on good to firm and dead ground. *S.
E. Sherwood*

RUBY LOOK 5 b.m. Green Ruby (USA) – Lookslike Reindeer (Bonne
Noel) [1992/3 16v² 22dᵖᵘ 22fᵖᵘ] sturdy mare: maiden pointer: runner-up in ?
weakly-contested maiden hurdle at Towcester in April: should stay further
than 2m. *N. A. Smith*

RUDDA CASS 9 b.g. Rapid River – Glaven (Blakeney) [1992/3 18g⁶]
poor handicapper on Flat, stays 1½m: poor form in novice hurdle at 67
Sedgefield in October. *Mrs V. A. Aconley*

RUDOLF 6 ch.h. Bustino – Joliette (Jimmy Reppin) [1992/3 16sᵖᵘ]
unfurnished horse with scope: second foal: dam fairly well 9f winner: –
showed nothing in novice hurdle in January on debut. *T. Thomson Jones*

RUE BALZAC (IRE) 5 ch.g. Deep Run – Woodcliffe (Harwell) [1992/3
F17d⁶] brother to winning chaser Deep Cliff: dam, lightly raced, from good –
jumping family: sixth in NH Flat race at Hereford in May: yet to race over
hurdles or fences. *N. A. Callaghan*

RUFFINSWICK 7 gr.g. Baron Blakeney – Indiscreet (Stupendous) c–
[1992/3 24vᵖᵘ] leggy, sparely-made gelding: poor novice hurdler: fell only –
start over fences: suited by test of stamina. *P. Leach*

RUFFTRADE 6 b.g. Sunley Builds – Caribs Love (Caliban) [1992/3
F16m F16g²] half-brother to fairly useful hurdler and winning chaser Tree

627

Poppy (by Rolfe): dam of little account: second in NH Flat race at Chepstow in June: yet to race over hurdles or fences. *C. P. E. Brooks*

RUFUS 7 ch.g. Cheval – Perdeal (Perspex) [1992/3 c26d² c24v² c27vF c105 c25sᵘʳ c24v² c27s* c26d² c21s*] workmanlike gelding: winning hurdler: – fair form in novice chases: successful at Newton Abbot in February and Hexham (visored) in May: sold to join B. Smart 20,000 gns Ascot June Sales: suited by test of stamina and plenty of give in the ground: jumps deliberately over fences. *J. A. C. Edwards*

RULING (USA) 7 b.h. Alleged (USA) – All Dance (USA) (Northern Dancer) [1992/3 16v⁴ 17s³ 17g 16d* 17mᵖᵘ 20f⁴ 16g³ 26sᵖᵘ] 165 §
'Ruling. A serious Champion Hurdle prospect. Third last two years. Quarter share for sale due to owner being disillusioned by racing's petty bureaucracy.' So ran an advertisement in the racing Press shortly before the Champion Hurdle. On the day though, a dispute with the Cheltenham management over complimentary badges apparently resolved, there was far more reason to be disillusioned with Ruling. Jumping poorly, he became tailed off after the third and was pulled up before the third last. It was suggested in some quarters that Ruling, an entire, might have been un-nerved by having to line up next to the mare Flakey Dove at the start. It's a possibility. What we do know, however, is that Ruling had looked a most arduous ride a lot earlier. His latest run at Cheltenham seemed to confirm the suspicion that, having curtailed his Flat career at an early stage by declining to enter the starting stalls, Ruling was now set on minimising his exertions in races over hurdles.
    In fairness to him, that run in the Champion Hurdle was easily his worst of the season. Returning from a carbon fibre implant operation, lack of fitness obviously contributed to his making so little impact on his first few appearances, though his last of sixteen in the Tote Gold Trophy appeared to demand some additional explanation. Ironically, considering what followed, and unfortunately for those who were encouraged sufficiently to back him down to 14/1 for the Champion, the unsatisfactory aspects of Ruling's character were put aside in his race immediately before Cheltenham, in virtually the last of the trials, when he registered his first victory since January 1991. It was an impressive win in style as well, Ruling storming ten lengths clear of his one serious rival Rodeo Star in the Countryside Select Hurdle at Haydock, though it was tempered by the fact that Ruling was meeting Rodeo Star on terms 24 lb better than in the Tote Gold Trophy. On form, Ruling's best efforts of 1992/3 came after Cheltenham in the Martell Aintree Hurdle and the Scottish Champion Hurdle. He was off the bridle at an early stage in both, always prominent when about three and a half lengths fourth to Morley Street at Aintree, then doing all his best work at the finish (having been detached in last place) when two lengths third to Staunch Friend at Ayr. On his final outing Ruling broke down in the Grande Course de Haies d'Auteuil.

		Alleged (USA) (b 1974)	Hoist The Flag (b 1968)	Tom Rolfe
Ruling (USA) (b.h. 1986)				Wavy Navy
			Princess Pout (b 1966)	Prince John
				Determined Lady
		All Dance (USA) (b 1978)	Northern Dancer (b 1961)	Nearctic
				Natalma
			All Rainbows (b 1973)	Bold Hour
				Miss Carmie

    Connections are now trying to find Ruling a place at stud. His high-class efforts to be third in two Champion Hurdles, the first as a novice, obviously make appeal, and he has a good Flat-race pedigree. His sire is the dual Arc de Triomphe winner Alleged, his maternal grandsire Northern Dancer, and his third dam is Miss Carmie, the progenitor of, among others, American champions Chris Evert, Chief's Crown and Winning Colors. The small, compact Ruling was effective at two and two and a half miles and acted on firm ground and good to soft; he had three runs on very soft ground and was well below form on all of them. The final positive point to make about Ruling is that he was best in blinkers, but basically the key to this

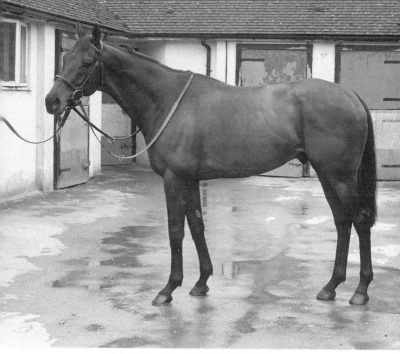

Iain MacDonald's and Jim Short's "Ruling"

horse's performances is not to be found in the form book. *R. F. Johnson Houghton*

RUMBELOW 4 b.c. Welsh Captain – Romana (Roman Warrior) [1992/3 17f² 18gᵖᵘ] lightly raced on Flat: poor second of 4 finishers in juvenile hurdle at Plumpton in August: tailed off when pulled up following month. *J. R. Jenkins*

RUMBLE (USA) 5 ch.g. Lugnaquilla – Sumba (Targowice (USA)) [1992/3 16d 17s² 17vᵖᵘ 16v 16mᵖᵘ] sturdy gelding: winner twice on Flat in USA: second in novice event at Wolverhampton in November, best effort over hurdles: ran as though something amiss last outing. *Andrew Turnell*

83

RUN AGAIN 8 br.g. Runnett – Bee Hawk (Sea Hawk II) [1992/3 18m 17d 21s] compact gelding: novice hurdler: probably stayed 2½m: dead. *R. Dickin*

–

RUN BY JOVE (USA) 10 gr.g. Northern Jove (CAN) – Running Eagle (USA) (Bald Eagle) [1992/3 c16m³] workmanlike, good-bodied gelding: winning hurdler/chaser: below-form third in selling handicap at Perth in August, only outing of season: stays 2¼m: acts on firm and dead ground: usually visored or blinkered in 1990/1, blinkered at Perth. *J. White*

c–
–

RUN FAST FOR GOLD 6 ch.m. Deep Run – Goldyke (Bustino) [1992/3 17dᶠ 17dᶠ 17s⁶ 16d 17g* 17f³] lengthy mare: poor hurdler: won

81

novice handicap at Taunton in March: good third in similar race on same course later in month: will stay further than 17f: acts on firm and probably on dead ground. *G. B. Balding*

RUN FOR FREE   9 b.g. Deep Run – Credit Card (Current Coin) [1992/3 **c163**
c24s* c24v* c30s* c24v² c27m c25f² c33g*]   –

'It ain't over till it's over' has become a well-worn battlecry in sport, encouraging a last-ditch effort from teams or individuals seemingly facing defeat. For the sporting journalist, there's no better story than the lost cause transformed into a great triumph. Like top weight Run For Free's amazing victory in the Stakis Scottish National. Left twenty to thirty lengths at the start after looking for a moment like refusing to race, Run For Free, normally a front runner, trailed the twenty other runners over the early fences. His participation looked a pointless exercise and his rider Mark Perrett reported afterwards that he seriously considered pulling up after a circuit, leading Martin Pipe to quip that if Perrett had been in radio contact he'd have been told to! But Perrett persevered, and Run For Free gradually worked his way back, surviving interference when his stable-companion Riverside Boy came down six out, and was close up turning into the home straight. Keeping on strongly, Run For Free just caught the leader Merry Master, who looked likely to hold on between the last two but lost impetus when meeting the last awkwardly. The winning margin was a neck and Run For Free, on whom Perrett rode a tremendous finish, had earned himself a special footnote in racing's history books.

Run For Free's achievement at Ayr was outstanding—he and Merry Master (who received 24 lb) finished twenty lengths clear of anything

Rehearsal Handicap Chase, Chepstow—
Run For Free beats his better-fancied stable-companion Miinnehoma

Coral Welsh National Handicap Chase, Chepstow —
Run For Free in splendid isolation

else—and it crowned a magnificent season. Run For Free's well-publicised wayward tendencies, which incidentally before Ayr had never included giving trouble at the start, had tended to overshadow his merit as a race-horse. He is only just below top class, better than his eighth in the Tote Cheltenham Gold Cup suggests; his below-form effort at Cheltenham is best forgotten as his saddle slipped early in the race. Run For Free was well worth his place in the Gold Cup field, though his proneness to mistakes and his unreliable steering—he tends to hang or veer left in a finish—tempered confidence in him. He continued on the upgrade, after being among the best of the previous season's staying novices, and won his first three races, the Edward Hanmer Memorial Chase at Haydock, and the Rehearsal Chase and the Coral Welsh National at Chepstow. The Coral Welsh National brought the best out of Run For Free who disposed of the opposition in a style reminiscent of Carvill's Hill's brilliant pillar-to-post victory in the race twelve months earlier. Run For Free, carrying 10-9, had a much easier task at the weights than Carvill's Hill, but he won in tremendous style, setting a sound pace and keeping up the gallop, despite blundering and almost parting company with his rider at the sixteenth, to win by eight lengths, virtually unchallenged from the home turn. Miinnehoma, runner-up in the Rehearsal Chase, closed up on Run For Free in the back straight but didn't last for long and it was another stable-companion Riverside Boy who stayed on for second. Miinnehoma finished third, and Bonanza Boy, a winner of the race twice, came home fourth to complete a clean sweep for Pond House stables. Michael Dickinson's feat of training the first five in the 1983 Cheltenham Gold Cup is unique in a top race, but there have been few other training feats comparable with Pipe's first four in the Welsh National. In Britain, you have to go back for a clean sweep to the 1822 St Leger when James Croft's four runners filled the first four places. Pipe himself had also saddled the first three in the Rehearsal Chase, a rare achievement in itself. Pipe, incidentally, had been due to saddle five runners in the Welsh National but top weight Chatam was withdrawn on the morning after knocking himself. To cap a splendid day, Pipe had four other winners at Chepstow.

Run For Free went up considerably in the weights after the Coral Welsh National and couldn't match Jodami in the Peter Marsh Chase at

Stakis Scottish National Handicap Chase, Ayr—
Run For Free recovers from a very slow start to pip Merry Master, the pair well clear

Mrs Millicent R. Freethy's "Run For Free"

Run For Free (b.g. 1984)	Deep Run (ch 1966)	Pampered King (b 1954)	Prince Chevalier
			Netherton Maid
		Trial By Fire (ch 1958)	Court Martial
			Mitrailleuse
	Credit Card (b 1971)	Current Coin (b 1963)	Hook Money
			Frances
		Tarkita (br 1966)	Black Tarquin
			Nikita

Haydock towards the end of January. Run For Free met Jodami, who had also progressed extremely well, on terms 13 lb worse than when they'd finished first and second in the Edward Hanmer. The most noticeable difference between the pair in the Peter Marsh was in their jumping. Whilst Jodami confirmed his continued progress with a polished round, Run For Free provided evidence, with a typically inconsistent jumping display, that he had probably reached the limits of his development as a chaser. Run For Free finished a good second, coming out the best horse at the weights, but provided further evidence of his waywardness when veering left under pressure after the last and running into the far running rail halfway up the run-in. Run For Free also tended to hang left on the flat when beaten a length and a half by Docklands Express—who'd finished fifteen lengths ahead of him in the Gold Cup—in the three-finisher Martell Cup Chase on firm ground at Aintree. Run For Free is by no means an easy ride—he wears a sliding bar bit and races only on left-handed tracks—but he is a strong-galloping type and a tough nut to crack granted a thorough test of stamina. He reaffirmed at Aintree that he acts on firm going but he's one to make a special note of when conditions are testing, which brings his abundant stamina fully into play. Races like the Welsh and Scottish Nationals, not forgetting the Grand National itself, are right up Run For Free's street. He should have another good season in 1993/4.

The lengthy, sparely-made Run For Free is bred to be a stayer, by champion National Hunt sire Deep Run out of the tough and genuine mare Credit Card who was placed in the Irish Grand National. Credit Card won on the Flat over a mile and a half and a mile and three quarters before embarking on a jumping career. She showed very useful form over hurdles and fences and continued racing until she was eight. Some believe that a long and hard racing career prejudices a mare's prospects at stud. Well, it didn't affect Credit Card who produced nine foals in thirteen years at stud before her death, the last of them a now-yearling filly by Orchestra. Credit Card's unraced four-year-old by Le Bavard was led out unsold at the 1993 Tattersalls Derby Sale. He's a full brother to Credit Call's first foal Bankers Benefit, a genuine and very useful staying hurdler/chaser who was runner-up in the Irish Grand National. Bankers Benefit and Run For Free are easily the best of Credit Card's offspring that have reached the racecourse. Her second foal Card Seller (by Le Bavard) won a point-to-point; her third Penny Opera (by Orchestra) won a minor race over hurdles; and her sixth Moneymore Again (by Furry Glen) was placed in a National Hunt Flat race. Credit Call's fifth foal the Torus filly Spin A Coin was unraced and is now at stud. Credit Call's two-year-old filly by Orchestra is called Brass Band. *M. C. Pipe*

RUN FOR NICK (FR) 5 b.g. Nikos – Run For Juliet (USA) (Model Fool) [1992/3 20m] leggy gelding: winning hurdler: stiff task only outing of season (March): races freely: will prove best at 2m: acts on any going: blinkered once. *Miss Z. A. Green* —

RUN LEAH RUN 14 b.g. Deep Run – Thrifty Pat (Even Money) [1992/3 c21vpu] strong gelding: winning hurdler/chaser: fairly useful form when winning 2 points in February: pulled up in hunter chase in April: stays well: acts on any going: suited by forcing tactics. *Miss Lucinda V. Russell* c– —

RUN MILADY 5 b.m. Blakeney – Bewitched (African Sky) [1992/3 25g 22dpu 21s 18d 22d4 22g5 21dpu 21g2] leggy mare: poor novice hurdler: beaten narrowly in seller at Hexham in May: probably stays 2¾m: acts on good to firm and soft ground: blinkered twice. *Mrs S. M. Austin* 68

RUNNING FORTUNE 8 b.m. Goldhills Pride – Kingdom Come (Klondyke Bill) [1992/3 18s 18d5] compact, workmanlike mare: novice hurdler/chaser: no longer of any account. *Mrs S. J. Smith* c– —

RUNNING LUCKY 6 ch.g. Le Moss – Run of Luck (Lucky Brief) [1992/3 22fpu 23s6] no sign of ability in novice hurdles: dead. *W. A. Stephenson* —

RUN OF GOLD 8 ch.m. Deep Run – The Ceiriog (Deep Diver) [1992/3 17m 18gF 20g 21spu] leggy mare: lightly raced and little sign of ability. *J. D. Roberts* —

RUN PET RUN 8 ch.m. Deep Run – Tierna's Pet (Laurence O) [1992/3 21srtr 25drtr c25g2 c28g* 21d2 c25g2 c21s6 c24d2 c25g*] workmanlike mare: modest novice hurdler: fair handicap chaser: won at Kelso (amateurs) in March and Hexham in May: suited by further than 2m and stays very well: acts on heavy going: refused to race first 2 outings, reformed character afterwards: front runner. *P. Monteith* c105 90

RUN TO FORM 8 br.g. Deep Run – Let The Hare Sit (Politico (USA)) [1992/3 21d6 24s c24s a20g4 c21f*] compact, workmanlike gelding: winning hurdler: fair chaser nowadays: won 3-runner handicap at Plumpton in March: stays 3m: probably acts on any going. *Mrs J. Pitman* c111 —

RUN UP THE FLAG 6 ch.g. Deep Run – Trianqo (Tarqogan) [1992/3 16m3 21d* 21s* 22v* 21d2 22s] well-made gelding: progressive form over hurdles when winning handicap at Warwick, minor event at Kempton and handicap at Sandown in first half of season: also ran well fifth start, but was well beaten last (February): will stay beyond 2¾m: acts on good to firm and heavy ground. *J. T. Gifford* 133

RUN WEST 12 b.g. Record Run – Lush Gold (Goldhill) [1992/3 c26g4 c26d4] workmanlike gelding: well beaten in hunter chases. *Mrs M. D. Rebori* c–

RUPPLES   6 b.g. Muscatite – Miss Annie (Scottish Rifle) [1992/3 c18m²   **c85**
c18d⁵ c16f c18m c16s² c17s⁵ c18d³ c17d³ c18m² c17g² c18s³ c20g c18d*   –
c18f⁶] workmanlike gelding: selling hurdler: modest handicap chaser: ran
creditably most starts in 1992/3 and won at Cartmel in May: stays 19f:
probably acts on any ground: usually blinkered in 1990/1: sketchy jumper:
often gets well behind. *M. C. Chapman*

RURAL CUSTOM   9 b.m. Country Retreat – Fenway (Troilus) [1992/3   **c–**
c22g³] poor pointer, winner in May: remote third in novice hunter chase at
Fakenham later in month. *Mrs Jane Cotton*

RUSHHOME   6 gr.m. Rushmere – Doon Silver (Doon) [1992/3 c21sᵖᵘ]   **c–**
well beaten in NH Flat race and when pulled up in a novice hunter chase. *P.
R. Rodford*

RUSHING WILD   8 b.g. Rushmere – Lady Em II (Lord of Verona)   **c172**
[1992/3 c26d* c30s* c25d² c27m² c29sᵖᵘ]
   Steeplechasing can be one of sport's most exciting spectacles; it can
also be one of its cruellest. When the Cheltenham Gold Cup runner-up
Rushing Wild suddenly lost his action and was pulled up on the second
circuit in the Irish Grand National it was natural to fear the worst. It transpired that he had suffered a pelvic injury serious enough to leave connections with no option but to have him put down. Like the Gold Cup winner
Jodami, Rushing Wild was an up-and-coming chaser who had progressed
extremely well. Stepping straight out of point-to-points (where he was
successful in six of his eight races), Rushing Wild burst onto the hunter

*Anthony Mildmay, Peter Cazalet Memorial Handicap Chase, Sandown—
Rushing Wild (near side) disputes the lead in the early stages*

chasing scene with a twenty-five-length victory in the Christies Foxhunter Challenge Cup at the 1992 Cheltenham Festival. Transferred to champion trainer Martin Pipe for the latest season, Rushing Wild was quick to make his mark in handicap company, following up an impressive all-the-way win at Wincanton with another runaway victory in the Anthony Mildmay, Peter Cazalet Memorial Handicap at Sandown in January which put him firmly in the Gold Cup picture. Rushing Wild turned the Sandown race into a procession from a mile out and won by twenty-five lengths from the 1992 Gold Cup winner Cool Ground who gave him 27 lb. On his only other outing before Cheltenham, Rushing Wild was beaten, starting odds on, by Country Member in the three-runner Agfa Diamond Chase, a limited handicap at Sandown in February. He was pushed out in the Gold Cup betting to around 10/1 after this defeat but ran far better than was generally appreciated at the time, facing a much stiffer task at the weights than in the Mildmay/Cazalet. The Gold Cup was only Rushing Wild's seventh outing in steeplechases. The pick of the paddock, looking superb, he ran a tremendous race at Cheltenham, leading from an early stage, jumping soundly and staying on strongly to go down by two lengths to Jodami, finishing clear of the remainder headed by Royal Athlete and the King George VI Chase winner The Fellow. Like Jodami, Rushing Wild seemed likely to improve further.

	Rushmere (ch 1967)	Blakeney (b 1966)	Hethersett Windmill Girl
Rushing Wild (b.g. 1985)		Omentello (b 1962)	Elopement Castelloza
	Lady Em II (ch 1967)	Lord of Verona (b 1948)	Dante Mulier Magnifica
		Emley	Hunsingore mare by Inchkeith

A big, powerful individual, Rushing Wild was a thorough stayer, suited by forcing tactics, who acted on good to firm and soft going. His achievements should give a boost to his sire Rushmere who had only a handful of runners in the latest season (Rushing Wild was his only winner). Rushmere was bred to stay and won at a mile and a quarter as a two-year-old, and at a mile and three quarters and two miles the following season (showing fairly useful form) before being sold out of Peter Walwyn's stable for 6,400 guineas to go jumping. Rushmere was successful twice as a juvenile hurdler for Gifford before being sent to the sales again, this time making 5,600 guineas to be trained by Atkins. Rushmere, who proved ideally suited by give in the ground, continued racing until breaking down on his only outing in 1980/1; he became inconsistent, but showed useful form at his best over hurdles at up to three miles and won two minor staying handicaps on the Flat as a six-year-old. Rushing Wild's dam, the non-thoroughbred Lady Em II, was unraced and comes from an undistinguished family. The best of her other offspring is the smart but unreliable chaser Ballet Lord (by Coliseum) who was trained by Neville Crump in the late-'seventies and early-'eighties, after being purchased as an unraced five-year-old when Crump spotted him competing in a three-day event in Yorkshire. *M. C. Pipe*

RUSSELL DALUS   6 b.g. Mandalus – Russell's Touch (Deep Run) [1992/3 16d* 16s⁶ 22vᵖᵘ 17g 16d³ 23m²] leggy, lengthy gelding: sold out of G. Balding's stable 39,000 gns Doncaster August Sales: won novice hurdle at Haydock in November: forced pace, ran well when placed on last 2 starts, blinkered on first occasion: stays 23f: acts on good to firm and dead going. *S. E. Sherwood*   100

RUSSELL ROVER   8 b. or br.g. Strong Gale – Cacador's Magnet (Chinatown) [1992/3 c21g* c16f⁶ c18mᵖᵘ c20sᵖᵘ c23f⁶] rangy, workmanlike gelding: tubed last outing: third foal: half-brother to quite useful hurdler Truth Be Told (by Proverb): dam Irish maiden hurdler: maiden pointer: won novice chase at Clonmel in June when trained by T. O'Callaghan: poor form in handicap chases in Britain, making mistakes. *G. A. Ham*   c?

RUSSIAN CASTLE (IRE)   4 b.g. Carlingford Castle – Pampered Russian (Deep Run) [1992/3 16s 16s 20d 22g² 16g³ 16f⁶] leggy, angular   84 gelding: first foal: dam unraced: juvenile hurdler: easily best effort when never-dangerous third at Ayr in April: should stay much further than 2m. *J. Wade*

RUSSIAN LION   12 br.g. Dubassoff (USA) – Tabellion (Tabbas) [1992/3 c21m3 c26d6 c28fur] tall gelding: poor maiden jumper. *Mrs F. M. Gray*   c–
–

RUSSIAN VENTURE   4 ch.g. Torus – Laurello (Bargello) [1992/3 aF16g3 F16dpu] fourth foal: half-brother to fairly useful Irish chaser Chattering (by Le Bavard): dam placed in novice hurdles at up to 3m: third in NH Flat race at Southwell in January: dead. *P. F. Nicholls*

RUSSIAN VISION   4 b.g. Petoski – Visible Form (Formidable (USA)) [1992/3 17g3 16d 16v3] smallish gelding: half-brother to winning hurdler Spofforth (by Jalmood): modest maiden on Flat, stays 1½m: poor form in juvenile hurdles in first half of season: blinkered last start. *A. A. Scott*   81

RUSSINSKY   6 b.m. Celio Rufo – Jeanarie (Reformed Character) [1992/3 21dpu 23g 16v5 16s3 17g3 16m4 21d2 24f4 23g2] angular mare: moderate novice hurdler: suited by a test of stamina: acts on firm and dead going. *G. C. Bravery*   85

RUSTIC AIR   6 ch.g. Crash Course – Country Tune (Prince Hansel) [1992/3 21m3 20s3 24s3 20g4 20d2 16d5 c16gur c23d*] lengthy gelding: modest novice hurdler: jumped soundly in the main and made all in novice chase at Market Rasen in February: needs further than 2m and stays 23f: acts on good to firm and soft ground: sometimes finds little: sure to improve over fences. *J. G. FitzGerald*   c90 p
95

RUSTIC BRIDGE   4 b.g. Celestial Storm (USA) – Travel Legend (Tap On Wood) [1992/3 F17g6] third living foal: dam won over 7f: well beaten in NH Flat race at Bangor in March: yet to race over hurdles. *P. Calver*

RUSTIC FLIGHT   6 ch.g. Rustingo – Emerald Flight (Cantab) [1992/3 F16d6 17s5 17g5 22dpu 20vpu] plain, workmanlike gelding: poor form in novice hurdles. *R. J. Eckley*   66

RUSTIC ROMANCE   5 b.m. Rolfe (USA) – Count On Me (No Mercy) [1992/3 F18g6] mid-division in 2 NH Flat races: yet to race over hurdles or fences. *R. J. Hodges*

RUST MOOR   6 ch.m. Rustingo – Foolish Hooley (Idiot's Delight) [1992/3 F17g6 F17v 16d 16s 16f4 16dF 17f] small mare: second foal: dam poor winning hurdler: no sign of ability. *R. J. Price*   –

RUST PROOF   6 gr.g. Rusticaro (FR) – Grecian Charter (Runnymede) [1992/3 17dF 17m] leggy gelding: half-brother to winning hurdler Princess Semele (by Imperial Fling): seems of little account. *K. White*   –

RUSTY BRIDGE   6 b.g. Rustingo – Bridge Ash (Normandy) [1992/3 c21s4 c25g2 c24s5 c25g4 c24f2 c26f5 c26g2] sturdy gelding: first foal: dam quite useful staying chaser: modest pointer, winner in May: poor form in hunter chases: stays 25f: acts on any ground. *J. I. Johnson*   c79

RUSTY RAILS   11 ch.g. Rustingo – La Chica (El Cid) [1992/3 c26m5] lengthy, rather plain gelding: novice hurdler/chaser: poor pointer. *G. J. Smith*   c–
–

RUSTY ROC   12 b.g. Rustingo – La Chica (El Cid) [1992/3 17g* 16d] lightly-made gelding: fair hurdler: didn't have to be at his best to land the odds in claimer at Taunton in November: well beaten in handicap following month: winning chaser: suited by around 2m: acts on any going: front runner: game. *M. W. Davies*   c–
104 +

RUTH'S GAMBLE   5 b.g. Kabour – Hilly's Daughter (Hillandale) [1992/3 16v 16s 17d 16g6 17g3] sparely-made gelding: modest and inconsistent handicapper on Flat: sold out of D. Chapman's stable 4,000 gns Newmarket Autumn Sales: poor novice hurdler: races at around 2m. *Mrs L. C. Jewell*   70

RUTHS PRIDE   8 ch.m. Amboise – Ruths Image (Grey Love) [1992/3 17g 16g2 17d 17d 17g5 16f3 17g4] small, lightly-made mare: selling hurdler: 75

637

Longley Hall of Fame Handicap Chase, Cheltenham—
Wingspan is about to unseat his rider, leaving Ryde Again clear

creditable efforts most outings in 1992/3: races only at around 2m: acts on firm ground. *G. M. Price*

RUTLAND GATE (NZ) 6 b.g. Gaiter (NZ) – Lady of Penmarric (NZ) (Le Fripon (NZ)) [1992/3 F16g* F17m] useful-looking New Zealand-bred gelding: won 22-runner NH Flat race at Kempton in February: still looked green when seventh in valuable event at Cheltenham in March: yet to race over hurdles or fences. *Mrs J. R. Renfree-Barons*

RUTLAND WATER (USA) 6 ch.g. Sharpen Up – Hemlock (USA) (Big Spruce (USA)) [1992/3 17vpu 16v² 18s] strong gelding: second in novice event at Windsor in February, easily best effort over hurdles: has run as though something amiss on his 3 other appearances. *R. Akehurst*   102

RU VALENTINO 9 ch.g. Deep Run – Tape Mary (Even Money) [1992/3 c21sF c21s³ c24d* c24g² c25m⁵ c27g² c25d] leggy gelding: fairly useful hurdler: won novice handicap chase at Ludlow in February: creditable efforts next 3 starts: stays well: yet to race on extremes of going, acts on any other: not yet an accomplished jumper of fences. *J. A. C. Edwards*   c106 –

RYCO 10 ch.g. Enryco Mieo – Teresa-Hernandez (Queen's Hussar) [1992/3 c21s c27v³ c21vpu c17v⁶] winning hurdler/pointer: best effort in steeplechases when third of 5 finishers in novice event at Fontwell in December: stays well: acts on any going. *Mrs M. E. Long*   c82 –

RYDAL PRIDE 8 b.g. Pry – Will Preach (Will Somers) [1992/3 c16m c21s⁵] lengthy gelding: poor novice hurdler/chaser: sold 1,700 gns Ascot June Sales. *J. T. Gifford*   c– –

RYDE AGAIN 10 ch.g. Celtic Cone – Rydewell (Blast) [1992/3 c21v² c21s* c20gF] lengthy, workmanlike gelding: very useful hurdler: showed himself as good as ever over fences when winning handicap at Cheltenham in January by 12 lengths: fell third only subsequent start: effective at around 2½m and stays well: suited by strong handling: blinkered last 2 starts 1990/1: normally jumps soundly. *Mrs J. Pitman*   c147 –

RYMASTER 6 b.g. Rymer – Asti Spumante (FR) (Fireside Chat (USA)) [1992/3 16m] tailed off in NH Flat race and a novice hurdle. *A. L. Forbes*   –

RYMER KING 11 b.g. Rymer – Belinda Pocket (Pampered King) [1992/3   c–
c28s⁶ c22vᵖᵘ c25mᵘʳ c26dᵖᵘ c25gᶠ] leggy, workmanlike gelding: has been   –
operated on for soft palate and tubed: fairly useful chaser at best: no worthwhile form in 1992/3: stays well: best form with give in the ground. *J. Chugg*

RYMOLBREESE 8 gr.m. Rymer – Moll (Rugantino) [1992/3 c16d⁶   c–
c21sᶠ c25dᵘʳ c19d⁵ c19m⁴] sparely-made, angular mare: poor novice   –
hurdler/chaser: has run in a seller. *A. P. James*

RYMSTER 10 b.g. Rymer – Funny Baby (Fable Amusant) [1992/3 c22g²]   c92
tall gelding: one-time useful hurdler: fair form in points in 1993, winning in   –
April: having second race in steeplechases and fair effort when second in
novice hunter chase at Fakenham previous month: stays 2¾m: acts on dead
going. *Mrs J. Read*

RYTON GUARD 8 br.g. Strong Gale – Gardez Le Reste (Even Money)   c83
[1992/3 c21d⁴ c20gᶠ c24g c24f³ c25m⁵] rather sparely-made gelding: –
moderate novice chaser: stays 3m: acts on firm and dead going. *S. Christian*

RYTON RUN 8 br.g. Deep Run – Money Spinner (Even Money) [1992/3   c72 x
c21sᵖᵘ c24f³ c25m³ c21mᵖᵘ c23f⁵ c21m⁴] lengthy gelding: poor novice   –
chaser: probably stays 25f: acts on hard ground: poor jumper. *Mrs S. M.
Odell*

S

SAAHI (USA) 4 b.c. Lyphard (USA) – Dumtadumtadum (USA) (Grey
Dawn II) [1992/3 16dᵖᵘ 17g⁵] compact colt: fair performer around 1m on Flat: –
showed nothing in juvenile hurdles in February. *C. Weedon*

SABAKI RIVER 9 br.g. Idiot's Delight – Keen Lass (Andrea Mantegna)   c114
[1992/3 c20d c16v² c21d⁴ 17s² 17s* 17f⁴ 17d³ 17g* 16f 20g* 23f⁴] leggy   128

Oxenton Handicap Hurdle, Cheltenham—Sabaki River is clear of Dextra Dove at the last

gelding: fairly useful handicap hurdler/chaser: successful over hurdles at Chepstow, Cheltenham and Exeter in second half of season: effective at around 2m with give in the ground and stays 2¾m: acts on any going: usually a front runner: tough and game. *Mrs J. G. Retter*

SABIN DU LOIR (FR) 14 ch.g. Go Marching (USA) – Star Light (FR) (Val de Loir) [1992/3 c20s³ c21v*] rather lightly-made gelding: very smart performer who won 8 races over hurdles and 13 over fences: gained last success in John Bull Chase at Wincanton in January, rallying in fine style to beat Ryde Again a neck: raced mainly around 2½m: acted on any going: game and genuine: tended to make the odd mistake: was suited by forcing tactics: has been retired. *M. C. Pipe*   **c151** –

SACRE D'OR (USA) 8 b.g. Lemhi Gold (USA) – Dedicated To Sue (USA) (Su Ka Wa) [1992/3 c21s* c21m⁴ c21d* c21s* c21v⁶ c20d² c21d² c21m* c20fᵖᵘ] workmanlike gelding: useful handicap chaser: trained until after sixth start by J. Mackie: successful at Uttoxeter, Bangor and Leicester in first half of season, and won Mildmay of Flete Challenge Cup at Cheltenham in March (by 2 lengths from Smartie Express): effective at 2m to 21f: acts on soft going and good to firm (never going well on firm last start): sound jumper: game. *N. Tinkler*   **c134** –

SACROSANCT 9 b.g. The Parson – Cahernane Girl (Bargello) [1992/3 c22g⁴ 25s* 21s² 21f² 25m*] sturdy, workmanlike gelding: fair hurdler: won handicaps at Perth (amateurs) in April and Uttoxeter in June: fourth in novice hunter chase at Nottingham in February on chasing debut: stays 25f: acts on any going. *K. C. Bailey*   **c78** p 109

SADDLER'S CHOICE 8 b.g. Buckskin (FR) – Lady Perry (David Jack) [1992/3 c24s³ c26v² c23v² c24s* c24d* c25d⁵ c25g⁵] big, lengthy gelding: fair hurdler at best: won novice chases at Ludlow (handicap) and Huntingdon in January: ran poorly last 2 starts: stays 3¼m: acts on heavy going: lazy sort who needs plenty of driving: sometimes let down by his jumping. *J. A. C. Edwards*   **c99** –

SAFARI KEEPER 7 b.g. Longleat (USA) – Garden Party (Reform) [1992/3 21g⁴ 22d⁴ 22d² 26s a20g⁶ a24g²] sparely-made gelding: novice selling hurdler: stays 3m: acts on dead ground and fibresand: tried blinkered: sometimes jumps none too fluently: inconsistent. *J. Norton*   65

SAFARI PARK 4 ch.f. Absalom – Nyeri (Saint Crespin III) [1992/3 18m² 18m² 16g 20g⁶] small filly: half-sister to a winning Italian jumper by Balidar: 73

*Mildmay of Flete Challenge Cup (Handicap Chase), Cheltenham—
Sacre d'Or takes the last ahead of Southern Minstrel and Smartie Express*

poor maiden on Flat: no better over hurdles: best efforts over 2¼m on good
to firm going: front runner. *B. S. Rothwell*

SAFE ARRIVAL (USA) 5 gr.m. Shadeed (USA) – Flyingtrip (USA)
(Vaguely Noble) [1992/3 17g 17g 16dᵖᵘ 17v⁵ 16s] leggy mare: poor novice
hurdler: sometimes blinkered, including last 2 starts: sold 2,300 gns
Newmarket July Sales. *T. Keddy* —

SAFETY (USA) 6 b.g. Topsider (USA) – Flare Pass (USA) (Buckpasser) **c87**
[1992/3 c17m* c16f* c18s³ c17gᵘʳ a22g a16g* a16g² c17mᵘʳ c18v³ c18f] 105
lengthy gelding: fair hurdler: won handicap at Lingfield in February: modest
chaser: won novice events at Newton Abbot and Plumpton early in season:
best at around 2m: acts on firm going and goes particularly well on equitrack
(below his best with plenty of give in the ground): blinkered nowadays: front
runner. *J. White*

SAFFAAH (USA) 6 ch.g. Secreto (USA) – Somebody Noble (USA) 111
(Vaguely Noble) [1992/3 17s² 16vᵖᵘ 17s 17m³ 21g] quite good-topped
gelding: fair hurdler: races freely and form only at around 2m: acts on soft
and good to firm going: sometimes wears tongue strap. *W. R. Muir*

SAGAMAN (GER) 7 b.g. Solo Dancer (GER) – Scholastika (GER) 126
(Alpenkonig (GER)) [1992/3 17g* 16g4] angular gelding: fairly useful
hurdler: reportedly injured when successful in handicap at Cheltenham in
October: showed nothing on next start 5 months later: stays 2½m: acts on
firm and dead ground (ran poorly on soft): visored once in 1989/90: has
looked a difficult ride. *K. R. Burke*

SAIF AL ADIL (IRE) 4 b.g. Reference Point – Hardihostess (Be My
Guest (USA)) [1992/3 17gᵖᵘ] fifth foal: half-brother to a poor Flat maiden by —
Persian Bold: dam, 7f winner at 2 yrs, stayed 1½m: behind when pulled up
in novice hurdle in May on debut. *Mrs R. Williams*

SAILOR BLUE 6 b.g. Julio Mariner – Blue Delphinium (Quorum) **c88** §
[1992/3 c18gᴿ c16s² c16vᵘʳ 18v⁵ 21s⁴ 20s 17d³ 21g* 18v³] leggy, 102 §
sparely-made gelding: fair hurdler: won handicap at Towcester in March:
form over fences only when second in handicap at Worcester in October:
effective from 2m to 21f: acts on good to firm and soft ground: blinkered
nowadays: sometimes looks reluctant over fences (did so final start).
Andrew Turnell

SAILOR BOY 7 b.g. Main Reef – Main Sail (Blakeney) [1992/3 a20g⁵
a20g² 21gᵖᵘ a24g⁶] smallish gelding: winning hurdler, only modest form in 87 §
1992/3: effective from 2¼m to 2¾m: goes well on equitrack: blinkered last
3 outings: reluctant, and one to treat with caution. *A. S. Reid*

SAILORS CHOICE 6 ch.g. Scallywag – Sailor's Sol (The Bo'sun) 75
[1992/3 17d⁵] half-brother to winning hurdlers Ashbury Lad (by Andrea
Mantegna) and Soldier Sahib (by Sahib): dam, half-sister to several winning
jumpers, was placed over 1½m: some promise when fifth of 12 in novice
hurdle at Perth in September, but wasn't seen out again: will stay 2½m. *J.
A. Hellens*

SAILOR'S DELIGHT 9 b.g. Idiot's Delight – Sarasail (Hitting Away) **c–**
[1992/3 c20m⁴] close-coupled gelding: carries condition: moderate chaser: —
in need of race in October: sold 5,800 gns in May: stays 2¾m: acts on firm
ground. *W. A. Stephenson*

SAILORS LUCK 8 b.g. Idiot's Delight – Sarasail (Hitting Away) [1992/3 **c94**
17v c16d* c16s² c16d³ c16m² c20mᵖᵘ] sparely-made gelding: moderate —
hurdler: won novice handicap chase at Windsor in January: ran well next 3
starts: suited by sharp 2m: acts on soft and good to firm going. *P. G. Murphy*

SAILOR'S ROSE 5 ch.m. Julio Mariner – Roseitess (Royal And Regal
(USA)) [1992/3 F16v F16s⁴ F17f⁴ 17m 17g 18dᵖᵘ] unfurnished mare: fifth 70
foal: half-sister to 6-y-o Rosemoss (by Le Moss), placed in NH Flat races:
dam won maiden hurdle in Ireland: showed a little ability in NH Flat races,
and in novice hurdles on last 2 starts: blinkered last outing (pulled hard). *M.
C. Pipe*

SAINT BENE'T (IRE) 5 b.g. Glenstal (USA) – Basilea (FR) (Frere Basile (FR)) [1992/3 18m² 18f³ 17m* 16d⁴ 18gᵖᵘ 18mᵖᵘ 17g 17g³ 17f²] workmanlike gelding: selling hurdler: won conditional jockeys handicap at Huntingdon (bought in 4,300 gns) in August: ran creditably when placed in late in season: stays 2¼m: acts on firm and good to soft ground: jumps well. *K. G. Wingrove* — 85

SAINT CIEL (USA) 5 b.h. Skywalker (USA) – Holy Tobin (USA) (J O Tobin (USA)) [1992/3 16d³ 16v⁶ 17g] neat horse: poor novice hurdler: has raced only at around 2m: probably acts on heavy ground: sketchy jumper: winner over 10.5f on Flat in 1993. *F. Jordan* — 80

SAINTE MARTINE 6 b.m. Martinmas – Petite Culotte (Lucky Brief) [1992/3 16mᶠ 17g³ 19m⁴] poor novice hurdler: in frame in early-season events at Hereford and Exeter: stays 19f: acts on good to firm ground. *Mrs A. Knight* — 72

SAINTHILLS SON 8 b.g. Dunphy – Sainthill (St Alphage) [1992/3 23dᵖᵘ 20s 23s a22g 21s³ 24fᵘʳ 22f⁴] lengthy, sparely-made gelding: plating-class novice hurdler: stays 2¾m: acts on any going. *M. Tate* — 67

SAINTLY LAD 11 b.g. Derrylin – Saintly Miss (St Paddy) [1992/3 16d*] strong gelding: has been fired: very lightly-raced hurdler: first race for almost 3 years, finished lame when winning selling hurdle at Towcester in October and wasn't offered for auction: blinkered only start in 1989/90. *P. D. Cundell* — 79

SAINTLY LASS 9 b.m. Derrylin – Saintly Miss (St Paddy) [1992/3 16v 18v⁶ 16fᵖᵘ] leggy mare: very lightly raced and has shown only a little ability over hurdles: retained 850 gns Ascot February Sales. *P. D. Cundell* — 71

SAINTLY PATH 10 ch.g. Deep Run – Shuil Le Dia (Kabale) [1992/3 17s⁶ 20d⁴ 16g 16s 20s³ 16g] strong, plain gelding: poor novice hurdler/chaser: stays 2½m: acts on soft going: poor jumper of fences. *W. G. Reed* — c– x 81

SAINT RUBY (IRE) 4 ch.g. Hard Fought – Maquillage (Manado) [1992/3 F17m] leggy, rather unfurnished gelding: third live foal: dam unraced: tailed off in NH Flat race at Cheltenham in April: sold 1,000 gns Ascot June Sales: yet to race over hurdles. *C. Weedon* — —

SAKIL (IRE) 5 b.h. Vision (USA) – Sciambola (Great Nephew) [1992/3 16v³ a16g⁴ a18g³ 20v⁶] poor novice hurdler: ran badly last start (January): stays 2¼m: acts on heavy going and equitrack. *S. Dow* — 78

SALAMANDER JOE 8 br.g. Salluceva – Fast And Clever (Clever Fella) [1992/3 c27d³ c24f c28d² c28m³ c26d⁶] leggy gelding: fair handicap chaser at best: off course over 5 months before running poorly last 2 starts: stays well: acts on firm and dead ground: makes mistakes: untrustworthy. *D. Nicholson* — c103 § —

SALAR'S SPIRIT 7 ch.g. Salmon Leap (USA) – Indigine (USA) (Raise A Native) [1992/3 17s³ 18m³ 17f⁴ 18g² 17sᵖᵘ 17g³ 17f⁵ 16f⁶] leggy gelding: poor novice hurdler: stays 2¼m: probably acts on any going. *W. G. M. Turner* — 69

SALCOMBE HARBOUR (NZ) 9 ch.g. English Harbour – Faux Leigh (NZ) (Harleigh) [1992/3 c21d² c24gᵖᵘ c23fᵖᵘ] lengthy gelding: second in hunter chase at Windsor in February, easily best effort of season: suited by around 2½m and give in the ground: usually visored or blinkered nowadays: jumps none too fluently: reluctant and unreliable. *H. M. Irish* — c90 § —

SALESMAN 6 b.g. Starch Reduced – Miss Purchase (Sterling Bay (SWE)) [1992/3 17gᵖᵘ 16g⁵ 16m] leggy gelding: little sign of ability over hurdles. *J. R. Bosley* — —

SALIC DANCE 5 b.h. Shareef Dancer (USA) – Sandy Island (Mill Reef (USA)) [1992/3 17vᵖᵘ 22m 26mᵖᵘ] small horse: has shown more temperament than ability over hurdles: visored last start. *G. A. Ham* — – §

SALINGER 5 b.g. Rousillon (USA) – Scholastika (GER) (Alpenkonig (GER)) [1992/3 16d⁵] leggy, angular gelding: placed over 1¼m on Flat: modest form when close fifth of 9 in slowly-run novice hurdle at Uttoxeter in October. *L. J. Codd* — 88 ?

SALLY FAY (IRE)   5 b.m. Fayruz – Trust Sally (Sallust) [1992/3 18spu]
close-coupled mare: no sign of ability over hurdles. *T. Kersey*   –

SALLY FORTH   7 b.g. Sallust – Sally Knox (Busted) [1992/3 16g⁴ 17m⁵]
good-topped gelding: poor novice selling hurdler: started slowly last outing   66
(August). *J. R. Bostock*

SALLY PIGTAILS   7 b.m. Broadsword (USA) – Panniers Premier
(Pannier) [1992/3 20m⁴] smallish, sparely-made mare: poor novice hurdler: 65
sold 1,650 gns Ascot December Sales: stays 2½m: acts on good to firm and
dead going. *A. J. Wilson*

SALLY'S GEM   8 b.g. Hasty Word – China Bank (Wrekin Rambler)   c108
[1992/3 c21v⁴ c24dpu c24d²] leggy, good-topped gelding: fair hurdler: 5/1   –
from 20/1, first form over fences and fair effort when clear second to
Flashthecash in novice handicap at Stratford in February: needs at least
2½m and stays 3m: acts on good to soft going: game front runner: should
win a race over fences. *J. White*

SALLY SOHAM (IRE)   5 b. or br.m. Kambalda – Riseaway (Raise You
Ten) [1992/3 17d 22sF 17g 17g⁵] angular mare: sister to fair staying hurdler   72
Kamrise: dam unraced: easily best effort over hurdles when fifth in maiden
at Plumpton in March: will stay beyond 17f. *F. Murphy*

SALMAN (USA)   7 b.g. Nain Bleu (FR) – H M S Pellinore (USA) (King
Pellinore (USA)) [1992/3 17d 16d 17g* 17g* 17dF 17m⁶] strong gelding: has   105
had soft palate operation: trained until after second start by S. Norton:
improved hurdler afterwards, successful in conditional jockeys novice
handicap at Fakenham and novice event at Bangor in March: races at around
2m: acts on good to firm going: headstrong and makes running. *Mrs V. C.
Ward*

SALMON DANCER (IRE)   4 b.c. Salmon Leap (USA) – Welsh Walk
(Welsh Saint) [1992/3 18mpu] leggy colt: poor maiden on Flat: showed   –
nothing in selling hurdle at Market Rasen in August: sold 950 gns
Doncaster November Sales. *M. F. Barraclough*

SALMONID   7 ch.g. Salmon Leap (USA) – Persian Polly (Persian Bold)
[1992/3 16dpu 16vpu 17g* 17m⁶ 16spu 16f 17mpu] stocky gelding: 50/1-winner   92
of novice hurdle at Huntingdon in February, easily best effort: likely to
prove suited by around 2m and a sound surface: takes good hold. *Miss K. S.
Allison*

SALMON STREAM (USA)   8 b.m. Irish River (FR) – Mary Deva   c–
(Dhaudevi (FR)) [1992/3 17m³] winning hurdler in 1988/9: very lightly raced   75
and first form since, including over fences, when third in seller at Newton
Abbot in August: sold 680 gns Doncaster September Sales: blinkered once.
J. White

SALTHORSE DELIGHT   5 b.m. Idiot's Delight – Lucys Willing (Will
Hays (USA)) [1992/3 F17m] angular mare: second foal: half-sister to 6-y-o
Robbie's Boy (by Sunley Builds): dam poor winning pointer: pulled hard and
finished tailed off in NH Flat race at Cheltenham in April: yet to race over
hurdles or fences. *C. P. E. Brooks*

SALUTING WALTER (USA)   5 b.g. Verbatim (USA) – Stage Hour
(USA) (Stage Director (USA)) [1992/3 17dpu 16s 16v 16f⁴ 18g² 16s⁶]   77
good-topped gelding: fair form at 1m to 1¼m on Flat at 3 yrs, below best in
1992: poor novice hurdler: stays 2¼m: probably acts on any going. *I.
Campbell*

SALVAGER   9 b.g. Balinger – Mahnaz (Deep Diver) [1992/3 17gpu 18dpu]
big, rangy, chasing type: very lightly raced and little sign of ability over   –
hurdles: sold to J. Poulton 1,650 gns Ascot November Sales: won a point in
April. *J. T. Gifford*

SAMMY HICK   4 ch.g. Venturesome – Our Maidie (Jolly Jet) [1992/3
16mpu] first foal: dam of little account: burly and green, virtually refused   –
second and soon pulled up in October on hurdling debut. *Alf Watson*

SAM PEPPER 7 ch.g. Turn Back The Time (USA) – Haselbech (Spartan
General) [1992/3 c24s^ur c23v^pu c24v^3 c27s^F c24f^3 c25s] angular, sparely-
made gelding: winning pointer: maiden hurdler/chaser. *Mrs S. M. Farr*

c–
–

SAM SHORROCK 11 b. or br.g. Vivadari – To Windward (Hard Tack)
[1992/3 c21d* c24s c26s^3 24v^5 c22v^pu c24v^5 c26g^5 c26d^pu c26d^2 c26v*
c24g^pu] chunky gelding: carries plenty of condition: moderate handicap
chaser: successful at Uttoxeter (conditional jockeys) in October and
Hereford in April: behind only outing over hurdles: thorough stayer: acts on
heavy going: often blinkered. *G. Thorner*

c98
–

SAM THE MAN 6 b.g. Aragon – First Temptation (USA) (Mr Leader
(USA)) [1992/3 22f^4 20g^pu 17d^6 18d 17v^5 17v^3 16v^F 18v] sparely-made
gelding: easily best effort over hurdles when third in conditional jockeys
selling handicap at Plumpton in November, finding little: likely to prove
best at around 2m: acts on heavy going: blinkered once. *J. Ffitch-Heyes*

76

SAMURAI GOLD (USA) 5 b.h. Golden Act (USA) – Taipan's Lady
(USA) (Bold Hour) [1992/3 16g] compact horse: one-time modest middle-
distance performer on Flat: sold out of P. Walwyn's stable 5,600 gns
Newmarket September Sales, resold 4,600 gns, probably for export, Ascot
February Sales: no aptitude for hurdling in novice event at Wincanton in
between. *C. James*

–

SANAWI 6 b.g. Glenstal (USA) – Russeting (Mummy's Pet) [1992/3 16f^3
17m* 16s^F] small gelding: selling handicap hurdler: bought in 4,250 gns
after winning at Stratford in October: barely stayed 19f: probably acted on
any going: blinkered once: dead. *P. D. Evans*

83

SANDAIG 7 b.g. Kemal (FR) – Pride of Croghan (Raise You Ten) [1992/3
c17g^F c17s^4 a16g^4 c17g^6 c21g^3] rangy gelding: novice hurdler/chaser:
blinkered, best effort over fences when second in novice handicap at
Worcester in April: stays 21f: acts on dead going. *K. C. Bailey*

c85
–

SAND-DOLLAR 10 ch.g. Persian Bold – Late Spring (Silly Season)
[1992/3 20f* 17g^4 17d^5 a20g^3 20d^6 20f^4] leggy gelding: fairly useful handicap
hurdler at best: won at Taunton in October: below form after next start:
stays 2½m: seems best on a sound surface, and acts on fibresand: held up. *J.
A. B. Old*

122 d

SANDEDGE 6 b.m. Major Domo – Hallo Cheeky (Flatbush) [1992/3
c25g^F] lengthy mare: second foal: half-sister to poor novice hurdler
Rosewell (by Liberated): dam, selling hurdler, stayed well: winning pointer:
fell second in hunter chase at Kelso in March. *G. F. White*

c–
–

SANDFORD SPRINGS (USA) 6 b.m. Robellino (USA) – Tiger Scout
(USA) (Silent Screen (USA)) [1992/3 20g^2 16v^2 20d^4 20d^4] workmanlike
mare: moderate novice hurdler: ran well first 2 starts, below form last 2:
needs testing conditions at 2m and should stay beyond 2½m: acts on heavy
going: wore hood once, blinkered last outing. *D. Burchell*

94

SANDFORTH WAY 4 b.f. Silly Prices – Socher (Anax) [1992/3 21s^pu]
second foal: dam, novice selling hurdler, sister to fairly useful chaser Earth
Works and half-sister to numerous other jumping winners, including smart
2m chaser Sea Merchant: tailed off when pulled up in selling hurdle at
Hexham in May. *Martyn Wane*

–

SANDHURST PARK 8 ch.g. Sandhurst Prince – Sandford Lass
(Sandford Lad) [1992/3 17v 17v c19s^6 16s^2 17s^6 21d^4 18s c18g^3] small,
angular gelding: modest hurdler nowadays: sold out of P. Murphy's stable
2,200 gns Doncaster March Sales after sixth start: third in novice chase at
Exeter in May: stays 19f: acts on heavy ground: blinkered fourth and last 2
outings, visored in between. *K. F. Clutterbuck*

c82
89

SAND KING (NZ) 7 gr.g. Beechcraft (NZ) – Gifted Girl (NZ) (Rich Gift)
[1992/3 16s^pu 16s 26s^3 22s 20d^6 22m^2 24g* 22f^pu] workmanlike .gelding:
modest hurdler: won novice handicap at Bangor in March: ran as though
something amiss next time: stays 3m: acts on good to firm ground:
blinkered last 3 starts: looks a difficult ride. *J. White*

88

SANDMOOR PRINCE 10 b.g. Grundy – Princesse du Seine (FR) (Val   c88
de Loir) [1992/3 c18f⁴ c20m c21dᵖᵘ 22sᵖᵘ c23m³ c20d³] leggy gelding: –
novice hurdler: modest handicap chaser: creditable third at Worcester and
Ludlow in the spring: stays 23f: acts on firm going and good to soft: trainer
ridden. *Dr P. Pritchard*

SANDRO 4 b.g. Niniski (USA) – Miller's Creek (USA) (Star de Naskra   75
(USA)) [1992/3 18g* 17g⁵ 18d* 17m⁵ 17v 17v³ 16v⁴ 17v 17sʳᵒ 16vᵖᵘ 16g 17g]
leggy gelding: maiden on Flat: successful in juvenile hurdles at Fontwell
(claimer, awarded race on technical grounds) and Exeter early in season:
sold out of J. Fanshawe's stable 7,200 gns Newmarket September Sales
after first win: well below form last 5 outings: stays 2¼m: acts on heavy
ground: usually blinkered: ran out ninth start. *R. J. Baker*

SANDSTONE ARCH 10 b.g. Niels – War Rain (Bahrain) [1992/3   c88
c21mᵖᵘ c25dᵖᵘ c25sᵖᵘ c24fᵘʳ c26m* c24f³ c23g* c21vᵖᵘ c26fF c24fᵖᵘ   –
c23mᵖᵘ] rangy gelding: won novice chases at Catterick in March and Kelso
in April: stiff tasks 3 of last 4 starts: stays 3¼m: acts on firm ground,
probably unsuited by heavy. *T. H. Caldwell*

SANDSUMO 6 ch.g. Sandhurst Prince – Mursuma (Rarity) [1992/3 20d   103
22s⁵ a20g³ 21v 16v⁶ 21fF] fair handicap hurdler: stayed 2½m: acted on good
to soft and good to firm ground, and on fibresand: dead. *M. H. Tompkins*

SANDUSKY (USA) 5 b.g. Al Nasr (FR) – Sandy Blue (USA) (Windy   –
Sands) [1992/3 F17gᵖᵘ] half-brother to several winners in USA, including
stakes winner Window Seat (by Super Concorde): pulled up in NH Flat race
in October: yet to race over hurdles or fences. *J. R. Jenkins*

SANDY ANDY 7 ch.g. Sandalay – Fort Etna (Be Friendly) [1992/3 F16d   c91 ?
c20g² c23dF c25sᵖᵘ c20g⁵ c23g⁴ c25g] lengthy ex-Irish gelding: half-
brother to 4 winning jumpers, including Irish hurdlers Slatt Noble (by Tall
Noble) and Blake's Beauty (by Sexton Blake): dam, sister to a winning
hurdler, 2-y-o 5f winner: won 4 points in 1992: modest novice chaser: best
effort second of 6 at Newcastle in November: trained until after first start by
P. Berry: stays 2½m: jumps none too fluently. *J. K. M. Oliver*

SANDY BEAU 7 ch.g. Beau Charmeur (FR) – Straight Sprite (Three   c87
Wishes) [1992/3 c21g c24m* c25dᵖᵘ c21dᵖᵘ c25mᵖᵘ] sturdy gelding: only   –
form in novice chases over 3m on good to firm ground, winning at Newcastle
in November: sold 7,100 gns Doncaster May Sales: likely to prove suited by
good test of stamina. *J. Hanson*

SANDY BIRD 6 b.g. Sandhurst Prince – Holywell (Wolver Hollow)   –
[1992/3 22sᵖᵘ] leggy ex-Irish gelding: third foal: half-brother to Irish Flat
winner Holly Bird (by Runnett): dam poor Flat maiden: poor maiden on Flat
and over hurdles. *T. Kersey*

SANDYBRAES 8 ch.g. Kambalda – Kinsella's Choice (Middle Temple)   c107 p
[1992/3 c21sᵘʳ c24d³ c24d³ c25g* c26s* c24mᵘʳ c24m*] lengthy gelding: –
winning hurdler in Ireland: successful in small fields for novice chases at
Bangor in March, Plumpton in April and Perth in May, first 2 handicaps:
stays 3¼m: acts on good to firm and soft going: on the upgrade. *D. Nicholson*

SANDY'S BEACON 8 b.g. Foggy Bell – Ditchling Beacon (High Line)   c92
[1992/3 c21g* c21d³] big, workmanlike gelding: lightly-raced winning   –
hurdler: successful in novice event at Sedgefield in October on chasing
debut: made mistakes when below that form in similar race on same course
later in month: stays 3m: acts on good to soft going. *J. G. FitzGerald*

SAN FERNANDO 7 b.g. Bulldozer – Burren Orchid (Will Hays (USA))   123
[1992/3 21g⁵ 17s*] rangy gelding: chasing type: handicap hurdler: fairly
useful form when winning handicap at Ascot in January: effective at around
2m when conditions are testing and stays 21f: acts on soft going. *J. T. Gifford*

SAN FRANCISCO JOE (USA) 9 b. or br.g. Plum Bold (USA) –   77
Destacion (USA) (Decimator (USA)) [1992/3 21dᵖᵘ a20g⁶ a22gᵖᵘ 18g 24sᵖᵘ
20s² a18g³] compact gelding: poor hurdler: placed in sellers last 2 starts,
best efforts of season: sold 3,100 gns Malvern June Sales: stays 2½m: acts

on good to firm and soft ground, and on fibresand: usually visored in 1991/2, blinkered fourth outing: sometimes looks less than keen. *A. W. Denson*

SANG DE FLEUR (FR) 6 br.g. Zino – Calamine (Hotfoot) [1992/3 F17m F16m] half-brother to French 9f winner Dismissed (by Brigadier Gerard): dam never ran: tailed off in NH Flat races at Doncaster in February and Nottingham (visored) in March: yet to race over hurdles or fences. *M. Avison*

SAN LORENZO (USA) 5 b.g. El Gran Senor (USA) – Wising Up (USA) (Smarten (USA)) [1992/3 16d* 16d³ 17d⁵ 17d* 16d⁴ 17s* 17s³ 17s⁵ 17f5 21m⁵ 22s⁴ 22mᶠ 16f* 17g³] close-coupled, well-made gelding: fairly useful handicap hurdler: won at Exeter, Wolverhampton and Huntingdon in first half of season and at Ludlow in May: effective at 2m and stays 21f: acts on any ground: blinkered twice in 1991/2: consistent. *K. C. Bailey* — 121

SANNDILA (IRE) 5 b.m. Lashkari – Santalina (Relko) [1992/3 16s* 18s* 16d⁵ 16d2 16g⁶ 18d* 16s] sparely-made mare: useful hurdler: won 2 minor events at Fairyhouse in November and one at Thurles in March: ran poorly on fifth (at Wincanton) and last starts: will stay further than 2¼m: acts on soft going: front runner. *P. J. Flynn, Ireland* — 133

SAN PIER NICETO 6 b.g. Norwick (USA) – Langton Herring (Nearly A Hand) [1992/3 17dᵖᵘ 18g 17d 17f⁴ 18m⁴] small, lengthy gelding: modest handicap hurdler: creditable efforts last 2 starts: stays 2¼m: probably acts on any going on turf (ran poorly on fibresand). *M. D. Hammond* — 89

SANSMOSS 8 ch.g. Le Moss – Coforta (The Parson) [1992/3 c22v⁴ c24sᵘʳ c25vᵖᵘ c25dᵖᵘ] lengthy, workmanlike gelding: maiden hurdler/chaser: no worthwhile form: sold 1,150 gns Ascot March Sales: blinkered last outing: poor jumper of fences. *D. Nicholson* — c– x, –

SANTANO 7 gr.g. Monsanto (FR) – Stance (Habat) [1992/3 c21mᴿ c22gᵖᵘ] poor pointer: no form in novice hunter chases: hampered and refused first outing. *N. J. Pewter* — c–, –

SANTARAY 7 ch.g. Formidable (USA) – Stockingful (Santa Claus) [1992/3 16sᵖᵘ 16s⁵] good-topped gelding: fair hurdler in 1991/2: ran as though something amiss in 1992/3: likely to prove best at 2m: best form on good ground (possibly unsuited by soft): wears a tongue strap. *J. Mackie* — –

SANTELLA BOBKES (USA) 8 b.h. Solford (USA) – Ambiente (USA) (Tentam (USA)) [1992/3 c21f⁴ 24gᵖᵘ c27m c24dᵖᵘ] good-topped horse: poor hurdler/chaser: stays well: acts on good to firm going: tried blinkered. *M. A. Barnes* — c–, –

SAOIRSE (IRE) 5 b.m. Horage – Teletype (Guillaume Tell (USA)) [1992/3 16s 16v* 18s 16v 18d⁵] ex-Irish mare: half-sister to Deliffin (by Wolverlife), winner at 2m on Flat and placed over hurdles: dam lightly-raced maiden: moderate form when winning maiden hurdle at Clonmel in December: trained until after fourth outing by D. P. Kelly: well beaten at Cartmel 4 months later: should stay beyond 2m: acts on heavy going. *D. Moffatt* — 95 ?

SARAH'S WROATH 8 b.g. Morston (FR) – All Our Yesterdays (Jimsun) [1992/3 20s³ 21s² 24v⁶ 25dᵖᵘ c22vᵖᵘ 20dᵖᵘ] small, angular gelding: has been tubed: poor novice hurdler: creditable efforts first 2 starts: made mistakes on chasing debut: stays 2½m: acts on soft and good to firm going. *M. Scudamore* — c–, 75

SARA LANE 9 ch.m. Sagaro – Maypole Lane (Grundy) [1992/3 22d² 22s⁶ 26g] lengthy mare: modest staying novice hurdler: no worthwhile form in novice chases: seemed to need plenty of give in the ground: blinkered 3 times: dead. *N. G. Ayliffe* — c–, 87

SARAVILLE 6 ch.m. Kemal (FR) – Golden Ingot (Prince Hansel) [1992/3 c20v c20s² c16sᶠ c19d² c21m* c18g² c23d* c27g* c26mᶠ] workmanlike ex-Irish mare: sister to winning jumpers Rossville and Richville: dam unraced: moderate hurdler: trained by J. Maxwell until after third outing: won mares novice chases at Wincanton and Worcester (handicap) in March and novice chase at Fontwell in April: would probably — c118 p, –

have finished very good third but for falling 2 out in novice handicap at Cheltenham later in April: probably needs further than 2¼m nowadays and stays well: acts on soft and good to firm going: type to improve further. *M. C. Pipe*

SARAZAR (USA) 4 ch.g. Shahrastani (USA) – Sarshara (Habitat) [1992/3 17f⁵] moderate form when placed in 1½m maidens on Flat in Ireland in 1992: favourite, fifth of 10 in maiden juvenile hurdle at Lingfield in March: should improve. *R. Akehurst*   80 p

SAREEN EXPRESS (IRE) 5 gr.g. Siberian Express (USA) – Three Waves (Cure The Blues (USA)) [1992/3 a16g² 16dᵖᵘ] sparely-made, dipped-backed gelding: novice hurdler: best effort when close second in claimer at Lingfield in March: won on Flat the following month: yet to race beyond 2m: acts well on equitrack: looks a difficult ride: blinkered twice. *Mrs J. C. Dawe*   77

SARGEANTS CHOICE 4 b.g. Le Solaret (FR) – Rose Dante (Tiran (HUN)) [1992/3 F14m] first foal: dam unraced: soundly beaten in NH Flat race at Market Rasen in March: yet to race over hurdles. *A. L. Forbes*

SARONA SMITH 6 ch.m. Alias Smith (USA) – Sarona (Lord of Verona) [1992/3 F17s 20s⁵ 20s 18d² 17d⁵ 18g³ 22dᵖᵘ 18d] smallish, good-topped mare: poor novice hurdler: should stay beyond 2¼m: acts on dead ground. *F. T. Walton*   78

SARTORIUS 7 b.g. Henbit (USA) – Salvationist (Mill Reef (USA)) [1992/3 17g 16d⁶ c16v* c17s³ c16d⁵ c19v²] rather sparely-made gelding: fair hurdler: won novice chase at Nottingham in December: also ran well when placed in similar races at Newcastle (valuable event) later in month and Fontwell in January: seems suited by an easy surface and acts on heavy ground. *T. Thomson Jones*   c99 +
                                                                                              –

SARUM PRINCE 7 b.g. Derring Rose – Come Now (Prince Hansel) [1992/3 22dᵖᵘ 20g⁶ 22sᵖᵘ] small, sturdy gelding: of little account. *R. Callow*   –

SASKIA'S HERO 6 ch.g. Bairn (USA) – Comtec Princess (Gulf Pearl) [1992/3 18d⁶ 16d 16s* a16g² 16s⁴ 18d⁶ 17f] good-topped gelding: modest hurdler: won novice event at Catterick in December: good second in similar race at Southwell in January: well below best last 3 outings, including in a seller: yet to race beyond 2¼m: acts on soft ground and fibresand, possibly unsuited by firm. *J. F. Bottomley*   93

SASKIA'S REPRIEVE 9 ch.g. Giacometti – Anjamadi (Buff's Own) [1992/3 16s 17s⁶ 22m 22f* 20m⁶] small, sparely-made gelding: moderate hurdler: won handicap at Huntingdon in May, best effort of season: stays 2¾m: unsuited by very soft going, acts on any other: effective with or without visor. *J. F. Bottomley*   94

SATIN D'OR 7 ch.m. Le Coq d'Or – Super Satin (Lord of Verona) [1992/3 c25g⁵] workmanlike mare: tailed off in NH Flat race in 1989/90: maiden pointer: jumped deliberately when well beaten in hunter chase at Kelso in March. *F. T. Walton*   c–

SATIN LOVER 5 ch.g. Tina's Pet – Canoodle (Warpath) [1992/3 17d* 17g* 17d* 17v* 16s* 17d* 17m³ 17f]   137
          Satin Lover's owner, a vice chairman of Newcastle United Football Club, had plenty to cheer about both on the football field and on the racecourse in 1992/3. Newcastle United became champions of the First Division while Satin Lover, who runs in the club colours of black and white stripes, won the first six of his eight races over hurdles. Such was Satin Lover's progress that connections did consider having a crack at the Champion Hurdle with him, but sensibly the Trafalgar House Supreme Novices' Hurdle was the race chosen for his appearance at the Cheltenham Festival. Satin Lover, sent off second favourite at 4/1 in the fifteen-runner field, lost his unbeaten record but acquitted himself really well. Pushed along from three out, he stayed on in good style to take third place behind Montelado and Lemon's Mill, finishing almost fifteen lengths behind the impressive winner. Satin Lover, who benefited from the strong gallop at

Cheltenham, didn't have the race run to suit him at Aintree on his only subsequent start. Waited with as usual, he lacked the pace to trouble the principals in a race run at just a fair gallop and was already held when blundering at the second last. It's possible that the very firm ground at Aintree was also against Satin Lover but we wouldn't want to put it any stronger than that. He's shown his form on firm ground on the Flat, while the going at Cheltenham was on the firm side of good. Satin Lover's wins, in novice events at Cheltenham (two of them), Ascot (also two), Kempton and Sandown, were gained on ground which ranged from good through to heavy. He put up his best performance during this period at Kempton on his fifth start, when holding the renewed challenge of Big Beat by half a length.

		Mummy's Pet (b 1968)	Sing Sing Money For Nothing
	Tina's Pet (b 1978)	Merry Weather (br 1971)	Will Somers Copper Sky
Satin Lover (ch.g. 1988)		Warpath (gr 1969)	Sovereign Path Ardneasken
	Canoodle (ch 1978)	Turtle Dove (ch 1972)	Gyr Jabula

Satin Lover, a close-coupled, good-topped gelding who usually impresses with his well-being, is by the smart sprinter Tina's Pet out of Canoodle, a fair winner at one and a half miles to two miles. Canoodle, a full sister to five winning jumpers including the smart hurdler Path of Peace, has bred two other winners. Her first foal Pathero (by Godswalk) was a moderate middle-distance stayer on the Flat, while her second foal Konig Germania (by Tender King) won in Norway. Satin Lover, a useful stayer on the Flat, was bought out of Reg Akehurst's stable shortly before finishing a very close third in the 1992 Northumberland Plate. While he's capable of winning a big handicap on the Flat, Satin Lover's prospects of doing the same over

Bonusphoto Novices' Hurdle, Kempton—
Satin Lover (right) has to fight hard to get the better of Big Beat

hurdles look even brighter in our opinion. Raced only at around two miles to date, Satin Lover is likely to prove as effective at two and a half. He's a sound jumper. *N. Tinkler*

SAUNDERS LASS 9 b.m. Hillandale – Portella (Porto Bello) [1992/3 c16v3] lengthy mare: poor handicap hurdler/novice chaser: creditable third at Uttoxeter in December: likely to prove best over a sharp 2m: acts on any going. *P. J. Bevan*

c82 –

SAUSALITO BOY 5 b.g. Idiot's Delight – Brown Sauce (Saucy Kit) [1992/3 22sF 16f 16s3 16v4 22v* 22s2 22m*] leggy, sparely-made gelding: won novice handicap hurdle at Sandown in January and novice event at Ludlow in March: will be suited by further than 2¾m: acts on good to firm and heavy ground: suited by forcing tactics: on the upgrade. *N. A. Twiston-Davies*

106 p

SAUVIGNON (IRE) 5 b.m. Alzao (USA) – Romanee Conti (Will Somers) [1992/3 17d 16d5 16s] compact mare: poor novice hurdler: sold 1,650 gns Ascot December Sales: likely to prove best at 2m: best effort on firm ground. *C. D. Broad*

69

SAVOY 6 ch.g. Callernish – Dream Daisy (Choral Society) [1992/3 20g6] third foal: brother to winning pointer Ned The Hall: dam winning Irish pointer: showed promise when sixth of 22 in novice hurdle at Doncaster in December: should do better. *G. Richards*

85 p

SAXON FAIR 4 ch.g. Saxon Farm – Fair Kitty (Saucy Kit) [1992/3 16d 16s 20g 18g] sparely-made gelding: fifth living foal: half-brother to Flat and hurdles winner Kitty Come Home (by Monsanto): dam, useful hurdler and fair chaser, stayed well: tailed off all starts over hurdles. *Mrs V. A. Aconley*

–

SAXON LAD (USA) 7 b.g. Lear Fan (USA) – Presto Youth (USA) (Youth (USA)) [1992/3 c17mF 18g] angular, lightly-made gelding: poor novice selling hurdler: fell first on chasing debut: blinkered last start. *G. P. Enright*

c– –

SAYANT 8 b.g. Sayyaf – Bodnant (Welsh Pageant) [1992/3 17d 17m*] sturdy gelding: carries condition: only second outing over hurdles since 1989/90 when winning seller at Bangor (no bid) in March: races only at around 2m: acts on good to firm going and fibresand. *W. Clay*

91

SAYH 4 b.g. Bluebird (USA) – Relfo (Relko) [1992/3 20s3 16s2 23m3] angular gelding: half-brother to several winners, including fair hurdler Frendly Fellow (by Grundy): fairly useful middle-distance winner on Flat in 1992: sold out of M. Jarvis' stable 9,000 gns Ascot November Sales: won juvenile hurdle at Kempton in December: also good efforts last 2 starts: suffering from throat infection when below form second outing: will prove suited by a test of stamina: acts on soft and good to firm going. *J. White*

108

SAY LITTLE 7 ch.g. Say Primula – Eliza de Rich (Spanish Gold) [1992/3 23d 21v3 24v5] workmanlike gelding: novice hurdler: third at Hexham in November, best effort: stays 21f. *G. M. Moore*

87

SAYMORE 7 ch.g. Seymour Hicks (FR) – Huahinee (FR) (Riverman (USA)) [1992/3 16s 16d4 16m4 17g2 17g* 17f5] smallish, sparely-made gelding: selling hurdler nowadays: bought in 3,000 gns after winning by 12 lengths at Bangor in April: races around 2m: acts on firm and dead ground: pulls hard: sometimes breaks blood vessels. *R. Hollinshead*

98

SAY NO MORE 7 b.g. Bold Champion – Scarlet Wind (Whistling Wind) [1992/3 c25d3 c22gpu] winning pointer in Ireland: showed nothing in hunter chases in February. *T. P. Tate*

c– –

SAYSANA 6 b.m. Sayf El Arab (USA) – Rosana Park (Music Boy) [1992/3 18gpu] no sign of ability in 2 races over hurdles, latter a seller. *A. Moore*

–

SAYYURE (USA) 7 b.g. Lydian (FR) – Periquito (USA) (Olden Times) [1992/3 25s* 24spu 25g3 25g3] sturdy, lengthy gelding: useful handicap hurdler: won at Kempton in December: ran creditably penultimate start: stays 25f: acts on any going: sometimes flashes tail under pressure: has broken blood vessels: jumps soundly. *T. Thomson Jones*

134

SCALISCRO 12 ch.g. Smokey Rockett – Rosamond (Spiritus) [1992/3 c19g3] big, angular gelding: poor novice hurdler/chaser. *Jonathan Ford*

c–
–

SCALLY'S COMET 4 ch.f. Scallywag – Stellify (Maris Piper) [1992/3 F16s 16d6 24g6] first foal: dam winning pointer: behind in NH Flat race at Bangor in February: sixth of 16 in maiden at Uttoxeter in April, first and easily better effort over hurdles: should be suited by further than 2m. *B. Preece*

75

SCALLY'S LADY 8 gr.m. Scallywag – Decipher (Broxted) [1992/3 18d 22g c19mur c17spu] leggy, sparely-made mare: poor novice hurdler/hunter chaser. *S. I. Pittendrigh*

c–
–

SCALP 'EM (IRE) 5 b.g. Commanche Run – Supremely Royal (Crowned Prince (USA)) [1992/3 17g3 18m6] workmanlike gelding: poor staying maiden on Flat: modest form when third in maiden at Plumpton in March on hurdling debut: ran poorly later in month: should stay further than 17f. *P. D. Evans*

83

SCARBA 5 b.g. Skyliner – Looking For Gold (Goldfella) [1992/3 16dur 16dpu 16g6 16g4 18mF 17gpu] close-coupled gelding: poor maiden on Flat: best effort over hurdles when fourth in novice event at Catterick in March. *D. T. Garraton*

86

SCARLET BERRY 5 br.m. Zambrano – Scarlet Letch (New Brig) [1992/3 20spu 18d 17d 20g3 27d] strong, compact mare: seventh foal: half-sister to winning staying hurdler/chaser Scarlet Terror (by Dynastic) and novice hurdler/chaser Scarlet Ember (by Nearly A Hand): dam quite useful staying chaser: little sign of ability in novice hurdles. *R. Brewis*

–

SCARLET EMBER 7 b.m. Nearly A Hand – Scarlet Letch (New Brig) [1992/3 c17d6 c16sF] workmanlike mare: novice hurdler/chaser, no worthwhile form. *R. Brewis*

c–
–

SCARLET EXPRESS 6 b.g. Precocious – Scarlet Slipper (Gay Mecene (USA)) [1992/3 17s* a20g2 24d4 17g2 a16gF3 22m 17g2 21d5 20m6 17gF] sparely-made gelding: modest handicap hurdler: won at Fakenham in December: also ran well when placed subsequently, but below best last 2 completed starts: has shown little over fences: stays 2½m: acts on good to firm, soft ground and fibresand: tried blinkered and visored. *B. Richmond*

c–
99

SCARNING DALE 10 b.g. Cawston's Clown – Within Bounds (Canisbay) [1992/3 20m c21g4 c24d c21spu c21gpu] lengthy, good-bodied gelding: winning hurdler/chaser: fourth in handicap over fences at Hexham in March, only form of season: stays 3m: acts on dead going (unsuited by soft). *W. Bentley*

c80
–

SCEPTICAL 5 b.g. Idiot's Delight – Lavilla (Tycoon II) [1992/3 17g] half-brother to winning hurdler Mister Half-Chance (by Nearly A Hand): dam, from excellent jumping family, showed no worthwhile form: showed nothing in novice hurdle at Newbury in February. *Andrew Turnell*

–

SCHERZO IMPROMPTU 4 ch.f. Music Boy – Law And Impulse (Roan Rocket) [1992/3 17spu] lightly raced and no form on Flat: tailed off when pulled up in juvenile hurdle at Newton Abbot in August. *L. G. Cottrell*

–

SCHIEHALLION 8 ch.m. Scallywag – Hardwick Sun (Dieu Soleil) [1992/3 c22dpu] angular mare: moderate hurdler, lightly raced: all but fell eleventh and soon pulled up in October on chasing debut: stays 2½m: acts on good to soft going. *J. M. Jefferson*

c–
–

SCHWANTZ 5 b.g. Exhibitioner – Hardirondo (Hardicanute) [1992/3 21m4] sturdy gelding: poor maiden over hurdles: sold 900 gns Ascot September Sales: best form at 2m: acts on good to firm and dead ground (ran poorly on fibresand). *W. T. Kemp*

–

SCHWEPPES TONIC 7 br.g. Persian Bold – Gay Shadow (Northfields (USA)) [1992/3 17s4 16spu 17g3 20v*] sparely-made gelding: modest hurdler: finished lame when very easy winner of selling hurdle (no bid) at Hereford in November: stays 2½m: acts on heavy going: visored second start. *William Price*

97

SCIACCA 6 ch.m. Dalsaan – Hill of Howth (Sassafras (FR)) [1992/3 17m* 17m* 17m 17vF 17d3 16d4] small, lengthy mare: modest form over hurdles: won seller at Bangor (bought in 3,750 gns) and claimer at Perth in August: good third in selling handicap at Plumpton in February: unlikely to stay much beyond 17f: probably acts on any going: held up. *C. Weedon* 91

SCOBIE BOY (IRE) 5 ch.g. Decent Fellow – Normazoo (Rhodomantade) [1992/3 F16s* F16g F17m] smallish gelding: first foal: dam won NH Flat race: won 18-runner NH Flat race at Nottingham in February: soundly beaten in similar races subsequently: yet to race over hurdles or fences. *C. R. Egerton*

SCOLE 8 b.g. Deep Run – Verbana (Boreen (FR)) [1992/3 c18g3 c23g* c21vur c20d3] angular gelding: novice hurdler: won novice chase at Worcester in October: fairly useful effort when third in quite valuable similar race at Aintree in November: likely to prove suited by test of stamina: acts on dead going: jumps soundly. *F. Murphy* c114 –

SCOOBY DOO 6 b.g. Le Bavard (FR) – Shule Doe (Royal Buck) [1992/3 21spu 20d 22g] leggy, angular non-thoroughbred gelding: fifth foal: dam ran once over hurdles in Ireland: signs of ability in Irish points in 1991, little over hurdles in Britain. *Mrs H. Bell* –

SCORPOTINA 4 b.f. Scorpio (FR) – Ablula (Abwah) [1992/3 F17d] fourth foal: half-sister to a poor maiden by Roscoe Blake: dam lightly raced: tailed off in NH Flat race at Hereford in May: yet to race over hurdles. *A. Bailey* –

SCOTONI 7 ch.g. Final Straw – Damiya (FR) (Direct Flight) [1992/3 17s2 c18f3 c19f* 21d5 c19dF c16v* c16vF c16s* c19m2 c16f3] close-coupled gelding: fair form over hurdles and fences: successful in novice chases at Fontwell and Lingfield in first half of season and Folkestone (handicap) in February: stays 19f: acts on any going. *R. J. O'Sullivan* c105 –

SCOTTISH FLING 9 ch.g. Imperial Fling (USA) – Relicia (Relko) [1992/3 16dpu 16spu 20gpu] lightly-raced novice hurdler: no show in 1992/3, including in a seller. *P. Beaumont* –

SCOTTISH GOLD 9 b.g. Sonnen Gold – Calaburn (Caliban) [1992/3 25gpu 24d] sturdy gelding: moderate hurdler at best: little sign of retaining ability in first half of 1992/3: stays 3m: acts on any going. *Miss L. A. Perratt* –

SCOTTISH PERIL 6 b.g. Mljet – Kumari Peril (Rebel Prince) [1992/3 16g6 21d5 20s 20m3 21g3] neat non-thoroughbred gelding: fourth foal: dam unraced: poor novice hurdler: will stay beyond 21f: best effort on dead ground. *R. Allan* 81

SCOTTISH REFORM 6 b.g. Night Shift (USA) – Molvitesse (Molvedo) [1992/3 c16dF c16d5 c21d* c21gur c21g2 c20mF] lengthy gelding: novice hurdler: won novice chase at Carlisle in April: went down narrowly in similar race at Hexham in May: stays 21f: acts on good to firm and dead ground. *J. J. O'Neill* c92 –

SCOTTISH RUBY 4 ch.g. Scottish Reel – Screenable (USA) (Silent Screen (USA)) [1992/3 17f5 18d5] leggy gelding: plating-class maiden on Flat: fifth at Huntingdon in September, first and better effort in selling hurdles in first half of season: sold 1,350 gns Doncaster January Sales. *C. Tinkler* 76

SCOTTON BANKS (IRE) 4 b.g. Le Moss – Boherdeel (Boreen (FR)) [1992/3 F16m4 F17d3 F16f5] seventh foal: dam maiden hurdler in Ireland: showed ability all 3 starts in NH Flat races in the spring: yet to race over hurdles. *M. H. Easterby*

SCRABBLE 4 ch.f. Scallywag – Word Game (Hasty Word) [1992/3 F17d] first foal: dam lightly-raced maiden hurdler/pointer: mid-division in NH Flat race at Ascot in April: yet to race over hurdles. *Mrs S. J. Smith* –

SCRAGGED OAK LASS 8 ch.m. Hell's Gate – Iris's Wish (Prince of Norway) [1992/3 18fpu 17fpu 22f] first foal: dam winning pointer: showed nothing in novice hurdles in May. *R. Dean* –

SCRIVEN BOY 6 b.g. Lafontaine (USA) – Miss Bula (Master Buck) [1992/3 16v 17dpu 22m6 24g3 22d] good-topped gelding: third of 6 finishers in novice handicap hurdle at Bangor in March, best effort: stays 3m: visored last start. *J. A. C. Edwards* — 78

SCRUMPY COUNTRY 8 b.g. Country Retreat – Windfall VI (Master Owen) [1992/3 c25v3] sturdy gelding: modest pointer: fair third in hunter chase at Towcester in February: looks a thorough stayer. *C. Marriott* — c82

SCRUTINEER (USA) 4 b.g. Danzig Connection (USA) – Script Approval (USA) (Silent Screen (USA)) [1992/3 17s* 16v4 17g 16g5 17m*] strong gelding: fairly useful middle-distance performer on Flat (suited by a sound surface) when trained by J. Gosden: won juvenile hurdles at Newbury in January and Wolverhampton in March: best effort fifth in valuable similar event at Kempton on fourth outing: will stay beyond 17f: has won on soft going, but best effort on good: wore tongue strap last 2 starts: sometimes finds little under pressure. *D. Nicholson* — 112

SCU'S LADY (IRE) 5 b.m. Mazaad – Lydja (Hethersett) [1992/3 18g6] small, sturdy mare: poor plater over hurdles: sold 1,500 gns Doncaster August Sales, resold 1,100 gns Doncaster March Sales: best form at 2m: acts on good to firm going. *M. F. Barraclough* — –

SEA BARN 10 ch.g. Julio Mariner – Zakyna (Charlottesville) [1992/3 17m* 17g*] tall, leggy gelding: poor maiden pointer: very lightly raced over hurdles: attracted no bid after winning selling handicap at Newton Abbot and novice seller at Hereford, both in March: should stay beyond 17f: acts on good to firm going. *P. J. Hobbs* — 91

SEA BREAKER (IRE) 5 b.g. Glow (USA) – Surfing (Grundy) [1992/3 22m* 22m* 22m* 22f2 22g 21g2 25dpu 17d6 17s] modest hurdler: beat small-field novice hurdles at Market Rasen and Worcester, and handicap at Huntingdon in August: ran creditably on occasions subsequently: effective at 2¾m and should stay 3m: acts on firm and dead ground: ungenuine: must be held up as long as possible. *D. E. Cantillon* — 97 §

SEA BUCK 7 b.g. Simply Great (FR) – Heatherside (Hethersett) [1992/3 c22vpu c24spu 25v3 26d3 22g* 21g3 22f2 25d2 24s 25g5 21f2 22d2 27g6] leggy gelding: fair handicap hurdler: won conditional jockeys event at Sandown in February: generally ran with credit subsequently: pulled up both outings over fences: stays well: probably acts on any going: sometimes visored in 1989/90: sometimes runs in snatches and needs plenty of driving. *G. B. Balding* — c– / 112

SEA CADET 5 ch.g. Precocious – Sea Power (Welsh Pageant) [1992/3 18s 17s 20dpu 17m4] sturdy, angular gelding: poor novice hurdler: best form at around 2m: acts on dead going. *K. Bishop* — –

SEA DRAGON 5 ch.m. Librate – La Chica (El Cid) [1992/3 aF16g F16s] compact mare: half-sister to fair hurdler and winning chaser Rusty Roc (by Rustingo) and a winning pointer by Saucy Kit: dam, 5f winner at 2 yrs, also successful over hurdles: soundly beaten in NH Flat races in March and April: sold 900 gns Malvern June Sales: yet to race over hurdles or fences. *M. W. Davies* — –

SEAGRAM (NZ) 13 ch.g. Balak – Llanah (NZ) (Bally Royal) [1992/3 c25d3 c28d3 c27dur c26vpu c30spu] smallish, workmanlike gelding: one-time smart and thoroughly genuine staying chaser: won 1991 Seagram Grand National at Liverpool: lost his enthusiasm and has been retired. *D. H. Barons* — c– / –

SEAGULL HOLLOW (IRE) 4 b.g. Taufan (USA) – Marthe Meynet (Welsh Pageant) [1992/3 16g 16d3 16g* 16s* 16g 18d* 18gpu 16g6] tall, leggy gelding: half-brother to useful jumper Antinous (by Hello Gorgeous) and winning hurdler Qurrat Al Ain (by Wolver Hollow): modest 6f winner on Flat: won juvenile hurdles at Catterick and Wetherby in first half of season and at Market Rasen in February: ran as though something amiss last 2 starts (found to be coughing after last): stays 2¼m: acts on soft ground. *M. H. Easterby* — 103

SEA ISLAND 9 b.m. Windjammer (USA) – Sule Skerry (Scottish Rifle) **c 122**
[1992/3 c27v³ c20s² c27s³ c24mᶠ] leggy, rather sparely-made mare: fairly –
useful handicap chaser: blinkered when running creditably last 2 completed
outings: stays 27f: acts on good to firm and heavy going: held up. *M. C. Pipe*

SEA LORD 4 b.g. Aragon – Floral (Floribunda) [1992/3 18m 16g] maiden
plater on Flat, suited by 1¼m: well beaten in selling hurdles in September –
and March. *K. W. Hogg, Isle of Man*

SEAN'S SCHOLAR (USA) 6 b.m. Kris S (USA) – Nalees Scholar
(USA) (Nalees Man (USA)) [1992/3 17g⁴] leggy, sparely-made mare: easily **79 +**
best effort over hurdles when second in minor event over 2½m on dead
going in 1991/2: gave strong impression she'll be suited by a return to
further than 17f when fourth at Huntingdon in February. *C. N. Allen*

SEA PATROL 6 b.g. Shirley Heights – Boathouse (Habitat) [1992/3
F16d³ F17v² F16v⁵ 16v⁴ 25d⁴ 22f*] leggy gelding: fifth foal: brother to Flat **88**
maiden Head of The River and half-brother to smart middle-distance stayer
Dry Dock (by High Line): dam, who stayed 1¼m, half-sister to Oaks winner
Bireme and high-class middle-distance stayer Buoy: won 4-runner novice
hurdle at Worcester in March: stays 2¾m (appeared not to stay 25f):
probably acts on any ground: blinkered last 2 starts. *M. C. Pipe*

SEA PET 4 b.f. Dubassoff (USA) – Palace Pet (Dragonara Palace (USA))
[1992/3 22s a22g⁵ 24g⁵ 20g⁶ 22m⁶ 22dᵖᵘ 25v⁵ 21g⁴] leggy filly: twice-raced **68**
on Flat: sold out of Miss G. Kelleway's stable 4,500 gns Doncaster October
Sales: poor form over hurdles, including in sellers: stays 3m: best on a
sound surface and acts on fibresand: blinkered sixth outing. *J. J. Birkett*

SEARCY 5 b.g. Good Times (ITY) – Fee (Mandamus) [1992/3 21f⁴ 18gʳᵗʳ
22g 17dᵖᵘ] sparely-made gelding: poor temperamental plater over hurdles: **68 §**
stays 21f: blinkered last outing: subsequently won 2 points. *Miss S. J. Wilton*

SEA SEARCH 6 ch.g. Deep Run – Gift Seeker (Status Seeker) [1992/3
16s⁶ 20g⁵ 22v⁴ 21f⁴ 22g⁵] well-made gelding: modest form in novice **88**
hurdles: stays 21f: acts on firm going, possibly unsuited by heavy. *N. J.
Henderson*

SEASIDE MINSTREL 5 ch.g. Song – Blackpool Belle (The Brianstan)
[1992/3 16g 17d] compact gelding: winning plater on Flat when trained by C. –
Hill: tailed off in 2 novice hurdles in October, second a seller. *R. J. Manning*

SEA TROUT 9 b.g. Kings Lake (USA) – Take Your Mark (USA) (Round
Table) [1992/3 21s 25s 22d 22d² 24d⁴ 22m* 26m 24s³ 22d² 21m] lengthy, **114**
quite good-topped gelding: fair hurdler: won handicap at Ludlow in March:
stayed 3m: acted on heavy and good to firm ground: dead. *C. H. Jones*

SEBEL HOUSE 10 b.g. Buckskin (FR) – Lulu Dee (Straight Deal) **c95**
[1992/3 c24d² c21s³] leggy, sparely-made gelding: moderate chaser: ran –
very well when second in amateurs event at Ludlow in November, poorly at
Bangor following month: stays 3m: acts on soft going: blinkered 3 times,
including both starts in 1992/3. *D. McCain*

SECOND CALL 4 ch.f. Kind of Hush – Matinata (Dike (USA)) [1992/3
18s* 17s 18v⁴ 17f* 17g⁵ 17g³ 18f*] compact filly: half-sister to promising **101**
Irish hunter chaser Kerry Orchid (by Absalom): modest performer, stays
1¼m, on Flat: sold out of H. Candy's stable 18,000 gns Newmarket Autumn
Sales: fair form over hurdles: won juvenile events at Folkestone and
Sandown (handicap) and novice event at Fontwell in 1992/3: sold to join T.
Forster 12,000 gns Ascot June Sales: stays 2¼m: acts on any going:
headstrong and makes running. *G. Harwood*

SECOND SCHEDUAL 8 b.g. Golden Love – Billeragh Girl (Nor- **c149**
mandy) [1992/3 16d² c16g² c20d⁴ c21v² c24d² c20g³ c21m* c25g2] **137**
The atmosphere at the Cheltenham Festival is something to savour,
made unique by the presence of so many Irish racegoers. Alas, Irish-trained
winners at the meeting have been in shorter supply than usual in recent
seasons, so few would begrudge the Irish their six winners at the latest
Festival. It equalled the total in 1978 and 1982 and was only one fewer than

the Irish best in recent years—seven in 1977. The Irish also had six first past the post in 1980 but Chinrullah and Tied Cottage were disqualified some time later. The revival in Irish fortunes could have something to do with the effects of the economic recession which has slowed down the flow of Ireland's best prospects to high-spending yards in Britain, a notable feature of National Hunt racing in the 'eighties. That said, the Irish total seemed to surprise even the most optimistic. Concern emanated almost daily from the leading Irish stables about the predictions of firmish going at Cheltenham, but for which confidence in Ireland's best would have been much higher. However, the myth that Cheltenham has to be a bog for Irish horses to do well was exposed by the victories of Montelado, Fissure Seal, Rhythm Section, Shawiya, Shuil Ar Aghaidh and Second Schedual.

Second Schedual was the only Irish-trained winner of a steeplechase at the Festival meeting, his triumph in the Cathcart Challenge Cup coming at the expense of a more fancied Irish runner, the favourite General Idea who conceded him 4 lb. Second Schedual dictated the pace all the way, jumping soundly, and kept on in typically genuine style to hold the strong challenge of General Idea from the last by a head. Second Schedual had made three previous visits to Britain earlier in the season, doing particularly well when fourth to Deep Sensation in the H & T Walker Gold Cup at Ascot in November and runner-up to Another Coral in the Tripleprint Gold Cup at Cheltenham in December. He was let down by his jumping, possibly unsettled after being hampered at an early fence, when a below-form third to Young Hustler and Cogent in the Arlington Premier Series Final at Newbury in February. The Cathcart was Second Schedual's only victory of the season but he kept his form throughout, and finished a very good second to Bishops Hall in the Pierse Contracting John P. Harty Memorial Handicap Chase at the big Punchestown meeting at the end of April on his only start after Cheltenham. Second Schedual usually races up with the pace, and is effective at two miles to twenty-five furlongs, and acts on soft going and good to firm. He's tough, genuine and consistent, and a sound jumper of fences who, judged on his effort on his reappearance, is capable of useful form over hurdles.

The big, strong Second Schedual fetched 12,000 guineas as an un-broken three-year-old at the Doncaster May Sales. His sire the smart stayer Golden Love, runner-up in the Goodwood Cup, was establishing himself as a fairly useful sire of jumpers but his dam the unraced Billeragh Girl had little to recommend her as a broodmare. She herself had been represented on the racecourse by Second Schedual's full brother Lover Bill who had shown only modest form over hurdles. Kilmanahan, the dam of Billeragh Girl, was

Cathcart Challenge Cup Chase, Cheltenham—
the sixth Irish success of the Festival meeting
as Second Schedual beats his compatriot General Idea

Mr Hugh McMahon's "Second Schedual"

Second Schedual (b.g. 1985)	Golden Love (b 1967)	Above Suspicion (b 1956)	Court Martial
			Above Board
		Syncopation (b 1958)	Infatuation
			Dinkie Melody
	Billeragh Girl (b 1978)	Normandy (b 1965)	Vimy
			Stone Crop
		Kilmanahan (b 1970)	Arctic Slave
			Saucy Vic

also unraced and hadn't bred a winner from nine foals, though she was a half-sister to the smart Irish hurdler Troyswood and several other winning jumpers. Second Schedual's dam has still to breed another winner, though Lover Bill was subsequently placed several times over fences and Second Schedual's year-younger half-sister Saucy Minstrel (by Black Minstrel) was runner-up in an Irish point-to-point. *A. L. T. Moore, Ireland*

SECOND TIME ROUND 10 bl.g. Genuine – Brinny River (Gail Star) [1992/3 c2 1m^{ur}] poor maiden jumper. *Mrs G. M. Gladders* c–
–

SECRET CASTLE 5 b.g. Castle Keep – Excavator Lady (Most Secret) [1992/3 F14d 17m⁵ 16m* 18d^F 16d² 18g⁵ 17m³] unfurnished gelding: won novice hurdle at Catterick in October: best efforts when placed subsequently, but finished tamely under pressure final start: will stay 2½m: acts on good to firm and dead ground. *M. H. Easterby* 95

SECRET DYNASTY 6 b.m. Dynastic – Thelmas Secret (Secret Ace) [1992/3 22g] of little account. *M. A. Barnes* –

SECRET FINALE 14 ro.g. Warpath – Fox Covert (Gigantic) [1992/3 22f⁶ 24g³ 26m^{pu} 22d 26s^{pu}] compact gelding: winning staying selling hurdler: no longer of any account: tried visored. *J. R. Fort* –

SECRET FOUR 7 b.g. My Top – Secret Top (African Sky) [1992/3 21g] rather sparely-made gelding: useful and genuine staying hurdler at best: well below form only outing of season (October): acts on firm and good to soft ground. *S. Christian* —

SECRET LIASON 7 b.g. Ballacashtal (CAN) – Midnight Mistress (Midsummer Night II) [1992/3 16m 16s 17d* 17d a16g³ 17g 16f 21m³ 20d⁵ 20m³] workmanlike gelding: modest handicap hurdler: won at Wolverhampton in November: in-and-out form afterwards: stays 21f: acts on good to firm and soft going: sometimes looks reluctant: below best when blinkered on 3 occasions. *K. S. Bridgwater* 99

SECRET RITE 10 ch.g. Kambalda – Deepdecending (Deep Run) [1992/3 c18d⁴ c24sᵖᵘ c26s² c16s² c18v⁵ c26sᵖᵘ c26gᵖᵘ c27d⁶] workmanlike gelding: modest handicap chaser: effective at 2m and stays 3¼m: acts on heavy and good to firm ground. *J. T. Gifford* c86 —

SECRET SCEPTRE 6 ch.g. Kambalda – Secret Suspicion (Above Suspicion) [1992/3 F16s 24s² 22d³ F16v* 20d⁵ 24d³ 22s] second foal: dam lightly-raced Irish maiden: won a point in 1991 and a NH Flat race at Down Royal in January: moderate novice hurdler: fair fifth at Ayr in February: stays 3m: acts on soft going. *I. R. Ferguson, Ireland* 88

SECRET SUMMIT (USA) 7 b.g. Diamond Shoal – Ygraine (Blakeney) [1992/3 18d* 16d² c17g⁴ c18d* c21s⁵ c16g* c18sᵘʳ c16g* c16mᵖᵘ] compact gelding: won claiming hurdle at Southwell in October and handicap chases at Market Rasen and Southwell (2, one a novice event) in the spring: should stay beyond 2¼m: acts on hard and dead ground: usually blinkered or visored: sketchy jumper: inconsistent, and sometimes finds little under pressure. *A. L. Forbes* c92 § 90 §

SECRET TURN (USA) 7 b.g. Secreto (USA) – Changing (USA) (Forli (ARG)) [1992/3 c16gᶠ] lengthy gelding: moderate novice hurdler: showed promise but jumped none too fluently in October on chasing debut: will stay 2½m. *Andrew Turnell* c91 —

SEDGE WARBLER 6 ro.m. Scallywag – Arctic Warbler (Deep Run) [1992/3 16s⁴ 16v² 21v³ 21v² 22mᵖᵘ] strong, rangy mare: moderate novice hurdler: ran creditably all completed starts in 1992/3: broke a blood vessel on final outing: stays 21f: acts on heavy going. *O. Sherwood* 93

SEE NOW 8 ch.g. Tumble Wind (USA) – Rosie O'Grady (Barrons Court) [1992/3 17m* 18hᵖᵘ 17s⁵ c20gᵖᵘ 17g 17d] lengthy gelding: selling hurdler: won at Newton Abbot (no bid) in August: ran poorly afterwards: no sign of ability only outing over fences: stays 2¼m: acts on soft going and good to firm: inconsistent. *Mrs A. Knight* c– 72

SEE WHAT I MEAN 6 ch.g. Le Bavard (FR) – Proximity (Gulf Pearl) [1992/3 23dᵖᵘ] second foal: dam won twice at 1½m on Flat: tailed off when pulled up in novice hurdle at Kelso in November: sold 4,100 gns in May. *W. A. Stephenson* —

SELF IMPORTANT (USA) 8 ch.g. Vigors (USA) – Dear Meme (USA) (Sir Gaylord) [1992/3 20g 24g] modest novice hurdler at best: lightly raced and no form for a long time: sometimes blinkered. *D. A. Nolan* —

SEMAPHORE HILL 9 b.g. Whistlefield – Border Beacon (News Item) [1992/3 c19sᵖᵘ c26vᵖᵘ c21vᶠ c16d] compact gelding: winning hurdler: novice chaser: no form since 1990/1: blinkered last 2 outings. *P. J. Hobbs* c– —

SEMINOLE PRINCESS 5 b.m. Ahonoora – Ballys Princess (Salvo) [1992/3 22f⁵ 16dᵘʳ 17v a16g a22g⁶ 22gᵖᵘ 17m] leggy, light-framed mare: bad maiden hurdler. *C. H. Jones* 61

SENATOR OF ROME 10 b.g. New Member – Romany Serenade (Romany Air) [1992/3 c24f⁴ c22f] well-made gelding: fair chaser at best: stayed 25f: acted on firm and dead ground: dead. *H. W. Wheeler* c–

SENATOR SNUGFIT (USA) 8 b.g. Shecky Greene (USA) – Sudden Splendor (USA) (Stage Door Johnny) [1992/3 c25s² c24sᵖᵘ c25s⁴ 21v⁵ 25d⁴] tall, lengthy, angular gelding: fairly useful chaser: ran well first outing in c116 —

1992/3, but showed nothing afterwards, including in handicap hurdles: stayed well: acted on heavy going: blinkered fourth outing: dead. *M. W. Easterby*

SENDAI 7 b.m. Le Moss – Dark Harbour (Deep Run) [1992/3 20d 21v² 20dF 26m³ 22m² 24fF] strong mare: type to make a chaser: fairly useful hurdler: good efforts when placed at Warwick in January and Cheltenham in March and April: effective at 2¾m and stays 3¼m: acts on heavy and good to firm going. *J. T. Gifford* — 128

SENEGALAIS (FR) 9 b.g. Quart de Vin (FR) – Divonne (FR) (Vieux Chateau) [1992/3 c21dur c24s⁵ 22v c25s⁴ c24dF c24vpu c20mF c21dur] leggy gelding: winning hurdler: poor novice chaser: sold 3,000 gns Ascot June Sales: probably stays 3m: acts on soft going: blinkered sixth and last outings. *S. Mellor* — c76 —

SENSEI 6 ch.g. Ovac (ITY) – Sweet Gum (USA) (Gummo (USA)) [1992/3 F16g⁵ F16g⁶ F19m 16g⁴ F17g 18d* 18d 20spu 18vpu] ex-Irish gelding: first foal: dam ran twice at 4 yrs: won maiden hurdle at Downpatrick in September: no form subsequently (trained until after eighth start by F. Berry): sold 1,800 gns Ascot 2nd June Sales: stays 2¼m: acts on dead ground: blinkered last outing. *R. T. Juckes* — 85

SEON 7 b.g. Furry Glen – St Moritz (Linacre) [1992/3 16f³ 20m⁴ 17m* 17g* 17m² 16m⁶ 18d² 17m² 16g* 16v* 17s⁴ 17s* 16d 17d³ 17g 17m⁴ 18g² 17f 18d⁵ 17d⁴ 16s⁶] smallish, workmanlike gelding: made into a fairly useful hurdler in first half of season and won handicaps at Carlisle, Kelso, Ayr, Hexham and Newcastle: fair efforts on occasions in second half: stays 2¼m: acts on any going: races prominently and jumps well: tough and genuine. *W. Bentley* — 117

SEQUESTRATOR 10 b.g. African Sky – Miss Redmarshall (Most Secret) [1992/3 17m⁶ 16f² 17m⁴ 17g² 16m 17g 17mpu] smallish gelding: poor hurdler: ran creditably second to fourth starts: best at around 2m: acts on firm going: front runner: visored once in 1990/1. *P. D. Evans* — 82

SERAPHIM (FR) 4 b.f. Lashkari – Sassika (GER) (Arratos (FR)) [1992/3 16s² 22d⁴ 18g* 18g* a20g² 18g⁴ 17m*] angular filly: poor form over middle distances on Flat: modest form over hurdles: successful in 2 juvenile claimers at Sedgefield in February (claimed out of T. Barron's stable £8,559 after latter) and novice claimer at Newcastle in March: stays 2½m: acts on soft and good to firm ground, and fibresand. *A. Harrison* — 97

SERDARLI 11 b.m. Miami Springs – Run Swift (Run The Gantlet (USA)) [1992/3 a18gpu c21mF c21f² c21f⁴ 21m⁶] leggy, narrow mare: produced a foal in 1987 and 1990: maiden hurdler/chaser: trained first start by M. Charles: easily best effort of season when second in handicap chase at Huntingdon in May: stays 21f: acts on firm ground. *M. J. Ryan* — c69 + —

SERGEANT LEMON 4 ch.g. Doulab (USA) – Rabuba (Connaught) [1992/3 18d] little form in 3 runs at 2 yrs: tailed off in juvenile hurdle at Sedgefield in November. *M. W. Easterby* — —

SERGEANT SILVER 8 gr.g. General Ironside – Coolentallagh (Perhapsburg) [1992/3 22g 22spu c24s⁵ c21s⁶ c26s⁵ c24dpu 24g²] lengthy gelding: poor novice hurdler/chaser: stays 3m: acts on soft going: blinkered last outing. *R. J. Eckley* — c– 65

SERIOUS HONOUR (SWE) 6 ch.g. Ballacashtal (CAN) – Blue Garter (Targowice (USA)) [1992/3 21mpu] leggy gelding: no sign of ability in novice hurdles: tried visored/blinkered. *J. Norton* — —

SERIOZHA 10 b.g. Cut Above – Anna Karenina (Princely Gift) [1992/3 c21gpu c20m c21d⁵ c18s⁴] good-bodied gelding: poor chaser: best form at 2½m: acts on firm going. *R. Curtis* — c– —

SERPHIL 5 ch.g. Prince Vandezee – Rostresse (Rosyth) [1992/3 17m 22d⁵ 21v* 26s² 22d² 28g⁴ 21s⁵] neat, good-quartered gelding: selling hurdler: won handicap at Hexham (no bid) in November: ran well next 2 outings: stays 3¼m: acts on good to firm and heavy going: blinkered last 4 starts: looks a difficult ride. *L. Lungo* — 80

SETAI'S PALACE   6 b.m. Royal Palace – Tagliatelle (Straight Lad) [1992/3 22d³ 21g³ 22m⁵ 22g*] lengthy, shallow-girthed mare: modest hurdler: won 19-runner maiden at Huntingdon in April: stays 2¾m: best efforts with give in the ground. *D. Nicholson*   94

SETTER COUNTRY   9 b.m. Town And Country – Top Soprano (High   c123 Top) [1992/3 c21d³ c18d⁴ c21g³ c17v* c16d* c16s³ c16d⁴ c17s³ c16g³ c17m⁵ – c16gᵘʳ 17g⁴ c16g⁴] close-coupled mare: winning hurdler: fairly useful chaser: won handicaps at Newton Abbot and Ascot in November: rather inconsistent form afterwards: effective from 2m to 2¹f: acts on any ground: genuine: usually jumps well. *R. J. Hodges*

SET THE STANDARDS (IRE)   5 b.g. Mazaad – Jupiter Miss (USA)   109 (Hawaii) [1992/3 16gᵘʳ 17s³ 28d⁴ 28g⁵ 24m³ 20g* 20m² 21mF] sturdy gelding: handicap hurdler: 33/1-winner at Ayr in March: good second at Newcastle later in month: stayed really well: probably acted on any going: usually ridden up with pace: dead. *A. C. Whillans*

SEVEN OF DIAMONDS   8 b.g. Comedy Star (USA) – Priceless Gem   c107 (Roi Soleil) [1992/3 c21d* c24g² c27m c24g²] big, lengthy gelding: winning – hurdler: useful hunter chaser: won at Wincanton in February: very good second at Kempton next time, below form subsequently: effective at 2¹f and stays 3m: acts on dead ground. *H. Wellstead*

SEVEN SONS   6 b.g. Absalom – Archaic (Relic) [1992/3 17m⁶ 20m] small gelding: moderate hurdler at best: tailed off both outings in 1992/3: – keen-going sort (has worn net muzzle), ideally suited by sharp 2m: acts on hard going. *W. G. M. Turner*

SEVENTH LOCK   7 b.g. Oats – Barge Mistress (Bargello) [1992/3   c77 c17d⁴] short-backed gelding: moderate hurdler: last of 4 finishers in novice – chase at Towcester in October: stays 2¾m: acts on heavy and good to firm ground and equitrack. *O. Sherwood*

SEVEN TOWERS (IRE)   4 b.g. Roselier (FR) – Ramble Bramble (Random Shot) [1992/3 F16g³] second foal: dam, lightly raced, from highly successful jumping family: third of 13 in NH Flat race at Ayr in March: yet to race over hurdles. *Mrs M. Reveley*

SEXTON   8 b.h. Beldale Flutter (USA) – Be Tuneful (Be Friendly) [1992/3 18s a22gᵖᵘ 16v 22s 25mᵖᵘ] smallish, compact horse: lightly-raced novice – selling hurdler: form only at around 2m: blinkered fourth outing. *N. G. Ayliffe*

SEXY MOVER   6 ch.g. Coquelin (USA) – Princess Sinna (Sun Prince)   99 [1992/3 17m³ 18d⁶ 21d* 20d⁵ 21m] small, sparely-made gelding: handicap hurdler: won amateurs event at Carlisle in November: ran creditably otherwise except for lack-lustre effort final start: better suited by around 2½m than 2m, and will stay further: acts on firm and dead going. *W. Storey*

SHAARID (USA)   5 b.g. El Gran Senor (USA) – Summer Silence (USA)   108 (Stop The Music (USA)) [1992/3 17d² 17d⁶] small gelding: fairly useful form over 9f on Flat at 3 yrs, winning first of 2 starts: sold out of H. Thomson Jones's stable 6,500 gns Newmarket December (1991) Sales: promising second in novice hurdle at Huntingdon in January, but failed to reproduce that effort when favourite for similar race at Hereford following month. *R. F. Johnson Houghton*

SHADANZA (IRE)   4 b.g. Shardari – Amanzi (African Sky) [1992/3 16g   81 17s³ 16sᵖᵘ] small, leggy, close-coupled gelding: half-brother to winning hurdler Captain My Captain (by Flash of Steel): modest middle-distance maiden on Flat: third of 16 in novice hurdle at Carlisle in January: ran poorly in seller following month. *A. P. Stringer*

SHADAYLOU (IRE)   4 ch.f. Standaan (FR) – Grande Madame (Monseigneur (USA)) [1992/3 17gᵖᵘ 16d⁵ 16gF] poor maiden on Flat and – seemed no better over hurdles: suffered a fatal fall at Ayr in October. *Miss L. A. Perratt*

SHADEUX   7 ch.g. Valiyar – A Deux (FR) (Crepello) [1992/3 22s 18d⁴   111 18s³ 18s⁴ 21s³ 25v 18s² 25mᵖᵘ] rather sparely-made gelding: fair handicap hurdler: trained until after second start by Mrs J. Wonnacott: easily best efforts of season on third and fifth outings: sold out of Mrs J. Retter's stable 4,000 gns Ascot February Sales after sixth: trained for next by P. Rich: needs testing conditions at around 2m and stays 3¼m: acts on any going: blinkered twice. *A. L. Forbes*

SHADOW BIRD 6 b.m. Martinmas – In The Shade (Bustino) [1992/3 17g] modest middle-distance performer on Flat, successful twice in 1992: behind in novice hurdle at Huntingdon in October. *G. A. Pritchard-Gordon*   –

SHADY ROAD 11 b.g. Laurence O – Aprils End (Star Signal) [1992/3 c16dF c16g] lengthy, workmanlike gelding: winning chaser: no worthwhile form in 1992/3: probably stays 2¾m: acts on soft going. *G. Richards*   c–
–

SHAFAYIF 4 ch.f. Ela-Mana-Mou – Rare Roberta (USA) (Roberto (USA)) [1992/3 18m* 17f[ro]] lengthy, sparely-made filly: middle-distance plater on Flat: sold out of B. Hanbury's stable 2,100 gns Newmarket July Sales: won selling hurdle (bought in 5,000 gns) at Market Rasen in August (saddle slipped): narrow leader when cocked jaw and ran out last in juvenile event at Plumpton later in month: sold 1,350 gns Ascot November Sales: not one to trust. *I. Campbell*   78 §

SHAFFIC (FR) 6 b.g. Auction Ring (USA) – Tavella (FR) (Petingo) [1992/3 21d6 17g2 16s4 20s4 20dF] neat gelding: fair novice hurdler: probably stays 2½m: acts on good to firm and probably soft going: sketchy jumper: runs in snatches: blinkered last start. *M. D. Hammond*   98

SHAHDJAT (IRE) 5 ch.m. Vayrann – Shahdiza (USA) (Blushing Groom (FR)) [1992/3 25d2 24s* 22d2 25s5 24g2 25f* 24s] sparely-made, angular mare: one-time useful stayer on Flat in Ireland: won novice hurdles at Chepstow in November and Newbury in March: suited by good test of stamina: probably acts on any going: blinkered last 2 starts: lazy and will prove best with strong handling. *K. C. Bailey*   101

SHAHMIRAJ 5 b.m. Final Straw – Palace Tor (Dominion) [1992/3 18m5 17mur 18m 17s3 18s 18d6 17d* 22g 16d 17m 22d2 22g] angular mare: trained until after fourth start by W. A. Stephenson, next 4 by P. Cheesbrough: won selling handicap hurdle at Carlisle (no bid) in February: good second in seller at Sedgefield in April, best effort subsequently: stays 2¾m: acts on soft going. *V. Thompson*   73

SHAKE TOWN (USA) 5 b.g. Caro – All Dance (USA) (Northern Dancer) [1992/3 16d2 17g 17m 16d 16m5 17g6] good-topped gelding: half-brother to high-class hurdler Ruling (by Alleged): fair handicapper on Flat, winner 3 times at 7f in 1991, below form in 1992: unlucky short-head second in novice event at Uttoxeter in October, easily best effort over hurdles: sold out of M. Tompkins' stable 5,000 gns Ascot December Sales after second start: visored first 2 outings, blinkered third: pulls hard: sketchy jumper. *J. Mackie*   94 d

SHAKIMA 12 br.g. Crash Course – Linmoss (Linacre) [1992/3 c27f5] handicap chaser: ran poorly in amateurs event in October, only outing of season: stays 3¼m: probably acts on any going. *K. C. Bailey*   c–
–

SHAKINSKI 4 gr.f. Niniski (USA) – Shakana (Grundy) [1992/3 17f 17gF] fair stayer at best on Flat: well beaten in novice hurdle at Huntingdon in March: dead. *M. J. Ryan*   –

SHALCHLO BOY 9 gr.g. Rusticaro (FR) – Mala Mala (Crepello) [1992/3 20d c23g4 c26gpu c17f2 c21spu c24g4] small, sturdy gelding: winning hurdler/chaser: fourth in amateurs handicap over fences at Worcester in March, second and best effort of season: trained first start Mrs J. Wonnacott: stays 3m: acts on hard and dead going: blinkered once: jumps none too fluently. *W. G. M. Turner*   c89
–

SHALOU 4 b.c. Forzando – Axe Valley (Royben) [1992/3 16g 17f6] smallish colt: useful plater on Flat, stays 1m: mid-division in juvenile claiming hurdle at Wincanton and juvenile seller at Taunton in October. *R. J. Hodges*   –

SHAMAALY BABY (USA) 5 ch.g. Northern Baby (CAN) – Shining Skin (USA) (Fappiano (USA)) [1992/3 17s^{pu} 17m^6 18s^{pu}] small, strong gelding: poor novice hurdler, has run in sellers: sold 1,600 gns Malvern June Sales. *D. McCain*   67

SHAMANA 7 b.m. Broadsword (USA) – Celestial Bride (Godswalk (USA)) [1992/3 c18d^2 c16d^2 c17v* c17s^{pu} c16v^4 c16d* c17m^2 c16g* c17m^4] lengthy, rather leggy mare: useful chaser: won handicaps at Cheltenham in December, Wolverhampton in February and Sandown in March: also good second to Space Fair in valuable similar event at Cheltenham in March: best at around 2m: acts on good to firm and heavy ground: sketchy jumper. *D. Nicholson*   c132 –

SHAMARPHIL 7 b.m. Sunyboy – Chaffcombe (Crozier) [1992/3 c24m^3 c23v^{ur} c27d^2] winning pointer: modest form when placed in hunter chases in April and May: stays 27f: acts on good to firm and dead going. *Miss Susan Pitman*   c76

SHAMBA MAJI 5 b.m. Meadowbrook – Fala Kalima (Sousa) [1992/3 F17m 16g 16g] leggy mare: tailed off in NH Flat races and novice hurdles. *S. J. Leadbetter*   –

SHANAGHEY WEST 9 b.g. Marshalsea – Kauai-Ka-Zum (Kauai King) [1992/3 c16v* c22v^{pu} c18m^4 c17g^4 c21f^4 c21g^F] workmanlike gelding: winning hurdler when trained in Ireland by I. Ferguson: poor form over fences, but was successful in 4-runner novice event at Lingfield in January: probably stays 2½m: acts on any ground: visored fifth start. *J. R. Jenkins*   c81 –

SHANAKEE 6 b.g. Wassl – Sheeog (Reform) [1992/3 17d^3] plating-class sprint form at best on Flat: promising third of 15 in novice hurdle at Wolverhampton in February. *K. S. Bridgwater*   91 p

SHANBALLY BOY 12 b.g. Random Shot – June's Slipper (No Argument) [1992/3 c25g^6] smallish, workmanlike gelding: winning chaser: tailed off in hunter chase in May: stays well: acts on heavy going and good to firm. *G. D. Hanmer*   c– –

SHANNAGARY 12 ch.g. Deep Run – Farranfore (Fortina) [1992/3 c21g^4 c21s^6] dipped-backed gelding: fair handicap chaser: no show in 2 outings in October: seems suited by around 2½m: acts on any going: has tended to hang right. *R. J. Hodges*   c– –

SHANNON GLEN 7 b.g. Furry Glen – Shannon Ville (Deep Run) [1992/3 c21d^3 c20d^5 c20d c21s^4 c21v* c20g^{pu}] lengthy gelding: fairly useful hurdler: best effort in novice chases when winning at Leicester in January: suited by around 2½m: acts on good to firm and heavy ground: blinkered last 2 outings: inconsistent. *Mrs J. Pitman*   c97 –

SHANNON JULIETTE 6 b.m. Julio Mariner – Craftsmans Made (Jimsun) [1992/3 23s^{pu} 19m^6 22d* 25s^{pu} 22v^F] smallish, sparely-made ex-Irish mare: third living foal: dam unraced sister to useful chasers Welsh Oak and Warner For Leisure: winning pointer: only form in novice hurdles when winning mares event at Wincanton in October: should stay beyond 2¾m: acts on dead ground. *D. R. Gandolfo*   79

SHANNON KING (IRE) 5 ch.g. Boyne Valley – Miss Royal (King's Company) [1992/3 F14d^2 18m^4 F10d 16g^3 16s^2 16d^3] tall, lengthy gelding: modest form when placed in novice hurdles: sold 6,000 gns Doncaster March Sales: acts on soft ground. *J. G. FitzGerald*   90

SHANNON RUN (IRE) 4 b.g. Celio Rufo – Annie Owen (Master Owen) [1992/3 F14m] non-thoroughbred gelding: seventh foal: half-brother to a lightly-raced novice hurdler by Over The River: dam unplaced in 2 NH Flat races and 2 maiden hurdles: soundly beaten in NH Flat race at Market Rasen in March: yet to race over hurdles. *O. Brennan*   –

SHARDRA 4 b.f. Sharrood (USA) – Dragonist (Dragonara Palace (USA)) [1992/3 17g^{pu} 17d 16d 17g^4 18m 16f^4 18v 17f] sparely-made filly: half-sister to several winners, including hurdler Arsonist (by Ardross): poor maiden on Flat, stays 9f: sold out of M. Camacho's stable 2,700 gns Doncaster August   67

Sales: juvenile selling hurdler: best effort over 2m on firm ground. *M. F. Barraclough*

SHARED FORTUNE (IRE)   5 b. or br.g. Strong Gale – Reaper's Run (Deep Run) [1992/3 F14d F17m 16d⁶ 26sᵖᵘ 24g c16mᵘʳ c20mᵖᵘ c17d c18sᶠ 17s⁶] half-brother to winning pointer Reaper's Castle (by Carlingford Castle): dam unraced half-sister to Fredcoteri: no worthwhile form over hurdles or fences: sold 1,550 gns Ascot June Sales: tried blinkered. *W. T. Kemp*   c–
 –

SHAREEF STAR   5 b.g. Shareef Dancer (USA) – Ultra Vires (High Line) [1992/3 16vᵖᵘ a18gᵖᵘ] small gelding: modest hurdler at best: showed nothing either outing in 1992/3: stays 2½m: acts on dead ground. *R. T. Juckes*   –

SHARP ANSWER   6 ch.g. Affirmed (USA) – Sharp Jose (USA) (Sharpen Up) [1992/3 21gᵖᵘ] tall, workmanlike gelding: showed signs of ability in novice hurdles in 1991/2: several mistakes only outing in 1992/3 (March). *B. Smart*   –

SHARPFORD   8 ch.g. Milford – Sharp And Sweet (Javelot) [1992/3 c21m⁵ c26dᵖᵘ] leggy gelding: tubed: poor plater over hurdles and fences: stays 2½m (not 3m): acts on firm and dead ground: sometimes blinkered. *D. W. Browning*   c–
 –

SHARPGUN (FR)   7 ch.g. Sharpo – Whitegun (FR) (Carwhite) [1992/3 17g² c16f⁵ c18g³ 17s⁴ c24mᵘʳ c21s⁴ 17s* 17v² 16v 17v³ 20v² 18s⁵ 20f⁵] leggy gelding: moderate hurdler/chaser: won selling handicap hurdle at Fakenham (no bid) in December: stays 2½m: probably acts on any ground: blinkered once: sometimes takes little interest: unreliable. *A. Moore*   c– §
 95 §

SHARP INVITE   6 ch.m. Sharpo – Invitation (Faberge II) [1992/3 16s 20v* 18d² 18d² 18v* 19v 18d² 16dᵘʳ 24d 16s* 16d⁶] half-sister to quite useful hurdler and winning chaser Quickstep (by Hotfoot): dam useful middle-distance performer and sister to Rheingold: useful hurdler: won handicaps at Clonmel, Navan and Fairyhouse (quite valuable event) in 1992/3: stays 2½m: acts on heavy going. *W. P. Mullins, Ireland*   133

SHARP ISSUE (USA)   5 ch.g. Diesis – Concentrate (USA) (Broadway Forli (USA)) [1992/3 24sᵖᵘ 16sᵖᵘ 18v 17s a22g] workmanlike gelding: of little account: blinkered last start. *M. C. Chapman*   –

Bisquit Cognac Handicap Hurdle, Fairyhouse—
the winner Sharp Invite (right) jumps the last alongside Atone
with the weakening Roman Forum just behind

SHARP PERFORMER (IRE) 4 br.g. Sharpo – Husnah (USA) (Caro) [1992/3 F14g³] lengthy gelding: second foal: dam fair stayer on Flat: third in 19-runner NH Flat race at Market Rasen in April: yet to race over hurdles. *K. C. Bailey*

SHARP PRINCE 4 ch.g. Sharpo – Jungle Queen (Twilight Alley) [1992/3 16d 16d 16s^bd 16f⁴] close-coupled gelding: closely related to Jungle Knife (by Kris) and half-brother to Jungle Jim (by Hotfoot), both of them very useful hurdlers: fair miler on Flat when trained by H. Cecil: bought for only 3,000 gns Newmarket Autumn Sales: poor form over hurdles. *S. E. Kettlewell*

76

SHARPRIDGE 9 ch.g. Nearly A Hand – Maria's Piece (Rose Knight) [1992/3 c20sᵖᵘ c20m² c18d⁴ c21f² c26gᴿ] rangy gelding: poor novice chaser: creditable second at Ludlow early in season and at Plumpton in March: tailed off when refused last on last start: stays 3m: acts on firm and good to soft going. *Mrs J. Pitman*

c84 –

SHARPSIDE 6 b.g. Broadsword (USA) – Moll (Rugantino) [1992/3 c18sᵖᵘ c16sᵘʳ 17fᵖᵘ] third foal: half-brother to poor novice hurdler/chaser Rymolbreese (by Rymer): dam, winning hurdler, stayed 21f: no sign of ability. *J. White*

c– –

SHARPTINO 4 ch.c. Bustino – Sharper Still (Sharpen Up) [1992/3 17sᶠ] smallish, workmanlike colt: modest maiden on Flat, no form in 1993 for S. Dow: better for race, showed signs of ability though behind when falling last in juvenile hurdle at Newbury in January: pulled hard. *R. Akehurst*

– p

SHARP TOP 5 b.m. Sharpo – Two High (High Top) [1992/3 17d*] workmanlike mare: half-sister to winning hurdler Always Alex (by Final Straw): modest winner from 1½m to 2m on Flat in 1992: won novice hurdle at Huntingdon in November, but wasn't seen out again: will stay further than 17f. *M. J. Ryan*

84

SHARRIBA 4 gr.f. Sharrood (USA) – Alsiba (Northfields (USA)) [1992/3 17vᶠ 16s⁵ 16v 17d* 17g⁴ 16f³ 17f⁴ 17g⁶] leggy filly: modest maiden on Flat, stays 9f: sold out of D. Elsworth's stable 3,200 gns Newmarket Autumn Sales: won juvenile hurdle at Stratford in February: vastly improved form when fourth in Glenlivet Anniversary Hurdle at Aintree in April on seventh start: ran respectably in juvenile handicap at Ascot later in April: should stay beyond 17f: successful on dead ground but best efforts on a sound surface. *G. L. Humphrey*

123

SHASHIKALA 5 ch.m. Enchantment – Ginara (Treason Trial) [1992/3 17vᵖᵘ 22vᵖᵘ 22dᵖᵘ] third foal: dam winning hurdler, suited by test of stamina: no sign of ability. *J. E. Collinson*

–

SHASTON 8 ch.g. Rolfe (USA) – Nicaline (High Line) [1992/3 23s⁴ 24v² 22d c20s c26v* c26d⁵ c26g* c24m³ c26dᵖᵘ] smallish, sparely-made gelding: fair hurdler: good second at Chepstow in December: won novice chase at Wincanton in January and handicap at Plumpton in March: well below form last 2 starts: well suited by a thorough test of stamina: acts on any going: best blinkered: none too consistent. *W. G. M. Turner*

c104 111

SHATRAVIV 5 b.m. Meadowbrook – M-N-Ms Lass (Workboy) [1992/3 F17d] second foal: dam poor plater at 2 yrs: seventh of 25 in NH Flat race at Carlisle in April: yet to race over hurdles or fences. *J. I. A. Charlton*

SHAWIYA (IRE) 4 b.f. Lashkari – Shaiyra (Relko) [1992/3 16s² 16s* 16d* 16s* 17m* 16g*] Thank heavens for Shawiya. Where the juvenile hurdlers were concerned the latest season would have been eminently forgettable without her. While it is true to say that she was only marginally superior to the other leading juveniles in a far-from-vintage year, saying so doesn't do justice to her achievements. Shawiya, successful in all but one of her six starts, became the first filly to win the Daily Express Triumph Hurdle, and the first winner of that race to go on to take Punchestown's Champion Four-Year-Old Hurdle.

141 p

Daily Express Triumph Hurdle, Cheltenham—
Shawiya (noseband) is pressed by the eventual third Major Bugler at the last

Shawiya was the pick of the four Irish challengers for the Daily Express Triumph Hurdle at Cheltenham in March, her form giving her an obvious chance in what looked a very open race. Missing from the line-up was Titled Dancer who had beaten Shawiya by a head at Navan in November, when both were running for the first time over hurdles. Shawiya easily turned the tables in a listed event at Fairyhouse eight days later, when they occupied the first two places, but after following up this success at Leopardstown Shawiya was then off the course for almost two months, reportedly because of a poisoned foot. On her return, at Punchestown, Shawiya was once again opposed by Titled Dancer, and the pair were involved in another tremendous battle. Shawiya prevailed by half a length, but she had a desperately hard race in the process and it came as no surprise when her rider Jason Titley was suspended for excessive use of the whip. The Irish champion Charlie Swan was on board Shawiya in her two subsequent races. For a while it was touch and go about their teaming up at Cheltenham, for Shawiya, who had bruised her near-fore hoof in a schooling bumper, wasn't passed fit to run until half past six on the morning of the Triumph Hurdle, the journey to England still to be made. Despite this set-back there seemed to be no lack of confidence behind Shawiya, who was sent off at 12/1, the same price as Her Honour and the Tote Placepot Hurdle winner Amazon Express. Only Beauchamp Grace and Indian Quest, first and second respectively in the Stroud Green Hurdle, started at shorter odds, the former the favourite at 13/2. Beauchamp Grace, along with several others in the field, failed to do herself justice on the firmish going. Shawiya, on the other hand, wasn't at all inconvenienced by conditions which were very different from those she'd encountered previously over hurdles. As usual she raced up with the pace, travelling strongly just behind the leader Mohana until moving smoothly into the lead three from home. Major Bugler joined Shawiya at the next, where there were around a dozen horses still in with a chance, and this pair began to get away from the pack on the run to the last. Shawiya's jockey didn't go for his whip until the run-in where his mount responded gamely to gain the upper hand, but she then tended to idle and it was only by three quarters of a length that she held the late challenge of Amazon Express, with Major Bugler a further two lengths back in third place just ahead of Judicial Field.

The first, third and fourth, along with Indian Quest and Clurican who finished in the mid-division, renewed rivalry in the Murphys Irish Stout Champion Four-Year-Old Hurdle at Punchestown six weeks later. Also in the thirteen-runner field were the Finale Junior Hurdle winner Dare To Dream, Shawiya's old rival Titled Dancer, who'd won the Glenlivet Anniversary Hurdle at Aintree on her most recent start, and Lemon's Mill, also successful at Aintree and earlier runner-up to Montelado in the Trafalgar House Supreme Novices' Hurdle at the Cheltenham Festival. The story of the race is easily told. Lemon's Mill, who started favourite, ensured it was truly run but she dropped out quickly when Shawiya moved smoothly past her going to two out, with only Titled Dancer and Judicial Field posing any sort of threat at that stage. However, Shawiya was soon well in command and she ran on strongly to win impressively by nine lengths from Titled Dancer with Judicial Field, who'd have finished a little closer but for mistakes at the last two flights, three and a half lengths further away in third. Indian Quest did best of the British challengers, staying on to take fourth place without ever looking likely to trouble the principals. Shawiya, though clearly thriving on racing, was given a well-earned break. Report had it that she was to be prepared for the Breeders' Cup Chase at Belmont Park in October. However, in late-July she was found to have a cyst in her throat and is now thought likely to miss virtually all the first half of the next season. All being well, she'll have the Champion Hurdles in Ireland and Britain as her main objectives. Better juvenile hurdlers than Shawiya have failed to make their presence felt in the top races in the following season. Shawiya, a leggy, angular filly rather lacking in scope, may not improve sufficiently to bridge the gap. But she will progress, and her toughness and enthusiasm, along with her sound jumping, will stand her in good stead when she takes on the more established performers.

Shawiya was bred by the Aga Khan whose studs have produced several other well-known jumpers in recent seasons, including Balasani, Chirkpar,

Murphys Irish Stout Champion Four-Year-Old Hurdle, Punchestown — this time Shawiya is clear at the final flight

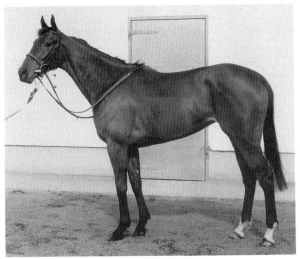

Miss G. Maher's "Shawiya"

Shawiya (IRE) (b.f. 1989)	Lashkari (b 1981)	Mill Reef (b 1968)	Never Bend Milan Mill
		Larannda (ch 1971)	Right Royal V Morning Calm
	Shaiyra (b 1977)	Relko (b 1960)	Tanerko Relance III
		Asharaz (gr 1967)	Sicambre Vareta

Rouyan and Mounamara, the last-named the winner of the Champion Four-Year-Old Hurdle in 1991. Successful in a mile-and-a-half maiden on the Flat for the Aga Khan, Shawiya was bought by her present connections for IR 12,000 guineas as a potential broodmare. The well-bred Shawiya should prove as valuable an asset at stud as she is on the racecourse. From the third crop of the Breeders' Cup Turf winner Lashkari, Shawiya is out of Shaiyra, an unraced half-sister to the high-class French stayer Shafaraz and daughter of a half-sister to Zeddaan, a brilliantly speedy two-year-old who won the Poule d'Essai des Poulains and Prix d'Ispahan at three. Shaiyra has bred numerous other winners, notably the smart miler Shaikiya (by Bold Lad (Ire)), the good French staying jumper Shaiykoun (by Tap On Wood) who had The Fellow behind him when winning the 1990 Grand Steeple-Chase d'Enghien, and Sheyrann (by Top Ville), a very useful hurdler in France and Germany in the latest season. The tough and genuine Shawiya, a credit to the family, has raced only at around two miles. She will certainly stay further, and the twenty-one furlongs of the Breeders' Cup Chase would have been within her compass. Shawiya acts on good to firm and soft going.
M. J. P. O'Brien, Ireland

SHAWWELL 6 gr.g. Alias Smith (USA) – Besciamella (Foggy Bell) [1992/3 20m^{pu} 21s^2 25d^6 20g^3 21g^{pu} 20m^2 21d^{pu}] tall, unfurnished gelding: 93

665

half-brother to winning hurdler Stagshaw Belle (by Royal Fountain): dam 2m hurdle winner: moderate form when placed in novice hurdles: should stay beyond 2 1f: acts on good to firm and soft ground. *J. I. A. Charlton*

SHAYNA MAIDEL 4 ch.f. Scottish Reel – Revisit (Busted) [1992/3 17d^{ur} 16s^F 16d⁵ 16g⁵ 17g⁵ 16g³ 17m³ 16g 17d⁴ 16m⁴ 17m⁵ 18v³] smallish filly: poor maiden on Flat: poor hurdler: sold out of Miss H. Knight's stable 900 gns Ascot December Sales after second start: will stay beyond 2 1/4m: acts on good to firm and heavy going. *J. J. Birkett*   84

SHEAN ALAINN (IRE) 5 b.m. Le Moss – Stable Lass (Golden Love) [1992/3 F16v² F16v² 21v* 21g^{pu} 25m] shallow-girthed mare: second foal: sister to useful hurdler Brackenfield: dam never ran: pulled up in a point in 1992: second in NH Flat race at Thurles in December when trained by M. O'Connor: won mares novice hurdle at Towcester in February in good style: ran poorly both subsequent starts: should stay beyond 2 1f: acts well on heavy going. *Mrs M. Reveley*   87 +

SHEDARBO 8 ch.g. Sagaro – Song of Grace (Articulate) [1992/3 c26m^{pu}] strong, rangy gelding: well beaten in novice hurdles: poor novice chaser (makes mistakes). *Ms Polly Gowers*   c– x   –

SHEEPHAVEN 9 b.g. Relkino – Suffolk Broads (Moulton) [1992/3 c23s³ c25s^{pu} c24d] rather leggy, angular gelding: in frame in maiden hurdles: first race since November, 1991, when creditable third in handicap chase at Worcester in March: failed to reproduce that form: stays 3m: acts on heavy and good to firm ground. *T. J. Etherington*   c102   –

SHEEP STEALER 5 gr.g. Absalom – Kilroe's Calin (Be Friendly) [1992/3 F16s F16d 16g* 17m⁶ 18d 17v³] workmanlike gelding: won novice hurdle at Catterick in March: ran creditably next and last outings: unlikely to stay beyond 17f: acts on good to firm ground. *J. G. FitzGerald*   88

SHEER ABILITY 7 b.g. Carlingford Castle – Auburn Queen (Kinglet) [1992/3 c21s^F c24s^F c24v² c22v* c22v*] lengthy gelding: maiden hurdler: won novice chases at Towcester in February and April: stays 3m: acts on heavy ground. *Mrs F. Walwyn*   c101   –

SHEER JEST 8 b.g. Mummy's Game – Tabasheer (USA) (Indian Chief II) [1992/3 c24g* c24g* c25m* c22m* c17m* c28f²]   c117 p

Sheer Jest's long winning run came to an end in the Horse And Hound Cup at Stratford on the last day of the season. A useful staying performance from Generals Boy did the trick, with Sheer Jest not at his best. The ten-length second pulled too hard in the small field early on, and although he moved up to deprive Generals Boy of the lead three out he gave way quickly going to the last. This reverse apart, the season went very well for Sheer Jest. The most important aspect of it was that he developed into one of the best hunter chasers around. A clash between him and Double Silk would have been worth going a long way to see. Their meeting was deferred when, in May, Sheer Jest was pulled out of the Cheltenham Champion Hunters' Chase in favour of an easier race on the same card which he won at 7/2 on. Thus far Sheer Jest has been less highly tried than Double Silk or most of the other leading hunters—the John Corbet Cup at Stratford is the most competitive race he's been in, and the Horse And Hound Cup the most valuable. The John Corbet Cup, subtitled Champion Novices' Hunters' Chase with some justification, was Sheer Jest's last race and second successive win in 1992; he beat Once Stung in a close finish, looking a fine recruit from the point-to-point field. The winning sequence in hunter chases took up again at Kempton in February and expanded through visits to Leicester, Nottingham, Stratford and the one already mentioned to Cheltenham before it ended at a total of seven. The race at Nottingham was one in the 'Rising Stars' series, and that's what he'd clearly become. Next time out, at Stratford in April, he gave his best, most impressive, display to date in inflicting a crushing defeat on the hitherto-unbeaten novice Ellerton Hill. The fifteen-length margin gives no idea of his superiority, for he was allowed to coast home after a superb exhibition of jumping apart from one early mistake and quickening on at the fifth last.

			Mummy's Pet	Sing Sing
		Mummy's Game	(b 1968)	Money For Nothing
		(b 1979)	Final Game	Pardao
Sheer Jest			(ch 1970)	Ankole
(b.g. 1985)			Indian Chief II	Pronto
		Tabasheer (USA)	(b 1965)	Coya Linda
		(b 1972)	Nearctara	Nearctic
			(b 1967)	Avatara

Sheer Jest is a half-brother to a winning jumper in Bloak Moss (by Cavo Doro) and is even more closely related to a dam of others in Tremellick (by Mummy's Pet), the dam of the useful pair Avro Anson and Lanhydrock. Tremellick was a five-furlong sprinter, as was another winner by Mummy's Pet out of the unraced Tabasheer, Karens Pet, and it's hard to see where Sheer Jest gets his stamina from. Perhaps from his maternal grandsire, the Argentinian Derby winner Indian Chief II who stayed comfortably beyond two miles. Neither the second nor third dams showed much. Sheer Jest is very versatile so far as distance is concerned. He failed to get the three and a half miles of the Horse And Hound Cup but that was because he wouldn't settle. The John Corbet Cup is run over the same course (remeasured at three and a half since 1992, having been thought to be three and a quarter). He showed himself effective at seventeen furlongs against a fair horse in Radio Cue at Cheltenham, and he has won at several distances between the two extremes (the race against Ellerton Hill was over two and three quarter miles). Whatever the distance Sheer Jest is held up, and usually he settles well enough. He acts on good to soft and good to firm ground; the Horse And Hound Cup was his first run on firm. A tall gelding, he is an accomplished jumper. *W. J. Warner*

SHEER POWER (IRE) 4 b.g. Exhibitioner – Quality Blake (Blakeney) [1992/3 17g³ 18g⁶ 18f 17mᶠ 17f] lengthy gelding: half-brother to several winners, including fairly useful hurdler/fair chaser Taelos (by Godswalk): dam won at up to 15f: poor form over hurdles: blinkered last start. *R. Rowe* — 54

SHEER STEEL 13 ch.g. Precipice Wood – Flora Finching (Fortina) [1992/3 c25f] leggy, angular gelding: poor chaser: sold out of J. Bukovets' stable 1,200 gns Ascot September Sales: suited by good test of stamina: acts on soft going: blinkered once: poor jumper. *T. D. B. Underwood* — c– x, –

SHEHEREZADE (IRE) 5 br.m. Asir – Alhamdulillah (Pry) [1992/3 21vᵖᵘ] half-sister to NH Flat winner Pameva (by Decent Fellow): dam, winning hurdler, stayed 3m: raced too freely and tailed off when pulled up in mares novice hurdle at Towcester in February. *C. R. Egerton* — –

SHEIKH'S PET 7 b.g. Mummy's Pet – Parlais (Pardao) [1992/3 c21mᵘʳ] neat gelding: novice selling hurdler: maiden pointer: unseated rider third in May on steeplechasing debut: best at around 2m: acts on soft and good to firm going and equitrack: best form blinkered. *F. R. Bown* — c–, –

SHEILAS HILLCREST 7 b.g. Hotfoot – Be Honest (Klairon) [1992/3 c23m³] big gelding: poor novice hurdler/chaser: not discredited only outing of season (August): probably stays 23f: seems suited by top-of-the-ground. *Mrs Y. E. Stapleton* — c73, –

SHEILOAN 4 b.f. Cruise Missile – Fair Princess (Quality Fair) [1992/3 F16g] non-thoroughbred filly: third foal: dam unraced: behind in NH Flat race at Kempton in February: sold 1,050 gns Ascot March Sales: yet to race over hurdles. *J. J. Bridger*

SHELLHOUSE (IRE) 5 ch.g. Deep Run – Miss Curraghmore (Little Buskins) [1992/3 F16g] second foal: dam fair Irish hurdler/chaser, successful at up to 2¾m: mid-division in NH Flat race at Kempton in February: yet to race over hurdles or fences. *N. J. Henderson*

SHELLY'S FOLLY 8 b.h. Music Boy – Gay Maria (Tacitus) [1992/3 17g 17m⁴ 16s 17fᵘʳ 16f* 17m² 16f 17dᵖᵘ] small, close-coupled horse: won novice selling hurdle at Towcester (bought in 3,000 gns) in May: poor efforts last 2 outings: stays 2¼m when conditions aren't testing: probably acts on any going: blinkered once. *R. J. Hodges* — 83

SHELTON ABBEY 7 br.g. The Parson – Herald Holidolly (New Member) [1992/3 c24gF c21m c24mur c21dbd c24mR 23s 28sur 26s2 28d2 28g* 24m2 25d 25s*] tall gelding: fair handicap hurdler: trained until after sixth outing by W. A. Stephenson: won at Sedgefield in March and Wetherby in April: hasn't taken to fences: sold 16,000 gns in May: stays well: acts on good to firm and soft going: to be trained by J. Hellens. *P. Cheesbrough*

cxx
106

SHEPHERD'S HYMN 12 ch.g. Cidrax (FR) – Lay Lady Lay (Celtic Ash) [1992/3 c27dpu] lengthy, plain gelding: fair chaser: stayed extremely well: acted on any going: suited by forcing tactics: was genuine: dead. *Mrs V. A. Aconley*

c–
–

SHERIFF'S BAND 6 ch.g. Posse (USA) – Willis (FR) (Lyphard (USA)) [1992/3 c25g* c25dF c25dpu c24g5 c27gpu] tall, leggy gelding: selling hurdler: won novice chase at Market Rasen in October: only other form when good fifth in novice handicap at Doncaster in January: sold 4,100 gns Doncaster May Sales: stays 25f: acts on heavy going. *M. H. Easterby*

c84
–

SHERMAGO 11 b.m. Humdoleila – Tartarbee (Charlottesville) [1992/3 c24g3 c24m* c25d4 c25g3 c24g5 c25g c26m3 c27g 25m3] rather sparely-made mare: selling hurdler: won poor novice chase at Carlisle in September: easily best subsequent effort fourth outing: stays 3m: acts on hard ground. *Mrs J. D. Goodfellow*

c77
63

SHERWOOD FOX 6 b.g. Sallust – Nicholette (Nicholas Bill) [1992/3 22dpu 22dpu 17s 18m5 c18mpu 20g] sturdy gelding: poor novice hurdler: won a point in March: no show in novice claimer on steeplechasing debut: blinkered last outing. *Mrs J. Wonnacott*

c–
–

SHE'S NO NUN 6 b.m. The Parson – Last Alliance (Honour Bound) [1992/3 F17d3] half-sister to winning jumpers Larchwood (by Precipice Wood) and Just As I Am (by Deep Run): dam never ran: third of 17 in NH Flat race at Hereford in May: yet to race over hurdles or fences. *S. Christian*

SHIKABELL 9 br.m. Kala Shikari – Betbellof (Averof) [1992/3 c19m6] leggy mare: lightly raced: winning hurdler: poor novice chaser: well beaten in selling handicap in February: likely to prove best at around 2m: acts on firm ground. *M. P. Muggeridge*

c–
–

SHILGROVE PLACE 11 ch.g. Le Bavard (FR) – Petmon (Eudaemon) [1992/3 23g 24d 20spu c24gF c20spu] good-topped gelding: fair hurdler at best and winning chaser: little sign of retaining ability in 1992/3: stays 2¾m, seemingly not 3m: acts on any going. *Mrs S. A. Bramall*

c–
–

SHILINSKI 6 b.g. Niniski (USA) – Sushila (Petingo) [1992/3 18mpu 21mpu] sparely-made gelding: winning staying hurdler, but ungenuine and one to steer well clear of: blinkered nowadays. *G. M. Moore*

– §

SHIMMERING SCARLET (IRE) 5 b.m. Glint of Gold – Scarlet Slipper (Gay Mecene (USA)) [1992/3 17m5 18f 17g5 16g a16g5 a20g* a20g2 a22g* 20m3 17g3 20m* 20f3 22f2 23f4] compact mare: modest hurdler: won novice handicaps at Lingfield (2) and Taunton (amateurs) in second half of season: stays 2¾m: acts on firm going and equitrack. *R. H. Buckler*

99

SHIMSHEK (USA) 9 b.g. Gold Stage (USA) – Marie de Retz (Reliance II) [1992/3 c22gF] big gelding: lightly-raced 2m hurdler: fair form in points in 1993, won twice in May: in third and pushed along when falling thirteenth in hunter chase at Fakenham 2 months earlier. *Mrs J. Read*

c–
–

SHINING ART 8 ch.g. Artaius (USA) – Moonlight Sonata (So Blessed) [1992/3 16d 20spu 22dpu] leggy gelding: modest novice hurdler in 1989/90: no sign of retaining ability in 1992/3: sold 2,000 gns Ascot February Sales: stays 3m: acts on heavy going. *D. McCain*

–

SHINING PENNY 6 b.g. Sunyboy – Quickapenny (Espresso) [1992/3 21g 21fpu] strong, good-topped gelding: fifth foal: half-brother to winning jumpers Sneakapenny (by Levanter) and Catchapenny (by True Song): dam, a useful hurdler and winning chaser, stayed well: no sign of ability either outing over hurdles. *M. J. Wilkinson*

–

SHIONA ANNE 9 b.m. Royal Fountain – Miss Craigie (New Brig) [1992/3 c20g³ c20s⁴ c21sᶠ c25g⁶ c21s] lengthy, workmanlike mare: novice hurdler: poor form when in frame in novice chases in November: should be suited by further than 2½m: acts on soft ground. *R. H. Goldie* c80 –

SHIREOAK'S FLYER 5 ch.g. Hell's Gate – Velocidad (Balidar) [1992/3 F17s 16s 22sᵖᵘ 18gᵖᵘ 18sᵖᵘ 23mᵖᵘ] tall gelding: first foal: dam winning sprinter: no sign of ability. *D. J. W. Edmunds* –

SHIRL 4 b.f. Shirley Heights – Bercheba (Bellypha) [1992/3 17m 18d³ 18g 18d 16s³ 16v⁵ a22g² 17f⁵ 21s⁴] compact filly: won 1½m seller on Flat in August: plating-class form over hurdles: best efforts at 2m with plenty of give in the ground. *G. F. H. Charles-Jones* 78

SHIRYON 8 b.g. Tickled Pink – Assel Zawie (Sit In The Corner (USA)) [1992/3 17v a22gᶠ 22vᵖᵘ a16gᶠ] leggy gelding: seems of little account. *Mrs A. Knight* –

SHOCKING TIMES 4 b.f. Skyliner – Mashin Time (Palm Track) [1992/3 17mᵖᵘ] plating-class sprint maiden on Flat: no promise in August on hurdling debut. *R. Simpson* –

SHOCK TACTICS 6 br.g. Capitano – Fused Light (Fury Royal) [1992/3 c21m⁵] useful-looking gelding: novice hurdler: remote last of 5 finishers in novice chase at Windsor in November: will stay beyond 21f: ran creditably when blinkered once. *Mrs F. Walwyn* c– –

SHOEHORN 6 br.g. Prince Tenderfoot (USA) – Relkalim (Relko) [1992/3 16f* 18s² 16s³ 17g 16d⁴] sparely-made gelding: modest 9f winner on Flat: claimed out of R. Peacock's stable £2,001 in September: won conditional jockeys handicap at Uttoxeter later in month and ran very well second and third starts: not seen out after October: stays 2¼m: acts on firm and soft ground. *D. T. Turner* 98

SHOOFE (USA) 5 ch.g. L'Emigrant (USA) – Bid For Manners (USA) (Raise A Bid (USA)) [1992/3 17g³ 21d² 20s³ 16g⁴] small, close-coupled gelding: fair stayer at best on Flat, winner in 1993: fair form in novice hurdles, best efforts on first 2 outings: stays 21f: acts on dead ground: jumps soundly: sold to join K. Morgan 6,400 gns Newmarket July Sales. *D. Morley* 99

SHOON WIND 10 b.g. Green Shoon – Gone (Whistling Wind) [1992/3 c25g⁴ c24g* c25s² c30s³ c25m⁵ c25g* c24f²] workmanlike gelding: fairly useful handicap chaser: won at Newcastle in November and Ayr in April: good second on former course in May: suited by a test of stamina: acts on any going: sometimes jumps sketchily. *M. D. Hammond* c125 –

SHOOTING LODGE (IRE) 5 b.g. High Line – Heather Croft (Kala Shikari) [1992/3 17m 20g] sturdy, lengthy gelding: poor novice hurdler: best effort over 2¾m on dead going. *J. R. Jenkins* –

SHOREHAM LADY 8 br.m. Strong Gale – Tarpon Springs (Grey Sovereign) [1992/3 17g 25d] lengthy mare: poor novice hurdler: stays 3m: acts on dead ground. *S. N. Cole* –

SHOTAWAY 6 b.m. Cruise Missile – Hold The Line (New Brig) [1992/3 aF16g F18g] second foal: dam won an Irish point: temperamental pointer: behind in NH Flat races in March: yet to race over hurdles or in a steeplechase. *N. R. Mitchell* –

SHOW THE FLAG 5 b.g. Beldale Flutter (USA) – Pretty Miss (So Blessed) [1992/3 17g⁴ 16v² 16v⁶ 22g⁴ 16f³ 17d³ 17f* 17f] modest hurdler: won maiden at Huntingdon in May: ran in seller previous 2 starts: effective at 2m and probably stays 2¾m: acts on any going: blinkered final outing (stumbled badly and run best ignored): pulls hard. *K. C. Bailey* 85

SHREWD GIRL (USA) 5 b.m. Sagace (FR) – Hydahs (USA) (Chieftain II) [1992/3 17m³ 18g⁶ 16d] poor middle-distance maiden on Flat: sold out of B. Hills's stable 2,700 gns Ascot July Sales: well beaten over hurdles: sold 3,200 gns Doncaster November Sales. *T. W. Cunningham* –

SHREWD JOHN 7 b.h. John French – Seal Shrew (Seaepic (USA)) [1992/3 16f⁵ 18m⁴ 16f⁴ 17d* 18d⁶ 16d³ 16d² 17s a16g⁴ 16d⁶ 16s] leggy horse: c– 82 §

poor hurdler: won novice event at Perth in September: in-and-out form subsequently: yet to complete over fences: form only at around 2m: acts on good to soft going: sometimes fails to go through with his effort. *R. D. E. Woodhouse*

SHRILL WHISTLE   10 ch.g. Whistlefield – Don's Double (Double Red)   c–
[1992/3 c17m^{pu}] pulled up both outings over hurdles and in a hunter chase: –
modest pointer. *Mrs L. A. Syckelmoore*

SHU FLY (NZ)   9 ch.g. Tom's Shu (USA) – Alycone (NZ) (Philoctetes)   c 128
[1992/3 17m^2 c16d^2 17s^4 c20m^2 c16d^3 c17g* 17m^{pu} c18g* c16f^2 c21m^{pu}]   128
smallish, sturdy gelding: fairly useful hurdler: trained by N. Smith first outing: won handicap chases at Taunton and Exeter (novices) in March: easily best effort and fairly useful performance when second to Valiant Boy in valuable event at Aintree following month: best form at up to 2¼m: acts on firm and dead ground: jumps soundly: sometimes finds little. *C. D. Broad*

SHUIL AR AGHAIDH   7 b.m. The Parson – Shuil Eile (Deep Run)
[1992/3 16g^4 24d* 19d^6 20s^2 26s^3 19v^{ro} 22s^2 25m*]   157
Shuil Ar Aghaidh was returned the longest-priced of the six Irish-trained winners at the Cheltenham Festival. Her odds of 20/1 for the Bonus-Print Stayers' Hurdle reflected not only doubts as to whether her best would be good enough but also whether she'd be seen at her best on the ground. Shuil Ar Aghaidh was in her second season over hurdles. As a novice she won four races in Ireland, including handicaps, and on her first visit to Britain finished a creditable sixth to My View in the Coral Golden Hurdle Final. Season 1992/3 hadn't been so successful, but she'd continued to progress since winning a handicap at Naas in October. In December she was sent over for the Youngmans Long Walk Hurdle at Ascot and acquitted herself well in the face of her stiffest task up to that point, finishing third to Vagog and Burgoyne, beaten only two and a half lengths and two lengths, looking a thorough stayer. A shot at another graded race at Navan in February resulted in a near-miss and another good performance—she went down by a head in dividing the useful Dee Ell and Bayrouge. The ground at Ascot and Navan was soft. Shuil Ar Aghaidh seldom ran on anything much

BonusPrint Stayers' Hurdle, Cheltenham—
Shuil Ar Aghaidh (No. 12) comes to lead at the last from the blinkered Pragada and Baydon Star

Mrs P. Kiely's "Shuil Ar Aghaidh"

different, and not once in her career over hurdles had she run on ground as firm as it was for the Stayers' Hurdle. So, how would she handle the conditions?

A similar question hung over the favourite Baydon Star and others in the twelve-runner race, Burgoyne, Pragada, Super Sense, Sweet Duke and, perhaps, Vagog. On form Burgoyne looked to have as good a chance as any in a no more than average Stayers' Hurdle. The field was weaker than the previous year's when he'd come fifth behind Nomadic Way, Trapper John, Ubu III and Crystal Spirit. Contrary to many expectations the race proved a true test of stamina, thanks to Pragada's jockey's awareness that his front-running mount's best chance lay in ensuring one. Pragada led to the last. He set a sound pace, but the field kept tidily together until starting down the hill for the second time. Shuil Ar Aghaidh, held up towards the back, was able to make smooth headway on the outside down the hill and she held a good place two out. The race looked wide open there with at least half a dozen still in with a chance, and just before Sweet Glow and Sweet Duke began to weaken between the last two flights there were still five almost in line abreast up front. Pragada rose at the last flanked by Shuil Ar Aghaidh and Baydon Star. On the flat Baydon Star cracked first. The challenge seemed to spur Pragada on, but gradually Shuil Ar Aghaidh began to get on top and she finished very strongly indeed to beat him on merit by two and a half lengths. She and Rose Ravine are the only mares to have won the Stayers' Hurdle in twenty-two runnings; their wins have come since the mares' 5 lb allowance was introduced at the beginning of 1983/4. On her only subsequent outing Shuil Ar Aghaidh appeared in a mile-and-a-half Flat race at Tipperary. She was up against some useful animals, and another stout

671

staying performance wasn't enough to get her into the first four. She has won on the level, but not outside Irish National Hunt Flat company.

Shuil Ar Aghaidh's pedigree has stamina written all over it. The dam's only previous runner Rawhide (by Buckskin) is a stayer, very useful over hurdles and fences at his best though not so good nowadays. Rawhide was a good fourth to Rolling Ball in the Sun Alliance Novices' Chase in 1991 and would probably have finished third to Omerta in the Irish Grand National the same season but for falling two out. A younger mare out of the dam, Another Shuil (by Duky), won a point-to-point in Ireland in April. The dam's full brother was no less a stayer than Why Forget, placed in a couple of Scottish Nationals, a Whitbread Gold Cup and a National Hunt Chase. This family has been prominent on the Irish jumping scene for generations. The three 'Shuils' on the bottom line of the extended pedigree all won over hurdles there, while both 'Eile' and 'Shee' won bumpers events as well.

Shuil Ar Aghaidh (b.m. 1986)	The Parson (b 1968)	Aureole (ch 1950)	Hyperion
			Angelola
		Bracey Bridge (b 1962)	Chanteur II
			Rutherford Bridge
	Shuil Eile (b 1978)	Deep Run (ch 1966)	Pampered King
			Trial By Fire
		Shuil Dubh (br 1966)	Black Tarquin
			Shuil Shee

The chances are we'll be seeing Shuil Ar Aghaidh more often in Britain. As a result of her improved form in the Stayers' Hurdle she'll be at the top of the Irish handicap, and opportunities for good horses outside handicaps are more plentiful here. Judged on her performance at Cheltenham she's certain to win more good long-distance hurdles. There isn't much of her—she's leggy and sparely made—but she's very tough and genuine. She possesses a fair turn of foot for a stayer. *P. Kiely, Ireland*

SHUIL SAOR 6 b.g. Fairbairn – Shuil Comeragh (Laurence O) [1992/3 c21g c20g6 c20d3 c20vur] leggy gelding: winning hurdler: modest form in novice chases: will stay beyond 2½m: acts on dead ground. *Mrs S. J. Smith* — c89 / –

SHUTAFUT 7 b.g. Tachypous – Declamation (Town Crier) [1992/3 18s 17d4 16d 22s c18gF c21f2] well-made gelding: lightly-raced novice hurdler, poor form: close second in novice handicap chase at Wincanton in May: stays 21f: acts on firm going. *Capt. T. A. Forster* — c89 / 72

SHUTTLECOCK STAR 11 b.g. Star Appeal – Bluets (USA) (Hitting Away) [1992/3 c26m6] neat gelding: winning selling hurdler: fair pointer: well beaten in hunter chases: stays 2¾m: best with plenty of give in the ground. *Miss Linda Morgan* — c– / –

SHUT UP 4 b.f. Kind of Hush – Creetown Lady (Creetown) [1992/3 16f2 18f] showed temperament prior to finishing behind only start on Flat, at 2 yrs: poor form in early-season juvenile hurdles, second of 3 at Hexham. *R. Allan* — ?

SIBERIAN BREEZE 5 gr.g. Siberian Express (USA) – Zepha (Great Nephew) [1992/3 17m5 17g* 16s 16m4 16m4] leggy gelding: poor hurdler: won conditional jockeys selling handicap at Bangor (no bid) in March: ran creditably fourth start: stays 2½m: acts on good to firm ground, below form on soft: blinkered last 2 outings. *J. A. Glover* — 82

SIBERIAN SWING 4 gr.f. Siberian Express (USA) – Swing Is Back (Busted) [1992/3 16m 17mpu] leggy, sparely-made filly: half-sister to winning hurdler Tyburn Lad (by Belfort): lightly-raced maiden on Flat and over hurdles (no promise). *J. D. Roberts* — –

SIBTON ABBEY 8 b.g. Strong Gale – Bally Decent (Wrekin Rambler) [1992/3 c26d4 c21g* c24g2 c25v* c27s* c30s4 c26s* c27m5 c29spu c30dpu] — c161 p / –

The gradually increasing impatience of the Jockey Club over 'the use of the whip' has led to its stewards handling what has become a burning issue with a notable lack of intelligence. For a decade or more the whip has frequently been in the racing news. Inconsistencies in local stewards' interpretations of the guidelines for its use have led to discontent among jockeys, and the publicity whenever a top jockey has been suspended has, generally speaking, tended to caricature racing as a cruel sport in which jockeys are out to win at whatever cost to the horse. The various attempts to deal with a relatively minor problem—for that is what it has always been—have done more damage to racing's public image over the years than the actions of any whip-happy jockey. Take the publicity surrounding the latest alterations to the guidelines which now suggest stewards consider holding an inquiry if a horse is hit more than five times (compared to the previous threshold of ten) after the penultimate obstacle. The chairman of the Jockey Club's Disciplinary Committee, Anthony Mildmay-White, and his officials sought to justify the unpopular tightening of the controls at a Press seminar in April. Videos were naively shown illustrating some of the uses of the whip that would be unacceptable under the re-drawn guidelines. Several of the videos featured the brilliant Adrian Maguire, who in the latest season became the youngest jump jockey to complete a century in a British season. Maguire's rise has been meteoric—from 7 lb claiming amateur to top professional in a little over two years—and it probably is only a matter of time before he becomes champion. Any horse Maguire rides gets the best of handling and he is particularly strong in a finish. To hear some of jumping's top jockeys—including, by implication, Maguire—labelled by Jockey Club officials at the seminar as 'hard men who abuse the whip and the horse' was outrageous. Naturally enough, the Press had a field day and Maguire, who took legal advice, received plenty of sympathy from fellow professionals. Mr Mildmay-White was moved to issue a statement saying that the Jockey Club 'very much regrets that Adrian Maguire has received this publicity'. There was no 'vendetta against Adrian Maguire'.

Maguire has served a number of suspensions for misuse of the whip but to describe his style as 'offensive'—a term used at the seminar for his riding of Sibton Abbey in the Hennessy Cognac Gold Cup—is a smear on a fine jockey. Maguire's dilemma is the same as that faced by any jockey; to get to the top, and to stay there, he has to ride better than his rivals which means doing his utmost, within the rules, to win. Maguire had over seven hundred rides in 1992/3 because he does just that. Using the whip makes most horses maintain their maximum effort and serves as a reminder to lazy ones; the whip does sometimes mark and occasionally cause damage to a horse, but effective use undoubtedly wins races. Maguire earned a much

Hennessy Cognac Gold Cup (Handicap Chase), Newbury—
40/1-shot Sibton Abbey (No. 13) wins from 21 lb out of the handicap

Timeform Hall of Fame Chase, Cheltenham—Sibton Abbey confirms his improvement, beating Another Coral (right), Cool Ground and Henry Mann

publicised suspension for excessive use of the whip after winning the 1992 Gold Cup by a short head on Cool Ground but his pragmatic reaction—'I wouldn't have won otherwise'—illustrated how ill-advised tight whip guide-lines would be. Another of the *Rules of Racing*, rule 151, places a jockey under an obligation to 'ensure that his horse is given a full opportunity to win or of obtaining the best possible placing'. That is surely the whole basis of racing, as of any highly competitive sport, and, in an all-out driving finish, no jockey worth his salt can be expected to throw a race away through fear of transgressing ambiguous whip guidelines. As we have said before, know-ing when and how frequently to use the whip is a matter of judgement—split-second judgement in a tight finish—and it's always wisest to give a top jockey the benefit of any doubt. No good jockey hits a horse any more than necessary and, in any case, he wouldn't be on the horse in the first place if his riding caused offence to owner and trainer (and he would risk not being on the horse again if his riding displeased). All cases involving alleged misuse of the whip should be judged on their merits. Hitting a horse at the wrong time (out of rhythm with its stride) or when it is obviously beaten and has nothing more to give should be treated quite differently from using the whip on a horse that is running on strongly in the closing stages of a race when maximum effort is required. The specifying of a figure for the number of times the whip can be used without risk of an inquiry is at the root of the trouble. Commonsense should apply. But, then, if the Jockey Club had used commonsense in dealing with this particular issue from the start, the guidelines—which, as well as being interpreted differently by different stewards, also sometimes seem to be interpreted as *rules*—wouldn't be providing the problems that they are.

Maguire's riding of Sibton Abbey in the Hennessy Cognac Gold Cup was studied by the Newbury stewards on the day. They decided Maguire had stayed within the guidelines as they stood then, though he had struck the horse more than the recommended ten times. This was sensible in our view, but as we said, the Jockey Club later saw fit to describe Maguire's riding in damning terms. Maguire's forceful riding had the desired effect on Sibton Abbey in that the horse responded with the utmost gameness to win a high-class renewal of the Hennessy by three quarters of a length from

Jodami. Sibton Abbey, a 40/1-outsider carrying 21 lb more than the weight allotted to him in the long handicap, made the immediate transition from a fairly useful chaser to a smart one. Most of the best-backed horses ran their race in the Hennessy and there was no doubting that Sibton Abbey, a winner at Worcester in October and Cheltenham (amateur riders event) in November, had put up a vastly improved display. Top weight The Fellow was six lengths behind Jodami in third with the previous year's winner Chatam fourth. Sibton Abbey ran well below his Hennessy form when fourth in the Anthony Mildmay, Peter Cazalet Memorial Handicap at Sandown on his next outing, but he'd reportedly missed some work and wasn't knocked about by his amateur rider. Smith Eccles took the mount when Sibton Abbey went on to Cheltenham in January for the Timeform Hall of Fame Chase, an aptly-named contest in that it attracted two Gold Cup winners (Cool Ground and Garrison Savannah), a Grand National winner (Party Politics), a Sun Alliance Chase winner (Miinnehoma) and a Mackeson and Tripleprint Gold Cup winner (Another Coral), as well as the Hennessy winner, meeting at level weights. Sibton Abbey, who started at 16/1 on this occasion, improved on his Hennessy form, running another thoroughly game and genuine race to win by three quarters of a length from Another Coral, with Cool Ground five lengths away in third. Smith Eccles, a late substitute when the booked jockey Murphy was injured in an earlier fall, rode at his most forceful on Sibton Abbey who had looked to be travelling worst of the leading three at the second last. Smith Eccles was criticised in some quarters for his use of the whip. 'What do I do? I gave the horse thirteen hits with the whip from the third last, and all the time he was responding and ran for me,' said Smith Eccles. 'I just don't believe he would have won had I ridden him any other way. And, rightly, I believe, that is why the stewards didn't have me in.' Some sets of stewards would undoubtedly have suspended Smith Eccles. Smith Eccles rode Sibton Abbey in his three remaining races, the first of them the Tote Cheltenham Gold Cup in which he kept on to finish a good fifth to Jodami after racing with the leaders from the start. Sibton Abbey's demanding season seemed to catch up with him after the Gold Cup and he was never going well in the Jameson Irish Grand National or the Whitbread Gold Cup, in both of which he was pulled up.

Sibton Abbey (b.g. 1985)	Strong Gale (br 1975)	Lord Gayle (b 1965)	Sir Gaylord
			Sticky Case
		Sterntau (br 1969)	Tamerlane
			Sterna
	Bally Decent (ch 1971)	Wrekin Rambler (ch 1963)	Pampered King
			Inquisitive Rose
		Bally Elegant (ch 1964)	Ballylinan
			Elegant Miss

Sibton Abbey, a lengthy gelding, is by that fine sire of chasers Strong Gale out of the Wrekin Rambler mare Bally Decent, who showed nothing on the racecourse—she ran in two maiden hurdles and a bumper—but has bred five other winners, including the brothers Ballywest and Ballylord (by Lord Ha Ha). Ballywest, a winning stayer on the Flat when he was fourth in the Irish Cesarewitch, showed fair form over hurdles at up to two and three quarter miles after appearing best at around two miles for most of his career; Ballylord, in training with J. J. O'Neill, is a fair winning hurdler who stays twenty-one furlongs. Bally Decent has had another winner by Lord Ha Ha, the modest mare Ballywho, successful in a bumper and a two-and-a-quarter-mile handicap on the Flat in Ireland. Bally Decent has also had two minor winners by Crozier, The Mighty Crozier, a bumper winner, and Fuller's Pride, winner of a maiden hurdle at Down Royal. Sibton Abbey is a thorough stayer, suited by forcing tactics; his Gold Cup performance confirmed that he acts on top-of-the-ground—he's won on firm—but it's worth emphasising that he acts particularly well in the mud. Sibton Abbey's good jumping also stands him in good stead. We're prepared to forgive him his two lack-lustre runs at the end of the season and predict that the best probably hasn't yet been seen of him. He's still young for a chaser and is sure to win more good races. *F. Murphy*

SIBYL O'DONNELL   6 b.m. Durandal – Seersucker (Dolman) [1992/3 16s^bd 17s] sparely-made mare: bad maiden hurdler. *K. S. Bridgwater*   –

SICILIAN MELODY   9 b.g. Grange Melody – Hiriwa (Diritto) [1992/3 c25d^pu] workmanlike gelding: poor novice jumper. *G. M. R. Coatsworth*   c–

SICILIAN SWING   8 b.g. Swing Easy (USA) – Mab (Morston (FR)) [1992/3 c17m^6 c18f^F] tall, leggy gelding: poor 2m novice hurdler/chaser: dead. *Mrs S. D. Williams*   c–
–

SIDE OF HILL   8 b.g. Furry Glen – Fiuggi (Majetta) [1992/3 c20s* c21v^4 c20v^3 c24d^ur c23g* c27m* c25f^4] sparely-made gelding: fair handicap chaser: won at Chepstow in December and Worcester (amateurs) and Newton Abbot in March: good fourth in valuable handicap at Aintree in April: stays well: acts on any going: sometimes wears a tongue strap. *M. C. Pipe*   c112

SIERRA SNOW   8 br.m. King of Spain – Snow Rum (Quorum) [1992/3 20g] workmanlike mare: poor and unreliable maiden (stays 1¼m) on Flat in 1989: tailed off in mares novice event in April on hurdling debut. *K. A. Morgan*   –

SIGNORE DE ANGLES   4 b.g. Sizzling Melody – Lady Lorelei (Derring-Do) [1992/3 18f^pu] poor plater at 2 yrs: behind when pulled up last in selling hurdle at Fontwell in October. *J. M. Bradley*   –

SIGNOR SASSIE (USA)   5 ch.h. The Minstrel (CAN) – Sahsie (USA) (Forli (ARG)) [1992/3 16s^3 16v^5 17s^3 22s^6 c16d^5 c21g^4 c20f^2 c21m^4] lengthy, good-topped horse: modest hurdler/novice chaser: stays 2½m: probably acts on any ground: has tongue tied down. *N. Tinkler*   c85
88

SIKERA SPY   11 b.m. Harvest Spirit – Ida Spider (Ben Novus) [1992/3 c21s^pu c22m^F c25d^5 c20g c25s^2 c30s* c25m* c25f^2 c25g*] rangy mare: fairly useful handicap chaser: won at Bangor in February, March and April: good second to Black Humour in strongly-run valuable handicap at Aintree on penultimate start: stays well: acts on soft ground, particularly well on a sound surface: bold jumper, prone to the odd mistake: races with zest and makes running: genuine. *Mrs A. R. Hewitt*   c120
–

SILENCE WILL SPEAK (IRE)   5 b.g. Taufan (USA) – Shopping (FR) (Sheshoon) [1992/3 F16d] half-brother to maiden Irish hurdler Graceful Fancy (by Carwhite): dam won over middle distances on Flat in France: tailed off in NH Flat race at Haydock in February: sold 1,300 gns Doncaster May Sales: yet to race over hurdles or fences. *N. Tinkler*   –

SILENT BRAVO   6 b.g. Ardross – Pampas Flower (Pampered King) [1992/3 aF16g^6 16g 20d 22g^3 22g 21f] tall, workmanlike gelding: poor form when third in novice hurdle at Huntingdon in April: stays 2¾m. *A. G. Blackmore*   80

SILENT CHANT   9 br.g. Smooth Stepper – Florimell (Shooting Chant) [1992/3 c23f^6 c21mF] smallish, angular gelding: lightly-raced handicap hurdler: ran in snatches but held a 4-length lead when falling 2 out in novice chase at Southwell in October: will stay 3m: acts on firm ground: blinkered nowadays. *D. J. G. Murray-Smith*   c82
–

SILENT RING (USA)   7 b. or br.g. Silent Cal (USA) – Rafters Ring (USA) (Delta Judge) [1992/3 22f 17m 21s c20f^pu 22m^pu] leggy gelding: winning hurdler/chaser: no form in 1992/3: probably stays 2¾m: acts on firm and dead ground: sometimes blinkered or visored (has won in both). *N. Waggott*   c–
–

SILK DEGREES   7 gr.g. Dunbeath (USA) – Bustling Nelly (Bustino) [1992/3 16g^F 20m^5 c17d* c17d* c21d^F] leggy gelding: fairly useful hurdler/chaser: won novice events over fences at Sedgefield and Kelso in April: in lead when falling 2 out in similar event at Perth in May: was effective at around 2m and stayed 3m: acted on firm and dead ground: dead. *W. Storey*   c119
–

SILK DYNASTY   7 b.g. Prince Tenderfoot (USA) – Mountain Chase (Mount Hagen (FR)) [1992/3 F10d a16g^2 a16g^pu 17g^pu] small gelding: poor   77 novice hurdler: creditable second in selling handicap at Southwell in February when trained by R. Hollinshead: showed nothing last 2 starts: best form at 2m: acts on firm going and fibresand. *J. Carden*

SILKEN SORCERER 5 b.g. Enchantment – Jamra (Upper Case (USA)) [1992/3 16g⁶] fifth foal: dam won 3 times at around 1m in Scandinavia: 25 lengths sixth of 16 in novice hurdle at Catterick in March. *J. H. Johnson* 73

SILKSTREAM 6 b.g. Millfontaine – Wraparound Sue (Touch Paper) [1992/3 17m c17gᶠ] sparely-made gelding: has shown only a little ability in novice hurdles: fell first on chasing debut. *B. Smart* c–
–

SILKY SIREN 4 b.f. Formidable (USA) – Smooth Siren (USA) (Sea Bird II) [1992/3 a16g 16sᵖᵘ] small, sturdy filly: modest on Flat (best blinkered): showed nothing in juvenile event and a seller (blinkered) over hurdles. *M. C. Pipe* –

SILLARS STALKER (IRE) 5 b.g. Stalker – Mittens (Run The Gantlet (USA)) [1992/3 21d* 22d* 20s² 20d* 22s 20g 21m²] leggy gelding: developed into a useful hurdler in 1992/3: won handicaps at Uttoxeter, Sedgefield and Doncaster in first half of season: amateur ridden, returned to form when very good second in competitive race at Cheltenham in March: effective at 2½m and will stay 3m: acts on good to firm and soft going: usually held up: on the upgrade. *Mrs J. R. Ramsden* 132 p

SILLY HABIT (USA) 7 b.m. Assert – Habitassa (Habitat) [1992/3 20g 26mᵖᵘ] smallish, sparely-made mare: of little account: visored last start. *H. J. Collingridge* –

SILVER AGE (USA) 7 b.h. Silver Hawk (USA) – Our Paige (USA) (Grand Revival (USA)) [1992/3 20g⁴ 20g⁴ 20f² 17d* 21d⁴ 20g⁴] leggy horse: handicap hurdler: won jockeys' challenge race at Chepstow in October: ran creditably next outing, poorly on last (November): stays 21f: acts on soft going and good to firm. *J. M. Bradley* 101

SILVER CONCORD 5 gr.g. Absalom – Boarding House (Shack (USA)) [1992/3 17mᵖᵘ] lengthy gelding: no sign of ability over hurdles: blinkered last time: sold 1,650 gns Doncaster October Sales. *G. M. Moore* –

SILVER FOR SURE 4 gr.g. Belfort (FR) – Moment's Pleasure (USA) (What A Pleasure (USA)) [1992/3 17dᵖᵘ 16vᵖᵘ] seventh foal: half-brother to –

Flat v Jump Jockeys Challenge Handicap Hurdle, Chepstow —
Michael Hills strikes a blow for the Flat jockeys aboard Silver Age

several poor Flat maidens: dam placed over 5f at 2 yrs: no sign of ability in 2 juvenile hurdles. *J. K. Cresswell*

SILVER HAZE 9 gr.g. Absalom – Chance Belle (Foggy Bell) [1992/3 c18m* c18m2 c16m3 c17f* c18s* c17fbd c16m5 c17d5 c17dur c17d6 c16d6 c16g3 c17g3 c16g3 c17m3 c16mF] workmanlike gelding: novice hurdler: won novice chases at Bangor (dead-heated), Hexham and Cartmel early in season (trained until after tenth start by W. A. Stephenson): also ran well in spring: best at around 2m: acts on any ground: blinkered twice. *J. Wade*
c89
–

SILVER HELLO 7 gr.g. Nishapour (FR) – Si (Ragusa) [1992/3 22f2 c25m* c24m5 c25gpu c26g4 c27m6] leggy gelding: maiden hurdler: moderate chaser: won at Market Rasen in September: good fourth at Carlisle in March, easily best effort afterwards: stays 3¼m: acts on firm ground. *Miss L. A. Perratt*
c98
83 +

SILVERHILLS 10 ch.g. Touch Paper – Rosie Probert (Captain's Gig (USA)) [1992/3 18f] big, strong, plain gelding: of little account. *T. B. Hallett*
c–
–

SILVERINO 7 gr.g. Relkino – Silver Tips (High Top) [1992/3 c24v* c25s3 c25d4 c27d4] lengthy gelding: winning hurdler: won novice handicap chase at Lingfield in January: ran well next and last starts: suited by thorough test of stamina: acts on heavy going: needs plenty of driving. *A. Moore*
c92 +
–

SILVER'S GIRL 8 b.m. Sweet Monday – Persian Silver (Cash And Courage) [1992/3 17spu 16d 20s 17s] sparely-made mare: poor novice hurdler: best efforts around 2m: yet to race on a firm surface. *D. Moffatt*
66

SILVER SHILLING 6 gr.g. Sonnen Gold – Continental Divide (Sharp Edge) [1992/3 F17m 23d 21v 21spu] leggy, lengthy gelding: behind in novice hurdles. *Mrs V. C. Ward*
–

SILVER STICK 6 gr.g. Absalom – Queen's Parade (Sovereign Path) [1992/3 22d* 21m*] leggy gelding: fair handicap hurdler: won at Sedgefield in September and Carlisle in October: should stay beyond 2¾m: probably acts on any ground: best blinkered. *M. W. Easterby*
106

SILVER STRINGS 13 b.g. Blakeney – Melody Hour (Sing Sing) [1992/3 17v5 22d6 a20g3 a22g2 a22gpu 17dF 21d 17f] sparely-made gelding: selling hurdler: ran creditably when placed twice at Southwell in January: below form subsequently: stays 2¾m: acts on good to firm, dead going and on fibresand: races up with pace. *B. Palling*
79

SIMMIE 8 b.g. Buckskin (FR) – Miss Dunbrody (Le Prince) [1992/3 17g 17d5 17d c24spu c22spu] leggy, lengthy gelding: novice hurdler: lightly raced and no form of late: tailed off when pulled up on both outings over fences: stays 2½m: acts on good to firm and soft going. *F. Murphy*
c–
–

SIMONE'S SON (IRE) 5 ch.g. Hatim (USA) – Simone's Luck (Malinowski (USA)) [1992/3 16m4 18m* 18g4 16f* 17g* 17m* 17m2 17m5 17m 16d* 17s3 17m2 16fur 17gbd] leggy gelding: had a good season and developed into a fair hurdler: won sellers at Market Rasen (bought in 5,200 gns) and Worcester (no bid) and handicaps at Stratford (ladies) and Bangor early in season, and handicap at Uttoxeter in March: races only around 2m: acts on firm and dead ground (below best on soft): blinkered nowadays: has turn of foot and often held up: tough. *G. Barnett*
113

SIMON JOSEPH 6 b. or br.g. Tower Walk – Lady Bess (Straight Lad) [1992/3 21d 16s3 16d4] big, lengthy, angular gelding: moderate novice hurdler: best efforts at 2m: acts on soft going. *Capt. T. A. Forster*
92

SIMPLE ARITHMETIC 5 ch.g. Southern Music – Graphics Eska (Jimmy Reppin) [1992/3 F16v* F16s4 F17f] well-made gelding: third foal: half-brother to maiden Irish jumper New Experience (by Smackover): dam, winning 2½m hurdler, half-sister to several winning jumpers, notably useful staying chaser Tartan Takeover and useful staying hurdler Graphics Solar: won NH Flat race at Uttoxeter in December: pulled hard when eighth of 15 in valuable similar event at Aintree in April: yet to race over hurdles or fences. *K. C. Bailey*

SIMPLE PLEASURE 8 b.g. Idiot's Delight – Kirkham Lass (Parasang) c 104
[1992/3 c16m 23d⁵ 22d⁶ c16g* c20d³ c17d* c20g³ c21g⁴ c21g² c21s² 25s³ 97
c21g* c22m⁴] smallish gelding: moderate hurdler/fair chaser: won handicap
chases at Edinburgh in December, Sedgefield (amateurs) in January and
Southwell in May: stays 25f: probably acts on any going: consistent. *Mrs M.
Stirk*

SIMPLY GEORGE 4 b.g. Simply Great (FR) – Grand Occasion (Great
Nephew) [1992/3 17m 17f³ a16g² a16g³ a16g⁵ 18g²] modest performer at 90
best on Flat: modest novice hurdler: ran creditably when second at Lingfield
in February and Fontwell in March: stays 2¼m: best form on good ground
and equitrack. *J. White*

SIMPLY IRIS 4 b.g. Simply Great (FR) – Be A Dancer (Be Friendly)
[1992/3 16g 16s² 16d 16s⁵ 16v³ 17s⁴] ex-Irish gelding: moderate 1½m 92 ?
winner on Flat in 1992: modest form at best over hurdles: trained until after
fifth start by N. McGrath. *F. J. O'Mahony*

SIMPLY JOYFUL 6 b.m. Idiot's Delight – Royal Pam (Pamroy) [1992/3 c–
F17g 22d 26d⁵ c21m^pu] fourth living foal: half-sister to poor novice –
hurdler/chaser Mountain Muse (by Sunyboy): dam, unraced, from
successful jumping family: no sign of ability. *P. J. Hobbs*

SIMPSON 8 ch.g. Royal Match – Black Penny (West Partisan) [1992/3
25g* 24d²] progressive hurdler, useful already: won handicap at Newbury 136 p
in February: good second in falsely-run similar event at Ascot 2 months
later: thorough stayer: acts on soft and good to firm ground: jumps to the
right: sure to win more races. *J. A. B. Old*

SIMWELL (IRE) 5 ch.g. Over The River (FR) – Fairyslave (Arctic
Slave) [1992/3 17s 17g] half-brother to 3 winning jumpers, all by Paddy's 79 p
Stream, including useful performer Arctic Stream: dam won over hurdles in
Ireland: showed plenty of promise in novice hurdle at Newbury in
November: below that form, soon off bridle, in similar event at Huntingdon
3 months later: will stay beyond 17f: acts on soft going: worth another
chance. *F. Murphy*

SINGERS IMAGE 4 br.g. Chief Singer – Little White Lies (Runnett)
[1992/3 17g^pu] angular gelding: modest 1m winner on Flat: behind when –
pulled up in juvenile hurdle at Newbury in November. *G. B. Balding*

SINGING DETECTIVE 6 gr.g. Absalom – Smoke Creek (Habitat)
[1992/3 a20g² a16g⁶ 16vpu 21g 25m⁵ 23m⁵ 20f² 22f³ 21m⁵] sturdy gelding: 71
poor novice hurdler: stays 2¾m: acts on firm, dead ground and equitrack:
sometimes visored. *P. M. McEntee*

SINGING GOLD 7 b.g. Gold Claim – Gellifawr (Saulingo) [1992/3 16v*
16mpu 16d6 17fpu] compact gelding: won weakly-contested maiden event at ?
Towcester in April, first outing over hurdles since 1989/90: no form
afterwards: should stay further than 2m: acts on heavy going: tried
blinkered (didn't wear them at Towcester): difficult to assess. *H. Sawyer*

SINGING REPLY (USA) 5 b.m. The Minstrel (CAN) – Bright Reply
(USA) (Gleaming (USA)) [1992/3 16v⁶ 16s⁴ 16v² 18m* 17f⁶ 16s 20m³] 78
sparely-made mare: poor maiden on Flat: won selling hurdle at Fontwell
(bought in 4,600 gns) in March: good third at Taunton (claimed by R. Price
£5,007) following month: stays 2½m: acts on good to firm and heavy going:
held up. *D. Marks*

SINGING SPEAR 8 gr.g. Abednego – Royal Banquet (Royal Buck) c76
[1992/3 c17s⁵ c21v⁴ c24v^pu c21g^F c21f³ c16g² c18s³] sturdy, workmanlike –
ex-Irish gelding: poor novice chaser: sold 3,500 gns Ascot June Sales:
blinkered once. *G. L. Humphrey*

SINGLESOLE 8 ch.g. Celtic Cone – Milly Kelly (Murrayfield) [1992/3 c 109
c25m* c25d* c24s* c24g^F 25s] small, strong gelding: winning hurdler: fair –
chaser: successful in handicaps over fences at Southwell, Wolverhampton
and Fakenham in first half of season: stays 25f: acts on good to firm and soft
ground: best blinkered: needs plenty of driving. *Mrs P. Sly*

John Hughes Memorial Trophy (Handicap Chase), Aintree—
four out and Sirrah Jay (right) disputes the lead with Channels Gate (No. 17)
and Western Legend, with Strong Gold just behind

SING THE BLUES 9 b.g. Blue Cashmere – Pulcini (Quartette) [1992/3 97 ?
a16g a18g3 a20g* a20g a18g4 16f5] rangy, rather sparely-made gelding:
modest hurdler: won handicap at Lingfield in January: below form
afterwards: stays 2½m: best on equitrack (has gained all 8 hurdling wins at
Lingfield). *C. J. Benstead*

SINGULAR RUN 7 b.g. Trojan Fen – Needy (High Top) [1992/3 18mpu] –
good-topped gelding: poor novice hurdler: dead. *Mrs J. C. Dawe*

SIOUX PERFICK 4 b.f. Blakeney – Siouxsie (Warpath) [1992/3 18g] of –
little account on Flat: no promise in selling hurdle in October: sold 750 gns
Doncaster November Sales. *C. W. Thornton*

SIR CRUSTY 11 br.g. Gunner B – Brazen (Cash And Courage) [1992/3 115
26d5 25s 22v3 25v6 25s3 24s 25g 25f2 26m] compact gelding: fair handicap
hurdler nowadays: poor efforts last 4 starts: suited by test of stamina: acts
on any going: usually soon off bridle nowadays. *O. O'Neill*

SIRE NANTAIS (FR) 9 br.g. Meisir (FR) – Farala (FR) (Faunus (FR)) c–
[1992/3 c24spu] leggy, workmanlike gelding: fairly useful chaser at best: –
pulled up last 3 starts, lame only outing in 1992/3: stays 25f: acts on heavy
going and good to firm. *J. Berry*

SIRISAT 9 ch.g. Cisto (FR) – Gay Ruin (Master Spiritus) [1992/3 c24spu c–
c25g c25mF c23gur c23fpu] tall gelding: modest hunter chaser: well beaten
in 1993: trained until after third start by K. Hollowell: stays 2¾m: acts on
good to firm ground. *John R. Upson*

SIR NODDY 10 ch.g. Tom Noddy – Pinzarose (Pinzan) [1992/3 c19v3 c93 x
c24spu c19m6 c25f4 c25gpu c26v c24f3 c26m4 c25dF] big, workmanlike –
gelding: modest chaser: in-and-out form in 1992/3: stays 25f: acts on any
ground: prone to bad mistakes. *C. J. Vernon Miller*

SIR PAGEANT 4 b.g. Pharly (FR) – National Dress (Welsh Pageant) 73
[1992/3 16s 17g3] half-brother to winning hurdler Top It All (by Song):
moderate maiden on Flat, stays 1½m: sold out of P. Cole's stable 12,500 gns
Newmarket Autumn Sales: easily better effort over hurdles when third in
novice event at Hereford in May. *K. S. Bridgwater*

SIR PETER LELY 6 b.g. Teenoso (USA) – Picture (Lorenzaccio) c100 +
[1992/3 c17d* c16m3 c17m2] tall, leggy gelding: fair hurdler: won novice –
chase at Hexham in October, and subsequently ran well at Wetherby and
Newcastle: not seen out after November: should stay 2½m: ran badly on

soft ground, acts on any other: jumps well: suited by forcing tactics: blinkered twice in 1991/2 and at Newcastle. *M. D. Hammond*

SIRRAH JAY   13 b. or br.g. Tug of War – Dellasville (Trouville) [1992/3   c112   §
c21s*c16g5c21d3c21dpuc21s3c21v4c20s3c21vpuc21v3c21v3c21s*c21m2
c21m4 c20f2 c22f* c20s4] compact, workmanlike gelding: fair handicap chaser: always to the fore and led again close home to win John Hughes Memorial Trophy at Aintree in April by a neck from Southern Minstrel: successful earlier at Newton Abbot and Lingfield: stays 2¾m: acts on any going: blinkered once: runs the odd bad race. *G. B. Balding*

SIR SPEEDY   10 b.g. Owen Anthony – Fair Georgina (Silver Cloud)
[1992/3 17m4 16d4] leggy, good-topped gelding: maiden pointer: 2m selling   79
hurdler: acts on any going: blinkered in 1992/3. *A. P. Stringer*

SISTERLY   7 b.m. Brotherly (USA) – Wee Jennie (Vimadee) [1992/3   c–
c26g5] winning pointer: tailed off in maiden hunter chase in May. *J. W. E. Weaver*

SISTER SHOT   5 br.m. Celtic Cone – Duckdown (Blast) [1992/3 18v]
plain, unfurnished mare: seventh foal: sister to Celtic Shot and half-sister to   67 p
winning Irish staying hurdler Magic Oats and 6-y-o Morshot (both by Oats): dam winning hurdler from good jumping family: some promise when seventh of 17 in mares novice hurdle at Fontwell in January. *C. P. E. Brooks*

SIXOFUS (IRE)   5 b. or br.g. Glenstal (USA) – Grace Darling (USA)
(Vaguely Noble) [1992/3 17m] quite modest 1m winner on Flat at 3 yrs, when   –
trained by R. Boss: tailed off in novice hurdle at Newton Abbot in August. *W. G. M. Turner*

SIXTH IN LINE (IRE)   5 ch.g. Deep Run – Yellow Lotus (Majority
Blue) [1992/3 17dF] rather unfurnished gelding: half-brother to several   –
winners, including jumper Natyapour (by Nishapour): dam winning hurdler: fell fourth in novice hurdle at Wolverhampton in February on debut. *Mrs V. S. Hickman*

SIZZLING AFFAIR   4 b.c. Sizzling Melody – Vivchar (Huntercombe)
[1992/3 17g5 17f 17g3 16s3 17s5] small colt: poor maiden on Flat: fair third in   92
juvenile hurdles at Newbury and Kempton in first half of season: ran in sellers first 2 starts. *T. Casey*

SKELTON LASS (IRE)   4 ch.f. Lord Chancellor (USA) – Juleith
(Guillaume Tell (USA)) [1992/3 aF16g F16g6] third foal: dam lightly-raced Irish maiden: showed little in NH Flat races: yet to race over hurdles. *J. Parkes*

SKERRY MEADOW   9 b.g. Anfield – Mi Tia (Great Nephew) [1992/3   c90
22m c26g4 c27spu c24m5 c27dpu c23g3 c28f5] compact gelding: fair hunter   –
chaser: third at Uttoxeter in May, best effort of season: stays 3¼m: acts on good to firm going. *O. J. Carter*

SKETCHER (NZ)   10 b.g. Candyboy (NZ) – Jezebel (NZ) (Ardistaan)   c87
[1992/3 c25s4] tall, leggy gelding: useful and game hurdler in 1989/90: first   –
form over fences (let down by jumping previously) when fourth at Towcester in November: stays well: best form on a soft surface. *D. H. Barons*

SKIDDAW CALYPSO   4 b.f. Grey Desire – Wyn-Bank (Green God)
[1992/3 F16d F17g] workmanlike filly: half-sister to fair chaser Roxall Clump (by Neltino): dam fair handicapper when in mood on Flat, won a 2m hurdle: tailed off in 2 NH Flat races: yet to race over hurdles. *S. G. Payne*

SKIDDAW SONG   5 b.m. Monsanto (FR) – Miss Diaward (Supreme
Sovereign) [1992/3 21spu] lengthy, leggy mare: no sign of ability over   –
hurdles. *S. G. Payne*

SKINNHILL   9 b.g. Final Straw – Twenty Two (FR) (Busted) [1992/3   c101   §
c21v3 c21d4 c21v2 c25m* c25g3 c26v6 c27d2 c27f4 c26m] close-coupled   –
gelding: fair handicap chaser when in mood: won at Wolverhampton in March: ran creditably when placed otherwise: effective at around 2½m and stays 27f: acts on any going: usually blinkered (visored once):

temperamental and best when having things all his own way. *T. Thomson Jones*

SKIPLAM WOOD 7 b.m. Cree Song – Mab (Morston (FR)) [1992/3 18g4] small, sparely-made mare: poor novice hurdler: finished badly lame in August, and wasn't seen out again: races keenly and unlikely to stay much beyond 2m. *S. G. Chadwick*

SKIPPERS QUAY 6 ch.g. Longleat (USA) – Orange Tip (Orange Bay) [1992/3 F17d 16s 17g 22gpu] lengthy, angular gelding: novice hurdler: no worthwhile form. *G. A. Pritchard-Gordon*

SKIPPING TIM 14 b.g. Deep Run – Skiporetta (Even Money) [1992/3 c27s* c21s* c25f6 c26d2 c21s2 c26d5 c21v* c20dpu c21v c21v2 c23d4 c19m* c27m* c26g* c27sur c21g* c24g* c26m3] lengthy, dipped-backed gelding: prolific winning chaser: won 8 times in 1992/3: successful at Newton Abbot (2 handicaps), Cheltenham (claimer), Fontwell (selling handicap and claimer), Hereford (claimer), Bangor (selling handicap, bought in 4,200 gns) and Exeter (claimer): stays 3¼m: acts on any going: races up with the pace: tough and genuine, and a credit to connections. *M. C. Pipe*

c114
–

SKIRCOAT GREEN 8 ch.g. Buckskin (FR) – Little Exchange (Laurence O) [1992/3 21d2 25v4 22v2 22d2 22g* 21s*] sparely-made gelding: fair form over hurdles: won maiden at Sedgefield in February and amateurs novice event at Wetherby in April: once-raced over fences: stays 25f: acts on heavy going: genuine and consistent: front runner. *P. Beaumont*

c–
101

SKITTLE ALLEY 7 b.g. Adonijah – Skittish (USA) (Far North (CAN)) [1992/3 16v4 16v5 21g] close-coupled, workmanlike gelding: modest hurdler, lightly raced: sold 1,750 gns Doncaster May Sales: seems best at around 2m: acts on heavy going, won NH Flat race on equitrack. *S. Mellor*

92

SKY CAT 9 b.g. Skyliner – Spring Kitten (Pitcairn) [1992/3 16g3 18m4] lightly-raced handicap hurdler: in frame in claimer at Southwell in August and seller at Sedgefield in September: stays 2¼m: best run on top-of-the-ground: may do best with exaggerated waiting tactics: blinkered last 4 outings. *C. Tinkler*

95

SKYLARKIN 7 ch.g. Karlinsky (USA) – Rose Cottage (Rose Knight) [1992/3 17d 20dpu] sixth foal: half-brother to 2 poor animals: shown quite modest hurdler: no sign of ability in novice hurdles in May: sold 1,100 gns Ascot 2nd June Sales. *F. Jordan*

SKY RECORD 4 b.g. Skyliner – On The Record (Record Token) [1992/3 16g 17g] small gelding: behind in sprint maiden on Flat in 1992: sold out of Miss S. Hall's stable 2,400 gns Doncaster November Sales: no sign of ability over hurdles in February. *D. Moffatt*

SKY VENTURE 9 ch.g. Paddy's Stream – Mijette (Pauper) [1992/3 c22s2 c24d5 c24spu c26dur c23gF c26gbd c24fur c25spu c24mpu] sturdy gelding: novice chaser, frequently let down by his jumping: only poor judged on most form: stays 3m: acts on soft ground. *C. C. Trietline*

c77 x

SLAUGHT SON (IRE) 5 br.g. Roselier (FR) – Stream Flyer (Paddy's Stream) [1992/3 F16g4 F16m6] second foal: half-brother to winning chaser Father Dowling (by Teofane): dam never ran: showed a little ability in NH Flat races in March: yet to race over hurdles or fences. *R. F. Fisher*

SLAVI (FR) 5 ch.m. Nikos – Srpkigna (FR) (Sanhedrin (USA)) [1992/3 17s* 17s* 16f3] sparely-made mare: fair hurdler: won handicap and claimer at Newton Abbot in August: creditable third in conditional jockeys handicap at Uttoxeter following month: sold only 1,000 gns Ascot February Sales: takes strong hold and best at around 2m: acts on any ground: usually held up, and has found little. *M. C. Pipe*

110

SLEEPLINE ROMANY 8 b.g. Buzzards Bay – Sleepline Comfort (Tickled Pink) [1992/3 c17s4 c16g4] rangy gelding: novice hurdler/chaser: no form. *T. Thomson Jones*

c–
–

SLEEPLINE ROYALE 7 ch.g. Buzzards Bay – Sleepline Princess (Royal Palace) [1992/3 17v2 18v* 17s4 17v* 17d5 17f 20fpu 16v3] leggy,

118

close-coupled gelding: fairly useful hurdler: won handicaps at Folkestone in January and Lingfield in February: best at around 2m: has won on firm going but probably needs plenty of give in the ground nowadays: usually soon off bridle, and best with strong handling. *T. Thomson Jones*

SLICE OF THE ACTION   10 b.g. Random Shot – Tangle Tut (Tangle) [1992/3 c24spu] angular gelding: once-raced over hurdles: poor winning pointer: no show in hunter chase in April on steeplechasing debut. *Owen Thomas*   c– –

SLIEVENAMADDY   9 br.g. Fidel – Culkeern (Master Buck) [1992/3 c20fpu] tall gelding: poor novice hurdler/chaser: stays 21f: acts on good to firm ground. *B. R. Summers*   c– –

SLIEVENAMON MIST   7 ch.g. Thatching – La Generale (Brigadier Gerard) [1992/3 F16g2 F16g6 F18s* 20s3 18v* 18d3 19s5 16d2] ex-Irish gelding: fourth foal: dam never ran: won NH Flat race at Fairyhouse in November: fairly useful form over hurdles: won maiden at Navan in December: below-form second in novice event at Wincanton in April on British debut (previously trained by D. Hughes): should stay beyond 2¼m: acts on heavy going. *K. C. Bailey*   119 ?

SLIPMATIC   4 b.f. Pragmatic – Slipalong (Slippered) [1992/3 F16g2 F18g2] second foal: dam fair hurdler/chaser, probably stayed 3m: second in quite well-contested mares NH Flat races in March: yet to race over hurdles. *P. J. Jones*

SLIPPERTON   6 b.g. Pollerton – June's Slipper (No Argument) [1992/3 16v6 16v 17g6 16spu 17g5] lengthy, deep-girthed gelding: poor novice hurdler: sold 3,400 gns Ascot June Sales: blinkered third and fourth starts (slowly away on latter occasion). *O. Sherwood*   80

SLIPPERY MAX   9 b.g. Nicholas Bill – Noammo (Realm) [1992/3 c16g2 c16f2 c17f2 c16g2 c16g c16v3 a18g c21g4 c17d3 c18d3 c22vF] leggy, sparely-made gelding: moderate hurdler/chaser: stays 2½m, at least when conditions aren't testing: acts on any going. *R. T. Juckes*   c86 –

SLY PROSPECT (USA)   5 ch.g. Barachois (CAN) – Miss Sly (USA) (Diamond Prospect (USA)) [1992/3 17m3 16m3 18g 16f3 16g6 17g] lengthy, rather plain gelding: 2m plater over hurdles: generally ran creditably in 1992/3 until tailed off last start (September): acts on firm going: best visored/blinkered. *K. White*   70

SMALLMEAD LAD   6 b.g. Teofane – Raise The Clouds (Silver Cloud) [1992/3 26dpu c20d6 c21m2 22dpu c20g5] smallish gelding: poor hurdler: easily best effort in novice chases when second at Worcester in March: stays 21f: acts on good to firm ground. *D. R. Gandolfo*   c86 –

SMALLWOOD WILLET   13 ch.g. Funny Man – Miss Fleece All (Tangle) [1992/3 c19vpu c21m5] lengthy gelding: poor novice hurdler/ winning chaser: stays 3m: acts on firm going. *T. J. Swaffield*   c– –

SMARTIE EXPRESS   11 b. or br.g. Pony Express – Spick And Span (Smartie) [1992/3 c19s3 c26d4 c16v2 c21d3 c21m* c21m* c21m2 c20f* c20s*] close-coupled gelding: fairly useful handicap chaser: won at Warwick in February, Wincanton and Newbury in March and Ludlow in April: also second to Sacre d'Or in Mildmay of Flete at Cheltenham: races mostly at around 2½m but stays 3m: acts on any going: jumps well: game and consistent. *R. J. Hodges*   c118 –

SMARTIE LEE   6 ch.m. Dominion – Nosy Parker (FR) (Kashmir II) [1992/3 23s a20gpu 21v4 20f4] small mare: moderate hurdler: should prove suited by further than 2½m: acts on firm ground. *P. F. I. Cole*   92

SMART IN SABLE   6 br.m. Roscoe Blake – Cool Down (Warpath) [1992/3 17dpu] placed in NH Flat races in 1991/2 but behind until pulled up 2 out in novice hurdle at Perth in September. *G. Richards*   –

SMART REBAL (IRE)   5 b.g. Final Straw – Tomfoolery (Silly Season) [1992/3 17g2] sturdy gelding: poor novice hurdler: creditable second in novice handicap at Hereford in October: probably stays 2½m. *J. Akehurst*   76

SMART WORK 5 ch.m. Giacometti – Highwood Princess (Crooner) [1992/3 18g^{pu} 20d 21d] angular mare: second foal: dam of no account: no better herself over hurdles: won a point in March. *J. E. Long* –

SMILES AHEAD 5 ch.g. Primo Dominie – Baby's Smile (Shirley Heights) [1992/3 16d* 20v^2 16v^4 21v^2 22d 22s^2 22v^5 21f] lengthy gelding: won novice handicap hurdle at Uttoxeter in November: creditable efforts when runner-up subsequently, well below form otherwise: stays 2¾m: acts on heavy going: wore net muzzle twice and visored 4 times in 1991/2. *P. J. Bevan* 97

SMILING CHIEF (IRE) 5 ch.g. Montelimar (USA) – Victa (Northfields (USA)) [1992/3 16d 17d^{ur} 16g^5 16d* 17s 18s] good-topped gelding: half-brother to winning hurdler Paris Trader (by Alias Smith): modest 1¼m winner on Flat when trained by C. Cyzer: confirmed promise when winning novice handicap hurdle at Wincanton in November, but ran poorly both subsequent starts: should stay further than 2m: acts on dead going: sometimes races with head high. *R. J. Hodges* 92

SMITH'S BAND (IRE) 5 b.g. Orchestra – Pollys Flake (Will Somers) [1992/3 F16g F17d] fourth foal: half-brother to Searcher (by Furry Glen), a NH Flat race winner and maiden hurdler/pointer: dam won 3 times over hurdles and was placed over fences in Ireland: soundly beaten in NH Flat races in February and April: yet to race over hurdles or fences. *Mrs J. Pitman*

SMITH'S GAMBLE 11 ch.g. General Ironside – Sayanarra (King's Leap) [1992/3 21d] strong, close-coupled gelding: winning hurdler/chaser: no show only outing of season (October): stays 2¾m: best form with give in the ground: sometimes let down by his jumping over fences. *J. White* c– –

SMITH TOO (IRE) 5 br.g. Roselier (FR) – Beau St (Will Somers) [1992/3 16d^3 17s^3 22v 24v^5 25g^2 24g* 25v^3 24f] close-coupled, unfurnished gelding: first foal: dam won 3 races over hurdles at around 2½m in Ireland: fair form over hurdles: won novice event at Towcester in March: stays 25f: best efforts on good ground. *Mrs J. Pitman* 102

SMITHY BEAR 11 b.g. Rupert Bear – Avonteous (Rockavon) [1992/3 c23m^5 c21g^{pu} c19d^{pu}] small gelding: poor hurdler/chaser: no form for long time: tried blinkered and visored. *K. S. Bridgwater* c– –

SMITHY'S CHOICE 11 b.g. Bonne Noel – Passage Falcon (Falcon) [1992/3 22f^{pu} 21d^{pu}] compact gelding: winning hurdler: novice chaser: has run only twice since 1988/9: usually blinkered, visored last 2 outings. *I. Anderson* c– –

SMOKE 7 gr.m. Rusticaro (FR) – Fire-Screen (Roan Rocket) [1992/3 21s] neat mare: poor middle-distance performer on Flat, placed several times in 1992: sold out of J. Parkes's stable 2,500 gns Doncaster March Sales: poor novice hurdler: only form over 2m on firm ground. *W. G. Reed* –

SMOKEBRIDGE GRAS 6 b.g. Pardigras – Stalbridge Smoke (Royal Smoke) [1992/3 F17g F17s^5 16v^{pu} 17s 17v^4 a18g^{pu} 17d] unfurnished gelding: first foal: dam, unraced, from successful jumping family: poor form at best over hurdles: likely to stay 2½m: acts on heavy going: blinkered last start: reluctant. *W. G. M. Turner* 71 §

SMOOTH ESCORT 9 b.g. Beau Charmeur (FR) – Wishing Trout (Three Wishes) [1992/3 c25s^6 c27v^2 c26s* c25d^3 c33g^F c26f^3] sparely-made, close-coupled gelding: fair chaser: won handicap at Folkestone in February: below-form third both subsequent completed outings: suited by a thorough test of stamina: acts on heavy and good to firm going: blinkered 3 times in 1991/2 and on last 4 starts. *Mrs D. Haine* c109

SMOOTH START 8 b.g. Smooth Stepper – Ardmoyne (Le Bavard (FR)) [1992/3 c21g^5 c21d^6 c20m^5] compact, workmanlike gelding: poor chaser: in frame in points in 1993: stays 3m: acts on firm and dead going: tried visored once. *A. P. James* c– –

SMULLYAN 11 b.g. Faraway Times (USA) – Wounded Knee (Busted) [1992/3 c18m⁴] lengthy, sparely-made gelding: winning pointer/hunter chaser: stayed 3m: acted on firm ground: blinkered once: dead. *B. Ellison*

    c–
    –

SNAKE EYE 8 b.g. Tina's Pet – Dingle Belle (Dominion) [1992/3 17mᵖᵘ 18d⁵ 25d⁶] small, strong gelding: poor novice hurdler/chaser: sold 1,000 gns Doncaster November Sales: barely stays 2m. *W. T. Kemp*

    c–
    –

SNAPPY'S BOY JOSH 4 b.g. Hotfoot – September Snap (Music Boy) [1992/3 16sᵖᵘ 17d 18s³ 16f 17f⁵] leggy gelding: poor novice hurdler: best efforts at 2m on firm ground. *P. J. Feilden*

    64

SNEAKAPENNY 11 ch.g. Levanter – Quickapenny (Espresso) [1992/3 c24m³ c25m⁵ c25d⁴ c26d⁶ 22d⁵] strong, workmanlike gelding: fair chaser: best effort in first half of season when third at Stratford in September: sold to Mrs Lucy Wadham 10,000 gns Ascot December Sales: successful in 5 points in 1993: stays well: acts on any going: tried blinkered: makes mistakes. *K. C. Bailey*

    c113 x
    –

SNEEK 5 gr.g. Belfort (FR) – Gold Duchess (Sonnen Gold) [1992/3 16gᵖᵘ] sparely-made gelding: lightly raced, no sign of ability. *Mrs V. A. Aconley*

    –

SNIPPETOFF 5 b.g. Dubassoff (USA) – Snippet (Ragstone) [1992/3 F17m] fourth foal: half-brother to 23f selling hurdle winner Snappit (by Billion): dam, from good family, of little account: behind in NH Flat race at Hereford in May: sold 1,700 gns Malvern June Sales: yet to race over hurdles or fences. *D. McCain*

SNITTON GATE 6 b.g. Roscoe Blake – Cala di Volpe (Hardiran) [1992/3 18g⁶] lengthy gelding: no form in 2 novice hurdles. *Martyn Meade*

    –

SNITTON LANE 7 b.m. Cruise Missile – Cala di Volpe (Hardiran) [1992/3 c21d⁴ c22v² c21s³ c20d* c21g* c21d c20s³ c20s⁵ c21d²] sturdy, workmanlike mare with scope: fair hurdler: successful in novice chases at Ludlow and Kempton (valuable event) in February and also ran very well on seventh outing: stays 21f: acts on heavy going: sometimes wears tongue strap: usually jumps soundly. *J. A. C. Edwards*

    c117
    –

SNOOKER TABLE 10 b.g. Ballymore – Northern Twilight (English Prince) [1992/3 18s⁴ 16gᵖᵘ a20g³ 20f³] leggy gelding: poor hurdler nowadays: trained first 2 outings by T. Hallett: novice chaser: stays 2½m: acts on firm and dead going: tried blinkered: poor jumper of fences. *Mrs J. Wonnacott*

    c– x
    79

SNOW BOARD 4 gr.g. Niniski (USA) – Troja (Troy) [1992/3 17f²] useful-looking gelding: has plenty of scope: changed hands 8,000 gns

    116 p

Mitsubishi Shogun 'Pendil' Trophy (Novices' Chase), Kempton—
Snitton Lane is a convincing winner from Atlaal

*Baileys Arkle Perpetual Challenge Cup (Novices' Chase), Leopardstown —
Soft Day takes the last between How's The Boss (left) and Killiney Graduate*

Newmarket September Sales: promising 3½ lengths second to Zamirah in
juvenile hurdle at Newbury in March: progressed into a fairly useful stayer
on Flat afterwards: will stay much further than 17f: sure to win races over
hurdles. *B. W. Hills*

SNOWGIRL (IRE)   5 gr.m. Mazaad – Rust Free (Free State) [1992/3
16d⁶] fair sprint handicapper at her best on Flat, when trained by J. Berry:
sixth of 11 in novice event at Edinburgh in January on hurdling debut. *Mrs E.
Slack*   73

SNOWSHILL SHAKER   4 b.g. Son of Shaka – Knight Hunter
(Skyliner) [1992/3 F 16s³ F 12d⁴ F 17f] leggy gelding: first foal: dam ran twice:
in frame in NH Flat races: yet to race over hurdles. *N. A. Twiston-Davies*

SNOWY LANE (IRE)   5 ch.g. Commanche Run – Lassalia (Sallust)
[1992/3 20g⁵ 21v² 17s² 21v 21g⁵ 26mF 22f⁵ 25f 24s* 22d 22m⁶ 24f³] smallish
gelding: fairly useful handicap hurdler: won at Chepstow in April: ran poorly
afterwards: stays 3m: acts on heavy ground, possibly unsuited by
top-of-the-ground: front runner: visored last 4 starts, blinkered previous
three. *M. C. Pipe*   123

SNUFFLE BABE (IRE)   5 br.g. Orchestra – Inny View (Master Buck)
[1992/3 F 16s² F 17g*] lengthy, rather unfurnished gelding with scope:
half-brother to winning Irish hurdler The Old Poacher (by Reformed
Character): dam, unraced, from good jumping family: odds on, won
11-runner NH Flat race at Carlisle in March: yet to race over hurdles or
fences. *Mrs M. Reveley*

SOCIAL CLIMBER   9 b. or br.g. Crash Course – What A Duchess
(Bargello) [1992/3 c21s⁵ c16v c21f⁶ c22m² c19s⁵ c18gF c17m⁴] strong,
lengthy gelding: winning hurdler: modest novice chaser: will stay beyond
2¾m: acts on soft and good to firm ground. *Andrew Turnell*   c90
–

SOCIETY BALL   6 b.m. Law Society (USA) – Mariakova (USA) (The
Minstrel (CAN)) [1992/3 25g⁵ 22s* 21spu] tall, good-topped mare: modest
1½m winner on Flat at 3 yrs: won seller at Fontwell (bought in 4,800 gns) in
November, easily best effort over hurdles: stays 2¾m: acts on soft ground:
blinkered last 2 outings. *N. Tinkler*   83

SOCKEM 6 b.g. Nordico (USA) – Floating Petal (Wollow) [1992/3 16s 18d^{pu} 20d^{pu} 17g^F] small, sparely-made gelding: no form over hurdles: headstrong. *C. N. Williams* —

SOCKS DOWNE 14 b. or br.g. Paddy's Stream – Kincsem (Nelcius) [1992/3 c26g^{pu} c21s^3 c21s^4 c21d^2 c21v^3 c21g^2 c19g^3 c22f^F] workmanlike gelding: moderate handicap chaser: suited by around 2½m, give in the ground and forcing tactics. *A. J. Chamberlain* **c89** —

SO DISCREET (USA) 5 b.g. Secreto (USA) – I'll Be Around (USA) (Isgala) [1992/3 19h* 17m* 22s* 25d^2] won novice hurdles at Exeter, Bangor (handicap) and Cartmel early in season: stays 2¾m (fair effort over 25f in September): probably acts on any ground: blinkered once. *J. White* 93

SOFT DAY 8 br.g. Strong Gale – Arctic Tack (Arctic Slave) [1992/3 c17s* c18d* c16d^2 c18s* c17d* c19d* c18s* c18s^F c16g^{pu}] deep-girthed gelding: useful hurdler: smart form in novice chases in 1992/3, winning at Galway, Gowran Park, Punchestown (twice) and Leopardstown (twice), last 3 victories in valuable events: stayed 19f: acted on soft going: dead. *A. L. T. Moore, Ireland* **c140** —

SO GIFTED 7 b.m. Niniski (USA) – Maybe So (So Blessed) [1992/3 c16m c21d^{pu}] leggy, angular mare: no sign of ability. *Mrs V. A. Aconley* **c–** —

SOHAIL (USA) 10 ch.g. Topsider (USA) – Your Nuts (USA) (Creme Dela Creme) [1992/3 c21m^2 c26g^5 c18m^6] leggy, good-topped gelding: fair chaser: ran poorly last 2 starts (not raced after September): stays 21f: acts on any going: pulls hard. *J. White* **c107** ? —

SOHRAB (IRE) 5 ch.g. Shernazar – On Show (Welsh Pageant) [1992/3 16d^6 17d^4 17s^5 17g^2 16d* 16g^2] good-topped gelding: trained until after third start by R. Callow: much improved afterwards, easily winning maiden hurdle at Uttoxeter in April: unlikely to stay much beyond 2m: acts on dead ground: tends to jump to his right: likely to progress further. *N. A. Twiston-Davies* 107 p

SOLAR CLOUD 11 ch.g. Northfields (USA) – Passing Fancy (USA) (Buckpasser) [1992/3 c21g^3 c21m* c25m^4 c19d c21v^2 c21s^2 c22g^4 c20m^4 c22f^{pu} 24g c21g^3 c21m^4] close-coupled, light-framed gelding: poor chaser: won handicap at Huntingdon in August: best at up to 2¾m: acts on any going: tried blinkered/visored (not in 1992/3): claimer ridden: tends to get behind: unreliable. *M. J. Charles* **c83** § — §

SOLAR GREEN 8 ch.g. Green Shoon – Solaranda (Green God) [1992/3 c16v c16v^{pu} c20m^{ur} c16m^F c24d^5 c19f^5 c21f^{pu}] workmanlike gelding: only a little sign of ability. *G. A. Ham* **c–** —

SOLAR NOVA 5 b.m. Sunley Builds – Damascus Star (Mandamus) [1992/3 F16m] third foal: dam unraced: mid-division in 17-runner NH Flat race at Nottingham in March: yet to race over hurdles or fences. *I. Park* —

SOLEIL DANCER (IRE) 5 b.g. Fairy King (USA) – Cooliney Dancer (Dancer's Image (USA)) [1992/3 16d^{ur} 17v^4 16s^3 17v^4 a16g^3 16d* 16f^3] sturdy, angular gelding: half-brother to winning hurdler Birmingham's Pride (by Indian King): useful miler at best on Flat when trained mainly by M. McCormack: easy winner of handicap hurdle at Windsor in February: will prove suited by around 2m: acts on heavy going. *D. M. Grissell* 107

SOLEMN MELODY 6 b.g. Jalmood (USA) – Garganey (USA) (Quack (USA)) [1992/3 17s^F 17g^{pu} 17v^{pu} a16g^{pu}] of little account: trained first 3 starts by Mrs J. Retter: sold 775 gns Ascot February Sales: blinkered once. *A. Barrow* —

SOLENT LAD 10 b.g. Undulate (USA) – River Palace (Royal Palace) [1992/3 26g^{pu} 22v^{pu} 22g^{pu} 21m 25m^{pu}] lengthy, workmanlike gelding: selling hurdler: winning chaser: sometimes blinkered/visored. *B. Stevens* **c–** —

SOLICITOR'S CHOICE 10 b.g. Cagirama – Girostar (Drumbeg) [1992/3 c22v^5 c16v^{pu} c20m^4 c20d^3 c20d c21f^3 c24m^5 c25g^4 c22m^3 c25m^{pu} c26m^3] lengthy, good-quartered gelding: poor novice chaser: stays 3¼m: acts on any going: blinkered final outing. *T. T. Bill* **c80** —

SOLIDASAROCK 11 ch.g. Hardboy – Limefield Rita (Mon Capitaine) **c118**
[1992/3 c25g⁵ c24d³ c24s² c21v³ c24d⁵ c24f* c26f*] strong, well-made –
gelding: fairly useful handicap chaser: won at Newbury and Wincanton in
the spring: stays 3¼m: acts on any going: usually jumps well. *R. Akehurst*

SOLID FUEL 7 ch.g. Le Bavard (FR) – Twilight Spring (Cantab) [1992/3
26s³ 25f³] angular gelding: modest handicap hurdler: not raced after 92
September: out-and-out stayer: probably acts on any ground. *D. Moffatt*

SOLID (IRE) 5 b.g. Glenstal (USA) – Reine de Chypre (FR) (Habitat)
[1992/3 17g³ a20g⁴ a20g³ a20g² 17g⁴ a18g²] small, sparely-made gelding: 81
poor hurdler: trained first start by J. Jenkins: stays 2½m: best form on
fibresand. *D. J. S. Cosgrove*

SOLID STEEL (IRE) 5 b.h. Flash of Steel – Bonny Brae (Cure The
Blues (USA)) [1992/3 22g³ 18d* 17d* 17v* 21s⁴ 18v⁴ 20v⁵ 17fF] 101
workmanlike horse: fair hurdler: won conditional jockeys novice selling
hurdle at Exeter and 2 selling handicaps at Plumpton (no bid each time) in
first half of season: stayed 2¾m: acted on heavy going: blinkered once,
visored once: dead. *A. Moore*

SOLITARY REAPER 8 b.g. Valiyar – Fardella (ITY) (Molvedo) [1992/3
17m 17m³ 16g² 17d 17s a20g 17d 22m 17g] leggy gelding: poor hurdler 75
nowadays: stays 2½m: acts on hard going. *C. R. Beever*

SOLO BUCK 7 b.m. Buckskin (FR) – Go-It-Alone (Linacre) [1992/3 22d⁶
18v³ 22vF 24spu 16s⁴ 22m] workmanlike mare: poor novice hurdler: stays 80
2¾m: best efforts on a yeilding surface: visored/blinkered last 2 outings. *A.
P. Jones*

SOLO CORNET 8 br.g. Furry Glen – Royal Willow (Royal Buck) [1992/3
16d⁴ 16d⁴ 16s² 16sF 17mF 16dpu 17spu] leggy, sparely-made gelding: modest 87
novice hurdler: sold 2,800 gns Doncaster May Sales: unlikely to stay
beyond 2m: acts on soft ground: weak finisher (prone to breaking blood
vessels). *J. G. FitzGerald*

SOME DAY SOON 8 b.g. Beau Charmeur (FR) – Our Day (Conte **c88**
Grande) [1992/3 c24vF4 c21f²] workmanlike gelding: once-raced hurdler: –
first form in novice chases when second at Sandown in March: should stay
beyond 21f: acts on firm going. *M. Bradstock*

SOME DO 11 br.g. Reformed Character – Rosie Hawkins (Raise You Ten) **c–** §
[1992/3 c26d c24spu c27v] good-topped gelding: winning staying chaser: –
lightly raced and no form since 1988/9. *J. C. McConnochie*

SOME DO NOT 9 b.g. Maculata – Ballynavin Money (Even Money) **c–**
[1992/3 16vpu 16s] sturdy gelding: winning hurdler: novice chaser: probably –
stays 3m: acts on good to firm and dead going. *W. Storey*

SOME OBLIGATION 8 b.g. Gleason (USA) – Happy Lass (Tarqogan) **c106** §
[1992/3 c19d* c24m² c27mpu c17d* c20d²] tall, workmanlike gelding: fair
chaser: won hunter chases at Hereford in February and Fakenham in April:
good second in handicap at Ludlow on final start: effective at 2m and stays
3m: acts on any going: turned it in second start and is one to treat with
caution. *John R. Upson*

SOMEONE BRAVE 5 b.g. Commanche Run – Someone Special
(Habitat) [1992/3 18m³ 18f² 25g* 18g²] small, sparely-made gelding: modest 89
middle-distance maiden at best on Flat: won novice hurdle at Southwell in
August: not raced after September: effective at 2¼m and stays 25f: acts on
firm ground. *Bob Jones*

SOME POSSE 11 b.g. Posse (USA) – Some Dame (FR) (Vieux Manoir) **c–**
[1992/3 c19s] sturdy gelding: maiden pointer: no sign of ability in hunter
chases. *P. G. Watkins*

SOMERBY 6 br.g. Tudorville – Nautique (Windjammer (USA)) [1992/3
20f 16d] leggy gelding: no sign of ability: sold 1,800 gns Doncaster May –
Sales. *J. Wharton*

SOMERSAULTING (IRE) 5 b.h. Jester – Gwen Somers (Will
Somers) [1992/3 22g² 23s² 22v⁵] leggy, sparely-made horse: moderate 93

novice hurdler: stays 23f: acts on soft ground: sometimes blinkered, visored final outing (December). *A. R. Davison*

SOME SPARE 14 b.g. Track Spare – Some Say (I Say) [1992/3 21g[pu]] small, plain gelding: novice hurdler, poor at best. *C. H. Jones* –

SOME-TOY 7 ch.g. Arkan – Cedar of Galaxy (Bauble) [1992/3 c21s[ur]] fair pointer: unseated rider first in novice hunter chase in February. *John Squire* c–

SONALTO 7 br.g. Noalto – Sanandrea (Upper Case (USA)) [1992/3 c16f[3] c23s[F] c26g[pu] c18d[pu] c17v[pu] 22m] sparely-made gelding: tubed: poor chaser: stays 25f: acts on firm and soft ground: sometimes visored/blinkered. *D. L. Williams* c74 –

SONEETO 7 b.g. Teenoso (USA) – Flying Bid (Auction Ring (USA)) [1992/3 18s] tall, leggy gelding: won 2m hurdle on equitrack in 1889/90: tailed off only outing since that season. *S. Woodman* –

SONG AN'DANCE MAN 10 ch.g. Gay Fandango (USA) – Callistro (Song) [1992/3 c17g[pu] c19g[6]] strong gelding: of little account: tried blinkered/visored. *Mrs A. E. Lee* c– –

SONG OF SIXPENCE (USA) 9 b.g. The Minstrel (CAN) – Gliding By (USA) (Tom Rolfe) [1992/3 17g[F] 18f[6] 17d[6] 17d 17s[2] 17g[4] 17m[4]] sturdy, good-bodied gelding: fair handicap hurdler nowadays: races only at around 2m: acts on good to firm and soft ground: held up. *I. A. Balding* 114

SONIC SIGNAL 7 b. or br.m. Trojan Fen – Danger Signal (Red God) [1992/3 22d 22v[5] 21s[pu]] neat mare: poor and inconsistent staying handicapper on Flat when trained by M. Haynes: well beaten in novice hurdles: blinkered final start. *W. G. Turner* –

SONNENKA 6 br.g. Sonnen Gold – Karlenka (Amboise) [1992/3 24g] no sign of ability in NH Flat race and a maiden hurdle. *R. R. Lamb* –

SONNY JAMES 9 b.g. Sunyboy – Lafitte (Lucky Sovereign) [1992/3 18s 25s[pu]] leggy, sparely-made gelding: no sign of ability in 3 starts over hurdles. *G. C. Maundrell* –

SONOFAGIPSY 9 b.g. Sunyboy – Zingarella (Romany Air) [1992/3 c26g*] fair pointer: won maiden hunter chase at Hereford in May: stays 3¼m: should improve. *J. W. Dufosee* c80 p

SON OF ANUN 4 ch.g. Norwick (USA) – Sister Rosarii (USA) (Properantes) [1992/3 aF16g[2] F16f[6]] fifth foal: half-brother to 1988 2-y-o 5f winner Annother Sigwells (by Ballacashtal): dam never ran: showed ability in NH Flat races: yet to race over hurdles. *W. G. M. Turner* –

SON OF IRIS 5 br.g. Strong Gale – Sprats Hill (Deep Run) [1992/3 F16s[2] F14m F17d[5]] second foal: half-brother to winning chaser Dunbrody Abbey (by Proverb): dam won two 3m chases after birth of first foal: showed ability in NH Flat races: yet to race over hurdles or fences. *Mrs M. Reveley* –

SONSIE MO 8 b.g. Lighter – Charlotte Amalie (No Mercy) [1992/3 c17g[2] c17g[4]c16g[F]c16s[4]c16g[2]c16g*c17d[2]c16m[3]c17m[F]c17g[4]c16s[3]c16f*c18d[ur]] sparely-made gelding: fair handicap chaser: won conditional jockeys events at Edinburgh in January and Wetherby in May: best at around 2m: acts on any going: consistent. *Mrs S. C. Bradburne* c101 –

SONS TONIMARA 8 ch.g. Don Enrico (USA) – Copper Sox (John's Pride) [1992/3 16s[pu] 16m 17d[pu] 16v[pu]] strong, lengthy gelding: of no account. *M. Scudamore* –

SOONER STILL 9 b.g. Tachypous – Sooner Or Later (Sheshoon) [1992/3 c26g[2] c25v[F] c25s c26d[2] c24d[6] c29v[pu] c24g[4] c24d[3] c23m[4] c25f c27d[2] c26m* c27d[3] c26m[5]] sparely-made, angular gelding: fair chaser nowadays: won handicap at Uttoxeter in May: thorough stayer: acts on any going: usually blinkered or visored. *J. A. C. Edwards* c105 –

SOOTHFAST (USA) 4 b.g. Riverman (USA) – Sookera (USA) (Roberto (USA)) [1992/3 17m[6] 16v* 16v[4] 17g] smallish gelding: half-brother to 4 Flat winners, including Durzi (by High Line), also placed over hurdles: dam won Cheveley Park Stakes: 1¼m winner on first of 2 starts on Flat in France at 3 95 +

yrs: won juvenile hurdle at Towcester in April: stiff task in handicap final start: yet to race beyond 17f: easily best efforts on heavy ground. *J. A. B. Old*

SOPHINI 5 b.m. State Diplomacy (USA) – Sophisticated (Bivouac) [1992/3 22s^{pu} 20m 21s 20m] rather plain mare: poor novice hurdler: best effort on second start. *Mrs A. Tomkinson* — 66

SORBIERE 6 b.g. Deep Run – Irish Mint (Dusky Boy) [1992/3 F19m* 20g² 20d³ 20s³ 21f*] first foal: dam, poor novice hurdler/chaser, half-sister to Corbiere: successful in NH Flat race at Naas in June (trained until after fourth start by E. Kearns) and maiden hurdle at Newbury in March: will stay further than 21f: probably acts on any ground: should progress. *N. J. Henderson* — 102 p

SORDIFA (IRE) 5 ch.g. Tate Gallery (USA) – Firdosa (Relic) [1992/3 16g 17d^{pu} 18m] small gelding: poor novice hurdler: races at around 2m: acts on good to firm ground: blinkered once. *Mrs D. F. Culham* — –

SOROPTIMIST (FR) 4 br.f. Groom Dancer (USA) – Coast Patrol (USA) (Cornish Prince) [1992/3 17g^{pu}] ex-French filly: second known foal: dam stakes winner in USA: lightly-raced maiden on Flat: no promise in early-season juvenile hurdle. *Martyn Meade* — –

SOUL AGREEMENT 6 b.g. Kemal (FR) – Agreement (Final Problem) [1992/3 24d²] tall, rather unfurnished gelding: ran very green when second of 7 in novice event at Market Rasen in February on hurdling debut: sure to improve. *Mrs S. A. Bramall* — 92 p

SOUND CARRIER (USA) 5 br.g. Lord Gaylord (USA) – Bright Choice (USA) (Best Turn (USA)) [1992/3 F17s³ 17s] big, leggy gelding with plenty of scope: third foal: half-brother to a winner on Flat in USA: dam minor stakes winner at around 1m in USA: third in NH Flat race at Newbury in January: showed little in novice hurdle following month. *O. Sherwood* — –

SOUND OF ISLAY 8 b.g. Deep Run – Sharpaway (Royal Highway) [1992/3 c22d^F 16g 23s⁴ 25v⁵ 21s^{pu}] useful-looking gelding: fair, but temperamental hurdler: fell second on chasing debut: sold 3,800 gns Ascot March Sales: best left alone. *Capt. T. A. Forster* — c– §§

SOUND OF JURA 8 b.g. Deep Run – Arctic Chatter (Le Bavard (FR)) [1992/3 c21d⁶ c24d³ c24s² c26v^{pu} c24s c25d⁶] workmanlike gelding: winning hurdler: modest novice chaser: sold 5,400 gns Ascot March Sales: stays 25f: acts on soft ground: not an accomplished jumper of fences. *Capt. T. A. Forster* — c88

SOUND PROFIT 5 ch.m. Scallywag – Night Profit (Carnival Night) [1992/3 16g^{pu} 20s 24g 18d 17d] compact mare: well beaten over hurdles. *W. G. Young* — –

SOUND REVEILLE 5 b.g. Relkino – Loughnavalley (Candy Cane) [1992/3 F16f] fifth foal: dam fairly useful 2m hurdler: behind in NH Flat race at Haydock in May: yet to race over hurdles or fences. *C. P. E. Brooks* — –

SOUSON (IRE) 5 b.g. Soughaan (USA) – Down The Line (Brigadier Gerard) [1992/3 17m³ 22f³] leggy, angular gelding: poor novice hurdler: not raced after September: stays 2¾m: acts on firm and dead ground: creditable efforts when blinkered twice. *M. W. Easterby* — 81

SOUTARI 5 br.g. Scorpio (FR) – Sousocks (Soueida) [1992/3 a16g^{pu}] pulled up both starts over hurdles. *M. McCormack* — –

SOUTER'S HILL (USA) 6 b.g. Temperence Hill (USA) – Kissapotamus (USA) (Illustrious) [1992/3 16g 16g 20g] leggy gelding: winning 2m hurdler: no worthwhile form in 1992/3. *T. Craig* — –

SOUTH BAR 8 gr.m. Scallywag – Erra (Romany Air) [1992/3 17s 17d] plain mare: no sign of ability in 3 races over hurdles. *R. G. Frost* — –

SOUTH CROSS (USA) 8 ch.g. Valdez (USA) – Blue Cross Nurse (USA) (Needles) [1992/3 c21m² c21d⁵ c22s⁵] sturdy gelding: poor chaser: broke blood vessel final outing (November): stays 2¾m: acts on any going: visored once. *G. M. Moore* — c87

SOUTHEND FLUTTER 6 b.h. Beldale Flutter (USA) – By The Lake (Tyrant (USA)) [1992/3 18gᵖᵘ] no sign of ability in NH Flat races, and a selling hurdle. *N. B. Mason*

–

SOUTHEND UNITED 7 b.g. Black Minstrel – Diamond Panes (Lock Diamond) [1992/3 c16vⁿ c16s⁶ c18vᵖᵘ c17v⁴ c19vᵖᵘ c16v⁵ c18g³ c16s* c16gᶠ c16m⁴ c16gᵖᵘ] lengthy gelding: novice hurdler: won novice chase at Ludlow in April and would have won novice handicap at Southwell next time but for falling last: ran poorly afterwards: best form at 2m: acts on soft going. *John R. Upson*

c96
–

SOUTHERLY BUSTER 10 b.g. Strong Gale – Southern Slave (Arctic Slave) [1992/3 c24sᵖᵘ c21dᵖᵘ] lengthy gelding: fairly useful chaser at up to 3m in 1990/1: showed nothing both outings since: blinkered twice. *O. Sherwood*

c–

SOUTHERLY GALE 6 b.g. Strong Gale – Chestnut Belle (Even Money) [1992/3 16d 21g] unfurnished gelding: well beaten on 2 outings over hurdles. *N. J. Henderson*

–

SOUTHERN MINSTREL 10 ch.g. Black Minstrel – Jadida (FR) (Yelapa (FR)) [1992/3 c21sᵖᵘ c17s³ c16sᵖᵘ c16s² c20d² c21s* c21m³ c22f² c25g] lengthy gelding: fairly useful handicap chaser nowadays: trained until after second start by W. A. Stephenson: won at Wetherby in March: afterwards placed in Mildmay of Flete at Cheltenham and John Hughes Memorial at Aintree: best at up to 2¾m: acts on any going. *P. Cheesbrough*

c116
–

SOUTH HARVEST 10 br.g. Oats – Roscrea (Ballymore) [1992/3 c21sᵖᵘ c21d⁵ c24dᵘʳ c24v³ c25dᵖᵘ c20f² c21f c24gᶠ] workmanlike gelding: modest novice chaser: best form around 2½m: acts on firm and dead ground, probably unsuited by heavy: visored sixth and seventh outings. *J. R. Jenkins*

c95

SOUTHOLT (IRE) 5 b.g. Deep Run – Girseach (Furry Glen) [1992/3 F16g² F17mᵖᵘ] smallish gelding: second foal: dam won on Flat and over hurdles in Ireland: second of 22 in NH Flat race at Kempton in February: pulled up in valuable event at Cheltenham following month: yet to race over hurdles or fences. *F. Murphy*

SOUTH SANDS 7 ch.g. Sayf El Arab (USA) – Collegian (Stanford) [1992/3 20gᵘʳ 16d 18s² 18s² 20s⁴ a16gᶠ 18dᵖᵘ] leggy gelding: moderate handicap hurdler: stays 21f: probably acts on any going: blinkered prior to 1992/3: races up with pace. *Mrs J. Wonnacott*

93

SOUTH STACK 7 b.g. Daring March – Lady Henham (Breakspear II) [1992/3 22mᶠ 20s² 1m² 21m⁶ 25g 22d⁴ 21d⁵ 21v² 22s* 26sᵖᵘ 20s⁶ 22d] leggy gelding: selling hurdler: won novice event at Sedgefield (no bid) in December: ran poorly afterwards: stays 2¾m: best form on a yielding surface. *Mrs S. J. Smith*

83

SOVEREIGN NICHE (IRE) 5 gr.g. Nishapour (FR) – Sovereign Flash (FR) (Busted) [1992/3 17d* 18d² 16s a16gᵖᵘ 17m 17f 17v³ 20m 17f⁵ 17d 17f⁶ 17fᵖᵘ] lengthy gelding: sold 5,800 gns Doncaster August Sales: selling hurdler: won at Wolverhampton (bought in 5,800 gns) in November: well below form most starts afterwards (sold out of Mrs J. Ramsden's stable 900 gns Ascot February Sales after fourth outing): stays 2¼m: acts on good to firm, heavy ground and fibresand: blinkered once, usually visored nowadays. *A. Barrow*

79 d

SOVEREIGNS MATCH 5 b.g. Royal Match – Sovereign's Folly (Sovereign Bill) [1992/3 F17s a18g³] no sign of ability. *G. A. Pritchard-Gordon*

–

SOVEREIGN SOUND 6 b.g. Town And Country – Top Soprano (High Top) [1992/3 c16g c21d c21s⁵ 21v³ 23s 16v 16m⁶ 21g³ 16v² 16g] strong, sturdy gelding: moderate handicap hurdler: poor novice chaser: stayed 21f: acted on heavy going: usually blinkered: dead. *Andrew Turnell*

c–
93

SOVIET RUN 6 b. or br.g. Deep Run – Russian Wings (Zabeg) [1992/3 21sᵖᵘ 16s] leggy, close-coupled gelding: no sign of ability. *M. D. Hammond*

–

691

SOYBEAN   9 gr.g. Ardross – Meanz Beanz (High Top) [1992/3 c23m⁵ c26m³ c27d⁴] smallish, workmanlike gelding: poor novice hurdler/chaser: stays 3¼m: acts on good to firm ground: blinkered once. *B. Smart*

c73 –

SPACE CAPTAIN   6 b.g. Star Appeal – Dovey (Welsh Pageant) [1992/3 18g*] lengthy, angular gelding: won 2 NH Flat races in 1991/2 and novice event at Cartmel in August on hurdling debut. *G. M. Moore*

100

SPACE FAIR   10 b.g. Space King – Katie Fare (Ritudyr) [1992/3 c20gᶠ c21d c17s³ c17m² c20m² c17m* c17m*]

c143 –

The Queen Mother Champion Chase is said to be the principal target of the useful handicapper Space Fair in the 1993/4 season. It's a pity he didn't contest the latest running of that event, for it was one of the weakest in the race's history and Space Fair, in cracking form at the time, probably wouldn't have been too far away. The Champion Chase will surely take more winning next time round and it is unlikely that Space Fair, who by then will be eleven years old, will have improved enough to be considered a leading contender for the race. That said, Space Fair should never be dismissed lightly when running at Cheltenham, for the course usually brings out the best in him. He excelled himself over hurdles there when twelfth to Kribensis in the 1990 Champion Hurdle, finished a good third in the 1992 Arkle Trophy Chase and, in the latest season, won two handicap chases, including the Grand Annual Challenge Cup at the Festival meeting in March. Space Fair stays two and a half miles, but a strongly-run contest at around two miles is ideal for him and he had those conditions in both the handicap chases. Ridden with more restraint than usual, Space Fair took up the running three out in the Grand Annual and between three out and two out in a fairly valuable event a month later. He kept on gamely under pressure to win by two lengths from Shamana in the former and by four lengths from Fragrant Dawn, who'd finished fourth in the Champion Chase, in the latter.

	Space King (b 1959)	King's Bench (b 1949)	Court Martial
			King's Cross
		Lunar Way (b 1954)	Solonaway
Space Fair (b.g. 1983)			Florida Moon
	Katie Fare (ch 1965)	Ritudyr (ch 1958)	King of The Tudors
			Scamal Fanach
		Kirghiz (b 1950)	Fastnet
			Kefana

Katie Fare, the dam of Space Fair, also won at Cheltenham. That was in 1973 when she completed a hat-trick of wins in hunter chases. Unlike Space Fair, Katie Fare, who died in 1987, was suited by a test of stamina. Of her other winning produce the fair chaser Fare Love (by Grey Love) barely stayed two and a half miles while Space Kate, a full sister to Space Fair, won a handicap hurdle over three and a quarter. The lengthy, workmanlike Space Fair has won on soft going but he goes particularly well on top-of-the-ground. A thoroughly genuine performer who jumps soundly, he'll continue to give a good account of himself. *R. Lee*

Cheltenham Grand Annual Chase Challenge Cup (Handicap), Cheltenham— Space Fair clears the last ahead of Storm Alert

Holman Cup (Handicap Chase), Cheltenham —
another typically good jump by Space Fair

SPACE PRINCE 12 b.g. Space King – Queens Purse (Lucky Sovereign) **c80**
[1992/3 c25d5 c19s4 c19v4 c26mur c26fpu] lengthy, rather sparely-made
gelding: maiden hunter chaser: stays 19f: acts on heavy ground. *R. A.
Phillips*

SPACIAL (USA) 9 b.g. Star Appeal – Abeer (USA) (Dewan (USA)) c–
[1992/3 c20s3 c20d c18g5 c19g5] tall gelding: fairly useful handicap chaser in –
1991/2: ran badly in 1992/3: effective from 2m to 2 1f: probably acts on any
going: blinkered final outing: sometimes hangs badly right, and is suited by
a right-handed track. *N. A. Gaselee*

SPAMBRUCO 9 gr.g. Jolly Me – Colourful Girl (Blue Streak) [1992/3 –
20gpu 16dpu] sparely-made gelding: fifth foal: dam, half-sister to Pegwell
Bay, pulled up lame only start: seems of little account. *H. J. Manners*

SPANISH BLAZE (IRE) 5 b.g. Spanish Place (USA) – The Blazing
Star (Proverb) [1992/3 F14m] fifth foal: half-brother to fairly useful Irish
staying chaser Rossi Novae (by Roselier) and winning jumper Jupiter's
Glory (by Derring Rose): dam winning Irish pointer: eighth of 20 in NH Flat
race at Market Rasen in March: sold 17,000 gns Doncaster May Sales: yet to
race over hurdles or fences. *J. Hanson*

SPANISH FAIR (IRE) 5 b.g. Spanish Place (USA) – Bonne Fair
(Bonne Noel) [1992/3 18g5 16g2 17m* 17d 17d4 16dF 17m2 21d4] tall, **93 p**
unfurnished gelding: first foal: dam unraced: won a point in Ireland in 1992
and novice hurdle at Newcastle in October: ran creditably last 3 starts:
trained until after fourth start by W. A. Stephenson: sold to Mrs S. Bramall
72,000 gns in May: stays 21f: acts on good to firm and dead ground: type to
progress. *P. Cheesbrough*

SPANISH SERVANT 8 ch.g. Don – Please Oblige (Le Levanstell) **120**
[1992/3 17d 22d3] good-bodied, workmanlike gelding: has been fired:
one-time useful hurdler: fairly useful effort when third in handicap at
Newton Abbot in April: stays 2¾m: acts on soft and good to firm ground. *P.
R. Hedger*

SPANISH WHISPER 6 b.g. Aragon – Whisper Gently (Pitskelly) **85 §**
[1992/3 16g4 17g6 17s a18g6 17g5 17g3 16g2 17d6 16g* 17g4] leggy gelding:
poor selling hurdler nowadays: won selling handicap at Hexham (bought in 2,400
gns) in May: races at around 2m: acts on firm and good to soft going:
inconsistent and sometimes looks reluctant. *J. R. Bostock*

SPARC A LIGHT 9 ch.g. Lighter – Spartaca (Spartan General) [1992/3 c–
c19spu] rangy gelding: modest pointer: yet to complete in steeplechases. *G.
Bodily*

SPARKLER GEBE 7 b.g. Be My Native (USA) – Siliferous (Sandy c–
Creek) [1992/3 c18gF c18gpu 17s2 23m* 22dbd 22v 20v4 22s a22g* a24g3] **91**
sparely-made gelding: modest hurdler: won conditional jockeys claimers at
Stratford in October and Lingfield (handicap) in February: no promise in
novice chases: stays 23f: acts on good to firm going (ran respectably on
heavy): best in blinkers: inconsistent and sometimes looks none too keen.
R. J. O'Sullivan

SPARKLING CONE 4 gr.g. Celtic Cone – Sparkling Time (USA)
(Olden Times) [1992/3 F17f3 F17m5] half-brother to useful staying hurdler
Coworth Park (by Wolver Hollow): dam ran twice at 2 yrs: showed ability in
NH Flat races at Hereford in May: yet to race over hurdles. *M. C. Pipe*

SPARKLING FLAME 9 b.g. Beau Charmeur (FR) – Shreelane c–
(Laurence O) [1992/3 c26gpu c27spu 24v2] tall, rather sparely-made gelding: **103**
one-time smart chaser: showed nothing first 2 starts 1992/3: second of 24 in
novice event at Worcester in January on hurdling debut: will stay beyond
25f: probably acts on heavy going. *N. J. Henderson*

SPARKLING SUNSET (IRE) 5 br.g. Strong Gale – Cherry Jubilee
(Le Bavard (FR)) [1992/3 17vF 17s2 16s2 17f2 20d3] lengthy, unfurnished **128**
gelding: second live foal: dam, from family of Arkle, is half-sister to several
winners, notably very useful jumper Randolph Place: useful novice over
hurdles: best effort when third to Hebridean at Ascot in April: better suited

by 2½m than 2m, and will stay further: seems suited by give in the ground: sure to win races. *N. J. Henderson*

SPARK OF PEACE 11 ch.g. Royal Match – Geneva (Linacre) [1992/3 c16v c21g⁵ c26dᵖᵘ c21sᵖᵘ] sturdy gelding: carries condition: winning 2m hurdler/chaser: no form in 1992/3: trained first start by M. Charles. *R. Brotherton* c–

SPARTAN CHIEF 12 ch.g. True Song – Silver Spartan (Spartan General) [1992/3 c25g⁴ c24f⁴] lengthy gelding: modest hunter chaser nowadays: suited by test of stamina: acts on firm going. *N. J. Jones* c83

SPARTAN DANCER 9 gr.g. Scallywag – Spartan Imp (Spartan General) [1992/3 c26d⁵ c28d⁵ c24s³ c24g⁴ c27gᵘʳ c24m⁴] rangy gelding: modest hunter chaser: trained first 2 starts of season by Mrs J. Retter: stays 3½m: acts on any going. *Mrs M. J. Trickey* c81

SPARTAN DREAM 6 b.g. Gabitat – Soldiers Dream (Spartan General) [1992/3 16sꟳ 17sᵖᵘ 25sᵖᵘ a20g³ a22gᵖᵘ] rangy, angular gelding: novice hurdler: no form: dead. *M. D. I. Usher* –

SPARTAN MAGIC 8 ch.g. Kinglet – Spartan's Lock (Spartan General) [1992/3 c21gꟳ c24mꟳ] behind in NH Flat races: fell both outings in novice chases. *R. Voorspuy* c–

SPARTAN RANGER 8 b.g. Lochnager – Spartan Flutter (Spartan General) [1992/3 c20gꟳ c20s² c25g⁵] big, rangy gelding: winning hurdler: second in novice chase at Carlisle in November: below that form in January: should be well suited by distances beyond 2½m: acts on soft ground. *M. D. Hammond* c88

SPARTAN SUN 6 ch.g. Sunyboy – Spartaca (Spartan General) [1992/3 F17g 18d] sparely-made gelding: fourth foal: dam of little account in points and hunter chases: behind in NH Flat race and novice hurdle early in season. *H. Willis* –

SPARTAN TIMES 9 b.g. Official – Pillbox (Spartan General) [1992/3 26d⁵] big, strong gelding: chasing type: fairly useful hurdler in 1990/1: first race since when fifth in handicap in January: suited by test of stamina: acts on soft going. *Capt. T. A. Forster* –

SPEAKERS CORNER 10 ch.g. Politico (USA) – Gusty Lucy (White Speck) [1992/3 c22f⁴] lengthy gelding: useful hunter chaser at best: respectable fourth in Martell Fox Hunters' at Aintree in April: stays 3¼m: acts on soft going, probably on firm: sometimes makes mistakes: usually front runner. *M. E. Sowersby* c98

SPECIAL ACCOUNT 7 b.g. Le Moss – Liffey's Choice (Little Buskins) [1992/3 19m 22g 24v* 25s* 25s⁶ 24s 24s⁴] leggy gelding: won novice hurdles at Worcester and Taunton (handicap) in first half of season: below form afterwards: suited by good test of stamina: acts on heavy going. *C. R. Barwell* 103

SPECTACULAR DAWN 4 gr.f. Spectacular Bid (USA) – Early Rising (USA) (Grey Dawn II) [1992/3 17v⁶ 16s* 17g² 17g] angular filly: fairly useful middle-distance stayer on Flat for J. Dunlop: won juvenile hurdle at Warwick in February: ran well afterwards, particularly in handicap final start: will stay at least 2½m: acts on soft going: should progress. *N. J. Henderson* 109 p

SPEED OIL 4 br.c. Java Tiger – Maydrum (Meldrum) [1992/3 16s] close-coupled, leggy colt: poor maiden on Flat, stays 1m: behind in juvenile hurdle at Wetherby in December. *R. Bastiman* –

SPEEDO MOVEMENT 4 ch.f. Scottish Reel – Third Movement (Music Boy) [1992/3 16s 16vᵖᵘ a16g³ a16g⁴] leggy filly: moderate staying maiden on Flat: poor form in juvenile hurdles: will stay beyond 2m: acts on fibresand. *B. A. McMahon* 84

SPEEDY SIOUX 4 ch.f. Mandrake Major – Sioux Be It (Warpath) [1992/3 16g* 16gꟳ 18g 16g 17g⁵ 17m⁶ 21g 25vᵖᵘ 22m⁵ 18v] sparely-made, angular filly: maiden plater on Flat, stays 1¼m: poor form over hurdles: won 76

juvenile claimer at Ayr in October: sold out of C. Thornton's stable 2,500 gns Doncaster November Sales before next start: stays 2¾m: acts on good to firm ground: usually blinkered nowadays. *S. G. Chadwick*

SPERRIN VIEW   7 ch.m. Fidel – Baroness Vimy (Barrons Court)   c–
[1992/3 c25mF 21mᵖᵘ 22m] ex-Irish mare: lightly-raced novice hurdler: sold   –
privately 1,850 gns Ascot 2nd June Sales: no form: fell on chasing debut: visored once. *J. Simmons*

SPIDERS DELIGHT   5 ch.g. Sula Bula – Spiders Web (Big Deal)
[1992/3 F17m³ 17mF] third foal: half-brother to 6-y-o Issyin (by Oats): dam   –
useful, most genuine and consistent chaser in her prime, effective from 2m to 3m: third in NH Flat race at Carlisle in October: narrow lead but weakening when falling 3 out in conditional jockeys novice hurdle at Newcastle following month. *P. Monteith*

SPIKEY (NZ)   7 b.g. Valuta – Sweet Canyon (NZ) (Headland II) [1992/3   c85 x
23s⁵ c17sᵖᵘ c24d³ c25d² c24f⁴ c25s⁵ c25gᵘʳ] workmanlike gelding: poor   –
novice hurdler: modest novice chaser: suited by test of stamina: acts on dead and firm ground: poor jumper of fences. *J. R. Jenkins*

SPINNING   6 b. or br.g. Glint of Gold – Strathspey (Jimmy Reppin)
[1992/3 17f³ 17m³ 17f* 16f*]   151 P
    What price Spinning for the next Champion Hurdle if the ground is as lively as it was for the last? He's an interesting horse and no mistake, pattern-race class on the Flat and now ready to move up from handicaps over hurdles. Spinning came to hurdling as a four-year-old in the spring of 1991 with a *Timeform* Flat rating of 107; few come with a higher one, but he'd also been proving a very difficult ride with a marked tendency to hang. On his hurdling debut he seemed to spoil his chance by pulling hard, and didn't reappear over timber until the last day of the year when, despite pulling again, he got off the mark in a novice event at Cheltenham. He hasn't looked back since under either code, and is much more amenable nowadays. That second season, 1991/2, he went on to finish a creditable third in the Imperial Cup following further wins in novice events at Kempton and Sandown, and returned to the Flat, he won the Bessborough Handicap at Royal Ascot and the Tote Gold Trophy and a listed race at Goodwood before finishing a good third in the Man o' War Stakes at Belmont.

Cordon Bleu Handicap Hurdle, Aintree—Spinning leaves his opponents toiling

Swinton Handicap Hurdle, Haydock —
another easy success for Spinning, who leads Jungle Knife over the last

Spinning began his latest hurdling campaign in another Imperial Cup. He finished third again, but was less than four lengths behind Olympian and would have gone close to beating him with clean jumps at the last two flights. The swift compensation predicted for him was delayed until Aintree by Thumbs Up and High Baron in the County Hurdle at Cheltenham where, backed down to 7/4 as though defeat in the big field was out of the question, he faded on the run-in having pulled his way into the lead at an early stage. Not even a rise in the weights could stop Spinning in the Cordon Bleu Handicap at Aintree; in fact he won so emphatically by eight lengths in a fast time that 10 lb more on his back would probably not have stopped him. He was on top four out, having stretched his nine opponents from the start, and he gave the jockey on the chasing Bollin Patrick no cause for optimism in the straight. They were a much stronger bunch that opposed Spinning in the Swinton Handicap Hurdle at Haydock in May. First run in 1978, when Royal Gaye beat a field that included the first four in the Champion Hurdle, the race has been one of the season's most important handicaps ever since. Prize money of nearly £40,000 attracted seventeen runners in 1993, headed by the Champion Hurdle ninth Jinxy Jack and seventh Flakey Dove. Spinning, receiving 12 lb from one and 7 lb from the other, started a heavily-backed favourite at 3/1. The previous week he'd finished third to Roll A Dollar and Assessor, beaten a neck and a head, in the even more valuable Sagaro Stakes over two miles on the Flat at Ascot. The Swinton Hurdle showed that he was still improving fast. On this occasion he wasn't allowed to go on until two out. As usual, Olympian attempted to run everything into the ground; Sabaki River and Canny Chronicle aided and abetted, with Spinning tucked in handy on the rails, travelling strongly under restraint. When given his head Spinning soon took charge of the race, and on the run home he remained in complete command, his jockey scarcely moving except to look round once at the four-length second Jungle Knife; Pontynys-wen, who'd led on sufferance three out when the front-runners weakened,

697

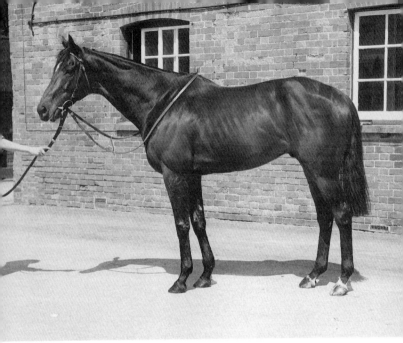

Mr Paul Mellon's "Spinning"

kept on for third place, a further six lengths back. Neither Jinxy Jack nor
Flakey Dove showed much.

Spinning (b. or br.g. 1987)	Glint of Gold (b 1978)	Mill Reef (b 1968)	Never Bend	
			Milan Mill	
		Crown Treasure (b 1973)	Graustark	
			Treasure Chest	
	Strathspey (ch 1976)	Jimmy Reppin (ch 1965)	Midsummer Night II	
			Sweet Molly	
		Strip The Willow (ch 1965)	Native Dancer	
			Near Miss	

As at Aintree, Spinning's time beat the course record. Ground
conditions were just right for breaking records, and Spinning has done
nearly all his racing over hurdles on that type of ground—firm or good to
firm. He hasn't raced on soft over hurdles and his record on the Flat
strongly advises caution should he ever do so. Spinning stays very well on
the Flat, but is perfectly at home at the minimum distance for hurdlers, as
were many Flat stayers before him, Royal Gait to name one. He takes a good
hold, so a good pace in his races is ideal. The well-made Spinning was bred
for the Flat, and although owner/breeder Paul Mellon is a keen supporter of
jumping on both sides of the Atlantic he was probably aiming for a Derby
winner when he arranged the mating between Glint of Gold and the useful
top-of-the-ground miler Strathspey, a full sister to the One Thousand
Guineas third Joking Apart. Spinning was Strathspey's last foal before she

698

appeared in the December Sales en-route for South Africa. Of the previous five to reach the racecourse only Spinning's year-younger sister Sun On The Spey failed to win. One of his close relatives, River Spey (by Mill Reef), won a listed race at Newbury and ran second in the Cheshire Oaks, while another by the same stallion, Dunninald, was almost as useful at up to a mile. *I. A. Balding*

SPINNING STEEL 6 b.g. Kinglet – Lasses Nightshade (Deadly Nightshade) [1992/3 16g⁴ 20g⁵ a20g⁵ c21gF c16m⁴ 16f* 17d³ 16f⁴ 20g] poor hurdler: won novice seller at Ludlow (no bid) in March: poor novice chaser: stays 2½m: acts on firm and dead going. *Martyn Meade*   c72 76

SPIN (NZ) 7 ch.g. Lakenheath (USA) – Casurina (NZ) (Oakville) [1992/3 F17s F16d 16spu a20gR] small, plain New Zealand-bred gelding: no sign of ability: refused final start. *D. Burchell*   – §

SPIN THE COIN 7 b.g. Scallywag – Furstin (Furry Glen) [1992/3 22mpu 17g⁵ 25vpu 22d⁴ 22f⁴ 23gF 25m] workmanlike gelding: poor novice hurdler: stays 2¾m: acts on firm and dead ground. *B. Preece*   72

SPIRITED HOLME (FR) 8 b.g. Gay Mecene (USA) – Lyphard's Holme (USA) (Lyphard (USA)) [1992/3 c21g⁵ c24g c25dpu] sturdy gelding: winning 2m hurdler/chaser: usually visored or blinkered. *D. L. Williams*   c– –

SPIRIT IN THE NITE (IRE) 4 b.g. Orchestra – Haut Lafite (Tamerlane) [1992/3 F17f² F17g² F17d] half-brother to several winners, including hurdler/chaser Camden Belle (by Camden Town): dam won at up to 1m in Ireland: second in NH Flat races at Sandown and Newbury in March: yet to race over hurdles. *J. T. Gifford*

SPIRIT LEVEL 5 ch.m. Sunley Builds – Tuneful Flutter (Orchestra) [1992/3 17spu 18s 18s⁵ 16g] sparely-made mare: novice hurdler: only form in seller on third outing: visored once. *J. R. Payne*   73

SPIRIT OF KIBRIS 8 ch.g. Quayside – Golden Shuil (Master Owen) [1992/3 16s* c17s² c16v² 16v⁴ c17sF c20f⁵ c19fpu c21f³] rather leggy, close-coupled gelding: fair hurdler: won handicap at Warwick in November: modest novice chaser: stays 2½m: suited by plenty of give in the ground: carries head high and sometimes fails to go through with effort: reportedly broke blood vessel penultimate start. *Mrs J. Pitman*   c97 § 104 §

SPIRITUALIST 7 ch.g. Simply Great (FR) – Parima (Pardao) [1992/3 21s³ 23m⁵ a16g⁴] angular gelding: very lightly-raced novice hurdler: poor form: stays 23f: acts on good to firm, soft ground and fibresand. *Mrs G. S. Plowright*   77

SPITFIRE JUBILEE 7 b.g. Chief Singer – Altana (Grundy) [1992/3 c19gur c24m⁴ c21m] well-made gelding: poor hurdler: novice hunter chaser: probably stays 3m: acts on firm and dead ground: blinkered twice. *Mrs L. A. Syckelmoore*   c83 –

SPLIT SECOND 4 b.g. Damister (USA) – Moment In Time (Without Fear (FR)) [1992/3 18m⁵ 18f² 16g² 18d² 18d 22d⁶ 20g] leggy gelding: no sign of ability on Flat for J. W. Watts: modest form when second in early-season juvenile hurdles: below form afterwards: should stay further than 2¼m: best effort on dead ground. *Mrs V. A. Aconley*   89

SPONSOR LIGHT 9 ch.g. Lighter – Sponsorship (Sparkler) [1992/3 21d c17v³ c17v² c17s⁶ c16g⁶] leggy, lengthy gelding: carries condition: winning hurdler: poor novice chaser: form only at around 2m: acts on heavy going. *J. L. Gledson*   c81 –

SPONTANEOUS PRIDE 5 b.g. Belfort (FR) – Seaknot (Perhapsburg) [1992/3 F17d] useful-looking gelding: sixth foal: half-brother to 3 poor animals: dam, well beaten in NH Flat race and only start over hurdles, sister to useful hurdler Sea Empress: eighth of 21 in NH Flat race at Sandown in October: yet to race over hurdles or fences. *K. C. Bailey*

SPOONHILL WOOD 7 ch.m. Celtic Cone – My Darling (Arctic Slave) [1992/3 c20v² c23vpu c20spu 22m² c23d⁶ c25s⁴ c18g² c23m³ c25mur]   c82 80 compact mare: poor novice hurdler/chaser: probably stays 3m: acts on good to firm and heavy ground: usually blinkered nowadays. *J. Wharton*

SPORTING IDOL   8 b.g. Mummy's Game – Village Idol (Blakeney) [1992/3 23g 21v^{pu}] leggy gelding: modest hurdler at best: ran badly in 1992/3: stays 2½m: acts on any going: blinkered once. *J. G. M. O'Shea*   –

SPORTING MARINER   11 b.g. Julio Mariner – Ma Griffe (Indian Ruler) [1992/3 c24s^4 c21d^{ur} c25g c27m^{pu}] rather sparely-made gelding: hunter chaser: no form in 1993: suited by test of stamina: probably acts on any ground: often a front runner. *D. R. Bloor*   c– –

SPORT LADY (USA)   4 b.f. Sportin' Life (USA) – Mazyoun (USA) (Blushing Groom (FR)) [1992/3 17v] fourth foal: half-sister to winning hurdler Eastern Whisper (by Arctic Tern): dam, placed at 6f and 7f, from family of Mysterious and J O Tobin: last in early-season juvenile hurdle on debut. *R. T. Juckes*   –

SPORT OF FOOLS (IRE)   4 b.f. Trojan Fen – Senouire (Shirley Heights) [1992/3 17v 17d* 17d* 22d 18g^2] plating-class maiden at 2 yrs: successful in 2 novice hurdles at Newton Abbot in April (first a claimer): good second in similar event at Exeter following month: should stay beyond 17f: acts on dead ground. *W. J. Reed*   99

SPORTSNEWS   11 b.g. New Member – Dicopin (Deauville II) [1992/3 c21m^4 c27d^F] workmanlike gelding: poor-jumping novice staying chaser: no form since 1989/90: sold 2,000 gns Malvern Junes Stakes: blinkered twice. *Mrs C. Lawrence*   c– x –

SPORTS VIEW   4 b.g. Mashhor Dancer (USA) – Persian Express (Persian Bold) [1992/3 17d^F 17d^6 16v^F 16s] compact gelding: modest staying maiden on Flat: easily best effort in juvenile hurdles on second start (not raced after December): yet to race beyond 17f: acts on dead going. *P. G. Murphy*   86

SPOTTED HEUGH   9 gr.g. Montreal Boy – Zo-Zo (Hamood) [1992/3 c21g^{pu}] bad maiden pointer: no show on steeplechasing debut. *C. Graham*   c–

SPREAD YOUR WINGS (IRE)   5 ch.m. Decent Fellow – The Wren's Nest (Wrekin Rambler) [1992/3 F16d^5 F18s^4] half-sister to winning Irish hurdler Le Roilelet (by Le Bavard): dam won on Flat and over hurdles in Ireland: signs of ability in NH Flat races: yet to race over hurdles or fences. *D. R. Gandolfo*

SPREE CROSS   7 b.g. Kemal (FR) – Danger Lady (Commando) [1992/3 c17d* c17g^F c21s^5 c16d* c17v^2 c16g^2 c17d^2 c16d^5 c16d^3 c16s*] sturdy gelding: fair handicap chaser: won at Hexham and Wetherby (trained until after then by W. A. Stephenson) in first half of season and Perth in April: sold 15,000 gns in May: pulls hard and best at around 2m: acts on heavy going. *P. Cheesbrough*   c110

SPRINGALEAK   8 b. or br.m. Lafontaine (USA) – Union Rules (Workboy) [1992/3 c24d^4 c25s^5 c24g^{pu}] leggy mare: winning hurdler: fairly useful chaser: ran badly last 2 starts: stays 25f: acts on any going: tends to run in snatches. *O. Sherwood*   c124 –

SPRING BASH   8 b.g. Crash Course – Spring Hat (Orchardist) [1992/3 24v^{pu} 21s 21v^{pu}] sparely-made gelding: very lightly-raced novice hurdler. *B. A. McMahon*   72

SPRING FLIGHT   10 b.g. Captain James – Late Swallow (My Swallow) [1992/3 22d^{pu} 16v 20d 17f^{pu}] close-coupled, smallish gelding: winning hurdler: trained first 2 starts by G. Charles-Jones: form only at 2m: probably acts on any ground. *R. Simpson*   71

SPRING FORWARD   9 b.h. Double Form – Forward Princess (USA) (Forward Pass) [1992/3 17d 17m^5 17f 20s a16g^{pu} 21f^6 21d] small, sparely-made horse: poor hurdler: sold out of R. Peacock's stable 950 gns Ascot March Sales after third start, out of Miss K. George's stable 1,200 gns Ascot May Sales after fifth: tried in blinkers and visor. *Mrs M. E. Long*   –

SPRING FUN 10 b.g. Over The River (FR) – Russian Fun (Zabeg) [1992/3 c27mᵖᵘ c27g⁵] sturdy gelding: winning hunter chaser: ran poorly in 1992/3: stays 25f. *H. Wellstead*

c82

SPRING GRASS 5 br.m. Pardigras – Spring River (Silly Season) [1992/3 F17f⁶] fifth foal: half-sister to a winner on Flat and 2 winning jumpers: dam in frame over 1½m and 2m: sixth of 15 in NH Flat race at Hereford in May: yet to race over hurdles or fences. *B. J. M. Ryall*

SPRINGHOLM 11 br.g. Mandalus – Lady Hiltop (Prince Hansel) [1992/3 c18m³ c18g³ c18s² c20s³ c20g³ c21f*] strong gelding: modest chaser nowadays: won 3-runner amateurs handicap at Sandown in March: stays 21f: probably acts on any going: races prominently and usually jumps well. *D. Nicholson*

c98
–

SPRINGLAKE'S LADY 7 b.m. Music Boy – North Pine (Import) [1992/3 17vᵖᵘ] sparely-made mare: of little account over hurdles, though won bad race in 1989/90: blinkered twice. *A. M. Forte*

–

SPRINGMOUNT 9 b.g. Mandalus – Jadini (Gombos (FR)) [1992/3 c24m⁴ c25gᵘʳ] strong ex-Irish gelding: poor form over hurdles: fourth in a hunter chase at Ludlow in March when trained by J. Swindells: subsequently won 2 points: stays 3m: acts on soft and good to firm ground. *Mrs Jan Wood*

c81
–

SPRINGVALE CRUSADE 10 b.g. Callernish – Harlem Lady (Arctic Slave) [1992/3 c21vᶠ c26dᵖᵘ 24g³ a24gᵖᵘ] small gelding: lightly-raced staying handicap hurdler: no form since 1990/1, including in novice chases: visored last 2 starts. *L. J. Codd*

c–
–

SPROWSTON BOY 10 ch.g. Dominion – Cavalier's Blush (King's Troop) [1992/3 21g⁴ 24m³] close-coupled, sparely-made gelding: usually unimpressive in appearance: quite useful handicap hurdler: finished lame on final start (February): stays 25f: acts on any going: jumps well: forces pace. *Miss L. A. Perratt*

126

SPRUCER 8 b.g. Prince Regent (FR) – Knollwood Court (Le Jean) [1992/3 c17s² c22s² c26sᵖᵘ] tall gelding: fair chaser: ran poorly final outing (December): effective at 2m when conditions are testing and stays 25f: best form with plenty of give in the ground. *Mrs I. McKie*

c107
–

SPUFFINGTON 5 b.g. Sula Bula – Pita (Raffingora) [1992/3 16v⁵ 18g²] good-topped gelding: fourth foal: dam plating-class maiden on Flat: close second in novice hurdle at Folkestone in February: will stay beyond 2¼m: will improve further and win a similar event. *J. T. Gifford*

95 p

SPUR BAY 6 b.g. Deep Run – Sweet Slievenamon (Arctic Slave) [1992/3 17dᶠ 16dᵖᵘ 16d] big, rather leggy gelding: disputing lead when falling 2 out in novice hurdle at Stratford in October, only sign of ability. *Mrs J. Pitman*

–

SPY HILL 7 b. or br.g. Over The River (FR) – Tarqogan's Rose (Tarqogan) [1992/3 c24g⁴ c27g³ c28gᵇᵈ c25m⁴ c25dᵖᵘ c24dᵖᵘ c26d² c26m*] tall, angular gelding: novice hurdler: modest chaser: blinkered only time, won novice event at Uttoxeter in June: stayed 27f: acted on good to firm and soft ground: dead. *Mrs S. A. Bramall*

c90
–

SPY'S DELIGHT 7 b.g. Idiot's Delight – Ida Spider (Ben Novus) [1992/3 c18mᶠ c16d⁴ c16v⁴ c17gᵖᵘ 16vᵖᵘ 16m] workmanlike, stocky gelding: novice hurdler, poor at best: no form over fences. *Mrs A. R. Hewitt*

c–
–

SQUADRON (CAN) 10 ch.g. Vice Regent (USA) – Quadrillion (USA) (Quadrangle) [1992/3 20mᵖᵘ] smallish, plain gelding: winning hurdler at up to 2¾m: yet to complete over fences: usually blinkered or visored. *B. Preece*

c–
–

SQUEEZE PLAY 8 b.g. Gleason (USA) – Cherry Leaf (Vulgan) [1992/3 c17f²] good-topped gelding: modest novice chaser: ran creditably in September: effective at around 2m and will probably stay 3m: probably acts on any ground: blinkered nowadays. *D. M. Grissell*

c88
–

SQUIBS HAM 6 b.g. Lighter – Gay Gussie (Bowsprit) [1992/3 17g] of little account. *G. Stickland*

–

SQUIRE SILK 4 b.g. Natroun (FR) – Rustle of Silk (General Assembly (USA)) [1992/3 F16d5 F17f] third foal: half-brother to winning hurdler Byzantine (by Damister): dam, modest maiden, from excellent family: signs of ability in NH Flat races: yet to race over hurdles. *Miss S. E. Hall*

SQUIRES PRIVILEGE (IRE) 5 b.g. Green Shoon – Road Scraper (Proverb) [1992/3 25g 21d 22s 25g4] rangy gelding: chasing type: third foal: brother to Irish novice jumper Cooladerra Lady: dam unraced: winning pointer in Ireland: poor novice hurdler: stays 25f: acts on dead ground. *J. J. O'Neill*　　69

SQUIRES TALE (IRE) 5 b.g. Kemal (FR) – Darren's Heather (Menelek) [1992/3 F16m* F17m3] workmanlike gelding with scope: fifth foal: half-brother to winning Irish hurdler Higcham (by Le Moss), who stays 3m: dam unraced: 33/1-winner of NH Flat race at Nottingham in March: third at Cheltenham following month: yet to race over hurdles or fences. *B. S. Rothwell*

SRADARA (IRE) 5 ch.m. Camden Town – Lisdoonvarna (Miami Springs) [1992/3 17dpu a16gpu] sturdy mare: first living foal: dam lightly-raced Irish maiden: showed nothing over hurdles. *T. Dyer*　　–

SRIVIJAYA 6 b.h. Kris – Princess Pati (Top Ville) [1992/3 16g 16s2 17g3 16d3 c16g* c16gF c17d2 c16gF 17m5 c17g] good-bodied horse: fair handicap hurdler: won novice chase at Catterick in February: races only at around 2m: probably acts on any going: blinkered once: usually held up and often finishes weakly. *Mrs M. Reveley*　　c104 113

STACKHOUSE BOY 4 b.g. Sweet Monday – City's Sister (Maystreak) [1992/3 16d 16s] tall, leggy gelding: third foal: brother to Sweet City and half-brother to Better Times Ahead (by Scallywag), both useful hurdlers and winning chasers: dam, winner at up to 13f on Flat and in frame at 2m over hurdles, from good jumping family: not at all knocked about when behind in juvenile hurdles around turn of year. *G. Richards*　　– p

STAGE PLAYER 7 b.g. Ile de Bourbon (USA) – Popkins (Romulus) [1992/3 20g 21s5 21g5 21f2 23mpu 21f2 21mpu] small, workmanlike gelding: fairly useful hurdler: pulled up lame on fifth and final starts: stays 3m: suited by a sound surface (acts on firm ground). *Miss S. J. Wilton*　　118

STAGGERING (IRE) 4 bl.f. Daring March – Sipped (Ballyciptic) [1992/3 F16m F16g5] half-sister to fair staying hurdlers Sip of Orange and Celtic Breeze and Irish NH Flat race winner I Am (all by Celtic Cone): dam, winning hurdler, stayed 3m: showed a little ability in NH Flat races: yet to race over hurdles. *M. P. Naughton*　　–

STAG NIGHT 4 ch.g. Good Times (ITY) – Deer Forest (Huntercombe) [1992/3 18gur 16spu] smallish, close-coupled gelding: of little account on Flat nowadays: sold out of C. Tinkler's stable 1,500 gns Doncaster June Sales: no sign of ability in selling hurdles: visored second outing. *A. W. Potts*　　–

STAGS FELL 8 gr.g. Step Together (USA) – Honey's Queen (Pals Passage) [1992/3 c21dF c17dF c16dF c21gF 21m c17s4 c18mF] leggy, rather angular gelding: fair chaser at up to 2½m at best: jumps badly and no longer worth a rating: blinkered once. *G. M. Moore*　　cxx –

STAGSHAW BELLE 9 b.m. Royal Fountain – Besciamella (Foggy Bell) [1992/3 23gur 23d6 c16g c17d3 c23d4 c20gF 22gpu] leggy, sparely-made mare: poor novice hurdler/chaser: stays 2¾m: acts on heavy going. *Mrs S. C. Bradburne*　　c83 –

STAMP DUTY 6 b.g. Sunyboy – Royal Seal (Privy Seal) [1992/3 17s5 20v6] rangy gelding: chasing type: lightly-raced novice hurdler, modest form: should stay beyond 21f: acts on soft ground. *N. J. Henderson*　　89

STAN CARTER 5 gr.g. Broadsword (USA) – Stancombe Lass (Rugantino) [1992/3 F18v6 aF16g 24v 22s 28mpu] sparely-made gelding: first foal: dam winning pointer/hunter chaser: no sign of ability. *C. Smith*　　–

STAND AT EASE 8 b.g. The Brianstan – Plush (Lombard (GER)) [1992/3 17m5] stocky gelding: poor novice hurdler: sold 2,500 gns Ascot　　–

September Sales: unlikely to stay much beyond 2m: probably acts on any going. *R. H. Buckler*

STANDISH 5 b.g. Starch Reduced – Rose Standish (Gulf Pearl) [1992/3 F16v 16fᵖᵘ] first foal: dam, winning stayer on Flat, poor novice over hurdles: no sign of ability. *B. P. J. Baugh* —

STANDSTILL 6 b.g. Broadsword (USA) – Hazeldean (St Paddy) [1992/3 17d 16g] lengthy gelding: 2m novice hurdler, modest at best: dead. *Mrs S. J. Smith* —

STANE STREET (IRE) 5 b.m. Gorytus (USA) – Tumble Ria (Tumble Wind (USA)) [1992/3 17m 21f] small, angular mare: winning selling hurdler: stiff tasks in 1992/3: stays 19f: best form with give in the ground. *R. T. Phillips* —

STANMAR LAD 4 ch.g. Stanford – Marcela (Reform) [1992/3 F14g] sturdy, compact gelding: half-brother to several winners, including fairly useful hurdlers Tern (by Blakeney) and Persian Style (by Persian Bold): dam useful winner over 6f at 2 yrs: well beaten in NH Flat race at Market Rasen in April: yet to race over hurdles. *D. Esden*

STAPLEFORD LADY 5 ch.m. Bairn (USA) – Marie Galante (FR) (King of The Castle (USA)) [1992/3 18f5 17d3 17g5 17v6 21v6 18s a22g4 23d6 22d 17s3 20m6 18mF] leggy, narrow mare: maiden plater over hurdles: probably stays 2½m and acts on any going: blinkered once. *R. J. Manning* | 68

STAR ACTOR 7 b.g. Pollerton – Play The Part (Deep Run) [1992/3 c21dF c25d3 c23gᵘʳ c32mᵘʳ] rangy gelding: maiden hurdler: fair novice chaser: will prove best at up to 3m: acts on dead ground: sketchy jumper. *N. J. Henderson* | c99 —

STAR BLEND 11 ch.g. Royal Blend – Star Speaker (Philemon) [1992/3 c27gᵖᵘ c21mᵖᵘ] very lightly raced and no sign of ability. *Mrs L. C. Jewell* | c– —

STAR CATCH 4 b.g. Skyliner – Let Slip (Busted) [1992/3 16g 16d] leggy, angular gelding: half-brother to winning 2m selling hurdler Susan Henchard (by Auction Ring): once-raced on Flat: poor form in juvenile hurdles in first half of season. *W. Carter* | 70

STAR CROSSED (NZ) 8 b.g. March Legend (NZ) – Etoile (NZ) (Star Performer) [1992/3 c22g6] smallish, well-made gelding: successful on Flat in New Zealand, and in a point in February: jumped none too fluently when sixth in novice hunter chase at Nottingham later in month. *S. A. Brookshaw* | c– p

STAREMBER LAD 9 b.g. New Member – Star Beauty (Jock Scot) [1992/3 c24s2] tall gelding: useful hunter chaser at best: respectable second at Chepstow in February: subsequently won 4 points: should stay beyond 3m: acts on soft going. *K. Cumings* | c99

STAR HILL 6 b.g. Star Appeal – Pook's Hill (High Top) [1992/3 17gᵖᵘ 17mᵖᵘ] one-time fairly useful miler on Flat: showed nothing over hurdles. *J. C. Poulton* | —

STARLAP 9 b.g. Pry – Soldier's Friend (King's Troop) [1992/3 c20g4 c21g2 c21g4 c19f3 c17m2 c17m* c18g2 c17d4] rangy gelding: moderate chaser: trained first 3 outings by Mrs A. Farrant: won handicap at Towcester in May: best at around 2m: acts on good to firm and dead ground: hooded final start (ran badly): often finishes weakly. *R. J. Hodges* | c94 —

STARMINE 7 ch.g. Jasmine Star – Creation Lady (Cavo Doro) [1992/3 22sᵖᵘ 20s c21s* c25sᵘʳ c27dᵘʳ c21d4 c26g4 c21g5] leggy gelding: no form over hurdles: won claiming chase at Leicester in January: below that form afterwards: should stay beyond 21f: acts on soft ground: sketchy jumper. *J. Parkes* | c95 —

STAR MOVER 4 ch.f. Move Off – Star Attention (Northfields (USA)) [1992/3 18m 17mᵇᵈ 18g 16s 18m 18d3] poor form at 2 yrs and over hurdles: half-sister to winning 2m hurdler Primrose Star (by Le Coq d'Or): poor form at 2 yrs and over hurdles: trained first 4 starts by W. A. Stephenson: sold 1,400 gns in May: best effort over 2¼m on dead ground. *P. Cheesbrough* | 76

STAR OF ITALY   6 b.g. Superlative – Arianna Aldini (Habitat) [1992/3 c85
c18d⁴ c16v* c16dᵇᵈ c19sᵖᵘ c16s³ c16v*] compact gelding: novice hurdler: –
won novice chases at Hereford in November (handicap) and April: likely to
prove best at around 2m: acts on heavy going. *Andrew Turnell*

STAR OF KUWAIT   9 b.m. Crooner – Miss Kuwait (The Brianstan) c78
[1992/3 a20g c24gᵘʳ c21m³ c24f⁴] leggy, sparely-made mare: winning –
hurdler: poor novice chaser: stays 21f: acts on any going: occasionally
blinkered. *K. O. Cunningham-Brown*

STAR OF OUGHTERARD   8 b.g. Horage – Corny Story (Oats) c–
[1992/3 c26vᵘʳ c27vᵘʳ c16v⁵ 22g⁴ 23mᵖᵘ 22dᵖᵘ 22f⁶ 21f] leggy gelding: 86
moderate hurdler: no form over fences: stays 2¾m: acts on hard going:
usually blinkered or visored: sometimes looks unenthusiastic. *T. P.
McGovern*

STAR OF OVAC   10 b.g. Ovac (ITY) – Petit Millie (Light Brigade) c–
[1992/3 c17mᵖᵘ] poor maiden jumper. *Grenville Richards* –

STAR OF SCREEN (USA)   13 b.g. Vaguely Noble – Slip Screen (USA) c– x
(Silent Screen (USA)) [1992/3 c26mᵖᵘ] leggy gelding: winning staying – x
chaser: sometimes blinkered: poor jumper. *J. C. S. Hickman*

STAR OF THE GLEN   7 b.g. Glenstal (USA) – Bamstar (Relko) [1992/3
17g³ 16g* 16m* 17g³ 16g² 16d* 17g 17s 16m* 16f² 17mˢᵘ 16fᵖᵘ] lengthy 121
gelding: fairly useful hurdler: won 2 races each at Ludlow and Wincanton in
1992/3: races around 2m nowadays: acts on firm and dead going: reluctant to
race when blinkered final start: held up. *Mrs J. Pitman*

STAR QUEST   6 b.h. Rainbow Quest (USA) – Sarah Siddons (FR) (Le
Levanstell) [1992/3 17s 21vᵖᵘ 21f⁵] leggy, lengthy horse: winning 2½m –
hurdler: no form in 1992/3. *J. R. Jenkins*

STAR'S DELIGHT   11 gr.g. John de Coombe – Vanity Surprise c?
(Blakeney) [1992/3 c16sᵖᵘ c16v³ c16d⁵ c16g⁴ c17mᶠ] leggy, lightly-made –
gelding: smart chaser at best: ran badly in 1992/3 (in frame in small fields):
stays 2½m: acts on heavy going and good to firm: usually jumps well: game.
M. C. Pipe

STARSTREAK   6 b.h. Comedy Star (USA) – Kochia (Firestreak) [1992/3
21m*] thrice-raced hurdler: easy winner of novice event at Perth in August: 95 +
stays 21f: acts on good to firm ground: blinkered on hurdling debut. *Mrs M.
Reveley*

STAR THYME   6 b.m. Point North – Floraventure (Floribunda) [1992/3
16s 16d⁵ 16m⁵] smallish, good-topped mare: first form over hurdles when 69
fifth in novice claimer in May on final start: wears tongue strap. *J. Mackie*

STAR TRACKER   6 br.m. Lochnager – Star Attention (Northfields c–
(USA)) [1992/3 17m⁴ 18d⁴ c16sᵖᵘ 18d] only form when last in early-season 77
selling hurdle on second start. *W. A. Stephenson*

STATAJACK (IRE)   5 b.g. King of Clubs – Statira (Skymaster) [1992/3
16d⁵ 17v⁵ 16d 17s³ 17d⁶] sparely-made gelding: fairly useful hurdler: races 117
at around 2m: probably acts on heavy going: usually blinkered nowadays:
carries head high and looks a difficult ride. *D. R. C. Elsworth*

STATED CASE   8 b.g. Beldale Flutter (USA) – High Point Lady (CAN) c–
(Knightly Dawn (USA)) [1992/3 28sᵖᵘ c24g⁵ 21v* 16d⁵ 16m⁶ 28g* 24g* 113
25d* 28m*] rather sparely-made gelding: fair hurdler nowadays: awarded
claimer at Towcester in February and successful in handicaps at Sedgefield
(2, one a seller (no bid)), Hexham and Carlisle in the spring: novice chaser:
needs further than 2m and stays very well: acts on heavy and good to firm
going: usually blinkered nowadays: none too fluent over fences. *M. H.
Easterby*

STATELY LOVER   10 b.g. Free State – Maid In Love (Sky Gipsy) c105
[1992/3 c26d³ c26s³ c21v⁵ c21vᶠ 22m² 22d⁶] big, rangy gelding: fair 108
hurdler/chaser: stays 3¼m: acts on good to firm and heavy going:
sometimes visored. *S. E. Sherwood*

'Certain Justice' Challenge Cup (Handicap Chase), Fontwell—
course specialist St Athans Lad makes all

STATE OF AFFAIRS 6 b.g. Free State – Trigamy (Tribal Chief) [1992/3 17s 17v⁴ 17v² 17s² 16s*] smallish gelding: modest middle-distance stayer on Flat: best effort over hurdles when easily winning novice handicap at Nottingham in February: raced only on soft and heavy ground. *C. A. Horgan*

96 p

ST ATHANS GIRL 10 b.m. Record Run – Greasby Girl (John Splendid) [1992/3 c19fᵖᵘ c16g⁶ c17sᵖᵘ] light-framed mare: of no account. *R. Curtis*

c–
–

ST ATHANS LAD 8 b.g. Crooner – Greasby Girl (John Splendid) [1992/3 c17m² c18f* c18g* c18f² c18g² c19f* c18d* c21sᵘʳ 18v 18g³ c19m* c18g* c18g* c19f* c18f*] good-bodied gelding: novice hurdler: much improved over fences and had a magnificent season, winning 4 novice events (2 of them handicaps) and 5 handicaps, all at Fontwell: stays 2½m: acts on any going: best blinkered nowadays: races freely and usually makes running: tough and genuine. *R. Curtis*

c121
85

STATION EXPRESS (IRE) 5 b.g. Rusticaro (FR) – Vallee d'O (FR) (Polyfoto) [1992/3 18dᵖᵘ 18g 18d* 18v⁵ a18g 18dᵇᵈ 18g 16g 18g⁴ 16g* 17g² 22m* 16g² 23f⁵] small, sparely-made gelding: selling hurdler: successful in handicaps (no bid) at Sedgefield in November, Hexham in March and Sedgefield (valuable event) in May: effective at 2m and stays 2¾m: acts on good to firm and dead ground: visored once. *B. Ellison*

78

STAUNCH FRIEND (USA) 5 b.g. Secreto (USA) – Staunch Lady (USA) (Staunchness) [1992/3 17g* 17d* 17s² 17s* 20g 17m 16g*]

164

If the Cheltenham National Hunt Festival ever was synonymous with the mud flying, it certainly isn't now. In the last ten years, our assessment of the going on Champion Hurdle day (sometimes at variance with the official description) has been once soft, once good to soft, four times good and four times good to firm. The seven years before that, contrastingly, saw two runnings on good to soft, two on soft and three on heavy ground. Conceptions of the ideal Cheltenham horse have had to be adjusted, not least those gained from the lengthy round of trials. One firmly in the Champion Hurdle reckoning at the turn of the year, when the ground was soft, was Staunch Friend. On heavy ground at Punchestown the previous April he'd looked a strong contender, the best of the 1991/2 batch of juveniles, when registering a facile twelve-length and nine-length victory over Muir Station and Duke of Monmouth in the Guinness Trophy Champion Four-Year-Old Hurdle. His four runs before Christmas in the latest season did little to temper enthusiasm for him; he was beaten only once. That was at the hands of Mighty Mogul in the Gerry Feilden at Newbury, the margin four lengths with Staunch Friend giving 3 lb and the pair fifteen lengths clear. Mighty Mogul's emergence as the season's top hurdler in the next month eased any disappointment with the result. More perturbing was the way in which Staunch Friend had seemed an assured winner, stalking Mighty Mogul until taking the last none too fluently and giving second-best almost immediately afterwards. The opposition was far less exacting for Staunch Friend's three successes and he started at odds on for all three. The Flavel-Leisure Four-Year-Old Hurdle at Newbury saw him hardly off the bridle to win by twelve lengths; he showed a clean pair of heels to Al Mutahm and Duke of Monmouth in a late sprint for the ASW Hurdle at Cheltenham; and the three-runner Horse Racing Abroad Hurdle at Chepstow had his superiority accurately reflected by a starting price of 5/1 on.

The first of those runs was on good ground, the remainder on a soft surface, and Staunch Friend looked as if he still had more to give. However, having stood at 10/1 for the Champion at New Year, Staunch Friend started the race as a 20/1-shot. This was one of the Champion Hurdles run on top-of-the-ground and confidence in him was further dented by his last of seven, well beaten, in a valuable race at Rome in January. We did not have a representative at Capannelle that day, so commenting on the state of the ground and explanations for his poor showing is problematical, but it was reported that Staunch Friend was never going well. We can well believe it, because that was certainly the case at Cheltenham; not counting the tailed-off Ruling, Staunch Friend was last by halfway, and remained there.

This year's Champion field was a pretty quirky collection, several of whom ended the season with badly tarnished reputations. Staunch Friend was threatening to become one of them as he lined up for the Friendly Hotels Scottish Champion Hurdle at Ayr, the field including four others from Cheltenham one month earlier in Royal Derbi (second), Flown (eighth), Jinxy Jack (ninth) and Ruling, and completed by the Tote Gold Trophy runner-up Native Mission. Flown gave a poor, moody display and Ruling another characterful performance, but this was Staunch Friend's moment of redemption. A good jump at the last in the back straight, the fourth last, saw him go a close second and at the second last he held a slight lead. Royal Derbi was moving well at that stage but his run petered out shortly afterwards and Native Mission emerged as the chief danger, neither

Friendly Hotels Scottish Champion Hurdle, Ayr—
Staunch Friend leads Native Mission over the last,
chased by Jinxy Jack (almost hidden) and Royal Derbi

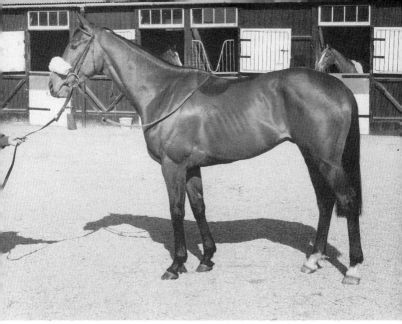

Mr B. Schmidt-Bodner's "Staunch Friend"

taking the last in his stride before Staunch Friend was driven out to
establish a length-and-a-half advantage at the line. Ruling, putting his best
foot forward far too late, was another half length back in third.

			Northern Dancer (b 1961)	Nearctic
Staunch Friend (USA) (b.g. 1988)	Secreto (USA) (b 1981)			Natalma
		Betty's Secret (ch 1977)		Secretariat
				Betty Loraine
	Staunch Lady (USA) (b 1968)	Staunchness (b 1962)		Bold Ruler
				Tiny Request
		Fee Fee Girl (ch 1961)		Johns Chic
				Sunny Boo

The ground at Ayr was good, and Staunch Friend's prospects almost
certainly depend on his having some give in the ground. He goes well when
conditions are very testing, and he should stay two and a half miles. Staunch
Friend's American Flat-race pedigree was described in *Chasers & Hurdlers
1991/2*. Staunch Lady had produced at least seven winners before him,
including the Grade 1-placed Sunny Bay (by Northern Baby) who has done
well at stud with the Prix d'Ispahan third Jalaajel and the very useful 1987
two-year-old Suntrap. Staunch Friend began his racing days carrying the
colours of Sheikh Mohammed trained by John Oxx in Ireland, and won a
maiden at Leopardstown. As to his future, the possibility of a campaign over
fences was mentioned by his trainer in the aftermath to the Scottish
Champion Hurdle. Staunch Friend obviously has the ability to win races in
that sphere, but the same can be said of him over hurdles where, on his day,
he isn't far off the best around. *M. H. Tompkins*

707

STAUNCH RIVAL (USA) 6 b.g. Sir Ivor – Crystal Bright (Bold Lad (IRE)) [1992/3 22g² 26g² 26g² 22d* 23s* 21s 25v 22m⁴ 24s 24g⁵ 24f4] neat gelding: fair handicap hurdler: won at Sandown (conditional jockeys) and Windsor in first half of season, and twice ran well in second half: will stay beyond 3m: acts on good to firm and soft ground. *G. Thorner*   114

STAY AWAKE 7 ch.g. Anfield – Djimbaran Bay (Le Levanstell) [1992/3 c18m³ c18m c18d⁶ c18m⁶ c18s² c16d² c16m⁶ 18m² 18d³ 16f* 16g*]lengthy, good-topped gelding: fair handicap hurdler/chaser: twice won by short head over hurdles at Wetherby in May: best at around 2m: probably acts on any going: blinkered twice in 1989/90, and on seventh outing (trained until after then by J. J. O'Neill): let down by his jumping over fences. *Mrs M. Reveley*   c101 x / 115

STAY ON TRACKS 11 gr.g. Roselier (FR) – Bee In Bonnet (Track Spare) [1992/3 c26sᶠ c25g⁴ c25g³ c27d⁴ c24spu c28d⁶ c25g⁴ c24d* c24m³ c33gpu] strong, compact gelding: fairly useful chaser nowadays: trained until after fourth outing by W. A. Stephenson: won handicap at Haydock in February: sold 13,000 gns in May: effective at 3m to 3½m: best with give in the ground: blinkered once. *P. Cheesbrough*   c118 / –

STAYWITHME 8 ch.g. Tumble Gold – Willetta (Will Somers) [1992/3 c26vpu c19vF c21spu] strong ex-Irish gelding: first foal: dam winning Irish pointer: showed nothing over fences. *R. J. O'Sullivan*   c–

ST BRAD (IRE) 5 ch.g. Sallust – Lohunda Lady (Ballymore) [1992/3 F16s] compact gelding: fourth foal: half-brother to 2 Flat winners and to winning Irish hurdler Muck 'N' Brass (by Welsh Saint): dam Irish Flat and hurdles winner: tailed off in NH Flat race at Warwick in February: yet to race over hurdles or fences. *O. Sherwood*

STEEL CONGRESS 6 gr.g. Godswalk (USA) – My First Lady (Ballymore) [1992/3 17m⁵ 16f 17m⁶ 16d² 20g⁵] sparely-made gelding: poor novice hurdler: sold out of D. Moffatt's stable 1,800 gns Doncaster October Sales after third start: best efforts at 2m on dead ground: dead. *J. J. Birkett*   74

STEEL DANCE 5 b.g. Mashhor Dancer (USA) – Damaska (USA) (Damascus (USA)) [1992/3 20v 18g⁴ 18g] rather sparely-made gelding: no form over hurdles. *Miss H. C. Knight*   –

STEELE JUSTICE 9 ch.g. Avocat – Strandhill (Bargello) [1992/3 c24m² c25m² c25g⁴] angular gelding: fairly useful hunter chaser: second at Edinburgh (to The Red One) and Kelso (to Davy Blake): stays 25f: acts on firm going. *W. Manners*   c99 / –

STEEL RIVER 6 b.h. Be My Native (USA) – Oystons Propweekly (Swing Easy (USA)) [1992/3 21vpu] leggy horse: lightly-raced novice hurdler, poor at best. *Bob Jones*   –

STEEPLE JACK 6 b.g. Pardigras – Mountain Mear (Giolla Mear) [1992/3 23s⁵ 22mpu] leggy gelding: modest hurdler: ran respectably in January, badly in March: stays 23f: acts on soft going, possibly unsuited by good to firm. *K. Bishop*   93

STEF THE GREEK 6 br.g. Teofane – Bee In Bonnet (Track Spare) [1992/3 18m² 17m³] close-coupled, sparely-made gelding: modest novice hurdler: stayed 2¼m: acted on good to firm ground: dead. *M. D. Hammond*   88

STE-JEN (IRE) 4 b.g. Stalker – Bellinor (Le Levanstell) [1992/3 18g* 17gᶠ 17g⁵ 16s 16s* 17s² 16s* 17g² 17m³] sparely-made gelding: twice-raced on Flat: won juvenile hurdle at Cartmel in August and 2 claimers at Leicester in February: ideally needs testing conditions at 2m and should stay beyond 2¼m: acts on soft and good to firm going. *G. M. Moore*   106

ST ENTON 8 b.g. Record Token – Nuse Avella (Jimsun) [1992/3 c25mpu] pulled up in a point and a novice hunter chase. *R. Green*   c–

STEPFASTER 8 gr.m. Step Together (USA) – Pollyfaster (Polyfoto) [1992/3 c21g² c20gur c25g² c21d³ c26spu c20gᶠ c24m² c21sᶠ c20g³ c21m⁴ c20g* c21lf³ c21lg⁶ c23m*] leggy mare: fair handicap chaser: trained until after fifth outing by W. A. Stephenson, sold out of P. Cheesbrough's stable 10,500 gns in May after twelfth: won at Market Rasen in April and June: c104 / –

effective at 2½m and probably stays 27f: acts on hard and dead going. *Miss L. C. Siddall*

STERLING BUCK (USA) 6 b.g. Buckfinder (USA) – Aged (USA) (Olden Times) [1992/3 16g² 17d 16m³ 16v⁴ c20dᵖᵘ 20d⁶ 17d 22f² 22mᵘʳ 22d 20m] leggy, close-coupled gelding: poor novice hurdler: once-raced over fences: stays 2¾m: probably acts on any ground: blinkered once. *G. H. Yardley*
c–
79

STEVE FORD 4 gr.g. Another Realm – Sky Miss (Skymaster) [1992/3 F16d⁶ F14m] half-brother to 3 winners, including fair 7f and 1m winner Emad (by Hot Spark): dam poor half-sister to very smart Flat performer Sexton Blake: showed a little ability in NH Flat races: yet to race over hurdles. *P. D. Evans*

STEVEYVUL 9 ro.h. Whistlefield – Persian Water (Waterfall) [1992/3 17s⁴ 17d*] lengthy, workmanlike horse: moderate hurdler, lightly raced: won handicap at Newton Abbot in April: fell only outing over fences: should stay beyond 17f: acts on firm and dead going, well beaten on soft. *O. O'Neill*
c–
98

STEY SUNY 6 ch.g. Sunyboy – Stey Brae (Malicious) [1992/3 19m] angular gelding: second foal: dam very lightly-raced novice hurdler: tailed off in early-season novice event on hurdling debut. *R. Dickin*
–

STILL DANCING 7 b.g. Bay Express – Liberation (Native Prince) [1992/3 17d 17f] of little account. *J. S. Hubbuck*
–

STILL HOPEFUL 4 b.f. Broadsword (USA) – Still Marching (Riboboy (USA)) [1992/3 F12d aF16g⁶ F14s] small, sparely-made filly: first foal: dam showed ability at 2 yrs: behind in NH Flat races. *P. S. Felgate*
–

STING IN THE TAIL 4 b.f. Scorpio (FR) – Polola (Aragon) [1992/3 18f 18gᵖᵘ] workmanlike filly: well beaten on Flat and over hurdles. *P. R. Hedger*
–

STIRLING EXPRESS 8 ch.g. Blue Refrain – Great Aunt Ivy (Bay Express) [1992/3 c17dᶠ c20gᵖᵘ c16sᶠ] lengthy gelding: fair chaser: probable winner when falling last at Catterick in December on final start: likely to prove best at up to 2½m: acts on any going: sketchy jumper. *J. Mackie*
c105
–

STIRRUP CUP 9 b.g. Majestic Maharaj – Gold Gift (Gold Rod) [1992/3 c26v* c26v* c28s* c27v* c25s* c23d* c25mᵖᵘ] leggy gelding: developed
c123 +
–

Singer & Friedlander Handicap Chase, Uttoxeter—
Stirrup Cup (No. 4) is all out to get the better of Kentish Piper

into a fairly useful chaser in 1992/3, winning novice event at Plumpton and handicaps on same course, Nottingham (2), Newton Abbot and Uttoxeter: stays well: acts well in the mud, probably unsuited by good to firm going: front runner: usually jumps well: a great credit to his trainer. *C. R. Egerton*

ST JOHN'S HILL 5 ch.g. Norwick (USA) – Dame Nellie (Dominion) [1992/3 F17g⁴ 17d 17g 16v⁶] small, sparely-made gelding: soundly beaten over hurdles. *R. J. Hodges*   –

ST LAYCAR 8 b.g. St Columbus – Lady Carinya (Heswall Honey) [1992/3 c26mᵇᵈ] modest pointer: brought down sixth in hunter chase in May. *G. B. Tarry*   c–

STONE MADNESS 9 br.m. Yukon Eric (CAN) – Mingwyn Wood (Pirate King) [1992/3 23s⁶ c21s 21vᵖᵘ] small mare: poor staying selling hurdler: no aptitude for chasing. *A. R. Davison*   c– x –

STONE WARRIOR 6 b.g. Claude Monet (USA) – My Haven (Godswalk (USA)) [1992/3 aF16g] second foal: half-brother to maiden plater Madonnina (by King of Spain): dam 2-y-o 7f winner: tailed off in NH Flat race at Southwell in February: sold 1,900 gns Doncaster May Sales: yet to race over hurdles or fences. *Mrs A. Swinbank*

STONEY BROOK 5 ch.g. Meadowbrook – True Friend (Bilsborrow) [1992/3 F16d³ F17g] good-topped gelding: half-brother to winning staying chaser Truely Royal (by Royal Fountain): dam winning hurdler: third in NH Flat race at Haydock in February: well beaten following month: yet to race over hurdles or fences. *A. Eubank*

STOP ON RED 6 b.g. Rainbow Quest (USA) – Danger Ahead (Mill Reef (USA)) [1992/3 16v 16vᵖᵘ 20f] leggy gelding: no sign of ability over hurdles. *A. J. Chamberlain*   –

STOPROVERITATE 4 ch.f. Scorpio (FR) – Luscinia (Sing Sing) [1992/3 16s 16s⁵ 16m⁶] workmanlike filly: half-sister to winning French jumper Junior Royal (by Ribero): fair at around 1m on Flat: poor form over hurdles: barely stays 2m. *S. G. Norton*   80

STORM ALERT 7 b.g. Strong Gale – Jet Travel (Deep Run) [1992/3 c18m* c16d* c16d* c16s* c17s* c16d* c17m³] lengthy gelding: progressive chaser, useful already: unbeaten in his first 6 races in 1992/3, in handicaps at Stratford, Warwick, Ludlow, Newbury and Sandown and minor event at Nottingham: third to Space Fair in valuable handicap at Cheltenham in March on final start: usually races at around 2m but should stay further: acts on good to firm and soft ground: sound jumper: has a turn of foot and is held up: genuine and consistent. *Andrew Turnell*   c143 p –

Elmbridge Handicap Chase, Sandown—the second last, where Storm Alert is still held up behind Fragrant Dawn

Lt. Col. W. Whetherly's "Storm Alert"

STORM DRUM 4 ch.g. Celestial Storm (USA) – Bushti Music (Bustino) [1992/3 a16g⁴ 17d³ 17s* 17s² 16f* 16m² 22f⁶] half-brother to winning staying hurdler Mandika (by Flash of Steel): modest middle-distance performer on Flat: sold out of P. Makin's stable 6,200 gns Newmarket Autumn Sales: won juvenile hurdle at Plumpton and novice hurdle at Ludlow in the spring: should stay beyond 17f (ran poorly over 2¾m): probably acts on any going: blinkered last 3 starts: races lazily. *K. C. Bailey*   **100**

STORM DUST 4 b.g. Celestial Storm (USA) – Mary Sunley (Known Fact (USA)) [1992/3 16g* 17dᵘʳ 17v² 17s⁴ 16d* 17m 17g³] small, light-bodied, close-coupled gelding: fair middle-distance performer on Flat: won juvenile hurdles at Kempton in October and Windsor in February: also ran very well when placed, in juvenile handicap at Ascot on final start: will stay beyond 17f: acts on heavy going, possibly unsuited by good to firm. *J. R. Fanshawe*   **129**

STORM FLIGHT 7 b.g. Strong Gale – Cacador's Magnet (Chinatown) [1992/3 c21dᴿ] sturdy gelding: well beaten in novice hurdles: refused third on chasing debut. *K. C. Bailey*   **c–** / **–**

STORMHEAD 5 ch.g. Move Off – Young Lamb (Sea Hawk II) [1992/3 17g⁵ 17v* 17s* 17g³ 22dᵖᵘ] unfurnished gelding: won novice hurdles at Newton Abbot in December and Ascot in January: ran as though something amiss final start: suited by testing conditions when racing at 2m and should stay further: acts on heavy going (won NH Flat race on firm): races up with pace. *O. Sherwood*   **108**

STORMING RUN (IRE) 5 b.g. Strong Gale – Beauty Run (Deep Run) [1992/3 21gᵖᵘ 16d] angular gelding: first foal: dam won NH Flat race and placed over hurdles in Ireland: no sign of ability. *P. T. Dalton*   **–**

STORM RISK 4 ch.c. Risk Me (FR) – Lightning Legend (Lord Gayle (USA)) [1992/3 17vᶠ 16sᵖᵘ a16g a16g] rather sparely-made colt: maiden on Flat: no form over hurdles. *J. C. Tuck*   **–**

STORM WARRIOR 8 b.g. Main Reef – Spadilla (Javelot) [1992/3 a18g^{ur} a18g^3 a24g 17d^5 a21g^5 21d^{pu}] leggy gelding: poor hurdler/novice chaser: stays 3m: acts on any going: wears blinkers: jumps fences poorly. *B. Preece* — c– x 73

STORMY DREAMS 8 b.m. Strong Gale – Dreamello (Bargello) [1992/3 c21g^F] rather lightly-built mare: winning hurdler: fatally injured on chasing debut: stayed 2¾m: acted on good to firm ground. *Mrs M. Reveley* — c–

STORMY FASHION 6 b.g. Strong Gale – Belle Chanel (Moyrath Jet) [1992/3 16v^{pu}] big, rangy gelding: chasing type with plenty of scope: first foal: dam, winning Irish hurdler/chaser, stayed 3m: pulled up in novice hurdle in January on debut. *M. McCormack* — –

STORMY PETREL (IRE) 4 br.f. Strong Gale – Gorryelm (Arctic Slave) [1992/3 F16m^5 F16g^4] sister to Irish NH Flat race winner Strong Hurricane, and half-sister to winning jumpers Simply Sally (by Over The River), The Cobalt Unit (by Deep Run) and Hillcrest Lady (by Kambalda): dam, a maiden, is daughter of a winning hurdler: signs of ability in late-season NH Flat races: yet to race over hurdles. *P. T. Walwyn* — –

STORMY SUNSET 6 br.m. Strong Gale – Last Sunset (Deep Run) [1992/3 17v^{pu} 22v^{pu} 16v 17d^5 18d^{bd} 17m^F] lengthy, unfurnished mare: would have finished second at Newton Abbot in May but for falling last, first form in novice hurdles. *W. W. Dennis* — 78

STORMY SWAN 7 ch.g. Deep Run – Sea Cygnet (Menelek) [1992/3 17d 21s 16s 22g^4] sturdy gelding: poor novice hurdler: first form on final start. *R. Mathew* — 69

ST PATRICK'S DAY 5 ch.g. Night Shift (USA) – Princess Lieven (Royal Palace) [1992/3 17g^3 17d^6 17d] leggy, workmanlike gelding: fair at best on Flat, stayed 1¼m: well beaten over hurdles: dead. *Andrew Turnell* — –

STRAIGHT BAT 10 b.g. Dragonara Palace (USA) – Camdamus (Mandamus) [1992/3 c21g^{pu}] lengthy gelding: poor novice hurdler/hunter chaser. *J. C. Collett* — c– –

STRAIGHT GOLD 8 ch.m. Vaigly Great – Merokette (Blast) [1992/3 a20g^{pu} 20f 27g^{pu}] smallish, angular mare: winning hurdler: showed nothing in 1992/3. *T. B. Hallett* — –

STRAIGHT LACED (USA) 6 b. or br.g. Alleged (USA) – Swoonmist (USA) (Never Bend) [1992/3 a18g^2 a20g^3 21d* 22f^2 22f^6] leggy gelding: fair handicap hurdler: won at Fakenham in April: stays 2¾m: acts on good to soft, firm going and equitrack: usually blinkered: reluctant, and sometimes needs plenty of driving. *P. C. Clarke* — 103 §

STRAIGHT PILOT 11 br.g. Ascertain (USA) – Lucky Flight (Lucky Leaprechaun) [1992/3 c27g* c27d^4] workmanlike gelding: fair hunter chaser: won at Sedgefield in March, better effort in 1992/3: stays well: acts on firm and dead ground. *David Ford* — c95

STRANDS OF GOLD 14 b.g. Le Coq d'Or – Sweet Fanny (Bitter Sweet) [1992/3 c27g^{pu}] strong, compact gelding: smart staying chaser at his best: hunter chaser nowadays: probably acts on any going. *R. J. Alford* — c– –

STRANGE WAYS 5 b.h. Reach – Burglar Tip (Burglar) [1992/3 F17m] half-brother to winning sprinters Loft Boy (by Cawston's Clown) and Long Arm of Th' Law (by Longleat): dam 5f winner: last of 15 in NH Flat race at Hereford in May: yet to race over hurdles or fences. *H. E. Haynes* — –

STRATFORD LADY 4 b.f. Touching Wood (USA) – Hawks Nest (Moulton) [1992/3 17s^2 16v^{pu} 17g^{bd}] close-coupled filly: untrustworthy maiden middle-distance plater on Flat: poor form only completed start in selling hurdles: blinkered last 2 starts. *J. A. Glover* — 66

STRATHBOGIE MIST (IRE) 5 br.g. Seclude (USA) – Devon Lark (Take A Reef) [1992/3 21s^{pu} 16s 22d 18m^6] close-coupled, plain gelding: fourth foal: half-brother to fairly useful hurdler/chaser Copper Mine (by Kambalda): dam won 2m maiden hurdle: bad novice hurdler. *J. Parkes* — 62

STRATHMORE LODGE 4 b.f. Skyliner – Coliemore (Coliseum) [1992/3 F16v F17g^3 F16f^3] seventh foal: half-sister to winning jumpers

Dubious Jake (by Dubassoff), More Distinct (by Class Distinction) and Ardlussa Bay (by Miramar Reef): dam won NH Flat race and 2m hurdle: third in NH Flat races in the North in the spring: yet to race over hurdles. *J. M. Jefferson*

STRATH ROYAL 7 b.g. Furry Glen – Last Princess (Le Prince) [1992/3 F18d² 16s⁴ 21s 16s* 16g³ 17f² 16m* 16s² 16m* 16d*] leggy gelding: won novice hurdles at Nottingham (2) and Towcester and handicap on latter course in second half of season, last win in good style: best form at 2m but should stay further: acts on soft and good to firm ground: sometimes sweating and edgy in preliminaries: potentially useful. *O. Brennan* — 118 p

STRAWBERRY FOOL 4 b.f. Idiot's Delight – Record Red (Record Run) [1992/3 F16spu] third foal: half-sister to poor novice hurdler Red Nest (by Nestor): dam poor maiden on Flat and over hurdles: pulled up in NH Flat race in January: yet to race over hurdles. *Mrs P. M. Joynes*

STRAW BLADE 7 ch.m. Final Straw – Little Niece (Great Nephew) [1992/3 17m⁴ 17spu 17m² 17g⁵ 17d⁴] sparely-made mare: selling hurdler nowadays: should stay beyond 17f: acts on firm and dead ground: tried in blinkers. *Mrs J. G. Retter* — 78

STRAW THATCH 4 b.g. Thatching – Lashing (USA) (Storm Bird (CAN)) [1992/3 16g³ 17g⁵ 16g³ 16g³ 17g 16g⁴] close-coupled gelding: fair at best at around 1m on Flat: modest form at best in juvenile hurdles: raced only on good ground and final starts. *R. Allan* — 93

STREETFIELD 6 b.m. Scallywag – Sunset Song (Song) [1992/3 16vᵖᵘ c16spu] lengthy, workmanlike mare: no sign of ability. *K. S. Bridgwater* — c–
–

STREET KID 5 b.g. Teenoso (USA) – Chalkey Road (Relko) [1992/3 17s² 16m² 22m* 20f] leggy gelding: fair handicap hurdler: won at Worcester in March: effective at 2m to 2¾m: acts on good to firm and soft going: sometimes wears tongue strap: races up with pace: sketchy jumper. *R. F. Johnson Houghton* — 108

STRELLEY PRINCE 6 br.g. Prince of Peace – Sweetcal (Caliban) [1992/3 20mꟳ 16s 16spu] small, lengthy gelding: poor form only completed start in novice hurdles. *Mrs S. J. Smith* — 78

STRIDING EDGE 8 ch.g. Viking (USA) – Kospia (King Emperor (USA)) [1992/3 17f* 17s³ 18g⁶ 17g 17m c17g* c16m⁶ c18d⁵ 21d 17mᵇᵈ 16f⁶ 17m] neat gelding: handicap hurdler: won at Plumpton in August: generally ran poorly afterwards: successful in novice chase at Fakenham in October: best at around 2m: acts on hard and dead ground: sometimes blinkered/ visored. *J. R. Jenkins* — c87
101 d

STRIKE IT RIGHT 8 b.g. Royal Match – Mrs Neddy (Super Song) [1992/3 c21dpu c24spu] good-bodied gelding: no sign of ability: sold 2,000 gns Doncaster January Sales: blinkered last 2 outings. *C. J. Vernon Miller* — c–
–

STRIKING IMAGE (IRE) 4 ch.f. Flash of Steel – Sister Sala (Double-U-Jay) [1992/3 17v⁶ 17d⁵ 17d] workmanlike filly: fair middle-distance performer at best on Flat: poor form in juvenile hurdles: likely to stay beyond 17f: acts on heavy going: sketchy jumper. *J. S. Moore* — 69

STROKED AGAIN 8 b.m. On Your Mark – Anniversary Waltz (Carnival Dancer) [1992/3 18fꟳ 19m 24d 18mꟳ 17s 16d⁴ 20m 21m 20m] leggy gelding: modest hurdler: trained until after fifth outing by M. Pipe: stays 3m: acts on firm and dead going: jumps sketchily. *B. Richmond* — 85

STRONG APPROACH 8 br.g. Strong Gale – Smart Fashion (Carlburg) [1992/3 c25g⁶ c21d⁵ c16d* c20d⁴ c20g² c20s² c21sꟳ c21m⁶] rather leggy gelding: fair handicap chaser: won at Carlisle in February: ran well next 3 starts: effective at 2m when conditions are testing and stays 3m well: acts on soft going: sound jumper. *J. I. A. Charlton* — c113

STRONG BEAU 8 br.g. Strong Gale – Red Pine (Khalkis) [1992/3 c22d* c21v² c20d² c24v³ c24s² c24s³ c25m* c25d⁶] tall, good-bodied gelding: fairly useful chaser: won novice event at Stratford in October and Fulke Walwyn Kim Muir Handicap (Amateur Riders, by 2½ lengths from Merano) — c123
–

Fulke Walwyn Kim Muir Challenge Cup Handicap Chase (Amateur Riders), Cheltenham—
Strong Beau (left) wears down Merano

at Cheltenham in March: will prove well suited by a thorough test of stamina: acts on good to firm and heavy going: best ridden up with pace: game. *D. Nicholson*

STRONG BOND   12 ch.g. Pablond – Windward II (Wood Cot) [1992/3 c25m³] winning hunter chaser: stays 25f: acts on firm going: blinkered only outing in 1992/3. *Mrs M. A. Cooke*   **c88**

STRONG BREEZE   9 br.g. Strong Gale – Salty Breeze (Pitpan) [1992/3 22d⁶ 20g² 20fF 24sᵖᵘ 16dᵖᵘ 16sᵖᵘ 16d 17m³ 22g c24mᵖᵘ] workmanlike gelding: poor novice jumper: stays 2½m: acts on good to firm ground. *C. L. Popham*   **c–** **74**

STRONG CHARACTER   7 b.g. Torus – La'bavette (Le Bavard (FR)) [1992/3 28g³] close-coupled gelding: no form over hurdles: won a point in April. *R. R. Lamb*   **–**

STRONG FANCY   10 br.g. Royal Match – Sugar Lump (Candy Cane) [1992/3 c20g⁵ c16s³ c20g⁴ c20d⁴ 20m³ 17m² c16g⁴ c16s² 22g² 22m] sturdy gelding: poor hurdler: moderate novice chaser: stays 2¾m: probably acts on any going: usually blinkered nowadays: possibly ungenuine. *S. E. Kettlewell*   **c85** **71**

STRONG FLAME (IRE)   4 br.g. Strong Gale – Hamers Flame (Green Shoon) [1992/3 F17m⁶ F14s³] fourth foal: half-brother to fair hurdler Notary-Nowell (by Deep Run): dam useful hurdler/fairly useful chaser in Ireland: third in NH Flat race at Market Rasen in April: yet to race over hurdles. *M. D. Hammond*

STRONG GOLD   10 b.g. Strong Gale – Miss Goldiane (Baragoi) [1992/3 c20g⁵ c21sᵖᵘ c26dᵖᵘ c21m³ c22f⁵] strong, lengthy gelding: fairly useful chaser at best: only fair form in 1992/3: barely stays 3m: probably acts on any going: usually blinkered. *Andrew Turnell*   **c108** **–**

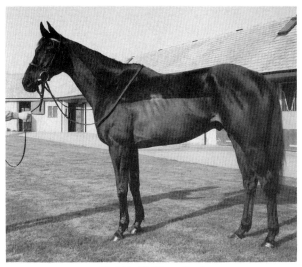

Mrs J. Mould's "Strong Beau"

STRONG JOHN (IRE) 5 b.h. Strong Gale – Deep Khaletta (Deep Run) [1992/3 17s² 17v² 17s 17dᵖᵘ 17d² 24gᵖᵘ 16m⁶] lengthy, unfurnished horse: third foal: half-brother to fair Irish hurdler Dont Rough It (by Pragmatic): dam, behind in NH Flat races and maiden hurdles, sister to several winning jumpers: moderate novice hurdler: should stay beyond 17f: acts on heavy ground. *F. Murphy*   90

STRONG MEASURE (IRE) 5 b.g. Strong Gale – Inch Tape (Prince Hansel) [1992/3 16g 20m⁶ 18m⁵] compact gelding: third live foal: half-brother to maiden hurdler/pointer Happy Paddy (by Paddy's Stream): dam unraced half-sister to several winning jumpers, including Gleann Buidhe, dam of Righthand Man: poor novice hurdler: should prove suited by a test of stamina. *P. Cheesbrough*   75

STRONG MEDICINE 6 b.g. Strong Gale – In The Forest (Crowded Room) [1992/3 17v³ 16v 17d³ 16f* 20g² 22f² 22f* 23f*] lengthy, workmanlike gelding: won novice hurdles at Windsor, Fontwell and Stratford (handicap) in second half of season: stays 23f: probably acts on any going: type to progress further. *K. C. Bailey*   109 p

STRONG SILVER (USA) 8 b.g. Silver Hawk (USA) – Brave Mimi (FR) (Lyphard (USA)) [1992/3 16s 17d 16d c16m⁴ c16sᵖᵘ c22mᵖᵘ c18m] sparely-made gelding: poor novice hurdler/chaser: best efforts at 2m: acts on dead and good to firm ground: blinkered last 2 outings. *R. Johnson*   c70 –

STRONG SOUND 6 b.g. Strong Gale – Jazz Music (Choral Society) [1992/3 c21m⁶ c21d* c21g³ c25d³ c24s² c23gᶠ c21s⁴] big, workmanlike gelding: won novice chase at Sedgefield early in season (trained until after fifth outing by W. A. Stephenson): no form in 2 runs in second half: stays 25f: acts on soft ground. *P. Cheesbrough*   c95

715

STRONG TRACE (IRE) 4 b.g. Strong Gale – Royal Inheritance (Will Somers) [1992/3 aF13g³ aF16g⁴] half-brother to Dorade (by Windjammer), winner of 7f seller on Flat: dam 6f winner at 2 yrs: in frame in NH Flat races at Lingfield: yet to race over hurdles. *S. Mellor*

STRONG VIEWS 6 b.g. Remainder Man – Gokatiego (Huntercombe) [1992/3 16m⁵ 17g* 18d* 16s² 16g 17g⁴ 17dᵖᵘ] tall, good-topped gelding: chasing type: fair handicap hurdler: won twice at Kelso in November: trained until after fourth outing by W. A. Stephenson: sold 33,000 gns in May: should stay further than 2¼m: acts on soft and good to firm ground: finds little off bridle and best with waiting tactics. *P. Cheesbrough*   109

STRUAN RUN (NZ) 6 br.g. Gaiter (NZ) – Lotsydamus (NZ) (Auk (USA)) [1992/3 18d 20vᵖᵘ] workmanlike gelding: novice hurdler: only form at 17f on dead ground (1991/2). *Capt. T. A. Forster*   –

STUDFORD 5 ch.g. Move Off – Sharenka (Sharpen Up) [1992/3 F18d⁵ 20dᵖᵘ 16vᵖᵘ 16s 16sᵖᵘ] smallish gelding: second foal: dam ran twice: no form in novice hurdles: tried blinkered. *M. W. Easterby*   –

STUNNING STUFF 8 b.g. Boreen (FR) – Mayfield Grove (Khalkis) [1992/3 c19m* c22d² c20g⁵] rangy ex-Irish gelding: maiden hurdler: won novice chase at Exeter in October: ran poorly on final start (February): will stay beyond 2¾m: acts on good to firm and dead going. *K. C. Bailey*   c101

STUPID CUPID 9 b.m. Idiot's Delight – Trianqo (Tarqogan) [1992/3 c21s⁵ c21v⁴ c19vᶠ c21v³ c16d⁴ c22g* c21dᵖᵘ c23dᵖᵘ 25g] lengthy mare: fairly useful hurdler at best: won novice chase at Nottingham in March: ran badly afterwards: needs further than 2m and stays 25f: acts on good to firm and heavy ground: not yet an accomplished jumper of fences. *R. Rowe*   c87

ST VILLE 7 b.g. Top Ville – Dame Julian (Blakeney) [1992/3 26d 28s* 26s⁴ a24g* a20g* 28g⁶ 25s] small gelding: fair hurdler: won handicaps at Sedgefield in December and Southwell in January and February (conditional jockeys): successful at 2½m but ideally suited by good test of stamina: acts on soft going and all-weather surfaces: usually blinkered prior to 1992/3. *J. W. Curtis*   102

STYLISH GENT 6 br.g. Vitiges (FR) – Squire's Daughter (Bay Express) [1992/3 18m² 16m³ 17mˢᵘ 18d² 17d 17g⁶ 18g a18g 16gᶠ 16m 17m 16g 16m 18v⁵] sturdy gelding: modest hurdler at best: claimed out of N. Tinkler's stable £5,100 after fourth outing: ran poorly afterwards: stays 2¼m: acts on good to firm and dead ground: tried blinkered. *J. J. Birkett*   95 d

STYLUS 4 ch.g. Sharpo – Pine Ridge (High Top) [1992/3 16s* 16d³ 16v² 17d*] sturdy, deep-bodied gelding: once-raced on Flat: won juvenile hurdle at Leicester (150/1) in February and novice event at Perth in May: good third in Petros Victor Ludorum Hurdle at Haydock in between: likely to prove best at around 2m: acts on soft going (below best on heavy). *D. Nicholson*   117

SUASANAN SIOSANA 8 b. or br.g. Frigid Aire – Efficiency (Pardao) [1992/3 c26gᵖᵘ 21g⁵] close-coupled, deep-girthed gelding: poor novice hurdler/chaser: tried blinkered: poor jumper: won a point in February. *John R. Upson*   c– x / – x

SUCCESSFUL MISSION 8 b.m. Ascertain (USA) – Mission Impossible (Raeburn II) [1992/3 16g] first foal: dam winning pointer: tailed off in novice hurdle at Hexham in March on debut. *P. Beaumont*   –

SUEZ CANAL (IRE) 4 b.g. Commanche Run – Sphinx (GER) (Alpenkonig (GER)) [1992/3 17m⁶ 17d⁶ 16d⁴ 16d⁴ 16s* 16v² 16s³ 16s³ 20g⁴ 16v³] angular gelding: fair stayer when in the mood on Flat: won juvenile hurdle at Warwick in January: ran creditably most other starts: needs testing conditions at 2m and should stay further: acts on heavy going: needs plenty of driving. *F. Jordan*   95

SUFFOLK ROAD 6 br.g. Yashgan – Maybird (Royalty) [1992/3 F17v F16d* 20s* 20d⁵ 19d⁴ 21v 24s* 24s] strong, good-bodied ex-Irish gelding: chasing type: brother to useful Irish hurdler Sheamy's Dream and half-brother to 3 minor winners: dam unraced: won NH Flat race at   108

Roscommon and maiden hurdle at Listowel (trained until after fifth start by J. Coogan) early in season and handicap at Worcester in February (ran poorly other 2 starts in Britain): suited by a test of stamina: acts on soft going. *R. Rowe*

SUGEMAR 7 ch.g. Young Generation – Jade Ring (Auction Ring (USA)) [1992/3 16m 22v²] compact gelding: modest middle-distance performer on Flat: sold out of J. Toller's stable 1,900 gns Newmarket Autumn Sales: second of 8 in novice hurdle at Cartmel in May. *M. C. Chapman* — 85

SUKAAB 8 gr.g. Nishapour (FR) – Nye (FR) (Sanctus II) [1992/3 22d² 26m 20m⁴ 22d 24g] workmanlike gelding: fairly useful handicap hurdler: ran badly last 2 starts: poor form in novice chases: stays 2¾m: acts on good to firm and soft ground: tried blinkered/visored in 1990/1. *B. J. M. Ryall* — c– 121

SUKEY TAWDRY 7 gr.m. Wassl – Jenny Diver (USA) (Hatchet Man (USA)) [1992/3 18g⁴ 18m⁶ 22sᵖᵘ 20s 24gᵖᵘ 16fᵖᵘ 20gᵖᵘ 22fᵘʳ 17fᵖᵘ] leggy mare: of little account nowadays: blinkered/visored occasionally. *R. A. Bennett* —

SULA 5 br.m. Sula Bula – Dusky Damsel (Sahib) [1992/3 21d 17sᵖᵘ 20g 16gᵖᵘ 16d 17f] unfurnished mare: half-sister to winning hurdler Country Damsel (by Town And Country): dam winning 2m hurdler: no form on Flat or over hurdles. *B. Mactaggart* —

SULAAH ROSE 4 b.f. Sula Bula – Dusky Damsel (Sahib) [1992/3 18fᵘʳ 16v 16g 17d 16gᵖᵘ] leggy, angular filly: no sign of ability. *Mrs J. Jordan* —

SULLI BOY (NOR) 8 b.g. Sparkling Boy – Lady Sullivan (Pitcairn) [1992/3 18f⁵ 17g³ 17d³ 17d⁴ 16s a16g⁵ 17d² 20g 17fᵖᵘ] smallish, dipped-backed gelding: fair handicap hurdler: pulled up lame final outing: stays 2½m: acts on firm and dead going. *Miss B. Sanders* — 113

SULTAN'S SON 7 b.g. Kings Lake (USA) – Get Ahead (Silly Season) [1992/3 22m² 21g² 24f⁴ 21g⁶ 21s² 20d⁵ 16m* 18g³ 17d* 17gᵘʳ 22f 20d⁴] sturdy gelding: successful in selling hurdles at Ludlow (conditional jockeys, bought in 2,000 gns) in March and Fakenham (handicap, no bid) in April: effective at 2m and should stay beyond 21f: acts on good to firm and soft ground: to be trained by K. Bridgwater. *John R. Upson* — 97

SULUK (USA) 8 b.h. Lypheor – Cheerful Heart (Petingo) [1992/3 a18g* a22g* a16g* a18g* a20g² a16g* a20g* a16g2] sparely-made horse: fair hurdler: does his racing on the fibresand at Southwell and has won 18 of his 21 starts there: successful in 1992/3 in 4 claimers and 2 sellers (bought in 5,800 gns then 5,000 gns): effective at 2m to 2¾m: usually drifts right in closing stages: jumps well: tough, genuine and consistent. *R. Hollinshead* — 113

SUM MEDE 6 b.g. King Persian – Brun's Toy (FR) (Bruni) [1992/3 a16gF 16g⁵ 16g⁵ 18g³ 17g] sparely-made gelding: poor hurdler: yet to race beyond 2¼m: acts on fibresand, raced only on good ground on turf: blinkered last 2 starts: looks none too keen. *B. S. Rothwell* — 82

SUMMER CRUISE 4 b.g. Slip Anchor – Enthralment (USA) (Sir Ivor) [1992/3 16v³] poor maiden on Flat nowadays: distant last in selling hurdle in February. *A. N. Lee* —

SUMMERHILL SCOOP 5 ch.g. Castle Keep – New Top (New Brig) [1992/3 18f⁵ 18d 20d] light-framed gelding: fifth foal: half-brother to winning hurdler Tip Top Lad (by Aragon): dam fairly useful staying hurdler: bad novice hurdler. *A. Moore* —

SUMMER SANDS 5 ch.m. Mummy's Game – Renira (Relkino) [1992/3 17g a18g a16g 16s] small mare: 2m novice over hurdles, poor at best: visored once: sold 1,500 gns Ascot February Sales. *J. L. Harris* —

SUN BALLAD 8 b.g. Ballad Rock – Sunny Eyes (Reliance II) [1992/3 21d] very big, lengthy gelding: no sign of ability over hurdles. *J. Mackie* —

SUNBEAM TALBOT 12 b.g. Sunyboy – Alfetta (Royal Highway) [1992/3 c26g* c28d* c27v⁵ c28s² c26v⁴ c26v² c27d² c25g³ c26d³ c27g³] small, sturdy gelding: fair chaser: successful in handicaps at Cheltenham (amateurs) and Stratford in October: generally ran creditably later on: — c113

717

*Baring Securities Tolworth Hurdle, Sandown—
the first two, Sun Surfer (right) and Dreamers Delight*

suited by a good test of stamina: acts on heavy going and good to firm. *A. P. Jones*

SUNDAY JIM   9 b.g. Jimsun – Berkeley Belle (Runnymede) [1992/3 c21s^{pu} c21m^{F3} 19f⁶ 22f⁴ 22f⁵ 21d^{pu}] strong, sturdy gelding: poor novice hurdler/chaser at best. *H. J. M. Webb*   c– –

SUNDAY PUNCH   7 b.g. The Parson – Darkina (Tarqogan) [1992/3 17d 21v⁵ 18f⁵] big gelding: chasing type: modest hurdler in 1991/2: no form in 1992/3: stays 2¾m: acts on good to firm and soft going. *J. T. Gifford*   –

SUNDAYSPORT SCOOP   8 b.g. Great Nephew – Heaven Knows (Yellow God) [1992/3 c26g c27g^{bd} c25m⁶ c27d⁶] small, stocky gelding: poor novice jumper: tried blinkered. *Mrs I. H. Hadden*   c– –

SUNKALA SHINE   5 ch.g. Kalaglow – Allander Girl (Miralgo) [1992/3 22s³] good-topped gelding: half-brother to several winners, including jumper Getting Plenty (by Oats): third in novice event at Nottingham in November on hurdling debut: modest form when placed on Flat in February and April: sure to improve. *J. G. FitzGerald*   84 p

SUNLEY BAY   7 gr.g. Sunley Builds – Menrise Bay (Menelek) [1992/3 16d⁵ 16d⁵ 20g² c20s³ c27v⁴ 21v³ 24s⁵ 22s² 21g⁵ 26s* 24s³ 24g⁴] good-topped ex-Irish gelding: first foal: dam winning Irish hurdler: trained until after third start by M. Hourigan: won novice hurdle at Hereford in April: also a fair performer over fences (still a maiden): probably needs   c103 112

718

further than 2½m when conditions aren't testing and stays well: acts on heavy going: usually blinkered nowadays. *P. F. Nicholls*

SUNLEY SPARKLE 5 b.m. Sunley Builds – Royal Darwin (Royal Palm) [1992/3 16g³ 17dᵘʳ 17g⁴ 17m⁴ 17m⁶ 20m 16f] close-coupled, angular mare: poor on Flat, stays 1m: poor novice hurdler: will prove suited by sharp 2m: acts on good to firm ground. *D. R. Gandolfo* — 66

SUNNYGIMBO 7 ch.g. Harvest Spirit – Jolly Music (Money Business) [1992/3 c18dᶠᵘʳ] brother to winning jumper Harvest Hymn and half-brother to several others: dam won 2m hurdle: failed to complete in points: jumped poorly on steeplechasing debut. *J. P. D. Elliott* — c–

SUNSET COURT 11 ch.g. Quayside – Shamrock Penny (Flyover) [1992/3 c21gᶠ] angular gelding: winning 2m hurdler: maiden pointer: fell on steeplechasing debut: dead. *R. H. Pike* — c–
–

SUNSET REINS FREE 8 b.g. Red Sunset – Free Rein (Sagaro) [1992/3 18m 18m⁵ 17m 18d] lengthy, angular gelding: handicap hurdler: poor form in 1992/3 (trained first 2 starts by J. Birkett): once-raced over fences: races at around 2m: acts on firm and dead going: visored once. *S. G. Payne* — c–
–

SUNSET ROCK 6 b.g. Red Sunset – Oileann Carrig (Pitcairn) [1992/3 16d* 16d² 16d²] tall, useful-looking gelding: chasing type: won novice hurdle at Catterick in November: second in novice handicaps in February: unlikely to stay beyond 2m at present: raced only on dead ground: should progress further. *J. G. FitzGerald* — 93 p

SUNSET STREET (IRE) 5 b.g. Bellypha – Sunset Reef (Mill Reef (USA)) [1992/3 16f] good-topped gelding: no sign of ability in 2 races over hurdles. *A. L. Forbes* — –

SUNSHINE BLUES 10 b.g. Sunyboy – Fatal Hour (Fate) [1992/3 22sᵖᵘ] tall gelding: lightly raced and no sign of ability. *Mrs F. Walwyn* — c–
–

SUNSTANE 9 ch.m. Sunyboy – Stanegate (Coliseum) [1992/3 c21sᵘʳ c24mᵖᵘ] lengthy, shallow-girthed mare: no sign of ability. *F. L. Matthews* — c–
–

SUN SURFER (FR) 5 ch.g. R B Chesne – Sweet Cashmere (FR) (Kashmir II) [1992/3 16d* 18d² 17d* 21s* 17v* 21s³ 21d⁴] sturdy gelding: fairly useful hurdler: successful in novice events at Wincanton and Stratford and minor event at Newbury prior to winning Baring Securities Tolworth Hurdle at Sandown in January by a neck from Dreamers Delight: ran poorly final outing (February): likely to prove suited by further than 2m and stays 21f: acts on heavy going: jumps well. *Capt. T. A. Forster* — 127

SUNY ZETA 9 b.m. Sunyboy – Blue Zeta (Bluerullah) [1992/3 18s 21s] strong mare: no sign of ability. *R. H. Goldie* — –

SUPER BEAUTY 4 b.f. Capricorn Line – Super Lady (Averof) [1992/3 18d 17g⁶] poor maiden on Flat, sold out of G. Balding's stable 750 gns Ascot July Sales: no sign of ability in juvenile hurdles. *Miss S. Waterman* — –

SUPER COIN 5 b.g. Scorpio (FR) – Penny Princess (Normandy) [1992/3 F16d⁴ F16s F16d 17m⁴ 22m] leggy gelding: third foal: dam, poor novice hurdler, is daughter of a poor sister to Pendil: fourth in novice hurdle at Bangor in March: tailed off next time: should stay beyond 17f: acts on good to firm ground. *D. McCain* — 77

SUPER DEB 6 ch.m. Superlative – Debutina Park (Averof) [1992/3 16sᵖᵘ 16vᵖᵘ 17dᵖᵘ] sturdy mare: fair sprinter at best: pulled up over hurdles, looking ungenuine: blinkered last 2 outings. *N. A. Twiston-Davies* — – §

SUPER FOUNTAIN 10 b.m. Royal Fountain – Super Satin (Lord of Verona) [1992/3 c23d² c24sᵖᵘ c24dᵖᵘ c28gᵖᵘ c27dᵖᵘ] lengthy mare: winning staying chaser: no form since 1990/1. *F. T. Walton* — c–
–

SUPER HEIGHTS 5 b.g. Superlative – Shadha (Shirley Heights) [1992/3 17vᵖᵘ 21vᵖᵘ] small gelding: poor and unreliable on Flat, stays 7f: sold out of Miss A. Whitfield's stable 920 gns Newmarket Autumn Sales: showed nothing in selling hurdles. *D. L. Williams* — –

Steel Plate And Sections Young Chasers' Qualifier, Ayr—
a third win for Superior Finish

SUPERIOR FINISH 7 br.g. Oats – Emancipated (Mansingh (USA)) **c133**
[1992/3 c21s4 c23v2 c24d2 c24v* c24s* c25m2 c25g*] tall, leggy gelding: –
fair hurdler: better over fences and won novice events at Kempton,
Leicester and Ayr and finished good second to Young Hustler in Sun
Alliance Chase at Cheltenham in second half of season: stays 25f: acts on
good to firm and heavy going: visored once: not yet an accomplished jumper
of fences. *Mrs J. Pitman*

SUPER MALT (IRE) 5 ch.m. Milk of The Barley – Super Amber
(Yellow God) [1992/3 18g2 17f5 18g4 21s*] leggy mare: improved form when **106**
winning conditional jockeys handicap hurdle at Newbury in November:
better suited by 21f than shorter: acts on any ground: tends to hang left.
Miss K. S. Allison

SUPER RITCHART 5 b.g. Starch Reduced – Karousa Girl (Rouser)
[1992/3 18m4 21d5 23s2 23s* 2 1v 23s 16s* 17s2 17d4] leggy, angular gelding: **108**
fair handicap hurdler: won at Wolverhampton in November and Leicester in
January: effective at 2m under testing conditions and stays 23f: best efforts
with give in the ground, though ran poorly on heavy: usually races
prominently: game. *B. Palling*

SUPER SANDY 6 ch.m. Import – Super Satin (Lord of Verona) [1992/3
17dpu] no sign of ability in NH Flat races and a novice hurdle. *F. T. Walton* –

SUPER SARENA (IRE) 4 b.f. Taufan (USA) – Stop The Cavalry
(Relko) [1992/3 17v6 21dpu 16d3 16d4 16gbd] rather sparely-made filly: **96**
staying maiden on Flat: modest form in juvenile hurdles: should stay beyond
2m: acts on heavy ground. *R. G. Frost*

SUPER SENSE 8 b.g. Pragmatic – Killonan Lass (The Parson) [1992/3 **c– x**
21s* 26s5 24s5 25m6 24s5] rangy gelding: useful hurdler: won handicap at **145**
Warwick in November: ran well afterwards: novice chaser, let down by his
jumping: suited by thorough test of stamina: acts on good to firm and soft
going: usually held up. *J. T. Gifford*

SUPER SHARP (NZ) 5 ch.g. Brilliant Invader (AUS) – Aspen Annie
(NZ) (Amalgam (USA)) [1992/3 F17m F16g* F17f] tall, plain gelding: trained
first start by N. Smith: won NH Flat race at Catterick in March: tailed off in
valuable similar event at Aintree following month: yet to race over hurdles
or fences. *C. D. Broad*

SUPER SPELL 7 ch.g. Smooth Stepper – Super Twig (Super Slip)
[1992/3 17d4 17s* 17v2 16s2 17sF] plain, rather leggy gelding: first foal: dam **108**

720

unraced: won novice hurdle at Bangor in November: ran well next 2 starts: will stay further than 17f: acts on heavy ground. *G. A. Ham*

SUPERVISION 5 b.g. Superlative – Something Casual (Good Times (ITY)) [1992/3 F17m] first foal: dam fair miler: tailed off in early-season NH Flat race: yet to race over hurdles or fences. *Mrs M. A. Kendall*

SUPPOSIN 5 b.g. Enchantment – Misty Rocket (Roan Rocket) [1992/3 F17m⁵ 16g⁶ 16g 16d 20g⁶] small, lightly-made gelding: first foal: dam winning selling hurdler: bad novice hurdler. *Mrs S. J. Smith* — 58

SUPREME BLUSHER 6 ch.m. Blushing Scribe (USA) – Yashama (Supreme Red) [1992/3 23dᵖᵘ 18d 18dᵖᵘ] small sharp mare: fifth foal: half-sister to fair hurdler/chaser The Slater (by Town And Country) and winning pointer/hunter chaser The Motcombe Oak (by Brotherly): dam never ran: no sign of ability in novice hurdles. *W. T. Kemp* — –

SUPREME KNIGHT 6 b.m. River Knight (FR) – Maber's Owen (Master Owen) [1992/3 F17s 16vᵖᵘ] sparely-made ex-Irish mare: first foal: dam unraced: no sign of ability. *R. C. Harper* — –

SUPREME WARRIOR 7 b.g. Simply Great (FR) – Sindo (Derring-Do) [1992/3 17s⁵ 18f 20g³ 21s⁶ 20f²] small gelding: poor novice hurdler nowadays: not raced after October: stays 21f: probably acts on any going: blinkered once. *J. P. Taplin* — 75

SURCOAT 6 b.h. Bustino – Mullet (Star Appeal) [1992/3 25vᵖᵘ 16d 17d⁵ 18g* 25m*] small, stocky horse: won novice handicap hurdles at Exeter and Taunton in the spring: stays 25f: acts on dead and good to firm ground. *R. J. Baker* — 91

SURELY GIFTED (IRE) 4 b.g. Sure Blade (USA) – Gift Wrapped (Wolver Hollow) [1992/3 18f⁵ 18dᵖᵘ 17fᵖᵘ] plating-class maiden on Flat: sold out of W. Muir's stable 1,300 gns Ascot June Sales: no sign of ability over hurdles: trained by W. G. Turner first 2 starts. *M. Williams* — –

SURE METAL 10 b.g. Billion – Sujini (Tycoon II) [1992/3 c17g³ c16g² c16d* c16s² c17v² c16s⁵] workmanlike, angular gelding: useful chaser: won handicap at Haydock (fourth course win) in November and ran creditably most other starts in 1992/3: stays 2½m: acts on good to firm and heavy going: front runner: rather erratic jumper of fences. *D. McCain* — c138 / –

SUREN 7 b. or br.g. Ela-Mana-Mou – Go Feather Go (USA) (Go Marching (USA)) [1992/3 20g⁴ 22s 23s 22d⁵ 23g⁵ 22m⁴ 22d⁵ 21dᵖᵘ] leggy gelding: moderate handicap hurdler: poor novice over fences: stays 2¾m: acts on dead ground and good to firm: sometimes blinkered. *C. Weedon* — c– / 89

SURE PRIDE (USA) 5 b.g. Bates Motel (USA) – Coquelicot (CAN) (L'Enjoleur (CAN)) [1992/3 18s 16s⁶ 16v⁶ 18v³ 17dᵘʳ 18m* 18m³ 17g⁶ 18g³ 20g*] rangy gelding: modest maiden on Flat: won claiming hurdle at Fontwell in February and novice event (easily) at Ascot in April: stays 2½m: best efforts on a sound surface, ran respectably on heavy. *A. Moore* — 105

SURE SHOT NORMAN 4 b.c. Song – Angel Drummer (Dance In Time (CAN)) [1992/3 20sᵖᵘ 17d] maiden plater on Flat, of little account nowadays: sold 1,000 gns Ascot November Sales: no sign of ability over hurdles. *G. H. Jones* — –

SURE TO WIN (IRE) 4 ch.g. Sure Blade (USA) – Mahabba (USA) (Elocutionist (USA)) [1992/3 16dᶠ 16g 17m⁴] modest performer on Flat: stays 1¼m: first form in novice hurdles on final start. *J. M. Carr* — 71

SURF BOAT 4 ch.f. Master Willie – Wave Dancer (Dance In Time (CAN)) [1992/3 20v 16d 18g² 16g³ 17mᵖᵘ] lengthy filly: modest middle-distance maiden on Flat: sold out of B. Hills's stable 5,600 gns Newmarket December Sales: poor novice hurdler: pulled up lame final start: best efforts at around 2m on good ground: blinkered last 3 starts. *N. Tinkler* — 78

SURJAY 8 b.g. Bustineto – Nenagh Belle (Dalesa) [1992/3 c22gᵘʳ] once-raced over hurdles: poor winning pointer: unseated rider on steeplechasing debut. *D. Mills* — c– / –

SUROT 7 b.m. Torus – Dizzy Dot (Bargello) [1992/3 c21d^ur 16v^pu 18m 21g^pu] workmanlike mare: first foal: half-sister to poor novice jumper Dizzy Dealer (by Le Bavard): dam never ran: unseated rider second on chasing debut: no sign of ability over hurdles. *Mrs J. Jordan*   c– –

SURPRISING SUE 6 b.m. Sula Bula – Astonish Me (Levanter) [1992/3 17g] lengthy, unfurnished mare: first foal: dam of little account: tailed off in early-season novice hurdle on debut. *A. P. Jones*   –

SUTTON LASS 10 ch.m. Politico (USA) – Selborne Lass (Deep Run) [1992/3 c25m^pu] sturdy mare: poor pointer: no sign of ability in 2 steeplechases. *R. C. Harper*   c– –

SWAGMAN (USA) 6 ch.g. Graustark – Mawgrit (USA) (Hoist The Flag (USA)) [1992/3 22d^5 16s 22s^pu] leggy gelding: novice hurdler: no form since 1990/1: poor jumper. *B. Richmond*   – x

SWAHILI RUN 5 ch.g. Ayyabaan – Nicolene (Nice Music) [1992/3 F16d^3 F16v F16s^4 a16g^3 18g^* 17g 16f^*] angular gelding: fifth foal: brother to 2 poor maiden jumpers: dam quite useful at up to 13f: won novice hurdles at Exeter and Wincanton in the spring: will stay beyond 2¼m: acts on firm going: front runner: likely to improve further. *M. C. Pipe*   103 p

SWALLOWFIELD 8 b.m. Wattlefield – Peperino (Relko) [1992/3 17v^pu a16g^pu] second foal: half-sister to winning hurdler Major Bush (by Julio Mariner): dam maiden half-sister to useful sprinter Shayboob: no sign of ability. *D. Welsh*   –

SWANK GILBERT 7 b.g. Balliol – Song To Singo (Master Sing) [1992/3 16m 17g 18m^pu 16g^4] close-coupled gelding: bad novice selling hurdler: tried blinkered. *T. A. K. Cuthbert*   58

SWAN'S APPROACH 10 b.g. Swan's Rock – Kilcairn Bridge (Lucifer (USA)) [1992/3 c21g^pu c21d^pu] winning ex-Irish pointer: no sign of ability in early-season novice chases. *D. R. Franks*   c–

SWAN STAR 4 br.f. Petong – Lewista (Mandrake Major) [1992/3 17f^pu] of little account on Flat nowadays: visored, no sign of ability in early-season juvenile selling hurdle. *G. Blum*   –

SWEATSHIRT 8 b.g. Leander – Roman Lilly (Romany Air) [1992/3 c22d* c22g^5] rangy gelding: fair hunter chaser: awarded race (hampered when beaten short head by Curaheen Boy) at Stratford in February: ran poorly later in month: stays 2¾m: acts on dead ground. *S. Pike*   c90

SWEET CITY 8 ch.g. Sweet Monday – City's Sister (Maystreak) [1992/3 17g 21d 21s 23s^6 17d* 17s^4 16d^4 c16d^5 24g 22g] workmanlike gelding: fairly useful hurdler nowadays: won conditional jockeys handicap at Kelso in December: winning chaser: stays 2½m: ideally suited by give in the ground (acts on heavy): tried blinkered/visored: poor jumper of fences: inconsistent. *G. Richards*   c– x 116 §

SWEET DUKE (FR) 6 b.g. Iron Duke (FR) – Sweet Virginia (FR) (Tapioca II) [1992/3 21g* 24s* 21g^2 26d^3 25v* 26s 24s^6 22s^2 25m^4 24s* 24d* 24f]   161

Peter Scudamore rode into retirement on a winner, Sweet Duke, in the Alpine Meadow Handicap Hurdle at Ascot the week after the Grand National. Scudamore, who stood a fair second to Dunwoody in the jockeys' table, explained his decision to 'get out while I'm still at the top and in one piece'. 'I'm sure some people might be critical of me packing up, thinking I should have carried on to the end of the season and tried to catch Richard for the championship,' he said. 'But I didn't really want to struggle on around the little tracks any more . . . . . jump racing is all about battling away on a rotten day at Worcester or in a novice chase in the cold at Devon, and they're hard days'. Scudamore's sudden retirement brought to an end a most successful career, one which put him, statistically, a distance clear of his contemporaries. No records last for ever, but Scudamore retired holding probably the three most important ones for a jumping jockey in Britain—the most championships (eight, one of them shared), the most winners in a

Letheby & Christopher Long Distance Hurdle, Ascot—Sweet Duke is impressive

season (221 in 1988/9) and the most winners in a career (generally quoted as 1,677, but in fact 1,678 since, as a result of a very late disqualification, Scudamore won 124 races in 1986/7, not 123 as in most of the reference books including *Chasers & Hurdlers 1986/87*). The 1992/3 season was the eighth in which Scudamore reached his century, another record. His prolonged domination produced many highlights—including Champion Hurdle victories on Celtic Shot and Granville Again and a brilliant Welsh National win on Carvill's Hill—but the fact that he never won the Gold Cup or the Grand National, jumping's two most glamorous events, undoubtedly contributed in part to his public image as a dedicated and uncomplicated professional lacking the charisma of his immediate predecessor as top jockey John Francome. But in all important respects Scudamore was the equal of Francome. He was cool and calculating, tactically sound and a superb judge of pace; he presented horses extremely well at the obstacles and had fewer falls than most, allying his skill with the strength and balance to survive mistakes that most others probably wouldn't have survived; and he was very strong in a finish. Scudamore may not have enjoyed a 'swashbuckling' image—he seemed all furrowed brow and concentration when interviewed—but he was a *great* champion nonetheless, who rarely lost a race he should have won. It could truly be said of Scudamore's retirement, as it could of Francome's, that it marked the end of an era.

The horse who gave Scudamore his final victory, Sweet Duke, had a magnificent season, starting off with early-season wins in handicaps at Perth and Chepstow and continuing on the upgrade, adding a more competitive handicap at Cheltenham to his tally in December, to graduate to championship standard as a staying hurdler. He came fourth in the Bonus-Print Stayers' Hurdle at the Festival meeting and then won the Letheby and Christopher Long Distance Hurdle at Ascot at the end of March, turning the tables on terms 7 lb better than at Cheltenham with the Stayers' Hurdle runner-up Pragada. Sweet Duke's victory under top weight in the Alpine

Meadow Handicap came a week later. Sweet Duke, a sound jumper of hurdles, is reportedly to go chasing in the next season and if he makes a smooth transition to jumping fences he is just the type to develop into a contender for the Sun Alliance Chase which his stable won in the latest season with Young Hustler. Like Young Hustler, Sweet Duke is very tough and genuine, and a great credit to his trainer. Sweet Duke acts on good to firm going but goes particularly well with give in the ground and acts on heavy. He usually races prominently.

Alpine Meadow Handicap Hurdle, Ascot—congratulations for Scudamore as he signs off with a win on Sweet Duke

Sweet Duke is a leggy gelding who doesn't carry much condition when in training. He was bred in France but began his career in National Hunt Flat races in Britain as a four-year-old, finishing runner-up to Dual Image in the Seagram Champion NH Flat race at Aintree on the second of two starts. Sweet Duke won two novice hurdles at Worcester in the first half of the next season when he put up his best effort to come second to Mighty Mogul in the

Andy Mavrou's "Sweet Duke"

Sweet Duke (FR) (b.g. 1987)	Iron Duke (FR) (b 1973)	Sicambre (br 1948)	Prince Bio
			Sif
		Insulaire (b 1966)	Aureole
			Ismene
	Sweet Virginia (FR) (br 1977)	Tapioca II (b 1953)	Vandale
			Semoule d'Or
		La Horse (b 1970)	White Label
			Noble Lady

Persian War Premier Novices' Hurdle at Chepstow. Sweet Duke's sire Iron Duke was a good French middle-distance horse and his dam Sweet Virginia won three times over jumps in France and is a half-sister to a number of other winning French jumpers, the most successful of them being the brothers Funny Horse and Dazzling Horse (by Carmarthen). Sweet Duke's lightly-raced grandam La Horse didn't win, tried on the Flat and over jumps, but his great grandam Noble Lady, from a well-known family belonging to the Volterras, was a minor winner on the Flat and a half-sister to Mme Volterra's top French stayer Pardallo II who won the 1968 Gold Cup at Royal Ascot and, incidentally, was also successful over hurdles. Sweet Duke's dam Sweet Virginia is also the dam of Sweet Easter, a filly by Jaazeiro who won six times on the Flat in France, and Sweet As Moss, a filly by Tip Moss who was placed over jumps in France. *N. A. Twiston-Davies*

SWEET FRIENDSHIP 5 b.m. Alleging (USA) – Child of Grace (King's Leap) [1992/3 F 17g] third live foal: half-sister to Amazing Silks (by Furry Glen), a winner on Flat and over hurdles: mid-division in 25-runner early-season NH Flat race: yet to race over hurdles or fences. *D. J. Wintle*

SWEET GEORGE 6 b.g. Ardross – Madam Slaney (Prince Tenderfoot (USA)) [1992/3 23vpu 20d5 21f*] rangy gelding: poor hurdler: won novice handicap at Newbury in March: stays 21f: acts on firm going. *N. J. Henderson* 79

SWEET GLOW (FR) 6 b.g. Crystal Glitters (USA) – Very Sweet (Bellypha) [1992/3 25g6 26d4 25s4 24s* 24d* 25gF 25m5 24s4 24g3 26s] 156
A very heavy fall at the last in the Rendlesham Hurdle at Kempton in February marked the end of a purple patch for Sweet Glow which had begun in the valuable Rosling King Hurdle at Ascot the previous month. He'd started the season slowly, giving the impression he might no longer be up to contesting top races, but he put up a smart performance to win the Rosling King, a handicap, by two and a half lengths and half a length from Grace Card and Dara Doone. He was conceding weight to the second and third, who finished clear of the rest of a good field. He followed up three weeks later in the four-runner Daily Telegraph Hurdle over the same course. As in the handicap he responded to a call for finishing speed. Boscean Chieftain's rider tried to steal the race in the home straight but Sweet Glow quickened impressively to get up by three lengths. Next came the Rendlesham Hurdle and the fall. Ridden by a 5-lb claimer unable to claim the allowance because of the race's value, he was disputing the lead with the eventual winner Baydon Star when it happened, in with every chance. Win or lose Sweet Glow would have run at least as well as ever he had stood up. First reports indicated that he'd received a shaking severe enough to threaten the chance of a rematch in the Stayers' Hurdle at Cheltenham. In the end he returned to finish fifth to Shuil Ar Aghaidh, and had three races after that but he wasn't seen at his best. His performance in the Long Distance Hurdle at Ascot in March was right out of character—lack-lustre, full of deliberate jumping. He shaped well in a handicap hurdle at Ascot the following month, finishing strongly into third place behind Buonarroti, beaten little more than two lengths having been set a great deal to do. Finally, he was well beaten in the strongly-contested Grande Course de Haies d'Auteuil in July.
Sweet Glow came to Britain by way of a French claiming race. He is well bred and used to be trained by Criquette Head, for whom he won over a mile at Compiegne and Saint-Cloud. He joined his present stable in October, 1990, having been claimed for the equivalent of £12,430 at Saint-Cloud, and he has improved in each season over hurdles since. Sweet Glow's grandam Very Charming is a sister to the outstanding racemare Dahlia. She won at a

mile and a quarter in France and has produced numerous winners, among them the very useful middle-distance colt Theatrical Charmer and his half-sister Very Sweet, Sweet Glow's dam, another mile-and-a-quarter winner. Sweet Glow is the second foal of his dam; the first, Sweet Lassie (by Posse), was a fair performer at around a mile in France who later won in the USA; the third, Kalgrey (by Kaldoun), has also shown form in both France and the USA, and is useful.

Sweet Glow (FR) (b.g. 1987)	Crystal Glitters (USA) (b 1980)	Blushing Groom (ch 1974)	Red God / Runaway Bride
		Tales To Tell (b 1967)	Donut King / Fleeting Doll
	Very Sweet (gr 1981)	Bellypha (gr 1976)	Lyphard / Belga
		Very Charming (ch 1974)	Vaguely Noble / Charming Alibi

Sweet Glow's sire Crystal Glitters won the Prix d'Ispahan twice and was best at up to nine furlongs, so all in all it is surprising that a horse of Sweet Glow's breeding should make his mark as a three-mile hurdler. However, speed is his main asset as a three-miler; he is not one who needs, or is even suited by, an out-and-out slog as, for example, a horse like Pragada is. Among his other assets are his toughness, the ability to show his form on any type of ground, and his surefootedness—he has fallen only the once, and that was the result of taking off only a fraction too soon. Sweet Glow has been tried in blinkers several times, but not since he ran very freely in them on his second start in Britain. *M. C. Pipe*

SWEETING 8 b.g. Lighter – Snare (Poaching) [1992/3 24vpu 23vpu c25dpu 20m4 28m3] leggy, lengthy gelding: poor novice hurdler: no form over fences: stays 3½m: form only on good to firm ground. *J. White* — c– 73

SWEET MARINER 7 ch.g. Julio Mariner – Sweet Bush (The Brianstan) [1992/3 22g] sparely-made gelding: of little account. *D. J. Wintle* — –

SWEET NOBLE (IRE) 4 ch.g. The Noble Player (USA) – Penny Candy (Tamerlane) [1992/3 16d2 16s2 16d6 18d3 a18g3 a16g5 20m3] workmanlike gelding: half-brother to 3 winners, notably high-class hurdler Corporal Clinger (by Bruni): poor maiden on Flat: poor form over hurdles: stays 2½m: acts on good to firm, soft ground and on fibresand: consistent. *J. G. FitzGerald* — 84

SWEET N' TWENTY 7 b.m. High Top – Royal Home (Royal Palace) [1992/3 16s3 18v 17s 20d* 20g2] sturdy, workmanlike mare: fairly useful hurdler: won conditional jockeys handicap at Ascot in February: stays 2½m: probably acts on any going on turf but ran poorly on all-weather: sometimes has tongue tied down. *M. C. Pipe* — 121

SWEET SCIMITAR 4 b.f. Broadsword (USA) – Saucy Linda (Saucy Kit) [1992/3 F16s] smallish, workmanlike filly: first foal: dam winning pointer: tailed off in mares NH Flat race at Ludlow in April: yet to race over hurdles. *P. J. Jones* — –

SWEET SINNY 7 b.m. Sweet Monday – Sinartra (Connaught) [1992/3 17dpu] once-raced on Flat (at 2 yrs): no sign of ability in novice event in November on hurdling debut. *Mrs A. R. Hewitt* — –

SWERVIN MERVIN 5 ch.g. Dominion – Brilliant Rosa (Luthier) [1992/3 17m4 18d4] leggy, lengthy gelding: half-brother to quite useful 2m hurdler Smart Performer (by Formidable): plating-class maiden at up to 1m at 3 yrs: poor form when fourth in novice hurdles in first half of season: likely to prove best at around 2m: acts on good to firm and dead ground: held up. *B. Ellison* — 80

SWIFT ASCENT (USA) 11 b.g. Crow (FR) – Barely Flying (USA) (Fleet Nasrullah) [1992/3 18gpu] tall, leggy gelding: 2m winning hurdler/novice chaser: no form since 1990/1. *A. Barrow* — c– / –

SWIFT CARRIAGE 7 br.m. Carriage Way – River Petterill (Another River) [1992/3 17m 16d4 18d 16d] lengthy, good-quartered mare: novice selling hurdler: has raced mainly at around 2m on dead ground. *W. Storey* — 72

SWIFT CONVEYANCE (IRE) 4 br.f. Strong Gale – Markree Castle (Pitpan) [1992/3 16g 17v³ 17s 16d⁵ 18d 16s⁶ 17m 17s⁵] lengthy, leggy, unfurnished filly: second foal: dam won over hurdles and fences in Ireland: poor form over hurdles: yet to race beyond 2¼m: best efforts on a yielding surface. *W. T. Kemp*   77

SWILLY EXPRESS 7 b.m. Ballacashtal (CAN) – Thunder Bay (Canisbay) [1992/3 19g⁴ 21s⁵ 21s³ 25s⁴ 25s c21dᵖᵘ] small, sturdy mare: fair handicap hurdler: no promise on chasing debut: stays 25f: seems suited by plenty of give in the ground. *S. Christian*   c–   102

SWINGTIME BELLE 6 b.m. Swing Easy (USA) – Betbellof (Averof) [1992/3 16mᵖᵘ 16f⁵ 16g⁵ 16gᵖᵘ 17m⁴ 17s⁴] leggy mare: bad selling hurdler nowadays: once-raced over fences: occasionally blinkered/visored. *M. W. Eckley*   c–   54

SWINHOE CROFT 11 b.g. Orange Bay – On A Bit (Mummy's Pet) [1992/3 c25s* c24d³ c27m⁶] leggy gelding: fairly useful hunter chaser: won at Bangor in February: creditable efforts afterwards (finished lame when sixth in Foxhunter Chase at Cheltenham final start): stays very well: acts on heavy and good to firm going: blinkered once: races up with the pace. *F. Lloyd*   c105   –

SWISS BEAUTY 5 b.m. Ballacashtal (CAN) – Cocked Hat Supreme (Uncle Pokey) [1992/3 17m² 22m³ 22f 21sᵖᵘ 17dᵖᵘ] lengthy mare: poor novice hurdler: best efforts at 2m on good to firm ground. *Miss Z. A. Green*   73

SWITCH 7 ch.g. Electric – Ominous (Dominion) [1992/3 18v* 22s³ 21s² c16v³ c24gᵘʳ] leggy, quite good-topped gelding: fairly useful hurdler: won handicap at Worcester in November: third in novice event at Warwick in January on chasing debut: unseated rider ninth following month: stays 21f: acts on good to firm and heavy ground: tends to jump left: sure to improve over fences. *C. P. E. Brooks*   c90 p   129

SWOOPING 8 b.g. Kings Lake (USA) – High Hawk (Shirley Heights) [1992/3 c21gᶠ] lengthy, rather dipped-backed gelding: modest pointer: second in 2½m novice hunter chase in 1992: fell seventh in March. *Mrs T. J. Hill*   c–   –

SWORD BEACH 9 ch.g. Scallywag – Bargello's Lady (Bargello) [1992/3 c21m³] workmanlike gelding: usually impresses in appearance: fairly useful chaser: shaped as though he'd retained most of his ability when third at Carlisle in March: effective at 2½m and stays 3m: probably best on a sound surface: visored once: jumps soundly: usually races up with pace. *M. H. Easterby*   c122   –

SWORD BRIDGE 6 b.m. Broadsword (USA) – Tye Bridge (Idiot's Delight) [1992/3 22mᵖᵘ] leggy mare: no form over hurdles. *D. H. Gibbon*   –

SWORDED KNIGHT 7 ch.g. Broadsword (USA) – Alan's Girl (Prince Hansel) [1992/3 c24dᶠ c20s⁵ c26vᵖᵘ 23s³ 25s 25dᵖᵘ] big, lengthy gelding: modest novice hurdler/chaser: stays 23f: acts on soft ground. *N. A. Gaselee*   c85   85

SYBILLIN 7 b.g. Henbit (USA) – Tea House (Sassafras (FR)) [1992/3 c16d* c16d* c17s* c16s* c16g* c16m³]   c156   –

Following favourites at the Cheltenham National Hunt Festival was a road to ruin: they all went down except Olympian, co-favourite for the Coral Cup, the third race on the middle day. As usual the racing over the three days was highly competitive, and only one runner started at odds on, that being Sybillin, 5/4 on to win the Waterford Castle Arkle Trophy. A high-class hurdler having his first season over fences, Sybillin already looked plenty good enough to run against the leading two-milers in the Queen Mother Champion Chase. So he was bound to be a warm order against seven novices in the Arkle, particularly as he'd recently given weight and a beating to Wonder Man, generally assumed to be his main rival. However, he gave his supporters little to cheer. He did draw out with Wonder Man and Travado down the hill and was still in with a chance two from home, but they left him behind on the last turn. He dropped away tamely up the hill, his head high and to one side, and trailed in third, twenty lengths behind second-placed Wonder Man, seemingly distressed. Sybillin hadn't impressed in the paddock and had clearly run way below his best. Straight afterwards his trainer commented, 'It was very disappointing but I'm not totally surprised after seeing the result of his blood test. It wasn't right at Nottingham last time but he got away with it. This was a harder race and he didn't.' He added that he wasn't satisfied with the results of tests on some of the stable's other horses. Trainglot's poor showing the next day added greatly to concern, and, although Aslan ran well in the bumper, Gold Options was withdrawn from the Gold Cup as a precaution. Another unfavourable blood test on Sybillin—the result came through at eleven o'clock on the morning of the race—caused his withdrawal from the Sandeman Maghull Novices' Chase at Aintree the following month, and the Arkle turned out to be his final race of the season. The usefulness of blood-testing as a means of assessing fitness in the racehorse has been a matter for some debate. There are trainers, including some of the profession's leading lights, who swear by regular testing. However, the fact that Sybillin could go out at Nottingham to record probably one of the best performances of the season by a novice supplies ammunition for its detractors. Peter Easterby once told the story in a *Timeform Interview* of how he had Sea Pigeon blood-tested after he disappointed him in the Royal Doulton Hurdle at Haydock. The results said the blood was 'all wrong'. There didn't seem much wrong with the horse to his trainer, though; he went ahead with plans to run him in the Chester Cup nine days later and Sea Pigeon won it for the second time.

Had Sybillin managed to win the Arkle we should be writing him up as the next champion two-mile chaser. Now, the lightly-raced Travado and Wonder Man must come into the reckoning as well, along with Viking Flagship too. All four rate as better prospects than any who contested a weak Queen Mother Champion Chase in 1993. It would still be anything but a surprise if Sybillin went right to the top over fences, such was the impression he made prior to Cheltenham. In that period he looked a natural as, one after the other, a novice chase at Uttoxeter, the Hurst Park Novices' Chase at Ascot, the Northumberland Gold Cup at Newcastle, the Victor Chandler Handicap at Ascot and the Nottinghamshire Novices' Chase fell to him. He was the same horse as he'd been at his best over hurdles, in that he

Northumberland Gold Cup Novices' Chase, Newcastle—
Sybillin (left) has too much speed for Dawson City

Victor Chandler Handicap Chase, Ascot—
Sybillin puts up an outstanding performance for a novice in beating Deep Sensation

jumped superbly, travelled strongly through the race and produced a
handsome turn of foot. Dawson City hardly got him off the bridle in a
moderately-run race at Newcastle. But good as Dawson City was, he was still
just another novice. The opposition was much more experienced, as well as
much stronger in depth, in the Victor Chandler and Sybillin seemed to have
a great deal on his plate. In winning by ten lengths from the H & T Walker
Gold Cup winner and eventual Champion Chase winner Deep Sensation he
posted credentials as solid as you would ever see from an Arkle candidate,
not to mention far more solid than are usually seen. He cruised up to the
leaders two out, flew the last and drew right away, being one of the few all
day to finish with any running in him. That win set up an intriguing clash in
the Nottinghamshire Novices' Chase with Wonder Man. Sybillin won

Nottinghamshire Novices' Chase, Nottingham—good jumping from Sybillin and Wonder Man

decisively by a length and a half conceding 3 lb, the remaining runners outclassed. Wonder Man made the running as usual. Sybillin moved up to track him from the ninth, challenged travelling the better in the straight and only needed to be pushed out after he quickened past on the run-in. Sybillin had matched Wonder Man's jumping and had shown easily the better turn of foot. So what went wrong at Cheltenham? It has to be said that 1992/3 was the fourth season in a row in which his season ended disappointingly. In 1989/90, when he ran eleven times and was leading juvenile hurdler, he finished well beaten at Auteuil over two and a half miles, a distance probably beyond him. In 1990/1, when he ran three times, he was pulled up before the last in the Champion Hurdle after travelling well to three out. In 1991/2, seen out five times, he lost his form after two runs and broke a blood vessel on his final start. Possibly his constitution isn't the most robust.

		Hawaii	Utrillo II
	Henbit (USA)	(b 1964)	Ethane
	(b 1977)	Chateaucreek	Chateaugay
Sybillin		(ch 1970)	Mooncreek
(b.g. 1986)		Sassafras	Sheshoon
	Tea House	(b 1967)	Ruta
	(ch 1980)	House Tie	Be Friendly
		(b 1975)	Mesopotamia

Sybillin is by the Derby winner Henbit, who has become regarded primarily as a jumping sire nowadays. The dam Tea House won at six furlongs and a mile in Ireland, showing useful form, and is out of another Irish one-mile winner, House Tie, a daughter of the Chesham Stakes winner Mesopotamia. Tea House made a good start as a broodmare, first producing Mr Sunday Sport, a prolific winner in Italy since he won twice in Britain as a two-year-old, then his brother Sybillin. And she followed with the Irish two-year-old seven-furlong winner Come To Tea (by Be My Guest) and the modest mile-and-a-half winner Sure Haven (by Sure Blade). Her foal of 1990 Butter Knife (also by Sure Blade) hasn't made the racecourse yet, but that of 1991, Danish (by Danehill), got off the mark first time of asking over six furlongs at Leopardstown in May.

Sybillin is best at a mile to a mile and a quarter on the Flat; he has been restricted to two miles for the last three jumping seasons, invariably held up to make the most of that turn of foot. A workmanlike gelding, he acts on any going. *J. G. FitzGerald*

SYD GREEN (IRE) 5 b.g. Green Shoon – Gone (Whistling Wind) [1992/3 F16s 22d^su 16d] rangy, unfurnished gelding: brother to staying jumpers Green Tops and Shoon Wind, latter fairly useful: dam maiden hurdler/pointer in Ireland: tailed off in novice hurdles. *R. F. Fisher* —

SYDMONTON 7 ch.g. Deep Run – Inaghmose (Pitpan) [1992/3 17s⁵ 20s⁶ 16g² 16v^pu 18d] angular gelding: fair hurdler: ran poorly last 2 outings: should stay beyond 17f: acts on soft ground. *N. J. Henderson* — 101

SYDNEY BARRY (NZ) 8 b.g. Tom's Shu (USA) – Avill Star (NZ) (Karayar) [1992/3 17s^pu 17d⁴ 19f^pu 17g* 17s^pu 17g^F 16v³ 16d⁵ 17d 22v a18g⁶ 20v² 20f* 17m*] compact gelding: won novice handicap hurdles at Hereford in September and May (2, both in good style): stays 2½m: probably acts on any going. *R. H. Buckler* — 83

SYLVIA BEACH 7 b.m. The Parson – Cyllevista (Menelek) [1992/3 16d 16s⁴ 16v³ 20m* 21g³ 22m] sparely-made mare: won mares novice hurdle at Hereford in March: little form in 2 starts after: should stay beyond 2½m: acts on good to firm and heavy going. *P. G. Murphy* — 89

SYMMETRICAL 4 ch.c. Kris – Flawless Image (USA) (The Minstrel (CAN)) [1992/3 17s] very lightly-raced maiden and no form on Flat: sold 2,100 gns Ascot November Sales: blinkered, behind in juvenile hurdle at Plumpton in April: sold 1,750 gns Ascot May Sales. *J. Akehurst* —

SYNDERBOROUGH LAD 7 ch.g. Rymer – Roman Lilly (Romany Air) [1992/3 c25d⁵ c21m] fair pointer: showed ability both starts in novice hunter chases: may do better. *S. Pike* — c73 p

T

TACTICAL MISSION (IRE) 5 b.g. Rainbow Quest (USA) – Our Village (Ballymore) [1992/3 22v² 20g* 21s³] lengthy gelding: fair stayer on Flat, goes well on fibresand: won novice hurdle at Doncaster in December: good third in handicap at Warwick following month: will stay beyond 2¾m: acts on heavy ground. *J. Akehurst*   103

TAFFY JONES 14 br.g. Welsh Pageant – Shallow Stream (Reliance II) [1992/3 c17m² c18m⁴ c16g c16g³ c18m² c16m⁵ c17v⁶ c16f² c19d⁶] smallish gelding: poor chaser: ran creditably when placed in 1992/3: stays 2½m: acts on hard and dead ground: visored once: unreliable jumper. *M. McCormack*   c78 x –

TAGMOUN CHAUFOUR (FR) 8 ch.g. Pavo Real (FR) – Bien Venue (FR) (Popof) [1992/3 c26v⁶] small, plain gelding: winning chaser: needed race only outing of season (January): thorough stayer: acts on soft going. *A. Barrow*   c– –

TAILSPIN 8 b.g. Young Generation – Mumtaz Flyer (USA) (Al Hattab (USA)) [1992/3 17sᵖᵘ 23m 18m⁴ 17m⁴ 18g 17d⁵ 17fᵖᵘ] lengthy gelding: novice plater over hurdles: usually blinkered nowadays. *Mrs J. Scrivens*   78 ?

TAKE BY STORM (IRE) 4 b.c. Bluebird (USA) – Laurel Express (Bay Express) [1992/3 16g³ 17v] lengthy, angular colt: fair middle-distance performer at best on Flat (below form in 1993): promising third in juvenile hurdle at Wetherby in October: failed to run up to that form in similar event at Cheltenham following month. *G. M. Moore*   101

TAKE CHANCES 5 ch.g. Town And Country – Festive Season (Silly Season) [1992/3 F16s⁶] good-topped gelding: third foal: brother to winning pointer Country Festival: dam winning pointer: backward, remote sixth of 22 in NH Flat race at Warwick in February: yet to race over hurdles or fences. *Mrs P. N. Dutfield*

TAKE ISSUE 8 b.g. Absalom – Abstract (French Beige) [1992/3 17d 20g⁶ 20f⁶] workmanlike gelding: fairly useful hurdler at best, no worthwhile form in 1992/3: stays 2½m: seems to act on any going: visored once (below form). *R. M. Flower*   –

TAKE IT IN CASH 4 ch.f. Ballacashtal (CAN) – Soft Secret (Most Secret) [1992/3 16s] workmanlike filly: modest sprint maiden on Flat: tailed off in juvenile hurdle at Nottingham in November, and is unlikely to stay 2m. *R. Dickin*   –

TAKEMETHERE 9 b.g. Decent Fellow – Mandaloch (Mandamus) [1992/3 c25d⁵ c20g c20g* c20m³ c20m³ c23s⁴ c21f² c18gF] workmanlike gelding: fair chaser: won handicap at Doncaster in January: best effort afterwards when second in similar event at Worcester in May: retained 8,000 gns Ascot June Sales: effective at around 2½m and barely stays 3m: acts well on a sound surface: sometimes finds little under pressure: sketchy jumper. *M. C. Pipe*   c104 –

TAKEOVER BID 9 b.g. Dramatic Bid (USA) – Sassenach Girl (Sassafras (FR)) [1992/3 c26m⁶] tall gelding: winning pointer: won hunter chase in 1991 but was tailed off in similar event in May: stays 3m. *S. H. Marriage*   c– –

TAKE STOCK 7 br.g. Callernish – Mojeli (Arapaho) [1992/3 18m 18g] lengthy gelding: no sign of ability in 3 runs over hurdles. *W. A. Stephenson*   –

TAKE THE BUCKSKIN 6 b.g. Buckskin (FR) – Honeyburn (Straight Rule) [1992/3 aF16g*] has been hobdayed: third foal: dam, lightly raced, from excellent jumping family which includes Deep Sensation, The Benign Bishop and Chandigar: won 15-runner NH Flat race at Southwell in January: yet to race over hurdles or fences. *T. Thomson Jones*

TAKE TWO 5 b.g. Jupiter Island – Dancing Daughter (Dance In Time (CAN)) [1992/3 16f⁴ 18f³ 18v* 17f*] sturdy gelding: fair hurdler: won selling handicap at Cartmel (bought in 2,600 gns) and claimer at Stratford late in   102 season, well-backed favourite both times: will prove best at around 2m: acts on any ground. *J. White*

TALAB   8 b.g. Beldale Flutter (USA) – Glen Dancer (Furry Glen) [1992/3 17v 16s⁵ a16g³ 17m⁶ 20m 20s⁶ 24g a16g⁶] sturdy gelding: poor hurdler: stays 2½m: acts on any going: blinkered once. *R. A. Bennett*   75

TALATON FLYER   7 b.g. Kala Shikari – Pertune (Hyperion's Curls) [1992/3 20mᵖᵘ 18f⁴ 19m⁶] workmanlike gelding: modest hurdler: not raced after September: stays 19f: acts on good to firm and dead ground. *P. J. Hobbs*   87

TALENTED TING (IRE)   4 ch.g. Hatim (USA) – An Tig Gaelige (Thatch (USA)) [1992/3 17s] strong gelding: half-brother to winning hurdler Tigest (by What A Guest): fairly useful at around 1¼m on Flat, visored when successful in 1993: well beaten in juvenile hurdle at Newcastle in December. *P. C. Haslam*   –

TALKING MONEY   9 ch.g. Quayside – Shuil Alainn (Levanter) [1992/3 18g³] smallish, workmanlike gelding: poor novice hurdler: remote third in seller at Fontwell in September, best effort. *M. P. Muggeridge*   76

TALLAND STREAM   6 b.g. Paddy's Stream – Mary May (Little Buskins) [1992/3 17d³ 16d³ 16d⁶ 18d] fourth foal: half-brother to winning jumpers Fast Study and Marys Course (both by Crash Course): dam winner on Flat and over hurdles in Ireland: easily best effort in novice hurdles when third at Ludlow in December on second outing: should stay beyond 2m: acts on dead ground. *Capt. T. A. Forster*   87

TALLYWAGGER   6 b.g. Mandalus – Boro Cent (Little Buskins) [1992/3 24d⁴ 24g⁴ 25g⁵ 24mF 28d* 22g³ 25g³ 24m* 25s⁶ a24g²] small, sparely-made, angular gelding: developed into a fairly useful handicap hurdler in 1992/3, winning at Hexham, Sedgefield and Newcastle: below best last 2 outings: suited by a good test of stamina: acts on dead and good to firm ground. *G. M. Moore*   127

TALUS   9 gr.g. Kalaglow – Helcia (Habitat) [1992/3 19m 18s⁶ 22s 20f³ 22s⁵ 18s⁴ 20v 23s a18g⁵ 20g c17gᵘʳ c21fF 20m 20sᵖᵘ] leggy, lengthy, angular gelding: poor hurdler: has failed to complete over fences: stays 2¾m: probably acts on any going: blinkered once, often visored. *J. R. Bosley*   c– 82

TAMARA'S GIFT   8 b.m. The Brianstan – Mandy's Gift (Mandamus) [1992/3 c21gF] poor maiden pointer: tailed off when falling in maiden hunter chase in May. *Mrs D. Cope*   c–

TAMAR LASS   8 b.m. Shaab – La Jolie Fille (Go Blue) [1992/3 c24s³ c23v² c27d³ c26g³] compact mare: winning pointer: only poor form when placed in hunter chases: stays 27f: acts on heavy ground. *Miss J. du Plessis*   c73

TAMBORITO (IRE)   4 b.g. Thatching – Vera Musica (USA) (Stop The Music (USA)) [1992/3 F17g F16g] good-topped gelding: first foal: dam ran in Italy: tailed off in NH Flat races at Doncaster in January and Catterick in March: yet to race over hurdles. *T. J. Naughton*   –

TAMMY MY GIRL   10 ch.m. Timolin (FR) – Teasemenot (Doubtless II) [1992/3 28gᵖᵘ c26dᵖᵘ c25v³ c25vᵖᵘ c25d* c26dᵖᵘ c25sF] leggy, close-coupled mare: won amateurs novice chase at Market Rasen in January: stays 25f: acts on dead ground: refused to race once and took no interest sixth outing. *P. Beaumont*   c87 §

TAMMY'S FRIEND   6 b.g. Deep Run – Cinderwood (Laurence O) [1992/3 20v³ c18s* c21d⁵ c21m* c21f² c24f*] well-made gelding: poor novice hurdler: better over fences and won maiden at Plumpton in April and novice handicaps at Uttoxeter and Huntingdon in May: has won over 2¼m, is better at 3m: probably acts on any going: should do well in long-distance handicap chases. *Mrs J. Pitman*   c102 p –

TANANA   4 b.f. Teenoso (USA) – La Nureyeva (USA) (Nureyev (USA)) [1992/3 17m² 17f] plating-class maiden on Flat: second in juvenile event at Huntingdon in August, easily better effort over hurdles: sold 920 gns Doncaster October Sales. *J. G. FitzGerald*   81

TANBER LASS 12 b.m. New Member – Santan (Dairialatan) [1992/3 c74
c26g³ c17sᵖᵘ c23g⁶ c17s³ c20m³ c21m c18m⁶ c24g c27f⁴] leggy, lengthy
mare: poor novice chaser: stays 3¼m: best form on a sound surface. *R. G.
Frost*

TANCRED GRANGE 4 ch.g. Prince Sabo – Carpadia (Icecapade
(USA)) [1992/3 16s a16g a16g a18g² a16gᵖᵘ] close-coupled gelding: modest 85
1m winner on Flat in 1992: sold out of Miss S. Hall's stable 6,100 gns
Doncaster October Sales: only form over hurdles when second in novice
event at Southwell in January: stayed 2¼m: acted on fibresand: dead. *B.
Preece*

TANDERAGEE 12 ch.m. Trasi's Son – Whitney (Venture VII) [1992/3 c–
21vpu c26vF c21spu c24vpu c24dpu] lengthy mare: seems of little account –
nowadays: blinkered last outing. *Mrs N. S. Sharpe*

TANFIRION BAY (IRE) 5 b.g. Whistling Deer – Alone All Alone
(Tanfirion) [1992/3 23spu a20g⁵] neat gelding: moderate handicap hurdler at –
best: below-form fifth at Lingfield in January: stays 2¾m: probably acts on
any going: visored once. *P. R. Hedger*

TANGLED STRING 9 b.g. Idiot's Delight – Heartstring (Fortissimo) c99
[1992/3 c24vpu c24s² c24vᵘʳ c24v⁶ c24g⁴ c23m⁶ c20s*] leggy gelding: –
novice hurdler: modest chaser: won 4-runner novice event at Chepstow in
April: stays 3m: acts on soft going: sketchy jumper. *C. C. Elsey*

TANGLE JIM 8 b.g. Jimsun – Spartangle (Spartan General) [1992/3 c–
c24mᵘʳ] fair pointer, winner 3 times in 1993: unseated rider seventh in April –
on steeplechasing debut. *M. J. Trickey*

TANGO'S DELIGHT 5 b.g. Idiot's Delight – Lucky Tango (Tangle)
[1992/3 F12d² F17m] useful-looking gelding with scope: half-brother to –
several winners, including useful hurdler Vivaque (by Bivouac): dam,
moderate staying hurdler/chaser, stayed 3m: second of 18 in NH Flat race at
Windsor in February: always behind in valuable event at Cheltenham in
March: yet to race over hurdles or fences. *D. R. C. Elsworth*

TANGO TOM 8 ch.g. New Member – Dance Partner (Manicou) [1992/3 c70
c24m⁵] fair pointer: only poor form when fifth of 7 finishers in hunter chase –
at Taunton in April. *R. J. Smith*

TANNINGTON 10 b.g. Deep Run – Kertina (Fortina) [1992/3 c24gF c–
c24dᵇᵈ c24spu] sparely-made gelding: maiden hurdler/chaser: dead. *F. –
Murphy*

TAPATCH (IRE) 5 b.h. Thatching – Knees Up (USA) (Dancing Champ
(USA)) [1992/3 16gF 16g* 16g⁵ 17m² 17f* 18m⁴ 17f* 16f⁶] close-coupled 111
horse: fair handicap hurdler: won at Edinburgh (amateurs) in December,
Huntingdon in March and Newcastle (gamely) in May: stays 17f: acts on
hard going: not a fluent jumper. *G. M. Moore*

TAP DANCING 7 ch.g. Sallust – Amorak (Wolver Hollow) [1992/3 20gpu
21f 25s² 25d³ 25d⁴ 26d 28vpu 24s⁶ 17d⁵] close-coupled gelding: modest 88
hurdler: ran creditably most completed starts in 1992/3: needs further than
17f and stays well: acts on any going: visored when successful. *J. Allen*

TAPESTRY DANCER 5 b.g. Lidhame – Royal Bat (Crowned Prince
(USA)) [1992/3 17m 17m⁶ 18g* 17d⁵ 18d⁴ 20vpu 17g⁶ 17f⁴ 16f⁶] close-coupled 76
gelding: won selling hurdle at Fontwell (no bid) in September: well below
form last 4 starts: stays 2¼m: acts on dead ground. *M. J. Haynes*

TARA BOY 8 b.g. Rusticaro (FR) – Flosshilde (Rheingold) [1992/3 c25g c84
c26g² c26d³ c21m*] leggy gelding: won novice hunter chase at Uttoxeter in –
June: sold 5,800 gns Malvern June Sales: stays 27f: acts on any ground:
sometimes blinkered. *W. D. Francis*

TARAMOSS 6 b.g. Le Moss – Birniebrig (New Brig) [1992/3 22s³ 25v⁴
24s*] rangy, good sort: chasing type: favourite, made all in maiden hurdle at 102
Hexham in May: stays 3m: acts on soft ground. *J. A. C. Edwards*

TARDA 6 ch.m. Absalom – Ixia (I Say) [1992/3 16m 18m⁶] angular mare:
modest 1m/1¼m performer on Flat, successful in 1992: very lightly raced 70

over hurdles: best effort when sixth of 19 in maiden at Market Rasen in May. *Mrs M. Reveley*

TAREESH 6 br.m. Fine Blade (USA) – Loch Gorman (Bargello) [1992/3 16v c21vᵖᵘ c16s⁵ 20m² 25g* 21gF 26s³ 26g³ 22f²] rather unfurnished mare with scope: fourth foal: dam, runner-up in Irish NH Flat race, well beaten in maiden hurdles: won novice hurdle at Southwell in March: also ran very well last 3 starts: novice chaser: stays 3¼m: probably acts on any going: blinkered sixth outing. *K. C. Bailey*   c– 94

TARGET MISSILE 6 ch.g. Leading Man – Kemoening (Falcon) [1992/3 F16s F16d 21d] unfurnished gelding: half-brother to several winning hurdlers, notably Triumph Hurdle winner Saxon Farm (by Hittite Glory): dam modest Flat maiden: still backward and green, showed nothing in novice hurdle at Uttoxeter in March. *D. McCain*   –

TARKOVSKY 8 b.g. Moorestyle – Fallen Rose (Busted) [1992/3 c24d⁴ c24sᵖᵘ 25v² 25g⁵ 24s⁶ 24g⁴ 20d³] compact, workmanlike gelding: modest form in 2 starts over fences: fair handicap hurdler on his day: suited by test of stamina and plenty of give in the ground: visored last 2 outings: sometimes looks unenthusiastic: inconsistent. *R. Lee*   c84 105 §

TARMON (IRE) 5 ch.g. Whistling Deer – Royal Performance (Klairon) [1992/3 20f 16g 17g 17sᵖᵘ a20gᵖᵘ 17d 20g c18g⁶] compact gelding: poor hurdler: little promise on chasing debut: stays 2½m: acts on firm going: often blinkered or visored. *A. Barrow*   c– –

TAROUDANT 6 b.g. Pharly (FR) – Melbourne Miss (Chaparral (FR)) [1992/3 22s] workmanlike gelding: winning hurdler: better for race, held up and never placed to challenge in handicap at Nottingham in February: very successful on Flat in 1993: should stay beyond 2¾m: should do well when returned to hurdling. *Mrs M. Reveley*   – p

TARQOGAN'S BEST 13 bl.g. Tarqogan – Balldado (Harwell) [1992/3 c22fR 22sᵖᵘ] tall, leggy gelding: fairly useful form when winning handicap chase on first start in 1990/1 (trained by M. Pipe), but has refused 5 times since (had done so 3 times in 1988/9 also): sometimes blinkered or visored: one to leave well alone. *R. Simpson*   c§§ §§

TARTAN TAILOR 12 b.g. Patch – Court Time (Arctic Time) [1992/3 c21m² c21m³ c16d³ c21g*] tall, close-coupled gelding: fairly useful chaser nowadays: made all in 3-finisher handicap at Perth in September: stays 3m: probably acts on any going: finds little: tried visored: unreliable. *G. Richards*   c116 § – §

TARTAN TORNADO 7 b.g. Strong Gale – Frankford Run (Deep Run) [1992/3 17d³ 17s⁶ c16s⁵ c16sᵖᵘ c17d⁴] strong, lengthy gelding: has scope: poor novice hurdler/chaser: sold 5,000 gns Doncaster May Sales: carries head high: visored second and fourth starts. *G. Richards*   c– 69

TARTAN TRADEMARK 11 ch.g. Deep Run – Golden Shuil (Master Owen) [1992/3 c21m⁵] fairly useful chaser on his day: needed race in handicap at Carlisle in March: stays 27f: acts on any going: often makes running: has broken blood vessels: evidently difficult to train. *G. Richards*   c– –

TARTAN TRADEWINDS 6 b.g. Strong Gale – Tipperary Special (Wrekin Rambler) [1992/3 F16g⁵ 17sF 16g⁵ 21m* 21d⁴ 17d³ 21gᵖᵘ] well-made gelding with scope: chasing type: half-brother to 4 winning jumpers, notably quite useful Irish chaser Istimewa (by Laurence O): dam, lightly raced, from successful jumping family: won novice hurdle at Carlisle in March: ran well next 2 starts, poorly last: likely to stay beyond 21f: acts on good to firm and dead going. *G. Richards*   98

TARTAN TRIX 10 b.g. Pitpan – Blue Trix (Blue Chariot) [1992/3 c24v* c26d* c27mᵖᵘ c20s⁴ c27g³ c33mᵖᵘ] strong, workmanlike gelding: useful hunter chaser nowadays: won at Lingfield and Plumpton in February: well below form afterwards: stays 3¼m: acts on heavy going, possibly unsuited by good to firm: sound jumper. *W. R. Hacking*   c111 –

TARTAN TYRANT 7 b.g. Tycoon II – Tina Fort (Fortina) [1992/3 c25gF c25s* c25g* c21d²] tall, good-topped gelding: brother to fairly useful chaser Tartan Takeover and half-brother to 3 other winning jumpers, notably   c103 p useful staying hurdler Graphics Solar (by Royal Palace): comfortable winner of novice chases at Wetherby and Ayr in March: creditable second in similar race at Carlisle following month: will stay beyond 25f: acts on soft going: not yet an accomplished jumper: should progress further. *G. Richards*

TARTAR TERTIUS 9 b.g. Balliol – Tartar Princess (Fury Royal) [1992/3 26gpu 18d5 17s4] lightly-made gelding: lightly-raced novice hurdler: only form for long time when fifth at Fontwell in October. *John Whyte* — 79

TASMIN GAYLE (IRE) 5 br.m. Strong Gale – Dame Sue (Mandamus) [1992/3 17m 17f 17d] third foal: sister to Irish novice hurdler Storm Rose and half-sister to winning hurdler Dont Tell The Wife (by Derring Rose) and Irish NH Flat winner Bawnrock (by Roselier): dam winner on Flat, over hurdles and over fences: well beaten in novice hurdles in spring. *R. Brewis* — –

TATTLEJACK (IRE) 5 ch.g. Le Bavard (FR) – Bonne Fille (Bonne Noel) [1992/3 F16d 22m6 22dpu] second live foal: dam well beaten in 3 Irish NH Flat races: little sign of ability. *N. A. Twiston-Davies* — –

TAUNTING (IRE) 5 b.g. Taufan (USA) – Dancing Decoy (Troy) [1992/3 a16g] leggy gelding: little promise over hurdles. *M. Blanshard* — –

TAURIAN PRINCESS 4 b.f. Electric – Facetious (Malicious) [1992/3 17m 17d5 16v* 16s a18g 17d4 17m 16m4] lengthy filly: half-sister to winning hurdler Facility Letter (by Superlative): no form on Flat: sold out of A. Lee's stable 1,700 gns Newmarket July Sales: won juvenile claiming hurdle at Nottingham in December: creditable efforts when fourth afterwards: likely to stay beyond 17f: acts on heavy and good to firm ground (ran poorly on fibresand). *W. Clay* — 74

TAURUS 7 br.g. Lucifer (USA) – Jane Eyre (Master Buck) [1992/3 16dF 16d 22d6] lengthy gelding: poor novice hurdler: best effort over 2m on good to firm ground. *Mrs J. Pitman* — –

TAWAFIJ (USA) 4 ch.c. Diesis – Dancing Brownie (USA) (Nijinsky (CAN)) [1992/3 16m 17g6] sturdy colt: sold out of H. Thomson Jones's stable 6,400 gns Newmarket Autumn Sales: fairly useful on Flat in 1993, twice a winner over 7f: showed promise both starts in juvenile hurdles earlier: will improve further. *R. Allan* — 85 p

TAWJIH (USA) 6 b.h. Lyphard's Wish (FR) – Chop Towhee (USA) (Hatchet Man (USA)) [1992/3 17d2] smallish horse: selling hurdler: creditable second at Plumpton in October: stays 2¼m: acts on soft ground: ran creditably visored once in 1991/2. *M. Madgwick* — 78

TAXI LAD 9 ch.g. Dublin Taxi – Midnight Pansy (Deadly Nightshade) [1992/3 25vpu 24dpu] tall, strong, short-backed gelding: winning hurdler: maiden chaser: very lightly raced and no form for a long time. *R. G. Brazington* — c–

TAX THE DEVIL 5 b.g. Nicholas Bill – Devils Alternative (Hotfoot) [1992/3 F17s* F17s aF16g5 18gpu] fifth foal: half-brother to plating-class Flat maiden Devils Dirge (by Song): dam, placed at 1½m, daughter of useful Heaven Knows: won NH Flat race at Huntingdon in December: tailed off when pulled up in novice event in April on hurdling debut. *S. Dow* — –

TAYLORMADE BOY 10 b.g. Dominion – Ash Gayle (Lord Gayle (USA)) [1992/3 16d2] leggy, sparely-made gelding: fair handicap hurdler at best: needed race when below-form second in seller at Catterick in November: stays 3m: acts on any going. *Denys Smith* — 91

TAYLORS CASTLE 6 b.m. Castle Keep – How Audacious (Hittite Glory) [1992/3 18fpu 17g4 18d5 17v 16s5 16d 16s4 17m5 18m] sparely-made mare: selling hurdler: barely stays 2m: acts on good to firm and soft ground. *S. N. Cole* — 81

TAYLORS PRINCE 6 ch.g. Sandhurst Prince – Maiden's Dance (Hotfoot) [1992/3 16sbd 17g a18g6 16vF 16g* 17s4] lengthy, rather sparely-made gelding: moderate hurdler: won novice handicap at Towcester in March: unlucky loser on same course time before: form only at 2m: acts on heavy going: visored last 3 starts. *H. J. Collingridge* — 91

TBILISI 6 b.g. Roscoe Blake – Big Maggie (Master Owen) [1992/3 c21gF] c–
failed to complete in points or a novice hunter chase. *Michael Mullineaux*

TEA-LADY (IRE) 5 b.m. Balinger – Wealthy (Gold Rod) [1992/3 F17g
17dᵖᵘ 17d² 16s⁶ a18gᵘʳ 17d⁴ 20m⁶] workmanlike mare: poor novice hurdler: 71
stays 2½m: acts on soft and good to firm going. *Mrs A. L. M. King*

TEAM CHALLENGE 11 ch.g. Laurence O – Maid O'The Wood (Prince c– §
Hansel) [1992/3 c24s⁵ c25g⁴ c22f c24g] deep-girthed gelding: handicap –
chaser, no form in 1992/3: to be trained by R. Lee in 1993/4: stays well:
probably acts on any going: usually blinkered or visored and has worn a
hood: usually a sound jumper: unreliable. *Mrs J. Pitman*

TEAPLANTER 10 b.g. National Trust – Miss India (Indian Ruler) c114 +
[1992/3 c21dᶠ c25g² c24g* c25d*] tall, strong gelding: smart hunter chaser
at best, winner of 13 of his 15 completed starts, including at Huntingdon in
April and Towcester in May: stays well: has won on firm ground, but seems
ideally suited by give: suited by forcing tactics. *Miss C. Saunders*

TEDS TACTICS 10 ch.g. New Member – Alice Clarke (Politico (USA)) –
[1992/3 16vᵖᵘ 17vᵖᵘ 18mᶠ] small, lengthy gelding: first foal: dam winning 2m
hurdler: no sign of ability over hurdles. *H. E. Haynes*

TEEGA SUKU 6 ch.g. Sula Bula – Tizziwizzy VII (Pedigree Unknown) –
[1992/3 F17g 18d 21s 22v 25sᵖᵘ] leggy non-thoroughbred gelding: no sign of
ability. *Mrs J. A. Young*

TEENAGE SCRIBBLER 8 br.g. Over The River (FR) – Balldado
(Harwell) [1992/3 21mᵖᵘ 16d*] big, lengthy, good-bodied gelding: sold out of 99
W. Kemp's stable 1,250 gns Ascot December Sales after first outing: has
evidently had training troubles and broke down when winning selling hurdle
at Catterick in February: stays 21f: acts on heavy going: front runner. *K. R.
Burke*

TEKLA (FR) 8 b.g. Toujours Pret (USA) – Hekla Des Sacart (FR)
(Laniste) [1992/3 16v⁶ 17s 20d] leggy, close-coupled gelding: winning
hurdler: sold out of J. FitzGerald's stable 9,000 gns Doncaster November
Sales: behind in mid-season handicaps: has raced only at around 2m: acts on
heavy going. *A. J. Chamberlain*

TEL E THON 6 b.g. Ela-Mana-Mou – Costa Rossa (ITY) (Welsh
Pageant) [1992/3 17f³ 17g* 20m* 17f³ 18f² 20d⁶ 17d⁴ 16f⁴ 17m⁶ 17d⁶ 18f⁴] 108
smallish gelding: fair handicap hurdler: successful twice at Plumpton early
in season: generally ran creditably afterwards: stays 2½m: acts on firm and
dead ground: usually blinkered or visored (visored when successful):
usually makes running. *P. J. Jones*

TELL YOU WHAT 8 ch.g. Crested Lark – Andromeda II (Romany Air) c–
[1992/3 c21dᵖᵘ c20dᵖᵘ c16s⁵ c17f⁵ c17f³ c17v² c17gᵘʳ c21fᵖᵘ] tall, lengthy –
gelding: poor winning hurdler: no form over fences (placed in two 3-runner
events): should stay beyond 2m: probably acts on any going. *T. Casey*

TELMAR SYSTEMS 4 b.g. Don Enrico (USA) – Russola (John de
Coombe) [1992/3 aF16gʳᵗʳ aF13g⁴ aF16g³ aF16g³] first foal: dam winning
hurdler: in frame in NH Flat races at Lingfield in February and March (2):
refused to start once: yet to race over hurdles. *K. T. Ivory*

TEMPELHOF (IRE) 4 b.c. Alzao (USA) – Konigin Kate (GER) (Authi)
[1992/3 16g⁴ 21f⁵] leggy colt: brother to very useful hurdler/promising 89
chaser Hawthorn Blaze: fair 1¼m winner on Flat in 1992: sold out of J.
Hills's stable 15,000 gns Newmarket Autumn Sales: modest form in juvenile
hurdle at Worcester and maiden hurdle at Newbury, both in March. *Miss
Jacqueline S. Doyle*

TEMPERING 7 b.g. Kris – Mixed Applause (USA) (Nijinsky (CAN))
[1992/3 16d⁶ 18g² a18g⁴] good-bodied gelding: poor novice hurdler: best 81 +
form at 2m: acts on dead going: sweated profusely in 1992/3: takes good hold
and makes running: prolific winner on all-weather at Southwell on Flat. *D.
W. Chapman*

TEMPLE GARTH 4 b.g. Baron Blakeney – Future Chance (Hopeful Venture) [1992/3 16s⁴ 16d 20g² 22g* 21d* 20f³] workmanlike gelding: half-brother to a minor sprint winner by Monsanto and a winner in Italy by Derrylin: dam, daughter of top-class sprinter Abelia, won over 1¾m: modest form over hurdles: odds on, made all in novice events at Sedgefield in March and Carlisle in April: will stay beyond 2¾m: acts on soft going (stiff task when well beaten on firm). *J. H. Johnson*   97

TEMPORALE 7 ch.h. Horage – Traminer (Status Seeker) [1992/3 17s³ 21f³ 21d* 18g* 21m⁴ a20gᶠ a20g a18g⁴ 20d 21d² 21d⁵ 22g³ 22m⁵ 21d⁶ 21m⁵] small, compact horse: modest hurdler: won 2 handicaps at Southwell in October: creditable efforts when placed in selling handicaps subsequently: stays 2¾m: acts on hard, dead ground and equitrack: tried in blinkers, better without. *K. R. Burke*   83

TEMPORARY 8 ch.g. Croghan Hill – Pejays Princess (Pumps (USA)) [1992/3 F16m⁵ 20g⁴ c20gpu 17v⁵ c24vpu c21f² c25spu c21d⁵] workmanlike ex-Irish gelding: trained until after third start by D. Kiely: poor novice hurdler/chaser: stays 21f: acts on firm ground. *R. G. Frost*   **c80**
80

TEN DEEP 8 ch.m. Deep Run – Tendale (Raise You Ten) [1992/3 16m 17m 17d⁵ 20m 17m³ 16m³] sparely-made mare: poor novice hurdler: barely stays 3m: acts on good to firm ground: sometimes unruly at start, and refused to race once. *G. W. Giddings*   65 §

TENDER LIGHT (BEL) 5 ch.m. Moulouki – Double Vitesse (Double Jump) [1992/3 18fᶠ] half-sister to several winners, including French 1000 Guineas third Speedy Girl (by Connaught) and selling hurdler Airlanka (by Corvaro): dam won at up to 1m at 2 yrs in France: collapsed and died approaching seventh in novice hurdle at Fontwell in October. *M. Madgwick*   –

TENESAINT 12 ch.g. St Columbus – Tenella (Wrekin Rambler) [1992/3 c24dur c25g* c25g* c25v* c27mpu] lengthy gelding: useful hunter chaser nowadays: won at Nottingham and Towcester (twice) by wide margins in 1993: broke down badly last outing: suited by 3m and more: acts on good to firm and heavy going. *C. R. Saunders*   **c112**

TEN HIGH (IRE) 4 b.f. Leap High (USA) – Another Decade (Daring Display (USA)) [1992/3 16dpu 17m⁶ 16gpu] small, lightly-made filly: inconsistent maiden on Flat: seems of little account on Flat and over hurdles. *J. Dooler*   –

TENNIS COACH 6 gr.g. Siberian Express (USA) – Net Call (Song) [1992/3 F17d⁴] fourth of 17 in NH Flat race at Doncaster in December: sold 3,000 gns Doncaster March Sales: yet to race over hurdles or fences. *M. D. Hammond*

TERAO 7 b.g. Furry Glen – Bodyline (Crash Course) [1992/3 c23vpu c27vur c21vᶠ c20g⁶] rangy gelding with scope: lightly raced and fairly useful hurdler: let down by his jumping over fences: in lead when falling 2 out in novice event won by Cogent at Kempton in January (would probably have shown fairly useful form): likely to stay 3m: acts on heavy ground. *M. C. Pipe*   **c128** x

TERNIMUS (USA) 6 ch.h. Arctic Tern (USA) – Lustrious (USA) (Delaware Chief (USA)) [1992/3 16f 23s⁴ 22g⁴ 26d⁵ 23d² 23s⁶ 22d 25v⁵ a22gᶠ] leggy horse: modest middle-distance stayer on Flat: poor form over hurdles: stayed 3¼m: acted on dead going: was sometimes blinkered: dead. *B. Preece*   76

TERRIBLE GEL (FR) 8 b.g. Raisingelle (USA) – Ina du Soleil (FR) (Or de Chine) [1992/3 c16s* c16mᶠ c17d* c17v⁵ c17s*] workmanlike, good-quartered gelding: fair hurdler/chaser: successful in novice events over fences at Southwell in September, Kelso in November and Sedgefield in December, last 2 handicaps: likely to prove best at around 2m: probably acts on any going. *Mrs M. Reveley*   **c102**
–

TERRIFORN 8 br.g. Northern Value (USA) – Sparkling Bell (Spartan General) [1992/3 21d 17s] leggy gelding: seems of little account over   **c–**
–

hurdles and in steeplechases: sold to Mrs R. Hurley 2,800 gns Ascot November Sales: won a point in April. *C. T. Nash*

TESEKKUREDERIM   6 b. or br.g. Blazing Saddles (AUS) – Rhein Symphony (Rheingold) [1992/3 25s⁴ 22g³ 23m³ 20d² 20s⁴ 23d² 20s²] leggy, angular gelding: has no off-eye: modest novice hurdler: has run in sellers: stays 25f: acts on good to firm and soft going. *W. Clay*   89

TEWTRELL LAD   10 ch.g. Paddy's Stream – May Foliage (Barman II) [1992/3 c27d⁴ c25sᵖᵘ c26dᵖᵘ 23fᵖᵘ] strong, workmanlike gelding: poor novice hurdler: modest handicap chaser at best: stayed well: acted on firm ground: dead. *J. G. M. O'Shea*   c– –

TEXAN BABY (BEL)   4 b.g. Baby Turk – Texan Rose (FR) (Margouillat (FR)) [1992/3 F16s* F16d² F17m F17f] big, rangy gelding: brother to French 1m to 10.5f winner Barabaros and half-brother to French 11f winner Martine Midy (by Lashkari): dam French 1½m winner later won over jumps: won NH Flat race at Warwick in February: second in similar race at Haydock later in month: towards rear in valuable events last 2 starts: yet to race over hurdles. *N. A. Twiston-Davies*

TEXAN CLAMOUR (FR)   5 b.g. Vacarme (USA) – Texan Maid (FR) (Targowice (USA)) [1992/3 17m²] easy winner of 3 selling hurdles in second half of 1991/2: good second in non-selling handicap at Newton Abbot in August, but wasn't seen out again: stays 2½m: acts on good to firm and dead ground. *J. S. Moore*   104

TEXAN TYCOON   5 b.g. Last Tycoon – High Move (High Top) [1992/3 17s² 17v⁵ 16v² 17g²] angular gelding: half-brother to winning hurdler High Bid (by Auction Ring): fair 1½m winner on Flat in 1992: runner-up in novice hurdles, showing quite useful form: will stay beyond 17f: acts on heavy going: blinkered once in 1991/2 (when racing in Ireland): well capable of winning a novice hurdle. *R. Akehurst*   114

TEXAS SCRAMBLE   4 b.g. Norwick (USA) – Orange Parade (Dara Monarch) [1992/3 17m³ 17g⁶ 17d⁶ 17f* 18d⁴ 16s* 16v³] lengthy gelding: plating-class maiden at 2 yrs: won selling hurdles at Taunton (no bid) and Exeter (sold out of C. Popham's stable 5,000 gns), and juvenile event at Haydock: also ran well final start (December): stays 2¼m: acts on any going. *B. P. J. Baugh*   99

TEX MEX (IRE)   5 b.g. Deep Run – Polar Bee (Gunner B) [1992/3 F17v⁶] first foal: dam won at 1¾m and 2m on Flat in Ireland: well-beaten sixth of 15 in NH Flat race at Newton Abbot in November: yet to race over hurdles or fences. *S. Mellor*

THAKAWAH   4 br.g. Green Desert (USA) – Index To Forli (USA) (Forli (ARG)) [1992/3 16dF] fair stayer on Flat: sold out of R. Armstrong's stable 14,000 gns Newmarket July Sales: tailed off when falling 3 out in novice hurdle in April: dead. *J. A. B. Old*   –

THAMESDOWN TOOTSIE   8 b.m. Comedy Star (USA) – Lizzie Lightfoot (Hotfoot) [1992/3 c21d³ c21g² c25dᵘʳ 28v c21s⁴ c24s² c26d³ c26g* c26g³ c21d c27v² c26f⁴] close-coupled mare: fair handicap hurdler at best: moderate form over fences: successful in handicap at Folkestone in February: easily best efforts afterwards when placed: suited by a good test of stamina: acts on heavy going and unsuited by firm. *A. P. Jones*   c87 –

THANKSFORTHEOFFER   5 b. or br.g. Buzzards Bay – Raise The Offer (Auction Ring (USA)) [1992/3 F17g⁵ 17d³ 20v³ 22v⁵ 20m⁶ 24f 24g⁴ 26g 22m³ 22f] unfurnished gelding: second foal: half-brother to a poor animal by Sayf El Arab: dam stayed well on Flat: poor novice hurdler: trained until after seventh outing by D. Wintle: effective at 17f and should stay beyond 2¾m: acts on good to firm and heavy going: blinkered last 2 starts. *I. R. Jones*   67

THARSIS   8 ch.g. What A Guest – Grande Promesse (FR) (Sea Hawk II) [1992/3 20g 22g 20f² 20m⁶ 24g⁴ 22g 25m⁵ 22m² 16g² 20m*] smallish, workmanlike gelding: modest hurdler nowadays: dead-heated for first with   97

John Shaw in handicap at Market Rasen in June: effective at 2½m and stays well: acts on firm and dead ground. *W. J. Smith*

THATCHER ROCK (NZ) 8 b.g. Le Grand Seigneur (CAN) – Lady Joelyn (NZ) (Noble Bijou (USA)) [1992/3 c21s5 c19s3 c18v* c21s2 c21g2 c24g* c21s* c20sbd c21v*] workmanlike gelding: winning hurdler: fair chaser: won conditional jockeys minor event at Fontwell, novice event at Fakenham and handicaps at Worcester (dead-heated) and Newton Abbot in second half of season: stays 3m: acts on good to firm and heavy going. *P. F. Nicholls* **c105**

THATS FOR SURE 12 gr.g. Idiot's Delight – Brinkwood (Precipice Wood) [1992/3 c26d6 c26spu c25vpu c27vpu] workmanlike gelding: winning hurdler/chaser: lightly raced and no form for long time. *J. T. Gifford* **c–**

THATS NOT GOSSIP 7 ch.g. Deep Run – Swinging Sovereign (Swing Easy (USA)) [1992/3 20gpu c21gpu c16mF] lengthy, angular gelding: no sign of ability: sold 2,000 gns Ascot 2nd June Sales. *S. I. Pittendrigh* **c–**

THATS THE BUSINESS 9 br.g. Milan – Laragh (Fray Bentos) [1992/3 c25sF c25vpu c21s2 c26v5 c26gpu c27m2 c24f* c23m c27g5 c23f5 c24g] good-bodied gelding: modest chaser: won 2-runner handicap at Huntingdon in March: sold 2,400 gns Ascot June Sales: stays 3¼m: probably acts on any ground: usually visored nowadays: sometimes looks reluctant. *G. B. Balding* **c89**

THE-ADSTONE-LODGE 5 ch.m. Royal Vulcan – Aqualon (Ballad Rock) [1992/3 16spu 18d] smallish, workmanlike mare: first foal: dam won twice at 1m in Ireland: no sign of ability in 2 novice hurdles in February. *John R. Upson* **–**

THE ALPINE AMAZON 5 b.m. Broadsword (USA) – Chalet Waldegg (Monsanto (FR)) [1992/3 18spu] angular mare: third of 4 in NH Flat race in 1991/2: showed little aptitude in novice seller in January on hurdling debut. *D. R. Gandolfo* **–**

THE ANTARTEX 10 gr.g. Vital Season – Rue Talma (Vigo) [1992/3 c21m2 c16g6 c30m2 c27d3 c20d4] leggy, workmanlike gelding: fairly useful chaser: ran well when placed in 1992/3: finished lame in December, and wasn't seen out again: effective at 2m when conditions are very testing and stays well: acts on heavy and good to firm ground. *G. Richards* **c119**

THE ANTIPODEAN (NZ) 9 ch.g. Royal Plume – Della Dossi (NZ) (Della Porta) [1992/3 c21spu c21spu c20d3 c24d6] lengthy gelding: winning hurdler: easily best effort in novice chases when staying-on third in 2½m novice handicap at Ludlow in December. *D. H. Barons* **c87**

THE BARREN ARCTIC 7 br.g. Baron Blakeney – Arctic Granada (Arctic Slave) [1992/3 c18dur c19gbd c18vF c18spu c18g5] smallish gelding: poor novice hurdler/chaser: let down by his jumping of fences. *R. H. Buckler* **c– x**

THE BLACK MONK (IRE) 5 ch.g. Sexton Blake – Royal Demon (Tarboosh (USA)) [1992/3 18m* 18f* 17g5 18d3 22g* 17dbd 16s* 21v* 18s* 21s* 18s3 20s5 22s3 21m2 21s4 22m* 20d2 20g* 27f3] smallish, close-coupled gelding: in tremendous form in 1992/3 and made into a fairly useful hurdler: won sellers at Exeter (2), Ludlow and Chepstow, claimers at Leicester and Exeter, and handicaps at Chepstow (conditional jockeys), Newton Abbot and Hereford: best form at 2½m to 2¾m: acts on any going: has won blinkered, visored nowadays: tough and genuine: held up. *M. C. Pipe* **125**

THE BLUE BOY (IRE) 5 ch.g. Tate Gallery (USA) – Blue Lookout (Cure The Blues (USA)) [1992/3 20s5 17mur 17f2 17d5 17f4 17f 17f] sparely-made gelding: fairly useful as a juvenile hurdler: only modest form at best in 1992/3, including in a seller: sold 4,400 gns Malvern June Sales: stays 2½m: goes well on top-of-the-ground: sometimes blinkered: usually makes running: looks unenthusiastic nowadays. *Mrs J. G. Retter* **91 §**

THE BUTLER 7 ch.g. Roman Warrior – Just Nicola (Eborneezer) [1992/3 c23vpu c21spu c21dF c21fpu c21m6 c21s c24mpu 22fpu] close-coupled gelding: poor novice hurdler/chaser. *Miss D. J. Baker* **c–**

Corcrain Enterprises Ltd's "The Committee"

THE CAN CAN MAN 6 b.g. Daring March – Dawn Ditty (Song) [1992/3
16m³ 17f² 18d⁴] tall gelding: one-time quite useful 7f/1m handicapper on   88
Flat: modest form when placed in novice hurdles at Ludlow and Huntingdon
in March: will prove best at 2m on a sound surface: acts on firm ground,
below form on dead. *M. Johnston*

THE CARROT MAN 5 ch.g. True Song – Minor Furlong (Native
Bazaar) [1992/3 F14s⁶] fourth foal: half-brother to a poor novice by Sunyboy:
dam never ran: well-beaten sixth in the NH Flat race at Market Rasen in
April: yet to race over hurdles or fences. *C. R. Egerton*

THE CHANCELLOR 7 b.g. Newski (USA) – Bonnie's Delight (Idiot's
Delight) [1992/3 F17d 20m⁴] rangy gelding with scope: second foal: dam,   80 +
tailed off in 2 selling hurdles, half-sister to very useful staying hurdler
Garliestown and good pointer/useful hurdler Glasserton: first race for 6
months, every chance when breaking down run-in in maiden hurdle at
Exeter in May. *Mrs J. G. Retter*

THE CHANGELING (IRE) 4 b.g. Celio Rufo – Ladycastle (Pitpan)
[1992/3 aF16g²] second foal: half-brother to useful hurdler/novice chaser
Rocco (by King's Ride): dam of little account over hurdles: second of 9 in
NH Flat race at Southwell in February: yet to race over hurdles. *G. C.
Bravery*

THE CHOODLER 6 b.m. Strong Gale – Cousin Clare (Pontifex (USA))
[1992/3 18h⁴] lengthy, sparely-made mare: of little account. *J. P. Taplin*   –

THE CITY MINSTREL 8 br.g. Black Minstrel – Miss Diga (Tarqogan)   c–
[1992/3 c24d⁵ c25g c24dᵖᵘ c23fᵖᵘ] well-made gelding: winning chaser: little   –

740

show in hunter chases in 1993: barely stays 3m: acts on heavy ground: sometimes hangs badly. *Stephen Bush*

THE COMMITTEE 10 b.g. Derring Rose – What A Whet (Fine Blade (USA)) [1992/3 c21d c24s c25s^{ur} c20s^F c24d^5 c26v^3 c25v^3 c24d^{bd} c24d^4 c25m^3 c29s] leggy, rather sparely-made gelding: useful chaser: creditable third in valuable amateurs handicap at Cheltenham in March: close fourth behind Esha Ness in void Martell Grand National: suited by good test of stamina: acts on any going. *J. H. Scott, Ireland*   c134 –

THE COUNTRY TRADER 7 br.g. Furry Glen – Lady Girand (Raise You Ten) [1992/3 21g^5 18g^{pu} 16g] tall, lengthy gelding: chasing type: poor form in novice hurdles: stays 21f: yet to race on top-of-the-ground. *G. Richards*   73

THE CUCKOO'S NEST 5 b.g. Precocious – Troy Moon (Troy) [1992/3 16s 17f^6] leggy gelding: modest front-running handicapper on Flat, stays 1m: sold out of C. Brittain's stable 6,600 gns Newmarket September Sales: tailed off in 2 novice hurdles in October: resold 1,750 gns Ascot March Sales. *M. Williams*   –

THE DECENT THING 10 br.g. Decent Fellow – Paperchain (Articulate) [1992/3 17d^5 22m^3] sturdy, workmanlike gelding: fairly useful hurdler: very lightly raced since 1988/9: showed he retains most of his ability when third at Cheltenham in April: will stay beyond 2¾m: acts on soft and good to firm going. *G. B. Balding*   118

THE DEMON BARBER 11 b.g. Fine Blade (USA) – Mingy (Della Strada) [1992/3 c25m* 25g^5 25g^4 25s^5 20d] leggy gelding: fairly useful hurdler: useful chaser, tends to make mistakes and did so when winning at Bangor in October: stays 3¼m: acts on good to firm and soft going. *G. Richards*   c131 x 127

THE DIFFERENCE 6 b.g. Cruise Missile – Brandy's Honour (Hot Brandy) [1992/3 25v 22d 25v^5 c26d^F c23d^F] leggy gelding: no sign of ability: blinkered last 2 outings. *C. Smith*   c– –

THE DOMINANT GENE 4 gr.c. Dominion – Judy's Dowry (Dragonara Palace (USA)) [1992/3 17s^2 17m^{pu} 16d^{pu}] good-bodied colt: maiden plater on Flat and over hurdles. *J. R. Jenkins*   ?

THE DRAGON MASTER 11 br.g. Pollerton – Glen Rambler (Wrekin Rambler) [1992/3 c17s^F c17v^4] tall, leggy gelding: one-time useful chaser: last of 4 finishers in handicap at Towcester in January: stays 2½m: acts on good to firm and soft going. *R. Waley-Cohen*   c–

THE ELOPER 5 b.g. Idiot's Delight – Night Action (Dusky Boy) [1992/3 F17d] seventh foal: half-brother to NH Flat race winner Warmonger (by Sunyboy) and to 2 poor novice hurdlers: dam never ran: mid-division in 17-runner NH Flat race at Hereford in May: yet to race over hurdles or fences. *Mrs I. McKie*

THE ENERGISER 7 ch.g. Energist – Be An Angel (Be Friendly) [1992/3 21s 22g^{pu} 24s^{pu} 25d^{pu}] plain gelding: fourth foal: half-brother to winning Irish chaser Glen Og Lane (by Glen Quaich) and novice jumper Kilcoursey (by Lucifer): dam unraced: no sign of ability over hurdles. *R. R. Lamb*   –

THE EVACUEE 5 gr.m. Rymer – Moll (Rugantino) [1992/3 F17m] leggy mare: signs of a little ability in 3 NH Flat races: yet to race over hurdles or fences. *A. P. James*

THE FELLOW (FR) 8 b.g. Italic (FR) – L'Oranaise (FR) (Paris Jour) [1992/3 20d* c22s* c27s^3 c24s* c27m^4 c30d^5 c22s^4 c29d^5]   c171 149

Predicting the outcome of Cheltenham's championship races has rarely been straightforward, and punters must have become used to having their fingers burned, particularly in the Gold Cup in which winning favourites have been few and far between. Defeat for The Fellow, a short-head runner-up in the two previous years, saved the bookmakers from a huge payout. The horse was one of the most heavily-backed favourites in the history of the race, starting at 5/4 after a string of big bets on the course including £10,500 to £6,000, £7,000 to £4,000 four times, £6,500 to £4,000 twice, £12,000 to £8,000, £7,500 to £5,000, £6,000 to £4,000 twice and, the biggest single bet, £22,000 to £16,000. The Fellow's backers knew their fate before the third last as the leaders got away from him; he stayed on in the straight but never looked like getting back on terms and was beaten nine and a half lengths by the winner Jodami. The Fellow had been very much the season's leading staying chaser up until Cheltenham and he looked a worthy favourite on the strength of his second successive victory in the King George VI Chase and a particularly meritorious weight-carrying performance in the Hennessy Cognac Gold Cup, on his two previous visits to Britain. The latest King George VI Chase wasn't a vintage edition and The Fellow, an even-money favourite, won by six lengths from Pat's Jester. His form in the Hennessy—a good third to Jodami and Sibton Abbey, conceding them 25 lb and 27 lb respectively—had made him look a good thing at Kempton with the main home-trained hope Remittance Man on the side-lines. The Fellow's victory in the King George was, in the end, gained impressively as he surged clear on the run-in, drifting left in the closing stages, after beginning a strong run from two out. Strangely, before asserting himself, the patiently-ridden The Fellow had for a moment looked in trouble, slipping further back, as the runners turned for home, his rider having kept him on the outside for most of the race before eventually launching his challenge very wide in the straight. The exaggerated tactics adopted by Kondrat at Kempton led to his being derided by some, his strongest critic being the television commentator John McCririck. McCririck's cultivated eccentricity has helped to make him famous but his attack on Kondrat's riding on *The Morning Line* did him no credit. John Francome and Peter Scudamore both did their best to defend Kondrat in the face of a particularly bombastic performance from McCririck.

The Fellow's trainer Francois Doumen, who has now won the King George VI Chase three times in the last six years, was responsible for the plan at Kempton which involved The Fellow racing wide 'to let him breathe easily as long as possible and to avoid the legs of falling horses'. The Fellow's rider also steered an intentionally wide course at Cheltenham but no-one could say the tactics contributed to The Fellow's downfall. Kondrat told the trainer that 'The Fellow did not like it when the leaders quickened a

King George VI Chase, Kempton—a repeat success for The Fellow (right); with him at the last are Pat's Jester and The Illywacker (blinkers)

Marquesa de Moratalla's "The Fellow"

		Italic (FR) (b 1974)	Carnaval (b 1963)	Fast Fox
				Cambre
The Fellow (FR) (b.g. 1985)			Bagheira (b 1967)	Pegomas
				Anabela
		L'Oranaise (FR) (b 1974)	Paris Jour (b 1962)	Herbager
				La Petite Hutte
			S'Agaro (b 1964)	Rely On Me
				Encore Une

mile from home', and, interestingly, Doumen reported afterwards the horse 'was not as tired as a beaten horse normally is and he recovered very quickly'. The signs seemed to be that The Fellow might be getting lazy or developing a few of his own ideas about the game. Although The Fellow is still young, confidence in his ability to match Wayward Lad's three King George victories, let alone Desert Orchid's four, was further undermined by his below-form fifth in the Whitbread Gold Cup at Sandown in late-April when he reportedly broke a blood vessel.

British racegoers saw as much of The Fellow in the latest season as their French counterparts. The Fellow won two valuable races in October at Auteuil before being sent over for the Hennessy, taking the two-and-a-half-mile Prix Carmarthen Hurdle (with his well-known stable-companions Ucello II and Ubu III third and fifth) and the Prix Heros XII Steeplechase over two and three quarters. His training after the Whitbread was geared to the Grand Steeple-Chase de Paris, before which he ran respectably to finish a close fourth to Ucello in what is usually the most important trial, the Prix

Millionaire over two and three quarter miles. In the Grand Steeple-Chase itself, however, The Fellow was beaten sixteen lengths by Ucello, managing only fifth and running a lack-lustre race into the bargain.

The leggy, rather lean-looking The Fellow, who was again superbly turned out for his races, is a French Saddlebred (selle francais) whose pedigree was covered in detail in *Chasers & Hurdlers 1991/92*. There's a significant addition to the information given there in that The Fellow's five-year-old full brother Al Capone II developed into one of the top steeplechasers in France in the latest season, finishing runner-up—ahead of The Fellow—in both the Prix Millionaire and the Grand Steeple-Chase de Paris. The Fellow's unraced dam L'Oranaise, a sister or half-sister to several winners including two that also won over jumps L'Oranais and Bel Oranais, has bred two other winning jumpers, including another of The Fellow's brothers, Quick Fellow, who was successful four times over fences and won on the Flat. The Fellow is effective at two and a half and two and three quarter miles and stays very well. He acts on heavy going and good to firm, and is a good jumper who is suited by waiting tactics. *F. Doumen, France*

THE FLY BOYS 11 ch.g. Sousa – Ravenna (Celtic Ash) [1992/3 17d³ 17mᵇᵈ] leggy gelding: poor hurdler/novice chaser: stayed 21f: acted on firm and good to soft going: blinkered once: was a sketchy jumper: dead. *B. Forsey*
c–
76

THE FLYING FOOTMAN 7 b.g. Furry Glen – Ballygoman Maid (Light Thrust) [1992/3 c16d³ c20sᶠ c17sᵖᵘ 22dᵖᵘ 17g⁶ 17g*] workmanlike gelding: trained until after third outing by J. McConnochie: poor form when winning novice handicap hurdle at Bangor in April: poor novice over fences: should stay beyond 17f. *D. Nicholson*
c84 ?
84

THE FORTIES 8 ch.g. Bybicello – Fanny Adams (Sweet Ration) [1992/3 c24s⁵ c33vᶠ c28sᵖᵘ] lengthy gelding: fair handicap chaser at best: shaped as though retaining ability first 2 starts but ran poorly on last (December): dyed-in-the-wool stayer: acts on soft ground and good to firm: usually a sound jumper. *T. T. Bill*
c–

THEFRIENDLYBARBER 10 gr.g. General Ironside – Aprils End (Star Signal) [1992/3 c26m⁵] close-coupled gelding: winning hunter chaser: no worthwhile form for a long time: stays 25f: acts on firm and dead ground. *Lady Susan Brooke*
c–
–

THE FRUIT 14 ch.g. Kambalda – Beautiful Night (Midsummer Night II) [1992/3 c25d⁵ c21gᵖᵘ c21f³ c21f³] tall, close-coupled gelding: poor chaser nowadays: stays 2½m: acts on firm going: poor jumper. *R. R. Ledger*
c77 x
–

THE GANNOCHY (USA) 7 ch.g. Coastal (USA) – Bright View (Hot Spark) [1992/3 17mᵖᵘ 17g⁴ 18sᵖᵘ 17s a20gᵖᵘ 17g] neat gelding: selling hurdler: no form in 1992/3: best around 2m: acts on firm ground: often finds little: blinkered or visored. *L. Wordingham*
– §

THE GLOW (IRE) 5 b.g. Glow (USA) – Full Choke (Shirley Heights) [1992/3 16s² 17v² 17v⁵ 17s² 16v² 22fF 20d* 20d⁶ 17g] rangy gelding with scope: chasing type: fairly useful form in novice hurdles in 1992/3, and won at Ascot in March: long way below form in valuable novice handicap at Cheltenham in April: better suited by 2½m than 2m: acts on heavy going. *D. R. C. Elsworth*
112

THE GOOFER 6 b.g. Be My Native (USA) – Siliferous (Sandy Creek) [1992/3 16d³] tall, leggy gelding: fair middle-distance performer, suited by soft going, on Flat: fair effort when third in well-contested novice hurdle at Haydock in December: looked promising but wasn't seen out again. *A. P. Stringer*
97

THE GORROCK 4 b.g. Petoski – Aquarula (Dominion) [1992/3 18dᵖᵘ 17dᵖᵘ 17s 24f 23mᵖᵘ] half-brother to winning hurdler To Be Fair (by Adonijah): seems of little account: visored second and third outings, blinkered last. *A. J. Chamberlain*
–

THE GREEN FOOL 6 ch.g. Southern Music – Random Thatch (Random Shot) [1992/3 20g³ 16g² 20s² 16d² 20d³ 20g 20m* 20g³ 16d² 21m³
113

18d* 17s⁵ 22g³ 17f^bd] workmanlike gelding: fair handicap hurdler: won at Edinburgh in February and Sedgefield in April: effective from 2m to 2¾m: acts on soft and good to firm going: tough and consistent. *V. Thompson*

THE GREEN STUFF   8 ch.g. Green Shoon – Cottage View (Golden   c110
Vision) [1992/3 c16v* c17v* c16v³ c16d⁴ c19m⁴ c20s³ c17m⁵] big, strong   –
gelding: has been hobdayed: fair handicap chaser: won at Lingfield and Towcester around turn of year: best effort subsequently when creditable third at Chepstow in April on penultimate start: stays 2½m: acts on any going. *John R. Upson*

THE GREY MONK (IRE)   5 gr.g. Roselier (FR) – Ballybeg Maid
(Prince Hansel) [1992/3 F17g⁵] leggy gelding: fifth foal: half-brother to 3 winning jumpers, including very useful Irish hurdler Princess Casilia (by Croghan Hill): dam never ran: fifth of 11 in NH Flat race at Carlisle in March: yet to race over hurdles or fences. *G. Richards*

THE GYMNAZIUM   8 b.m. Oats – Old Hand (Master Owen) [1992/3
24v^pu 16f⁵] angular mare: no promise in novice hurdles. *J. Pilkington*   –

THE HALF WIT   7 br.g. Layal – Lady Matilda VII (Pedigree Unknown)
[1992/3 17g^pu] tall, good-topped gelding: lightly-raced novice hurdler. *J. R.*   –
Bosley

THE HEALY   6 b.m. Blushing Scribe (USA) – Smitten (Run The Gantlet
(USA)) [1992/3 18d] small, sparely-made mare: poor novice hurdler: tailed   –
off in seller in September: best at 2m on top-of-the-ground: sometimes blinkered or visored. *G. M. R. Coatsworth*

THE HIDDEN CITY   7 b.g. Lord Ha Ha – Night Moves (Garda's
Revenge (USA)) [1992/3 17m⁵ 16f⁶ 17s 20g 16d*^dis 17v⁶ 20s 16d 17f⁵ 17g⁵   82
20m⁶ 21d] small gelding: poor hurdler: trained first 4 outings by R. Manning: first past post in seller at Ludlow (no bid) in November but disqualified on technical grounds: best form at around 2m: acts on good to firm and dead ground: blinkered once. *C. C. Trietline*

THE HOLY GOLFER   6 br.g. Avocat – Taitu (Menelek) [1992/3 21d 17s   c–
c20d c16v^pu 17g⁵ a20g⁶ a16g 17f⁴ 16f² 17d⁶ 16d³ 17f* 17m] leggy gelding: 72
seventh foal: half-brother to a poor animal by Belfalas: dam never ran: maiden pointer in Ireland in 1992: generally ran creditably in 1992/3, and won conditional jockeys novice selling handicap hurdle at Hereford (no bid) in May: no form in novice chases: effective at 2m and stays 21f: probably acts on any going. *D. R. Gandolfo*

THE HUCKLEBUCK   8 ch.g. Buckskin (FR) – Iron Star (General   cxx
Ironside) [1992/3 c23g⁵ c27s^ur c23g^ur c26g⁶] lengthy, angular gelding: bad   – x
novice chaser, jumps poorly and is probably ungenuine: tried blinkered. *R.*
Dickin

THE HUMBLE TILLER   10 b.g. Rarity – Bardicate (Bargello) [1992/3   c– x
c25d⁵ c27d⁵] leggy gelding: winning hurdler: poor staying chaser: below
form in October: acts on any going: wore hood once. *C. T. Nash*

THE ILLYWHACKER   8 b.g. Dawn Review – Trucken Queen   c150
(Harwell) [1992/3 c18g⁴ c21g* c20d⁵ c21v^bd c24s³ c20s⁵ c21g* c21mF] tall,
leggy gelding: useful hurdler: smart over fences: won handicap at Wincanton in November and Cavalier Chase at Worcester (by ½ length from Young Hustler) in March: ran very well when 13 lengths third in King George VI Chase at Kempton in between: effective at 2½m and stayed 3m: probably acted on any going: best blinkered (visored once): was sometimes let down badly by his jumping: dead. *Mrs J. Pitman*

THE JET SET   6 b.g. Corvaro (USA) – Broomfield Ceili (Northfields
(USA)) [1992/3 16s] compact gelding: lightly-raced novice hurdler: poor   –
form. *Mrs J. Pitman*

THE JOGGER   8 b.g. Deep Run – Pollychant (Politico (USA)) [1992/3   c89 x
c24m² c23vF c21mF c27dF] maiden hunter chaser: has the ability to win a   –
race but frequently let down by his jumping: stays 3m: acts on good to firm and heavy going: tried blinkered over hurdles. *E. Retter*

THE KIMBLER 5 ch.g. Lir – Kimberley Ann (St Columbus) [1992/3   c–
c27d^{ur} c18g^F] first foal: dam lightly-raced half-sister to several winning
jumpers: second in a point in March: hasn't got beyond the first in
steeplechases. *B. R. J. Young*

THE KINGS SECRET 9 br.g. Torus – Candy Princess (Candy Cane)   c–
[1992/3 c17m⁵ c18f^{pu}] first foal: dam won 2½m hurdle in Ireland: runner-up   –
in 2 points in Ireland in 1990: no form over hurdles or in novice chases: tried
blinkered: dead. *Dr P. Pritchard*

THE LADY'S PARTNER 11 br.g. Fine Blade (USA) – Owenette   c83
(Master Owen) [1992/3 c25g] poor novice chaser: sold 2,700 gns Ascot 2nd   –
June Sales: stays well: acts on firm ground: sometimes blinkered. *S. I.
Pittendrigh*

THE LAST EMPRESS (IRE) 5 b.m. Last Tycoon – Beijing (USA)
(Northjet) [1992/3 17s] fair stayer on Flat when trained by P. Cole: showed   –
only a little promise in novice hurdle at Wolverhampton in November. *A. S.
Reid*

THE LAST MISTRESS 6 b.m. Mandalus – Slinky Persin (Jupiter   c66 +
Pluvius) [1992/3 16g 20s⁵ 22g² c20g² c22s^F c22d 22s 22d] sparely-made   92
ex-Irish mare: moderate novice hurdler, no form in Britain: poor novice
chaser: trained until after sixth start by W. Roper: stays 2¾m. *D. J. Wintle*

THE LAST TUNE 9 b.m. Gunner B – Tempest Girl (Caliban) [1992/3   c–
c20s^F] angular, workmanlike mare: winning hurdler: poor novice chaser: –
will stay beyond 2½m: acts on soft going. *B. A. McMahon*

THE LAST WASHER (IRE) 4 b.g. Mazaad – Gigo Jive (Jukebox)
[1992/3 17m⁶] poor plater on Flat, stays 7f: well beaten in juvenile hurdle at   –
Huntingdon in August: sold 1,200 gns Newmarket September Sales, resold
1,850 gns Ascot March Sales and again for 1,300 gns Ascot May Sales. *M. H.
Tompkins*

THE LAUGHING LORD 7 b.g. Lord Ha Ha – Celtic Serenity   c94
(Proverb) [1992/3 21m⁵ 22g⁴ 23g* 23d c21v² c21d³ c20d* c25m⁵ c23g²   107
c25g⁴ 21g²] leggy gelding: fair handicap hurdler: won amateurs event at
Kelso in October (trained until after next start by W. A. Stephenson): won
novice chase at Haydock in February: generally below form afterwards:
changed hands 17,000 gns in May after tenth outing: stays 23f well: acts on
any going. *P. Cheesbrough*

THE LEGGETT 10 b.g. Faraway Times (USA) – Mrs McNicholas   c112 §
(Tudor Music) [1992/3 c24s³ c26s^{pu} c21v c26v^{pu} c21s c27d^{ro} c21m⁵ c25f^F   –
c26g* c24d c26m⁵ c27d^{ro} c24g² c19d²] rather sparely-made gelding: fair
chaser nowadays: won handicap at Exeter in March: generally ran with
credit when completing subsequently: effective at 2½m and stays well: acts
on any going: free-going sort, best allowed to race up with pace: blinkered
last 3 outings: sometimes runs out. *M. C. Pipe*

THE LIGHTER SIDE 7 br.g. Comedy Star (USA) – Moberry   c84
(Mossberry) [1992/3 c20m^{ur} c27s⁶ c21s c25d⁵ c24s³ c24g⁶ c23d² c21g³   –
c21g^{pu}] compact gelding: moderate hurdler, successful 6 times at
Southwell: poor novice chaser: stays 3m: best on sound surface or
fibresand: not discredited when blinkered once. *M. J. Charles*

THE LINK MAN 6 b.g. Mandalus – Mariners Chain (Walshford) [1992/3   c–
16d⁶ c24m^F 26g^{pu} 22g⁴ 20m³ 23f* 22v* 18d³ 23m⁵] workmanlike gelding: 79
won novice handicap hurdles at Stratford in March and Newton Abbot
(conditional jockeys) in April: fell first on chasing debut: effective at 2¼m
and should stay beyond 23f: acts on any ground. *Miss Jacqueline S. Doyle*

THE-LOG-MAN (IRE) 4 b.g. On Your Mark – Mishcasu (Majority
Blue) [1992/3 aF16g] 3,000Y: sixth foal: brother to 2-y-o 5f winner Sheen   –
Cleen Lad and half-brother to 1m winner Shy Dolly (by Cajun): dam 9f
winner: soundly beaten in NH Flat race at Lingfield in January: yet to race
over hurdles. *W. G. M. Turner*

THE MAJOR GENERAL 6 b.g. Pollerton – Cornamucla (Lucky Guy)
[1992/3 23m] second live foal: half-brother to winning Irish hurdler   –

Ballinderry Glen (by Furry Glen): dam won NH Flat race and a point: well beaten in novice hurdle at Stratford in May. *G. Richards*

THE MALAKARMA   7 b.g. St Columbus – Impinge (USA) (Impressive   c 108
(USA)) [1992/3 c24g* c25d² c25d² c28f⁶] rangy, useful-looking gelding: won hunter chase at Leicester in March: excellent second, clear of remainder, at Ascot and Towcester in May: should stay long distances: acts on dead ground, possibly unsuited by firm: wears tongue strap. *Mrs I. McKie*

THE MASTER GUNNER   9 ch.g. Gunner B – Major Isle (Major   c 103
Portion) [1992/3 17v⁴ c21d⁴ c19sᵘʳ c21d² c21d² c20g*] workmanlike   –
gelding: fair hurdler: improved effort in novice chases when winning at Ascot by 20 lengths: stays 21f: acts on soft going. *K. C. Bailey*

THE MEDICINE MAN   6 b.g. Little Wolf – Annie Panny (Take A Reef)
[1992/3 17gᵖᵘ 18gᶠ] compact gelding: of no account. *Dr P. Pritchard*   –

THE MILLWRIGHT   6 b.g. Milford – Laureppa (Jimmy Reppin) [1992/3
F16d 16d⁴ 16v] rangy gelding: better effort in novice hurdles when fourth of   85
18 at Ludlow in December: made mistakes when tailed off only subsequent start: will be suited by further than 2m. *S. Mellor*

THE MINDER (FR)   6 b. or br.g. Miller's Mate – Clarandal (Young
Generation) [1992/3 17s³ 18s³ 17v⁴ 17s* 20d 17g⁴ 17m² 17s² 18d]   86
sparely-made gelding: won novice handicap hurdle at Taunton in January: creditable efforts when second afterwards: stays 2½m: acts on heavy and good to firm ground. *G. F. Edwards*

THE MINE CAPTAIN   6 b.g. Shaab – Bal Casek (New Linacre) [1992/3
aF16g* aF16g* 17g² 21g³ 18g² 18g³ 17g 16m] leggy gelding: won NH Flat   93
races at Lingfield in January and February: modest novice at best over hurdles: below form last 3 outings: stays 21f: yet to race on a soft surface. *F. J. O'Mahony*

THE MOSSES   8 br.g. Kinglet – Yutoi Lady (Arctic Slave) [1992/3 c25m⁵   c–
c26dᵖᵘ c22vᵖᵘ c26dᵖᵘ] lengthy gelding: modest chaser in 1991/2: no form in   –
1992/3: stays 3m well: acts on soft going. *Capt. T. A. Forster*

THE MRS   7 b.m. Mandalus – Barrowvale (Valerullah) [1992/3 16d 18s⁵
22s*] workmanlike mare: half-sister to fairly useful jumper Devil's Valley   79
(by Lucifer) and to a winning pointer: dam, winning hurdler, from family of good 2m chaser Straight Fort: best effort over hurdles when winning novice event at Nottingham in November: will stay beyond 2¾m: acts on soft going. *J. W. Mullins*

THEM TIMES (IRE)   4 b.f. Petorius – Atropine (Beldale Flutter
(USA)) [1992/3 17v 17d 17g⁴ 16f³ 16f⁵ 17d] sparely-made filly: modest form   68 ?
at around 1m on Flat in Ireland in 1992, when trained by L. Browne: juvenile selling hurdler: acts on firm ground. *F. Jordan*

THE NASH   6 ch.g. Joshua – Dawn Affair (Entanglement) [1992/3 20g
16sᵖᵘ] close-coupled gelding: no sign of ability. *J. Mulhall*   –

THE NEW WIFE   6 b.m. Latest Model – Arctic Caper (Pardigras)   c–
[1992/3 17g 18g c16dᶠ] leggy, rather unfurnished mare: no sign of ability   –
over hurdles: fell fifth on chasing debut. *J. S. King*

THE NIGELSTAN   12 b.g. Fine Blade (USA) – Owenette (Master   c 106
Owen) [1992/3 c24dᵖᵘ c24g³ c24f*] leggy gelding: fair chaser: won handicap   –
at Stratford in June: stays 3m: has won on soft ground, but best form on a sound surface: visored once: sometimes makes mistakes. *P. R. Hedger*

THE OIL BARON   7 gr.g. Absalom – Ruby's Chance (Charlottesville)   c–
[1992/3 c21sᵖᵘ] leggy gelding: novice selling hurdler: jumped poorly in   –
August on chasing debut: best at around 2m: acts on dead ground. *R. P. C. Hoad*

THEO'S FELLA   9 br.g. Decent Fellow – Scottish Vulgan (Vulgan)   c88
[1992/3 c24m³ c20g²] angular, workmanlike gelding: winning hurdler: modest form when placed in novice chases at Stratford and Ascot in April: stays 3m: acts on firm and dead ground. *G. B. Balding*

THE OVERTRUMPER 6 b.g. Buzzards Bay – Nahawand (High Top) [1992/3 F16d 17d 17d⁶ 17d 17g 16dᵇᵈ] compact gelding: second foal: brother to Dehar Boy, a poor maiden on Flat and over hurdles: dam, plater, stayed 7f: no sign of ability. *Graeme Roe* —

THE PAPPARAZI 13 ch.g. Boreen (FR) – Marble Owen (Master Owen) [1992/3 23s 21s⁴] strong gelding: lightly-raced handicap hurdler: showed he still retains ability when fourth in handicap at Warwick in January: once-raced over fences: stays 3m: acts on soft going. *B. J. Curley* c–
106

THE PATTERS MAGIC 6 ch.g. Cardinal Flower – Carlins Daughter (Carlin) [1992/3 18g³ 17d⁴ 16m] close-coupled gelding: poor novice hurdler: stays 2¼m: best form with give in the ground. *M. D. Hammond* 79

THE PEDLAR 5 ch.m. Riberetto – Scally Jenks (Scallywag) [1992/3 17gᵖᵘ] first foal: dam unraced: tailed off when pulled up in novice hurdle at Hereford in May on debut. *K. White* —

THE PERFECT GENT 4 b.g. Rymer – Its Now Up To You (Deep Run) [1992/3 F18s 16mᵖᵘ 22dᵖᵘ] lengthy, unfurnished gelding: first foal: dam unraced daughter of a fair hurdler: no sign of ability. *E. F. Birchall* —

THE POINT IS 6 ch.g. Major Point – Babble (Forlorn River) [1992/3 18g c21d⁵c16d c20sᵘʳ a18g³ 16m³ 17m² 16f³ 16m³] leggy gelding: modest novice hurdler/chaser: best at around 2m: acts on firm going. *F. J. Yardley* c–
86

THE PORTSOY LOON 6 b.g. Miami Springs – Glittering Gem (Silly Season) [1992/3 16s⁴ 21d⁶] big, lengthy gelding with scope: better effort in novice hurdles when sixth at Uttoxeter (still green) in March: should do better. *G. Thorner* 84 p

THE PRIDE OF POKEY 9 br.m. Uncle Pokey – Vikrom (Menelek) [1992/3 c24m² c21g⁵ c25g⁵] good-topped, workmanlike mare: poor novice hunter chaser: stays 3m: acts on good to firm and soft ground. *Miss C. E. J. Dawson* c68

THE PRINCESSOFSPEED 5 b.m. Bay Express – La Jeunesse (Young Generation) [1992/3 22sᵖᵘ 17dᵖᵘ] sparely-made mare: of little account over hurdles and temperamental to boot. *A. M. Forte* – §

THE PRUSSIAN (USA) 7 b.h. Danzig (USA) – Miss Secretariat (USA) (Secretariat (USA)) [1992/3 17sᵖᵘ 17sᵖᵘ 17d a20g² a16g⁶ a22gᵘʳ a20g³ a24gᶠ 17g⁵] rangy horse: useful middle-distance performer on Flat in 1990 when trained by M. Stoute: poor form at best over hurdles: stays 2½m: form only on equitrack: sketchy jumper. *K. G. Wingrove* 78

THE PURSEWARDEN 10 b.g. Down The Hatch – Miss Sonnet (Master Owen) [1992/3 c21mᵖᵘ] workmanlike gelding: winning hurdler: poor novice chaser: sold 1,700 gns Ascot June Sales: should stay beyond 2¼m: yet to race on very soft going, acts on any other. *Mrs F. Walwyn* c–

THE QUAKER 7 ch.m. Oats – Malford Lass (Paveh Star) [1992/3 22d 26d] angular mare: no sign of ability. *R. Hawker* –

THE QUIET GENIUS 6 b.m. Reesh – Gay Ribbon (Ribero) [1992/3 F16s 21sᵖᵘ 23g⁶] leggy mare: second in 2 NH Flat races: little show in novice hurdles. *M. D. Hammond* –

THE RAMBLING MAN 6 b.g. Pitpan – Chammyville (Chamier) [1992/3 16g 16g 21d c20gᶠ] well-made gelding: poor form over hurdles: made mistakes and was behind when falling 3 out in maiden chase at Edinburgh in December: should stay well. *G. Richards* c–
75

THE REAL UNYOKE 8 b. or br.g. Callernish – Tudor Dancer (Balidar) [1992/3 c18d⁴ c19s* c25v⁶ c24d* c22d² c32mᵖᵘ c25vᵖᵘ] workmanlike gelding: fair chaser: won novice event at Naas and handicap at Leopardstown in December: made numerous mistakes and tailed off when pulled up in valuable amateurs event at Cheltenham in March on penultimate start: should stay beyond 3m: acts on soft going. *J. A. Berry, Ireland* c113

THE RED ONE 9 b.g. Derring Rose – Fairy Island (Prince Hansel) [1992/3 c25d* c24m* c27mᵇᵈ c24f* c25sᵖᵘ c25g* c25gᶠ c24mᵖᵘ] smallish, c110
–

workmanlike gelding: fair chaser: successful in hunter events at Wetherby and Edinburgh in February and novice events at Stratford in March and Market Rasen in April: was suited by around 3m: acted on firm and good to soft ground: dead. *P. R. Haley*

THE RIGHT GUY 8 ch.g. Regular Guy – Vulgan's Law (Vulgan) [1992/3 c25g^F c26d^{ur} c25s⁴] big, workmanlike gelding: winning pointer: moderate form when fourth in maiden hunter chase at Hexham in April. *P. Needham*

    c80
    –

THE SCREAMIN DEMON 10 ch.g. Le Moss – Gallant Breeze (USA) (Mongo) [1992/3 c26m⁴] lengthy gelding: poor form in hunter chases: ran well at Hereford in March: stays 3¼m: acts on dead and good to firm ground. *Lee Bowles*

    c75

THE SLATER 8 ch.g. Town And Country – Yashama (Supreme Red) [1992/3 c16s² c16s* c16d⁴ c19s² c16d² c16m^F c18g²] leggy gelding: fair hurdler: won novice chase at Warwick in November: better form afterwards, and ran very well in valuable event at Cheltenham in March until falling 3 out: effective at 2m, barely stays 19f: acts on good to firm and soft ground: usually jumps soundly: should do well in handicap chases. *W. G. M. Turner*

    c106 +
    –

THE STOAT 6 ch.m. Oats – Ivy Hill (Cantab) [1992/3 17d 26g^{pu}] half-sister to winning chaser Red Rondo (by Rontino) and novice hurdler Cantantivy (by Idiot's Delight): dam won a point: poor novice hurdler: dead. *Miss L. C. Plater*

    61

THE STRAY BULLETT 10 gr.g. Gunner B – Grey Miss (Grey Sovereign) [1992/3 c19s^{pu}] no promise on hurdling debut in March, 1992: pulled up and dismounted before sixth in novice hunter chase in April. *A. M. Forte*

    c–
    –

THE SWINGE 6 b.g. Thatching – Hi Gorgeous (Hello Gorgeous (USA)) [1992/3 17d^{pu}] compact gelding: more sign of temperament than ability over hurdles: tried blinkered. *A. J. K. Dunn*

    – §

THE TALKER 8 b.g. Le Bavard (FR) – Oona Ogan (Tarqogan) [1992/3 c25g^{pu}] rangy gelding: winning pointer: poor novice steeplechaser: stayed 3m: acted on dead going: dead. *R. J. Weaver*

    c–

THE TARTAN DYER 6 b.g. Kambalda – Moongello (Bargello) [1992/3 23d 17d 17d 27d] unfurnished gelding: brother to winning jumper Height of Fun and half-brother to 2 others: dam unraced: poor form in novice hurdles: sold 10,000 gns Doncaster May Sales. *G. Richards*

    64

THE TARTAN SPARTAN 9 ch.g. McIndoe – Themopolli (Spartan General) [1992/3 c25g⁴ c26d³] big, good-topped gelding: poor novice hurdler: modest chaser: better effort of season when third in handicap at Uttoxeter in March: suited by test of stamina: acts on good to firm and dead going: twice blinkered. *M. J. Wilkinson*

    c86
    –

THE TITAN GHOST 4 ch.c. Nicholas Bill – Holloway Wonder (Swing Easy (USA)) [1992/3 16s² 16d 16v³ a16g 17v⁴ 16d⁵ 22g 22g² 17g³ 17d* 16f 20g^{pu}] workmanlike colt with scope: modest maiden on Flat: sold out of B. McMahon's stable 1,950 gns Doncaster October Sales: modest form over hurdles: didn't need to be at his best to win amateurs maiden at Carlisle in April: best form at around 2m: acts on heavy ground, possibly unsuited by firm: blinkered final outing. *S. Coathup*

    92

THE TONDY (IRE) 5 gr.g. Godswalk (USA) – Miss Kirby (Town Crier) [1992/3 16d^{pu}] fourth foal: half-brother to a Flat winner in Belgium by Tender King: dam poor Irish Flat maiden: tailed off when pulled up in maiden hurdle at Edinburgh in January. *N. Bycroft*

    –

THE ULTIMATE BUCK 11 b.g. Buckskin (FR) – Royal Gertrude (Royal Buck) [1992/3 c27d^{pu}] poor pointer: no promise in hunter chases. *Mrs P. Visick*

    c–

THE UNDERGRADUATE 14 gr.g. Scallywag – Mrs Cantab (Cantab) [1992/3 c26g^{ur}] rangy gelding: inconsistent novice hunter chaser: stays

    c– x
    –

well: acts on heavy going: usually makes mistakes: usually blinkered nowadays. *C. C. Trietline*

THE VATMAN COMETH 8 b.g. Lafontaine (USA) – Sugar Lump (Candy Cane) [1992/3 c20g6 c25gur c23vpu] leggy, workmanlike gelding: modest novice hurdler in 1989/90: would probably have put up a fair performance and finished second but for unseating rider 2 out in novice chase at Wolverhampton in November: will probably stay 25f. *John R. Upson*   c95 / –

THE WALTZING MOUSE 10 b.g. Strong Gale – Tip Your Toes (Prince Tenderfoot (USA)) [1992/3 c24g c25mF4 c26g3 c25g3] short-legged gelding: modest form in hunter chases: stays 3¼m: looked none too keen when blinkered first start. *Miss E. M. Powell*   c79 / –

THE WHIP 6 ch.g. Fine Blade (USA) – Phayre Vulgan (Vulgan) [1992/3 18s6 18m 22g6] unfurnished gelding: novice hurdler: best effort when sixth over 2¾m at Fontwell in April. *D. M. Grissell*   77

THE WHIRLIE WEEVIL 5 gr.m. Scallywag – Primrose Wood (Precipice Wood) [1992/3 F17s 16g 18dF] useful-looking mare with scope: first foal: dam won numerous races over hurdles and fences at up to 3m, showing fairly useful form: close up and travelling well when falling 3 out in novice hurdle at Kelso in February, first sign of ability: bred to stay very well: should do better. *G. Richards*   – p

THE WIDGET MAN 7 b.g. Callernish – Le Tricolore Token (Pedigree Unknown) [1992/3 21s6 20d6 25s6 25s4 c21v3 c22v2 c27g* c25f4] lengthy, angular gelding: useful hurdler: comfortably landed the odds in novice chase at Fontwell in March: finished lame when good last of 4 in valuable novice chase at Aintree in April: effective at around 2½m and stays well: acts on firm and soft ground: tail swisher and sometimes looks none too keen: not yet an accomplished jumper of fences. *J. T. Gifford*   c119 / 142

THE WRENS DEN 8 b.m. Le Moss – The Wren's Nest (Wrekin Rambler) [1992/3 25gpu 25s 18d] sturdy, lengthy mare: poor novice hurdler. *E. M. Caine*   –

THEY ALL FORGOT ME 6 b.g. Tender King – African Doll (African Sky) [1992/3 c17g5 c19m2 c21f2 c17g4 c26d4 c21g2 c17m c21f2 c24g c17d3] leggy gelding: moderate handicap chaser: ran creditably most starts in 1992/3: suited by a good gallop at 2m and stays 3¼m: acts on any ground: blinkered once. *T. Casey*   c86 / –

THE YANK 7 b. or br.g. Deroulede – Determined Lady (Distinctly (USA)) [1992/3 c21m2 c24g2 c25g4 c24g* c24g6 c24d* c24m*] small gelding: winning hurdler: won novice chases at Edinburgh in December, January and February, first and last handicaps, second a claimer: suited by a good test of stamina: acts on good to soft and firm going: blinkered/visored nowadays. *M. D. Hammond*   c95 / –

THEYDON PRIDE 4 ch.g. Oats – Cavaleuse (Runnett) [1992/3 17v5] first foal: dam poor Flat maiden: well beaten in 7-runner juvenile hurdle at Newton Abbot in November. *J. Simmons*   –

THE YOKEL 7 b.g. Hays – Some Dame (Will Somers) [1992/3 c21vpu c21m5 c22mpu] poor novice hurdler/chaser. *J. Mackie*   c– / –

THE YOMPER (FR) 11 ch.g. Arctic Tern (USA) – Grundylee (FR) (Grundy) [1992/3 17v4 18v 17v5 18s6 18g2 20s3 22g 17dpu] rather sparely-made gelding: selling hurdler nowadays: stays 2½m: acts on any going: front runner: tried visored and blinkered. *R. Curtis*   85

THIBAAIN (USA) 5 b.g. El Gran Senor (USA) – Catherine's Bet (USA) (Grey Dawn II) [1992/3 19m2 21d4] lengthy gelding: fair 1¾m winner on Flat in 1991: moderate form when in frame in novice hurdles at Exeter in September and Kempton following month. *J. White*   90

THIKA 7 b.m. Sunyboy – Bush Lady (Flatbush) [1992/3 25dpu c23vpu c21dF c21mpu] probably of little account: tried blinkered. *J. A. Pickering*   c– / –

THINKING TWICE (USA) 4 ch.c. Kris – Good Thinking (USA) (Raja Baba (USA)) [1992/3 18s3 17s6 16g2 17g2 18d* 16f*] sturdy colt: has had a   123 p tie-back operation: fair middle-distance performer on Flat: sold out of P. Harris' stable 13,000 gns Newmarket Autumn Sales: took well to hurdling and won handicaps at Punchestown in April and Haydock (juvenile) following month: retained 32,000 gns Doncaster May Sales: will stay 2½m: acts on firm and dead ground: genuine. *N. J. Henderson*

THIN RED LINE 9 b. or br.g. Brigadier Gerard – Golden Keep (Worden II) [1992/3 18m3 22m5 c21mur 17g5 17g5 16s5 21d 18s6 16d2 17s 16s2 17d 20f6] leggy gelding: modest hurdler: unseated rider first on chasing debut: stays 2½m: probably acts on any going: blinkered or visored: best waited with: inconsistent and sometimes irresolute: not one to trust. *J. R. Jenkins*

c–
90 §

THIRD IN LINE 10 ch.g. Proverb – Snipkin (Straight Lad) [1992/3 c26dpu] sparely-made gelding: fairly useful chaser at best: showed little in December: will stay beyond 25f: goes well on sound surface: blinkered once in 1988/9: usually a front runner. *Mrs V. S. Hickman*

c–
–

THIRD ROSE 7 b.m. Riberetto – Red Rose III (St Elmo) [1992/3 F17m6 F17s] non-thoroughbred mare: dam winning pointer: signs of ability in NH Flat races at Carlisle in October and November: yet to race over hurdles or fences. *A. Eubank*

THIRTY ALL 8 b.g. Rymer – Mystic Match (Rubor) [1992/3 c21mF c25gpu c24m4 c24m2] big, plain gelding: won 3 of his 5 completed starts in points in 1992, showing fair form: first form in novice chases when second at Newcastle in November. *J. E. Brockbank*

c83

THIS NETTLE DANGER 9 b.g. Kambalda – Golden Goose (Prince Hansel) [1992/3 24g4 21gF 21d4 24v3 21s4 22d4 22s4 16s5 24f* 26f* 27g3 25m] leggy, workmanlike gelding: won handicap hurdles at Towcester (novices) and Huntingdon in May: good third at Stratford later in May: tailed off last start: novice chaser: stays 27f: acts on any going: poor jumper of fences. *O. Brennan*

c– x
96

THISONESFORALICE 5 b.g. Lochnager – Bamdoro (Cavo Doro) [1992/3 17m 16g 16g] sturdy gelding: poor and inconsistent performer on Flat, stays 9f: poor form over hurdles. *A. Harrison*

68

THISTLEHOLM 7 ro.g. Hello Handsome – Private Path (Warpath) [1992/3 21m* 22g3 21spu] big, lengthy gelding: fair handicap hurdler: won at Carlisle in September: ran well when third at Ayr in October, but poorly

107

Hell Nook Four Years Old Handicap Hurdle, Haydock —
left to right, Bold Boss, Thinking Twice (winner) and Batabanoo fight it out

only subsequent start (6 months later): should stay beyond 2¾m: acts on good to firm and dead going. *W. M. Nelson*

THISTLE MONARCH   8 b.g. Rontino – Lavender Blue (Silly Season) [1992/3 16g 17s* 25s* 20s² 22g* 24s⁶] rangy gelding: chasing type: improved hurdler in 1992/3, successful in novice events at Carlisle, Wetherby and Ayr: not seen out after February: has won at 17f but is much better suited by a good test of stamina: acts on soft ground. *G. Richards*   118

THISTLE PRINCESS   4 gr.f. Belfort (FR) – Rueful Lady (Street-fighter) [1992/3 F16d F16s] second foal: dam, winning hurdler, stayed 21f: mid-field in NH Flat races at Ayr in January and Bangor in February: yet to race over hurdles. *G. Richards*

THOMAS RAND   4 b.g. Macmillion – Play It Sam (Mandamus) [1992/3 F16d⁴ F17d] second living foal: brother to 5-y-o Ross Graham: dam of little account: fourth in NH Flat race at Hexham in March, easily better effort: yet to race over hurdles. *M. Dods*

THOMAS THE TANK   9 ch.g. Palm Track – Galah Bird (Darling Boy) [1992/3 16v² 22gᵖᵘ] stocky gelding: only sign of ability over hurdles when second in novice event at Hexham in December: should prove suited by further than 2m: acts on heavy ground. *R. H. Goldie*   81

THOR STONE   5 gr.m. Southern Music – Di's Wag (Scallywag) [1992/3 17d 16s 16s 21sᵖᵘ 17d 21s] angular mare: little worthwhile form over hurdles. *E. H. Owen jun*   –

THORVALORE   5 b.g. Kabour – Wind And Reign (Tumble Wind (USA)) [1992/3 F14d F17s F16d] second live foal: dam poor maiden plater on Flat: tailed off in NH Flat races: yet to race over hurdles or fences. *W. M. Nelson*

THREEBUCK CREEK (USA)   4 b.g. Topsider (USA) – Three Tails (Blakeney) [1992/3 17gᵖᵘ 16f 17f⁶ 17g 24dᵖᵘ] smallish, round-barrelled gelding: first foal: dam high-class middle-distance performer: little worthwhile form over hurdles. *R. Ingram*   –

THREEOUTOFFOUR   8 b.g. Milford – Smiling (Silly Season) [1992/3 c16m⁴ c21g*] leggy, workmanlike gelding: quite useful hurdler: jumped soundly when winning novice chase at Wetherby in October: looked sure to progress but wasn't seen out again: stays 25f: yet to race on heavy going, acts on any other. *O. Brennan*   c104 +
–

THREE STRONG (IRE)   4 br.g. Strong Gale – Mellie (Impecunious) [1992/3 F16m³ F16g] second foal: half-brother to novice hurdler Grazember (by Oats): dam useful staying hurdler: showed ability in NH Flat races: yet to race over hurdles. *J. H. Johnson*

THRESHFIELD (USA)   7 b.h. Northern Prospect (USA) – French Cutie (USA) (Vaguely Noble) [1992/3 17g⁶] fair handicapper on Flat, successful at up to 1m: sixth of 12 in novice event at Huntingdon in October, only outing over hurdles. *B. J. Curley*   78

THRILL SEEKER (IRE)   4 b.f. Treasure Kay – Traminer (Status Seeker) [1992/3 16v 18g⁵] small filly: half-sister to modest hurdler Temporale (by Horage): placed over 1m on Flat in Ireland when trained by W. Roper: always behind in juvenile hurdles at Towcester and Market Rasen (claimer) in April. *M. H. Tompkins*   –

THROW A SIX   7 b.g. Capricorn Line – Greek Glance (Athenien II) [1992/3 21m⁴] half-brother to poor novice hurdler/chaser Balinglance (by Balinger): dam of little account: remote fourth in weak novice hurdle at Carlisle in October. *Mrs S. A. Ward*

THROW AWAY LINE   4 bl.f. Petorius – Corsage (FR) (Nureyev (USA)) [1992/3 16sᵖᵘ] leggy filly: poor miler on Flat: jumped poorly and tailed off when pulled up in juvenile hurdle at Wetherby in March. *R. E. Barr*   –

THUHOOL   5 b.g. Formidable (USA) – Wurud (USA) (Green Dancer (USA)) [1992/3 20g 16g 20d⁴ 18d 17v² 16s⁴ 17d³ 18s* 16d³ 16s² 18v² 18s² 18g* 18g² 16s³] good-topped gelding: usually looks very well: fair hurdler: won handicaps at Folkestone in December and February (novices): ran well   99

Tote County Handicap Hurdle, Cheltenham—Thumbs Up and Spinning (far side) at the last

in novice events last 2 starts: stays 2¼m: suited by give in the ground and acts on heavy ground: tough and consistent. *R. Rowe*

THUMBS UP 7 b.g. Fidel – Misclaire (Steeple Aston) [1992/3 17s* 17s² 22v² 17v³ 16s* 17m*] sturdy gelding: successful in novice hurdles at Chepstow and Worcester prior to winning County Hurdle (Handicap) at Cheltenham in March by 6 lengths from High Baron, travelling well throughout and showing much improved form: ideally suited by around 2m: 128 p

Mr Michael Buckley's "Thumbs Up"

has won on soft going, best run on good to firm: tends to idle in front and suited by waiting tactics: capable of further improvement. *N. J. Henderson*

THUNDERBIRD ONE (USA)   4 b.g. Star de Naskra (USA) – Grande Couture (USA) (Miswaki (USA)) [1992/3 16s³ a16g* 16m] leggy gelding: middle-distance performer on Flat: won novice hurdle at Southwell in February: will stay beyond 2m: acts on soft going and fibresand. *Denys Smith*   88

THUNDER BUG (USA)   5 ch.m. Secreto (USA) – Followeveryrainbow (USA) (Mehmet (USA)) [1992/3 18f⁴ 17g⁴ 17m² 19f⁴ 17s³ 17v⁵ 17m* 17f² 26spu 20f⁴ 23f³] leggy, sparely-made mare: won novice handicap hurdle at Hereford in March: good second at Chepstow later in month, easily best subsequent effort: best form at around 2m: acts on any going. *A. P. James*   90

THUNDER (IRE)   5 b.g. Sexton Blake – White Huntress (Jaazeiro (USA)) [1992/3 F17m³ F17g³] rangy, unfurnished gelding: third of 17 in NH Flat races at Bangor and Hereford in October: yet to race over hurdles or fences. *J. M. Bradley*

THYMON THE HORTH   4 ch.g. Hotfoot – Delta Wind (Tumble Wind (USA)) [1992/3 F16m] second foal: dam showed a little ability at 2 yrs: behind in NH Flat race at Nottingham in March: yet to race over hurdles. *T. G. Mills*

THYNE RUN (IRE)   5 b.g. Good Thyne (USA) – Oweena Run (Deep Run) [1992/3 22g 20mpu 21dpu] unfurnished gelding: second foal: dam unraced: showed nothing in novice hurdles in March and April. *J. H. Johnson*   –

TIANANMEN SQUARE (IRE)   5 b.g. Dominion – Oriental Star (Falcon) [1992/3 16s* 16v*]   141 p

Enough was seen of Tiananmen Square in the very short time he was on view to identify him as one of the best Irish prospects, as long as he can put his training difficulties behind him. He ran only twice, justifying favouritism in a maiden hurdle at Fairyhouse and a novice hurdle at Navan on consecutive Saturdays in December. He started at 3/1 on in a field of twenty-two at Fairyhouse on his jumping debut. The field at Navan was smaller but considerably stronger, with other last-time-out winners Bayrouge, Bucks-Choice and Friends of Gerald among the opposition. The race came to the boil two flights out, where Bayrouge and Tiananmen Square, having kept well in touch, made their challenge to the front-running Bucks-Choice. Approaching the last Tiananmen Square and Bayrouge looked to have it between them, then Tiananmen Square quickened on to win by two lengths. Bucks-Choice finished fifteen lengths further back, keeping Friends of Gerald out of third place. Reportedly the winner was slightly lame on his off-hind afterwards. His performance earned him a 33/1 quote for the Champion Hurdle, but over the next two months intermittent muscle problems behind put the date of his next appearance in doubt, and eventually time ran out.

Tiananmen Square (IRE) (b.g. 1988)	Dominion (b 1972)	Derring-Do (b 1961)	Darius
			Sipsey Bridge
		Picture Palace (b 1961)	Princely Gift
			Palais Glide
	Oriental Star (b 1973)	Falcon (b 1964)	Milesian
			Pretty Swift
		Coming-Of-Age (b 1967)	Majority Blue
			Welsh Star

Obviously Tiananmen Square had a big reputation when he went to Fairyhouse. He'd built it in National Hunt Flat races during 1991/2. He was all the rage for the inaugural Tote Festival Bumper at Cheltenham in 1992 after two wins in Ireland, and ran well there, only to be beaten ten lengths by Montelado. The defeat, his only one to date, he avenged by two and a half lengths in the corresponding Punchestown feature when receiving weight off his rival. He is, incidentally, one of only two horses to have beaten Montelado so far—the other is Bayrouge. Tiananmen Square's pedigree is a cut above that of the average bumpers horse. His dam Oriental Star had a *Timeform* rating of 94 as a three-year-old; she won seven races altogether,

Thomastown Maiden Hurdle, Fairyhouse — Tiananmen Square (C. Swan) at 3/1 on

at five furlongs to a mile and a half, for Michael Stoute's stable. She is a half-sister to the good middle-distance colt Gay Lemur, while both her dam and grandam were winning two-year-olds. Dominion, who died in February, proved an eminently versatile sire, getting tough, fast two-year-olds as well as jumpers like Hopscotch, Capability Brown and Sprowston Boy. Oriental Star has produced some versatile performers, among them Folkland (by Auction Ring) and Biras Creek (by Sandy Creek) who won on the Flat and over jumps, and Oregon Trail (also by Auction Ring) a fair middle-distance maiden on the Flat who went on to take the Arkle Chase in 1986; Geostar (by Runnett) became a winner over jumps after failing to make the grade on the Flat. Three of the four foals mentioned stayed at least three miles, the other, Biras Creek, appeared not to stay two and a half. Tiananmen Square has been raced exclusively at two miles. He impresses as a horse with a good turn of foot and plenty of speed for a hurdler but it is most unlikely that two miles will be his limit. A smallish gelding, he acts on heavy going. *N. Meade, Ireland*

TIARUM 11 b.g. Tiran (HUN) – Contessa (HUN) (Peleid) [1992/3 17m 19h⁵ c17s² c17d⁵ 22dᵖᵘ c21fF] small, lightly-made gelding: poor hurdler/ maiden chaser: sold out of G. Ham's stable 1,250 gns Ascot December Sales after fourth start: stays 21f: probably acts on any going: blinkered once. *N. B. Thomson* — c84 —

TIBBS INN 4 ch.g. Adonijah – Historia (Northfields) (USA) [1992/3 16gˢᵘ 16g 16vᵖᵘ 16sᵖᵘ 18s⁶ 16m 17gF 18v⁴] close-coupled gelding: twice-raced at 2 yrs: would have shown easily best form over hurdles but for falling last in novice event at Stratford in May. *C. Smith* — 89 ?

TIBBY HEAD (IRE) 5 b.g. Lyphard's Special (USA) – Deer Park (FR) (Faraway Son (USA)) [1992/3 16fᵖᵘ] plating-class maiden on Flat: behind when pulled up in novice hurdle at Worcester in September. *J. Mackie* —

Woodchester Credit Lyonnais Downshire Handicap Hurdle, Punchestown—
Time For A Run leads on the bridle at the last; behind him, left to right,
are Atone, Lady Olein and Eyelid

TIBER RUN   8 ch.g. Deep Run – Trattoria (Espresso) [1992/3 22s 21m^{pu} 22g^{pu} 28g^{pu}] little sign of ability over hurdles or fences: trained until after second start by S. Payne. *T. J. Carr*   c– –

TICONDEROGA   7 b.g. Broadsword (USA) – Little Primrose (Master Owen) [1992/3 c16d^{pu} c18s^F c17g^3 c16m^6] tall gelding: modest novice hurdler: poor novice chaser: should stay further than 17f: acts on good to firm ground: blinkered last outing. *D. Nicholson*   c– –

TIDAL RIVER   4 gr.f. Absalom – Ebb And Flo (Forlorn River) [1992/3 17g^6 16g^{bd} 18g^4 16d^5 18d 18d] half-sister to quite useful jumpers Connaught River (by Connaught) and Rivers Edge (by Sharpen Up): poor maiden on Flat and over hurdles: has run in sellers. *Denys Smith*   64

TIGER CLAW (USA)   7 b.g. Diamond Shoal – Tiger Scout (USA) (Silent Screen (USA)) [1992/3 17m 16s 17s^F] leggy, sparely-made gelding: fair hurdler in 1991/2: well below form in 1992/3: races only at around 2m: acts on firm going: tried blinkered/visored, better form without. *R. J. Hodges*   –

TIGERS PET   9 b.g. Tina's Pet – Too Do (Manado) [1992/3 c21m^3 c21g* c21m^2 c21f* c19g^2 c17g^2 c19g c21g^4] sparely-made gelding: fair handicap chaser: won at Southwell and Worcester early in season: first race for nearly 6 months, creditable second at Sedgefield in March, below best last 2 starts: stays 21f: acts on firm and dead ground. *W. H. Bissill*   c101 –

TIGH-NA-MARA   5 b.m. Miramar Reef – Charlie's Sunshine (Jimsun) [1992/3 F14s^5] fourth foal: sister and half-sister to poor animals: dam, winning hurdler, stayed 23f: fifth of 15 in NH Flat race at Market Rasen in April: yet to race over hurdles or fences. *D. T. Garraton*   –

TILDEBO   9 b.g. Ile de Bourbon (USA) – Thereby (Star Moss) [1992/3 c16g^5 16f^{pu} c16d^{rtr} c17m c20f^{pu}] strong, lengthy gelding: fair performer when in the mood: very unreliable at start in 1992/3 (trained until after third outing by J. Webber): successful with and without blinkers: one to avoid. *R. T. Phillips*   c§§ §§

TILDEN PARK   7 b.m. Bustineto – Moycarkey (Raise You Ten) [1992/3 c21m^4 c21g^R] leggy mare: poor maiden hurdler: selling handicap chaser: broke down in August, and wasn't seen out again: stays 2½m: acts on good to firm and dead going: sometimes blinkered. *P. J. Bevan*   c– –

TILT TECH FLYER   8 b.g. Windjammer (USA) – Queen Kate (Queen's Hussar) [1992/3 18v^4 16s 17v^3 18s] tall, leggy gelding: fair hurdler: creditable efforts when in frame in handicaps at Worcester in November and Lingfield in December: stays 2¼m: acts on heavy going. *J. Akehurst*   107

TIMANFAYA 6 b.g. Sparkling Boy – Easterly Gael (Tudor Music) [1992/3 16g² 16g 16s 20g³ 17g³] plain gelding: modest novice hurdler: creditable efforts when placed in 1992/3: stays 2½m: acts on dead ground. *Mrs D. F. Culham*   84

TIME FOR A RUN 6 b.g. Deep Run – Hourly Rate (Menelek) [1992/3 16v* 18d² 16s² 16d*] good-bodied gelding: chasing type: second foal: dam, winning hurdler, half-sister to useful hurdler Glassilaun: won both starts in NH Flat races: has taken well to hurdling, and won maiden at Navan in January and 17-runner handicap at Punchestown in April: will stay beyond 2¼m: acts on heavy going: useful already and looks sure to go on to better things. *E. J. O'Grady, Ireland*   131 p

TIMELLS BROOK 5 gr.g. Balinger – Cherry Meringue (Birdbrook) [1992/3 F17v F16d] first foal: dam showed little in points: well beaten in NH Flat races in November and December: yet to race over hurdles or fences. *R. G. Frost*

TIME MODULE 9 b.g. Latest Model – Gemini Miss (My Swanee) [1992/3 c17vᵖᵘ c24sᵖᵘ c24sᵖᵘ c27vᶠ c24vᵖᵘ] sturdy gelding: poor novice hurdler/chaser: sometimes visored. *D. D. Scott*   c–
–

TIMES ARE HARD 9 b.g. Bay Express – Raffinrula (Raffingora) [1992/3 16s⁶ 16m] sparely-made gelding: winning 2m hurdler: well beaten in 2 handicaps in October: best form on good ground. *C. A. Smith*   –

TIME SLOT (USA) 6 ch.g. Secreto (USA) – Ebbing Tide (USA) (His Majesty (USA)) [1992/3 17gᵖᵘ 16s 17s⁶ 16d a16g⁵] well-made gelding: poor novice hurdler: sold 1,650 gns Doncaster May Sales. *J. C. McConnochie*   –

TIME STAR (NZ) 9 br.g. Drums of Time (USA) – Crescent Star (NZ) (Persian Garden) [1992/3 c19g⁴ c19sᵖᵘ] workmanlike gelding: poor novice hurdler/chaser: stays 2½m: best form with give in the ground: sometimes looks none too keen. *D. J. Caro*   c–
–

TIM SOLDIER (FR) 6 ch.g. Tip Moss (FR) – Pali Dancer (FR) (Green Dancer (USA)) [1992/3 c16d⁶ c21s⁵ c20sᶠ c21s* c20d⁵ c25mᶠ c26d⁴ c25sᵖᵘ c21gᵖᵘ] leggy, light-framed gelding: fair hurdler at best: lucky winner of novice handicap chase at Bangor in February: creditable fourth in valuable similar race at Uttoxeter in March: stays 3¼m: acts on any going: blinkered once in 1991/2: poor jumper. *M. F. Barraclough*   c88 x
–

TIMURS DOUBLE 12 b.g. Double Form – Timur's Daughter (Tamerlane) [1992/3 16v 17g² 16d⁵ 21m 17d⁵ 21s³ 22g⁶] rangy gelding: fair handicap hurdler on his day: best effort of season on second start: maiden chaser: needs a testing 2m and stays 2¾m: suited by give in the ground and acts on heavy: blinkered once. *Major W. N. Sample*   c–
102

TIMURS LUCK 7 b.g. Lochnager – Timur's Daughter (Tamerlane) [1992/3 20vᵖᵘ] big gelding: poor novice hurdler: stays 2½m: acts on good to firm ground: jumps none too fluently. *T. H. Caldwell*

TINA'S ANGEL 6 b.m. Martinmas – Tina's Magic (Carnival Night) [1992/3 16g⁵ 17m 17m³ 17dᵖᵘ] leggy, sparely-made mare: poor 2m maiden plater over hurdles: trained until after third start by M. Muggeridge. *J. S. Moore*   69

TINA'S GAME 5 ch.m. Mummy's Game – Mantina (Bustino) [1992/3 21g 17s⁴ 16sᵖᵘ 16s 16m 17d⁶ 16gᵖᵘ] lengthy mare: plating-class maiden on Flat and over hurdles. *A. P. Stringer*   63

TINAS LAD 10 b.g. Jellaby – Arbatina (Sallust) [1992/3 c20m⁶ c21g⁴ c18d* c17gᶠ c16sᵖᵘ c18d⁵ c16f² c16f* c17m⁵ c16m⁴] workmanlike gelding: fair handicap chaser on his day: won at Stratford in November and Ludlow in March: effective from 2m to 2½m: acts on firm and dead ground: front runner: runs occasional lack-lustre races (reportedly breaks blood vessels) and sometimes finishes weakly. *J. A. C. Edwards*   c105
–

TINA'S MISSILE 6 b.g. Cruise Missile – Tina's Gold (Goldhill) [1992/3 16sᶠ 17dᵖᵘ 18d³ 17m³ 16d³] lengthy, unfurnished gelding: moderate novice hurdler: will stay beyond 2¼m: acts on good to firm and dead going. *R. Lee*   84

Mitsubishi Shogun Trophy (Handicap Chase), Doncaster—
Tinryland (left) and Space Fair have a ding-dong battle

TINDARI (FR)   5 ch.g. Vacarme (USA) – Yseult (FR) (Olantengy (FR)) [1992/3 21d² 20s² 24g* 24d* 25d*] workmanlike gelding: progressive form over hurdles in 1992/3 and won maiden event and handicap at Edinburgh and conditional jockeys handicap at Carlisle: quite useful effort in last named on final start (February): suited by test of stamina: best form with give in the ground: on the upgrade. *J. M. Jefferson*   117

TINGLE BROOK   9 br.g. Paddy's Stream – Yvonne's Fancy (Continuation) [1992/3 c21gᵖᵘ c25gᵖᵘ c25s] leggy gelding: poor maiden jumper. *Miss C. Bell*   c–
–

TINKER DAN   5 br.g. Kirchner – Rose Mulholland (Lombard (GER)) [1992/3 16s 16m 17s] sturdy gelding: first foal: dam, behind in NH Flat race, fell only outing over hurdles: has shown little over hurdles. *P. J. Jones*   –

TINRYLAND   9 b.g. Prince Regent (FR) – Tonduff Star (Royal Highway) [1992/3 c20g⁶ c21d³ c17m* c24g c21m⁵ c16g⁵] sturdy, close-coupled gelding: useful handicap chaser: won at Doncaster in January by a head from Space Fair: ran as though something amiss afterwards: effective from 2m to 21f, and should stay 3m: acts on good to firm and dead going (possibly unsuited by soft): often hangs left. *N. J. Henderson*   c141
–

TIP IT IN   4 gr.g. Le Solaret (FR) – Alidante (Sahib) [1992/3 18m⁵ 16d⁵ 18d⁶ 18v* a16g² a18g⁴ 18g² 17f² 17m 16s⁵] small, lengthy, lightly-made gelding: won novice selling handicap hurdle at Market Rasen (bought in 3,000 gns) in December: ran well in novice handicaps next 4 starts: will stay beyond 2¼m: acts on any turf ground and fibresand: game. *A. Smith*   86

TIP NAP   5 b.g. Pitpan – Miss Metro (Upper Case (USA)) [1992/3 17gᵖᵘ 20mᵖᵘ 18m] lengthy, angular gelding: no sign of ability over hurdles. *Mrs S. J. Smith*   –

TIPPING TIM 8 b.g. King's Ride – Jeanarie (Reformed Character) **c153**
[1992/3 c24s⁴ c21g* c25g* c21d* c21v³ c24s c24v⁵ c27m]   –
    Tipping Tim wasn't seen at his best in his last three races, the King
George VI Chase at Kempton, the Peter Marsh Chase at Haydock and the
Cheltenham Gold Cup. Reportedly he pulled some back muscles at Kempton and was difficult to get right afterwards. Report also had it that he broke
a blood vessel in the Gold Cup. Considering the nature of his task he ran
respectably there, jumping well and showing prominently until outpaced
from three out. Prior to the King George Tipping Tim had done nothing but
improve and he is still young enough—the same age as Jodami—to bounce
back after a summer's rest, though he has plenty more improving to do
before he can be considered in the top flight.
    Tipping Tim's best form to date is in handicaps, the Mackeson Gold
Cup and the Tripleprint Gold Cup run at Cheltenham in November and
December respectively; he won the first and finished third in the other, a
race previously known as the A.F. Budge Gold Cup. However, he also has a
win to his name already in a Grade 2 conditions event, the Tetley Bitter
Charlie Hall Chase at Wetherby in late-October. Tipping Tim had the edge
in fitness on some of his rivals that day and was receiving 8 lb from two of
them, Pat's Jester and Cool Ground. He came to the last looking as if he
might be held by Pat's Jester, having thrown down a determined challenge
from two out, but he produced the better jump and snatched a narrow lead
which he held to the line under hard driving. After this performance Tipping
Tim started the heavily-backed 11/2 favourite for a highly competitive
Mackeson. He was obviously improving; equally obviously, he needed to be,
not least because he was 11 lb worse off with Another Coral, the previous
year's winner whom he'd beaten seven lengths in a handicap at Cheltenham in the first half of October when Another Coral had been making his
seasonal reappearance. Another Coral started only half a point longer,
sharing second favouritism with the top weight, the previous year's A.F.
Budge winner Kings Fountain. One reason for the weight of money for the
favourite, back to two and a half miles from three miles, was the promise of a
true test of stamina at the trip, given the competitive field and soft
conditions underfoot. Sure enough, he got a true test, with a good pace set at

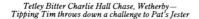

Tetley Bitter Charlie Hall Chase, Wetherby—
Tipping Tim throws down a challenge to Pat's Jester

Mackeson Gold Cup Handicap Chase, Cheltenham—
another big prize goes Tipping Tim's way

first by Sirrah Jay, taken up by Howe Street at the fourth, then carried on by Brandeston when Howe Street unseated at the tenth. And Tipping Tim finished the race very strongly. Dropped out, he made steady progress on the inside down the far side, hit the front over the second last, forged clear of the three others still in with a chance on the home turn, and ran on to win most decisively by seven lengths and a short head from Another Coral and Beech Road. Kings Fountain fell at the fourth last when close up, travelling well. The Tripleprint Gold Cup saw Tipping Tim a further 8 lb worse off with

Mrs J. Mould's "Tipping Tim"

760

Another Coral; by now he had the mark of a very useful chaser and carried top weight of 12-0. He ran a creditable third to Another Coral in the heavy ground, reproducing Mackeson form with him at the revised weights in going down by eight lengths. Brought to have every chance, he came under pressure at the second last and couldn't quite get to grips with the winner who'd led three out.

		Rarity	Hethersett
Tipping Tim (b.g. 1985)	King's Ride (b 1976)	(b 1967)	Who Can Tell
		Ride	Sovereign Path
		(b 1966)	Turf
	Jeanarie (b 1977)	Reformed Character	Reliance II
		(br 1970)	No Saint
		Jeanette Marie	Fighting Don
		(br 1966)	Quetta

Tipping Tim is the first foal of his dam, the maiden Jeanarie; the third foal Russinsky (by Celio Rufo) was placed in several novice hurdles in the latest season; the fifth, Tipping Tim's brother Topping Tom, is in training with Twiston-Davies. Tipping Tim's grandam Jeannette Marie and great-grandam Quetta were better broodmares than they were racemares and each produced several winners, the pick of Jeannette Marie's being the useful chaser Bold Argument and the late-developing staying chaser Camelot Knight, a close relative of Tipping Tim since he's also by King's Ride. An unraced sister of Jeannette Marie, First Adventure, is the dam of the 1973 Arkle Trophy winner Denys Adventure.

In Captain Dibble, Dakyns Boy and Tipping Tim, the Twiston-Davies stable has three likely Grand National candidates. Tipping Tim, effective at two and a half miles to three and a quarter miles has disappointed on his two starts over further but was out of form on the first occasion and probably past his best on the second (in the 1992 Whitbread Gold Cup). A work-manlike, lengthy gelding, he jumps very soundly, is tough and genuine and almost certainly acts on any going. There is a chance that a left-handed track suits him best. *N. A. Twiston-Davies*

TIPP MARINER 8 ch.g. Sandalay – Knockbawn Lady (Push On) [1992/3 c21d³ c26vᵖᵘ c19sᶠ c26d* c26dᵖᵘ c26dᵖᵘ] rangy gelding: winning hurdler: won novice chase at Wincanton in February: ran poorly both starts afterwards, blinkered on last: suited by a test of stamina nowadays: acts on soft going: jumps fences soundly in the main. *S. E. Sherwood*   c95 –

TIP THE DOVE 4 br.f. Riberetto – Nimble Dove (Starch Reduced) [1992/3 F16g F18g³] lengthy, unfurnished filly: third foal: half-sister to winning hurdler Sally's Dove (by Celtic Cone): dam, fairly useful staying hurdler, from very successful jumping family: showed ability in mares NH Flat races in March: yet to race over hurdles. *R. J. Price*

TIP TOP LAD 6 b.g. Aragon – New Top (New Brig) [1992/3 18s⁴ 17vᶠ 18v 17f*] rangy gelding: modest form when winning novice handicap hurdle at Lingfield in March: should stay beyond 2¼m: best effort on firm ground. *D. M. Grissell*   97

TIRLEY MAN 9 ch.g. Stan Flashman – Gamefull Gipsy (Welton Gameful) [1992/3 c17gᵖᵘ] leggy gelding: failed to complete in points and a hunter chase. *D. E. S. Smith*   c–

TIRLEY MISSILE 7 ch.g. Cruise Missile – Tic-On-Rose (Celtic Cone) [1992/3 c21s³ c21g⁶] sparely-made gelding: first foal: dam winning hurdler: winning pointer: signs of ability in hunter chases, but wandered badly and looked irresolute last outing: one to treat with caution. *F. G. Smith*   c82 §

TITIAN GIRL 4 ch.f. Faustus (USA) – Redhead (Hotfoot) [1992/3 16s⁴ 16s⁴ 17s 16s 22s 16g⁴ 16g⁶] sparely-made filly: of little account on Flat: modest plater over hurdles: acts on soft going: blinkered all bar fifth start. *Miss L. C. Siddall*   75

TITLED DANCER (IRE) 4 ch.f. Where To Dance (USA) – Lady Broke (Busted) [1992/3 16s* 16s² 16d² 16v* 16d 16s² 17f* 16g²]   132 p
    The two most valuable races run in Britain confined to juvenile hurdlers fell to Irish-trained runners, both of them fillies, Shawiya taking

the Daily Express Triumph Hurdle and Titled Dancer the Glenlivet Anniversary Hurdle. Both races were substandard, the latter noticeably so. The firm ground at Aintree was partly responsible for a field of only eight in the Glenlivet, the smallest turnout since the same number contested the inaugural running in 1976 when it was won by another Irish challenger Cooch Behar. The race lacked quality as well as quantity. The Victor Ludorum Hurdle winner Bold Boss, whose form was no more than useful, was sent off clear favourite at 13/8. Next in the betting at 9/2 came Titled Dancer and Zamirah, the latter beaten at long odds on in her previous race, followed by Her Honour, Kadi and Dominant Serenade, who'd finished ninth, tenth and twelfth respectively in the Triumph Hurdle. Titled Dancer, running on a firm surface for the first time over hurdles, handled the ground well. She travelled strongly just off the steady gallop set by Zamirah, and was able to take up a handy position when Her Honour increased the pace at the last flight in the back straight, four from home. Poised to challenge at the third last, where Bold Boss was under pressure and losing touch, Titled Dancer enjoyed an uninterrupted run up the far rail, moved smoothly into the lead at the next and began to forge clear under pressure. Two lengths ahead starting up the run-in, Titled Dancer then began to idle and at the line had only half a length to spare over the rallying Her Honour. Winning the Glenlivet isn't Titled Dancer's sole claim to fame, for she's also the only horse to have beaten the season's leading juvenile Shawiya over hurdles. Titled Dancer achieved that feat at Navan in November when the pair, both running for the first time over hurdles, were separated by a head. Shawiya had the better of the argument in three subsequent meetings, Titled Dancer getting closest to her at Punchestown in January. Titled Dancer, who'd won on that course in the meantime, went down by half a length after putting in a persistent challenge from before two out. But she was unable to trouble Shawiya and was beaten nine lengths when the pair met for the final time, again at Punchestown, in the Champion Four-Year-Old Hurdle in April. Titled Dancer ran right up to her best in finishing second, one place ahead of the Triumph Hurdle fourth Judicial Field, the result leaving no-one in any doubt that Shawiya is her superior at present.

Titled Dancer is by the beautifully-bred Where To Dance, who went to stud as an unraced three-year-old in 1988 and died in South Africa the

Glenlivet Anniversary 4-Y-O Hurdle, Aintree—
Titled Dancer has the measure of Her Honour

Mrs Padraig Nolan's "Titled Dancer"

Titled Dancer (IRE) (ch.f. 1989)	Where To Dance (USA) (b 1985)	Northern Dancer (b 1961)	Nearctic Natalma
		Where You Lead (ch 1970)	Raise A Native Noblesse
	Lady Broke (ch 1980)	Busted (b 1963)	Crepello Sans Le Sou
		Sahibs Daughter (b 1974)	Sahib Roman Nose

following year. Titled Dancer's dam Lady Broke, also unraced, is a half-sister to three winners, one of them a jumper, in Italy. The second dam Sahib's Daughter, a fairly useful winner at up to seven furlongs, is a half-sister to Stella Roma, dam of the useful staying chasers Androma and Bigsun. Titled Dancer, a fair winner over a mile and a half on the Flat, has raced only at around two miles over hurdles. In our opinion she'll be seen to even better advantage over longer distances. A workmanlike filly with scope, Titled Dancer looks the type to progress and she should make up into a very useful performer. She acts on any going. *J. G. Coogan, Ireland*

TITUS ANDRONICUS 6 b.g. Oats – Lavilla (Tycoon II) [1992/3 c21s^{pu} c22v^F c25v^F c21g^3 c24g^6 c22g^6 c21g^4 c17m^3 c22m^2] strong, lengthy gelding: modest maiden jumper: stays 2¾m: acts on good to firm ground: blinkered once: sketchy jumper. *N. A. Gaselee*   **c83 –**

TITUS GOLD 8 b.g. Sonnen Gold – Chemin de Guerre (Warpath) [1992/3 16s* 17d³ 16v³] leggy gelding: fair handicap hurdler: first outing since 1989/90, won at Uttoxeter in October: good third at Wolverhampton in November, below form following month: best around 2m with plenty of give in the ground: successful blinkered/visored and not. *W. Clay*   **107**

Bic Razor Lanzarote Handicap Hurdle, Kempton—no danger to Tomahawk

TOAD ALONG 8 b.g. Daring March – Fille de Phaeton (Sun Prince) [1992/3 c16s⁵ c18dᵖᵘ c17g⁶ 16g⁶] big gelding: winning 2m hurdler/chaser: showed nothing in 1992/3: sometimes wears a tongue strap. *J. Webber*   c–
–

TOASTER CRUMPET 4 b.g. Seymour Hicks (FR) – Lady Letitia (Le Bavard (FR)) [1992/3 F16d F17g] third foal: dam, winning Irish hurdler, half-sister to Wayward Lad: tailed off in NH Flat races at Ayr (trained by D. McCain) in January and Carlisle in March: sold 1,700 gns Doncaster May Sales: yet to race over hurdles. *G. Richards*

TOBIN BRONZE 6 b.g. Sexton Blake – Pampered Julie (Le Bavard (FR)) [1992/3 F16s⁵ F16d 21d⁶] first foal: dam well beaten in Irish NH Flat races: signs of ability in NH Flat races and a novice hurdle in second half of season: likely to do better. *M. D. Hammond*   – p

TOBY HENRY 5 b.g. Jalmood (USA) – Wave Dancer (Dance In Time (CAN)) [1992/3 16g 16d 17g⁵ 18sᵖᵘ] smallish, sturdy gelding: novice hurdler: ran poorly in 1992/3. *N. A. Gaselee*   –

TOCHENKA 9 ch.m. Fine Blue – Authors Daughter (Charlottown) [1992/3 c26d* c27g* c23g² c24f⁵] strong, workmanlike mare: winning hurdler: much improved form over fences when winning handicaps at Hereford and Fontwell in April: good second in similar race at Worcester later in month but ran poorly last start: stays well: acts on firm and dead ground: has run blinkered (not in 1992/3). *N. A. Twiston-Davies*   c100
–

TOI MARINE 8 b.g. Deep Run – Owens Toi (Master Owen) [1992/3 a16g a20g] leggy gelding: successful pointer: poor maiden hurdler: headstrong, and looks a difficult ride. *A. A. Hambly*   63

TOMAHAWK 6 ch.g. Be My Guest (USA) – Siouan (So Blessed) [1992/3 16gF 17d 17s 16v* 17g] leggy gelding: useful hurdler: trained until after second start by R. Holder: won Bic Razor Lanzarote Handicap Hurdle at Kempton in January in good style: ran well in Tote Gold Trophy at Newbury following month, only subsequent start: best at around 2m: acts on good to firm and heavy going: takes good hold and races up with pace. *P. G. Murphy*   133

TOMALLEY 9 b.g. Reformed Character – High Jean (Arrigle Valley) [1992/3 c19gᵘʳ] temperamental maiden pointer: tailed off when unseating rider in hunter chase at Fontwell in March. *P. F. Henderson*   c–

TOM BIR 11 ch.g. Deep Run – Clontinty Queen (Laurence O) [1992/3 c21d⁴] workmanlike gelding: fair handicap chaser at best: in need of race in September, only start in 1992/3: stays 3m (not 3¼m in testing conditions): acts on any going. *Andrew Turnell*   c–

TOM CLAPTON 6 b.g. Daring March – Embroideress (Stanford) [1992/3 17m*] leggy, workmanlike gelding: fair hurdler: claimed for £9,100 after winning claimer at Newton Abbot in August by 12 lengths and   108

subsequently won on Flat in Italy: stays 19f: best form on ground no softer than dead: usually makes running. *M. C. Pipe*

TOM FURZE   6 b.g. Sula Bula – Bittleys Wood (Straight Lad) [1992/3 20d 16m3] fifth foal: dam once-raced daughter of very useful pointer Orchid Moor: easily better effort in novice hurdles when third of 5 finishers at Towcester in May: should stay beyond 2m: acts on good to firm going. *J. A. B. Old*   80

TOM PENNY   11 b.g. Tom Noddy – Pennyworth (Brightworthy) [1992/3 F13m c17s3] fair pointer in 1990: very lightly raced since: second run in a steeplechase when showing nothing in a novice event at Chepstow in April. *Mrs R. Harry*   c–

TOMPET   7 b.g. Le Bavard (FR) – Swanny Jane (Bargello) [1992/3 c23g3 c24m* c24g2 c26d3 c25s6 c26d c25dur c24d5 c24g* c26m5 c24gF c25d4] lengthy, workmanlike gelding: moderate form over fences: won novice event at Stratford in October and handicap at Taunton in April: suited by a good test of stamina: acts on good to firm and not discredited on dead going: blinkered twice. *N. A. Twiston-Davies*   c92 –

TOM'S APACHE   4 br.g. Sula Bula – Tom's Nap Hand (Some Hand) [1992/3 17g 16g] leggy gelding: lightly-raced maiden on Flat: well beaten in juvenile hurdles at Cheltenham in October and Windsor in November. *Billy Williams*   –

TOM TOWLEY   7 b.g. Reformed Character – Darwin Tulip (Campaign) [1992/3 22gur 20m4 20m4 18g4 25spu 22g] lightly-made gelding: poor novice hurdler: stays 2½m: acts on soft and good to firm ground. *A. Smith*   76

TOM TROUBADOUR   10 b. or br.g. Black Minstrel – Graceland (Golden Love) [1992/3 c25m3] big, rangy gelding: fairly useful chaser: not disgraced in October: stays 3m: acts on firm going. *J. T. Gifford*   c– –

TONKAWA   8 b.g. Indian King (USA) – Lady Tycoon (No Mercy) [1992/3 22d3 24g3 22g] good-bodied gelding: one-time winning stayer on Flat for G. Harwood: best effort in novice hurdles when third over 3m at Market Rasen in October: sold 1,100 gns Ascot May Sales. *J. M. Bradley*   92

TONY MURPHYS LADY   7 b. or br.m. Over The River (FR) – Salty Sea (Sir Herbert) [1992/3 18v 22g] plain mare: second foal: sister to winning Irish pointer Dashing Brook: dam, behind in 3 Irish NH Flat races, half-sister to 2 winning jumpers: behind in novice hurdles at Fontwell in January and April. *John R. Upson*   –

TONY'S DELIGHT (IRE)   5 b.g. Krayyan – Tinas Image (He Loves Me) [1992/3 17dpu 17mpu] unfurnished gelding: has scope: fairly useful form at up to 9f on Flat in Ireland when trained by K. Prendergast: shaped very well in novice event at Newbury in February on hurdling debut but raced too freely and jumped sketchily both subsequent outings. *G. B. Balding*   94 +

TOO CLEVER BY HALF   5 b.g. Pragmatic – Acushla Macree (Mansingh (USA)) [1992/3 F17d F17f6 F16f6] first foal: dam winning hurdler: sixth in NH Flat races at Sandown in March and Haydock in May: yet to race over hurdles or fences. *R. F. Johnson Houghton*   –

TOODLEOO   4 ch.f. Kings Lake (USA) – Boo (Bustino) [1992/3 F16s6] third living foal: dam staying daughter of half-sister to Warpath and Dakota: well beaten in NH Flat race at Bangor in February: sold 1,150 gns Doncaster March Sales: yet to race over hurdles. *C. W. Thornton*   –

TOOGOOD TO BE TRUE   5 br.g. Sonnen Gold – Lady Relka (Relko) [1992/3 F18d4 20d6 22s 16s* 18d* 22g] tall, leggy gelding: has scope: NH Flat race winner: fair hurdler: won novice events at Catterick in January and Sedgefield in April: best form at around 2m (never going well over 2¾m on last start, subsequently found to be coughing): acts on soft going. *M. H. Easterby*   99

TOOMUCH TOOSOON (IRE)   5 b.g. Glenstal (USA) – Star of India (General Assembly (USA)) [1992/3 16m5] poor form when fifth in two 2m novice hurdles: sold 1,500 gns Ascot May Sales. *S. Christian*   70

TOOTING TIMES 7 ch.g. Leading Man – Saucy (Saucy Kit) [1992/3 c25s^{ur}] temperamental maiden pointer: behind when unseating rider in maiden hunter chase at Hexham in April. *M. McCarthy*

c–

TOP BRASS (IRE) 5 ch.g. Orchestra – Lady Norefield (Milan) [1992/3 16s^5 16v^4] rangy gelding: second foal: dam winning Irish pointer: won only start in Irish points (March, 1992): sold 19,000 gns Doncaster May (1992) Sales: showed ability in mid-season novice hurdles at Nottingham and Wincanton: will prove suited by further than 2m: likely to improve again. *K. C. Bailey*

86 p

TOPCLIFFE 6 b.m. Top Ville – Sandford Lady (Will Somers) [1992/3 20s] leggy mare: poor novice hurdler: best effort over 25f on good ground. *Mrs V. A. Aconley*

–

TOPFORMER 6 gr.g. Highlands – Umtali (Boreen (FR)) [1992/3 16d 16g^4 16s 20g^2 21f] rangy, angular gelding: best effort over hurdles when second in novice handicap at Edinburgh in February: better suited by 2½m than shorter. *F. Watson*

84

TOPHARD 7 b.g. Lyphard's Special (USA) – Tomard (Thatching) [1992/3 26g^4 c17d^{ur} c16g^6 26d^{pu} 16s^6 17d] sparely-made gelding: poor novice hurdler/chaser: stays well: acts on firm and dead ground: often visored or blinkered. *R. Lee*

c–
–

TOP IT ALL 5 b.g. Song – National Dress (Welsh Pageant) [1992/3 22m^4 23g22g^{ur}21d^{3}18d^{3}c21s^{3}c21v^{F}a22g$^c17s^{ur}c21f^{2}c21f^{2}c24g^2] workmanlike gelding: winning hurdler: modest novice chaser: stays 21f: probably acts on any ground: blinkered 4 times, including last 3 starts. *M. J. Ryan*

c82
71

TOP JAVALIN (NZ) 6 ch.g. Veloso (NZ) – Buena Vista (AUS) (Buena Shore (USA)) [1992/3 22s^2 25g^3 21s 24v* 22v^3 25s^3 22s 25g^2 24s* 24d] smallish, lengthy gelding: handicap hurdler: won at Chepstow (amateurs) in December and Worcester (improved effort and fairly useful performance, trotting up) in March: ran poorly last outing: suited by a good test of stamina: yet to race on ground firmer than good, acts well in the mud. *D. H. Barons*

129 +

Whitbread Gold Cup (Handicap Chase), Sandown—
Givus A Buck and Topsham Bay have it between them . . . . .

TOP MOUNT   6 ch.g. Avocat – Kala Lady (Kala Shikari) [1992/3 25spu
20gpu] unfurnished gelding: second live foal: dam unraced half-sister to 2
winning jumpers: won a point in Ireland in 1992: has shown nothing over
hurdles. *J. A. Hellens*   –

TOP SCALE   7 b.g. Tower Walk – Singing High (Julio Mariner) [1992/3
18m* 17d] good-bodied gelding: poor handicapper on Flat, stays 11f: won
conditional jockeys novice event at Market Rasen in August on hurdling
debut: sold out of W. Haigh's stable 18,000 gns Doncaster November Sales:
well-beaten last of 9 in much more competitive race at Ascot in February. *K.
C. Bailey*   81 +

TOPSHAM BAY   10 b.g. Proverb – Biowen (Master Owen) [1992/3   c148
c25d4 c28d4 c27sur c30spu c25g3 c29dpu c27m c27f* c30d*]   –
     The last fence at Sandown is only two-hundred-and-twenty yards from
the post but the stiff uphill finish has given rise to many a dramatic finale.
The season's last big steeplechase the Whitbread Gold Cup, in particular,
has maintained its grip on racegoers and televiewers by acquiring a
reputation for exciting finishes. It has lately become known for producing
controversial ones too. For the second time in three years the first past the
post lost the race in the stewards' room after deviating and hampering the
second after the final fence. The Sandown track widens significantly after
the last and horses often come off a straight line, as did Givus A Buck in the
latest edition. He hung left after coming under the whip and gave Topsham
Bay, with whom he'd drawn clear from three out, a hefty bump. There was
only a head between the pair at the line and, although some were surprised
at the outcome, the stewards had little option but to reverse the placings.
The decision gave Topsham Bay his second successive victory in the race.
The third and fourth home were Cahervillahow and Docklands Express who
had fought out the finish in 1991 when Cahervillahow, drifting right and
carrying Docklands Express with him, had been disqualified in what must
have been a much more borderline decision. For Topsham Bay, hobdayed

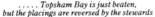

*. . . . . Topsham Bay is just beaten,
but the placings are reversed by the stewards*

after his Whitbread success in 1992, it was the sort of climax that, for a good part of the season, had seemed most unlikely. Topsham Bay was slow to come to hand—it took two or three races before he reached peak fitness—and he didn't begin to show any signs of returning to form until a fair third to Wont Be Gone Long at Sandown in mid-February. Two outings later, he was outclassed in the Tote Cheltenham Gold Cup but very much took the eye in the paddock, impressing with his well-being. Topsham Bay started 10/1 in the Whitbread. On his previous start he'd beaten his only opponent in course-record time when winning the Paul Croucher Memorial Trophy at Newbury in March for the second year running.

Topsham Bay (b.g. 1983)	Proverb (ch 1970)	Reliance II (b 1962)	Tantieme
			Relance III
		Causerie (br 1961)	Cagire II
			Happy Thought
	Biowen (br 1974)	Master Owen (b 1956)	Owen Tudor
			Miss Maisie
		Own Blend (br 1955)	Monsieur L'Amiral
			Sailors Maid

The unraced Master Owen mare Biowen, the dam of Topsham Bay, was also represented in the latest Whitbread field by the fairly useful Fifth Amendment (by The Parson) who was campaigned mostly in hunter chases, winning twice, in the latest season. Biowen has produced two other winning jumpers, the useful Mixed Blends (also by The Parson), successful over hurdles and fences, and the fair hurdler Pollen Bee (by Pollerton), both of them stayers like Topsham Bay and Fifth Amendment. The big, strong Topsham Bay needs a thorough test of stamina. He acts on firm and dead ground, and is a very sound jumper. He is reportedly to be aimed at the Grand National in the next season and has the credentials to go well in that race. *D. H. Barons*

TOP SPIN 4 b.c. Niniski (USA) – Spin (High Top) [1992/3 17d^{2} 17v^{2} 17s 17g^{4} 16g^{2} 17m] good-topped colt: useful but inconsistent middle-distance 126
stayer on Flat: sold out of R. Hern's stable 52,000 gns Newmarket Autumn Sales: fairly useful form when runner-up in valuable juvenile hurdles at Lingfield in December and Kempton (beaten neck by Amazon Express) in February on second and fifth starts: no other comparable form: will stay further than 17f: acts on heavy going (never going well on good to firm). *J. R. Jenkins*

TOP VILLAIN 7 b.g. Top Ville – Swan Ann (My Swanee) [1992/3 18s^{5} c–
16s^{4} 16g^{3} a16g^{5} c17g^{5} c16m^{5}] angular gelding: moderate hurdler: reportedly 97
finished lame final start (second outing over fences): seemed not to stay 2½m in testing conditions: acts on good to firm going: blinkered twice in 1990/1: sometimes looks ungenuine. *B. S. Rothwell*

TOP WAVE 5 br.g. High Top – Sea Fret (Habat) [1992/3 17s^{6} 16d* 17g^{6} 16s 16s 16s 16v* 16v^{5} 16s 20v^{6} 20g^{5}] ex-Irish gelding: staying handicapper 111
on Flat: fair form over hurdles, winning maiden at Roscommon in October and handicap at Punchestown in December: trained until after tenth start by J. McLoughlin: ran poorly at Ayr in April on British debut: should stay beyond 2m: acts on heavy going: blinkered fifth to tenth starts. *N. J. Henderson*

TORANFIELD 9 b.g. Monksfield – Toranquine (FR) (Right Royal V) c–
[1992/3 c24d c21d] leggy gelding: useful chaser at best: below form both –
starts in 1992/3, reportedly injuring near-fore in Mackeson Gold Cup at Cheltenham in November on second: ideally suited by further than 2m and stays 2½m: acts on heavy going and good to firm: usually front runner. *F. Lennon, Ireland*

TORKABAR (USA) 8 ch.h. Vaguely Noble – Tarsila (High Top) [1992/3
24v^{rtr}] smallish horse: modest staying hurdler on his day: often refuses to §§
race (did so in December on only outing of season): blinkered twice: has been ridden in spurs: one to leave well alone. *D. L. Williams*

TORRENT BAY 11 b.g. Roselier (FR) – Peaceful Girl (Keep The Peace) c93
[1992/3 c24d^{2} c22g^{3} c21g^{F}] strong, workmanlike gelding: fair form when –

placed in hunter chases at Ludlow and Fakenham (jumped none too fluently) in February: stays 3m: acts on good to firm and soft going. *C. R. Egerton*

TORT 9 b.g. Le Moss – Steady Flow (Reliance II) [1992/3 c25d* c28dpu c103 x c26spu c25v3 c24s2 c25gpu c25gur c26fpu c25d3 c24f] lengthy gelding: fair handicap chaser: won at Towcester in October: creditable efforts when placed afterwards: should be suited by very long distances: acts on good to firm and heavy going: makes mistakes. *P. T. Dalton*

TORWADA 10 b.g. Troy – Miss By Miles (Milesian) [1992/3 18gwd] – sturdy gelding: fairly useful hurdler in 1990/1: rider instructed not to race by owner/trainer at Fontwell in September (withdrawn under starters orders): stays 2½m: acts on heavy going: jumps less than fluently. *B. J. Curley*

TOSS THE DICE 4 ch.g. Risk Me (FR) – Curfew (Midsummer Night II) 93 [1992/3 17d2 16gF] workmanlike gelding: modest performer on Flat, best at up to 1m: modest form when second in juvenile hurdle at Stratford in February: fell third in seller following month (claimed by Mrs J. Carr Evans £5,050). *M. H. Tompkins*

TOTHEWOODS 5 b.g. The Parson – Elsea Wood (Eborneezer) [1992/3 F17s4] half-brother to NH Flat race winner Deep In The Wood (by Deep Run), winning pointer Wood By Wood (by Precipice Wood) and 7-y-o Carling Wood (by Carlingford Castle): dam moderate hunter chaser: fourth of 14 in NH Flat race at Newbury in January: yet to race over hurdles or fences. *A. J. Wilson*

TOUCHED BY LOVE 5 b.g. Touching Wood (USA) – Secret Valentine – (Wollow) [1992/3 18spu] small, close-coupled gelding: selling hurdler: deteriorated after fourth start 1991/2, and showed nothing in September: blinkered last 4 outings. *Miss S. J. Wilton*

TOUCHING STAR 8 b.g. Touching Wood (USA) – Beaufort Star (Great c94 Nephew) [1992/3 c16s3 c18s3 c16s2 c17g5 c16v3 c16g2 c17sur c17m6 c20f2 – c18g2 c18f2] close-coupled gelding: novice hurdler: moderate chaser: stays 2½m: acts on any ground: successful with and without blinkers. *P. J. Hobbs*

TOUCHING TIMES 5 b.g. Touching Wood (USA) – Pagan Deity 59 (Brigadier Gerard) [1992/3 18dF 17s 16v6] sparely-made gelding: poor novice selling hurdler: acts on soft ground: winner over 2m on Flat in 1993. *J. C. Gillen*

TOUCH 'N' PASS 5 ch.g. Dominion – Hanglands (Bustino) [1992/3 84 18dpu 17s4 18v6 a20g 18d 22dur 17d2 22g* 28g2 24gF 22d6 22m4] neat gelding: selling hurdler: won handicap at Sedgefield (no bid) in February: below form last 2 completed outings: suited by a test of stamina: best on a sound surface: front runner: blinkered second start. *R. O'Leary*

TOUCH OF ELEGANCE 8 gr.m. Marching On – Supremelos – (Supreme Sovereign) [1992/3 19m 22v a22gpu] of little account. *M. C. Pipe*

TOUCH OF WINTER 7 b. or br.g. Strong Gale – Ballyhoura Lady c83 x (Green Shoon) [1992/3 c25sur c27s4 c25gF 26g2 25d3 25v6 a20g*] leggy, 99 angular gelding: modest form over hurdles: didn't have to be at his best when easily landed the odds in maiden event at Lingfield in January: usually let down by his jumping, and only poor form, over fences: stays well: acts on dead ground and equitrack. *K. C. Bailey*

TOUCH TRICKY 5 b.m. Capricorn Line – Levanter Rose (Levanter) 69 [1992/3 18f 17d 18g 17g6 22g6 20f*] second foal: dam of little account: poor form over hurdles, best effort when winning novice event at Taunton in October: stays 2½m: acts on firm going: takes good hold, and is held up. *Mrs S. D. Williams*

TOUGH COOKIE 8 gr.g. Lochnager – Jovenita (High Top) [1992/3 c87 c16m* c16g6 c17m4 c17dpu] workmanlike gelding: lightly-raced novice – hurdler: won maiden chase at Edinburgh in February, best effort over fences: races only at around 2m: acts on good to firm and dead going. *R. Allan*

TOURAQUE (FR) 8 b.g. Caerleon (USA) – Ange Gris (USA) (Grey
Dawn II) [1992/3 21dpu 17m] smallish, good-quartered gelding: bad novice
hurdler. *Mrs D. F. Culham*   –

TOUREEN PRINCE 10 b.g. Cheval – Lauregeen (Laurence O) [1992/3   **c107 +**
c27m⁴ c20s* c25g*] good-bodied gelding: useful hunter chaser nowadays: –
won at Ascot and Bangor in April, latter impressively: effective at 2½m and
stays 25f (not 27f): acts on any going: blinkered once: should win more
hunter chases. *Miss H. C. Knight*

TOUR EIFFEL 6 b.g. High Line – Gay France (FR) (Sir Gaylord)
[1992/3 17m 16d⁶ 17d 24gsu] smallish gelding: useful 1½m winner on Flat
for H. Cecil in 1990: no worthwhile form in novice hurdles: blinkered,
destroyed after breaking leg at Edinburgh in February. *R. C. Armytage*   –

TOUT DE VAL 4 b.f. Tout Ensemble – Julie Emma (Farm Walk) [1992/3
18fur 17mpu] sixth reported foal: dam winning selling hurdler: no promise in
early-season juvenile hurdles. *R. J. Hodges*   –

TOWNY BOY 7 b.g. Camden Town – Serenesse (Habat) [1992/3 17f*
17s² 17m* 18gpu] smallish, workmanlike gelding: selling handicap hurdler: **90**
won at Plumpton in August (retained 3,300 gns) and September (no bid):
destroyed after breaking a leg at Fontwell later in September: stayed 2¼m,
not 2½m: acted on firm and soft ground. *Mrs L. Clay*

TRADERS DREAM 4 b.g. Superlative – Divine Thought (Javelot)
[1992/3 16s a16g⁵ a16gpu] half-brother to useful chaser Field Conqueror (by   **62**
Busted) and fair hurdler Inde Pulse (by Troy): modest maiden on Flat: poor
form in juvenile hurdles: sold 2,500 gns Doncaster March Sales. *T.
Thomson Jones*

Tote Jackpot Handicap Hurdle, Sandown—
Trainglot (noseband) and Sweet Duke come over the last together

Coventry City Novices' Trial Hurdle, Warwick — Trainglot readily lands the odds

TRADER TYE (IRE) 5 b.g. Buckskin (FR) – Hunter's Pet (Cracksman)
[1992/3 F17s² 20vᵖᵘ] IR 20,000Y: good-topped gelding: fourth foal: dam,
unraced, from family of Gaye Brief and Gaye Chance: second in NH Flat race
at Huntingdon in December: no promise in novice hurdle at Lingfield
following month. *F. Murphy*   –

TRAINGLOT 6 ch.h. Dominion – Mary Green (Sahib) [1992/3 20g³ 20g*
16s* 22s* 21m* 21mᵖᵘ] small, leggy horse: developed into a useful novice
hurdler in 1992/3, successful at Edinburgh, Nottingham, Sandown (Tote
Jackpot Handicap, by 6 lengths from Sweet Duke) and Warwick: pulled up in
early stages last start (something looked amiss): will stay beyond 2¾m:
acts on good to firm and soft ground. *J. G. FitzGerald*   129

TRAIN ROBBER 8 b.g. Sharp Deal – Biggsie's Bird (Even Money)   **c89**
[1992/3 c20sᵖᵘ c19m² c21m⁴ 22d 17m] leggy gelding: novice hurdler/chaser: **114**
ran very well (long way out of handicap) in County Hurdle at Cheltenham in
March on last start (never dangerous): seems best at up to 2½m: probably
acts on any ground. *W. G. McKenzie-Coles*

TRANSMIT 6 b. or br.g. Pitskelly – Lydian Lady (Junius (USA)) [1992/3
21d 20s⁴ 17s⁶ 16s 21g⁴ 21gᶠ] leggy gelding: modest handicap hurdler: **93**
running creditably when falling 2 out at Towcester in March: stays 21f: acts
on good to firm and dead ground: sometimes has tongue tied down. *A. Bailey*

TRAP DANCER 5 gr.g. Mashhor Dancer (USA) – Patraana (Nishapour
(FR)) [1992/3 F16d F17d 18g⁵ 17d⁵ 18d⁴] second foal: dam unraced: best   **91**
effort in novice hurdles when fourth of 6 at Cartmel in May: stays 2¼m: acts
on dead ground. *B. Mactaggart*

TRAPRAIN LAW 10 b.g. Politico (USA) – Pops Girl (Deep Run) [1992/3   **c101**
c21d⁶ c28sᶠ c24g* c20g³ c20s³ c24dᵖᵘ c24mᵘʳ] lengthy gelding: fair chaser: –
won handicap at Edinburgh in December: stayed 3m: acted on soft going:
jumped soundly: dead. *W. G. Reed*

TRAUMATIC LAURA 8 gr.m. Pragmatic – Trim (Miralgo) [1992/3   **c79**
c17g² c21s³ c17s c25gᵖᵘ] workmanlike mare: poor novice hurdler/chaser,   –

771

lightly raced: effective at around 2m and probably stays 3m: acts on soft going: blinkered twice. *Mrs S. Taylor*

TRAVADO   7 br.g. Strong Gale – Adelina (Athenius) [1992/3 c17g* c16d^{bd}   **c152** p
c17s* c16v* c16m*]   —

Katabatic and Waterloo Boy couldn't go on indefinitely. However, their sharp decline in the latest season was accompanied by the timely appearance of a number of potential replacements in the top two-mile to two-and-a-half-mile chasing divisions. Three of the most promising of them, Travado, Wonder Man and Sybillin, filled the first three places in the two-mile novices' championship race at Cheltenham in March, the Waterford Castle Arkle Challenge Trophy. Beforehand Sybillin had obvious claims and he started a shade of odds on in the field of eight. He had given Wonder Man weight and a beating at Nottingham on their latest outing and was undefeated in five races over fences. He and Wonder Man, three times a winner over fences, had shown very smart form as hurdlers and had accumulated a wealth of experience between them. Travado was a different type. He was raced only sparingly before being sent chasing, making his debut in National Hunt Flat company as a five-year-old then having four runs over hurdles the following season, 1991/2. He won the National Hunt Flat race and the first two over hurdles, and ran creditably when more highly tried, on his final start beating a lot more than beat him in the Sun Alliance Novices' Hurdle.

Sent chasing, Travado took to it very well and earned his place in the Arkle field with stylish wins in a couple of novice events at Newbury and another at Kempton. On the latter course, in January, he came up against Atlaal, a horse who had finished second to Wonder Man at Kempton the previous month. Travado shaped just as convincingly as Wonder Man did against Atlaal, and was on his way to a ten-length-plus win when Atlaal fell at the last. Travado was progressing despite a nasty experience at Cheltenham on his second start, where he was brought down at the seventh and received such a blow to the head that one eye was closed for nearly a month. Unsettled by a blunder at the first, he hadn't jumped well that day but otherwise his jumping was of a high standard for a novice. In the Arkle, Travado, held up in touch, going smoothly, jumped very well apart from one mistake at the second last. By then the race already looked to lie between Sybillin, Wonder Man and Travado, the first three in the betting and the only

Waterford Castle Arkle Challenge Trophy Chase, Cheltenham—
Travado (No. 4) jumps upsides Wonder Man at the last

runners shorter than 20/1. They'd drawn away down the hill from Valiant Boy, Winnie the Witch and Atlaal (Irish challenger Galevilla Express fell four out, The Slater three out). Wonder Man led, as he had from the start, and after Travado's mistake he threatened to take a grip as Sybillin began to show signs of distress. However, Travado responded gamely to being shaken up and was back in a position to challenge Wonder Man going to the last. An excellent leap there helped him into the lead and although Wonder Man fought back strongly he held on by a length.

None of the Arkle principals ran again. In their absence fourth-placed Valiant Boy took the two-mile novice chase at Aintree with a useful effort. The Arkle looks good form even though Sybillin, who trailed in twenty lengths adrift in third, clearly wasn't himself. Sybillin's performance in winning at Ascot (the Victor Chandler) and Nottingham rate as the best of the season over the distance by a novice chaser. That of Travado and Wonder Man in the Arkle wouldn't be far behind, and with normal improvement all three horses should be up to challenging strongly for top honours in 1993/4. Travado, of course, may well show more than normal improvement in view of the fact that he has had so little racing.

Travado (br.g. 1986)	Strong Gale (br 1975)	Lord Gayle (b 1965)	Sir Gaylord
			Sticky Case
		Sterntau (br 1969)	Tamerlane
			Sterna
	Adelina (b 1967)	Athenius (ch 1959)	Aureola
			Pensacola
		Artist's Impression (br 1956)	Artist's Son
			Garrenroe

Mrs Michael Ennever's "Travado"

Travado was bought as a four-year-old for 24,000 guineas at the Doncaster Sales. He is by Katabatic's sire Strong Gale out of Irish point-to-point winner Adelina, the dam of minor winners previously, Flat or jumps, in Royal Deal (by King's Leap), I'm Serious and Pitalina (both by Pitpan), Short Memories (by Quisling) and Ann's Prince (by Ragapan). The family is a long-established one in Irish jumping. Perhaps its best-known member in recent years before Travado came along was the top hunter chaser Eliogarty, whose great grandam is also Garrenroe. The Flat and hurdles winner Garrenroe produced three winners, all of whom, including the smart hurdler/chaser Forgotten Dreams and the disqualified Irish Cesarewitch winner Ballyknock, were full brothers to Travado's grandam Artist's Impression.

Good chasers come in all shapes and sizes. Travado has quality written all over him, he's a grand sort physically. As far as his distance and ground requirements are concerned, he is effective at two miles to two and a half miles and has already shown he acts on good to firm and heavy. He is genuine, too, and will prove hard to beat in the next season. *N. J. Henderson*

TRAVAIL TEMPORAIRE 7 b.g. Kambalda – Lady Serene (Le Tricolore) [1992/3 22g² 24f² 22g 26g c20dᶠ c24s³ c26vᶠ c25v³ c24gᵖᵘ c25d c21v⁴ c27g³] sparely-made gelding: novice hurdler/chaser: sold out of N. Twiston-Davies' stable 2,400 gns Doncaster March Sales after tenth start: ran very well over fences last outing: thorough stayer: probably acts on any going: blinkered fourth and ninth starts: usually looks ungenuine. *T. H. Caldwell*   **c94** §   **89** §

TRAVEL BOUND 8 b.g. Belfalas – Sugar Shaker (Quisling) [1992/3 c23s⁴ c25dᵖᵘ 25s³ 28dᵖᵘ c20s] close-coupled gelding: poor novice hurdler/chaser: stays 3m: acts on soft ground: visored first 2 outings. *E. J. Alston*   **c78**   **78**

TRAVELLER'S TRIP 12 ch.g. Royal Trip – Bohemian Girl (Pardao) [1992/3 c21g⁵ c20f⁴ c18g³ c18g³ c21gᵖᵘ c18mᶠ] leggy, workmanlike gelding: poor hurdler/maiden chaser: stayed 2½m: acted on any going. *J. Mackie*   **c74**   –

TRAVELLING WRONG 7 b.g. Strong Gale – Evening Society (Even Money) [1992/3 c24d* c24s* c26v* c24s³ c24g* c25f⁴ c32m³] big, rangy, good sort: has plenty of scope: half-brother to 3 winning jumpers, including very useful hunters Green Bay (by Green Shoon) and It's The Only Way (by Laurence O), and to dam of Another Coral: dam winning hurdler: winning pointer in Ireland: winner of novice chases at Chepstow, Newbury and Cheltenham in first half of season and handicap at Newbury in February: ran well but jumped none too fluently in second half of race in amateur events on last 2 starts: stays very well: acts on any going: front runner. *D. Nicholson*   **c115**

TRAVEL MYTH 5 ch.m. Bairn (USA) – Travel Legend (Tap On Wood) [1992/3 17g] rangy mare: poor novice hurdler: tailed off only outing of season (September). *R. G. Frost*   –

TRAVEL OVER 12 b.g. Over The River (FR) – Kincsem (Nelcius) [1992/3 c21g⁴ c25m³] big, strong, rangy gelding: carries condition: fairly useful chaser: ran creditably in October: reportedly broke blood vessel when below best over 4 months later: stays 3¼m: acts on heavy and good to firm going: races up with pace. *R. Lee*   **c121**

TRAVISTOWN 11 b.g. Grange Melody – Ednamore (Vulgan) [1992/3 c24f⁶ c21gᵖᵘ c26gᵖᵘ] quite good-topped gelding: poor novice chaser: blinkered twice. *Mrs J. E. Hawkins*   **c–**   –

TREASSOWE MARINER 5 br.g. Julio Mariner – House Breaker (Burglar) [1992/3 17s 16vᵖᵘ] sturdy gelding: third foal: dam winning selling hurdler/pointer: no sign of ability in 2 novice hurdles. *A. Moore*   –

TREASURE BEACH 4 ch.g. Dublin Lad – Melowen (Owen Dudley) [1992/3 17mᵘʳ 18gᵖᵘ 16g 16gᵖᵘ] rather leggy, workmanlike gelding: poor maiden on Flat for M. Brittain: sold 1,200 gns Doncaster June Sales: no sign of ability in juvenile hurdles in first half of season. *K. A. Linton*   –

TREASURE COURT 6 b.g. Mummy's Treasure – Julia Too (Golden Horus) [1992/3 16s^{pu} a16g^{pu}] leggy gelding: lightly raced and no sign of ability. *P. Burgoyne* –

TREASURE RUN 6 ch.g. Deep Run – Castle Treasure (Perspex) [1992/3 F18s 16s 22d] half-brother to winning jumpers Proplus and Missing Man (both by Proverb): dam never ran: remote seventh of 18 in NH Flat race at Exeter in January: well beaten in novice hurdles at Worcester in February and March. *J. S. King* –

TREBONKERS 9 b.g. Treboro (USA) – Sally Conkers (Roi Lear (FR)) [1992/3 23g^4 22g 23g^3 26m 22d 28s 20d^4 25d 24m^5 25g^4 25d^5 25v^4 25m^6] leggy gelding: poor hurdler: maiden chaser: stays 3m: seems to act on any going: tried visored: unreliable. *Miss L. A. Perratt* c–
– §

TRECOMETTI 5 b.m. Giacometti – Balitree (Balidar) [1992/3 F16g 18d] leggy, lengthy mare: half-sister to winning jumper Trewithien (by Air Trooper): dam won over hurdles: well beaten in NH Flat race in March and a mares novice hurdle in April. *D. H. Barons* –

TREE POPPY 10 b.m. Rolfe (USA) – Caribs Love (Caliban) [1992/3 20v^3 20v^2 21s^6 c21v^4 21s^3] workmanlike mare: winning chaser: fairly useful handicap hurdler: best effort of season when second at Lingfield in December: barely stays 3m: suited by an easy surface and acts on heavy ground. *C. P. E. Brooks* c–
118

TREMBALINO 5 b.g. Tremblant – Balinese (Balidar) [1992/3 17s^4 17g 16f 17g^3 16g 17m 17s^{pu} 16s^5 17s a16g^5] compact gelding: selling hurdler: raced only at around 2m: acted on dead ground: blinkered twice: dead. *P. R. Rodford* 68

TREMENDOUS (USA) 5 b.g. Spectacular Bid (USA) – Returned Conqueror (USA) (Danzig (USA)) [1992/3 21d 16v a16g^{pu}] well-made gelding: showed nothing in novice hurdles. *J. Norton* –

Brigadier C. B. Harvey's "Travelling Wrong"

TRENDY AUCTIONEER (IRE) 5 b.g. Mazaad – Trendy Princess (Prince Tenderfoot (USA)) [1992/3 16s a16g a16g⁶ a22g 17d⁶ 17g* 17g* 20m 17f 18v 17f*] angular gelding: poor form on Flat for M. Pipe: sold out of J. Moore's stable 1,800 gns Ascot November Sales: selling hurdler: changed hands 1,650 gns Ascot February Sales: won handicaps at Plumpton in March (no bid) and April (bought in 3,200 gns) and Stratford (bought in 4,750 gns) in June: best form at around 2m: acts on firm ground: blinkered once, visored nowadays. *Mrs L. C. Jewell*   75

TRENTSIDE MIST 5 b.g. Laxton – Trent Lane (Park Lane) [1992/3 17d³ 17gᵖᵘ 16s 18d 16s³] workmanlike gelding: poor novice hurdler: has run in a seller. *C. Smith*   72

TRENTSIDE VALOUR 8 b.g. Tudorville – Trent Valley (Grey Mirage) [1992/3 22d⁴ 16vᵖᵘ c17sᵖᵘ c26sᵖᵘ 20d⁶ 22mᵖᵘ c21g³ c25m³ c25mᵖᵘ 26d⁴] leggy, plain gelding: poor novice hurdler/chaser: stays 25f: acts on good to firm and heavy going: usually visored or blinkered. *C. Smith*   c77 –

TRES AMIGOS 6 b.g. Norwick (USA) – Safeguard (Wolver Hollow) [1992/3 c17f* c21d³ c23g² c26d* c26s⁴ c20d² c21m² c20f² c20g³ c21m* c25m²] tall, leggy gelding: winning hurdler: fair chaser: won novice event at Sedgefield and handicap at Catterick in first half of season and handicap at Sedgefield in May: effective at 2½m and stays 3¼m: probably acts on any going: usually races up with the pace: tough and consistent. *J. H. Johnson*   c103 –

TRESIDDER 11 b.g. Connaught – Twenty Two (FR) (Busted) [1992/3 c16m³ c16g⁵ c18d⁶ c16d³ c16g⁶ c17d⁵ c16f* c17m* c17f²] leggy, sparely-made gelding: fair handicap chaser nowadays: successful at Worcester and Sedgefield in March: good second at Huntingdon in May: best form at around 2m: acts on any going: usually held up. *M. W. Easterby*   c108 –

TRESILLIAN BAY 8 b.g. Torus – Ivory Silk (Shantung) [1992/3 22s] third foal: dam Irish maiden on Flat and over jumps: better for race, well beaten in novice hurdle at Nottingham in November on debut. *Mrs M. Reveley*

TREVADLOCK 4 b.f. Creetown – Storm Vogel (Stupendous) [1992/3 F16s F17m] good-bodied filly: half-sister to some poor performers: dam won on Flat and over hurdles in Ireland: well beaten in NH Flat races in the spring: yet to race over hurdles. *R. Hollinshead*

TREVAYLOR (NZ) 9 ch.g. Rapier II – Regal Bride (NZ) (Regalis) [1992/3 17v³] leggy, lengthy gelding: poor maiden hurdler: creditable third at Newton Abbot in December: fair and progressive chaser in 1991/2: takes strong hold and will prove best at around 2m: acts on heavy going. *P. J. Hobbs*   c– 83

TREVVEETHAN (IRE) 4 ch.g. On Your Mark – Carrick Slaney (Red God) [1992/3 16s 16s⁶ 18d 18gᵖᵘ 16s⁴ 16d²] workmanlike gelding: half-brother to winning Irish hurdler Redundant Squire (by English Prince): no sign of ability on Flat: modest juvenile hurdler: best efforts last 2 starts: should stay beyond 2m: acts on soft ground. *Mrs S. M. Austin*   87

TREYFORD 13 ch.g. Deep Run – Bunkilla (Arctic Slave) [1992/3 c21s⁵ c23g²] tall, short-coupled gelding: hunter chaser nowadays: fair form when second at Uttoxeter in May: stays 23f: acts on firm and dead going. *Anthony M. Steel*   c91 –

TRIBAL RULER 8 b.g. Prince Tenderfoot (USA) – Candolcis (Candy Cane) [1992/3 c22d⁴ c26m⁴ c24d³ c24d²] leggy, good-topped gelding: moderate handicap chaser: creditable second at Carlisle in February: stays 25f: acts on any going, except perhaps heavy: has run well when sweating, and for amateur: usually races up with pace. *D. McCain*   c86 –

TRIBUTE TO DAD 6 b.g. Aragon – Bourienne (Bolkonski) [1992/3 17m 17d⁴ᵈⁱˢ 16d³ 18d⁴ 20s⁵] sparely-made gelding: poor novice selling hurdler: ran consistently in 1992/3, though looked none too keen last start (December): stays 2½m: probably acts on any going: blinkered twice. *Mrs S. J. Smith*   70

TRICYCLING (IRE) 5 b.g. Flash of Steel – Stradavari (Stradavinsky) [1992/3 16g 20gᵖᵘ] leggy gelding: poor novice hurdler: pulled up lame in January, and wasn't seen out again: suited by 2½m: possibly unsuited by heavy going, acts on fibresand: blinkered last 3 starts 1991/2. *P. Monteith* — 74

TRI FOLENE (FR) 7 b.m. Nebos (GER) – Jefty (FR) (Jefferson) [1992/3 c21d* c21g³ c21gᵖᵘ c20s² c27v³ c21sᵖᵘ c21s⁵ c21s⁴ c27f* c23m³] close-coupled, angular mare: fairly useful chaser on her day: won handicap at Cheltenham in September and amateurs chase at Fontwell (didn't need to be at best) in May: effective at 21f and stays 27f: acts on any going: blinkered or visored nowadays: irresolute and one to treat with caution. *M. C. Pipe* — c118 §

TRILL ALONG 7 ch.g. Longleat (USA) – Cabaletta (Double Jump) [1992/3 16g⁴ 16d 16g 17m] big, lengthy gelding: poor novice hurdler: best form on a sound surface: reportedly broke down final outing: reportedly retired. *M. D. Hammond* — 82

TRIMLOUGH 8 b.g. Trimmingham – Lougharue (Deep Run) [1992/3 c16f⁴ c18m* c18dᶠ c16d* c16d* c17d³ c16v² c16d* c16fᵘʳ c16f³ c16g*] good-bodied gelding: quite useful hurdler/chaser: won novice events over fences at Bangor, Wolverhampton and Catterick in first half of season and Uttoxeter (handicap) in February and handicap at Worcester in April: also ran particularly well when close third in valuable event at Aintree on penultimate outing: races only around 2m: jumps fences soundly: usually races prominently. *P. T. Dalton* — c127

TRING PARK 7 b.g. Niniski (USA) – Habanna (Habitat) [1992/3 22mᵖᵘ] workmanlike gelding: winning 2m hurdler: no promise in 2 runs since 1990/1: sold 1,650 gns Ascot September Sales: subsequently failed to complete in 4 points: blinkered once. *R. Curtis* — —

TRIPLE TOP 8 b.g. High Top – Dalmally (Sharpen Up) [1992/3 16d⁶ 17dᵖᵘ 17g 17d 16g] lengthy, workmanlike gelding: winning hurdler: no form after first start in 1992/3: likely to stay beyond 2m: acts on good to firm ground: visored third and fourth outings. *K. White* — —

TRIPWIRE 10 b.g. Homing – Ambuscade (Relko) [1992/3 c24d⁶] fairly useful 2-y-o winner: maiden pointer: tailed off in April on steeplechasing debut. *C. R. Mason* — c—

TRISTAN'S COMET 6 br.g. Sayf El Arab (USA) – Gleneagle (Swing Easy (USA)) [1992/3 a16g² a16g³ a18g² a16gᶠ a20g³ 16dᵘʳ 21dᵘʳ a16g²] leggy gelding: modest hurdler: ran poorly last start, creditably on his other completed starts in 1992/3: effective from 2m to 2½m: acts on fibresand. *J. L. Harris* — 89

TRISTIORUM 6 ch.g. Crofthall – Annie-Jo (Malicious) [1992/3 20sᵘʳ 20gᵖᵘ] lengthy, sparely-made gelding: of no account: blinkered. *S. B. Avery* — —

TROJAN CALL 6 b. or br.g. Trojan Fen – Breezy Answer (On Your Mark) [1992/3 c21d* c21vᶠ c21v² c21dᶠ 23d⁶] strong, close-coupled gelding: winning hurdler: successful in handicap chase at Plumpton in October on chasing debut: good second in amateurs handicap at Folkestone in January: may stay beyond 21f: acts on heavy going: irresolute. *R. Rowe* — c84 §

TRONCHETTO (IRE) 4 b.g. Shernazar – Idle Days (Hittite Glory) [1992/3 17d⁵ 17g⁴ 22m* 22d² 20g³ 21gᶠ 21g⁶ 22m*] smallish gelding: modest middle-distance stayer on Flat: sold out of Sir Mark Prescott's stable 9,400 gns Ascot June (1992) Sales: won maiden hurdle at Sedgefield in March and novice hurdle at Market Rasen in June: stays 2¾m: acts on good to firm and dead ground: blinkered last 2 outings. *J. J. O'Neill* — 103

TROODOS 7 b.g. Worlingworth – My Polyanna (Polyfoto) [1992/3 22g* 22d³ 26s⁵ 26s³ 28g*] leggy gelding: modest hurdler: won handicaps at Sedgefield in October and February: retained 11,500 gns Doncaster May Sales: suited by a good test of stamina: acts on soft ground. *Mrs S. M. Austin* — 99

TROOPER THORN 9 b.g. Cool Guy (USA) – Mother Machree (Bing II) [1992/3 17f 16g⁵] angular, sparely-made gelding: modest novice hurdler at best: poor form in 1992/3: has raced mainly at around 2m: acts on firm ground. *S. I. Pittendrigh* — 74

TROPENNA 10 b.g. Bybicello – Highmoor Lass (Rubor) [1992/3 22s^{pu} 25d⁶ 28g c21m⁶ c21g c24d] big, workmanlike gelding: novice hurdler/ winning chaser, poor form: probably stays 3m: acts on firm ground. *J. L. Goulding* — c– –

TROPICAL ACE 6 b.m. Final Straw – Rampage (Busted) [1992/3 23s³ 21v^{pu} 22d⁶ 22s² 25d²] workmanlike mare: poor form in varied company over hurdles, including selling: stays 25f: acts on soft ground. *R. Voorspuy* — 80

TROPICAL MIST (FR) 13 b. or br.g. Faraway Son (USA) – Tropical Cream (USA) (Creme Dela Creme) [1992/3 27m 26g] leggy, narrow gelding: staying handicap hurdler/chaser: no form for a long time: often blinkered/ visored. *G. A. Ham* — c– –

TROPNEVAD 5 ch.g. Alias Smith (USA) – Confident Girl (Quorum) [1992/3 F14d⁴ F16m⁶ F17f 17d 17s] workmanlike gelding: half-brother to 4 winning hurdlers, notably useful Irish performer Natural Ability (by Billion): dam suited by 7f and 1m: has shown a little ability in NH Flat races, none over hurdles: visored last outing. *J. M. Jefferson* —

TROUBADOUR BOY 7 b.g. Rymer – Sweet Linda (Saucy Kit) [1992/3 c21d^{co} c21d⁵ c24s^R c27v^{bd} c24v^{pu} c26s^F] lengthy gelding: poor novice hurdler/chaser: sold 2,600 gns Doncaster May Sales: probably stays 3¼m and acts on heavy going: sometimes visored. *T. Thomson Jones* — c81 ?

TROUT ANGLER 12 br.g. Rarity – Gun Tana (FR) (Tanerko) [1992/3 c24s^{pu}] leggy gelding: staying handicap chaser: has lost his form. *Miss P. O'Connor* — c– –

TRUBLION (FR) 8 b.g. Cherubin (FR) – Mirella II (FR) (Clairon (BEL)) [1992/3 17d] rangy, good-looking gelding: winning hurdler: always behind only outing of season (November): won novice handicap chase in 1991/2 (needs to improve his jumping over fences): stays 3m: acts on soft ground, unsuited by good to firm. *S. Mellor* — c– –

TRUE BRAVE (USA) 5 b.h. Dancing Brave (USA) – True Lady (USA) (Le Fabuleux) [1992/3 18d² 18d³ 20d² 21v* 26s 18s⁶ 20d⁴ 20v³ 21d⁴ 22d³ 26s²] leggy horse: smart hurdler: won very valuable 4-y-o event at Auteuil in November: ran well most starts afterwards (in Italian Champion Hurdle on eighth outing), especially when second to Ubu III in Grande Course de Haies d'Auteuil final start: long way below form at Ascot on fifth outing (weakened quickly 3 out): stays 3¼m: acts on heavy going: jumps soundly. *F. Doumen, France* — 156

TRUE BRIT (FR) 9 ch.g. Grundy – Charlotteen (Charlottown) [1992/3 18g³ 21f⁵ 25s^{pu} 20f⁵] plain gelding: winning pointer: poor selling hurdler: stays 2½m: probably acts on any going. *A. J. K. Dunn* — 78

TRUE DILEMMA 6 b.g. Salluceva – True Or False (Varano) [1992/3 28g² 25s a24g⁵ a24g⁶ 26s⁶ 28g^{pu}] sturdy gelding: poor staying novice hurdler: second in novice handicap at Sedgefield in October, easily best effort of season. *A. Fowler* — 68

TRUE FAIR 10 b.g. Balinger – Aberfair (Honour Bound) [1992/3 c25g^F c20f² c25m^{pu} c21g³] workmanlike gelding: modest novice hurdler/chaser: probably stays 3m: acts on firm ground. *G. F. White* — c91 –

TRUE HOLLOW 11 ch.g. True Song – Wilspoon Hollow (Wolver Hollow) [1992/3 c21m c26g⁴ c25d] big, leggy gelding: bad novice jumper: makes mistakes. *Mrs P. M. Pile* — c– x

TRUE LOOP 11 ch.g. True Song – Loophole (London Gazette) [1992/3 c22g^{pu}] workmanlike, good-quartered gelding: winning hurdler: modest novice chaser in 1990/1: showed nothing in hunter chase at Nottingham in February: stays well: acts on any going: blinkered once. *F. M. Barton* — c– –

TRUELY ROYAL 9 b.g. Royal Fountain – True Friend (Bilsborrow) [1992/3 c24s³ c25g^F c26s² c25d⁵ c25d³ c26g* c24m³ c24d² c24s⁴ c26d⁴] workmanlike gelding: moderate chaser: won novice handicap at Catterick in March: creditable efforts next 3 starts: suited by good test of stamina: acts on heavy and good to firm going. *J. I. A. Charlton* — c94 –

TRUE MEASURE 6 b.m. Kala Shikari – Fair Measure (Quorum) [1992/3 c26m3] smallish mare: once-raced over hurdles: won a point in April: poor form when third in novice hunter chase at Folkestone later in month. *J. Best*

c73
–

TRUE STEEL 7 b.g. Deep Run – Aran Tour (Arapaho) [1992/3 16fpu] tall, lengthy gelding: moderate novice hurdler at best: claimed 5,200 gns after pulling up in a seller in May: stays 2¾m: best efforts on dead going. *C. P. E. Brooks*

–

TRUE STORM 4 b.f. True Song – Kitengi (Elf-Arrow) [1992/3 F16m] third foal: sister to a poor animal: dam won her only 2 completed outings in points: well beaten in NH Flat race at Warwick in May: yet to race over hurdles. *J. L. Spearing*

–

TRUFORU 8 b.g. Creative Plan (USA) – The Music Lady (Tudor Music) [1992/3 24spu] rangy, rather plain ex-Irish gelding: lightly-raced maiden pointer: tailed off when pulled up in novice event in April on hurdling debut. *P. R. Rodford*

–

TRUMP 4 b.g. Last Tycoon – Fleeting Affair (Hotfoot) [1992/3 17g4 17m 17s 16d* 20g* 21d* 18d3] workmanlike gelding: first foal: dam, winning stayer on Flat, sister to Flown: successful over middle distances on Flat: won novice handicap hurdles at Edinburgh in January and February and at Carlisle in April: will stay beyond 21f: acts on dead ground: game. *C. Parker*

101

TRUMPET 4 ch.g. Dominion – Soprano (Kris) [1992/3 17d5 17d2 17d5 16m 17m2 21d4] good-topped gelding: modest middle-distance stayer on Flat: modest form over hurdles: gave a temperamental display last outing: should stay beyond 17f: acts on good to firm and dead ground: visored third start (ran well): swishes tail. *J. G. M. O'Shea*

87 §

TRUMPET PLAYER 10 b.g. Trombone – Linda Lovelace (Ragusa) [1992/3 c25gpu] leggy, workmanlike gelding: placed in points: modest novice hurdler/chaser: bit backward only outing of season (October): looks an out-and-out stayer: acts on soft going: blinkered final start 1990/1. *P. M. Rich*

c–
–

TRUST DEED (USA) 5 ch.g. Shadeed (USA) – Karelia (USA) (Sir Ivor) [1992/3 17v 21v5 18s4 18s4 18v6 a24g* a24g3 27d5] compact gelding: poor hurdler: won novice claimer at Southwell in February: stays 3m: acts on any ground: sometimes blinkered or visored. *Mrs A. Knight*

77

TRUSTINO 5 b.m. Relkino – Game Trust (National Trust) [1992/3 F17v 17g] non-thoroughbred mare: first foal: dam fair hunter chaser: behind in NH Flat race at Hereford in November and novice hurdle at Stratford in May. *C. T. Nash*

–

TRUST THE GYPSY 11 br.g. National Trust – Zingarella (Romany Air) [1992/3 c17g* c19g* c17d2 c21f2] leggy gelding: fairly useful hunter chaser: won at Leicester and Fontwell in March: stays 21f: acts on dead ground, not discredited on firm on last outing. *J. W. Dufosee*

c102
–

TRUSTY FRIEND 11 b.g. True Song – Princess Camilla (Prince Barle) [1992/3 c26g2 c25g4 c27vF c28s c24dur c24s3 c27d] big, leggy gelding: fair chaser: creditable efforts when in frame in 1992/3: sold 4,000 gns Ascot June Sales: stays well: acts well on heavy going: tried blinkered and visored. *J. A. C. Edwards*

c107
–

TRUTH BE TOLD 9 ch.g. Proverb – Cacador's Magnet (Chinatown) [1992/3 25v2 22s*] workmanlike gelding: progressive hurdler, fairly useful form when winning handicap at Nottingham in February, wasn't seen out again: lightly-raced novice chaser: suited by test of stamina: acts on heavy going: usually held up. *J. T. Gifford*

c–
125 p

TRYING AGAIN 5 b.g. Northern Game – Wood Heath (Heres) [1992/3 F16v F16m F17d2 F17d4] unfurnished gelding: second foal: dam, unraced, from family of smart hunter Lizzy The Lizard: in frame in NH Flat races at Ascot and Sandown in April: yet to race over hurdles or fences. *D. R. Gandolfo*

–

TRY LEGUARD (IRE) 4 gr.c. Try My Best (USA) – Crown Coral (Main Reef) [1992/3 17dᵖᵘ 16gᵖᵘ 17vᶠ 17s] neat colt: modest 7f performer on Flat: has shown no aptitude for hurdling. *J. S. Moore* — x

TRY ME NOW 7 b.g. Try My Best (USA) – Sapientia (FR) (Prudent II) [1992/3 c21f⁵ c21f⁶] compact gelding: poor chaser: lightly raced: takes strong hold and suited by sharp 2m: acts on firm ground: needs to improve his jumping. *Miss E. M. England* c–

TRYUMPHANT LAD 9 gr.g. Roselier (FR) – Blackbog Lass (Le Tricolore) [1992/3 c24v³ c26f* c27f⁶] lengthy, sparely-made gelding: fair hunter chaser: won 3-finisher event at Plumpton in March by 20 lengths: well below best last outing: stays 3¼m: acts on any going: blinkered 3 times in 1990/1. *M. J. Deasley* c99 —

TSAR ALEXIS (USA) 5 br.h. Topsider (USA) – Evening Silk (USA) (Damascus (USA)) [1992/3 18d 17v 17s a22g] angular horse: poor form over hurdles, including in sellers: blinkered last 5 starts of 1991/2. *C. L. Popham* 68

TUDOR DA SAMBA 4 b.g. Sizzling Melody – La Belle Princesse (Royal Match) [1992/3 17s* 18s² 16s* 17d⁵ 20g⁵ 16m⁴ 18g* 17m* 21s* 20m² 18fᵖᵘ] leggy, sparely-made gelding: modest staying maiden on Flat: sold out of J. Fanshawe's stable 2,200 gns Newmarket Autumn Sales: won selling hurdles at Taunton (2), Leicester, Exeter and Chepstow in 1992/3: stays 21f: acts on good to firm and soft going: usually makes running: blinkered or visored: sometimes wears tongue strap: jumps sketchily. *M. C. Pipe* 113

TUDOR FABLE (IRE) 5 b.g. Lafontaine (USA) – Welsh Pride (Welsh Saint) [1992/3 17s⁴ 21g⁴ 22f³ 17g⁴] strong, attractive gelding: chasing type: modest form in novice hurdles: stays 2¾m: probably acts on any ground. *N. J. Henderson* 92

TUDOR IVY 5 b.m. Sacrilege – Penny's Daughter (Angus) [1992/3 F16s F17m 17g⁵] small mare: first reported foal: dam, lightly raced and no form, is sister to winning hurdler/chaser Shotang: well beaten in NH Flat races and a novice hurdle (at Hereford in May). *C. F. C. Jackson*

TUESDAY BROWN 9 b.m. Monsanto (FR) – Friday Brown (Murrayfield) [1992/3 16vᵖᵘ 17dᵖᵘ] lengthy mare: no sign of ability in novice hurdles. *P. J. Hobbs* —

TUFFNUT GEORGE 6 ch.g. True Song – Arenig (New Member) [1992/3 c20g² c22d4 c20dᶠ c20d4 c21g² c22g² c24fᵘʳ c22g⁴ c20fᵖᵘ c23m⁵ c25mᵘʳ 23f] leggy, angular gelding: moderate novice hurdler/chaser: stays 2¾m: acts on good to firm and dead ground: sometimes looks irresolute: visored seventh to tenth starts. *J. A. Pickering* c90 —

TUFTER'S GARTH 8 b. or br.g. Maculata – Magic Minstrel (Pitpan) [1992/3 c26mᵖᵘ] workmanlike gelding: poor maiden hurdler/pointer: blinkered once in 1991/2. *Mrs M. Rigg* c–

TUG OF GOLD 8 gr.g. Tug of War – Grey Squirrell (Golden Gorden) [1992/3 c26d* c24d⁶ c23d³] leggy, close-coupled gelding: useful handicap chaser: won Fulke Walwyn Kim Muir Chase at Cheltenham in 1991/2: lightly raced in 1992/3 (successful at Uttoxeter in October): stayed well: acted on any going: game: sound jumper: dead. *D. Nicholson* c132 —

TUGRA (FR) 5 b.m. Baby Turk – Ramsar (Young Emperor) [1992/3 17m 16v 17d] smallish mare: poor maiden on Flat and over hurdles: headstrong. *G. M. Moore* 57

TUKUM 5 ch.g. Crofthall – Harome (Workboy) [1992/3 21gᵘʳ] lengthy, workmanlike gelding: first foal: dam third in a selling hurdle: in need of run, showed nothing in novice hurdle at Wetherby in October on debut. *G. Fleming*

TULAPET 4 gr.f. Mansingh (USA) – Iridium (Linacre) [1992/3 a16gᵖᵘ] little worthwhile form on Flat: no sign of ability in claiming hurdle at Lingfield in January: sold 2,700 gns Ascot March Sales. *S. Dow* —

TULFARRIS 6 b. or br.g. Glenstal (USA) – Trusted Maiden (Busted) [1992/3 20m⁵] leggy gelding: quite moderate novice hurdler: form only at —

2m (beaten long way out in 2½m seller in September): acts on soft ground. *M. D. Hammond*

TUMBLE TIME 9 b.g. Tumble Wind (USA) – Odette Odile (Home Guard (USA)) [1992/3 c21g⁴ c17m⁴] sturdy gelding: poor novice hunter chaser: stays 25f: acts on good to firm ground: blinkered over hurdles. *Ms Polly Gowers*
c–
–

TUMBRIL 8 ch.g. Legal Tender – Cartwheel (Escart III) [1992/3 c26mᵖᵘ] tall, leggy gelding: little worthwhile form in 2 races over hurdles: modest pointer, winner in February: behind until pulled up in hunter chase later in month. *Mrs J. Marles*
c–
–

TUNS HILL 11 ch.g. True Song – Aggreccles (Aggressor) [1992/3 c23m c26v³] small, deep-girthed gelding: winning hurdler/chaser: third at Hereford in April, better effort of season: stays 3¼m: acts on heavy going: blinkered once. *R. Dickin*
c93
–

TURBULENT WIND 6 b.m. Strong Gale – Knock Off (Arctic Slave) [1992/3 17g 16s F16d c16s⁴ c20v³ c16s² c19s* c20vᵖᵘ c21dᵖᵘ] non-thoroughbred mare: half-sister to several winners over jumps, including fair hurdler/chaser Wicket (by Deep Run): dam, placed over hurdles, from good jumping family: no worthwhile form over hurdles: better over fences and won mares novice event at Naas in January: pulled up last 2 starts, in valuable mares novice handicap at Uttoxeter on final outing: should stay beyond 2½m: acts on soft going. *A. L. T. Moore, Ireland*
c95
–

TURF DANCER 6 b.m. Anfield – Cachucha (Gay Fandango (USA)) [1992/3 22m²] plating-class middle-distance maiden on Flat: finished lame when second of 4 finishers in novice event at Worcester in August on hurdling debut. *P. C. Haslam*
81

TURF RUN 6 br.g. Deep Run – Tranquil Love (Ardoon) [1992/3 16s 17vᵖᵘ] compact gelding: novice hurdler: well beaten in 1992/3: takes good hold. *Miss B. Sanders*
–

TURNBERRY DAWN 11 ch.g. Fair Turn – Shuil Alainn (Levanter) [1992/3 c24m c26dᵖᵘ c24vᶠ c24vᵖᵘ c24d³ c24f³] leggy, workmanlike gelding: moderate handicap chaser nowadays: third in small fields in the spring: stays 3¼m: acts on firm and dead going. *T. B. Hallett*
c95 ?
–

TURN'EM BACK JACK (CAN) 10 ch.g. Lord Durham (CAN) – Irish Molly (CAN) (George Royal) [1992/3 c21vᵖᵘ c21sᵘʳ c20d⁵ c21m³ c21m* c21g²] workmanlike gelding: winning hurdler: won novice handicap chase at Wolverhampton in March: good second in similar event at Bangor following month: seems to act on any going: blinkered 4 times in 1986/7: front runner: sketchy jumper. *A. Bailey*
c85
–

TURNING TRIX 6 b.g. Buckskin (FR) – Merry Run (Deep Run) [1992/3 20g² 17s⁴ 21g² 24sᵖᵘ 24g⁵] rangy, rather plain gelding: fair form when in frame in novice hurdles: ran poorly last 2 starts: stays 21f. *S. E. Sherwood*
101

TURN NOW 6 b. or br.g. Petorius – Millers Lady (Mill Reef (USA)) [1992/3 16f] leggy gelding: no sign of ability in 2 outings over hurdles. *O. O'Neill*
–

TUROLDUS (FR) 8 b.g. Toujours Pret (USA) – Katy Collonge (FR) (Trenel) [1992/3 18sᵖᵘ 18m] strong, workmanlike gelding: modest novice hurdler/chaser: no show in 2 races in spring: stays 2¾m. *Mrs S. J. Smith*
c–
–

TURTLE BEACH 4 ch.g. Primo Dominie – Double Finesse (Double Jump) [1992/3 16sᵖᵘ] half-brother to fair jumper Admirals All (by Julio Mariner): modest on Flat, stays 1m: sold out of A. Scott's stable 4,200 gns Newmarket Autumn Sales: pulled hard and no promise in juvenile hurdle at Warwick in February. *C. C. Elsey*
–

TUSKY 5 ch.g. Prince Sabo – Butosky (Busted) [1992/3 16g² 16g² 16s⁴ 16d³] good-topped gelding: type to carry condition: half-brother to winning hurdler Bush Hill (by Beldale Flutter): modest and inconsistent miler on Flat: sold out of M. Camacho's stable 8,400 gns Doncaster November Sales:
92

moderate form when placed in mid-season novice hurdles: has raced only at 2m with give in the ground. *G. M. Moore*

TUXFORD 13 b.g. Crozier – Dairyguard (Tynwald) [1992/3 c24gᵖᵘ] rangy c– gelding: lightly raced: poor novice chaser: stays 3m: acts on hard ground. *J. G. O'Neill*

TV PITCH (FR) 5 b.m. Fast Topaze (USA) – Allatum (USA) (Alleged (USA)) [1992/3 22m² 22d⁴ 16g⁶ 16g⁴ 22s 20m³ 25d 22g 17f⁶ 16g⁴] leggy, 98 sparely-made mare: modest handicap hurdler: stays 2¾m: best efforts on a sound surface: inconsistent. *D. Lee*

TWIN OAKS 13 br.g. Raise You Ten – En Clair (Tarqogan) [1992/3 c29s* c157 c27sᵖᵘ c24d* c20s⁴ c24v⁴ c29dᵖᵘ] big, rangy, good sort: useful hurdler: – high-class chaser at best: had a magnificent record at Haydock and gained last 8 wins there, including in 1991 Greenalls Gold Cup and 1992 Peter Marsh Chase: smart form when successful in handicap in November and Tommy Whittle Chase (by 12 lengths from Pat's Jester) in December: retired after being pulled up lame in February: stayed long distances: was suited by an easy surface and acted on heavy ground: usually raced up with pace: jumped well. *G. Richards*

TWIN STATES 4 b.g. State Diplomacy (USA) – Malmo (Free State) [1992/3 F16v] second foal: dam barely stayed 2m over hurdles: eighth of 16 in NH Flat race at Uttoxeter in April: yet to race over hurdles. *J. R. Turner*

TWIST 'N' SCU 5 ch.g. Prince Sabo – Oranella (Orange Bay) [1992/3 F14d 16sᵖᵘ 24sᵖᵘ] tall, leggy gelding: second foal: dam, daughter of a useful winner in Italy, winner at up to 2¼m on Flat: no sign of ability in novice hurdles. *N. A. Twiston-Davies*

TWO JOHN'S (IRE) 4 b. or br.g. King's Ride – No Honey (Dual) [1992/3 F16g³] brother to smart hurdler Carobee and useful hurdler Alekhine and half-brother to several winning jumpers, including useful hurdler Winter Squall (by Celio Rufo): dam unraced half-sister to several winners, including jumper Highway Dual: strong-finishing third of 22 in NH Flat race at Kempton in February: yet to race over hurdles. *P. F. Nicholls*

Tommy Whittle Chase, Haydock—another win over the course for Twin Oaks

TWO STEP RHYTHM   9 gr.g. Neltino – Niagara Rhythm (Military)   c?
[1992/3 c22mᵘʳ c21d⁴] rather angular gelding: fair chaser: looked likely
winner when unseating rider first of 2 starts in 1992/3: should prove suited
by further than 2½m: acts on good to soft going, probably on good to firm:
sketchy jumper. *J. C. McConnochie*

TWO WAY MIRROR (IRE)   5 ch.g. Double Schwartz – Alice Kyteler   87
(Crepello) [1992/3 17d⁶ 18gᵖᵘ 16m 16f²] leggy ex-Irish gelding: half-brother
to several winners, including useful Irish staying chaser Rust Never Sleeps
(by Jaazeiro): dam Irish 9f winner: first worthwhile form on final start over
hurdles. *R. G. Frost*

TYDELMORE   9 b.g. Tycoon II – Delcombe (Cracksman) [1992/3 17gᵖᵘ]   –
pulled up in a point in 1992 and a novice hurdle (saddle slipped) in May. *B.
Preece*

TYMPANIST   5 b.m. Relkino – Melodist (Menelek) [1992/3 21g 21sᵖᵘ]   –
small, sturdy mare: half-sister to poor novice hurdler Jack Dash (by Celtic
Cone): dam half-sister to several winning jumpers, including very smart
performer Dramatist: no sign of ability over hurdles. *J. E. Brockbank*

TYNRON DOON   4 b.g. Cragador – Bel Esprit (Sagaro) [1992/3 17d³   84
16s² 16s⁴ 17v⁴ 16s² 21s²] smallish, sturdy gelding: 1m plater on Flat: poor
form over hurdles: stays 21f: acts on soft going: blinkered fourth start (ran
respectably). *D. J. Wintle*

TYRED N'SNOOKERD   9 b.g. Le Johnstan – Dobella (Sovereign Lord)   c–
[1992/3 c20sᵖᵘ c21dᵖᵘ] leggy, workmanlike gelding: winning hurdler: pulled   –
up all 3 outings over fences: probably stays 3m: acts on good to firm and
dead going: sometimes blinkered or visored. *P. R. Hedger*

TYRIAN   6 b.m. Elegant Air – Character Builder (African Sky) [1992/3   –
a16g] of no account: tried blinkered. *R. J. Baker*

TYRONE BRIDGE   7 b.g. Kings Lake (USA) – Rhein Bridge   153 §
(Rheingold) [1992/3 17v⁴ 20d³ 25s* 26s⁴ 24d³ 25mᵖᵘ] leggy gelding: smart
hurdler: awarded Akzo Long Distance Hurdle at Newbury in November,
having been hampered by neck winner Burgoyne: in frame in valuable
contests at Ascot afterwards: suited by a good test of stamina: acts on good
to firm and heavy going: often blinkered prior to 1992/3: jumps none too
fluently: moody and inconsistent. *M. C. Pipe*

TYRONE FLYER   4 b.c. Celestial Storm (USA) – Dance A Jig (Dance In   –
Time (CAN)) [1992/3 18fᵖᵘ] modest 7f performer on fibresand, winner in
March for Miss G. Kelleway: blinkered, no promise in early-season juvenile
hurdle. *M. C. Pipe*

U

UBERTO II (FR)   7 ch.g. Quart de Vin (FR) – Juyola (FR) (Francois   c–
Saubarer) [1992/3 c16gꟻ c18m c21gᵖᵘ] leggy gelding: winning 2½m chaser
in France: no form in Britain: dead. *Martyn Meade*

UBU III (FR)   7 b.g. Maiymad – Isis VIII (FR) (Or de Chine) [1992/3 20d⁵   c160
c25d³ 24v⁴ c22s² c22d* c22d* 22d² 22d² 26s*]   160
   The weekend after The Fellow finished fourth in the Gold Cup, trainer
Doumen spoke of plans to run him next in either the Irish Grand National or
the Whitbread Gold Cup. He explained, 'There is no point in running him in
Paris as I have three top-class chasers to run there already in Ubu III, Ucello
II and Voretin'. It was no more than the truth. All three enjoyed a good
season in top company in Paris, particularly Ubu and Ucello who between
them rounded off by lifting the two most important jumping prizes in
France, the Grande Course de Haies d'Auteuil and the Grand Steeple-Chase
de Paris.
   The Grande Course is regarded as the French Champion Hurdle, and
Ubu is, in fact, a top-class hurdler as well as chaser, probably the best

all-rounder in action in Europe at present. His form over the French brush hurdles is rather better than he showed in a welcome visit to Britain in 1992 when he finished six lengths behind Nomadic Way, third promoted to second, in the Stayers' Hurdle at Cheltenham. Following his return to France that season he won his first Grande Course de Haies d'Auteuil, having come a close third in the Grand Steeple-Chase de Paris only a fortnight earlier. In 1992/3 he continued to mix hurdling and chasing, and prior to the build-up towards his second Grande Course he won feature chases at Auteuil in March and April, the Prix Troytown and the Prix Murat, respectively earning the equivalent of £43,200 and £54,750. In both races he showed himself slightly superior to Voretin. Good horse that he is, Ubu started only second favourite for the Grande Course, run on the first Saturday in July and worth the equivalent of £71,200 to the winner. There was a red-hot favourite for the fourteen-runner race, Royal Chance. Unbeaten in 1993, Royal Chance had twice got the better of Ubu at level weights over hurdles since the latter ran in the Prix Murat, by two lengths in the Prix Leon Rombaud at Auteuil in May and by three in the Prix La Barka over the same course in June. However, that was over two and three quarter miles. Royal Chance seemed not to stay the extra half-mile of the Grande Course and finished only fifth. He certainly didn't see the trip out like Ubu, who ran on very strongly from the second last to hold off Doumen's second string True Brave ridden out by two and a half lengths. The numerically-strong British challenge foundered. Eighth-placed Lord Relic (27/1) ran respectably considering his inexperience and will do better another year; Sweet Glow (89/1) and Ruling (70/1) were never in the hunt, the latter returning injured. Hopefully, owners on this side of the Channel

Marquesa de Moratalla's "Ubu III"

won't be too discouraged. The French can be beaten in their own backyard, as Dawn Run showed in the Grande Course in 1984. Gaye Chance and For Auction ran into a place in the two previous years, as more recently did the American horse Flatterer.

Ubu III (FR) (b.g. 1986)	Maiymad (br 1977)	Rheingold (br 1969)	Faberge II Athene
		Miss Melody (b 1970)	Tudor Melody The Veil
	Isis VIII (FR) (b 1974)	Or de Chine (b 1960)	Chingacgook Orbela
		Diane (ch 1969)	Vieux Chateau Kali

The workmanlike Ubu is by Valfinet's sire Maiymad out of Isis VIII, a French Saddlebred (selle francais) who won on the Flat and over jumps there. Ubu stays much better than Valfinet is ever likely to, and he seems suited by two and three quarter miles and more nowadays. He does most of his racing on an easy surface and handles the mud very well. What a splendid horse to own! His owner, by the way, is in the enviable position of having Ucello, The Fellow and Sybillin besides. *F. Doumen, France*

UCELLO II (FR)   7 b.g. Quart de Vin (FR) – Judy (FR) (Laniste (FR))   **c163**
[1992/3 20d² 20d³ c28v* c22vᶠ c22s* c29s*]   146

Ucello II, a horse who has long had the reputation of being better than his stable-companion The Fellow, showed himself just about the best chaser in France in 1992/3 in the course of gaining three wins from three completed starts over fences. His wins included one in the top chase of the autumn season at Auteuil, the Prix La Haye Jousselin in November (where he beat another good-class Doumen-trained chaser Voretin two lengths), and another in the biggest prize of all, the Grand Steeple-Chase de Paris, there in June. Ucello's best form is not the equal of The Fellow's but with the latter seemingly not at that level in 1993, Ucello had much the better record in France in the latest season. Ucello has a different style from The Fellow: he is a bold-jumping, front-running chaser who acts well on heavy ground. He is effective from just beyond two miles to three miles five furlongs, the distance of the Grand Steeple-Chase.

The Grand Steeple-Chase had been regarded in the French Press as Ucello's destiny since he won seven out of seven chases as a four-year-old, earning, understandably, rave notices, but 1993 represented Ucello's third attempt at the Grand Steeple-Chase. He'd fallen in 1991, the year The Fellow won, and had been beaten half a length in 1992 by the surprise winner El Triunfo with Ubu III, known in Britain as a high-class staying hurdler, in third (it is not unusual for French jumpers to mix hurdling and chasing—Ucello himself ran twice over hurdles in France in the autumn, showing very useful form). As in 1992, when he beat El Triunfo conceding weight, Ucello won the principal trial for the Grand Steeple-Chase, the Prix Millionaire II at Auteuil over two and three quarter miles. In 1992, however, he'd had one run prior to the Millionaire after his winter break; this time he had none. It can certainly be argued that his programme in 1993 served him better on the big day. In the latest Millionaire he beat six of the eight who were to oppose him in the Grand Steeple-Chase but the outcome was not conclusive. He beat Utin du Moulin by half a length, with The Fellow's brother Al Capone II and The Fellow himself close behind, Voretin in fifth the equal of Ucello at the weights. The Grand Steeple-Chase showed decisively who was the best. Ucello, challenged for the lead for a long way by Al Capone, dominated the final mile of the race and, though Voretin tried to challenge, Ucello won by six lengths from Al Capone who stayed on to retake second from Voretin; the last-named was a length away in third. The Fellow, beaten sixteen lengths, was a lack-lustre fifth.

It's unfortunate that racegoers have not yet had the opportunity to see Ucello in Britain. His style of racing could make him an exciting prospect in the King George for example. It was planned to run him in the SGB Chase at Ascot before Christmas but that was abandoned after a heavy fall in the Prix Georges Courtois in early-December. Doumen's immediate reaction after the Grand Steeple-Chase was to suggest that Ucello would be kept for the

Grand Steeple-Chase de Paris, Auteuil—the bold-jumping front-runner Ucello

top French prizes in 1993/4 and, indeed, there is little but prestige to encourage top French jumpers to race in Britain. The inferior prize money, the cost of travelling and unfamiliar obstacles all stand in the way of greater competition between British, Irish and Continental jumpers. There is undoubtedly scope for initiatives to boost competition—a series similar to the Sport of Kings Challenge would surely have greater success than that Anglo-American contest, and some sort of incentive for success, in a series of linked races, or for best cumulative record in a series of races would be another possibility—the Irish Gold Cup, Cheltenham Gold Cup and Grand Steeple-Chase de Paris present themselves as an obvious triple crown.

		Quart de Vin (FR) (b 1972)	Devon (ch 1958)	Worden II
Ucello II (FR) (b.g. 1986)				Sees
			Quartelette (b 1963)	Tantieme
				Quaker Girl
		Judy (FR) (b 1968)	Laniste (bl 1963)	Tarquin
				Louisianne II
			Upsala III (b 1964)	Verdi
				Lakme II

Ucello II, a leggy gelding, is, like so many of the French jumpers, including The Fellow, a non-thoroughbred, a selle francais. He is by the thoroughbred Quart de Vin who also sired the Sun Alliance Chase winner Rolling Ball. Quart de Vin was a stayer on the Flat and a good hurdler. Ucello's dam Judy, placed once over fences in the Provinces, produced two winners prior to Ucello—Palencia (by Taj Dewan) won on the Flat and over jumps while Ucello's brother Tivoli is a winner over fences. Judy is a sister to Doumen's first King George winner Nupsala, who was also twice a Grand Steeple-Chase runner-up. Judy's dam Upsala II won once on the Flat and twelve times over fences. *F. Doumen, France*

UCKERBY MOOR 4 b.g. Reesh – Neringulla (African Sky) [1992/3 F16s 16s] leggy gelding: third foal: half-brother to a poor performer by Longleat: dam unraced: behind in NH Flat race and a juvenile hurdle in January: modest form at around 7f on Flat in 1993. *W. L. Barker* —

UFANO (FR) 7 b.g. Toujours Pret (USA) – Osca (FR) (Taj Dewan) [1992/3 c22d c25s c26v4 c24v6 c24d4 c27dpu] sturdy gelding: poor novice chaser: stays 3¼m: acts on heavy ground. *Capt. T. A. Forster* c74 —

UFFMOOR LADY   7 b.m. Torus – Red Aster (St Alphage) [1992/3 17s^{pu} 16g^{pu}] sparely-made mare: half-sister to novice chaser Redally (by Ballymore): dam won on Flat: no sign of ability in novice hurdles. *K. S. Bridgwater*   –

ULLSWATER   7 b.g. Wassl – Dignified Air (FR) (Wolver Hollow) [1992/3 18m* 16g^{pu} 17g^5 c16d^6 17s^2 17s^6 a18g^6 16v^6 22s^6 c21f^5] close-coupled gelding: poor hurdler: won handicap at Worcester in August: tailed off both outings over fences: stays 2½m: probably acts on any ground: blinkered once. *A. S. Reid*   c– 80

ULURU (IRE)   5 b.g. Kris – Mountain Lodge (Blakeney) [1992/3 21s^2 21s 21v^6 16m^3 16g^3 16d^2 16s^2] small, compact gelding: one-time useful middle-distance performer on Flat: sold out of Mrs J. Ramsden's stable 5,800 gns Newmarket Autumn Sales: modest novice hurdler: best form at 2m but well worth another try at around 2½m: acts on good to firm and soft ground. *C. T. Nash*   83

UMBRELLA GIRL   9 br.m. Creative Plan (USA) – Carambola (Hul A Hul) [1992/3 17s] lightly-made mare: novice hurdler/chaser: lightly raced and no form since 1990/1. *A. P. James*   c– –

UNASSUMING   5 ch.g. Vaigly Great – Petard (Mummy's Pet) [1992/3 17g 20g 17d^{pu}] lengthy gelding: 2m novice plater over hurdles: tried visored. *J. A. Pickering*   –

UNCERTAIN   5 ch.h. Noalto – Paridance (Doudance) [1992/3 17d^{pu}] lightly raced and no form on Flat: no sign of ability in early-season novice hurdle. *D. Haydn Jones*   –

UNCERTAIN TIMES   6 ch.g. Sunley Builds – Winter Gala (Monksfield) [1992/3 F17f] first foal: dam no sign of ability in 2 races: seventh of 18 in NH Flat race at Sandown in March: yet to race over hurdles or fences. *R. Rowe*   –

UNCLE ELI   10 br.g. Rolfe (USA) – Dirrie Star (Dunoon Star) [1992/3 c16v^F c16s^2 c20s^4 c21g*] leggy, close-coupled gelding: fairly useful chaser: won handicap at Kempton in February: stays 21f: acts on heavy going: poor jumper. *P. J. Hobbs*   c123 x

UNCLE ERNIE   8 b.g. Uncle Pokey – Ladyfold (Never Dwell) [1992/3 F10d* c21s^{F4} c16s^3 c17m^5] workmanlike gelding: very useful chaser: creditable third in valuable limited handicap at Sandown in December: ran poorly following month: had won celebrity race on Flat at Wetherby on reappearance: best form at around 2m: probably acts on any going: usually jumps well: held up. *J. G. FitzGerald*   c145 –

UNCLE MOGY   7 ch.g. Monsanto (FR) – Primrolla (Relko) [1992/3 c16d^2 c16m^{ur} c18g* c19s^3 c16g^{pu}] lengthy, workmanlike gelding: winning hurdler: won novice chase at Bangor in March: pulled up lame final start: sold to join P. Hobbs 3,000 gns Ascot June Sales: stays 19f: acts on soft ground. *D. Nicholson*   c93

UNCLE RAGGY   10 b.g. Monksfield – Lorna Doone (Raise You Ten) [1992/3 c27g^2 c33m^3] rangy gelding: fair hunter chaser nowadays: needs a thorough test of stamina: acts on firm and dead going: blinkered twice. *J. White*   c87 –

UNCLES-LAD   5 b.g. Uncle Pokey – Poppy Pin (Country Retreat) [1992/3 16g^{pu} 16d 24g] unfurnished gelding: no sign of ability. *R. C. Armytage*   –

UNDER OFFER   12 br.g. Rhodomantade – Blue Flash (Blue Lightning) [1992/3 c24s^2 c24s^5 c26v* c24v^4 c26d^3 c21g^2 c26d^2 c26d^3 c27d^5] leggy, lengthy gelding: modest handicap chaser on his day: won amateurs event at Wincanton in January: suited by test of stamina: acts on heavy going and good to firm: wears blinkers: front runner: not one to rely on. *J. S. King*   c90 §

UNDERWAY (FR)   7 b.g. Djarvis (FR) – Jamaica (FR) (Tryptic) [1992/3 c24g^{pu} c21g^{pu}] smallish, sturdy gelding: of little account. *Fred Kirby*   c– –

UNDERWYCHWOOD (IRE) 5 b.g. Try My Best (USA) – Sooner Or Later (Sheshoon) [1992/3 16g 16d 16v³ 24s⁴ 22s³ 20s⁴ 24d 22d 23g⁵] ex-Irish gelding: half-brother to several winners, including fairly useful staying hurdler/chaser Sooner Still (by Tachypous): dam lightly-raced half-sister to Oaks-placed Suni and Media Luna: modest novice hurdler at best: trained until after seventh outing by A. Maxwell: ran poorly in Britain: effective at 2m under testing conditions and stays 3m: acts on heavy going. *P. Burgoyne*　　97 ?

UNEX-PLAINED 10 b.g. Last Fandango – Miss Pinkerton (Above Suspicion) [1992/3 c17d⁵ c16s⁴ c21s⁴ c21d⁴ c21g⁶ c21g² c21v³ c21m² c21f⁴] smallish, workmanlike gelding: modest chaser nowadays: trained until after seventh outing by G. Moore: stays 21f: acts on heavy and good to firm ground: blinkered once. *M. R. Channon*　　c90 –

UNHOLY ALLIANCE 6 b.g. Carlingford Castle – Rambling Love (Golden Love) [1992/3 F16d⁵ F17d⁶ 16g² 22g* 24f* 20g³ 22g* 22g* 20g³ 26dʳᵗʳ 25f⁴] workmanlike ex-Irish gelding: first foal: dam winning Irish pointer and in frame in steeplechases: trained until after third outing by M. Morris: won novice hurdles at Fontwell, Worcester and Cheltenham (2) early in season: good fourth in quite valuable event at Aintree in April (first race for around 5 months): stays well: acts on firm ground: refused to race tenth outing. *K. C. Bailey*　　119 §

UNICOL 11 ch.g. Manado – Ragatina (Ragusa) [1992/3 c21d⁴ c29s⁵] good-bodied gelding: winning staying chaser: lightly raced and no form since 1989/90: blinkered once. *D. McCain*　　c– –

UNINSURED 4 b.f. Hadeer – Standard Breakfast (Busted) [1992/3 18sᵖᵘ 16s] second foal: dam disappointed after winning over 1½m on debut: showed nothing over hurdles. *Mrs D. Haine*　　–

UNION CASTLE 7 ch.g. Carlingford Castle – Fair Invader (Brave Invader (USA)) [1992/3 23s² 22d⁴ 22g 25d⁴] heavy-topped gelding: chasing type: novice hurdler, modest at best: ran poorly last 2 outings: sold 8,000 gns Ascot June Sales: stays 23f: acts on soft ground: visored final start: jumps none too fluently. *J. A. C. Edwards*　　88

UNION QUAY 9 ch.g. Quayside – Reaper's Own (Master Owen) [1992/3 c21s c22gᵖᵘ c24g] workmanlike gelding: poor novice hunter chaser: stays 3¼m: acts on firm ground. *N. J. Pewter*　　c–

UNKNOWN CHALLENGER (IRE) 5 ch.g. Kemal (FR) – Therene (Levanter) [1992/3 F16m²] third foal: dam unplaced in Irish NH Flat races: second in 24-runner NH Flat race at Warwick in May: yet to race over hurdles or fences. *O. Sherwood*　　–

UNPAID MEMBER 9 b.g. Moorestyle – Sunningdale Queen (Gay Fandango (USA)) [1992/3 a20g c18gᶠ] sparely-made gelding: no form over hurdles since 1990/1: poor novice chaser: stays 2¾m: probably acts on any going: sometimes blinkered. *J. Wharton*　　c– –

UNSHAKEABLE 7 b.g. Oats – Another Breeze (Deep Run) [1992/3 c20sᶠ c20sᶠ] strong, lengthy, good sort: fairly useful hurdler: fell both outings over fences: stayed 3m: acted on soft going: dead. *N. A. Gaselee*　　c– –

UN SOUVERAIN 5 b.g. Kenmare (FR) – Serenita (FR) (Lyphard (USA)) [1992/3 20m* 20m⁶ 24fᵖᵘ] close-coupled, angular gelding: won novice hurdle at Bangor in July (saddle slipped over 3m in August): best efforts on a sound surface. *W. Bentley*　　86

UP ALL NIGHT 4 b.f. Green Desert (USA) – Vielle (Ribero) [1992/3 16g 18s⁶ a16g 17dᶠ 17g⁶] of little account on Flat nowadays: poor juvenile hurdler: would have run best race but for falling fourth start. *R. Curtis*　　77 ?

UP AND COMING 10 b.g. Avocat – Cummin Hill (Wrekin Rambler) [1992/3 c26vᵖᵘ c25gᵖᵘ c26g² c24dᵖᵘ c26mᵖᵘ] strong gelding: one-time fairly useful chaser: fair form when second at Exeter in March, only completed start of 1992/3: stays 3¼m: acts on firm and dead going: sometimes wears tongue strap: possibly none too genuine. *N. J. Henderson*　　c108 –

788

UP-A-POINT 8 gr.g. Rusticaro (FR) – Malmsey (Jukebox) [1992/3 c19g⁴ c16g⁵ c17v* c16dᵘʳ c18v⁶ c16v³ c16v³ c18g³ c17dᶠ] leggy gelding: fair handicap chaser: won conditional jockeys event at Cheltenham in December: best up to 2¼m: probably acted on any going: dead. *P. J. Hobbs*   **c105**

UPSTANDING 11 b.g. Latest Model – Calamity (Haven) [1992/3 c25f⁴ c24g² c21s⁴ c27s³ c25d³ c25m* c23gᵖᵘ] deep-girthed, workmanlike gelding: handicap chaser: finished alone at Wolverhampton in March: stayed 3¼m: acted on any ground: ungenuine: dead. *N. H. Davis*   **c86 §**

UP TO ME (FR) 10 gr.g. Crystal Palace (FR) – Felicite (FR) (Tapioca II) [1992/3 16vᵖᵘ 18s 21g 18g 22dᵖᵘ] angular gelding: no sign of ability: blinkered once. *R. M. Flower*   –

UPTON LASS (IRE) 4 b.f. Crash Course – Gorrue Lady (Furry Glen) [1992/3 17s 17d⁵ 16v] unfurnished filly: third foal: dam unraced: no sign of ability. *Andrew Turnell*   –

UPWELL 9 b.g. Tanfirion – Debnic (Counsel) [1992/3 28sᵖᵘ 20d 28d⁵ c20gᵖᵘ c21g⁴ c27m⁵] lengthy, sparely-made gelding: winning hurdler: poor novice chaser: stays well: acts on firm ground. *R. Johnson*   c– –

UP YONDER 9 ch.g. Moor House – Peggy Jet (Willipeg) [1992/3 c20sᵖᵘ] leggy, workmanlike gelding: no sign of ability: dead. *P. Beaumont*   c– –

URANUS COLLONGES (FR) 7 b.g. El Badr – Flika (FR) (Verdi) [1992/3 F16d² F17d* c26s* c25s²] very tall, leggy gelding: half-brother to a winner on Flat in France by Quart de Vin: won NH Flat race at Doncaster in December and novice chase at Catterick (very easily) in January: creditable second in novice chase at Wetherby in March: will prove suited by a thorough test of stamina: acts on soft ground: sure to improve further. *J. G. FitzGerald*   **c103 p**

URBAN COWBOY 6 b.g. Town And Country – Ginnett (Owen Anthony) [1992/3 16d² 18d³ 22dᶠ 22d² 22s³ 20g³ 20d] sparely-made gelding: moderate novice hurdler: stays 2¾m: acts on soft ground. *C. James*   **95**

URBAN SURFER 9 b.g. Le Bavard (FR) – Reynella (Royal Buck) [1992/3 22m³ c21gᵖᵘ c24s⁴] lengthy gelding: poor novice hurdler/chaser: trained until after second start by J. White: stays 2½m: acts on dead ground: blinkered once. *Mrs Caroline Dix*   c– –

URIZEN 8 ch.g. High Line – Off The Reel (USA) (Silent Screen (USA)) [1992/3 c25s³ c25d⁵ c26dᶠ] close-coupled gelding: one-time fairly useful hurdler: modest form in novice chases in 1992/3: stays 3m: acts on firm and good to soft ground: a difficult ride nowadays. *J. A. C. Edwards*   **c89** –

URON V (FR) 7 b.g. Cap Martin (FR) – Jolivette (FR) (Laniste) [1992/3 21s³ 24s³ 26s² 28g³ 25s²] neat gelding: fair hurdler: suited by long distances and plenty of give in the ground. *M. D. Hammond*   **104**

URSHI-JADE 5 b.m. Pennine Walk – Treeline (High Top) [1992/3 17d 16sᶠ 17s⁶ 17s⁴ 22v⁵ a20g⁵] smallish, angular mare: no form on Flat: maiden plater over hurdles: stays 2¾m: acts on heavy ground: visored fourth start (fair effort). *K. White*   **67**

USHAK 5 b. or br.g. Baby Turk – Persian Carpet (FR) (Kalamoun) [1992/3 17m⁵ 16s⁴ 17gᵖᵘ] poor novice hurdler: pulled up lame final outing (October): yet to race beyond 17f: probably acts on any ground. *J. Webber*   **90**

USHERS ISLAND 7 br.g. Sandalay – Star Luck (Star Signal) [1992/3 F20g* F20g² c20gᶠ 22d c20s⁵ c20d³ c20s c18sᵘʳ F20d c33g² c32m* c25f*] lengthy ex-Irish gelding: won NH Flat race at Leopardstown in August: well beaten over hurdles: trained until after ninth outing by T. Walsh: fair chaser: won National Hunt Chase (Amateur Riders) at Cheltenham in March and novice event at Wetherby (hung left) in May, former by short head from Claxton Greene: suited by long distances: best form on a sound surface. *J. H. Johnson*   **c113** –

UTRILLO (USA) 4 b.c. Dahar (USA) – Waltz Me Sue (USA) (Olden Times) [1992/3 17g² 17g⁵ 16s 17f³ 22vᵖᵘ] leggy colt: maiden on Flat: modest form over hurdles: form only at 2m on a sound surface. *B. J. Curley*   **88**

V

VADO VIA 5 b.m. Ardross – Brigado (Brigadier Gerard) [1992/3 24d*   119
22d* 22v* 24s3 24d3 22v* 24s 25v4 24s5 22d2] leggy mare: fairly useful
hurdler: won handicaps at Haydock (conditional jockeys), Nottingham and
twice at Newton Abbot (two amateur events) in first half of season: also ran
well in second half: stays 3m: acts on heavy going: held up: tough, genuine
and consistent. *D. J. Wintle*

VAGOG 8 b.g. Glint of Gold – Vadrouille (USA) (Foolish Pleasure (USA))   156
[1992/3 26d* 25v2 26s* 24vpu 25mpu] small, lightly-made gelding: smart
hurdler: successful in handicap at Cheltenham and Youngmans Long Walk
Hurdle at Ascot in first half of season, latter by 2½ lengths from Burgoyne:
ran badly afterwards: needs a thorough test of stamina: successful on firm
going but best form with plenty of give: suited by forcing tactics: wears
blinkers. *M. C. Pipe*

VAIGLY FINE 6 b.m. Vaigly Great – Juju (Dragonara Palace (USA))   –
[1992/3 17d] no sign of ability. *J. I. A. Charlton*

VAIGLY MASON 4 b.g. Vaigly Great – Hunslet (Comedy Star (USA))   83
[1992/3 16mF 18d 16d 17s 18d2 16s2] leggy gelding: third foal: dam, 7f
winner, is sister to high-class hurdler Starfen: placed at up to 7f at 2 yrs:
best efforts over hurdles when second in selling handicap hurdles in
January: will prove best at around 2m: acts on soft ground: blinkered fourth
outing. *M. H. Easterby*

VAIN PRINCE 6 b.h. Sandhurst Prince – Vain Deb (Gay Fandango   c113
(USA)) [1992/3 c17f* c17d2 c16mro c16d4 c17m* c18s* c20d2 c16g3 c16m2   –
c16m2 c17g3 c16s* c16gF c16f2] leggy horse: fairly useful hurdler: won
novice chases at Huntingdon, Newcastle and Market Rasen in first half of
season and handicap at Wetherby in April: should stay beyond 2¼m:
probably acts on any going: blinkered twelfth and thirteenth starts:
consistent. *N. Tinkler*

VALASSY 10 b.g. Northern Value (USA) – Plum Sassy (Prince   c76
Tenderfoot (USA)) [1992/3 c27s5 c26d6 c23g c26dur c27g3 c26m c25dpu]   –
lengthy gelding: poor handicap chaser nowadays: stays well: acts on heavy
going and good to firm. *J. A. C. Edwards*

Murphy's Handicap Hurdle, Cheltenham—Vagog is unchallenged

VALATCH 5 ch.g. Valiyar – Love Match (USA) (Affiliate (USA)) [1992/3 22dF 16s⁶ 22g 17f] big, good-topped gelding: poor novice hurdler: easily best run at 2m on soft ground. *J. L. Harris* 68

VAL DE RAMA (IRE) 4 b.g. Lafontaine (USA) – Port Magee (Royal Highway) [1992/3 17g] smallish, workmanlike gelding: half-brother to winning Irish jumpers Where's The Other (by Three Legs) and Royal Optimist (by Prince Regent): dam fair miler: last in juvenile hurdle at Newcastle in November: sold to D. Smith 8,100 gns in May. *W. A. Stephenson* –

VALE OF SECRECY 12 b.g. The Parson – Arctic Rhapsody (Bargello) [1992/3 24d 21s⁶ 21s⁵ 22g] rather lightly-made gelding: winning staying hurdler/chaser: no form since early 1991/2: changed hands 1,700 gns Doncaster January Sales after second start. *R. F. Fisher* c–
 –

VALFINET (FR) 6 b.g. Maiymad – Oland (FR) (Saumon (FR)) [1992/3 17d* 17v* 16s* 17s* 17s² 16g* 17m] 156

By his own admission Peter Scudamore found it very difficult to choose between mounts for the Champion Hurdle. In the end he plumped correctly for Granville Again ahead of Valfinet. Valfinet's chief claims lay in that he'd been in tremendous form all season, right through January and February while his stable companion had been off the track, and had shown a phenomenal amount of improvement, progressing from 110-rated handicapper to pattern-race winner in the space of three months. But it remained to be seen how effective his trail-blazing style of running would be in the Champion Hurdle, especially with similar types in the big field; and also how effective he would be on the firmish ground. He led the race until going to the fifth, never managing to establish much of an advantage over Flown and Jinxy Jack, then gradually faded, ultimately beating only Staunch Friend and Ruling home. We never thought Valfinet would be capable of leading throughout but expected him to last much longer; that he was probably below his best raises serious doubts about his ability to handle the ground.

Valfinet wasn't seen out again. Despite coming away from Cheltenham empty-handed he was retired for the season with earnings of £58,616, all win money except for the £3,060 which went with second place in the Agfa Hurdle at Sandown in February. Prior to the Agfa Hurdle, a recognised trial, Valfinet was exploited in handicaps, running off a mark that always underestimated his rate of improvement. He had to battle to land the William Hill Handicap Hurdle at Sandown second time up, coming back at Kilcash on the

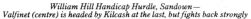

William Hill Handicap Hurdle, Sandown—
Valfinet (centre) is headed by Kilcash at the last, but fights back strongly

Kingwell Hurdle, Wincanton—Valfinet is too strong for Kribensis

flat despite being hampered. Otherwise, in the Whitbread White Label
Handicap at Cheltenham and less valuable events at Haydock and Taunton,
he was worth double or more his clear winning margins. There was no
telling how good he was from these handicap performances. The Agfa
Hurdle turned out a difficult race to assess—a five-runner affair with
Morley Street virtually pulled up and 33/1-shot Mole Board swooping from
nowhere to win by six lengths after Valfinet had set a scorching pace to the
last. All the same, the result could not be interpreted as in any way
uncomplimentary to Valfinet, and when again put on trial in the Grade 2
Kingwell Hurdle at Wincanton in February he started at odds on to beat one
of the Champion Hurdle favourites Muse, plus Gran Alba, Sanndila,
Kribensis and Exact Analysis. The race turned out less of a trial than
anticipated when Muse failed to give his running, but Valfinet could do no
more than win convincingly. He led from the start and when pressed by
Kribensis he found extra to pull away by five lengths.

  Valfinet was imported from France after running third on his jumping
debut in a four-year-old hurdle at Clairefontaine in October 1991. That same
year he'd won four middle-distance races on the Flat for the stable of L.
Audon, the last of them one of some importance at Longchamp confined to
French non-thoroughbreds (the Grand Prix des A.Q.P.S.). Valfinet's dam
Oland is a French Saddlebred, a breed British jumping is becoming increasingly aware of, but his sire Maiymad is a thoroughbred. Maiymad is also the
sire of the good French horse Ubu III who ran in the Stayers' Hurdle at
Cheltenham in 1992. Maiymad showed very useful form over middle
distances in his racing days; on one occasion he came out a better horse at
the weights than leading jumping sire Strong Gale in the Prix Ridgway at
Deauville. Oland's dam Islande is a winner-producer, and she herself won
on the Flat and over jumps in France.

		Rheingold	Faberge II
	Maiymad	(br 1969)	Athene
	(br 1977)	Miss Melody	Tudor Melody
Valfinet (FR)		(b 1970)	The Veil
(b.g. 1987)		Saumon	Hodell
	Oland (FR)	(ch 1972)	Sinella
	(ch 1980)	Islande	Laniste
		(b 1974)	Tahiti

  Don't bother looking for stamina in Valfinet's pedigree. He's a two-
miler, a tremendously-enthusiastic front runner who jumps well. He'll be a
great sight when he goes over fences. He should win more good races over
hurdles first, although a Champion Hurdle is likely to be beyond him unless
the small fields of the 'seventies return. A tall, leggy gelding, Valfinet has
shown all his form on an easy surface and acts well on soft and heavy. *M. C.
Pipe*

VALIANT BOY 7 b.g. Connaught – Irish Amber (Amber Rama (USA))   c135
[1992/3 c16m² c16s* c21gᵖᵘ c16m⁴ c16f* c18g* c16g⁴] tall gelding: fairly   –
useful hurdler: very useful form in novice chases in 1992/3, winning PML
Lightning Novices' Chase at Ascot in January and Sandeman Maghull
Novices' Chase at Aintree in April, latter by a head from Shu Fly, getting up
near finish: well below form on final 2 starts, though won 3-runner event at
Bangor later in April: stays 2½m: probably acts on any ground: blinkered
once: broke blood vessel third start: game and genuine. *S. E. Kettlewell*

VALIANT DASH 7 b.g. Valiyar – Dame Ashfield (Grundy) [1992/3 26m³
21d⁵ 26d⁵ 20g² 20d²] close-coupled gelding: fair hurdler: stays 3¼m: yet to   111
race on heavy going, acts on any other: usually races up with pace. *S. E.
Kettlewell*

VALIANT WARRIOR 5 br.g. Valiyar – Jouvencelle (Rusticaro (FR))
[1992/3 21m* 20g⁶ 20d⁶] leggy gelding: won novice hurdle at Wetherby in   101 §
October: ran poorly afterwards and looked most ungenuine final start
(December): stays 21f: acts on good to firm and dead going: front runner: not
one to trust. *M. D. Hammond*

VALIANT WORDS 6 br.g. Valiyar – Wild Words (Galivanter) [1992/3
16s] useful-looking gelding: half-brother to winning hurdler Jakaroo (by
Sahib): middle-distance performer on Flat, poor nowadays: showed nothing
in novice event at Kempton in December on hurdling debut. *R. Akehurst*

VALKYRIE REEF 4 ch.f. Miramar Reef – Private Sue (Brigadier
Gerard) [1992/3 16f³ 18mᵖᵘ 18f⁵ 18d* 16g 18d] leggy filly: poor maiden on   82
Flat: won novice selling hurdle at Sedgefield (no bid) in September: well
below form in juvenile events afterwards: sold 2,500 gns Ascot November
Sales: yet to race beyond 2¼m: acts on dead ground. *Denys Smith*

VALLEY OF TIME (FR) 5 br.m. In Fijar (USA) – Vallee Sarthoise
(FR) (Val de Loir) [1992/3 16g] workmanlike mare: poor novice hurdler: yet   –
to race beyond 2m: acts on good to firm ground. *D. A. Nolan*

VALMARANDA (USA) 5 ch.m. Sir Ivor – Sweetsider (USA) (Topsider
(USA)) [1992/3 16s* 16sᵖᵘ 21d 16sᵖᵘ 17s⁴ 20g 21g 17m 17m⁵] workmanlike   86
ex-Irish mare: third foal: sister to hurdles-placed Cellatica and half-sister to
a winner in USA by Drone: dam won at about 9f at 2 yrs: modest hurdler:
won maiden at Sligo in August: trained until after third start by

*Sandeman Maghull Novices' Chase, Aintree —
left to right, Valiant Boy, Shu Fly and Trimlough*

M. McCausland: fair efforts in Britain: form only at around 2m: acts on soft and good to firm ground. *D. Moffatt*

VALNAU (FR) 6 b.g. Grandchant (FR) – Matale (FR) (Danoso) [1992/3 21s 20mᵇᵈ] stocky, plain gelding: little sign of ability: blinkered last 3 starts. *M. C. Pipe* –

VALSEUR (USA) 4 ch.c. Lyphard (USA) – Vachti (FR) (Crystal Palace (FR)) [1992/3 18g 28m* 22d* 25v* 22g5 22m3 25m*] smallish, good-bodied colt: modest stayer on Flat: successful in 2 novice selling hurdles at Sedgefield (no bid either time) and a claiming handicap and selling handicap (bought in 4,800 gns) at Perth in second half of season: stays 3½m: acts on good to firm and heavy ground: usually races up with pace. *L. Lungo* 95

VALTAKI 8 b.g. Valiyar – Taqa (Blakeney) [1992/3 17m3 17m 16f4 18s6] neat gelding: modest hurdler: once-raced over fences: races at around 2m: acts well on firm ground: sometimes wears blinkers/tongue strap: occasionally reluctant to race, and not to be trusted. *L. J. Codd* c– 88 §

VALUED FRIEND (USA) 5 b.g. Ziggy's Boy (USA) – Tuvalu (USA) (Our Native (USA)) [1992/3 22g4 19m] leggy gelding: poor novice hurdler: sold 500 gns Ascot November Sales: stays 2¾m: acts on firm ground and equitrack. *J. J. Bridger* –

VA LUTE (FR) 9 b.g. No Lute (FR) – Viverba (FR) (Sanctus II) [1992/3 a18g*] small, lightly-made gelding: fair hurdler: won claimer at Lingfield in February: best at around 2m: probably acts on any going. *P. F. Nicholls* 101 +

VANBOROUGH LAD 4 b.g. Precocious – Lustrous (Golden Act (USA)) [1992/3 18sF] angular gelding: modest at up to 1¼m on Flat: well beaten when falling last in juvenile hurdle at Folkestone in February. *M. J. Haynes* –

VANBRUGH'S ROOM 5 ch.g. Smackover – Klairove (Averof) [1992/3 F14d F17s 16dᵖᵘ] second foal: brother to 5f seller winner Klairover: dam fair hurdler: no sign of ability. *R. D. E. Woodhouse* –

VAN DYKE BROWN 12 b.g. Gay Mecene (USA) – Latin Melody (Tudor Melody) [1992/3 c22g4 c22g*] fair pointer: finished lame when winning novice hunter chase at Fakenham in May: stays 2¾m. *W. A. Wales* c82

VANISKI 6 b.g. Niniski (USA) – Voltigeuse (USA) (Filiberto (USA)) [1992/3 22d5 25m3 24g3 24gᵖᵘ] light-framed, leggy, plain gelding: moderate novice hurdler: stays 25f: acts on good to firm going: visored once. *Mrs Barbara Waring* 99

VANTARD 11 ch.g. Le Bavard (FR) – Miss Hereford (Hereford) [1992/3 c18m5 c23f4 c18d3 c18m c16g6 c25gᵖᵘ] sparely-made gelding: poor chaser: stays 3m: acts on firm and dead ground: usually blinkered. *Mrs J. Jordan* c75 –

VANUATU (IRE) 4 b.f. Orchestra – Owey (Sovereign Gleam) [1992/3 16vᵖᵘ 16mᵖᵘ 17d] sparely-made filly: sister to very smart chaser Pat's Jester: no form on Flat or over hurdles. *T. Thomson Jones* –

VARECK II (FR) 6 b.g. Brezzo (FR) – Kavala II (FR) (Danoso) [1992/3 F17d] modest pointer: blinkered, behind in NH Flat race at Hereford in May: yet to race over hurdles or in a steeplechase. *M. C. Pipe* –

VASILIEV 5 b.g. Sadler's Wells (USA) – Poquito Queen (CAN) (Explodent (USA)) [1992/3 17d5 16s2 17g4 16d 17g3] leggy gelding: fair novice hurdler when in the mood: yet to race beyond 17f: acts on soft ground: often visored or blinkered: reluctant, and one to treat with caution. *J. P. Leigh* 101 §

VATACAN BANK 8 b.g. The Parson – Little Credit (Little Buskins) [1992/3 c25sᵖᵘ c24vᵖᵘ] leggy, workmanlike gelding: pulled up in novice chases: blinkered once. *O. Sherwood* c–

VA UTU 5 b.g. Balliol – Flame (Firestreak) [1992/3 17g5 16d3 17s3 16g2 17s4 17s4 16f2 17f* 16g4 16f2 17m 18m] close-coupled gelding: modest handicap hurdler: won at Lingfield in March: stays 19f: probably acts on any ground, ran particularly well on equitrack in 1991/2: tough and consistent. *M. R. Channon* 93

VAYRUA (FR) 8 ch.g. Vayrann – Nabua (FR) (Le Fabuleux) [1992/3 c21g   **c103**
c21d² c20d⁶ c16s² c17s² c17s⁴ c25s³ c21gᵖᵘ] good-topped gelding: one-time   –
useful hurdler: fair novice chaser: not raced after February: ideally suited
by around 2½m: best form on an easy surface: suited by forcing tactics:
sketchy jumper. *J. A. Hellens*

VAZON BAY 9 b.g. Deep Run – Fair Argument (No Argument) [1992/3   **c95**
21g c20s² c21f⁴] strong, rangy gelding: one-time useful hurdler: moderate   –
novice chaser: stays 2½m: probably acts on any ground: blinkered. *Mrs J.
Pitman*

VAZON EXPRESS 7 b.g. Le Bavard (FR) – Grangecon Express (Bonne   c–
Noel) [1992/3 26d c23gᵖᵘ 18gᵖᵘ 17g⁵ 16mᵖᵘ 20g²21d] sparely-made, angular   73
gelding: poor novice hurdler: pulled up on chasing debut: stays 2¾m: acts
on firm and dead ground: visored once. *P. T. Dalton*

VEE TEE 7 b.g. Tug of War – Lager (Prince Hansel) [1992/3 c16s⁵ c16dF   c–
c17dF c17dᵖᵘ c16s⁶ c27g] long-backed gelding: of little account. *V.
Thompson*

VELEDA II (FR) 6 ch.g. Olmeto – Herbe Fine (FR) (Francois Saubaber)
[1992/3 23gᵇᵈ 21g² 22f* 21m 25sᵖᵘ] big, leggy, angular gelding: chasing   90
type: modest hurdler: won novice event at Huntingdon in March: ran poorly
afterwards: should stay beyond 2¾m: acts on firm going. *Mrs S. A. Bramall*

VELOCE (IRE) 5 b.g. Kafu – Joanns Goddess (Godswalk (USA)) [1992/3
17sᵖᵘ] neat gelding: very tough and quite useful on Flat, winner at 7f and 1m   –
in 1993: no promise in novice event at Wolverhampton in January on
hurdling debut. *A. Bailey*

VELVETEEN BOY 5 b.g. Enchantment – Penny Bazaar (Native
Bazaar) [1992/3 16d 17d⁵] leggy gelding: no sign of ability in 2 races on Flat   –
or in novice hurdles. *T. W. Donnelly*

VERBAL WARNING 5 gr.g. Move Off – Millisles (Pongee) [1992/3
18dᵖᵘ 21sᵖᵘ] second foal: dam of little account: seems little better himself: –
trained by A. Batey first start. *W. Storey*

VERITATE 9 b.m. Roman Warrior – Empress of England (Constable)   c– x
[1992/3 25g³ 24f⁵ c23g⁵] lengthy, workmanlike mare: poor novice   71
hurdler/chaser: stays 3m: acts on good to firm and dead ground: visored
once: poor jumper of fences. *M. J. Wilkinson*

VERMONT MAGIC 5 b.g. Elegant Air – Jove's Voodoo (USA)
(Northern Jove (CAN)) [1992/3 17dᵖᵘ 17sᵖᵘ 17fᵘʳ] half-brother to winning   –
hurdlers Zamore and Spirit Away (both by Dominion): one-time fair
performer on Flat when trained by Lord Huntingdon: showed nothing over
hurdles: trained by R. Hodges first 2 starts. *M. C. Pipe*

VERSAILLESPRINCESS 5 b.m. Legend of France (USA) –
Naamullah (Reform) [1992/3 17dᵖᵘ 16sᵖᵘ] lengthy mare: second foal: dam   –
never ran: no sign of ability in novice hurdles. *K. O. Cunningham-Brown*

VERY CHEERING 10 b.g. Gleason (USA) – Cherry Joy (Bally Joy)   c79 x
[1992/3 c24dᵖᵘ c24g³ c26sF c24gˢᵘ] plain gelding: poor novice chaser: stays   –
3m: best effort on good ground: poor jumper. *Mrs S. J. Smith*

VERY EVIDENT (IRE) 4 b.g. Glenstal (USA) – Royal Daughter (High
Top) [1992/3 20s³ 16s⁶ 16s⁴ a16gᵖᵘ 22d 16g 21gᵖᵘ] lengthy, workmanlike   90 d
gelding: disappointing middle-distance maiden on Flat: sold out of B. Hills's
stable 9,200 gns Newmarket Autumn Sales: modest form on debut over
hurdles: ran poorly, including in seller, afterwards: pulled up, reportedly
lame, final start: best effort at 2½m on soft going. *R. O'Leary*

VERY TOUCHING 8 gr.g. Touch Paper – Sally Stanford (Daring   c–
Display (USA)) [1992/3 c21gF] compact gelding: modest novice hunter   –
chaser: sold 6,200 gns Malvern February Sales: should stay beyond 2½m:
acts on dead ground. *Mrs C. M. Clifford*

VERY VERY ORDINARY 7 b.g. Furry Glen – Very Very (Vulgan)   c137 p
[1992/3 c21d⁴ c21d³ c22s* c26v³ c20s² c25s* c25d* c27mᵖᵘ c25f³]
Very Very Ordinary was thrown in at the deep end on his last two
starts—in the Tote Cheltenham Gold Cup and the Martell Cup at Aintree—

Crispin Chase (Handicap), Ascot—Calapaez (grey) and Very Very Ordinary jump the last together

and it showed. But his performances took nothing away from the very good impression he'd been creating in handicaps. He'd looked likely to progress following a fairly successful first season over fences in 1991/2, and after opening his account in the latest season at Towcester in November he went from strength to strength. Good runs in handicaps at Cheltenham in December and Newbury in January (second to Another Coral) preceded two impressive victories at Ascot, in the First National Chase in January and the Crispin Chase in February. Very Very Ordinary, who is usually held up, has an excellent turn of foot for a stayer, and he was confidently ridden on both occasions, confirming himself still very much on the upgrade when winning the Crispin Chase from Calapaez and Cache Fleur, facing a considerably stiffer task than when winning the First National Chase. Whether or not Very Very Ordinary—described by his trainer as 'far and away the fastest horse I've had anything to do with'—proves up to taking on the best is a matter for conjecture. He's reportedly being aimed at the King George VI Chase on Boxing Day but, presumably, he'll pick up the thread in handicaps beforehand. He's the sort to keep improving and stay ahead of the handicapper and looks the type who would get into a race like the Hennessy on a handy mark.

		Wolver Hollow (b 1964)	Sovereign Path
Very Very Ordinary (b.g. 1986)	Furry Glen (b 1971)		Cygnet
		Cleftess (br 1956)	Hill Gail
			Cleft
	Very Very (ch 1967)	Vulgan (b 1943)	Sirlan
			Vulgate
		Merry Palm (br 1960)	Merry Boy
			Solar Palm

The tall, angular Very Very Ordinary was named by John Upson—'I name my horses spontaneously'—after he had read a story in an Irish newspaper that John Costello, who used to train at Highfields, had said he'd trained an 'ordinary' horse called Zeta's Lad which had won five novice chases. 'When the Costellos, who are my mentors, sold Zeta's Lad to my wife Diane he was described by them as "the best horse she'd ever buy"', Upson explained in a *Timeform Interview*. 'So I couldn't resist the name Very Very Ordinary for a horse I thought was the best young horse I'd owned'. Like most of the horses at Highfields, Very Very Ordinary is jumping bred. He is by the Irish Two Thousand Guineas winner Furry Glen who died in 1987 but has had plenty of success as a sire of jumpers. Very Very Ordinary's unraced dam Very Very is a sister to a poor winning stayer on the Flat called Valuable and is a half-sister to two winning chasers, the fairly useful Inishowen and the modest Merry Missus (the dam of Scottish

National runner-up Merry Master). Very Very has bred three other winning chasers, the very useful Fauloon and the fairly useful Parish Rigged (both by Master Buck) and the fair Bobby Kelly (by Le Bavard), all of whom were well suited by a test of stamina. Very Very Ordinary stays well but is effective at two and a half miles when conditions are testing. He acts well in the mud and is game and genuine. *John R. Upson*

VIA CAVOUR (USA) 4 gr.c. Green Dancer (USA) – Princess Verna (USA) (Al Hattab (USA)) [1992/3 aF16g4] half-brother to 2 winners in USA: dam lightly-raced maiden: distant fourth in NH Flat race at Southwell in February: yet to race over hurdles. *M. W. Easterby*

VIAGGIO 5 b.g. High Line – Al Washl (USA) (The Minstrel (CAN)) [1992/3 16d5 17d2 17v* 18s 16spu] lengthy ex-Irish horse: won novice hurdle at Newton Abbot in December: ran poorly afterwards: poor form on Flat in 1993: should stay beyond 17f: acts on heavy ground: blinkered once: sometimes wears tongue strap. *J. Akehurst* 97

VIARDOT (IRE) 4 b.c. Sadler's Wells (USA) – Vive La Reine (Vienna) [1992/3 16v2 17s* 17s* 17m] angular colt: won novice hurdle at Wolverhampton in January and juvenile event at Sandown in February: never dangerous in Daily Express Triumph Hurdle at Cheltenham on final start: sold to join Mrs M. Reveley's stable 18,000 gns Doncaster May Sales, and fairly useful 1½m winner in July: will stay beyond 17f: acts on heavy going: likely to make a useful handicap hurdler. *M. C. Pipe* 123 p

Sheikh Ahmed Bin Saeed Al-Maktoum's "Viardot"

VICARIDGE 6 b.g. The Parson – Streamon (Rapid River) [1992/3 20m 17s⁵ c20gᵖᵘ] good-topped gelding with plenty of scope: lightly-raced novice hurdler: running promising first race over fences in novice event at Newcastle in February when pulled up after a bad mistake 6 out (disputing lead): should do better. *R. Brewis* — c– p 72

VICEROY GEM (IRE) 5 ch.g. Sallust – Gang Plank (Tower Walk) [1992/3 17g⁴ 16d] close-coupled gelding: modest hurdler at best: poor form in 1992/3: trained first start by R. Holder: races at around 2m: acts on good to firm and heavy ground. *P. G. Murphy* — 82

VICEROY JESTER 8 br.g. Jester – Midnight Patrol (Ashmore (FR)) [1992/3 18d² 18v⁵ 22v⁵ 20s* 16s 21vᵖᵘ 20d⁵] lengthy, workmanlike gelding: fairly useful handicap hurdler: trained first 2 starts by G. Balding: won amateurs event at Ascot in December: ran badly afterwards: only poor form in novice chases: stays 2½m: acts on any going: visored twice. *P. G. Murphy* — c– 123

VICOMPT DE VALMONT 8 b.g. Beau Charmeur (FR) – Wish Again (Three Wishes) [1992/3 c21d² c24s⁴ 25v c26d* c26g⁵ c27g⁵] leggy gelding: fair hurdler at best: won novice chase at Plumpton in February: sold 12,000 gns Ascot June Sales: suited by a test of stamina: acts on soft ground: usually blinkered: inconsistent and ungenuine. *N. J. Henderson* — c90 § – §

VICTOR BRAVO (NZ) 6 br.g. War Hawk – Regal Command (NZ) (First Consul (USA)) [1992/3 21g³ 23d⁶] compact gelding: fair hurdler: ran creditably in 2 starts in October: stays 3m: acts on dead going. *N. A. Gaselee* — 105

VICTORIA'S DELIGHT 6 br.m. Idiot's Delight – Hasty Dawn (Dawn Review) [1992/3 17mᵖᵘ 19h⁴] smallish, lengthy mare: of little account: visored final start. *Mrs P. M. Joynes* — –

VICTOR ROMEO 4 b.g. Nomination – Be My Sweet (Galivanter) [1992/3 16d⁶ 17d] leggy gelding: irresolute winning plater on Flat, best at around 1m: poor form in 2 selling hurdles in October. *R. C. Spicer* — 60

VICTORY ANTHEM 7 ch.g. Tug of War – Anvil Chorus (Levanter) [1992/3 c18gᶠ c18mᵘʳ 17dᶠ 18s⁵ a16g² a16g* 16m² 17f⁴ 16fᵖᵘ 17g²] lengthy gelding: moderate handicap hurdler: sold out of N. Henderson's stable 5,000 gns Ascot November Sales after fourth start: won at Lingfield in January: let down by his jumping in 2 runs over fences: races only at around 2m: acts on good to firm ground and equitrack. *P. C. Clarke* — c– 95

VICTORY GATE (USA) 8 b.g. Lydian (FR) – Pago Miss (USA) (Pago Pago) [1992/3 c21sᶠ c24dᵖᵘ c24v⁵ c26dᶠ c24g³ c26s²] leggy, workmanlike gelding: one-time fair hurdler: poor novice chaser: stays 3¼m: yet to race on firm going, acts on any other: tried blinkered: sketchy jumper of fences. *A. Moore* — c74 –

VICTORY WIND 8 ch.g. Asdic – Cool Wind (Windjammer (USA)) [1992/3 c20gᵘʳ c16gᵖᵘ c16gᶠ 17m c16gᵖᵘ] workmanlike gelding: 2m novice hurdler/chaser, poor at best. *T. Morton* — c– –

VIDEO DEALER 5 b.g. Aragon – Ginnies Pet (Compensation) [1992/3 18m] close-coupled gelding: novice selling hurdler: maiden pointer. *C. L. Popham* — –

VIENNA WOODS 6 b.g. Elegant Air – Grace Note (Parthia) [1992/3 F16d* F18v* 16s² 16d 18d] sturdy gelding: half-brother to numerous winners, including 5 hurdlers: dam useful sprinter: won NH Flat races at Catterick and Market Rasen in first half of season: second in novice hurdle at Catterick in January, but failed to confirm that promise: likely to stay 2½m: acts on soft going. *J. G. FitzGerald* — 95

VIKING FLAGSHIP 6 b.g. Viking (USA) – Fourth Degree (Oats) [1992/3 c16sᶠ c16d* c16d* c17s* c16d* c17s* c16d* c16g*] — c144 p –

With its generous prize money and promise of good jumping ground, the Punchestown late-April fixture offers a real incentive these days to keep horses on the go after Cheltenham and Aintree are over, and leading British stables have been showing increasing interest. The visitors experienced mixed fortunes there in 1993 but on the positive side managed to come away with three wins, two of them provided by Viking Flagship, an absentee from Cheltenham and Aintree because of the going. He made up for lost opportunities by taking the first day's £21,782 BMW Drogheda Chase and the third day's £16,188 Bank of Ireland Colliers Novice Chase, both over two miles. Viking Flagship is a fine prospect, possibly even another Waterloo Boy for his trainer. Largely as a result of missing the big meetings in Britain he hasn't been so highly tried as some of his contemporaries—Sybillin, Travado and Wonder Man for instance—but seems sure to be taking on the best of them at some stage in the next season, very likely on handicap terms initially.

Following a last-fence fall, when in command, in a novice event at Nottingham in February on his chasing debut Viking Flagship, quite useful over hurdles, was kept busy learning his new trade. Before the month-end he'd gone the rounds to Wolverhampton, to Leicester, then to Wincanton to contest other minor novice events. The fall hadn't affected his confidence; he jumped boldly, and for the most part accurately, winning all three races without much fuss, twice starting odds on. He started odds on again when next seen out at Chepstow in April, opposed by Atlaal and three long-shots. The steady gallop allowed him little opportunity to show his full superiority, but he seemed to have taken Atlaal's measure when that horse departed at the last and left him a distance clear. So to Punchestown, and Viking Flagship's first handicap chase. He was out of the handicap along with five of the seven other runners; 6 lb out in fact, yet started 5/4 favourite. The two in it, Cyphrate and Good For A Laugh, put up no sort of resistance to Viking Flagship and Foulksrath Castle who pulled well clear in the straight. Viking Flagship made two or three mistakes on the way round and seemed in danger of defeat going to the second last; but a good jump there followed by another at the last helped see him home by two and a half lengths. Progressive as this performance confirmed Viking Flagship to be, the race for the Bank of Ireland Chase was billed primarily as a domestic affair between How's The Boss and Soft Day. However, the clash between two of Ireland's best novices ended at the second fence, when Soft Day broke a hind leg. How's The Boss himself injured a shoulder during the race, and even the best of the home contingent on the afternoon, Galevilla Express, failed to hit top form. The main challenge to Viking Flagship came from another improving sort, Antonin, the horse who had finished second behind him at Leicester. Antonin set a strong pace to the small field and kept in

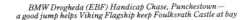

BMW Drogheda (EBF) Handicap Chase, Punchestown—
a good jump helps Viking Flagship keep Foulksrath Castle at bay

Bank of Ireland Colliers Novice Chase, Punchestown —
a second win at the meeting for Viking Flagship

front until approaching the last where Viking Flagship, having turned in a better round of jumping than on the Tuesday, caught him before going on to score comfortably by four lengths. The pair finished clear of the others, led by Galevilla Express and the Aintree winner Valiant Boy.

		Northern Dancer (b 1961)	Nearctic
	Viking (USA) (ch 1977)		Natalma
		Paddy's Song (b 1961)	Chanteur II
Viking Flagship (b.g. 1987)			Birthday Wood
		Oats (b 1973)	Northfields
	Fourth Degree (br 1980)		Arctic Lace
		Puzzes Times (b 1969)	Olden Times
			Puzzesca

Viking Flagship was no stranger to the Irish tracks. He was trained over there at two and three, and reached the frame a few times on the Flat before being sent to Pipe for hurdling. His present owner Graeme Roach, a licence-holder at the time, acquired him after the horse's fourth win on the trot for Pipe as a juvenile, ran him without success in the Champion Four-Year-Old Hurdle at Punchestown, then put him into Nicholson's charge for the 1991/2 season. Viking Flagship's sire Viking stood in Ireland for a while, but failed to catch on and was exported to Denmark in 1988. By Northern Dancer out of the 1964 Cheshire Oaks winner, he won four races at up to nine furlongs in the USA, the best of them in allowance company. Viking Flagship's tail-female line is North American in the second and third generation, though Puzzes Times, out of a winner in the USA, actually raced in France (she won a nine-furlong handicap at Maisons-Laffitte) and produced several winners there on the Flat and over jumps. Viking Flagship's dam never ran. He is her second foal, following Don Vincento (by Don),

Roach Foods Ltd's "Viking Flagship"

the subject of a controversial stewards inquiry at Bangor in March and successful favourite for a maiden hurdle at Ballinrobe next time out. Don Vincento is a thorough stayer. On the other hand none of Viking Flagship's trainers has seen a need to run him beyond seventeen furlongs: he is a horse with a good turn of foot who races up with the pace. One day he will be given his chance and probably show he can stay a bit further, but two-mile chases are likely to be his only targets in 1993/4. Physically Viking Flagship is best described as neat; not very big, but sufficiently robust to run twice over fences in three days. Although pulled out on account of the ground at Cheltenham and Aintree, he has one fair performance to his credit on good to firm. He certainly handles soft ground, and he won on the Lingfield equi-track as a juvenile. He is genuine and consistent. *D. Nicholson*

VIKING ROCKET 9 ch.m. Viking (USA) – Calcine (Roan Rocket) c– [1992/3 c24gF] sparely-made, rather plain mare: fair chaser: close second – when falling 5 out at Newcastle in November: stays 25f: best form with give in the ground: genuine. *C. Parker*

VIKING VENTURE 8 ch.g. Viking (USA) – Mattira (FR) (Rheffic (FR)) – [1992/3 20gpu 17vpu 23spu a16g a18g a20g] small gelding: fair hurdler at around 2m at best: no form in 1992/3: tried visored: sold 625 gns Ascot February Sales. *Mrs L. C. Jewell*

VILCOE BAY 6 b.g. Roscoe Blake – Vilmainder (Remainder) [1992/3 17s a16g a20g2 a20g5 a18g2 a16g2 a20g4 26mpu] compact gelding: poor novice 78 hurdler: stays 2½m: best form on fibresand. *B. A. McMahon*

VILLAGE DANCER 6 b.g. Creetown – Autumn Ballet (Averof) [1992/3 – 17gpu] plain, close-coupled gelding: first foal: dam winning 2½m hurdler: soundly beaten only outing on Flat and when pulled up in early-season novice hurdle. *A. J. Wight*

VILLAGE KID 4 br.g. Another Realm – Village Lass (No Mercy) [1992/3 – F17d] eighth foal: half-brother to Flat winners Sunapa's Owlet (by Derrylin) and Village Pet (by Tina's Pet): dam never ran: mid-division in 17-runner NH Flat race at Hereford in May: well beaten on Flat following month: yet to race over hurdles. *P. R. Hedger*

VILLAGE PET 5 b.h. Tina's Pet – Village Lass (No Mercy) [1992/3 – 17m5] inconsistent sprinter on Flat, modest at best: tailed off in early-season claimer on hurdling debut: sold 725 gns Ascot September Sales. *P. J. Hobbs*

VILLAGE REINDEER (NZ) 6 b.g. Le Grand Seigneur (CAN) – Riggane (NZ) (Reindeer) [1992/3 21g5 22s2 23d3 25g* 25g2 25f 25s5] 116 angular gelding: fairly useful handicap hurdler: won at Nottingham in March: ran poorly last 2 outings: stays 25f: possibly needs give in the ground, and acts on heavy going. *P. Calver*

VILLA PARK 11 b.g. Varano – Fethard Flirt (Furry Glen) [1992/3 22v4 c– 22g a24g4 20s5] tall gelding: poor hurdler nowadays: unseated rider both 83 starts over fences: stays 2¾m: acts on any going. *G. Wareham*

VILLA RECOS 8 b.g. Deep Run – Lovely Colour (Shantung) [1992/3 c92 17d4 17d3 20g5 17f c16s2 c21gpu 21m] workmanlike gelding: fairly useful 125 § hurdler: second in novice event at Ludlow in April on chasing debut: ran poorly next time: stays 2½m: acts on good to firm and soft ground: blinkered once: sometimes looks ungenuine and best treated with caution. *Mrs J. Pitman*

VILLA TARANTO 8 b.m. Ashmore (FR) – Gunnard (Gunner B) [1992/3 – § 16srtr 18spu] lengthy mare: no sign of ability: refused to race once. *Mrs B. Brunt*

VINCANTO 11 ch.g. Orchestra – Subiaco (Yellow River) [1992/3 c17mR c§§ c23f5 c27spu c21fpu] lengthy gelding: moderate chaser at up to 2½m in – 1991/2: no form in 1992/3: sold 1,400 gns Ascot September Sales: unenthusiastic and one to leave alone nowadays. *M. C. Pipe*

VINTAGE CROP   6 ch.g. Rousillon (USA) – Overplay (Bustino) [1992/3 17m6]   159 p

The race-sponsor's Vintage Crop was well backed for the Smurfit Champion Hurdle despite his palpable lack of experience and despite training problems which had been partly responsible for keeping him off the course since he'd trotted up by eight lengths in the Cesarewitch in October. For a horse whose hurdling experience amounted to two winning starts in Irish maiden and novice company sixteen months in the past, Vintage Crop showed up remarkably well against Granville Again and the rest. He came sixth, beaten under nine lengths, and would have been placed higher, probably even have threatened the winner, except for bad mistakes at the last two flights. As he went to the second last he looked still full of running, having moved easily just behind the leaders all the way, but he almost fell at the last. This is a top-class hurdler in the making, and one with prospects of surpassing the individual achievements of Major Rose, Flash Imp and Nomadic Way, Cesarewitch winners who all ran second in the Champion Hurdle. Vintage Crop was denied the opportunity of adding to his hurdling experience in 1992/3 by the lure of the Ascot Gold Cup. When put back to the Flat in the spring he failed to strike the sort of form required to win that event, and although he was sent to Royal Ascot with a recent win at Leopardstown behind him he never threatened to finish better than a modest sixth to Drum Taps. He improved on his Ascot form afterwards, winning a listed race at the Curragh.

Vintage Crop's sire Rousillon was exported to Japan from the National Stud in 1990 when his first runners were only three-year-olds. Among the best milers of his generation, Rousillon has proved quite a strong influence for stamina, but few of his offspring have made any impression on jumps

Dr Michael Smurfit's "Vintage Crop"

racing so far. The dam Overplay showed useful middle-distance form on the Flat for Vintage Crop's stable after finishing a good fourth in the Irish One Thousand Guineas, and has enjoyed a successful career at stud. At least four of her other foals have won at home or abroad; her three-year-old of 1992, Over The Run (by Commanche Run), won three times over seven furlongs in Japan. The second dam, the miler Melodramatic, was every bit as good a racemare as Overplay; she finished third in the Coronation Stakes at Royal Ascot. Her dam Irish Flight, a maiden, was a half-sister to two classic-placed colts, the 1959 Two Thousand Guineas third Carnoustie and the 1963 Irish St Leger third Philemon.

Vintage Crop (ch.g. 1987)	Rousillon (USA) (b 1981)	Riverman (b 1969)	Never Bend
			River Lady
		Belle Dorine (b or br 1977)	Marshua's Dancer
			Palsy Walsy
	Overplay (b 1978)	Bustino (b 1971)	Busted
			Ship Yard
		Melodramatic (b 1970)	Tudor Melody
			Irish Flight

Vintage Crop had no difficulty going the pace in the Champion Hurdle. His showing in the race, and that of the likes of Major Rose, Flash Imp, Nomadic Way and, let's not forget, Royal Gait and Sea Pigeon, is a warning against presuming that a horse capable of winning over extreme distances on the Flat will need further than two miles to bring out the best in him over hurdles. Flash Imp, in fact, showed himself clearly better at two than two and a half and didn't stay three. However, there seems no reason to suppose that Vintage Crop won't stay significantly beyond the two and a quarter miles he's so far tackled over hurdles, if asked. He's likely to be asked in the Aintree Hurdle, if not before. Vintage Crop, a lengthy gelding, lightly made by jumping standards, has won on dead ground and run very well on good to firm over hurdles. Connections said before the Gold Cup (run on soft) that they were of the opinion that he needed top-of-the-ground conditions to show his best. However, while it's true he had them for the Cesarewitch, he started favourite for that race on the strength of a good fifth on soft in the Irish St Leger. *D. K. Weld, Ireland*

VIRGINIA'S BAY 7 b.g. Uncle Pokey – Carnation (Runnymede) [1992/3 c21m⁵] sturdy, workmanlike gelding: winning 2m hurdler: well beaten in steeplechases: tried visored/blinkered. *M. McCarthy* — c– –

VIRIDIAN 8 b.g. Green Shoon – Cahermore Ivy (Perspex) [1992/3 22mᵖᵘ c25gᵖᵘ c23f* c24g⁶] workmanlike gelding: fair handicap chaser: trained until after second outing by Mrs A. King: won at Worcester in May, only form of 1992/3: stays 25f: probably acts on any going: unreliable. *E. T. Buckley* — c108 § –

VIRKON VENTURE (IRE) 5 b.g. Auction Ring (USA) – Madame Fair (Monseigneur (USA)) [1992/3 16s² 17s³ 17v⁵ 16v² 16v³ 17g⁶] leggy gelding: one-time fairly useful performer at around 1¼m on Flat: modest novice hurdler: ran badly final outing: likely to stay beyond 17f: acts on heavy ground. *M. H. Tompkins* — 94

VISAGA 7 b.g. King's Ride – Subiacco (Yellow River) [1992/3 18g² 22s 20g c24s⁵ c24dᵘʳ c25gᵖᵘ] rangy gelding: novice hurdler/chaser: probably stays 3m and acts on soft ground: broke blood vessel final start. *D. Nicholson* — c76 91

VISCOUNT TULLY 8 b.g. Blakeney – Cymbal (Ribero) [1992/3 24gᶠ 22s 23g² 22s⁴] close-coupled gelding: fair handicap hurdler: not raced after October: stays 23f: acts on soft going: sometimes hangs left: unreliable. *C. F. C. Jackson* — 105 §

VISION OF FREEDOM (IRE) 5 b.g. Vision (USA) – Captive Audience (Bold Lad (IRE)) [1992/3 a16g⁴ a16gᶠ 17s⁵ 17m* 17d⁵ 20g⁵] poor form around 1m on Flat: best effort over hurdles when winning maiden at Taunton in April: ran in sellers first 2 starts: likely to prove best at around 2m: acts on good to firm ground. *W. J. Reed* — 92

VITAL SCORE 7 b.g. Vital Season – Tia Song (Acrania) [1992/3 16d 17s 21v 17v c17s⁴ c21f³] close-coupled gelding: no sign of ability. *J. S. King* — c– –

VITAL WITNESS (CAN) 6 b.g. Val de L'Orne (FR) – Friendly Witness (USA) (Northern Dancer) [1992/3 16s⁴ 22s² 23s³ 24d² 22s² 21g 26m] leggy, workmanlike gelding: fairly useful handicap hurdler: should stay beyond 3m: acts on soft going. *K. A. Morgan* — 115

VITAL WONDER 5 ch.g. Vital Season – Honey Wonder (Winden) [1992/3 F16g F17f³ F17d²] half-brother to winning jumpers Honeydew Wonder (by Idiot's Delight) and Wonder Bee (by Grandiose), former a useful hurdler: dam unraced: placed in NH Flat races at Sandown in March and April: yet to race over hurdles or fences. *D. R. C. Elsworth* —

VIVA BELLA (FR) 6 b.g. Cap Martin (FR) – Moldau (FR) (Francois Saubaber) [1992/3 c24dᵖᵘ c25d⁶ c25sᵖᵘ c23d³ c21s* c27d² c27gᵘʳ c25sᵖᵘ c21m c24dᵖᵘ] leggy novice hurdler: won novice chase at Carlisle in January: poor efforts last 3 starts: stays 27f: acts on soft ground: often blinkered: sound jumper. *Mrs S. A. Bramall* — c94 —

VODKA FIZZ 8 ch.g. Don – Doon Royal (Ardoon) [1992/3 17v 17s 16v c21v² c18m* c21m³ c19f⁴] angular, workmanlike gelding: one-time fair hurdler: won novice chase at Fontwell in February: stays 21f: acts on heavy and good to firm going (ran poorly on firm). *J. T. Gifford* — c92 —

VOLCANIC DANCER (USA) 7 b.g. Northern Baby (CAN) – Salva (USA) (Secretariat (USA)) [1992/3 21v⁵ 21sᵖᵘ 24dʳᵗʳ] strong, compact gelding: fair staying hurdler in 1991/2: ran badly in 1992/3: blinkered once: refused to race final start: one to leave alone. *J. Mackie* — §

VOLPEDO (USA) 6 ch.g. Secreto (USA) – Votre Altesse (FR) (Riverman (USA)) [1992/3 21s³ 18d 22d] compact gelding: poor novice hurdler: stays 2¾m: acts on soft ground: sometimes wears tongue strap and a brush pricker. *R. J. Manning* —

VOMERO (NZ) 8 gr.m. Church Parade – Loobagh (NZ) (Polar Route (NZ)) [1992/3 19fᵖᵘ 22v⁴ 21v⁵ a20g* a20g⁴ a20g³] lengthy mare: modest hurdler: won maiden claimer at Lingfield in January: fell both starts over fences: stays 2¾m: acts on heavy going and equitrack: visored once: inconsistent and sometimes looks irresolute. *P. F. Nicholls* — c– 88 §

VULCAN BELLE 6 b.m. Royal Vulcan – Star Shell (Queen's Hussar) [1992/3 F16s] third foal: sister to Irish NH Flat race-placed Royal Mountbrowne: dam never ran: tailed off in NH Flat race at Nottingham in February: yet to race over hurdles or fences. *B. S. Rothwell* —

VULGAN WARRIOR 11 b.g. Vulgan Slave – Belgrave Queen (Sheshoon) [1992/3 c28gᵖᵘ c25m c25g] tall, lengthy gelding: fairly useful staying chaser in 1990/1: no form in 1992/3. *S. Christian* — c– —

VULPIN DE LAUGERE (FR) 6 b.g. Olmeto – Quisling II (FR) (Trenel (FR)) [1992/3 F16s 21g 20mᵖᵘ] tall, close-coupled gelding: showed nothing over hurdles. *Mrs S. A. Bramall* —

VULRORY'S CLOWN 15 b.g. Idiot's Delight – Vulrory (Vulgan) [1992/3 c25mᵘʳ c23s* c25dᶠ c22s³ c20g⁶ c19m* c20f³ c18sᵖᵘ c17m² c18g* c18f³] workmanlike gelding: modest chaser: won claimers at Market Rasen in September, Catterick in March and Stratford in May: effective at around 2m and stays 23f: acts on any going: usually a bold jumper: suited by forcing tactics: tends to sweat: genuine. *O. Brennan* — c90 —

W

WAAZA (USA) 4 b.g. Danzig Connection (USA) – Nishig (USA) (Naskra (USA)) [1992/3 17d 17g⁴ 16sᵖᵘ 17m⁴ 16f³] lengthy, good-topped gelding: poor performer at up to 11f on Flat nowadays: poor form over hurdles: acts on good to firm ground: flashes tail: blinkered third and fourth outings. *Miss L. C. Siddall* — 76

WABWOM 4 b.g. Dunbeath (USA) – Lunar Shamal-Gal (Tumble Wind (USA)) [1992/3 F16s aF16g 18mᵖᵘ] compact gelding: second foal: dam fair —

2-y-o 5f winner: no sign of ability: sold 1,800 gns Doncaster June Sales. *J. A. Glover*

WADELEY 6 br.g. Strong Gale – Shady Doorknocker (Mon Capitaine) [1992/3 22s4 26d* 21d3] workmanlike gelding with scope: won novice hurdle at Wolverhampton in February: creditable third at Carlisle 2 months later: likely to prove suited by a good test of st .mina: acts on dead ground: should improve. *J. A. C. Edwards*   101 p

WADSWICK COUNTRY 6 b.m. Sunyboy – Pollys Owen (Master Owen) [1992/3 F17v] third foal: dam, winning hurdler/chaser, stayed well: tailed off in NH Flat race at Hereford in November: yet to race over hurdles or fences. *R. Barton*

WAIT YOU THERE (USA) 8 b.g. Nureyev (USA) – Ma Mere L'Oie (FR) (Lightning (FR)) [1992/3 c 16s4 c20d] leggy gelding: fair chaser at best: ran badly in 1992/3: stays 25f, at least when conditions aren't testing: acts on any going. *H. Alexander*   c–
–

WAKASHAN 5 b.h. Dancing Brave (USA) – Lady Moon (Mill Reef (USA)) [1992/3 20s2 20v4 22s4 26g3] leggy, quite good-topped horse: has been hobdayed and had a soft palate and tie-back operations: novice hurdler: easily best effort in valuable event on third outing: sold 2,100 gns Ascot March Sales: stays 2¾m: probably best with plenty of give in the ground: wears tongue strap. *K. A. Morgan*   116 ?

WAKI GOLD (USA) 6 ch.g. Miswaki (USA) – Sainte Croix (USA) (Nijinsky (CAN)) [1992/3 16g 17d 16g c16g5] strong gelding: poor form in novice hurdles and on chasing debut: won over 1¼m on Flat in May. *R. J. Hodges*   c–
–

WALDORF T BEAGLE 7 b.g. Buckskin (FR) – Arctic Alice (Brave Invader (USA)) [1992/3 22s5 25d c24g2 c26gpu c26dF 27d4] lengthy gelding: poor novice hurdler/chaser: sold 1,050 gns Ascot May Sales: stays well: acts on soft ground and fibresand: blinkered final start. *C. R. Egerton*   c82
79

WALKERS POINT 7 b.g. Le Moss – Saltee Star (Arapaho) [1992/3 F21g 20g F18g3 F16g* 20g6 c18spu 18d 23m 20d5] ex-Irish gelding: won NH Flat race at Roscommon in August: no form over hurdles: showed nothing on chasing debut: trained until after seventh start by M. O'Toole. *J. A. C. Edwards*   c–
–

WALKING ON WATER 4 ch.g. Celestial Storm (USA) – Maiden Pool (Sharpen Up) [1992/3 17s3] fair at up to 1¼m on Flat (inconsistent and not an easy ride, goes well blinkered or visored): demoted after finishing second of 4 in early-season juvenile hurdle. *R. F. Johnson Houghton*   ?

WALKING SAINT 6 b.m. Godswalk (USA) – Saintly Tune (Welsh Saint) [1992/3 18m4 18m5 17m 17gpu 16d 18m4 17gpu 16dpu] neat mare: poor performer on Flat nowadays and over hurdles. *Graeme Roe*   61

WALK IN RHYTHM 12 b.g. Tower Walk – Maiden d'Or (Songedor) [1992/3 c19vpu] well-made gelding: hunter chaser: stays 25f: acts on firm and soft going. *Mrs A. Price*   c–
–

WALLANGRIFF 5 ch.g. Noalto – Concern (Brigadier Gerard) [1992/3 18spu 16vpu] workmanlike gelding: modest sprint winner at best on Flat: no promise over hurdles. *D. J. S. Cosgrove*   –

WALLISTRANO 6 br.g. Indian King (USA) – Kilistrano (Capistrano) [1992/3 22g6 16s4 20g] big gelding: chasing type: very lightly-raced novice hurdler: easily best effort when fourth at Ludlow in April: acts on soft ground. *John R. Upson*   81

WALLY WREKIN 10 ch.g. Peter Wrekin – Winning Venture (Eastern Venture) [1992/3 c25s2] compact gelding: second in maiden hunter chase at Hexham in April: stays 25f: acts on soft ground. *Mrs P. A. Powley*   c84
–

WALREDDON DOVE 5 b.m. Cruise Missile – Blue Heather (Langton Heath) [1992/3 F17v F17v6 22s5 21g 22m5] second foal by a thoroughbred stallion: dam unraced: poor form in novice hurdles. *S. C. Horn*   74

WALTON MELODY 6 ch.m. Kabour – Straight Melody (Highland Melody) [1992/3 21mpu 16spu] smallish, quite good-topped mare: third living foal: dam never ran: pulled up in novice hurdles. *P. Salmon* –

WALTON THORNS 5 b.g. Leading Man – Jacqueline Jane (David Jack) [1992/3 F14g2] half-brother to quite useful hurdler/chaser Silver Wind (by Broxted): dam unraced sister to fair chaser Dawn Breaker: gambled-on favourite, second in 19-runner NH Flat race at Market Rasen in April: yet to race over hurdles or fences. *C. R. Egerton*

WANG HOW 5 b.g. Nishapour (FR) – Killifreth (Jimmy Reppin) [1992/3 F16d5] fourth foal: half-brother to a 5f winner by Good Times: dam fairly useful 1½m winner: fifth of 20 finishers in NH Flat race at Hexham in March: yet to race over hurdles or fences. *C. W. Thornton*

WANNEROO (IRE) 4 b.g. Lord Ha Ha – Queen's Gala (Gala Performance (USA)) [1992/3 17g6] sparely-made gelding: first foal: dam unplaced in Irish NH Flat races: sixth in juvenile hurdle at Newcastle in November: dead. *R. R. Lamb* 80

WAR BEAT 5 b.g. Wolver Heights – Branitska (Mummy's Pet) [1992/3 20m3 22g* 20m3 20g a20gF a20g5 20m 24g5 16m] workmanlike, stocky gelding: modest form at best over hurdles: won novice event at Worcester in August: generally poor efforts afterwards: stays 2¾m: acts on good to firm and dead going and fibresand. *B. P. J. Baugh* 88 d

WAR COUNSEL (FR) 5 b.g. Leading Counsel (USA) – Tripolizza (FR) (Abdos) [1992/3 18d4 21d4 22gF] smallish gelding: retained 6,200 gns Doncaster November Sales: modest novice hurdler: stays 21f: acts on dead going. *Mrs D. Haine* 90

WAR DANCER 11 ch.g. Tug of War – Cacadors Polly (Juvenile Court) [1992/3 c16sF c16v5 c16vpu c17d5] good-topped gelding: winning hurdler: poor maiden chaser: best form at around 2m: acts on dead going. *M. Castell* c74 –

WARFIELD 6 b.g. Glint of Gold – Alys (Blakeney) [1992/3 17g] unfurnished ex-French gelding: second foal: dam French 1m to 1¼m winner: one-time useful stayer on Flat: eleventh of 20 in useful novice event at Newbury in February on hurdling debut: likely to do better. *P. F. Nicholls* – p

WAR HEAD 10 b.g. Warpath – Foil (Bleep-Bleep) [1992/3 c25spu c24g] workmanlike gelding: poor novice chaser. *M. D. Hammond* c– –

WARLEGGAN 12 br.g. Star Appeal – Dauphiness (Supreme Sovereign) [1992/3 c25m4 c26g* c26g6 c20dpu c26fF] leggy gelding: fair handicap chaser: won at Hereford in October: ran poorly afterwards: stays 3¼m: acts on firm and dead going. *G. A. Ham* c112 –

WARNER FORPLEASURE 7 b.g. Lighter – Gay Park (Pardigras) [1992/3 17spu c18g 22f* 24f 16s 22s4 c18m c16m] leggy gelding: modest hurdler: won seller at Worcester (no bid) in March: no form over fences: sold 1,650 gns Ascot June Sales: stays 2¾m: acts on firm and dead ground: usually blinkered. *P. J. Hobbs* c– 81

WARNER FOR WINNERS 7 b.g. Roman Warrior – Cala Conta (Deep Run) [1992/3 c25dpu c26vpu c26g* c26m6 c24m5 c21f*] strong, sturdy gelding: winning hurdler: successful in novice handicap chases at Plumpton and Warwick in the spring: stays 3¼m: probably acts on any going. *P. J. Hobbs* c91 –

WARNER'S END 12 ch.g. Legal Tender – Yoriet (Hornet) [1992/3 c21g6 c22s5] robust gelding: moderate handicap chaser: not raced after November: effective at around 2½m and stays well: acts on soft and good to firm going: front runner: blinkered nowadays. *J. Webber* c95 –

WARRIORS CODE 10 ch.g. Roman Warrior – Rose's Code (True Code) [1992/3 c16s4 a20g c26gF c25gR] lengthy, workmanlike gelding: winning staying hurdler (best form at Southwell): no form over fences: very temperamental. *D. T. Todd* c§§ –

WARRIOR'S PROMISE 8 ch.g. Mansingh (USA) – Pegs Promise (Tumble Wind (USA)) [1992/3 c21d c24m c24fᵖᵘ] rather sparely-made gelding: novice hurdler/chaser: blinkered final outing: unreliable at start: one to avoid. *D. L. Williams*　　**c§§**
　　§§

WASHAKIE 8 gr.g. Warpath – Super Satin (Lord of Verona) [1992/3 c24m* c25gᵘʳ] lengthy, good-topped gelding: winning hurdler: won hunter chase at Newcastle in March: will stay beyond 3m: acts on hard going. *F. T. Walton*　　**c93**
　　–

WASHINGTONCROSSING 7 ch.g. Over The River (FR) – Rather Grand (Will Somers) [1992/3 c18d³ c21dᶠ c21v* c21v* c20g*] strong, stocky gelding: maiden hurdler: progressive form when successful in good style in novice chases at Lingfield (2) and Newbury in second half of season (not raced after February): will stay much further than 21f: acts on heavy going: races prominently: jumps well: sure to win more races and is one to follow. *Andrew Turnell*　　**c117** P
　　–

WASSLS MILLION 7 b.g. Wassl – Black Crow (Sea Hawk II) [1992/3 16d 17g² 16s 17f³] small, sparely-made gelding: poor novice hurdler: trained until after second start by W. Price: raced only at around 2m: acts on firm going: tried blinkered. *T. Morton*　　69

WASTEOFTIME 6 ch.m. Le Bavard (FR) – Pirgo (Sweet Revenge) [1992/3 F16s a20gᵘʳ] angular mare: first foal: dam maiden hurdler/chaser: well beaten in NH Flat race in April: unseated rider first in novice hurdle following month. *E. T. Buckley*　　–

WATER CARRIER 6 b.g. Henbit (USA) – Aquaria (Double-U-Jay) [1992/3 17sᵖᵘ 17g 20dᵖᵘ] of little account: blinkered final outing. *W. G. Turner*　　–

Pell-mell Partners' "Washingtoncrossing"

WATERCOURSE 9 b.g. Henbit (USA) – Fountain (Reform) [1992/3 c27mᵖᵘ] leggy Irish gelding: one-time fairly useful hurdler: novice steeplechaser: tailed off when pulled up in valuable hunter chase at Cheltenham in March: stays 3m: acts on soft going, probably unsuited by a sound surface. *P. J. P. Doyle, Ireland*

c–
–

WATERFORD CASTLE 6 b.g. Le Bavard (FR) – Bob's Hansel (Prince Hansel) [1992/3 23s⁴ 20v⁵ 21g 21f² 23mᵖᵘ 24g] useful-looking gelding: brother to winning jumpers Habton Whin and That's Serious and half-brother to other winning jumpers, including fairly useful Its A Cracker (by Over The River): dam, from good jumping family, placed in bumpers: modest novice hurdler: stays 23f: probably acts on any going: may do better over fences. *N. A. Gaselee*

90

WATERLOO BOY 10 ch.g. Deep Run – Sapphire Red (Red Alert) [1992/3 c18d* c16s* c16s² c17g* c16m⁶ c20fᵖᵘ]

c159 ?
–

Part of the appeal of racing over jumps is that many of its top performers return year after year. Waterloo Boy is one who has become an 'old friend', a grand type who has been thoroughly genuine and reliable. However, he's now approaching the autumn of his career and backers should treat him with caution following poor runs in the Queen Mother Champion Chase and the Mumm Melling Chase, in the second of which he was pulled up after breaking blood vessels. Waterloo Boy had looked to have a good chance in the latest Queen Mother Champion Chase but ran as if something was amiss, jumping sketchily for him and being ridden along some way from home before trailing in a distant last of six finishers behind Deep Sensation. It was Waterloo Boy's fifth consecutive appearance at the Cheltenham Festival meeting, at which he had won the Arkle Challenge Trophy and been placed in three runnings of the Queen Mother Champion Chase. There'd been little in his record before Cheltenham to suggest Waterloo Boy's imminent fall from grace. He'd given a most uncharacteristic display—jumping badly—when going down by ten lengths to Katabatic in the Castleford Chase at Wetherby, but had won his three other races. He beat Katabatic in the Plymouth Gin Haldon Gold Cup at Exeter on his reappearance—his first victory over that horse in seven meetings—and

Game Spirit Chase, Newbury—
Waterloo Boy, Katabatic and Cyphrate in the order they finished

Mr M. R. Deeley's "Waterloo Boy"

beat him again, in receipt of 3 lb, in the Game Spirit Chase at Newbury in February, winning the race for the second year in a row. Waterloo Boy's other victory came in the Mitsubishi Shogun Tingle Creek Trophy, a valuable limited handicap at Sandown in December which he had also won the previous year. He put up a typically game performance under 12-0, looking to have it all on from three out, but responding magnificently under pressure to hold off his main challengers Deep Sensation, who received 21 lb, and Uncle Ernie, who received 10 lb, by two and a half lengths and a length. Waterloo Boy's victories in the latest season took his career tally over fences to fifteen; he's also won the Castleford Chase twice and the Victor Chandler Handicap.

		Pampered King	Prince Chevalier
	Deep Run	(b 1954)	Netherton Maid
	(ch 1966)	Trial By Fire	Court Martial
Waterloo Boy		(ch 1958)	Mitrailleuse
(ch.g. 1983)		Red Alert	Red God
	Sapphire Red	(ch 1971)	Ashton Jane
	(ch 1977)	Sapphire Lady	Majority Blue
		(b 1968)	Sayann

The compact, well-made Waterloo Boy was hobdayed before the 1991/2 season. A full account of his pedigree antecedents has been given in previous editions of *Chasers & Hurdlers*. Waterloo Boy's sire Deep Run gets winners over all distances but his unraced dam was sprint bred, by a Stewards' Cup winner out of a five-furlong winner. Waterloo Boy has made his name as a two-miler but has shown his form at two and a half. He is usually a good jumper and acts on any going. *D. Nicholson*

WATER ORCHID 8 b.g. Lafontaine (USA) – Johnnie's Lass (Menelek) [1992/3 c21spu c16spu] big, workmanlike gelding: moderate novice chaser at best: stays 2½m: acts on dead going. *D. McCain*   c–
–

WATERSFORD KNIGHT 7 b.g. Baron Blakeney – Golden Acorn c78
(Twelve Oaks) [1992/3 22v c18s⁴ c25d^F c25f c25g⁴ 21s^{pu}] workmanlike –
ex-Irish gelding: second foal: half-brother to a poor animal by Crooner: dam
never ran: poor maiden hurdler/chaser: dead. *J. W. Mullins*

WATERSMEET DOWN 10 ch.g. Carlburg – Brians Vulgan (Vulgan) c88
[1992/3 c25f⁵ c21g² c26g^{pu}] modest chaser at best: off course after October –
until distant third in a point in April: stays 3m: acts on hard going: usually
blinkered. *P. J. Hobbs*

WATERTIGHT (USA) 8 b.g. Affirmed (USA) – Brookward (USA) c90
(Stevward) [1992/3 c21d* c21v* c21s^F] rather leggy, sparely-made gelding: –
modest chaser: won handicaps at Sedgefield in October and Hexham in
November: stayed 3m: acted well on heavy going: dead. *Mrs M. Reveley*

WATSON HOUSE 5 b.g. Palm Track – Maydrum (Meldrum) [1992/3
17d 21g⁴ 24m⁴] leggy gelding: poor novice hurdler: probably stays 3m: acts 77
on heavy and good to firm ground. *B. Mactaggart*

WAVE HILL 4 b.g. Sizzling Melody – Trikymia (Final Straw) [1992/3
18g^{pu}] fairly useful miler on Flat, winner in June, 1993: pulled up in novice –
hurdle in April. *P. R. Hedger*

WAVE MASTER 6 b.g. Chief Singer – Sea Fret (Habat) [1992/3 17g
17v^{pu}] close-coupled gelding: 2m novice selling hurdler: ran badly in 1992/3: –
blinkered once. *R. J. Hodges*

WAVE TO ME 4 ch.g. Risk Me (FR) – Songs Jest (Song) [1992/3 18m^{pu}]
of little account: dead. *N. Tinkler* –

WAXING LYRICAL 6 b.m. Noalto – Honey To Spare (Track Spare)
[1992/3 18m^{pu}] leggy mare: lightly raced and of little account. *J. L. Eyre* –

WAY CLEAR 10 b.m. Bulldozer – Welsh Wise (Welsh Saint) [1992/3 c72
c25s³ c25d⁴ c26m^{ur}] leggy, sparely-made mare: novice hunter chaser: poor –
form in 1993: will stay beyond 25f: acts on dead and good to firm ground. *J.
Meddings*

WAYLON 5 b.g. Dunbeath (USA) – Heavenly Gaze (FR) (Gay Mecene
(USA)) [1992/3 F14d 17s^{pu} 17d^{pu}] pulled up both starts over hurdles, –
blinkered on second occasion. *J. J. O'Neill*

WAY OF LIFE (FR) 8 ch.g. No Lute (FR) – My Beloved (FR) c95
(Margouillat (FR)) [1992/3 c16d⁵ c21v² c16s⁴ c20m^{pu} c22f^F] tall, lengthy –
gelding: novice hurdler: modest chaser: form in 1992/3 only on second start:
will stay beyond 21f: acts on good to firm and heavy ground: sound jumper:
twice whipped round at start. *S. Mellor*

WAYSIDE 11 br.g. Smokey Rockett – Rosamond (Spiritus) [1992/3 c17d⁶ c–
c21m^{pu}] leggy gelding: poor novice hurdler/chaser: stays 25f: acts on firm –
going. *V. Thompson*

WAYWARD EDWARD 7 ch.g. Takachiho – Portate (Articulate) c–
[1992/3 c17f^F c16s⁵ 16d 16g⁵ 16d⁵ c25v^F 16s² 16s a22g² a22g⁶ c27g^F 24d⁴ 76
21g 22m² 22f 21g^{bd}] sparely-made gelding: poor novice hurdler: no form
over fences: stays 2¾m: acts on good to firm, soft going and fibresand:
blinkered last 3 outings. *Mrs S. Lamyman*

WAYWARD SON 4 gr.g. Risk Me (FR) – Mummy's Chick (Mummy's
Pet) [1992/3 16g^{pu} 16s 18v⁵ 17s^{pu} 17f^{pu}] of little account on Flat nowadays –
and over hurdles: trained by T. Etherington first 4 starts, blinkered final
one. *J. J. Bridger*

WAYWARD WIND 9 b.g. Rymer – Willow Wind (Tumble Wind (USA)) c–
[1992/3 c21g] leggy ex-Irish gelding: poor novice jumper. *B. A. McGarrigle* –

WEAPON EXHIBITION 6 ch.m. Exhibitioner – Weapon (Prince Ippi
(GER)) [1992/3 20m] leggy mare: poor novice hurdler: placed in points in –
1993: blinkered once. *G. A. Ham*

WEAREAGRANDMOTHER 6 b.m. Prince Tenderfoot (USA) – Lady
Bettina (Bustino) [1992/3 18d⁶ 18s²] leggy, sparely-made mare: poor 77

hurdler nowadays: finished lame final start (November): stays 2½m: possibly needs give in the ground: usually visored in 1991/2. *P. M. Rich*

WEARSIDE   5 ch.g. Noalto – Shela (Sheshoon) [1992/3 aF16g aF16g] third foal: dam of little account: tailed off in NH Flat races at Southwell: yet to race over hurdles or fences. *Denys Smith*

WEDNESDAYS AUCTION (IRE)   5 b.h. Mazaad – Happy Always (Lucky Wednesday) [1992/3 17d] lightly raced on Flat, modest 9f winner at best: sold out of B. Hanbury's stable 2,100 gns Newmarket Autumn Sales: tailed off in novice event in January on hurdling debut. *R. Rowe*   –

WEEKDAY CROSS (IRE)   5 b.g. Taufan (USA) – Isoldes Tower (Balliol) [1992/3 16d 17d6 16d3 16s3 17s4 a16g 17g* 17g2 17m4 16m2 17m6 17g2] good-bodied gelding: modest hurdler: won selling handicap at Fakenham (no bid) in February: races at around 2m: best efforts on a sound surface: usually held up. *J. R. Jenkins*   90

WEEKEND GIRL   4 b.f. Vorvados – Mrs Scattercash (Northfields (USA)) [1992/3 17mur 16d 17s a16g] small, sparely-made filly: probably of little account: sold 1,300 gns Malvern June Sales. *W. M. Brisbourne*   –

WEE MACGREGOR   5 ch.g. Gypsy Castle – Secret Storm (Secret Ace) [1992/3 F17m F17s 16g 23d] small, lightly-made gelding: second live foal: dam unraced: tailed off in novice hurdles. *L. Lungo*   –

WEE WILLIE DICKINS   6 b.g. Homeboy – Time of Your Life (Mount Hagen (FR)) [1992/3 F16d 17s6 16v] angular, workmanlike gelding: has scope: half-brother to Charlie Dickins (by Free State), a winner on Flat and over hurdles: dam never ran: behind in NH Flat race and novice hurdles. *S. Mellor*   –

WEE WIZARD (IRE)   4 br.g. Tender King – Zanskar (Godswalk (USA)) [1992/3 16g 16d6 16g3 16g 16d3 16s6 16s4 16s2 16d3 16g3 16s* 18d2] poor maiden on Flat: modest form over hurdles: trained until after eighth start by P. O'Leary: won juvenile event at Wetherby in April: ran well in handicap next time: will stay beyond 2¼m: acts on soft going. *M. A. Barnes*   91

WEIGHT PROBLEM   16 ch.g. Proverb – Queen of Killonan (Ossian II) [1992/3 c25dpu] sturdy gelding: poor staying chaser: usually blinkered or visored. *P. J. Bevan*   c– –

WEIRPOOL   11 ch.g. Le Bavard (FR) – Vulplume (Vulgan) [1992/3 c20gpu] rangy gelding: fair staying chaser at best: no form since 1989/90. *Mrs S. Clarke*   c– –

WELCOME TIDINGS   9 b.m. Record Run – Glanfield (Eborneezer) [1992/3 c17v4 c18v4] tall, leggy mare: poor novice chaser at best. *M. J. Bolton*   c– –

WELKNOWN CHARACTER   11 b.g. Reformed Character – Daybrook Venture (Daybrook Lad) [1992/3 c21g* c26d2 c21g2 c25d* c26d4 c21d5 c21m2 c22fF c26dpu] smallish gelding: fairly useful handicap chaser: won at Wincanton and Ascot in first half of season: ran very well seventh start (March): effective at 21f to 3¼m: acts on firm and dead ground: blinkered once: jumps well: usually races prominently. *P. F. Nicholls*   c119 –

WELL AND TRULY   6 b.m. Rousillon (USA) – Altana (Grundy) [1992/3 17s4] sparely-made mare: novice hurdler: stays 2½m: acts on dead, good to firm ground and equitrack: 1½m winner on Flat in January. *B. A. McMahon*   –

WELLANE BOY (IRE)   5 ch.g. Orchestra – Marians Pride (Pry) [1992/3 17s5 20s 25d] leggy gelding: first foal: dam winning hurdler/chaser at up to 3m in Ireland: no worthwhile form in novice hurdles. *Martyn Meade*   –

WELL BRIEFED   6 br.g. Miner's Lamp – In Brief (Lucky Brief) [1992/3 c21mpu] sturdy, compact gelding: fair hurdler: pulled up in novice event in September on chasing debut: sold 4,400 gns in May: stays 3m when conditions aren't testing: acts on firm going and probably unsuited by soft. *W. A. Stephenson*   c– –

WELL DELAYED 8 br.m. Kambalda – Candy Slam (Candy Cane) [1992/3 c25g³] sparely-made mare: fair pointer: poor form in novice hunter chases: will stay long distances: acts on dead going. *C. W. Sanders*   c65

WELL DONE RORY 4 b.g. Homeboy – Star Flower (Star Appeal) [1992/3 17d⁶ 16f⁶ 16m² 18v* 18m*] small, leggy gelding: soundly beaten on Flat: won late-season juvenile hurdles at Cartmel (maiden) and Market Rasen (seller, bought in 3,000 gns): will stay at least 2½m: acts on heavy and good to firm ground. *J. White*   89

WELLINGTON BROWN 9 b.g. Faraway Times (USA) – Chevulgan (Cheval) [1992/3 c22dᵖᵘ] leggy, good-topped gelding: very useful hunter chaser in 1992: ran poorly in February (including in a point): stays 25f: acts well on a firm surface. *Mrs H. Trigg*   c– –

WELLWOTDOUTHINK 7 b.m. Rymer – Doubly Royal (Royal Buck) [1992/3 16g*] angular, workmanlike mare: won 3 NH Flat races in 1991/2 and 7-runner novice hurdle at Ayr in November: created most favourable impression when accounting for Frickley by 7 lengths at Ayr, jumping fast and fluently and scoring with consummate ease: kept off course by viral infection afterwards: a very exciting prospect, sure to win more races. *Mrs M. Reveley*   92 P

WELL WRAPPED 9 b.g. Arapaho – Arctic Amoroso (Arctic Slave) [1992/3 c21d* c21g* c21d*] lengthy gelding: fairly useful handicap chaser: won at Southwell and Wolverhampton (twice) in the autumn: effective around 2½m, should stay 3m: acts on soft going: front runner: jumps very well. *Miss H. C. Knight*   c127 –

WELSH BARD 9 b.g. Welsh Saint – Songorella (Song) [1992/3 c17vᵘʳ c16s³ c16s² c16s³ c17s⁴ c16vF] leggy, good-topped gelding: fairly useful chaser on his day: best at 2m: acts on heavy and good to firm ground: tried visored and blinkered. *C. P. E. Brooks*   c124 –

WELSH COMMANDER 10 b.g. Welsh Chanter – Black Barret (Bargello) [1992/3 c21f²] sturdy, workmanlike gelding: moderate hurdler/novice chaser: finished lame in 2-runner race in March: suited by test of stamina: best form on good going: blinkered once. *T. J. Etherington*   c?

WELSH COTTAGE 6 b.h. Balinger – Sunny Cottage (Sunyboy) [1992/3 16g 22v⁴ 22vF 22m³ 22g²] deep-girthed horse: modest novice hurdler: will stay beyond 2¾m: acts on heavy going. *J. T. Gifford*   91

The Rip Handicap Chase, Ascot—Welknown Character leads throughout

WELSH LUSTRE (IRE) 4 b.f. Mandalus – Grease Pot (Gala Performance (USA)) [1992/3 F17g³ F16s³ F17m⁶] lengthy filly: third foal: dam lightly-raced sister to very useful staying chaser Greasepaint: showed ability in all 3 NH Flat races in the spring: yet to race over hurdles. *D. Nicholson*

WELSHMAN 7 ch.g. Final Straw – Joie de Galles (Welsh Pageant) [1992/3 17g² 17d⁴ 22v 21dᵖᵘ 20f3] compact gelding: quite useful handicap hurdler: creditable efforts when placed in 1992/3: should stay beyond 21f: acts on heavy and good to firm going: tough and game. *M. Blanshard* — 129

WELSHMAN'S GULLY 9 ch.g. Jasmine Star – Malibu Lady (Ragapan) [1992/3 c21m*] workmanlike gelding: novice hurdler: won novice hunter chase at Folkestone in May: should stay beyond 21f: acts on good to firm going. *Mrs D. B. A. Silk* — c80 –

WELSH SINGER 7 ch.g. Celtic Cone – Madam Butterfly (Deep Run) [1992/3 17d² F17s* 19m³ 18f* 17g³ 17d² 17s⁶ 16s² 16d⁶ 18m⁴ 18g⁴] sturdy, lengthy gelding: won NH Flat race at Tralee in August and novice hurdle at Fontwell in October: ran creditably when placed afterwards: stays 19f: probably acts on any going: blinkered twice. *P. R. Hedger* — 95

WENDY JANE 8 b.m. Relkino – Syltung (Shantung) [1992/3 c21m] modest pointer: behind in novice hunter chase in May. *J. Best* — c–

WENLOCK SCALLY 5 gr.m. Scallywag – Mountainette (Peter Wrekin) [1992/3 F16d F16sᵖᵘ] good-topped mare: fourth foal: half-sister to novice selling hurdler Ricardo Boots (by Remainder Man): dam half-sister to a winning hurdler: little sign of ability in NH Flat races: dead. *J. H. Peacock* — –

WENRISC 6 ch.m. Boreen (FR) – Right Chimes (Even Money) [1992/3 21v⁵ 21v⁵ 22d 21v⁵ 26g⁶] workmanlike mare: poor novice hurdler: stays 21f: best efforts on heavy ground. *D. Nicholson* — 77

WENSLEYDALE WILLIAM 7 ch.g. Tudorville – Kingsfold Flash (Warpath) [1992/3 21dᵖᵘ] workmanlike gelding: winning hurdler: once-raced over fences: sold 1,320 gns Doncaster November Sales, resold 1,750 gns same venue in May: suited by around 2½m: best form on dead ground: blinkered once. *C. W. Thornton* — c– –

WESSEX WARRIOR 7 b.g. Anfield – Achiever (Tarqogan) [1992/3 18d⁴ 16g⁵ 19gᵖᵘ a20g⁴ a20g a16gᵖᵘ 17f* 20m² 16vᵖᵘ 17m] deep-girthed gelding: modest hurdler: no bid after winning selling handicap at Lingfield in March: ran very well next time: stays 2½m: best form on top-of-the-ground. *D. R. Laing* — 98

WEST AUCKLAND 4 br.g. Silly Prices – Elitist (Keren) [1992/3 16dF 17dᵖᵘ 16d] no sign of ability on Flat or over hurdles. *N. Chamberlain* — –

WEST BAY 7 b.g. Kemal (FR) – Northern Push (Push On) [1992/3 18s 21s⁶ 22dʳᵒ 18v⁵ a20g² a18gᵖᵘ 18g 20m⁵ 22f*] compact gelding: poor hurdler: won amateurs novice handicap at Worcester in May: stays 2¾m: acts on any going: temperamental (has run out). *T. Thomson Jones* — 78 §

WEST ENDER 10 gr.g. Pongee – Three Oaks (Drumbeg) [1992/3 c25g* c24g* c26s² c25s* c21s* c24m] lengthy, workmanlike gelding: fair handicap chaser: won twice at both Market Rasen and Huntingdon in first half of season: ran poorly final start (January): effective at around 2½m and stays 3¼m: acts on good to firm and soft ground: suited by forcing tactics: jumps soundly. *J. M. Jefferson* — c113 –

WESTERN DANCER 12 b.g. Free State – Polyandrist (Polic) [1992/3 23s 20s 23v³ 22g] compact gelding: lightly-raced novice hurdler: stays 23f: acts on heavy going. *C. A. Horgan* — 84

WESTERN DIVIDE (USA) 8 b.g. Sharpen Up – River Nile (USA) (Damascus (USA)) [1992/3 17d 16g] small, stocky gelding: winning 2m selling hurdler: no form since 1989/90: tried blinkered. *J. Perrett* — –

WESTERN LEGEND 9 ch.g. Proverb – Calamity Jane (Never Dwell) [1992/3 c26dᵖᵘ c21v⁵ c21s⁴ c21g* c22g² c22f⁶] workmanlike gelding: fairly — c115 –

useful chaser: won amateurs handicap at Wincanton in February: fair efforts afterwards: stays 2¾m: acts on soft and good to firm going: forces pace: sometimes breaks blood vessels. *P. F. Nicholls*

WESTERN TRUCE   10 b.g. Genuine – Wesco (Golden Love) [1992/3 c20gpu c25gpu c25mpu] workmanlike gelding: winning chaser in Ireland: no form in Britain: blinkered final outing. *J. Webber*   c–

WESTHOLME (USA)   5 ch.g. Lyphard's Wish (FR) – Shroud (USA) (Vaguely Noble) [1992/3 16d⁴ 17d² 16s⁵ 17s⁴] lengthy, sparely-made gelding: fair middle-distance performer on Flat: modest novice hurdler: will stay beyond 17f: acts on soft ground: ungenuine. *M. H. Easterby*   94 §

WEST LODGE LADY   8 ch.m. Crooner – Rose of France (Grand Roi) [1992/3 22v⁴ c20m³] small, angular mare: no form over hurdles or in a novice chase: twice blinkered. *N. B. Thomson*   c–

WEST MONKTON   7 ch.g. Croghan Hill – Cora Gold (Goldhill) [1992/3 18mur 18gpu a20g 18d 22f] sparely-made gelding: novice hurdler, poor at best: trained until after third start by T. Forster. *C. T. Nash*   –

WEST ORIENT   8 b.g. Strong Gale – Bean Giolla (Giolla Mear) [1992/3 20g⁵ 16s 20mro 22spu c16gF c16v³ c16s⁶ c16mF] rangy gelding: lightly-raced novice hurdler, poor form: modest novice at best over fences: pulls hard and forces pace (will probably prove best at around 2m): acts on heavy ground: ran out once. *Mrs H. Parrott*   c93 ?

WEST STREET   9 br.g. Arapaho – Paddys Flyer (Paddy's Stream) [1992/3 c21m* c21g* c24g⁵] quite good-topped gelding: fairly useful hunter chaser: successful in novice events at Warwick and Uttoxeter in May: stays 3m: acts on good to firm ground: front runner. *Richard Mathias*   c95

WESTWARD DRIFT   8 ch.g. Paddy's Stream – Quay Blues (Quayside) [1992/3 c20gpu c24gpu] leggy, lengthy gelding: seems of little account. *F. Jestin*   c–

WESTWELL BOY   7 b.g. Kambalda – Lady Ashton (Anthony) [1992/3 c23gF c22sF c24gpu 28g⁴ 25sF 25m] big, rangy, good sort: modest hurdler: no form over fences: best form short of 3m on a sound surface. *P. Beaumont*   c–

WEST WITH THE WIND   6 b. or br.g. Glint of Gold – Mighty Fly (Comedy Star (USA)) [1992/3 21g⁵ 18d⁴ 16g⁵ 17d² 16g 16s 20d] strong gelding: moderate handicap hurdler: stays 2½m: acts on soft and good to firm going. *M. Dods*   98

WETANDRY   8 b.g. Foggy Bell – Fair Ches (Pedigree Unknown) [1992/3 17dpu 20m⁴ 16vpu 16vpu] of no account. *C. H. Jones*   –

WHAAT FETTLE   8 br.g. Strong Gale – Double Century (Double-U-Jay) [1992/3 c24d³ c25g* c25g* c25g* c25d² c28s² c28d* c28d⁴ c33gur c28g⁴ c34dpu c33g c23d³] lengthy gelding: has been hobdayed: fairly useful chaser: won 4 handicaps at Kelso in first half of season: every chance when unseating rider 2 out in valuable event at Newcastle in February: ran poorly last 4 starts: stays 4m: acts on soft and good to firm ground: front runner: jumps soundly. *G. Richards*   c123

WHASSAT   9 b.g. Saher – Whisht (Raise You Ten) [1992/3 17dpu] sturdy, good-bodied gelding: poor hurdler: ran badly early in season: best form at around 2m: acts on good to firm ground. *M. P. Muggeridge*   –

WHAT A CARD   5 b.m. Myjinski (USA) – Ventrex (Henry The Seventh) [1992/3 18m] small, sparely-made mare: novice selling hurdler: best form at 2m: acts on hard ground and fibresand: visored once. *R. Johnson*   –

WHAT A MISS   6 ch.m. Move Off – Vinovia (Ribston) [1992/3 17m⁶ 18g 18g³] leggy, lightly-made mare: first sign of ability when third in claiming hurdle at Kelso in October: sold 3,400 gns in May. *W. A. Stephenson*   80

WHAT A NOBLE   7 ch.g. Deep Run – What A Duchess (Bargello) [1992/3 24m 19m³ 20g³ 19m² 23g⁶ 24s⁴ 23v² 25d⁵] sparely-made gelding: sixth foal: half-brother to winning jumpers Eastshaw and Social Climber (both by Crash Course), former useful: dam unraced, from excellent jumping family, including L'Escargot: modest novice hurdler: trained until   98 fourth outing by A. L. T. Moore in Ireland: easily best effort in Britain second at Folkestone in January: stays well: acts on good to firm and heavy ground. *T. J. Etherington*

WHAT A TO DO 9 b.g. Le Bavard (FR) – Alfie's Wish (Three Wishes) [1992/3 c26g⁴ c22s⁴ c24s⁴ c27v* c26vᵘʳ] close-coupled gelding: maiden hurdler: lightly-raced modest chaser: won amateurs handicap at Fontwell in January: out-and-out stayer: acts on heavy going. *Capt. T. A. Forster*   c92

WHATCOMESNATURALLY (USA) 4 ch.f. Arctic Tern (USA) – Reina Real (ARG) (Escudo Real) [1992/3 18g⁵ 18s² 16m⁴ 18d⁶ 17s⁴ 20d 22g] poor maiden on Flat: sold out of J. Hills's stable 2,600 gns Newmarket July Sales: poor juvenile hurdler: trained until after third outing by M. Chapman: should be suited by further than 2¼m: acts on good to firm and soft ground. *M. D. Hammond*   83

WHAT DO YOU THINK 5 ch.m. Battle Hymn – Kimble Girl (Some Hand) [1992/3 F16s F16g] second foal: dam placed over 5f at 2 yrs: well beaten in NH Flat races: yet to race over hurdles or fences. *G. Thorner*

WHATEVER YOU LIKE 9 b.g. Deep Run – Garravogue (Giolla Mear) [1992/3 c16s* c16v⁴ c17m c18d³] tall gelding: fairly useful handicap chaser: won at Warwick in November: ran poorly next 2 starts, fair effort final one: sold to join P. Nicholls 12,500 gns Doncaster May Sales: effective at 2m and stays 2½m: acts on soft going: sometimes wears a tongue strap. *N. J. Henderson*   c124

WHAT IF 9 ch.m. Nicholas Bill – Starproof (Comedy Star (USA)) [1992/3 16s* 16g⁵ 17m⁴ 16v* 21m⁶ 16mᵖᵘ] leggy, close-coupled mare: modest hurdler: won claimer at Nottingham in February and handicap at Towcester in April: pulled up reportedly lame final start: fell both outings in novice chases: effective at 2m, barely stays 2¾m: probably acts on any going: sometimes breaks blood vessels. *O. Brennan*   c– 98

WHATMORECANIASKFOR (IRE) 5 ch.m. Le Bavard (FR) – Blackrath Girl (Bargello) [1992/3 16s 16s 17v 16d 20s 21gᵖᵘ 22s⁵ 20mᶠ] sparely-made mare: fourth foal: sister to a novice jumper and half-sister to 2 others: dam unraced: poor novice hurdler: best effort over 2m on soft ground: visored last 2 outings. *G. F. H. Charles-Jones*   63

WHAT'S IN ORBIT 8 br.g. Strong Gale – Jet Travel (Deep Run) [1992/3 c17g² c16gᶠ c16d² c19d²] rather leggy, good-topped ex-Irish gelding: novice hurdler: fair novice chaser: not raced after November: stays 19f: acts on heavy ground: blinkered last 2 starts: sketchy jumper: rather temperamental. *P. F. Nicholls*   c107

WHATS THE CRACK 10 b.g. The Parson – Mighty Crack (Deep Run) [1992/3 c26d³] angular gelding: useful chaser: creditable third in handicap at Cheltenham in September: should stay further than 3¼m: acts on good to firm and dead ground: sometimes hangs under pressure: sound jumper: blinkered twice. *D. Nicholson*   c136

WHATS YOUR PROBLEM 10 b.g. Buckskin (FR) – Laurenca (Laurence O) [1992/3 c24d⁵ c19s⁵ c21g³ c20dᵖᵘ] lengthy, good sort: fair handicap chaser: stays 3m: acts on soft going, ran poorly on good to firm. *Miss H. C. Knight*   c100

WHEAL PROSPER 8 b.g. Strong Gale – Kells Bay (Deep Run) [1992/3 c27vᶠ c21v³ c24vᵖᵘ c30sᵖᵘ] sturdy, lengthy gelding: fair pointer in 1992: lightly raced in steeplechases: would have won novice event at Newton Abbot in December but for falling last: no form afterwards: stays 27f: acts on heavy ground. *P. F. Nicholls*   c87 ?

WHEELER'S WONDER (IRE) 4 br.f. Sure Blade (USA) – Querida (Habitat) [1992/3 17vᵘʳ 17s 16d² 16g⁵ 16m* 16m² 17s*] small, leggy filly: poor maiden on Flat: sold out of N. Wright's stable 800 gns Newmarket Autumn Sales: won novice hurdles at Wincanton (claimer) and Chepstow (3-runner event) in the spring: will prove best at around 2m: has won on good to firm going, easily best form on soft: amateur ridden. *B. J. Llewellyn*   109

WHEELIES NEWMEMBER 10 ch.g. New Member – Idyll-Liquor c85
(Narrator) [1992/3 c2 1m² c20f³ c25g⁶ c21gᵘʳ] leggy gelding: hunter chaser: –
stays 2 1f: acts on hard ground. *Mrs A. Hamilton*

WHERE ARE WE 7 b. or br.g. Cure The Blues (USA) – Kachela
(Kalamoun) [1992/3 22sᵖᵘ 16dᵖᵘ 16f 17f 17g] angular ex-Irish gelding: –
second foal: half-brother to a winner in Sweden by Bold Lad: dam well
beaten on Flat: poor maiden on Flat and over hurdles. *D. L. Williams*

WHERES YU TOO 6 ch.g. Blushing Scribe (USA) – Golderama (Golden
Dipper) [1992/3 a16g a22gᵖᵘ] probably of little account. *P. R. Rodford* –

WHICH WAY NOW 12 b.g. Mandamus – Manimay (Manicou) [1992/3 c96
c24v⁵ c26d5 c26m² c26g⁶] rangy gelding: fairly useful hunter chaser: stays –
3¼m: possibly unsuited by heavy going, acts on any other. *Mrs S. Clarke*

WHIPPERS DELIGHT (IRE) 5 ch.g. King Persian – Crashing Juno
(Crash Course) [1992/3 17d⁴ 16v⁴ 20v 18s² 17v² a16g² a16g² a16g² a18g² 101
16d* 16d4] leggy gelding: fair hurdler: improved form when winning claimer
at Uttoxeter in March: form only at around 2m: acts on heavy ground and
equitrack: races with zest and makes running: jumps well: splendidly tough
and genuine. *G. F. H. Charles-Jones*

WHIRLING CONE 8 b.g. Celtic Cone – Toumanova (High Line) c91
[1992/3 c25gᶠ c20d² c20g²] workmanlike gelding: novice hurdler/chaser: –
stayed 2½m: acted on dead ground: dead. *B. S. Rothwell*

WHISKEY BLUES 8 b.g. Cure The Blues (USA) – Ozone (Auction c–
Ring (USA)) [1992/3 17g 17d 17d 16s⁶ 17sᵖᵘ a16g³ a16g⁵ a18g a18g 17g⁵ 17d 68
c17g⁴ c23mᵖᵘ c2 1fᵖᵘ 17g⁶] leggy gelding: poor hurdler: showed nothing over
fences: best at around 2m: acts on firm ground and fibresand: sometimes
blinkered. *B. Richmond*

WHISKY RYE 6 b.g. Rymer – Upham Reunion (Paridel) [1992/3 16s]
rather unfurnished gelding: tailed off in NH Flat races and a novice hurdle. –
S. E. Sherwood

WHISPERING STEEL 7 b.g. Furry Glen – Shady Grove (Deep Run) c120 P
[1992/3 c 16g⁶ c24d* c20s* c24d* c20s* c25d*]

The strength in depth of chasing talent trained in the North hasn't
been greater since the heady days of the late-'seventies and early-'eighties
when Peter Easterby and Michael Dickinson each won three trainers'
championships. Gold Cup winner Jodami and the top staying novice Cab On
Target will continue to provide formidable opposition for the big southern
yards in the championship races. And it wouldn't be a surprise if Whispering
Steel, who missed his intended engagement in the Sun Alliance Chase
because of the firmish going, gave the North another good-class performer
in the next season. Whispering Steel wasn't seen out after an impressive
win in the West of Scotland Pattern Novices' Chase at Ayr at the end of
January, a victory which extended his winning sequence to five. He'd looked
more impressive with every race—his earlier victories coming in novice
chases and an Arlington qualifier, all at Haydock—and had gone from
looking 'an above-average novice' to 'a most promising recruit'. Whispering
Steel's form—he beat Candy Tuff by three lengths at Ayr—left him with
plenty to find against some of those he'd have taken on at the Cheltenham
Festival. But he'd given the impression in most of his races of having a good
deal in reserve and looked sure to go on to much better things. His sound,
bold jumping was another thing likely to stand him in good stead against the
best of the southern novices. Whispering Steel now looks well-nigh certain
to show much improved form in the next season and is very much one to
keep on the right side. Front-running Whispering Steel stays well and acts
on soft going, but he doesn't *need* a thorough test of stamina to be seen to
best advantage and is capable of winning races at two and a half miles.

The workmanlike Whispering Steel is very much a chasing type on
looks, though he still retains a rather leggy appearance. Whispering Steel is
bred for jumping too, by the successful sire Furry Glen out of the unraced
Deep Run mare Shady Grove, and he was bought for 12,500 guineas as an

Arlington Premier Series Chase (Qualifier), Haydock—
Whispering Steel's fourth win in a row over the course

Whispering Steel (b.g. 1986)	Furry Glen (b 1971)	Wolver Hollow (b 1964)	Sovereign Path
			Cygnet
		Cleftess (br 1956)	Hill Gail
			Cleft
	Shady Grove (ch 1980)	Deep Run (ch 1966)	Pampered King
			Trial By Fire
		Land (b 1968)	Baldric II
			Queen of Helena

unbroken three-year-old at the prestigious Derby Sale. Whispering Steel is Shady Grove's second foal, her first, also by Furry Glen, being the Irish two-and-a-half-mile chase winner Knox Court. Whispering Steel's grandam Land bred numerous winners including Major Land, a winner on the Flat and over jumps in Italy, Tisdall's Grove, a fairly useful winner on the Flat and successful over hurdles in Ireland, and the fair handicap chaser Mountebor. *G. Richards*

WHISTLE BLOWER   8 ch.g. Le Bavard (FR) – Grangeclare Lady (Menelek) [1992/3 c24s³ c26vᵖᵘ c21dᵖᵘ] tall, lengthy gelding: modest novice chaser: stays 3m: acts on soft ground: sometimes breaks blood vessels. *Miss H. C. Knight*   c82 –

WHISTLING BUCK (IRE)   5 br.g. Whistling Deer – Buck Ends (Master Buck) [1992/3 F17d³ F16d* F17s F17m] tall, narrow gelding: first foal: dam winning Irish hurdler: won NH Flat race at Ludlow in December: well beaten in better races afterwards: yet to race over hurdles or fences. *R. Rowe*

WHITE DIAMOND   5 b.g. Touching Wood (USA) – Dimant Blanche (USA) (Gummo (USA)) [1992/3 F17m* F16g³ F17m] lengthy gelding: second foal: dam 5f winner: won NH Flat race at Carlisle in October: third in similar event at Catterick 5 months later: yet to race over hurdles or fences. *Mrs A. Swinbank*

WHITEWEBB 6 br.g. Carwhite – Mrs Webb (Sonnen Gold) [1992/3 16g⁴ 16s* 16d 16s 16d⁵ 20m² 16s⁴ 18m³ 16g*] leggy, sparely-made gelding: modest handicap hurdler: won at Catterick in December and Hexham in May: suited by stiff test at 2m and should stay at least 2½m: acts on soft and good to firm ground: mainly visored in 1991/2 and was on sixth and seventh outings. *B. W. Murray* 88

WHITWOOD 8 b.g. Hasty Word – Minetta (Neron) [1992/3 c20d* c20dᵖᵘ] strong gelding: lightly raced: fair hurdler: won novice chase at Market Rasen in November: broke blood vessel later in month: will stay 3m: acts on soft going. *Mrs M. Reveley* c102 –

WHITWORTH GREY 5 gr.g. Marching On – Grey Morley (Pongee) [1992/3 16m 16d⁶ 17s⁵ 22sᵖᵘ] lengthy, angular gelding: plating-class maiden on Flat and over hurdles: blinkered/visored last 2 starts. *M. Dods* –

WHO'S IN CHARGE 9 b.g. Proverb – I'm Grannie (Perspex) [1992/3 c18m c21f⁶ c21f² c24d⁵ c17g⁵ c17d] big, rangy gelding: unenthusiastic and inconsistent staying chaser: retained 1,450 gns Doncaster May Sales. *G. M. R. Coatsworth* c85 §

WHO SIR 7 br.g. Callernish – Ingenious (Indigenous) [1992/3 21s⁶ 25d⁵ 21d⁵ 24s⁴] strong, sturdy gelding: chasing type: poor form in novice hurdles: stays 25f: acts on soft ground. *J. J. O'Neill* 78

WHO'S NEXT 5 b.g. Oats – Kaotesse (Djakao (FR)) [1992/3 20v³] workmanlike gelding with scope: NH Flat race winner: poor form in 2 races over hurdles. *J. R. Jenkins* 65

WHO'S TEF (IRE) 5 b.g. Muscatite – Eternal Optimist (Relko) [1992/3 18s⁴ 18m* 17f* 16g³] sparely-made gelding: modest handicapper on Flat, stays 1¼m: won maiden hurdle at Market Rasen and novice event at Huntingdon in May: yet to race beyond 2¼m: acts on firm going. *M. H. Easterby* 106

WHOSTHAT 7 b.g. Politico (USA) – Muffler (Haris II) [1992/3 26sᵖᵘ] leggy gelding: half-brother to winning pointers Granger (by Grangerullah) and Miss Mufsi (by One Day Soon): dam third in novice hurdle: no sign of ability in novice hurdle in January on debut. *R. R. Lamb* –

WHY NOT EQUINAME 5 ch.g. Buckskin (FR) – Rednael (Leander) [1992/3 23g 16d⁶ 16g⁶ 21d] long-backed gelding: poor novice hurdler: should stay further than 2m: best effort on good ground. *J. H. Johnson* 75

WHY NOT FLOPSY 8 b.m. Quayside – Realinda (Realm) [1992/3 c27gᵖᵘ] workmanlike mare: little sign of ability. *A. Charles-Jones* c–

WHY RUN 8 ch.h. Le Moss – Why Ask (Deep Run) [1992/3 c26dᵘʳ c22vᵖᵘ] good-topped horse: winning hurdler: showed nothing in novice chases: should stay beyond 2¹f: acts on soft going. *D. J. G. Murray-Smith* c– –

WHY SO HASTY 12 b.g. Proverb – Well Caught (Golden Vision) [1992/3 F10d 17s⁶ 22s c33v⁴ c28s³ c23d² c24vᵖᵘ c25s] leggy, sparely-made gelding: maiden hurdler: modest handicap chaser: stays well: acts on any going. *M. C. Chapman* c91

WIBBLE-WABBLE 7 ch.g. Longleat (USA) – Ebb And Flo (Forlorn River) [1992/3 c23dᶠ c26mᵘʳ c21gᵖᵘ c19vᵖᵘ] lengthy, workmanlike gelding: no sign of ability over hurdles or fences: sold 1,100 gns Doncaster August Sales: poor jumper of fences. *F. L. Matthews* c– x –

WICKET 8 b.m. Deep Run – Knock Off (Arctic Slave) [1992/3 c21s* c23gᶠ c21d³ 22s³ 25g⁶ 21f c25mᵘʳ c22gᴿ] smallish, sturdy mare: fair handicap hurdler: won novice chase at Worcester in February: refused first final outing: stays 25f: probably acts on any going. *M. J. Wilkinson* c90 106

WICKFIELD LAD 10 gr.g. Owen Anthony – Dumbella (Dumbarnie) [1992/3 17v 17v 22s a20g⁴ a22g⁵ 23d⁶ c17f² c20fᵘʳ c19m³ c20s⁵ c18gᵖᵘ c18f] smallish, lengthy gelding: poor novice hurdler/chaser: stays 2½m: acts on firm going and equitrack. *D. J. Deacon* c82 71

WICKFIELD SINGER 4 b.c. Chief Singer – Peaceful (Crepello) [1992/3 F16s³ F16g] half-brother to 4 Flat winners, including Denston (by

Moulton), also a winning hurdler/chaser, and to winning pointer Crown Eyeglass (by Niniski): dam, from excellent Flat family, fairly useful winner at up to 1¼m: third in NH Flat race at Ludlow in January: soundly beaten in similar race at Kempton following month: yet to race over hurdles. *N. A. Twiston-Davies*

WICK POUND   7 b.g. Niniski (USA) – Hors Serie (USA) (Vaguely Noble) [1992/3 c19m³ c21du c21d* c20d⁴ c20mF c21g² c21d* c24mF c18gF] sparely-made gelding: fair hurdler: won novice chases at Kempton in October and Wincanton in April: suited by around 2½m: acts on dead ground, particularly well on equitrack: best in blinkers: sketchy jumper of fences. *J. A. B. Old*   c108 –

WIDE BOY   11 b.g. Decoy Boy – Wide of The Mark (Gulf Pearl) [1992/3 c17gF c16g⁴ c17d² c16d³ c18v² c20s² c17s² c21s* c20s² c18d4] smallish, strong gelding: fairly useful handicap chaser: dead-heated at Worcester in March: stays 2 1f: probably acts on any going: usually jumps well. *P. J. Hobbs*   c120 –

WIGTOWN BAY   10 br.g. Young Nelson – Bonnie Bladnoch (Lord of Verona) [1992/3 c21f3 c21dpu c26dpu c25d⁴ c22s² c20g c20m² c21g² c21d* c23g c21f⁴ c21m²] plain gelding: moderate handicap chaser: fortunate winner at Uttoxeter in April: usually races at around 2½m but probably stays 3¼m: acts on any going: poor jumper. *J. Mackie*   c94 x

WILCO   4 ch.g. Bay Express – Solo Singer (Song) [1992/3 18f] second foal: dam half-sister to smart French jumper Khorassan: sprint maiden on Flat: tailed off in juvenile hurdle: sold 1,200 gns Ascot September Sales. *Andrew Turnell*   –

WILD AND LOOSE   5 b.g. Precocious – Regain (Relko) [1992/3 17sur 17v 16vpu 16g⁵] workmanlike gelding: half-brother to winning hurdler White River (by Pharly): one-time fairly useful performer at up to 1¼m on Flat: poor novice hurdler: acts on heavy ground: sold 3,200 gns Ascot June Sales. *D. R. C. Elsworth*   85

WILD ATLANTIC   10 b.g. Welsh Saint – Stonebow Lady (Windjammer (USA)) [1992/3 c17d³ c16m⁵ c17dF c24d² c25d⁵ c22g c16g⁴ c21mpu c17g² c18sur] strong, compact gelding: modest novice chaser: effective at around 2m and stays 3m: acts on dead and good to firm going: sometimes wears tongue strap: jumps none too fluently. *Mrs S. J. Smith*   c86 –

WILD BRAMBLE (IRE)   5 ch.m. Deep Run – Bramble Leaf (Even Money) [1992/3 F17v* F17g⁴ 21v² 21s² 21g⁶ 21v*] lengthy, rather unfurnished mare: sister to useful staying chaser The Builder and half-sister to winning hurdlers Frank Be Lucky (by Mandalus) and Brunoni (by Ovac): dam pulled up only outing over fences: winning Irish pointer: successful in NH Flat race at Hereford in November and mares novice hurdles at Uttoxeter in January and April: should stay beyond 21f: acts on heavy ground: forces pace: should continue on the upgrade. *Mrs M. Reveley*   101 p

WILD CHILD   10 b.m. Grey Ghost – Girl Sunday (Derek H) [1992/3 c21s³ c25m4] sturdy mare: modest hunter chaser: stays 25f: acts on good to firm and soft ground. *H. S. Fletcher*   c84 –

WILD FORTUNE   11 b.g. Free Boy – Hopeful Fortune (Autre Prince) [1992/3 c25dpu] fair pointer: tailed off when pulled up in hunter chase in March on steeplechasing debut. *P. Baring*   c–

WILD ILLUSION   9 ch.g. True Song – Fused Light (Fury Royal) [1992/3 c26m*] fairly useful pointer: won hunter chase at Cheltenham in May: stays 3¼m: acts on good to firm ground. *Miss Jennifer Pidgeon*   c101

WILD MIDNIGHT   11 b.g. Beau Charmeur (FR) – Our Day (Conte Grande) [1992/3 28d 23s] good-topped gelding: third foal: brother and half-brother (by Le Patron) to winning pointers: dam never ran: tailed off in 2 novice hurdles. *D. R. Franks*   –

WILDNITE   9 b.g. Whealden – Melinite (Milesian) [1992/3 c26mF] compact gelding: modest pointer: no sign of ability otherwise. *Miss L. Robbins*   c–

WILL BONNY (NZ) 6 br.g. Val Dansant (CAN) – Tobacco Road (NZ) (Crown Lease) [1992/3 F17d F17v 17v^{pu} 18g^{pu} 18g^{pu}] short-backed, leggy New Zealand-bred gelding: no sign of ability. *D. C. Jermy* —

WILLESDON (USA) 9 ch.h. Reviewer (USA) – Dona Maya (USA) (Reviewer (USA)) [1992/3 18h* 18f^6 18f] smallish, sparely-made horse: poor handicap hurdler: won at Exeter in August: not raced after September: races only at around 2m: yet to race on heavy going, acts on any other. *A. Barrow* 82

WILLIAMSFIELD 8 gr.g. Kafu – Royal Bundle (Crowned Prince (USA)) [1992/3 18m c18d3 c18s^6 c17v^{pu}] lengthy gelding: of little account: poor jumper of fences. *C. James* c– x —

WILLIE BUDGET 4 b.g. Master Willie – Cash Limit (High Top) [1992/3 13g^6 F17d^{pu}] half-brother to several winners, including hurdler Hand In Glove (by Star Appeal): dam lightly-raced maiden: little show in NH Flat races: dead. *A. G. Blackmore* —

WILLIE McGARR (USA) 8 ch.g. Master Willie – Pay T V (USA) (T V Commercial (USA)) [1992/3 c22g3] sparely-made gelding: modest novice hunter chaser: stays 25f: acts on dead going: showed temperament over hurdles. *Mrs D. Thomas* c85 – §

WILLIE SPARKLE 7 b.g. Roi Guillaume (FR) – Adamay (Florescence) [1992/3 17d^2 17g^2 18d^2 18s^2 17d^3 20s^3 16d* 20d^2 16d^F 17m 17g^3 20g* 21s^2] leggy gelding: fairly useful handicap hurdler: won at Ayr in January (conditional jockeys) and April: stays 21f: acts on good to firm and soft ground: tough and consistent. *Mrs S. C. Bradburne* 115

WILL JAMES 7 ch.g. Raga Navarro (ITY) – Sleekit (Blakeney) [1992/3 16g 17m 16s^4 17d^5 17d^2 16f^F 17g^3 17m^3 16f^6 17m^5] strong gelding: modest hurdler nowadays: races only at around 2m: acts on dead and firm ground: usually blinkered. *C. J. Drewe* 85

WILLOW BELLE (IRE) 5 b.m. Bustineto – Light Belle (Light Brigade) [1992/3 F16v^{pu} 16g 16f a18g^F] third living foal: dam never ran: of little account. *E. T. Buckley* —

WILLOW BLUE 6 gr.g. Full of Hope – Paddock Princess (Dragonara Palace (USA)) [1992/3 18s 17g] leggy gelding: of little account: visored once. *T. P. McGovern* —

WILLOW HOLDING 8 b.g. Some Hand – Catherines April (Fez) [1992/3 c23g^F c21m^{ur} c25d^{pu} 24g3] lengthy gelding: poor novice hurdler: failed to complete over fences: sold 1,500 gns Doncaster January Sales: probably stays 3m: acts on dead ground. *Mrs A. Swinbank* c– x 73

WILL'S BOUNTY 10 b.g. Tudor Treasure – Silva (Spartan General) [1992/3 17g^6 16g^3 16m^4 c16s^4 c16v^2 c18d^3 c16s^3 c18d^F 16m] sparely-made gelding: poor novice hurdler/winning chaser: best at around 2m: probably acts on any going. *J. Colston* c84 77

WILLSFORD 10 b.g. Beau Charmeur (FR) – Wish Again (Three Wishes) [1992/3 21v* c24d^4 c29d^3 c34d c33g] workmanlike gelding: useful hurdler/ chaser: won handicap hurdle at Warwick in January: best effort over fences afterwards when third in valuable handicap at Haydock in February: stays extremely well: needs plenty of give in the ground: usually wears blinkers: broke blood vessel once: lazy sort who needs plenty of driving. *Mrs J. Pitman* c130 134

WILL SHE WONT SHE 7 ch.m. Remainder Man – Russellia (Red God) [1992/3 16g^6 16v 16d^4 c16f^{pu} 17d^2 18g] workmanlike mare: poor novice hurdler: no promise on chasing debut: best form at around 2m on an easy surface. *R. G. Frost* c– 81

WILLUBELONG 4 ch.g. Move Off – Scally's Girl (Scallywag) [1992/3 22g] first foal: dam never ran: behind in novice hurdle at Sedgefield in March. *W. Raw* —

WILTOSKI 5 b.g. Petoski – Cojean (USA) (Prince John) [1992/3 16g 26d^4 a24g^6 26d^6 28g^{pu} 17f^2 22g^4 18f^2 20m^2 17g^2 17f^3] leggy, angular gelding: 88

selling hurdler: effective at 2m and probably stays 3¼m: acts on firm and dead ground: usually blinkered or visored. *I. Campbell*

WILTSHIRE YEOMAN 13 ch.g. Derrylin – Ribo Pride (Ribero) [1992/3 17g⁶ c17vᴿ 17v 16d³ a16g⁴ a24g] leggy, angular gelding: poor hurdler/novice chaser: best form at around 2m: acts on heavy going. *P. Hayward*   c–
84

WIMBLEBALL 13 b. or br.h. Sunrising – Polly Wall (Live Spirit) [1992/3 c21vᵖᵘ c26g⁵ c19m⁴ c17dᵘʳ] small horse: poor chaser: stays 3¼m: acts on any going. *J. R. Payne*   c75
–

WIMBORNE 8 b. or ro.g. What A Guest – Khadija (Habat) [1992/3 c16sꟳ c17d³ c16mꟳ c16gᵖᵘ c17d³ c16dꟳ 26sᵖᵘ c16gᵖᵘ] leggy, workmanlike gelding: selling hurdler: poor novice chaser: races mainly at around 2m: acts on good to firm and dead ground: sometimes wears tongue strap: poor jumper of fences. *Mrs S. J. Smith*   c78 x
–

WINABUCK 10 ch.g. Buckskin (FR) – Mistic Breeze (Master Owen) [1992/3 c23m* 24g⁴ c21d⁵ c25d³ c22sᵘʳ c21sꟳ c24sᵘʳ c21v* c21dꟳ c24m 23g⁵ c22fᵇᵈ c21dꟳ] rangy, workmanlike gelding: winning hurdler: fair chaser: successful in handicaps at Worcester (fourth course win) and Uttoxeter in first half of season: stays 3¼m: acts on good to firm and heavy going: usually blinkered nowadays: poor jumper: inconsistent. *R. Dickin*   c114 x
–

WIND FORCE 8 br.g. Strong Gale – Richest (Richboy) [1992/3 c25m* c21gᵘʳ c21m* c16m* c21g* c16s² c25sᵖᵘ c20g* c20f* c21f*] rangy gelding: progressive handicap chaser, useful already: won at Bangor, Carlisle (twice) and Wetherby in first half of season and at Ayr, Aintree (by 15 lengths from Guiburn's Nephew) and Uttoxeter in the spring: effective at 2m and stays 25f: probably acts on any going: jumps boldly and is inclined to odd bad mistake: genuine. *G. Richards*   c137 p
–

WINDS OF WAR 8 br.g. Strong Gale – Kind Rose (Royal And Regal (USA)) [1992/3 20d² 16g² F16v* 20s⁵ 18d³ 16v⁴ 16d* 17m 16s² 16d⁴] good-topped, workmanlike gelding: chasing type: second foal: brother to Young Gale, winner on Flat and over hurdles in Ireland: dam 1¼m winner in Ireland: won NH Flat race at Clonmel in November and dead-heated for first place in maiden hurdle at Leopardstown in February: ran creditably last 3 starts, including in Trafalgar House Supreme Novices' Hurdle at Cheltenham on eighth: stays 2½m: acts on good to firm and soft ground. *M. F. Morris, Ireland*   128

WINDSOR HIGHNESS 6 ch.m. Glenstal (USA) – Mrs Simpson (USA) (Windsor Ruler (USA)) [1992/3 17d² 17g* 18d² 17g² 16m⁵ 17d⁶ 18s⁵ 17s a16g³ a16g 18mᵖᵘ] sparely-made mare: poor hurdler: won selling handicap at Stratford (sold out of M. Muggeridge's stable 5,800 gns) in September: raced at around 2m: acted on soft ground: dead. *K. G. Wingrove*   81

WINDSOR PARK (USA) 7 br.g. Bold Forbes (USA) – Round Tower (High Top) [1992/3 17m² 18h² 16m² 16f⁴ 18f⁴ 20m* 18s⁴] leggy gelding: moderate hurdler: won handicap at Market Rasen in September: stays 21f: acts on hard and dead going. *K. S. Bridgwater*   97

WINDY WAYS 8 br.g. Strong Gale – Woodville Grove (Harwell) [1992/3 c26vᵖᵘ c27s⁴ c25s³ c25g* c34dᵖᵘ c24sꟳ c26f²] big, rangy gelding: fairly useful chaser: won handicap at Towcester in March: ran creditably final start: stays very well: probably acts on any ground: jumps boldly. *N. J. Henderson*   c124

WIN ELECTRIC 7 br.m. Down The Hatch – Claddagh Pride (Bargello) [1992/3 c25sᵘʳ c25d³ c27s⁶ c27gᵖᵘ c23dᵖᵘ] leggy, lightly-made mare: no form over hurdles or in steeplechases: tried blinkered. *Mrs R. G. Henderson*   c–
–

WINGCOMMANDER EATS 8 b.g. Nishapour (FR) – Rhodie Blake (Blakeney) [1992/3 16m* 21m³ c17s³ 18f³ c16g² c17fꟳ 22g⁶ 17m⁶ 18m⁶ c18g⁴] compact gelding: modest hurdler: won selling handicap at Worcester (bought in 2,600 gns) in August: modest novice chaser: stays 21f: probably acts on any going: blinkered last 2 outings over hurdles. *P. J. Hobbs*   c86
95

Tote 7th Race Handicap Chase, Aintree — Wind Force wins in tremendous style

WINGS OF FREEDOM (IRE)   5 b.g. Fairy King (USA) – Wingau   104
(FR) (Hard To Beat) [1992/3 20m* 22f3 17d6 18v6 20v2 17s3 20d4 16g* 17m
16v4 22m3 21m2 22f*] lengthy, quite good-topped gelding: fair handicap
hurdler: won at Bangor (novices) in September, Towcester in March and
Worcester in May: will stay beyond 2¾m: creditable efforts on heavy going,
best form on top-of-the-ground: tough and consistent. *J. R. Jenkins*

WINGSPAN (USA)   9 b.g. Storm Bird (CAN) – Miss Renege (USA)   c147 ?
(Riva Ridge (USA)) [1992/3 c21sur c21dF c21d4 c17f4 c16mpu c16s*] small   –
gelding: very useful chaser at best: running well when unseating rider first
start: below form after, including when winning claimer at Plumpton in
April: effective from 2m to 21f: acts on any going: races up with pace: usually
makes the odd mistake. *M. C. Pipe*

WINNIE LORRAINE   8 b.m. St Columbus – Win Green Hill (National   c67
Trust) [1992/3 c21f3 c26g4] leggy mare: modest pointer: novice hunter
chaser: stays 3¼m: acts on firm ground. *H. Wellstead*

WINNIE THE WITCH   9 b.m. Leading Man – Star Ruler (Indian Ruler)   c109 +
[1992/3 c21d* c16s* c21s3 c16s* c16dF c16d2 c16m5 c21d6 c21f6]   –
shallow-girthed mare: useful hurdler: won novice chases at Warwick (2) in
first half of season and Nottingham in January: good fifth in Arkle Chase at
Cheltenham on seventh start, but ran poorly final two: stays 21f: probably
acts on any going: jumps soundly: game. *K. S. Bridgwater*

WINNING CALL   6 b.m. Kinglet – Game Bid (Laurence O) [1992/3 16v
22m] small, plain mare: first foal: dam, winning hurdler/chaser, stayed well: –
tailed off in novice hurdles: sold 1,150 gns Ascot March Sales: blinkered on
debut. *H. Willis*

WINNING DANCER   10 b.g. Dance In Time (CAN) – Ravenshead   c–
(Charlottown) [1992/3 17vpu c19v6 c17v c19m5 c16spu] sparely-made   –
gelding: poor hurdler/novice chaser: stayed 2½m: acted on heavy and good
to firm going: dead. *Miss L. Bower*

WINNINGTONRIG   5 b.g. Lochnager – Singing High (Julio Mariner)   68
[1992/3 16g 16g 17g 16m 23mpu] smallish gelding: second foal: half-brother
to Flat and hurdles winner Top Scale (by Tower Walk): dam won over 1m:
poor form over hurdles: best form at around 2m on good ground. *A. C.
Whillans*

WINNOWING (IRE)   5 b.m. Strong Gale – Dusty Hall (Saint Denys)   – p
[1992/3 F17s3 17dF 22d] unfurnished mare: second foal: half-sister to
winning hurdler Off Piste (by Deep Run): dam unraced half-sister to
top-class hurdler Aonoch: third in NH Flat race: never dangerous, not
knocked about, in mid-divison in 23-runner mares novice hurdle at
Wincanton in February: should improve. *C. P. E. Brooks*

WINSOME GRAIN   4 ch.f. Gorytus (USA) – Some Dame (Will Somers)   69
[1992/3 16g 16g 16s5] close-coupled, workmanlike filly: half-sister to several
Flat winners and to useful chaser For The Grain (by Nishapour): dam,
half-sister to high-class Record Run, won over 1¼m: poor form first 2 starts
over hurdles. *Miss L. A. Perratt*

WINTER BELLE (USA)   5 b.g. Sportin' Life (USA) – Belle O'Reason
(USA) (Hail To Reason) [1992/3 F16d* F17m3 F16g3] good-bodied gelding:
half-brother to several winners in USA: dam gained 2 of her 7 wins in USA in
stakes races: won NH Flat race at Leopardstown in December: third in
valuable similar events at Cheltenham (tended to hang left) in March and
Punchestown in April: yet to race over hurdles or fences. *P. Prendergast,
Ireland*

WINTERBOURNE ABBAS (IRE)   4 gr.g. Treasure Kay – Snow   118
Maid [1992/3 16g 16d5 16d5 16s* 16s4 16d5 16v2 16s 17m] leggy,
workmanlike gelding: fair middle-distance maiden on Flat: won juvenile
hurdle at Fairyhouse in November: behind in Daily Express Triumph
Hurdle at Cheltenham on final start: yet to race beyond 17f: acts on heavy
going: blinkered last 3 starts, best effort on first occasion. *T. M. Walsh,
Ireland*

WINTER LIGHTNING 4 b.f. Dominion – Shaft of Sunlight (Sparkler) [1992/3 16m 18f⁴ 17m⁵ 17mᶠ 17d2 17g⁶ 18g2 22d⁶ 16d3] small, light-framed filly: modest stayer on Flat for P. Walwyn: modest form at best over hurdles: ran badly in sellers last 2 starts: should prove well suited by further than 2¼m: acts on dead ground. *D. J. Wintle*   85

WINTER OATS 6 b.g. Oats – Mangro (Mandamus) [1992/3 16f 2 1s] close-coupled gelding: no form over hurdles: trained first start by B. Wilkinson. *S. E. Kettlewell*   –

WINTER SQUALL (IRE) 5 gr.g. Celio Rufo – No Honey (Dual) [1992/3 F 17d 17s⁵ 16s* 17s* 16g2 17m* 17f⁵]   136 p

As one door closes another opens. Soon after it became known that their highly promising hurdler Carobee was out for the season through injury, David Nicholson's stable had the good fortune to acquire Carobee's year-younger half-brother Winter Squall. Winter Squall, successful on the first of his two starts in National Hunt Flat races for Mrs Pitman in 1991/2, had a couple of outings for Stan Mellor before joining Nicholson. Unfortunately the horse's saddle slipped in another National Hunt Flat race on his reappearance, and a week later he finished only fifth in a novice hurdle at Chepstow. However, Winter Squall, like his owner's other horses Baydon Star, Mighty Mogul and Wonder Man, enjoyed great success after joining Nicholson. While not quite so good as Carobee, Winter Squall did at least emulate his half-brother by winning the valuable novice hurdle run at Chepstow in March. Winter Squall, with victories at Ludlow and Sandown under his belt, started favourite for the Beaufort Hurdle, as it is now known, and was almost as impressive as Carobee had been twelve months earlier. Taking up the running four out, Winter Squall quickened clear without having to be at all hard ridden and won by twelve lengths from Pharly Story. Winter Squall, like Carobee, made one further appearance in the Seagram Top Novices' Hurdle at Aintree. As a result of his Chepstow win Winter Squall had to carry the maximum 8 lb penalty in this event, but unlike Carobee he was unable to defy it. Winter Squall ran his best race, though, in finishing around three lengths fifth to Roll A Dollar, and he'd probably have finished a length closer but for being bumped on the run-in. Roll A Dollar also inflicted the only other defeat on Winter Squall during the latter's time with Nicholson, giving him 4 lb and a three-length beating at Kempton in February.

Beaufort Hurdle, Chepstow—Winter Squall is impressive

Mrs Shirley Robins' "Winter Squall"

Winter Squall (IRE) (gr.g. 1988)	Celio Rufo (gr 1980)	Warpath (br 1969)	Sovereign Path
			Ardneasken
		Counter Coup (gr 1970)	Busted
			Alborada
	No Honey (br 1977)	Dual (b 1958)	Chanteur II
			Duplicity
		Honey High (b 1955)	Honeyway
			High Trial

Winter Squall's dam No Honey is proving to be a gold mine, and any of her unraced produce to go through the sale ring can be virtually guaranteed to realise a high price. The latest to be sold was Two John's (by King's Ride) who fetched 58,000 guineas as an unbroken three-year-old at the 1992 Doncaster May Sales. A full brother to Carobee and to the ill-fated Alekhine, one of the best two-mile novice hurdlers of 1988/9, Two John's has already shown promise, finishing strongly into third of twenty-two in a National Hunt Flat race at Kempton in February on his only start. Waiting in the wings are a three-year-old full brother to Winter Squall and a two-year-old by Persian Mews. No Honey, who has also produced the winning pointer No Bees (by Reformed Character), is an unraced sister to five winners, among them the very useful middle-distance stayer Alloway Lad and the successful hurdler/chaser/point-to-pointer Highway Dual. Winter Squall, from the second crop of the Italian St Leger winner Celio Rufo, has raced only at around two miles but he will stay further. Although he put up his best performance on firm ground, he gained his first two wins over hurdles on soft and the probability is that he acts on any. The tall, unfurnished Winter Squall has scope for further improvement over hurdles, but his future lies over fences. *D. Nicholson*

WINTERS SOVEREIGN   13 br.g. Sovereign King – Wintersbrig (New   c–
Brig) [1992/3 c27gpu] strong, good-bodied gelding: winning staying hunter   –
chaser: tried blinkered. *Mrs Janine M. Mills*

WISE CUSTOMER   9 ch.g. Deep Run – Clontinty Queen (Laurence O)
[1992/3 20d 23g² 22d² 22d⁴] well-made, compact gelding: modest hurdler: 97
stays 23f: acts on dead ground. *Miss T. A. White*

WISE GAMBOL   14 b.g. Gambling Debt – Nutkin (Roan Rocket) [1992/3   c81
c17d⁴] leggy gelding: winning hunter chaser: barely stays 3m: acts on any
going. *Simon J. Stearn*

WISHING GATE (USA)   5 br.g. Gate Dancer (USA) – Meditation
(USA) (Private Thoughts (USA)) [1992/3 F17s 16g⁴ 20g² 24g* 20m² 24m*   104
20f²] sturdy gelding: won maiden hurdle at Edinburgh in February and
novice hurdle at Newcastle in March: will stay beyond 3m: acts on firm
ground. *M. D. Hammond*

WITCHES COVEN   4 gr.f. Sharrood (USA) – Tricky (Song) [1992/3 18v
16m 24spu] sparely-made filly: modest 1¾m winner on Flat in 1992 for M.   –
Bell: well beaten over hurdles: pulls hard: sold 1,300 gns Newmarket July
Sales. *Mrs A. Knight*

WITH IMPUNITY   4 br.g. Sula Bula – Sleepline Comfort (Tickled Pink)
[1992/3 aF16g] fourth foal: half-brother to 8-y-o Sleepline Romany (by
Buzzards Bay): dam 5f seller winner at 2 yrs: showed nothing in NH Flat
race at Southwell in February: yet to race over hurdles. *T. Thomson Jones*

WITHY BANK   11 b.g. Blakeney – Chiltern Lass (High Hat) [1992/3 c21d   c–
c26sF] small gelding: fair chaser: suited by test of stamina: acted on good to   –
firm and soft going: blinkered once: dead. *Mrs S. J. Smith*

WITNEY GIRL   7 ch.m. Le Bavard (FR) – Flying Pegus (Beau Chapeau)
[1992/3 22s 21v 25v 23s⁶ 25d⁶] sturdy, lengthy mare: poor novice hurdler: 69
thorough stayer: acts on soft ground. *J. C. McConnochie*

WODEHOUSE   8 b.g. Sunyboy – Flammula (Wrekin Rambler) [1992/3
16v 16sco 26spu] big, rangy gelding: very lightly-raced novice over hurdles,
showing poor form at best. *J. R. Bosley*

WOLFHANGAR   11 ch.g. Decent Fellow – Vaguely Vulgan (Vulgan)   c–
[1992/3 c16s⁵ c17m] lengthy, workmanlike gelding: fair 2m chaser in   –
1989/90: no form since. *Miss C. J. E. Caroe*

WOLF'S DEN   4 ch.g. Fools Holme (USA) – Tralee Falcon (Falcon)
[1992/3 F16g F16d] half-brother to several minor winners: dam fair sprinter:
tailed off in NH Flat races: yet to race over hurdles. *P. Spottiswood*

WOLFSVILLE   5 b.g. Little Wolf – Perryville (New Brig) [1992/3 20spu
20g] workmanlike gelding: fourth live foal: dam lightly-raced novice
hurdler: no sign of ability in novice hurdles. *R. R. Lamb*

WOLF WOOD   5 ch.m. Little Wolf – Nightwood (Sparkler) [1992/3 16d]
lengthy mare: tailed off only outing on Flat and in a novice selling hurdle. *S.*   –
Christian

WOLVER RUN   8 b.g. Furry Glen – Roselita (Deep Run) [1992/3 c24m⁴   c–
17m⁵] ex-Irish gelding: fair hurdler/moderate chaser at best: sold out of W.   –
Browne's stable 8,600 gns Doncaster August Sales after first start: stays
2¾m: acts on soft going. *D. Moffatt*

WOMAN OF THE ROAD   7 b.m. Boreen (FR) – Lady Darnley
(Supreme Sovereign) [1992/3 21spu] lengthy mare: sixth reported foal: –
half-sister to 2 poor animals: dam behind in maiden hurdle on only outing:
little promise in points and a novice hurdle. *D. J. Wintle*

WONDERFULL POLLY (IRE)   5 ch.m. Pollerton – Wonderful Lilly
(Prince Hansel) [1992/3 F16v F16g] second reported foal: dam fair Irish
hurdler, successful at up to 2½m: well beaten in NH Flat races: yet to race
over hurdles or fences. *P. F. Nicholls*

WONDER MAN (FR)   8 ch.g. The Wonder (FR) – Juvenilia (FR) (Kash-   c151
mir II) [1992/3 c16d* c16s* c16d* c16d² c16g² c16m²]   –
   It was good to see hurdlers of the calibre of Cab On Target, Sybillin
and Wonder Man come through in their first season over fences. In their

different ways they should all go on to fill a gap in the higher ranks of chasing. Sybillin and Wonder Man are two-milers with sights set on the Queen Mother Champion Chase. You'd have to say right now that of the pair Sybillin looks the better prospect for the event, but unquestionably Wonder Man has winning a big prize in him. Wonder Man won several big prizes as a hurdler, including the Welsh Champion Hurdle in 1990/1, the season he also finished seventh of twenty-four behind Morley Street in the Champion Hurdle. He made only one appearance in 1991/2, winning a minor race at Warwick in November. Subsequently he was switched from the care of his first trainer, Mrs Pitman, to that of his present one and sent chasing. There wasn't much between Wonder Man and Sybillin as hurdlers, and as 1992/3 moved on the pair of them came to be regarded as the leading British hopes for the two-mile novices' chase at the Cheltenham Festival, the Arkle Challenge Trophy. That was certainly the situation when they met in the Nottinghamshire Novices' Chase at Nottingham in February about three weeks before the Arkle, when the 5/2-on Sybillin won by a length and a half, conceding 3 lb. Wonder Man put in a good round of jumping out in front, but was caught and outpaced on the flat. By that time Wonder Man had established himself as a bold jumper of fences who, as over hurdles, travelled strongly from the start. He was inclined to make the odd full-blooded mistake, though. Such a one almost cost him his unbeaten record after impressive wins at Wolverhampton and Sandown, when at Kempton in December he was cruising to victory over Atlaal and the rest of a fair field until he ploughed through the last and was forced to scramble home. And there was no coming back from a similar error two out when 4/1 on against the same horse at Ascot on his fourth start; handed the initiative Atlaal stayed in front, jumping the last the better, too. Encouragingly, Wonder Man handled the big Cheltenham fences impeccably on his first sight of them in the Arkle, and he ran a fine race to finish a length second to Travado, the pair of them well clear of an out-of-sorts Sybillin. He set a fair

Bonusfilm Novices' Chase, Kempton—
the winner Wonder Man (right) and Atlaal at the fourth last

Mrs Shirley Robins' "Wonder Man"

pace, increased the tempo from four out so that all except Travado were shaken off by the home turn, and while unable to match the winner over the last he kept on strongly up the hill, getting the trip as well as he's ever done.

Wonder Man (FR) (ch.g. 1985)	The Wonder (FR) (br 1978)	Wittgenstein (b 1971)	Roi Dagobert Stavroula
		The Lark (gr 1972)	Lanark Norman Lass
	Juvenilia (FR) (b 1975)	Kashmir II (b or br 1963)	Tudor Melody Queen of Speed
		Trasimene (b 1970)	Fine Top Cerisoles II

Wonder Man came to jumping by way of the Flat in France, where he was successful at up to nine furlongs. He also had a few runs on the Flat over here. His dam has produced several winners in France, among the others being a jumper called Comeri (by Phaeton). Juvenilia, a daughter of the mile-and-a-half winner Trasimene and a granddaughter of the Prix de Diane winner Cerisoles, won over five furlongs in France as a two-year-old. Wonder Man, a tall, lengthy gelding, has made good physical progress down the years and is now much stronger than when he appeared not to get home in the Triumph Hurdle on his only run on heavy going. He has plenty of form on soft and has run well in both his races on good to firm, the latest the Arkle. *D. Nicholson*

WONT BE GONE LONG 11 b.g. The Parson – Most Seen (Mustang)   c128
[1992/3 c21s⁵ c25g* c33g c26m⁴] tall, leggy gelding: fairly useful chaser: –
won handicap at Sandown in February: ran badly afterwards: stays very
well: suited by a firm surface: sound jumper. *N. J. Henderson*

WOODBURY GIRL 6 b.m. Quayside – Wrekenogan (Tarqogan)   78
[1992/3 20d⁴ 24s³ 22d a20g⁵] workmanlike ex-Irish mare: fourth foal:

half-sister to maiden hurdler/chaser Hursthill (by Pollerton) and fair Irish hurdler Cooleogan (by Proverb): dam, unraced half-sister to fair jumper Parsons Law, out of half-sister to Ekbalco: poor maiden hurdler: stays 3m: acts on heavy ground and fibresand: blinkered final start (January). *Mrs A. L. M. King*

WOODEN BEAR 10 ch.g. Orchestra – Release Record (Jukebox) [1992/3 c20gF c21gpu] strong gelding: no sign of ability. *G. B. Barlow*   c–

WOODGATE 12 ch.g. Quayside – Owen Money (Master Owen) [1992/3 c25d3 c27v c24v4] smallish, sparely-made gelding: fairly useful but unreliable handicap chaser at best: only worthwhile form in 1992/3: needs a thorough test of stamina: acts on heavy going: blinkered once. *Capt. T. A. Forster*   c–

WOODLAND FLOWER 8 b.m. Furry Glen – Quetta's Dual (Dual) [1992/3 c24g4 c27vpu c24gpu c25g* c26g2 c24d2] leggy mare: winning hurdler: won novice chase at Wolverhampton in March: ran well in handicaps afterwards: suited by a test of stamina: acts on heavy going: jumps soundly: blinkered last 3 outings: occasionally looks irresolute. *O. Sherwood*   c95

WOODLANDS BOY (IRE) 5 b.g. Hawaiian Return (USA) – Annie Sue VI (Snuff Matter) [1992/3 22v6 22v c16v4 c19v2 c25sF 22g4] non-thoroughbred gelding: third foal: dam won 4¼m hunter chase in Ireland: novice hurdler/chaser: clear second when falling 4 out in quite valuable race over fences at Ascot in April: will prove suited by test of stamina: acts on soft ground: should win a novice chase. *T. J. Etherington*   c95   80

WOODLANDS CROWN 10 ch.g. Milford – Town Girl (Town Crier) [1992/3 18m c16dF] workmanlike gelding: no form over hurdles: beaten when falling 3 out on chasing debut. *D. C. Tucker*   c–

WOODLANDSFOR POWER 7 ch.g. St Columbus – Spartella (Spartan General) [1992/3 20g c23mF c26gF c23gpu] rather sparely-made gelding: winning pointer: of little account otherwise. *P. A. Pritchard*   c–

WOODLANDS GENHIRE 8 ch.g. Celtic Cone – Spartella (Spartan General) [1992/3 c25s5 c26vpu c25s4 c25d3 c26g4 c25g* c26mpu] leggy, workmanlike gelding: modest chaser: won handicap at Towcester in March: needs a thorough test of stamina and give in the ground. *P. A. Pritchard*   c92

WOODLANDS GENPOWER 11 b.g. Celtic Cone – April Sovereign (Lucky Sovereign) [1992/3 26dpu 21s 24s 21gpu] compact gelding: moderate staying hurdler at best: ran poorly in 1992/3: maiden chaser: probably best without visor. *P. A. Pritchard*   c–

WOODLANDS POWER 5 b.g. Celtic Cone – Surely Right (Giolla Mear) [1992/3 F16m] second foal: dam winning pointer: behind in NH Flat race at Warwick in May: yet to race over hurdles or fences. *P. A. Pritchard*

WOODSIDE HEATH 6 ch.g. King Persian – Saga's Humour (Bustino) [1992/3 16g 20v 17v3 a16g 23v2 22s4 22g 21f5] close-coupled, rather sparely-made gelding: moderate novice hurdler: stays 23f: acts on heavy ground. *J. S. Moore*   89

WOODURATHER 7 br.g. Touching Wood (USA) – Rather Warm (Tribal Chief) [1992/3 17v3 16gF] small gelding: fairly useful hurdler at best: respectable third in February: best form at around 2m: acts on good to firm and heavy going. *M. C. Pipe*   115

WOODY WILL 7 b.g. Mandalus – Woodville Grove (Harwell) [1992/3 c16v2 c21spu c16d3 c21m* c21v2 c21dF c21m2 c24m4] lengthy gelding: maiden hurdler: won novice chase at Worcester in March: ran creditably when second afterwards, including in handicap: should stay beyond 21f: acts on good to firm and heavy ground. *O. Sherwood*   c95

WORDY'S WONDER 5 b.m. Welsh Captain – Lydia II (Neckar) [1992/3 F14s* a18g6 17g4 18dpu] leggy, angular mare: 33/1-winner of NH Flat race at   72

Market Rasen in November: poor form over hurdles: best effort on good ground. *L. Wordingham*

WORKAMIRACLE   6 b.m. Teamwork – Armagnac Princess (Armagnac Monarch) [1992/3 17s^{pu}] first foal: dam very useful staying chaser: no sign of ability in early-season claiming hurdle on debut. *R. G. Frost*   –

WORLD WITHOUT END (USA)   4 ch.g. World Appeal (USA) – Mardie's Bid (USA) (Raise A Bid (USA)) [1992/3 F17d^2 F14g^5] leggy gelding: fifth foal: half-brother to 4 winners in USA: dam won 6 races in USA: showed ability in NH Flat races in April: yet to race over hurdles. *S. G. Norton*

WORTHY KNIGHT   12 ch.g. Dubassoff (USA) – Quidsworth (Trullah) [1992/3 c21m^{pu}] neat gelding: fair handicap chaser in 1991/2: pulled up, reportedly lame, in August: best at around 2½m: acts on any going with possible exception of heavy: sometimes makes mistakes. *J. R. Jenkins*   c–   –

WOTAMONA   5 b.m. Another Realm – Meadow Wood (Meadow Court) [1992/3 a18g^5 a20g 16d a18g^{ur} 20g 22f^6 18g^5] sparely-made mare: poor maiden hurdler: stays 2¼m: acts on good to firm ground and fibresand: jumps none too fluently. *B. Palling*   64

WOT PET   10 b.g. Crozier – Annies Pet (Normandy) [1992/3 c28g^F c27d^5 c26d^3 c25s] deep-girthed gelding: maiden hunter chaser: well beaten in 1993: stays well. *T. M. Gibson*   c–

WREKIN COLLEGE   5 b.g. Sonnen Gold – Wrekinianne (Reform) [1992/3 16v^4 16v 16d^4 23d^{pu} 16g^5 17f^5] angular gelding: poor novice hurdler: should stay beyond 2m: acts on heavy going. *D. R. Gandolfo*   70

WREKIN HILL   11 b.g. Duky – Cummin Hill (Wrekin Rambler) [1992/3 c25s^3 c25m^2 c24m^3 c27d^4 c25g* c22f c25s^3 c21s^2] big, rangy gelding: fair chaser: trained until after fourth outing by W. A. Stephenson: won handicap at Ayr in March: sold to J. White 9,000 gns in May: stays 27f: acts on any going: tried blinkered in 1990/1. *P. Cheesbrough*   c109   –

WREKIN WARRIOR   8 b.g. Coded Scrap – Miss Denetop (Eborneezer) [1992/3 c21m^{pu}] tall, leggy, lengthy gelding: of little account over hurdles: maiden pointer: no show in novice hunter chase in June. *A. L. Wallace*   c–   –

WRETS   4 b.g. Kalaglow – Hayley Warren (Habitat) [1992/3 17s 17d^{pu} 16m^{pu}] lengthy, angular gelding: fair form at up to 1¼m on Flat: sold 6,400 gns Newmarket Autumn Sales: no form over hurdles. *Mrs P. M. Joynes*   –

WRIST WATCH   4 gr.g. Alias Smith (USA) – Time-Table (Mansingh (USA)) [1992/3 F17s aF16g^6 17g^{pu} 20d^{pu} 21s^{pu}] sturdy gelding: fifth foal: dam modest 6f winner: no sign of ability: sold 2,500 gns Ascot June Sales: blinkered fourth start. *T. M. Jones*   –

WRITE THE MUSIC   12 b.g. Riboboy (USA) – Zither (Vienna) [1992/3 c25d^5] compact gelding: winning staying hurdler/novice hunter chaser: usually visored or blinkered: poor jumper of fences: faint-hearted. *Capt V. Lloyd-Davies*   c88   x   – §

WRITTEN AGREEMENT   5 ch.g. Stanford – Covenant (Good Bond) [1992/3 17s^4] of little account. *R. E. Peacock*   –

WYCLIFFE   5 ch.g. Dunbeath (USA) – Blakewood (Blakeney) [1992/3 18d 16s^4 17s^2 17d^5 18m^2 17f^4] workmanlike gelding: half-brother to fair hurdler Starwood (by Star Appeal): lightly-raced maiden on Flat: poor novice hurdler: should stay beyond 2¼m: probably acts on any ground: forces pace. *N. B. Mason*   83

WYJUME (IRE)   4 b.f. Phardante (FR) – Adare Lady (Varano) [1992/3 F16f^3 F17m] unfurnished filly: sixth foal: half-sister to very smart staying hurdler and winning chaser Pragada (by Pragmatic): dam ran twice: third of 6 in NH Flat race at Wincanton in March: mid-division in similar race at Cheltenham in April: yet to race over hurdles. *J. T. Gifford*

WYLAM   6 b.g. What A Guest – Wish You Wow (Wolver Hollow) [1992/3 c21m* c21d^4 c21m^3] sparely-made gelding: winning hurdler: lucky winner of 3-finisher novice chase at Southwell in October: good third at Windsor in   c87   –

November: stays 21f: acts on good to firm going: usually visored in 1990/1.
G. H. Eden

Y

YAAFOOR (USA) 4 b.g. Northern Baby (CAN) – Second Glance (USA) (Big Burn (USA)) [1992/3 17v³ 16d³ 16m⁶ 18g⁶ 17g 18f⁵] lengthy gelding: maiden on Flat: sold out of A. Scott's stable 4,600 gns Newmarket July Sales: poor juvenile hurdler at best: well below form in sellers last 2 starts: acts on good to firm and heavy ground: blinkered twice. *P. R. Hedger* — 77

YAAKUM 4 b.g. Glint of Gold – Nawadder (Kris) [1992/3 16v a16g²] made running when second of 15 in juvenile hurdle at Southwell in January: won over 2m on Flat in 1993 (visored). *J. E. Banks* — 87

YAHEEB (USA) 9 b.h. Alleged (USA) – Rissa (USA) (Nijinsky (CAN)) [1992/3 c20s* c22v³ c18d⁴ c16d² c18m⁶ c16d] small, sturdy horse: one-time smart hurdler: won novice chase at Carlisle in November: well below form last 2 outings: probably needs further than 2m nowadays and stays 3m: acts on good to firm and heavy ground: best on right-handed courses. *M. W. Easterby* — c98 —

YAMANOUCHI 9 b.g. Hard Fought – Noreena (Nonoalco (USA)) [1992/3 18g 16g⁶ 16d⁵ 17d 20g² 18g⁴ 16d³ 17g] neat gelding: moderate hurdler: poor novice chaser: stayed 2½m: acted on firm going: dead. *D. Moffatt* — c– 90

YANBU 8 b.g. Artaius (USA) – Belle Bretonne (Celtic Ash) [1992/3 c19h⁴ 22d² 18f 17s⁴ 23m⁶ 17v 25s 18s⁶ 17m⁶ 22s² 27dᵖᵘ] smallish gelding: selling hurdler: well beaten only outing over fences: sold out of C. Popham's stable 2,000 gns Ascot September Sales after fifth start: stays 2¾m: best with plenty of give in the ground: usually blinkered: ungenuine. *J. P. Taplin* — c– 85 §

YANKEE FLYER 6 b.m. Henbit (USA) – Yankee Special (Bold Lad (IRE)) [1992/3 16f 17s⁴ 18v 16s 16d F13m⁵] small, sparely-made mare: selling hurdler: barely stays 2m in testing conditions: acts on soft ground: blinkered final start over hurdles. *Miss S. J. Wilton* — 65

YANKEE RHYTHM 9 br.g. Ascertain (USA) – Jungle Rhythm (Drumberg) [1992/3 c25g³] modest and temperamental pointer: remote third in novice hunter chase at Bangor in April. *Miss K. Bryan* — c–

YASHEEN (IRE) 4 b.f. Yashgan – Shirleen (Daring Display (USA)) [1992/3 F16g F16s⁶] good-topped filly: half-sister to several winners, including fairly useful 7f performer Superoo (by Superlative): dam won in Italy: sixth of 17 finishers in NH Flat race at Ludlow in April: yet to race over hurdles. *D. J. Wintle* —

YASLOU 6 ch.g. Yashgan – Lough Graney (Sallust) [1992/3 22s 26g⁵ 18d* 23g] compact gelding: 33/1, won conditional jockeys novice handicap hurdle at Exeter in April, only form of 1992/3: stays 2½m: acts on soft going. *W. R. Muir* — 79

YELLOW PANSY 6 ch.m. Don Enrico (USA) – Pansy Rock (Roxy (FR)) [1992/3 F16g] smallish, lengthy mare: second foal: dam, daughter of a fair hurdler, well beaten in novice hurdles: tailed off in NH Flat race at Worcester in March: yet to race over hurdles or fences. *Mrs N. S. Sharpe* —

YELLOW SPRING 8 b.g. Buckskin (FR) – Carrigello (Bargello) [1992/3 22v⁶ 21g* 21m³] leggy gelding: useful handicap hurdler: won at Kempton in February: good third to Olympian in valuable event at Cheltenham following month: should stay beyond 21f: acts on firm and dead ground. *D. M. Grissell* — 131

YEOMAN WARRIOR 6 b.g. Tug of War – Annies Pet (Normandy) [1992/3 16v⁵ 17s⁶ 21sᶠ 18g 22d² 22m⁴] lengthy, good sort with plenty of scope: chasing type: brother to useful Irish jumper Fissure Seal: modest — 99 novice hurdler: will stay further than 2¾m: acts on good to soft and good to firm going: should win a race or two. *R. Rowe*

YIMKIN BOOKRA 5 b.g. Nomination – Top Stream (Highland Melody) [1992/3 16s³ 17d⁴ 18s³ 17g⁴ 17g] smallish, sturdy gelding: modest maiden on Flat and over hurdles: will stay beyond 2¼m: easily best efforts on soft ground: blinkered last 2 starts. *W. R. Muir* — 97

YIRAGAN 11 ch.g. Cantab – Foreverusa (Poona) [1992/3 c24d^ur c27v c29g³ c34d⁶ c24s⁴ c24d⁶] leggy, sparely-made gelding: fair chaser: suited by a thorough test of stamina: acts on heavy and good to firm going: blinkered last 2 starts (below form): usually jumps well. *D. H. Barons* — c112 –

YORK IMPERIAL 12 br.g. Belfalas – Regency Princess (Prince Regent (FR)) [1992/3 c21g² c26d*] lengthy, angular gelding: hunter chaser: won maiden at Carlisle in April by 20 lengths: stays 3¼m: acts on good to firm and soft going: blinkered once. *Mrs R. Spencer* — c93 –

YORKSHIRE GALE 7 br.g. Strong Gale – Mio Slipper (Sole Mio (USA)) [1992/3 17g^ur 21s* 22v* 21s³ 21g 25f³] workmanlike gelding: chasing type: won novice hurdles at Newbury and Cheltenham in first half of season: ran poorly last 2 starts: effective at 21f and should stay 3m: acts on heavy going. *J. T. Gifford* — 115

YORKSHIRE HOLLY 10 br.g. Bivouac – Holly Doon (Doon) [1992/3 21g³ 23g² c24f² c21g* c22m⁴] small gelding: smart hurdler at best: successful in novice chase at Sedgefield in March: stayed well: acted on heavy going: dead. *R. S. Wood* — c87 127

YORKSHIREMAN (USA) 8 ch.g. Our Native (USA) – Queen Vega (USA) (Te Vega) [1992/3 c18d⁵ c24s³ c23d^ur c26d c25g⁶ c20s² c20d*] close-coupled gelding: fairly useful hurdler: fair chaser: won handicap at Ludlow in April: effective at 2½m and stays 3m: acts on soft going: sometimes has tongue tied down: makes mistakes. *J. A. Glover* — c103 x –

YOU'LL DO 10 b.g. Billion (USA) – Keino (Kautokeino (FR)) [1992/3 c24fF c21f5] workmanlike gelding: poor maiden hurdler/chaser. *J. F. Symes* — c– –

YOUNG ALFIE 8 b.g. Neltino – Anglophil (Philemon) [1992/3 c17s⁴] big, plain gelding: poor novice hurdler/chaser: stays 3m: acts on soft and good to firm going: blinkered last 3 starts. *J. F. Panvert* — c75 –

YOUNG BENZ 9 ch.g. Young Generation – Cavalier's Blush (King's Troop) [1992/3 c21s³ c16s⁴ c21s³ c20d³ c16v* c17d³] tall gelding: useful chaser: very easy winner of 4-runner handicap at Haydock in January: stays 2½m: acts on heavy going: tried blinkered and visored: often jumps none too fluently. *M. H. Easterby* — c141 –

YOUNG GALA 4 b.f. Young Man (FR) – Spring Gala (Ancient Monro) [1992/3 17g^ur] angular filly: fifth foal: half-sister to winning jumpers Galadine (by Gaberdine) and Gala Loch (by Lochnager): dam tailed-off last only start: little aptitude for hurdling in juvenile event at Kelso in March. *S. G. Payne* — –

YOUNG GEORGE 6 b.g. Camden Town – Young Grace (Young Emperor) [1992/3 18g 16m] leggy, close-coupled gelding: poor novice hurdler: raced only at around 2m: best form on good ground. *M. Dods* — –

YOUNG HUSTLER 6 ch.g. Import – Davett (Typhoon) [1992/3 c22m² c21m* c23gF c21g* c23v⁴ c20d c21v² c24s* c26v* c24m* c21d* c20g* c21g² c25m* c25f³] — c149

There was an unfamiliar name at the top of the trainers' table in mid-November. Nigel Twiston-Davies, in only his fourth season as a full licence holder, held a useful lead over the usual pacesetters, Gordon Richards and Martin Pipe. The splendid progress of Twiston-Davies through the training ranks became one of the stories of the season, with the achievements of such as Captain Dibble, Dakyns Boy, Gaelstrom, Sweet Duke, Tipping Tim and Young Hustler eventually earning him third place to Pipe and David Nicholson in the table of leading trainers. Young Hustler was the most successful horse to represent the yard, winning eight races worth over

Great Yorkshire Handicap Chase, Doncaster—
the novice Young Hustler isn't troubled by his much more experienced rivals

£115,000. Like most of his stable's inmates, Young Hustler was kept on the go. He had fifteen races from the first week in September to the Grand National meeting at Aintree in April, winning on courses as diverse as Bangor and Cheltenham, and on going of practically every description. Sharp track or galloping track, top-of-the-ground or the mud, it made no difference to

Scilly Isles Novices' Chase, Sandown—Young Hustler leads from Fighting Words
and Gay Ruffian (No. 6) in the back straight

834

the tough and versatile Young Hustler who proved effective at two and a half miles to three and a quarter.

Young Hustler started in lowly company, getting off the mark in a novice chase at Bangor in September after being beaten at odds on in his first race over fences at Stratford earlier in the month. After adding a victory at Cheltenham in October Young Hustler progressed to better races. He didn't prove up to the tasks at first, finishing behind the good recruit Barton Bank in the Aga Worcester Novice Chase (fourth) and the Pat Taaffe Novice Chase at Cheltenham (second) and being well beaten, from nearly two stone out of the handicap and starting at 100/1, when the only novice to contest the H & T Walker Gold Cup at Ascot. But Young Hustler was much improved after the turn of the year, and after winning a novice chase at Newbury and a handicap at Wincanton, he collected three valuable prizes in as many Saturdays, the Great Yorkshire Chase at Doncaster, the Scilly Isles Novices' Chase at Sandown and the Arlington Premier Chase Final at Newbury. Improvement in Young Hustler's jumping went hand in hand with his progressive form and after his clear-cut victories at Doncaster (where he turned a competitive handicap into a procession from five out), Sandown and Newbury, he began to look a good prospect for the Sun Alliance Chase at the Festival meeting. Young Hustler's performance at the beginning of March in the Cavalier Chase at Worcester, where the King George VI Chase third The Illywhacker narrowly denied him a six-timer, strengthened his credentials for Cheltenham. He started 9/4 second favourite behind Barton Bank in a field of eight in which only Young Hustler, Barton Bank and the Reynoldstown Chase winner Capability Brown looked to have the potential to reach greater heights over fences. Young Hustler and Capability Brown, both front runners, set a blistering gallop, clear of the rest, until Capability Brown parted company with his rider at the fourteenth of the nineteen fences. Young Hustler was then able to get a breather but gave the impression that his gruelling battle for the lead with Capability Brown had taken its toll as Scudamore nursed him home from the turn for a three-length win from Superior Finish, with the 100/1-shot It's A Cracker fifteen lengths further back in third. Barton Bank was a big disappointment, in trouble before halfway and pulled up with a broken blood vessel. Young Hustler's sound jumping and his experience stood him in good stead in the Sun Alliance but he met his match in the Mumm Mildmay Chase at Aintree where Cab On Target, a young chaser with more size and scope, put up a performance that left few under any illusions about the identity of the

Arlington Premier Series Chase Final, Newbury — Young Hustler's winning run continues; Cogent (right) and Second Schedual battle for the minor places

Sun Alliance Novices' Chase, Cheltenham—
the high point of Young Hustler's magnificent season; Superior Finish is in pursuit

season's leading staying novice chaser. Young Hustler started favourite, conceding 6 lb to Cab On Target, but he was no match for the winner from some way out, eventually finishing third, beaten also by Forest Sun. Young Hustler ran a little below form in the Mumm Mildmay Chase but even at his best he'd have faced a well-nigh impossible task at the weights against a most impressive winner.

Young Hustler (ch.g. 1987)	Import (ch 1971)	Porto Bello (ch 1965)	Floribunda
			Street Song
		Immortelle (ch 1960)	Never Say Die
			Thunder
	Davett (b 1969)	Typhoon (br 1958)	Honeyway
			Kingsworthy
		Phrygia (ch 1956)	Mossborough
			Lenaea

The smallish, workmanlike Young Hustler is by the very good sprinter Import, winner of the Wokingham and the Stewards' Cup, out of the genuine and durable middle-distance handicapper Davett. Davett, a fairly useful performer at her best, was still winning races at seven on the Flat in Scotland and the North and she was placed over hurdles before being retired to stud. Davett was a half-sister to Cullen, who won the Great Metropolitan Handicap on the Flat and was a useful staying hurdler, and to another genuine staying handicapper on the Flat, Quarry Wood, the dam of Champion Stakes and Benson And Hedges Gold Cup winner Cormorant Wood and of Supreme Novices Hurdle and Scottish Champion Hurdle winner River Ceiriog. Davett, who is now dead, had eight foals, easily the best of them before Young Hustler being the useful if rather unreliable chaser The Divider (by Leander) who was effective at two miles and stayed three. Young Hustler's four-year-old full brother, Davett's last foal, reportedly may go point-to-pointing in the Borders in the next season. Young Hustler, himself, looks set for another good campaign. Horses with his ability, cast-iron constitution and zest for racing aren't kept out of the winner's circle for long. His legion of admirers will wish him well. *N. A. Twiston-Davies*

YOUNG MARINER 6 b.g. Julio Mariner – Petite Mandy (Mandamus) [1992/3 F16d] third foal: dam useful pointer/hunter chaser: well beaten in

Mr G. M. MacEchern's "Young Hustler"

NH Flat race at Ludlow in December: yet to race over hurdles or fences. *W. Price*

YOUNG MINER 7 ch.g. Monksfield – Tassel Tip (Linacre) [1992/3 c25s c26vpu c25s2 c25v4 c24s3 c24dbd c25d2 c25m* c26dpu] strong, compact gelding: winning hurdler: modest form over fences: won novice chase at Market Rasen in March: blinkered, ran poorly next time: out-and-out stayer: acts on heavy and good to firm ground. *Mrs T. J. McInnes Skinner* **c89 –**

YOUNG MORETON 9 b.g. Young Generation – Kissimmee (FR) (Petingo) [1992/3 c25spu] smallish, workmanlike gelding: novice hurdler/chaser: no form since 1987/8. *G. A. Pritchard-Gordon* **c– –**

YOUNG PARSON 7 b.g. The Parson – Dadooronron (Deep Run) [1992/3 16d6 16g5 20s5] smallish gelding: poor form in novice hurdles: stays 2½m: acts on soft ground. *E. H. Owen jun* **79**

YOUNG POKEY 8 b.g. Uncle Pokey – Young Romance (King's Troop) [1992/3 c21g c16d3 c16g* c17m4 c16f3 c16gpu] rangy gelding: useful chaser: won handicap at Sandown in February: in frame in valuable events at Cheltenham and Aintree afterwards: ran poorly final start: best at around 2m: acts on good to firm and dead ground: fluent jumper: races up with pace. *O. Sherwood* **c140 –**

YOUNG SNUGFIT 9 ch.g. Music Boy – Sinzinbra (Royal Palace) [1992/3 c16spu c17m6 c17gur c16g4 c16mpu] big, lengthy gelding: very smart chaser at best: well below form in 1992/3 (close last of 4 in minor event at Kempton): best around 2m: acts on any going: blinkered twice: jumps well: suited by forcing tactics. *O. Sherwood* **c? –**

YOUNG TY 9 br.g. Lighter – Star of Tycoon (Tycoon II) [1992/3 c20m* c20g*] angular gelding: useful hurdler for Dr J. Robinson in 1990/1: **c98 p –**

successful in novice chases at Doncaster in January and Ayr following month: stays 2½m: acts on any going: jumps soundly in main: should progress over fences. *Mrs M. Reveley*

YOUNG WARRIOR 9 ch.g. Roman Warrior – Teenager (Never Say c–
Die) [1992/3 c19g⁶ c21dᵖᵘ c25gᵖᵘ] leggy, plain gelding: handicap chaser: no
form since 1990/1: usually blinkered: sold out of Miss H. Knight's stable
1,400 gns Ascot November Sales after second start: dead. *Simon de Burgh*

YOZZER HUGHES 8 br.g. Tumble Wind (USA) – Miss Britain (Tudor c–
Melody) [1992/3 18g²] leggy, workmanlike gelding: modest hurdler/novice 94
chaser: stays on any going. *T. B. Hallett*

YUVRAJ 9 b.g. Final Straw – Never Never Land (Habitat) [1992/3 17gᵖᵘ]
compact gelding: lightly-raced hurdler: best at 2m: acts on soft, good to firm –
going and all-weather surfaces: blinkered once. *B. J. McMath*

Z

ZAFRA 5 b.m. Dunbeath (USA) – White's Ferry (Northfields (USA))
[1992/3 22f³] third in early-season novice claimer at Fontwell, better effort 67
over hurdles. *G. F. H. Charles-Jones*

ZAGAZIG (USA) 10 b.g. Chieftain II – I'll Take It (USA) (Royal Levee c–
(USA)) [1992/3 20v c16v⁶ c16v⁶ c16v³] workmanlike gelding: modest
hurdler at best: poor novice chaser: sold 825 gns Ascot February Sales: best –
at 2m: probably acts on any going. *A. Moore*

ZAMANAYN (IRE) 5 gr.g. Mouktar – Zariya (USA) (Blushing Groom
(FR)) [1992/3 16g 17f⁶] lightly-raced novice hurdler: only form on first start. 84
John R. Upson

ZAM BEE 7 gr.g. Zambrano – Brown Bee III (Marcus Superbus) [1992/3 c98
c25g³ c25d² c25g² c25sᵖᵘ c26s⁴ c25d² c20g* c25s³ c20m³ c20f⁶ c21s* c20f⁴ –
c22m³ c21g*] lengthy gelding: modest chaser: won novice event at
Newcastle and 2 handicaps at Hexham in second half of season: effective at
2½m and stays 25f: probably acts on any ground. *W. G. Reed*

ZAMIL (USA) 8 b.g. Lyphard (USA) – Wayward Lass (USA) (Hail The c101
Pirates (USA)) [1992/3 c21s³ c20d⁴ c16v* c21v* c21sᶠ c21sᵖᵘ c16d²]
good-topped gelding: fair hurdler: won novice chases at Uttoxeter and –
Newton Abbot in first half of season: creditable second at Uttoxeter in
February: effective at 2m and stays 21f: best form with give in the ground
and acts on heavy. *K. R. Burke*

ZAMIRAH (IRE) 4 b.f. Trojan Fen – Sweet Pleasure (Sweet Revenge)
[1992/3 16s⁴ 16d* 17f* 17m² 17f⁶] lengthy filly: fair middle-distance 121
performer on Flat when trained by G. Wragg: fairly useful form over
hurdles: won juvenile events at Wincanton in February and Newbury in
March: ran well afterwards, sixth of 8 in valuable contest at Aintree final
start: will stay beyond 17f: acts on firm and dead ground: front runner:
sometimes makes mistakes. *N. A. Twiston-Davies*

ZAM'S SLAVE 8 gr.m. Zambrano – Cool Date (Arctic Slave) [1992/3 c–
c24m c25gᶠ c27gᵖᵘ c24m c21vᵖᵘ] compact mare: poor chaser: trained until
after third outing by J. Charlton: stays 25f: acts on hard ground: usually –
amateur ridden. *Miss P. Robson*

ZANY GIRL 6 b.m. Idiot's Delight – Noble Leaf (Sahib) [1992/3 F16s
22fᵖᵘ 17dᵖᵘ] third foal: sister to NH Flat race winner Zanyman: dam –
lightly-raced novice hurdler: no sign of ability. *Mrs A. Barclay*

ZANYMAN 7 b.g. Idiot's Delight – Noble Leaf (Sahib) [1992/3 21d³]
smallish gelding: NH Flat race winner: looked a stayer when third in novice 90
hurdle at Kempton in October. *J. A. C. Edwards*

ZEALOUS KITTEN (USA) 5 ch.m. The Minstrel (CAN) – Zealous
Cat (USA) (Cougar (CHI)) [1992/3 18s⁵ 20s³ 17s* 16v² 17dᶠ] leggy mare: 104
rarely takes the eye: fair hurdler: won handicap at Wolverhampton in

January: effective from 2m to 2½m: acts on heavy ground: game and consistent. *R. J. Price*

ZEPHYR NIGHTS (USA)   6 b.g. Grey Dawn II – Vaslava (Habitat)   c–
[1992/3 c24sᵖᵘ] leggy gelding: poor novice hurdler: acts on good to firm and   –
dead ground: blinkered twice: won a point in April: no show in hunter chase
later in month. *T. L. Jones*

ZEST FOR LIFE   7 ch.g. Quayside – Orange Sprite (The Last Hurrah)
[1992/3 17d² 22d³] tall gelding: lightly-raced novice hurdler: sold 1,600 gns   84
Ascot March Sales: stays 2¾m: acts on dead going. *D. Nicholson*

ZETA'S LAD   10 ch.g. Over The River (FR) – Zeta's Daughter (Master   c 149
Owen) [1992/3 c23v* c24d* c26v* c24d* c24g* c29s³]   –
Zeta's Lad is a prime example of the type of horse his trainer favours
buying, an Irish National Hunt-bred with a long-term future as a chaser.
Bought as a three-year-old, he really came to himself at ten, making up into
a smart staying chaser. Zeta's Lad remained in Ireland to develop after his
purchase, and won a National Hunt Flat race and a maiden hurdle there in
1987/8. He went straight over fences in Britain in 1988/9 and by the end of
that season had won five of his ten races in minor company. Then came a
set-back. Following two wins in handicaps in 1989/90 he injured a leg in the
Scottish Grand National. As a result he had to be given a year off. On his
return in 1991/2 he usually ran well, but his form settled at a middle level;
when put in against good horses in an attempt to follow up stable-companion
Nick The Brief's successes in the Hennessy Cognac Gold Cup at Leopardstown he started at 33/1 and looked well out of his depth.
Zeta's Lad was back in Ireland eleven months later, in January 1993
that is, for the Telecom Eireann Thyestes Handicap Chase at Gowran Park,
a National trial. It was his third race of the latest season, and already the
evidence pointed to his being an improved horse. Not so much the evidence
of his first-time-out win at Uttoxeter in December, more his game neck win
from Le Piccolage in a strongly-run race at Kempton later in the month. The
Thyestes amply confirmed as much, as Zeta's Lad got up on the post from
Ebony Jane. Three out of three soon became four out of four when Espy was
beaten two and a half lengths in the Fairlawne Chase, a good quality

*Telecom Eireann Thyestes Handicap Chase, Gowran Park—
Zeta's Lad (right) and Ebony Jane give their all*

Racing Post Handicap Chase, Kempton—
Zeta's Lad wins from Docklands Express and Bradbury Star (left)

conditions race at Windsor, making Zeta's Lad one of the most interesting candidates for the valuable Racing Post Chase at Kempton in February. However, further improvement seemed essential there if he were to maintain his winning run off the handicap mark he'd been given. He had the same weight as the 11/4 favourite Bradbury Star; he started at 11/1, while another five of the twelve runners, Blazing Walker, Gold Options, Romany King, Tinryland and Mr Entertainer were shorter. The race turned out to be a familiar one round Kempton, more of a test of speed than stamina with a good proportion of the field still in with a shout turning for home. Bradbury Star led into the final straight attended closely by the previous year's winner Docklands Express and Zeta's Lad. On the outside of the three Zeta's Lad was travelling very well under restraint. His usual jockey Robbie Supple holds him for a late run, and John White, deputizing on this occasion, had clearly been well briefed. The three horses stayed together until touching down over the last, where Zeta's Lad produced easily the best turn of foot to go on and win by a length and a neck, just pushed out with hands and heels, from Docklands Express and Bradbury Star. After this performance Zeta's Lad became a leading fancy for the Grand National on the same mark, and was vying with Party Politics and Romany King for favouritism at Aintree at the time of the first false start. He completed a circuit before being pulled up, in mid-division. He ran a good race when favourite for the Irish Grand National at Fairyhouse nine days later, finishing third behind Ebony Jane, beaten five and a half lengths by the one-length winner who was 6 lb better off than in the Thyestes Chase. However, he came under pressure before the second last and faded out of second place on the flat. His trainer thinks that the circuit of Aintree might have taken a bit too much out of him and intends going straight to Fairyhouse next time.

Zeta's Lad (ch.g. 1983)	Over The River (FR) (ch 1974)	Luthier (b or br 1965)	Klairon
			Flute Enchantee
		Medenine (b 1967)	Prudent II
			Ma Congaie
	Zeta's Daughter (b 1971)	Master Owen (b 1956)	Owen Tudor
			Miss Maisie
		Black Zeta (b 1965)	Black Tarquin
			Southern Zeta

If the name Zeta's Lad has a familiar ring to it the reader will probably be old enough to have been racing in the 'seventies, when another Zeta, Zeta's Son, was around. Zeta's Son, another smart staying chaser with a turn of foot, winner of the Hennessy Gold Cup and the Anthony Mildmay, Peter Cazalet Memorial in 1976/7, was out of Southern Zeta. Zeta's Lad's gran-dam, the unraced Black Zeta, was his half-sister. Black Zeta produced several minor jumping winners. Zeta's Daughter wasn't among them—she never raced—but she left her mark at stud. Besides Zeta's Lad she is the dam of Sea Splash (by Menelek), Baltard (by Bargello), Little Chippings and Give Her The Boot (both by Little Buskins) and Erostin Floats (by Paddy's Stream), all of them jumping winners if you count Baltard's three point-to-points.

In spite of his age and his achievements already, there is a chance that the best is still to come from Zeta's Lad. He seems sure to win more good handicap chases over three miles or more. Genuine and consistent, and a very dependable jumper, he has so far shown that he can act on ground as different as good to firm and heavy. He has an excellent turn of foot and is best waited with. *John R. Upson*

ZEUS 9 ch.g. Morston (FR) – Fodens Eve (Dike (USA)) [1992/3 24g⁴ 21d 17d⁶ 23d 22d⁶ 21m 23f] lengthy, good-topped gelding: of little account nowadays. *G. Fierro*   –

ZILLJO'S-STAR 6 b.g. Strong Gale – Rosie O'Grady (Barrons Court) [1992/3 21m⁴ 25g³ 21d5] workmanlike gelding: moderate novice hurdler: stayed 21f: acted on good to firm ground: dead. *J. H. Johnson*   93

ZINGER 5 b.g. Lucky Wednesday – Starkist (So Blessed) [1992/3 16d] sparely-made gelding: of little account: sold 1,050 gns Doncaster June Sales. *T. Fairhurst*   –

ZUKO (CHI) 12 b.g. Kimono (CHI) – La Saudade (CHI) (Candaules) [1992/3 c21d c25s⁶ c24v⁶ c21g³ c25s²] compact gelding: one-time useful chaser: stayed 25f: acted on any going: sound jumper: dead. *Mrs S. J. Smith*   c100 –

ZULU 5 b.h. Idiot's Delight – Take My Hand (Precipice Wood) [1992/3 F18d 24g⁶ 22g] fifth foal: half-brother to winning jumpers Contact Kelvin (by Workboy), Gunner Mac (by Gunner B) and D C Flyer (by Record Token): dam poor maiden: poor form over hurdles, better effort at 3m. *N. B. Mason*   74

ZULU (FR) 8 b.h. Zino – Marilu (FR) (Luthier) [1992/3 16d 17s 17v³ 17v a16g⁵ 17s] smallish, angular horse: poor hurdler nowadays: raced only at around 2m: acts on any going. *G. A. Ham*   72

ZUMMERSET (NZ) 11 b.g. Star Wolf – Homunga Miss (NZ) (Masthead) [1992/3 c18g⁵ c21d⁴ c19s⁶ c16dᵖᵘ c24d⁴ c20d c17fᵖᵘ] compact gelding: winning chaser: no form in 1992/3: sometimes breaks blood vessels: sketchy jumper: blinkered once. *A. Barrow*   c– –

ERRATA & ADDENDA

'CHASERS & HURDLERS 1991/92'

Bellezza	mare, not gelding
Kristenson	trainer Mrs L. Stone
Monk's Mistake	rated—over hurdles
Seaton Girl	rated 81 over hurdles
Tri Folene (Fr)	won her 3 *completed* starts
P839	Scudamore's total for 1986/7 is 124 (21.45%)

BIG RACE RESULTS 1992/93

Prize money for racing in Ireland has been converted to £ Sterling at the exchange rate current at the time of the race. The figures are correct to the nearest £.

1   UNITED HOUSE   2m
CONSTRUCTION CHASE
(HANDICAP) (5yo +)
£16,155   Ascot   21 October

Katabatic 9-12-0 SMcNeill...... **1**
Campsea-Ash 8-10-7
DMurphy........................ 2½.2
Hogmanay (Can) 10-10-7
HDavies 3.3
Moment of Truth 8-10-7
BStorey 2½.4
Sirrah Jay 12-10-7
AMaguire 3½.5
Master Rajh 8-10-13
MMLynch 4.6

2/1 KATABATIC, 9/4 Master Rajh, 5/2 Moment of Truth, 10/1 Sirrah Jay, 12/1 Hogmanay, 40/1 Campsea-Ash
Pell-mell Partners (Andrew Turnell)
6ran 3m57.64 (Good)

2   DESERT ORCHID   2m5f
SOUTH WESTERN PATTERN
CHASE (Gr 2) (5yo +)
£15,625   Wincanton   22 October

Remittance Man 8-11-8
RDunwoody **1**
Kings Fountain 9-11-8
PScudamore 12.2
Setter Country 8-10-9
WIrvine 25.3
Norton's Coin 11-11-8
GMcCourt 12.4

4/11 REMITTANCE MAN, 5/2 Kings Fountain, 16/1 Norton's Coin, 40/1 Setter Country
Mr J. E. H. Collins (N. J. Henderson)
4ran 5m16.20 (Good to Soft)

3   TOTE WEST   3m1f
YORKSHIRE HURDLE
(Gr 2) (4yo +)
£7,845   Wetherby   31 October

Burgoyne 6-11-0 LWyer.......... **1**
Nomadic Way (USA) 7-11-7
JOsborne 5.2
Better Times Ahead 6-11-4
NDoughty......................... 4.3
Everaldo (Fr) 8-11-0
JRKavanagh 7.4
Tallywagger 5-11-0
JCallaghan 2.5
Sweet Glow (Fr) 5-11-0
PScudamore 8.6
Mils Mij 7-11-2 MrWHurst ...hd.7
Fettuccine 8-11-0
MrAThornton 1½.8
Judges Fancy 8-11-0 AMaguire.. f

11/10 Nomadic Way, 4/1 BURGOYNE, 9/2 Sweet Glow, 13/2 Everaldo, 14/1 Fettuccine, 20/1 Better Times Ahead, 33/1 Judges Fancy, Mils Mij, 50/1 Tally-wagger
Mr P. D. Savill (M. H. Easterby) 9ran 6m02.96 (Good)

4   TETLEY BITTER   3m110y
CHARLIE HALL CHASE
(Gr 2) (5yo +)
£12,440   Wetherby   31 October

Tipping Tim 7-11-2
CLlewellyn........................ **1**
Pat's Jester 9-11-10
NDoughty........................ nk.2
Ida's Delight 13-11-2
PNiven 20.3
Cool Ground 10-11-10
AMaguire 3½.4
Cahervillahow 8-11-2
LCusack 2.5
Old Applejack 12-11-2
PMcWilliams 1½.6
Kildimo 12-11-2
RichardGuest dist.7

9/4 Cahervillahow, 11/4 TIPPING TIM, 7/2 Pat's Jester, 5/1 Cool Ground, 16/1 Kildimo, Old Applejack, 33/1 Ida's Delight
Mrs J. Mould (N. A. Twiston-Davies)
7ran 6m22.16 (Good)

5   PLYMOUTH GIN   2¼m
HALDON GOLD CHALLENGE
CUP CHASE (Gr 2) (5yo +)
£11,250   Exeter   3 November

Waterloo Boy 9-11-6
RDunwoody **1**
1*   **Katabatic** 9-11-6 LHarvey ... 5.2
Golden Freeze 10-11-0
MPitman 12.3
2³   Setter Country 8-10-9
WIrvine 8.4
1³   Hogmanay (Can) 10-11-0
HDavies 15.5

2/5 Katabatic, 11/4 WATERLOO BOY, 25/1 Golden Freeze, Hogmanay, 80/1 Setter Country
Mr M. R. Deeley (D. Nicholson) 5ran 4m23.75 (Good to Soft)

6   TOTE SILVER   2½m110y
TROPHY (HANDICAP
HURDLE) (4yo +)
£15,281   Chepstow   7 November

Mighty Mogul 5-10-12
RDunwoody **1**

Petosku 4-10-2
  PScudamore **4.2**
  Dara Doone 6-11-2 HDavies **4.3**
3³ Better Times Ahead 6-11-9
  NDoughty........................... ¾.4
  Annicombe Run 8-10-6
  CLlewellyn...........................7.5
  The Widget Man 6-11-7
  PHide ¾.6
  Top Javalin (NZ) 5-9-12
  RGreene............................sh.7
  Derab (USA) 6-10-12
  BPowell..............................hd.8
  Needwood Muppet 5-10-0
  LHarvey 3.9
  Bollin Patrick 7-10-12
  LWyer 15.10
  Pactolus (USA) 9-11-3
  MAFitzgerald 15.11
  Black Sapphire 5-10-10
  SSmithEccles.................. 15.12
  Belafonte 5-10-0 NMann............ f

11/8 MIGHTY MOGUL, 9/2 Bollin
Patrick, 8/1 Dara Doone, Petosku, 12/1
Belafonte, Better Times Ahead, 16/1
Annicombe Run, Needwood Muppet,
20/1 The Widget Man, 33/1 Black Sap-
phire, Derab, Pactolus, Top Javalin
  Mrs Shirley Robins (D. Nicholson)
13ran 5m06.78 (Soft)

7 STEEL PLATE AND   3m 1f
  SECTIONS YOUNG CHASERS
  CHAMPIONSHIP FINAL
  (LIMITED HANDICAP)
  (5, 6, 7 and 8yo)
£13,420 Cheltenham 13 November
  Bradbury Star 7-11-12
  DMurphy.............................. **1**
  Whaat Fettle 7-10-5
  MMoloney........................¾.2
  Le Piccolage 8-10-5
  RDunwoody dh.2
  Glenbrook d'Or 8-10-5
  LHarvey 12.4
  Takemethere 8-10-5
  JLower..............................dist.5
  Ok Corral (USA) 5-10-2
  BClifford ½.6

1/2 BRADBURY STAR, 9/2 Whaat
Fettle, 5/1 Le Piccolage, 20/1 Glenbrook
d'Or, 33/1 Takemethere, 66/1 Ok Corral
  Mr James Campbell (J. T. Gifford)
6ran 6m37.70 (Good to Soft)

8 MACKESON GOLD 2½m 110y
  CUP HANDICAP CHASE
  (Gr 3) (5yo +)
£32,332 Cheltenham 14 November
4* **Tipping Tim** 7-10-10
  CLlewellyn............................ **1**
  Another Coral 9-10-8
  RDunwoody **7.2**
  Beech Road 10-10-6
  RichardGuest sh.3

General Idea 7-11-7
  BSheridan 5.4
  Brandeston 7-10-1
  DMurphy........................... 12.5
  Edberg 8-10-6 GMcCourt 8.6
  Space Fair 9-10-0 JOsborne . nk.7
  Toranfield 8-10-6
  NWilliamson 2.8
  Nos Na Gaoithe 9-10-1
  RGarritty.......................dist.9
2² Kings Fountain 9-11-10 ATory .. f
  Milford Quay 9-10-13
  PScudamore .... f
  Howe Street 9-10-0 AOrkney .. ur
5³ Golden Freeze 10-10-10
  MPitman ....pu
  Monumental Lad 9-9-7
  DLeahy.................................pu
1 Sirrah Jay 12-10-4 JFrost ....pu
  Gale Again 5-10-2 CGrant........pu

11/2 TIPPING TIM, 6/1 Another Coral,
Kings Fountain, 15/2 Edberg, 9/1 Gale
Again, 12/1 Brandeston, General Idea,
Milford Quay, 14/1 Beech Road, Toran-
field, 16/1 Space Fair, 25/1 Golden
Freeze, Howe Street, 33/1 Nos Na
Gaoithe, Sirrah Jay, 100/1 Monumental
Lad
  Mrs J. Mould (N. A. Twiston-Davies)
16ran 5m 19.48 (Good to Soft)

9 CORAL-ELITE 2m 110y
  HURDLE (4yo +)
£23,165 Cheltenham 15 November
  Morley Street 8-11-8
  RDunwoody **1**
  Granville Again 6-11-2
  PScudamore **1.2**
  Oh So Risky 5-11-5 PHolley. **2.3**
  Tyrone Bridge 6-11-2
  DMurphy.............................3.4

3/5 Granville Again, 8/5 MORLEY
STREET, 9/1 Oh So Risky, Tyrone
Bridge
  Michael Jackson Bloodstock Ltd (G.
B. Balding) 4ran 4m26.63 (Heavy)

10 EDWARD HANMER 3m
  MEMORIAL CHASE
  (LIMITED HANDICAP) (5yo +)
£9,968 Haydock 18 November
  Run For Free 8-11-0
  PScudamore **1**
  Jodami 7-11-5 MDwyer **3.2**
  Romany King 8-11-10
  RichardGuest 25.3
  Knight Oil 9-10-7
  MRichards..........................10.4

11/8 RUN FOR FREE, 13/8 Romany
King, 3/1 Jodami, 20/1 Knight Oil
  Mrs Millicent R. Freethy (M. C. Pipe)
4ran 6m26.55 (Soft)

11 RACECALL ASCOT 2½m
  HURDLE (Gr 2) (4yo +)
£14,318 Ascot 20 November
  Muse 5-11-0 PHolley **1**

843

9* **Morley Street** 8-11-10
RDunwoody hd.2
9 **Tyrone Bridge** 6-11-0
MFoster 8.3
Lift And Load (USA) 5-11-0
GMcCourt 2½.4
6³ Dara Doone 6-11-0 AMaguire .5.5
6 The Widget Man 6-11-0
DMurphy.............................5.6
Grey Salute (Can) 9-11-0
GBradley ....pu

2/5 Morley Street, 7/1 Tyrone Bridge, 9/1 MUSE, 16/1 Lift And Load, 20/1 The Widget Man, 25/1 Dara Doone, 100/1 Grey Salute
White Horse Racing Ltd (D. R. C. Elsworth) 7ran 4m54.43 (Good to Soft)

12 H & T WALKER 2m3f110y
GOLD CUP CHASE
(LIMITED HANDICAP)
(Gr 2) (5yo +)
£27,440 Ascot 21 November
Deep Sensation 7-11-2
DMurphy.............................. 1
Danny Harrold 8-10-13
SMcNeill 2.2
7* **Bradbury Star** 7-12-0
EMurphy ½.3
Second Schedual 7-11-2
CSwan 1.4
The Illywhacker 7-11-2
MPitman 4.5
Cyphrate (USA) 6-11-9
PScudamore 30.6
Young Hustler 5-10-7
DBridgwater 1½.7
Sabaki River 8-10-7
MAFitzgerald 25.8
8³ Beech Road 10-11-4
RichardGuest...................... ur
Far Senior 6-10-12 ATory ....pu

3/1 Bradbury Star, 5/1 Second Schedual, 11/2 DEEP SENSATION, The Illywhacker, 8/1 Danny Harrold, 9/1 Beech Road, Cyphrate, 12/1 Far Senior, 50/1 Sabaki River, 100/1 Young Hustler
Mr R. F. Eliot (J. T. Gifford) 10ran 5m01.59 (Good to Soft)

13 LADBROKE 2m110y
NOVEMBER HANDICAP
HURDLE (4yo +)
£17,200 Liverpool 21 November
Baydon Star 5-10-1
RDunwoody 1
Jungle Knife 6-11-2
SSmithEccles.................... 7.2
Jinxy Jack 8-12-0
NDoughty........................... 3.3
Welshman 6-10-7
DGallagher.........................3.4
6 Bollin Patrick 7-10-4
LWyer 20.5
Triple Top 7-10-0 AO'Hagan ...pu

evens BAYDON STAR, 7/2 Jungle Knife, 4/1 Jinxy Jack, 8/1 Bollin Patrick, 9/1 Welshman, 100/1 Triple Top
Mrs Shirley Robins (D. Nicholson) 6ran 4m01.15 (Good to Soft)

14 CROWTHER HOMES 3m3f
BECHER CHASE (HANDICAP)
(6yo +)
£20,019 Liverpool 21 November
4 **Kildimo** 12-10-3 LWyer 1
Four Trix 11-10-0 DByrne.... 7.2
The Antartex 9-10-1
RDunwoody 1½.3
Stay On Tracks 10-10-0
CGrant nk.4
Interim Lib 9-10-3
MrJBradburne 30.5
4 Cool Ground 10-12-0 AMaguire . f
Seagram (NZ) 12-10-0
NHawke .... ur
City Entertainer 11-10-1
MrDMcCain ....pu
John O'Dee 9-9-7
MrPaulMurphy ....pu

9/4 Cool Ground, 9/2 Stay On Tracks, 5/1 The Antartex, 6/1 Four Trix, Seagram, 9/1KILDIMO, 16/1InterimLib,33/1City Entertainer, John O'Dee
Lady Harris (Mrs S. J. Smith) 9ran 7m15.28 (Good to Soft)

15 PETERBOROUGH 2½m110y
CHASE (Gr 2) (5yo +)
£11,142 Huntingdon 24 November
2* **Remittance Man** 8-11-9
RDunwoody 1
Emsee-H 7-11-1 AMaguire .. 7.2
8 **Sirrah Jay** 12-11-1 JFrost. dist.3
Uncle Ernie 7-11-5
MDwyer dist.4

1/5 REMITTANCE MAN, 4/1 Uncle Ernie, 33/1 Emsee-H, Sirrah Jay
Mr J. E. H. Collins (N. J. Henderson) 4ran 5m10.83 (Soft)

16 BONUSPRINT GERRY 2m110y
FEILDEN HURDLE
(Gr 2) (4yo +)
£9,620 Newbury 28 November
6* **Mighty Mogul** 5-11-3
RDunwoody 1
Staunch Friend (USA) 4-11-6
PScudamore 4.2
11 **Lift And Load (USA)** 5-11-6
DMurphy........................... 15.3
Seon 6-11-0 LWyer 3½.4
Flown 5-11-6 JOsborne sh.5
Duke of Monmouth (USA)
4-11-6 MRichards 15.6

5/4 Staunch Friend, 11/8 MIGHTY MOGUL, 9/1 Duke of Monmouth, 14/1 Lift And Load, 16/1 Flown, 50/1 Seon
Mrs Shirley Robins (D. Nicholson) 6ran 4m05.86 (Soft)

17   AKZO LONG   3m110y
        DISTANCE
        HURDLE
        (Gr 2) (4yo +)
£9,500   Newbury   28 November
3*   **Burgoyne** 6-11-4 LWyer **1**
11³   **Tyrone Bridge** 6-11-0
        RDunwoody nk.**2**
        Ambuscade (USA) 6-11-0
        MDwyer 10.**3**
3   Sweet Glow (Fr) 5-11-0
        PScudamore 25.**4**
        Gaelstrom 5-10-13
        CLlewellyn.........................15.**5**
11   The Widget Man 6-11-0
        DMurphy.........................dist.**6**
        Sir Crusty 10-11-0
        VSlattery nk.**7**
        Officer Cadet 5-11-0
        DMorris 15.**8**
3²   Nomadic Way (USA) 7-11-7
        JOsborne dist.**9**
6/4 Nomadic Way, 11/4 Burgoyne, 6/1 TYRONE BRIDGE, 7/1 Ambuscade, 9/1 Gaelstrom, 14/1 Sweet Glow, The Widget Man, 100/1 Officer Cadet, Sir Crusty
   Mr Paul Green (M. C. Pipe) 9ran 6m20.04 (Soft)

18   HENNESSY COGNAC 3¼m110y
        GOLD CUP
        HANDICAP CHASE
        (Gr 3) (5yo +)
£36,160   Newbury   28 November
        Sibton Abbey 7-10-0
        AMaguire **1**
10²   **Jodami** 7-10-2 MDwyer ¾.**2**
        The Fellow (Fr) 7-11-13
        AKondrat............................ 6.**3**
        Chatam (USA) 8-11-4
        PScudamore 1½.**4**
        Gambling Royal 9-10-0
        RDunwoody 6.**5**
        Rowlandsons Jewels 11-10-0
        DGallagher.......................25.**6**
        Captain Dibble 7-10-4
        CLlewellyn.......................25.**7**
        Twin Oaks 12-11-6 NDoughty .pu
        Party Politics 8-10-13
        DMurphy...............................pu
        Sparkling Flame 8-10-6
        JWhite ....pu
        Bishops Hall 6-10-0
        NWilliamson ....pu
        Latent Talent 8-10-0
        JOsborne ....pu
        Mr Boston 7-10-0 STurner ......pu
10/3 Jodami, 9/2 Captain Dibble, Chatam, 5/1 The Fellow, 13/2 Gambling Royal, 11/1 Twin Oaks, 12/1 Latent Talent, Party Politics, 25/1 Bishops Hall, 40/1 SIBTON ABBEY, 50/1 Mr Boston, Rowlandsons Jewels, Sparkling Flame
   Mr G. A. Hubbard (F. Murphy) 13ran 7m01.01 (Soft)

19   BELLWAY HOMES   2m110y
        'FIGHTING FIFTH' HURDLE
        (Gr 2) (4yo +)
£9,500   Newcastle   28 November
        Halkopous 6-11-0
        SSmithEccles........................ **1**
        Royal Derbi 7-11-8 CGrant .. 6.**2**
        Corrin Hill 5-11-0 PNiven . 1½.**3**
        Coulton 5-11-4 GMcCourt 8.**4**
        Bold Ambition 5-11-0
        SusanKersey 10.**5**
        Able Player (USA) 5-11-0
        DBentley........................30.**6**
7/4 Coulton, HALKOPOUS, 9/4 Royal Derbi, 25/1 Able Player, 66/1 Corrin Hill, 150/1 Bold Ambition
   Mr Athos Christodoulou (M. H. Tompkins) 6ran 4m03.28 (Good)

20   REHEARSAL CHASE   3m
        (LIMITED HANDICAP)
        (Gr 2) (5yo +)
£15,970   Chepstow   5 December
10*   **Run For Free** 8-10-7
        MPerrett **1**
        Miinnehoma 9-10-7
        PScudamore 12.**2**
        Bonanza Boy 11-10-7
        HDavies 8.**3**
14   Cool Ground 10-11-13
        AMaguire 25.**4**
4/7 Miinnehoma, 3/1 RUN FOR FREE, 5/1 Cool Ground, 22/1 Bonanza Boy
   Mrs Millicent R. Freethy (M. C. Pipe) 4ran 6m38.97 (Heavy)

21   WILLIAM HILL   2m110y
        HANDICAP HURDLE
        (Gr 3) (4yo +)
£20,750   Chepstow   5 December
        Valfinet (Fr) 5-10-2 JLower **1**
        Kilcash (Ire) 4-10-10
        MRichards......................... ½.**2**
        Maamur (USA) 4-10-0
        DJBurchell 1½.**3**
        King Credo 7-10-13
        JOsborne 8.**4**
        Egypt Mill Prince 6-11-0
        MPitman 12.**5**
        Jopanini 7-10-10
        RDunwoody 2½.**6**
        Easy Buck 5-10-9 CMaude....hd.**7**
13²   Jungle Knife 6-11-10
        SSmithEccles 25.**8**
        One More Dream 5-10-13
        JFrost ....pu
        Miss Bobby Bennett 5-10-9
        MFoster ....pu
5/4 VALFINET, 7/2 Jopanini, 13/2 Kilcash, 10/1 Egypt Mill Prince, 12/1 Jungle Knife, 14/1 Easy Buck, One More Dream, 16/1 King Credo, 50/1 Maamur, Miss Bobby Bennett
   Mr Frank A. Farrant (M. C. Pipe) 10ran 4m09.84 (Heavy)

22   MITSUBISHI SHOGUN   2m
TINGLE CREEK TROPHY
(LIMITED HANDICAP CHASE)
(Gr 2) (5yo +)
£12,260   Sandown   5 December

5*	**Waterloo Boy** 9-12-0	
	RDunwoody 1	
12*	Deep Sensation 7-10-7	
	DMurphy 2½.2	
15	Uncle Ernie 7-11-4 MDwyer 1.3	
	Mr Felix 6-10-7 BPowell 20.4	
8	Edberg 8-10-7 AOrkney 8.5	

7/4 Deep Sensation, 15/8 Uncle Ernie, 11/4 WATERLOO BOY, 8/1 Edberg, 66/1 Mr Felix

Mr M. R. Deeley (D. Nicholson) 5ran 4m08.56 (Soft)

---

23   DURKAN BROTHERS   2½m
INTERNATIONAL
PUNCHESTOWN CHASE
(Gr 2) (5yo +)
£12,727   Punchestown   6 December

	Gold Options 10-11-4	
	MDwyer 1	
8	General Idea 7-12-0	
	BSheridan hd.2	
	Garamycin 10-12-0	
	AMaguire 9.3	
4	Cahervillahow 8-11-4	
	LPCusack ¾.4	
	Firions Law 7-12-0 MFlynn .. sh.5	
	Blitzkreig 9-11-4	
	CO'Dwyer 20.6	
	Rust Never Sleeps 8-11-4	
	GMO'Neill .... f	
	The Committee 9-11-4 CFSwan f	
	Feroda 11-11-11 TJTaaffe ....pu	

5/2 Cahervillahow, 4/1 General Idea, 9/2 Garamycin, 13/2 Feroda, 8/1 Blitzkreig, 10/1 Firions Law, GOLD OPTIONS, 20/1 Rust Never Sleeps, The Committee

Mr J. McCaghy (P. D. McCreery) 9ran 5m48.60 (Soft)

---

24   TOMMY WHITTLE   3m
CHASE (5yo +)
£10,114   Haydock   9 December

18	**Twin Oaks** 12-11-2	
	RDunwoody 1	
4²	Pat's Jester 9-11-10	
	NDoughty 12.2	
	Espy 9-11-2 GBradley 15.3	
14*	Kildimo 12-11-2 JCallaghan .. 12.4	
	Old Road (USA) 6-10-12	
	NWilliamson ....pu	

5/4 TWIN OAKS, 11/8 Pat's Jester, 13/2 Kildimo, 12/1 Espy, 66/1 Old Road

Mr J. N. G. Moreton (G. Richards) 5ran 6m29.48 (Good to Soft)

---

25   ARLINGTON BULA   2m 1f
HURDLE (Gr 2) (4yo +)
£21,475   Cheltenham   12 December

19*	Halkopous 6-11-2 AMaguire ... 1	

9²	**Granville Again** 6-11-8	
	PScudamore 10.2	
11²	**Morley Street** 8-11-8	
	RDunwoody 6.3	
9³	Oh So Risky 5-11-8 PHolley.. nk.4	
	Kribensis 8-11-0 DMurphy ... 10.5	
	Boro Smackeroo 7-11-4	
	AOrkney 3½.6	

7/4 Granville Again, 15/8 Morley Street, 3/1 Oh So Risky, 8/1 HALKOPOUS, 25/1 Kribensis, 200/1 Boro Smackeroo

Mr Athos Christodoulou (M. H. Tompkins) 6ran 4m23.91 (Heavy)

---

26   TRIPLEPRINT GOLD   2m5f
CUP (HANDICAP CHASE)
(Gr 3) (5yo +)
£31,715   Cheltenham   12 December

8²	**Another Coral** 9-11-4	
	RDunwoody 1	
12	**Second Schedual** 7-11-0	
	AMaguire 5.2	
8*	**Tipping Tim** 7-12-0	
	CLlewellyn 3.3	
	Freeline Finishing 8-10-11	
	BPowell 2½.4	
	For The Grain 8-10-11	
	GMcCourt 2.5	
	Sacre d'Or (USA) 7-10-5	
	CHawkins 2.6	
	Elfast 9-11-2 MMLynch 30.7	
8	Milford Quay 9-11-9	
	PScudamore .... f	
12	The Illywhacker 7-11-0	
	MPitman ....bd	
8	Nos Na Gaoithe 9-10-6	
	RGarritty ....pu	

9/2 Sacre d'Or, Tipping Tim, 5/1 Second Schedual, 11/2 ANOTHER CORAL, 8/1 The Illywhacker, 9/1 Milford Quay, 10/1 Freeline Finishing, 12/1 For The Grain, 20/1 Nos Na Gaoithe, 25/1 Elfast

Mr M. R. Deeley (D. Nicholson) 10ran 5m35.37 (Heavy)

---

27   YOUNGMANS LONG   3m 1f110y
WALK HURDLE
(Gr 1) (4yo +)
£23,191   Ascot   19 December

	Vagog 7-11-7 MFoster 1	
17*	Burgoyne 6-11-7 LWyer 2½.2	
	Shuil Ar Aghaidh 6-11-2	
	AMaguire 2.3	
17²	Tyrone Bridge 6-11-7	
	RDunwoody 4.4	
	Super Sense 7-11-7	
	DMurphy 2.5	
11*	Muse 5-11-7 PHolley 5.6	
	True Brave (USA) 4-11-7	
	RDuchene 20.7	
	Sweet Duke (Fr) 5-11-7	
	PScudamore dist.8	
	Piper's Son 6-11-7 GBradley ...pu	

10/3 Burgoyne, 4/1 Muse, 9/2 True Brave, 5/1 Tyrone Bridge, 15/2 VAGOG,

11/1 Super Sense, Sweet Duke, 14/1 Shuil Ar Aghaidh, 50/1 Piper's Son

Mr M. A. Swift (M. C. Pipe) 9ran 6m 18.50 (Soft)

28	SGB HANDICAP CHASE (5yo +)		3m 110y
£24,338	Ascot	19 December	
18	**Captain Dibble** 7-10-1 CLlewellyn		**1**
20[2]	**Miinnehoma** 9-10-8 PScudamore		2½.**2**
18	**Rowlandsons Jewels** 11-10-0 DGallagher		20.**3**
10[3]	Romany King 8-10-7 GBradley		3½.4
24	Kildimo 12-10-5 LWyer		30.5
	Parsons Green 8-10-0 JRKavanagh		30.6
20	Cool Ground 10-12-0 AMaguire		nk.7
18	Gambling Royal 9-10-0 RDunwoody		ur

7/4 Miinnehoma, 3/1 Gambling Royal, 4/1 Romany King, 7/1 CAPTAIN DIBBLE, 16/1 Parsons Green, 20/1 Kildimo, Rowlandsons Jewels, 25/1 Cool Ground

Mrs R. Vaughan (N. A. Twiston-Davies) 8ran 6m25.40 (Soft)

29	FROGMORE HANDICAP CHASE (5yo +)		2m
£10,143	Ascot	19 December	
12	**Cyphrate (USA)** 6-11-2 PScudamore		**1**
	Last 'o' The Bunch 8-10-11 NDoughty		3½.**2**
5	**Setter Country** 8-10-0 WIrvine		15.**3**
	Young Benz 8-11-2 LWyer		3.4
	Poetic Gem 7-10-0 AMaguire		20.5
	Ardbrin 9-10-1 DMurphy		½.6
	Redundant Pal 9-12-0 JRailton		pu

7/4 Last 'o' The Bunch, 10/3 Young Benz, 9/2 CYPHRATE, 6/1 Ardbrin, 7/1 Setter Country, 16/1 Redundant Pal, 25/1 Poetic Gem

Alias Smith & Jones Racing (M. C. Pipe) 7ran 4m02.76 (Soft)

30	NORTHUMBERLAND 2m 110y GOLD CUP NOVICES' CHASE (Gr 2) (4yo +)		
£14,416	Newcastle	19 December	
	Sybillin 6-11-7 CGrant		**1**
	Dawson City 5-11-7 RGarritty		4.**2**
	Sartorius 6-11-7 HDavies		1½.**3**
	Vayrua (Fr) 7-11-7 AOrkney		1½.4
	Military Honour 7-11-7 MrSSwiers		¾.5

Sponsor Light 8-11-7 TReed 20.6
Traumatic Laura 7-11-2 DBentley 2½.7

10/11 Dawson City, 15/8 SYBILLIN, 6/1 Sartorius, 33/1 Vayrua, 40/1 Military Honour, 100/1 Traumatic Laura, 200/1 Sponsor Light

Marquesa de Moratalla (J. G. FitzGerald) 7ran 4m24.25 (Soft)

31	TRIPLEPRINT FELTHAM NOVICES' CHASE (Gr 1) (5yo +)		3m
£24,763	Kempton	26 December	
	Dakyns Boy 7-11-7 PScudamore		**1**
	Ardcroney Chief 6-11-7 MRichards		dist.**2**
	Barton Bank 6-11-7 RDunwoody		f
	Forest Sun 7-11-7 AMaguire		f
	Casting Time (NZ) 8-11-7 HDavies		pu

evens Barton Bank, 7/4 Forest Sun, 9/2 DAKYNS BOY, 50/1 Ardcroney Chief, 150/1 Casting Time

Mr Alan Parker (N. A. Twiston-Davies) 5ran 6m 19.50 (Soft)

32	KING GEORGE VI CHASE (Gr 1) (5yo +)		3m
£44,500	Kempton	26 December	
18[3]	**The Fellow (Fr)** 7-11-10 AKondrat		**1**
24[2]	**Pat's Jester** 9-11-10 NDoughty		6.**2**
26	**The Illywhacker** 7-11-10 MPitman		7.**3**
12[3]	Bradbury Star 7-11-10 DMurphy		15.4
22*	Deep Sensation 7-11-10 RDunwoody		1½.5
	Docklands Express 10-11-10 ATory		25.6
26[3]	Tipping Tim 7-11-10 CLlewellyn		dist.7
8	Kings Fountain 9-11-10 PScudamore		ur

evens THE FELLOW, 9/2 Bradbury Star, 8/1 Kings Fountain, 9/1 Docklands Express, 10/1 Pat's Jester, 12/1 Deep Sensation, 16/1 Tipping Tim, 20/1 The Illywhacker

Marquesa de Moratalla (F. Doumen) 8ran 6m 14.54 (Soft)

33	FINALE JUNIOR HURDLE (Gr 1) (3yo)		2m 110y
£15,655	Chepstow	28 December	
	Dare To Dream (Ire) 11-0 DBridgwater		**1**
	Mohana 10-9 JLower		¾.**2**
	Major Bugler (Ire) 11-0 AMaguire		10.**3**

Bold Boss 11-0 NBentley.... 1½.4
Eden's Close 11-0
SSmithEccles.................. 2½.5
Palacegate King 11-0
DBentley............................4.6
Liability Order 11-0 NMann...30.7
Second Call 10-9 MPerrett.... ¾.8
Top Spin 11-0 DGallagher.......6.9
Perforate 11-0 WMcFarland ....pu
Genie Spirit 10-9 CLlewellyn...pu

11/4 Major Bugler, 9/2 Bold Boss, DARE
TO DREAM, Mohana, 10/1 Second Call,
Top Spin, 16/1 Liability Order, Palace-
gate King, 20/1 Eden's Close, 50/1 Genie
Spirit, Perforate
Miss Judy Smith (R. Akehurst) 11ran
4m15.34 (Soft)

34   CORAL WELSH   3m5f110y
      NATIONAL (HANDICAP
      CHASE) (Gr 3) (5yo +)
£24,872   Chepstow   28 December
20*   Run For Free 8-10-9
      MPerrett 1
      Riverside Boy 9-10-0
      MFoster 8.2
28²   Miinnehoma 9-10-11
      JLower................................ 5.3
20³   Bonanza Boy 11-10-9
      SSmithEccles.................. 3½.4
28*   Captain Dibble 7-10-8
      CLlewellyn....................... nk.5
      Belmount Captain 7-10-0
      AMaguire nk.6
      Just So 9-10-2 SBurrough 20.7
      Merry Master 8-10-0
      GeeArmytage........................... f
      Pharoah's Laen 11-10-0
      BPowell...............................pu
      Givus A Buck 9-10-0 PHolley ..pu
      Foyle Fisherman 13-10-0
      EMurphy..............................pu

11/4 Miinnehoma, RUN FOR FREE, 4/1
Belmount Captain, 5/1 Captain Dibble,
10/1 Merry Master, 20/1 Bonanza Boy,
Givus A Buck, 25/1 Just So, 50/1
Riverside Boy, 66/1 Pharoah's Laen,
100/1 Foyle Fisherman
Mrs Millicent R. Freethy (M. C. Pipe)
11ran 8m08.89 (Soft)

35   BONUSPRINT CHRISTMAS 2m
      HURDLE (Gr 1) (4yo +)
£31,430   Kempton   28 December
16*   Mighty Mogul 5-11-7
      RDunwoody 1
16   Flown 5-11-7 JOsborne......... 5.2
25²   Granville Again 6-11-7
      PScudamore 3.3
21   King Credo 7-11-7 HDavies ..10.4
25   Oh So Risky 5-11-7 GBradley .6.5
25   Kribensis 8-11-7 DMurphy.....6.6
      Gran Alba (USA) 6-11-7
      GMcCourt dist.7
      Regent Lad 8-11-7 JFrost......30.8

11/10 Granville Again, 3/1 MIGHTY
MOGUL, 7/1 Oh So Risky, 9/1 Gran Alba,
10/1 Flown, 12/1 Kribensis, 33/1 King
Credo, 200/1 Regent Lad
Mrs Shirley Robins (D. Nicholson)
8ran 3m49.84 (Good to Soft)

36   CASTLEFORD CHASE   2m
      (Gr 1) (5yo +)
£27,546   Wetherby   28 December
5²   Katabatic 9-11-10 SMcNeill.... 1
22*   Waterloo Boy 9-11-10
      PNiven 10.2
25   Boro Smackeroo 7-11-10
      AOrkney..........................3½.3

10/11 Waterloo Boy, evens KATABA-
TIC, 16/1 Boro Smackeroo
Pell-mell Partners (Andrew Turnell)
3ran 4m09.96 (Soft)

37   ERICSSON CHASE   3m
      (Gr 1) (5yo +)
£32,692 Leopardstown 28 December
23²   General Idea 7-11-11
      BSheridan 1
23   Cahervillahow 8-12-0
      LPCusack 2.2
23³   Garamycin 10-12-0
      CFSwan 9.3
18   Bishops Hall 6-11-11
      THorgan 12.4
23   The Committee 9-12-0
      JPBanahan........................9.5
      Final Tub 9-12-0 APowell ... 1½.6
23   Feroda 11-12-0 TJTaaffe.......15.7
      Laura's Beau 8-12-0
      CO'Dwyer 1½.8
      Deep Bramble 5-11-9
      KFO'Brien .... f
23   Firions Law 7-12-0 MFlynn .....pu

9/4 GENERAL IDEA, 7/2 Garamycin,
4/1 Firions Law, 5/1 Cahervillahow, 16/1
Bishops Hall, Feroda, Laura's Beau,
20/1 Deep Bramble, Final Tub, 50/1 The
Committee
Dr Michael Smurfit (D. K. Weld) 10ran
6m33.60 (Good to Soft)

38   BOOKMAKERS HURDLE   2m
      (Gr 2) (4yo +)
£15,797 Leopardstown 30 December
      Novello Allegro (USA) 4-11-2
      CFSwan 1
      Muir Station (USA) 4-11-2
      KFO'Brien hd.2
      Crowded House (Ire) 4-11-2
      RDunwoody 4.3
      Royal Gait 9-12-0 GMcCourt ..2.4
      Sanndila (Ire) 4-10-11
      MDuffy............................6.5
      Cock Cockburn 6-11-7
      DHO'Connor......................6
      Nilousha 5-11-2 APowell 7

11/10 Royal Gait, 5/1 Sanndila, 6/1
Crowded House, NOVELLO ALLE-

848

GRO, 7/1 Muir Station, 14/1 Cock
Cockburn, 50/1 Nilousha
Mrs Rita Polly (N. Meade) 7ran
3m54.30 (Good to Soft)

39	CHEVELEY PARK STUD	2m
	NEW YEAR'S DAY HURDLE	
	(LIMITED HANDICAP) (4yo +)	
£8,403	Windsor	1 January
27	**Muse** 6-11-5 AProcter	1
13*	**Baydon Star** 6-11-2	
	RDunwoody	1.2
16³	**Lift And Load** (USA) 6-10-7	
	DMurphy	nk.3
16	Duke of Monmouth (USA)	
	5-11-3 MRichards	20.4
	Pontynyswen 5-10-7	
	DJBurchell	8.5
21	Jungle Knife 7-10-11	
	AMaguire	7.6
	Cheerful Times 10-10-0	
	GRobertson	10.7
	Present Times 7-10-7	
	GLMoore	10.8
	Tiger Claw (USA) 7-10-7	
	ILawrence	6.9

evens Baydon Star, 5/1 Jungle Knife, Lift
And Load, 13/2 MUSE, 7/1 Duke of
Monmouth, 66/1 Cheerful Times, Pon-
tynyswen, Tiger Claw, 150/1 Present
Times
White Horse Racing Ltd (D. R. C.
Elsworth) 9ran 4m00.95 (Soft)

40	CHALLOW HURDLE	2m5f
	(Gr 1) (4yo +)	
£15,875	Newbury	2 January
	Lord Relic (NZ) 7-11-7	
	PScudamore	1
17	Gaelstrom 6-11-2	
	CLlewellyn	10.2
	Yorkshire Gale 7-11-7	
	DMurphy	25.3
	Mr Matt (Ire) 5-11-7	
	PeterHobbs	4.4
	Irish Bay 7-11-7	
	RDunwoody	10.5
19³	Corrin Hill 6-11-7 AMaguire	pu
	Glen Lochan (NZ) 8-11-7	
	JOsborne	pu

15/8 LORD RELIC, 2/1 Glen Lochan, 8/1
Corrin Hill, Irish Bay, 11/1 Gaelstrom,
16/1 Yorkshire Gale, 20/1 Mr Matt
Mrs H. J. Clarke (M. C. Pipe) 7ran
5m 10.30 (Soft)

41	MANDARIN	3¼m110y
	HANDICAP CHASE (6yo +)	
£7,304	Newbury	2 January
18²	**Jodami** 8-12-0 MDwyer	1
	Esha Ness 10-10-9	
	BdeHaan	2½.2
	Sea Island 9-10-2	
	PScudamore	4.3
	Windy Ways 8-10-4	
	RDunwoody	4.4

	Keep Talking 8-10-13	
	SSmithEccles	sh.5
	Bonsai Bud 10-10-1	
	DGallagher	sh.6
	Logamimo 7-10-4	
	ALarnach	2½.7
	Boraceva 10-10-8 JFrost	3½.8
	Ask Frank 7-10-0 AMaguire	½.9
	Country Member 8-10-11	
	LHarvey	½.10
28	Parsons Green 9-10-12	
	JRKavanagh	f
	Topsham Bay 10-11-10	
	HDavies	ur
	Pamber Priory 10-10-1	
	GRowe	ur

9/4 JODAMI, 3/1 Country Member, 8/1
Keep Talking, 10/1 Sea Island, 12/1 Ask
Frank, Bonsai Bud, 14/1 Windy Ways,
16/1 Logamimo, 20/1 Parsons Green,
25/1 Boraceva, Esha Ness, Pamber
Priory, 33/1 Topsham Bay
Mr J. N. Yeadon (P. Beaumont) 13ran
7m02.24 (Soft)

42	MITSUBISHI SHOGUN	2½m
	NEWTON CHASE	
	(Gr 1) (5yo +)	
£30,987	Haydock	9 January
23*	**Gold Options** 11-11-10 LWyer	1
36*	**Katabatic** 10-11-10	
	SMcNeill	3.2
32	**Kings Fountain** 10-11-10	
	ATory	2½.3
24*	Twin Oaks 13-11-10	
	GMcCourt	8.4
	Multum In Parvo 10-11-10	
	NWilliamson	dist.5
29²	Last 'o' The Bunch 9-11-10	
	NDoughty	pu

4/5 Katabatic, 7/2 Kings Fountain, Twin
Oaks, 12/1 Last 'o' The Bunch, 14/1
GOLD OPTIONS, 50/1 Multum In Parvo
Mr J. McCaghy (J. G. FitzGerald) 6ran
5m28.83 (Soft)

43	BARING SECURITIES	2m110y
	TOLWORTH HURDLE	
	(Gr 1) (4yo +)	
£15,850	Sandown	9 January
	Sun Surfer (Fr) 5-11-7	
	CLlewellyn	1
	Dreamers Delight 7-11-7	
	RDunwoody	nk.2
	Thumbs Up 7-11-7	
	JRKavanagh	10.3
	Big Beat (USA) 5-11-7	
	PHolley	4.4
	Texan Tycoon 5-11-7	
	HDavies	1½.5
	Poors Wood 6-11-7	
	EMurphy	dist.6
	Leotard 6-11-7 JOsborne	pu

6/4 Big Beat, 4/1 Dreamers Delight, 7/1
SUN SURFER, 8/1 Texan Tycoon, 9/1

Leotard, 12/1 Thumbs Up, 14/1 Poors Wood

Mr Simon Sainsbury (Capt. T. A. Forster) 7ran 4m13.50 (Heavy)

44	ANTHONY MILDMAY, PETER CAZALET MEMORIAL HANDICAP CHASE (5yo +)	3m5f110y	
£14,070	Sandown	9 January	
	Rushing Wild 8-10-1		
	PScudamore		1
28	**Cool Ground** 11-12-0		
	AMaguire	25.2	
	Nick The Brief 11-10-11		
	RSupple	25.3	
18*	Sibton Abbey 8-10-3		
	MrPaulMurphy	2.4	
28	Kildimo 13-10-0		
	MAFitzgerald	30.5	
	Duntree 8-10-1 RDunwoody	ur	
	Brown Windsor 11-10-11		
	JOsborne	pu	
41	Topsham Bay 10-10-6		
	HDavies	pu	
14	Seagram (NZ) 13-10-0 DTegg	pu	
41	Keep Talking 8-10-3		
	SSmithEccles	pu	
	Ghofar 10-10-0 BPowell	ref	

evens RUSHING WILD, 11/2 Sibton Abbey, 13/2 Keep Talking, 9/1 Duntree, 16/1 Cool Ground, 20/1 Brown Windsor, Ghofar, 25/1 Topsham Bay, 33/1 Kildimo, Nick The Brief, 66/1 Seagram

Hunt & Co (Bournemouth) Ltd (M. C. Pipe) 11ran 7m57.97 (Soft)

45	THE LADBROKE (LIMITED HANDICAP HURDLE) (Gr 1) (4yo +)	2m	
£37,717	Leopardstown	9 January	
	Glencloud (Ire) 5-10-13		
	GMO'Neill		1
21²	**Kilcash (Ire)** 5-11-5		
	MRichards	nk.2	
	Atone 6-10-6 KFO'Brien	sh.3	
	Native Mission 6-11-4		
	MDwyer	½.4	
	Eyelid 7-11-10 CFSwan	1.5	
	Ink By The Drum (USA)		
	5-10-8 THorgan	nk.6	
	Alterezza (USA) 6-10-13		
	JHShortt	1.7	
	Bitofabanter 6-11-7		
	FWoods	2½.8	
	Tawney Flame 7-10-8		
	JTitley	nk.9	
	Natural Ability 8-11-11		
	MDuffy	1.10	
	Fay Lin 6-10-0 PMcWilliams	2.11	
	Keppols Prince 6-10-7		
	KMorgan	1½.12	
	Naiysari (Ire) 5-10-1		
	MFlynn	2½.13	
	Nordic Gayle 6-10-0		
	NByrne	1½.14	
	Killiney Graduate 7-11-0		
	SHO'Donovan	1½.15	
	Persuasive 6-10-1		
	MrMBuckley	½.16	
	Mr Greenfield 9-10-4		
	JMagee	12.17	
	Statajack (Ire) 5-10-7		
	AProcter	1.18	
	Rising Waters (Ire) 5-10-13		
	CO'Dwyer	1½.19	
	Master Swordsman (USA)		
	10-11-0 MissCHutchinson	2.20	
	Back Door Johnny 7-11-5		
	LPCusack	4.21	
38	Cock Cockburn 7-11-8		
	DHO'Connor	f	
	Lady Olein (Ire) 5-11-5		
	JPBanahan	f	
	Larnaca 6-11-5 MrAJMartin	f	
	Random Prince 9-11-4 HRogers	f	

6/1 Eyelid, 8/1 Bitofabanter, 9/1 Kilcash, Native Mission, 10/1 Fay Lin, 12/1 Tawney Flame, 14/1 Alterezza, Atone, Cock Cockburn, Lady Olein, 16/1 Ink By The Drum, 20/1 GLENCLOUD, Larnaca, Rising Waters, 25/1 Natural Ability, 33/1 Back Door Johnny, Keppols Prince, 40/1 Statajack, 66/1 Mr Greenfield, Naiysari, Nordic Gayle, Persuasive, Random Prince, 100/1 Killiney Graduate, Master Swordsman

Mr D. Tierney (N. Meade) 25ran 3m59.93 (Good to Soft)

46	VICTOR CHANDLER HANDICAP CHASE (Gr 2) (5yo +)	2m	
£22,528	Ascot	16 January	
30*	**Sybillin** 7-10-10 MDwyer		1
32	**Deep Sensation** 8-10-11		
	DMurphy	10.2	
	Fragrant Dawn 9-10-4		
	PHolley	7.3	
29*	Cyphrate (USA) 7-11-1		
	PScudamore	8.4	
	Sure Metal 10-10-8		
	GMcCourt	10.5	
	Al Hashimi 9-10-9		
	CLlewellyn	8.6	
	Boutzdaroff 11-10-4		
	AMaguire	4.7	
23	Blitzkreig 10-11-7		
	CO'Dwyer	10.8	
26	Freeline Finishing 9-10-4		
	RDunwoody	f	
	Young Snugfit 9-11-10		
	JOsborne	pu	
	Star's Delight 11-11-7		
	MPerrett	pu	

5/2 Cyphrate, 9/2 SYBILLIN, 5/1 Deep Sensation, 6/1 Blitzkreig, 7/1 Freeline Finishing, 20/1 Sure Metal, Young Snugfit, 25/1 Boutzdaroff, 33/1 Al Hashimi, Fragrant Dawn, Star's Delight

Marquesa de Moratalla (J. G. FitzGerald) 11ran 4m01.25 (Soft)

47   JIM ENNIS   2m7f110y
CONSTRUCTION PREMIER
LONG DISTANCE HURDLE
(Gr 2) (5yo +)
£9,380   Haydock   23 January

Pragada 10-11-10 PScudamore **1**
6   **Better Times Ahead** 7-11-3
    NDoughty 5.**2**
27²   **Burgoyne** 7-11-7 MDwyer . 30.**3**
    Belvederian 6-11-3
    LCusack 10.**4**
27*   Vagog 8-11-10 MFoster .... pu
17³   Ambuscade (USA) 7-11-3
    RHodge .... pu
    Lafkadio 6-11-3
    WWorthington .... pu

9/4 Vagog, 5/2 Burgoyne, 9/2 Belvederian, 13/2 PRAGADA, 8/1 Ambuscade,
Better Times Ahead, 100/1 Lafkadio
    Mrs Margaret McGlone (M. C. Pipe)
7ran 6m 18.45 (Heavy)

48   HAYDOCK PARK   2m
CHAMPION HURDLE TRIAL
(Gr 2) (5yo +)
£9,500   Haydock   23 January

13³   **Jinxy Jack** 9-11-7 NDoughty ... **1**
19   **Coulton** 6-11-10
    CLlewellyn ½.**2**
19²   **Royal Derbi** 8-11-10
    MPerrett 15.**3**
    Ruling (USA) 7-11-3
    MDwyer 10.**4**
    Rodeo Star (USA) 7-11-3
    GMcCourt 15.**5**

9/4 JINXY JACK, 11/4 Coulton, 3/1 Royal
Derbi, 4/1 Ruling, 11/1 Rodeo Star
    Mrs B. M. McKinney (G. Richards)
5ran 4m01.53 (Heavy)

49   PETER MARSH CHASE   3m
(LIMITED HANDICAP)
(Gr 2) (5yo +)
£15,570   Haydock   23 January

41*   **Jodami** 8-11-2 MDwyer **1**
34*   **Run For Free** 9-11-10
    MPerrett 2.**2**
42*   **Gold Options** 11-11-5
    PScudamore 4.**3**
42   Twin Oaks 13-11-5
    NDoughty 12.**4**
32   Tipping Tim 8-11-0
    CLlewellyn 5.**5**
    Why So Hasty 12-10-10
    WWorthington .... pu

5/4 JODAMI, 11/4 Run For Free, 9/2
Twin Oaks, 7/1 Gold Options, Tipping
Tim, 200/1 Why So Hasty
    Mr J. N. Yeadon (P. Beaumont) 6ran
6m48.61 (Heavy)

50   BIC RAZOR LANZAROTE   2m
HANDICAP HURDLE (4yo +)
£15,500   Kempton   23 January

Tomahawk 6-10-0 DMurphy ... **1**

Nijmegen 5-10-0 JOsborne. 12.**2**
Avro Anson 5-10-10
    DByrne 2½.**3**
Bibendum 7-10-0
    MMLynch 2½.**4**
Qualitair Sound (Ire) 5-10-10
    JJQuinn 6.**5**
39   Jungle Knife 7-11-10
    JRKavanagh 30.**6**
    Ilewin 6-10-0 MAhern 30.**7**
    Calicon 7-10-10 JFrost .... pu
    Martha's Son 6-10-9 BPowell .. pu
    Here He Comes 7-10-9
    HDavies .... pu

5/2 Here He Comes, 9/2 Nijmegen, 5/1
Avro Anson, Martha's Son, 8/1 Qualitair
Sound, 12/1 Calicon, TOMAHAWK, 14/1
Jungle Knife, 40/1 Bibendum, 100/1
Ilewin
    Charles Saunders & Partners (P. G.
Murphy) 10ran 4m08.63 (Heavy)

51   WEST OF SCOTLAND   3m 1f
PATTERN NOVICES' CHASE
(Gr 2) (5yo +)
£9,544   Ayr   30 January

Whispering Steel 7-11-9
    NDoughty **1**
Candy Tuff 7-11-5 PNiven 3.**2**
Eastern Oasis 10-11-5
    PWilliams 8.**3**
3   Mils Mij 8-11-5 TReed 1½.**4**
    Truely Royal 9-11-5
    BStorey 20.**5**
    Island Gale 8-11-5
    PWaggott 10.**6**
    Kilclooney Forrest 11-11-5
    ALarnach .... f

8/11 WHISPERING STEEL, 7/2 Candy
Tuff, 4/1 Mils Mij, 16/1 Eastern Oasis,
50/1 Kilclooney Forrest, 66/1 Island
Gale, Truely Royal
    Mr J. Michael Gillow (G. Richards)
7ran 6m33.92 (Good to Soft)

52   TIMEFORM   3m 1f110y
HALL OF FAME CHASE
(6yo +)
£10,309   Cheltenham   30 January

44   **Sibton Abbey** 8-11-12
    SSmithEccles **1**
26*   **Another Coral** 10-11-12
    RDunwoody ¾.**2**
44²   **Cool Ground** 11-11-12
    AMaguire 5.**3**
    Henry Mann 10-11-3
    MAFitzgerald 4.**4**
    Garrison Savannah 10-11-12
    MPitman 12.**5**
34³   Miinnehoma 10-11-12
    MPerrett .... pu
18   Party Politics 9-11-12
    GMcCourt .... pu

5/2 Cool Ground, 11/4 Miinnehoma, 9/2
Another Coral, 13/2 Garrison Savannah,

12/1 Henry Mann, 16/1 Party Politics, SIBTON ABBEY

Mr G. A. Hubbard (F. Murphy) 7ran 7m06.90 (Soft)

---

53   WYKO POWER   2m5f110y
TRANSMISSION HURDLE
(Gr 1) (4yo +)
£26,917   Cheltenham   30 January

39*	**Muse** 6-11-8 PHolley **1**
17	**Nomadic Way (USA)** 8-11-8
	GMcCourt 25.2
	Mudahim 7-11-8 DTegg 30.3
35*	Mighty Mogul 6-11-8
	RDunwoody ....pu

4/9 Mighty Mogul, 11/4 MUSE, 15/2 Nomadic Way, 33/1 Mudahim

White Horse Racing Ltd (D. R. C. Elsworth) 4ran 5m40.59 (Soft)

---

54   MITSUBISHI SHOGUN   2m110y
TROPHY (HANDICAP CHASE)
(5yo +)
£7,180   Doncaster   30 January

	Tinryland 9-10-8 JRKavanagh . **1**
8	**Space Fair** 10-9-12
	RGreene........................... hd.2
36³	**Boro Smackeroo** 8-10-5
	AOrkney........................... 5.3
46	Al Hashimi 9-10-10 CFSwan . 10.4
22³	Uncle Ernie 8-11-11
	MDwyer 10.5
46	Young Snugfit 9-12-0
	JOsborne 5.6
	Clay County 8-10-2
	MMoloney ½.7
	Nohalmdun 10-10-0 DByrne . 12.8

11/8 Uncle Ernie, 5/1 TINRYLAND, 11/2 Space Fair, 13/2 Boro Smackeroo, 7/1 Young Snugfit, 9/1 Clay County, 14/1 Al Hashimi, 33/1 Nohalmdun

Mr Michael Buckley (N. J. Henderson) 8ran 3m56.78 (Good to Firm)

---

55   GREAT YORKSHIRE   3m
CHASE (HANDICAP) (5yo +)
£19,691   Doncaster   30 January

12	**Young Hustler** 6-10-0
	DBridgwater **1**
	Otterburn House 9-10-2
	MDwyer 5.2
28³	**Rowlandsons Jewels** 12-11-3
	DGallagher........................ 8.3
18	Latent Talent 9-11-4
	JOsborne 3.4
41²	Esha Ness 10-10-13 BdeHaan 5.5
41	Parsons Green 9-11-2
	JRKavanagh nk.6
	West Ender 10-10-0 LHarvey .7.7
	Winabuck 10-9-9
	DMeredith 3½.8
28	Gambling Royal 10-11-11
	CFSwan........................... 10.9
	Catch The Cross 7-10-7
	MFoster .... f
41³	Sea Island 9-10-6 JLower .... f

	Errant Knight 9-9-11
	MHourigan .... ur
12²	Danny Harrold 9-11-7
	SMcNeill ....pu
34	Pharoah's Laen 12-11-2
	GBradley ....pu

3/1 Otterburn House, 9/2 YOUNG HUSTLER, 9/1 Danny Harrold, Esha Ness, Sea Island, 10/1 Gambling Royal, 11/1 Catch The Cross, 12/1 West Ender, 14/1 Rowlandsons Jewels, 16/1 Latent Talent, 20/1 Errant Knight, Parsons Green, 50/1 Pharoah's Laen, Winabuck

Mr G. M. MacEchern (N. A. Twiston-Davies) 14ran 5m59.48 (Good to Firm)

---

56   BAILEYS ARKLE   2m3f
PERPETUAL CHALLENGE
CUP (Gr 2) (6yo +)
£9,099   Leopardstown   31 January

	Soft Day 8-12-0 TJTaaffe **1**
	How's The Boss 7-12-0
	MDwyer 1½.2
45	**Killiney Graduate** 7-11-6
	NWilliamson 3.3
	Galevilla Express 6-11-5
	CNBowens sh.4
	The Illiad 12-11-2 MFlynn 15.5
	King of The Gales 6-11-10
	CFSwan .... f

11/8 How's The Boss, 6/4 SOFT DAY, 7/1 Galevilla Express, The Illiad, 16/1 King of The Gales, 20/1 Killiney Graduate

Mr F. Conroy (A. L. T. Moore) 6ran 4m56.05 (Good to Soft)

---

57   AIG EUROPE CHAMPION   2m
HURDLE (Gr 1) (4yo +)
£33,242   Leopardstown   31 January

48³	**Royal Derbi** 8-11-10 DMurphy **1**
38*	**Novello Allegro (USA)**
	5-11-6 CFSwan................ 2½.2
38²	**Muir Station (USA)** 5-11-6
	KFO'Brien ¾.3
	Irish Peace (Ire) 5-11-6
	MDwyer nk.4
	Gaelic Myth (USA) 6-11-10
	CO'Dwyer 3.5
45	Natural Ability 8-11-10
	GMO'Neill........................ nk.6
	Autumn Gorse (Ire) 4-10-12
	BSheridan ½.7
	Chirkpar 6-11-10
	LPCusack........................ 2½.8
25*	Halkopous 7-11-10
	AMaguire 3½.9
45	Lady Olein (Ire) 5-11-1
	JPBanahan.........................6.10
38³	Crowded House (Ire) 5-11-6
	RDunwoody .... f

4/5 Halkopous, 6/1 Novello Allegro, 7/1 Crowded House, 15/2 Autumn Gorse, 9/1 Muir Station, 14/1 ROYAL DERBI, 16/1 Chirkpar, 20/1 Irish Peace, 40/1

Gaelic Myth, Lady Olein, 50/1 Natural Ability

Mr M. Tabor (N. A. Callaghan) 11ran
3m54.40 (Good to Soft)

| 58 | HAROLD CLARKE LEOPARDSTOWN CHASE | 3m |

(Gr 2) (5yo +)
£12,637   Leopardstown   31 January

37[3]	**Garamycin** 11-12-0 BSheridan **1**
	Ebony Jane 8-10-7	
	RDunwoody ½.**2**
	Joe White 7-10-2 CFSwan ... ¾.**3**
	For William 7-10-0	
	KFO'Brien nk.4
	Jamalade 7-11-3 DMurphy ..dist.5
37	Final Tub 10-10-10	
	CO'Dwyer 8.6
44[3]	Nick The Brief 11-12-0	
	RSupple................................6.7
	Lanigans Wine 11-10-0	
	APowell...............................7.8
	Dagwood 8-10-0 DTEvans......... f
37	The Committee 10-11-1	
	AMaguire ....bd
	Rawhide 9-10-10 LPCusack.....pu

7/2 Ebony Jane, GARAMYCIN, 11/2 Jamalade, 13/2 Nick The Brief, 7/1 Final Tub, Joe White, 12/1 For William, The Committee, 16/1 Dagwood, Rawhide, 25/1 Lanigans Wine

P. G. Garahy (W. Deacon) 11ran
6m30.35 (Good to Soft)

| 59 | PHILIP CORNES SADDLE OF GOLD STAYERS' NOVICES' HURDLE (5yo +) | 3m |

£10,755   Chepstow   6 February

	Brackenfield 7-11-5 PNiven ... **1**
40[2]	**Gaelstrom** 6-11-2	
	DBridgwater 1½.**2**
	Lo Stregone 7-11-5	
	GMcCourt 20.3
	Mr Flanagan 7-11-0	
	GBradley 10.4
	Sunley Bay 7-11-0	
	MAFitzgerald......................8.5
	Thistle Monarch 8-11-5	
	NDoughty...........................20.6
	Special Account 7-11-5	
	NMann 10.7
	Aahsaylad 7-11-5 BClifford......pu
	Beautiful Dream 5-10-12	
	PeterHobbs ....pu
	Solo Buck 7-10-9 DGallagher...pu

10/3 BRACKENFIELD, 7/2 Lo Stregone, 4/1 Gaelstrom, 5/1 Aahsaylad, Thistle Monarch, 16/1 Beautiful Dream, Sunley Bay, 25/1 Mr Flanagan, 50/1 Special Account, 100/1 Solo Buck

Mr Guy Faber (Mrs M. Reveley) 10ran
6m22.01 (Soft)

| 60 | SCILLY ISLES NOVICES' CHASE | 2½m 110y |

(Gr 1) (5yo +)
£19,110   Sandown   6 February

55*	**Young Hustler** 6-11-6	
	CLlewellyn............................ **1**
30[2]	**Dawson City** 6-11-6 LWyer.. 5.**2**
	Fighting Words 7-11-6	
	PHide nk.3
	Gay Ruffian 7-11-6	
	PScudamore ¾.4
	Phils Pride 9-11-6 MDwyer 7.5
31	Forest Sun 8-11-6 AMaguire ..4.6
	Retail Runner 8-11-6	
	EMurphy 1½.7
	Camelot Knight 7-11-6	
	JOsborne 5.8
	Lake Teereen 8-11-6	
	TGrantham........................30.9
	Edimbourg 7-11-6	
	MHourigan 10.10
	Dubacilla 7-11-1 SBurrough ....ur

5/2 YOUNG HUSTLER, 7/2 Dawson City, 6/1 Forest Sun, Gay Ruffian, 7/1 Retail Runner, 14/1 Lake Teereen, 16/1 Dubacilla, Fighting Words, 20/1 Phils Pride, 25/1 Camelot Knight, 100/1 Edimbourg

Mr G. M. MacEchern (N. A. Twiston-Davies) 11ran 5m20.10 (Good to Soft)

| 61 | TOTE JACKPOT HANDICAP HURDLE | 2¾m |

(Gr 3) (4yo +)
£13,550   Sandown   6 February

	Trainglot 6-10-2 MDwyer **1**
27	**Sweet Duke (Fr)** 6-11-4	
	CLlewellyn......................... 6.**2**
	Peanuts Pet 8-11-2	
	JOsborne 2.3
	Balasani (Fr) 7-11-9	
	MPerrett 2½.4
	Fairfields Cone 10-9-11	
	WMarston 1½.5
	Northern Village 6-9-10	
	ADicken 15.6
	Sillars Stalker (Ire) 5-10-3	
	AMaguire sh.7
	Calabrese 8-10-10	
	RDunwoody 5.8
	Bollin William 5-11-10	
	LWyer 2.9
	Holy Joe 11-11-5 LHarvey ..hd.10
	Ketti 8-11-0 HDavies........ 3½.11
6	Belafonte 6-9-13	
	MHourigan 2.12
	Run Up The Flag 6-10-8	
	PHide ½.13
	Beebob 5-11-0	
	PScudamore 30.14
	Be My Habitat 4-9-7	
	AScholes ....pu

7/2 TRAINGLOT, 4/1 Sillars Stalker, 6/1 Run Up The Flag, 9/1 Sweet Duke, 10/1 Bollin William, 12/1 Ketti, 14/1 Holy Joe, Peanuts Pet, 16/1 Beebob, 20/1 Balasani,

Belafonte, Calabrese, 25/1 Northern Village, 40/1 Fairfields Cone, 100/1 Be My Habitat

Marquesa de Moratalla (J. G. FitzGerald) 15ran 5m31.08 (Soft)

62	AGFA DIAMOND	3m110y
	CHASE (LIMITED HANDICAP)	
	(Gr 2) (5yo +)	
£20,581	Sandown	6 February
41	**Country Member** 8-10-7	
	LHarvey 1	
44*	**Rushing Wild** 8-12-0	
	PScudamore 6.2	
34	**Captain Dibble** 8-11-6	
	CLlewellyn......................... 3.3	

8/15 Rushing Wild, 10/3 COUNTRY MEMBER, 9/2 Captain Dibble

Mrs C. C. Williams (Andrew Turnell) 3ran 6m26.95 (Good to Soft)

63	AGFA HURDLE (5yo +) 2m110y	
£10,114	Sandown	6 February
	Mole Board 11-10-9	
	CLlewellyn.......................... 1	
21*	**Valfinet (Fr)** 6-11-0	
	PScudamore 6.2	
48	**Ruling (USA)** 7-10-9	
	MDwyer 20.3	
35	Gran Alba (USA) 7-11-10	
	SMcNeill 15.4	
25³	Morley Street 9-11-10	
	RDunwoody dist.5	

6/5 Valfinet, 15/8 Morley Street, 9/2 Ruling, 14/1 Gran Alba, 33/1 MOLE BOARD

Mr W. E. Sturt (J. A. B. Old) 5ran 4m06.71 (Soft)

64	MARSTON MOOR CHASE 2m5f	
	(LIMITED HANDICAP)	
	(Gr 2) (5yo +)	
£15,228	Wetherby	6 February
	Armagret 8-10-7 DByrne 1	
46²	**Deep Sensation** 8-10-11	
	DMurphy......................... 2½.2	
	Blazing Walker 9-12-0	
	CGrant hd.3	
	Joyful Noise 10-10-10	
	TJarvis 20.4	
42³	Kings Fountain 10-11-8	
	ATory 10.5	
37	Feroda 12-10-12 TJTaaffe.......... f	
	Wingspan (USA) 9-10-11JFrost f	
42	Multum In Parvo 10-10-7	
	NWilliamson ....pu	

15/8 Deep Sensation, 10/3 Kings Fountain, 7/2 Wingspan, 10/1 Blazing Walker, Feroda, 11/1 Multum In Parvo, 16/1 Joyful Noise, 25/1 ARMAGRET

Mrs R. M. Wilkinson (B. E. Wilkinson) 8ran 5m31.58 (Good to Soft)

65	JAMES CAPEL NOVICES'	2m
	CHASE (5yo +)	
£9,990	Ascot	10 February
	Atlaal 8-11-4 JOsborne 1	

Wonder Man (Fr) 8-11-12
RDunwoody ¾.2
Mr Jamboree 7-11-4
PScudamore 20.3
Nadiad 7-11-4 GMcCourt........ 1.4

1/4 Wonder Man, 5/1 ATLAAL, 14/1 Mr Jamboree, 33/1 Nadiad

Mr Oliver Donnelly (J. R. Jenkins) 4ran 4m03.88 (Good to Soft)

66	DAILY TELEGRAPH	3m
	HURDLE (5yo +)	
£11,988	Ascot	10 February
17	**Sweet Glow (Fr)** 6-11-0	
	PScudamore 1	
	Boscean Chieftain 9-11-0	
	MAFitzgerald..................... 3.2	
27	**Tyrone Bridge** 7-11-10	
	RDunwoody 12.3	
	Celtic Chief 10-11-10	
	JLower..........................dist.4	

4/6 SWEET GLOW, 13/8 Tyrone Bridge, 16/1 Celtic Chief, 25/1 Boscean Chieftain

Fairlord Wholesale Confectioners Ltd (M. C. Pipe) 4ran 5m52.76 (Good to Soft)

67	CRISPIN CHASE	3m110y
	(HANDICAP) (5yo +)	
£13,710	Ascot	10 February
	Very Very Ordinary 7-11-3	
	AMaguire 1	
	Calapaez 9-11-0	
	MRichards...................... 2½.2	
	Cache Fleur (Fr) 7-10-13	
	PScudamore 1½.3	
	Ross Venture 8-11-0	
	JOsborne 12.4	
55³	Rowlandsons Jewels 12-11-4	
	DGallagher.........................5.5	
44	Kildimo 13-11-2 LWyer 30.6	
	Mutare 8-12-0 RDunwoody .... f	

15/8 VERY VERY ORDINARY, 4/1 Cache Fleur, 5/1 Calapaez, 6/1 Mutare, 9/1 Rowlandsons Jewels, 20/1 Kildimo, Ross Venture

Mrs Wendy Cohen (John R. Upson) 7ran 6m25.37 (Good to Soft)

68	REYNOLDSTOWN	3m110y
	NOVICES' CHASE	
	(Gr 2) (5yo +)	
£14,743	Ascot	10 February
	Capability Brown 6-11-5	
	PScudamore 1	
31*	**Dakyns Boy** 8-11-12	
	CLlewellyn...................... 10.2	
	Channels Gate 9-11-5	
	JOsborne 30.3	
	Silverino 7-11-5 GLMoore ..dist.4	

evens Dakyns Boy, 11/8 CAPABILITY BROWN, 8/1 Channels Gate, 33/1 Silverino

Mr David S. Lewis (M. C. Pipe) 4ran 6m23.99 (Good to Soft)

69   SIDNEY BANKS   2m5f110y
MEMORIAL NOVICES'
HURDLE (4yo +)
£7,068   Huntingdon   11 February

Hebridean 6-11-4
RDunwoody **1**
High Alltitude (Ire) 5-11-2
CGrant **12.2**
Grand Hawk (USA) 5-11-2
PScudamore **2.3**
Wakashan 5-11-2 ASSmith ...10.4
Dennington (Ire) 5-11-2
AMaguire dist.5
Cambo (USA) 7-11-4
DSkyrme ¾.6
Big Chance 4-10-5 JStenning ...pu

11/8 Grand Hawk, 2/1 High Alltitude, 7/2
HEBRIDEAN, 18/1 Wakashan, 33/1
Dennington, 50/1 Big Chance, Cambo
    Mr P. A. Deal (D. Nicholson) 7ran
5m 19.45 (Soft)

70   RACING IN WESSEX   2m5f
CHASE (5yo +)
£5,248   Wincanton   11 February

Cherrykino 8-11-6 HDavies.... **1**
32   **Bradbury Star** 8-12-0
EMurphy **2.2**
52   **Garrison Savannah** 10-12-0
MPitman **15.3**
64   Wingspan (USA) 9-11-6
JFrost 4.4
Cavvies Clown 13-11-2
GBradley 6.5
Golden Celtic 9-11-6
JOsborne ....pu

7/4 CHERRYKINO, 2/1 Bradbury Star,
9/2 Garrison Savannah, Wingspan, 33/1
Cavvies Clown, 40/1 Golden Celtic
    Anne Duchess of Westminster (Capt.
T. A. Forster) 6ran 5m31.15 (Good to
Soft)

71   GAME SPIRIT CHASE   2m 1f
(Gr 2) (5yo +)
£15,570   Newbury   13 February
36²   **Waterloo Boy** 10-11-7
RDunwoody **1**
42²   **Katabatic** 10-11-10
SMcNeill **1.2**
46   **Cyphrate (USA)** 7-11-7
PScudamore **12.3**
64   Feroda 12-11-3 CFSwan 25.4
54   Young Snugfit 9-11-3
JOsborne .... ur

8/11 Katabatic, 9/4 WATERLOO BOY,
9/1 Cyphrate, 14/1 Young Snugfit, 33/1
Feroda
    Mr M. R. Deeley (D. Nicholson) 5ran
4m21.55 (Good)

72   ARLINGTON PREMIER   2½m
SERIES CHASE FINAL (6yo +)
£20,618   Newbury   13 February
60*   **Young Hustler** 6-11-0
CLlewellyn........................... **1**

Cogent 9-11-0 SMcNeill........ **4.2**
26²   **Second Schedual** 8-11-7
CFSwan.............................. **1.3**
12   Beech Road 11-11-7 JFrost ...20.4
26   Milford Quay 10-11-7
PScudamore 12.5
29   Poetic Gem 8-11-7
AMaguire 20.6
Miami Bear 7-11-7 PeterHobbs . f
Ryde Again 10-11-7 MPitman .... f
Little-Nipper 8-11-0
RDunwoody .... ur

2/1 YOUNG HUSTLER, 9/4 Ryde Again,
6/1 Second Schedual, 7/1 Cogent, 12/1
Beech Road, Milford Quay, 14/1 Little-
Nipper, 66/1 Poetic Gem, 100/1 Miami
Bear
    Mr G. M. MacEchern (N. A. Twiston-
Davies) 9ran 5m 18.57 (Good)

73   TOTE GOLD TROPHY   2m 110y
HANDICAP HURDLE
(Gr 3) (4yo +)
£33,800   Newbury   13 February
35   **King Credo** 8-10-0 AMaguire .. **1**
45   **Native Mission** 6-10-1
MDwyer **5.2**
45   **Bitofabanter** 6-9-7
PCarberry **4.3**
39³   Lift And Load (USA) 6-10-4
SMcNeill 2.4
Flakey Dove 7-10-0 DTegg. 1½.5
48   Rodeo Star (USA) 7-10-4
GMcCourt ½.6
61   Balasani (Fr) 7-10-0
MPerrett hd.7
50*   Tomahawk 6-10-0
CLlewellyn...................... 1½.8
50   Here He Comes 7-9-7
JMcCarthy 4.9
50   Qualitair Sound (Ire) 5-10-0
JJQuinn........................... 1½.10
45*   Glencloud (Ire) 5-10-0
CFSwan.............................6.11
Galaxy High 6-10-0
JRKavanagh 3.12
57*   Royal Derbi 8-10-8
RDunwoody ¾.13
16   Seon 7-10-0 JOsborne 1½.14
Noble Insight 6-9-7
LReynolds nk.15
63³   Ruling (USA) 7-12-0
HDavies 1½.16

11/2 Royal Derbi, 13/2 Bitofabanter,
Flakey Dove, Lift And Load, Native
Mission, 7/1 Balasani, 10/1 KING
CREDO, 14/1 Glencloud, 16/1 Rodeo
Star, Tomahawk, 20/1 Here He Comes,
25/1 Ruling, 33/1 Galaxy High, Qualitair
Sound, 66/1 Seon, 100/1 Noble Insight
    Mr G. Gornall (S. Woodman) 16ran
3m59.54 (Good)

74   HENNESSY COGNAC   3m
GOLD CUP (Gr 1) (5yo +)
£44,005   Leopardstown   14 February
49*   **Jodami** 8-12-0 MDwyer **1**

18 **Chatam (USA)** 9-12-0
PScudamore hd.2
37* **General Idea** 8-12-0
BSheridan dist.3
58 The Committee 10-12-0
AMaguire 1½.4
37² Cahervillahow 9-12-0
LPCusack 20.5
River Tarquin 9-12-0 KMorgan . f
58 Jamalade 7-12-0 RDunwoody...pu
11/8 JODAMI, 5/2 Chatam, 3/1 General Idea, 13/2 Cahervillahow, 33/1 River Tarquin, 40/1 The Committee, 50/1 Jamalade
Mr J. N. Yeadon (P. Beaumont) 7ran 6m25.84 (Good to Soft)

75 PERSIAN WAR 2½m110y
PREMIER NOVICES'
HURDLE (Gr 2) (4yo +)
£6,304 Chepstow 20 February
69² **High Alltitude (Ire)** 5-11-9
NBentley................................ 1
Castle Courageous 6-11-9
EMurphy............................. 3.2
Now Your Talkin 7-11-9
MrTJenks............................. 10.3
43* Sun Surfer (Fr) 5-11-12
CLlewellyn........................ 12.4
Crystal Cone 7-11-6
DSalter dist.5
9/4 Now Your Talkin, 5/2 Sun Surfer, 11/4 HIGH ALLTITUDE, 10/3 Castle Courageous, 50/1 Crystal Cone
Mr B. Batey (G. M. Moore) 5ran 5m11.70 (Good to Soft)

76 TOTE CITY TRIAL 2m
HURDLE (LIMITED
HANDICAP) (4yo +)
£4,760 Nottingham 20 February
48² **Coulton** 6-12-0 MDwyer 1
39 **Duke of Monmouth (USA)**
5-11-6 RDunwoody 2.2
40 **Corrin Hill** 6-10-7
GMcCourt 15.3
39 Cheerful Times 10-10-7
TWall.................................8.4
What If 9-10-7 ASSmith 8.5
4/7 COULTON, 3/1 Duke of Monmouth, 6/1 Corrin Hill, 40/1 What If, 66/1 Cheerful Times
Mr M. G. St Quinton (M. W. Easterby) 5ran 4m21.25 (Good)

77 NOTTINGHAMSHIRE 2m
NOVICES' CHASE
(Gr 2) (5yo +)
£7,760 Nottingham 20 February
46* **Sybillin** 7-11-12 MDwyer 1
65² **Wonder Man (Fr)** 8-11-9
RDunwoody 1½.2
Vain Prince 6-11-5
GMcCourt dist.3
Fine Harvest 7-11-5 TWall . 1½.4
Past Glories 10-11-5 HDavies ... f

2/5 SYBILLIN, 5/2 Wonder Man, 20/1 Vain Prince, 33/1 Past Glories, 100/1 Fine Harvest
Marquesa de Moratalla (J. G. FitzGerald) 5ran 3m58.39 (Good)

78 FAIRLAWNE CHASE 3m
(5yo +)
£8,208 Windsor 20 February
Zeta's Lad 10-11-4
JRKavanagh 1
24³ **Espy** 10-11-8 GBradley 2½.2
Repeat The Dose 8-11-12
JOsborne hd.3
Willsford 10-11-4 MPitman...15.4
Killbanon 11-11-8 SMcNeill....... f
7/4 Willsford, ZETA'S LAD, 5/1 Repeat The Dose, 6/1 Espy, 16/1 Killbanon
Mrs Diane Upson (John R. Upson) 5ran 6m09.99 (Good to Soft)

79 BALTINGLASS HURDLE 2m
(4yo)
£4,358 Punchestown 21 February
Shawiya (Ire) 10-7 JTitley 1
Titled Dancer (Ire) 10-7
JHShortt............................ ½.2
Green Glen (USA) 10-5
NWilliamson 8.3
Yukon Gold (Ire) 10-5
MFlynn..............................13.4
Pennine Tune (Ire) 10-9
KFO'Brien 3½.5
Garboni (USA) 10-5 APowell 6
Thatcherise (Ire) 10-4
RDunwoody 7
Aegean Fanfare (Ire) 10-9
CFSwan 8
Stark Contrast (USA) 10-5
FWoods 9
Winterbourne Abbas (Ire) 10-9
BSheridan 10
Rainbow Valley (Ire) 10-9
CO'Dwyer ....pu
7/4 SHAWIYA, 4/1 Pennine Tune, 7/1 Titled Dancer, Yukon Gold, 8/1 Aegean Fanfare, 9/1 Green Glen, Thatcherise, 10/1 Stark Contrast, 14/1 Winterbourne Abbas, 16/1 Rainbow Valley, 20/1 Garboni
Miss G. Maher (M.J.P. O'Brien) 11ran 4m07.95 (Soft)

80 KINGWELL HURDLE 2m
(Gr 2)(4yo +)
£11,060 Wincanton 25 February
63² **Valfinet (Fr)** 6-11-2
PScudamore 1
35 **Kribensis** 9-11-2
RDunwoody 5.2
53* Muse 6-11-10 PHolley 15.3
63 Gran Alba (USA) 7-11-10
GMcCourt 15.4
Exact Analysis (USA) 7-11-2
GUpton................................20.5

38   Sanndila (Ire) 5-10-11
      AMaguire 20.6
4/5 VALFINET, 7/4 Muse, 12/1 Gran
Alba, Sanndila, 16/1 Kribensis, 150/1
Exact Analysis
  Mr Frank A. Farrant (M. C. Pipe) 6ran
3m45.62 (Good)

81   JIM FORD   3m1f110y
      CHALLENGE CUP CHASE
      (5yo+)
£9,870   Wincanton   25 February
70   **Cavvies Clown** 13-11-2
      GBradley 1
70³   **Garrison Savannah** 10-11-12
      MPitman 2.2
52³   **Cool Ground** 11-11-12
      AMaguire 2½.3
44   Ghofar 10-11-2 HDavies dist.4
evens Cool Ground, 7/4 Garrison Savannah, 6/1 CAVVIES CLOWN, 12/1 Ghofar
  Mrs J. Ollivant (Mrs J. Pitman) 4ran
6m50.77 (Good to Soft)

82   PETROS VICTOR   2m
      LUDORUM HURDLE (4yo)
£7,115   Haydock   27 February
33   **Bold Boss** 11-10 MDwyer........ 1
      Glaisdale (Ire) 11-4
      HDavies 5.2
      Stylus 11-4 CLlewellyn......... 4.3
33²   Mohana 10-13 PScudamore 8.4
      Co-Chin (Ire) 11-4 DJMoffatt..8.5
      Merry Scorpion 11-4
      ALarnach..........................dist.6
33   Liability Order 11-4 PNiven.....pu
5/2 Mohana, 3/1 Glaisdale, 7/2 BOLD
BOSS, 4/1 Stylus, 12/1 Co-Chin, 25/1
Liability Order, 40/1 Merry Scorpion
  Mr John Robson (G. M. Moore) 7ran
3m52.84 (Good to Soft)

83   EAST LANCS CHASE   2½m
      (6yo+)
£10,114   Haydock   27 February
8   **Gale Again** 6-11-4 KJohnson ... 1
72   **Milford Quay** 10-11-4
      PScudamore 3.2
      Carbisdale 7-11-0 PNiven 5.3
      Strong Approach 8-11-0
      BStorey 6.4
72   Miami Bear 7-11-0 AJones .... f
5/4 Milford Quay, 9/4 GALE AGAIN, 3/1
Carbisdale, 9/1 Strong Approach, 33/1
Miami Bear
  Mr P. Piller (P. Cheesbrough) 5ran
5m19.40 (Good to Soft)

84   GREENALLS GOLD   3½m110y
      CUP (HANDICAP CHASE)
      (5yo+)
£27,017   Haydock   27 February
52   **Party Politics** 9-11-7
      CLlewellyn............................ 1

      Fiddlers Pike 12-10-0
      MrsRHenderson 4.2
78   **Willsford** 10-10-0
      BdeHaan 2½.3
34²   Riverside Boy 10-10-4
      PScudamore 5.4
      Plenty Crack 10-10-0 BStorey ... f
49   Twin Oaks 13-11-3 NDoughty .pu
55²   Otterburn House 9-10-1
      MDwyer ....pu
44   Topsham Bay 10-10-9
      HDavies ....pu
67   Kildimo 13-10-0 JCallaghan .....pu
3/1 Otterburn House, 7/2 Riverside Boy,
Twin Oaks, 6/1 Topsham Bay, 8/1 Plenty
Crack, 10/1 Willsford, 16/1 Fiddlers Pike,
PARTY POLITICS, 33/1 Kildimo
  Mrs David Thompson (N. A. Gaselee)
9ran 7m32.68 (Good to Soft)

85   DOVECOTE NOVICES'   2m
      HURDLE (Gr 2) (4yo+)
£6,555   Kempton   27 February
      Roll A Dollar 7-11-7
      GLMoore.............................. 1
      Winter Squall (Ire) 5-11-3
      RDunwoody 3.2
      Cabochon 6-11-7 JFrost.....2½.3
      Peaceman 7-11-3
      EMurphy 1½.4
43   Big Beat (USA) 5-11-7
      PHolley 25.5
      Arcot 5-11-3 SDWilliams 8.6
      Pay Homage 5-11-3
      DMurphy............................4.7
      Aude La Belle (Fr) 5-10-12
      SMcNeill 12.8
      Highland Spirit 5-10-12
      JLower..................................8.9
15/8 Winter Squall, 9/2 Arcot, 6/1 ROLL
A DOLLAR, 13/2 Cabochon, 8/1 Big
Beat, 14/1 Peaceman, 16/1 Highland
Spirit, 20/1 Pay Homage, 33/1 Aude La
Belle
  Mr K. Higson (D. R. C. Elsworth) 9ran
3m46.95 (Good)

86   TOTE PLACEPOT   2m
      HURDLE (Gr 2) (4yo)
£10,100   Kempton   27 February
      Amazon Express 10-12
      JOsborne 1
33   **Top Spin** 10-12 LWyer nk.2
33   **Eden's Close** 11-2
      RCampbell........................ 12.3
      Kiveton Tycoon (Ire) 10-12
      SDWilliams nk.4
      Scrutineer 10-12
      RDunwoody 2½.5
      Eid (USA) 10-12 JRailton ¾.6
      Ivor's Flutter 10-12 PHolley ...2.7
      Great Max (Ire) 10-12
      DMurphy............................8.8
      Cariboo Gold (USA) 10-12
      SMcNeill 15.9

857

Bo Knows Best (Ire) 10-12
AMaguire 25.10
Desert Force (Ire) 10-12
BClifford ....pu
Precious Wonder 10-12
MHourigan ....pu

7/2 Ivor's Flutter, 9/2 Bo Knows Best, 11/2 Great Max, 13/2 Kiveton Tycoon, 7/1 Scrutineer, 8/1 Eden's Close, Top Spin, 12/1 AMAZON EXPRESS, 33/1 Cariboo Gold, Desert Force, 66/1 Eid, 100/1 Precious Wonder
Mrs Jill Moss (R. Akehurst) 12ran 3m47.66 (Good)

87   RACING POST CHASE   3m
      (HANDICAP) (Gr 3) (5yo +)
£28,110   Kempton   27 February
78*   **Zeta's Lad** 10-10-10 JWhite..... 1
32   **Docklands Express** 11-12-0
      JOsborne 1½.2
70²   **Bradbury Star** 8-10-10
      DMurphy...........................nk.3
      Royal Athlete 10-10-10
      MPitman 7.4
49³   Gold Options 11-11-8 LWyer ..3.5
64³   Blazing Walker 9-11-13
      CGrant 4.6
28   Romany King 9-10-13
      AMaguire 1.7
      Mr Entertainer 10-10-0
      JRKavanagh 2.8
67²   Calapaez 9-10-0 SMcNeill.......4.9
67   Rowlandsons Jewels 12-10-0
      DGallagher.....................20.10
54*   Tinryland 9-10-7
      RDunwoody 30.11
64   Joyful Noise 10-10-7 TJarvis ....ur

11/4 Bradbury Star, 4/1 Blazing Walker, 15/2 Gold Options, 8/1 Romany King, Tinryland, 10/1 Mr Entertainer, 11/1 ZETA'SLAD, 14/1 Calapaez, 20/1 Docklands Express, 25/1 Royal Athlete, 33/1 Rowlandsons Jewels, 66/1 Joyful Noise
Mrs Diane Upson (John R. Upson) 12ran 5m55.96 (Good)

88   RENDLESHAM   3m110y
      HURDLE (Gr 2) (4yo +)
£10,380   Kempton   27 February
39²   **Baydon Star** 6-11-9
      RDunwoody 1
      Grace Card 7-11-5 PNiven . 30.2
      Sayyure (USA) 7-11-5
      SSmithEccles................. dist.3
66*   Sweet Glow (Fr) 6-11-12
      DRichmond .... f

10/11BAYDONSTAR, 11/4 Sweet Glow, 10/3 Grace Card, 14/1 Sayyure
Mrs Shirley Robins (D. Nicholson) 4ran 6m01.07 (Good)

89   CAVALIER CHASE   2½m110y
      (Gr 2) (5yo +)
£16,225   Worcester   3 March
32³   **The Illywhacker** 8-11-10
      MPitman 1

72*   **Young Hustler** 6-11-10
      PScudamore ½.2
60³   **Fighting Words** 7-11-3
      PHide 30.3
87   Joyful Noise 10-11-3
      TJarvis dist.4

4/5 Young Hustler, 5/2 THE ILLY-WHACKER, 3/1 Fighting Words, 33/1 Joyful Noise
Mr J. Hitchins (Mrs J. Pitman) 4ran 5m16.20 (Good)

90   BERKSHIRE HURDLE   2m5f
      (Gr 2) (4yo +)
£9,440   Newbury   6 March
73   **Lift And Load (USA)** 6-11-12
      DMurphy................................ 1
73   **Flakey Dove** 7-11-4 DTegg.. 6.2
61   **Ketti** 8-11-0 MrGLewis 8.3
73   Royal Derbi 8-11-12
      RDunwoody 6.4
      Crystal Spirit 6-11-12 JFrost....ur

10/11Flakey Dove, 4/1 Crystal Spirit, 9/2 LIFT AND LOAD, 5/1 Royal Derbi, 33/1 Ketti
Mrs P. Jubert (R. Hannon) 5ran 5m09.86 (Firm)

91   BEAUFORT HURDLE   2m110y
      (5yo)
£12,575   Chepstow   13 March
85²   **Winter Squall (Ire)** 11-5
      RDunwoody 1
      Pharly Story 11-5
      PScudamore 12.2
      River Island (USA) 11-5
      CLlewellyn........................ ½.3
      Fotoexpress 11-5
      MrCBurnett-Wells..............4.4
      Book of Music (Ire) 11-5
      DMurphy 1½.5
      Oatis Regrets 11-5
      JOsborne ½.6
      Brandon Prince (Ire) 11-5
      SEarle 15.7
      Cru Exceptionnel 11-5
      PeterHobbs............................. f

5/4 WINTER SQUALL, 10/3 Oatis Regrets, 11/2 Pharly Story, 13/2 Brandon Prince, 16/1 Cru Exceptionnel, 20/1 Book of Music, 25/1 Fotoexpress, River Island
Mrs Shirley Robins (D. Nicholson) 8ran 3m55.40 (Good to Firm)

92   SUNDERLANDS   2m110y
      IMPERIAL CUP
      (HANDICAP HURDLE) (4yo +)
£20,399   Sandown   13 March
      Olympian 6-10-0 PScudamore 1
      Gymcrak Stardom 7-10-10
      LWyer 3.2
      Spinning 6-11-8
      RDunwoody ¾.3
50³   Avro Anson 5-11-10 DByrne...4.4

San Lorenzo (USA) 5-10-5
SMcNeill 7.5
Kalogy 6-11-1
MAFitzgerald.................. 2½.6
Keen Vision (Ire) 5-10-0
PeterHobbs nk.7
Bookcase 6-10-10 PHolley ...12.8
50²   Nijmegen 5-11-2 MDwyer 3.9
73   Seon 7-10-9 NBentley...........4.10
Sleepline Royale 7-10-9
GBradley...........................3.11
Villa Recos 8-11-3
MPitman ¾.12
73   Noble Insight 6-10-7
MPerrett 1.13
61   Beebob 5-11-7 JLower ....pu
Sulli Boy (Nor) 8-10-3
DGallagher...........................pu

6/4 OLYMPIAN, 11/2 Spinning, 9/1
Gymcrak Stardom, 10/1 Avro Anson,
Nijmegen, 12/1 Kalogy, Keen Vision,
16/1 San Lorenzo, 20/1 Bookcase, 25/1
Sulli Boy, 33/1 Villa Recos, 40/1 Beebob,
Seon, Sleepline Royale, 66/1 Noble
Insight
  M. & N. Plant Ltd (M. C. Pipe) 15ran
3m42.03 (Firm)

93   TRAFALGAR HOUSE   2m110y
    SUPREME NOVICES'
    HURDLE (Gr 1) (4yo +)
£30,014   Cheltenham   16 March
    Montelado 6-11-8 CSwan 1
    Lemon's Mill (USA) 4-10-9
      PScudamore 12.2
    Satin Lover 5-11-8
      GMcCourt 2½.3
    Boro Eight 7-11-8
      AMaguire 3½.4
57   Gaelic Myth (USA) 6-11-8
      DMurphy...........................2.5
    Frickley 7-11-8 NDoughty......1.6
    Winds of War 8-11-8
      LCusack 3½.7
    Aiybak (Ire) 5-11-8
      BSheridan 3½.8
43   Leotard 6-11-8 JOsborne 4.9
    Maestroso (Ire) 4-11-0
      SMcNeill 3½.10
    Cyprus (Fr) 5-11-8
      SCurran 2½.11
    Almanzora 9-11-8 MPitman ..3.12
76³   Corrin Hill 6-11-8 PNiven ...20.13
43²   Dreamers Delight 7-11-8
      RDunwoody .... f
    Tony's Delight (Ire) 5-11-8
      GBradley...............................pu

7/2 Boro Eight, 4/1 Satin Lover, 5/1
MONTELADO, 13/2 Frickley, 10/1
Gaelic Myth, Lemon's Mill, 16/1
Dreamers Delight, Leotard, 25/1 Corrin
Hill, 50/1 Aiyback, Winds of War, 66/1
Almanzora, 200/1 Cyprus, Maestroso,
Tony's Delight
  Mr F. O. Hannon (P. J. Flynn) 15ran
3m50.62 (Good to Firm)

94   WATERFORD   2m
    CASTLE
    ARKLE CHALLENGE
    TROPHY CHASE
    (Gr 1) (5yo +)
£40,680   Cheltenham   16 March
    Travado 7-11-8 JOsborne 1
77²   **Wonder Man (Fr)** 8-11-8
      RDunwoody 1.2
77*   **Sybillin** 7-11-8 MDwyer 20.3
    Valiant Boy 7-11-8 RGarritty ..8.4
    Winnie The Witch 9-11-3
      DBridgwater 3.5
65*   Atlaal 8-11-8 GBradley 1½.6
    The Slater 8-11-8 PHolley .... f
56   Galevilla Express 6-11-3
      CBowens................................. f

4/5 Sybillin, 7/2 Wonder Man, 5/1
TRAVADO, 20/1 Galevilla Express,
Winnie The Witch, 25/1 Atlaal, 66/1
Valiant Boy, 100/1 The Slater
  Mrs Michael Ennever (N. J. Hender-
son) 8ran 3m56.67 (Good to Firm)

95   SMURFIT   2m110y
    CHAMPION HURDLE
    CHALLENGE
    TROPHY
    (Gr 1) (4yo +)
£84,734   Cheltenham   16 March
35³   **Granville Again** 7-12-0
      PScudamore 1
90   **Royal Derbi** 8-12-0
      MPerrett 1.2
57   **Halkopous** 7-12-0
      AMaguire 2½.3
73*   King Credo 8-12-0 HDavies....3.4
35   Oh So Risky 6-12-0 PHolley....2.5
    Vintage Crop 6-12-0
      BSheridan hd.6
90²   Flakey Dove 7-11-9
      CLlewellyn......................... ½.7
35²   Flown 6-12-0 RDunwoody ... nk.8
48*   Jinxy Jack 9-12-0 NDoughty....2.9
45   Eyelid 7-12-0 CSwan.............3.10
80²   Kribensis 9-12-0 DMurphy nk.11
63   Morley Street 9-12-0
      GBradley...........................2.12
76*   Coulton 6-12-0 MDwyer.... 3½.13
    Athy Spirit 8-12-0 KO'Brien .7.14
76²   Duke of Monmouth (USA) 5-12-0
      GMcCourt 5.15
80*   Valfinet (Fr) 6-12-0 JLower ..7.16
16²   Staunch Friend (USA) 5-12-0
      JOsborne 17
73   Ruling (USA) 7-12-0 PNiven...pu

7/2 Flown, 13/2 GRANVILLE AGAIN,
9/1 Coulton, Halkopous, Vintage Crop,
10/1 Oh So Risky, 14/1 Ruling, 16/1
Kribensis, Valfinet, 20/1 King Credo,
Morley Street, Staunch Friend, 25/1
Duke of Monmouth, Jinxy Jack, 50/1
Eyelid, Flakey Dove, Royal Derbi, 200/1
Athy Spirit
  Mr Eric Scarth (M. C. Pipe) 18ran
3m51.83 (Good to Firm)

96	RITZ CLUB NATIONAL	3m 1f
	HUNT HANDICAP CHASE	
	(5yo +)	
£28,383	Cheltenham	16 March
34	**Givus A Buck** 10-10-8	
	PHolley	1
62*	**Country Member** 8-11-5	
	LHarvey	sh.2
41	**Boraceva** 10-10-2	
	AMaguire	nk.3
67³	Cache Fleur (Fr) 7-10-8	
	PScudamore	2.4
	Shoon Wind 10-10-4	
	PNiven	dist.5
81*	Cavvies Clown 13-11-10	
	GBradley	ur
	Stirrup Cup 9-10-5 JOsborne	pu

5/4 Country Member, 5/1 Stirrup Cup, 11/2 GIVUS A BUCK, 10/1 Boraceva, Cache Fleur, Cavvies Clown, 12/1 Shoon Wind

Mr K. Costello (D. R. C. Elsworth) 7ran 6m14.77 (Good to Firm)

97	FULKE WALWYN	3m 1f
	KIM MUIR CHALLENGE CUP	
	HANDICAP CHASE	
	(AMATEUR RIDERS) (5yo +)	
£17,103	Cheltenham	16 March
	Strong Beau 8-9-8 MrTJenks.. 1	
	Merano (Fr) 10-10-11	
	MrSSwiers	2½.2
74	**The Committee** 10-11-10	
	MrPGraffin	12.3
	Re-Release 8-9-7	
	MrGLewis	12.4
55	Esha Ness 10-11-0	
	MrPFenton	1.5
34	Merry Master 9-11-2	
	MrMArmytage	nk.6
	Vulgan Warrior 11-10-0	
	MrMRimell	30.7
	Larksmore 8-9-8	
	MissSWallin	8.8
10	Knight Oil 10-10-10	
	MrJDurkan	nk.9
	Allezmoss 7-10-12 MrJBerry	f
	Roc de Prince (Fr) 10-11-9	
	MrAJMartin	ur
	Cythere 9-10-0	
	MrTMcCarthy	ur

5/1 Esha Ness, 11/2 Merano, 6/1 STRONG BEAU, 13/2 Allezmoss, 7/1 Merry Master, 8/1 Cythere, 9/1 The Committee, 10/1 Knight Oil, 14/1 Re-Release, Roc de Prince, 33/1 Vulgan Warrior, 66/1 Larksmore

Mrs J. Mould (D. Nicholson) 12ran 6m12.10 (Good to Firm)

98	AMERICAN EXPRESS	3¼m
	GOLD CARD HANDICAP	
	HURDLE (FINAL) (4yo +)	
£20,858	Cheltenham	16 March
	Fissure Seal 7-11-4 CSwan	1
	Jakarrdi 7-11-1 MPitman .. 2½.2	

	Sendai 7-10-10 PHide	3.3
	Acrow Line 8-10-0	
	DJBurchell	2.4
	Manenda 6-10-1	
	RDunwoody	½.5
	Kings Rank 8-11-0	
	DRichmond	6.6
	Jimbalou 10-10-2 RJBeggan	2.7
47	Lafkadio 6-10-0	
	WWorthington	nk.8
	Sea Trout 9-10-1 GUpton	nk.9
	Cairncastle 8-10-7 HDavies.. 2.10	
	Sukaab 8-10-13 CLlewellyn ½.11	
	Furry Baby 6-10-1	
	AMaguire	1½.12
85³	Cabochon 6-11-8	
	PScudamore	4.13
	Vital Witness (Can) 6-10-6	
	ASSmith	1½.14
	Midland Glenn 9-11-10	
	AMulholland	1½.15
	Ferromyn 8-11-5	
	CO'Dwyer	2½.16
6	Pactolus (USA) 10-11-9	
	GMcCourt	5.17
	Petty Bridge 9-11-8	
	RBellamy	5.18
	Lesbet 8-10-8 PHolley	¾.19
17	Sir Crusty 11-10-7	
	MAFitzgerald	6.20
	Bean King 7-11-3 JRKavanagh... f	
	Snowy Lane (Ire) 5-11-1 JLower f	

4/1 Cabochon, 10/1 Manenda, Sendai, Sukaab, 11/1 Ferromyn, 12/1 Cairncastle, Jakarrdi, 14/1 FISSURE SEAL, Furry Baby, Pactolus, Petty Bridge, Sea Trout, 16/1 Vital Witness, 20/1 Jimbalou, 25/1 Bean King, Kings Rank, Snowy Lane, 33/1 Midland Glenn, Sir Crusty, 50/1 Lesbet, 100/1 Acrow Line, Lafkadio

Delton Syndicate (H. de Bromhead) 22ran 6m31.09 (Good to Firm)

99	SUN ALLIANCE	2m5f
	NOVICES' HURDLE (Gr 1)	
	(4yo +)	
£30,135	Cheltenham	17 March
59²	**Gaelstrom** 6-11-2 CLlewellyn. 1	
	Cardinal Red 6-11-7	
	BdeHaan	2½.2
40*	**Lord Relic (NZ)** 7-11-7	
	PScudamore	1½.3
	Giventime 5-11-7 LHarvey. 1½.4	
45³	Atone 6-11-7 CSwan	1.5
	Martomick 6-11-2 JRailton	7.6
	Bucks-Choice 6-11-7	
	AMullins	3.7
69*	Hebridean 6-11-7	
	RDunwoody	8.8
47	Belvederian 6-11-7	
	LCusack	¾.9
	Bally Clover 6-11-7	
	JRKavanagh	1½.10
	Hillwalk 7-11-7 DMorris... 1½.11	
75³	Now Your Talkin 7-11-7	
	GMcCourt	1.12
	Hurdy 6-11-7 GBradley	3.13

860

Pectorus (Ire) 5-11-7
MFoster 10.14
61 Be My Habitat 4-10-12
PNiven 30.15
Captain My Captain (Ire) 5-11-7
DianeClay 7.16
Bedfield (Ire) 5-11-7
BMurphy 4.17
Beauchamp Express 6-11-7
JOsborne ....pu
61* Trainglot 6-11-7 MDwyer........pu

5/2 Lord Relic, 4/1 Hebridean, 6/1 Atone,
7/1 Trainglot, 10/1 Belvederian, Bucks-
Choice, 14/1 Giventime, 16/1 GAEL-
STROM, 33/1 Now Your Talkin, 40/1
Bally Clover, 50/1 Hurdy, Martomick,
66/1 Pectorus, 100/1 Beauchamp
Express, Hillwalk, 150/1 Be My Habitat,
Cardinal Red, 300/1 Bedfield, Captain
My Captain

Mrs J. K. Powell (N. A. Twiston-
Davies) 19ran 4m59.37 (Good to Firm)

100 SUN ALLIANCE CHASE   3m 1f
(Gr 1) (5yo +)
£42,570   Cheltenham   17 March
89² **Young Hustler** 6-11-4
PScudamore 1
Superior Finish 7-11-4
MPitman 3.2
Its A Cracker 9-11-4
MrJBerry.......................... 15.3
Annio Chilone 7-11-4 PHide ...6.4
Ru Valentino 9-11-4
NWilliamson 15.5
Ashfold Copse 7-11-4 MPerrett. f
68* Capability Brown 6-11-4
AMaguire .... ur
31 Barton Bank 7-11-4
RDunwoody ....pu

7/4 Barton Bank, 9/4 YOUNG
HUSTLER, 5/1 Ashfold Copse, 7/1
Capability Brown, 10/1 Superior Finish,
33/1 Annio Chilone, Ru Valentino, 100/1
Its A Cracker

Mr G. M. MacEchern (N. A. Twiston-
Davies) 8ran 6m11.69 (Good to Firm)

101 CORAL CUP   2m5f
(HANDICAP HURDLE)
(5yo +)
£36,546   Cheltenham   17 March
92* **Olympian** 6-10-0 PScudamore 1
61 **Sillars Stalker (Ire)** 5-9-8
MrRHale 2½.2
Yellow Spring 8-10-5
PeterHobbs 5.3
Abnegation 8-10-5 DMurphy ..5.4
92 San Lorenzo (USA) 5-10-0
SMcNeill sh.5
61 Belafonte 6-10-4 GBradley 1.6
73 Balasani (Fr) 7-11-12
PNiven nk.7
Metal Oiseau (Ire) 5-10-0
ACharlton.............................7.8
Andermatt 6-10-1
NWilliamson 2½.9

45 Alterezza (USA) 6-11-5
BSheridan 12.10
6 Annicombe Run 9-10-1
MAFitzgerald....................1.11
Bishops Island 7-11-0
RDunwoody 3.12
NickleJoe 7-10-0
DGallagher........................30.13
61³ Peanuts Pet 8-11-3
GMcCourt 1½.14
Celcius 9-9-7 TDascombe.....1.15
Gallateen 5-10-9 NDoughty....... f
61 Fairfields Cone 10-9-11
DMeredith .... ur
Fox Chapel 6-10-2 MDwyer.....ur
Andrew's First 6-10-2
CLlewellyn...........................bd
Prime Display (USA) 7-11-5
JOsborne ....pu
40 Irish Bay 7-10-5 CSwan ....pu

4/1 Andrew's First, OLYMPIAN, 10/1
NickleJoe, 12/1 Abnegation, 14/1 Ander-
matt, Gallateen, 16/1 Balasani, Bishops
Island, 20/1 Annicombe Run, Yellow
Spring, Sillars Stalker, Yellow Spring, 25/1
Alterezza, Fox Chapel, Peanuts Pet,
33/1 Metal Oiseau, Prime Display, San
Lorenzo, 40/1 Belafonte, 50/1 Fairfields
Cone, 100/1 Celcius

M. & N. Plant Ltd (M. C. Pipe) 21ran
4m57.11 (Good to Firm)

102 QUEEN MOTHER   2m
CHAMPION CHASE
(Gr 1) (5yo +)
£63,694   Cheltenham   17 March
64² **Deep Sensation** 8-12-0
DMurphy 1
71³ **Cyphrate (USA)** 7-12-0
PScudamore ¾.2
71² **Katabatic** 10-12-0 SMcNeill. 2.3
46³ Fragrant Dawn 9-12-0
PHolley 6.4
54³ Boro Smackeroo 8-12-0
AOrkney............................15.5
71* Waterloo Boy 10-12-0
RDunwoody dist.6
1 Moment of Truth 9-12-0
GMcCourt .... f
70 Wingspan (USA) 9-12-0
JFrost ....pu
71 Young Snugfit 9-12-0
JOsborne ....pu

6/5 Katabatic, 7/4 Waterloo Boy, 11/1
DEEP SENSATION, 14/1 Cyphrate,
16/1 Young Snugfit, 25/1 Fragrant Dawn,
50/1 Boro Smackeroo, Moment of Truth,
100/1 Wingspan

Mr R. F. Eliot (J. T. Gifford) 9ran
3m56.52 (Good to Firm)

103 NATIONAL HUNT CHASE   4m
CHALLENGE CUP
(AMATEUR RIDERS) (5yo +)
£15,140   Cheltenham   17 March
Ushers Island 7-12-4
MrNWilson........................... 1

861

Claxton Greene 9-12-7
  MrMArmytage sh.2
Travelling Wrong 7-12-7
  MrJDurkan 1.3
Gold Cap (Fr) 8-12-4
  MrGLewis 1½.4
Brief Case 7-12-4
  MrPGraffin......................dist.5
Emily's Star 6-12-2 MrTJenks ... f

68³ Channels Gate 9-12-7
  MrPFenton .... ur
Star Actor 7-12-0 MrCVigors... ur
Miss Shaw 7-11-9
  MrMWilding......................... ur
Rocket Launcher 7-12-7
  MrMBatters ....pu
Carrickrovaddy 7-12-0
  MrAJMartin ....pu
The Real Unyoke 8-12-7
  MrDPMurphy ....pu
Nebraska 7-12-4
  MrDJDonegan ....pu

100/30 Claxton Greene, 11/2 Travelling
Wrong, 7/1 The Real Unyoke, 15/2
USHERS ISLAND, 8/1 Gold Cap, 9/1
Rocket Launcher, 10/1 Channels Gate,
14/1 Star Actor, 16/1 Brief Case, Emily's
Star, 20/1 Carrickrovaddy, Nebraska,
100/1 Miss Shaw
  Mr R. W. L. Bowden (J. H. Johnson)
13ran 8m23.60 (Good to Firm)

104 MILDMAY OF FLETE 2½m110y
     CHALLENGE CUP
     HANDICAP CHASE
     (5yo +)
£25,499   Cheltenham   17 March
26   Sacre d'Or (USA) 8-11-0
       GMcCourt 1
     Smartie Express 11-10-0
       MAFitzgerald.................... 2.2
     Southern Minstrel 10-10-0
       CGrant 2½.3
     Bel Course 11-9-11
       WMarston dist.4
     Plat Reay 9-10-0 SMcNeill hd.5
     Kentish Piper 8-10-4
       DMurphy......................... nk.6
8   Howe Street 10-11-4
       AOrkney.......................... 1½.7
     Belstone Fox 8-10-3
       RDunwoody dist.8
15² Emsee-H 8-10-13
       SSmithEccles...................... ur
83² Milford Quay 10-11-10 JFrost ..pu
78³ Repeat The Dose 8-11-8
       JOsborne ....pu

4/1 Kentish Piper, 5/1 Belstone Fox, 7/1
Repeat The Dose, SACRE D'OR,
Southern Minstrel, 8/1 Howe Street, 9/1
Emsee-H, 10/1 Smartie Express, 12/1
Milford Quay, 33/1 Plat Reay, 50/1 Bel
Course
  Mrs D. Wright (N. Tinkler) 11ran
5m04.02 (Good to Firm)

105 DAILY EXPRESS   2m 1f
     TRIUMPH HURDLE
     (Gr 1) (4yo)
£25,340   Cheltenham   18 March
79* Shawiya (Ire) 10-9 CSwan 1
86* Amazon Express 11-0
       SMcNeill ¾.2
33³ Major Bugler (Ire) 11-0
       AMaguire 2.3
     Judicial Field (Ire) 11-0
       BSheridan ¾.4
     Loshian (Ire) 10-9
       THorgan 1½.5
86   Kiveton Tycoon (Ire) 11-0
       SDWilliams 4.6
86   Bo Knows Best (Ire) 11-0
       MAFitzgerald..................... ½.7
86   Ivor's Flutter 11-0 PHolley. 2½.8
     Her Honour 10-9
       PScudamore ¾.9
     Kadi (Ger) 11-0
       GMcCourt 1½.10
     Indian Run (Ire) 11-0
       WIrvine nk.11
     Dominant Serenade 11-0
       PNiven hd.12
     Indian Quest 11-0
       JRKavanagh hd.13
     Viardot (Ire) 11-0 MDwyer .dh.13
     Clurican (Ire) 11-0
       WMarston 1.15
     Holy Wanderer (USA) 11-0
       GUpton...........................3.16
     Beauchamp Grace 10-9
       RDunwoody nk.17
     Robingo (Ire) 11-0 JLower 2.18
79   Winterbourne Abbas (Ire) 11-0
       NWilliamson 3½.19
82   Mohana 10-9 MFoster sh.20
86³ Eden's Close 11-0
       DMurphy........................ ½.21
86² Top Spin 11-0 GBradley nk.22
     Storm Dust 11-0
       SSmithEccles................... ½.23
86   Eid (USA) 11-0 JRailton 10.24
     Dissimulateur (Fr) 11-0
       JOsborne 25.25

13/2 Beauchamp Grace, 11/1 Indian
Quest, 12/1 Amazon Express, Her
Honour, SHAWIYA, 14/1 Dominant
Serenade, Judicial Field, Storm Dust,
16/1 Bo Knows Best, Major Bugler, Top
Spin, 20/1 Kadi, Loshian, Robingo, 25/1
Viardot, 33/1 Dissimulateur, Kiveton
Tycoon, 40/1 Clurican, Eden's Close,
Holy Wanderer, Indian Run, Ivor's
Flutter, Mohana, 66/1 Winterbourne
Abbas, 200/1 Eid
  Miss G. Maher (M. J. P. O'Brien)
25ran 3m59.73 (Good to Firm)

106 BONUSPRINT   3m 110y
     STAYERS' HURDLE
     (Gr 1) (4yo +)
£43,435   Cheltenham   18 March
27³ Shuil Ar Aghaidh 7-11-5
       CSwan 1

47* **Pragada** 10-11-10
MPerrett 2½.2
88* **Baydon Star** 6-11-10
RDunwoody 3.3
61² Sweet Duke (Fr) 6-11-10
DBridgwater 8.4
88 Sweet Glow (Fr) 6-11-10
PScudamore sh.5
27 Super Sense 8-11-10 PHide ..12.6
90 Crystal Spirit 6-11-10 JFrost.15.7
57 Chirkpar 6-11-10 LCusack......4.8
47³ Burgoyne 7-11-10 AMaguire 15.9
90³ Ketti 8-11-5 HDavies..........10.10
66³ Tyrone Bridge 7-11-10
GMcCourt ....pu
47 Vagog 8-11-10 MFoster...........pu

3/1 Baydon Star, 4/1 Sweet Glow, 5/1
Crystal Spirit, 11/2 Burgoyne, 9/1 Pra-
gada, 14/1 Chirkpar, Vagog, 16/1 Tyrone
Bridge, 20/1 SHUIL AR AGHAIDH, 25/1
Super Sense, 33/1 Sweet Duke, 100/1
Ketti

Mrs P. Kiely (P. Kiely) 12ran 5m43.19
(Good to Firm)

---

107 TOTE   3¼m110y
CHELTENHAM GOLD CUP
CHASE (Gr 1) (5yo +)
£99,448   Cheltenham   18 March
74* **Jodami** 8-12-0 MDwyer 1
62² **Rushing Wild** 8-12-0
RDunwoody 2.2
87 **Royal Athlete** 10-12-0
BdeHaan 7.3
32* The Fellow (Fr) 8-12-0
AKondrat ½.4
52* Sibton Abbey 8-12-0
SSmithEccles......................4.5
87² Docklands Express 11-12-0
JOsborne ¾.6
81² Garrison Savannah 10-12-0
MPitman 10.7
49² Run For Free 9-12-0
MPerrett 5.8
81³ Cool Ground 11-12-0
AMaguire 3½.9
49 Tipping Tim 8-12-0
DBridgwater 2½.10
74² Chatam (USA) 9-12-0
PScudamore 8.11
84 Topsham Bay 10-12-0
JFrost hd.12
74 Cahervillahow 9-12-0
CSwan ¾.13
Black Humour 9-12-0 GBradley f
70* Cherrykino 8-12-0 HDavies....... f
67* Very Very Ordinary 7-12-0
RSupple ....pu

5/4 The Fellow, 8/1 Docklands Express,
JODAMI, 10/1 Chatam, 11/1 Run For
Free, Rushing Wild, 14/1 Cahervillahow,
16/1 Cherrykino, 22/1 Sibton Abbey, 25/1
Garrison Savannah, Tipping Tim, 50/1
Cool Ground, 66/1 Black Humour, Royal
Athlete, Very Very Ordinary, 200/1
Topsham Bay

Mr J. N. Yeadon (P. Beaumont) 16ran
6m34.55 (Good to Firm)

---

108 CHRISTIES   3¼m110y
FOXHUNTER CHASE
CHALLENGE CUP (5yo +)
£15,920   Cheltenham   18 March
Double Silk 9-12-0
MrRTreloggen 1
Kerry Orchid 5-11-4
MrAJMartin.................... 1½.2
Once Stung 7-12-0
MrJGreenall 5.3
Toureen Prince 10-12-0
MrJMPritchard 12.4
Moorcroft Boy 8-12-0
MrTJenks........................... ½.5
Swinhoe Croft 11-12-0
MrCStockton 1.6
Seven of Diamonds 8-12-0
MrMBatters 20.7
Radical Views 8-12-0
MrEBailey............................... f
Randolph Place 12-12-0
MrIStark .... ur
The Red One 9-12-0
MrSSwiers ....bd
Duncan 8-12-0
MrMArmytage ....pu
Watercourse 9-12-0
MissLEADoyle ....pu
Some Obligation 8-12-0
MrTByrne ....pu
40 Glen Lochan 13-12-0
MrNTutty............................pu
Holy Foley 11-12-0
MrNHarris ....pu
Sporting Mariner 11-12-0
MrPHarding-Jones..............pu
Spring Fun 10-12-0
MrMGMiller ....pu
Tartan Trix 10-12-0
MrPHacking.........................pu

11/2 Kerry Orchid, The Red One, 6/1
Toureen Prince, 7/1 Radical Views, 8/1
Once Stung, 11/1 Seven of Diamonds,
Tartan Trix, 12/1 DOUBLE SILK, 14/1
Watercourse, 16/1 Moorcroft Boy, 20/1
Randolph Place, 33/1 Duncan, Holy
Foley, 40/1 Swinhoe Croft, 50/1 Glen
Lochan, Some Obligation, 100/1 Spring
Fun, 300/1 Sporting Mariner

Mr R. C. Wilkins (R. C. Wilkins) 18ran
6m40.06 (Good to Firm)

---

109 CHELTENHAM   2m110y
GRAND ANNUAL CHASE
CHALLENGE CUP
(HANDICAP) (5yo +)
£24,094   Cheltenham   18 March
54² **Space Fair** 10-11-1 AMaguire . 1
Shamana 7-10-9
RDunwoody 2.2
Storm Alert 7-11-7
SMcNeill 1.3
Young Pokey 8-11-10
JOsborne 12.4

29³ Setter Country 9-10-3
   WIrvine 20.5
   Private Audition 11-9-7
   MrPaulMurphy 25.6
   Acre Hill 9-10-10 CSwan........ 15.7
   Whatever You Like 9-10-8
   JRKavanagh 12.8
46 Star's Delight 11-11-2
   GMcCourt .... f
   Alkinor Rex 8-10-6 MPerrett..... f
   Sonsie Mo 8-9-11 PWilliams ...... f
   Gabish 8-9-11 MHourigan ....pu

11/4 Storm Alert, 5/1 SPACE FAIR,
Young Pokey, 13/2 Shamana, 10/1 What-
ever You Like, 11/1 Setter Country, 12/1
Acre Hill, Alkinor Rex, 20/1 Private
Audition, Star's Delight, 66/1 Sonsie Mo,
200/1 Gabish
  Osborne House Limited (R. Lee)
12ran 3m59.52 (Good to Firm)

---

110 CATHCART CHALLENGE 2m5f
    CUP CHASE (6yo +)
£26,040   Cheltenham   18 March
72³ **Second Schedual** 8-11-3
   AMaguire 1
74³ **General Idea** 8-11-7
   BSheridan hd.2
64* **Armagret** 8-11-3 DByrne 6.3
60 Forest Sun 8-11-0 GBradley 1.4
87 Tinryland 9-11-7
   RDunwoody dist.5
89* The Illywhacker 8-11-7
   MPitman .... f
   Among Friends 8-11-0
   WMcFarland ....bd

5/2 General Idea, 3/1 The Illywhacker,
5/1 Tinryland, 11/2 Armagret, 6/1
SECOND SCHEDUAL, 14/1 Forest Sun,
80/1 Among Friends
  Mr Hugh McMahon (A. L. T. Moore)
7ran 5m09.81 (Good to Firm)

---

111 TOTE COUNTY   2m 1f
    HANDICAP HURDLE (Gr 3)
    (5yo +)
£22,805   Cheltenham   18 March
43³ **Thumbs Up** 7-10-2
   RDunwoody 1
   High Baron 6-10-9
   MHourigan 6.2
92³ **Spinning** 6-10-10 JFrost 1.3
   Hashar (Ire) 5-10-1 PHolley . ½.4
   Done Instantly 8-10-6
   NWilliamson 1½.5
   Assuring (Ire) 5-11-0
   KO'Brien..............................1.6
73³ Bitofabanter 6-11-5
   PCarberry hd.7
   Train Robber 8-10-0
   WIrvine 2½.8
   Dancing Paddy 5-10-3
   DO'Sullivan........................6.9
   Mubadir (USA) 5-11-0
   CSwan 2.10

   Doran's Town Lad 6-10-10
   AMullins 2½.11
   Wings of Freedom (Ire) 5-10-0
   DGallagher......................hd.12
   Good For A Loan 6-10-0
   AMaguire 1½.13
   Willie Sparkle 7-9-12
   PWilliams nk.14
73 Glencloud (Ire) 5-11-6
   GMO'Neill....................... 10.15
   Masai Mara (USA) 5-10-2
   JRKavanagh 3½.16
   Pardon Me Sir 9-11-2
   SHodgson..........................6.17
   Diamond Cut (Fr) 5-11-0
   GMcCourt 12.18
   Duharra (Ire) 5-10-11
   BSheridan .... ur
   Shu Fly (NZ) 9-10-9 GBradley .pu
   Rowlandsons Gems 8-9-7
   DSalter.................................pu

7/4 Spinning, 8/1 High Baron, Mubadir,
10/1 Bitofabanter, Shu Fly, 12/1 Masai
Mara, 14/1 Dancing Paddy, 16/1 Good For
A Loan, THUMBS UP, 20/1 Assuring,
Glencloud, 25/1 Duharra, Hashar, 33/1
Diamond Cut, Done Instantly, Doran's
Town Lad, 50/1 Willie Sparkle, 100/1
Rowlandsons Gems, 200/1 Pardon Me
Sir, Train Robber, Wings of Freedom
  Mr Michael Buckley (N. J. Hender-
son) 21ran 3m55.60 (Good to Firm)

---

112 TETLEY BITTER   4¼m
    MIDLANDS NATIONAL
    (HANDICAP CHASE) (6yo +)
£23,456   Uttoxeter   20 March
   Mister Ed 10-10-3 DMorris.... 1
   Into The Red 9-10-9
   BClifford 15.2
   Do Be Brief 8-10-0
   BdeHaan 8.3
   Dandy Minstrel 9-10-0
   DBridgwater 4.4
84² Fiddlers Pike 12-11-7
   MrsRHenderson 2.5
   Yiragan 11-10-8 NHawke.... 1½.6
   Crawford Says 8-10-10
   PMcWilliams.................... nk.7
41 Bonsai Bud 10-10-11
   DGallagher......................3½.8
84³ Willsford 10-11-6 MPitman.... 10.9
   False Economy 8-10-4
   NWilliamson 2½.10
   Proplus 11-10-0 JRKavanagh ...11
   Farm Week 11-10-2 SHodgson 12
   Goodshot Rich 9-10-9
   GBradley .... f
41 Windy Ways 8-11-0
   RDunwoody ....pu
d-h72² Whaat Fettle 8-10-8
   MMoloney ....pu
   Auction Law (NZ) 9-9-13
   RDavis.................................pu
   Ace of Spies 12-10-3
   RGarritty.............................pu

4/1 Into The Red, 9/2 Windy Ways, 8/1 Whaat Fettle, 9/1 Crawford Says, 10/1 Dandy Minstrel, 11/1 Fiddlers Pike, 12/1 Do Be Brief, Willsford, 14/1 Auction Law, 16/1 False Economy, 20/1 Farm Week, 25/1 MISTER ED, 33/1 Bonsai Bud, 40/1 Goodshot Rich, 50/1 Proplus, Yiragan, 66/1 Ace of Spies

The Talking Horse Partnership (R. Curtis) 17ran 8m46.34 (Good to Soft)

113	LETHEBY & CHRISTOPHER LONG DISTANCE HURDLE (Gr 2) (4yo +)	3m
£12,980	Ascot	31 March
106	Sweet Duke (Fr) 6-11-3 CLlewellyn	1
106²	Pragada 10-11-10 MPerrett	7.2
106	Crystal Spirit 6-11-10 JFrost	4.3
106	Sweet Glow (Fr) 6-11-7 DRichmond	8.4
106	Super Sense 8-11-3 PHide	2½.5
90*	Lift And Load (USA) 6-11-10 DMurphy	pu
	Castle Secret 7-11-3 DJBurchell	pu

7/4 Pragada, 5/1 SWEET DUKE, Sweet Glow, 11/2 Crystal Spirit, 6/1 Lift And Load, 10/1 Super Sense, 33/1 Castle Secret

Mr Andy Mavrou (N. A. Twiston-Davies) 7ran 5m54.57 (Soft)

114	SEAGRAM TOP NOVICES' HURDLE (Gr 2) (4yo +)	2m110y
£9,964	Aintree	1 April
85*	Roll A Dollar 7-11-6 PHolley	1
93	Gaelic Myth (USA) 6-11-2 DMurphy	hd.2
	Land Afar 6-11-2 AWebb	¾.3
93	Frickley 7-11-6 NDoughty	1½.4
91*	Winter Squall (Ire) 5-11-10 RDunwoody	2½.5
93	Dreamers Delight 7-11-2 RBellamy	2½.6
	Lyn's Return (Ire) 4-10-10 DGallagher	8.7
93³	Satin Lover 5-11-6 GMcCourt	1.8
85	Peaceman 7-11-2 EMurphy	ro

9/4 ROLL A DOLLAR, 9/2 Satin Lover, Winter Squall, 11/2 Gaelic Myth, 13/2 Frickley, 11/1 Dreamers Delight, 20/1 Peaceman, 25/1 Lyn's Return, 50/1 Land Afar

Mr K. Higson (D. R. C. Elsworth) 9ran 3m49.38 (Firm)

115	SANDEMAN MAGHULL NOVICES' CHASE (Gr 2) (5yo +)	2m
£16,147	Aintree	1 April
94	Valiant Boy 7-11-10 RGarritty	1

111	Shu Fly (NZ) 9-11-3 JacquiOliver	hd.2
	Trimlough 8-11-3 NMann	nk.3
	Billy Bathgate 7-11-3 CSwan	2.4
	Montpelier Lad 6-11-3 NDoughty	15.5
104	Belstone Fox 8-11-3 RDunwoody	pu
	Dante's Inferno 7-11-3 TReed	pu

11/4 Montpelier Lad, 9/2 Dante's Inferno, 5/1 Belstone Fox, 13/2 Billy Bathgate, 7/1 Shu Fly, 9/1 Trimlough, 12/1 VALIANT BOY

Mr Roy Chadwick (S. E. Kettlewell) 7ran 3m51.66 (Firm)

116	MARTELL CUP CHASE (Gr 2) (5yo +)	3m 1f
£33,564	Aintree	1 April
107	Docklands Express 11-11-5 JOsborne	1
107	Run For Free 9-11-5 MPerrett	1½.2
107	Very Very Ordinary 7-11-5 RSupple	dist.3
96	Cavvies Clown 13-11-5 GBradley	ur

5/4 Run For Free, 6/4 DOCKLANDS EXPRESS, 15/2 Very Very Ordinary, 8/1 Cavvies Clown

Mr R. H. Baines (K. C. Bailey) 4ran 6m08.10 (Firm)

117	JOHN HUGHES MEMORIAL TROPHY CHASE (HANDICAP) (5yo +)	2¾m
£21,658	Aintree	1 April
15³	Sirrah Jay 13-10-0 AMaguire	1
104³	Southern Minstrel 10-10-5 CGrant	nk.2
26	Nos Na Gaoithe 10-10-12 RGarritty	8.3
103	Channels Gate 9-10-0 NWilliamson	hd.4
	Strong Gold 10-10-5 SMcNeill	1½.5
	Western Legend 9-10-11 MDwyer	8.6
	Boom Time 8-10-6 CSwan	¾.7
	Wrekin Hill 11-10-9 KJohnson	10.8
	Team Challenge 11-11-6 MPitman	2.9
	Our Fellow 11-9-11 MHourigan	15.10
	On The Hooch 8-9-11 PWilliams	8.11
	Captain Brandy 8-11-10 KO'Brien	1.12
14	Interim Lib 10-10-8 MrJBradburne	10.13
	Lumberjack (USA) 9-11-8 JOsborne	f
	Welknown Character 11-10-9 MAFitzgerald	f
	Way of Life (Fr) 8-10-0 SEarle	f

865

Socks Downe 14-10-0 AWebb.... f
81 Ghofar 10-11-6 HDavies ....pu
104 Bel Course 11-9-11
WMarston3 ....pu
Solar Cloud 11-9-12
JudyDavies............................pu
55 Winabuck 10-10-6
WHumphreys.......................bd
Over The Deel 7-10-0
MrAThornton ....ur
Tarqogan's Best 13-10-9
BClifford ....ref

7/1 Southern Minstrel, Wellknown
Character, 8/1 Interim Lib, 9/1 Strong
Gold, Western Legend, 10/1 Channels
Gate, 12/1 Boom Time, 14/1 Lumberjack,
16/1 Captain Brandy, SIRRAH JAY,
Wrekin Hill, 20/1 Ghofar, 25/1 Nos Na
Gaoithe, On The Hooch, 33/1 Bel
Course, Over The Deel, Team Chal-
lenge, Winabuck, 66/1 Way of Life, 100/1
Our Fellow, Socks Downe, Solar Cloud,
200/1 Tarqogan's Best
Elias Gale Racing (G. B. Balding)
23ran 5m26.79 (Firm)

118 GLENLIVET   2m110y
ANNIVERSARY 4-Y-O
HURDLE (Gr 2) (4yo)
£24,624   Aintree   1 April
79² **Titled Dancer (Ire)** 10-9
JShortt.................................. 1
105 **Her Honour** 10-9
PScudamore ½.2
Nadjati (USA) 11-0 PHolley. 1.3
Sharriba 10-9 AWebb 3½.4
105 Dominant Serenade 11-0
PNiven ¾.5
Zamirah (Ire) 10-9
CLlewellyn...................... nk.6
105 Kadi (Ger) 11-0
RDunwoody nk.7
82* Bold Boss 11-0 MDwyer nk.8
13/8 Bold Boss, 9/2 TITLED DANCER,
Zamirah, 11/2 Her Honour, 8/1 Kadi, 10/1
Dominant Serenade, 25/1 Nadjati, 100/1
Sharriba
Mrs Padraig Nolan (J. G. Coogan) 8ran
3m53.32 (Firm)

119 PERRIER JOUET CHASE   3m1f
(HANDICAP) (5yo +)
£8,115   Aintree   2 April
107 **Black Humour** 9-12-0
GBradley 1
Sikera Spy 11-10-6
RBellamy 3.2
Rocktor (NZ) 8-10-12
JFrost 4.3
Side of Hill 8-10-5 MPerrett....3.4
Antrim County 8-10-0
TJMitchell 3.5
Raglan Road 9-10-0 PHolley . 12.6
Sooner Still 9-10-2
NWilliamson dist.7
83³ Carbisdale 7-11-11 PNiven ......pu

River House 11-9-13
MrAThornton ....pu
112 Proplus 11-10-0 JOsborne ....pu
97 Re-Release 8-9-9 DRichmond . ur
4/1 Sikera Spy, 9/2 BLACK HUMOUR,
5/1 Rocktor, 7/1 Carbisdale, 9/1 Side of
Hill, 11/1 River House, 14/1 Antrim
County, Sooner Still, 16/1 Re-Release,
33/1 Proplus, 40/1 Raglan Road
R. E. A. Bott (Wigmore St) Ltd (C. P.
E. Brooks) 11ran 6m06.79 (Firm)

120 MUMM MELLING CHASE 2½m
(Gr 1) (5yo +)
£43,720   Aintree   2 April
102* **Deep Sensation** 8-11-10
DMurphy.............................. 1
29 **Redundant Pal** 10-11-10
JRailton 8.2
87 **Gold Options** 11-11-10
LWyer hd.3
102 Waterloo Boy 10-11-10
RDunwoody ....pu
7/4 DEEP SENSATION, Waterloo Boy,
9/4 Gold Options, 25/1 Redundant Pal
Mr R. F. Eliot (J. T. Gifford) 4ran
4m57.04 (Firm)

121 MUMM MILDMAY CHASE 3m1f
(NOVICES') (Gr 2) (5yo +)
£20,976   Aintree   2 April
Cab On Target 7-11-3 PNiven. 1
110 **Forest Sun** 8-11-3
GBradley 12.2
100* **Young Hustler** 6-11-9
PScudamore 6.3
17 The Widget Man 7-11-3
DMurphy........................25.4
47² Better Times Ahead 7-11-3
NDoughty............................pu
11/8 Young Hustler, 15/8 CAB ON
TARGET, 11/2 Forest Sun, 10/1 Better
Times Ahead, 16/1 The Widget Man
Mrs J. G. Fulton (Mrs M. Reveley)
5ran 6m03.47 (Firm)

122 MARTELL FOX   2¾m
HUNTERS' CHASE (6yo +)
£10,887   Aintree   2 April
108* **Double Silk** 9-12-0
MrRTreloggen 1
Dark Dawn 9-12-0
MrJGreenall 6.2
Mandraki Shuffle 11-12-0
MrAHarvey 7.3
Speakers Corner 10-12-0
MrMSowersby 15.4
Bob Tisdall 14-12-0
CaptAOgden....................2½.5
Mount Argus 11-12-0
MrSBrookshaw 1½.6
Golden Minstrel 14-12-0
MissAEmbiricos hd.7
Knockelly Castle 13-12-0
MrJTrice-Rolph 3½.8

866

Gadbrook 11-12-0
MrMArmytage 2.9
Lacidar 13-12-0
MrAThornton 5.10
Harley 13-12-0 MrDMcCain .7.11
Renagown 10-12-0
MrSBrisby...................... 1½.12
Double Turn 12-12-0
MrPHarding-Jones.............2.13
Bold King's Hussar 10-12-0
MissAPlunkett...................3.14
Blue Dart 13-12-0
MrDAlers-Hankey............6.15
Bartres 14-12-0 MrJDurkan .5.16
Polygonum 11-12-0
MrWBurnell.......................3.17
Gee-A 14-12-0
MrPaulMurphy 3.18
Senator of Rome 10-12-0
MrMHarris........................1.19
Aherlow Glen 9-12-0
MrDPipe 4.20
Elvercone 12-12-0
CaptAWoodward nk.21
Noel Luck 13-12-0
MrMPhillips 22
Curaheen Boy 13-12-0
MissJButler...........................pu
Forest Ranger 11-12-0
MrRMcGrath .... ur
Faaris 12-12-0 MrCNewport...... f
Glenavey 12-12-0 MrPHacking . f
Kings Wild 12-12-0 MrSBush .... f

5/2 DOUBLE SILK, 7/1 Dark Dawn, 8/1
Mount Argus, Speakers Corner, 14/1
Glenavey, Knockelly Castle, 16/1
Gee-A, 20/1 Lacidar, Renagown, 25/1
Aherlow Glen, Curaheen Boy, Faaris,
Gadbrook, 33/1 Forest Ranger, Man-
draki Shuffle, Polygonum, 50/1 Bartres,
Bob Tisdall, Bold King's Hussar, Double
Turn, Senator of Rome, 66/1 Golden
Minstrel, Harley, 100/1 Blue Dart,
Elvercone, King's Wild, Noel Luck
     Mr R. C. Wilkins (R. C. Wilkins) 27ran
5m26.79 (Firm)

123   ODDBINS HURDLE   2½m
         (HANDICAP) (4yo +)
£11,429   Aintree   2 April
101   Gallateen 5-10-11 NDoughty .. 1
101*   Olympian 6-11-1
         PScudamore 3½.2
13   Welshman 7-10-12
         DGallagher.......................3½.3
       Mizyan (Ire) 5-10-3 CGrant ..hd.4
       Mister Major 5-10-0
         AMaguire nk.5
       Oneupmanship 8-10-12
         HDavies 8.6
92²   Gymcrak Stardom 7-10-7
         LWyer 2.7
       Child of The Mist 7-10-6
         RDunwoody 6.8
       Bellezza 6-10-2 GLMoore.....20.9
       Street Kid 5-10-0
         MrGJohnsonHoughton 3.10

61   Bollin William 5-11-10
         RGarritty.............................2.11
       Macedonas 5-10-0 CSwan........12

2/1 Olympian, 4/1 Gymcrak Stardom, 5/1
Oneupmanship, 10/1 Welshman, 11/1
Mizyan, 12/1 GALLATEEN, 14/1
Bellezza, Bollin William, 16/1 Child of
The Mist, 20/1 Macedonas, Mister
Major, Street Kid
     Mr E. R. Madden (G. Richards) 12ran
4m37.08 (Firm)

124   BELLE EPOQUE   3m110y
         SEFTON NOVICES' HURDLE
         (Gr 2) (4yo +)
£7,650   Aintree   2 April
99²   Cardinal Red 6-11-4 BdeHaan 1
99*   Gaelstrom 6-11-5
         PScudamore 1½.2
       As Du Trefle (Fr) 5-11-7
         JLower.............................. 20.3
       Unholy Alliance 6-11-4
         ATory 2.4
       Banaiyka (Ire) 4-10-5
         CSwan 25.5
99   Now Your Talkin 7-11-7
         RDunwoody ....pu

13/8 Gaelstrom, 4/1 Banaiyka, CARDI-
NAL RED, 5/1 As du Trefle, 7/1 Now
Your Talkin, 12/1 Unholy Alliance
     Mrs F. Walwyn (Mrs F. Walwyn) 6ran
5m50.80 (Firm)

125   CORDON BLEU   2m110y
         HANDICAP HURDLE (5yo +)
£15,440   Aintree   3 April
111³   Spinning 6-10-7 JFrost 1
13   Bollin Patrick 8-10-1
         LWyer 8.2
       Nikitas 8-10-0 SMcNeill 7.3
111   Done Instantly 8-10-0
         CSwan hd.4
95   Jinxy Jack 9-12-0 NDoughty....6.5
73   Qualitair Sound (Ire) 5-10-0
         JJQuinn.............................4.6
92   Noble Insight 6-9-9
         DRichmond 25.7
       Albertito (Fr) 6-9-11
         SWynne 3½.8
95   Duke of Monmouth (USA) 5-11-7
         JOsborne 1.9
45   Larnaca 6-10-7 AMaguire . 2½.10

13/8 SPINNING, 4/1 Jinxy Jack, 11/2
Done Instantly, 10/1 Qualitair Sound,
11/1 Duke of Monmouth, 12/1 Larnaca,
20/1 Albertito, Bollin Patrick, 33/1 Nikitas, 50/1 Noble Insight
     Mr Paul Mellon (I. A. Balding) 10ran
3m44.57 (Firm)

126   MARTELL AINTREE   2m
         CHASE (LIMITED HANDICAP)
         (Gr 2) (5yo +)
£22,904   Aintree   3 April
46   Boutzdaroff 11-10-7 MDwyer. 1
102

	Fragrant Dawn 9-10-10	
	PHolley	2½.2
109	Young Pokey 8-11-8	
	JOsborne	6.3
42	Last 'o' The Bunch 9-11-2	
	NDoughty	3½.4
102²	Cyphrate (USA) 7-11-10	
	PScudamore	7.5
102	Boro Smackeroo 8-11-0	
	AOrkney	pu

2/1 Fragrant Dawn, 9/4 Cyphrate, 6/1 Young Pokey, 8/1 Boro Smackeroo, 9/1 BOUTZDAROFF, 10/1 Last 'o' The Bunch

Robinson Publications Limited (J. G. FitzGerald) 6ran 3m45.87 (Firm)

127	MARTELL AINTREE HURDLE (Gr 1) (4yo +)	2½m
£29,693	Aintree	3 April
95	**Morley Street** 9-11-7	
	GBradley	1
95*	**Granville Again** 7-11-7	
	PScudamore	1½.2
95	Flown 6-11-7 RDunwoody	2.3
95	Ruling (USA) 7-11-7	
	PNiven	hd.4
57	Crowded House (Ire) 5-11-7	
	AMaguire	30.5
57²	Novello Allegro (USA) 5-11-7	
	CSwan	12.6

10/11 Granville Again, 7/2 Flown, 6/1 MORLEY STREET, 15/2 Novello Allegro, 16/1 Ruling, 25/1 Crowded House

Michael Jackson Bloodstock Ltd (G. B. Balding) 6ran 4m38.63 (Firm)

128	MARTELL GRAND NATIONAL CHASE (HANDICAP) (Gr 3) (7yo +)	4½m
	Aintree	3 April
97	**Esha Ness** 10-10-0 JWhite	1
107	Cahervillahow 9-10-11	
	CSwan	1½.2
87	Romany King 9-10-7	
	AMaguire	2.3
97³	The Committee 10-10-0	
	NWilliamson	½.4
96*	Givus A Buck 10-10-0	
	PHolley	12.5
	On The Other Hand 10-10-3	
	NDoughty	6
37	Laura's Beau 9-10-0	
	CO'Dwyer	7
107³	Royal Athlete 10-10-4 BdeHaan	f
112	Farm Week 11-10-1 SHodgson	f
	Senator Snugfit (USA) 8-10-0	
	PeterHobbs	f
	Paco's Boy 8-10-0 MFoster	f
104	Howe Street 10-10-0 AOrkney	f
46	Sure Metal 10-10-0 SJO'Neill	f
	The Gooser 10-10-0 KO'Brien	f
117	Interim Lib 10-10-4	
	MrJBradburne	ur

	Quirinus (Cze) 11-11-10	
	JBrecka	pu
107	Garrison Savannah 10-11-8	
	MPitman	pu
62³	Captain Dibble 8-10-8	
	PScudamore	pu
	Direct 10-10-3 PNiven	pu
112*	Mister Ed 10-10-0 DMorris	pu
14	Stay On Tracks 11-10-0	
	KJohnson	pu
	Travel Over 12-10-2	
	MrMArmytage	pu
	David's Duky 11-10-0	
	MBrennan	pu
	New Mill House 10-10-0	
	THorgan	pu
87	Rowlandsons Jewels 12-10-0	
	DGallagher	pu
84	Riverside Boy 10-10-0	
	MPerrett	pu
87*	Zeta's Lad 10-10-4 RSupple	pu
84*	Party Politics 9-11-2	
	CLlewellyn	pu
34	Bonanza Boy 12-10-0	
	SMcNeill	ref
89	Joyful Noise 10-10-1 TJarvis	ref
97	Roc de Prince (Fr) 10-10-6	
	GMcCourt	dns
107	Chatam (USA) 9-11-7	
	JLower	dns
	Formula One 11-10-0	
	JudyDavies	dns
117³	Nos Na Gaoithe 10-10-2	
	RGarritty	dns
	Wont Be Gone Long 11-10-1	
	RDunwoody	dns
84	Kildimo 13-10-0 LWyer	dns
55	Latent Talent 9-10-2	
	JOsborne	dns
	Royle Speedmaster 9-10-5	
	MrJDurkan	dns
117	Tarqogan's Best 13-10-0	
	BClifford	dns

7/1 Party Politics, 15/2 Romany King, Zeta's Lad, 17/2 Royal Athlete, 9/1 Captain Dibble, 10/1 Garrison Savannah, 16/1 Givus A Buck, Wont Be Gone Long, 20/1 Laura's Beau, On The Other Hand, 25/1 Cahervillahow, Mister Ed, The Committee, 28/1 Chatam, Latent Talent, Riverside Boy, 40/1 Kildimo, 50/1 ESHA NESS, Rowlandsons Jewels, Stay On Tracks, Sure Metal, The Gooser, 66/1 Howe Street, New Mill House, Nos Na Gaoithe, Roc de Prince, 100/1 Bonanza Boy, David's Duky, Direct, Paco's Boy, Travel Over, 150/1 Joyful Noise, 200/1 Farm Week, Formula One, Interim Lib, Royle Speedmaster, Senator Snugfit, 300/1 Quirinus, 500/1 Tarqogan's Best

The odds are those generally available at the time of the first false start. No starting prices were returned. The race was declared void after the second false start

Distances are those taken by Timeform

Esha Ness's time was 9m01.13 (Firm)

129   LILY TREE NOVICES'   2½m
      HURDLE (4yo +)
£3,191   Ascot   7 April
99   **Hebridean** 6-11-12
      RDunwoody 1
      Boycott 6-11-7 GUpton **4.2**
      Sparkling Sunset (Ire) 5-11-7
      JOsborne **1.3**
98   Cabochon 6-11-7 JFrost nk.4
69[3] Grand Hawk (USA) 5-11-7
      PScudamore 15.5
      The Glow (Ire) 5-11-7
      PHolley 3.6
      Royal Piper (NZ) 6-11-7
      LHarvey 1½.7
99   Be My Habitat 4-11-0
      PNiven 15.8
      Maneree 6-11-2 MPerrett 4.9
59   Mr Flanagan 7-11-7
      GBradley 8.10
      Oats N Barley 4-10-7
      TThompson 5.11
      Dunmaglass 6-11-0 SArnold ....pu
      Early Man 6-11-7 PeterHobbs .pu
      Gort 5-11-4 MHourigan ....pu
      Mad Thyme 6-11-7 DMurphy ..pu
      Neat And Tidy 8-11-7
      CMaude................................pu
      Double The Black 8-11-2
      MrJBeardsall.......................pu
      All Talk No Action (Ire) 4-11-0
      EMurphy ....pu
      Far View (Ire) 4-10-7
      SCurran ....pu

100/30 HEBRIDEAN, 4/1 Cabochon, 9/2
Grand Hawk, 10/1 The Glow, 12/1
Sparkling Sunset, 14/1 Boycott, Early
Man, Mr Flanagan, Royal Piper, 16/1
Gort, 20/1 Maneree, 25/1 Mad Thyme,
33/1 All Talk No Action, Be My Habitat,
66/1 Double The Black, Dunmaglass,
Far View, Neat And Tidy, Oats N Barley
    Mr P. A. Deal (D. Nicholson) 19ran
4m55.78 (Good to Soft)

130   ALPINE MEADOW   3m
      HANDICAP HURDLE (4yo +)
£5,380   Ascot   7 April
113* **Sweet Duke (Fr)** 6-12-0
      PScudamore 1
      Simpson 8-10-13
      CLlewellyn......................... 4.2
      Bollinger 7-10-9
      DMurphy......................... 1½.3
66[2] Boscean Chieftain 9-11-0
      MAFitzgerald....................sh.4
101 Prime Display (USA) 7-11-0
      JOsborne 15.5
101 Irish Bay 7-10-2 RDunwoody..6.6
6   Top Javalin (NZ) 6-10-0
      RDavis...............................3.7
      Bonanza 6-10-8 PNiven 30.8
      Threebuck Creek (USA) 4-10-2
      SArnold ....pu

5/2 SWEET DUKE, 100/30 Top Javalin,
7/2 Simpson, 7/1 Boscean Chieftain, 8/1
Bollinger, 14/1 Irish Bay, 25/1 Bonanza,
33/1 Prime Display, 400/1 Threebuck
Creek
    Mr Andy Mavrou (N. A. Twiston-
Davies) 9ran 5m54.06 (Good to Soft)

131   JAMESON GOLD CUP   2m
      HURDLE (Gr 2) (5yo +)
£11,616   Fairyhouse   12 April
      Princess Casilia 8-11-9
      MrWPMullins 1
93   **Winds of War** 8-11-8 CSwan. **8.2**
57[3] **Muir Station (USA)** 5-11-13
      KFO'Brien ¾.3
      Sylvia Fox 6-11-3
      RDunwoody 12.4
93   Boro Eight 7-11-11 AMaguire.2.5
114[2] Gaelic Myth (USA) 6-11-8
      CO'Dwyer 6
      Maramouresh (Ire) 5-11-3
      FWoods 7
      Wallys Run 6-11-6 DTEvans......8

evens Boro Eight, 100/30 Muir Station,
4/1 Gaelic Myth, 8/1 Sylvia Fox, 10/1
PRINCESS CASILIA, 14/1 Wallys Run,
Winds of War, 50/1 Maramouresh
    Mr M. F. O'Dowd (W. P. Mullins) 8ran
4m11.70 (Soft)

132   JAMESON IRISH GRAND   3m5f
      NATIONAL CHASE
      HANDICAP (Gr 1) (4yo +)
£58,788   Fairyhouse   12 April
58[2] **Ebony Jane** 8-10-7 CSwan....... 1
23   **Rust Never Sleeps** 9-10-6
      AJO'Brien........................ **1.2**
128 **Zeta's Lad** 10-11-5
      RSupple........................... 4½.3
97   Allezmoss 7-10-0 FWoods 9.4
58   For William 7-10-0
      KFO'Brien 4.5
112 Crawford Says 8-10-0
      PMcWilliams nk.6
58[3] Joe White 7-10-0 PCarberry....2.7
      Mass Appeal 8-10-1 BSheridan..8
128 The Committee 10-10-9
      JShortt......................................9
      Ounavarra Creek 8-10-0
      HRogers 10
58   Dagwood 8-10-0 DTEvans.......11
128 Laura's Beau 9-10-8
      CO'Dwyer 12
37   Bishops Hall 7-10-3 JTitley......13
107 Cool Ground 11-11-12
      AMaguire .... f
      Gerties Pride 9-10-0 CO'Brien .. f
      Lamh Eile 10-10-0 TJMitchell ... f
      Inch Lady 8-10-0 THorgan .... f
      Kindly King 9-10-0 JMagee........ f
128 Royal Athlete 10-10-13
      MPitman .... ur
      Rossi Novae 10-10-0 MDuffy ... ur
117 Captain Brandy 8-10-0
      MrFJFlood..............................co
98   Ferromyn 8-10-0
      MrSRMurphy.......................co

107² Rushing Wild 8-12-0
RDunwoody ....pu
128 The Gooser 10-10-4
SHO'Donovan ....pu
74 River Tarquin 9-11-0
KMorgan ....pu
107 Sibton Abbey 8-11-13
SSmithEccles ....pu
Haki Saki 7-10-3 GMO'Neill ....pu

11/2 Zeta's Lad, 6/1 EBONY JANE,
Rushing Wild, 13/2 Royal Athlete, 12/1
Cool Ground, For William, Sibton
Abbey, 14/1 Laura's Beau, 16/1 River
Tarquin, 20/1 Allezmoss, Bishop's Hall,
Captain Brandy, Haki Saki, The Com-
mittee, 25/1 Ferromyn, Mass Appeal,
33/1 Joe White, The Gooser, 50/1 Craw-
ford Says, 66/1 Dagwood, Inch Lady,
Ounavarra Creek, Rust Never Sleeps,
100/1 Kindly King, Lamh Eile, Rossi
Novae, 150/1 Gertie's Pride
Mr James Lynch (F. Flood) 27ran
7m59.80 (Soft)

133 POWER GOLD CUP   2¼m
CHASE (Gr 1) (5yo +)
£17,470   Fairyhouse   13 April
56² **How's The Boss** 7-11-7
MDwyer 1
94 **Galevilla Express** 6-11-2
CNBowens 6.2
Lasata 8-11-7 CSwan 9.3
Lady Bye-Bye 7-10-9
JMDonnelly 20.4
Out of Court 8-11-7
BSheridan dist.5
56* Soft Day 8-11-7 TJTaaffe .... f

11/10 Soft Day, 7/4 HOW'S THE BOSS,
5/1 Galevilla Express, 12/1 Lasata, 20/1
Out of Court, 40/1 Lady Bye-Bye
Mr Edward Farrell (J. Brassil) 6ran
4m50.00 (Soft)

134 FESTIVAL NOVICES'   2½m
HURDLE (Gr 3) (5yo +)
£6,900   Fairyhouse   14 April
99 **Belvederian** 6-12-0 CSwan 1
131³ **Muir Station (USA)** 5-11-13
KFO'Brien 7.2
Fantus 6-11-4 MDwyer 4.3
131* Princess Casilia 8-11-9
MrWPMullins 1.4
99 Bucks-Choice 6-12-0
AMullins 13.5
Merciful Hour 6-11-8
TJTaaffe 20.6
Tout Va Bien (Ire) 5-11-2
PCarberry 3.7
Buckminster 6-11-11
GMO'Neill............................pu

5/4 Bucks-Choice, 9/2 BELVEDERIAN,
5/1 Muir Station, Princess Casilia, 6/1
Buckminster, 12/1 Merciful Hour, 20/1
Tout Va Bien, 33/1 Fantus
Mr A. J. O'Reilly (M. F. Morris) 8ran
5m10.10 (Soft)

135 FRIENDLY HOTELS   2m
SCOTTISH CHAMPION
HURDLE (Gr 2) (4yo +)
£9,465   Ayr   16 April
95 **Staunch Friend (USA)** 5-11-10
AMaguire 1
73² **Native Mission** 6-11-2
MDwyer 1½.2
127 **Ruling (USA)** 7-11-6
PNiven ½.3
125 Jinxy Jack 9-11-6 NDoughty....2.4
95² Royal Derbi 8-11-10
DMurphy hd.5
127³ Flown 6-11-10 RDunwoody 6.6

9/4 Royal Derbi, 7/2 Flown, 5/1
STAUNCH FRIEND, 6/1 Ruling, 13/2
Native Mission, 8/1 Jinxy Jack
Mr B. Schmidt-Bodner (M. H. Tomp-
kins) 6ran 3m40.68 (Good)

136 EDINBURGH WOOLLEN 2½m
MILL'S FUTURE CHAMPION
NOVICES' CHASE (Gr 1)
(5yo +)
£18,840   Ayr   17 April
121* **Cab On Target** 7-11-8
PNiven 1
Persian House 6-11-8
AMaguire 8.2
115 **Montpelier Lad** 6-11-8
RDunwoody 20.3
Mackinnon 8-11-8
NDoughty....................20.4
No More The Fool 7-11-8
MMoloney.....................20.5
50 Bibendum 7-11-8 PeterHobbs ... f
72² Cogent 9-11-8 SMcNeill .... f

4/9 CAB ON TARGET, 4/1 Cogent, 9/1
Bibendum, 10/1 Montpelier Lad, 16/1
Persian House, 25/1 Mackinnon, 66/1
No More The Fool
Mrs J. G. Fulton (Mrs M. Reveley)
7ran 4m55.40 (Good)

137 STAKIS SCOTTISH   4m 1f
NATIONAL (HANDICAP
CHASE) (Gr 3) (5yo +)
£29,700   Ayr   17 April
116² **Run For Free** 9-11-10
MPerrett 1
97 **Merry Master** 9-10-0
GeeArmytage.................. nk.2
128 **Mister Ed** 10-10-0
DMorris 20.3
128* Esha Ness 10-10-0 JWhite ¾.4
Beau Charm 9-10-0 BStorey ...2.5
96³ Boraceva 10-10-0
AMaguire 15.6
112 Whaat Fettle 8-10-0
MMoloney...................... 2½.7
128 Party Politics 9-11-5
DMurphy..........................7.8
Off The Bru 8-10-0
MrJBradburne.....................7.9
112 Willsford 10-10-0 BdeHaan...1.10
97 Cythere 9-9-12 PHide.........sh.11
128 Wont Be Gone Long 11-10-1
RDunwoody 10.12

870

128	Riverside Boy 10-10-0 JLower... f
	Smooth Escort 9-10-0 CGrant ... f
68[2]	Dakyns Boy 8-10-1
	CLlewellyn............................ur
55	Parsons Green 9-10-0 CSwan..ur
44	Duntree 8-10-4 HDavies..........ur
116	Cavvies Clown 13-10-7
	MPitman ....pu
	Abercromby Chief 8-10-0
	AOrkney................................pu
128	Stay On Tracks 11-10-0
	KJohnson ....pu
128	Latent Talent 9-10-0
	JOsborne ....pu

9/2 Dakyns Boy, 11/2 Party Politics, 6/1
RUN FOR FREE, 10/1 Wont Be Gone
Long, 11/1 Latent Talent, Riverside Boy,
12/1 Mister Ed, 14/1 Esha Ness, 18/1
Boraceva, 20/1 Parsons Green, Wills-
ford, 22/1 Cavvies Clown, 28/1 Merry
Master, 33/1 Duntree, Whaat Fettle,
40/1 Off The Bru, 50/1 Smooth Escort,
Stay On Tracks, 66/1 Cythere, 250/1
Beau Charm, 300/1 Abercromby Chief
  Mrs Millicent R. Freethy (M. C. Pipe)
21ran 8m18.17 (Good)

138	E.B.F. 'NATIONAL HUNT' 2m1f
	NOVICES' HURDLE FINAL
	(HANDICAP) (Gr 3)
	(5, 6 and 7yo)
£14,900	Cheltenham 21 April
	Country Lad (Ire) 5-10-7
	SMcNeill 1
	Le Metayer (Fr) 5-11-7
	JRailton 10.2
	Benjamin 5-10-11
	CLlewellyn......................2½.3
43	Poors Wood 6-11-4
	DMurphy........................nk.4
	Chuck Curley (USA) 5-10-8
	EMurphy 1½.5
	Ask The Governor 7-10-8
	AMaguire 3.6
	The Mine Captain 6-9-9
	RFarrant nk.7
	Munka 7-10-4 PeterHobbs . 1½.8
	Amtrak Express 6-11-4
	RDunwoody 1½.9
	Full O'Praise (NZ) 6-10-7
	CGrant 5.10
	Northern Saddler 6-10-9
	WIrvine 8.11
129	The Glow (Ire) 5-11-5
	AProcter5 ....2.12
	Swahili Run 5-11-3 MFoster.1.13
91	Fotoexpress 5-11-4
	MrCBurnett-Wells..........hd.14
	Pontoon Bridge 6-10-8
	MPerrett 2.15
	Goldingo 6-10-4 RDavis......¾.16
	Martrajan 6-10-0 BdeHaan .sh.17
	James The First 5-11-3
	MAFitzgerald....................4.18

9/2 Chuck Curley, 13/2 Amtrak Express,
7/1 Le Metayer, 10/1 Ask The Governor,
Munka, 12/1 Poors Wood, 14/1 James The

First, 16/1 Fotoexpress, Northern
Saddler, Pontoon Bridge, 20/1 Full
O'Praise, 25/1 Benjamin, Goldingo,
Swahili Run, The Glow, 33/1 COUNTRY
LAD, Martrajan, The Mine Captain
  Mrs Robina Pattison (Mrs S. D.
Williams) 18ran 4m00.56 (Good)

139	S.W. SHOWERS 2m5f
	SILVER TROPHY CHASE
	(Gr 2) (5yo +)
£15,550	Cheltenham 21 April
72	**Beech Road** 11-11-0
	RDunwoody 1
87	**Calapaez** 9-11-0 AMaguire..¾.2
102[3]	**Katabatic** 10-11-7
	SMcNeill sh.3
120[3]	Gold Options 11-11-7
	MDwyer dist.4

4/5 Katabatic, 100/30 Gold Options, 5/1
BEECH ROAD, 10/1 Calapaez
  Mr Tony Geake (G. B. Balding) 4ran
5m12.75 (Good)

140	WHITBREAD 3m5f110y
	GOLD CUP
	(HANDICAP CHASE)
	(Gr 3) (5yo +)
£57,400	Sandown 24 April
	Order as they passed the post
128	**Givus A Buck** 10-10-0
	PHolley 1
107	**Topsham Bay** 10-10-1
	RDunwoody hd.2
128[2]	**Cahervillahow** 9-10-1
	CSwan 10.3
116*	Docklands Express 11-11-5
	JOsborne 2.4
107	The Fellow (Fr) 8-11-13
	AKondrat.........................15.5
128	Garrison Savannah 10-10-9
	MPitman 20.6
128	Rowlandsons Jewels 12-10-0
	MAFitzgerald....................20.7
128	Captain Dibble 8-10-5
	CLlewellyn........................¾.8
132	Sibton Abbey 8-10-12
	SSmithEccles......................pu
128	David's Duky 11-10-0
	NWilliamson ....pu
112	Fiddlers Pike 12-10-0
	MrsRHenderson ....pu
	Fifth Amendment 8-10-0
	BdeHaan ....pu
117	Over The Deel 7-10-0
	KJohnson ....pu

7/2 The Fellow, 9/2 Cahervillahow, 5/1
Garrison Savannah, 11/2 Captain Dibble,
6/1 Docklands Express, 15/2 Sibton
Abbey, 10/1 TOPSHAM BAY, 20/1 Givus
A Buck, 25/1 Rowlandsons Jewels, 50/1
Fiddlers Pike, 66/1 David's Duky, 150/1
Fifth Amendment, 200/1 Over The Deel
  Sir Eric Parker (D. H. Barons) 13ran
7m27.43 (Good to Soft)

871

141   COUNTRY PRIDE   2m
      CHAMPION NOVICES'
      HURDLE (Gr 1) (5yo +)
£16,188   Punchestown   27 April
      Bayrouge (Ire) 5-11-8
         RDunwoody 1
134   **Princess Casilia** 8-11-9
         MrWPMullins 4.2
134   **Bucks-Choice** 6-12-0
         AMullins 25.3
131² Winds of War 8-12-0 CSwan ..hd.4
131   Wallys Run 6-12-0
         DTEvans 25.5
      Vienna Shop (Ire) 5-11-13
         BSheridan 15.6
131   Boro Eight 7-12-0 THorgan 7
      Big Matt (Ire) 5-11-13
         CO'Dwyer .... f

11/4 Boro Eight, 7/2 BAYROUGE,
Princess Casilia, 5/1 Bucks-Choice, 8/1
Winds of War, 12/1 Big Matt, 16/1 Wallys
Run, 50/1 Vienna Shop
      Mr Joseph Crowley (Mrs Ann
O'Brien) 8ran 4m05.37 (Good to Soft)

142   BMW DROGHEDA (E.B.F.) 2m
      HANDICAP CHASE
      (Gr 2) (4yo +)
£21,782   Punchestown   27 April
      Viking Flagship 6-10-7
         RDunwoody 1
      Foulksrath Castle 9-10-7
         KMorgan 2½.2
      Buckboard Bounce 7-10-7
         KFO'Brien 25.3
      Good For A Laugh 9-10-11
         TJTaaffe 8.4
56³   Killiney Graduate 7-10-7
         FWoods 12.5
133³ Lasata 8-10-7 THorgan dist.6
126   Cyphrate (USA) 7-12-0
         CSwan ....pu
      Third Quarter 8-10-7
         CO'Dwyer .... f

5/4 VIKING FLAGSHIP, 7/2 Cyphrate,
9/2 Foulksrath Castle, 8/1 Buckboard
Bounce, 10/1 Killiney Graduate, 12/1
Good For A Laugh, 16/1 Lasata, Third
Quarter
      Roach Foods Limited (D. Nicholson)
8ran 4m14.79 (Good to Soft)

143   MURPHYS IRISH STOUT   2m
      CHAMPION HURDLE
      (Gr 1) (4yo)
£26,980   Punchestown   29 April
105* **Shawiya (Ire)** 4-10-9 CSwan ... 1
118* **Titled Dancer (Ire)** 4-10-9
         JShortt................................. 9.2
105   Judicial Field (Ire) 4-11-0
         BSheridan 3½.3
105   Indian Quest 4-11-0
         CLlewellyn........................4.4
79³   Green Glen (USA) 4-11-0
         NWilliamson 1½.5

105   Clurican (Ire) 4-11-0
         RDunwoody 6
93²   Lemon's Mill (USA) 4-10-9
         MPerrett 7
      Murahin (USA) 4-11-0
         CO'Dwyer 8
      Currency Basket (Ire) 4-11-0
         PMcWilliams 9
      Private Guy (Ire) 4-11-0
         APowell 10
33*   Dare To Dream (Ire) 4-11-0
         DBridgwater 11
79   Pennine Tune (Ire) 4-11-0
         KFO'Brien 12
105³ Major Bugler (Ire) 4-11-0
         GBradley ....pu

7/4 Lemon's Mill, 11/4 SHAWIYA, 13/2
Dare To Dream, 7/1 Titled Dancer, 10/1
Judicial Field, Major Bugler, 14/1 Indian
Quest, Pennine Tune, 20/1 Private Guy,
25/1 Green Glen, 33/1 Clurican, Currency Basket, Murahin
      Miss G. Maher (M. J. P. O'Brien)
13ran 3m48.06 (Good)

144   BANK OF IRELAND   2m
      COLLIERS NOVICE CHASE
      (Gr 3) (5yo +)
£16,188   Punchestown   29 April
142* **Viking Flagship** 6-12-0
         RDunwoody 1
      Antonin (Fr) 5-11-7
         JHBurke 4.2
133² Galevilla Express 6-11-6
         CNBowens 15.3
115* Valiant Boy 7-12-0
         RGarritty 12.4
      Billy Bligh 8-11-4
         CO'Dwyer 4½.5
133   Lady Bye-Bye 7-11-3
         JMDonnelly............................6
133* How's The Boss 7-12-0 CSwan ..7
133   Soft Day 8-12-0 TJTaaffe ....pu

2/1 How's The Boss, Soft Day, 4/1
VIKING FLAGSHIP, 10/1 Valiant Boy,
12/1 Galevilla Express, 14/1 Antonin,
16/1 Billy Bligh, 66/1 Lady Bye-Bye
      Roach Foods Limited (D. Nicholson)
8ran 4m05.53 (Good)

145   DEAN MOOR LONG   2m7f110y
      DISTANCE HURDLE (5yo +)
£10,885   Haydock   3 May
130   **Boscean Chieftain** 9-11-0
         MAFitzgerald........................ 1
124* **Cardinal Red** 6-11-0
         BdeHaan 3½.2
113³ **Crystal Spirit** 6-11-0
         JFrost ¾.3
113² Pragada 10-11-4 RDunwoody .7.4
106   Burgoyne 7-11-0
         AMaguire 1½.5
21   Jopanini 8-11-0 BSheridan 5.6
130* Sweet Duke (Fr) 6-11-4
         CLlewellyn........................4.7

872

7/4 Crystal Spirit, 3/1 Pragada, 7/2 Sweet
Duke, 6/1 Cardinal Red, 8/1 Burgoyne,
25/1 BOSCEAN CHIEFTAIN, Jopanini
    Miss Christine Olds (Mrs J. G. Retter)
7ran 5m32.10 (Firm)

146	SWINTON HANDICAP	2m

HURDLE (Gr 3) (4yo +)
£23,765   Haydock   3 May

125*	**Spinning** 6-11-0 JFrost **1**
50	**Jungle Knife** 7-10-11
	AMaguire **4**.2
39	**Pontynyswen** 5-10-0
	DJBurchell **6**.3
45	Persuasive 6-9-9
	MrMBuckley................... 1½.4
111	Bitofabanter 6-10-12
	TJTaaffe 5.5
125³	Nikitas 8-9-9 JMcCarthy 2½.6
	Admiralty Way 7-10-0
	DianeClay nk.7
	Deb's Ball 7-10-6 DJMoffatt. nk.8
21	Easy Buck 6-10-2 CMaude....hd.9
114³	Land Afar 6-10-4 AWebb ¾.10
	King's Shilling (USA) 6-9-11
	VSlattery3 .... ¾.11
123²	Olympian 6-10-3
	RDunwoody 7.12
12	Sabaki River 9-10-0
	MAFitzgerald...................5.13
95	Flakey Dove 7-11-7
	MrDDuggan 3.14
135	Jinxy Jack 9-11-12
	NDoughty...........................1.15
	Canny Chronicle 5-11-0
	PNiven 1½.16
	Simone's Son (Ire) 5-9-7
	DMeade................................. ur

3/1 SPINNING, 5/1 Olympian, 6/1 Bitofabanter, 8/1 Land Afar, 10/1 Easy Buck,
11/1 Jungle Knife, 16/1 Canny Chronicle,
Deb's Ball, Flakey Dove, Jinxy Jack, 20/1
King's Shilling, Sabaki River, 25/1 Pontynyswen, 33/1 Persuasive, 40/1 Nikitas,
50/1 Simone's Son, 66/1 Admiralty Way
    Mr Paul Mellon (I. A. Balding) 17ran
3m33.30 (Firm)

INDEX TO
BIG RACE RESULTS

Aahsaylad 59
Abercromby Chief 137
Able Player 19
Abnegation 101
Ace of Spies 112
Acre Hill 109
Acrow Line 98
Admiralty Way 146
Aegean Fanfare 79
Aherlow Glen 122
Aiybak 93
Albertito 125
Al Hashimi 46, 54
Alkinor Rex 109
Allezmoss 97, 132
All Talk No Action 129
Almanzora 93
Alterezza 45, 101
Amazon Express
86*, 105²
Ambuscade 17³, 47
Among Friends 110
Amtrak Express 138
Andermatt 101
Andrew's First 101
Annicombe Run 6, 101
Annio Chilone 100
Another Coral
8², 26*, 52²
Antonin 144²
Antrim County 119
Arcot 85
Ardcroney Chief 31²
Ardbrin 29
Armagret 64*, 110³
As du Trefle 124³
Ashfold Copse 100
Ask Frank 41
Ask The Governor 138
Assuring 111
Athy Spirit 95
Atlaal 65*, 94
Atone 45³, 99
Auction Law 112
Aude La Belle 85
Autumn Gorse 57
Avro Anson 50³, 92

Back Door Johnny 45
Balasani 61, 73, 101
Bally Clover 99
Banaiyka 124
Barton Bank 31, 100
Bartres 122
Baydon Star
13*, 39², 88*, 106³
Bayrouge 141*
Bean King 98
Beauchamp Express 99
Beauchamp Grace 105
Beau Charm 137
Beautiful Dream 59
Bedfield 99

Beebob 61, 92
Beech Road
8³, 12, 72, 139*
Belafonte 6, 61, 101
Bel Course 104, 117
Bellezza 123
Belmount Captain 34
Belstone Fox 104, 115
Belvederian ..47, 99, 134*
Be My Habitat 61, 99, 129
Benjamin 138³
Better Times Ahead
3³, 6, 47², 121
Bibendum 50, 136
Big Beat 43, 85
Big Chance 69
Big Matt 141
Billy Bathgate 115
Billy Bligh 144
Bishops Hall .. 18, 37, 132
Bishops Island 101
Bitofabanter
45, 73³, 111, 146
Black Humour ..107, 119*
Black Sapphire 6
Blazing Walker 64³, 87
Blitzkreig 23, 46
Blue Dart 122
Bob Tisdall 122
Bo Knows Best ... 86, 105
Bold Ambition 19
Bold Boss 33, 82*, 118
Bold King's Hussar 122
Bollinger 130³
Bollin Patrick .. 6, 13, 125²
Bollin William 61, 123
Bonanza 130
Bonanza Boy 20³, 34, 128
Bonsai Bud 41, 112
Bookcase 92
Book of Music 91
Boom Time 117
Boraceva 41, 96³, 137
Boro Eight 93, 131, 141
Boro Smackeroo
25, 36³, 54³, 102, 126
Boscean Chieftain
66², 130, 145*
Boutzdaroff 46, 126*
Boycott 129²
Brackenfield 59*
Bradbury Star
7*, 12³, 32, 70², 87³
Brandeston 8
Brandon Prince 91
Brief Case 103
Brown Windsor 44
Buckboard Bounce 142³
Buckminster 134
Bucks-Choice
99, 134, 141³
Burgoyne
3*, 17*, 27², 47³, 106, 145

Cabochon 85³, 98, 129
Cab On Target 121*, 136*
Cache Fleur 67³, 96
Cahervillahow 4, 23,
37², 74, 107, 128², 140³
Cairncastle 98
Calabrese 61
Calapaez 67², 87, 139²
Calicon 50
Cambo 69
Camelot Knight 60
Campsea Ash 1²
Candy Tuff 51²
Canny Chronicle 146
Capability Brown
68*, 100
Captain Brandy .. 117, 132
Captain Dibble 18, 28*,
34, 62³, 128, 140
Captain My Captain 99
Carbisdale 83³, 119
Cardinal Red
99², 124*, 145²
Cariboo Gold 86
Carrickrovaddy 103
Casting Time 31
Castle Courageous 75²
Castle Secret 113
Catch The Cross 55
Cavvies Clown
70, 81*, 96, 116, 137
Celcius 101
Celtic Chief 66
Channels Gate
68³, 103, 117
Chatam ..18, 74², 107, 128
Cheerful Times 39, 76
Cherrykino 70*, 107
Child of The Mist 123
Chirkpar 57, 106
Chuck Curley 138
City Entertainer 14
Claxton Greene 103²
Clay County 54
Clurican 105, 143
Co-Chin 82
Cock Cockburn 38, 45
Cogent 72², 136
Cool Ground 4, 14, 20,
28, 44², 52³, 81³, 107, 132
Corrin Hill
19³, 40, 76³, 93
Coulton... 19, 48², 76*, 95
Country Lad 138*
Country Member
41, 62*, 96²
Crawford Says ... 112, 132
Crowded House
38³, 57, 127
Cru Exceptionnel 91
Crystal Cone 75
Crystal Spirit
90, 106, 113³, 145³

874

Curaheen Boy............. 122
Currency Basket........ 143
Cyphrate.........12, 29*, 46,
71³, 102², 126, 142
Cyprus.......................... 93
Cythere 97, 137

Dagwood 58, 132
Dakyns Boy 31*, 68², 137
Dancing Paddy............. 111
Dandy Minstrel 112
Danny Harrold.......12², 55
Dante's Inferno 115
Dara Doone..............6³, 11
Dare To Dream..33*, 143
Dark Dawn................ 122²
David's Duky..... 128, 140
Dawson City 30², 60²
Deb's Ball 146
Deep Bramble 37
Deep Sensation 12*, 22*,
32, 46², 64², 102*, 120*
Dennington 69
Derab.............................. 6
Desert Force 86
Diamond Cut 111
Direct 128
Dissimulateur 105
Do Be Brief 112³
Docklands Express
32, 87², 107, 116*, 140
Dominant Serenade
105, 118
Done Instantly.... 111, 125
Doran's Town Lad 111
Double Silk 108*, 122*
Double The Black 129
Double Turn 122
Dreamers Delight
43², 93, 114
Dubacilla 60
Duharra 111
Duke of Monmouth
16, 39, 76², 95, 125
Duncan 108
Dunmaglass 129
Duntree................44, 137

Early Man 129
Eastern Oasis 51³
Easy Buck.............21, 146
Ebony Jane.........58², 132*
Edberg........................8, 22
Eden's Close.33, 86³, 105
Edimbourg 60
Egypt Mill Prince......... 21
Eid 86, 105
Elfast 26
Elvercone 122
Emily's Star 103
Emsee-H 15², 104
Errant Knight 55
Esha Ness
..41², 55, 97, 128*, 137
Espy....................24³, 78²
Everaldo 3
Exact Analysis............. 80
Eyelid 45, 95

Faaris........................... 122
Fairfields Cone......61, 101
False Economy........... 112
Fantus 134³
Farm Week......... 112, 128
Far Senior 12
Far View 129
Fay Lin 45
Feroda 23, 37, 64, 71
Ferromyn 98, 132
Fettuccine 3
Fiddlers Pike
84², 112, 140
Fifth Amendment....... 140
Fighting Words.... 60³, 89³
Final Tub 37, 58
Fine Harvest................. 77
Firions Law............23, 37
Fissure Seal................ 98*
Flakey Dove
73, 90², 95, 146
Flown
16, 35², 95, 127³, 135
Forest Ranger 122
Forest Sun
31, 60, 110, 121²
Formula One............... 128
For The Grain 26
For William 58, 132
Fotoexpress 91, 138
Fox Chapel.................. 101
Foyle Fisherman 34
Fragrant Dawn
46³, 102, 126²
Freeline Finishing..26, 46
Frickley.................93, 114
Full o' Praise 138
Furry Baby.................... 98

Gabish 109
Gadbrook..................... 122
Gaelic Myth
57, 93, 114², 131
Gaelstrom
17, 40², 59², 99*, 124²
Galaxy High 73
Gale Again 8, 83*
Galevilla Express
56, 94, 133², 144³
Gallateen 101, 123*
Gambling Royal 18, 28, 55
Garamycin....23³, 37³, 58*
Garboni........................ 79
Garrison Savannah
52, 70³, 81², 107, 128, 140
Gay Ruffian 60
Gee-A 122
General Idea
8, 23², 37*, 74³, 110²
Genie Spirit 33
Gerties Pride 132
Ghofar..............44, 81, 117
Giventime 99
Givus A Buck
34, 96*, 128, 140*
Glaisdale......................82²

Glenavey 122
Glenbrook d'Or.............. 7
Glencloud......45*, 73, 111
Glen Lochan 40, 108
Gold Cap 103
Golden Celtic 70
Golden Freeze...........5³, 8
Golden Minstrel 122
Goldingo 138
Gold Options.......23*, 42*,
49³, 87, 120³, 139
Good For A Laugh 142
Good For A Loan 111
Goodshot Rich 112
Gort 129
Grace Card................... 88²
Gran Alba.........35, 63, 80
Grand Hawk........69³, 129
Granville Again
9², 25², 35³, 95*, 127²
Great Max 86
Green Glen 79³, 143
Grey Salute.................. 11
Gymcrak Stardom
92², 123

Haki Saki..................... 132
Halkopous
19*, 25*, 57, 95³
Harley.......................... 122
Hashar......................... 111
Hebridean ...69*, 99, 129*
Henry Mann 52
Here He Comes 50, 73
Her Honour.......105, 118²
High Alltitude......69², 75*
High Baron 111²
Highland Spirit 85
Hillwalk 99
Hogmanay 1³, 5
Holy Foley 108
Holy Joe 61
Holy Wanderer 105
Howe Street ...8, 104, 128
How's The Boss
56², 133*, 144
Hurdy 99

Ida's Delight 4³
Ilewin.......................... 50
Inch Lady 132
Indian Quest 105, 143
Indian Run 105
Ink By The Drum 45
Interim Lib....14, 117, 128
Into The Red 112²
Irish Bay 40, 101, 130
Irish Peace................... 57
Island Gale 51
Its A Cracker............. 100³
Ivor's Flutter 86, 105

Jakarrdi........................98²
Jamalade................58, 74
James The First 138
Jimbalou 98
Jinxy Jack
13³, 48*, 95, 125, 135, 146

Jodami 10², 18², 41*, 49*, 74*, 107*
Joe White 58³, 132
John O'Dee 14
Jopanini...................21, 145
Joyful Noise
64, 87, 89, 128
Judges Fancy 3
Judicial Field 105, 143³
Jungle Knife
13², 21, 39, 50, 146²
Just So 34

Kadi 105, 118
Kalogy 92
Katabatic 1*, 5², 36*, 42², 71², 102³, 139³
Keen Vision 92
Keep Talking 41, 44
Kentish Piper 104
Keppols Prince 45
Kerry Orchard 108²
Ketti 61, 90³, 106
Kilcash................ 21², 45²
Kilclooney Forrest 51
Kildimo............4, 14*, 24, 28, 44, 67, 84, 128
Killbanon 78
Killiney Graduate
45, 56³, 142
Kindly King............... 132
King Credo
21, 35, 73*, 95
King of The Gales........ 56
Kings Fountain
2², 8, 32, 42³, 64
Kings Rank 98
King's Shilling 146
Kings Wild 122
Kiveton Tycoon....86, 105
Knight Oil 10, 97
Knockelly Castle 142
Kribensis...25, 35, 80², 95

Lacidar........................ 122
Lady Bye-Bye..... 133, 144
Lady Olein 45, 57
Lafkadio................... 47, 98
Lake Teereen 60
Lamh Eile 132
Land Afar 114³, 146
Lanigans Wine.............. 58
Larksmore.................... 97
Larnaca................45, 125
Lasata 133³, 142
Last o' The Bunch
29², 42, 126
Latent Talent
18, 55, 128, 137
Laura's Beau 37, 128, 132
Le Metayer 138²
Lemon's Mill 93², 143
Leotard 43, 93
Le Piccolage .... 7²ᵈ⁻ʰᵗ
Lesbet 98
Liability Order 33, 82
Lift And Load
11, 16³, 39³, 73, 90*, 113

Little-Nipper 72
Logamimo 41
Lord Relic 40*, 99³
Loshian 105
Lo Stregone 59³
Lumberjack 117
Lyn's Return.............. 114

Maamur 21³
Macedonas 123
Mackinnon 136
Mad Thyme 129
Maestroso 93
Major Bugler
33³, 105³, 143
Mandraki Shuffle 122³
Manenda...................... 98
Maneree 129
Maramouresh............... 131
Martha's Son 50
Martomick 99
Martrajan.................... 138
Masai Mara 111
Mass Appeal 132
Master Rajh 1
Master Swordsman 45
Merano 97²
Merciful Hour 134
Merry Master
34, 97, 137²
Merry Scorpion 82
Metal Oiseau 101
Miami Bear 72, 83
Midland Glenn............. 98
Mighty Mogul
6*, 16*, 35*, 53
Miinnehoma
20², 28², 34³, 52
Milford Quay
8, 26, 72, 83², 104
Military Honour........... 30
Mils Mij...................3, 51
Miss Bobby Bennett.... 21
Miss Shaw.................. 103
Mister Ed 112*, 128, 137³
Mister Major................ 123
Mizyan........................ 123
Mohana.........33², 82, 105
Mole Board.............. 63*
Moment of Truth ... 1, 102
Montelado 93*
Montpelier Lad..115, 136³
Monumental Lad 8
Moorcroft Boy 108
Morley Street
9*, 11², 25³, 63, 95, 127*
Mount Argus 122
Mr Boston.................... 18
Mr Entertainer 87
Mr Felix 22
Mr Flanagan 59, 129
Mr Greenfield............. 45
Mr Jamboree..............65³
Mr Matt...................... 40
Mubadir 111
Mudahim 53³
Muir Station
38², 57³, 131³, 134²

Multum In Parvo....42, 64
Munka 138
Murahin...................... 143
Muse
11*, 27, 39*, 53*, 80³
Mutare........................... 67

Nadiad.......................... 65
Nadjati 118³
Naiysari 45
Native Mission
45, 73², 135²
Natural Ability 45, 57
Neat And Tidy........... 129
Nebraska 103
Needwood Muppet........ 6
New Mill House 128
Nickle Joe 101
Nick The Brief 44³, 58
Nijmegen 50², 92
Nikitas 125³, 146
Nilousha 38
Noble Insight ..73, 92, 125
Noel Luck 122
Nohalmdun.................. 54
Nomadic Way...3², 17, 53²
No More The Fool..... 136
Nordic Gayle................ 45
Northern Saddler...... 138
Northern Village........... 61
Norton's Coin 2
Nos Na Gaoithe
8, 26, 117³, 128
Novello Allegro
38*, 57², 127
Now Your Talkin
75³, 99, 124

Oatis Regrets............... 91
Oats N Barley............. 129
Officer Cadet 17
Off The Bru 137
Oh So Risky9³, 25, 35, 95
O K Corral 7
Old Applejack 4
Old Road 24
Olympian
92*, 101*, 123², 146
Once Stung 108³
One More Dream........ 21
Oneupmanship 123
On The Hooch............ 117
On The Other Hand .. 128
Otterburn House...55², 84
Ounavarra Creek........ 132
Our Fellow................. 117
Out of Court 133
Over The Deel ... 117, 140

Paco's Boy 128
Pactolus...................6, 98
Palacegate King.......... 33
Pamber Priory 41
Pardon Me Sir 111
Parsons Green 28, 41, 55, 137
Party Politics
18, 52, 84*, 128, 137

876

Past Glories 77
Pat's Jester 4², 24², 32²
Pay Homage 85
Peaceman.............85, 114
Peanuts Pet 61³, 101
Pectorus.......................... 99
Pennine Tune.......79, 143
Perforate 33
Persian House 136²
Persuasive 45, 146
Petosku 6²
Petty Bridge 98
Pharly Story.............91²
Pharoah's Laen.......34, 55
Phils Pride 60
Piper's Son................... 27
Plat Reay 104
Plenty Crack................ 84
Poetic Gem 29, 72
Polygonum 122
Pontoon Bridge 138
Pontynyswen 39, 146³
Poors Wood 43, 138
Pragada
    47*, 106², 113², 145
Precious Wonder......... 86
Present Times............. 39
Prime Display 101, 130
Princess Casilia
    131*, 134, 141²
Private Audition 109
Private Guy................ 143
Proplus 112, 119

Qualitair Sound
    50, 73, 125
Quirinus 128

Radical Views 108
Raglan Road................ 119
Rainbow Valley............. 79
Randolph Place........... 108
Random Prince............. 45
Rawhide......................... 58
Redundant Pal 29, 120²
Regent Lad 35
Remittance Man ...2*, 15*
Renagown 122
Repeat The Dose
    78³, 104
Re-Release...........97, 119
Retail Runner 60
Rising Waters 45
River House 119
River Island 91³
Riverside Boy
    34², 84, 128, 137
River Tarquin 74, 132
Robingo 105
Roc de Prince.......97, 128
Rocket Launcher........ 103
Rocktor.................... 119³
Rodeo Star 48, 73
Roll A Dollar........85*, 114
Romany King
    10³, 28, 87, 128³
Rossi Novae 132
Ross Venture............... 67

Rowlandsons Gems.... 111
Rowlandsons Jewels ... 18,
    28³, 55³, 67, 87, 128, 140
Royal Athlete
    87, 107³, 128, 132
Royal Derbi......... 19², 48³,
    57*, 73, 90, 95², 135
Royal Gait 38
Royal Piper 129
Royle Speedmaster ... 128
Ruling
    48, 63³, 73, 95, 127, 135³
Run For Free 10*, 20*,
    34*, 49², 107, 116², 137*
Run Up The Flag 61
Rushing Wild
    44*, 62², 107², 132
Rust Never Sleeps
    23, 132²
Ru Valentino 100
Ryde Again 72

Sabaki River 12, 146
Sacre d'Or...........26, 104*
San Lorenzo..........92, 101
Sanndila...................38, 80
Sartorius.....................30³
Satin Lover 93³, 114
Sayyure 88³
Scrutineer 86
Seagram 14, 44
Sea Island..............41³, 55
Sea Trout 98
Second Call 33
Second Schedual
    12, 26², 72³, 110*
Senator of Rome 122
Senator Snugfit........... 128
Sendai 98³
Seon..................16, 73, 92
Setter Country
    2³, 5, 29³, 109
Seven of Diamonds 108
Shamana 109²
Sharriba 118
Shawiya ...79*, 105*, 143*
Shoon Wind.................. 96
Shu Fly...............111, 115²
Shuil Ar Aghaidh
    27³, 106*
Sibton Abbey 18*, 44,
    52*, 107, 132, 140
Side of Hill................. 119
Sikera Spy............... 119²
Sillars Stalker 61, 101²
Silverino 68
Simone's Son 146
Simpson..................... 130²
Sir Crusty 17, 98
Sirrah Jay .. 1, 8, 15³, 117*
Sleepline Royale......... 92
Smartie Express........ 104²
Smooth Escort............ 137
Snowy Lane 98
Socks Downe.............. 117
Soft Day.........56*, 133, 144
Solar Cloud 117
Solo Buck...................... 59

Some Obligation 108
Sonsie Mo................... 109
Sooner Still 119
Southern Minstrel
    104³, 117²
Space Fair 8, 54², 109*
Sparkling Flame 18
Sparkling Sunset 129³
Speakers Corner 122
Special Account 59
Spinning
    92³, 111³, 125*, 146*
Sponsor Light 30
Sporting Mariner........ 108
Spring Fun 108
Star Actor 103
Stark Contrast 79
Star's Delight........46, 109
Statajack 45
Staunch Friend
    16², 95, 135*
Stay On Tracks
    14, 128, 137
Stirrup Cup 96
Storm Alert............... 109³
Storm Dust 105
Street Kid 123
Strong Approach......... 83
Strong Beau 97*
Strong Gold................ 117
Stylus.........................82³
Sukaab....................... 98
Sulli Boy.................... 92
Sunley Bay.................. 59
Sun Surfer.........43*, 75
Superior Finish......... 100²
Super Sense..27, 106, 113
Sure Metal 46, 128
Swahili Run................ 138
Sweet Duke 27, 61²,
    106, 113*, 130*, 145
Sweet Glow 3, 17,
    66*, 88, 106, 113
Swinhoe Croft............ 108
Sybillin.30*, 46*, 77*, 94³
Sylvia Fox 131

Takemethere 7
Tallywagger 3
Tarqogan's Best . 117, 128
Tartan Trix 108
Tawney Flame............. 45
Team Challenge 117
Texan Tycoon............. 43
Thatcherise................. 79
The Antartex 14³
The Committee 23, 37,
    58, 74, 97³, 128, 132
The Fellow
    18³, 32*, 107, 140
The Glow 129, 138
The Gooser.........128, 132
The Illiad.................... 56
The Illywacker
    12, 26, 32³, 89*, 110
The Mine Captain 138
The Real Unyoke 103
The Red One.............. 108

The Slater 94
The Widget Man
       6, 11, 17, 121
Third Quarter 142
Thistle Monarch 59
Threebuck Creek 130
Thumbs Up ....43[3], 111*
Tiger Claw 39
Tinryland 54*, 87, 110
Tipping Tim
     4*, 8*, 26[3], 32, 49, 107
Titled Dancer
       79[2], 118*, 143[2]
Tomahawk 50*, 73
Tony's Delight.............. 93
Top Javalin 6, 130
Topsham Bay
     41, 44, 84, 107, 140[2]
Top Spin ....33, 86[2], 105
Toranfield...................... 8
Toureen Prince 108
Tout Va Bien.............. 134
Trainglot 61*, 99
Train Robber 111
Traumatic Laura........... 30
Travado 94*
Travelling Wrong ...... 103[3]
Travel Over 128
Trimlough .... 115[3]
Triple Top.................... 13
True Brave 27
Truely Royal................. 51
Twin Oaks
       18, 24*, 42, 49, 84
Tyrone Bridge
   9, 11[3], 17[2], 27, 66[3], 106

Uncle Ernie .... 15, 22[3], 54
Unholy Alliance 124
Ushers Island 103*

Vagog.............27*, 47, 106
Vain Prince ....77[3]
Valfinet..21*, 63[2], 80*, 95
Valiant Boy 94, 115*, 144
Vayrua 30
Very Very Ordinary
       67*, 107, 116[3]
Viardot........................... 105
Vienna Shop................. 141
Viking Flagship
       142*, 144*
Villa Recos 92
Vintage Crop................. 95
Vital Witness 98
Vulgan Warrior 97

Wakashan 69
Wallys Run........... 131, 141
Watercourse................ 108
Waterloo Boy 5*, 22*,
      36[2], 71*, 102, 120
Way of Life 117
Welknown Character . 117
Welshman ....13, 123[3]
West Ender................... 55
Western Legend......... 117

Whaat Fettle
       7[2d-ht], 112, 137
Whatever You Like.... 109
What If 76
Whispering Steel........ 51*
Why So Hasty............... 49
Willie Sparkle 111
Willsford 78, 84[3], 112, 137
Winabuck 55, 117
Winds of War
       93, 131[2], 141
Windy Ways..........41, 112
Wings of Freedom...... 111
Wingspan.........64, 70, 102
Winnie The Witch........ 94
Winterbourne Abbas
       79, 105
Winter Squall
       85[2], 91*, 114
Wonder Man 65[2], 77[2], 94[2]
Wont Be Gone Long
       128, 137
Wrekin Hill 117

Yellow Spring .... 101[3]
Yiragan 112
Yorkshire Gale ....40[3]
Young Benz 29
Young Hustler 12, 55*,
   60*, 72*, 89[2], 100*, 121[3]
Young Pokey .....109, 126[3]
Young Snugfit
     46, 54, 71, 102
Yukon Gold.................. 79

Zamirah 118
Zeta's Lad
       78*, 87*, 128, 132[3]

INDEX TO PHOTOGRAPHS

PORTRAITS & SNAPSHOTS

Horse		Breeding	Copyright	Page
Amazon Express	4 b.c	Siberian Express – Thalestris (Mill Reef)	*Rex Coleman*	37
Annio Chilone	7 b.h	Touching Wood – Alpine Alice (Abwah)	*Rex Coleman*	42
Another Coral	10 br.g	Green Shoon – Myralette (Deep Run)	*Dinah Nicholson*	45
Atlaal	8 b.g	Shareef Dancer – Anna Paola (Prince Ippi)	*John Crofts*	58
Autumn Gorse	4 ch.g	Salmon Leap – Nous (Le Johnstan)	*Jacqueline O'Brien*	61
Balasani	7 b.h	Labus – Baykara (Direct Flight)	*Bernard Parkin*	64
Barton Bank	7 br.g	Kambalda – Lucifer's Daughter (Lucifer)	*Dinah Nicholson*	72
Baydon Star	6 br.g	Mandalus – Leuze (Vimy)	*Dinah Nicholson*	76
Bayrouge	5 br.m	Gorytus – Bay Tree (Relko)	*Jacqueline O'Brien*	79
Beauchamp Grace	4 b.f	Ardross – Buss (Busted)	*Dinah Nicholson*	81
Belvederian	6 b.g	Deep Run – Arctic Shine (Arctic Slave)	*Jacqueline O'Brien*	87
Black Humour	9 b.g	Buckskin – Artiste Gaye (Artist's Son)	*W. W. Rouch & Co*	97
Boro Eight	7 b.g	Deep Run – Boro Nickel (Nicolaus)	*Jacqueline O'Brien*	108
Brackenfield	7 ch.g	Le Moss – Stable Lass (Golden Love)	*Alec Russell*	113
Bradbury Star	8 b.g	Torus – Ware Princess (Crash Course)	*Rex Coleman*	115
Bucks-Choice	6 b.g	Buckskin – Ursula's Choice (Cracksman)	*Jacqueline O'Brien*	123
Cabochon	6 b.g	Jalmood – Lightning Legacy (Super Concorde)	*Bernard Parkin*	129
Cab On Target	7 br.g	Strong Gale – Smart Fashion (Carlburg)	*Alec Russell*	132
Capability Brown	6 b.g	Dominion – Tomfoolery (Silly Season)	*Bernard Parkin*	140
Captain Dibble	8 b.g	Crash Course – Sailor's Will (Laurence O)	*Dinah Nicholson*	143
Cardinal Red	6 b.g	The Parson – Rose Ravine (Deep Run)	*W. W. Rouch & Co*	147
Castle Courageous ...	6 b.g	Castle Keep – Peteona (Welsh Saint)	*Rex Coleman*	152
Chatam	9 b.g	Big Spruce – Cristalina (Green Dancer)	*Bernard Parkin*	164
Cogent	9 b.g	Le Bavard – Cottstown Breeze (Autumn Gold)	*Dinah Nicholson*	175
Country Member	8 ch.g	New Member – Romany Serenade (Romany Air)	*Dinah Nicholson*	189
Crystal Spirit	6 b.g	Kris – Crown Treasure (Graustark)	*W. W. Rouch & Co*	195
Cyphrate	7 b/br.g	Saint Cyrien – Euphrate (Royal And Regal)	*Bernard Parkin*	198
Dagobertin	7 ch.g	Roi Dagobert – Regalla (Viceregal)	*Bernard Parkin*	199

879

Dakyns Boy	8 ch.g	Deep Run – Mawbeg Holly (Golden Love)	*Dinah Nicholson*	201
Dare To Dream	4 b.g	Baillamont – Tears of Allah (Troy)	*Rex Coleman*	207
Deep Heritage	7 ch.g	Deep Run – Bunkilla (Arctic Slave)	*Jacqueline O'Brien*	214
Deep Sensation	8 ch.g	Deep Run – Bannow Bay (Arctic Slave)	*Rex Coleman*	218
Duke of Monmouth ...	5 b.g	Secreto – Queen For The Day (King Emperor)	*Camilla Horn*	241
Ebony Jane	8 br.m	Roselier – Advantage (Perspex)	*Jacqueline O'Brien*	248
Egypt Mill Prince	7 b.g	Deep Run – Just Darina (Three Dons)	*W. W. Rouch & Co*	250
Esha Ness	10 b.g	Crash Course – Beeston (Our Babu)	*W. W. Rouch & Co*	262
Eyelid	7 b.h	Roscoe Blake – Pie Eye (Exbury)	*Jacqueline O'Brien*	265
Flashing Steel	8 b.g	Broadsword – Kingsfold Flash (Warpath)	*Jacqueline O'Brien*	283
Fragrant Dawn	9 br.g	Strong Gale – Aridje (Mummy's Pet)	*W. W. Rouch & Co*	294
Gaelic Myth	6 b.g	Nijinsky – Irish Valley (Irish River)	*Jacqueline O'Brien*	302
Gaelstrom	6 b.m	Strong Gale – Armonit (Town Crier)	*Dinah Nicholson*	304
Galevilla Express	6 br.m	Strong Gale – Canute Villa (Hardicanute)	*Jacqueline O'Brien*	307
Gay Ruffian	7 b.g	Welsh Term – Alcinea (Sweet Revenge)	*Bernard Parkin*	311
General Idea	8 ch.g	General Assembly – Idealist (Busted)	*Jacqueline O'Brien*	313
Glaisdale	4 b.g	Lomond – Glass Slipper (Relko)	*John Crofts*	321
Glencloud	5 b.g	Glenstal – Clouded Issue (Manado)	*Jacqueline O'Brien*	323
Grand Hawk	5 b.g	Silver Hawk – Ginger Lass (Elocutionist)	*Bernard Parkin*	332
Granville Again	7 ch.g	Deep Run – High Board (High Line)	*Bernard Parkin*	335
Hawthorn Blaze	7 br.g	Alzao – Konigin Kate (Authi)	*Bernard Parkin*	350
Hebridean	6 b.g	Norwick – Pushkar (Northfields)	*Dinah Nicholson*	352
Her Honour	4 b.f	Teenoso – Burning Ambition (Troy)	*Bernard Parkin*	356
How's The Boss	7 b.g	Ragapan – Barradan Lass (Deep Run)	*Jacqueline O'Brien*	369
Indian Quest	4 b.g	Rainbow Quest – Hymettus (Blakeney)	*W. W. Rouch & Co*	376
Jodami	8 b.g	Crash Course – Masterstown Lucy (Bargello)	*Alec Russell*	395
Judicial Field	4 b.g	Law Society – Bold Meadows (Persian Bold)	*Jacqueline O'Brien*	399
Katabatic	10 br.g	Strong Gale – Garravogue (Giolla Mear)	*Dinah Nicholson*	408
Kerry Orchid	5 gr.g	Absalom – Matinata (Dike)	*Jacqueline O'Brien*	413
Land Afar	6 b.g	Dominion – Jouvencelle (Rusticaro)	*Dinah Nicholson*	429

Lemon's Mill	4 b.f	Roberto – Mill Queen (Mill Reef)	*Bernard Parkin* 437
Lord Relic	7 b.g	Zamazaan – Morning Order (Bismark)	*Bernard Parkin* 449
Mohana	4 br.f	Mashhor Dancer – The Ranee (Royal Palace)	*Bernard Parkin* 495
Montelado	6 b.g	Montelimar – Misippus (Green God)	*Jacqueline O'Brien* 501
Morley Street	9 ch.g	Deep Run – High Board (High Line)	*Bernard Parkin* 506
Muir Station	5 b.h	Darby Creek Road – Donna Inez (Herbager)	*Jacqueline O'Brien* 514
Novello Allegro	5 b.g	Sir Ivor – Tants (Vitiges)	*Jacqueline O'Brien* 538
Party Politics	9 br.g	Politico – Spin Again (Royalty)	*W. W. Rouch & Co* 559
Pragada	10 b.g	Pragmatic – Adare Lady (Varano)	*Bernard Parkin* 577
Princess Casilia	8 ch.m	Croghan Hill – Ballybeg Maid (Prince Hansel)	*Jacqueline O'Brien* 581
Roll A Dollar	7 b.g	Spin of A Coin – Handy Dancer (Green God)	*W. W. Rouch & Co* 613
Royal Athlete	10 ch.g	Roselier – Darjoy (Darantus)	*W. W. Rouch & Co* 620
Royal Derbi	8 b.g	Derrylin – Royal Birthday (St Paddy)	*John Crofts* 623
Ruling	7 b.h	Alleged – All Dance (Northern Dancer)	*W. W. Rouch & Co* 629
Run For Free	9 b.g	Deep Run – Credit Card (Current Coin)	*Bernard Parkin* 633
Second Schedual	8 b.g	Golden Love – Billeragh Girl (Normandy)	*Jacqueline O'Brien* 655
Shawiya	4 b.f	Lashkari – Shaiyra (Relko)	*Jacqueline O'Brien* 665
Shuil Ar Aghaidh	7 b.m	The Parson – Shuil Eile (Deep Run)	*Jacqueline O'Brien* 671
Spinning	6 b/br.g	Glint of Gold – Strathspey (Jimmy Reppin)	*W. W. Rouch & Co* 698
Staunch Friend	5 b.g	Secreto – Staunch Lady (Staunchness)	*John Crofts* 707
Storm Alert	7 b.g	Strong Gale – Jet Travel (Deep Run)	*Dinah Nicholson* 711
Strong Beau	8 br.g	Strong Gale – Red Pine (Khalkis)	*Dinah Nicholson* 715
Sweet Duke	6 b.g	Iron Duke – Sweet Virginia (Tapioca II)	*Dinah Nicholson* 724
The Committee	10 b.g	Derring Rose – What A Whet (Fine Blade)	*Jacqueline O'Brien* 740
The Fellow	8 b.g	Italic – L'Oranaise (Paris Jour)	*John Crofts* 743
Thumbs Up	7 b.g	Fidel – Misclaire (Steeple Aston)	*Fiona Vigors* 753
Tipping Tim	8 b.g	King's Ride – Jeanarie (Reformed Character)	*Dinah Nicholson* 760
Titled Dancer	4 ch.f	Where To Dance – Lady Broke (Busted)	*Jacqueline O'Brien* 763
Travado	7 br.g	Strong Gale – Adelina (Athenius)	*Fiona Vigors* 773
Travelling Wrong	7 b.g	Strong Gale – Evening Society (Even Money)	*Dinah Nicholson* 775
Ubu III	7 b.g	Maiymad – Isis VIII (Or de Chine)	*John Crofts* 784

Viardot	4 b.c	Sadler's Wells – Vive La Reine (Vienna)	*Bernard Parkin*	797
Viking Flagship	6 b.g	Viking – Fourth Degree (Oats)	*Dinah Nicholson*	801
Vintage Crop	6 ch.g	Rousillon – Overplay (Bustino)	*Jacqueline O'Brien*	802
Washingtoncrossing	7 ch.g	Over The River – Rather Grand (Will Somers)	*Dinah Nicholson*	808
Waterloo Boy	10 ch.g	Deep Run – Sapphire Red (Red Alert)	*Dinah Nicholson*	810
Winter Squall	5 gr.g	Celio Rufo – No Honey (Dual)	*Dinah Nicholson*	826
Wonder Man	8 ch.g	The Wonder – Juvenilia (Kashmir II)	*Dinah Nicholson*	829
Young Hustler	6 ch.g	Import – Davett (Typhoon)	*Dinah Nicholson*	837

RACE PHOTOGRAPHS

Race and Meeting	*Copyright*	*Page*
Agfa Diamond Handicap Chase (Sandown)	*George Selwyn*	188
Agfa Hurdle (Sandown)	*George Selwyn*	496
A.I.G. Europe Champion Hurdle (Leopardstown)	*Maymes Ansell*	622
Albert Bartlett & Sons 'Future Champions' Novices' Hurdle (Ayr)	*Alec Russell*	112
Alpine Meadow Handicap Hurdle (Ascot)	*Ed Byrne*	724
American Express F.X. Veterans Chase (Warwick)	*George Selwyn*	229
American Express Gold Card Handicap Hurdle Final (Cheltenham)	*Caroline Norris*	278
Anthony Mildmay, Peter Cazalet Memorial Handicap Chase (Sandown)	*George Selwyn*	635
Arlington Bula Hurdle (Cheltenham)	*George Selwyn*	345
Arlington Premier Series Chase Final (Newbury)	*Ed Byrne*	835
Arlington Premier Series Chase (Qualifier) (Chepstow)	*Chepstow Racecourse*	484
Arlington Premier Series Chase (Qualifier) (Haydock)	*Alec Russell*	818
Aspiring Champions Novices' Chase (Chepstow)	*Chepstow Racecourse*	138
Baileys Arkle Perpetual Challenge Cup (Novices' Chase) (Leopardstown)	*Caroline Norris*	686
Bank of Ireland Colliers Novice Chase (Punchestown)	*Maymes Ansell*	800
Baring Securities Tolworth Hurdle (Sandown)	*W. Everitt*	718
Beachley Handicap Chase (Chepstow)	*Chepstow Racecourse*	570
Beaufort Hurdle (Chepstow)	*Ed Byrne*	825
Belle Epoque Sefton Novices' Hurdle (Aintree)	*Alec Russell*	146
Bellway Homes Fighting Fifth Hurdle (Newcastle)	*Alec Russell*	344
Berkshire Hurdle (Newbury)	*George Selwyn*	440
Betterton Chase (Newbury)	*Ed Byrne*	182
Bet With The Tote Novices' Handicap Chase (Final) (Uttoxeter)	*Ed Byrne*	154
Bic Razor Lanzarote Handicap Hurdle (Kempton)	*George Selwyn*	764
Bisquit Cognac Handicap Hurdle (Fairyhouse)	*Maymes Ansell*	661
BMW Drogheda (EBF) Handicap Chase (Punchestown)	*Ed Byrne*	799
Bollinger Champagne Novices' Handicap Chase (Ascot)	*George Selwyn*	333
Bonusfilm Novices' Chase (Kempton)	*George Selwyn*	828
Bonusphoto Novices' Hurdle (Kempton)	*George Selwyn*	648
BonusPrint Christmas Hurdle (Kempton)	*Ed Byrne*	483
BonusPrint Handicap Hurdle (Kempton)	*George Selwyn*	530
BonusPrint Stayers' Hurdle (Cheltenham)	*Caroline Norris*	670
Bookmakers Hurdle (Leopardstown)	*Caroline Norris*	537

Bradstock Insurance Novice Chase (Punchestown)	*Maymes Ansell*	290
Cathcart Challenge Cup Chase (Cheltenham)	*Caroline Norris*	654
'Certain Justice' Challenge Cup (Handicap Chase) (Fontwell)	*Ed Byrne*	705
Challow Hurdle (Newbury)	*Ed Byrne*	448
Charisma Gold Cup Chase (Kempton)	*W. Everitt*	269
Charles Sidney Novices' Hurdle (Doncaster)	*Alec Russell*	298
Cheltenham Grand Annual Chase Challenge Cup (Handicap) (Cheltenham)	*John Crofts*	692
Cheveley Park Stud New Year's Day Hurdle (Limited Handicap) (Windsor)	*Ed Byrne*	516
Chivas Regal Amateur Riders Novices' Handicap Chase (Aintree)	*Alec Russell*	284
Christies Foxhunter Challenge Cup (Cheltenham)	*John Crofts*	234
Clark Whitehill Juvenile Novices' Hurdle (Cheltenham)	*George Selwyn*	355
Constant Security Handicap Chase (Doncaster)	*Alec Russell*	618
Coral Cup (Handicap Hurdle) (Cheltenham)	*George Selwyn*	545
Coral-Elite Hurdle (Cheltenham)	*George Selwyn*	504
Coral Welsh National Handicap Chase (Chepstow)	*George Selwyn*	631
Cordon Bleu Handicap Hurdle (Aintree)	*Alec Russell*	696
Coventry City Novices' Trial Hurdle (Warwick)	*Ed Byrne*	771
Crispin Chase (Handicap) (Ascot)	*George Selwyn*	796
Crowther Homes Becher Handicap Chase (Aintree)	*George Selwyn*	415
Crudwell Cup (Handicap Chase) (Warwick)	*Ed Byrne*	106
Culroy Novices' Chase (Ayr)	*Alec Russell*	137
Daily Express Triumph Hurdle (Cheltenham)	*Ed Byrne*	663
Dalrymple Novices' Hurdle (Ayr)	*Alec Russell*	458
Dean Moor Long Distance Hurdle (Haydock)	*Alec Russell*	109
Deloitte And Touche Novice Hurdle (Leopardstown)	*Caroline Norris*	107
Dennys Juvenile Hurdle (Leopardstown)	*Maymes Ansell*	60
Dipper Novices' Chase (Newcastle)	*Alec Russell*	211
Dovecote Novices Hurdle (Kempton)	*Ed Byrne*	612
East Lancs Chase (Haydock)	*Alec Russell*	305
EBF Johnstown Hurdle (Naas)	*Caroline Norris*	59
EBF 'National Hunt' Novices' Handicap Hurdle (Final) (Cheltenham)	*Alec Russell*	187
EBF Novices' Chase Series Final (Fairyhouse)	*Caroline Norris*	282
Edinburgh Woollen Mill's Future Champion Novices' Chase (Ayr)	*Alec Russell*	131
Elmbridge Handicap Chase (Sandown)	*George Selwyn*	710
Emblem Chase (Kempton)	*Ed Byrne*	256
Ericsson Chase (Leopardstown)	*Caroline Norris*	312
Evesham Conditional Jockeys' Novices' Hurdle (Cheltenham)	*Alec Russell*	428
Fairview New Homes Novices' Chase (Ascot)	*Ed Byrne*	377
Festival Novices' Hurdle (Fairyhouse)	*Maymes Ansell*	86
Finale Junior Hurdle (Chepstow)	*George Selwyn*	206
Findus Handicap Chase (Leopardstown)	*Caroline Norris*	608
1st Choice Novices' Hurdle (Leopardstown)	*Caroline Norris*	78
Fitzpatricks Hotel Group Chase (Leopardstown)	*Maymes Ansell*	368
Flat v Jump Jockeys Challenge Handicap Hurdle (Chepstow)	*George Selwyn*	677
Flowers Original Handicap Chase (Cheltenham)	*George Selwyn*	85
Food Brokers 'Finesse' Four Years Old Hurdle (Cheltenham)	*George Selwyn*	459
Forgive'N Forget Novices' Chase (Doncaster)	*Alec Russell*	130
Friendly Hotels Scottish Champion Hurdle (Ayr)	*Alec Russell*	706
Fulke Walwyn Kim Muir Challenge Cup Handicap Chase (Amateur Riders) (Cheltenham)	*George Selwyn*	714
Fulwell Handicap Chase (Kempton)	*George Selwyn*	51
Game Spirit Chase (Newbury)	*George Selwyn*	809
George Duller Handicap Hurdle (Cheltenham)	*George Selwyn*	478
Glenlivet Anniversary 4-Y-O Hurdle (Aintree)	*Alec Russell*	762
Grand Steeple-Chase de Paris (Auteuil)	*Ed Byrne*	786
Godiva Kingmaker Novices' Chase (Warwick)	*George Selwyn*	285
Golden Eagle Novices' Chase (Ascot)	*Ed Byrne*	47
Great Yorkshire Handicap Chase (Doncaster)	*Alec Russell*	834
Greenalls Gold Cup (Handicap Chase) (Haydock)	*Alec Russell*	558

Grosvenor Insurance Handicap Chase (Ascot)	*George Selwyn*	601
Grouse Handicap Chase (Newcastle)	*Alec Russell*	476
Guinness Festival Bumper (Cheltenham)	*George Selwyn*	602
H & T Walker Gold Cup (Handicap Chase) (Ascot)	*George Selwyn*	215
Harold Clarke Leopardstown Chase (Leopardstown)	*Caroline Norris*	309
Haydock Park Champion Hurdle Trial (Haydock)	*Alec Russell*	389
Heineken Gold Cup Chase (Handicap) (Punchestown)	*Caroline Norris*	279
Hell Nook Four Years Old Handicap Hurdle (Haydock)	*Alec Russell*	751
Hennessy Cognac Gold Cup (Handicap Chase) (Newbury)	*George Selwyn*	673
Hennessy Cognac Gold Cup (Leopardstown)	*Maymes Ansell*	393
Holman Cup (Handicap Chase) (Cheltenham)	*George Selwyn*	693
Horse And Hound Grand Military Gold Cup (Sandown)	*Ed Byrne*	547
100 Pipers Hurdle (Handicap) (Aintree)	*George Selwyn*	41
Irish National Novices' Hurdle Series Final (Punchestown)	*Maymes Ansell*	122
Jack Brown Handicap Chase (Chepstow)	*George Selwyn*	225
Jameson Gold Cup (Novices' Hurdle) (Fairyhouse)	*Caroline Norris*	580
Jameson Irish Grand National (Fairyhouse)	*Caroline Norris*	247
Jim Ennis Construction Premier Long Distance Hurdle (Haydock)	*Alec Russell*	576
Jim Ford Challenge Cup (Chase) (Wincanton)	*George Selwyn*	156
John Hughes Grand National Trial Chase (Chepstow)	*Chepstow Racecourse*	273
John Hughes Memorial Trophy (Handicap Chase) (Aintree)	*George Selwyn*	680
Kepak Boyne EBF Hurdle (Navan)	*Caroline Norris*	212
Kestrel Handicap Hurdle (Ascot)	*George Selwyn*	229
King George VI Chase (Kempton)	*George Selwyn*	742
Kingwell Hurdle (Wincanton)	*George Selwyn*	792
Ladbroke Racing Handicap Hurdle (Haydock)	*Alec Russell*	40
Leigh Handicap Chase (Haydock)	*Alec Russell*	432
Letheby & Christopher Long Distance Hurdle (Ascot)	*George Selwyn*	723
Liverpool Novices' Handicap Hurdle (Aintree)	*Alec Russell*	539
Longley Hall of Fame Handicap Chase (Cheltenham)	*George Selwyn*	638
Mackeson Gold Cup Handicap Chase (Cheltenham)	*George Selwyn*	760
Mandarin Handicap Chase (Newbury)	*George Selwyn*	391
Marston Moor Chase (Limited Handicap) (Wetherby)	*Alec Russell*	53
Martell Aintree Chase (Limited Handicap) (Aintree)	*Alec Russell*	111
Martell Aintree Hurdle (Aintree)	*Ed Byrne*	505
Martell Cup Chase (Aintree)	*Ed Byrne*	228
Martell Fox Hunters' Chase (Aintree)	*George Selwyn*	235
Martell Grand National Handicap Chase (Aintree)	*George Selwyn*	258
Martell Grand National Handicap Chase (Aintree)	*George Selwyn*	258
Martell Grand National Handicap Chase (Aintree)	*Alec Russell*	260
Martell Grand National Handicap Chase (Aintree)	*Liverpool Daily Post & Echo*	261
Martell Mersey Novices' Hurdle (Aintree)	*George Selwyn*	436
Mildmay of Flete Challenge Cup (Handicap Chase) (Cheltenham)	*John Crofts*	640
Mitsubishi Shogun Golden Miller Trophy (Handicap Chase) (Cheltenham)	*Ed Byrne*	439
Mitsubishi Shogun Newton Chase (Haydock)	*Alec Russell*	328
Mitsubishi Shogun Trophy (Handicap Chase) (Doncaster)	*Alec Russell*	758
Mitsubishi Shogun Trophy Handicap Chase (Uttoxeter)	*Ed Byrne*	314
Mitsubishi Shogun 'Pendil' Trophy (Novices' Chase) (Kempton)	*Ed Byrne*	685
Mumm Melling Chase (Aintree)	*Ed Byrne*	217
Mumm Mildmay Novices' Chase (Aintree)	*Ed Byrne*	130
Murphy's Handicap Hurdle (Cheltenham)	*George Selwyn*	791
Murphys Irish Stout Champion Four-Year-Old Hurdle (Punchestown)	*Caroline Norris*	664
Narraghmore Handicap Chase (Punchestown)	*Maymes Ansell*	327
'National Spirit' Challenge Trophy Hurdle (Fontwell)	*Ed Byrne*	287
Northumberland Gold Cup Novices' Chase (Newcastle)	*Alec Russell*	728
Nottinghamshire Novices' Chase (Nottingham)	*Ed Byrne*	729
No 1 Bourbon Street Champion National Hunt Flat (Aintree)	*Ed Byrne*	522

Oddbins Handicap Hurdle (Aintree)	Ed Byrne	307
Ostler Handicap Chase (Chepstow)	*Chepstow Racecourse*	341
Oxenton Handicap Hurdle (Cheltenham)	George Selwyn	639
Peregrine Handicap Chase (Ascot)	Ed Byrne	134
Perrier Jouet Chase (Handicap) (Aintree)	Alec Russell	96
Persian War Premier Novices' Hurdle (Chepstow)	*Chepstow Racecourse*	359
Peterborough Chase (Huntingdon)	Ed Byrne	599
Peter Marsh Handicap Chase (Haydock)	Alec Russell	392
Petros Victor Ludorum Hurdle (Haydock)	Alec Russell	102
Pierse Contracting John P. Harty Memorial Handicap Chase (Punchestown)	Caroline Norris	94
Power Gold Cup Chase (Fairyhouse)	Maymes Ansell	368
P.Z. Mower EBF Chase (Thurles)	Caroline Norris	343
Queen Mother Champion Chase (Cheltenham)	Alec Russell	216
Racing Post Handicap Chase (Kempton)	Ed Byrne	840
Regency Hurdle (Warwick)	Ed Byrne	280
Rehearsal Handicap Chase (Chepstow)	George Selwyn	630
Rendlesham Hurdle (Kempton)	George Selwyn	75
Reynoldstown Novices' Chase (Ascot)	George Selwyn	139
Ritz Club National Hunt Handicap Chase (Cheltenham)	John Crofts	319
Rocking Horse Nursery Handicap Chase (Newbury)	Ed Byrne	555
Saint Systems Risograph Hurdle (Doncaster)	Alec Russell	226
Sandeman Maghull Novices' Chase (Aintree)	Ed Byrne	793
Scilly Isles Novices' Chase (Sandown)	George Selwyn	834
Seagram Top Novices' Hurdle (Aintree)	Alec Russell	612
Sean Macklin Champion Hunters' Chase (Punchestown)	Ed Byrne	412
Sea Pigeon Handicap Hurdle (Doncaster)	Alec Russell	586
SGB Handicap Chase (Ascot)	George Selwyn	142
Shoveler Novices' Hurdle (Newcastle)	Alec Russell	50
Singer & Friedlander Handicap Chase (Uttoxeter)	Alec Russell	709
Smurfit Champion Hurdle Challenge Trophy (Cheltenham)	George Selwyn	334
South Wales Electricity Handicap Chase (Chepstow)	*Chepstow Racecourse*	296
Stakis Scottish National Handicap Chase (Ayr)	Alec Russell	632
Stanley Leisure Children In Need Novices' Chase (Aintree)	Alec Russell	210
Steel Plate And Sections Young Chasers Championship Final (Limited Handicap) (Cheltenham)	Ed Byrne	114
Steel Plate And Sections Young Chasers Novices' Chase (Qualifier) (Cheltenham)	George Selwyn	291
Steel Plate And Sections Young Chasers' Qualifier (Ayr)	Alec Russell	720
Sun Alliance Novices' Chase (Cheltenham)	John Crofts	836
Sun Alliance Novices' Hurdle (Cheltenham)	Alec Russell	303
Sunderlands Imperial Cup (Handicap Hurdle) (Sandown)	Ed Byrne	544
Swinton Handicap Hurdle (Haydock)	Alec Russell	697
S. W. Showers Silver Trophy Chase (Cheltenham)	George Selwyn	82
Tattersalls Mares Only Novices' Chase Final (Uttoxeter)	Ed Byrne	239
Telecom Eireann Thyestes Handicap Chase (Gowran Park)	Maymes Ansell	839
Tetley Bitter Charlie Hall Chase (Wetherby)	Alec Russell	759
Tetley Bitter Midlands National (Handicap Chase) (Uttoxeter)	Ed Byrne	492
The Ladbroke (Leopardstown)	Caroline Norris	322
The Rip Handicap Chase (Ascot)	George Selwyn	813
Thomastown Maiden Hurdle (Fairyhouse)	Caroline Norris	755
Timeform Hall of Fame Chase (Cheltenham)	George Selwyn	674
Tommy Whittle Chase (Haydock)	Alec Russell	782
Tote Cheltenham Gold Cup (Cheltenham)	Caroline Norris	394
Tote City Trial Handicap Hurdle (Nottingham)	Ed Byrne	186
Tote County Handicap Hurdle (Cheltenham)	John Crofts	753
Tote Credit Handicap Hurdle (Windsor)	Ed Byrne	619
Tote Eider Handicap Chase (Newcastle)	Alec Russell	378
Tote Gold Trophy (Handicap Hurdle) (Newbury)	George Selwyn	417

Tote Jackpot Handicap Hurdle (Sandown)	*George Selwyn*	770
Tote Placepot Hurdle (Kempton)	*Ed Byrne*	36
Tote 7th Race Handicap Chase (Aintree)	*Alec Russell*	823
Tote Silver Trophy (Handicap Hurdle) (Chepstow)	*Chepstow Racecourse*	481
Tote West Yorkshire Hurdle (Wetherby)	*Alec Russell*	126
Trafalgar House Supreme Novices' Hurdle (Cheltenham)	*Caroline Norris*	500
Tripleprint Feltham Novices' Chase (Kempton)	*Ed Byrne*	200
Tripleprint Gold Cup (Handicap Chase) (Cheltenham)	*Ed Byrne*	44
United House Construction Handicap Chase (Ascot)	*George Selwyn*	406
Victor Chandler Handicap Chase (Ascot)	*George Selwyn*	729
Waterford Castle Arkle Challenge Trophy Chase (Cheltenham)	*Ed Byrne*	772
Waterloo Hurdle (Haydock)	*Alec Russell*	482
Welsh Handicap Hurdle (Chepstow)	*Chepstow Racecourse*	223
Wensleydale Hurdle (Wetherby)	*Alec Russell*	221
Whitbread Gold Cup (Handicap Chase) (Sandown)	*Ed Byrne*	766
Whitbread Gold Cup (Handicap Chase) (Sandown)	*George Selwyn*	767
Whitlenge Novices' Chase (Warwick)	*Ed Byrne*	71
William Hill Handicap Hurdle (Sandown)	*Racing Post*	791
William Hill Handicap Hurdle (Uttoxeter)	*Ed Byrne*	498
Woodchester Credit Lyonnais Downshire Handicap Hurdle (Punchestown)	*Ed Byrne*	756
Wyko Power Transmission Hurdle (Cheltenham)	*George Selwyn*	517
Yorkshire Handicap Hurdle (Doncaster)	*Alec Russell*	384

1992/93 STATISTICS

The following tables show the leading owners, trainers, jockeys, amateur riders, horses and sires of winners during the 1992/93 season, under Jockey Club Rules. Some of the tables are reproduced by permission of **The Sporting Life.**

OWNERS

		Horses	Races Won	Stakes £
1.	Mrs J. Mould	9	18	145,788
2.	Mrs Shirley Robins	12	16	144,375
3.	R. F. Eliot	2	4	137,700
4.	Marquesa de Moratalla	5	12	128,302
5.	J. N. Yeadon	2	4	125,142
6.	G. M. MacEchern	1	8	116,202
7.	Pell-Mell Partners	22	27	114,062
8.	G. A. Hubbard	31	23	105,277
9.	P. Piller	27	33	90,433
10.	Eric Scarth	1	1	84,734
11.	Mrs Millicent R. Freethy	1	4	80,510
12.	M & N Plant Ltd	4	10	76,720

TRAINERS

		Horses	Races Won	Stakes £
1.	M. C. Pipe	143	194	808,012
2.	D. Nicholson	73	100	492,480
3.	N. A. Twiston-Davies	63	76	451,332
4.	G. Richards	88	104	327,714
5.	J. T. Gifford	67	49	285,899
6.	J. G. FitzGerald	66	62	260,812
7.	Mrs M. Reveley	91	90	250,548
8.	N. J. Henderson	77	53	242,924
9.	G. B. Balding	52	38	212,445
10.	K. C. Bailey	63	57	170,188
11.	P. Beaumont	22	19	162,642
12.	A. Turnell	35	37	161,247

SIRES OF WINNERS

		Individual Winners	Races Won	Stakes £
1.	Deep Run (1966)	51	94	622,660
2.	Strong Gale (1975)	43	96	479,293
3.	Crash Course (1971)	10	16	192,552
4.	The Parson (1968)	28	54	185,261
5.	Furry Glen (1971)	24	57	170,902
6.	Over The River (1974)	20	34	146,486
7.	High Line (1966)	6	15	129,895
8.	Buckskin (1973)	20	36	120,845
9.	Import (1971)	1	8	116,202
10.	Glint of Gold (1978)	7	19	115,441
11.	Ardross (1976)	16	37	102,526
12.	Kambalda (1970)	12	34	101,859

JOCKEYS

		1st	2nd	3rd	Unpl	Total Mts	Per Cent
1.	R. Dunwoody	173	120	89	357	739	23.4
2.	P. Scudamore	129	75	47	165	416	31.0
3.	A. Maguire	124	118	97	383	722	17.2
4.	P. Niven	108	62	52	164	386	28.0
5.	J. Osborne	102	71	61	266	500	20.4
6.	G. McCourt	70	61	61	238	430	16.3
7.	N. Doughty	69	36	33	125	263	26.2
8.	C. Llewellyn	68	43	50	251	412	16.5
9.	M. Dwyer	61	58	47	150	316	19.3
10.	C. Grant	58	56	49	256	419	13.8
11.	M. A. Fitzgerald	54	51	50	271	426	12.7
12.	Peter Hobbs	51	49	37	181	318	16.0

AMATEUR RIDERS

		1st	2nd	3rd	Unpl	Total Mts	Per Cent
1.	A. Thornton	26	27	12	81	146	17.8
2.	T. Jenks	20	18	19	71	128	15.6
3.	S. Swiers	12	6	3	37	58	20.7
4.	J. Greenall	12	6	2	7	27	44.4
5.	M. Buckley	9	8	8	21	46	19.6
6.	J. Durkan	9	8	6	47	70	12.9
7.	C. Burnett-Wells	9	7	6	32	54	16.7
8.	T. Byrne	9	7	2	30	48	18.8

HORSES

		Races Won	Stakes £
1.	Deep Sensation (8 yrs) ch.g. Deep Run – Bannow Bay	3	134,854
2.	Jodami (8 yrs) b.g. Crash Course – Masterstown Lucy	3	122,322
3.	Young Hustler (6 yrs) ch.g. Import – Davett	8	116,202
4.	Granville Again (7 yrs) ch.g. Deep Run – High Board	1	84,734
5.	Run For Free (9 yrs) b.g. Deep Run – Credit Card	4	80,510
6.	Mighty Mogul (5 yrs) ch.g. Good Thyne – Deep Shine	5	67,385
7.	Topsham Bay (10 yrs) b.g. Proverb – Biowen	2	62,416
8.	Olympian (6 yrs) ch.g. High Line – Elysian	3	59,890
9.	Valfinet (6 yrs) b.g. Maiymad – Oland	5	55,556
10.	Sybillin (7 yrs) b.g. Henbit – Tea House	5	55,116
11.	Sibton Abbey (8 yrs) b.g. Strong Gale – Bally Decent	4	53,639
12.	Morley Street (9 yrs) ch.g. Deep Run – High Board	2	52,858

Timeform

The
Champions

from the 'Chasers & Hurdlers' series

Champion Jumper

1975/76	Night Nurse	**178**
1976/77	Night Nurse	**182**
1977/78	Monksfield	**177**
1978/79	Monksfield	**180**
1979/80	Sea Pigeon	**175**
1980/81	Little Owl	**176**
1981/82	Silver Buck	**175**
1982/83	Badsworth Boy	**179**
1983/84	Dawn Run	**173**
1984/85	Burrough Hill Lad	**184**
1985/86	Dawn Run	**167**
1986/87	Desert Orchid	**177**
1987/88	Desert Orchid	**177**
1988/89	Desert Orchid	**182**
1989/90	Desert Orchid	**187**
1990/91	Morley Street	**174**
1991/92	Carvill's Hill	**182**
1992/93	Jodami	**174p**

Best Two-Mile Chaser

75/76	Lough Inagh	**167**	84/85	Bobsline	**164 +**
76/77	Skymas	**156**	85/86	Dawn Run	**167**
77/78	Tingle Creek	**154**	86/87	Pearlyman	**171**
78/79	Siberian Sun	**151**	87/88	Pearlyman	**174**
79/80	I'm A Driver	**163**	88/89	Desert Orchid	**182**
80/81	Anaglogs Daughter	**171**	89/90	Desert Orchid	**187**
81/82	Rathgorman	**170**	90/91	Desert Orchid	**178**
82/83	Badsworth Boy	**179**	91/92	Remittance Man	**173**
83/84	Badsworth Boy	**177**	92/93	Katabatic	**161?**

Best Staying Chaser

75/76	Captain Christy	**182**	84/85	Burrough Hill Lad	**184**
76/77	Bannow Rambler	**163**	85/86	Burrough Hill Lad	**183**
77/78	Midnight Court	**164**	86/87	Desert Orchid	**177**
78/79	Gay Spartan	**166**	87/88	Desert Orchid	**177**
79/80	Silver Buck	**171**	88/89	Desert Orchid	**182**
80/81	Little Owl	**176**	89/90	Desert Orchid	**187**
81/82	Silver Buck	**175**	90/91	Desert Orchid	**178**
82/83	Bregawn	**177**	91/92	Carvill's Hill	**182**
83/84	Burrough Hill Lad	**175**	92/93	Jodami	**174p**

Best Novice Chaser

75/76	Bannow Rambler	**152p**	84/85	Drumadowney	**159**
76/77	Tree Tangle	**159§**	85/86	Pearlyman	**150**
77/78	The Dealer	**145**	86/87	Kildimo	**151p**
78/79	Silver Buck	**151**	87/88	Danish Flight	**156p**
79/80	Anaglogs Daughter	**156**	88/89	Carvill's Hill	**169p**
80/81	Clayside	**145**	89/90	Celtic Shot	**152p**
81/82	Brown Chamberlin	**147p**	90/91	Remittance Man	**153p**
82/83	Righthand Man	**150**	91/92	Miinnehoma	**152p**
83/84	Bobsline	**161p**	92/93	Sybillin	**156**

Best Hunter Chaser

75/76	Otter Way	**143**	84/85	Further Thought	**141**
76/77	Under Way	**124**	85/86	Ah Whisht	**148**
77/78	Spartan Missile	**133**	86/87	Observe	**146**
78/79	Spartan Missile	**133 +**	87/88	Certain Light	**147**
79/80	Rolls Rambler	**132**	88/89	Call Collect	**142p**
80/81	Spartan Missile	**169**	89/90	Mystic Music	**143**
81/82	Compton Lad	**142**	90/91	Mystic Music	**143?**
82/83	Eliogarty	**147**	91/92	Rushing Wild	**127p**
83/84	Venture To Cognac	**149**	92/93	Double Silk	**122p**

Best Two-Mile Hurdler

75/76	Night Nurse	**178**	84/85	Browne's Gazette	**172**
76/77	Night Nurse	**182**	85/86	See You Then	**173**
77/78	Monksfield	**177**	86/87	See You Then	**173**
78/79	Monksfield	**180**	87/88	Celtic Shot	**170**
79/80	Sea Pigeon	**175**	88/89	Beech Road	**172**
80/81	Sea Pigeon	**175**	89/90	Kribensis	**169**
81/82	For Auction	**174**	90/91	Morley Street	**174**
82/83	Gaye Brief	**175**	91/92	Granville Again	**165p**
83/84	Dawn Run	**173**	92/93	Mighty Mogul	**170**

Best Staying Hurdler

75/76	Comedy of Errors	**170**	84/85	Bajan Sunshine	**162**
76/77	Night Nurse	**182**	85/86	Gaye Brief	**167**
77/78	Monksfield	**177**	86/87	Galmoy	**165**
78/79	Monksfield	**180**	87/88	Galmoy	**160**
79/80	Pollardstown	**167**	88/89	Rustle	**169**
80/81	Daring Run	**171+**	89/90	Trapper John	**159**
81/82	Daring Run	**171**	90/91	King's Curate	**164**
82/83	Gaye Brief	**175**	91/92	Nomadic Way	**162**
83/84	Dawn Run	**173**	92/93	Sweet Duke	**161**

Best Novice Hurdler

75/76	Grand Canyon	**159**	85/86	River Ceiriog	**158p**
76/77	Outpoint	**154**	86/87	The West Awake	**153p**
77/78	Golden Cygnet	**176**	87/88	Carvill's Hill	**157p**
78/79	Venture To Cognac	**162**	88/89	Sondrio	**152p**
79/80	Slaney Idol	**143**		Wishlon	**152+**
80/81	Dunaree	**159**	89/90	Regal Ambition	**151**
81/82	Angelo Salvini	**149**	90/91	Ruling	**167**
82/83	Dawn Run	**168**	91/92	Royal Gait	**164p**
83/84	Desert Orchid	**158**	92/93	Montelado	**150P**
84/85	Asir	**148p**			

Best Juvenile Hurdler

75/76	Valmony	**157**	84/85	Out of The Gloom	**151**
76/77	Meladon	**149**	85/86	Dark Raven	**153p**
77/78	Major Thompson	**144**	86/87	Aldino	**154**
78/79	Pollardstown	**141**	87/88	Kribensis	**143p**
79/80	Hill of Slane	**144**	88/89	Royal Derbi	**144**
80/81	Broadsword	**144**	89/90	Sybillin	**138**
81/82	Shiny Copper	**141**	90/91	Oh So Risky	**149p**
82/83	Sabin du Loir	**147p**	91/92	Staunch Friend	**151p**
83/84	Northern Game	**142**	92/93	Shawiya	**141p**

FIXTURES 1993/94

(a)   Denotes all-weather jumping meeting
(aF)   Denotes all-weather Flat meeting
* Denotes evening meeting

October

1	Fri	Hexham
2	Sat	Chepstow, Kelso, Uttoxeter
4	Mon	Plumpton, Southwell
5	Tue	Newton Abbot
6	Wed	Towcester
7	Thu	Ludlow, Wincanton
8	Fri	Carlisle, Market Rasen
9	Sat	Ayr, Bangor, Worcester
11	Mon	Carlisle, Fontwell
12	Tue	Sedgefield
13	Wed	Exeter, Uttoxeter, Wetherby
14	Thu	Hexham, Taunton
15	Fri	Ludlow
16	Sat	Kelso, Kempton, Southwell, Stratford
18	Mon	Fakenham
19	Tue	Plumpton
20	Wed	Cheltenham, Newcastle
21	Thu	Wincanton
22	Fri	Exeter, Newbury
23	Sat	Catterick, Huntingdon, Worcester
25	Mon	Southwell
26	Tue	Newton Abbot
27	Wed	Fontwell, Sedgefield
28	Thu	Kempton, Stratford
29	Fri	Bangor, Wetherby
30	Sat	Ascot, Warwick, Wetherby

November

1	Mon	Plumpton, Southwell (aF)
2	Tue	Exeter
3	Wed	Haydock, Kelso, Uttoxeter
4	Thu	Lingfield (aF), Uttoxeter, Wincanton
5	Fri	Hexham, Market Rasen
6	Sat	Chepstow, Newcastle, Sandown
8	Mon	Carlisle, Southwell (aF)
9	Tue	Fontwell, Sedgefield, Southwell
10	Wed	Lingfield (aF), Newbury, Worcester
11	Thu	Kelso, Taunton, Towcester
12	Fri	Ayr, Cheltenham, Huntingdon
13	Sat	Ayr, Cheltenham, Lingfield (aF), Nottingham, Windsor
15	Mon	Leicester, Plumpton
16	Tue	Newton Abbot, Southwell (aF), Warwick, Wetherby
17	Wed	Haydock, Hereford, Kempton, Southwell
18	Thu	Haydock, Ludlow, Wincanton
19	Fri	Ascot, Leicester, Sedgefield
20	Sat	Aintree, Ascot, Catterick, Market Rasen, Towcester
22	Mon	Catterick, Folkestone, Southwell (aF)

December

1	Wed	Catterick, Huntingdon, Southwell (aF)
2	Thu	Lingfield (aF), Uttoxeter, Windsor
3	Fri	Exeter, Hereford, Nottingham, Sandown
4	Sat	Chepstow, Sandown, Towcester, Wetherby
6	Mon	Edinburgh, Ludlow
7	Tue	Plumpton, Sedgefield
8	Wed	Haydock, Lingfield (aF), Worcester
9	Thu	Fakenham, Haydock, Taunton
10	Fri	Cheltenham, Doncaster, Hexham
11	Sat	Cheltenham, Doncaster, Edinburgh, Lingfield
13	Mon	Newton Abbot, Warwick
14	Tue	Folkestone, Southwell (aF)
15	Wed	Bangor, Exeter, Lingfield (aF)
16	Thu	Kelso, Southwell (aF), Towcester
17	Fri	Catterick, Market Rasen, Uttoxeter
18	Sat	Ascot, Lingfield (aF), Nottingham, Uttoxeter
20	Mon	Edinburgh, Lingfield
21	Tue	Hereford, Lingfield (aF)
22	Wed	Hexham, Ludlow, Southwell
27	Mon	Ayr, Hereford, Huntingdon, Kempton, Market Rasen, Newton Abbot, Sedgefield, Wetherby, Wincanton
28	Tue	Chepstow, Kempton, Wetherby
29	Wed	Newcastle, Plumpton, Southwell, Stratford
30	Thu	Carlisle, Fontwell, Taunton, Warwick
31	Fri	Catterick, Folkestone, Leicester, Newbury

January

1	Sat	Catterick, Lingfield (aF), Newbury, Nottingham, Southwell (aF)
3	Mon	Ayr, Cheltenham, Exeter, Leicester, Windsor, Wolverhampton (aF)

4	Tue	Lingfield (aF), Newton Abbot
5	Wed	Lingfield, Sedgefield, Southwell (a)
6	Thu	Lingfield (a), Market Rasen, Worcester
7	Fri	Edinburgh, Southwell (aF), Towcester
8	Sat	Haydock, Lingfield (aF), Sandown, Warwick
10	Mon	Lingfield, Wolverhampton (aF)
11	Tue	Chepstow, Leicester, Lingfield (aF)
12	Wed	Kelso, Lingfield (a), Plumpton, Southwell (a)
13	Thu	Lingfield (a), Wetherby, Wincanton
14	Fri	Ascot, Edinburgh, Southwell (aF)
15	Sat	Ascot, Lingfield (aF), Newcastle, Warwick
17	Mon	Carlisle, Fontwell, Wolverhampton (aF)
18	Tue	Folkestone, Lingfield (aF)
19	Wed	Ludlow, Southwell (a), Windsor
20	Thu	Ayr, Lingfield (a), Taunton
21	Fri	Catterick, Kempton, Southwell (aF)
22	Sat	Catterick, Haydock, Kempton, Lingfield (aF), Market Rasen
24	Mon	Leicester, Lingfield, Wolverhampton (aF)
25	Tue	Chepstow, Lingfield (aF), Nottingham
26	Wed	Sedgefield, Southwell (a)
27	Thu	Huntingdon, Lingfield (a), Newton Abbot
28	Fri	Doncaster, Southwell (aF), Uttoxeter, Wincanton
29	Sat	Ayr, Cheltenham, Doncaster, Lingfield (aF)
31	Mon	Plumpton, Wolverhampton (aF)

February

1	Tue	Lingfield (aF), Nottingham, Sedgefield
2	Wed	Leicester, Southwell (a), Windsor
3	Thu	Edinburgh, Lingfield (a), Towcester
4	Fri	Kelso, Lingfield, Southwell (aF)
5	Sat	Chepstow, Lingfield (aF), Sandown, Stratford, Wetherby
7	Mon	Fontwell
8	Tue	Carlisle, Lingfield (aF), Warwick
9	Wed	Ascot, Ludlow, Southwell (a)
10	Thu	Huntingdon, Lingfield (a), Wincanton
11	Fri	Bangor, Newbury, Southwell (aF)
12	Sat	Ayr, Catterick, Lingfield (aF), Newbury, Uttoxeter
14	Mon	Hereford, Plumpton, Wolverhampton (aF)
15	Tue	Lingfield (aF), Newton Abbot, Towcester
16	Wed	Folkestone, Sedgefield, Southwell (a), Worcester

17	Thu	Leicester, Lingfield (a), Sandown, Taunton
18	Fri	Edinburgh, Fakenham, Sandown, Southwell (aF)
19	Sat	Chepstow, Lingfield (aF), Newcastle, Nottingham, Windsor
21	Mon	Fontwell
22	Tue	Huntingdon, Lingfield (aF), Sedgefield
23	Wed	Doncaster, Folkestone, Southwell (a), Warwick
24	Thu	Catterick, Lingfield (a), Wincanton
25	Fri	Haydock, Kempton, Southwell (aF)
26	Sat	Edinburgh, Haydock, Kempton, Lingfield (aF), Market Rasen
28	Mon	Leicester, Plumpton, Wolverhampton (aF)

March

1	Tue	Lingfield (aF), Nottingham
2	Wed	Southwell (a), Wetherby, Worcester
3	Thu	Lingfield (a), Ludlow, Taunton, Warwick
4	Fri	Kelso, Newbury, Southwell (aF)
5	Sat	Doncaster, Hereford, Lingfield (aF), Newbury, Stratford
7	Mon	Doncaster, Windsor
8	Tue	Leicester, Lingfield (a), Sedgefield
9	Wed	Bangor, Catterick, Folkestone, Southwell (a)
10	Thu	Carlisle, Towcester, Wincanton
11	Fri	Ayr, Market Rasen, Sandown
12	Sat	Ayr, Chepstow, Sandown, Southwell
14	Mon	Plumpton, Taunton
15	Tue	Cheltenham, Lingfield (aF), Sedgefield
16	Wed	Cheltenham, Huntingdon, Newton Abbot
17	Thu	Cheltenham, Hexham
18	Fri	Fakenham, Lingfield
19	Sat	Chepstow, Lingfield, Newcastle, Uttoxeter
21	Mon	Newcastle, Plumpton
22	Tue	Fontwell, Newcastle, Nottingham
23	Wed	Exeter, Kelso, Worcester
24	Thu	Stratford, Wincanton
25	Fri	Ludlow, Newbury
26	Sat	Bangor, Lingfield (aF), Newbury, Sedgefield
28	Mon	Hexham
29	Tue	Sandown
30	Wed	Ascot, Worcester

April

2	Sat	Carlisle, Newton Abbot, Plumpton, Towcester, Uttoxeter
4	Mon	Carlisle, Chepstow, Fakenham, Hereford, Huntingdon, Market Rasen, Newton Abbot, Plumpton, Towcester, Uttoxeter, Wetherby, Wincanton
5	Tue	Chepstow, Wetherby

6 Wed	Ascot, Ludlow
7 Thu	Aintree
8 Fri	Aintree, Lingfield (aF)
9 Sat	Aintree, Hereford
11 Mon	Kelso
12 Tue	Sedgefield
13 Wed	Worcester
14 Thu	Ayr
15 Fri	Ayr, Taunton*
16 Sat	Ayr, Bangor, Stratford
19 Tue	Newton Abbot
20 Wed	Cheltenham, Perth
21 Thu	Fontwell, Perth
22 Fri	Ludlow*, Perth, Taunton*
23 Sat	Hexham*, Market Rasen, Sandown, Worcester*
25 Mon	Hexham*, Southwell (aF)
26 Tue	Ascot*, Huntingdon*
27 Wed	Cheltenham*, Exeter, Kelso
29 Fri	Bangor*, Newton Abbot, Sedgefield*
30 Sat	Hereford, Hexham*, Plumpton*, Uttoxeter

May

2 Mon	Exeter, Fontwell, Haydock, Ludlow, Southwell, Towcester
3 Tue	Newton Abbot
4 Wed	Wetherby*
5 Thu	Sedgefield*, Uttoxeter*
6 Fri	Market Rasen*, Wincanton*
7 Sat	Newcastle*, Warwick*, Worcester
9 Mon	Southwell (aF)
10 Tue	Chepstow, Folkestone*, Towcester*
11 Wed	Hereford, Perth*, Southwell
12 Thu	Huntingdon*, Newton Abbot*, Perth
13 Fri	Stratford*
14 Sat	Bangor
17 Tue	Cheltenham*
18 Wed	Sedgefield, Worcester
19 Thu	Exeter, Perth*, Uttoxeter*
20 Fri	Fakenham*, Stratford*
21 Sat	Southwell*, Warwick*
24 Tue	Southwell (aF)
25 Wed	Cartmel
26 Thu	Hereford
27 Fri	Towcester*
28 Sat	Cartmel, Hexham, Southwell (aF)
30 Mon	Cartmel, Fontwell, Hereford, Hexham*, Huntingdon, Uttoxeter, Wetherby

June

2 Thu	Uttoxeter
3 Fri	Southwell (aF), Stratford*
4 Sat	Market Rasen*, Stratford

895

TIMEFORM AT CHELTENHAM

HALF PRICE DAY AT THE RACES

Timeform are once again sponsoring a race at the home of National Hunt racing and its customers can join in the day with an exclusive half price package.

The Timeform Hall of Fame Chase will be run at Cheltenham on Saturday January 29th as part of a high class card. Last year's race produced a select field and a thrilling finish with Hennessy winner Sibton Abbey just holding off Another Coral.

Timeform can offer its customers half price admission to the Members Enclosure (usually £15) and a half price Timeform Race Card (usually £5). A day at Cheltenham for just £10!

Further details will be announced nearer the day.

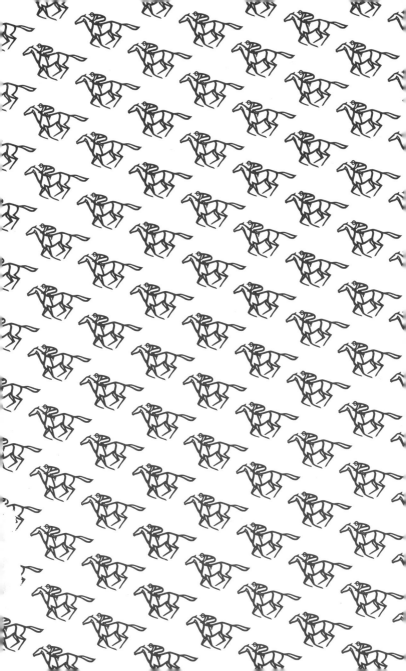